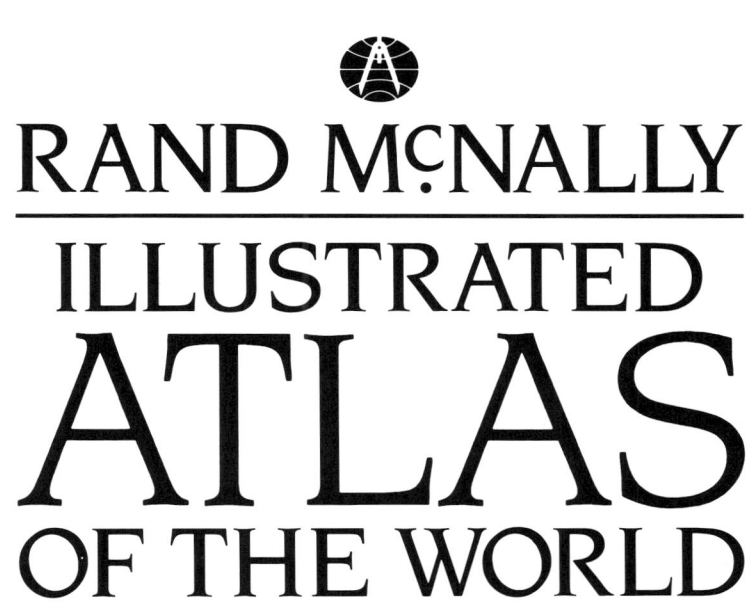

RAND McNALLY

ILLUSTRATED
ATLAS
OF THE WORLD

ILLUSTRATED
ATLAS
OF THE WORLD

 RAND McNALLY & COMPANY

CHICAGO • NEW YORK • SAN FRANCISCO

ILLUSTRATED ATLAS OF THE WORLD
Copyright © 1992 by Rand McNally & Company
1994 Revised Edition

All rights reserved.

Published by Blitz Editions
an imprint of
Bookmart Limited
Registered Number 2372865
Trading as Bookmart Limited
Desford Road
Enderby
Leicester
LE9 5AD

ISBN 1 85605 359 8

Pages 1 through 240 and
A·1 through A·144 from
The Great Geographical Atlas
Copyright © 1992 Instituto Geografico De Agostini

Library of Congress Cataloging-in-Publication Data
Rand McNally and Company.
    Illustrated atlas of the world. — 1994 rev. ed.
        p.   cm.
    Shows changes to Czechoslovakia, Yugoslavia, and Eritrea.
    Title on added t.p.: Rand McNally illustrated atlas of the world.
    Includes indexes.
    ISBN 0-528-83492-4
    1. Atlases.   I. Title.   II. Title: Rand McNally illustrated atlas
of the world.   III. Title: Atlas of the world.
G1021.R185   1993   < G&M >
912—dc20   93-504
                                    CIP
                                    MAP

Printed in Spain

Jacket photo Comstock/Hartman-Dewitt
Title page photo by Ray Atkeson

CONTENTS

Our Planet Earth Section

Maps

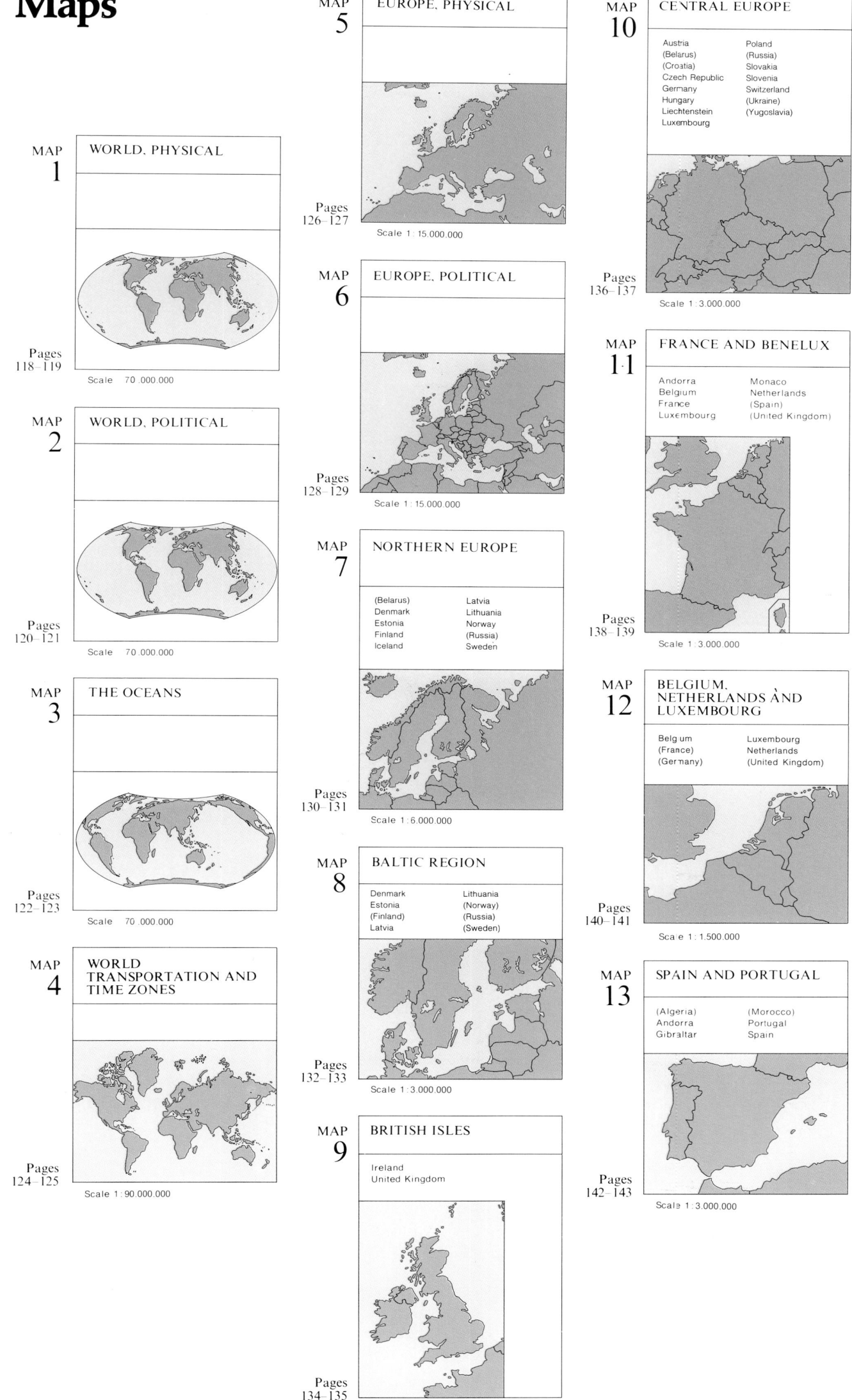

MAP 1 — WORLD, PHYSICAL
Pages 118–119
Scale 70.000.000

MAP 2 — WORLD, POLITICAL
Pages 120–121
Scale 70.000.000

MAP 3 — THE OCEANS
Pages 122–123
Scale 70.000.000

MAP 4 — WORLD TRANSPORTATION AND TIME ZONES
Pages 124–125
Scale 1:90.000.000

MAP 5 — EUROPE, PHYSICAL
Pages 126–127
Scale 1:15.000.000

MAP 6 — EUROPE, POLITICAL
Pages 128–129
Scale 1:15.000.000

MAP 7 — NORTHERN EUROPE
(Belarus) — Latvia
Denmark — Lithuania
Estonia — Norway
Finland — (Russia)
Iceland — Sweden
Pages 130–131
Scale 1:6.000.000

MAP 8 — BALTIC REGION
Denmark — Lithuania
Estonia — (Norway)
(Finland) — (Russia)
Latvia — (Sweden)
Pages 132–133
Scale 1:3.000.000

MAP 9 — BRITISH ISLES
Ireland
United Kingdom
Pages 134–135
Scale 1:3.000.000

MAP 10 — CENTRAL EUROPE
Austria — Poland
(Belarus) — (Russia)
(Croatia) — Slovakia
Czech Republic — Slovenia
Germany — Switzerland
Hungary — (Ukraine)
Liechtenstein — (Yugoslavia)
Luxembourg
Pages 136–137
Scale 1:3.000.000

MAP 11 — FRANCE AND BENELUX
Andorra — Monaco
Belgium — Netherlands
France — (Spain)
Luxembourg — (United Kingdom)
Pages 138–139
Scale 1:3.000.000

MAP 12 — BELGIUM, NETHERLANDS AND LUXEMBOURG
Belgium — Luxembourg
(France) — Netherlands
(Germany) — (United Kingdom)
Pages 140–141
Scale 1:1.500.000

MAP 13 — SPAIN AND PORTUGAL
(Algeria) — (Morocco)
Andorra — Portugal
Gibraltar — Spain
Pages 142–143
Scale 1:3.000.000

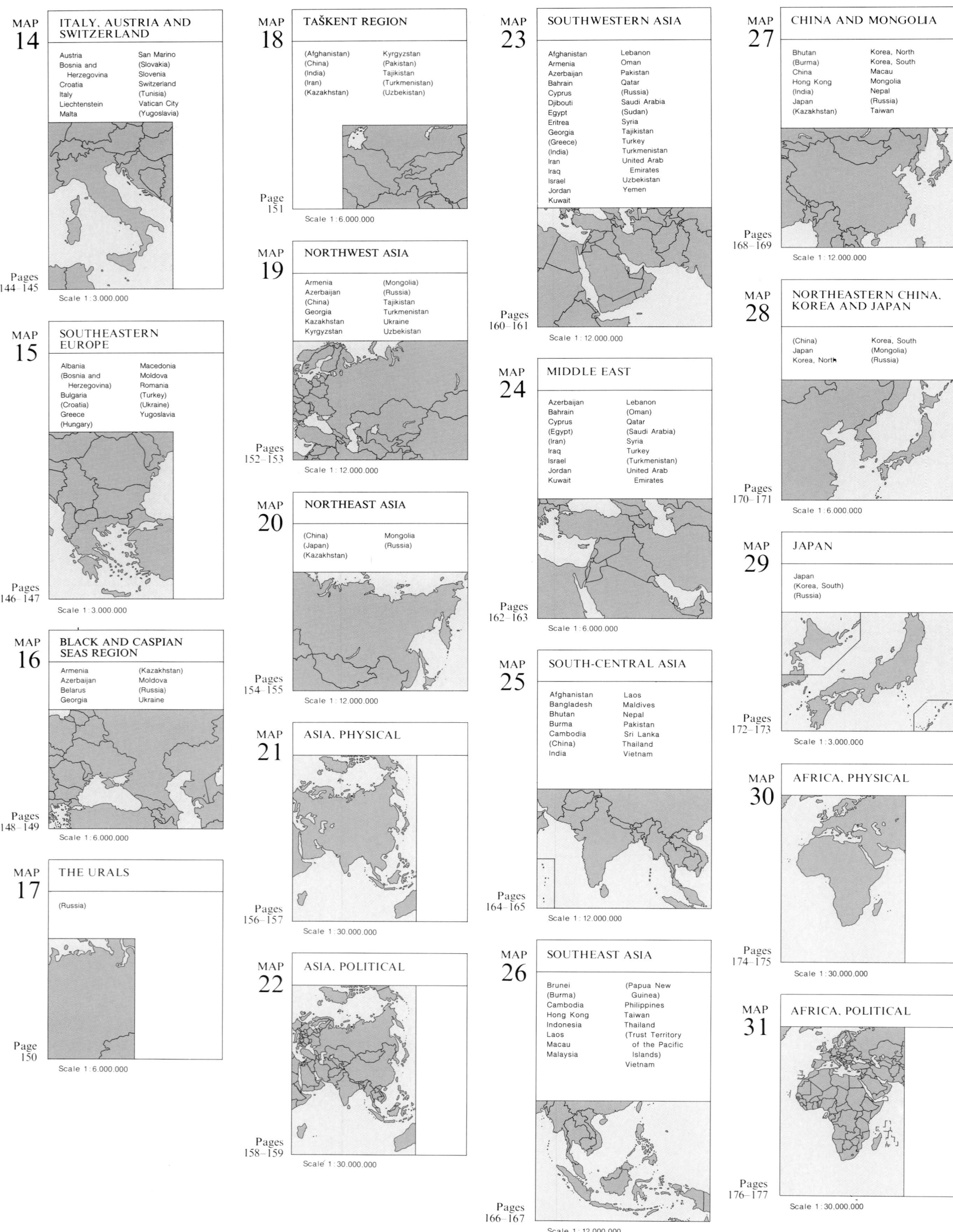

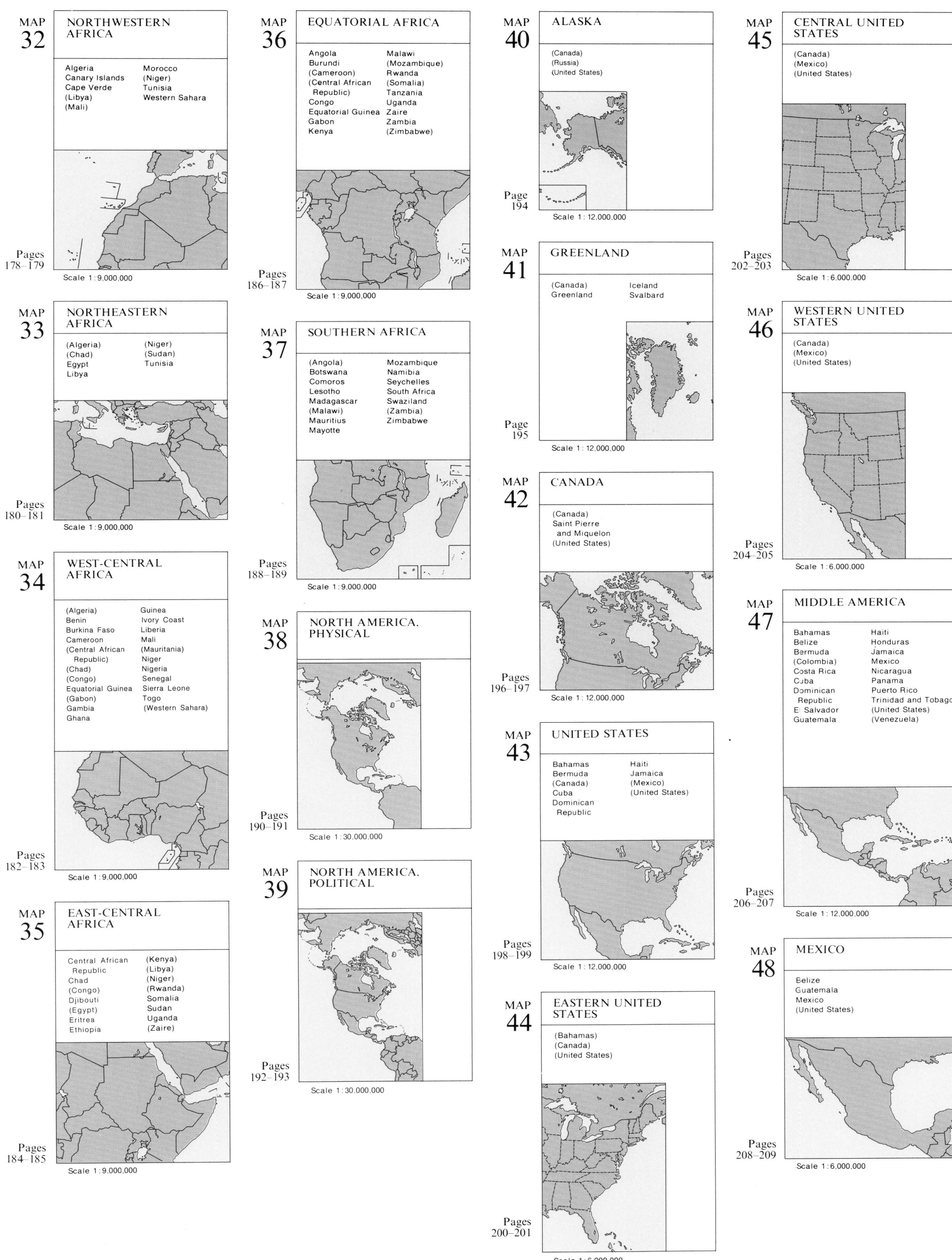

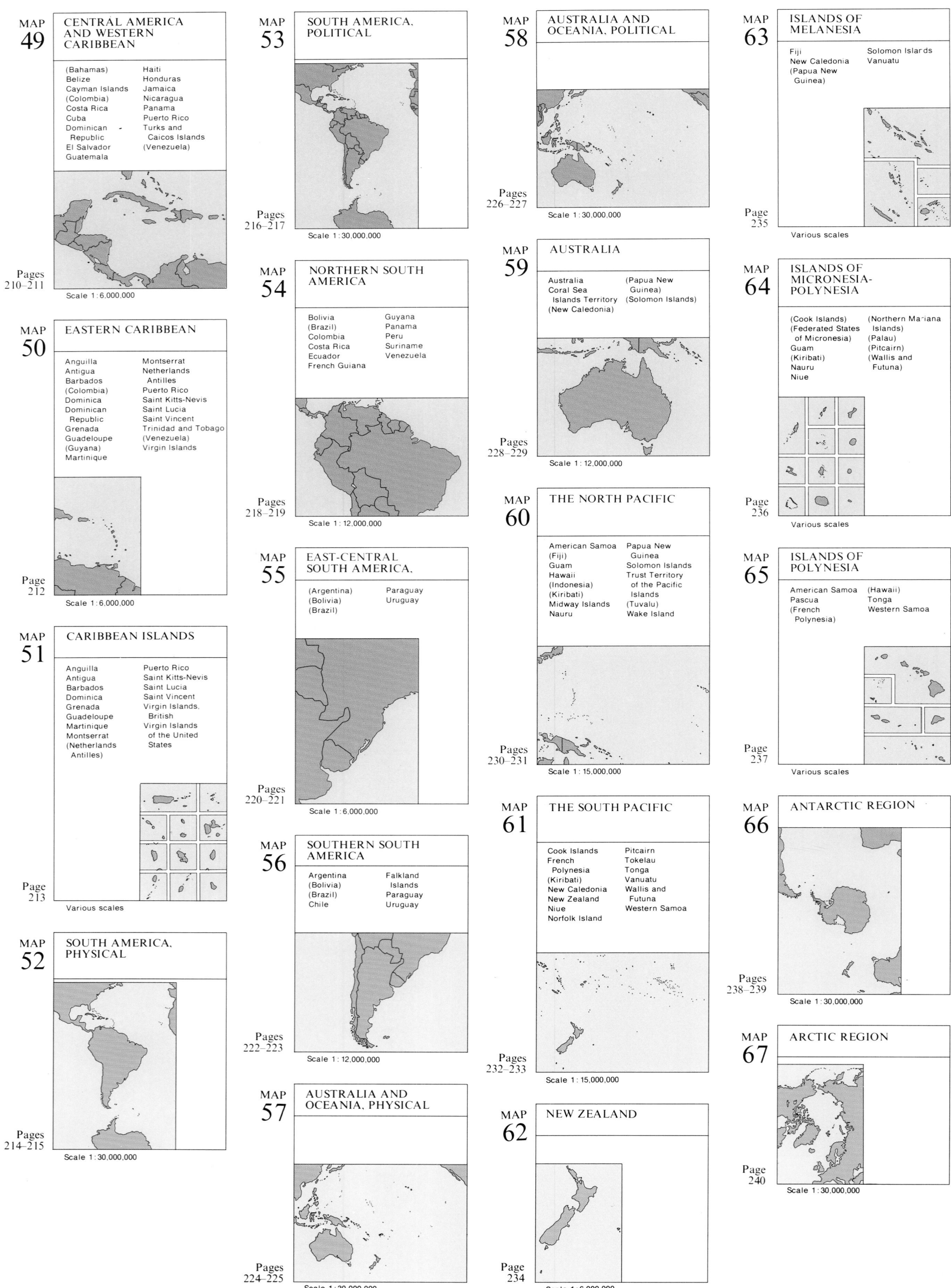

VIII

Our Planet Earth Section

Part 1

THE EARTH AND THE UNIVERSE

How the universe began · Earth's place in the Solar System
How the Earth became fit for life
Man looks at Earth from outer space

CREATION AND DESTRUCTION

Violent activity pervades our universe and has done so ever since the primordial fireball of creation. Evidence of violence comes from radio telescopes scanning the farthest reaches: entire galaxies may be exploding, torn apart by gravitational forces of unimaginable power. Some very large stars may burst apart in supernovas, spraying interstellar space with cosmic debris. From this violence new stars and new planets are constantly being formed throughout the universe.

The Big Bang theory (left) of the origin of the universe envisages all matter originating from one point in time and space—a point of infinite density. In the intensely hot Big Bang all the material that goes to make up the planets, stars and galaxies that we see now began to expand outward in all directions. This expansion has been likened to someone blowing up a balloon on which spots have been painted. As the air fills and expands the balloon, the spots get farther away from each other. Likewise, clusters of galaxies that formed from the original superdense matter began, and continue, to move away from neighboring clusters. The Big Bang generated enormous temperatures and the remnants of the event still linger throughout space. A leftover, background radiation provides a uniform and measurable temperature of 3°C. It is generally believed that the universe will continue to expand into complete nothingness.

Stars vary enormously in size, temperature and luminosity. The largest, so-called red giants like Antares (1)—the biggest yet known—or Aldebaran (2), are nearing the end of their lives: diminishing nuclear "fuel" causes their thinning envelopes to expand. Rigel (3) is many times brighter than our Sun (4)—a middle-aged star—but both are so-called main-sequence stars. Epsilon Eridani (5) is rather like the Sun. Wolf 359 (6) is a red dwarf.

Our Solar System was formed from a collapsing cloud of gas and dust (A). Collapse made the center hotter and denser (B) until nuclear reactions started. Heat blew matter from the heart of the now flattened, spinning disc (C). Heavier materials condensed closest to the young Sun, now a hot star, eventually forming the inner ring of planets; the lighter ones accumulated farther out, making up the atmosphere and composition of the giant outer planets (D).

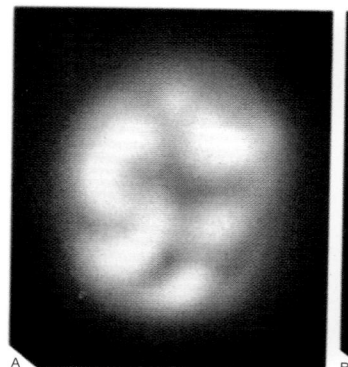
A

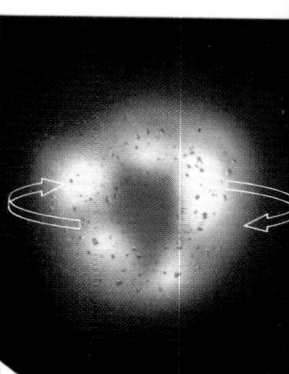
B

Billions of galaxies exist outside our own Milky Way, each thousands of light-years across and filled with millions of stars. Found in clusters, they are either elliptical or spiral in form. The clusters recede from each other following the space-time geometry, as established by Hubble in 1929, proving that the universe is expanding.

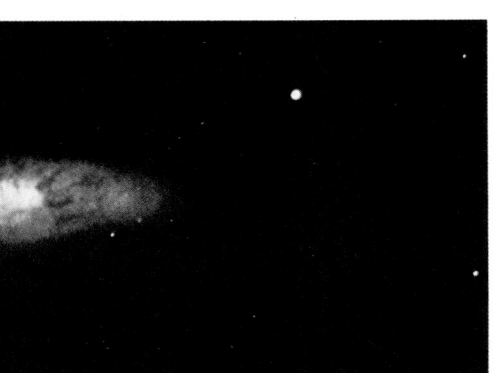

The "exploding" galaxy M82 may be an example of the violence of our universe. Clouds of hydrogen gas, equivalent in mass to 5,000,000 suns, have been ejected from the nucleus at 160 km (100 miles) per second. Black holes may cause the explosions, when gravity sucks in all matter, so that even light cannot escape.

Our own cluster of galaxies (below), the Local Group (A), consists of about 30 members, weakly linked by the force of gravity. Earth lies in the second-largest galaxy, the Milky Way (B)—here shown edge-on and at an angle—which is a spiral galaxy of about 100,000 million stars. Its rotating "arms" are great masses of clouds, dust and stars that sweep around a dense nucleus. In the course of this new stars are regularly created from dust and gas. Our Sun (S) lies 33,000 light-years from the nucleus and takes 225 million years to complete an orbit. The Andromeda Galaxy (C), known to astronomers as M31, is the largest of our Local Group. It too is a spiral, and lies about two million light-years away. Roughly 130,000 light-years in diameter, it appears as a flattened disc, and indicates how our galaxy would look if viewed from outside. Two smaller elliptical galaxies, M32 and NGC 205, can also be seen.

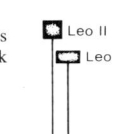

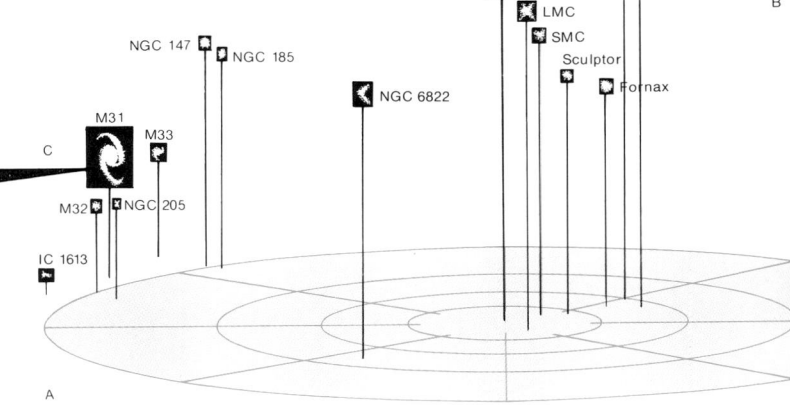

Stars are being born (left) in the Great Nebula of Orion, visible from Earth. The brilliant light comes from a cluster of very hot young stars, the Trapezium, surrounded by a glowing aura of hydrogen gas. Behind the visible nebula there is known to be a dense cloud where radio astronomers have detected emissions from interstellar molecules, and have identified high-density globules. These probably indicate that stars are starting to form.

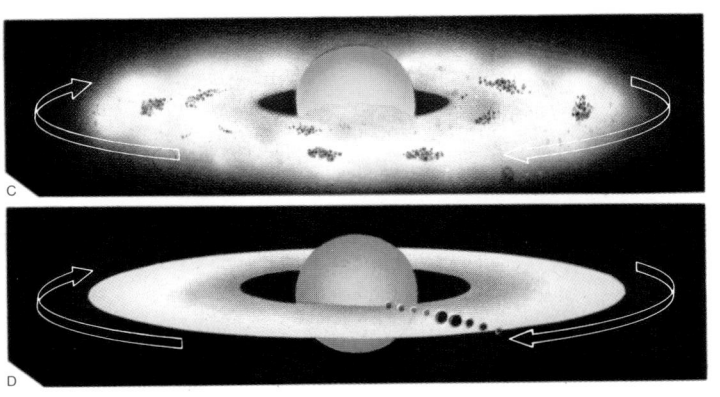

The Making of the Universe

Most astronomers believe that the universe began in a great explosion of matter and energy – the "Big Bang" – about 15,000 million years ago. This event was implied by Einstein's theory of general relativity, as well as by more recent astronomical observations and calculations. But the clinching evidence came in 1965, when two American radio astronomers discovered a faint, uniform, background radiation which permeated all space. This they identified as the remnants of the primordial Big Bang.

The generally accepted explanation for the so-called "cosmic microwave" background, detected by American astronomers Arno Penzias and Robert Wilson, is indeed that it is the echo of the Big Bang itself, the radio noise left over from the fireball of creation. In recognition of their discovery, Penzias and Wilson shared a Nobel Prize in 1978.

The Big Bang has also been identified by astronomers in other ways. All the evidence shows that the universe is expanding, and its constituent parts—clusters of galaxies, each containing thousands of millions of stars like our Sun—are moving away from each other at great speeds. From this and other evidence scientists deduce that long ago the galaxies must have been closer together, in a superdense phase, and that at some time in the remote past all the material in the universe must have started spreading out from a single point. But this "single point" includes not only all three-dimensional matter and space but also the dimension of time, as envisioned in Einstein's revolutionary concept of space-time. Einstein's theory of relativity describes the phenomenon, not in terms of galaxies moving through space in

then reused to form new stars and planets.

Thus, from the debris of such explosions new stars can form to repeat the creative cycle, and at each stage more of the heavy elements are produced. Today's heavenly bodies are very much the products of stellar violence in the universe, and indeed the universe itself is now seen to be an area of violent activity. During the past two decades the old idea of the universe as a place of quiet stability has been increasingly superseded by evidence of intense activity on all scales. Astronomers have identified what appear to be vast explosions involving whole galaxies, as well as those of individual stars.

Black holes
The evidence of just why these huge explosions occur is often hard to obtain, because the exploding galaxies may be so far away that light from them takes millions of years to reach telescopes on Earth. But it is becoming increasingly accepted by astronomers that such violent events may be associated with the presence of black holes at the centers of some galaxies.

These black holes are regions in which matter has become so concentrated that the force of gravity makes it impossible for anything—even light itself—to escape. As stars are pulled into super-massive black holes they are torn apart by gravitational forces, and their material forms into a swirling maelstrom from which huge explosions can occur. Collapse into black holes, accompanied by violent outbursts from the maelstrom, may be the ultimate fate of all matter in the universe. For our own Solar System, however, such a fate is far in the future: the Sun in its present form is believed to have enough "fuel" to keep it going for at least another 5,000 million years.

A star is born
The origins of the Earth and the Solar System are intimately connected with the structure of our own galaxy, the Milky Way. There are two main types of galaxies: flattened, disc-shaped spiral galaxies (like the Milky Way), and the more rounded elliptical galaxies, which range in form from near spheres to cigar shapes. The most important feature of a spiral galaxy is that it is rotating, a great mass of stars sweeping around a common center. In our galaxy the Sun, located some way out from the galaxy's center, takes about 225 million years to complete one circuit, called a cosmic year.

New stars are born out of the twisting arms of a spiral galaxy, with each arm marking a region of debris left over from previous stellar explosions. These arms are in fact clouds of dust and gas, including nitrogen and oxygen. As the spiral galaxy rotates over a period of millions of years, the twisting arms are squeezed by a high-density pressure wave as they pass through the cycle of the cosmic year. With two main spiral arms twining around a galaxy such as our own, large, diffuse clouds get squeezed twice during each orbit around the center of the galaxy.

Even if one orbit takes as long as hundreds of millions of years, a score or more squeezes have probably occurred since the Milky Way was first formed thousands of millions of years ago. At a critical point, such repeated squeezing increases the density of a gas cloud so much that it begins to collapse rapidly under the inward pull of its own gravity. A typical cloud of this kind contains enough material to make many stars. As it breaks up it collapses into smaller clouds—which are also collapsing—and these become stars in their own right.

Our own Solar System may have been formed in this way from such a collapsing gas cloud, which went on to evolve into the system of planets that we know today.

Nucleus (N)   Sun (S)

100,000 light-years

Exploding space
The original material of the universe was hydrogen, the simplest of all elements. Nuclear reactions that occurred during the superdense phase of the Big Bang converted about 20 percent of the original hydrogen into helium, the next simplest element. So the first stars were formed from a mixture of about 80 percent hydrogen and 20 percent helium. All other matter in the universe, including the atoms of heavier elements such as carbon and oxygen—which help to make up the human body or the pages of this book—has been processed in further nuclear reactions. The explosion of a star—a relatively rare event called a supernova—scatters material across space, briefly radiating more energy than a trillion suns and ejecting matter into the cosmic reservoir of interstellar space. This is

the expansion, but as being carried apart by the expansion of space-time itself. Space-time may be imagined as a rubber sheet speckled with paint blobs (galaxies), which move apart as the rubber sheet expands.

Galaxies consist of star systems, dust clouds and gases formed from the hot material exploding outward from the original cosmic fireball. Our own Milky Way system, the band of light that stretches across the night sky, is typical of many galaxies, containing millions of stars slowly rotating around a central nucleus.

Earth in the Solar System

The Sun is an ordinary, medium-sized star located some two-thirds of the way from the center of our galaxy, the Milky Way. Yet it comprises more than 99 percent of the Solar System's total mass and provides all the light and heat that make life possible on Earth. This energy comes from nuclear reactions that take place in the Sun's hot, dense interior. The reactions convert hydrogen into helium, with the release of vast amounts of energy – the energy that keeps the Sun shining.

Nuclear reactions in the Sun's core maintain a temperature of some 15,000,000°C and this heat prevents the star from shrinking. The surface temperature is comparatively much lower —a mere 6,000°C. Thermonuclear energy-generating processes cause the Sun to "lose" mass from the center at the rate of four million tonnes of hydrogen every second. This mass is turned into energy (heat), and each gram of matter "burnt" produces the heat equivalent of 100 trillion electric fires. The Sun's total mass is so great, however, that it contains enough matter to continue radiating at its present rate for several thousand million years before it runs out of "fuel."

The Sun's retinue
The Solar System emerged from a collapsing gas cloud. In addition to the Sun there are at least nine planets, their satellites, thousands of minor planets (asteroids), comets and meteors. Most stars occur in pairs, triplets or in even more complicated systems, and the Sun is among a minority of stars in being alone except for its planetary companions. It does seem, however, that a single star with a planetary system offers the greatest potential for the development of life. When there are two or more stars in the same system, any planets are likely to have unstable orbits and to suffer from wide extremes of temperature.

The Solar System's structure is thought to be typical of a star that formed in isolation. As the hot young Sun threw material outward, inner planets (Mercury, Venus, Earth and Mars) were left as small rocky worlds, whereas outer planets (Jupiter, Saturn, Uranus and Neptune) kept their lighter gases and became huge "gas giants." Jupiter has two and a half times the mass of all the other planets put together. Pluto, a small object with a strange orbit, which sometimes carries it within the orbit of Neptune, is usually regarded as a ninth planet, but some astronomers consider it to be an escaped moon of Neptune or a large asteroid.

Planetary relations
Several planets are accompanied by smaller bodies called moons or satellites. Jupiter and Saturn have at least 17 and 22 respectively, whereas Earth has its solitary Moon. Sizes vary enormously, from Ganymede, one of Jupiter's large, so-called Galilean satellites, which has a diameter of 5,000 km (3,100 miles), to Mars' tiny Deimos, which is only 8 km (5 miles) across.

The Earth's Moon is at an average distance of 384,000 km (239,000 miles) and has a diameter of 3,476 km (2,160 miles). Its mass is $\frac{1}{81}$ of the Earth's. Although it is referred to as the Earth's satellite, the Moon is large for a secondary body. Some astronomers have suggested that the Earth/Moon system is a double planet. Certain theories of the origins of the Moon propose that it was formed from the solar nebula in the same way as the Earth was and very close to it. The Moon takes 27.3 days to orbit the Earth—exactly the same time that it takes to rotate once on its axis. As a result, it presents the same face to the Earth all the time.

Our planet's orbit around the Sun is not a perfect circle but an ellipse and so its distance from the Sun varies slightly. More importantly, the Earth is tilted, so that at different times of the year one pole or another "leans" toward the Sun. Without this tilt there would be no seasons. The angle of tilt is not constant: over tens of thousands of years the axis of the Earth "wobbles" like a slowly spinning top, so that the pattern of the seasons varies over the ages. These changes have been linked to recent ice ages, which seem to occur when the northern hemisphere has relatively cool summers.

Patterns of time
The Earth's movements on its axis and around the Sun give us our basic measurements of time—the day and the year—as well as setting the rhythm of the seasons and the ice ages. One rotation of the Earth on its axis—the time from one sunrise to the next—originally defined the day, and the time taken for one complete orbit around the Sun defined the year. Today, however, scientists define both the day and the year in terms of time units "counted" by precision instruments called atomic clocks.

A third basic rhythm is set not by the Sun but by the Moon, which runs through a cycle of phases $29\frac{1}{2}$ days long. This is the basis of the calendar month. But just as the modern calendar cannot cope with months $29\frac{1}{2}$ days long, so too it would have trouble with the precise year, which is, inconveniently, just less than $365\frac{1}{4}$ days long. This is the reason for leap years, by means of which an extra day is added to the month of February every fourth year.

Even this system does not keep the calendar exactly in step with the Sun. Accordingly, the leap year is left out in the years which complete centuries, such as 1900, but retained when they divide exactly by 400. The year 2000 will, therefore, be a leap year. With all these corrections, the average length of the calendar year is within 26 seconds of the year defined by the Earth's movements around the Sun. Thus the calendar will be one day out of step with the heavens in the year 4906.

Cosmic rubble
The other planets are too small and too far away to produce noticeable effects on the Earth, but the smallest members of the Sun's family, the asteroids, can affect us directly. Some of them have orbits that cross the orbit of the Earth around the Sun. From time to time they penetrate the Earth's atmosphere: small fragments burn up high in the atmosphere as meteors, whereas larger pieces may survive to strike the ground as meteorites. These in fact provide an echo of times gone by. All the planets, as the battered face of the Moon shows, suffered collisions from many smaller bodies in the course of their evolution from the collapsing pre-solar gas cloud.

Eclipses occur because the Moon, smaller than the Sun, is closer to Earth and looks just as big. This means that when all three are lined up the Moon can blot out the Sun, causing a solar eclipse. When the Earth passes through the main shadow cone, or umbra, the eclipse is total; in the area of partial shadow, or penumbra, a partial eclipse is seen. A similar effect is produced when Earth passes between the Moon and the Sun, causing a lunar eclipse. At most full moons, eclipses do not occur; the Moon passes either above or below the Earth's shadow, because the Moon's orbit is inclined at an angle of 5° to the orbit of the Earth.

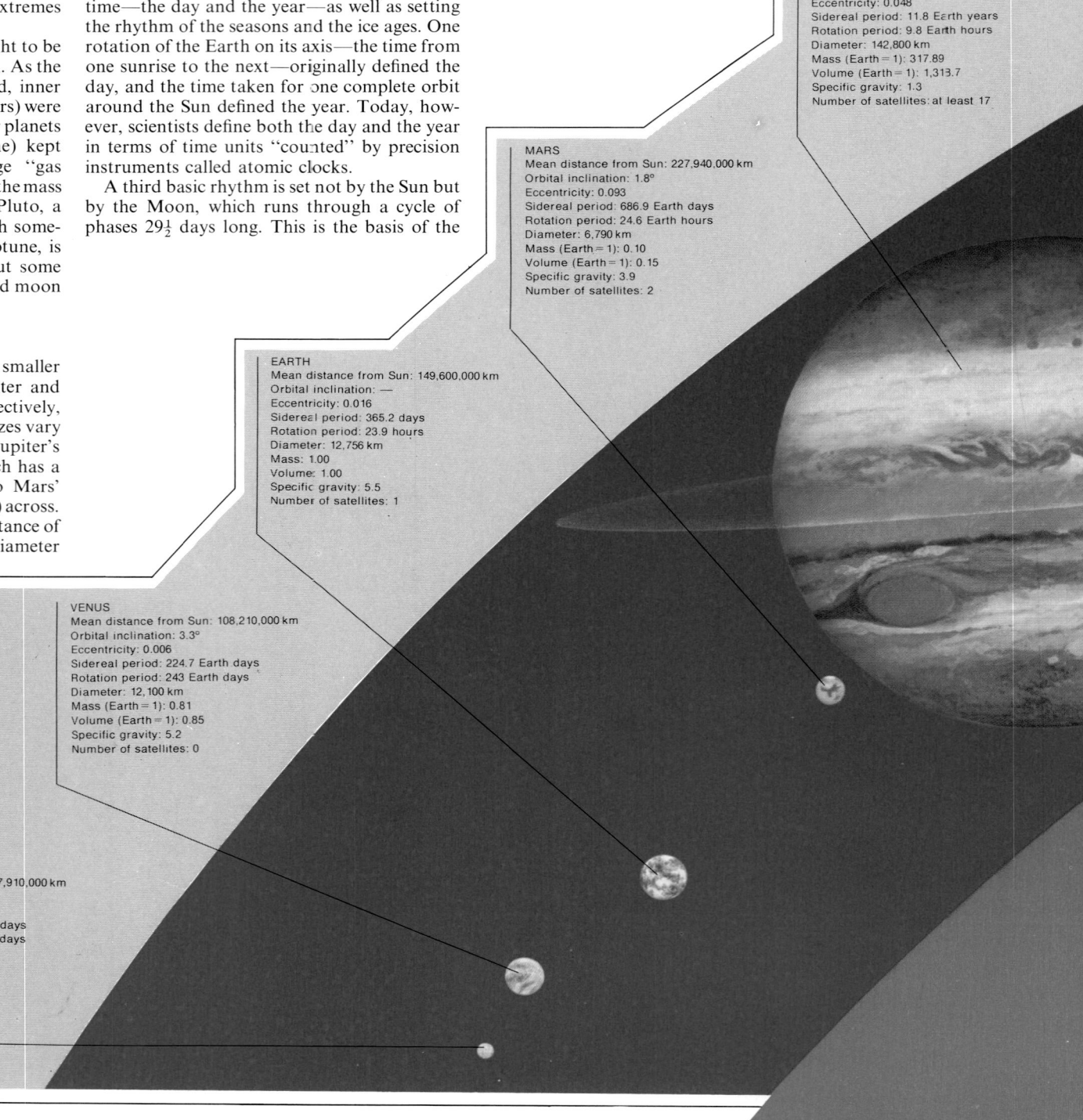

JUPITER
Mean distance from Sun: 778,340,000 km
Orbital inclination: 1.3°
Eccentricity: 0.048
Sidereal period: 11.8 Earth years
Rotation period: 9.8 Earth hours
Diameter: 142,800 km
Mass (Earth = 1): 317.89
Volume (Earth = 1): 1,313.7
Specific gravity: 1.3
Number of satellites: at least 17

MARS
Mean distance from Sun: 227,940,000 km
Orbital inclination: 1.8°
Eccentricity: 0.093
Sidereal period: 686.9 Earth days
Rotation period: 24.6 Earth hours
Diameter: 6,790 km
Mass (Earth = 1): 0.10
Volume (Earth = 1): 0.15
Specific gravity: 3.9
Number of satellites: 2

EARTH
Mean distance from Sun: 149,600,000 km
Orbital inclination: —
Eccentricity: 0.016
Sidereal period: 365.2 days
Rotation period: 23.9 hours
Diameter: 12,756 km
Mass: 1.00
Volume: 1.00
Specific gravity: 5.5
Number of satellites: 1

VENUS
Mean distance from Sun: 108,210,000 km
Orbital inclination: 3.3°
Eccentricity: 0.006
Sidereal period: 224.7 Earth days
Rotation period: 243 Earth days
Diameter: 12,100 km
Mass (Earth = 1): 0.81
Volume (Earth = 1): 0.85
Specific gravity: 5.2
Number of satellites: 0

MEMBERS OF THE SOLAR SYSTEM
The Sun has nine planetary attendants. They are best compared in terms of orbital data (distance from the Sun, inclination of orbit to the Earth's orbit, and eccentricity, which means the departure of a planet's orbit from circularity); planetary periods (the time for a planet to go around the Sun—sidereal periods, and the time it takes for one axial revolution—the rotation period); and physical data (equatorial diameter, mass, volume and density or specific gravity—the weight of a substance compared with the weight of an equal volume of water).

Scale
Diameter of Sun: 1,400,000 km

MERCURY
Mean distance from Sun: 57,910,000 km
Orbital inclination: 7°
Eccentricity: 0.205
Sidereal period: 87.9 Earth days
Rotation period: 58.7 Earth days
Diameter: 4,870 km
Mass (Earth = 1): 0.05
Volume (Earth = 1): 0.05
Specific gravity: 5.5
Number of satellites: 0

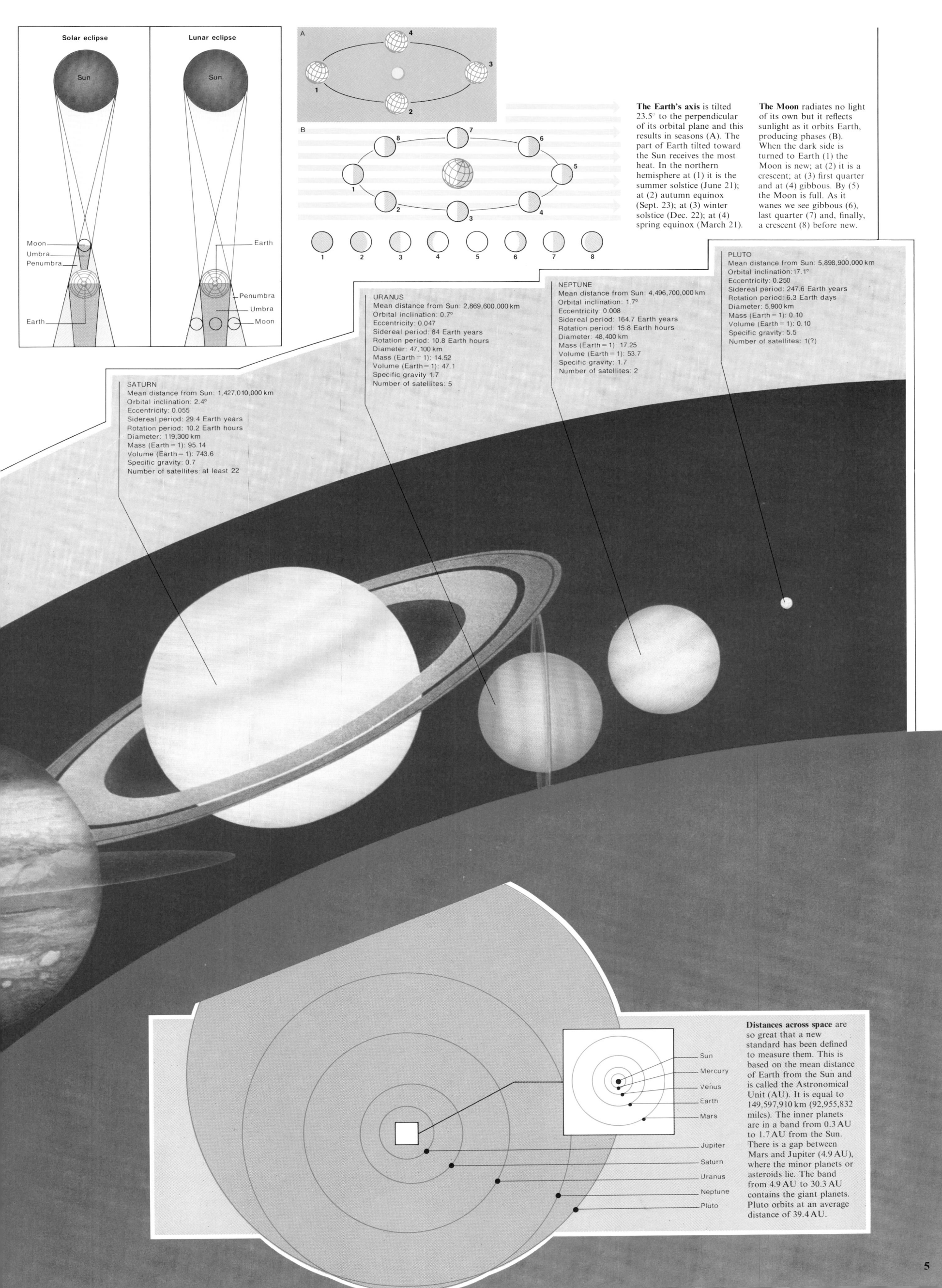

Solar eclipse

Sun

Moon
Umbra
Penumbra

Earth

Lunar eclipse

Sun

Earth

Penumbra
Umbra
Moon

A

4
3
1
2

B

8   7   6
1   5
2   4
3

1 2 3 4 5 6 7 8

The Earth's axis is tilted 23.5° to the perpendicular of its orbital plane and this results in seasons (A). The part of Earth tilted toward the Sun receives the most heat. In the northern hemisphere at (1) it is the summer solstice (June 21); at (2) autumn equinox (Sept. 23); at (3) winter solstice (Dec. 22); at (4) spring equinox (March 21).

The Moon radiates no light of its own but it reflects sunlight as it orbits Earth, producing phases (B). When the dark side is turned to Earth (1) the Moon is new; at (2) it is a crescent; at (3) first quarter and at (4) gibbous. By (5) the Moon is full. As it wanes we see gibbous (6), last quarter (7) and, finally, a crescent (8) before new.

PLUTO
Mean distance from Sun: 5,898,900,000 km
Orbital inclination: 17.1°
Eccentricity: 0.250
Sidereal period: 247.6 Earth years
Rotation period: 6.3 Earth days
Diameter: 5,900 km
Mass (Earth = 1): 0.10
Volume (Earth = 1): 0.10
Specific gravity: 5.5
Number of satellites: 1(?)

NEPTUNE
Mean distance from Sun: 4,496,700,000 km
Orbital inclination: 1.7°
Eccentricity: 0.008
Sidereal period: 164.7 Earth years
Rotation period: 15.8 Earth hours
Diameter: 48,400 km
Mass (Earth = 1): 17.25
Volume (Earth = 1): 53.7
Specific gravity: 1.7
Number of satellites: 2

URANUS
Mean distance from Sun: 2,869,600,000 km
Orbital inclination: 0.7°
Eccentricity: 0.047
Sidereal period: 84 Earth years
Rotation period: 10.8 Earth hours
Diameter: 47,100 km
Mass (Earth = 1): 14.52
Volume (Earth = 1): 47.1
Specific gravity 1.7
Number of satellites: 5

SATURN
Mean distance from Sun: 1,427,010,000 km
Orbital inclination: 2.4°
Eccentricity: 0.055
Sidereal period: 29.4 Earth years
Rotation period: 10.2 Earth hours
Diameter: 119,300 km
Mass (Earth = 1): 95.14
Volume (Earth = 1): 743.6
Specific gravity: 0.7
Number of satellites: at least 22

Sun
Mercury
Venus
Earth
Mars

Jupiter
Saturn
Uranus
Neptune
Pluto

Distances across space are so great that a new standard has been defined to measure them. This is based on the mean distance of Earth from the Sun and is called the Astronomical Unit (AU). It is equal to 149,597,910 km (92,955,832 miles). The inner planets are in a band from 0.3 AU to 1.7 AU from the Sun. There is a gap between Mars and Jupiter (4.9 AU), where the minor planets or asteroids lie. The band from 4.9 AU to 30.3 AU contains the giant planets. Pluto orbits at an average distance of 39.4 AU.

Earth as a Planet

Viewed from space, the Earth appears to be an ordinary member of the group of inner planets orbiting the Sun. But the Earth is unique in the Solar System because it has an atmosphere that contains oxygen. It is the nature of this surrounding blanket of air that has allowed higher life forms to evolve on Earth and provides their life-support system. At the same time the atmosphere acts as a shield to protect living things from the damaging effects of radiation from the Sun.

Any traces of gas that may have clung to the newly formed Earth were soon swept away into space by the heat of the Sun before it attained a stable state powered by nuclear fusion. Farther out in the Solar System, the Sun's heat was never strong enough to blow these gases away into space, so that even today the giant planets retain atmospheres composed of these primordial gases—mostly methane and ammonia.

The evolution of air
Until the Sun "settled down," Earth was a hot, airless ball of rock. The atmosphere and oceans—like the atmospheres of Venus and Mars—were produced by the "outgassing" of material from the hot interior of the planet as the crust cooled. Volcanoes erupted constantly and produced millions of tonnes of ash and lava. They also probably yielded, as they do today, great quantities of gas, chiefly carbon dioxide, and water vapor. A little nitrogen and various sulphur compounds were also released. Other things being equal, we would expect rocky planets, like the young Earth, to have atmospheres rich in carbon dioxide and water vapor. Venus and Mars do indeed have carbon dioxide atmospheres today, but the Earth now has a nitrogen/oxygen atmosphere. This results from the fact that life evolved on Earth, converting the carbon dioxide to oxygen and storing carbon in organic remains such as coal. Some carbon dioxide was also dissolved in the oceans. The Earth's oxygen atmosphere is a clear sign of life; the carbon dioxide atmospheres of Venus and Mars suggest the absence of life. Why did the Earth begin to evolve in a different way from the other inner planets?

When the Sun stabilized, Earth, Venus and Mars started off down the same evolutionary road, and carbon dioxide and water vapor were the chief constituents of the original atmospheres. On Venus the temperature was hot enough for the water to remain in a gaseous form, and both the water vapor and carbon dioxide in the Venusian atmosphere trapped heat by means of the so-called "greenhouse effect." In this process, radiant energy from the Sun passes through the atmospheric gases and warms the ground. The warmed ground re-radiates heat energy, but at infrared wavelengths, with the result that carbon dioxide and water molecules absorb it and stop it escaping from the planet. Instead of acting like a window, the atmosphere acts like a mirror for outgoing energy. As a result, the surface of Venus became hotter still. Today the surface temperature has stabilized at more than 500°C.

Mars, farther out from the Sun than Earth, was never hot enough for the greenhouse effect to dominate. The red planet once had a much thicker atmosphere than it does today, but, being smaller than the Earth, its gravity is too weak to retain a thick atmosphere. As a result, the planet cooled into a frozen desert as atmospheric gases escaped into space. Mars then, in fact, suffered a climatic change. At one time—hundreds of millions of years ago—there must have been running water because traces of old riverbeds still scar the Martian surface. Today, however, Mars has a thin atmosphere of carbon dioxide and surface temperatures below zero.

Earth—the ideal home
On Earth conditions were just right. Water stayed as a liquid and formed the oceans, while some carbon dioxide from outgassing went into the atmosphere, and some dissolved in the oceans. The resulting modest greenhouse effect

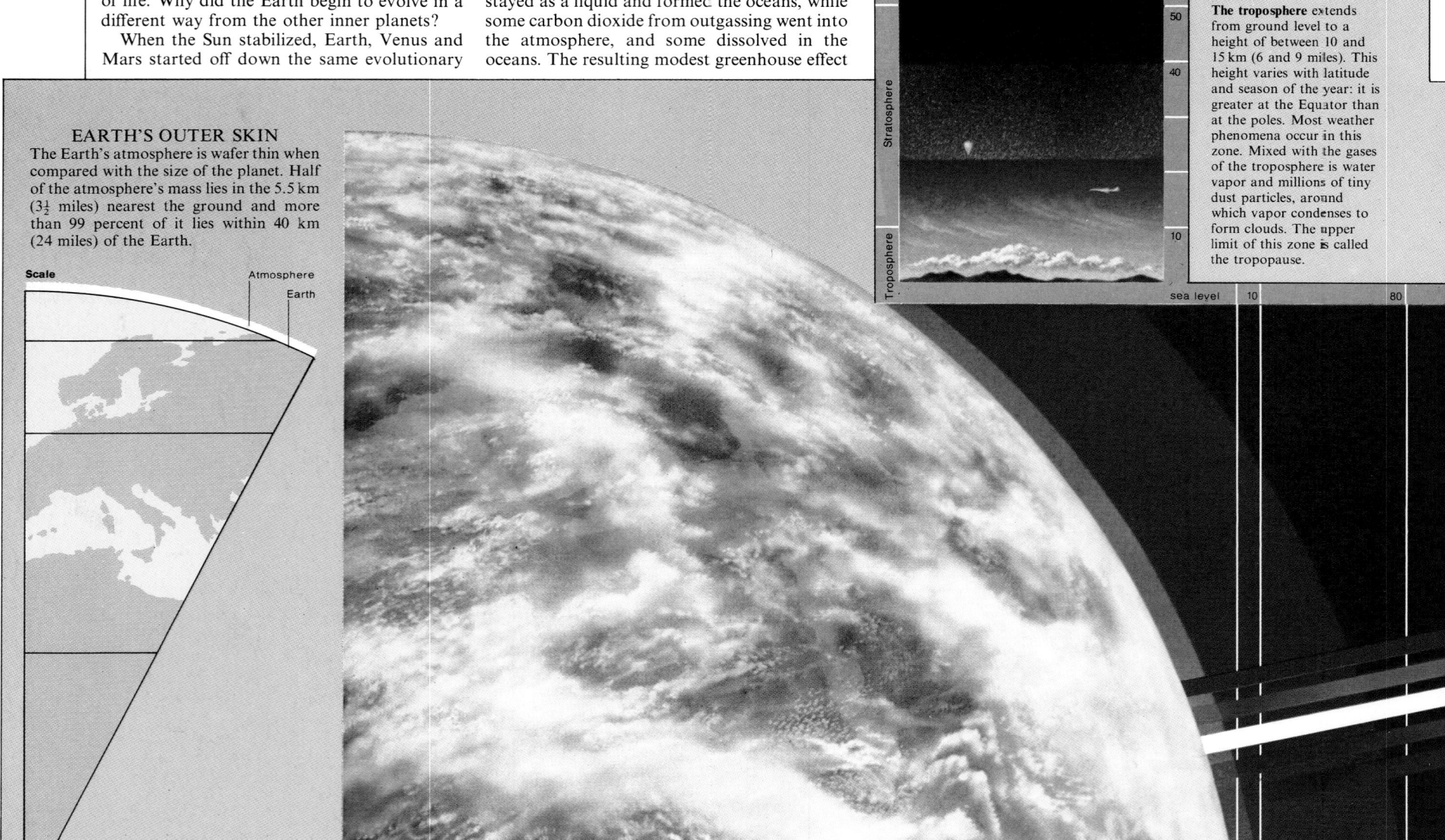

EARTH'S OUTER SKIN
The Earth's atmosphere is wafer thin when compared with the size of the planet. Half of the atmosphere's mass lies in the 5.5 km (3½ miles) nearest the ground and more than 99 percent of it lies within 40 km (24 miles) of the Earth.

Scale

Atmosphere

Earth

Earth's radius: 6,378 km

Earth reduced by 90% in proportion to this scale

210 km

160

Thermosphere

Mesosphere

Stratosphere

80

50

40

Troposphere

10

sea level   10   80

The **thermosphere** extends from 80 km (50 miles) up to 400 km (250 miles). Within this zone temperatures rise steadily with height to as much as 1,650°C (3,000°F), but the air is so thin that temperature is not a meaningful concept. At this height the air is mostly composed of nitrogen molecules to a height of 200 km (125 miles), when oxygen molecules become the dominant constituent.

The **mesosphere** is between 50 and 80 km (30 and 50 miles) above ground level. The stratopause is its lower limit and the mesopause its upper. This zone of the atmosphere is mainly distinguished by its ever decreasing temperatures and, unlike the stratosphere, it does not absorb solar energy.

The **stratosphere** is the level above the troposphere and extends as far as 50 km (30 miles). The chemical composition of the air up to this height is nearly constant and, in terms of volume, it is composed of nitrogen (78%) and oxygen (20%). The rest is mostly argon and other trace elements. The percentage of carbon dioxide (0.003) is small but crucial because this gas absorbs heat. There is virtually no water vapor or dust in this region of the atmosphere, but it does include the ozone layer, which is strongest between 20 km (12 miles) and 40 km (24 miles) high.

The **troposphere** extends from ground level to a height of between 10 and 15 km (6 and 9 miles). This height varies with latitude and season of the year: it is greater at the Equator than at the poles. Most weather phenomena occur in this zone. Mixed with the gases of the troposphere is water vapor and millions of tiny dust particles, around which vapor condenses to form clouds. The upper limit of this zone is called the tropopause.

Stratosphere and Mesosphere

Troposphere

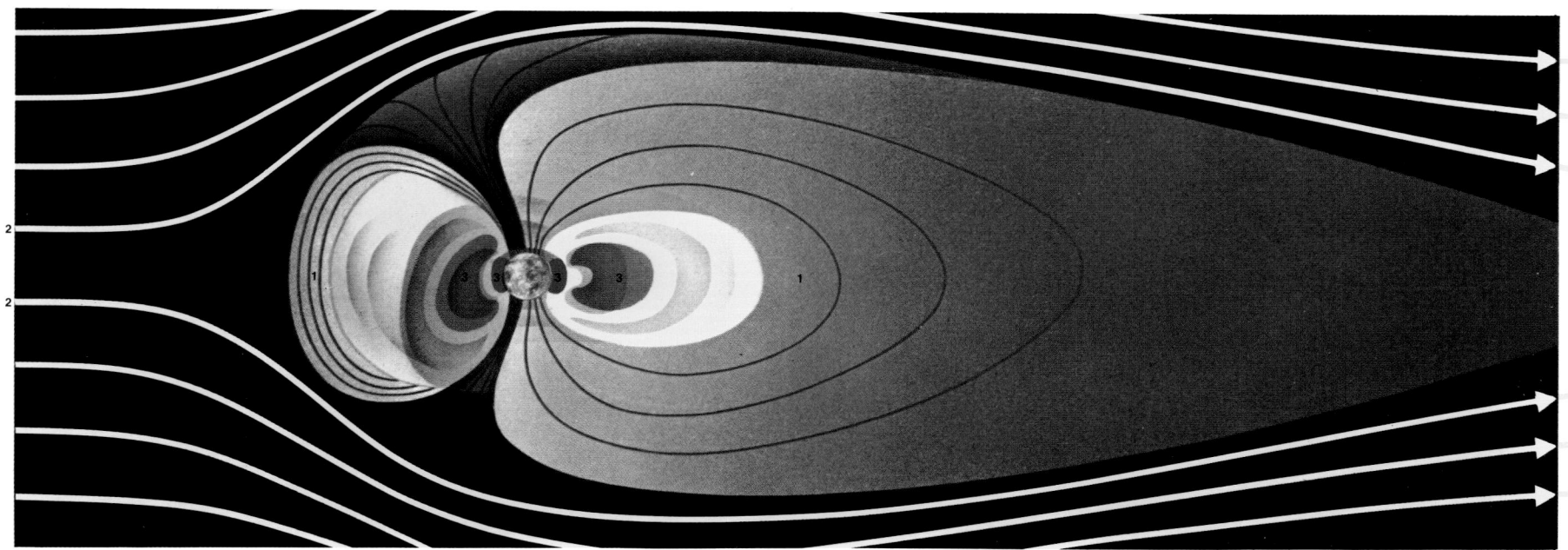

was compensated for by the formation of shiny white clouds of water droplets which reflected some of the Sun's radiation back into space. Our planet stabilized with an average temperature of 15°C. This proved ideal for the emergence of life, which evolved first in the seas and then moved onto land, converting carbon dioxide into oxygen as it did so.

In any view from space, planet Earth is dominated by water—in blue oceans and white clouds—and water is the key to life as we know it. Animal life—oxygen-breathing life—could only evolve after earlier forms of life had converted the atmosphere to an oxygen-rich state. The nature of the air today is a product of life as well as being vital to its existence.

An atmospheric layer cake

Starting at ground level, the first zone of the atmosphere is the troposphere, kept warm near the ground by the greenhouse effect but cooling to a chilly −60°C at an altitude of 15 km (9 miles). Above the troposphere is a warming layer, the stratosphere, in which energy from the Sun is absorbed and temperatures increase to reach 0°C at an altitude of 50 km (30 miles). The energy—in the form of ultraviolet radiation—is absorbed by molecules of ozone, a form of oxygen. Without the ozone layer in the atmosphere, ultraviolet rays would penetrate the

The Earth's magnetic field behaves as if there were a huge bar magnet placed inside the globe, with its magnetic axis tilted at a slight angle to the geographical north–south axis. The speed of rotation of the liquid core differs from that of the mantle, producing an effect like a dynamo (below). The region in which the magnetic field extends beyond the Earth is the magnetosphere (1). Streams of charged particles (2) from the Sun distort its shape into that of a teardrop. Zones of the magnetosphere include the Van Allen Belts (3), which are regions of intense radioactivity where magnetic particles are "trapped."

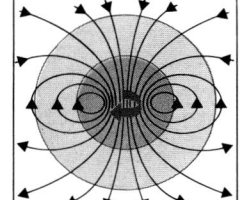

ground and sterilize the land surface: without life, there would be no oxygen from which an ozone layer could form.

Above the stratosphere, another cooling layer, the mesosphere, extends up to 80 km (50 miles), at which point the temperature has fallen to about −100°C. Above this level the gases of the atmosphere are so thin that the standard concept of temperature is no real guide to their behavior, and from the mesosphere outwards the atmosphere is best described in terms of its electrical properties.

In the outer layers of the atmosphere, the Sun's energy is absorbed by individual atoms in such a way that it strips electrons off them, leaving behind positively charged ions, which give the region its name—the ionosphere. A few hundred kilometers above the Earth's surface, gravity is so feeble that electromagnetic forces begin to determine the behavior of the charged particles, which are shepherded along the lines of force in the Earth's magnetic field. Above 500 km (300 miles), the magnetic field is so dominant that yet another region, the magnetosphere, is distinguished. This is the true boundary between Earth and interplanetary space.

The magnetosphere has been likened to the hull of "spaceship Earth." Charged particles (the solar wind) streaming out from the Sun are deflected around Earth by the magnetosphere

like water around a moving ship, while the region of the Earth's magnetic influence in space trails "downstream" away from the Sun like the wake of a ship. The Van Allen Belts, at altitudes of 3,000 and 15,000 km (1,850 and 9,300 miles) are regions of space high above the Equator where particles are trapped by the magnetic field. Particles spilling out of the belts spiral towards the polar regions of Earth, producing the spectacle of the auroras—the northern and southern lights. The Earth and Mercury are the only inner planets with magnetospheres such as this. The cause of the Earth's magnetism is almost certainly the planet's heavy molten core, which is composed of magnetic materials.

The Earth's atmosphere exhibits a great variety of characteristics on a vertical scale. As well as variations of temperature and the electrical properties of the air, there are differences in chemical composition—in the mixture of gases and water vapor—according to altitude. The Earth's gravitational pull means that air density and pressure decrease with altitude. Pressure of about 1,000 millibars at sea level falls to virtually nothing (10^{-42} millibars) by a height of 700 km (435 miles) above the Earth. All these factors, and their interrelationships, help to maintain the Earth's atmosphere as a protective outer covering or radiation shield and an essential life-support system.

The ionosphere is another name for the atmospheric layer beyond 80 km (50 miles). The region is best described in terms of the electrical properties of its constituents rather than by temperature. It is here that ionization occurs. Gamma and X-rays from the Sun are absorbed by atoms and molecules of nitrogen and oxygen and, as a result, each molecule or atom gives up one or more of its electrons, thus becoming a positively charged ion. These ions reflect radio waves and are used to bounce back radio waves transmitted from the surface of the Earth.

The exosphere is the layer above the thermosphere and it extends from 400 km (250 miles) up to about 700 km (435 miles), the point at which, it may be said, space begins. It is almost a complete vacuum because most of its atoms and molecules of oxygen escape the Earth's gravity.

The magnetosphere includes the exosphere, but it extends far beyond the atmosphere—to a distance of between 64,000 and 130,000 km (40,000 and 80,000 miles) above the Earth. It represents the Earth's external magnetic field and its outer limit is called the magnetopause.

The atmosphere protects the Earth from harmful solar radiation and also from bombardment by small particles from space. Most meteors (particles orbiting the Sun) burn up in the atmosphere, but meteorites (debris of minor planets) reach the ground. Of all incoming solar radiation, only visible light, radio waves and infrared rays reach the surface of Earth. X-rays are removed in the ionosphere, and ultraviolet and some infrared radiations are filtered out in the stratosphere. Studies of such radiations have, therefore, to be made from observatories in space.

| 160 | 240 | 320 | 400 | 480 | 560 | 640 | 720 kilometers |

Thermosphere/Ionosphere   Exosphere/Magnetosphere   Space

Man Looks at the Earth

Orbiting satellites keep a detailed watch on the Earth's land surface, oceans and atmosphere, feeding streams of data to meteorologists, geologists, oceanographers, farmers, fishermen and many others. Some information would be unobtainable by any other means. Surveys from orbit are quicker and less expensive than from aircraft, for example, because a satellite can scan a much larger area. And, surprisingly enough, certain features on the ground are easier to see from space.

Landsat (A) circles Earth 14 times every 24 hours at a height of 920 km (570 miles). Every 25 seconds it surveys 34 250 sq km (13,225 sq miles).

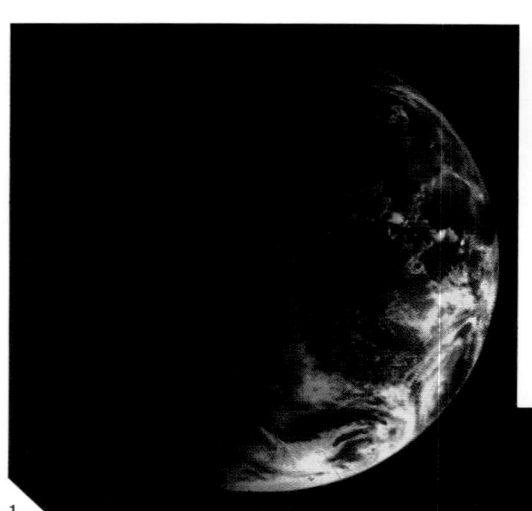

MAPPING AND MEASURING
Man has been looking at Earth from satellites since the beginning of the 1960s, and has firmly established the value of surveys from space to those engaged in a variety of earthly pursuits. Chief of these activities are resource management, ranging from monitoring the spread of deserts and river silting to locating likely mineral deposits; environmental protection, which includes observing delicate ecosystems and natural disasters; and a whole range of mapping and land-use planning.

Satellites give us a greater overview of numerous aspects of life on Earth than any earthbound eye could see.

Of all the information gleaned from satellites, accurate weather forecasts are of particular social and economic value. The first weather satellite was Tiros 1 (Television and Infrared Observation Satellite), launched by the United States in 1960. By the time Tiros 10 ceased operations in 1967, the series had sent back more than half a million photographs, firmly establishing the value of satellite imagery.

Tiros was superseded by the ESSA (Environmental Science Services Administration) and the NOAA (National Oceanic and Atmospheric Administration) satellites. These orbited the Earth from pole to pole, and they covered the entire globe during the course of a day. Other weather satellites, such as the European Meteosat, are placed in geostationary orbit over the Equator, which means they stay in one place and continually monitor a single large region.

Watching the weather
In addition to photographing clouds, weather satellites monitor the extent of snow and ice cover, and they measure the temperature of the oceans and the composition of the atmosphere. Information about the overall heat balance of our planet gives clues to long-term climatic change, and includes the effects on climate of human activities such as the burning of fossil fuels and deforestation.

Infrared sensors allow pictures to be taken at night as well as during the day. The temperature of cloud tops, measured by infrared devices, is a guide to the height of the clouds. In a typical infrared image, high clouds appear white because they are the coldest, lower clouds and land areas appear gray, and oceans and lakes are black. Information on humidity in the atmosphere is provided by sensors tuned to wavelengths between 5.5 and 7 micrometers, at which water vapor strongly absorbs the radiation.

To "see" inside clouds, where infrared and visible light cannot penetrate, satellites use sensors tuned to short-wavelength radio waves (microwaves) around the 1.5 centimeter wavelength. These sensors can reveal whether or not clouds will give rise to heavy rainfall, snow or hail. Microwave sensors are also useful for locating ice floes in polar regions, making use of the different microwave reflections from land ice, sea ice and open water.

Satellites that send out such pictures are in relatively low orbits, at a height of about 1,000 km (620 miles), and they pass over each part of the Earth once every 12 hours. But to build up a global model of the Earth's weather and climate, meteorologists need continual information on wind speed and direction at various levels in the atmosphere, together with temperature and humidity profiles. This data is provided by geostationary satellites. Cloud photographs taken every half-hour give information on winds, and computers combine this with temperature and humidity soundings to give as complete a model as is possible of the Earth's atmosphere.

Increasing attention is also being paid to the Earth's surface, notably by means of a series of satellites called Landsat (originally ERTS or Earth Resource Technology Satellites), the first of which was launched by the United States in 1972. The third and current Landsat is in a similar pole-to-pole orbit as the weather satellites, but its cameras are more powerful and they make more detailed surveys of the Earth. Landsat rephotographs each part of the Earth's surface every 18 days.

How to map resources
The satellite has two sensor systems: a television camera, which takes pictures of the Earth using visible light; and a device called a multispectral scanner, which scans the Earth at several distinct wavelengths, including visible light and infrared. Data from the various channels of the multispectral scanner can be combined to produce so-called false-color images, in which each wavelength band is assigned a color (not necessarily its real one) to emphasize features of interest.

An important use of Landsat photographs is for making maps, particularly of large countries with remote areas that have never been adequately surveyed from the ground. Several countries, including Brazil, Canada and China, have set up ground stations to receive Landsat data directly. Features previously unknown or incorrectly mapped, including rivers, lakes and glaciers, show up readily on Landsat images. Urban mapping and hence planning are aided by satellite pictures that can distinguish areas of industry, housing and open parkland.

Landsat photographs have also proved invaluable for agricultural land-use planning.

They are used for estimates of soil types and for determining land-use patterns. Areas of crop disease or dying vegetation are detectable by their different colors. Yields of certain crops such as wheat can now be accurately predicted from satellite imagery, so that at last it is becoming possible to keep track of the worldwide production of vital food crops. Fresh water, too, is one of our most valuable resources, and knowing its sources and seasonal variation is vital to irrigation projects.

Finally, the geologist and mineral prospector have benefited from remote sensing. Features such as fault lines and different types of sediments and rocks show up clearly on Landsat pictures. This allows geologists to select promising areas in which the prospector can look for mineral deposits.

Another way to study the Earth is by bouncing radar beams off it. Radar sensing indicates the nature of soil or rock on land and movement of water at sea, for example. This was not done by Landsat, but by equipment aboard the United States' Skylab and by a short-lived American satellite called Seasat. The former Soviet Union included Earth surveying in its Salyut program, and resource mapping is also a feature of the spacelab aboard the American space shuttle. All these activities help man to manage the limited resources on our planet and to preserve the environment.

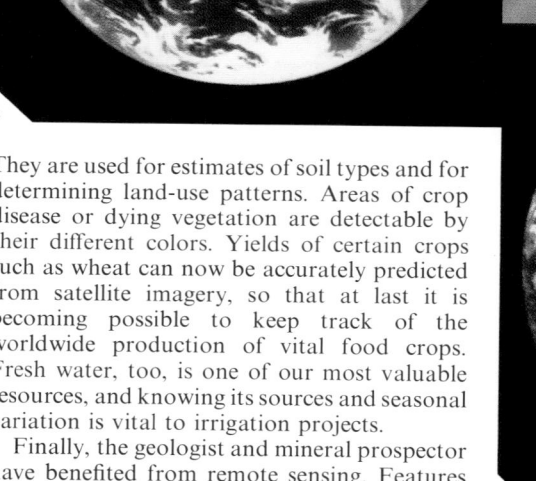

A **multispectral scanner** (B) has an oscillating mirror (1) that focuses visible and near infrared radiation on to a detector (2). This converts the intensity of the radiation into a voltage. An electronics unit (3) turns the voltage pattern into a series of digitized numbers that can be fed into a computer.

The numbers (C) are then transmitted back to a receiving station (D) as a radio frequency at the rate of 15 million units a second. The numbers are translated back into the digital voltage pattern and converted by computer (E) into the equivalent binary numbers, each of which represents a color.

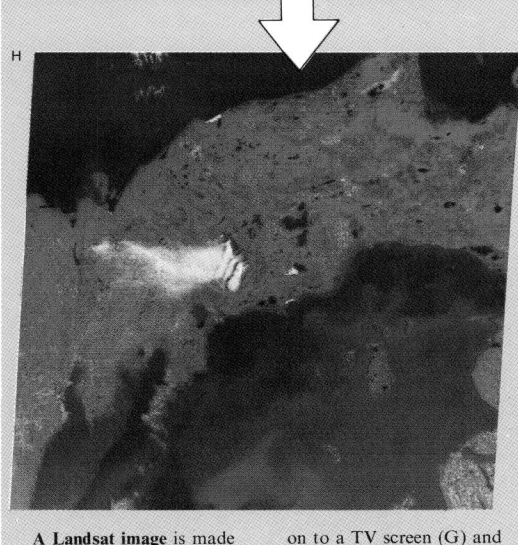

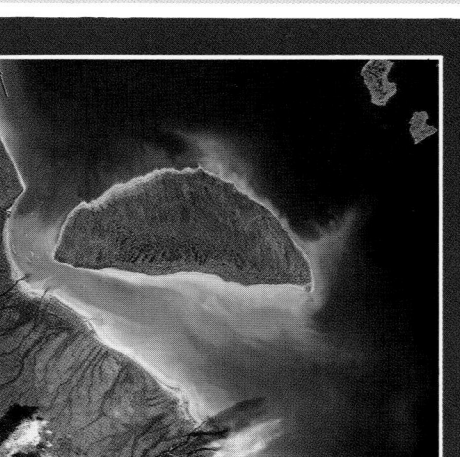
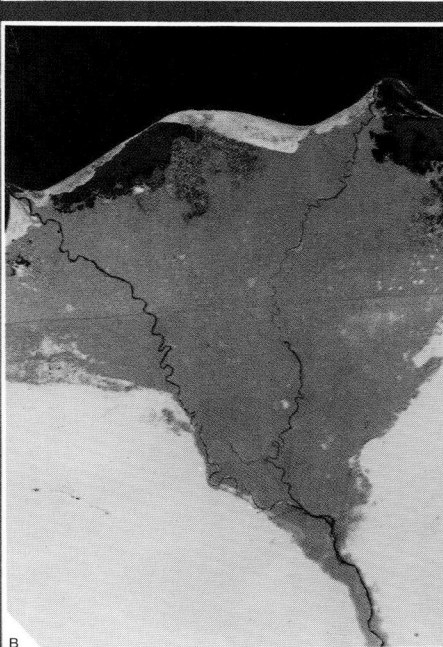

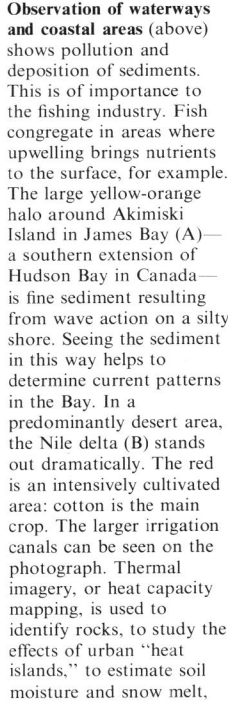

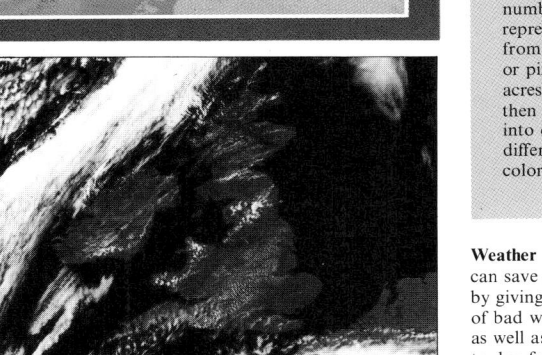
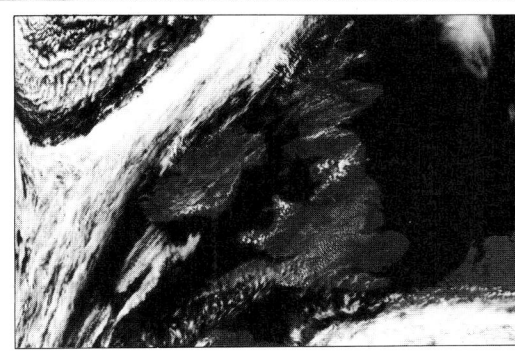

A Landsat image is made up of very many points, each of which is obtained by means of the procedure described above. Each number in the image (F) represents the radiation from a small area of land, or pixel, 0.44 hectares (1.1 acres) in size. A computer then translates the numbers into different colors, or different shades of one color, which are projected on to a TV screen (G) and the image is seen for the first time. Finally, photographs of this false-color image are produced (H). This picture, showing a forest fire in the Upper Peninsula, Michigan, is of use to those engaged in forest management. Other satellite data of use in forestry include types of trees, patterns of growth and the spread of disease.

Observation of waterways and coastal areas (above) shows pollution and deposition of sediments. This is of importance to the fishing industry. Fish congregate in areas where upwelling brings nutrients to the surface, for example. The large yellow-orange halo around Akimiski Island in James Bay (A)— a southern extension of Hudson Bay in Canada— is fine sediment resulting from wave action on a silty shore. Seeing the sediment in this way helps to determine current patterns in the Bay. In a predominantly desert area, the Nile delta (B) stands out dramatically. The red is an intensively cultivated area: cotton is the main crop. The larger irrigation canals can be seen on the photograph. Thermal imagery, or heat capacity mapping, is used to identify rocks, to study the effects of urban "heat islands," to estimate soil moisture and snow melt,

and to map shallow ground water. In this photograph of the northeast coast of North America (C) purple represents the coldest temperatures—in Lakes Erie and Ontario. The coldest parts of the Atlantic Ocean are deep blue, whereas warmer waters near the coast are light blue. Green is the warmer land, but also the Gulf Stream in the lower right part of the image. Brown, yellow and orange represent successively warmer land surface areas. Red is hot regions around cities and coal-mining regions found in eastern Pennsylvania (to the upper left of center in the picture); and, finally, gray and white are the very hottest areas—the urban heat islands of Baltimore, Philadelphia and New York City. Black areas in the upper left are cold clouds. The temperature range of the image is about 30°C (55°F).

Weather satellite imagery can save lives and property by giving advance warning of bad weather conditions, as well as providing day-to-day forecasts. This Tiros image (left) shows a cold front moving west of Ireland with low-level wave clouds over southern and central England. There are low-pressure systems over northern France and to the northwest of Ireland.

The Earth seen from space shows phases just like the Moon, Mercury and Venus do to us. These dramatic photographs were taken from a satellite moving at 35,885 km (22,300 miles) above South America at 7.30 am (1), 10.30 am (2), noon (3), 3.30 pm (4) and at 10.30 pm (5), and clearly show the Earth in phase.

LANDSAT AND THE FARMER

sown	grows		dormant				grows			ripe	harvest
Sep	Oct	Nov	Dec	Jan	Feb	Mar	Apr	May	Jun	Jul	Aug

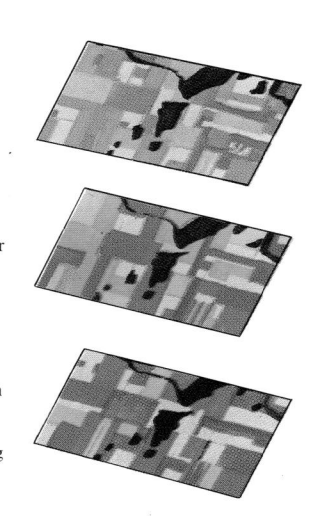

Agriculturists benefit from "multitemporal analysis" by satellites (left). This is the comparison of data from the same field recorded on two or more dates. It is also able to differentiate crops, which may have an identical appearance, or signature, on one day, but on another occasion exhibit different rates of growth. The pattern of growth is different for small grains than most other crops. A "biowindow" is the period of time in which vegetation is observed. These three biowindows (right) show the emergence and ripening (light blue to red to dark blue) of wheat in May, July and August.

Part 2

MAKING AND SHAPING THE EARTH

The structure and substance of the Earth
Forces that move continents · Forces that fashion Earth's landscapes
How man has changed the face of the Earth

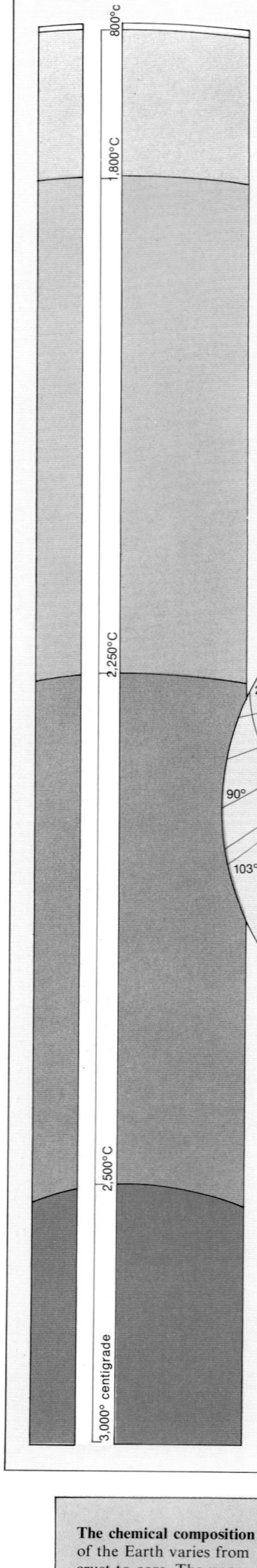

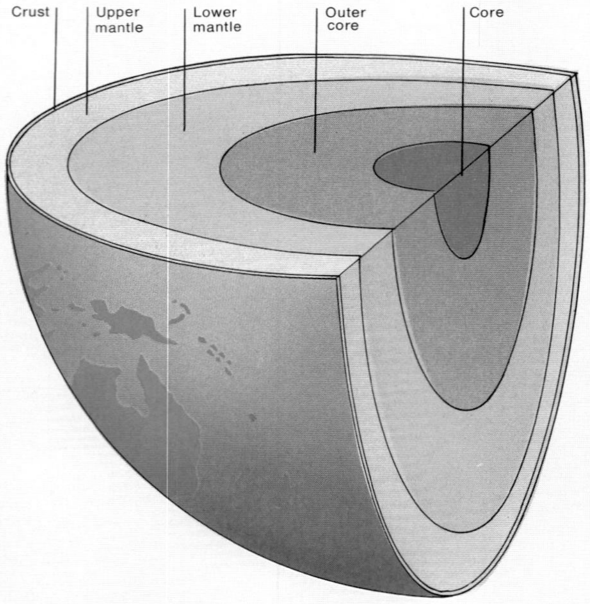

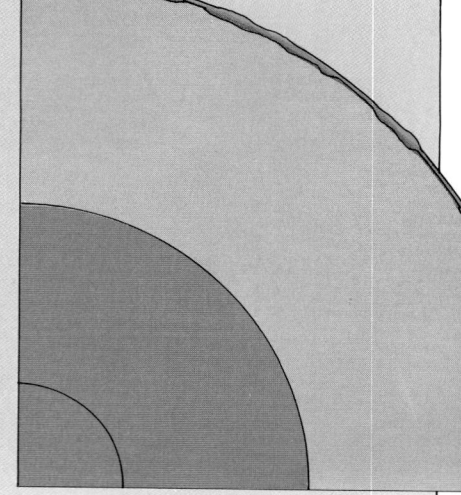

Crust | Upper mantle | Lower mantle | Outer core | Core

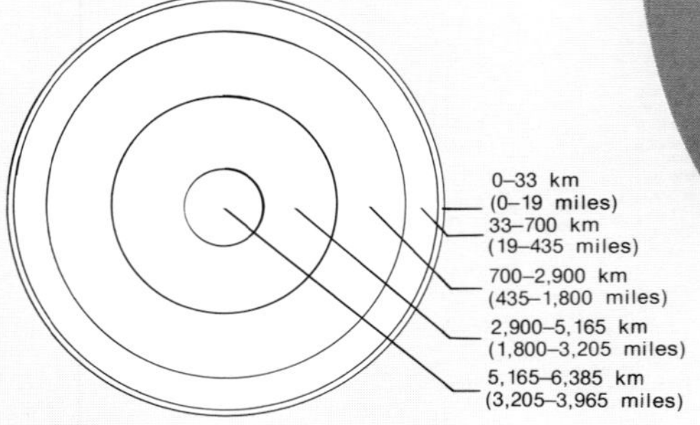

0–33 km
(0–19 miles)
33–700 km
(19–435 miles)
700–2,900 km
(435–1,800 miles)
2,900–5,165 km
(1,800–3,205 miles)
5,165–6,385 km
(3,205–3,965 miles)

The internal structure of the Earth, in its simplest form, is composed of a crust, a mantle with an upper and lower layer, and a core, which has an inner region. Temperatures in the Earth increase with depth, as is observed in a deep mine shaft or bore-hole, but the prediction of temperatures within the Earth is made difficult by the fact that different rocks conduct heat at different rates: rock salt, for example, has 10 times the heat conductivity of coal. Also, estimates have to take into account the abundance of heat-generating atoms in a rock. Radioactive atoms are concentrated toward the Earth's surface so the planet has, in effect, a thermal blanket to keep it warm. The temperature at the center of the Earth is believed to be approximately 3,000°C (5,400°F).

A NEW GEOLOGY

A revolution in geological thinking during the first half of this century transformed man's ideas about the structure of the planet Earth. The science of palaeomagnetism, which studies the magnetic properties of rocks and the history of the Earth's magnetic field, and later the new science of marine geology, contributed greatly to the refinement of theories such as continental drift. Man has even looked beyond the Earth for knowledge of this planet's innermost depths.

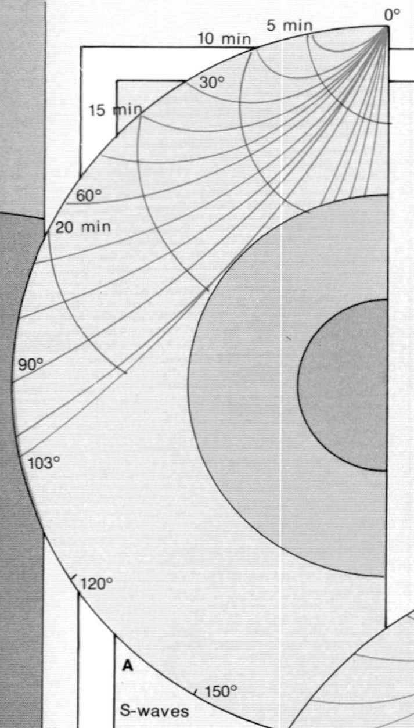

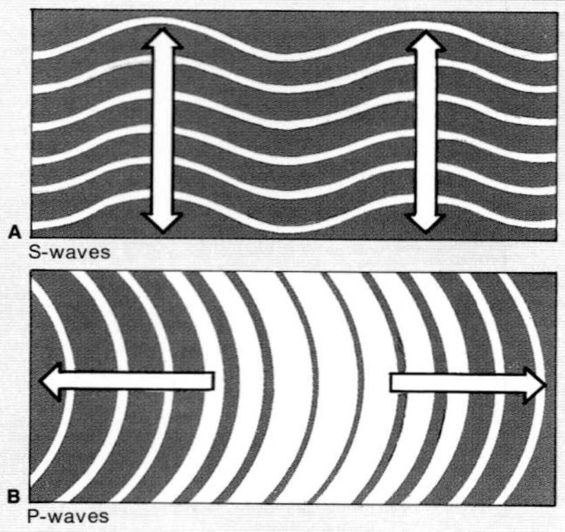

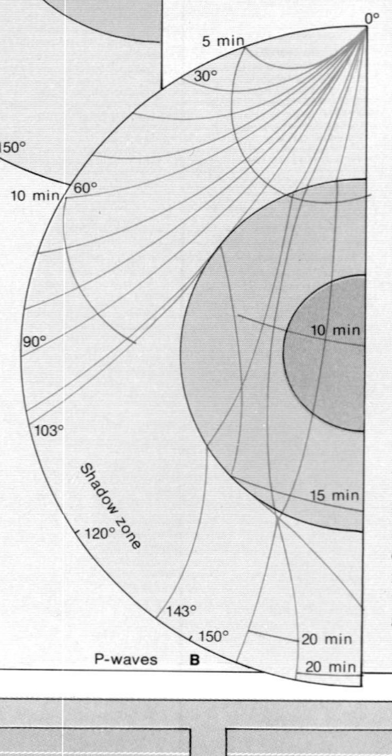

800°C
1,800°C
2,250°C
2,500°C
3,000° centigrade

S-waves

P-waves

A
S-waves

B
P-waves

By plotting the pathways of shock waves propagated by an earthquake it is possible to construct a kind of X-ray picture of the Earth's interior. Seismic waves (blue lines) travel at different speeds through materials of different density. (Red lines represent distance traveled by waves during certain time intervals.) Secondary, shear or S-waves cause particles of rock to vibrate vertically. Primary, or P-waves are compressional and cause rock movement backwards and forwards. S-waves can only pass through solids (as can be seen in A) whereas P-waves pass through gases, liquids and solids (as seen in B). They increase in speed as they pass through the denser mantle and core. The region where no earthquake waves reach the surface is an earthquake shadow zone.

Shadow zone

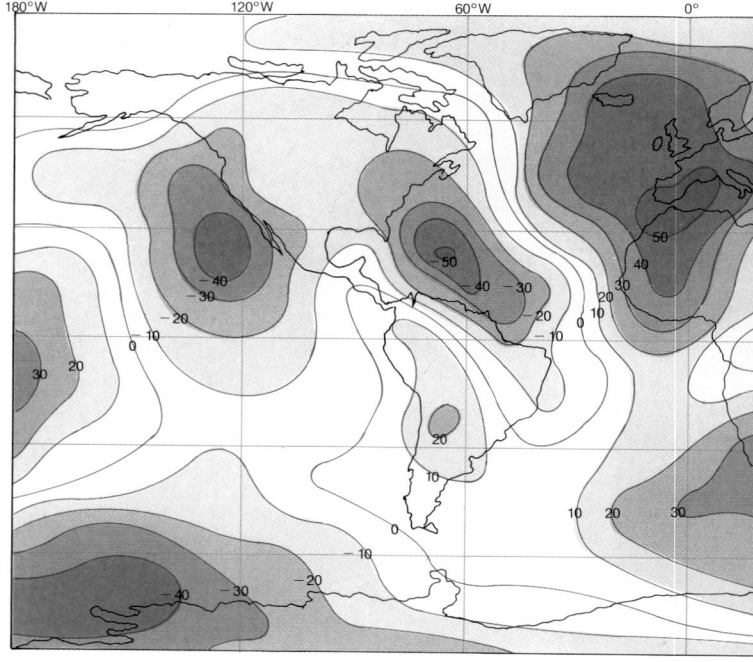

180°W | 120°W | 60°W | 0°

A Silicon
B Aluminum
C Iron
D Calcium
E Magnesium
F Nickel
G Other

The chemical composition of the Earth varies from crust to core. The upper crust of continents (sial) is mainly granite, rich in aluminum and silicon, whereas oceanic crust (sima) is largely basalt, made of magnesium and silicon. The mantle is composed of rocks that are rich in magnesium and iron silicates, whereas the core, it is believed, is made of iron and nickel oxides.

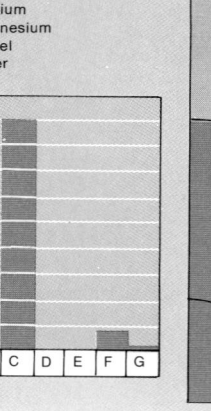

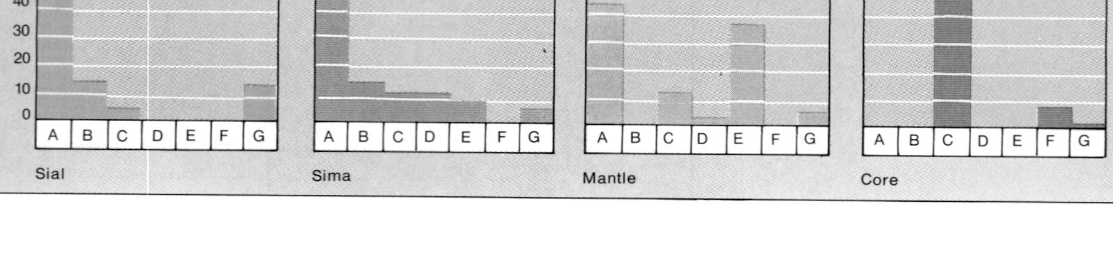

Sial | Sima | Mantle | Core

%
90
80
70
60
50
40
30
20
10

A B C D E F G

Earth's Structure

The Earth is made up of concentric shells of different kinds of material. Immediately beneath us is the crust; below that is the mantle; and at the center of the globe is the core. Knowledge of the internal structure of Earth is the key to an understanding of the substances of Earth and an appreciation of the forces at work, not only deep in the center of the planet but also affecting the formation of surface features and large-scale landscapes. The workings of all these elements are inextricably linked.

A 17th-century diagram of the Earth shows an internal structure of fire and subterranean rivers.

Our knowledge of the Earth is largely restricted to the outer crust. The deepest hole that man has drilled reaches only 10 km (6 miles)—less than 1/600th of the planet's radius—and so our knowledge about the rest of the Earth has had to come via indirect means: by the study of earthquake waves, and a comparison between rocks on Earth and those that make up meteorites—small fragments of asteroids and other minor planetary bodies that originated from similar materials to the Earth.

The Earth's crust
The outermost layer of the Earth is called the crust. The crust beneath the oceans is different from the material that makes up continental crust. Ocean crust is formed at mid-ocean ridges where melted rocks (magma) from the mantle rise up in great quantities and solidify to form a layer a few kilometers thick over the mantle. As this ocean crust spreads out from the ridge it becomes covered with deep-ocean sediments. The ocean crust was initially called "sima," a word made up from the first two letters of the characteristic elements—silicon and magnesium. Sima has a density of 2.9 gm/cc (1 gm/cc is the density of water).

Continental crust was named "sial"—from silicon and aluminum, the most abundant elements. Sial is lighter than sima with a density of 2.7 gm/cc. The continental crust is like a series of giant rafts, 17 to 70 km (9–43 miles) thick. As a result of numerous collisions and breakages, these continental rafts have been bulldozed into their present shape, but they have been forming for at least 4,000 million years. The oldest known rocks, in Greenland, are 3,750 million years old, which is only about 800 million years younger than the Earth itself. The complex history of the continents' evolution over this vast time span makes construction of an ideal cross section difficult, but the rocks of the lower two-thirds of the crust appear to be denser (2.9 gm/cc) than the upper levels.

The Moho, or Mohorovičić discontinuity, discovered in 1909, marks the base of the crust and the beginning of the mantle rocks, where the density increases from 2.9 to 3.3 gm/cc. The Moho is at an average depth of 10 km (6 miles) under the sea and 35 km (20 miles) below land.

The mantle
Our knowledge of the mantle comes from mantle rocks that are sometimes brought to the surface. These are even more enriched in magnesium oxides than the sima, with lesser amounts of iron and calcium oxides. The uppermost mantle to a depth of between 60 and 100 km (40–60 miles), together with the overlying crust, forms the rigid lithosphere, which is divided into plates. Below this is a pasty layer, or asthenosphere, extending to a depth of 700 km (435 miles). The upper mantle is separated from the lower mantle by another discontinuity where the density of the rock increases from 3.3 to 4.3 gm/cc.

Scientists now believe that the mantle is the planetary motor force behind the movements of the continents. By studying in detail the chemistry of the volcanic rocks that have come directly from the mantle, they have gathered much information about this mantle motor. The rocks that come up along oceanic ridges and form new oceanic crust reveal by their chemical composition that they have formed from mantle that has undergone previous melting. By contrast, islands such as Hawaii and Iceland have formed from mantle material that, for the most part, has never been melted before. One explanation for these chemical observations is that, while the top 700 km (435 miles) of the mantle region is moving in accordance with movement of the plates, the mantle beneath it is moving independently and sending occasional rivers of unaltered material through the surface to form islands like volcanic Hawaii.

The core
Structurally, the most important boundary in the Earth lies at a depth of 2,900 km (1,800 miles) below the surface, where the rock density almost doubles from about 5.5 to 9.9 gm/cc. This is known as the Gutenberg discontinuity and was discovered in 1914. Below this level the material must have the properties of a liquid since certain earthquake waves cannot penetrate it. Scientists infer from the composition of meteorites, some of which are composed of iron and nickel, that this deep core material is composed largely of iron, with some nickel and perhaps lighter elements such as silicon. The processes involved in the formation of a planet have been compared to the separation of the metals (the core) from the slag (the mantle and crust) in a blast furnace.

The core has a radius of 3,485 km (2,165 miles) and makes up only one-sixth of the Earth's volume, yet it has one-third of its mass. In the middle of the liquid outer core there is an even denser ball with a radius of 1,220 km (760 miles)—two-thirds the size of the Moon—where, under intense pressure, the metals have solidified. The inner core is believed to be solid iron and nickel and is 20 percent denser (12–13 gm/cc) than the surrounding liquid.

Electric currents in the core are the only possible source of the Earth's magnetic field. This drifts and alters in a way which could arise only from some deeply buried fluid movement. At the top of the core, the pattern of the field moves about 100 m (330 ft) west each day. Every million years or so during the Earth's history, the north–south magnetic poles have switched so that compasses pointed south, not north.

The dynamo that generates magnetism and its strange variations is still not fully understood. Motion in the core may be powered by giant slabs of metal that crystallize out from the liquid and sink to join the inner core. Our knowledge of the Earth's structure has increased greatly over the last 50 years, but many intriguing questions remain to be answered.

The Earth is not a sphere but an ellipsoid (below) that is flattened at the poles, where the radius is 6,378 km (3,960 miles), and bulging at the Equator, where the radius is 6,536 km (4,060 miles). This results from the Earth's rapid rotation. But, rather than a perfect ellipsoid, the true shape is a "geoid"—the actual shape of sea level—which is lumpy, with variations away from ellipsoid of up to 80 m (260 ft) (left). This reflects major variations in density in Earth's outer layers.

60°E   120°E   180°E

The Earth as a Geoid

The Earth's magnetic field is strongest at the poles and weakest in equatorial regions. If the field were simply like a bar magnet inside the globe, lines of intensity would mirror lines of latitude; but the field is inclined at an angle of 11° to the Earth's axis. The geomagnetic poles are similarly inclined and they do not coincide with the geographic poles. In reality, the field is much more complex than that of a bar magnet. In addition, over long periods of time, the magnetic poles and the north–south orientation of the field change slowly. The strength of the Earth's magnetic field is measured in units called oersteds.

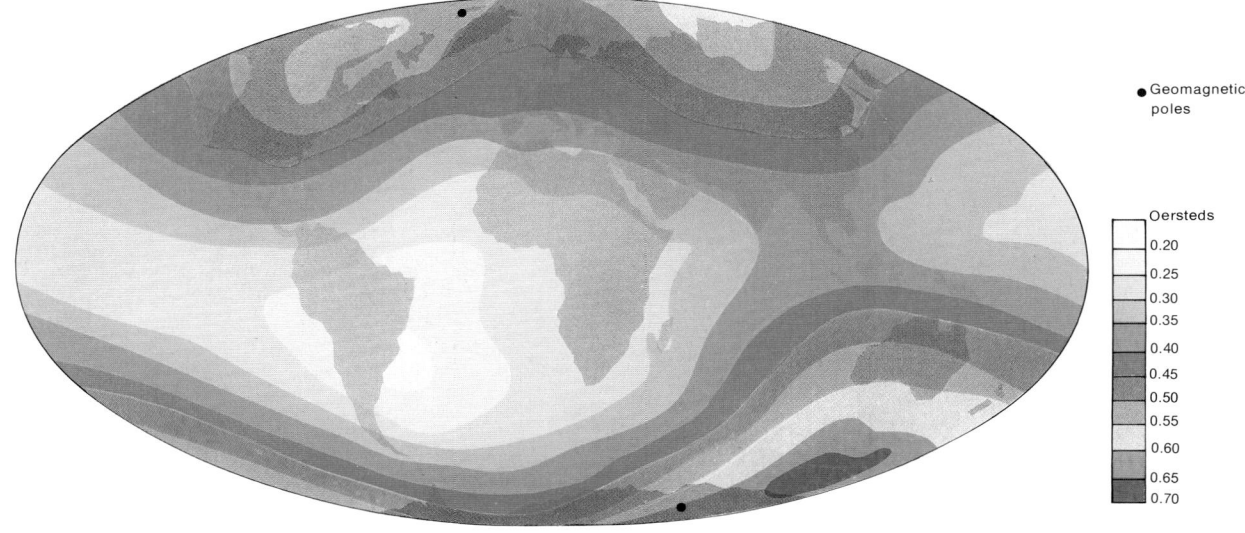

● Geomagnetic poles

Oersteds
0.20
0.25
0.30
0.35
0.40
0.45
0.50
0.55
0.60
0.65
0.70

Earth's Moving Crust

The top layer of the Earth is known as the lithosphere and is composed of the crust and the uppermost mantle. It is divided into six major rigid plates and several smaller platelets that move relative to each other, driven by movements that lie deep in the Earth's liquid mantle. The plate boundaries correspond to the zones of earthquakes and the sites of active volcanoes. The concept of plate tectonics – that the Earth's crust is mobile despite being rigid – emerged in the 1960s and helped to confirm the early twentieth-century theory of continental drift proposed by Alfred Wegener.

THE DYNAMIC EARTH
As early as the 17th century, the English philosopher Francis Bacon noted that the coasts on either side of the Atlantic were similar and could be fitted together like pieces of a jigsaw puzzle. Three hundred years later Alfred Wegener proposed the theory of continental drift, but no one would believe the Earth's rigid crust could move. Today, geological evidence has provided the basis for the theory of plate tectonics, which demonstrates that the Earth's crust is slowly but continually moving.

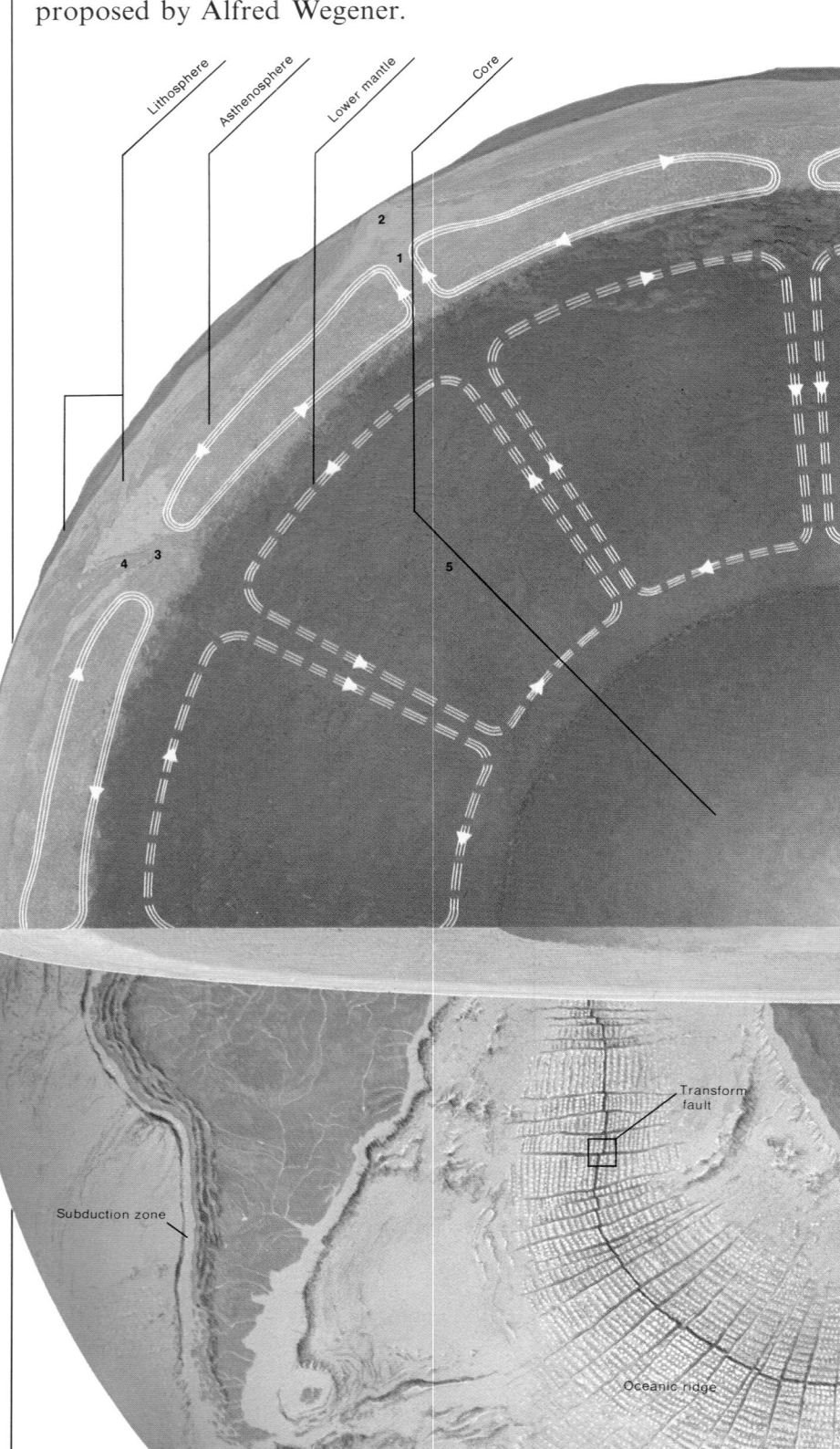

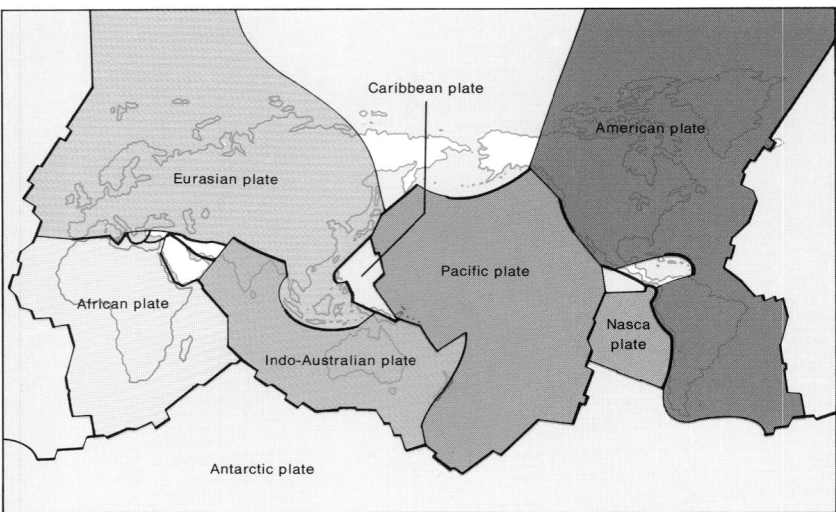

Earth's lithosphere—the rocky shell, or crust—is made up of six major plates and several smaller platelets, each separated from each other by ridges, subduction zones or transcurrent faults. The plates grow bigger by accretion along the mid-ocean ridges, are destroyed at subduction zones beneath the trenches, and slide beside each other along the transcurrent faults. The African and Antarctic plates have no trenches along their borders to destroy any of their crust, so they are growing bigger. This growth is compensated by the subduction zone that is developing to the north of the Tonga Islands and subduction zones in the Pacific. Conversely, the Pacific and Indo-Australian plates are shrinking. Along the plate boundaries magma wells up from the mantle to form volcanoes. Here, too, are the origins of earthquakes as the plates collide or slide slowly past each other.

The motor that drives the lithospheric plates is found deep in the mantle. The simplified model at the top of the globe shows how this may work. Due to temperature differences in the mantle, slow convection currents circulate. Where two current cycles move upwards together and separate (1), the plates bulge and move apart along mid-ocean ridges (2). Where there is a downward moving current (3), the plates move together and sometimes one slips under the other to form a subduction zone (4). Another model proposes that the convection currents are found deep in the mantle (5). Only time and more research, however, will reveal the true mechanism of plate movement.

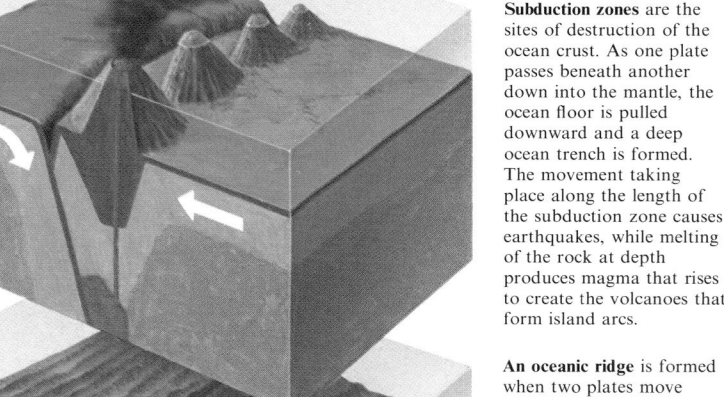

Subduction zones are the sites of destruction of the ocean crust. As one plate passes beneath another down into the mantle, the ocean floor is pulled downward and a deep ocean trench is formed. The movement taking place along the length of the subduction zone causes earthquakes, while melting of the rock at depth produces magma that rises to create the volcanoes that form island arcs.

An oceanic ridge is formed when two plates move away from each other. As they move, molten magma from the mantle forces its way to the surface. This magma cools and is in turn injected with new magma. Thus the oceanic ridge is gradually forming the newest part of Earth's crust.

Transform, or transcurrent, faults are found where two plates slide past each other. They may, for example, link two parts of a ridge (A, B). A study of the magnetic properties of the seabed may suggest a motion shown by the white arrows, but the true movements of the plates are shown by the red arrows. The transform fault is active only between points (2) and (3). Between points (1) and (2) and between (3) and (4) the scar of the fault is healed and the line of the fault is no longer a plate boundary.

The early evidence for continental drift was gathered by Alfred Wegener, a German meteorologist. He noticed that the coastlines on each side of the Atlantic Ocean could be made to fit together, and that much of the geological history of the flanking continents—shown by fossils, structures and past climates—also seemed to match. Wegener compared the two sides of the Atlantic with a sheet of torn newspaper and reasoned that if not just one line of print but 10 lines match then there is a good case for arguing that the two sides were once joined. Yet for 50 years continental drift was generally considered to be a fanciful dream.

Seafloor spreading
In the 1950s the first geological surveys of the oceans began, and a 60,000 km (37,200 mile) long chain of mountains was discovered running down the center of the Atlantic Ocean, all round the Antarctic, up to the Indian Ocean, into the Red Sea and up the Eastern Pacific Ocean into Alaska. Along the axis of this mid-ocean ridge system there was often a narrow, deep rift valley. In places this ridge was offset along sharp fractures in the ocean floor.

The breakthrough in developing the global plate tectonic theory came with the first large-scale survey of the ocean floor. Magnetometers, which were developed during World War II for tracking submarines, showed the ocean floor to be magnetically striped. The ocean floor reveals magnetic characteristics because the ocean crust basalts are full of tiny crystals of the magnetic mineral magnetite. As the basalt cooled, the magnetic field of these crystals aligned itself with the Earth's magnetic field. This would be insignificant if it were not for the fact that the magnetic pole of the Earth has switched from north to south at different times in the past. Half the magnetite compasses of the ocean floor point south rather than north.

In the middle 1960s, two Cambridge geophysicists, Drummond Matthews and Fred Vine, noticed that the pattern of stripes was symmetrical around the mid-ocean ridge. Such an extraordinary and unlikely symmetry could mean only one thing—any two matching stripes must originally have been formed together at the mid-ocean ridge and then moved away from each other as newer crust formed between them to create new stripes. It was soon calculated that the North Atlantic Ocean was growing wider by about 2 cm ($\frac{3}{4}$ in) a year. At last, drifting continents was accepted.

Consumption of the seafloor
Seafloor spreading soon became included in an even more sensational model—plate tectonics. If the oceans are growing wider, then either the whole planet is expanding or the spreading ocean floor is consumed elsewhere. In the late 1950s a global network of seismic stations had been set up to monitor nuclear explosions and earthquakes. For the first time the positions of all earthquakes could be accurately defined.

It was found that the zones of earthquake activity were predominantly narrow, following the mid-ocean ridges and extending along the rim of the Pacific, beneath the island arcs of the

West Pacific and beneath the continental margins in the East Pacific as well as underlying the Alpine-Himalayan Mountain Belt. The seismic zones around the Pacific dipped away from the ocean and continued to depths as great as 700 km (430 miles). They intercepted the surface at the curious arc-shaped deep-ocean trenches. It had been known for 20 years that the pull of gravity over these trenches is strangely reduced, so to survive they must continually be dragged downwards. Here was the site of ocean-floor consumption—now known as a subduction zone. Subduction zones must be efficient at consuming ocean crust because no known ocean crust is older than 200 million years—less than five percent of Earth's lifetime.

The oceanic lithosphere (the Earth's rocky crust) is extraordinarily rigid. Even where the oceanic lithosphere becomes consumed within subduction zones it still maintains its rigidity. As it bends down into the Earth it tends to corrugate, forming very long folds. These corrugations give rise to the pattern of chains of deep-ocean trenches and chains of volcanic islands formed above the subduction zone.

As oceanic lithosphere grows older it cools, contracts and sinks. From the depth of the ocean floor it is possible to make an accurate estimate of the age of the crust beneath. Even the steepness of the subduction zone is a function of the age, and therefore the density, of the lithosphere. The oldest crust provides the strongest downward pull and hence the steepest angle of dip of the subduction zone.

As well as the spreading ridges (constructive margins) and the subduction zones (destructive margins) there is another kind of plate boundary (conservative margins), where the plates slip past one another along a major fault such as the San Andreas Fault of California.

The past positions of the continents
Continental drift is thus the result of the creation and destruction of oceanic lithosphere, but only the continents can record the oceanic plate motions taking place more than 200 million years ago. The discovery of ancient lines of subduction zone volcanoes can testify to the destruction of long-gone oceans. One particularly important technique for finding the positions of the continents is to study the magnetism of certain rocks, particularly lavas, that record the position of the north–south magnetic poles at the time when the rock cooled. If the rock "compass" points, for example, west, then the continent must have rotated by 90°. The vertical dip of the rock compass can reveal the approximate latitude of the rock at its formation (the dip increases from horizontal at the Equator to vertical at the magnetic poles).

As longitude is entirely arbitrary (defined on the position of Greenwich) one can only hope to gain the relative positions of the continents with regard to one another. The best additional information is provided by studies of fossils—if the remains of shallow-water marine organisms are very different they must have been separated by an ocean. The full impact of continental drift on the development of land animals and plants is only beginning to be realized.

THE DRIFTING CONTINENTS
It is now accepted that the continents have changed their positions during the past millions of years, and by studying the magnetism preserved in the rocks the configuration of the continents has been plotted for various geological times. The sequence of continental drifting, illustrated below, begins with one single landmass—the so-called supercontinent Pangaea—and the ancestral Pacific Ocean, called the Panthalassa Ocean. Pangaea first split into a northern landmass called Laurasia and a southern block called Gondwanaland, and subsequently into the continents we see today. The maps illustrate the positions of the continents in the past, where they are now and their predicted positions in 50 million years' time.

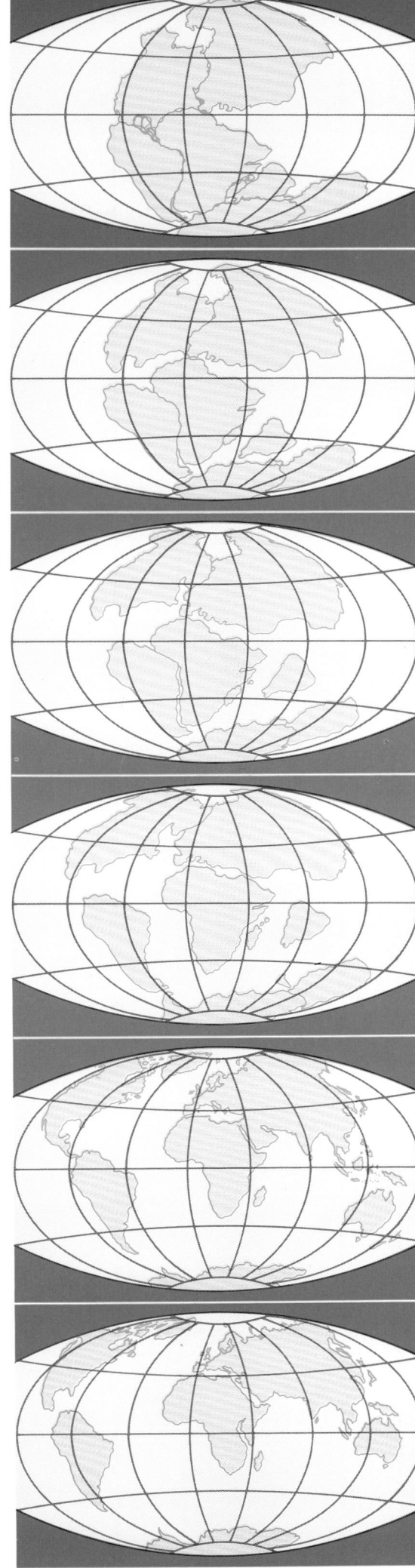

225 million years ago one large landmass, the supercontinent Pangaea, exists and Panthalassa forms the ancestral Pacific Ocean. The Tethys Sea separates Eurasia and Africa and forms an ancestor of the Mediterranean Sea.

180 million years ago Pangaea splits up, the northern block of continents, Laurasia, drifts northwards and the southern block, Gondwanaland, begins to break up. India separates and the South American–African block divides from Australia–Antarctica. New ocean floor is created between the continents.

135 million years ago the Indian plate continues its northward drift and Eurasia rotates to begin to close the eastern end of the Tethys Sea. The North Atlantic and the Indian Ocean have opened up and the South Atlantic is just beginning to form.

65 million years ago Madagascar has split from Africa and the Tethys Sea has closed, with the Mediterranean Sea opening behind it. The South Atlantic Ocean has opened up considerably, but Australia is still joined to the Antarctic and India is about to collide with Asia.

The present day: India has completed its northward migration and collided with Asia, Australia has set itself free from Antarctica, and North America has freed itself from Eurasia to leave Greenland between them. During the past 65 million years (a relatively short geological span of time) nearly half of the present-day ocean floor has been created.

50 million years in the future, Australia may continue its northward drift, part of East Africa will separate from the mainland, and California west of the San Andreas Fault will separate from North America and move northwards. The Pacific Ocean will become smaller, compensating for the increase in size of both the Atlantic and Indian oceans. The Mediterranean Sea will disappear as Africa moves to the north.

Magnetic surveys of the seabed helped build the plate tectonics theory. Research vessels equipped with magnetometers sailed back and forth over a mid-ocean ridge and recorded the varying magnetism of the seabed. The Earth's magnetic pole has switched from north to south at different times in the past, and this mapping revealed a striped magnetic pattern on the seabed. It was noticed that the stripes on either side of the ridge were symmetrical. The explanation was that the matching stripes must have formed together and moved apart as more crust was injected between them—a notion that was subsequently supported by dating of the seafloor.

3   2   1   0   1   3

Time in millions of years

Folds, Faults and Mountain Chains

The continents are great rafts of lighter rock that float in the mantle of the Earth. When drifting continents collide, great mountain chains are thrown up as the continental crust is forced to thicken to absorb the impact of the collision. The highest mountains are formed out of thick piles of sediment that are built up from the debris of erosion constantly washed off the land and deposited on the continental margins. Through the massive deformations of rock faults and folds these remains of old mountains become recycled, thus building new mountains from the remains of old ones.

For the formation of mountain ranges such as the Appalachians or the Himalayas, or the Caledonian mountain chain of Norway, Scotland and Newfoundland, the pattern of development is very much the same. First, a widening ocean with passive margins is located between two continents.

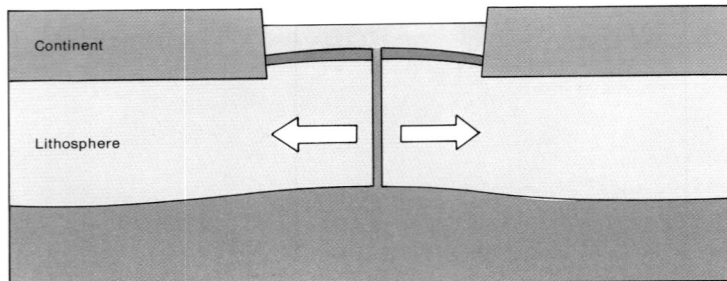

As more ocean floor is created the continents move farther apart, and at the edge of each continent sediment accumulates from the debris of erosion. These piles of thick sediment are known as sedimentary basins.

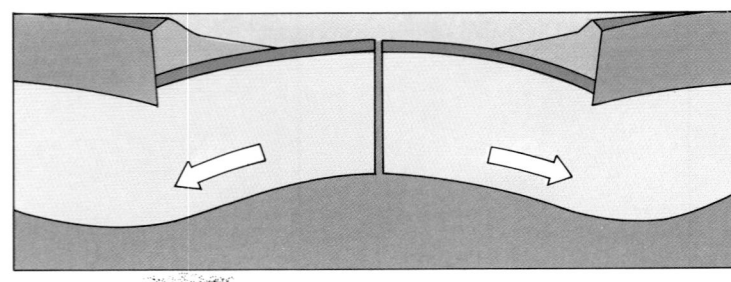

For the formation of the Appalachians, the ancestral Atlantic Ocean began to close, a subduction zone was formed at the ocean–continent boundary, and the oceanic lithosphere began to be absorbed into the mantle. Magma intruded to form granite "plutons" and volcanoes, and much of the sedimentary basin was metamorphosed.

The ocean continued to close until North America and Africa were joined together, further compressing the sediments in the sedimentary basin at the passive ocean margin. The two continents were joined like this between 350 and 225 million years ago.

About 180 million years ago, after the original Appalachians had been worn down in size, the present Atlantic Ocean opened along a new break in the continental crust, offset from the line of the original mountains. As the continents split, so the crust became stretched along great curved faults.

Parts of the ancient Appalachian mountains have been eroded to sea level, leaving the Appalachians, that formed on the edge of the old continent, inland.

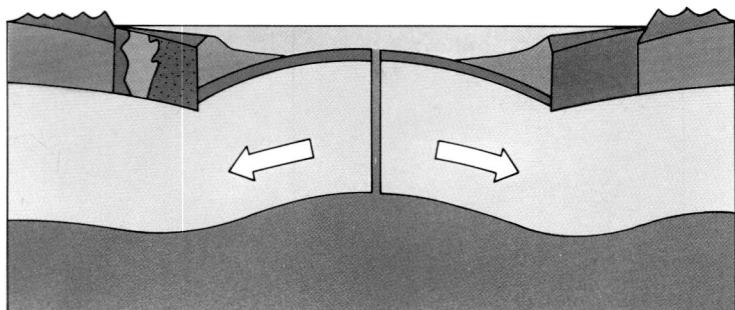

- Continental shelf
- Granite
- Metamorphic rock
- Sediment
- Ocean crust

BIRTH AND DEATH OF A MOUNTAIN

Mountains are thrust upward by the pressure exerted by the moving plates of the Earth's crust, and are formed out of the sediments that have been eroded from the continental masses. Young mountains are lofty and much folded, but the agents of erosion and weathering soon begin to reduce their height, and over many millions of years the mountain range is eroded to sea level. This eroded material accumulates in the sea at the edge of the continents and becomes the building material for another phase of mountain building.

ISOSTASY

The continents float in the Earth's mantle, and because they are only slightly less dense (2.67 g/cc compared to 3.27 g/cc), 85% of their bulk lies below sea level. Thus the higher the mountain the deeper the mountain root. And as the crust can exist only to a maximum depth of about 70 km (43 miles) before it is liquefied in the mantle, mountains can never rise above a maximum of 10 km (6 miles) above sea level.

Folds are generally related to underlying faults. The commonest simple folds are monoclines, formed when a single fault exhibits underlying movement. With continued movement a simple symmetrical anticline (1) may fold unevenly to form an asymmetric anticline (2). More movement bends the strata further into a recumbent fold (3) and eventually the strata break to form an overthrust fold (4). Over a long period an overthrust fold may be pushed many kilometers from its original position to form a nappe (5). Faults are generally of three kinds: faults of tension known as normal faults, when one block drops down (6); faults of horizontal shear (7), known as strike-slip faults; and faults of compression (8), known as thrust faults.

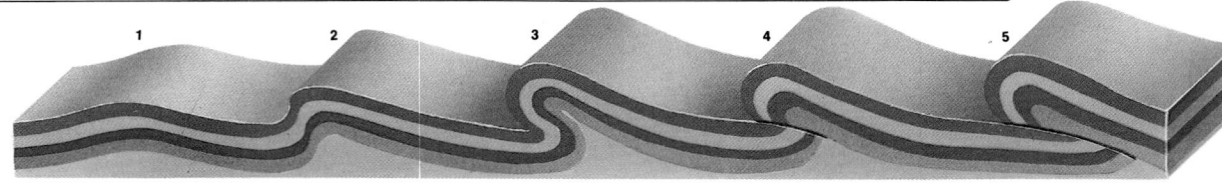

Continents float in the Earth's mantle like icebergs in the sea—more than four-fifths of their bulk lies beneath the surface. The continental crust is 28 km (17 miles) thick at sea level, and where mountains rise above this level there is a corresponding thickening in the crust beneath. The maximum thickness of crust is 70 km (43 miles), so mountains can only ever rise to a maximum height of approximately 10 km (6 miles) above sea level. This relation between upper and underlying crust is known as isostasy, or state of equal pressure.

As mountains become eroded, the process of isostatic rebound allows them to recover about 85 cm (34 in) for every 1 meter (40 in) removed. When, after about 100 million years, a major mountain range has been eroded down to sea level, the rocks exposed at the surface are those that were 15–25 km (9–15 miles) underground when the mountains were at their highest. Such rocks are coarsely crystalline, and make up the fabric of the old, tough continental crust.

Sedimentary basins

As early as the nineteenth century it was noticed that the biggest mountains formed where there had previously been the thickest pile of sediments. According to the principle of isostasy, a thick pile of sediments can form only where the Earth's crust is thin and sinking. The Aegean Sea in the eastern Mediterranean, for example, is at present being pulled apart, and therefore becoming thinner. Over the next few million years, as the Aegean crust sinks, a thick pile of sediments—a sedimentary basin—will accumulate. Most sedimentary basins are at present shallow seas, and form the continental shelves. The depth of water over these shelf seas has been determined by the erosion that accompanied the lowest sea levels of the past 100 million years—about 140 m (460 ft) below the present sea level.

Mountain building

When continents collide, it is the regions of stretched crust that are the first to absorb some of the impact. Such a former sedimentary basin is being turned into the Zagros Mountains of southwestern Iran as Arabia advances northeastward into Asia. The individual blocks of continental crust appear to be sliding back along curved faults, and the sediments that have built up over the thinned crust are now being forced into folds.

Early in the life of such a sedimentary basin sea water may become cut off from the ocean and evaporate to form extensive deposits of salt. Such salt deposits reduce friction and allow the folded pile of sediments overlying the continental blocks to become disconnected and to slide up to 100 km (62 miles) away from the collision zone. In the Zagros Mountains this process has only just begun, but in older mountain ranges, such as the Canadian Rockies or the European Alps, the formation of nappes—disconnected sediment piles forced ahead of the main compression zone—has been widespread.

As mountain ranges often form out of the sedimentary basins along the boundaries between a continent and the ocean, new mountains tend to add on to the fringes of the continents. In North America, for example, the oldest remnants of ranges that make up large tracts of the Canadian shield are found in the center of the continent, while the process of mountain building is continuing in the west.

Other continents show a more complex pattern of mountain ranges through subsequent phases of splitting and amalgamation, and the Himalayas and the Urals have formed where smaller continents have come together to make up the continent of Asia.

The boundary between the continent and the ocean along the western coast of the Atlantic Ocean is not a plate boundary and is therefore termed passive, in contrast to active boundaries such as the eastern coast of the Pacific Ocean, where the ocean plate is moving down into the mantle at a subduction zone beneath the Andean mountain chain. The highest Andean mountains are tall volcanoes of andesite (formed from magmas pouring off the underlying subduction zone). The bulk of the mountain range consists of enormous underground batholiths, in which the magma has solidified before being able to erupt, and compressed and uplifted sedimentary basins formed along the continental margin.

The crustal region immediately beyond the volcanoes that form above subduction zones, however, is very often in tension and in the process of being pulled apart. This appears to be caused by mantle material being dragged down with the oceanic lithosphere. Small ocean basins, such as the Sea of Japan, may open up under such conditions.

Folds and faults

When movement of the Earth's crust has taken place along a planar fracture through sedimentary rocks, it can be easily identified by the breaks in the layers, and such planes of movement are known as faults. Folds form where rock layers bend rather than break. Generally, faults form when rocks are brittle, and folds are found when rocks are plastic.

Sediments close to the surface are often so soft that they behave plastically, as do rocks at depths greater than 15–20 km (9–12 miles), where the continental crust is of sufficiently high temperature and pressure for slow rock flow to take place. Thus most continental faults are found between these levels. All major folds found in soft sediments apparently have a fault of some kind beneath them, and it is the failure of the fault to pass right through to the surface that creates the fold.

Folds are often extremely complicated and some geologists have tended to describe them in extraordinary detail, but in fact they are little more than brush strokes in the overall picture. Pre-existing faults beneath the folds tend to determine the folds' orientation. Once a continental fault has formed, it provides a plane of weakness wherever the continental crust is subject to stress. Many faults around the Mediterranean Sea came into existence during a period of tension, and these are now being reactivated and produce the large earthquakes associated with the continuing collision of Africa with Europe.

At the end of all the complications and intricacies of continental collision, the final phase of mountain building—that involving uplift—remains perhaps the least understood. In the last two million years, for example, while man has been increasingly active on Earth, 2,500,000 sq km (almost 1,000,000 sq miles) of Tibet has risen 4,000 m (2 miles). But the origin of such gigantic and rapid movement lies within the Earth's mantle.

The highest mountains are the product of continental collisions. As the rocks are squeezed, folded and faulted, the original continental crust becomes shortened and thickened. Although the overall extent and height of mountain chains is controlled by mountain building, the whole range can only be viewed from a spacecraft. For the earthbound mountain visitor the familiar shapes of peaks and valleys are those formed by mountain destruction (1). Snow at high altitudes consolidates to form ice that moves slowly downhill in the form of glaciers. To wear away a mountain range at an average of 5 km (3 miles) above sea level requires the removal of more than 20 km (12 miles) of rock, as the thick continental crust that floats in the underlying mantle rises to compensate for the loss of surface mass. Half-eroded mountains (2), such as the Appalachians, pictured above, may linger on for tens of millions of years until, like large regions of the Canadian interior, the mountains are all eroded away and only the hard crystalline surface rocks that were once buried 20 km (12 miles) underground remain (3).

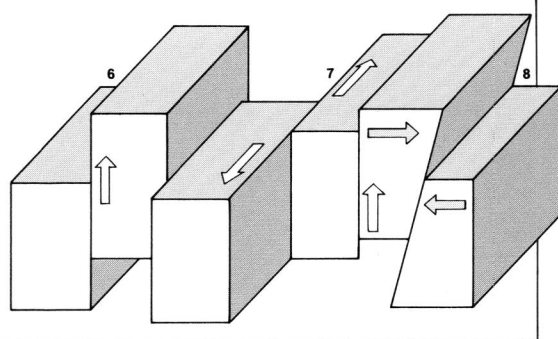

Rock Formation and History

All the rocks on Earth are interrelated through the rock cycle – a never-ending chain of processes that forms and modifies rocks and minerals on the Earth's surface, in its crust and in the mantle. These events are powered both by energy from the Sun and the heat of the Earth itself, and the processes include the forces of nature – from wind and water to the movements of the continents. This geological cycle of creation and destruction is one of the most distinctive features of our planet. Each feature of geological activity, each agent of landscape-making is but a stage of the continuing rock cycle.

CONSTANT CHANGE

The processes of formation and destruction of the three basic rock types—igneous, sedimentary and metamorphic—are linked in an interminable cycle of change. Igneous rocks are thrown up from inside the Earth, are eroded and eventually laid down as sediments. As accumulated sediments sink into the Earth, they are changed by heat and pressure—metamorphosed—before surfacing again in the processes of mountain building.

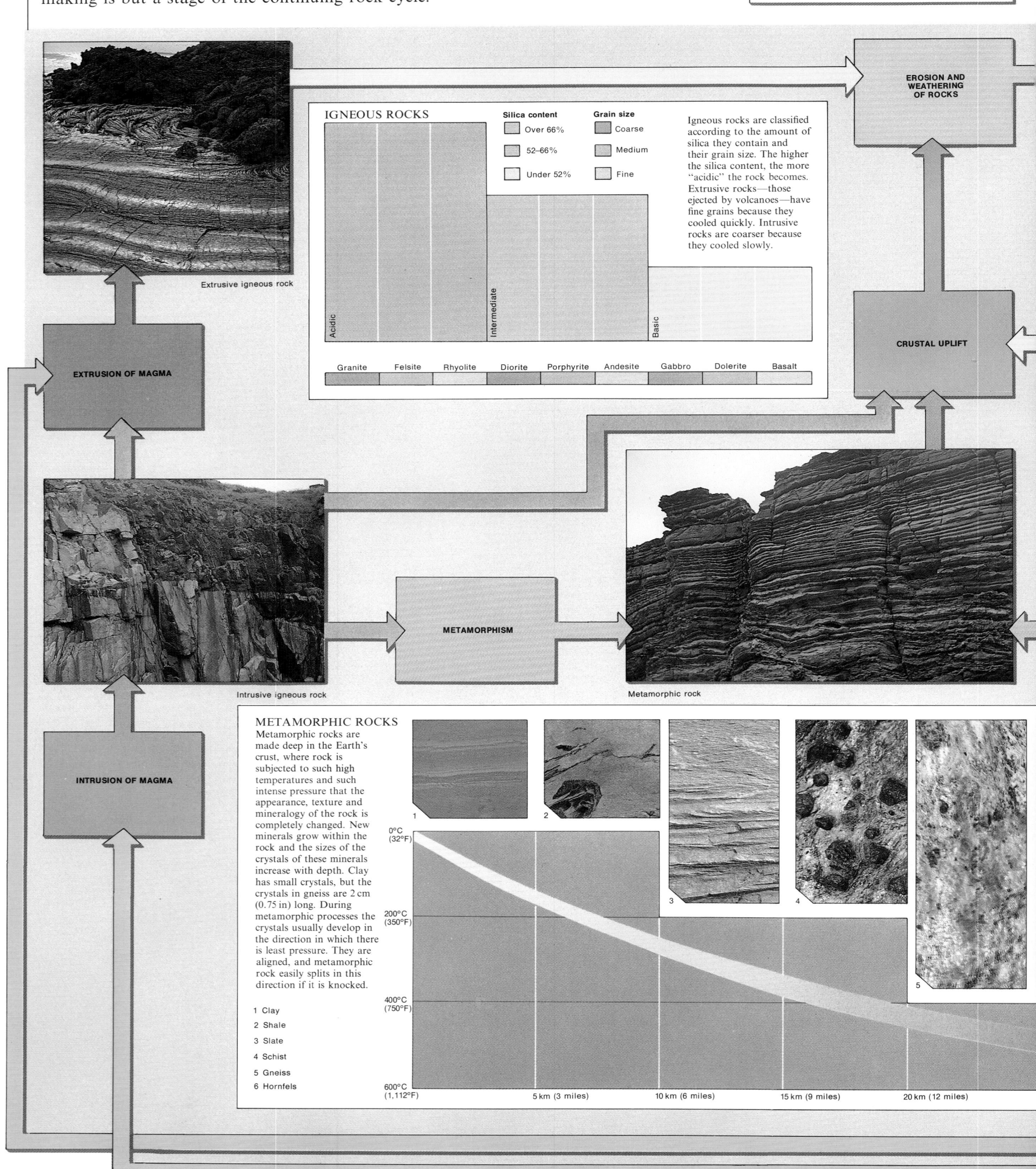

Extrusive igneous rock

EROSION AND WEATHERING OF ROCKS

EXTRUSION OF MAGMA

IGNEOUS ROCKS

Silica content
- Over 66%
- 52–66%
- Under 52%

Grain size
- Coarse
- Medium
- Fine

Igneous rocks are classified according to the amount of silica they contain and their grain size. The higher the silica content, the more "acidic" the rock becomes. Extrusive rocks—those ejected by volcanoes—have fine grains because they cooled quickly. Intrusive rocks are coarser because they cooled slowly.

Acidic — Intermediate — Basic

Granite | Felsite | Rhyolite | Diorite | Porphyrite | Andesite | Gabbro | Dolerite | Basalt

CRUSTAL UPLIFT

INTRUSION OF MAGMA

Intrusive igneous rock

METAMORPHISM

Metamorphic rock

METAMORPHIC ROCKS

Metamorphic rocks are made deep in the Earth's crust, where rock is subjected to such high temperatures and such intense pressure that the appearance, texture and mineralogy of the rock is completely changed. New minerals grow within the rock and the sizes of the crystals of these minerals increase with depth. Clay has small crystals, but the crystals in gneiss are 2 cm (0.75 in) long. During metamorphic processes the crystals usually develop in the direction in which there is least pressure. They are aligned, and metamorphic rock easily splits in this direction if it is knocked.

1 Clay
2 Shale
3 Slate
4 Schist
5 Gneiss
6 Hornfels

0°C (32°F)
200°C (350°F)
400°C (750°F)
600°C (1,112°F)

5 km (3 miles) | 10 km (6 miles) | 15 km (9 miles) | 20 km (12 miles)

SEDIMENTARY ROCKS

Sediments can be turned into rock by means of three main processes. Cementation is the term used when water percolates between grains of sand. As it does so, any iron oxide, silica or calcium carbonate that were in solution are deposited in thin layers around the grains, thus cementing them into a hard sandstone (1). As more sediment is laid down, the increasing weight of the sediments on top exerts pressure on the underlying layers. Water is squeezed out and a dense rock is formed (2) by the process of compaction. This is the way clay becomes mudstone. Finally, during mountain-building processes forces are exerted on rock minerals that cause them to recrystallize into a solid mass of rock (3) that has no spaces between its mineral constituents.

Sedimentary rock

25 km (15 miles)   30 km (18 miles)

All the rocks on Earth are formed at one stage or another in what is known as the rock cycle. All high ground on the continents suffers erosion; the eroded material is transported and deposited on lower ground; in time, these sediments may be elevated by mountain-building processes and so, in turn, become eroded. If, between their formation and destruction, sediments pass deep into the Earth's crust, they may be transformed by heat or pressure into metamorphic rock; or, at even greater depths, they may melt to form yet another kind of rock—igneous rock.

Materials at the bottom of a thick pile of sediments may be heated enough to melt. If this material then cools and solidifies underground, it is called plutonic rock. Sometimes, however, it escapes to the surface by means of a short cut—a volcano—to become part of the rock cycle. On the other hand, some sediments are lost off the edge of the continents on to the deep ocean floor, and they disappear into the mantle of the Earth by means of the downward movements of the oceanic crust. A measure of the difference between the input and the output of the continental rock cycle is a measure of how fast the continental crust is increasing or decreasing. Scientists believe it is increasing—at a rate of between 0.1 and 1.0 cu km a year.

Types of rock

The range of rock types found on the continents has been classified under three headings: sedimentary, igneous and metamorphic. Sedimentary rocks include all those formed at low temperatures on the Earth's surface; igneous rocks have all solidified from molten rock, or magma; and metamorphic rocks are sedimentary or igneous rocks that have changed their nature under conditions of high temperature and pressure.

There is a certain amount of difficulty in defining the boundaries between the different types. Ash formed from solidified magma falling out of the air after a volcanic eruption is igneous, but what if it should move downhill in a mudslide? If a metamorphic rock is deeply buried it may start to melt and form a "migmatite," which is part liquid and part solid. Is this igneous? And where does the boundary lie between a deeply buried sediment and a metamorphic rock? Coal seams that have been thoroughly metamorphosed from their original peat deposits are found as layers in unaltered sandstones. This classification does, however, provide a useful preliminary guide to understanding the nature of different types of rock.

Rock types are defined by studying their texture, the way they were formed, and their composition. There are interesting textural similarities between evaporites—salt deposits formed as an inland sea dries up—and some plutonic igneous rocks. Both have crystallized directly from a liquid. There are similarities between sandstones and plutonic "cumulates," which form at the base of enormous magma reservoirs where strong magma currents deposit thick layers of crystals. So rock types must be defined in terms of more than just texture.

Rock formation

The simplest sedimentary rocks are those made up of whole fragments of eroded material. "Scree" deposits that accumulate at the base of a cliff or a steep valley side from angular rock fragments that have broken off the rock face above can make a sedimentary "breccia." A rock made from rounded stream pebbles is a "conglomerate." Further erosion reduces the rock into three components: dissolved ions (atoms with an electrical charge) such as those of calcium or magnesium; mineral grains (sand) that cannot be broken down chemically, such as quartz; and a variety of minerals containing sheet-like layers of silicate and alumina (silicon and aluminum oxides)—the minerals that are often the main constituents of clays.

A river carrying these minerals first deposits the sand, and then the clay, while the dissolved ions pass out into the sea, where some are absorbed by living organisms and used to construct protective shells and rigid skeletons. When the creatures die, the shells and bones again become part of the rock cycle, building up great thicknesses of limestone.

Igneous rocks are chemically far more complex than are sedimentary rocks, but are texturally simpler. The slower the magma cools, the larger are the crystals that form within it. If it cools too quickly it may not crystallize at all, forming instead a super-cooled liquid, or glass. A plutonic igneous rock—one cooled deep underground—is coarse grained; a volcanic rock is fine grained. A rock can, however, have both large and small crystals, testifying to a more complex history.

The most striking feature of Earth magmas is their uniformity. With few exceptions, they are all rich in silica. The greater the silica content, the higher their viscosity (resistance to flowing). Those rich in silica tend to solidify underground. The complex chemistry of magmas comes from the melting of the variety of minerals making up the mantle.

The chemistry of metamorphic rocks is like that of their igneous or sedimentary starting materials. As these become more deeply buried and heated, the constituent minerals grow larger. A mudstone metamorphoses to a slate, then to a schist and finally a gneiss. The "slatiness" or "schistosity" of these rocks is provided by micas and other sheet-shaped mineral grains. Such minerals require abundant alumina to form. If this is not present in the starting rock, it will be metamorphosed into more granular material.

A record in the rocks

Rocks contain an unwritten history of the Earth. Sedimentary rocks hold information about climates of the past and fossil relics of organisms that lived when the sediments were laid down. Igneous rocks record periods of crustal activity that relate to the movements of the continents; and metamorphic rocks indicate periods of uplift that exposed previously buried rock. From such information it is possible to construct a geological time scale. Although fossils are a useful means of correlating one pile of sediment with another, good fossils go back only 600 million years. Earlier organisms are believed to have been soft bodied and were not easily fossilized.

The only complete time scale comes from the radioactive "clocks" in many igneous and metamorphic rocks. Certain forms of natural elements, or isotopes, are unstable and emit energy. By measuring the amount of "daughter" atoms that have been formed by the radioactive decay of a larger "parent" atom, it is possible to determine the age of a rock and events in the history of its formation. The dating of rocks from radioactive decay has thus enabled a true time scale for the history of the Earth to be constructed.

Earth's Minerals

Minerals are the basic ingredients of the Earth, from crust to core. They make up not only the ores on which man has based much of his technology, and the gemstones which he values for their beauty or rarity, but also the components of rocks, pebbles and sands. Two million years ago minerals – in the form of stones – provided early man with his first tools. Today, man's use of minerals, such as uranium for nuclear power or silicon for microcomputers, is revolutionizing our lives.

SUBSTANCES OF THE EARTH
Minerals are made up of chemical elements, arranged according to various crystal structures. Man's chief interest in minerals has been as precious stones and, increasingly, as a resource in the form of useful metal ores. But of the 2,500 minerals so far identified, the majority are rock-forming substances—the material components of the Earth. Relatively infrequent geological processes over vast time spans are responsible for concentrating minerals dispersed through rocks into richer deposits, and it is these economically important ores that have provided man with his supply of workable mineral resources through the ages.

Minerals, and the metals derived from them, have always had an inherent fascination for man, as well as providing the basis for his technology. Gold in particular, which was worked in Egypt as early as 5000 BC, still retains its mysterious attraction. Because of its chemical inactivity it is imperishable, immutable and nontarnishing, and has served as the basis of world trade for almost 2,000 years. Copper has been smelted since the early part of the third millennium BC, to be replaced eventually by harder alloys. Arsenical bronze, for instance, bridged the gap between the Copper and Bronze ages (bronze is an alloy of copper and tin). More complex technology was needed for the working of iron, which began c.1100 BC, whereas brass (an alloy of copper and zinc) did not appear until Roman times.

Although the steel-making process had its roots in antiquity, it was not until the nineteenth century that new techniques changed man's attitude to minerals. Before the modern age of plastics, the capacity to produce steel was the hallmark of industrial development, and together with coal it formed the linchpin of western industrial progress. Today minerals have come to assume their greatest importance as exploitable—but nonrenewable—resources.

Components of the Earth
The terms "mineral," "rock" and "stone" are often used interchangeably, but in fact all rocks are made up of minerals, which are natural and usually inorganic substances with a particular chemical makeup and crystal structure.

Certain stones have properties that satisfy basic human needs for beauty and color. Some possess a flashing sparkle, others have special optical characteristics such as refraction and dispersion ("fire"), or contain inclusions that give rise to phenomena like the "asterism" found in sapphires. About 100 such minerals are classified as gemstones and valued for their beauty, durability or rarity.

Most minerals occur as either pure (ore) deposits or mixed with other minerals in rocks—an economically important difference. Their exploitation has been vastly extended in recent decades through our greater understanding of the mineral-forming processes that take place in the Earth's crust. All mineral ores result from a separation process in which a mineral-rich solution separates into its various components according to the temperature, pressure and composition of the original mixture. Precipitation is the simplest kind of separation, as when calcium salts separate from circulating groundwater to yield stalactites and stalagmites in caves, in the form of calcite crystals.

Mineral formation
Most deposits of metallic ores originate in the intense physicochemical activity that takes place at the boundaries between the Earth's huge crustal plates. Very high concentrations of minerals occur in association with warm solutions coming from springs in the seabed, notably along the spreading zones in the southeastern Pacific Ocean, the Red Sea, the African Rift Valley and the Gulf of Aden. This process also occurs in shallow-water volcanic areas, as near the Mediterranean island of Thira and the submarine volcano of Bahu Wuhu, Indonesia. Cold seawater penetrates the crust and leaches out minerals from the basalts of these "hot spots," returning to the surface of the seabed as hot springs. The minerals then precipitate in the cold, oxygen-rich seawater.

Mineral separation may also occur when part of the deep-seated magma forces its way into the upper layers of the Earth's crust and begins to cool. The great plugs of magma that form the rock kimberlite, in which diamonds are found, must have come from a depth of at least 100 km (62 miles). If the magma reaches the surface through fissures as extrusive rocks, the pattern of minerals in the surrounding rocks is also changed by a process called contact metamorphism, with various bands or zones of minerals occurring at various distances from the contact boundary.

As rocks become weathered, mineral concentrations that resist weathering may be left. Alternatively, all the weathered materials may be transported by running water, becoming concentrated as they are sorted out according to their different densities. Gold is the best-known example of this alluvial type of mineral deposit—known as a placer deposit. If the minerals are washed into the sea, they may be distributed over deltas or over the seafloor, but when this happens the concentrations of minerals are usually very low.

Mineral energy
Fossil fuels such as coal and petroleum are major mineral sources of energy. But with the twentieth-century discovery of nuclear fission, uranium also became an important energy resource. The richest deposits occur, as with other minerals, as veins deposited in fractures by hot-water movements. These deposits, consisting of a uranium oxide called pitchblende were the first to be mined, for example at Joachimstal (Czech Republic), Great Bear Lake (Canada) and Katanga (Zaire). Weathered products of such rocks, redeposited as sandstones, also contain uranium, as in Wyoming (USA) and in the Niger basin. In many respects uranium is similar to silver: both occur with similar geological abundance, their ores are enriched about 2,000 times during processing, and the metals are recovered by using chemicals to dissolve the metal selectively and then by "stripping" the metal from the solution.

MINERALS FROM THE OCEAN
Ocean sediments that originally came from land contain organic matter that absorbs the oxygen in the sediments. As a result, solutions of minerals such as manganese and iron are released, seeping upwards through the debris. When they come in contact with the oxygen in seawater they are precipitated, condensing into so-called "manganese" nodules in amounts that may eventually prove to be a valuable source of mineral wealth. Metallic elements also accumulate very slowly from the seawater itself.

METAL-RICH BRINES
Scientists have recently discovered deep hollows on the floor of the Red Sea and other similar enclosed basins connected with rift valleys. These prevent normal circulation of water and form undersea pools of hot, high-density brines. The brines contain sulphur and other minerals in very high concentrations, and overlie sediments rich in metals such as zinc, copper, lead, silver and gold. Hot springs in fissures below the pools escape into them, carrying up solutions of the metallic minerals which combine with sulphur to create a concentrated broth rich in metals.

METALS FROM THE INTERIOR
Rift zones on the bed of the Pacific Ocean, where the Earth's crustal plates are slowly separating, provide sensational visual evidence of metallic ores in the actual process of creation. Seawater percolates through the fractured surface to the molten rock below, where it leaches out the soluble metallic components, erupting in superheated hydrothermal springs to form geysers of mineral-rich water. Oxygen in the cold water of the sea-floor causes the minerals to condense out, precipitating in plumes of dark powder. Continental drift, collision and sedimentation over millions of years will eventually incorporate these deposits into the landmasses.

Uranium, chromium and many other minerals are widely distributed through the Earth's crust, but they are valuable as a resource only if the technology exists to extract them economically. In mineral development, the high-grade ores are worked out first, followed by the poorer deposits if demand remains or increases. With uranium, the low-grade deposits contain more of the total quantity of the mineral, but these are worth exploiting because of uranium's importance and because the technology exists. Chromium, on the other hand, is currently extracted only from high-grade ores. Large deposits of low-grade ores do exist, but technology for exploiting them economically has not yet been developed.

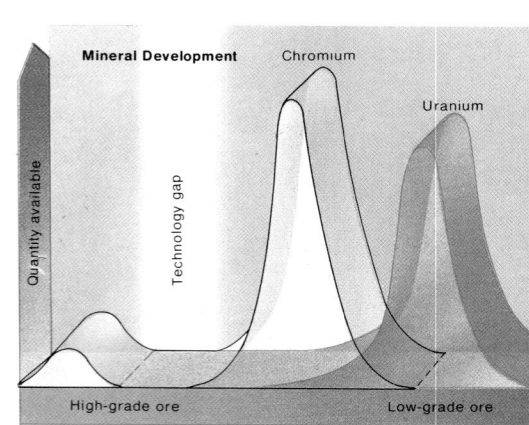

Mineral Development

Chromium

Uranium

Quantity available

Technology gap

High-grade ore

Low-grade ore

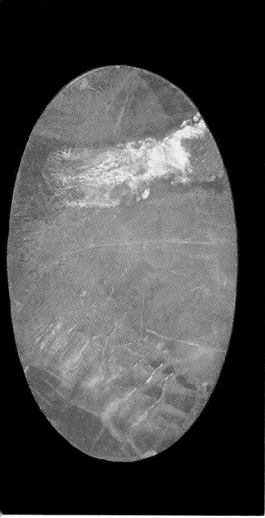

Opal (above), a silica mineral, often contains impurities which give it a range of colors. These flash and change according to the angle of vision, a result of the interference of light along minute internal cracks in the stone.

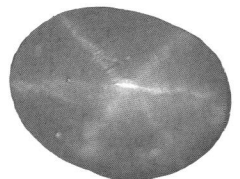

Sapphire gemstone (left), a form of the dull gray mineral corundum (below), owes its color to inclusions of titanium and iron.

MINERALS IN THE SERVICE OF MAN

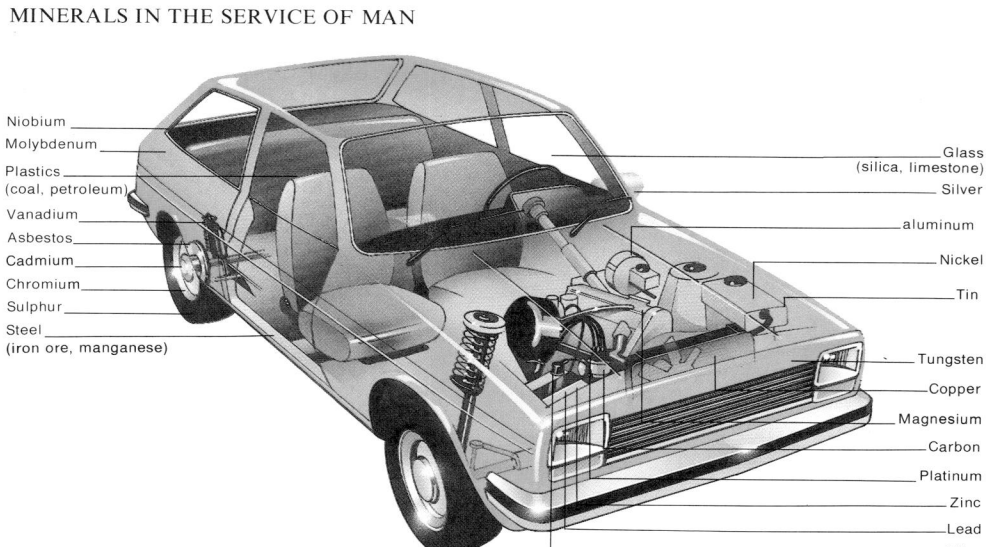

Niobium
Molybdenum
Plastics (coal, petroleum)
Vanadium
Asbestos
Cadmium
Chromium
Sulphur
Steel (iron ore, manganese)

Glass (silica, limestone)
Silver
aluminum
Nickel
Tin
Tungsten
Copper
Magnesium
Carbon
Platinum
Zinc
Lead
Mica

The modern automobile makes use of a whole alphabet of minerals in its composition, from aluminum to zinc. The importance of plastics, made from petroleum and coal, is constantly increasing, but the need for specialist metals is as great as ever. Cadmium, for example, is used in electro-plating; carbon goes into making electrodes and graphite seals; transistors and electric contact points require platinum; sulphur is present in vulcanizing rubber and lubricants; lamp filaments contain tungsten. Of basic metals, iron and steel still account for almost three-quarters of the total quantity of the metals used; lead for 1.19 percent and copper for only 0.94 percent. But the amount of useful metal is often a small fraction of the rock that has to be mined and processed. A copper ore, for instance, only yields about 0.7 percent of metal, so to equip a single car's radiator with copper well over one and a half tonnes of rock will have to be excavated, of which 99.3 percent will simply be discarded.

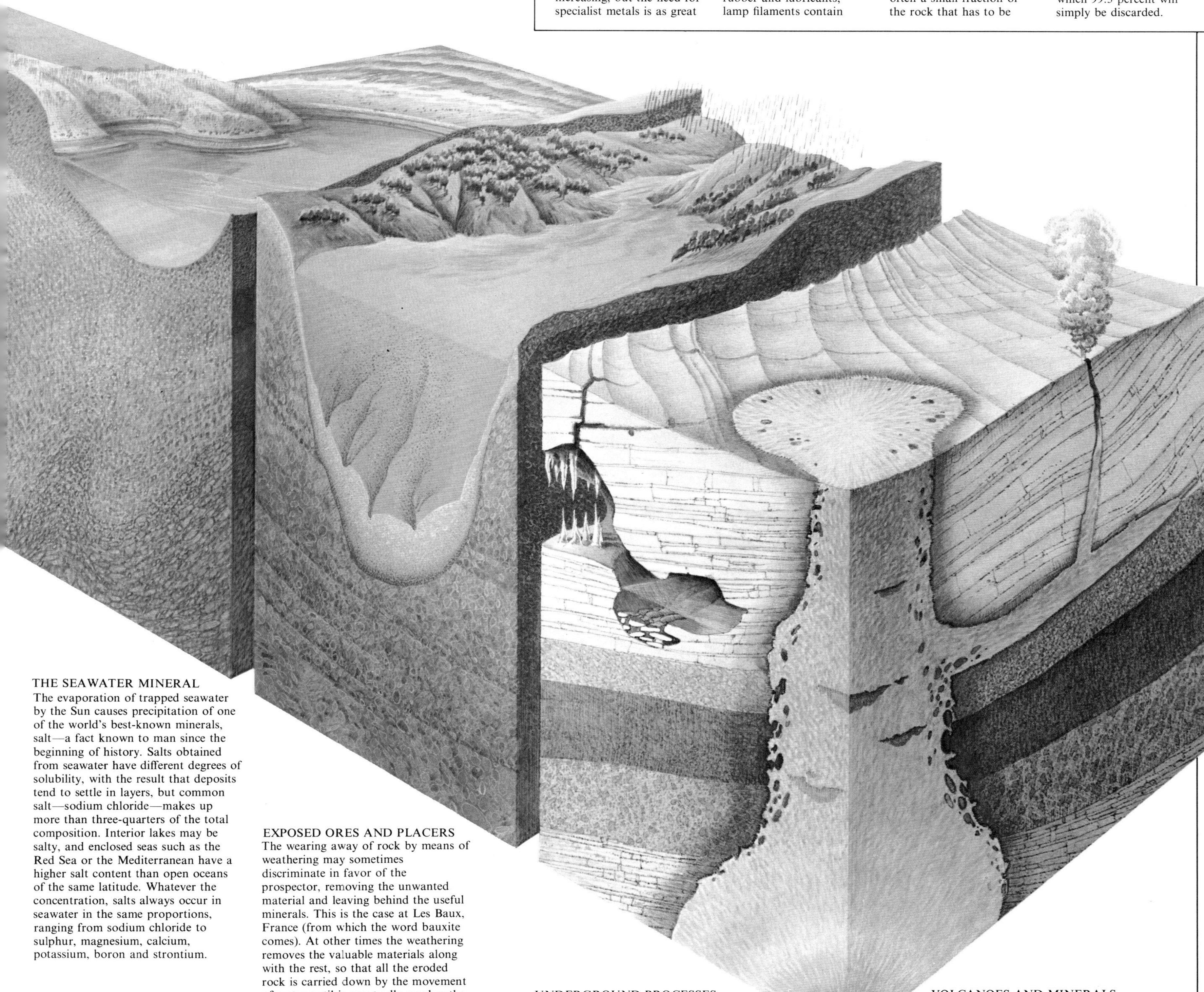

THE SEAWATER MINERAL
The evaporation of trapped seawater by the Sun causes precipitation of one of the world's best-known minerals, salt—a fact known to man since the beginning of history. Salts obtained from seawater have different degrees of solubility, with the result that deposits tend to settle in layers, but common salt—sodium chloride—makes up more than three-quarters of the total composition. Interior lakes may be salty, and enclosed seas such as the Red Sea or the Mediterranean have a higher salt content than open oceans of the same latitude. Whatever the concentration, salts always occur in seawater in the same proportions, ranging from sodium chloride to sulphur, magnesium, calcium, potassium, boron and strontium.

EXPOSED ORES AND PLACERS
The wearing away of rock by means of weathering may sometimes discriminate in favor of the prospector, removing the unwanted material and leaving behind the useful minerals. This is the case at Les Baux, France (from which the word bauxite comes). At other times the weathering removes the valuable materials along with the rest, so that all the eroded rock is carried down by the movement of water until it eventually reaches the sea. So-called "placer" deposits occur where the heavier particles of minerals have become separated, accumulating as deposits of mineral sand and concentrating in riverbeds or estuaries. Gold is the best-known example of this alluvial type of deposit, but tin and other minerals are also found as placers in many parts of the world.

UNDERGROUND PROCESSES
Limestone rock, formed from calcium carbonate, is dissolved by seeping water containing carbon dioxide from the air and the soil. The subsurface water may create vast networks of underground caverns in the limestone, and as the water slowly evaporates it leaves deposits of calcium carbonate, forming stalactites and stalagmites.

VOLCANOES AND MINERALS
Volcanic magma penetrating the Earth's crust may form important mineral deposits. On cooling, the heavy or "basic" minerals are the first to crystallize and sink to the bottom. The minerals may also separate out chemically. The intense heat affects surrounding rocks, causing mineral changes in banded zones.

Earthquakes and Volcanoes

Earthquakes and volcanic eruptions challenge man's faith in the stability of the world, but these violent releases of energy testify to our planet's ever-dynamic activity. Earthquakes are caused when the rigid crust is driven past or over itself by underlying movements that extend deep into the Earth's mantle. Stress builds up until it exceeds the strength of the rocks, when there follows a sudden movement. Volcanoes occur where molten rock, or magma, from the mantle forces its way to the surface through lines of weakness in the crust, often at the lithospheric plate boundaries.

The Earth's crust generally breaks along pre-existing planes of weakness, or faults. Such breakages give rise to an "explosive" release of stress that is familiar to surface dwellers as the vibrations of an earthquake.

Not all earthquakes, however, take place along pre-existing faults, otherwise no new faults would be generated. Many recent large earthquakes have been located immediately north of the Tonga Islands because a giant rent is developing through previously unbroken ocean crust. The crust to the south is being swallowed down into the mantle and that to the north continues at the surface to be subducted farther to the west. Once a fault has formed, however, it remains a plane of weakness even though the two sides tend to become partly resealed, so that when movement does occur there is a considerable release of energy.

Measuring earthquakes

Earthquakes are quantified in two ways. The actual energy release (magnitude) at the source of the earthquake (the focus) is measured on the Richter scale, a log scale where every unit of increase represents approximately 24 times the energy release. A magnitude 7 earthquake is roughly equivalent to the explosion of a one megaton nuclear bomb (one million tonnes of TNT). The strongest earthquake recorded this century was a magnitude 8.5 event in Alaska in 1964. Earthquakes as they are perceived are measured on the Modified Mercalli scale by their impact in terms of the amount of surface destruction. A medium-size earthquake under a town, such as that beneath Tangshan, China, in 1976 which killed more than a quarter of a million people, might record higher on the Mercalli scale than the Alaska event, which affected a large but sparsely populated region.

The magnitude of the earthquake depends on the frictional resistance that has to be overcome before movement can take place. This total frictional resistance, therefore, increases with the area of the fault plane. So the bigger the fault plane that moves, the bigger the earthquake. The largest earthquakes occur on wide fault planes that dip at a very shallow angle and can pass through a great deal of relatively shallow crust that will not deform plastically.

Earthquakes are unlikely to occur where rocks are plastic and can flow to accommodate the buildup of stress. Some faults, such as the San Andreas Fault in the western United States, pass from brittle rocks into a plastic zone at depths of only a few kilometers. Therefore, the next San Francisco earthquake cannot be as great as the 1964 Alaskan one, although this may be of little comfort to the potential victims. Along some sections of the San Andreas Fault the plastic zone comes directly to the surface, and motion occurs without large earthquakes.

Earthquake prediction is still in its infancy, although it is recognized that a number of phenomena may occur before a major earthquake—the ground may swell, the electrical conductivity of groundwater may change, and the water height of wells may rapidly alter.

How volcanoes are formed

Volcanoes, although spectacular, are safer than earthquakes. While an average of 20,000 people are killed each year in earthquakes, only about 400 are killed by volcanoes; and many of the victims die from starvation due to crop failure after heavy ash falls.

Volcanoes are formed when molten rock (magma) escapes through the Earth's crust to the Earth's surface. Most of this magma forms within the upper mantle between 30 and 100 km (20–60 miles) underground. The temperature increases with depth between 20° and 50°C per

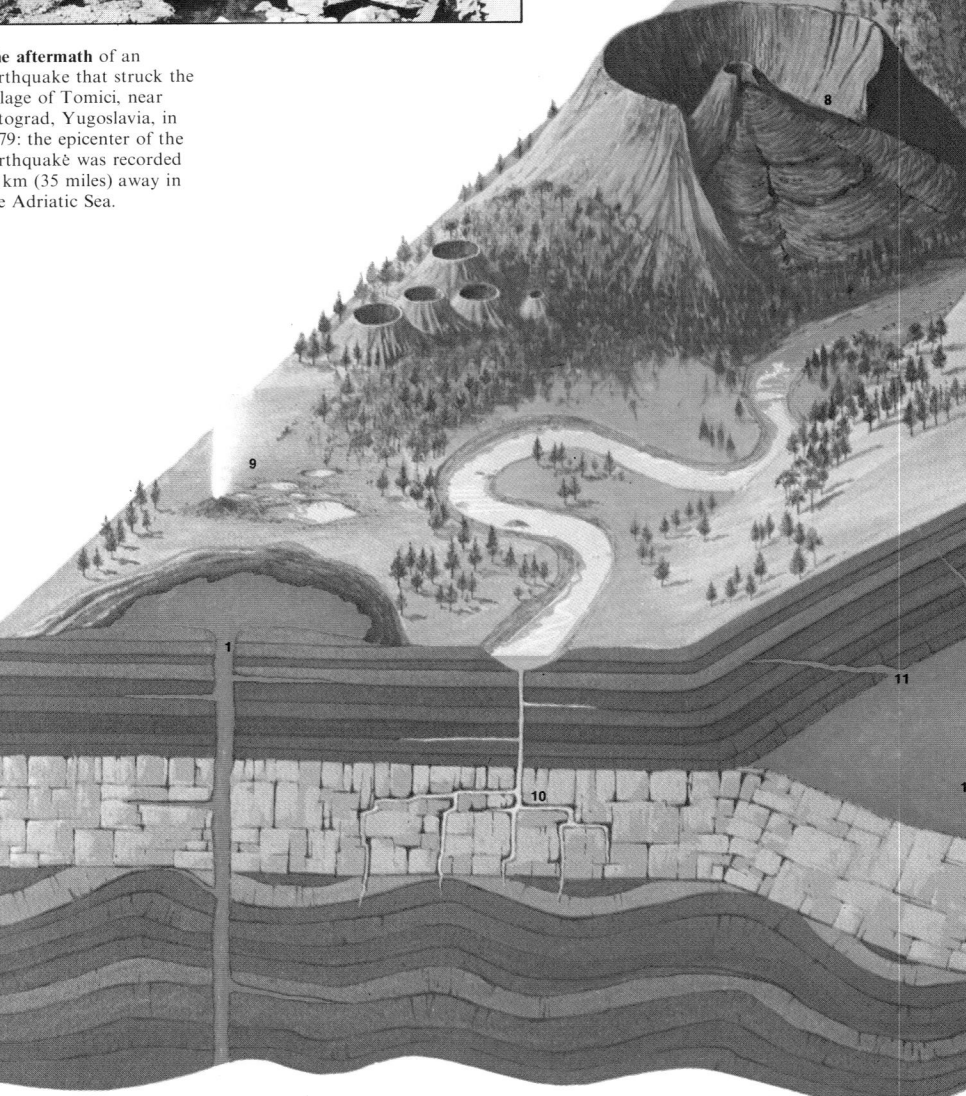

The aftermath of an earthquake that struck the village of Tomici, near Titograd, Yugoslavia, in 1979: the epicenter of the earthquake was recorded 55 km (35 miles) away in the Adriatic Sea.

Earthquakes occur when slabs of the Earth's crust move in relation to each other. The focus of the earthquake is the point where movement occurs (1), and the epicenter is the point on the surface directly above it (2). Blue lines represent zones of surface damage as measured on the Modified Mercalli scale.

km (35°–90°F per 3,250 ft) from the crust to the mantle, but even so the rocks are normally not hot enough to melt.

Basaltic magmas, found along mid-ocean spreading ridges and oceanic islands, are formed when hot, deep mantle rises and, on reduction of pressure, begins to melt. Such "basic" magmas generally have low silica and water content, a high temperature and flow easily—often, as in Hawaii, "quietly erupting" to form volcanoes with very gentle gradients known as shield volcanoes. Silica-rich magma forms under continental crust. Ocean crust sucks up water after it has formed at the oceanic spreading ridges and much of this water later becomes taken with the crust down a subduction zone, where it helps to lower the melting point of both mantle and ocean-crust rocks.

By the time these magmas reach the surface they are cooler and have a higher water content than basalts. These "intermediate" or andesite magmas are also more viscous (less willing to

flow) because they contain more silica. The eruptions are more explosive as the water and other gases dissolve out of the magma as it approaches the surface, and the lava remains close to the volcanic vent, building up the archetypal steep-sided conical stratified volcano, such as Mount Fujiyama in Japan. Sometimes the conical form may be destroyed in catastrophic eruptions, as has happened at Mount St Helens in the United States.

The most violent of all eruptions are found where magmas from the mantle have penetrated and melted a great thickness of continental rocks, so as to create highly viscous silica- and water-rich "acid" magmas. As such magmas approach the surface they may turn into a red-hot froth that blasts out from fissures to cover enormous areas in a volcanic material known as ignimbrite. The most extensive eruption known to have occurred in the past 2,000 years was probably on Mount Taupo, on North Island, New Zealand. In AD 150 it discharged some

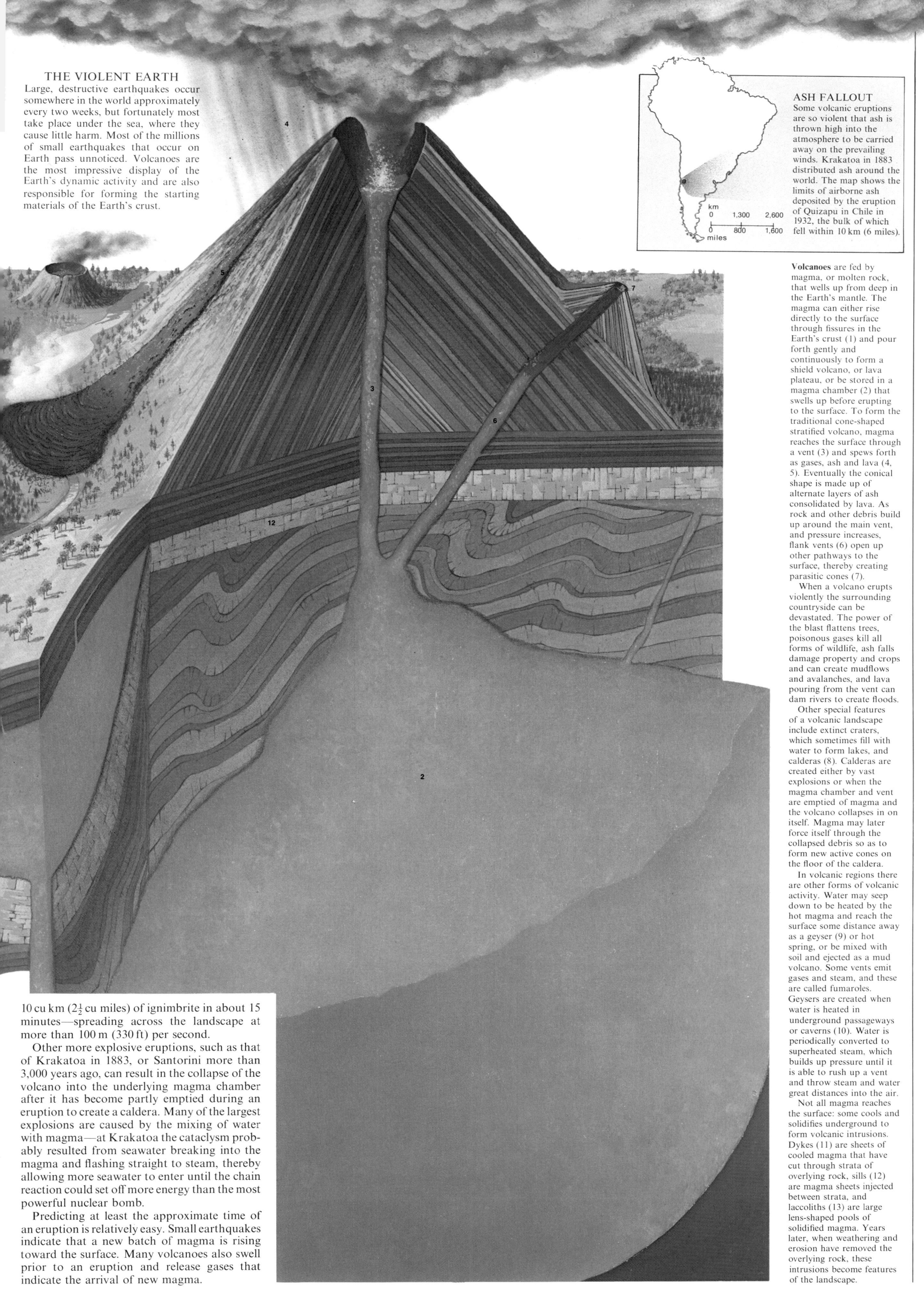

THE VIOLENT EARTH

Large, destructive earthquakes occur somewhere in the world approximately every two weeks, but fortunately most take place under the sea, where they cause little harm. Most of the millions of small earthquakes that occur on Earth pass unnoticed. Volcanoes are the most impressive display of the Earth's dynamic activity and are also responsible for forming the starting materials of the Earth's crust.

Volcanoes are fed by magma, or molten rock, that wells up from deep in the Earth's mantle. The magma can either rise directly to the surface through fissures in the Earth's crust (1) and pour forth gently and continuously to form a shield volcano, or lava plateau, or be stored in a magma chamber (2) that swells up before erupting to the surface. To form the traditional cone-shaped stratified volcano, magma reaches the surface through a vent (3) and spews forth as gases, ash and lava (4, 5). Eventually the conical shape is made up of alternate layers of ash consolidated by lava. As rock and other debris build up around the main vent, and pressure increases, flank vents (6) open up other pathways to the surface, thereby creating parasitic cones (7).

When a volcano erupts violently the surrounding countryside can be devastated. The power of the blast flattens trees, poisonous gases kill all forms of wildlife, ash falls damage property and crops and can create mudflows and avalanches, and lava pouring from the vent can dam rivers to create floods.

Other special features of a volcanic landscape include extinct craters, which sometimes fill with water to form lakes, and calderas (8). Calderas are created either by vast explosions or when the magma chamber and vent are emptied of magma and the volcano collapses in on itself. Magma may later force itself through the collapsed debris so as to form new active cones on the floor of the caldera.

In volcanic regions there are other forms of volcanic activity. Water may seep down to be heated by the hot magma and reach the surface some distance away as a geyser (9) or hot spring, or be mixed with soil and ejected as a mud volcano. Some vents emit gases and steam, and these are called fumaroles. Geysers are created when water is heated in underground passageways or caverns (10). Water is periodically converted to superheated steam, which builds up pressure until it is able to rush up a vent and throw steam and water great distances into the air.

Not all magma reaches the surface: some cools and solidifies underground to form volcanic intrusions. Dykes (11) are sheets of cooled magma that have cut through strata of overlying rock, sills (12) are magma sheets injected between strata, and laccoliths (13) are large lens-shaped pools of solidified magma. Years later, when weathering and erosion have removed the overlying rock, these intrusions become features of the landscape.

10 cu km (2½ cu miles) of ignimbrite in about 15 minutes—spreading across the landscape at more than 100 m (330 ft) per second.

Other more explosive eruptions, such as that of Krakatoa in 1883, or Santorini more than 3,000 years ago, can result in the collapse of the volcano into the underlying magma chamber after it has become partly emptied during an eruption to create a caldera. Many of the largest explosions are caused by the mixing of water with magma—at Krakatoa the cataclysm probably resulted from seawater breaking into the magma and flashing straight to steam, thereby allowing more seawater to enter until the chain reaction could set off more energy than the most powerful nuclear bomb.

Predicting at least the approximate time of an eruption is relatively easy. Small earthquakes indicate that a new batch of magma is rising toward the surface. Many volcanoes also swell prior to an eruption and release gases that indicate the arrival of new magma.

The Oceans

Earth is the water planet. Of all the planets of the solar system only the Earth has abundant liquid water, and 97 percent of this surface water is found in the seas and oceans. The water of the oceans appears to be passive and unchanging, whereas the rain and rivers seem active, but this is far from true. In reality the oceans are a turmoil of giant sluggish rivers – far larger than any of the land rivers – and of circulating surface currents that are driven by the prevailing winds.

No topographic map of the Earth can be drawn unless there is some kind of base line from which to measure depths and heights. This base line has always been taken as the level of the sea, yet the sea is perpetually changing level. One can choose some kind of average to call "sea level," but even today different countries have defined that base line in different ways. The currents found within the sea itself can also give the water surface a slope—the calm Sargasso Sea off the northern coast of South America is, for example, about 1.5 m (5 ft) higher than the water to the west adjacent to the Gulf Stream.

Waves

The changes in the level of the sea, at its surface, provide the most familiar image of motion within the waters. Various changes take place over many different time periods, but the most rapid are those that we call waves.

Waves are produced by the wind moving over the water and catching on the surface. They can move at between 15 and 100 km/hr (10–60 mph) and wave crests may be separated by up to 300 m (1,000 ft) in the open ocean. In general, the greater the wavelength, the faster the wave's speed and the farther the distance traveled by the wave. Waves that have traveled a long way from the winds that created them are known as swell. Without the wind continually pushing them they become symmetrical and smooth. Wind waves produce spilling breakers more like the rapids of a mountain torrent, whereas swell produces giant plunging breakers.

A combination of strong winds and low atmospheric pressure associated with storms can cause yet another kind of wave, known as a storm surge. A storm surge is formed by the water being driven ahead of the wind, and rising as the atmospheric pressure weighing down on the water decreases. Where storms drive water into funnel-shaped coasts, the water can rise more than 10 m (33 ft) above normal sea level, flooding large areas of low-lying land at the head of the bay. Venice, the Netherlands and Bangladesh have been particularly subject to destructive storm surges. Other catastrophic changes in sea level have their origins in the seabed. These are tsunamis (Japanese for "high-water in the harbor") and are generally triggered by underwater earthquakes that suddenly raise or lower large areas of the seafloor.

Tides

As the Earth orbits around the Sun the water in the oceans experiences a changing pull of gravity from both the Moon and the Sun. The Sun is overhead once a day, and because the Moon is itself orbiting the Earth, it is overhead once every 24 hours 50 minutes. The pull of gravity from the Sun is less than half that from the Moon, and so it is the Moon that sets the rhythm of the water movements we call tides. The variation in gravitational pull from the Moon is extremely small, however, and even if the whole of the Earth were covered with deep water a tide of only about 30 cm (12 in) would be produced, rushing around the world keeping pace with the circling Moon. Yet the tides in shallow coastal regions are often very much higher than this—for example, up to 18 m (60 ft) in the Bay of Fundy, Canada. The seas and bays with the highest tides are located where the whole mass of water is resonating—rebounding backwards and forwards like water in a bath, as the smaller tides in the outlying oceans push it twice each day.

The Bay of Fundy experiences a particularly high tidal range because it happens to have a resonant frequency—a range of movement—very close to the 12½-hour frequency between tides. Large enclosed seas such as the Mediterranean have very small tides because there is no outside push from an ocean to set them resonating. In contrast, where water movement associated with the tides passes through a narrow channel it can produce tidal currents of up to 30 km/hr (19 mph), such as the famous maelstrom of northern Norway.

After these relatively short-lived disturbances the sea returns to its normal, or at least to its average, level again. When the total volume of free water at the Earth's surface alters, or when the shapes of the ocean basins vary, the sea level itself may start to wander.

How does the volume of water vary? It can be buried in rocks—but the steam clouds above volcanoes return such water so it is normally recycled rather than lost. Some vapor can be broken down through radiation in the upper atmosphere and the hydrogen lost to outer space, but this is relatively insignificant. Or it can be frozen and stacked up on land in the form of ice—this is significant as we are still living in an ice age. The lowest ice-age sea levels produced beaches at about 130 m (430 ft) below present sea level, and the low-lying coastal regions of that period have now become flooded to form the continental shelves.

The salt content of the oceans

Average ocean water contains about 35 parts per 1,000 of salts which include 14 elements in concentrations greater than 1 part per million—the most abundant being sodium and chlorine. Where there is considerable surface evaporation, for example in enclosed seas such as the Dead Sea, the salt concentration builds up and the water becomes denser. Where the sea-surface is turning to ice the salt also becomes concentrated in the water.

The coldest, saltiest ocean water comes from the Antarctic. As it is also the densest it hugs the ocean bottom as it flows northwards, reaching as far as the latitudes of Spain. A similar current from the Arctic is slightly lighter and therefore rides above it—but traveling southwards, as far as the southern Atlantic. A second slightly lighter body of Antarctic water rides above the Arctic water—again traveling northwards. Where these water movements meet each other they rise up, bringing to the surface oxygenated water that can support a profusion of life in oceans that have been compared to a desert because of their lack of biological activity. Unlikely as it seems, it is the icy, stormy, polar waters that provide the lungs of the oceans.

Both the Sun and the Moon exert gravitational pull on the water in the oceans, but the pull of the Sun is less than half that of the Moon. It is the Moon, therefore, that sets the rhythm of the tides. Because the Moon orbits the Earth every 24 hours and 50 minutes, the time of high or low tide advances approximately an hour each day. When the Moon is in its first and last quarters (1, 3) it forms a right angle with the Earth and the Sun and the gravitational fields are opposed, thus causing only a small difference between high and low tide. These are called neap tides. When the Sun, Moon and Earth lie in a straight line (2, 4), at the full and the new Moon, then the high tides become higher and the low tides lower. These are the spring tides. The graph illustrates tidal range over a period of a month.

Depth in meters
0 1 2 3 4 5 6 7 8

Neap tide

Spring tide

Neap tide

Spring tide

Depth in meters

0
1,000
2,000
3,000
4,000
5,000
6,000
7,000
8,000

1 Continent
2 Continental shelf
3 Continental slope
4 Continental rise
5 Submarine canyon
6 Abyssal plain
7 Abyssal hills
8 Mid-ocean ridge
9 Oceanic trench
10 Island arc
11 Continental sea

THE CHANGING OCEANS

Nearly two-thirds of the Earth's surface is covered by the seas and oceans and this great expanse of water is continually in movement. The most familiar movements are waves formed by the wind and the rising and falling tides that respond to the position of the Moon. But even greater movements take place. Currents driven by prevailing winds form whirlpools an ocean in width, and below the surface flow great rivers of colder water. Sea level is also rising as ice melts from the polar caps.

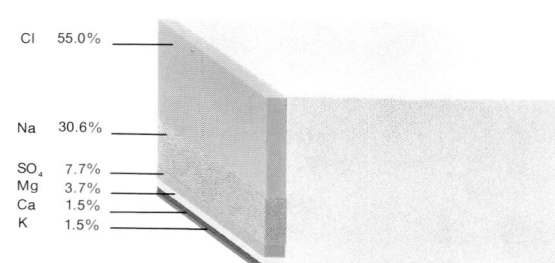

Cl	55.0%
Na	30.6%
SO₄	7.7%
Mg	3.7%
Ca	1.5%
K	1.5%

Seawater is about 96% pure water and the rest is made up of dissolved salts. Many elements are present in minute quantities, but only chlorine (Cl), sodium (Na), sulphate (SO_4), magnesium (Mg), calcium (Ca) and potassium (K) appear in concentrations of more than 1% of the total dissolved salts.

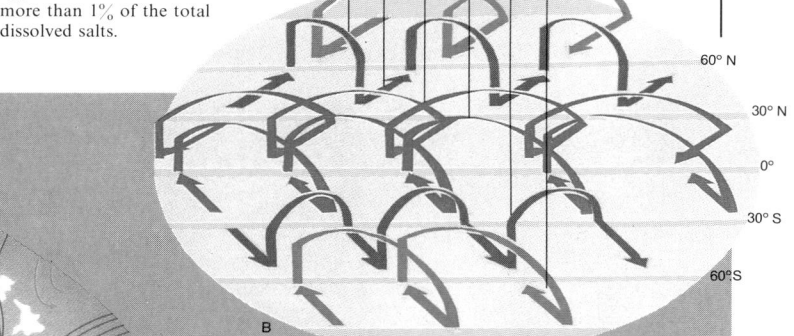

The surface currents of the world's oceans (A) are driven by the prevailing winds (B). The winds and the spinning motion of the Earth drive the currents into gyres—massive whirlpools the width of an ocean. These gyres draw warm water away from the Equator and pull cold polar waters towards it. The centers of gyres are characterized by areas of high pressure, around which winds circulate. Because the Earth is spinning, gyres formed in the northern hemisphere rotate in a clockwise direction, whereas those of the southern hemisphere turn anticlockwise. In all, there are five major gyres, made up of the 38 major named currents. The formation of warm (red) and cold (blue) surface currents is not difficult to understand, given the regions from which they flow. However, even in temperate and subtropical regions, the warm waters of the oceans' surfaces have a permanent layer of cold water beneath them. This cold layer has been formed in the polar regions, where, as the ocean waters have been chilled, they have sunk and then spread out into all the other major ocean basins of the world. The warm subtropical and temperate waters float like an oil slick, from 10 m to 550 m (33–1,900 ft) thick, on top of this cold layer. There is very little mixing between the two layers because the warm water is lighter than the cold water.

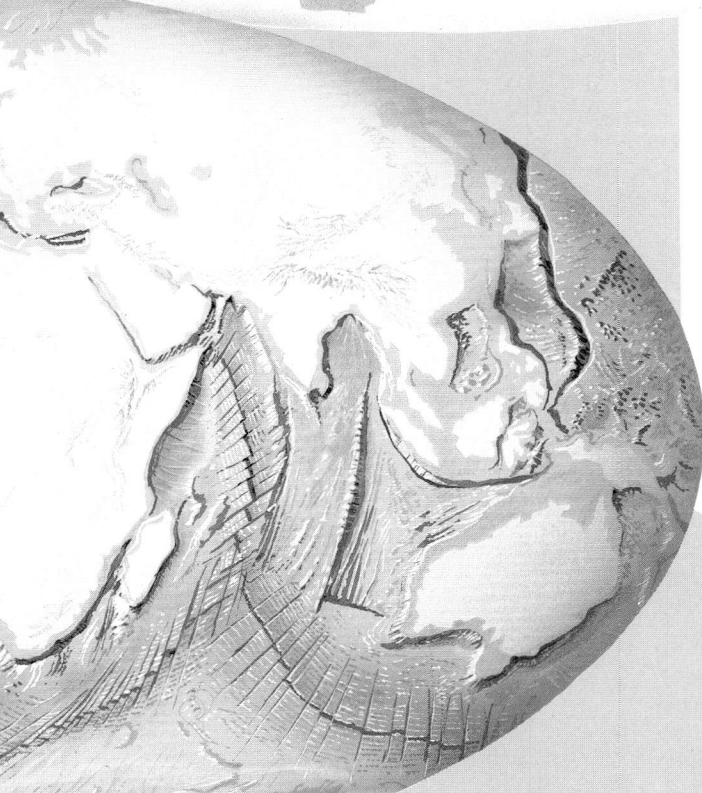

The seabed, more uniform than the land surface, also contains a landscape of underwater features that resemble the plains, valleys and mountains of the continents. Off the edge of continents lie the flat, shallow continental shelves, which are bounded by the steeper incline of the continental slope, which meets the true ocean floor at the continental rise.

Here deep submarine canyons may be found. These seem to be in a process of continual erosion from turbidity currents. River water pouring into major estuaries and carrying sediment can also scour out the slope—especially during periods of low sea level. The abyssal plain is rarely interrupted by volcanic hills and

mountains. The largest chains are at the mid-ocean ridge, where two crustal plates are moving apart and new ocean floor is being created. At some ocean margins deep trough-shaped valleys or trenches are the sites of ocean floor consumption at a subduction zone. The volcanic island arcs that form behind it sometimes isolate a continental sea.

Much of the Earth's water is locked up as ice and stacked on the land. As the ice melts the sea level rises. Only 20,000 years ago the sea level was a full 100 m (330 ft) lower than it is today, and the continental shelves were dry land. About 10,000 years ago the sea level was rising as fast as 3 cm (1 in) each year. Today the melting ice is causing the sea level to rise about 1 mm (0.04 in) each year: only a small increment, but if all the ice melted, the sea level would rise by about 60 m (197 ft) and would flood many of the world's major cities.

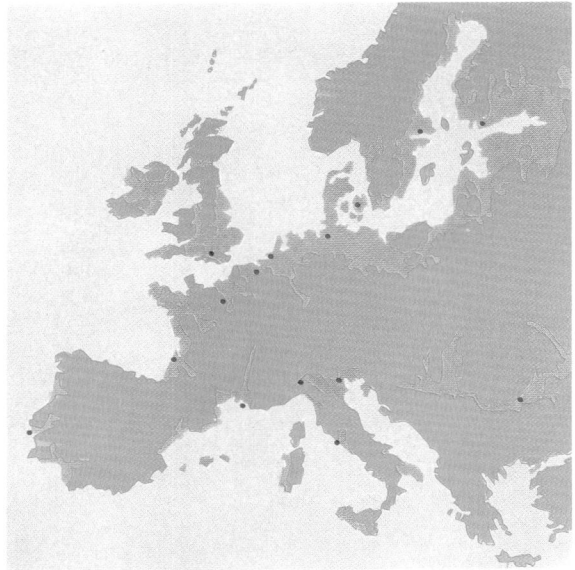

- ⬤ < 60 m
- ⬤ > 60 m
- • Major cities

TSUNAMIS

Tsunamis are generated by massive underwater earthquakes (A) and are common around the Pacific. They can travel at more than 700 km/hr (435 mph) and individual waves may occur at intervals of 15 minutes, or 200 km (125 miles). Low-lying atolls of the Pacific have extremely steep sides underwater, and are generally unharmed, but the gently shelving islands such as Hawaii slow down the tsunami and build it into a giant wave 30 m (100 ft) or more in height. This map plots the hourly position of a tsunami that originated south of Alaska.

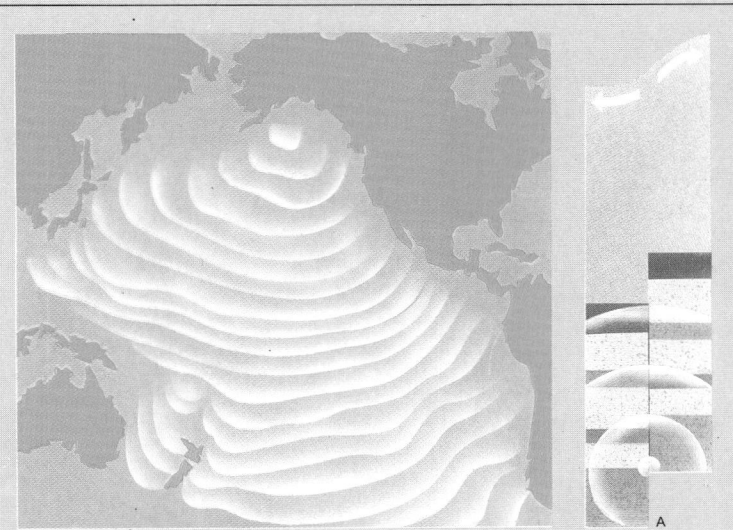

Landscape-makers: Water

Of all the natural agents of erosion at work on the Earth's surface, water is probably the most powerful. Many of the finer details of the landscape, from the contouring of hills and valleys to the broad spread of plains, are the work of water. In recent years we have come to understand more fully the subtle factors at work in a river, for example, as it deepens mountain gorges or builds up sedimentary layers in its approach to the sea. The full force of a waterfall, the instability of a meandering stream, the multiple layering of river terraces – all are features of this most versatile landscape-maker.

Ninety-seven percent of the world's water is in the oceans, another two percent is locked up in the ice caps of Greenland and Antarctica, which leaves one percent only on the surface of Earth, under the ground and in the air. The importance of this one percent is, however, inestimable: most life forms could not exist without it, and yet at the same time many are threatened by it, in the form of flood and storm.

The Sun's energy "powers" the evaporation of water from the oceans. Water vapor then circulates in the atmosphere and is precipitated as rain or snow over land, from which it eventually drains back to the oceans. This is the vast, never-ending water cycle. Water in the air that falls as, for example, rain is replaced on average every 12 days. The total water supply remains constant and is believed to be exactly the same as it was 3,000 million years ago.

From raindrops to rivers

Rain falling on to the surface of the land has a great deal of energy: large drops may hit the ground with a terminal velocity of about 35 km/hr (20 mph). If the rain falls on bare soil, it splashes upwards, breaking off and transporting tiny fragments of soil, which come to rest downhill. Vegetation-covered soil breaks the impact and some of the rain may evaporate without ever reaching the ground.

Soil is rather like a sponge. If the holes or pores are very small, rain finds it difficult to penetrate and water runs over the surface of the soil. If the pores are large, rain infiltrates, filling up the pore spaces. Soils that are thin, have low infiltration rates, or already have a lot of water in them, are very susceptible to overland flow. The water may then concentrate into a channel called a gully, and this can have a dramatic effect upon the landscape. The creation of gullies, together with the splash effect, leads to soil erosion. The problem is particularly severe in semiarid regions, where rainfall is sporadic but intense, vegetation is sparse and overgrazing is common. In extreme cases, badlands are formed and by this time recuperation of the land is impossible or is prohibitively expensive.

Where the infiltration rate is high, water percolates through the soil and eventually into the bedrock. There are two well-defined regions, the saturated and the unsaturated. The upper limit of the saturated zone is the water table. Beneath this, water moves at a rate of a few meters a day, but in rocks such as limestone it can move much more quickly along cracks and joints. In most rock types there are some soluble components which are removed as water continually flows through. In limestone regions, the dissolution of calcium salts results in spectacular cave formations.

Groundwater often provides a vital source for domestic consumption. In porous materials, especially chalk, water is stored in large quantities. Such strata are called aquifers and in some areas, notably North Africa, it is believed that water being pumped up now resulted from rainfall when the climate was wetter tens of thousands of years ago.

Water from a number of sources—from overland flow, soil seepage and springs draining aquifers—produces the flow in rivers. Groundwater appears days or even weeks after a heavy rainfall, but overland flow reaches the channel in hours, producing the sudden peak in flow that may cause flooding and occasionally great damage farther downstream. Flood waves usually rise quickly in mountain areas and the wave moves downstream as the river collects more and more water from its tributaries. Eventually, although the volume continues to increase downstream, the flood wave becomes broader and flatter, so it moves more slowly and causes less damage. The most serious floods occur after intense rainfall on already saturated soils where upland rivers issue on to plains.

Rivers at work

The work of a river from its source to its mouth involves three processes, the first of which is erosion. This includes corrasion, or abrasion— the grinding of rocks and stones against the river's banks and bed—which produces both

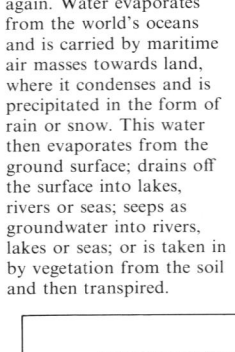

The hydrological cycle involves a vast transfer of water from sea to air to land, and back to sea again. Water evaporates from the world's oceans and is carried by maritime air masses towards land, where it condenses and is precipitated in the form of rain or snow. This water then evaporates from the ground surface; drains off the surface into lakes, rivers or seas; seeps as groundwater into rivers, lakes or seas; or is taken in by vegetation from the soil and then transpired.

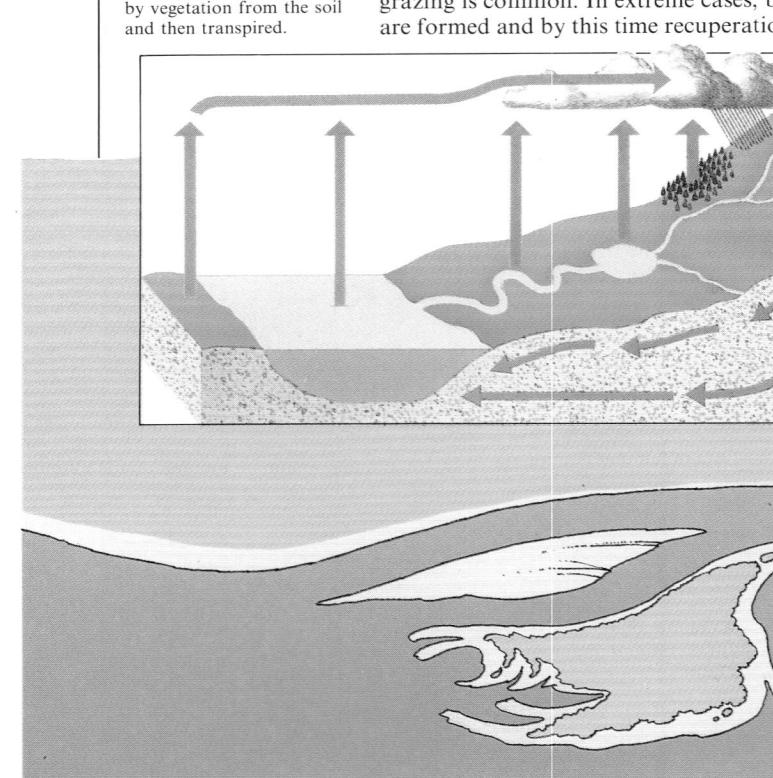

When a river reaches the sea, providing the coast is sheltered and the sea is shallow with no strong currents, its speed is checked and material is deposited (1). The river then forms distributaries (2) in order to continue its flow to the sea. A delta forms its characteristic fan shape (3) as it grows sideways and seawards. A river needs active erosion in its upper course in order to form a delta.

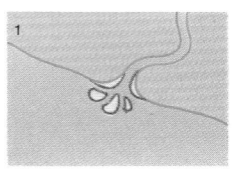
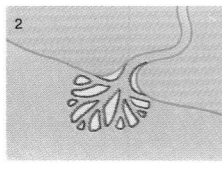
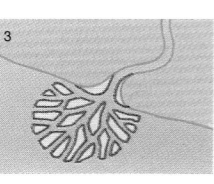

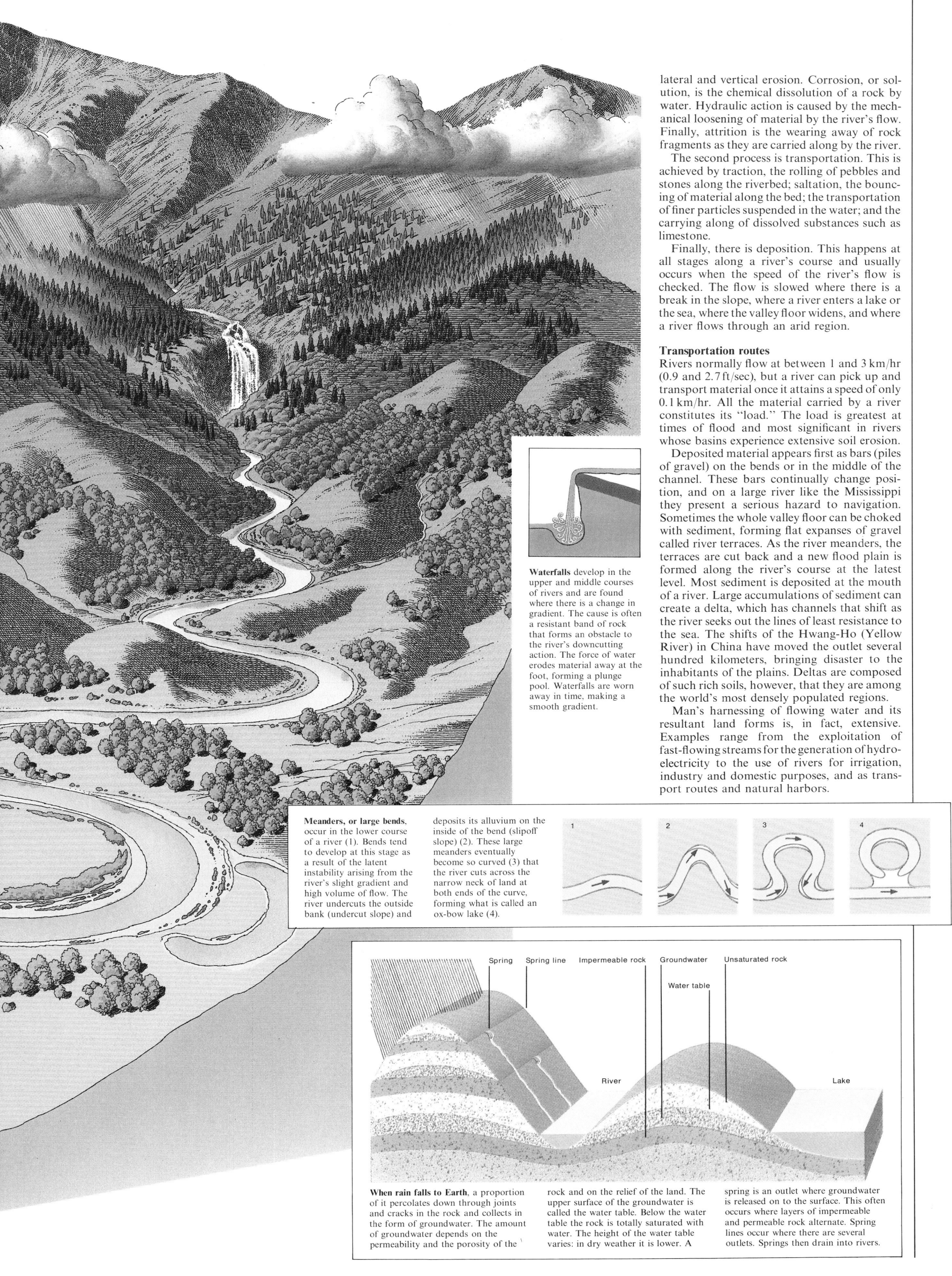

lateral and vertical erosion. Corrosion, or solution, is the chemical dissolution of a rock by water. Hydraulic action is caused by the mechanical loosening of material by the river's flow. Finally, attrition is the wearing away of rock fragments as they are carried along by the river.

The second process is transportation. This is achieved by traction, the rolling of pebbles and stones along the riverbed; saltation, the bouncing of material along the bed; the transportation of finer particles suspended in the water; and the carrying along of dissolved substances such as limestone.

Finally, there is deposition. This happens at all stages along a river's course and usually occurs when the speed of the river's flow is checked. The flow is slowed where there is a break in the slope, where a river enters a lake or the sea, where the valley floor widens, and where a river flows through an arid region.

Transportation routes
Rivers normally flow at between 1 and 3 km/hr (0.9 and 2.7 ft/sec), but a river can pick up and transport material once it attains a speed of only 0.1 km/hr. All the material carried by a river constitutes its "load." The load is greatest at times of flood and most significant in rivers whose basins experience extensive soil erosion.

Deposited material appears first as bars (piles of gravel) on the bends or in the middle of the channel. These bars continually change position, and on a large river like the Mississippi they present a serious hazard to navigation. Sometimes the whole valley floor can be choked with sediment, forming flat expanses of gravel called river terraces. As the river meanders, the terraces are cut back and a new flood plain is formed along the river's course at the latest level. Most sediment is deposited at the mouth of a river. Large accumulations of sediment can create a delta, which has channels that shift as the river seeks out the lines of least resistance to the sea. The shifts of the Hwang-Ho (Yellow River) in China have moved the outlet several hundred kilometers, bringing disaster to the inhabitants of the plains. Deltas are composed of such rich soils, however, that they are among the world's most densely populated regions.

Man's harnessing of flowing water and its resultant land forms is, in fact, extensive. Examples range from the exploitation of fast-flowing streams for the generation of hydroelectricity to the use of rivers for irrigation, industry and domestic purposes, and as transport routes and natural harbors.

Waterfalls develop in the upper and middle courses of rivers and are found where there is a change in gradient. The cause is often a resistant band of rock that forms an obstacle to the river's downcutting action. The force of water erodes material away at the foot, forming a plunge pool. Waterfalls are worn away in time, making a smooth gradient.

Meanders, or large bends, occur in the lower course of a river (1). Bends tend to develop at this stage as a result of the latent instability arising from the river's slight gradient and high volume of flow. The river undercuts the outside bank (undercut slope) and deposits its alluvium on the inside of the bend (slipoff slope) (2). These large meanders eventually become so curved (3) that the river cuts across the narrow neck of land at both ends of the curve, forming what is called an ox-bow lake (4).

When rain falls to Earth, a proportion of it percolates down through joints and cracks in the rock and collects in the form of groundwater. The amount of groundwater depends on the permeability and the porosity of the rock and on the relief of the land. The upper surface of the groundwater is called the water table. Below the water table the rock is totally saturated with water. The height of the water table varies: in dry weather it is lower. A spring is an outlet where groundwater is released on to the surface. This often occurs where layers of impermeable and permeable rock alternate. Spring lines occur where there are several outlets. Springs then drain into rivers.

Landscape-makers: Ice and Snow

A series of glacial periods has punctuated the Earth's history for the last two million years. During the last glacial, the ice covered an area nearly three times larger than that covered by ice sheets and glaciers today. Its remnants are still found in the ice caps of the world: most present-day glacial ice is in Antarctica and Greenland in two great ice sheets which together contain about 97 percent of all the Earth's ice. The rest is in glaciers in Iceland, the Alps and other high mountain chains.

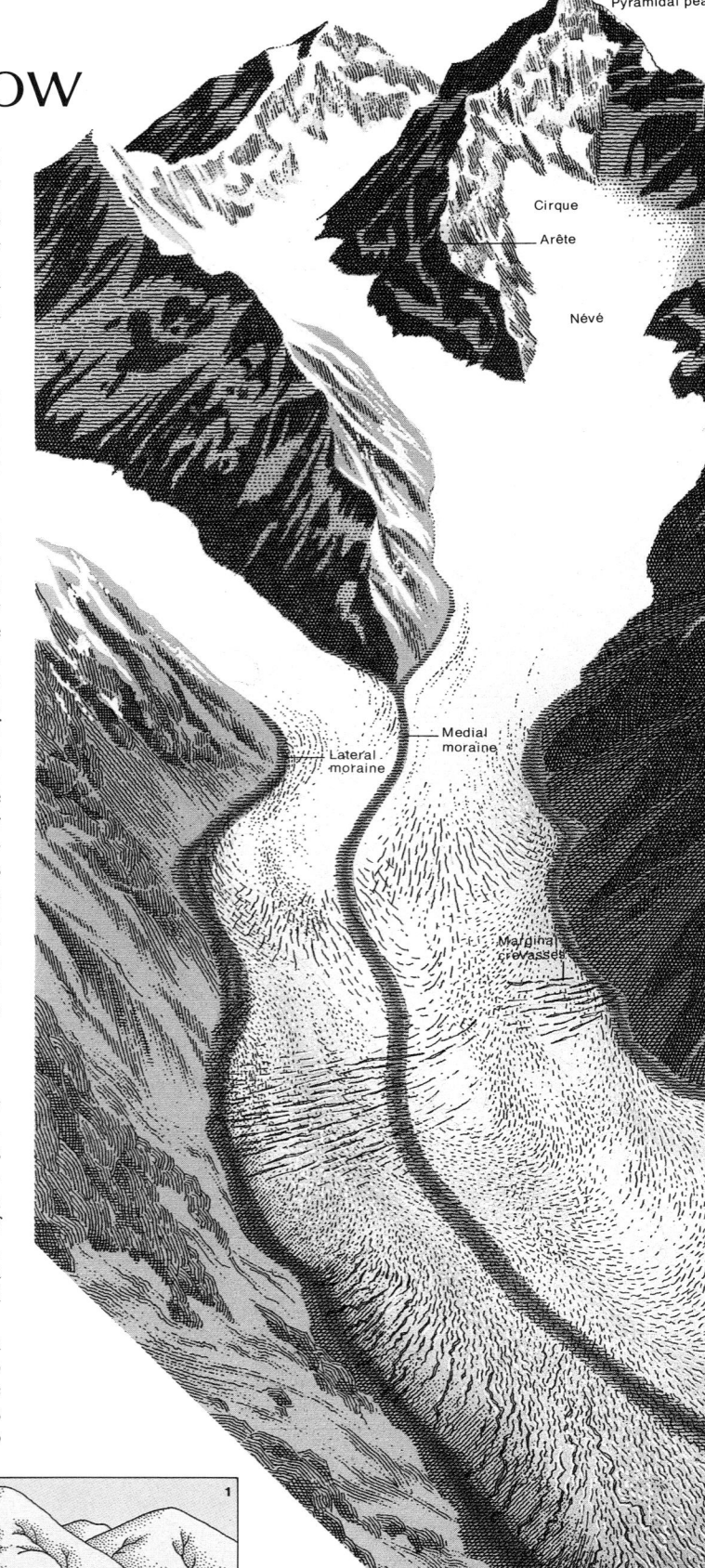

Pyramidal peak
Cirque
Arête
Névé
Medial moraine
Lateral moraine
Marginal crevasses

During the Earth's major glacial periods, ice sheets almost as big as that of present-day Antarctica spread over the northern part of North America, reaching as far south as the Ohio River, and over northern Europe as far south as southern England, the Netherlands and southern Poland. Today glacial activity is more restricted, but the mechanisms by which it carves dramatic features of the Earth's landscape remain the same.

Types of glacier

There are six main types of ice mass: cirque glaciers, which occupy basin-shaped depressions in mountain areas; valley glaciers; piedmont glaciers, in which the ice spreads in a lobe over a lowland; floating ice tongues and ice shelves; mountain ice caps; and ice sheets. Climate and relief are responsible for these differences, but glaciers can also be classified according to their internal temperatures.

Cold glaciers are those in which the ice temperature is below freezing point and they are frozen to the rock beneath. This condition, which hinders the movement of glaciers, exists in many parts of Antarctica and Greenland, where air temperatures are low, as well as at high altitudes in some lower-latitude mountain regions. Temperate glaciers, on the other hand, show internal temperatures at or close to the melting point of ice. Unlike cold glaciers, they are not frozen to the rock beneath and can therefore slide over it. Ice melts on the surface of the glacier when the weather is warm, and underneath the glacier as it is warmed by geothermal heat from inside the Earth. Streams collecting meltwater may flow over, through or under the ice and emerge at the ice edge. In other glaciers, cold ice may overlie temperate ice.

Glaciers are formed from snow that, as it accumulates year after year, becomes compacted, turning first into "névé" or "firn" and eventually, after several years or even decades, into glacial ice. This process of accumulation is offset by ablation, through which ice is lost by

melting, evaporation or, in glaciers that end in the sea or in lakes, by calving. If accumulation exceeds ablation, the glacier increases in size; conversely, if ablation is higher, the glacier shrinks and eventually disappears.

Glaciers move because of the force of gravity. The fastest-moving glaciers, for example those of coastal Greenland which descend steeply from areas of great accumulation, move at speeds of more than 20 m (65 ft) a day. A few meters a day is more common, however. Some glaciers move exceptionally quickly in surges, which usually last for a few weeks; rates of more than 100 m (330 ft) a day have been recorded. At the other extreme, some glaciers or parts of glaciers—the central zones of ice sheets and ice caps for example—are virtually motionless. When the ice in a glacier is subject to pressure or tension—as it flows down a valley, for example—it behaves rather like a plastic substance and changes its shape to fit the contours of the valley. Part or all of the movement of a glacier is accomplished by means of this internal deformation. In temperate glaciers, or glaciers whose lower layers are temperate, there is also basal sliding. Movement of a glacier produces cracks or crevasses in areas where stress exceeds the strength of the ice.

The work of glaciers

Glaciers and ice sheets can profoundly modify the landscape by both erosion and deposition. Measured rates of erosion of bedrock may be as much as several millimeters a year. Rock surfaces are scratched, or striated, and worn down by the constant grinding action (abrasion) of rock fragments embedded in the base of the ice. The extreme pressure of thick glacial ice on a basal boulder has been known to rupture solid bedrock beneath it.

The products of bedrock erosion range from fine clays and silts produced by abrasion, to large boulders picked up and transported by the ice. Some rocks have been carried hundreds of kilometers, from southern Scandinavia to

A U-shaped valley, such as Langdale (below) in the English Lake District, is a clear indication of a glaciated past. The floor is quite flat and the valley sides rise steeply from it.

A crevasse (below left) is created by stress within a glacier. Internally, the ice is rather like plastic but its surface is rigid and brittle. This causes tension and cracking on the surface.

This erratic (below right) is made of Silurian grit, yet it sits on a limestone perch. Ice left Yorkshire 20,000 years ago, since when the limestone surface has been lowered by solution.

Before the onset of glaciation a mountain region is often sculpted largely by the work of rivers and the processes of weathering. The hills are rounded and the valleys are V-shaped (1). During a period of glacial activity, valleys become filled with snow and eventually

glaciers and, after thousands of years, the region shows a typically glaciated landscape (2). When the ice has finally disappeared there remains a glacial trough (3) with hanging valleys, truncated spurs, waterfalls and all the landforms associated with deposition of material.

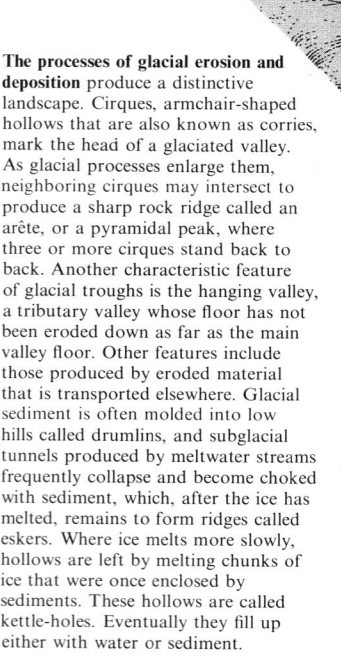

The processes of glacial erosion and deposition produce a distinctive landscape. Cirques, armchair-shaped hollows that are also known as corries, mark the head of a glaciated valley. As glacial processes enlarge them, neighboring cirques may intersect to produce a sharp rock ridge called an arête, or a pyramidal peak, where three or more cirques stand back to back. Another characteristic feature of glacial troughs is the hanging valley, a tributary valley whose floor has not been eroded down as far as the main valley floor. Other features include those produced by eroded material that is transported elsewhere. Glacial sediment is often molded into low hills called drumlins, and subglacial tunnels produced by meltwater streams frequently collapse and become choked with sediment, which, after the ice has melted, remains to form ridges called eskers. Where ice melts more slowly, hollows are left by melting chunks of ice that were once enclosed by sediments. These hollows are called kettle-holes. Eventually they fill up either with water or sediment.

eastern England, for example, and such far-traveled rocks are termed erratics. The finer sediments, compacted at the base of the glacier by the weight of the overlying ice, form till or boulder clay.

The surface of a glacier is often strewn with rock debris, which either rests on the ice or is within the glacier and revealed as the ice melts. Lateral moraines consist of rock debris that has accumulated along the sides of the glacier as a result of rockfall from, and erosion of, the valley sides. Where two glaciers join, the inner lateral moraines merge to form a medial moraine. In the ablation zone, the surface of the glacier becomes increasingly laden with debris "melting out" so that the ice may become completely buried. At the end of the glacier all rock debris is dumped, forming a terminal moraine.

Meltwater streams pouring out from glaciers or flowing in tunnels beneath them can be powerful agents of erosion and can transport large quantities of sediment. Bedrock surfaces become potholed and carved by channels that are eroded with great speed. As the streams emerge from the edge of the ice, they carry with them and deposit vast quantities of sand and gravel which form flood plains (outwash plains). Alternatively, meltwater streams may deposit sediment between the edge of the glacier and valley side, leaving a "kame terrace" when the ice finally melts. Meltwater streams feeding glacial lakes that are dammed by a glacier or moraine, for example, construct deltas of sand and gravel and lay down finer sediments (varved clays) on the lake floor.

Snow processes

Snow plays a smaller part than glacial ice in landform sculpture. Its most important role is in avalanches, which, in mountain regions, regularly bring down thousands of tonnes of rock debris. The mixture of snow, rock and other debris forms avalanche boulder tongues on the flat ground where the avalanche comes to rest and the snow melts. Gullies (avalanche chutes) on mountain slopes are swept clean of loose debris several times a year and they are gradually enlarged. Snow patches that remain stationary on more gentle slopes or in hollows encourage rock weathering under and around them. Such a process, termed nivation, may lead to deepening and enlargement of hollows and further snow accumulation. This is one way in which new glaciers are formed.

A glaciated valley exhibits a distinctive shape and profile. A cross section shows a U-shape, while longitudinally the valley floor is marked by a series of rocky steps and basins. The zone of accumulation is characterized by a cirque, in which snow collects to produce a firn field. A bergschrund is a type of crevasse that opens up near the top of the firn field where the head of the glacier is pulled away from the cirque walls. A rock step is where the gradient becomes much steeper. The speed of the ice flow is accelerated and consequent tension within the ice creates a number of deep crevasses called an ice fall. The zone of ablation has large accumulations of various kinds of rock debris.

Glacial erosion of rock surfaces is typified by a roche moutonnée, a resistant rock hummock that lies in the path of the ice. The upstream side is smooth as a result of abrasion by rock debris that is frozen into the base of the glacier. This debris scratches and scrapes rock, producing striations. The downstream side is rough as a result of ice plucking. Meltwater removes the small blocks of rock.

A great variety of material arrives at the terminus or snout of a glacier—ranging from large blocks of rock and boulders to very finely ground rock "flour." All the material is dropped in a haphazard way as the ice melts. The mixture of clay and boulders is termed glacial till. If the ice margin remains stationary, till accumulates to form a terminal moraine. If the snout recedes continuously, no ridge forms.

Landscape-makers: The Seas

The coastline is both the birthplace and the graveyard of the land. Over tens of thousands of years, geological uplift of a continent, or a fall in sea level, may create an emerging fringe of new land, whereas a period of submergence drowns the coasts and floods the adjacent river valleys, destroying land but producing some of the most attractive coastal landscapes. More rapid are the changes brought about by the sea itself. Erosion of coastal rocks or beaches can cut back the coastline at a rate of several meters a year, whereas other coastlines are built up at a comparable rate from marine sediments.

Changing coastlines are apparent on a human time scale. In temperate latitudes, beaches tend to be combed down and narrowed by winter waves, only to be restored during the calmer weather of summer. They may be lost one week and replenished the next, demonstrating an invaluable ability to recover from the wounds of all but the most devastating storms. Cliffs are generally much less dynamic, particularly if composed of resistant rock, but any loss that they suffer is permanent because there is no process that is capable of rebuilding them.

Coasts vary greatly around the world. Tropical areas often have wide beaches made up of fine material which in many cases forms broad mangrove swamps that collect sediment and build up the coast. In more exposed tropical zones coral reefs are common, either fringing the shore or (particularly where the sea level is rising) separated from the shore by a lagoon to give a barrier reef. Continued submergence of a small island surrounded by such a reef may produce an atoll. In contrast, Arctic beaches are narrow and coarse, and may be icebound for up to 10 months each year. Recession of soft rock cliffs results more from melting of ice in the ground than from wave erosion.

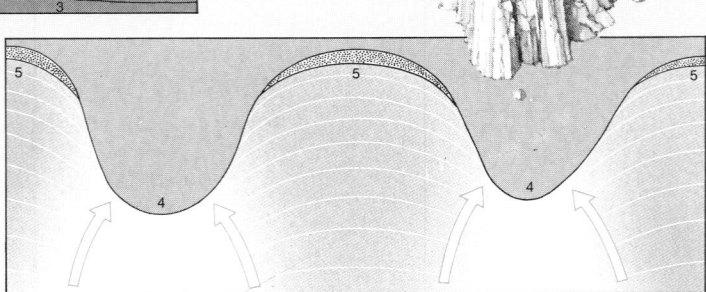

Cliffs are attacked by waves at the zone that lies between high tide (HT) and low tide (LT). The rate of erosion depends on the strength and jointing pattern of the rock and the angle at which the strata are presented to the sea. Erosion begins when water and rocks are hurled at the cliff and new fragments are broken off. The pressure of the water also compresses air in joints and cracks to shatter the rock face. As the base of the cliff is attacked, a notch (1) may be cut, and as this is made deeper the cliff above collapses. Eventually a wave-cut platform (2) is created, the top of which is

exposed at low tide. The debris from the cliff is carried along the coast or deposited offshore (3). The shallow seabed now slows down incoming waves: they attack the cliff (4), but their energy is reduced. In calm water, for example at the head of a bay (5), wave energy is diffused and light material such as sand is deposited as beaches.

Waves at work

Across great expanses of open ocean energy is transferred from the wind to the sea surface to produce waves, thus fueling the machine that ultimately creates the coast. Originating as waves with heights of up to 20 or even 30 m (65–100 ft), they lose part of their energy quite rapidly as they travel, and once they have been reduced in height to the lower but more widely spaced ocean swell, they continue to travel across enormous distances.

The coasts of western Europe receive waves produced almost 10,000 km (6,200 miles) away off Cape Horn, and swell reaching California has sometimes crossed more than 11,000 km

THE SEA COAST

The coastline is continually changing, whether day by day as the tides sift and sort the sand and shingle on the beaches, or over tens of thousands of years as the erosive power of waves carves out headlands and bays. And over millions of years the coastline is subjected to major changes of sea level, whether it is the land uplifting or sinking, or the sea itself rising or receding. Today, interference by man can damage the coast. Dam building and river-channel engineering drastically reduce the amount of sediment reaching the coast; and sea walls built to protect the coast and groynes constructed to retard sand removal both pose a long-term threat to adjacent coasts, which become starved of the sediment that previously supplied their beaches.

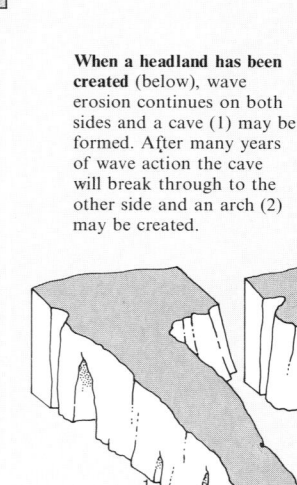

When a headland has been created (below), wave erosion continues on both sides and a cave (1) may be formed. After many years of wave action the cave will break through to the other side and an arch (2) may be created.

Light material such as mud, sand and shingle is carried by the sea. Waves tend to push the particles obliquely up a beach (right), but the backwash moves the material down again at right-angles to the shore. Thus the materials move in a zigzag fashion along the beach (1). This is known as longshore drift. When the load-carrying capacity of the waves is reduced for any reason, the material is deposited and forms a variety of features. The largest beaches (2) are found in the calmest waters such as in bays or at river mouths, with the finest grains sorted out nearest to the sea and larger pebbles

stranded higher up. Spits (3) and bars (4) are sand ridges deposited across a bay or river mouth. When one end of the ridge is attached to the land it is called a spit. Spits are very often shaped like a hook as waves are refracted around the tip of land. Bars are formed where sand is deposited in shallow water offshore across the entrances to bays and run parallel to the coastline. Dunes, pictured above, are formed when sand on the beach is driven inland by onshore winds. Very often they isolate flooded land behind them to form coastal features such as salt marshes and mud flats.

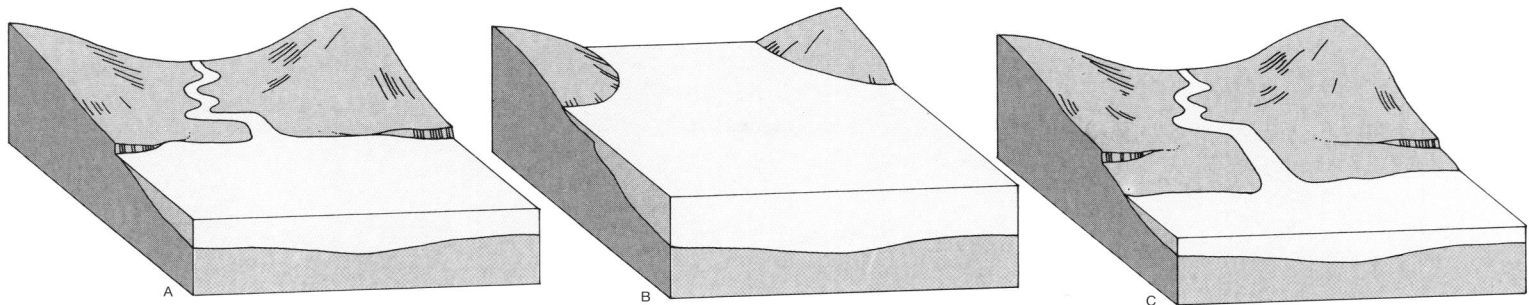

There are two major kinds of coastline—coastlines of submergence and coastlines of emergence. They are created by either a sinking or an uplift of the land, or by a change in sea level. A coastline with wave-cut cliffs and a river valley (A), for example, that experiences a rise in sea level will produce a new coastline (B) with a drowned estuary, coastal uplands isolated as islands, and a submerged coastal plain. The same coastline subjected to a drop in sea level (C) results in an extended river, abandoned cliffs far inland, and a raised beach that forms a new coastal plain.

(6,800 miles) of the Pacific from the storm belt south of New Zealand. The waves thus act as a giant conveyor for the energy that is finally used up in a few seconds of intense activity. Few other natural systems gather their energy so widely and then concentrate it so effectively.

A ball floating on the sea surface shows that, although a passing wave form moves forward, the water (and ball) follow a near-circular path and end up almost where they started. Beneath the surface the water follows similar orbits, but the amount of movement becomes progressively less with depth, until it dies out altogether. The greater the wavelength (the distance between crests) the greater is the depth of disturbance.

Long-swell waves approaching a gentle shore start disturbing the seabed far from the coast and these waves slow up, pack closer together and increase in height until they become unstable, thus producing the spilling white surf that carries much sediment to build up wide sandy beaches. Shorter local storm waves disturb the water to less depth, and thus reach much closer inshore before they interact with the seabed. Such waves do not therefore break until they plunge directly down on to the beach, leading to severe erosion, which results in the production of steep pebble beaches.

Waves slow up in shallow water, and so an undulating seabed causes their crests to bend and change their direction of approach. As a result, waves converge toward headlands (where their erosional attack is concentrated),

but they diverge as they enter bays, spreading out their energy and encouraging the deposition of the sediment they carry across the seabed close inshore. The high-energy waves at the headlands remove any rock fragments that become detached and transport them to the beaches that form at the bayheads.

Erosional coasts

Much of the local variability of coastal scenery results from differing rates of erosion on different types of rock. Bays are cut back rapidly into soft rocks such as clay, sand or gravel. Headlands are evidence that the sea takes longer to remove higher areas of harder rock such as granite or limestone. Despite the enormous power of storm waves, erosion of resistant rocks is slow and relies on any weakness that the sea can exploit.

Joints, faults and bedding planes are etched out by the water and by rock fragments hurled against them by breaking waves. Air compressed into such crevices by water pressure widens and deepens them into cracks and then into caves. In this way a solid cliff face can be eroded to form the great variety of features.

Resistant rocks can form steep, simple cliffs of great height—more than 600 m (2,000 ft) in some places—and the sea may have to undercut them to produce collapse and retreat. Cliffs of weaker rocks rarely reach 100 m (330 ft) in height and are more rapidly eroded by atmospheric processes, by running water and by

landslips. There the role of the sea is largely confined to removing the rock debris from the foot of the cliff. Soft rock cliffs are gently sloping but complex in form.

Coasts of deposition

Although waves bend as they approach the shore, they rarely become completely parallel to the coastline. Wave crests drive sediment obliquely toward the beach, whereas the troughs carry it back directly offshore down the beach slope. In this way, sand and pebbles are transported in a zigzag motion, called longshore drift, away from the areas where they are produced. One such source of material is cliff erosion, but on average about 95 percent of the material moving on to beaches was originally carried to the coast by rivers.

Beaches are built up wherever longshore drift is impeded (for example, by a headland) or where wave and current energy is reduced (as at the head of a bay). An abundant supply of sediment may build a sandbar across the mouth of a bay or in shallow water offshore. Where the coast changes direction, longshore drift may continue in its original direction and build a spit out from the land. Depositional features may become strengthened by vegetation. Plants may take root and bind together newly deposited sediments, but they constitute relatively delicate coasts that are vulnerable to erosion if for any reason they are not continually supplied with fresh deposits of sediment.

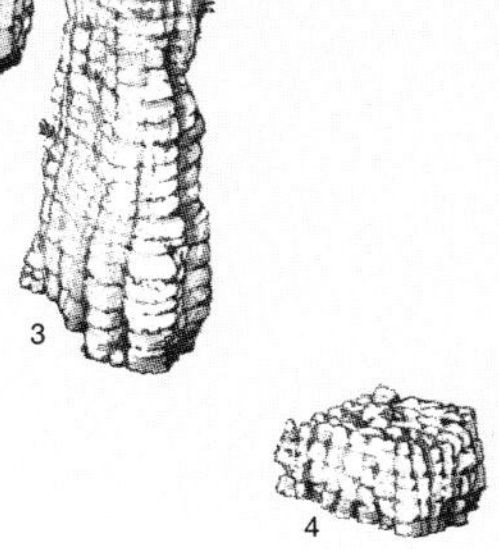

Further wave erosion (above) causes the roof of the arch to collapse, leaving an isolated column of rock called a stack (3). Another cave, and then an arch, may be formed behind the stack, which itself may be eroded to a short stump (4).

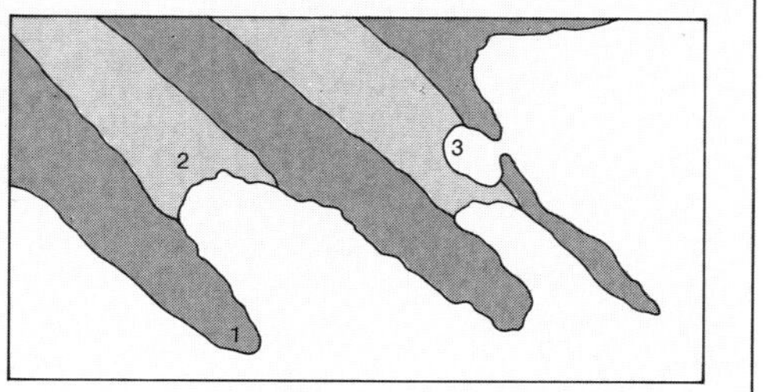

Headlands alternating with bays are found where bands of strong (1) and weak (2) rocks meet the coast at an angle and there is a varied resistance to erosion. The bays are first carved out of the softer rock, leaving the waves to attack the headlands of hard rock. If, in contrast, the strata lie parallel to the coast, then the hard rock has few irregular indentations except where the sea has broken through to the soft rock behind and has scoured out a cove (3).

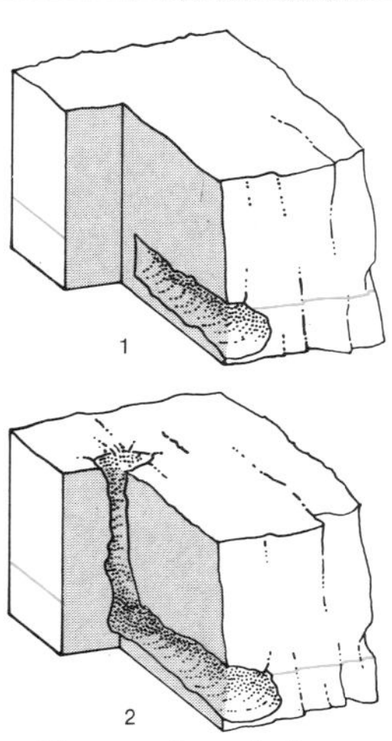

Gloups are formed when waves first erode a cave, then extend it backward as a long shaft running into the cliff (1). If the roof collapses at one point, a blowhole, or gloup (2), is formed. If the whole roof collapses, a deep cleft called a geo is created.

Waves are generated by wind on the surface of the sea. It is the shape of the wave that travels forward—the individual water particles move in near-circular orbits. Disturbance diminishes with depth to about half a wavelength. Waves break when they strike a sloping shore, and the wave height is about the same as the depth of the water.

Landscape-makers: Wind and Weathering

Winds are part of the global circulation of air and they can affect landforms wherever surface material is loose and unprotected by vegetation. The effects of a strong wind are a familiar sight—whether in the dust clouds that rise from a plowed field after a dry spell, or in the sand swept along the beach on a windy day. Weathering is the disintegration and decomposition of rocks through their exposure to the atmosphere. It includes the changes that destroy the original structure of rocks, and few on the Earth's surface have not been weathered at one time or another in the history of our evolving landscape.

Active and fixed dunes in Africa and western Asia

Fixed sand dunes

Active sand dunes

Sand dunes cover only 20 percent of the world's deserts, and tend to be concentrated in a small number of sand seas, or ergs, such as the Erg Bourharet in Algeria (above). Longitudinal, or seif, dunes (below) are long, narrow ridges that lie parallel to the direction of prevailing winds. Surface heating and wind flow produce vertical spiraling motions of air.

Direction of wind

Most sand seas today are being actively molded by winds. The landscape has long been shaped by wind, and some dune fields produced in dry climates in the distant past may be "fossilized" now by soils and vegetation cover. Desertification often occurs where this vegetation is disturbed by man.

EROSION AND WEATHERING

Winds result from the differential heating of regions of the globe. They act indirectly as agents of erosion through water or waves, but they also directly affect the surface of the Earth, molding landforms either by erosion or deposition. The nature of weathering processes and the rate at which they operate depend upon climate, the properties of the rock and the conditions of the biosphere. Both wind erosion and the various weathering processes are significant landscape-makers.

Many rocks are formed deep in the Earth, where they are in equilibrium with the forces that created them. If they become exposed at the surface, they are in disequilibrium with atmospheric forces. This brings about the changes—adjustments to atmospheric and organic agents—that we call weathering. Products of weathering are moved by agents of erosion, one of which is the wind. Where the surface is protected, for example by vegetation, the wind has little effect, but where strong winds attack loose surface material that is unprotected, erosion, abrasion and deposition may occur, producing characteristic landforms.

How wind shapes the surface

Strong winds occur in many places, but nowhere are they more effective in forming the surface of the land than in deserts, where their work is largely unhindered by vegetation. There the wind can pick up material and then, charged with sand particles, blast away at the ground, carrying away the debris and depositing it. Many notorious desert winds are associated with sand movement and dust storms—the harmattan of West Africa and the sirocco of the Middle East, for example.

Wind erosion occurs where winds charged with sand attack soils or rock. Dry soils may be broken up and the resulting debris, which includes soil nutrients, is carried away as dust. This poses a serious problem, especially when arid and semiarid lands experience drought. Wind erosion involving the lifting and blowing away of loose material from the ground surface is called deflation.

Erosion by sand and rock fragments carried by winds is called abrasion. In this way winds erode individual surface pebbles into distinctive shapes known as ventifacts. They can also mold larger rock masses into aerodynamic shapes known as yardangs—features that often look rather like upturned rowing boats. Some of these features are so large that they have been identified only since satellite photographs have become available. Finally, winds erode by attrition, which involves the mutual wearing down of particles as they are carried along.

Winds can transport material in three different ways. They can lift loose, sand-sized particles into the air and carry them downwind along trajectories that resemble those of ballistic missiles: the particles rise steeply and descend along gentle flight paths. This produces a bouncing movement known as saltation in a layer extending approximately 1 m (3 ft) above the

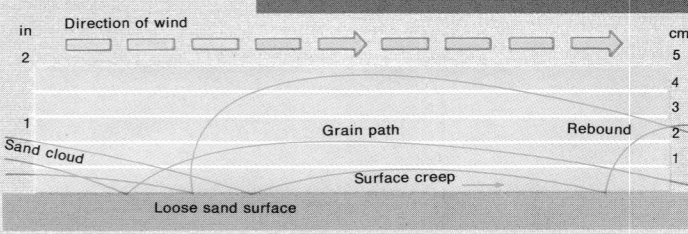

in 2

Direction of wind

Grain path   Rebound

Sand cloud

Surface creep

Loose sand surface

cm 5 4 3 2 1

Sand particles move in a series of long jumps—a process called saltation. Particles describe a curved path (above), the height and length of which depends upon the mass of the grain, the wind velocity and the number of other particles moving around. Saltation only occurs in a layer extending up to approximately 1 m (3 ft) above the ground surface. Sand grains moving in this way are also responsible for the abraded base of features such as pedestal rocks (right). These landforms are weathered first—for example by the crystallization of salts—and are then eroded by the sand-laden winds.

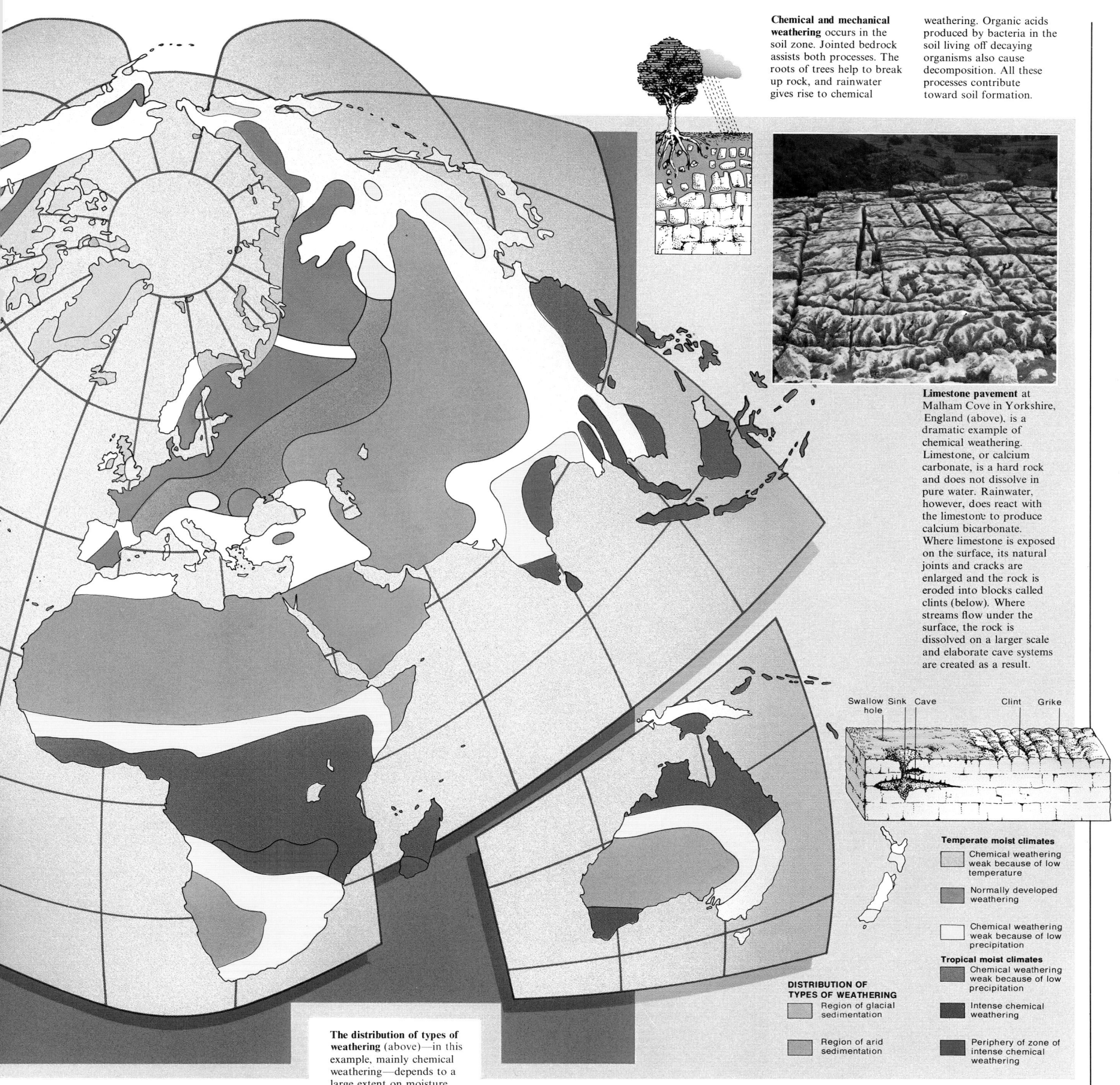

The distribution of types of weathering (above)—in this example, mainly chemical weathering—depends to a large extent on moisture and temperature. When classifying regions with different rates of chemical weathering in terms of climatic zones, many areas of the world can be placed into one of two principal categories: tropical moist climates and temperate moist climates. The white areas on the map are mountain ranges or regions of tectonic activity where there is no appreciable weathering mantle.

ground. As the bouncing particles strike the surface, they push other particles along the ground (creep or drift). Fine particles that are disturbed by saltation rise up into the airflow and are carried away as dust (suspension).

The materials eroded and transported by winds must eventually come to rest in features of deposition, the most extensive of which are sand dunes. Sand seas at first sight appear to be random and complex, rather like a choppy ocean, but their features generally fall into three size groups: small ripples, which have a wavelength of up to 3 m (10 ft) and a height of 20 cm (8 in); dunes, with a wavelength of 20–300 m (65–1,000 ft) and a height of up to 30 m (68 ft); and sand mountains or "draa," which have a wavelength of 1–3 km (0.6–1.5 miles) and rise to a height of up to 200 m (650 ft). Within each size group various forms can be explained in terms of the nature of the sand and the kinds of winds that blow over it. Where winds blow consistently from one direction, long linear dunes form parallel or transverse to the wind direction. Where sand supply is limited, horned "barchan" dunes may form. If winds blow from several directions during a year, then star-shaped dunes and other complex patterns appear. Sand dunes are also common along the

shorelines of large lakes and the world's oceans, where onshore winds can pile quite extensive areas of loose drifting sand.

Agents of weathering

Weathering takes two forms: mechanical weathering breaks up rock without altering its mineral constituents, whereas chemical weathering changes in some way the nature of mineral crystals. One agent of mechanical weathering is temperature change. It used to be thought that rocks disintegrated as a result of a huge daily range of temperature (thermal weathering). Despite travelers' tales of rocks splitting in the desert night with cracks like pistol shots, there is little evidence to support this view. In the presence of water, however, alternate heating and cooling of rocks does result in fracture. Frost is also an effective rock breaker. The freezing of water and expansion of ice in the cracks and pores of rocks create disruptive pressures; alternate freezing and thawing eventually causes pieces of rock to break off in angular fragments. Finally, the roots of plants and trees grow into the joints of rock and widen them, thus loosening the structure of the rock. Animals burrowing through the soil can have a similar effect on rocks.

Chemical and mechanical weathering can work hand in hand. In arid regions, for example, the crystallization of salts results in the weathering of rock. As water evaporates from the rock surface, salt crystals grow (from minerals dissolved in the water) in small openings in the rock. In time these crystals bring to bear enough pressure to break off rock fragments from the parent block.

Chemical weathering is most effective in humid tropical climates, however, and it usually involves the decomposition of rocks as a result of their exposure to air and rainwater, which contains dissolved chemicals. Carbon dioxide from the air, for example, becomes dissolved in rainwater, making it into weak carbonic acid. This reacts with minerals such as calcite, which is found in many rocks. Similarly, rocks can be oxidized by oxygen in the air. This happens to rocks that contain iron, for example, if they are exposed on the surface: a reddish iron oxide is produced which causes the rocks to crumble.

Over many thousands, even millions, of years, the processes of mechanical and chemical weathering have affected many of the rocks on the Earth's surface. When rocks are weakened in such a way, they then fall prey to the agents of erosion—water, ice, winds and waves.

Landscape-makers: Man

Man has done much to reshape the face of the planet since his first appearance on Earth more than two million years ago. Early man did little to harm the environment but, with the rise of agriculture, the landscape began to change. An increasing population and the growth of urban settlements gradually created greater demands for agricultural land and living space. But industrialization during the last 200 years has had the biggest impact. Man's search for and exploitation of the Earth's resources has to a large extent transformed the natural landscape and at the same time created totally artificial man-made environments.

Man's major impact on the landscape has been through forest clearance. He made the first attack on natural forests about 8,000 years ago in Neolithic times in northern and western Europe, as revealed by the changing composition of tree pollen deposited in bogs. After Roman times, especially in the Mediterranean region, there was another spate of forest clearance, so that by the Middle Ages little original forest survived in the Old World. As population and emigration increased, it was the turn of trees in the New World and Africa to fall before the axe and plow. Man's present voracious appetite for timber and its products could, if unchecked, clear most of the Earth's great forests by the end of this century.

Forest clearance not only changes the appearance of the landscape but can alter the balance of nature within a region. The hydrological cycle may be affected, and soil erosion may be increased, which in turn chokes rivers with sediment and leads to the silting up of harbors and estuaries. The coastal area of Valencia in Spain, for example, has widened by nearly 4 km (2.5 miles) since Roman times, much of which can be accounted for by forest clearance, and subsequent soil erosion and the deposition of the material by rivers as they near the sea. Reafforestation of an area can reduce soil erosion and the threat of flooding. Landscape management can reduce wind speeds: for example, shelter belts in the Russian steppes have been planted over distances of more than 100 km (62 miles).

Water management
The second great impact of man has been on the waterways of the world. The most spectacular changes are caused by the construction of dams to make vast new lakes. Such projects have frequently had effects far beyond those originally anticipated. The Aswan High Dam on the River Nile was completed in 1970, creating Lake Nasser and making possible the irrigation of an additional 550,000 hectares (1,358,000 acres) in upper Egypt. But some would argue that the dam holds back silt from the rivers and stores it in the lake, a fact that has seriously reduced the rate of silting in the Nile delta. This has resulted in increased salinity and some loss of fertility of the soil, as well as changes to the delta's coastline. The storage of silt in Lake Nasser has caused increased erosion of the riverbed downstream and the undermining of the foundations of bridges and barrages.

Other man-made changes to rivers include straightening and canalization, usually for

Massive power plants (left) symbolize man's modifications to the landscape in modern, industrialized society. Demand for energy and mineral resources has led to the creation of huge holes in the ground like this borax mine (below left) in the Mojave desert in California. The open pit is 100 m (330 ft) deep, 1,460 m (4,800 ft) long and 915 m (3,000 ft) wide. In opening up resource areas in Brazil, the Trans-Amazonian highway has disturbed the forest (below).

Hong Kong's bustling waterfront (below) captures the true essence of urban man. If space is in short supply, he expands his world vertically and maximizes his use of every square meter. Central business districts in the world's major cities reflect this concern with space.

flood protection, but also to prevent the channel from shifting. As long ago as the third millennium BC, during the reign of Emperor Yao, a hydraulic engineer was apparently appointed to control the wandering course of the Hwang-Ho (Yellow River), and the system he devised survived for at least 1,500 years. Even so, over the centuries, the river has changed course radically, and today measures are still being taken to control the fine sediment that the river carries and the flooding caused by its deposition. The Missouri River in the United States is estimated to erode material from an area of about 3,680 hectares (9,000 acres) annually over a length of 1,220 km (758 miles). It is little wonder that engineers attempt to control rivers by means of realignment or try to "train" a river's flow by using concrete stays.

New land from old

The continuing pressure of population on food resources and the need to create new agricultural land illustrate still further the impact of man as a landscape shaper. As part of irrigation projects land is often leveled and new waterways are created in the form of canals. Pakistan has one of the most extensive man-made irrigation systems in the world. It controls almost completely the flow of the Indus, Sutlej and Punjab rivers through some 640 km (400 miles) of linking canals.

A huge demand for rice in many parts of southeastern Asia has led to farmers terracing steep slopes on many mountainous islands. In the Netherlands, about one-third of the entire cultivated area of the country is land that has been reclaimed from the sea. In the future more grandiose schemes are likely. Any large-scale expansion of agricultural land in the former Soviet Union will be mainly dependent on water supply. There have been plans since the 1930s to divert northward-flowing rivers to irrigated areas in the south and west. This idea, which might become a reality by the turn of the century, could have serious implications for the waters of the Arctic Ocean. If the amount of fresh water flowing into the ocean is reduced, salinity will increase, thus affecting the melting of ice floes and, consequently, sea level.

Man has also made his mark along the coastlines, from small-scale measures, such as the construction of groynes—wooden piles that reduce the amount of sand that is transported along the beach by wave action—to large-scale man-made harbors.

Modern man, the urban dweller of the machine age, has brought great changes to the face of the landscape. The need for materials for the construction of the urban fabric has led to the creation of huge quarries, in which building stone and road-building materials are extracted from the ground. Demand for energy and minerals leads to extensive modification of the landscape, especially where mineral deposits are near the surface and can be extracted by open-cast mining. The largest holes on Earth (excluding ocean basins) are those that result from the extraction of fuel (coal) and minerals.

The side effects of mining can be detrimental to the environment. Land may subside and despoilation of the landscape by slag heaps, for example, is considerable. Escaping coal dust can suffocate vegetation in a mining area, and gases given off during some mining operations can also damage plant and animal life.

Reclamation of spoiled areas is obligatory in many countries. Old open-cast workings are often filled with water to be used for recreational facilities, and slag heaps are treated and planted with vegetation: research has produced certain strains of plants that will grow even in the most acidic soils.

The true impact of man

During the last hundred years or so man has become much more aware of his role as an agent of landscape creation and destruction. The significance of man the landscape-maker, in comparison with slow, natural changes, is the speed with which he effects transformation, the sheer amount of energy which he can apply to a relatively small area, and the selectiveness and determination with which he applies that energy. Man's increased impact has not been a smooth and continuous process: it has occurred at different rates in different places and at different times. While it can be argued that some landscapes have been constructed which themselves conserve and often beautify the natural environment, man's active role has primarily been destructive: he has transformed the Earth's surface, perhaps irreversibly.

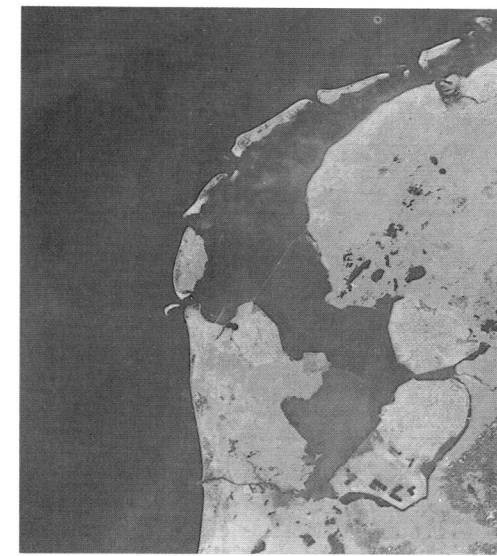

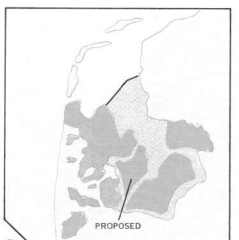

Man-made environments have become increasingly complex and large scale. Highway construction—this vast interchange (left) is in Chicago—is typical of the extensive use of land for modern transport systems alone. The acreage of land use classified as urban continues to increase. Man's endeavors to make still more land available for his many purposes have extended to cultivating previously inhospitable desert lands (above). More than half the land in Israel is naturally unproductive because of its aridity. By means of elaborate water carriage and storage schemes and scientifically researched irrigation projects, the desert has been totally transformed from a barren wasteland into intensively cultivated fields. Output from agriculture can also be increased by terracing. In densely populated areas, or mountainous regions, as in Luzon in the Philippines (right), man's skillful landscaping has completely reshaped the topography.

Part 3

THE EMERGENCE OF LIFE

How life on Earth began and developed
How life has evolved and spread over the planet
How man came to inherit the Earth

THE STAGES OF LIFE
Simple organic molecules, the precursors of life, could certainly have evolved in Earth's primitive atmosphere. Energy from the Sun, volcanoes and electric storms had the power to combine the basic chemicals into the amino acids and other molecules that are the constituents of living matter, forming droplets of "pre-life" in pools and on shorelines. Concentrations of droplets collected around some minerals, coagulating in a "soup" of long-chain polymers—proteins and nucleic acids which together form the living cell. Thus far have scientists re-created life's origins, but the combining of proteins and nucleic acids into a living unit remains to be achieved.

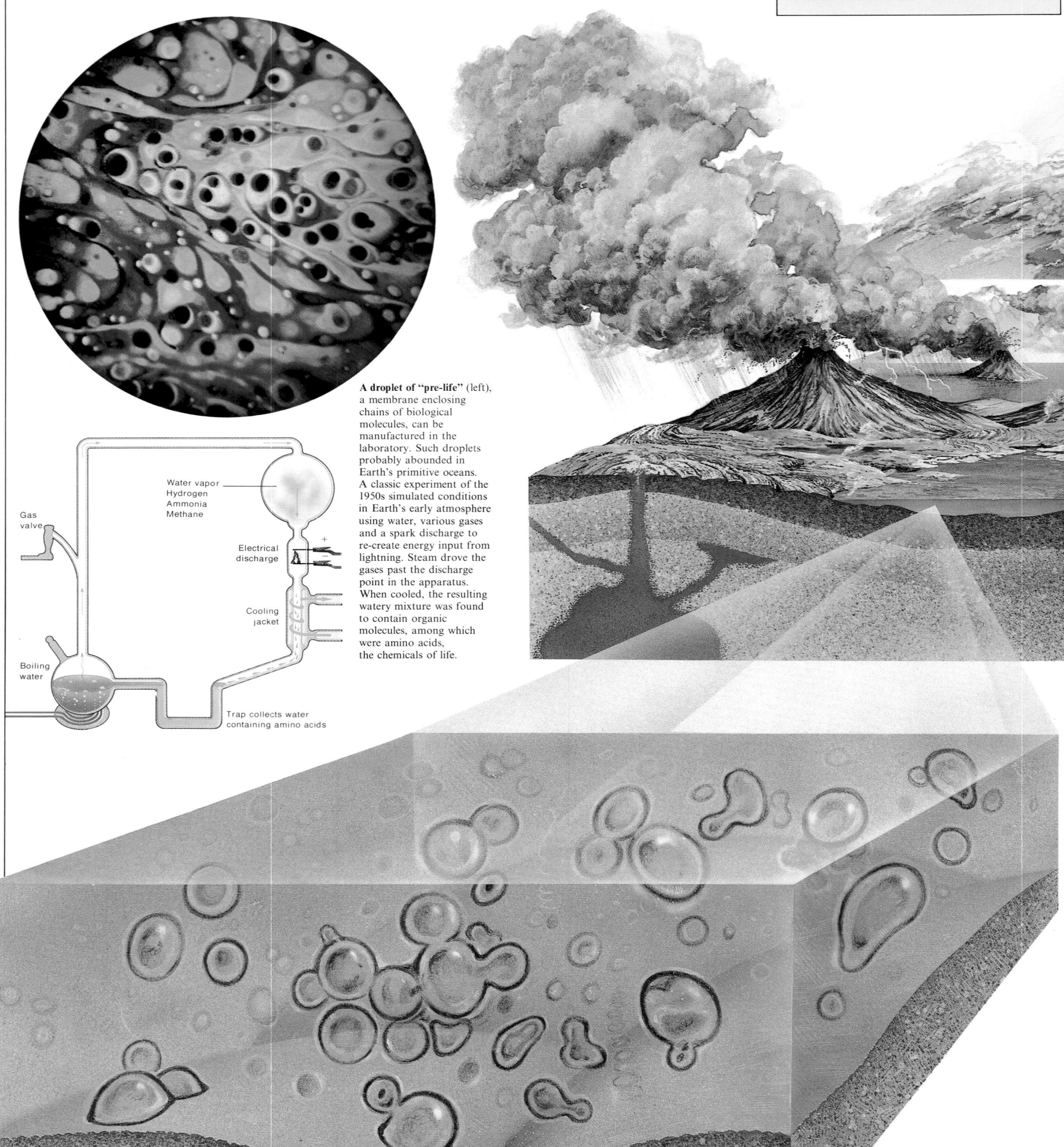

A droplet of "pre-life" (left), a membrane enclosing chains of biological molecules, can be manufactured in the laboratory. Such droplets probably abounded in Earth's primitive oceans. A classic experiment of the 1950s simulated conditions in Earth's early atmosphere using water, various gases and a spark discharge to re-create energy input from lightning. Steam drove the gases past the discharge point in the apparatus. When cooled, the resulting watery mixture was found to contain organic molecules, among which were amino acids, the chemicals of life.

Gas valve

Water vapor
Hydrogen
Ammonia
Methane

Electrical discharge

Cooling jacket

Boiling water

Trap collects water containing amino acids

LIFE BEGINS
A "primordial soup" of organic molecules, each separated from the water by a membrane, formed thick concentrations in Earth's shallow pools. From these evolved the long-chain polymers that form proteins and nucleic acids in every living cell.

The Source of Life

Life may have come to Earth from outer space – some meteorites contain life-like organic molecules – but the basic constituents of life, the biochemical structures called proteins and nucleic acids, could just as well have formed on Earth itself. By simulating possible primitive conditions on Earth, and applying a likely energy source, American scientists of the 1950s manufactured, from inorganic substances, the amino acids that form the subunits of all living things.

THE RADIANT SUN
A dense atmosphere of water vapor and various gases—but not oxygen—formed round the cooling planet Earth after its creation 4,600 million years ago. Oxygen in the atmosphere would have prevented the evolution of life from nonliving organic matter by blocking the Sun's ultraviolet radiation (which may have provided energy for the forming of organic compounds), and free oxygen would also have destroyed such compounds as they began to accumulate.

THE PRIMITIVE ATMOSPHERE
Volcanic eruptions drove water vapor and gases into the atmosphere of the young Earth; lightning and other discharges of atmospheric electricity accompanied the torrential rain; dissolved minerals collected in the pools. These were some of the preconditions for life on Earth, whereby mixtures of organic compounds in water may have combined to form more complex units essential for life.

Water played a key part in the creation of life on Earth. At first the temperature of the newly formed planet was far too high for water to exist in a liquid state. Instead, it formed a dense atmosphere of steam, which, as the Earth cooled, condensed into droplets of rain that poured down for perhaps thousands of years. This torrential, thundery rain eroded the land and dissolved the minerals, which collected in pools on the surface.

Earth's original atmosphere was also very different from today's. Most importantly, it contained no free oxygen, the gas which makes air-breathing life possible; the primitive atmosphere was composed of carbon monoxide, carbon dioxide, hydrogen and nitrogen. But the absence of oxygen created two conditions that are essential if life is to evolve. First, without oxygen the atmosphere could have no layer of ozone (an oxygen compound), which now acts as a barrier to most of the Sun's high-energy radiation (mainly ultraviolet light). Second, the absence of free oxygen meant that any complex chemicals that might be formed would not immediately break down again. Thus the molecules of life could form.

The chemistry of life

Life may be distinguished from nonlife in three ways: living organisms are able to increase the complexity of their parts through synthetic, self-building reactions; they obtain and use energy by breaking down chemical compounds; and they can make new copies of themselves.

It is the combined properties of the chemicals

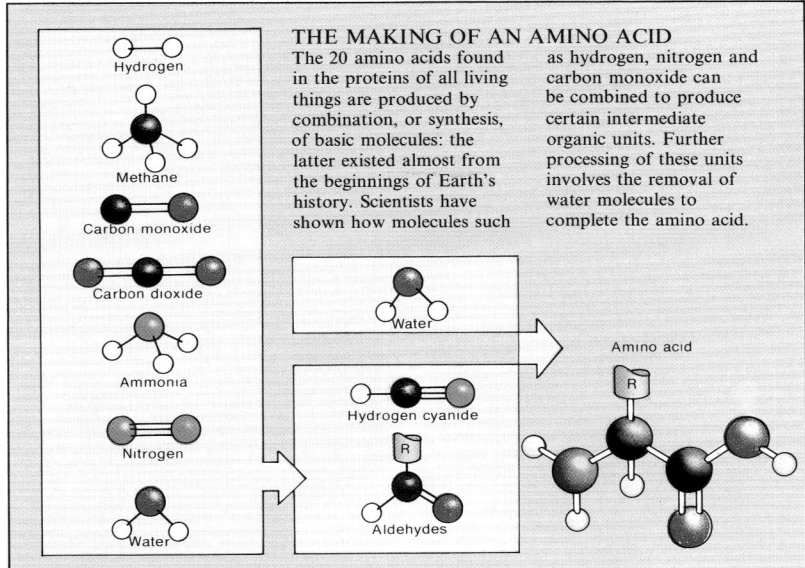

THE MAKING OF AN AMINO ACID
The 20 amino acids found in the proteins of all living things are produced by combination, or synthesis, of basic molecules: the latter existed almost from the beginnings of Earth's history. Scientists have shown how molecules such as hydrogen, nitrogen and carbon monoxide can be combined to produce certain intermediate organic units. Further processing of these units involves the removal of water molecules to complete the amino acid.

Hydrogen

Methane

Carbon monoxide

Carbon dioxide

Ammonia

Nitrogen

Water

Water

Hydrogen cyanide

Aldehydes

Amino acid

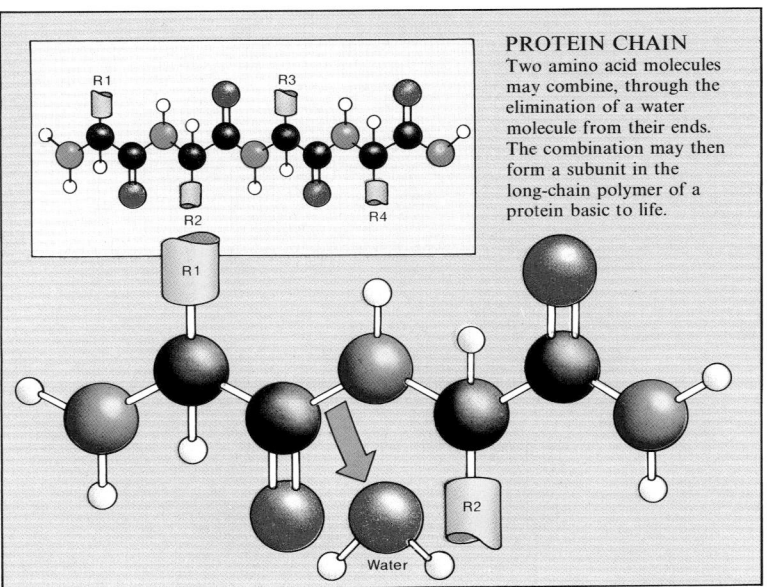

PROTEIN CHAIN
Two amino acid molecules may combine, through the elimination of a water molecule from their ends. The combination may then form a subunit in the long-chain polymer of a protein basic to life.

R1 R3
R2 R4
R1
R2
Water

of life that make them so special, not just the chemicals themselves. Experiments in the last few decades have given us a very good idea of how life could have arisen from the simple, nonliving chemicals which compose it. In the early 1950s, Harold Urey and Stanley Miller simulated the atmosphere of a primitive world by filling a flask with water, ammonia, methane and hydrogen. They supplied it with energy in the form of heat and an electric spark—to simulate lightning—and the experiment was left to run for a week.

Analyzing the mixture formed, they found it contained many chemicals that are associated with living things, particularly nitrogen compounds called amino acids—the really important chemicals of life. Further experiments brought together other gas mixtures, including the one that is now thought to have covered the young Earth, and these gave similar results, as long as there was no free oxygen present. The resulting mixture of organic compounds in water came to be known as the "primordial

soup," and it is from this "soup" that life may have emerged.

Miller and Urey had shown that the basic substances of life can be derived from a primitive atmosphere. But there are still large gaps in our understanding of how these substances became more organized and self-regulating: in other words, how they became alive. More complex molecular structures somehow developed through the linking up of the basic units to form long, chain-like sequences of larger units, called polymers. But how this happened is still not fully understood.

The two most important classes of biological molecules are proteins and nucleic acids, both of which are polymers. Proteins are the building materials of living matter, the chief components of muscles, skin and hair. They also form enzymes—the chemicals that control biochemical reaction in living cells. Nucleic acids—DNA (deoxyribonucleic acid) and RNA (ribonucleic acid)—are so called because they are found in the central nuclei of cells. They are the cell's genetic material, the raw stuff of heredity. They act as the memories and the messengers of life, storing information in units called genes, and releasing that information to the cells when it is needed. Nucleic acids can reproduce themselves and, without this ability, life would not exist or continue.

The basic units that link together to form proteins are amino acids, and all proteins in living organisms are made up of just 20 different amino acids. In chemical terms, a protein molecule is a polymer consisting of a long chain of amino acid units joined together in a particular sequence, and the code to this sequence is held by DNA.

How living chemicals joined

Experiments with simulated primordial conditions have produced many amino acids other than the 20 commonly found in proteins. All amino acids (and other types of chemicals) tend to "stick" onto the surface of clay, but those 20 found in proteins stick particularly well to clays rich in the metal nickel. This suggests that the first proteins may have been formed in pools or on the fringes of seas, where the primordial soup was in contact with nickel-rich clays. There heat from the Sun or a volcano could have combined the amino acids to form a primitive protein.

The four classes of chemicals that form the basic components of nucleic acids have also, like the amino acids, been "cooked up" in a primordial soup, and they too will stick to clay to form long-chain polymers. And, just as nickel-rich clays are best at absorbing the amino acid constituents of protein, so clays rich in zinc absorb the building blocks of nucleic acids. This suggests that such clays could have been the birthplace of genes, which are the "messengers" of inheritance.

However, the coupling of proteins and nucleic acids, which together form the living cell, has yet to be explained, and it is improbable that proteins or nucleic acids alone could have provided the basis for life.

The Russian biochemist I. A. Oparin has shown that, in water, solutions of polymers (such as proteins) have a tendency to form droplets surrounded by an outer membrane very like that which encloses living cells. As these droplets grow by absorbing more polymers, some split in two when they become too large for stability. If such a droplet had protein enzymes to harness energy and make more polymers, and if it had nucleic acids with instructions for making those proteins, and if each new droplet received a complete copy of the nucleic acid instructions, the droplet would be alive—it would be a living cell.

The Structure of Life

All life forms stem from a single cell, and every cell contains in its nucleus instructions for the re-creation of the organism of which it forms a part. These are encoded in chromosomes, which contain the miraculous molecular substance of DNA, sectioned into units of heredity called genes. The genetic code determines in detail the physical characteristics of an individual creature, so that variations in DNA cause variations in the individual. Scientists believe that it is the interaction of the individual variation with the environment that ultimately leads to the evolution of the similar, interbreeding groups of creatures that are known as species.

THE HIDDEN SECRET
Dramatic discoveries in recent decades have revolutionized biology, the primary life science. Scientists can now trace parts of the genetic blueprint that lays down the pattern for every form of life, linking the large-scale unfolding of species that we know as evolution with the ultramicroscopic activity of the molecules within the nucleus of every cell. This may be the secret behind the rich diversity of life on Earth.

Deoxyribonucleic acid (DNA) consists of a "backbone" of alternating sugar and phosphate molecules, and to each sugar is attached one of four nitrogenous bases (adenine, guanine, thymine and cytosine, or A, G, T, C). A single gene might contain 2,000 of these bases, and in the body cell of a human being the 46 chromosomes (thread-like bodies of DNA and protein) run to 3,000 million bases. The sequence of these bases stores the information for making amino acids into proteins, just as the sequence of letters in this sentence stores the information for making a particular verbal structure. But the DNA alphabet has only four letters (A, G, T, C).

The thread of life
DNA is a double molecule, resembling a twisted ladder, its two main strands twining around each other to form the famous double helix. The strands are linked by pairs of bases—A and T, or G and C—whose shape is such that each pair fits together neatly, like pieces of a jigsaw, to form the rungs of the DNA ladder. As a result, the information on the strands can be duplicated by "unzipping" the double helix and making new strands by using the old ones as templates. DNA stores, duplicates and passes on the information that makes life alive.

Cells multiply by splitting in two, and each newly made cell thus gets instructions for its existence by the mechanism of heredity, the gene. But heredity is a word more often applied to the passing on of DNA from an organism to its offspring. In sexual reproduction the offspring gets some of the DNA (usually half) from one parent, and the rest from the other, ending up with a unique mix all of its own.

The laws of heredity
Man has long known that characteristics can be passed on from one generation to the next, for he has been selectively breeding crops and animals for thousands of years. However, it was not until the mid-nineteenth century that an obscure Austrian monk, Gregor Mendel (1822–84), discovered the laws that govern inheritance, and his work was ignored until the beginning of the twentieth century, when more powerful microscopes made possible the direct observation of the cell.

Mendel experimented with pea plants because they had easily recognizable traits, and because, although normally self-fertilizing, they could be cross-fertilized with pollen from a different plant. Mendel made many crosses between different pure-bred plants and found that in the offspring, or hybrids, some characters always prevailed over others: red flowers over white, tall plants over short, and so on. He called the prevailing characters dominant, and the nonprevailing characters recessive. He then let the first-generation hybrids self-fertilize, and found not only that the recessive traits reappeared in the hybrids' offspring, but also that they reappeared in a constant proportion of three dominant to one recessive; the second generation contained three times as many red-flowered peas as white-flowered peas.

To explain his results, Mendel proposed that each plant had two hereditary "factors"— today called alleles—for each character, and that the dominant factor suppressed the recessive factor. If a plant inherited both a dominant and a recessive factor, the dominant one would prevail. Only if both factors were recessive would the recessive character be apparent. Mendel found many other pairs of traits where one form was dominant and the other recessive. He established that permutations arising from the crossing of the two first-generation hybrids allows the dominant gene to be present in three out of four crosses in the second generation; but

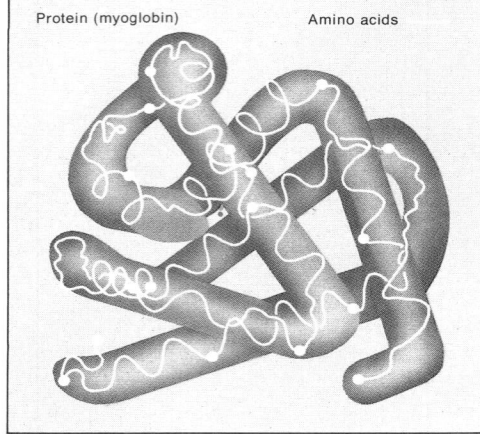

Genes

Protein (myoglobin)   Amino acids

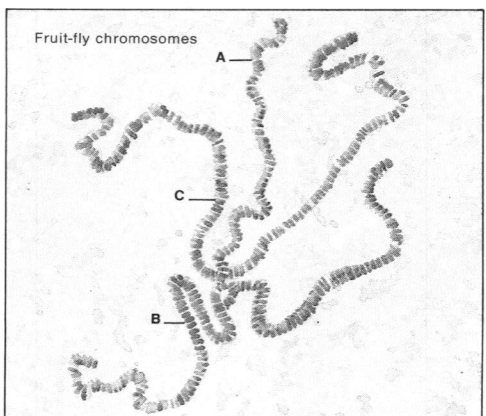

Fruit-fly chromosomes

A

C

B

Chromosomes

Cell

The cell is the basic unit of all life, and every cell contains in its nucleus the thread-like structures, called chromosomes, that control heredity. Each species has its own number of chromosomes, and the number is always the same for that species. Chromosomes are sectioned into genes, units of heredity made of DNA molecules. DNA acts like a code, specifying the order and number of amino acids that make up proteins— the organic compounds characteristic of all life.

Chromosomes (below left) of the fruit fly, much magnified, show bands of DNA arranged in sections that correspond exactly with specific genes, the chemical units of heredity. The proof of this correspondence came when the American geneticist Hermann Muller introduced the use of ionizing radiation to damage the fruit flies' chromosomes at ultra-microscopic points, causing precise point mutations in offspring of parents whose DNA had been damaged at the places indicated. Random mutations may occur in any organism, and not only as a result of radiation. A gradual accumulation of minor mutations may lead to evolutionary change.

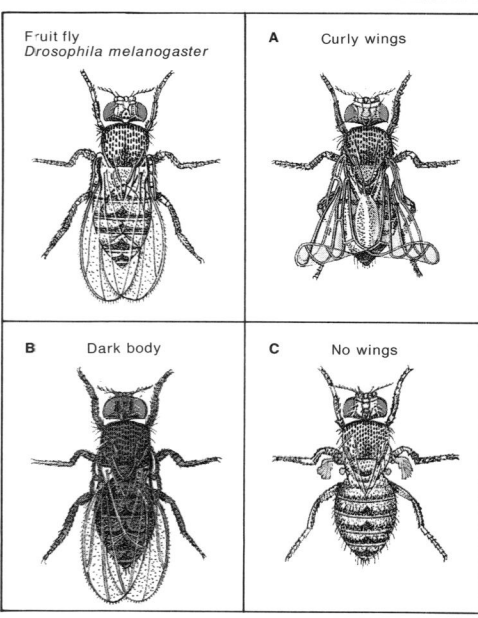

Fruit fly
Drosophila melanogaster

A   Curly wings

B   Dark body

C   No wings

in the fourth cross, only the two recessive alleles of the genes are present. So there is always a three-to-one ratio of dominant to recessive.

Theories of evolution
Mendel's work was of course unknown to his contemporaries, Charles Darwin and Alfred Russel Wallace, who even then were providing solutions to the major mystery of biology—the way that species evolve, change and develop over time. Evolution was not a new idea in Darwin's day. In 1809 the French naturalist Jean-Baptiste Lamarck had proposed a theory of the inheritance of acquired characteristics, suggesting that new habits learned by an organism in response to environmental change may become physically incorporated in the animal's descendants. For instance, the fact that the ancestral giraffe had to stretch its neck to reach food might give its offspring long necks to enable them to reach food more easily. Less satisfactory than the "natural selection" theory of Darwin and Wallace (who independently reached the same conclusion), Lamarckism founders on the fact that there is no genetic mechanism enabling acquired characters to pass on in this way.

Darwin's theory of natural selection has three key elements: all individuals vary, and some variations are passed on to the next generation; the gap between the potential and the actual number of offspring reproduced by organisms is very wide and implies that not all will survive; organisms best adapted to the environment will survive, their offspring will have been selected, and the favorable variation

will spread through the population, perhaps eventually changing it.

Genetic variation, the mainspring of natural selection, is reflected in variations of DNA, the material substance of heredity. Changes in the order of DNA's nitrogenous bases—called mutations—produce changes in the proteins which are usually, but not always, harmful. More important than these is the effect of genes recombining in sexually reproduced offspring.

Sexual reproduction provides the offspring with two sets of DNA, one from each parent. The processes that give rise to a half-set of chromosomes in a sperm or egg shuffle and recombine the genes on each chromosome to provide new combinations. Then, when sperm and egg fuse together at fertilization, the half-sets come together and even more combinations are produced. The world's enormous diversity of life can be explained in terms of a struggle that favors certain genetic combinations.

Iiwi
Vestiaria coccinea

Apapane
Himatione sanguinea

Laysan finch
Psittirostra cantans

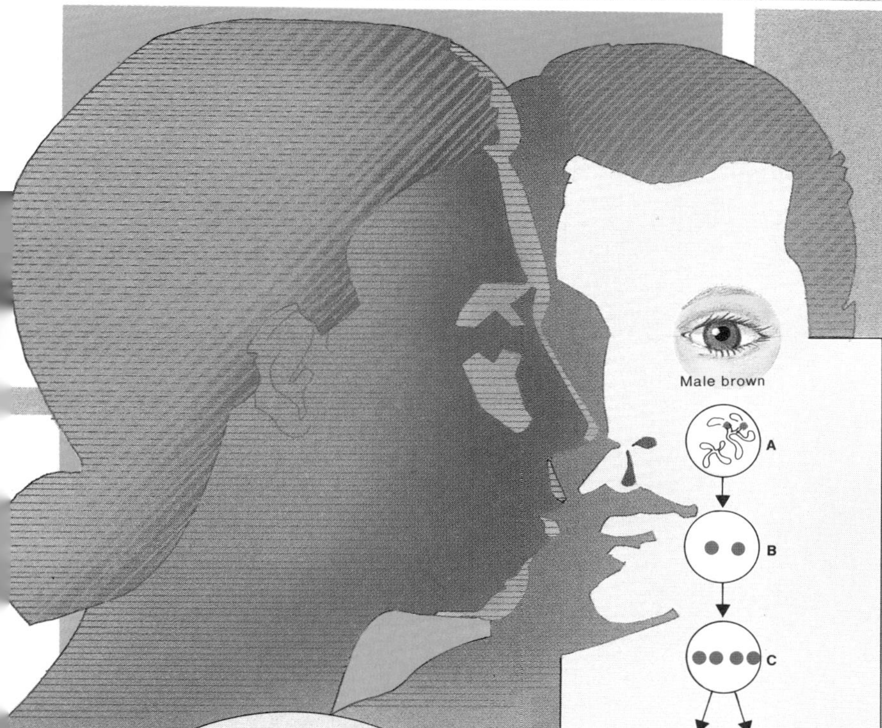

Some human traits, such as eye color, are inherited as single factors (below). In such cases one gene is dominant over the other, recessive, gene, and the gene giving a brown eye color is always dominant over that which gives a blue eye color. The chromosomes carrying eye-color genes (A) pair (B) and duplicate (C, D) before dividing twice (E, F) in the process known as meiosis, or reduction division. This ensures that the offspring gets half the chromosomes from the male and half from the female parent, so each new cell gets both genes when sperm and egg unite. But because brown-eye genes are dominant over blue, all offspring have brown eyes, with the blue-eye gene hidden. But if two brown-eyed parents carry recessive blue-eye genes, half the male sperm cells have blue-eye genes, and the female eggs carry a gene for either blue or brown eyes. So the two recessive genes have a one-in-four chance of being combined to produce a blue-eyed child, no brown-eye genes being present.

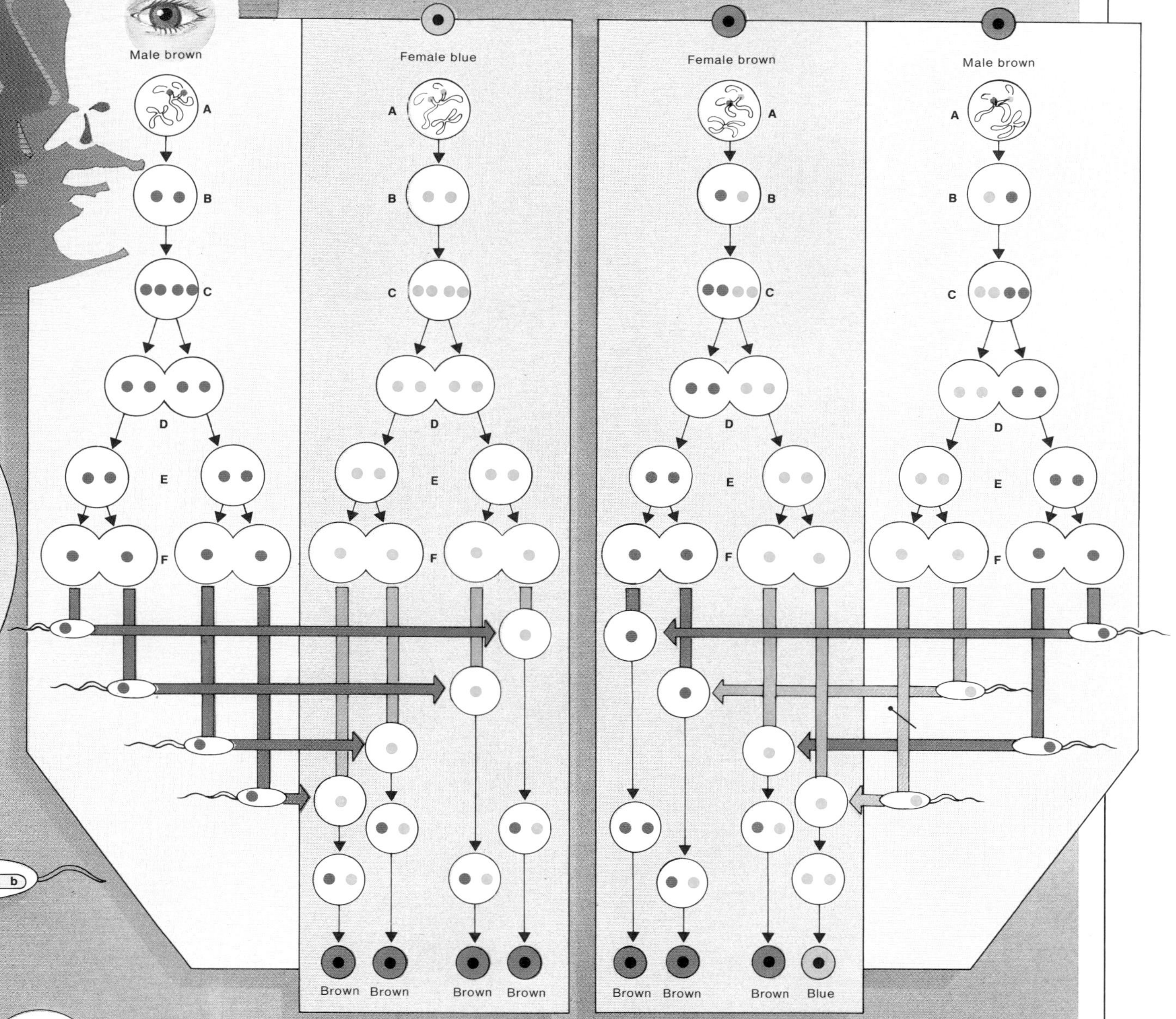

Male brown · A B C D E F
Female blue · A B C D E F
Female brown · A B C D E F
Male brown · A B C D E F

Brown Brown Brown Brown Brown Brown Brown Blue

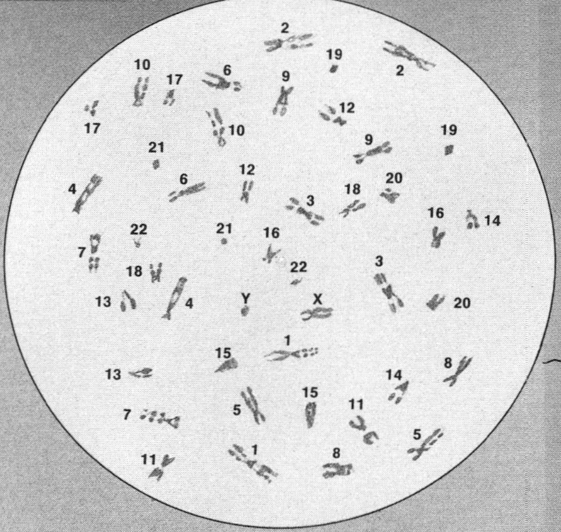

A human body cell (above) contains 46 chromosomes—22 matching pairs and the chromosomes (X, Y) which determine sex. Males have X and Y, females X and X. In sexual reproduction (right) traits carried by the male sperm and the female egg combine in the zygote, the fertilized egg from which all new life starts. All growth is the result of repeated cell division, or mitosis, where the nucleus forms paired chromosomes that duplicate themselves; the cell splits, and the chromosomes re-form in the nucleus of the new cells. Sex cells are produced by reduction division, or meiosis, with each cell taking only one from each pair of chromosomes, which exchange corresponding segments in the process called recombination. The genes are thus reshuffled at each generation, so that new combinations of gene traits are available for selection each time meiosis takes place. The result is genetic diversity, with many possibilities for the species to adapt to a changing environment.

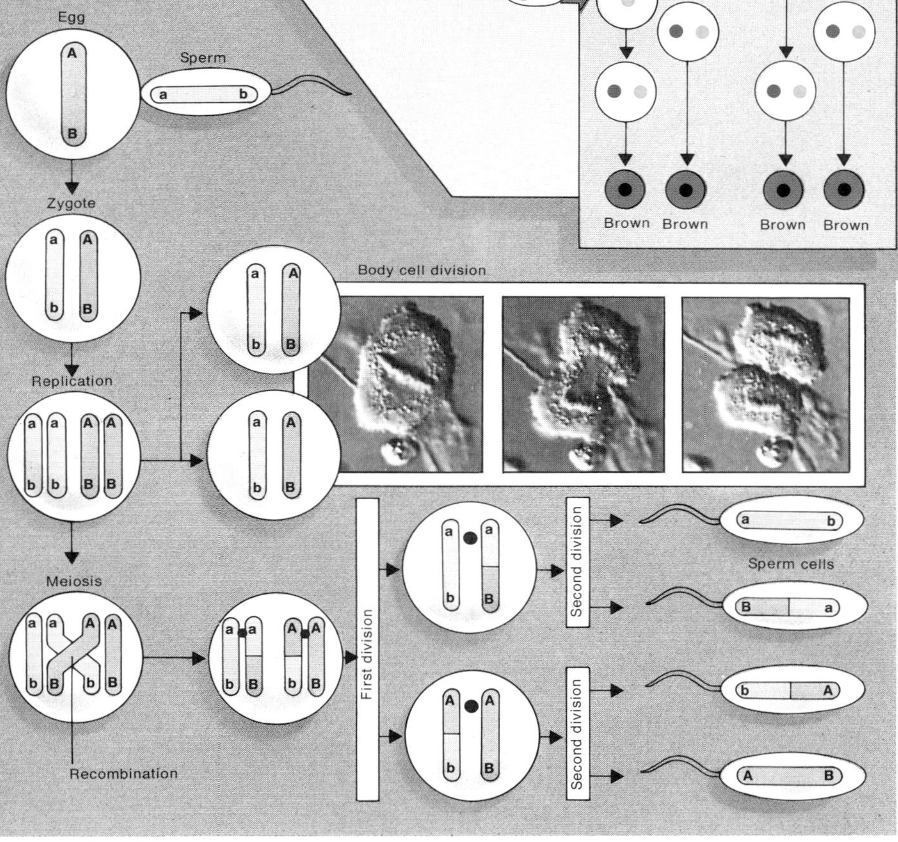

Egg
Sperm
Zygote
Replication
Body cell division
Meiosis
First division
Second division
Sperm cells
Recombination

VARIANT FORMS

Dark forms of many insects, such as the peppered moth *Biston betularia*, have developed widely in industrial areas of the world since the industrial age. The dark variant, resulting from a single genetic mutation, escapes the eye of predators against the black, lichen-free bark of soot-darkened trees (top), whereas the typical pale form is very conspicuous. In rural, unpolluted areas where tree trunks are light and lichen covered (bottom) the well-concealed pale form is much commoner. *Biston*'s rapid evolutionary response is remarkable: in 1849 only one dark example was recorded at Manchester, England, but by 1900 98% of the moths caught in the area were of the dark type. A similar change occurred in other industrial areas, during the period when the most coal was being burned and the population was most rapidly expanding. But with today's clean-air laws the number of pale moths in these areas is once again on the increase.

A diversity of forms (left) has stemmed from a single ancestor of the Hawaiian honeycreeper, which now numbers 14 species. These have adapted in their mid-Pacific isolation to fill niches usually taken by other birds, ranging from the nectar-feeding iiwi to the Laysan finch with its thick beak for cracking seeds, and the short-billed apapane, which includes insects in its diet. But the honeycreepers' success in divergence may have led to overspecialization, with at least eight species now extinct. The Australian marsupial mouse and the Indian spiny mouse (right) look very similar, due to the fact that they fill similar ecological niches, but they belong to groups evolving separately for almost 100 million years.

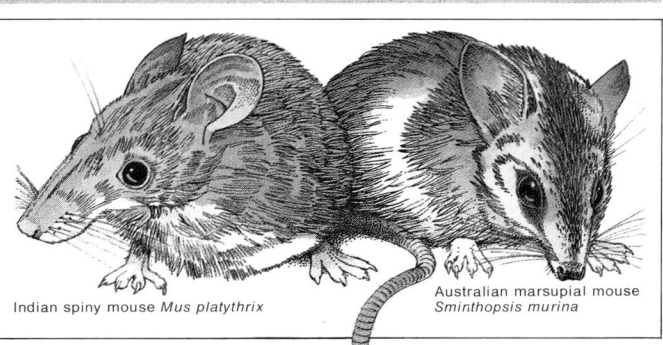

Indian spiny mouse *Mus platythrix*

Australian marsupial mouse *Sminthopsis murina*

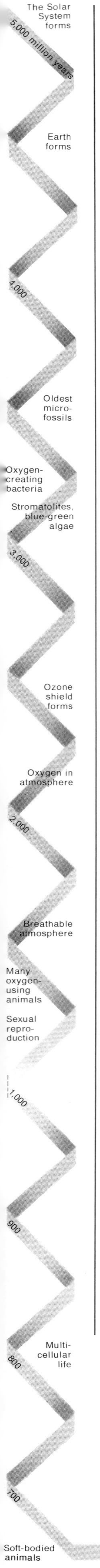

Earliest Life Forms

Earth's original atmosphere lacked oxygen, without which there could be no survival for air-breathing creatures. This vital gas was supplied by life itself, in the form of microscopic organisms that flourished in the atmosphere of the time and emitted oxygen as "waste." In this way a breathable atmosphere built up; increasingly complex life forms were able to develop in the seas; early plants and insects gained a foothold on the shores; and, finally, larger animals could survive on land.

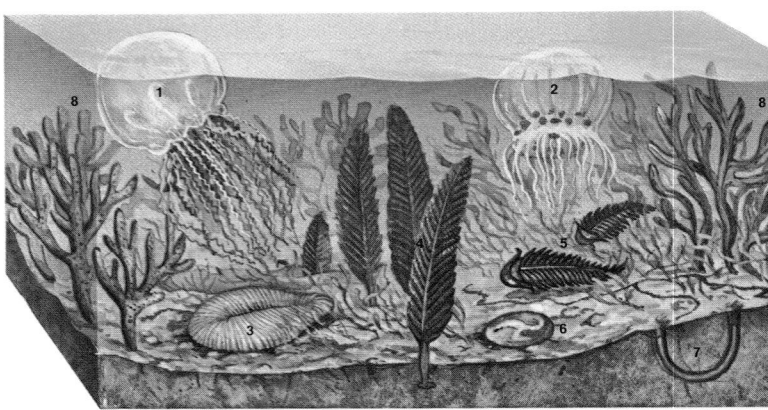

A BREATHABLE ATMOSPHERE

Without oxygen, life as we know it could not exist; yet Earth's original atmosphere contained practically none. The oxygenation of the atmosphere was the work of the planet's first life—primeval bacteria and algae. Of these, some released oxygen as waste while consuming carbon dioxide or nitrogen in photosynthesis. Colonies of algae forming stromatolites ("stony carpets") generated even more oxygen, but this was first taken up by ocean rocks, visible today as "banded iron formations." Once all the ocean rocks were oxidized, an oxygen-rich atmosphere could develop, with an ozone layer to filter out harmful radiation from the Sun.

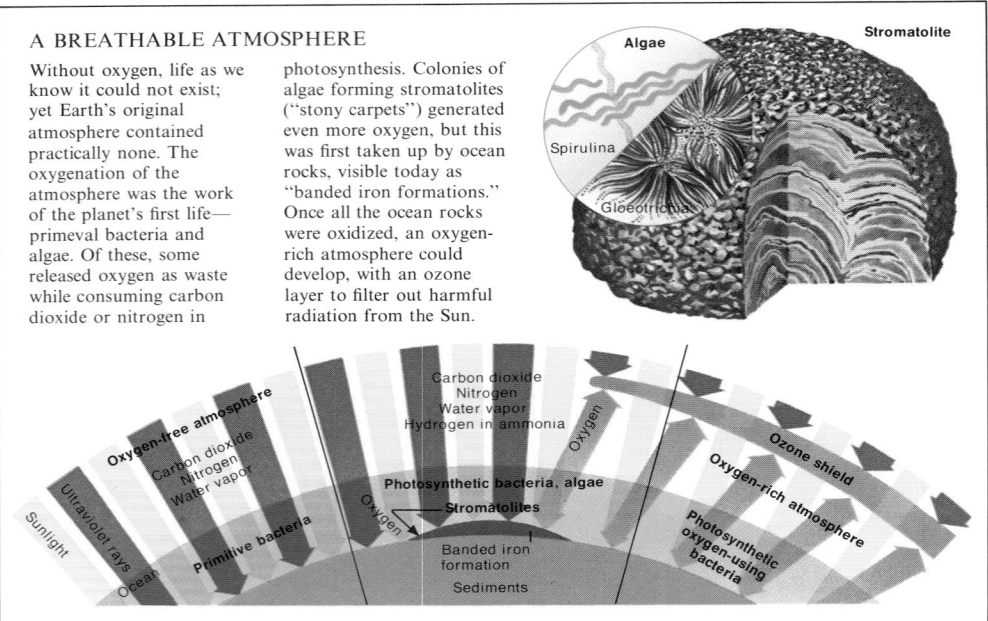

THE FIRST SHELLED CREATURES

These evolved (right) in the seas when conditions allowed soft-bodied life to form protective casings. In the fossil record of 550 million years ago, soft and shelled forms are found. The trilobites (1, 2, 3)—a now extinct order of woodlouse-like animals—dominated the scene, but other early arthropods (4) included a possible insect ancestor (5), and there may even have been an ancestor to fish (6) Sponges (7), crinoids (8), early molluscs (9), bristleworms (10) and lamp-shells (11) were plentiful, but other creatures (12) are bewilderingly strange.

Scientists have identified bacteria-like microfossils in the rocks that were formed more than 3,500 million years ago. Some of these organisms appear to have been capable of photosynthesis—the process of utilizing sunlight, water and carbon dioxide for "food," with release of oxygen as the vitally important by-product. As a result, surplus oxygen very gradually accumulated in the Earth's atmosphere, forming an upper-atmosphere shield of ozone (which kept out damaging ultraviolet radiation from the Sun) and providing an oxygen-rich atmosphere in which breathing life could develop.

At least five types of microfossil have been found in ancient sediments of Western Australia, aged about 3,560 million years, and these provide the earliest evidence of life so far discovered. Other early proof of life comes from the so-called "stromatolites," some of which may date back as far as 3,400 million years. These curious columns, growing in warm, shallow waters, are formed of blue-green algae which have entrapped chalky sediments, bacteria and other microfossils. Their study is made easier by the fact that similar structures have developed at later geological times, and some are even being formed at the present day.

Living below the surface of the water and not initially reliant on oxygen for life, such bacteria and algae were shielded from the Sun's ultraviolet rays as they imperceptibly altered the Earth's atmosphere. For hundreds of millions of years life of this kind persisted, with few obvious developments or changes.

Breathing life

About 1,800 million years ago, the effects of these microscopic photosynthesizers became dramatically apparent in the "rusting" of the ocean sediments, when the red color of the rocks being formed at that time indicates that there was enough free oxygen on Earth to bring about the process known as oxidation. Once the ocean rocks capable of absorbing oxygen had done so, forming the red "banded iron formations" known to geologists, oxygen could enter the atmosphere in ever greater quantities.

It has been estimated that a breathable atmosphere existed on Earth about 1,700 million years ago, and aerobic (oxygen-using) organisms first became abundant not very long afterwards. These organisms were single celled, and it may have been almost 1,000 million years before multicellular animals evolved. The fossilized remains of animals alive 800 million years ago have been found in many parts of the world, but it is not yet known whether multicellular animals had a long history before these earliest known forms, or whether they had developed and radiated rapidly from a creature capable of feeding as well as photosynthesizing.

One of the earliest collections of animals of this type was discovered in the Ediacara Sandstones of the Flinders Range in Australia, where some 650 million years ago the rocks once formed part of an ancient beach. Here a spectacular collection of soft-bodied animals, similar to today's coelenterates (such as jellyfish) and worms, was washed ashore and preserved in silt from the nearby shallow sea. Comparable, mainly floating forms have been found in other parts of the world in rocks dating from between 650 and 580 million years ago.

The first vertebrates

One of the most important changes in animal life seems to have occurred about 580 million years ago. At that date many creatures evolved hard, protective shells, which also acted as areas of muscle attachment and as support for their bodies—in other words, as external skeletons. Hard shells were more easily preserved as fossils than the soft bodies of earlier animals, so rich collections have been recovered from rocks of the Cambrian Period, beginning 580 million years ago, as well as from later strata.

The first fish-like animals—the earliest true vertebrates—are found in rocks of the Ordovician Period, from about 500 million years ago, and these were in many ways very similar to the lampreys and hagfishes of today. But unlike them, these ancient creatures were heavily armored with external bone. They must have been poor swimmers, living mainly on the seabed and filtering edible particles from the sediments, which they sucked into their jawless mouths. From them arose true fishes, with backbones, jaws and teeth, and they came to replace the less efficient earlier forms.

During the Devonian Period, about 400 million years ago, the fishes diversified greatly, adapting to fit all kinds of aquatic environments. Some grew to a huge size, such as *Dunkleosteus*, which achieved a length of up to 9 m (29 ft 7 in), although it belonged to a group of fishes that retained heavy armor. Some of these curious creatures probably used their stilt-like pectoral fins to hitch themselves across the beds of the pools in which they lived.

From water to land

The fishes that teemed in the seas and fresh waters of the Devonian world found their way into difficult environments such as swamps and oasis pools, where there was a danger of drying out in the warmer weather. Many of these fishes had rudimentary lungs, and one group developed powerful jointed fins.

Such marginal habitats were not ideal for fishes, but they were nevertheless rich in species, and it is from them that the first land vertebrates developed. When the water dried up they survived, for their strong fins held them up so that they did not flop over helplessly.

They found themselves in a new, dry world, but one which was already inhabited, at least round the water's edges, with plants related to modern liverworts, mosses and club mosses. There were also numerous invertebrate animals such as millipedes, spiders and wingless insects. These plants and animals provided shelter and food, so that the environment was not wholly hostile to larger animals.

The first steps on land probably took the form of strong flexions of the body—desperate swimming movements which swung the fins forward, pegging the animal's position in the drying mud. But in a very short time geologically, animals had evolved in which the rays of the lobe fins had vanished, leaving stubby legs with which the animals—no longer fishes but amphibians —could haul themselves over land. But they still had to return to water to breed and lay eggs.

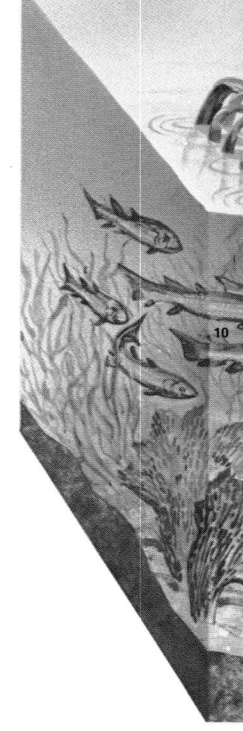

THE FIRST AMPHIBIANS

Amphibians (1) emerged some 345 million years ago (right), inhabiting swampy environments with luxuriant vegetation—club mosses and ferns (2, 3) that made up the early coal forests. Lungfish (4) were well adapted to life in oxygen-poor waters, but the move to land was probably made by related fish with a passage linking nostrils to throat—*Eusthenopteron* (5). Land offered food (6, 7, 8) and suitably damp conditions for a possibly stranded aquatic animal.

Palaeozoic				Mesozoic		Cenozoic	
500	400	300		200		100	0

Millions of years ago

A timescale of life on Earth emerges from the record of fossils embedded in rock strata. Major breaks in faunas (animal assemblages) separate eras coinciding roughly with periods of intense mountain-building activity. These eras are broken down into geological periods, which are separated by lesser faunal breaks and which are generally named from the area where rocks of that age were first discovered. The geological eras and periods do not imply particular rock types.

Left margin timeline:

The Solar System forms

5,000 million years

Earth forms

4,000

Oldest microfossils

Oxygen-creating bacteria

Stromatolites, blue-green algae

3,000

Ozone shield forms

Oxygen in atmosphere

2,000

Breathable atmosphere

Many oxygen-using animals

Sexual reproduction

1,000

900

800

Multi-cellular life

700

Soft-bodied animals

Bottom timeline:

| 600 | Shelled/skeletal animals | CAMBRIAN | 550 | First fishes | ORDOVICIAN |

THE AGE OF JELLYFISH

Jellyfish (left) and other soft-bodied animals flourished in the pre-Cambrian seas, more than 600 million years ago. The forms of one group, imprinted on sand, have been preserved as fossils in the Australian Ediacara Sandstones. They include varieties similar to modern jellyfish (1, 2); worm-like crawlers (3); sea pens (4) very like modern types; segmented worms (5); "three-legged" creatures like no known animal (6); and sand casts of burrowing worms (7).

LIFE ON SEA AND LAND

For more than half the Earth's existence, its atmosphere has been hostile to air-breathing life. Then, about 1,600 million years ago, the photosynthesizing action of minute organisms built up enough free oxygen in the atmosphere for more complex oxygen-dependent forms to develop. The first multicellular life led to the soft-bodied animals of the pre-Cambrian time—worms, jellyfish and sea pens. About 580 million years ago many animals developed hard parts, including shells. Over 1,200 new marine species date from this period, and the evolutionary explosion came to fill the Earth's seas with fishes. Some of these had powerful jointed fins and rudimentary lungs, and lived in swamps where primitive plants and insects had already made the move to land. As the pools dwindled the stranded animals could survive by breathing air.

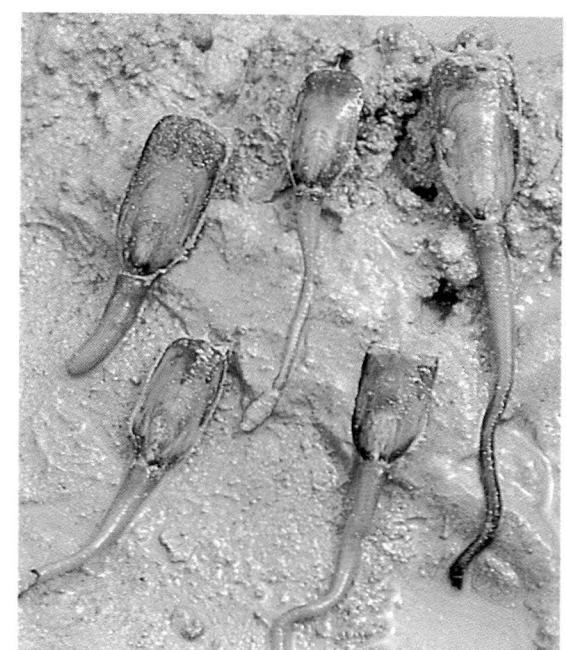

LIVING FOSSILS

Some life forms that emerged 570 million years ago have survived virtually unchanged to the present day. These "living fossils" include *Lingula* (left), today found in warm, brackish coastal waters, poor in oxygen and unsuited to most life, off the Pacific and Indian oceans. *Neopilina* (below), a primitive marine mollusc first found alive in 1952, has features unlike other molluscs but suggesting much closer affinities with the annelids (worms) and arthropods (insects, crabs, etc.).

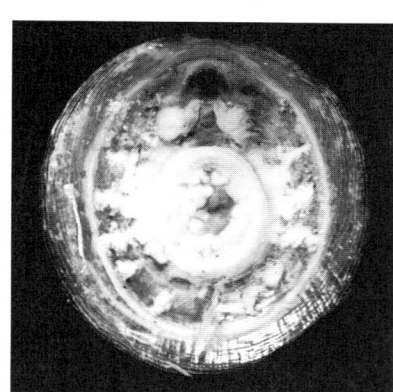

THE AGE OF JELLYFISH	THE AGE OF FISHES
1 Jellyfish (*Ediacaria*)	1 Primitive plant (*Nematophyton*)
2 Jellyfish (*Medusina*)	2 Psilophite plant (*Asteroxylon*)
3 Flatworm (*Dickinsonia costata*)	3 Psilophite plant (*Rhynia*)
4 Sea pens (*Rangea, Charnia*)	4 Primitive insect (*Rhyniella*)
5 Segmented worms (*Spriggina floundersi*)	5 Placoderm fish (*Bothriolepis*)
6 Unknown animal (*Tribrachidium*)	6 Placoderm fish (*Phyllolepis*)
7 Burrowing worm (fossil casts)	7 Placoderm fish (*Dunkleosteus*)
8 Sponges and algae (hypothetical)	8 Early shark (*Cladoselache*)
	9 Lunglish (*Dipterus*)
	10 Lobe-fin fish (*Osteolepis*)
	11 Crustacean (*Montecaris*)

THE FIRST SHELLED CREATURES	THE FIRST AMPHIBIANS
1 Trilobites (*Waptia*)	1 Amphibian (*Ichthyostega*)
2 Trilobites (*Marella splendens*)	2 Club moss (*Cyclostigma*)
3 Trilobite (*Olenoides serratus*)	3 Fern (*Pseudosporochnus*)
4 Primitive arthropod (*Perspicaris dictynna*)	4 Lunglish (*Scaumenacia*)
5 Primitive arthropod (*Aysheaia pedunculata*)	5 Rhipidistian fish (*Eusthenopteron*)
6 Ancestral lancelet fish (*Branchiostoma*)	6 Millipede (*Acantherpestes ornatus*)
7 Sponge (*Vauxia*)	7 Early scorpion (*Palaeophonus*)
8 Crinoids (*Echmatocrinus*)	8 Spider-like creature (*Palaeocharinoides*)
9 Mollusc (*Wiwaxia*)	9 Small plant (*Sciadophyton*)
10 Bristleworm (*Nereis*)	
11 Brachiopod (*Lingulella*)	
12 Unknown animal (*Hallucigenia sparsa*)	

THE AGE OF FISHES

Fishes (left) filled the brackish Devonian waters, about 350 million years ago, while primitive plants and insects had pioneered the land. Giant weeds (1) grew above muddy waters, and vascular plants (2, 3) colonized the shores, sheltering early insects (4). Primitive fishes (5, 6, 7) remained, but ray-finned types (8)—ancestors of modern fish—were dominant. However, it was from the lobe-finned fishes (9, 10) that the first land vertebrates emerged.

The Age of Reptiles

When the Carboniferous Period began, the world was already populated with animals and plants of many kinds. The oceans were full of fishes, invertebrates and aquatic plants. The land, meanwhile, was producing dramatic new species: giant mosses and ferns, spiders and insects and, most important of all, the rapidly evolving amphibians. These creatures were taking the first evolutionary steps on a path that would lead to some of the most remarkable creatures ever to live – the dinosaurs.

The broad, low-lying, swampy plains of the late Carboniferous provided ideal conditions for the world's early plants. They spread and diversified, and some of them grew to enormous size. Giant club mosses, huge horsetails and luxuriant tree ferns took on the proportions of modern-day trees and formed the world's first forests. These new forests were full of animal life: primitive spiders and scorpions hunting their prey, giant dragonflies hovering over the marshy waters and other insects scavenging or hunting on the mossy forest floor or in the branches of the "trees." In the huge coal-forest swamps, the most advanced of all animals, the amphibians, were rapidly evolving. Some of these would ultimately return to life in the water. But others were developing stronger legs and were becoming better able to cope with an existence on dry land.

It was from this second group that the reptiles evolved—the first animals to be equipped with waterproof skins. Unlike their amphibian ancestors, they could stay out of the water indefinitely without losing their body fluids through their skins. They were no longer tied to the water's edge and the pattern of life was revolutionized. The world was soon inhabited by the first wave of land vertebrates—reptiles, which then rapidly diversified.

Included among these first reptiles were creatures known as sailbacks. They had a row of long, bony spines that supported a great fin running down from the back of their heads to the base of their tails. This whole apparatus functioned as a heat-exchange organ: the fin absorbed heat from the atmosphere in the early, cooler parts of the day, when the animal was cold, and blushed off warmth later, when it became overheated. Unlike the cold-blooded reptiles, sailbacked reptiles could, to a certain extent, regulate their body temperatures.

Mammal-like reptiles

It was only about 50 million years later, however, that animals skeletally identical to mammals were found throughout the world. Almost certainly these creatures had a degree of warmbloodedness. But they were all rather small—the biggest was no larger than a domestic cat—and this may account for their decline. They were destined to be overshadowed for many millions of years by the dinosaurs.

The late Triassic Period, about 200 million years ago, is marked by a sudden decline in the

THE RULING REPTILES

Seymouria and other advanced amphibians evolved to form the first reptiles, such as *Scutosaurus*. From these a multitude of adaptations evolved. Some herbivores, such as *Corythosaurus*, developed 2,000 or more teeth, to help them consume tough, fibrous food plants. Another herbivorous group attained enormous size—*Brachiosaurus* weighed as much as 80 tonnes—and this may have been an adaptation to regulate body temperature (large objects lose and gain heat more slowly than small objects). Another adaptation, but one that developed mainly in the carnivores, was that of offensive weaponry: *Deinonychus* had a huge sickle-shaped claw on each hind foot and the later *Tyrannosaurus* combined a massive body with a jagged mouthful of 60 teeth. Armor plating was a defensive adaptation, produced by herbivores such as *Triceratops*, whereas speed of movement was developed both by some herbivores and by small carnivores such as *Struthiomimus*.

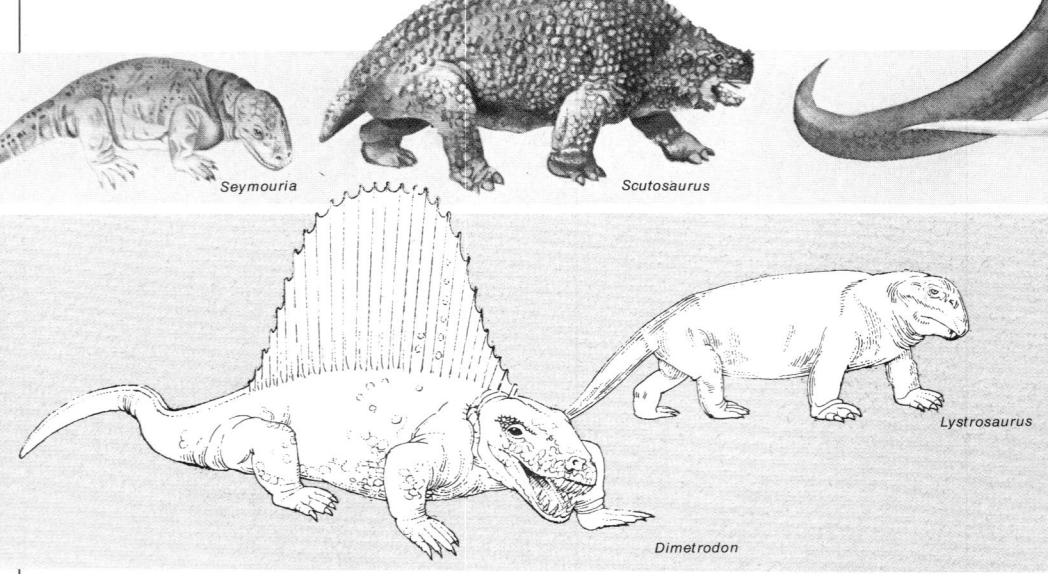

Corythosaurus

Seymouria

Scutosaurus

Deinonychus

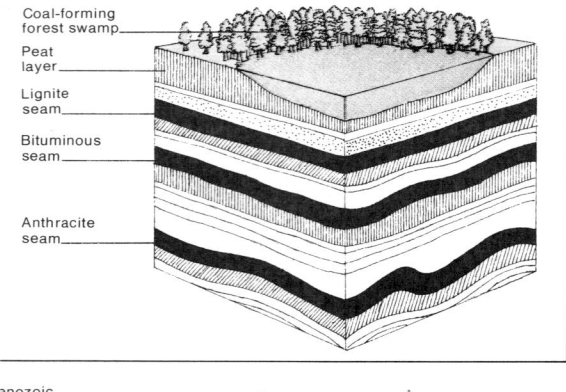

Dimetrodon

Lystrosaurus

THE MAMMAL LINE

Sailbacks such as *Dimetrodon* mark the beginning of mammal history. These reptiles had developed the first method of regulating body temperature—each was equipped with a large fin on its back which acted as a heat-exchange organ, a living solar panel. From these strange creatures, para-mammals such as *Lystrosaurus* evolved, animals with many mammal-like features. Some of the later members of this group, such as *Thrinaxodon*, probably even had fur on their bodies. Then, about 200 million years ago, the first true warm-blooded mammals, such as *Morganucodon*, developed. But by this time the group as a whole was declining in response to reptilian competition. Mammals would have to wait 140 million years before becoming successful again.

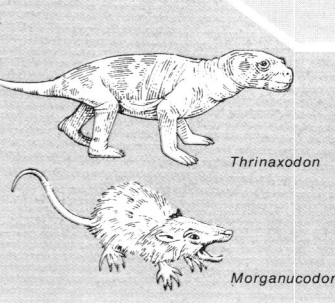

Thrinaxodon

Morganucodon

COAL FORMATION

Coal consists of carbon from plant remains and most of it was formed in the swamp-forests from which reptiles emerged. First, peat formed from rotted vegetation. Sea levels rose, ocean covered the peat bogs and marine sediments were laid down. The resulting pressure converted peat to coal. The cycle recurred and the deepest coal seams were compressed and hardened.

Coal-forming forest swamp
Peat layer
Lignite seam
Bituminous seam
Anthracite seam

Palaeozoic			Mesozoic		Cenozoic
500	400	300	200	100	0

Millions of years ago

Three geological eras mark the evolution of life on Earth. It was the Mesozoic era, beginning 230 million years ago, that spanned the age of reptiles. Until then, throughout the Palaeozoic era, life had been slowly evolving from the primitive organisms that appeared 400 million years earlier.

By the Mesozoic, the earliest reptiles had developed. Among their descendants were dinosaurs and early representatives of the mammalian line. Mammals, however, would have to wait another 165 million years, until the Cenozoic, before they achieved dominance.

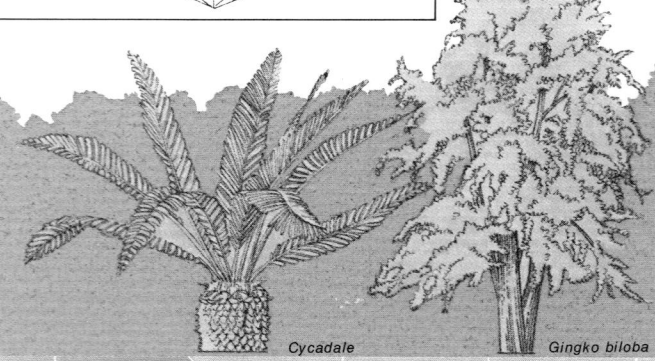

Cycadale

Gingko biloba

The plant communities underwent as many developments in the course of the Mesozoic era as did the reptiles. The end of the Palaeozoic saw changes in climate—the Permian Period was much drier than the Carboniferous. Giant horsetails, ferns and club mosses that had formed the world's first forests gave way to other types of plant: early conifers and their relatives

(the gymnosperms) came to the fore. These new species, such as the Cycadales, had evolved a new, improved method of reproduction—using seeds not spores. By Jurassic times, the climate had changed again and the moist conditions supported dense forests of ferns and of conifers. The final major Mesozoic development took place in Cretaceous times, when the flowering plants evolved.

CARBONIFEROUS 300   Earliest reptiles **PERMIAN** Early conifers   250   First radiation of reptiles **TRIASSIC**   First mammals Se

40

EVOLUTION AND ADAPTATION

Once their amphibian ancestors had crawled from the swamps, reptiles rapidly evolved and developed a remarkable range of adaptations: they took to the air, invaded the seas and held dominion over the land. By early Jurassic times, they had firmly established their claim to the title Ruling Reptiles. Another group of early reptile descendants led to the mammals, and although these were long overshadowed by the dinosaurs, they were destined to rise to dominance.

mammal-like reptiles and by the extraordinary evolutionary radiation of the so-called Archosaurs ("ruling reptiles"). These began to fill every available ecological niche. They evolved into carnivores, herbivores and omnivores. They included the Crocodilians, which adapted to a life in the water; the flying pterosaurs, which were the first vertebrates to fly, and, most important of all, the dinosaurs, whose evolutionary reign over the land was to endure for the next 140 million years.

Dinosaurs adapted well to life on the land. They developed "fully erect" limbs (not unlike those of the later higher mammals) rather than the splayed legs found in most other reptiles. The new position of their limbs, which gave them the necessary mobility on dry land, was also accompanied by a general increase in size. But the dinosaurs were not the only land reptiles of the time; many other forms, including tortoises, snakes and lizards, were also carving their niches during the Mesozoic era.

Similarly, the pterosaurs did not remain the only creatures of the sky. By 170 million years ago, birds in the form of claw-winged *Archaeopteryx* had evolved, and these were to prove a serious challenge to the primitive winged reptiles which had poor flying abilities.

Aquatic reptiles

Just as the land and the air were rapidly inhabited by newly evolving forms, so the water produced many new developments. Several of the Mesozoic reptiles began to adapt to aquatic life in ways often parallel to present-day mammals: the long-necked, fish-eating plesiosaurs led a life much like that of seals; the larger

pliosaurs had a streamlined shape similar to that of certain whales; some mollusc-eating placodonts could be likened to the walrus; and the elegant icthyosaurs were in many ways like dolphins. Large invertebrates were also found in the seas. The most dramatic of these were the ammonites—shelled relatives of the octopus—some of which grew to more than 2 m (6 ft) in size. Among fishes a new type emerged, the Teleosts, and these were destined to become the dominant fishes of the modern world.

Wholesale extinction

At the end of the Cretaceous Period, the reptiles were flourishing. Then suddenly, 65 million years ago, a catastrophe occurred. Virtually every species, including all the large animals, were wiped out. Throughout the Mesozoic, a series of dinosaurs and other reptiles had been evolving and slowly becoming extinct, but they were always replaced by other species. This wholesale extinction was unprecedented.

The cause of the catastrophe is unknown, but since the nature of the Earth itself was unchanged, it seems likely that some outside phenomenon was responsible. One theory suggests that a large meteorite collided with the Earth, throwing enough dust into the atmosphere to blot out the sun for several years—long enough to kill almost all the green plants on land and in the sea. If this was the case, only small animals that fed on carrion, decaying vegetation, seeds or nuts could hope to survive. Whatever the cause, the reign of the reptiles was at an end, leaving the small, adaptable mammals and birds to recolonize the virtually empty planet during the Cenozoic era.

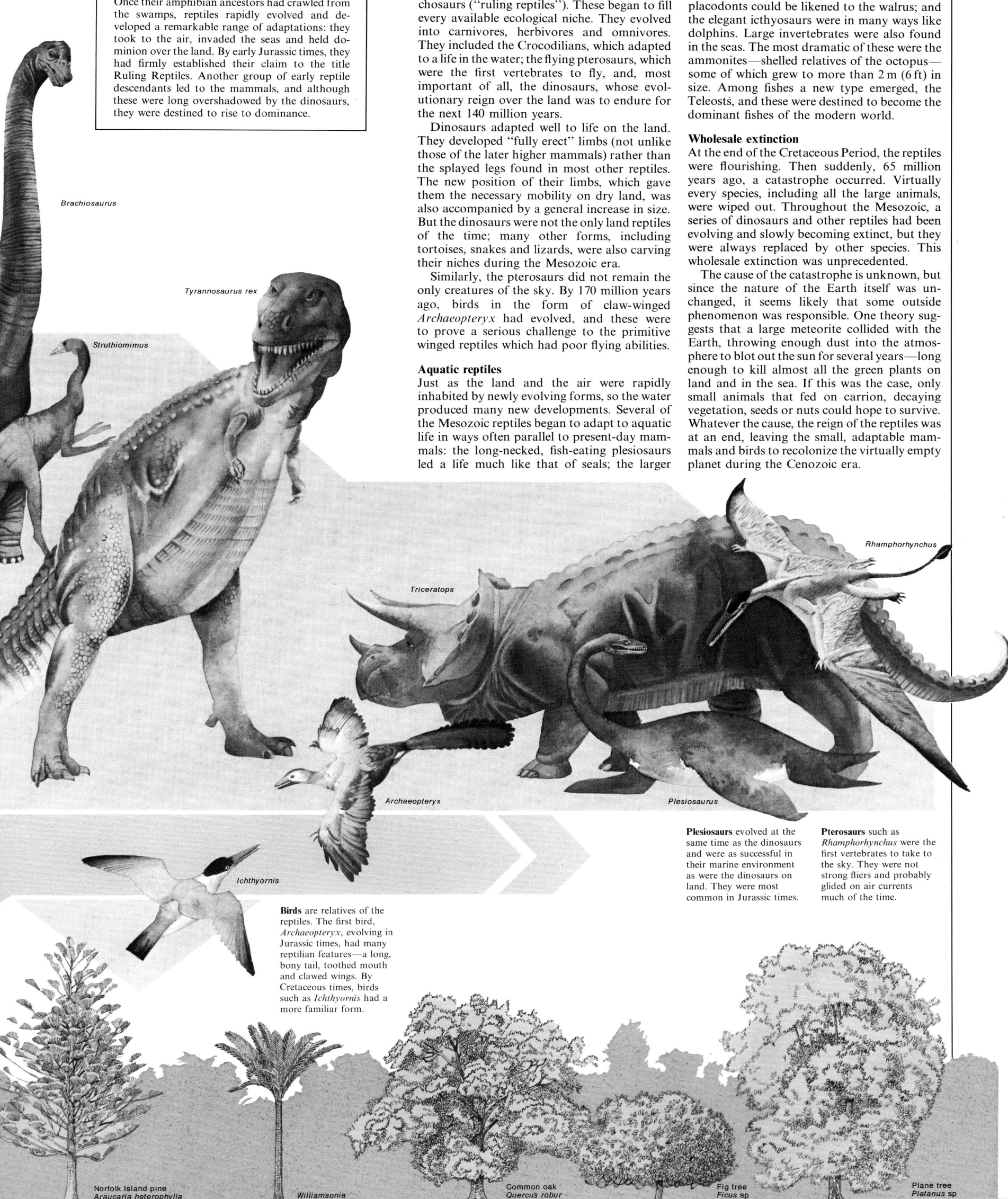

Brachiosaurus

Tyrannosaurus rex

Struthiomimus

Rhamphorhynchus

Triceratops

Archaeopteryx

Plesiosaurus

Ichthyornis

Plesiosaurs evolved at the same time as the dinosaurs and were as successful in their marine environment as were the dinosaurs on land. They were most common in Jurassic times.

Pterosaurs such as *Rhamphorhynchus* were the first vertebrates to take to the sky. They were not strong fliers and probably glided on air currents much of the time.

Birds are relatives of the reptiles. The first bird, *Archaeopteryx*, evolving in Jurassic times, had many reptilian features—a long, bony tail, toothed mouth and clawed wings. By Cretaceous times, birds such as *Ichthyornis* had a more familiar form.

Norfolk Island pine
Araucaria heterophylla

Williamsonia

Common oak
Quercus robur

Fig tree
Ficus sp

Plane tree
Platanus sp

adiation of reptiles **JURASSIC** First birds   150   **CRETACEOUS** First flowering plants   100 First modern fishes   Extinction of dinosaurs

41

The Age of Mammals

After the time of the great dying, 65 million years ago, reptiles never regained the importance they had achieved during the Mesozoic era. A new era, the Cenozoic, had begun. On the continental landmasses, mammals and birds, newly released from 160 million years of reptilian domination, began to occupy their niches in the rich, empty habitats. They flourished and diversified, and the cold-blooded reptiles became second-class citizens in a world of warm-blooded animals.

While reptiles still dominated the world, during the late Mesozoic, a new group of mammals had arisen. These were the first creatures on Earth to give birth to fully formed, live young. Until this time, the most advanced of the mammals had been marsupials whose young were still virtually embryos at birth and had to develop in the mother's pouch, or marsupium. The new mammals had evolved a more sophisticated system—the mother retained the fetus safely inside her body until it was fully formed, nourishing it during this time through a special organ, the placenta, developed during pregnancy. These mammals, the placentals, were destined to become the major mammalian group.

Although all the Mesozoic placentals were small, they had already evolved into a number of different forms that existed alongside the dinosaurs. Besides the insectivores, which were the ancestral type, they included early representatives of the Primates (precursors of modern monkeys and apes), the Carnivores, and the now extinct Condylarthrans (primitive hoofed mammals). When suddenly, 65 million years ago, there was no longer competition from the large land reptiles, these early groups rapidly evolved and extravagant forms developed.

But just as the first reptiles had passed through an early evolution, largely to be replaced by a second evolutionary wave, so the first large mammals were, in many cases, superseded by other, more successful lines. In the earliest part of the Cenozoic era, the different groups of placentals, although not closely related, all tended to be heavy limbed and heavy tailed and to walk on the whole length of their feet (as do modern bears) or on thick, stubby toes. These ungainly, thickset mammals soon died out. Some became extinct because their descendants, more efficiently adapted to their environment, overtook and replaced them. Others, such as the powerful taeniodonts and the large rodent-like tillodonts, seem to have been evolutionary blind alleys.

Spectacular developments

It was the Oligocene Period, 36 million years ago, that saw the end of most of these early essays in mammalian gigantism, but, in many parts of the world, they were replaced by others just as spectacular. In South America, the giant sloths and glyptodonts (massive relatives of the armadillos) survived until comparatively recently. The ground sloths, at least, were contemporaries of the first men on the continent.

As each group of early mammals evolved, during the early and middle part of the Cenozoic era, many of their developments closely reflected changes taking place in their environment. The first horse-like creature, for example, was *Hyracotherium*, also called *Eohippus* or "dawn horse." It lived 54 million years ago and was a small, multi-toed creature, well adapted to its densely forested habitat. The teeth of its descendants gradually changed in size and complexity, but it was not until the Miocene Period, nearly 20 million years later, that any radical alterations took place. This was the time when grasses (the Gramineae), until then a rare family of plants, came to the fore. The world's plains suddenly became clothed in a food plant very suitable for the attention of grazing creatures such as the early horses.

Animals of the grasslands

Horses and many other animals moved from the forests to make use of this new and abundant food supply. Once on the plains, different adaptations for survival were required: high-crowned teeth to deal with tough grasses; limbs enabling the animal to run tirelessly without extra, unwanted weight from supporting side toes (which were lost); large eyes capable of seeing for long distances and placed far back on the head for detecting predators approaching from any direction (as a result of which, however, the ability to judge distances ahead had to be sacrificed). Thus, the modern horses are plains-dwelling animals, perfectly adapted to their present way of life.

Mammals reached the climax of diversity during the Pliocene Period, 10 million years ago. But in the following period, the Pleistocene, ice sheets swept down from the polar regions and from the high mountains of the north, bringing massive and sudden changes to the ecology of virtually every region in the world. This dramatic disturbance to the environment brought extinction to an enormous number of species.

The survivors consisted mainly of the smaller species. Unfortunately for many of them, however, they included *Homo sapiens*. Man rose to success at the end of the Pleistocene and has, in the last 10,000 years, taken dominion over virtually every part of the world. During this time, he has proved far more destructive to other animal species than any natural force has ever been. More than 5,000 years ago, the giant sloths may have been a dying species, but there is no doubt that early human hunters hurried on their extinction. Since then, the list of species eliminated by man has grown ever longer. Today the human race is causing the extinction of both animals and plants at a rate comparable to that of 65 million years ago, when some dramatic natural catastrophe swept the dinosaurs from the face of the world. Unless man, the super-efficient species, can curb his numbers and his destructive activities, a new age of dying may soon be upon the world.

By early Cenozoic times, many forms had evolved from the insectivorous mammals of the Mesozoic Period. *Miacis*, *Hyaenodon* and *Oxyaena* were flesh eaters. Plant-eating mammals, such as Taeniodonts, *Arsinoitherium* and *Phenacodus* (one of the first hoofed mammals), had also evolved, while other early forms, such as *Andrewsarchus*, were omnivorous. The early Primates, however, remained insect eaters for millions of years.

EARLY STAGES

Miacis

Andrewsarchus

Hyaenodon

D'atryma

Euryapteryx

CENOZOIC BIRDS

Giant flightless birds came to the fore more than once during the Cenozoic era. *Diatryma*, a massive, flesh-eating bird, ruled the North American grasslands in early Cenozoic times, while mammals were still small, fairly primitive and easily dominated. *Euryapteryx* and its relatives (the moas) evolved in New Zealand, where, because there were no mammals, they filled an empty ecological niche.

The Carnivores diversified into two major types—the cats and their kin (Aeluroidea), and the dogs and their relatives (Arctoidea). During the Oligocene Period, about 36 million years ago, Aeluroidea gave rise not only to early relatives of modern cats, such as sabre-toothed *Hoplophoneus*, but also to two other families, the civets and the hyenas. At the same time, Arctoidea also diversified and produced the dogs, weasels, bears and racoons. It was a complex group, with many forms that were later to become extinct—the massive bear-dogs, such as *Daphoenus*, for example, which lived during the Miocene Period. Cats and dogs evolved to exploit different habitats. The cats adapted to life in forests, and learned to hide and then stalk and ambush their prey. Dogs evolved as plains animals, and used pack-hunting techniques to catch fleet-footed, grassland animals.

Perissodactyls and Artiodactyls were two important groups that evolved from the primitive hoofed mammals; Perissodactyls had an odd number of toes on each foot, Artiodactyls had an even number. These two groups suffered very different fortunes. Artiodactyls are still at the height of their success; the early stock produced the modern pig, camel, deer, giraffe, hippopotamus, antelope, sheep, goat and cow. Perissodactyls, however, are in decline and the only survivors are the horse, rhinoceros and tapir. But they were once important and many, now-extinct, kinds such as *Moropus* and *Brontotherium* existed alongside more familiar types such as *Hyracotherium*. Few remained after the Pliocene Period, however. This was when the Artiodactyls came to the fore. They, too, had had casualties—the pig-like *Archaeotherium* was by then extinct—but many other Artiodactyls, such as the early giraffe, *Palaeotragus*, were evolving. Most important, however, was small *Archaeomeryx*, for it had developed the key to Artiodactyl success—it was a ruminant and this enabled it to make the best possible use of the world's new grasslands.

Palaeozoic			Mesozoic		Cenozoic
500	400	300	200	100	0

Millions of years ago

Three geological eras mark the slow evolution of life on Earth. The Palaeozoic era, 570 million years ago, saw the appearance of the first primitive life forms. By the end of the era, 340 million years later, the reptiles had evolved and the following Mesozoic era was the age of reptilian domination. This reign over the land ended 65 million years ago as the Cenozoic era began. Then mammals came to the fore and the age of mammalian dominance of the world had dawned.

EARLY GRASSES

Grasses first appeared in the densely forested lands of 60 million years ago. Probably similar to the sedges (right) found in wet woodland areas today, they offered an attractive meal to many mammals. But it was not until the Miocene Period, when a change in climate reduced forest cover, that grasses became widespread. Then many forest creatures migrated to grassland areas.

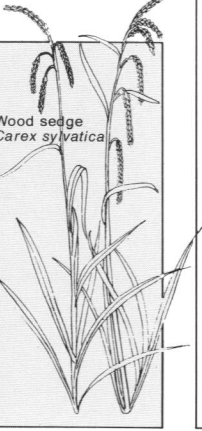

Wood sedge
Carex sylvatica

THE MARSUPIALS

Thylacosmilus and mouse-like *Argyrolagus* were two of the many forms of marsupial mammal that evolved in Cenozoic times in South America. Almost everywhere else, the marsupials, unable to compete with their more efficient placental cousins, met with an early extinction. But in two remote regions—South America (then separate from North America) and Australia—there was no competition from placentals, and there the marsupials flourished.

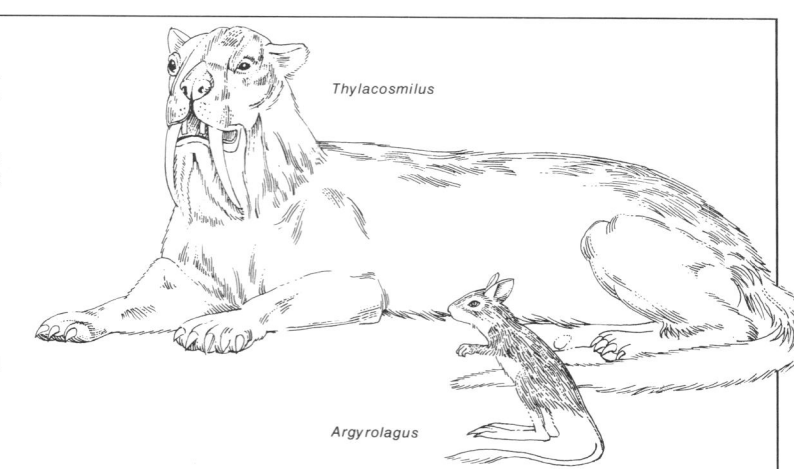

Thylacosmilus

Argyrolagus

TERTIARY	First radiation of mammals and birds			Forest horses				Second radiation of mammals
Palaeocene		60	Eocene		50		40	Oligocene

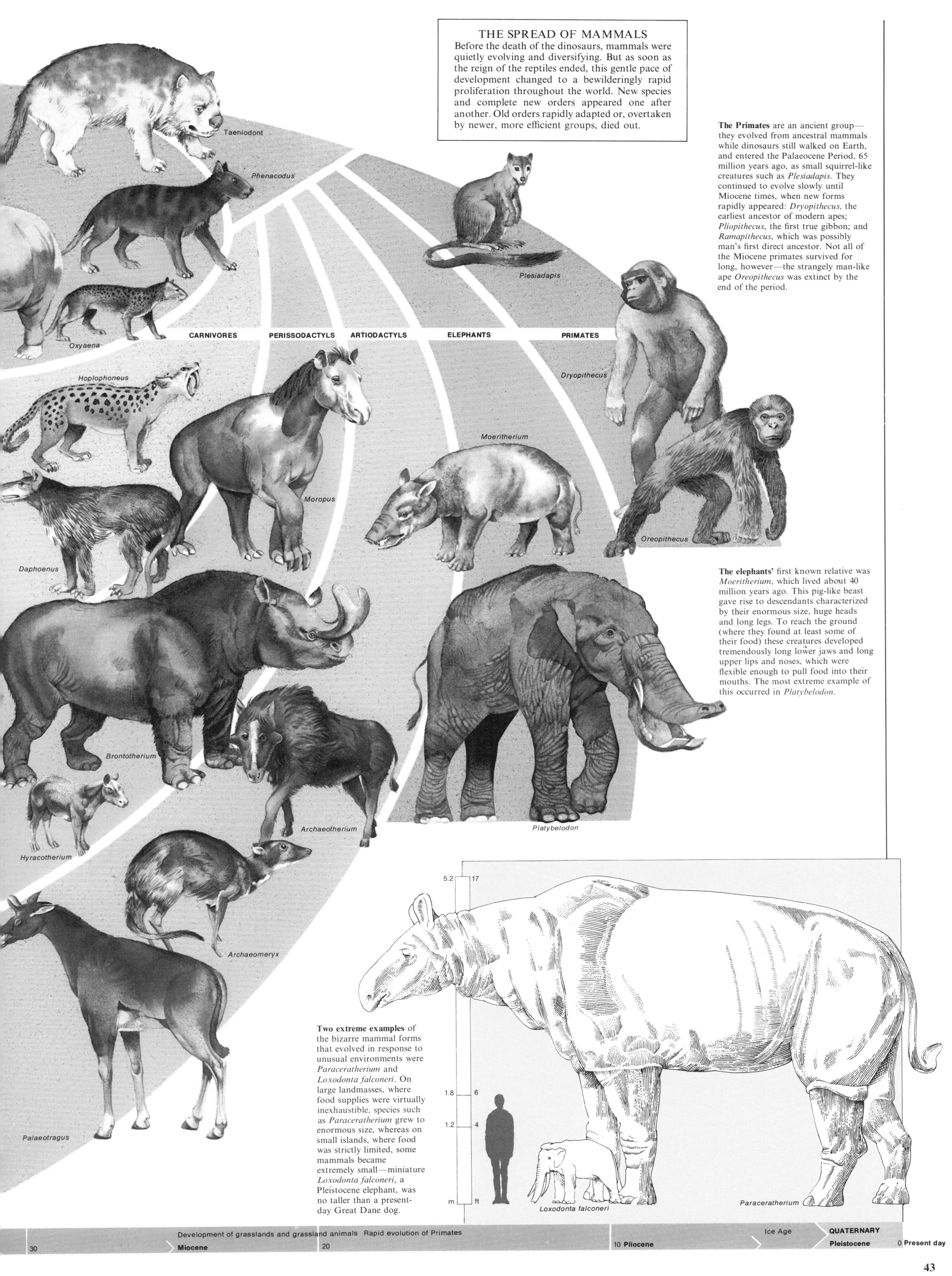

THE SPREAD OF MAMMALS

Before the death of the dinosaurs, mammals were quietly evolving and diversifying. But as soon as the reign of the reptiles ended, this gentle pace of development changed to a bewilderingly rapid proliferation throughout the world. New species and complete new orders appeared one after another. Old orders rapidly adapted or, overtaken by newer, more efficient groups, died out.

The Primates are an ancient group—they evolved from ancestral mammals while dinosaurs still walked on Earth, and entered the Palaeocene Period, 65 million years ago, as small squirrel-like creatures such as *Plesiadapis*. They continued to evolve slowly until Miocene times, when new forms rapidly appeared: *Dryopithecus*, the earliest ancestor of modern apes; *Pliopithecus*, the first true gibbon; and *Ramapithecus*, which was possibly man's first direct ancestor. Not all of the Miocene primates survived for long, however—the strangely man-like ape *Oreopithecus* was extinct by the end of the period.

Taeniodont

Phenacodus

Plesiadapis

Oxyaena

| CARNIVORES | PERISSODACTYLS | ARTIODACTYLS | ELEPHANTS | PRIMATES |

Hoplophoneus

Dryopithecus

Moropus

Moeritherium

Oreopithecus

Daphoenus

The elephants' first known relative was *Moeritherium*, which lived about 40 million years ago. This pig-like beast gave rise to descendants characterized by their enormous size, huge heads and long legs. To reach the ground (where they found at least some of their food) these creatures developed tremendously long lower jaws and long upper lips and noses, which were flexible enough to pull food into their mouths. The most extreme example of this occurred in *Platybelodon*.

Brontotherium

Archaeotherium

Hyracotherium

Platybelodon

Archaeomeryx

Two extreme examples of the bizarre mammal forms that evolved in response to unusual environments were *Paraceratherium* and *Loxodonta falconeri*. On large landmasses, where food supplies were virtually inexhaustible, species such as *Paraceratherium* grew to enormous size, whereas on small islands, where food was strictly limited, some mammals became extremely small—miniature *Loxodonta falconeri*, a Pleistocene elephant, was no taller than a present-day Great Dane dog.

Palaeotragus

Loxodonta falconeri

Paraceratherium

Development of grasslands and grassland animals   Rapid evolution of Primates

| 30 | **Miocene** | 20 | 10 **Pliocene** | Ice Age **QUATERNARY** | 0 **Present day** |
| | | | | **Pleistocene** | |

Spread of Life

Different parts of the Earth have their own characteristic groups of animals, and this pattern of distribution caused nineteenth-century zoologists to divide the world into zoogeographical regions. Charles Darwin suggested how these assemblages of animals may have come about by the process of evolution. But we now know that movements of the Earth's land surfaces are also responsible for the present-day distribution of many of the world's animal species and groups.

The evolution of a major group of animals, such as the reptiles or the mammals, tends to follow a set pattern in five stages. First the original ancestral group spreads out, with each sub-group adapting to its environment. This process, called adaptive radiation, results in a variety of different kinds of animals, each suited to life in a particular niche or habitat—determined largely by food supply and environmental conditions. The different kinds then move into all of the areas they can reach in which the environment is right, producing the second stage of widespread distribution.

Competition for food or living space, or changes in climate may then cause some forms to decline and disappear from parts of the range, resulting in a third stage of discontinuous distribution. Any further reduction leads to isolated relict populations—the fourth stage—in which the animal exists only in one or two limited areas. The final stage is extinction.

In all distribution patterns, however, there is not only an ecological element but also a historical one, with past events determining where animals are and where they are not. There are thus two basic types of distribution: continuous, where the area is not interrupted by an insurmountable barrier (such as a mountain range), and discontinuous, where the area of distribution is subdivided and there is no way that members of one group can interchange with members of another.

One of these factors—the earliest and most important—is the (continuing) movement of the Earth's tectonic plates. This caused the supercontinent Pangaea to break up, probably in the Triassic Period (225–180 million years ago), and the continental masses to drift apart to their present positions. New oceans developed, separating the Americas from the Euro-African block and splitting both from Antarctica. Madagascar and Australia became islands, India moved north from Africa to join the Asian block, and mountain ranges such as the Alps, Andes, Rockies and Himalayas were thrown up. As a result, animal types that had already evolved on Pangaea or its fragments before they had significantly separated (i.e. all the major invertebrate groups and most of the earlier vertebrates) can be expected to exist on all the present-day continents.

Bridging the continents

Independently of these activities, ice ages occurred from time to time, resulting in the vast accumulations of ice at the poles and a consequent general lowering of the sea level by as much as 100 m (330 ft). This temporarily exposed the previously submerged continental shelves, providing additional land for colonization, and new corridors that linked existing areas, such as the land bridge that appeared between Alaska and Siberia.

Groups that had evolved after the breakup of Pangaea, e.g. the hare, squirrel and dog families, made use of land bridges as the climate allowed, and came to occupy more than one continent. Flying animals—birds and bats—also made intercontinental crossings and established themselves on both sides of oceans, although a surprising number of these have remained very restricted in distribution. But most animals have to stay where they are because of special dietary or environmental requirements, or because they are "trapped" on islands, such as Madagascar and Australia, and cannot get off. These areas have the most distinctive faunas in the world.

Barriers and corridors

The extent to which an expanding group can spread from its original area depends on whether there are barriers, such as mountain ranges, deserts or seas, or corridors that link major areas in which the animals can live. Different animals have different environmental requirements, and so a topographical feature that is a barrier for one may be a corridor for another.

The dispersal of many animals is achieved by "hopping" from lake to lake across a continent, or from island to island across a sea. Some, such as insects, are good at this, whereas others, such as land mammals, are bad. Thus a considerable range of weevils (Curculionidae) are found on islands from New Caledonia to the Marquesas, some 6,500 km (4,000 miles) across the southern Pacific Ocean, whereas the marsupials of the region are concentrated in Australia, Papua New Guinea and a few adjacent islands, with only one genus reaching the Celebes and none crossing Wallace's Line into Borneo.

An example of colonization by "hopping" is seen on the volcanic island of Krakatoa near Java, which exploded in 1883 destroying all life. Within 25 years there were 263 species of animals on the island. Most were insects, but there were three species of land snails, two species of reptiles and 16 of birds. In another 22 years, 46 species of vertebrates had arrived, including two species of rats.

The effect of man

Animal distribution cannot be considered merely as a natural phenomenon, because it has been greatly and increasingly modified by man's impact on the environment. Agricultural practice has made large sections of the land area unsuitable for many of the animals that originally lived there, notably through the clearing of forests and the draining of marshes.

Man has also introduced animals, either deliberately or accidentally, to regions where they were not endemic. The rabbit in Australia and the deer in New Zealand were both deliberately introduced, but rats, cockroaches and many other animals have been accidentally transported throughout the world on ships and aircraft. The enormous growth in human population has driven many animals from their natural homes and into more remote environments, such as mountains. Indeed, in the past century human interference has altered the pattern of animal distribution more drastically than any topographic or climatic change.

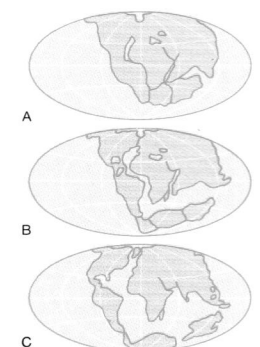

Earth's original single landmass, Pangaea (A), probably began to break up more than 200 million years ago. Species that had already evolved diversified on the Noah's Arks of the drifting supercontinents (B), called Laurasia and Gondwanaland. As the process continued (C), related animals flourished in the separated continents of the southern hemisphere.

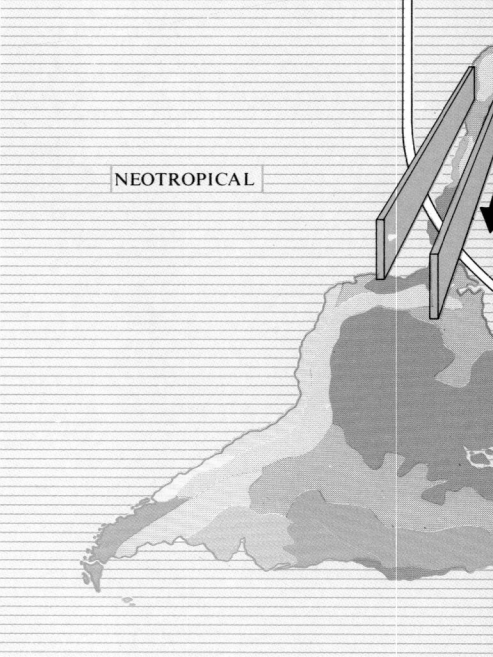

NEOTROPICAL

PATTERNS OF ANIMALS
Over the ages the shape of the Earth has changed. Whole continents have moved; mountains and deserts have grown; land bridges between continents have opened and closed. These events, together with food supply, climate and other animals, account for the present natural pattern of life in the six zoogeographical regions, each containing a unique mix of animals. But man's activities have drastically affected this natural distribution in all parts of the world.

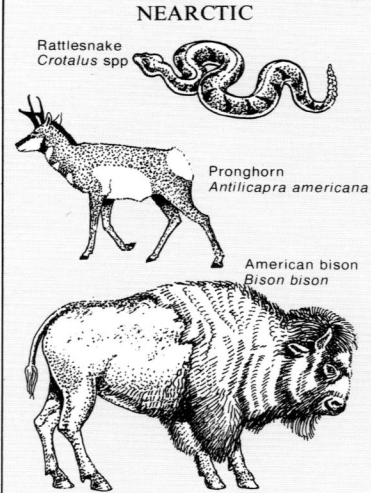

NEARCTIC

Rattlesnake
Crotalus spp

Pronghorn
Antilicapra americana

American bison
Bison bison

NEOTROPICAL

Two-toed sloth
Choloepus didactylus

Marmoset
Callithrix jacchus

Crested seriema
Cariama cristata

The Nearctic or "New North" region covers all of North America, from the highlands of Mexico in the south to Greenland and the Aleutian Islands in the north. Its climate and vegetation resemble that of the Palearctic region, and many of its mammals crossed over from the Palearctic via the Bering land bridge, which linked Siberia and Alaska when the sea level was lower. Animals unique to the Nearctic group include the pronghorn, an antelope-like mammal that inhabits the grasslands and plains of western and central America, and the bison, another large mammal that inhabits the prairies. Several species of rattlesnake also belong to the Nearctic group, although they are not exclusive to this region.

The Neotropical or "New Tropical" region consists of South America, the West Indies and most of Mexico. The climate and vegetation are mostly tropical—only the southern tip is in the temperate zone—and it is linked to the Nearctic by the Central American corridor. The Neotropical region has more distinctive families than any other. These include, among mammals, the sloth, which inhabits the tropical forests and has adapted to an upside-down existence. Among birds, the long-legged crested seriema is also unique to the region. Neotropical monkeys, such as the marmoset, have lateral-facing nostrils, which distinguish them from their downward-nosed relatives found in the Old World.

Land routes around the world have altered with the ages, sometimes allowing invaders to penetrate new lands, or closing to form natural sanctuaries for less efficient animals. The Central American isthmus (A) opened South America to placental mammals from the north. The Sahara desert closed most of Africa (B) to Eurasian species. Asia and Australia (C) share "island hoppers" in the transitional zones, but sea barriers have kept the regions separate.

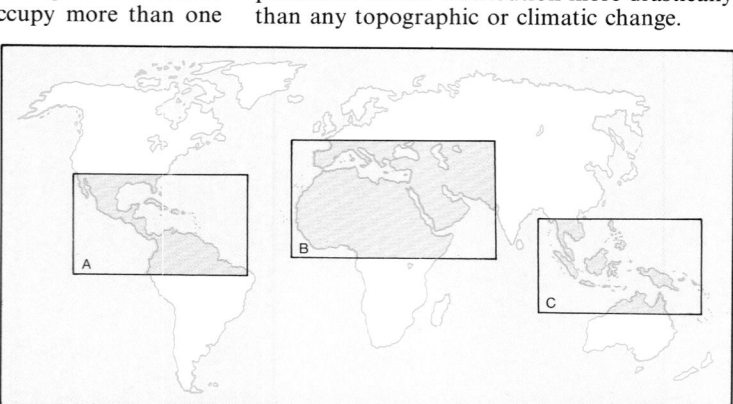

A land bridge between the Americas emerged about three million years ago, breaking the long isolation of the south. The primitive pouched mammals which had developed there were now threatened by more advanced mammals from the north, and many extinctions followed. Northern invaders included peccaries, raccoons and a llama-like camelid. But members of the armadillo and opossum families were successful in making their way to the northern region.

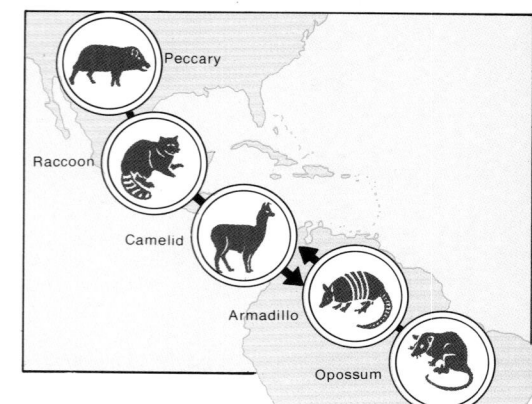

Peccary

Raccoon

Camelid

Armadillo

Opossum

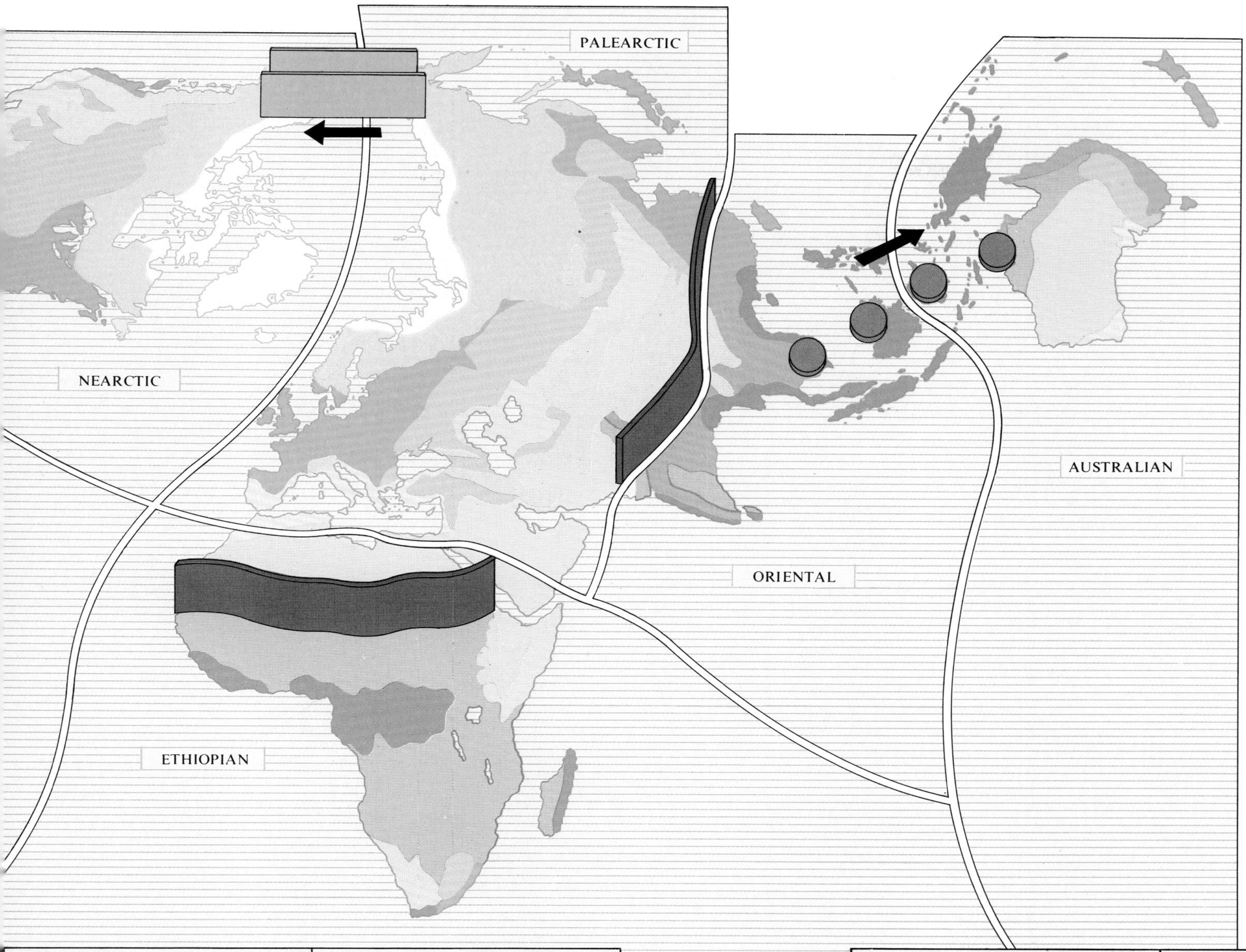

PALEARCTIC

NEARCTIC

AUSTRALIAN

ORIENTAL

ETHIOPIAN

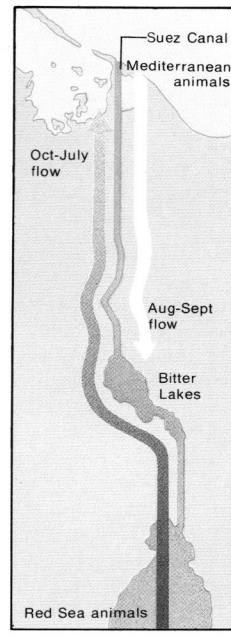

Suez Canal
Mediterranean
animals

Oct-July
flow

Aug-Sept
flow

Bitter
Lakes

Red Sea animals

The man-made filter of the Suez Canal, cut in 1869, is an animal corridor between the Mediterranean and Red Sea. But movement is mainly from the latter, for the channel passes through the hot, salty Bitter Lakes, favoring animals adapted to these conditions, and the current flows northwards for 10 months of the year. However, not all the 130 invading species are likely to survive Mediterranean conditions.

PALEARCTIC

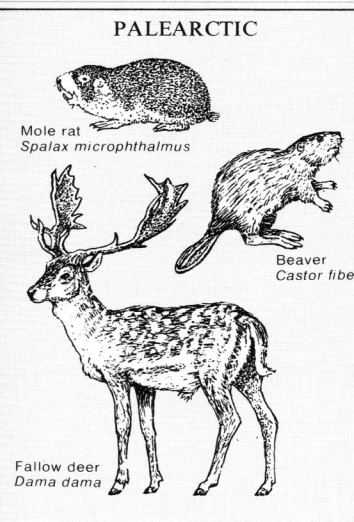

Mole rat
Spalax microphthalmus

Beaver
Castor fiber

Fallow deer
Dama dama

The Palearctic or "Old North" region covers the entire northerly part of the Old World, with seas to the north, east and west. To the south, the Sahara desert and the Himalaya mountains form barriers that separate the Palearctic from the Ethiopian and Oriental regions, although these regions are all part of the same landmass. One of the few species of mammals unique to the Palearctic is the Mediterranean mole rat, a thick-furred rodent. Another Palearctic rodent, the beaver, is shared with the Nearctic region. Fallow deer occur throughout Europe. They have been introduced by man into many other parts of the world, but their origin is almost certainly Mediterranean.

ETHIOPIAN

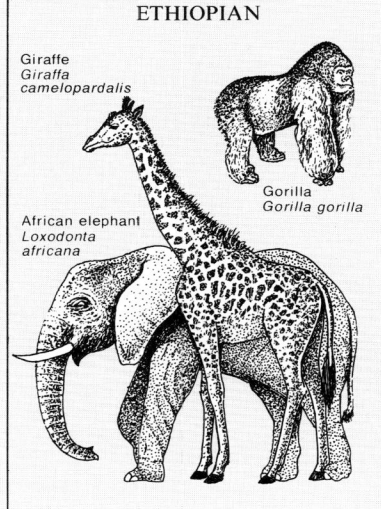

Giraffe
Giraffa
camelopardalis

Gorilla
Gorilla gorilla

African elephant
Loxodonta
africana

The Ethiopian region includes southern Arabia as well as all Africa south of the Sahara. It resembles in many ways the Neotropical region and is almost as rich in unique families. Its fauna also has much in common with the Oriental region. Unique mammals include the giraffe, at 5.5 m (18 ft) the tallest of living land animals, which inhabits the savanna. The region also supports two of the world's four great apes, the gorilla and the chimpanzee, which are found in the forests of western and central Africa. (The other great apes, the orangutan and the gibbon, are Oriental.) The African elephant is distinguished from its Indian relative by its greater size and by its huge ears and massive tusks.

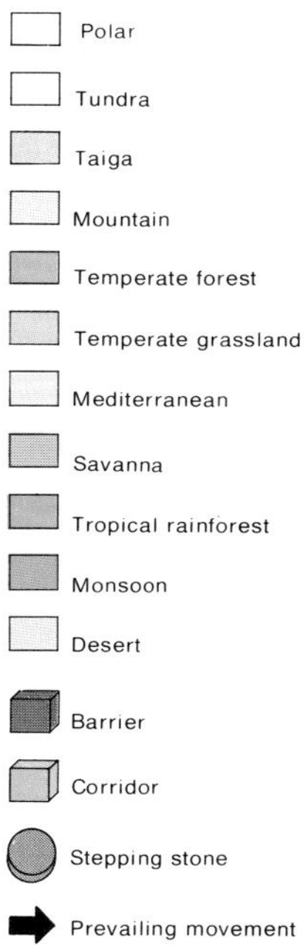

☐	Polar
☐	Tundra
☐	Taiga
☐	Mountain
▨	Temperate forest
▨	Temperate grassland
▨	Mediterranean
▨	Savanna
▨	Tropical rainforest
▨	Monsoon
☐	Desert
▧	Barrier
▧	Corridor
●	Stepping stone
➜	Prevailing movement

ORIENTAL

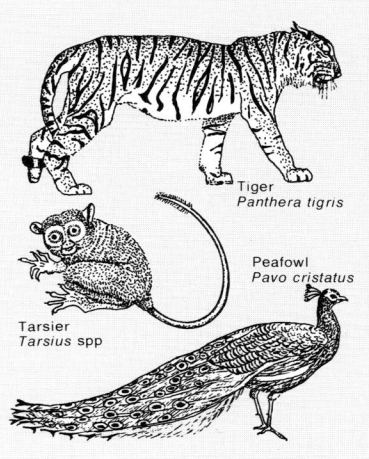

Tiger
Panthera tigris

Peafowl
Pavo cristatus

Tarsier
Tarsius spp

The Oriental region includes India, southern China, southeastern Asia and part of Malaysia. It is bounded to the north by the Himalayas and on either side by ocean, and is separated from the Australian region by a line known as Wallace's Line. It shares a quarter of its mammal families with Africa, but has more primates than any other region. The tarsier, a small relative of the monkey, is unique to southeastern Asia and represents an important early stage of primate evolution. The tiger was once widespread, but its natural habitats are steadily diminishing and the tiger itself is in danger of extinction by man. The peacock is one of the region's many brilliantly colored birds.

AUSTRALIAN

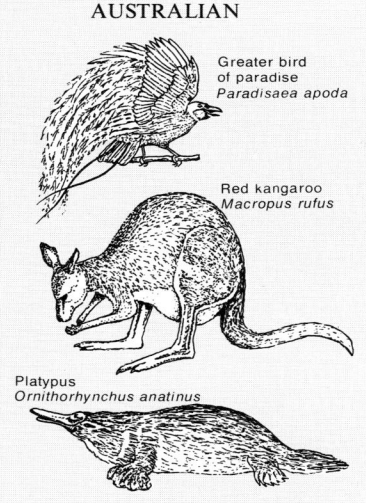

Greater bird
of paradise
Paradisaea apoda

Red kangaroo
Macropus rufus

Platypus
Ornithorhynchus anatinus

The Australian region is unique in having no land connection with any other region. Its native fauna has developed in isolation from the rest of the world for at least 50 million years. Most of the mammals are marsupial—animals such as the kangaroo that carry their young in a pouch. Even more of a biological curiosity than the marsupials is the duckbilled platypus, a monotreme or egg-laying mammal. It lives along the banks of streams in Australia and Tasmania, and lays small, leathery eggs like those of snakes and turtles, but it is a true mammal and nurses its young with milk. Some 13 bird families are unique to the region, including the magnificent bird of paradise.

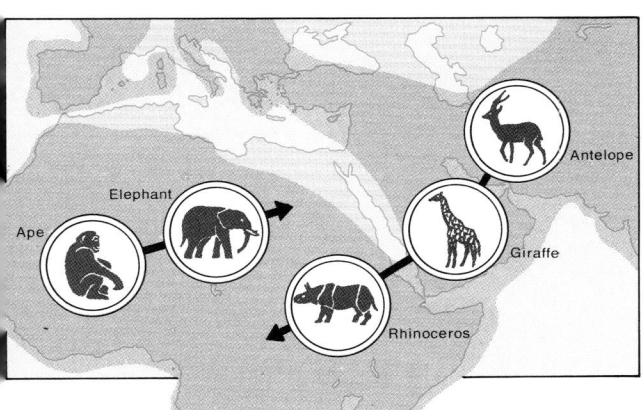

Antelope

Elephant

Ape

Giraffe

Rhinoceros

A desert barrier gradually began to form in northern Africa about nine million years ago, replacing the forest corridor between the Ethiopian and Palearctic regions. During the change, many animals typical of the African plains moved in from the north, including ancestors of today's antelopes, giraffes and rhinoceroses. But African animals also moved up north: early elephants and, much later, apes, which may have been precursors of modern man.

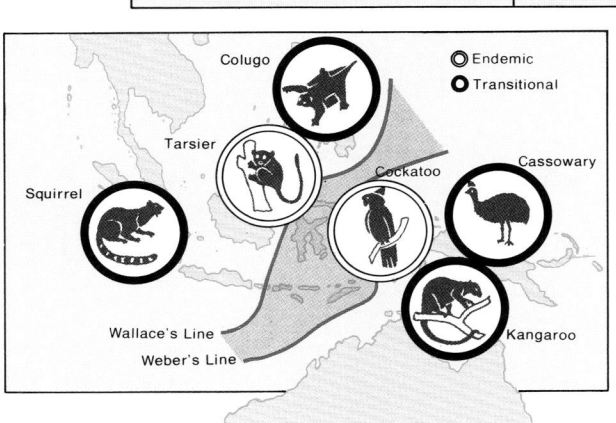

Colugo

Tarsier

Squirrel

Cockatoo

Cassowary

Kangaroo

Wallace's Line

Weber's Line

◉ Endemic
◯ Transitional

The transitional area of "Wallacea" contains animals from both the Oriental and Australian regions, bounded by Wallace's and Weber's Lines, but few have crossed to the other region. Some Oriental mammals, such as tarsiers, are found in Wallacea, but the gliding colugo and varieties of squirrel are not. The Australian cockatoo has reached the transition area, but the flightless cassowary and the tree kangaroo have not.

Spread of Man

Modern Man, *Homo sapiens sapiens*, has proved a highly successful animal since his emergence some 50,000 years ago: today more than 4,000 million members of this subspecies of the *Homo* (Man) group occupy the Earth, living in even the most inhospitable regions. But the fossil record shows that man's lineage goes back millions of years, with different stages of development leading to a greater control of the environment, and with climate itself helping man's ultimate domination of Earth.

Man's lineage may go back at least 14 million years to a small woodland creature known as *Ramapithecus* (Rama's ape). Since the first discoveries of *Ramapithecus* in the Indian subcontinent, its fossils have come to light in many parts of the world, including China, eastern Europe, Turkey and eastern Africa. Fossil remains show that it survived for several million years until, about eight million years ago, there is a tantalizing gap in the fossil record. Then, about four and a half million years later (according to recent discoveries in eastern Africa), we have solid evidence of an upright hominid— a member of man's zoological family. This is "Lucy," a fossil skeleton found in 1973 by Donald Johanson and Tom Gray, and subsequently classified with many other finds as *Australopithecus afarensis*.

This may be man's ancestral "rootstock," but a little later there existed two kinds of "ape-man" (*Australopithecus*), and our own direct ancestor Handy Man (*Homo habilis*). Datable volcanic ash found with the fossils provides a time scale and indicates that, about two million years ago, ape-man and "true" man lived side by side in the lush grassland that then covered the eastern African plains.

One and a half million years ago, according to the fossil evidence, there was again only one hominid species. The varieties of australopithecines had died out, and Handy Man (*Homo habilis*) had apparently evolved into Upright Man (*Homo erectus*). Remains of Upright Man have been found in many regions of the world, from various parts of Africa and Europe to China and Indonesia, although not in the Americas. But there is reason to believe that it was in Africa, well over one million years ago, that he evolved from his ancestor, and began a very gradual expansion out of the continent.

Upright Man had about one million years to spread across the Old World, adapting as he did so to local conditions, just as people of today are adapted in their various ways. He was a nomadic hunter gatherer, socially organized in groups. His skills included the use of fire and cooking, as well as the making of quite large structures out of wood. Recent discoveries suggest that, during the million years of his existence, *Homo erectus* gradually evolved into the next stage of man – *Homo sapiens*.

The next step is revealed most clearly in fossils from more than 100,000 to less than 50,000 years ago. Called Neanderthal Man in Europe, Solo Man in Indonesia, and Rhodesian Man in southern Africa, these types of human being were all descendants of *Homo erectus*.

Variable in brain size, but with prominent eyebrow ridges and receding jaws, they may have been dead ends on the evolutionary road; or some may have led to, or been incorporated in, Modern Man (*Homo sapiens sapiens*).

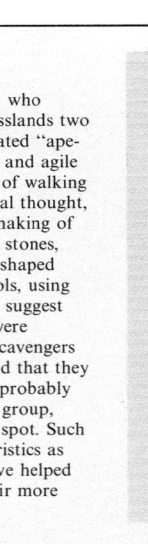

THE AFRICAN CRADLE
Handy Man (*Homo habilis*), who shared the East African grasslands two million years ago with a related "ape-man" species, was a slender and agile creature with a human way of walking and a capacity for conceptual thought, as evidenced in systematic making of tools. Handy Man collected stones, often from far away, and reshaped them into purpose-made tools, using other stones. Fossil remains suggest that these earliest humans were efficient hunters as well as scavengers of larger predators' kills, and that they brought food to campsites, probably sharing it among the whole group, rather than eating it on the spot. Such specifically human characteristics as the sharing of food may have helped our ancestors to survive their more primitive hominid relations.

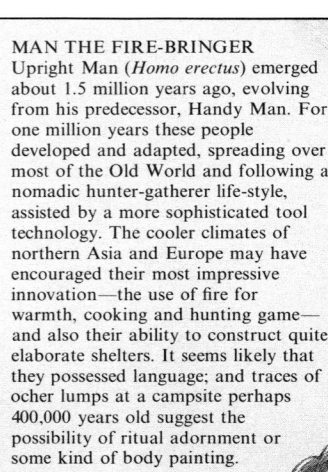

MAN THE FIRE-BRINGER
Upright Man (*Homo erectus*) emerged about 1.5 million years ago, evolving from his predecessor, Handy Man. For one million years these people developed and adapted, spreading over most of the Old World and following a nomadic hunter-gatherer life-style, assisted by a more sophisticated tool technology. The cooler climates of northern Asia and Europe may have encouraged their most impressive innovation—the use of fire for warmth, cooking and hunting game— and also their ability to construct quite elaborate shelters. It seems likely that they possessed language; and traces of ocher lumps at a campsite perhaps 400,000 years old suggest the possibility of ritual adornment or some kind of body painting.

THE HUMANIZING OF MAN
Modern man's predecessor, although called Wise Man (*Homo sapiens*), was long regarded as more brutish than human. But widespread finds have now changed this image, as can be seen in an old and an updated reconstruction of the same Neanderthal skull (right). Many scientists believe that these people showed a human concern for each other, burying their dead with ceremonial reverence, and looking after disabled members of the group. In their Neanderthal form they inhabited Europe and the Middle East from about 100,000 to 40,000 years ago, and were perhaps adapted to ice-age conditions. *Homo sapiens* counterparts of Neanderthal Man also occur in Africa and southeastern Asia.

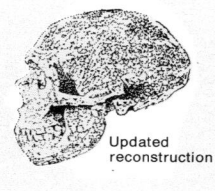
Updated reconstruction

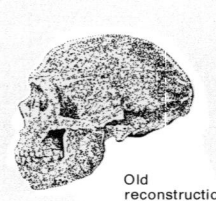
Old reconstruction

The burial of a Neanderthal man took place 60,000 years ago at Shanidar in the Iraq highlands. Fossil traces suggest that the body was laid on a bed of branches, and that flowers were brought to the grave and placed deliberately around the body. The flowers included many varieties still known locally for their medicinal properties. Ritual burials occur at many Neanderthal sites, from the Pyrenees to northern Asia, and indicate a sensitivity that contradicts Neanderthal man's traditional image.

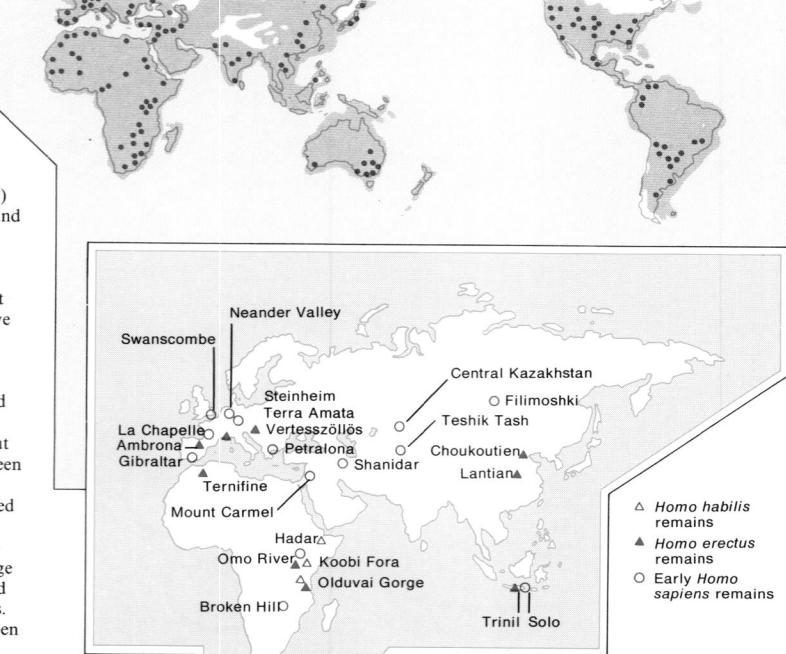

The spread of man (right) from the African heartland of Handy Man (*Homo habilis*) probably began about one million years ago. Remains of Upright Man (*Homo erectus*) have been found all over the Old World, and show a gradual physical and cultural evolution toward a later *Homo sapiens* ancestor, beginning about 350,000 years ago. Between 70,000 and 12,000 years ago, glacial periods locked up the sea water as ice (top), lowering sea levels and opening a land bridge to America that was used by later nomadic peoples. But they had to cross open sea to reach Australia.

Land areas c. 19,000 years ago
Ice sheets c. 19,000 years ago
• *Homo sapiens sapiens* remains

Neander Valley
Swanscombe
Steinheim
Terra Amata
Vértesszöllös
La Chapelle
Ambrona
Gibraltar
Petralona
Ternifine
Mount Carmel
Hadar
Omo River
Koobi Fora
Olduvai Gorge
Broken Hill
Central Kazakhstan
Filimoshki
Teshik Tash
Choukoutien
Shanidar
Lantian
Trinil Solo

△ *Homo habilis* remains
▲ *Homo erectus* remains
○ Early *Homo sapiens* remains

THE AGE OF ART
Toward the end of the last Ice Age, from about 35,000 years ago, truly modern humans began to depict their world in wonderfully vivid terms. The age of art may have reached its peak at Lascaux, France, some 15,000 years ago, but less well-preserved cave paintings from Africa show that the artistic impulse was equally present elsewhere. Called Cro-Magnon Man in Europe, these people spread to all parts of the world, crossing to the Americas by way of the Bering land bridge (when ice locked up the water of the straits), and even venturing over the seas to Australia. Physically these people were just like present-day humans. They led a nomadic, hunter-gathering life, living in large, organized groups, hunting such animals as mammoths, reindeer, bison and horses, and using a technology, as well as an artistry, far in advance of anything previously developed.

Fossils almost four million years old, found since 1973, may mark the ancestral "rootstock" of humanity, but the earliest form of true man is thought to be *Homo habilis*, who shared his African habitat with "ape-man" relatives some two million years ago. His successor, *Homo erectus*, spread over Asia and Europe, evolving gradually into modern man's predecessors, creatures whose large brow ridges belie many typically human characteristics. These were replaced by Modern Man.

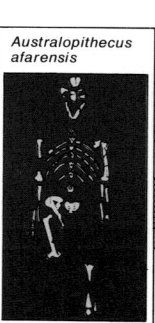
Australopithecus afarensis

3 million years ago

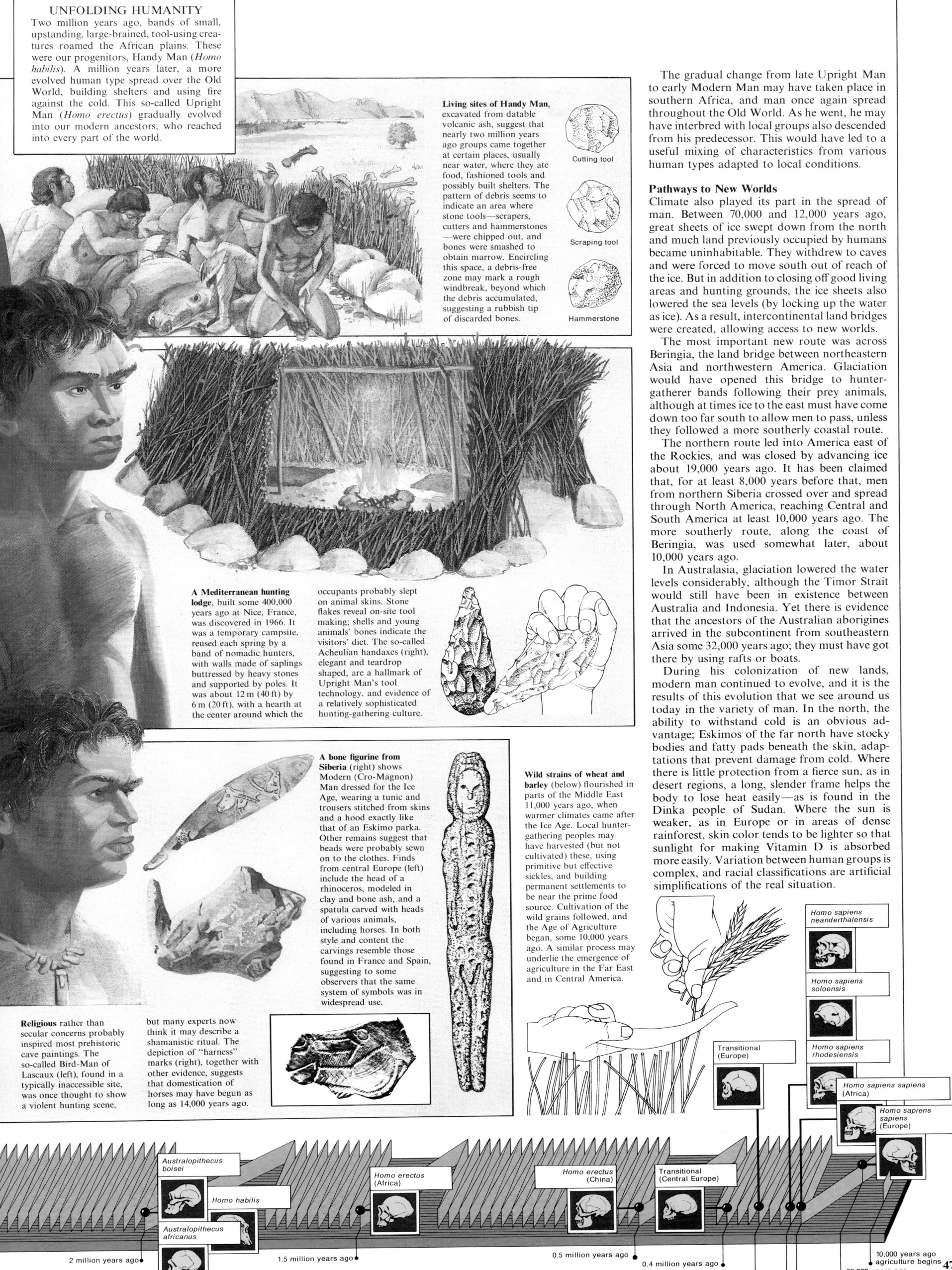

UNFOLDING HUMANITY

Two million years ago, bands of small, upstanding, large-brained, tool-using creatures roamed the African plains. These were our progenitors, Handy Man (*Homo habilis*). A million years later, a more evolved human type spread over the Old World, building shelters and using fire against the cold. This so-called Upright Man (*Homo erectus*) gradually evolved into our modern ancestors, who reached into every part of the world.

Living sites of Handy Man, excavated from datable volcanic ash, suggest that nearly two million years ago groups came together at certain places, usually near water, where they ate food, fashioned tools and possibly built shelters. The pattern of debris seems to indicate an area where stone tools—scrapers, cutters and hammerstones—were chipped out, and bones were smashed to obtain marrow. Encircling this space, a debris-free zone may mark a rough windbreak, beyond which the debris accumulated, suggesting a rubbish tip of discarded bones.

Cutting tool

Scraping tool

Hammerstone

A Mediterranean hunting lodge, built some 400,000 years ago at Nice, France, was discovered in 1966. It was a temporary campsite, reused each spring by a band of nomadic hunters, with walls made of saplings buttressed by heavy stones and supported by poles. It was about 12 m (40 ft) by 6 m (20 ft), with a hearth at the center around which the occupants probably slept on animal skins. Stone flakes reveal on-site tool making; shells and young animals' bones indicate the visitors' diet. The so-called Acheulian handaxes (right), elegant and teardrop shaped, are a hallmark of Upright Man's tool technology, and evidence of a relatively sophisticated hunting-gathering culture.

A bone figurine from Siberia (right) shows Modern (Cro-Magnon) Man dressed for the Ice Age, wearing a tunic and trousers stitched from skins and a hood exactly like that of an Eskimo parka. Other remains suggest that beads were probably sewn on to the clothes. Finds from central Europe (left) include the head of a rhinoceros, modeled in clay and bone ash, and a spatula carved with heads of various animals, including horses. In both style and content the carvings resemble those found in France and Spain, suggesting to some observers that the same system of symbols was in widespread use.

Wild strains of wheat and barley (below) flourished in parts of the Middle East 11,000 years ago, when warmer climates came after the Ice Age. Local hunter-gathering peoples may have harvested (but not cultivated) these, using primitive but effective sickles, and building permanent settlements to be near the prime food source. Cultivation of the wild grains followed, and the Age of Agriculture began, some 10,000 years ago. A similar process may underlie the emergence of agriculture in the Far East and in Central America.

Religious rather than secular concerns probably inspired most prehistoric cave paintings. The so-called Bird-Man of Lascaux (left), found in a typically inaccessible site, was once thought to show a violent hunting scene, but many experts now think it may describe a shamanistic ritual. The depiction of "harness" marks (right), together with other evidence, suggests that domestication of horses may have begun as long as 14,000 years ago.

The gradual change from late Upright Man to early Modern Man may have taken place in southern Africa, and man once again spread throughout the Old World. As he went, he may have interbred with local groups also descended from his predecessor. This would have led to a useful mixing of characteristics from various human types adapted to local conditions.

Pathways to New Worlds

Climate also played its part in the spread of man. Between 70,000 and 12,000 years ago, great sheets of ice swept down from the north and much land previously occupied by humans became uninhabitable. They withdrew to caves and were forced to move south out of reach of the ice. But in addition to closing off good living areas and hunting grounds, the ice sheets also lowered the sea levels (by locking up the water as ice). As a result, intercontinental land bridges were created, allowing access to new worlds.

The most important new route was across Beringia, the land bridge between northeastern Asia and northwestern America. Glaciation would have opened this bridge to hunter-gatherer bands following their prey animals, although at times ice to the east must have come down too far south to allow men to pass, unless they followed a more southerly coastal route.

The northern route led into America east of the Rockies, and was closed by advancing ice about 19,000 years ago. It has been claimed that, for at least 8,000 years before that, men from northern Siberia crossed over and spread through North America, reaching Central and South America at least 10,000 years ago. The more southerly route, along the coast of Beringia, was used somewhat later, about 10,000 years ago.

In Australasia, glaciation lowered the water levels considerably, although the Timor Strait would still have been in existence between Australia and Indonesia. Yet there is evidence that the ancestors of the Australian aborigines arrived in the subcontinent from southeastern Asia some 32,000 years ago; they must have got there by using rafts or boats.

During his colonization of new lands, modern man continued to evolve, and it is the results of this evolution that we see around us today in the variety of man. In the north, the ability to withstand cold is an obvious advantage; Eskimos of the far north have stocky bodies and fatty pads beneath the skin, adaptations that prevent damage from cold. Where there is little protection from a fierce sun, as in desert regions, a long, slender frame helps the body to lose heat easily—as is found in the Dinka people of Sudan. Where the sun is weaker, as in Europe or in areas of dense rainforest, skin color tends to be lighter so that sunlight for making Vitamin D is absorbed more easily. Variation between human groups is complex, and racial classifications are artificial simplifications of the real situation.

Homo sapiens neanderthalensis

Homo sapiens soloensis

Homo sapiens rhodesiensis

Transitional (Europe)

Homo sapiens sapiens (Africa)

Homo sapiens sapiens (Europe)

Australopithecus boisei

Homo habilis

Australopithecus africanus

Homo erectus (Africa)

Homo erectus (China)

Transitional (Central Europe)

2 million years ago

1.5 million years ago

0.5 million years ago

0.4 million years ago

250,000 years ago

100,000 years ago

50,000 years ago

35,000 years ago

10,000 years ago agriculture begins

47

Part 4

THE DIVERSITY OF LIFE
Earth's habitats from the Poles to the Equator
Plants and animals of the Earth's natural regions
Man the preserver and man the destroyer

WEATHER STATIONS

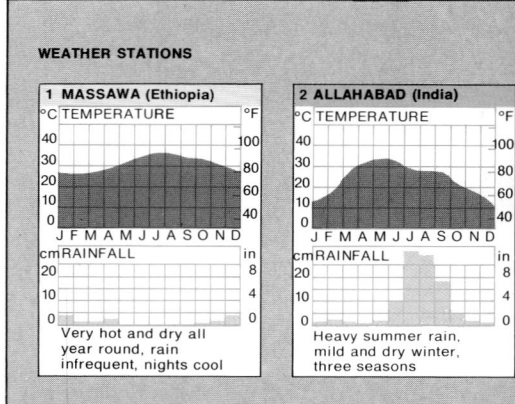

1 MASSAWA (Ethiopia)

°C TEMPERATURE °F

J F M A M J J A S O N D

cmRAINFALL in

Very hot and dry all year round, rain infrequent, nights cool

2 ALLAHABAD (India)

°C TEMPERATURE °F

J F M A M J J A S O N D

cmRAINFALL in

Heavy summer rain, mild and dry winter, three seasons

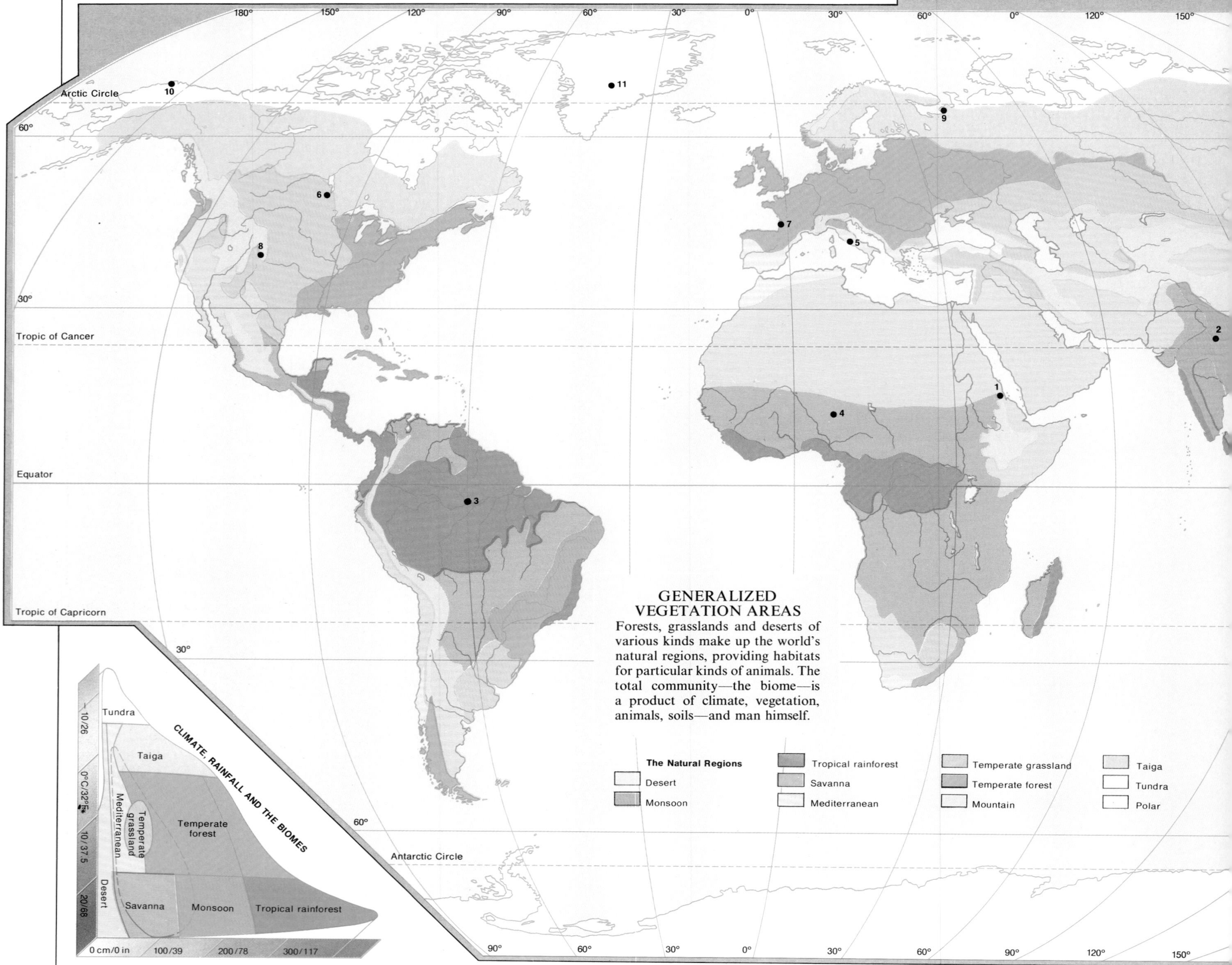

GENERALIZED VEGETATION AREAS

Forests, grasslands and deserts of various kinds make up the world's natural regions, providing habitats for particular kinds of animals. The total community—the biome—is a product of climate, vegetation, animals, soils—and man himself.

The Natural Regions

- Desert
- Monsoon
- Tropical rainforest
- Savanna
- Mediterranean
- Temperate grassland
- Temperate forest
- Mountain
- Taiga
- Tundra
- Polar

CLIMATE, RAINFALL AND THE BIOMES

Tundra

Taiga

Mediterranean

Temperate grassland

Temperate forest

Desert

Savanna

Monsoon

Tropical rainforest

10/26 — 0°C/32°F — 10/37.5 — 20/68

0 cm/0 in — 100/39 — 200/78 — 300/117

Temperature and rainfall (above) govern the world's zones of plant and animal life. Dryness prevents tree growth both in icy tundra and in hot deserts. Wetter conditions cause savannas and grasslands to yield to forest biomes, tropical or temperate (the dotted line indicates zones within which variations occur).

A broad correlation (below) between soil types, climate and vegetation areas shows the interconnections that define the biomes. The soil of the biome is related to climatic conditions and is also modified by plant and animal activity, but soil types are not necessarily confined to any one particular biome.

SOIL AND THE BIOMES

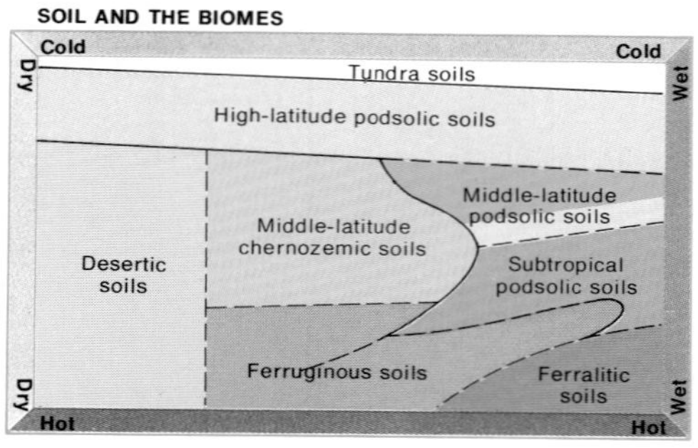

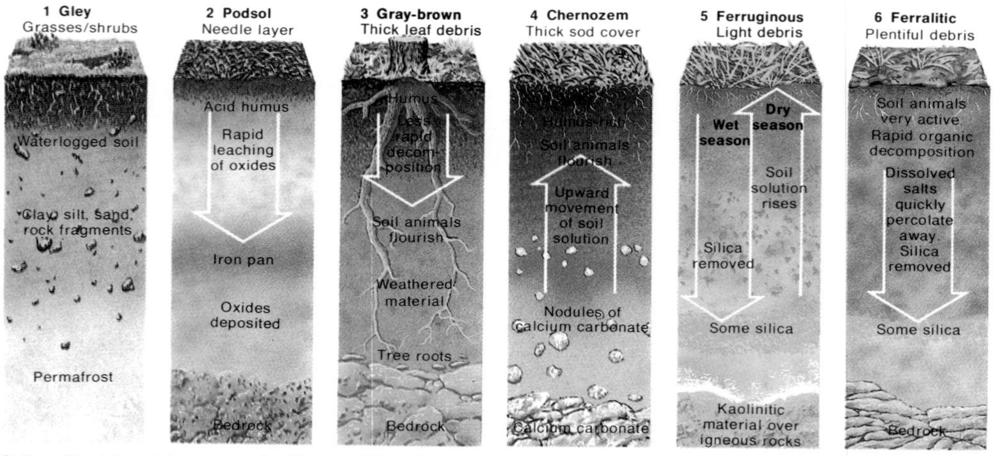

Cold — Cold — Dry — Wet

Tundra soils

High-latitude podsolic soils

Middle-latitude chernozemic soils

Middle-latitude podsolic soils

Middle-latitude podsolic soils

Subtropical podsolic soils

Desertic soils

Ferruginous soils

Ferralitic soils

Dry — Hot — Wet

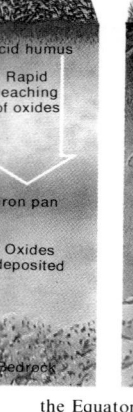

1 Gley
Grasses/shrubs

Waterlogged soil

Clay silt, sand, rock fragments

Permafrost

2 Podsol
Needle layer

Acid humus

Rapid leaching of oxides

Iron pan

Oxides deposited

Bedrock

3 Gray-brown
Thick leaf debris

Humus

Rapid decomposition

Soil animals flourish

Weathered material

Tree roots

Bedrock

4 Chernozem
Thick sod cover

Soil animals flourish

Upward movement of soil solution

Nodules of calcium carbonate

Calcium carbonate

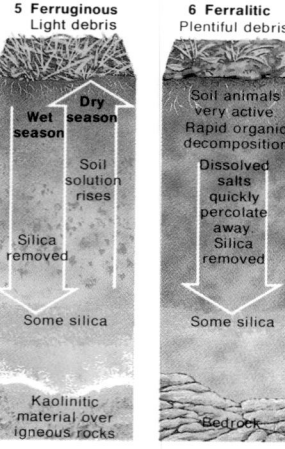

5 Ferruginous
Light debris

Wet season

Dry season

Soil animals flourish

Soil solution rises

Silica removed

Some silica

Kaolinitic material over igneous rocks

6 Ferralitic
Plentiful debris

Soil animals very active

Rapid organic decomposition

Dissolved salts quickly percolate away. Silica removed

Some silica

Bedrock

Soil profiles (above) from surface to bedrock reflect the influence of climate and vegetation on the rock. Depths vary from 1 m in the tundra to 30–40 m at the Equator. Waterlogged gley (1) may form above tundra permafrost. Podsol (2) is typical of taiga forests, where spring snow-melt is heavily leached through a needle layer, sometimes forming an iron "pan." Gray-brown forest soil (3) has rich, organic humus, as has chernozem (4), the typical temperate grassland soil. Ferruginous soils (5) occur in dry-season tropical climates (monsoon, savanna), and ferralitic soils (6) where there is constant rainfall.

ECOSYSTEM DYNAMICS

An ecosystem consists of a group of organisms and its physical environment. A marshland ecosystem from North America (right) shows the dynamic interactions between plant and animal communities and their habitats, which include climate, soil and water. The energy and food in the system initially derive from the Sun—the main energy source for living things, notably plants. Plants are food for herbivores, on land and in water; herbivores are food for carnivores; decomposers (bacteria and fungi) nourish plants, breaking down dead bodies into compounds.

Earth's Natural Regions

Geographers have long looked for ways of classifying conditions such as climate, soil and vegetation to describe the general similarities and differences from area to area throughout the world. By identifying distinctive patterns of climate and vegetation they have provided a convenient global division into natural regions or biomes. And recent developments in ecology – the study of plants and animals in relation to their environments – have given such divisions a greater depth.

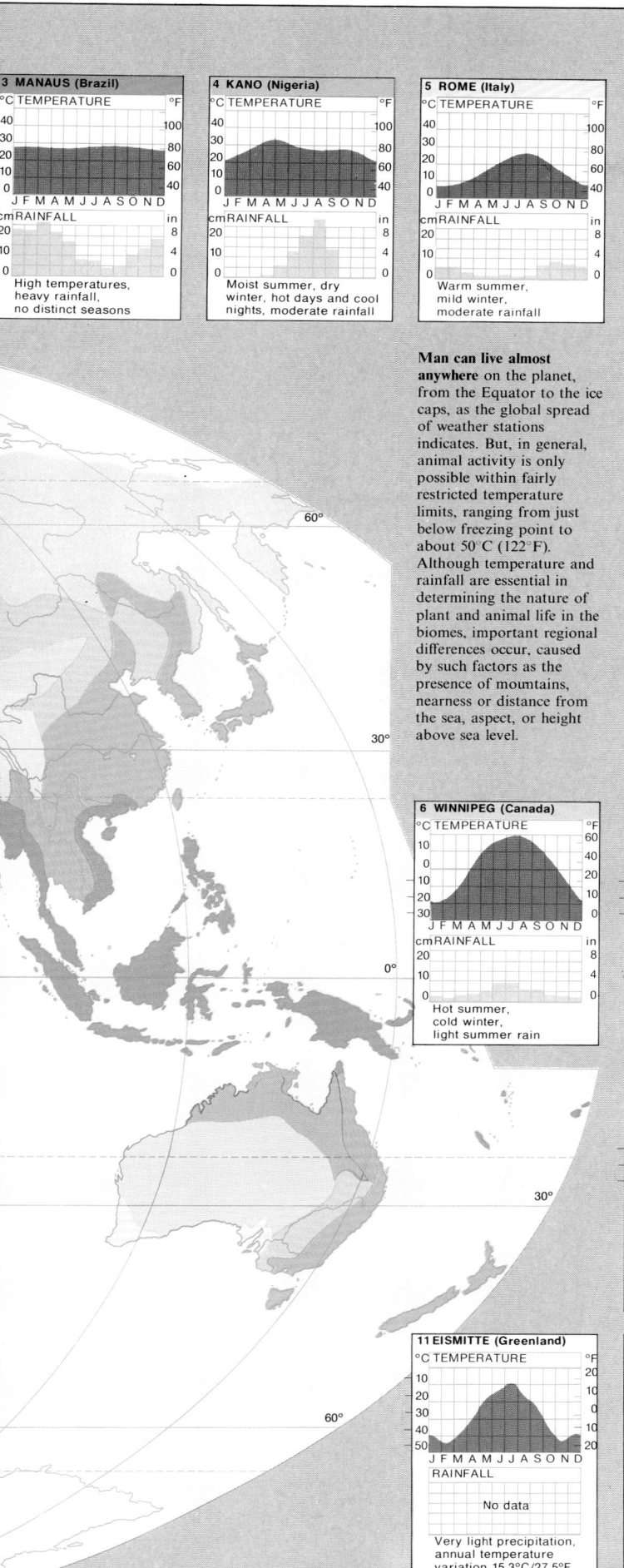

3 MANAUS (Brazil)
°C TEMPERATURE °F
40 / 100
30 / 80
20 / 60
10 / 40
0
J F M A M J J A S O N D
cm RAINFALL in
20 / 8
10 / 4
0 / 0
High temperatures, heavy rainfall, no distinct seasons

4 KANO (Nigeria)
°C TEMPERATURE °F
40 / 100
30 / 80
20 / 60
10 / 40
0
J F M A M J J A S O N D
cm RAINFALL in
20 / 8
10 / 4
0 / 0
Moist summer, dry winter, hot days and cool nights, moderate rainfall

5 ROME (Italy)
°C TEMPERATURE °F
40 / 100
30 / 80
20 / 60
10 / 40
0
J F M A M J J A S O N D
cm RAINFALL in
20 / 8
10 / 4
0 / 0
Warm summer, mild winter, moderate rainfall

Man can live almost anywhere on the planet, from the Equator to the ice caps, as the global spread of weather stations indicates. But, in general, animal activity is only possible within fairly restricted temperature limits, ranging from just below freezing point to about 50°C (122°F). Although temperature and rainfall are essential in determining the nature of plant and animal life in the biomes, important regional differences occur, caused by such factors as the presence of mountains, nearness or distance from the sea, aspect, or height above sea level.

6 WINNIPEG (Canada)
°C TEMPERATURE °F
10 / 60
0 / 40
10 / 20
20 / 10
30 / 0
J F M A M J J A S O N D
cm RAINFALL in
20 / 8
10 / 4
0 / 0
Hot summer, cold winter, light summer rain

7 BORDEAUX (France)
°C TEMPERATURE °F
10 / 60
0 / 40
10 / 20
20 / 10
30 / 0
J F M A M J J A S O N D
cm RAINFALL in
20 / 8
10 / 4
0 / 0
Warm summer, mild winter, four distinct seasons

8 PIKE'S PEAK (USA)
°C TEMPERATURE °F
10 / 60
0 / 40
10 / 20
20 / 10
30 / 0
J F M A M J J A S O N D
cm RAINFALL in
20 / 8
10 / 4
0 / 0
4,300 m (14,111ft) Temperature decreases with increasing altitude

9 ARKHANGELSK (RUSSIA)
°C TEMPERATURE °F
10 / 60
0 / 40
10 / 20
20 / 10
30 / 0
J F M A M J J A S O N D
cm RAINFALL in
20 / 8
10 / 4
0 / 0
Short summer, long and cold winter, light summer rain

10 BARROW (Alaska)
°C TEMPERATURE °F
10 / 60
0 / 40
10 / 20
20 / 10
30 / 0
J F M A M J J A S O N D
cm RAINFALL in
20 / 8
10 / 4
0 / 0
Brief summer, very long and cold winter, very light rainfall

11 EISMITTE (Greenland)
°C TEMPERATURE °F
10 / 20
20 / 10
30 / 0
40 / 10
50 / 20
J F M A M J J A S O N D
RAINFALL
No data
Very light precipitation, annual temperature variation 15.3°C/27.5°F

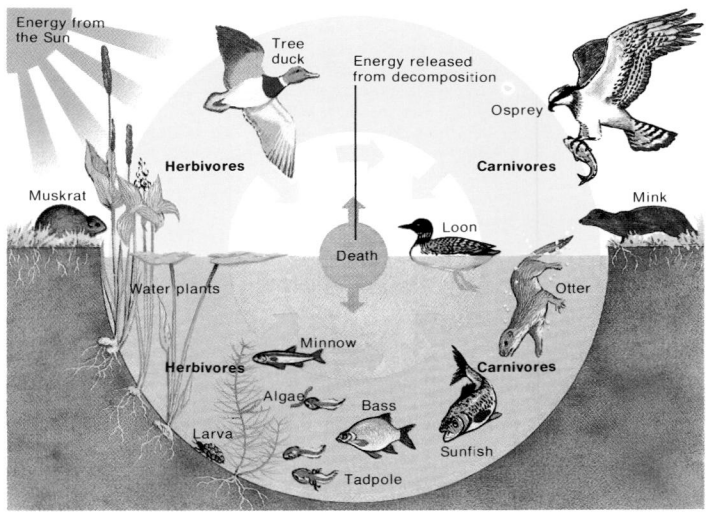

Energy from the Sun
Tree duck
Energy released from decomposition
Osprey
Herbivores
Carnivores
Muskrat
Mink
Loon
Death
Otter
Water plants
Minnow
Herbivores
Carnivores
Algae
Bass
Larva
Sunfish
Tadpole

Divisions according to climate were first suggested by the Greek philosopher Aristotle, and his ideas were still in use until about 100 years ago. Aristotle posited a number of climatic zones—called torrid, temperate and frigid—defined by latitude. But with time it became increasingly apparent that the complex distribution of atmospheric pressure, winds, rainfall and temperature could not be related to such a simple frame. Nineteenth-century scientists divided the world into 35 climatic provinces. Then in 1900 the German meteorologist Wladimir Köppen produced a more sophisticated climatic classification based on temperature and moisture conditions related to the needs of plants. At about the same time other scientists studied the distribution of vegetation types throughout the world. These studies together provided the basis for much of the later work on climatic regions.

An important step forward was made in 1904 by the British geographer A. J. Herbertson. He argued that subdivision of physical environments should take into account the distribution of the various phenomena as they related to each other. He conceived the idea of *natural regions*, each with "a certain unity of configuration (relief), climate and vegetation." His final classification contained four groups or regions: Polar Types, Cool Temperate Types, Warm Temperate Types and Tropical Hot Lands. Herbertson's scheme, controversial at first, was later much used for teaching geography.

Ecology

Meanwhile the study of environmental problems had been advanced by the idea of *ecology*, the relationship of living things between each other and their surroundings. The term was first used in 1868 by Ernst Haeckel, the German biologist, but it was not until the end of the nineteenth century that scientists really began to study life forms in relation to their habitat. In addition to the central ideas of interdependence between the members of plant and animal communities and between the community and the physical environment, there now came the suggestion that communities develop in a sequence that leads to a "climax"—a final step of equilibrium or balance. Their climax stage depends on conditions of climate or soil.

Later the British botanist A. G. Tansley, a leading exponent of ecological thinking, introduced the term *ecosystem* to describe a group of living organisms and its effective environment. Tansley's definition of 1935 referred to the whole system, including "not only the organism complex, but also the whole complex of physical factors forming what we call the environment of the biome." The idea became very influential and has been used in the social sciences as well as in the natural ones. But it is difficult to apply in practice, partly because of the highly complex and often diverse interactions that take place in different parts of the ecosystem.

Ecologists have developed special methods and have given particular attention to the ways in which energy is transferred within the system. The term *biome* refers to the whole complex of organisms, both animals and plants, that live together naturally as a society. By *environment* is meant all the external conditions that affect the life and development of an organism.

Biomes

The biomes shown on the map are broadly drawn generalizations. They should be regarded as idealized regions, within which many local variations may exist—for example, of climate or soil conditions. On a larger scale such features as mountain ranges may cause variations at a regional level. Scientists have tried to work out "hierarchies" that include many levels or orders of scale leading to the major climatic-vegetation realms or biomes. These realms give a broad picture that is useful at the world level of scale, and which forms a starting point for further analysis. Any map of the biomes has to have lines to indicate the boundaries of each region, but these too are generalizations. Although climate and vegetation do sometimes change abruptly from place to place, more often there are transitional zones, and the boundaries on the maps give the broad locations of these.

Herbertson's concept of natural regions attempted also to take account of the influence of man as an important factor in the environment. But he was not totally successful in including man in his analysis, no doubt because of the complexity of the problems involved and because of the immense influence that man has had upon the natural vegetation of the world. The cutting of forests, the drainage and reclamation of land, the introduction, use and spread of cultivated plants, the domestication of animals, the development of sophisticated systems of agriculture and many other actions all create, over large areas of the biomes, landscapes that are more man-made than natural.

Resource systems

An idea that clarifies the study of the interrelations of societies and environments, and the ways in which these change with the passage of time, is that of the *resource system*. This is a model of a population of human beings and their social and economic characteristics, including their technical skills and resources, together with those aspects of the natural environment that affect them and which they influence. The model includes the sequences by which natural materials are obtained, transformed and used. It tries to show how societies are organized according to their natural resources, the effects of that use, and the ways in which natural conditions limit or expand the life and work of the society. But it is easier to apply such a model to societies that have direct relations with natural conditions, through farming, fishing or forestry, than to great urban–industrial complexes.

The sections that follow present a picture of the diversity of habitats from ice caps to equatorial forests, the principal ways man has modified the environment and the problems of maintaining healthy resource systems.

Climate and Weather

The pattern of world climates depends largely on great circulations of air in the atmosphere. These movements of air are driven by energy from the Sun, and they transfer surplus heat from the tropics to the polar regions. Over a long period of time – such as months, seasons or years – they create the climate. Over a short period – day by day, or week by week – they form the weather. Together, climate and weather are among the most significant natural components of the world's diverse environments.

The world's tropical zones receive more heat from the Sun than they re-emit into space, and so their land and sea surfaces become warm. The polar regions, on the other hand, emit more radiation than they receive, and so they become cold. Warm air is less dense than cold air, and this means that atmospheric pressure becomes low at the Equator and high at the poles. As a result, a circulation of air—both vertical and horizontal—is set up. But because of the Earth's rotation and the distribution of land and sea there is not a simple air circulation pattern in each hemisphere; winds are deflected to the right in the northern hemisphere and to the left in the southern hemisphere, a phenomenon known as the Coriolis effect.

A climatic patchwork

When warm air rises it expands and cools and the water vapor it is carrying condenses to form clouds. For this reason heavy, showery rain is frequent in the belt of rising air near the Equator. In the subtropical zones (where the air is sinking), clouds evaporate and the weather is fine. Air moves out of the subtropical high-pressure belts in the lower atmosphere. Some of it flows towards the poles and meets colder air, flowing out of the polar high-pressure region, in a narrow zone called the polar front. This convergence of air is concentrated around low-pressure systems known as depressions.

The pattern of climates does not remain constant throughout the year because of seasonal changes in the amount of radiation from the Sun—the "fuel" of the atmospheric engine. In June, when the northern hemisphere is tilted towards the Sun, the radiation is at a maximum at latitude 23°N and all the climatic belts shift northwards. In December it is summer in the southern hemisphere and all the belts move southwards.

Climate is also affected by the distribution of land and sea across the globe. The temperature of the land changes more quickly than that of

TYPES OF WEATHER

There is a constant flow of air between the world's polar and tropical regions, and this has a prime effect on the weather in other regions. In the high and middle latitudes cold and warm fronts succeed each other, and along coasts sea fogs often form. In temperate and tropical regions thunderstorms are frequent, and the tropics are characterized by the turbulent storms known as hurricanes in the Caribbean area and typhoons in the Pacific.

POLAR WEATHER

Weather in high latitudes is marked by consistently low temperatures—on the ice caps temperatures are nearly always below freezing. At the poles the sun never rises for six months of the year and for the remaining six months it never sets. Even in summer it stays low on the horizon and its rays are so slanted that they bring very little warmth. On the tundra the temperature rises above freezing for a few months in summer, but severe frosts are likely to occur at any time. As well as being bitterly cold, polar weather is predominantly dry. The lower the temperature the less moisture the air can contain. Clouds, when they form, are high, thin sheets of cirrostratus. Composed of ice crystals, they often produce a halo effect around the sun. Snow, when it falls, is usually dry and powdery.

DEPRESSIONS

Low-pressure weather systems, or depressions, form when polar and subtropical air masses converge. Cloud and rain usually occur at the boundary, or front, of the different air masses. Seen in cross section, a fully developed depression shows both warm (A) and cold (B) fronts. As the wave of warm air rises over the cold, its moisture condenses into the "layered" clouds that usually precede a warm front. Behind the warm front, cold air forces under the warm air, producing the wedge-shaped cold front.

FOG

Fogs form as a result of the condensation of water vapor in the air; they may occur when warm, moist air is cooled by its passage over a cold surface. Off the coast of California, for example, air near the surface of the sea is cooled by the cold California current and sea fog is frequent. The air at higher levels is still warm and acts like a lid over the fog, and mountains prevent the fog from dispersing in an easterly direction. Fumes and smoke are trapped by this temperature inversion, creating the notorious Los Angeles smog.

THUNDERSTORMS

These develop when air is unstable to a great height. Particularly violent storms occur when cold, dry air masses meet warm, moist air, causing the latter to rise rapidly. As the warm air surges upwards it cools and its moisture condenses into cumulonimbus, or thunder, clouds. Flat cloud tops mark the level where stable air occurs again. Quickly moving raindrops and hail in the clouds become electrically charged and cause lightning, and the explosion of heated air along the path of the flash creates the sound wave that is heard as thunder.

HURRICANES

These are tropical storms on a vast scale that build up over warm oceans. Their core is an area of low pressure around which large quantities of warm, moist air are carried to the high atmosphere at great speed. The Earth's rotation is responsible for the huge swirling movement: in the northern hemisphere the movement is anticlockwise, in the southern hemisphere it is clockwise. Towering bands of clouds produce torrential rain. The central region, or "eye," of a hurricane, however, has light winds, clear skies and no rainfall.

THE WORLD'S CLIMATIC REGIONS

Climate is the characteristic weather of a region over a long period of time. It is often described in terms of average monthly and yearly temperatures and rainfall. These in turn depend largely on latitude, which determines whether a region is basically hot or cold and whether it has pronounced seasonal changes. Climate is also influenced by prevailing winds, by ocean currents and by geographical features such as the distribution of land and water. Highland climates are influenced by altitude and are always cooler than those of nearby lowland regions. Tropical climates are always warm. Near the Equator rain falls for most of the year, but towards the subtropics the wet and dry seasons are more marked. Temperate climates reflect the conflict between warm and cold air masses. They range from the Mediterranean type with hot, dry summers and mild, moist winters to the cooler, wetter climates of higher latitudes. The subarctic is mainly cold and humid; polar climates are always cold and mainly dry.

Types of Climate

- Polar
- Subarctic
- Cool temperate
- Warm temperate
- Dry
- Tropical
- Highland

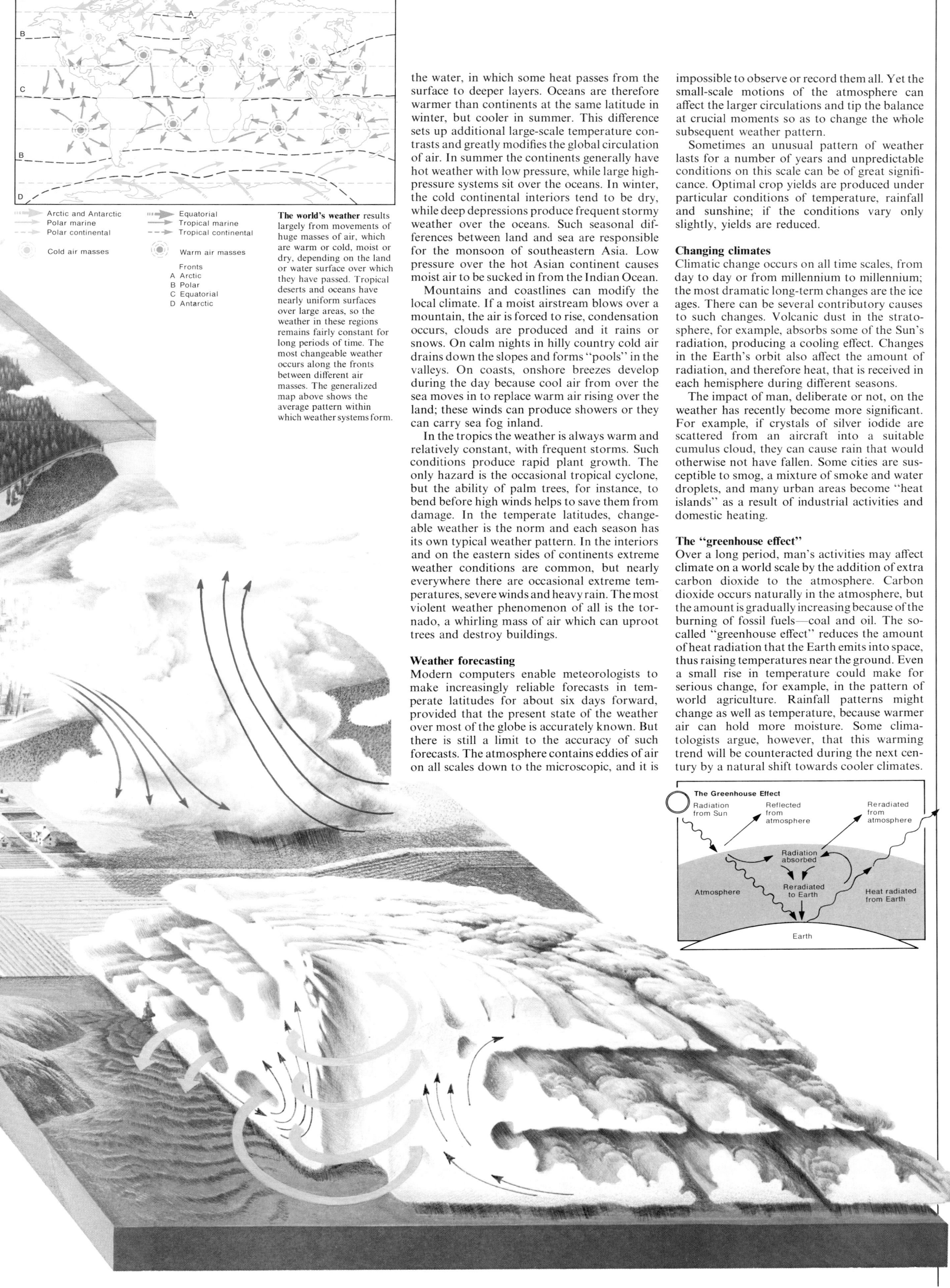

Arctic and Antarctic
Polar marine
Polar continental

Cold air masses

Equatorial
Tropical marine
Tropical continental

Warm air masses

Fronts
A Arctic
B Polar
C Equatorial
D Antarctic

The world's weather results largely from movements of huge masses of air, which are warm or cold, moist or dry, depending on the land or water surface over which they have passed. Tropical deserts and oceans have nearly uniform surfaces over large areas, so the weather in these regions remains fairly constant for long periods of time. The most changeable weather occurs along the fronts between different air masses. The generalized map above shows the average pattern within which weather systems form.

the water, in which some heat passes from the surface to deeper layers. Oceans are therefore warmer than continents at the same latitude in winter, but cooler in summer. This difference sets up additional large-scale temperature contrasts and greatly modifies the global circulation of air. In summer the continents generally have hot weather with low pressure, while large high-pressure systems sit over the oceans. In winter, the cold continental interiors tend to be dry, while deep depressions produce frequent stormy weather over the oceans. Such seasonal differences between land and sea are responsible for the monsoon of southeastern Asia. Low pressure over the hot Asian continent causes moist air to be sucked in from the Indian Ocean.

Mountains and coastlines can modify the local climate. If a moist airstream blows over a mountain, the air is forced to rise, condensation occurs, clouds are produced and it rains or snows. On calm nights in hilly country cold air drains down the slopes and forms "pools" in the valleys. On coasts, onshore breezes develop during the day because cool air from over the sea moves in to replace warm air rising over the land; these winds can produce showers or they can carry sea fog inland.

In the tropics the weather is always warm and relatively constant, with frequent storms. Such conditions produce rapid plant growth. The only hazard is the occasional tropical cyclone, but the ability of palm trees, for instance, to bend before high winds helps to save them from damage. In the temperate latitudes, changeable weather is the norm and each season has its own typical weather pattern. In the interiors and on the eastern sides of continents extreme weather conditions are common, but nearly everywhere there are occasional extreme temperatures, severe winds and heavy rain. The most violent weather phenomenon of all is the tornado, a whirling mass of air which can uproot trees and destroy buildings.

Weather forecasting
Modern computers enable meteorologists to make increasingly reliable forecasts in temperate latitudes for about six days forward, provided that the present state of the weather over most of the globe is accurately known. But there is still a limit to the accuracy of such forecasts. The atmosphere contains eddies of air on all scales down to the microscopic, and it is

impossible to observe or record them all. Yet the small-scale motions of the atmosphere can affect the larger circulations and tip the balance at crucial moments so as to change the whole subsequent weather pattern.

Sometimes an unusual pattern of weather lasts for a number of years and unpredictable conditions on this scale can be of great significance. Optimal crop yields are produced under particular conditions of temperature, rainfall and sunshine; if the conditions vary only slightly, yields are reduced.

Changing climates
Climatic change occurs on all time scales, from day to day or from millennium to millennium; the most dramatic long-term changes are the ice ages. There can be several contributory causes to such changes. Volcanic dust in the stratosphere, for example, absorbs some of the Sun's radiation, producing a cooling effect. Changes in the Earth's orbit also affect the amount of radiation, and therefore heat, that is received in each hemisphere during different seasons.

The impact of man, deliberate or not, on the weather has recently become more significant. For example, if crystals of silver iodide are scattered from an aircraft into a suitable cumulus cloud, they can cause rain that would otherwise not have fallen. Some cities are susceptible to smog, a mixture of smoke and water droplets, and many urban areas become "heat islands" as a result of industrial activities and domestic heating.

The "greenhouse effect"
Over a long period, man's activities may affect climate on a world scale by the addition of extra carbon dioxide to the atmosphere. Carbon dioxide occurs naturally in the atmosphere, but the amount is gradually increasing because of the burning of fossil fuels—coal and oil. The so-called "greenhouse effect" reduces the amount of heat radiation that the Earth emits into space, thus raising temperatures near the ground. Even a small rise in temperature could make for serious change, for example, in the pattern of world agriculture. Rainfall patterns might change as well as temperature, because warmer air can hold more moisture. Some climatologists argue, however, that this warming trend will be counteracted during the next century by a natural shift towards cooler climates.

The Greenhouse Effect
Radiation from Sun
Reflected from atmosphere
Reradiated from atmosphere
Radiation absorbed
Atmosphere
Reradiated to Earth
Heat radiated from Earth
Earth

Resources and Energy

Resources, it has been said, comprise mankind's varying needs from generation to generation and are valued because of the uses societies can make of them. They represent human appraisals and are the products of man's ingenuity and experience. While natural resources remain vitally important in themselves, they must always be regarded as the rewards of human skill in locating, extracting and exploiting them. The development of resources depends on many factors, including the existence of a demand, adequate transport facilities, the availability of capital and the accessibility, quality and quantity of the resource itself.

The world's extraction of its resources highlights the inequality of their distribution. Each resource shown on the map is attributed to the three countries with the largest production percentages of that commodity. So, in 1976, the three leading bauxite producers were Australia (26.69%), Jamaica (14.19%) and Rep. of Guinea (13.9%). Usually, the larger and more wealthy a state the greater its monopoly of resources—although the tiny Pacific island of New Caledonia produces more than 14% of the world's nickel. China is reputed to mine 75% of the world's tungsten and to be increasing its oil supply rapidly. Energy consumption figures are for the year 1976, since when there have been some outstanding changes to patterns of availability, perhaps most noticeably in Britain's new-found oil and gas surplus. Bahrain and Tobago, too small to be shown on this map, also have surpluses of energy production.

A dictionary defines the term "resource" as "a means of aid or support," implying anything that lends support to life or activity. Man has always assessed nature with an eye to his own needs, and it is these varying needs that endow resources with their usefulness. Fossil fuels such as oil have lain long in the Earth, but it was not until about 1900 that the large-scale needs fostered by the rising demands of motor vehicles led to the development of new techniques for locating and extracting this raw material. Today oil has also become precious in the manufacture of a wide variety of industrial products, which themselves are resources that are much used by other industries.

The nature of resources
Resources can be most usefully classified in two groups: "renewable" and "nonrenewable." The latter is composed of materials found at or near the Earth's surface, which are sometimes known as "physical" resources. They include such essential minerals as uranium, iron, copper, nickel, bauxite, gold, silver, lead, mercury and tungsten. Oil, coal and natural gas are the principal nonrenewable fuel and energy resources, but after they have been used for producing heat or power their utility is lost and part of the geological capital of 325 million years of history is gone for ever. Some minerals such as iron and its product, steel, can be recycled and renewed, however. "Renewable" resources are basically biological, being the food and other vegetable matter which life needs to sustain human needs. Provided soil quality is maintained, their productivity may even be increased as better strains of plants and breeds of animals are developed.

Work has long been in progress to improve renewable resources, and has moved forward to manufacturing vegetable-flavored protein (VFP) from soybeans as a meat substitute and to viable experiments to extract protein from leaves. In Brazil, many cars have been converted to run successfully on alcohol extracted from sugar. One renewable resource—the tree—can be closely related to other resources: some conservationists are alarmed at the overuse of firewood as a source of fuel and energy in the semiarid areas of Africa. This may be an important factor in increasing the tendency for the deserts to spread in that continent, and in such a situation there is a new realization of the concept of closely managing resources such as soil, timber and fisheries. This is partly because we have a clearer understanding of the ecology of vegetation and the important interdependence of climate, soil, plants and animal life. Much, however, remains to be done.

The politics of nonrenewable resources
Today we are naturally troubled about the availability of natural resources. Oil is a prime cause for concern. Although many believe that production will grow until the mid-2020s and that new oil reserves will be discovered, oil's scarcity, based on a growing rate of demand and increasingly wasteful use, is now widely accepted. Because, like many resources, it is unevenly distributed, those countries with large and accessible supplies—such as the members of OPEC—have used their political power on a number of occasions to raise oil's price, with adverse effects on the economies of most importers. Ironically, these substantial price rises have had the effect of stimulating exploration and development in many new areas; there are already signs of increased production in China.

Other nonrenewable resources are also distributed unevenly, but have not been mined on any scale comparable with their availability; vast reserves of coal in the former Soviet Union and China have not been worked on any scale resembling their known extent.

New energy sources
As resources such as oil become less available and more expensive, the renewable resources of power such as water, wind, waves and solar energy, all of which are currently under study or development, will receive new injections of capital. Attention will also have to be paid to more widespread nuclear energy production. Energy has been called "the ultimate resource," and it is imperative that we make wise provisions for its future availability.

Future resources
It has been calculated that within four years of the launch of Sputnik I, more than 3,000 products resulting from space research were put into commercial production. These included new alloys, ceramics, plastics, fabrics and chemical compounds. Satellite developments have meant that land use can now be measured quickly and potential mineral sources closely identified. A satellite capable of converting solar power to electricity and contributing to the Earth's energy deficit has been widely discussed, while the Moon and planets have been mooted as future possible sources of minerals.

Conclusions
Resources are, in the main, the products of man's skill, ingenuity and expertise, and their widespread use, as in the case of timber and iron for shipbuilding, became apparent only as man's needs for them became clear. Our forebears were once concerned about the availability of flint, seaweed, charcoal and natural rubber; countries even went to war over supplies of spices. Today our requirements are slightly different—we no longer depend only on local sites for resources, and improved transport facilities and appropriate technologies have lowered the costs of obtaining materials for manufacture.

Nevertheless, the principles remain the same. A continual search for new resources capable of exploitation and wide application must be maintained, together with a close regard for the value of the renewable resources such as animal and vegetable products required to support man in his search for new resources. Perhaps the most vital consideration is the need for wise policies of conservation relating to the proven reserves of nonrenewable resources still in the ground, and the careful future use of such valuable deposits known or thought to exist.

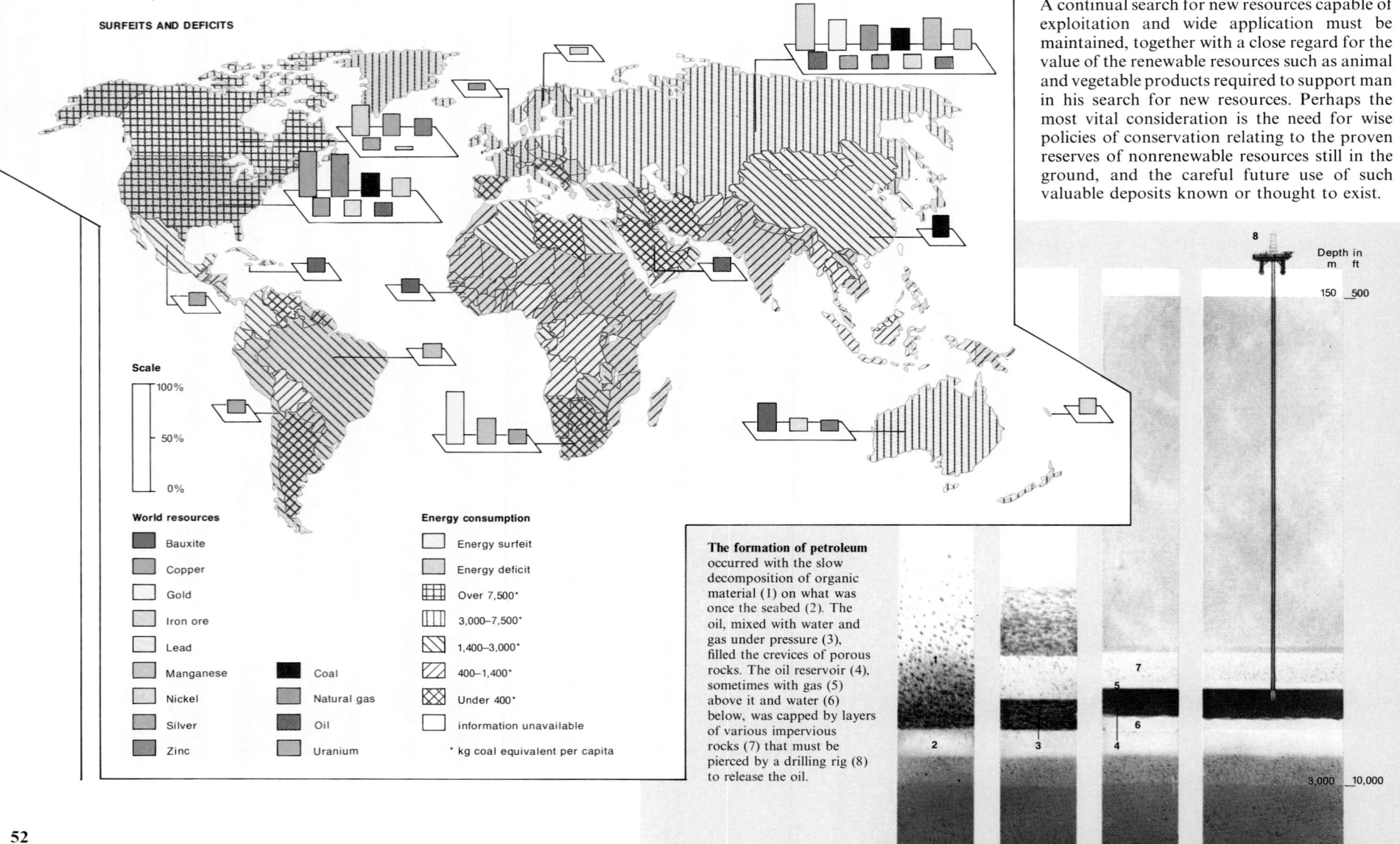

SURFEITS AND DEFICITS

Scale

100%

50%

0%

World resources
- Bauxite
- Copper
- Gold
- Iron ore
- Lead
- Manganese
- Nickel
- Silver
- Zinc
- Coal
- Natural gas
- Oil
- Uranium

Energy consumption
- Energy surfeit
- Energy deficit
- Over 7,500*
- 3,000–7,500*
- 1,400–3,000*
- 400–1,400*
- Under 400*
- information unavailable

* kg coal equivalent per capita

The formation of petroleum occurred with the slow decomposition of organic material (1) on what was once the seabed (2). The oil, mixed with water and gas under pressure (3), filled the crevices of porous rocks. The oil reservoir (4), sometimes with gas (5) above it and water (6) below, was capped by layers of various impervious rocks (7) that must be pierced by a drilling rig (8) to release the oil.

Depth in
m   ft

150   500

3,000   10,000

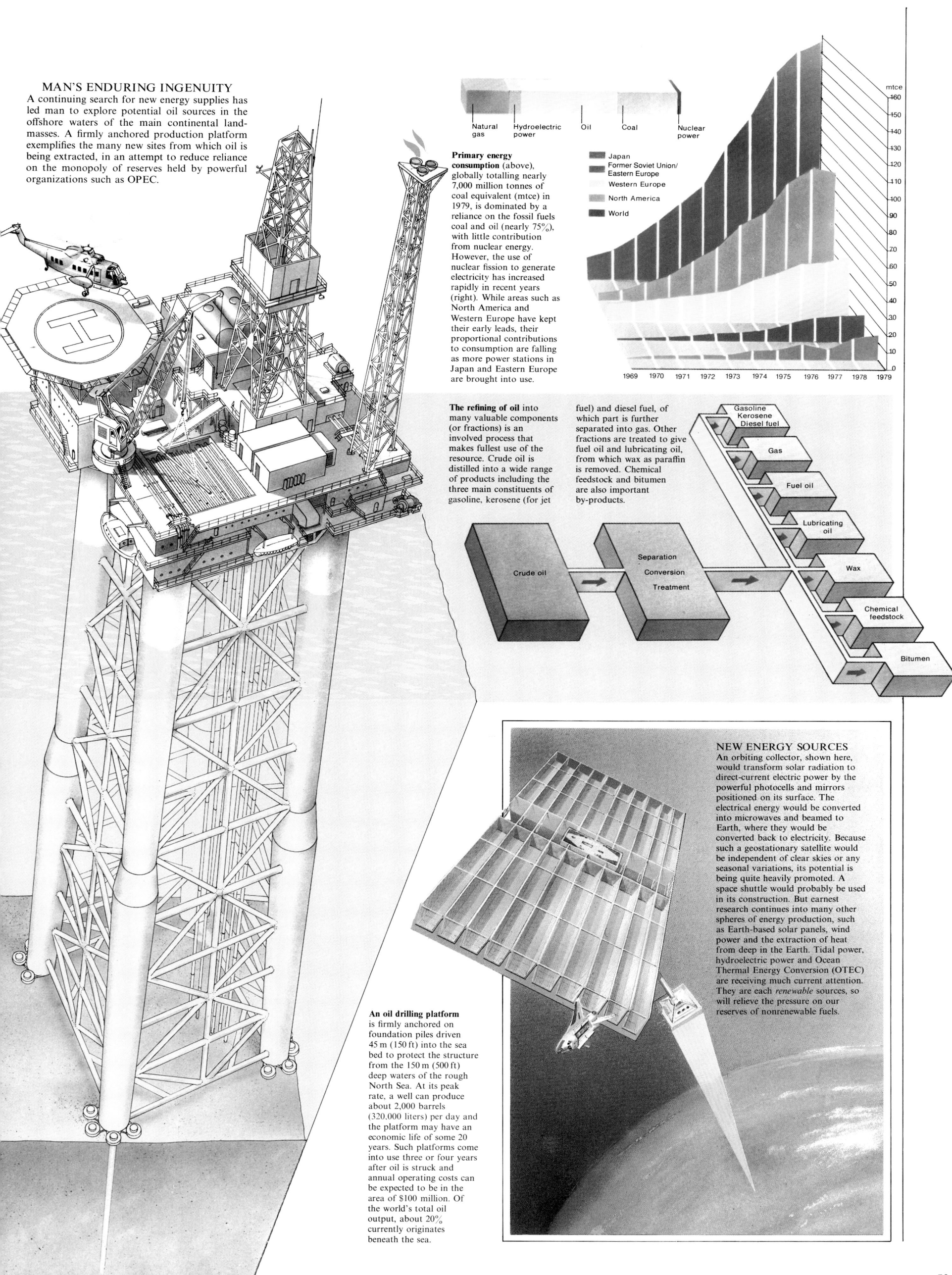

MAN'S ENDURING INGENUITY

A continuing search for new energy supplies has led man to explore potential oil sources in the offshore waters of the main continental landmasses. A firmly anchored production platform exemplifies the many new sites from which oil is being extracted, in an attempt to reduce reliance on the monopoly of reserves held by powerful organizations such as OPEC.

Natural gas   Hydroelectric power   Oil   Coal   Nuclear power

Japan
Former Soviet Union/ Eastern Europe
Western Europe
North America
World

mtce

Primary energy consumption (above), globally totalling nearly 7,000 million tonnes of coal equivalent (mtce) in 1979, is dominated by a reliance on the fossil fuels coal and oil (nearly 75%), with little contribution from nuclear energy. However, the use of nuclear fission to generate electricity has increased rapidly in recent years (right). While areas such as North America and Western Europe have kept their early leads, their proportional contributions to consumption are falling as more power stations in Japan and Eastern Europe are brought into use.

1969 1970 1971 1972 1973 1974 1975 1976 1977 1978 1979

The refining of oil into many valuable components (or fractions) is an involved process that makes fullest use of the resource. Crude oil is distilled into a wide range of products including the three main constituents of gasoline, kerosene (for jet fuel) and diesel fuel, of which part is further separated into gas. Other fractions are treated to give fuel oil and lubricating oil, from which wax as paraffin is removed. Chemical feedstock and bitumen are also important by-products.

Crude oil → Separation Conversion Treatment →

Gasoline Kerosene Diesel fuel
Gas
Fuel oil
Lubricating oil
Wax
Chemical feedstock
Bitumen

An oil drilling platform is firmly anchored on foundation piles driven 45 m (150 ft) into the sea bed to protect the structure from the 150 m (500 ft) deep waters of the rough North Sea. At its peak rate, a well can produce about 2,000 barrels (320,000 liters) per day and the platform may have an economic life of some 20 years. Such platforms come into use three or four years after oil is struck and annual operating costs can be expected to be in the area of $100 million. Of the world's total oil output, about 20% currently originates beneath the sea.

NEW ENERGY SOURCES

An orbiting collector, shown here, would transform solar radiation to direct-current electric power by the powerful photocells and mirrors positioned on its surface. The electrical energy would be converted into microwaves and beamed to Earth, where they would be converted back to electricity. Because such a geostationary satellite would be independent of clear skies or any seasonal variations, its potential is being quite heavily promoted. A space shuttle would probably be used in its construction. But earnest research continues into many other spheres of energy production, such as Earth-based solar panels, wind power and the extraction of heat from deep in the Earth. Tidal power, hydroelectric power and Ocean Thermal Energy Conversion (OTEC) are receiving much current attention. They are each *renewable* sources, so will relieve the pressure on our reserves of nonrenewable fuels.

Population Growth

Every minute of every day, more than 250 children are born into the world. The Earth's population now stands at about 4,300 million and is continuing to grow extremely rapidly. The problems associated with such growth are enormous – already, about two-thirds of the world's people are underfed, according to United Nations' recommended standards of nutrition. And an even greater number live in very poor housing conditions, have inadequate access to medical facilities, receive little or no education and, at present, have no hope of improving their lot. As yet, there are no simple or immediate solutions.

Average annual population growth rate 1970–1978

- 3% and over
- 2.5% to less than 3%
- 2% to less than 2.5%
- 1.0% to less than 2%
- Less than 1%
- Information unavailable

World population (millions)

World population
Projected world population

If the world's population continues to grow at its present rate, by the year 2000 there could be more than 6,400 million people on Earth (above). Such growth rates are only a recent phenomenon—for most of mankind's existence on Earth the numbers grew slowly (right). Then in the late 18th century, scientific and industrial developments and the discovery of new food sources (the prairies of the New World) raised living standards. Death rates declined and populations grew rapidly.

THE MULTIPLYING PROBLEMS

Populations are increasing most rapidly in the world's poorer nations. Poverty, in fact, seems to be at the heart of many of the complex interrelated problems created by rapid population growth. Poor countries, for example, are the least able to feed increasing numbers of people, while at the same time their lack of educational and medical facilities means that family planning is often inadequate and birth rates remain relatively high.

In 1830, there were only about 1,000 million people on Earth. By 1930, this figure had doubled. And by 1975, it had doubled again. If the present rate of increase continues, it will have doubled again by the year 2020.

This may not happen—it is extremely difficult to predict how world population will behave. What is certain is that it will continue to increase and, moreover, that this increase will not be evenly distributed. Since more than 50 percent of the human race lives in Asia, it is inevitable that the largest population increases will take place there. In fact, by the year 2000, the population of Asia may well have grown from about 2,000 million to more than 3,600 million. Substantial increases, of 400 million or more, will probably also occur in Africa, and Latin America is growing equally quickly.

In more prosperous North America and Europe, however, population growth seems to be stabilizing as women have fewer children and families become smaller—several countries, such as West Germany, now record a zero population growth rate. The poorer countries, the so-called Third World, are therefore gaining, and will probably continue to gain, an increasing share of the world's people. In 1930, about 64 percent of the human race lived in the poor countries of Asia, Africa and Latin America. By 1980, this proportion had increased to more than 75 percent. Population growth in these regions is creating enormous problems. It is estimated that there are now

more than 800 million people living in absolute poverty in the developing world, and these numbers can but increase as populations swell.

An obvious solution is to reduce birth rates, but this cannot be achieved quickly. In much of Africa and Asia, a very high proportion of the population is made up of young people who are, or soon will be, of childbearing age. Population increases are therefore inevitable. This will probably change as family planning becomes more widespread and women have fewer children, but such relief lies in the future and is likely to affect the poorest countries last. The most pressing problem for the growing numbers of impoverished people today is that of hunger.

Food – the fundamental problem

In theory, no food supply problem should exist—already enough food is produced in the world to feed a population of 5,500 million people. In fact, however, two-thirds of this food is consumed by the rich industrialized nations, and supplies are not reaching many of those in need. The developed nations dominate world food markets because developing nations, and people within those nations, are too poor to buy food, and are themselves unable to produce sufficient quantities to feed their growing populations. The answer to undernutrition and malnutrition lies largely in raising the incomes of poor peoples and improving distribution of supplies of food.

At a local level, food produced or imported

by developing countries must reach those in need at a price they can afford. One way of doing this is to encourage the rural poor to produce their own food. Small-scale, intensively farmed plots often prove to be the most efficient form of agriculture in areas where labor is plentiful. At present, many of the rural poor are either without land, or hold plots on extremely unfavorable terms of tenancy. By providing land, appropriate technology (small-scale, inexpensive farming equipment such as windpumps to draw water for irrigation), financial aid and information and education, small farmers could be helped to farm their land as effectively and efficiently as possible.

At a national level, too, developing countries must become more self-sufficient in food. This has already been achieved in some countries. India, although at one time heavily dependent upon imports of one of its staple foodstuffs—rice—has now increased production on such a scale that imports are no longer necessary. Unfortunately, for many developing countries this is not the case. Zaire, for example, was once an exporter of food. Today the country can no longer produce enough to keep pace with the demands of its own expanding population. At a world level, food production must be maintained as well, for unless production is kept high, prices are unstable and at times of bad harvests the poorer nations cannot afford to import essential supplies.

Food alone, however, is not enough to solve

FEEDING THE WORLD

How are the growing numbers of people on Earth to be fed when millions are already undernourished? In the short term, the food problem could be solved by improving distribution of supplies that are already available. But the world can also be made to produce more food. Fertilizers and pest control can make land more productive and genetic engineering could produce higher-yielding and more nutritious crops.

The world will have to produce more food than it does today (below) if future populations are to be fed. At present, large areas of the Earth's land surface cannot be farmed—they are either too cold, dry, marshy, mountainous or forested. Cultivatable areas could be extended, given the necessary investment.

THE HEALTH OF NATIONS

Many developing nations are severely short of medical and welfare facilities for their growing populations. Yet these are the very countries with high incidences of disease—mainly because of malnutrition, lack of clean water supplies, and inadequate and overcrowded housing. Furthermore, without health services family planning facilities are not widely available, and expanding populations continue to strain existing resources.

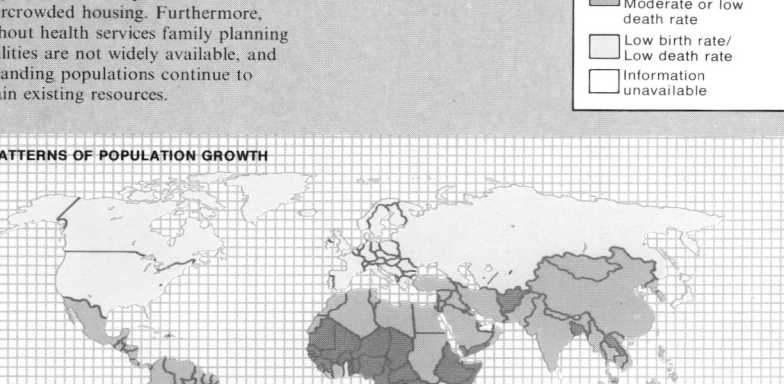

Birth and Death Rates
- High birth rate/ High death rate
- High birth rate/ Moderate or low death rate
- Low birth rate/ Low death rate
- Information unavailable

THE NONPRODUCTIVE LANDS

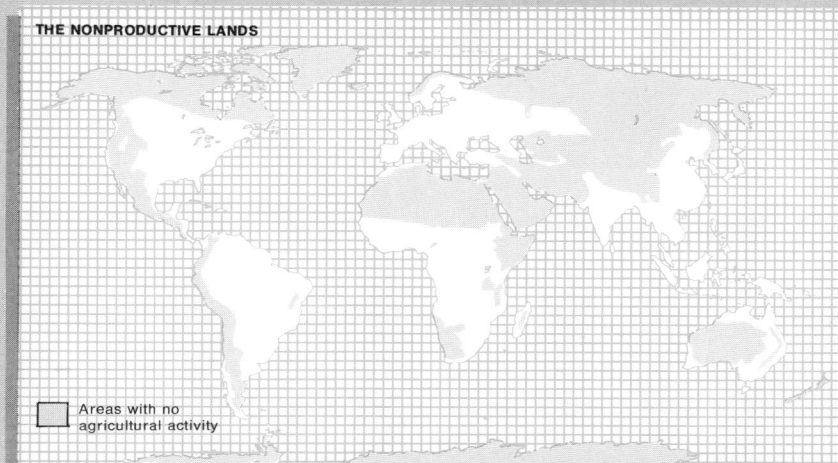

Areas with no agricultural activity

FOOD CONSUMPTION

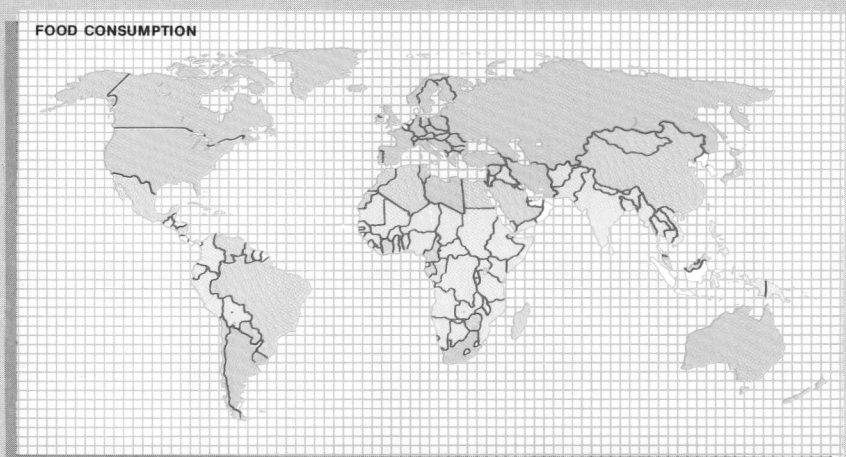

Calories per capita
- Less than 95% of needs
- 95% to 115% of needs
- More than 115% of needs
- Information unavailable

Malnutrition is widespread throughout the developing nations of Africa, Asia and South America. The problem is made worse by the fact that populations in these countries are growing more rapidly than anywhere else in the world.

PATTERNS OF POPULATION GROWTH

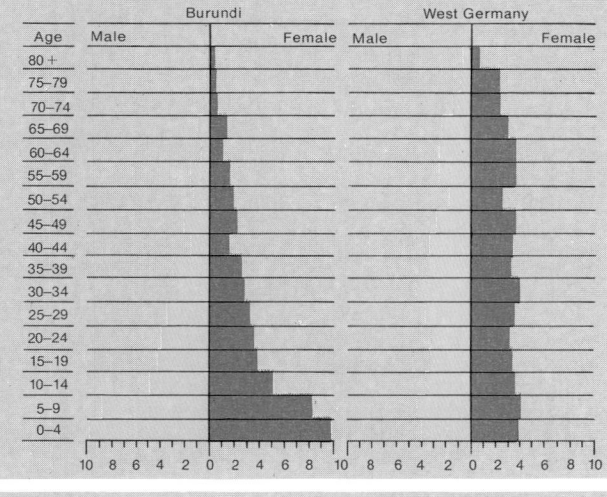

As a country's health facilities improve, its mortality rates decline. Birth rates, however, do not immediately fall (above). Thus, ironically, an improvement in facilities at first exacerbates the problem of rapid growth in population. A country with a declining death rate and a high birth rate gains an increasing percentage of young people who are, or will be, of child-bearing age. Population pyramids (right) plot the percentage balance between age and youth in a nation.

the problems created by population growth. Broadly based economic development, such as in manufacturing and industry, is essential if developing countries are to have the income and other resources to enable them to cope with their evergrowing numbers of people.

Economic growth

To achieve economic development, certain obstacles must be overcome. First, the Third World needs energy supplies at a price it can afford, for, with the exception of Nigeria and the now-rich Middle East, most developing regions are woefully short of the energy resources needed to fuel growth. Second, for sustained economic development a skilled labor force is required, as are educational facilities to provide the necessary skills from within the nations themselves. Third, investment is required to enable developing nations to exploit the resources they do have—minerals, for example. And this investment must be on terms that are as beneficial to the developing nations as they are to powerful multinational organizations that frequently fund such projects. Finally, and most important, more enlightened social and political outlooks are needed within many countries if their growing populations of impoverished people are to benefit from any economic development and consequent increase in national wealth.

It has been said that wealth is the best method of contraception and, judging by the history of population growth in the rich industrialized nations, this seems to be the case. If it is, economic development of the Third World may well alleviate many of the problems created by population growth.

INCOME

When the income level of a population is raised sufficiently, it seems that birth rates ultimately decline. This has been the pattern that has emerged in the Western world. If this is the case, then economic development of the Third World countries could eventually help to stabilize world population growth, as well as provide nations with the means to cope. It could also help provide for their growing numbers.

Gross National Product per capita 1978 ($US)
- Less than $300
- $300 to $699
- $700 to $2,999
- $3,000 to $6,999
- $7,000 and over
- Information unavailable

POVERTY AND WEALTH

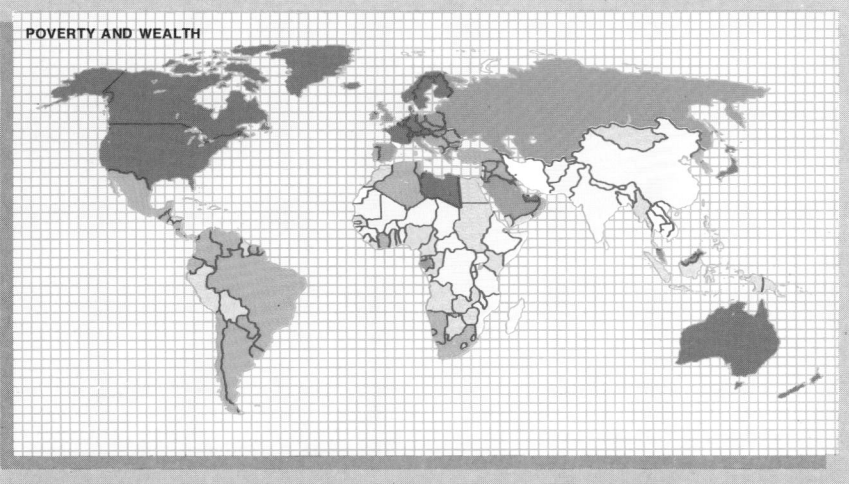

A nation's Gross National Product (GNP), when divided by the number of its population, gives some indication of the relative wealth (or poverty) of its people. But because national wealth is not evenly distributed in many countries (particularly in South America), this figure can conceal the extreme poverty of very large numbers of a nation's people.

EDUCATIONAL RESOURCES

Education is essential if the people of the developing world are to be equipped to improve their lot. Basic education on health and hygiene could dramatically reduce the incidence of disease; education about birth control would help lower birth rates; agricultural advice could help the rural poor to produce more food. Finally, general schooling is required to provide skilled labor.

ILLITERACY

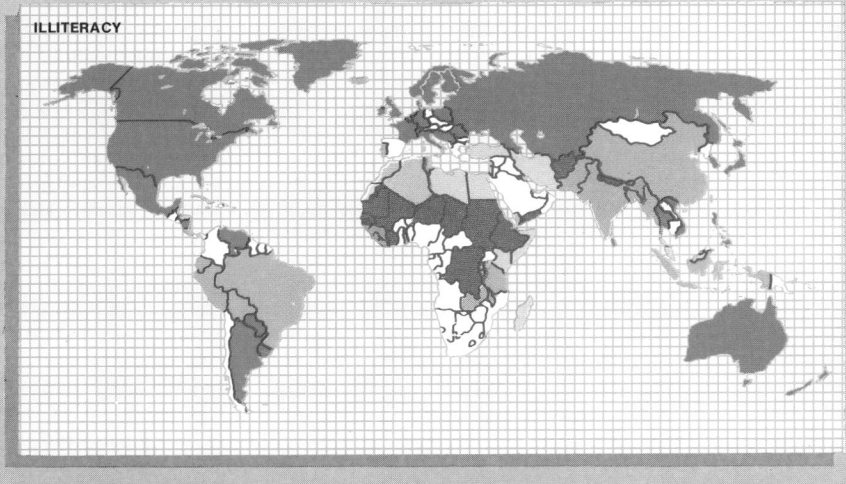

Illiteracy rate
- 80% and over
- 60% to less than 80%
- 40% to less than 60%
- 20% to less than 40%
- Less than 20%
- Information unavailable

Literacy rates are in fact improving in developing countries and national expenditure on schools is growing more quickly than is population. Two major problems are, first, the social traditions that severely restrict the number of girls attending school and, second, the reluctance of many rural poor to send to school children who provide valuable manual labor on the land.

Human Settlement

Man is naturally a gregarious animal. As an agriculturist he first settled in small communities, but it was not long before the emergence of towns and cities. Now nearly half the world's people live in these larger settlements, and by the year 2000, for the first time in history, more people will live in cities than in the countryside. Cities have grown up for various reasons, and are unevenly distributed across the world; but it is in the developing countries that the most rapid rates of urban growth are today taking place.

THE DISTRIBUTION OF POPULATION

Human settlement is highly uneven because it is related to many social and topographical factors. At first, man was tied to the sites of his crops and the grazing land of his cattle; life in nonrural centers only became a typical feature of population development as specialized services came into demand and towns and cities arose to support these needs. But during the 20th century there has been a vast increase in urban populations, particularly in Third World countries.

City life has a long and varied history going back to the early population centers of the Tigris–Euphrates, Indus and Nile valleys. Administrative and political needs led to the development of capital cities. Some, like London and Paris, evolved on conveniently located river crossings; others, such as Canberra, Islamabad and Brasilia, have locations that were deliberately planned.

Types of towns and cities
Market towns were established to exchange produce and, as trade expanded, hierarchies of service centers became established. These ranged from small "central places" that supplied rural areas with simple goods and services from elsewhere, to large cities that provided highly specialized services. Through such centrally placed systems, rural areas became connected with major industrialized areas. Mining towns such as Johannesburg, South Africa, and Broken Hill, Australia, sprang up as man began to exploit the Earth's mineral resources, their locations determined by the presence of rich ore deposits. Fishing ports and settlements dependent on forestry fall into the same group.

Increasing specialization, exemplified by the Black Country, England, and the Ruhr, West Germany, was a feature of European industrial development in the eighteenth and nineteenth centuries, and was based on the availability of capital investment and the presence of sources of fuel and power, especially water and steam power. Such industrialized cities relied on newly developed forms of transport to bring in new materials and to carry away manufactured products. Chicago is a good example of the relationship between the development of rail and water routes and the growth of a city as a market, agricultural processing and manufacturing center. As transport developed, further specialized centers concentrated on locomotive, ship or aircraft construction.

Uneven settlement patterns
Across the world, density and distribution of population are uneven. The land surface of the Earth as a whole has a density of 28 people per sq km (73 per sq mile) although Manhattan, for example, has 26,000 per sq km (63,340 per sq mile) and Australia has only 1.5 per sq km (4 per sq mile). In Brazil, towns and cities are mostly sited in the rich southeast, in contrast to a sparseness of settlement in its interior. Contrasts also occur between Mediterranean North Africa and the deserted Sahara to the south; or Canada of the St. Lawrence and the Canadian Shield to the north. Here the causes are not hard to find: extremes of climate, terrain and vegetation form effective barriers to settlement. Geographers estimate that two-thirds of the world's population lives within 500 km (310 miles) of the sea.

Any true consideration of human settlements must, however, be placed within the context of the economic, political and social systems in which they have evolved. Physical considerations alone cannot fully explain the urban concentrations of Western Europe, Japan or the northeastern USA, or the comparative absence of cities elsewhere. Only 5 percent of Malawi's and 4.7 percent of New Guinea's populations live in towns, while the percentage is 87, in Belgium the percentage is 87, in Australia 86, in the UK 78 and in the USA 73.5. The figure for Norway is only 42 percent. Urbanization is a varied phenomenon and cities grow for many reasons.

The attractions of the city
Cities have always acted as magnets to poor or unemployed rural populations, and migrations from the countryside have assisted high rates of

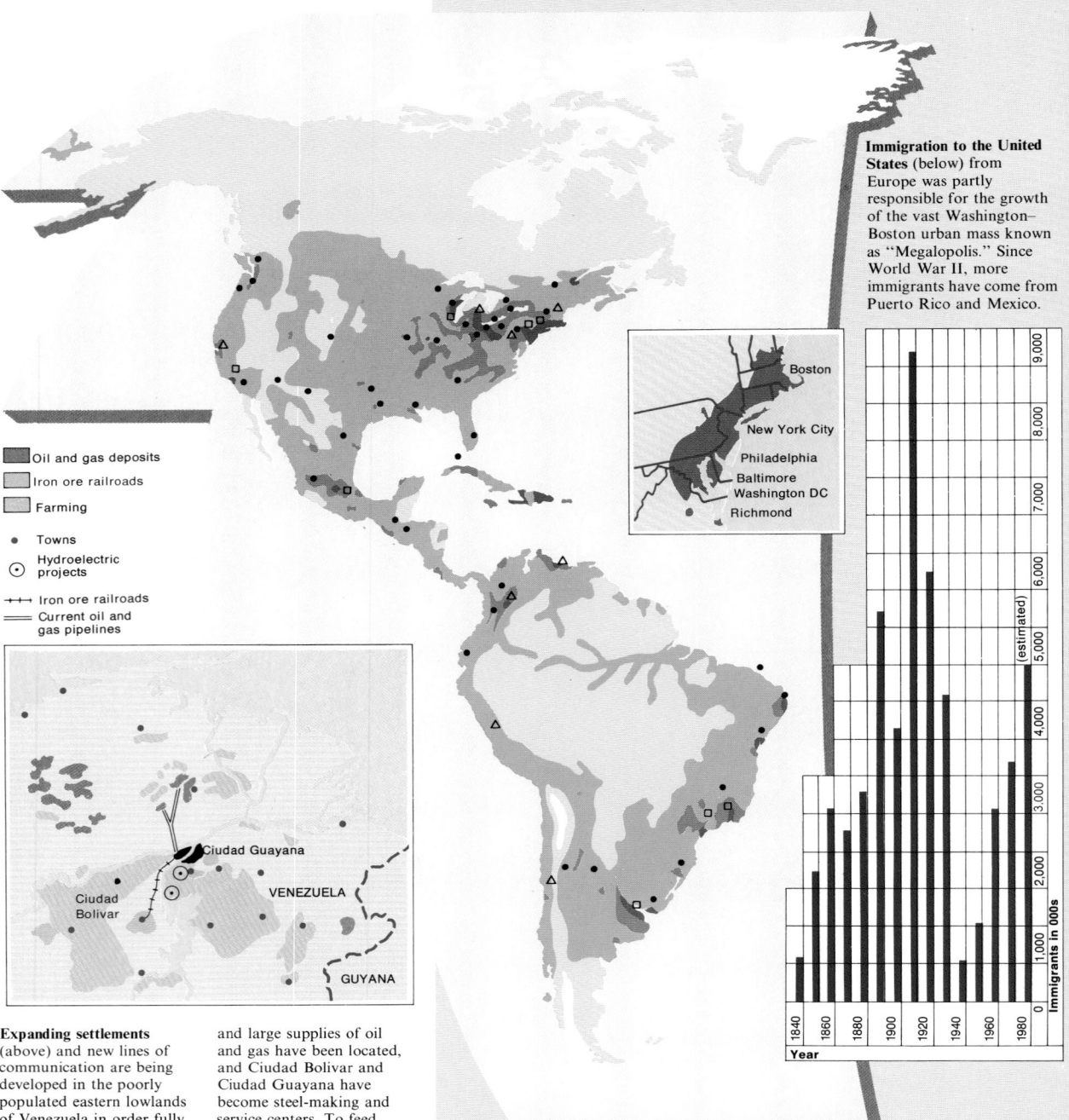

Oil and gas deposits
Iron ore railroads
Farming
• Towns
⊙ Hydroelectric projects
＋＋＋ Iron ore railroads
＝＝ Current oil and gas pipelines

Ciudad Guayana
Ciudad Bolivar
VENEZUELA
GUYANA

Expanding settlements (above) and new lines of communication are being developed in the poorly populated eastern lowlands of Venezuela in order fully to exploit the resources being discovered there. Huge deposits of iron ore and large supplies of oil and gas have been located, and Ciudad Bolivar and Ciudad Guayana have become steel-making and service centers. To feed the people of these new settlements, agriculture has been greatly expanded.

Boston
New York City
Philadelphia
Baltimore
Washington DC
Richmond

Immigration to the United States (below) from Europe was partly responsible for the growth of the vast Washington–Boston urban mass known as "Megalopolis." Since World War II, more immigrants have come from Puerto Rico and Mexico.

city growth. Very large cities—Tokyo, New York and Los Angeles—are still found in the northern world, but many cities with far faster growth rates are sited in the Third World, especially in Asia. There the total number of inhabitants living in towns and cities is still much lower than in Europe, but centers such as Shanghai, Karachi, Bandung, New Delhi, Seoul, Jakarta and Manila are among the world's most rapidly expanding urban centers. Perhaps as many as a third of these city dwellers in Asia, Africa and Latin America put up with makeshift housing in shanty towns that present enormous problems of health, sanitation, education and unemployment: city growth in the developing world is a daunting prospect.

People on the move
In the past, one solution to population pressure on the land could be found in the migrations which occurred on a large scale from Asia into Europe, from Europe to the Americas and Australasia, and from China into southeastern Asia. But as claims are being made on almost every habitable area of the Earth, mass migrations have largely declined in importance. Many nations restrict movement to or from

their countries. Australia has strict immigration quotas; Vietnam restricts emigration for largely ideological reasons. Large movements of labor still take place, however, from the poorer regions of the Mediterranean to the industrial cities of France and Germany. Migrant workers from neighboring countries in Africa also play an essential part in the mining economy of South Africa.

New trends in urbanization
In many industrialized countries, a strong process of decentralization is leading to reductions in the populations of cities and corresponding increases in those of the suburbs and beyond. In 1951 the geographer Jean Gottman showed how groups of city regions tend to form chains of functionally linked cities, to which he gave the term "megalopolis." His prime example was Megalopolis, USA, stretching from north of Boston to south of Washington DC. Similar settlements occur in the Tokyo–Yokohama–Osaka area of Japan and the Ruhr megalopolis of northwestern Europe. Ultimately, equally drastic and large-scale patterns are likely to emerge in the already overcrowded human settlements of the Third World.

Migrating refugees, the world total of which increases on average by 2,000–3,000 every day, can affect settlement patterns. The Ugandan children (below) fled to the northern province of Karamoja in the wake of the 1979 war with Tanzania and the resultant famine that occurred in much of Uganda.

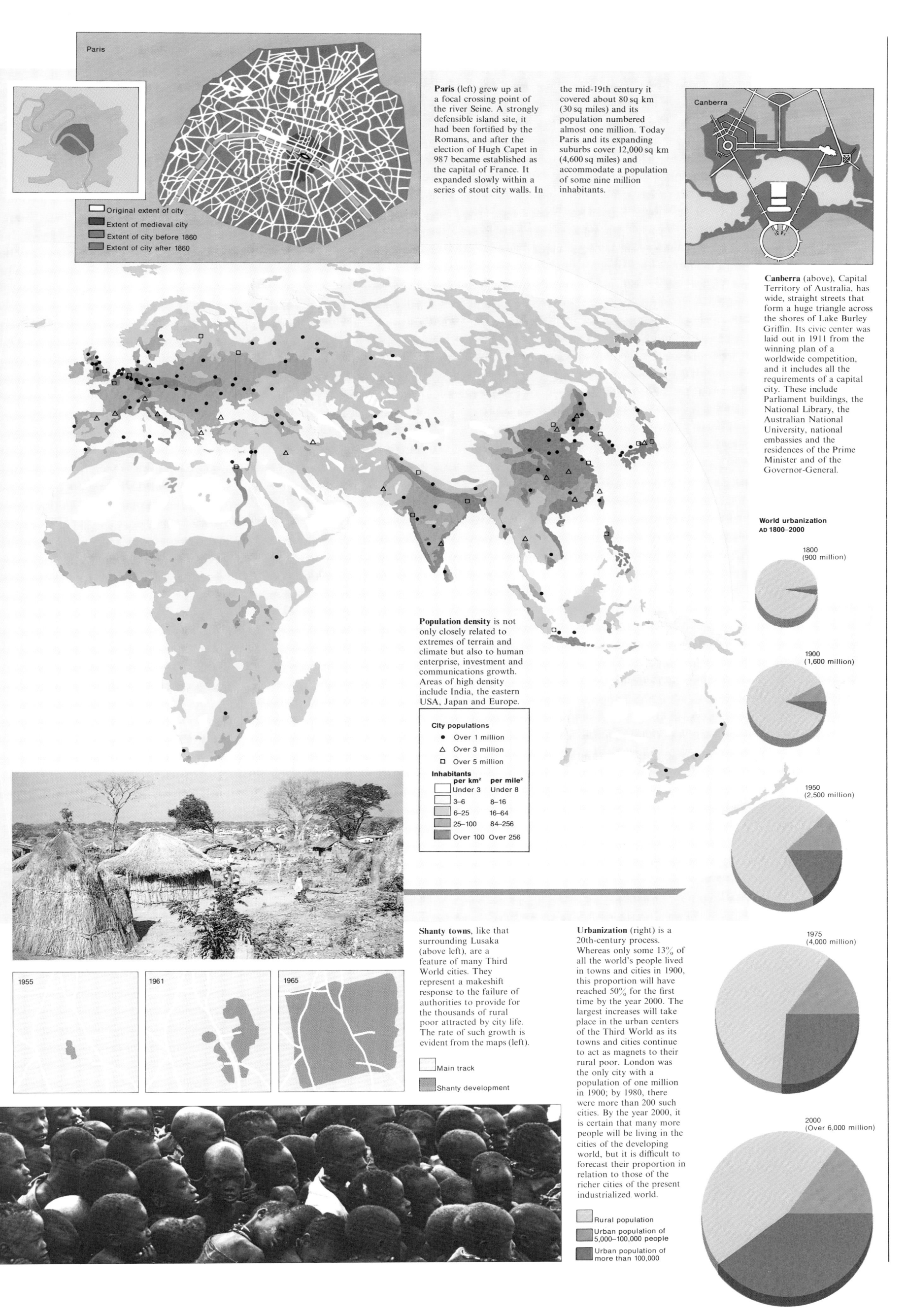

Paris

Original extent of city
Extent of medieval city
Extent of city before 1860
Extent of city after 1860

Paris (left) grew up at a focal crossing point of the river Seine. A strongly defensible island site, it had been fortified by the Romans, and after the election of Hugh Capet in 987 became established as the capital of France. It expanded slowly within a series of stout city walls. In the mid-19th century it covered about 80 sq km (30 sq miles) and its population numbered almost one million. Today Paris and its expanding suburbs cover 12,000 sq km (4,600 sq miles) and accommodate a population of some nine million inhabitants.

Canberra

Canberra (above), Capital Territory of Australia, has wide, straight streets that form a huge triangle across the shores of Lake Burley Griffin. Its civic center was laid out in 1911 from the winning plan of a worldwide competition, and it includes all the requirements of a capital city. These include Parliament buildings, the National Library, the Australian National University, national embassies and the residences of the Prime Minister and of the Governor-General.

Population density is not only closely related to extremes of terrain and climate but also to human enterprise, investment and communications growth. Areas of high density include India, the eastern USA, Japan and Europe.

City populations
- Over 1 million
△ Over 3 million
□ Over 5 million

Inhabitants

per km²	per mile²
Under 3	Under 8
3–6	8–16
6–25	16–64
25–100	84–256
Over 100	Over 256

World urbanization
AD 1800–2000

1800 (900 million)

1900 (1,600 million)

1950 (2,500 million)

1975 (4,000 million)

2000 (Over 6,000 million)

Shanty towns, like that surrounding Lusaka (above left), are a feature of many Third World cities. They represent a makeshift response to the failure of authorities to provide for the thousands of rural poor attracted by city life. The rate of such growth is evident from the maps (left).

1955   1961   1965

Main track
Shanty development

Urbanization (right) is a 20th-century process. Whereas only some 13% of all the world's people lived in towns and cities in 1900, this proportion will have reached 50% for the first time by the year 2000. The largest increases will take place in the urban centers of the Third World as its towns and cities continue to act as magnets to their rural poor. London was the only city with a population of one million in 1900; by 1980, there were more than 200 such cities. By the year 2000, it is certain that many more people will be living in the cities of the developing world, but it is difficult to forecast their proportion in relation to those of the richer cities of the present industrialized world.

Rural population
Urban population of 5,000–100,000 people
Urban population of more than 100,000

Trade and Transport

It is a commonplace that we live in a "shrinking" world. During the last century the development of communications has been so rapid that man appears almost to have conquered the challenge of distance; but such a concept depends on the kind of area to be covered and the cost of transporting goods in relation to their value, bulk and perishability. People, goods and services become accessible by trade. Transport makes trade possible: trade's demands lead to improvements in transport.

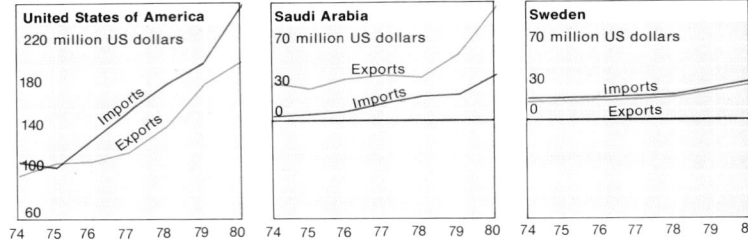

Exports in millions of US dollars (A)

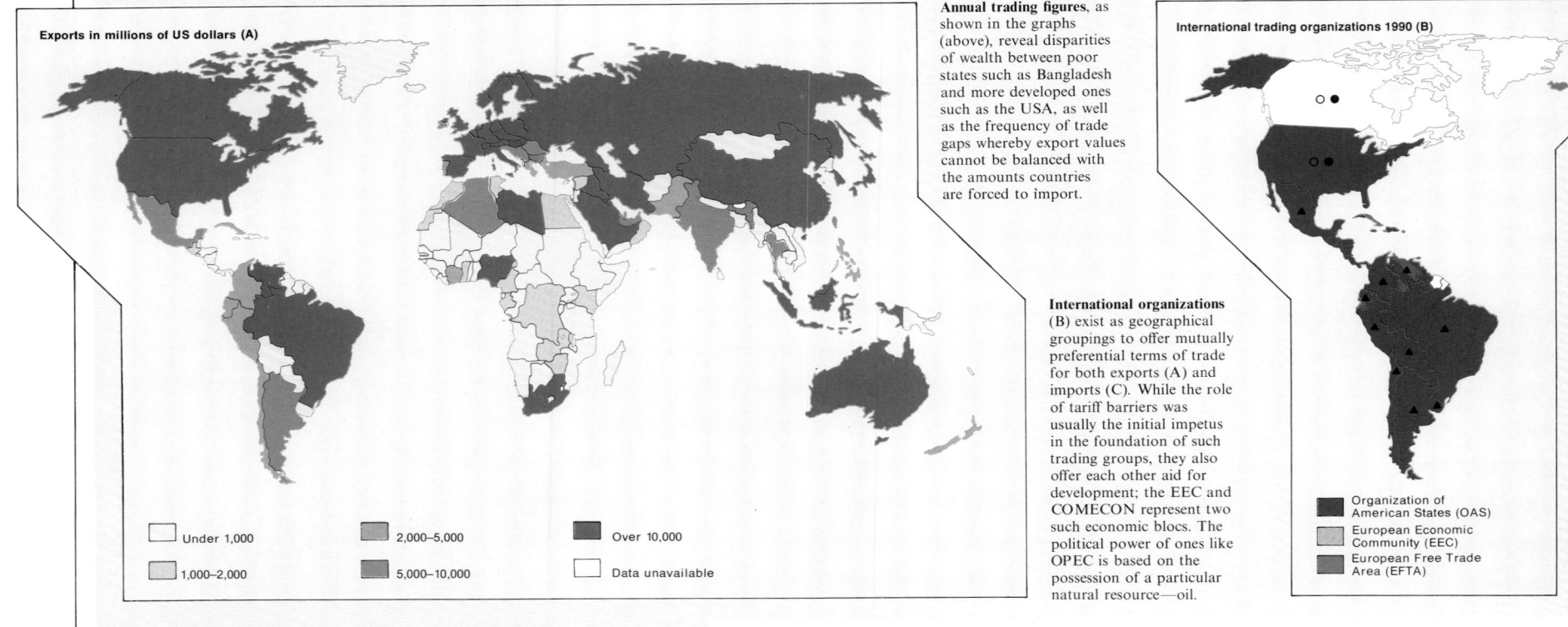

Annual trading figures, as shown in the graphs (above), reveal disparities of wealth between poor states such as Bangladesh and more developed ones such as the USA, as well as the frequency of trade gaps whereby export values cannot be balanced with the amounts countries are forced to import.

International trading organizations 1990 (B)

International organizations (B) exist as geographical groupings to offer mutually preferential terms of trade for both exports (A) and imports (C). While the role of tariff barriers was usually the initial impetus in the foundation of such trading groups, they also offer each other aid for development; the EEC and COMECON represent two such economic blocs. The political power of ones like OPEC is based on the possession of a particular natural resource—oil.

- Under 1,000
- 1,000–2,000
- 2,000–5,000
- 5,000–10,000
- Over 10,000
- Data unavailable

- Organization of American States (OAS)
- European Economic Community (EEC)
- European Free Trade Area (EFTA)

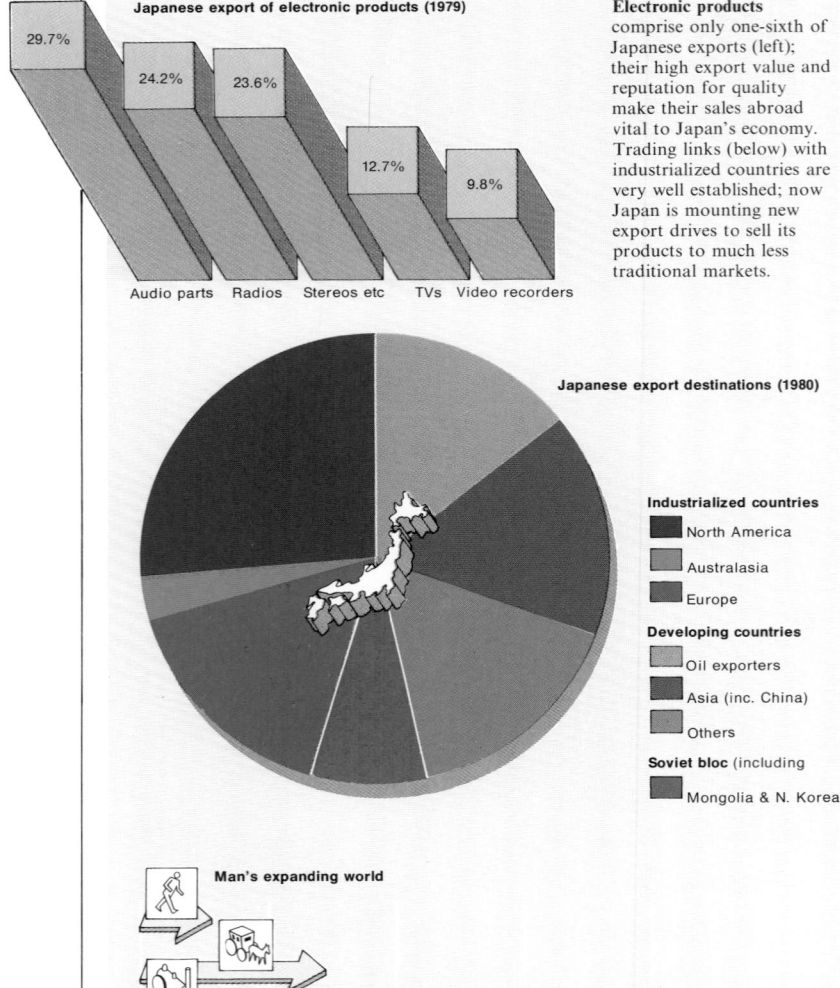

Japanese export of electronic products (1979)

29.7% | 24.2% | 23.6% | 12.7% | 9.8%

Audio parts | Radios | Stereos etc | TVs | Video recorders

Electronic products comprise only one-sixth of Japanese exports (left); their high export value and reputation for quality make their sales abroad vital to Japan's economy. Trading links (below) with industrialized countries are very well established; now Japan is mounting new export drives to sell its products to much less traditional markets.

Japanese export destinations (1980)

Industrialized countries
- North America
- Australasia
- Europe

Developing countries
- Oil exporters
- Asia (inc. China)
- Others

Soviet bloc (including
- Mongolia & N. Korea)

Man's expanding world

It is only a little more than two centuries since navigators completed the mapping of the world's major landmasses and much less since the mapping of the continental interiors was completed—even today some gaps still remain. Canals like the Suez (1869) and Panama (1915) reduced the extent of long sea voyages—the Suez Canal shortened the distance from northwestern Europe to India by 15,000 km (9,300 miles)—so that in transport terms, the various parts of the world became more accessible, especially as steamships and motor vessels replaced sailing ships, and time distances were reduced still further by the airplane.

Locational advantages

Inland waterways, roads and railroads opened up new areas for mining or specialized agriculture, and created opportunities for the manufacture of goods and for the distribution of the finished products. The contrast, however, between locations such as London, Tokyo or Chicago (which are accessible to all forms of transport) and parts of South America where modern transport hardly penetrates, has become much more marked over the years. New transport developments tend to connect major centers first of all, and thus increase their already high locational status.

Such developments must nevertheless be seen in the light of the demand for communications and trade between different points, the nature of the goods being carried and the actual cost of transport. Transport improvements have allowed different parts of the world to share ideas

and products; ironically, they have also made such places more dissimilar, since each area of the Earth has had the chance to specialize in the services it can provide most efficiently.

Specialization of area

Before the widespread development of canals and railroads, road transport was expensive and towns and villages tended to be more self-sufficient. Railroads played a vital role in reducing transport costs in relation to distance and in providing an opportunity for different areas to specialize. After the emergence of railroad networks in North America, specialized areas of agricultural production quickly developed because they were well adjusted to the climatic conditions needed for growing maize (corn), cotton, fruit and fresh vegetables for the new urban markets. In the southern hemisphere, steamships and the introduction of refrigeration enabled meat, butter and cheese to be kept fresh on their journeys to the north.

This concept of specialization of area is basic to world trading patterns, since regions tend to concentrate on commodities and services that they can exchange for other specialized goods and products from other regional or world markets. Countries and areas do best when they concentrate on products for which they have comparative cost advantages in terms of the presence of natural resources, the availability of the skills to develop them, and a demand for the products. Enterprise in adapting natural conditions for the production of goods at competitive price levels is also important. Settlers in New

Technological change in transport has resulted in important reductions in the cost of trade. A man trading on foot might travel half the area a

draft horse could cover in a 12-hour day, but it was the acceptance of steam after *The Rocket* (1829) that made trade more reliable and greatly

expanded the potential for international commerce. Modern jet airliners can easily fly thousands of kilometers in half a day, and while they are being

used more and more for freight, most bulk freight is still carried by train or by specialized cargo vessel. The graph below plots changing transport technology.

0 | 120 | 240 | 360 | 480 | 600 | 720 | 840 | 960 | 1,080 | 1,200 | 1,320 | 1,440 | 1,560

Kilometers traveled in 12 hours

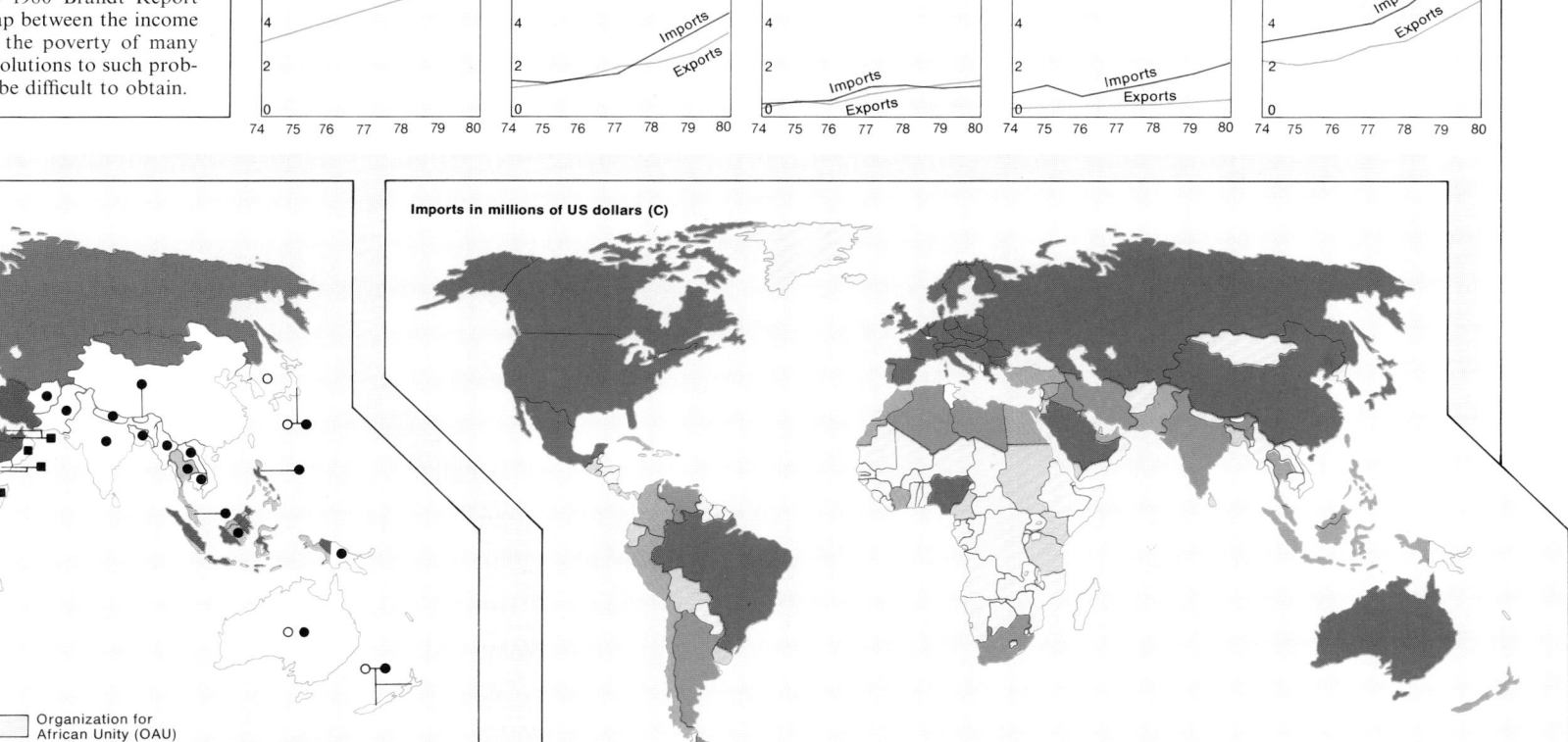

Imports in millions of US dollars (C)

Council for Mutual Economic Aid (COMECON)
Organization of Petroleum Exporting Countries (OPEC)
Association of South-East Asian Nations (ASEAN)
Organization for African Unity (OAU)
▲ Latin American Free Trade Association (LAFTA)
■ Arab League (AL)
○ Colombo Plan
● Organization for Economic Cooperation and Development (OECD)

Under 1,000
1,000–2,000
2,000–5,000
5,000–10,000
Over 10,000
Data unavailable

Zealand, for example, had little hesitation in clearing the prevailing tussock grass to create a new pastoral environment for their large-scale production of sheep and dairy products.

In the real world, however, there are many impediments to the operation of a free market system, and it is unwise for states like New Zealand to assume that they will always dominate Commonwealth dairy trade.

Impediments to free markets
Countries erect protectionist tariff barriers to assist their home industries and/or to obtain extra revenue. Import or export quotas may be imposed, and trade agreements with other countries give special preference to certain commodities. Problems arise from the exchange of currencies and their fluctuations in value. Tariff barriers may be erected for political, welfare or defense reasons. Sometimes special measures may be adopted to encourage the internal production of certain goods rather than obtaining them more cheaply from abroad, and such methods may be economically important to a new country that has always relied on the export of raw materials for its income but now wishes domestically to manufacture previously imported goods.

Political ties are vital to the groupings of certain countries. For reasons of international politics, countries such as those of the Soviet bloc trade with each other rather than with the outside world; and historical links, as between the UK and the Commonwealth, France and her ex-colonies, and Spain and Portugal with

Latin America, are also influential. The European Economic Community (EEC) is composed of countries that have formed a strong bloc among the developed countries.

Rich man, poor man
The developed countries of "the North" have more than 80 percent of the world's manufacturing income but only a quarter of its population, whereas the poorer peoples of "the South" number 3,000 million and receive only a fifth of world income. Attempts have been made to obtain a better economic balance. The 1948 General Agreement on Tariffs and Trade (GATT) and the United Nations Conference on Trade and Development (UNCTAD) provided mechanisms for multinational trade negotiations, and the World Bank and the International Monetary Fund (IMF) together with the 1960 International Development Association (IDA) have all provided easier loans for less developed states.

The widening gap between rich and poor countries has led to understandable demands for a new international order calling for basic changes in the structure of world production, aid and trade, and the transfer of resources. The 1980 Independent Commission on International Development Issues (The Brandt Commission) advocated just such a transfer to the Third World. But during a major world recession there seems little sign of any international political will strong enough to take action on the scale needed to solve the problems that contrasts in wealth and poverty involve.

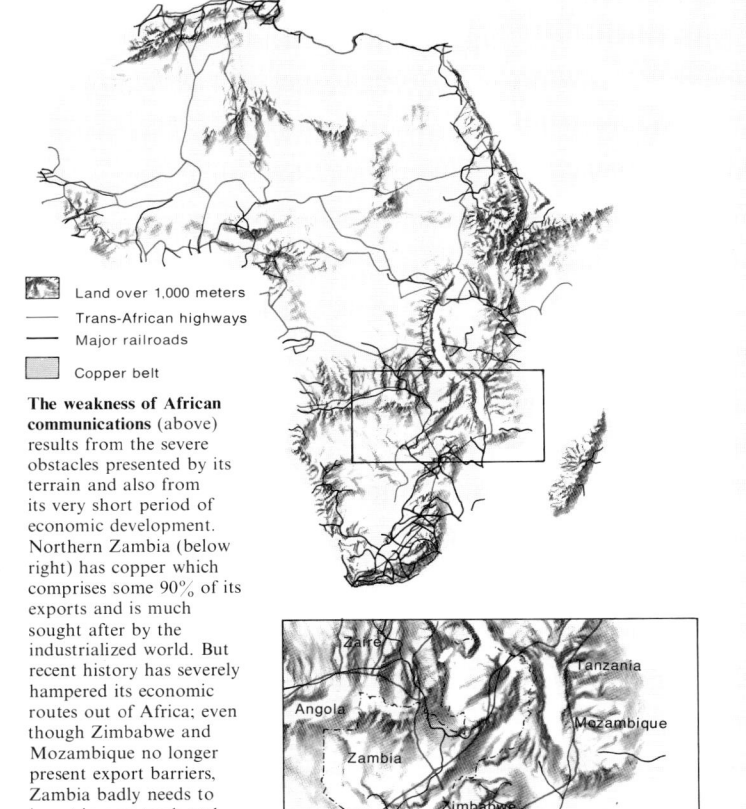

Land over 1,000 meters
Trans-African highways
Major railroads
Copper belt

The weakness of African communications (above) results from the severe obstacles presented by its terrain and also from its very short period of economic development. Northern Zambia (below right) has copper which comprises some 90% of its exports and is much sought after by the industrialized world. But recent history has severely hampered its economic routes out of Africa; even though Zimbabwe and Mozambique no longer present export barriers, Zambia badly needs to invest in new track and rolling stock.

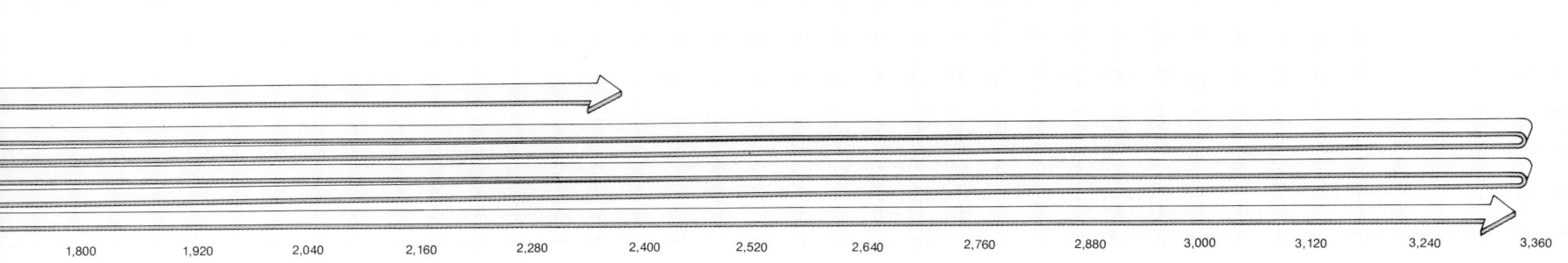

1,800   1,920   2,040   2,160   2,280   2,400   2,520   2,640   2,760   2,880   3,000   3,120   3,240   3,360

Polar Regions

Sunless in winter, and capped with permanent land ice and shifting sea ice, the world's polar regions present an image of intense and everlasting cold. But permanent ice caps have been the exception rather than the rule in the 4,600 million years of Earth's history. The most recent intensification of the present ice age (which began at least two million years ago) reached its maximum about 20,000 years ago and still continues to fluctuate. Polar conditions preclude all but the toughest life forms on land, but the plankton-rich waters attract many animals, and man is beginning to exploit the polar regions' potential.

There have been about a dozen ice ages since the world began. During the intervening periods there was still a zonal pattern of world temperatures, with hot equatorial regions and cooler poles. But the ice caps, which are both chilling and self-sustaining, were absent altogether—the poles being cold temperate rather than icebound. The shiny ice surfaces of today's poles reflect more than 90 percent of the solar radiation which reaches them from the low-angled summer sun, while in winter the sun never rises at all. Thus the regions are now permanently ice capped.

Antarctica, the great southern polar continent, lies under an ice mantle 14 million sq km (5.4 million sq miles) in area, and sometimes more than 4,000 m (13,000 ft) thick. Many of its neighboring islands also carry permanent ice. In the Arctic, the three islands of Greenland lie under a pall of ice of subcontinental size, more than 1.8 million sq km (700,000 sq miles) in area and up to 3,000 m (9,800 ft) thick.

The ice cover of polar seas varies. The central core of the Arctic Ocean carries a mass of permanent pack ice, slowly circulating within the polar basin, which is added to each winter by a belt of ice forming over the open sea. Currents and winds break this up to form pack ice that also circulates, gradually melting in summer or drifting south. Antarctica too is surrounded by fast ice, which breaks up in spring to form a broad belt of persistent pack ice. Circulating slowly about the continent, the pack ice forms huge gyres spreading far to the north, dotted with tabular bergs that have broken away from the continental ice sheet.

The frozen land
In the present glacial phase, the ice caps reached their farthest spread about 20,000 years ago, and then began the retreat which brought them, some 10,000 to 12,000 years ago, to their current position and size. Since then the climate of the polar regions has been both warmer and colder than it is at the present time.

The coldness of the poles is caused by the tilt of the Earth's axis, which prevents sunlight from reaching them at all in the winter. Even in summer, little heat is received from the sun because of the low angle at which its rays reach the surface; much even of this is reflected away by the ice.

Arctic summer

Arctic spring

Arctic winter

Arctic autumn

The fluctuating nature of the polar climates creates very difficult conditions for plants and animals. Very little will grow on the terrestrial ice caps, but water scarcity rather than cold is the most important factor inhibiting plant growth: the small patches of lichens, algae and mosses that occur on rock faces and nunataks (points of rock jutting above the land ice) are usually in the path of a snowmelt runnel. Vegetation patches sometimes contain tiny populations of insects and mites, which may be active for only a few days each year when the sun warms them from a state of dormancy.

However, these tiny scattered plant communities appear all over Antarctica wherever rock surfaces break through the ice cap, and have been seen less than 300 km (190 miles) from the South Pole, and on peaks 2,000 m (6,600 ft) above sea level. Insects and mites occur within 600 km (380 miles) of the Pole itself. In specially favored positions on the Antarctic Peninsula and the offshore islands, carpets of moss and grasses may be seen. Conditions around the northern terrestrial ice cap are similar, with aridity, strong winds and cold discouraging all but the hardiest plants and the smallest, toughest animal colonies.

The frozen seas
The marine ice caps, by contrast, are relatively lively places, especially during summer, when days are long and the sea ice is patchy. Water-lanes between floes are often rich in microscopic algae and the minute zooplanktonic animals that feed on them. These animals in turn attract fish, sea birds and seals in their thousands, as well as whales—including the largest baleen species. Some of the richest patches of sea are close to islands where strong currents stir the water and bring nutrients to the surface, and these attract semipermanent populations of seals and birds. The birds breed on the island cliffs and feed in the sheltered waters among the ice; the seals may breed on the ice itself, producing their pups on a floating nursery where food is close at hand.

Different species of seals are found on inshore and offshore ice environments. In the Arctic, bearded and ringed seals, which produce their young in spring as the inshore ice begins to break up, are often preyed upon by floe-riding polar bears; Eskimos too prize both species for their meat, blubber and skins. Farther out on the offshore pack ice live hooded and harp seals, where their pups are safe from all but the shipborne commercial hunters. In the Antarctic, Weddell seals are the inshore species, whereas crabeater and Ross seals prefer the distant pack ice. Crabeaters, which feed largely on planktonic krill (once thought to be crab larvae), are probably the most numerous of all seal species, with a population estimated at 10 to 15 million.

Sea ice in the north provides a precarious platform on which coastal human populations of the Arctic, such as Eskimos, can extend their winter hunting range. When the land is snowbound and animals are scarce, the sea may still provide food for hunters skilled in fishing, and in stalking seals to their breathing holes.

Nonindigenous inhabitants of the ice caps have greatly increased in recent years, following the discovery and exploitation of oil in the north, as well as other valuable minerals in both the regions. Scientists and technicians today occupy bases and weather stations which in some cases, such as the Amundsen-Scott at the South Pole, are several decades old and have to be maintained by means of aircraft.

EARTH'S FROZEN LIMITS
The permanent ice around Earth's poles covers whole oceans, as well as landmasses of immense size. These ice sheets fluctuate, and on land may be thousands of meters thick, sometimes covering all but the highest mountains, and allowing hardly any life. In the circumpolar seas, however, conditions encourage a very rich growth of plankton, and this supports a plentiful and varied range of wildlife. Man, too, is active in the Arctic, where there are indigenous populations. But in the far south the presence of man is confined to scientists and their support groups. The Antarctic Treaty of 1959 has reserved the continent for nonpolitical scientific use.

THE FAR SOUTH

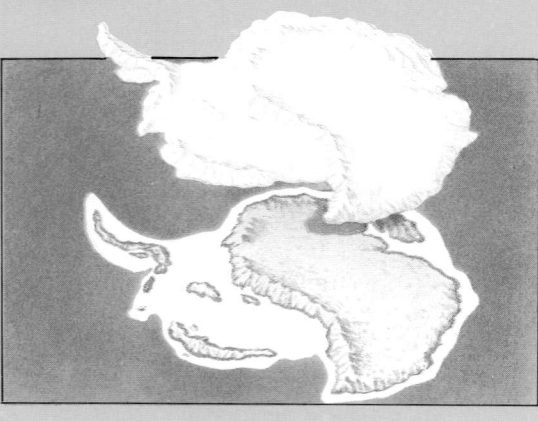

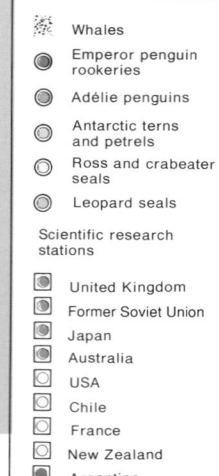

A crushing weight of ice (above) permanently covers the continent and seas of Antarctica, forcing much of the land below sea level. The Antarctic convergence (right), the line at which northern and southern water masses meet, marks a sharp change in temperature and marine life. Especially in areas of upwelling, nutrients make these waters rich in plankton. This feeds a multitude of shrimp-like krill that provide food for a huge number of other animals—fish, penguins, flying birds, seals and whales. The Antarctic landmass allows little natural life, but since the 1959 Antarctic Treaty it has proved to be an area of international scientific cooperation.

Whales

Emperor penguin rookeries

Adélie penguins

Antarctic terns and petrels

Ross and crabeater seals

Leopard seals

Scientific research stations

United Kingdom
Former Soviet Union
Japan
Australia
USA
Chile
France
New Zealand
Argentina

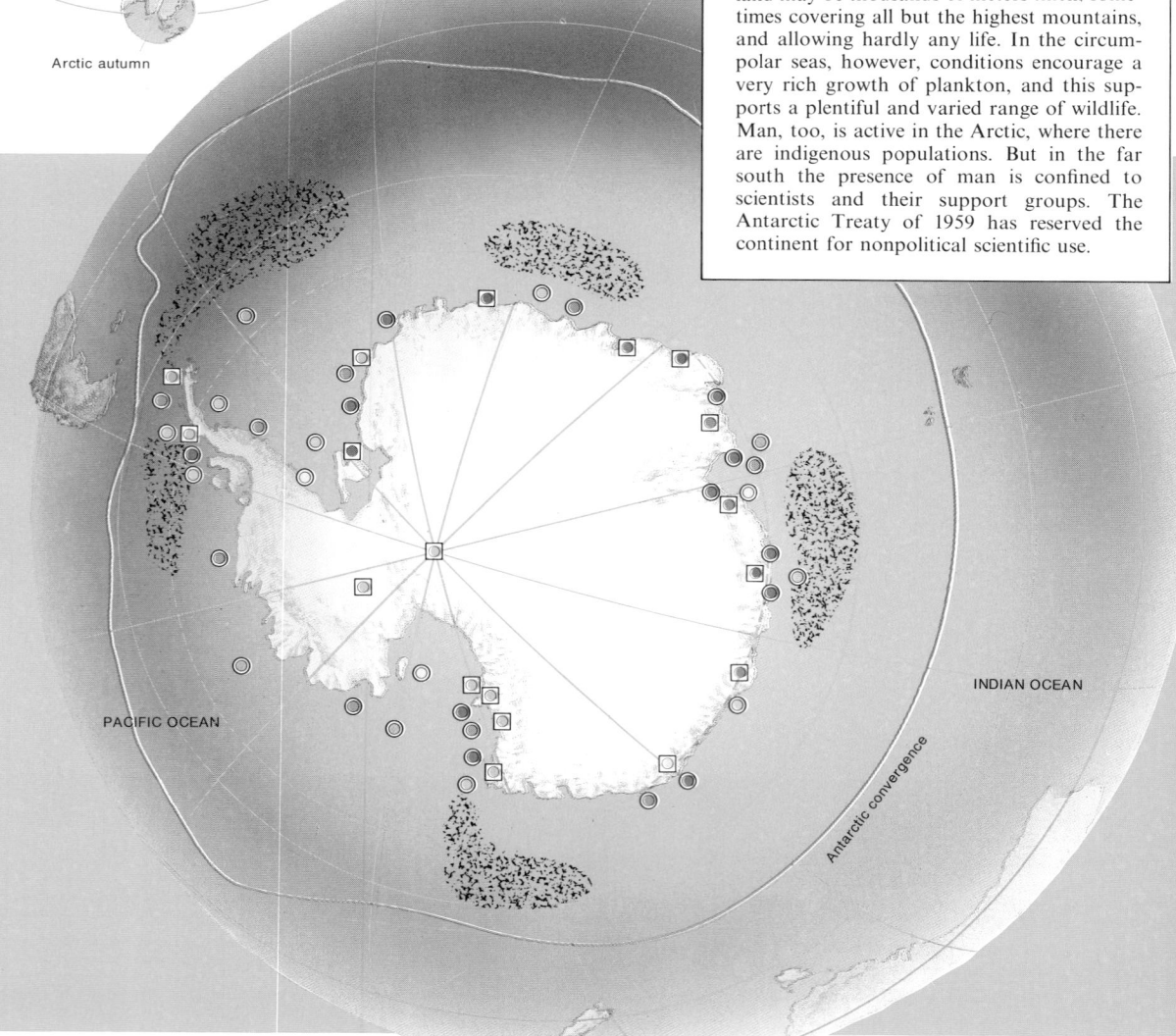

ATLANTIC OCEAN

INDIAN OCEAN

PACIFIC OCEAN

Antarctic convergence

THE FAR NORTH

Pleistocene ice sheet	Iceberg tracks	Limit of pack ice	
Iceberg source	Approx. iceberg limit		

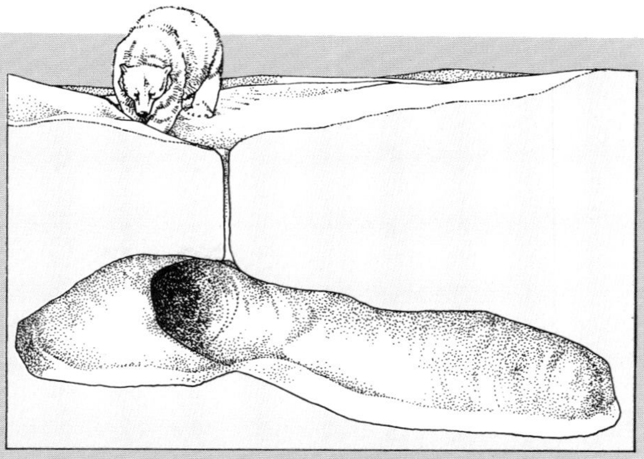

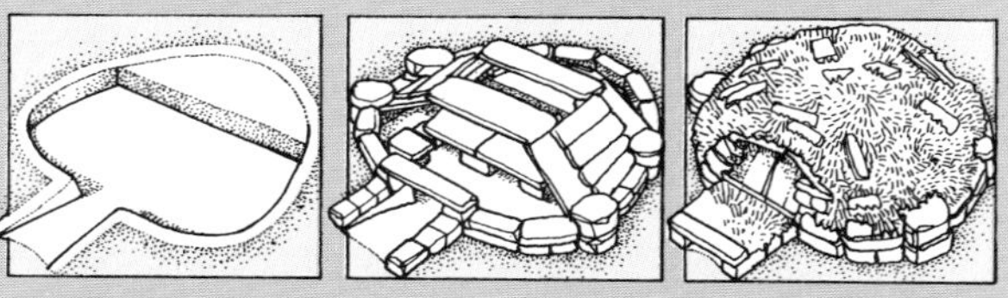

An underground shelter against the winter is built by both men and bears in the polar regions. The bear's den (left) is prepared by a pregnant female for the delivery of her cubs, but may be used by other females and some males. The Inuit *igdlu* (below left) is a semipermanent winter house with an approaching passage and a sleeping platform cut from the earth. The largest roof slabs are then erected, the outside walls are built, and the structure is sealed with turfs to keep in the heat.

Hunting seals has always been an essential activity for indigenous Arctic peoples (above), who rely on them for food, fuel and clothing. Use of the gun for subsistence purposes has had a far less drastic effect than the industrial killing, or culling, of baby seals for their fur (left) in North America.

The frozen seas yield to modern technology as man develops the Arctic's vast potential. The Soviet nuclear icebreaker *Lenin* (left) clears a way for commercial shipping. The US nuclear submarine *Nautilus* has pioneered a shortened route under the North Pole (below).

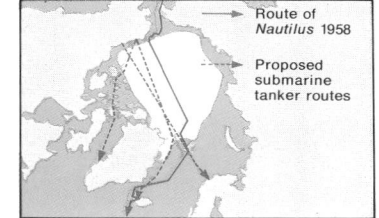

Route of *Nautilus* 1958	
Proposed submarine tanker routes	

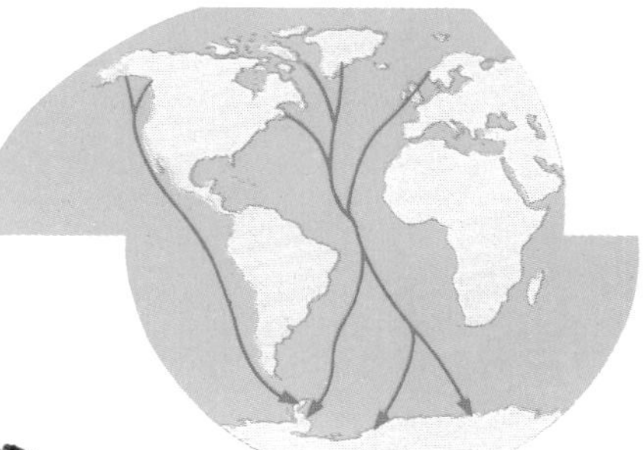

Huge sheets of sea ice cover the Arctic ocean basin; land ice covers most of Greenland and the northern edges of North America and Eurasia. Less than 20,000 years ago land ice extended as far south as London in the UK and New Jersey in the USA. Many scientists believe that we are still between two periods of glacial activity. Desolate in winter, the Arctic bursts into life during the short summer; but the breakup of ice may send bergs south into the path of transatlantic shipping.

MIGRATION

Of all migrant birds, the Arctic tern travels the farthest. It breeds in the high Arctic of Europe and North America and then, as winter approaches, migrates 17,000 km (11,000 miles) to the krill-rich waters of the Antarctic. It thus regularly packs two summers into a single year.

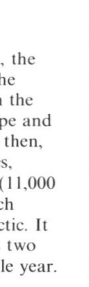

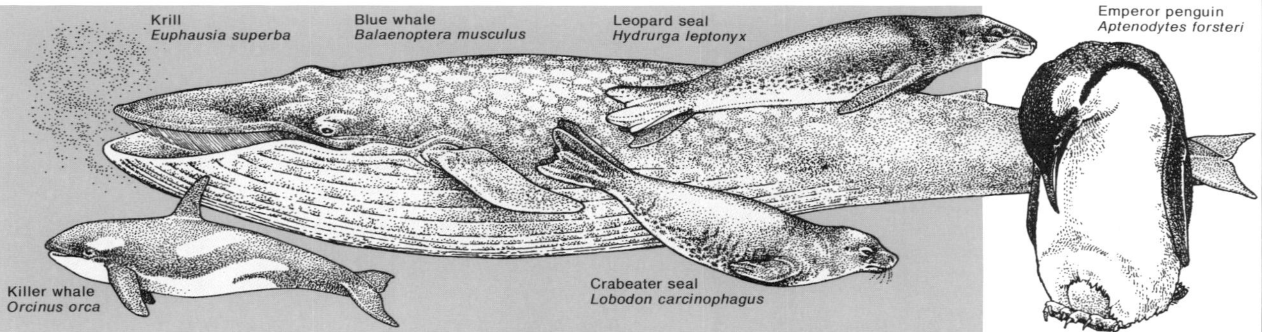

Krill
Euphausia superba

Blue whale
Balaenoptera musculus

Leopard seal
Hydrurga leptonyx

Emperor penguin
Aptenodytes forsteri

Killer whale
Orcinus orca

Crabeater seal
Lobodon carcinophagus

Countless tiny shrimp-like krill (above), yielding up to 1,350 million tonnes a year, are the chief food source of Antarctic waters and could possibly be used for human needs. Krill eaters include the blue whale, which can eat as much as three tonnes a day, and the crabeater seal. Among the Antarctic carnivores, the leopard seal preys mainly on penguins, and the killer whale on seals and penguins.

The South Pole, scene of Scott's tragic expedition of 1912 (left), is now the site of one of Antarctica's many scientific research stations (right). The bleak region may eventually yield a vast supply of mineral and other resources.

The emperor penguin (above) endures the rigors of the Antarctic winter on sea ice close to the continent in order to breed. Once the female has laid her single egg, the male starts the 64-day incubation through the midwinter darkness, carrying and incubating the egg on the top of his feet. This arduous regime ensures that young chicks, hatched in spring, avoid attacks from skuas, and benefit from better weather during their summer development. Penguins are one of the several kinds of wingless birds to have evolved in the southern hemisphere; but of all birds the emperor penguin is best adapted to the harsh polar environment of the Antarctic region.

Tundra and Taiga

Tundra is land that has been exposed for only about 8,000 years, since the retreat of the ice caps, and only relatively recently occupied by plants. In consequence, few plants and animals have yet had time to adapt to the virtually soilless and treeless environment. The less rigorous conditions of neighboring taiga forest allow a longer growing season and a somewhat wider range of species. The delicately balanced ecology of both areas is being increasingly threatened, however, by the activities of man.

"Tundra," from a Lapp word meaning "rolling, treeless plain," defines the narrow band of open, low ground that surrounds the Arctic Ocean. It lies north of the line beyond which the temperature of the warmest month usually fails to reach 10°C (50°F). North of this trees do not generally grow well, so the line forms a natural frontier between tundra and the broad band of coniferous forest that circles the northern hemisphere to its south between about 60°N and 48°N. This forest, forming the world's largest and most uninterrupted area of vegetation, is usually referred to by its Russian name of "taiga."

Cheerless landscapes

The tundra presents a desolate and restrictive environment for most of the year: in winter there are several months of semidarkness. While there is considerable variation in the climates of places at the same latitude, temperatures average only −5°C (23°F) and are well below freezing for many months of the year. Frost-free days are restricted to a few weeks in midsummer and even then, although days are warmer, the sun is never high in the sky. Nearly all tundra has been free from ice for only a few thousand years. As a result, it either has no soil at all or has developed only a thin covering of

sandy, muddy or peaty soil, successfully colonized by only a few types of plants.

Trimmed by such grazing animals as hares, musk oxen and reindeer or caribou, and by strong winds carrying abrasive rock dust and ice particles, typical tundra vegetation forms a low, patchy mat a few centimeters deep. Much of it grows on permafrost — ground that thaws superficially in summer but remains perennially frozen beneath the surface. Here drainage is poor, shallow ponds are frequent and the scanty soils tend to be waterlogged and acidic. Nevertheless, a small number of grasses, sedges, mosses and marsh plants may grow well and the summer tundra in flower can be an impressive sight. Knee-high forests of dwarf birch, willow and alder grow in valleys sheltered from the strong and biting wind.

The taiga also is a dark and monotonous habitat. Again, while there is a good deal of variation in climatic conditions, on average the region has somewhat milder summers than the tundra with mean average temperatures of 2–6°C (34–42°F), less wind and a slightly longer growing season. The taiga is mostly older than the tundra, and its soils have had longer to mature. They support a small number of tree species, with coniferous spruce, pine, fir and

larch predominating. Short-season broadleaves such as willows, alders, birches and poplars tend to occur on the better soils of river valleys and the edges of forest lakes.

Animals of the far north

The number of animal species supported throughout the year by tundra and taiga is also comparatively small, with interdependent populations that may fluctuate wildly from season to season. In winter both tundra and taiga are silent, although far from deserted. Mice, voles and lemmings remain active, living in tunnels under the snow, which keeps them well insulated from the wind and subzero temperatures. Above the snow Arctic hares forage; they tend to gather in snow-free areas where food can still be found. Arctic foxes are mainly tundra animals and the musk oxen, too, winter on high, exposed tundra where their dense, shaggy coats protect them from the worst

The circumpolar north that surrounds the permanently frozen ice cap is dominated by tundra—open plain that remains snowfree for only several months in the summer—and taiga, the vast coniferous forest stretching right round the northern hemisphere. The Siberian taiga, for example, is one-third larger than the entire United States.

□ Tundra   □ Taiga

Producers
■ USSR
■ USA

Man's pursuit of resources has accelerated in the past two decades, with the former Soviet Union drastically increasing its outflow of both oil and gas since 1970. North American output has lagged far behind, mainly because the need for exploration and exploitation has only recently become important. In all tundra and taiga areas, gas did not start flowing until the early 1960s. The former Soviet Union's coal output has been rising steadily while that of North America has fluctuated. (In these figures, North America is composed of Alaska and the Yukon and Northwest territories. The former Soviet Union is more loosely defined as "regions of the far north".)

Oil ('000 tonnes)
Coal ('000 tonnes)
Natural gas (1,000,000,000 cu m)
1960 1965 1970 1975

Pollution of Lake Baikal, the world's deepest freshwater lake, is being increasingly threatened by man's indifference to its unique position as a freshwater reservoir. Increasing exploitation of the Siberian taiga for minerals and timber has led to the pollution of the 300 or so rivers discharging effluents into the lake.

Siberian spruce
Picea obovata

Common crossbill
Loxia curvirostra

Adaptation to severe cold by trees of the taiga includes their conical forms that allow snow to be shed easily, and narrow needle-leaves that reduce water loss to a minimum. Seeds are protected by closed woody cones; opened by crossbills, they provide a constant supply of food during winter.

Reindeer or caribou
Rangifer tarandus

Raven
Corvus corax

January

February

Arctic fox
Alopex lagopus

March

April

Capercaillie
Tetrao urogallus

May

Snowy owl
Nyctea scandiaca

June

Brown lemming
Lemmus lemmus

Arctic skua
Stercorarius parasiticus

Movement in these regions takes many directions. The capercaillie spends all winter in the taiga, where it thrives on the abundant conifer needles, buds and shoots. Some move southward into deciduous woods during the summer months. The Arctic skua breeds on the tundra but moves to the warmer oceans in winter, while the tundra movements of the all-scavenging raven and the snowy owl are governed by those of their

prey. The raven picks clean the carcasses left by other predators; the snowy owl feeds on small rodents such as mice and lemmings, as does the Arctic fox. Lemmings remain static and inconspicuous in normal years but some populations expand rapidly every third or fourth year, leading to mass local migration in every direction, possibly caused by an abundance of vegetation that encourages more frequent breeding.

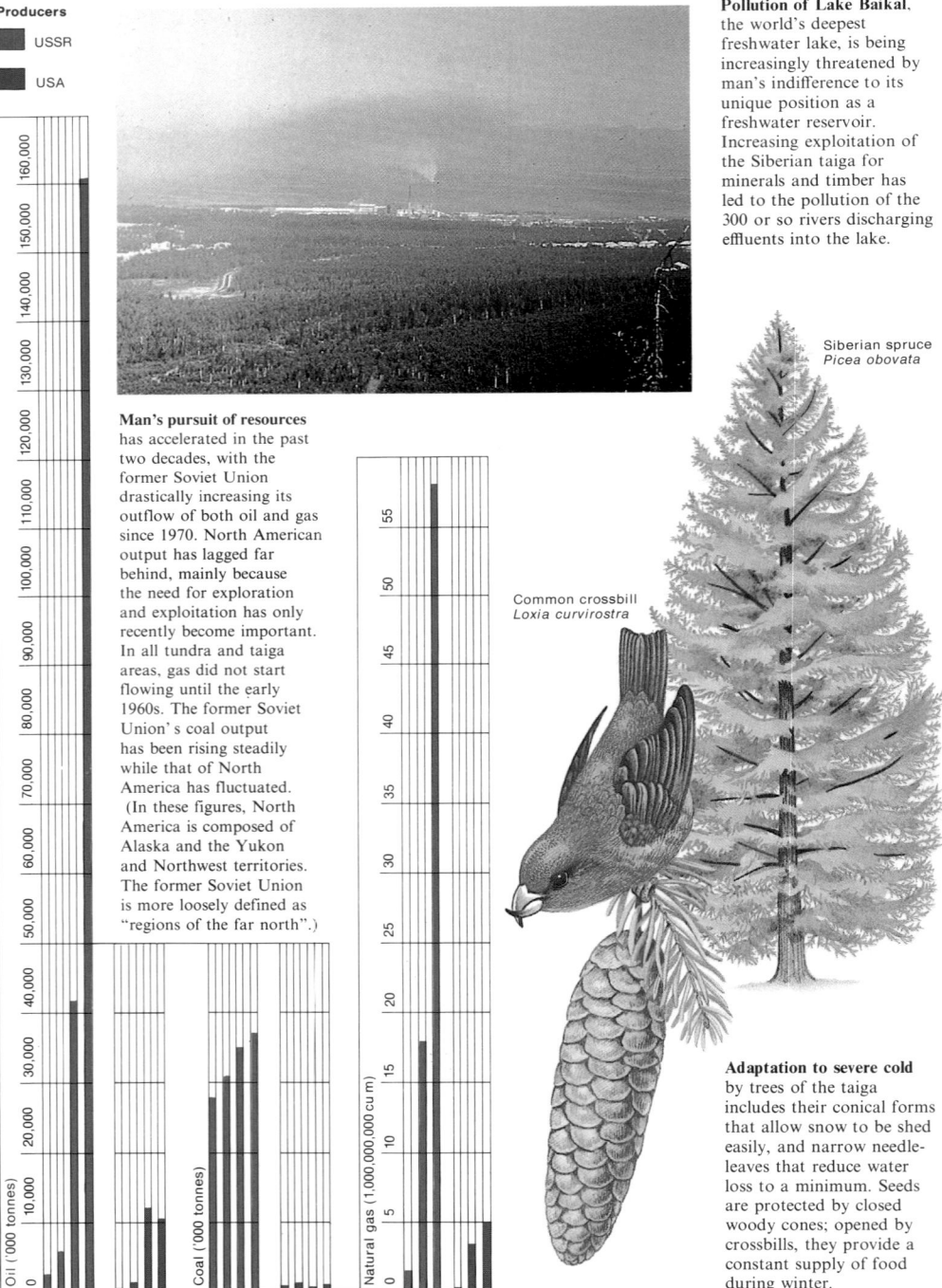

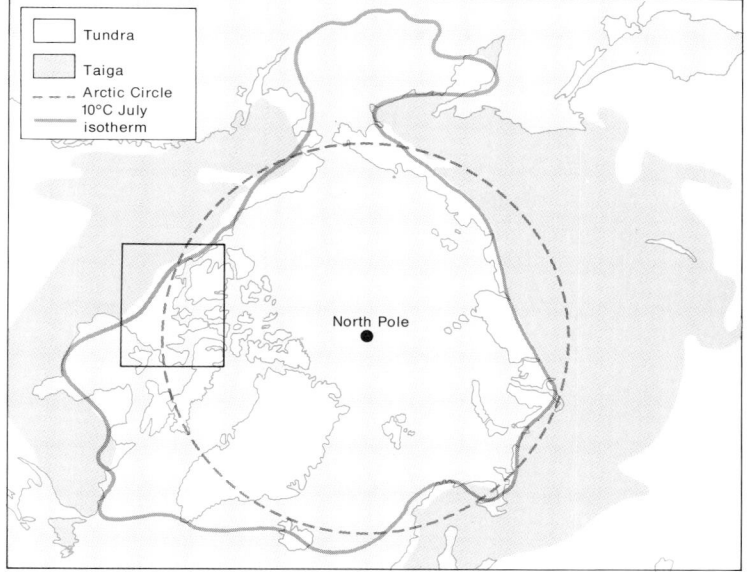

The rough boundary between the tundra and taiga—the tree line—approximates to the 10°C July isotherm, the climatic point north of which trees fail to grow successfully. Seasonal caribou migration in the Canadian barren grounds (boxed) is shown in the main diagram (below). Such migration is also undertaken by reindeer in northern Eurasia.

The summer tundra—seen here in Swedish Lapland—provides a wide cover of low plants including "reindeer mosses" and other lichens. Grazing reindeer return minerals to the soil. Shallow ponds form as the frozen ground above the permafrost thaws for a few months in summer. Mountains stay partly snow covered in the warmest weather and are a prominent physical feature of the tundra.

weather. Bears, badgers, beavers and squirrels are common taiga mammals. Elk and reindeer (in North America, moose and caribou) winter in the shelter of the taiga; wolves are mostly woodland animals in winter, following their prey to the open tundra in spring. Red foxes, coyotes, mink and wolverines also move to the tundra in summer.

Snow buntings, ptarmigans and snowy owls live on the tundra throughout the coldest months and are fully adapted to life there. Crossbills and capercaillies are among taiga residents, equipped to live on its abundant conifer buds, seeds and needles. Enormous populations of migrant birds, especially water birds and waders, fly north to both tundra and taiga with the spring thaw. Waxwings, bramblings, siskins and redpolls leave their temperate latitudes to feed on the lush and fast-growing vegetation and the profusion of insects that appear as soon as the snows begin to melt.

Man in the northlands

These circumpolar regions separate the world's greatest centers of population. They are now crisscrossed with air routes. A total population of about nine million people currently inhabits the tundra and taiga. Numbers have been increased by the immigration of technicians and administrators during the last few decades; oil prospecting and mining, forest exploitation and other activities of these newcomers is altering the seminomadic lives of the million or so aboriginal peoples such as the Khanty (Ostyaks) and Nentsy (Samoyeds) of Russia, the Samer (Lapps) of Scandinavia and Russia, and the Inuit (formerly Eskimos) of North America. New roads, exploitation of minerals and forests, and pipeline construction have disrupted the migration of their reindeer (caribou) and their land has been appropriated for hydroelectric schemes.

In the taiga, Russia is constructing railroads and towns and extracting huge amounts of timber; they have prospected widely and successfully for gold, nickel, iron, tin, mica, diamonds and tungsten, and have discovered vast reserves of oil and natural gas in western Siberia. Alaskan oil, discovered in 1968, now flows across the state at 54–62°C (130–145°F), and to protect the permafrost from this heat the pipeline has had to be elevated for half its 1,300 km (800 mile) length. The pipe's route to the ice-free port of Valdez has interfered with the migration of caribou; hunting and other pressures have led to a drop in their population from three million to some 200,000 in about 30 years. Only official protection has saved the musk ox from a similar fate. These bleak areas are so vast and inhospitable that living space there will never be threatened. However, if only on a local scale, their ecologies are under increasing pressure from man.

Many Norwegian Lapps (or Samer) derive their income from reindeer, which they domesticated many centuries ago to provide meat, milk and skins. Now they follow them through the seasons along well-worn and familiar routes. Such nomadic life styles are becoming rarer as Samer settle down.

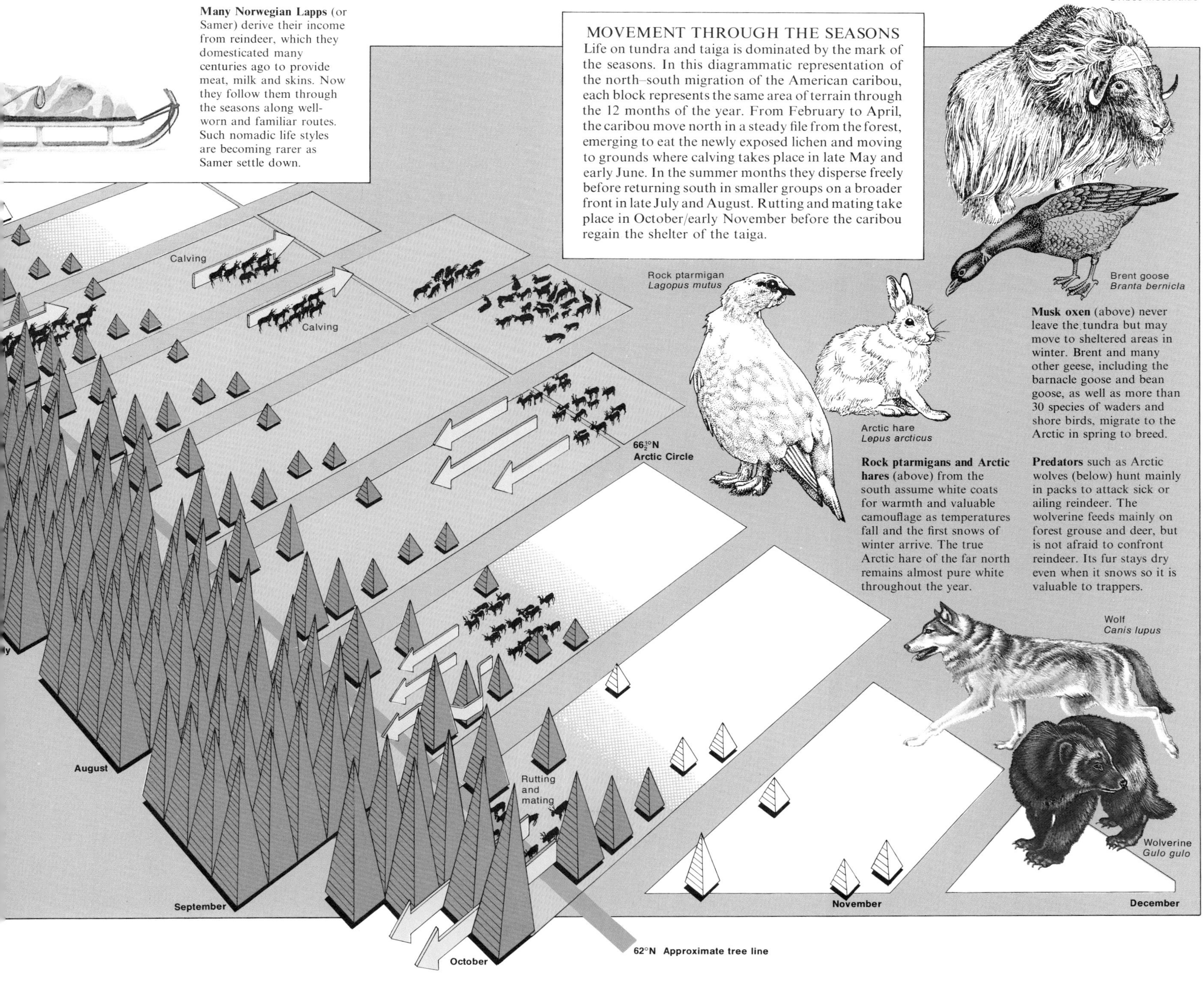

MOVEMENT THROUGH THE SEASONS

Life on tundra and taiga is dominated by the mark of the seasons. In this diagrammatic representation of the north–south migration of the American caribou, each block represents the same area of terrain through the 12 months of the year. From February to April, the caribou move north in a steady file from the forest, emerging to eat the newly exposed lichen and moving to grounds where calving takes place in late May and early June. In the summer months they disperse freely before returning south in smaller groups on a broader front in late July and August. Rutting and mating take place in October/early November before the caribou regain the shelter of the taiga.

Musk ox
Ovibos moschatus

Rock ptarmigan
Lagopus mutus

Brent goose
Branta bernicla

Arctic hare
Lepus arcticus

Musk oxen (above) never leave the tundra but may move to sheltered areas in winter. Brent and many other geese, including the barnacle goose and bean goose, as well as more than 30 species of waders and shore birds, migrate to the Arctic in spring to breed.

Rock ptarmigans and Arctic hares (above) from the south assume white coats for warmth and valuable camouflage as temperatures fall and the first snows of winter arrive. The true Arctic hare of the far north remains almost pure white throughout the year.

Predators such as Arctic wolves (below) hunt mainly in packs to attack sick or ailing reindeer. The wolverine feeds mainly on forest grouse and deer, but is not afraid to confront reindeer. Its fur stays dry even when it snows so it is valuable to trappers.

Wolf
Canis lupus

Wolverine
Gulo gulo

Calving

Calving

66½°N
Arctic Circle

August

September

October

Rutting and mating

November

December

62°N Approximate tree line

Temperate Forests

At one time, dense, primeval forests blanketed large areas of North America, Europe and eastern Asia. Almost all of the trees that flourished in these temperate regions were deciduous – they shed their leaves in autumn, stood bare branched through winter and produced new foliage every spring. Little of this forest now exists. The few remaining pockets, however, still provide habitats for a large range of shade-loving plants: lichens and fungi, tree-hugging mosses, scrambling creepers and shrubs. And this vegetation in turn provides sanctuary for a surprisingly wide variety of forest creatures.

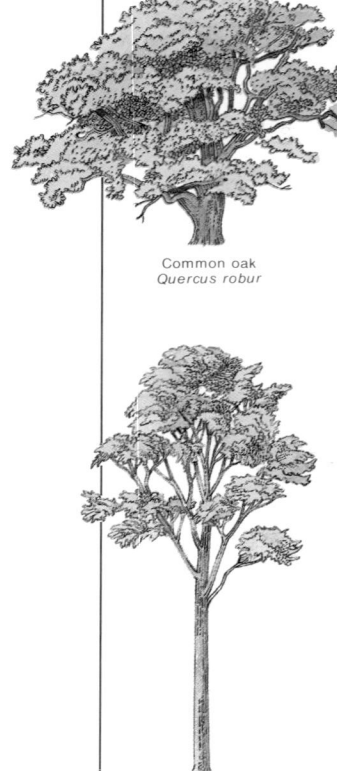

Common oak
Quercus robur

Silver beech
Nothofagus menziesii

Deciduous trees such as the oak (top) make up the temperate forests in cooler temperate regions. In milder, wetter climates, where the seasons are less distinct, evergreens such as southern beech (above) are typical temperate species.

The greater part of the temperate forest zone lies in the northern hemisphere, where winter soil temperatures reduce the ability of plants to absorb water. Hence the trees tend to shed their leaves, which use up moisture through evaporation. In the southern hemisphere, however, the temperate latitudes encourage a type of rainforest in such areas as southern Chile, Tasmania, New Zealand and parts of southeastern Australia. Here the climate is maritime, often with high rainfall and frequent fogs, and evergreen rather than deciduous types of trees grow. Temperate rainforests also occur in the northern hemisphere, in China and in northwestern and northeastern North America.

Deciduous forest consists of a mixture of trees, sometimes with one variety predominant. In central Europe, beech is the leading—and sometimes the only—tree species, whereas oaks mixed with other species made up the forest farther west and east. In North America, beech and maple were once extensive.

The climate in temperate forest zones varies sharply according to seasons—summers tend to be warm, winters moderately cold, and rainfall fairly regular. In fact, the seasonal rhythm is a central feature of temperate forests, and it affects the entire ecosystem—the whole community of plants and animals found there. Soils are generally of the fertile "brown earth" type: the leaf litter of deciduous forests in particular breaks down easily, and is quickly worked into the soil by burrowing animals such as earthworms. In wetter or rockier regions, the soil is more "podsolic"—bleached, sandy and less fertile than the true brown earths.

After the ice

Two million years ago, a series of ice sheets began to extend into the temperate latitudes. In Europe, species moving south before the advancing cold were cut off from the warmer climates by the east–west run of mountains. As a result, many varieties of plants and animals

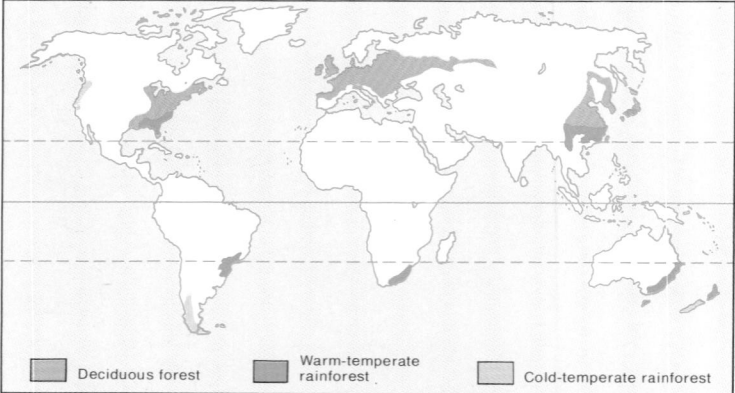

Deciduous forest	Warm-temperate rainforest	Cold-temperate rainforest

Natural distribution: in the northern hemisphere's temperate zone deciduous forests occur in the cooler areas—in eastern USA, northeastern China, Korea, the northern parts of Japan's Honshu island and western Europe. These forests only give way to evergreens in the warmer and wetter parts of the zone. In the southern hemisphere, the climate is generally rather milder throughout the temperate zone and so there are virtually no deciduous forests. Evergreen forests, however, can be found in southeastern South Africa, Chile, New Zealand, Australia and Tasmania.

were killed off. Species were reduced still further in islands such as Britain, where the newly formed barriers of the English Channel, Irish Sea and North Sea made recolonization even more difficult after the ice had retreated.

Eastern Asia was one of the few areas in the world that escaped the extreme climatic changes of the ice ages and therefore its temperate forests, unlike those of Europe, still contain an enormous variety of tree species. North America also fared better than Europe, for although glaciers at one time extended deep into the continent, the north–south direction of the mountain ranges allowed relatively easy migration of trees southwards as the climate worsened. Hence most species survived and were able to reoccupy their former territories when the ice retreated. As a result, some 40 species of deciduous trees occur in the North American forests, and contribute to the spectacular display of color during the autumn, notably in

the eastern USA. But a combination of climatic change and, more recently and importantly, of intense human activity, has meant that the remnants of temperate forest seen today differ greatly from the original forest in both composition and form. Only in remote regions such as the southern Appalachian Mountains do substantial areas of the original forest survive. Elsewhere, regrowth has occurred, but much of this is essentially scrub woodland.

The forest structure

Mature temperate deciduous forest is made up of distinct horizontal layers, particularly where the dominant tree is the oak, which allows enough light for a rich shrub layer to grow beneath it. The largest trees, such as oak, maple or ash, may be 25–50 m (80–160 ft) tall, and beneath them grows a prominent layer of smaller trees such as hazel, hornbeam or yew. Lower down again, a varied ground cover of perennial herbs, ferns, lichens and mosses flourishes in the comparative dampness of the forest floor. Because the trees are bare of leaves in winter, many of the plants growing on the forest floor take advantage of the warmth and light of spring to flower early in the year before the main trees come into full leaf and prevent the sun from reaching them. Various woody climbers, such as ivy and honeysuckle, are also present, growing over the trees and shrubs.

Much of the food supply in temperate forests is locked up in the trees themselves, but the annual fall of leaves in the deciduous forests produces a soil rich in nourishment. This supports a vast quantity of life, ranging in size from earthworms and insects to microscopic bacteria of the soil. The death of individual trees and branches also releases the food supply back to the earth. In shady, damp locations, insects, fungi, bacteria and other decomposing agents break down the leaves and other plant and animal debris more quickly, returning them to the soil as food for new plants.

Creatures of the forest

Temperate forests once contained many varieties of animal life, including several species of large animals. Herbivores such as wild oxen, wood bison, elk and moose ate grass and leaves; scavengers such as wild pigs rooted in the forest floor; predators such as wolves preyed on the other animals. Most of these have now been hunted to extinction by man or are extremely rare. Smaller animals still survive in comparatively large numbers, and include squirrels, chipmunks and raccoons, hedgehogs, wood mice, badgers and foxes.

The bird life of temperate forests is very diverse. Some species are insect eaters, exploring the bark and crevices for insects and grubs. Others, such as the wood pigeon, concentrate on seeds. Yet others, like the tawny owl, are predators. Complex interactions between predators and prey have developed at all levels of the forest, from the high canopy to the rotting ground litter, with each group evolving more efficient techniques of capture or escape in a kind of evolutionary race for survival.

The invertebrate insect life is also extremely varied and numerous, and forms a key component of the ecosystem. Oaks are particularly rich in insect life, and more than 100 species of moths feed on their leaves.

The plant and animal life of the temperate forest is remarkably rich and plentiful. And yet it is only a fraction of what once existed. Ever since man has occupied these regions he has found them so useful to his needs that he has long since cleared most of the original tree cover, replaced it with "civilization" and, in the process, destroyed innumerable species of forest wildlife.

THE SEASONAL CYCLE

It is the cycle of the four seasons that gives the temperate deciduous forest its distinctive character. All animals and plants have adapted their ways of life to cope with the seasonal changes in heat, light, moisture and food. The yearly shedding and regrowth of the forest's leaves is one of the most striking and important of adaptations to the seasonal cycle and one that affects all other life in the forest. In summer the leafy canopy of the trees blocks out the sunlight from the forest floor and creates unsuitable conditions for many other plants to flourish. When the leaves fall they form a layer over the soil and provide winter protection for the plant roots and hibernating animals beneath the ground. Finally, once the dead leaves have been broken down, they give fertility to the soil and provide food for future generations of plants.

SPRING

Between February and April, the low spring sun climbs steadily higher in the sky and, streaming through the still leafless branches of the trees, falls more directly on the forest floor, warming the soil and melting the last frosts. As soon as the days become warmer the sluggish sap in the trees begins to flow more quickly, carrying nutrients to the branches, where leaf buds start to form.

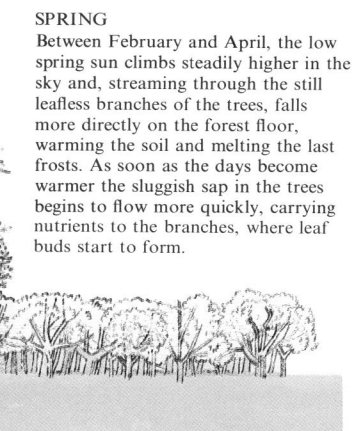

Bluebell
Endymion non-scriptus

Hepatica
Hepatica nobilis

Small plants of the forest floor, such as European bluebells and hepaticas taking advantage of the warm soil and plentiful light, flower in spring.

Forest insects emerge in spring, some, such as the emperor moth, from their winter cocoons, some from hibernation and some newly hatched from eggs.

Small emperor moth
Saturnia pavonia

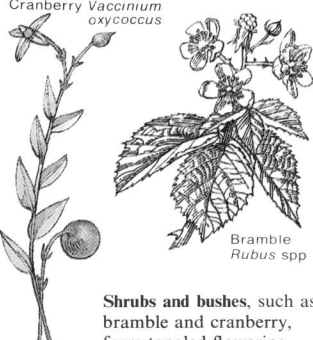

European blackbird *Turdus merula*

Birds building nests in early spring make use of the forest's winter litter—broken twigs, dead leaves and dried grasses all serve as construction materials.

Woodchuck *Marmota monax*

Western European hedgehog
Erinaceus europaeus

White-tailed deer
Odocoileus virginianus

New plant growth and the increase in insects provide food for such animals as the North American woodchuck and the European hedgehog that wake thin and hungry from months of hibernation. Deer and other non-hibernating animals are also weak and thin—indeed many may have died during the harsh weather. The spring birth of young, however, soon restores their numbers.

SUMMER

By early summer the leaves of the trees are fully grown. They form a dense canopy, blocking out the sun and cooling the soil of the forest floor. Most of the small ground plants have long since finished flowering, but their leaves remain green and they continue actively storing food in their roots ready for their rapid spring growth.

Cranberry *Vaccinium oxycoccos*

Bramble
Rubus spp

Shrubs and bushes, such as bramble and cranberry, form tangled flowering masses wherever sunlight manages to filter through the forest's gloomy canopy.

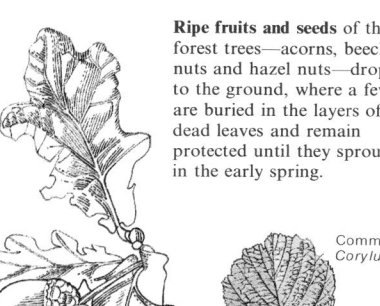

Hordes of insects inhabit the forest in summer, living off the vast supply of food plants. The European stag beetle feeds on the sap of chestnut and oak trees.

Stag beetle
Lucanus cervus

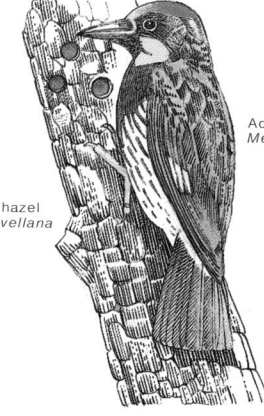

Willow warbler
Phylloscopus trochilus

The North American pewee and the willow warbler are two of the forest's many summer visitors that feed on the insect population. Some seed-eating birds, finches for example, also take advantage of this summer food supply.

Eastern wood pewee
Contopus virens

Hazel mouse
Muscardinus avellanarius

The hazel mouse protects its young by raising them in a summer nest, which it builds in a tree: almost every creature in the forest is viewed as a source of food by some other animal and the young litters are particularly at risk.

AUTUMN

As the autumn days grow shorter and cooler the forest foliage begins to turn color; the trees are responding to the drop in temperature and are cutting off the food supply to their leaves, which lose their green color and fall to the ground, forming a thick carpet on the forest's floor. Rain, frost, insects, earthworms and fungi then break down the leaves, making them part of the fertile forest soil.

Oak
Quercus spp

Ripe fruits and seeds of the forest trees—acorns, beech nuts and hazel nuts—drop to the ground, where a few are buried in the layers of dead leaves and remain protected until they sprout in the early spring.

Common hazel
Corylus avellana

Preparing for winter, the acorn woodpecker stores seeds in holes that it drills in tree trunks. Chipmunks hide supplies of nuts in their winter nests.

Acorn woodpecker
Melanerpes formicivorus

Eastern chipmunk
Tamias striatus

American black bear
Ursus americanus

The black bear of North America, like other winter hibernators, consumes vast quantities of food during autumn to build up its winter stores of food in the form of body fat.

WINTER

By winter, only evergreen shrubs and a few small hardy plants remain green. Many of the plants of the forest floor lose their green leaves during the first deep frost. The leaves of the trees still lie rotting on the bare ground, but within the soil, beneath the protective layers of leaf litter, plants are growing and spring flowers are developing buds.

Late-fruiting plants, such as holly, mistletoe and dog rose, provide food for winter residents of the temperate forest such as the European hawfinch.

Hawfinch
Coccothraustes coccothraustes

Holly
Ilex spp

European woodcock
Scolopax rusticola

Woodcocks are insect-eaters. They can survive winter by prizing insects from the soil with their long beaks, providing that the ground is not too deeply frozen.

North American screech owl
Otus asio

Owls and foxes remain fairly active in winter, regularly leaving their nests or lairs to catch small animals or birds that are also in search of food.

Red fox
Vulpes vulpes

European badger
Meles meles

European badgers, like racoons, opossums, bears and skunks, are "shallow" hibernators. On mild winter days they wake and go to search for food.

THE EVERGREEN TEMPERATE RAINFORESTS

There are two main kinds of temperate rainforest, the warm temperate, such as can still be found on North Island, New Zealand (left), and the cold temperate, such as that of the Chilean coast. Both of these kinds of forest have one major feature in common: they have enough water for even the most moisture-greedy plants, such as mosses and ferns, to grow throughout the year. The animal life of the forest is also affected by the abundance of rain, so that snails, slugs, frogs and other water-loving creatures flourish. Most temperate rainforest is of the warm-temperate kind, normally found on the edges of subtropical regions, and the vegetation, with palms, lianas,

bamboos, as well as ferns and mosses, is similar to, although less rich than, the tropical rainforest's vegetation. The cold-temperate rainforests grow in cooler regions but their coastal position means that the climate is milder and wetter than inland (where deciduous trees dominate). Their vegetation is less lush and less varied than the warm-temperate forests, but mosses and ferns grow in abundance. Broad-leaved evergreens, such as New Zealand's southern beech, are the most common trees of these forests, although on the northwestern coast of North America Douglas firs and other conifers outnumber the broad-leaved evergreen species.

Man and the Temperate Forests

Temperate forests have suffered enormously at the hands of man. For the great civilizations of China, Europe and, later, North America the forests not only yielded cropland for expanding populations but also contributed materials and fuel for early technologies. More recently the demands of industry have reduced the forests still further. But today, scientists believe that this depleted resource could again play an important role in providing energy, food and materials for future generations.

PERMANENT SETTLEMENT
The Bronze Age and, later, the Iron Age laid the foundations of Chinese and Western civilizations. The forest shrank as permanent settlements grew (3) and, with the use of metals and improved technology, agricultural land was extended (4). But the forest was recognized as an important resource and areas were protected. Management techniques were introduced that, especially in medieval Europe, changed dense forest to coppice woods (5).

EARLY INDUSTRIAL TIMES
Sources of cropland and timber had been discovered in the New World, but in the Far East and Europe forests were drastically reduced. Virtually no Chinese forest remained, and in Europe nations began importing timber to serve growing industrial needs (6). To help solve shortages, plantations were established on country estates (7), which were often landscaped into parkland and planted with introduced species of trees (8).

PREHISTORIC FORESTS
Hunter gatherers made clearings in the forest when they cut brushwood for building shelters and for fuel (1): human impact on the temperate forest was small. But 7,000 years ago in Europe, 6,000 years ago in eastern Asia and 1,000 years ago in eastern North America, the first farming communities of the temperate forest (2) began to clear larger pockets of forest to provide land for crops and timber for houses and tools.

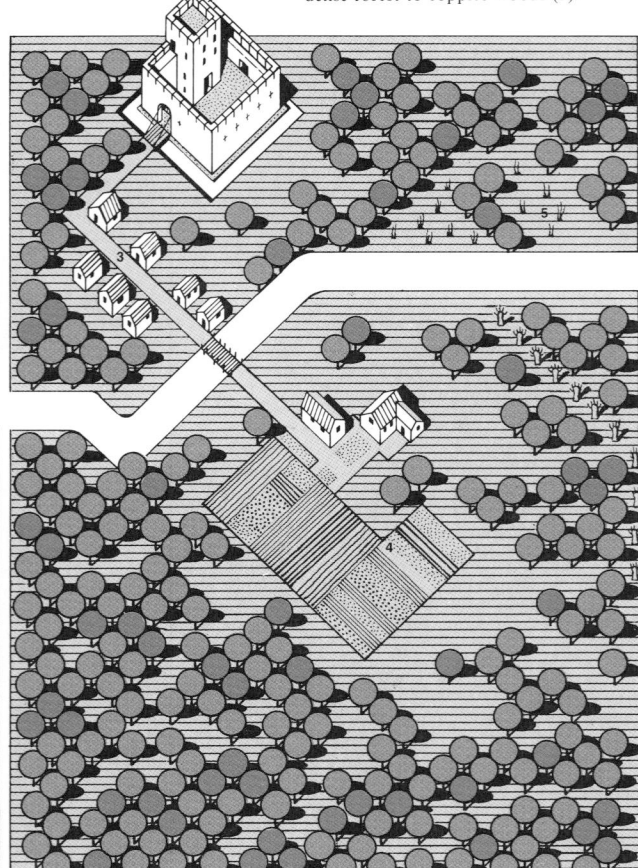

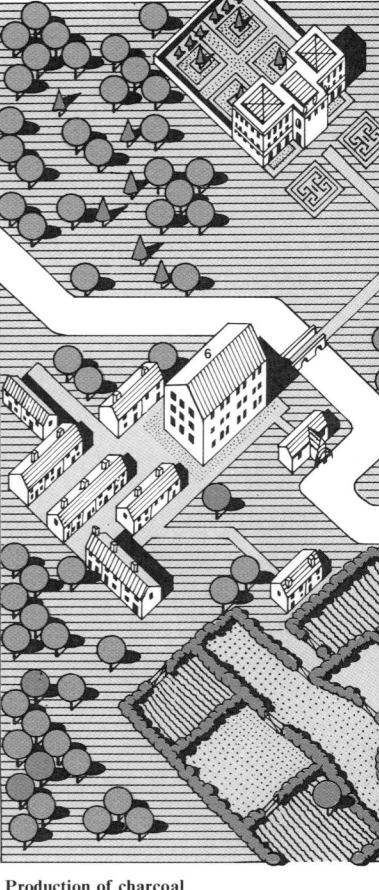

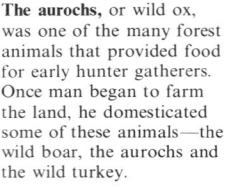
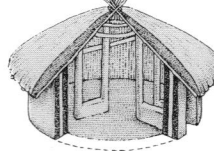

The aurochs, or wild ox, was one of the many forest animals that provided food for early hunter gatherers. Once man began to farm the land, he domesticated some of these animals—the wild boar, the aurochs and the wild turkey.

The dwellings of the late Neolithic Chinese were relatively sophisticated, reflecting an increasingly settled way of life that was soon to alter the landscape as forests were felled to provide building materials and land to plant crops.

The fortified villages and the farms of the Eastern Woodland Indians were set in semipermanent clearings cut in the North American forest. Before European settlement, however, human populations were small and deforestation was negligible.

Grain harvesting is depicted in a Chinese tomb image. By the 1st century AD, China contained nearly 60 million people, and agriculture, along with stock raising and metal mining, was drastically depleting the tree cover.

Coppicing and pollarding allowed continual cropping of forests. Branches were cut from trees, the bases of which were left to regrow shoots. This technique reduced the density of tree cover, encouraging a richer growth of ground plants.

Coppicing

Pollarding

Production of charcoal (below), which was a basic raw material for smelting in early industrial times, was responsible for much deforestation of the land.

Human interference with the forests goes back deep into prehistory. There is evidence that fire was used to stampede hunted animals in southern Europe as long as 400,000 years ago. Human populations, while they remained small, had only a slight effect on the vast stretches of primeval forest. Even so, hunting practices and the use of fire to clear land reduced some of the forests of Europe and Asia even before the invention of agriculture. In the New World, too, Eastern Woodland Indians had already affected the North American forests, and early Maori hunters had burned much of the tree cover of New Zealand by the time Europeans arrived.

Nevertheless it was the development of agriculture in Neolithic (New Stone Age) times that had the first really destructive effect on the temperate forests. Clearings were made for crops and the felled trees provided fuel and building material for the new communities. Large forest animals suffered as well, some (such as deer) being hunted for food and others (such as wolves) because they threatened grazing animals. But it was the population increase resulting from the new, settled way of life that caused the extension of man-made cropland deep into former forests.

With man's development of metals, more forests were destroyed: wood and charcoal were used for smelting and the new iron tools made tree clearance easier and more thorough. Firing of forests was also a familiar military ploy, used by such warriors as the Romans.

Medieval woodlands
By medieval times, large tracts of forest had been cleared in Europe and in the Far East, although in the former area there remained extensive royal hunting forest reserves. Local woodlands were carefully managed to serve the needs of the community; the techniques used included pollarding and coppicing.

Pollarding involved the cropping of main branches at a certain height above ground. In coppicing, the "coppice with standards" method was used to harvest the smaller species, such as hazel and hornbeam, whereas the standards (such as oaks) were cut on a longer rotation of 100 years or so. Alternatively, the oak itself could be part of the coppice crop, its stems being cut near ground level so that shoots arose from the stump, to be cut 10 to 20 years later. For local communities, industries and cities, forests provided a variety of materials for building, tanning and fencing, as well as dye-stuffs, charcoal and domestic fuel.

The growth of the iron and shipbuilding industries in the sixteenth century devastated so much woodland and forest that in many regions good timber became scarce and had to be imported from considerable distances. The pressure on woodland continued until the production of coke and cheap coal brought some relaxation, but by the early twentieth century the coppice system had broken down and management of Europe's woodlands had largely been abandoned. In Europe the poor state of the deciduous forests was further worsened by two world wars. Many countries have since set up organizations with the specific task of building reserves of timber. Economic pressures, however, have led to the planting mainly of quick-growing conifers, rather than typical trees of the temperate deciduous forest.

New World forests
The migrants who settled in the New World were the descendants of the people who had largely destroyed the forests of Europe. Confronted by the temperate deciduous forests of eastern North America, they virtually continued where they had left off. Tracts were cleared to create arable and range land and to provide the massive amounts of timber needed for the colonization, industrialization and urbanization of North America. With the opening of the prairie lands for agriculture, however,

Disturbance to the natural vegetation has occurred throughout the temperate forest zone. Exploitation of this biome's greatest resource, its agricultural potential, has been one of the major causes of deforestation. The only forests that have escaped major disturbance are in remote areas, too rocky or too steep for cultivation. Today, intensive farming is still a major economic activity of the temperate forest regions. But farmland is not the only important resource to have disturbed the forests. Mining for key minerals such as copper, iron and coal, all of which made possible the development of Western and Chinese civilization, has also contributed to destruction of the forest cover. For centuries the forests provided man with food, fuel and materials, but, ironically, it has been the removal of the forest that has enabled man to exploit the most important of these regions' resources.

THE CHANGING LANDSCAPE

Mankind has been occupying the temperate forest regions for many thousands of years, at first with little effect on the natural forest ecology. But during the last 2,000 years human activity has destroyed the original tree cover at an accelerating pace. As populations increased and economies developed —at different rates in the three major regions— forests disappeared to be replaced by farms, cities, industries and communications networks. Today, scarcely any of the original forest cover remains.

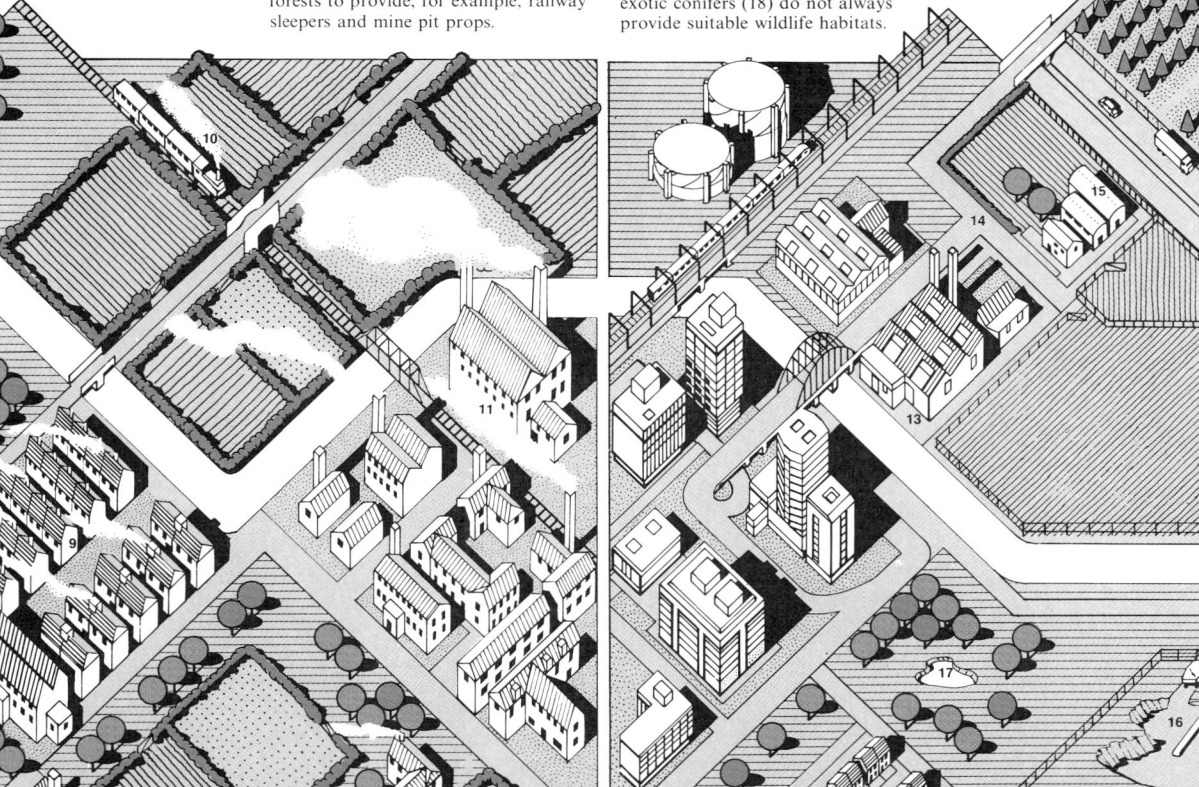

THE 19TH CENTURY
The Industrial Revolution developed in Europe and the New World, large towns and cities sprang up (9), pushing back the woodlands and forests still farther. This process was aided by the spreading network of railroads (10). Coke, iron and other minerals were replacing timber products as raw materials for growing industries (11), but demands were still made on the forests to provide, for example, railway sleepers and mine pit props.

FORESTS TODAY
The 20th century has seen an increasing trend towards urbanization in areas that were once temperate forest. Housing complexes (12) and new factory sites (13) cover large areas, while roadbuilding (14), industrial agriculture (15) and open-cast mining (16) destroy remaining woodland. Leisure areas (17) and nature reserves protect some woods, but plantations of exotic conifers (18) do not always provide suitable wildlife habitats.

Early pioneers in the USA (below) transformed forestland as they moved west. By 1830 most of the eastern forests had been felled for settlement.

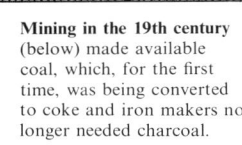

Mining in the 19th century (below) made available coal, which, for the first time, was being converted to coke and iron makers no longer needed charcoal.

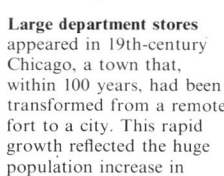

Large department stores appeared in 19th-century Chicago, a town that, within 100 years, had been transformed from a remote fort to a city. This rapid growth reflected the huge population increase in many 19th-century towns.

A reafforestation scheme (below) was set up in China in 1950 to replant areas that lost their original forest cover many centuries ago. Similar projects are under way in many other temperate forest regions.

The European wood bison has escaped extinction because one herd of the animals has lived, for centuries, in a royal hunting reserve. Today, wildlife parks throughout temperate regions protect endangered forest species.

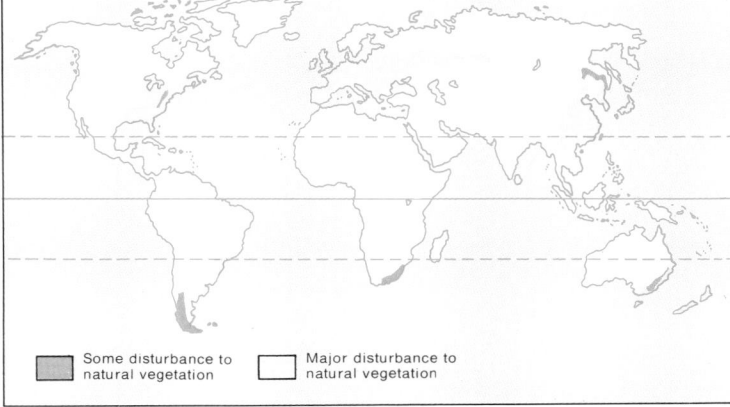

Some disturbance to natural vegetation

Major disturbance to natural vegetation

the pressures shifted, some of the east coast deciduous forest grew up again, and it is possible that parts of the eastern USA may have nearly as much forest cover now as when the settlers first arrived. Nevertheless, other areas of forestland have been destroyed in recent decades by strip mining and the creation of a vast road and rail network. In the southern hemisphere, especially in the last 200 years, the temperate rainforests of Australia and New Zealand have been subjected to much the same pattern of events, although on a smaller and somewhat less devastating scale.

Conservation
Today the general need to preserve and extend the woodlands is clearly recognized, but great uncertainty exists about their future. The demand for hardwoods for veneers, quality papermaking and furniture still exceeds supply. Oak is still the preferred material for some types of boat building and, especially in Europe, for joinery work. But one of the major difficulties with forestry as a land use is forecasting future trends within the industry, largely as a result of the long-term nature of the crop—hardwood trees planted today will not yield their timber until well into the next century. Government tax policies can be all important in deciding whether the majority of woodlands are, or will

continue to be, sound economic investments.
Temperate forests and woodlands still exist in sizeable quantities in central Europe and the USA, but many of today's plots, particularly in western Europe, are far too small for efficient conservation of plant and animal life, and are isolated from other woods. As a result, successful breeding and exchange of genetic material is very difficult, especially when modern agriculture is rapidly destroying the linking corridors of hedgerows. The use of woodlands for recreation is also presenting considerable problems. Controlling agencies have been formed to cope with leisure demands, and a start has been made in the multiple use of forests for recreation, conservation and timber felling, but progress still needs to be made in harmonizing these potentially conflicting interests. Meanwhile, natural expanses of woodland and forest are still being lost to agricultural and urban expansion and to plantations of nonnative conifers.
Temperate forests are a biologically efficient form of land use. In terms of biomass—the amount of living material (animal and plant) in any one area—they could still play an important role in the provision of food, materials and even renewable energy. Thus on scientific, economic and aesthetic grounds a strong case can be made for immediate conservation measures.

Mediterranean Regions

Forests of evergreen trees once covered much of the Mediterranean regions. They flourished in spite of the hot, rainless summer months – as the original plant life, they had evolved to survive such harsh conditions. Man, however, has proved to be a greater threat than the climate. He introduced domestic animals and cleared the land to grow crops; the natural vegetation was burned, browsed and plowed into nonexistence. Man's activities left behind tracts of impoverished soil which rapidly became scrubland. Today, scrub is the most typical vegetation in all the Mediterranean climate zones throughout the world.

CONVERGENCE
Isolated from each other by enormous areas of land and ocean, regions with a Mediterranean type of climate rarely have any plant species in common. But, by a process known as "convergent evolution," the plant communities in each of these areas have produced remarkably similar responses to their similar environments. This can be seen in the conifer communities, the broad-leaved evergreen trees, and in the various hardy shrubs and ground plants typical of each of the regions.

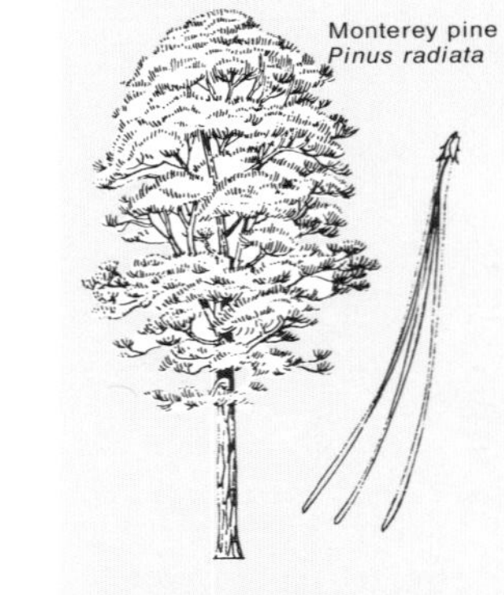

Monterey pine
Pinus radiata

California's Monterey pine and other Mediterranean conifers—South African podocarps and Chile pines, for example—have needle-shaped leaves that prevent rapid loss of water from such trees during drought.

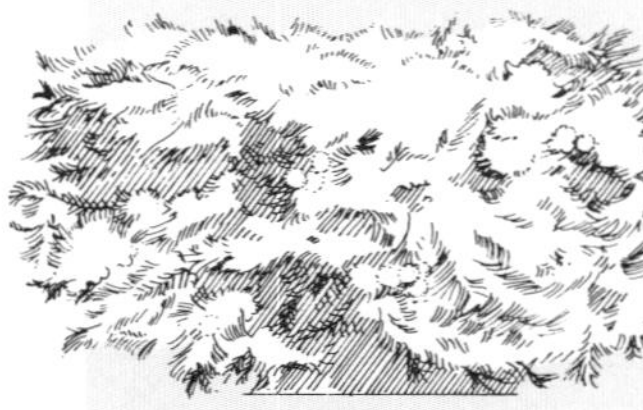

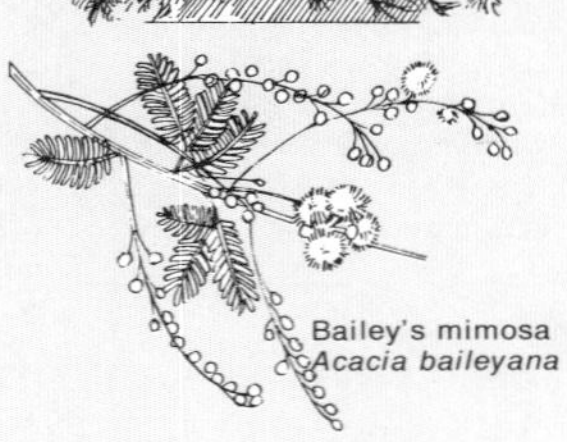

Bailey's mimosa
Acacia baileyana

Nonconiferous evergreens such as Australia's acacias and eucalypts, Chile's *quillajas* and California's evergreen oaks are typical Mediterranean trees. Their leathery leaves limit summer moisture loss.

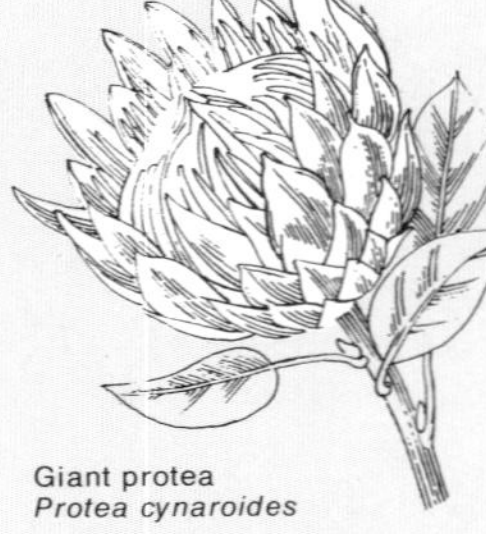

Giant protea
Protea cynaroides

Shrubs and ground plants show various adaptations to drought. South African proteas and Europe's laurel have thick evergreen leaves. Narrow leaves and water-storing roots are other common adaptations.

Long, hot, dry summers and warm, moist winters form the seasonal rhythm of the "Mediterranean" year. This climatic pattern can be found in small areas of nearly every continent in the world, typically on the western side of landmasses and in the mild, temperate latitudes. North America's "Mediterranean" is in California, South America's occurs in Chile and Africa's lies at the southern tip of Cape Province. Australia has two small "Mediterranean" areas, one on the southern coast and one on the western. Europe's Mediterranean region, which has given its name to this climate, covers much of the southern part of the continent and extends into northern Africa.

Wherever Mediterranean conditions prevail, the native plant life has adapted to survive the scanty annual rainfall and the long summer droughts. Some species have developed deep root systems that can tap low summer water tables, and many of the ground plants—such as bulbs and aromatic herbs—grow vigorously only in early summer while rain still moistens the soil. But it is the broad-leaved evergreens with their drought-resistant leaves that are the most typical of the Mediterranean areas.

This natural pattern of vegetation has been drastically altered by man. In southern Europe in particular, almost all the original evergreen forests have long since been destroyed and thickets of fast-growing, tough scrub plants have grown up in their place. This scrub, which once probably covered only small areas, is now so widespread that it is considered the most typically Mediterranean of all kinds of vegetation. It is the *maquis* of France, the *macchia* of Italy and the *mattoral* of Spain. A similar type of vegetation (although containing different species) can also be found in South Africa's fynbos, in California's chapparal, and in Australia's tracts of natural mallee scrub.

Classical land use
Southern Europe, with its long history of human settlement, farming and pastoralism, is the most altered of all the Mediterranean regions. Over the centuries vast tracts of original vegetation have been removed, either by farmers (for crop growing) or by grazing animals. And, particularly on the steep slopes and rocky outcrops, this has resulted in extensive deterioration and erosion of the soil. Agriculture generally has less serious effects upon the vegetation than has animal grazing. Mankind has learned, over many hundreds of years, which are the most suitable crops for the various soils, terrain and climatic conditions of the region. The Mediterranean "triad" of wheat on the lowlands and olives and vines on the hills has been a successful combination since Classical times.

Pastoral plundering of the land, however, has more serious consequences. The virtually omnivorous goat is particularly damaging and can strip a whole forest of its foliage, bark, shrubs, ground plants and grass. After such an assault the vegetation rarely returns to its former condition; normally, a scrubby growth of kermes oak and shrubs springs up to form a typical maquis-type vegetation.

The rise and fall of each great Mediterranean civilization has seen forests destroyed in one area after another. The Greek colonization of southern Italy was provoked by deforestation and soil erosion in Attica. The Romans extended clearance north to the Po valley and into eastern Tunisia. From the seventh century onwards, Muslims made great inroads into the forests of North Africa as well as southern and eastern Spain; and in the north of Spain and southern France, medieval monks cleared forested valleys. During the seventeenth and eighteenth centuries large areas of Provence and Italy were cleared to plant vines and this process continued in the 1800s, when the great wine-producing areas of Languedoc and Algeria were established. During this time the iron industries of Spain and northern Italy, with their growing need for charcoal, were adding to the destruction. Recent reafforestation efforts have been puny compared to past degradation.

Protected species
But throughout this history of forest removal some tree species have been protected. These have been the natural tree crops that have, at times, supported complete peasant economies. The chestnut forests of Corsica, for example, sustained a large rural population until this century; the chestnuts provided flour for bread and fodder for pigs. In Portugal and Sardinia the cork-oak forests are still important today.

It is the olive, however, symbol of peace and of New Testament landscapes, that is the Mediterranean's most characteristic tree crop. Of all the Mediterranean plants, it is the most perfectly adapted to its environment, with its deep roots to search out scarce water and its hard, shiny leaves to conserve what it finds. In fact, the summer drought is essential to olive growers for it encourages the build-up of oil in the fruit. Paradoxically, however, the olive—like the vine, the fig and many other "Mediterranean" crops—did not originate in the Mediterranean but was introduced from Asia Minor.

In spite of massive destruction of the natural landscape, mankind has learned many valuable lessons during his occupation of this region. Ideas that were to become important in laying the foundations of sound land management policy were developed in the Mediterranean area. Hillside terracing, irrigation, crop rotation and manuring were all, from necessity, practiced from early times. The flourishing agricultural industries of the world's other Mediterranean regions—the wine industry of California, the vast soft-fruit plantations of Australia and the citrus industry of South Africa—all owe a considerable debt to the generations of farmers who learned to exploit the red soils of the Mediterranean basin.

The Mediterranean regions occur between the latitudes 30° and 40°, on the western and southwestern sides of the continents. These areas are affected in summer by the high-pressure systems of nearby desert regions, and in winter by wet, low-pressure systems brought in from the oceans and over the land by the prevailing Westerlies. This distinct seasonal shifting of major influences on the climate produces the hot, waterless summers and warm, moist, sometimes stormy winters typical of the Mediterranean climate.

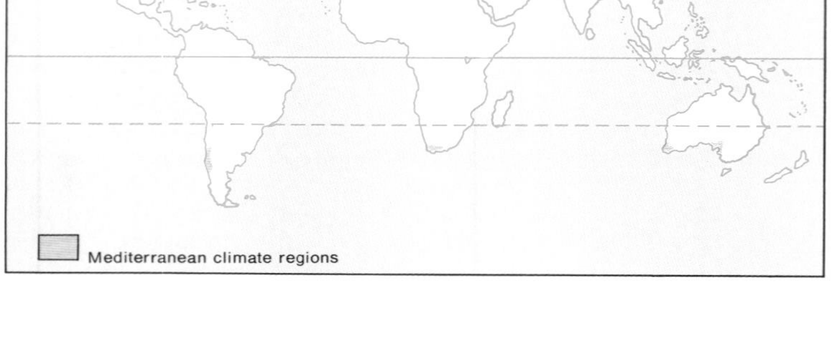

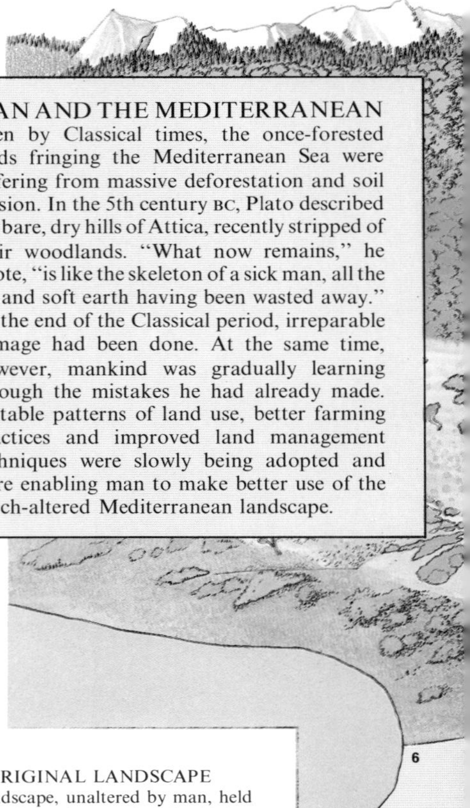

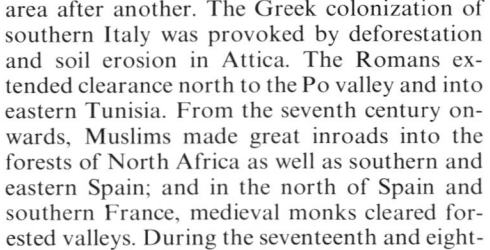

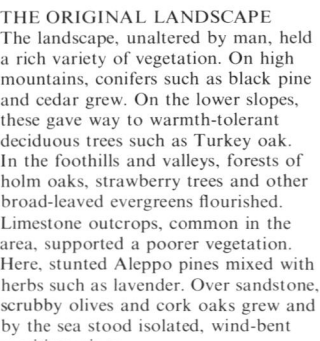

MAN AND THE MEDITERRANEAN
Even by Classical times, the once-forested lands fringing the Mediterranean Sea were suffering from massive deforestation and soil erosion. In the 5th century BC, Plato described the bare, dry hills of Attica, recently stripped of their woodlands. "What now remains," he wrote, "is like the skeleton of a sick man, all the fat and soft earth having been wasted away." By the end of the Classical period, irreparable damage had been done. At the same time, however, mankind was gradually learning through the mistakes he had already made. Suitable patterns of land use, better farming practices and improved land management techniques were slowly being adopted and were enabling man to make better use of the much-altered Mediterranean landscape.

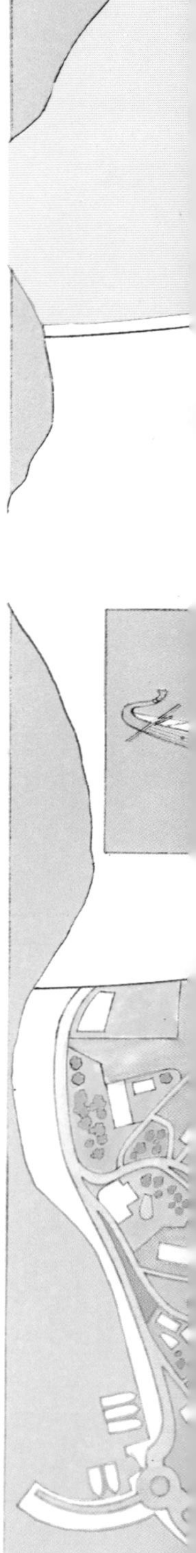

THE ORIGINAL LANDSCAPE
The landscape, unaltered by man, held a rich variety of vegetation. On high mountains, conifers such as black pine and cedar grew. On the lower slopes, these gave way to warmth-tolerant deciduous trees such as Turkey oak. In the foothills and valleys, forests of holm oaks, strawberry trees and other broad-leaved evergreens flourished. Limestone outcrops, common in the area, supported a poorer vegetation. Here, stunted Aleppo pines mixed with herbs such as lavender. Over sandstone, scrubby olives and cork oaks grew and by the sea stood isolated, wind-bent maritime pines.

THE CLASSICAL AGE
Civilizations followed one after another, each taking its toll of the environment. In the mountains, forests were felled, the tall, straight conifers sought after by shipbuilders such as the Phoenicians, and deciduous hardwood timber in demand for charcoal to fuel growing industries. Some replanting did take place, especially as groves of crop trees such as chestnuts. Below in the foothills, agriculture and the grazing of animals had destroyed vast areas of natural forest. Terracing techniques, however, helped to stop soil erosion, and irrigation reached the height of its Classical art with Roman aqueducts and canals. Tree crops, such as olives, were found best suited to the thin hill soils. On the plains, especially where alluvial soils had been deposited, cereals were grown. Meanwhile, towns sprang up and the coastline became densely populated as ships and ports were built and sea trade grew. Exotic food plants, such as pomegranate trees, citron trees and vines, were brought into the region by merchant seamen.

THE MEDITERRANEAN TODAY
The region today bears the scars of many centuries of human activity. The once-forested mountains will never return to their former state, although some regrowth and some replanting (mostly with introduced tree species) has occurred. As in Classical times, hillsides are terraced and planted with vines and fruit trees. But with modern irrigation and fertilizing, land is less readily exhausted and abandoned now. On the plains, native shrubs, such as lavender, are commercially cultivated and grain is widely grown, particularly durum wheat used for making pasta. Cork oaks are planted, especially over dry sandstone areas, but indigenous vegetation has not suffered by this—scrubby woodland is more widespread than ever and can be found throughout the landscape. Perhaps the single most important part of the Mediterranean basin today is the coastline, for this has produced the region's major modern industry—tourism.

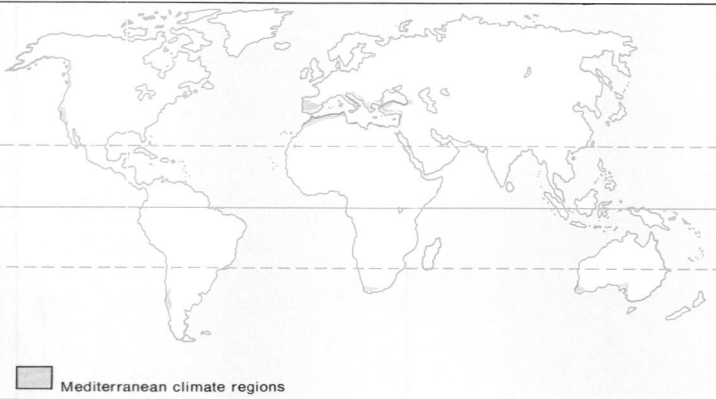

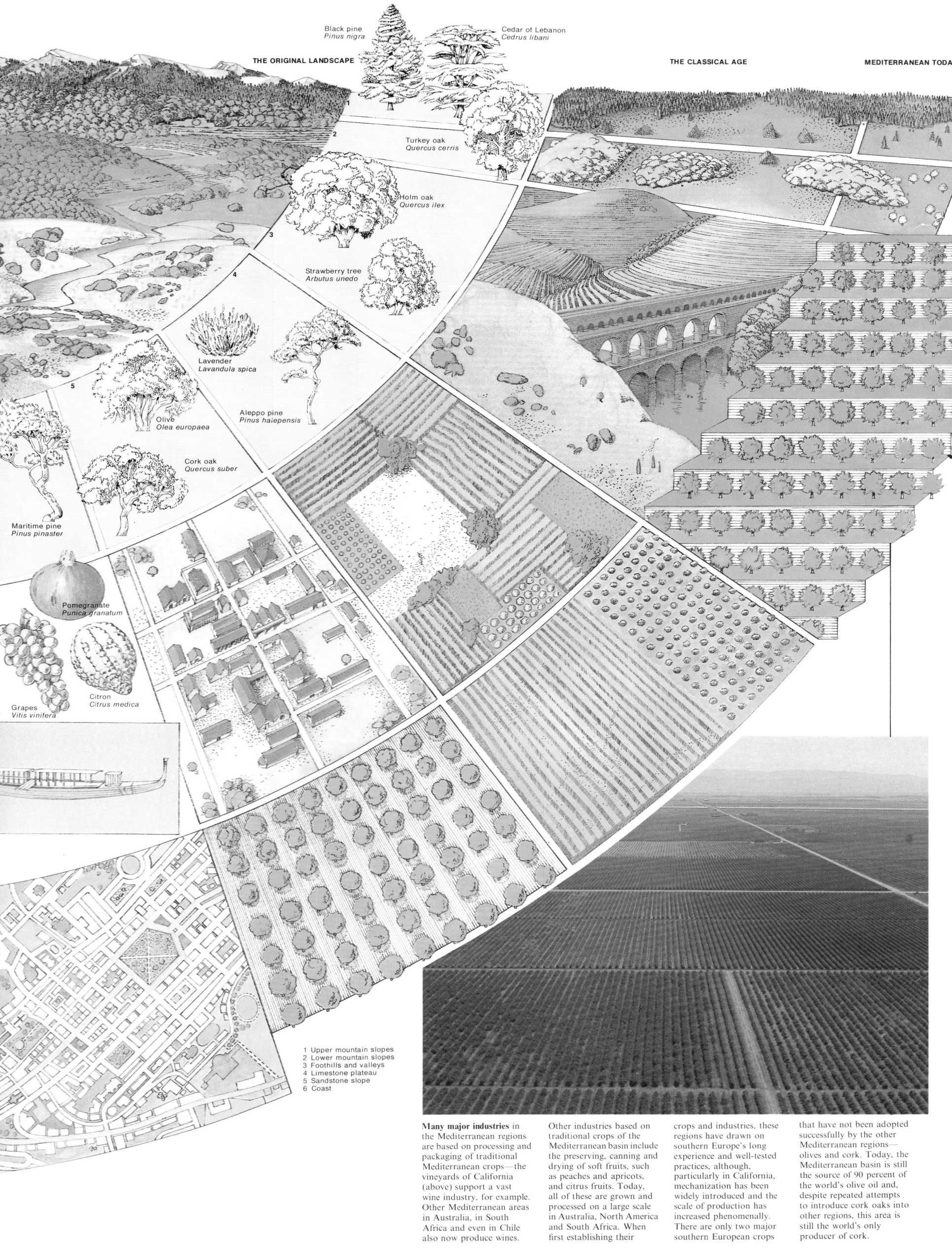

Black pine
Pinus nigra

Cedar of Lebanon
Cedrus libani

Turkey oak
Quercus cerris

Holm oak
Quercus ilex

Strawberry tree
Arbutus unedo

Lavender
Lavandula spica

Aleppo pine
Pinus halepensis

Olive
Olea europaea

Cork oak
Quercus suber

Maritime pine
Pinus pinaster

Pomegranate
Punica granatum

Citron
Citrus medica

Grapes
Vitis vinifera

1 Upper mountain slopes
2 Lower mountain slopes
3 Foothills and valleys
4 Limestone plateau
5 Sandstone slope
6 Coast

Many major industries in the Mediterranean regions are based on processing and packaging of traditional Mediterranean crops—the vineyards of California (above) support a vast wine industry, for example. Other Mediterranean areas in Australia, in South Africa and even in Chile also now produce wines.

Other industries based on traditional crops of the Mediterranean basin include the preserving, canning and drying of soft fruits, such as peaches and apricots, and citrus fruits. Today, all of these are grown and processed on a large scale in Australia, North America and South Africa. When first establishing their

crops and industries, these regions have drawn on southern Europe's long experience and well-tested practices, although, particularly in California, mechanization has been widely introduced and the scale of production has increased phenomenally. There are only two major southern European crops

that have not been adopted successfully by the other Mediterranean regions— olives and cork. Today, the Mediterranean basin is still the source of 90 percent of the world's olive oil and, despite repeated attempts to introduce cork oaks into other regions, this area is still the world's only producer of cork.

Temperate Grasslands

Compared with other flowering plants, grasses are newcomers to the Earth. They appeared only 60 million years ago, but since then they have proved to be an extremely successful family of plants. Today, the grasses dominate large areas of the world's natural vegetation and play a vital part in the intricate balance of plant and animal life in these regions. In spite of the inroads made by man, vast stretches of original grassland still cover the interiors of the North American and Eurasian landmasses.

The prairies of North America and the steppes of Eurasia extend far into the interiors of the northern continents. These are the best known and the most extensive of the world's temperate grasslands. The southern hemisphere, however, has examples in the veld of South Africa and the pampas of South America. Extensive grasslands also occur in southern Australia, although these are sometimes described as semiarid scrub because of the high average temperatures and the prolonged droughts in the region.

Temperate grasslands probably developed wherever the rainfall was too low to support forest and too high to result in semiarid regions, conditions found typically in the interiors of large continents. Continental interiors tend to be somewhat drier than coastal regions, but they are also characterized by extreme changes in temperature from one season to the next. In the North American grasslands, for example, winter temperatures may fall well below freezing whereas summer temperatures of 38°C (100°F) are not unusual. And these sharp fluctuations in seasonal temperature greatly influence how much of the rainfall is made available to plants. In summer particularly, when most of the rain falls, high temperatures, strong winds and lack of protective tree cover cause much of the moisture to evaporate before it can be absorbed into the soil.

Climatic conditions are not the only factor responsible for the distribution and form of the temperate grasslands. There are many pointers that indicate the importance of fire in determining their continuing existence and their extent. Natural fires, caused by lightning and fueled by the dry summer grasses, have always been a feature of these regions, but more recently, man-made fires have been crucial in fixing the boundary between forest and grassland.

Trees and shrubs frequently invade the margins of grasslands, but whenever there is a fire few of them survive. Grasses, however, have certain characteristics that enable them to withstand the potentially destructive impact of fire. The growing point of grasses is at the base of the leaves, close to the ground, and so destruction of the leaves above this point does not interrupt growth—in fact it may stimulate it. These same characteristics also serve to protect grasses from destruction by grazing animals. The large animals of these lands, such as the North American bison and the Eurasian horse, are able to crop the grasses without permanently damaging their food supply.

Grazers and predators

Large migrating herbivores with a strong herd instinct characterize one of the major types of temperate grassland animal. In the North American grasslands the bison (which may have numbered 60 million before being virtually exterminated by settlers) and the antelope-like pronghorn were the major examples of large herbivores. In Eurasia large herds of saiga antelopes, wild horses and asses at one time roamed the steppes, although they too have suffered from human activities, as has South America's largest grassland herd animal, the pampas deer. As these herds of grazing animals have been reduced, so have the carnivorous animals of the grasslands that preyed upon them. At one time, however, these predators played an important part in protecting the grasslands by continually keeping the numbers of grazing herd animals in check.

Saiga
Saiga tatarica

American bison
Bison bison

European hare
Lepus europaeus

Guanaco
Lama guanicoe

Springhaas
Pedetes cafer

RUNNING AND LEAPING HERBIVORES

Maned wolf
Chrysocyon brachyurus

Plains wolf
Canis lupus nubilus

Coyote
Canis latrans

RUNNING CARNIVORES

Prairie dog
Cynomys ludovicianus

European souslik
Citellus citellus

Viscacha
Lagostomus maximus

Marsupial mole
Notoryctes typhlops

SMALL BURROWING ANIMALS

Pampas cat
Lynchailurus pajeros

Black-footed ferret
Mustela nigripes

Marbled polecat
Vormela peregusna

Gopher snake
Pituophis melanoleucus

SMALL CARNIVORES

The dominant native species of grass varies from area to area. In the undisturbed prairies, for example, tall bluestem and Indian grass grow in the east and in wet central lowlands and mix with switch grass in drier parts. Farther west and on high land in the east, little bluestem and also western wheatgrass grow. June grass grows in the north, and buffalo grass and blue grama grow farthest west.

Many flowering herbs grow in the grasslands and have developed resistance to summer droughts: Russian tarragon has narrow leaves to help prevent moisture evaporation; rhizomes and bulbs, such as Eurasia's iris and anemone, store water in their specialized "root" systems.

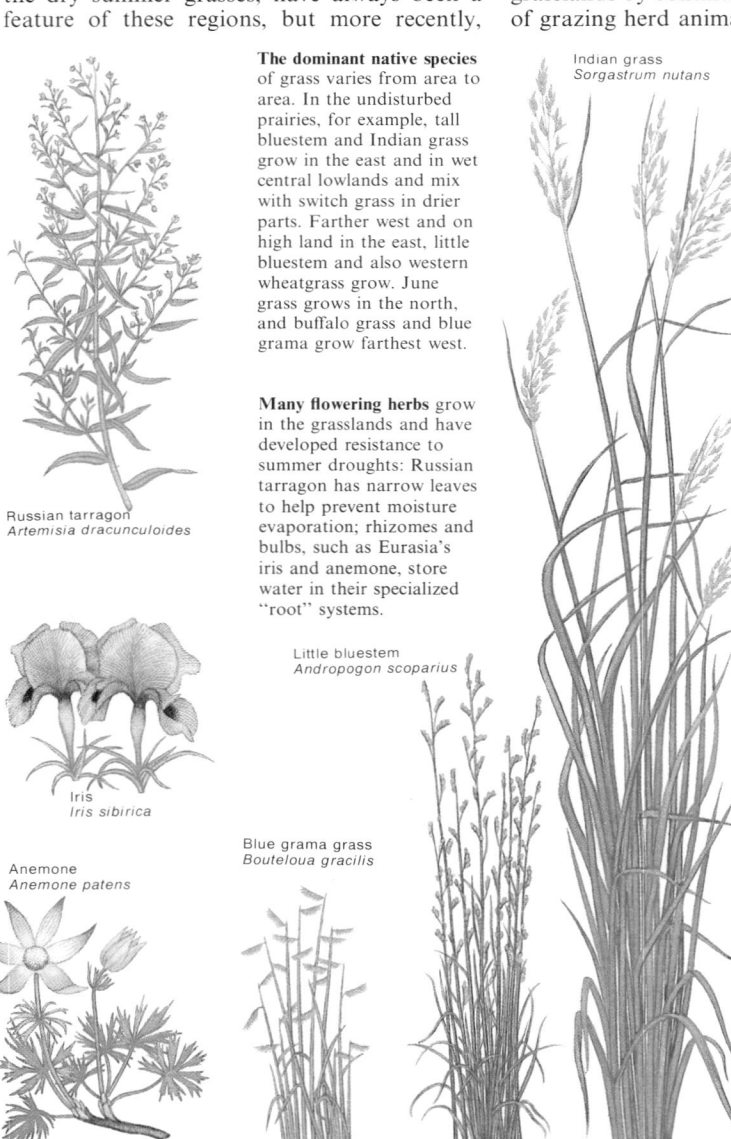

Russian tarragon
Artemisia dracunculoides

Iris
Iris sibirica

Anemone
Anemone patens

Indian grass
Sorgastrum nutans

Little bluestem
Andropogon scoparius

Blue grama grass
Bouteloua gracilis

The natural distribution of the temperate grasslands is dictated mainly by rainfall: most occur in continental interiors where there is too little rain for forest but enough to prevent desert from forming. Between these limits the large range in rainfall allows three main types of grassland: tall grass in wetter areas, mid-grass, and short grass in drier parts. The largest grasslands exist in North America, Eurasia, South America, in Australia's Murray–Darling river basin and on the South African plateau.

Short-grass regions | Mid-grass regions | Tall-grass regions

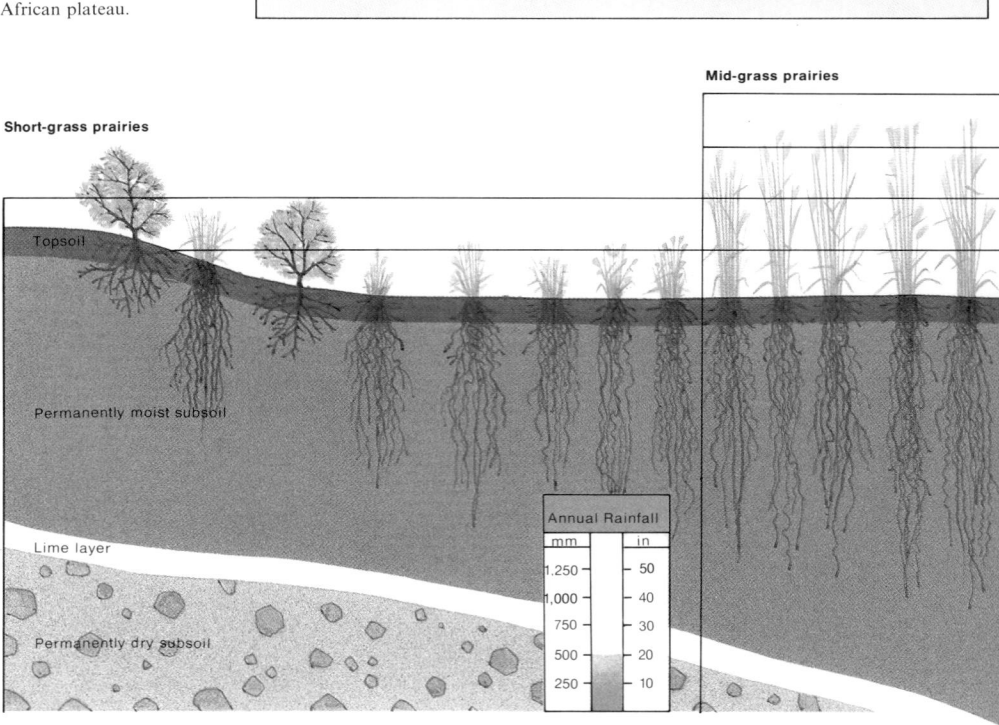

Short-grass prairies

Mid-grass prairies

Topsoil

Permanently moist subsoil

Lime layer

Permanently dry subsoil

Annual Rainfall

mm	in
1,250	50
1,000	40
750	30
500	20
250	10

GRASSLAND ADAPTATION

Animals of these regions have had to adapt to a difficult environment: vast, treeless expanses of grass offer little protection from harsh weather or predators. Different animals have found various answers to the problem and a clearly defined pattern of these adaptations can be traced throughout the grasslands.

Running and leaping herbivores survive because of their ability to move faster than a pursuer. The larger animals such as the Eurasian saiga, North America's bison and pronghorn and the guanaco of South America are runners. The leaping herbivores are usually smaller creatures that escape danger by bounding away to boltholes. They include the European hare and the African springhaas.

Running carnivores follow, and prey on, running and leaping herbivores. These animals, such as the coyote and the now extinct plains wolf of North America, and South America's maned wolf, also depend on speed—to enable them to catch their prey.

Small burrowing animals hide from predators by digging under the ground. Some, such as Australia's marsupial mole, spend most of their lives below ground. Others, such as the European souslik, South America's viscacha and North America's prairie dog, live and sleep under the ground but come to the surface to find food.

Small carnivores concentrate on the burrowers as their main source of food. They either, like the pampas cat, rely on surprise attack of their prey, or, like Eurasia's marbled polecat and the grasslands' many kinds of snake, depend on their long, lithe shape to follow creatures into their burrows.

Two distinctive types of grassland bird can be distinguished: the sky birds, which spend long periods of time on the wing, and the ground birds.

Birds of the sky include songbirds such as the skylark which, having no perch from which to proclaim its territory, sings in the sky, and birds of prey such as Eurasia's tawny eagle and North America's red-tailed hawk and prairie falcon, which ride the thermals scanning the ground for their prey.

Ground birds rarely take to the wing, although none has actually lost the ability to fly when necessary. They include birds such as the New World sage grouse and burrowing owl (which lives below ground in abandoned prairie dog burrows), the black grouse of Eurasia and songbirds such as North America's meadowlark.

Insects and other invertebrates have developed many different survival techniques. Some use camouflage: the praying mantis resembles a leaf bud and the tumble bug is the color of the dark grassland soil. Grasshoppers are miniature leaping herbivores and earthworms are small-scale versions of the grassland burrowers.

Skylark
Alauda arvensis

Red-tailed hawk
Buteo jamaicensis

Tawny eagle
Aquila rapax

Prairie falcon
Falco mexicanus

BIRDS OF THE SKY

Western meadowlark
Sturnella neglecta

Burrowing owl
Speotyto cunicularia

Sage grouse
Centrocercus urophasianus

Black grouse
Lyurus tetrix

GROUND BIRDS

Tumble bug
Canthonlaevis drury

Praying mantis
Mantis religiosa

Lubber grasshopper
Romalea microptera

INSECTS AND OTHER INVERTEBRATES

Common earthworm
Lumbricus terrestris

Another major type of animal found in the temperate grasslands, and one that is better adapted to survive man's activities, is the small, burrowing animal, for example the prairie dog and the gopher of North America, the viscacha of South America and the little ground squirrel known as the souslik in Eurasia.

Unlike the large herd animals, these creatures tend not to migrate. Many of them live together in complex, permanent, underground communities. The colonial "townships" of the prairie dog, for example, may house more than one million individuals, which each year excavate vast quantities of the grassland soil. This has considerable effect upon the structure of the soil. By bringing up earth from lower layers to the surface, these animals are responsible for changing the mineral content of certain areas of topsoil. This then encourages isolated pockets of different plant species to flourish.

A third group of grassland animals, consisting of insects and other invertebrates such as earthworms, has an even more important effect upon the soil. They live in or on the soil and play a vital role in maintaining grassland fertility. These creatures may be herbivores, carnivores or primary (first stage) decomposers (which break down such material as dead grass and animal remains). These three types of activity allow a complete range of organic matter to be processed and incorporated into the earth, where it is further broken down by the second-stage decomposers, the countless millions of soil bacteria. In this way nutrients continuously flow back to the earth and restore its fertility.

Fertile black earths

The topsoil of temperate grassland regions, therefore, contains large amounts of organic material, which is produced every year and is quickly incorporated into the soil. The low and intermittent rainfall and the protective cover of grasses mean that the topsoil undergoes little chemical leaching, a process in which minerals are removed and carried down to lower layers by rainfall percolating through the earth. The soils are thus dark in color, generally fertile and of the "black earth" type ("chernozem" in Russian) which is, at least at first, capable of producing high yields of crops.

The most suitable and most widely grown crops are, predictably, the cultivated grasses, and it is these grasses that provide more food for mankind (either directly as grain or indirectly as animal fodder) than any other source. The temperate grassland biome is therefore an important agricultural resource. Undisturbed natural grasslands, however, are also valuable resources. They need to be preserved both for the information that they can provide about how complex communities of wildlife function efficiently, and because, as a rich source of genetic material, they hold many of the answers to the major agricultural problems that probably lie ahead for the human race.

A typical cross section, based on the North American prairies, shows temperate grasslands in relation to rainfall. Annual rainfall determines the depth of the permanently moist subsoil, which in turn dictates the length to which grass roots can grow. Tall grasses have deep root systems and need a considerable depth of moist subsoil. As the rainfall decreases, they gradually give way to shorter grass species. Short grasses require less water and their shallower roots are well suited to drier regions. On dry margins, desert plants start to dominate, and on the wet margins, trees appear.

Tall-grass prairies

cm	ft
215	7
180	6
150	5
120	4
90	3
60	2
30	1
0	0

Annual Rainfall	
mm	in
1,250	50
1,000	40
750	30
500	20
250	10

Annual Rainfall	
mm	in
1,250	50
1,000	40
750	30
500	20
250	10

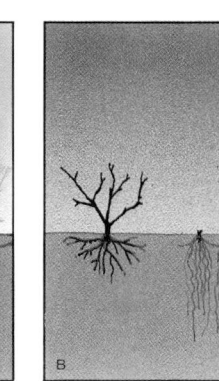
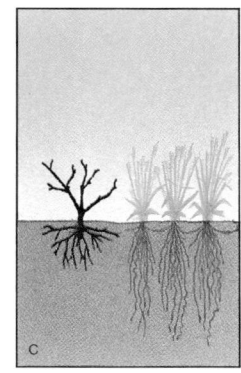
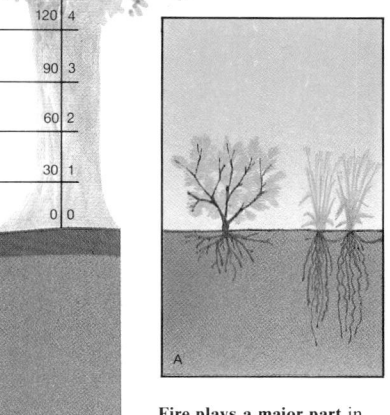

A

B

C

Fire plays a major part in fixing and maintaining the natural boundaries of the temperate grasslands, where tree saplings and shrubs are continually attempting to invade (A). Man-made fires are recent phenomena, natural fires have always occurred. In summer, low-pressure systems build up in continental interiors, causing violent electrical storms. The dry sward of summer grass is easily ignited by lightning and fire is quickly spread by wind. Shrubs and saplings are killed or badly damaged by fire, but grasses, with their growing points close to the soil, remain unharmed (B). They may even benefit from this "pruning" and grow more quickly. Some species grow new buds from their underground shoots. Removal of the main shoot may encourage growth of "tillers" (shoots growing out sideways), which then increase the spread of the grasses as they begin to invade the area left vacant by the dead, or slowly recuperating, shrubs (C).

Man and the Temperate Grasslands

The vast areas of temperate grassland lay virtually empty until the end of the eighteenth century. Over the next 125 years they were occupied by millions of people, most of them migrants from overcrowded Europe. By 1914, the grasslands had become the granaries and the stockyards of the world. Today, they are still the most important food-producing regions on Earth and their riches, properly distributed, are the world's first reserve against the possibility of a hungry future for the human race.

The great nineteenth-century migration to the grasslands proved of immense significance to the human race. It meant that, within a single century, the area of productive land available was suddenly enlarged by thousands of millions of hectares. In all of mankind's history, such a thing had never happened before.

But before the grasslands could be occupied a number of major problems had to be solved. First, in order to reach these regions it was almost always necessary to travel deep into the continental interiors, and there were few navigable rivers and no mechanized forms of transportation for early pioneers. Second, with virtually no indigenous population, newcomers had to learn by their mistakes how best to exploit the new and unfamiliar environment. Third, even if settlers succeeded in using the land, they still had to find markets for their produce.

A number of technological developments, however, that took place in the nineteenth century provided the right combination of circumstances for the opening up of the grasslands. The Industrial Revolution in Europe produced the steamship and the railway locomotive, which created both a means of travel to and from these distant parts and an internal transport system for moving produce to ports and markets. It also produced the kind of machinery needed to plow and farm the great new open spaces; it made it possible for one family to cultivate an area 50 times as large as that which most farmers had known in Europe. Industrialization also threw thousands of Europeans out of work, and therefore provided a large supply of eager migrants. And it crowded further thousands into cities, thus creating vast markets for the settlers' produce.

It was the coming together of these various circumstances that acted as the catalyst and converted, for example, the Russian penetration of the Eurasian steppes in the late eighteenth

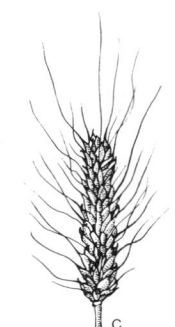
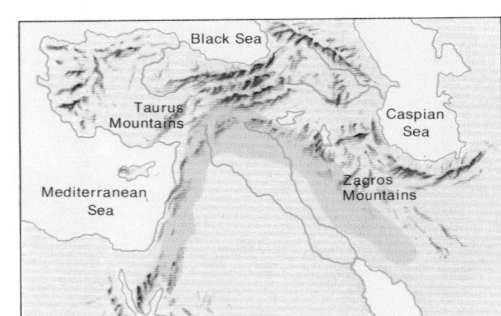

THE CRADLE OF AGRICULTURE

Stands of wild einkorn (A), emmer wheat (B) and wild barleys can be seen today in the grassy foothills that flank the Taurus and the Zagros mountains, and the uplands of northern Israel. It was in this region 10,000 years ago that the world's earliest farmers gathered seeds from these species and sowed the first crops. Wild einkorn is probably the oldest of all wheats and the parent of every modern variety—including the most important and most widely grown kind of grain in the world today, common bread wheat (C).

GRASSLAND EXPLOITATION

Today, temperate grasslands provide mankind with a superabundance of food. But the vast potential of these regions was not exploited until the mid-19th century, when mass migration by Europeans, combined with new technology, allowed full-scale development and settlement.

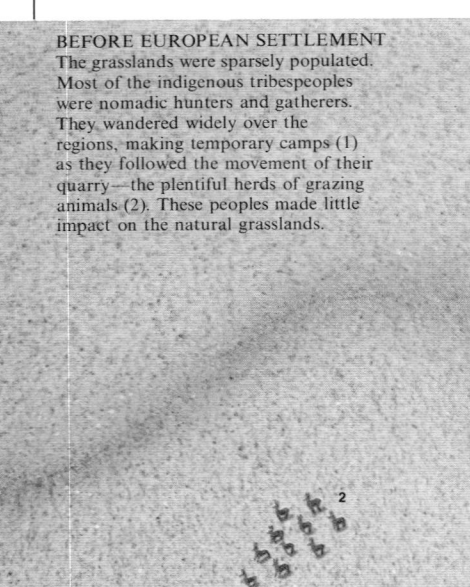

BEFORE EUROPEAN SETTLEMENT
The grasslands were sparsely populated. Most of the indigenous tribespeoples were nomadic hunters and gatherers. They wandered widely over the regions, making temporary camps (1) as they followed the movement of their quarry—the plentiful herds of grazing animals (2). These peoples made little impact on the natural grasslands.

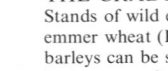

GRASSLAND SETTLERS
Early pioneers relied on animal-drawn transport (3), primitive farm tools (4) and unpredictable free-range livestock grazing (5). During the 19th century, farming became more productive: better equipment cultivated larger areas (6); barbed wire made stock raising efficient (7); railways and the telegraph improved communication (8).

Tehuelche Indians (above) adopted horses for hunting from early Spanish settlers to the pampas. In South Africa and North America, too, the introduced horse became a valued asset for grassland hunters. For people of the Eurasian steppes, for example the Mongols (right), native horses have always been culturally important.

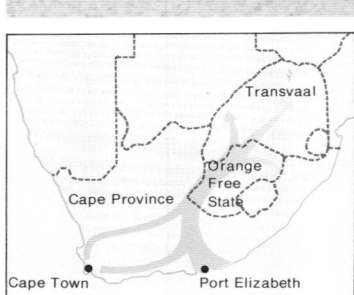

The **South African veld** was first settled by Europeans after 1836 (left). Dutch farmers (Boers), rejecting British rule of the Cape Colony, trekked north in search of new land. Moving into the Transvaal they discovered rich grassland, recently emptied of its original inhabitants, who had fled to escape the aggressive attentions of neighboring Zulus.

Vaqueros were the original cowboys (left). Tending herds of cattle for the missionaries in 18th-century California, they developed techniques and traditions that served hundreds of later cowboys working the prairie ranges. In other grassland regions, as free-range stock raising became important, similar "cowboy" professions evolved—the Australian stockman and the gaucho of South America.

century into the explosive movement of hundreds of thousands of settlers a few years later. In the USA, too, by the year 1850, settlement had reached and then rapidly crossed the Mississippi. In the Argentine, genuine colonization of the pampas had begun, in South Africa, the Boers had reached the high veld, and in Australia pioneer settlers were moving outwards from the various areas of coastal settlement into the scrub grasslands of the interior.

Farmers or ranchers?

The fundamental question posed for these settlers was whether their newly found land should be used for crops or for livestock. Most grasslands have a dry edge and a wet edge, and it was therefore sensible to use the drier parts for stock raising and the wetter parts for cultivation. But the question was complicated by the fact that most of the newcomers were cultivators, and also that the line dividing dry from wet was vague—worse, it shifted from year to year.

Early attempts to define the dividing line tended to be ignored by the settlers themselves, and they pushed the limit of cultivation into areas where plowing the soil led to its destruction. Several generations of farmers had to learn this bitter lesson, and they learned only slowly: the worst disasters on the American grasslands occurred in the 1930s and created the infamous

Dust Bowl region in the dry grasslands of the Midwest. Similarly, the Soviet Virgin Lands Program for growing cereal crops on the dry steppes was established in 1954 and is still experiencing difficulties.

Special methods are required both for farming and for ranching the grasslands successfully. Farming has to take account of the open, treeless surface, the scanty and variable rainfall and the comparatively shallow topsoil. To minimize the risk of soil erosion, farmers plant windbreaks, plow fields along the contour, and protect the soil with a covering of the previous year's stubble and by planting cover crops in rotation with cereals. Ranchers, too, have learned to live with variable rainfall. They build stock ponds, irrigate areas of fodder crops to be used as a reserve in dry years and avoid overstocking and consequent overgrazing, which destroys the quality of the grass.

Food for the world

Today, the world's principal trading supplies of cereals and meat flow from these lands, over the networks of railway which link the grasslands to mill towns, slaughter yards and ports of shipment such as Adelaide in Australia, Buenos Aires in Argentina and Montreal in Canada. Without these links to large towns, the grasslands would be of little value, for even

today their populations are sparse and the local markets are relatively insignificant.

Throughout most of the world, however, the human population continues to soar and it remains to be seen whether the grasslands can continue to supply these growing numbers with food. Undoubtedly, the output of cereals and meat can be increased, although at considerable cost in fertilizers, new crop strains, more irrigation and more machines. On the other hand, the problem at present is not mainly one of production, nor will it be in the near future. The land can produce more, but there is no point in doing so unless the yields can be made available where they are most needed.

The world's hungry people live in other regions, many of them in countries that are unable to afford imported food supplies, particularly during those years when prices are high. The major importers of temperate grassland produce are the rich industrialized nations, such as those of western Europe. Furthermore, much of the grain imported by these countries is not consumed by humans but used to feed stalled, beef-producing cattle—a highly inefficient way of using these supplies. Consequently, unless producer nations and wealthy importing nations can create a system for produce to reach those in need of it, extra output from the grasslands will be irrelevant.

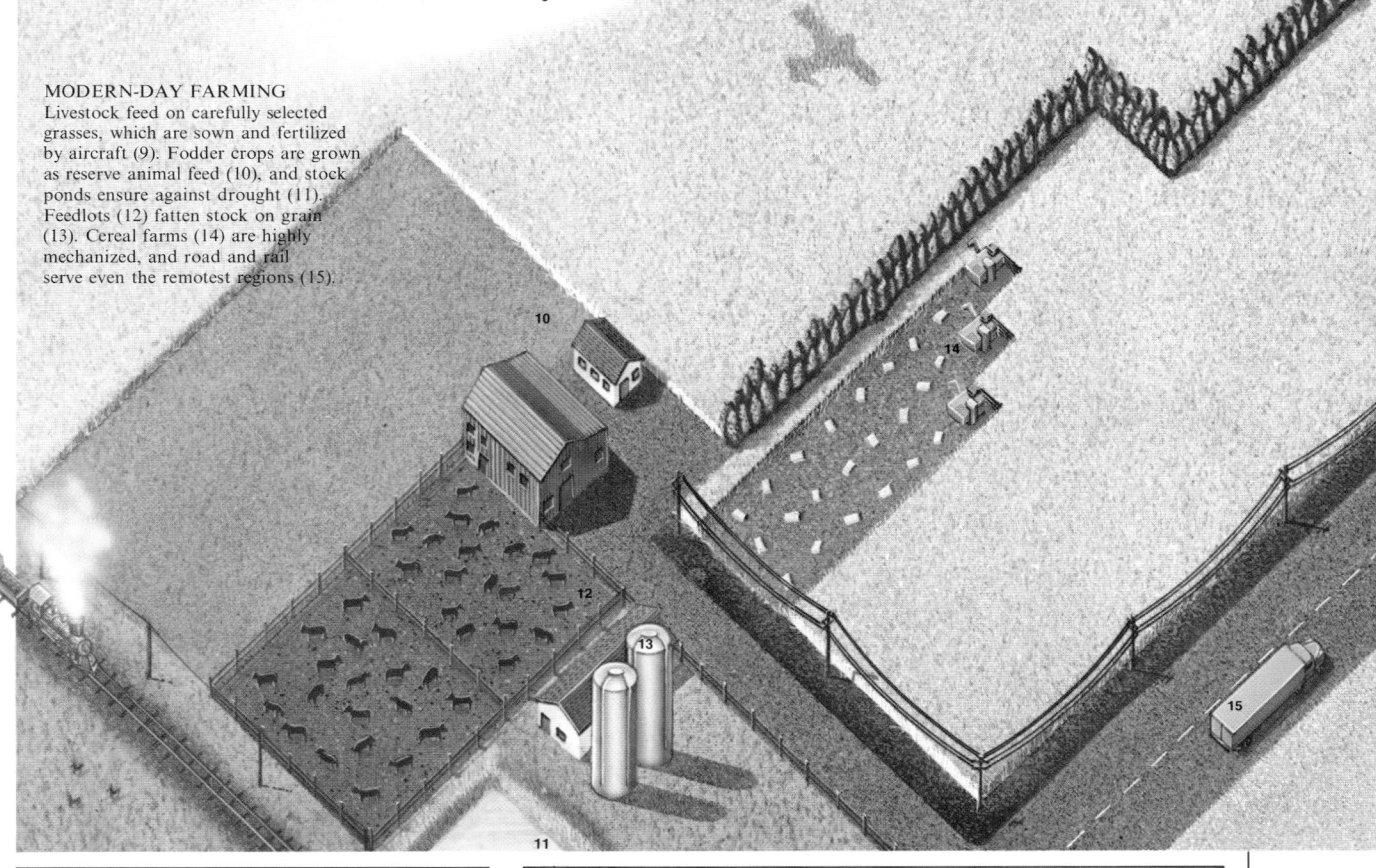

MODERN-DAY FARMING
Livestock feed on carefully selected grasses, which are sown and fertilized by aircraft (9). Fodder crops are grown as reserve animal feed (10), and stock ponds ensure against drought (11). Feedlots (12) fatten stock on grain (13). Cereal farms (14) are highly mechanized, and road and rail serve even the remotest regions (15).

The steam-driven plow (below) went through many developments to reduce its unwieldiness and heaviness. The version produced in 1858 used a traction engine and pulley wheel system. The plow was drawn back and forth between these by a power-driven cable. This design was, however, superseded by the steam tractor, which, although unsuited to small European fields, was ideal for drawing multifurrow plows across the grasslands.

Sand-smothered farms in the heart of the Dust Bowl were rapidly abandoned during the 1930s and 40s (above). This was one costly lesson that man had to learn in the process of developing the grasslands. Traditionally grazing land, the western part of the prairies was first plowed this century. Years of drought arrived, crops died and the desert encroached.

World cereal supplies flow from temperate grasslands (right). North America is the most important producing region, for although almost all nations produce grain, few can grow enough to feed their populations and even fewer have any surplus to export or hold in reserve against poor harvests. But North America, with its prairie cornfields and its small population, exports many millions of tonnes.

World grain-trading regions
- Africa
- North America
- South America
- Asia
- Western Europe
- Australia and New Zealand
- Former Soviet Union / Eastern Europe

Net exports

Net imports

Million tonnes

110
100
90
80
70
60
50
40
30
20
10
0

1934–1948   1948–1952   1960   1970   1979

0
10
20
30
40
50
60

Deserts

Much of the Earth's land surface is so short of water that it is defined as desert. Not all deserts are hot, sandy wastelands; some are cold, some are rocky, but all lack moisture for most of the year. Even so, a surprising variety of plants and animals have adapted to these hostile environments. Plants have developed ingenious ways of surviving long periods of drought, and many desert animals shelter during the intense heat of the day, emerging only at night to feed.

LIFE IN THE DESERT
The overriding need to obtain and conserve water dictates the pattern of desert life. Many plants close their pores during the day and most daytime creatures limit their activity to early morning and late afternoon. At night the temperature drops sharply and dew provides welcome moisture. Some plants bloom at night, and the desert is alive with insects, night-hunting birds, reptiles and small mammals.

DESERTS BY DAY

Many birds are at home in the desert. The lanner falcon of Africa and Asia gets all the moisture it needs from its diet of small birds and rodents. Sandgrouse live in the open deserts of Eurasia and North Africa; mainly seed eaters, they must make long flights each day to find water. Roadrunners, in American deserts, hunt insects, lizards and small rattlesnakes.

Lanner falcon
Falco biarmicus

Pallas's sandgrouse
Syrrhaptes paradoxus

Roadrunner
Geococcyx californianus

Large mammals are nomadic and obtain most of the moisture they need from plants. Camels can go for long periods without food or water because their humped back stores fat which can be drawn on when food is scarce, and water stored in their body tissues prevents dehydration. Addax antelopes survive entirely on plants. They roam remote parts of the Sahara, their broad hooves enabling them to travel easily over soft sand. Gazelles rely on speed. Small and fleet footed, they are able to disperse quickly over great distances to find food and water.

Arabian camel
Camelus dromedarius

Asian camel
Camelus bactrianus

Addax antelope
Addax nasomaculatus

Dorcas gazelle
Gazella dorcas

Insects and reptiles are well adapted to desert life. Desert locusts, when overpopulation threatens their food supply, change from a solitary to a swarming migratory form. Harvester ants store seeds against times of drought; desert tortoises withstand drought by becoming torpid. Lizards are cold blooded and need the sun to warm them, but must shelter from the intense heat of midday. The thorny devil, a small Australian ant-eating lizard, is protected from potential predators by its prickly scales.

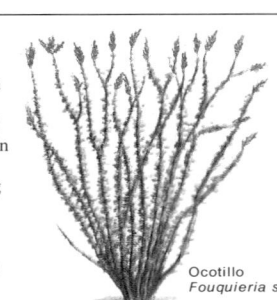

Desert locust
Schistocerca gregaria

swarming adult

solitary hopper

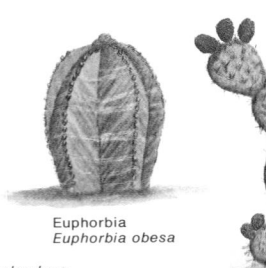

Harvester ants
Pogonomyrmex sp

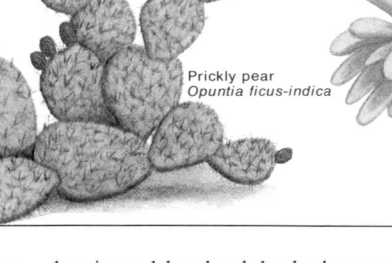

Desert tortoise
Gopherus polyphemus

Thorny devil
Moloch horridus

Gridiron-tailed lizard
Callisaurus draconoides

Desert plants have evolved various ways of coping successfully with drought. The ocotillo of southwestern America sheds its leaves, reducing its need for water. Euphorbias, and cacti such as the prickly pear, store water in their stems. Blue kleinia, a South African succulent, has a waxy coating that limits water loss. Agaves mature very slowly, building up reserves of food and water in their leaves before they flower. Esparto, a needlegrass, is typical of many desert grasses.

Ocotillo
Fouquieria splendens

Euphorbia
Euphorbia obesa

Prickly pear
Opuntia ficus-indica

Blue kleinia
Senecio articulatus

Agave
Agave americana

Deserts occur where rainfall is low and infrequent and where any moisture quickly evaporates or disappears instantly into the parched ground. In the driest deserts, rainfall rarely exceeds 100 mm (4 in) a year, and is so unreliable that some places may have no rain for 10 years or more. These are deserts in the truest sense of the word: harsh wildernesses that are almost totally without life. Regions with less than 255 mm (10 in) of rain a year are generally classified as arid and those with less than 380 mm (15 in) as semiarid.

Hot deserts have very high daytime temperatures in summer, although they drop sharply at night, and the winters are relatively mild. In the so-called cold deserts the summers are hot but the winters are so cold that temperatures may fall as low as $-30°C$ ($-22°F$).

Desert climates and landscapes
In the subtropical latitudes, swept by hot, drying winds, high-pressure weather systems prevent rain clouds from forming. In these regions, rain comes only from local storms or follows low-pressure weather systems (often seasonal) when they move in across the desert. Large areas of central Asia have become desert because they are so far from the sea that clouds have shed all their rain before they reach them. Other deserts occur because mountains cut them

off from moisture-bearing winds. The Andes, for example, shelter the drylands of Argentina, and a high sierra stops rain from reaching the Mojave and Great Basin deserts of North America. Rain is also rare on the western sides of continents where cold ocean currents flow from the polar regions towards the Equator.

Desert climates vary not only from place to place but also with time. Over short periods rainfall is much less predictable than it is in temperate regions and droughts are frequent. Some droughts, such as those that occur along the southern fringe of the Sahara, are so severe that it may seem that the climate has changed permanently. But most droughts are short-lived and are followed by years of normal (although sparse) rainfall. Over longer periods of time, however, desert climates do change. Prehistoric cave drawings in the Saharan highlands, for example, show that elephants, rhinoceroses and even hippopotamuses—animals that are at home in wetter climates—lived in these now dry, barren uplands in a more moist period between 7,000 and 4,000 years ago.

Desert landscapes also vary enormously. They are as contrasted as the Colorado canyon country of the United States and the sandy wastes of the Middle East, but most include one or more of several basic features: steep, rocky mountain slopes, broad plains, basin floors

dominated by dry lake beds or sand seas, and canyon-like valleys. In low-lying areas, evaporation sometimes leaves a glistening residue of salt. Where there is soil, it is often sandy or consists of little more than fragmented rock, and because plant life is usually sparse there is little or no humus to enrich the ground.

Where water is life
Plant growth depends on water, and desert plants are usually widely spaced to reduce competition for what little moisture is available. Many plants rely on short, sharp rainstorms; others make use of dew and grow in locations, such as crevices in rocks, where water can accumulate. Some complete their life cycle in a single wet season, producing seeds that lie dormant during the following drought and germinate only when enough moisture is available for them to grow. These are the ephemerals that carpet the desert with a brief but brilliant display of flowers shortly after rain has fallen.

Most desert plants, however, are able to tolerate or resist drought. These are the xerophytes ("dry plants") and phreatophytes ("deep-water plants"). Xerophytic trees and shrubs have a wide-spreading network of shallow roots that take in water from a large area of ground. Many xerophytes also limit the amount of water

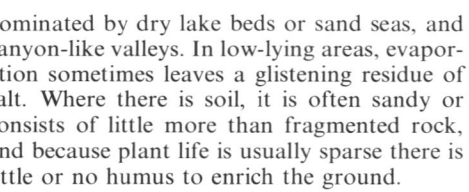

Esparto grass
Stipa tenacissima

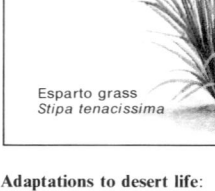

Adaptations to desert life: kangaroo rats, jerboas and gerbils (A) make prodigious leaps with their long back legs to escape predators, and some desert lizards (B) run at high speed on their hind legs when pursued, using their tail for balance. Spadefoot toads have scoop-like hind feet with which they dig burrows to avoid the intense heat of day. Skinks use flattened toes fringed with scales to "swim" through the sand. Fan-toed geckos have toes that spread into fans at the tips, enabling them to walk easily on sand dunes, and the Namib palmate gecko has webbed feet that support it on loose sand.

The saguaro dominates the desert landscapes of Mexico and southern America. Immensely slow growing, it can take 200 years to reach its full height, and more than four-fifths of its weight may be water stored in its stem to be used in times of drought. To minimize water loss, it opens its pores only at night to absorb carbon dioxide and to help radiate heat accumulated by day.

Five great arid regions are bordered by semi-arid steppe and scrub. Cold deserts—the Gobi in central Asia, the Great Basin in North America and the Patagonian Desert in South America—lie in the higher latitudes. Cold ocean currents also affect climate, causing fogs to form over coastal deserts in southwest Africa, South America and Baja California, Mexico.

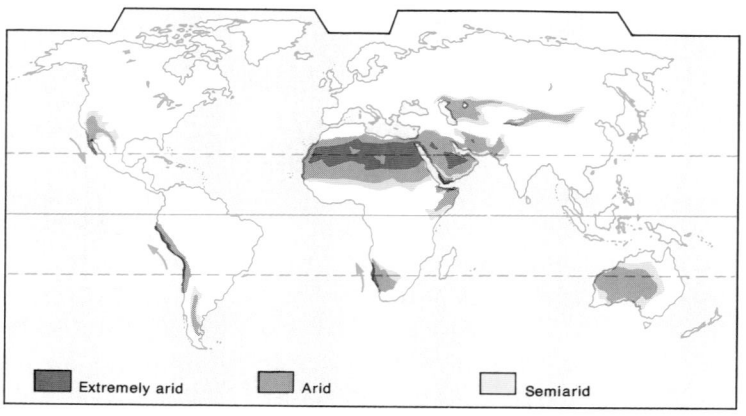

Extremely arid Arid Semiarid

DESERTS BY NIGHT

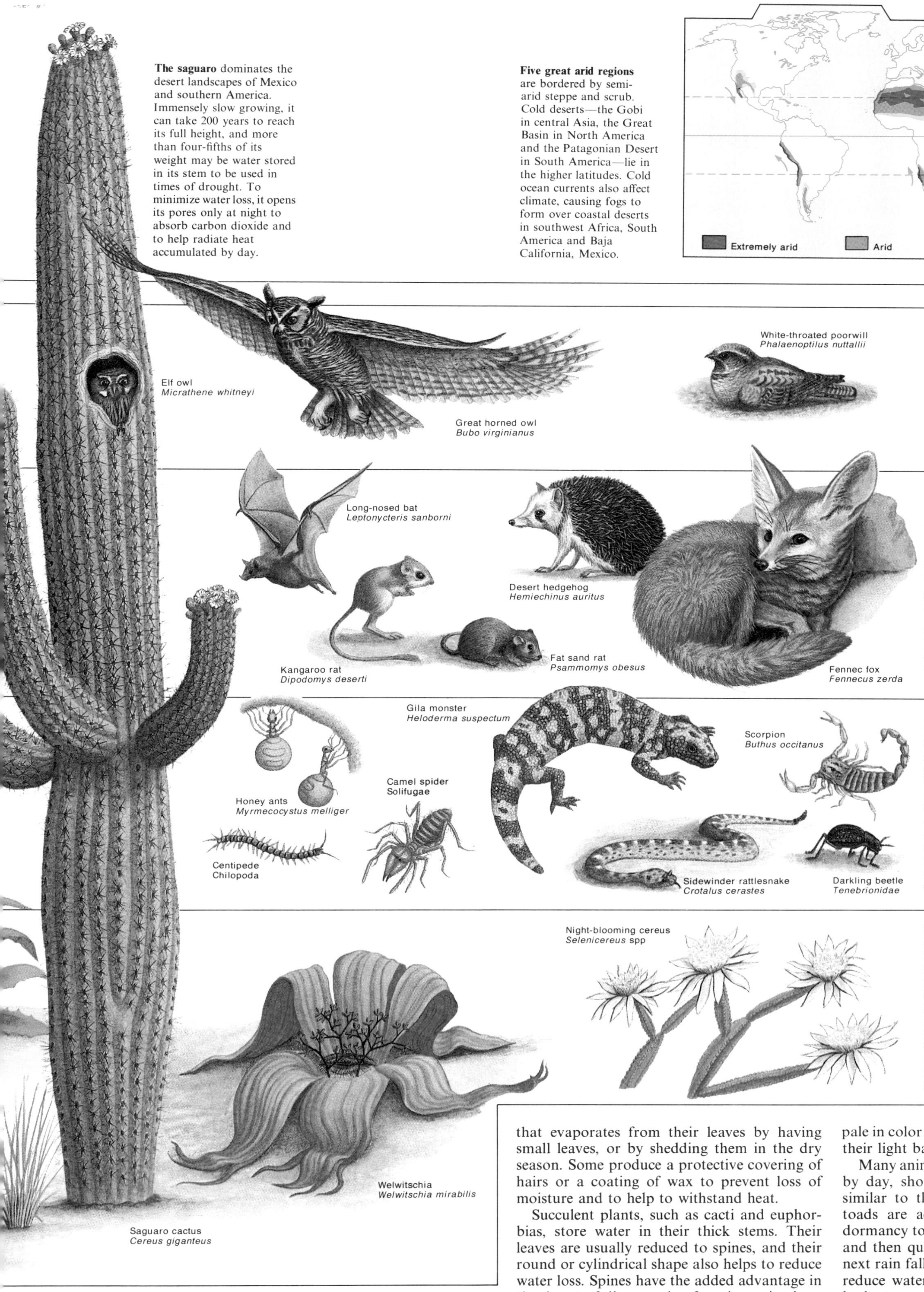

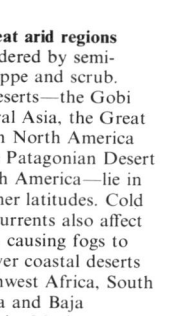

Elf owl
Micrathene whitneyi

Great horned owl
Bubo virginianus

White-throated poorwill
Phalaenoptilus nuttallii

Owls and nightjars hunt under cover of darkness. Elf owls shelter by day, emerging at dusk to catch insects, and great horned owls often come into the desert at night to hunt. The poorwill, a small desert nightjar, is known to American Indians as "the sleeper." An insect eater, it sometimes survives the rigors of winter, when food is scarce, by hibernating.

Long-nosed bat
Leptonycteris sanborni

Desert hedgehog
Hemiechinus auritus

Kangaroo rat
Dipodomys deserti

Fat sand rat
Psammomys obesus

Fennec fox
Fennecus zerda

Most small animals are active at night. Nectar-eating bats visit plants that blossom at night, pollinating the flowers while they feed. American kangaroo rats obtain water from a dry diet of seeds and conserve moisture by producing very concentrated urine. The sand rat of North Africa feeds on salty succulents and excretes great quantities of extremely salty urine. Hedgehogs are mainly insect eaters; the long ears of desert species help to disperse body heat. The Saharan fennec, the smallest type of desert fox, hunts lizards, rodents and locusts.

Gila monster
Heloderma suspectum

Scorpion
Buthus occitanus

Camel spider
Solifugae

Honey ants
Myrmecocystus melliger

Centipede
Chilopoda

Sidewinder rattlesnake
Crotalus cerastes

Darkling beetle
Tenebrionidae

Among insects and other invertebrates the hunt for food intensifies at night. Honey ants gather nectar; centipedes and camel spiders hunt insects. The gila monster, a poisonous American lizard, eats centipedes, eggs and sometimes other lizards, and uses its tail to store fat. The sidewinder, a small rattlesnake, is active mainly at night, leaving its distinctive parallel tracks in the sand. Scorpions emerge from their burrows to stalk insects and spiders, and darkling beetles feed on dry, decomposing vegetation.

Night-blooming cereus
Selenicereus spp

Welwitschia
Welwitschia mirabilis

Saguaro cactus
Cereus giganteus

Some desert plants are nocturnal, in the sense that they bloom only at night or make use of the dew that forms when the temperature falls. The welwitschia, unique to the Namib Desert in southwest Africa, has broad, sprawling leaves on which moisture condenses at night. The night-blooming cereus of the American deserts flowers for a single night in summer. Like other nocturnal plants, its flowers are luminously pale and strongly scented to attract pollinating night insects.

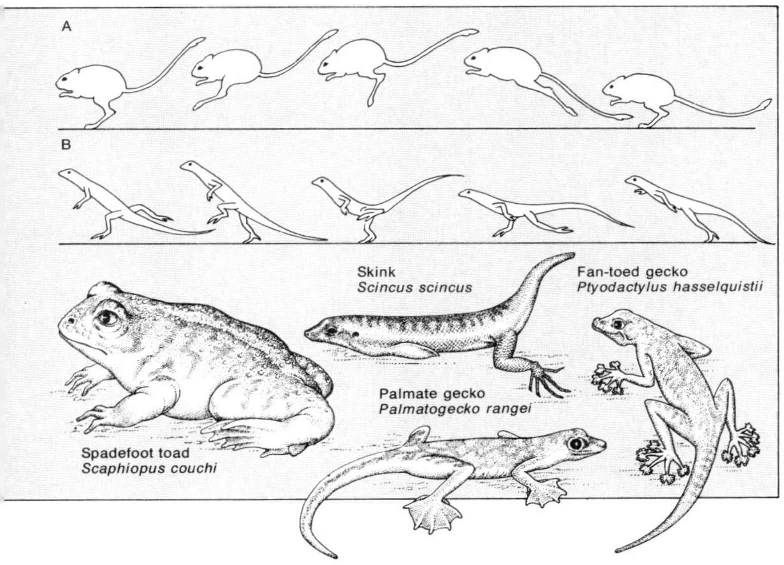

A

B

Skink
Scincus scincus

Fan-toed gecko
Ptyodactylus hasselquistii

Palmate gecko
Palmatogecko rangei

Spadefoot toad
Scaphiopus couchi

that evaporates from their leaves by having small leaves, or by shedding them in the dry season. Some produce a protective covering of hairs or a coating of wax to prevent loss of moisture and to help to withstand heat.

Succulent plants, such as cacti and euphorbias, store water in their thick stems. Their leaves are usually reduced to spines, and their round or cylindrical shape also helps to reduce water loss. Spines have the added advantage in the desert of discouraging foraging animals.

The drought-resisting phreatophytes—date palms, mesquite and cottonwood trees, for example—have a similar variety of adaptations to dry conditions, but their most typical feature is a long tap root that draws water from great depths. Many plants can also tolerate the presence of salt in the soil. These are the halophytes ("salt plants") such as saltbush and other small shrubs that grow in and around salt pans.

The struggle to survive

Animals, too, need to obtain and conserve water at all costs and to be able to adjust to extremes of temperature. Most are small enough to shelter under stones or in burrows during the intense heat of day; others survive adverse conditions by becoming dormant or by migrating. For most desert creatures it is also an advantage to be inconspicuous, and many are

pale in color so that they are hard to see against their light background of sand or stones.

Many animals, especially those that are active by day, show adaptations that are strikingly similar to those of desert plants. Frogs and toads are activated by rain, emerging from dormancy to feed and mate in temporary pools and then quickly burying themselves until the next rain falls. Mammals have hairy coats that reduce water loss and also help to keep their body temperature at a tolerable level. Most desert insects have a waxy coating that serves much the same purpose.

Some geckos and other lizards store food, in the form of fat, in their tails, and camels store fat in their humped backs to sustain them when food is scarce. Honey ants force-feed nectar to some members of the colony, creating living "honey pots" for the rest of the community to feed from in times of drought. Many creatures are able to survive on the moisture contained in their food, and rarely need to drink. Most desert dwellers also have extremely efficient kidneys that produce very concentrated urine, so that little or no moisture is lost in the process.

Man enjoys no such advantages. Nevertheless, he still seeks to live in deserts, as he has for thousands of years, and the pressures he exerts on the environment may well have irrevocably changed much of the world's desert landscapes.

Man and the Deserts

Water is the key to man's survival in deserts: where water has been available, great civilizations have flourished, and man's dream of making the desert bloom has become a reality. More recently, discoveries of great mineral wealth have spurred the opening up of some of Earth's most inhospitable regions. But while man's ingenuity has made many deserts both habitable and productive, the human tendency to increase the extent of deserts has become a problem of international proportions.

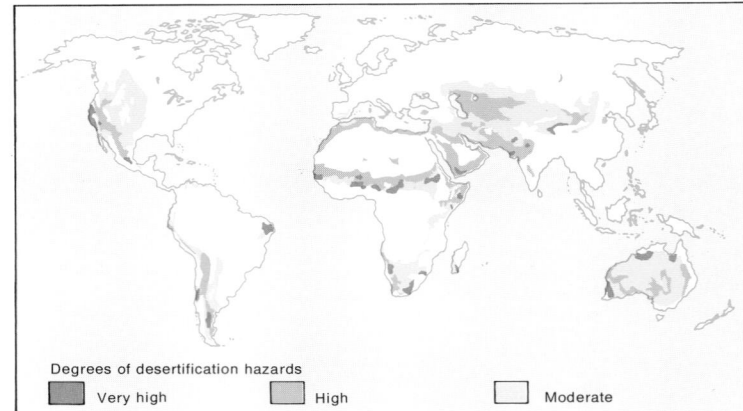

Degrees of desertification hazards

Very high   High   Moderate

Given water, much is possible, and not surprisingly man has tended to settle where water is most readily available: along the courses of rivers (such as the Nile) that rise outside the desert, and around oases fed by springs or by wells that tap groundwater supplies. But desert rainfall is so unreliable that often runoff and spring flow are uncertain in quantity and timing. Much groundwater is either also unreliable or it is fossil water that has accumulated in the geological past and is not being replenished by today's rainfall. Thus in areas such as southern Libya and some of the oasis settlements of the Arabian Gulf, and in America's arid west, groundwater is a nonrenewable resource that is being rapidly depleted.

Making water go farther
Man has also used great ingenuity to secure water supplies and to transport them to where they are needed. Runoff from flash floods that follow rare desert storms may be collected in channels and distributed to crops in nearby fields, and terracing slopes to trap runoff is a traditional way of obtaining the maximum benefit from limited rainfall. Reservoirs, ranging from the small night tanks of the southern Atacama desert in Chile to the massive artificial lakes along the Colorado river in the United States, store seasonally or perennially unreliable runoff. Also, surface runoff may be increased by reducing the permeability of runoff surfaces, a

solution engineered by the Nabataeans in the Negev desert more than 2,000 years ago and being reemployed by the Israelis today.

The transport of water is a fundamental desert activity. Open canals are typical, usually carrying water to irrigated fields—a practice used throughout the fertile crescent of Mesopotamia more than 8,000 years ago and still widespread today. A striking alternative are the ancient qanats, which limit the evaporation of water while it is in transit. Qanats are still found in the Middle East, although today pipelines are increasingly used.

Ultimately the conversion of salt water to fresh water may ensure plentiful supplies for many desert regions. The process is expensive, but large-scale desalination has already become a reality in some affluent communities such as oil-rich Saudi Arabia and Kuwait. Increasing emphasis is also being placed on more efficient use of existing freshwater supplies: in Egypt and Israel, waste water from towns is being purified and recycled for use in agriculture.

Cultivating the desert
The successful control of water has enabled large areas of otherwise arid and semiarid land to be made productive. The Egyptian civilization along the Nile depended, and still depends, on the management of seasonal floodwaters. In North America, the large-scale, long-distance piping of water has made central

Desertification—the advance of desert areas across the Earth—now affects more than 30 million sq km (12 million sq miles) and deserts are continuing to expand at an alarming rate. In recent years, on the southern edge of the Sahara alone, as much as 650,000 sq km (250,900 sq miles) of land that was once productive have been lost, and in places there is little left to show where the Sahara ends and the Sahel–Sudan region begins. Intense and often inappropriate human pressures are major causes, frequently aggravated by drought: overcultivating vulnerable land, chopping down trees for fuelwood and grazing too many livestock, especially on the margins of arid lands.

THE SHIFTING SANDS

Recent decades have seen unprecedented changes in the world's deserts. Increasing pressure on the environment, especially from pastoralists and farmers, has caused extensive damage and a rapid expansion of barren land. In many desert regions, nomadism has long been the only way in which man could survive, except in oases. Today, even these traditional ways of life are changing as the exploitation of oil and other mineral resources, and the introduction of new agricultural techniques, are drawing many of the deserts into a spectacular new age of development.

The traditional pastoral response to limited water supplies and forage in desert regions is nomadic livestock herding, still practiced by the Tuareg of the northern Sahara (right) and by tribal groupings in Mongolia (left). The nomadic way of life has, however, become severely restricted in recent years. Long-distance migrations are often incompatible with the requirements of the modern state, and the poor rewards no longer match the incentives to settle in towns and cities.

Oases have provided welcome refuges in deserts since ancient times. Secure water supplies from wells or springs make settled life possible in the midst of the most arid landscapes. Many oases are intensively cultivated with three tiers of vegetation: tall date palms shade orchards of citrus fruits, apricots, peaches, pomegranates and figs, and both palms and orchard trees shade the ground crops of vegetables and cereals. Irrigation channels distribute water to the desert soils, which are frequently rich in plant foods although they lack humus. Windbreaks help to protect cultivated land from erosion and from migrating dunes, although many oases are losing the battle with encroaching sands and the oasis people are leaving to find work in the oil fields.

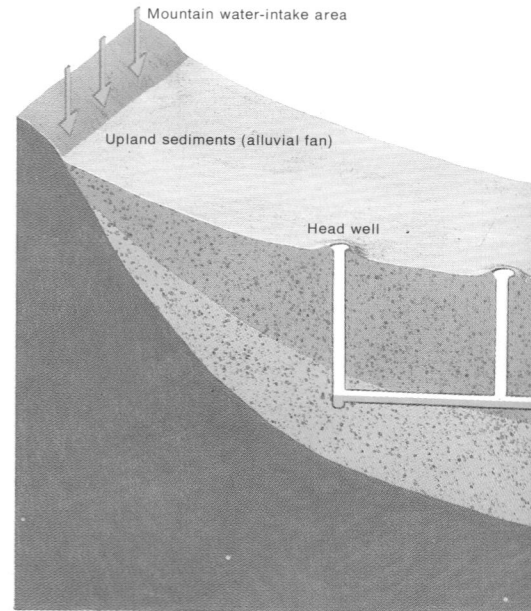

Mountain water-intake area

Upland sediments (alluvial fan)

Head well

California the most productive agricultural region in the world. But while irrigation can bring enormous benefits, it can also create problems. Too much water causes waterlogging of the land, and where water evaporates in the dry desert air, concentrations of dissolved salts build up in the soil.

Farming without irrigation is possible only where rainfall, although meager, is sufficient to sustain crops with a short growing season. Soil moisture is conserved by using dry surface mulches, by fallowing and crop rotation, by planting seeds sparsely and by controlling weeds. Geneticists are also producing new varieties of cereal crops that can survive for weeks without water. Dry farming, however, is precarious. Especially at times of drought it can cause serious problems of soil erosion, chiefly by the action of wind.

Man the desert maker
The extension of dry farming into unsuitable regions, and waterlogging and the accumulation of salts in irrigated areas, are major causes of desertification—the spread of deserts into formerly habitable land. Other major causes are the overgrazing of livestock on land with too little forage and the removal of trees and shrubs for firewood by communities that have no alternative fuel supply. A sequence of drier than normal years does the rest.

Many scientists believe that desertification can be reversed, provided the pressures on the land are reduced sufficiently to allow vegetation to recover. But desertification affects such huge areas, often crossing national frontiers, that broad-scale, international cooperation is needed to coordinate reductions in population and livestock pressures and to improve understanding of drought.

In some countries the battle against desertification has already begun. In China, extensive planting of drought-tolerant trees has created windbreaks to control sand movement and to protect farmland. In Algeria, a broad belt of trees has been planted to keep the Sahara at bay, and in Iran, advancing dunes have been halted by spraying them with petroleum residue: when the spray dries it forms a mulch that retains moisture and allows vegetation to grow, and much desert land has been reclaimed.

The deserts' riches
The exploitation of resources has also led to an "opening up" of many deserts. The rushes for precious metals in Arizona, Australia and South Africa started man's development of these regions in the nineteenth century. Some minerals, such as the evaporite deposits of Searles Basin in California and the nitrates of the Atacama desert in Chile, are actually products of the arid environment.

A resource that deserts also possess in abundance is solar power, and in many hot, dry regions the heat of the sun is used to evaporate mineral-rich solutions of salts, as well as being harnessed as a source of energy. Sunshine and the dry, clear air are also drawing ever-increasing numbers of tourists to the "sun cities" of the western United States and to Saharan oases, which were, until recently, only remote desert outposts.

No resource, however, has created as much attention or wealth as has oil. Oil has transformed the fortunes of several desert nations and provided an economic boom that has led to rapid industrialization and spectacular urban growth. The benefits of such growth in terms of affluence are substantial. The problems—the weakening of traditional desert societies, the submerging of traditional cities in the concrete labyrinths of modern complexes, and the precariousness of prosperity that is based on finite resources—are also clear.

Mineral wealth provides a powerful incentive for man's development of arid lands, and today the flow of oil rather than water is often a measure of a desert nation's prosperity. In some of the world's most desolate regions, flares signal the presence of modern "oases" where fossil fuels are being extracted—products, like the fossil waters that are sometimes trapped in the same sedimentary rocks, of the desert's geological past. Uranium, another mineral "fuel," also often lies beneath desert sands. Arid environments may also provide a rich harvest of other minerals: potash, phosphates and nitrates, valuable sources of commercial fertilizers; gypsum, manganese and salt; and borax, source of the element boron, used in nuclear reactors.

A "plastic" revolution has helped transform much of Israel's desert hinterland into productive farmland. Plastic cloches, plastic mulches and greenhouses trap moisture and reduce evaporation, and water trickled through thin plastic tubes irrigates the plants' roots with a minimum of wastage. Such innovative agricultural techniques enable Israel to produce most of its own food requirements, and fruit and vegetables grown in the relatively mild desert winters are also exported to Europe, where they command high prices.

One of the most ingenious ways man has devised of bringing water to desert regions is by the ancient underground system known as the qanat. Invented by the Persians in the first millennium BC, qanats tap groundwater in upland sediments and carry it by gravity to the surface on lower land. The head well is dug first, sometimes to a depth of 100 m (330 ft), until water is reached. A line of shafts is then sunk to provide ventilation and to give access to the channel being tunneled below. Work begins at the mouth end, and a typical channel is 10–20 km (6–12 miles) long when completed, depending on the depth of the head well and the slope of the land. Its slight gradient ensures that water flows freely but gently down to ground level. Surface canals then divert the water to where it is needed. Thousands of such qanats are still in use, their routes marked by mounds of excavated debris.

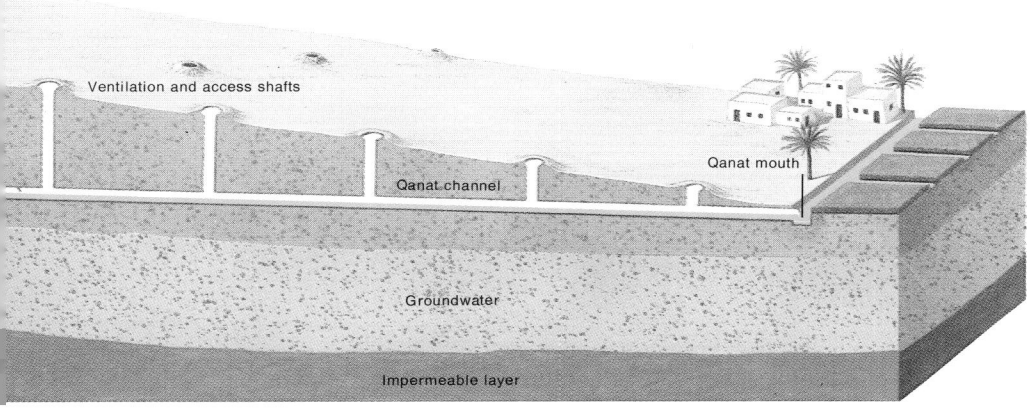

Ventilation and access shafts

Qanat mouth

Qanat channel

Groundwater

Impermeable layer

Guayule
Parthenium argentatum

Jojoba
Simmondsia californica

"Rubber" dandelion
Taraxacum kok-saghyz

Many desert plants have a bright future when they are grown on a commercial scale. Oil from the bean-like seeds of the jojoba plant, native to America's arid southwest, is remarkably similar to oil from sperm whales and has a multitude of uses, particularly as a high-grade industrial lubricant. Other promising plants are the latex-yielding guayule shrub of American and Mexican deserts, and a variety of dandelion from central Asia, both of which are being cultivated as a source of rubber.

Savannas

Between the tropical rainforest and desert regions lie large stretches of savanna, which are characterized by seasonal rainfall and long periods of drought. Those nearest to the forests usually take the form of open woodland, whereas those nearest to the deserts consist of widely scattered thorn scrub or tufts of grass. Unlike temperate grasslands, where the summers are hot but the winters are cold, savanna regions are always warm and in the wet season rain falls in heavy tropical downpours.

The most extensive areas of savanna are in Africa, north and south of the rainforest, and in South America, where the two main regions are the *llanos* of Venezuela, north of the Amazon rainforest, and the *campos* of Brazil in the south. Smaller areas of savanna also occur in Australia, India and southeastern Asia.

Savannas range from thickly wooded grasslands to almost treeless plains. Some are the result of man's destruction of the forest, and most are maintained in their present state by the high incidence of fire, both natural and man-made. The grasses tend to be taller and coarser than their temperate counterparts and they grow in tufts rather than as a uniform ground cover. In areas of high rainfall some grasses grow up to 4.5 m (15 ft) tall. Trees and bushes are usually widely spaced so that they do not compete with each other for water in the dry season. Humid, or moist, savannas experience 3 to 5 dry months a year, dry savannas 6 to 7 months, and thornbush savannas 8 to 10 months. Rainfall also varies widely, from more than 1,200 mm (47 in) a year in humid savannas to as little as 200 mm (8 in) where the savanna merges into desert.

Types of savannas

Humid woodland savanna presents an abrupt contrast to the rainforest. Trees tend to be scattered and some are so low growing that they are dwarfed by the tall grass that springs up during the summer rains. In the dry season the grass fuels fierce fires, which destroy all except thick-barked, large-leaved deciduous trees. Consequently, the proportion of fire-resistant trees and shrubs is large, and the grass quickly regenerates with the coming of the next rains.

In Africa this type of savanna is known as Guinea savanna north of the rainforest and as miombo savanna south of the rainforest. In South America it is known as *campo cerrado*, from the Portuguese words meaning field (*campo*) and dense. (*Campos sujos* are *campos* in which stretches of open grassland predominate and *campos limpos* are grasslands from which trees are entirely absent.) The *llanos*, or plains, of northern South America are grasslands interspersed with forests and swamps.

North of the Guinea savanna in Africa lies a belt known as Sudan savanna. The annual rainfall is in the range 500 to 1,000 mm (20–40 in) and the dry season lasts from October to April. This is typical dry savanna. Tall grasses between 1 and 1.5 m (3–5 ft) form an almost continuous ground cover and acacias and other thorny trees dot the landscape, together with branching dôm palms and massive water-storing baobab trees. Because of the interrupted tree cover the old name given to many savannas of this type was orchard steppe, and this description gives a good idea of the countryside. Like the humid woodland savannas it is maintained by regular burning of the grass in the dry season, and there is a delicate

balance and interaction between climate, soil, vegetation, animals and fire. On the desert margins the grasses grow in short tufts and the scattered acacias are seldom more than 3 m (10 ft) tall. The scrub and grasses are too widely dispersed for fires to spread, and this type of savanna is modified not by fire but by aridity and blistering heat.

Thorn-scrub and thorn-forest savannas frequently form transitional zones between tropical forests and grasslands. The *caatinga*, or "light forest," of northeastern Brazil is a typical thorn-forest savanna. Long, hot, dry seasons alternate with erratic downpours of rain, and the rate of evaporation is high. Drought-resisting trees and thorny shrubs mix with bromeliads, cacti and palm trees.

Abundance of life

No other environment supports animals so spectacular in size and so immense in numbers as do the African savannas. In spite of the concentration of animal life, however, competition for food is not severe. Each species has its own preferences and feeds from different levels of the vegetation. Giraffes and elephants can easily reach the upper branches of trees, antelopes feed on bushes at different heights from the ground, zebras and impalas eat the grasses and warthogs root for the underground parts of plants. With the onset of the dry season, massed herds assemble for the great migrations that are a major part of savanna life, moving to areas where rain has recently fallen and new grass is plentiful.

Following the grazing animals are the large predators: the lions, leopards and cheetahs. Wild dogs hunt in packs, and the scavengers—jackals, hyenas and vultures—move in to dispose of the remains of the kill.

The savannas of South America and Australia are much poorer in animal species. The only mammal of any size on the South American savanna is the elusive, nocturnal maned wolf, which eats almost anything from small animals to wild fruit. On the Australian savanna the largest inhabitant is the kangaroo, and the prime predator—apart from man—is the dingo, or native dog.

Many of the resident savanna birds are ground-living species such as the ostrich in Africa and its counterparts, the rhea in South America and the emu in Australia. The warm African climate attracts large numbers of visiting birds, which migrate each year across the Sahara to escape from the severe winter of the northern hemisphere.

For many thousands of years man has lived in harmony with the savanna. Within the last century, however, and in recent decades in particular, the savanna has come under increasing pressure. Inevitably, there is competition between the needs of the environment and those of the human population, and the future of the savanna is very much in the balance.

On each side of the Equator are broad tracts of tropical grassland known as savannas. In these regions there are distinct wet and dry seasons and temperatures are high all the year round, seldom falling below 21°C (70°F). Rain falls mainly in the hottest months, whereas the cooler months are generally dry. Thorn-scrub and thorn-forest savannas occur where the rainfall is more erratic; they have relatively little grass cover, and trees and bushes can tolerate long periods of drought.

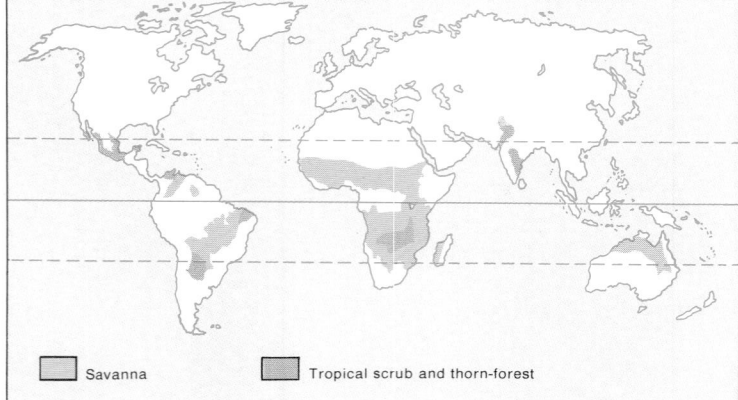

Savanna

Tropical scrub and thorn-forest

THE AFRICAN SAVANNA

More than a third of Africa is savanna, the vast parklike plains and gently rolling foothills providing the setting for a supreme wildlife spectacle. Vegetation is the basis of the immense wealth of animal life. It supports the large herds of grazing animals, and they return nutrients to the grassland in their droppings. The plant eaters, in turn, provide food for the hunters and for the scavengers that play an indispensable role by keeping the savanna free from carrion. Most of the plant-eating animals are agile and swift-footed, which enables them to escape from their enemies, and live in herds, which also provides some protection in the open habitat. Many of the animals, both predators and prey, are camouflaged: stripes or spots, at a distance, help to break up their outline; dappled markings merge with the pattern of sunlight and shade in the undergrowth; and tawny colors make them difficult to see against a background of dry grass.

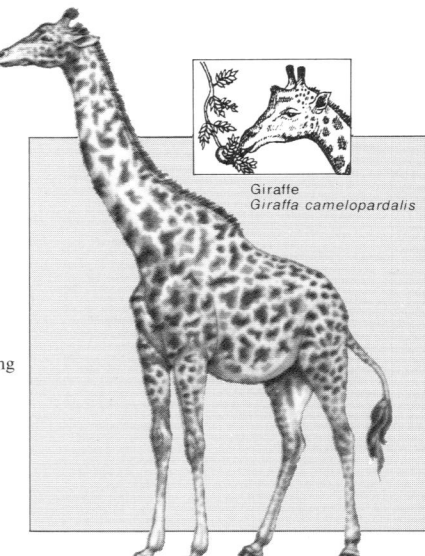

THE PLANT EATERS
Most plant eaters have adapted to feeding at a particular level of the vegetation. Giraffes browse on acacia tips that other animals cannot reach and elephants use their trunks to tear down succulent branches and leaves, although both feed on low-growing vegetation when it is easily available. Elephants will also uproot trees to gather leaves that are otherwise out of reach. The black rhinoceros plucks low-growing twigs and leaves by grasping them with its upper lip (the white rhinoceros has a broad, square mouth for grazing on grass). Eland often use their horns to collect twigs by twisting and breaking them. Zebra, wildebeest, topi and gazelle all graze on the same grasses, but at different stages of the plants' growth.

Giraffe
Giraffa camelopardalis

HUNTERS OF THE PLAINS
The plant eaters provide rich hunting for the carnivores. Lions kill the largest prey and hunt in family groups; the lioness usually makes the kill but the male is the first to eat. The leopard is a solitary hunter. It lies in ambush or stalks its prey, mainly at night, in brush country where it has ground cover. Cheetahs are the swiftest of all the hunters. They usually hunt in pairs in open grassland, stalking their prey and then charging in a lightning-fast sprint. Hunting dogs travel in well-organized packs. They exhaust their quarry by chasing it to a standstill and attacking as a team. Whereas lions, leopards and cheetahs usually kill by leaping for the neck or throat, packs of hunting dogs characteristically attack from the rear.

Lion
Panthera leo

THE SCAVENGERS
When the hunters have eaten, the scavengers move in. Jackals, small and quick, make darting runs to snatch titbits while packs of hyenas use their powerful bone-crushing jaws to demolish the bulk of the carcass. Hyenas are the most voracious of the carnivores, often driving the primary predator from its kill. Vultures are frequently the first to see a kill as they circle high in the sky, but must await their turn to feed on the skin and scraps because their descent attracts the more aggressive scavengers. Carrion beetles, carrion flies and the larvae of the horn-boring moth dispose of what is left. Most of the large scavengers, particularly the hyenas, also do their own hunting, singling out prey that is small, weak or sickly.

Jackal
Canis aureus

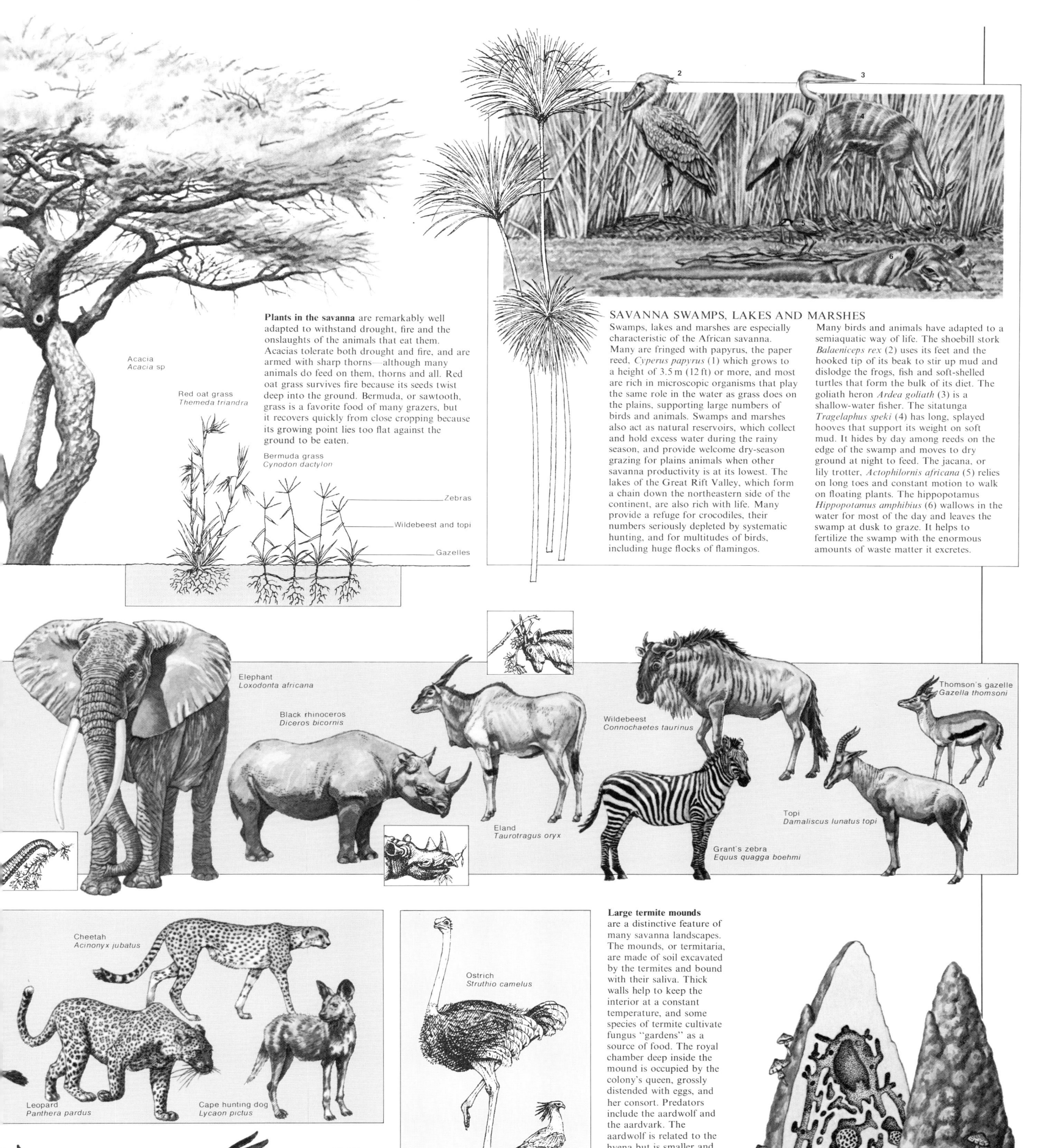

Plants in the savanna are remarkably well adapted to withstand drought, fire and the onslaughts of the animals that eat them. Acacias tolerate both drought and fire, and are armed with sharp thorns—although many animals do feed on them, thorns and all. Red oat grass survives fire because its seeds twist deep into the ground. Bermuda, or sawtooth, grass is a favorite food of many grazers, but it recovers quickly from close cropping because its growing point lies too flat against the ground to be eaten.

Acacia
Acacia sp

Red oat grass
Themeda triandra

Bermuda grass
Cynodon dactylon

Zebras

Wildebeest and topi

Gazelles

SAVANNA SWAMPS, LAKES AND MARSHES

Swamps, lakes and marshes are especially characteristic of the African savanna. Many are fringed with papyrus, the paper reed, *Cyperus papyrus* (1) which grows to a height of 3.5 m (12 ft) or more, and most are rich in microscopic organisms that play the same role in the water as grass does on the plains, supporting large numbers of birds and animals. Swamps and marshes also act as natural reservoirs, which collect and hold excess water during the rainy season, and provide welcome dry-season grazing for plains animals when other savanna productivity is at its lowest. The lakes of the Great Rift Valley, which form a chain down the northeastern side of the continent, are also rich with life. Many provide a refuge for crocodiles, their numbers seriously depleted by systematic hunting, and for multitudes of birds, including huge flocks of flamingos.

Many birds and animals have adapted to a semiaquatic way of life. The shoebill stork *Balaeniceps rex* (2) uses its feet and the hooked tip of its beak to stir up mud and dislodge the frogs, fish and soft-shelled turtles that form the bulk of its diet. The goliath heron *Ardea goliath* (3) is a shallow-water fisher. The sitatunga *Tragelaphus speki* (4) has long, splayed hooves that support its weight on soft mud. It hides by day among reeds on the edge of the swamp and moves to dry ground at night to feed. The jacana, or lily trotter, *Actophilornis africana* (5) relies on long toes and constant motion to walk on floating plants. The hippopotamus *Hippopotamus amphibius* (6) wallows in the water for most of the day and leaves the swamp at dusk to graze. It helps to fertilize the swamp with the enormous amounts of waste matter it excretes.

Elephant
Loxodonta africana

Black rhinoceros
Diceros bicornis

Eland
Taurotragus oryx

Wildebeest
Connochaetes taurinus

Grant's zebra
Equus quagga boehmi

Topi
Damaliscus lunatus topi

Thomson's gazelle
Gazella thomsoni

Cheetah
Acinonyx jubatus

Leopard
Panthera pardus

Cape hunting dog
Lycaon pictus

Ostrich
Struthio camelus

Secretary bird
Sagittarius serpentarius

LONG-LEGGED BIRDS
The ostrich, up to 2.4 m (8 ft) tall, can see for great distances across the plains and can outrun most of its enemies. Its territory is often shared with grazing animals, such as wildebeest, which take advantage of the ostrich's keen sight to alert them to danger. The secretary bird (so-called because of its quill-like crest) strides through the grass hunting small mammals, insects and snakes; it kills snakes by battering them with its powerful, long-clawed feet.

White-backed vulture
Pseudogyps africanus

Carrion beetle

Carrion fly

Spotted hyena
Crocuta crocuta

Horn-boring moth larva

Large termite mounds are a distinctive feature of many savanna landscapes. The mounds, or termitaria, are made of soil excavated by the termites and bound with their saliva. Thick walls help to keep the interior at a constant temperature, and some species of termite cultivate fungus "gardens" as a source of food. The royal chamber deep inside the mound is occupied by the colony's queen, grossly distended with eggs, and her consort. Predators include the aardwolf and the aardvark. The aardwolf is related to the hyena but is smaller and has weak jaws; it digs the termites out of their mound and scoops them up with its long sticky tongue. The aardvark, distantly related to the elephant, uses its powerful hoof-like claws to break into termite nests.

Aardwolf
Proteles cristatus

Aardvark
Orycteropus afer

Man and the Savannas

In their natural state, savannas are among the most strikingly productive of all Earth's regions. Before the coming of man they supported a wealth of animal life that has seldom been surpassed. As yet they are relatively undeveloped, but many of them lie in areas where the pressures of population growth are becoming increasingly acute. Wisely used, they offer great hope for the future, both as cattle lands and for the cultivation of food crops. But without proper management savannas can rapidly turn into wasteland, and man will be the poorer for the loss of such a great natural resource.

Throughout much of the savannas the climate is semiarid and the soils tend to be poor: stripped of their plant cover, they bake hard and crack during the long months of hot sunshine, and during the wet season they often become waterlogged or are washed away by the rains. Man's indiscriminate use of fire, unwise agricultural methods and the unrestricted grazing of domestic animals have already led to much soil loss, and erosion is widespread in tropical Africa, Asia, South America and Australia.

Systematic burning has long been practiced by the people of the savannas. Large areas are burned each year to clear land for agriculture or to remove dead grass and encourage a fresh growth to feed livestock. The resulting ash provides much-needed nutrients for crops, and the grasses rapidly produce new green shoots that provide a rich pasture for domestic herds. But although the short-term effects may be beneficial, repeated burning is harmful to the vegetation, the animals and the soil.

Trees are always more or less damaged by fire. Their trunks become twisted and gnarled, fresh shoots are killed and young trees are prevented from growing. Constant burning can destroy some species altogether, and when they disappear so too does the wildlife that depends on them for food and shelter.

Grasses, on the other hand, may be encouraged by burning, and the lush new growth that springs up when the first rains break the long dry season provides welcome nourishment for domestic herds and game animals alike. But whereas game animals move freely over the range, cropping grasses at various stages of growth, cattle tend to feed on grass only in the neighborhood of wells and other sources of drinking water. They may trample the soil and continue to graze the same area until the grass is completely suppressed.

The hazards of large projects

Cultivation in marginal areas that are unsuited to intensive agriculture also contributes to the impoverishment of the savanna. The Sahel and Sudan savannas on the fringes of the Sahara are particularly vulnerable to large-scale development projects that fail to take account of local climate and soil. Mechanized agriculture in fragile areas bordering the desert may well lead to soil erosion and dustbowl conditions, and large-scale irrigation schemes often result in waterlogging and an accumulation of salts in the soil. Cultivation in the savannas requires understanding and care. Many smaller schemes are safer—and usually more productive—than a few large ones, but not all planners yet realize that agricultural methods that are effective in temperate regions seldom come up to expectations in tropical climates.

Man first inhabited the savannas, as he did many other regions of the world, as a hunter and gatherer. He took from the land only what he needed from day to day, and although he used fire as a hunting tool, his impact was little more than that of any other savanna inhabitant. In East Africa, groups of nomadic Hadza (left) still hunt game and collect roots, fruit and the honey of wild bees, building grass huts as temporary shelters.

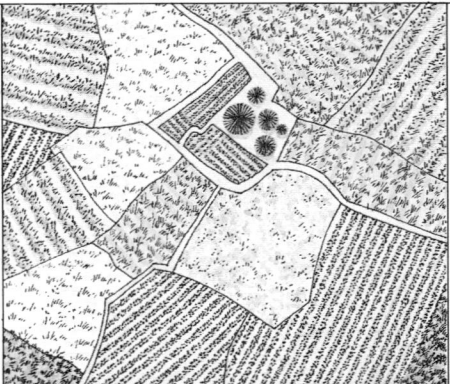

Small farms are scattered over much of the savannas. Plots close to houses are farmed continuously; beyond them lie the main fields, where periods of cultivation are usually followed by periods of fallow. Maize, millet and peanuts are the main food crops, and early and late crops are sometimes sown on the same plot to extend the growing season. Most of the work is done by hand, and any surplus to a family's needs is sold.

THE VULNERABLE WILDERNESS

Nowhere has man's impact on the tropical grasslands been felt more keenly than in Africa, although much of what is happening in Africa is happening also in savannas elsewhere. The majority of the people still live on the land, where the determining factor is the length and severity of the annual dry season. In the moister savannas the people are primarily cultivators, while in savannas that are too dry to sustain agriculture the main occupation is raising livestock. Most of the savannas are as yet sparsely settled, but competition is inevitably growing between man and wildlife, particularly in Africa, for the remaining tracts of relatively untouched wilderness.

The development of mineral resources and industries has led to an increasing movement of people—mainly young adults—from rural areas to towns and mining centers, attracted by opportunities for work—often at the expense of agriculture, since the heavy work of farming is left to the women, old people and children. Mining enterprises such as those in the Zambian Copper Belt (above), may recruit large labor forces from the surrounding countryside. Mining also dramatically alters the landscape, especially where the bedrock containing the ore reaches the surface and is quarried in huge terraces. The need for electricity to power mining and other industries leads, in turn, to the development of hydroelectric schemes, many of which entail resettling people whose villages are flooded by the creation of large artificial lakes.

Large areas of savanna have been set aside in East and Central Africa, and to a lesser extent in South America and Australia, as national parks and reserves where the landscape is kept intact and animals can be studied in their natural habitats. In Africa, observation platforms are frequently built close to waterholes where animals congregate to drink, and wardens use light aircraft to patrol the vast areas involved. Camel units are also used to patrol near-desert regions where much of the wildlife flourishes. Animals, such as elephants, whose numbers can grow out of control in the protected environment of the reserves are culled by licensed hunters to prevent the vegetation being destroyed. Culling maintains the health of the community as a whole and is also an economic source of meat in many countries where the people are short of protein foods.

Similarly, the introduction of European breeds of cattle into the savannas has not been an unqualified success. Not only are these breeds more susceptible to tropical pests and diseases than are the local varieties, but they are also adversely affected by the hot climate and their productivity is greatly reduced. In Africa and Brazil, native breeds are replacing more recent importations, and their productivity is being enhanced by selective breeding. In Australia, where most of the cattle are of British stock, tropical zebu, or humped cattle, are being introduced into the herds.

In the future, much more of the savanna may be developed as ranch lands, because the temperate grasslands will become less able to support enough animals to satisfy the world demand for meat. The *llanos* of Venezuela, the *campos* of Brazil and the tropical grasslands of Argentina and Australia already carry large herds of beef cattle. Throughout the savannas, however, ranching is still hampered by lack of water, poor natural pasture and remoteness from markets. In Africa, where herding is mainly nomadic, the sinking of wells by government organizations is changing the traditional ways of life, and cattle raising on a commercial

scale is likely to become increasingly important. In Africa, too, the conservation and controlled cropping of game animals could become one of the most productive—and constructive—forms of land use.

Game as a resource

The value of game animals as a source of food is considerable. Buffaloes, for example, and kangaroos in Australia, can thrive on natural grasses that will not even maintain the weight of domestic stock, and they show greater gains in weight than African and European cattle on most forms of vegetation, while several species of antelopes can survive on a water ration that is wholly inadequate for cattle.

In recent years attention has been directed toward the economics of controlled cropping of wild game, and of ranching animals such as eland, which can be kept as if they were domesticated stock and can convert poor pasture into excellent meat. Game animals are also more resistant than cattle to the tsetse fly, which infests large areas of Africa and transmits the disease trypanosomiasis (known as nagana in cattle and as sleeping sickness in man).

But for the most part game animals are still

considered to be a nuisance by man, and it is perhaps fortunate that by denying much of the savanna to domestic animals—and to man—the tsetse fly has preserved these regions from exploitation at the expense of the game. Many countries have also set aside large tracts of savanna as national parks and game reserves, where the natural environment is preserved and the wildlife can thrive.

Safeguarding the savanna

At a time when the pressure of the expanding human population calls for the development of areas hitherto uninhabited or only sparsely populated, it may seem paradoxical to maintain that the development of national parks and nature reserves is essential to the welfare of mankind. The aim of game conservation, however, is not simply to preserve rare or unusual animals for the enjoyment of posterity, or even for their scientific interest. It is to ensure that the land is put to its most economic and efficient use. The next few decades will show whether the savannas of the world will be developed into major sources of food and revenue for the countries that own them, or whether they will be misused and degraded into desert.

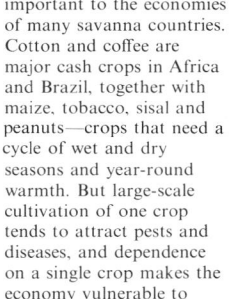

Commercial agriculture is important to the economies of many savanna countries. Cotton and coffee are major cash crops in Africa and Brazil, together with maize, tobacco, sisal and peanuts—crops that need a cycle of wet and dry seasons and year-round warmth. But large-scale cultivation of one crop tends to attract pests and diseases, and dependence on a single crop makes the economy vulnerable to fluctuating world prices.

Cattle rearing takes the place of cultivation in areas that are too dry to be cropped successfully. In Africa, people such as the Masai are nomadic herders, moving their cattle long distances in search of pasture. Wealth is counted in terms of the numbers rather than the quality of the cattle they own, but improved management of their herds and better control of animal diseases are now making their cattle much more productive.

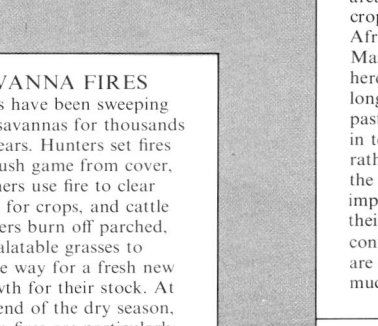

SAVANNA FIRES
Fires have been sweeping the savannas for thousands of years. Hunters set fires to flush game from cover, farmers use fire to clear land for crops, and cattle owners burn off parched, unpalatable grasses to make way for a fresh new growth for their stock. At the end of the dry season, when fires are particularly fierce, large areas of savanna lie under a thin haze of smoke.

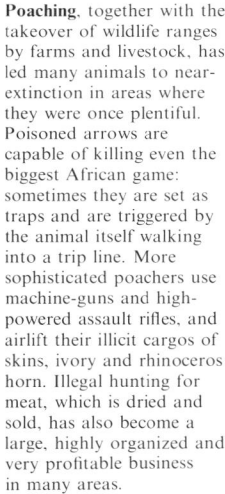

Poaching, together with the takeover of wildlife ranges by farms and livestock, has led many animals to near-extinction in areas where they were once plentiful. Poisoned arrows are capable of killing even the biggest African game: sometimes they are set as traps and are triggered by the animal itself walking into a trip line. More sophisticated poachers use machine-guns and high-powered assault rifles, and airlift their illicit cargos of skins, ivory and rhinoceros horn. Illegal hunting for meat, which is dried and sold, has also become a large, highly organized and very profitable business in many areas.

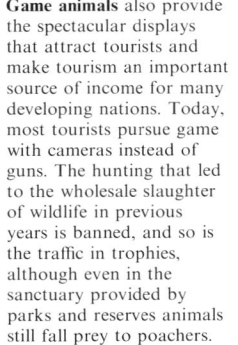

Game animals also provide the spectacular displays that attract tourists and make tourism an important source of income for many developing nations. Today, most tourists pursue game with cameras instead of guns. The hunting that led to the wholesale slaughter of wildlife in previous years is banned, and so is the traffic in trophies, although even in the sanctuary provided by parks and reserves animals still fall prey to poachers.

Animals are frequently transferred from areas where they are at risk to safer areas such as game parks and reserves. In Kenya, helicopters came to the rescue of a herd of rare antelopes when their range was threatened by a proposed irrigation scheme and moved them to Tsavo National Park. Animals are also moved to introduce new blood to small, isolated herds or to restock areas from which they have been lost.

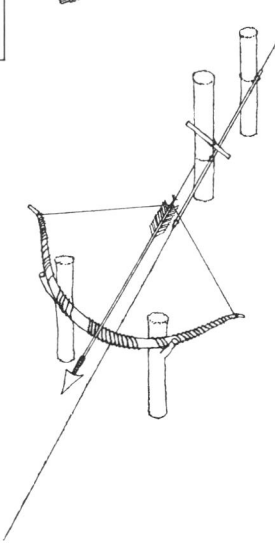

Tropical Rainforests

Tropical rainforests, extremely rich in both plant and animal life, consist of a series of layered or stratified habitats. These range from the dark and humid forest floor through a layer of shrubs to the emerging tops of the scattered giant trees towering above the dense main canopy of the forest. Each layer of vegetation is a miniature life zone containing a wide selection of animal species. These can be divided into a number of ecological groups according to their various ways of life, and many have evolved special adaptations to enable them to make maximum use of the plentiful food supply surrounding them.

Crested tree swift
Hemiprocne longipennis

Crowned eagle
Stephanoaetus coronatus

Tropical rainforests occur only in the regions close to the Equator; they have a heavy rainfall and a uniformly hot and moist climate. There are slightly more of these forests in the northern half of the world than in the southern half and they occur at altitudes of up to 1,500 m (5,000 ft). Temperatures are normally between 24°C and 30°C (77°–86°F) and rarely fall below 21°C (70°F) or rise above 32°C (90°F). The skies are often cloudy and the rain falls more or less evenly throughout the year. Rainfall is usually more than 2,000 mm (78 in) a year and is never less than 1,500 mm (59 in). A distinctive feature of this tropical, humid climate is that the average daily temperature range is much greater than the range between the hottest and coolest months.

A stratified habitat

There are usually three to five overlapping layers in the mature tropical rainforest. The tallest trees (called "emergents") rise above a closed, dense canopy formed by the crowns of less tall trees, which nevertheless can reach more than 40 m (130 ft) tall. Below this canopy is a third or middle layer of trees—the understory; their crowns do not meet but they still form a dense layer of growth about 5–20 m (16–65 ft) tall. The fourth layer consists of woody shrubs of varying heights between 1–5 m (3–16 ft). The bottom layer comprises decomposers (fungi) that rarely reach 50 cm (20 in) in height.

Although the trees are so tall, few of them have really thick trunks. Nearly all are evergreens, shedding their dark, leathery leaves and growing new ones continuously. Many of the larger species grow buttresses—thin, triangular slabs of hardwood that spread out from the bases of their trunks. These support the trees, so removing the need for a heavy outlay of energy and resources on deep root systems. Hanging lianas (vines), thin and strong as rope, vanish like cables into the mass of foliage. They are especially abundant on riverbanks, where the canopy of trees is thinner; their leaves and flowers appear only among the treetops.

Epiphytes—plants that grow on other plants but do not take their nourishment from them—festoon the trunks and branches of trees, and up to 80 may grow on a single tree. They include many kinds of orchid and bromeliad. Their aerial roots make use of a humus substitute derived from the remains of other plants, often

Moth orchid
Phalaenopsis sanderana

Tropical rainforests are located in the hot and wet equatorial lands of Latin America, West Africa, Madagascar and Asia. These areas have consistently high temperatures throughout the year and receive high rainfall from the moist and unstable winds blowing in from the oceans.

The hummingbird numbers about 300 species, most of which are confined to the forests of South America. It is renowned for its ability to hover while gathering nectar, a feat achieved by the almost 180° rotations of its wings, which beat rapidly more than 80 times per second.

Tropical rainforests

brought together by ants. The bases of their leaves may be broad and bowl shaped and collect and hold water; they also provide homes for a variety of insects and reptiles.

Rainforest soils are not as fertile as might be supposed by the luxuriance of their vegetation. On the contrary, the silicates and compounds necessary for plant growth are leached away by the rain to leave red or yellow soils of poor quality. This process, known as laterization, is widespread in the humid tropics. Humus is rapidly broken down by bacteria, fungi and termites, while earthworms, which in more temperate regions normally contribute to the mixing of humus with mineral particles, are usually absent.

In rainforests there are often up to 25 different tree species on a single hectare of land (60 species to the acre). Most temperate forests have only a fifth of this number, with nothing like the abundance of plants that grow in the tropics. This incredible variety supports—directly or indirectly—a corresponding variety of animal species which has an abundant food supply because the forest never ceases to be productive. This is why most mammals do not move far; they stay where their food grows.

Life in the canopy

The dense leaves and branches of the canopy provide the most food and so support the greatest number of species. Macaws and toucans (from the American tropics) and parrots and trogons (which live in forests throughout the tropics) eat the fruit growing in the

THE LAYERS OF THE FOREST

Stratification—the existence of distinct layers of forest vegetation—is especially pronounced in the tropics, where there are usually five main storys. These can overlap greatly and may vary in height from area to area. The large differences between the layers present many varied habitats and ecological niches for a very wide range of animals.

CANOPY LAYER

This dense story exerts a powerful influence on the levels below since its trees, which grow between 20 m (65 ft) and 40 m (130 ft) tall, form such a thick layer of vegetation that they cut off sunlight from the forest below. The canopy is noted for the diversity of its fauna. Many birds and animals are adapted to running along branches to get the flowers, fruits or nuts that form their diets. The pointed tips of canopy leaves encourage rapid drainage.

Sacred langur
Presbytis entellus

Tree shrew
Tupaia glis

MIDDLE LAYER

This understory comprises trees from 5 m (16 ft) to 20 m (65 ft) tall whose long, narrow crowns do not become quite so dense as those of the canopy. There is very often no clear distinction, however, between this level and the canopy. Middle-layer trees are strong enough to bear large animals such as leopards that spend part of their lives on the ground. Epiphytes are plentiful in this layer.

Leopard
Panthera pardus

Pouched tree frog
Gastrotheca ovifera

Orang-utan
Pongo pygmaeus

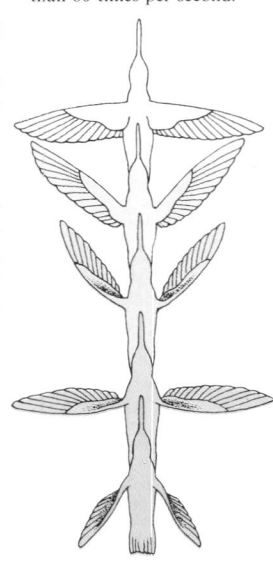

Flowering plants of the forest include epiphytes such as bromeliads and orchids like the species of *Phalaenopsis* illustrated here. Epiphytes grow on other plants such as trees where they can receive sunlight and are nourished by humus in the bark. Many epiphytic orchids have swellings in their roots or at the bases of their leaves where water can be stored. Seventy species of *Phalaenopsis* grow in southeast Asian forests and *P. sanderana*, one of the most beautiful, was first discovered in the Philippines in 1882.

SHRUB LAYER

The vegetation of this level is sparse in comparison with that above it and consists of treelets and woody shrubs that rarely reach 5 m (16 ft). These grow up in any available space between the abundant boles of large trees. Life in this story exists equally well at ground level.

Four-striped squirrel
Funisciurus lemniscatus

Oriental civet
Viverra tangalunga

Tree pangolin
Manis tricuspis

GROUND LAYER

Shade-tolerant herbs, ferns and tree seedlings represent the only flora at ground level; there is no grass there. Light is less than one percent of full daylight so that many mammals are well camouflaged in the gloom, whereas others have compact bodies to facilitate movement through the undergrowth. Ants and termites are well adapted to the high humidity and darkness of the forest floor. Fungi and a host of invertebrates quickly break down the litter of rotting leaves, fruit and fallen branches to provide vital nutrients for the fast-growing trees of the tropical rainforest.

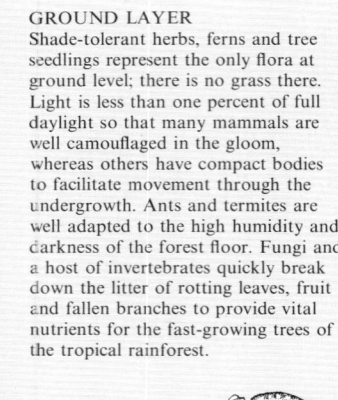

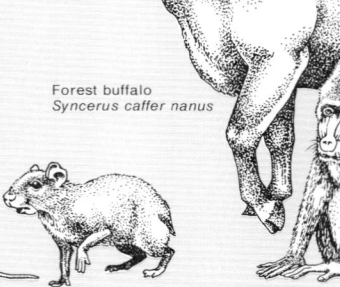

Okapi
Okapia johnstoni

Forest buffalo
Syncerus caffer nanus

Indian tiger
Panthera tigris tigris

Malayan tapir
Tapirus indicus

Congo forest mouse
Deomys ferrugineus

Short-eared elephant shrew
Macroscelides proboscideus

Orange-rumped agouti
Dasyprocta aguti

Mandrill
Mandrillus sphinx

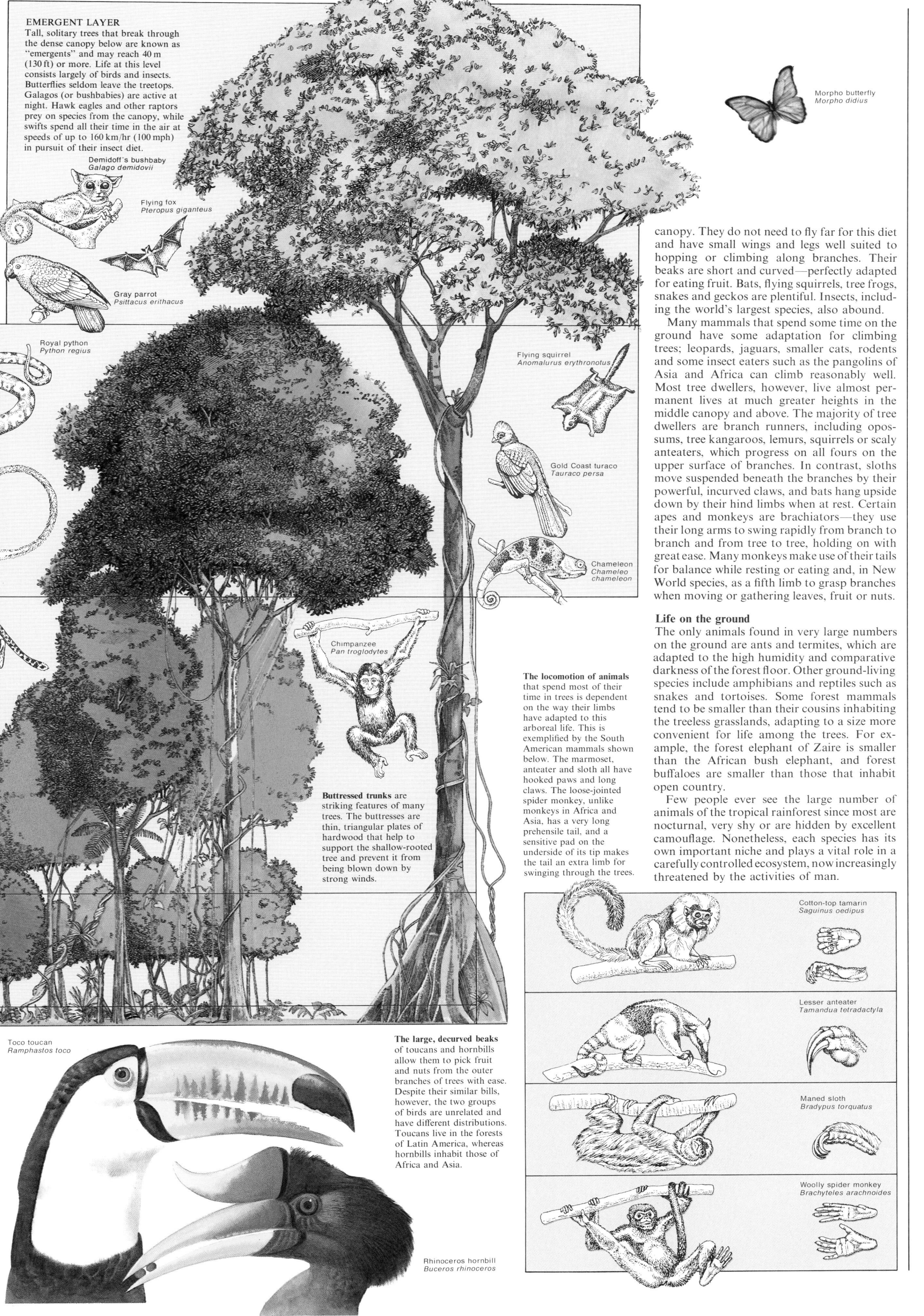

Tall, solitary trees that break through the dense canopy below are known as "emergents" and may reach 40 m (130 ft) or more. Life at this level consists largely of birds and insects. Butterflies seldom leave the treetops. Galagos (or bushbabies) are active at night. Hawk eagles and other raptors prey on species from the canopy, while swifts spend all their time in the air at speeds of up to 160 km/hr (100 mph) in pursuit of their insect diet.

Demidoff's bushbaby
Galago demidovii

Flying fox
Pteropus giganteus

Gray parrot
Psittacus erithacus

Morpho butterfly
Morpho didius

Royal python
Python regius

Flying squirrel
Anomalurus erythronotus

Gold Coast turaco
Tauraco persa

Chameleon
Chameleo chameleon

Chimpanzee
Pan troglodytes

Buttressed trunks are striking features of many trees. The buttresses are thin, triangular plates of hardwood that help to support the shallow-rooted tree and prevent it from being blown down by strong winds.

The locomotion of animals that spend most of their time in trees is dependent on the way their limbs have adapted to this arboreal life. This is exemplified by the South American mammals shown below. The marmoset, anteater and sloth all have hooked paws and long claws. The loose-jointed spider monkey, unlike monkeys in Africa and Asia, has a very long prehensile tail, and a sensitive pad on the underside of its tip makes the tail an extra limb for swinging through the trees.

canopy. They do not need to fly far for this diet and have small wings and legs well suited to hopping or climbing along branches. Their beaks are short and curved—perfectly adapted for eating fruit. Bats, flying squirrels, tree frogs, snakes and geckos are plentiful. Insects, including the world's largest species, also abound.

Many mammals that spend some time on the ground have some adaptation for climbing trees; leopards, jaguars, smaller cats, rodents and some insect eaters such as the pangolins of Asia and Africa can climb reasonably well. Most tree dwellers, however, live almost permanent lives at much greater heights in the middle canopy and above. The majority of tree dwellers are branch runners, including opossums, tree kangaroos, lemurs, squirrels or scaly anteaters, which progress on all fours on the upper surface of branches. In contrast, sloths move suspended beneath the branches by their powerful, incurved claws, and bats hang upside down by their hind limbs when at rest. Certain apes and monkeys are brachiators—they use their long arms to swing rapidly from branch to branch and from tree to tree, holding on with great ease. Many monkeys make use of their tails for balance while resting or eating and, in New World species, as a fifth limb to grasp branches when moving or gathering leaves, fruit or nuts.

Life on the ground
The only animals found in very large numbers on the ground are ants and termites, which are adapted to the high humidity and comparative darkness of the forest floor. Other ground-living species include amphibians and reptiles such as snakes and tortoises. Some forest mammals tend to be smaller than their cousins inhabiting the treeless grasslands, adapting to a size more convenient for life among the trees. For example, the forest elephant of Zaire is smaller than the African bush elephant, and forest buffaloes are smaller than those that inhabit open country.

Few people ever see the large number of animals of the tropical rainforest since most are nocturnal, very shy or are hidden by excellent camouflage. Nonetheless, each species has its own important niche and plays a vital role in a carefully controlled ecosystem, now increasingly threatened by the activities of man.

Cotton-top tamarin
Saguinus oedipus

Lesser anteater
Tamandua tetradactyla

Maned sloth
Bradypus torquatus

Woolly spider monkey
Brachyteles arachnoides

Toco toucan
Ramphastos toco

The large, decurved beaks of toucans and hornbills allow them to pick fruit and nuts from the outer branches of trees with ease. Despite their similar bills, however, the two groups of birds are unrelated and have different distributions. Toucans live in the forests of Latin America, whereas hornbills inhabit those of Africa and Asia.

Rhinoceros hornbill
Buceros rhinoceros

Man and the Tropical Rainforests

Every three seconds a portion of original rainforest the size of a football field disappears as man fells the trees and extends his cultivation. Although tropical conditions allow rapid regrowth of secondary forest, the loss of primary forest is destroying thousands of plant and animal species that will never again be seen on Earth. Even by conservative estimates, it is likely that all the world's primary tropical forest will have disappeared within 85 years unless the trend is reversed.

A DIMINISHING RESOURCE
This idealized tract of rainforest includes many of the activities of man that are daily endangering the survival of the forest. Shifting "slash-and-burn" cultivation and excessive logging present the greatest threats. Antidotes such as reafforestation have so far made very little headway.

The activities of man have only recently begun to threaten the tropical rainforest. Since pre-historic times, forests have offered shelter to people who, lacking any knowledge of agriculture, have existed as hunters and gatherers. They used only stone and wooden weapons such as bows and arrows to kill their animal prey, and collected berries, fruit and honey from their surroundings. Their influence on the forest environment was minimal and today a few races such as African pygmies and the Punans of Borneo still live in such a simple state of balance with nature. The Punans, for example, have no permanent homes, but use leaves and branches to construct temporary shelters that are used for only a few weeks before being abandoned. The pygmies build similar homes.

Shifting agriculture
Most forest dwellers, however, live in more permanent settlements and grow most of their food in forest clearings they have made. Such people are expert at chopping down trees in order to set fire to them, and this "slash-and-burn" farming results in small areas littered with charred logs and stumps whose ashes enrich the ground. Crops such as wild tapioca (cassava or manioc) are widely grown, but after a year or two the soil loses the little fertility it once had so that a new tract of forest has to be cleared and burned. Such shifting agriculture provides food for more than 200 million inhabitants of the Third World. As a farming system it has been used throughout the world for more than 2,000 years. When there were few farmers per kilometer the land was allowed to lie fallow for at least 10 years so that the soil could recover. Today, however, population pressures are so great that fallow periods have been drastically reduced and a swift repetition of slash-and-burn degrades and removes nutrients from the soil.

Effects on world climate
Tropical forest floors seldom have deep layers of humus so that, once trees are removed, the shallow topsoil is exposed and soon becomes eroded. In turn, this reduces the capacity of the ground to retain moisture, and without this sponge-like effect runoff can become very erratic and lead to floods, such as those that frequently occur in India and Bangladesh. Estuary sedimentation is often greatly increased

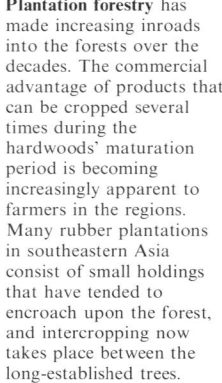
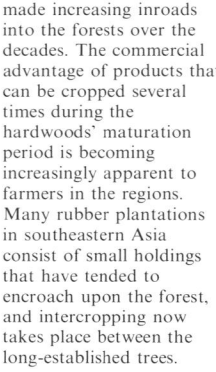

Living in harmony with the forest are small groups of hunter gatherers who mainly live on a flesh diet, killing their prey with bows and arrows. Nuts and berries supplement this diet, and leaves gathered from the immediate jungle cover their temporary dome-shaped shelters. These are abandoned as an area becomes exhausted and the tribe moves on. Twenty or so pygmies need about 500 sq km (200 sq miles) to support themselves.

Selective logging by gangs of men seeking out the straightest and most valuable hardwood species has been the most common form of tree extraction, even though 75 percent of the canopy might have to be destroyed to remove just a few important trees. Today heavy axes are being replaced by power saws that have no difficulty in cutting down the large buttresses that were once left behind.

Plantation forestry has made increasing inroads into the forests over the decades. The commercial advantage of products that can be cropped several times during the hardwoods' maturation period is becoming increasingly apparent to farmers in the regions. Many rubber plantations in southeastern Asia consist of small holdings that have tended to encroach upon the forest, and intercropping now takes place between the long-established trees.

Shifting cultivation converts thousands of square kilometers of primary forest to substandard cultivation every year. Forest is cleared by slash-and-burn, the resulting fertile clearing is cropped with staples such as manioc, and then left to degrade to secondary forest once the ash-strewn ground has lost its poor fertility. Inevitably, the ground becomes permanently degraded. One encouraging antidote to the futility of such shifting agriculture is the recent strategy of agroforestry (as used by countries such as Nigeria and Thailand), which encourages the planting of fast-growing trees at the same time as the farmer's normal crops. Such intercropping offers considerable financial incentives to the small itinerant farmer.

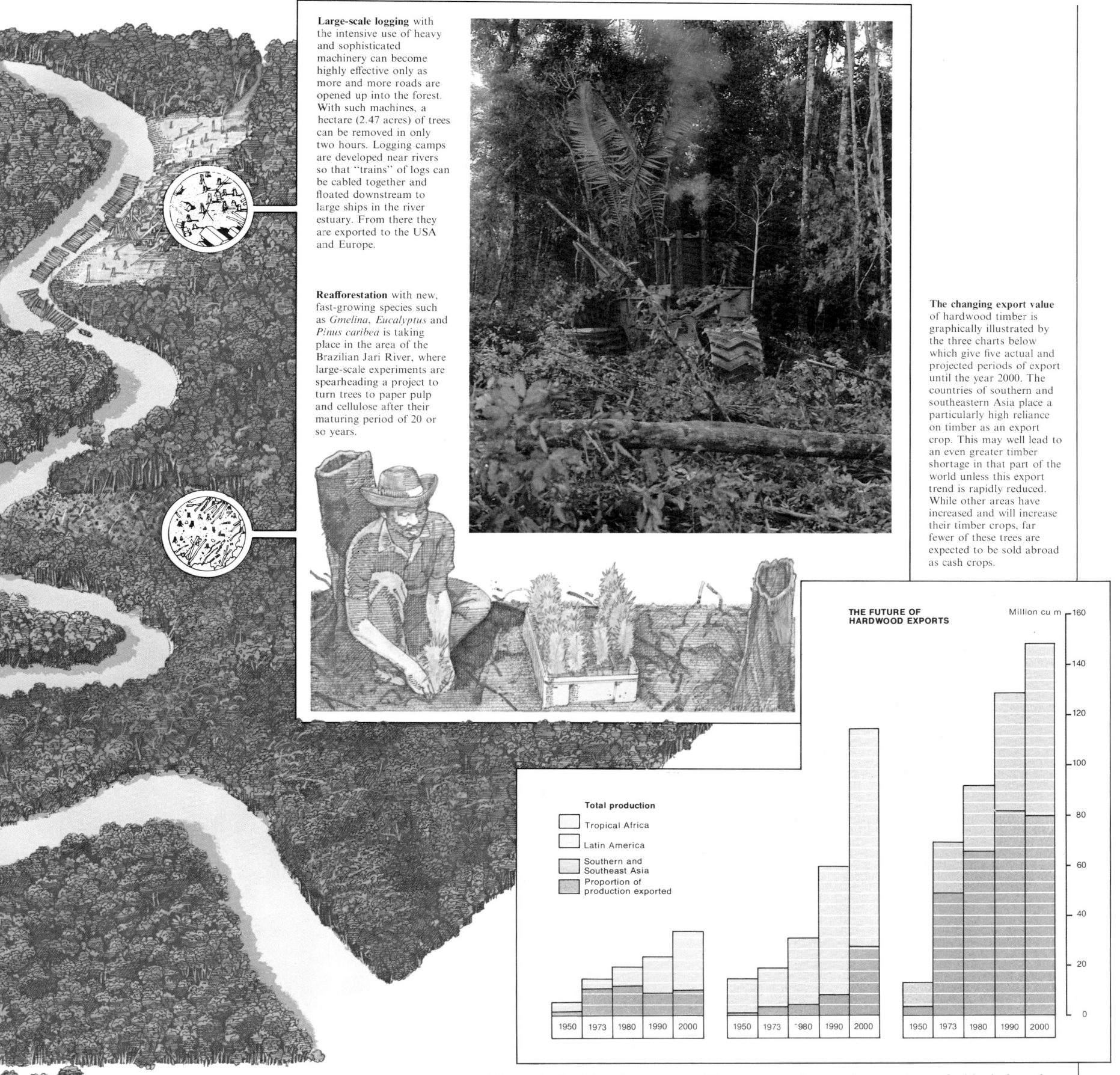

Large-scale logging with the intensive use of heavy and sophisticated machinery can become highly effective only as more and more roads are opened up into the forest. With such machines, a hectare (2.47 acres) of trees can be removed in only two hours. Logging camps are developed near rivers so that "trains" of logs can be cabled together and floated downstream to large ships in the river estuary. From there they are exported to the USA and Europe.

Reafforestation with new, fast-growing species such as *Gmelina*, *Eucalyptus* and *Pinus caribea* is taking place in the area of the Brazilian Jari River, where large-scale experiments are spearheading a project to turn trees to paper pulp and cellulose after their maturing period of 20 or so years.

The changing export value of hardwood timber is graphically illustrated by the three charts below which give five actual and projected periods of export until the year 2000. The countries of southern and southeastern Asia place a particularly high reliance on timber as an export crop. This may well lead to an even greater timber shortage in that part of the world unless this export trend is rapidly reduced. While other areas have increased and will increase their timber crops, far fewer of these trees are expected to be sold abroad as cash crops.

THE FUTURE OF HARDWOOD EXPORTS

Million cu m

Total production
- Tropical Africa
- Latin America
- Southern and Southeast Asia
- Proportion of production exported

1950 1973 1980 1990 2000 | 1950 1973 1980 1990 2000 | 1950 1973 1980 1990 2000

as the forest topsoil is simply washed away by torrential rain. In parts of Asia, deforestation has caused changes in water flow that have interfered with the production of new high-yield rice crops.

Tropical forests contain an enormous store of carbon, and some authorities believe that its release into the air (as carbon dioxide) when the forest is burned down may be as great in volume as that released by the rest of the world's fossil fuels. The higher proportion of carbon dioxide in the atmosphere may lead to an increase in global temperatures, especially at the poles. Trees also release oxygen into the air through photosynthesis, and some scientists have estimated that half of the world's oxygen is derived from this source. Others estimate that half of the rainfall of the Amazon basin is generated by the forest itself, so that any great reduction in tree cover would turn Amazonia into a much drier region.

Threats to Amazonia
Much attention has been paid to the situation of Amazonia, covering as it does some 6.5 million sq km (2½ million sq miles). In an attempt to give better access to timber and mineral reserves, the Brazilian government's building of the TransAmazonian Highway (3,000 km or 1,860 miles long) has opened the way to deforestation, and settlers have been encouraged to make small holdings on the cleared forest beside the road. Between 1966 and 1978, the government calculated that farmers and big business interests had turned 80,000 sq km (31,000 sq miles) of forest into grazing land for 6 million cattle intended for hamburgers. However, like the wholesale extraction of timber, this has proved to be of doubtful economic value. Because costs rise steeply as less accessible areas are tapped, expenses tend to eliminate logging profits.

Threats in Africa
Even greater threats to tropical forest land have come from less cautious and realistic governments, such as that of Ivory Coast. There neither shifting agriculture nor excessive logging for valuable export sales appear to be under any sort of control. Accordingly, between 1966 and 1974, the area of forest declined from 156,000 sq km (60,000 sq miles) to 54,000 sq km (20,000 sq miles), much of the latter being secondary forest that can never be returned to its original status. Like many other developing countries, Ivory Coast has been more keen to cut down and export its profitable timbers than to think about protecting its invaluable forest environment. Inevitably, forest farmers move into cleared areas and often establish plantation cash crops such as coffee, cocoa and rubber, while the establishment of national parks to curtail depletion has often had very little profitable effect. The Malaysian rainforest is also disappearing rapidly, through widescale logging and open-cast mining for bauxite (aluminum ore).

A large proportion of the world's rainforest occurs in tropical countries faced with severe problems of population control. It is therefore inevitable that the pressures on such forests will be great. Human interference does more than merely destroy the primary forest, to be replaced in time by secondary growth; more importantly, the wholesale removal of trees also drastically reduces the vast genetic reservoir contained in the number of plant and animal species the forests harbor. This in itself is a sound ecological argument for preserving forests and for reversing current trends towards monoculture in the tropics. All the warnings about forest depletion appear to be clear, yet there seems little hope that man will heed them until it is too late.

Monsoon Regions

The word monsoon often conjures up the image of torrential rain and steaming tropical jungles. Yet such a view is misleading, for very great contrasts occur in the regions of the tropical world with a monsoon climate. What distinguishes monsoon regions is not so much the amount of rainfall or the permanently high temperatures, but the dramatic contrast between seasons, with an extended dry season as an essential feature. And in fact the word monsoon derives from the Arabic word for season.

THE SEASON OF RAIN
Life in the monsoon regions balances on the expectation of seasonal heavy rain. In much of India, for instance, 85 percent of the annual rainfall occurs during the limited monsoon periods, and humans as well as plants and animals depend on it wholly. About half the world's people live in these regions, in communities whose rhythm of life necessarily reflects the rains' seasonal nature.

This contrast between wet and dry seasons reflects the reversals of winds over sea and land, which in the northern hemisphere blow from the northeast in the dry winter season, and from the southwest in the wet summer periods.

The monsoon regions occur most widely in southern, southeastern and eastern Asia to the south of latitude 25°N, and in western and central Africa north of the Equator, but there are also smaller regions with a characteristically monsoon climate in eastern Africa, northern Australia and central America. Despite the similar overall climatic pattern, however, the monsoon regions are otherwise very diverse.

Before human settlement the original vegetation of the monsoon regions reflected the dominance of an extended dry season followed by a period of violent rainfall. Typical forest cover was provided by the sal (*Shorea robusta*) deciduous forest, which adjusts to extended periods of moisture deficiency by shedding its leaves. However, within the monsoon region rainfall varies from 200 mm (8 in) a year to more than 20,000 mm (800 in), and the rainy periods may vary between three and nine months.

The range of vegetation found in the monsoon regions reflects this diversity. Where tropical rainforest alters to monsoon forest, as in eastern Java, there is a sharp fall in the total number of plant and animal species, and species adapted to endure seasonal drought begin to be seen. At the other extreme of rainfall the forest thins and shades into semidesert vegetation in India's northwest. But if there is a "type" of monsoon vegetation it is tropical deciduous forest, with sal as the dominant species.

As well as contrasts in climate, the monsoon regions also exhibit pronounced changes in temperature and vegetation as a result of variations in altitude. The Western Ghats of India and the foothills of the Himalayas in Assam both rise to more than 2,500 m (8,200 ft). Temperatures decrease sharply at such altitudes with corresponding changes in vegetation. In southern India on the Nilgiri Hills a wet temperate forest is characteristic, with an intermingling of temperate and tropical species. Magnolias, planes and elms all grow there.

Agriculture in monsoon regions

Despite its extensive area there is no part of the monsoon world that is untouched by man and by man's activities. In southern Asia, agricultural activity can be traced back at least 5,000 years, and there have been agricultural settlements throughout the monsoon regions for at least 1,500 years. Man's activity and the grazing of domesticated animals have interfered with, and progressively modified, the natural vegetation. The range of species indicates that, in the whole of the monsoon biome, there is now virtually no primary forest left. The pace of man's interference has speeded up considerably over the last 100 years. As a result, less than 10 percent of the land in southern Asia is now forested, and other parts of the monsoon

Many parts of the world experience "monsoon" winds, blowing from sea to land in summer, and from land to sea in winter; but typical monsoon vegetation is most clearly seen in the regions of southeastern Asia and the Indian subcontinent. In climatic terms, however, the monsoon circulation of seasonal wind reversals, with wetter summers and dry winters, also affects considerable areas of Africa, South America and northern Australia.

☐ Annual rainfall more than 500 mm (20 in), with wet and dry seasons

regions are similarly losing their forest cover.

Many of today's farming methods incorporate traditional cultivation practices, but there have also been very significant changes in recent decades. Traditional agriculture in the monsoon regions has been developed to take into account the seasonal nature of its rainfall pattern and the total rainfall received. The fundamental role of water throughout the region and the absence of low temperatures have placed great importance on either cultivating crops that can tolerate the seasonal rainfall pattern, or on providing irrigation.

Through most of southern Asia, overwhelmingly the most populous of the monsoon regions, the most important single crop is rice, which covers about one-third of the total cultivated area. Rice needs a great deal of water and for this reason is grown mainly in areas of high irrigation, such as the delta lands of the southern and eastern coasts of India, and in areas where rainfall is more than 1,500 mm (59 in) a year. Its cultivation creates a very distinctive landscape as a result of the fact that rice must spend much of its growing period with a few centimeters of water over the soil.

Rice cultivation gives the monsoon regions their characteristic pattern of paddy fields, but other cereal crops such as wheat, the millets and sorghum are also very important. These can tolerate far drier conditions than can rice and occur in areas such as central India or upland Thailand, where uncertain and less abundant rainfall puts a premium on drought tolerance.

Even with traditional crops, man has often interfered extensively with the environment in order to increase yields and attempt to guarantee successful cropping. Traditional irrigation schemes range from diverting rivers at times of flood, in order to lead water to dry land, to digging wells and building small reservoirs. But recent technological developments have brought a new dimension to agricultural activity in the monsoon regions. Large-scale dam and irrigation canal schemes have become important in Africa as well as in monsoon Asia. The introduction and speed of electric or diesel "pumpsets" have transformed well irrigation in regions with extensive groundwater. The

Heat differences in the atmosphere cause the seasonal wind reversals (left) characteristic of monsoon circulation. In January the northern hemisphere is tilted away from the sun, and cold, dry winds blow from the central Asian landmass toward the Equator. Here they change direction (an effect of the Earth's rotation), converge with other winds, and drop their rain. In July the situation is reversed when the heated Asian landmass attracts a flow of cooler air from the equatorial oceans, which moves northward with the sun. The moist air condenses on reaching land, and the monsoon rains descend.

reliable water supply that irrigation can give has brought in its train the opportunity for farmers to adopt a wide range of new farming practices. Chemical fertilizers and new strains of seed have made possible great increases in the productivity of the land in many parts of the monsoon regions, but their use is generally restricted to areas of reliable water supply.

Subsistence cultivation over thousands of years has been by far the most important element in the transformation of the landscape and vegetation of the monsoon world, but the introduction of plantation cultivation during the last centuries has also had a major effect. Tea plantations, for instance, have led to the almost total replacement of natural vegetation in the hills of southern India and Sri Lanka.

Populations in all the countries of the monsoon regions are rapidly increasing, and demands for economic development are constantly growing, placing increasing pressures on the environment, pressures which to date have seemed almost irresistible.

DISAPPEARING ANIMALS
The dwindling wildlife of southeastern Asia includes species that may be regarded locally as pests—a fact that makes their protection difficult outside game reserves. Animals such as the tiger and the wild pig are doubly threatened as human cultivation spreads into the natural habitat: their hunting and foraging grounds are reduced, and their destruction of crops or livestock provides villagers with an obvious incentive for killing them in order to protect their own livelihoods.

Tiger
Panthera tigris

Wild pig
Sus scrofa

SELF-SUFFICIENCY IN CHINA
Local materials are turned into saleable products at a ratan factory in southern China. This factory is not owned by the state but by the village-sized brigade responsible for the manufacturing. The brigade functions as a smaller economic unit within the Ting Chow people's commune of 20 to 30 villages, but is encouraged to act independently, owning what it creates. The commune takes care of such matters as waterways—it contains 82 km (51 miles) of canals.

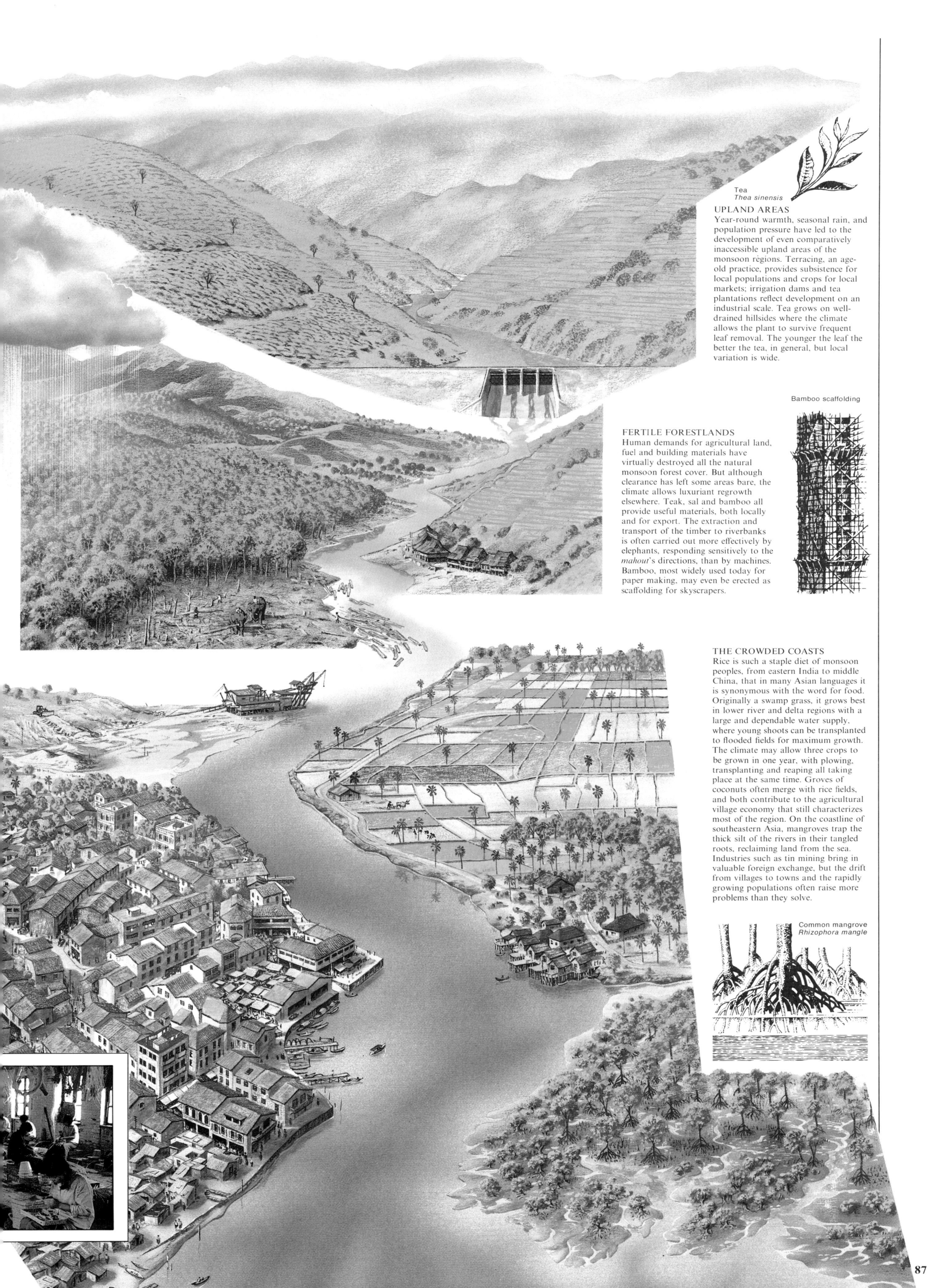

Tea
Thea sinensis

UPLAND AREAS

Year-round warmth, seasonal rain, and population pressure have led to the development of even comparatively inaccessible upland areas of the monsoon regions. Terracing, an age-old practice, provides subsistence for local populations and crops for local markets; irrigation dams and tea plantations reflect development on an industrial scale. Tea grows on well-drained hillsides where the climate allows the plant to survive frequent leaf removal. The younger the leaf the better the tea, in general, but local variation is wide.

Bamboo scaffolding

FERTILE FORESTLANDS

Human demands for agricultural land, fuel and building materials have virtually destroyed all the natural monsoon forest cover. But although clearance has left some areas bare, the climate allows luxuriant regrowth elsewhere. Teak, sal and bamboo all provide useful materials, both locally and for export. The extraction and transport of the timber to riverbanks is often carried out more effectively by elephants, responding sensitively to the *mahout*'s directions, than by machines. Bamboo, most widely used today for paper making, may even be erected as scaffolding for skyscrapers.

THE CROWDED COASTS

Rice is such a staple diet of monsoon peoples, from eastern India to middle China, that in many Asian languages it is synonymous with the word for food. Originally a swamp grass, it grows best in lower river and delta regions with a large and dependable water supply, where young shoots can be transplanted to flooded fields for maximum growth. The climate may allow three crops to be grown in one year, with plowing, transplanting and reaping all taking place at the same time. Groves of coconuts often merge with rice fields, and both contribute to the agricultural village economy that still characterizes most of the region. On the coastline of southeastern Asia, mangroves trap the thick silt of the rivers in their tangled roots, reclaiming land from the sea. Industries such as tin mining bring in valuable foreign exchange, but the drift from villages to towns and the rapidly growing populations often raise more problems than they solve.

Common mangrove
Rhizophora mangle

Mountain Regions

A quarter of Earth's land surface lies at heights of 1,000 m (3,300 ft) or more above sea level. But the highland regions are thinly populated by man, who is, generally speaking, a lowland dweller (most major population centers are less than 100 m (330 ft) above sea level). Some formerly lowland animals have fled from man to the harsh refuge of the mountains, joining with specially adapted plants and wildlife, but today man himself is finding the highland regions increasingly useful and desirable.

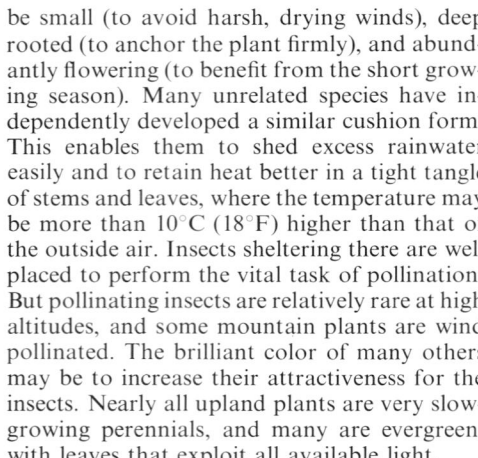
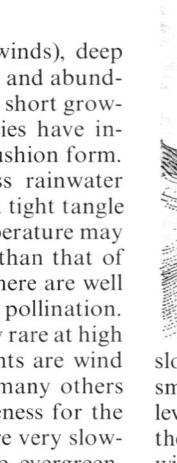

The world's highest mountain peaks rise to almost 9.6 km (6 miles) above sea level, but these heights are small compared to the total diameter of the Earth. The rough surface of an orange would have mountains higher than the Himalayas if scaled up to world size. But mountain environments, although they vary enormously from system to system, all tend to demand remarkable endurance and adaptability from the plants and animals that inhabit them.

Altitude rather than geological variation determines conditions of life on mountains. The temperature falls by 2°C with every 300 m (3.4°F every 1,000 ft)—hence the snowcapped beauty of the heights—and life forms must be adapted to increasingly harsh conditions as height increases. As a result, zones of different life occur at different levels, from tropical forests (at the base of low-latitude mountains) to arctic-type life in the zone of ice and snow at the summit. The latitude of the mountain affects the heights to which these zones extend: trees occur at 2,300 m (7,500 ft) in the southern Alps, whereas farther north, in central Sweden, trees cannot survive above 1,000 m (3,300 ft).

Life at the top
The specially adapted plant and animal life of the mountains occurs above the tree line, for here the variations in living conditions reach their greatest extremes. A plant that has found a foothold on a bare rock face may have to endure intense heat, even where the average temperature is low, when the summer sun blazing through the clear air warms the slabs to tropical temperatures. But when that part of the mountain falls into shadow, the temperature decreases very rapidly, often assisted by the high winds that blow almost constantly throughout the year in many mountain areas.

Soil necessary for plant life develops with the breakdown of the rock through the agency of water, frost and ice. Lichens, whose acids may aid in this destruction, can survive at very high levels, and as they die may add some humus to the newly forming soil. This may first accumulate in sheltered places where plants requiring high humidity, such as mosses and filmy ferns, are found. Flowering plants follow where a greater depth of soil has formed, although some grow in cracks between rocks.

Flowering plants of the mountains all tend to be small (to avoid harsh, drying winds), deep rooted (to anchor the plant firmly), and abundantly flowering (to benefit from the short growing season). Many unrelated species have independently developed a similar cushion form. This enables them to shed excess rainwater easily and to retain heat better in a tight tangle of stems and leaves, where the temperature may be more than 10°C (18°F) higher than that of the outside air. Insects sheltering there are well placed to perform the vital task of pollination. But pollinating insects are relatively rare at high altitudes, and some mountain plants are wind pollinated. The brilliant color of many others may be to increase their attractiveness for the insects. Nearly all upland plants are very slow-growing perennials, and many are evergreen, with leaves that exploit all available light.

Some large animals, such as the ibex or the Rocky Mountain goat, are adapted to spend their lives among the rocks and slopes. These stocky creatures, with hooves that act rather like suction cups, produce their summer young in the security of the heights, although in winter they descend to the shelter of the upper forests. Among smaller mammals, most of which are rodents, some dig burrows in which they hibernate through the winter. Others have very thick insulating coats, and may stay awake through the coldest weather in burrows under the snow.

Refugees from the lowlands
Some mountain animals, particularly carnivorous mammals and birds, have been driven by human persecution into remote mountain fastnesses. Many birds of prey, which could otherwise survive well in lowland areas, have their last strongholds among the mountains. They survive by feeding on small rodents, many of which are extremely wary. Some upland birds feed on insects or on seeds, but their number is comparatively small. The Alpine chough is one of the most interesting of mountain birds, for it has learned to find food among the scraps provided by climbers and skiers, whom it often follows to very high altitudes.

Insects and other small invertebrates, like their Arctic counterparts, may take several years to mature. Some are wingless, and many tend to fly low in order not to be blown away from their home range. Jumping spiders have been seen at heights of 6,700 m (22,000 ft) on the

LIFE ON THE HEIGHTS
Mountain climates become colder the higher one goes. This change in conditions creates distinctive horizontal zones of plant and animal life, although the pattern may vary according to the latitude and aspect of a mountain. Some life forms manage to eke out a precarious existence even on the roof of the world. Lower down, the brief growing season encourages a short burst of plant and animal activity above the timber line, conspicuous for the brightly colored summer flowers. Man mainly inhabits the lower slopes and valleys. He exploits mountain resources but rarely lives on the inhospitable heights.

slopes of Mount Everest, where they exist on small flies and springtails, but even above this level springtails and glacier "fleas" occur where there are no plants, apparently surviving on wind-blown insects and pollen grains.

Man and the mountains
The remote beauty of the mountains has led many peoples to identify them as the abode of the gods, but man himself prefers to live in the more convenient lowlands. The rarefied atmosphere of the heights makes physical work difficult, although some mountain-dwelling peoples have developed adaptations of the blood system to enable them to carry scarce oxygen more efficiently. The short growing season prevents cultivation of all but the hardiest cereal crops, and most uplanders rely on their livestock—cattle, sheep, llamas or yaks—for their existence. The animals are often driven to high pasture during the summer, descending to the valleys in the winter.

Modern, urbanized man finds the beauty and freshness of mountains increasingly attractive. Climbers have invaded most of the world's mountain regions, and in winter hosts of skiers flock to the resorts. Many important wildlife sanctuaries and national parks, particularly in the United States, are in mountain areas.

Lowland populations often rely on the pure mountain streams for both water and energy. Whole upland valleys are sometimes flooded to store water for distant conurbations. And the forceful flow of the water as it descends from the snow-fed heights is frequently harnessed to produce electricity for entire regions hundreds of kilometers away. The clear mountain air also offers the best conditions for astronomical observation, and most observatories today are built in dry, cloudless mountain areas.

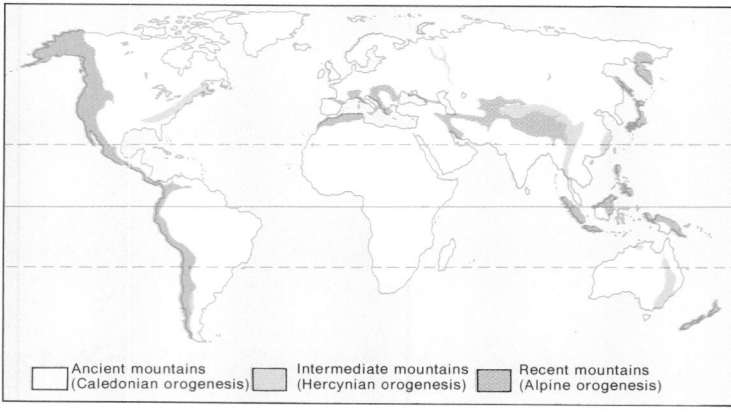

Activity in Earth's crust has produced mountains in every continent (left). Some thrust up sharply, while older mountains have been eroded to rounded shapes. The Scottish Highlands were made by mountain-building forces 400 million years ago (170 million years before the Appalachians and the Urals). The Rockies are 70 million years old and the Alps 15 million years old.

Ancient mountains (Caledonian orogenesis) | Intermediate mountains (Hercynian orogenesis) | Recent mountains (Alpine orogenesis)

Many peoples have believed that the gods have their abodes in the high places of the world. Tibet (above), one of the highest and most mountainous of all countries, has a large number of religious sites. Modern man also finds the clear, dry air suitable for the study of heavenly bodies: most modern observatories, such as Kitt Peak, USA (right), are built on mountain sites far from cities.

MOUNTAIN ADAPTATIONS

Saussurea
Saussurea tridactyla

Alpine soldanella
Soldanella alpina

Ingenious adaptations to harsh mountain conditions have been evolved by many plants, most of which have tiny cells with thick sap that does not freeze easily. Saussurea masks itself with white hair to reduce evaporation from the leaf surface. Alpine soldanellas are active even under snow, pushing up their flowers before the thaw.

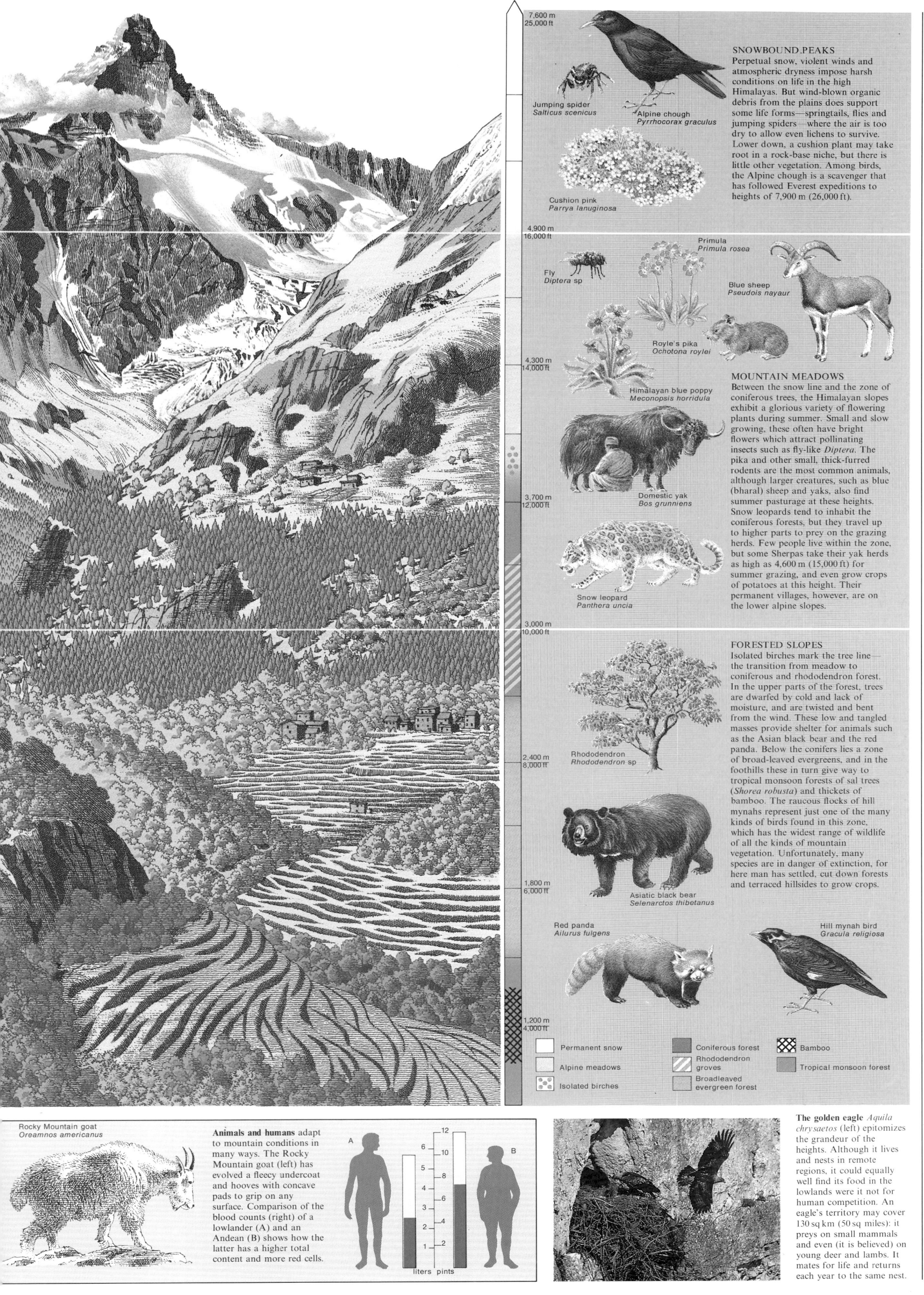

7,600 m
25,000 ft

Jumping spider
Salticus scenicus

Alpine chough
Pyrrhocorax graculus

Cushion pink
Parrya lanuginosa

SNOWBOUND PEAKS

Perpetual snow, violent winds and atmospheric dryness impose harsh conditions on life in the high Himalayas. But wind-blown organic debris from the plains does support some life forms—springtails, flies and jumping spiders—where the air is too dry to allow even lichens to survive. Lower down, a cushion plant may take root in a rock-base niche, but there is little other vegetation. Among birds, the Alpine chough is a scavenger that has followed Everest expeditions to heights of 7,900 m (26,000 ft).

4,900 m
16,000 ft

Fly
Diptera sp

Primula
Primula rosea

Blue sheep
Pseudois nayaur

Royle's pika
Ochotona roylei

Himalayan blue poppy
Meconopsis horridula

Domestic yak
Bos grunniens

4,300 m
14,000 ft

Snow leopard
Panthera uncia

MOUNTAIN MEADOWS

Between the snow line and the zone of coniferous trees, the Himalayan slopes exhibit a glorious variety of flowering plants during summer. Small and slow growing, these often have bright flowers which attract pollinating insects such as fly-like *Diptera*. The pika and other small, thick-furred rodents are the most common animals, although larger creatures, such as blue (bharal) sheep and yaks, also find summer pasturage at these heights. Snow leopards tend to inhabit the coniferous forests, but they travel up to higher parts to prey on the grazing herds. Few people live within the zone, but some Sherpas take their yak herds as high as 4,600 m (15,000 ft) for summer grazing, and even grow crops of potatoes at this height. Their permanent villages, however, are on the lower alpine slopes.

3,700 m
12,000 ft

3,000 m
10,000 ft

FORESTED SLOPES

Isolated birches mark the tree line—the transition from meadow to coniferous and rhododendron forest. In the upper parts of the forest, trees are dwarfed by cold and lack of moisture, and are twisted and bent from the wind. These low and tangled masses provide shelter for animals such as the Asian black bear and the red panda. Below the conifers lies a zone of broad-leaved evergreens, and in the foothills these in turn give way to tropical monsoon forests of sal trees (*Shorea robusta*) and thickets of bamboo. The raucous flocks of hill mynahs represent just one of the many kinds of birds found in this zone, which has the widest range of wildlife of all the kinds of mountain vegetation. Unfortunately, many species are in danger of extinction, for here man has settled, cut down forests and terraced hillsides to grow crops.

Rhododendron
Rhododendron sp

2,400 m
8,000 ft

Asiatic black bear
Selenarctos thibetanus

1,800 m
6,000 ft

Red panda
Ailurus fulgens

Hill mynah bird
Gracula religiosa

1,200 m
4,000 ft

☐ Permanent snow

☐ Alpine meadows

☐ Isolated birches

▨ Coniferous forest

▨ Rhododendron groves

☐ Broadleaved evergreen forest

▨ Bamboo

▨ Tropical monsoon forest

Rocky Mountain goat
Oreamnos americanus

Animals and humans adapt to mountain conditions in many ways. The Rocky Mountain goat (left) has evolved a fleecy undercoat and hooves with concave pads to grip on any surface. Comparison of the blood counts (right) of a lowlander (A) and an Andean (B) shows how the latter has a higher total content and more red cells.

liters pints

The golden eagle *Aquila chrysaetos* (left) epitomizes the grandeur of the heights. Although it lives and nests in remote regions, it could equally well find its food in the lowlands were it not for human competition. An eagle's territory may cover 130 sq km (50 sq miles): it preys on small mammals and even (it is believed) on young deer and lambs. It mates for life and returns each year to the same nest.

Freshwater Environments

Broad, muddy rivers, fast-running streams, miniature ponds and deep, ancient lakes all provide their own distinctive environments for populations of animals and colonies of aquatic plants. And in spite of the fact that these, the world's freshwater systems, contain only a minute proportion of the Earth's total supplies of water, the remarkable variety and richness of the wildlife they support make them among the most valuable and significant of all the world's natural habitats.

Fresh water is never really pure for, like sea water, and indeed like all other natural waters, it contains various dissolved minerals. Fresh water differs from seawater only in the relatively low concentrations of the minerals it contains. But these mineral traces are extremely important; they provide essential nutrients without which freshwater plants could not exist. And without plant life, there would be virtually no animal life either.

Not all parts of every freshwater system are rich in both plants and animals. Large, deep lakes are very similar to oceans—no light can penetrate their gloomy depths, and few plants can live in these conditions. The surface waters, on the other hand, where light is plentiful, teem with microscopic floating plants, mainly single-celled algae such as desmids and diatoms. The edges of lakes provide a different set of conditions again, for here the water is shallow and light can penetrate right through it. Plants can take root in the silt on the bottom, grow up through the water and thrust their leaves out into the light and air. Edges of lakes and, for the same reasons, the waters of small ponds are usually full of such plant life, which in turn supports many freshwater animals.

Running waters
Just as the still waters of lakes and ponds offer a variety of habitats, so the running waters of rivers support many different forms of life, each adapted to the particular conditions of its environment. In the upper reaches, where rivers are scarcely more than upland streams, water is fast flowing and clear of silt. Few plants, except close-clinging mosses, can gain a hold on the bare stony bottom and most of the fish are well muscled and strong bodied to enable them to withstand the constant tug of the current. As a river swells to form a mature lowland water course, however, it becomes slower moving and the water is warmer and richer in nutrients. Plants grow readily in these lower reaches and provide a supply of food for aquatic animals.

With such a wide range of conditions, freshwater environments support an enormous variety of animal life—insects, fishes, amphibians, reptiles, mammals and birds. In some ways insects are the most important of all these creatures: freshwater systems contain more insects and other invertebrates, representing a greater variety of species, than any other kind of animal. Furthermore, these, the smallest representatives of the freshwater animal world, provide one of the most important links in the complex freshwater food chain.

Insects may be the most numerous, but fishes are probably the most familiar of all freshwater creatures, and they certainly show some of the greatest varieties of adaptations to the many different habitats. Their sizes vary from the tiny, 14 mm ($\frac{1}{2}$ in) of the virtually transparent dwarf goby fish found in small streams and lakes in the Philippines to the 4 m (14 ft) of the arapaima found in deep rivers in tropical South America. Their feeding habits vary from those of the ferocious carnivorous piranha of South America to those of the North American paddle fish which, although more than three times the size of the largest piranha, feed solely on microscopic organisms which they filter from the water with their specially adapted throats.

The breeding habits of freshwater fish also vary widely, from the carefully maternal instincts of the African mouthbreeding cichlids—these retain the developing eggs safely in their mouths until the offspring hatch—to the rather more common ejection of eggs into the water, where their fertilization and survival is simply left to chance. Other adaptations include the ability to breathe air (as does the African lungfish), to leap waterfalls (a common practice among migrating salmon) and to emit an electric shock of up to 600 volts (an adaptation of the South American electric eel).

Creatures of the water's edge
Of all the other major groups of animals, amphibians (such as frogs and toads) are probably the most reliant on freshwater systems. Because their skins must not dry out and they have to lay their eggs in water, few amphibians can venture far from the water's edge. And because they cannot tolerate the salt in seawater (it causes them to lose their body fluids through their skins) they are totally dependent upon fresh water for their existence. Reptiles, rather less typical of freshwater environments, range in size from miniature North American terrapins to the giant crocodiles that live along the banks of the Nile. Freshwater mammals, on the other hand, with the considerable exception of the hippopotamus, all tend to be rather small creatures such as otters, beavers, coypus, aquatic moles and water shrews.

Birds are another important group of freshwater creatures. Although few birds are truly aquatic an enormous number of species live in or near freshwater systems and take advantage of the various food supplies: the plants and fish within the waters; the bankside vegetation and small animal life; and the many forms of freshwater insects. Marshes and swamps, for example, provide some of the richest bird habitats in the world.

Also numbered among the species dependent on Earth's freshwater systems is man. And although strictly a nonaquatic, land-living animal, man uses more fresh water than any other creature. His needs seem to be inexhaustible as he harnesses, channels, diverts and often pollutes freshwater systems throughout the world. Unfortunately, the vast requirements of the human race are not always compatible with the rather more humble needs of all other species that depend upon fresh water.

Volume of Lakes in cu km (cu miles)

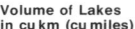

Huron, North America
3,447 (827)

Nyasa, Africa
8,373 (2,009)

Superior, North America
12,153 (2,916)

Tanganyika, Africa
19,418 (4,659)

Baikal, Asia
23,260 (5,581)

Discharge of Rivers in cu m (cu ft) per second

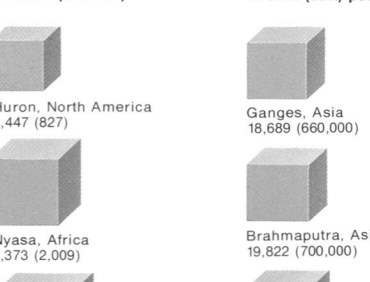

Ganges, Asia
18,689 (660,000)

Brahmaputra, Asia
19,822 (700,000)

Yangtze, Asia
21,804 (770,000)

Congo, Africa
39,644 (1,400,000)

Amazon, South America
212,376 (7,500,000)

The five largest lakes in the world hold more than 53% of all fresh water that flows over the land. The rest of the world's lakes account for another 45%.

The world's largest river, the Amazon, discharges more than one-fifth of all fresh water that flows from the mouths of the world's rivers into the oceans.

THE UPPER REACHES Here, water flows rapidly. Tumbling over bare rocks and stones, it is chilly, oxygen-rich and free of silt. Bird life attracted to these reaches includes the sure-footed dipper, which walks the stream bed hunting for caddis larvae. Slightly farther downstream, but where the river is still narrow and easily dammed, beavers are found. Few plants can live within the water, but river crowfoot has feathery underwater leaves that remain intact where most other plants would be shredded by the current. Many fish, such as trout, have streamlined bodies to offer the least resistance to the stream's pull, while others survive on the bottom by bracing against the rocks—the bullhead, for example. Insects have various means of anchoring themselves to the stream bed—blackfly larvae have hooks to fix themselves to pebbles.

Dipper
Cinclus cinclus

Beaver
Castor fiber

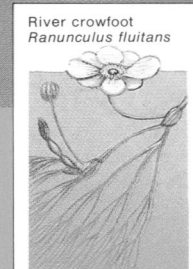

River crowfoot
Ranunculus fluitans

Brown trout
Salmo trutta

Blackfly larvae
Simulium spp

Bullhead
Cottus bairdi

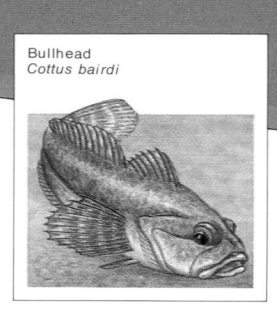

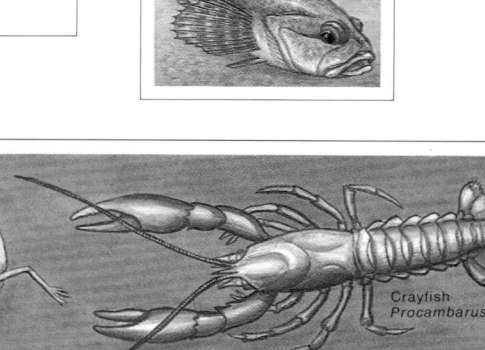

Cave salamander
Proteus anguinus

Blindfish
Typhlichthys sp

Crayfish
Procambarus sp

THE LIFE OF A RIVER

As a river makes its way from its upland source to the sea, it gradually changes its character. And at every stage in its progress, the animals and plants that inhabit the riverbanks and the waters reflect these changes by their adaptations to their environments. Most distinctive and dramatic are those adaptations produced in the wildlife of the upper and lower river reaches.

African spoonbill
Platalea alba

Southern painted turtle
Chrysemys picta dorsalis

THE LOWER REACHES

The slowly flowing river and its muddy banks are rich in animals and plants. Many birds live along the water's edge; spoonbills wade in the shallows, filtering food from the water with their beaks. The banks, fringed with reedmaces and other plants, provide habitats for many reptiles, such as the American painted turtle, and mammals, such as the platypus. Plants also grow on the water—they range from large waterlilies to tiny algae that are food for river fishes: Africa's upside-down-feeding catfish, for example. In these waters, mammals as well as fish are to be found—Amazonian manatees live entirely aquatic lives. The plentiful river plants, such as curled pondweed, provide food for water snails and other herbivores, and cover for predators such as pike. Crustacea and insects living in the silt of the riverbed are food for bottom-feeding fish such as the strange-looking North American paddle fish.

LAKES: CHANGE AND EVOLUTION

No two lakes are alike: each is virtually a self-contained world for its population of aquatic animals and plants. Furthermore, no individual lake remains the same for long: in every lake, slow, inexorable changes in conditions are gradually but constantly changing the balance of species inhabiting the lake bed, the bankside and the water.

Changing conditions may be caused by one of several processes. Accumulating sediments, one of the most common of these processes, may eliminate a lake altogether. The water becomes shallower as sediments thicken (1) and these sediments are then added to and consolidated by water plants taking root. Ultimately, land plants (2) invade the area.

Lakes develop their own peculiar species when the aquatic wildlife that evolves within them has no means of migrating to other freshwater systems to interbreed. The world's only existing species of freshwater seal, for example, is found in just one lake—isolated Lake Baikal in Asia.

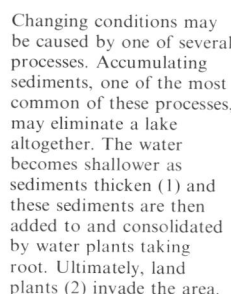

Baikal seal
Phoca sibirica

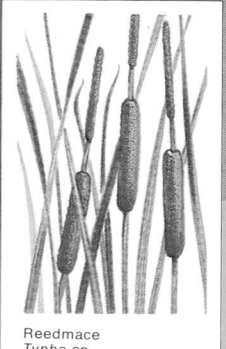

Reedmace
Typha sp

Platypus
Ornithorhynchus anatinus

Waterlily
Nymphaea sp

African catfish
Synodontis batensoda

Amazonian manatee
Trichechus inunguis

Curled pondweed
Potamogeton crispus

White ramshorn snail
Planorbis albus

DARK WATERS

Underground rivers that flow through many of the world's cave systems support surprising numbers of creatures that have adapted to the permanent darkness. Many of these, such as the American cave crayfish, have lost the coloration of their surface-living kin. Some, such as Kentucky blind fishes, no longer possess eyes. Some salamanders are sighted and black when born, but become blind and colorless by adulthood.

Pike
Esox lucius

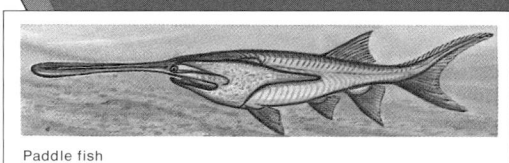

Paddle fish
Polyodon spathula

Spectacled caiman
Caiman crocodilus

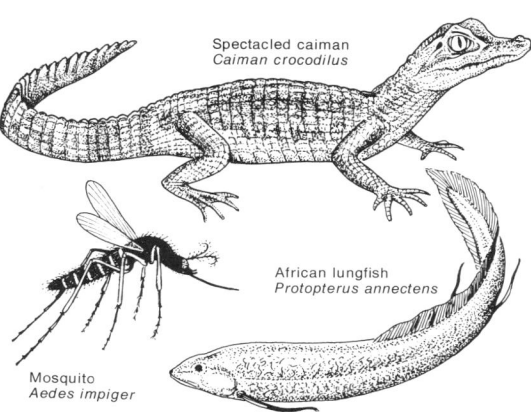

African lungfish
Protopterus annectens

Mosquito
Aedes impiger

WETLANDS

Marshes and swamps are the richest of freshwater habitats. Wading birds, such as Asia's painted stork *Ibis leucocephalus* (above), are particularly common. Reptiles include caimans, which lay their eggs in swamps' warm, rotting vegetation. Of the many insects, mosquitoes are probably the most numerous, and of the many fishes, African lungfish are perhaps best adapted to life in wetlands. They survive drought, when marshes dry up, by their ability to breathe air.

Man and the Freshwater Environments

From earliest times, man has been finding new uses for and making new demands upon the world's freshwater resources. Today, the whole of modern society depends upon a vast supply to serve its agricultural, industrial, domestic and other needs. To meet the ever-growing demand for water, man has performed remarkable engineering feats: altering the courses of rivers, creating and destroying lakes, drowning valleys and tapping water sources that lie deep within the Earth.

Water is essential to human life. Simply to remain alive, an active adult living in a temperate climate needs a liquid intake of about two liters (3½ pints) every day. In warmer climates, the body's fluid requirements are even greater. Consequently, man has always been tied to reliable sources of drinking water—rivers, springs, lakes and ponds—and the availability of these, until very recently, has dictated the routes of all his wanderings and determined the sites of all his settlements.

From the time of the earliest human settlements, however, man has looked upon freshwater systems not simply as a source of drinking water but also as an increasingly useful resource for a multitude of other purposes. Today, water enters into virtually every aspect of modern life, and enormous quantities are used in agriculture, in industry, in the home, in the production of energy, for transport and for recreation.

The farmer's resource

Of all the major activities that rely on fresh water, agriculture is by far the world's largest consumer. In much of Europe and North America, rainfall is usually plentiful and lack of sufficient water for crops is rarely a problem. But in other parts of the world the climate simply does not produce enough rainfall and water shortages are a perennial problem. There, irrigation is not just a sophisticated technique to improve the yields and increase the varieties of crops grown; it is, and always has been, an essential element of agriculture.

Methods of irrigation range from small-scale devices—such as miniature windpumps—used in many developing countries simply to lift water from rivers for bankside crops, to vast dams, reservoirs and canal systems such as the Indus River project in Pakistan, which irrigates 10 million hectares (25 million acres) of land.

Traditional irrigation techniques usually involve using open channels or furrows for conducting water to fields. But one of the major problems with these, particularly in hot climates, is that much of the water evaporates and is lost before it can be used. Several new techniques, such as sprinklers and drip-feed systems, have recently been developed, however, to help make more efficient use of available supplies.

Although the most severe water deficiencies are experienced in the dry subtropical and tropical regions of the world, the temperate regions of North America and Europe, in spite of their relatively wet climates, do suffer shortages. Large towns and cities rarely have enough locally available rainfall or river flow to satisfy both domestic demand and the insatiable needs of industry. In the developed nations, industry consumes more water than any other activity.

Industrial demands

Fresh water is not only an integral part of almost every manufacturing process, it has other important industrial uses. As a source of power, it has been used since the early days of civilization—water wheels were one of man's first industrial inventions. Today, these simple devices are rarely seen in industrial societies, but water power is more important than ever before. Giant dams allow enormous volumes of water to be controlled and the power harnessed to drive turbines and generate electricity.

Freshwater systems have also, for centuries, provided industry with an important means of transporting its goods, and canal systems are still an essential part of industrial infrastructure in many countries of the world: the Europa Canal, when completed, will link three of Europe's major rivers, the Rhine, Main and Danube, and so form a continuous waterway running east–west across the breadth of Europe.

THE VERSATILE RESOURCE

Every day, more than seven trillion liters (12 trillion pints) of water are removed from the world's freshwater systems. Almost all of this water is then directed to one of four destinations—some is destined for industry, a certain amount is piped to towns and cities for use in public services and in homes, some is fed to agricultural regions, and the rest is stored in reservoirs for future use.

INDUSTRY 19.5%

DOMESTIC 4.4%

AGRICULTURE 73.8%

RESERVOIRS 2.3%

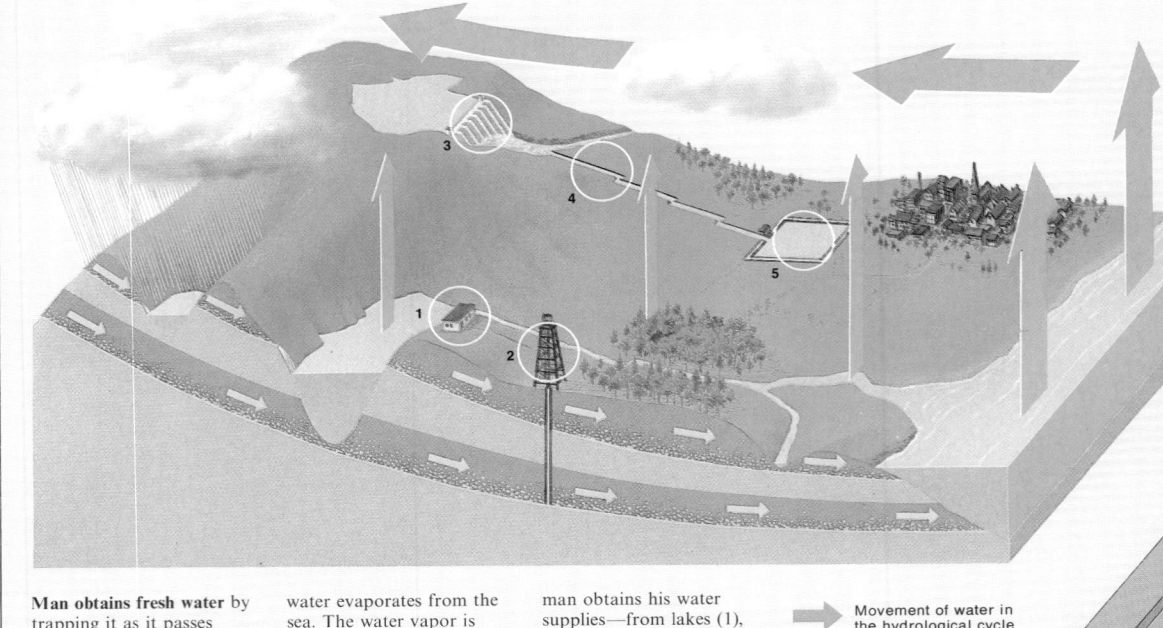

Man obtains fresh water by trapping it as it passes through one of the stages in the hydrological cycle—the never-ending circulation of Earth's waters from the ocean, to the atmosphere, to land. This cycle can be traced from the point at which water evaporates from the sea. The water vapor is blown across the land and falls as rain, hail or snow. Some then evaporates, but the rest completes the cycle by flowing over the land or through the soil or rocks back to the sea. It is at this point in its journey that man obtains his water supplies—from lakes (1), boreholes and wells (2) and dammed rivers (3). These supplies are then either used locally, or are transported by pipe or canal (4) to reservoirs (5) where they are stored ready for distribution.

→ Movement of water in the hydrological cycle

▨ Water-bearing rock

Already, the finished sections of the canal are carrying oil, chemicals, fertilizers, coal, coke and building materials to and from some of Europe's major industrial regions.

Many of Europe's waterways date back to the great canal-building days of the Industrial Revolution. Although a few of these are still used for commerce, many are today considered too narrow to transport economical quantities of goods. Some, however, are now finding a role to play in one of the world's fastest-growing new industries—the leisure market. Today, canals provide a wide range of aquatic activities for holiday makers, tourists and sportsmen.

Recreation and sport

Freshwater systems throughout the world, in fact, are rapidly being recognized and developed as major recreational resources. Lakes and reservoirs are stocked with fish for anglers, silted waterways are dredged to provide sailing and swimming facilities, and old quarries and open-cast workings are landscaped and flooded to provide entirely new freshwater systems purely for leisure pursuits. The projects not only help to rejuvenate previously misused land, they also provide significant incomes to otherwise underdeveloped areas, especially highland regions that are too remote to attract other industries, and are unsuitable for farming.

Unfortunately, however, few of the world's freshwater systems can continue indefinitely to absorb the ever-growing demands that are being made upon them. Overuse of water resources is already a problem and has led to the pollution and destruction of many water systems—in some places overtapping has lowered water tables so drastically that rivers and lakes have been permanently destroyed. Although steps have been taken to protect certain waterways, legislation to guard against misuse and overuse is costly, time consuming and, inevitably, comes up against vested interests. Nevertheless, stringent conservation measures are becoming increasingly necessary if society is to maintain one of its most precious resources.

RESERVOIRS

About 70 trillion liters (15 trillion gallons) of fresh water are held in storage during any one year. Reservoirs ensure a continuous supply of water in spite of the inevitable seasonal fluctuations in demand and in the natural supply from rivers and rainfall. And where reservoirs are formed by damming rivers, there are additional benefits—the vast quantities of water held can be controlled and the power used to generate electricity. The Kariba Dam in Zimbabwe (right) has the potential for producing 8,500 million kilowatt hours of electrical power every year.

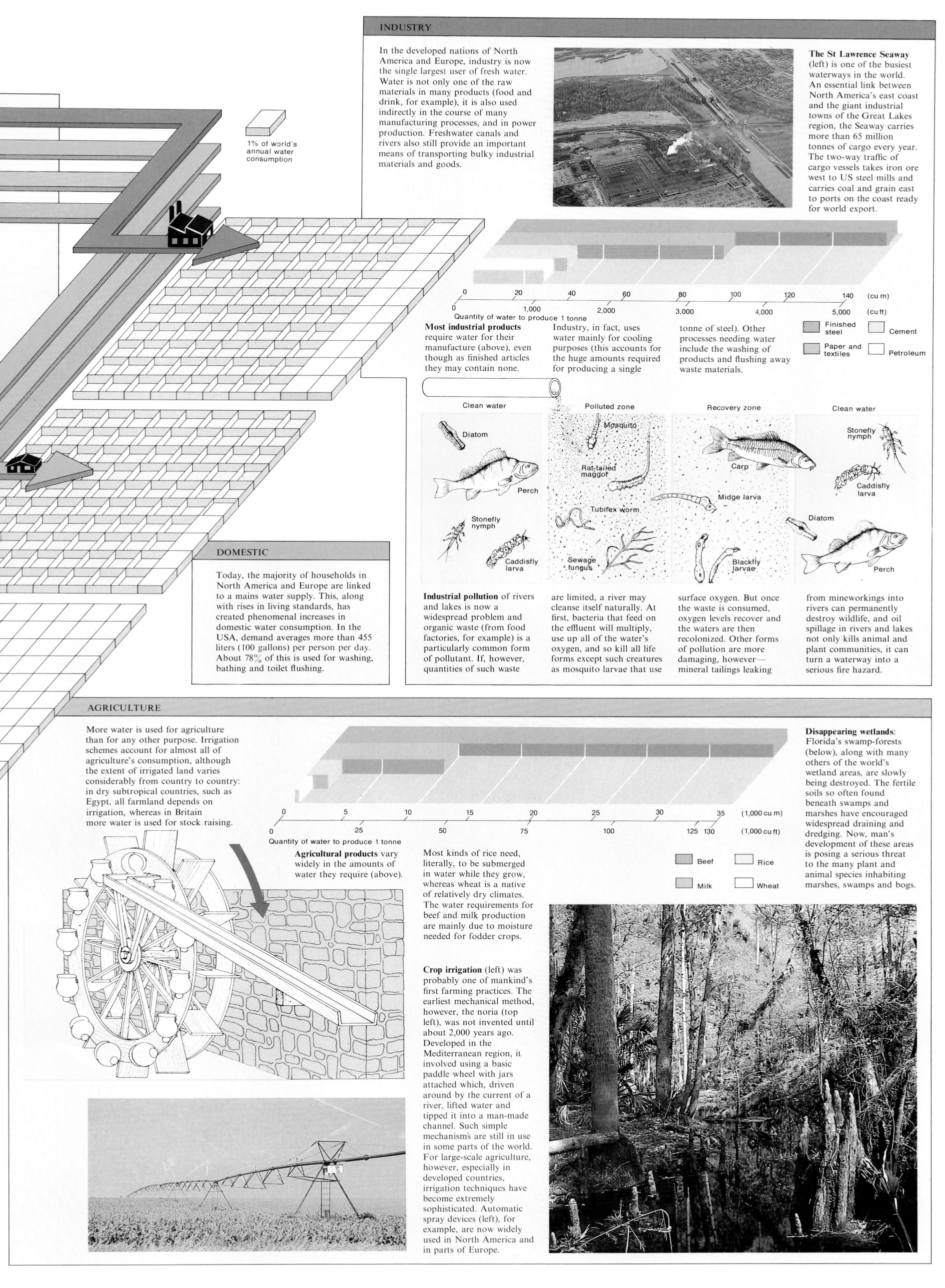

INDUSTRY

In the developed nations of North America and Europe, industry is now the single largest user of fresh water. Water is not only one of the raw materials in many products (food and drink, for example), it is also used indirectly in the course of many manufacturing processes, and in power production. Freshwater canals and rivers also still provide an important means of transporting bulky industrial materials and goods.

The St Lawrence Seaway (left) is one of the busiest waterways in the world. An essential link between North America's east coast and the giant industrial towns of the Great Lakes region, the Seaway carries more than 65 million tonnes of cargo every year. The two-way traffic of cargo vessels takes iron ore west to US steel mills and carries coal and grain east to ports on the coast ready for world export.

1% of world's annual water consumption

Quantity of water to produce 1 tonne			
0 20 40 60 80 100 120 140 (cu m)			
0 1,000 2,000 3,000 4,000 5,000 (cu ft)			

Finished steel · Paper and textiles · Cement · Petroleum

Most industrial products require water for their manufacture (above), even though as finished articles they may contain none.

Industry, in fact, uses water mainly for cooling purposes (this accounts for the huge amounts required for producing a single tonne of steel). Other processes needing water include the washing of products and flushing away waste materials.

Clean water — Diatom, Perch, Stonefly nymph, Caddisfly larva

Polluted zone — Mosquito, Rat-tailed maggot, Tubifex worm, Sewage fungus

Recovery zone — Carp, Midge larva, Blackfly larvae

Clean water — Stonefly nymph, Caddisfly larva, Diatom, Perch

Industrial pollution of rivers and lakes is now a widespread problem and organic waste (from food factories, for example) is a particularly common form of pollutant. If, however, quantities of such waste are limited, a river may cleanse itself naturally. At first, bacteria that feed on the effluent will multiply, use up all of the water's oxygen, and so kill all life forms except such creatures as mosquito larvae that use surface oxygen. But once the waste is consumed, oxygen levels recover and the waters are then recolonized. Other forms of pollution are more damaging, however— mineral tailings leaking from mineworkings into rivers can permanently destroy wildlife, and oil spillage in rivers and lakes not only kills animal and plant communities, it can turn a waterway into a serious fire hazard.

DOMESTIC

Today, the majority of households in North America and Europe are linked to a mains water supply. This, along with rises in living standards, has created phenomenal increases in domestic water consumption. In the USA, demand averages more than 455 liters (100 gallons) per person per day. About 78% of this is used for washing, bathing and toilet flushing.

AGRICULTURE

More water is used for agriculture than for any other purpose. Irrigation schemes account for almost all of agriculture's consumption, although the extent of irrigated land varies considerably from country to country: in dry subtropical countries, such as Egypt, all farmland depends on irrigation, whereas in Britain more water is used for stock raising.

Quantity of water to produce 1 tonne			
0 5 10 15 20 25 30 35 (1,000 cu m)			
0 25 50 75 100 125 130 (1,000 cu ft)			

Beef · Milk · Rice · Wheat

Agricultural products vary widely in the amounts of water they require (above).

Most kinds of rice need, literally, to be submerged in water while they grow, whereas wheat is a native of relatively dry climates. The water requirements for beef and milk production are mainly due to moisture needed for fodder crops.

Crop irrigation (left) was probably one of mankind's first farming practices. The earliest mechanical method, however, the noria (top left), was not invented until about 2,000 years ago. Developed in the Mediterranean region, it involved using a basic paddle wheel with jars attached which, driven around by the current of a river, lifted water and tipped it into a man-made channel. Such simple mechanisms are still in use in some parts of the world. For large-scale agriculture, however, especially in developed countries, irrigation techniques have become extremely sophisticated. Automatic spray devices (left), for example, are now widely used in North America and in parts of Europe.

Disappearing wetlands: Florida's swamp-forests (below), along with many others of the world's wetland areas, are slowly being destroyed. The fertile soils so often found beneath swamps and marshes have encouraged widespread draining and dredging. Now, man's development of these areas is posing a serious threat to the many plant and animal species inhabiting marshes, swamps and bogs.

Seawater Environments

The oceans form by far the largest of the world's habitable environments, covering almost three-quarters of the Earth's surface at an average depth of more than 3,500 m (11,500 ft). Little more than a century ago, scientists believed that the deep sea's low temperatures, perpetual darkness and immense pressures made life in these regions completely untenable. But we now know that animals live at all depths in the ocean, even at the bottom of trenches more than 11,000 m (36,000 ft) deep.

THE PATTERN OF MARINE LIFE
The distribution of life in the seas is like an inverted pyramid whose broad base is formed by billions of minute single-celled plants—the phytoplankton. Plants need sunlight and nutrient salts, so phytoplankton occurs only in the upper, sunlit layers and where salts are present. Elsewhere, the distribution of marine life thins out rapidly.

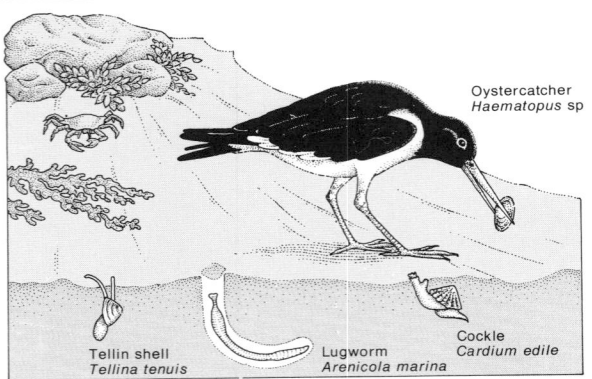

Shore life belongs to both land and sea, and thus has to cope with a wide range of conditions. Seaweeds get all their food from the sea and are quite unlike land plants. Many animals take refuge below the surface: tellin shell molluscs sift food particles through special "lips"; lugworms swallow sand, digesting any organic matter; cockles take in food and eject waste through two siphons. Some birds have bills adapted for opening bivalve molluscs.

Oystercatcher *Haematopus* sp

Tellin shell *Tellina tenuis*
Lugworm *Arenicola marina*
Cockle *Cardium edile*

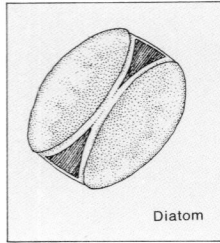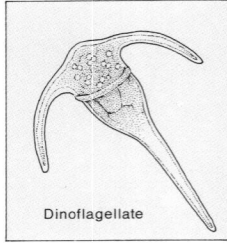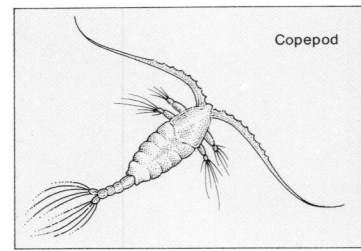

Marine plant life consists largely of diatoms—minute single-celled specks, each enclosed in a lidded box of silicon. Dinoflagellates, classed as plants but able to swim, dominate warmer waters. Both are food for copepods, the flea-sized grazers whose total weight, in the North Sea alone, is some seven million tonnes.

Diatom
Dinoflagellate
Copepod

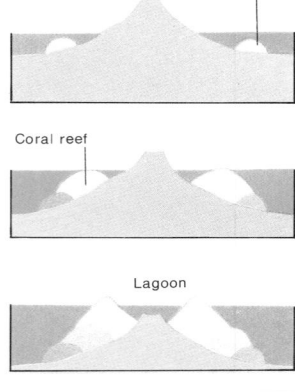

A coral atoll, forming in warm shallow water round an extinct volcano, makes up a living aquarium for thousands of tropical marine life forms. Countless billions of tiny polyps, each secreting a hard, calcareous skeleton, form the first layer of the reef, but die as the volcano gradually sinks. Their skeletons provide a base for further layers of corals, which enclose the sinking island to create a shallow, salt water lagoon. Different coral species in the same reef provide homes for a great variety of life.

Volcanic island   Coral

Coral reef

Lagoon

Life is by no means evenly distributed throughout the oceans, either vertically or horizontally. The great majority of marine creatures are concentrated in the upper few hundred meters, for the biological organization of life in the seas, as on land, depends on photosynthesis (the process by which plants use the Sun's energy to combine carbon dioxide and water to produce more complex compounds). This near-surface layer is the euphotic ("well-lighted") zone.

Some of the Sun's rays are reflected from the surface of the sea, and those that penetrate are scattered and absorbed as they pass through the water, so that even in the clearest oceanic water there is insufficient light to support photosynthesis at depths greater than about 100 m (330 ft). In turbid inshore regions, where the water is less clear, this near-surface layer may be reduced to a very few meters. So the large seaweeds that anchor themselves to the seabed are restricted to the small areas of the sea where the water is sufficiently shallow to allow them to photosynthesize. Of much greater importance over most of the oceans are the tiny floating plants of the phytoplankton, which live suspended in the sunlit surface layers.

Pastures of the sea
Phytoplankton, like all plant life, requires not only sunlight for survival but also adequate supplies of nutrient salts and chemical trace elements. River waters carry down considerable quantities of dissolved mineral salts and other

matter, so that high levels of phytoplankton production may occur locally around major estuaries. But a far more important source of nutrient supply to the euphotic zone is the recycling of salts that have sunk into the deeper layers, locked up in the bodies of plants and animals or in their fecal pellets.

In those areas of the oceans that overlie the continental shelves (about six percent of the total), the depth is nowhere more than about 200 m (650 ft), and the nutrient-rich bottom water is fairly readily brought back to the surface by currents and the stirring effect of storms. This stirring can reach much greater depths in near-polar latitudes, where the "water column" is not layered by temperature but remains more or less uniformly cold from top to bottom. In the Antarctic, cold (and therefore heavy) surface water sinks and is replaced by nutrient-rich water that may surface from depths of 1,000 m (3,300 ft).

In subtropical and tropical regions of the open ocean, where the warm surface layer is only a few tens of meters deep, the temperature falls rapidly with depth. There is little exchange between deep and shallow layers, and the euphotic zone receives an adequate supply of nutrient salts only in certain areas. These occur between westward-flowing and eastward-flowing currents in each of the major oceans. The Earth's rotation causes these currents to diverge so as to create an upwelling of nutrient-rich water along their common boundaries.

Finally, in restricted coastal regions of the tropics and subtropics the local climatic conditions cause an offshore movement of surface water, which is again replaced by upwelling nutrient-rich deep water. The central oceanic regions, including the deep blue subtropical waters, are in effect the deserts of the sea.

Sea grazers and carnivores
The abundance of animals in the oceans closely follows that of the plants. But very few of the larger marine animals can feed directly on the phytoplankton because the individual plants are so small—often only a fraction of a millimeter across. Instead, the phytoplankton supports an amazingly diverse community of planktonic animals, which also spend their lives in mid-water and are swept along by the ocean currents. This community, the zooplankton, includes many different protozoans (single-celled animals), crustaceans, worms and molluscs, and also the juvenile stages of fishes and of many invertebrate animals that live as adults on the seabed. Most members of the zooplankton are very small and many of them graze on the phytoplankton. But some planktonic animals, particularly among the jellyfish and salps, may be a meter or more across and are voracious carnivores feeding on their planktonic neighbors. In turn, the zooplankton provides food for many of the active swimmers such as the fishes and baleen whales, while at the top of the food chain are larger carnivores including

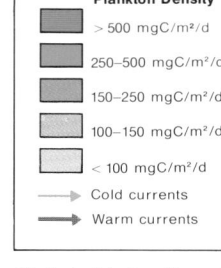

Plankton Density

- > 500 mgC/m²/d
- 250–500 mgC/m²/d
- 150–250 mgC/m²/d
- 100–150 mgC/m²/d
- < 100 mgC/m²/d
- → Cold currents
- ⇒ Warm currents

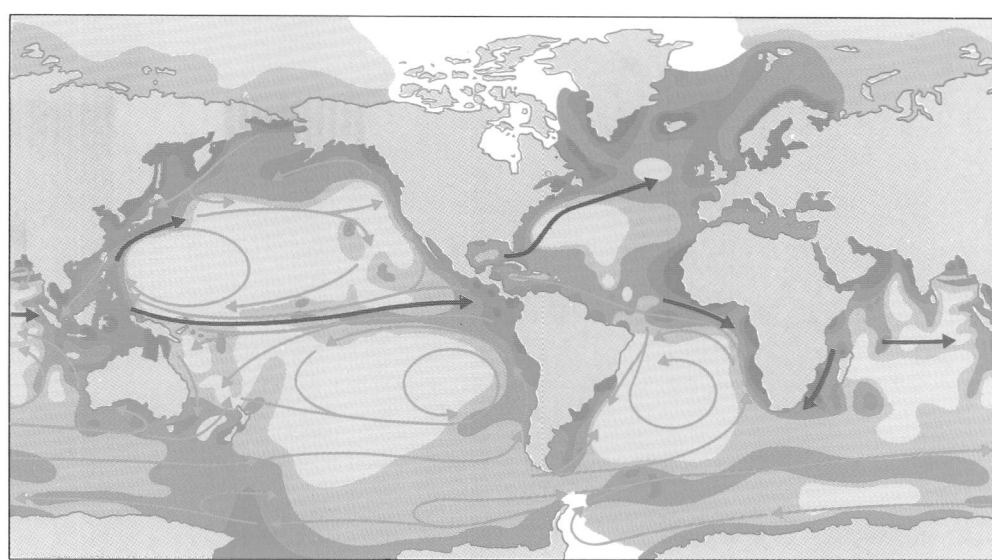

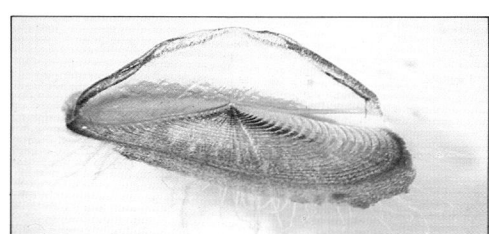

The by-the-wind sailor, *Velella*, is a so-called colonial animal, consisting of a whole collection of animals that function as a single individual. The gas-filled float of its body carries a vertical sail to catch the wind, and below dangle a group of modified polyps specialized for particular roles such as deterrence, reproduction, feeding and digesting.

Phytoplanktonic cells need not only sunlight but also nutrient salts, and so they are restricted to areas where these are available: coastal regions, high latitudes (particularly the Antarctic), narrow tongues extending across the tropical regions of the main ocean basins, and a number of subtropical upwelling regions.

Zones of life (below) extend from the teeming euphotic ("well-lighted") layer to the sparsely populated bathypelagic ("deep-sea") depths, while benthic ("bottom") life occurs at all seabed levels. Phytoplankton (plant life) (1) dictates the pattern of the rest, flourishing where surface conditions allow nutrient salts to well up from lower depths. Herbivores such as minute zooplankton (2) provide food for a host of surface-layer life, which in turn feeds larger predators. Dead animals and fecal pellets fall to lower levels, where they sustain life, but in far smaller quantity.

1 Phytoplankton
2 Zooplankton
3 Blue whale *Balaenoptera musculus*
4 Herring *Clupea harengus*
5 Gray seal *Halichoerus grypus*
6 Bluefin tuna *Thunnus thynnus*
7 Bottlenosed dolphin *Tursiops truncatus*
8 Mackerel *Scomber scomber*
9 Common squid *Loligo* spp
10 White shark *Carcharodon carcharias*
11 Hatchet fish *Argyropelecus hemigymnus*
12 Giant squid *Architeuthis* spp
13 Sea anemone *Cerianthus orientalis*
14 Tripod fish *Benthosaurus grallator*
15 Scarlet shrimp *Notostomus longirostris*
16 Angler fish *Linophryne bicornis*
17 Brittle star *Ophiothrix fragilis*
18 Sea cucumber class Holothuroidea

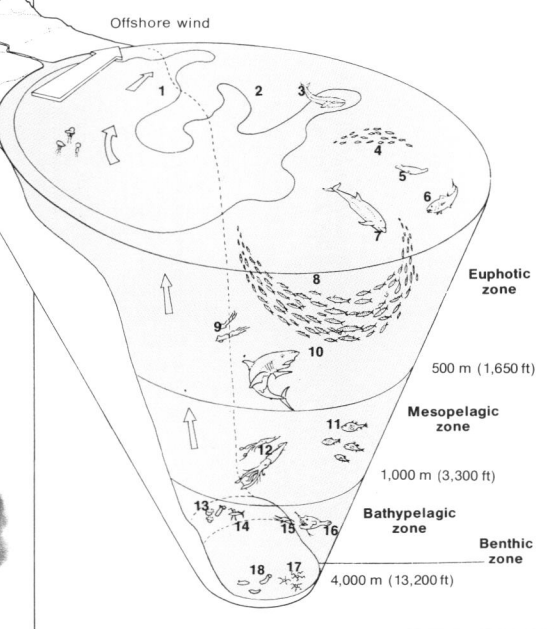

Offshore wind

Euphotic zone

500 m (1,650 ft)

Mesopelagic zone

1,000 m (3,300 ft)

Bathypelagic zone

Benthic zone

4,000 m (13,200 ft)

Bizarre life forms new to science live in the sunless depths, where plumes of hot mineral-rich water gush through deep-sea vents in the Earth's crust. These oases of life support huge, gutless tubeworms more than 1.5 m (5 ft) long, which appear to take food particles from the hot vents through blood-red tentacles. Other creatures include blind crabs and large white clams.

sharks, tuna-like fishes and toothed whales.

Beneath the euphotic zone, of course, there can be no herbivores at all, although some animals that spend the daylight hours in the deeper layers move upwards at night to feed in the plankton-rich surface waters. All of the permanent members of the deep-living communities are dependent for food upon material that sinks or is carried downwards from the euphotic zone. Many of them feed on dead animal remains and fecal material as it sinks through the water column or after it reaches the seabed. These detritus eaters in turn support the predatory carnivores that feed upon the detritivores or upon each other.

In shallow areas the food material that reaches the bottom supports complex communities, notably the rich and varied groups of invertebrates and fishes associated with coral reefs. In the deep sea, however, where the euphotic zone is separated from the seabed by several kilometers of water, much of the sinking material is recycled within the water column and relatively little reaches the bottom. Life on the deep-sea floor therefore becomes more and more sparse with increasing depth, but in recent years scientists have discovered that this community includes a surprising number of fishes, some many meters in length. So far man's knowledge of these deep-sea communities is relatively meager, but with our increasing use of the deep oceans we may need to know much more about the life in this environment.

95

Man and the Seawater Environments

For thousands of years man has used the oceans as a source of food and other materials, and as a repository for wastes. But only in the last 100 years have technological advances and fast-growing human populations had a significant effect, to a point where overfishing and pollution are becoming a cause for concern. Harvesting of krill and seaweeds may ease the pressure on traditional seafoods, but legal restrictions on dumping of wastes or on overfishing are notoriously hard to enforce.

Until about the middle of the nineteenth century the seas had always seemed to be a boundless source of food and of income for fishermen who were brave enough to face the elements with their relatively small sailing ships and primitive gear. But once fishing vessels began to be fitted with steam engines in the 1880s they became relatively independent of the weather, while improvements in the fishing gear itself, such as steam-powered winches in trawling and harpoon guns in whaling, made the whole business of fishing much more efficient.

At first these advances resulted in enormous increases in catches, but in many fisheries this was rapidly followed by a distressing fall in the catch per unit of effort—that is, it was becoming more and more difficult in successive years to catch the same amount of fish as before. In most fisheries the initial response to this situation was to increase the size and number of fishing vessels and to search for new fishing grounds. But as the fishing pressure on the stocks increased, with smaller fish being captured, often before they were able to reproduce, the catch per unit of effort frequently continued to fall.

In many cases attempts were made to counter the effects of overfishing by introducing regulations to control the mesh size of the nets, so allowing the small fish to escape; by establishing closed seasons or quotas of fish which might legitimately be taken from a particular fishing ground in any one year; or even, as in the case of the British herring fishery in the late 1970s, by imposing a complete ban on fishing. Moral questions also sometimes intervene, as in whaling operations, which, many conservationists believe, have driven some species close to extinction despite attempts to rationalize the fisheries.

Fisheries in decline

The North Sea trawl fishery, the first to be affected by the new technology in the nineteenth century, has been declining in terms of catch per unit of effort since the early decades of this century. Dramatic but short-lived improvements after the "closed seasons" of the two world wars proved that fishing pressure had a serious effect on stocks, but by the 1970s many North Sea fishing ports had become almost deserted. This decline put pressure on more distant fishing grounds used by European fishermen, and recent decades have been marked by a series of fishing disputes, with nations fighting for the continued existence of their fisheries despite clear evidence that there are not enough catchable fish to satisfy everyone.

A similar story of declining catches during the present century could be told of many of the old-established fisheries around the world, but at the same time the demand for fish in a protein-hungry world has increased. To satisfy this demand the total annual world catch increased by about seven percent from the end of World War II until the early 1970s, by this time reaching a figure of around 60–70 million tonnes. But this increase was achieved only by exploiting previously unfished stocks or new geographical areas. Such an increase cannot go on indefinitely, for we are rapidly running out of "new" areas and some of the new fisheries have already shown the same symptoms of overfishing as the older ones—and sometimes even more dramatically.

New foods from the sea

The indications are that the present total catch is close to the maximum that can be obtained from relatively conventional fisheries even with careful management, and that, to increase the total, or even to sustain it, we must look to completely new sources such as krill, the shrimp-like food of the whalebone whales.

Estimates of the sustainable annual catch of krill in the Antarctic range from about 50 to 500 million tonnes, that is up to about seven times as much as the current total from all other fisheries put together. Of course, the use of such an enormous quantity of small crustaceans would present considerable problems. Part of it might be converted into a protein-rich paste for human consumption, but much would be used indirectly as a feed for farm animals.

Many larger seaweeds are already cropped in several parts of the world, particularly in Japan, and are used not only for human food but also for animal food and in many industrial processes. About one million tonnes of seaweed are taken each year, but because seaweeds grow naturally only in relatively shallow areas of the oceans this figure could probably not be significantly increased using natural populations. However, seaweeds can be grown artificially on frames floating over deep water. Experiments suggest that, by enriching the surface layers through artificial upwelling of nutrient-rich deep water, each square kilometer of such a floating seaweed farm could produce enough food to feed 1,000–2,000 people, and enough energy and other products to satisfy the needs of a further 1,000. With an estimated 260 million sq km (100 million sq miles) of "arable" surface, the seas might thus support up to 10 times the present world population.

Polluted waters

Of course, the present century has seen an increase not only in what man takes out of the sea but also in the harmful substances that he throws into it. Not only oil but many other substances are dumped into the seas accidentally or intentionally, usually either in the discharged effluent from industrial plant or as a result of agricultural chemicals being leached into rivers and thence into the ocean. In many cases the amounts are very small compared with the amounts present in the oceans as a whole; the problem is that they are usually released, and accumulate, in restricted inshore areas near which we live and from which we obtain most of our sea-caught food.

Since the 1930s there have been both national and international attempts to control pollution by legislation, and since 1958 a series of United Nations conferences has sought agreement on many aspects of international maritime law, including pollution. Despite many prophecies of imminent doom, it does not seem that marine pollution yet poses any general threat to humanity. Nevertheless, with ever-increasing industrialization and the production of more and more toxic materials, including radioactive wastes, it is essential that we monitor the effects of man's activities on the ocean.

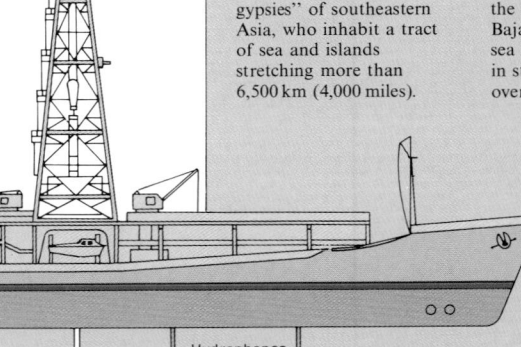

The ocean is home to the Bajau (above), the "sea gypsies" of southeastern Asia, who inhabit a tract of sea and islands stretching more than 6,500 km (4,000 miles).

Each group has its own clan pattern, blazoned on the sails of their *praus*. The Bajau may live on the open sea in clusters of boats, or in stilt-house villages built over estuaries.

Drilling derrick

Hydrophones

THE MARINE RESOURCES

Modern technology has enabled man to expand his age-old exploitation of the seas to the limit in some areas, and a need for the careful management of our marine resource is imperative. But in some fields, such as energy and the extraction of fresh water, the seas may yield inexhaustible riches.

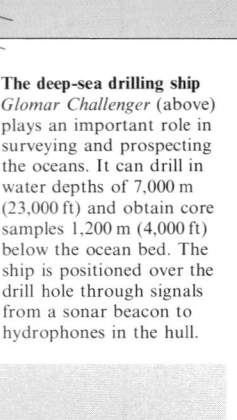

The deep-sea drilling ship *Glomar Challenger* (above) plays an important role in surveying and prospecting the oceans. It can drill in water depths of 7,000 m (23,000 ft) and obtain core samples 1,200 m (4,000 ft) below the ocean bed. The ship is positioned over the drill hole through signals from a sonar beacon to hydrophones in the hull.

Sonar beacons

Core sample tube

Drilling head

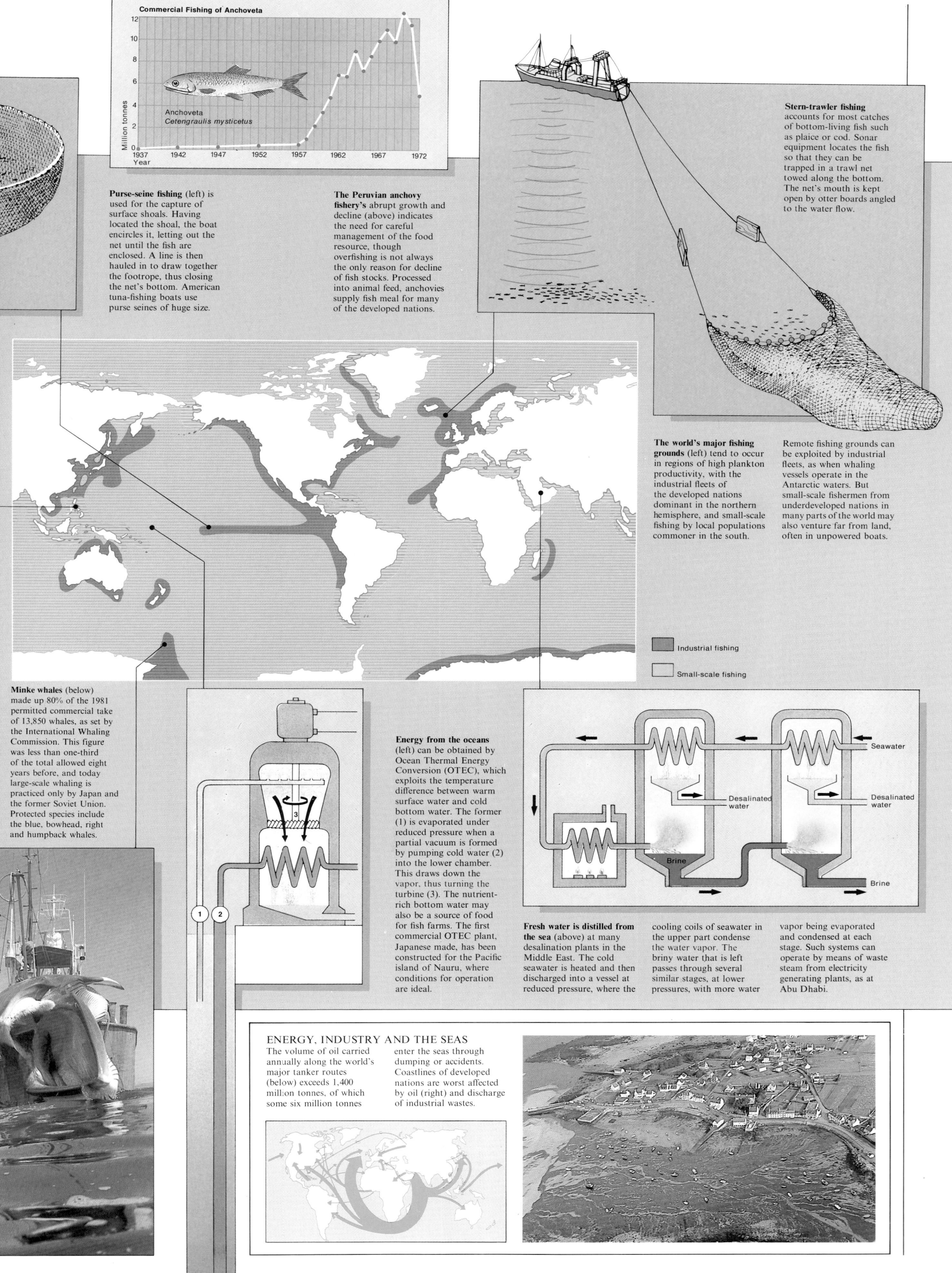

Commercial Fishing of Anchoveta

Anchoveta
Cetengraulis mysticetus

Purse-seine fishing (left) is used for the capture of surface shoals. Having located the shoal, the boat encircles it, letting out the net until the fish are enclosed. A line is then hauled in to draw together the footrope, thus closing the net's bottom. American tuna-fishing boats use purse seines of huge size.

The Peruvian anchovy fishery's abrupt growth and decline (above) indicates the need for careful management of the food resource, though overfishing is not always the only reason for decline of fish stocks. Processed into animal feed, anchovies supply fish meal for many of the developed nations.

Stern-trawler fishing accounts for most catches of bottom-living fish such as plaice or cod. Sonar equipment locates the fish so that they can be trapped in a trawl net towed along the bottom. The net's mouth is kept open by otter boards angled to the water flow.

The world's major fishing grounds (left) tend to occur in regions of high plankton productivity, with the industrial fleets of the developed nations dominant in the northern hemisphere, and small-scale fishing by local populations commoner in the south.

Remote fishing grounds can be exploited by industrial fleets, as when whaling vessels operate in the Antarctic waters. But small-scale fishermen from underdeveloped nations in many parts of the world may also venture far from land, often in unpowered boats.

Industrial fishing

Small-scale fishing

Minke whales (below) made up 80% of the 1981 permitted commercial take of 13,850 whales, as set by the International Whaling Commission. This figure was less than one-third of the total allowed eight years before, and today large-scale whaling is practiced only by Japan and the former Soviet Union. Protected species include the blue, bowhead, right and humpback whales.

Energy from the oceans (left) can be obtained by Ocean Thermal Energy Conversion (OTEC), which exploits the temperature difference between warm surface water and cold bottom water. The former (1) is evaporated under reduced pressure when a partial vacuum is formed by pumping cold water (2) into the lower chamber. This draws down the vapor, thus turning the turbine (3). The nutrient-rich bottom water may also be a source of food for fish farms. The first commercial OTEC plant, Japanese made, has been constructed for the Pacific island of Nauru, where conditions for operation are ideal.

Seawater

Desalinated water

Desalinated water

Brine

Brine

Fresh water is distilled from the sea (above) at many desalination plants in the Middle East. The cold seawater is heated and then discharged into a vessel at reduced pressure, where the cooling coils of seawater in the upper part condense the water vapor. The briny water that is left passes through several similar stages, at lower pressures, with more water vapor being evaporated and condensed at each stage. Such systems can operate by means of waste steam from electricity generating plants, as at Abu Dhabi.

ENERGY, INDUSTRY AND THE SEAS

The volume of oil carried annually along the world's major tanker routes (below) exceeds 1,400 million tonnes, of which some six million tonnes enter the seas through dumping or accidents. Coastlines of developed nations are worst affected by oil (right) and discharge of industrial wastes.

Part 5

UNDERSTANDING MAPS
What maps are and how they are made
New horizons and latest developments in maps and mapmaking
How to read the language of maps

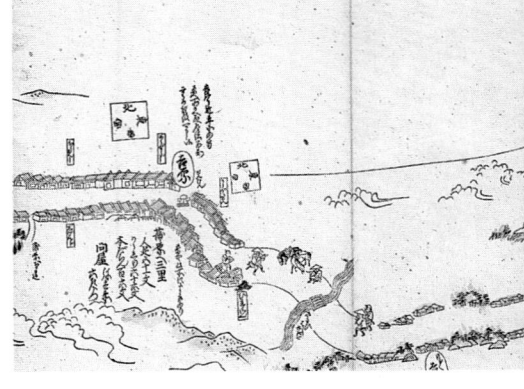

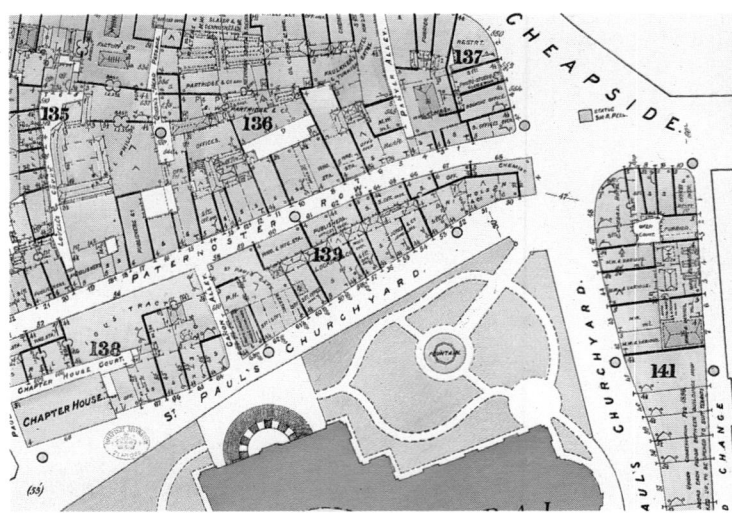

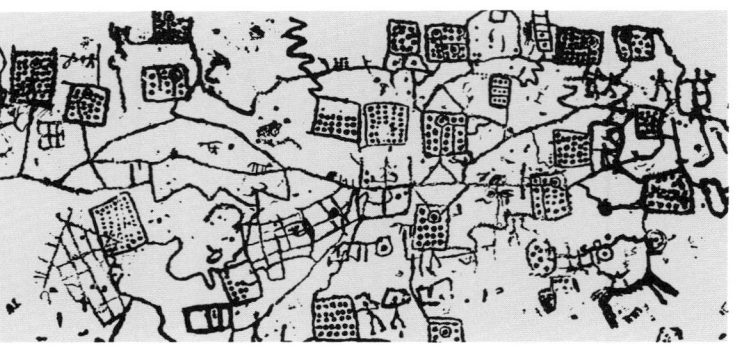

Elegant road maps with pictorial and geographical features have been produced by many different cultures. The woodcut map of the Tōkaidō (detail above), the great Japanese highway, 555 km (345 miles) long, between Edo (Tokyo) and Kyoto, was drawn as a panorama by the famous artist Moronobu in 1690. Its pictorial details do not prevent it being an accurate representation of the road's track. A Mexican map of the Tepetlaoztoc valley (right) drawn in 1583 marks roads with footprints between parallel lines, and hill ranges with wavy lines. Symbols in panels represent place-names.

Maps defining territory and ownership are almost as old as the human territorial instinct itself. The rock-carving maps of the Val Camonica, Italy (above), dating from the second and first millennia BC, show stippled square fields, paths, river lines, houses, and even humans and animals. It is uncertain whether their purpose was legal, but the need to establish ownership is a basic function of many maps, as seen in a detail from Goad's 19th-century insurance map of London (left), where every occupation is recorded.

America first appears as a separate continent (below) in an inset to Martin Waldseemüller's world map of 1507, with the two hemispheres facing each other. Presiding over the Old World is Claudius Ptolemy, the 2nd-century geographer whose remarkably scientific maps, copied and recopied over a thousand years, were revised and emended by Waldseemüller to show some of the results of Portuguese exploration. His New World counterpart is the Italian Amerigo Vespucci, one of the early explorers of the continent, after whom it was named. This is the first map to show the Pacific (not yet named) as an ocean between America and Asia. The west coast of South America, still to be explored by Europeans, seems to be inspired guesswork. The island between the landmasses is Cipango (Japan) known from Marco Polo.

The earliest surviving Chinese globe (above) was made in 1623 by two Jesuit missionaries, probably for the emperor of China. The long legend in Chinese expresses terms and ideas derived from early Chinese cosmology. It describes the Earth as "floating in the Heavens like the yolk of an egg . . . with all objects having mass tending toward its center"—one of the first known references to gravity.

High-altitude photography (left) allows accurate updating of topographic maps (right), while data gathering by satellites (above) expands the range. Landsat satellites carry electronic remote-sensing equipment that detects the energy emitted by surface materials and translates it into images. Healthy plants may show as bright red, sparse vegetation as pink, barren lands as light gray, and urban areas as green or dark gray. The folded shape of the Appalachians (1) is clearly seen; the Canada–US border (2) is revealed by land-use patterns; silt from the Mississippi (3) builds up the delta. Sudan irrigation (4) shows up as brilliant red.

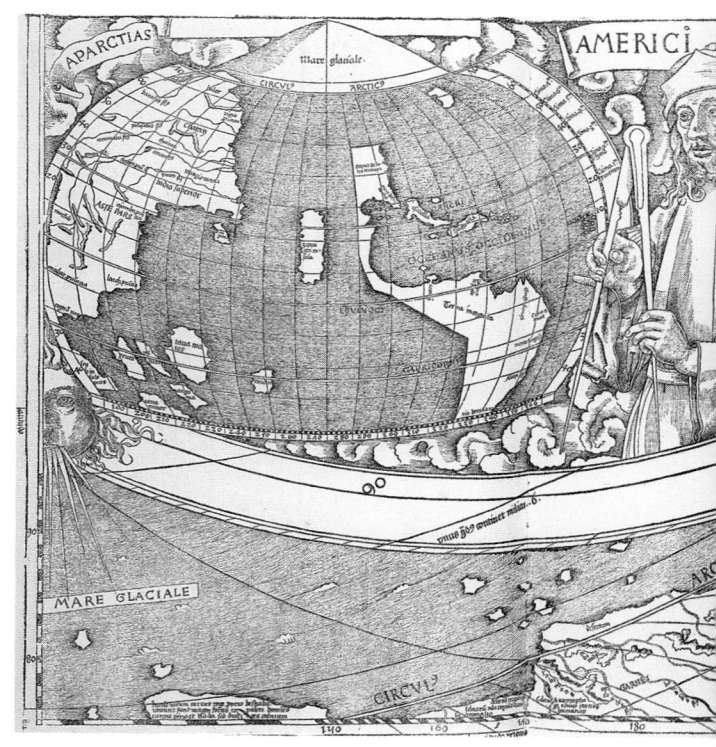

Mapping, Old and New

Mapmaking must have its origins in the earliest ages of human history, since people of preliterate as well as literate cultures possess an innate skill in map drawing. This innate capacity is further indicated by the ease with which almost anyone can sketch in the sand or on paper simple directions for showing the way. But maps may also define territory and express man's idea of the world in graphic representation. Today, modern technology has vastly extended the scope of cartography.

Many non-European cultures developed ingenious route-map techniques: the North American Indians, for example, made sketch maps of routes on birch bark. These were diagrammatic maps in which directions and distances were not accurate but relationships were true, as in New York Subway or London Underground maps. The people of the Marshall Islands in the western Pacific made route maps over the seas, depicting the direction of the main seasonal wave swells in relation to the islands.

Although maps of routes are the simplest type of map in concept, they developed complex forms as cartography progressed. A road map of the whole Roman Empire, drawn about AD 280, survives today in a thirteenth-century copy known as the Peutinger Table. Hernando Cortes, the Spanish conqueror, made his way across Mexico in the 1520s with the help of preconquest Mexican maps painted on cloth. These showed roads with double lines or colored bands marked with footprints. Another type of map is the strip map depicting a single road along its entire length. Pictorial maps of the Tōkaidō highway from Edo to Kyoto in Japan, made from a survey of 1651, were popular in the Edo period of Japanese history.

Nautical charts evolved as a special type of direction-finding map to meet the needs of seamen. Those of the late Middle Ages came to be known as "portolan" charts, from the word "portolani," or sailing directions. They showed the sea and adjacent coasts superimposed on a network of radiating compass lines.

Territorial maps

Another basic type of map derives from man's sense of territorial possession. The earliest example of a "cadastral" plan (a map showing land parcels and property boundaries) appears to be that preserved as rock carvings at Bedolina in Val Camonica in northern Italy. However, in the ancient civilizations of Mesopotamia and Egypt, land surveying had become an established profession by 2000 BC. An idea of what Egyptian surveyors' plans of 1000 BC were like can be seen from the "Fields of the Dead" representing the Egyptians' idea of life after death. These show plots of land surrounded by water and intersected by canals. The Romans used cadastral surveys to determine land ownership and assess tax liability.

Another form of map showing territorial demarcations is the map of administrative units. The Chinese in the thirteenth century AD were making official district maps to help in the organization of grain supplies and the collection of taxes. Many of their gazetteers (fang chih), written in the form of local geographies and

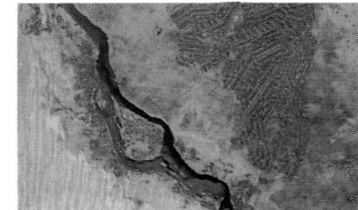

histories from the eleventh century onward, were illustrated with maps. Political maps showing the boundaries of states were increasingly significant in European cartography from the sixteenth century onward.

A third major class of map is the general or topographical map expressing man's perception of the world, its regions and its place in the universe. A Babylonian world map of the seventh century BC is drawn on a clay tablet and shows the Earth as a circular disc surrounded by the Earthly Ocean. With the ancient Greeks, geography developed on scientific principles. The treatise on mapmaking by Claudius Ptolemy (AD 87–150), later known as the *Geographia*, was the most famous cartographic text of the period. It influenced the Arabic geographers of the Middle Ages, notably Muhammad Ibn Muhammad, Al-Idrisi (1099–1164), and with the revival of Ptolemy in fifteenth-century Europe became one of the major works of the Renaissance. Published, with engraved maps, at Bologna in 1477, the *Geographia* ranks as the first printed atlas in the western world. The invention of techniques of engraving in wood and copper facilitated a wide diffusion of geographical knowledge through the mappublishing trade. The first atlas made up of modern maps to a uniform design was Abraham Ortelius's *Theatrum Orbis Terrarum* published at Antwerp in 1570. From 1492, when Martin Behaim made his "Erdapfel" at Nürnberg, globes also became popular, and globemakers vied with each other to make larger and more elaborate ones to keep pace with the growth of knowledge about the world.

Over the last two hundred years cartography has made rapid and remarkable advances. Observatories built in Paris in 1671 and at Greenwich in 1675 enabled the location of places to be established more exactly with the use of astronomical tables. Improvements in surveying instruments facilitated more accurate and rapid land survey. France was the pioneer in establishing (from 1679 onward) a national survey on a geometrical basis of triangulation. By the end of the eighteenth century national surveys on small and medium scales had been begun by most European countries. In the United States the Geological Survey was set up in 1879 to undertake the topographical and geological mapping of the country.

Mapping today

Since World War II cartographic techniques have undergone a revolution. The use of air survey and photogrammetry has made it possible to map most of the Earth's surface. Electronic distance measurement by laser or light beams in surveying, and digital computers in mapping, are among the most recent advances in methods. Mosaics or air photography are used to produce orthophoto maps which can supplement or substitute for the conventional topographic map. Artificial satellites and manned space craft make it possible to provide a world-wide framework of geodetic networks.

Earth Resource Technology Satellites (ERTS) imagery has made it possible to map mountain ranges in Africa and features on the surface of Antarctica that were hitherto unknown. The imagery is made available by means of remote-sensing instruments, carried by the satellites, that are sensitive to invisible portions of the electromagnetic spectrum—longer and shorter wavelengths than can be sensed by the human eye. Remote-sensing instruments usually work in the infrared bands. They can also pick up the energy emitted by all types of surface material—rocks, soils, vegetation, water and man-made structures—and produce photographs or images from it.

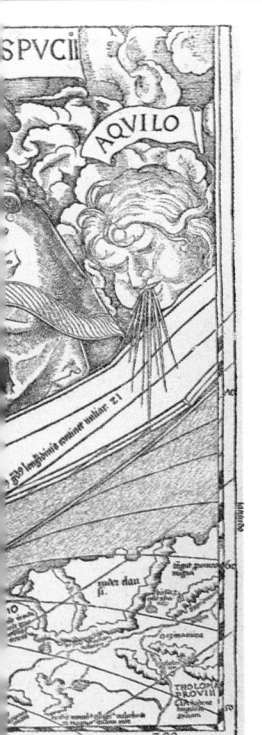

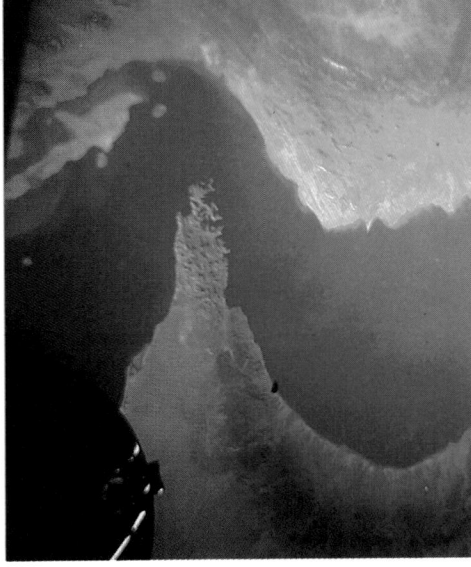

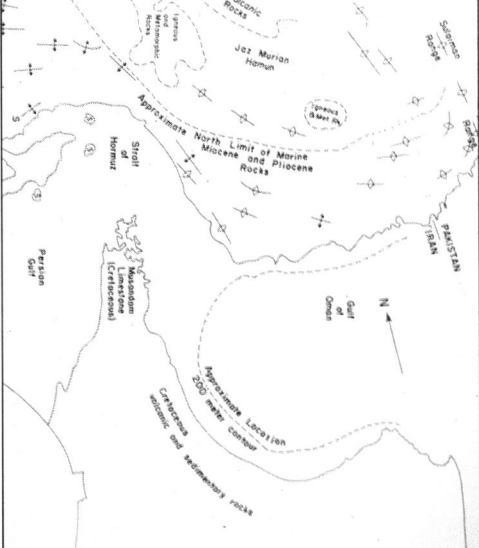

Space technology helps cartographers to map even interior details of the planet: its geology and mineral wealth. A photo (below) taken from Gemini 12 at an altitude of 272 km (168 miles) forms the basis of a geologic sketch map of SW Asia (below right), showing the oil-rich area around the region between the Persian Gulf and the Gulf of Oman. The symbol S on the map indicates salt plugs; diamonds show fold trends; double-headed arrows anticlines.

The Language of Maps

Mapmakers for more than 4,000 years have tried to find the best way to represent the shape and features of the three-dimensional Earth on two-dimensional paper, parchment and cloth. The measurement of distance and direction is a basic requirement for accurate surveys, but until about 1800 theoretical understanding of the method was well in advance of the technical equipment available. Today the use of lasers and light beams sometimes takes the place of direct measurement on the ground.

A reference system must be used to show distance and direction correctly in the construction of maps. The simplest type is the rectangular or square grid. The Chinese mapmaker Pei Xin made a map with a grid in about AD 270, and this system remained in continuous use in China until modern times. The Roman system of centuriation, a form of division of public lands on a square or rectangular basis, was also a "coordinate" system starting from a point of origin at the intersection of two perpendicular axes. Roman surveyors' maps, dating from the first century AD, are the earliest known European maps based on a grid system.

Latitude and longitude

Makers of small-scale regional maps and of world maps in early times also had to take account of the fact that the Earth is a sphere. The Greeks derived from the Babylonians the idea of dividing a circle into 360 degrees. In the second century BC the Greek geographer Eratosthenes (c. 276–194 BC) was the first to calculate the circumference of the globe and was reported to have made a world map based on the concept of the Earth's sphericity. From this the Greeks went on to develop the system of spherical coordinates which remains in use today. The poles at each end of the Earth's axis provide reference points for the Earth in its rotation in relation to the celestial sphere. Parallel circles around the Earth are degrees of latitude and express the idea of distance north or south of the Equator. Lines of longitude running north and south through the poles express east–west distances. One meridian is chosen as the meridian of origin, known as the prime meridian.

Whereas latitude from early times could be observed from the height of the Sun or (in the northern hemisphere) from the position of the Pole Star at night, accurate observations of longitude were not possible until the middle of the eighteenth century, when the chronometer was invented and more accurate astronomical tables were provided. In 1884 most countries agreed, at an international conference in Washington DC, to adopt the prime meridian through the Royal Greenwich Observatory in England and to calculate longitude to 180 degrees east and west of Greenwich.

Projection and distortion

The mathematical system by which the spherical surface of the Earth is transferred to the plane surface of a map is called a map projection. The Greek geographer Ptolemy gave instructions in his geographical treatise of AD 150 for the construction of two projections. When the *Geographia* was revised in Europe in the fifteenth century, and navigators began sailing across the oceans, mapmakers devised new projections more appropriate to the expanding geographical knowledge of the world. The Dutch geographer Gerard Mercator invented the projection named after him, applying it to his world chart of 1569. This cylindrical projection, in which all points are at true compass courses from each other, was of great benefit to navigators and is still one of the most commonly used projections. Another advance was made when Johann Heinrich Lambert of Alsace (1728–1777) invented the azimuthal equal-area projection, in which the sizes of all areas are represented on the projection in correct proportion to one another, and the conformal projection, in which at any point on the map the scale is constant in all directions.

Since all projections involve deformation of the geometry of the globe, the cartographer has to choose the one that best suits the purpose of his map. "Conformal" or "orthomorphic" projections, in which angular relations (or shape) are preserved, are widely used for the construction of topographical maps. "Equivalent" or "equal-area" projections retain relative sizes and are particularly useful for general reference maps displaying economic, historical, political and other geographical phenomena.

Since the mid-fifteenth century, European mapmakers have generally arranged their maps with north at the top of the sheet. Earlier maps, however, were not standardized in this way. The circular world maps of the Middle Ages were orientated with east at the top, because this was where the terrestrial paradise was traditionally sited. Indeed, the word "orientation" originally meant the arrangement of something so as to face east.

Map scale

Scale is another basic property of a map. The scale of a map is the ratio of the distance on the map to the actual distance represented. Whereas the Babylonians, Egyptians, Greeks and Romans drew surveys to scale, in medieval Europe mapmakers used customary methods of estimating. The earliest known local map since Roman times which is drawn to scale (it displays a scale bar) is a plan of Vienna, 1422.

Projection, grid, orientation and scale form the framework of a map. The language of maps in concept and content is much more complex. To represent the surface of the Earth on a map, the cartographer must select and generalize from a vast quantity of material, using symbols and conventional signs as codes.

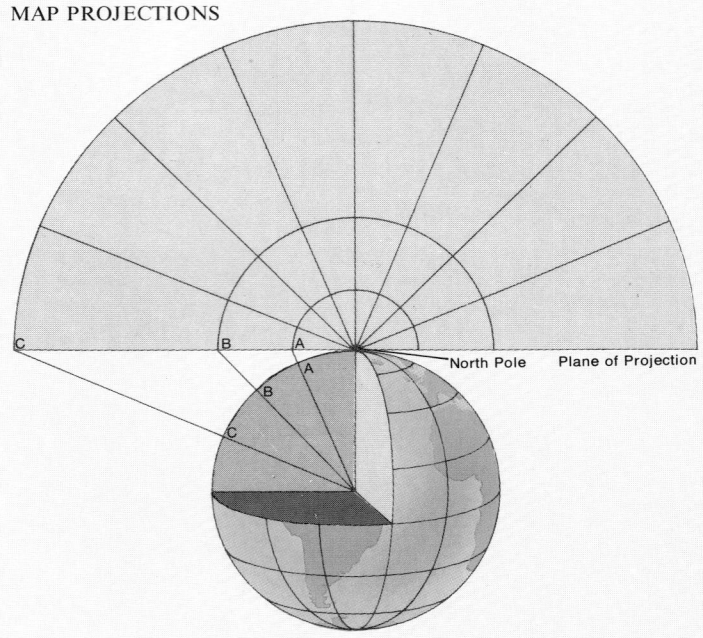

MAP PROJECTIONS

North Pole   Plane of Projection

The Lambert Equal-Area Projection, used in this atlas, may be visualized as a flat plane placed at a tangent to the globe, with the lines of longitude appearing as straight lines extending from the point of tangency, the North Pole (above). Deformation increases away from this point (below).

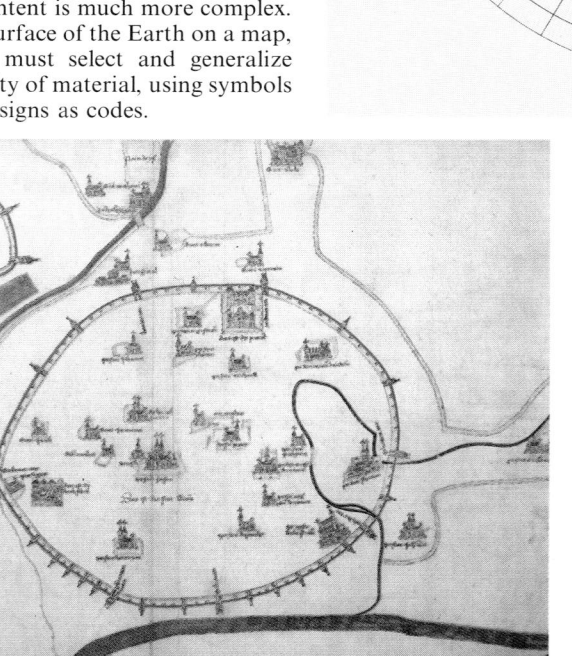

Map scales express the relationship between a distance measured on the map and the true distance on the ground. A plan of Vienna (left), originally made in 1422, is drawn in the bird's-eye-view style typical of early medieval town plans. But the scale bar at its foot shows that it has been explicitly drawn to scale, indicating that the concept of a uniform scale had been grasped in medieval Europe.

Direction and distance are concepts used in the relative location of two or more points (below). These concepts are organized according to a general frame of reference, with direction following the grid system of coordinates. Thus places shown in (A) can be precisely located in terms of longitude and of latitude (B), with the degrees further subdivided into one-sixtieths of minutes.

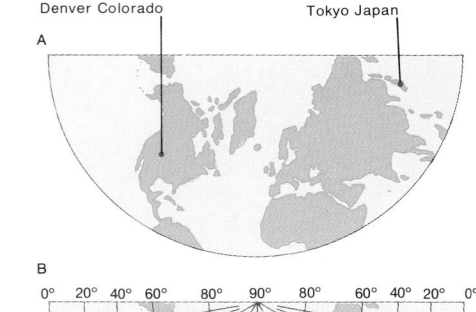

Denver Colorado

Tokyo Japan

A

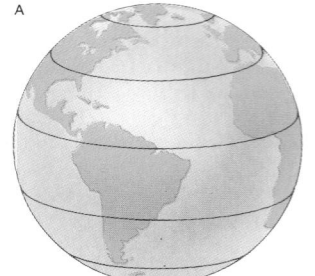
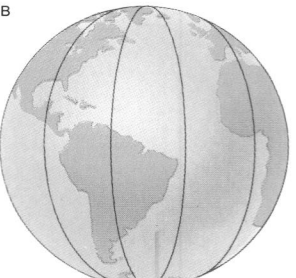
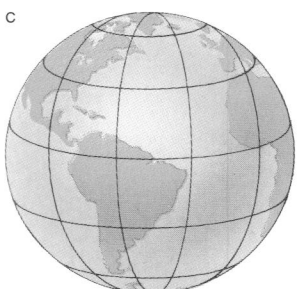

A   B   C

Superimposed on the globe (left), lines of latitude (A) and longitude (B) allow every place to be exactly located in terms of a coordinate system (C). The parallels of latitude measure distance from 0° to 90° north and south of the Equator. The meridians of longitude measure distance from 0° to 180° east and west of a "prime meridian" at Greenwich.

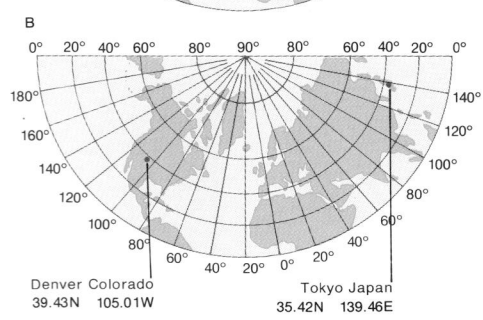

B

0° 20° 40° 60° 80° 90° 80° 60° 40° 20° 0°
180°   140°
160°   120°
140°   100°
120°   80°
100°   60°
80°   60° 40° 20° 0° 20° 40°

Denver Colorado
39.43N   105.01W

Tokyo Japan
35.42N   139.46E

The Hammer Projection (far right), developed from the Lambert Projection of one hemisphere (right), is designed to show the whole world in a single view, and is used in this atlas in a version modified by Wagner and known as the Hammer-Wagner Projection. The Earth appears as an ellipse because the lines of longitude are plotted at twice their horizontal distance from the center line, and numbered at twice their previous values. The central meridian is half the length of the Equator.

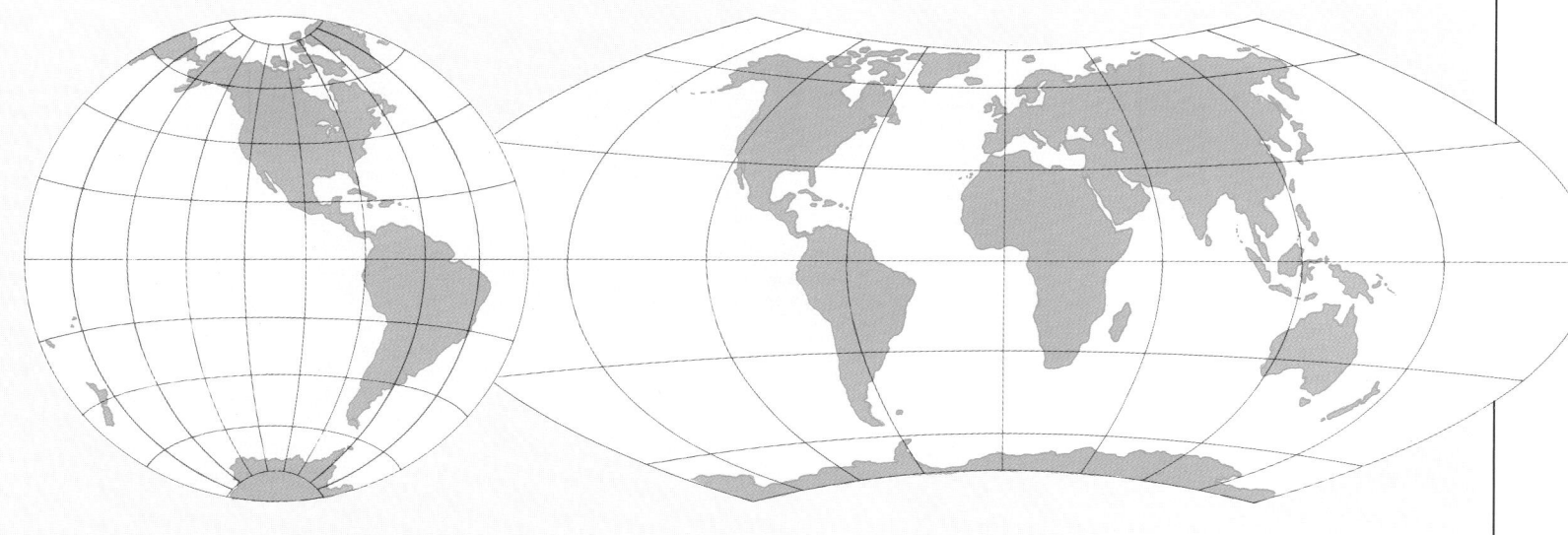

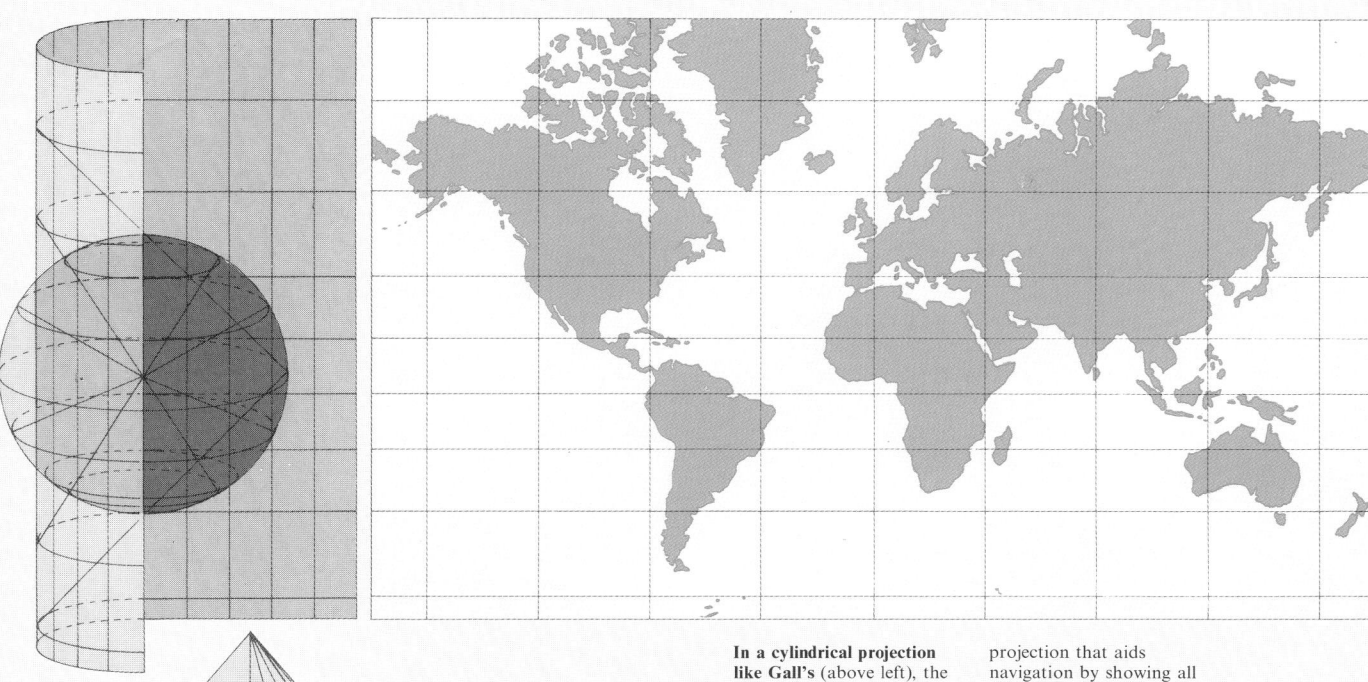

Photogrammetric plotting instruments (above) are now used in the preparation of large-scale accurate topographic maps. These are sophisticated machines that provide very precise measurements, plotting the map data in orthogonal projection.

In a cylindrical projection like Gall's (above left), the sphere is "unwrapped" on to a cylinder, making a complete transformation to a flat surface. Mercator's Projection (above), devised in 1569, is a cylindrical projection that aids navigation by showing all compass directions as straight lines. A projection (below), based on Peters', distorts shape to show land surface area ratios, emphasizing the Third World.

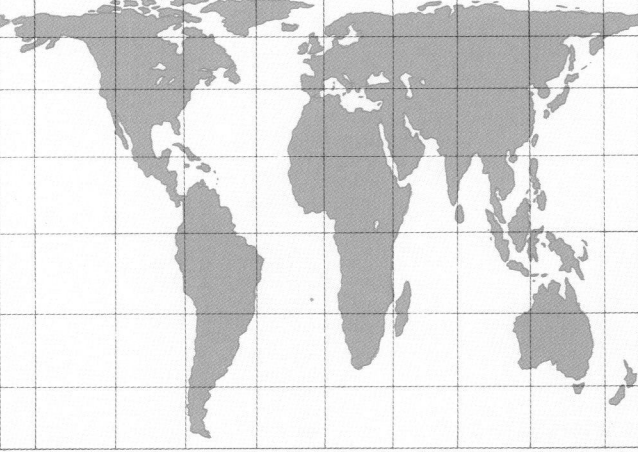

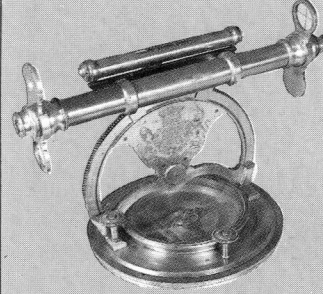

The theodolite (above), a basic surveying instrument dating back to the 16th century, can measure angles and directions horizontally and vertically. A swivel telescope with cross-hairs inside it permits accurate alignment, and it may be used in the field.

Delisle's Conic Projection (right), used in this atlas, intersects the globe at two points (above). Distortion is least at the parallels where the cone "touches" the globe, increasing with distance from them. Thus it is good for mid-latitudes.

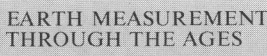

EARTH MEASUREMENT THROUGH THE AGES

Surveying—the technique of making accurate measurements of the Earth's surface—is as old as civilization and has been an essential element in mankind's development of his environment. The need to establish land boundaries arose at least 3,500 years ago in the fertile valleys of the Nile, Tigris and Euphrates rivers. Man's urge to explore and to describe the world also led to the development of instruments determining position, distance and direction. The astrolabe, sometimes called the world's oldest scientific instrument, may date to the 3rd century BC. Today's techniques make increasing use of computers.

An Egyptian wall painting (left) from the middle of the second millennium BC shows what appears to be the measurement of a grain field by means of a rope with knots at regular intervals on its length.

The astrolabe (right), used in classical times to observe the positions of celestial bodies, became a navigational instrument in the Middle Ages, when it was developed to permit establishment of latitude.

How to Use Maps

Today maps play a role more important than ever before in increasing our knowledge of the Earth, its regions and peoples. How maps communicate knowledge is now a subject of scientific study. The process comprises the collection and mapping of the data and the reading of the map. In this final stage the map user is all important. Through him the map is transformed into an image in the mind, and the effectiveness of the map depends on the reader being able to understand it.

The cartographer's map has to convey an objective picture of reality. To compile the map the cartographer selects and generalizes information, taking into account the purpose of his map. If he is making a topographical reference map, he has to reduce the three-dimensional landforms of the Earth on to the flat surface of the map. He adds cultural detail such as towns, roads and railroads, and features not apparent to the eye, such as administrative boundaries. On the topographical base map he adds appropriate place-names, using typefaces which reflect their class and significance. All this requires the classification of phenomena, with emphasis to direct the reader's attention.

Themes and symbolization

The cartographer who seeks not merely to represent visible features but to convey geographical ideas about specific phenomena uses the techniques of thematic cartography, where the emphasis is on one or two elements, or themes. Maps today provide one of the most effective means of communicating many kinds of data and ideas relating to the world and its peoples. Their extensive use makes them an important force in education, planning, recreation and in many other human affairs.

The map is designed in code, with symbols to represent features, and a legend, or key, to explain them. There are three types of symbol: point, line and area. Point symbols usually denote places, which may be distinguished into classes by the shape, color and size of the symbol. Line symbols express connections, such as roads or traffic flow, and they may also define and distinguish areas. Area symbols in which variations of color are often combined with patterns of lines or dots are used to depict spatial phenomena, such as types of soil, vegetation and density of population.

How much detail can be shown on a map will depend on its scale, which controls the process of generalization. Scale expresses the relationship of the distance on the map to the distance on the Earth, with the distance on the map always given as the unit 1. It is denoted in various ways: as a representative fraction such as 1:1,000,000; as a written statement; or by means of a graph or bar. Some map scales have become widely used and are generally familiar to map users. The scale 1:25,000 is ideal for walkers and relief can be shown in detail. That of 1:50,000 is a typical medium scale for national surveys. The publication of an international map of the world on a scale of one to

one million (1:1,000,000) has been in progress since 1909. On this scale 1 mm represents 1 km on the ground. The regional maps of countries in this atlas are drawn on scales of 1:6,000,000, 1:3,000,000 and 1:1,500,000; those of the continents are at 1:30,000,000 and 1:15,000,000. The Map Section index maps show the arrangement.

Terrain depiction

Since the early days of map making in ancient Chinese and classical Greek and Roman civilizations, map makers have been concerned to show the configuration of the land. For many centuries they symbolized mountains and hills by pictorial features often looking like caterpillars or sugar loaves. As topographical mapping developed in Europe from the seventeenth century onward, new techniques were devised to improve the visual impression of the features and to depict them accurately in terms of height and location. The system of hachuring (shading with fine parallel or crossed lines), first used in 1674, gives a good idea of relief but not of height. The use of contours, which became general from the nineteenth century onward, is more exact in representing actual elevation, but for many regions, especially those of irregular relief, the appearance of the land is lost.

The addition of hypsometric tints (tints between contours which show elevation) helps clarify the elevation. Applying shadows to the form of the land through the process called hill shading or relief shading creates a visual impression of the configuration of the land surface. Hypsometric tints combined with hill shading gives both elevation information and surface form of the area being depicted, leading to an almost three-dimensional effect.

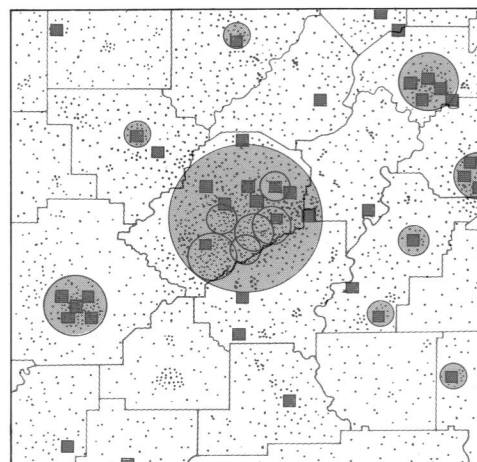
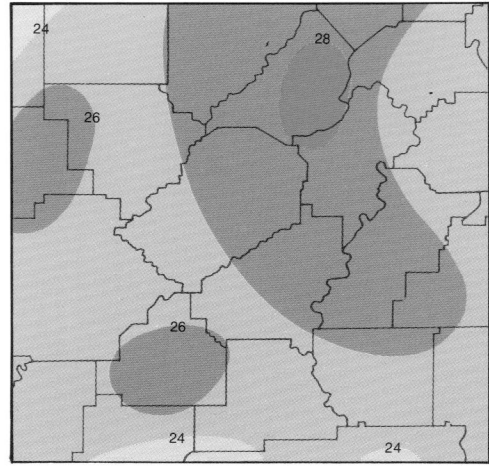

Maps are classed (right) as either general (A) or thematic (B,C). The purpose of a general reference map is to provide locational information, showing how the positions of various geographical phenomena relate to each other. Thematic maps concentrate on a particular type of information, or theme, such as the distribution of people (B) or rainfall (C), and are generally based on statistical data.

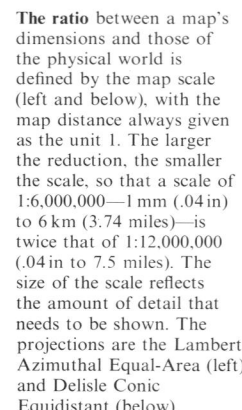

The ratio between a map's dimensions and those of the physical world is defined by the map scale (left and below), with the map distance always given as the unit 1. The larger the reduction, the smaller the scale, so that a scale of 1:6,000,000—1 mm (.04 in) to 6 km (3.74 miles)—is twice that of 1:12,000,000 (.04 in to 7.5 miles). The size of the scale reflects the amount of detail that needs to be shown. The projections are the Lambert Azimuthal Equal-Area (left) and Delisle Conic Equidistant (below).

Scale 1:12,000,000

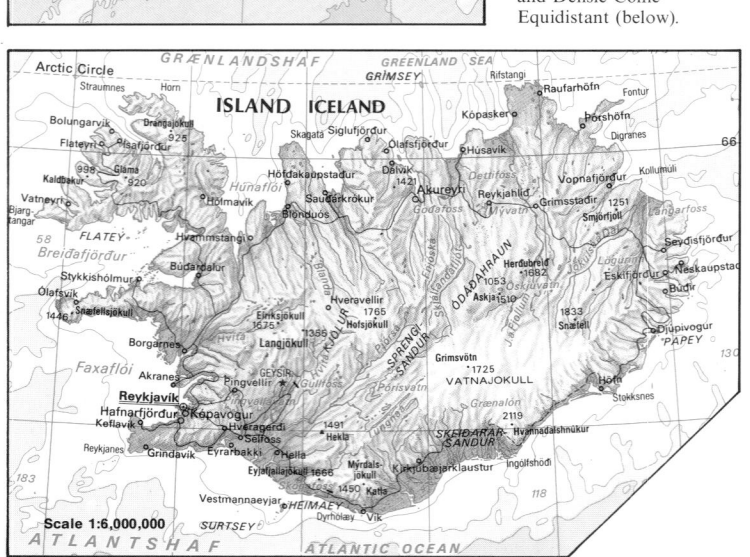

Scale 1:6,000,000

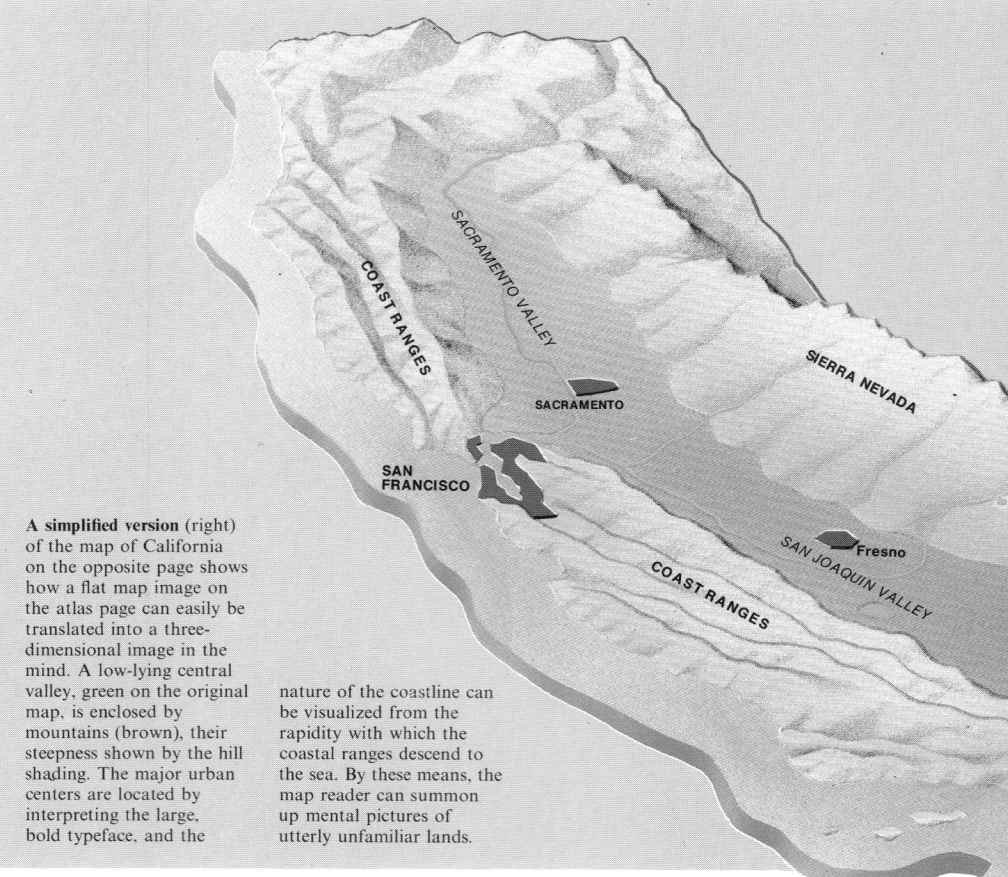

A simplified version (right) of the map of California on the opposite page shows how a flat map image on the atlas page can easily be translated into a three-dimensional image in the mind. A low-lying central valley, green on the original map, is enclosed by mountains (brown), their steepness shown by the hill shading. The major urban centers are located by interpreting the large, bold typeface, and the

nature of the coastline can be visualized from the rapidity with which the coastal ranges descend to the sea. By these means, the map reader can summon up mental pictures of utterly unfamiliar lands.

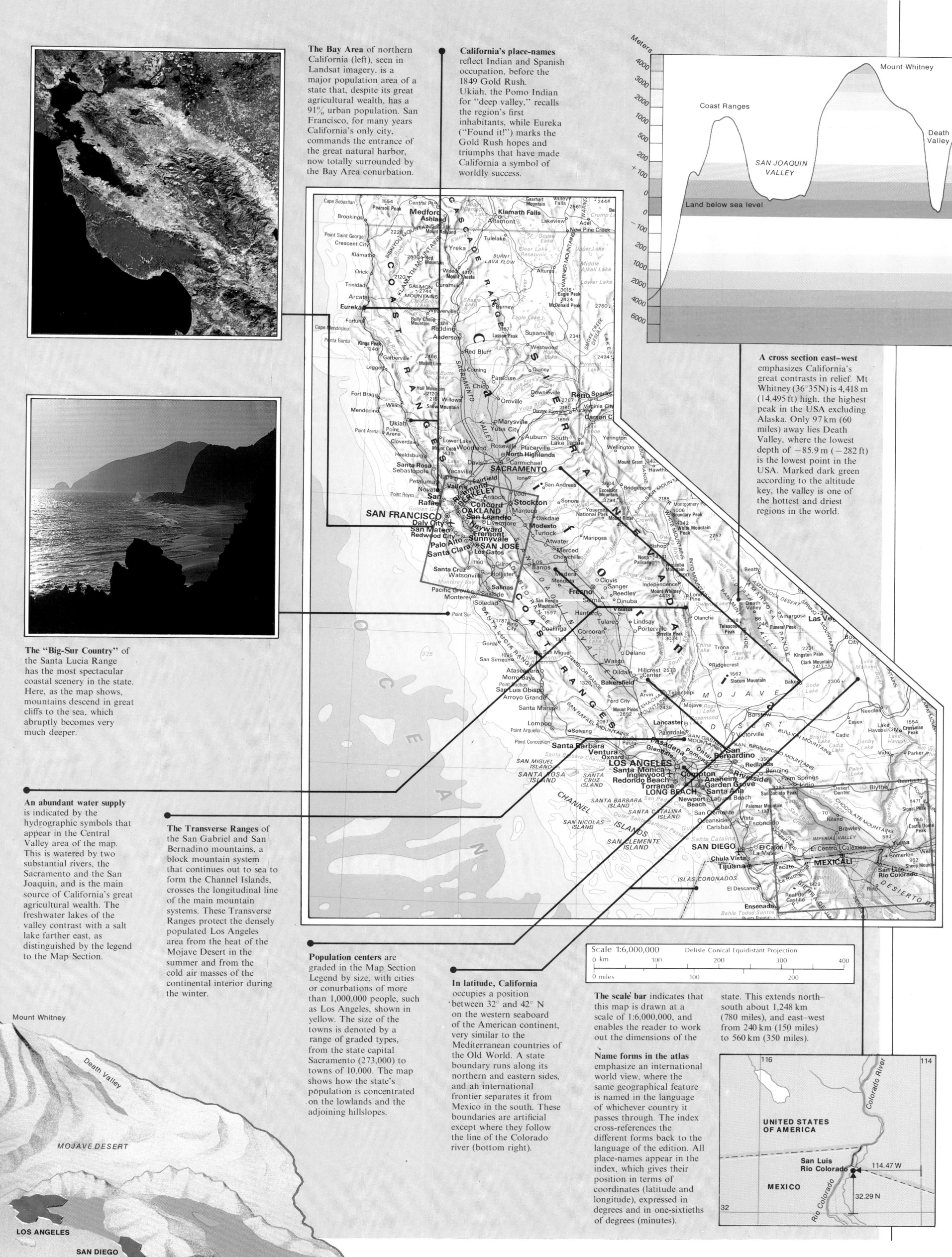

The Bay Area of northern California (left), seen in Landsat imagery, is a major population area of a state that, despite its great agricultural wealth, has a 91% urban population. San Francisco, for many years California's only city, commands the entrance of the great natural harbor, now totally surrounded by the Bay Area conurbation.

California's place-names reflect Indian and Spanish occupation, before the 1849 Gold Rush. Ukiah, the Pomo Indian for "deep valley," recalls the region's first inhabitants, while Eureka ("Found it!") marks the Gold Rush hopes and triumphs that have made California a symbol of worldly success.

A cross section east–west emphasizes California's great contrasts in relief. Mt Whitney (36°35N) is 4,418 m (14,495 ft) high, the highest peak in the USA excluding Alaska. Only 97 km (60 miles) away lies Death Valley, where the lowest depth of −85.9 m (−282 ft) is the lowest point in the USA. Marked dark green according to the altitude key, the valley is one of the hottest and driest regions in the world.

The "Big-Sur Country" of the Santa Lucia Range has the most spectacular coastal scenery in the state. Here, as the map shows, mountains descend in great cliffs to the sea, which abruptly becomes very much deeper.

An abundant water supply is indicated by the hydrographic symbols that appear in the Central Valley area of the map. This is watered by two substantial rivers, the Sacramento and the San Joaquin, and is the main source of California's great agricultural wealth. The freshwater lakes of the valley contrast with a salt lake farther east, as distinguished by the legend to the Map Section.

The Transverse Ranges of the San Gabriel and San Bernadino mountains, a block mountain system that continues out to sea to form the Channel Islands, crosses the longitudinal line of the main mountain systems. These Transverse Ranges protect the densely populated Los Angeles area from the heat of the Mojave Desert in the summer and from the cold air masses of the continental interior during the winter.

Population centers are graded in the Map Section Legend by size, with cities or conurbations of more than 1,000,000 people, such as Los Angeles, shown in yellow. The size of the towns is denoted by a range of graded types, from the state capital Sacramento (273,000) to towns of 10,000. The map shows how the state's population is concentrated on the lowlands and the adjoining hillslopes.

In latitude, California occupies a position between 32° and 42° N on the western seaboard of the American continent, very similar to the Mediterranean countries of the Old World. A state boundary runs along its northern and eastern sides, and an international frontier separates it from Mexico in the south. These boundaries are artificial except where they follow the line of the Colorado river (bottom right).

The scale bar indicates that this map is drawn at a scale of 1:6,000,000, and enables the reader to work out the dimensions of the state. This extends north–south about 1,248 km (780 miles), and east–west from 240 km (150 miles) to 560 km (350 miles).

Name forms in the atlas emphasize an international world view, where the same geographical feature is named in the language of whichever country it passes through. The index cross-references the different forms back to the language of the edition. All place-names appear in the index, which gives their position in terms of coordinates (latitude and longitude), expressed in degrees and in one-sixtieths of degrees (minutes).

Scale 1:6,000,000   Delisle Conical Equidistant Projection

0 km   100   200   300   400

0 miles   100   200

UNITED STATES OF AMERICA

MEXICO

San Luis Rio Colorado

114.47 W

32.29 N

Mount Whitney

Death Valley

MOJAVE DESERT

LOS ANGELES

SAN DIEGO

ACKNOWLEDGMENTS

Senior Executive Art Editor
Michael McGuinness

Executive Editor
James Hughes

Coordinating Editor
Dian Taylor

Editors
Lesley Ellis
Judy Garlick
Ken Hewis

Art Editor
Mike Brown

Designers
Sue Rawkins
Lisa Tai

Picture Researcher
Flavia Howard

Researchers
Nicholas Law
Nigel Morrison
Alicia Smith

Editorial Assistant
Barbara Gish

Proofreader
Kathie Gill

Indexers
Hilary and Richard Bird

Production Controller
Barry Baker

Typesetting by Servis Filmsetting
Limited, Manchester, England

Reproduction by Gilchrist
Brothers Limited, Leeds, England

CONTRIBUTORS AND CONSULTANTS

GENERAL CONSULTANT
Professor Michael Wise, CBE, MC, BA, PhD, D.Univ, Professor of
Geography, London School of Economics and Political Science

EDITORIAL CONSULTANT
John Clark

Frances Atkinson, BSc

British Museum (Natural History), Botany Library

Robert W. Bradnock, MA, PhD, Lecturer in Geography with special
reference to South Asia at the School of Oriental and African
Studies, University of London

Michael J. Bradshaw, MA, Principal Lecturer in Geography, College
of St Mark and St John, Plymouth

Dr J. M. Chapman, BSc, ARCS, PhD, MIBiol, Lecturer in Biology,
Queen Elizabeth College, University of London

Dr Jeremy Cherfas, Departmental Demonstrator in Zoology, Oxford
University

Dr M. J. Clark, Senior Lecturer in Geomorphology, Geography
Department, Southampton University

J. L. Cloudsley-Thompson, MA, PhD(Cantab), DSc(Lond),
Hon DSc(Khartoum), Professor of Zoology, Birkbeck College,
University of London

Professor R. U. Cooke, Department of Geography, University
College, London

Professor Clifford Embleton, MA, PhD, Department of Geography,
King's College, University of London

Dr John Gribbin, Physics Consultant to *New Scientist* magazine

Dr John M. Hellawell, BSc, PhD, FIBiol, MIWES, Principal,
Environmental Aspects, Severn Trent Water Authority, Birmingham

Dr Garry E. Hunt, BSc, PhD, DSc, FRAS, FRMetS, FIMA, MBCS,
Head of Atmospheric Physics, Imperial College, London

David K. C. Jones, Lecturer in Geography, London School of
Economics and Political Science

Dr Russell King, Department of Geography, University of Leicester

Dr D. McNally, Assistant Director, University of London
Observatory

Meteorological Office, Berkshire

Dr Robert Muir Wood, PhD

Dr B. O'Connor, Department of Geography, University of London

J. H. Paterson, MA, Professor of Geography in the University of
Leicester

Dr Nigel Pears, Department of Geography, University of Leicester

Joyce Pope, BA

Dr A. L. Rice, Institute of Oceanographic Sciences, Wormley, Surrey

Ian Ridpath, science writer and broadcaster

Royal Geographical Society

Helen Scoging, BSc, Department of Geography, London School of
Economics and Political Science

Bernard Stonehouse, DPhil, MA, BSc, Chairman, Post-Graduate
School of Environmental Science, University of Bradford

Dr Christopher B. Stringer, PhD, Senior Scientific Officer,
Palaeontology Department, British Museum (Natural History)

J. B. Thornes, Professor of Physical Geography and Head of
Department, Bedford College, University of London

UN Information Office and Library

Professor J. E. Webb, DSc, *Emeritus*, Department of Zoology,
Westfield College, University of London

Peter B. Wright, BSc, MPhil

UNDERSTANDING MAPS
Helen Wallis, MA, DPhil, FSA, The Map Librarian, British Library

A great many other individuals, organizations, and institutions have
given invaluable advice and assistance during the preparation of this
Our Planet Earth Section and the publishers wish to extend their
thanks to them all.

ILLUSTRATION CREDITS

Maps in the Our Planet Earth Section by Creative Cartography Limited
unless otherwise specified. Map of the world's climatic regions, page 50,
adapted from *An Introduction to Climate* 4th edition by Trewartha/
Elements of Geography by G. T. Trewartha, A. H. Robinson and
E. H. Hammond © McGraw-Hill Book Co., N.Y., 1967. Used with
permission of McGraw-Hill Book Co. Map diagram page 101 (bottom)
courtesy Doctor Arno Peters.

2–3 *Exploding universe* Product Support (Graphics); *others* Quill.
4–5 Bob Chapman. **6–7** Bob Chapman. **8–9** Mick Saunders;
Landsat diagrams Gary Marsh; *biowindows* Chris Forsey. **10–11**
Mick Saunders. **12–13** Bob Chapman. **14–15** *Diagrams* Chris Forsey;
mountain sequence Donald Myall. **16–17** Colin Salmon. **18–19** Peter
Morter; *graph* Mick Saunders; *car* Peter Owen. **20–21** Bob
Chapman; *diagram* Chris Forsey; *map* Colin Salmon. **22–23** Chris
Forsey (*including maps*). **24–25** Brian Delf. **26–27** Brian Delf.
28–29 Dave Etchell/John Ridyard. **30–31** Creative Cartography Ltd.
32–33 Mick Saunders. **34–35** Chris Forsey; *experiment* Gary Hincks;
others Mick Saunders. **36–37** Chris Forsey; *fruit flies, birds and mice*
Donald Myall. **38–39** Chris Forsey; *time scale* Mick Saunders;
stromatolite and diagram Garry Hincks. **40–41** Donald Myall;
time scale Mick Saunders. **42–43** Donald Myall; *time scale* Mick
Saunders. **44–45** Creative Cartography Ltd. **46–47** Donald Myall;
diagram Kai Choi; *skulls* Jim Robins. **48–49** Creative Cartography
Ltd. **50–51** Peter Morter; *diagram* Marilyn Clark. **52–53** Kai Choi.
54–55 Creative Cartography Ltd. **56–57** Creative Cartography Ltd.
58–59 Creative Cartography Ltd. **60–61** Creative Cartography Ltd;
illustrations Jim Robins. **62–63** *Migration diagram and graph* Kai
Choi; *illustrations* Coral Mula. **64–65** Donald Myall. **66–67**
Landscape diagram Bill le Fever; *illustrations* Russell Barnett. **68–69**
Donald Myall. **70–71** Jim Robins; *bottom left* Andrew
Macdonald. **72–73** Rory Kee; *bottom left* Russell Barnett; *plow*
Kai Choi; *grains and graph* Creative Cartography Ltd. **74–75** Bob
Bampton/The Garden Studio; *animal adaptations* Russell Barnett.
76–77 Donald Myall; *qanat* Bob Chapman. **78–79** David Ashby.
80–81 David Ashby. **82–83** Coral Mula; *trees, orchid, toucan and
hornbill* Donald Myall. **84–85** Jim Robins. **86–87** Creative
Cartography Ltd. **88–89** Brian Delf; *blood counts diagram* Colin
Salmon. **90–91** Bob Chapman; *animals and plants* Rod Sutterby.
92–93 Kai Choi; *hydrological cycle* Bob Chapman. **94–95** Andy
Farmer; *shore and plant life* Russell Barnett; *coral atoll* Colin
Salmon. **96–97** Creative Cartography Ltd. **98–99** *Topographic maps*
Rand McNally; *sketch map* Space Frontiers Ltd. **100–101** *Diagrams*
Creative Cartography Ltd. **102–103** *Maps* Istituto Geografico De
Agostini; Rand McNally; *diagrams* Creative Cartography Ltd.

PICTURE CREDITS

Credits read from top to bottom and from left to right on each page. Images that extend over two pages are credited to the left-hand page only.

2 US Naval Observatory; California Institute of Technology and Carnegie Institution of Washington. **3** Both pictures from Royal Observatory, Edinburgh. **8** All pictures from NASA. **9** All pictures from NASA except top and top right, courtesy of Garry Hunt, Laboratory of Planetary Atmospheres, University College, London. **14–15** Maurice and Sally Landre/Colorific! **16–17** All pictures courtesy of Dr Basil Booth, Geoscience Features. **18** Institute of Geological Sciences. **19** Paul Brierley; Institute of Geological Sciences. **20** Camera Press, London. **26** Barnaby's Picture Library; Barnaby's Picture Library; Institute of Geological Sciences. **28** Dr Alan Beaumont. **30** Tom Sheppard/Robert Harding Picture Library; Professor Ronald Cooke. **31** Institute of Geological Sciences. **32** Stuart Windsor; Sefton Photo Library, Manchester; Rio Tinto Zinc; Douglas Botting; Aspect Picture Library. **33** NASA; Mireille Vautier; Explorer/Vision International. **34** Paul Brierley. **37** Paediatric Research Unit, Guy's Hospital Medical School; Dr Laurence Cook, Zoology Department, University of Manchester. **39** Both pictures from British Museum (Natural History). **46** Colophoto Hans Hinz. **47** Dr P. G. Bahn, School of Archaeology and Oriental Studies, University of Liverpool/Musée des Antiquités Nationales, St. Germain-en-Laye. **56** UNICEF (Photo no. 8675 by H. Dalrymple). **57** Dr A. M. O'Connor, Department of Geography, University College, London. **61** International Fund for Animal Welfare; K. Kunov/Novosti Press Agency; Popperfoto; Charles Swithinbank. **62** Alan Robson. **63** Gösta Hakansson/Frank Lane Agency. **65** G. R. Roberts. **67** Anglo-Chinese Educational Trust; Aerofilms. **69** Ted Streshinsky. **72** Engraving from *At Home with the Patagonians.* **73** The Mansell Collection. **76** J. Bitsch/Zefa; Penny Tweedie/Colorific! **77** Alan Hutchison Library; Bill Holden/Zefa. **80** Syndication International; Gerald Cubitt/Bruce Coleman Ltd; Bruce Coleman Ltd. **81** Alan Hutchison Library; R. and M. Borland/Bruce Coleman Ltd; M. P. Kahl/Bruce Coleman Ltd; Jan and Des Bartlett/Bruce Coleman Ltd. **84** J. von Puttkamer/Alan Hutchison Library. **85** Marion Morrison. **86–87** Richard and Sally Greenhill. **88** Alan Hutchison Library; The Association of Universities for Research in Astronomy, Inc. **89** Gunter Ziesler/Bruce Coleman Ltd. **91** Mike Price/Bruce Coleman Ltd. **92** Ian Murphy. **93** Paolo Koch/Vision International; J. Allan Cash; M. Timothy O'Keefe/Bruce Coleman Ltd. **94** Heather Angel. **95** Institute of Oceanographic Sciences. **96** Fritz Prenzel/Bruce Coleman Ltd; Gordon Williamson/Bruce Coleman Ltd. **97** Martin Rogers/Susan Griggs Agency. **98** British Library; British Museum; Centro Camuno di Studi Preistorici; British Library; NASA; NASA; Rand McNally; British Museum. **99** British Museum; NASA; NASA; Rand McNally; Space Frontiers Ltd; Paul G. Lowman/NASA Goddard SFC/Space Frontiers Ltd. **100** Historisches Museum, Vienna. **101** Hunting Surveys Ltd; Michael Holford/Science Museum, London; Michael Holford; Michael Holford/Science Museum, London. **103** Space Frontiers Ltd; F. Damm/Zefa.

Page numbers in *italic* refer to the illustrations and their captions.

**Cartographic and
Geographic Director**
Giuseppe Motta

**Geographic
Research**
G. Baselli
M. Colombo

**Toponymy and
Translation**
C. Carpine
M. Colombo
H. R. Fischer
R. Nuñez de las Cuevas
Rand McNally
Cartographic Research Staff
I. Straube

**Computerized
Data Organization**
C. Bardesono
E. Ciano
G. Comoglio
E. Di Costanzo

Index
S. Osnaghi
T. Tomasini

**Cartographic
Editor**
V. Castelli

**Cartographic
Compilation**
G. Albera
L. Cairo
C. Camera
G. Conti
G. Fizzotti
G. Gambaro
M. Mochetti
O. Passarelli
M. Peretti
G. Rassiga
A. Saino
F. Valsecchi

**Terrain
Illustration**
S. Andenna
E. Ferrari

**Cartographic
Production**
F. Tosi
G. Capitini
A. Carnero

Filmsetting
S. Fiorini
P. L. Gatta
E. Geranio
G. Ghezzi
L. Lorena
R. Martelli
E. Morchio
M. Morganti
C. Pezzana
P. Uglietti
D. Varalli

**Photographic
Processing**
G. Fracassina
G. Klaus
L. Mella

Coordination
S. Binda
L. Pasquali
G. Zanetta

The editors wish to thank the many organizations, institutions and individuals who have given their valuable help and advice during the preparation of this International Map Section. Special thanks are extended to the following:

Agenzia Novosti, Rome, Italy
D. Arnold, Acting Chief of Documentation and Terminology Section, United Nations, New York, USA
Australian Bureau of Statistics, Brisbane, Australia
J. Breu, United Nations Group of Experts on Geographical Names, Vienna, Austria
Bureau Hydrographique International, Monaco, Principality of Monaco
Canada Map Office, Ottawa, Canada
Cartactual, Budapest, Hungary
Census and Statistical Department, Tripoli, Libya
Central Bureau of Statistics, Accra, Ghana
Central Bureau of Statistics, Jerusalem, Israel
Central Bureau of Statistics, Ministry of Economic Planning and Development, Nairobi, Kenya
Central Department of Statistics, Riyadh, Saudi Arabia
Central Statistical Board of the USSR, Moscow, USSR
Central Statistical Office, London, UK
Centro de Informaçao e Documentaçao Estadística, Rio de Janeiro, Brazil
Committee for the Reform of Chinese Written Language, Peking, China
Danmark Statistik, Copenhagen, Denmark
Defense Mapping Agency, Distribution Office for Latin America, Miami, USA
Defense Mapping Agency, Washington DC, USA
Department of National Development and Energy, Division of National Mapping, Belconnen ACT, Australia
Department of State Coordinator for Maps and Publications, Washington DC, USA
Department of State Map Division, Sofia, Bulgaria
Department of Statistics, Wellington, New Zealand
Direcçao Nacional de Estadística, Maputo, Mozambique
Dirección de Cartografía Nacional, Caracas, Venezuela
Dirección de Estadística y Censo de la Repubblica de Panamá, Panama
Dirección General de Estadística, Mexico City, Mexico
Dirección General de Estadística y Censos, San Salvador, El Salvador
Direcţia Centrala de Statistică, Bucharest, Romania
Directorate of National Mapping, Kuala Lumpur, Malaysia
Directorate of Overseas Surveys, London, UK
Elaborazione Dati e Disegno Automatico, Torino, Italy
Federal Office of Statistics, Lagos, Nigeria
Federal Office of Statistics, Prague, Czechoslovakia
Geographical Research Institute, Hungarian Academy of Sciences, Budapest, Hungary
Geological Map Service, New York, USA
G. Gomez de Silva, Chief Conference Services Section, United Nations Environment Programme, New York, USA
Government of the People's Republic of Bangladesh, Statistics Division, Ministry of Planning, Dacca, Bangladesh
High Commissioner for Trinidad and Tobago, London, UK
L. Iarotski, World Health Organization, Geneva, Switzerland Information Division, Valletta, Malta
Institut für Angewandte Geodäsie, Frankfurt, West Germany
Institut Géographique, Abidjan, Ivory Coast
Institut Géographique du Zaïre, Kinshasa, Zaïre
Institut Géographique National, Brussels, Belgium
Institut Géographique National, Paris, France
Institut Haïtien de Statistique, Port-au-Prince, Haiti
Institut National de Géodésie et Cartographie, Antananarivo, Madagascar
Institut National de la Statistique, Tunis, Tunisia
Institute of Geography, Polish Academy of Sciences, Warsaw, Poland
Instituto Geográfico Militar, Buenos Aires, Argentina
Instituto Nacional de Estadística, La Paz, Bolivia
Instituto Nacional de Estadística, Madrid, Spain
Istituto Centrale di Statistica, Rome, Italy
Istituto Geografico Militare, Florence, Italy
Istituto Idrografico della Marina, Genoa, Italy
Landesverwaltung des Fürstentums, Vaduz, Liechtenstein
Ministère des Affaires Economiques, Brussels, Belgium
Ministère des Ressources Naturelles, des Mines et des Carrières, Kigali, Rwanda
Ministère des Travaux Publics, des Transports et de l'Urbanisme, Ouagadougou, Upper Volta
Ministry of Finance, Department of Statistics and Research, Nicosia, Cyprus

Ministry of Lands, Housing and Urban Development, Surveys and Mapping Division, Dar es Salaam, Tanzania
Ministry of the Interior, Jerusalem, Israel
National Census and Statistics Office, Manila, Philippines
National Central Bureau of Statistics, Stockholm, Sweden
National Geographic Society, Washington DC, USA
National Institute of Polar Research, Tokyo, Japan
National Ocean Survey, Riverdale, Maryland, USA
National Statistical Institute, Lisbon, Portugal
National Statistical Office, Zomba, Malawi
National Statistical Service of Greece, Athens, Greece
J. Novotny, Prague, Czechoslovakia
Office Nationale de la Recherche Scientifique et Technique, Yaoundé, Cameroon
Officina Comercial del Gobierno de Colombia, Rome, Italy
Ordnance Survey of Ireland, Dublin, Ireland
Österreichisches Statistisches Zentralamt, Vienna, Austria
Państwowe Przedsiebiorstwo Wydawnictw Kartograficznych, Warsaw, Poland
Scott Polar Research Institute, University of Cambridge, Cambridge, UK
Secrétariat d'Etat au Plan, Algiers, Algeria
Servicio Geografico Militar, Montevideo, Uruguay
Z. Shiying, Research Institute of Surveying and Mapping, Peking, China
Statistisches Bundesamt, Wiesbaden, West Germany
Statistisk Sentralbyrå, Oslo, Norway
Survey and National Mapping Department, Kuala Lumpur, Malaysia
Ufficio Turismo e Informazioni della Turchia, Rome, Italy
United States Board on Geographic Names, Washington DC, USA
M. C. Wu, Chinese Translation Service, United Nations, New York, USA
Z. Youguang, Committee for the Reform of Chinese Written Language, Peking, China

The editors are also grateful for the assistance provided by the following embassies, consulates and official state representatives:

Angolan Embassy, Rome
Australian Embassy, Rome
Austrian Embassy, Rome
Embassy of Bangladesh, Rome
Embassy of Botswana, Brussels
Brazilian Embassy, Rome
British Embassy, Rome
Burmese Embassy, Rome
Embassy of Cameroon, Rome
Embassy of Cape Verde, Lisbon
Consulate of Chad, Rome
Chilean Embassy, Rome
Embassy of the People's Republic of China in Italy, Rome
Danish Embassy, Rome
Embassy of El Salvador, Rome
Ethiopian Embassy, Rome
Finnish Embassy, Rome
Embassy of the German Democratic Republic, Rome
Greek Embassy, Rome
Honduras Republic Embassy, Rome
Hungarian Embassy, Rome
Consulate General of Iceland, Rome
Embassy of India, Rome
Embassy of the Republic of Indonesia, Rome
Embassy of the Islamic Republic of Iran, Rome

Irish Embassy, Rome
Embassy of Israel, Rome
Japanese Embassy, Rome
Korean Embassy, Rome
Luxembourg Embassy, Rome
Embassy of Malta, Rome
Mexican Embassy, Rome
Moroccan Embassy, Rome
Netherlands Embassy, Rome
Embassy of New Zealand, Rome
Embassy of Niger, Rome
Embassy of Pakistan, Rome
Peruvian Embassy, Rome
Philippine Embassy, Rome
Romanian Embassy, Rome
Somali Embassy, Rome
South African Embassy, Rome
Spanish Embassy, Rome
Consulate General of Switzerland, Milan
Royal Thai Embassy, Rome
Consulate of Upper Volta, Rome
Uruguay Embassy, Rome
Embassy of the Socialist Republic of Vietnam in Italy, Rome
Permanent Mission of Yemen to United Nations Educational, Scientific and Cultural Organization, Paris

INTERNATIONAL MAP SECTION

Hydrographic and Topographic Features
Symboles hydrographiques et morphologiques
Gewässer- und Geländeformen
Idrografia, Morfologia
Hidrografía y morfología

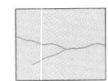
River, Stream
Cours d'eau permanent
Ständig wasserführender Fluß
Corso d'acqua perenne
Corriente de agua de régimen permanente

Lake
Lac d'eau douce
Süßwassersee
Lago d'acqua dolce
Lago de agua dulce

Rocks
Ecueils, Roches
Klippen, Felsriffe
Scogli, Rocce
Escollos, Rocas

Summer Limit of Pack-Ice
Limite du pack en été
Packeisgrenze im Sommer
Limite estivo del pack ghiacciato
Límite estival de banco de hielo

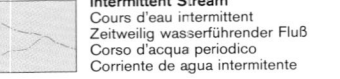
Intermittent Stream
Cours d'eau intermittent
Zeitweilig wasserführender Fluß
Corso d'acqua periodico
Corriente de agua intermitente

Intermittent Lake
Lac d'eau douce temporaire
Zeitweiliger Süßwassersee
Lago d'acqua dolce periodico
Lago de agua dulce intermitente

Reef, Atoll
Barrière, Atoll
Riff, Atoll
Barriera, Atollo
Barrera de arrecifes

Winter Limit of Pack-Ice
Limite du pack en hiver
Packeisgrenze im Winter
Limite invernale del pack ghiacciato
Límite invernal de banco de hielo

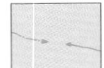
Disappearing Stream
Perte de cours d'eau
Versickernder Fluß
Corso d'acqua che si inabissa
Corriente de agua que desaparece

Salt Lake
Lac d'eau salée
Salzsee
Lago d'acqua salata
Lago de agua salada

Mangrove
Mangrove
Mangrove
Mangrovie
Manglar

Limit of Icebergs
Limite des glaces flottantes
Treibeisgrenze
Limite dei ghiacci alla deriva
Límite de hielo a la deriva

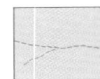
Undefined or Fluctuating River Course
Cours d'eau incertain
Fluß mit veränderlichem Lauf
Fiume dal corso incerto
Corriente de agua incierta

Intermittent Salt Lake
Lac d'eau salée temporaire
Zeitweiliger Salzsee
Lago d'acqua salata periodico
Lago de agua salada intermitente

Continental Ice-cap
Glacier continental
Inlandeis, Gletscher
Ghiacciaio continentale
Glaciar continental

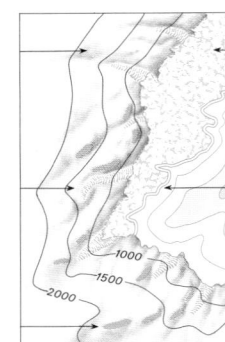
Ice Shelf
Banquise
Schelfeis oder Eisschelf
Banchisa polare (Ice-shelf)
Banquisa

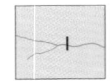
Waterfall, Rapids, Cataract
Chute, Rapide, Cataracte
Wasserfall, Stromschnelle, Katarakt
Cascata, Rapida, Cateratta
Cascada, Rapido, Catarata

Dry Lake Bed
Lac asséché
Trockener Seeboden
Alveo di lago asciutto
Lecho de lago seco

Glacial Tongue
Langue glaciaire
Gletscherzunge
Lingua di ghiaccio
Lengua de glaciar

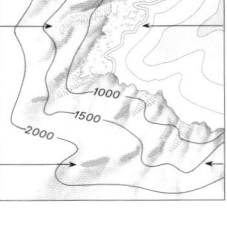
Limit of Ice Shelf
Limite de la banquise
Schelfeisgrenze
Limite della banchisa
Límite de la banquisa

Canal
Canal
Kanal
Canale
Canal

Lake Surface Elevation
Cote du lac au-dessus du niveau de la mer
Höhe des Seespiegels
Altitudine del lago
Elevación de lago sobre el nivel del mar

Rocky Areas (Antarctica)
Règion de roches (Antarctique)
Eisfreie Gebiete, Gebirge (Antarktika)
Aree rocciose (Antartide)
Area rocosa (Antártida)

Contour Lines in Continental Ice
Courbes de niveau dans les régions glaciaires
Höhenlinien auf vergletschertem Gebiet
Curve altimetriche nelle aree ghiacciate
Curvas de nivel en áreas heladas

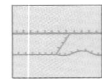
Navigable Canal
Canal navigable
Schiffbarer Kanal
Canale navigabile
Canal navegable

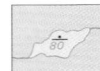
Lake Depth
Profondeur du lac
Seetiefe
Profondità del lago
Profundidad del lago

Defined Shoreline
Trait de côte définie
Küsten- oder Uferlinie
Linea di costa definita
Línea de costa definida

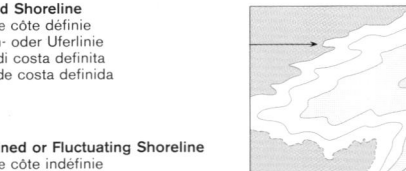
Bathymetric Contour
Courbe bathymétrique
Tiefenlinie
Curva batimetrica
Curva batimétrica

Swamp
Marais
Sumpf
Palude d'acqua dolce
Pantano

Sand Area
Région de sable, Désert
Sandgebiet, Sandwüste
Area sabbiosa, Deserto
Zona arenosa, desierto

Undefined or Fluctuating Shoreline
Trait de côte indéfinie
Unbestimmte oder veränderliche Uferlinie
Linea di costa indefinita
Línea de costa indefinida

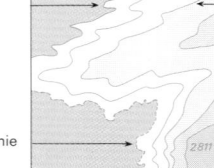
Depth of Water
Valeur de sonde
Tiefenzahl
Quota batimetrica
Cota batimétrica

Salt Marsh
Marais d'eau salée
Salzsumpf
Palude d'acqua salata
Pantano de agua salada

Sandbank, Sandbar
Banc de sable
Sandbank
Bassofondo sabbioso
Banco submarino de arena

Mountain Range
Chaîne de montagnes
Bergkette
Catena di monti
Cadena montañosa

Mountain
Mont
Berg, Bergmassiv
Monte
Monte

Salt Pan
Marais salant
Salzpfanne
Salina
Salina

Port Facilities
Installations portuaires
Hafenanlagen
Impianti portuali
Instalaciones portuarias

Elevation
Cote, Altitude
Höhenzahl
Quota altimetrica
Cota altimétrica

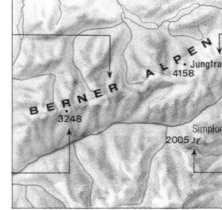
Mountain Pass, Gap
Passage, Col, Port
Paß, Joch, Sattel
Passo, Colle, Valico
Paso, Collado, Puerto de montaña

Key to Elevation and Depth Tints
Hypsométrie, Bathymétrie
Höhenstufen, Tiefenstufen
Altimetria, Batimetria
Altimetría, Batimetría

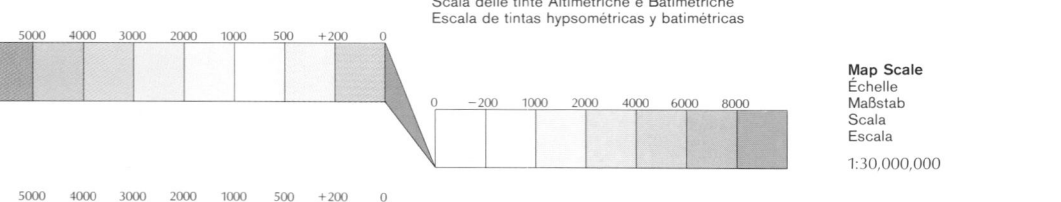

Scales in Metric and English Measures
Échelle des teintes hypsométriques et bathymétriques
Farbskala der Höhen- und Tiefenstufen
Scala delle tinte Altimetriche e Batimetriche
Escala de tintas hipsométricas y batimétricas

Land Elevation Below Sea Level
Dépression et cote au-dessous du niveau de la mer
Senke mit Tiefenzahl unter dem Meeresspiegel
Depressione e quota sotto il livello del mare
Depresión y elevación bajo el nivel del mar

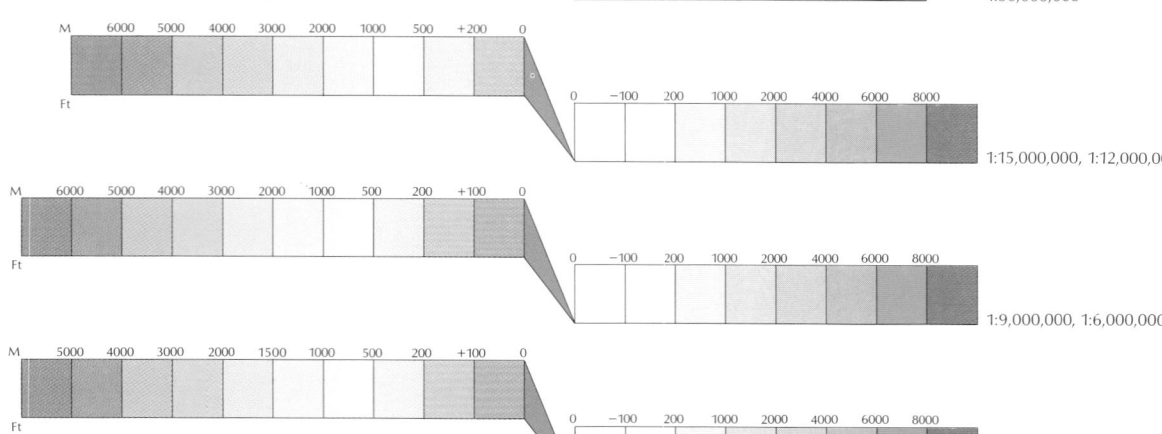

Map Scale
Échelle
Maßstab
Scala
Escala

1:30,000,000

1:15,000,000, 1:12,000,000

1:9,000,000, 1:6,000,000

1:3,000,000, 1:1,500,000
1:600,000, 1:300,000

Map Projections
Projections cartographiques
Kartennetzentwürfe
Proiezioni cartografiche
Proyecciones cartográficas

The projections appearing in this atlas have been plotted by computer

Les réseaux des projections ont été obtenus par élaboration automatique à partir de formules mathématiques

Die Kartennetze aller im Atlas vorkommenden Abbildungen wurden mit Hilfe der Datenverarbeitung (EDV) völlig neu errechnet

I disegni delle proiezioni presenti in quest'opera sono stati realizzati interamente ex-novo con l'uso del computer e del plotter a partire dalle formule matematiche

El reticulado de las proyecciones (redes geográficas) incluidas en esta obra han sido obtenidas por proceso automático a partir de las formulas matemáticas

114

The meanings of the symbols on the Legend pages are in English, French, German, Italian, and Spanish languages to permit the interpretation of the maps by a broad readership.

Boundaries, Capitals
Frontières, Soulignements / Confini, Sottolineature
Grenzen, Unterstreichungen / Límites, Subrayados

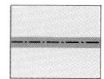

Defined International Boundary
Frontière internationale définie
Staatsgrenze
Confine di Stato definito
Límite de Nación definido

Second-order Political Boundary
Frontière d'État fédéré, Région
Bundesstaats-, Regionsgrenze
Confine di Stato federato, Regione
Límite de Estado federado, Región

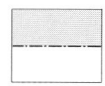

International Boundary (Continent Maps)
Frontière internationale (Continents)
Staatsgrenze (Erdteilkarten)
Confine di Stato (Carte dei Continenti)
Límite de Nación (Continentes)

Third-order Political Boundary
Frontière de Province, Comté, Bezirk
Provinz-, Grafschafts-, Bezirksgrenze
Confine di Provincia, Contea, Bezirk
Límite de Provincia, Condado, Bezirk

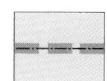

Undefined International Boundary
Frontière internationale indéfinie
Nicht genau festgelegte Staatsgrenze
Confine di Stato indefinito
Límite de Nación indefinido

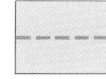

Administrative District Boundary
Frontière de Circonscription
Kreisgrenze
Confine di Circondario
Límite de Circunscripción administrativa

International Ocean Floor Boundary Defined by Treaty or Bilateral Agreement

Frontière d'état en mer définie par traités et conventions bilatéraux

Durch Verträge festgelegte Staatsgrenze im Meeresgebiet

Confine di Stato nel mare definito da trattati e convenzioni bilaterali

Límite de Nación en el Mar definido por los tratados bilaterales

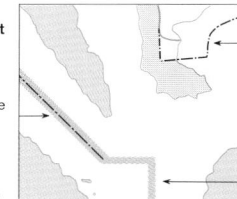

International Ocean Floor Boundary
Frontière d'état en mer
Staatsgrenze im Meeresgebiet
Confine di Stato nel mare
Límite de Nación en el mar

Undefined Ocean Floor Boundary
Frontière indéfinie d'état tracée en meer
Unbstimmte Staatsgrenze im Meeresgebiet
Confine di Stato indefinito nel mare
Límite indefinido de Nación en el mar

ROMA — **National Capital**
Capitale d'État
Hauptstadt eines unabhängigen Staates
Capitale di Stato
Capital de Nación

Kristiansand — **Third-order Capital**
Capitale de Province, Comté, Bezirk
Provinz-, Grafschafts-, Bezirkshauptstadt
Capoluogo di Provincia, Contea, Bezirk
Capital de Provincia, Condado, Bezirk

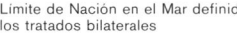

LYON — **Dependency or Second-order Capital**
Capitale d'État fédéré, Région
Bundesstaats-, Regionshauptstadt
Capitale di Stato federato, Regione
Capital de Estado federado, Región

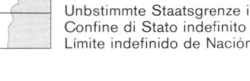

Anadyr — **Administrative District Capital**
Capitale de Circonscription
Kreishauptstadt
Capoluogo di Circondario
Capital de Circunscripción administrativa

Other Symbols
Symboles divers / Simboli vari
Sonstige Zeichen / Signos varios

LUTON AIRPORT — **International Airport**
Aéroport international
Internationaler Flughafen
Aeroporto internazionale
Aeropuerto internacional

SANTAS CREUS — **Church, Monastery, Abbey**
Monastère, Eglise, Abbaye
Kloster, Kirche, Abtei
Monastero, Chiesa, Abbazia
Monasterio, Iglesia, Abadía

Lighthouse
Phare
Leuchtturm
Faro
Faro

DAMPIERRE — **Castle**
Château
Burg, Schloß
Castello
Castillo

BUI DAM — **Dam**
Barrage
Staudamm, Staumauer
Diga artificiale, Sbarramento
Presa

PAESTUM — **Ruin, Archeological Site**
Ruine, Centre archéologique
Ruine, Archäologisches Zentrum
Rovina, Zona archeologica
Ruina, Zona arqueológica

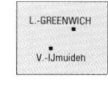

L.-GREENWICH, V.-IJmuiden — **Section of a City**
Faubourg
Stadt- oder Ortsteil
Sobborgo urbano
Suburbio

MOLENS VAN KINDERDIJK — **Monument, Historic Site, etc.**
Monument
Denkmal
Monumento
Monumento

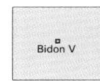

Bidon V — **Uninhabited Locality, Hamlet**
Ville inhabitée, Ferme, Hameau
Unbewohnte Stadt, Gehöft, Weiler
Città disabitata, Fattoria, Nucleo di case
Ciudad despoblada, Granja, Casar

HADRIAN'S WALL — **Wall**
Muraille
Wall, Mauer
Vallo, Muraglia
Muralla

Bi'r Nāhid — **Periodically Inhabited Oasis**
Oasis habitées périodiquement
Zeitweilig bewohnte Oase
Oasi periodicamente abitate
Oasis periodicamente habitados

GIANT'S CAUSEWAY — **Point of Interest**
Curiosité
Sehenswürdigkeit
Curiosità
Curiosidad

Casey (Australia) — **Scientific Station**
Base géophysique
Geophysikalische Beobachtungsstation
Base geofisica
Base geofísica

CUEVAS DE ARTÁ — **Cave**
Grotte, Caverne
Höhle
Grotta, Caverna
Cueva, Gruta

Populated Places
Population / Popolazione
Bevölkerung / Población

Continent Maps
Cartes des Continents / Carte dei Continenti
Erdteilkarten / Mapas de Continentes
< 25 000
25 000-100 000
100 000-250 000
250 000-1 000 000
> 1 000 000

Regional Maps
Cartes à plus grande échelle / Carte di sviluppo
Karten größeren Maßstabs / Mapas a gran escala
< 10 000
10 000-25 000
25 000-100 000
100 000-250 000
250 000-1 000 000
> 1 000 000

Symbols represent population of inhabited localities
Les symboles représentent le nombre d'habitants des localités
Die Signaturen entsprechen der Einwohnerzahl des Ortes
I simboli sono relativi al valore demografico dei centri abitati
Los símbolos son proporcionales a la población del lugar

Town area symbol represents the shape of the urban area
Le petit plan de la ville reproduit la configuration de l'aire urbaine
Die Plansignatur stellt die Gestalt des Stadtgebietes dar
La piantina della città rappresenta la configurazione dell'area urbana
El pequeño plano de la ciudad representa la forma del area urbana

Transportation
Communications / Comunicazioni
Verkehrsnetz / Comunicaciones

Primary Railway
Chemin de fer principal
Hauptbahn
Ferrovia principale
Ferrocarril principal

Secondary Railway
Chemin de fer secondaire
Sonstige Bahn
Ferrovia secondaria
Ferrocarril secundario

Motorway, Expressway
Autoroute
Autobahn
Autostrada
Autopista

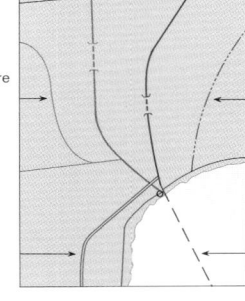

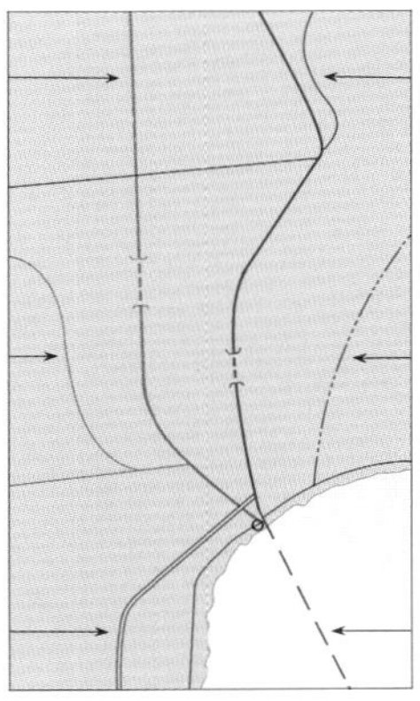

Road
Route de grande communication, Autres Routes
Fernverkehrsstraße, andere Straßen
Strada principale, Altre Strade
Carretera principal, Otras Carreteras

Trail, Caravan Route
Piste, Voie caravanière
Wüstenpiste, Karawanenweg
Pista nel deserto, Carovaniera
Pista en el desierto, Vía de Carabanas

Ferry, Shipping Lane
Bac, Ligne maritime
Fähre, Schiffahrtslinie
Traghetto, Linea di navigazione
Transbordador (Ferry), Línea de navegación

Type Styles
Caractères utilisés pour la toponymie / Caratteri usati per la toponomastica
Zur Namenschreibung verwendete Schriftarten / Caracteres utilizados para la toponimia

ITALY / Hessen / RIBE — **Political Units**
Etat, Dépendance, Division administrative
Staat, abhängiges Gebiet, Verwaltungsgliederung
Stato, Dipendenza, Divisione amministrativa
Nación, Dependencia, Division administrativa

Ankaratra / Monte Bianco / Tsiafajavona / Ngorongoro Crater / Nevado del Tolima / Kings Peak — **Small Mountain Range, Mountain, Peak**
Petit massif, Mont, Cime
Bergmassiv, Berg, Gipfel
Piccolo gruppo montuoso, Monte, Vetta
Macizo pequeño, Monte, Cima

LABRADOR SEA / Gulf of Alaska / Hudson Bay / Estrecho de Magallanes — **Sea, Gulf, Bay, Strait**
Mer, Golfe, Baie, Détroit
Meer, Golf, Bucht, Meeresstraße
Mare, Golfo, Baia, Stretto
Mar, Golfo, Bahía, Estrecho

SAXONY / THRACE / SUSSEX — **Historical or Cultural Region**
Région historique ou culturelle
Historische oder Kulturlandschaft
Regione storico - culturale
Región histórica y cultural

Cabo de São Vicente / Land's End / Mizen Head / Point Conception / Col de la Perche / Passo della Cisa — **Cape, Point, Pass**
Cap, Pointe, Passe
Kap, Landspitze, Paß
Capo, Punta, Passo
Cabo, Punta, Paso

West Mariana Basin / Galapagos Fracture Zone / Mid-Atlantic Ridge — **Undersea Features**
Formes du relief sous-marin
Formen des Meeresbodens
Forme del rilievo sottomarino
Formas del relieve submarino

PATAGONIA / BASSIN DE RENNES / PENÍNSULA DE YUCATÁN — **Physical Region (plain, peninsula)**
Région physique (plaine, péninsule)
Landschaft (Ebene, Halbinsel)
Regione fisica (pianura, penisola)
Región natural (llanura, península)

MAHÉ / ALDABRA ISLANDS / CORSE / CHANNEL ISLANDS / SULU ARCHIPELAGO — **Island, Archipelago**
Ile, Archipel
Insel, Archipel
Isola, Arcipelago
Isla, Archipiélago

Tarfaya / Tombouctou / Agadir / Nouakchott / BRAZZAVILLE / CASABLANCA — **Size of type indicates relative importance of inhabited localities**

La dimension des caractères indique l'importance d'une localité

Die Schriftgröße entspricht der Gesamtbedeutung des Ortes

La grandezza del carattere è proporzionale all'importanza della località

La dimensión de los caracteres de imprenta indica la importancia de la localidad

PYRENEES / CUMBRIAN MOUNTAINS / SIERRA DE GÁDOR / LA SILA — **Mountain Range**
Chaîne de montagnes
Bergkette, Gebirge
Catena di monti
Cadena montañosa

Thames / Po / Victoria Falls / Lotagipi Swamp / Göta kanal / Lago Maggiore — **River, Waterfall, Cataract, Canal, Lake**
Fleuve, Chute d'eau, Cataracte, Canal, Lac
Fluß, Wasserfall, Katarakt, Kanal, See
Fiume, Cascata, Cateratta, Canale, Lago
Río, Cascada, Catarata, Canal, Lago

INDEX MAPS

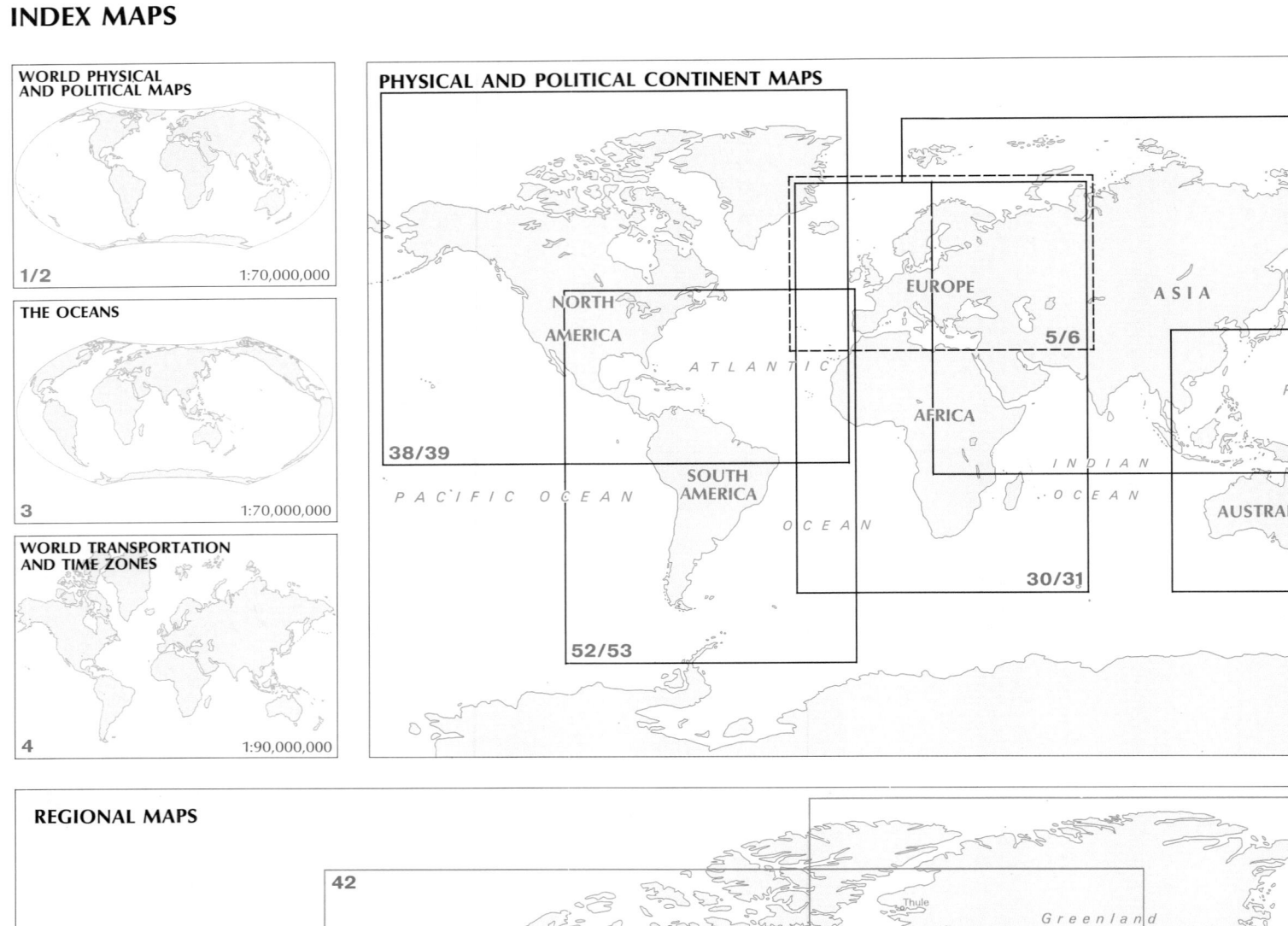

WORLD PHYSICAL AND POLITICAL MAPS

1/2   1:70,000,000

THE OCEANS

3   1:70,000,000

WORLD TRANSPORTATION AND TIME ZONES

4   1:90,000,000

PHYSICAL AND POLITICAL CONTINENT MAPS

21/22

NORTH AMERICA

EUROPE

ASIA

5/6

ATLANTIC

PACIFIC OCEAN

AFRICA

38/39

INDIAN

SOUTH AMERICA

OCEAN

AUSTRALIA AND OCEANIA

PACIFIC OCEAN

OCEAN

30/31

57/58

52/53

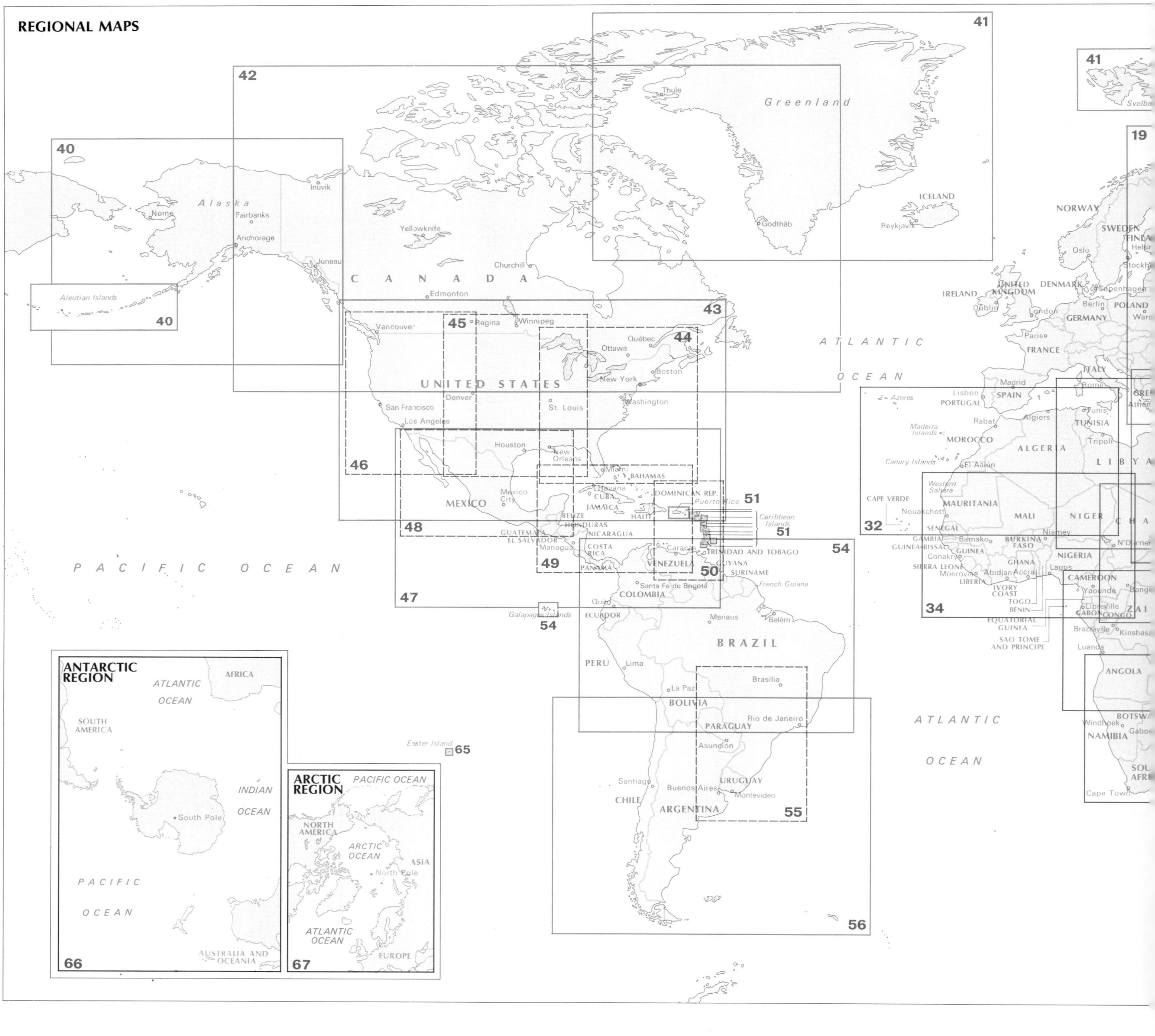

REGIONAL MAPS

41

42

41

40

Greenland

Thule

19

Alaska

Inuvik

ICELAND

NORWAY

Nome

Fairbanks

Godthåb

SWEDEN FINLA

Anchorage

Yellowknife

Reykjavík

Oslo

Helsi

Juneau

Stockh

Aleutian Islands

CANADA

Churchill

IRELAND

UNITED DENMARK

KINGDOM

Copenhagen

40

Edmonton

Dublin

London

Berlin POLAND

GERMANY

Warsa

45

Regina

Winnipeg

ATLANTIC

Paris

43

Québec

44

FRANCE

Vancouver

Ottawa

ITALY

UNITED STATES

New York

OCEAN

Rom

Boston

Lisbon

Madrid

GRE

Azores

PORTUGAL

SPAIN

Ath

Denver

Washington

Algiers

Tunis

San Francisco

St. Louis

Madeira

Rabat

TUNISIA

Los Angeles

Islands

MOROCCO

Tripoli

46

Houston

ALGERIA

LIBYA

New

Canary Islands

El Aaiún

Orleans

Miami

BAHAMAS

Western

CAPE VERDE

Sahara

MAURITANIA

Mexico

Havana

CUBA

DOMINICAN REP.

51

Nouakchott

MALI

NIGER

CHA

City

JAMAICA

Puerto Rico

MEXICO

BELIZE

HAITI

Caribbean

Islands

51

SENEGAL

Bamako

Niamey

N'Djame

48

HONDURAS

GUATEMALA

NICARAGUA

32

GAMBIA

BURKINA

FASO

NIGERIA

GUINEA-BISSAU

GUINEA

EL SALVADOR

Managua

54

SIERRA LEONE

GHANA

Conakry

CAMEROON

49

COSTA

RICA

TRINIDAD AND TOBAGO

Monrovia

Abidjan Accra

Yaound

PANAMA

GUYANA

IVORY

Lagos

Caracas

VENEZUELA

SURINAME

34

COAST

TOGO

Bang

PACIFIC

OCEAN

50

French Guiana

BENIN

ZAI

47

Santa Fe de Bogotá

EQUATORIAL

GUINEA

Brazzaville

GABON

CONGO

Kinshasa

COLOMBIA

SAO TOME

Libreville

Quito

AND PRINCIPE

ECUADOR

Luanda

Galapagos Islands

Manaus

Belém

54

BRAZIL

ANGOLA

PERÚ

Lima

ANTARCTIC REGION

AFRICA

Brasília

ATLANTIC

Easter Island

65

BOTSWA

OCEAN

La Paz

ATLANTIC

SOUTH

AMERICA

BOLIVIA

Rio de Janeiro

Windhoek

Gaboi

NAMIBIA

PARAGUAY

PACIFIC

INDIAN

ARCTIC REGION

PACIFIC OCEAN

Asunción

OCEAN

South Pole

OCEAN

NORTH

AMERICA

ARCTIC

OCEAN

Santiago

URUGUAY

SOU

Buenos Aires

Montevideo

Cape Tow

ASIA

PACIFIC

North Pole

CHILE

ARGENTINA

55

OCEAN

ATLANTIC

OCEAN

66

ATLANTIC

OCEAN

67

EUROPE

AUSTRALIA AND

OCEANIA

56

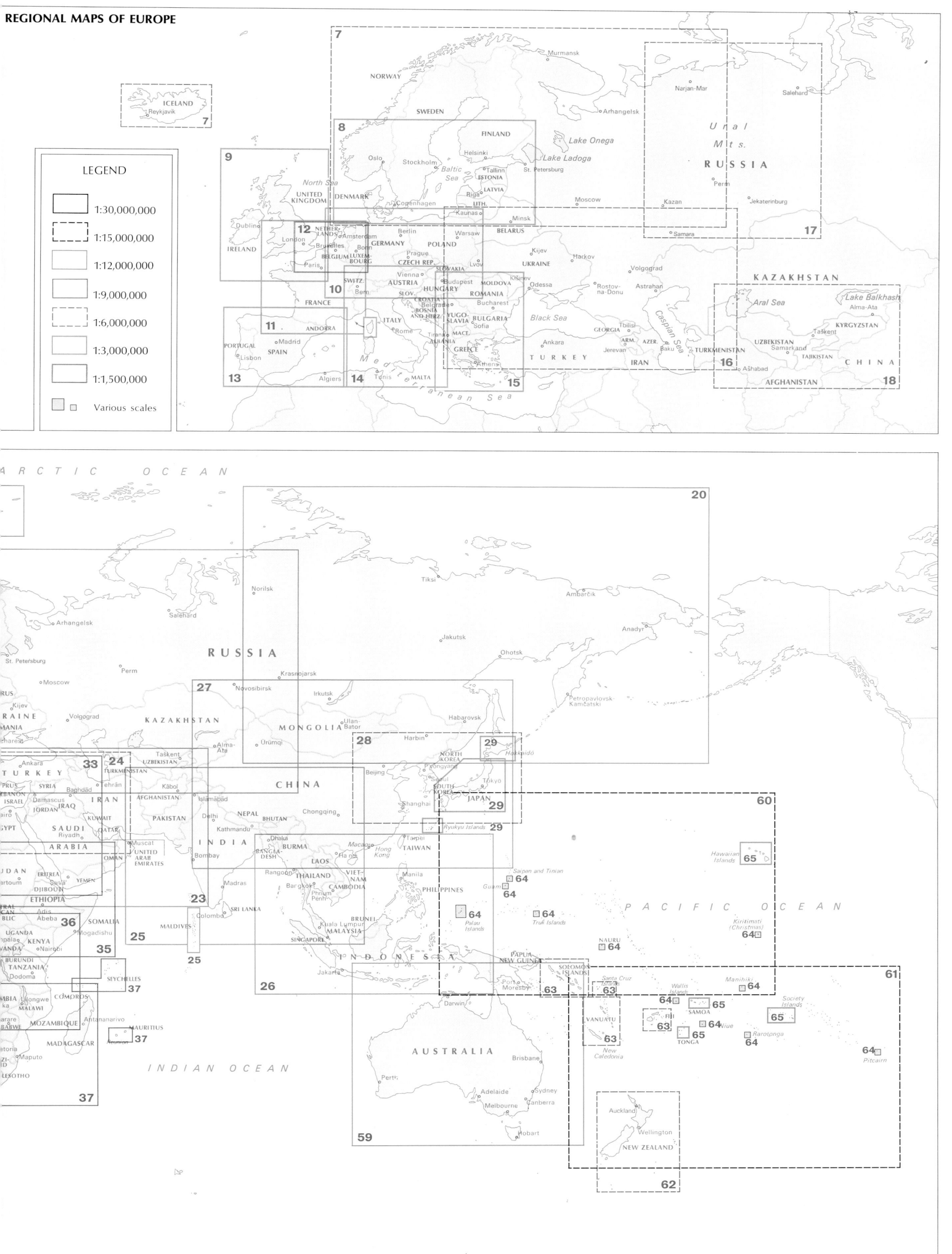

Map 1 **WORLD, PHYSICAL**

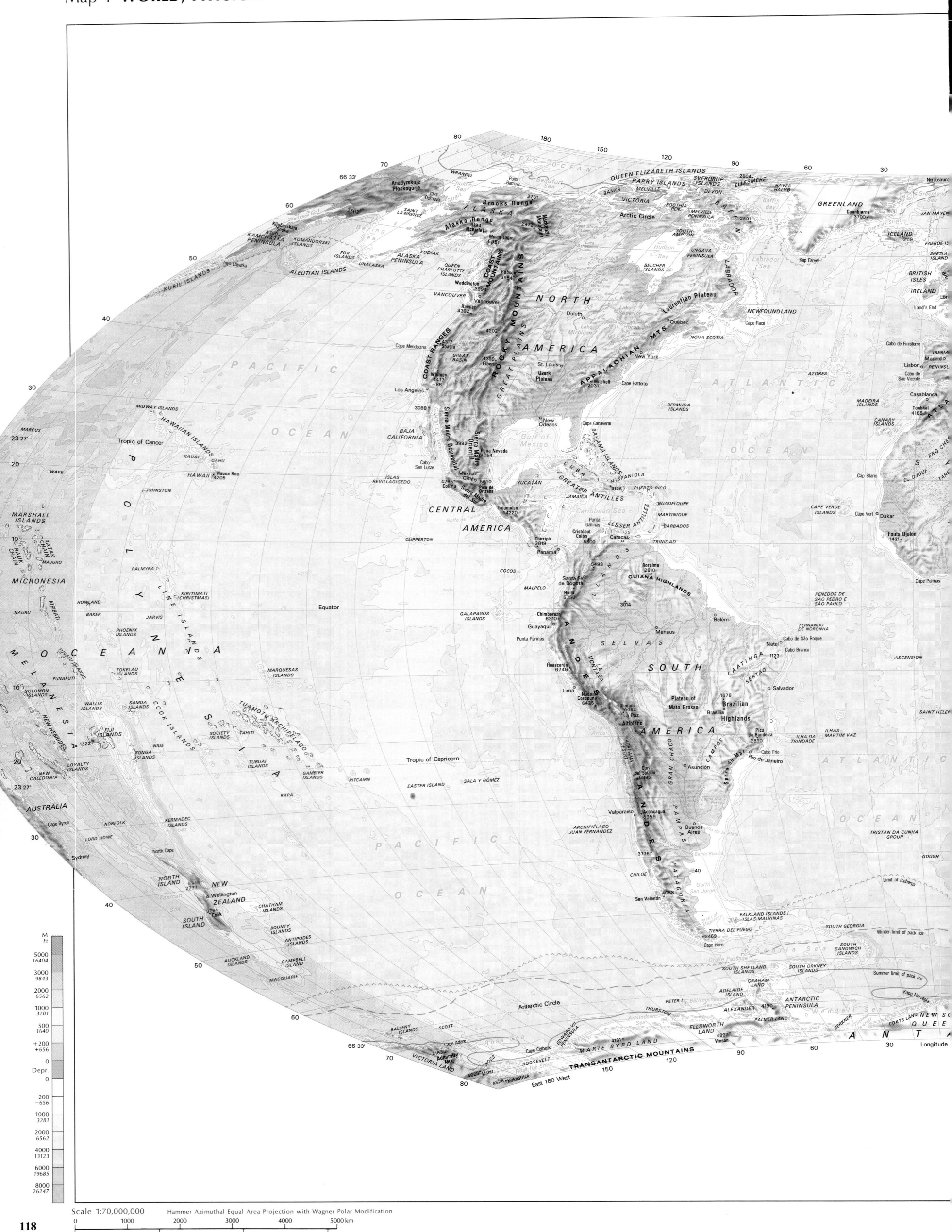

ARCTIC OCEAN

WRANGEL
Point Barrow
Beaufort Sea
QUEEN ELIZABETH ISLANDS
SVERDRUP ISLANDS
2604 ELLESMERE
NORDAUSTLANDET
Anadyrskoje Ploskogorje
66 33'
BANKS
MELVILLE
PARRY ISLANDS
HAYES HALVØ
GREENLAND
Gunnbjørns 3700
JAN MAYEN
SAINT LAWRENCE
Chukchi Sea
Bering Strait
ALASKA
Brooks Range
2761
VICTORIA
BOOTHIA PEN.
MELVILLE PENINSULA
DEVON
Baffin Bay
2591
ICELAND
2119
KAMCHATKA PENINSULA
KOMANDORSKI ISLANDS
Gulf of Alaska
Alaska Range
2972
Mackenzie Mountains
Arctic Circle
SOUTHAMPTON
Hudson Bay
Kap Farvel
FAERØE IS.
SHETLAND ISLANDS
Mys Lopatka
Mount Logan 6051
Mount McKinley
BRITISH ISLES
KURIL ISLANDS
FOX ISLANDS
KODIAK
UNALASKA
ALASKA PENINSULA
QUEEN CHARLOTTE ISLANDS
COAST MOUNTAINS
Waddington 3994
BELCHER ISLANDS
UNGAVA PENINSULA
LABRADOR
Labrador Sea
IRELAND
ALEUTIAN ISLANDS
VANCOUVER
Vancouver
Rainier 4392
ROCKY MOUNTAINS
NORTH
Lake Winnipeg
Lake Superior
LAURENTIAN PLATEAU
Quebec
NEWFOUNDLAND
Cape Race
Land's End
Cape Mendocino
Robson 3954
GREAT PLAINS
AMERICA
Lake Huron
Lake Michigan
APPALACHIAN MTS.
NOVA SCOTIA
Cabo de Finisterre
IBERIAN
Whitney 4417
Shasta
4202
GREAT BASIN
4399
Elbert 4399
St. Louis
Ozark Plateau
Mitchell 2037
New York
Cape Hatteras
AZORES
Madrid
Lisbon
PENINS
COAST RANGES
Los Angeles
SIERRA NEVADA
3088
Peña Nevada 4054
BERMUDA ISLANDS
Cabo de São Vicente
MADEIRA ISLANDS
Casablanca
Toubkal 4165
MIDWAY ISLANDS
HAWAIIAN ISLANDS
Tropic of Cancer
BAJA CALIFORNIA
SIERRA MADRE ORIENTAL
New Orleans
Cape Canaveral
BAHAMA ISLANDS
CANARY ISLANDS
MARCUS 23 27'
KAUAI
OAHU
Cabo San Lucas
Mexico City
Pico de Orizaba 5610
Gulf of Mexico
CUBA
HISPANIOLA
PUERTO RICO
Cap Blanc
EL DJOUF
ERG CHE
WAKE
HAWAII
Mauna Kea 4205
SIERRA MADRE DEL SUR
4285 Colima
GREATER ANTILLES
JAMAICA
GUADELOUPE
MARTINIQUE
Cape Verde
Cape Vert
Dakar
20
JOHNSTON
Golfo de Tehuantepec
YUCATÁN
Tajumulco 4220
BARBADOS
Fouta Djalon 1421
MARSHALL ISLANDS
10
PALMYRA
CENTRAL
Punta Gallinas
LESSER ANTILLES
RATAK CHAIN
MAJURO
LINE ISLANDS
KIRITIMATI (CHRISTMAS)
CLIPPERTON
AMERICA
Chirripó 3819
Cristóbal Colón 5800
Caracas
TRINIDAD
MICRONESIA
HOWLAND
BAKER
JARVIS
Panama
5493
Roraima 2810
GUIANA HIGHLANDS
PENEDOS DE SÃO PEDRO E SÃO PAULO
NAURU
KIRIBATI
COCOS
MALPELO
Santa Fé de Bogotá
3014
SELVAS
FERNANDO DE NORONHA
ASCENSION
PHOENIX ISLANDS
Equator
GALÁPAGOS ISLANDS
Chimborazo 6310
Guayaquil
Manaus
Belém
Cabo de São Roque
Natal
Cabo Branco
P O L Y N E S I A
Punta Pariñas
Huascarán 6746
SOUTH
CAATINGA
1123
SAINT HELE
M E L A N E S I A
O C E A N I A
TOKELAU ISLANDS
MARQUESAS ISLANDS
Lima
SERTÃO
SOLOMON ISLANDS
SAMOA ISLANDS
WALLIS ISLANDS
Nudo de Cerezuela 6425
AMERICA
Plateau of Mato Grosso
1678
Salvador
NEW HEBRIDES
FUNAFUTI
COOK ISLANDS
NIUE
SOCIETY ISLANDS
Tahiti
TUAMOTU ARCHIPELAGO
Illimani 6462
La Paz
Brasília
Brazilian Highlands
1322
FIJI ISLANDS
TONGA ISLANDS
TUBUAI ISLANDS
Altiplano
CAMPOS
Pico da Bandeira 2890
ILHA DA TRINDADE
ILHAS MARTIM VAZ
LOYALTY ISLANDS
Tropic of Capricorn
GAMBIER ISLANDS
PITCAIRN
EASTER ISLAND
SALA Y GÓMEZ
GRAN CHACO
Cabo Frio
Rio de Janeiro
ATLANTIC
NEW CALEDONIA
20
RAPA
Asunción
Ojos del Salado 6893
SIERRA DO MAR
23 27'
AUSTRALIA
Aconcagua 6959
PAMPAS
Buenos Aires
TRISTAN DA CUNHA GROUP
Cape Byron
ARCHIPIÉLAGO JUAN FERNÁNDEZ
Valparaíso
3776
PATAGONIA
Bahía Blanca
GOUGH
NORFOLK
LORD HOWE
KERMADEC ISLANDS
North Cape
CHILOÉ
40
Golfo San Jorge
FALKLAND ISLANDS
ISLAS MALVINAS
Sydney
Tasman Sea
NORTH ISLAND
2797
NEW ZEALAND
Wellington
4058
San Valentín
Limit of icebergs
SOUTH ISLAND
3764 Cook
CHATHAM ISLANDS
TIERRA DEL FUEGO
2469
SOUTH GEORGIA
Winter limit of pack ice
BOUNTY ISLANDS
ANTIPODES ISLANDS
Cape Horn
Drake Passage
SOUTH SANDWICH ISLANDS
50
AUCKLAND ISLANDS
CAMPBELL ISLAND
SOUTH SHETLAND ISLANDS
SOUTH ORKNEY ISLANDS
Summer limit of pack ice
MACQUARIE
BALLENY ISLANDS
SCOTT
GRAHAM LAND
ADELAIDE ISLAND
PETER I
Bellingshausen Sea
ANTARCTIC PENINSULA
Weddell Sea
Kapp Norvegia
Cape Adare
EDWARD VII PENINSULA
THURSTON
ALEXANDER
PALMER LAND
COATS LAND
NEW S
QUEE
Antarctic Circle
60
ELLSWORTH LAND
4181
4190
ANT A
66 33'
Cape Colbeck
MARIE BYRD LAND
4897 Vinson
30
Longitude
VICTORIA LAND
4025 Lister
ROSS
Ross Ice Shelf
ROOSEVELT
TRANSANTARCTIC MOUNTAINS
120
90
60
Admiralty Mts.
4528 Kirkpatrick
120
150
80
East 180 West

M Ft
5000 16404
3000 9843
2000 6562
1000 3281
500 1640
+200 +656
0 0
Depr.
0
−200 −656
1000 3281
2000 6562
4000 13123
6000 19685
8000 26247

Scale 1:70,000,000   Hammer Azimuthal Equal Area Projection with Wagner Polar Modification

0   1000   2000   3000   4000   5000 km
0   1000   2000   3000 miles

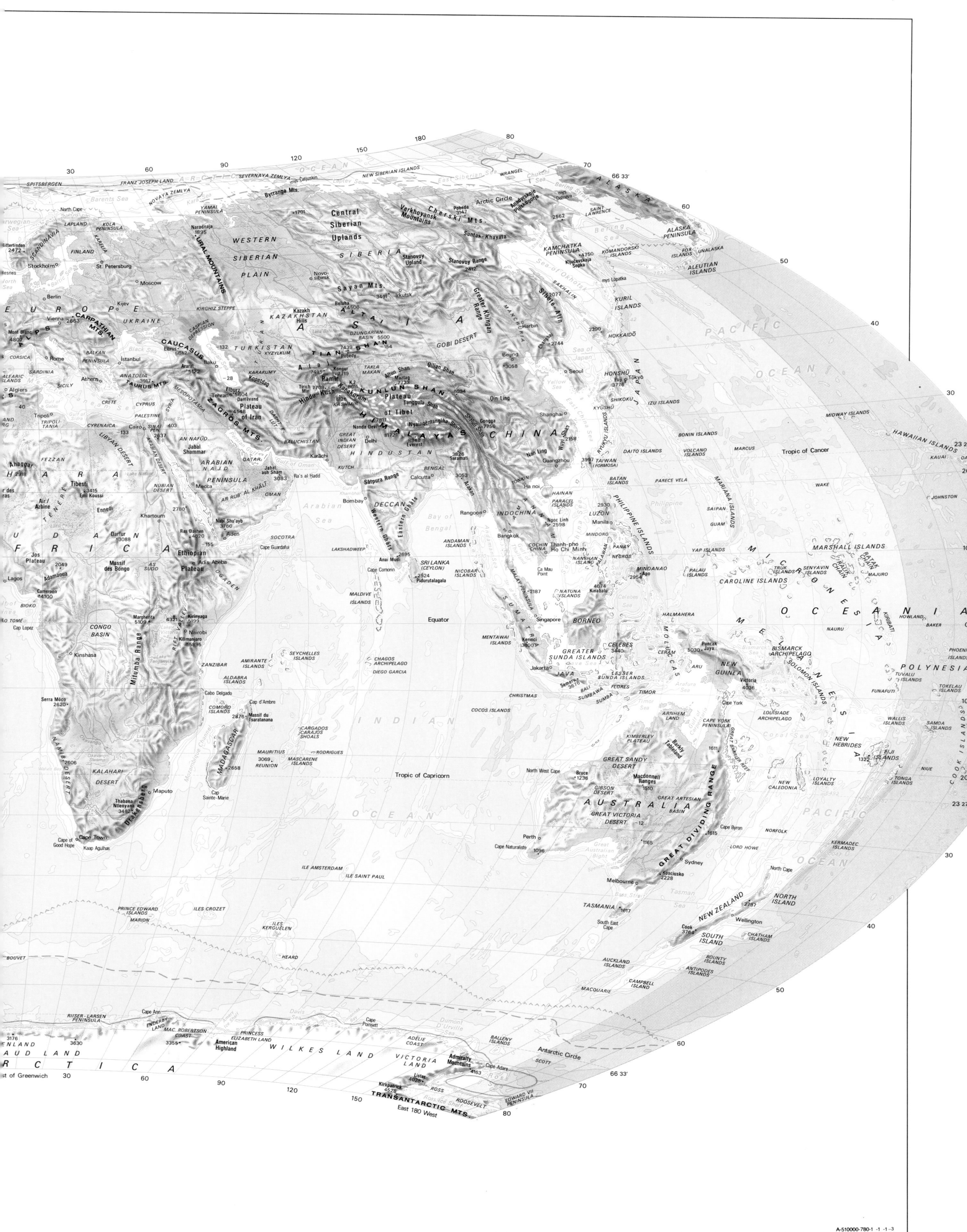

Map 2 **WORLD, POLITICAL**

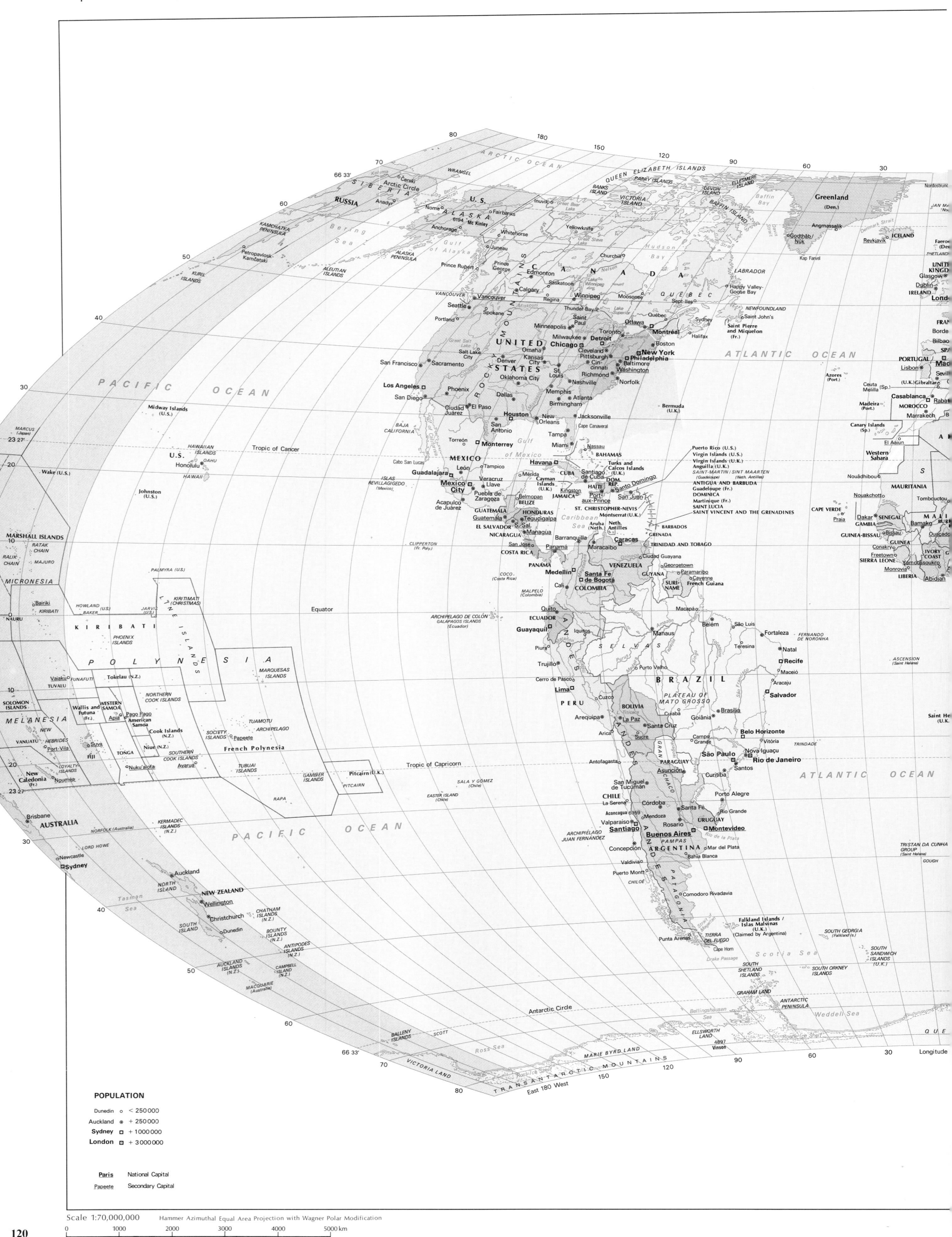

POPULATION

Dunedin ○ < 250 000
Auckland ⊙ + 250 000
Sydney ☐ + 1 000 000
London ⊡ + 3 000 000

Paris National Capital

Papeete Secondary Capital

Scale 1:70,000,000   Hammer Azimuthal Equal Area Projection with Wagner Polar Modification

0   1000   2000   3000   4000   5000 km

0   1000   2000   3000 miles

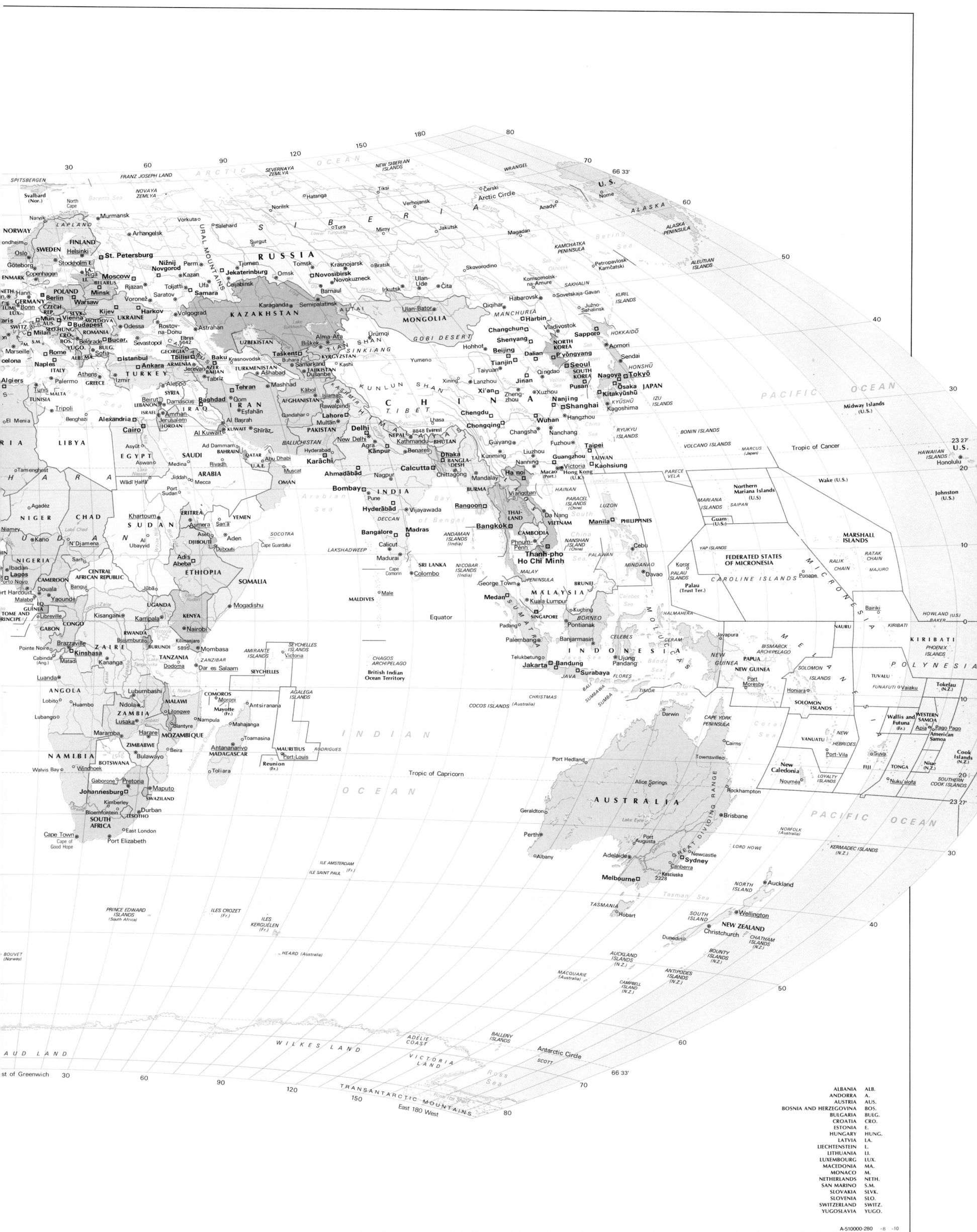

ALBANIA	ALB.
ANDORRA	A.
AUSTRIA	AUS.
BOSNIA AND HERZEGOVINA	BOS.
BULGARIA	BULG.
CROATIA	CRO.
ESTONIA	E.
HUNGARY	HUNG.
LATVIA	LA.
LIECHTENSTEIN	L.
LITHUANIA	LI.
LUXEMBOURG	LUX.
MACEDONIA	MA.
MONACO	M.
NETHERLANDS	NETH.
SAN MARINO	S.M.
SLOVAKIA	SLVK.
SLOVENIA	SLO.
SWITZERLAND	SWITZ.
YUGOSLAVIA	YUGO.

A-510000-280 -8 -10

Map 3 **THE OCEANS**

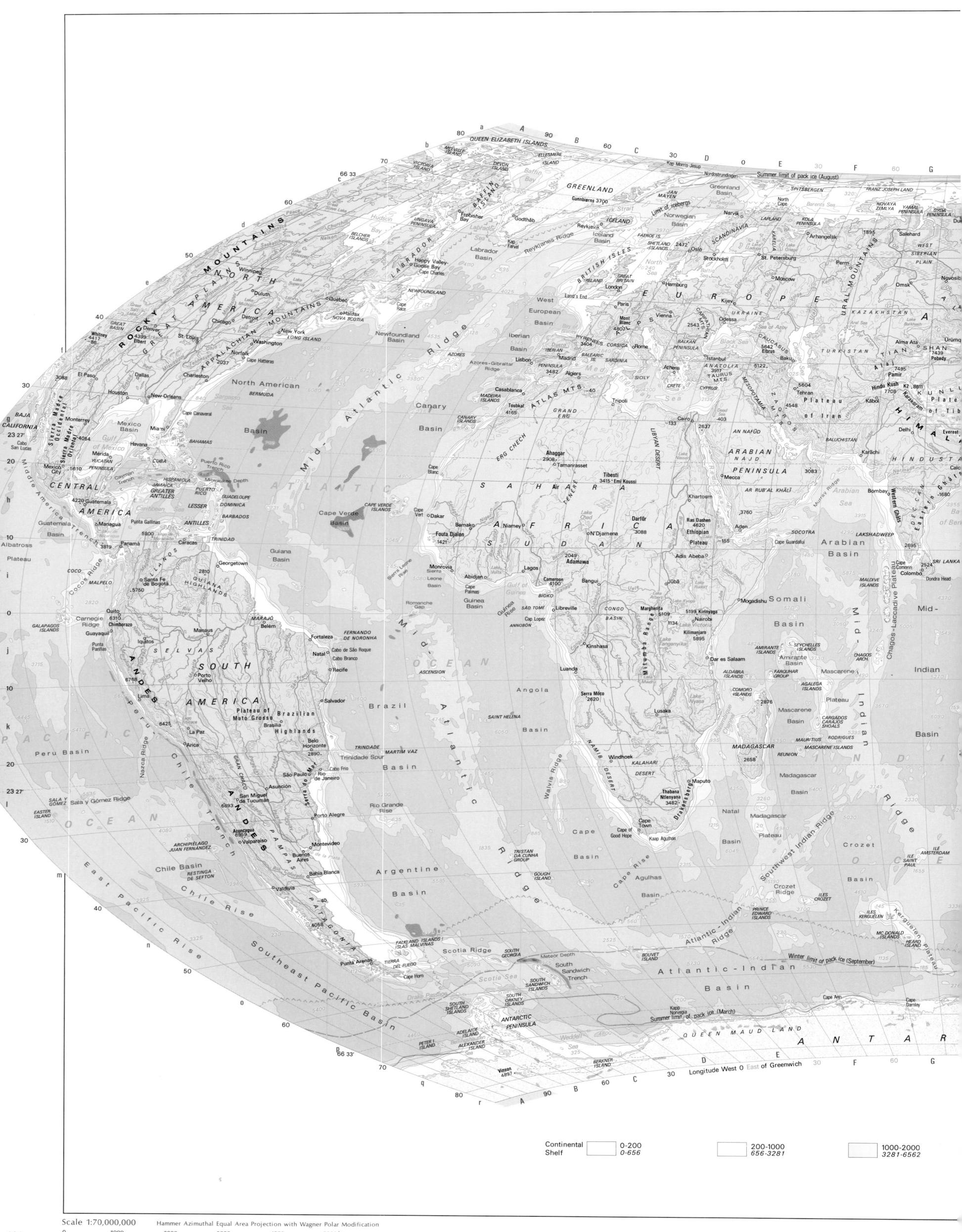

| Continental Shelf | 0-200 0-656 | | 200-1000 656-3281 | 1000-2000 3281-6562 |

Scale 1:70,000,000   Hammer Azimuthal Equal Area Projection with Wagner Polar Modification

| 0 | 1000 | 2000 | 3000 | 4000 | 5000 km |

| 0 | 1000 | 2000 | 3000 miles |

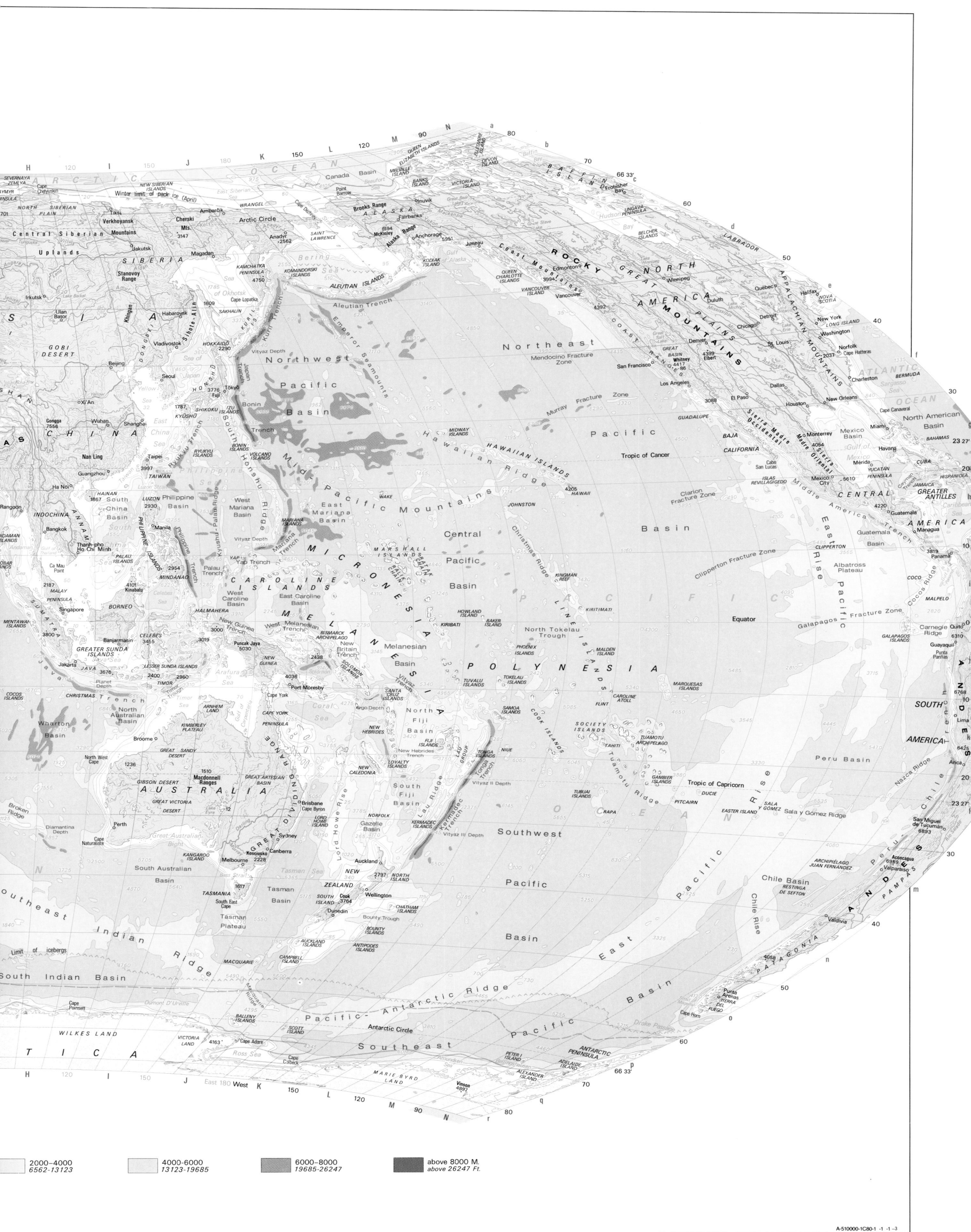

2000-4000
6562-13123

4000-6000
13123-19685

6000-8000
19685-26247

above 8000 M.
above 26247 Ft.

A-510000-1C80-1 -1 -1 -3

Map 4 **WORLD TRANSPORTATION AND TIME ZONES**

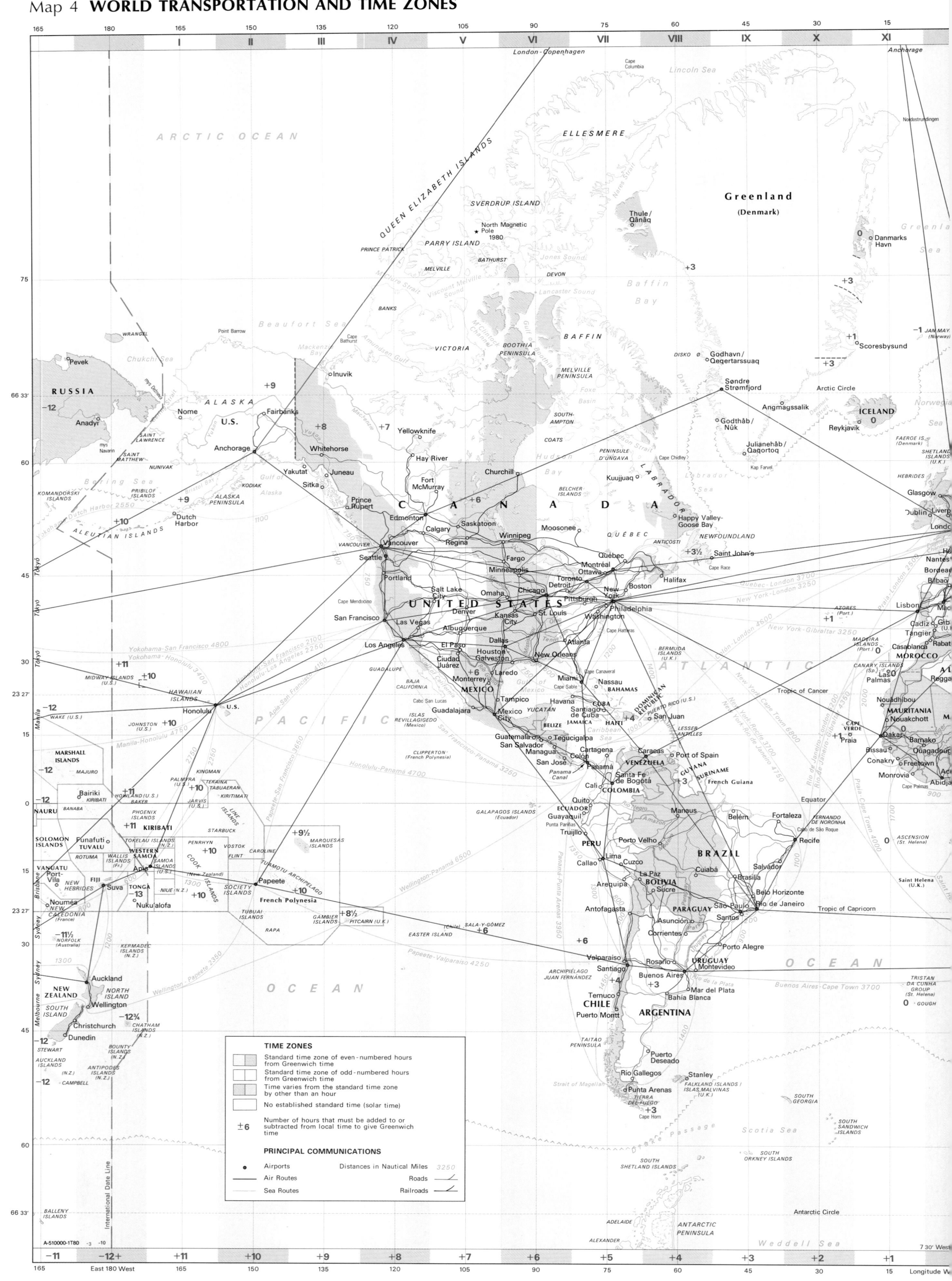

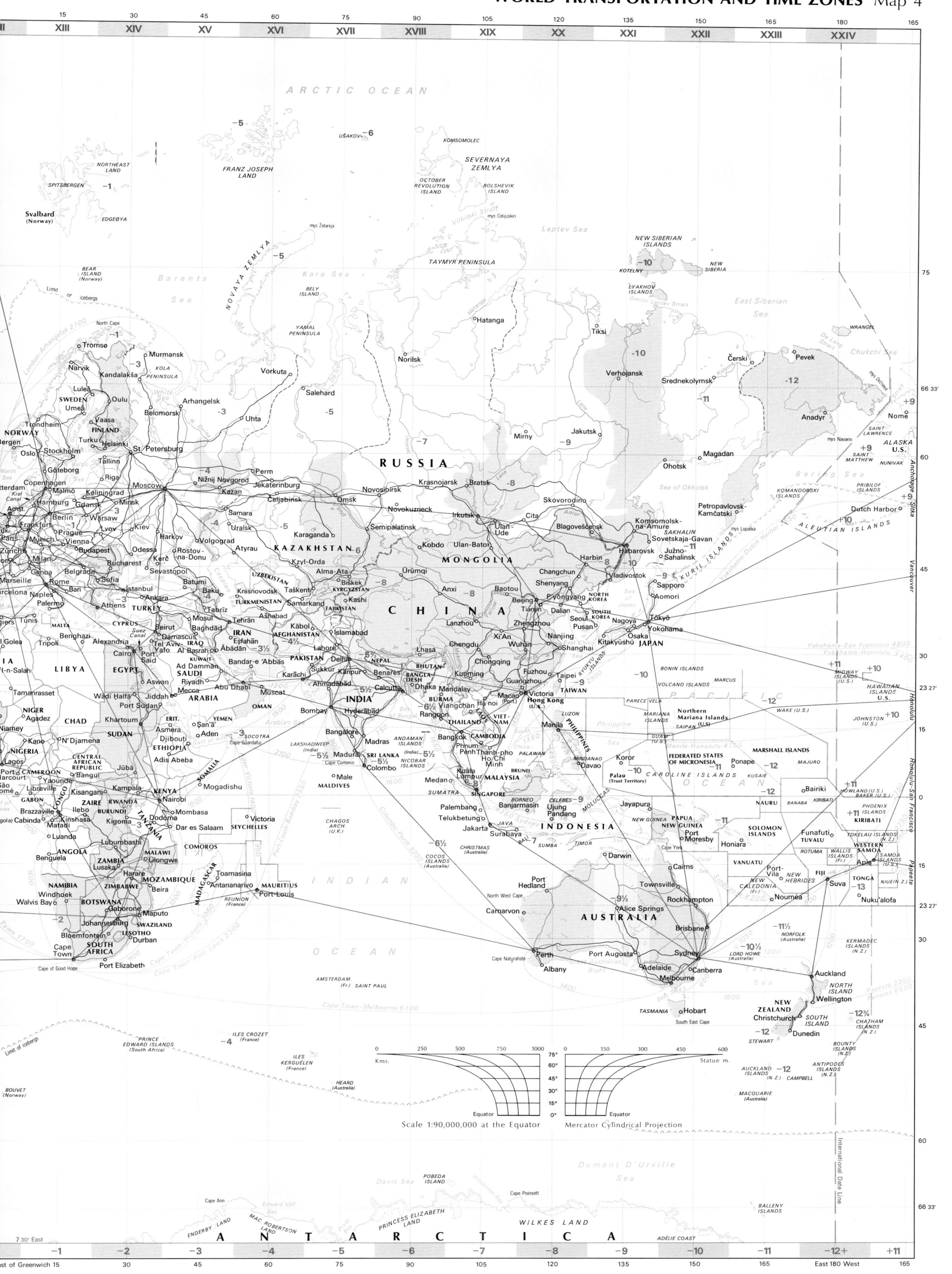

Scale 1:90,000,000 at the Equator Mercator Cylindrical Projection

Map 5 **EUROPE, PHYSICAL**

Scale 1:15,000,000

Lambert Azimuthal Equal Area Projection

Longitude East 0 of Greenwich

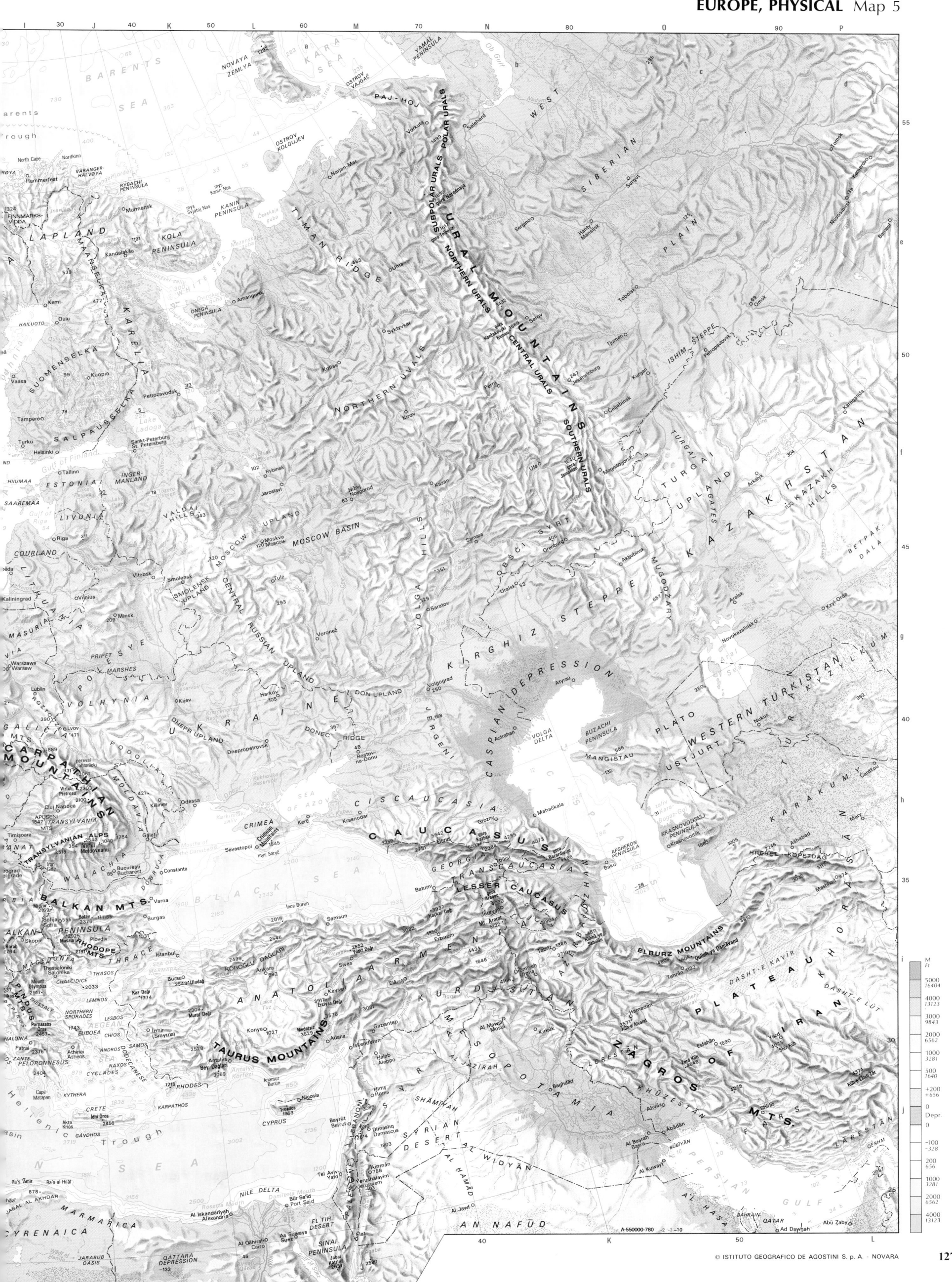

Map 6 **EUROPE, POLITICAL**

KING CHRISTIAN IX LAND

Greenland
(Den.)

KING FREDERIK VI COAST

Nanortalik
Frederikshåb
Narssaq
Julianehåb

3700

Scoresbysund

a

Greenland Sea

BEAR ISLAND
(Norway)

Denmark Strait

Scoresby Sund

JAN MAYEN
(Norway)

VESTERÅLEN

Tromsø

d

55

Ísafjörður
Horn

Akureyri

ICELAND

VATNAJÖKULL 2119
Hvannadalshnúkur

Seydisfjördur

Arctic Circle

Narvik

LOFOTEN

Bodø

Mo i Rana

e

Norwegian Sea

Thorshavn

Faeroe Islands
(Den.)

FØROYAR / FÆRØERNE

SHETLAND ISLANDS

ROCKALL

NORWAY

Namsos

Storuman

SCANDINAVIA

50

Kristiansund

Molde

Trondheim

Ålesund

Østersund

Härnösand

SWEDEN

Dombås
Glittertind 2472

Sundsvall

Bergen

Gjøvik

Falun

Gävle

Haugesund

Drammen

Oslo

Stavanger

Skien

Moss

Karlstad

Västerås

Uppsala

Kristiansand

Lindesnes

Örebro

Stockholm

ORKNEY ISLANDS

Thurso

Norrköping

Linköping

Göteborg

Jönköping

GOTLAND

f

North Sea

HEBRIDES

Inverness

Aberdeen

Kattegat

Växjö

ÖLAND

45

Glasgow

Dundee

Edinburgh

Newcastle upon Tyne

Carlisle

DENMARK

Ålborg

Frederikshavn

Helsingborg

Kalmar

Karlskrona

Herning

Århus

BORNHOLM (Den.)

IRELAND

Sligo

Galway

Belfast

Londonderry

Middlesbrough

Esbjerg

København
Copenhagen

Malmö

Trelleborg

Kolding

Odense

Flensburg

Limerick

Dublin

Manchester

Leeds

UNITED KINGDOM

Kingston-upon-Hull

Kiel

Lübeck

Rostock

Stralsund

Gdynia

Gdańsk (Danzig)

Waterford

Wexford

Liverpool

Sheffield

Nottingham

Bremerhaven

Hamburg

Szczecin
Stettin

Bydgoszcz

Mizen Head

Cork

Fishguard

Leicester

Birmingham

Norwich

Groningen

Bremen

Hannover

Berlin

Poznań

POLAND

Swansea

Cardiff

Bristol

Ipswich

's-Gravenhage

Amsterdam

NETHERLANDS

Osnabrück

Essen

Magdeburg

Wrocław
Breslau

Celtic Sea

Land's End

ISLES OF SCILLY

Exeter

Plymouth

Southampton

Brighton

London

Dover

Den Haag

Rotterdam

Antwerpen

BELGIUM

Brussel
Bruxelles

Dortmund

Düsseldorf

Köln Cologne

Bonn

GERMANY

Leipzig

Dresden

Chemnitz

Erfurt

Wałbrzych

Częstochowa

Katowice

Ostrava

English Channel

Penzance

Cherbourg

Le Havre

Amiens

Lille

Liège

Luxembourg

LUXEMBOURG

Wiesbaden

Frankfurt

Würzburg

Nürnberg

CZECH REP.

Praha
Prague

Plzeň

Brno

40

Pointe de Saint-Mathieu

Brest

CHANNEL ISLANDS (U.K.)

Saint-Malo

Caen

Rouen

Reims

Metz

Saarbrücken

Mannheim

Stuttgart

Regensburg

SLOVAKIA

Bratislava

Lorient

Rennes

Le Mans

Troyes

Nancy

Strasbourg

Freiburg

Augsburg

München
Munich

Linz

Wien
Vienna

Győr

Budapest

Angers

Paris

Orléans

Dijon

Mulhouse

Basel

Zürich

Vaduz

LIECHTENSTEIN

Innsbruck

Salzburg

AUSTRIA

Graz

Székesfehérvár

HUNGARY

Nantes

FRANCE

Tours

Bourges

Besançon

Bern

SWITZERLAND

Lausanne

Genève

Klagenfurt

Balaton

Pécs

La Rochelle

Poitiers

Clermont-Ferrand

Lyon

Mont Blanc 4807

Bolzano

SLOVENIA

Trieste

Ljubljana

Zagreb

La Coruña

Cabo de Finisterre

Limoges

Saint-Étienne

Grenoble

Milano
Milan

Brescia

Verona

Venezia
Venice

Rijeka

CROATIA

Osijek

Novi Sad

h

Azores
(Portugal)

GRACIOSA

SÃO JORGE

TERCEIRA

PICO

Angra do Heroísmo

FAIAL

SÃO MIGUEL

Ponta Delgada

SANTA MARIA

Vigo

Oviedo

Gijón

Santander

San Sebastián

Bayonne

Bordeaux

Bay of Biscay

Braga

Porto

León

Burgos

Pamplona

Toulouse

PYRENEES

Pico de Aneto 3404

ANDORRA

Andorra la Vella

Montpellier

Nîmes

Avignon

Marseille

Perpignan

Toulon

Monts Dore

Monaco

Nice

Genova
Genoa

Torino
Turin

La Spezia

Parma

Bologna

Livorno
Leghorn

Firenze
Florence

Perugia

Ancona

SAN MARINO

Pola

Zadar

Split

BOSNIA AND HERZEGOVINA

Sarajevo

Dubrovnik

Podgorica

Shkodër

i

PORTUGAL

Coimbra

Salamanca

Valladolid

Zaragoza
Saragossa

Tarragona

Cabo de Creus

Barcelona

Castellón de la Plana

Toledo

Valencia

BALEARIC ISLANDS

MINORCA

Palma

MAJORCA

IBIZA

CORSICA (Fr.)

Ajaccio

Bastia

LIGURIAN Sea

Sassari

Olbia

Nuoro

ITALY

VATICAN CITY

Roma
Rome

L'Aquila

Pescara

Foggia

Bari

ALBANIA

Tirana

Lisboa
Lisbon

Setúbal

Madrid

SPAIN

Évora

Badajoz

Albacete

Murcia

Alicante

Cartagena

SARDINIA

Cagliari

Tyrrhenian Sea

Napoli
Naples

Salerno

Brindisi

Taranto

Lecce

Cabo de São Vicente

Faro

Huelva

Córdoba

Sevilla

Granada

Mulhacén 3482

Almería

Cosenza

Ionian Sea

30

MADEIRA ISLANDS

Funchal

PORTO SANTO

ILHAS DESERTAS

Cádiz

Algeciras

Gibraltar (U.K.)

Tanger
Tangier

Ceuta (Spain)

Tétouan

Málaga

ISLA DE ALBORÁN (Spain)

Melilla (Spain)

Palermo

Trapani

Mt. Etna 3323

Messina

Reggio di Calabria

SICILY

Catania

Siracusa

Catanzaro

ILHAS SELVAGENS

Madeira
(Portugal)

Larache

Ksar el Kebir

Oran

Mostaganem

Al Jazā'ir
Algiers

Bejaïa

Jijel

Skikda

Annaba

Bizerte

Cap Bon

Nabūl

Tūnis

PANTELLERIA (Italy)

ISOLE PELAGIE (Italy)

KERKENNAH ISLANDS

Valletta

MALTA

LA PALMA

Canary Islands
(Spain)

GOMERA

HIERRO

TENERIFE

Santa Cruz de Tenerife

GRAN CANARIA

Las Palmas de Gran Canaria

LANZAROTE

FUERTEVENTURA

Casablanca

Rabat

Kenitra

Meknès

Fès

Sidi Bel Abbès

Relizane

Blida

Tizi Ouzou

Sétif

Guelma

Constantine

Süsah
Sousse

j

Safi

El Jadida

Oued Zem

Taza

Oujda

Saïda

Tiaret

Batna

Tébessa

Gafsa

Essaouira

Beni Mellal

MOROCCO

Marrakech

ATLAS MOUNTAINS

Djelfa

Qafşah

TUNISIA

Tarābulus
Tripoli

Al Khums

Agadir

Sidi Ifni

Tiznit

Jebel Toubkal 4165

ALGERIA

Laghouat

Biskra

Al Qayrawān

Qābis

DJERBA

Medanīyīn

Goulimine

Ar Rachidiya

Aïn Sefra

Ghardaïa

Ouargla

Medanīyīn

Gharyān

Mişrātah

El Aaiún

Tarfaya

Zagora

Béchar

Abadla

Ghadāmis

Mizdah

Gulf of Sidra

25

Western Sahara

Semara

Tindouf

Tabelbala

Timimoun

ERG OCCIDENTAL

GRAND ERG OCCIDENTAL

El Goléa

Beni Abbès

Hassi Messaoud

GRAND ERG ORIENTAL

Chott Melrhir

Nālūt

Adh Dhahibāt

Az Zāwiyah

TRIPOLITANIA

Surt

Bani Walid

al Qaddāhīyah

LIBYA

Dakhla

El Aaiún

Scale 1:15,000,000 Lambert Azimuthal Equal Area Projection

0   200   400   600   800   1000 km

0   250   500 miles

Longitude East 10 of Greenwich

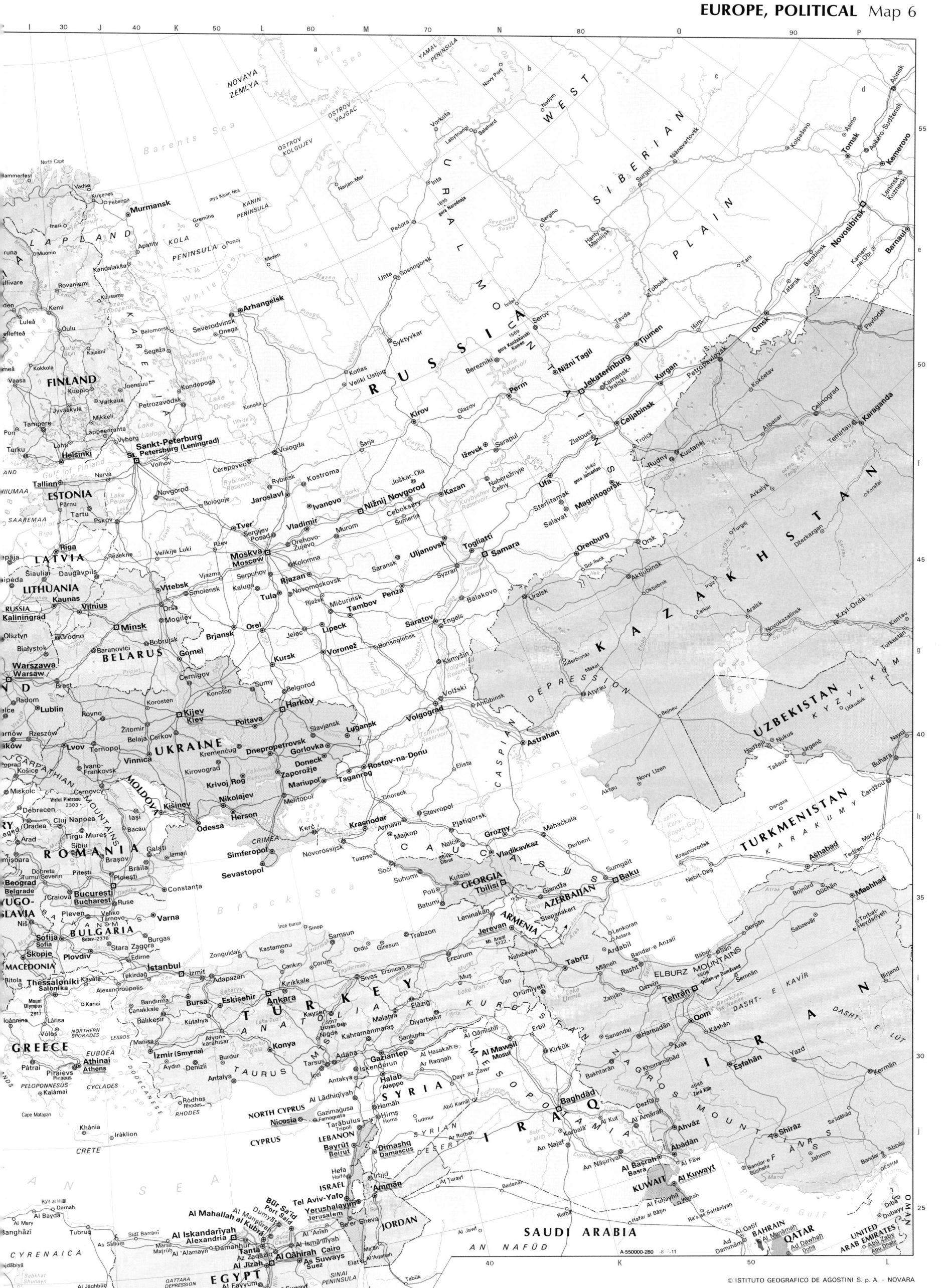

Map 7 **NORTHERN EUROPE**

Inset map (a)

ÍSLAND ICELAND

GRÆNLANDSHAF / GREENLAND SEA
GRÍMSEY
Arctic Circle

Reykjavík · Hafnarfjörður · Kópavogur · Keflavík
Akureyri · Húsavík · Siglufjörður · Ólafsfjörður
Vatnajökull · Langjökull · Hofsjökull
Vestmannaeyjar · HEIMAEY · SURTSEY
FAXAFLÓI · Breiðafjörður · FLATEY

ATLANTSHAF / ATLANTIC OCEAN
Long. West 20 of Greenwich

West 0 East

Main map

NORGE / NORWAY
SVERIGE / SWEDEN
SUOMI / FINLAND
DANMARK / DENMARK
DEUTSCHLAND / GERMANY
POLSKA / POLAND
EESTI / ESTONIA
LATVIJA / LATVIA
LIETUVA / LITHUANIA
BYELARUS / BELARUS
ROSSIJA / RUSSIA

FINNMARK · FINNMARKSVIDDA · LAPPI · LAPPLAND
NORRBOTTEN · VÄSTERBOTTEN · NORRLAND
LOFOTEN · VESTERÅLEN
MØRE OG ROMSDAL · SØR-TRØNDELAG · NORD-TRØNDELAG
NORDLAND · HEDMARK · OPPLAND · BUSKERUD
HORDALAND · SOGN OG FJORDANE · ROGALAND
TELEMARK · VEST-AGDER · AUST-AGDER
VESTFOLD · ØSTFOLD · AKERSHUS
JÄMTLAND · VÄSTERNORRLAND · GÄVLEBORG
KOPPARBERG · VÄRMLAND · VÄSTMANLAND
UPPSALA · SÖDERMANLAND · ÖSTERGÖTLAND
SKARABORG · ÄLVSBORG · BOHUS · HALLAND
JÖNKÖPING · KRONOBERG · KALMAR · GOTLAND
BLEKINGE · KRISTIANSTAD · MALMÖHUS · SMÅLAND · GÖTALAND
VAASA / VASA · OULU · KESKI-SUOMI · KYMI
HÄME · TURKU / ÅBO · PORI · MIKKELI
AHVENANMAA / ÅLAND

Oslo · Bergen · Trondheim · Stavanger · Kristiansand · Drammen
Tromsø · Narvik · Bodø · Kiruna · Gällivare
Stockholm · Göteborg · Uppsala · Västerås · Örebro · Norrköping
Linköping · Jönköping · Malmö · Helsingborg · Lund
Helsinki / Helsingfors · Turku / Åbo · Tampere / Tammerfors
Oulu / Uleåborg · Vaasa / Vasa · Kuopio · Jyväskylä
København / Copenhagen · Odense · Ålborg · Århus · Esbjerg
Hamburg · Bremen · Hannover · Berlin · Lübeck · Kiel · Rostock
Szczecin / Stettin · Gdańsk / Danzig · Gdynia · Bydgoszcz
Kaliningrad · Klaipéda · Kaunas · Vilnius
Tallinn · Tartu · Rīga · Liepāja · Daugavpils
Minsk · Pskov

NORSKE-HAVET / NORWEGIAN SEA
NORDSJØEN / NORTH SEA
Skagerrak · Kattegat
ØSTERSJÖN / BALTIC SEA · Bottniska viken
BORNHOLM (Denmark) · ÖLAND · GOTLAND · ÅLAND
SAAREMAA · HIIUMAA · Gulf of Riga

Scale and legend

M / Ft
2000 / 6562
1000 / 3281
500 / 1640
200 / 656
+100 / +328
0
Depr.
0
−100 / −328
200 / 656
1000 / 3281
2000 / 6562

Scale 1:6,000,000
Delisle Conic Equidistant Projection

0 100 200 300 400 km
0 100 200 miles

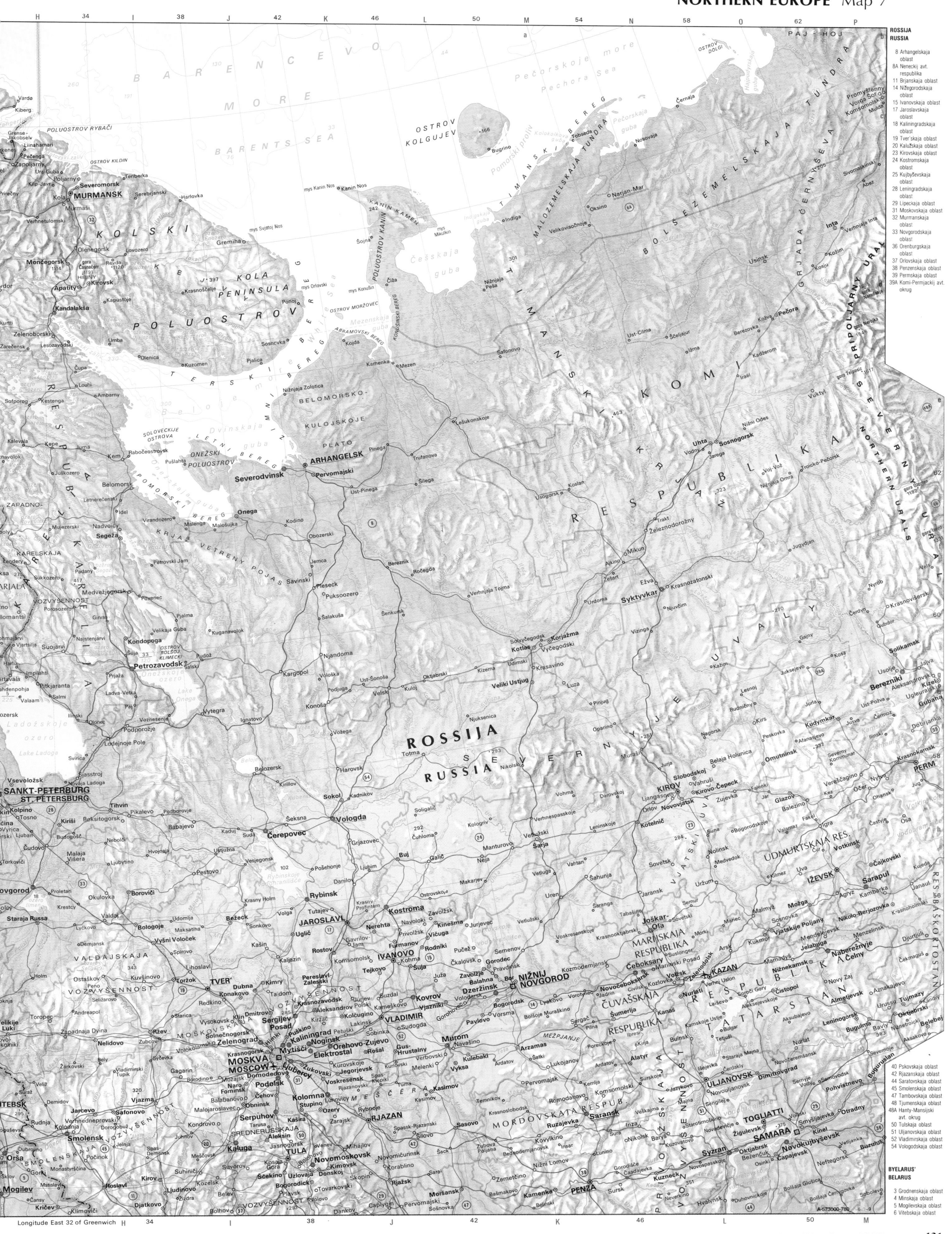

ROSSIJA
RUSSIA

8 Arhangelskaja oblast
8A Neneckij avt. respublika
11 Brjanskaja oblast
14 Nižegorodskaja oblast
15 Ivanovskaja oblast
17 Jaroslavskaja oblast
18 Kaliningradskaja oblast
19 Tver'skaja oblast
20 Kalužskaja oblast
23 Kirovskaja oblast
24 Kostromskaja oblast
25 Kujbyševskaja oblast
28 Leningradskaja oblast
29 Lipeckaja oblast
31 Moskovskaja oblast
32 Murmanskaja oblast
33 Novgorodskaja oblast
35 Orenburgskaja oblast
36 Orlovskaja oblast
37 Orlovskaja oblast
38 Penzenskaja oblast
39 Permskaja oblast
39A Komi-Permjackij avt. okrug

40 Pskovskaja oblast
42 Rjazanskaja oblast
44 Saratovskaja oblast
45 Smolenskaja oblast
47 Tambovskaja oblast
48A Hanty-Mansijskij avt. okrug
50 Tulskaja oblast
51 Uljanovskaja oblast
52 Vladimirskaja oblast
54 Vologodskaja oblast

BYELARUS'
BELARUS

3 Grodnenskaja oblast
4 Minskaja oblast
5 Mogilevskaja oblast
6 Vitebskaja oblast

Map 8 **BALTIC REGION**

Scale 1:3,000,000

Delisle Conic Equidistant Projection

0 50 100 150 200 km

0   50   100 miles

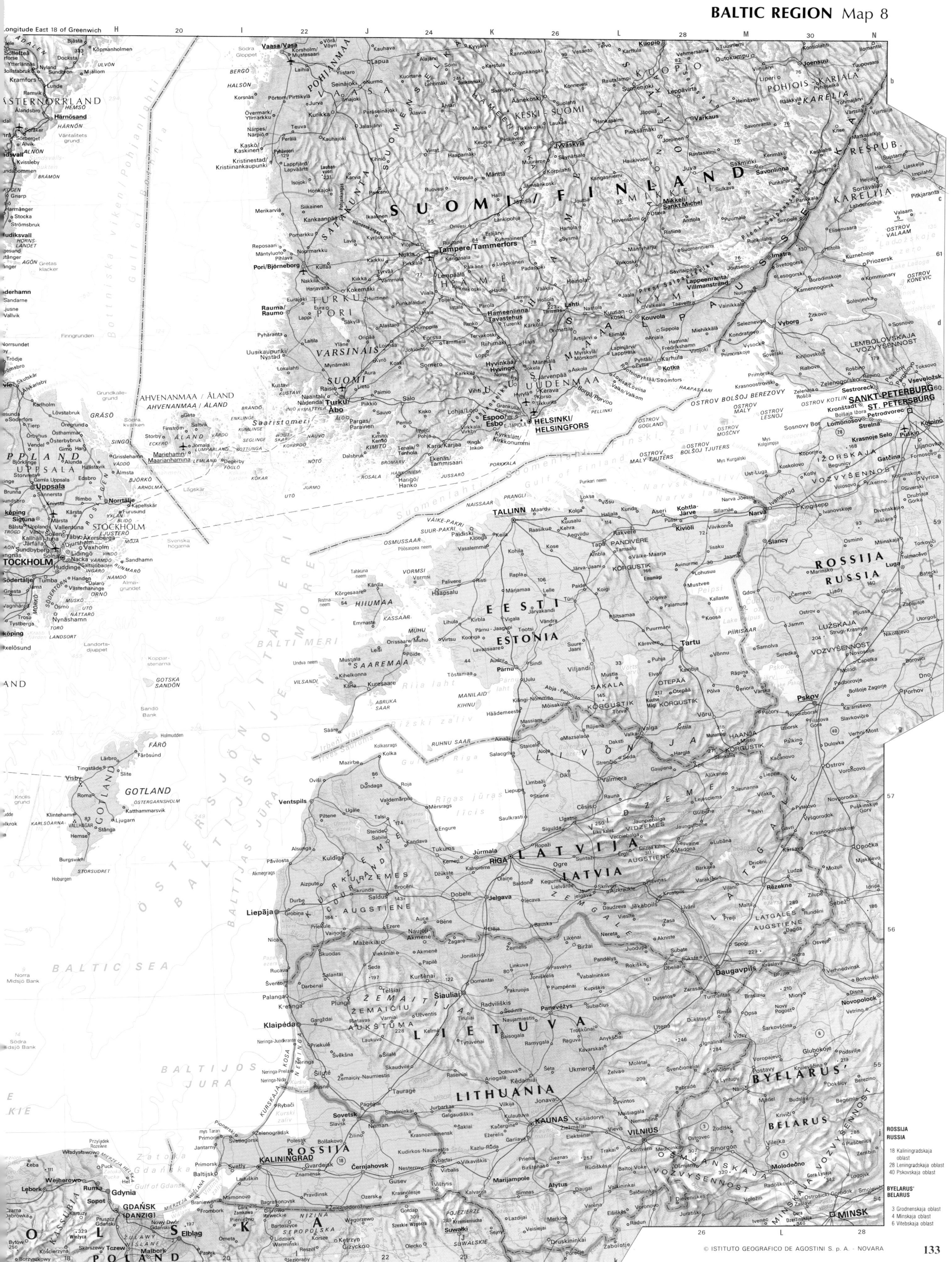

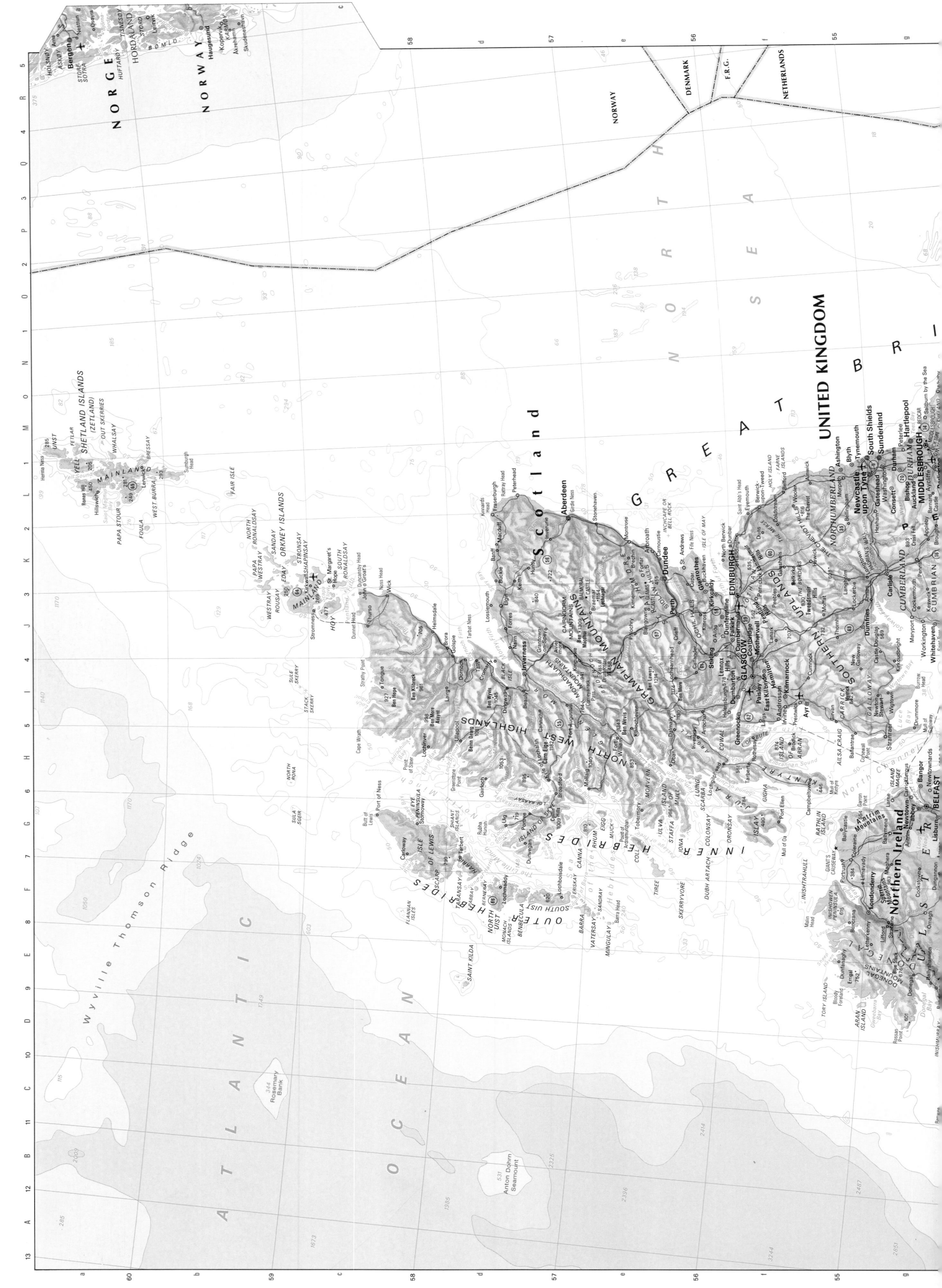

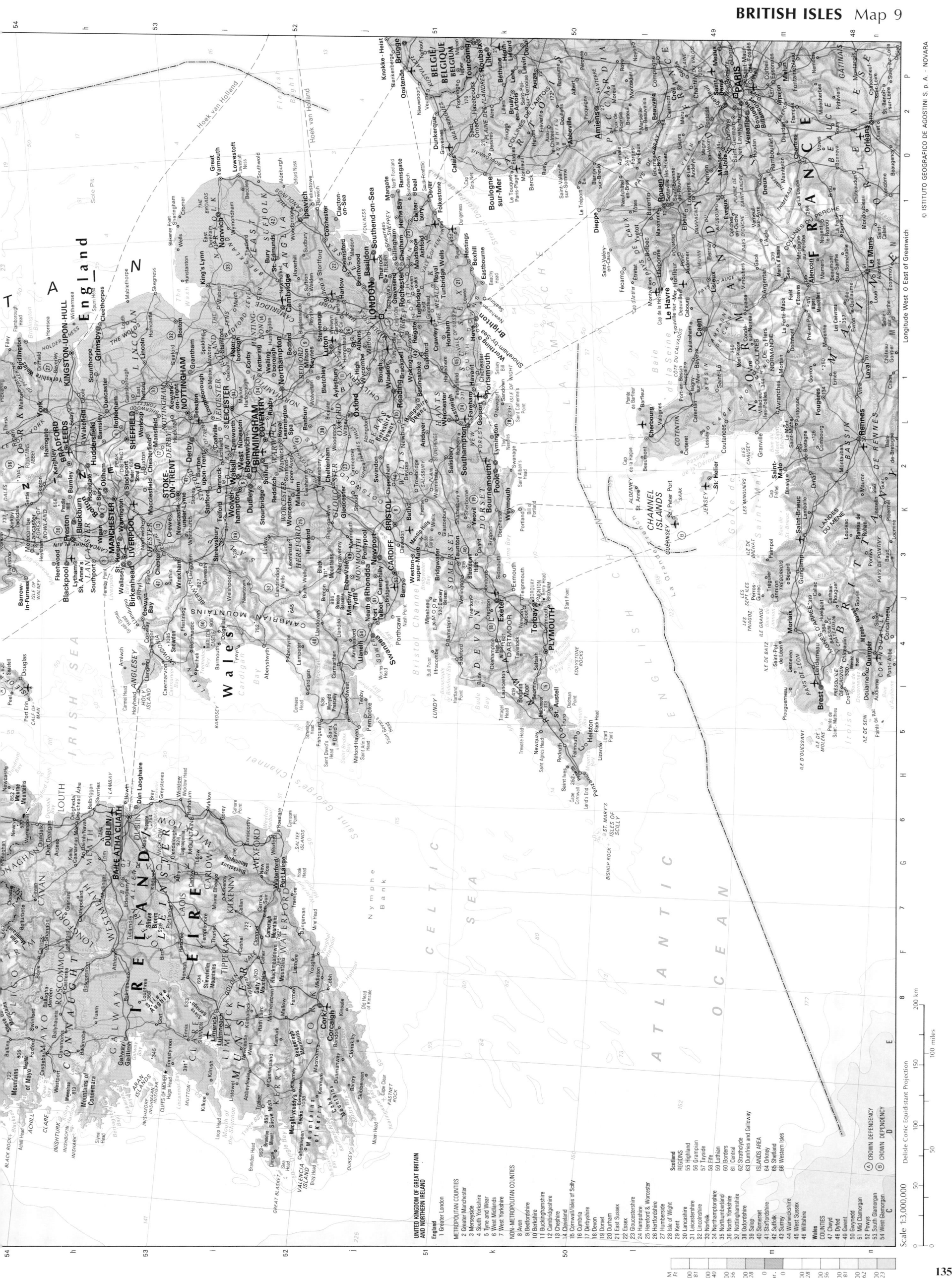

UNITED KINGDOM OF GREAT BRITAIN AND NORTHERN IRELAND

England

METROPOLITAN COUNTIES
2 Greater Manchester
3 Merseyside
4 South Yorkshire
5 Tyne and Wear
6 West Midlands
7 West Yorkshire

NON-METROPOLITAN COUNTIES
8 Avon
9 Bedfordshire
10 Berkshire
11 Buckinghamshire
12 Cambridgeshire
13 Cheshire
14 Cleveland
15 Cornwall/Isles of Scilly
16 Cumbria
17 Derbyshire
18 Devon
19 Dorset
20 Durham
21 East Sussex
22 Essex
23 Gloucestershire
24 Hampshire
25 Hereford & Worcester
26 Hertfordshire
27 Humberside
28 Isle of Wight
29 Kent
30 Lancashire
31 Leicestershire
32 Lincolnshire
33 Norfolk
34 Northamptonshire
35 Northumberland
36 North Yorkshire
37 Nottinghamshire
38 Oxfordshire
39 Salop
40 Somerset
41 Staffordshire
42 Suffolk
43 Surrey
44 Warwickshire
45 West Sussex
46 Wiltshire

Wales

COUNTIES
47 Clwyd
48 Dyfed
49 Gwent
50 Gwynedd
51 Mid Glamorgan
52 Powys
53 South Glamorgan
54 West Glamorgan

Scotland

REGIONS
55 Highland
56 Grampian
57 Tayside
58 Fife
59 Lothian
60 Borders
61 Central
62 Strathclyde
63 Dumfries and Galloway

ISLANDS AREA
64 Orkney
65 Shetland
66 Western Isles

Ⓐ CROWN DEPENDENCY
Ⓑ CROWN DEPENDENCY

Scale 1:3,000,000

Delisle Conic Equidistant Projection

200 km

100 miles

135

Map 10 CENTRAL EUROPE

DEUTSCHLAND
GERMANY

LÄNDER
1 Brandenburg
2 Mecklenburg-
  Vorpommern
3 Sachsen
4 Sachsen-Anhalt
5 Thüringen

Scale 1:3,000,000   Delisle Conic Equidistant Projection

J Longitude East 14 of Greenwich K

ROSSIJA
RUSSIA
18 Kaliningradskaja
  oblast

UKRAJINA
UKRAINE
9 Ivano-Frankovskaja
  oblast
13 Lvovskaja oblast
17 Rovenskaja oblast
11 Ternopolskaja oblast
21 Volynskaja oblast
23 Zakarpatskaja oblast

BYELARUS'
BELARUS
1 Brestskaja oblast
3 Grodnenskaja oblast

ČESKÁ REPUBLIKA
CZECH REPUBLIC
A Hlavní město Praha
1 Středočeský kraj
2 Jihočeský kraj
3 Západočeský kraj
4 Severočeský kraj
5 Východočeský kraj
6 Jihomoravský kraj
7 Severomoravský kraj

SLOVENSKÁ REPUBLIKA
SLOVAKIA
B Hlavní město
  Bratislava
8 Západoslovenský kraj
9 Středoslovenský kraj
10 Východoslovenský
  kraj

POLSKA
POLAND
WOJEWÓDZTWA
1 Biała Podlaska
2 Białystok
3 Bielsko
4 Bydgoszcz
5 Chełm
6 Ciechanów
7 Częstochowa
8 Elbląg
9 Gdańsk
10 Gorzów
11 Jelenia Góra
12 Kalisz
13 Katowice
14 Kielce
15 Konin
16 Koszalin
17 Kraków
18 Krosno
19 Legnica
20 Leszno
21 Łódź
22 Łomża
23 Lublin
24 Nowy Sacz
25 Olsztyn
26 Opole
27 Ostrołęka
28 Piła
29 Piotrków
30 Płock
31 Poznań
32 Przemyśl
33 Radom
34 Rzeszów
35 Siedlce
36 Sieradz
37 Skierniewice
38 Słupsk
39 Suwałki
40 Szczecin
41 Tarnobrzeg
42 Tarnów
43 Toruń
44 Wałbrzych
45 Warszawa
46 Włocławek
47 Wrocław
48 Zamość
49 Zielona Góra

MAGYARORSZÁG
HUNGARY
MEGYEI VÁROSOK
A Budapest
B Debrecen
C Győr
D Miskolc
E Pécs
F Szeged

MEGYÉK
1 Bács-Kiskun
2 Baranya
3 Békés
4 Borsod-Abaúj-
  Zemplén
5 Csongrád
6 Fejér
7 Győr-Moson-
  Sopron
8 Hajdú-Bihar
9 Heves
10 Komárom-
  Esztergom
11 Nógrád
12 Pest
13 Somogy
14 Szabolcs-Szatmár-
  Bereg
15 Jász-Nagykun-
  Szolnok
16 Tolna
17 Vas
18 Veszprém
19 Zala

Map 11 **FRANCE AND BENELUX**

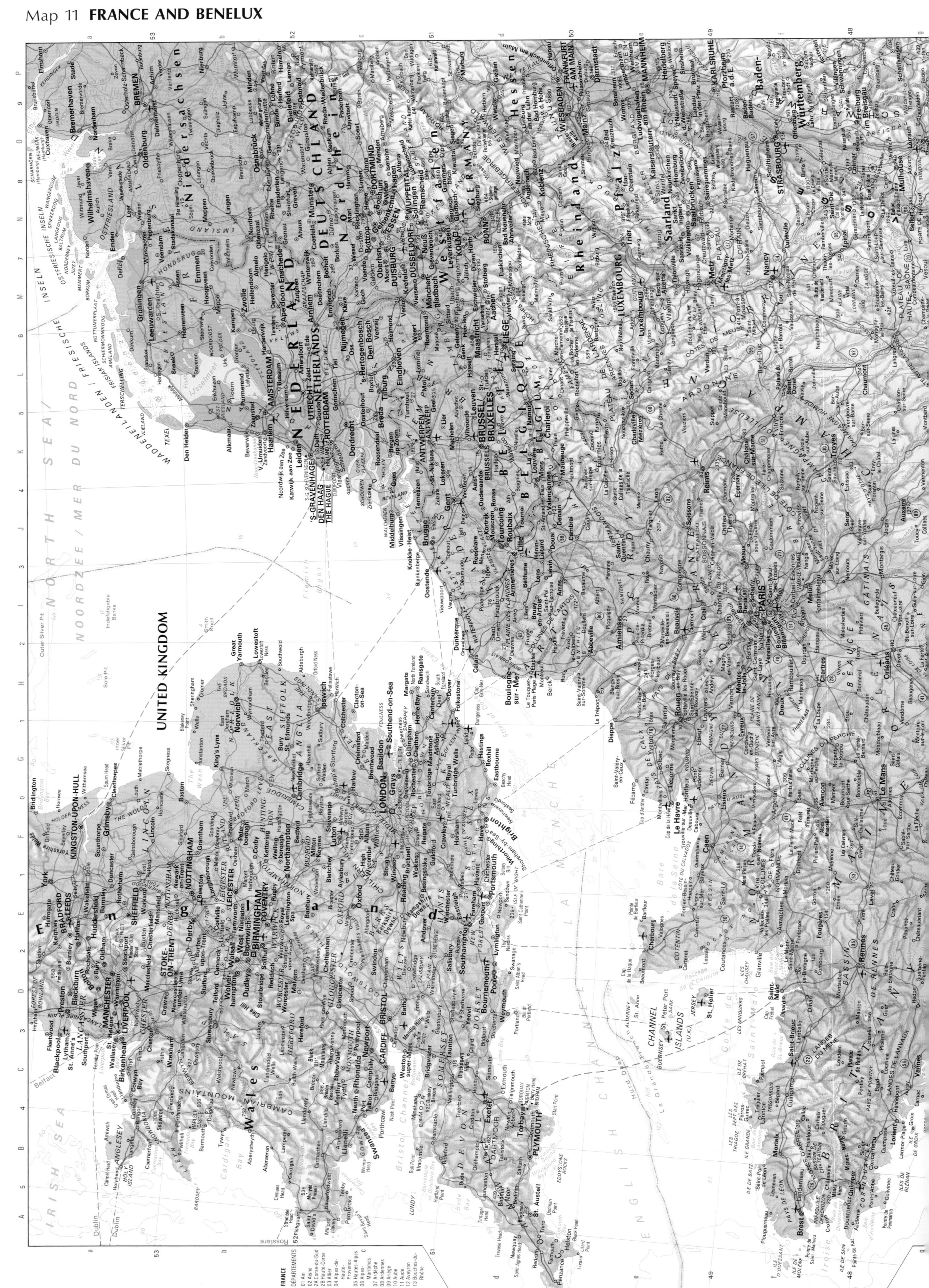

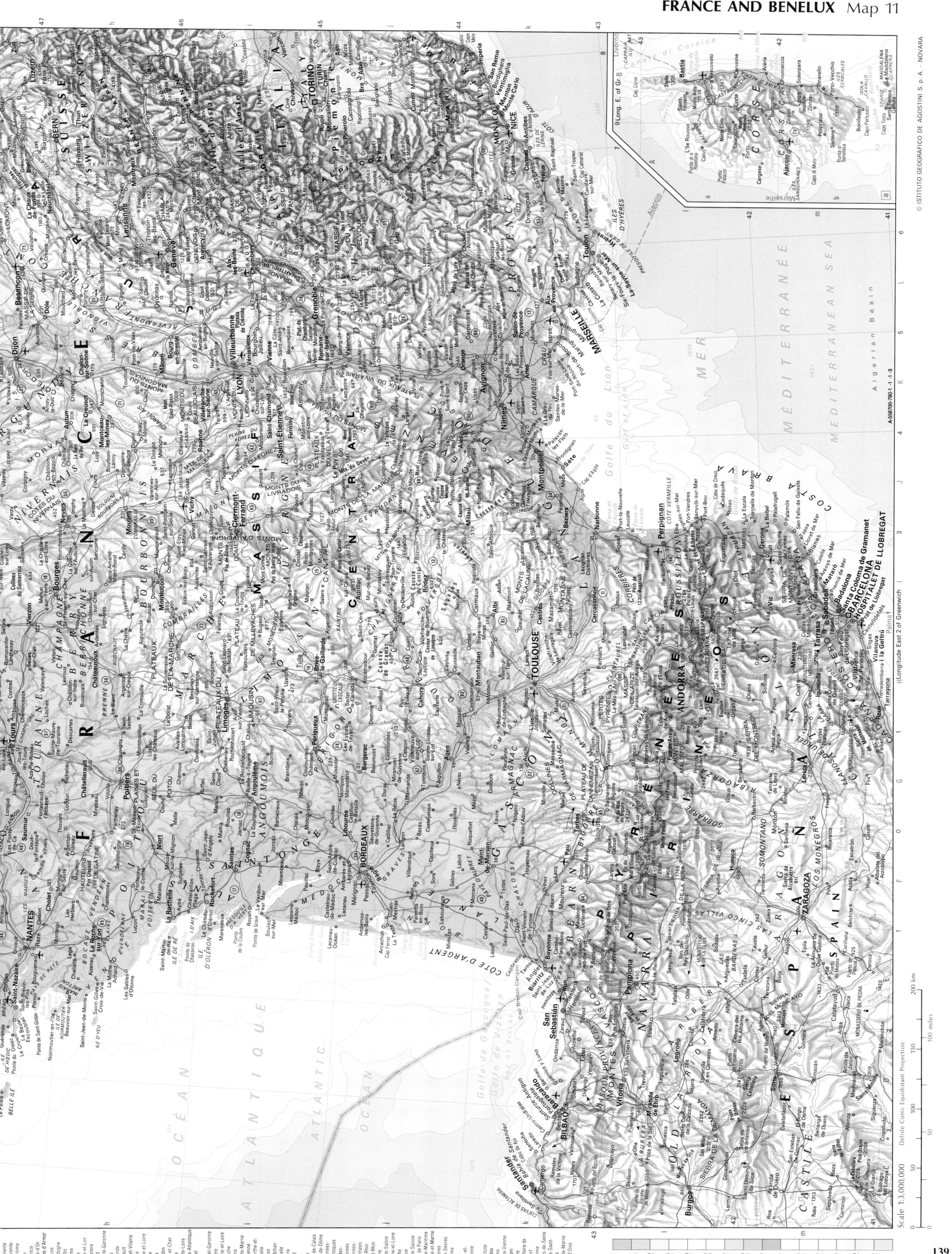

Scale 1:3,000,000

Delisle Conic Equidistant Projection

139

Map 12 **BELGIUM, NETHERLANDS AND LUXEMBOURG**

UNITED KINGDOM

NEDE

NETH

England

NORTH SEA / NOORDZEE /
MER DU NORD

'S-GRAVENHA

Flemish Bight

ZEELAND

ENGLISH CHANNEL / LA MANCHE

FRANCE
DEPARTEMENTOS
75 Ville de Paris
92 Hauts-de-Seine
93 Seine-Saint-Denis
94 Val-de-Marne

FRANCE

PARIS

Scale 1:1,500,000   Delisle Conic Equidistant Projection

0   25   50   75   100 km
0   25   50 miles

Map 12

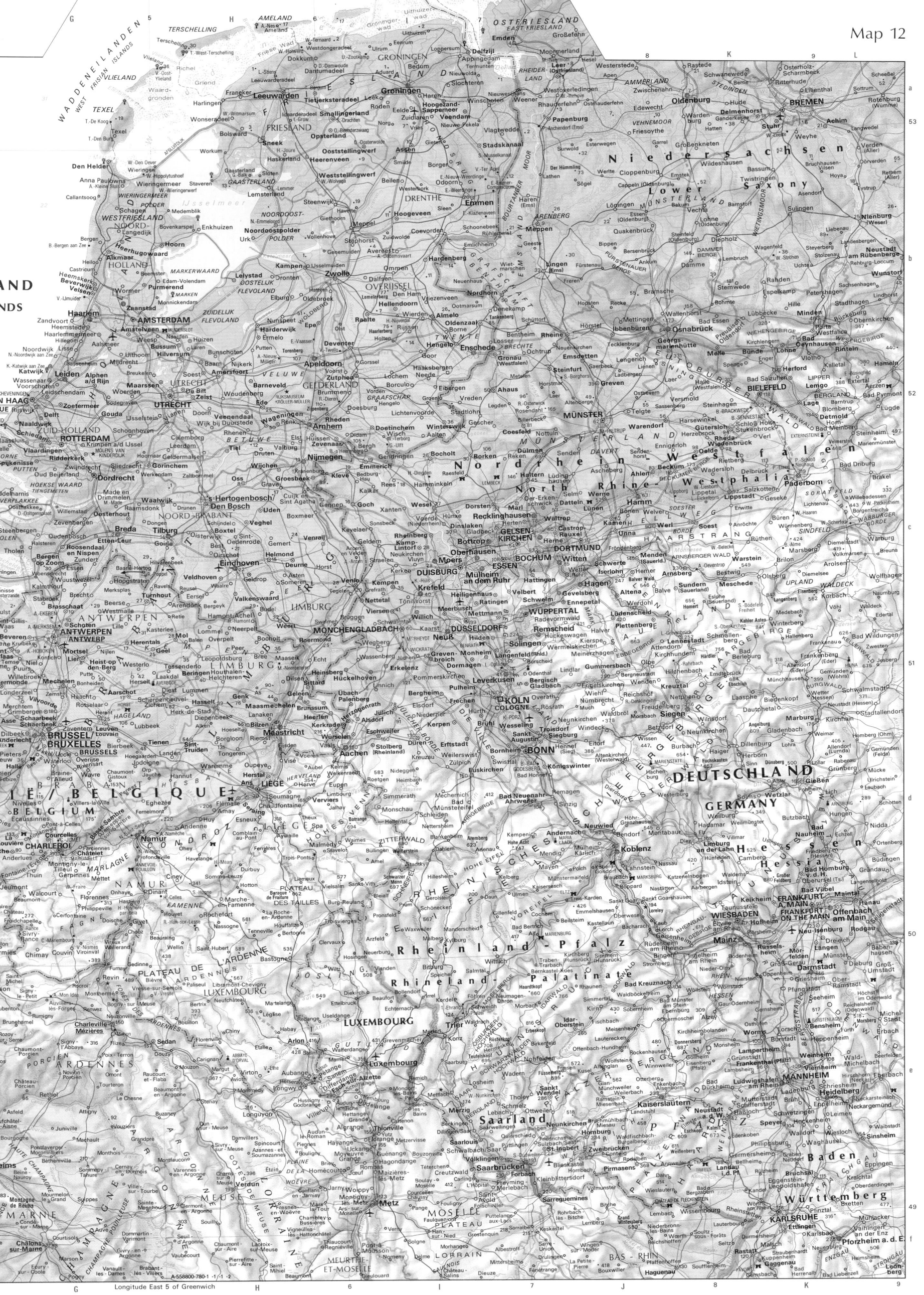

Map 13 **SPAIN AND PORTUGAL**

Longitude West 5 of Greenwich

Scale 1:3,000,000   Delisle Conic Equidistant Projection

0   50   100   150   200 km

0   50   100 miles

Map 14 **ITALY, AUSTRIA AND SWITZERLAND**

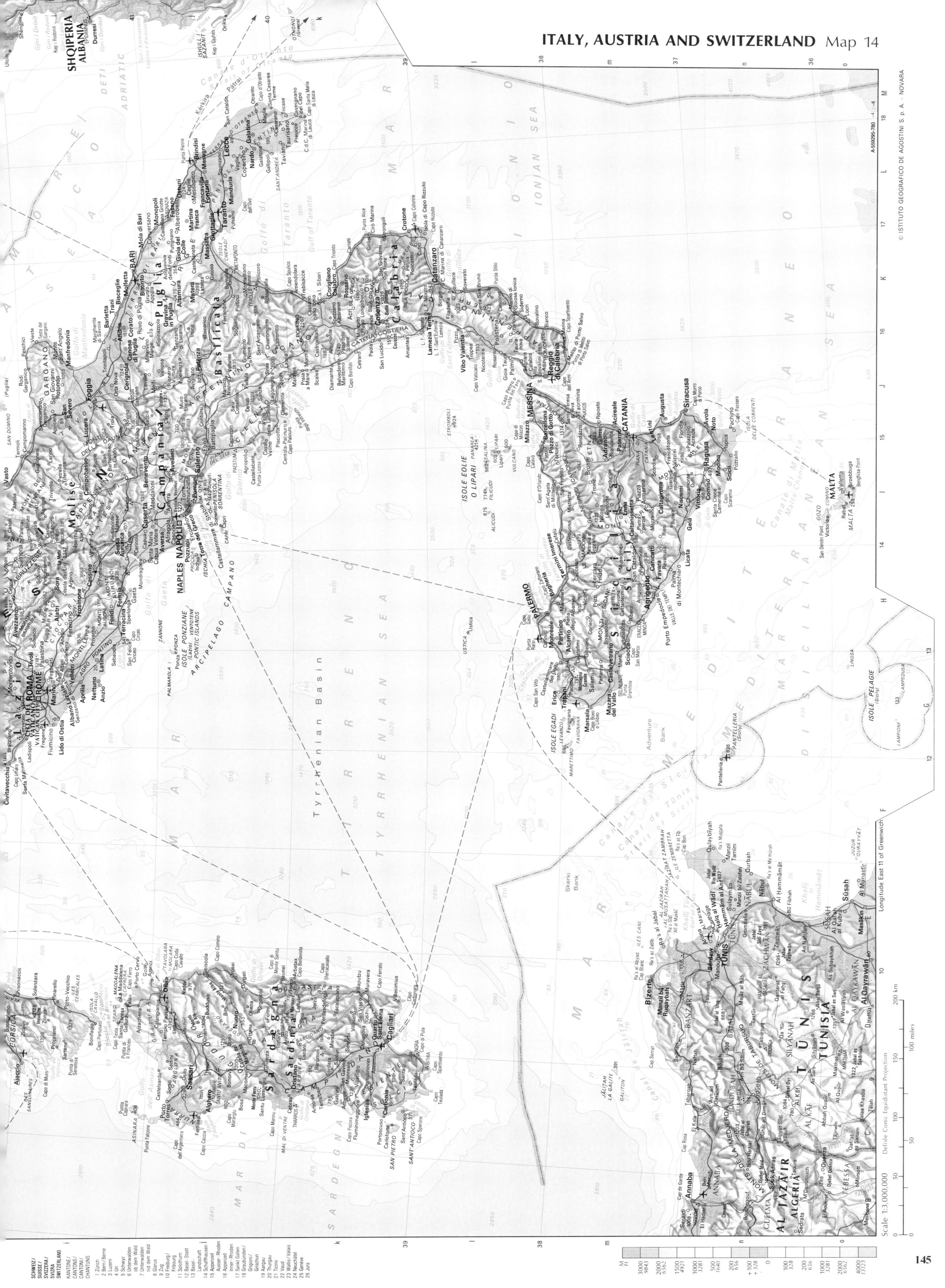

SHQIPERIA
ALBANIA

ADRIATIC SEA

ADRIATICO

IONIAN SEA

Puglia

BARI

Taranto

Gulf of Taranto

Golfo di Taranto

Basilicata

Foggia

Molise

Calabria

Catanzaro

Crotone

Reggio di Calabria

MESSINA

Campania

NAPLES NAPOLI

Salerno

CATANIA

Siracusa

Ragusa

SORRENTINA

TYRRHENIAN SEA

Tyrrhenian Basin

Sicilia

PALERMO

MALTA

LAZIO

CITTÀ DEL ROMA
VATICAN CITY ROME

ISOLE PONZIANE
VENTOTENE
PONTIC ISLANDS

ARCIPELAGO
CAMPANO

MAR TIRRENO

Corsica

Sardegna
Sardinia

Sassari

Oristano

Cagliari

MAR DI SARDEGNA

ISOLE PELAGIE
(SICILY)

PANTELLERIA

MEDITERRANEAN SEA

Canale di Sicilia
Canal de Sicile
Strait of Sicily

MARE MEDITERRANEO

TUNIS

TUNISIA

ALGERIA

AL JAZĀ'IR

Annaba

Longitude East 11 of Greenwich

Delisle Conic Equidistant Projection

Scale 1:3,000,000

© ISTITUTO GEOGRAFICO DE AGOSTINI S.p.A - NOVARA

A-569295-780 -4 -6

Map 15 **SOUTHEASTERN EUROPE**

Map 15

Map 16 **BLACK AND CASPIAN SEAS REGION**

M
Ft
5000
16404
4000
13123
3000
9843
2000
6562
1000
3281
500
1640
200
656
+100
+328
0
Depr.
0
−100
−328
200
656
1000
3281
2000
6562

Scale 1:6,000,000   Delisle Conic Equidistant Projection

0   100   200   300   400 km
0   100   200 miles

148

Map 17 **THE URALS**

ROSSIJA
RUSSIA

8 Arhangelskaja oblast
8A Neneckij avt. respublika
12 Čeljabinskaja oblast
14 Gorkovskaja oblast
23 Kirovskaja oblast
24 Kostromskaja oblast
25 Kujbiševskaja oblast
26 Kurganskaja oblast
35 Omskaja oblast
36 Orenburgskaja oblast
39 Permskaja oblast
39A Komi-Permjackij avt. okrug
44 Saratovskaja oblast
46 Jekaterinburgskaja oblast
48 Tjumenskaja oblast
48A Hanty-Mansijskij avt. okrug
48B Jamalo-Neneckij respublika
51 Uljanovskaja oblast
54 Vologodskaja oblast

QAZAQSTAN
KAZAKHSTAN

3 Celinogradskaja oblast
10 Kokčetavskaja oblast
11 Kustanajskaja oblast
15 Severo-Kazahstanskaja oblast
17 Turgajskaja oblast

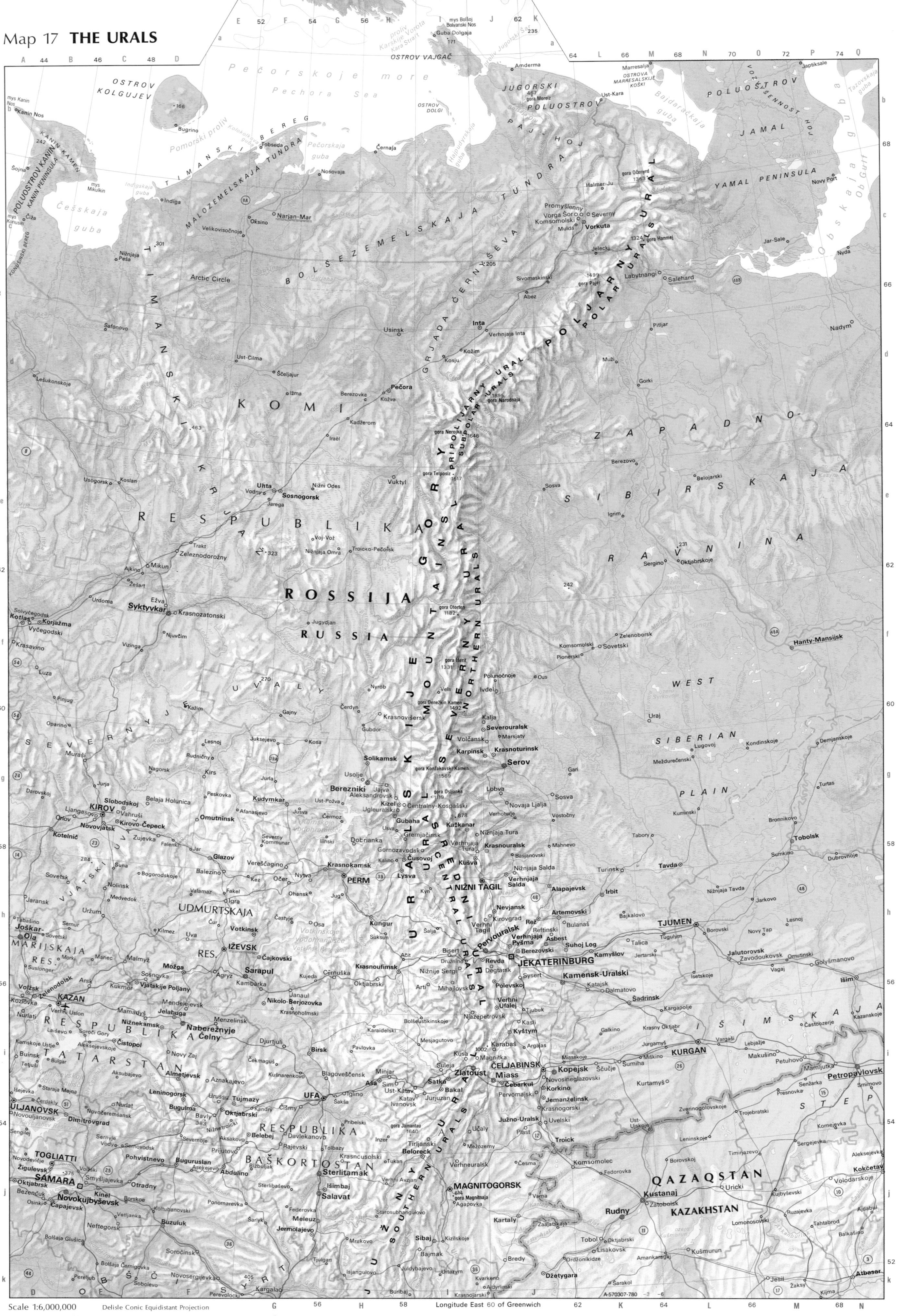

Scale 1:6,000,000   Delisle Conic Equidistant Projection

Longitude East 60 of Greenwich

0   100   200   300   400 km
0   100   200 miles

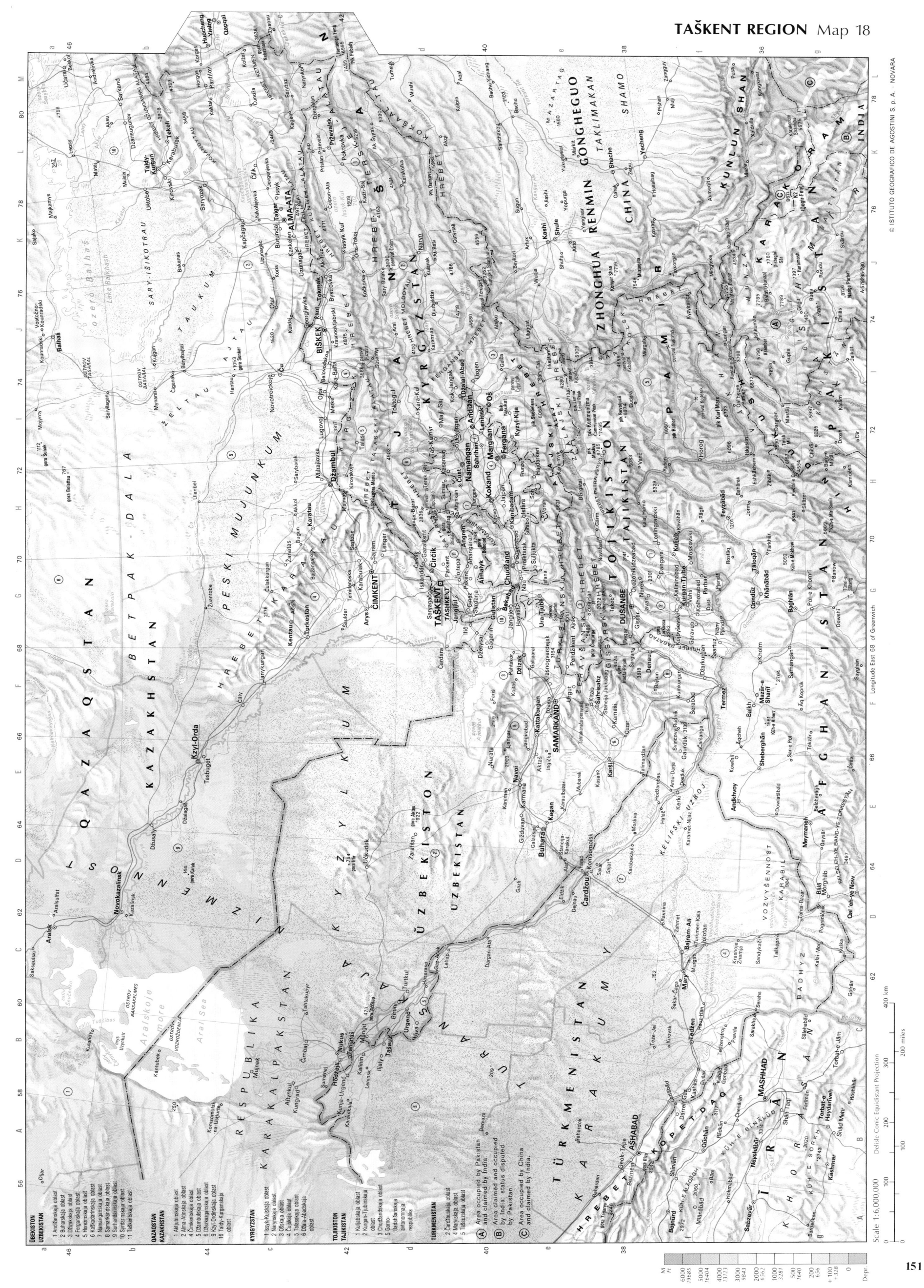

© ISTITUTO GEOGRAFICO DE AGOSTINI S.p.A. - NOVARA

Scale 1:6.000.000

Delisle Conic Equidistant Projection

Map 19

ROSSIJA
RUSSIA

3 Krasnodarski kraj
3A Adygeja, respublika
6 Stavropolski kraj

6A Karačajevo-
Čerkesskaja
respublikas
8 Arhangelskaja
oblast
8A Neneckij avt.res.
9 Astrahanskaja
oblast
10 Belgorodskaja obl.
11 Brjanskaja obl.
12 Čeljabinskaja obl.
14 Nižegorodskaja
oblast
16 Ivanovskaja obl.
17 Jaroslavskaja obl.
18 Kaliningradskaja
oblast
19 Tver'skaja obl.
22 Kalužskaja obl.
23 Kirovskaja obl.
24 Kostromskaja obl.
25 Kujbyševskaja
oblast
26 Kurganskaja obl.
27 Kurskaja obl.
28 Leningradskaja
oblast
30 Lipeckaja obl.
31 Moskovskaja obl.
32 Murmanskaja obl.
33 Novgorodskaja
oblast
35 Omskaja obl.
36 Orenburgskaja
oblast
37 Orlovskaja obl.
38 Penzenskaja obl.
39 Permskaja obl.
39A Komi-Permjackij
avt. okr.
40 Pskovskaja obl.
41 Rostovskaja obl.
42 Rjazanskaja obl.
44 Saratovskaja obl.
45 Smolenskaja obl.
46 Jekaterinburgskaja
oblast
47 Tambovskaja obl.
48 Tjumenskaja obl.
48A Hanty-Mansijski
avt. okr.
50 Tulskaja obl.
51 Uljanovskaja obl.
52 Vladimirskaja obl.
53 Volgogradskaja
oblast
54 Vologodskaja obl.
55 Voronežskaja obl.

UKRAYINA
UKRAÏNE

1 Čerkasskaja obl.
2 Černigovskaja obl.
3 Černovickaja obl.
4 Dnepropetrovskaja
oblast
5 Doneckaja obl.
6 Harkovskaja obl.
7 Hersonskaja obl.
8 Hmelnickaja obl.
9 Ivano-Frankovskaja
oblast
10 Kijevskaja obl.
11 Kirovogradskaja
oblast
12 Krym, respublika
13 Lvovskaja obl.
14 Nikolajevskaja
oblast
15 Odesskaja obl.
16 Poltavskaja obl.

Scale 1:12,000,000   Delisle Conic Equidistant Projection

0   200   400   600   800 km

0   200   400 miles

152

Longitude East 55 of Greenwich

The Commonwealth of Independent States (CIS) was created by republics of the former Soviet Union.

UKRAYINA
UKRAINE
17 Rovenskaja obl.
18 Sumskaja obl.
19 Ternopolskaja obl.
20 Vinnickaja obl.
21 Volynskaja obl.
22 Vorošilovgradskaja oblast
23 Zakarpatskaja obl.
24 Zaporožskaja obl.
25 Žitomirskaja obl.

BYELARUS'
BELARUS
1 Brestskaja obl.
2 Gomelskaja obl.
3 Grodnenskaja obl.
4 Minskaja obl.
5 Mogilevskaja obl.
6 Vitebskaja obl.

ÜZBEKISTON
UZBEKISTAN
1 Andižanskaja obl.
2 Buharskaja obl.
3 Džizakskaja obl.
4 Ferganskaja obl.
5 Horezmskaja obl.
6 Kaškadarinskaja oblast
7 Namanganskaja oblast
8 Samarkandskaja oblast
9 Surhandarinskaja oblast
10 Syrdarinskaja obl.
11 Taškentskaja obl.

QAZAQSTAN
KAZAKHSTAN
1 Aktjubinskaja obl.
2 Alma-Atinskaja oblast
3 Celinogradskaja obl.
4 Čimkentskaja obl.
5 Džambulskaja obl.
6 Džezkazganskaja oblast
7 Alyrauskaja obl.
8 Karagandinskaja oblast
9 Kzyl-Ordinskaja oblast
10 Kokčetavskaja oblast
11 Kustanajskaja obl.
12 Mangyšlakskaja oblast
13 Pavlodarskaja obl.
14 Semipalatinskaja obl.
15 Severo-Kazahstanskaja obl.
16 Taldy-Kurganskaja oblast
17 Turgajskaja obl.
18 Uralskaja obl.
19 Vostočno-Kazahstanskaja obl.

SAKARTVELO
GEORGIA
1 Jugo Osetija

AZÄRBAYJAN
AZERBAIJAN
1 Nagorno-Karabah

KYRGYZSTAN
1 Issyk-Kulskaja oblast
2 Narynskaja obl.
3 Ošskaja obl.
4 Čujskaja oblast
5 Talasskaja obl.
6 Džalal-Abadskaja oblast

TOJIKISTON
TAJIKISTAN
1 Kuljabskaja obl.
2 Kurgan-Tjubinskaja oblast
3 Chudžandskaja obl.
5 Gorno-Badahšanskaja avt. respublika

TÜRKMENISTAN
2 Čardžouskaja obl.
3 Balkanskaja oblast
4 Maryjskaja obl.
5 Tašauzskaja obl.

M ft	
6000	19685
5000	16404
4000	13123
3000	9843
2000	6562
1000	3281
500	1640
+200	+656
0 Depr.	0
−100	−328
200	656
1000	3281
2000	6562

Map 20

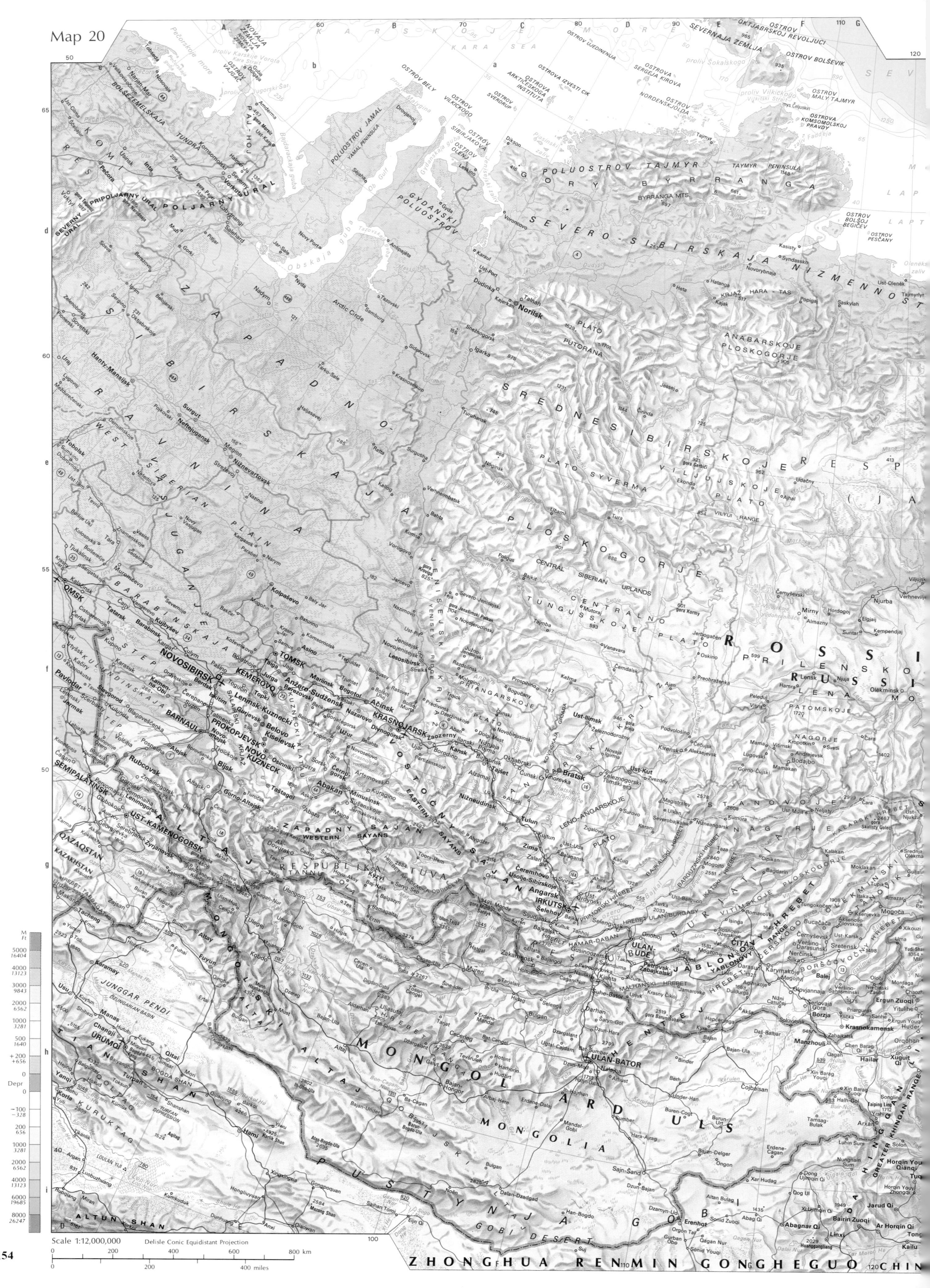

Scale 1:12,000,000

Delisle Conic Equidistant Projection

The Commonwealth of
Independent States (CIS)
was created by republics
of the former Soviet Union.

ROSSIJA
RUSSIA

1 Altajski kraj
1A Gornyj Altaj, respublika
2 Habarovski kraj
2A Evrejskaja avt.
    respublika
4 Krasnojarski kraj
4A Hakasija, respublika
5 Primorski kraj
7 Amurskaja oblast
8A Neneckij avt.
    respublika
15 Čitinskaja oblast
16 Irkutskaja oblast
16A Ust-Ordynski
    Burjatski avt. okrug
21 Kamčatskaja oblast
21A Korjakski avt.
    okrug
22 Kemerovskaja
    oblast
30 Magadanskaja
    oblast
30A Čukotski avt. okrug
34 Novosibirskaja
    oblast
35 Omskaja oblast
43 Sahalinskaja oblast
48 Tjumenskaja oblast
48A Hanty-Mansijski
    avt. okrug
48B Jamalo-Neneckij
    respublika
49 Tomskaja oblast

QAZAQSTAN
KAZAKHSTAN

13 Pavlodarskaja
    oblast
14 Semipalatinskaja
    oblast
19 Vostočno-
    Kazahstanskaja
    oblast

Ostrov Kunašir, ostrov Šikotan, ostrov
Iturup and Malaja Kurilskaja Grjada,
occupied since 1945,
are claimed by Japan pending a final
peace treaty.

Longitude East 150 of Greenwich

A-579395-780   -3 - -4

© ISTITUTO GEOGRAFICO DE AGOSTINI S. p A. - NOVARA

155

Map 21 **ASIA, PHYSICAL**

PACIFIC

Aleutian Trench

ALEUTIAN ISLANDS

Bonin Trench

Kuril Trench

KURIL ISLANDS

HOKKAIDO

HONSHU

SIHOTE-ALIN

KAMCHATKA PENINSULA

SREDINNY HREBET

KORJAKSKOJE NAGORJE

KOLYMA RANGE

EASTERN SIBERIA

CHERSKI MOUNTAINS

VERKHOYANSK MOUNTAINS

STANOVOY RANGE

ALDAN MOUNTAINS

LENA MOUNTAINS

STANOVOY UPLAND

MANCHURIA

GREATER KHINGAN RANGE

LESSER KHINGAN RANGE

ALASKA RANGE

BROOKS RANGE

ALASKA

SEWARD PENINSULA

KENAI PENINSULA

ALEUTIAN RANGE

ALASKA PENINSULA

KODIAK

Gulf of Alaska

Bering Sea

Bering Strait

Chukchi Sea

NORTH SIBERIAN PLAIN

CENTRAL SIBERIAN UPLAND

YENISEY RIDGE

EASTERN SAYANS

TANNUOLA

KHANGAI MTS.

MONGOLIAN ALTAI

GOBI DESERT

ORDOS

TAIHANG SHAN

ARCTIC OCEAN

Canada Basin

Makarov Basin

Lomonosov Ridge

North Pole

Eurasia Basin

Nansen Cordillera

Fram Basin

QUEEN ELIZABETH ISLANDS

ELLESMERE ISLAND

DEVON

BAFFIN

VICTORIA

BANKS

MELVILLE ISLAND

PRINCE PATRICK

AXEL HEIBERG

SVERDRUP ISLANDS

GREENLAND

KING CHRISTIAN IX LAND

KING CHRISTIAN X LAND

KING FREDERIK VI COAST

NEW SIBERIAN ISLANDS

ANJOU ISLANDS

LYAKHOV ISLANDS

SEVERNAYA ZEMLYA

KOMSOMOLEC ISLAND

BOLSHEVIK ISLAND

OCTOBER REVOLUTION ISLAND

PIONEER ISLAND

TAYMYR PENINSULA

BYRRANGA MOUNTAINS

GYDA PENINSULA

YAMAL PENINSULA

NOVAYA ZEMLYA

FRANZ JOSEPH LAND

SPITSBERGEN

BEAR ISLAND

Barents Sea

Kara Sea

Laptev Sea

East Siberian Sea

WRANGEL

WEST SIBERIAN PLAIN

Arctic Circle

URAL MOUNTAINS

KAZAKHSTAN

KAZAKH HILLS

TIAN SHAN

TARIM BASIN

DZUNGARIAN BASIN

ALTAI

WESTERN ALTAI

TURFAN DEPRESSION

EASTERN TURKISTAN

BEI SHAN

NAN SHAN

TIMAN RIDGE

NORTHERN UVALS

KOLA PENINSULA

KARELIA

LAPLAND

SCANDINAVIA

SVEALAND

GOTALAND

Norwegian Sea

Greenland Sea

Denmark Strait

ICELAND

Reykjanes Ridge

Mid-Atlantic Ridge

ATLANTIC OCEAN

Iceland Basin

Rockall Rise

FAEROE ISLANDS

SHETLAND ISLANDS

ORKNEY ISLANDS

BRITISH ISLES

GREAT BRITAIN

IRELAND

ENGLAND

North Sea

Baltic Sea

Gulf of Bothnia

MOSCOW BASIN

VALDAI HILLS

CENTRAL RUSSIAN UPLAND

VOLHYNIA

UKRAINE

PODOLIA

POLESYE

POLAND

POMERANIA

SILESIA

SUDETEN

BOHEMIA

BOHEMIAN FOREST

FRIESLAND

FLANDERS

VOSGES

MASSIF CENTRAL

BRITTANY

JURA

ALPS

APENNINES

CORSICA

SARDINIA

CARPATHIAN MTS.

BALKAN MTS.

BALKAN PENINSULA

THRACE

MACEDONIA

PINDUS MTS.

CRETE

CYPRUS

ANATOLIA

TAURUS MTS.

Black Sea

CRIMEA

CISCAUCASIA

CAUCASUS

TRANSCAUCASUS

ARMENIA

KURDISTAN

ZAGROS

MESOPOTAMIA

AL JAZIRAH

SYRIAN DESERT

NILE DELTA

Caspian Sea

CASPIAN DEPRESSION

Volga Delta

KIRGHIZ STEPPE

USTYURT PLATEAU

KARA KUM

KYZYL KUM

WESTERN TURKISTAN

Mediterranean Sea

Adriatic Sea

Aral Sea

KAZAKH HILLS

© ISTITUTO GEOGRAFICO DE AGOSTINI S.p.A. - NOVARA

Scale 1:30,000,000   Lambert Azimuthal Equal Area Projection

Map 22 ASIA, POLITICAL

© ISTITUTO GEOGRAFICO DE AGOSTINI S. p. A. - NOVARA

A-515200-280 —8-1-10

Scale 1:30,000,000

Lambert Azimuthal Equal Area Projection

Longitude East 80 of Greenwich

Map 23 **SOUTHWESTERN ASIA**

Scale 1:12,000,000   Delisle Conic Equidistant Projection

0   200   400   600   800 km

0   200   400 miles

AFGHANISTAN

VELĀYAT

1 Badakhshan
2 Bādghīsāt
3 Baghlān
4 Balkh
5 Bāmīān
6 Farāh
7 Fāryāb
8 Ghazni
9 Ghowr
10 Helmand
11 Herāt
12 Jowzjān
13 Kābol
14 Kāpīsā
15 Konarha
16 Laghmān
17 Lowgar
18 Nangarhār
19 Nīmrūz
20 Orūzgān
21 Paktiā
22 Parvān
23 Qandahār
24 Qondūz
25 Samangān
26 Takhār
27 Vardak
28 Zābol

ĪRĀN

OSTĀN

1 Āzarbāijān-e Gharbī
2 Āzarbāijān-e Sharqī
3 Bakhtarān
4 Boyer Ahmadī-e
   Kohkīlūyeh
5 Būshehr
6 Chahār Mahāl-e
   Bakhtīārī
7 Esfahān
8 Fārs
9 Gīlān
10 Hamadān
11 Hormozgān
12 Īlām
13 Kermān
14 Khorāsān
15 Khūzestān
16 Kordestān
17 Lorestān
18 Markazī
19 Māzandarān
20 Semnān
21 Sīstāne-e
   Balūchestān
22 Yard
23 Zanjān

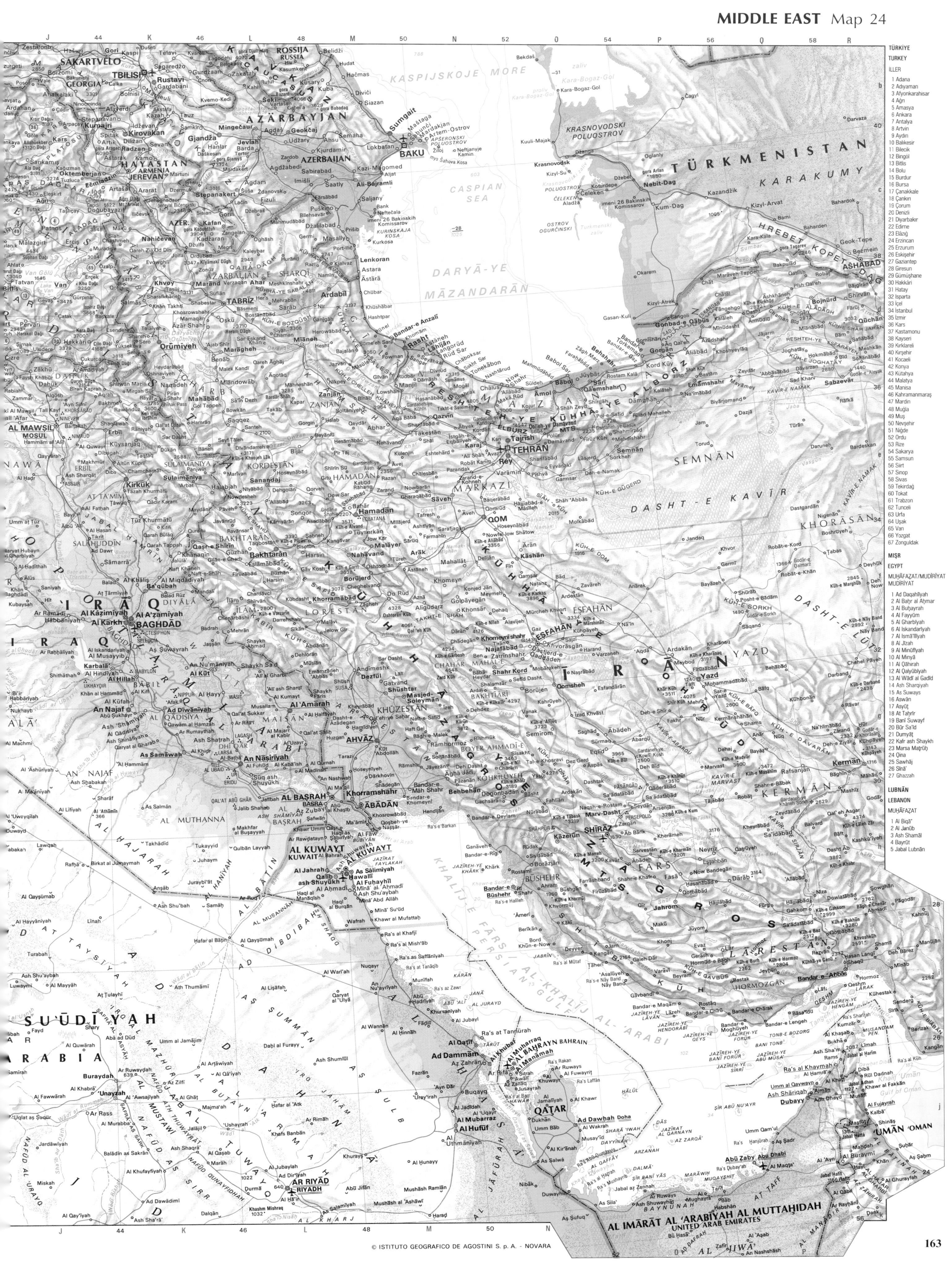

TÜRKIYE
TURKEY

ILLER

1 Adana
2 Adıyaman
3 Afyonkarahisar
4 Ağrı
5 Amasya
6 Ankara
7 Antalya
8 Artvin
9 Aydın
10 Balıkesir
11 Bilecik
12 Bingöl
13 Bitlis
14 Bolu
15 Burdur
16 Bursa
17 Çanakkale
18 Çankırı
19 Çorum
20 Denizli
21 Diyarbakır
22 Edirne
23 Elazığ
24 Erzincan
25 Erzurum
26 Eskişehir
27 Gaziantep
28 Giresun
29 Gümüşhane
30 Hakkâri
31 Hatay
32 Isparta
33 İçel
34 Istanbul
35 İzmir
36 Kars
37 Kastamonu
38 Kayseri
39 Kırklareli
40 Kırşehir
41 Kocaeli
42 Konya
43 Kütahya
44 Malatya
45 Manisa
46 Kahramanmaraş
47 Mardin
48 Muğla
49 Muş
50 Nevşehir
51 Niğde
52 Ordu
53 Rize
54 Sakarya
55 Samsun
56 Sirt
57 Sinop
58 Sivas
59 Tekirdağ
60 Tokat
61 Trabzon
62 Tunceli
63 Urfa
64 Uşak
65 Van
66 Yozgat
67 Zonguldak

MIŞR

EGYPT

MUHĀFAZĀT/MUDĪRĪYAT
MUDĪRĪYAT

1 Ad Daqahliyah
2 Al Bahr al Ahmar
3 Al Buhayrah
4 Al Fayyūm
5 Al Gharbiyah
6 Al Iskandarīyah
7 Al Ismā'īlīyah
8 Al Jīzah
9 Al Minūfīyah
10 Al Minyā
11 Al Qāhirah
12 Al Qalyūbīyah
13 Al Wādī al Gadīd
14 Ash Sharqīyah
15 As Suways
16 Aswān
17 Asyūt
18 At Tahrīr
19 Banī Suwayf
20 Būr Sa'īd
21 Dumyāt
22 Kafr ash Shaykh
23 Marsā Matrūh
24 Qina
25 Sawhāj
26 Sīnā'
27 Ghazzah

LUBNĀN

LEBANON

MUHĀFAZĀT

1 Al Biqā'
2 Al Janūb
3 Ash Shamāl
4 Bayrūt
5 Jabal Lubnān

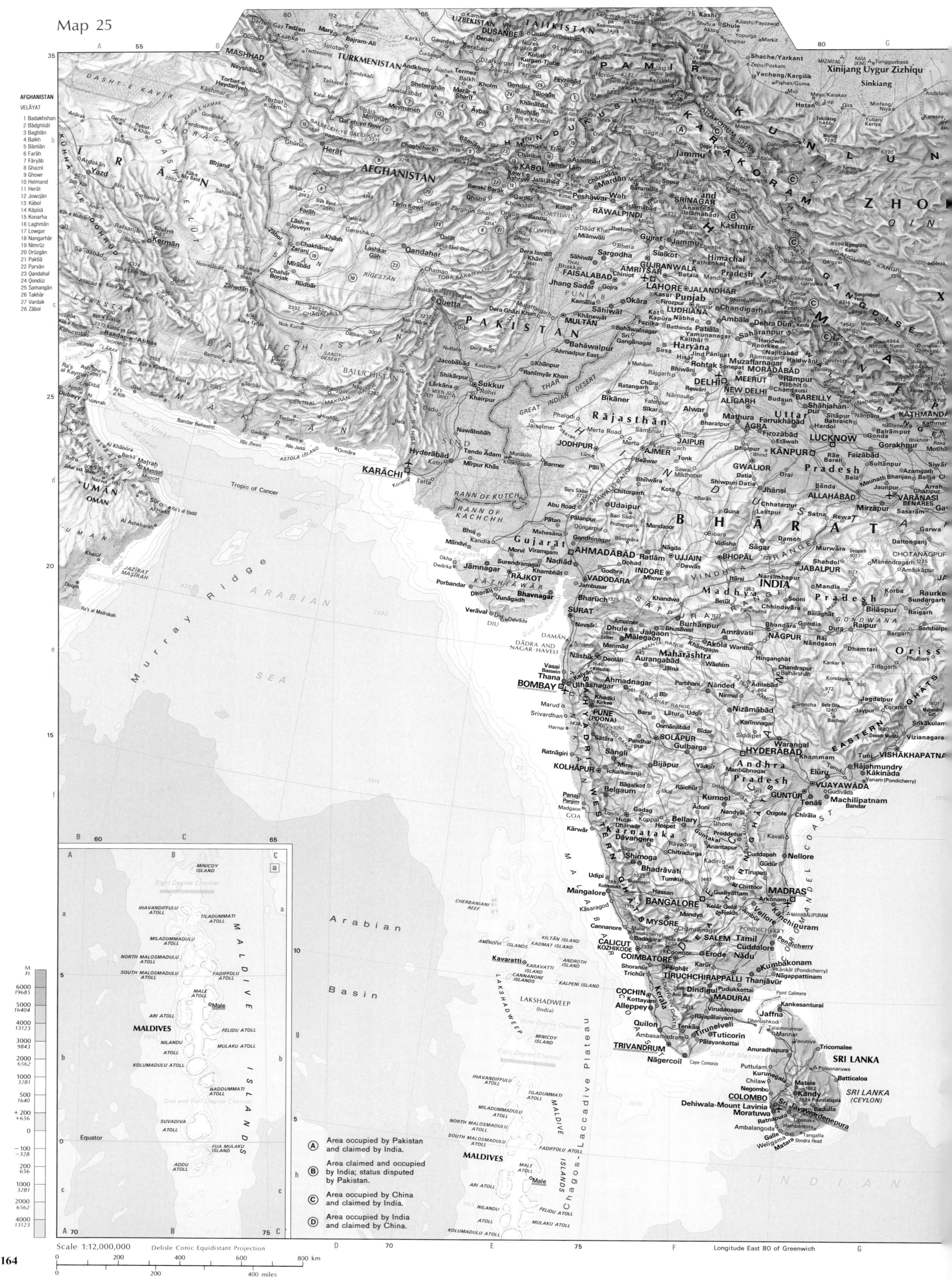

Map 25

AFGHANISTAN
VELĀYAT

1 Badakhshan
2 Bādghīsāt
3 Baghlān
4 Balkh
5 Bāmīān
6 Farāh
7 Fāryāb
8 Ghaznī
9 Ghowr
10 Helmand
11 Herāt
12 Jowzjān
13 Kābol
14 Kāpīsā
15 Konarha
16 Laghmān
17 Lowgar
18 Nangarhār
19 Nīmrūz
20 Orūzgān
21 Paktiā
22 Parvān
23 Qandahār
24 Qondūz
25 Samangān
26 Takhār
27 Vardak
28 Zābol

MALDIVES

Ⓐ Area occupied by Pakistan and claimed by India.

Ⓑ Area claimed and occupied by India; status disputed by Pakistan.

Ⓒ Area occupied by China and claimed by India.

Ⓓ Area occupied by India and claimed by China.

Scale 1:12,000,000
Delisle Conic Equidistant Projection

0   200   400   600   800 km

0   200   400 miles

Longitude East 80 of Greenwich

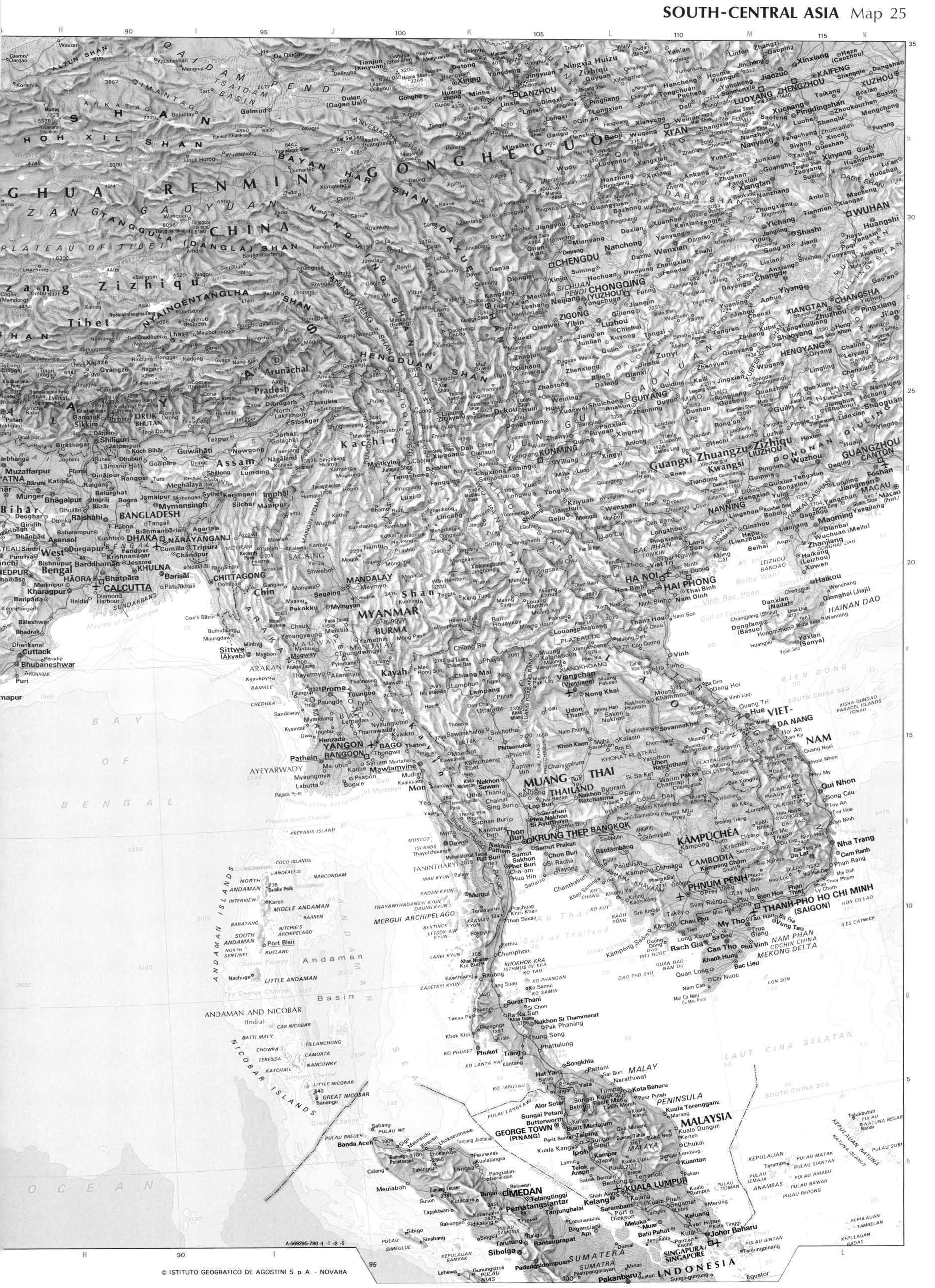

Map 26 **SOUTHEAST ASIA**

Scale 1:12,000,000 at the Equator

Mercator Cylindrical Projection

Longitude East 110 of Greenwich

A-569800-780-2 -2 -2 -2

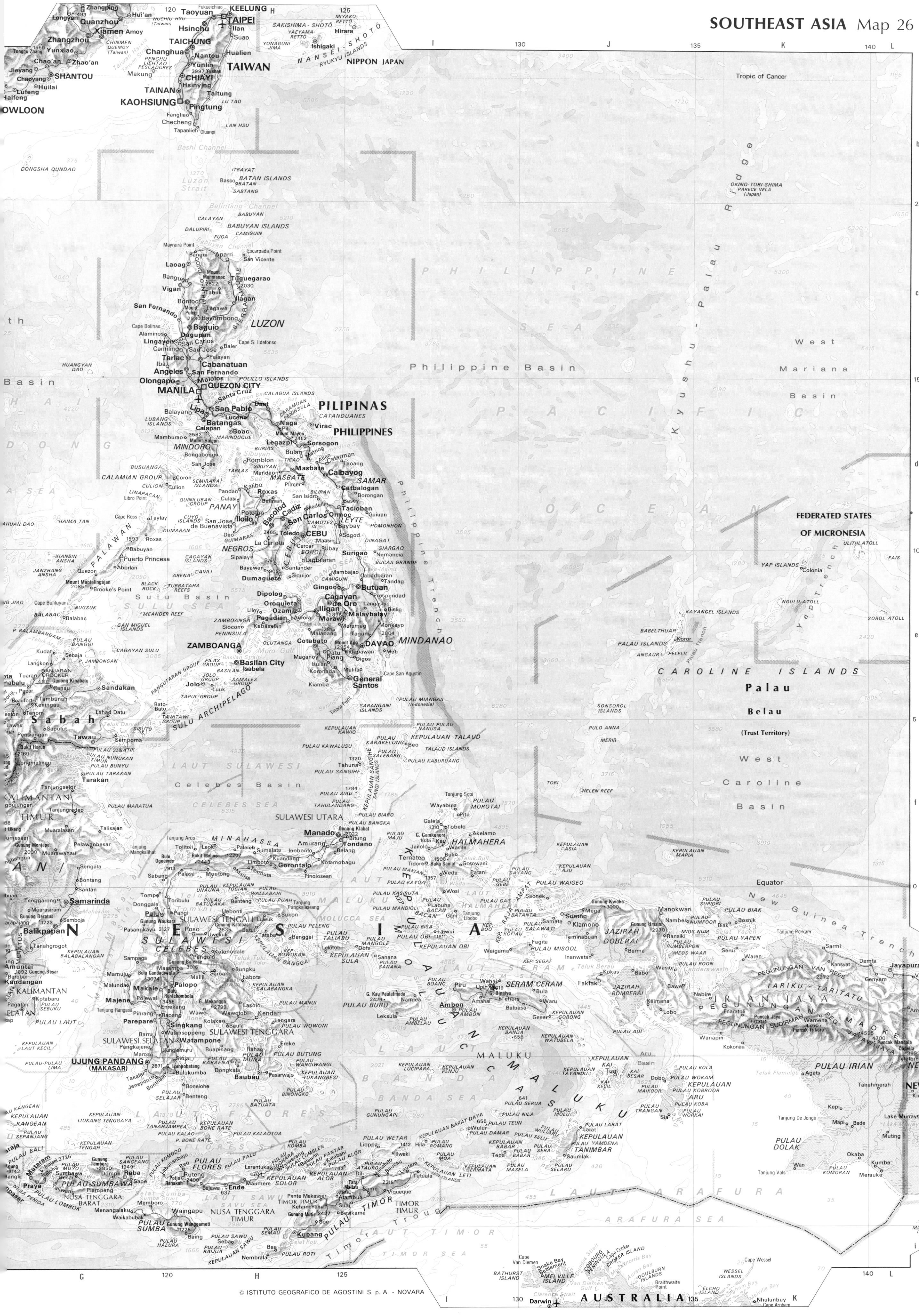

TAIWAN
TAIPEI
KEELUNG
TAICHUNG
CHIAYI
TAINAN
KAOHSIUNG

NIPPON JAPAN

Tropic of Cancer

BATAN ISLANDS
BABUYAN ISLANDS

LUZON
Laoag
Vigan
Baguio
Dagupan
Lingayen
Tarlac
Angeles
Olongapo
MANILA
QUEZON CITY
Santa Cruz
Lipa
Batangas
Calapan

PILIPINAS
PHILIPPINES

MINDORO
Legazpi
Sorsogon
Naga
Virac
CATANDUANES

MASBATE
Calbayog
Catbalogan
SAMAR
Tacloban
Roxas
PANAY
Iloilo
Bacolod
Cadiz
San Carlos
Ormoc
LEYTE
CEBU
Toledo
NEGROS
Dumaguete
Surigao
BOHOL
Tagbilaran

PALAWAN
Puerto Princesa

FEDERATED STATES
OF MICRONESIA

YAP ISLANDS

Dipolog
Cagayan de Oro
Oroquieta
Ozamiz
Iligan
Pagadian
Malaybalay
Marawi
ZAMBOANGA
Cotabato
DAVAO
MINDANAO
Digos
General Santos
Basilan City
Isabela
Jolo
SULU ARCHIPELAGO

PACIFIC OCEAN

Philippine Basin

PHILIPPINE SEA

CAROLINE ISLANDS
Palau
Belau
(Trust Territory)

West Caroline Basin

PALAU ISLANDS
Koror

Sabah
Sandakan
Tawau
Tarakan

Celebes Basin
CELEBES SEA
LAUT SULAWESI

KEPULAUAN TALAUD
TALAUD ISLANDS

SULAWESI UTARA
Manado
Tondano
Gorontalo
MINAHASSA
HALMAHERA
Ternate
Tidore

KALIMANTAN TIMUR
Samarinda
Balikpapan

INDONESIA

SULAWESI TENGAH
Palu
Poso

New Guinea Trench

IRIAN JAYA
Jayapura
PEGUNUNGAN
Manokwari
Sorong
JAZIRAH DOBERAI

SERAM CERAM
Fakfak
Ambon
PULAU BURU
PULAU SERAM

CELEBES
SULAWESI
Makale
Palopo
Majene
Parepare
Singkang
Watampone
SULAWESI TENGGARA
Kendari
UJUNG PANDANG
(MAKASAR)

MALUKU

PAPUA
NEW GUINEA
PULAU IRIAN

BANDA SEA
LAUT BANDA

KEPULAUAN ARU

KEPULAUAN TANIMBAR
Saumlaki

LAUT FLORES
FLORES
PULAU FLORES
Ende
Maumere
PULAU SUMBAWA
Bima
Mataram
PULAU LOMBOK
PULAU BALI
NUSA TENGGARA TIMUR
Waingapu
PULAU SUMBA

TIMOR TIMUR
PULAU TIMOR

ARAFURA SEA
LAUT ARAFURA

TIMOR SEA
LAUT TIMOR

Kupang

Darwin

AUSTRALIA

MELVILLE ISLAND

Map 27 **CHINA AND MONGOLIA**

Legend:

(A) Area occupied by Pakistan and claimed by India.

(B) Area claimed and occupied by India; status disputed by Pakistan.

(C) Area occupied by China and claimed by India.

(D) Area occupied by India and claimed by China.

Scale 1:12,000,000   Delisle Conic Equidistant Projection

0   200   400   600   800 km

0   200   400 miles

Elevation key (M / ft):
6000 / 19685
5000 / 16404
4000 / 13123
3000 / 9843
2000 / 6562
1000 / 3281
500 / 1640
+ 200 / +656
Depr.
− 100 / −328
200 / 656
1000 / 3281
2000 / 6562
4000 / 13123
6000 / 19685
8000 / 26247

ROSSIJA
RUSSIA CITA
ULAN-UDE

HEILONGJIANG

GOBI

NEI Mongol Zizhiqu
Inner Mongolia

HEGUO

BAOTOU

HOHHOT DATONG

BEIJING PEKING

TIANJIN (TIENTSIN)

TANGSHAN

HEBEI

SHIJIAZHUANG

TAIYUAN

SHANXI

HANDAN

JINAN (TSINAN)

SHANDONG SHANTUNG PENINSULA

QINGDAO (TSINGTAO)

LUOYANG ZHENGZHOU

XI'AN

HENAN

KAIFENG

XUZHOU

LIANYUNGANG (XINPU)

JIANGSU

BENGBU

HUAINAN

NANJING (NANKING)

WUXI SUZHOU

SHANGHAI

HEFEI

ANHUI

HUBEI

WUHAN

HANGZHOU

ZHEJIANG

NANCHANG

HUNAN

CHANGSHA

JIANGXI

HENGYANG

GUIZHOU

NANLING

GUANGDONG

GUANGZHOU CANTON

LIUZHOU

KWANGSI

MACAU Macao (Port.)

NEW KOWLOON VICTORIA Hong Kong (U.K.)

HAINAN DAO

HAINAN

NAN HAI SOUTH CHINA SEA

South China Sea

HARBIN

QIQIHAR

CHANGCHUN

JILIN

SHENYANG

FUSHUN

ANSHAN

LIAONING

DALIAN

Bo Hai Gulf of Chihli

MUDANJIANG

VLADIVOSTOK

CHŎNGJIN

NORTH KOREA

P'YŎNGYANG

SEOUL SŎUL INCH'ŎN

TAEJŎN

TAEHAN-MIN'GUK SOUTH KOREA

TAEGU

KWANGJU PUSAN

HUANG HAI / HWANG-HAE YELLOW SEA

CHEJU-DO

HOKKAIDŌ

SAPPORO

HAKODATE

AOMORI

AKITA

SENDAI

NIPPON JAPAN

NIIGATA

NAGANO

TŌKYŌ YOKOHAMA

NAGOYA

KYŌTO ŌSAKA KŌBE NARA

HIROSHIMA

KITAKYŪSHŪ FUKUOKA

NAGASAKI KUMAMOTO

KAGOSHIMA

KYŪSHŪ

SHIKOKU

HONSHŪ

Japan Basin

SEA OF JAPAN

DONG HAI / HIGASHI-SHINA-KAI EAST CHINA SEA

RYUKYU ISLANDS NANSEI-SHOTŌ

NAHA

TAICHUNG

T'AIPEI KEELUNG

TAIWAN

TAINAN

KAOHSIUNG

PACIFIC OCEAN

Tropic of Cancer

PHILIPPINE SEA

BATAN ISLANDS

BABUYAN ISLANDS

LUZON

PILIPINAS PHILIPPINES

ZHONGHUA RENMIN GONGHEGUO

CHINA

1 Beijing Shi
2 Shanghai Shi
3 Tianjin Shi

Map 28 **NORTHEASTERN CHINA, KOREA AND JAPAN**

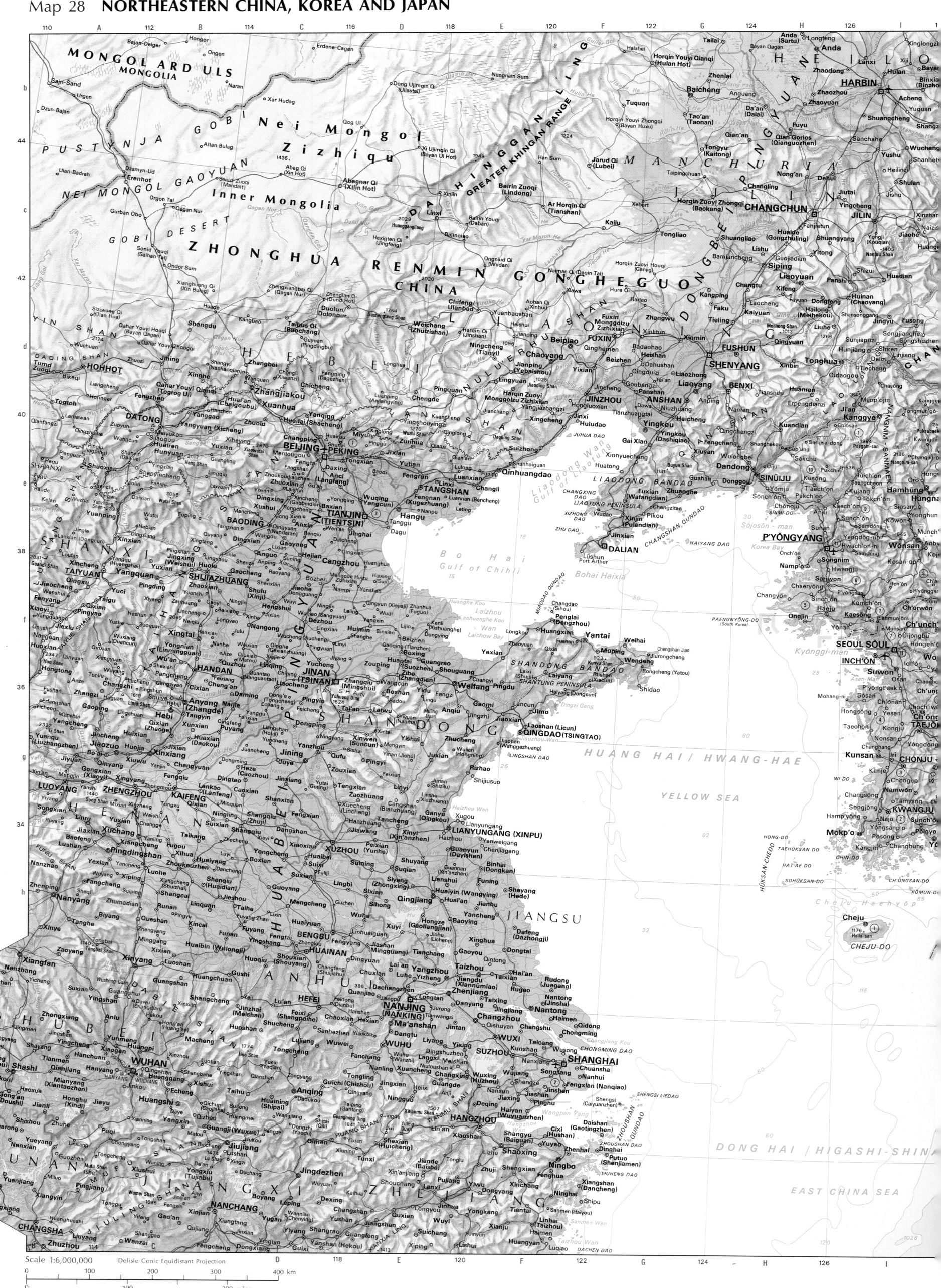

Scale 1:6,000,000   Delisle Conic Equidistant Projection

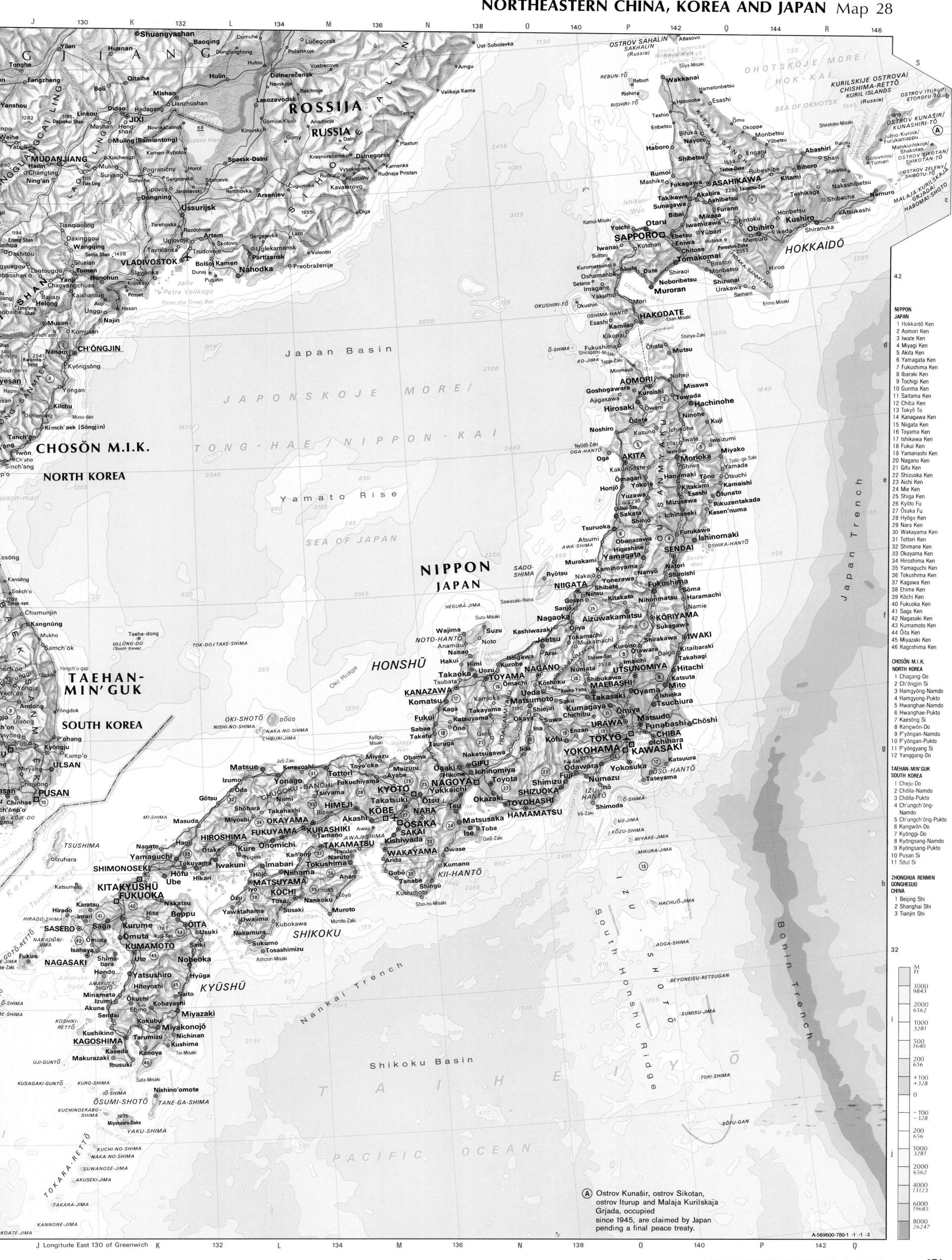

Map 29 JAPAN

Longitude East 144 of Greenwich

OHOTSKOJE MORE

HOK-KAI

SEA OF OKHOTSK

Ostrov Kunasir, ostrov Sikotan, ostrov
Iturup, and Malaja Kurilskaja Grjada,
occupied since 1945, are claimed by
Japan pending a final peace treaty.

KURILSKIJE OSTROVA/
CHISHIMA-RETTŌ
KURIL ISLANDS

OSTROV
ITURUP/
ETOROFU-TŌ

ROSSIJA
RUSSIA

OSTROV KUNAŠIR

KUNASHIRI-TŌ

OSTROV
ŠIKOTAN/
SHIKOTAN-TŌ

MALAJA KURILSKAJA
GRJADA/

HABOMAI-SHOTŌ

NIPPON-KAI

SEA OF JAPAN

REBUN-TŌ
RISHIRI-TŌ

Wakkanai

Monbetsu

Abashiri

ASAHIKAWA

KITAMI-SANCHI

KONSEN-
DAICHI

Nemuro
NEMURO-
HANTŌ

Kushiro

SAPPORO

Obihiro

HOKKAIDŌ

TOKACHI-
HEIYA

HIDAKA-
SANMYAKU

OSHIMA-HANTŌ

Muroran

HAKODATE

MATSUMAE-
HANTŌ

KITA - TAIHEIYŌ

PACIFIC OCEAN

Oki Ridge

Oki Trench

HONSHŪ

DŌGO
DŌZEN
OKI-SHOTŌ
CHIBURI-JIMA
NAKA-NO-SHIMA

HONSHŪ

SHIMOKITA-HANTŌ

Mutsu

TSUGARU-HANTŌ

AOMORI

Misawa

HONSHŪ

Nankai Trough

SHIMANE-HANTŌ

Matsue
Yonago
Tottori

KYOTO

IZUMO

ŌKU-SANCHI

TANBA-
SANCHI

TAEHAN - MIN'GUK

Masan
Chinhae
Kimhae
Tongnae
PUSAN

SOUTH KOREA

HIROSHIMA

OKAYAMA

HIMEJI

KŌBE
ŌSAKA
SAKAI

KURASHIKI

FUKUYAMA

TAKAMATSU

WAKAYAMA

TSUSHIMA

KAMINO-SHIMA
SHIMONO-
SHIMA

Korea Strait

Taehan-Haehyŏp/
Tsushima-Kaikyō

SHIMONOSEKI

Yamaguchi

KITAKYŪSHŪ
Ube

Kure

MATSUYAMA

KŌCHI

SHIKOKU-SANCHI

Tokushima

SHIKOKU

FUKUOKA

KYŪSHŪ-
SANCHI

ŌITA

Beppu

TSUKUSHI-SANCHI

SASEBO

KUMAMOTO

NAGASAKI

GOTŌ-RETTŌ

KŌSHIKI-
RETTŌ

EAST CHINA SEA

HIGASHI-SHINA KAI

KYŪSHŪ

Miyazaki

KAGOSHIMA

SATSUMA-
HANTŌ

Scale 1:3,000,000   Delisle Conic Equidistant Projection

0   50   100   150   200 km

0   50   100 miles

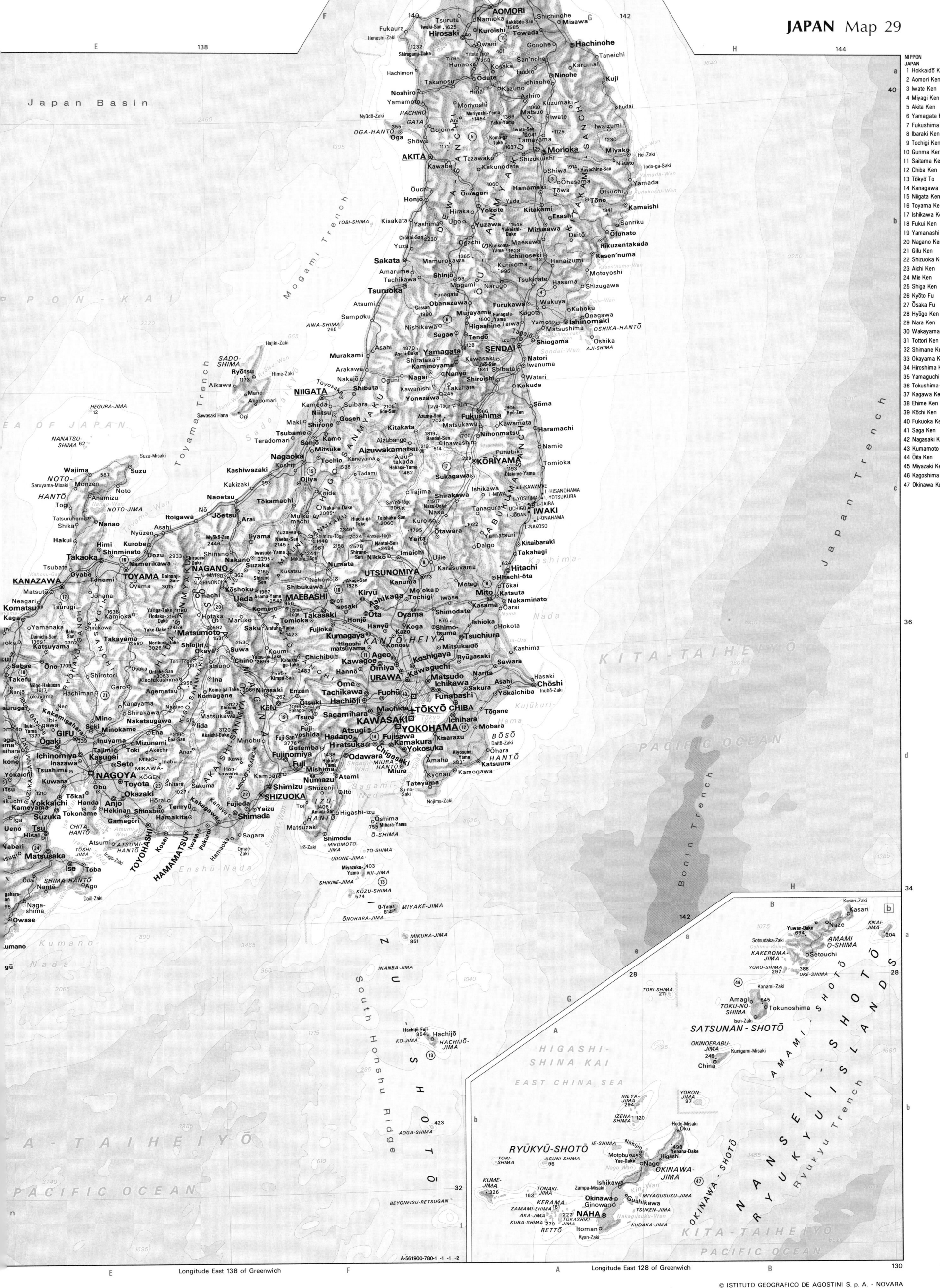

Japan Basin

Mogami Trench

*NIPPON
JAPAN*
1 Hokkaidō Ken
2 Aomori Ken
3 Iwate Ken
4 Miyagi Ken
5 Akita Ken
6 Yamagata Ken
7 Fukushima Ken
8 Ibaraki Ken
9 Tochigi Ken
10 Gunma Ken
11 Saitama Ken
12 Chiba Ken
13 Tōkyō To
14 Kanagawa Ken
15 Niigata Ken
16 Toyama Ken
17 Ishikawa Ken
18 Fukui Ken
19 Yamanashi Ken
20 Nagano Ken
21 Gifu Ken
22 Shizuoka Ken
23 Aichi Ken
24 Mie Ken
25 Shiga Ken
26 Kyōto Fu
27 Ōsaka Fu
28 Hyōgo Ken
29 Nara Ken
30 Wakayama Ken
31 Tottori Ken
32 Shimane Ken
33 Okayama Ken
34 Hiroshima Ken
35 Yamaguchi Ken
36 Tokushima Ken
37 Kagawa Ken
38 Ehime Ken
39 Kōchi Ken
40 Fukuoka Ken
41 Saga Ken
42 Nagasaki Ken
43 Kumamoto Ken
44 Ōita Ken
45 Miyazaki Ken
46 Kagoshima Ken
47 Okinawa Ken

SEA OF JAPAN

NIPPON-KAI

Toyama Trench

SADO-SHIMA

Japan Trench

KITA-TAIHEIYŌ

PACIFIC OCEAN

Bonin Trench

South Honshu Ridge

HIGASHI-SHINA KAI

EAST CHINA SEA

SATSUNAN-SHOTŌ

AMAMI-SHOTŌ

NANSEI-SHOTŌ

RYŪKYŪ ISLANDS

Ryukyu Trench

RYŪKYŪ-SHOTŌ

OKINAWA-SHOTŌ

KITA-TAIHEIYŌ

PACIFIC OCEAN

A-561900-780-1 -1 -1 -2

Map 30 **AFRICA, PHYSICAL**

Map 30

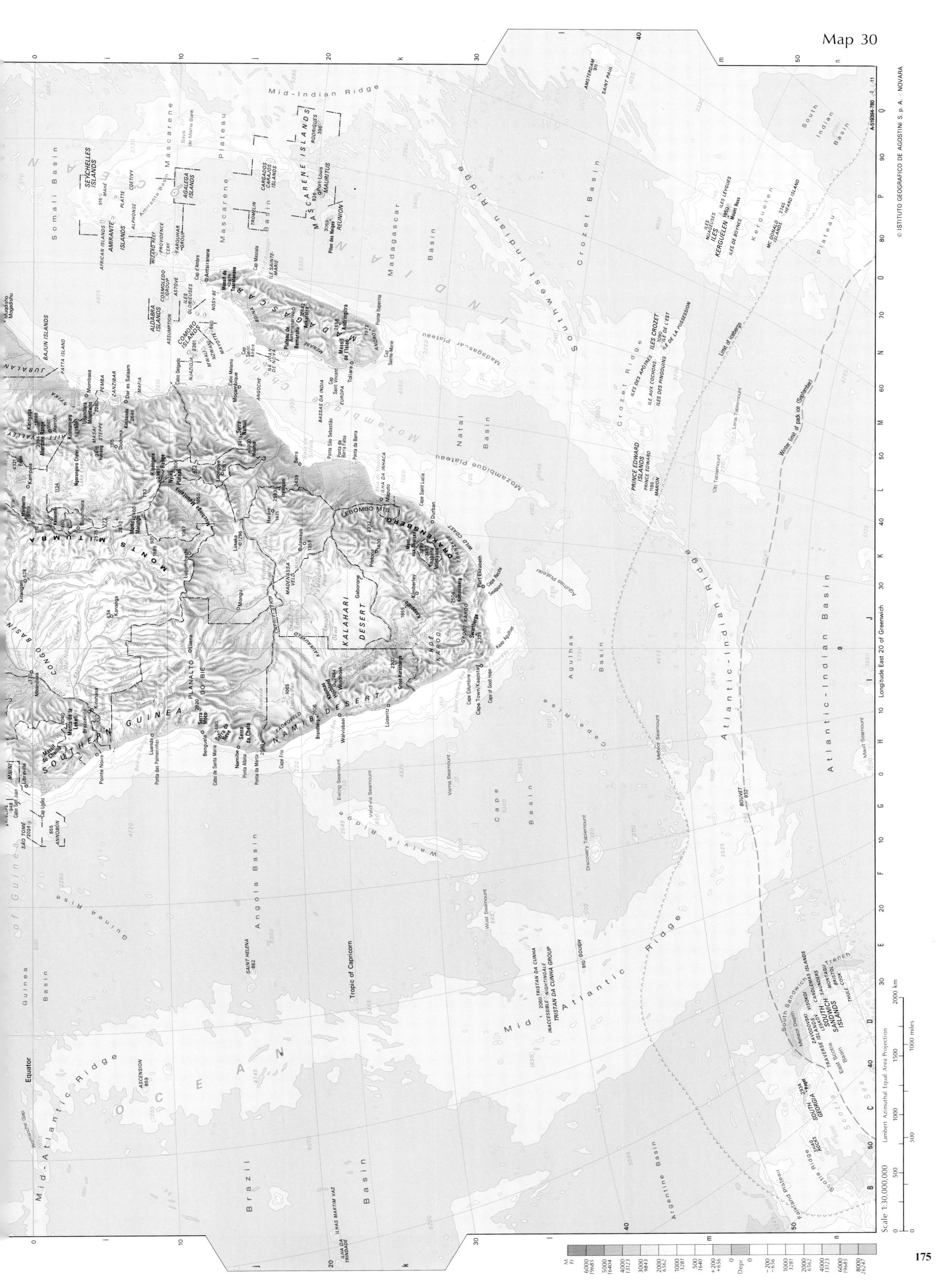

Map 31 **AFRICA, POLITICAL**

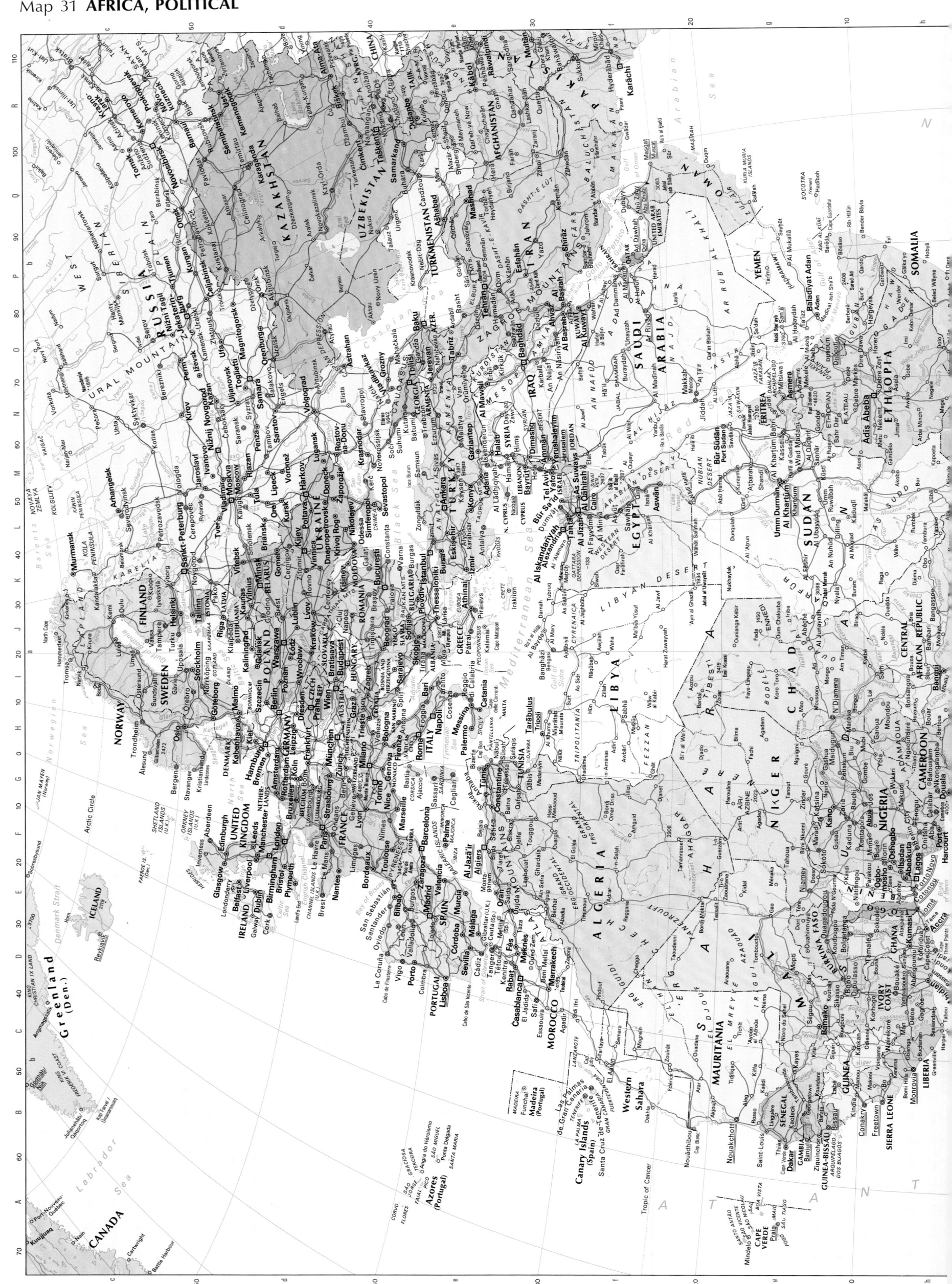

Map 31

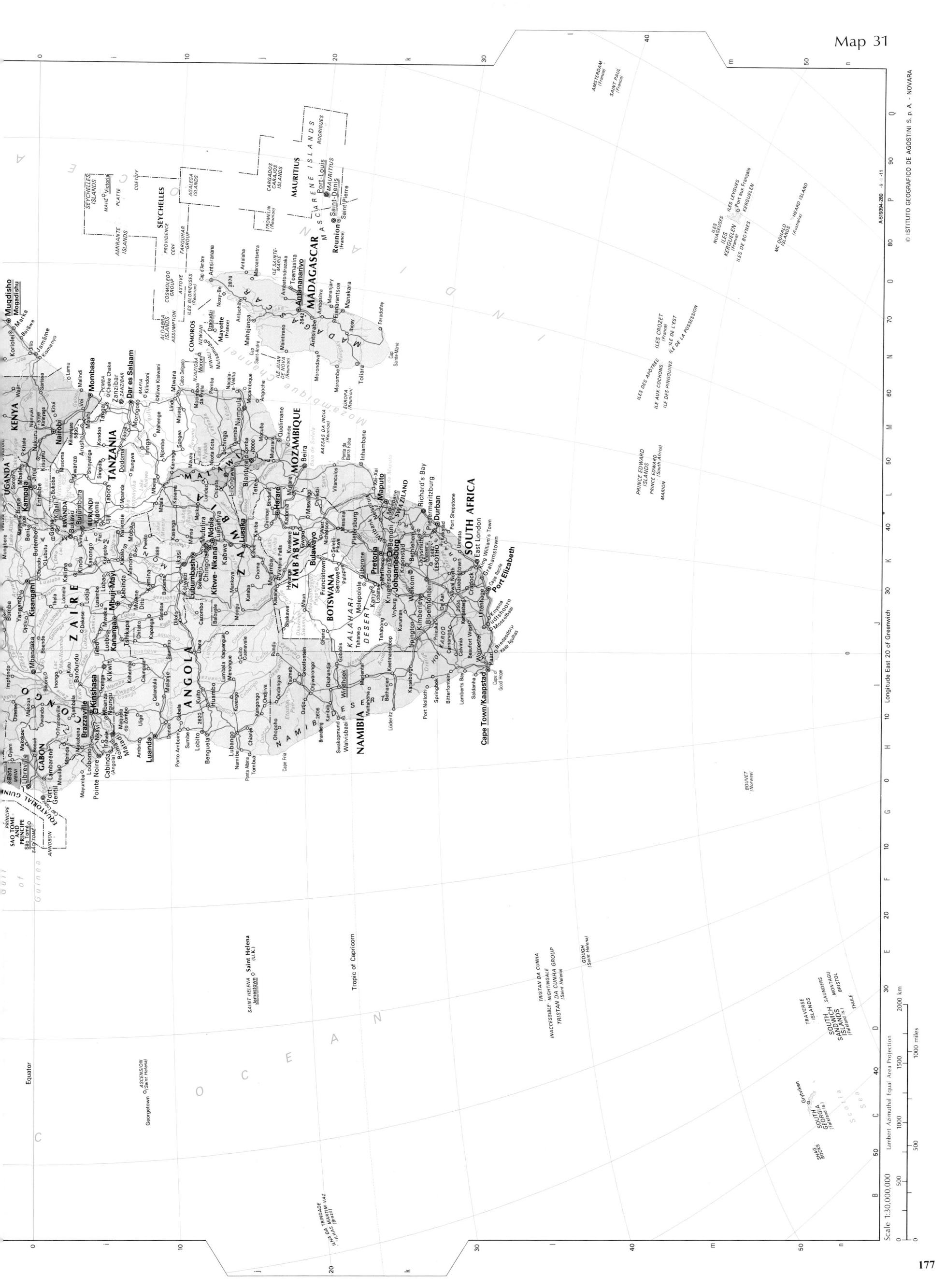

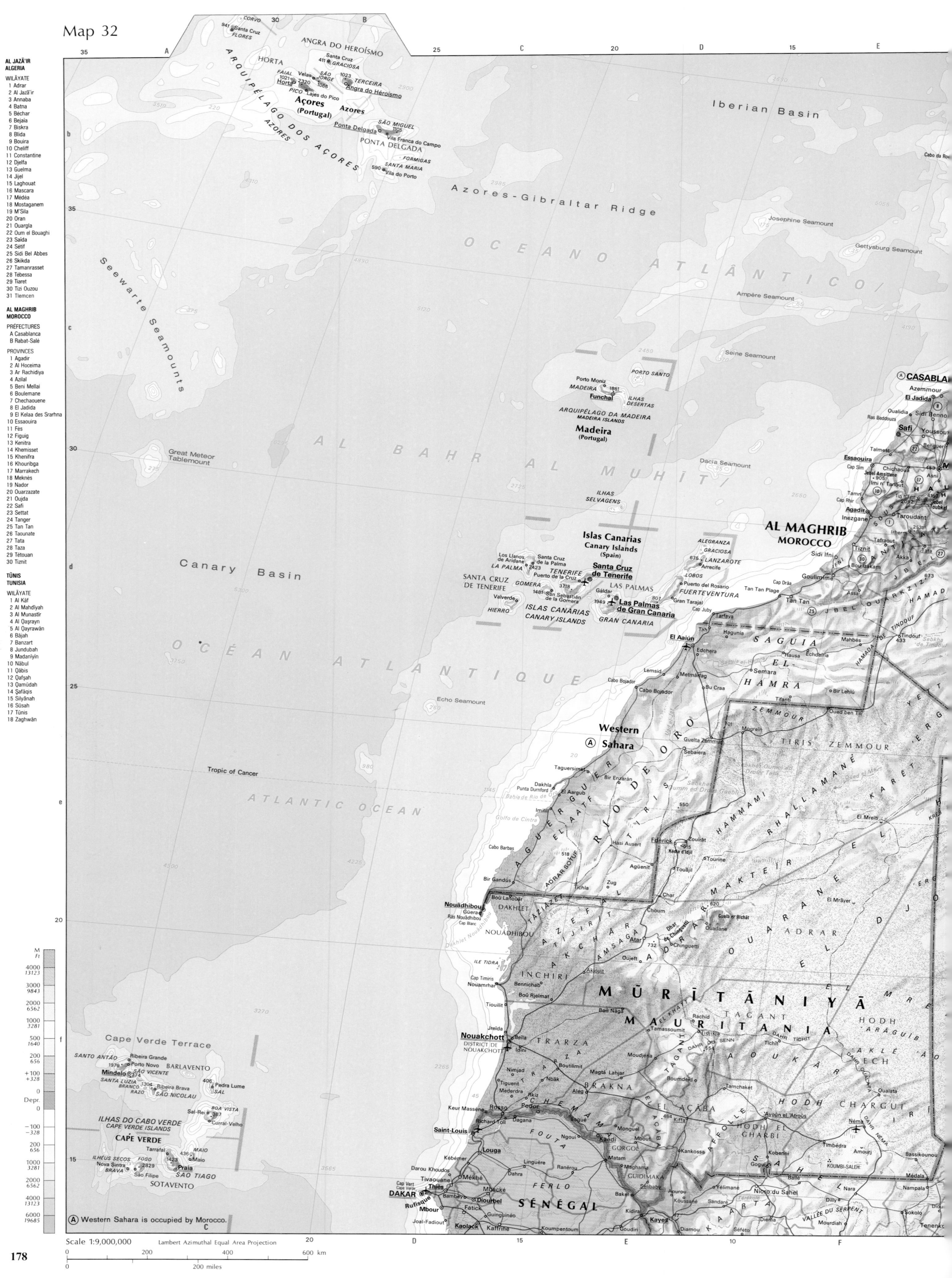

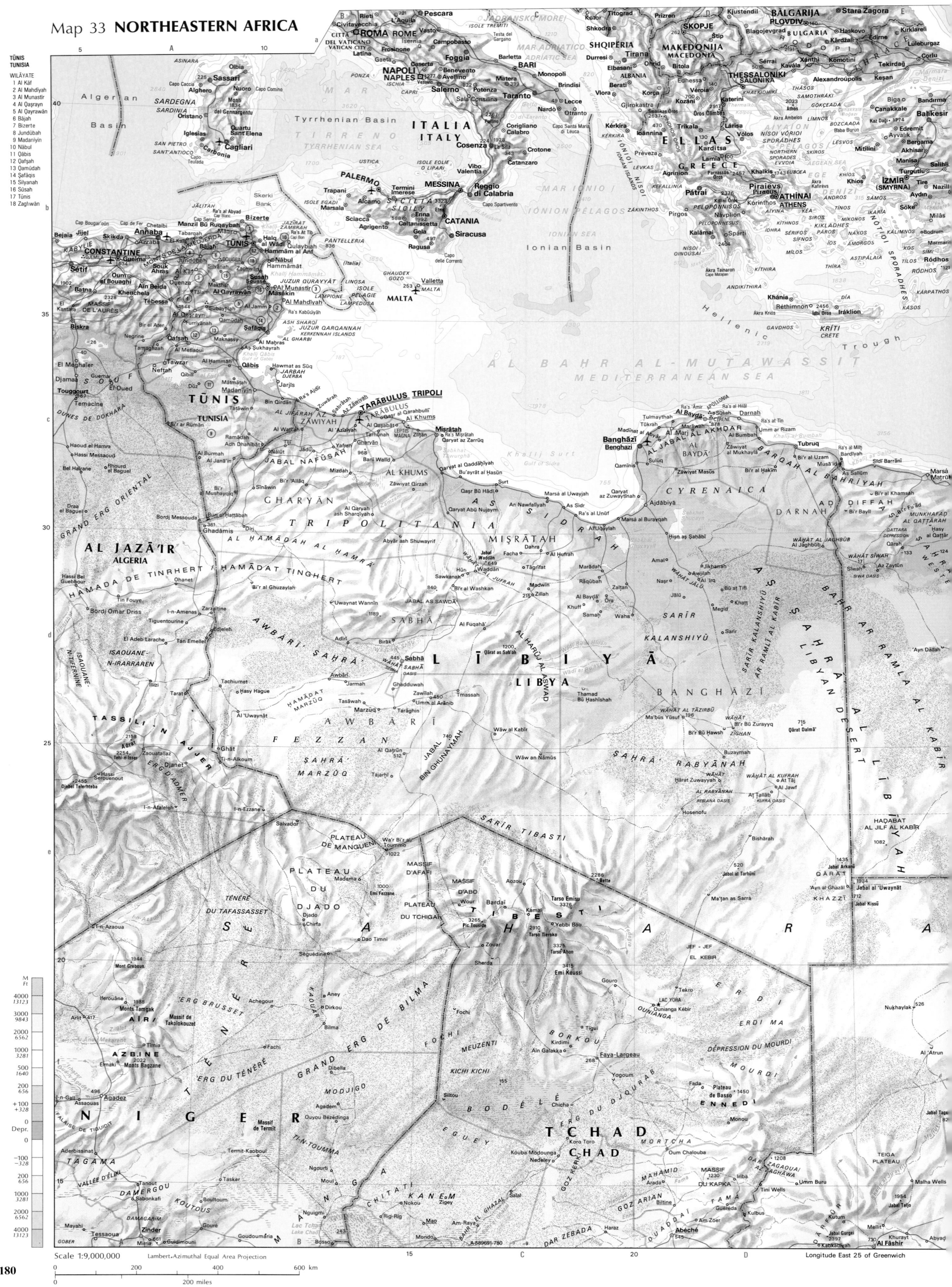

Map 33 **NORTHEASTERN AFRICA**

TŪNIS
TUNISIA
WILĀYATE
1 Al Kāf
2 Al Mahdīyah
3 Al Munastir
4 Al Qaṣrayn
5 Al Qayrawān
6 Bājah
7 Bizerte
8 Jundūbah
9 Madanīyin
10 Nābul
11 Qābis
12 Qafṣah
13 Qamūdah
14 Ṣafāqis
15 Silyānah
16 Sūsah
17 Tūnis
18 Zaghwān

ITALIA
ITALY

GREECE
ELLAS

BULGARIJA
BULGARIA

MEDITERRANEAN SEA
AL BAHR AL-MUTAWASSIT

AL JAZĀ'IR
ALGERIA

LĪBIYĀ
LIBYA

TŪNIS
TUNISIA

TRIPOLITANIA

FEZZAN

CYRENAICA

S A H A R A

NIGER

TCHAD
CHAD

M
Ft
4000 13123
3000 9843
2000 6562
1000 3281
500 1640
200 656
+ 100 +328
Depr. 0
− 100 −328
200 656
1000 3281
2000 6562
4000 13123

Scale 1:9,000,000
Lambert-Azimuthal Equal Area Projection
Longitude East 25 of Greenwich

0 200 400 600 km
0 200 miles

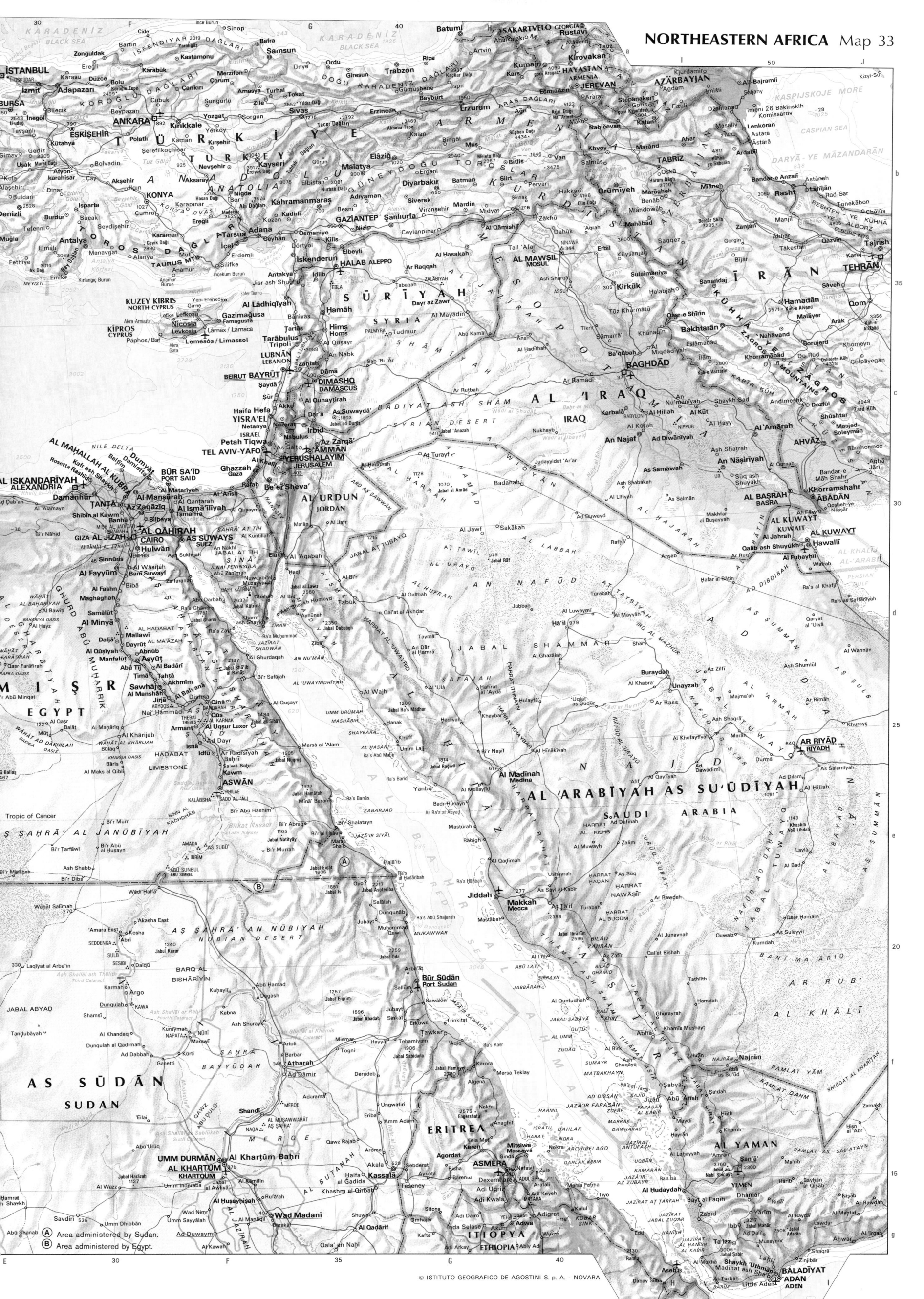

(A) Area administered by Sudan.
(B) Area administered by Egypt.

Map 34 **WEST-CENTRAL AFRICA**

LIBERIA
COUNTIES
1 Bong
2 Cape Mount
3 Grand Bassa
4 Grand Gedeh
5 Lofa
6 Maryland
7 Montserrado
8 Nimba
9 Sinoe

CÔTE D'IVOIRE
IVORY COAST
DÉPARTEMENTS
1 Abengourou
2 Abidjan
3 Aboisso
4 Adzopé
5 Agboville
6 Biankouma
7 Bondoukou
8 Bongouanou
9 Bouaflé
10 Bouaké
11 Bouna
12 Boundiali
13 Dabakala
14 Daloa
15 Danané
16 Dimbokro
17 Divo
18 Ferkessédougou
19 Gagnoa
20 Guiglo
21 Issia
22 Katiola
23 Korhogo
24 Lakota
25 Man
26 Mankono
27 Odienné
28 Oumé
29 Sassandra
30 Séguéla
31 Soubré
32 Tengréla
33 Touba
34 Zuénoula

BURKINA FASO
DÉPARTEMENTS
1 Centre
2 Centre-Est
3 Centre-Nord
4 Centre-Ouest
5 Est
6 Hauts-Bassins
7 Komoé
8 Nord
9 Sahel
10 Sud-Ouest
11 Volta Noire

TOGO
RÉGIONS
1 Centre
2 Kara
3 Maritime
4 Plateaux
5 Savanes

BÉNIN
PROVINCES
1 Atakora
2 Atlantique
3 Borgou
4 Mono
5 Ouémé
6 Zou

M / Ft
3000 / 9843
2000 / 6562
1000 / 3281
500 / 1640
200 / 656
100 / +328
0
−100 / −328
200 / 656
1000 / 3281
2000 / 6562
4000 / 13123
6000 / 19685

Ⓐ Federal Capital Territory
Ⓑ The political subdivisions shown for Guinea represent statistical areas and are not recognized for administrative purposes.

Scale 1:9,000,000   Lambert Azimuthal Equal Area Projection
0   200   400   600 km
0   200 miles

Longitude West 5 of Greenwich

A-589495-780-1 -1 -1 -2

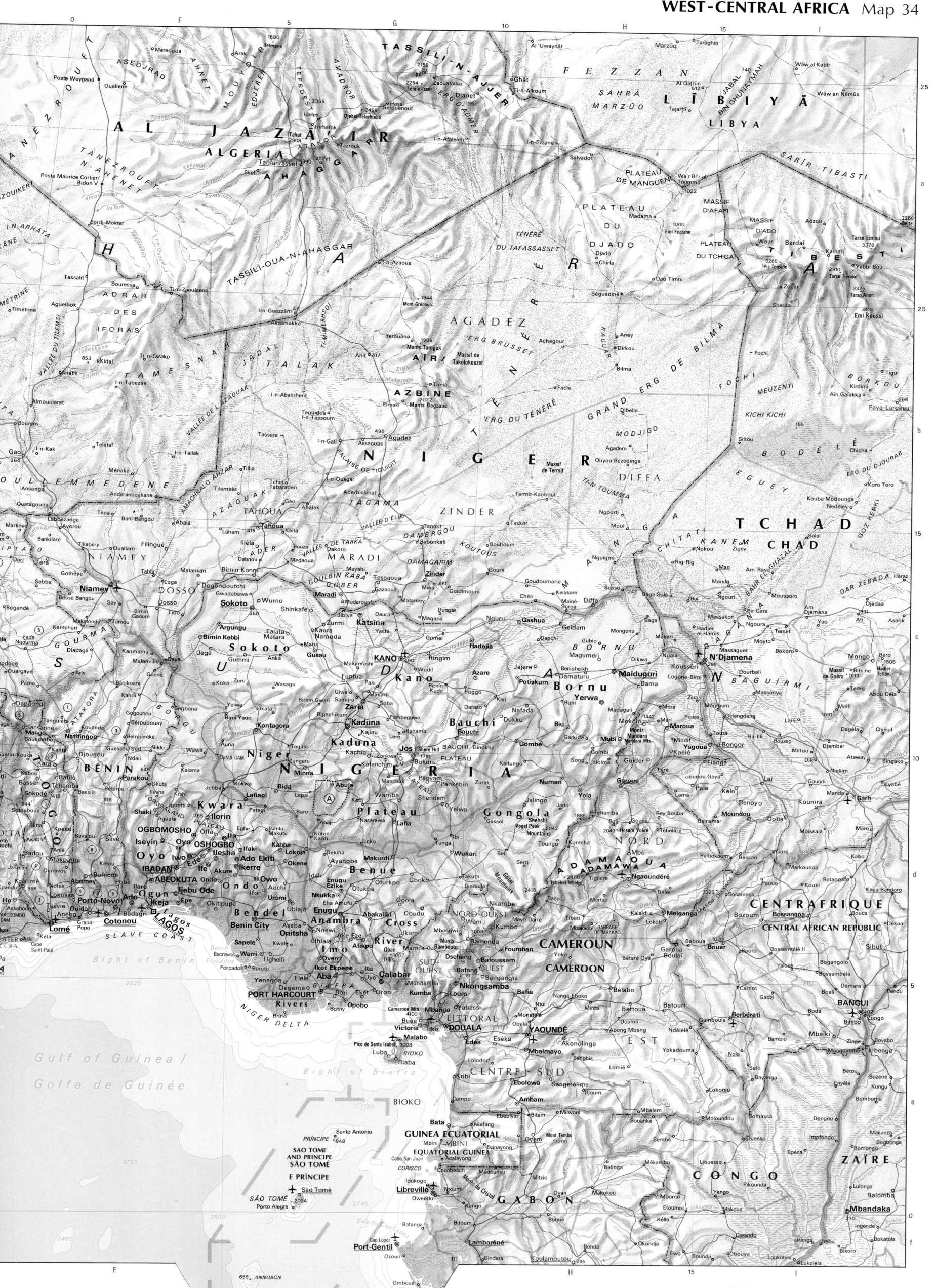

Map 35 **EAST-CENTRAL AFRICA**

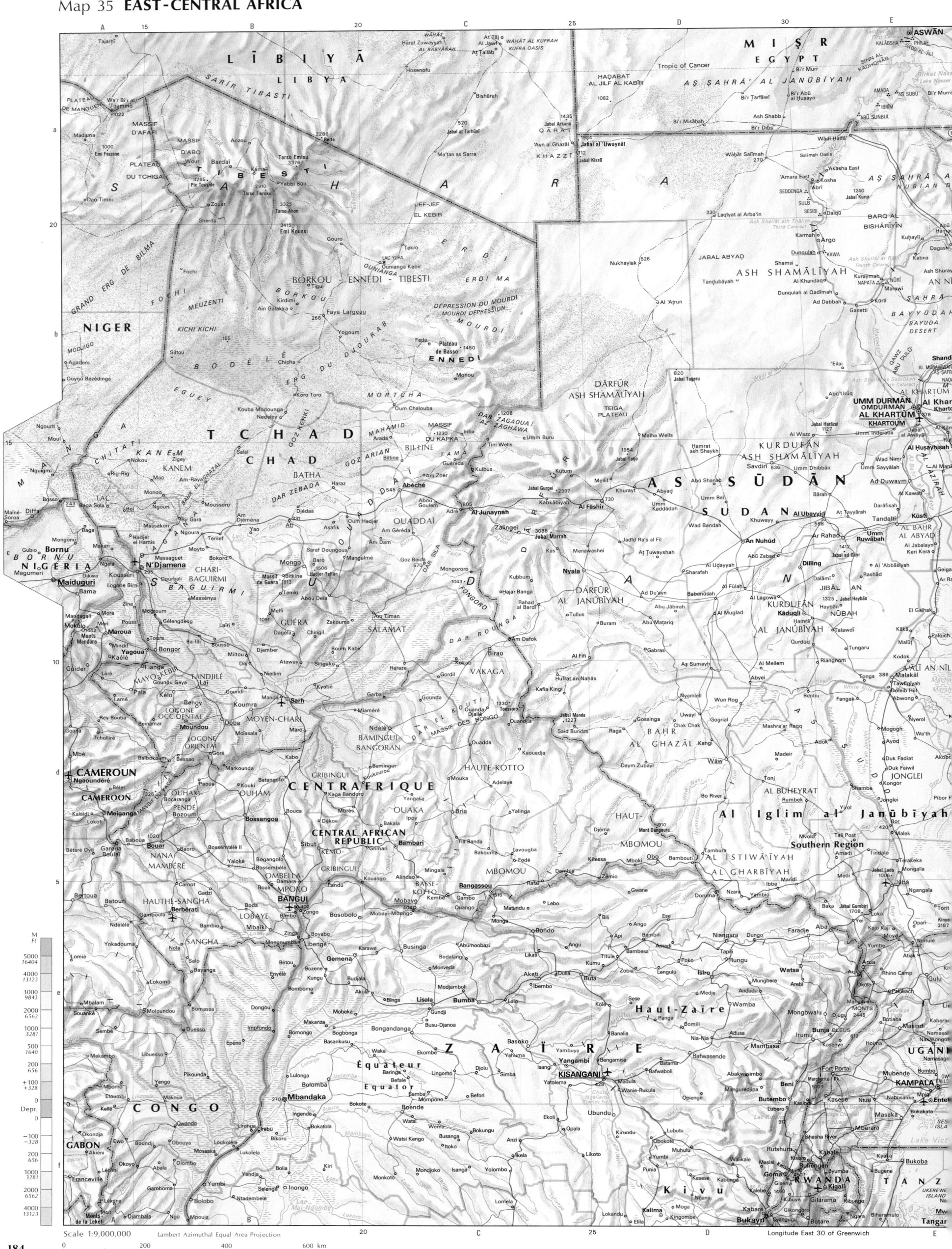

Scale 1:9,000,000

Lambert Azimuthal Equal Area Projection

Longitude East 30 of Greenwich

Ⓐ Area administered by Sudan
Ⓑ Area administered by Egypt

Map 36 **EQUATORIAL AFRICA**

Scale 1:9,000,000   Lambert Azimuthal Equal Area Projection

0   200   400   600 km

0   200 miles

Map 37 **SOUTHERN AFRICA**

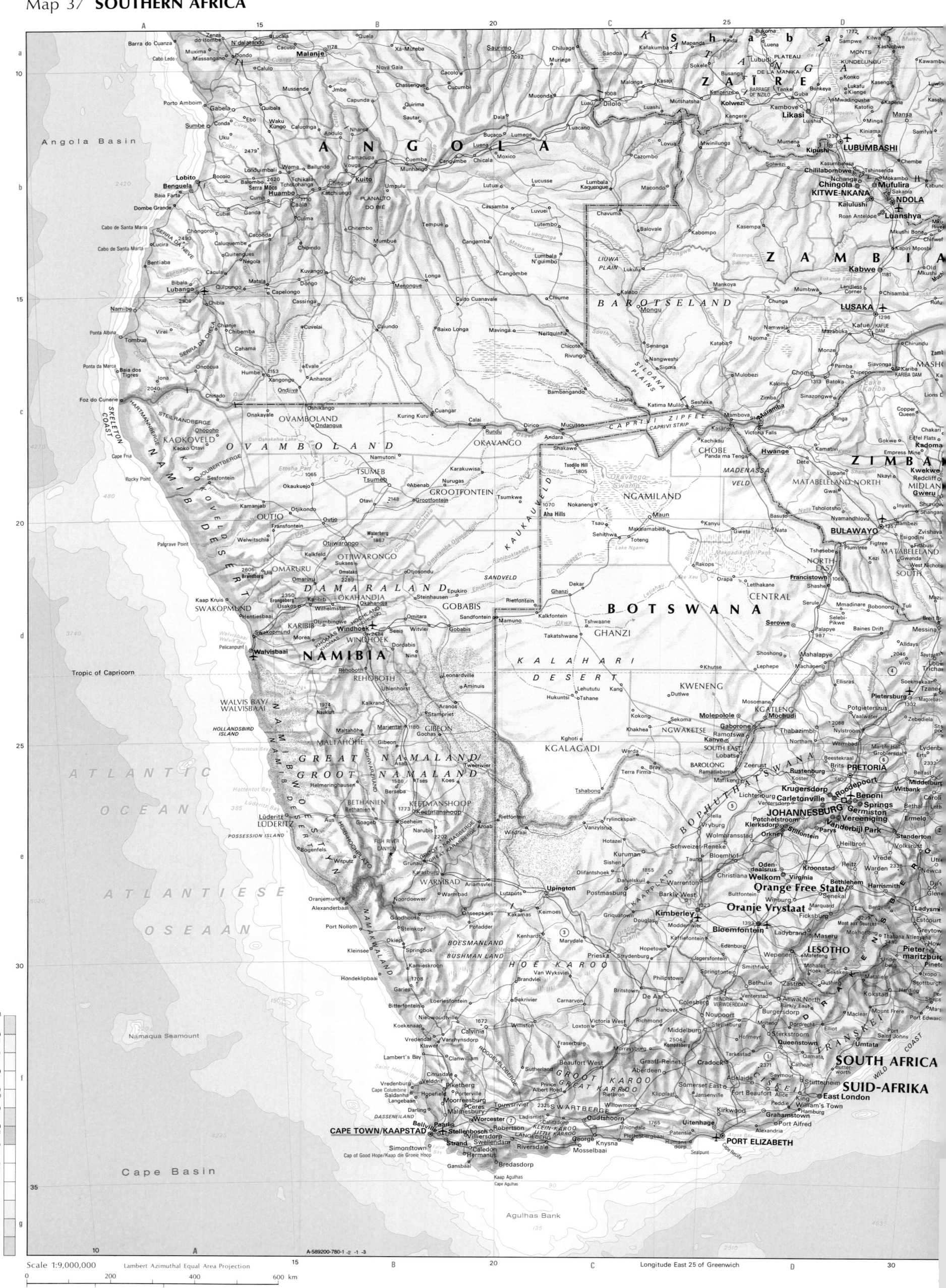

Scale 1:9,000,000   Lambert Azimuthal Equal Area Projection   Longitude East 25 of Greenwich

A-589200-780-1 -2 -1 -3

SEYCHELLES

ALDABRA ISLANDS
WEST ISLAND   MIDDLE ISLAND
SOUTH ISLAND   ALDABRA
ASSUMPTION   GROUP
ISLAND
COSMOLEDO
GROUP
ASTOVE
ISLAND

ARCHIPEL DES COMORES / COMORO ISLANDS

Mitsamiouli
NJAZIDJA   Moroni
RÉCIF VAILHEU   Foumbouni
MWALI   Mutsamudu
Fomboni   NZWALI
COMORES /   MAYOTTE
COMOROS   MAHORÉ
Mayotte
(France)

ILES GLORIEUSES
(Reunion)

BANC DU BISSON

BANC DU GEYSER

Cap d'Ambre

ANTSIRANANA

Montagne d'Ambre
Anivorano Nord
Ambilobe   Vohémar
NOSY LAVA
NOSY MITSIO   Sosumav
NOSY-BE
Nosy-Be   Ambanja   ANTSIRANANA
MASSIF DU
ILES RADAMA   TSARATANANA
Maromandia   Sambava
NOSY LAVA   Analalava   Antsohihy   Andapa   Antalaha

MADAGASIKARA

MADAGASCAR

SOUTH AFRICA
SUID-AFRIKA
MAGISTERIAL
DISTRICTS
1 Eastern Cape
2 Eastern Transvaal
3 Northern Cape
4 Northern Transvaal
5 North West
6 Pretoria-
  Witwatersrand-
  Vereeniging
7 Western Cape

OCÉANO ÍNDICO / OCÉAN INDIEN

INDIAN OCEAN / INDIESE OSEAAN

Natal Basin

Mozambique Plateau

Madagascar Plateau

SEYCHELLES ISLANDS

BIRD ISLAND   DENIS ISLAND

PRASLIN ISLAND
SILHOUETTE ISLAND   LA DIGUE ISLAND
916   Victoria
MAHÉ ISLAND

AFRICAN ISLANDS
REMIRE REEF
BENJAMEN   D'ARROS ISLAND
ISLAND   BOUQUET ISLAND
POIVRE ISLANDS   ILE DES ROCHES
ETOILE CAY   PLATTE ISLAND
AMIRANTE ISLANDS
BOUDEUSE CAY   MARIE LOUISE
ILE DES NOEUF   ISLAND
ALPHONSE ISLAND
BIJOUTIER ISLAND   COETIVY ISLAND
SAINT FRANÇOIS
ISLAND

INDIAN OCEAN

Amirante Basin

MAURITIUS
Port-Louis   MAURITIUS
Beau-Bassin   Flacq
Curepipe
Mahébourg
Saint-Denis
Saint-Paul
Saint-Benoit
Saint-Pierre   Piton des Neiges
RÉUNION   Saint-Joseph
Réunion
(France)

ILES MASCAREIGNES/
MASCARENE ISLANDS

ALDABRA ISLANDS
WEST ISLAND   WIZARD REEF
MIDDLE ISLAND
SOUTH ISLAND
ALDABRA
ASSUMPTION   GROUP
ISLAND
COSMOLEDO
GROUP
ASTOVE
ISLAND

SEYCHELLES

SAINT PIERRE
ISLAND
PROVIDENCE
ISLAND
CERF ISLAND
FARQUHAR
GROUP   NORTH ISLAND
GOELETTE ISLAND   SOUTH ISLAND

AGALEGA ISLANDS
(Mauritius)

Amirante Trench

Longitude East 50 of Greenwich

Map 38 **NORTH AMERICA, PHYSICAL**

© ISTITUTO GEOGRAFICO DE AGOSTINI S. p. A. - NOVARA

Scale 1:30,000,000

Lambert Azimuthal Equal Area Projection

A-530000-780-1-1-1-8

Map 39 **NORTH AMERICA, POLITICAL**

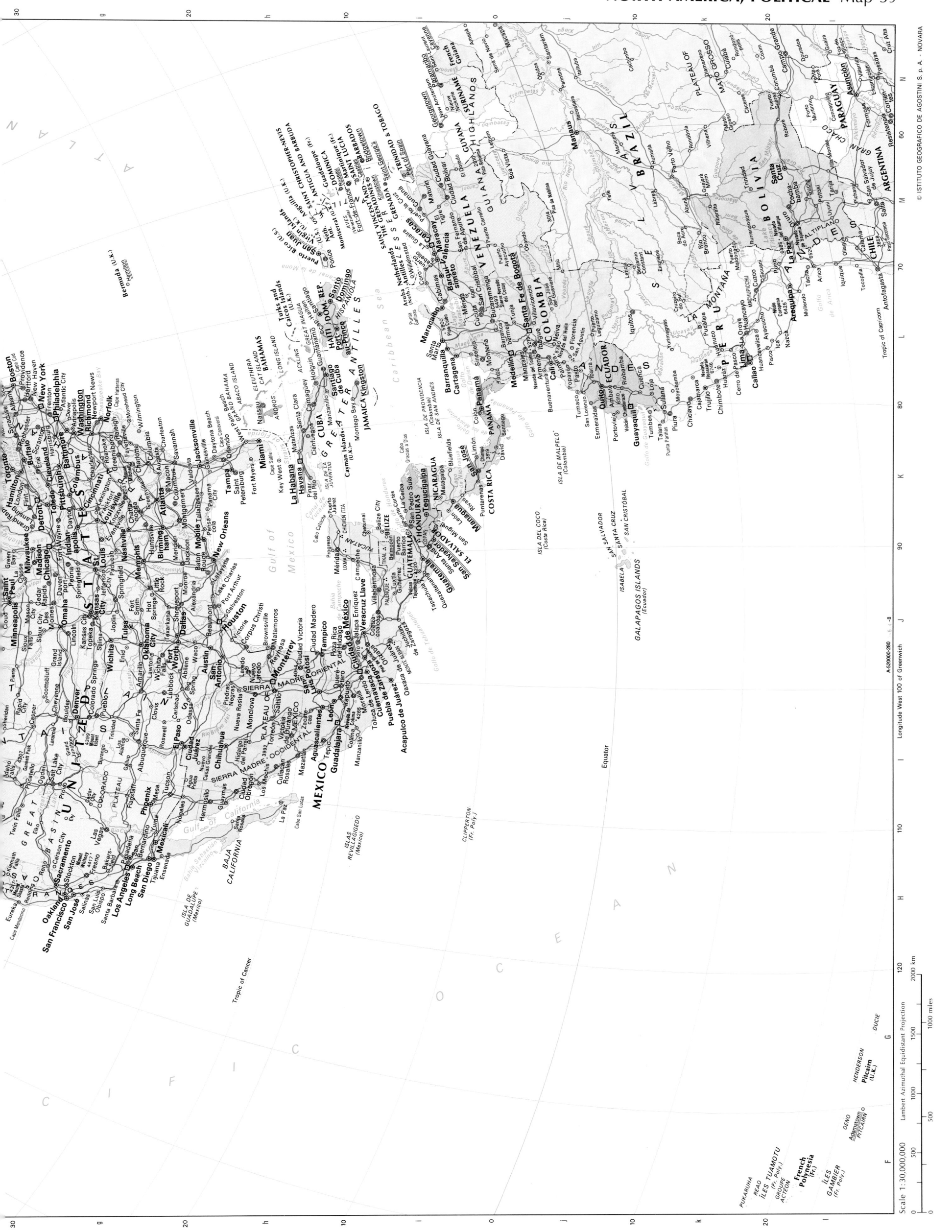

Scale 1:30,000,000   Lambert Azimuthal Equidistant Projection

Longitude West 100 of Greenwich

A-500000-280   -5.1-8

Map 40 **ALASKA**

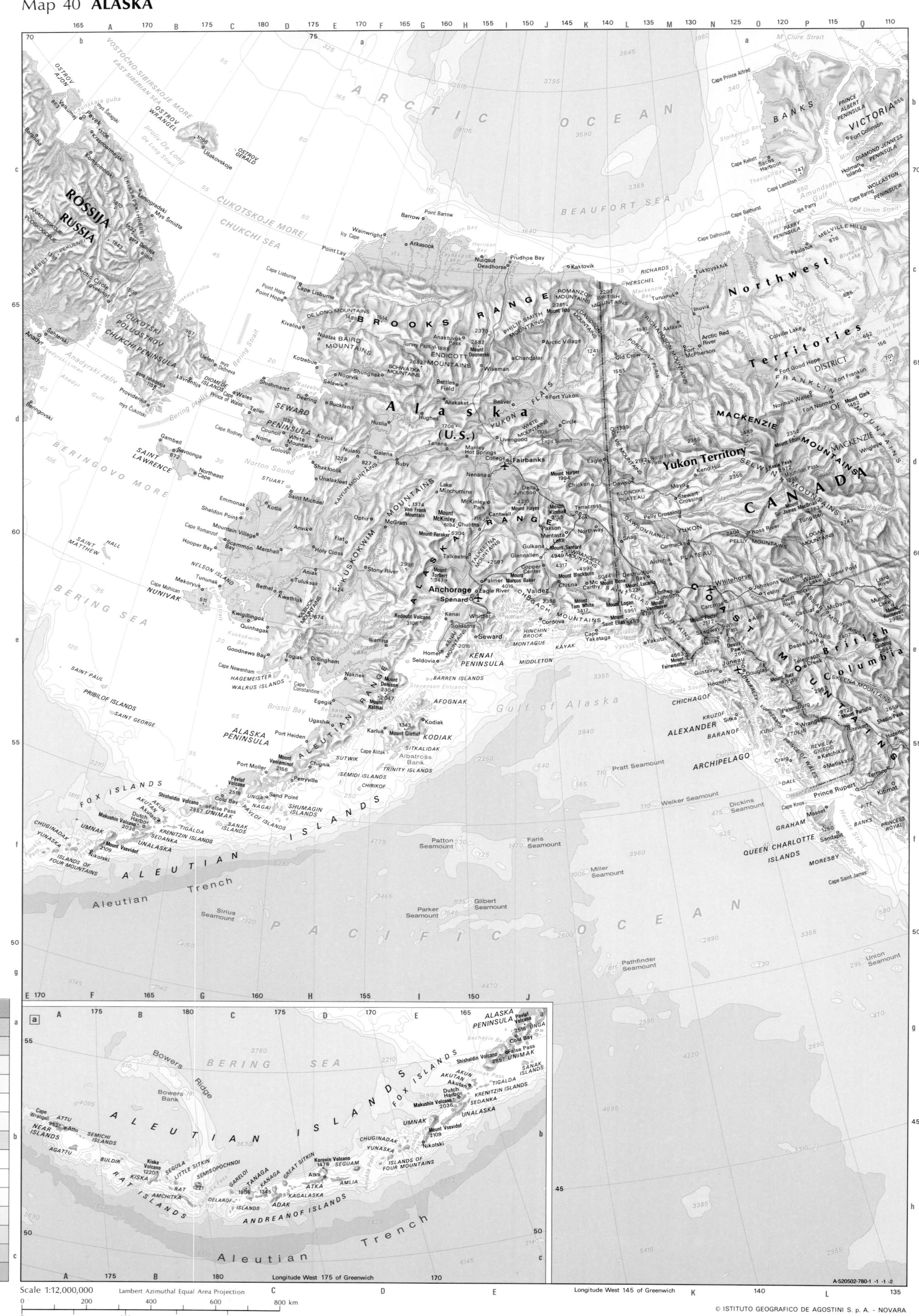

ARCTIC OCEAN

BEAUFORT SEA

CHUKCHI SEA

ROSSIJA
RUSSIA

CUKOTSKI
POLUOSTROV
CHUKCHI PENINSULA

BROOKS RANGE

DE LONG MOUNTAINS

ENDICOTT MOUNTAINS

SCHWATKA MOUNTAINS

Northwest Territories

MACKENZIE MOUNTAINS

CANADA

Yukon Territory

BERINGOVO MORE

SAINT LAWRENCE

SEWARD PENINSULA

Alaska (U.S.)

YUKON FLATS

Fairbanks

Anchorage

BERING SEA

NUNIVAK

NELSON ISLAND

KUSKOKWIM MOUNTAINS

ALASKA RANGE

Mount McKinley 6194

Mount Foraker 5304

TALKEETNA MOUNTAINS

WRANGELL MOUNTAINS

CHUGACH MOUNTAINS

Valdez

KENAI PENINSULA

Seward

British Columbia

COAST MOUNTAINS

Juneau

ALEXANDER ARCHIPELAGO

Sitka

ALASKA PENINSULA

KODIAK

Gulf of Alaska

ALEUTIAN RANGE

FOX ISLANDS

UNIMAK

UNALASKA

ALEUTIAN ISLANDS

Aleutian Trench

PACIFIC OCEAN

Patton Seamount

Parker Seamount

Sirius Seamount

Faris Seamount

Gilbert Seamount

Welker Seamount

Dickins Seamount

Pratt Seamount

QUEEN CHARLOTTE ISLANDS

Pathfinder Seamount

Union Seamount

a

BERING SEA

Bowers Ridge

Bowers Bank

ALEUTIAN ISLANDS

NEAR ISLANDS

RAT ISLANDS

ANDREANOF ISLANDS

Aleutian Trench

ALASKA PENINSULA

FOX ISLANDS

UNIMAK

UNALASKA

ISLANDS OF FOUR MOUNTAINS

M
ft
5000 16404
4000 13123
3000 9843
2000 6562
1000 3281
500 1640
200 656
0
100 328
200 656
1000 3281
2000 6562
4000 13123
6000 19685

Scale 1:12,000,000
Lambert Azimuthal Equal Area Projection

0   200   400   600   800 km
0   200   400 miles

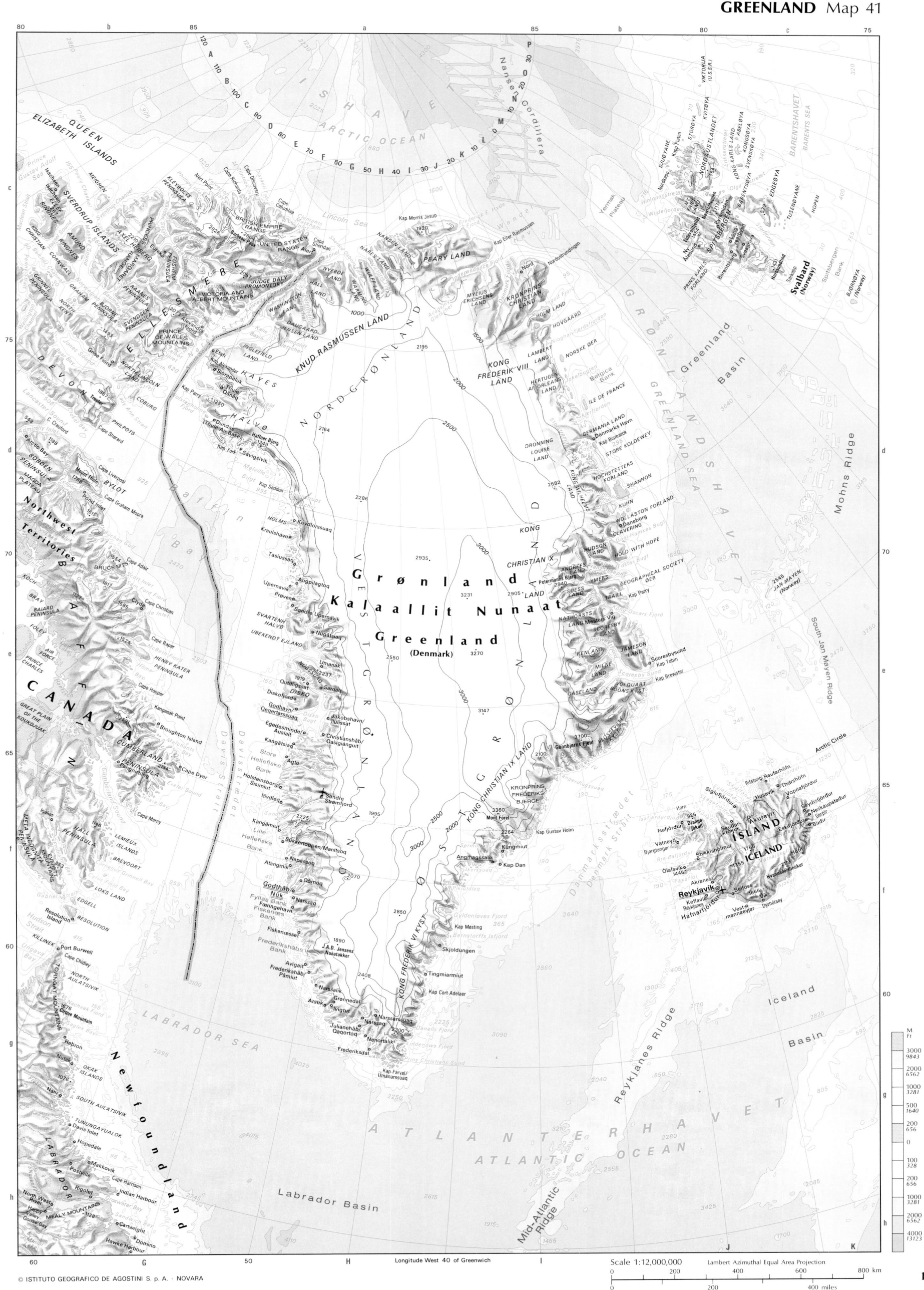

Scale 1:12,000,000   Lambert Azimuthal Equal Area Projection

Longitude West 40 of Greenwich

Map 42 **CANADA**

Scale 1:12,000,000   Lambert Azimuthal Equal Area Projection

Longitude West 100 of Greenwich

M	Ft
5000	16404
4000	13123
3000	9843
2000	6562
1000	3281
500	1640
200	656
0	0
100	328
200	656
1000	3281
2000	6562
4000	13123

0   200   400   600   800 km

0   200   400 miles

Map 43 **UNITED STATES**

British Columbia
VANCOUVER ISLAND
VANCOUVER
Washington
SEATTLE
Tacoma
Olympia
Spokane
PORTLAND
Oregon
Alberta
CALGARY
Medicine Hat
Lethbridge
Saskatchewan
Saskatoon
Regina
Moose Jaw
Manitoba
WINNIPEG
Brandon
Montana
Great Falls
Helena
Butte
Billings
North Dakota
Bismarck
Minot
Grand Forks
Fargo
Idaho
Boise
Idaho Falls
Twin Falls
Wyoming
Casper
Cheyenne
South Dakota
Rapid City
Pierre
Sioux Falls
ROCKY MOUNTAINS
Nevada
Reno
Carson City
Utah
Salt Lake City
Provo
Ogden
California
SAN FRANCISCO
OAKLAND
SACRAMENTO
SAN JOSE
Fresno
Bakersfield
LOS ANGELES
Long Beach
San Diego
Tijuana
MEXICALI
GREAT BASIN
Las Vegas
Henderson
Arizona
PHOENIX
Mesa
Tucson
Colorado
DENVER
Colorado Springs
Pueblo
Nebraska
OMAHA
Lincoln
Kansas
Wichita
Topeka
Oklahoma
OKLAHOMA CITY
Tulsa
New Mexico
Albuquerque
Santa Fe
El Paso
CIUDAD JUÁREZ
Texas
FORT WORTH
DALLAS
AUSTIN
SAN ANTONIO
HOUSTON
Corpus Christi
Laredo
CHIHUAHUA
Hermosillo
Ciudad Obregón
Culiacán
Durango
Mazatlán
MONTERREY
Saltillo
Torreón
Matamoros
Reynosa
Ciudad Victoria
TAMPICO
SIERRA MADRE OCCIDENTAL
SIERRA MADRE ORIENTAL
SAN LUIS POTOSÍ
GUADALAJARA
León
Aguascalientes
Zacatecas
Querétaro
Morelia
CIUDAD DE MÉXICO
MEXICO CITY
PUEBLA DE ZARAGOZA
VERACRUZ LLAVE
Orizaba

PACIFIC OCEAN
OCÉANO PACÍFICO
Tropic of Cancer
Clarion Fracture Zone

BAJA CALIFORNIA
La Paz
Cabo San Lucas

Scale 1:12,000,000
Lambert Azimuthal Equidistant Projection
Longitude West 100 of Greenwich

M / Ft	
5000 / 16404	
4000 / 13123	
3000 / 9843	
2000 / 6562	
1000 / 3281	
500 / 1640	
200 / +656	
0	
Depr.	
−100 / −328	
200 / 656	
1000 / 3281	
2000 / 6562	
4000 / 13123	
6000 / 19685	
8000 / 26247	

0 200 400 600 800 km
0 200 400 miles

Map 44

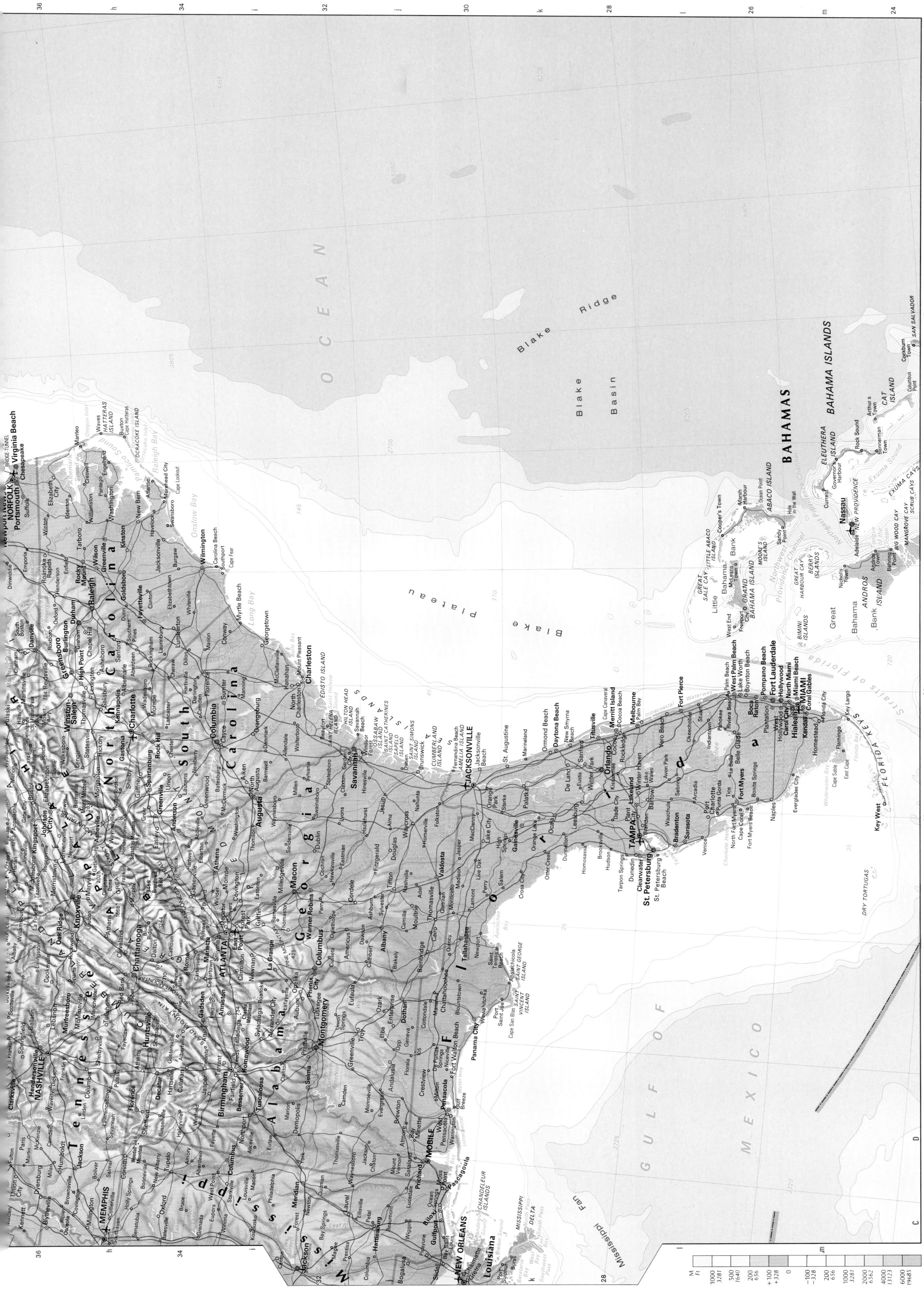

OCEAN

Blake Ridge

Blake Basin

Blake Plateau

BAHAMAS

BAHAMA ISLANDS

Bahama Islands

Longitude West 78° of Greenwich

ELEUTHERA

NEW PROVIDENCE

Nassau

ANDROS ISLAND

ABACO ISLAND

GRAND BAHAMA ISLAND

GREAT ABACO

LITTLE ABACO

Little Bahama Bank

Great Bahama Bank

BIMINI ISLANDS

BERRY ISLANDS

CAT ISLAND

SAN SALVADOR

Columbus Point

Northwest Providence Channel

Straits of Florida

Virginia Beach
NORFOLK
Portsmouth
Chesapeake
Suffolk

HATTERAS ISLAND
Cape Hatteras
OCRACOKE ISLAND
Waves
Buxton
Manteo
Oregon Inlet

Raleigh Bay
Cape Lookout
Morehead City
New Bern
Pamlico Sound
Albemarle Sound
Elizabeth City
Edenton
Williamston

Onslow Bay

Wilmington
Jacksonville
Burgaw
Southport
Cape Fear

North Carolina
Raleigh
Durham
Chapel Hill
Greensboro
Winston Salem
High Point
Burlington
Rocky Mount
Wilson
Goldsboro
Greenville
Kinston
Fayetteville
Lumberton

South Carolina
Columbia
Charleston
North Charleston
Mount Pleasant
Florence
Sumter
Orangeburg
Myrtle Beach
Georgetown
Long Bay

EDISTO ISLAND
HILTON HEAD ISLAND
Beaufort

Georgia
Savannah
Augusta
Macon
Columbus
Albany
Valdosta
Warner Robins
Dublin
Americus
Athens

OSSABAW ISLAND
SAINT CATHERINES ISLAND
SAPELO ISLAND
CUMBERLAND ISLAND
SAINT SIMONS ISLAND
AMELIA ISLAND
Brunswick
Waycross

Florida
JACKSONVILLE
Jacksonville Beach
St. Augustine
Ormond Beach
Daytona Beach
New Smyrna Beach
Titusville
Cape Canaveral
Merritt Island
Cocoa Beach
Melbourne
Palm Bay
Vero Beach
Fort Pierce
West Palm Beach
Palm Beach
Boca Raton
Pompano Beach
Fort Lauderdale
Hollywood
North Miami
MIAMI
Miami Beach
Hialeah
Coral Gables
Kendall
Homestead
Key Largo
Florida Keys
Key West
DRY TORTUGAS

ORLANDO
Sanford
Winter Park
Kissimmee
Lakeland
Winter Haven
Plant City
TAMPA
St. Petersburg
Clearwater
Bradenton
Sarasota
Venice
Fort Myers
Cape Coral
Naples
Port Charlotte
Punta Gorda
Arcadia
Sebring
Belle Glade
Lake Okeechobee
Everglades City
Cape Sable
Florida Bay

Gainesville
Ocala
Leesburg
Lake City
Live Oak
Tallahassee
Panama City
Fort Walton Beach
Pensacola
Apalachicola
SAINT GEORGE ISLAND
SAINT VINCENT ISLAND
Cape San Blas

GULF OF MEXICO

Alabama
Birmingham
Montgomery
Mobile
Prichard
Tuscaloosa
Bessemer
Gadsden
Huntsville
Decatur
Florence
Anniston
Selma
Dothan
Enterprise
Troy
Phenix City
Tuskegee
Opelika
Auburn

Tennessee
NASHVILLE
MEMPHIS
Chattanooga
Knoxville
Johnson City
Kingsport
Murfreesboro
Jackson
Columbia
Cleveland

Mississippi
Jackson
Hattiesburg
Biloxi
Gulfport
Meridian
Laurel
Tupelo
Columbus
Greenville
Pascagoula

Louisiana
NEW ORLEANS
Bogalusa
Slidell

CHANDELEUR ISLANDS
MISSISSIPPI DELTA
MISSISSIPPI FAN

Great Smoky Mts.
Appalachian
Blue Ridge
Piedmont

Scale 1:6,000,000
Delisle Conic Equidistant Projection

0   100   200   300   400 km
0   100   200 miles

© ISTITUTO GEOGRAFICO DE AGOSTINI S. p. A. - NOVARA

M Ft
1000 3281
500 1640
200 656
+100 +328
0
−100 −328
200 656
1000 3281
2000 6562
4000 13123
6000 19685

Map 45

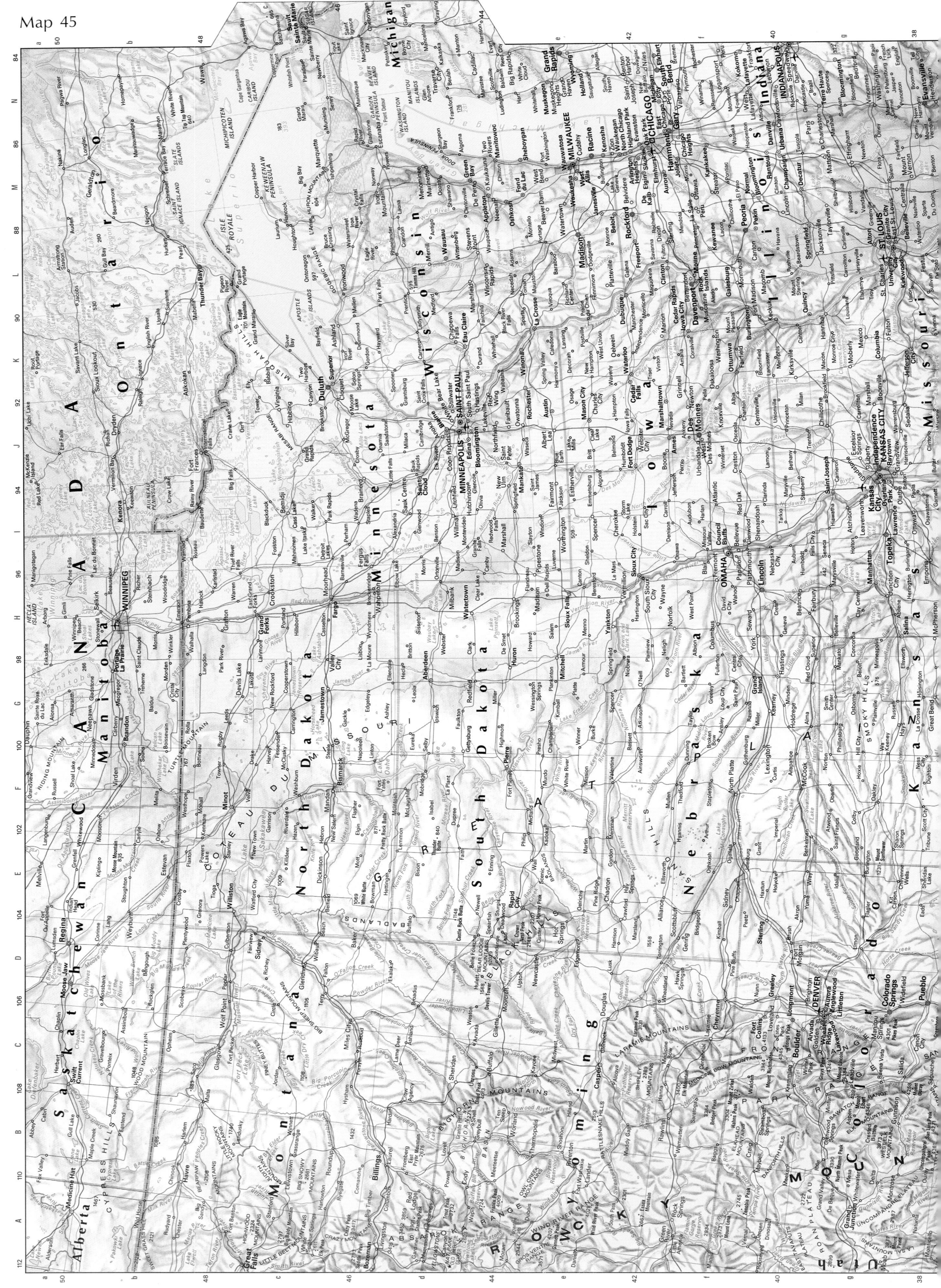

© ISTITUTO GEOGRAFICO DE AGOSTINI S. p. A. - NOVARA

Kentucky · Tennessee · Mississippi · Alabama · Arkansas · Louisiana · Oklahoma · Texas · New Mexico

MEXICO · Sonora · Chihuahua · Coahuila · Nuevo León · Tamaulipas · Durango · Sinaloa

SIERRA MADRE ORIENTAL · SIERRA MADRE OCCIDENTAL

GULF OF MEXICO · MISSISSIPPI DELTA · CHANDELEUR ISLANDS

NASHVILLE · MEMPHIS · Little Rock · North Little Rock · Hot Springs National Park · Fort Smith · Springfield · TULSA · Tulsa · WICHITA · Enid · OKLAHOMA CITY · Stillwater · Norman · Lawton · Wichita Falls · Amarillo · Lubbock · Midland · Odessa · El Paso · CIUDAD JUAREZ · Las Cruces · Albuquerque · Santa Fe · Roswell · Carlsbad · Abilene · San Angelo · FORT WORTH · DALLAS · Denton · Irving · Garland · Mesquite · Waco · Temple · Killeen · AUSTIN · SAN ANTONIO · HOUSTON · Galveston · Beaumont · Port Arthur · Corpus Christi · Laredo · Nuevo Laredo · Brownsville · Matamoros · McAllen · Reynosa · Eagle Pass · Piedras Negras · MONTERREY · Saltillo · Torreón · Gómez Palacio · Shreveport · Alexandria · Lake Charles · Baton Rouge · NEW ORLEANS · Metairie · Gulfport · Biloxi · MOBILE · Jackson · Vicksburg · Natchez · Hattiesburg · Meridian · Columbus · Tupelo

Longitude West 98 of Greenwich · Delisle Conic Equidistant Projection · Scale 1:6,000,000

400 km · 300 · 200 miles · 100

203

Map 46 **WESTERN UNITED STATES**

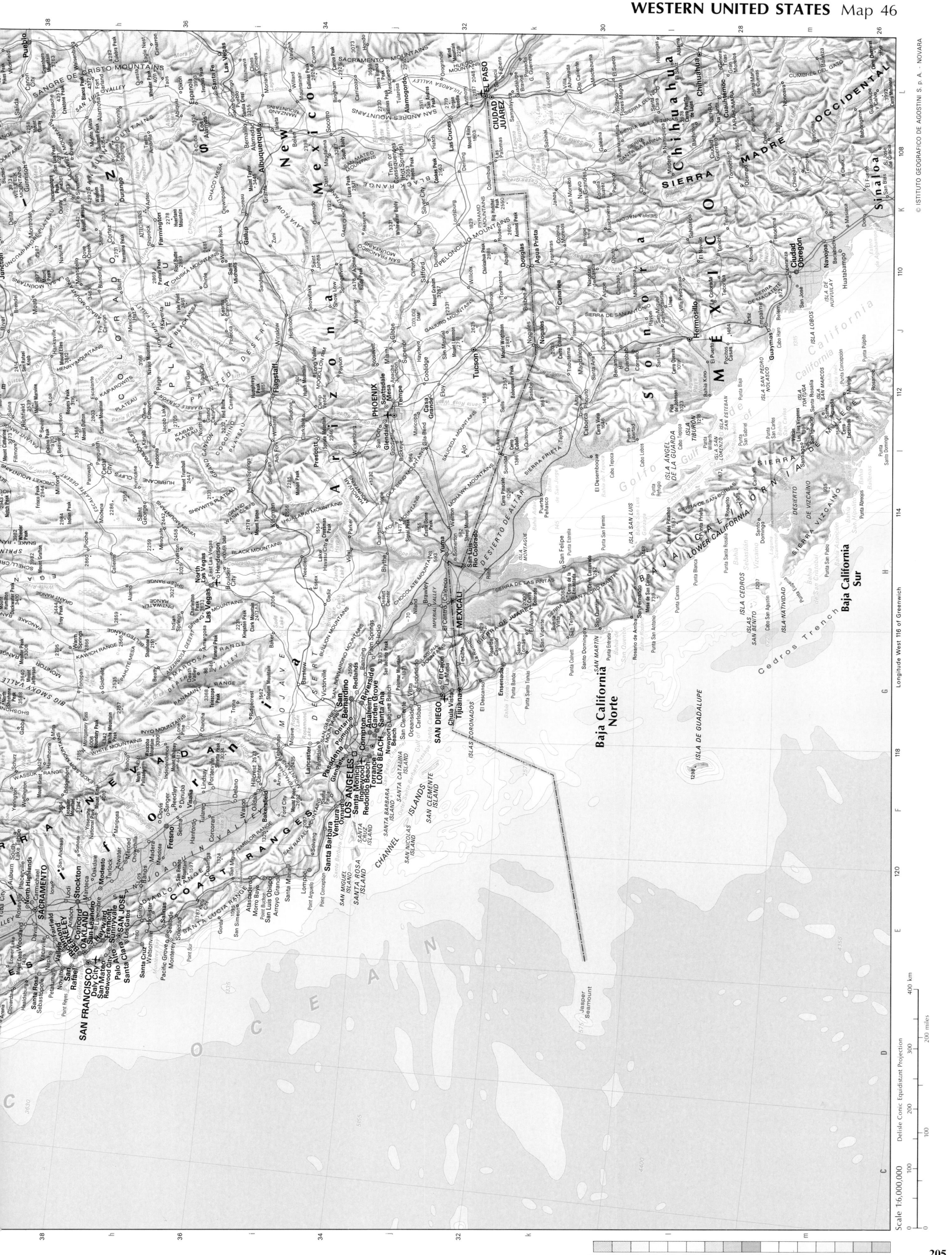

Scale 1:6,000,000

Delisle Conic Equidistant Projection

Longitude West 116 of Greenwich

Map 47 **MIDDLE AMERICA**

MÉXICO

ESTADOS

D.F. Distrito Federal
1 Aguascalientes
2 Baja California Norte
3 Baja California Sur
4 Campeche
5 Coahuila
6 Colima
7 Chiapas
8 Chihuahua
9 Durango
10 Guanajuato
11 Guerrero
12 Hidalgo
13 Jalisco
14 México
15 Michoacán
16 Morelos
17 Nayarit
18 Nuevo León
19 Oaxaca
20 Puebla
21 Querétaro
22 Quintana Roo
23 San Luis Potosí
24 Sinaloa
25 Sonora
26 Tabasco
27 Tamaulipas
28 Tlaxcala
29 Veracruz
30 Yucatán
31 Zacatecas

UNITED STATES

California · Arizona · New Mexico · Texas · Oklahoma · Kansas · Missouri · Arkansas · Louisiana · Mississippi · Tennessee

LOS ANGELES · San Diego · Tijuana · Mexicali · PHOENIX · Tucson · El Paso · CIUDAD JUÁREZ · Albuquerque · OKLAHOMA CITY · TULSA · FORT WORTH · DALLAS · AUSTIN · SAN ANTONIO · HOUSTON · Galveston · Corpus Christi · MEMPHIS · Little Rock · Shreveport · Baton Rouge · NEW ORLEANS · MOBILE · Jackson

BAJA CALIFORNIA · Ensenada · Hermosillo · Guaymas · Ciudad Obregón · CHIHUAHUA · Los Mochis · Guasave · La Paz · Culiacán Rosales · Mazatlán · Durango · Torreón · Gómez Palacio · Saltillo · MONTERREY · Matamoros · Reynosa · Nuevo Laredo · Monclova · Ciudad Victoria · Tepic · GUADALAJARA · León · Aguascalientes · SAN LUIS POTOSÍ · Querétaro · TAMPICO · Ciudad Madero · Puerto Vallarta · Morelia · CIUDAD DE MÉXICO / MEXICO CITY · Toluca de Lerdo · PUEBLA DE ZARAGOZA · Cuernavaca · VERACRUZ LLAVE · Orizaba · Jalapa Enríquez · Acapulco de Juárez · Chilpancingo de los Bravos · Oaxaca de Juárez · MÉRIDA · Campeche · Chetumal · Villahermosa · Coatzacoalcos · Minatitlán · Tuxtla Gutiérrez · San Cristóbal de las Casas · Tapachula · Quezaltenango

Gulf of Mexico / Golfo de México · Mexico Basin · Campeche Bank · PENÍNSULA DE YUCATÁN

OCÉANO PACÍFICO · PACIFIC OCEAN · Albatross Plateau · Guatemala Basin · Middle America Trench · Middle America Ridge · Cedros Trench · Rosa Seamount · Mathematicians Seamounts · ISLAS REVILLAGIGEDO (México) · ÎLE CLIPPERTON (Fr. Poly.) · ISLA DE GUADALUPE (México)

GUATEMALA · EL SALVADOR · SAN SALVADOR · Santa Ana · BELIZE · HONDURAS

M ft	
5000 / 16404	
4000 / 13123	
3000 / 9843	
2000 / 6562	
1000 / 3281	
500 / 1640	
+200 / +656	
0	
Depr.	
−100 / −328	
200 / 656	
1000 / 3281	
2000 / 6562	
4000 / 13123	
6000 / 19685	
8000 / 26247	

Scale 1:12,000,000
Lambert Azimuthal Equal Area Projection
0 200 400 600 800 km
0 200 400 miles

Longitude West 90 of Greenwich

A-530000-780-1 -1 -1 -3

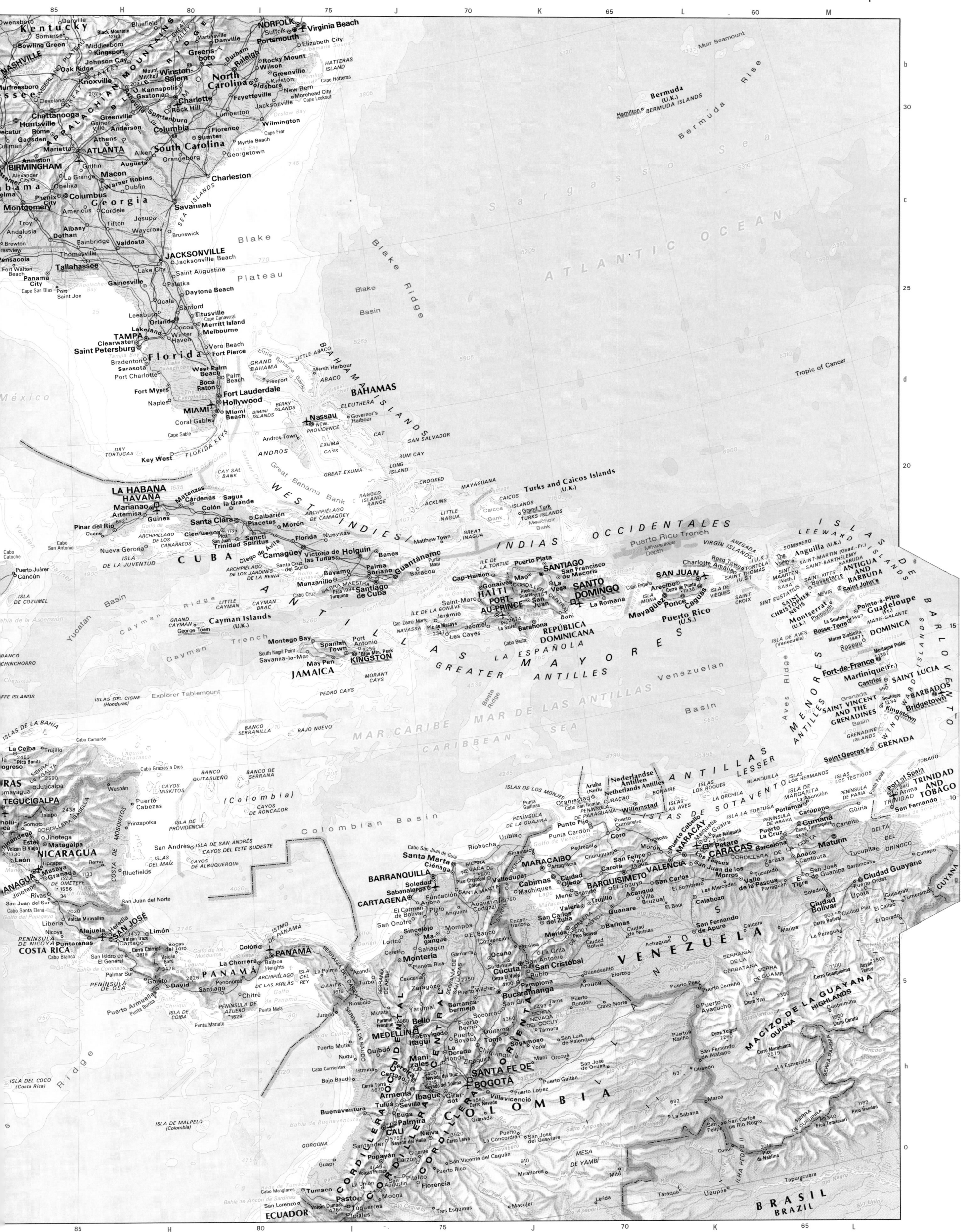

Scale 1:6,000,000   Delisle Conic Equidistant Projection

0   100   200   300   400 km

0   100   200 miles

208

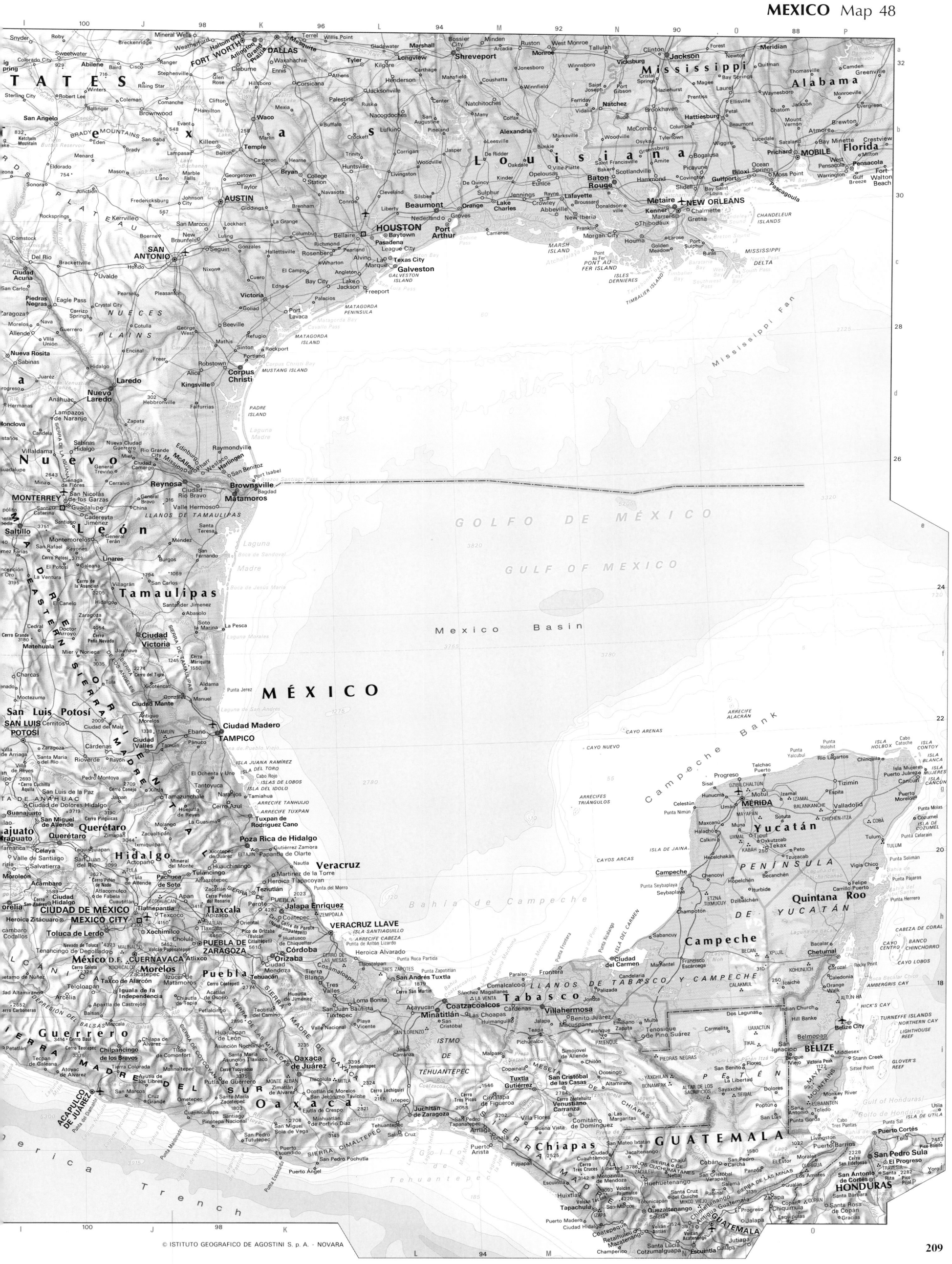

Map 49 CENTRAL AMERICA AND WESTERN CARIBBEAN

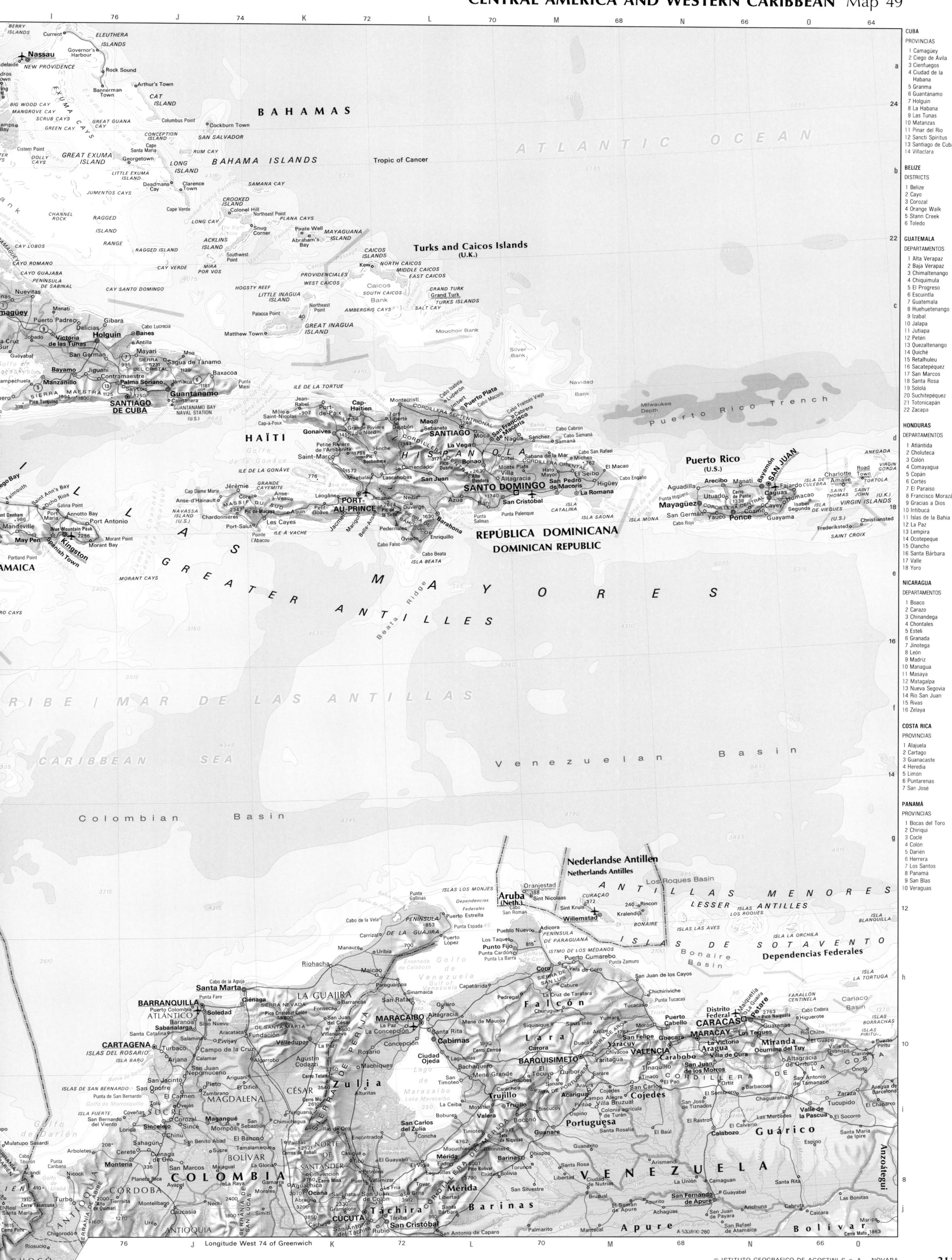

Map 50 **EASTERN CARIBBEAN**

Scale 1:6,000,000   Delisle Conic Equidistant Projection

0   100   200   300   400 km

0   100   200 miles

Longitude West of 64 of Greenwich

A-533900-280

© ISTITUTO GEOGRAFICO DE AGOSTINI S. p A. - NOVARA

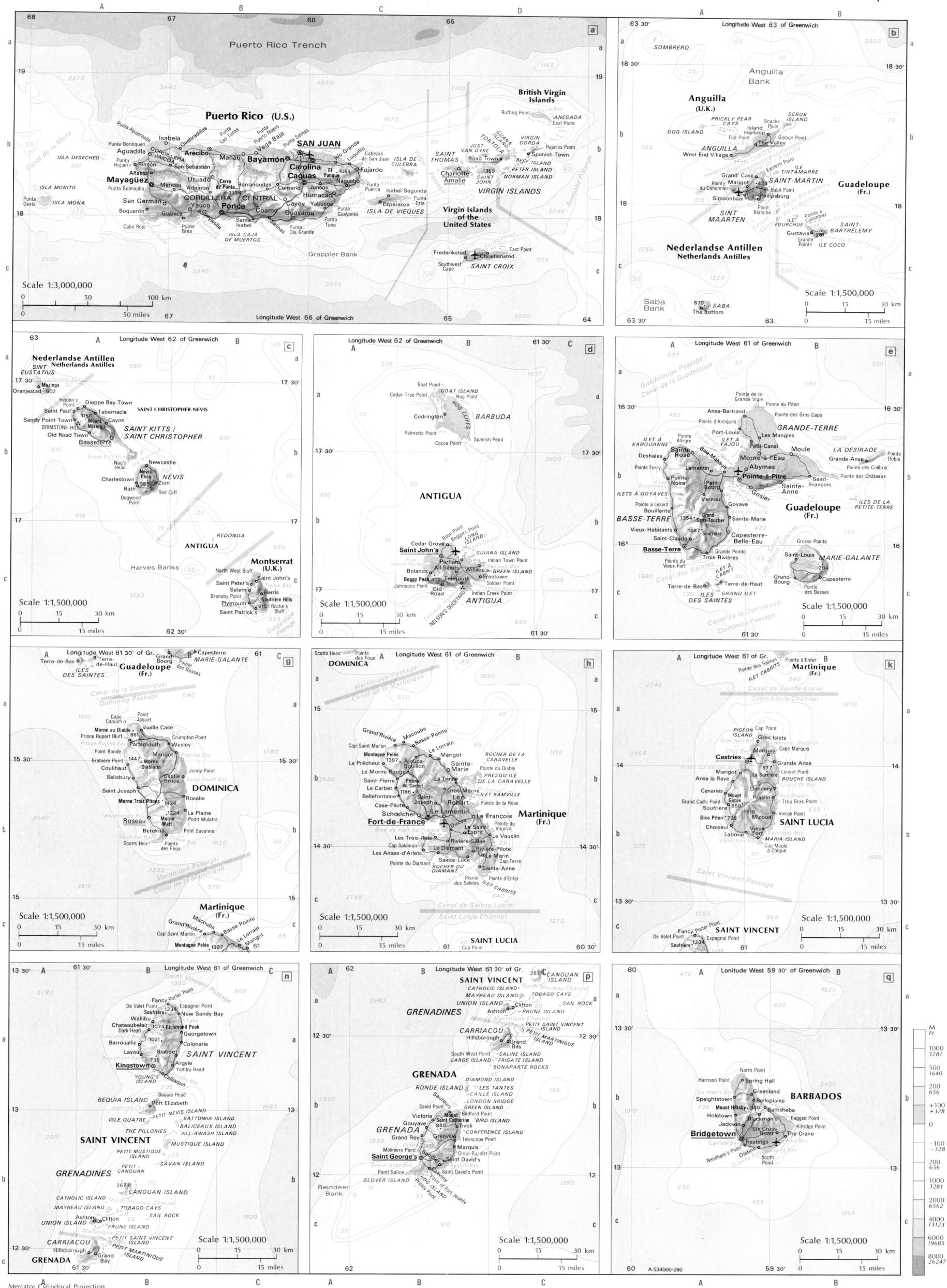

Map 52

SOUTH AMERICA, PHYSICAL

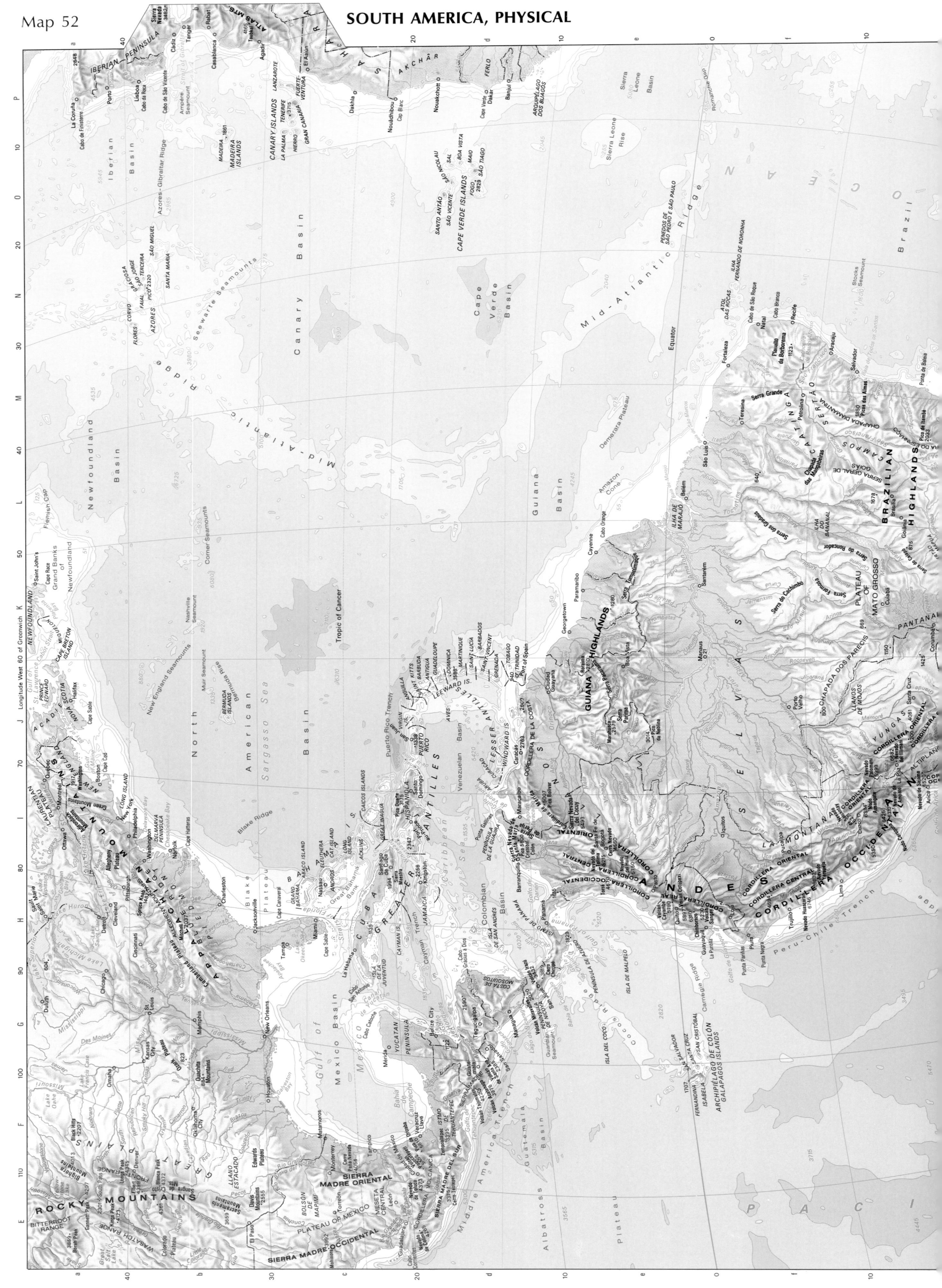

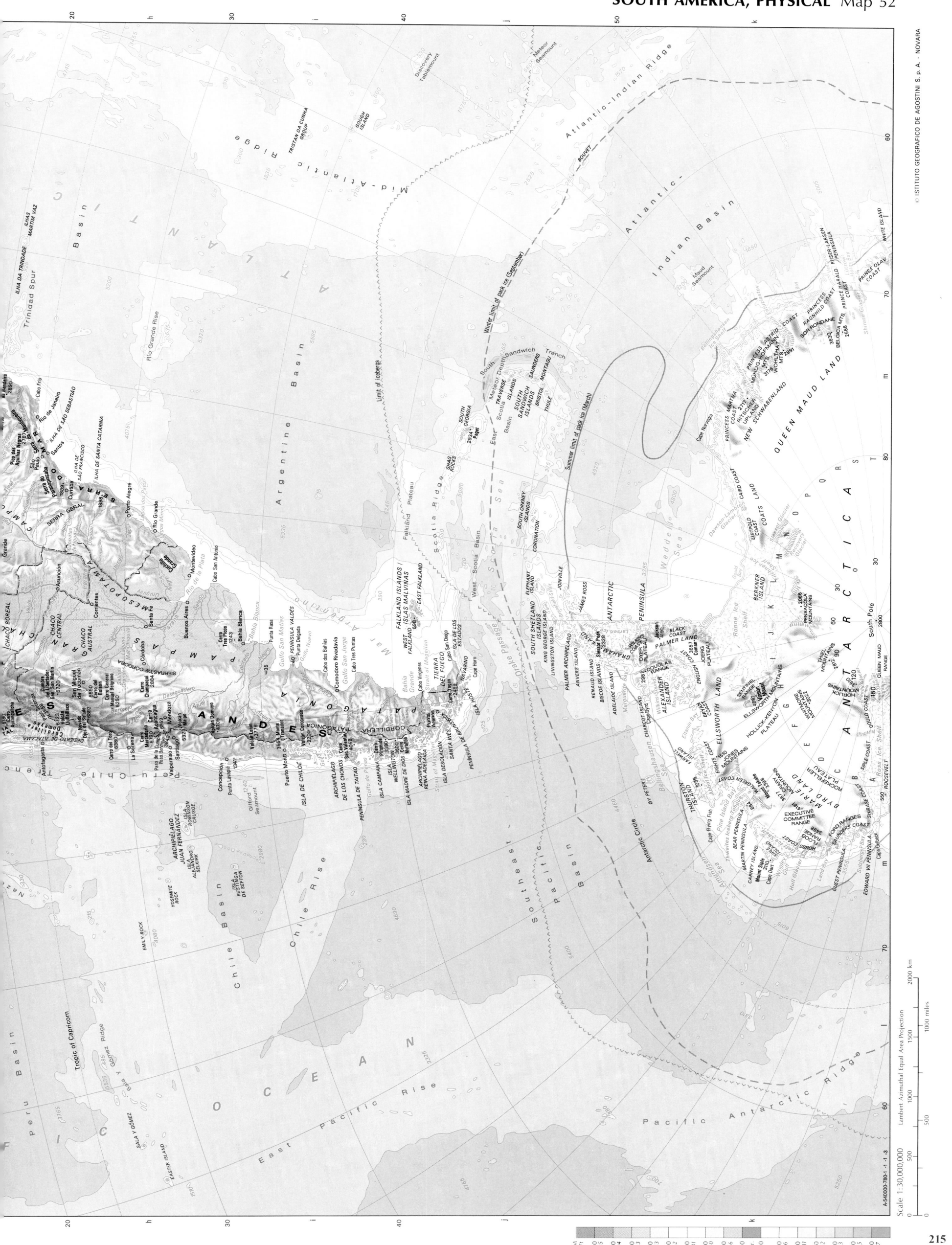

Scale 1:30,000,000

Lambert Azimuthal Equal Area Projection

A-540000-7801-1-1-3

Map 53

SOUTH AMERICA, POLITICAL

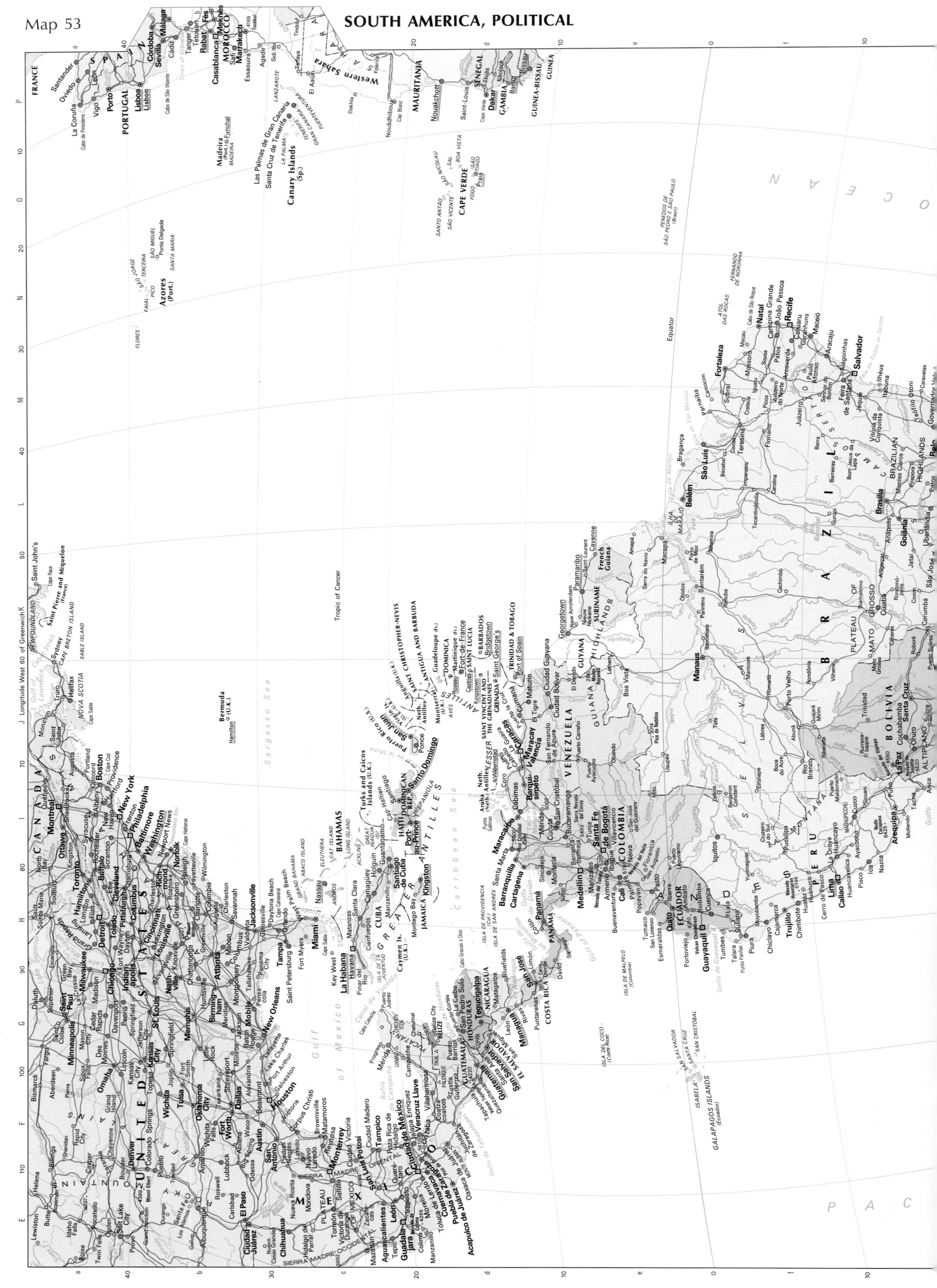

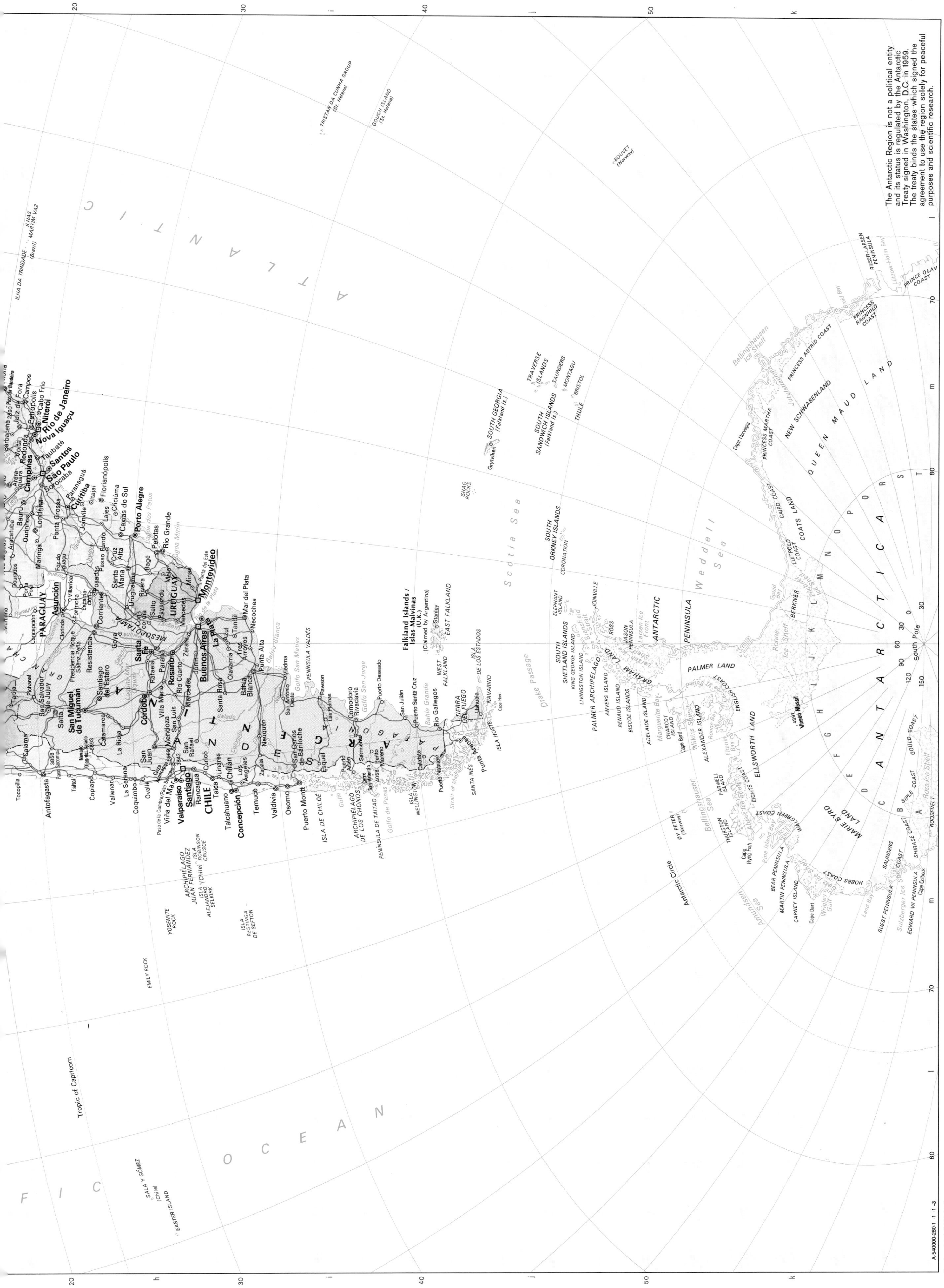

The Antarctic Region is not a political entity and its status is regulated by the Antarctic Treaty signed in Washington, D.C. in 1959. The treaty binds the states which signed the agreement to use the region solely for peaceful purposes and scientific research.

© ISTITUTO GEOGRAFICO DE AGOSTINI S.p.A. - NOVARA

Scale 1:30,000,000

Lambert Azimuthal Equal Area Projection

A-540000-280-1 -1 -1 -3

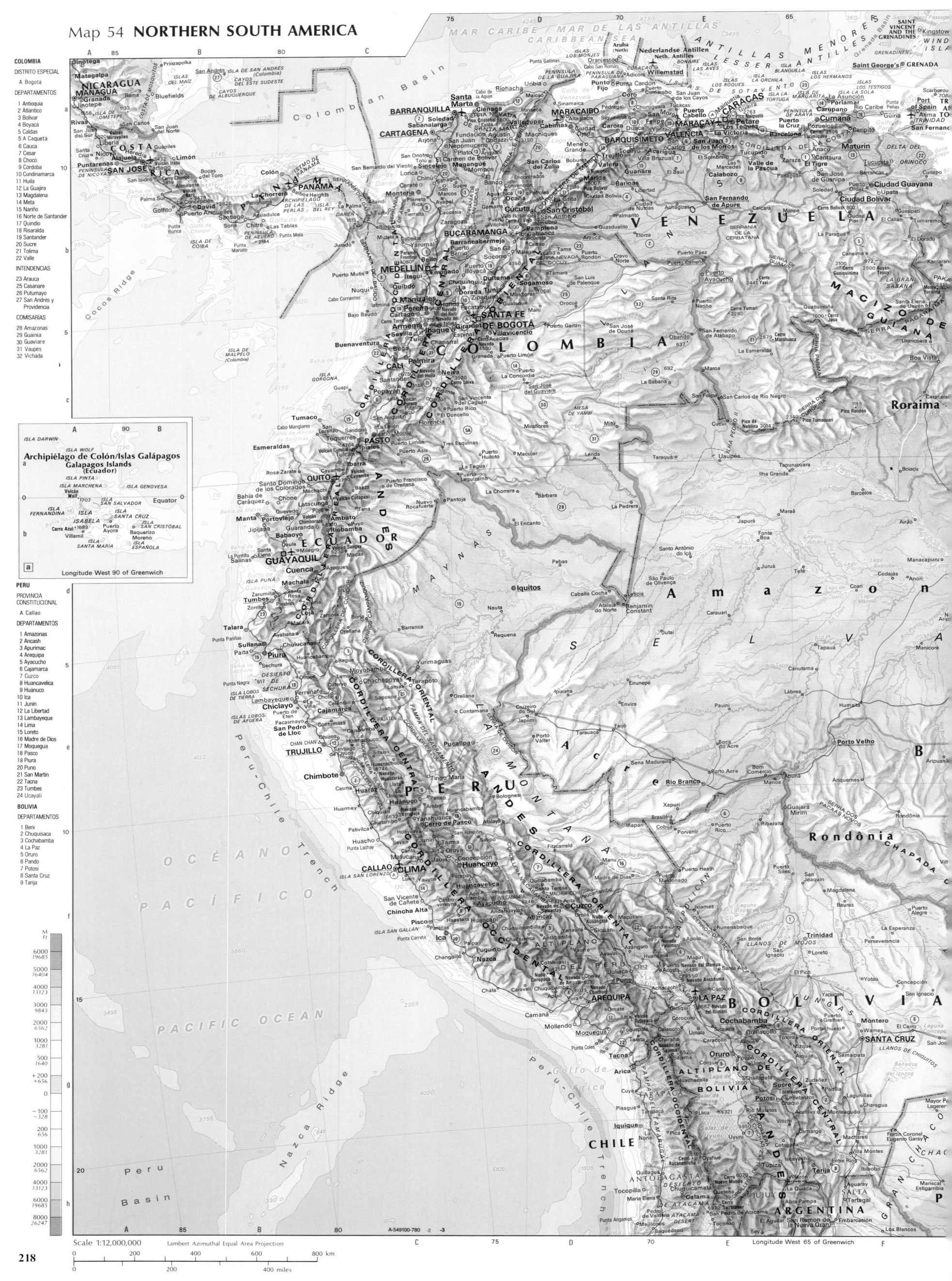

Map 54 **NORTHERN SOUTH AMERICA**

COLOMBIA

DISTRITO ESPECIAL
A Bogota

DEPARTAMENTOS
1 Antioquia
2 Atlántico
3 Bolívar
4 Boyacá
5 Caldas
5 A Caquetá
6 Cauca
7 Cesar
8 Chocó
9 Córdoba
10 Cundinamarca
11 Huila
12 La Guajira
13 Magdalena
14 Meta
15 Nariño
16 Norte de Santander
17 Quindío
18 Risaralda
19 Santander
20 Sucre
21 Tolima
22 Valle

INTENDENCIAS
23 Arauca
25 Casanare
26 Putumayo
27 San Andrés y Providencia

COMISARÍAS
28 Amazonas
29 Guainía
30 Guaviare
31 Vaupés
32 Vichada

PERU

PROVINCIA CONSTITUCIONAL
A Callao

DEPARTAMENTOS
1 Amazonas
2 Ancash
3 Apurímac
4 Arequipa
5 Ayacucho
6 Cajamarca
7 Cuzco
8 Huancavelica
9 Huánuco
10 Ica
11 Junín
12 La Libertad
13 Lambayeque
14 Lima
15 Loreto
16 Madre de Dios
17 Moquegua
18 Pasco
19 Piura
20 Puno
21 San Martín
22 Tacna
23 Tumbes
24 Ucayali

BOLIVIA

DEPARTAMENTOS
1 Beni
2 Chuquisaca
3 Cochabamba
4 La Paz
5 Oruro
6 Pando
7 Potosí
8 Santa Cruz
9 Tarija

ISLA DARWIN
ISLA WOLF
Archipiélago de Colón/Islas Galápagos
Galápagos Islands
(Ecuador)

ISLA PINTA
ISLA MARCHENA   ISLA GENOVESA
Volcán Wolf 1707
ISLA SAN SALVADOR   Equator
ISLA FERNANDINA   ISLA SANTA CRUZ   ISLA SAN CRISTÓBAL
Cerro Azul 1689   Puerto Ayora   Baquerizo Moreno
Villamil   ISLA SANTA MARÍA   ISLA ESPAÑOLA

Longitude West 90 of Greenwich

Scale 1:12,000,000
Lambert Azimuthal Equal Area Projection

Map 55 **EAST-CENTRAL SOUTH AMERICA**

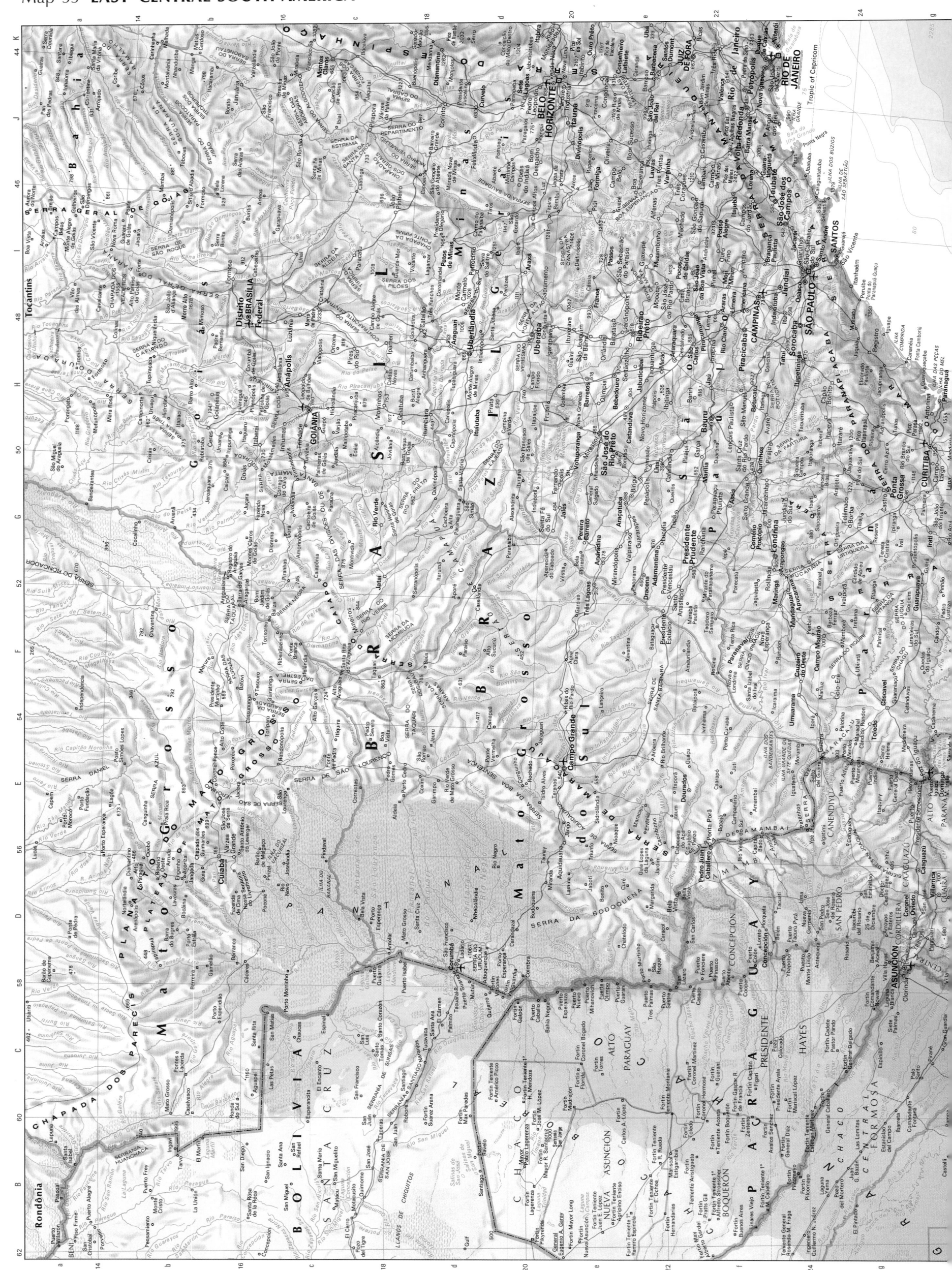

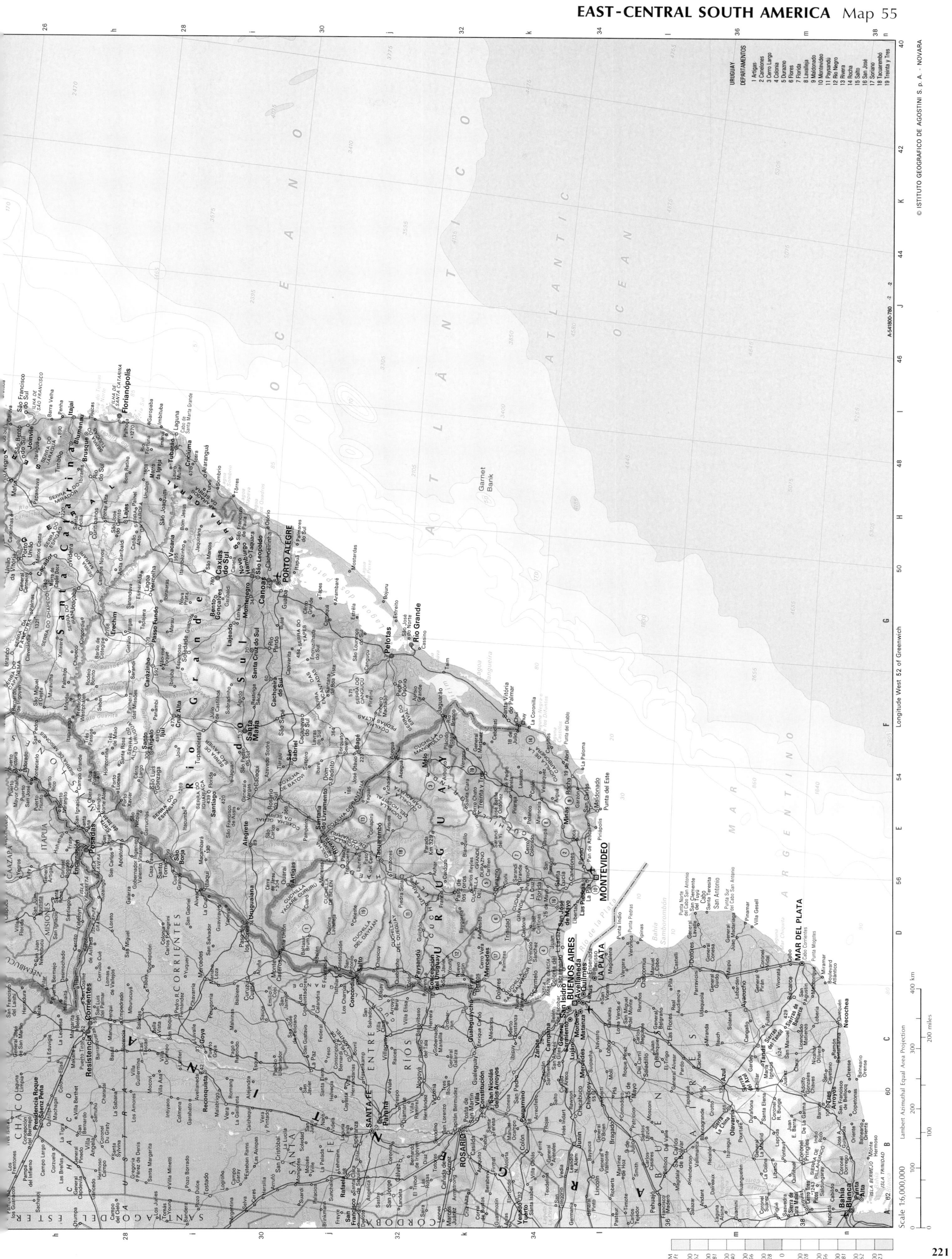

URUGUAY
DEPARTAMENTOS

1 Artigas
2 Canelones
3 Cerro Largo
4 Colonia
5 Durazno
6 Flores
7 Florida
8 Lavalleja
9 Maldonado
10 Montevideo
11 Paysandú
12 Río Negro
13 Rivera
14 Rocha
15 Salto
16 San José
17 Soriano
18 Tacuarembó
19 Treinta y Tres

Scale 1:6,000,000

Lambert Azimuthal Equal Area Projection

Longitude West 52 of Greenwich

Map 56 **SOUTHERN SOUTH AMERICA**

CHILE
REGIÓN
METROPOLITANA
A Santiago
REGIONES
1 Tarapacá
2 Antofagasta
3 Atacama
4 Coquimbo
5 Aconcagua
6 Libertador General
  Bernardo O'Higgins
7 Maule
8 Bio Bio
9 Araucania
10 Los Lagos
11 Aisén del General
   Carlos Ibáñez del
   Campo
12 Magallanes y
   Antártica Chilena

ARGENTINA
A CAPITAL FEDERAL
PROVINCIAS
1 Buenos Aires
2 Catamarca
3 Chaco
4 Chubut
5 Córdoba
6 Corrientes
7 Entre Rios
8 Formosa
9 Jujuy
10 La Pampa
11 La Rioja
12 Mendoza
13 Misiones
14 Neuquén
15 Rio Negro
16 Salta
17 San Juan
18 San Luis
19 Santa Cruz
20 Santa Fe
21 Santiago del Estero
22 Tierra del Fuego
23 Tucumán

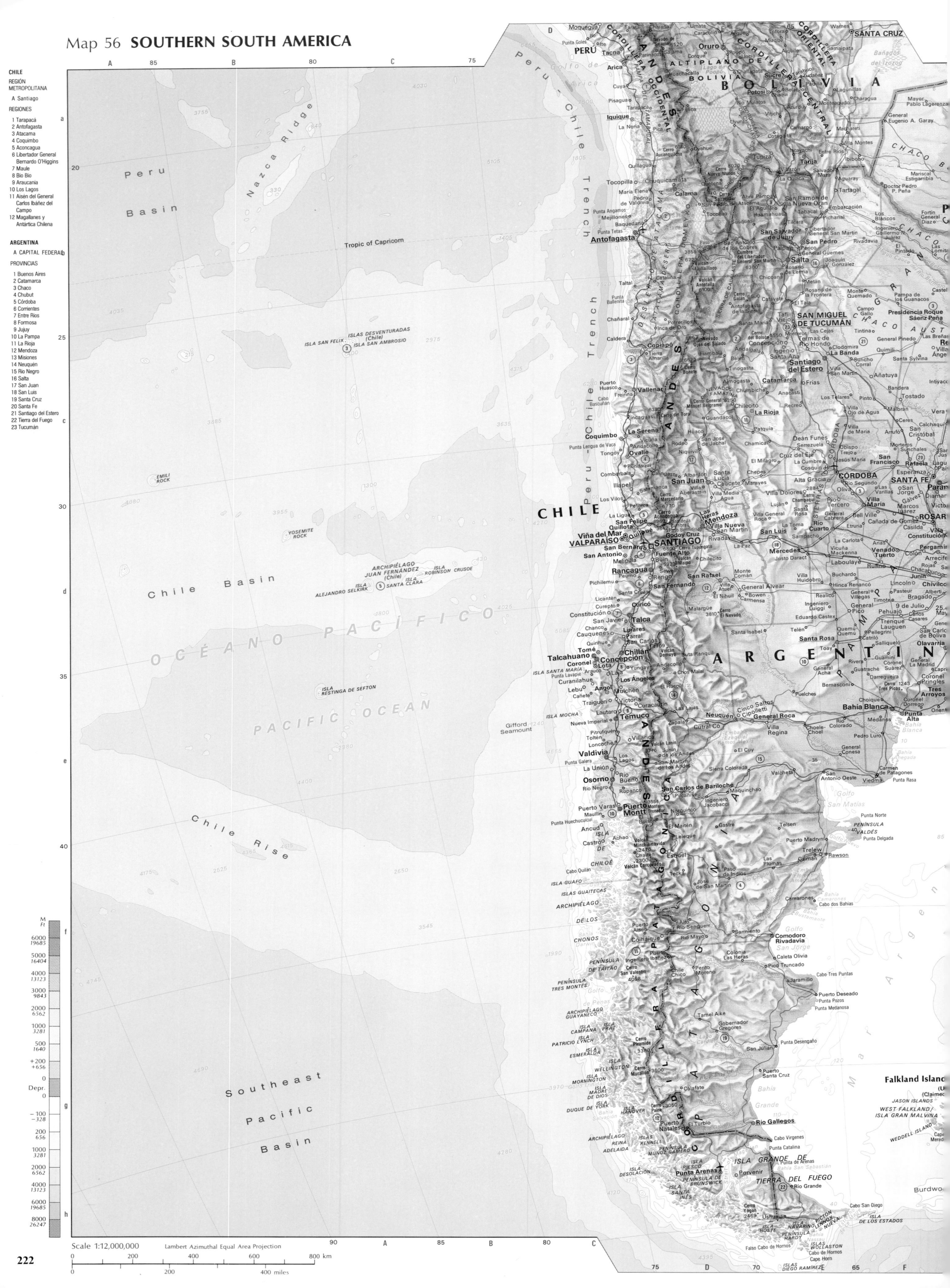

Scale 1:12,000,000   Lambert Azimuthal Equal Area Projection

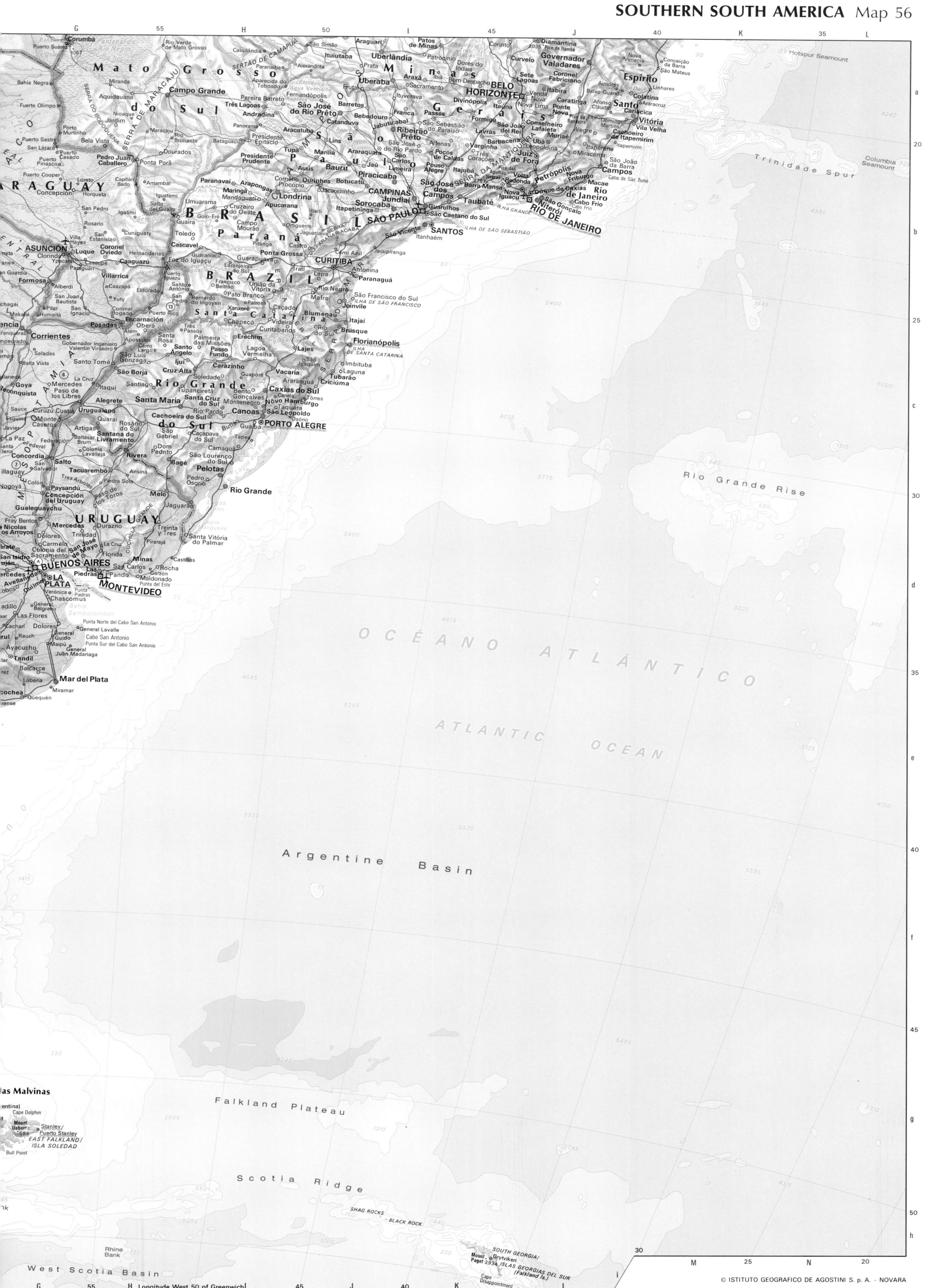

Map 57 **AUSTRALIA AND OCEANIA, PHYSICAL**

Scale 1:30,000,000   Lambert Azimuthal Equal Area Projection

Map 58 **AUSTRALIA AND OCEANIA, POLITICAL**

CHINA
JAPAN
SOUTH KOREA
TAIWAN
PHILIPPINES
VIET-NAM
LAOS
THAILAND
CAMBODIA
MALAYSIA
BRUNEI
INDONESIA
PAPUA NEW GUINEA
AUSTRALIA
NEW ZEALAND

Northern Mariana Islands (U.S.)
Guam (U.S.)
MARSHALL ISLANDS
FEDERATED STATES OF MICRONESIA
CAROLINE ISLANDS
Palau (Trust Territory)
MICRONESIA
MELANESIA
POLYNESIA
SOLOMON ISLANDS
VANUATU
NEW CALEDONIA (France)
FIJI
TUVALU
KIRIBATI
NAURU / NAOERO
NEW HEBRIDES

South China Sea
Philippine Sea
East China Sea
Celebes Sea
Banda Sea
Arafura Sea
Coral Sea
Tasman Sea
INDIAN OCEAN
PACIFIC OCEAN

GREAT SANDY DESERT
GREAT VICTORIA DESERT
GIBSON DESERT
SIMPSON DESERT
TANAMI DESERT
NULLARBOR PLAIN
ARNHEM LAND
KIMBERLEY
CAPE YORK PENINSULA
TASMANIA

NORTH ISLAND
SOUTH ISLAND

Sydney
Melbourne
Brisbane
Perth
Adelaide
Canberra
Auckland
Wellington
Christchurch

Tōkyō
Yokohama
Ōsaka
Shanghai
Guangzhou (Canton)
Hong Kong
Manila
Quezon City
Jakarta
Port Moresby
Nouméa

Scale 1:30,000,000   Lambert Azimuthal Equal Area Projection

0   500   1000   1500   2000 km
0   500   1000 miles

Longitude East 170 of Greenwich

UNITED STATES

San Luis
Obispo
Santa Barbara
Los Angeles
Long Beach
San Bernardino
Tijuana
Ensenada

Bakersfield
Pasadena
Phoenix
San Diego
Mexicali

Santa
Rosalia

ISLA DE
GUADALUPE
(Mexico)

BAJA
CALIFORNIA

La Paz

Cabo San Lucas

Yuma
Nogales
Agua
Prieta

Tucson

Hermosillo

Guaymas

Ciudad
Obregón

Los Mochis

Culiacán
Rosales

El Paso
Ciudad
Juárez

Casas Grandes

Chihuahua

Hidalgo
del Parral

MEXICO

Durango

Mazatlán

Odessa
Big
Spring

Piedras
Negras

Nueva
Rosita

Monclova

Torreón

Victoria

Tropic of Cancer

ISLAS
REVILLAGIGEDO
(Mexico)

Midway Islands
(U.S.)
() PEARL AND HERMES
KURE

LISIANSKI
LAYSAN
MARO
GARDNER
PINNACLES
FRENCH FRIGATE
SHOALS
NECKER
NIHOA

HAWAIIAN ISLANDS

Hawaii
(U.S.)

NIIHAU
KAUAI
KAULA
OAHU
Honolulu
LANAI
MOLOKAI
MAUI
KAHOOLAWE
Hawi
Hilo

HAWAII

Johnston
(U.S.)

Tropic of Cancer

CLIPPERTON
(French Polynesia)

PACIFIC OCEAN

KINGMAN
(U.S.)
PALMYRA
(U.S.)

TERAINA
(WASHINGTON)
TABUAERAN
(FANNING)

KIRITIMATI
(CHRISTMAS)

HOWLAND
(U.S.)
BAKER
(U.S.)

JARVIS
(U.S.)

Equator

WINSLOW
PHOENIX ISLANDS
KANTON
MCKEAN
BIRNIE
ENDERBURY
RAWAKI
(PHOENIX)
NIKUMARORO
(GARDNER)
ORONA
(HULL)
MANRA
(SYDNEY)
CARONDELET

KIRIBATI

MALDEN

STARBUCK

VOSTOK

CAROLINE

FLINT

LINE ISLANDS

POLYNESIA

Tokelau (New Zealand)
ATAFU
TOKELAU
ISLANDS
NUKUNONU
FAKAOFO

RAKAHANGA
MANIHIKI
PENRHYN

PUKAPUKA

EIAO
NUKU HIVA
MARQUESAS
UA HUKA
UA POU
HIVA OA
TAHUATA
ISLANDS
FATU HIVA

WESTERN
SAMOA
d Futuna
nce)
Mata-Utu
WALLIS
UVÉA
FUTUNA
ALOFI

SAMOA ISLANDS
SAVAI'I
Apia
UPOLU
Pago Pago
TUTUILA

MANUA
ISLANDS

SWAINS

NORTHERN
COOK ISLANDS

NASSAU

SUWARROW

MANIHI
MATAIVA
RANGIROA
APATAKI
ARATIKA
TAKUME
FANGATAU
ÎLES DU
ROI GEORGES
PUKAPUKA

TUAMOTU

ARCHIPELAGO

ÎLES DU
DÉSAPPOINTEMENT

TONGA
FONUALEI
NIUAFO'OU
TAFAHI
NIUATO PUTAPU
VAVA'U
GROUP
HA'APAI
GROUP
KOTU GROUP
NOMUKA GROUP
TONGATAPU
GROUP
Nuku'alofa
ATA
MINERVA REEFS

American
Samoa
(U.S.)

Cook Islands
(New Zealand)

PALMERSTON

ANTIOPE
Alofi
Niue
(New Zealand)

AITUTAKI
MANUAE
TAKUTEA
MITIARO
ATIU
MAUKE

BEVERIDGE

SOUTHERN
COOK
ISLANDS
MARIA
Avarua
Rarotonga

MANGAIA

LEEWARD
ISLANDS
MOTU
ONE
MANUAE
MAUPIHAA
MAUPITI
BORA-BORA
HUAHINE
RAIATEA
Moorea
SOCIETY ISLANDS
WINDWARD ISLANDS
TETIAROA
Papeete
TAHITI

ÎLES PALLISER

KAUKURA
FAKARAVA
TAHANEA
MARUTEA
MOTUTUNGA
RAVAHERE
HAO
MANUANGI
VAHITAHI

MAKEMO
FAKAHINA
TATAKOTO
AMANU
PUKARUHA
REAO

French
Polynesia

HEREHERETUE
ÎLES DU DUC
DE GLOUCESTER
TUREIA
GROUPE
ACTÉON
MARUTEA

RIMATARA
RURUTU
TUBUAI
RAEVAVAE
MARIA
TEMATANGI
MORANE
FAGATAUFA
MURUROA
MANGAREVA
GAMBIER
ISLANDS
TEMOE

TUBUAI
ISLANDS

RAPA
ÎLOTS
DE BASS

OENO
HENDERSON
DUCIE
PITCAIRN
Adamstown
Pitcairn
(U.K.)

Tropic of Capricorn

RAOUL
CAULEY
RTIS
KERMADEC
ISLANDS
(New Zealand)
L'ESPERANCE ROCK

RINGGOLD
ISLES
ORN
ANDS
LAU
GROUP
ONO-I-LAU

SALA Y GÓMEZ
(Chile)
EASTER ISLAND
(Chile)

ERNEST
LEGOUVE

MARIA THERESA

CHATHAM ISLANDS
(New Zealand)
HATHAM
PITT

A-590000-280-2 -2 -2 -3

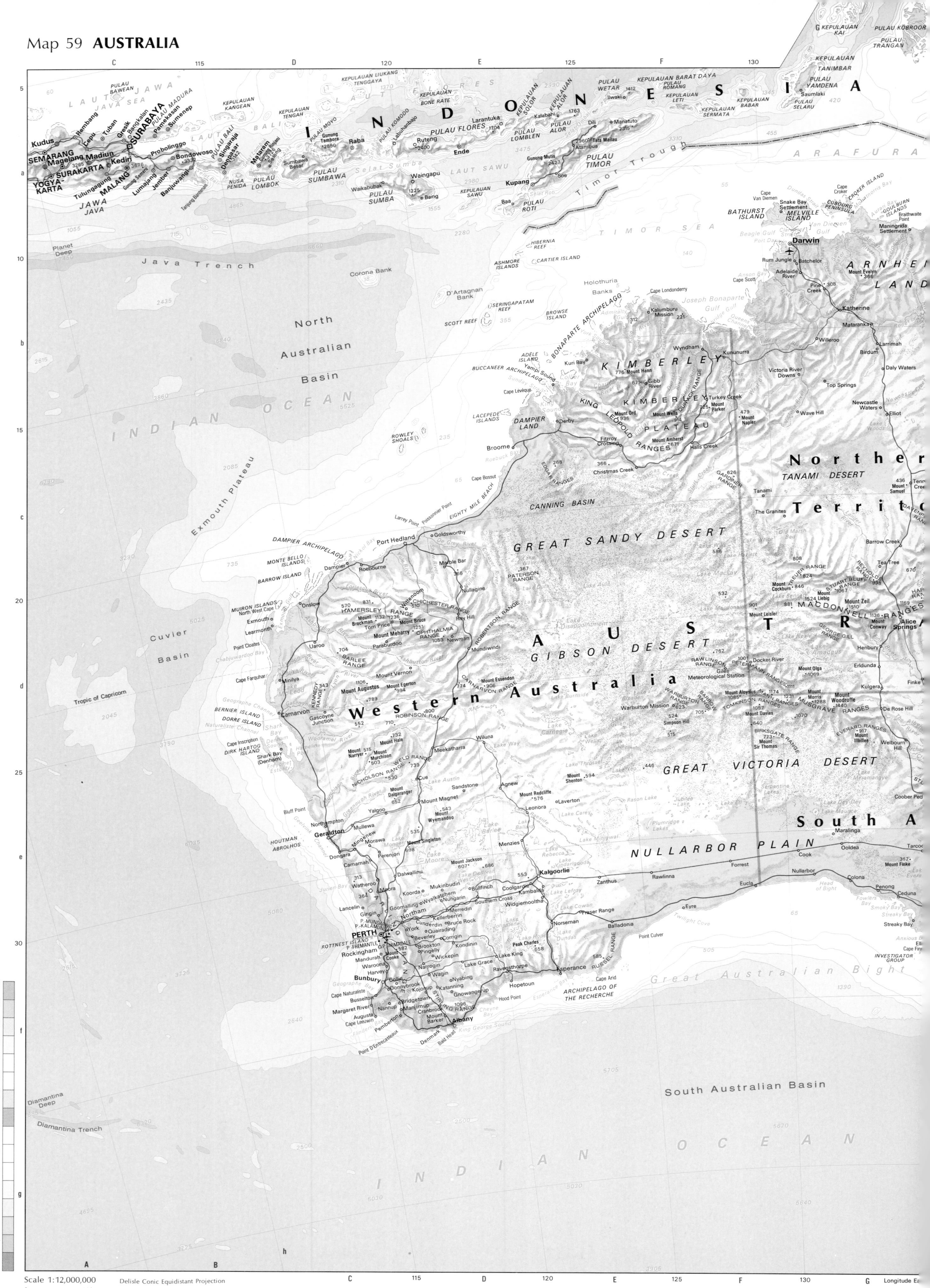

Map 59 **AUSTRALIA**

G KEPULAUAN KAI
PULAU KOBROOR
KEPULAUAN
TRANGAN

INDONESIA

KEPULAUAN BARAT DAYA
PULAU WETAR
PULAU ROMANG
PULAU LETI
KEPULAUAN BABAR
PULAU SERMATA
PULAU SELARU
KEPULAUAN TANIMBAR
PULAU YAMDENA
Saumlaki

KEPULAUAN LIUKANG TENGGAYA
KEPULAUAN BONE RATE
Iwaki
Manatuto
KEPULAUAN SOLOR
KEPULAUAN ALOR
Dili
Tata Mailau
PULAU TIMOR
Soe
ARAFURA

LAUT JAWA
Java Sea
PULAU BAWEAN
Rembang
Cepu
Tuban
Gresik
SURABAYA
PULAU MADURA
Pamekasan
Sumenep
Kudus
SEMARANG
Magelang Madiun
Kediri
SURAKARTA
YOGYAKARTA
Tulungagung
MALANG
Lumajang Jember
Banjuwangi
Bondowoso
Probolinggo
JAWA
Java

LAUT BALI
PULAU BALI
NUSA PENIDA
PULAU LOMBOK
Mataram
PULAU SUMBAWA
Bima
Raba
Sumbawa Besar
PULAU FLORES
Ruteng
Ende
Larantuka
PULAU LOMBLEN
Atambua
Kupang
PULAU ROTI
Baing
Waingapu
PULAU SUMBA
Waikabubak
KEPULAUAN SAWU
Baa
PULAU SAWU
LAUT SAWU
Selat Sumba
Selat Roti
Selat Sape

Cape Van Diemen
BATHURST ISLAND
Snake Bay Settlement
MELVILLE ISLAND
COBURG PENINSULA
Cape Croker
CROKER ISLAND
GOULBURN ISLANDS
Braithwaite Point
Maningrida Settlement

TIMOR SEA
Timor Trough
Timor Trench

Darwin
Rum Jungle
Batchelor
Mount Evelyn
Pine Creek
Katherine
ARNHEM LAND

Cape Scott
Adelaide River
Cape Van Diemen
Beagle Gulf
Port Darwin

HIBERNIA REEF
ASHMORE ISLANDS
CARTIER ISLAND
Cape Londonderry
SERINGAPATAM REEF
Holothuria Banks
SCOTT REEF
BROWSE ISLAND
Kalumburu Mission
Joseph Bonaparte Gulf
Wyndham
Kununurra
Willeroo
Larrimah
Birdum
Victoria River Downs
Top Springs
Daly Waters
Newcastle Waters
Wave Hill
Elliot

North Australian Basin

Java Trench
Planet Deep
Corona Bank
D'Artagnan Bank

INDIAN OCEAN

BONAPARTE ARCHIPELAGO
ADELE ISLAND
KIMBERLEY
Kuri Bay
Mount Hann
KING LEOPOLD RANGES
KIMBERLEY PLATEAU
Gibb River
Mount Ord
Mount Wells
Turkey Creek
Mount Parker
Mount Napier
Mount Amherst
Derby
Fitzroy Crossing
Halls Creek
Cape Leveque
DAMPIER LAND
LACEPEDE ISLANDS
BUCCANEER ARCHIPELAGO
Yampi Sound
Broome
Christmas Creek
Tanami
TANAMI DESERT
GARDNER RANGE
Mount Samuel
Barrow Creek
Tea Tree
The Granites

NORTHERN TERRITORY

ROWLEY SHOALS
Cape Bossut
EIGHTY MILE BEACH
Larrey Point
Frostmaster Point
Goldsworthy
Port Hedland
GREAT SANDY DESERT
PATERSON RANGE
CANNING BASIN
Lake Mackay
Lake Disappointment
HELLER RANGE
MACDONNELL RANGES
Alice Springs
Mount Zeil
Mount Liebig
Mount Conway
Henbury
Kulgera
Finke
De Rose Hill

Exmouth Plateau

DAMPIER ARCHIPELAGO
MONTE BELLO ISLANDS
BARROW ISLAND
Dampier
Roebourne
Marble Bar
Nullagine
CHICHESTER RANGE
HAMERSLEY RANGE
Mount Bruce
Tom Price
Mount Meharry
OPHTHALMIA RANGE
Newman
ROBERTSON RANGE
ROBINSON RANGE
CARNARVON RANGE
Mount Essendon
AUSTRALIA
GIBSON DESERT
RAWLINSON RANGE
Docker River
Mount Olga
Meteorological Station
WARBURTON RANGES
Warburton Mission
TOMKINSON RANGES
MUSGRAVE RANGES
PETERMANN RANGES
Mount Davies
BIRKSGATE RANGE
Mount Sir Thomas
EVERARD RANGES
Mount Illbillee
Welbourn Hill

MUIRON ISLANDS
North West Cape
Exmouth
Learmonth
Point Cloates
Cuvier Basin
Onslow
Uaroo
Minilya
GARLEE RANGE
Mount Vernon
Mount Augustus
Mount Egerton
KENNEDY RANGE
Gascoyne Junction
Carnarvon
ROBINSON RANGE
Mundiwindi
Wiluna
Lake Carnegie
Lake Way
Western Australia
Mount Shenton
GREAT VICTORIA DESERT

BERNIER ISLAND
DORRE ISLAND
DIRK HARTOG ISLAND
Cape Inscription
Shark Bay (Denham)
Useless Loop
Bluff Point
Mount Narryer
Mount Murchison
Mount Hale
ROBINSON RANGE
NICHOLSON RANGE
WELD RANGE
Meekatharra
Cue
Sandstone
Agnew
Mount Redcliffe
Laverton
Leonora
Lake Carey
GREAT VICTORIA DESERT
South Australia
Maralinga

Tropic of Capricorn

Northampton
Mullewa
Yalgoo
Mount Magnet
Mount Wydgee
Lake Austin
Lake Barlee
Menzies
Lake Rebecca
Lake Carnegie
Coober Pedy

Geraldton
Dongara
HOUTMAN ABROLHOS
Mingenew
Morawa
Perenjori
Mount Singleton
Lake Moore
Mount Jackson
Dalwallinu
Southern Cross
Kalgoorlie
Coolgardie
Widgiemooltha
Zanthus
Rawlinna
NULLARBOR PLAIN
Forrest
Cook
Ooldea
Nullarbor

Lancelin
Gingin
Wongan Hills
Goomalling
Northam
Cunderdin
Merredin
Kellerberrin
Bruce Rock
Mukinbudin
Wyalkatchem
Nungarin
Bullfinch
Kambalda
Norseman
Balladonia
Eucla
Head of Bight
Penong
Ceduna
Streaky Bay

PERTH
FREMANTLE
ROTTNEST ISLAND
GARDEN ISLAND
Rockingham
Mandurah
Armadale
Kelmscott
Pinjarra
York
Beverley
Brookton
Pingelly
Corrigin
Kondinin
Narrogin
Wagin
Lake Grace
Lake King
Peak Charles
Esperance
Cape Arid
ARCHIPELAGO OF THE RECHERCHE
Great Australian Bight
INVESTIGATOR GROUP
Cape Finniss

Bunbury
Collie
Harvey
Donnybrook
Kojonup
Katanning
Nyabing
Gnowangerup
Ravensthorpe
Hopetoun
Hood Point
Cape Naturaliste
Busselton
Margaret River
Nannup
Bridgetown
Manjimup
STIRLING RANGE
Mount Barker
Albany
King George Sound
Augusta
Cape Leeuwin
Pemberton
Denmark
Bald Head
Cheyne Beach

South Australian Basin

Diamantina Deep
Diamantina Trench

INDIAN OCEAN

Scale 1:12,000,000
Delisle Conic Equidistant Projection

0 200 400 600 800 km
0 200 400 miles

228

M Ft
4000 13123
3000 9843
2000 6562
1000 3281
500 1640
+ 200 +656
Depr.
− 100 −328
200 656
1000 3281
2000 6562
4000 13123
6000 19685
8000 26247

Longitude East

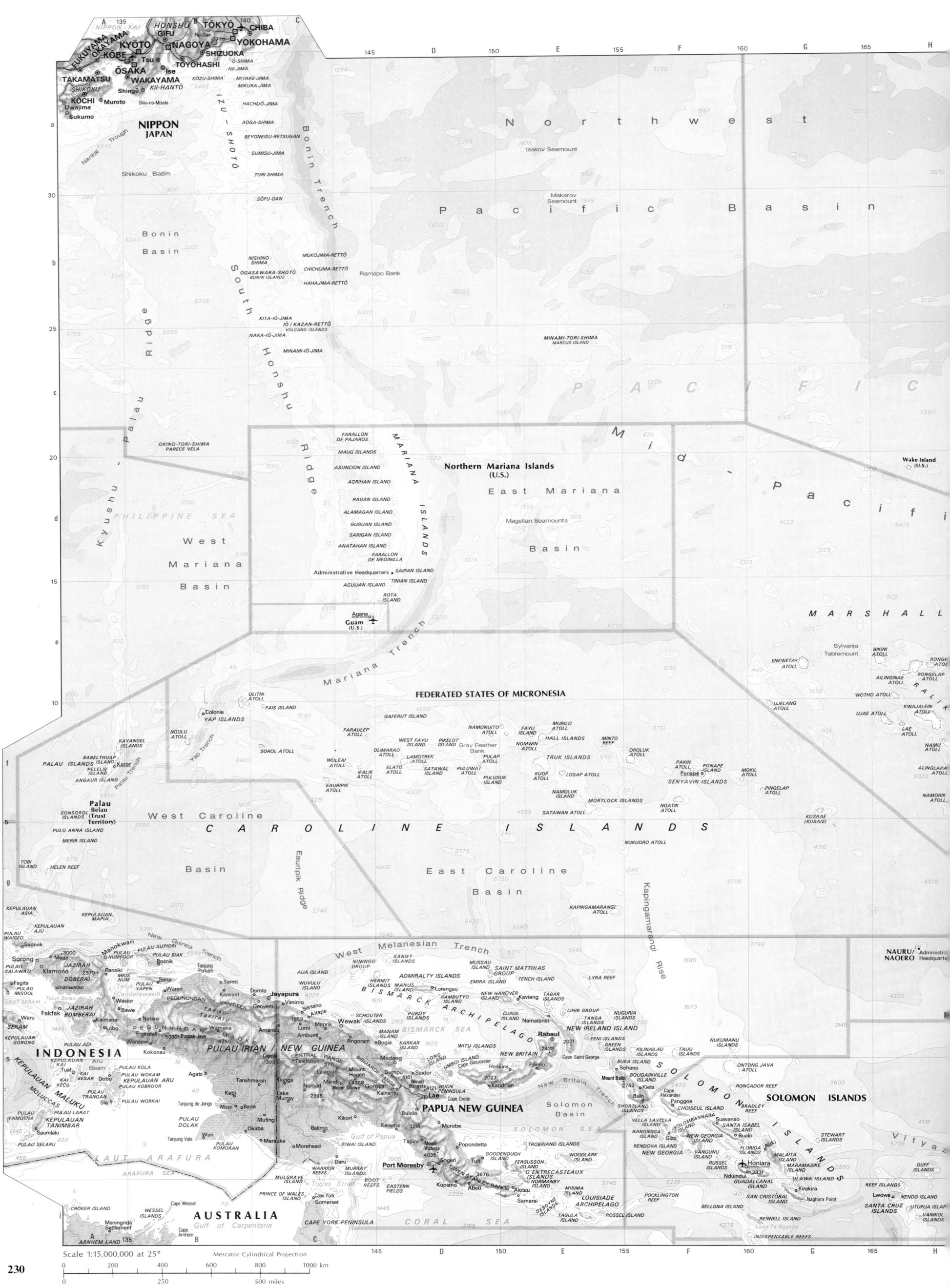

Scale 1:15,000,000 at 25°

Mercator Cylindrical Projection

230

0   200   400   600   800   1000 km

0   250   500 miles

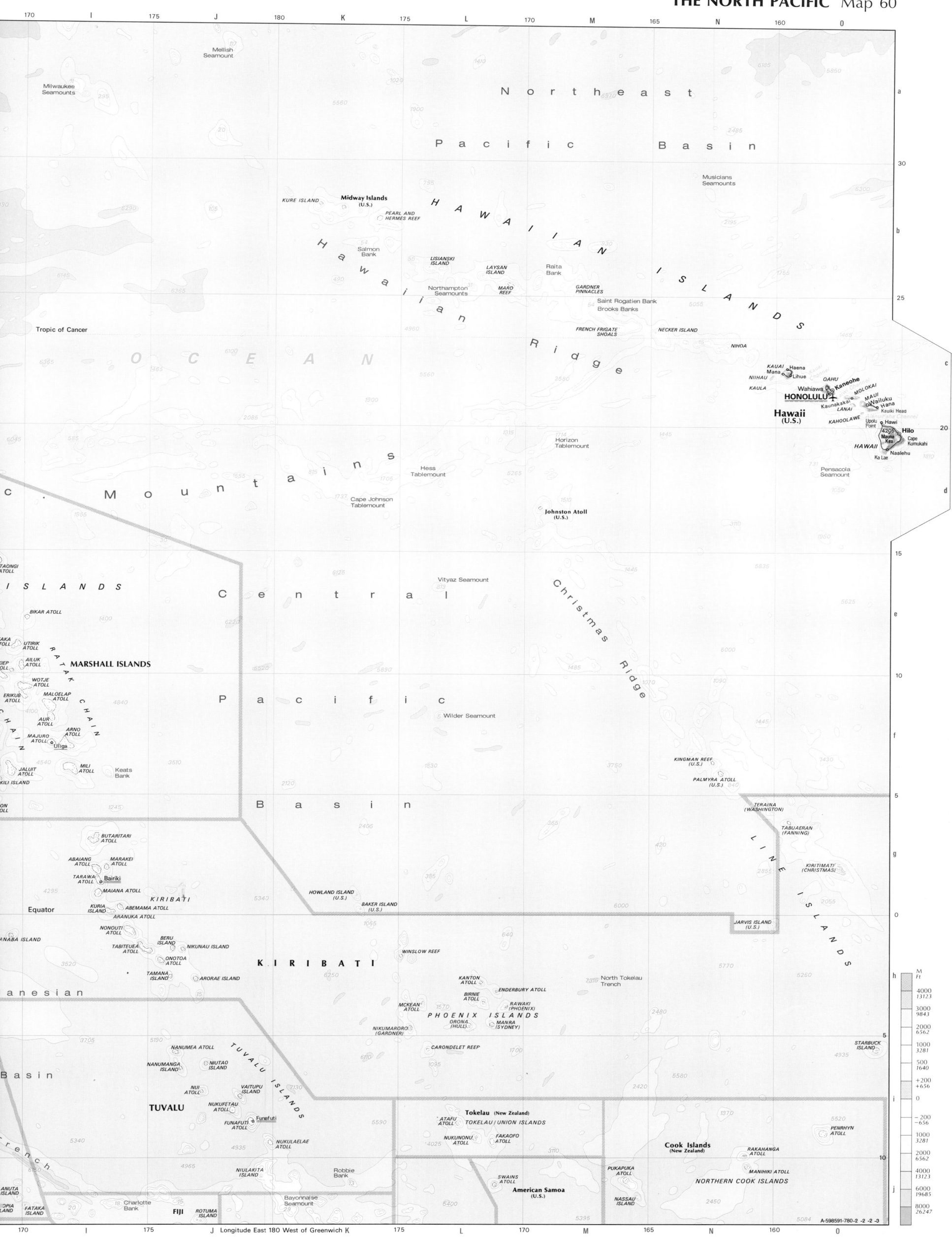

170 · I · 175 · J · 180 · K · 175 · L · 170 · M · 165 · N · 160 · O

Mellish
Seamount

Milwaukee
Seamounts

N o r t h e a s t

P a c i f i c   B a s i n

30

KURE ISLAND   Midway Islands
(U.S.)
PEARL AND
HERMES REEF

Musicians
Seamounts

H A W A I I A N   I S L A N D S

Salmon
Bank

LISIANSKI
ISLAND   LAYSAN
ISLAND   Raita
Bank

25

Northampton
Seamounts   MARO
REEF   GARDNER
PINNACLES
Saint Rogatien Bank
Brooks Banks

Tropic of Cancer

O C E A N

FRENCH FRIGATE
SHOALS   NECKER ISLAND

NIHOA

KAUAI Haena
Mana
OAHU
NIIHAU   Lihue   Wahiawa Kaneohe
MOLOKAI
KAULA   Kaunakakai MAUI
HONOLULU   LANAI   Wailuku Hana
Kauiki Head
Upolu Hawi
KAHOOLAWE   Point
Hawaii   Mauna Hilo
(U.S.)   HAWAII Kea   Cape
Ka Lae Naalehu Kumukahi

c

20

Horizon
Tablemount

Hess
Tablemount

d

Cape Johnson
Tablemount   Johnston Atoll
(U.S.)

Pensacola
Seamount

15

ISLANDS   C e n t r a l

Vityaz Seamount

BIKAR ATOLL

TAKA
ATOLL
UTIRIK
ATOLL
AILUK
ATOLL   MARSHALL ISLANDS
WOTJE
ATOLL
ERIKUB
ATOLL MALOELAP
ATOLL
AUR
ATOLL   ARNO
ATOLL
Uliga

P a c i f i c

Christmas Ridge

e

10

Wilder Seamount

f

KINGMAN REEF
(U.S.)

JALUIT
ATOLL   MILI
ATOLL   Keats
Bank
KILI ISLAND

PALMYRA ATOLL
(U.S.)

5

BON
TOLL

B a s i n

TERAINA
(WASHINGTON)

TABUAERAN
(FANNING)

BUTARITARI
ATOLL

ABAIANG
ATOLL   MARAKEI
ATOLL
TARAWA
ATOLL Bairiki
MAIANA ATOLL   KIRIBATI
KURIA
ISLAND ABEMAMA ATOLL
ARANUKA ATOLL

HOWLAND ISLAND
(U.S.)   BAKER ISLAND
(U.S.)

KIRITIMATI
(CHRISTMAS)

L
I
N
E

I
S
L
A
N
D
S

Equator

JARVIS ISLAND
(U.S.)

0

ANABA ISLAND

NONOUTI
ATOLL
BERU
ISLAND
TABITEUEA
ATOLL   NIKUNAU ISLAND
ONOTOA
ATOLL
TAMANA
ISLAND ARORAE ISLAND

K I R I B A T I

Winslow Reef

lanesian

KANTON
ATOLL
BIRNIE
ATOLL   ENDERBURY ATOLL
MCKEAN
ATOLL   RAWAKI
(PHOENIX)
P H O E N I X   I S L A N D S
NIKUMARORO   ORONA   MANRA
(GARDNER)   (HULL)   (SYDNEY)

North Tokelau
Trench

h

5

Basin

CARONDELET REEF

STARBUCK
ISLAND

TUVALU ISLANDS

NANUMEA ATOLL
NANUMANGA
ISLAND   NIUTAO
ISLAND
NUI
ATOLL   VAITUPU
ISLAND
TUVALU   NUKUFETAU
ATOLL
FUNAFUTI Funafuti
ATOLL

ATAFU
ATOLL   Tokelau (New Zealand)
TOKELAU / UNION ISLANDS
NUKUNONU   FAKAOFO
ATOLL   ATOLL

PENRHYN
ATOLL

NIULAKITA
ISLAND

Robbie
Bank

French

ANUTA
ISLAND
OPIA
LAND FATAKA
ISLAND   Charlotte
Bank   FIJI   ROTUMA
ISLAND

Bayonnaise
Seamount

SWAINS
ATOLL

American Samoa
(U.S.)

PUKAPUKA
ATOLL

NASSAU
ISLAND

Cook Islands
(New Zealand)

RAKAHANGA
ATOLL

MANIHIKI ATOLL

NORTHERN COOK ISLANDS

j

10

170 · I · 175 · J · Longitude East 180 West of Greenwich K · 175 · M · 165 · N · 160 · O

M ft	
4000	13123
3000	9843
2000	6562
1000	3281
500	1640
+200	+656
0	
- 200	- 656
1000	3281
2000	6562
4000	13123
6000	19685
8000	26247

A-598591-780-2 -2 -2 -3

Map 61 **THE SOUTH PACIFIC**

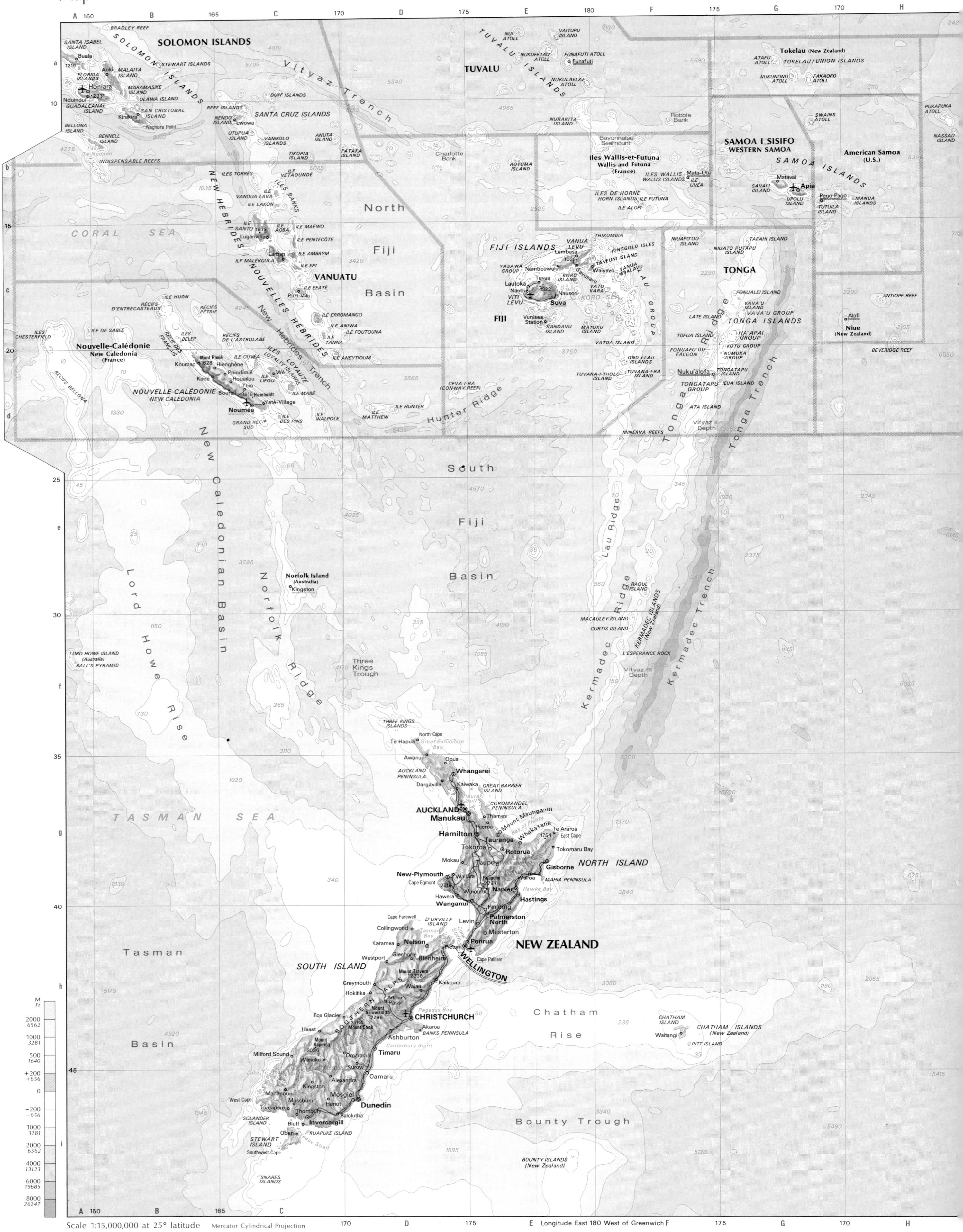
SOLOMON ISLANDS
SOLOMON ISLANDS
BRADLEY REEF
SANTA ISABEL ISLAND
Buala
STEWART ISLANDS
FLORIDA ISLANDS
Auki
MALAITA ISLAND
Honiara
MARAMASIKE ISLAND
2331
Nduindui
GUADALCANAL ISLAND
ULAWA ISLAND
Kirakira
SAN CRISTOBAL ISLAND
Naghora Point
BELLONA ISLAND
RENNELL ISLAND
Lake Te-Nggano
INDISPENSABLE REEFS
Vityaz Trench
DUFF ISLANDS
REEF ISLANDS
NENDO ISLAND
Lwowa
SANTA CRUZ ISLANDS
UTUPUA ISLAND
VANIKOLO ISLANDS
ANUTA ISLAND
TIKOPIA ISLAND
FATAKA ISLAND
TUVALU
TUVALU ISLANDS
NUI ATOLL
VAITUPU ISLAND
NUKUFETAU ATOLL
FUNAFUTI ATOLL
Funafuti
NUKULAELAE ATOLL
NURAKITA ISLAND
Robbie Bank
Bayonnaise Seamount
Charlotte Bank
ROTUMA ISLAND
Iles Wallis-et-Futuna
Wallis and Futuna
(France)
ILES WALLIS WALLIS ISLANDS
Mata-Utu
ILE UVEA
ILES DE HORNE HORN ISLANDS
ILE FUTUNA
ILE ALOFI
Tokelau (New Zealand)
ATAFU ATOLL
TOKELAU / UNION ISLANDS
NUKUNONU ATOLL
FAKAOFO ATOLL
SWAINS ATOLL
PUKAPUKA ATOLL
NASSAU ISLAND
SAMOA I SISIFO
WESTERN SAMOA
SAMOA ISLANDS
American Samoa
(U.S.)
Matavai
SAVAI'I ISLAND
Apia
UPOLU ISLAND
Pago Pago
TUTUILA ISLAND
MANUA ISLANDS
CORAL SEA
NEW HEBRIDES / NOUVELLES HÉBRIDES
ILES TORRÈS
ILES BANKS
ILE VETAOUNDÉ
VANUA LAVA
ILE LAKON
ILE SANTO
1879
Luganville
ILE AOBA
ILE MAÉWO
ILE PENTECÔTE
ILE AMBRYM
Lamap
ILF MALÉKOULA
ILE EPI
VANUATU
ILE EFATÉ
Port-Vila
ILE ERROMANGO
ILE ANIWA
ILE FOUTOUNA
ILE TANNA
ILE ANEYTIOUM
North Fiji Basin
FIJI ISLANDS
VANUA LEVU
THIKOMBIA
Lambasa
RINGGOLD ISLES
TAVEUNI ISLAND
YASAWA GROUP
Nambouwalu
Waiyevo
VANUA MBALAVU
Lautoka
Tavua
KORO ISLAND
Nandi
1322
Nausori
VITI LEVU
Suva
KORO SEA
FIJI
Vunisea Station
KANDAVU ISLAND
MATUKU ISLAND
VATOA ISLAND
LAU GROUP
ONO-I-LAU ISLANDS
TUVANA-I-THOLO ISLAND
TUVANA-I-RA ISLAND
CEVA-I-RA (CONWAY REEF)
Hunter Ridge
ILE HUNTER
ILE MATTHEW
ILE WALPOLE
NIUAFO'OU ISLAND
TAFAHI ISLAND
NIUATO PUTAPU ISLAND
TONGA
FONUALEI ISLAND
VAVA'U ISLAND
VAVA'U GROUP
LATE ISLAND
TONGA ISLANDS
TOFUA ISLAND
HA'APAI GROUP
KOTU GROUP
FONUAFO'OU FALCON
NOMUKA GROUP
Nuku'alofa
TONGATAPU ISLAND
TONGATAPU GROUP
'EUA ISLAND
ATA ISLAND
Vityaz II Depth
MINERVA REEFS
Tonga Ridge
Tonga Trench
ANTIPOPE REEF
Alofi
Niue
(New Zealand)
BEVERIDGE REEF
ILE HUON
RÉCIFS D'ENTRECASTEAUX
RÉCIFS PÉTRIE
ILES CHESTERFIELD
ILE DE SABLE
ILES BELEP
RÉCIFS DE L'ASTROLABE
Nouvelle-Calédonie
New Caledonia
(France)
Mont Panié
1628
ILE OUVÉA
ILES LOYAUTÉ LOYALTY ISLANDS
Koumac
Hienghène
ILE LIFOU
Poindimié
Koné
Houailou
Wé
Thio
NOUVELLE-CALÉDONIE
NEW CALEDONIA
Bourail
1618 Humboldt
ILE MARÉ
Yaté-Village
Nouméa
GRAND RÉCIF SUD
ILE DES PINS
RÉCIFS BELLONA
New Hebrides Trench
New Caledonian Basin
South Fiji Basin
Lord Howe Rise
Norfolk Ridge
Norfolk Island
(Australia)
Kingston
LORD HOWE ISLAND
(Australia)
BALL'S PYRAMID
Three Kings Trough
Lau Ridge
RAOUL ISLAND
KERMADEC ISLANDS
(New Zealand)
MACAULEY ISLAND
CURTIS ISLAND
L'ESPERANCE ROCK
Vityaz III Depth
Kermadec Ridge
Kermadec Trench
TASMAN SEA
Tasman Basin
THREE KINGS ISLANDS
North Cape
Te Hapua
Great Exhibition Bay
Awanui
Opua
AUCKLAND PENINSULA
Whangarei
Dargaville
Kaiwaka
GREAT BARRIER ISLAND
Hauraki Gulf
COROMANDEL PENINSULA
AUCKLAND
Manukau
Thames
Mount Maunganui
Paeroa
Bay of Plenty
Whakatane
Te Araroa
East Cape
1754
Hamilton
Tauranga
Tokoroa
Rotorua
Tokomaru Bay
Mokau
Taupo
Gisborne
NORTH ISLAND
New-Plymouth
Waitara
Cape Egmont
2518
Ruapehu
2797
Wairoa
MAHIA PENINSULA
Hawera
Waiouru
Napier
Hawke Bay
Wanganui
Hastings
Feilding
Palmerston North
Levin
Masterton
Porirua
NEW ZEALAND
WELLINGTON
Cape Palliser
Cape Farewell
Collingwood
D'URVILLE ISLAND
Tasman Bay
Cook Strait
Karamea
Nelson
Picton
Blenheim
Glenhope
Westport
SOUTH ISLAND
Greymouth
Mount Travers 2338
Waiau
Kaikoura
Hokitika
SOUTHERN ALPS
Arthur's Pass
Pegasus Bay
Fox Glacier
Mount Arrowsmith 2795
CHRISTCHURCH
3764 Mount Cook
Haast
Akaroa
BANKS PENINSULA
Mount Aspiring 3036
Ashburton
Canterbury Bight
Milford Sound
Wanaka
Omarama
Timaru
Lake Te Anau
Kingston
Alexandra
Oamaru
Manapouri
Mosgiel
West Cape
Mossburn
Dunedin
Tuatapere
Thornbury
Heriot
Balclutha
SOLANDER ISLAND
Invercargill
Bluff
Oban
RUAPUKE ISLAND
Foveaux Strait
STEWART ISLAND
Southwest Cape
SNARES ISLANDS
Chatham Rise
CHATHAM ISLAND
CHATHAM ISLANDS
(New Zealand)
Waitangi
PITT ISLAND
Bounty Trough
BOUNTY ISLANDS
(New Zealand)
M
Ft
2000 6562
1000 3281
500 1640
+200 +656
0
−200 −656
1000 3281
2000 6562
4000 13123
6000 19685
8000 26247
Longitude East 180 West of Greenwich

Scale 1:15,000,000 at 25° latitude Mercator Cylindrical Projection

0 200 400 600 800 1000 km

0 250 500 miles

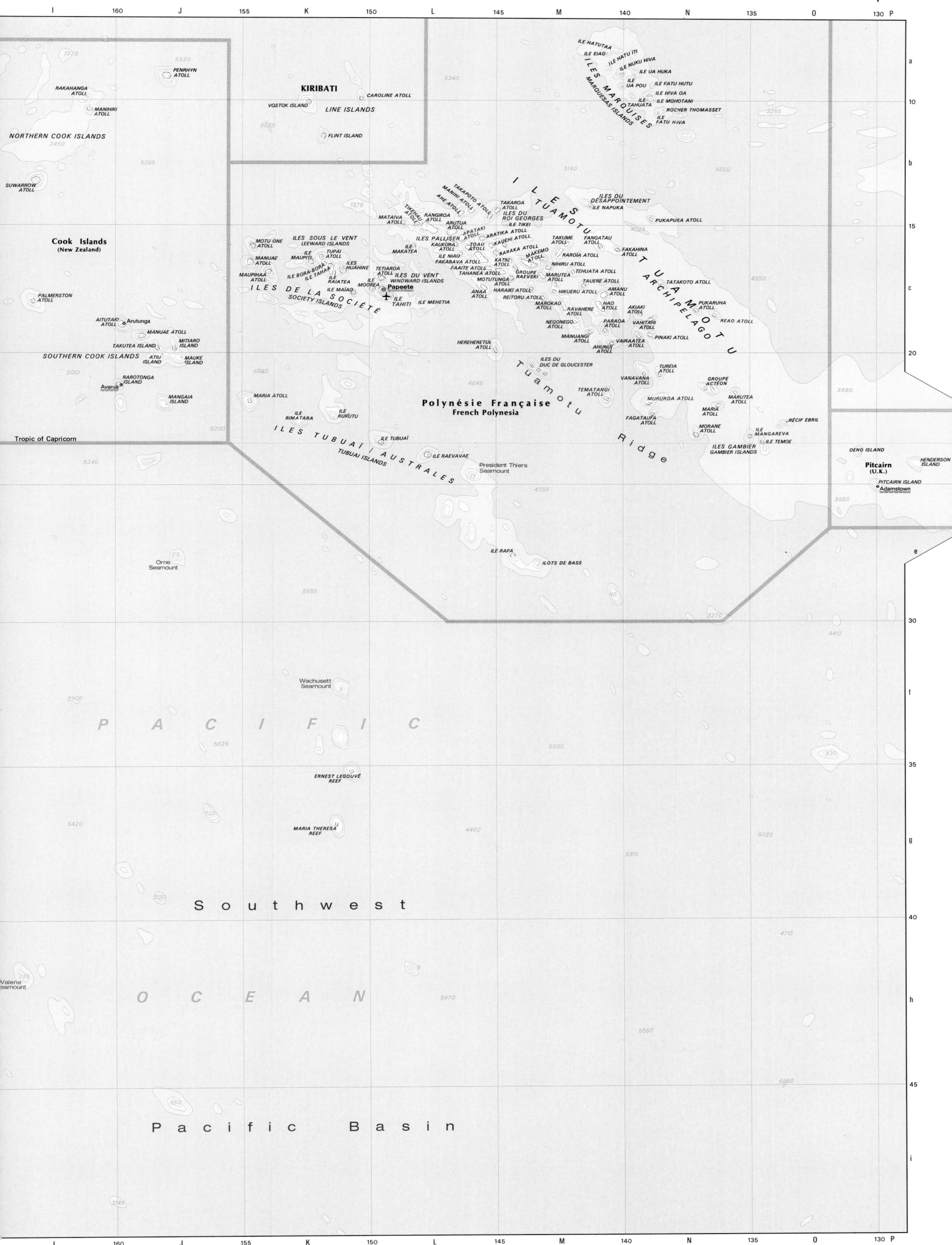

KIRIBATI

Caroline Atoll

Vostok Island

Line Islands

Flint Island

ILE HATUTAA
ILE EIAO
ILE HATU ITI
ILE NUKU HIVA
ILE UA HUKA
ILE UA POU
ILE FATU HUTU
ILE HIVA OA
ILE TAHUATA
ILE MOHOTANI
ROCHER THOMASSET
ILE FATU HIVA

ILES MARQUISES
MARQUESAS ISLANDS

RAKAHANGA
ATOLL

PENRHYN
ATOLL

MANIHIKI
ATOLL

NORTHERN COOK ISLANDS

SUWARROW
ATOLL

Cook Islands
(New Zealand)

PALMERSTON
ATOLL

AITUTAKI
ATOLL   Arutunga

MANUAE ATOLL

TAKUTEA ISLAND

MITIARO
ISLAND

SOUTHERN COOK ISLANDS

ATIU
ISLAND

MAUKE
ISLAND

RAROTONGA
ISLAND

Avarua

MANGAIA
ISLAND

Tropic of Capricorn

I L E S   T U A M O T U

TAKAPOTO ATOLL
MANIHI ATOLL
AHE ATOLL
TAKAROA
ATOLL
ILES DU
ROI GEORGES
ILE TIKEI
MATAIVA
ATOLL
TIKEHAU
ATOLL
RANGIROA
ATOLL
ARUTUA
ATOLL
APATAKI
ATOLL
ARATIKA ATOLL
KAUKURA
ATOLL
TOAU
ATOLL
KAUEHI ATOLL
TAKUME
ATOLL
FANGATAU
ATOLL
ILES DU
DESAPPOINTEMENT
ILE NAPUKA
PUKAPUKA ATOLL

ILES SOUS LE VENT
LEEWARD ISLANDS
MOTU ONE
ATOLL
MANUAE
ATOLL
MAUPIHAA
ATOLL
ILE
MAUPITI
TUPAI
ATOLL
ILE
MAKATEA
ILE BORA-BORA
ILE TAHAA
ILE
RAIATEA
ILES
HUAHINE
ILE MAIAO
ILE
MOOREA
TETIAROA
ATOLL
ILES DU VENT
WINDWARD ISLANDS
Papeete
ILE
TAHITI
ILE MEHETIA
ILE NIAU
FAKARAVA ATOLL
FAAITE ATOLL
TAHANEA ATOLL
KATIU
ATOLL
MAKEMO
ATOLL
GROUPE
RAEVSKI
MOTUTUNGA
ATOLL
MARUTEA
ATOLL
RAROIA ATOLL
NIHIRU ATOLL
TEHUATA ATOLL
FAKAHINA
ATOLL
TATAKOTO ATOLL
ANAA
ATOLL
HARAIKI ATOLL
REITORU ATOLL
HIKUERU ATOLL
TAUERE ATOLL
AMANU
ATOLL
PUKARUHA
ATOLL
MAROKAU
ATOLL
HAO
ATOLL
AKIAKI
ATOLL
REAO ATOLL
HEREHERETUE
ATOLL
NEGONEGO
ATOLL
RAVAHERE
ATOLL
PARAOA
ATOLL
VAHITAHI
ATOLL
PINAKI ATOLL
MANUANGI
ATOLL
AHUNUI
ATOLL
VAIRAATEA
ATOLL

ILES DE LA SOCIÉTÉ
SOCIETY ISLANDS

ILES PALLISER
ATOLL

T U A M O T U   A R C H I P E L A G O

Tuamotu Ridge

ILES DU
DUC DE GLOUCESTER
TUREIA
ATOLL
VANAVANA
ATOLL
GROUPE
ACTÉON
TEMATANGI
ATOLL
MURUROA ATOLL
MARUTEA
ATOLL
FAGATAUFA
ATOLL
MARIA
ATOLL
RÉCIF EBRIL
MORANE
ATOLL
ILE MANGAREVA
ILE TEMOE
ILES GAMBIER
GAMBIER ISLANDS

Polynésie Française
French Polynesia

MARIA ATOLL

ILE
RIMATARA
ILE
RURUTU
ILE TUBUAÏ
ILE RAEVAVAE

I L E S   T U B U A Ï   /   A U S T R A L E S
TUBUAI ISLANDS

President Thiers
Seamount

ILE RAPA
ILOTS DE BASS

OENO ISLAND
HENDERSON
ISLAND

Pitcairn
(U.K.)

PITCAIRN ISLAND
Adamstown

Orne
Seamount

Wachusett
Seamount

ERNEST LEGOUVÉ
REEF

MARIA THERESA
REEF

P A C I F I C

S o u t h w e s t

O C E A N

Valerie
Seamount

P a c i f i c   B a s i n

Map 62 **NEW ZEALAND**

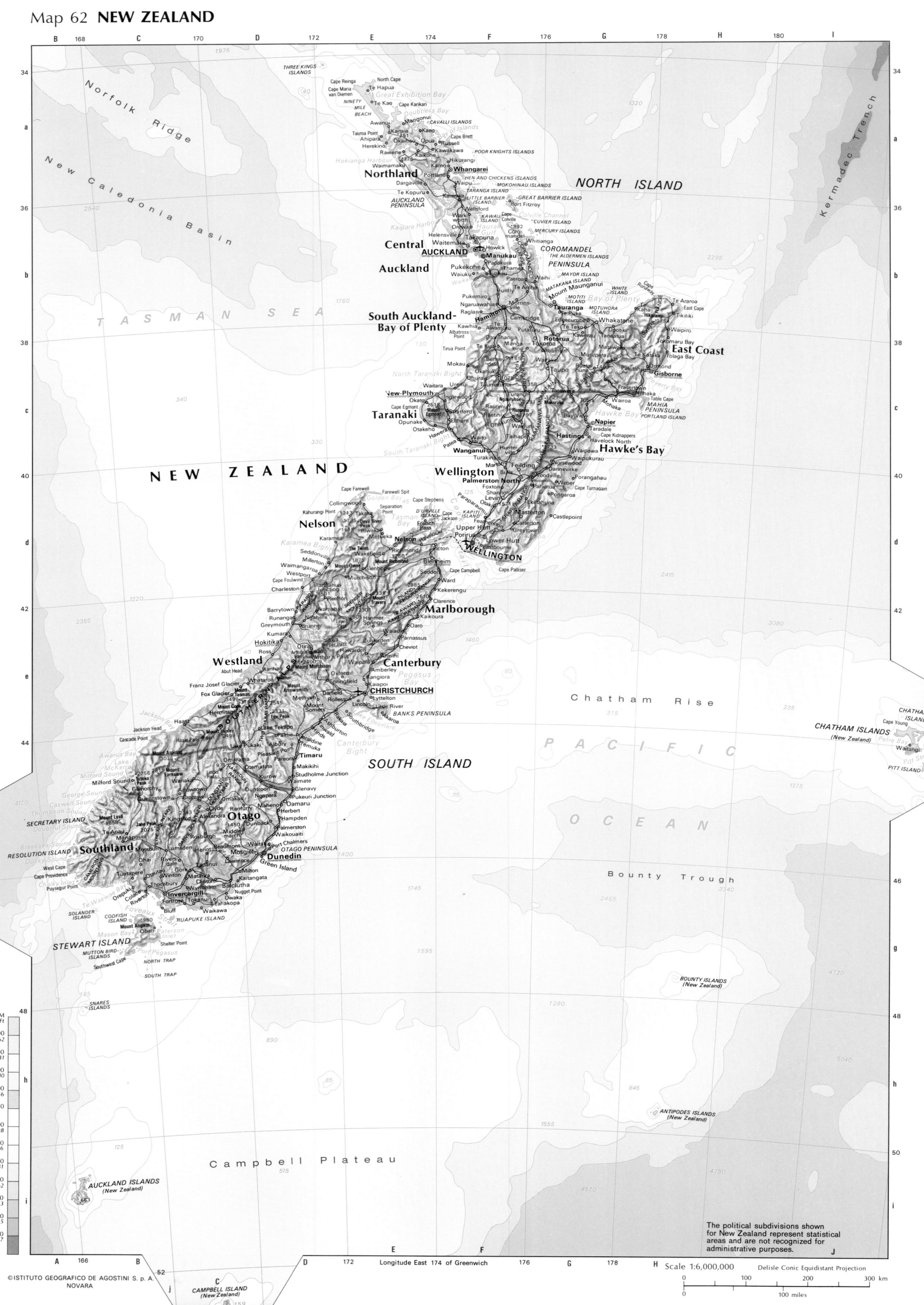

NORTH ISLAND

TASMAN SEA

Northland

Central
AUCKLAND

Auckland

South Auckland-
Bay of Plenty

COROMANDEL
PENINSULA

East Coast

Gisborne

New Plymouth

Taranaki

Napier

Hastings

Hawke's Bay

Wanganui

NEW ZEALAND

Wellington
Palmerston North

Nelson

Upper Hutt
WELLINGTON

Marlborough

Westland

Canterbury

Hokitika

CHRISTCHURCH

Chatham Rise

CHATHAM
ISLAND

CHATHAM ISLANDS
(New Zealand)

P A C I F I C

Timaru

SOUTH ISLAND

O C E A N

Otago

B o u n t y   T r o u g h

Southland

Invercargill

Dunedin

STEWART ISLAND

BOUNTY ISLANDS
(New Zealand)

SNARES
ISLANDS

ANTIPODES ISLANDS
(New Zealand)

C a m p b e l l   P l a t e a u

AUCKLAND ISLANDS
(New Zealand)

The political subdivisions shown
for New Zealand represent statistical
areas and are not recognized for
administrative purposes.

Norfolk Ridge

New Caledonia Basin

Kermadec Trench

CAMPBELL ISLAND
(New Zealand)

Longitude East 174 of Greenwich

Scale 1:6,000,000   Delisle Conic Equidistant Projection

0   100   200   300 km

0   100 miles

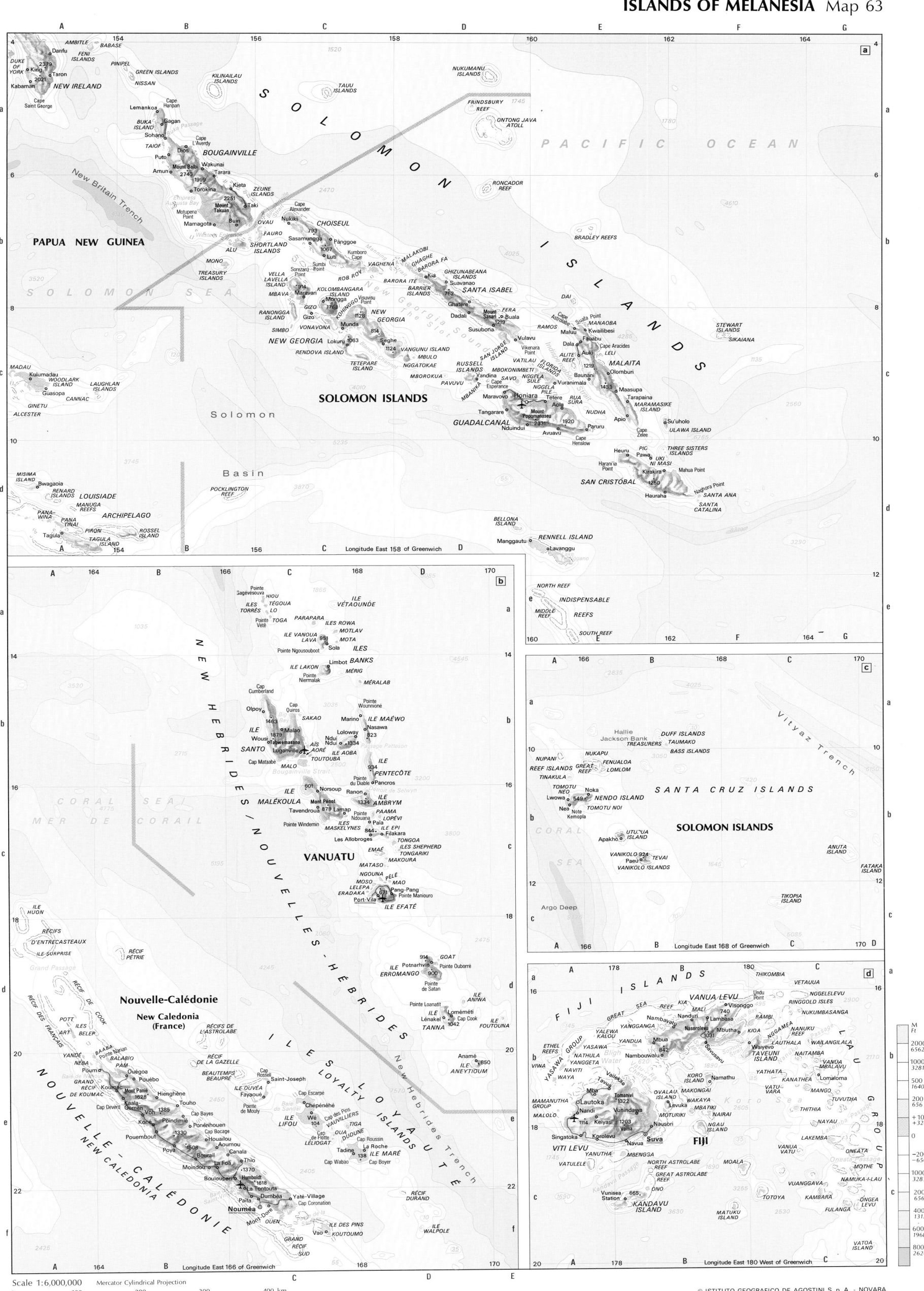

Scale 1:6,000,000   Mercator Cylindrical Projection

0   100   200   300   400 km

0   100   200 miles

Map 64 ISLANDS OF MICRONESIA-POLYNESIA

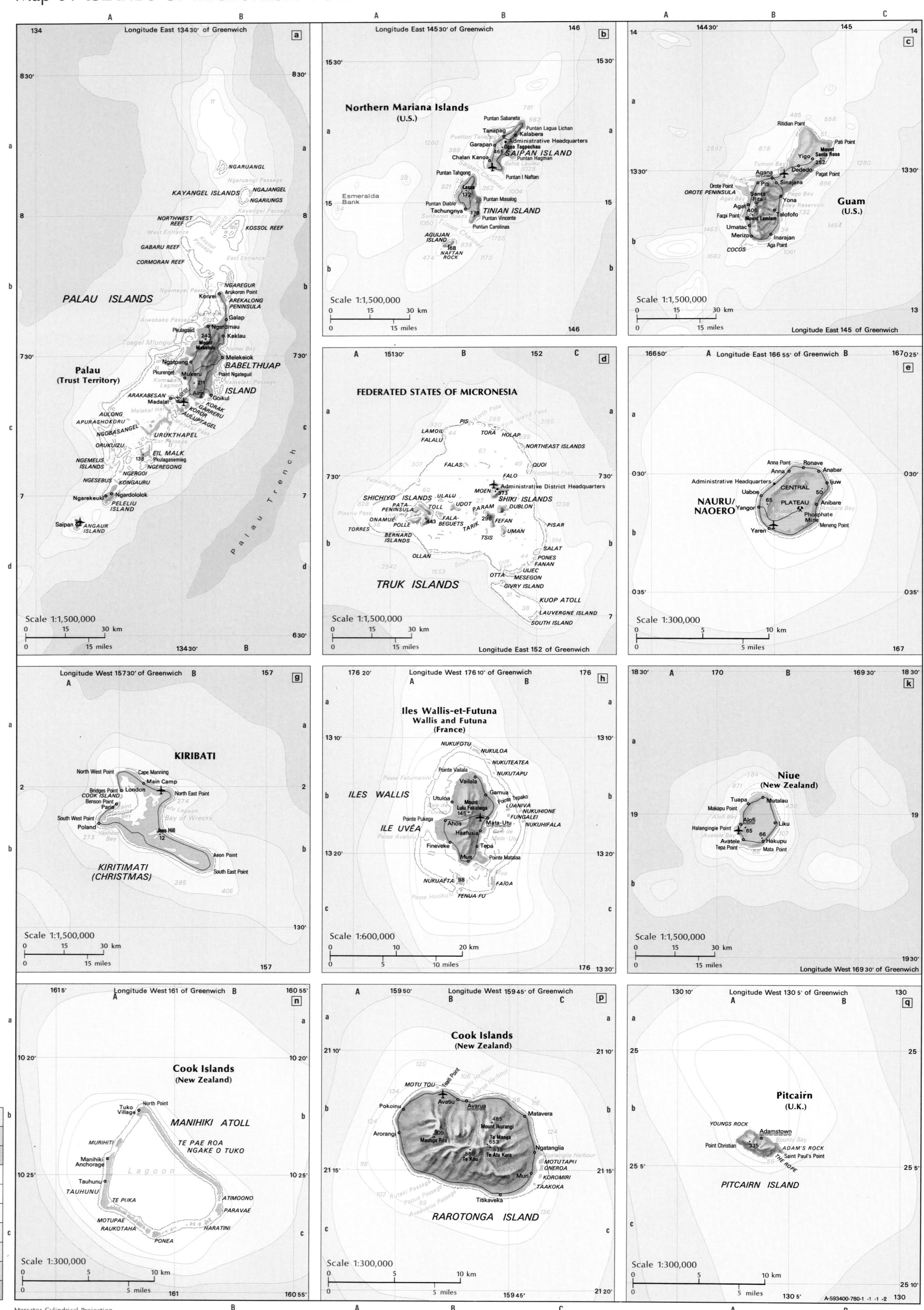

Mercator Cylindrical Projection

© ISTITUTO GEOGRAFICO DE AGOSTINI S. p. A. - NOVARA

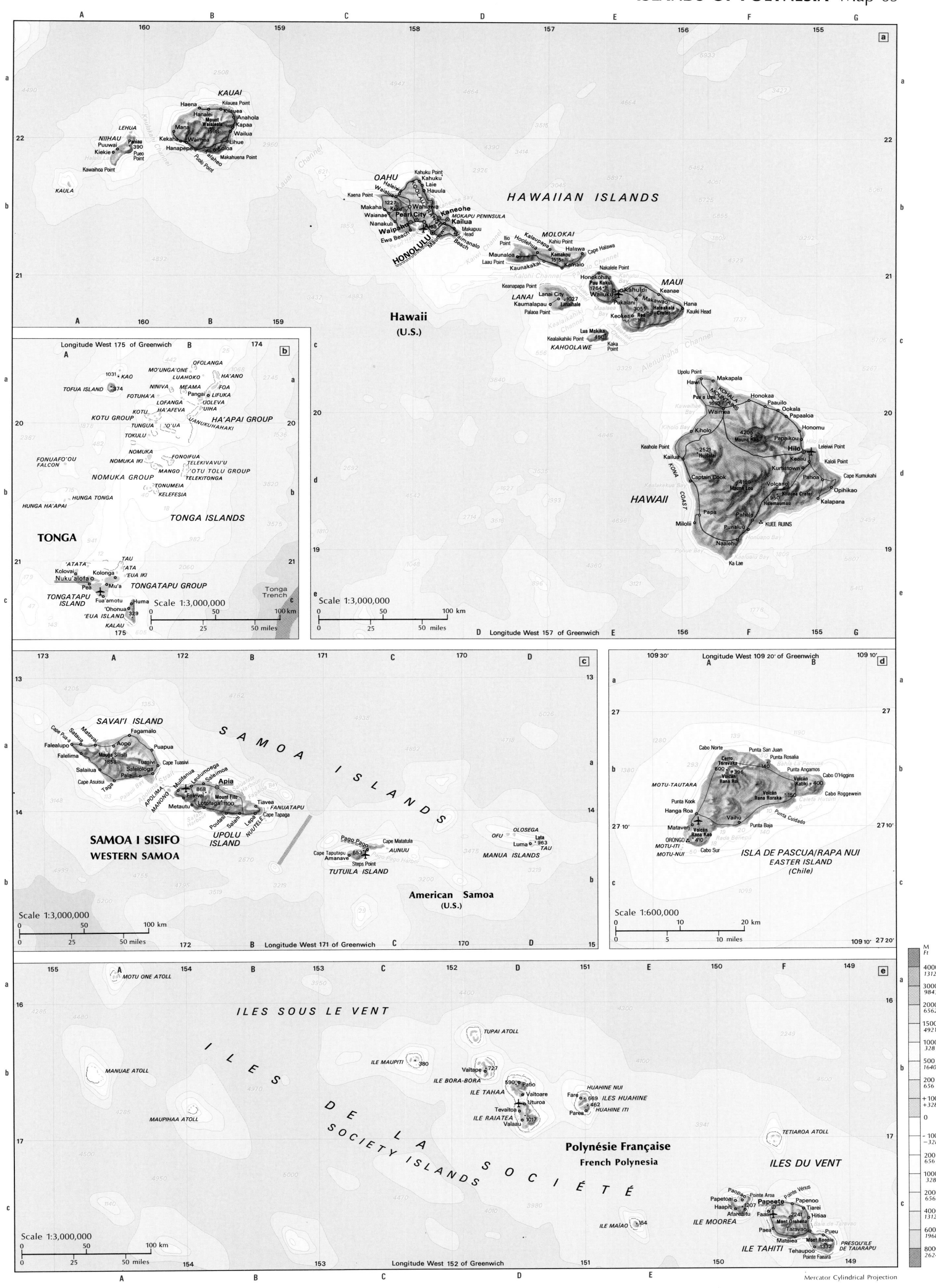

Mercator Cylindrical Projection

© ISTITUTO GEOGRAFICO DE AGOSTINI S. p. A. - NOVARA

Map 66 **ANTARCTIC REGION**

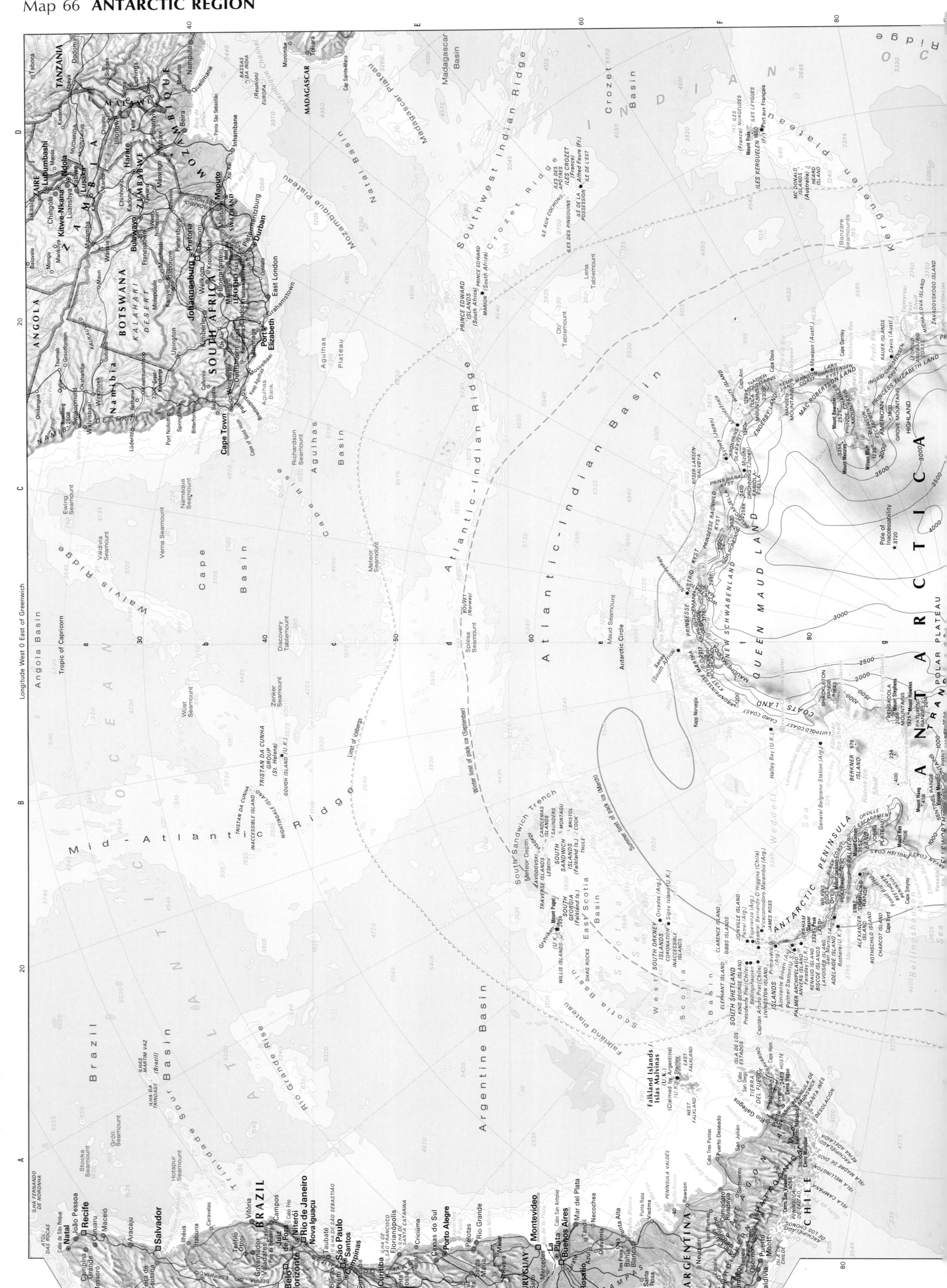

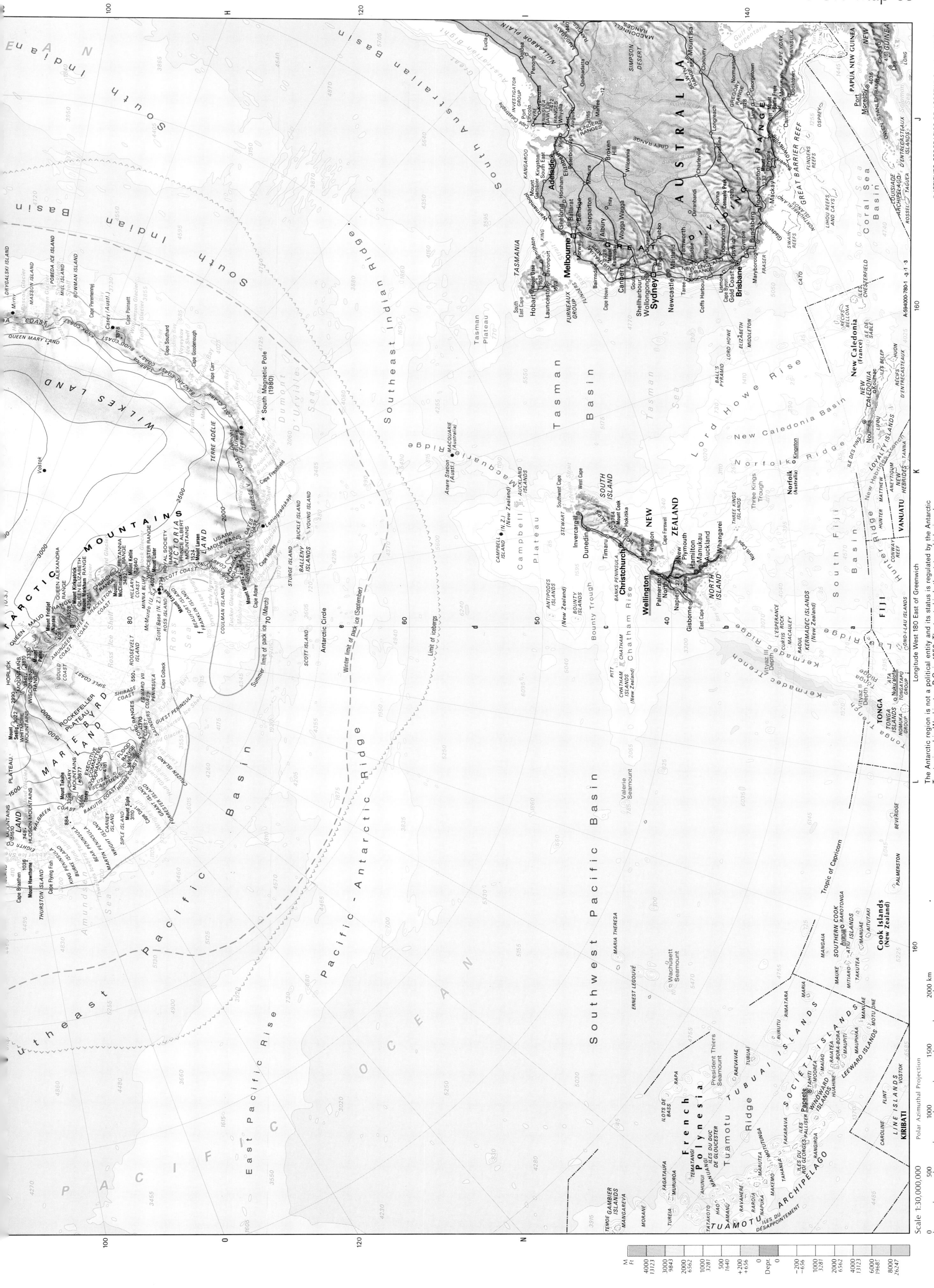

WILKES LAND

South Indian Basin

South Indian Basin

South Australian Basin

AUSTRALIA

Adelaide

Melbourne

TASMANIA

Hobart

Canberra

Sydney

Newcastle

Wollongong

Brisbane

Tasman Basin

Tasman Sea

Lord Howe Rise

New Caledonia (France)

New Caledonia Basin

Norfolk Ridge

Norfolk (Australia)

VANUATU

NEW ZEALAND

SOUTH ISLAND

NORTH ISLAND

Christchurch

Wellington

Dunedin

Auckland

Campbell Plateau

Chatham Rise

FIJI

South Fiji Basin

Kermadec Ridge

TONGA

Antarctic Circle

TRANSANTARCTIC MOUNTAINS

VICTORIA LAND

TERRE ADÉLIE

South Magnetic Pole (1980)

Dumont D'Urville Sea

Ross Sea

Ross Ice Shelf

MARIE BYRD LAND

Amundsen Sea

Southeast Indian Ridge

Pacific-Antarctic Ridge

East Pacific Rise

Pacific-Antarctic Ridge

SOUTHWEST PACIFIC BASIN

Southwest Pacific Basin

PACIFIC OCEAN

Tropic of Capricorn

French Polynesia

TUAMOTU ARCHIPELAGO

TUBUAI ISLANDS

Cook Islands (New Zealand)

SOCIETY ISLANDS

Papeete

KIRIBATI

Scale 1:30,000,000

Polar Azimuthal Projection

Longitude West 180 East of Greenwich

© ISTITUTO GEOGRAFICO DE AGOSTINI S.p.A. - NOVARA

Map 67 **ARCTIC REGION**

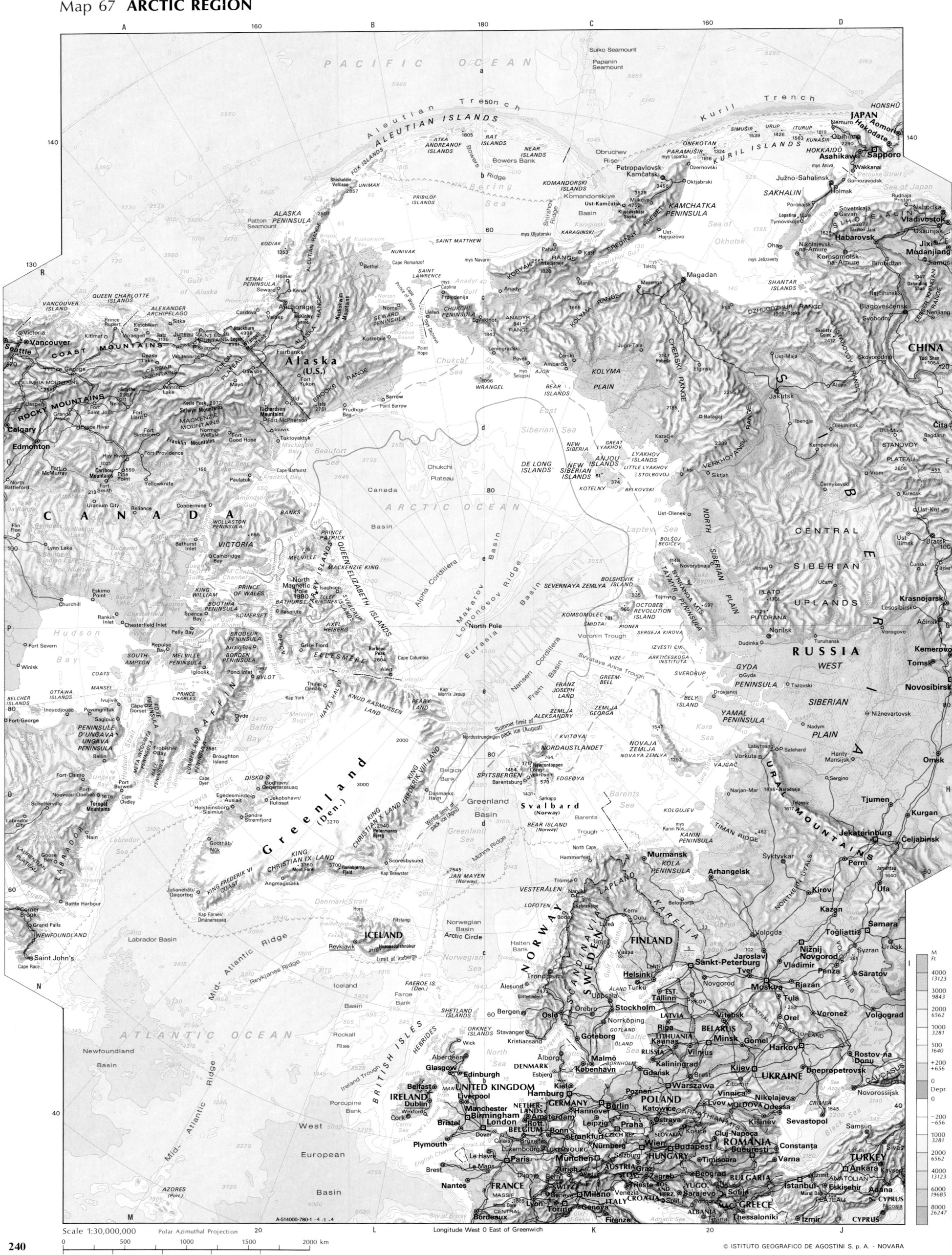

Scale 1:30,000,000   Polar Azimuthal Projection

A-514000-780-1 -4 -1 -4   Longitude West 0 East of Greenwich

© ISTITUTO GEOGRAFICO DE AGOSTINI S.p.A. - NOVARA

GEOGRAPHICAL INFORMATION AND INTERNATIONAL MAP INDEX

World Nations

This table gives the area, population, population density, form of government, capital and location of every country in the world.

Area figures include inland water.

The populations are estimates made by Rand McNally on the basis of official data, United Nations estimates and other available information.

Besides specifying the form of government for all political areas, the table classifies them into five groups according to their political status. Units labeled

A are independent sovereign nations. Units labeled *B* are independent as regards internal affairs, but for purposes of foreign affairs they are under the protection of another country. Units labeled *C* are colonies, overseas territories, dependencies, etc. of other countries. Units labeled *D* are states, provinces or other major administrative subdivisions of important countries. Units in the table with no letter designations are regions, islands or other areas that do not constitute separate political units by themselves.

Map Plate numbers refer to the International Map section of the atlas.

Country, Division, or Region English (Conventional)	Local Name	Area km²	Area sq mi	Population 1/1/93	Population Density per km²	Population Density per sq mi	Form of Government and Political Status	Capital	Continent and Map Plate
Afars and Issas, see Djibouti	…	…	…						…
† AFGHANISTAN	Afghānestān	652,225	251,826	16,290,000	25	65	Islamic republic	A Kābol	Asia … 23
Africa		30,300,000	11,700,000	668,700,000	22	57			Africa … 30-31
Alabama	Alabama	135,775	52,423	4,128,000	30	79	State (U.S.)	D Montgomery	N. Amer. … 44
Alaska	Alaska	1,700,139	656,424	564,000	0.3	0.9	State (U.S.)	D Juneau	N. Amer. … 40
† ALBANIA	Shqiperia	28,748	11,100	3,305,000	115	298	Republic	A Tirana	Europe … 15
Alberta	Alberta	661,190	255,287	2,839,000	4.3	11	Province (Canada)	D Edmonton	N. Amer. … 42
† ALGERIA	Al Jazā'ir	2,381,741	919,595	26,925,000	11	29	Provisional military government	A Al Jazā'ir (Algiers)	Africa … 32
American Samoa	American Samoa (English) / Amerika Samoa (Samoan)	199	77	52,000	261	675	Unincorporated territory (U.S.)	C Pago Pago	Oceania … 65
Andaman and Nicobar Islands	Andaman and Nicobar Islands	8,293	3,202	302,000	36	94	Territory (India)	D Port Blair	Asia … 25
ANDORRA	Andorra	453	175	56,000	124	320	Coprincipality (Spanish and French protection)	B Andorra la Vella	Europe … 13
† ANGOLA	Angola	1,246,700	481,354	10,735,000	8.6	22	Republic	A Luanda	Africa … 36
ANGUILLA	Anguilla	91	35	7,000	77	200	Dependent territory (U.K. protection)	B The Valley	N. Amer. … 51
Anhui	Anhui	139,000	53,668	58,440,000	420	1,089	Province (China)	D Hefei	Asia … 28
Antarctica	…	14,000,000	5,400,000	(1)	…	…			Antarctica … 66
† ANTIGUA AND BARBUDA	Antigua and Barbuda	442	171	77,000	174	450	Parliamentary state	A St. John's	N. Amer. … 51
Arabian Peninsula	…	3,010,000	1,160,000	35,848,000	12	31			Asia … 23
† ARGENTINA	Argentina	2,780,400	1,073,519	32,950,000	12	31	Republic	A Buenos Aires and Viedma (2)	S. Amer. … 56
Arizona	Arizona	295,276	114,006	3,872,000	13	34	State (U.S.)	D Phoenix	N. Amer. … 46
Arkansas	Arkansas	137,742	53,182	2,410,000	17	45	State (U.S.)	D Little Rock	N. Amer. … 45
† ARMENIA	Hayastan	29,800	11,506	3,429,000	115	298	Republic	A Jerevan	Asia … 16
ARUBA	Aruba	193	75	65,000	337	867	Self-governing territory (Netherlands protection)	B Oranjestad	N. Amer. … 49
Ascension	Ascension	88	34	1,200	14	35	Dependency (St. Helena)	C Georgetown	Africa … 30-31
Asia	…	44,900,000	17,300,000	3,337,800,000	74	193			Asia … 21-22
† AUSTRALIA	Australia	7,682,300	2,966,155	16,965,000	2.2	5.7	Federal parliamentary state	A Canberra	Oceania … 59
Australian Capital Territory	Australian Capital Territory	2,400	927	282,000	118	304	Territory (Australia)	D Canberra	Oceania … 59
† AUSTRIA	Österreich	83,856	32,377	7,899,000	94	244	Federal republic	A Wien (Vienna)	Europe … 14
† AZERBAIJAN	Azärbayjan	86,600	33,436	7,510,000	87	225	Republic	A Baku	Asia … 16
Azores	Açores	2,247	868	261,000	116	301	Autonomous region	D Ponta Delgada	Europe … 32
Baden-Wurttemberg	Baden-Württemberg	35,751	13,804	9,798,000	274	710	State (Germany)	D Stuttgart	Europe … 10
† BAHAMAS	Bahamas	13,939	5,382	265,000	19	49	Parliamentary state	A Nassau	N. Amer. … 47
† BAHRAIN	Al Baḥrayn	691	267	561,000	812	2,101	Monarchy	A Al Manāmah (Manama)	Asia … 24
Balearic Islands	Islas Baleares	5,014	1,936	743,000	148	384	Province (Spain)	D Palma	Europe … 13
Baltic Republics	…	174,000	67,182	8,154,000	47	121			Europe … 8
† BANGLADESH	Bangladesh	143,998	55,598	120,850,000	839	2,174	Republic	A Dhaka	Asia … 25
† BARBADOS	Barbados	430	166	258,000	600	1,554	Parliamentary state	A Bridgetown	N. Amer. … 51
Bavaria	Bayern	70,554	27,241	11,430,000	162	420	State (Germany)	D München (Munich)	Europe … 10
† BELARUS	Byelarus'	207,600	80,155	10,400,000	50	130	Republic	A Minsk	Europe … 16
† BELGIUM	Belgique (French) / België (Flemish)	30,518	11,783	10,030,000	329	851	Constitutional monarchy	A Bruxelles (Brussels)	Europe … 12
† BELIZE	Belize	22,963	8,866	186,000	8.1	21	Parliamentary state	A Belmopan	N. Amer. … 49
Benelux	…	74,968	28,945	25,612,000	342	885	Economic union		Europe … 12
† BENIN	Bénin	112,600	43,475	5,083,000	45	117	Republic	A Porto-Novo and Cotonou	Africa … 34
Berlin	Berlin	883	341	3,475,000	3,935	10,191	State	D Berlin	Europe … 10
Bermuda	Bermuda	54	21	60,000	1,111	2,857	Dependent territory (U.K.)	C Hamilton	N. Amer. … 47
† BHUTAN	Druk	46,500	17,954	1,680,000	36	94	Monarchy (Indian protection)	B Thimphu	Asia … 25
Bioko	Bioko	2,017	779	75,000	37	96	Province of Equatorial Guinea	D Malabo	Africa … 34
† BOLIVIA	Bolivia	1,098,581	424,165	7,411,000	6.7	17	Republic	A La Paz and Sucre	S. Amer. … 54
Borneo, Indonesian	Kalimantan	539,460	208,287	9,458,000	18	45	Part of Indonesia (4 provinces)		Asia … 26
† BOSNIA AND HERZEGOVINA	Bosna i Hercegovina	51,129	19,741	4,375,000	86	222	Republic	A Sarajevo	Europe … 14
† BOTSWANA	Botswana	582,000	224,711	1,379,000	2.4	6.1	Republic	A Gaborone	Africa … 37
Brandenburg	Brandenburg	29,060	11,220	2,690,000	93	240	State (Germany)	D Potsdam	Europe … 10
† BRAZIL	Brasil	8,511,996	3,286,500	159,630,000	19	49	Federal republic	A Brasília	S. Amer. … 54-56
Bremen	Bremen	404	156	687,000	1,700	4,404	State (Germany)	D Bremen	Europe … 10
British Columbia	British Columbia (English) / Colombie-Britannique (French)	947,800	365,948	3,665,000	3.9	10	Province (Canada)	D Victoria	N. Amer. … 42
British Indian Ocean Territory	British Indian Ocean Territory	60	23	(1)	…	…	Dependent territory (U.K.)	C …	Africa … 22
† BRUNEI	Brunei	5,765	2,226	273,000	47	123	Monarchy	A Bandar Seri Begawan	Asia … 26
† BULGARIA	Balgarija	110,912	42,823	8,842,000	80	206	Republic	A Sofija (Sofia)	Europe … 15
† BURKINA FASO	Burkina Faso	274,200	105,869	9,808,000	36	93	Provisional military government	A Ouagadougou	Africa … 34
† BURMA	Myanmar	676,577	261,228	43,070,000	64	165	Provisional military government	A Yangon (Rangoon)	Asia … 25
† BURUNDI	Burundi	27,830	10,745	6,118,000	220	569	Republic	A Bujumbura	Africa … 36
California	California	424,002	163,707	31,310,000	74	191	State (U.S.)	D Sacramento	N. Amer. … 46
† CAMBODIA	Kâmpŭchéa	181,035	69,898	8,928,000	49	128	Transitional government	A Phnum Pénh (Phnom Penh)	Asia … 26
† CAMEROON	Cameroon (English) / Cameroun (French)	475,442	183,569	12,875,000	27	70	Republic	A Yaoundé	Africa … 34
† CANADA	Canada	9,970,610	3,849,674	30,530,000	3.1	7.9	Federal parliamentary state	A Ottawa	N. Amer. … 42
Canary Islands	Islas Canarias	7,273	2,808	1,613,000	222	574	Part of Spain (2 provinces)		Africa … 32
† CAPE VERDE	Cabo Verde	4,033	1,557	404,000	100	259	Republic	A Praia	Africa … 32
Cayman Islands	Cayman Islands	259	100	29,000	112	290	Dependent territory (U.K.)	C Georgetown	N. Amer. … 49
Celebes	Sulawesi	189,216	73,057	12,995,000	69	178	Part of Indonesia (4 provinces)		Asia … 26
† CENTRAL AFRICAN REPUBLIC	Centrafrique	622,984	240,535	3,068,000	4.9	13	Republic	A Bangui	Africa … 35
Central America	…	520,000	200,000	30,402,000	58	152			N. Amer. … 49
Ceylon, see Sri Lanka	…	…	…	…	…	…			…
† CHAD	Tchad	1,284,000	495,755	5,297,000	4.1	11	Republic	A N'Djamena	Africa … 35

Country, Division, or Region English (Conventional)	Local Name	Area km²	Area sq mi	Population 1/1/93	Population Density per km²	Population Density per sq mi	Form of Government and Political Status	Capital	Continent and Map Plate	
CHANNEL ISLANDS	. . .	194	*75*	143,000	737	*1,907*	Dependent territory (U.K.)	*B* . . .	Europe	9
† CHILE	Chile	756,626	*292,135*	13,635,000	18	*47*	Republic	*A* Santiago	S. Amer.	56
† CHINA (excl. Taiwan)	Zhongguo Renmin Gongheguo	9,556,100	*3,689,631*	1,179,030,000	123	*320*	Socialist republic	*A* Beijing (Peking)	Asia	27
China (Nationalist), see Taiwan	. . .	. . .	. . .	. . .	. . .	. . .	. . .	. . .	. . .	. . .
Christmas Island	Christmas Island	135	*52*	900	6.7	*17*	External territory (Australia)	*C* Flying Fish Cove	Oceania	26
Cocos (Keeling) Islands	Cocos (Keeling) Islands	14	*5.4*	500	36	*93*	Territory (Australia)	*C* . . .	Oceania	22
† COLOMBIA	Colombia	1,141,748	*440,831*	34,640,000	30	*79*	Republic	*A* Santa Fe de Bogotá	S. Amer.	54
Colorado	Colorado	269,620	*104,100*	3,410,000	13	*33*	State (U.S.)	*D* Denver	N. Amer.	45
Commonwealth of Independent States	. . .	22,031,200	*8,506,294*	281,640,000	13	*33*	Alliance of sovereign states	. . . Minsk	Eur.-Asia	. . .
Commonwealth of Nations	. . .	29,230,000	*11,320,000*	1,498,930,000	51	*132*	. . .	. . . London	. . .	. . .
† COMOROS (excl. Mayotte)	Al-Qumur (Arabic) / Comores (French)	2,235	*863*	503,000	225	*583*	Federal Islamic republic	*A* Moroni	Africa	37
† CONGO	Congo	342,000	*132,047*	2,413,000	7.1	*18*	Republic	*A* Brazzaville	Africa	36
Connecticut	Connecticut	14,358	*5,544*	3,358,000	234	*606*	State (U.S.)	*D* Hartford	N. Amer.	44
COOK ISLANDS	Cook Islands	236	*91*	18,000	76	*198*	Self-governing territory (New Zealand protection)	*B* Avarua	Oceania	61
Coral Sea Islands Territory	Coral Sea Islands Territory	2.6	*1.0*	(1)	. . .	. . .	External territory (Australia)	*C* . . .	Oceania	59
Corsica	Corse	8,720	*3,367*	255,000	29	*76*	Part of France	*D* . . .	Europe	11
† COSTA RICA	Costa Rica	51,100	*19,730*	3,225,000	63	*163*	Republic	*A* San José	N. Amer.	49
Côte d'Ivoire, see Ivory Coast	. . .	. . .	. . .	. . .	. . .	. . .	. . .	. . .	. . .	. . .
† CROATIA	Hrvatska	56,538	*21,829*	4,793,000	85	*220*	Republic	. . . Zagreb	Europe	14
† CUBA	Cuba	110,861	*42,804*	10,900,000	98	*255*	Socialist republic	*A* La Habana (Havana)	N. Amer.	49
Curacao	Curaçao	444	*171*	146,000	329	*854*	Division of Netherlands Antilles (Neth.)	*D* Willemstad	N. Amer.	49
† CYPRUS	Kípros (Greek) / Kıbrıs (Turkish)	5,896	*2,276*	527,000	89	*232*	Republic	*A* Nicosia (Levkosía)	Asia	24
CYPRUS, NORTH	Kuzey Kıbrıs	3,355	*1,295*	193,000	58	*149*	Republic	*A* Nicosia (Lefkoşa)	Asia	24
† CZECH REPUBLIC	Česká Republika	78,864	*30,450*	10,335,000	131	*339*	Republic	*A* Praha (Prague)	Europe	10
Delaware	Delaware	6,447	*2,489*	692,000	107	*278*	State (U.S.)	*D* Dover	N. Amer.	44
† DENMARK	Danmark	43,093	*16,638*	5,169,000	120	*311*	Constitutional monarchy	*A* København (Copenhagen)	Europe	8
Denmark and Possessions	. . .	2,220,092	*857,182*	5,275,000	2.4	*6.2*	. . .	. . .	. . .	. . .
District of Columbia	District of Columbia	177	*68*	590,000	3,333	*8,676*	Federal district (U.S.)	*D* Washington	N. Amer.	44
† DJIBOUTI	Djibouti	23,200	*8,958*	396,000	17	*44*	Republic	*A* Djibouti	Africa	35
† DOMINICA	Dominica	790	*305*	88,000	111	*289*	Republic	*A* Roseau	N. Amer.	51
† DOMINICAN REPUBLIC	República Dominicana	48,442	*18,704*	7,591,000	157	*406*	Republic	*A* Santo Domingo	N. Amer.	49
† ECUADOR	Ecuador	283,561	*109,484*	11,055,000	39	*101*	Republic	*A* Quito	S. Amer.	54
† EGYPT	Mişr	1,001,449	*386,662*	57,050,000	57	*148*	Socialist republic	*A* Al Qāhirah (Cairo)	Africa	33
Ellis Islands, see Tuvalu	. . .	. . .	. . .	. . .	. . .	. . .	. . .	. . .	. . .	. . .
† EL SALVADOR	El Salvador	21,041	*8,124*	5,635,000	268	*694*	Republic	*A* San Salvador	N. Amer.	49
England	England	130,478	*50,378*	48,235,000	370	*957*	Administrative division (U.K.)	*D* London	Europe	9
† EQUATORIAL GUINEA	Guinea Ecuatorial	28,051	*10,831*	394,000	14	*36*	Republic	*A* Malabo	Africa	36
ERITREA	Eritrea	93,679	*36,170*	3,425,000	37	*95*	Republic	*A* Asmera	Africa	35
† ESTONIA	Eesti	45,100	*17,413*	1,613,000	36	*93*	Republic	*A* Tallinn	Europe	8
† ETHIOPIA	Itiopya	1,157,603	*446,953*	51,715,000	45	*116*	Transitional military government	*A* Ādīs Ābeba (Addis Ababa)	Africa	35
Eurasia	. . .	54,800,000	*21,100,000*	4,032,700,000	74	*191*	. . .	. . .	. . .	. . .
Europe	. . .	9,900,000	*3,800,000*	694,900,000	70	*183*	. . .	. . .	Europe	5-6
European Community	. . .	4,070,000	*1,570,000*	346,800,000	85	*221*	. . .	. . . Brussels (Bruxelles)	Europe	5-6
FAEROE ISLANDS	Føroyar	1,399	*540*	49,000	35	*91*	Self-governing territory (Danish protection)	*B* Thorshavn	Europe	6
Falkland Islands (3)	Falkland Islands (English) / Islas Malvinas (Spanish)	12,173	*4,700*	2,100	0.2	*0.4*	Dependent territory (U.K.)	*C* Stanley	S. Amer.	56
† FIJI	Fiji (French) / Viti (Fijian)	18,274	*7,056*	754,000	41	*107*	Republic	*A* Suva	Oceania	63
† FINLAND	Suomi (Finnish) / Finland (Swedish)	338,145	*130,559*	5,074,000	15	*39*	Republic	*A* Helsinki (Helsingfors)	Europe	7
Florida	Florida	170,313	*65,758*	13,630,000	80	*207*	State (U.S.)	*D* Tallahassee	N. Amer.	44
† FRANCE (excl. Overseas Departments)	France	547,026	*211,208*	57,570,000	105	*273*	Republic	*A* Paris	Europe	11
France and Possessions	. . .	666,866	*257,476*	59,617,000	89	*232*	. . .	. . . Paris	. . .	. . .
French Guiana	Guyane Française	91,000	*35,135*	131,000	1.4	*3.7*	Overseas department (France)	*C* Cayenne	S. Amer.	54
French Polynesia	Polynésie Française	3,521	*1,359*	208,000	59	*153*	Overseas territory (France)	*C* Papeete	Oceania	61
French West Indies	. . .	2,880	*1,112*	785,000	273	*706*	. . .	. . .	N. Amer.	50
Fujian	Fujian	120,000	*46,332*	31,160,000	260	*673*	Province (China)	*D* Fuzhou	Asia	27
† GABON	Gabon	267,667	*103,347*	1,115,000	4.2	*11*	Republic	*A* Libreville	Africa	36
Galapagos Islands	Archipiélago de Colón (Islas Galápagos)	7,964	*3,075*	8,500	1.1	*2.8*	Province (Ecuador)	*D* Baquerizo Moreno	S. Amer.	54
† GAMBIA	Gambia	10,689	*4,127*	916,000	86	*222*	Republic	*A* Banjul	Africa	34
Gansu	Gansu	450,000	*173,746*	23,280,000	52	*134*	Province (China)	*D* Lanzhou	Asia	27
Georgia	Georgia	153,953	*59,441*	6,795,000	44	*114*	State (U.S.)	*D* Atlanta	N. Amer.	44
GEORGIA	Sakartvelo	69,700	*26,911*	5,593,000	80	*208*	Provisional military government	*A* Tbilisi	Asia	16
† GERMANY	Deutschland	356,955	*137,822*	80,590,000	226	*585*	Federal republic	*A* Berlin and Bonn	Europe	10
† GHANA	Ghana	238,533	*92,098*	16,445,000	69	*179*	Provisional military government	*A* Accra	Africa	34
Gibraltar	Gibraltar	6.0	*2.3*	32,000	5,333	*13,913*	Dependent territory (U.K.)	*C* Gibraltar	Europe	13
Gilbert Islands, see Tuvalu	. . .	. . .	. . .	. . .	. . .	. . .	. . .	. . .	. . .	. . .
Great Britain, see United Kingdom	. . .	. . .	. . .	. . .	. . .	. . .	. . .	. . .	. . .	. . .
† GREECE	Ellas	131,957	*50,949*	10,075,000	76	*198*	Republic	*A* Athínai (Athens)	Europe	15
GREENLAND	Kalaallit Nunaat (Inuit) / Grønland (Danish)	2,175,600	*840,004*	57,000	. . .	*0.1*	Self-governing territory (Danish protection)	*B* Godthåb (Nūk)	N. Amer.	41
† GRENADA	Grenada	344	*133*	97,000	282	*729*	Parliamentary state	*A* St. George's	N. Amer.	51
Guadeloupe (incl. Dependencies)	Guadeloupe	1,780	*687*	413,000	232	*601*	Overseas department (France)	*C* Basse-Terre	N. Amer.	51
Guam	Guam	541	*209*	143,000	264	*684*	Unincorporated territory (U.S.)	*C* Agana	Oceania	64
Guangdong	Guangdong	178,000	*68,726*	65,380,000	367	*951*	Province (China)	*D* Guangzhou (Canton)	Asia	27
† GUATEMALA	Guatemala	108,889	*42,042*	9,705,000	89	*231*	Republic	*A* Guatemala	N. Amer.	49
GUERNSEY (incl. Dependencies)	Guernsey	78	*30*	58,000	744	*1,933*	Crown dependency (U.K. protection)	*B* St. Peter Port	Europe	9
† GUINEA	Guinée	245,857	*94,926*	7,726,000	31	*81*	Provisional military government	*A* Conakry	Africa	34
† GUINEA-BISSAU	Guiné-Bissau	36,125	*13,948*	1,060,000	29	*76*	Republic	*A* Bissau	Africa	34
Guizhou	Guizhou	170,000	*65,637*	33,745,000	199	*514*	Province (China)	*D* Guiyang	Asia	27
† GUYANA	Guyana	214,969	*83,000*	737,000	3.4	*8.9*	Republic	*A* Georgetown	S. Amer.	54
Hainan	Hainan	34,000	*13,127*	6,820,000	201	*520*	Province (China)	*D* Haikou	Asia	27
† HAITI	Haïti	27,750	*10,714*	6,509,000	235	*608*	Provisional military government	*A* Port-au-Prince	N. Amer.	49
Hamburg	Hamburg	755	*292*	1,657,000	2,195	*5,675*	State (Germany)	*D* Hamburg	Europe	10
Hawaii	Hawaii	28,313	*10,932*	1,159,000	41	*106*	State (U.S.)	*D* Honolulu	N. Amer.	60
Hebei	Hebei	190,000	*73,359*	63,500,000	334	*866*	Province (China)	*D* Shijiazhuang	Asia	28
Heilongjiang	Heilongjiang	469,000	*181,082*	36,685,000	78	*203*	Province (China)	*D* Harbin	Asia	27
Henan	Henan	167,000	*64,479*	88,890,000	532	*1,379*	Province (China)	*D* Zhengzhou	Asia	27
Hessia	Hessen	21,114	*8,152*	5,766,000	273	*707*	State (Germany)	*D* Wiesbaden	Europe	10
Hispaniola	La Española	76,192	*29,418*	14,100,000	185	*479*	. . .	. . .	N. Amer.	49

Country, Division, or Region English (Conventional)	Local Name	Area km²	Area sq mi	Population 1/1/93	Population Density per km²	Population Density per sq mi	Form of Government and Political Status	Capital	Continent and Map Plate
Holland, see Netherlands	...	...	...	...	...	...	...	...	...
† HONDURAS	Honduras	112,088	*43,277*	5,164,000	46	*119*	Republic	*A* Tegucigalpa	N. Amer. 49
Hong Kong	Hong Kong (English) / Xianggang (Chinese)	1,072	*414*	5,580,000	5,205	*13,478*	Chinese territory under British administration	*C* Victoria (Hong Kong)	Asia 27
Hubei	Hubei	187,400	*72,356*	56,090,000	299	*775*	Province (China)	*D* Wuhan	Asia 27
Hunan	Hunan	210,000	*81,081*	63,140,000	301	*779*	Province (China)	*D* Changsha	Asia 27
† HUNGARY	Magyarország	93,033	*35,920*	10,305,000	111	*287*	Republic	*A* Budapest	Europe 10
† ICELAND	Ísland	103,000	*39,769*	260,000	2.5	*6.5*	Republic	*A* Reykjavík	Europe 7
Idaho	Idaho	216,456	*83,574*	1,026,000	4.7	*12*	State (U.S.)	*D* Boise	N. Amer. 46
Illinois	Illinois	150,007	*57,918*	11,640,000	78	*201*	State (U.S.)	*D* Springfield	N. Amer. 45
† INDIA (incl. part of Jammu and Kashmir)	India (English) / Bhārat (Hindi)	3,203,975	*1,237,062*	873,850,000	273	*706*	Federal republic	*A* New Delhi	Asia 25
Indiana	Indiana	94,328	*36,420*	5,667,000	60	*156*	State (U.S.)	*D* Indianapolis	N. Amer. 44
† INDONESIA	Indonesia	1,948,732	*752,410*	186,180,000	96	*247*	Republic	*A* Jakarta	Asia 26
Inner Mongolia	Nei Mongol Gaoyuan	1,183,000	*456,759*	22,340,000	19	*49*	Autonomous region (China)	*D* Hohhot	Asia 27
Iowa	Iowa	145,754	*56,276*	2,821,000	19	*50*	State (U.S.)	*D* Des Moines	N. Amer. 45
† IRAN	Īrān	1,638,057	*632,457*	60,500,000	37	*96*	Islamic republic	*A* Tehrān	Asia 23
† IRAQ	Al ʿIrāq	438,317	*169,235*	18,815,000	43	*111*	Republic	*A* Baghdād	Asia 24
† IRELAND	Ireland (English) / Éire (Gaelic)	70,285	*27,137*	3,525,000	50	*130*	Republic	*A* Dublin (Baile Átha Cliath)	Europe 9
ISLE OF MAN	Isle of Man	572	*221*	70,000	122	*317*	Crown dependency (U.K. protection)	*B* Douglas	Europe 9
† ISRAEL (excl. Occupied Areas)	Yisra'el (Hebrew) / Isrā'īl (Arabic)	20,770	*8,019*	4,593,000	221	*573*	Republic	*A* Yerushalayim (Jerusalem)	Asia 24
Israeli Occupied Areas (4)	...	7,632	*2,947*	2,461,000	322	*835*	None	...	Asia 24
† ITALY	Italia	301,277	*116,324*	56,550,000	188	*486*	Republic	*A* Roma (Rome)	Europe 14
† IVORY COAST	Côte d'Ivoire	322,500	*124,518*	13,765,000	43	*111*	Republic	*A* Abidjan and Yamoussoukro (2)	Africa 34
† JAMAICA	Jamaica	10,991	*4,244*	2,412,000	219	*568*	Parliamentary state	*A* Kingston	N. Amer. 49
† JAPAN	Nippon	377,801	*145,870*	124,710,000	330	*855*	Constitutional monarchy	*A* Tōkyō	Asia 29
Java	Jawa	132,187	*51,038*	107,580,000	814	*2,108*	Part of Indonesia (5 provinces)	...	Asia 26
JERSEY	Jersey	116	*45*	85,000	733	*1,889*	Crown dependency (U.K. protection)	*B* St. Helier	Europe 9
Jiangsu	Jiangsu	102,600	*39,614*	69,730,000	680	*1,760*	Province (China)	*D* Nanjing (Nanking)	Asia 28
Jiangxi	Jiangxi	166,600	*64,325*	39,270,000	236	*610*	Province (China)	*D* Nanchang	Asia 27
Jilin	Jilin	187,000	*72,201*	25,630,000	137	*355*	Province (China)	*D* Changchun	Asia 27
Johnston Atoll	Johnston Atoll	1.3	*0.5*	1,400	1,077	*2,800*	Unincorporated territory (U.S.)	*C* ...	Oceania 60
† JORDAN (excl. West Bank)	Al Urdun	91,000	*35,135*	3,632,000	40	*103*	Constitutional monarchy	*A* 'Ammān	Asia 24
Kansas	Kansas	213,110	*82,282*	2,539,000	12	*31*	State (U.S.)	*D* Topeka	N. Amer. 45
Kashmir, Jammu and	Jammu and Kashmir	222,236	*85,806*	11,565,000	52	*135*	Disputed territory (India and Pakistan)	*D* ...	Asia 25
† KAZAKHSTAN	Qazaqstan	2,717,300	*1,049,156*	17,190,000	6.3	*16*	Republic	*A* Alma-Ata	Asia 19
Kentucky	Kentucky	104,665	*40,411*	3,745,000	36	*93*	State (U.S.)	*D* Frankfort	N. Amer. 44
† KENYA	Kenya	582,646	*224,961*	26,635,000	46	*118*	Republic	*A* Nairobi	Africa 36
Kerguelen Islands	Iles Kerguélen	6,993	*2,700*	200	...	*0.1*	Territory (France)	*C* ...	S. Amer. 30-31
KIRIBATI	Kiribati	811	*313*	76,000	94	*243*	Republic	*A* Bairiki	Oceania 60
† KOREA, NORTH	Chosŏn Minjujuŭi Inmīn Konghwaguk	120,538	*46,540*	22,450,000	186	*482*	Socialist republic	*A* P'yŏngyang	Asia 28
† KOREA, SOUTH	Taehan-min'guk	99,016	*38,230*	43,660,000	441	*1,142*	Republic	*A* Sŏul (Seoul)	Asia 28
Korea (entire)	...	219,554	*84,770*	66,110,000	301	*780*	...	...	Asia 28
† KUWAIT	Al Kuwayt	17,818	*6,880*	2,388,000	134	*347*	Constitutional monarchy	*A* Al Kuwayt (Kuwait)	Asia 24
Kwangsi	Guangxi Zhuangzu Zizhiqu	236,300	*91,236*	43,975,000	186	*482*	Autonomous region (China)	*D* Nanning	Asia 27
† KYRGYZSTAN	Kyrgyzstan	198,500	*76,641*	4,613,000	23	*60*	Republic	*A* Biškek	Asia 18
Labrador	Labrador	292,218	*112,826*	36,000	0.1	*0.3*	Part of Newfoundland province (Canada)	...	N. Amer. 42
† LAOS	Lao	236,800	*91,429*	4,507,000	19	*49*	Socialist republic	*A* Viangchan (Vientiane)	Asia 26
Latin America	...	20,500,000	*7,900,000*	461,900,000	23	*58*	...	...	N.A.,S.A. 52-53
† LATVIA	Latvija	63,700	*24,595*	2,737,000	43	*111*	Republic	*A* Rīga	Europe 8
† LEBANON	Lubnān	10,400	*4,015*	3,467,000	333	*864*	Republic	*A* Bayrūt (Beirut)	Asia 24
† LESOTHO	Lesotho	30,355	*11,720*	1,873,000	62	*160*	Constitutional monarchy under military rule	*A* Maseru	Africa 37
Liaoning	Liaoning	145,700	*56,255*	41,035,000	282	*729*	Province (China)	*D* Shenyang (Mukden)	Asia 28
† LIBERIA	Liberia	99,067	*38,250*	2,869,000	29	*75*	Republic	*A* Monrovia	Africa 34
† LIBYA	Lībiyā	1,759,540	*679,362*	4,552,000	2.6	*6.7*	Socialist republic	*A* Ṭarābulus (Tripoli)	Africa 33
† LIECHTENSTEIN	Liechtenstein	160	*62*	30,000	188	*484*	Constitutional monarchy	*A* Vaduz	Europe 14
† LITHUANIA	Lietuva	65,200	*25,174*	3,804,000	58	*151*	Republic	*A* Vilnius	Europe 8
Louisiana	Louisiana	134,275	*51,843*	4,282,000	32	*83*	State (U.S.)	*D* Baton Rouge	N. Amer. 45
Lower Saxony	Niedersachsen	47,349	*18,282*	7,420,000	157	*406*	State (Germany)	*D* Hannover	Europe 10
† LUXEMBOURG	Luxembourg (French) / Lezebuurg (Luxembourgish)	2,586	*998*	392,000	152	*393*	Constitutional monarchy	*A* Luxembourg	Europe 12
Macao	Macau	17	*6.6*	477,000	28,059	*72,273*	Chinese territory under Portuguese administration	*C* Macau	Asia 27
MACEDONIA	Makedonija	25,713	*9,928*	2,179,000	85	*219*	Republic	*A* Skopje	Europe 15
† MADAGASCAR	Madagasikara	587,041	*226,658*	12,800,000	22	*56*	Republic	*A* Antananarivo	Africa 37
Madeira	Madeira	794	*307*	284,000	358	*925*	Autonomous region (Portugal)	*D* Funchal	Europe 32
Maine	Maine	91,653	*35,387*	1,257,000	14	*36*	State (U.S.)	*D* Augusta	N. Amer. 44
† MALAWI	Malaŵi	118,484	*45,747*	9,691,000	82	*212*	Republic	*A* Lilongwe	Africa 36
Malaya	Semenanjung Malaysia	131,598	*50,810*	15,335,000	117	*302*	Part of Malaysia (11 states)	*D* ...	Asia 26
† MALAYSIA	Malaysia	334,758	*129,251*	18,630,000	56	*144*	Federal constitutional monarchy	*A* Kuala Lumpur	Asia 26
† MALDIVES	Maldives	298	*115*	235,000	789	*2,043*	Republic	*A* Male	Asia 25
† MALI	Mali	1,248,574	*482,077*	8,754,000	7.0	*18*	Republic	*A* Bamako	Africa 34
† MALTA	Malta	316	*122*	360,000	1,139	*2,951*	Republic	*A* Valletta	Europe 14
Manitoba	Manitoba	649,950	*250,947*	1,221,000	1.9	*4.9*	Province (Canada)	*D* Winnipeg	N. Amer. 42
Maritime Provinces	...	134,590	*51,965*	1,983,000	15	*38*	...	...	N. Amer. 42
† MARSHALL ISLANDS	Marshall Islands	181	*70*	51,000	282	*729*	Republic (U.S. protection)	*A* Uliga	Oceania 60
Martinique	Martinique	1,100	*425*	372,000	338	*875*	Overseas department (France)	*C* Fort-de-France	N. Amer. 51
Maryland	Maryland	32,135	*12,407*	4,975,000	155	*401*	State (U.S.)	*D* Annapolis	N. Amer. 44
Massachusetts	Massachusetts	27,337	*10,555*	6,103,000	223	*578*	State (U.S.)	*D* Boston	N. Amer. 44
† MAURITANIA	Mūrītāniyā (Arabic) / Mauritanie (French)	1,025,520	*395,956*	2,092,000	2.0	*5.3*	Republic	*A* Nouakchott	Africa 32
† MAURITIUS (incl. Dependencies)	Mauritius	2,040	*788*	1,096,000	537	*1,391*	Republic	*A* Port-Louis	Africa 37
Mayotte (5)	Mayotte	374	*144*	89,000	238	*618*	Territorial collectivity (France)	*C* Dzaoudzi and Mamoudzou (2)	Africa 37
Mecklenburg-Vorpommern	Mecklenburg-Vorpommern	23,835	*9,203*	2,000,000	84	*217*	State (Germany)	*D* Schwerin	Europe 10
† MEXICO	México	1,967,183	*759,534*	86,170,000	44	*113*	Federal republic	*A* Ciudad de México (Mexico City)	N. Amer. 48
Michigan	Michigan	250,738	*96,810*	9,488,000	38	*98*	State (U.S.)	*D* Lansing	N. Amer. 44
† MICRONESIA, FEDERATED STATES OF	Federated States of Micronesia	702	*271*	117,000	167	*432*	Republic (U.S. protection)	*A* Ponape	Oceania 60
Middle America	...	2,710,000	*1,050,000*	151,200,000	56	*144*	...	...	N. Amer. 47
Midway Islands	Midway Islands	5.2	*2.0*	500	96	*250*	Unincorporated territory (U.S.)	*C* ...	Oceania 60
Minnesota	Minnesota	225,182	*86,943*	4,513,000	20	*52*	State (U.S.)	*D* St. Paul	N. Amer. 45
Mississippi	Mississippi	125,443	*48,434*	2,616,000	21	*54*	State (U.S.)	*D* Jackson	N. Amer. 45
Missouri	Missouri	180,546	*69,709*	5,231,000	29	*75*	State (U.S.)	*D* Jefferson City	N. Amer. 45

| Country, Division, or Region | | Area | | Population | Population Density per | | Form of Government | | | Continent and |
English (Conventional)	Local Name	km²	sq mi	1/1/93	km²	sq mi	and Political Status		Capital	Map Plate
† MOLDOVA	Moldova	33,700	13,012	4,474,000	133	344	Republic	A	Kišinev (Kishinev)	Europe 16
MONACO	Monaco	1.9	0.7	31,000	16,316	44,286	Constitutional monarchy	A	Monaco	Europe 11
† MONGOLIA	Mongol Ard Uls	1,566,500	604,829	2,336,000	1.5	3.9	Republic	A	Ulan-Bator (Ulaanbaatar)	Asia 27
Montana	Montana	380,850	147,046	821,000	2.2	5.6	State (U.S.)	D	Helena	N. Amer. 46
Montenegro	Crna Gora	13,812	5,333	650,000	47	122	Republic (Yugoslavia)	D	Titograd	Europe 15
Montserrat	Montserrat	102	39	13,000	127	333	Dependent territory (U.K.)	C	Plymouth	N. Amer. 51
† MOROCCO (excl. Western Sahara)	Al Maghrib	446,550	172,414	27,005,000	60	157	Constitutional monarchy	A	Rabat	Africa 32
† MOZAMBIQUE	Moçambique	799,380	308,642	15,795,000	20	51	Republic	A	Maputo	Africa 37
† NAMIBIA	Namibia	824,272	318,254	1,580,000	1.9	5.0	Republic	A	Windhoek	Africa 37
NAURU	Nauru (English) / Naoero (Nauruan)	21	8.1	10,000	476	1,235	Republic	A	Domaneab	Oceania..... 64
Navassa Island	Navassa Island	4.9	1.9	(1)	...	...	Unincorporated territory (U.S.)	C	...	N. Amer. 49
Nebraska	Nebraska	200,358	77,358	1,615,000	8.1	21	State (U.S.)	D	Lincoln	N. Amer. 45
† NEPAL	Nepāl	147,181	56,827	20,325,000	138	358	Constitutional monarchy	A	Kathmāṇḍaū	Asia 25
† NETHERLANDS	Nederland	41,864	16,164	15,190,000	363	940	Constitutional monarchy	A	Amsterdam and 's-Gravenhage (The Hague)	Europe 12
NETHERLANDS ANTILLES	Nederlandse Antillen	800	309	191,000	239	618	Self-governing territory (Netherlands protection)	B	Willemstad	N. Amer. 50
Nevada	Nevada	286,368	110,567	1,308,000	4.6	12	State (U.S.)	D	Carson City	N. Amer. 46
New Brunswick	New Brunswick (English) / Nouveau-Brunswick (French)	73,440	28,355	824,000	11	29	Province (Canada)	D	Fredericton	N. Amer. 42
New Caledonia	Nouvelle-Calédonie	19,058	7,358	177,000	9.3	24	Overseas territory (France)	C	Nouméa	Oceania..... 63
New England	New England	186,472	71,997	13,488,000	72	187	Part of U.S. (6 states)	...	...	N. Amer. 43
Newfoundland	Newfoundland (English) / Terre-Neuve (French)	405,720	156,649	641,000	1.6	4.1	Province (Canada)	D	St. John's	N. Amer. 42
Newfoundland (island)	Newfoundland (English) / Terre-Neuve (French)	108,860	42,031	605,000	5.6	14	Part of Newfoundland province (Canada)	......		N. Amer. 42
New Hampshire	New Hampshire	24,219	9,351	1,154,000	48	123	State (U.S.)	D	Concord	N. Amer. 44
New Hebrides, see Vanuatu	...	...	...	...	...	...	....	...	...	....
New Jersey	New Jersey	22,590	8,722	7,898,000	350	906	State (U.S.)	D	Trenton	N. Amer. 44
New Mexico	New Mexico	314,939	121,598	1,590,000	5.0	13	State (U.S.)	D	Santa Fe	N. Amer. 45
New South Wales	New South Wales	801,600	309,500	5,770,000	7.2	19	State (Australia)	D	Sydney	Oceania..... 59
New York	New York	141,089	54,475	18,350,000	130	337	State (U.S.)	D	Albany	N. Amer. 44
† NEW ZEALAND	New Zealand	270,534	104,454	3,477,000	13	33	Parliamentary state	A	Wellington	Oceania..... 62
† NICARAGUA	Nicaragua	129,640	50,054	3,932,000	30	79	Republic	A	Managua	N. Amer. 49
† NIGER	Niger	1,267,000	489,191	8,198,000	6.5	17	Provisional military government	A	Niamey	Africa 34
† NIGERIA	Nigeria	923,768	356,669	91,700,000	99	257	Provisional military government	A	Lagos and Abuja	Africa 34
Ningsia	Ningxia Huizu Zizhiqu	66,400	25,637	4,820,000	73	188	Autonomous region (China)	D	Yinchuan	Asia 27
NIUE	Niue	258	100	1,700	6.6	17	Self-governing territory (New Zealand protection)	B	Alofi	Oceania..... 64
Norfolk Island	Norfolk Island	36	14	2,600	72	186	External territory (Australia)	C	Kingston	Oceania..... 61
North America	...	24,700,000	9,500,000	438,200,000	18	46	....	......		N. Amer. 38-39
North Borneo, see Sabah	...	...	...	...	...	...				....
North Carolina	North Carolina	139,397	53,821	6,846,000	49	127	State (U.S.)	D	Raleigh	N. Amer. 44
North Dakota	North Dakota	183,123	70,704	632,000	3.5	8.9	State (U.S.)	D	Bismarck	N. Amer. 45
Northern Ireland	Northern Ireland	14,121	5,452	1,604,000	114	294	Administrative division (U.K.)	D	Belfast	Europe 9
NORTHERN MARIANA ISLANDS	Northern Mariana Islands	477	184	48,000	101	261	Commonwealth (U.S. protection)....	B	Saipan (island)	Oceania..... 60
Northern Territory	Northern Territory	1,346,200	519,771	176,000	0.1	0.3	Territory (Australia)	D	Darwin	Oceania· 59
North Rhine-Westphalia	Nordrhein-Westfalen	34,068	13,154	17,420,000	511	1,324	State (Germany)	D	Düsseldorf	Europe 10
Northwest Territories	Northwest Territories (English) / Territoires du Nord-Ouest (French)	3,426,320	1,322,910	61,000	...	...	Territory (Canada)	D	Yellowknife	N. Amer. 42
† NORWAY (incl. Svalbard and Jan Mayen)	Norge	386,975	149,412	4,308,000	11	29	Constitutional monarchy	A	Oslo	Europe 7
Nova Scotia	Nova Scotia (English) / Nouvelle-Écosse (French)	55,490	21,425	1,007,000	18	47	Province (Canada)	D	Halifax	N. Amer. 42
Oceania (incl. Australia)	...	8,500,000	3,300,000	26,700,000	3.1	8.1				Oceania..... 57-58
Ohio	Ohio	116,103	44,828	11,025,000	95	246	State (U.S.)	D	Columbus	N. Amer. 44
Oklahoma	Oklahoma	181,049	69,903	3,205,000	18	46	State (U.S.)	D	Oklahoma City	N. Amer. 45
† OMAN	'Umān	212,457	82,030	1,617,000	7.6	20	Monarchy	A	Masqaṭ (Muscat)	Asia 23
Ontario	Ontario	1,068,580	412,581	11,265,000	11	27	Province (Canada)	D	Toronto	N. Amer. 42
Oregon	Oregon	254,819	98,386	2,949,000	12	30	State (U.S.)	D	Salem	N. Amer. 46
Orkney Islands	Orkney Islands	976	377	20,000	20	53	Part of Scotland (U.K.)	D	Kirkwall	Europe 9
Pacific Islands, Trust Territory of the, see Palau	...	...	...	...	...	...	....	......		....
† PAKISTAN (incl. part of Jammu and Kashmir)	Pākistān	879,902	339,732	123,490,000	140	363	Federal Islamic republic	A	Islāmābād	Asia 25
PALAU	Palau (English) / Belau (Palauan)	508	196	16,000	31	82	Under U.S. administration	B	Koror	Oceania..... 60
† PANAMA	Panamá	75,517	29,157	2,555,000	34	88	Republic	A	Panamá	N. Amer. 49
† PAPUA NEW GUINEA	Papua New Guinea	462,840	178,704	3,737,000	8.1	21	Parliamentary state	A	Port Moresby	Oceania..... 60
† PARAGUAY	Paraguay	406,752	157,048	5,003,000	12	32	Republic	A	Asunción	S. Amer. 56
Peking	Beijing	16,800	6,487	11,290,000	672	1,740	Autonomous city (China)	D	Beijing (Peking)	Asia 28
Pennsylvania	Pennsylvania	119,291	46,058	12,105,000	101	263	State (U.S.)	D	Harrisburg	N. Amer. 44
† PERU	Perú	1,285,216	496,225	22,995,000	18	46	Republic	A	Lima	S. Amer. 54
† PHILIPPINES	Pilipinas (Pilipino) / Philippines (English)	300,000	115,831	65,500,000	218	565	Republic	A	Manila	Asia 26
Pitcairn (incl. Dependencies)	Pitcairn	49	19	50	1.0	2.6	Dependent territory (U.K.)	C	Adamstown	Oceania..... 61
† POLAND	Polska	312,683	120,728	38,330,000	123	317	Republic	A	Warszawa (Warsaw)	Europe 10
† PORTUGAL	Portugal	91,985	35,516	10,660,000	116	300	Republic	A	Lisboa (Lisbon)	Europe 13
Prairie Provinces	Prairie Provinces	1,963,470	758,100	5,159,000	2.6	6.8	Part of Canada (3 provinces)	......		N. Amer. 42
Prince Edward Island	Prince Edward Island (English) / Île-du Prince-Édouard (French)	5,660	2,185	152,000	27	70	Province (Canada)	D	Charlottetown	N. Amer. 42
PUERTO RICO	Puerto Rico	9,104	3,515	3,594,000	395	1,022	Commonwealth (U.S. protection)....	B	San Juan	N. Amer. 51
† QATAR	Qaṭar	11,427	4,412	492,000	43	112	Monarchy	A	Ad Dawḥah (Doha)	Asia 24
Qinghai	Qinghai	720,000	277,994	4,585,000	6.4	16	Province (China)	D	Xining	Asia 27
Quebec	Québec	1,540,680	594,860	7,725,000	5.0	13	Province (Canada)	D	Québec	N. Amer. 42
Queensland	Queensland	1,727,200	666,876	3,000,000	1.7	4.5	State (Australia)	D	Brisbane	Oceania..... 59
Reunion	Réunion	2,510	969	633,000	252	653	Overseas department (France)	C	Saint-Denis	Africa 37
Rhineland-Palatinate	Rheinland-Pfalz	19,849	7,664	3,771,000	190	492	State (Germany)	D	Mainz	Europe 10
Rhode Island	Rhode Island	4,002	1,545	1,026,000	256	664	State (U.S.)	D	Providence	N. Amer. 44
Rhodesia, see Zimbabwe	...	...	...	...	...	...				....
Rodrigues	Rodrigues	104	40	40,000	385	1,000	Part of Mauritius	......		Africa 30-31
† ROMANIA	România	237,500	91,699	23,200,000	98	253	Republic	A	Bucureşti (Bucharest)	Europe 15
† RUSSIA	Rossija	17,075,400	6,592,849	150,500,000	8.8	23	Republic	A	Moskva (Moscow)	Eur., Asia .. 19-20
Russia in Europe	...	3,955,818	1,527,350	106,980,000	27	70	....	......		Europe 19

Country, Division, or Region English (Conventional)	Local Name	Area km²	Area sq mi	Population 1/1/93	Population Density per km²	Population Density per sq mi	Form of Government and Political Status	Capital	Continent	Map Plate
†RWANDA	Rwanda	26,338	*10,169*	7,573,000	288	*745*	Provisional military government	A Kigali	Africa	36
Saarland	Saar	2,570	*992*	1,085,000	422	*1,094*	State (Germany)	D Saarbrücken	Europe	10
Sabah	Sabah	73,711	*28,460*	1,544,000	21	*54*	State (Malaysia)	D Kota Kinabalu	Asia	26
†ST. CHRISTOPHER-NEVIS	St. Christopher-Nevis	269	*104*	40,000	149	*385*	Parliamentary state	A Basseterre	N. Amer.	51
St. Helena (incl. Dependencies)	St. Helena	314	*121*	7,000	22	*58*	Dependent territory (U.K.)	C Jamestown	Africa	31
†ST. LUCIA	St. Lucia	616	*238*	153,000	248	*643*	Parliamentary state	A Castries	N. Amer.	51
St. Pierre and Miquelon	St.-Pierre et Miquelon	242	*93*	7,000	29	*75*	Territorial collectivity (France)	C Saint-Pierre	N. Amer.	42
†ST. VINCENT AND THE GRENADINES	St. Vincent and the Grenadines	388	*150*	116,000	299	*773*	Parliamentary state	A Kingstown	N. Amer.	51
†SAN MARINO	San Marino	61	*24*	23,000	377	*958*	Republic	A San Marino	Europe	14
†SAO TOME AND PRINCIPE	São Tomé e Príncipe	964	*372*	134,000	139	*360*	Republic	A São Tomé	Africa	34
Sarawak	Sarawak	129,449	*49,981*	1,751,000	14	*35*	State (Malaysia)	D Kuching	Asia	26
Sardinia	Sardegna	24,090	*9,301*	1,681,000	70	*181*	Autonomous region (Italy)	D Cagliari	Europe	14
Saskatchewan	Saskatchewan	652,330	*251,866*	1,099,000	1.7	*4.4*	Province (Canada)	D Regina	N. Amer.	42
†SAUDI ARABIA	Al ʻArabīyah as Suʻūdīyah	2,149,690	*830,000*	15,985,000	7.4	*19*	Monarchy	A Ar Riyāḍ (Riyadh)	Asia	23
Saxony	Sachsen	18,338	*7,080*	4,993,000	272	*705*	State (Germany)	D Dresden	Europe	10
Saxony-Anhalt	Sachsen-Anhalt	20,444	*7,893*	3,021,000	148	*383*	State (Germany)	D Magdeburg	Europe	10
Scandinavia	. . .	1,320,000	*510,000*	23,479,000	18	*46*	. . .	. . .	Europe	7
Schleswig-Holstein	Schleswig-Holstein	15,730	*6,073*	2,643,000	168	*435*	State (Germany)	D Kiel	Europe	10
Scotland	Scotland	78,789	*30,421*	5,145,000	65	*169*	Administrative division (U.K.)	D Edinburgh	Europe	9
†SENEGAL	Sénégal	196,712	*75,951*	7,849,000	40	*103*	Republic	A Dakar	Africa	34
Serbia	Srbija	88,361	*34,116*	10,020,000	113	*294*	Republic (Yugoslavia)	D Belgrade (Beograd)	Europe	15
†SEYCHELLES	Seychelles	453	*175*	70,000	155	*400*	Republic	A Victoria	Africa	37
Shaanxi	Shaanxi	205,000	*79,151*	34,215,000	167	*432*	Province (China)	D Xi'an (Sian)	Asia	27
Shandong	Shandong	153,000	*59,074*	87,840,000	574	*1,487*	Province (China)	D Jinan	Asia	27
Shanghai	Shanghai	6,200	*2,394*	13,875,000	2,238	*5,796*	Autonomous city (China)	D Shanghai	Asia	28
Shanxi	Shanxi	156,000	*60,232*	29,865,000	191	*496*	Province (China)	D Taiyuan	Asia	27
Shetland Islands	Shetland Islands	1,433	*553*	22,000	15	*40*	Part of Scotland (U.K.)	D Lerwick	Europe	9
Sichuan	Sichuan	570,000	*220,078*	111,470,000	196	*507*	Province (China)	D Chengdu	Asia	27
Sicily	Sicilia	25,709	*9,926*	5,270,000	205	*531*	Autonomous region (Italy)	D Palermo	Europe	14
†SIERRA LEONE	Sierra Leone	72,325	*27,925*	4,424,000	61	*158*	Transitional military government	A Freetown	Africa	34
†SINGAPORE	Singapore (English) / Singapura (Malay)	636	*246*	2,812,000	4,421	*11,431*	Republic	A Singapore	Asia	26
Sinkiang	Xingiang Uygur Zizhiqu	1,600,000	*617,764*	15,755,000	9.8	*26*	Autonomous region (China)	D Ürümqi	Asia	27
†SLOVAKIA	Slovenská Republika	49,035	*18,933*	5,287,000	108	*279*	Republic	A Bratislava	Europe	10
†SLOVENIA	Slovenija	20,251	*7,819*	1,965,000	97	*251*	Republic	A Ljubljana	Europe	14
†SOLOMON ISLANDS	Solomon Islands	28,370	*10,954*	366,000	13	*33*	Parliamentary state	A Honiara	Oceania	63
†SOMALIA	Soomaaliya	637,657	*246,201*	6,000,000	9.4	*24*	None	A Muqdisho (Mogadishu)	Africa	35
†SOUTH AFRICA	South Africa (English) / Suid-Afrika (Afrikaans)	1,220,018	*471,090*	42,407,000	35	*90*	Republic	A Pretoria, Cape Town, and Bloemfontein	Africa	37
South America	. . .	17,800,000	*6,900,000*	310,700,000	17	*45*	. . .	. . .	S. Amer.	52-53
South Australia	South Australia	984,000	*379,925*	1,410,000	1.4	*3.7*	State (Australia)	D Adelaide	Oceania	59
South Carolina	South Carolina	82,898	*32,007*	3,616,000	44	*113*	State (U.S.)	D Columbia	N. Amer.	44
South Dakota	South Dakota	199,745	*77,121*	718,000	3.6	*9.3*	State (U.S.)	D Pierre	N. Amer.	45
South Georgia (incl. Dependencies)	South Georgia	3,755	*1,450*	(1)	. . .	. . .	Dependent territory (U.K.)	C . . .	S. Amer.	56
South West Africa, see Namibia	. . .	. . .	. . .	. . .	. . .	. . .	. . .	. . .	. . .	. . .
†SPAIN	España	504,750	*194,885*	39,155,000	78	*201*	Constitutional monarchy	A Madrid	Europe	13
Spanish North Africa (6)	Plazas de Soberanía en el Norte de África	32	*12*	144,000	4,500	*12,000*	Five possessions (Spain)	C . . .	Africa	13
Spanish Sahara, see Western Sahara	. . .	. . .	. . .	. . .	. . .	. . .	. . .	. . .	. . .	. . .
†SRI LANKA	Sri Lanka	64,652	*24,962*	17,740,000	274	*711*	Socialist republic	A Colombo and Sri Jayawardenapura	Asia	25
†SUDAN	As Sūdān	2,505,813	*967,500*	28,760,000	11	*30*	Provisional military government	A Al Kharṭūm (Khartoum)	Africa	35
Sumatra	Sumatera	473,606	*182,860*	36,455,000	77	*199*	Part of Indonesia (7 provinces)	. . .	Asia	26
†SURINAME	Suriname	163,820	*63,251*	413,000	2.5	*6.5*	Republic	A Paramaribo	S. Amer.	54
†SWAZILAND	Swaziland	17,364	*6,704*	925,000	53	*138*	Monarchy	A Mbabane and Lobamba	Africa	37
†SWEDEN	Sverige	449,964	*173,732*	8,619,000	19	*50*	Constitutional monarchy	A Stockholm	Europe	7
SWITZERLAND	Schweiz (German) / Suisse (French) / Svizzera (Italian)	41,293	*15,943*	6,848,000	166	*430*	Federal republic	A Bern (Berne)	Europe	14
†SYRIA	Sūrīyah	185,180	*71,498*	14,070,000	76	*197*	Socialist republic	A Dimashq (Damascus)	Asia	24
TAIWAN	Taiwan	36,002	*13,900*	20,985,000	583	*1,510*	Republic	A Taipei	Asia	27
†TAJIKISTAN	Tojikiston	143,100	*55,251*	5,765,000	40	*104*	Republic	A Dušanbe (Dushanbe)	Asia	18
†TANZANIA	Tanzania	945,087	*364,900*	28,265,000	30	*77*	Republic	A Dar es Salaam and Dodoma (2)	Africa	36
Tasmania	Tasmania	67,800	*26,178*	456,000	6.7	*17*	State (Australia)	D Hobart	Oceania	59
Tennessee	Tennessee	109,158	*42,146*	5,026,000	46	*119*	State (U.S.)	D Nashville	N. Amer.	44
Texas	Texas	695,676	*268,601*	17,610,000	25	*66*	State (U.S.)	D Austin	N. Amer.	45
†THAILAND	Muang Thai	513,115	*198,115*	58,030,000	113	*293*	Constitutional monarchy	A Krung Thep (Bangkok)	Asia	26
Thuringia	Thüringen	16,251	*6,275*	2,734,000	168	*436*	State (Germany)	D Erfurt	Europe	10
Tibet	Xizang Zizhiqu	1,220,000	*471,045*	2,235,000	1.8	*4.7*	Autonomous region (China)	D Lhasa	Asia	27
Tientsin	Tianjin	11,300	*4,363*	9,170,000	812	*2,102*	Autonomous city (China)	D Tianjin (Tientsin)	Asia	28
†TOGO	Togo	56,785	*21,925*	4,030,000	71	*184*	Provisional military government	A Lomé	Africa	34
Tokelau	Tokelau	12	*4.6*	1,800	150	*391*	Island territory (New Zealand)	C . . .	Oceania	61
TONGA	Tonga	747	*288*	103,000	138	*358*	Constitutional monarchy	A Nukuʻalofa	Oceania	61
†TRINIDAD AND TOBAGO	Trinidad and Tobago	5,128	*1,980*	1,307,000	255	*660*	Republic	A Port of Spain	N. Amer.	50
Tristan da Cunha	Tristan da Cunha	104	*40*	300	2.9	*7.5*	Dependency (St. Helena)	C Edinburgh	Africa	30-31
†TUNISIA	Tunisie (French) / Tūnis (Arabic)	163,610	*63,170*	8,495,000	52	*134*	Republic	A Tūnis	Africa	32
†TURKEY	Türkiye	779,452	*300,948*	58,620,000	75	*195*	Republic	A Ankara	Eur.,Asia	24
Turkey in Europe	. . .	23,764	*9,175*	8,805,000	371	*960*	. . .	. . .	Europe	24
†TURKMENISTAN	Türkmenistan	488,100	*188,456*	3,884,000	8.0	*21*	Republic	A Ašhabad	Asia	19
Turks and Caicos Islands	Turks and Caicos Islands	500	*193*	13,000	26	*67*	Dependent territory (U.K.)	C Grand Turk	N. Amer.	49
TUVALU	Tuvalu	26	*10*	10,000	385	*1,000*	Parliamentary state	A Funafuti	Oceania	60
†UGANDA	Uganda	241,139	*93,104*	17,410,000	72	*187*	Republic	A Kampala	Africa	36
†UKRAINE	Ukrayina	603,700	*233,090*	51,990,000	86	*223*	Republic	A Kijev (Kiev)	Europe	16
†UNITED ARAB EMIRATES	Al Imārāt al ʻArabīyah al Muttaḥidah	83,600	*32,278*	2,590,000	31	*80*	Federation of monarchs	A Abū Ẓaby (Abu Dhabi)	Asia	23
†UNITED KINGDOM	United Kingdom	244,154	*94,269*	57,890,000	237	*614*	Constitutional monarchy	A London	Europe	9
United Kingdom and Possessions	. . .	259,753	*100,291*	63,860,000	246	*637*	. . .	. . .	. . .	. . .
†UNITED STATES	United States	9,809,431	*3,787,425*	256,420,000	26	*68*	Federal republic	A Washington	N. Amer.	43
United States and Possessions	. . .	9,820,617	*3,791,744*	260,380,000	27	*69*	. . .	. . .	. . .	. . .
Upper Volta, see Burkina Faso	. . .	. . .	. . .	. . .	. . .	. . .	. . .	. . .	. . .	. . .
†URUGUAY	Uruguay	177,414	*68,500*	3,151,000	18	*46*	Republic	A Montevideo	S. Amer.	55
Utah	Utah	219,902	*84,904*	1,795,000	8.2	*21*	State (U.S.)	D Salt Lake City	N. Amer.	46
†UZBEKISTAN	Ŭzbekiston	447,400	*172,742*	21,885,000	49	*127*	Republic	A Taškent (Tashkent)	Asia	19
†VANUATU	Vanuatu	12,190	*4,707*	157,000	13	*33*	Republic	A Port-Vila	Oceania	63

Country, Division, or Region		Area		Population	Population Density per		Form of Government	Capital	Continent and
English (Conventional)	Local Name	km²	sq mi	1/1/93	km²	sq mi	and Political Status		Map Plate
VATICAN CITY	Città del Vaticano	0.4	0.2	800	2,000	4,000	Monarchical-sacerdotal state	A Vatican City	Europe 14
† VENEZUELA	Venezuela	912,050	352,145	19,085,000	21	54	Federal republic	A Caracas	S. Amer. 54
Vermont	Vermont	24,903	9,615	590,000	24	61	State (U.S.)	D Montpelier	N. Amer. 44
Victoria	Victoria	227,600	87,877	4,273,000	19	49	State (Australia)	D Melbourne	Oceania 59
† VIETNAM	Viet Nam	330,036	127,428	69,650,000	211	547	Socialist republic	A Ha Noi	Asia 26
Virginia	Virginia	110,771	42,769	6,411,000	58	150	State (U.S.)	D Richmond	N. Amer. 44
Virgin Islands of the United States	Virgin Islands	344	133	104,000	302	782	Unincorporated territory (U.S.)	C Charlotte Amalie	N. Amer. 51
Virgin Islands, British	British Virgin Islands	153	59	13,000	85	220	Dependent territory (U.K.)	C Road Town	N. Amer. 51
Wake Island	Wake Island	7.8	3.0	200	26	67	Unincorporated territory (U.S.)	C . . .	Oceania 60
Wales	Wales	20,766	8,018	2,906,000	140	362	Administrative division (U.K.)	D Cardiff	Europe 9
Wallis and Futuna	Îles Wallis et Futuna	255	98	17,000	67	173	Overseas territory (France)	C Mata-Utu	Oceania 61
Washington	Washington	184,674	71,303	5,052,000	27	71	State (U.S.)	D Olympia	N. Amer. 46
Western Australia	Western Australia	2,525,500	975,101	1,598,000	0.6	1.6	State (Australia)	D Perth	Oceania 59
Western Sahara	. . .	266,000	102,703	200,000	0.8	1.9	Occupied by Morocco	C El Aaiún	Africa 32
† WESTERN SAMOA	Western Samoa (English) / Samoa i Sisifo (Samoan)	2,831	1,093	197,000	70	180	Constitutional monarchy	A Apia	Oceania 65
West Indies	West Indies (English) / Indias Occidentales (Spanish)	235,000	91,000	34,627,000	147	381	. . . .	. . . . . .	N. Amer. 47
West Virginia	West Virginia	62,759	24,231	1,795,000	29	74	State (U.S.)	D Charleston	N. Amer. 44
Wisconsin	Wisconsin	169,653	65,503	5,000,000	29	76	State (U.S.)	D Madison	N. Amer. 45
Wyoming	Wyoming	253,349	97,818	462,000	1.8	4.7	State (U.S.)	D Cheyenne	N. Amer. 46
† YEMEN	Al Yaman	527,968	203,850	12,215,000	23	60	Republic	A San'a'	Asia 23
YUGOSLAVIA	Jugoslavija	102,173	39,449	10,670,000	104	270	Republic	A Beograd (Belgrade)	Europe 14-15
Yukon Territory	Yukon Territory	483,450	186,661	31,000	0.1	0.2	Territory (Canada)	D Whitehorse	N. Amer. 42
Yunnan	Yunnan	394,000	152,124	38,450,000	98	253	Province (China)	D Kunming	Asia 27
† ZAIRE	Zaïre	2,345,095	905,446	39,750,000	17	44	Republic	A Kinshasa	Africa 36
† ZAMBIA	Zambia	752,614	290,586	8,475,000	11	29	Republic	A Lusaka	Africa 36
Zanzibar	Zanzibar	2,461	950	434,000	176	457	Part of Tanzania	. . . Zanzibar	Africa 36
Zhejiang	Zhejiang	101,800	39,305	43,150,000	424	1,098	Province (China)	D Hangzhou	Asia 27
† ZIMBABWE	Zimbabwe	390,759	150,873	10,000,000	26	66	Republic	A Harare	Africa 37
WORLD	. . .	150,100,000	57,900,000	5,477,000,000	36	95	. . . .	. . . . . .	 1-2

† Member of the United Nations (1992).
. . . None, or not applicable.
(1) No permanent population.
(2) Future capital.
(3) Claimed by Argentina.
(4) Includes West Bank, Golan Heights, and Gaza Strip.
(5) Claimed by Comoros.
(6) Comprises Ceuta, Melilla, and several small islands.

World Geographical Tables

The Earth: Land and Water

	Total Area km²	Total Area sq mi	Area of Land km²	Area of Land sq mi	%	Area of Oceans and Seas km²	Area of Oceans and Seas sq mi	%
Earth	510,100,000	197,100,000	150,100,000	57,900,000	29.4	360,200,000	139,100,000	70.6
N. Hemisphere	255,050,000	98,500,000	106,571,000	41,109,000	41.6	148,762,600	57,448,300	58.4
S. Hemisphere	255,050,000	98,500,000	43,529,000	16,791,000	17.0	211,437,400	81,651,700	83.0

The Continents

Continent	Area km² sq mi	Population Estimate (1/1/93)	Population per km² sq mi	Mean Elevation m ft	Highest Elevation m/ft	Lowest Elevation m/ft (below sea level)	Highest Recorded Temperature °C/°F	Lowest Recorded Temperature °C/°F
Europe	9,900,000 / 3,800,000	694,700,000	70 / 183	300 / 980	gora Elbrus, Russia 5,642/18,510	Caspian Sea, Asia-Europe −28/−92	Sevilla, Spain 50°/122°	Ust-Ščugor, Russia −55°/−67°
Asia	44,900,000 / 17,300,000	3,337,800,000	74 / 193	910 / 3,000	Everest, China-Nepal 8,848/29,028	Dead Sea, Israel-Jordan −403/−1,322	Tirat Zevi, Israel 54°/129°	Ojmjakon and Verkhoyansk, Russia −68°/−90°
Africa	30,300,000 / 11,700,000	668,700,000	22 / 57	580 / 1,900	Kilimanjaro, Tanzania 5,895/19,340	Lac Assal, Djibouti −157/−515	Al 'Azīzīyah, Libya 58°/136°	Ifrane, Morocco −24°/−11°
North America	24,700,000 / 9,500,000	438,200,000	18 / 46	610 / 2,000	Mt. McKinley, U.S. 6,194/20,320	Death Valley, U.S. −86/−282	Death Valley, U.S. 57°/134°	Northice, Greenland −66°/−87°
South America	17,800,000 / 6,900,000	310,700,000	17 / 45	550 / 1,800	Cerro Aconcagua, Argentina 6,960/22,835	Salinas Chicas −42/−138	Rivadavia, Argentina 49°/120°	Sarmiento, Argentina −33°/−27°
Oceania, incl. Australia	8,500,000 / 3,300,000	26,700,000	3 / 8	.... /	Mt. Wilhelm, Papua New Guinea 4,509/14,793	Lake Eyre, Australia −12/−39	Cloncurry, Australia 53°/128°	Charlotte Pass, Australia −22°/−8°
Australia	7,682,300 / 2,966,155	16,965,000	2 / 6	300 / 1,000	Mt. Kosciusko, Australia 2,228/7,310	Lake Eyre, Austraila −12/−39	Cloncurry, Australia 53°/128°	Charlotte Pass, Australia −22°/−8°
Antarctica	14,000,000 / 5,400,000	....	... / ...	1,830 / 6,000	Vinson Massif 4,897/116,06	sea level	Vanda Station 15°/59°	Vostok −89°/−129°
World	150,100,000 / 57,900,000	5,477,000,000	36 / 95	.... /	Everest, China-Nepal 8,848/29,028	Dead Sea, Israel-Jordan −403/−1,322	Al 'Azīzīyah, Libya 58°/136°	Vostok −89°/−129°

Principal Mountains

Mountain	Country	Height m	Height ft
Europe			
Elbrus, gora	△Russia	5,642	18,510
Dyhtau, gora	Russia	5,204	17,073
Blanc, Mont	△France-△Italy	4,807	15,771
Rosa, Monte	Italy-△Switzerland	4,634	15,203
Matterhorn	Italy-Switzerland	4,478	14,692
Grossglockner	△Austria	3,797	12,457
Teide, Pico de	△Spain (Canary Is.)	3,718	12,198
Aneto, Pico de	Spain	3,404	11,168
Etna	Italy	3,323	10,902
Zugspitze	Austria-△Germany	2,963	9,721
Ólimbos, Óros	△Greece	2,917	9,570
Corno Grande	Italy	2,912	9,554
Gerlachovský štít	△Slovakia	2,663	8,737
Glittertind	△Norway	2,472	8,110
Kebnekaise	△Sweden	2,111	6,926
Narodnaja, gora	Russia	1,895	6,217
Nevis, Ben	△United Kingdom	1,343	4,406
Asia			
Everest	△China-△Nepal	8,848	29,028
K2 (Qogir Feng)	China-△Pakistan	8,611	28,250
Kānchenjunga	△India-Nepal	8,598	28,208
Makālu	China-Nepal	8,481	27,825
Dhaulāgiri	Nepal	8,172	26,810
Annapurna	Nepal	8,078	26,504
Muztag	China	7,723	25,338
Tirich Mīr	Pakistan	7,690	25,230
Kommunizma, pik (Communism Peak)	△Tajikistan	7,495	24,590
Pobedy, pik	China-Russia	7,439	24,406
Damāvand, Qolleh-ye	△Iran	5,604	18,386
Ağrı Dağı, Büyük (Mt. Ararat)	△Turkey	5,122	16,804
Jaya, Puncak	△Indonesia	5,030	16,503
Ključevskaja Sopka, vulkan	Russia	4,750	15,584
Kinabalu, Gunong	△Malaysia	4,101	13,455
Yushan	△Taiwan	3,997	13,114
Fuji-San	△Japan	3,776	12,388
Nabī Shu'ayb, Jabal an	△Yemen	3,760	12,336
Apo, Mt.	△Philippines	2,954	9,692
Shaykh, Jabal ash- (Mt. Hermon)	Lebanon-△Syria	2,814	9,232
Mayon, Mt.	Philippines	2,462	8,077
Chili-san	△South Korea	1,915	6,283
Meron, Hare	△Israel	1,208	3,963

Mountain	Country	Height m	Height ft
Africa			
Kilimanjaro	△Tanzania	5,895	19,340
Kirinyaga (Mt. Kenya)	△Kenya	5,199	17,058
Margherita	△Uganda-△Zaire	5,109	16,762
Ras Dashan Terara	△Ethiopia	4,620	15,158
Toubkal, Jebel	△Morocco	4,165	13,665
Cameroon, Mt.	△Cameroon	4,100	13,451
North America			
McKinley, Mt.	△United States	6,194	20,320
Logan, Mt.	△Canada	5,951	19,524
Orizaba, Pico de	△Mexico	5,610	18,406
Popocatépetl, Volcán	Mexico	5,452	17,887
Whitney, Mt.	United States	4,417	14,491
Elbert, Mt.	United States	4,399	14,433
Rainier, Mt.	United States	4,392	14,410
Shasta, Mt.	United States	4,317	14,162
Pikes Pk.	United States	4,301	14,110
Tajumulco, Volcán	△Guatemala	4,220	13,845
Mauna Kea	United States	4,205	13,796
Grand Teton	United States	4,197	13,770
Waddington, Mt.	Canada	3,994	13,104
Robson, Mt.	Canada	3,954	12,972
Chirripó, Cerro	△Costa Rica	3,819	12,530
Gunnbjørns Fjeld	△Greenland	3,700	12,139
Duarte, Pico	△Dominican Rep.	3,175	10,417
Mitchell, Mt.	United States	2,037	6,684
Marcy, Mt.	United States	1,629	5,344
South America			
Aconcagua, Cerro	△Argentina	6,960	22,835
Ojos del Salado, Nevado	Argentina-△Chile	6,863	22,516
Huascarán, Nevado	△Peru	6,746	22,133
Illimani, Nevado del	△Bolivia	6,682	21,923
Chimborazo, Volcán	△Ecuador	6,310	20,702
Cristóbal Colón, Pico	△Colombia	5,800	19,029
Neblina, Pico da	△Brazil-Venezuela	3,014	9,888
Oceania			
Wilhelm, Mt.	△Papua New Guinea	4,509	14,793
Cook, Mt.	△New Zealand	3,764	12,349
Kosciusko, Mt.	△Australia	2,228	7,310
Antarctica			
Vinson Massif	△Antarctica	4,897	16,066
Kirkpatrick, Mt.	Antarctica	4,528	14,856

△ Highest mountain in country.

Oceans, Seas, and Gulfs

Name	Area km²	sq mi	Greatest Depth m	ft
Pacific Ocean	165,200,000	63,800,000	11,020	36,155
Atlantic Ocean	82,400,000	31,800,000	9,220	30,249
Indian Ocean	74,900,000	28,900,000	7,450	24,442
Arctic Ocean	14,000,000	5,400,000	5,450	17,881
Arabian Sea	3,864,000	1,492,000	5,800	19,029
South China Sea	3,447,000	1,331,000	5,560	18,241
Caribbean Sea	2,753,000	1,063,000	7,680	25,197
Mediterranean Sea	2,505,000	967,000	5,020	16,470
Bering Sea	2,269,000	876,000	4,096	13,438
Bengal, Bay of	2,173,000	839,000	5,258	17,251
Okhotsk, Sea of	1,603,000	619,000	3,372	11,063
Norwegian Sea	1,546,000	597,000	4,020	13,189
Mexico, Gulf of	1,544,000	596,000	4,380	14,370
East China Sea	1,248,000	482,000	4,424	14,514
Hudson Bay	1,230,000	475,000	259	850

Waterfalls

Waterfall	Country	River	Height m	ft
Angel	Venezuela	Churún	972	3,189
Tugela	South Africa	Tugela	948	3,110
Yosemite	United States	Yosemite Creek	739	2,425
Sutherland	New Zealand	Arthur	579	1,900
Gavarnie	France	Gave de Pau	421	1,381
Lofoi	Zaire	Lofoi	384	1,260
Krimml	Austria	Krimml	381	1,250
Takakkaw	Canada	Yoho	380	1,248
Staubbach	Switzerland	Staubbach	305	1,001
Mardalsfoss	Norway	. . .	297	974
Gersoppa	India	Sharavati	253	830
Kaieteur	Guyana	Potaro	247	810

Principal Rivers

River	Continent	Length km	mi
Nile	Africa	6,671	4,145
Amazon-Ucayali	South America	6,400	4,000
Yangtze (Chang Jiang)	Asia	6,300	3,900
Yellow (Huang He)	Asia	5,464	3,395
Ob-Irtyš	Asia	5,410	3,362
Río de la Plata-Paraná	South America	4,876	3,030
Congo (Zaire)	Africa	4,700	2,900
Paraná	South America	4,500	2,800
Amur (Heilong Jiang)	Asia	4,416	2,744
Lena	Asia	4,400	2,700
Mekong	Asia	4,200	2,600
Niger	Africa	4,200	2,600
Jenisej	Asia	4,092	2,543
Mississippi	North America	3,779	2,348
Missouri	North America	3,726	2,315
Volga	Europe	3,531	2,194
São Francisco	South America	3,199	1,988
Rio Grande	North America	3,034	1,885
Indus	Asia	2,900	1,800
Danube	Europe	2,858	1,776
Yukon	North America	2,849	1,770
Brahmaputra	Asia	2,849	1,770
Salween (Thanlwin)	Asia	2,816	1,750
Zambezi	Africa	2,700	1,700
Tocantins	South America	2,639	1,640
Orinoco	South America	2,600	1,600
Paraguay	South America	2,591	1,610
Amudarja	Asia	2,540	1,578
Murray	Australia	2,520	1,566
Ganges	Asia	2,511	1,560
Euphrates	Asia	2,430	1,510
Ural	Asia	2,428	1,509
Arkansas	North America	2,348	1,459
Colorado	North America (U.S.-Mex.)	2,334	1,450
Syrdarja	Asia	2,205	1,370
Tarim	Asia	2,137	1,328
Orange	Africa	2,100	1,300
Negro	South America	2,100	1,300
Irrawaddy (Ayeyarwady)	Asia	2,100	1,300
Red	North America	2,044	1,270
Columbia	North America	2,000	1,200
Xingu	South America	1,979	1,230
Ucayali	South America	1,963	1,220
Saskatchewan-Bow	North America	1,939	1,205
Peace	North America	1,923	1,195
Tigris	Asia	1,899	1,180
Sungari	Asia	1,835	1,140
Pechora	Europe	1,809	1,124
Limpopo	Africa	1,800	1,100
Snake	North America	1,670	1,038

Principal Islands

Island	Area km²	sq mi	Highest Point Name	m	ft
Grønland (Greenland)	2,175,600	840,000	Gunnbjørns Fjeld	3,700	12,139
New Guinea	800,000	309,000	Puncak Jaya	5,030	16,503
Borneo	744,100	287,300	Gunong Kinabalu	4,101	13,455
Madagascar	587,000	227,000	Maromokotro	2,876	9,436
Baffin Island	507,451	195,928	Unnamed	2,591	8,501
Sumatera (Sumatra)	473,606	182,860	Gunung Kerinci	3,800	12,467
Honshū	230,966	89,176	Fuji-San	3,776	12,388
Great Britain	229,978	88,795	Ben Nevis	1,343	4,406
Victoria Island	217,291	83,897	Mt. Bumpus	655	2,149
Ellesmere Island	196,236	75,767	Barbeau Peak	2,604	8,543
Sulawesi (Celebes)	189,216	73,057	Bulu Rantekombola	3,455	11,335
South Island	149,883	57,870	Mt. Cook	3,764	12,349
Jawa (Java)	132,187	51,038	Gunung Semeru	3,676	12,060
North Island	114,669	44,274	Mt. Ruapehu	2,797	9,177
Cuba	110,800	42,800	Pico Turquino	1,994	6,542
Newfoundland	108,860	42,031	Unnamed	814	2,670
Luzon	104,688	40,420	Mt. Pulog	2,930	9,613
Ísland (Iceland)	103,000	39,800	Hvannadalshnúkur	2,119	6,952
Mindanao	94,630	36,537	Mt. Apo	2,954	9,692
Ireland	84,400	32,600	Carrauntoohil	1,038	3,406
Hokkaidō	83,515	32,245	Taisetsu-Zan	2,290	7,513
Novaja Zemlja (Novaya Zemlya)	82,600	31,900	Unnamed	1,547	5,075
Sahalin, ostrov (Sakhalin)	76,400	29,500	gora Lopatina	1,609	5,279
Hispaniola	76,000	29,300	Pico Duarte	3,175	10,417
Banks Island	70,028	27,038	Unnamed	747	2,451
Tasmania	67,800	26,200	Mt. Ossa	1,617	5,305
Sri Lanka	64,600	24,900	Pidurutalagala	2,524	8,281
Devon Island	55,247	21,331	Unnamed	1,887	6,191
Tierra del Fuego, Isla Grande de	48,200	18,600	Cerro Yogan	2,469	8,100

Major Lakes

Lake	Location	Area km²	sq mi	Depth m	ft
Caspian Sea	Asia-Europe	370,990	143,240	1,025	3,363
Superior, L.	Canada-U.S.	82,100	31,700	406	1,332
Victoria, L.	Africa	69,463	26,820	85	279
Aral'skoje more (Aral Sea)	Asia	64,100	24,700	68	223
Huron, L.	Canada-U.S.	60,000	23,000	229	750
Michigan, L.	U.S.	57,800	22,300	282	924
Tanganyika. L.	Africa	31,986	12,350	1,463	4,800
Bajkal, ozero (L. Baikal)	Russia	31,500	12,200	1,620	5,315
Great Bear Lake	Canada	31,326	12,095	413	1,356
Nyasa, L.	Africa	28,878	11,150	695	2,280
Great Slave Lake	Canada	28,568	11,030	614	2,015
Erie, L.	Canada-U.S.	25,667	9,910	62	204
Winnipeg, L.	Canada	24,387	9,416	28	92
Ontario, L.	Canada-U.S.	19,529	7,540	243	798
Balhaš, ozero (L. Balkhash)	Kazakhstan	18,300	7,100	26	85
Chad, L.	Africa	16,300	6,300	7	24
Onežskoje ozero (L. Onega)	Russia	9,720	3,753	127	417
Eyre, L.	Australia	9,500	3,700	1	4
Titicaca, Lago	Bolivia-Peru	8,300	3,200	302	990
Nicaragua, Lago de	Nicaragua	8,158	3,150	70	230
Mai-Ndombe, Lac	Zaire	8,000	3,100	11	36
Athabasca, L.	Canada	7,935	3,064	124	407
Reindeer Lake	Canada	6,650	2,568	219	720
Tônlé Sab, Bœng	Cambodia	6,500	2,500	12	39
Rudolf, L.	Ethiopia-Kenya	6,405	2,473	219	720
Torrens, L.	Australia	5,900	2,300	*	*
Albert, L.	Uganda-Zaire	5,594	2,160	51	168
Vänern	Sweden	5,584	2,156	99	325

* Intermittently dry lake

Drainage Basins

Name	Continent	Area km²	sq mi
Amazon	South America	6,151,000	2,375,000
Congo (Zaire)	Africa	3,823,000	1,476,000
Mississippi-Missouri	North America	3,230,000	1,247,000
Río de la Plata-Paraná	South America	3,100,000	1,197,000
Ob'-Irtyš	Asia	2,989,000	1,154,000
Nile	Africa	2,802,000	1,082,000
Lena	Asia	2,489,000	961,000
Amur-Argun	Asia	2,051,000	792,000
Niger	Africa	1,891,000	730,000
Yangtze (Chang Jiang)	Asia	1,826,000	705,000
Mackenzie	North America	1,572,000	607,000
Volga	Europe	1,360,000	525,000
Zambezi	Africa	1,331,000	514,000
St. Lawrence	North America	1,303,000	503,000

World Geographical Tables

Historical Population of the World

AREA	1650	1750	1800	1850	1900	1914	1920	1939	1950	1993
Europe	*100,000,000*	*140,000,000*	*190,000,000*	265,000,000	400,000,000	470,000,000	453,000,000	526,000,000	530,000,000	694,700,000
Asia	*335,000,000*	*476,000,000*	*593,000,000*	754,000,000	932,000,000	1,006,000,000	1,000,000,000	1,247,000,000	1,418,000,000	3,337,800,000
Africa	*100,000,000*	*95,000,000*	*90,000,000*	95,000,000	118,000,000	130,000,000	140,000,000	170,000,000	199,000,000	668,700,000
North America	*5,000,000*	*5,000,000*	*13,000,000*	39,000,000	106,000,000	141,000,000	147,000,000	186,000,000	219,000,000	438,200,000
South America	*8,000,000*	*7,000,000*	*12,000,000*	20,000,000	38,000,000	55,000,000	61,000,000	90,000,000	111,000,000	310,700,000
Oceania, incl. Australia	*2,000,000*	*2,000,000*	*2,000,000*	2,000,000	6,000,000	8,000,000	9,000,000	11,000,000	13,000,000	26,700,000
Australia					4,000,000	5,000,000	6,000,000	7,000,000	8,000,000	16,965,000
World	*550,000,000*	*725,000,000*	*900,000,000*	1,175,000,000	1,600,000,000	1,810,000,000	1,810,000,000	2,230,000,000	2,490,000,000	5,477,000,000

Figures in italics represent very rough estimates.

Largest Countries: Population

Country	Population 1/1/93
1. China	1,179,030,000
2. India	873,850,000
3. United States	256,420,000
4. Indonesia	186,180,000
5. Brazil	159,630,000
6. Russia	150,500,000
7. Japan	124,710,000
8. Pakistan	123,490,000
9. Bangladesh	120,850,000
10. Nigeria	91,700,000
11. Mexico	86,170,000
12. Germany	80,590,000
13. Vietnam	69,650,000
14. Philippines	65,500,000
15. Iran	60,500,000
16. Turkey	58,620,000
17. Thailand	58,030,000
18. United Kingdom	57,890,000
19. France	57,570,000
20. Egypt	57,050,000
21. Italy	56,550,000
22. Ukraine	51,990,000
23. Ethiopia	51,715,000
24. South Korea	43,660,000
25. Burma	43,070,000
26. South Africa	42,407,000
27. Zaire	39,750,000
28. Spain	39,155,000
29. Poland	38,330,000
30. Colombia	34,640,000
31. Argentina	32,950,000
32. Canada	30,530,000
33. Sudan	28,760,000
34. Tanzania	28,265,000
35. Morocco	27,005,000
36. Algeria	26,925,000
37. Kenya	26,635,000
38. Romania	23,200,000
39. Peru	22,995,000
40. North Korea	22,450,000
41. Uzbekistan	21,885,000
42. Taiwan	20,985,000
43. Nepal	20,325,000
44. Venezuela	19,085,000
45. Iraq	18,815,000

Largest Countries: Area

Country	km²	sq mi
1. Russia	17,075,400	*6,592,849*
2. Canada	9,970,610	*3,849,674*
3. United States	9,809,431	*3,787,425*
4. China	9,556,100	*3,689,631*
5. Brazil	8,511,996	*3,286,500*
6. Australia	7,682,300	*2,966,155*
7. India	3,203,975	*1,237,062*
8. Argentina	2,780,400	*1,073,519*
9. Kazakhstan	2,717,300	*1,049,156*
10. Sudan	2,505,813	*967,500*
11. Algeria	2,381,741	*919,595*
12. Zaire	2,345,095	*905,446*
13. Greenland	2,175,600	*840,004*
14. Saudi Arabia	2,149,690	*830,000*
15. Mexico	1,967,183	*759,534*
16. Indonesia	1,948,732	*752,410*
17. Libya	1,759,540	*679,362*
18. Iran	1,638,057	*632,457*
19. Mongolia	1,566,500	*604,829*
20. Peru	1,285,216	*496,225*
21. Chad	1,284,000	*495,755*
22. Niger	1,267,000	*489,191*
23. Mali	1,248,574	*482,077*
24. Angola	1,246,700	*481,354*
25. South Africa	1,220,118	*471,090*
26. Ethiopia	1,157,603	*446,953*
27. Colombia	1,141,748	*440,831*
28. Bolivia	1,098,581	*424,165*
29. Mauritania	1,025,520	*395,956*
30. Egypt	1,001,449	*386,662*
31. Tanzania	945,087	*364,900*
32. Nigeria	923,768	*356,669*
33. Venezuela	912,050	*352,145*
34. Pakistan	879,902	*339,732*
35. Namibia	824,272	*318,254*
36. Mozambique	799,380	*308,642*
37. Turkey	779,452	*300,948*
38. Chile	756,626	*292,135*
39. Zambia	752,614	*290,586*
40. Burma	676,577	*261,228*
41. Afghanistan	652,225	*251,826*
42. Somalia	637,657	*246,201*
43. Central African Republic	622,984	*240,535*
44. Ukraine	603,700	*233,090*
45. Madagascar	587,041	*226,658*

Smallest Countries: Population

Country	Population 1/1/93
1. Vatican City	800
2. Niue	1,700
3. Anguilla	7,000
4. Nauru	10,000
Tuvalu	10,000
5. Palau	16,000
6. Cook Islands	18,000
7. San Marino	23,000
8. Liechtenstein	30,000
9. Monaco	31,000
10. St. Christopher-Nevis	40,000
11. Northern Mariana Islands	48,000
12. Faeroe Islands	49,000
13. Marshall Islands	51,000
14. Andorra	56,000
15. Greenland	57,000
16. Guernsey	58,000
17. Aruba	65,000
18. Isle of Man	70,000
Seychelles	70,000
19. Kiribati	76,000
20. Antigua and Barbuda	77,000
21. Jersey	85,000
22. Dominica	88,000
23. Grenada	97,000
24. Tonga	103,000
25. St. Vincent and the Grenadines	116,000
26. Micronesia, Federated States of	117,000
27. Sao Tome and Principe	134,000
28. St. Lucia	153,000
29. Vanuatu	157,000
30. Belize	186,000
31. Netherlands Antilles	191,000
32. Cyprus, North	193,000
33. Western Samoa	197,000
34. Maldives	235,000
35. Barbados	258,000
36. Iceland	260,000
37. Bahamas	265,000
38. Brunei	273,000
39. Malta	360,000
40. Solomon Islands	366,000
41. Luxembourg	392,000
42. Equatorial Guinea	394,000
43. Djibouti	396,000

Smallest Countries: Area

Country	km²	sq mi
1. Vatican City	0.4	*0.2*
2. Monaco	1.9	*0.7*
3. Nauru	21	*8.1*
4. Tuvalu	26	*10*
5. San Marino	61	*24*
6. Guernsey	78	*30*
7. Anguilla	91	*35*
8. Jersey	116	*45*
9. Liechtenstein	160	*62*
10. Marshall Islands	181	*70*
11. Aruba	193	*75*
12. Cook Islands	236	*91*
13. Niue	258	*100*
14. St. Christopher-Nevis	269	*104*
15. Maldives	298	*115*
16. Malta	316	*122*
17. Grenada	344	*133*
18. St. Vincent and the Grenadines	388	*150*
19. Barbados	430	*166*
20. Antigua and Barbuda	442	*171*
21. Andorra	453	*175*
Seychelles	453	*175*
22. Northern Mariana Islands	477	*184*
23. Palau	508	*196*
24. Isle of Man	572	*221*
25. St. Lucia	616	*238*
26. Singapore	636	*246*
27. Bahrain	691	*267*
28. Micronesia, Federated States of	702	*271*
29. Tonga	747	*288*
30. Dominica	790	*305*
31. Netherlands Antilles	800	*309*
32. Kiribati	811	*313*
33. Sao Tome and Principe	964	*372*
34. Faeroe Islands	1,399	*540*
35. Mauritius	2,040	*788*
36. Comoros	2,235	*863*
37. Luxembourg	2,586	*998*
38. Western Samoa	2,831	*1,093*
39. Cyprus, North	3,355	*1,295*
40. Cape Verde	4,033	*1,557*
41. Trinidad and Tobago	5,128	*1,980*
42. Brunei	5,765	*2,226*
43. Cyprus	5,896	*2,276*

Highest Population Densities

Country	Density per km²	sq mi	Country	Density per km²	sq mi
1. Monaco	16,316	*44,286*	16. Tuvalu	385	*1,000*
2. Singapore	4,421	*11,431*	17. San Marino	377	*958*
3. Vatican City	2,000	*4,000*	18. Netherlands	363	*940*
4. Malta	1,139	*2,951*	19. Aruba	337	*867*
5. Bangladesh	839	*2,174*	20. Lebanon	333	*864*
6. Bahrain	812	*2,101*	21. Japan	330	*855*
7. Maldives	789	*2,043*	22. Belgium	329	*851*
8. Guernsey	744	*1,933*	23. St. Vincent and the Grenadines	299	*773*
9. Jersey	733	*1,889*	24. Rwanda	288	*745*
10. Barbados	600	*1,554*	25. Grenada	282	*729*
11. Taiwan	583	*1,510*	Marshall Islands	282	*729*
12. Mauritius	537	*1,391*	26. Sri Lanka	274	*711*
13. Nauru	476	*1,235*	27. India	273	*706*
14. Korea, South	441	*1,142*	28. El Salvador	268	*694*
15. Puerto Rico	395	*1,022*	29. Trinidad and Tobago	255	*660*

Lowest Population Densities

Country	Density per km²	sq mi	Country	Density per km²	sq mi
1. Greenland	...	*0.1*	16. Niue	6.6	*17*
2. Mongolia	1.5	*3.9*	17. Bolivia	6.7	*17*
3. Namibia	1.9	*5.0*	18. Mali	7.0	*18*
4. Mauritania	2.0	*5.3*	19. Congo	7.1	*18*
5. Australia	2.2	*5.7*	20. Saudi Arabia	7.4	*19*
6. Botswana	2.4	*6.1*	21. Oman	7.6	*20*
7. Iceland	2.5	*6.5*	22. Turkmenistan	8.0	*21*
Suriname	2.5	*6.5*	23. Belize	8.1	*21*
8. Libya	2.6	*6.7*	Papua New Guinea	8.1	*21*
9. Canada	3.1	*7.9*	24. Angola	8.6	*22*
10. Guyana	3.4	*8.9*	25. Russia	8.8	*23*
11. Chad	4.1	*11*	26. Somalia	9.4	*24*
12. Gabon	4.2	*11*	27. Algeria	11	*29*
13. Central African Republic	4.9	*13*	28. Norway	11	*29*
14. Kazakhstan	6.3	*16*	29. Zambia	11	*29`*
15. Niger	6.5	*17*			

... Less than 0.1

Major Metropolitan Areas of the World

This table lists the major metropolitan areas of the world according to their estimated population on January 1, 1993. For convenience in reference, the areas are grouped by major region with the total for each region given. The number of areas by population classification is given in parentheses with each size group.

For ease of comparison, each metropolitan area has been defined by Rand McNally according to consistent rules. A metropolitan area includes a central city, neighboring communities linked to it by continuous built-up areas, and more distant communities if the bulk of their population is supported by commuters to the central city. Some metropolitan areas have more than one central city; in such cases each central city is listed.

SIZE	ANGLO AMERICA	LATIN AMERICA	WESTERN EUROPE	EASTERN EUROPE/ RUSSIA	WEST ASIA	EAST ASIA	AFRICA/OCEANIA
Over 15,000,000 (6)	New York	Ciudad de México (Mexico City) São Paulo				Ōsaka-Kōbe-Kyōto Sŏul (Seoul) Tōkyō-Yokohama	
10,000,000- 15,000,000 (13)	Los Angeles	Buenos Aires Rio de Janeiro	London Paris	Moskva (Moscow)	Bombay Calcutta Delhi-New Delhi	Jakarta Manila Shanghai	Al-Qāhirah (Cairo)
5,000,000- 10,000,000 (21)	Chicago Philadelphia-Trenton- Wilmington San Francisco- Oakland-San Jose	Lima Santa Fe de Bogotá Santiago	Essen-Dortmund- Duisburg (Ruhr Area)	Sankt-Peterburg (St. Petersburg)	Dhaka (Dacca) İstanbul Karāchi Madras Tehrān	Beijing (Peking) Krung Thep (Bangkok) Nagoya Tianjin (Tientsin) T'aipei Victoria (Hong Kong)	Johannesburg Lagos
3,000,000- 5,000,000 (37)	Boston Dallas-Fort Worth Detroit-Windsor Houston Miami-Fort Lauderdale Montréal San Diego-Tijuana Toronto Washington	Belo Horizonte Caracas Guadalajara Porto Alegre	Barcelona Berlin Madrid Milano (Milan) Roma (Rome)	Athínai (Athens) Kijev (Kiev)	Ahmadābād Baghdād Bangalore Hyderābād Lahore	Guangzhou (Canton) Pusan Shenyang (Mukden) Singapore Thanh Pho Ho Chi Minh (Saigon) Wuhan Yangon (Rangoon)	Al-Iskandarīyah (Alexandria) Casablanca Kinshasa Melbourne Sydney
2,000,000- 3,000,000 (64)	Atlanta Baltimore Cleveland Minneapolis-St. Paul Phoenix Pittsburgh St. Louis Seattle-Tacoma	Fortaleza La Habana (Havana) Medellín Monterrey Recife Salvador San Juan Santo Domingo	Amsterdam Birmingham Bruxelles (Brussels) Frankfurt am Main Hamburg Leeds-Bradford Lisboa (Lisbon) Liverpool Manchester München (Munich) Napoli (Naples) Stuttgart Wien (Vienna)	Bucureşti (Bucharest) Budapest Char'kov (Kharkov) Doneck-Makejevka Katowice-Bytom- Gliwice Nižnij Novgorod (Gorkiy) Warszawa (Warsaw)	Ankara Baku Colombo Dimashq (Damascus) İzmir Kānpur Pune (Poona) Taškent	Bandung Changchun Chengdu (Chengtu) Chongqing (Chungking) Dalian (Dairen) Fukuoka Harbin Kuala Lumpur Nanjing (Nanking) P'yongyang Sapporo-Otaru Surabaya Taegu Xi'an (Sian)	Abidjan Adis Abeba Al-Kharṭūm-Umm Durmān (Khartoum- Omdurman) Cape Town Durban El Djazaïr (Algiers)
1,500,000- 2,000,000 (48)	Cincinnati Denver El Paso-Ciudad Juárez Portland Vancouver	Brasília Cali Curitiba Guatemala Guayaquil Montevideo San José	Glasgow København (Copenhagen) Köln (Cologne) Mannheim Stockholm	Beograd (Belgrade) Dnepropetrovsk Jekaterinburg (Sverdlovsk) Minsk Novosibirsk	'Amman Ar-Riyad (Riyadh) Bayrūt (Beirut) Chittagong Faisalabad Ḥalab (Aleppo) Jaipur Jiddah Kābol (Kabul) Lucknow Mashhad Nāgpur Rāwalpindi- Islāmābād Surat Tbilisi Tel Aviv-Yafo	Hiroshima-Kure Jinan (Tsinan) Kaohsiung Kitakyūshū- Shimonoseki Medan Qingdao (Tsingtao) Taiyuan	Accra Dakar Rabat-Salé
1,000,000- 1,500,000 (119)	Buffalo-Niagara Falls- St. Catharines Columbus Hartford-New Britain Indianapolis Kansas City Milwaukee New Orleans Norfolk-Newport News Sacramento St. Petersburg- Clearwater San Antonio	Asuncíon Barranquilla Belém Campinas Córdoba Goiânia La Paz Manaus Maracaibo Puebla Quito Rosario San Salvador Santos Valencia Vitória	Antwerpen (Antwerp) Dublin (Baile Átha Cliath) Düsseldorf Hannover Helsinki Lille-Roubaix Lyon Marseille Newcastle-Sunderland Nürnberg Porto Rotterdam Sevilla Torino (Turin) Valencia	Čel'abinsk (Chelyabinsk) Łódź Kazan' Kraków Krasnojarsk Odessa Omsk Perm Praha (Prague) Rīga Rostov-na-Donu Samara (Kuybyshev) Saratov Sofija (Sofia) Ufa Volgograd Voronež	Adana Agra Allahābād Al-Kuwayt (Kuwait) Alma-Ata Asansol Bhopāl Cochin Coimbatore Esfahān Indore Jerevan Ludhiāna Madurai Patna Shīrāz Tabrīz Vadodara Vārānasi (Benares) Vishākhapatnam	Anshan Baotou Changsha Fushun Guiyang Hangzhou Ha Noi Jilin (Kirin) Kunming Kwangju Lanzhou Nanchang Palembang Qiqihar (Tsitsihar) Semarang Sendai Shijiazhuang Shizuoka-Shimizu Taejŏn Tangshan Ujung Pandang Ürümqi Zhengzhou Zibo	Adelaide Antananarivo Brisbane Dar es Salaam Douala Harare Ibadan Kampala Luanda Lusaka Maputo Nairobi Perth Pretoria Ṭarābulus (Tripoli) Tunis
Total by region (308)	38	42	41	33	57	64	33

Populations of Major Cities

The largest and most important of the world's major cities are listed in the following table. Also included are some smaller cities because of their regional significance.

Local official name forms have been used throughout the table. When a commonly used "conventional" name form exists, it has been featured within parentheses, following the official name. Each city name is followed by the English name of its country. Names in the United States, the United Kingdom, and Canada are further distinguished by the name of the state, region, or province in which they are located.

Many cities have population figures within parentheses following the country name. These are metropolitan populations, comprising the central city and its suburbs. When a city is within the metropolitan area of another city the name of the metropolitan central city is specified in parentheses preceded by a *. The symbol † identifies a political district population which includes some rural population. For these cities the estimated city population has been based upon the district figure.

The population of each city has been dated for ease of comparison. The date is followed by a letter designating: Census (C) or Official Estimate (E).

City and Country	Population	Date
Aachen, Germany (535,000) ...	233,255	89E
Ābādān, Iran	296,081	76C
Abidjan, Ivory Coast	1,950,000	83E
Abū Ẓaby (Abu Dhabi), United Arab Emirates	242,975	80C
Acapulco [de Juárez], Mexico	301,902	80C
Accra, Ghana (1,250,000)	949,113	87C
Adana, Turkey	931,555	90C
Ad Dawḥah (Doha), Qatar (310,000)	217,294	86E
Addis Ababa, see Ādīs Ābeba		
Adelaide, Australia (1,036,747)	12,340	89E
Aden, see Baladiyad 'Adan		
Ādīs Ābeba (Addis Ababa), Ethiopia (1,760,000)	1,686,300	88E
Agana, Guam (44,000)	896	80C
Āgra, India (955,684)	899,195	91C
Aguascalientes, Mexico	293,152	80C
Ahmadābād, India (3,297,655)	2,872,865	91C
Ahvāz, Iran	579,826	86C
Akita, Japan	302,359	90C
Akron, Oh., U.S. (*Cleveland)	223,019	90C
Albany, N.Y., U.S. (874,304) ...	101,082	90C
Al Baṣrah, Iraq	616,700	85E
Albuquerque, N.M., U.S. (480,557)	384,736	90C
Aleppo, see Halab		
Alexandria, see Al Iskandarīyah		
Algiers, see Al Jazā'ir		
Al Iskandarīyah (Alexandria), Egypt (3,350,000)	2,917,327	86C
Al Jazā'ir (Algiers), Algeria (2,547,983)	1,507,241	87E
Al Jīzah (Giza), Egypt (*Al Qāhirah)	1,870,508	86C
Al Kharṭūm (Khartoum), Sudan (1,450,000)	476,218	83C
Al Kuwayt (Kuwait), Kuwait (1,375,000)	44,335	85C
Allahābād, India (858,213)	806,447	91C
Alma-Ata, Kazakhstan (1,190,000)	1,128,000	89C
Al Madīnah (Medina), Saudi Arabia	290,000	80E
Al Maḥallah al Kubrā, Egypt	358,844	86C
Al Manāmah (Manama), Bahrain (224,643)	115,054	81C
Al Manṣurah, Egypt (375,000)	316,870	86C
Al Mawṣil (Mosul), Iraq	570,926	85E
Al Qāhirah (Cairo), Egypt (9,300,000)	6,052,836	86C
Amagasaki, Japan (*Ōsaka) ...	498,998	90C
'Ammān, Jordan (1,450,000) ...	936,300	89E
Amritsar, India	709,456	91C
Amsterdam, Netherlands (1,860,000)	696,500	89E
Anchorage, Ak., U.S.	226,338	90C
Andorra la Vella, Andorra	20,437	91E
Ankara, Turkey (2,650,000) ...	2,553,209	90C
Annaba (Bône), Algeria	305,526	87C
Anshan, China	1,330,000	88E
Antananarivo, Madagascar ...	663,000	85E
Antwerpen (Antwerp), Belgium (1,100,000)	479,748	87E
Apia, Western Samoa	33,170	81C
Arequipa, Peru (446,942)	108,023	81C
Arhangelsk, Russia	416,000	89C
Arnhem, Netherlands (296,362)	129,000	89E
Ar Riyāḍ (Riyadh), Saudi Arabia	1,250,000	80E
Asansol, India (763,845)	261,836	91C
Ašhabad, Turkmenistan	398,000	89C
As Suways (Suez), Egypt	326,820	86C
Astrahan, Russia	509,000	89C
Asunción, Paraguay (700,000)	477,100	85E
Athínai (Athens), Greece (3,027,331)	885,737	81C
Atlanta, Ga., U.S. (2,833,511)	394,017	90C
Auckland, New Zealand (850,000)	149,046	86C
Augsburg, Germany (405,000)	247,731	89E
Austin, Tx., U.S. (781,572)	465,622	90C
Baghdād, Iraq	3,841,268	87C
Bakhtarān, Iran	560,514	86C
Baku, Azerbaijan (2,020,000)	1,150,000	89C
Baladiyat 'Adan (Aden), Yemen (318,000)	176,100	84E
Balikpapan, Indonesia (†279,852)	208,040	80C
Baltimore, Md., U.S. (2,382,172)	736,014	90C
Bamako, Mali	646,163	87C
Bandar Seri Begawan, Brunei (64,000)	22,777	81C
Bandung, Indonesia (1,800,000)	1,633,000	85E
Bangalore, India (4,086,548)	2,650,659	91C
Banghāzī (Benghazi), Libya ...	466,250	88E
Bangkok, see Krung Thep		
Bangui, Cen. Afr. Rep.	473,817	84E
Banjul, Gambia (95,000)	44,188	83C
Barcelona, Spain (4,040,000)	1,714,355	88C
Barnaul, Russia (665,000)	602,000	89C
Barquisimeto, Venezuela	497,635	81C
Barranquilla, Colombia (1,140,000)	899,781	85C
Basel, Switzerland (575,000) ...	169,587	90E
Basse-Terre, Guadeloupe (26,000)	13,656	82C
Basseterre, St. Chris.-Nevis ..	14,725	80C
Baton Rouge, La., U.S. (528,264)	219,531	90C
Bayrūt (Beirut), Lebanon (1,675,000)	509,000	82E
Beijing (Peking), China (7,320,000)	6,710,000	88E
Beirut, see Bayrūt		
Belém, Brazil (1,200,000)	1,116,578	85E
Belfast, N. Ire., U.K. (685,000)	303,800	87E
Belgrade, see Beograd		
Belize City, Belize	47,000	85E
Belmopan, Belize	4,500	85E
Belo Horizonte, Brazil (2,950,000)	2,114,429	85E
Benares, see Vārānasi		
Bengbu, China (†612,600)	403,900	86E
Benxi, China	860,000	88E
Beograd (Belgrade), Yugoslavia (1,400,000)	1,130,000	87E
Bergamo, Italy (345,000)	118,959	87E
Berlin, Germany (3,825,000) ...	3,352,848	89E
Bern (Berne), Switzerland (298,363)	134,393	90E
Bhopal, India	1,063,662	91C
Bielefeld, Germany (515,000)	311,946	89E
Bilbao, Spain (985,000)	384,733	88E
Billings, Mt., U.S. (113,419) ...	81,151	90C
Birmingham, Eng., U.K. (2,675,000)	1,013,995	81C
Birmingham, Al., U.S. (907,810)	265,968	90C
Biškek Kirghizia	616,000	89C
Bissau, Guinea-Bissau	125,000	88C
Blackpool, Eng., U.K. (280,000)	146,297	81C
Bloemfontein, South Africa (235,000)	104,381	85C
Bogor, Indonesia (560,000) ...	246,946	80C
Boise, Id., U.S. (205,775)	125,738	90C
Bologna, Italy (525,000)	432,406	87E
Bombay, India (12,571,720)	9,909,547	91C
Bonn, Germany (570,000)	282,190	89E
Bordeaux, France (640,012) ...	208,159	82C
Boston, Ma., U.S. (4,171,643)	574,283	90C
Brasília, Brazil	1,567,709	85E
Bratislava, Slovakia	442,999	90E
Braunschweig, Germany (330,000)	253,794	89E
Brazzaville, Congo	585,812	84C
Bremen, Germany (800,000) ...	5,325,058	89E
Brest, France (201,145)	156,060	82C
Bridgetown, Barbados (115,000)	7,466	80C
Brighton, Eng., U.K. (420,000)	134,581	81C
Brisbane, Australia (1,273,511)	744,828	89E
Bristol, Eng., U.K. (630,000) ...	413,861	81C
Bruxelles / Brussel (Brussels), Belgium (2,385,000)	136,920	87E
Bucaramanga, Colombia (550,000)	352,326	85C
Bucureşti (Bucharest), Romania (2,275,000)	1,989,823	86E
Budapest, Hungary (2,565,000)	2,016,132	90E
Buenos Aires, Argentina (10,750,000)	2,922,829	80C
Buffalo, N.Y., U.S. (1,189,288)	328,123	90C
Bujumbura, Burundi	273,000	86E
Bulawayo, Zimbabwe	429,000	83E
Burlington, Vt., U.S. (131,439)	39,127	90C
Bursa, Turkey	838,323	90C
Būr Sa'īd (Port Said), Egypt ...	399,793	86C
Cádiz, Spain (240,000)	156,591	88E
Cagliari, Italy (305,000)	220,574	87E
Cairo, see Al Qāhirah		
Calcutta, India (11,605,833) ...	4,388,262	91C
Calgary, Alta., Can. (671,326)	636,104	86C
Cali, Colombia (1,400,000) ...	1,350,565	85C
Calicut (Kozhikode), India (800,913)	419,531	91C
Callao, Peru (*Lima)	264,133	81C
Campinas, Brazil (1,125,000)	841,016	85E
Canberra, Australia (271,362)	247,194	86C
Cannes, France (295,525)	72,259	82C
Canton, see Guangzhou		
Cape Town, South Africa (1,790,000)	776,617	85C
Caracas, Venezuela (3,600,000)	1,816,901	81C
Cardiff, Wales, U.K. (625,000)	262,313	81C
Cartagena, Colombia	531,426	85C
Casablanca, Morocco (2,475,000)	2,139,204	82C
Castries, St. Lucia	53,933	87E
Catania, Italy (550,000)	372,486	87E
Cayenne, French Guiana	38,091	82C
Cebu, Philippines (720,000) ...	610,000	90C
Čeljabinsk (Chelyabinsk), Russia (1,325,000)	1,143,000	89C
Chandīgarh, India (574,646) ...	502,992	91C
Changchun, China (†2,000,000)	1,822,000	88E
Changshu, China (†998,000)	281,300	86E
Changzhou, China	522,700	86E
Chao'an, China (†1,214,500)	265,400	86E
Charleston, W.V., U.S. (250,454)	57,287	90C
Charlotte, N.C., U.S. (1,162,093)	395,934	90C
Chattanooga, Tn., U.S. (433,210)	152,466	90C
Chengdu, China (†2,960,000)	1,884,000	88E
Chiba, Japan (*Tōkyō)	829,467	90C
Chicago, Il., U.S. (8,065,633)	2,783,726	90C
Chiclayo, Peru (279,527)	213,095	81C
Chihuahua, Mexico	385,603	80C
Chittagong, Bangladesh (1,391,877)	980,000	81C
Ch'ŏngjin, N. Korea	490,000	81E
Chongqing (Chungking), China (†2,890,000)	2,502,000	88E
Chŏnju, S. Korea	426,473	85C

City and Country	Population	Date
Christchurch, New Zealand (320,000)	168,200	86C
Chungking, see Chongqing		
Cincinnati, Oh., U.S. (1,744,124)	364,040	90C
Ciudad de México, Mexico (14,100,000)	8,831,079	80C
Ciudad Juárez, Mexico (*El Paso)	544,496	80C
Clermont-Ferrand, France (256,189)	147,361	82C
Cleveland, Oh., U.S. (2,759,823)	505,616	90C
Cochin, India (1,139,543)	564,038	91C
Coimbatore, India (1,135,549)	853,402	91C
Cologne, see Köln		
Colombo, Sri Lanka (2,050,000)	683,000	86E
Columbia, S.C., U.S. (453,331)	98,052	90C
Columbus, Oh., U.S. (1,377,419)	632,910	90C
Conakry, Guinea	800,000	86E
Concepción, Chile (675,000)	267,891	82C
Constanța, Romania	327,676	86E
Constantine, Algeria	440,842	87C
Córdoba, Argentina (1,070,000)	993,055	80C
Córdoba, Spain	302,301	88E
Cotonou, Benin	478,000	84E
Coventry, Eng., U.K. (645,000)	318,718	81C
Cúcuta, Colombia (445,000)	379,478	85C
Cuernavaca, Mexico	192,770	80C
Curitiba, Brazil (1,700,000)	1,279,205	85E
Cusco, Peru (184,550)	89,563	81C
Dakar, Senegal	1,447,642	88C
Dalian (Lüda), China	2,280,000	88E
Dallas, Tx., U.S. (3,885,415)	1,006,877	90C
Dandong, China	579,800	86E
Danzig, see Gdańsk		
Daqing, China (†880,000)	640,000	88E
Dar es Salaam, Tanzania	1,300,000	84E
Darmstadt, Germany (305,000)	136,067	89E
Datong, China (†1,040,000)	810,000	88E
Davao, Philippines (†850,000)	569,300	90C
Dayton, Oh., U.S. (951,270)	182,044	90C
Delhi, India (8,375,188)	7,174,755	91C
Denver, Co., U.S. (1,848,319)	467,610	90C
Des Moines, Ia., U.S. (392,928)	193,187	90C
Detroit, Mi., U.S. (4,665,236)	1,027,974	90C
Dhaka, Bangladesh (3,430,312)	2,365,695	81C
Dhānbād, India (817,549)	151,334	91C
Dimashq (Damascus), Syria (1,950,000)	1,326,000	88E
Djibouti, Djibouti	120,000	76E
Dnepropetrovsk, Ukraine (1,600,000)	1,179,000	89C
Doneck, Ukraine (2,200,000)	1,110,000	89C
Dongguan, China (†1,208,500)	254,900	86E
Dortmund, Germany (*Essen)	587,328	89E
Douala, Cameroon	1,029,731	86E
Dresden, Germany (670,000)	518,057	89E
Dublin (Baile Átha Cliath), Ireland (1,140,000)	502,749	86C
Duisburg, Germany (*Essen)	527,447	89E
Durban, South Africa (1,550,000)	634,301	85C
Dušanbe, Tajikistan	595,000	89C
Düsseldorf, Germany (1,190,000)	569,641	89E
Ecatepec de Morelos, Mexico (*Ciudad de México)	741,821	80C
Edinburgh, Scot., U.K. (630,000)	433,200	89E
Edmonton, Alta., Can. (785,465)	573,982	86C
El Paso, Tx., U.S. (1,211,300)	515,342	90C
Enschede, Netherlands (288,000)	145,200	89E
Erbīl, Iraq	333,903	85E
Eşfahān (Isfahan), Iran (1,175,000)	986,753	86C
Essen, Germany (4,950,000)	620,594	89E
Faisalabad, Pakistan	1,104,209	81C
Fargo, N.D., U.S (153,296)	74,111	90C
Fès, Morocco (535,000)	488,823	82C
Firenze (Florence), Italy (640,000)	425,835	87E
Florianópolis, Brazil (365,000)	178,400	85E
Fortaleza, Brazil (1,825,000)	1,582,414	85E
Fort-de-France, Martinique (116,017)	99,844	82C
Fort Worth, Tx., U.S. (*Dallas)	447,619	90C
Frankfurt am Main, Germany (1,855,000)	625,258	89E
Freetown, Sierra Leone (525,000)	469,776	85C
Fukuoka, Japan (1,750,000)	1,237,107	90C
Funabashi, Japan (*Tōkyō)	533,273	90C
Funafuti, Tuvalu	2,191	79C
Fushun, China	1,290,000	88E
Fuxian, China (†960,700)	246,200	86E
Fuxin, China	700,000	88E
Fuzhou, China (†1,240,000)	910,000	88E
Gaborone, Botswana	107,677	87E
Gdańsk (Danzig), Poland (909,000)	461,500	89E
General Sarmiento, Argentina (*Buenos Aires)	502,926	80C
Genève (Geneva), Switzerland (470,000)	165,404	90E
Genova (Genoa), Italy (805,000)	727,427	87E
Gent (Ghent), Belgium (465,000)	233,856	87E
Georgetown, Cayman Islands	13,700	88E
Georgetown, Guyana (188,000)	78,500	83E
George Town (Pinang), Malaysia (495,000)	248,241	80C
Gifu, Japan	410,318	90C
Giza, see Al Jīzah		
Glasgow, Scot., U.K. (1,800,000)	695,630	89E
Godthåb (Nûk), Greenland	12,217	90E
Goiânia, Brazil (990,000)	923,333	85E
Gorki, see Nižnij Novgorod		
Göteborg, Sweden (710,894)	431,840	90E
Granada, Spain	263,334	88E
Graz, Austria (325,000)	243,166	81C
Grenoble, France (392,021)	156,637	82C
Guadalajara, Mexico (2,325,000)	1,626,152	80C
Guadalupe, Mexico (*Monterrey)	370,524	80C
Guangzhou (Canton), China (†3,420,000)	3,100,000	88E
Guarulhos, Brazil (*São Paulo)	571,700	86E
Guatemala, Guatemala (1,400,000)	1,057,210	89E
Guayaquil, Ecuador (1,580,000)	1,572,615	87C
Guilin, China (†457,500)	342,200	86E
Guiyang, China (†1,430,000)	1,030,000	88E
Gujranwala, Pakistan (658,753)	600,993	81C
Gwalior, India (720,068)	692,982	91C
Haicheng, China (†984,800)	210,700	86E
Haikou, China (†289,600)	209,200	86E
Hai Phong, Vietnam (†1,447,523)	351,919	89C
Halab (Aleppo), Syria (1,261,000)	1,261,000	88E
Halifax, N.S., Can. (295,990)	113,577	86C
Hamamatsu, Japan	534,624	90C
Hamburg, Germany (2,225,000)	1,603,070	89E
Hamilton, Bermuda (15,000)	1,676	85E
Hamilton, Ont., Can. (557,029)	306,728	86C
Handan, China (†1,030,000)	870,000	88E
Hannover, Germany (1,000,000)	498,495	89E
Ha Noi (Hanoi), Vietnam (1,275,000)	905,939	89C
Hāora (Howrah), India (*Calcutta)	946,732	91C
Harare, Zimbabwe (890,000)	681,000	83E
Harbin, China	2,710,000	88E
Harkov, Ukraine (1,940,000)	1,611,000	89C
Hartford, Ct., U.S. (1,085,837)	139,739	90C
Havana, see La Habana		
Ḥefa (Haifa), Israel (435,000)	222,600	89E
Hefei, China (†930,000)	740,000	88E
Hegang, China	588,300	86E
Helsinki, Finland (1,040,000)	490,034	88E
Hibli, India	647,640	91C
Ḥims (Homs), Syria	447,000	88E
Hiroshima, Japan (1,575,000)	1,085,677	90C
Hohhot, China (†830,000)	670,000	88E
Hong Kong, see Victoria		
Honiara, Solomon Is.	30,413	86C
Honolulu, Ha., U.S. (836,231)	365,272	90C
Houston, Tx., U.S. (3,711,043)	1,630,553	90C
Huainan, China (†1,110,000)	700,000	88E
Hyderābād, India (4,280,261)	2,991,884	91C
Ibadan, Nigeria	1,144,000	87E
Ilorin, Nigeria	380,000	87E
Inch'ŏn, S. Korea (*Seoul)	1,628,000	89E
Indianapolis, In., U.S. (1,249,822)	731,327	90C
Indore, India (1,104,065)	1,086,673	91C
Irkutsk, Russia	626,000	89C
Isfahan, see Eşfahān		
Islāmābād, Pakistan (*Rāwalpindi)	204,364	81C
İstanbul, Turkey (7,550,000)	6,748,435	90C
Iževsk, Russia	635,000	89C
İzmir, Turkey (1,900,000)	1,762,849	90C
Jabalpur, India (887,188)	739,961	91C
Jackson, Ms., U.S. (395,396)	196,637	90C
Jacksonville, Fl., U.S. (906,727)	635,230	90C
Jaipur, India (1,514,425)	1,454,678	91C
Jakarta, Indonesia (10,000,000)	9,200,000	89E
Jamshedpur, India (834,535)	461,212	91C
Jaroslavl, Russia	633,000	89C
Jekaterinburg, Russia (1,620,000)	1,367,000	89C
Jerevan, Armenia (1,315,000)	1,199,000	89C
Jiaozuo, China (†509,900)	335,400	86E
Jīddah, Saudi Arabia	1,300,000	80E
Jinan, China (†2,140,000)	1,546,000	88E
Jinzhou, China (†810,000)	710,000	88E
Jixi, China (†820,000)	700,000	88E
João Pessoa, Brazil (550,000)	348,500	85E
Jodhpur, India	648,621	91C
Johannesburg, South Africa (3,650,000)	632,369	85C
Kābol, Afghanistan	1,424,400	88E
Kagoshima, Japan	536,685	90C
Kaifeng, China (†629,100)	458,800	86E
Kaliningrad, Russia	401,000	89C
Kampala, Uganda	1,008,707	90E
Kano, Nigeria	538,300	87E
Kānpur, India (2,111,284)	1,958,282	91C
Kansas City, Mo., U.S. (1,566,280)	435,146	90C
Kaohsiung, Taiwan (1,845,000)	1,342,797	88E
Karāchi, Pakistan (5,300,000)	4,901,627	81C
Karaganda, Kazakhstan	614,000	89C
Karl-Marx-Stadt, Germany (450,000)	311,765	89E
Kāthmāndau, Nepal (320,000)	235,160	81C
Katowice, Poland (2,778,000)	365,800	88E
Kawasaki, Japan (*Tōkyō)	1,173,606	60C
Kayseri, Turkey	416,276	90C
Kazan, Russia (1,140,000)	1,094,000	89C
Keelung (Chilung), Taiwan	348,541	88E
Kemerovo, Russia	520,000	89C
Khartoum, see Al Kharṭūm		
Khulna, Bangladesh	648,359	81C
Kiel, Germany (335,000)	240,675	89E
Kigali, Rwanda	181,600	83E
Kijev (Kiev), Ukraine (2,900,000)	2,587,000	89C
Kingston, Jamaica (770,000)	646,400	87E
Kingston-upon-Hull, Eng., U.K. (350,000)	322,144	81C
Kingstown, St. Vin. and the Gren. (28,936)	19,028	87E
Kinshasa, Zaire	3,000,000	86E
Kisangani (Stanleyville), Zaire	282,650	84C
Kišinev, Moldavia	665,000	89C
Kitakyūshū, Japan (1,525,000)	1,026,467	90C
Kitchener, Ont., Can. (311,195)	150,604	86C
Kitwe-Nkana, Zambia (283,962)	207,500	80C
Knoxville, Tn., U.S. (604,816)	165,121	90C
Kōbe, Japan (*Ōsaka)	1,477,423	90C
København (Copenhagen), Denmark (1,685,000)	466,723	90E
Köln (Cologne), Germany (1,760,000)	937,482	89E
Kowloon, Hong Kong (*Victoria)	774,781	88C
Kraków, Poland (828,000)	743,700	89E
Krasnodar, Russia	620,000	89C
Krasnojarsk, Russia	912,000	89C
Krivoj Rog, Ukraine	713,000	89C
Krung Thep (Bangkok), Thailand (7,025,000)	5,845,152	89E
Kuala Lumpur, Malaysia (1,475,000)	919,610	80C
Kujbyšev, see Samara		
Kumamoto, Japan	579,305	90C
Kumasi, Ghana (600,000)	385,192	87C
Kunming, China (†1,550,000)	1,310,000	88E
Kuwait, see Al Kuwayt		
Kwangju, S. Korea (975,000)	1,165,000	89E
Kyōto, Japan (*Ōsaka)	1,461,140	90C
Lagos, Nigeria (3,800,000)	1,213,000	87E
La Habana (Havana), Cuba (2,125,000)	2,036,800	87E
Lahore, Pakistan (3,025,000)	2,707,215	81C
Lansing, Mi., U.S. (432,674)	127,321	90C
Lanzhou, China (†1,420,000)	1,297,000	88E
La Paz, Bolivia	1,057,200	88E
La Plata, Argentina (*Buenos Aires)	477,175	80C
Las Palmas de Gran Canaria, Spain (†366,347)	319,000	88E
Las Vegas, Nv., U.S. (741,459)	258,295	90C
Lausanne, Switzerland (263,442)	122,600	90E
Leeds, Eng., U.K. (1,540,000)	445,242	81C
Le Havre, France (254,595)	199,388	82C

Metropolitan area populations are shown in parentheses.
⋆ City is located within the metropolitan area of another city; for example, Kyōto, Japan is located in the Ōsaka metropolitan area.
† Population of entire municipality or district, including rural area.

C Census
E Official estimate

City and Country	Population	Date
Leicester, Eng., U.K. (495,000)	324,394	81C
Leipzig, Germany (700,000)	545,307	89E
Leningrad, see Sankt-Peterburg		
León, Mexico	593,002	80C
Leshan, China (†972,300)	307,300	86E
Lexington, Ky., U.S. (348,428)	225,366	90C
Libreville, Gabon	235,700	85E
Liège, Belgium (750,000)	200,891	87E
Lille, France (1,020,000)	168,424	82C
Lilongwe, Malawi	233,973	87C
Lima, Peru (4,608,010)	371,122	81C
Linyi, China (†1,365,000)	190,000	86E
Linz, Austria (355,000)	199,910	81C
Lisboa (Lisbon), Portugal (2,250,000)	807,167	81C
Little Rock, Ar., U.S. (513,117)	175,795	90C
Liuzhou, China	680,000	88E
Liverpool, Eng., U.K. (1,525,000)	538,809	81C
Ljubljana, Slovenia (†316,607)	233,200	87E
Łódź, Poland (1,061,000)	851,500	89E
Lomas de Zamora, Argentina (*Buenos Aires)	510,130	80C
Lomé, Togo	400,000	81C
London, Ont., Can. (342,302)	269,140	86C
London, Eng., U.K. (11,100,000)	6,574,009	81C
Los Angeles, Ca., U.S. (14,531,529)	3,485,398	90C
Louisville, Ky., U.S. (952,662)	269,063	90C
Luanda, Angola	1,459,900	89E
Lubumbashi, Zaire	543,268	84C
Lucknow, India (1,642,134)	1,592,010	91C
Ludhiāna, India	1,012,062	91C
Luoyang, China (1,090,000)	760,000	88E
Lusaka, Zambia	535,830	80C
Luxembourg, Luxembourg (136,000)	76,130	85E
Lvov, Ukraine	790,000	89C
Lyon, France (1,275,000)	413,095	82C
Madison, Wi., U.S. (367,085)	191,262	90C
Madras, India (5,361,468)	3,795,028	91C
Madrid, Spain (4,650,000)	3,102,846	88E
Madurai, India (1,093,702)	951,696	91C
Magdeburg, Germany (400,000)	290,579	89E
Magnitogorsk, Russia	440,000	89C
Makkah (Mecca), Saudi Arabia	550,000	80E
Malabo, Equatorial Guinea	31,630	83C
Málaga, Spain	574,456	88E
Malang, Indonesia	547,000	83E
Male, Maldives	46,334	85E
Malmö, Sweden (445,000)	232,908	90E
Managua, Nicaragua	682,000	85E
Manama, see Al Manāmah		
Manaus, Brazil	809,914	85E
Manchester, Eng., U.K. (2,775,000)	437,612	81C
Manchester, N.H., U.S. (147,809)	99,567	90C
Mandalay, Burma	532,949	83E
Manila, Philippines (6,800,000)	1,587,000	90C
Manizales, Colombia (330,000)	299,352	85C
Mannheim, Germany (1,400,000)	300,468	89E
Maputo, Mozambique	1,069,727	89E
Maracaibo, Venezuela	890,643	81C
Mar del Plata, Argentina	414,696	80C
Mariupol', Ukraine	517,000	89C
Marrakech, Morocco (535,000)	439,728	82C
Marseille, France (1,225,000)	874,436	82C
Maseru, Lesotho	109,382	86C
Masqaṭ (Muscat), Oman	50,000	81E
Mbabane, Swaziland	38,290	86C
Mbuji-Mayi, Zaire	423,363	84C
Medan, Indonesia	2,110,000	85E
Medellín, Colombia (2,095,000)	1,468,089	85C
Medina, see Al Madīnah		
Meknès, Morocco (375,000)	319,783	82C
Melbourne, Australia (3,039,100)	55,300	89E
Memphis, Tn., U.S. (981,747)	610,337	90C
Mendoza, Argentina (650,000)	119,088	80C
Mexicali, Mexico (365,000)	341,559	80C
Mexico City, see Ciudad de México		
Miami, Fl., U.S. (3,192,582)	358,548	90C
Middlesbrough (Teesside), Eng., U.K. (580,000)	158,516	81C
Milano (Milan), Italy (3,750,000)	1,495,260	87E
Milwaukee, Wi., U.S. (1,607,183)	628,088	90C
Minneapolis, Mn., U.S. (2,464,124)	368,383	90C
Minsk, Byelorussia (1,650,000)	1,589,000	89C
Mobile, Al., U.S. (476,923)	196,278	90C
Mombasa, Kenya	537,000	90E
Mönchengladbach, Germany (410,000)	252,910	89E
Monrovia, Liberia	465,000	86E
Monterrey, Mexico (2,015,000)	1,090,009	80C
Montevideo, Uruguay (1,550,000)	1,251,647	85C
Montgomery, Al., U.S. (292,517)	187,106	90C
Montréal, Que., Can. (2,921,357)	1,015,420	86C
Morón, Argentina (*Buenos Aires)	598,420	80C
Moroni, Comoros	23,432	90C
Moskva (Moscow), Russia (13,100,000)	8,769,000	89C
Mudanjiang, China	650,000	88E
Multān, Pakistan (732,070)	696,316	81C
München (Munich), Germany (1,955,000)	1,211,617	89E
Münster, Germany	248,919	89E
Muqdisho (Mogadishu), Somalia	600,000	84E
Murcia, Spain (†314,124)	149,800	88E
Murmansk, Russia	468,000	89C
Mysore, India (652,246)	480,006	91C
Naberežnyje Čelny (Brežnev), Russia	501,000	89C
Nagasaki, Japan	444,616	90C
Nagoya, Japan (4,800,000)	2,154,664	90C
Nāgpur, India (1,661,409)	1,622,225	91C
Nairobi, Kenya	1,505,000	90E
Nanchang, China (†1,260,000)	1,090,000	88E
Nancy, France (306,982)	96,317	82C
Nanjing (Nanking), China	2,390,000	88E
Nanning, China (†1,000,000)	720,000	88E
Nantes, France (464,857)	240,539	82C
Napoli (Naples), Italy (2,875,000)	1,204,211	87E
Nashville, Tn., U.S. (985,026)	487,969	90C
Nassau, Bahamas	135,000	82E
Natal, Brazil	510,106	85E
N'Djamena, Chad	500,000	88E
Netzahualcóyotl, Mexico (*Ciudad de México)	1,341,230	80C
Newark, N.J., U.S. (*New York)	275,221	91C
Newcastle, Australia (425,610)	130,940	89E
Newcastle upon Tyne, Eng., U.K. (1,300,000)	199,064	81C
New Delhi, India (*Delhi)	294,149	91C
New Kowloon, Hong Kong (*Victoria)	1,526,910	88C
New Orleans, La., U.S. (1,238,816)	496,938	90C
Newport, Wales, U.K. (310,000)	115,896	81C
New York, N.Y., U.S. (18,087,251)	7,322,564	90C
Niamey, Niger	398,265	88C
Nice, France (449,496)	337,085	82C
Nicosia, Cyprus (185,000)	48,221	82E
Nikolajev, Ukraine	503,000	89C
Ningbo, China (†1,050,000)	570,000	88E
Niterói, Brazil (*Rio de Janeiro)	441,684	85E
Nižnij Novgorod, Russia (2,025,000)	1,438,000	89C
Norfolk, Va., U.S. (1,396,107)	261,229	90C
North York, Ont., Can. (*Toronto)	556,297	86C
Nottingham, Eng., U.K. (655,000)	273,300	81C
Nouakchott, Mauritania	285,000	87E
Nouméa, New Caledonia (88,000)	65,110	89C
Nova Iguaçu, Brazil (*Rio de Janeiro)	592,800	85E
Novokuzneck, Russia	600,000	89C
Novosibirsk, Russia (1,600,000)	1,436,000	89C
Nuku'alofa, Tonga	21,265	86C
Nürnberg, Germany (1,030,000)	480,078	89E
Odessa, Ukraine (1,185,000)	1,115,000	89C
Ogbomosho, Nigeria	582,900	87E
Okayama, Japan	593,742	90C
Oklahoma City, Ok., U.S. (958,839)	444,719	90C
Omaha, Nb., U.S. (618,262)	335,796	90C
Omdurman, see Umm Durmān		
Omsk, Russia (1,175,000)	1,148,000	89C
Oran, Algeria	628,558	87C
Orenburg, Russia	547,000	89C
Orlando, Fl., U.S. (1,072,748)	164,693	91C
Orūmīyeh, Iran	300,746	86C
Ōsaka, Japan (16,450,000)	2,623,831	90C
Osasco, Brazil (*São Paulo)	591,568	85E
Oshogbo, Nigeria	380,800	87E
Oslo, Norway (720,000)	452,415	87E
Ostrava, Czechoslovakia (760,000)	331,557	90E
Ottawa, Ont., Can. (819,263)	300,763	86C
Ouagadougou, Burkina Faso	441,514	85C
Palembang, Indonesia	874,000	83E
Palermo, Italy	723,732	87E
Palma, Spain (†314,608)	249,000	88E
Panamá, Panama (770,000)	411,549	90C
Papeete, French Polynesia (80,000)	23,555	88C
Paramaribo, Suriname (296,000)	241,000	88E
Paris, France (9,775,000)	2,078,900	87E
Patna, India (1,098,572)	916,980	91C
Peking, see Beijing		
Penza, Russia	543,000	89C
Perm, Russia (1,160,000)	1,091,000	89C
Perth, Australia (1,158,387)	82,413	89E
Peshāwar, Pakistan (566,248)	506,896	81C
Philadelphia, Pa., U.S. (5,899,345)	1,585,577	90C
Phnum Pénh, Cambodia	700,000	86E
Phoenix, Az., U.S. (2,122,101)	900,013	90C
Pingxiang, China (†1,286,700)	368,700	86E
Pittsburgh, Pa., U.S. (2,242,798)	369,879	90C
Ploiești, Romania (310,000)	234,886	86E
Plovdiv, Bulgaria	364,162	89E
Pointe-à-Pitre, Guadeloupe (83,000)	25,310	82C
Port-au-Prince, Haiti (880,000)	797,000	87E
Port Elizabeth, South Africa (690,000)	272,844	85C
Port Harcourt, Nigeria	327,300	87E
Portland, Me., U.S. (215,281)	64,358	90C
Portland, Or., U.S. (1,477,895)	437,319	90C
Port-Louis, Mauritius (420,000)	139,730	87E
Port Moresby, Papua New Guinea	152,100	87E
Porto (Oporto), Portugal (1,225,000)	327,368	81C
Porto Alegre, Brazil (2,600,000)	1,272,121	85E
Port of Spain, Trinidad and Tobago (370,000)	50,878	90C
Porto-Novo, Benin	164,000	84E
Port Said, see Būr Sa'īd		
Portsmouth, Eng., U.K. (485,000)	174,218	81C
Port-Vila, Vanuatu (23,000)	18,905	89C
Poznań, Poland (672,000)	586,500	89E
Praha (Prague), Czech Republic (1,325,000)	1,215,656	90E
Praia, Cape Verde	61,797	90C
Pretoria, South Africa (960,000)	443,059	85C
Providence, R.I., U.S. (1,141,510)	160,728	90C
Puebla [de Zaragoza], Mexico (1,055,000)	835,759	90C
Pune, India (2,485,014)	1,559,558	91C
Pusan, S. Korea (3,800,000)	3,773,000	89E
P'yŏngyang, N. Korea (1,600,000)	1,283,000	80E
Qingdao, China	1,300,000	88E
Qiqihar, China (†1,330,000)	1,180,000	88E
Qom, Iran	543,139	86C
Québec, Que., Can. (603,267)	164,580	86C
Quetta, Pakistan (285,719)	244,842	81C
Quezon City, Philippines (*Manila)	1,632,000	90C
Quilmes, Argentina (*Buenos Aires)	446,587	80C
Quito, Ecuador (1,300,000)	1,137,705	87C
Rabat, Morocco (980,000)	518,616	82C
Rājkot, India (651,007)	556,137	91C
Raleigh, N.C., U.S. (735,480)	207,951	90C
Rānchī, India (614,454)	598,498	91C
Rangoon, see Yangon		
Rāwalpindi, Pakistan (1,040,000)	457,091	81C
Recife, Brazil (2,625,000)	1,287,623	85E
Reno, Nv., U.S. (254,667)	133,850	90C
Reykjavík, Iceland (137,941)	93,425	87E
Ribeirão Prêto, Brazil	383,125	85E
Richmond, Va., U.S. (865,640)	203,056	90C
Rio de Janeiro, Brazil (10,150,000)	5,603,388	85E
Riverside, Ca., U.S. (*Los Angeles)	226,505	90C
Riyadh, see Ar Riyāḍ		
Rjazan, Russia	515,000	89C
Rochester, N.Y., U.S. (1,002,410)	231,636	90C
Roma (Rome), Italy (3,175,000)	2,815,457	87E
Rosario, Argentina (1,045,000)	938,120	80C
Rostov-na-Donu, Russia (1,165,000)	1,020,000	89C
Rotterdam, Netherlands (1,110,000)	576,300	89E
Rouen, France (379,879)	101,945	82C
Rouseau, Dominica	9,348	84E

City and Country	Population	Date
Sacramento, Ca., U.S. (1,481,102)	369,365	90C
Safāqis, Tunisia (310,000)	231,911	84C
Saigon, see Ho Chi Minh		
St. Catharines, Ont., Can. (343,258)	123,455	86C
St.-Étienne, France (317,228)	204,955	82C
St. George's, Grenada (25,000)	4,788	81C
St. John's, Antigua and Barbuda	24,359	77E
St. Louis, Mo., U.S. (2,444,099)	396,685	90C
St. Paul, Mn., U.S. (*Minneapolis)	272,235	90C
St. Petersburg, Fl., U.S. (*Tampa)	238,629	90C
Sakai, Japan (*Ōsaka)	807,859	90C
Salem, India (573,685)	363,934	91C
Salt Lake City, Ut., U.S. (1,072,227)	159,936	90C
Salvador, Brazil (2,050,000)	1,804,438	85E
Samara, Russia (1,505,000)	1,257,000	89C
Samarkand, Uzbekistan	366,000	89C
Şan'ā', Yemen	427,150	90E
San Antonio, Tx., U.S. (1,302,099)	935,933	90C
San Diego, Ca., U.S. (2,949,000)	1,110,549	90C
San Francisco, Ca., U.S. (6,253,311)	723,959	90C
San José, Costa Rica (670,000)	278,600	88C
San Jose, Ca., U.S. (*San Francisco)	782,248	90C
San Juan, Puerto Rico (1,775,260)	424,600	80C
Sankt-Peterburg, Russia (5,825,000)	4,456,000	89C
San Luis Potosí, Mexico (470,000)	362,371	80C
San Miguel de Tucumán, Argentina (525,000)	392,888	80C
San Salvador, El Salvador (920,000)	462,652	85E
San Sebastián, Spain (285,000)	177,622	88E
Santa Fe de Bogotá, Colombia (4,260,000)	3,982,941	85C
Santiago, Chile (4,100,000)	232,667	82C
Santo André, Brazil (São Paulo)	635,129	85E
Santo Domingo, Dominican Rep.	1,313,172	81C
Santos, Brazil (1,065,000)	460,100	85E
São Bernardo do Campo, Brazil (*São Paulo)	562,485	85E
São Luís, Brazil (600,000)	227,900	85E
São Paulo, Brazil (15,175,000)	10,063,110	85E
São Tomé, Sao Tome and Prin.	17,380	70C
Sapporo, Japan (1,900,000)	1,671,765	90C
Sarajevo, Bosnia and Herzegovina (†479,688)	341,200	87E
Saratov, Russia (1,155,000)	905,000	89C
Sargodha, Pakistan (291,362)	231,895	81C
Savannah, Ga., U.S. (242,622)	137,560	90C
Scarborough, Ont., Can. (*Toronto)	484,676	86C
Seattle, Wa., U.S. (2,559,164)	516,259	90C
Semarang, Indonesia	1,206,000	83E
Semipalatinsk, Kazakhstan	334,000	89C
Sendai, Japan (1,175,000)	918,378	90C
Seoul, see Sŏul		
Sevilla (Seville), Spain (945,000)	663,132	88E
's-Gravenhage (The Hague), Netherlands (770,000)	443,900	89E
Shanghai, China (9,300,000)	7,220,000	88E
Shantou, China (†790,000)	560,000	88E
Sheffield, Eng., U.K. (710,000)	470,685	81C
Shenyang (Mukden), China (†4,370,000)	3,910,000	88E
Shīrāz, Iran	848,289	86C
Shizuoka, Japan (975,000)	472,199	90C
Shubrā al Khaymah, Egypt (*Al Qāhirah)	710,794	86C
Sialkot, Pakistan (302,009)	258,147	81C
Singapore, Singapore (3,025,000)	2,685,400	89E
Sioux Falls, S.D., U.S. (123,809)	100,814	90C
Sofija (Sofia), Bulgaria (1,205,000)	1,136,875	89E
Solāpur, India (620,499)	603,870	91C
Sŏul (Seoul), S. Korea (15,850,000)	10,522,000	89E
Southampton, Eng., U.K. (415,000)	211,321	81C
Soweto, South Africa (*Johannesburg)	521,948	85C
Springfield, Il., U.S. (189,550)	105,227	90C
Springfield, Ma., U.S. (529,519)	156,983	90C
Srīnagar, India (606,002)	594,775	81C
Stalingrad, see Volgograd		
Stockholm, Sweden (1,449,972)	672,187	90E
Stoke-on-Trent, Eng., U.K. (440,000)	272,446	81C
Strasbourg, France (400,000)	248,712	82C
Stuttgart, Germany (1,925,000)	562,658	89E
Suez, see As Suways		
Suichang, China (†2,216,500)	363,500	86E
Suixian, China (†1,281,600)	187,700	86E
Surabaya, Indonesia	2,345,000	85E
Surakarta, Indonesia (575,000)	491,000	83E
Surat, India (1,517,076)	149,643	91C
Suva, Fiji (141,273)	69,665	86C
Suzhou, China	740,000	88E
Swansea, Wales, U.K. (275,000)	172,433	81C
Sydney, Australia (3,623,550)	9,800	89E
Syracuse, N.Y., U.S. (659,864)	163,860	90C
Szczecin, Poland (449,000)	409,500	89E
Tabrīz, Iran	971,482	86C
Tacoma, Wa., U.S. (*Seattle)	176,664	90C
Taegu, S. Korea	2,207,000	89E
Taejŏn, S. Korea	1,041,000	89E
Tai'an, China (†1,325,400)	215,900	86E
Taichung, Taiwan	715,107	85E
Tainan, Taiwan	656,927	88E
Taipei, Taiwan (6,130,000)	2,637,100	88E
Taiyuan, China (†1,980,000)	1,700,000	88E
Tallinn, Estonia	482,000	89C
Tampa, Fl., U.S. (2,067,959)	280,015	90C
Tampico, Mexico (435,000)	267,957	80C
Tanger (Tangier), Morocco (370,000)	266,346	82C
Tangshan, China (†1,440,000)	1,080,000	88E
Tanṭā, Egypt	334,505	86C
Ṭarābulus (Tripoli), Libya	591,062	88E
Taškent (Tashkent), Uzbekistan (2,325,000)	2,073,000	89C
Tbilisi, Georgia (1,460,000)	1,260,000	89C
Tegucigalpa, Honduras	551,606	88C
Tehrān, Iran (7,500,000)	6,042,584	86C
Tel Aviv-Yafo, Israel (1,735,000)	317,800	89E
Teresina, Brazil (525,000)	425,300	85E
Thanh Pho Ho Chi Minh (Saigon), Vietnam (3,300,000)	2,796,229	89C
The Hague, see s'-Gravenhage		
Thessaloníki, Greece (706,180)	406,413	81C
Thimphu, Bhutan	12,000	82E
Thunder Bay, Ont., Can. (122,217)	112,272	86C
Tianjin (Tientsin), China (†5,540,000)	4,950,000	88E
Tianshui, China (†953,200)	209,500	86E
Tijuana, Mexico (*San Diego)	429,500	80C
Tirana, Albania	238,100	89C
Tiruchchirāppalli, India (711,120)	386,628	91C
Tlalnepantla, Mexico (*Ciudad de México)	778,173	80C
Togliatti (Stavropol), Russia	630,000	89C
Tōkyō, Japan (27,700,000)	8,163,127	90C
Tomsk, Russia	502,000	89C
Torino (Turin), Italy (1,550,000)	1,035,565	87E
Toronto, Ont., Can. (3,427,168)	612,289	86C
Torreón, Mexico (575,000)	328,086	80C
Toulon, France (410,393)	179,423	82C
Toulouse, France (541,271)	347,995	82C
Tours, France (262,786)	132,209	82C
Tripoli, see Ṭarābulus		
Trivandrum, India (825,682)	523,733	91C
Trujillo, Peru (354,301)	202,469	81C
Tsun Wan, Hong Kong (*Victoria)	514,241	88C
Tucson, Az., U.S. (666,880)	405,390	90C
Tula, Russia (640,000)	540,000	89C
Tulsa, Ok., U.S. (708,954)	367,302	90C
Tūnis, Tunisia (1,225,000)	596,654	84C
Tver', Russia	451,000	89C
Ufa, Russia (1,100,000)	1,083,000	89C
Ujung Pandang (Makasar), Indonesia	841,000	83E
Ulan-Bator, Mongolia	548,400	89E
Ulsan, S. Korea	551,014	85C
Umm Durmān (Omdurman), Sudan (*Khartoum)	526,287	83C
Utrecht, Netherlands (518,779)	230,700	89E
Vadodara (Baroda), India (1,115,390)	1,021,084	91C
Vaduz, Liechtenstein	4,874	90E
Valencia, Spain (1,270,000)	743,933	88E
Valletta, Malta (215,000)	9,210	89E
Valparaíso, Chile (675,000)	265,355	82C
Vancouver, B.C., Can. (1,380,729)	431,147	86C
Vārānasi (Benares), India (1,026,467)	925,962	91C
Venezia (Venice), Italy (420,000)	88,700	87E
Veracruz [Llave], Mexico (385,000)	284,822	80C
Vereeniging, South Africa (525,000)	60,584	85C
Verona, Italy	259,151	87E
Viangchan (Vientiane), Laos	377,409	85C
Victoria, B.C., Can. (255,547)	66,303	86C
Victoria, Hong Kong (4,770,000)	1,175,860	88C
Victoria, Seychelles	23,000	84E
Vienna, see Wien		
Vientiane, see Viangchan		
Vilnius, Lithuania	582,000	89C
Vishākhapatnam, India (1,051,918)	750,024	91C
Vitória, Brazil (735,000)	201,500	85E
Vladivostok, Russia	648,000	89C
Volgograd (Stalingrad), Russia (1,360,000)	999,000	89C
Volta Redonda, Brazil (375,000)	219,267	85E
Voronež, Russia	887,000	89C
Vorošilovgrad, Ukraine	497,000	89C
Warszawa (Warsaw), Poland (2,323,000)	1,651,200	89E
Washington, D.C., U.S. (3,923,574)	606,900	90C
Weifang, China (†1,042,200)	312,500	86E
Wellington, New Zealand (350,000)	137,495	86C
Wichita, Ks., U.S. (485,270)	304,011	90C
Wien (Vienna), Austria (1,875,000)	1,482,800	88E
Wiesbaden, Germany (795,000)	254,209	89E
Willemstad, Netherlands Antilles (130,000)	31,883	81C
Wilmington, De., U.S. (*Philadelphia)	71,529	90C
Windhoek, Namibia	114,500	88E
Windsor, Ont., Can. (253,988)	193,111	86C
Winnipeg, Man., Can. (625,304)	594,551	86C
Wrocław, Poland	637,400	89E
Wuhan, China	3,570,000	88E
Wuppertal, Germany (830,000)	371,283	89E
Wuxi, China	880,000	88E
Wuxing (Huzhou), China (†964,400)	208,500	86E
Xiamen, China (†546,400)	343,700	86E
Xi'an, China (†2,580,000)	2,210,000	88E
Xiaogan, China (†1,204,400)	125,500	86E
Xining, China	620,000	88E
Xuzhou, China	860,000	88E
Yancheng, China (†1,251,400)	258,400	86E
Yangon, Burma (2,800,000)	2,705,039	83C
Yaoundé, Cameroon	653,670	86C
Yerushalayim (Jerusalem), Israel (530,000)	493,500	87E
Yichun, China	840,000	88E
Yokohama, Japan (*Tōkyō)	3,220,350	90C
Yulin, China (†1,228,800)	115,600	86E
Zagreb, Croatia	697,925	87E
Zanzibar, Tanzania	133,000	84E
Zaozhuang, China (†1,592,000)	292,200	86E
Zaporožje, Ukraine	884,000	89C
Zaragoza (Saragossa), Spain	582,239	88E
Zhangjiakou, China (†640,000)	500,000	88E
Zhengzhou, China (†1,580,000)	1,150,000	88E
Zhongshan, China (†1,059,700)	238,700	86E
Zibo, China (†2,370,000)	840,000	88E
Zurich, Switzerland (870,000)	342,861	90E

Metropolitan area populations are shown in parentheses.
* City is located within the metropolitan area of another city; for example, Kyōto, Japan is located in the Ōsaka metropolitan area.
† Population of entire municipality or district, including rural area.

C Census
E Official estimate

A • 15

Transliteration Systems

Toponymy: Criteria Used for the Writing of Names on the Maps

The language of geography is a language which defines geographic features in universally recognized terms. In creating this language, toponymy experts and cartographers have confronted complex problems in finding terms which are universally acceptable. So that the reader can fully understand the maps in this atlas, here is a brief explanation of how the toponyms (place-names for geographic features) have been written, particularly those relating to regions or countries where the Roman alphabet is not used. Among these are the Slavic-speaking nations such as Russia, Yugoslavia and Bulgaria; and China and Japan, which use ideographic characters. Of the European countries, Greece has its own alphabet, which is totally different from the Roman alphabet. Many of the Islamic countries use Arabic, with variations derived from local dialects.

There are two basic systems for Romanizing writing. The first is by phonetic transcription, using combinations of different alphabetical signs for each language when the phonetic sound in other languages should be maintained. For example, the Italian sound "sc" (which must be followed by an "e" or "i" to remain soft) in French is "ch," in English is "sh," and in German is "sch."

The second system is transliteration, in which the words, letters or characters of one language are represented or spelled in the letters or characters of another language.

Chinese, Japanese and Arabic Languages

Various Asian and African countries use non-Roman forms in their writing. For example, the Chinese and Japanese languages use ideographic characters instead of an alphabet, and these ideographic characters are transformed into the Roman alphabet through phonetic transcription. Until recently, one of the methods used for transforming Chinese was the Wade-Giles system, named for its English authors. Used in this atlas is the Pinyin system, which was approved by the Chinese government in 1958 and has been incorporated into the official maps of the People's Republic of China. The Pinyin system also has been adopted by the United States Board on Geographic Names and is used in official United Nations documents. The Pinyin names, however, often are accompanied by the Wade-Giles form, as the latter was widely known.

In Japan, ideographic characters are used, although the Roman alphabet is used in many Japanese scientific works. Japan uses two principal systems for standardizing names. They are the Kunreisiki, used by the government in official publications, and the Hepburn method. Adopted for this atlas is the Hepburn method, the system used in international English-language publications and by the United States Board on Geographic Names.

Romanization of the Arabic alphabet, which is used in many Islamic countries, is by transliteration. Since English and French are still used as international languages in many Arab countries, the name forms proposed by the major English and French sources have been taken into consideration. Generally, the systems proposed by the United States Board on Geographic Names and the Permanent Committee on Geographical Names have been used for most Asian countries and Arab-speaking countries.

Greek, Russian and Other Slavic Languages

Practically all written languages in Europe use the Roman alphabet. The differences in phonetics and grammar are shown by the use of diacritical marks and by groupings of consonants, vocals and syllables which give meaning to the various tones in the language. According to a centuries-old tradition, each written language maintains its formal characters, using the translated form rather than the phonetic transcription when a geographical term must be given in another language. This system, therefore, makes it more a translation than a transliteration.

In the Aegean area, Greek and the Greek alphabet are particularly significant because of historical links to the beginning of European civilization. The 1962 United States Board on Geographic Names and the Permanent Committee on Geographical Names systems, based on modern Greek pronunciation, have been used in transcribing toponyms from official sources for these maps. (The table that follows has an example indicating essential norms for Romanizing the modern Greek alphabet.)

A different situation arises in countries using the Cyrillic alphabet. Six principal Slavic languages using this alphabet are Russian, Byelorussian, Ukrainian, Bulgarian, Serbian, and Macedonian. The Cyrillic alphabet also is used by some non-Slavic people of the former Soviet Union. The nomenclature of these regions has been transliterated in accordance with the system proposed by the International Organization for Standardization, taking into consideration sounds and letters and uses of the diacritical marks normal in Slavic languages. The International Organization for Standardization method is accepted and used in bibliographical works and international documents. (The table which follows gives the relationship between the letters of the Cyrillic and Roman alphabets for the above six languages.)

Special Cases: Conventional Forms and Multilinguals

Cartographic nomenclature generally derives from the official nomenclature of the sovereign and nonsovereign countries, although a number of cases need explanation.

In numerous situations, English conventional forms are used along with the local or conventional name in referring to a geographical entity used outside the official English language area. For example, Vienna, Prague, Copenhagen and Moscow are English forms for Wien, Praha, København and Moskva, respectively. There are cases, however, where the conventional or historical form commonly used in English cartography has been applied with the same meaning. Thus, Peking and Nanking are the English conventional forms for Beijing and Nanjing, while Tsinan, Tientsin and Mukden are the former conventional spellings or names for Jinan, Tianjin and Shenyang, respectively. Other examples are Saigon, the former name for Ho Chi Minh, Vietnam; and Bangkok, the name for Krung Thep, which is used in Thailand.

The lack of reliable data for countries, especially ex-colonies without a firm national cartographic tradition, has made it necessary to utilize mapping skills of former colonial nations such as France, the United Kingdom and Belgium. A lack of data has led to the adoption of French and British forms in many areas, as these two languages are widely used for official purposes.

Another special case is that of the multilingual areas. Many countries and areas officially recognize two or more written and spoken languages; therefore, all of the principal written forms appear on the maps. This is true, for example, of Belgium where the official languages are French and Dutch (e.g. Bruxelles/Brussel) and of Italian regions such as Valle d'Aosta and Alto Adige, where French, German and Italian are used (e.g. Aosta/Aoste) (Bolzano/Bozen).

In preparing this atlas, each of these special cases has been taken into full consideration within the limits of the scale, space and readability of the maps.

Transliteration of the Cyrillic Alphabet
(International System—ISO)

Cyrillic Letter		Roman Letter		Cyrillic Letter		Roman Letter	
А	а	a		О	о	o	
Б	б	b		П	п	p	
В	в	v		Р	р	r	
Г	г	g		С	с	s	
Д	д	d		Т	т	t	
Е	е	e	initially, after a vowel or after the mute sign "Ъ", becomes "je"	У	у	u	
				Ф	ф	f	
				Х	х	h	
Ё	ё	ë		Ц	ц	c	
Ж	ж	ž		Ч	ч	č	
З	з	z		Ш	ш	š	
И	и	i		Щ	щ	šč	
Й	й	j	not written if preceded by "И" or "Ы"	Ъ	ъ	—	not written
				Ы	ы	y	
К	к	k		Ь	ь	—	not written
Л	л	l		Э	э	e	
М	м	m		Ю	ю	ju	
Н	н	n		Я	я	ja	

Transcription of Modern Greek
(U.S. B. G. N./P.C.G.N.)

Greek Letter (or combination)		Roman Letter (or combination)		Greek Letter (or combination)		Roman Letter (or combination)	
Α	α	a			μπ	b	beginning a word
	αι	ai				mb	within a word
	αυ	av		Ν	ν	n	
Β	β	v			ντ	d	beginning a word
Γ	γ	g				nd	within a word
	γγ	ng		Ξ	ξ	x	
	γκ	g	beginning a word	Ο	ο	o	
					οι	oi	
		ng	within a word		ου	ou	
Δ	δ	d		Π	π	p	
Ε	ε	e		Ρ	ρ	r	
	ει	i		Σ	σ	s	
	ευ	ev			ς	s	ending a word
Ζ	ζ	z		Τ	τ	t	
Η	η	i			τζ	tz	
	ηυ	iv		Υ	υ	i	
Θ	θ	th			υι	i	
Ι	ι	i		Φ	φ	f	
Κ	κ	k		Χ	χ	kh	
Λ	λ	l		Ψ	ψ	ps	
Μ	μ	m		Ω	ω	o	

The "Geographical Glossary" lists the principal geographical terms used on the maps. All of these terms, including abbreviations, prefixes and suffixes, appear in the cartographic table as they appear on the maps. Terms are listed in accordance with the English alphabet, without consideration of diacritical marks on letters or of particular groups of letters.

Prefixes and suffixes relating to principal names or forming part of geographical toponyms are followed or preceded by a dash and the language to which they refer: e.g. Chi-/Dan. (Chi, a Danish prefix, means large); -bor/Slvn. (-bor, a Slovakian suffix, means city). Suffixes can also appear as words in themselves. In this case, the suffix and primary word are coupled together: e.g. Berg, -berg (Berg, which means mountain, can be used alone or as part of another word, such as Hapsberg).

Certain terms are followed or preceded by their abbreviation used on the maps. Both instances are listed: e.g. Fjord, Fj. and Fj., Fjord.

All geographical terms are identified by the language or languages to which each belongs. The language or languages in italics follows the term: e.g. Abbey/Eng.; -bad/Nor., Dut., Swed., Germ. Each term is translated into a corresponding English term or terms.

Below is a table identifying the abbreviations of various language names used on the maps. Note that certain abbreviations represent a group of languages, instead of one language: e.g. Ural. is the abbreviation for Uralic, a group word for Udmurt, Komi, and Nenets.

Alt. = Altaic (Turkmen, Tatar, Bashkir, Kazakh, Karalpak, Nogai, Kirghiz, Uzbek, Uigur, Altaic, Yakut, Khakass)
Ban. = Bantu (KiSwahili, ChiLuba, Lingala, KiKongo)
Cauc. = Caucasian (Chechen, Ingush, Kalmuck, Georgian)
Iran. = Iranian (Baluchi, Tagus)
Mel. = Melanesian (Fijian, New Caledonian, Micronesian, Nauruan)
Mong. = Mongolian (Buryat, Khalka Mongol)
Poly. = Polynesian (Maori, Samoan, Tongan, Tahitian, Hawaiian)
Sah. = Saharan (Kanuri, Tubu)
Som. = Somalian (Somali, Galla)
Sud. = Sudanese (Peul, Ehoué, Mossi, Yoruba, Ibo)
Ural. = Uralic (Udmurt, Komi, Nenets).

Because of their technical application to geography, some geographical terms may not fully correspond with the meaning given for them in some dictionaries.

Abbreviations of Language Names

Abbreviations in English	English	Abbreviations in English	English	Abbreviations in English	English	Abbreviations in English	English	Abbreviations in English	English	Abbreviations in English	English
Afr.	Afrikaans	Bulg.	Bulgarian	Fr.	French	Khm.	Khmer	Pers.	Persian	Som.	Somalian
A.I.	American Indian	Burm.	Burmese	Gae.	Gaelic	Kor.	Korean	Pol.	Polish	Sp.	Spanish
Alb.	Albanian	Cat.	Catalan	Georg.	Georgian	K.S.	Khoi-San	Poly.	Polynesian	Sud.	Sudanese
Alt.	Altaic	Cauc.	Caucasian	Germ.	German	Laot.	Laotian	Port.	Portuguese	Swa.	Swahili
Amh.	Amharic	Chin.	Chinese	Gr.	Greek	Lapp.	Lappish	Prov.	Provençal	Swed.	Swedish
Ar.	Arabic	Cz.	Czech	Hebr.	Hebrew	Latv.	Latvian	Rmsh.	Romansh	Tam.	Tamil
Arm.	Armenian	Dan.	Danish	Hin.	Hindi	Lith.	Lithuanian	Rom.	Romanian	Thai	Thai
Az.	Azerbaidzhani	Dut.	Dutch	Hung.	Hungarian	Mal.	Malay	Rus.	Russian	Tib.	Tibetan
Ban.	Bantu	Eng.	English	Icel.	Icelandic	Malag.	Malagasy	Sah.	Saharan	Tur.	Turkish
Bas.	Basque	Esk.	Eskimo	Indon.	Indonesian	Mel.	Melanesian	S.C.	Serbo-Croatian	Ural.	Uralic
Beng.	Bengali	Est.	Estonian	Ir.	Irish	Mong.	Mongolian	Sin.	Sinhalese	Urdu	Urdu
Ber.	Berber	Far.	Faroese	Iran.	Iranian	Nep.	Nepalese	Slvk.	Slovak	Viet.	Vietnamese
Br.	Breton	Finn.	Finnish	It.	Italian	Nor.	Norwegian	Slvn.	Slovene	Wall.	Walloon
		Fle.	Flemish	Jap.	Japanese	Pash.	Pashto			Wel.	Welsh

Glossary of Geographical Terms

Local Form	English	Local Form	English	Local Form	English	Local Form	English
A		Ait / Ar.; Ber.	sons	Ard- / Gae.	high	Badwëynta / Som.	ocean
		Aivi, -aivi / Lapp.	mountain	Areg / Ar.	dune	Badyarada / Som.	gulf
A- / Ban.	people	Ak / Tur.	white	Areia / Port.	beach	Baeg / Kor.	white
A' / Icel.	river	'Aklé / Ar.	dunes	Arena / Sp.	beach	Bæk / Dan.	brook
Å / Dan.; Nor.; Swed.	stream	Akmeņs / Latv.	stone	Argent / Fr.	silver	Bælt / Dan.	strait
a., an / Germ.	on	Ákra / Gr.	point	Arhipelag / Rus.	archipelago	Bagni / It.	thermal springs
Aa / Germ.	stream	Akti / Gr.	coast	Arkhaios / Gr.	old, antique	Baharu / Mal.	new
Aache / Germ.	stream	Ala / Malag.	forest	Arm / Eng.; Germ.	branch	Bahia / Port.	bay
Aaiún / Ar.	springs	Ala / Finn.	low, lower	Arquipélago / Port.	archipelago	Bahia / Sp.	bay
Aan / Dut.; Fle.	on	Alan / Tur.	field	Arr., Arroyo / Sp.	stream	Bahir / Ar.	river, lake, sea
Āb / Pers.	stream	Alb / Rom.	white	Arrecife / Sp.	reef	Bahr / Ar.	river, lake, sea
Ābād / Pers.	city, town	Albo / Sp.	white	Arroio / Port.	stream	Bahr / Ar.	wadi
Abad, -abad / Pers.	city, town	Albufera / Sp.	lagoon	Art / Tur.	pass, watershed	Bahrat / Ar.	lake
Ābār / Ar.	spring	Alcalá / Sp.	castle	Aru / Sin.; Tam.	river	Bahri / Ar.	north, northern
Abbadia / It.	abbey	Alcázar / Sp.	castle	Ås / Dan.; Nor.; Swed.	hills	Bahrī / Ar.	north
Abbaye / Fr.	abbey	Aldea / Sp.	village	Asfar / Ar.	yellow	Bahrīyah / Ar.	northern
Abbazia / It.	abbey	Alföld / Hung.	lowland	Asif / Ber.	river	Bai / Chin.	white
Abbi / Amh.	great	Ali / Amh.	mountain	Asky / Alt.	lower	Bǎi / Rom.	thermal springs
Abd / Ar.	servant	Alia / Poly.	stream	Áspros / Gr.	white	Baia / Port.	bay
Abeba / Amh.	flower	Alin / Mong.	range	Assa / Ber.	wadi	Baie / Fr.	bay
Aber / Br.; Wel.	estuary	Alm / Germ.	mountain	Atalaya / Sp.	frontier	Baigne / Fr.	seaside resort
Abhang / Germ.	slope		pasture	Áth / Gae.	ford	Baile / Gae.	city, town
Abū / Ar.	father, master	Alor / Mal.	river	Átha / Gae.	ford	Bain / Fr.	thermal springs
Abyad / Ar.	white	Alp / Germ.	mountain	Atol / Port.	atoll	Bains / Fr.	thermal springs
Abyaḍ / Ar.	white		pasture	Au / Germ.	meadow	Baixo / Port.	low, lower
Abyār / Ar.	well	Alpe / Germ.; Fr.; It.	mountain	Aue / Germ.	irrigated field	Bajan / Mong.	rich
Abyss / Eng.	ocean depth, deep		pasture	Aust / Nor.	east	Bajo / Sp.	low
Ach / Germ.	stream	Alps / Eng.	mountains	Austur / Icel.	east	Bajrak / Alb.	tribe
Achaïf / Ar.	dunes	Alsó / Hung.	low, lower	Ava / Poly.	canal	Bakhtīyārī / Pers.	western
Ache / Germ.	stream	Alt / Germ.	old	Aven / Fr.	doline, sink	Bakki / Icel.	hill
Achter / Afr.; Dut.; Fle.	back	Altin / Tur.	lower	Awa / Poly.	bay	Bālā / Pers.	high
Acqua / It.	water	Altiplano / Sp.	plateau	Àyios / Gr.	saint	Bald / Eng.	peak
Açu / A.I.	great	Alto / Sp.; It.; Port.	high	'Ayn / Ar.	spring, well	Balka / Rus.	gorge
Açude / Port.	reservoir, dam	Altopiano / It.	plateau	'Ayoún / Ar.	springs, wells	Balkan / Bulg.; Tur.	mountain range
Ada / Tur.	island	Älv / Swed.	river	'Ayoûn / Ar.	spring	Ballin / Gae.	mouth
Adalar / Tur.	archipelago	Am / Kor.	mountain, peak	Aza / Ber.	wadi	Ballon / Fr.	dome
Adasr / Tur.	island	Amane / Ber.	water	Azraq / Ar.	light blue	Bally / Gae.	city, town
Addis / Amh.	new	Amba / Amh.	mountain	Azul / Port.; Sp.	light blue	Balta / Rom.	marsh
Adi / Amh.	village	Ambato / Malag.	rock	Azur / Fr.	light blue	Báltos / Gr.	marsh
Adrar / Ber.	mount, mountains	An / Gae.	of			Ban / Laot.	village
		An, a. / Germ.	on			Bana / Jap.	promontory
Aéroport / Fr.	airport	Ana / Poly.	grotto	**B**		Baña / Slvk.	mine
Aeroporto / It.; Port.	airport	Anatolikós / Gr.	eastern			Bañados / Sp.	marsh
Aeropuerto / Sp.	airport	Äng / Swed.	meadow	B., Bay / Eng.	bay	Banc / Fr.	bank
Af / Som.	mouth, gorge	Angra / Port.	bay, anchorage	b., bei / Germ.	by	Banco / It.; Sp.	bank
Afsluitdijk / Dut.	dam	Ani- / Malag.	center	B., Bucht / Germ.	bay	Band / Pers.	dam, mountain range
Agadir / Ber.	castle	Áno / Gr.	upper	Ba / Sud.	river	Bandao / Chin.	peninsula
Aǧiz / Tur.	mouth	Ānou / Ber.	well	Ba- / Ban.	people	Bandar / Ar.; Mal.; Pers.	port, market
Agro / Sp.; It.	plain	Anse / Fr.	inlet	Ba / Mel.	hill, mountain	Bang / Indon.; Mal.	stream
Agua / Sp.	water	Ant- / Malag.	center	Baai / Afr.	bay	Bangou / Sah.	well
Aguja / Sp.	needle	Ao / Chin.; Khm.; Thai	gulf	Bab / Ar.	gate	Banhado / Port.	marsh
Agulha / Port.	needle, promontory	'Âouâna / Ar.	well	Bac / Viet.	north	Bani / Ar.	sons
Ahal / Georg.	new	Apǎ / Rom.	water	Bach / Germ.	brook, torrent	Banja / Bulg.; S.C.; Slvn.	thermal springs
Aḥmar / Ar.	red	'Aqabat / Ar.	pass	Bacino / It.	reservoir	Banjaran / Mal.	mountain range
Ahrāmāt / Ar.	pyramids	Aqueduc / Fr.	aqueduct	Back / Eng.	ridge	Banka / Rus.	sandbank
Ahzar / Ber.	wadi	Ar / Mong.	north	Back / Swed.	brook	Banke / Dan.	bank
Aigialós / Gr.	coast	Ar / Sin.; Tam.	river	Bäck / Swed.	brook	Baño / Sp.	thermal springs
Aigue / Prov.	water	'Arâguïb / Ar.	hills	Backe / Swed.	brook	Banský / Cz.	upper
Aiguille / Fr.	needle	Arba / Amh.	mount	Bad, -bad / Dan.; Germ.; Nor.; Swed.	thermal springs	Bánya / Hung.	mine
Ain / Ar.	spring	Arbore / Rom.	tree			Bar / Gae.	peak
		Archipiélago / Sp.	archipelago	Baden, -baden / Germ.	thermal springs	Bar / Eng.	sandbar
		Arcipelago / It.	archipelago	Bādiyat / Ar.	desert		
		Ard / Ar.	region				

Geographical Glossary

Local Form	English
Bar / Hin.	great
Bāra / Hin.	great
Bara / S.C.	pond
Barā / Urdu	great
Baraji / Tur.	dam
Barat / Indon.; Mal.	west, western
Barkas / Lith.	castle, city, town
Barlovento / Sp.	windward
Barq / Ar.	hill
Barra / Port.; Sp.	bar, bank
Barrage / Fr.	dam
Barragem / Port.	reservoir
Barranca / Sp.	gorge
Barranco / Port.; Sp.	gorge
Barre / Fr.	bar
Barun / Mong.	western
Bas / Fr.	low
-bas / Rus.	reservoir
Bassa / Port.	flat
Bassejn / Rus.	reservoir
Bassin / Fr.	basin
Bassure / Fr.	flat
Bassurelle / Fr.	flat
Bašta / S.C.	garden
Bataille / Fr.	battle
Batalha / Port.	battle
Batang / Indon.; Mal.	river
Batha / Sah.	stream
Baţīn / Ar.	depression
Bāţlāq / Pers.	marsh
Batu / Mal.	rock
Bayan / Mong.	rich
Bayır / Tur.	mountain, slope
Bayou / Fr.	branch, stream
Bayt / Ar.	house
Bazar / Pers.	market
Be / Malag.	great
Beau / Fr.	beautiful
Becken / Germ.	basin
Bed / Eng.	river bed
Beek / Dut.	creek
Be'er / Hebr.	spring
Bei / Chin.	north
Bei, b. / Germ.	by
Beida / Ar.	white
Beinn / Gae.	mount
Bel / Ar.	son
Bel / Bulg.	white
Bel / Tur.	pass
Beled / Ar.	village
Belen / Tur.	mount
Belet / Ar.	village
Beli / S.C.; Slvn.	white
Beli / Tur.	pass
Bellah / Sah.	well
Belogorje / Rus.	mountains
Belt / Dan.; Germ.	strait
Bely /.Rus.	white
Bély / Cz.	white
Ben / Ar.	son
Ben / Gae.	mount
Bender / Pers.	port, market
Bendi / Tur.	dam
Beni / Ar.	son
Beo / S.C.	white
Bereg / Rus.	bank
Berg, -berg / Afr.; Dut.; Fle.; Germ.; Nor.; Swed.	mount
Berge / Afr.	mountain
Bergen / Dut.; Fle.	dunes
Bergland / Germ.	upland
Bermejo / Sp.	red
Besar / Mal.	great
Betsu / Jap.	river
Betta / Tam.	mountain
Bhani / Hin.	community
Bharu / Mal.	new
Bheag / Gae.	little
Bīābān / Pers.	desert
Biały / Pol.	white
Bianco / It.	white
Bien / Viet.	lake
Bight / Eng.	bay
Bijeli / S.C.	white
Bill / Eng.	promontory
Bilo / S.C.	range
Bilý / Cz.	white
Binnen / Dut.; Fle.; Germ.	inner
Biqā' / Ar.	valley
Bir / Ar.	well
Bi'r / Ar.	well
Birkat / Ar.	pond
Bistrica / Bulg.; S.C.; Slvn.	stream
Bjarg / Icel.	rock
Bjerg / Dan.	mount
Bjeshkët / Alb.	mountain pasture
Blaauw / Afr.	blue
Blanc / Fr.	white
Blanco / Sp.	white
Blau / Germ.	blue
Bleu / Fr.	blue
Bluff / Eng.	cliff
Bo- / Ban.	people
Bo / Chin.	white
Bo / Swed.	habitation
Boca / Sp.	gap, mouth
Bôca / Port.	gap, mouth
Bocage / Fr.	forest
Bocca / It.	gap, pass
Bocchetta / It.	gap, pass
Bodden / Germ.	bay, lagoon
Boden / Germ.	soil
Bœng / Khm.	lake, marsh
Bog / Eng.	marsh
Bogaz / Alt.; Az.; Tur.	strait
Bogāzi / Tur.	strait
Bogdo / Mong.	high
Bogen / Nor.	bay
Bois / Fr.	forest
Boka / S.C.	channel
Boloto / Rus.	marsh
Bolšoj / Rus.	great
Bolsón / Sp.	basin
Bom / Port.	good
Bong / Kor.	peak
Bongo / Malag.	upland
Bor / Cz.; Rus.	coniferous forest
Bór / Pol.	forest
-bor / Slvn.	city, town
Bóras / Gr.	north
Börde / Germ.	fertile plain
Bordj / Ar.	fort
Bóreios / Gr.	northern
Borg, -borg / Dan.; Nor.; Swed.	castle
Borgo / It.	village
Born / Germ.	spring
Bory / Pol.	forest
Bosch / Dut.; Fle.	forest
Bosco / It.	wood
Bosque / Sp.	forest
Bosse / Fr.	hill
Botn / Nor.	bay
Bou / Fr.	father, master
Bouche / Fr.	mouth
Boula / Sud.	well
Bourg / Fr.	city, town
Bourne, - bourne / Eng.	frontier
Boven / Afr.	upper
Boz / Tur.	grey
Bozorg / Pers.	great
Brána / Cz.	gate
Braña / Sp.	mountain pasture
Branche / Fr.	branch
Branco / Port.	white
Braţul / Rom.	branch
Bravo / Sp.	wild
Brazo / Sp.	branch
Brdo / Cz.; S.C.	hill
Bre / Nor.	glacier
Bredning / Dan.	bay
Breg / Alb.; Bulg.; S.C.	hill, coast
Brjag / Bulg.	bank
Bro / Dan.; Nor.; Swed.	bridge
Brod / Bulg.; Cz.; Rus.; S.C.; Slvk.; Slvn.	ford
Bród / Pol.	ford
Bron / Afr.	spring
Bronn / Germ.	spring
Bru / Nor.	bridge
Bruch / Germ.	peat-bog
Bruchzone / Germ.	fracture zone
Bruck, -bruck / Germ.	bridge
Brücke / Germ.	bridge
Brug / Dut.; Fle.	bridge
Brugge / Dut.; Fle.	bridge
Bruk / Nor.	factory
Brunn / Swed.	spring
-brunn / Germ.	spring
Brunnen / Germ.	spring
Brygg / Swed.	bridge
Brzeg / Pol.	coast
Bü / Ar.	father, master
Bucht, B. / Germ.	bay
Bugt / Dan.	bay
Buhayrat / Ar.	lake, lagoon
Bühel / Germ.	hill
Bühl / Germ.	hill
Buhta / Rus.	bay
Bukit / Mal.	mountain, peak
Buku / Indon.	hill, mountain
Bukt / Nor.; Swed.	bay
Bulag / Mong.; Tur.	spring
Bulak / Mong.; Tur.	spring
Būlāq / Tur.	spring
Bult / Afr.	hill
Bulu / Indon.	mountain
Bur / Som.	mount
Bür / Ar.	port
Burg, - burg / Afr.; Ar.; Dut.; Eng.; Germ.	castle
Burgh / Eng.	city, town
Burgo / Sp.	village
Burha / Hin.	old
Buri / Thai	city, town
Burj / Ar.	village
Burn / Eng.	stream
Burnu / Tur.	promontory
Burqat / Ar.	mount, marsh
Burun / Tur.	cape
Busen / Germ.	bay
Busu / Ban.	land
Būtat / Ar.	lake, pond
Butte / Eng.; Fr.	flat-topped hill
Büyük / Tur.	great
By / Eng.	near
By, -by / Dan.; Nor.; Swed.	city, town
Bystrica / Cz.; Slvk.	stream
Bystrzyca / Pol.	stream

C

Local Form	English
C., Cap / Cat.; Fr.; Rom.	cape
C., Cape / Eng.	cape
C., Colle / It.	pass
Caatinga / A.I.	forest
Cabeça / Port.	peak
Cabeço / Port.	peak
Cabeza / Sp.	peak
Cabezo / Sp.	peak, mountain
Cabo / Port.; Sp.	cape
Cachoeira / Port.	waterfall, rapids
Cachopo / Port.	reef
Cadena / Sp.	range
Caer / Wel.	castle
Cagan / Cauc.; Mong.	white
Cairn / Gae.	hill
Čáj / Az.; Tur.	river
Cajdam / Mong.	salt marsh
Caka / Chin.	lake
Cala / Sp.; It.	inlet
Calar / Sp.	plateau
Caldas / Sp.; Port.	thermal springs
Caleta / Sp.	inlet
Camp / Cat.; Fr.; Eng.	field
Campagna / It.	plain
Campagne / Fr.	plain
Campo / Sp.; It.; Port.	field
Cañada / Sp.	gorge, ravine
Canale / It.	canal, channel
Caño / Sp.	branch
Cañón / Sp.	gorge
Canyon / Eng.	gorge
Cao / Viet.	mountain
Cap, C. / Cat.; Fr.; Rom.	cape
Car / Gae.	castle
Càrn / Gae.	peak
Carrera / Sp.	road
Carrick / Gae.	rock
Casale / It.	hamlet
Cascada / Sp.	waterfall
Cascata / It.	waterfall
Castel / It.	castle
Castell / Cat.	castle
Castello / It.	castle
Castelo / Port.	castle
Castillo / Sp.	castle
Castro / Sp.; It.	village
Catarata / Sp.	cataract
Catena / It.	mountain range
Catinga / Port.	degraded forest
Cauce / Sp.	river bed
Causse / Fr.	highland
Cava / It.	stone quarry
Çay / Tur.	river
Cay / Eng.	islet, island
Caye / Fr.	island
Cayo / Sp.	islet, island
Ceann / Gae.	promontory
Centralny / Rus.	middle
Čeren / Alb.	black
Černi / Bulg.	black
Černý / Cz.	black
Čěrny / Rus.	black
Cerrillo / Sp.	hill
Cerrito / Sp.	hill
Cerro / Sp.; Port.	hill, mountain
Cêrro / Port.	hill, mountain
Červen / Bulg.	red
Červony / Rus.	red
Cetate / Rom.	city, town
Chaco / Sp.	scrubland
Chāh / Pers.	well
Chaïf / Ar.	dunes
Chaîne / Fr.	mountain range
Champ / Fr.	field
Chang / Chin.	highland
Chapada / Port.	highland
Chapadão / Port.	highland
Château / Fr.	castle
Châtel / Fr.	castle
Chāy / Tur.	river
Chedo / Kor.	archipelago
Chenal / Fr.	canal
Cheng / Chin.	city, town, wall
Cheon / Kor.	city, river
Chergui / Ar.	eastern
Cherry, -cherry / Hin.; Tam.	city, town
Chew / Amh.	salt mine, salt
Chhâk / Khm.	bay
Chhotla / Hin.	little
Chi- / Ban.	great
Chi / Chin.	marsh, lake
Chi / Kor.	lake, pond
Chi- / Swa.	land
Chiang / Thai	city, town
Chico / Sp.	little
Chine / Eng.	ridge
Ch'on / Kor.	station
Ch'ŏn / Kor.	river
Chŏsuji / Kor.	reservoir
Chott / Ar.	salt marsh
Chu / Chin.; Viet.	mountain, hill
Chuôr phnum / Khm.	mountain range
Chute / Fr.	waterfall
Chutes / Fr.	waterfalls
Cidade / Port.	city, town
Ciems / Latv.	village
Čierny / Slvk.	black
Cime / Fr.	peak
Cîmp / Rom.	field
Cimpie / Rom.	plain
Cinco / Sp.; Port.	five
Citeli / Georg.	red
Città / It.	city, town
Ciudad / Sp.	city, town
Ckali / Georg.	water
Ckaro / Georg.	spring
Co / Chin.	lake
Col / Cat.; Fr.	pass
Colina / Port.; Sp.	hill
Coll / Cat.	hill
Collado / Sp.	pass
Colle, C. / It.	pass
Collina / It.	hill
Colline / Fr.	hill
Colonia / Sp.; It.	colony
Coma / Sp.	hill country
Comb / Eng.	basin
Comba / Sp.	basin
Combe / Fr.	basin
Comté / Fr.	county, shire
Con / Viet.	island
Conca / It.	depression
Condado / Sp.	county, shire
Cone / Eng.	volcanic cone
Cône / Fr.	volcanic cone
Contraforte / Port.	front range
Cordal / Sp.	crest
Cordilheira / Port.	mountain range
Cordillera / Sp.	mountain range
Coring / Chin.	lake
Corixa / A.I.	stream
Corno / It.	peak
Cornone / It.	peak
Corrente / It.; Port.	stream
Corriente / Sp.	stream
Costa / Sp.; It.; Port.	coast
Côte / Fr.	coast
Coteau / Fr.	height, slope
Coxilha / Port.	ridge
Craig / Gae.	rock
Cratère / Fr.	crater
Cresta / Sp.; It.	crest
Crêt / Fr.	crest
Crête / Fr.	crest
Crkva / S.C.	church
Crni / S.C.; Slvn.	black
Crven / S.C.	red
Csatorna / Hung.	canal
Cuchilla / Sp.	ridge
Cuenca / Sp.	basin
Cuesta / Sp.	escarpment
Cueva / Sp.	cave
Čuka / Bulg.; S.C.	peak
Čukur / Tur.	well
Cu Lao / Viet.	island
Cumbre / Sp.	peak
Cun / Chin.	village
Cura / A.I.	stone
Curr / Alb.	rock
Cy., City / Eng.	city, town
Czarny / Pol.	black

D

Local Form	English
Da / Chin.	great
Da / Viet.	mountain, peak
Daal / Dut.; Fle.	valley
Daba / Mong.	pass
Daba / Som.	hill
Daban / Chin.; Mong.	pass
Dae / Kor.	great
Dağ / Tur.	mountain
Dağ., Daği / Tur.	mountain
Dāgh / Pers.; Tur.	mountain
Daği, Dağ. / Tur.	mountain
Dağları / Tur.	mountain range
Dahar / Ar.	hill
Dahr / Ar.	plateau, escarpment
Dai / Chin.; Jap.	great
Daiet / Ar.	marsh
Dak / Viet.	stream
Dake / Jap.	mountain
Dakhla / Ar.	depression
Dakhlet / Ar.	depression, bay
Dal, -dal / Afr.; Dan.; Dut.; Eng.; Nor.; Swed.	valley
Dala / Alt.	steppe, plain
Dalaj / Mong.	lake, sea
Dalan / Mong.	wall
Dallol / Sud.	valley, torrent
Dalur / Icel.	valley
Damm / Germ.	dam
Dan / Kor.	point

Local Form	English
Danau / *Indon.*	lake
Danda / *Nep.*	mountains
Dao / *Chin.*	island, peninsula
Dao / *Viet.*	island
Dar / *Ar.*	house, region
Dar / *Swa.*	port
Dara / *Tur.*	torrent, valley
Darb / *Ar.*	track
Darja / *Alt.*	river, sea
Darya, Daryā / *Pers.*	river, sea
Daryācheh / *Pers.*	lake, sea
Daš / *Alt.; Az.*	rock
Dasht / *Pers.*	desert, plain
Dawḥat / *Ar.*	bay
Dayr / *Ar.*	convent
De / *Sp.; Fr.*	of
Deal / *Rom.*	hill
Dearg / *Gae.*	red
Debre / *Amh.*	hill, monastery
Dega / *Som.*	stone
Deh / *Pers.*	village
Dēḥ / *Som.*	stream
Deich / *Germ.*	dike
Dél / *Hung.*	south
Delft / *Dut.; Fle.*	deep
Delger / *Mong.*	wide, market
-den / *Eng.*	city, town
Deniz / *Tur.*	sea
Denizi / *Tur.*	sea
Dent / *Fr.*	peak
Deo / *Laot.; Viet.*	pass
Dépression / *Fr.*	depression
Depressione / *It.*	depression
Der / *Som.*	high
Dera / *Hin.; Urdu*	temple
Derbent / *Tur.*	gorge, pass
Dere / *Tur.*	river, valley
Désert / *Fr.*	desert
Desfiladero / *Sp.*	pass
Desh / *Hin.*	land, country
Desierto / *Sp.*	desert
Det / *Alb.*	sea
Détroit / *Fr.*	strait
Deux / *Fr.*	two
Dezh / *Pers.*	castle
Dhar / *Ar.*	heights, hills
Dhār / *Hin.; Urdu*	mountain
Dhitikós / *Gr.*	western
Dien / *Khm.; Viet.*	rice-field
Diep / *Dut.; Fle.*	deep, strait
Dijk, -dijk / *Dut.; Fle.*	dam
Ding / *Chin.*	mountain, peak
Dique / *Sp.*	dam
Di Sopra / *It.*	upper
Di Sotto / *It.*	lower
Distrito / *Sp.; Port.*	district
Diu / *Hin.*	island
Diz / *Pers.*	castle
Djebel / *Ar.*	mountain
Dji / *Ban.*	water
Djup / *Swed.*	deep
Do / *Kor.*	Island
Do / *S.C.*	valley
Dō / *Jap.*	island, administrative division
Dōho / *Som.*	valley
Doi / *Thai*	mountain, peak
Dol / *Bulg.; Cz.; Rus.; S.C.*	valley
Doł / *Pol.*	valley
Dolen / *Bulg.*	low
Dolgi / *Rus.*	long
Dolina / *Bulg.; Cz.; Pol.; Rus.; S.C.; Slvn.*	valley
Dolni / *Bulg.*	low
Dolni / *Pol.*	lower
Dolny / *Pol.*	lower
Domb / *Hung.*	hill
Dôme / *Fr.*	dome
Dong / *Chin.; Viet.*	east
Dong / *Kor.*	city, town
Dong / *Thai*	mountain
Dong / *Viet.*	marsh, plain
Donji / *S.C.*	low, lower
Dorf, -dorf / *Germ.*	village
Doroga / *Rus.*	road
Dorp, -dorp / *Afr.; Dut.; Fle.*	village
Dos / *Rom.*	ridge
Dos / *Sp.*	two
Douarn / *Br.*	land
Dougou / *Sud.*	settlement
Doukou / *Sud.*	settlement
Down / *Eng.*	hill
Drâa / *Ar.*	dunes, hills
Dracht / *Germ.*	sandbank
Draw / *Eng.*	ravine, valley
Drif / *Afr.*	ford
Drift / *Afr.*	ford
Droichead / *Gae.*	bridge
Droûs / *Ar.*	crest
Dry / *Pash.*	river
Dubh / *Gae.*	black
Dugi / *S.C.*	long
Dugu / *Sud.*	settlement
Dun / *Gae.*	castle
Duna / *Sp.; It.*	dune
Düne / *Germ.*	dune
Dungar / *Hin.*	mountain
Dūngar / *Hin.*	mountain
Duong / *Viet.*	stream
Durchbruch / *Germ.*	gorge
Ḍurg / *Hin.*	castle
-durga / *Hin.*	castle
Duży / *Pol.*	great
Dvor / *Cz.*	court
Dvorec / *Rus.*	castle
Dvůr / *Cz.*	castle
Dwór / *Pol.*	court
Džebel / *Bulg.*	mountain
Dzong / *Tib.*	fort, monastery

E

Local Form	English
Ea / *Thai*	river
Eau / *Fr.*	water
Ebe / *Ban.*	forest
Ebene / *Germ.*	plain
Eck / *Germ.*	point
Eclusa / *Sp.*	lock
Écluse / *Fr.*	lock
Écueil / *Fr.*	cliff
Edeien / *Ber.*	sand desert
Edjérir / *Ber.*	wadi
Egg / *Germ.; Nor.*	crest, point
Eglab / *Ar.*	hills
Ehi / *Sah.*	mountain
Eid / *Nor.*	isthmus
Eiland / *Afr.*	island
Eisen / *Germ.*	iron
Eisenerz / *Germ.*	iron ore
El / *Amh.*	well
Elv, -elv / *Nor.*	river
Embalse / *Sp.*	reservoir
Embouchure / *Fr.*	mouth
Emi / *Sah.*	mountain
En / *Fr.*	in
Ende / *Germ.*	end
Enneri / *Sah.*	stream
Ennis / *Gae.*	island
Enseada / *Port.*	Bay, inlet
Ensenada / *Sp.*	bay, inlet
Ér / *Hung.*	stream
Erdö / *Hung.*	forest
Erg / *Ar.*	sand desert
Erz / *Germ.*	ore
Espigão / *Port.*	plateau
Ēstān / *Pers.*	land
Este / *Sp.*	east
Estero / *Sp.*	estuary, marsh
Estrecho / *Sp.*	strait
Estreito / *Port.*	strait
Estuaire / *Fr.*	estuary
Estuário / *Port.*	estuary
Estuario / *Sp.; It.*	estuary
Észak / *Hung.*	north
Étang / *Fr.*	pond
Ewaso / *Ban.*	river
Ey / *Icel.*	island
Eyja / *Icel.*	island
Eyjar / *Icel.*	islands
Eylandt / *Dut.*	island
Ežeras / *Lith.*	lake
Ezers / *Latv.*	lake

F

Local Form	English
Fa / *Mel.*	stream
Falaise / *Fr.*	cliff
Fall, -fall / *Germ.; Eng.; Swed.*	waterfall
Falls / *Eng.*	waterfall
Falu / *Hung.*	village
-falva / *Hung.*	village
Fan / *Sah.*	village
Faraglione / *It.*	cliff
Farallón / *Sp.*	cliff
Faro / *Sp.; It.*	lighthouse
Farvand / *Dan.*	strait
Fehér / *Hung.*	white
Fehn / *Germ.*	peat fen, peat-bog
Fekete / *Hung.*	black
Feld / *Dan.; Germ.*	field
Fell / *Eng.*	upland moor
Fell / *Icel.*	mountain
Fels / *Germ.*	rock
Fen / *Eng.*	marsh, peat-bog
Feng / *Chin.*	mountain, peak
Feste / *Germ.*	fort
Festung / *Germ.*	fort
Fier / *Rom.*	iron
Firn / *Germ.*	snow-field
Firth / *Eng.*	estuary, fjord
Fiume / *It.*	river
Fjäll / *Swed.*	mountain
Fjärd / *Swed.*	fjord
Fjell / *Nor.*	mountain
Fjöll / *Icel.*	mountain
Fjord, Fj. / *Dan.; Nor.; Swed.*	fjord
Fjörður / *Icel.*	fjord, bay
Fleuve / *Fr.*	river
Fließ / *Germ.*	torrent
Fljót / *Icel.*	river
Flói / *Icel.*	bay, gulf
Floresta / *Sp.; Port.*	forest
Flow / *Eng.*	strait
Flughafen / *Germ.*	airport
Fluß / *Germ.*	river
Fo / *Mel.*	stream
Foa / *Mel.*	stream
Foa / *Poly.*	cove
Foce / *It.*	mouth
Föld / *Hung.*	plain
Fonn / *Nor.*	glacier
Fontaine / *Fr.*	fountain
Fonte / *It.; Port.*	spring
Fontein / *Afr.; Dut.*	spring
Foort / *Afr.; Dut.*	ford
Forca / *It.*	pass
Forcella / *It.*	defile
Ford / *Rus.*	fjord
Förde / *Germ.*	fjord, gulf
Foreland / *Eng.*	promontory
Foresta / *It.*	forest
Forêt / *Fr.*	forest
Fors / *Swed.*	rapids, waterfall
Forst / *Germ.; Dut.*	forest
Forte / *It.; Port.*	fort
Fortin / *Sp.*	fort
Fosa / *Sp.*	trench
Foss / *Icel.; Nor.*	rapids, waterfall
Fossé / *Fr.*	trench
Foum / *Ar.*	pass
Fourche / *Fr.*	pass
Foz / *Sp.; Port.*	mouth
Frei / *Germ.*	free
Fronteira / *Port.*	frontier
Frontera / *Sp.*	frontier
Frontón / *Sp.*	promontory
Fuente / *Sp.*	spring
Fuerte / *Sp.*	fort
Fuji / *Jap.*	mountain
Fūlat / *Ar.*	marsh
Furt / *Germ.*	ford
Fushë / *Alb.*	plain

G

Local Form	English
G., Gora / *Bulg.; Rus.; S.C.*	mountain, hill
G., Gunung / *Indon.*	mountain
Ga / *Jap.*	bay
Ga / *Mel.*	mountain, peak
Gabel / *Germ.*	pass
Gaissa / *Lapp.*	mountain
Gala / *Sin.; Tam.*	mountain
Gam / *Hin.; Urdu*	village
Gamle / *Nor.; Swed.*	old
Gana / *Sud.*	little
Gang / *Germ.*	passage
Gang / *Chin.*	port, bay
Gang / *Kor.*	stream, bay
Gang / *Tib.*	glacier
Ganga / *Hin.*	river
Ganj / *Hin.; Urdu*	market
-gaon / *Hin.*	city, town
Gaoyuan / *Chin.*	plateau
Gap / *Kor.*	point
Gar / *Hin.*	house
Gara / *Bulg.*	station
Gara / *Ar.*	hills, range
Gară / *Rom.*	station
Garaet / *Ar.*	marsh, intermittent lake
Garam / *Beng.; Hin.; Urdu*	village
-gard / *Pol.*	city, town
Gård, -gård / *Dan.; Nor.; Swed.*	farmhouse
Gardaneh / *Pers.*	pass
Gare / *Fr.*	railway station
Garet / *Ar.*	hill
Garh, -garh / *Hin.; Urdu*	castle
Garhi / *Hin.; Nep.; Urdu*	fort
Garten / *Germ.*	garden
Gat / *Dan.; Fle.; Dut.*	strait
Gata / *Jap.*	bay, lake
Gau, -gau / *Germ.*	district
Gäu, -gäu / *Germ.*	district
Gavan / *Rus.*	port
Gave / *Bas.*	torrent
Gawa / *Jap.*	river
Geb., Gebirge / *Germ.*	mountain range
Gebergte / *Afr.; Dut.*	mountain range
Gebirge, Geb. / *Germ.*	mountain range
Geç., Geçit / *Tur.*	pass
Geçidi / *Tur.*	pass
Geçit, Geç. / *Tur.*	pass
Geysir / *Icel.*	geyser
Ghar / *Hin.; Urdu*	house
Ghar / *Pash.*	mountain, mountain range
Gharbīyah / *Ar.*	western
Ghat / *Hin.; Nep.; Urdu*	pass
Ghubbat / *Ar.*	bay
Ghurd / *Ar.*	dune
Gi / *Kor.*	peninsula
Giang / *Viet.*	stream
Giri / *Hin.; Urdu*	mountain, hill
Girlo / *Rus.*	branch
Gjebel / *Ar.*	mountain
Gji / *Alb.*	bay
Glace / *Fr.*	ice
Glaciar / *Sp.*	glacier
Glacier / *Eng.; Fr.*	glacier
Glen / *Gae.*	valley
Gletscher / *Germ.*	glacier
Gobi / *Mong.*	desert
Godār / *Pers.*	ford
Gok / *Kor.*	river
Gök / *Tur.*	blue
Gol / *Cauc.; Mong.*	river
Göl / *Tur.*	lake
Gola / *It.*	gorge
Gold / *Germ.; Eng.*	gold
Golet / *S.C.*	mountain
Golf / *Germ.*	gulf
Golfe / *Fr.*	gulf
Golfete / *Sp.*	inlet
Golfo / *Sp.; It.; Port.*	gulf
Goljam / *Bulg.*	great
Gölü / *Tur.*	lake
Gong / *Tib.*	high
Gonggar / *Tib.*	mountain
Gongo / *Ban.*	mountain
Góra / *Pol.*	mountain
Gora, G. / *Bulg.; Rus.; S.C.*	mountain, hill
Gorica / *S.C.; Slvn.*	hill
Gorje / *S.C.*	mountain range
Gorlo / *Rus.*	gorge
Gorm / *Gae.*	blue
Gorni / *Bulg.; S.C.; Slvn.*	upper
Gornji / *S.C.; Slvn.*	upper
Górny / *Pol.*	high
Gorod / *Rus.*	city, town
Gorodok / *Rus.*	village
Gorski / *Bulg.*	upper
Gory / *Rus.*	mountains
-gou / *Chin.*	river
Goulbi / *Sud.*	river, lake
Goulbin / *Sud.*	wadi
Goulet / *Fr.*	gap
Gour / *Ar.*	hills, range
Gourou / *Sud.*	wadi
Goz / *Sah.*	dune
Graafschap / *Dut.*	county, shire
Graben / *Germ.*	ditch, canal
Gracht / *Dut.*	canal
Grad, -grad / *Bulg.; Rus.; S.C.; Slvn.*	city, town, castle
Gradac / *S.C.*	castle
Gradec / *Bulg.*	village
Gradec / *Slvn.*	castle
Græn / *Icel.*	green
Gran / *Sp.; It.*	great
Grande / *Sp.; It.; Port.*	great
Grao / *Cat.; Sp.*	gap
Grat / *Germ.*	crest
Grève / *Fr.*	beach
Grind / *Germ.*	peak
Grjada / *Rus.*	range
Gród, -gród / *Pol.*	castle, city, town
Grön / *Icel.*	green
Grond / *Afr.*	soil
Gronden / *Dut.; Fle.*	flat
Groot / *Afr.; Dut.; Fle.*	great
Groß / *Germ.*	great
Grotta / *It.*	grotto
Grotte / *Fr.; Germ.*	grotto
Grube / *Germ.*	mine
Grün / *Germ.*	green
Grunn / *Nor.*	ground
Gruppe / *Germ.*	mountain system
Gruppo / *It.*	mountain system
Gua / *Mal.*	cave
Guaçu / *A.I.*	great
Guan / *Chin.*	pass
Guazú / *A.I.*	great
Guba / *Rus.*	bay
Guchi / *Jap.*	strait
Guelb / *Ar.*	hill, mountain
Guelta / *Ar.*	well
Guic / *Br.*	village
Güney / *Tur.*	south, southern
Gunong / *Mal.*	mountain
Guntō / *Jap.*	archipelago
Gunung, G. / *Indon.*	mountain
Guo / *Chin.*	state, land
Gur / *Rom.*	mountain
Guri / *Jap.*	cliff
Gurud / *Ar.*	hills, dunes
Gyár / *Hung.*	factory

H

Local Form	English
Haag / *Dut.; Fle.*	hedge
-håb / *Dan.*	port
Haḍabat / *Ar.*	highland
Hadd / *Ar.*	point
Hadjer / *Ar.*	hill, mountain
Hae / *Kor.*	bay, sea
Haehyeop / *Kor.*	strait

Geographical Glossary

Local Form	English
Haf / *Icel.*	sea
Ḩafar / *Ar.*	well
Hafen / *Germ.*	port
Haff / *Germ.*	lagoon
Hafir / *Ar.*	spring, ditch
Hafnar / *Icel.*	port
Hāfūn / *Som.*	bay
Hage / *Dan.*	point
Hage / *Dut.; Fle.*	hedge
Hågna / *Swed.*	peak
Hai / *Chin.*	sea, lake, bay
Hain / *Germ.*	forest
Haixia / *Chin.*	strait
Ḩajar / *Ar.*	hill, mountain
Hajar / *Ar.*	hill country
Halbinsel / *Germ.*	peninsula
Halma / *Hung.*	hill
Halom / *Hung.*	hill
Halq / *Ar.*	gap
Hals / *Nor.*	peninsula
Halvø / *Dan.*	peninsula
Halvøy / *Nor.*	peninsula
Hama / *Jap.*	beach
Hamāda / *Ar.*	rocky desert
Ḩamādah / *Ar.*	plateau
Ḩamādat / *Ar.*	plateau
Hammam / *Ar.*	thermal springs
Ḩammām / *Ar.*	well
Hamn / *Nor.; Swed.*	port
Hamrā' / *Ar.*	red
Hāmūn / *Jap.*	salt lake
Hana / *Jap.*	cape
Hana / *Poly.*	bay
Hane / *Tur.*	house
Hang / *Kor.*	port
Hank / *Ar.*	escarpment, plateau
Hantō / *Jap.*	peninsula
Har / *Hebr.*	mountain
Hara / *Mong.*	black
Harar / *Swa.*	well
Ḩarrah / *Ar.*	lava field
Ḩarrat / *Ar.*	lava field
Hasi / *Ar.*	well
Ḩasi / *Ar.*	well
Hassi / *Ar.*	well
Ḩasy / *Ar.*	well
Haug / *Nor.*	hill
Haupt- / *Germ.*	principal
Haure / *Lapp.*	lake
Haus / *Germ.*	house
Hausen / *Germ.*	village
Haut / *Fr.*	high
Hauteur / *Fr.*	hill
Hauts Plateaux / *Fr.*	highlands
Hauz / *Pers.*	reservoir
Hav / *Dan.; Nor.; Swed.*	sea, gulf
Haven / *Eng.; Fle.; Dut.*	port
Havn / *Dan.; Nor.*	port
Havre / *Fr.*	port
Hawr / *Ar.*	lake, marsh
Ház / *Hung.*	house
-háza / *Hung.*	house
Hazm / *Ar.*	height, mountain range
He / *Chin.*	river
Head / *Eng.*	headland
Hed / *Dan.; Swed.*	heath
Hegy / *Hung.*	mountain
Hegység / *Hung.*	mountain
Hei / *Nor.*	heath
Heide / *Germ.*	heath
Heijde / *Dut.; Fle.*	heath
Heilig / *Germ.*	saint
Heim, -heim / *Germ.; Nor.*	house
Heiya / *Jap.*	plain
-hely / *Hung.*	locality
Hem / *Swed.*	home
Hen / *Br.*	old
Higashi / *Jap.*	east, eastern
Hima / *Hin.*	ice
Himal / *Nep.*	peak
Hisar / *Tur.*	castle
Ho / *Chin.*	reservoir, river
Ho / *Kor.*	river, reservoir
Hō / *Jap.*	mountain
Hoch / *Germ.*	high, upper
Hochland / *Germ.*	highland
Hochplato / *Afr.*	highland
Hodna / *Ar.*	highland
Hoek / *Dut.; Fle.*	cape
Hof / *Dut.; Germ.*	court
Höfn / *Icel.*	port
Høg / *Nor.*	peak
Hög / *Swed.*	mountain
Hogna / *Nor.*	peak
Höhe / *Germ.*	peak
Høj / *Dan.*	hill
Hoj / *Ural.*	mountain range
Hok / *Jap.*	north
Hoku / *Jap.*	north, northern
Holm / *Dan.; Nor.; Swed.*	island
Holz / *Germ.*	forest
Hon / *Viet.*	island, point
Hong / *Chin.; Viet.*	red
Hono / *Poly.*	bay, anchorage
Hoog / *Afr.; Dut.; Fle.*	high
Hook / *Eng.*	point
Hoorn / *Afr.; Dut.; Fle.*	cape, point

Local Form	English
Hora / *Cz.; Slvk.*	point
Horn / *Eng.; Germ.; Icel.; Nor.; Swed.*	point
Horni / *Cz.*	high
Horný / *Slvk.*	upper
Horst / *Germ.*	mountain
Horvot / *Hebr.*	ruins
Hory / *Cz.; Slvk.*	mountain range
Hout / *Dut.; Fle.*	forest
Hovd, -hovd / *Dan.; Nor.*	cape
Ḩowz / *Pers.*	basin
Hrad / *Cz.; Slvk.*	castle, city, town
Hradiště / *Cz.*	citadel
Hřeben / *Cz.*	crest
Hrebet / *Rus.*	mountain range
Hu / *Rmsh.*	lake
Huang / *Chin.*	yellow
Hude / *Germ.*	pasture
Huerta / *Sp.*	market garden
Hügel / *Germ.*	hill
Hügelland / *Germ.*	hill country
Huis, -huis / *Afr.; Dut.; Fle.*	house
Huisie / *Afr.*	house
Huizen, -huizen / *Dut.*	houses
Huk / *Afr.; Dan.; Swed.*	cape
Hum / *S.C.*	hill
Hurst / *Eng.*	grove
Hus / *Dut.; Nor.; Swed.*	house
Huta / *Pol.; Slvk.*	hut
Hütte / *Germ.*	hut
Hver / *Icel.*	crater
Hvit / *Icel.*	white
Hvost / *Rus.*	spit

I

Local Form	English
I., Island / *Eng.*	island
Ierós / *Gr.*	holy
Igarapé / *A.I.*	river
Ighazer / *Ber.*	torrent
Ighil / *Ber.*	hill
Iguidi / *Ber.*	dunes
Ih / *Mong.*	great
Ike / *Jap.*	pond
Ile / *Fr.*	island
Ilha / *Port.*	island
Iller / *Tur.*	administrative division
Ilot / *Fr.*	islet
Imi / *Ar.*	spring
I-n / *Ber.*	well
Inch / *Gae.*	island
Inder / *Dan.; Nor.*	inner
Indre / *Nor.*	inner
Inferiore / *It.*	lower
Inish / *Gae.*	island
Insel / *Germ.*	island
Insulă / *Rom.*	island
Inver / *Gae.*	mouth
Irhazér / *Ber.*	wadi
Irmak / *Tur.*	river
'Irq / *Ar.*	dunes
Is / *Nor.*	glacier
Ís / *Icel.*	ice
Isblink / *Dan.*	glacier
Ishi / *Jap.*	rock
Iske / *Alt.*	old
Isla / *Sp.*	island
Iso / *Finn.*	great
Iso / *Jap.*	cliff
Isola / *It.*	island
Isthmós / *Gr.*	isthmus
Istmo / *Sp.; It.*	isthmus
Ita / *A.I.*	stone
Itä / *Finn.*	east
Itivdleq / *Esk.*	isthmus
Iwa / *Jap.*	rock, cliff
Iztočni / *Bulg.*	eastern
Izvor / *Bulg.; Rom.; S.C.; Slvn.*	spring

J

Local Form	English
J., Jazīrat / *Ar.*	island
J., Jiang / *Chin.*	river
Jabal / *Ar.*	mountain
Jaha / *Ural.*	river
Jam / *Ural.*	lake, river
Jama / *Rus.*	cave
Jan / *Alt.*	great
Janga / *Tur.*	north
Jangi / *Alt.; Iran.*	new
Janūbīyah / *Ar.*	southern
Jar / *Rus.*	bank
Järv / *Est.*	lake
Järve / *Finn.*	lake
Järvi / *Finn.*	lake
Jasirēd / *Som.*	island
Jaun / *Latv.*	new
Jaur / *Lapp.*	lake
Jaure / *Lapp.*	lake
Javr / *Lapp.*	lake
Javrre / *Lapp.*	lake
Jazā'ir / *Ar.*	islands
Jazīrat, J. / *Ar.*	island
Jazovir / *Bulg.*	reservoir
Jbel / *Ar.*	mountain
Jebel / *Ar.*	mountain
Jedid / *Ar.*	new
Jedo / *Kor.*	archipelago
Jezero / *S.C.; Slvn.*	lake
Jezioro / *Pol.*	lake
Jhil / *Hin.; Urdu*	lake
Jian / *Chin.*	mountain
Jiang, J. / *Chin.*	river
Jiao / *Chin.*	cape, cliff
Jibāl / *Ar.*	mountain
Jih / *Cz.*	south
Jima / *Jap.*	island
Jin / *Kor.*	cove
Jing / *Chin.*	spring
Jisr / *Ar.*	bridge
Joch / *Germ.*	pass
Jõgi / *Est.*	river
Jøkel / *Nor.*	glacier
Joki / *Finn.*	river
Jokka / *Lapp.*	river
Jökull / *Icel.*	glacier
Jord, -jord / *Nor.*	earth
Ju / *Ural.*	river
Judeţ / *Rom.*	district
Jugan / *Ural.*	river
Jura / *Lith.*	sea
Jūra / *Latv.*	sea
Jūras Līcis / *Latv.*	bay
Jūrmala / *Latv.*	beach
Jurt / *Cauc.*	village
Južni / *Bulg.; S.C.; Slvn.*	southern
Južny / *Rus.*	southern
Juzur / *Ar.*	islands

K

Local Form	English
Ka / *Poly.*	lake
Kaap / *Afr.*	cape
Kabīr / *Ar.*	great
Kae / *Kor.*	inlet
Kāf / *Ar.*	peak, mountain
Kafr / *Ar.*	village
Kaga / *Ban.*	hills, mountain range
Kahal / *Ar.*	plateau, escarpment
Kai / *Jap.*	sea
Kaikyō / *Jap.*	strait
Kaise / *Lapp.*	mountain
Kal / *Pers.*	stream
Kala / *Az.; Kor.*	fort
Kala / *Finn.*	river
Kala / *Hin.*	black
Kala / *Tur.*	castle
Kalaa / *Ar.*	castle
Kalaki / *Georg.*	city, town
Kale / *Tur.*	castle
Kali / *Hin.*	black
Kali / *Indon.; Mal.*	bay, river
Kallio / *Finn.*	rock
Kaln / *Latv.*	mountain
Kalós / *Gr.*	beautiful, good
Kamen / *Bulg.; Rus.; S.C.; Slvn.*	mountain, peak
Kámen / *Cz.*	rock
Kameň / *Slvk.*	rock
Kami / *Jap.*	upper
Kamień / *Pol.*	rock
Kamm / *Germ.*	crest
Kamp / *Germ.*	field
Kâmpóng / *Khm.*	village
Kámpos / *Gr.*	field
Kampung / *Indon.; Mal.*	village
Kan.; Kanal / *Alb.; Dan.; Germ.; Nor.; Rus.; S.C.; Slvn.; Swed.; Tur.*	canal, channel
Kanaal / *Dut.; Fle.*	canal
Kanał / *Pol.*	canal
Kanal, Kan. / *Alb.; Dan.; Germ.; Nor.; Rus.; S.C.; Slvn.; Swed.; Tur.*	canal, channel
Kand, -kand / *Pers.; Tur.*	city, town
Kang / *Chin.; Kor.*	bay, river
Kangas / *Fle.*	heath
Kange / *Esk.*	east
Kangri / *Tib.*	snow-capped mountain
Kantara / *Ar.*	bridge
Kaôh / *Khm.*	island
Kap / *Dan.; Germ.*	cape
Kapija / *S.C.*	gate, gorge
Kapp / *Nor.*	cape
Kar / *Tib.*	white
Kar / *Ural.*	city, town
Kara / *Tur.*	black
Karang / *Indon.; Mal.*	sandbank, cliff
Kari / *Finn.*	cliff
Kariba / *Ban.*	gorge
Kariet / *Ar.*	village
Karki / *Finn.*	peninsula
Kastel / *Germ.*	castle
Kástron / *Gr.*	fort, city, town
Káto / *Gr.*	lower
Kaupstadur / *Icel.*	city, town
Kaupunki / *Finn.*	city, town
Kavīr / *Pers.*	salt desert
Kawa / *Jap.*	river
Kawm / *Ar.*	hill
Kebir / *Ar.*	great
Kedi / *Georg.*	mountain range
Kédia / *Ar.*	mountain, plateau
Kedim / *Ar.*	old
Kef / *Ar.*	mountain
Kefála / *Gr.*	mountain, peak
Kefar / *Hebr.*	village
Kei / *Jap.*	river
Kelet / *Hung.*	east
Ken / *Gae.*	cape
Kent / *Alt.; Iran.; Tur.*	city, town
Kenya / *Swa.*	fog
Kep / *Alb.*	cape
Kep., Kepulauan / *Mal.*	archipelago
Kepulauan, Kep. / *Mal.*	archipelago
Kereszt / *Hung.*	cross
Kerk / *Dut.; Fle.*	church
Keski / *Finn.*	middle
Kette / *Germ.*	mountain range
Keur / *Sud.*	village
Key / *Eng.*	coral island
Kha / *Tib.*	valley
Khal / *Hin.*	canal
Khalīj / *Ar.*	gulf
Khand / *Hin.*	district
Khao / *Thai*	hill, mountain
Kharābeh / *Pers.*	ruins
Khashm / *Ar.*	promontory
Khatt / *Ar.*	wadi
Khawr / *Ar.*	mouth, bay
Khazzān / *Ar.*	dam
Khemis / *Ar.*	fifth
Khersónisos / *Gr.*	peninsula
Khirbat / *Ar.*	ruins
Khlong / *Thai*	stream, mouth
Khokhok / *Thai*	isthmus
Khor / *Ar.*	mouth, bay
Khóra / *Gr.*	land
Khorion / *Gr.*	village
Khowr / *Pers.*	bay
Khrisós / *Gr.*	gold
Ki- / *Ban.*	little
Kibali / *Sud.*	river
Kil / *Gae.*	church
Kilde / *Dan.*	spring
Kilima / *Swa.*	mountain
Kill / *Gae.*	strait
Kilwa / *Ban.*	lake
Kin / *Gae.*	cape
Kinn / *Nor.*	cape, point
Kirche / *Germ.*	church
Kirk / *Eng.*	church
Kis / *Hung.*	little
Kisiwa / *Swa.*	island
Kita / *Jap.*	north, northern
Kızıl / *Tur.*	red
Klein / *Afr.; Dut.; Germ.*	little
Kliff / *Germ.*	cliff
Klint / *Dan.*	reef
Klip / *Afr.; Dut.*	rock, cliff
Klit / *Dan.*	dune
Kloof / *Afr.; Dut.*	gorge
Kloster / *Dan.; Germ.; Nor.; Swed.*	convent
Knob / *Eng.*	mountain
Knock / *Gae.*	mountain, hill
Ko / *Jap.*	bay, lake, little
Ko / *Sud.*	stream
Ko / *Thai*	island, point
Købing / *Dan.*	town
Kogel / *Germ.*	dome
Kōgen / *Jap.*	plateau
Koh / *Hin.; Pers.*	mountain, mountain range
Kol / *Alt.*	river, valley
Kol / *Alt.; Tur.*	lake
Koll / *Nor.*	peak
Kólpos / *Gr.*	gulf
Kong / *Dan.; Nor.; Swed.*	king
Kong / *Indon.; Mal.*	mountain
Kong / *Viet.*	mountain, hill
Konge / *Ban.*	river
König / *Germ.*	king
Koog / *Germ.*	polder
Kop / *Afr.*	hill
Kopec / *Cz.; Slvk.*	hill
Kopf / *Germ.*	peak
Köping / *Swed.*	town
Köprü / *Tur.*	bridge
Körfezi / *Tur.*	gulf
Korfi / *Gr.*	rock
Koro / *Mel.*	mountain, island
Koro / *Sud.*	old
Koru / *Tur.*	forest
Kosa / *Rus.*	spit
Koška / *Rus.*	cliff
Koski / *Finn.*	rapids
Kosui / *Jap.*	lake
Kot / *Urdu*	castle
Kota / *Mal.*	city, town
Kotal / *Pash.; Pers.*	pass
Kotar / *S.C.*	cultivated area
Kotlina / *Pol.*	basin

Local Form	English
Kotlovina / Rus.	basin, plain
Kou / Chin.	mouth, pass
Kourou / Sud.	well
Kowr / Pers.	river
Kowtal / Pers.	pass
Koy / Tur.	bay
Köy / Tur.	village
Kraal / Afr.	village
Kraina / Pol.	land
Kraj / Rus.; S.C.	land
Kraj / Rus.	administrative division
Krajina / S.C.	land
Krak / Ar.	hill, castle
Krans / Afr.	mountain
Kras / S.C.; Slvn.	karst landscape
Krasny / Rus.	red
Kreb / Ar.	hills, mountain range
Kriaž / Ar.	mountain range
Krš / S.C.	karst area, limestone area
Krung / Thai	city, town
Ksar / Ar.	castle
Ksour / Ar.	fortified village
Ku- / Ban.	river branch
Kuala / Mal.	river, mouth
Kubra / Ar.	bridge
Küçük / Tur.	little
Kuduk / Tur.	spring
Küh / Pers.	mountain
Kühhā / Pers.	mountain range
Kul / Alt.; Iran.; Tur.	lake
Kulam, -kulam / Hin.; Tam.	pond
Kulle / Swed.	hill
Kulm / Germ.	peak
Kultuk / Rus.	bay
Kum / Tur.	dunes, sand desert
Kuppe / Germ.	dome, seamount
Kurayb / Ar.	hill
Kurgan / Alt.	hill
Kurgan / Tur.	fort
Kuro / Jap.	black
Kurort / Bulg.; Germ.; Rus.	spa
Kust / Dut.; Fle.	coast
Kust- / Swed.	coast
Küste / Germ.	coast
Kút / Hung.	spring
Kuyu / Tur.	spring
Kvemo / Georg.	low, lower
Kwa / Ban.	village
Kylä / Finn.	village
Kyle / Gae.	strait, channel
Kyō / Jap.	strait
Kyrka / Swed.	church
Kyst / Dan.; Nor.	coast
Kyun / Burm.	island
Kyūryō / Jap.	hills, mountains
Kyzyl / Tur.	red
Kzyl / Tur.	red

L

Local Form	English
L., Lake, Lago / Eng.; It.; Port.; Sp.	lake
La / Tib.	pass
Laagte / Afr.	stream, valley
Labuan / Indon.; Mal.	bay, port
Lac / Fr.	lake
Lach / Som.	stream, wadi
Lacul / Rom.	lake
Lae / Poly.	cape, point
Laem / Thai	bay, port
Låg / Nor.; Swed.	low, lower
Lag / Swed.	stream, wadi
Läge / Swed.	beach
Lagh / Som.	stream, wadi
Lago, L. / It.; Port.; Sp.	lake
Lagoa / Port.	lagoon
Laguna / Alb.; It.; Rus.; Sp.	lagoon, lake
Lagune / Fr.	lagoon
Laht / Est.	bay
Lahti / Finn.	bay, gulf
Laks / Finn.	bay
Lalla / Ar.	saint
Lampi / Finn.	pond
Lande / Fr.	heath
Lang / Afr.; Dut.; Germ.	long
Lang / Viet.	village
Lao / Chin.	old
Lapa / Poly.	mountain range, peak
Largo / Port.; Sp.	basin
Las / Pol.	forest
Las, Lãs / Som.	well
Laut / Mal.	sea
Law / Gae.	hill, mountain
Lázně / Cz.	thermal springs
Lednik / Rus.	glacier
Leite / Germ.	coast
Lekh / Nep.	mountain range

Local Form	English
Les / Bulg.; Cz.; Rus.; Slvk.	forest
Leso / Rus.	forested
Levante / It.; Sp.	eastern
Levkós / Gr.	white
Levy / Rus.	left
Lha / Tib.	temple
Lhari / Hin.; Nep.	mountain
Lho / Tib.	south
Lido / It.	sandbar
Liedao / Chin.	archipelago
Liehtao / Chin.	archipelago
Liels / Latv.	great
Lilla / Swed.	little
Lille / Dan.; Nor.	little
Liman / Alb.; Rus.; Tur.	lagoon, bay
Liman / Tur.	bay, port
Limin / Gr.	port
Limni / Gr.	lake
Ling / Chin.	mountain range, peak
Linna / Finn.	castle
Liqen / Alb.	lake
Lithos / Gr.	stone
Litoral / Port.; Sp.	littoral
Litorale / It.	littoral
Llan / Wel.	church
Llano / Sp.	plain
Llanura / Sp.	plain
Lo- / Ban.	river
Loch / Gae.	lake, inlet
Loch / Germ.	grotto
Loka / Slvn.	forest
Loma / Sp.	hill
Long / Indon.	stream
Loo / Dut.; Fle.	clearing
Lough / Gae.	lake
Loutrá / Gr.	thermal springs
Ložbina / Rus.	depression
Lu- / Ban.	river
Lua / Ban.	river
Lua / Mel.	island, reef
Lua / Poly.	crater
Luang / Thai	yellow
Luch / Germ.	peat-bog
Lücke / Germ.	pass
Lug / Rus.	meadow
Luka / S.C.; Slvn.	port
Lule / Lapp.	east, eastern
Lum / Alb.	river
Lund / Dan.; Swed.	forest
Lung / Rom.	long
Lung / Tib.	valley
Luoto / Finn.	shoal
Lurg / Pers.	salt flat
Lut / Pers.	desert

M

Local Form	English
M., Monte / It.; Port.; Sp.	mountain
Ma / Ar.	water
Ma- / Ban.	people
Maa / Est.; Finn.	island, land
Ma'arrat / Ar.	height
Machi / Jap.	district
Macizo / Sp.	massif
Madhya / Hin.	central
Madīnah / Ar.	city, town
Madīq / Ar.	strait
Mado / Swa.	well
Madu / Tam.	pond
Mae / Thai	stream
Mae nam / Thai	stream, mouth
Magh / Gae.	plain
Mägi / Est.	mountain
Măgura / Rom.	height
Mahā / Hin.	great
Mahal / Hin.; Urdu	palace
Mai / Amh.; Ban.	stream
Majdan / S.C.	quarry
Mäki / Finn.	mountain, hill
Makrós / Gr.	long
Mala / Hin.; Tam.	mountain
Malai / Hin.; Tam.	mountain
Malal / A.I.	fence
Malhão / Port.	dome
Mali / Alb.	mountain
Mali / S.C.; Slvn.	little
Malki / Bulg.	little
Malla / Tam.	mountain
Maly / Rus.	little
Malý / Cz.; Slvk.	little
Maly / Pol.	little
Man / Kor.	bay
Manastir / Bulg.; S.C.	monastery
Manche / Fr.	channel
Mar / It.; Port.; Sp.	sea
Mar / Tib.	red
Mar / Ural.	city, town
Marais / Fr.	marsh
Marché / Fr.	market
Mare / Fr.	pond
Mare / It.; Rom.	sea
Mare / Rom.	great
Marea / Rom.	sea
Marécage / Fr.	marsh
Marios / Lith.	reservoir

Local Form	English
Marisma / Sp.	marsh
Mark / Dan.; Nor.; Swed.	land
Markt / Germ.	market
Marsa / Ar.	anchorage, bay
Marsch / Germ.	marsh
Maru / Jap.	mountain
Mas / Prov.	farmhouse
Maşabb / Ar.	mouth
Mashra' / Ar.	landing, pier
Masivul / Rom.	massif
Massiv / Germ.; Rus.	massif
Mata / Poly.	point
Mata / Port.; Sp.	forest
Mata / Som.	waterfall
Mato / Port.; Sp.	forest
Matsu / Jap.	point
Mauna / Poly.	mountain
Mávros / Gr.	black
Mayo / Sud.	river
Maza / Lith.	little
Mazar / Pers.; Tur.	sanctuary
Mazs / Latv.	little
Me / Khm.	river
Me / Mel.	hill, mountain
Me / Thai	great
Medina / Ar.	city, town
Medjez / Ar.	ford
Meer / Dut.; Fle.	lake
Meer / Germ.	lake, sea
Megálos / Gr.	great
Mégas / Gr.	great
Megye / Hung.	district
Mélas / Gr.	black
Melkosopočnik / Rus.	hill country
Mellan / Swed.	central
Men / Chin.	gate, channel
Ménez / Br.	mountain
Menzel / Ar.	bivouac
Meos / Indon.	island
Mer / Fr.	sea
Mercato / It.	market
Merdja / Ar.	lagoon, marsh
Meri / Est.; Finn.	sea
Meridional / Rom.; Sp.	southern
Merin / A.I.	little
Merja / Ar.	lagoon, marsh
Mers / Ar.	port
Mersa / Ar.	port
Mesa / Sp.	mesa, tableland
Meseta / Sp.	plateau
Mésos / Gr.	central
Mesto / Bulg.; S.C.; Slvk.; Slvn.	city, town
Město / Cz.	city, town
Mestre / Port.	principal
Meydan / Tur.	square
Mezad / Hebr.	castle
Mező / Hung.	field
Mgne., Montagne / Fr.	mountain
Mgnes., Montagnes / Fr.	mountains
Miao / Chin.	temple
Miasto / Pol.	city, town
Mic / Rom.	little
Middel / Afr.; Dut.; Fle.	middle
Midi / Fr.	noon, south
Między / Pol.	central
Miedzyrzecze / Pol.	interfluve
Mierzeja / Pol.	sand spit
Mifraz / Hebr.	bay, gulf
Miftah / Ar.	gorge
Mikrós / Gr.	little
Mina / Port.; Sp.	mine
Minā' / Ar.	port
Minami / Jap.	south, southern
Minamoto / Jap.	spring
Minato / Jap.	port
Mine / Jap.	peak
Mirim / A.I.	little
Misaki / Jap.	cape
Mittel- / Germ.	middle
Mo / Chin.	sand desert
Mo / Nor.; Swed.	heath
Moana / Poly.	lake
Mogila / Bulg.; Rus.	hill
Moku / Poly.	island
Mølle / Dan.	mill
Monasterio / Sp.	monastery
Mond / Afr.; Dut.; Fle.	mouth
Mong / Burm.; Thai; Viet.	city, town
Moni / Gr.	monastery
Mont / Cat.; Fr.	mountain
Montagna / It.	mountain
Montagne, Mgne. / Fr.	mountain
Montagnes, Mgnes. / Fr.	mountains
Montaña / Sp.	mountain
Monte, M. / It.; Port.; Sp.	mountain
Monts, Mts. / Fr.	mountains
Moos / Germ.	moor
Mór / Gae.	great
More / Bulg.; Rus.; S.C.	sea
More / Gae.	great
Mori / Jap.	mountain, forest
Morne / Fr.	mountain
Moron / Mong.	river
Morro / Port.; Germ.	hill, peak
Morrón / Sp.	mountain
Morze / Pol.	sea

Local Form	English
Most / Bulg.; Cz.; Pol.; Rus.; S.C.; Slvn.	bridge
Moto / Jap.	spring
Motte / Fr.	hill
Motu / Mel.; Poly.	island, rock
Moutier / Fr.	monastery
Movilă / Rom.	hill
Moyen / Fr.	central
Mta / Georg.	mountain
Mts., Monts, Mountains / Eng.; Fr.	mountains
Muang / Laot.; Thai	city, town, land
Muara / Indon.; Mal.	mouth
Muela / Sp.	mountain
Mühle / Germ.	mill
Mui / Mel.	point
Mui / Viet.	point, cape
Muiden / Dut.; Fle.	mouth
Muir / Gae.	sea
Mukh / Hin.	mouth
Mull / Gae.	promontory
Münde / Germ.	mouth
Mündung / Germ.	mouth
Municipiul / Rom.	commune
Munkhafaḍ / Ar.	depression
Münster / Germ.	monastery
Munte / Rom.	mountain
Muntelé / Rom.	mountain
Munţii / Rom.	mountain range
Muren / Mong.	river
Mushāsh / Ar.	spring
Muz / Tur.	ice
Muztagh / Tur.	snow-capped mountain
Mwambo / Ban.	rock, cliff
Myit / Burm.	stream
Mynydd / Wel.	mountain
Myo / Burm.	city, town
Mýri / Icel.	marsh
Mys / Rus.	cape

N

Local Form	English
Na / Cz.; Pol.; Rus.; S.C.; Slvn.	on
Nab / Ar.	spring
Nad / Cz.; Pol.; Rus.	on
Nada / Jap.	bay, sea
Nadi, -nadi / Hin.; Urdu	river
Næs / Dan.	point
Nafūd / Ar.	dunes
Nag / Tib.	black
Nagar, -nagar / Hin.; Tib.	city, town
Nagaram / Hin.; Tam.	city, town
Nagorje / Rus.	plateau, mountains
Nagy / Hung.	great
Nahr / Ar.	river
Naikai / Jap.	sea
Naka / Jap.	central
Nakhon / Thai	city, town
Nam / Burm.; Laot.; Thai	river
Nam / Kor.	south
Namakzar / Pers.	salt desert
Nan / Chin.	south
Narrows / Eng.	strait
Narssaq / Esk.	plain, valley
Näs / Swed.	cape
Nationalpark / Swed.; Germ.	national park
Nau / Lith.	new
Nauja / Lith.	new
Navolok / Rus.	cape, promontory
Ne / Jap.	cliff
Neder / Fle.; Dut.	low
Neem / Est.	cape
Negro / Port.; Sp.	black
Negru / Rom.	black
Nehir / Tur.	river
Nei / Chin.	inner
Nene, -nene / Ban.	great
Néos / Gr.	new
Nero / It.	black
Nes / Icel.; Nor.	cape
Ness / Gae.	promontory
Neu / Germ.	new
Neuf / Fr.	new
Nevado / Sp.	snow-capped mountain
Nez / Fr.	cape
Ngok / Viet.	mountain, peak
Ngolo / Ber.	great
Ni / Kor.	village
Niecka / Pol.	basin
Niemi / Finn.	peninsula
Nieuw / Fle.; Dut.	new
Nij / Dut.	new
Nīl / Hin.	blue
Nishi / Jap.	west
Niski / Pol.	lower
Nisko / S.C.	low
Nisoi / Gr.	islands
Nisos / Gr.	island
Nizina / Pol.	lowland
Nížina / Cz.	depression
Nizký / Cz.	low, lower

Geographical Glossary

Local Form	English
Nizmennost / *Rus.*	lowland, depression
Nižni / *Rus.*	low, lower
Nižný / *Slvk.*	low, lower
No / *Mel.*	stream
Nock / *Gae.*	ridge
Noir / *Fr.*	black
Non / *Thai*	hill
Nong / *Thai*	lake, marsh
Noord / *Afr.; Fle.; Dut.*	north
Noordoost / *Afr.; Fle.; Dut.*	northeast
Nor / *Arm.*	new
Nord / *Fr.; It.; Germ.*	north
Nördlich / *Germ.*	northern
Nørdre / *Dan.; Nor.*	northern
Norra / *Swed.*	northern
Nørre / *Dan.*	northern
Norte / *Sp.*	north
Nos / *Bulg.; Rus.; S.C.; Slvn.*	cape
Nosy / *Malag.*	island
Nótios / *Gr.*	southern
Nou / *Rom.*	new
Novi / *Bulg.; S.C.; Slvn.*	new
Novo / *Port.*	new
Novy / *Rus.*	new
Nový / *Cz.; Slvk.*	new
Now / *Pers.*	new
Nowy / *Pol.*	new
Nudo / *Sp.*	mountain
Nuevo / *Sp.*	new
Nui / *Viet.*	mountain
Numa / *Jap.*	marsh, lake
Nummi / *Finn.*	heath
Nunatak / *Esk.*	peak
Nuovo / *It.*	new
Nur / *Chin.*	lake
Nusa / *Mal.*	island
Nut, -nut / *Nor.*	peak
Nuwara / *Sin.; Tam.*	city, town
Nuwe / *Afr.*	new
Nyanza / *Ban.*	water, river, lake
Nyasa / *Ban.*	lake
Nyeong / *Kor.*	pass
Nyika / *Ban.*	upland
Nyŏng / *Kor.*	mount, pass
Nyugat / *Hung.*	west

O

Local Form	English
Ō / *Jap.*	great
Ó / *Hung.*	old
Ö / *Swed.*	island
Ø, -ø / *Dan.; Nor.*	island
Öar / *Swed.*	islands
Ober / *Germ.*	upper
Oblast / *Rus.*	province
Obo / *Mong.*	mountain, hill
Occidental / *Fr.; Rom.; Sp.*	western
Océan / *Fr.*	ocean
Océano / *Sp.*	ocean
Oceano / *It.; Port.*	ocean
Ocnă / *Rom.*	salt mine
Odde / *Dan.; Nor.*	promontory
Oeste / *Port.; Sp.*	west
Oever / *Fle.; Dut.*	bank
Oewer / *Afr.*	bank
Oie / *Germ.*	islet
Ojos / *Sp.*	spring
Oka / *Jap.*	coast
Oke / *Sud.*	height
Okean / *Rus.*	ocean
Oki / *Jap.*	bay
Okrug / *Rus.*	district
Ola / *Alt.*	city, town
Omuramba / *K.S.*	stream
Onder / *Afr.*	under
Oni / *Malag.*	river
Oos / *Afr.*	east
Oost / *Fle.; Dut.*	east
Oostelijk / *Dut.*	eastern
Opatija / *Slvn.*	abbey
Or / *Fr.*	gold
Oraş / *Rom.*	city, town
Óri / *Gr.*	mountains
Oriental / *Fr.; Port.; Rom.; Sp.*	eastern
Orientale / *It.*	eastern
Orilla / *Sp.*	bank
Órmos / *Gr.*	bay
Óros / *Gr.*	mountain
Ország / *Hung.*	land
Ort / *Germ.*	cape
Orta / *Tur.*	central
Orto / *Alt.*	central
Oseaan / *Afr.*	ocean
Ōshima / *Jap.*	large island
Ost / *Dan.; Germ.*	east
Öst / *Swed.*	east
Ostān, -ostān / *Pers.*	province
Øster / *Dan.; Nor.*	east, eastern
Öster / *Swed.*	east, eastern
Östlich / *Germ.*	eastern
Ostrog / *Rus.*	castle
Ostrov / *Rus.*	island
Ostrovul / *Rom.*	island
Ostrów / *Pol.*	island
Ostrvo / *S.C.*	island
Otok / *S.C.; Slvn.*	island
Otrog / *Rus.*	front range (mountains)
Oua / *Mel.*	stream
Ouar / *Ar.*	rocky desert
Oud / *Fle.; Dut.*	old
Oued / *Ar.*	wadi
Ouest / *Fr.*	west
Ouled / *Ar.*	son
Oum / *Ar.*	mother
Ouro / *Port.*	gold
Outu / *Poly.*	cape
Ova / *Ban.*	people
Ova / *Tur.*	plain
Ovasi / *Tur.*	plain
Øver / *Nor.*	over
Över / *Swed.*	over
Övre / *Swed.*	over
Øy / *Dan.; Nor.*	island
oz., Ozero / *Rus.*	lake
Ozek / *Alt.*	hollow
Ozera / *Rus.*	lakes
Ozero, oz. / *Rus.*	lake

P

Local Form	English
P., Pulau / *Mal.; Indon.*	island
Pää / *Finn.*	principal
Pad / *Rus.*	valley
Padang / *Indon.*	plain
Padiş / *Rom.*	upland
Padół / *Pol.*	valley
Pădure / *Rom.*	forest
Pahorek / *Cz.*	hill
Pahorkatina / *Cz.*	plateau, hills
Pais / *Port.; Sp.*	land, country
Pak / *Thai*	mouth
Pala / *It.*	peak
Palaiós / *Gr.*	old
Palanka / *S.C.*	village
Pali / *Poly.*	cliff
-palli / *Hin.*	village
Pampa / *Sp.*	plain, prairie
Panda / *Swa.*	junction
Panev / *Cz.*	basin
Pantanal / *Sp.*	swamp
Pantano / *Sp.*	swamp, lake
Pao / *Mel.*	hill
Pará / *A.I.*	river
Paramera / *Sp.*	desert highland
Páramo / *Sp.*	moor
Paraná / *A.I.*	river
Parbat / *Hin.; Urdu*	mountain
Parc / *Fr.*	park
Parco / *It.*	park
Parco Nazionale / *It.*	national park
Pardo / *Port.*	grey
Parque / *Sp.*	park
Parque Nacional / *Sp.; Port.*	national park
Pas / *Fr.; Rom.*	pass, strait
Pasaje / *Sp.*	passage
Pasir / *Mal.*	sand, beach
Paso / *Sp.*	pass
Passágem / *Port.*	passage
Passe / *Fr.*	pass
Passo / *It.; Port.*	pass
Pasul / *Rom.*	pass
Patak / *Hung.*	stream
Patam, -patam / *Hin.*	city, town
Patnā / *Hin.*	city, town
Patnam, -patnam / *Hin.*	city, town
Pattinam, -pattinam / *Hin.*	city, town
Pays / *Fr.*	land, country
Pazar / *Tur.*	market
Pea / *Est.*	cape
Pech / *Cat.*	hill
Pedhiás / *Gr.*	plain
Pedra / *Port.*	rock, mountain
Peg., Pegunungan / *Mal.; Indon.*	mountain range
Pegunungan, Peg. / *Mal.; Indon.*	mountain range
Pélagos / *Gr.*	sea
Pele / *Poly.*	peak, hill
Pen / *Br.*	principal
Pen / *Br.; Gae.*	cape, mountain
Peña / *Sp.*	peak
Pendi / *Chin.*	basin
Pendiente / *Sp.*	slope
Penha / *Port.*	peak
Península / *Port.; Sp.*	peninsula
Péninsule / *Fr.*	peninsula
Penisola / *It.*	peninsula
Peñon / *Sp.*	rock, island
Pente / *Fr.*	slope
Perekop / *Rus.*	channel
Pereval / *Rus.*	pass
Perevoz / *Rus.*	ford
Pertuis / *Fr.*	strait
Peščara / *S.C.*	sandy soil
Peski / *Rus.*	sand desert
Petit / *Fr.*	little
Pétra / *Gr.*	rock
Phanom / *Thai; Khm.*	mountain range, mountain
Phau / *Laot.*	mountain
Phnum / *Khm.*	hill, mountain
Phu / *Viet.*	mountain, hill
Phum / *Thai*	forest
Phumĭ / *Khm.*	village
Pi / *Chin.*	cape
Piana, Pianura / *It.*	plain
Piano / *It.*	plain
Piatră / *Rom.*	stone
Pic / *Cat.; Fr.*	peak
Picacho / *Sp.*	peak
Piccolo / *It.*	little
Pico / *Port.; Sp.*	peak
Piedra / *Sp.*	rock, cliff
Pietra / *It.*	stone
Pieve / *It.*	parish
Pik / *Rus.*	peak
Pils / *Latv.*	city, town
Pinar / *Sp.*	pine forest
Pingyuan / *Chin.*	plain
Pioda / *It.*	crest
Pirgos / *Gr.*	tower, peak
Pīsh / *Pers.*	anterior, before
Pitkä / *Finn.*	great
Piton / *Fr.*	mountain, peak
Piz / *Rmsh.*	peak
Pizzo / *It.*	peak
Pjasăci / *Bulg.*	beach
Plaat / *Fle.; Dut.*	sandbank
Plage / *Fr.*	beach
Plaine / *Fr.*	plain
Plan / *Fr.*	plain
Planalto / *Port.*	plateau
Planina / *Bulg.*	mountain
Plano / *Sp.*	plain
Plas / *Dut.; Fle.*	lake, marsh
Plato / *Bulg.; Rus.*	plateau
Platosu / *Tur.*	plateau
Platte / *Germ.*	plain, plateau
Plav / *S.C.*	blue
Plavnja / *Rus.*	marsh
Playa / *Sp.*	beach
Ploskogorje / *Rus.*	plateau
Plou / *Br.*	church
Po / *Kor.*	port
Po / *Chin.*	lake, white
P'o / *Kor.*	bay, lake
Poa / *Mel.*	hill
Poarta / *Rom.*	pass
Poartă / *Rom.*	gate
Pobla / *Cat.*	village
Pobrzeże / *Pol.*	littoral, coast
Poço / *Port.*	well
Poço / *Port.*	point
Pod / *Cz.; Pol.; Rus.; S.C.; Slvn.*	bridge
Podkamenny / *Rus.*	stony
Poggio / *It.*	hill
Pohja / *Finn.*	north, northern
Pohjois- / *Finn.*	north
Pojezierze / *Pol.*	lake region
Pol / *Pers.*	bridge
Pol, -pol / *Rus.*	city, town
Pola / *Port.; Sp.*	village
Polder / *Fle.; Dut.*	reclaimed land
Pole / *Pol.*	field
Pólis / *Gr.*	city, town
Poljana / *Bulg.; Rus.; S.C.; Slvn.*	field, terrace
Poljarny / *Rus.*	polar
Polje / *S.C.; Slvn.*	valley, field, basin
Poluostrov / *Rus.*	peninsula
Pomorije / *Bulg.*	littoral
Pomorze / *Pol.*	littoral
Ponente / *It.*	western
Pont / *Cat.; Fr.*	bridge
Ponta / *Port.*	point
Ponte / *It.; Port.*	bridge
Póntos / *Gr.*	sea
Poort / *Afr.; Fle.; Dut.*	pass
Pore, -pore / *Hin.; Urdu*	city, town
Porog / *Rus.*	rapids
Porte / *Fr.*	gate
Portile / *Rom.*	gorge
Portillo / *Sp.*	pass
Portiţa / *Rom.*	small gate
Porto / *It.*	port
Pôrto / *Port.*	port
Posht / *Pers.*	back, posterior
Potjo / *Indon.*	peak
Potok / *Bulg.; Cz.; Pol.; Rus.; S.C.; Slvn.*	stream
Póvoa / *Port.*	village
Pozo / *Sp.*	well
Pozzo / *It.*	well
Pradesh / *Hin.*	region, state
Prado / *Sp.*	meadow
Praia / *Port.*	beach
Prato / *It.*	meadow
Pré / *Fr.*	meadow
Prealpi / *It.*	prealps
Presa / *Sp.*	reservoir
Presqu'île / *Fr.*	peninsula
Prêto / *Port.*	black
Priehradní nádrž / *Cz.*	reservoir
Pripoljarny / *Rus.*	subpolar
Pristan / *Rus.*	port
Prohod / *Bulg.*	pass
Proliv / *Rus.*	strait
Promontoire / *Fr.*	promontory
Průchod / *Cz.*	pass
Przedgorze / *Pol.*	front range (mountains)
Przełęcz / *Pol.*	pass
Przemysł / *Pol.*	industry
Przylądek / *Pol.*	cape
Pua / *Mel.*	hill
Puebla / *Sp.*	village
Puente / *Sp.*	bridge
Puerto / *Sp.*	port, pass
Puig / *Cat.*	peak
Puits / *Fr.*	well
Pul / *Pash.*	bridge
Pulau, P. / *Mal.; Indon.*	island
Pulau Pulau / *Mal.*	islands
Pulo / *Mal.; Indon.*	island
Puna / *A.I.*	upland
Puncak / *Indon.*	mountain
Punjung / *Mal.; Indon.*	mountain
Punt / *Afr.*	point
Punta / *It.; Sp.*	point
Pur, -pur / *Hin.; Urdu*	city, town
-pura / *Hin.; Urdu*	city, town
Pura / *Indon.*	city, town, temple
Puri, -puri / *Hin.; Urdu*	city, town
Pus / *Alb.*	spring
Pušča / *Rus.*	forest
Pustynja / *Rus.*	desert
Puszcza / *Pol.*	heath
Puszta / *Hung.*	lowland
Put / *Afr.*	well
Put / *Rus.; S.C.*	road
Putra, -putra / *Hin.*	son
Puu / *Poly.*	mountain, volcano
Puy / *Fr.*	peak
Pwell / *Wel.*	pond
Pyeong / *Kor.*	plain
Pyhä / *Finn.*	saint

Q

Local Form	English
Qagan / *Mong.*	white
Qala / *Pash.*	fortified town
Qal'at / *Ar.*	castle
Qalb / *Ar.*	hill
Qalīb / *Ar.*	spring
Qalīq / *Ar.*	spring
Qanāt / *Ar.*	canal
Qantara / *Ar.*	bridge
Qaqortoq / *Esk.*	white
Qar / *Som.*	mountain
Qara / *Pers.*	black
Qarah / *Tur.*	black
Qārat / *Ar.*	height, mountain
Qāret / *Ar.*	village, hill
Qaryah / *Ar.*	village
Qaryat / *Ar.*	village
Qaṣr / *Ar.*	castle
Qawz / *Ar.*	dunes
Qeqertarssuaq / *Esk.*	peninsula
Qezel / *Tur.*	red
Qi / *Chin.*	river
Qing / *Chin.*	blue, green
Qiryat / *Hebr.*	city, town
Qolleh / *Pers.*	mountain, peak
Qu / *Chin.*	river, canal
Quan dao / *Viet.*	islands
Quebracho / *Sp.*	stream
Quebrada / *Sp.*	gorge, stream
Quedas / *Port.*	waterfalls
Qulbān / *Ar.*	well
Qundao / *Chin.*	archipelago
Qūr / *Ar.*	height, hill
Qytet / *Alb.*	city, town
Qyteti / *Alb.*	city, town

R

Local Form	English
R., Rio, River / *Eng.; Sp.*	river
Rada / *It.; Sp.*	anchorage
Rade / *Fr.*	anchorage
Rags / *Latv.*	cape
Rahad / *Ar.*	lake, pond
Rajon / *Rus.*	district
Rak / *Fle.; Dut.*	strait
Rakai / *Poly.*	reef
Ramla / *Ar.*	sand
Rancho / *Port.; Sp.*	farm, ranch
Rand / *Afr.; Germ.*	escarpment
Range / *Eng.*	mountain range
Rann / *Urdu*	marsh
Rano / *Malag.*	water
Ranta / *Finn.*	bank, beach
Rapide / *Fr.*	rapids
Ras / *Amh.*	peak
Rās / *Ar.*	point, cape

Local Form	English
Ras, Rås / Ar.	promontory, peak
Råsiga / Som.	promontory
Rass / Ar.	promontory, peak
Rassa / Lapp.	mountain
Råth / Gae.	castle
Raunina / Bulg.; Rus.	plain
Raz / Fr.	strait
Razliv / Rus.	flood plain
Récif / Fr.	reef
Recife / Port.	reef
Reede / Germ.; Dut.; Slvn.	anchorage
Reek / Afr.; Gae.	mountain range
Reg / Pash.	dunes
Région / Fr.	region
Rei / Port.	king
Reka / Bulg.; Rus.; S.C.; Slvn.	river
Řeka / Cz.	river
Réma / Gr.	torrent
Renne / Dan.; Nor.	deep
Reprêsa / Port.	dam, reservoir
Represa / Sp.	dam, reservoir
República / Port.; Sp.	republic
République / Fr.	republic
Rés., Réservoir / Fr.	reservoir
Res., Reservoir / Fr.	reservoir
Réservoir, Rés. / Fr.	reservoir
Reshteh / Pers.	mountain range
Respublika / Rus.	republic
Restinga / Port.	cliff, sandbank
Retsugan / Jap.	reef
Rettō / Jap.	archipelago
Rev / Dan.; Nor.; Swed.	reef
Rey / Sp.	king
Ri / Tib.	mountain
Ria / Sp.	estuary
Riacho / Port.	stream
Rialto / It.	plateau
Rialto / It.	rise
Riba / Port.	bank
Ribeira / Port.	river
Ribeirão / Port.	stream
Ribeiro / Port.	stream
Ribera / Sp.	coast
Ribnik / Slvn.	pond
Rid / Bulg.	mountain range
Rif / Icel.	cliff
Riff / Germ.	reef
Rīg / Pash.	dunes
Rijeka / S.C.	river
Rimāl / Ar.	sand desert
Rincón / Sp.	peninsula between two rivers
Ring / Tib.	long
Rinne / Germ.	trench
Rio / Port.	river
Rio, R. / Sp.	river
Riu / Rom.	river
Riva / It.	bank
Rive / Fr.	bank
Rivera / Sp.	brook, stream
Rivier, -rivier / Afr.; Dut.; Fle.	river
Riviera / It.	coast
Rivière / Fr.	river
Roads / Eng.	anchorage
Roc / Fr.	rock
Roca / Port.; Sp.	rock
Rocca / It.	castle
Roche / Fr.	rock
Rocher / Fr.	rock
Rock / Eng.	rock
Rod / Pash.	river
Rode / Germ.	tilled soil
Rodnik / Rus.	spring
Rog / Rus.; S.C.; Slvn.	peak
Roi / Fr.	king
Rojo / Sp.	red
Roque / Sp.	rock
Rot / Germ.	red
Roto / Poly.	lake
Rouge / Fr.	red
Równina / Pol.	plain
Rt / S.C.; Slvn.	cape
Ru / Tib.	mountain
Ruck / Germ.	ridge
Rücken / Germ.	ridge
Rud / Pers.	river
Ruda / Cz.; Slvk.	mine
Ruda / Pol.	ore
Rūdbār / Pers.	river
Rudha / Gae.	point
Rudnik / Rus.; S.C.; Slvn.	mine
Rug / Fle.; Dut.	ridge
Ruggen / Afr.	ridge
Ruina / Sp.	ruins
Ruine / Fr.; Dut.; Germ.	ruins
Rujm / Ar.	hill
Run / Eng.	stream

S

Local Form	English
S., See / Germ.	lake, sea
Saar / Est.	island

Local Form	English
Saari / Finn.	island
Sabbia / It.	sand
Sabkhat / Ar.	salt flat, salt marsh
Sable / Fr.; Eng.	beach
Sacca / It.	anchorage
Saco / Port.	bay
Sad / Cz.; Slvk.	park
Sad / Pers.	wall
Sadd / Ar.; Pers.	cataract, dam
Safid / Pash.; Urdu; Hin.	white
Şafrā' / Ar.	desert
Sāgar / Hin.	reservoir
Saguia / Ar.	irrigation canal
Sahara / Ar.	desert
Sahel / Ar.	plain, coast
Sahr / Iran.	city, town
Şaḥrā' / Ar.	desert
Said / Ar.	sweet
Saj / Alt.	stream, valley
Saki / Jap.	point
Sala / Latv.; Lith.	island
Saladillo / Sp.	salt desert
Salar / Sp.	salt lake
Sale / Ural.	village
Salina / It.; Sp.	salt flat, salt marsh
Saline / Dut.; Fr.; Germ.	salt flat, salt marsh
Salmi / Finn.	strait
Salseleh-ye Küh / Pers.	mountain range
Salto / Port.; Sp.	waterfall, rapids
Salz / Germ.	salt
Samudera / Indon.	ocean
Samudra / Hin.	lake
Samut / Thai	sea
San / Jap.; Kor.	mountain
San / It.; Sp.	saint
Sanchi / Jap.	mountain range
Sand / Dan.; Eng.; Nor.; Swed.; Germ.	beach
Šand / Mong.	spring
Sandur / Icel.	sand
Sank / Pers.	rock
Sankt, St. / Germ.; Swed.	saint
Sanmaeg / Kor.	mountain range
Sanmyaku / Jap.	mountain range
Sansanné / Sud.	campsite
Santo / It.; Port.; Sp.	saint
Santuario / It.	sanctuary
São / Port.	saint
Sar / Pers.	cape; peak
Šar / Rus.; Tur.	strait
Saraf / Ar.	well
Sari / Finn.	island
Sari / Tur.	yellow
Sarīr / Ar.	rocky desert
Sary / Tur.	yellow
Sasso / It.	stone
Sat / Rom.	village
Sattel / Germ.	pass
Saurum / Latv.	strait
Schleuse / Germ.	lock
Schloß / Germ.	castle
Schlucht / Germ.	gorge
Schnee / Germ.	snow
Schwarz / Germ.	black
Scoglio / It.	cliff
Se / Jap.	bank, shoal
Sebkha / Ar.	salt flat
Sebkhet / Ar.	salt flat
Sed / Ar.	dam
Seda / Ural.	mountain
See, S. / Germ.	lake, sea
Sefra / Ar.	yellow
Segara / Indon.	lagoon
Şehir / Tur.	city, town
Seki / Jap.	dam
Selat / Mal.; Indon.	strait
Selatan / Indon.	southern
Selkä / Finn.	ridge, lake
Sella / It.	pass
Selo / Bulg.; Rus.; S.C.; Slvn.	village
Selsela Kohe / Pers.	mountain range
Selva / It.; Sp.	forest
Semenanjung / Mal.	peninsula
Sen / Jap.	mountain
Seong / Kor.	castle
Sep / Alt.	canal
Serīr / Ar.	rocky desert
Serra / Cat.; Port.	mountain range
Serra / It.	mountain
Serranía / Sp.	mountain range
Sertão / Port.	steppe
Seto / Jap.	strait
Sett., Settentrionale / It.	northern
Settentrionale, Sett. / It.	northern
Seuil / Fr.	sill
Sev / Arm.	black
Sever / Rus.	north
Severny / Rus.	northern
Sfint / Rom.	saint
Sfîntu / Rom.	saint
Sgeir / Gae.	cliff
Sha'b / Ar.	cliff
Shahr / Pers.; Hin.	city, town
Sha'īb / Ar.	stream
Shallāl / Ar.	cataract

Local Form	English
Shām / Ar.	north; northern
Shamo / Chin.	sand desert
Shan / Chin.	mountain, mountain range
Shan / Gae.	old
Shand / Mong.	spring
Shankou / Chin.	pass
Shaqq / Ar.	wadi
Sharm / Ar.	bay
Sharqī / Ar.	east, eastern
Sharqīyah / Ar.	eastern
Shatt / Ar.	river, salt lake
Shatt / Tur.	stream
Shën / Alb.	saint
Sheng / Chin.	province
Shi / Chin.	city, town
Shibīn / Ar.	village
Shih / Chin.	rock
Shima / Jap.	island
Shimo / Jap.	lower
Shin / Jap.	new
Shō / Jap.	island
Shotō / Jap.	archipelago
Shū / Jap.	administrative division
Shui / Chin.	river
Shuiku / Chin.	reservoir
Shur / Pers.	salt
Sidhiros / Gr.	iron
Sidi / Ar.	master
Sieben / Germ.	seven
Sierra / Sp.	mountain range
Sikt / Ural.	village
Sillon / Fr.	furrow
Šine / Mong.	new
Sink / Eng.	depression
Sinn / Ar.	point
Sint / Dut.; Fle.	saint
Sirt / Tur.	mountain range
Sirtlar / Tur.	mountain range
Sistema / It.; Sp.	mountain system
Sīyāh / Pers.	black
Sjø / Nor.	lake
Sjö / Swed.	lake, sea
Skag / Icel.	peninsula
Skala / Bulg.; Rus.	rock
Skála / Slvk.	rock
Skar / Nor.	pass
Skär / Swed.	cliff
Skeir / Gae.	cliff
Skerry / Gae.	cliff
Skog / Nor.; Swed.	forest
Skóg / Icel.	forest
Skov / Dan.; Nor.	forest
Slatina / S.C.; Slvn.	mineral water
Slätt / Swed.	plain
Slieve / Gae.	mountain
Slot / Dut.; Fle.	castle
Slott / Nor.; Swed.	castle
Slough / Eng.	creek, pond, marsh
Sluis / Dut.; Fle.	sluice
Små / Swed.	little
Sne / Nor.	snow
Sneeuw / Afr.; Dut.	snow
Snežny / Rus.	snowy
Snø / Nor.	snow
So / Kor.	little
Sø / Dan.; Nor.	lake; sea
So / Ural.	passage
Söder / Swed.	south
Södra / Swed.	southern
Solončak / Rus.	salt flat
Sommet / Fr.	peak
Son / Viet.	mountain
Sønder / Dan.; Nor.	southern
Søndre / Dan.	southern
Sone / Jap.	bank
Song / Viet.	river
Sopka / Rus.	volcano
Sopočnik / Rus.	mountain system
Soprana / It.	upper
Šor, Sor / Alt.	salt marsh
Sos / Rus.	upon
Sotavento / Sp.	leeward
Sotoviento / Sp.	leeward
Sottana / It.	lower
Souk / Ar.	market
Souq / Ar.	market
Sour / Ar.	rampart
Source / Eng.; Fr.	spring
Souto / Port.	forest
Spitze / Germ.	peak
Spruit / Afr.	current
Sreden / Bulg.	central
Sredni / Rus.	central
Średni / Pol.	central
Srednji / S.C.; Slvn.	central
St., Saint, Sankt / Eng.; Fr.; Germ.; Swed.	saint
Stadhur / Icel.	city, town
Stadt, -stadt / Germ.	city, town
Stag / Eng.	city, town
Stagno / It.	pond
-stan / Hin.; Pers.; Urdu	land
Star / Bulg.	old
Stari / S.C.; Slvn.	old

Local Form	English
Stary / Pol.; Rus.	old
Starý / Cz.; Slvk.	old
Stat / Afr.; Dan.; Fle.; Nor.; Dut.; Swed.	city, town
Stathmós / Gr.	railway station
Stausee / Germ.	reservoir
Stavrós / Gr.	cross
Sted / Dan.; Nor.	place
Stedt / Germ.	place
Stein, -stein / Nor.; Germ.	stone
Sten / Nor.; Swed.	stone
Stena / S.C.; Slvn.	rock
Stěna / Cz.	mountain range
Stenón / Gr.	strait, pass
Step / Rus.	steppe
-sthān / Hin.; Pers.; Urdu	land
Stift / Germ.	foundation
Štít / Cz.; Slvk.	peak
Stock / Germ.	massif
Stok / Pol.	slope
Stor / Dan.; Nor.; Swed.	great
Store / Dan.	great
Stræde / Dan.	strait
Strana / Rus.	land
Strand / Germ.; Nor.; Swed.; Afr.; Dan.	beach
Straße / Germ.	street, road
Strath / Gae.	valley
Straum / Nor.; Swed.	stream
Středni / Cz.	central
Středný / Slvk.	central
Strelka / Rus.	spit
Stret / Nor.	strait
Stretto / It.	strait
Strom / Germ.	stream
Strøm / Nor.	stream
Ström / Swed.	stream
Stroom / Dut.	stream
Su / Jap.	sandbank
Su / Tur.	river
Suando / Finn.	pond
Suid / Afr.	south
Suidō / Jap.	strait
Sul / Port.	south
Sund / Dan.; Nor.; Swed.; Germ.	strait
Sungai / Mal.	river
Sunn / Nor.	south
Sūq / Ar.	market
Sur / Fr.	on
Sur / Sp.	south
Surkh / Pers.	red
Suu / Finn.	mouth, river mouth
Suur / Cat.	great
Svart / Nor.; Swed.	black
Sveti / S.C.; Slvn.	saint
Swa / Ban.	great
Swart / Afr.	black
Święty / Pol.	saint
Syrt / Alt.	ridge
Szállás / Hung.	village
Szczyt / Pol.	peak
Szeg / Hung.	bend
Székes / Hung.	residence
Szent / Hung.	saint
Sziget / Hung.	river island

T

Local Form	English
Tadi / Ban.	rock, cliff
Tae / Kor.	great
Tafua / Poly.	mountain
Tag / Alt.; Tur.	mountain
Tahta / Ar.	lower
Tahti / Ar.	lower
Tai / Chin.; Jap.	great
Taipale / Finn.	isthmus
Tajga / Rus.	forest
Take / Jap.	mountain
Tal / Germ.	valley
Tala / Mong.	plain, steppe
Tala / Ber.	spring
Tall / Ar.	hill
Talsperre / Germ.	dam
Tam / Viet.	stream
Tamgout / Ber.	peak
Tan / Chin.; Kor.	sandbank
Tana / Malag.	city, town
Tanana / Malag.	city, town
Tandjung / Mal.	cape, point
Tanezrouft / Ber.	desert
Tang / Tib.	upland
Tangeh / Pers.	strait
Tanjong / Mal.	cape, point
Tanjung, Tg. / Indon.	cape, point
Tanout / Ber.	well
Tao / Chin.	island
Taourirt / Ber.	peak
Targ / Pol.	market
Tärg / Bulg.	market
Tarn / Eng.	glacial lake
Tarso / Sah.	crater
Taš / Alt.	stone

Geographical Glossary

Local Form	English	Local Form	English	Local Form	English	Local Form	English
Tassili / Ber.	upland	Uebi / Som.	river	Vidda / Nor.	upland	Woḍa / Pol.	water
Tau / Tur.	mountain	Új- / Hung.	new	Vidde / Nor.	upland	Woestyn / Afr.	desert
Taung / Burm.	mountain	Ujście / Pol.	mouth	Viejo / Sp.	old	Wold / Dut.; Fle.; Eng.	forest
Ṭawïl / Ar.	hill	Ujung / Indon.	point, cape	Vier / Germ.	four	Wörth / Germ.	river island
Tégi / Sah.	hill	Ul / Chin.; Mong.	mountain, mountain range	Viertel / Germ.	quarter	Woud / Dut.; Fle.	forest
Teguidda / Ber.	well			Vieux / Fr.	old	Wschodni / Pol.	eastern
Tehi / Ber.	pass, mountain	Ula / Mong.	mountain range	Vig / Dan.	bay	Wysoczyzna / Pol.	upland
Teich / Germ.	pond	Ulan / Mong.	red	Vík / Icel.; Nor.; Swed.	gulf, bay	Wysoki / Pol.	upper
Tell / Tur.	hill	Uls / Mong.	state	Vila / Port.	city, town	Wyspa / Pol.	island
Telok / Mal.	bay, port	Umi / Jap.	bay	Villa / Sp.	city, town	Wyżyna / Pol.	highland
Teluk / Mal.	bay, port	Umm / Ar.	mother, spring	Ville, -ville / Eng.; Fr.	city, town	Wzgórze / Pol.	hill
Tempio / It.	temple	Umne / Mong.	south	Vinh / Viet.	bay		
Ténéré / Ber.	rocky desert	Under / Mong.	mountain, peak	Virful / Rom.	peak, mountain		
Tengah / Indon.; Mal.	central					**X**	
Tepe / Tur.	hill	Ungur / Alt.	cave	Virta / Finn.	river		
Tepesi / Tur.	hill	Unter-, U. / Germ.	under, lower	Višni / Rus.	high	Xi / Chin.	west
Termas / Sp.	thermal springs	Upar / Hin.	river	Visok / S.C.	high	Xia / Chin.	gorge, strait
Terme / It.	thermal springs	'Uqlat / Ar.	well	Viz / Hung.	water	Xian / Chin.	county, shire
Terra / It.; Dut.	land, earth	Ür / Tam.	city, town	Viztároló / Hung.	reservoir	Xiang / Chin.	village
Terrazzo / It.	guyot, tablemount	Ura / Jap.	bay, coast	Vlakte / Dut.; Fle.	plain	Xiao / Chin.	little
		Ura / Alt.	depression	Vlei / Afr.	pond	Xin / Chin.	new
Terre / Fr.	land, earth	Urd / Mong.	south	Vliet / Dut.; Fle.	river	Xu / Chin.	island
Teso / Cat.	hill	Uru / Tam.	city, town	Vloer / Afr.	depression		
Téssa / Ber.	wadi, depression	Ušće / S.C.	mouth	Voda / Bulg.; Cz.; Rus.; S.C.; Slvn.	water		
Testa / It.	point	Uske / Alt.	upper			**Y**	
Tête / Fr.	peak	Ust / Rus.	mouth	Vodny put / Rus.	stream, canal		
Tetri / Georg.	white	Ústí / Cz.	mouth	Vodohranilišče, vdhr. / Rus.	reservoir	Yam / Hebr.	lake, sea
Teu / Poly.	reef	Ustup / Rus.	terrace			Yama / Jap.	mountain
Teze / Alt.	new	Utan / Indon.; Mal.	forest	Vodopad / Rus.	waterfall	Yan / Chin.	mountain
Tg., Tanjung / Indon.	cape, point	Utara / Indon.	north, northern	Volcan / Fr.	volcano	Yang / Chin.	strait, ocean
Thaba / Ban.	mountain			Volcán / Sp.	volcano	Yani / Tur.	new
Thabana / Ban.	mountain	Uusi / Finn.	new	Voll / Nor.	meadow	Yar / Tur.	gorge
Thal / Germ.	valley	Uval / Rus.	height	Vórios / Gr.	northern	Yarimada / Tur.	peninsula
Thálassa / Gr.	sea	Úval / Cz.	mountain	Vorota / Rus.	gate	Yazı / Tur.	plain
Thale / Thai	lagoon	'Uwaynāt / Ar.	well	Vorrás / Gr.	north	Yegge / Sah.	well
Thamad / Ar.	well	Uzboj / Alt.	river bed	Vostočny / Rus.	eastern	Yeni / Tur.	new
Theós / Gr.	god	Uzun / Tur.	long	Vostok / Rus.	east	Yeon / Kor.	sea
Thermes / Fr.	thermal springs	Užürekis / Lith.	gulf	Vötn / Icel.	lake, water	Yeong / Kor.	mountain
Thog / Tib.	high, upper			Vož / Ural.	mouth	Yeşil / Tur.	green
Tian / Chin.	field			Vozvyšennost / Rus.	upland	Ylä / Finn.	upper
Tiefe / Germ.	deep	**V**		Vpadina / Rus.	depression	Yli- / Finn.	upper
Tierra / Sp.	land, earth			Vrah / Bulg.	peak	Yō / Jap.	ocean
Timur / Indon.; Mal.	eastern	Va / Alb.	ford	Vrata / Bulg.; S.C.; Slvn.	pass	Yobe / Sud.	great
Tind / Nor.	mountain	Va / Ural.	water, river	Vrch / Cz.; Slvk.	mountain	Yŏm / Kor.	island
Tinto / Sp.	black	Vaara / Finn.	mountain	Vrch / S.C.; Slvn.	peak	Yoma / Burm.	mountain range
Tirg / Rom.	market	Väärti / Finn.	bay	Vrchni / Cz.	upper	Yŏn / Kor.	lake, pond
Tis / Amh.	new	Vad / Rom.	ford	Vrchovina / Cz.	upland	Yŏng / Kor.	mountain, peak
Tizgui / Ber.	forest	Vær / Nor.	port	Vulcan / Rom.; Rus.	volcano	Ytter / Nor.; Swed.	outer
Tizi / Ber.	pass	Våg / Nor.	bay	Vulcano / It.	volcano	Yttre / Swed.	outer
Tjåkko / Lapp.	mountain	Vähä / Finn.	little	Vulkan / Germ.; Rus.	volcano	Yu / Chin.	old
Tjärn / Swed.	tarn, glacial lake	Väike / Est.	little	Vuopio / Lapp.	bend	Yu / Chin.	island
		Väin / Est.	strait	Vuori / Finn.	rock	Yu / Jap.	thermal spring
Tji / Mal.	stream	Val / Fr.; It.	valley	Východný / Cz.	eastern	Yüan / Chin.	spring, river
To / Kor.	island	Val / Rom.; Rus.	wall	Vyšný / Slvk.	upper	Yunhe / Chin.	canal
To / Mel.	stream	Valico / It.	pass	Vysoki / Rus.	high		
Tō / Jap.	island	Vall / Cat.	valley	Vysoky / Cz.; Slvk.	high		
Tó / Hung.	lake	Vall / Swed.	pasture	Vyšši / Cz.	high	**Z**	
To / Ural.	lake	Valle / It.; Sp.	valley				
Tobe / Tur.	hill	Vallée / Fr.	valley			Zāb / Ar.	river
Tofua / Poly.	mountain	Vallei / Afr.	valley	**W**		Zachodni / Pol.	western
Tog / Som.	valley	Vallo / It.	wall			Zaki / Jap.	cape
Tōge / Jap.	pass	Valta / Finn.	cape	W., Wādī / Ar.	wadi	Zalew / Pol.	gulf
Tokoj / Alt.	forest	Váltos / Gr.	marsh	Wa / Ban.	people	Zaliv / Bulg.; Rus.; S.C.; Slvn.	gulf
Tônle / Khm.	stream, lake	Valul / Rom.	wall	Wabe / Amh.	stream		
Tope / Dut.	peak	Vann / Dan.; Nor.	water, lake	Wad / Ar.	wadi	Zaljev / Slvn.	bay
Toplice / S.C.; Slvn.	thermal springs	Vanua / Mel.	land	Wad / Dut.	tidal flat	Zámek / Cz.	castle
Topp / Nor.	peak	Vár / Hung.	fort	Wādī, W. / Ar.	wadi	Zan / Jap.	mountain
Tor / Gae.	rock	Vara / Finn.	mountain	Wāḥāt / Ar.	oasis	Zand / Dut.; Fle.	sand
Tor / Germ.	gate	Varoš / S.C.	city, town	Wai / Mel.; Poly.	stream	Zandt / Dut.; Fle.	sand
Torbat / Pers.	tomb	Város / Hung.	city, town	Wal / Afr.	wall	Zangbo / Chin.	river
Törl / Germ.	pass	Varre / Lapp.	mountain	Wala / Hin.	mountain range	Zapad / Rus.	west
Torp / Swed.	hut	Vary / Cz.	spring	Wald / Germ.	forest	Zapaden / Bulg.	western
Torre / Cat.; It.; Sp.; Port.	tower	Vas / S.C.; Slvn.	village	Wan / Burm.	village	Zapadni / S.C.; Slvn.	western
Torrente / It.; Sp.	torrent, stream	Vásár / Hung.	market	Wan / Chin.; Jap.	bay	Západní / Cz.	western
		Väst / Swed.	west	Wand / Germ.	bluff	Zapadny / Rus.	western
Tossa / Cat.	mountain, peak	Väster / Swed.	western	War / Som.	pond	Zapovednik / Rus.	reserve
Tota / Sin.	port	Vatn / Icel.; Nor.	lake	Wâr / Ar.	desert	Zatoka / Pol.	gulf
Tour / Fr.	tower	Vatten / Swed.	water, lake	-waram / Hin.; Tam.	village	Zavod / Rus.	roadstead
Traforo / It.	tunnel	Vatu / Mel.; Poly.	island, reef	Wasser / Germ.	water	Zāwiyat / Ar.	monastery
Träsk / Swed.	lake	Vdhr., Vodohranilišče / Rus.	reservoir	Wat / Pol.	wall	Zdrój / Pol.	thermal springs
Trg / S.C.	market			Wat / Thai	church	Ze / Jap.	islet
Trog / Germ.	trough, trench	Vechiu / Rom.	old	Waterval / Afr.; Dut.	waterfall	Zee / Dut.; Fle.	sea
Trois / Fr.	three	Vecs / Latv.	old	Watt / Germ.	tidal flat	Zelëny / Rus.	green
Trung / Viet.	central	Veen / Dut.; Fle.	moor	Wāw / Ar.	oasis	Žem / Lith.	land, country
Tse / Tib.	peak, point	Vega / Sp.	irrigated crops	Weald / Eng.	wooded country	Zemé / Cz.; Slvk.	land, country
Tsi / Chin.	pond	Veld / Afr.; Dut.; Fle.	field	Webi / Som.	stream	Zemlja / Rus.	land
Tskali / Georg.	river	Veli / S.C.; Slvn.	great	Weg / Germ.	way, road	Zen / Jap.	mountain
Tsu / Jap.	bay	Velik / Bulg.	great	Wei / Chin.	cape, point	Zhan / Chin.	mountain
Tulül / Ar.	hills	Veliki / Rus.; S.C.; Slvn.	great	Weide / Germ.	pasture	Zhen / Chin.	market
Tünel / Pers.	tunnel	Veliký / Cz.	great	Weiler / Germ.	village	Zhong / Chin.	central
Tunturi / Lapp.	mountain, tundra	Vel'ky / Slvk.	great	Weiß / Germ.	white	Zhou / Chin.	quarter, district
		Vella / Cat.	old	Weon / Kor.	field		
Tur'ah / Ar.	irrigation canal	Ver / Ural.	forest	Wer / Som.	pond	Zhuang / Chin.	village
Turm / Germ.	tower	Verde / It.; Sp.	green	Werder / Germ.	river island	Ziemia / Pol.	land
Turn / Rom.	tower	Verh / Rus.	peak	Werk / Germ.	factory	Zigos / Gr.	pass
Turó / Cat.	dome	Verhni / Rus.	upper	Wes / Afr.	west	Zipfel / Germ.	tip, point
Tuz / Tur.	salt	Verk / Swed.	factory	Westlich / Germ.	western	Ziwa / Swa.	marsh
Týn / Cz.	fortress	Vermelho / Port.	red	Westr- / Sca.	western	Zizhiqu / Chin.	autonomous region
		Vert / Fr.	green	Wēyn / Som.	great		
		Ves / Cz.	village	Wēyne / Som.	great	Zlato / Bulg.	gold
U		Vesi / Finn.	water, lake	Wick / Eng.	village	Zuid / Dut.; Fle.	south
		Vest / Dan.; Nor.	west	Wiek / Germ.	bay	Zuidelijk / Dut.	southern
U., Unter-, Upon / Eng.; Germ.	under, lower	Vester / Dan.; Nor.	western	Wielki / Pol.	great	Żuława / Pol.	marsh
		Vestur / Icel.	west	Wieś / Pol.	village	Zun / Mong.	east
Uaimh / Gae.	cave	Vetta / It.	summit	Wijk / Dut.; Fle.	quarter, district	Zwart / Dut.	black
Uchi / Jap.	bay	Viaduc / Fr.	viaduct			Zwei / Germ.	two
Udde / Swed.	cape			-willer / Germ.	village		
Údolní nádrž / Cz.	reservoir						

International Map Index

All of the toponyms (place-names) which appear on the maps are listed in the International Map Index. Each entry includes the following: Place-name and, where applicable, other forms by which it is written or known; a symbol, where applicable, indicating what kind of feature it is; the number of the map on which it appears; and the map-reference letters and geographical coordinates indicating its location on the map.

Toponyms

Each toponym, or place-name, is written in full, with accents and diacritical marks. Since many countries have more than one official language, many of these forms are included on the maps. For example, many Belgian place-names are listed as follows: Bruxelles/Brussel; Antwerpen/Anvers, and vice versa, Brussel/Bruxelles; Anvers/Antwerpen. In Italy, certain regions have a special status—they are largely autonomous and officially bilingual. As a result, Index listings appear as follows: Aosta/Aoste; Alto Adige/Sud Tirol, and vice versa. One name, however, may be the only name on the map.

In China, the written forms of commonly used regional languages have been taken into account. These forms are enclosed in parenthesis following the official name: e.g. Xiangshan (Dancheng). However, when the regional is listed first, it is linked to the official name with an →: e.g. Dancheng→Xiangshan. The same style is used for former or historical name forms: e.g. Rhodesia→Zimbabwe and Zimbabwe (Rhodesia).

Place-names for major features (countries, major cities, and large physical features), where applicable, include the English conventional form identified by (EN) and linked in the local name or names with an = sign: e.g. Italia=Italy (EN), and vice versa, Italy (EN)=Italia. Former English names are linked in the Index to the conventional form by an →.

Symbols

The last component with the place-name is a symbol, where applicable, specifying the broad category of the feature named. A table preceding the Index lists all of the symbols used and their meanings; this information also appears as a footnote on each page of the Index. Place-names without symbols are cities and towns.

Alphabetization

Place-names are listed in English alphabetical order—26 letters, from A to Z—because of its international usage. Names including two or more words are listed alphabetically according to the first letter of the word: e.g. De Ruyter is listed under D; Le Havre is listed under L. Names with the prefix Mc are listed as if spelled Mac. The generic portion of a name (lake, sierra, mountain, etc.) is placed after the name: e.g. Lake Erie is listed as Erie, Lake; Sierra Morena is listed as Morena, Sierra. In Spanish, "ch" and "ll" groups and the letter "n" are included respectively under C, L, and N, without any distinction.

The same place-name sometimes is listed in the Index several times. It may because of the various translations of a name, or it may be that several places have the same name.

Various translations of a name appear as follows:

Danube (EN)=Dunav   Danube (EN)=Donau
Danube (EN)=Dunărea   Danube (EN)=Dunaj

Several places with the same name appear as follows; however, only in these cases is the location—abbreviated and enclosed in brackets—included. A table of these abbreviations precedes the Index.

Abbeville [U.S.]   Aberdeen [Scot.-U.K.]
Abbeville [Fr.]   Aberdeen [N.C.-U.S.]
Aberdeen [S. Afr.]

Map Number

Each map in the atlas is identified by a number. Where multiple maps are on one page, each map is additionally identified by a boxed letter in the upper-right-hand corner of the map. In the Index listing following the place-name and its variations in language and spelling, where applicable, is the number of the map on which it appears. If the map is one of several on a page, the Index listing includes the map number and letter.

Although a place-name may appear on one or more maps, it is indexed to only one map. Most places are indexed to the regional maps. However, if a place-name appears on either the physical or political continental maps, it is indexed to one of the two types of map. For example, a river or mountain would be indexed to a physical continental map; a city or state would be indexed to a political continental map.

Map-Reference Letters and Geographical Coordinates

The next elements in the Index listing are the map-reference letters and the geographical coordinates, respectively, locating the place on the map.

Map-reference letters consist of a capital and a lowercase letter. Capital letters are across the top and bottom of the maps; lowercase letters are down the sides. The map-reference letters assigned to each place-name refer to the location of the name within the area formed by grid lines connecting the geographical coordinates on either sides of the letters.

Geographical coordinates are the latitude (N for North, S for South) and longitude (E for East, W for West) expressed in degrees and minutes and based on the prime meridian, Greenwich.

Map-reference letters and coordinates for extensive geographical features, such as mountain ranges and countries, are given for the approximate central point of the area. Those for waterways, such as canals and rivers, are given for the mouth of the river, the point where it enters another river or where the feature reaches the map margin. On this page are sample maps showing points to which features are indexed according to map-reference letters and coordinates.

On most maps there is not enough space to place all of the names of administrative subdivisions. In these cases the location of the place is shown on the map by a circled letter or number and the place-name and circled letter or number are listed in the map margin. The map-reference numbers and coordinates for these places refer to the location of the circled letter or number on the map.

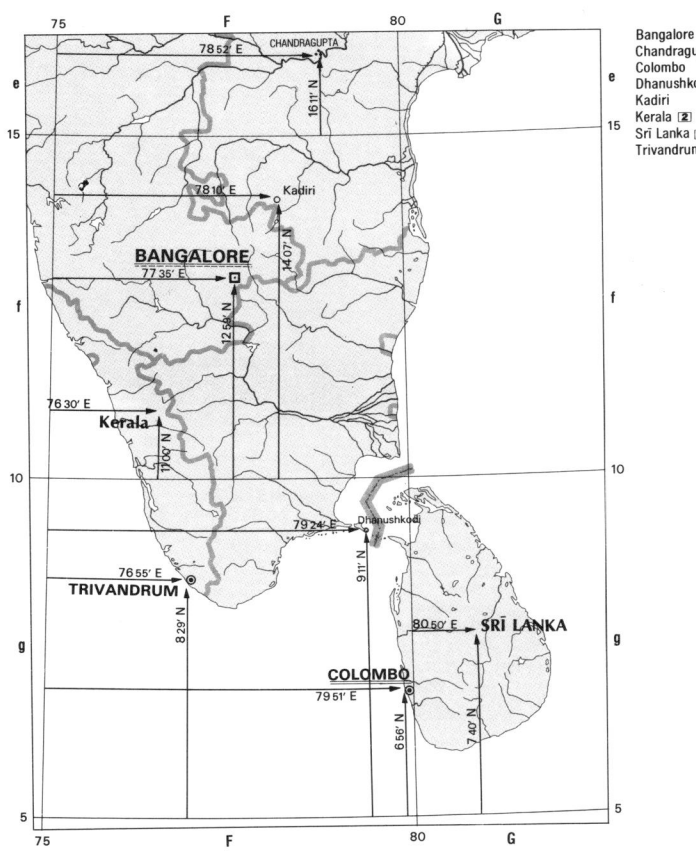

Bangalore	25	Ff	12°59'N 77°35'E
Chandragupta ⊡	35	Fe	16°11'N 78°52'E
Colombo	25	Fg	6°56'N 79°51'E
Dhanushkodi	25	Fg	9°11'N 79°24'E
Kadiri	25	Ff	14°07'N 78°10'E
Kerala ☒	25	Ff	11°00'N 76°30'E
Sri Lanka ⊡	25	Gg	7°40'N 80°50'E
Trivandrum	25	Fg	8°29'N 76°55'E

Alaska ☒	38	Dc	65°00'N 153°00'W
Alaska, Gulf of- ◖	38	Ed	58°00'N 146°00'W
Alexander Archipelago ◻	38	Fd	56°30'N 134°00'W
Barrow, Point- ▶	38	Db	71°23'N 156°30'W
Bering Strait ☒	38	Cc	65°30'N 169°00'W
Coast Mountains ☒	38	Gd	55°00'N 129°00'W
Kodiak ◉	38	Dd	57°30'N 153°30'W
Yukon ☒	38	Cc	62°33'N 163°59'W

List of Abbreviations

Afg. Afghanistan
Afr. Africa
Agl. Anguilla
Ak.-U.S. Alaska, U.S.
Al.-U.S. Alabama, U.S.
Alb. Albania
Alg. Algeria
Alta.-Can. Alberta, Canada
Am. Sam. American Samoa
And. Andorra
Ang. Angola
Ant. Antarctica
Ar.-U.S. Arkansas, U.S.
Arg. Argentina
Asia Asia
Atg. Antigua and Barbuda
Aus. Austria
Austl. Australia
Az.-U.S. Arizona, U.S.
Azr. Azores
Bah. Bahamas
Bar. Barbados
B.A.T. British Antarctic Territory
B.C.-Can. British Columbia, Canada
Bel. Belgium
Ben. Benin
Ber. Bermuda
Bhr. Bahrain
Bhu. Bhutan
Blz. Belize
Bnd. Burundi
Bngl. Bangladesh
Bol. Bolivia
Bots. Botswana
Braz. Brazil
Bru. Brunei
Bul. Bulgaria
Bur. Burma
Burkina Burkina Faso
B.V.I. British Virgin Islands
Ca.-U.S. California, U.S.
Cam. Cameroon
C. Amer. Central America
Can. Canada
Can. Is. Canary Islands
C.A.R. Central African Republic
Cay. Is Cayman Islands
Chad Chad
Chan. Is. Channel Islands
Chile Chile
China China
Co.-U.S. Colorado, U.S.
Cocos Is. Cocos Islands
Col. Colombia
Con. Congo
Cook Cook Islands
Cor. Sea Is. Coral Sea Islands
C.R. Costa Rica
Ct.-U.S. Connecticut, U.S.
Cuba Cuba
C.V. Cape Verde
Cyp. Cyprus
Czech. Czech Republic

D.C.-U.S. District of Columbia, U.S.
De.-U.S. Delaware, U.S.
Den. Denmark
Dji. Djibouti
Dom. Dominica
Dom. Rep. Dominican Republic
Ec. Ecuador
Eg. Egypt
El Sal. El Salvador
Eng.-U.K. England, U.K.
Eq. Gui. Equatorial Guinea
Est. Estonia
Eth. Ethiopia
Eur. Europe
Falk. Is. Falkland Islands
Far. Is. Faeroe Islands
Fiji Fiji
Fin. Finland
Fl.-U.S. Florida, U.S.
Fr. France
Fr. Gui. French Guiana
Fr. Poly. French Polynesia
F.S.M. Federated States of Micronesia
Ga.-U.S. Georgia, U.S.
Gabon Gabon
Gam. Gambia
Geor. Georgia
Ger. Germany
Ghana Ghana
Gib. Gibraltar
Grc. Greece
Gren. Grenada
Grld. Greenland
Guad. Guadeloupe
Guam Guam
Guat. Guatemala
Gui. Guinea
Gui. Bis. Guinea Bissau
Guy. Guyana
Haiti Haiti
Hi.-U.S. Hawaii, U.S.
H.K. Hong Kong
Hond. Honduras
Hun. Hungary
Ia.-U.S. Iowa, U.S.
I.C. Ivory Coast
Ice. Iceland
Id.-U.S. Idaho, U.S.
Il.-U.S. Illinois, U.S.
In.-U.S. Indiana, U.S.
India India
Indon. Indonesia
I. of M. Isle of Man
Iran Iran
Iraq Iraq
Ire. Ireland
Isr. Israel
It. Italy
Jam. Jamaica
Jap. Japan
Jor. Jordan
Kam. Cambodia
Kenya Kenya
Ker. Is. Kermadec Islands

Kir. Kiribati
Ks.-U.S. Kansas, U.S.
Kuw. Kuwait
Ky.-U.S. Kentucky, U.S.
La.-U.S. Louisiana, U.S.
Laos Laos
Lat. Latvia
Lbr. Liberia
Leb. Lebanon
Les. Lesotho
Lib. Libya
Liech. Liechtenstein
Lith. Lithuania
Lux. Luxembourg
Ma.-U.S. Massachusetts, U.S.
Mac. Macao
Mad. Madagascar
Mala. Malaysia
Mald. Maldives
Mali Mali
Malta Malta
Man.-Can. Manitoba, Canada
Mar. Is. Marshall Islands
Mart. Martinique
Maur. Mauritius
May. Mayotte
Mco. Monaco
Md.-U.S. Maryland, U.S.
Me.-U.S. Maine, U.S.
Mex. Mexico
Mi.-U.S. Michigan, U.S.
Mid. Is. Midway Islands
Mn.-U.S. Minnesota, U.S.
Mo.-U.S. Missouri, U.S.
Mong. Mongolia
Mont. Montserrat
Mor. Morocco
Moz. Mozambique
Ms.-U.S. Mississippi, U.S.
Mt.-U.S. Montana, U.S.
Mtna. Mauritania
Mwi. Malawi
Nam. Namibia
N. Amer. North America
Nauru Nauru
N.B.-Can. New Brunswick, Canada
Nb.-U.S. Nebraska, U.S.
N.C.-U.S. North Carolina, U.S.
N. Cal. New Caledonia
N.D.-U.S. North Dakota, U.S.
Nep. Nepal
Neth. Netherlands
Neth. Ant. Netherlands Antilles
Newf.-Can. Newfoundland, Canada
N.H.-U.S. New Hampshire, U.S.
Nic. Nicaragua
Nig. Nigeria
Niger Niger

N. Ire.-U.K. Northern Ireland, U.K.
N.J.-U.S. New Jersey, U.S.
N. Kor. North Korea
N.M.-U.S. New Mexico, U.S.
N. M. Is. Northern Mariana Islands
Nor. Norway
Nor. I. Norfolk Island
N.S.-Canada Nova Scotia, Canada
Nv.-U.S. Nevada, U.S.
N.W.T.-Can. Northwest Territories, Canada
N.Y.-U.S. New York, U.S.
N.Z. New Zealand
Ocn. Oceania
Oh.-U.S. Ohio, U.S.
Ok.-U.S. Oklahoma, U.S.
Oman Oman
Ont.-Ont. Ontario, Canada
Or.-U.S. Oregon, U.S.
Pa.-U.S. Pennsylvania, U.S.
Pak. Pakistan
Pal. Palau
Pan. Panama
Pap. N. Gui. Papua New Guinea
Par. Paraguay
Pas. Pascua
P.E.I.-Can. Prince Edward Island, Canada
Peru Peru
Phil. Philippines
Pit. Pitcairn
Pol. Poland
Port. Portugal
P.R. Puerto Rico
Qatar Qatar
Que.-Can. Quebec, Canada
Reu. Reunion
R.I.-U.S. Rhode Island, U.S.
Rom. Romania
Rwn. Rwanda
S. Afr. South Africa
S. Amer. South America
Sao T.P. Sao Tome and Principe
Sask.-Can. Saskatchewan, Canada
Sau. Ar. Saudi Arabia
S.C.-U.S. South Carolina, U.S.
Scot.-U.K. Scotland, U.K.
S.D.-U.S. South Dakota, U.S.
Sen. Senegal
Sey. Seychelles
Sing. Singapore
S. Kor. South Korea
S.L. Sierra Leone
S. Lan. Sri Lanka
S.M. San Marino
S.N.A. Spanish North Africa
Sol. Is. Solomon Islands
Som. Somalia
Sp. Spain

St. C.N. Saint Christopher-Nevis
St. Hel. Saint Helena
St. Luc. Saint Lucia
St. P.M. Saint Pierre and Miquelon
St. Vin. Saint Vincent and the Grenadines
Sud. Sudan
Sur. Suriname
Sval. Svalbard
Swe. Sweden
Switz. Switzerland
Syr. Syria
Tai. Taiwan
Tan. Tanzania
T.C. Is. Turks and Caicos Islands
Thai. Thailand
Tn.-U.S. Tennessee, U.S.
Togo Togo
Ton. Tonga
Trin. Trinidad and Tobago
T.T.P.I. Trust Territory of the Pacific Islands
Tun. Tunisia
Tur. Turkey
Tuv. Tuvalu
Tx.-U.S. Texas, U.S.
U.A.E. United Arab Emirates
Ug. Uganda
U.K. United Kingdom
Ukr. Ukraine
Ur. Uruguay
U.S. United States
Ut.-U.S. Utah, U.S.
Va.-U.S. Virginia, U.S.
Van. Vanuatu
V.C. Vatican City
Ven. Venezuela
Viet. Vietnam
V.I.U.S. Virgin Islands of the U.S.
Vt.-U.S. Vermont, U.S.
Wa.-U.S. Washington, U.S.
Wake Wake Island
Wales-U.K. Wales, U.K.
W.F. Wallis and Futuna
Wi.-U.S. Wisconsin, U.S.
W. Sah. Western Sahara
W. Sam. Western Samoa
W.V.-U.S. West Virginia, U.S.
Wy.-U.S. Wyoming, U.S.
Yem. Yemen
Yugo. Yugoslavia
Yuk.-Can. Yukon, Canada
Zaire Zaire
Zam. Zambia
Zimb. Zimbabwe

List of Symbols

Plains and Associated Features
- Plain, Basin, Lowland
- Delta
- Salt Flat

Valleys and Depressions
- Valley, Gorge, Ravine, Canyon
- Cave, Crater, Quarry
- Karst Features
- Depression
- Polder, Reclaimed Marsh

Vegetational Features
- Desert, Dunes
- Forest, Woods
- Heath, Steppe, Tundra, Moor
- Oasis

Political/Administrative Units
- 1 Independent Nation
- 2 State, Canton, Region
- 3 Province, Department, County, Territory, District
- 4 Municipality
- 5 Colony, Dependency, Administered Territory

Geographical Regions
- Continent
- Physical Region
- Historical or Cultural Region

Mountain Features
- Mount, Mountain, Peak
- Volcano
- Hill
- Mountains, Mountain Range
- Hills, Escarpment
- Plateau, Highland, Upland
- Pass, Gap

Coastal Features
- Cape, Point
- Coast, Beach
- Cliff
- Peninsula, Promontory
- Isthmus
- Sandbank, Tombolo, Sandbar

Islands Rocks, Reefs
- Island
- Atoll
- Rock, Reef
- Islands, Archipelago
- Rocks, Reefs
- Coral Reef

Hydrographic Features
- Well, Spring
- Geyser, Fumarole
- River, Stream, Brook
- Waterfall, Rapids, Cataract
- River Mouth, Estuary
- Lake
- Salt Lake
- Intermittent Lake, Dry Lake Bed
- Reservoir, Artificial Lake
- Swamp, Marsh, Pond
- Irrigation Canal, Navigable Canal, Ditch, Aqueduct

Ice Features
- Glacier, Snowfield
- Ice Shelf, Pack Ice

Marine Features
- Ocean
- Sea
- Gulf, Bay
- Strait, Fjord, Sea Channel
- Lagoon, Anchorage

Submarine Features
- Bank, Shoal
- Seamount
- Rise, Plateau, Tablemount
- Seamount Chain, Ridge
- Platform, Shelf
- Basin, Depression
- Escarpment, Slope, Sea Scarp
- Fracture
- Trench, Abyss, Valley, Canyon

Other Features
- National Park, Nature Reserve
- Scenic Area, Point of Interest
- Recreation Site, Sports Arena
- Cave, Cavern
- Historic Site, Memorial, Mausoleum, Museum
- Ruins
- Wall, Walls, Tower, Castle, Fortress
- Church, Abbey, Cathedral, Sanctuary
- Temple, Synagogue, Mosque
- Research or Scientific Station
- Airport, Heliport
- Port, Dock
- Lighthouse
- Mine
- Tunnel
- Dam, Bridge

A

Å 7 Cc 67.53N 12.59 E
Aa [Eur.] 12 Ic 51.50N 6.25 E
Aa [Fr.] 11 Ic 51.01N 2.06 E
Aa [Fr.] 12 Dd 50.44N 2.18 E
Aa [Ger.] 12 Kb 52.07N 8.41 E
Aa [Ger.] 12 Jb 52.15N 7.18 E
Aachen 10 Cf 50.46N 6.06 E
Aalen 10 Gh 48.50N 10.06 E
A'âlî an Nîl 35 Ed 9.15N 33.00 E
Aalsmeer 12 Gb 52.15N 4.45 E
Aalst/Alost 11 Kd 50.56N 4.02 E
Aalten 12 Ic 51.55N 6.35 E
Aalter 12 Fc 51.05N 3.27 E
Äänekoski 7 Fe 62.36N 25.44 E
Aa of Weerijs 12 Gc 51.35N 4.46 E
Aar 12 Kd 50.23N 8.00 E
Aarau 14 Cc 47.25N 8.02 E
Aarbergen 12 Kd 50.13N 8.03 E
Aare 14 Cc 47.37N 8.13 E
Aargau 14 Cc 47.30N 8.10 E
Aarlen/Arlon 11 Le 49.41N 5.49 E
Aarschot 11 Kd 50.59N 4.50 E
Aat/Ath 11 Jd 50.38N 3.47 E
Aazanèn 13 Ii 35.06N 3.02W
Āb 24 Md 36.00N 48.05 E
Aba [Nig.] 31 Hh 5.07N 7.22 E
Aba [Zaire] 31 Hk 3.52N 30.14 E
Aba/Ngawa 27 He 32.55N 101.45 E
Abā ad Dūd 24 Ki 27.02N 44.04 E
Abā as Su'ūd 23 Ff 17.28N 44.06 E
Abacaxis, Rio- 54 Gd 3.54S 58.50W
Abaco Island 38 Lg 26.25N 77.10W
Abacou, Pointe l'- 49 Kd 18.03N 73.47W
Abadab, Jabal- 35 Fb 18.53N 35.59 E
Ābādān 22 Gf 30.10N 48.50 E
Ābādeh [Iran] 23 Hc 31.10N 52.37 E
Ābādeh [Iran] 24 Oh 29.08N 52.52 E
Abadiânia 55 Hc 16.06S 48.48W
Abadla 32 Ge 31.01N 2.43W
Abaeté 55 Jd 19.09S 45.27W
Abaeté, Rio- 55 Jd 18.02S 45.12W
Abaetetuba 54 Id 1.42S 48.54W
Abagnar Qi (Xilin Hot) 22 Ne 43.58N 116.08 E
Abag Qi (Xin Hot) 27 Jc 44.01N 114.59 E
Abai 55 Eh 26.01S 55.57W
Abaiang Atoll 57 Id 1.51N 172.58 E
Abaj 19 Hf 49.38N 72.50 E
Abaji 34 Gd 8.28N 6.57 E
Abajo Mountains 46 Kh 37.50N 109.25W
Abakaliki 34 Gd 6.20N 8.03 E
Abakan 20 Ef 53.43N 91.30 E
Abakan 22 Ld 53.43N 91.26 E
Abakwasimbo 36 Eb 0.36N 28.43 E
Abala [Con.] 36 Cc 1.21S 15.30 E
Abala [Niger] 34 Fc 14.56N 3.26 E
Abalak 34 Gb 15.27N 6.17 E
Aban 20 Ee 56.40N 96.10 E
Abancay 54 Df 13.35S 72.55W
Abancourt 12 De 49.42N 1.46 E
Abanga 36 Bb 0.13N 10.28 E
Abano Terme 14 Fe 45.21N 11.47 E
Ābār al Jidd 24 Hf 32.50N 39.50 E
Abarqū 23 Hc 31.08N 53.17 E
Abarqu, Kavīr-e- 24 Og 31.00N 53.50 E
Abashiri 27 Pc 44.01N 144.17 E
Abashiri-Gawa 29a Db 43.56N 144.09 E
Abashiri-Ko 29a Da 44.00N 144.10 E
Abashiri-Wan 29a Da 44.00N 144.35 E
Abasolo 48 Je 24.04N 98.22W
Abatski 19 Hd 56.18N 70.28 E
Abau 60 Dj 10.11S 148.42 E
Abava 7 Eh 57.06N 21.54 E
Abay=Blue Nile (EN) 30 Kg 15.38N 32.31 E
Abaya, Lake- 30 Kh 6.20N 37.55 E
Abaza 20 Ef 52.39N 90.06 E
Abbadia San Salvatore 14 Fh 42.53N 11.41 E
Abbah Quşūr 14 Co 35.57N 8.50 E
Āb Bārīk 24 Oh 29.45N 52.37 E
'Abbāsābād 24 Qd 36.20N 56.25 E
Abbekås 8 Ei 55.24N 13.36 E
Abberton Reservoir 12 Cc 51.50N 0.55 E
Abbeville [Fr.] 11 Hd 50.06N 1.50 E
Abbeville [La.-U.S.] 45 Jl 29.58N 92.08W
Abbeville [S.C.-U.S.] 44 Fh 34.10N 82.23W
Abbey 46 Ka 50.43N 108.45W
Abbeyfeale/Mainistir na Féile 9 Di 52.24N 9.18W
Abbiategrasso 14 Ce 45.24N 8.54 E
Abbot, Mount- 59 Jd 20.03S 147.45 E
Abbot Ice Shelf 66 Pf 72.45S 96.00W
'Abd Al 'Azīz, Jabal- 24 Id 36.25N 40.20 E
'Abd al Kūrī 21 Hh 12.12N 52.13 E
Ābdānān 24 Lf 32.57N 47.26 E
Abdul Ghadir 35 Gc 10.42N 42.59 E
Abdulino 19 Fe 53.42N 53.38 E
Abe, Lake- 35 Gc 11.10N 41.45 E
Abéché 31 Jg 13.49N 20.49 E
Abeek 12 Hc 51.15N 6.00 E
Abe-Gawa 29 Fd 34.55N 138.22 E
Abeløya 41 Pc 79.00N 30.15 E
Abelvær 7 Cd 64.44N 11.11 E
Abemama Atoll 57 Id 0.21N 173.51 E
Abenab 37 Bc 19.12S 18.06 E
Abengourou 34 Ed 6.35N 3.25W
Abengourou 31 Gh 6.44N 3.29W
Åbenrå 7 Bi 55.02N 9.26 E
Åbenrå Fjord 8 Ci 55.05N 9.35 E
Abeokuta 31 Hh 7.09N 3.21 E
Āb-e-Pany 23 If 37.06N 68.20 E
Aberayron 9 Ii 52.15N 4.15W
Aberdare Range 30 Ki 0.25S 36.38 E
Aberdeen [Id.-U.S.] 46 Ie 42.57N 112.50W
Aberdeen [Md.-U.S.] 44 If 39.30N 76.14W
Aberdeen [Ms.-U.S.] 45 Lj 33.49N 88.33W
Aberdeen [N.C.-U.S.] 44 Hh 35.08N 79.26W
Aberdeen [S.Afr.] 37 Cf 32.29S 24.03 E
Aberdeen [Scot.-U.K.] 6 Fd 57.10N 2.04W
Aberdeen [S.D.-U.S.] 39 Je 45.28N 98.29W
Aberdeen [Wa.-U.S.] 43 Cb 46.59N 123.50W
Aberdeen Lake 42 Hd 64.28N 99.00W
Abergavenny 9 Kj 51.50N 3.00W
Aberystwyth 9 Ii 52.25N 4.05W
Abetone 14 Ef 44.08N 10.40 E
Abez 19 Gb 66.32N 61.46 E
Abhā 22 Gh 18.13N 42.30 E
Abhainn an Chláir/Clare 9 Dh 53.20N 9.03W
Abhainn an Lagáin/Lagan 9 Hg 54.37N 5.53W
Abhainn na Bandan/Bandon 9 Ej 51.40N 8.30W
Abhainn na Deirge/Derg 9 Fg 54.40N 7.25W
Abhar 24 Md 36.02N 49.45 E
Abhar 23 Gb 36.09N 49.13 E
Abhazskaja respublika 19 Eg 43.00N 41.10 E
Abibe, Serrania de- 54 Cb 8.00N 76.30W
Abidjan 31 Gh 5.19N 4.02W
Abidjan 34 Ed 5.30N 4.30W
Abilene [Ks.-U.S.] 45 Hg 38.55N 97.13W
Abilene [Tx.-U.S.] 39 Jf 32.27N 99.44W
Abingdon 9 Lj 51.41N 1.17W
Abinsk 16 Kg 44.52N 38.10 E
Abiquiu 45 Ch 36.12N 106.19W
Abiquiu Reservoir 45 Ch 36.18N 106.32W
Abisko 7 Eb 68.20N 18.51 E
Abitibi 42 Jf 51.04N 80.55W
Abitibi, Lake- 38 Le 48.42N 79.45W
Abiy Adi 35 Fc 13.37N 39.01 E
Abiyata, Lake- 35 Fd 7.38N 38.36 E
Abja-Paluoja 8 Kf 58.02N 25.14 E
Abnūb 33 Fd 27.16N 31.09 E
Åbo/Turku 6 Ic 60.27N 22.17 E
Abo, Massif d'- 35 Ba 21.41N 16.08 E
Abóboras, Serra das- 55 Jc 16.12S 44.35W
Abodo 35 Ed 7.50N 34.25 E
Aboisso 34 Ed 5.28N 3.02W
Aboisso 34 Ed 5.28N 3.12W
Abomey 31 Hh 7.11N 1.59 E
Abong Mbang 34 He 3.59N 13.11 E
Abony 10 Pi 47.11N 20.00 E
Aborigen, Pik- 20 Jd 62.05N 149.10 E
Aborlar 26 Ge 9.26N 118.33 E
Aborrebierg 8 Ej 54.59N 12.32 E
Abou Deia 35 Bc 11.27N 19.17 E
Abou Goulem 35 Cc 13.37N 21.38 E
Abovjan 16 Ni 40.14N 44.37 E
Abrād, Wādī- 23 Gf 15.51N 46.05 E
Abraham's Bay 49 Kb 22.21N 72.55W
Abramovski Bereg 7 Kc 66.25N 43.05 E
Abrántes 13 De 39.28N 8.12W
Abra Pampa 56 Gb 22.43S 65.42W
Abrego 49 Ki 8.04N 73.14W
Abreojos, Punta- 47 Bc 26.42N 113.35W
'Abrī 35 Ea 20.48N 30.20 E
Abrolhos, Arquipélago dos- 54 Kg 18.00S 38.40W
Abrud 15 Gc 46.16N 23.04 E
Abruka, Ostrov-/Abruka Saar 8 Jf 58.08N 22.25 E
Abruka Saar/Abruka, Ostrov- 8 Jf 58.08N 22.25 E
Abruzzi 14 Hh 42.20N 13.45 E
Absaroka Range 43 Fc 44.45N 109.50W
Abtenau 14 Hc 47.33N 13.21 E
Abū, Ḩād, Wādī- 24 Ei 27.46N 33.30 E
Abū ad Duhūr 24 Ge 35.44N 37.02 E
Abū 'Alī 24 Mi 27.20N 49.33 E
Abū al Khaşīb 24 Lg 30.27N 47.59 E
Abū an Na'am 24 Hj 25.14N 38.49 E
Abū 'Arīsh 23 Ff 16.58N 42.50 E
Abū Ballaş 33 Ee 24.26N 27.39 E
Abū Daghmah 24 Hd 36.25N 38.15 E
Abū Darbah 24 Fd 28.29N 33.20 E
Abu Dhabi (EN)=Abū Zaby 22 Hg 24.28N 54.22 E
Abū Ḩadrīyah 24 Mi 27.20N 48.58 E
Abū Ḩamad 31 Kg 19.32N 33.19 E
Abū Ḩammād 24 Dg 30.32N 31.40 E
Abū Ḩarbah, Jabal- 24 Ei 27.17N 33.13 E
Abū Ḩashā'ifah, Khalīj- 24 Bg 31.16N 27.25 E
Abuja 31 Hh 9.10N 7.11 E
Abū Jābirah 35 Dc 11.04N 26.51 E
Abū Jifān 24 Lj 24.31N 47.43 E
Abū Kabīr 24 Dg 30.44N 31.40 E
Abū Kamāl 23 Fc 34.27N 40.55 E
Abukuma-Gawa 29 Gb 38.06N 140.52 E
Abukuma-Sanchi 29 Gc 37.20N 140.45 E
Abū Latt 33 Hf 19.58N 40.08 E
Abū Libdah, Khashm- 33 Ie 22.58N 46.13 E
Abū Maţāriq 35 Dc 10.58N 26.17 E
Abu Mendi 35 Fc 11.47N 35.42 E
Abumonbazi 36 Db 3.42N 22.10 E
Abū Muḩarrik, Ghurd- 33 Ed 27.00N 30.00 E
Abū Musā, Jazīreh-ye- 23 Id 25.52N 55.03 E
Abunā 52 Jf 9.42S 65.23W
Abunā, Rio- 52 Jf 9.41S 65.23W
Abune Yosef 35 Fc 12.09N 39.12 E
Abū Qīr 24 Dg 31.19N 30.04 E
Abū Qīr, Khalīj- 24 Dg 31.20N 30.15 E
Abū Qumayyis, Ra's- 24 Nj 24.34N 51.30 E
Abu Road 25 Ed 24.29N 72.47 E
Abū Sawmah, Ra's- 24 Ei 26.51N 33.59 E
Abu Shanab 35 Dc 13.57N 27.47 E
Abu Simbel (EN)=Abū Sumbul 33 Fe 22.22N 31.38 E
Abū Şukhayr 24 Kg 31.52N 44.27 E
Abū Sumbul=Abu Simbel (EN) 33 Fe 22.22N 31.38 E
Abuta 28 Pc 42.31N 140.46 E
Abut Head 62 De 43.06S 170.15 E
Abū Tīj 33 Fd 27.02N 31.19 E
Abū Ţurţūr, Jabal- 24 Cj 25.20N 30.00 E
Abū'Urūq 35 Eb 15.54N 30.27 E
Abuyemeda 35 Fc 10.38N 39.43 E
Abū Zabad 35 Dc 12.21N 29.15 E
Abū Zaby=Abu Dhabi (EN) 22 Hg 24.28N 54.22 E
Abū Zanīmah 33 Fd 29.03N 33.06 E
Abwong 35 Ed 9.07N 32.12 E
Åby 8 Gf 58.40N 16.11 E
Abyaḍ 35 Dc 13.46N 26.28 E
Abyaḍ, Al Baḩr al-=White Nile (EN) 30 Kg 15.38N 32.31 E
Abyaḍ, Al Baḩr al-=White Nile (EN) 35 Ec 12.40N 32.30 E
Abyaḍ, Ar Ra's al- 23 Ee 23.32N 38.32 E
Abyaḍ, Jabal- 35 Db 18.55N 28.40 E
Abyaḍ, Ra's al-=Blanc, Cape- (EN) 30 He 37.20N 9.50 E
Abyār Alī 24 Hj 24.25N 39.33 E
Abyār ash Shuwayrif 33 Bd 29.59N 14.16 E
Åbybro 7 Bh 57.09N 9.45 E
Abydos 33 Fd 26.11N 31.55 E
Abyei 35 Dd 9.36N 28.26 E
Ābyek 24 Nd 36.02N 50.31 E
Abymes 51e Ab 16.16N 61.31W
Acacias 54 Dc 3.59N 73.47W
Academy Gletscher 41 Ib 81.45N 33.35W
Acadie 38 Me 46.00N 65.00W
Acaill/Achill 9 Dh 54.00N 10.00W
Acajutla 49 Cg 13.36N 89.50W
Acalayong 34 Ge 1.05N 9.40 E
Acámbaro 47 Dd 20.02N 100.44W
Acandi 54 Cb 8.31N 77.17W
Acaponeta 47 Cd 22.30N 105.22W
Acaponeta, Rio- 48 Gf 22.20N 105.37W
Acapulco de Juárez 39 Jh 16.51N 99.55W
Acará 54 Id 1.57S 48.11W
Acarai, Serra- 54 Gc 1.50N 57.40W
Acaraú 54 Jd 2.53S 40.07W
Acaray, Rio- 55 Eg 25.29S 54.42W
Acari, Rio- [Braz.] 54 Ge 5.18S 59.42W
Acari, Rio- [Braz.] 55 Jb 16.00S 45.03W
Acarigua 54 Eb 9.33N 69.12W
Acatenango, Volcán- 38 Jh 14.30N 91.40W
Acatlán de Osorio 48 Jh 18.12N 98.03W
Acayucan 47 Fe 17.57N 94.55W
Accéglio 14 Af 44.28N 7.00 E
Aččitau, Gora- 18 Cc 42.07N 60.31 E
Accomac 44 Jg 37.43N 75.40W
Accra 31 Gh 5.33N 0.13W
Acebal 55 Bk 33.14S 60.50W
Acebuches 48 Hc 28.15N 102.43W
Aceguá [Braz.] 55 Ej 31.52S 54.09W
Aceguá [Ur.] 55 Ej 31.52S 54.12W
Aceh 26 Cf 4.10N 96.50 E
Acerenza 14 Jj 40.48N 15.56 E
Acerra 14 Ij 40.57N 14.22 E
Achacachi 54 Eg 16.03S 68.43W
Achaguas 54 Eb 7.46N 68.14W
Achaïf, 'Erg- 34 Ea 20.49N 4.34W
Achao 56 Ff 42.28S 73.30W
Achegour 34 Hb 19.03N 11.53 E
Acheng 27 Mb 45.32N 126.56 E
Acheux-en-Amiénois 12 Ed 50.04N 2.32 E
Achiet-le-Grand 12 Ed 50.08N 2.47 E
Achill/Acaill 9 Dh 54.00N 10.00W
Achilleion 15 Cj 39.34N 19.55 E
Achill Head/Ceann Acla 9 Ch 53.59N 10.13W
Achim 10 Fc 53.02N 9.01 E
Achim 35 Bb 15.53N 19.31 E
Achterwasser 10 Jb 54.00N 13.57 E
Acı Gölü 24 Cd 37.50N 29.54 E
Ačinsk 22 Ld 56.17N 90.30 E
Acıpayam 24 Cd 37.25N 29.22 E
Acireale 14 Jm 37.37N 15.10 E
Aciş 15 Fb 47.32N 22.47 E
Ačisaj 18 Gc 43.33N 68.53 E
Acit 17 Hh 56.48N 57.54 E
Acit-Nur 27 Fb 49.30N 90.30 E
Acklins 38 Lg 22.25N 74.00W
Acklins, The Bight of- 49 Jb 22.30N 74.15W
Acle 12 Db 52.38N 1.33 E
Acobamba 54 Df 12.48S 74.34W
Acolin 11 Jh 46.49N 3.23 E
Aconcagua 56 Fd 32.15S 70.50W
Aconcagua, Cerro- 52 Ji 32.39S 70.00W
Açor, Serra de- 13 Ed 40.13N 7.48W
Açores=Azores (EN) 31 Ee 38.30N 28.00W
Açores, Arquipélago dos-=Azores (EN) 30 Ee 38.30N 28.00W
Acorizal 55 Db 15.12S 56.22W
Acoyapa 49 Eh 11.58N 85.10W
Acquapendente 14 Fh 42.44N 11.52 E
Acquasanta Terme 14 Hh 42.46N 13.24 E
Acquasparta 14 Gh 42.41N 12.33 E
Acquaviva delle Fonti 14 Kj 40.54N 16.50 E
Acqui Terme 14 Cf 44.41N 8.28 E
Acraman, Lake- 59 Hf 32.05S 135.25 E
Acre 54 Ee 9.00S 70.00W
Acre, Rio- 52 Jf 8.45S 67.22W
Acri 14 Kk 39.29N 16.23 E
Actéon, Groupe- 57 Ng 21.20S 136.30W
Actopan 48 Jg 20.16N 98.56W
Açu 54 Ke 5.34S 36.54W
Acuña 55 Di 29.55S 57.58W
Ada [Ghana] 34 Fd 5.47N 0.38 E
Ada [Ok.-U.S.] 43 He 34.46N 96.41W
Ada [Yugo.] 15 Dd 45.48N 20.08 E
Adaba 35 Fd 7.03N 39.31 E
'Adād 35 Hd 8.23N 46.48 E
'Adāle 35 Gd 9.45N 44.41 E
Adair, Bahia- 48 Cb 31.30N 113.50W
Adair, Cape- 42 Kb 71.31N 71.24W
Adaja 13 Hc 41.32N 4.52W
Adak 40a Cb 51.45N 176.40W
Adalar 15 Mi 40.52N 29.07 E
'Adale 35 He 2.46N 46.20 E
Ådalen 8 Ga 63.20N 17.30 E
Adalselv 8 Dd 60.04N 10.11 E
Adam, Mount- 56 Hh 51.34S 60.04W
Adamantina 55 Ge 21.42S 51.04W
Adamaoua=Adamawa (EN) 30 Ih 7.00N 15.00 E
Adamawa (EN)=Adamaoua 30 Ih 7.00N 15.00 E
Adamello 14 Ed 46.09N 10.30 E
Adamovka 16 Ud 51.32N 59.59 E
Adams 45 Le 43.58N 89.49W
Adams, Mount- 43 Cb 46.12N 121.28W
Adams Lake 46 Fa 51.13N 119.33W
Adams River 42 Ff 50.54N 119.33W
Adam's Rock 64q Ab 25.04S 130.05W
Adamstown 58 Ng 25.04S 130.05W
Adamuz 13 Hf 38.02N 4.31W
Adana 22 Ff 37.01N 35.18 E
Adapazarı 24 Db 40.46N 30.24 E
Adarama 35 Eb 17.05N 34.54 E
Adarān, Jabal- 33 Ig 13.46N 45.08 E
Adare, Cape- 66 Kf 71.17S 170.14 E
Adavale 59 Ie 25.55S 144.36 E
Adda [It.] 5 Gf 45.08N 9.53 E
Adda [Sud.] 35 Cd 9.51N 24.50 E
Aḍ Ḍab'ah 33 Ec 31.02N 28.26 E
Ad Dabbah 35 Eb 18.03N 30.57 E
Ad Dafinah 33 He 23.18N 41.58 E
Aḍ Ḍafrah 24 Ok 23.25N 53.25 E
Ad Dahnā' 21 Gg 24.30N 48.10 E
Addala-Šuhgelmeer, Gora- 16 Oh 42.20N 46.15 E
Aḍ Ḍāli' 33 Hg 13.42N 44.44 E
Ad Damazin 35 Ec 11.49N 34.23 E
Ad Dāmir 35 Eb 17.35N 33.58 E
Ad Dammām 22 Hg 26.26N 50.07 E
Ad Dār al Ḩamrā' 23 Ed 27.19N 37.44 E
Ad Dawādimī 23 Fe 24.28N 44.18 E
Ad Dawḩah=Doha (EN) 22 Hg 25.17N 51.32 E
Ad Dawr 24 Je 34.27N 43.47 E
Ad Dayr 33 Fd 25.20N 32.35 E
Ad Dibdibah 24 Lh 28.00N 46.30 E
Aḍ Ḍiffah 33 Ec 30.30N 25.30 E
Ad Dikākah 35 Ib 19.25N 51.30 E
Ad Dilam 23 Ge 23.59N 47.10 E
Ad Dindar 35 Ec 13.20N 34.05 E
Ad Dir'īyah 24 Lj 24.48N 46.32 E
Ad Dissān 33 Hf 16.56N 41.41 E
Addis Zemen 35 Fc 12.05N 37.44 E
Ad Dīwānīya 23 Fc 31.59N 44.56 E
Addu Atoll 21 Jj 0.25S 73.10 E
Ad Du'ayn 35 Dc 11.26N 26.09 E
Ad Duwayd 24 Jg 30.13N 42.18 E
Ad Duwaym 35 Ec 14.00N 32.19 E
Adel [Ga.-U.S.] 44 Fj 31.18N 83.25W
Adel [Or.-U.S.] 46 Fe 42.11N 119.54W
Adelaide [Austl.] 58 Eh 34.56S 138.36 E
Adelaide [Bah.] 44 Im 25.00N 77.31W
Adelaide [S.Afr.] 37 Df 32.42S 26.20 E
Adelaide Island 66 Qe 67.15S 68.30W
Adelaide Peninsula 42 Hc 68.05N 97.50W
Adelaide River 58 Ef 13.15S 131.06 E
Adelaye 35 Cd 7.07N 22.49 E
Adelboden 14 Bd 46.30N 7.33 E
Adèle Island 59 Ec 15.30S 123.10 E
Adélie, Terre- 66 Ie 67.00S 139.00 E
Ademuz 13 Kd 40.04N 1.17W
Aden (EN)=Baladiyat 'Adan 22 Gh 12.46N 45.01 E
Aden, Gulf of- 30 Lg 12.00N 48.00 E
Aden, Gulf of- (EN)='Adméd, Badyarada- 30 Lg 12.00N 48.00 E
Adenau 12 Id 50.23N 6.56 E
Ader 34 Fc 14.10N 5.05 E
Aderbissinat 34 Gb 15.37N 7.52 E
Adhan, Jabal- 24 Qj 25.27N 56.13 E
Adh Dhahībāt 32 Jc 32.01N 10.42 E
Adh Dhayd 24 Pj 25.17N 55.53 E
Adhélfi 15 Gj 39.08N 23.59 E
Adhelfoi 15 Jm 36.25N 26.37 E
'Adhriyāt, Jibāl- al- 24 Gg 30.25N 36.48 E
Adi, Pulau- 26 Jg 4.18S 133.26 E
Adiaké 34 Ed 5.16N 3.17W
Adi Arkay 35 Fc 13.31N 38.00 E
Adicora 54 Ea 11.57N 69.48W
Adi Dairo 35 Fc 14.21N 38.12 E
Adigala 35 Gc 10.24N 42.18 E
Adige/Etsch 5 Hf 45.10N 12.20 E
Adigrat 35 Fc 14.16N 39.28 E
Adi Keyeh 35 Fc 14.48N 39.23 E
Adi Kwala 35 Fc 14.37N 38.51 E
Ādīlābād 25 Fe 19.40N 78.32 E
Adīrī 31 If 27.30N 13.16 E
Adirondack Mountains 38 Le 44.00N 74.00W
Adis Abeba 31 Kh 9.01N 38.46 E
Adis Alem 35 Fd 9.03N 38.24 E
Adi Ugri 35 Fc 14.53N 38.49 E
Adiyaman 23 Eb 37.46N 38.17 E
Adjud 15 Kc 46.06N 27.10 E
Adjuntas 51a Bb 18.09N 66.43W
'Adméd, Badyarada-=Aden, Gulf of- (EN) 30 Lg 12.00N 48.00 E
Admer, Erg d'- 32 Ie 24.12N 9.10 E
Admiralty 40 Me 57.50N 134.30W
Admiralty Bay 51n Ba 13.00N 61.16W
Admiralty Gulf 59 Fb 14.20S 125.50 E
Admiralty Inlet 42 Ib 72.30N 86.00W
Admiralty Islands 57 Fe 2.10S 147.00 E
Admiralty Mountains 66 Kf 71.45S 168.30 E
Admont 14 Ic 47.34N 14.27 E
Ado 34 Fd 6.36N 2.56 E
Ado Ekiti 34 Gd 7.38N 5.13 E
Adok 35 Ed 8.11N 30.19 E
Adolfo Gonzales Chaves 55 Bn 38.02S 60.06W
Adolfo López Mateos, Presa- 48 Fe 25.05N 107.20W
Adonara, Pulau- 26 Hh 8.20S 123.10 E
Ādoni 25 Fe 15.38N 77.17 E
Adra 13 Ih 36.44N 3.01W
Adrano 14 Im 37.40N 14.50 E
Adrar 30 Ff 20.30N 13.30W
Adrar 31 Gf 27.54N 0.17W
Adrar 30 Hf 25.12N 8.10 E
Adrar [Alg.] 32 Gd 27.00N 1.00W
Adrar [Mtna.] 32 Ee 21.00N 11.00W
Adré 35 Cc 13.28N 22.12 E
Adria 14 Ge 45.03N 12.03 E
Adrian 44 Ee 41.54N 84.02W
Adrianópolis 55 Hg 24.41S 48.50W
Adriatic, Deti-=Adriatic Sea (EN) 5 Hg 43.00N 16.00 E
Adriatico, Mar-=Adriatic Sea (EN) 5 Hg 43.00N 16.00 E
Adriatic Sea (EN)=Adriatic, Deti- 5 Hg 43.00N 16.00 E
Adriatic Sea (EN)=Adriatico, Mar- 5 Hg 43.00N 16.00 E
Adriatic Sea (EN)=Jadransko More 5 Hg 43.00N 16.00 E
Aduard 12 Ia 53.15N 6.25 E
Adula 14 Dd 46.30N 9.05 E
Adulis 35 Fb 15.15N 39.37 E
Adur 12 Bd 50.49N 0.16W
Adusa 36 Eb 1.23N 28.01 E
Adventure Bank (EN) 14 Gm 37.20N 12.10 E
Adwa 31 Kg 14.10N 38.55 E
Adyča 21 Pc 68.13N 135.03 E
Adygalah 20 Jd 62.57N 146.25 E
Adygeja, respublika 19 Eg 44.30N 40.05 E
Adžarskaja respublika 19 Eg 41.40N 42.10 E
Adzopé 34 Ed 6.15N 3.45W
Adzopé 34 Ed 6.06N 3.52W
Adzva 17 Ic 66.36N 59.28 E
Aegean Sea (EN)=Aiyaion Pélagos 5 Ih 39.00N 25.00 E
Aegean Sea (EN)=Ege Denizi 5 Ih 39.00N 25.00 E
Aegina (EN) = Aiyina 15 Gl 37.40N 23.30 E
Aegviidu 8 Ke 59.17N 25.37 E
Aeon Point 64g Bb 1.46N 157.11W
Aerfort na Sionainne/Shannon 9 Ei 52.42N 8.57W
Ærø 8 Dj 54.55N 10.20 E
Ærøskøbing 8 Dj 54.53N 10.25 E
Aerzen 12 Lb 52.02N 9.16 E
Afafi, Massif d'- 34 Ha 22.15N 15.00 E
'Afak 24 Kf 32.04N 45.15 E
Afanasjevo 7 Mg 58.54N 53.16 E
Afareaitu 65e Fc 17.33S 149.47W
Afars and Issas→Djibouti 31 Lg 11.30N 43.00 E
Aff 11 Dg 47.43N 2.07W
Affollé 30 Fg 16.55N 10.25W
Affrica, Scoglio d'- 14 Eh 42.20N 10.05 E
Afghanistan 22 If 33.00N 65.00 E
Afgōye 35 He 2.09N 45.07 E
'Afif 23 Fe 23.55N 42.56 E
Afikpo 34 Gd 5.53N 7.55 E
Afipski 16 Kg 44.52N 38.50 E
Aflou 32 Hc 34.07N 2.06 E
Afmadōw 35 Ge 0.29N 42.06 E
Afognak 40 Ie 58.15N 152.30W
Afonso Cláudio 54 Jh 20.05S 41.08W
Afon Teifi 9 Ii 52.06N 4.43W
Afon Tywi 9 Ij 51.40N 4.15W
Afragola 14 Ij 40.55N 14.18 E
Afrērā, Lake- 35 Gc 13.20N 41.03 E
Africa 30 Jh 10.00N 22.00 E
African Islands 30 Mi 4.53S 53.24 E
Afşin 24 Gc 38.36N 36.55 E
Afsluitdijk 11 La 53.00N 5.15 E
Afton 46 Je 42.44N 110.56W
Afuá 54 Hd 0.10S 50.23W
'Afula 24 Ff 32.36N 35.17 E
Afyonkarahisar 22 Ff 38.45N 30.40 E
Agadem 31 Ig 16.50N 13.17 E
Agadez 31 Hg 16.58N 7.59 E
Agadez 34 Hb 19.45N 10.15 E
Agadir 31 Ge 30.25N 9.37W
Agadir 32 Fc 30.00N 9.00W
Agadyr 19 Hf 48.17N 72.53 E
Agalega Islands 30 Mj 10.24S 56.30 E
Agalta, Sierra de- 47 Ge 15.00N 85.53W
Agan 19 Hc 61.23N 74.35 E
Agana 58 Fc 13.28N 144.45 E
Agano-Gawa 28 Of 37.57N 139.07 E
Aga Point 64c Bb 13.14N 144.43 E
Agapovka 17 Ij 53.18N 59.10 E
Agaro 35 Fd 7.53N 36.36 E
Agartala 22 Lg 23.49N 91.16 E
Agassiz Pool 45 Ib 48.20N 95.58W
Agat 64c Bb 13.23N 144.39 E
Agat Bay 64c Bb 13.24N 144.39 E
Agats 58 Ee 5.33S 138.08 E
Agattu 40a Ab 52.25N 173.35 E
Agawa Bay 44 Eb 47.22N 84.33W
Agawa Bay 44 Eb 47.20N 84.42W
Agboville 34 Ed 5.56N 4.13W
Agboville 34 Ed 6.00N 4.15W
Agdam 19 Eh 39.58N 46.57 E
Agdaš 16 Oi 40.38N 47.29 E
Agde 11 Jk 43.19N 3.28 E
Agde, Cap d'- 11 Jk 43.16N 3.30 E
Agder 8 Cf 58.25N 8.15 E
Agdz 32 Fc 30.27N 7.56W
Agdžabedi 16 Oi 40.03N 47.28 E
Agematsu 29 Ed 35.47N 137.41 E
Agen 11 Gj 44.12N 0.38 E
Ageo 29 Fd 35.58N 139.36 E
Agepsta, Gora- 16 Lh 43.32N 40.30 E
Ager 14 Hb 48.05N 13.51 E
Agere Mariam 35 Fd 5.39N 38.15 E
Agersø 8 Di 55.10N 11.10 E
Agger 12 Jd 50.48N 7.11 E
Āghā Jārī 23 Gc 30.42N 49.50 E
Aghireşu 15 Gc 46.53N 23.15 E
Agiabampo, Estero de- 48 Ed 26.15N 109.15W
Ağın 24 Hc 38.57N 38.43 E

Index Symbols

1 Independent Nation
2 State, Region
3 District, County
4 Municipality
5 Colony, Dependency
Continent
Physical Region
Historical or Cultural Region
Mount, Mountain
Volcano
Hili
Mountains, Mountain Range
Hills, Escarpment
Plateau, Upland
Pass, Gap
Plain, Lowland
Delta
Salt Flat
Valley, Canyon
Crater, Cave
Karst Features
Depression
Polder
Desert, Dunes
Forest, Woods
Heath, Steppe
Oasis
Cape, Point
Coast, Beach
Cliff
Peninsula
Isthmus
Sandbank
Island
Atoll
Rock, Reef
Islands, Archipelago
Rocks, Reefs
Coral Reef
Well, Spring
Geyser
River, Stream
Waterfall Rapids
River Mouth, Estuary
Lake
Salt Lake
Intermittent Lake
Reservoir
Swamp, Pond
Canal
Glacier
Ice Shelf, Pack Ice
Ocean
Sea
Gulf, Bay
Strait, Fjord
Lagoon
Bank
Seamount
Tablemount
Ridge
Shelf
Basin
Escarpment, Sea Scarp
Fracture
Trench, Abyss
National Park, Reserve
Point of Interest
Recreation Site
Cave, Cavern
Historic Site
Ruins
Wall, Walls
Church, Abbey
Temple
Scientific Station
Airport
Port
Lighthouse
Mine
Tunnel
Dam, Bridge

Aginskoje 20 Gf 51.03N 114.33 E
Agnew 59 Ee 28.01S 120.30 E
Agnibilékrou 34 Ed 7.08N 3.12W
Agnita 15 Hd 45.58N 24.37 E
Agno 14 Fe 45.32N 11.21 E
Agnone 14 Ii 41.48N 14.22 E
Ago 29 Ed 34.19N 136.50 E
Agoare 34 Fd 8.30N 3.25 E
Agogna 14 Ce 45.04N 8.54 E
Agön 8 Gc 61.35N 17.25 E
Agordat 31 Kg 15.32N 37.53 E
Agordo 14 Gd 46.17N 12.02 E
Agout 11 Hk 43.47N 1.41 E
Āgra 22 Jg 27.11N 78.01 E
Agrahanski Poluostrov 16 Oh 43.45N 47.35 E
Agramunt 13 Nc 41.47N 1.06 E
Agreda 13 Kc 41.51N 1.56W
Ağrı 23 Fb 39.44N 43.03 E
Ağrı Daği = Mount Ararat (EN) 21 Gf 39.40N 44.24 E
Agričaj 16 Oi 41.17N 46.43 E
Agrigento 6 Hh 37.19N 13.34 E
Agrihan Island 57 Fc 18.46N 145.40 E
Agrij 15 Gb 47.15N 23.16 E
Agrinion 15 Ek 38.38N 21.25 E
Agropoli 14 Ij 40.21N 14.59 E
Agro Pontino 14 Gi 41.25N 12.55 E
Agryz 7 Mh 56.31N 53.01 E
Agto 41 Ge 67.37N 53.49W
Agua Brava, Laguna- 48 Gf 22.10N 105.32W
Agua Caliente, Cerro- 47 Cc 26.27N 106.12W
Aguachica 54 Db 8.18N 73.38W
Agua Clara 55 Fe 20.27S 52.52W
Aguada de Pasajeros 49 Gb 22.23N 80.51W
Aguadez, Irhazer Oua-n- 34 Gb 17.28N 6.26 E
Aguadilla 49 Nd 18.26N 67.09W
Aguadulce 49 Gi 8.15N 80.33W
Agua Fria River 46 Ij 33.23N 112.21W
Agua Limpa, Rio- 55 Gb 14.58S 51.20W
Aguán, Río- 49 Ef 15.57N 85.44W
Aguanaval, Río- 48 Hf 25.28N 102.53W
Aguapeí 55 Cc 16.12S 59.43W
Aguapeí, Rio- 56 Jb 21.03S 51.47W
Aguapeí, Rio- 55 Cb 15.53S 58.25W
Agua Prieta 39 If 31.18N 109.34W
Aguaray 56 Hb 22.16S 63.44W
Aguaray Guazú, Río- [Par.] 55 Dg 24.05S 56.40W
Aguaray Guazú, Río- [Par.] 55 Dg 24.47S 57.19W
Aguasay 50 Eh 9.25N 63.44W
Aguascalientes 39 Ig 21.53N 102.18W
Aguascalientes 47 Dd 22.00N 102.30W
Aguasvivas 13 Lc 41.20N 0.25W
Agua Verde, Rio- 55 Da 13.42S 56.43W
Agua Vermelha, Represa- 56 Ja 19.53S 50.17W
Agudo [Braz.] 55 Fi 29.38S 53.15W
Agudo [Sp.] 13 Hf 38.59N 4.52W
Agueda 13 Fc 41.02N 6.56W
Águeda 13 Dd 40.34N 8.27W
Aguelhok 34 Fb 19.28N 0.51 E
Aguenit 32 Ee 22.11N 13.08W
Aguerguer 30 Ff 23.09N 16.01W
Aguijan Island 57 Fc 14.51N 145.34 E
Aguilar de Campóo 13 Hb 42.48N 4.16W
Aguilar de la Frontera 13 Hg 37.31N 4.39W
Aguilas 13 Kg 37.24N 1.35W
Aguililla 48 Hh 18.44N 102.44W
Aguirre, Río- 50 Fh 8.28N 61.02W
Aguja, Cabo de la- 54 Da 11.21N 73.59W
Agujereada, Punta- 51a Ab 18.31N 67.08W
Agul 20 Ee 55.40N 95.45 E
Agulhas, Cape-(EN) = Agulhas, Kaap- 30 Jl 34.50S 20.00 E
Agulhas, Kaap- = Agulhas, Cape-(EN) 30 Jl 34.50S 20.00 E
Agulhas Negras, Pico das- 52 Lh 22.23S 44.38W
Agulhas Plateau (EN) 30 Jm 40.00S 26.00 E
Agung, Gunung- 26 Gh 8.21S 115.30 E
Aguni-Shima 27 Mf 26.35N 127.15 E
Agupey, Rio- 55 Di 29.07S 56.36W
Agustin Codazzi 54 Da 10.02N 73.15W
Ağva 24 Cb 41.05N 29.50 E
Ahaggar 30 Hf 23.10N 5.50 E
Ahaggar, Tassili-oua-n- 30 Hf 20.30N 5.00 E
Aha Hills 37 Cc 19.45S 21.10 E
Ahalcihe 19 Eg 41.38N 42.59 E
Ahalkalaki 19 Eg 41.25N 43.29 E
Ahangaran 18 Gd 40.57N 69.37 E
Ahar 23 Gb 38.28N 47.04 E
Ahat 15 Mk 38.39N 29.47 E
Ahaus 10 Cd 52.04N 7.00 E
Ahe Atoll 57 Mf 14.30S 146.18W
Ahenet, Tanezrouft-n- 32 He 22.00N 1.00 E
Ahini 20 Ff 53.18N 105.01 E
Ahipara 62 Ea 35.10S 173.09 E
Ahja Jõgi 8 Lf 58.19N 27.15 E
Ahlat 24 Jc 38.45N 42.29 E
Ahlen 10 De 51.45N 7.55 E
Ahmadābād 22 Jg 23.02N 72.37 E
Ahmadī 24 Qi 27.56N 56.42 E
Ahmadnagar 25 Ee 19.05N 74.44 E
Ahmadpur East 25 Ec 29.09N 71.16 E
Ahmar 30 Lh 9.23N 41.13 E
Aḥmar, Al Baḥr al- = Red Sea (EN) 30 Kf 25.00N 38.00 E
Ahmeta 16 Nh 42.02N 45.11 E
Ahmetli 15 Kk 38.31N 27.57 E
Ahnet 32 He 24.35N 3.15 E
Ahoa 64h Ab 13.17S 176.12W
Ahome 48 Ee 25.55N 109.11W
Ahon, Tarso- 35 Ba 20.23N 18.18 E
Ahr 10 Df 50.33N 7.17 E
Ahram 24 Nh 28.52N 51.16 E
Ahrāmāt al Jīzah 33 Fd 29.55N 31.05 E
Ahrensburg 10 Gc 53.41N 10.15 E
Ahrgebirge 12 Id 50.31N 6.54 E
Ahse 12 Jc 51.42N 7.51 E
Ahsu 16 Pi 40.35N 48.26 E
Āhtäri 7 Ee 62.02N 21.20 E
Ahtärinjarvi 8 Kb 62.40N 24.05 E
Ähtävänjoki 7 Fe 63.38N 22.48 E
Ahtopol 15 Kg 42.06N 27.57 E
Ahtuba 5 Kf 46.42N 48.00 E
Ahtubinsk 6 Kf 48.14N 46.14 E
Ahtyrka 19 De 50.19N 34.55 E
Ahuacapán 49 Cg 13.55N 89.51W
Ahuazotepec 48 Jg 20.03N 98.09W
Ahunui Atoll 57 Mf 19.35S 140.28W
Åhus 7 Di 55.55N 14.17 E
Ahvāz 22 Gf 31.19N 48.42 E
Ahvenanmaa/Åland 7 Ef 60.15N 20.00 E
Ahvenanmaa/Åland = Aland Islands (EN) 5 Hc 60.15N 20.00 E
Ahvenanmeri 8 Hd 60.00N 19.30 E
Aḥwar 23 Gg 13.31N 46.42 E
Aibag Gol 28 Ad 41.42N 110.24 E
Aibetsu 29a Cb 43.55N 142.33 E
Aichach 10 Hh 48.28N 11.08 E
Aichi Ken 28 Ng 35.00N 137.07 E
Aiea 65a Db 21.23N 157.56W
Aigle 14 Ad 46.20N 6.59 E
Aigoual, Mont- 11 Jj 44.07N 3.35 E
Aiguá 55 El 34.12S 54.45W
Aigues 11 Kj 44.07N 4.43 E
Aigues-Mortes 11 Kk 43.34N 4.11 E
Aiguilles 11 Mj 44.47N 6.52 E
Aiguillon 11 Gj 44.18N 0.21 E
Aigurande 11 Hh 46.26N 1.50 E
Ai He 28 Hd 40.13N 124.30 E
Aihui (Heihe) 22 Od 50.13N 127.26 E
Aikawa 29 Fb 38.02N 138.14 E
Aiken 43 Ke 33.34N 81.44W
Ailao Shan 27 Hg 23.15N 102.20 E
Ailette 12 Fe 49.35N 3.10 E
Ailinginae Atoll 57 Hc 11.08N 166.24 E
Aillte an Mhothair/Moher, Cliffs of- 9 Di 52.58N 9.27W
Ailly-le-Haut-Clocher 12 Dd 50.05N 1.59 E
Ailly-sur-Noye 12 Ee 49.45N 2.22 E
Ailsa Craig 9 Hf 55.16N 5.07W
Ailuk Atoll 57 Hc 10.20N 169.56 E
Aim 20 Ie 58.48N 134.12 E
Aimogasta 56 Gc 28.33S 66.49W
Aimorés 54 Jg 19.30S 41.04W
Ain 11 Lh 46.10N 5.20 E
Ain 11 Li 45.48N 5.10 E
Ainazi/Ajnazi 7 Fh 57.52N 24.25 E
Ain Beïda 32 Ib 35.48N 7.24 E
Ain Beni Mathar 32 Gc 34.01N 2.01W
Ain Bessem 13 Ph 36.18N 3.40 E
Ain Boucif 13 Pi 35.53N 3.09 E
Ain Defla 13 Nh 36.16N 1.58 E
Ain el Berd 13 Li 35.21N 0.31W
Ain el Hammam 13 Qh 36.34N 4.19 E
Ain el Turck 13 Li 35.44N 0.46W
Ain Galakka 35 Bb 18.05N 18.31 E
Ainos Óros 15 Dk 38.07N 20.40 E
Ain Oulmene 13 Ri 35.55N 5.18 E
Ain Oussera 13 Oi 35.27N 2.54 E
Ain Sefra 31 Ge 32.45N 0.35W
Ainsworth 45 Ge 42.33N 99.52W
Ain Taghrout 13 Rh 36.08N 5.05 E
Ain Tedeles 13 Mh 36.00N 0.18 E
Ain Témouchent 32 Gb 35.18N 1.08W
Ain Tolba 13 Ki 35.15N 1.15W
Aioi 29 Dd 34.49N 134.28 E
Aiquile 54 Eg 18.10S 65.10W
Air/Azbine 30 Hg 18.00N 8.30 E
Airabu, Pulau- 26 Ef 2.46N 106.14 E
Airai 64a Bc 7.21N 134.34 E
Airaines 12 De 49.58N 1.57 E
Airão 54 Fd 1.56S 61.22W
Airbangis 26 Cf 0.12N 99.23 E
Airdrie 46 Ha 51.18N 114.02W
Aire 11 Id 50.38N 2.24 E
Aire [Eng.-U.K.] 9 Mh 53.44N 0.54W
Aire [Fr.] 11 Ke 49.19N 4.49 E
Aire, Canal d'- 11 Id 50.38N 2.25 E
Aire, Isla del- 13 Qe 39.47N 4.16 E
Aire-sur-l'Adour 11 Fk 43.42N 0.16W
Air Force 42 Kc 67.55N 74.05W
Airolo 14 Cd 46.33N 8.35 E
Ais 63b Cb 15.26S 167.15 E
Aisch 10 Hg 49.46N 11.01 E
Aisén del General Carlos Ibáñez del Campo 56 Fg 46.00S 73.00W
Aishihik 42 Dd 61.34N 137.30W
Ai-Shima 29 Bd 34.30N 131.18 E
Aisne 11 Je 49.30N 3.30 E
Aisne 11 Ie 49.26N 2.50 E
Aisne à la Marne, Canal de l'- 11 Je 49.24N 3.55 E
Aïssa, Djebel- 32 Gc 32.51N 0.30W
Aitana, Pico- 13 Lf 38.39N 0.16W
Aitape 60 Ch 3.08S 142.21 E
Aitolikón 15 Ek 38.26N 21.21 E
Aitutaki Atoll 57 Lf 18.52S 159.45W
Ait Youssef ou Ali 13 Ii 35.09N 3.55W
Aiud 15 Gc 46.18N 23.43 E
Aiviekste 7 Fh 56.36N 25.44 E
Aiviekste/Ajviekste 7 Fh 56.36N 25.44 E
Aiwokako Passage 64a Bb 7.39N 134.33 E
Aix, Ile d'- 11 Eh 46.01N 1.10W
Aix-en-Provence 11 Lk 43.32N 5.26 E
Aixe-sur-Vienne 11 Hi 45.48N 1.08 E
Aix-les-Bains 11 Li 45.42N 5.55 E
Aiyaion Pélagos = Aegean Sea (EN) 5 Ih 39.00N 25.00 E
Aiyina 15 Gl 37.45N 23.26 E
Aiyina = Aegina (EN) 15 Gl 37.40N 23.30 E
Aiyinion 15 Fi 40.30N 22.33 E
Aiyion 15 Fk 38.15N 22.05 E
Aizawl 25 Id 23.44N 92.43 E
Aizenay 11 Eh 46.44N 1.37W
Aizpute/Ajzpute 7 Eh 56.45N 21.39 E
Aizubange 29 Fc 37.34N 139.49 E
Aizutakada 29 Fc 37.29N 139.48 E
Aizuwakamatsu 28 Of 37.30N 139.56 E
Ajā', Jabal- 24 Ii 27.30N 41.30 E
'Ajab Shīr 24 Kd 37.28N 45.54 E
Ajaccio 6 Gg 41.55N 8.44 E
Ajaccio, Golfe d'- 11a Ab 41.50N 8.41 E
Ajaguz 22 Ke 47.58N 80.27 E
Ajakli 20 Eb 70.13N 95.55 E
Ajan 20 Fe 59.38N 106.45 E
Ajan 20 Ie 56.27N 138.10 E
Ajanka 20 Ld 63.40N 167.30 E
Ajanta Range 25 Fd 20.30N 76.00 E
Ajat 17 Kj 52.54N 62.50 E
Ajax Peak 46 Id 45.20N 113.40W
Ajdābiyā 31 Je 30.46N 20.14 E
Ajdabul 19 Ge 52.42N 69.01 E
Ajdar 16 Ke 48.42N 39.13 E
Ajdar, Solončak- 18 Fd 40.50N 66.50 E
Ajdovščina 14 He 45.53N 13.53 E
Ajdyrlinski 17 Ij 52.03N 59.50 E
Ajhal 20 Gc 66.00N 111.32 E
Ajigasawa 28 Pd 40.47N 140.12 E
Aji-Shima 29 Gb 38.15N 141.30 E
Ajjer, Tassili-n- 30 Hf 25.30N 9.00 E
Ajka 10 Ni 47.06N 17.34 E
Ajke, Ozero- 16 Vd 50.55N 61.35 E
Ajkino 17 De 62.15N 49.56 E
'Ajlūn 24 Ff 32.20N 35.45 E
'Ajmah, Jabal al- 24 Fh 29.12N 34.02 E
'Ajmān 23 Id 25.25N 55.27 E
Ajmer 22 Jg 26.27N 74.38 E
Ajnaži/Ainaži 7 Fh 57.52N 24.25 E
Ajni 18 Ge 39.23N 68.36 E
Ajo 43 Ee 32.22N 112.52W
Ajo, Cabo de- 13 Ia 43.31N 3.35W
Ajon, Ostrov- 21 Sc 69.50N 168.40 E
Ajoupa-Bouillon 51h Ab 14.50N 61.08W
Ajsary 19 He 53.05N 71.00 E
Ajtos 15 Kg 42.42N 27.15 E
Aju, Kepulauan- 26 Jf 0.28N 131.03 E
'Ajūz, Jabal al- 24 Dj 25.49N 30.43 E
Ajviekste 7 Fh 56.36N 25.44 E
Ajviekste 7 Fh 56.36N 25.44 E
Ajzkraukle (Stučka) 7 Fh 56.36N 25.17 E
Ajzpute/Aizpute 7 Eh 56.45N 21.39 E
Akaba 34 Fd 7.57N 1.03 E
Akabira 28 Qc 43.30N 142.04 E
Akabli 32 Hd 26.42N 1.22 E
Akademika Obručeva, Hrebet- 20 Ef 51.30N 96.45 E
Akadomari 29 Fc 37.54N 138.24 E
Aka-Gawa 29 Fb 38.54N 139.50 E
Akagi-San 29 Fc 36.33N 139.11 E
Akaishi-Dake 29 Fd 35.27N 138.09 E
Akaishi-Sanmyaku 29 Fd 35.25N 138.10 E
Akajaure 7 Dc 67.42N 17.30 E
Aka-Jima 29b Ab 26.14N 127.17 E
Akaki 35 Fd 8.51N 38.48 E
Akala 35 Fb 15.38N 36.12 E
Akan 29a Db 43.08N 144.07 E
Akan-Gawa 29a Db 43.02N 144.16 E
Akar 24 Dc 38.38N 31.06 E
Akarnaniká Óri 15 Dk 38.45N 21.00 E
Akaroa 61 Dh 43.48S 172.59 E
Akasaki 29 Cd 35.31N 133.38 E
'Akasha East 35 Ea 21.05N 30.43 E
Akashi 28 Mg 34.38N 134.59 E
Akbaba Tepe 24 Hc 39.32N 39.33 E
Akbajtal, Pereval- 19 Hh 38.31N 73.41 E
Akbou 13 Qh 36.28N 4.32 E
Akbulak 19 Fe 51.03N 55.37 E
Akbura 18 Id 40.34N 72.45 E
Akçaabat 24 Hb 40.59N 39.34 E
Akçadağ 24 Gc 38.21N 37.59 E
Akçakale 24 Hd 36.41N 38.56 E
Akçakara Daği 24 Ic 38.40N 40.52 E
Akçakoca 24 Db 41.05N 31.09 E
Akçaova [Tur.] 15 Mh 41.03N 29.57 E
Akçaova [Tur.] 15 Ll 37.30N 28.02 E
Akčatau 19 Hf 47.59N 74.02 E
Akçay 15 Ll 37.50N 28.15 E
Akçay 15 Mm 36.36N 29.45 E
Akchâr 30 Ff 20.20N 14.28W
Ak Dağ [Tur.] 24 Ib 40.35N 41.46 E
Ak Dağ [Tur.] 23 Cb 36.32N 29.34 E
Akdağ [Tur.] 24 Gd 37.53N 37.56 E
Akdağ [Tur.] 24 Fb 40.57N 35.55 E
Akdağ [Tur.] 24 Cc 39.15N 28.49 E
Akdağ [Tur.] 15 Ll 37.42N 28.56 E
Akdağ [Tur.] 15 Mk 38.18N 29.58 E
Akdağ [Tur.] 15 Jk 38.33N 26.30 E
Ak Dağlar 24 Gc 39.30N 36.00 E
Ak Dağlar 24 Ic 38.40N 40.12 E
Akdağmadeni 24 Fc 39.40N 35.54 E
Akdeniz = Mediterranean Sea (EN) 5 Hh 35.00N 20.00 E
Ak-Dovurak 20 Ef 51.10N 90.40 E
Akechi 29 Ed 35.18N 137.22 E
Ake Eze 34 Gd 5.55N 7.40 E
Akera 16 Oj 39.09N 46.48 E
Åkersberga 8 He 59.29N 18.18 E
Akershus 7 Cf 60.00N 11.10 E
Aketi 31 Jh 2.44N 23.46 E
Akharnai 15 Gk 38.05N 23.44 E
Akhdar, al Jabal al- 21 Hg 23.30N 57.00 E
Akhḍar, Al Jabal al- 30 Je 32.30N 21.30 E
Akhḍar, Wādī al- 24 Gh 28.35N 36.35 E
Akhelóös 15 Ej 38.18N 21.10 E
Akhisar 23 Cb 38.55N 27.51 E
Akhmīm 33 Fd 26.34N 31.44 E
Akhtarīn 24 Gd 36.31N 37.20 E
Aki 29 Ce 33.30N 133.53 E
Akiaki Atoll 61 Nc 18.30S 139.12W
Akiéni 36 Bc 1.11S 13.53 E
Akimiski 38 Kd 53.00N 81.20W
Akimovka 16 If 46.42N 35.09 E
Aki-Nada 29 Cd 34.05N 132.40 E
Åkirkeby 8 Fi 55.04N 14.56 E
Akita 22 Qf 39.43N 140.07 E
Akita Ken 28 Pe 39.45N 140.20 E
Akjoujt 31 Fg 19.44N 14.22W
Akka 32 Fd 29.25N 8.15W
Akkanburluk 17 Mj 52.46N 66.35 E
'Akko 23 Ec 32.55N 35.05 E
Akkol 18 Hc 43.25N 70.47 E
Akköy 24 Bd 37.29N 27.15 E
Akkystau 19 Ff 47.17N 51.03 E
Aklavik 42 Dc 68.14N 135.02W
Aklé Mseïguilé 34 Eb 16.20N 4.45W
Akmené/Akmene 8 Jh 56.14N 22.43 E
Akmenrags/Akmeņrags 8 Ih 56.54N 20.55 E
Akmenrags/Akmenrags 8 Ih 56.54N 20.55 E
Akmeqit 27 Cd 37.05N 76.55 E
Akniste 8 Kh 56.10N 25.54 E
Akō 29 Dd 34.45N 134.23 E
Akobo 30 Kh 7.48N 33.03 E
Akobo 31 Kh 7.47N 33.01 E
Akola 22 Jg 20.44N 77.00 E
Akonolinga 34 He 3.46N 12.15 E
Akosombo Dam 34 Fd 6.16N 0.03 E
Akpatok 42 Kd 60.24N 68.05W
Akqi 27 Cc 40.50N 78.01 E
Ákra Ámbelos 15 Gj 39.56N 23.56 E
Ákra Kambanós 15 Hl 37.59N 24.45 E
Akranes 7a Ab 64.19N 22.06W
Ákra Spathí 15 Gl 37.27N 23.31 E
Åkrehamn 7 Ag 59.16N 5.11 E
Akritas, Ákra- = Akritas, Cape- (EN) 15 Em 36.43N 21.53 E
Akritas Cape- (EN) = Akritas, Ákra- 15 Em 36.43N 21.53 E
Akron [Co.-U.S.] 45 Ef 40.10N 103.13W
Akron [Oh.-U.S.] 43 Kc 41.04N 81.31W
Akrotiri 24 Ee 34.36N 32.57 E
Akša 20 Gf 50.17N 113.17 E
Aksaj 16 Oh 43.32N 46.55 E
Aksaj 19 Fe 51.13N 53.01 E
Aksaj 16 Kf 47.15N 39.52 E
Aksakal 15 Li 40.09N 28.07 E
Aksakovo 17 Gi 54.02N 54.09 E
Aksaray 23 Db 38.23N 34.03 E
Aksay 27 Fd 39.28N 94.15 E
Akşehir 23 Db 38.21N 31.25 E
Akşehir Gölü 24 Dc 38.30N 31.28 E
Akseki 24 Dd 37.02N 31.48 E
Aksenovo-Zilovskoje 20 Gf 53.00N 117.35 E
'Aks-e Rostam 24 Ph 28.23N 54.52 E
Aksoran, Gora 19 Hf 48.25N 75.30 E
Akstafa 16 Ni 41.13N 45.27 E
Akstafa 16 Ni 41.06N 45.28 E
Aksu [China] 22 Ke 41.09N 80.15 E
Aksu 19 He 52.28N 71.59 E
Aksu 18 Lb 45.34N 79.30 E
Aksu 19 Hf 46.20N 78.15 E
Aksu [Tur.] 15 Ll 37.56N 28.56 E
Aksu [Tur.] 24 Dd 36.51N 30.54 E
Aksuat 19 If 47.48N 82.50 E
Aksubajevo 7 Mi 54.52N 50.50 E
Aksu He 21 Ke 40.28N 80.52 E
Aksum 35 Fc 14.07N 38.45 E
Ak-Šyjrak 18 Ld 41.49N 78.44 E
Aktag 27 Dd 36.45N 84.40 E
Aktaš 20 Df 50.18N 87.44 E
Aktaš 19 Gh 39.55N 65.53 E
Aktau 19 He 50.16N 73.07 E
Aktau (Ševčenko) 22 He 43.35N 51.05 E
Aktau, Gora- 19 Gg 41.45N 64.30 E
Aktjubinsk 6 Le 50.17N 57.10 E
Aktjubinskaja Oblast 19 Ff 48.00N 58.00 E
Ak-Tjuz 18 Kc 42.50N 76.07 E
Akto 27 Cd 39.05N 76.02 E
Aktogaj 19 Hf 47.01N 79.40 E
Akula 36 Db 2.22N 20.11 E
Akun 40a Eb 54.12N 165.35W
Akune 28 Kh 32.01N 130.11 E
Akure 34 Gd 7.15N 5.12 E
Akureyri 6 Eb 65.40N 18.06W
Akuseki-Jima 28 Jj 29.28N 129.33 E
Akutan 40a Eb 54.10N 165.55W
Akutan 40a Eb 54.08N 165.46W
Akyab ↓ Sittwe 22 Lg 20.09N 92.54 E
Akyazı 24 Db 40.41N 30.37 E
Akžajkyn, Ozero- 18 Fb 44.55N 67.45 E
Akžal 19 If 49.13N 81.30 E
Ål 8 Cd 60.38N 8.34 E
Alà, Monti di- 14 Dj 40.35N 9.16 E
Alabama 38 Kf 31.08N 87.57W
Alabama 43 Je 32.50N 87.30W
Al'Abbāsīyah 35 Ec 12.10N 31.18 E
Alaca 24 Fb 40.10N 34.51 E
Alaçam Dağlari 15 Lj 39.20N 28.32 E
Alaçan 24 Fb 41.37N 35.37 E
Alaçati 15 Jk 38.16N 26.23 E
Aladağ 24 Jc 43.35N 39.20 E
Ala Dağ [Tur.] 24 Jb 40.11N 42.49 E
Ala Dağ [Tur.] 24 Ed 37.58N 32.04 E
Alādāgh, Kūh-e- 24 Qd 37.13N 57.30 E
Ala Dağları 24 Fd 37.55N 35.13 E
Aladža 16 Rj 39.21N 53.12 E
Aladža Manastir 15 Lf 43.17N 28.01 E
Alagir 16 Nh 43.01N 44.12 E
Alagna Valsesia 14 Be 45.51N 7.56 E
Alagnon 11 Ji 45.27N 3.19 E
Alagoas 54 Ke 9.30S 36.30W
Alagoinhas 53 Mg 12.07S 38.26W
Alagón 13 Kc 41.46N 1.07W
Alagón 13 Fe 39.44N 6.53W
Ala Gou 27 Ec 42.42N 89.12 E
Alahanpanjang 26 Dg 1.05S 100.47 E
Alahärmä 7 Fe 63.14N 22.51 E
Al Aḥmadī 24 Mh 29.05N 48.04 E
Alaid, Vulkan 20 Kf 50.50N 155.33 E
Alajärvi 7 Fe 63.00N 23.49 E
Alajku 19 Hg 40.18N 74.29 E
Alajski Hrebet 21 Jf 39.45N 72.30 E
Alajuela 49 Eh 10.30N 84.30W
Alajuela 47 Hf 10.01N 84.13W
Alajuela, Lago- 49 Hi 9.05N 79.24W
Alakol, Ozero- 21 Ke 46.05N 81.50 E
Alakurtti 7 Hc 66.59N 30.20 E
Alalakeiki Channel 65a Ec 20.35N 156.30W
Al 'Alamayn 31 Je 30.49N 28.57 E
Alalau, Rio- 54 Fd 0.30S 61.10W
Al Amādīyah 24 Jd 37.06N 43.29 E
Alamagan Island 57 Fc 17.36N 145.50 E
Al 'Amārah 23 Gc 31.50N 47.09 E
'Alam ar Rūm, Ra's- 24 Bg 31.22N 27.21 E
Alāmarvdasht 24 Oi 27.52N 52.34 E
Alamashindo 35 Ge 4.51N 42.04 E
Alamata 35 Fc 12.25N 39.37 E
Alameda 45 Ci 35.11N 106.37W
Alaminos 26 Gc 16.10N 119.59 E
Al 'Āmirīyah 24 Cg 31.01N 29.48 E
Alamito Creek 45 Dl 29.31N 104.17W
Alamitos, Sierra de los- 48 Hd 26.20N 102.15W
'Alāmo 35 Ge 4.23N 43.09 E
Alamo 46 Hh 37.22N 115.10W
Alamogordo 43 Fe 32.54N 105.57W
Alamos 47 Cc 27.01N 108.56W
Alamos, Sierra- 48 Gc 28.25N 105.00W
Alamosa 43 Fd 37.28N 105.52W
Al Anbār 24 If 34.00N 42.00 E
Åland/Ahvenanmaa 7 Ef 60.15N 20.00 E
Åland/Ahvenanmaa = Aland Islands (EN) 5 Hc 60.15N 20.00 E
Aland Islands (EN) = Ahvenanmaa/Åland 5 Hc 60.15N 20.00 E
Aland Islands (EN) = Åland/Ahvenanmaa 5 Hc 60.15N 20.00 E
Ålandsbro 8 Gb 62.40N 17.50 E
Ålandshav 8 Hd 60.00N 19.30 E
Alange 13 Ff 38.47N 6.15W
Alanje 49 Fi 8.24N 82.33W
Alanya 23 Db 36.33N 32.01 E
Alaotra, Lac- 37 Hc 17.30S 48.30 E
Alapaha River 44 Fj 30.26N 83.06W
Alapajevsk 19 Gd 57.52N 61.42 E
Alaplı 24 Db 41.08N 31.25 E
Al 'Aqabah = Aqaba (EN) 23 Dd 29.31N 35.00 E
Al 'Aqabah aş Şaghīrah 24 Ej 24.14N 32.53 E
Al 'Arabīyah As-Su'ūdīyah = Saudi Arabia (EN) 22 Gg 25.00N 45.00 E
Alarcón, Embalse de- 13 Je 39.45N 2.20W
Al 'Arīsh 33 Fc 31.08N 33.48 E
Al 'Armah 24 Lj 25.30N 46.30 E
Al Artāwīyah 24 Ki 26.30N 45.20 E
Alas, Selat- 26 Gh 8.40S 116.40 E
Al 'Aşab 24 Pk 23.20N 54.10 E
Alaşehir 24 Cc 38.21N 28.32 E
Al Ashkharah 23 Ie 21.47N 59.30 E
Al 'Āshūrīyah 24 Jg 31.02N 43.05 E
Alaska 40 Ic 65.00N 153.00W
Alaska 38 Dc 65.00N 153.00W
Alaska, Gulf of- 38 Ed 58.00N 146.00W
Alaska Peninsula 38 Dd 57.00N 158.00W
Alaska Range 38 Ec 62.30N 150.00W
Alassio 14 Cf 44.00N 8.10 E
Alastaro 8 Jd 60.57N 22.51 E
Alat 18 De 39.26N 63.48 E
Alataw Shan 27 Cb 45.00N 80.00 E
Alataw Shankou = Dzungarian Gate (EN) 21 Ke 45.25N 82.25 E
Al 'Athāmīn 24 Jg 30.35N 43.40 E
Alatri 14 Hi 41.43N 13.21 E
Al 'Aţrun 31 Jg 18.11N 26.36 E
Alatyr 7 Li 54.52N 46.36 E
Alatyr 19 Ee 54.50N 46.36 E
Álava 13 Jb 42.50N 2.45W
Alava, Cape- 46 Cb 48.10N 124.43W
Alaverdi 19 Eg 41.08N 44.37 E
Alavijeh 24 Nf 33.03N 51.05 E
Alavo/Alavus 7 Fe 62.35N 23.37 E
Alavus/Alavo 7 Fe 62.35N 23.37 E
Al 'Awāliq 23 Gg 14.15N 46.30 E
Al 'Awāriq 35 Ha 20.25N 48.40 E
Al 'Awsajīyah 24 Ki 26.04N 44.08 E
'Ālayh 24 Ff 33.48N 35.36 E
Al 'Ayn [Sau.Ar.] 24 Hj 25.04N 38.06 E
Al 'Ayn [U.A.E.] 24 Pj 24.13N 55.45 E
Alayor 13 Qe 39.56N 4.08 E
Al 'Ayyōţ 24 Dh 29.37N 31.15 E
Al A'zamīyah 24 Kf 33.23N 44.22 E
Alazani 16 Oi 41.03N 46.40 E
Alazeja 20 Kb 70.55N 153.40 E
Al'Azīzīyah 33 Bc 32.32N 13.01 E
Alazores, Puerto de los- 13 Hg 37.05N 4.15W
Alb [Ger.] 12 Ke 49.04N 8.20 E
Alb [Ger.] 10 Ei 47.35N 8.08 E
Alba 15 Gc 46.08N 23.30 E
Alba 14 Cf 44.42N 8.02 E
Alba Adriatica 14 Hh 42.50N 13.56 E
Al Bāb 24 Gd 36.22N 37.31 E
Albac 15 Fc 46.27N 22.58 E
Albacete 6 Fh 38.59N 1.51W
Albacete 13 Kf 38.50N 2.00W
Al Badārī 33 Fd 26.59N 31.25 E
Alba de Tormes 13 Gd 40.49N 5.31W
Al Badi 33 Ie 22.02N 46.34 E
Al Bādi 24 Ie 35.56N 41.32 E
Ålbæk 8 Dg 57.36N 10.25 E
Ålbæk Bugt 8 Dg 57.35N 10.30 E
Al Bahrah 24 Lh 29.40N 47.52 E
Al Baḥr al Aḥmar 35 Fb 19.50N 35.30 E
Al Baḥrayn 21 Hg 26.00N 50.30 E

Index Symbols

Independent Nation
State, Region
District, County
Municipality
Colony, Dependency
Continent
Physical Region
Historical or Cultural Region
Mount, Mountain
Volcano
Hill
Mountains, Mountain Range
Hills, Escarpment
Plateau, Upland
Pass, Gap
Plain, Lowland
Delta
Salt Flat
Valley, Canyon
Crater, Cave
Karst Features
Depression
Polder
Desert, Dunes
Forest, Woods
Heath, Steppe
Oasis
Cape, Point
Coast, Beach
Cliff
Peninsula
Isthmus
Sandbank
Island
Atoll
Rock, Reef
Islands, Archipelago
Rocks, Reefs
Coral Reef
Well, Spring
Geyser
River, Stream
Waterfall Rapids
River Mouth, Estuary
Lake
Salt Lake
Intermittent Lake
Reservoir
Swamp, Pond
Canal
Glacier
Ice Shelf, Pack Ice
Ocean
Sea
Gulf, Bay
Strait, Fjord
Lagoon
Bank
Seamount
Tablemount
Ridge
Shelf
Basin
Escarpment, Sea Scarp
Fracture
Trench, Abyss
National Park, Reserve
Point of Interest
Recreation Site
Cave, Cavern
Historic Site
Ruins
Wall, Walls
Church, Abbey
Temple
Scientific Station
Airport
Port
Lighthouse
Mine
Tunnel
Dam, Bridge

Al Baḩrayn=Bahrain (EN) [1] 22 Hg 26.00N 50.29 E
Albaida 13 Lf 38.51N 0.31W
Alba Iulia 15 Gc 46.04N 23.35 E
Albalate del Arzobispo 13 Lc 41.07N 0.31W
Al Balyanā 24 Fc 26.14N 32.00 E
Alban 11 Ik 43.54N 2.28 E
Albanel, Lac- 42 Kf 51.05N 73.05W
Albani, Colli- 14 Gi 41.45N 12.45 E
Albania (EN)=Shqipëria [1] 6 Hg 41.00N 20.00 E
Albano, Lago- 14 Gi 41.45N 12.40 E
Albano Laziale 14 Gi 41.44N 12.39 E
Albany 38 Kd 52.17N 81.31W
Albany [Austl.] 58 Ch 35.02S 117.53 E
Albany [Ga.-U.S.] 43 Ke 31.35N 84.10W
Albany [Ky.-U.S.] 44 Eg 36.42N 85.08W
Albany [N.Y.-U.S.] 39 Le 42.39N 73.45W
Albany [Or.-U.S.] 43 Cc 44.38N 123.06W
Alba Posse 55 Eh 27.33S 54.42W
Albarche 13 He 39.58N 4.46W
Albardón 56 Gd 31.26S 68.32W
Albarracín 13 Kd 40.25N 1.26W
Albarracín, Sierra de- 13 Kd 40.30N 1.30W
Al Başalīyah Qiblī 24 Ej 25.06N 32.47 E
Al Başrah [3] 24 Lg 30.30N 47.27 E
Al Başrah=Basra (EN) 22 Gf 30.30N 47.47 E
Al Baţḩā' 24 Kg 31.07N 45.54 E
Al Bāţin 24 Lh 29.00N 46.35 E
Al Bāţinah 21 Hg 23.45N 57.20 E
Albatross Bank (EN) 40 Ie 56.10N 152.20W
Albatross Bay 59 Ib 12.45S 141.43 E
Albatross Plateau (EN) 3 Mi 10.00N 103.00W
Albatross Point 62 Fc 38.07S 174.40 E
Al Batrūn 24 Fe 34.15N 35.39 E
Al Bawīţī 33 Ed 28.21N 28.52 E
Al Bayāḑ 21 Gg 22.00N 47.00 E
Al Bayḑā' [3] 33 Dc 32.00N 21.30 E
Al Bayḑā' 33 Cd 28.21N 18.58 E
Al Bayḑā' 31 Je 32.46N 21.43 E
Al Bayḑā' 33 Ig 13.58N 45.35 E
Albegna 14 Fh 42.30N 11.11 E
Albemarle 44 Gh 35.21N 80.12W
Albemarle Sound 43 Ld 36.03N 76.12W
Albenga 14 Cf 44.03N 8.13 E
Alberdi 56 Ic 26.10S 58.09W
Albères, Chaîne des- 11 Il 42.28N 2.56 E
Albères, Montes-/Les Alberes 11 Il 42.28N 2.56 E
Albergaria-a-Velha 13 Dd 40.42N 8.29W
Alberique 13 Le 39.07N 0.31W
Alberobello 14 Lj 40.47N 17.16 E
Albert 11 Id 50.00N 2.39 E
Albert, Canal-/Albert Kanaal =Albert Canal (EN) 11 Ld 50.39N 5.37 E
Albert, Lake- [Afr.] 30 Kh 1.40N 31.00 E
Albert, Lake- [Or.-U.S.] 46 Ee 42.38N 120.13W
Albert, Lake- (EN)=Mobuto Sese Seko, Lac- 30 Kh 1.40N 31.00 E
Alberta [3] 42 Gf 55.00N 115.00W
Albert Canal (EN)=Albert, Canal-/Albert Kanaal 11 Ld 50.39N 5.37 E
Albert Canal (EN)=Albert Kanaal/Albert, Canal- 11 Ld 50.39N 5.37 E
Albert Edward, Mount- 59 Ja 8.23S 147.27 E
Albert Edward Bay 42 Hc 69.35N 103.10W
Alberti 56 He 35.02S 60.16W
Albertirsa 10 Pi 47.15N 19.37 E
Albert Kanaal/Albert, Canal- =Albert Canal (EN) 11 Ld 50.39N 5.37 E
Albert Lea 43 Ic 43.39N 93.22W
Albert Nile 30 Kh 3.36N 32.02 E
Albertville [Al.-U.S.] 44 Dh 34.16N 86.12W
Albertville [Fr.] 11 Mi 45.41N 6.23 E
Albestroff 12 If 48.56N 6.51 E
Albi 11 Ik 43.56N 2.09 E
Albia 45 Jf 41.02N 92.48W
Al Bid' 24 Fh 28.28N 35.01 E
Albina 54 Hb 5.30N 54.03W
Albina, Ponta- 30 Ij 15.51S 11.44 E
Albino 14 De 45.46N 9.47 E
Albion [Mi.-U.S.] 44 Ed 42.15N 84.45W
Albion [Nb.-U.S.] 45 Hf 41.42N 98.00W
Albion [N.Y.-U.S.] 44 Hd 43.15N 78.12W
Al Biqā' 24 Ge 34.10N 36.10 E
Al Bi'r 23 Ed 28.51N 36.15 E
Al Bi'r al Jadīd 23 Ed 26.01N 38.29 E
Al Birk 23 Ff 18.13N 41.33 E
Albis 14 Cc 47.20N 8.30 E
Albo, Monte- 14 Dj 40.32N 9.35 E
Albocácer/Albocasser 13 Md 40.21N 0.02 E
Albocasser/Albocácer 13 Md 40.21N 0.02 E
Alborán, Isla de- 5 Fh 35.58N 3.02W
Alboran Basin (EN) 13 Ii 36.00N 4.00W
Ålborg 6 Gd 57.03N 9.56 E
Ålborg Bugt 7 Ch 56.45N 10.30 E
Alborz, Reshteh-ye- Kūhhā-ye-=Elburz Mountains (EN) 21 Hf 36.00N 53.00 E
Albox 13 Jg 37.23N 2.08W
Albret, Pays d'- 11 Fj 44.10N 0.20W
Ālbū 'Alī 24 Je 34.49N 43.35 E
Albufeira 13 Dg 37.05N 8.15W
Albū Gharz, Sabkhat- 24 Ie 34.45N 41.15 E
Al Buheyrat [3] 35 Dd 7.00N 29.30 E
Al Bumbah 33 Dc 32.13N 23.00 E
Albuñol 13 Ih 36.47N 3.12W
Albuquerque [Braz.] 55 Dd 19.23S 57.26W
Albuquerque [N.M.-U.S.] 39 If 35.05N 106.40W
Albuquerque, Cayos de- 47 Hf 12.10N 81.50W
Al Burayj 24 Ge 34.15N 36.46 E
Al Buraymī 23 Ie 24.15N 55.45 E
Al Burmah 32 Ic 31.45N 9.02 E
Alburquerque 13 Fe 39.13N 7.00W
Albury [Austl.] 58 Fh 36.05S 146.55 E
Albury [N.Z.] 62 Df 44.14S 170.53 E
Al Buţanah 30 Kg 15.00N 35.00 E
Al Buţayn 24 Kj 25.52N 45.50 E
Alby 8 Fb 62.30N 15.28 E
Alcácer do Sal 13 Df 38.22N 8.30W
Alcáçovar 13 Df 38.25N 8.13W
Alcalá de Chivert 13 Md 40.18N 0.14 E
Alcalá de Guadaira 13 Gg 37.20N 5.50W
Alcalá de Henares 13 Id 40.29N 3.22W
Alcalá del Júcar 13 Ke 39.12N 1.26W
Alcalá de los Gazules 13 Gh 36.28N 5.44W
Alcalá del Río 13 Gg 37.31N 5.59W
Alcalá la Real 13 Ig 37.28N 3.56W
Alcamo 14 Gm 37.59N 12.58 E
Alcanandre 13 Mc 41.37N 0.12 E
Alcañices 13 Fc 41.42N 6.21W
Alcañiz 13 Lc 41.03N 0.08W
Alcántara 13 Fe 39.43N 6.53W
Alcântara 54 Jd 2.24S 44.24W
Alcantara 14 Jm 37.49N 15.16 E
Alcántara, Embalse de- 13 Fe 39.45N 6.48W
Alcantarilla 13 Kg 37.58N 1.13W
Alcaraz 13 Jf 38.40N 2.29W
Alcaraz, Sierra de- 13 Jf 38.35N 2.25W
Alcaudete 13 Hg 37.36N 4.05W
Alcázar de San Juan 13 Ie 39.24N 3.12W
Alcester 63a Ac 9.33S 152.25 E
Alčevsk (Kommunarsk) 16 Ke 48.27N 38.52 E
Alcira/Alzira 13 Le 39.09N 0.26W
Alcobaça [Braz.] 54 Kg 17.30S 39.13W
Alcobaça [Port.] 13 De 39.33N 8.59W
Alcobendas 13 Id 40.32N 3.38W
Alcoi/Alcoy 13 Lf 38.42N 0.28W
Alcolea del Pinar 13 Jc 41.02N 2.28W
Alcorta 55 Bk 33.32S 61.07W
Alcoutim 13 Eg 37.28N 7.28W
Alcova 46 Le 42.37N 106.36W
Alcoy/Alcoi 13 Lf 38.42N 0.28W
Alcubierre, Sierra de- 13 Lc 41.44N 0.29W
Alcudia 13 Pe 39.52N 3.07 E
Alcudia, Bahía de-/Alcúdia, Badia d'- 13 Pe 39.48N 3.13 E
Alcudia, Sierra de- 13 Hf 38.35N 4.35W
Aldabra Group 37b Ab 9.25S 46.22 E
Aldabra Islands 30 Li 9.25S 46.22 E
Aldama [Mex.] 48 Jf 22.55N 98.04W
Aldama [Mex.] 47 Cc 28.51N 105.54W
Aldan 22 Od 58.37N 125.24 E
Aldan 20 Hd 63.20N 129.25 E
Aldan 21 Oc 63.28N 129.35 E
Aldan Plateau (EN)= Aldanskoje Nagorje 21 Od 57.30N 127.30 E
Aldanskoje Nagorje=Aldan Plateau (EN) 21 Od 57.30N 127.30 E
Aldarhan 27 Gb 47.42N 96.36 E
Alde 12 Db 52.10N 1.32 E
Aldeburgh 9 Oi 52.09N 1.35 E
Aldeia 55 Ed 18.12S 55.10W
Aldeia, Serra da- 55 Ic 17.00S 46.50W
Alderney 9 Kl 49.43N 2.12W
Aldershot 12 Bc 51.15N 0.46W
Alderson 46 Ja 50.18N 111.26W
Aledo 45 Kf 41.12N 90.45W
Aleg 31 Fg 17.03N 13.53W
Alegranza 32 Ed 29.23N 13.30W
Alegre 54 Jh 20.46S 41.32W
Alegre, Rio- 55 Cb 15.14S 59.58W
Alegrete 56 Ic 29.46S 55.46W
Alej 20 Df 52.50N 83.35 E
Alejandra 55 Ci 29.54S 59.50W
Alejandro Selkirk, Isla- 52 Hi 33.45S 80.46W
Alejsk 20 Df 52.28N 82.45 E
Aleksandrija 16 He 48.40N 33.07 E
Aleksandrov 19 Dd 56.25N 38.42 E
Aleksandrov Gaj 19 Ee 50.08N 48.32 E
Aleksandrovka 16 He 48.59N 32.13 E
Aleksandrovsk 17 Hg 59.10N 57.35 E
Aleksandrovskoje 16 Mg 44.39N 43.00 E
Aleksandrovsk-Sahalinsk 22 Qd 50.54N 142.10 E
Aleksandrów Kujawski 10 Od 52.52N 18.42 E
Aleksandrów Łódzki 10 Pe 51.49N 19.19 E
Aleksandry, Zemlja- 21 Ga 80.45N 46.00 E
Aleksejevka 19 If 48.26N 85.40 E
Aleksejevka 19 He 51.58N 70.59 E
Aleksejevka 17 Nj 53.31N 69.28 E
Aleksejevka 19 De 50.39N 38.42 E
Aleksejevsk 20 Fe 57.50N 108.23 E
Aleksejevskoje 7 Mi 55.19N 50.03 E
Aleksin 16 Jb 54.31N 37.07 E
Aleksinac 15 Ef 43.32N 21.43 E
Alem 56 Ic 27.31S 55.15W
Ålem 7 Dh 56.57N 16.23 E
Alem Maya 35 Gd 9.27N 41.58 E
Ålen 8 Db 62.51N 11.17 E
Alençon 11 Gf 48.26N 0.05 E
Alenquer 54 Hd 1.56S 54.46W
Alenuihaha Channel 60 Oc 20.26N 156.00W
Alépé 34 Ed 5.30N 3.39W
Aleppo (EN)=Ḩalab 22 Ff 36.12N 37.10 E
Aléria 11a Ba 42.06N 9.31 E
Aléria, Plaine d'- 11a Ba 42.05N 9.30 E
Alert 39 Ma 82.30N 62.00W
Alert Bay 46 Ba 50.35N 126.55W
Alès 11 Kj 44.08N 4.05 E
Aleşd 15 Fb 47.04N 22.25 E
Alessandria 14 Cf 44.54N 8.37 E
Ålestrup 8 Ch 56.42N 9.30 E
Ålesund 6 Gc 62.28N 6.09 E
Aleutian Basin (EN) 40 Ad 57.00N 177.00 E
Aleutian Islands 38 Bd 52.00N 176.00W
Aleutian Range 38 Dd 59.00N 155.00W
Aleutian Trench (EN) 3 Je 51.00N 179.00 E
Alexander, Cape- 60 Fi 6.35S 156.30 E
Alexander, Kap- 41 Ec 78.10N 72.45W
Alexander Archipelago 38 Fd 56.30N 134.00W
Alexanderbaai 37 Be 28.40S 16.30 E
Alexander City 43 Je 32.56N 85.57W
Alexander Island 66 Qe 71.00S 70.00W
Alexandra 61 Ci 45.15S 169.24 E
Alexandra Fiord 42 Ka 79.17N 75.00W
Alexandretta (EN)=İskenderun 22 Ff 36.37N 36.07 E
Alexandretta, Gulf of- (EN) =İskenderun Körfezi 23 Eb 36.30N 35.40 E
Alexándria 15 Fi 40.38N 22.27 E
Alexandria [Austl.] 59 Hc 19.05S 136.40 E
Alexandria [La.-U.S.] 39 Jf 31.18N 92.27W
Alexandria [Mn.-U.S.] 43 Hb 45.53N 95.22W
Alexandria [Rom.] 15 If 43.59N 25.20 E
Alexandria [S.Afr.] 37 Df 33.39S 26.24 E
Alexandria [Va.-U.S.] 44 If 38.49N 77.06W
Alexandria (EN)=Al Iskandarīyah [Eg.] 31 Je 31.12N 29.54 E
Alexandria Bay 44 Jc 44.20N 75.55W
Alexandrina, Lake- 59 Hg 35.25S 139.10 E
Alexandrita 54 Hg 19.42S 50.27W
Alexandroúpolis 6 Ig 40.51N 25.52 E
'Aleyak, Godār-e- 24 Qd 36.30N 57.45 E
Alf 10 Df 50.03N 7.07 E
Alfabia, Sierra de- 13 Oe 39.45N 2.48 E
Alfambra 13 Kd 40.21N 1.07W
Al Fardah 35 Hc 14.51N 48.26 E
Alfaro 13 Kb 42.11N 1.45W
Al Fāshir 31 Jg 13.38N 25.21 E
Al Fashn 33 Fd 28.49N 30.54 E
Alfatar 15 Kf 43.57N 27.17 E
Al Fathah 24 Je 35.04N 43.34 E
Al Fāw 23 Gd 29.58N 48.29 E
Al Fawwārah 24 Ji 26.03N 43.05 E
Al Fayyūm 31 Kf 29.19N 30.58 E
Alfbach 12 Jd 50.03N 7.08 E
Alfeld 10 Fe 51.59N 9.50 E
Alfenas 54 Ih 21.26S 45.57W
Al Fifi 35 Dc 10.03N 25.01 E
Alfiós 15 El 37.37N 21.27 E
Alföld 5 If 47.15N 20.25 E
Alfonsine 14 Gf 44.30N 12.03 E
Alford 12 Ca 53.15N 0.11 E
Ålfotbreen 8 Ac 61.45N 5.40 E
Alfreton 12 Aa 53.06N 1.23W
Alfta 7 Df 61.21N 16.05 E
Al Fuḩayḩīl 23 Gd 29.05N 48.08 E
Al Fuḩūd 24 Lg 30.58N 46.43 E
Al Fujayrah 23 Id 25.06N 56.21 E
Al Fūlah 35 Dc 11.48N 28.24 E
Al Fuqahā' 33 Cd 27.50N 16.21 E
Al Furāt=Euphrates (EN) 21 Gf 31.00N 47.25 E
Al Fuwayriţ 24 Ni 26.02N 51.22 E
Alga 19 Ff 49.55N 57.20 E
Algador 13 Ie 39.55N 3.53W
Al Gārah 24 Ih 29.52N 40.15 E
Algarås 8 Ff 58.48N 14.14 E
Ålgård 8 Af 58.46N 5.51 E
Algarrobo 49 Jh 10.12N 74.04W
Algarve 13 Dg 37.10N 8.15W
Algarve 5 Fh 37.10N 8.15W
Algeciras 6 Fh 36.08N 5.30W
Algeciras, Bahía de- 13 Gh 36.09N 5.25W
Algena 35 Fb 17.20N 38.34 E
Algeria (EN)=Al Jazā'ir [1] 31 Hf 28.00N 3.00 E
Algerian Basin (EN) 5 Gh 39.00N 5.00 E
Al Gharaq as Sulţānī 24 Dh 29.08N 30.42 E
Al Gharbī 32 Jc 34.40N 11.13 E
Al Ghāţ 24 Ki 26.00N 45.03 E
Al Ghaydah 23 Hf 16.12N 52.15 E
Alghero 14 Cj 40.33N 8.19 E
Alghero, Rada d'- 14 Cj 40.35N 8.20 E
Älghult 8 Fg 57.01N 15.34 E
Al Ghurāb 24 Dj 25.20N 30.20 E
Al Ghurayfah 24 Qk 23.59N 56.29 E
Al Ghurdaqah 33 Fd 27.14N 33.50 E
Algiers (EN)=Al Jazā'ir 31 He 36.47N 3.03 E
Algiers (EN)=Al Jazā'ir [3] 32 Hb 36.35N 3.00 E
Algoa Bay 30 Jl 33.50S 25.50 E
Algodoeiro, Serra do- 55 Jc 16.30S 44.45W
Algoma 45 Md 44.36N 87.27W
Algoma Uplands 44 Fb 47.00N 83.35W
Algona 45 Ie 43.04N 94.14W
Algonquin Park 44 Hc 45.27N 78.26W
Algrange 12 Ie 49.21N 6.03 E
Al Ḩabakah 24 Jh 29.51N 42.16 E
Al Ḩadd 23 Ie 22.29N 59.58 E
Al Ḩadīdah 23 Ia 21.31N 50.28 E
Al Ḩadīthah 23 Fc 34.07N 42.23 E
Al Ḩadīthah 24 Gg 31.28N 37.08 E
Al Ḩaḑr 24 Je 35.35N 42.44 E
Al Haffah 24 Ge 35.35N 36.02 E
Al Ḩahjarah 23 Fc 30.25N 44.30 E
Al Ḩā'ir 24 Lj 24.23N 46.50 E
Al Ḩajar 35 Hb 16.08N 47.50 E
Al Hajar 23 Ie 23.15N 57.30 E
Al Halfāyah 24 Lg 31.49N 47.26 E
Alhama 13 Kb 42.11N 1.45W
Al Ḩamād 21 Ff 32.00N 39.30 E
Alhama de Granada 13 Ih 37.00N 3.59W
Alhama de Murcia 13 Kg 37.51N 1.25W
Alhamilla, Sierra- 13 Jh 36.58N 2.20W
Al Ḩammāh 32 Ic 33.54N 9.48 E
Al Ḩammām [Eg.] 24 Cg 30.50N 29.23 E
Al Ḩammām [Iraq] 24 Kg 31.08N 44.04 E
Al Ḩamrā' 24 Pj 25.42N 55.47 E
Al Ḩanīyah 24 Kh 29.10N 45.50 E
Al Ḩarrah 24 Ch 28.20N 29.07 E
Al Ḩarrah 24 Hg 31.00N 38.40 E
Al Harūj al Aswad 30 If 27.00N 17.10 E
Al Ḩasā 24 Fg 30.49N 35.59 E
Al Hasā' 21 Gg 26.35N 48.10 E
Al Ḩasakah 23 Fb 36.29N 40.45 E
Al Ḩasan 24 Je 34.39N 43.43 E
Al Ḩasānī 24 Gj 24.58N 37.05 E
Alhaurín el Grande 13 Hh 36.38N 4.41W
Al Ḩawāmidīyah 24 Dh 29.54N 31.15 E
Al Ḩawātah 35 Ec 13.25N 34.38 E
Al Ḩawjā' 24 Hh 28.59N 38.34 E
Al Hawrah 35 Hc 13.49N 47.35 E
Al Ḩayy 23 Gc 32.10N 46.03 E
Al Ḩayz 33 Ed 28.02N 28.39 E
Al Hibāk 23 He 20.20N 53.10 E
Al Ḩijāz 21 Fg 24.30N 38.30 E
Al Ḩillah 33 Ie 23.50N 46.51 E
Al Ḩillah 23 Fc 32.29N 44.25 E
Al Ḩinākīyah 23 Fe 24.51N 40.31 E
Al Hindiyah 24 Kf 32.32N 44.13 E
Al Ḩinnāh 24 Mi 26.56N 48.45 E
Al Hirmil 24 Ge 34.23N 36.23 E
Al Hoceima 32 Gb 35.15N 3.55W
Al Hoceima [3] 32 Gb 35.00N 4.15W
Alhucemas, Peñón de- 13 Ii 35.13N 3.53W
Al Ḩudaydah 22 Gh 14.48N 42.57 E
Al Hufrah 33 Cd 29.30N 17.55 E
Al Hufrah 23 Ed 28.49N 38.15 E
Al Hufūf 22 Gg 25.22N 49.34 E
Al Ḩūj 24 Hh 29.00N 38.25 E
Al Ḩunayy 24 Mj 24.48N 48.45 E
Al Ḩuşayḩişah 35 Ec 14.44N 33.18 E
Al Ḩuwaimī 23 Fg 13.58N 47.40 E
Al Ḩuwayyiţ 24 Ij 25.36N 40.23 E
Al Ḩyyānīyah 24 Jh 28.42N 42.18 E
'Alīābād [Iran] 23 Id 28.37N 55.51 E
'Alīābād [Iran] 24 Le 35.04N 46.58 E
'Alīābād [Iran] 24 Nd 36.37N 51.33 E
Alīābād 24 Pd 36.56N 54.50 E
Alīābād, Kūh-e- 23 Hc 34.13N 50.46 E
Aliaga 13 Ld 40.40N 0.42W
Aliağa 24 Bc 38.48N 26.59 E
Aliákmon 15 Fi 40.30N 22.40 E
'Alī al Gharbī 24 Lf 32.27N 46.41 E
'Alī ash Sharqī 24 Lf 32.07N 46.44 E
Ali-Bajramly 19 Eh 39.55N 48.57 E
Alibej, Ozero- 15 Nd 45.50N 30.00 E
Alibey Adasi 15 Jj 39.20N 26.38 E
Alibo 35 Fd 9.53N 37.05 E
Alibori 34 Fc 11.56N 3.17 E
Alibunar 15 Dd 45.04N 20.58 E
Alicante 6 Fh 38.21N 0.29W
Alicante [3] 13 Lf 38.30N 0.30W
Alicante, Golfo de- 13 Lf 38.20N 0.15W
Alice [S.Afr.] 37 Df 32.47S 26.50 E
Alice [Tx.-U.S.] 43 Hf 27.45N 98.04W
Alice, Punta- 14 Lk 39.12N 17.09 E
Alice Springs 58 Eg 23.42S 133.53 E
Aliceville 44 Ci 33.08N 88.09W
Alicudi 14 Il 38.30N 14.20 E
Alīgarh 22 Jg 28.02N 78.17 E
Alīgūdarz 24 Mf 33.24N 49.41 E
Alihe→Oroqen Zizhiqi 27 La 50.35N 123.42 E
Alijó 13 Ec 41.16N 7.28W
Alijos, Rocas- 47 Ad 24.57N 115.44W
'Al Ijūq, Kūh-e- 24 Ng 31.30N 51.45 E
Al Ikhwān 21 Hh 12.08N 53.10 E
Al Ikhwān 24 Fi 26.19N 34.52 E
Alima 30 Ii 1.36S 16.36 E
Al Imārāt al 'Arabīyah al Muttaḩidah=United Arab Emirates (EN) [1] 22 Hg 24.00N 54.00 E
Alimiá 15 Km 36.16N 27.43 E
Alindao 35 Cd 5.02N 21.13 E
Alinglapalap Atoll 57 Hd 7.08N 168.16 E
Alingsås 7 Ch 57.56N 12.31 E
Aliquippa 44 Ge 40.38N 80.16W
Al 'Irāq=Iraq (EN) [1] 22 Gf 33.00N 44.00 E
Al'Irq 33 Dd 29.01N 21.31 E
Al 'Irqah 23 Gg 13.40N 47.18 E
Ali-Sabjeh 35 Gc 11.08N 42.43 E
'Alī Shāh 'Avaz 24 Ne 35.39N 51.04 E
Al Iskandarīyah [Eg.] = Alexandria (EN) 31 Je 31.12N 29.54 E
Al Iskandarīyah [Iraq] 24 Kf 32.53N 44.21 E
Aliskerovo 20 Lc 67.52N 167.40 E
Al Ismā'īlīyah=Ismailia (EN) 33 Fc 30.35N 32.16 E
Al Istiwā'īyah al Gharbīyah [3] 35 Dd 5.20N 28.30 E
Al Istiwā'īyah al Sharkīyah [3] 35 Ed 5.20N 33.50 E
Alistráti 15 Gh 41.04N 23.58 E
Alitak, Cape- 40 Ie 56.51N 154.21W
Alite Reef 63a Ec 8.53S 160.38 E
Alitus/Alytus 19 Ce 54.25N 24.08 E
Alivérion 15 Hk 38.25N 24.02 E
Aliwal North 31 Jl 30.44S 26.40 E
Al Jabalayn 35 Ec 12.36N 32.48 E
Al Jadīdah [Eg.] 24 Cj 25.34N 28.51 E
Al Jadīdah [Sau.Ar.] 24 Mj 25.39N 49.32 E
Al Jafr 24 Gg 30.18N 36.13 E
Al Jāfūrah 35 Ia 23.25N 50.17 E
Al Jāfūrah 24 Nj 25.00N 50.15 E
Al Jaghbūb 31 Jf 29.45N 24.31 E
Al Jahrah 23 Gc 29.20N 47.40 E
Al Jalāmīd 24 Hg 31.17N 40.06 E
Al Jamalīyah 24 Nj 25.37N 51.05 E
Al Jamm 32 Jb 35.18N 10.43 E
Al Janā'in 32 Jc 31.44N 10.09 E
Aljat 16 Pj 39.58N 49.27 E
Al Jawf [Lib.] 31 Jf 24.12N 23.18 E
Al Jawf [Sau.Ar.] 22 Fg 29.50N 39.52 E
Al Jazā'ir=Algeria (EN) [1] 31 Hf 28.00N 3.00 E
Al Jazā'ir=Algiers (EN) [3] 32 Hb 36.35N 3.00 E
Al Jazā'ir=Algiers (EN) 31 He 36.47N 3.03 E
Al Jazā'ir-El Harrach 13 Ph 36.43N 3.08 E
Al Jazīrah 35 Ec 14.40N 33.30 E
Al Jazīrah [Asia] 21 Gf 35.10N 42.00 E
Al Jazīrah [Sud.] 30 Kg 14.25N 33.00 E
Aljezur 13 Dg 37.19N 8.48W
Aljibe 13 Gh 36.31N 5.37W
Al Jifārah 30 Ie 32.30N 11.45 E
Al Jiwā' 23 He 23.00N 54.00 E
Al Jīzah=Giza (EN) 31 Ke 30.01N 31.13 E
Al Jubayl 23 Gd 27.01N 49.40 E
Al Jubaylah 24 Lj 24.54N 46.27 E
Al Junaynah [Sau.Ar.] 33 He 20.17N 42.48 E
Al Junaynah [Sud.] 31 Jg 13.27N 22.27 E
Al Juraid 24 Mi 27.11N 49.52 E
Aljustrel 13 Dg 37.52N 8.10W
Alka 40a Db 52.15N 174.30W
Al Kaba'ish 24 Lg 30.58N 47.00 E
Al Kāf [3] 32 Ib 36.00N 9.00 E
Al Kāf 32 Ib 36.11N 8.43 E
Alkali Lake 46 Ff 41.42N 119.50W
Al Kamāsin 23 Fe 20.25N 44.48 E
Al Kāmilīn 35 Eb 15.05N 33.11 E
Al Karak 24 Fg 31.11N 35.42 E
Al Karkh 24 Kf 33.20N 44.20 E
Al Karnak 33 Fd 25.43N 32.39 E
Al Kawah 35 Ec 13.44N 32.30 E
Al Kāẓimīyah 24 Kf 33.22N 44.20 E
Alken 12 Hd 50.52N 5.18 E
Al Khabrā' 23 Fd 26.04N 43.33 E
Al Khābūra 23 Ie 23.50N 57.18 E
Al-Khalīj al- 'Arabi=Persian Gulf (EN) 21 Hg 27.00N 51.00 E
Al Khalīl 24 Fg 31.32N 35.06 E
Al Khālis 24 Kf 33.51N 44.32 E
Al Khandaq 35 Eb 18.36N 30.34 E
Al Khārijah 31 Kf 25.26N 30.33 E
Al Kharj 24 Lj 24.10N 47.30 E
Al Kharţūm=Khartoum (EN) [3] 35 Eb 15.50N 33.00 E
Al Kharţūm=Khartoum (EN) 31 Kg 15.36N 32.32 E
Al Kharţūm Baḩrī= Khartoum North (EN) 31 Kg 15.38N 32.33 E
Al Khaşab 24 Qi 26.12N 56.15 E
Al Khaţţ 24 Qk 25.37N 56.01 E
Al Khawr 23 Hd 25.40N 51.30 E
Al Khidr 24 Kg 31.12N 45.33 E
Al Khubar 23 Hd 26.17N 50.12 E
Al Khufayfīyah 23 Fe 24.55N 44.42 E
Al Khums [3] 33 Bc 31.20N 14.10 E
Al Khums 31 Ie 32.39N 14.16 E
Al Khunn 35 Ha 23.18N 49.15 E
Al Khuwayr 24 Ni 26.04N 51.05 E
Al Kidn 35 Ia 22.30N 54.00 E
Al Kilḩ Sharq 24 Ej 25.03N 32.52 E
Alkionidhon, Kólpos- 15 Fk 38.05N 23.00 E
Al Kır'ānah 24 Nj 25.00N 51.03 E
Alkmaar 11 Kb 52.37N 4.44 E
Al Kūfah 24 Kf 32.02N 44.24 E
Al Kumayt 24 Lf 32.02N 46.52 E
Al Kuntillah 33 Fc 30.00N 34.41 E
Al Kushḩ 24 Ei 26.14N 32.05 E
Al Kut 23 Gc 32.30N 45.49 E
Al Kuwayt=Kuwait (EN) [1] 22 Gg 29.30N 47.45 E
Al Kuwayt=Kuwait (EN) 22 Gg 29.20N 47.59 E
Al Labbah 24 Ih 29.20N 41.30 E
Al Lādhiqīyah=Latakia (EN) 22 Ff 35.31N 35.07 E
Allagash River 44 Mb 47.05N 69.20W
Al Lagowa 35 Dc 11.24N 29.08 E
Allahābād 22 Kg 25.27N 81.51 E
Allah-Jun 20 Id 60.27N 134.57 E
Allah-Jun 20 Id 61.08N 137.59 E
Allahüekber DaGı 24 Jb 40.35N 42.32 E
Allakaket 40 Ic 66.34N 152.41W
Allanmyo 25 Je 19.22N 95.13 E
Allariz 13 Eb 42.11N 7.48W
All-Awash Island 51n Bb 12.55N 61.10W
Alldays 37 Dd 22.41S 29.06 E
Ålleberg 8 Ef 58.08N 13.36 E
Allegan 44 Ed 42.32N 85.51W
Allegheny Mountains 38 Lf 38.30N 80.00W
Allegheny Plateau 38 Le 41.30N 78.00W
Allegheny Reservoir 44 He 42.00N 78.56W
Allegheny River 43 Lc 40.27N 80.00W
Allègre, Pointe- 51e Ab 16.22N 61.45W
Allen 26 Hd 12.30N 124.17 E
Allen, Bog of- 9 Gh 53.20N 7.00W
Allen, Lough-/Loch Aillionn 9 Eg 54.08N 8.08W
Allendale 44 Gi 33.01N 81.19W
Allende 47 Dc 28.20N 100.51W
Allendorf (Eder) 12 Kc 51.02N 8.40 E
Allendorf (Lumda) 12 Kd 50.41N 8.50 E
Allentown 43 Lc 40.37N 75.30W
Alleppey 22 Ji 9.29N 76.19 E
Aller 10 Fd 52.57N 9.11 E
Allevard 11 Mi 45.24N 6.04 E
Allgäuer Alpen 10 Gi 47.20N 10.25 E
Alliance [Nb.-U.S.] 43 Gc 42.06N 102.52W
Alliance [Oh.-U.S.] 44 Ge 40.56N 81.06W
Allier [3] 11 Ih 46.30N 3.00 E
Allier 5 Gf 46.57N 3.05 E
Al Lifīyah 23 Fc 30.35N 43.09 E
Al Lişāfah 24 Li 27.37N 46.52 E
Alliston 44 Hc 44.09N 79.52W
Al Līth 23 Fe 20.09N 40.16 E
Alloa 9 Je 56.07N 3.49W
Allonnes 11 Gg 47.58N 0.09 E
Allos 11 Mj 44.14N 6.38 E
All Saints 51d Bb 17.03N 61.48W
Al Luḩayyah 23 Ff 15.43N 42.42 E
Al Luwaymī 23 Fd 27.54N 42.22 E
Alm 14 Hb 48.05N 13.55 E
Alma [Ga.-U.S.] 44 Fj 31.33N 82.28W
Alma [Mi.-U.S.] 44 Ed 43.23N 84.39W
Alma [Nb.-U.S.] 45 Gf 40.06N 99.22W
Alma [Que.-Can.] 42 Kg 48.32N 71.40W
Alma-Ata 22 Je 43.15N 76.57 E
Alma-Atinskaja Oblast [3] 19 Hg 44.00N 77.00 E
Almada 13 Cf 38.41N 9.09W
Almadén 13 Hf 38.46N 4.50W
Al Madīnah [Iraq] 24 Lg 30.57N 47.16 E
Al Madīnah [Sau.Ar.] = Medina (EN) 22 Fg 24.28N 39.36 E
Al Madīnah al Fikrīyah 24 Di 27.56N 30.49 E
'Al Madōw 35 Hc 10.59N 48.42 E
Al Mafraq 24 Gf 32.21N 36.12 E
Al Maghrib=Morocco (EN) [1] 31 Ge 32.00N 5.50W
Almagro 13 If 38.53N 3.43W
Almagrundet 8 He 59.06N 19.00 E

Index Symbols

[1] Independent Nation
[2] State, Region
[3] District, County
[4] Municipality
[5] Colony, Dependency
Continent
Physical Region
Historical or Cultural Region
Mount, Mountain
Volcano
Hill
Mountains, Mountain Range
Hills, Escarpment
Plateau, Upland
Pass, Gap
Plain, Lowland
Delta
Salt Flat
Valley, Canyon
Crater, Cave
Karst Features
Depression
Polder
Desert, Dunes
Forest, Woods
Heath, Steppe
Oasis
Cape, Point
Coast, Beach
Cliff
Peninsula
Isthmus
Sandbank
Island
Atoll
Rock, Reef
Islands, Archipelago
Rocks, Reefs
Coral Reef
Well, Spring
Geyser
River, Stream
Waterfall Rapids
River Mouth, Estuary
Lake
Salt Lake
Intermittent Lake
Reservoir
Swamp, Pond
Canal
Glacier
Ice Shelf, Pack Ice
Ocean
Sea
Gulf, Bay
Strait, Fjord
Lagoon
Bank
Seamount
Tablemount
Ridge
Shelf
Basin
Escarpment, Sea Scarp
Fracture
Trench, Abyss
National Park, Reserve
Point of Interest
Recreation Site
Cave, Cavern
Historic Site
Ruins
Wall, Walls
Church, Abbey
Temple
Scientific Station
Airport
Port
Lighthouse
Mine
Tunnel
Dam, Bridge

Al Maḩallah al Kubrá 33 Fc 30.58N 31.10 E
Al Maḩārīq 33 Fd 25.37N 30.39 E
Al Mahdīyah 32 Jb 35.30N 11.04 E
Al Mahdīyah [3] 32 Jb 35.35N 11.00 E
Al Maḩfid 33 Ig 14.03N 46.55 E
Al Mahrah 23 Hf 16.56N 52.15 E
Al Maḩras 32 Jc 34.32N 10.30 E
Al Majarr al Kabīr 24 Lg 31.34N 47.10 E
Almajului, Munţii- 15 Fe 44.43N 22.12 E
Al Maks al Qiblī 33 Fe 24.35N 30.38 E
Almalyk 19 Gg 40.49N 69.38 E
Al Manādir 24 Pk 23.10N 55.10 E
Al Manāmah=Manama (EN) 22 Hg 26.13N 50.35 E
Al Manāqil 35 Ec 14.15N 32.59 E
Almanor, Lake- 46 Ef 40.15N 121.08W
Almansa 13 Kf 38.52N 1.05W
Almansa, Puerto de- 13 Lf 38.49N 0.58W
Al Manshāh 33 Fd 26.28N 31.48 E
Almansor 13 Df 38.56N 8.54W
Al Manşūrah 33 Fc 31.03N 31.23 E
Al Manzilah 24 Dg 31.09N 31.56 E
Almanzor, Pico de- 13 Gd 40.15N 5.18W
Almanzora 13 Jg 37.21N 2.08W
Al Ma'qil 24 Lg 30.33N 47.48 E
Al Maqnah 24 Fh 28.24N 34.45 E
Al Maqta' 24 Pj 24.25N 54.29 E
Almar 13 Gd 40.54N 5.29W
Al Marāghah 24 Di 26.42N 31.36 E
Al Marsá 14 En 36.53N 10.20 E
Al Mary 31 Je 32.30N 20.54 E
Almaş 15 Gb 47.14N 23.19 E
Almas, Picos de- 52 Lg 13.33S 41.56W
Almas, Rio das- 54 If 14.35S 49.02W
'Al Maskād 35 Hc 11.18N 49.41 E
Al Maţarīyah 33 Fc 31.11N 32.02 E
Al Mawşil=Mosul (EN) 22 Gf 36.20N 43.08 E
Al Mayādīn 24 Ie 35.01N 40.27 E
Al Mayyāh 24 Ji 27.51N 42.47 E
Almazán 13 Jc 41.29N 2.32W
Al Mazār 24 Eg 31.23N 33.23 E
Almazny 20 Gd 62.19N 114.04 E
Almazora 13 Le 39.57N 0.03W
Al Mazra'ah 24 Fg 31.16N 35.31 E
Alme, Brilon- 12 Kc 51.27N 8.37 E
Almeida 13 Fc 41.16N 6.04W
Almeirim [Braz.] 54 Hd 1.32S 52.34W
Almeirim [Port.] 13 De 39.12N 8.38W
Al Mellem 35 Dd 9.49N 28.45 E
Almelo 11 Mb 52.21N 6.39 E
Almenara, Sierra de la- 13 Kg 37.35N 1.31W
Almendra, Embalse de- 13 Fc 41.13N 6.10W
Almendralejo 13 Ff 38.41N 6.24W
Almeria [3] 13 Jg 37.10N 2.20W
Almeria 6 Fh 36.50N 2.27W
Almeria, Golfo de- 13 Jh 36.46N 2.30W
Almetjevsk 19 Fe 54.54N 52.20 E
Al Metlaoui 32 Ic 34.20N 8.24 E
Älmhult 7 Dh 56.33N 14.08 E
Almijara, Sierra de- 13 Ih 36.55N 3.55W
Almina, Punta- 13 Gi 35.54N 5.17W
Al Minyā [Eg.] 24 Dh 29.45N 31.18 E
Al Minyā [Eg.] 31 Kf 28.06N 30.45 E
Al Miqdādīyah 24 Kf 33.59N 44.56 E
Almirante 49 Fi 9.18N 82.24W
Almirante Brown 66 Qe 64.53S 62.53W
Almirós 15 Fj 39.11N 22.46 E
Almiroú, Órmos- 15 Hn 35.23N 24.20 E
Almodôvar 13 Dg 37.31N 8.04W
Almodóvar del Campo 13 Hf 38.43N 4.10W
Almodóvar del Río 13 Gg 37.48N 5.01W
Almonte 13 Fg 37.15N 6.31W
Almonte 13 Fe 39.42N 6.28W
Almora 25 Fc 29.37N 79.40 E
Almoustarat 34 Fb 17.22N 0.07 E
Älmsta 8 He 59.58N 18.48 E
Al Mubarraz 23 Gd 25.25N 49.35 E
Al Mudawwarah 24 Fh 29.19N 35.59 E
Al Mudhari, Rujm- 24 Hf 32.45N 39.08 E
Al Mughayrā' [Sau.Ar.] 24 Gh 29.17N 37.41 E
Al Mughayrā' [U.A.E.] 24 Oj 24.05N 53.32 E
Al Muglad 31 Jg 11.02N 27.44 E
Al Muḩarraq 24 Ni 26.16N 50.37 E
Al Mukallā 22 Gh 14.32N 49.08 E
Al Mukhā 23 Fg 13.19N 43.15 E
Al Munastīr [3] 32 Jb 35.40N 10.50 E
Al Munastīr 32 Jb 35.47N 10.50 E
Almuñécar 13 Ih 36.43N 3.41W
Al Murabba' 24 Kj 25.43N 44.18 E
Almus 24 Gb 40.23N 36.55 E
Al Musannāh 24 Lh 29.02N 47.12 E
Al Muşawwarāt aş Şafra' 35 Eb 16.25N 33.22 E
Al Musayjid 24 Hj 24.05N 39.06 E
Al Musayyib 24 Kf 32.47N 44.18 E
Al Mustawī 24 Kj 25.55N 44.40 E
Al Muthanna [3] 24 Kg 30.50N 45.20 E
Al Muwayh 33 He 22.45N 41.35 E
Al Muwaylih 24 Fi 27.41N 35.28 E
Alnön 8 Gb 62.25N 17.25 E
Alnwick 9 Lf 55.25N 1.42W
Ålö 8 Jd 60.20N 22.15 E
Aloândia 55 Hc 17.43S 49.29W
Alofi 58 Kf 19.03S 169.56W
Alofi, Ile- 57 Jf 14.19S 178.02W
Alofi Bay 64k Bb 19.01S 169.56W
Aloja 7 Fh 57.44N 24.59 E
Along 25 Ic 28.10N 94.46 E
Alönnisos 15 Gj 39.13N 23.55 E
Alonsa 45 Ga 50.47N 99.00W
Alonso, Rio- 55 Gg 24.05S 51.35W
Alor, Kepulauan- 26 Hh 8.15S 124.30 E
Alor, Pulau- 21 Oj 8.15S 124.45 E
Alora 13 Hh 36.48N 4.42W
Alor Setar 22 Mi 6.07N 100.22 E
Alost/Aalst 11 Kd 50.56N 4.02 E
Alotau 60 Ej 10.31S 150.43 E
Aloysius, Mount- 59 Fe 26.00S 128.34 E
Alpen = Alps (EN) 5 Gf 46.25N 10.00 E
Alpena 43 Kb 45.04N 83.26W
Alpera 13 Kf 38.58N 1.13W
Alpes=Alps (EN) 5 Gf 46.25N 10.00 E
Alpes Bernoises/Berner Alpen=Bernese Alps (EN) 14 Bd 46.25N 7.30 E
Alpes Cottiennes 14 Af 44.45N 7.00 E
Alpes de Haute-Provence [3] 11 Lj 44.10N 6.00 E
Alpes Grées/Alpi Graie 14 Be 45.30N 7.10 E
Alpes Mancelles 11 Ff 48.25N 0.10W
Alpes Maritimes 14 Bf 44.15N 7.10 E
Alpes-Maritimes [3] 11 Nk 44.00N 7.10 E
Alpes Pennines/Alpi Pennine 14 Bd 46.05N 7.50 E
Alpes Valaisannes/Walliser Alpen 14 Bd 46.10N 7.30 E
Alpha Cordillera (EN) 67 Re 85.30N 125.00W
Alphen aan der Rijn 12 Gb 52.08N 4.42 E
Alphonse Island 30 Mi 7.00S 52.45 E
Alpi=Alps (EN) 5 Gf 46.25N 10.00 E
Alpi Apuane 14 Ef 44.05N 10.20 E
Alpi Aurine 10 Hi 47.00N 11.55 E
Alpi Carniche 14 Gd 46.40N 13.00 E
Alpi Cozie 14 Af 44.45N 7.00 E
Alpi Graie/Alpes Grées 14 Be 45.30N 7.10 E
Alpi Lepontine 14 Cd 46.25N 8.40 E
Alpi Liguri 14 Cf 44.10N 8.05 E
Alpi Marittime 14 Bf 44.15N 7.10 E
Alpine [Az.-U.S.] 46 Kj 33.51N 109.09W
Alpine [Tx.-U.S.] 43 Ge 30.22N 103.40W
Alpine [Wy.-U.S.] 46 Je 43.15N 110.59W
Alpi Orobie 14 Dd 46.00N 10.00 E
Alpi Pennine/Alpes Pennines 14 Bd 46.05N 7.50 E
Alpi Retiche=Rhaetian Alps (EN) 14 Dd 46.30N 10.00 E
Alpi Ticinesi 14 Cd 46.20N 8.45 E
Alpi Venoste 10 Gj 46.45N 10.55 E
Alprech, Cap d'- 12 Dd 50.42N 1.34 E
Alps (EN) = Alpen 5 Gf 46.25N 10.00 E
Alps (EN)=Alpes 5 Gf 46.25N 10.00 E
Alps (EN)=Alpi 5 Gf 46.25N 10.00 E
Al qa 'Āmīyāt 35 Hb 18.50N 48.30 E
Al Qābil 24 Pk 23.56N 55.49 E
Al Qaḑārif 31 Kg 14.02N 35.24 E
Al Qaḑīmah 33 Ee 22.21N 39.09 E
Al Qādisīya [3] 24 Kg 31.50N 45.00 E
Al Qādisīya 24 Kg 31.42N 44.28 E
Al Qadmūs 24 Ge 35.05N 36.10 E
Al Qaffāy 24 Nj 24.35N 51.44 E
Al Qāhirah=Cairo (EN) 31 Ke 30.03N 31.15 E
Al Qāhirah-Imbabah 33 Fc 30.05N 31.13 E
Al Qāhirah-Mişr al Jadīdah 33 Fc 30.06N 31.20 E
Al Qā'īyah 24 Ki 26.27N 45.35 E
Al Qal'ah al Kubrá 14 Eo 35.52N 10.32 E
Al Qalībah 23 Ed 28.24N 37.42 E
Al Qāmishlī 23 Fb 37.02N 41.14 E
Al Qanţarah 33 Fc 30.52N 32.19 E
Al Qaryah ash Sharqīyah 33 Bc 30.24N 13.36 E
Al Qaryatayn 24 Ge 34.14N 37.14 E
Al Qaşab 24 Kj 25.18N 45.30 E
Al Qaşabāt 33 Bc 32.35N 14.03 E
Al Qa'şah 24 Ch 28.25N 28.56 E
Al Qash 35 Fb 16.48N 35.51 E
Al Qaşr 33 Ed 25.42N 28.53 E
Al Qaşrayn 32 Ib 35.11N 8.48 E
Al Qaşrayn [3] 32 Ib 35.15N 9.00 E
Al Qaţīf 24 Mi 26.33N 50.00 E
Al Qaţrānī 24 Gg 31.15N 36.03 E
Al Qaţrūn 33 Be 24.56N 14.38 E
Al Qay'īyah 24 Fe 24.18N 43.30 E
Al Qayrawān 32 Jb 35.41N 10.07 E
Al Qayrawān [3] 32 Ib 35.30N 10.00 E
Al Qayşūmah [Sau.Ar.] 24 Jh 29.11N 42.58 E
Al Qayşūmah [Sau.Ar.] 23 Gd 28.16N 46.03 E
Alqōsh 24 Jd 36.44N 43.06 E
Al Qubayyāt 24 Ge 34.34N 36.17 E
Al Qunayţirah 23 Ec 33.07N 35.49 E
Al Qunfudhah 23 Ff 19.08N 41.05 E
Al Qurayyah 24 Gh 28.45N 36.12 E
Al Qurnah 24 Lg 31.00N 47.26 E
Al Quşaymah 33 Fc 30.40N 34.22 E
Al Quşayr [Eg.] 31 Kf 26.06N 34.17 E
Al Quşayr [Syr.] 24 Ge 34.31N 36.35 E
Al Qūşīyah 33 Fd 27.26N 30.49 E
Al Quşūr 14 Co 35.54N 8.53 E
Al Quţayfah 24 Gf 33.44N 36.36 E
Al Quwārah 24 Ji 26.47N 43.28 E
Al Quwayr 24 Jd 36.03N 43.30 E
Al Quzah 35 Hb 15.06N 49.08 E
Als 8 Ci 55.00N 9.55 E
Alsace 11 Nf 48.30N 7.30 E
Alsace, Ballon d'- 11 Mg 47.50N 6.51 E
Alsasua 13 Jb 42.54N 2.10W
Alsdorf 12 Id 50.53N 6.10 E
Alsea River 46 Cd 44.26N 124.05W
Alsenz 12 Je 49.49N 7.51 E
Alsfeld 10 Ff 50.45N 9.16 E
Alsina, Laguna- 55 Am 36.52S 62.07W
Alsten 7 Cd 65.57N 12.36 E
Alsterån 8 Gh 56.55N 16.26 E
Alsunga 8 Ig 57.02N 21.28 E
Alta 7 Fb 69.58N 23.14 E
Altaelva 7 Fb 69.58N 23.23 E
Altafjorden 7 Fa 70.12N 23.06 E
Altagracia 54 Da 10.07N 71.14W
Alta Gracia 56 Hd 31.40S 64.26W
Altagracia de Orituco 50 Ch 9.52N 66.23W
Altai (EN)= Altay Shan 21 Le 46.30N 93.00 E
Altaj 22 Le 46.20N 96.17 E
Altaj 21 Kd 51.30N 90.00 E
Altajski 20 Df 51.58N 85.30 E
Altajski Kraj [3] 20 Df 52.00N 82.30 E
Altamaha River 43 Ke 31.19N 81.17W
Altamira 53 Kf 3.12S 52.12W
Altamira, Cuevas de- 13 Ha 43.23N 4.05W
Altamira, Sierra de- 13 Ge 39.35N 5.10W
Altamirano 48 Mi 16.53N 92.09W
Altamont 46 Ee 42.12N 121.44W
Altamura 14 Kj 40.49N 16.33 E
Altamura, Isla de- 48 Ee 25.00N 108.10W
Altan Bulag 27 Jc 44.19N 113.28 E
Altan-Emel → Xin Barag Youqi 27 Kb 48.41N 116.47 E
Altan Xiret→Ejin Horo Qi 27 Id 39.31N 109.45 E
Altar 48 Db 30.43N 111.44W
Altar, Desierto de- 38 Hf 31.50N 114.15W
Altar, Rio- 48 Db 30.39N 111.55W
Altar de los Sacrificios 49 Be 16.28N 90.32W
Altata 47 Cd 24.38N 107.55W
Alta Verapaz [3] 49 Bf 15.40N 90.00W
Altavista 44 Hg 37.07N 79.18W
Altay 22 Ke 47.52N 88.07 E
Altay Shan=Altai (EN) 21 Le 46.30N 93.00 E
Altdorf 14 Cd 46.53N 8.40 E
Altea 13 Lf 38.36N 0.03W
Altena 10 De 51.18N 7.40 E
Altenberge 12 Jb 52.03N 7.28 E
Altenburg 10 If 50.59N 12.27 E
Altenglan 12 Je 49.33N 7.28 E
Altenkirchen (Westerwald) 12 Jd 50.42N 7.39 E
Alter do Chão 13 Ee 39.12N 7.40W
Altevatnet 7 Eb 68.32N 19.30 E
Altındağ 24 Ec 39.56N 32.52 E
Altinoluk 15 Jj 39.34N 26.44 E
Altinova 15 Jj 39.13N 26.47 E
Altıntaş 24 Dc 39.04N 30.07 E
Altinyayla 15 Mm 36.59N 29.33 E
Altkirch 11 Ng 47.37N 7.15 E
Altmark 10 Hd 52.40N 11.20 E
Altmühl 10 Hh 48.55N 11.52 E
Alto, Morro- 55 Ib 13.46S 46.50W
Alto, Pico- 54 Kd 4.20S 39.00W
Alto Alentejo 13 Ef 38.50N 7.40W
Alto Araguaia 54 Hg 17.19S 53.12W
Alto Coité 55 Eb 15.47S 54.20W
Alto Garças 55 Fc 16.56S 53.32W
Alto Longá 54 Je 5.15S 42.12W
Alto Molócuè 37 Fc 15.38S 37.42 E
Altomonte 14 Kk 39.42N 16.08 E
Alton [Eng.-U.K.] 12 Bc 51.08N 0.59W
Alton [Il.-U.S.] 43 Id 38.54N 90.10W
Altona, Hamburg- 10 Fc 53.33N 9.57 E
Altoona 43 Lc 40.32N 78.23W
Alto Paraguai 54 Gf 14.30S 56.31W
Alto Paraguay [3] 55 Ce 21.00S 59.00W
Alto Paraíso de Goiás 55 Ib 14.12S 47.38W
Alto Paraná [3] 55 Eg 25.00S 54.50W
Alto Parnaíba 54 Ie 9.06S 45.57W
Alto Purús, Rio- 54 De 9.34S 70.36W
Alto Rio Senguerr 56 Fg 45.02S 70.50W
Altos 54 Jd 5.03S 42.28W
Alto Sucuriú 55 Fd 19.19S 52.47W
Altötting 10 Ih 48.14N 12.41 E
Alto Uruguai, Serra do- 55 Fh 27.35S 53.40W
Altun Ha 49 Ce 17.50N 88.20W
Āltūn Kūprī 24 Ke 35.45N 44.09 E
Altun Shan 21 Kf 38.00N 88.00 E
Alturas 43 Cc 41.29N 120.32W
Alturitas 49 Ki 9.45N 72.25W
Altus 43 He 34.38N 99.20W
Altynkan 18 Hd 41.03N 70.43 E
Altynkul 18 Bc 43.07N 58.55 E
Alu 63a Bb 7.05S 155.47 E
Al 'Ubaylah 35 Ia 21.59N 50.57 E
Al Ubayyiḑ 31 Kg 13.11N 30.13 E
Alucra 24 Hb 40.20N 38.46 E
Al 'Udaysāt 24 Ej 25.35N 32.29 E
Al Uḑayyah 35 Dc 12.03N 28.17 E
Alūksne/Aluksne 7 Gh 57.26N 27.01 E
Aluksne/Alūksne 7 Gh 57.26N 27.01 E
Aluksnes Ozero 8 Lg 57.22N 27.10 E
Aluksne Ozero/Alūksnes Ezers 8 Lg 57.22N 27.10 E
Alūksnes Ezers/Aluksne Ozero 8 Lg 57.22N 27.10 E
'Alūla 35 Ic 11.58N 50.48 E
Al 'Ulá 23 Ed 26.37N 37.52 E
Al Umm 33 Hf 18.18N 40.45 E
Alunda 8 Hd 60.04N 18.05 E
Alupka 19 Dg 44.24N 34.03 E
Al'Uqaylah 33 Cc 30.16N 19.12 E
Al 'Uqaylat 24 Ii 26.43N 41.43 E
Al 'Uqayr 24 Nj 25.39N 50.13 E
Al Uqşur=Luxor (EN) 33 Fd 25.41N 32.39 E
Al Urayq 24 Hh 29.00N 39.10 E
Al Urdun=Jordan (EN) [1] 22 Ff 31.00N 36.00 E
Al 'Urūq al Mu'Tariḑah 35 Ia 21.00N 54.00 E
Ālūs 24 Je 34.02N 42.26 E
Alušta 19 Dg 44.42N 34.20 E
Al 'Uthmānīyah 24 Mj 25.15N 49.22 E
Al'Uwaynāt 33 Bd 25.48N 10.33 E
Al 'Uwaynidhīyah 24 Gi 26.38N 36.05 E
Al 'Uwayqīlah 24 Jg 30.21N 42.14 E
Al 'Uyūn 24 Hj 24.33N 39.35 E
Al Uzayin 24 Ke 34.02N 44.20 E
Al 'Uzayr 24 Lg 31.19N 47.25 E
Alva 43 Hd 36.48N 98.40W
Alva 13 Dd 40.18N 8.15W
Alvand, Kūh-e- 24 Me 34.41N 48.28 E
Älvängen 8 Eg 57.56N 12.09 E
Alvaro Obregón, Presa 48 Ed 28.00N 109.45W
Alvdal 7 Ce 62.07N 10.39 E
Älvdalen 8 Ed 60.30N 13.00 E
Älvdalen 7 Df 61.14N 14.02 E
Alvear 55 Di 29.06S 56.33W
Alvelos, Serra de- 13 De 39.55N 8.01W
Alvesta 7 Dh 56.54N 14.33 E
Ålvik 8 Gb 62.25N 17.24 E
Ålvik 7 Bf 60.26N 6.26 E
Alvin 45 Il 29.25N 95.15W
Älvkarleby 7 Df 60.34N 17.27 E
Alvord Valley 46 Fe 42.45N 118.25W
Alvøy 8 Ad 60.35N 4.50 E
Älvros 8 Fb 62.03N 14.39 E
Älvsborg [2] 7 Cg 58.00N 12.30 E
Älvsbyn 7 Ed 65.40N 21.00 E
Al Wāḩidī 23 Gg 14.20N 47.50 E
Al Wajh 22 Fg 26.14N 36.28 E
Al Wakrah 24 Nj 25.10N 51.36 E
Al Wannān 24 Mi 26.55N 48.24 E
Alwar 25 Fc 27.34N 76.36 E
Al Warī'ah 24 Li 27.50N 47.29 E
Al Wāsiţah 33 Fd 29.20N 31.12 E
Al Waslātīyah 14 Do 35.51N 9.35 E
Al Watī'ah 33 Bc 32.28N 11.46 E
Al Wazz 35 Eb 15.01N 30.10 E
Al Widyān 21 Gf 31.10N 40.45 E
Alxa Youqi (Ehen Hudag) 27 Hd 39.12N 101.40 E
Alxa Zuoqi (Bayan Hot) 27 Id 38.50N 105.32 E
Al Yaman = Yemen (EN) 22 Gh 15.00N 44.00 E
Al Yaman ad Dimuqrāţīyah → Yemen (EN) 22 Gh 15.00N 44.00 E
Alyangula 59 Hb 13.50S 136.25 E
Alygdžer 20 Ef 53.38N 98.16 E
Alymka 17 Ng 59.01N 68.40 E
Alytus/Alitus 19 Ce 54.25N 24.08 E
Alz 10 Ih 48.10N 12.48 E
Alzamaj 20 Ee 55.33N 98.39 E
Alzey 10 Eg 49.45N 8.07 E
Alzira/Alcira 13 Le 39.09N 0.26W
Amachkalo Ahzar 34 Fb 15.30N 3.20 E
Amacuro, Rio- 54 Fb 8.32N 60.28W
Amada 33 Fe 22.45N 32.10 E
Amadeus, Lake- 57 Eg 24.50S 130.45 E
Amadi [Sud.] 35 Ed 5.31N 30.20 E
Amadi [Zaire] 36 Eb 3.35N 26.47 E
Amadjuak Lake 42 Kd 64.55N 71.00W
Amadora 13 Cf 38.45N 9.14W
Amadror 32 Ie 24.50N 6.25 E
Amadror 32 Id 26.00N 5.21W
Amagasaki 29 Dd 34.42N 135.25 E
Amager 8 Ei 55.35N 12.35 E
Amagi [Jap.] 29 Be 33.26N 130.39 E
Amagi [Jap.] 29b Bb 27.47N 128.52 E
Amagi-San 29 Fd 34.51N 139.00 E
Amaha 29 Fd 35.13N 139.51 E
Amahai 26 Ig 3.20S 128.55 E
Amain, Monts d'- 11 Gf 48.39N 0.20 E
Amajac, Rio- 48 Jg 21.15N 98.46W
Amakusa-Nada 28 Jh 32.25N 129.40 E
Amakusa-Shotō 28 Kh 32.22N 130.12 E
Amal 33 Dd 29.25N 21.10 E
Åmal 7 Cg 59.03N 12.42 E
Amalfi 14 Ij 40.38N 14.36 E
Amaliás 15 El 37.48N 21.21 E
Amalner 25 Fd 21.03N 75.04 E
Amambai 55 Ef 23.05S 55.13W
Amambai, Rio- 55 Ff 23.22S 53.56W
Amambai, Serra de- 55 Ef 23.10S 55.30W
Amambay [3] 55 Df 23.00S 56.00W
Amami Islands (EN)= Amami-Shotō 21 Og 28.16N 129.21 E
Amami-Ō-Shima 27 Mf 28.15N 129.20 E
Amami-Shotō=Amami Islands (EN) 21 Og 28.16N 129.21 E
Amân 8 Fc 61.12N 14.45 E
Amanã, Lago- 54 Fd 2.35S 64.40W
Amana, Rio- 50 Eh 9.45N 62.39W
Amanave 65c Cb 14.19S 170.49W
Amangeldy 19 Ge 50.10N 65.13 E
Amankaragaj 17 Lj 52.27N 64.08 E
Amantea 14 Kk 39.07N 16.08 E
Amanu Atoll 57 Mf 17.48S 140.46W
Amanzimtoti 37 Ef 30.05S 30.53 E
Amapá 53 Ke 2.03N 50.48W
Amapá 54 Hc 1.30N 52.00W
Amapala 49 Dg 13.17N 87.40W
Amara' 15 Ke 44.37N 27.19 E
Amara 30 Kg 11.30N 37.45 E
Amaradia 15 Ge 44.22N 23.43 E
'Amara East 35 Ea 20.48N 30.23 E
Amarante [Braz.] 54 Je 6.14S 42.50W
Amarante [Port.] 13 Dc 41.16N 8.05W
Amaranth 45 Ga 50.36N 98.43W
Amargosa 46 Gh 36.18N 116.25W
Amargosa Desert 46 Gh 36.40N 116.30W
Amargosa Range 46 Gh 36.30N 116.45W
Amargosa River 46 Gh 36.13N 116.48W
Amarillo 39 If 35.13N 101.49W
Amárion 15 Hn 35.14N 24.39 E
Amarume 29 Fb 38.50N 139.54 E
Amasra 24 Eb 41.45N 32.34 E
Amasya 23 Ea 40.39N 35.51 E
Amathus 24 Ee 34.42N 33.08 E
Amatique, Bahia de- 49 Cf 15.55N 88.45W
Amatlán de Cañas 48 Gg 20.52N 104.27W
Amatrice 14 Hh 42.38N 13.17 E
Amaurilandia 55 Ff 22.10S 52.38W
Amay 12 Hd 50.33N 5.19 E
Amazar 20 Hf 53.54N 120.57 E
Amazon (EN)=Amazonas, Rio- (Solimões) 52 Lf 0.10S 49.00W
Amazon, Mouths of the- (EN) 52 Le 0.10S 49.00W
Amazonas [Braz.] [2] 54 Fd 5.00S 63.00W
Amazonas [Col.] [2] 54 Dd 1.00S 72.00W
Amazonas [Peru] [2] 54 Ce 5.00S 77.00W
Amazonas [Ven.] [2] 54 Ec 3.30N 66.00W
Amazonas, Rio-=Amazon (EN) 52 Lf 0.10S 49.00W
Amazonas, Rio- (Solimões) =Amazon (EN) 52 Lf 0.10S 49.00W
Amazon Cone (EN) 52 Ke 4.30N 52.00W
Amba Ferit 35 Fc 10.55N 38.55 E
Ambāla 25 Fb 30.21N 76.50 E
Ambalangoda 25 Gg 6.14N 80.03 E
Ambalavao 37 Hd 21.50S 46.57 E
Ambam 34 He 2.23N 11.17 E
Ambanja 37 Hb 13.39S 48.27 E
Ambarčik 22 Sc 69.39N 162.20 E
Ambarès-et-Lagrave 11 Fj 44.55N 0.29W
Ambargasta, Salinas de- 56 Hc 29.20S 64.30W
Ambarny 19 Db 65.54N 33.41 E
Ambasamudram 25 Fg 8.42N 77.28 E
Ambato 53 If 1.15S 78.37W
Ambato-Boéni 37 Hc 16.28S 46.40 E
Ambatofinandrahana 37 Hd 20.33S 46.47 E
Ambatolampy 37 Hc 19.23S 47.25 E
Ambatondrazaka 31 Lj 17.48S 48.26 E
Ambatosoratra 37 Hc 17.36S 48.32 E
Ambelau, Pulau- 26 Ig 3.51S 127.12 E
Amberg 10 Hg 49.27N 11.52 E
Ambergris Cay 49 Dd 18.03N 87.56W
Ambergris Cays 49 Lc 21.18N 71.37W
Ambérieu-en-Bugey 11 Li 45.57N 5.21 E
Amberley [Eng.-U.K.] 12 Bd 50.55N 0.32W
Amberley [N.Z.] 62 Ee 43.09S 172.45 E
Ambert 11 Ji 45.33N 3.45 E
Ambikāpur 25 Gd 23.07N 83.12 E
Ambila 37 Hd 21.58S 47.59 E
Ambilobe 37 Hb 13.11S 49.03 E
Ambitle 63a Aa 4.05S 153.40 E
Ambjörby 8 Ed 60.30N 13.10 E
Ambla 8 Ke 59.10N 25.44 E
Amblève 11 Ld 50.28N 5.36 E
Amblève/Amel 12 Id 50.21N 6.09 E
Ambo 54 Cf 10.07S 76.10W
Amboasary Sud 37 He 25.01S 46.23 E
Ambodifototra 37 Hc 16.58S 49.52 E
Ambohimahasoa 37 Hd 21.08S 47.12 E
Ambohimanarina 37 Hc 18.52S 47.29 E
Ambohitralanana 37 Ic 15.15S 50.28 E
Amboise 11 Gg 47.25N 0.59 E
Ambon 58 De 3.43S 128.12 E
Ambon, Pulau- 26 Ig 3.40S 128.10 E
Ambongo 37 Gc 16.50S 45.00 E
Amboseli, Lake- 36 Gc 2.37S 37.08 E
Ambositra 31 Lk 20.30S 47.14 E
Ambovombe 37 He 25.09S 46.06 E
Ambre, Cap d'-=Ambre, Cape d'-(EN) 30 Lj 11.57S 49.17 E
Ambre, Cape d'-(EN)= Ambre, Cap d'- 30 Lj 11.57S 49.17 E
Ambre, Montagne d'- 37 Hb 12.30S 49.10 E
Ambriz 31 Ii 7.50S 13.08 E
Ambrolauri 16 Mh 42.31N 43.05 E
Ambrym, Ile- 57 Hf 16.15S 168.07 E
Ambunti 60 Ch 4.14S 142.50 E
Āmbūr 25 Ff 12.47N 78.42 E
Amchitka 40a Bb 51.30N 179.00 E
Amchitka Pass 40a Cb 51.30N 179.30W
Am Dafok 35 Cc 10.28N 23.17 E
Am Dam 35 Cc 12.46N 20.29 E
Amded 32 He 22.10N 3.15 E
Amderma 19 Gb 69.45N 61.39 E
Am Djéména 35 Bc 13.06N 17.19 E
Amdo 27 Fe 32.29N 91.47 E
Ameca 47 Dd 20.33N 104.02W
Ameca, Rio- 48 Gg 20.41N 105.18W
Amel/Amblève 12 Id 50.21N 6.09 E
Ameland 12 Ha 53.26N 5.48 E
Ameland 11 La 53.25N 5.45 E
Ameland- Nes 12 Ha 53.26N 5.48 E
Amelia Island 44 Gj 30.37N 81.27W
Amélie-les-Bains-Palaloa 11 Il 42.28N 2.40 E
Amendola 14 Hh 42.59N 13.21 E
Amendolara 14 Kk 39.57N 16.35 E
'Āmerī 24 Nh 28.30N 51.05 E
Americana 55 If 22.45S 47.20W
American Falls 46 Ie 42.47N 112.51W
American Falls Reservoir 46 Ie 43.00N 113.00W
American Fork 46 Jf 40.23N 111.48W
American Highland 66 Ff 72.30S 78.00 E
American Samoa [5] 58 Kf 14.50S 170.00W
Americus 43 Ke 32.04N 84.14W
Amersfoort 11 Lb 52.09N 5.24 E
Amery Ice Shelf 66 Fe 69.30S 72.00 E
Ames 43 Ic 42.02N 93.37W
Amfilokhia 15 Ek 38.52N 21.10 E
Amfissa 15 Fk 38.32N 22.23 E
Amfreville-la-Campagne 12 Ce 49.13N 0.57 E
Amga 20 Id 60.52N 131.50 E
Amga 21 Pc 62.40N 134.59 E
Amgalang→Xin Barag Zuoqi 27 Kb 48.13N 118.14 E
Am Géréda 35 Cc 12.52N 21.10 E
Amgu 28 Nb 45.51N 137.41 E
Amguema 20 Nc 68.03N 177.55W
Amguid 32 Id 26.30N 5.36 E
Amguid 31 Hf 26.26N 5.22 E
Amgun 21 Pd 52.56N 139.40 E
Amherst 42 Lg 45.49N 64.14W
Amherst, Mount- 59 Fc 18.11S 126.59 E
Amherst Island 44 Ic 44.12N 76.42W
Amiata, Monte- 14 Fh 42.53N 11.37 E
Amiens 6 Gf 49.54N 2.18 E
Āmij, Wādī- 24 If 33.48N 41.46 E
Amik Gölü 24 Gd 36.22N 36.17 E
Amik Oölü 24 Gd 36.15N 36.12 E
Amili 25 Jc 28.26N 95.52 E
Amindīvi Islands 25 Ef 11.23N 72.23 E
Aminuis 37 Bd 23.43S 19.21 E
'Āmir, Ra's- 30 Je 32.57N 21.43 E
Amirante Islands 30 Mi 6.00S 53.10 E
Amirante Trench (EN) 37 Bb 6.00S 52.30 E
Amisk Lake 42 Hf 54.35N 102.15W
Amistad, Presa de la- 45 Fl 28.34N 101.15W
Amistad Reservoir 43 Gf 28.34N 101.15W
Amite 45 Kk 30.44N 90.30W
Amlekhganj 25 Gc 27.17N 84.59 E
Amlia 40a Db 52.06N 173.30W
Amlwch 9 Ih 53.25N 4.20W

Index Symbols

- [1] Independent Nation
- [2] State, Region
- [3] District, County
- [4] Municipality
- [5] Colony, Dependency
- Continent
- Physical Region
- Historical or Cultural Region
- Mount, Mountain
- Volcano
- Hill
- Mountains, Mountain Range
- Hills, Escarpment
- Plateau, Upland
- Pass, Gap
- Plain, Lowland
- Delta
- Salt Flat
- Valley, Canyon
- Crater, Cave
- Karst Features
- Depression
- Polder
- Desert, Dunes
- Forest, Woods
- Heath, Steppe
- Oasis
- Cape, Point
- Coast, Beach
- Cliff
- Peninsula
- Isthmus
- Sandbank
- Island
- Atoll
- Rock, Reef
- Islands, Archipelago
- Rocks, Reefs
- Coral Reef
- Well, Spring
- Geyser
- River, Stream
- Waterfall Rapids
- River Mouth, Estuary
- Lake
- Salt Lake
- Intermittent Lake
- Reservoir
- Swamp, Pond
- Canal
- Glacier
- Ice Shelf, Pack Ice
- Ocean
- Sea
- Gulf, Bay
- Strait, Fjord
- Lagoon
- Bank
- Seamount
- Tablemount
- Ridge
- Shelf
- Basin
- Escarpment, Sea Scarp
- Fracture
- Trench, Abyss
- National Park, Reserve
- Point of Interest
- Recreation Site
- Cave, Cavern
- Historic Site
- Ruins
- Wall, Walls
- Church, Abbey
- Temple
- Scientific Station
- Airport
- Port
- Lighthouse
- Mine
- Tunnel
- Dam, Bridge

'Amm Adām	35	Fb	16.22N	36.09 E
'Ammān	22	Ff	31.57N	35.56 E
Ammanford	9	Jj	51.48N	3.59W
Ammarnäs	7	Dd	65.58N	16.12 E
Åmmeberg	8	Ff	58.52N	15.00 E
Ammer	10	Hi	47.57N	11.08 E
Ammerån	8	Ga	63.09N	16.13 E
Ammerland	10	Dc	53.15N	8.00 E
Ammersee	10	Hi	48.00N	11.08 E
Ammi-Moussa	13	Ni	35.52N	1.07 E
Ammokhostos → Famagusta (EN)	23	Dc	35.07N	33.57 E
Amnja	17	Me	63.45N	67.07 E
Amnok-kang	27	Ld	39.55N	124.20 E
Āmol	23	Hb	36.23N	52.20 E
Amolar	55	Dd	18.01S	57.30W
Amorgós	15	Im	36.50N	25.53 E
Amorgós	15	Im	36.50N	25.59 E
Amorinópolis	55	Gc	16.36S	51.08W
Amory	45	Lj	33.59N	88.29W
Amos	42	Jg	48.34N	78.07W
Amot [Nor.]	8	Be	59.35N	8.00 E
Amot [Nor.]	7	Bg	59.54N	9.54 E
Amotfors	8	Ee	59.46N	12.22 E
Amoucha	13	Rh	36.23N	5.25 E
Amouliani	15	Gi	40.20N	23.55 E
Amour, Djebel-	32	Hc	33.45N	1.45 E
Amourj	32	Ff	16.10N	7.35W
Ampanihy	37	Gd	24.40S	44.45 E
Amparafaravola	37	Hc	17.36S	48.12 E
Amparo	55	If	22.42S	46.47W
Amper	10	Hh	48.10N	11.50 E
Ampère Seamount (EN)	5	Eh	35.05N	12.13W
Amphitrite Point	46	Cb	48.56N	125.35W
Amposta	13	Md	40.43N	0.35 E
Ampthill	12	Bb	52.02N	0.29W
Ampurdán/L'Empordà	13	Ob	42.12N	2.45 E
Ampurias	13	Pb	42.10N	3.05 E
Amqui	44	Na	48.28N	67.26W
'Amrān	23	Ff	15.41N	43.55 E
Amrāvati	22	Jg	20.56N	77.45 E
Am-Raya	35	Bc	14.05N	16.30 E
Amritsar	22	Jf	31.35N	74.53 E
Amrum	8	Cj	54.40N	8.20 E
Amsaga	32	Ee	20.07N	14.10W
Amsittene, Jebel-	32	Fc	31.11N	9.40W
Amstel	12	Gb	52.22N	4.56 E
Amstelveen	12	Gb	52.18N	4.53 E
Amsterdam	30	Ol	37.57S	77.40 E
Amsterdam [Neth.]	6	Ge	52.22N	4.54 E
Amsterdam [N.Y.-U.S.]	44	Jd	42.56N	74.12W
Amsterdam-Rijnkanaal	12	Hc	51.57N	5.25 E
Amstetten	14	Ib	48.07N	14.52 E
Am Timan	31	Jg	11.02N	20.17 E
Amūd, Jabal al-	23	Ec	30.59N	39.20 E
Āmūdā	24	Id	37.05N	40.54 E
Amu-Darja	18	Ef	37.57N	65.15 E
Amudarja=Amu Darya (EN)	21	He	43.40N	59.01 E
Āmū Daryā=Amu Darya (EN)	21	He	43.40N	59.01 E
Amu Darya (EN)=Amudarja	21	He	43.40N	59.01 E
Amu Darya (EN)=Āmū Daryā	21	He	43.40N	59.01 E
Amudat	36	Fb	1.58N	34.56 E
Amukta Pass	40a	Db	52.25N	172.00W
Amun	63a	Ba	5.57S	154.45 E
Amund Ringnes	42	Ha	78.15N	97.00W
Amundsen	66	Ee	66.55S	50.00 E
Amundsen Coast	66	Mg	85.30S	159.00W
Amundsen Glacier	66	Mg	85.35S	159.00W
Amundsen Gulf	38	Gb	71.00N	124.00W
Amundsen-Scott Station	66	Bg	90.00S	0.00
Amundsen Sea (EN)	66	Of	72.30S	112.00W
Amungen	8	Fc	61.10N	15.40 E
Amuntai	22	Nj	2.26S	115.15 E
Amur	21	Qd	52.56N	141.10 E
'Amūr, Wādī-	35	Eb	18.56N	33.34 E
Amurang	26	Hf	1.11N	124.35 E
Amursk	20	If	50.16N	136.55 E
Amurskaja Oblast [3]	20	Hf	54.00N	128.00 E
Amurzet	20	Ig	47.41N	131.07 E
Amvrakia, Gulf of- (EN)=Amvrakikós Kólpos	15	Dk	39.00N	21.00 E
Amvrakikós Kólpos=Amvrakia, Gulf of- (EN)	15	Dk	39.00N	21.00 E
Amvrosijevka	16	Kf	47.44N	38.31 E
Am Zoer	35	Cc	14.13N	21.23 E
Anaa Atoll	61	Lc	17.25S	145.30W
Anabar	64e	Ba	0.29S	166.57 E
Anabar	21	Nb	73.08N	113.36 E
Anabarskoje Ploskogorje	21	Mc	70.00N	108.00 E
An Abhainn Dubh/Blackwater	9	Gh	53.39N	6.43W
An Abhainn Mhór/Blackwater [Ire.]	9	Fj	51.51N	7.50W
An Abhainn Mhór/Blackwater [N.Ire.-U.K.]	9	Gg	54.30N	6.35W
Anabuki	29	Dd	34.02N	134.11 E
Anaçasti	56	Gc	28.49S	65.30W
Anaco	54	Fb	9.27N	64.28W
Anaconda	43	Eb	46.08N	112.57W
Anacortes	46	Db	48.30N	122.37W
Anadarko	45	Gi	35.04N	98.15W
Anadolu=Anatolia (EN)	21	Ff	39.00N	35.00 E
Anadyr	21	Tc	64.55N	176.05 E
Anadyr	22	Tc	64.45N	177.29 E
Anadyr Gulf (EN)=Anadyrskij Zaliv	21	Uc	64.00N	179.00W
Anadyr Range (EN)=Anadyrskoje Ploskogorje	21	Tc	67.00N	174.00 E
Anadyrskij Liman	20	Md	64.30N	178.00 E
Anadyrskij Zaliv=Anadyr Gulf (EN)	21	Uc	64.00N	179.00W
Anadyrskoje Ploskogorje=Anadyr Range (EN)	21	Tc	67.00N	174.00 E
Anáfi	15	Im	36.22N	25.47 E
Anaghit	35	Fb	16.20N	38.39 E
Anagni	14	Hi	41.44N	13.09 E
'Ānah	23	Fc	34.28N	41.56 E
Anaheim	46	Gj	33.51N	117.57W
Anahola	65a	Ba	22.09N	159.19W
Anáhuac	48	Id	27.14N	100.09W
Anahuac, Meseta de-	47	Dd	21.30N	101.00W
An Aird/Ards Peninsula	9	Hg	54.30N	5.30W
Anaj Mudi	21	Jh	10.10N	77.04 E
Anaktuvuk Pass	40	Ic	68.10N	151.50W
Analalava	37	Hb	14.38S	47.45 E
Analavelona	37	Gd	22.37S	44.10 E
Ana Maria, Golfo de-	49	Hc	21.25N	78.40W
Anambas, Kepulauan-=Anambas Islands (EN)	21	Mi	3.00N	106.00 E
Anambas Islands (EN)=Anambas, Kepulauan-	21	Mi	3.00N	106.00 E
Anambra [2]	34	Gd	6.30N	7.30 E
Anamé	63b	De	20.08S	169.49 E
Anamizu	28	Nf	37.14N	136.54 E
Anamur	23	Db	36.06N	32.50 E
Anamur Burun	23	Db	36.03N	32.48 E
Anan [Jap.]	28	Mh	33.55N	134.39 E
Anan [Jap.]	29	Ed	35.19N	137.48 E
Anane, Djebel-	13	Mi	35.12N	0.47 E
Ananes	15	Hm	36.31N	24.08 E
Ananjev	16	Ff	47.43N	29.59 E
Anankwin	25	Je	15.41N	97.59 E
Anantapur	25	Ff	14.41N	77.36 E
Anantnāg (Islāmābād)	25	Fb	33.44N	75.09 E
Anapa	19	Dg	44.53N	37.19 E
Anapo	14	Jm	37.03N	15.16 E
Anápolis	53	Lg	16.20S	48.58W
Anapu, Rio-	54	Hd	2.15S	51.30W
Anār	23	Ic	30.53N	55.18 E
Anārak	23	Hc	33.20N	53.42 E
Anare Station	66	Jd	54.30S	158.55 E
Anaro, Rio-	49	Lj	7.48N	70.12W
Añasco	51a	Ab	18.17N	67.10W
Anatahan Island	57	Fc	16.22N	145.40 E
Anatolia (EN)=Anadolu	21	Ff	39.00N	35.00 E
Anatoliki Rodhópi	15	Ih	41.44N	25.31 E
Añatuya	56	Hc	28.28S	62.50W
Anauá, Rio-	54	Fc	0.58N	61.21W
Anazarba	24	Fd	37.15N	35.45 E
An Baile Meánach/Ballymena	9	Gg	54.52N	6.17W
An Bhanna/Bann	9	Gf	55.10N	6.46W
An Bhearú/Barrow	9	Gi	52.10N	7.00W
An Bhinn Bhuí/Benwee Head	9	Dg	54.21N	9.48W
An Bhograch/Boggeragh Mountains	9	Ei	52.05N	9.00W
An Bhóinn/Boyne	9	Gh	53.43N	6.15W
An Bhrosnach/Brosna	9	Fh	53.13N	7.58W
An Blascaod Mór/Great Blasket	9	Ci	52.05N	10.32W
Anbyŏn	28	Ie	39.02N	127.32 E
An Cabhán/Cavan [2]	9	Fh	53.55N	7.30W
An Cabhán/Cavan	9	Fg	54.00N	7.21W
An Caisleán Nua/Newcastle	9	Hg	54.12N	5.54W
An Caisleán Nua/Newcastle West	9	Di	52.27N	9.03W
An Caisleán Riabhach/Castlerea	9	Eh	53.46N	8.29W
An Caoláire Rua/Killary Harbour	9	Dh	53.38N	9.55W
Ancares, Sierra de-	13	Fb	42.46N	6.54W
Ancash [2]	54	Ce	9.30S	77.45W
Ancenis	11	Eg	47.22N	1.10W
An Chathair/Caher	9	Fi	52.22N	7.55W
An Cheacha/Caha Mountains	9	Dj	51.45N	9.45W
Anchorage	39	Ec	61.13N	149.53W
An Chorr Chríochach/Cookstown	9	Gg	54.39N	6.45W
Anci (Langfang)	27	Kd	39.29N	116.40 E
An Clár/Clare [2]	9	Ei	52.50N	9.00W
An Cóbh/Cóbh	9	Ej	51.51N	8.17W
Ancohuma, Nevado-	54	Eg	15.51S	68.36W
Ancona	6	Hg	43.38N	13.30 E
Ancón de Sardinas, Bahia de-	54	Cc	1.30N	79.50W
Ancre	11	Ie	49.54N	2.28 E
Ancuabe	37	Fb	12.58S	39.51 E
Ancud	56	Ff	41.52S	73.50W
Ancud, Golfo de-	56	Ff	42.05S	73.00W
Anda	27	Mb	46.24N	125.20 E
Anda (Sartu)	28	Ha	46.35N	125.00 E
Andacollo [Arg.]	56	Fe	37.11S	70.41W
Andacollo [Chile]	56	Fd	30.14S	71.06W
Andahuaylas	54	Df	13.39S	73.23W
An Daingean/Dingle	9	Ci	52.08N	10.15W
Andalgalá	56	Gc	27.36S	66.19W
Åndalsnes	7	Be	62.34N	7.42 E
Andalucia=Andalusia (EN)	13	Hg	37.30N	4.30W
Andalucia=Andalusia (EN)	5	Fh	37.30N	4.30W
Andalusia	43	Je	31.19N	86.29W
Andalusia (EN)=Andalucia	13	Hg	37.30N	4.30W
Andalusia (EN)=Andalucia	5	Fh	37.30N	4.30W
Andaman and Nicobar [3]	25	If	12.30N	92.45 E
Andaman Basin (EN)	21	Lh	10.00N	94.00 E
Andaman Islands	21	Lh	12.30N	92.43 E
Andaman Sea (EN)	21	Lh	10.00N	95.00 E
Andamooka	59	Hf	30.27S	137.12 E
'Andān, Wādī-	23	Ie	21.05N	58.23 E
Andant	55	Am	36.34S	62.07W
Andapa	37	Hb	14.38S	49.33 E
Andara	37	Cc	18.03S	21.27 E
Andelle	12	De	49.19N	1.14 E
Andenes	7	Db	69.19N	16.08 E
Andenne	12	Hd	50.29N	5.06 E
Andenne-Naméche	12	Hd	50.28N	5.00 E
Andéramboukane	34	Fb	15.26N	3.02 E
Anderlecht	12	Gd	50.50N	4.18 E
Anderlues	12	Gd	50.24N	4.16 E
Andermatt	14	Cd	46.38N	8.37 E
Andernach	10	Df	50.26N	7.24 E
Andernos-les-Bains	11	Ej	44.44N	1.06W
Anderson	42	Ec	69.42N	129.01W
Anderson [Ca.-U.S.]	46	Df	40.27N	122.18W
Anderson [In.-U.S.]	43	Jc	40.10N	85.41W
Anderson [S.C.-U.S.]	43	Ke	34.30N	82.39W
Anderstorp	8	Eg	57.17N	13.38 E
Andes (EN)=Andes, Cordillera de los-	52	Jh	20.00S	67.00W
Andes, Cordillera de los-=Andes (EN)	52	Jh	20.00S	67.00W
Andevoranto	37	Hc	18.48S	49.02 E
Andfjorden	7	Db	69.10N	16.20 E
Andhra Pradesh [3]	25	Fe	16.00N	79.00 E
Andía, Sierra de-	13	Kb	42.45N	2.00W
Andikhásia Óri	15	Ej	39.47N	21.55 E
Andikira	15	Fk	38.23N	22.38 E
Andikithira=Andikithira (EN)	15	Gn	35.52N	23.18 E
Andikithira (EN)=Andikithira	15	Gn	35.52N	23.18 E
Andikithiron, Stenón-	15	Gn	35.45N	23.25 E
Andilamena	37	Hc	17.01S	48.32 E
Andilanatoby	37	Hc	17.56S	48.14 E
Andimeshk	24	Mf	32.27N	48.21 E
Andimilos	15	Hm	36.47N	24.14 E
Andiparos	15	Il	37.00N	25.03 E
Andipaxoi	15	Dj	39.08N	20.14 E
Andipsara	15	Ik	38.33N	25.24 E
Andir He	27	Dd	38.00N	83.36 E
Andirin	24	Gd	37.34N	36.20 E
Andirlangar	27	Dd	37.36N	83.50 E
Andirrion	15	Ek	38.20N	21.46 E
Anditilos	15	Km	36.22N	27.28 E
Andižan	22	Je	40.45N	72.22 E
Andižanskaja Oblast [3]	19	Hg	40.45N	72.20 E
Andkhvoy	23	Kb	36.56N	65.08 E
Andŏng	27	Md	36.36N	128.44 E
Andorra (Valls d'Andorra) [1]	6	Gg	42.30N	1.30 E
Andorra la Vella	6	Gg	42.31N	1.31 E
Andover	9	Lj	51.13N	1.28W
Andøya	7	Db	69.08N	15.54 E
Andradas	55	If	22.05S	46.35W
Andradina	56	Jb	20.54S	51.23W
Andraitx	13	Oe	39.35N	2.25 E
Andreanof Islands	38	Bd	52.00N	176.00W
Andreapol	7	Hh	56.39N	32.16 E
Andrées Land	41	Jd	73.20N	26.30W
Andrejevka	19	If	45.47N	80.35 E
Andrejevka	16	Je	49.32N	36.40 E
Andrejevo-Ivanovka	15	Nb	47.31N	30.21 E
Andrejevsk	20	Ge	58.10N	114.15 E
Andrelândia	55	Je	21.44S	44.18W
Andresito	55	Dk	33.08S	57.09W
Andrespol	10	Pe	51.43N	19.40 E
Andrews	45	Ej	32.19N	102.33W
Andria	14	Ki	41.13N	16.17 E
Andriamena	37	Hc	17.28S	47.29 E
Andriba	37	Hc	17.36S	46.53 E
Andrijevica	15	Cg	42.44N	19.48 E
Andringitra	30	Lk	22.20S	46.55 E
Andrítsaina	15	El	37.29N	21.54 E
Androka	37	Gd	24.59S	44.04 E
Andropov → Rybinsk	6	Jd	58.03N	38.52 E
Ándros	5	Ih	37.50N	24.50 E
Andros	38	Lg	24.25N	78.00W
Ándros	15	Hl	37.50N	24.56 E
Androscoggin River	44	Md	43.55N	69.55W
Androssan	9	If	55.40N	4.55W
Andros Town	47	Id	24.43N	77.47W
Androth Island	25	Ef	10.50N	73.41 E
Androy	30	Lk	25.00S	45.40 E
Andruševka	16	Fe	49.59N	29.01 E
Andrychów	10	Pg	49.52N	19.21 E
Andselv	7	Eb	69.04N	18.30 E
Andudu	36	Eb	2.29N	28.41 E
Andújar	13	Hf	38.03N	4.04W
Andulo	36	Ce	11.28S	16.43 E
Andu Tan	26	Fe	7.35N	114.15 E
Anduze	11	Jj	44.03N	3.59 E
An Earagail/Errigal	9	Ef	55.02N	8.07W
Aneby	8	Fg	57.50N	14.48 E
Anéfis	34	Fb	18.03N	0.36 E
Anegada	47	Le	18.45N	64.20W
Anegada, Bahia-	47	Hf	40.15S	62.15W
Anegada Passage	47	Le	18.30N	63.40W
Aného	34	Fd	6.14N	1.36 E
An Éirne/Erne	9	Eg	54.30N	8.15W
An Eithne/Inny	9	Fh	53.35N	7.50W
An Eoghanach/Annalee	9	Fg	54.02N	7.25W
Anet	12	Df	48.51N	1.26 E
Aneto, Pico de-	5	Gg	42.38N	0.40 E
Aney	34	Hb	19.24N	12.56 E
Aneytioum, Ile-	57	Hg	20.12S	169.49 E
An Feabhal	9	Ff	55.04N	7.15W
An Fhéil/Feale	9	Di	52.28N	9.40W
An Fheoir/Nore	9	Gi	52.25N	6.58W
Angamos, Punta- [Chile]	56	Fb	23.01S	70.32W
Angamos, Punta- [Pas.]	65d	Bb	27.04S	109.17W
Angara	21	Ld	58.06N	93.00 E
Angarsk	22	Md	52.34N	103.54 E
Angarski, Pereval-	16	Ig	44.47N	34.25 E
Angarski Krjaž	20	Fe	57.30N	103.00 E
Angathonisi	15	Jl	37.28N	27.00 E
Angaur Island	57	Ed	6.54N	134.09 E
Ånge	7	De	62.31N	15.37 E
Ånge	8	Fa	63.27N	14.03 E
An Gearran/Garron Point	9	Hf	55.05N	5.58W
Angel, Cerro-	48	Hf	22.49N	102.34W
Ángel, Salto-=Angel Falls (EN)	52	Je	5.57N	62.30W
Angelburg	12	Kd	50.47N	8.25 E
Angel de la Guarda, Isla-	47	Bc	29.20N	113.25W
Angeles	26	Hc	15.09N	120.35 E
Angeles, Sierra de los-	48	Jf	23.10N	99.20W
Angel Falls (EN)=Ángel, Salto-	52	Je	5.57N	62.30W
Angel Falls (EN)=Churún Merú	52	Je	5.57N	62.30W
Ängelholm	7	Ch	56.15N	12.51 E
Angélica	55	Bj	31.33S	61.33W
Angeln	10	Fb	54.40N	9.45 E
Ängelsberg	8	Ge	59.58N	16.02 E
Anger	35	Fd	9.40N	36.06 E
Angereb	35	Fc	13.44N	36.28 E
Ångermanälven	5	Hc	62.48N	17.56 E
Angermünde	10	Jc	53.02N	14.00 E
Angers	6	Ff	47.28N	0.33W
Angkor	25	Kf	13.26N	103.52 E
Angikuni Lake	42	Hd	62.10N	99.55W
Angistrion	15	Gl	37.40N	23.20 E
Anglem, Mount-	62	Bg	46.44S	167.54 E
Anglés	13	Oc	41.57N	2.39 E
Anglesey	5	Fe	53.18N	4.20W
Anglet	11	Ek	43.29N	1.32W
Angleton	45	Il	29.10N	95.26W
Anglin	11	Gh	46.42N	0.52 E
Anglona	14	Cj	40.45N	8.45 E
Angmagssalik	67	Mc	65.45N	37.30W
Ango	36	Eb	4.02N	25.52 E
Angoche	31	Kj	16.12S	39.54 E
Angoche, Ilha-	30	Kj	16.20S	39.51 E
Angol	56	Fe	37.48S	72.43W
Angola [1]	31	Ij	12.30S	18.30 E
Angola	44	Ee	41.38N	85.00W
Angola Basin (EN)	3	Ek	15.00S	3.00 E
Angoram	60	Ch	4.04S	144.04 E
Angostura	48	Ee	25.22N	108.11W
Angostura, Presa de la-	48	Mi	16.30N	92.30W
Angostura, Salto-	54	Dc	2.43N	70.57W
Angostura Reservoir	45	Ee	43.18N	103.27W
Angoulême	11	Gi	45.39N	0.09 E
Angoumois	11	Fi	45.30N	0.10W
Angra do Heroismo [3]	32	Bb	38.42N	27.15W
Angra do Héroismo	31	Ee	38.39N	27.13W
Angra dos Reis	55	Jf	23.00S	44.18W
Angren	19	Hg	41.03N	70.10 E
Angu	36	Db	3.33N	24.28 E
Anguang	28	Gb	45.36N	123.48 E
Anguilla [5]	39	Mh	18.15N	63.05W
Anguilla	38	Mh	18.15N	63.05W
Anguilla, Canal de l'-=Anguilla Channel (EN)	51b	Ab	18.09N	63.04W
Anguilla Bank (EN)	51b	Ab	18.30N	63.03W
Anguilla Cays	49	Hb	23.31N	78.33W
Anguilla Channel (EN)=Anguilla, Canal de l'-	51b	Ab	18.09N	63.04W
Anguli Nur	28	Cd	41.23N	114.30 E
Anguo	28	Ce	38.25N	115.20 E
Anhanca	36	Cf	16.47S	15.33 E
Anhanguera	55	Hd	18.21S	48.17W
An Hoa	25	Le	15.46N	108.03 E
Anholt	7	Ch	56.40N	11.35 E
Anhua (Dongping)	27	Jf	28.27N	111.15 E
Anhui Sheng (An-hui Sheng)=Anhwei (EN) [2]	27	Ke	32.00N	117.00 E
An-hui Sheng → Anhui Sheng=Anhwei (EN) [2]	27	Ke	32.00N	117.00 E
Anhwei (EN)=Anhui Sheng (An-hui Sheng) [2]	27	Ke	32.00N	117.00 E
Anhwei (EN)=An-hui Sheng → Anhui Sheng [2]	27	Ke	32.00N	117.00 E
Ani	29	Gb	39.59N	140.25 E
Aniak	40	Hd	61.34N	159.30W
An Iarmhí/Westmeath [2]	9	Fh	53.30N	7.30W
Anibare	64e	Bb	0.32S	166.57 E
Anibare Bay	64e	Bb	0.32S	166.57 E
Aniche	12	Fd	50.20N	3.15 E
Anidros	15	Im	36.37N	25.41 E
Anié	34	Fd	7.45N	1.12 E
Anie, Pic d'-	11	Fl	42.57N	0.43W
Aniene	14	Gi	41.56N	12.30 E
Anijangying → Luanping	28	Dd	40.55N	117.19 E
Anikščiaj/Anykščiai	7	Fi	55.31N	25.08 E
Animas Peak	45	Bk	31.35N	108.47W
Anina	15	Ed	45.05N	21.51 E
Anita Garibaldi	55	Gh	27.37S	51.05W
Anittepe	15	Kh	41.21N	27.42 E
Aniva	20	Jg	46.41N	142.35 E
Aniva, Zaliv-	20	Jg	46.20N	142.40 E
Anivorano Nord	37	Hb	12.43S	49.12 E
Aniwa, Ile-	57	Hf	19.16S	169.35 E
Anizy-le-Château	12	Fe	49.30N	3.27 E
Anjala	7	Gf	60.41N	26.50 E
Anji	28	Ei	30.39N	119.41 E
Anjiang → Qianyang	27	Jf	27.19N	110.13 E
Anjō	29	Ed	34.57N	137.05 E
Anjou	11	Fg	47.20N	0.30W
Anjou, Ostrova-=Anjou Islands (EN)	21	Qb	75.30N	143.00 E
Anjouan → Nzwani	30	Lj	12.15S	44.25 E
Anjou Islands (EN)=Anjou, Ostrova-	21	Qb	75.30N	143.00 E
Anjozorobe	37	Hc	18.24S	47.52 E
Anju	27	Md	39.37N	125.40 E
Anjuj	20	Ig	49.20N	136.20 E
Anjujski Hrebet	20	Lc	67.20N	166.00 E
Anjuou, Val d'-	11	Fg	47.25N	0.15W
Anka	34	Gc	12.07N	5.55 E
Ankang (Xing'an)	22	Mf	32.37N	109.03 E
Ankara	22	Ff	39.56N	32.52 E
Ankaratra	30	Lj	19.25S	47.12 E
Ankarsrum	7	Dh	57.42N	16.19 E
Ankavandra	37	Hc	18.45S	45.18 E
Ankazoabo	37	Gd	22.16S	44.30 E
Ankazobe	37	Hc	18.17S	47.05 E
Ankeny	45	Jf	41.44N	93.36W
Ankhor	35	Hc	10.47N	46.18 E
Anklam	10	Jc	53.52N	13.42 E
Ankober	35	Fd	9.40N	39.44 E
Ankoro	36	Ed	6.45S	26.57 E
Ankum	12	Jb	52.33N	7.53 E
An Laoi/Lee	9	Ej	51.55N	8.30W
Anlong	27	If	25.02N	105.30 E
An Longfort/Longford [2]	9	Fh	53.40N	7.40W
An Longfort/Longford	9	Fh	53.44N	7.47W
An Lorgain/Lurgan	9	Gg	54.28N	6.20W
Anlu	27	Je	31.12N	113.46 E
An Mhí/Meath [2]	9	Gh	53.35N	6.40W
An Muaidh/Moy	9	Dg	54.12N	9.08W
An Mhuir Cheilteach=Celtic Sea (EN)	5	Fe	51.00N	7.00W
An Muileann gCearr/Mullingar	9	Fh	53.32N	7.20W
An Muirthead/Mullet Peninsula	9	Cg	54.15N	10.04W
Ånn	7	Ce	63.15N	12.35 E
Ånn	8	Ea	63.19N	12.33 E
Ann, Cape- [Ant.]	66	Ee	66.10S	51.22 E
Ann, Cape- [Ma.-U.S.]	44	Ld	42.39N	70.38W
Anna [Il.-U.S.]	45	Lh	37.28N	89.15W
Anna [Nauru]	64e	Ba	0.29S	166.56 E
Anna	19	Ee	51.29N	40.26 E
Annaba	31	He	36.54N	7.46 E
Annaba [3]	32	Ib	35.35N	8.00 E
An Nabaţiyah at Taḩtā	24	Gf	33.23N	35.29 E
Annaberg-Buchholz	10	If	50.34N	13.00 E
An Nabī Şāliḩ	24	Eh	28.38N	33.59 E
An Nabk	23	Ec	34.01N	36.44 E
An Nabk Abū Qaşr	24	Hg	30.21N	38.34 E
An Nafīḑah	14	En	36.08N	10.23 E
An Nafūd	21	Gg	28.30N	41.00 E
An Najaf	22	Gf	31.59N	44.20 E
An Najaf [3]	24	Kg	31.20N	44.07 E
An Nakhl	33	Fd	29.55N	33.45 E
Annalee/An Eoghanach	9	Fg	54.02N	7.25W
Annam (EN)=Trung Phan	21	Me	15.00N	108.00 E
Annamitique, Chaîne-	25	Le	17.00N	106.00 E
Annan	9	Jg	54.59N	3.16W
Annan	9	Jg	55.00N	3.16W
Anna Paulowna	12	Gb	52.52N	4.52 E
Anna Paulowna-Kleine Sluis	12	Gb	52.52N	4.52 E
Anna Point	64e	Ba	0.29S	166.57 E
Annapolis	39	Lf	38.59N	76.30W
Annapolis Royal	44	Oc	44.45N	65.31W
Annapurna	21	Kg	28.34N	83.50 E
Ann Arbor	43	Kc	42.18N	83.45W
Anna Regina	50	Gi	7.16N	58.30W
An Nás/Naas	9	Gh	53.13N	6.39W
An Nashshāsh	24	Pk	23.05N	54.02 E
An Nashwah	24	Lg	30.49N	47.36 E
An Nāşirīyah	23	Gc	31.02N	46.16 E
An Nasser	24	Ej	24.36N	32.58 E
An Nawfalīyah	33	Cc	30.47N	17.50 E
Annecy	11	Mi	45.54N	6.07 E
Annecy, Lac d'-	11	Mi	45.51N	6.11 E
Annemasse	11	Mh	46.12N	6.15 E
Annevoie-Rouillon	12	Gd	50.21N	4.50 E
An Nīl [3]	35	Ea	20.10N	33.00 E
An Nīl al Azraq [3]	35	Ed	12.20N	34.15 E
Anning	27	Hg	24.58N	102.29 E
Anniston	43	Je	33.40N	85.50W
Annobón	30	Hi	1.32S	5.38 E
Annonay	11	Ki	45.14N	4.40 E
Annotto Bay	49	Id	18.16N	76.46W
An Nu'ayrīyah	24	Mi	27.28N	48.27 E
An Nuhūd	31	Jg	12.42N	28.26 E
An Nu' Mān	24	Fi	27.06N	35.46 E
An Nu'mānīyah	24	Kf	32.32N	45.25 E
Annweiler am Trifels	12	Je	49.12N	7.58 E
Anoia/Noya	13	Nc	41.28N	1.56 E
Anoka	45	Jd	45.11N	93.23W
An Ómaigh/Omagh	9	Fg	54.36N	7.18W
Anori	54	Fd	3.47S	61.38W
Anosyennes, Chaînes-	37	Hd	24.20S	47.00 E
Ānou Makarene	35	Gb	18.07N	7.35 E
Áno Viánnos	15	In	35.03N	25.25 E
Anóyia	15	Hn	35.15N	24.54 E
Anping [China]	28	Ce	38.13N	115.32 E
Anping [China]	28	Gd	41.10N	123.25 E
An Pointe/Warrenpoint	9	Gg	54.06N	6.15W
Anpu	27	Ig	21.30N	110.00 E
Anpu Gang	27	Ig	21.25N	109.40 E
Anqing	22	Nf	30.32N	116.59 E
Anqiu	28	Ef	36.25N	119.12 E
An Ráth/Ráth Luirc	9	Ei	52.21N	8.41W
An Ribhéar/Kenmare River	9	Dj	51.50N	9.50W
Anröchte	12	Kc	51.34N	8.20 E
Ans	12	Hd	50.39N	5.32 E
Anşāb	23	Fd	29.11N	44.43 E
Ansauvillers	12	Ee	49.34N	2.24 E
Ansbach	10	Gg	49.18N	10.35 E
An Sciobairín/Skibbereen	9	Dj	51.33N	9.15W
An Seancheann/Kinsale, Old Head of-	9	Ej	51.36N	8.32W
Anse-à-Veau	49	Kd	18.30N	73.19W
Anse-Bertrand	51e	Ab	16.29N	61.31W
Anse-d'Hainault	49	Jd	18.30N	74.27W
Anse la Raye	51k	Ab	13.57N	61.03W
Anshan	22	Oe	41.08N	122.59 E
Anshun	22	Mg	26.15N	105.58 E
Ansina	56	Id	31.54S	55.28W
Ansley	45	Gf	41.18N	99.23W
Anson Bay	59	Gb	13.20S	130.05 E
Ansongo	34	Fb	15.40N	0.31 E
An Srath Bán/Strabane	9	Fg	54.49N	7.27W
Anta	54	Df	13.29S	72.09W

Index Symbols

[1] Independent Nation
[2] State, Region
[3] District, County
[4] Municipality
[5] Colony, Dependency
Continent
Physical Region
Historical or Cultural Region
Mount, Mountain
Volcano
Hill
Mountains, Mountain Range
Hills, Escarpment
Plateau, Upland
Pass, Gap
Plain, Lowland
Delta
Salt Flat
Valley, Canyon
Crater, Cave
Karst Features
Depression
Polder
Desert, Dunes
Forest, Woods
Heath, Steppe
Oasis
Cape, Point
Coast, Beach
Cliff
Peninsula
Isthmus
Sandbank
Island
Atoll
Rock, Reef
Islands, Archipelago
Rocks, Reefs
Coral Reef
Well, Spring
Geyser
River, Stream
Waterfall Rapids
River Mouth, Estuary
Lake
Salt Lake
Intermittent Lake
Reservoir
Swamp, Pond
Canal
Glacier
Ice Shelf, Pack Ice
Ocean
Sea
Gulf, Bay
Strait, Fjord
Lagoon
Bank
Seamount
Tablemount
Ridge
Shelf
Basin
Escarpment, Sea Scarp
Fracture
Trench, Abyss
National Park, Reserve
Point of Interest
Recreation Site
Cave, Cavern
Historic Site
Ruins
Wall, Walls
Church, Abbey
Temple
Scientific Station
Airport
Port
Lighthouse
Mine
Tunnel
Dam, Bridge

Antabamba	54	Df	14.19S	72.55W
Antakya=Antioch (EN)	23	Eb	36.14N	36.07 E
Antalaha	31	Mj	14.55S	50.15 E
Antalya	22	Ff	36.53N	30.42 E
Antalya, Gulf of- (EN)=Antalya Körfezi	23	Db	36.30N	31.00 E
Antalya Körfezi=Antalya, Gulf of- (EN)	23	Db	36.30N	31.00 E
An Tan	25	Le	15.26N	108.39 E
Antananarivo	31	Lj	18.55S	47.30 E
Antananarivo [3]	37	Hc	19.00S	46.40 E
Antanimora	37	Hd	24.48S	45.39 E
An tAonach/Nenagh	9	Ei	52.52N	8.12W
Antarctica (EN)	66	Bg	90.00S	0.00
Antarctic Peninsula (EN)	66	Qe	69.30S	65.00W
Antas, Cachoeira das-	55	Ha	13.06S	48.09W
Antas, Rio das-	55	Gi	29.04S	51.21W
An Teampall Mór/Templemore	9	Fi	52.48N	7.50W
Antela, Laguna de-	13	Eb	42.07N	7.41W
Antelao	14	Gd	46.27N	12.16 E
Antelope Creek	46	Me	43.29N	105.23W
Anten	8	Ef	58.03N	12.30 E
Antequera [Par.]	55	Dg	24.08S	57.07W
Antequera [Sp.]	13	Hg	37.01N	4.33W
Anthony	45	Cj	32.00N	106.34W
Anti-Atlas	30	Ge	30.00N	8.30W
Antibes	11	Nk	43.55N	7.07 E
Antibes, Cap d'-	11	Nk	43.32N	7.07 E
Antica, Isla-	50	Eg	10.24N	62.43W
Anticosti, Ile d'-	38	Me	49.30N	63.00W
Antigo	45	Ld	45.09N	89.09W
Antigonish	42	Lg	45.37N	61.58W
Antigua	38	Mh	17.03N	61.48W
Antigua and Barbuda	39	Mh	17.03N	61.48W
Antigua Guatemala	47	Ff	14.34N	90.44W
Antiguo Cauce del Río Bermejo	56	Hc	25.39S	60.11W
Antiguo Morelos	48	Jf	22.30N	99.05W
Antilla	49	Jc	20.50N	75.45W
Antillas, Mar de las-/Caribe, Mar-=Caribbean Sea (EN)	38	Lh	15.00N	73.00W
Antillas Mayores=Greater Antilles (EN)	38	Lh	20.00N	74.00W
Antillas Menores=Lesser Antilles (EN)	38	Mh	15.00N	61.00W
Antilles, Mer des-/Caraïbe, Mer-=Caribbean Sea (EN)	38	Lh	15.00N	73.00W
An tInbhear Mór/Arklow	9	Gi	52.48N	6.09W
Antioch	46	Eg	38.00N	121.49W
Antioch (EN)=Antakya	23	Eb	36.14N	36.07 E
Antioche, Pertuis d'-	11	Eh	46.05N	1.20W
Antiope Reef	57	Kf	18.18S	168.40W
Antioquia [2]	54	Cb	7.00N	75.30W
Antipajëta	20	Cc	69.09N	77.00 E
Antipodes Islands	57	Ii	49.40S	178.50 E
Antiques, Pointe d'-	51e	Ab	16.26N	61.33W
An t-Iúr/Newry	9	Gg	54.11N	6.20W
Antler River	45	Fb	49.08N	101.00W
Antlers	45	Ii	34.14N	95.37W
Antofagasta [2]	56	Gb	23.30S	69.00W
Antofagasta	53	Ih	23.39S	70.24W
Antofagasta de la Sierra	56	Gc	26.04S	67.25W
Antofalla, Salar de-	56	Gc	25.44S	67.45W
Antofalla, Volcán-	56	Gc	25.34S	67.55W
Antoing	12	Fd	50.34N	3.27 E
Antón	49	Gi	8.24N	80.16W
Anton Dohrn Seamount (EN)	9	Cd	57.30N	11.00W
Antongil, Baie d'-	30	Lj	15.45S	49.50 E
Antonina	56	Kc	25.27S	48.43W
Antônio João	55	Ef	23.15S	55.31W
Antonito	45	Dh	37.05N	106.00W
Antón Lizardo, Punta de-	48	Lh	19.03N	95.58W
Antony	12	Ef	48.45N	2.18 E
Antopol	10	Ud	52.12N	24.53 E
Antracit	16	Ke	48.06N	39.06 E
Antreff	12	Ld	50.52N	9.15 E
Antrim/Aontroim	9	Gg	54.43N	6.13W
Antrim Mountains	9	Gf	55.00N	6.10W
Antrodoco	14	Hh	42.25N	13.05 E
Antsakabary	37	Hc	15.03S	48.56 E
Antsalova	37	Gc	18.42S	44.33 E
Antseranana [3]	37	Hb	13.40S	49.15 E
An tSionainn/Shannon	5	Fe	52.36N	9.41W
Antsirabe	31	Lj	19.51S	47.01 E
Antsiranana	31	Lj	12.17S	49.17 E
An tSiúir/Suir	9	Gi	52.15N	7.00W
Antsla	7	Gh	57.52N	26.33 E
An tSláine/Slaney	9	Gi	52.21N	6.30W
Antsohihy	31	Lj	14.52S	47.58 E
An tSuca/Suck	9	Eh	53.16N	8.03W
Anttola	8	Lc	61.35N	27.39 E
Antu (Songjiang)	28	Jc	42.33N	128.20 E
An Tuc	25	Lf	13.57N	108.39 E
Antufash, Jazīrat-	33	Hf	15.42N	42.25 E
An Tulach/Tullow	9	Gi	52.48N	6.44W
An Tulach Mhór/Tullamore	9	Fh	53.16N	7.30W
Antwerp (EN)=Antwerpen/Anvers	6	Ge	50.38N	5.34 E
Antwerp (EN)=Anvers/Antwerpen	6	Ge	50.38N	5.34 E
Antwerpen [3]	12	Gc	51.10N	4.30 E
Antwerpen/Anvers=Antwerp (EN)	6	Ge	50.38N	5.34 E
Antwerpen-Ekeren	11	Kc	51.17N	4.25 E
Antwerpen-Hoboken	12	Gc	51.10N	4.21 E
Antwerpen-Merksem	12	Gc	51.15N	4.27 E
Antykan	20	If	54.55N	135.13 E
An Uaimh/Navan	9	Gh	53.39N	6.41W
Anuradhapura	25	Gg	8.21N	80.23 E
Anuta Island	57	Hf	11.38S	169.50 E
Anvers/Antwerpen=Antwerp (EN)	6	Ge	50.38N	5.34 E
Anvers Island	66	Qe	64.33S	63.35W
Anvik	40	Gd	62.40N	160.12W
Anxi	22	Le	40.30N	96.00 E
Anxiang	27	Jf	29.26N	112.11 E
Anxin	28	Ce	38.55N	115.56 E
Anxious Bay	59	Gf	33.25S	134.35 E
Anyang (Zhangde)	22	Nf	36.01N	114.25 E
A'nyêmaqen Shan	21	Lf	34.30N	100.00 E
Anyi	28	Cj	28.50N	115.31 E
Anykščiai/Anikščjaj	7	Fi	55.31N	25.08 E
Anyva, Mys-	20	Jg	46.00N	143.25 E
Anza	14	Ce	46.00N	8.17 E
Anze	28	Bf	36.09N	112.14 E
Anzegem	12	Fd	50.50N	3.28 E
Anžero-Sudžensk	22	Kd	56.07N	86.00 E
Anzi	36	Dc	0.52S	23.24 E
Anzio	14	Gi	41.27N	12.37 E
Anzoátegui [2]	54	Fb	9.00N	64.30W
Anzob, Pereval-	18	Ge	39.07N	68.53 E
Aoba, Ile-	61	Cc	15.25S	167.50 E
Ao Ban Don	25	Jg	9.20N	99.25 E
Aoga-Shima	27	Oe	32.30N	139.50 E
Aohan Qi (Xinhui)	28	Ec	42.18N	119.53 E
Aoiz	13	Kb	42.47N	1.22W
Aoji	28	Kc	42.31N	130.24 E
Aola	63a	Ec	9.32S	160.29 E
Aomen/Macau=Macao (EN) [5]	22	Ng	22.10N	113.33 E
Aomen/Macau=Macao (EN)	27	Jg	22.12N	113.33 E
Aomori	22	Qe	40.49N	140.45 E
Aomori Ken [2]	28	Pd	40.40N	140.40 E
Aono-Yama	29	Bd	34.27N	131.48 E
Aontroim/Antrim	9	Gg	54.43N	6.13W
Aopo	65c	Aa	13.29S	172.30W
Aôral, Phnum-	25	Kf	12.02N	104.10 E
Aoré	63b	Cb	15.35S	167.10 E
Aosta / Aoste	14	Be	45.44N	7.20 E
Aosta, Val d'-	14	Be	45.45N	7.20 E
Aoste / Aosta	14	Be	45.44N	7.20 E
Aouk, Bahr-	30	Ih	8.51N	18.53 E
Aoukalé	35	Cd	9.10N	20.30 E
Aoukâr [Afr.]	32	Ge	24.00N	2.30W
Aoukâr [Mtna.]	30	Gg	17.30N	9.30W
Aoulef	32	Hd	26.58N	1.05 E
Aoumou	63b	Be	21.24S	165.49 E
Aourou	34	Cc	14.28N	11.34W
Aoya	29	Cd	35.32N	133.59 E
Aozou	31	If	21.49N	17.25 E
Apa, Rio-	56	Ib	22.06S	58.00W
Apača	20	Kf	52.50N	157.10 E
Apache	46	Kk	31.44N	109.07W
Apache Junction	46	Jj	33.26N	111.32W
Apahida	15	Gc	46.49N	23.45 E
Apakho	63c	Bb	11.25S	166.32 E
Apalachee Bay	38	Kg	29.30N	84.00W
Apalachicola	44	Ek	29.44N	84.59W
Apalachicola River	44	Ek	29.44N	84.59W
Apan	48	Jh	19.43N	98.25W
Apaporis, Río-	52	Jf	1.23S	69.25W
Aparecida do Taboado	54	Hg	20.05S	51.05W
Aparri	22	Oh	18.22N	121.39 E
Apataki Atoll	57	Mf	15.26S	146.20W
Apatin	15	Bd	45.40N	18.59 E
Apatity	6	Jb	67.34N	33.18 E
Apatzingán de la Constitucion	47	De	19.05N	102.21W
Apaxtla de Castrejón	48	Jh	18.09N	99.52W
Ape	7	Gh	57.32N	26.42 E
Apeldoorn	11	Lb	52.13N	5.58 E
Apeldoorn-Nieuw Milligen	12	Hb	52.14N	5.45 E
Apen	12	Ja	53.13N	7.48 E
Apennines (EN) = Appennini	5	Hg	43.00N	13.00 E
Apere, Río-	54	Ef	13.44S	65.18W
Aphrodisias	24	Cd	37.45N	28.40 E
Api	21	Kf	30.00N	80.57 E
Api	36	Eb	3.40N	25.26 E
Apia	58	Jf	13.50S	171.44W
Apiacás, Serra dos-	54	Gf	10.15S	57.15W
Apio	63a	Ec	9.39S	161.23 E
Apipé Grande, Isla-	55	Di	27.30S	56.54W
Apizaco	48	Jh	19.25N	98.09W
Aplao	54	Dc	16.05S	72.31W
Apo, Mount-	21	Oi	6.59N	125.16 E
Apodi	54	Ke	5.39S	37.48W
Apolda	10	He	51.01N	11.30 E
Apolima	65c	Aa	13.49S	172.07W
Apolima Strait	65c	Aa	13.50S	172.10W
Apollo Bay	59	Ig	38.45S	143.40 E
Apollonia [Alb.]	15	Ci	40.43N	19.27 E
Apollonia [Lib.]	33	Dc	32.54N	21.58 E
Apolo	54	Ef	14.43S	68.31W
Apón, Río-	49	Kh	10.06N	72.23W
Apopka, Lake-	44	Gk	28.37N	81.38W
Aporé	55	Fd	18.58S	52.01W
Aporé, Rio-	52	Kg	19.27S	50.57W
Apostle Islands	43	Ib	46.50N	90.30W
Apostoles	56	Ic	27.55S	55.46W
Apostolovo	16	Hf	47.39N	33.43 E
Apoteri	54	Gc	4.02N	58.34W
Apôtres, Iles des-	30	Mm	45.40S	50.20 E
Appalachia	44	Fg	36.54N	82.48W
Appalachian Mountains	38	Lc	41.00N	77.00W
Äppelbo	8	Ed	60.30N	14.00 E
Appennini = Apennines (EN)	5	Hg	43.00N	13.00 E
Appennino Abruzzese	14	Hh	42.00N	13.55 E
Appennino Calabro	14	Kl	39.00N	16.30 E
Appennino Campano	14	Ii	40.50N	14.45 E
Appennino Ligure	14	Cf	44.30N	9.00 E
Appennino Lucano	14	Jj	40.30N	16.00 E
Appennino Tosco-Emiliano	14	Fg	44.00N	11.30 E
Appennino Umbro-Marchigiano	14	Gg	43.20N	12.55 E
Appenzell	14	Dc	47.20N	9.25 E
Appenzell Ausser-Rhoden [2]	14	Dc	47.20N	9.20 E
Appenzell Inner-Rhoden [2]	14	Dc	47.15N	9.25 E
Appingedam	12	Ia	53.19N	6.52 E
Appleby	9	Kg	54.36N	2.29W
Appleton	43	Jc	44.16N	88.25W
Appomattox	44	Hg	37.21N	78.51W
Apra Harbor	64c	Bb	13.27N	144.38 E
Apricena	14	Ji	41.47N	15.27 E
Aprilia	14	Gi	41.36N	12.39 E
Apšeronsk	19	Dg	44.27N	39.44 E
Apšeronski Poluostrov=Apsheron Peninsula (EN)	5	Lg	41.00N	50.50 E
Apsheron Peninsula (EN)=Apšeronski Poluostrov	5	Lg	41.00N	50.50 E
Apt	11	Lk	43.53N	5.24 E
Apucarana	56	Jb	23.33S	51.29W
Apuoarana, Serra da-	55	Gf	23.50S	51.20W
Apuka	20	Ld	60.23N	169.45 E
Apuka	20	Ld	60.25N	169.35 E
Apulia (EN) = Puglia [2]	14	Ki	41.15N	16.15 E
Apurashokoru	64a	Ac	7.17N	134.18 E
Apure [2]	54	Eb	7.10N	68.50W
Apure, Río-	52	Je	7.37N	66.25W
Apurimac [2]	54	Df	14.00S	73.00W
Apurímac, Río-	52	Ig	12.17S	73.56W
Apurito	50	Bi	7.56N	68.27W
Apuseni, Munţii-=Apuseni Mountains (EN)	5	If	46.30N	22.30 E
Apuseni Mountains (EN)=Apuseni, Munţii-	5	If	46.30N	22.30 E
Āq	24	Kc	38.59N	45.27 E
Āqā	24	Me	35.00N	47.00 E
Aqaba (EN)=Al 'Aqabah	23	Dd	29.31N	35.00 E
Aqaba, Gulf of- (EN)='Aqabah, Khalīj al-	30	Kf	29.00N	34.40 E
Āqā Bāba	24	Md	36.20N	49.46 E
'Aqabah, Khalīj al-=Aqaba, Gulf of- (EN)	30	Kf	29.00N	34.40 E
Āqcheh	23	Kb	36.56N	66.11 E
'Aqdā	24	Of	32.26N	53.37 E
'Aqīq	35	Fb	18.14N	38.12 E
Aqitag	27	Fc	41.49N	90.38 E
Āqotāq	24	Ld	37.10N	47.05 E
Āq Qal'eh	24	Pd	37.01N	54.30 E
Aqqikkol Hu	27	Ed	37.00N	88.20 E
'Aqrah	24	Jd	36.45N	43.54 E
Aqrin, Jabal-	24	Hg	31.32N	38.18 E
Āq Şū	24	Ke	34.35N	44.31 E
Aquidabã, Rio-	55	De	20.58S	57.50W
Aquidabán, Río-	55	Df	23.11S	57.32W
Aquidauana	54	Gh	20.28S	55.48W
Aquidauana, Rio-	54	Gg	19.44S	56.50W
Aquidauna, Serra de-	55	Ee	20.50S	55.30W
Aquiles Serdán	48	Gc	28.36N	105.53W
Aquin	49	Kd	18.16N	73.24W
Aquitaine, Bassin d'-=Aquitane Basin (EN)	5	Fg	44.00N	0.10W
Aquitane Basin (EN)=Aquitaine, Bassin d'-	5	Fg	44.00N	0.10W
Ara	13	Mb	42.25N	0.09 E
'Arab, Baḩr al-	30	Jh	9.02N	29.28 E
'Arab, Khalīj al-	33	Ec	30.55N	29.05 E
'Arab, Shaţţ al-	21	Gf	30.28N	47.59 E
'Arabah, Wādī-	24	Eh	29.07N	32.39 E
'Arabah, Wādī al-	24	Fg	30.58N	32.24 E
Arabatskaja Strelka, Kosa-	16	Ig	45.40N	35.05 E
'Arabestān	24	Mg	30.30N	50.00 E
Arabian Basin (EN)	3	Gh	11.30N	65.00 E
Arabian Desert (EN)=Sharqīyah, Aş Şaḩrā' ash-	30	Kf	28.00N	32.00 E
Arabian Peninsula (EN)	21	Gg	25.00N	45.00 E
Arabian Sea (EN)	21	Ih	15.00N	65.00 E
Araç	24	Eb	41.15N	33.21 E
Aracá, Rio-	54	Fd	0.25S	62.55W
Aracaju	53	Mg	10.55S	37.04W
Aracataca	49	Jh	10.35N	74.13W
Aracati	54	Kd	4.34S	37.46W
Araçatuba	53	Kh	21.12S	50.25W
Aracena	13	Fg	37.53N	6.33W
Aracena, Sierra de-	13	Fg	37.56N	6.50W
Aracides, Cape-	63a	Ec	8.39S	161.01 E
Aracruz	54	Jg	19.49S	40.16W
Araçuaí	54	Jg	16.52S	42.04W
Arad	6	If	46.11N	21.19 E
'Arad	24	Fg	31.15N	35.13 E
Arad [2]	15	Ec	46.11N	21.25 E
Arada	35	Cb	15.01N	20.40 E
'Arādah	35	Ia	22.59N	53.26 E
Arafali	35	Fb	15.04N	39.45 E
Ara Fana	35	Gd	6.01N	41.11 E
Arafune-Yama	29	Fc	36.12N	138.38 E
Arafura, Laut-=Arafura Sea (EN)	57	Ee	9.00S	133.00 E
Arafura, Sea (EN)=Arafura, Laut-	57	Ee	9.00S	133.00 E
Aragac, Gora-	5	Kg	40.31N	44.10 E
Aragarças	53	Kg	15.55S	52.15W
Aragón	13	Kb	42.13N	1.44W
Aragón	5	Fg	41.00N	1.00W
Aragón	13	Lc	41.00N	1.00W
Aragona	14	Hm	37.24N	13.37 E
Aragua [2]	54	Eb	10.00N	67.10W
Araguacema	54	Ie	8.50S	49.34W
Aragua de Barcelona	50	Dh	9.28N	64.49W
Aragua de Maturín	50	Eh	9.58N	63.29W
Araguaia, Rio-	52	Lf	5.21S	48.41W
Araguaiana	55	Gb	16.49S	53.05W
Araguaina	54	Ie	7.12S	48.12W
Araguao, Boca-	54	Fb	9.17N	60.48W
Araguao, Caño-	50	Fh	9.15N	60.50W
Araguapiche, Punta-	50	Fh	9.29N	60.56W
Araguari	54	Ig	18.38S	48.11W
Araguari, Rio- [Braz.]	52	Le	1.15N	49.55W
Araguari, Rio- [Braz.]	55	Hd	18.21S	48.40W
Araguatins	54	Ie	5.38S	48.07W
Arâguîb	32	Ff	18.50N	7.45W
Aragvi	16	Ni	41.50N	44.43 E
Arai	28	Of	37.09N	138.06 E
Árainn/Inishmore	9	Dh	53.07N	9.45W
Árainn Mhór/Aran Island	9	Ef	55.00N	8.30W
Araioses	54	Jd	2.53S	41.55W
Arāk	22	Gf	34.05N	49.41 E
Arak	32	Hd	25.18N	3.45 E
Arakabesan	64a	Ac	7.21N	134.27 E
Arakan [2]	25	Ie	19.00N	94.15 E
Arakan Yoma	21	Lh	19.00N	94.40 E
Arakawa	29	Fb	38.09N	139.25 E
Ara-Kawa [Jap.]	29	Fb	38.09N	139.23 E
Ara-Kawa [Jap.]	29	Fc	37.11N	138.15 E
Árakhthos	15	Ej	39.01N	21.03 E
Araks	21	Gf	39.56N	48.20 E
Aral [China]	27	Dc	40.38N	81.24 E
Arai	19	Hg	41.48N	74.25 E
Aral Sea (EN)=Aralskoje More	21	He	45.00N	60.00 E
Aralsk	22	Ie	46.48N	61.40 E
Aralskoje More=Aral Sea (EN)	21	He	45.00N	60.00 E
Aralsor, Ozero-	16	Pe	49.05N	48.15 E
Aralsulfat	19	Gf	46.50N	61.59 E
Aramac	59	Jd	22.59S	145.14 E
Arambaré	55	Gj	30.55S	51.29W
Ārān	24	Ne	34.03N	51.30 E
Aranda de Duero	13	Ic	41.41N	3.41W
Arandelovac	15	De	44.18N	20.35 E
Arandilla	13	Ic	41.40N	3.41W
Aran Island/Arainn Mhór	9	Dh	53.07N	9.43W
Aran Islands	9	Ef	55.00N	8.30W
Aranjunez	13	Id	40.02N	3.36W
Aranos	37	Bd	24.09S	19.09 E
Arañuelo, Campo-	13	Ge	39.55N	5.30W
Aranuka Atoll	57	Id	0.11N	173.36 E
Arao	29	Be	32.59N	130.27 E
Araouane	31	Gg	18.53N	3.35W
Arapahoe	45	Gf	40.18N	99.54W
Arapey Grande, Rio-	55	Dj	30.55S	57.49W
Arapiraca	54	Ke	9.45S	36.39W
Arápis, Ákra-	15	Gi	40.27N	24.00 E
Arapkir	24	Hc	39.03N	38.30 E
Arapoim, Rio-	55	Kb	15.45S	43.39W
Arapongas	56	Jb	23.23S	51.27W
Arapoti	55	Hg	24.08S	49.50W
'Ar'ar	24	Ig	30.59N	41.02 E
'Ar'ar, Wādī	24	Jg	31.23N	42.26 E
Araranguá	56	Kc	28.56S	49.29W
Araraquara	53	Lh	21.47S	48.10W
Araras	55	If	22.22S	47.23W
Araras, Açude-	54	Jd	4.20S	40.30W
Araras, Serra das-	55	Fd	18.45S	53.30W
Ararat	19	Eh	39.50N	44.43 E
Ararat [Austl.]	59	Ig	37.17S	142.56 E
Ararat, Mount- (EN)=Büyük Ağri Daği	21	Gf	39.40N	44.24 E
Arari	54	Jd	3.28S	44.47W
Arari, Lago-	54	Id	0.37S	49.07W
Aras	21	Gf	39.56N	48.20 E
Aras Dağları	24	Jc	40.00N	43.00 E
Aratika Atoll	57	Mf	15.32S	145.32W
Aratürük/Yiwu	27	Fc	43.15N	94.35 E
Arauca [2]	54	Db	6.30N	71.00W
Arauca	54	Db	7.03N	70.47W
Arauca, Rio-	52	Je	7.24N	66.35W
Araucania [2]	56	Fe	37.50S	73.15W
Arauco	56	Fe	37.15S	73.19W
Araure	50	Bh	9.38N	69.15W
Aravaca, Madrid-	13	Id	40.27N	3.47W
Aravis	11	Mi	45.53N	6.28 E
Arawalli Range	21	Jg	25.00N	73.30 E
Araxá	54	Ig	19.35S	46.55W
Áraxos, Ákra-	15	Ek	38.10N	21.23 E
Araya	50	Dg	10.34N	64.15W
Araya, Peninsula de-	54	Fa	10.35N	64.00W
Arba	13	Kc	41.52N	1.18W
Arba'āt	35	Fb	19.50N	37.03 E
Arba'īn, Darb al-	24	Di	26.40N	30.50 E
Arbaj-Here	27	Hb	46.15N	102.48 E
Arba Minch	31	Kh	5.59N	37.38 E
'Arbat	24	Ke	35.25N	45.35 E
Arbatax	14	Dk	39.56N	9.42 E
Arboga	7	Dg	59.24N	15.50 E
Arbogaån	8	Ge	59.26N	16.04 E
Arbois	11	Lh	46.54N	5.46 E
Arboletes	49	Ii	8.52N	76.25W
Arbolito	55	Ek	32.39S	54.15W
Arbon	14	Dc	47.30N	9.25 E
Arbore	15	Ib	47.44N	25.56 E
Arborea	14	Ck	39.46N	8.35 E
Arborea	14	Ck	39.50N	8.50 E
Arborg	45	Ha	50.55N	97.15W
Arbrå	7	Dc	61.29N	16.23 E
Arbroath	9	Ke	56.34N	2.35W
Arbus	14	Ck	39.32N	8.36 E
Arc [Fr.]	11	Mi	45.34N	6.12 E
Arc [Fr.]	11	Lk	43.31N	5.07 E
Arcachon	11	Ej	44.39N	1.10W
Arcachon, Bassin d'-	11	Ej	44.42N	1.09W
Arcadia [Fl.-U.S.]	44	Gl	27.14N	81.52W
Arcadia [La.-U.S.]	45	Jj	32.33N	92.55W
Arcagly-Ajat	17	Jj	53.00N	61.50 E
Arcas, Cayos-	47	Fd	20.12N	91.58W
Arcata	46	Cf	40.52N	124.05W
Arcelia	48	Ih	18.17N	100.16W
Arcen, Areen en Velden-	12	Ic	51.28N	6.11 E
Arcevia	14	Gg	43.30N	12.56 E
Archangel (EN)=Arhangelsk	6	Kc	64.34N	40.32 E
Archaringa Creek	59	He	28.15S	135.15 E
Archer River	59	Ib	13.28S	141.41 E
Archer's Post	36	Gb	0.39N	37.41 E
Archidona	13	Hg	37.05N	4.23W
Arcidosso	14	Fh	42.52N	11.33 E
Arcipelago Campano	5	Hg	40.30N	13.20 E
Arcipelago Toscano=Tuscan Archipelago (EN)	5	Hg	42.45N	10.20 E
Arcis-sur-Aube	11	Kf	48.32N	4.08 E
Arciz	16	Fg	45.59N	29.27 E
Arco [Id.-U.S.]	46	Ie	43.38N	113.18W
Arco [It.]	14	Ee	45.55N	10.53 E
Arconce	11	Jh	46.27N	4.00 E
Arcos	55	Je	20.17S	45.32W
Arcos de Jalón	13	Jc	41.13N	2.16W
Arcos de la Frontera	13	Gh	36.45N	5.48W
Arcos de Valdevez	13	Dc	41.51N	8.25W
Arcoverde	53	Mf	8.25S	37.04W
Arctic Bay	39	Kb	73.02N	85.11W
Arctic Ocean	67	Be	85.00N	170.00 E
Arctic Ocean (EN)=Ishavet	67	Be	85.00N	170.00 E
Arctic Ocean (EN)=Severny Ledovity Okean	67	Be	85.00N	170.00 E
Arctic Red River	42	Ec	67.27N	133.45W
Arctic Red River	42	Ec	67.22N	133.30W
Arctic Village	40	Jc	68.08N	145.19W
Arda [Eur.]	15	Jh	41.39N	26.29 E
Arda [It.]	14	Ee	45.02N	10.02 E
Ardabīl [Iran]	22	Gf	38.15N	48.18 E
Ardabīl [Iraq]	24	Ie	34.24N	40.59 E
Ardahan	24	Jb	41.07N	42.41 E
Ardakāh	23	Hc	32.19N	53.59 E
Ardakān	24	Og	30.16N	52.01 E
Ardal	24	Ng	31.59N	50.39 E
Ardales	13	Hh	36.52N	4.51W
Ardalsfjorden	8	Bc	61.15N	7.30 E
Årdalstangen	7	Bf	61.14N	7.43 E
Ardanuç	24	Jb	41.08N	42.03 E
Ardatov	7	Ki	55.17N	43.12 E
Ardatov	7	Li	54.53N	46.13 E
'Arde	35	Hd	9.58N	46.04 E
Ardèche	11	Kj	44.16N	4.39 E
Ardèche [3]	11	Kj	44.40N	4.20 E
Ardee/Béal Átha Fhirdhia	9	Gh	53.52N	6.33W
Ardencaple Fjord	41	Jd	75.15N	20.10W
Ardenne, Plateau de l'-/Ardennen, Plateau van der-=Ardennes (EN)	5	Ge	50.10N	5.45 E
Ardennen, Plateau van der-/Ardenne, Plateau de l'-=Ardennes (EN)	5	Ge	50.10N	5.45 E
Ardennes [3]	11	Ke	49.40N	4.40 E
Ardennes (EN)=Ardenne, Plateau de l'-/Ardennen, Plateau van der-	5	Ge	50.10N	5.45 E
Ardennes (EN)=Ardennen, Plateau van der-/Ardenne, Plateau de l'-	5	Ge	50.10N	5.45 E
Ardennes, Canal des-	11	Ke	49.26N	4.02 E
Ardennes, Forêt des-	12	Ge	49.48N	4.50 E
Ardentes	11	Hh	46.45N	1.50 E
Ardeşen	24	Ib	41.12N	41.00 E
Ardestān	24	Of	33.22N	52.23 E
Árdhas	15	Jh	41.39N	26.29 E
Ardila	13	Ef	38.12N	7.28W
Ard Mhacha/Armagh	9	Gg	54.21N	6.39W
Ardmore	43	He	34.10N	97.08W
Ardnamurchan, Point of-	9	Ge	56.45N	6.30W
Ardon	16	Nh	43.07N	44.13 E
Ardooie	12	Fd	50.59N	3.12 E
Ardre	12	Fe	49.18N	3.40 E
Ardres	12	Dd	50.51N	1.59 E
Ards Peninsula/An Aird	9	Hg	54.30N	5.30W
Ar Dub'al Khālī	21	Hg	21.00N	51.00 E
Ardud	15	Fb	47.38N	22.53 E
Arebi	36	Eb	2.50N	29.38 E
Arecibo	47	Ke	18.28N	66.43W
Areen en Valden	12	Ic	51.28N	6.11 E
Areen en Velden-Arcen	12	Ic	51.28N	6.11 E
Arëgala/Ariogala	8	Ji	55.13N	23.30 E
Areia, Ribeirão da-	55	Jc	16.07S	45.52W
Areia Branca	54	Kd	4.57S	37.08W
Arekalong Peninsula	64a	Bb	7.40N	134.38 E
Aremberg	12	Id	50.25N	6.49 E
Arena	26	He	9.14N	120.46 E
Arena, Point-	43	Cd	38.57N	123.44W
Arena, Punta-	47	Cd	23.30N	109.30W
Arena de la Ventana, Punta-	47	Cd	24.04N	109.52W
Arenápolis	54	Gf	14.26S	56.49W
Arenas, Cayo-	47	Fd	22.08N	91.24W
Arenas, Punta de-	56	Gh	53.09S	68.13W
Arenas de San Pedro	13	Gd	40.12N	5.05W
Arenberg	12	Jb	52.42N	7.20 E
Arendal	7	Bg	58.27N	8.48 E
Arendonk	12	Hc	51.19N	5.05 E
Arénys de Mar/Arenys de Mar	13	Oc	41.35N	2.33 E
Arenys de Mar/Arénys de Mar	13	Oc	41.35N	2.33 E
Areópolis	15	Fm	36.40N	22.23 E
Areq, Sebkha bou-	13	Ji	35.10N	2.45W
Arequipa	53	Ig	16.24S	71.33W
Arequipa [2]	54	Dg	16.00S	72.30W
Arequito	55	Bk	33.09S	61.28W
Arero	35	Fe	4.44N	38.50 E
Ares, Muela de-	13	Ld	40.28N	0.07W
Åreskutan	8	Ea	63.26N	13.06 E
Åreskutan	7	Ce	63.24N	13.06 E
Arévalo	13	Hc	41.04N	4.43W
Arezzo	14	Fg	43.25N	11.53 E
Arga	13	Kb	42.18N	1.47W
Argajas	17	Ji	55.31N	60.55 E
Argamasilla de Alba	13	Ie	39.07N	3.06W
Argan	27	Ec	40.09N	88.22 E
Arganda	13	Id	40.18N	3.26W
Arga-Sala	20	Gc	68.37N	112.05 E
Argelès-Gazost	11	Fk	43.01N	0.06W
Argelès-sur-Mer	11	Jl	42.33N	3.01 E
Argens	11	Mk	43.24N	6.44 E

Index Symbols

[1] Independent Nation
[2] State, Region
[3] District, County
[4] Municipality
[5] Colony, Dependency
Continent
Physical Region
Historical or Cultural Region
Mount, Mountain
Volcano
Hill
Mountains, Mountain Range
Hills, Escarpment
Plateau, Upland
Pass, Gap
Plain, Lowland
Delta
Salt Flat
Valley, Canyon
Crater, Cave
Karst Features
Depression
Polder
Desert, Dunes
Forest, Woods
Heath, Steppe
Oasis
Cape, Point
Coast, Beach
Cliff
Peninsula
Isthmus
Sandbank
Island
Atoll
Rock, Reef
Islands, Archipelago
Rocks, Reefs
Coral Reef
Well, Spring
Geyser
River, Stream
Waterfall Rapids
River Mouth, Estuary
Lake
Salt Lake
Intermittent Lake
Reservoir
Swamp, Pond
Canal
Glacier
Ice Shelf, Pack Ice
Ocean
Sea
Gulf, Bay
Strait, Fjord
Lagoon
Bank
Seamount
Tablemount
Ridge
Shelf
Basin
Escarpment, Sea Scarp
Fracture
Trench, Abyss
National Park, Reserve
Point of Interest
Recreation Site
Cave, Cavern
Historic Site
Ruins
Wall, Walls
Church, Abbey
Temple
Scientific Station
Airport
Port
Lighthouse
Mine
Tunnel
Dam, Bridge

Argent, Côte d'- 11 Ej 44.00N 1.30W
Argenta 14 Ff 44.37N 11.50 E
Argentan 11 Ff 48.45N 0.01W
Argentario, Monte- 14 Fh 42.24N 11.09 E
Argentat 11 Hi 45.06N 1.56 E
Argentera 14 Bf 44.10N 7.18 E
Argenteuil 11 If 48.57N 2.15 E
Argentiera, Capo dell'- 14 Cj 40.44N 8.08 E
Argentina 55 Ai 29.33S 62.17W
Argentina [1] 53 Ji 34.00S 64.00W
Argentine Basin (EN) 3 Cn 45.00S 45.00W
Argentino, Lago- 52 Ik 50.13S 72.25W
Argentino, Mar- 52 Kj 46.00S 59.40W
Argenton 11 Fg 47.05N 0.13W
Argenton-Château 11 Fh 46.59N 0.27W
Argenton-sur-Creuse 11 Hh 46.35N 1.31 E
Arges 15 Jd 44.04N 26.37 E
Arges [2] 15 Hd 45.00N 24.50 E
Arghandāb 23 Jc 31.27N 64.23 E
Argo 35 Eb 19.31N 30.25 E
Argo Depth (EN) 3 Jk 12.10S 165.40W
Argolikós Kólpos = Argolis, Gulf of- (EN) 15 Fl 37.20N 22.55 E
Argolis, Gulf of- (EN) = Argolikós Kólpos 15 Fl 37.20N 22.55 E
Argonne 12 He 49.30N 5.00 E
Argonne 11 Ke 49.30N 5.00 E
Argos 15 Fl 37.38N 22.44 E
Árgos Orestikón 15 Ei 40.30N 21.16 E
Argostólion 15 Dk 38.11N 20.29 E
Arguedas 13 Kb 42.10N 1.36W
Argueil-Fry 12 De 49.37N 1.31 E
Arguello, Point- 46 Ei 34.35N 120.39W
Arguenon 11 Df 48.35N 2.13W
Argun 16 Nh 43.16N 45.52 E
Argun 21 Od 53.20N 121.28 E
Argungu 34 Fc 12.45N 4.31 E
Argyle 51n Ba 13.10N 61.10W
Argyle, Lake- 57 Df 16.15S 128.40 E
Argyll 9 Ie 56.20N 5.00W
Arhangelsk = Archangel (EN) 6 Kc 64.34N 40.32 E
Arhangelskaja Oblast [3] 19 Ec 63.30N 43.00 E
Arhara 20 Ig 49.30N 130.09 E
Arhavi 24 Ib 41.22N 41.16 E
Arholma 8 He 59.50N 19.05 E
Ar Horqin Qi (Tianshan) 27 Lc 43.55N 120.05 E
Århus [2] 8 Dh 56.10N 10.15 E
Århus 6 Hd 56.09N 10.13 E
Århus Bugt 8 Dh 56.10N 10.20 E
Arhust 27 Ib 47.42N 107.50 E
Ariadnoje 28 Lb 45.08N 134.25 E
Ariake-Kai 28 Kh 32.55N 130.27 E
Ariamsvlei 37 Be 28.08S 19.50 E
Ariano Irpino 14 Ji 41.09N 15.05 E
Ariari, Rio- 54 Dc 2.35N 72.47W
Arias 56 Hd 33.38S 62.25W
Ari Atoll 25a Bb 3.30N 72.45 E
Aribinda 34 Ec 14.14N 0.52W
Arica 53 Ig 18.29S 70.20W
Arica, Golfo de- 52 Ig 18.30S 70.30W
Arichuna 50 Ci 7.42N 67.08W
Arid, Cape- 59 Ef 34.00S 123.09 E
Arida 28 Mg 34.05N 135.07 E
Arida-Gawa 29 Dd 34.05N 135.06 E
Aridhaia 15 Fi 40.59N 22.04 E
Ariège 11 Hk 43.31N 1.25 E
Ariège [3] 11 Hk 43.00N 1.30 E
Ariel 55 Cm 36.32S 59.54W
Arieş 15 Gc 46.26N 23.59 E
Ariguani 54 Db 9.50N 74.01W
Ariguani, Rio- 49 Ki 9.35N 73.46W
Arīḩā [Jor.] 24 Fg 31.52N 35.27 E
Arīḩā [Syr.] 24 Ge 35.48N 36.36 E
Arikaree River 45 Ff 40.01N 101.56W
Arikawa 29 Ae 32.59N 129.07 E
Arilje 15 Df 43.45N 20.06 E
Arima 54 Fa 10.38N 61.17W
Arinos 55 Ib 15.55S 46.04W
Arinos, Rio- 52 Kg 10.25S 58.20W
Arinos Novo, Rio- 55 Db 14.13S 56.01W
Ariogala/Arėgala 8 Ji 55.13N 23.30 E
Aripuanā 54 Fe 9.10S 60.38W
Aripuanā, Rio- 52 Jf 5.07S 60.24W
Ariquemes 54 Fe 9.56S 63.04W
Arisa 35 Gc 11.11N 41.38 E
'Arish, Wādī al- 24 Eg 31.09N 33.49 E
Arismendi 49 Mi 8.29N 68.22W
Arita 29 Ae 33.11N 129.52 E
Aritzo 14 Dk 39.57N 9.12 E
Arixang/Wenquan 27 Dc 44.59N 81.04 E
Ariza 13 Jc 41.19N 2.03W
Arizaro, Salar de- 56 Gb 24.42S 67.45W
Arize, Massif de l'- 11 Hl 42.50N 1.30 E
Arizona [2] 43 Ee 34.00N 112.00W
Arizpe 48 Db 30.20N 110.10W
Årjäng 7 Cg 59.23N 12.08 E
Arjeplog 7 Dc 66.03N 17.54 E
Arjo 35 Fd 8.45N 36.30 E
Arjona 54 Ca 10.15N 75.21W
Arkadak 19 Ee 51.58N 43.28 E
Arkadelphia 43 Ie 34.07N 93.04W
Arkalyk 22 Id 50.13N 66.50 E
Arkansas 38 Jf 33.48N 91.04W
Arkansas [2] 43 Id 34.50N 93.40W
Arkansas City 43 Hd 37.04N 97.02W
Arkanū, Jabal- 33 De 22.15N 24.45 E
Arkatag 21 Kf 36.45N 89.10 E
Arkhángelos 15 Lm 36.12N 28.08 E
Árki 15 Jl 37.22N 26.45 E
Arklow/An tInbhear Mór 9 Gi 52.48N 6.09W
Arkona, Kap- 10 Jb 54.41N 13.26 E
Arkonam 25 Ff 13.06N 79.40 E
Arkösund 8 Gf 58.30N 16.56 E
Arkoúdhion 15 Dk 38.33N 20.43 E
Arktičeskoga Instituta, Ostrova- = Arkticheski Institut Islands (EN) 20 Da 75.20N 81.50 E
Arkticheski Institut Islands (EN) = Arktičeskoga Instituta, Ostrova- 20 Da 75.20N 81.50 E
Arlan, Gora- 16 Sj 39.43N 54.40 E
Arlanza 13 Hb 42.06N 4.09W
Arlanzón 13 Hb 42.03N 4.17W
Arlberg 14 Ec 47.08N 10.12 E
Arles 11 Kk 43.40N 4.38 E
Arlington [Or.-U.S.] 46 Ed 45.46N 120.13W
Arlington [Tx.-U.S.] 45 Hj 32.44N 97.07W
Arlington [Va.-U.S.] 43 Ld 38.52N 77.05W
Arlington Heights 45 Me 42.05N 87.59W
Arlit 31 Hg 19.00N 7.38 E
Arlon/Aarlen 11 Le 49.41N 5.49 E
Arlöv 8 Ei 55.39N 13.05 E
Arly 34 Fc 11.35N 1.28 E
Armagh/Ard Mhacha 9 Gg 54.21N 6.39W
Armagnac 11 Gk 43.45N 0.10 E
Armagnac, Collines de l'- 11 Gk 43.30N 0.30 E
Armah, Wādī- 23 Hf 18.12N 51.02 E
Arman 20 Ke 59.43N 150.12 E
Armançon 11 Jg 47.57N 3.30 E
Armandale, Perth- 59 Df 32.09S 116.00 E
Armant 33 Fd 25.37N 32.32 E
Armáthia 15 Jn 35.26N 26.52 E
Armavir 6 Kf 45.00N 41.08 E
Armenia 53 Ie 4.31N 75.41W
Armenia (EN) = Ermenistan 23 Fb 39.10N 43.00 E
Armenia (EN) = Ermenistan 21 Gf 39.10N 43.00 E
Armenia (EN) = Hayastan 19 Eg 40.00N 45.00 E
Armentières 11 Id 50.41N 2.53 E
Armeria 48 Gh 18.56N 103.58W
Armi, Capo dell'- 14 Jm 37.57N 15.41 E
Armidale 58 Gh 30.31S 151.39 E
Armisvesi 8 Lb 62.30N 26.35 E
Armjansk 16 Hf 46.05N 33.41 E
Armjanskaja Sovetskaja Socialističeskaja Respublika → Hayastan 19 Eg 40.00N 45.00 E
Armjanskaja SSR/Haikakan Sovetaken Socialistakan Respublika → Hayastan 19 Eg 40.00N 45.00 E
Armjanskaja SSR → Hayastan 19 Eg 40.00N 45.00 E
Armoricain, Massif- = Armorican Massif (EN) 5 Ff 48.00N 3.00W
Armorican Massif (EN) = Armoricain, Massif- 5 Ff 48.00N 3.00W
Armour 45 Ge 43.19N 98.21W
Arm River 46 Ma 50.46N 105.00W
Armstrong [Arg.] 55 Bk 32.47S 61.36W
Armstrong [B.C.-Can.] 46 Fa 50.27N 119.12W
Armstrong [Ont.-Can.] 42 If 50.18N 89.02W
Ārmūdiū 24 Qd 37.15N 56.05 E
Armutçuk Dağ 15 Ki 40.05N 27.23 E
Armutlu 15 Li 40.31N 28.50 E
Armutova 15 Jj 39.23N 26.50 E
Arnaia 15 Gi 40.29N 23.36 E
Arnaud 42 Kd 60.00N 69.55W
Arnautis, Akrōtērion- 24 Ee 35.06N 32.17 E
Arnay-le-Duc 11 Kg 47.08N 4.29 E
Arnedo 13 Jb 42.13N 2.06W
Årnes 7 Cf 60.09N 11.28 E
Arnhem 11 Lc 51.59N 5.55 E
Arnhem, Cape- 57 Ef 12.21S 136.21 E
Arnhem Bay 59 Hb 12.20S 136.10 E
Arnhem Land 57 Ef 13.10S 134.30 E
Arno 14 Eg 43.41N 10.17 E
Arno Atoll 57 Id 7.05N 171.41 E
Arnold 12 Aa 53.00N 1.08W
Arnon 11 Ig 47.13N 2.01 E
Arnøy 7 Ea 70.08N 20.36 E
Arnprior 44 Ic 45.26N 76.21W
Arnsberg 10 Ee 51.23N 8.05 E
Arnsberger Wald 12 Kc 51.26N 8.10 E
Arnsberg-Oeventrop 12 Kc 51.24N 8.08 E
Arnsburg 12 Kd 50.29N 8.48 E
Arnstadt 10 Gf 50.50N 10.57 E
Aro, Rio- 50 Di 8.01N 64.11W
Aroa 50 Bg 10.26N 68.54W
Aroa, Pointe- 65e Fc 17.28S 149.46W
Aroa, Rio- 50 Bg 10.41N 68.18W
Aroa, Sierra de- 50 Bg 10.15N 68.55W
Aroab 37 Be 26.47S 19.40 E
Aroánia Óri 15 Fl 37.57N 22.13 E
Aroche 13 Fg 37.57N 6.57W
Aroche, Pico de- 13 Ff 38.01N 6.56W
Aroeira 55 Ee 21.41S 54.25W
Arolsen 10 Ff 51.22N 9.01 E
Aroma 35 Fb 15.49N 36.08 E
Aron 11 Jh 46.50N 3.27 E
Arona 14 Ce 45.46N 8.34 E
Aroostook River 44 Nb 46.48N 67.45W
Arorae Island 57 Ie 2.38S 176.49 E
Arorangi 64p Bb 21.13S 159.49W
Aros, Rio- 48 Ec 29.30N 109.15W
Arosa 14 Dd 46.47N 9.40 E
Arosa, Ria de- 13 Db 42.28N 8.57W
Aros Papigochic, Rio- 48 Ec 29.09N 108.35W
Årøsund 8 Ci 55.15N 9.43 E
Arouca 13 Dd 40.56N 8.15W
Arpaçay 24 Jb 40.45N 43.25 E
Arpajon 11 If 48.35N 2.15 E
Arpino 14 Hi 41.39N 13.36 E
Arquata Scrivia 14 Cf 44.41N 8.53 E
Arque 54 Eg 17.48S 66.23W
Arques-la-Bataille 12 De 49.53N 1.08 E
Ar Rachidiya 32 Gc 31.55N 4.40W
Ar Rachidiya [3] 32 Gc 31.00N 4.00W
Ar Radīsiyah Baḩrī 33 Fe 24.57N 32.53 E
Arrah 25 Gc 25.34N 84.40 E
Ar Rahad 35 Ec 12.43N 30.39 E
Ar Rahad 30 Kg 14.28N 33.31 E
Arraias 54 If 12.56S 46.57W
Arraias, Rio- [Braz.] 54 Hf 11.10S 53.35W
Arraias, Rio- [Braz.] 55 Ia 12.28S 47.18W
Arraiolos 13 Ef 38.43N 7.59W
Ar Ramādī 23 Fc 33.25N 43.17 E
Ar Ramlah 24 Fh 29.32N 35.57 E
Ar Ramlī al Kabīr 33 Dd 26.30N 22.10 E
Arran, Island of- 9 Hf 55.35N 5.15W
Ar Rank 35 Ec 11.45N 32.48 E
Ar Raqqah 23 Eb 35.56N 39.01 E
Arras 11 Id 50.17N 2.47 E
Ar Rāshidah 24 Cj 25.35N 28.56 E
Ar Rass 24 Jj 25.52N 43.28 E
Ar Rastān 24 Ge 34.55N 36.44 E
Arrats 11 Gj 44.06N 0.52 E
Ar Rawḑah [Sau.Ar.] 33 He 21.16N 42.50 E
Ar Rawḑatayn 24 Lh 29.53N 47.44 E
Ar Rayhānī 24 Pk 23.37N 55.58 E
Arrecife 32 Ed 28.57N 13.32W
Arrecife Alacrán 47 Gd 22.24N 89.42W
Arrecifes 56 Hd 34.03S 60.07W
Arrecifes, Rio- 55 Ck 33.46S 59.31W
Arrée, Montagnes d'- 11 Cf 48.26N 3.55W
Arresø 8 Ei 55.55N 12.05 E
Arriaga 48 Mi 16.14N 93.54W
Ar Rifā'ī 24 Lg 31.43N 46.07 E
Ar Rihāb 24 Kg 30.52N 45.30 E
Ar Rimāh 24 Lj 25.34N 47.09 E
Ar Rimāl 21 Hg 22.00N 52.50 E
Ar Riyāḑ = Riyadh (EN) 22 Gg 24.38N 46.43 E
Arrochar 9 Ie 56.12N 4.45W
Arroio Grande 55 Fk 32.14S 53.05W
Arrojado 55 Ja 13.29S 44.37W
Arrojado, Rio- 55 Ja 13.24S 44.20W
Arromanches-les-Bains 12 Be 49.20N 0.37W
Arros 11 Gk 43.40N 0.02 E
Arroscia 14 Cg 44.03N 8.11 E
Arroux 11 Jh 46.29N 3.58 E
Arrow, Lough-/Loch Arabhach 9 Eg 54.05N 8.20W
Arrowsmith, Mount- 61 Dh 43.21S 170.59 E
Arrowtown 62 Cf 44.56S 168.50 E
Arroyo Barú 55 Cj 31.52S 58.26W
Arroyo de la Luz 13 Fe 39.29N 6.35W
Arroyo Grande 46 Ei 35.07N 120.34W
Arroyos y Esteros 55 Dg 25.04S 57.06W
Arruda 55 Db 15.02S 56.07W
Arrufó 55 Bj 30.15S 61.45W
Ar Rumaythah 24 Kg 31.32N 45.12 E
Ar Ruq'ī 24 Lh 29.01N 46.33 E
Ar Ruşāfah 24 He 35.02N 36.17 E
Ar Ruşayriş 31 Kg 11.51N 34.23 E
Ar Ruţbah 23 Fc 33.02N 40.17 E
Ar Ruwayḑah 24 Ki 26.23N 44.14 E
Ar Ruways [Qatar] 23 Hd 26.08N 51.13 E
Ar Ruways [U.A.E.] 23 He 24.08N 52.45 E
Ar Ruzayqāt 24 Ej 25.35N 32.28 E
Års 8 Ch 56.48N 9.32 E
Arsenjān 24 Oh 29.56N 53.18 E
Arsenjev 20 Ih 44.12N 133.20 E
Arsi [3] 35 Fd 7.10N 40.00 E
Arsk 7 Lh 56.07N 49.52 E
Årskogen 8 Gb 62.05N 17.20 E
Arslanköy 24 Fd 37.01N 34.17 E
Ars-sur-Moselle 12 Ie 49.05N 6.04 E
Arsuk 41 Hf 61.11N 48.30W
Årsunda 8 Gd 60.32N 16.44 E
Art 63b Ad 19.43S 163.39 E
Artà 13 Pe 39.42N 3.21 E
Arta 35 Gc 11.31N 42.50 E
Árta 15 Dj 39.09N 20.59 E
Artà, Cuevas de- 13 Pe 39.40N 3.24 E
Artašat 16 Nj 39.59N 44.33 E
Arteaga 48 Hh 18.28N 102.25W
Artem 20 Ih 43.23N 132.10 E
Artemisa 47 Hd 22.49N 82.46W
Artemón 15 Hm 36.57N 24.43 E
Artem-Ostrov 19 Fg 40.28N 50.18 E
Artemovsk 20 Ef 54.23N 93.30 E
Artemovsk 16 Ke 48.33N 38.03 E
Artemovski 17 Jh 57.25N 61.58 E
Artesa de Segre 13 Nc 41.54N 1.03 E
Artesia 43 Ge 32.51N 104.24W
Arthur 45 Ff 41.35N 101.31W
Arthur Creek 59 Hd 23.00S 136.58 E
Arthur River 59 Ih 41.00S 144.55 E
Arthur's Pass 61 Dh 42.57S 171.34 E
Arthur's Pass 62 De 42.54S 171.34 E
Arthur's Town 49 Ja 24.38N 75.32W
Arti 17 Ih 56.26N 58.32 E
Artibonite, Rivière de l'- 49 Kd 19.15N 72.47W
Artigas 56 Id 30.42S 56.28W
Artigas [2] 55 Dj 30.35S 57.00W
Artijarvi/Artsjö 8 Ld 60.45N 26.05 E
Artik 16 Mi 40.36N 43.58 E
Artillery Lake 42 Gd 63.08N 107.45W
Artois 11 Id 50.10N 2.30 E
Artois, Collines de l'- 11 Id 50.30N 2.15 E
Artoli 35 Eb 18.19N 33.54 E
Artsjö/Artjarvi 8 Ld 60.45N 26.05 E
Artux 27 Cd 39.40N 76.10 E
Artvin 23 Fa 41.11N 41.49 E
Artyk 20 Jd 64.12N 145.15 E
Aru 36 Fb 2.52N 30.51 E
Aru, Kepulauan- = Aru Islands (EN) 57 Ee 6.00S 134.30 E
Arua 31 Kh 3.01N 30.55 E
Aruanā 55 Gb 14.54S 51.05W
Aruba 54 Ea 12.30N 70.00W
Aruba 39 Lh 12.30N 71.00W
Aru Islands (EN) = Aru, Kepulauan 57 Ee 6.00S 134.30 E
Arukoron Point 64a Bb 7.43N 134.38 E
Arun 9 Mk 50.48N 0.33W
Arunāchal Pradesh [3] 25 Ic 27.50N 94.50 E
Arundel 12 Bd 50.51N 0.33W
Arun He 27 Lb 47.36N 124.06 E
Arun Qi 27 Lb 48.09N 123.29 E
Arus, Tanjung- 26 Hf 1.24N 125.06 E
Arusha [3] 36 Gc 3.30S 36.00 E
Arusha 31 Ki 3.22S 36.41 E
Arutua Atoll 61 Lc 15.18S 146.44W
Arutunga 61 Jc 18.52S 159.46W
Aruwimi 30 Jh 1.13N 23.36 E
Arvada [Co.-U.S.] 45 Dg 39.50N 105.05W
Arvada [Wy.-U.S.] 46 Ld 44.40N 106.03W
Arve 11 Mh 46.12N 6.08 E
Arvert, Presqu'île d'- 11 Ei 45.45N 1.05W
Arvida 42 Kg 48.26N 71.11W
Arvidsjaur 7 Ed 65.35N 19.10 E
Arvika 7 Cg 59.39N 12.36 E
Årviksand 7 Ea 70.12N 20.32 E
Arvin 46 Fi 35.12N 118.50W
Aryānah 14 En 36.52N 10.11 E
Arys 18 Gc 42.48N 68.15 E
Arys 19 Gg 42.26N 68.48 E
Arys, Ozero- 18 Fb 45.50N 66.20 E
Arz 11 Dg 47.39N 2.06W
Arzachena 14 Di 41.05N 9.23 E
Arzamas 19 Ed 55.23N 43.50 E
Arzanah 24 Oj 24.47N 52.34 E
Aržano 14 Kg 43.35N 16.59 E
Arzew 32 Gb 35.51N 0.19W
Arzew, Golfe d'- 13 Li 35.50N 0.10W
Arzew, Salines d'- 13 Li 35.42N 0.18W
Arzfeld 12 Id 50.05N 6.16 E
Arzgir 19 Ef 45.22N 44.13 E
Arzúa 13 Db 42.56N 8.09W
As 12 Hc 51.01N 5.35 E
Ås 8 De 59.40N 10.48 E
Aš 10 If 50.13N 12.12 E
Aša 19 Fd 55.02N 57.18 E
Aså 8 Dg 57.09N 10.25 E
Asab 37 Be 25.29S 17.59 E
Asaba 34 Gd 6.11N 6.45 E
Asad, Buḩayrat al- 24 He 35.57N 38.10 E
Asadābād [Afg.] 23 Lc 34.52N 71.09 E
Asadābād [Iran] 24 Me 34.47N 48.07 E
Asafik 35 Bc 13.10N 19.26 E
Asahi [Jap.] 29 Fb 38.15N 139.30 E
Asahi [Jap.] 29a Ca 44.08N 142.35 E
Asahi [Jap.] 29 Gd 35.43N 140.35 E
Asahi [Jap.] 29 Ec 36.57N 137.34 E
Asahi-Dake 29 Fb 38.16N 139.55 E
Asahi-Gawa 29 Cd 34.36N 133.58 E
Asahikawa 22 Qe 43.46N 142.22 E
Asaka-Drainage 29 Gc 37.30N 140.15 E
Asale, Lake- 35 Gc 14.00N 40.20 E
'Asalūyeh 24 Oi 27.28N 52.37 E
Asama-Yama 28 Of 36.27N 138.30 E
Asan-Man 28 If 36.56N 126.51 E
Asansol 22 Kg 23.41N 86.59 E
Asarna 7 De 62.39N 14.21 E
Asarum 8 Fh 56.12N 14.50 E
'Asäyr = Guardafui, Cape- (EN) 30 Mg 11.49N 51.15 E
Asayta 35 Gc 11.33N 41.27 E
Asbest 17 Jh 57.01N 61.31 E
Asbestos 44 Lc 45.46N 71.57W
Asbe Teferi 35 Gd 9.05N 40.51 E
Asbury Park 44 Je 40.14N 74.01W
Ascension 30 Fi 7.57S 14.22W
Ascensión, Bahía de la- 47 Ge 19.40N 87.30W
Ascensión, Bahía de la- 48 Ph 19.40N 87.30W
Ascensión, Laguna de la- 48 Fb 31.05N 107.55W
Aschaffenburg 10 Fg 49.59N 9.09 E
Ascheberg 12 Jc 51.47N 7.37 E
Aschendorf (Ems), Papenburg- 12 Ja 53.04N 7.22 E
Aschersleben 10 He 51.45N 11.28 E
Aščikol, Ozero- 18 Fb 45.05N 67.20 E
Aščiozek 16 Pe 49.12N 48.06 E
Ascoli Piceno 14 Hh 42.51N 13.34 E
Ascoli Satriano 14 Ji 41.12N 15.34 E
Ascot 12 Bc 51.24N 0.40W
Aseb 31 Lg 13.00N 42.44 E
Åseda 7 Dh 57.10N 15.20 E
Asedjrad 30 Hf 24.42N 1.40 E
Asekejevo 16 Rc 53.36N 52.51 E
Asela 31 Kh 7.58N 39.08 E
As Ela 35 Gc 11.06N 42.06 E
Åsele 7 Dd 64.10N 17.20 E
Åsen [Nor.] 7 Ce 63.36N 11.03 E
Åsen [Swe.] 7 Cf 61.17N 13.50 E
Asendabo 35 Fd 9.47N 37.36 E
Asendorf 12 Kb 52.46N 9.00 E
Asenovgrad 15 Hg 42.01N 24.52 E
Åsensbruk 8 Ef 58.48N 12.25 E
Åseral 8 Bf 58.37N 7.25 E
Aseri/Azeri 7 Gg 59.29N 26.51 E
Asfeld 12 Ge 49.28N 4.07 E
Aşfūn al Maţā'inah 24 Ej 25.23N 32.32 E
Åsgårdstrand 8 De 59.21N 10.28 E
Ashabad 22 Hf 37.57N 58.23 E
Ashanti [3] 34 Ed 6.45N 1.30W
Ashburn 44 Fj 31.43N 83.39W
Ashburton 61 Dh 43.54S 171.45 E
Ashburton River 57 Cg 21.40S 114.56 E
Ashdod 24 Fg 31.49N 34.39 E
Ashdown 45 Ij 33.41N 94.08W
Asheboro 44 Hh 35.42N 79.49W
Ashcroft 46 Ea 50.43N 121.17W
Asheville 43 Kd 35.34N 82.33W
Ashford 9 Nj 51.09N 0.53 E
Ashford Airport 12 Cc 51.10N 0.59 E
Ash Fork 46 Ii 35.13N 112.29W
Ashibetsu 28 Qc 43.31N 142.11 E
Ashikaga 29 Fc 36.21N 139.27 E
Ashington 9 Lf 55.11N 1.34W
Ashiro 29 Ga 40.06N 141.01 E
Ashiya 29 Be 33.53N 130.40 E
Ashizuri-Misaki 28 Lh 32.44N 133.01 E
Ashkal, Qar'at al- 14 Dm 37.10N 9.40 E
Āshkhāneh 24 Qd 37.28N 57.00 E
Ashland [Ks.-U.S.] 45 Gh 37.11N 99.46W
Ashland [Ky.-U.S.] 43 Kd 38.28N 82.38W
Ashland [Mt.-U.S.] 46 Ld 45.35N 106.16W
Ashland [Oh.-U.S.] 44 Fe 40.52N 82.19W
Ashland [Or.-U.S.] 43 Cc 42.12N 122.42W
Ashland [Wi.-U.S.] 43 Ib 46.35N 90.53W
Ashland, Mount- 46 De 42.05N 122.43W
Ashley 45 Gc 46.02N 99.22W
Ashmore Islands 57 Df 12.15S 123.05 E
Ashmūn 24 Dg 30.18N 30.58 E
Ashoro 29a Cb 43.14N 143.31 E
Ashqelon 24 Fg 31.40N 34.35 E
Ash Shabakah 24 Jg 30.49N 43.39 E
Ash Shabb 33 Ee 22.19N 29.46 E
Ash Sha'ib 24 Gh 28.59N 37.07 E
Ash Sha'm 23 Id 26.02N 56.05 E
Ash Shamālīyah [3] 35 Db 18.40N 30.00 E
Ash 'Shāmīyah 24 Kg 31.57N 44.36 E
Ash Shāmīyah 24 Lg 30.15N 46.55 E
Ash Shaqq 24 Lh 28.20N 47.30 E
Ash Shaqrā' 23 Gd 25.15N 45.15 E
Ash Sha'rā' 24 Kj 24.16N 44.11 E
Ash Sharīqah 23 Id 25.22N 55.23 E
Ash Sharqāţ 23 Fb 35.27N 43.16 E
Ash Sharqī 32 Jc 34.45N 11.15 E
Ash Sharqī 24 Ge 34.00N 36.30 E
Ash Sharqīyah 23 Ie 22.15N 58.30 E
Ash Shatrah 24 Lg 31.25N 46.10 E
Ash Shawbak 24 Fg 30.32N 35.34 E
Ash Shaykh Ḩumayd 24 Fh 28.07N 34.34 E
Ash Shifā 24 Fh 28.30N 35.30 E
Ash Shiḩr 23 Gg 14.44N 49.35 E
Ash Shināfīyah 24 Kg 31.35N 44.39 E
Ash Shu'aybah [Kuw.] 24 Mh 29.03N 48.08 E
Ash Shu'aybah [Sau.Ar.] 24 Ji 27.53N 42.43 E
Ash Shu'bah 24 Kh 28.54N 44.44 E
Ash Shumlūl 24 Li 26.31N 47.20 E
Ash Shuqayq 23 Ff 17.44N 42.01 E
Ash Shurayk 35 Eb 18.48N 33.34 E
Ash Shuwayhāt 24 Oj 24.05N 52.28 E
Ash Shuwaykh 24 Lh 29.21N 47.55 E
Ashtabula 43 Kc 41.53N 80.47W
Ashtabula, Lake- 45 Hc 47.11N 97.58W
Ashtīyān 24 Me 34.30N 49.55 E
Ashton [Id.-U.S.] 46 Jd 44.04N 111.27W
Ashton [St.Vin.] 51n Bb 12.36N 61.27W
Ashuanipi 42 Kf 52.55N 66.00W
Ashuanipi Lake 42 Kf 52.45N 66.10W
Asia 21 Ke 40.00N 85.00 E
Asia, Kepulauan- 26 Jf 1.03N 131.18 E
Asiago 14 Fe 45.52N 11.30 E
Asiago, Altopiano di- 14 Fe 45.54N 11.30 E
Asilah 32 Fb 35.28N 6.02W
Asinara 5 Gg 41.04N 8.15 E
Asinara, Golfo dell'- 14 Cj 41.00N 8.35 E
Asino 20 De 56.58N 86.09 E
'Asīr 23 Ff 19.00N 42.00 E
Aškadar 17 Hi 53.37N 56.01 E
Aşkale 24 Ic 39.55N 40.42 E
Askanija-Nova 16 Hf 46.27N 33.52 E
Asker 8 De 59.50N 10.26 E
Askersund 7 Dg 58.53N 14.54 E
Askī Al Mawşil 24 Jd 36.34N 42.42 E
Askim [Nor.] 8 De 59.35N 11.10 E
Askim [Swe.] 8 Dg 57.38N 11.56 E
Áskion Óros 15 Ei 40.22N 21.34 E
Askiz 20 Ef 53.08N 90.32 E
Askja 5 Eb 65.03N 16.48W
Askola 8 Kd 60.32N 25.36 E
Asköping 8 Ge 59.09N 16.04 E
Askøy 8 Ad 60.30N 5.05 E
Askøy 8 Ad 60.24N 5.11 E
Askrova 8 Ac 61.30N 4.55 E
Askvoll 7 Af 61.21N 5.04 E
Asl 24 Eh 29.30N 32.43 E
Aslanapa 15 Mj 39.13N 29.52 E
Asmara (EN) = Asmera 31 Kg 15.19N 38.57 E
Asmera = Asmara (EN) 31 Kg 15.19N 38.57 E
Åsnen 8 Fh 56.40N 14.40 E
Asni 32 Fc 31.15N 7.59W
Asnières-sur-Seine 12 Ef 48.55N 2.17 E
Aso 14 Hg 43.06N 13.51 E
Aso 29 Be 32.58N 131.02 E
Asola 14 Ee 45.13N 10.24 E
Asosa 31 Kg 10.02N 34.32 E
Aso-San 29 Be 32.53N 131.06 E
Asoteriba, Jabal- 35 Fa 21.51N 36.30 E
Asouf Mellene 32 Hd 25.40N 2.08 E
Asō-Wan 29 Ad 34.20N 129.15 E
Aspās 24 Og 30.40N 52.24 E
Aspe 13 Lf 38.21N 0.46W
Aspen 43 Fd 39.11N 106.49W
Aspermont 45 Fj 33.08N 100.14W
Aspiring, Mount- 61 Ch 44.23S 168.44 E
Aspromonte 14 Jl 38.10N 16.00 E
Assa 32 Fd 28.37N 9.25W
Aş Şadr 23 He 24.40N 54.41 E
Aş Şaff 24 Dh 29.34N 31.17 E
Aş Şāfī 24 Fg 31.02N 35.28 E
As Safīrah 24 Gd 36.04N 37.22 E
Aş Şaḩm 24 Qj 24.10N 56.53 E
Assahoun 34 Fd 6.27N 0.55 E
Aş Şa'īd 30 Kf 26.00N 32.00 E
Assal, Lac- 35 Gc 11.40N 42.22 E
As Salamīyah [Sau.Ar.] 23 Ge 24.12N 47.23 E
As Salamīyah [Syr.] 24 Ge 35.01N 37.03 E
Aş Şāliḩīyah 24 Ie 34.44N 40.45 E
As Sallūm 31 Je 31.34N 25.09 E
As Salmān 24 Kg 30.26N 44.30 E
As Salt 24 Ff 32.03N 35.44 E
As Salwá 23 He 24.45N 50.49 E

Index Symbols

[1] Independent Nation
[2] State, Region
[3] District, County
[4] Municipality
[5] Colony, Dependency
Continent
Physical Region
Historical or Cultural Region
Mount, Mountain
Volcano
Hill
Mountains, Mountain Range
Hills, Escarpment
Plateau, Upland
Pass, Gap
Plain, Lowland
Delta
Salt Flat
Valley, Canyon
Crater, Cave
Karst Features
Depression
Polder
Desert, Dunes
Forest, Woods
Heath, Steppe
Oasis
Cape, Point
Coast, Beach
Cliff
Peninsula
Isthmus
Sandbank
Island
Atoll
Rock, Reef
Islands, Archipelago
Rocks, Reefs
Coral Reef
Well, Spring
Geyser
River, Stream
Waterfall Rapids
River Mouth, Estuary
Lake
Salt Lake
Intermittent Lake
Reservoir
Swamp, Pond
Canal
Glacier
Ice Shelf, Pack Ice
Ocean
Sea
Gulf, Bay
Strait, Fjord
Lagoon
Bank
Seamount
Tablemount
Ridge
Shelf
Basin
Escarpment, Sea Scarp
Fracture
Trench, Abyss
National Park, Reserve
Point of Interest
Recreation Site
Cave, Cavern
Historic Site
Ruins
Wall, Walls
Temple
Scientific Station
Airport
Port
Lighthouse
Mine
Tunnel
Dam, Bridge

Assam 21 Lg 26.50N 94.00 E
Assam 25 Ic 26.00N 93.00 E
Assamakka 34 Gb 19.21N 5.38 E
As Samawah 23 Gc 31.18N 45.17 E
As Sanām 35 Ia 22.00N 51.10 E
Assaouas 34 Gb 16.52N 7.27 E
As Sars 14 Dn 36.05N 9.01 E
As Sayl al Kabīr 33 He 21.38N 40.25 E
Asse 12 Gd 50.56N 4.12 E
Asse 11 Lk 43.53N 5.53 E
Assebroek, Brugge- 12 Fc 51.12N 3.16 E
Assekkâraï 34 Fb 15.50N 2.52 E
Assemini 14 Dk 39.17N 9.01 E
Assen 11 Ma 53.00N 6.34 E
Assenede 12 Fc 51.14N 3.45 E
Assens 8 Ci 55.16N 9.55 E
As Sıbā'īyah 24 Ej 25.11N 32.41 E
As Sidr 31 Ie 30.39N 18.22 E
As Sidrah=Sirte Desert (EN) 30 Ie 30.30N 17.30 E
As Sila' 23 He 24.02N 51.46 E
As Simbillāwayn 24 Dg 30.53N 31.27 E
Assiniboia 42 Gg 49.38N 105.59W
Assiniboine 38 Je 49.53N 97.08W
Assiniboine, Mount- 38 Hd 50.52N 115.39W
Assis 56 Jb 22.40S 50.25W
Assisi 14 Gg 43.04N 12.37 E
Aßlar 12 Kd 50.36N 8.28 E
Assos 15 Jj 39.31N 26.20 E
As Sślimīyah 24 Mh 29.20N 48.04 E
As Subaykhah 14 Eo 35.56N 10.01 E
As Subū' 33 Fe 22.45N 32.34 E
As Sūdān=Sudan (EN) 31 Jg 15.00N 30.00 E
As Sudd 30 Kh 8.00N 31.00 E
As Sufāl 35 Hc 14.06N 48.43 E
Aş Şufuq 24 Nk 23.52N 51.45 E
Aş Şukhayrah 32 Jc 34.17N 10.06 E
As Sukhnah 24 He 34.52N 38.52 E
As Sulaymī 24 Ii 26.17N 41.21 E
As Sulayyil 23 Ge 20.27N 45.34 E
Aş Şulb 24 Mj 25.42N 48.25 E
Aş Sumayḩ 35 Dd 9.49N 27.39 E
Aş Şummān 33 Ie 23.00N 48.00 E
Aş Şummān 24 Li 27.00N 47.00 E
Assumption Island 30 Li 9.45S 46.30 E
As Sūq 33 He 21.54N 42.03 E
Assur 24 Je 35.25N 43.16 E
Aş Şuwār 24 Ie 35.30N 40.39 E
As Suwaydā' 23 Ec 32.42N 36.34 E
Aş Şuwayrah 24 Kf 32.55N 44.47 E
As Suways=Suez (EN) 31 Kf 29.58N 32.33 E
Astakidha 15 Jn 35.53N 26.50 E
Astakós 15 Ek 38.32N 21.05 E
Āstāneh [Iran] 24 Md 37.17N 49.59 E
Āstāneh [Iran] 24 Mf 33.53N 49.22 E
Āstārā 23 Gb 38.26N 48.52 E
Astara 6 Kh 38.28N 48.52 E
Aštarak 16 Ni 40.16N 44.18 E
Asten 12 Hc 51.24N 5.45 E
Asti 14 Cf 44.54N 8.12 E
Astico 14 Fe 45.37N 11.37 E
Astipálaia 15 Jm 36.33N 26.21 E
Astipálaia 15 Jm 36.35N 26.20 E
Asto, Monte- 11a Ba 42.30N 9.15 E
Astola Island 25 Cc 25.07N 63.51 E
Astorga 13 Fb 42.27N 6.03W
Astoria 43 Cb 46.11N 123.50W
Åstorp 8 Eh 56.08N 12.57 E
Astove Island 30 Lj 10.06S 47.45 E
Astrahan 6 Kf 46.21N 48.03 E
Astrahanskaja Oblast 19 Ef 47.10N 47.30 E
Astrolabe, Cape- 63a Ec 8.20S 160.34 E
Astrolabe, Récifs de l'- 57 Hf 19.49S 165.35 E
Astudillo 13 Hb 42.12N 4.18W
Asturias 13 Ga 43.20N 6.00W
Asuisui, Cape- 65c Aa 13.47S 172.29W
Asunción 53 Kh 25.16S 57.40W
Asunción, Bahia- 48 Bd 27.05N 114.10W
Asunción, Cerro de la- 48 Je 24.15N 99.56W
Asuncion Island 57 Fc 19.40N 145.24 E
Asunción Mita 49 Cf 14.20N 89.43W
Asunción Nochixtlán 48 Ki 17.28N 97.14W
Asunden 8 Fg 58.00N 15.50 E
Åsunden 8 Eg 57.44N 13.22 E
Aswa 36 Fb 3.43N 31.55 E
Aswān 31 Kf 24.05N 32.53 E
Aswān, Sadd al-=First Cataract (EN) 30 Kf 24.01N 32.52 E
Asyūţ 31 Kf 27.11N 31.11 E
Asyūţī, Wādī al- 24 Di 27.10N 31.16 E
Aszód 10 Pi 47.39N 19.30 E
'Ata 65b Bc 21.03S 174.59W
Atacama 56 Gc 27.30S 70.00W
Atacama, Desierto de-=Atacama Desert (EN) 52 Jh 22.30S 69.15W
Atacama, Salar de- 52 Jh 23.30S 68.15W
Atacama Desert (EN)=Atacama, Desierto de- 52 Jh 22.30S 69.15W
Atacama Trench (EN) 3 Nm 30.00S 73.00W
Atafu Atoll 57 Je 8.33S 172.30W
Atagaj 20 Ee 55.06N 99.25 E
Ata Island 57 Jg 21.03S 175.00W
Atakor 30 Hf 23.13N 5.40 E
Atakora 34 Fc 10.00N 1.35 E
Atakora 34 Fc 10.45N 1.30 E
Atakpamé 31 Hh 7.32N 1.08 E
Atalaia do Norte 54 Dd 4.20S 70.12W
Atalándi 15 Fk 38.39N 23.00 E
Atalaya 54 Df 10.44S 73.45W
Atalayasa 13 Nf 38.55N 1.15 E
Atambua 26 Hh 9.07S 124.54 E
Atami 29 Fd 35.05N 139.02 E
Atangmik 41 Gf 64.53N 52.00W
Aţâr 31 Ff 20.30N 13.03W
Atas-Bogdo-Ula 27 Gc 43.20N 96.30 E
Atascadero 46 Ei 35.29N 120.41W
Atasu 19 Hf 48.42N 71.38 E
'Atata 65b Ac 21.03S 175.15W
Atatürk Barajı 24 Hd 37.30N 38.30 E
Atauro, Pulau 26 Ih 8.13S 125.35 E
Atáviros 15 Km 36.12N 27.52 E
Ataway 35 Bd 9.59N 18.38 E
Atbara 35 Eb 17.40N 33.56 E
'Aţbarah 30 Kg 17.40N 33.56 E
'Aţbarah 31 Kg 17.42N 33.59 E
Atbasar 22 Id 51.48N 68.20 E
At-Baši 19 Hg 41.08N 75.51 E
Atça 15 Ll 37.53N 28.13 E
Atchafalaya Bay 43 If 29.25N 91.20W
Atchison 43 Hd 39.34N 95.07W
Atebubu 34 Ed 7.45N 0.59W
Ateca 13 Kc 41.20N 1.47W
Aterno 14 Hh 42.11N 13.51 E
Atessa 14 Ih 42.04N 14.27 E
Ath/Aat 11 Jd 50.38N 3.47 E
Athabasca 38 Hd 58.40N 110.50W
Athabasca 42 Gf 54.43N 113.17W
Athabasca, Lake- 38 Id 59.07N 110.00W
Athamánon, Óri- 15 Ej 39.27N 21.08 E
Athamánon Óri 15 Ej 39.27N 21.08 E
Athens [Al.-U.S.] 44 Dh 34.48N 86.58W
Athens [Ga.-U.S.] 43 Ke 33.57N 83.23W
Athens [Oh.-U.S.] 44 Ff 39.20N 82.06W
Athens [Tn.-U.S.] 44 Eh 35.28N 84.35W
Athens [Tx.-U.S.] 45 Ij 32.12N 95.51W
Athens (EN) = Athínai 6 Ih 37.59N 23.44 E
Athéras 15 Jl 37.38N 26.15 E
Atherton 59 Jc 17.16S 145.29 E
Athi 36 Gc 2.59S 38.31 E
Athies-sous-Laon 12 Fe 49.34N 3.41 E
Athínai = Athens (EN) 6 Ih 37.59N 23.44 E
Athi River 36 Gc 1.27S 36.59 E
Athis-de-l'Orne 12 Bf 48.49N 0.30W
Athlone/Baile Átha Luain 9 Fh 53.25N 7.56W
Athol 44 Kd 42.36N 72.14W
Áthos 15 Hi 40.10N 24.20 E
Athos, Mount- (EN)=Áyion Óros 15 Hi 40.15N 24.15 E
Ath Thamad 24 Fh 29.41N 34.18 E
Ath Thumāmī 24 Ki 27.42N 44.59 E
Athus, Aubange- 12 He 49.34N 5.50 E
Athy 9 Gi 53.00N 7.00W
Ati 31 Ig 13.13N 18.20 E
Atiak 36 Fb 3.16N 32.07 E
Atiamuri 62 Gc 38.23S 176.02 E
Atibaia, Rio- 55 If 22.42S 47.17W
Atienza 13 Jc 41.12N 2.52W
Atikokan 42 Ig 48.45N 91.37W
Atikonak Lake 42 Lf 52.40N 64.35W
Atimoono 64n Bc 10.26S 160.58W
Atitlán, Lago de- 49 Bf 14.42N 91.12W
Atitlán, Volcán- 47 Ff 14.35N 91.11W
Atiu Island 57 Lg 20.02S 158.07W
'Atk, Wādī al- 24 Li 26.03N 46.30 E
Atka 38 Bd 52.15N 174.30W
Atka [Ak.-U.S.] 40a Db 52.12N 174.12W
Atka 20 Kd 60.49N 151.58 E
Atka Iceport 66 Bf 70.35S 7.45W
Atkarsk 19 Ee 51.52N 44.59 E
Atkasook 40 Hb 70.28N 157.24W
Atkinson 45 Ge 42.32N 98.59W
Atlacomulco de Fabela 48 Jh 19.48N 99.53W
Atlanta [Ga.-U.S.] 39 Kf 33.45N 84.23W
Atlanta [Mi.-U.S.] 44 Ec 45.00N 84.09W
Atlanta [Tx.-U.S.] 45 Ij 33.07N 94.10W
Atlanterhavet=Atlantic Ocean (EN) 3 Di 2.00N 25.00W
Atlantic [Ia.-U.S.] 45 If 41.24N 95.01W
Atlantic [N.C.-U.S.] 44 Ih 34.54N 76.20W
Atlantic City 39 Lf 39.27N 74.35W
Atlantic Coastal Plain 38 Lf 34.00N 79.00W
Atlantic-Indian Basin (EN) 3 Eo 60.00S 15.00 E
Atlantic-Indian Ridge (EN) 3 Eo 52.00S 25.00 E
Atlántico 54 Da 10.40N 75.00W
Atlántico, Océano-=Atlantic Ocean (EN) 3 Di 2.00N 25.00W
Atlântico, Oceano-=Atlantic Ocean (EN) 3 Di 2.00N 25.00W
Atlantic Ocean 3 Di 2.00N 25.00W
Atlantic Ocean (EN)=Atlanterhavet 3 Di 2.00N 25.00W
Atlantic Ocean (EN)=Atlântico, Oceano- 3 Di 2.00N 25.00W
Atlantic Ocean (EN)=Atlántico, Océano- 3 Di 2.00N 25.00W
Atlantic Ocean (EN)=Atlantiese Oseaan 3 Di 2.00N 25.00W
Atlantic Ocean (EN)=Atlantique, Océan- 3 Di 2.00N 25.00W
Atlantic Ocean (EN)=Atlantshaf 3 Di 2.00N 25.00W
Atlantic Ocean (EN)=Muhīt, Al Baḩr al- 3 Di 2.00N 25.00W
Atlántida 49 Df 15.30N 87.00W
Atlantiese Oseaan=Atlantic Ocean (EN) 3 Di 2.00N 25.00W
Atlantique 34 Fd 6.35N 2.15 E
Atlantique, Océan-=Atlantic Ocean (EN) 3 Di 2.00N 25.00W
Atlantshaf=Atlantic Ocean (EN) 3 Di 2.00N 25.00W
Atlas=Atlas Mountains (EN) 30 Ge 32.00N 2.00W
Atlas Mountains (EN)=Atlas 30 Ge 32.00N 2.00W
Atlasova, Ostrov- 20 Kf 50.50N 155.25 E
Atlasovo 20 Jg 46.00N 142.09 E
Atlas Saharien=Saharan Atlas (EN) 30 He 34.00N 2.00 E
Atlas Tellien=Tell Atlas (EN) 30 He 36.00N 2.00 E
Atlin 42 Ee 59.35N 133.42W
Atlin Lake 42 Ee 59.35N 133.43W
Atlixco 47 Ee 18.54N 98.26W
Atløy 8 Ac 61.20N 4.55 E
Atmore 44 Dj 31.02N 87.29W
Atna 8 Dc 61.44N 10.49 E
Atna Peak 42 Ef 53.57N 128.04W
Atō 29 Bd 34.24N 131.43 E
Atoka 45 Hi 34.23N 96.08W
Átokos 15 Dk 38.29N 20.49 E
Atotonilco el Alto 48 Hg 20.33N 102.31W
Atoui, Khatt- 32 De 20.04N 15.58W
Atouila, 'Erg- 30 Gf 21.15N 3.20W
Atoyac, Río- 48 Ki 16.30N 97.31W
Atoyac de Alvarez 48 Ii 17.12N 100.26W
Atrak 21 Hf 37.23N 53.57 E
Ätran 7 Ch 56.53N 12.30 E
Atrato, Río- 52 Ie 8.17N 76.58W
Atrek 21 Hf 37.23N 53.57 E
Atri 14 Hh 42.35N 13.59 E
Atsugi 29 Fd 35.26N 139.20 E
Atsukeshi 28 Rc 43.02N 144.51 E
Atsukeshi-Wan 29a Db 43.00N 144.45 E
Aţsumi [Jap.] 28 Oe 38.37N 139.35 E
Atsumi [Jap.] 29 Ed 34.37N 137.05 E
Atsumi-Hantō 29 Ed 34.40N 137.15 E
Atsumi-Wan 29 Ed 34.45N 137.15 E
Atsuta 29a Bb 43.24N 141.25 E
Atsutoko 29a Db 43.15N 145.13 E
Aţ Ţaff 23 He 23.55N 54.25 E
Aţ Ţafīlah 24 Fg 30.50N 35.36 E
Aţ Ţā'if 22 Gg 21.16N 40.25 E
At Tāj 33 De 24.13N 23.18 E
Attalla 44 Dh 34.01N 86.05W
Aţ Ţallāb 33 De 24.01N 23.10 E
At Ta'mīm 24 Ke 36.00N 44.00 E
Attapu 25 Lf 14.48N 106.50 E
Aţ Ţārmīyah 24 Kf 33.40N 44.24 E
Attawapiskat 38 Kd 52.57N 82.18W
Attawapiskat 39 Kd 52.55N 82.26W
Attawapiskat Lake 42 If 52.15N 87.50W
Aţ Ţawīl 24 Hh 29.20N 39.35 E
At Taysīyaḩ 24 Jh 28.00N 44.00 E
Aţ Ţayyārah 35 Ec 13.12N 30.47 E
Attendorn 12 Jc 51.07N 7.54 E
Attersee 14 Hc 47.55N 13.33 E
Attert 12 Ie 49.49N 6.05 E
Attica 44 De 40.17N 87.15W
Attichy 12 Fe 49.25N 3.03 E
Attigny 12 Ge 49.29N 4.35 E
At Tīh Desert (EN)=Tīh, Şaḩrā' at- 33 Fc 30.05N 34.00 E
Attikamagen Lake 42 Ke 55.00N 66.30W
Attleboro 44 Le 41.56N 71.17W
Attleborough 12 Db 52.31N 1.01 E
Attre 12 Fd 50.37N 3.50 E
Attu 40a Ab 52.56N 173.15 E
Attu 40a Ab 52.55N 173.00 E
Aţ Ţulayhī 24 Ki 27.33N 44.08 E
Aţ Ţūr 24 Eh 28.14N 33.37 E
Aţ Ţurayf 23 Ec 31.44N 38.33 E
At Turbah 23 Fg 12.40N 43.30 E
Aţ Ţuwayshah 35 Dc 12.21N 26.32 E
Åtvidaberg 7 Dg 58.12N 16.00 E
Atwater 46 Eh 37.21N 120.36W
Atwood 45 Fg 39.45N 101.03W
Atyrau (Gurjev) 6 Lf 47.07N 51.56 E
Atyrauskaja oblast 19 Ff 47.30N 52.00 E
Auasbila 49 Ef 14.52N 84.40W
Auatu 35 Gd 7.17N 41.03 E
Auau Channel 65a Ec 20.51N 156.45W
Aubagne 11 Lk 43.17N 5.34 E
Aubange 12 He 49.35N 5.48 E
Aubange-Athus 12 He 49.34N 5.50 E
Aube 11 Jf 48.34N 3.43 E
Aube 11 Kf 48.15N 4.05 E
Aubel 12 Hd 50.42N 5.51 E
Aubenas 11 Kj 44.37N 4.23 E
Aubenton 12 Ge 49.50N 4.12 E
Aubetin 12 Ff 48.49N 3.01 E
Aubigny-en-Artois 12 Ed 50.21N 2.35 E
Aubigny-sur-Nère 11 Ig 47.29N 2.26 E
Aubin 11 Ij 44.32N 2.15 E
Aubrac, Monts d'- 11 Ij 44.38N 3.00 E
Aubry, Lake - 42 Ec 67.25N 126.30W
Auburn [Al.-U.S.] 44 Ei 32.36N 85.29W
Auburn [Ca.-U.S.] 46 Eg 38.54N 121.04W
Auburn [In.-U.S.] 44 Ee 41.22N 85.04W
Auburn [Me.-U.S.] 44 Lc 44.06N 70.14W
Auburn [Nb.-U.S.] 45 If 40.23N 95.51W
Auburn [N.Y.-U.S.] 44 Id 42.57N 76.34W
Auburn [Wa.-U.S.] 46 Dc 47.18N 122.13W
Auburn Range 59 Ke 25.10S 150.30 E
Aubusson 11 Ii 45.57N 2.10 E
Aucanquilcha, Cerro- 52 Jh 21.14S 68.28W
Auce 8 Jh 56.28N 22.50 E
Auch 11 Gk 43.39N 0.35 E
Auchel 12 Ed 50.30N 2.28 E
Auchi 34 Gd 7.04N 6.16 E
Auckland 58 Ih 36.52S 174.45 E
Auckland Islands 57 Hi 50.35S 166.00 E
Auckland Peninsula 62 Eb 36.15S 174.00 E
Aude 11 Jk 43.13N 3.14 E
Aude 11 Ik 43.05N 2.30 E
Auden 45 Ma 50.13N 87.47W
Audenarde/Oudenaarde 11 Jd 50.51N 3.36 E
Audierne 11 Bf 48.01N 4.32W
Audierne, Baie d'- 11 Bg 47.57N 4.28W
Audincourt 11 Mg 47.29N 6.50 E
Audo 35 Gd 6.09N 41.53 E
Audresselles 12 Dd 50.49N 1.35 E
Audru 8 Kf 58.20N 24.19 E
Audruicq 12 Ed 50.53N 2.05 E
Audubon 45 If 41.43N 94.55W
Audun-le-Roman 12 He 49.22N 5.53 E
Audun-le-Tiche 12 He 49.28N 5.57 E
Aue 10 If 50.35N 12.42 E
Aue [Ger.] 10 Fd 52.33N 9.05 E
Aue [Ger.] 12 Kb 52.16N 8.59 E
Auerbach 10 If 50.31N 12.24 E
Auezov 19 If 49.40N 81.40 E
Auffay 12 De 49.43N 1.06 E
Augathella 58 Fg 25.48S 146.35 E
Auge, Pays d'- 11 Ge 49.05N 0.10 E
Augpilagtoq 41 Gd 72.45N 55.35W
Augrabies Falls 30 Jk 28.35S 20.23 E
Augsburg 6 Hf 48.22N 10.53 E
Augusta [Ar.-U.S.] 45 Ki 35.17N 91.22W
Augusta [Austl.] 58 Ch 34.10S 115.10 E
Augusta [Ga.-U.S.] 39 Kf 33.29N 81.57W
Augusta [It.] 14 Jm 37.13N 15.13 E
Augusta [Ks.-U.S.] 45 Hh 37.41N 96.58W
Augusta [Me.-U.S.] 39 Me 44.19N 69.47W
Augusta [Mt.-U.S.] 46 Ic 47.30N 112.24W
Augusta, Golfo di- 14 Jm 37.10N 15.15 E
Augustów 10 Sc 53.51N 22.59 E
Augustowski, Kanał- 10 Tc 53.54N 23.26 E
Augustus, Mount- 57 Cg 24.20S 116.50 E
Auki 58 He 8.45S 160.42 E
Auld, Lake- 59 Ed 22.30S 123.45 E
Aulla 14 Df 44.12N 9.58 E
Aulne 11 Bf 48.17N 4.16W
Aulneau Peninsula 45 Ib 49.23N 94.29W
Aulnoye-Aymeries 12 Fd 50.12N 3.50 E
Aulong 64a Ac 7.17N 134.17 E
Ault 12 Dd 50.06N 1.27 E
Auluptagel 64a Ac 7.19N 134.29 E
Aulus-les-Bains 11 Hl 42.48N 1.20 E
Aumale 11 He 49.46N 1.45 E
Auna 34 Fc 10.11N 4.43 E
Aunay-sur-Odon 12 Be 49.01N 0.38W
Auneuil 12 Ee 49.22N 2.00 E
Auning 7 Ch 56.26N 10.23 E
Aunis 11 Fh 46.10N 1.00W
Aunuu 65c Cb 14.17S 170.33W
Auob 30 Jk 26.27S 20.38 E
Aura 8 Jd 60.36N 22.34 E
Aurangābād 25 Fe 19.53N 75.20 E
Aurari Bay 59 Gb 11.40S 133.40 E
Aur Atoll 57 Id 8.16N 171.06 E
Auray 11 Dg 47.40N 2.59W
Aurdal 7 Bf 60.56N 9.24 E
Aure 11 Ee 49.20N 1.07W
Aure [Nor.] 7 Be 63.13N 8.32 E
Aure [Nor.] 8 Bb 62.24N 6.36 E
Aurejärvi 8 Jb 62.05N 23.25 E
Aurès, Massif de l'- 30 He 35.14N 6.10 E
Aurich 10 Dc 53.28N 7.29 E
Aurillac 11 Ij 44.55N 2.27 E
Aurlandsfjorden 8 Bc 61.05N 7.05 E
Aurlandsvangen 7 Bf 60.54N 7.11 E
Auron 11 Mj 44.12N 6.56 E
Auron 11 Ig 47.06N 2.24 E
Aurora [Co.-U.S.] 43 Gd 39.44N 104.52W
Aurora [Il.-U.S.] 43 Jc 42.46N 88.19W
Aurora [Mo.-U.S.] 45 Jh 36.58N 93.43W
Aurora [Phil.] 26 He 7.57N 123.36 E
Aurora do Norte 55 Ia 12.38S 46.23W
Aursjøen 8 Cb 62.20N 8.40 E
Aursunden 8 Db 62.40N 11.40 E
Aurukun Mission 59 Ib 13.19S 141.45 E
Aurunci, Monti- 14 Hi 41.20N 13.40 E
Aus 37 Be 26.40S 16.15 E
Au Sable River 44 Fc 44.25N 83.20W
Ausangate, Nudo- 52 Ig 13.47S 71.13W
Ausiait/Egedesminde 67 Nc 68.50N 52.45W
Ausoni, Monti- 14 Hi 41.25N 13.20 E
Aust-Agder 7 Bg 58.50N 8.00 E
Austfonna 41 Oc 79.55N 25.00 E
Austin [Mn.-U.S.] 43 Ic 43.40N 92.59W
Austin [Nv.-U.S.] 43 Dd 39.30N 117.04W
Austin [Tx.-U.S.] 39 Jf 30.16N 97.45W
Austin, Lake- 59 De 27.40S 118.00 E
Austral, Chaco- 52 Jh 25.00S 61.00W
Australes, Iles-/Tubuaï, Iles-=Tubuai Islands (EN) 57 Lg 23.00S 150.00W
Australia 57 Eg 25.00S 135.00 E
Australia 58 Eg 25.00S 135.00 E
Australian Alps 57 Fh 37.00S 148.00 E
Australian Capital Territory 59 Jg 35.30S 149.00 E
Austria (EN) = Österreich 6 Hf 47.30N 14.00 E
Austvågøy 7 Db 68.20N 14.36 E
Autazes 54 Gd 3.35S 59.08W
Autheuil-Authouillet 12 De 49.06N 1.17 E
Authie 11 Hd 50.21N 1.38 E
Autlán de Navarro 47 De 19.46N 104.22W
Autun 11 Kh 46.57N 4.18 E
Auve 12 Ge 49.02N 4.42 E
Auvergne 11 Ii 45.20N 3.00 E
Auvergne, Monts d'- 11 Ii 45.30N 2.45 E
Auvézère 11 Gi 45.12N 0.50 E
Auvillers-lès-Forges-Mon Idée 12 Ge 49.52N 4.21 E
Auxerre 11 Jg 47.48N 3.34 E
Auxi-le-Château 11 Id 50.14N 2.07 E
Auxois 11 Kg 47.20N 4.30 E
Auxonne 11 Lg 47.12N 5.23 E
Auyán-Tepuy 54 Fb 5.55N 62.32W
Auzances 11 Ih 46.01N 2.30 E
Avaavaroa Passage 64p Bc 21.16S 159.47W
Availles-Limouzine 11 Gh 46.07N 0.39 E
Avala 15 De 44.42N 20.31 E
Avaldsnes 8 Ae 59.21N 5.16 E
Avallon 11 Jg 47.29N 3.54 E
Avalon Peninsula 42 Mg 47.30N 53.30W
Avana 64p Cb 21.14S 159.41W
Avaré 55 Hf 23.05S 48.55W
Avarua 58 Lg 21.12S 159.46W
Avarua Harbour 64p Bb 21.11S 159.46W
Avatele 64k Bb 19.06S 169.55W
Avatele Bay 64k Bb 19.05S 169.56W
Avatiu 64p Bb 21.12S 159.47W
Avatiu Harbour 64p Bb 21.11S 159.47W
Avatolu, Passe- 64h Ab 13.19S 176.14W
Ávdhira 15 Hi 40.59N 24.57 E
Ave 13 Dc 41.20N 8.45W
Aveh 24 Ne 34.47N 50.25 E
Aveh, Gardaneh-ye- 24 Me 35.32N 49.09 E
Aveiro 13 Dd 40.45N 8.30W
Aveiro [Braz.] 54 Gd 3.15S 55.10W
Aveiro [Port.] 13 Dd 40.38N 8.39W
Āvej 24 Me 35.34N 49.13 E
Avelgem 12 Fd 50.46N 3.26 E
Avellaneda [Arg.] 56 Ic 29.07S 59.40W
Avellaneda [Arg.] 56 Id 34.39S 58.23W
Avellino 14 Ij 40.54N 14.47 E
Aven Armand 11 Jj 44.15N 3.22 E
Averbode 12 Gc 51.02N 4.59 E
Avereest 12 Ib 52.37N 6.27 E
Avereest-Dedemsvaart 12 Ib 52.37N 6.27 E
Averøya 7 Be 63.00N 7.35 E
Aversa 14 Ij 40.58N 14.12 E
Avesnes-le-Compte 12 Ed 50.17N 2.32 E
Avesnes-les-Aubert 12 Fd 50.12N 3.23 E
Avesnes-sur-Helpe 11 Jd 50.07N 3.56 E
Aves Ridge (EN) 47 Lf 14.00N 63.30W
Avesta 7 Df 60.09N 16.12 E
Aveyron 11 Hj 44.05N 1.16 E
Aveyron 11 Ij 44.15N 2.30 E
Avezzano 14 Hh 42.02N 13.25 E
Avgan 15 Mk 38.25N 29.24 E
Avgó [Grc.] 15 In 35.36N 25.34 E
Avgó [Grc.] 15 Jn 35.55N 26.30 E
Aviemore 9 Jd 57.12N 3.50W
Avigait 41 Gf 62.15N 50.00W
Avigliano 14 Jj 40.44N 15.43 E
Avignon 6 Gg 43.57N 4.49 E
Ávila 13 Hd 49.39N 4.42W
Ávila 13 Hd 40.35N 5.00W
Ávila, Sierra de- 13 Gd 40.35N 5.08W
Avilés 13 Ga 43.33N 5.55W
Avinurme 8 Lf 58.55N 26.50 E
Avion 12 Ed 50.24N 2.50 E
Ávios Theódhoros 15 Gn 35.32N 23.56 E
Avioth 12 He 49.34N 5.24 E
Avis 13 Ee 39.03N 7.53W
Avisio 14 Fd 46.07N 11.05 E
Avize 12 Gf 48.58N 4.01 E
Avlaka Burun 15 Ii 40.07N 25.40 E
Avola [B.C.-Can.] 46 Fa 51.47N 119.19W
Avola [It.] 14 Jn 36.54N 15.08 E
Avon 9 Kj 51.30N 2.30W
Avon [Eng.-U.K.] 9 Kj 51.59N 2.10W
Avon [Eng.-U.K.] 9 Kj 51.30N 2.43W
Avon [Eng.-U.K.] 9 Lk 50.43N 1.46W
Avon Downs 58 Eg 20.05S 137.30 E
Avon Park 44 Gl 27.36N 81.31W
Avon River 59 Df 31.40S 116.07 E
Avranches 11 Ef 48.41N 1.22W
Avre [Fr.] 11 Ie 49.53N 2.20 E
Avre [Fr.] 11 Hf 48.47N 1.22 E
Avrig 15 Hd 45.43N 24.23 E
Avron 11 Ki 45.15N 4.50 E
Avşa Adasi 15 Ki 40.30N 27.30 E
Avuavu 63a Ec 9.50S 160.23 E
Awaji 28 Mg 34.35N 135.01 E
Awaji-Shima 28 Mg 34.25N 134.50 E
'Awālī 24 Ni 26.05N 50.33 E
Awanui 61 Dg 35.03S 173.15 E
Awara Plain 36 Hb 3.45N 41.07 E
Aware 35 Gd 8.14N 44.10 E
Awarua Bay 62 Cf 44.20S 168.05 E
Awasa 31 Kh 7.02N 38.29 E
Awash 30 Lg 11.12N 41.40 E
Awash 35 Gd 8.59N 40.10 E
Awa-Shima 28 Oe 38.27N 139.14 E
Awaso 34 Ed 6.14N 2.16W
Awat 27 Dc 40.38N 80.22 E
Awata 35 Fe 4.45N 39.26 E
Awatere 62 Fd 41.36S 174.10 E
Awbārī 31 If 26.35N 12.46 E
Awbārī 33 Bd 26.35N 12.46 E
Awbārī' Şaḩrā' 30 If 27.30N 11.30 E
Awdēgle 35 Ge 1.58N 44.51 E
Awe, Loch- 9 He 56.15N 5.15W
Awjilah 31 Jf 29.06N 21.17 E
Axel 12 Fc 51.16N 3.54 E
Axel Heiberg 38 Ja 80.30N 92.00W
Axim 34 Ee 4.52N 2.14W
Axiós 15 Fi 40.35N 22.50 E
Axixá 54 Jd 2.51S 44.04W
Ax-les-Thermes 11 Hl 42.43N 1.50 E
Ayabaca 54 Cd 4.38S 79.43W
Ayabe 28 Mg 35.18N 135.15 E
Ayachi, Ari n'- 32 Gc 32.30N 4.50W
Ayacucho 54 Df 14.00S 74.00W
Ayacucho [Arg.] 56 Ie 37.09S 58.29W
Ayacucho [Peru] 53 Ig 13.07S 74.13W
Ayakita-Gawa 29 Bf 31.58N 131.23 E
Ayakkum Hū 27 Ed 37.30N 89.20 E
Ayamé 34 Ed 5.37N 3.11W
Ayamonte 13 Eg 37.13N 7.24W
Ayancık 24 Fb 41.57N 34.36 E
Ayangba 34 Gd 7.31N 7.08 E
Ayapel 54 Cb 8.18N 75.08W
Ayas 24 Eb 40.01N 32.21 E
Ayaviri 54 Df 14.52S 70.35W
Āybak 23 Kb 36.16N 68.01 E
Aybastı 24 Gb 40.41N 37.24 E
Aycliffe 9 Lg 54.36N 1.34W
'Aydim, Wādī- 35 Ib 18.08N 53.08 E
Aydın 23 Cb 37.51N 27.51 E
Aydincik 24 Ed 36.08N 33.17 E
Aydın Dağları 24 Bc 38.00N 28.00 E
Aydingkol Hu 27 Ec 42.40N 89.15 E
Aydinkent 24 Ed 37.06N 31.36 E
Aydos Dağı 24 Fd 37.21N 34.22 E
Ayerbe 13 Lb 42.17N 0.41W
Ayer Hitam 26 Df 1.55N 103.11 E

Index Symbols

- 1 Independent Nation
- 2 State, Region
- 3 District, County
- 4 Municipality
- 5 Colony, Dependency
- Continent
- Physical Region
- Historical or Cultural Region
- Mount, Mountain
- Volcano
- Hill
- Mountains, Mountain Range
- Hills, Escarpment
- Plateau, Upland
- Pass, Gap
- Plain, Lowland
- Delta
- Salt Flat
- Valley, Canyon
- Crater, Cave
- Karst Features
- Depression
- Polder
- Desert, Dunes
- Forest, Woods
- Heath, Steppe
- Oasis
- Cape, Point
- Coast, Beach
- Cliff
- Peninsula
- Isthmus
- Sandbank
- Island
- Atoll
- Rock, Reef
- Islands, Archipelago
- Rocks, Reefs
- Coral Reef
- Well, Spring
- Geyser
- River, Stream
- Waterfall Rapids
- River Mouth, Estuary
- Lake
- Salt Lake
- Intermittent Lake
- Reservoir
- Swamp, Pond
- Canal
- Glacier
- Ice Shelf, Pack Ice
- Ocean
- Sea
- Gulf, Bay
- Strait, Fjord
- Lagoon
- Bank
- Seamount
- Tablemount
- Ridge
- Shelf
- Basin
- Escarpment, Sea Scarp
- Fracture
- Trench, Abyss
- National Park, Reserve
- Point of Interest
- Recreation Site
- Cave, Cavern
- Historic Site
- Ruins
- Wall, Walls
- Church, Abbey
- Temple
- Scientific Station
- Airport
- Port
- Lighthouse
- Mine
- Tunnel
- Dam, Bridge

Ayeyarwady 25 Ie 17.00N 95.00 E
Ayeyarwady = Irrawaddy (EN) 21 Lg 15.50N 95.06 E
Ayiá 15 Fj 39.43N 22.46 E
Ayia Marina 15 Jl 37.09N 26.52 E
Ayiásos 15 Jj 39.06N 26.22 E
Áyion Óros=Athos, Mount- (EN) [2] 15 Hi 40.15N 24.15 E
Áyios Evstrátios 15 Hj 39.31N 25.00 E
Áyios Ioánnis, Ákra- 15 In 35.20N 25.46 E
Áyios Kírikos 15 Jl 37.35N 26.14 E
Áyios Minás 15 Jl 37.36N 26.34 E
Áyios Nikólaos 15 In 35.11N 25.43 E
Áyios Yeóryios 15 Gl 37.28N 23.56 E
Aykota 35 Fb 15.10N 37.03 E
Aylesbury 9 Mj 51.50N 0.50W
Ayllón, Sierra de- 13 Ic 41.15N 3.25W
Aylmer Lake 42 Gd 64.05N 108.30W
Aylsham 12 Db 52.47N 1.15 E
Ayna 13 Jf 38.33N 2.05W
'Aynabo 35 Hd 8.57N 46.30 E
'Ayn ad Darāhim 14 Cn 36.47N 8.42 E
'Ayn al Baydā 24 Ge 34.32N 37.55 E
'Ayn al Ghazāl [Eg.] 24 Dj 25.46N 30.38 E
'Ayn al Ghazāl [Lib.] 31 Jf 21.50N 24.55 E
'Ayn al Shigi 24 Ci 27.01N 28.02 E
'Ayn al Wādī 24 Ci 27.23N 28.13 E
'Ayn Bū Sālim 14 Cn 36.37N 8.59 E
'Ayn Dāllah 33 Ed 27.19N 27.20 E
'Ayn Dār 24 Mj 25.58N 49.14 E
'Ayn Dīwār 24 Jd 37.17N 42.11 E
'Ayn Ilwān 24 Dj 25.44N 30.25 E
'Ayn Khalīfah 24 Bi 26.46N 27.47 E
'Ayn Sifnī 24 Jd 36.42N 43.21 E
'Ayn Sukhnah 33 Fd 29.30N 32.10 E
'Aynūnah 23 Ed 28.05N 35.08 E
Ayod 35 Ed 8.08N 31.24 E
Ayora 13 Ke 39.04N 1.03W
Ayorou 34 Fc 14.44N 0.55 E
'Ayoûn el 'Atroûs 31 Gg 16.38N 9.36W
Ayr 9 If 55.29N 4.28W
Ayr [Austl.] 59 Jc 19.35S 147.24 E
Ayr [Scot.-U.K.] 9 If 55.28N 4.38W
Ayre, Point of- 9 Ig 54.26N 4.22W
Ayrolle, Étang de l'- 11 Jk 43.16N 3.30 E
Aysha 35 Gc 10.45N 42.35 E
Aytré 11 Eh 46.08N 1.06W
Ayutla 48 Jg 20.07N 104.22W
Ayutla de los Libres 48 Ji 16.54N 99.13W
Ayvacık 24 Gb 41.00N 36.45 E
Ayvacık 15 Jj 39.36N 26.24 E
Ayvalık 23 Cb 39.18N 26.41 E
Aywaille 12 Hd 50.28N 5.40 E
Āzādshahr 24 Pd 37.05N 55.08 E
Azahar, Costa del- 13 Me 39.58N 0.01 E
Azaila 13 Lc 41.17N 0.29W
Azambuja 13 De 39.04N 8.52W
Azamgarh 25 Gc 26.04N 83.11 E
Azángaro 54 Df 14.55S 70.13W
Azannes-et-Soumazannes 12 He 49.18N 5.28 E
Azaouâd=Azaouad (EN) 30 Gg 19.00N 3.00W
Azaouad (EN)=Azaouâd 30 Gg 19.00N 3.00W
Azaouak 34 Fb 15.30N 3.18 E
Azaouak 30 Hg 15.20N 4.55 E
Azaouak, Vallée de l'- 30 Hg 17.30N 3.40 E
Azar 34 Fb 16.02N 4.04 E
Āzarbāijān-e Gharbī [3] 23 Fb 37.00N 45.00 E
Āzarbāijān-e Sharqī [3] 23 Gb 37.00N 47.00 E
Azarbajčan SSR → Azärbayjan 19 Eg 40.30N 47.30 E
Azärbayjan = Azerbaijan (EN) 19 Eg 40.30N 47.30 E
Azare 34 Hc 11.41N 10.12 E
Āzār Shahr 24 Kd 37.45N 45.59 E
Azay-le-Rideau 11 Gg 47.16N 0.28 E
A 'zāz 24 Gd 36.35N 37.03 E
Azazga 13 Qh 36.44N 4.22 E
Azbine/Aïr 30 Hg 18.00N 8.30 E
Azdaak, Gora- 16 Ni 40.13N 44.59 E
Azdavay 24 Eb 41.39N 33.18 E
Azefal 30 Ff 21.00N 14.45W
Azeffoun 13 Qh 36.53N 4.25 E
Azemmour 32 Fc 33.17N 8.21W
Azerbaijan (En) = Azärbayjan 19 Eg 40.30N 47.30 E
Azerbajdžanskaja Sovetskaja Socialističeskaja Respublika → Azärbayjan 19 Eg 40.30N 47.30 E
Azerbajdžanskaja SSR/ Azarbaijčan Sovet Socialistik Respublicasy → Azärbayjan 19 Eg 40.30N 47.30 E
Azerbajdžanskaja SSR → Azärbayjan 19 Eg 40.30N 47.30 E
Azeri/Aseri 7 Gg 59.29N 26.51 E
Azevedo Sodré 55 Ej 30.04S 54.36W
Azezo 35 Fc 12.33N 37.25 E
Azilal [3] 32 Fc 32.09N 6.05W
Azilal 32 Fc 31.58N 6.35W
Aznā 24 Mf 33.56N 49.24 E
Aznakajevo 7 Mi 54.56N 53.04 E
Azogues 54 Cd 2.44S 78.48W
Azores (EN)=Açores [5] 31 Ee 38.30N 28.00W
Azores (EN)=Açores, Arquipélago dos- 30 Ee 38.30N 28.00W
Azores-Gibraltar Ridge (EN) 3 Df 37.00N 16.00W
Azoum, Bahr- 30 Jg 10.53N 20.15 E
Azov 19 Df 47.05N 39.25 E
Azov, Sea of- (EN)= Azovskoje More 5 Jf 46.00N 36.00 E
Azovskoje More=Azov, Sea of- (EN) 5 Jf 46.00N 36.00 E
Azpeitia 13 Ja 43.11N 2.16W
Azrak, Bahr- 35 Bc 10.50N 19.50 E
Azraq, Al Baḥr al-=Blue Nile (EN) 30 Kg 15.38N 32.31 E
Azraq ash Shīshān 24 Gg 31.50N 36.49 E
Azrou 32 Fc 33.26N 5.13W
Aztec 45 Ch 36.49N 107.59W
Aztec Ruins 46 Kh 36.51N 108.10W
Azua 49 Ld 18.27N 70.44W
Azuaga 13 Gf 38.16N 5.41W
Azuar 13 Ie 39.08N 3.36W
Azuero, Peninsula de- = Azuero Peninsula (EN) 38 Ki 7.40N 80.30W
Azuero Peninsula (EN)= Azuero, Peninsula de- 38 Ki 7.40N 80.30W
Azul 53 Ki 36.45S 59.50W
Azul, Arroyo del- 55 Cm 36.15S 59.07W
Azul, Cerro- 54a Ab 0.54S 91.21W
Azul, Cordillera- 54 Ce 8.30S 76.00W
Azul, Rio- 48 Oi 17.54N 88.52W
Azul, Serra- 55 Eb 14.50S 54.50W
Azul, Sierras del- 55 Cm 37.02S 59.55W
Azūm 35 Cc 10.53N 20.15 E
Azuma-San 29 Gc 37.44N 140.08 E
Azur, Côte d'- 11 Mk 43.30N 7.00 E
Azurduy 54 Fg 19.59S 64.29W
Azzaba 32 Ib 36.44N 7.06 E
Az Zāb al Kabīr 23 Fb 36.00N 43.21 E
Az Zāb aṣ Ṣaghīr 23 Fb 35.12N 43.25 E
Az Zabdānī 24 Gf 33.43N 36.05 E
Az Zabū 24 Ch 28.22N 28.56 E
Az Ẓafīr 23 Ff 19.57N 41.30 E
Az Zaghāwa 35 Cb 15.15N 23.14 E
Az Ẓāhirah 24 Qk 23.30N 56.15 E
Az Zallāq 24 Ni 26.03N 50.29 E
Az Zaqāzīq 33 Fc 30.35N 31.31 E
Az Zarqā' 24 Oj 24.53N 53.04 E
Az Zarqā' 24 Gf 32.05N 36.06 E
Az Zāwiyah [3] 33 Bc 32.40N 12.10 E
Az Zāwiyah 33 Bc 32.45N 12.44 E
Az Zaytūn 33 Ed 29.09N 25.47 E
Azzel Matti, Sebkha- 30 Hf 26.00N 0.55 E
Az Zilfī 24 Ki 26.18N 44.48 E
Az Zubayr 24 Lg 30.23N 47.43 E

B

Baa 26 Hi 10.43S 123.03 E
Baaba 63b Ae 20.03S 163.58 E
Ba'ādwēyn 35 Hd 7.12N 47.24 E
Bá an Daingin/Dingle Bay 9 Ci 52.05N 10.15W
Baar 10 Ei 48.00N 8.30 E
Baarle-Hertog 12 Gc 51.27N 4.56 E
Baarn 12 Hb 52.14N 5.17 E
Baas, Bassure de- 12 Dd 50.30N 1.15 E
Bāb 24 Ok 23.55N 53.45 E
Baba 35 Bd 6.25N 17.07 E
Baba 15 Ei 40.55N 21.10 E
Baba Burun [Tur.] 24 Db 41.18N 31.26 E
Baba Burun [Tur.] 24 Bc 39.29N 26.04 E
Babadağ 15 Ll 37.48N 28.52 E
Baba Dağ 15 Mm 36.32N 29.10 E
Babadag 15 Le 44.54N 28.43 E
Babadag, Gora- 16 Pi 41.01N 48.29 E
Babaeski 24 Bb 41.26N 27.06 E
Bābā-Ḥeydar 24 Nf 32.20N 50.28 E
Babajevo 19 Dd 59.24N 35.55 E
Babajtag, Gora- 18 Hd 41.13N 70.16 E
Babajurt 16 Oh 43.35N 46.47 E
Bāb el Māndab=Bab el Mandeb (EN) 30 Lg 12.35N 43.25 E
Babanūsah 35 Dc 11.20N 27.48 E
Babao → Qilian 27 Hd 38.14N 100.15 E
Babaoyo 54 Cd 1.50S 79.30W
Babar, Kepulauan- 26 Ih 7.50S 129.45 E
Babar, Pulau- 57 De 7.55S 129.45 E
Babase 63a Aa 4.01S 153.42 E
Babatag, Hrebet- 18 Ge 38.00N 68.10 E
Babati 36 Gc 4.13S 35.45 E
Babbitt 43 Ib 47.43N 91.57W
B'abdā 24 Ff 33.50N 35.32 E
Bab el Mandeb (EN)=Bāb al Māndab 30 Lg 12.35N 43.25 E
Babelthuap Island 57 Ed 7.30N 134.36 E
Babenhausen [Ger.] 10 Gh 48.09N 10.15 E
Babenhausen [Ger.] 12 Ke 49.58N 8.57 E
Babeni 15 He 44.59N 24.15 E
Baberton 44 Ge 41.02N 81.38W
Bá Bheanntrai/Bantry Bay 9 Dj 51.38N 9.48W
Babian Jiang=Black River (EN) 21 Mg 20.17N 106.34 E
Babil [3] 24 Kf 32.40N 44.50 E
Babine Lake 42 Ef 54.45N 126.00W
Babino Polje 14 Lh 42.43N 17.33 E
Babit Point 51b Ab 18.03N 63.02W
Babo 26 Jg 2.33S 133.25 E
Bābol 23 Hb 36.34N 52.42 E
Babol Sar 24 Od 36.43N 52.39 E
Baboquivari Peak 46 Jk 31.46N 111.35W
Babor, Djebel- 13 Rh 36.32N 5.28 E
Baborigame 48 Fd 26.27N 107.16W
Baboua 35 Ad 5.48N 14.49 E
Babozero, Ozero- 7 Ic 66.30N 37.25 E
Babu → Hexian 27 Jg 24.28N 111.34 E
Babuna 15 Eh 41.30N 21.40 E
Babuyan 26 Hc 19.32N 121.57 E
Babuyan 26 Gd 10.01N 118.58 E
Babuyan Channel 26 Hc 18.44N 121.40 E
Babuyan Islands 21 Oh 19.15N 121.40 E
Babylon 23 Fc 32.32N 44.25 E
Bač 15 Cd 45.23N 19.14 E
Bacabachi 48 Ed 26.55N 109.24W
Bacabal 53 Lf 4.14S 44.47W
Ba-Cagan 27 Gb 45.40N 99.30 E
Bacajá, Rio- 54 Hd 3.25S 51.50W
Bacalar 48 Oh 18.43N 88.27W
Bacalar, Laguna de- 48 Oh 18.43N 88.22W
Bacalar Chico, Boca- 49 Dd 18.12N 87.53W
Bacan, Kepulauan- 26 Ig 0.35S 127.30 E
Bacan, Pulau- 26 Ig 0.35S 127.30 E
Bacău [2] 15 Jc 46.36N 27.00 E
Bacău 6 If 46.34N 26.54 E
Baccarat 11 Mf 48.27N 6.45 E
Bacchiglione 14 Ge 45.11N 12.14 E
Baceşti 15 Kc 46.51N 27.14 E
Bachaquero 49 Li 9.56N 71.08W
Bacharach 12 Jd 50.04N 7.46 E
Bacheli 25 Ge 18.40N 81.15 E
Bachiniva 48 Fc 28.45N 107.15W
Bachu/Maralwexi 27 Cd 39.46N 78.15 E
Back 38 Jd 67.15N 95.15W
Bačka 15 Cd 45.50N 19.30 E
Bac Kan 25 Ld 22.08N 105.49 E
Bačka Palanka 15 Cd 45.15N 19.22 E
Bačka Topola 15 Cd 45.49N 19.39 E
Bäckefors 8 Ef 58.48N 12.10 E
Bäckhammar 8 Fe 59.10N 14.11 E
Backnang 10 Fh 48.57N 9.26 E
Bačkovski Manastir 15 Hh 41.56N 24.51 E
Bac Lieu 25 Lg 9.17N 105.43 E
Bac Ninh 25 Ld 21.11N 106.03 E
Bacolet 51p Bb 12.02N 61.41W
Bacolod 22 Oh 10.40N 122.57 E
Bac-Phan=Tonkin (EN) 21 Mg 22.00N 105.00 E
Bacqueville, Lac- 42 Ke 58.00N 74.00W
Bacqueville-en Caux 12 Ce 49.47N 1.00 E
Bácsalmás 10 Pj 46.08N 19.20 E
Bács-Kiskun [2] 10 Pj 46.30N 19.25 E
Bacton 12 Db 52.51N 1.28 E
Bād 23 Hc 33.41N 52.01 E
Badagara 25 Ff 11.36N 75.35 E
Badagri 34 Fd 6.25N 2.53 E
Badain Jaran Shamo 21 Me 40.20N 101.40 E
Badajós, Lago- 54 Fd 3.15S 62.45W
Badajoz 6 Fh 38.53N 6.58W
Badajoz [3] 13 Ff 38.40N 6.10W
Badakhshan [3] 23 Lb 36.45N 72.00 E
Badalona 13 Oc 41.27N 2.15 E
Badanah 23 Fc 30.59N 41.02 E
Badaohao 28 Fd 41.50N 121.59 E
Badas, Kepulauan- 26 Ef 0.35N 107.06 E
Bad Aussee 14 Hc 47.36N 13.47 E
Bad Axe 44 Fd 43.48N 83.00W
Bad Bergzabern 10 Dg 49.06N 8.00 E
Bad Berleburg 12 Kc 51.04N 8.24 E
Bad Bertrich 12 Jd 50.03N 7.02 E
Bad Bramstedt 10 Fc 53.55N 9.53 E
Bad Brückenau 10 Ff 50.18N 9.45 E
Badda 35 Fd 7.55N 39.23 E
Baddo 25 Cc 27.59N 64.21 E
Bad Doberan 10 Hb 54.06N 11.54 E
Bad Driburg 12 Lc 51.44N 9.01 E
Bad Düben 10 Ie 51.36N 12.35 E
Bad Dürkheim 12 Ke 49.28N 8.12 E
Bade 26 Kh 7.10S 139.35 E
Bademli 15 Lk 38.04N 28.04 E
Baden [Aus.] 14 Kb 48.01N 16.14 E
Baden [Switz.] 14 Cc 47.28N 8.18 E
Baden-Baden 10 Eh 48.45N 8.15 E
Badenoch 9 Je 56.50N 4.00W
Baden-Württemberg [2] 10 Eh 48.30N 9.00 E
Bad Essen 12 Kb 52.19N 8.20 E
Bad Freienwalde 10 Kd 52.47N 14.02 E
Badgastein 14 Hc 47.07N 13.08 E
Bādghīsat [3] 23 Jc 35.00N 63.45 E
Bad Gleichenberg 14 Jd 46.52N 15.54 E
Bad Godesberg, Bonn- 10 Df 50.41N 7.09 E
Bad Hall 14 Ib 48.02N 14.12 E
Bad Harzburg 10 Ge 51.53N 10.34 E
Bad Herrenalb 12 Kf 48.48N 8.25 E
Bad Hersfeld 10 Ff 50.52N 9.42 E
Bad Homburg 10 Ef 50.13N 8.37 E
Bad Honnef 12 Jd 50.38N 7.12 E
Bá Dhún na nGall/Donegal Bay 5 Fe 54.30N 8.30W
Badhyz 18 Cg 35.50N 62.00 E
Badiraguato 48 Fe 25.22N 107.31W
Bad Ischl 14 Hc 47.43N 13.37 E
Bad Kissingen 10 Gf 50.12N 10.05 E
Bad Kreuznach 10 Dg 49.50N 7.52 E
Badlands [S.D.-U.S.] 45 Ee 43.30N 102.20W
Badlands [U.S.] 43 Gb 46.45N 103.30W
Bad Langensalza 10 Ge 51.06N 10.39 E
Bad Lautenberg am Harz 10 Ge 51.38N 10.28 E
Bad Liebenwerda 10 Je 51.31N 13.24 E
Bad Liebenzel 12 Kf 48.46N 8.44 E
Bad Mergentheim 10 Fg 49.29N 9.46 E
Bad Mondorf/Mondorf-les-Bains 12 Ie 49.30N 6.17 E
Bad Münster am Stein Ebernburg 12 Je 49.49N 7.51 E
Bad Münstereifel 12 Id 50.34N 6.45 E
Bad Muskau 10 Ke 51.33N 14.43 E
Bad Nauheim 12 Kd 50.22N 8.45 E
Bad Neuenahr-Ahweiler 10 Df 50.33N 7.08 E
Bad Neustadt an der Saale 10 Gf 50.20N 10.13 E
Bad Oeynhausen 12 Kb 52.12N 8.48 E
Bad Oldesloe 10 Gc 53.49N 10.23 E
Ba Don 25 Le 17.45N 106.27 E
Badou [China] 28 Df 36.27N 117.56 E
Badou [Togo] 34 Fd 7.35N 0.36 E
Bad Pyrmont 10 Fe 51.59N 9.15 E
Bad Ragaz 14 Dc 47.00N 9.30 E
Badrah 24 Kf 33.06N 45.58 E
Bad Reichenhall 10 Ii 47.44N 12.53 E
Badr Ḥunayn 23 Ee 23.44N 38.46 E
Bad River 45 Fd 44.22N 100.22W
Bad Salzuflen 12 Kb 52.05N 8.46 E
Bad Salzungen 10 Gf 50.49N 10.14 E
Bad Schwartau 10 Gc 53.55N 10.42 E
Bad Segeberg 10 Gc 53.56N 10.19 E
Bad Tölz 10 Hi 47.46N 11.34 E
Badulla 25 Gg 6.59N 81.03 E
Bad Wildungen 10 Fe 51.07N 9.07 E
Bad Wimpfen 10 Fg 49.14N 9.08 E
Baena 13 Hg 37.37N 4.19W
Baeza [Ec.] 54 Cd 0.28S 77.53W
Baeza [Sp.] 13 Ig 37.59N 3.28W
Baf/Paphos 24 Ee 34.50N 32.35 E
Bafang 34 Hd 5.09N 10.11 E
Bafatá 31 Fg 12.10N 14.40W
Bafélé 34 Cc 10.09N 10.08W
Baffin 38 Mc 68.00N 70.00W
Baffin Bay 38 Mb 73.00N 65.00W
Bafia 34 He 4.45N 11.14 E
Bafilo 34 Fd 9.21N 1.16 E
Bafing [Afr.] 30 Fg 13.49N 10.50W
Bafing [I.C.] 34 Dd 7.52N 7.07W
Bafoulabé 34 Cc 13.48N 10.50W
Bafoussam 31 Ih 5.28N 10.25 E
Bāfq 23 Ic 31.35N 55.24 E
Bāfq, Kūh-e- 24 Pg 31.20N 55.10 E
Bafra 23 Ea 41.34N 35.56 E
Bāft 24 Qh 29.14N 56.38 E
Bafwaboli 36 Eb 0.39N 26.10 E
Bafwasende 36 Eb 1.05N 27.16 E
Baga 34 Hc 13.06N 13.50 E
Bagaces 49 Eh 10.31N 85.15W
Bagagem, Rio- 55 Ha 13.58S 48.21W
Bagajevski 16 Lf 47.19N 40.25 E
Bāgalkot 25 Fe 16.11N 75.42 E
Bagamoyo 36 Gd 6.26S 38.54 E
Bagansiapi-Api 26 Df 2.09N 100.49 E
Bağarasi 15 Kl 37.42N 27.33 E
Baga Sola 35 Ac 13.32N 14.19 E
Bagata 36 Cc 3.44S 17.57 E
Bagdad 48 Ke 25.57N 97.09W
Bagdarin 20 Gf 54.30N 113.36 E
Bagdati (Majakovski) 16 Mh 42.02N 42.47 E
Bağdere 24 Ic 38.10N 40.45 E
Bagé 53 Ki 31.20S 54.06W
Bages et de Sigean, Étang de- 11 Jk 43.05N 3.01 E
Baggs 46 Lf 41.02N 107.39W
Bágh Baile na Sgealg/ Ballinskelligs Bay 9 Cj 51.50N 10.15W
Baghdād [3] 24 Kf 33.18N 44.36 E
Baghdād 22 Gf 33.21N 44.23 E
Baghdādī, Ra's- 24 Fj 24.40N 35.06 E
Bāgh-e Chenār 24 Qh 28.11N 56.54 E
Bāgh-e-Malek 24 Mg 31.32N 49.55 E
Bagheria 14 Hl 38.05N 13.30 E
Bāghīn 23 Ic 30.12N 56.48 E
Baghlān [3] 23 Kb 35.45N 69.00 E
Baghlān 23 Kb 36.13N 68.46 E
Bāglung 25 Gc 28.16N 83.36 E
Bagn 8 Cd 60.49N 9.34 E
Bagnara Calabra 14 Jl 38.17N 15.48 E
Bagnères-de-Bigorre 11 Gk 43.04N 0.09 E
Bagnères-de-Luchon 11 Gl 42.47N 0.36 E
Bagni di Lucca 14 Ef 44.01N 10.35 E
Bagno di Romagna 14 Fg 43.50N 11.57 E
Bagnolo Mella 14 Ee 45.26N 10.10 E
Bagnols-sur-Cèze 11 Kj 44.10N 4.37 E
Bago 22 Lh 17.30N 96.30 E
Bagoé 30 Gg 12.36N 6.34W
Bagolino 14 Ee 45.49N 10.28 E
Bagrationovsk 8 Ij 54.23N 20.40 E
Bagrax/Bohu 27 Ec 41.58N 86.29 E
Bagrax Hu/Bosten 21 Ke 42.00N 87.00 E
Bagua 54 Ce 5.40S 78.31W
Baguio 22 Oh 16.25N 120.36 E
Baguirmi 30 Ig 11.40N 16.20 E
Bagzane, Monts- 30 Hg 17.43N 8.45 E
Bahama Islands 38 Lg 24.15N 76.00W
Bahamas [1] 39 Lg 24.15N 76.00W
Bahamas, Canal Viejo de-= Old Bahama Channel (EN) 49 Ib 22.30N 78.05W
Bahār 24 Me 34.54N 48.26 E
Baharampur 25 Hd 24.06N 88.15 E
Baharden 19 Fh 38.28N 57.28 E
Bahardok 19 Fh 38.51N 58.24 E
Baharīyah, Wāḥāt al- 33 Ed 28.10N 29.00 E
Bahariya Oasis (EN)= Baḥarīyah, Wāḥāt al- 33 Ed 28.15N 28.57 E
Bahaur 26 Fg 3.20N 114.00 E
Bahāwalnagar 25 Ec 29.59N 73.16 E
Bahāwalpur 22 Jg 29.24N 71.41 E
Bahčisaraj 16 Hg 44.45N 33.51 E
Bahę 24 Gd 37.14N 36.34 E
Bahi 36 Gd 5.39S 35.19 E
Bahia [2] 54 Jf 12.00S 42.00W
Bahia, Islas de la- 47 Ge 16.20N 86.30W
Bahia Blanca 53 Ji 38.44S 62.16W
Bahia de Caráquez 54 Bd 0.37S 80.25W
Bahia Kino 47 Bc 28.50N 111.55W
Bahia Negra 56 Ib 20.15S 58.12W
Bahias, Cabo dos- 52 Jj 44.55S 65.32W
Bahij 24 Cg 30.56N 29.35 E
Bahinga 36 Ed 5.57S 27.06 E
Bahi Swamp 36 Gd 6.05S 35.10 E
Bahlui 15 Kb 47.08N 27.44 E
Bahmač 19 De 51.11N 32.50 E
Bahoruco, Sierra de- 49 Ld 18.10N 71.25W
Bahraich 25 Gc 27.35N 81.36 E
Bahrain (EN)=Al Baḥrayn [1] 22 Hg 26.00N 50.29 E
Baḥr al Ghazāl [3] 35 Dd 8.15N 26.50 E
Bahr ar Ramla al Kabīr 33 Ed 27.00N 26.00 E
Baḥrayn, Khalij al- 24 Nj 25.45N 50.40 E
Bahr Dar 31 Kg 11.36N 37.22 E
Bahta 20 Dd 62.20N 89.15 E
Bahusi 15 Jc 46.43N 26.42 E
Baia 15 Le 44.43N 28.40 E
Baia de Aramă 15 Fe 45.00N 22.50 E
Baia de Fier 15 Gd 45.10N 23.46 E
Baia dos Tigres 36 Bf 16.35S 11.43 E
Baia Farta 36 Be 12.37S 13.26 E
Baia Mare 15 Gb 47.40N 23.35 E
Baião 54 Id 2.41S 49.41W
Baia Sprie 15 Gb 47.40N 23.42 E
Baibiene 55 Ci 29.36S 58.10W
Baïbokoum 35 Bd 7.45N 15.41 E
Baicheng 22 Oe 45.34N 122.49 E
Baicheng/Bay 27 Dc 41.46N 81.52 E
Băicoi 15 Id 45.02N 25.51 E
Băiculeşti 15 Hd 45.04N 24.42 E
Baidoa (EN) = Isha Baydabo 31 Lh 3.04N 43.48 E
Baidou 35 Cd 5.52N 20.41 E
Baie-Comeau 39 Me 49.13N 68.10W
Baie-Mahault 50 Fd 16.16N 61.35W
Baie-Saint-Paul 42 Kg 47.27N 70.30W
Baie-Trinité 44 Na 49.24N 67.19W
Baie Verte 42 Lg 49.55N 56.11W
Baiguan → Shangyu 28 Fi 30.01N 120.53 E
Baihe 27 Je 32.46N 110.06 E
Bai He [China] 28 Bh 32.10N 112.20 E
Bai He [China] 28 Dd 40.43N 116.33 E
Baikal, Lake- (EN)=Bajkal, Ozero- 21 Md 53.00N 107.40 E
Baikal Range (EN)= Bajkalski Hrebet 21 Md 55.00N 108.40 E
Baile an Chaistil/ Ballycastle 118 Gf 55.12N 6.15W
Baile an Róba/Ballinrobe 118 Dh 53.37N 9.13W
Baile Átha Cliath/Dublin [2] 9 Gh 53.20N 6.15W
Baile Átha Cliath/Dublin 6 Fe 53.20N 6.15W
Baile Átha Luain/Athlone 9 Fh 53.25N 7.56W
Baile Átha Troim/Trim 9 Gh 53.34N 6.47W
Băile Borşa 15 Hb 47.41N 24.43 E
Baile Brigin/Balbriggan 9 Gh 53.37N 6.11W
Băile Govora 15 Hd 45.05N 24.11 E
Baile Locha Riach/Loughrea 9 Eh 53.12N 8.34W
Baile Mhistéala/ Mitchelstown 9 Ei 52.16N 8.16W
Bailén 13 If 38.06N 3.46W
Baile na Mainistreach/ Newtownabbey 9 Hg 54.42N 5.54W
Baile Nua na hArda/ Newtownards 9 Hg 54.36N 5.41W
Băile Olăneşti 15 Hd 45.12N 24.14 E
Băileşti 15 Ge 44.01N 23.21 E
Bailleul 12 Ce 49.12N 0.26 E
Bailleul 12 Ed 50.44N 2.44 E
Ba Illi 35 Bc 10.31N 16.29 E
Bailong Jiang 27 Ie 32.42N 105.15 E
Bailundo 36 Ce 12.10S 15.56 E
Baima 27 He 33.05N 100.29 E
Bain 12 Ba 53.04N 0.12W
Bainbridge 43 Ke 30.54N 84.34W
Bain-de-Bretagne 11 Eg 47.50N 1.41W
Baines Drift 37 Dd 22.30S 28.43 E
Baing 26 Hi 10.14S 120.34 E
Baingoin 27 Ee 31.36N 89.48 E
Baiquan 27 Mb 47.38N 126.04 E
Bā'ir 24 Gg 30.46N 36.41 E
Bā'ir, Wādī- 24 Gg 31.12N 37.31 E
Baird 45 Gj 32.24N 99.24W
Baird Inlet 40 Gd 60.45N 164.00W
Baird Mountains 40 Gc 67.35N 161.30W
Baird Peninsula 42 Jc 69.00N 75.15W
Bairiki 58 Id 1.20N 173.01 E
Bairin Youqi (Daban) 27 Kc 43.30N 118.37 E
Bairin Zuoqi (Lindong) 27 Kc 43.59N 119.22 E
Bairnsdale 58 Fh 37.50S 147.38 E
Bais 26 He 9.35N 123.07 E
Bai Shan 27 Fc 40.53N 93.48 E
Baisogala/Bajsogala 8 Ji 55.35N 23.44 E
Baitou Shan 21 Oe 42.00N 128.00 E
Baitoushan Tian Chi 28 Jc 42.00N 128.03 E
Baixiang 28 Cf 37.29N 114.44 E
Baixo Alentejo 13 Dg 37.55N 8.10W
Baixo Guandu 54 Jg 19.31S 41.01W
Baixo Longa 36 Cf 15.42S 18.38 E
Baiyanghe 27 Ec 43.12N 88.28 E
Baiyü 27 Ge 31.13N 98.51 E
Baja 10 Oj 46.11N 18.58 E
Baja, Punta- [Mex.] 48 Dc 28.25N 111.45W
Baja, Punta- [Pas.] 65d Ab 27.10S 109.22W
Baja California=Lower California (EN) 38 Hg 28.00N 112.00W
Baja California Sur [2] 47 Bd 25.50N 111.50W
Bājah [3] 32 Ib 36.30N 9.30 E
Bājah 32 Ib 36.44N 9.11 E
Bajalān 24 Md 37.18N 48.47 E
Bajan 27 Jb 49.15N 111.58 E
Bajanaul 19 He 50.47N 75.42 E
Bajandaj 20 Ff 53.04N 105.30 E
Bajan-Delger 27 Jb 45.55N 112.15 E
Bajangol 20 Ff 50.40N 103.25 E
Bajan-Hongor 22 Me 46.20N 100.40 E
Bajan-Ula [Mong.] 27 Jb 49.07N 112.45 E
Bajan-Ula [Mong.] 27 Gb 47.05N 95.15 E
Bajan-Under 27 Gc 44.45N 98.45 E
Baja Verapaz [3] 49 Bf 15.05N 90.20W
Bajawa 26 Hh 8.47S 120.59 E
Bajčunas 16 Rf 47.17N 53.03 E
Bajdarackaja Guba 20 Bc 69.00N 67.30 E
Bajdarata 17 Nb 68.12N 68.18 E
Bajdrag Gol 27 Hb 45.10N 100.45 E
Bājgīrān 24 Rd 37.36N 58.24 E
Baj-Haak 20 Ef 51.07N 94.34 E
Bajiazi 28 Jc 42.41N 129.13 E
Bajina Bašta 15 Cf 43.58N 19.34 E
Bajkal 20 Ff 51.53N 104.47 E
Bajkal, Ozero-=Baikal, Lake- (EN) 21 Md 53.00N 107.40 E
Bajkalovo 17 Kh 57.24N 63.40 E
Bajkalsk 20 Ff 51.30N 104.05 E
Bajkalski Hrebet=Baikal Range (EN) 21 Md 55.00N 108.40 E
Bajkit 20 Ed 61.41N 96.25 E
Bajkonur 19 Gf 47.50N 66.07 E
Bajmak 19 Fe 52.36N 58.19 E
Bajmba, Mount- 59 Ke 29.20S 152.05 E
Bajmok 15 Cd 45.58N 19.26 E
Bajo Baudó 54 Cc 4.58N 77.22W

Index Symbols

[1] Independent Nation
[2] State, Region
[3] District, County
[4] Municipality
[5] Colony, Dependency
Continent
Physical Region
Historical or Cultural Region
Mount, Mountain
Volcano
Hill
Mountains, Mountain Range
Hills, Escarpment
Plateau, Upland
Pass, Gap
Plain, Lowland
Delta
Salt Flat
Valley, Canyon
Crater, Cave
Karst Features
Depression
Polder
Desert, Dunes
Forest, Woods
Heath, Steppe
Oasis
Cape, Point
Coast, Beach
Cliff
Peninsula
Isthmus
Sandbank
Island
Atoll
Rock, Reef
Islands, Archipelago
Rocks, Reefs
Coral Reef
Well, Spring
Geyser
River, Stream
Waterfall Rapids
River Mouth, Estuary
Lake
Salt Lake
Intermittent Lake
Reservoir
Swamp, Pond
Canal
Glacier
Ice Shelf, Pack Ice
Ocean
Sea
Gulf, Bay
Strait, Fjord
Lagoon
Bank
Seamount
Tablemount
Ridge
Shelf
Basin
Escarpment, Sea Scarp
Fracture
Trench, Abyss
National Park, Reserve
Point of Interest
Recreation Site
Cave, Cavern
Historic Site
Ruins
Wall, Walls
Church, Abbey
Temple
Scientific Station
Airport
Port
Lighthouse
Mine
Tunnel
Dam, Bridge

Bajo Boquete 49 Fi 8.46N 82.26W
Bajram-Ali 19 Gh 37.39N 62.12 E
Bajram Curri 15 Dg 42.21N 20.04 E
Bajsogala/Baisogala 8 Ji 55.35N 23.44 E
Bajsun 18 Fe 38.14N 67.12 E
Bajun Islands 30 Li 0.50S 42.15 E
Bajžansaj 18 Gc 43.13N 69.56 E
Baka 35 Ee 4.33N 30.05 E
Bakacak 15 Ki 40.12N 27.05 E
Bakadžicite 15 Jg 42.25N 26.43 E
Bakal 19 Fe 54.56N 58.48 E
Bakala 35 Cd 6.11N 20.22 E
Bakanas 19 Hg 44.48N 76.15 E
Bakar 14 Ie 45.18N 14.32 E
Bakčar 20 De 57.01N 82.10 E
Bake 26 Dg 3.03S 100.16 E
Bakel 34 Cc 14.54N 12.27W
Baker [Ca.-U.S.] 46 Gi 35.15N 116.02W
Baker [La.-U.S.] 45 Kk 30.35N 91.10W
Baker [Mt.-U.S.] 43 Gb 46.22N 104.17W
Baker [Or.-U.S.] 43 Dc 44.47N 117.50W
Baker, Mount- 43 Cb 48.47N 121.49W
Baker Island 57 Jd 0.15N 176.27W
Baker Lake 39 Jc 64.10N 95.30W
Baker Lake 38 Jc 64.10N 95.30W
Bakersfield 39 Hf 35.23N 119.01W
Bā Kēv 25 Lf 13.42N 107.12 E
Bakhma 24 Kd 36.38N 44.17 E
Bakhtarān (Kermānshāh) 22 Gf 34.19N 47.04 E
Bakhtarān [3] 23 Gc 34.15N 47.20 E
Bakhtegān, Daryācheh-ye 24 Ph 29.20N 54.05 E
Bakhūn, Kūh-e- 23 Id 27.56N 56.18 E
Bakir 24 Bc 38.55N 27.00 E
Bakırköy, İstanbul 15 Li 40.59N 28.52 E
Baklan 15 Ml 37.58N 29.36 E
Bako 35 Fd 7.19N 35.08 E
Bako [Eth.] 35 Fd 9.05N 37.07 E
Bako [Eth.] 35 Fd 5.50N 36.37 E
Bakony = Bakony Mountains (EN) 5 Hf 47.15N 17.50 E
Bakony Mountains (EN) = Bakony 5 Hf 47.15N 17.50 E
Bakool [3] 35 Ge 4.10N 43.50 E
Bakouma 35 Cd 5.42N 22.47 E
Bakoye 34 Cc 13.49N 10.50W
Bakpulād 24 Qc 38.10N 57.00 E
Baksan 16 Mh 43.40N 43.28 E
Baksan 16 Nh 43.42N 44.03 E
Baku 6 Kg 40.23N 49.51 E
Bakum 12 Kb 52.44N 8.11 E
Bakungan 26 Cf 2.56N 97.30 E
Bakuriani 16 Mi 41.43N 43.31 E
Bakutis Coast 66 Of 74.45S 120.00W
Balā 24 Ec 39.34N 33.08 E
Bala, Cerros de- 54 Ef 14.30S 67.40W
Balabac 26 Ge 7.59N 117.04 E
Balabac 26 Ge 7.57N 117.01 E
Balabac, Selat- = Balabac Strait (EN) 21 Ni 7.40N 117.00 E
Balabac Strait (EN) = Balabac, Selat- 21 Ni 7.40N 117.00 E
Ba'labakk 24 Ge 34.00N 36.12 E
Balabalangan, Kepulauan- 26 Gg 2.20S 117.25 E
Balaban Dağı 24 Hb 40.28N 39.15 E
Balabanovo 16 Jb 55.11N 36.40 E
Balabio 63b Be 20.07S 164.11 E
Balaci 15 He 44.21N 24.55 E
Bal'ad 35 He 2.22N 45.24 E
Balad 24 Ke 34.01N 44.01 E
Balādīn as Sakrān 24 Kj 25.12N 44.37 E
Baladiyat 'Adan = Aden (EN) 22 Gh 12.46N 45.01 E
Balad Rūz 24 Kf 33.42N 45.05 E
Balagannoje 20 Je 59.43N 149.15 E
Balagansk 20 Ff 53.58N 103.02 E
Bālāghāt 25 Gd 21.48N 80.11 E
Bālāghāt Range 25 Fe 18.45N 76.30 E
Balagne 11a Aa 42.35N 8.50 E
Balaguer 13 Mc 41.47N 0.49 E
Balahna 7 Kh 56.31N 43.37 E
Balahta 20 Ee 55.24N 91.37 E
Balaka 36 Fe 14.59S 34.57 E
Balaklava 16 Hg 44.31N 33.34 E
Balakleja 19 Df 49.27N 36.52 E
Balakovo 6 Ke 52.02N 47.45 E
Balama 37 Fb 13.16S 38.36 E
Balambangam, Pulau- 26 Ge 7.17N 116.55 E
Bālā Morghāb 23 Jb 35.35N 63.20 E
Balan Dağı 15 Lm 36.52N 28.20 E
Balankanche 48 Og 20.45N 88.30W
Balasan 26 Hd 11.28N 123.05 E
Balasore → Bāleshwar 25 Hd 21.30N 86.56 E
Balašov 19 Ee 51.33N 43.10 E
Balassagyarmat 10 Ph 48.05N 19.18 E
Balāţ 33 Ed 25.33N 29.16 E
Balaton 5 Hf 46.50N 17.45 E
Balatonfüred 10 Nj 46.57N 17.53 E
Balatonkeresztúr 10 Nj 46.42N 17.23 E
Balaurin 26 Hh 8.15S 123.43 E
Bălăuseri 15 Hc 46.24N 24.41 E
Balayan 26 Hd 13.57N 120.44 E
Balazote 13 Jf 38.53N 2.08W
Balbi, Mount- 60 Ei 5.55S 154.59 E
Balboa Heights 47 Ig 8.57N 79.33W
Balbriggan/Baile Brigin 9 Gh 53.37N 6.11W
Balby 8 Ei 55.40N 13.20 E
Balcarce 56 Ie 37.50S 58.15W
Balcarce, Sierras de- 55 Cm 37.50S 58.40W
Bălceşti 15 Ge 44.37N 23.57 E
Balčik 15 Lf 43.25N 28.10 E
Balclutha 61 Ci 46.14S 169.44 E
Bald Eagle Mountain 44 Ie 41.00N 77.45W
Bald Head 59 Dg 35.07S 118.01 E
Bald Knob 44 Hg 37.56N 79.51W
Bald Knob 45 Ki 35.19N 91.34W
Baldo, Monte- 14 Ee 45.40N 10.50 E
Baldock 12 Bc 51.59N 0.11W
Baldone 8 Kh 56.41N 24.22 E
Baldur 45 Gb 49.23N 99.15W
Baldwin 44 Ed 43.54N 85.51W
Baldy Peak 43 Fe 33.55N 109.35W
Bale [3] 35 Gd 6.00N 41.00 E
Bâle/Basel 6 Gf 47.30N 7.30 E
Baleares [3] 13 Oe 39.30N 3.00 E
Balearic Islands (EN) = Baleares, Islas-/Balears, Illes- 5 Gh 39.30N 3.00 E
Balearic Islands (EN) = Balears, Illes-/Baleares, Islas- 5 Gh 39.30N 3.00 E
Balears, Illes-/Baleares, Islas- = Balearic Islands (EN) 5 Gh 39.30N 3.00 E
Balease, Gunung- 26 Hg 2.24S 120.33 E
Baleia, Ponta de- 52 Mg 17.40S 36.07W
Baleine, Rivière à la- 42 Ke 58.15N 67.38W
Balej 20 Gf 51.35N 116.38 E
Balen 12 Hc 51.10N 5.09 E
Baler 26 Hc 15.46N 121.34 E
Bāleshwar 25 Hd 21.30N 86.56 E
Balezino 19 Fd 57.59N 53.02 E
Balfate 49 Df 15.48N 86.25W
Bălgarija = Bulgaria (EN) [1] 6 Ig 43.00N 25.00 E
Balgazyn 20 Ef 50.58N 95.12 E
Balguntay 27 Ec 42.45N 86.18 E
Balḩāf 23 Fg 13.58N 48.11 E
Balhaš 22 Je 46.49N 74.59 E
Balhaš, Ozero- = Balkhash, Lake- (EN) 21 Je 46.00N 74.00 E
Balho 35 Gc 12.00N 42.10 E
Balholm 7 Bf 61.12N 6.33 E
Bali [3] 26 Gh 8.30S 115.00 E
Bali, Laut- = Bali Sea (EN) 21 Nj 7.45S 115.30 E
Bali, Pulau- 21 Nj 8.20S 115.00 E
Bali, Selat- = Bali Strait (EN) 26 Fh 8.18S 114.25 E
Baliceaux Island 51n Bb 12.57N 61.08W
Baliem 26 Kg 4.25S 138.59 E
Balige 26 Cf 2.20N 99.04 E
Balikesir 23 Cb 39.39N 27.53 E
Balık Gölü 24 Jc 39.45N 43.36 E
Balīkh, Nahr- 24 He 36.05N 39.10 E
Balikpapan 22 Nj 1.17S 116.50 E
Balimbing 26 Dh 5.55S 104.34 E
Balimo 60 Ci 8.03S 142.56 E
Balingen 10 Eh 48.17N 8.51 E
Balinqiao 28 Ec 43.16N 118.38 E
Balintang Channel 26 Hc 19.49N 121.40 E
Bali Sea (EN) = Bali, Laut- 21 Nj 7.45S 115.30 E
Bali Strait (EN) = Bali, Selat- 26 Fh 8.18S 114.25 E
Balitung, Palau- 21 Mj 2.50S 107.55 E
Baliza 55 Fc 16.15S 52.25W
Balk, Gaasterland- 12 Hb 52.54N 5.36 E
Balkan Mountains (EN) = Stara Planina 5 Ig 43.15N 25.00 E
Balkan Peninsula (EN) 5 Ig 41.30N 23.00 E
Balkanskaja oblast 19 Fh 39.50N 55.00 E
Balkašino 19 Ge 52.32N 68.46 E
Balkh 23 Kb 36.46N 66.54 E
Balkh [3] 23 Kb 36.30N 67.00 E
Balkhash, Lake- (EN) = Balhaš, Ozero- 21 Je 46.00N 74.00 E
Balladonia 59 Ef 32.27S 123.51 E
Ballagen 7 Db 68.20N 16.50 E
Ballaghaderreen/Bealach an Doirin 9 Eh 53.55N 8.35W
Ballantrae 9 If 55.06N 5.00W
Ballantyne Strait 42 Ga 77.30N 115.00W
Ballarat 58 Fh 37.34S 143.52 E
Ballard, Lake- 59 Ee 29.25S 120.55 E
Ballé 34 Db 15.20N 8.36W
Ballenas, Bahía- 48 Cd 26.45N 113.25W
Ballenas, Canal de- 48 Cc 29.10N 113.25W
Ballenero, Canal- 56 Fh 54.50S 71.00W
Ballenita, Punta- 56 Fc 25.46S 70.44W
Balleny Islands 66 Ke 66.35S 162.50 E
Balleroy 12 Be 49.11N 0.50W
Balleza 48 Fd 26.57N 106.21W
Balli 15 Ki 40.50N 27.03 E
Ballia 25 Gc 25.45N 84.10 E
Ballina 59 Ke 28.52S 153.33 E
Ballina/Béal an Átha 9 Dg 54.07N 9.09W
Ballinasloe/Béal Átha na Sluaighe 9 Eh 53.20N 8.13W
Ballinger 45 Gk 31.44N 99.57W
Ballinrobe/Baile an Róba 9 Dh 53.37N 9.13W
Ballinskelligs Bay/Bágh Baile na Sgealg 9 Cj 51.50N 10.15W
Ballshi 15 Ci 40.36N 19.44 E
Ball's Pyramid 57 Gh 31.45S 159.15 E
Ballycastle/Baile an Chaistil 9 Gf 55.12N 6.15W
Ballyhaunis/Béal Átha hAmhnais 9 Eh 53.46N 8.46W
Ballymena/An Baile Meánach 9 Gg 54.52N 6.17W
Ballyshannon/Béal Átha Seanaidh 9 Eg 54.30N 8.11W
Balmazújváros 10 Ri 47.37N 21.21 E
Balmoral Castle 9 Jd 57.02N 3.15W
Balneario Orense 55 Cn 38.49S 59.46W
Balneario Oriente 55 Bn 38.55S 60.32W
Balombo 36 Be 12.21S 14.43 E
Balonne River 57 Fg 28.47S 147.56 E
Balota, Virful- 15 Gd 45.18N 23.53 E
Balovale 31 Jj 13.33S 23.07 E
Balrāmpur 25 Gc 27.26N 82.11 E
Balranald 59 If 34.38S 143.33 E
Balş 15 He 44.21N 24.06 E
Balsas [Braz.] 54 Ie 7.31S 46.02W
Balsas [Mex.] 48 Jh 18.00N 99.47W
Balsas, Depresión del- 48 Ih 18.00N 100.10W
Balsas, Rio- [Mex.] 38 Ih 17.55N 102.10W
Balsas, Rio- [Pan.] 49 Ii 8.15N 77.59W
Balsas, Rio das- [Braz.] 54 Ie 9.58S 47.52W
Balsas, Rio das- [Braz.] 54 Je 7.14S 44.33W
Bålsta 8 Ge 59.35N 17.30 E
Balsthal 14 Bc 47.19N 7.42 E
Balta 16 Ff 47.57N 29.38 E
Baltanás 13 Hc 41.56N 4.15W
Baltasar Brum 56 Id 30.44S 57.19W
Baltaţi 15 Kb 47.13N 27.09 E
Baltic Sea (EN) = Baltijas Jūra 5 Hd 57.00N 19.00 E
Baltic Sea (EN) = Baltijos Jura 5 Hd 57.00N 19.00 E
Baltic Sea (EN) = Balti Meri 5 Hd 57.00N 19.00 E
Baltic Sea- (EN) = Baltiskoje More 5 Hd 57.00N 19.00 E
Baltic Sea (EN) = Bałtyckie, Morze- 5 Hd 57.00N 19.00 E
Baltic Sea (EN) = Itämeri 5 Hd 57.00N 19.00 E
Baltic Sea (EN) = Östersjön 5 Hd 57.00N 19.00 E
Baltic Sea (EN) = Østersøen 5 Hd 57.00N 19.00 E
Baltic Sea (EN) = Ostsee 5 Hd 57.00N 19.00 E
Baltijas Jūra = Baltic Sea (EN) 5 Hd 57.00N 19.00 E
Baltijos Jura = Baltic Sea (EN) 5 Hd 57.00N 19.00 E
Baltijsk 19 Be 54.40N 19.58 E
Baltijskaja Grjada 7 Fi 55.00N 25.00 E
Baltīm 33 Fc 31.33N 31.05 E
Balti Meri = Baltic Sea (EN) 5 Hd 57.00N 19.00 E
Baltimore 39 Lf 39.17N 76.37W
Baltiskoje More = Baltic Sea (EN) 5 Hd 57.00N 19.00 E
Baltit (Hunza) 25 Ea 36.20N 74.40 E
Baltoj Voke 8 Kj 54.24N 25.16 E
Baltrum 10 Dc 53.44N 7.23 E
Bałtyckie, Morze- = Baltic Sea (EN) 5 Hd 57.00N 19.00 E
Baluarte, Rio- 48 Ff 22.49N 106.02W
Baluchistān = Baluchistan (EN) 21 Ig 28.00N 63.00 E
Baluchistān = Baluchistan (EN) [3] 25 Cc 28.00N 63.00 E
Baluchistan (EN) = Baluchistān [3] 25 Cc 28.00N 63.00 E
Baluchistan (EN) = Baluchistān 21 Ig 28.00N 63.00 E
Balupe 8 Lh 56.54N 27.02 E
Balurghat 25 Hc 25.13N 88.46 E
Balvard 24 Qh 29.25N 56.06 E
Balve 12 Jc 51.20N 7.52 E
Balver Wald 12 Jc 51.21N 7.51 E
Balvi/Balvy 7 Gh 57.08N 27.20 E
Balvy/Balvi 7 Gh 57.08N 27.20 E
Balya 24 Bc 39.45N 27.35 E
Balygyčan 20 Kd 64.00N 154.10 E
Balykši 16 Qf 47.02N 51.55 E
Bām 24 Qd 36.58N 57.59 E
Bam 23 Id 29.06N 58.21 E
Bama 34 Hc 11.31N 13.41 E
Bamaji Lake 45 Ka 51.09N 91.25W
Bamako 31 Gg 12.38N 8.00W
Bamako [3] 34 Dc 13.00N 8.00W
Bamba 34 Eb 17.02N 1.24W
Bambama 36 Bc 2.32S 13.33 E
Bambana, Rio- 49 Fg 13.27N 83.50W
Bambangando 36 Df 16.59S 20.57 E
Bambari 31 Jh 5.45N 20.40 E
Bamberg 10 Gg 49.42N 10.52 E
Bambesa 36 Eb 3.28N 25.43 E
Bambesi 35 Ed 9.45N 34.44 E
Bambey 34 Bc 14.42N 16.28W
Bambezi 37 Dc 19.57S 28.55 E
Bambili 36 Eb 3.39N 26.07 E
Bambio 35 Be 3.54N 16.59 E
Bamboi 34 Ed 8.10N 2.02W
Bambouti 35 Dd 5.24N 27.12 E
Bambouto, Monts- 30 Ih 5.44N 10.04 E
Bambui 55 Je 20.01S 45.58W
Bam Co 27 Fe 31.15N 90.32 E
Bamenda 34 Hd 5.56N 10.10 E
Bāmīān [3] 23 Kc 34.45N 67.15 E
Bāmīān 23 Kc 34.50N 67.50 E
Bamiancheng 28 Gc 43.15N 124.00 E
Bamiantong → Muling 28 Kb 44.55N 130.32 E
Bamingui 35 Cd 7.34N 20.11 E
Bamingui 30 Ih 8.33N 19.05 E
Bamingui-Bangoran [3] 35 Cd 7.50N 20.15 E
Bampūr 23 Jd 27.12N 60.27 E
Bampūr 23 Id 27.18N 59.06 E
Banaadir 30 Lh 1.00N 44.00 E
Banaadir [3] 35 He 2.00N 45.15 E
Banaba Island 57 He 0.52S 169.35 E
Banabuiú, Açude- 54 Ke 5.20S 39.00W
Banagi 36 Fc 2.16S 34.51 E
Banalia 36 Eb 1.33N 25.20 E
Banamba 34 Dc 13.32N 7.27W
Bananal, Ilha do- [Braz.] 52 Kg 11.30S 50.15W
Bananal, Ilha do- [Braz.] 55 Dc 17.05S 56.25W
Bananga 25 Ig 6.57N 93.54 E
Banarli 15 Kh 41.04N 27.20 E
Banās 25 Fc 25.54N 76.45 E
Banās, Ra's- 30 Kf 23.54N 35.48 E
Banat 5 If 45.30N 21.00 E
Banat 15 Dd 45.30N 21.00 E
Banaz 24 Cc 38.46N 29.46 E
Banaz 24 Cc 38.12N 29.14 E
Banbar 27 Fe 30.48N 94.52 E
Banbridge/Droichead na Banna 9 Gg 54.21N 6.16W
Banbury 9 Li 52.04N 1.20W
Banco, Punta- 49 Fi 8.23N 83.09W
Bancroft 44 Ic 45.03N 77.51W
Bānda 25 Gc 25.29N 80.20 E
Banda, Kepulauan- = Banda Islands (EN) 26 Ig 4.35S 129.55 E
Banda, Laut- = Banda Sea (EN) 57 De 5.00S 128.00 E
Banda, Punta- 48 Ab 31.45N 116.45W
Banda Aceh 22 Li 5.34N 95.20 E
Bandai-San 29 Gc 37.38N 140.04 E
Banda Islands (EN) = Banda, Kepulauan- 26 Ig 4.35S 129.55 E
Bandak 8 Ce 59.25N 8.15 E
Bandama 30 Gh 5.10N 4.58W
Bandama Blanc 34 Dd 6.54N 5.31W
Bandar Beheshtī 23 Jd 25.18N 60.37 E
Bandar-e 'Abbās 22 Hg 27.11N 56.17 E
Bandar-e Anzalī 23 Gb 37.28N 49.27 E
Bandar-e Būshehr 22 Hg 28.59N 50.50 E
Bandar-e Chīrū 24 Oi 26.43N 53.43 E
Bandar-e Deylam 23 Hg 30.05N 50.07 E
Bandar-e-Gaz 24 Od 36.47N 53.59 E
Bandar-e-Khomeynī 24 Mg 30.25N 49.08 E
Bandar-e Lengeh 23 Hd 26.33N 54.53 E
Bandar-e Māh Shahr 23 Gc 30.33N 49.12 E
Bandar-e Maqām 23 Hd 26.56N 53.29 E
Bandar-e Moghūyeh 24 Pi 26.35N 54.31 E
Bandar-e-Rīg 24 Nh 29.29N 50.38 E
Bandar-e-Torkeman 23 Gf 30.45N 51.33 E
Bandar Seri Begawan 22 Ni 4.53N 114.56 E
Banda Sea (EN) = Banda, Laut- 57 De 5.00S 128.00 E
Bande 13 Eb 42.02N 7.58W
Bandeira, Pico da- 52 Lh 20.26S 41.47W
Bandeirantes 55 Ga 13.41S 50.48W
Bandeirantes, Ilha dos- 55 Ff 23.22S 53.50W
Bandera 56 Hc 28.54S 62.16W
Bandera, Alto- 49 Ld 18.49N 70.37W
Banderas, Bahía de- 47 Cd 20.40N 105.25W
Bandiagara 34 Ec 14.20N 3.37W
Bandiat 11 Gi 45.46N 0.20 E
Bandırma 23 Ca 40.20N 27.58 E
Bandirma Körfezi 15 Ki 40.25N 28.00 E
Bandol 11 Lk 43.08N 5.45 E
Bandon 46 Ce 43.07N 124.25W
Bandon/Abhainn na Bandan 9 Ej 51.40N 8.30W
Bandon/Droichead na Bandan 9 Ej 51.45N 8.45W
Ban Don, Ao- 25 Jg 9.20N 99.25 E
Bandundu [2] 36 Cc 5.00S 17.00 E
Bandundu 31 Ii 3.18S 17.20 E
Bandung 22 Mj 6.54S 107.36 E
Bāneh 24 Ke 35.59N 45.53 E
Banes 47 Id 20.58N 75.43W
Banff [Alta.-Can.] 42 Ff 51.10N 115.34W
Banff [Scot.-U.K.] 9 Kd 57.40N 2.31W
Banfora 34 Ec 10.38N 4.46W
Banga 36 Dd 5.57S 20.28 E
Bangalore 22 Jh 12.59N 77.35 E
Bangangté 34 Hd 5.09N 10.31 E
Bangar 26 Gf 4.43N 115.04 E
Bangassou 31 Jh 4.44N 22.49 E
Bangeta, Mount- 60 Di 6.16S 147.04 E
Banggai 26 Hg 1.34S 123.30 E
Banggai, Kepulauan- = Banggai Archipelago (EN) 26 Hg 1.30S 123.15 E
Banggai, Selat- 26 Hg 1.55S 124.00 E
Banggai Archipelago (EN) = Banggai, Kepulauan- 26 Hg 1.30S 123.15 E
Banggi, Pulau- 26 Ge 7.17N 117.12 E
Banghāzī = Benghazi (EN) 31 Je 32.07N 20.04 E
Banghāzī = Benghazi (EN) [3] 33 Dd 27.00N 20.30 E
Bangka, Pulau- [Indon.] 26 If 1.48N 125.09 E
Bangka, Pulau- [Indon.] 21 Mj 2.15S 106.00 E
Bangka, Selat- = Bangka Strait (EN) 26 Eg 2.20S 105.45 E
Bangkalan 26 Fh 7.02S 112.44 E
Bangka Strait (EN) = Bangka, Selat- 26 Eg 2.20S 105.45 E
Bangkinang 26 Df 0.21N 101.02 E
Bangko 26 Dg 2.05S 102.17 E
Bangkok (EN) = Krung Thep 22 Mh 13.45N 100.31 E
Bangladesh [1] 22 Kg 24.00N 90.00 E
Bangli 26 Gh 8.27S 115.21 E
Bangolo 34 Dd 7.01N 7.09W
Bangong Co 27 Ce 33.45N 79.15 E
Bangor [Me.-U.S.] 43 Nc 44.49N 68.47W
Bangor [Wales-U.K.] 9 Ih 53.13N 4.08W
Bangor/Beannchar 9 Hg 54.40N 5.40W
Bangoran 35 Bd 8.42N 19.06 E
Bangsund 7 Cd 64.24N 11.24 E
Bangu 36 Dd 9.05S 23.44 E
Bangued 26 Hc 17.36N 120.37 E
Bangui [C.A.R.] 31 Ih 4.22N 18.35 E
Bangui [Phil.] 26 Hc 18.32N 120.46 E
Bangweulu, Lake- 30 Jj 11.05S 29.45 E
Bangweulu Swamps 36 Fe 11.30S 30.15 E
Banhā 33 Fc 30.28N 31.11 E
Ban Houayxay 25 Kd 20.18N 100.26 E
Bani 30 Gg 14.30N 4.12W
Bani 47 Je 18.17N 70.20W
Bani, Jbel- 30 Gf 28.30N 9.00W
Bani Bangou 34 Fb 15.03N 2.42 E
Banie 10 Kc 53.08N 14.38 E
Banifing 34 Dc 12.43N 6.25W
Banī Forūr, Jazīreh-ye- 24 Pi 26.07N 54.28 E
Banihal Pass 25 Fb 33.15N 75.09 E
Banija 14 Ke 45.10N 16.10 E
Banikoara 34 Fc 11.18N 2.26 E
Banī ma 'Āriḍ 33 Ie 20.42N 47.42 E
Banī Mazār 33 Fd 28.30N 30.48 E
Banī Muḩammadīyāt 24 Di 27.17N 31.05 E
Banī Suwayf 33 Fd 29.05N 31.05 E
Banī Tonb 24 Pi 26.12N 54.56 E
Banī Walīd 33 Bc 31.46N 13.59 E
Bāniyās 23 Ec 33.15N 35.41 E
Banja 15 Hg 42.33N 24.50 E
Banja Koviljača 15 Ce 44.30N 19.11 E
Banja Luka 14 Lf 44.46N 17.10 E
Banjarmarsin 22 Nj 3.20S 114.35 E
Banjul 31 Fg 13.27N 16.35W
Bank 16 Pj 39.27N 49.14 E
Bankas 34 Ec 14.05N 3.31W
Bankeryd 8 Fg 57.51N 14.07 E
Banket 37 Ec 17.23S 30.24 E
Bankhead Lake 44 Di 33.30N 87.15W
Bankilaré 34 Fc 14.35N 0.44 E
Bankja 15 Gg 42.42N 23.08 E
Ban Kongmi 25 Lf 14.31N 106.55 E
Banks [Can.] 38 Gb 73.15N 121.30W
Banks [Can.] 42 Ef 53.25N 130.10W
Banks, Iles- = Banks Islands (EN) 57 Hf 13.50S 167.35 E
Banks Island 59 Ib 10.10S 142.15 E
Banks Islands (EN) = Banks, Iles- 57 Hf 13.50S 167.35 E
Banks Lake 46 Fc 47.45N 119.15W
Banks Peninsula 57 Ii 43.40S 172.40 E
Banks Strait 59 Jh 40.40S 148.10 E
Bann/An Bhanna 9 Gf 55.10N 6.46W
Ban Na San 25 Jg 8.53N 99.17 E
Bannerman Town 44 Im 24.09N 76.09W
Banning 46 Gj 33.56N 116.52W
Bannock Range 46 Ie 42.30N 112.20W
Bannu 25 Eb 32.59N 70.36 E
Bañolas/Banyoles 13 Ob 42.07N 2.46 E
Bánovce nad Bebravou 10 Oh 48.44N 18.15 E
Banqiao 27 Hf 25.28N 104.02 E
Banská Bystrica 10 Ph 48.44N 19.09 E
Banská Štiavnica 10 Oh 48.27N 18.55 E
Bansko 15 Gh 41.50N 23.29 E
Bānswāra 25 Ed 23.33N 74.27 E
Banta 35 Ge 1.13N 42.30 E
Bantenan, Tanjung- 26 Fh 8.47S 114.33 E
Bantry/Beanntraí 9 Dj 51.41N 9.27W
Bantry Bay/Bá Bheanntraí 9 Dj 51.38N 9.48W
Bañuela 13 Hf 38.24N 4.11W
Banyak, Kepulauan- = Banyak Islands (EN) 26 Cf 2.10N 97.15 E
Banyak Islands (EN) = Banyak, Kepulauan- 26 Cf 2.10N 97.15 E
Banyo 34 Hd 6.45N 11.49 E
Banyoles/Bañolas 13 Ob 42.07N 2.46 E
Banyuls-sur-Mer 11 Jl 42.29N 3.08 E
Banyuwangi 22 Nj 8.12S 114.21 E
Banzare Coast 66 Ie 67.00S 126.00 E
Banzare Seamounts (EN) 66 Df 58.50S 77.44 E
Banzart [3] 32 Ib 37.00N 9.30 E
Banzart = Bizerte (EN) 31 He 37.17N 9.52 E
Banzart, Buḩayrat- 14 Dm 37.11N 9.52 E
Bao'an 27 Jg 22.35N 114.10 E
Bao'an → Zhidan 27 Id 36.48N 108.46 E
Baochang → Taibus Qi 27 Kc 41.55N 115.22 E
Baode 27 Jd 38.59N 111.07 E
Baodi 28 De 39.43N 117.18 E
Baoding 22 Nf 38.47N 115.30 E
Baofeng [China] 27 Je 33.48N 113.14 E
Baofeng [China] 28 Bh 33.52N 113.04 E
Baoji 22 Mf 34.26N 107.12 E
Baokang 27 Je 31.49N 111.13 E
Baokang → Horqin Zuoyi Zhongqi 27 Lc 44.06N 123.19 E
Bao Loc 25 Lf 11.32N 107.48 E
Baoqing 27 Nb 46.20N 132.11 E
Baoro 35 Bd 5.40N 15.58 E
Baoshan 22 Lg 25.09N 99.12 E
Baotou 22 Me 40.38N 110.00 E
Baoulé [Afr.] 30 Gg 12.35N 6.34W
Baoulé [Mali] 30 Gg 13.33N 9.54W
Baoying 28 Eh 33.15N 119.18 E
Bapaume 11 Id 50.06N 2.51 E
Baqên (Dartang) 27 Fe 31.58N 94.00 E
Bāqerābād 24 Ne 34.56N 50.50 E
Ba'qūbah 23 Fc 33.45N 44.38 E
Baquedano 56 Gb 23.20S 69.51W
Bar 12 Ge 49.42N 4.50 E
Bar 16 Ee 49.02N 27.40 E
Bar [Yugo.] 15 Cg 42.05N 19.06 E
Barabai 26 Gg 2.35S 115.23 E
Barabevú 55 Bk 33.20S 61.52W
Barabinsk 22 Jd 55.21N 78.21 E
Barabinskaja Step 20 Ce 55.00N 79.00 E
Baraboo 45 Le 43.28N 89.45W
Baracaldo 13 Ja 43.18N 2.59W
Baracoa 47 Jd 20.21N 74.30W
Bărăganului, Cîmpia- 15 Ke 44.55N 27.15 E
Baragoi 36 Gb 1.47N 36.47 E
Bārāh 35 Ec 13.42N 30.22 E
Barahona 47 Je 18.12N 71.06W
Barak 24 Gd 36.51N 37.59 E
Baraka 35 Fb 18.13N 37.35 E
Barakah 35 Fb 18.13N 37.35 E
Barakāt 35 Ec 14.20N 33.36 E
Barakī Barak 23 Kc 33.58N 68.58 E
Baram 26 Ff 4.36N 113.59 E
Baram 26 Ff 4.36N 113.58 E
Baramanni 50 Gi 7.50N 59.13W
Barama River 50 Gi 7.40N 59.15W
Barāmūla 25 Eb 34.12N 74.21 E
Bāran 25 Fc 25.06N 76.31 E
Baran 7 Hi 54.29N 30.19 E
Baraniha 20 Lc 68.31N 168.25 E
Baranja 14 Me 46.00N 18.30 E
Baranoa 49 Jh 10.49N 75.03W
Baranof 40 Le 57.00N 135.00W

Index Symbols

[1] Independent Nation
[2] State, Region
[3] District, County
[4] Municipality
[5] Colony, Dependency
Continent
Physical Region
Historical or Cultural Region
Mount, Mountain
Volcano
Hill
Mountains, Mountain Range
Hills, Escarpment
Plateau, Upland
Pass, Gap
Plain, Lowland
Delta
Salt Flat
Valley, Canyon
Crater, Cave
Karst Features
Depression
Polder
Desert, Dunes
Forest, Woods
Heath, Steppe
Oasis
Cape, Point
Coast, Beach
Cliff
Peninsula
Isthmus
Sandbank
Island
Atoll
Rock, Reef
Islands, Archipelago
Rocks, Reefs
Coral Reef
Well, Spring
Geyser
River, Stream
Waterfall Rapids
River Mouth, Estuary
Lake
Salt Lake
Intermittent Lake
Reservoir
Swamp, Pond
Canal
Glacier
Ice Shelf, Pack Ice
Ocean
Sea
Gulf, Bay
Strait, Fjord
Lagoon
Bank
Seamount
Tablemount
Ridge
Shelf
Basin
Escarpment, Sea Scarp
Fracture
Trench, Abyss
National Park, Reserve
Point of Interest
Recreation Site
Cave, Cavern
Historic Site
Ruins
Wall, Walls
Church, Abbey
Temple
Scientific Station
Airport
Port
Lighthouse
Mine
Tunnel
Dam, Bridge

Baranoviči	6	Ie	53.08N	26.02 E
Baranovka	16	Ed	50.18N	27.41 E
Baranya [2]	10	Oj	46.05N	18.15 E
Barão de Capanema	55	Da	13.19S	57.52W
Barão de Cotegipe	55	Fh	27.37S	52.23W
Barão de Grajaú	54	Je	6.45S	43.01W
Barão de Melgaço	54	Gg	16.13S	55.58W
Baraque de Fraiture	11	Ld	50.15N	5.45 E
Baratang	25	If	12.13N	92.45 E
Barataria Bay	45	Ll	29.22N	89.57W
Barat Daya, Kepulauan-	21	Oj	7.25S	128.00 E
Barāwe	31	Lh	1.09N	44.03 E
Barbacena	53	Lh	21.14S	43.46 E
Barbacoas [Ven.]	49	Li	9.49N	70.03W
Barbacoas [Ven.]	50	Ch	9.29N	66.58W
Barbacoas, Bahía de-	49	Jh	10.10N	75.35W
Barbado, Rio-	55	Cb	15.12S	58.58W
Barbados [1]	39	Nh	13.10N	59.32W
Barbados	38	Nh	13.10N	59.32W
Barbados Ridge (EN)	50	Gf	12.45N	59.35W
Barbagia	14	Dj	40.10N	9.10 E
Barbar	35	Eb	18.01N	33.59 E
Bárbara	54	Dd	0.52S	72.30W
Barbaros	15	Ki	40.54N	27.27 E
Barbas, Cabo-	32	De	22.18N	16.41W
Barbastro	13	Mb	42.02N	0.08 E
Barbate de Franco	13	Gh	36.12N	5.55W
Barbeau Peak	38	La	81.54N	75.01W
Barbeton	37	Ee	25.48S	31.03 E
Barbezieux	11	Fi	45.28N	0.09W
Barbourville	44	Fg	36.52N	83.53W
Barboza Ferraz	55	Fg	24.04S	52.03W
Barbuda	38	Mh	17.38N	61.48W
Barcaldine	58	Fg	23.33S	145.17 E
Barcarrota	13	Ff	38.31N	6.51W
Barcău	15	Ec	46.59N	21.07 E
Barcellona Pozzo di Gotto	14	Jl	38.09N	15.13 E
Barcelona [3]	13	Nc	41.40N	2.00 E
Barcelona [Sp.]	6	Gg	41.23N	2.11 E
Barcelona [Ven.]	54	Fa	10.08N	64.42W
Barcelonnette	11	Mj	44.23N	6.39 E
Barcelos [Braz.]	54	Fd	0.58S	62.57W
Barcelos [Port.]	13	Dc	41.32N	8.37W
Barcin	10	Nd	52.52N	17.57 E
Barcoo River	59	Ie	25.30S	142.50 E
Barcs	10	Nk	45.58N	17.28 E
Barda	16	Oi	40.25N	47.05 E
Bardagé	35	Ba	22.06N	16.28 E
Bardaï	31	If	21.21N	16.59 E
Bardār Shāh	24	Ld	36.45N	47.15 E
Bārdaw	14	En	36.49N	10.08 E
Barddhamān	25	Hd	23.15N	87.51 E
Bardejov	10	Rg	49.18N	21.16 E
Bārḍēre	31	Lh	2.20N	42.20 E
Bardeskan	24	Qe	35.12N	57.58 E
Bardīyah	33	Ed	31.46N	25.06 E
Bardonecchia	14	Ae	45.05N	6.42 E
Bardsey	9	Ii	52.45N	4.45W
Bardstown	44	Eg	37.49N	85.28W
Barēda	31	Mg	11.52N	51.03 E
Bareilly	22	Jg	28.25N	79.23 E
Barencevo More=Barents Sea (EN)	67	Jd	74.00N	36.00 E
Barentin	11	Ge	49.33N	0.57 E
Barentsburg	67	Kd	78.04N	14.14 E
Barentshav=Barents Sea (EN)	67	Jd	74.00N	36.00 E
Barentsøya	41	Oc	78.27N	21.15 E
Barents Sea (EN)= Barencevo More	67	Jd	74.00N	36.00 E
Barents Sea (EN)= Barentshav	67	Jd	74.00N	36.00 E
Barents Trough (EN)	5	Ia	73.00N	29.00 E
Barentu	35	Fb	15.06N	37.36 E
Barfleur	11	Ee	49.40N	1.15W
Barfleur, Pointe de-	11	Ee	49.42N	1.16W
Barga	22	Kf	30.48N	81.17 E
Bārgāl	35	Ic	11.18N	51.07 E
Bargarh	25	Gd	21.20N	83.37 E
Barguelonne	11	Gj	44.07N	0.50 E
Barguzin	20	Ff	53.27N	108.58 E
Barguzinski Hrebet	20	Ff	54.30N	110.00 E
Bar Harbor	44	Mc	44.23N	68.13W
Barhi	25	Hd	24.18N	85.25 E
Bari [3]	35	Hd	10.00N	50.00 E
Bari	6	Hg	41.08N	16.51 E
Bari, Terra di-	14	Kj	41.05N	16.50 E
Ba Ria	25	Lf	10.30N	107.10 E
Barīdī, Ra's-	24	Gj	24.17N	37.31 E
Barika	13	Ri	35.22N	5.05 E
Barīm	33	Hg	12.39N	43.25 E
Barima, Río-	50	Fh	8.35N	60.25W
Barima River	50	Fh	8.35N	60.25W
Barinas	54	Db	8.38N	70.12W
Barinas [2]	54	Eb	8.10N	70.00W
Baring, Cape-	42	Fb	70.01N	117.28W
Baringa	36	Db	0.45N	20.52 E
Barinitas	49	Li	8.45N	70.25W
Baripāda	25	Hd	21.56N	86.43 E
Bariri	55	Hf	22.04S	48.44W
Bariri, Represa-	55	Hf	22.21S	48.39W
Bārīs	33	Fe	24.40N	30.36 E
Bari Sādri	25	Ed	24.25N	74.28 E
Barisāl	25	Id	22.42N	90.22 E
Barisan, Pegunungan-= Barisan Mountains (EN)	21	Mj	3.00S	102.15 E
Barisan Mountains (EN)= Barisan, Pegunungan-	21	Mj	3.00S	102.15 E
Barito	21	Nj	3.32S	114.29 E
Barjols	11	Lk	43.33N	6.00 E
Barkā'	23	Ie	23.35N	57.55 E
Barkam	27	He	31.45N	102.32 E
Barkan, Ra's-e-	24	Mg	30.01N	49.35 E
Barkava	8	Lh	56.40N	26.45 E
Barkley, Lake-	43	Jd	36.40N	87.55W
Barkley Sound	46	Cb	48.53N	125.20W
Barkly East	37	Df	30.58S	27.33 E
Barkly Tableland	57	Ef	19.00S	138.00 E
Barkly West	37	Ce	28.05S	24.31 E
Barkol	27	Fc	43.35N	92.51 E
Barkol Hu	27	Fc	43.40N	92.39 E
Barlavento [3]	32	Cf	16.10N	24.40W
Bar-le-Duc	11	Lf	48.47N	5.10 E
Barlee, Lake-	57	Cg	29.10S	119.30 E
Barlee Range	59	Dd	23.35S	116.00 E
Barletta	14	Ki	41.19N	16.17 E
Barlinek	10	Lc	53.00N	15.12 E
Barlovento, Islas de-= Windward Islands (EN)	38	Mh	15.00N	61.00W
Barma	26	Jg	1.54S	133.00 E
Barmer	25	Ec	25.45N	71.23 E
Barmera	59	If	34.15S	140.28 E
Barmouth	9	Ii	52.43N	4.03W
Barnard Castle	9	Lg	54.33N	1.55W
Barnaul	22	Kd	53.22N	83.45 E
Barnes Ice Cap	42	Kc	70.00N	73.30W
Barnesville [Ga.-U.S.]	44	Ei	33.04N	84.09W
Barnesville [Mn.-U.S.]	45	Hc	46.39N	96.25W
Barnet, London-	12	Bc	51.39N	0.12W
Barneveld	12	Hb	52.08N	5.34 E
Barnim	10	Jd	52.40N	13.45 E
Barnsley	9	Lh	53.34N	1.28W
Barnstaple	9	Ij	51.05N	4.04W
Barnstaple (Bideford Bay)	9	Ij	51.05N	4.20W
Barnstorf	12	Kb	52.43N	8.30 E
Barntrup	12	Lc	51.59N	9.07 E
Barnwell	44	Gi	33.14N	81.21W
Baro	30	Kh	8.26N	33.14 E
Baro [Chad]	35	Bc	12.12N	18.58 E
Baro [Nig.]	34	Gd	8.36N	6.25 E
Baronnies	11	Lj	44.15N	5.30 E
Barora Fa	63a	Db	7.30S	158.20 E
Barora Ite	63a	Db	7.36S	158.24 E
Barotseland	36	Df	15.05S	24.00 E
Barqah=Cyrenaica (EN)	33	Dc	31.00N	22.30 E
Barqah=Cyrenaica (EN)	30	Je	31.00N	23.00 E
Barqah, Jabal al-	24	Ej	24.24N	32.34 E
Barqah al Bahrīyah= Marmarica (EN)	30	Je	31.40N	24.30 E
Barqū, Jabal-	14	Dn	36.04N	9.37 E
Barques, Pointe aux-	44	Fc	44.04N	82.58W
Barquisimeto	53	Jd	10.04N	69.19W
Barr	11	Nf	48.24N	7.27 E
Barr, Ra's al-	24	Nj	25.47N	50.34 E
Barra	53	Lg	11.05S	43.10W
Barra	9	Fd	57.00N	7.30W
Barra, Ponta da-	30	Kk	23.47S	35.32 E
Barra, Sound of-	9	Fd	57.10N	7.20W
Barraba	59	Kf	30.22S	150.36 E
Barra Bonita, Represa-	55	Hf	22.38S	48.20W
Barra de Navidad	47	De	19.12N	104.41W
Barra do Bugres	54	Gg	15.05S	57.11W
Barra do Corda	54	Ie	5.30S	45.15W
Barra do Cuanza	36	Bd	9.18S	13.09 E
Barra do Dande	36	Bd	8.28S	13.22 E
Barra do Garças	54	Hg	15.53S	52.15W
Barra Falsa, Ponta da-	30	Kk	22.55S	35.37 E
Barra Head	9	Fe	56.46N	7.36W
Barra Mansa	54	Jh	22.32S	44.11W
Barrāmīyah, Wādī al-	24	Ej	25.00N	33.23 E
Barranca	54	Cd	4.50S	76.42W
Barrancabermeja	53	Ie	7.03N	73.52W
Barrancas [Col.]	49	Kh	10.57N	72.50W
Barrancas [Ven.]	54	Fb	8.42N	62.11W
Barrancas, Arroyo-	55	Cj	30.19S	59.25W
Barranco	55	Db	15.56S	57.41W
Barrancos	13	Ff	38.08N	6.59W
Barranqueras	56	Ic	27.29S	58.56W
Barranquilla	53	Id	10.59N	74.48W
Barranquitas	51a	Bb	18.12N	66.23W
Barra Patuca	49	Ef	15.50N	84.17W
Barras	54	Jd	4.15S	42.18W
Barra Velha	55	Hh	26.39S	48.43W
Barre	44	Kc	44.12N	72.30W
Barreira	55	Db	15.24S	57.52W
Barreiras	53	Lg	12.08S	45.00W
Barreirinha	54	Gd	2.47S	57.03W
Barreirinhas	54	Jd	2.45S	42.50W
Barreiro	13	Cf	38.40N	9.04W
Barreiro, Rio-	55	Fb	15.43S	52.45W
Barreiro Grande	55	Jd	18.12S	45.10W
Barreiros	54	Ke	8.49S	35.12W
Barren	25	If	12.16N	93.51 E
Barren, Iles-	37	Gc	18.25S	43.40 E
Barren Islands	40	Ie	58.55N	152.15W
Barretos	56	Kb	20.33S	48.33W
Barrie	42	Jh	44.24N	79.40W
Barrier Bay	66	Ge	67.45S	81.10 E
Barrier Islands	63a	Db	7.44S	158.32 E
Barrington Tops	59	Kf	32.00S	151.28 E
Barro Alto	55	Hb	15.04S	48.58W
Barrois, Plateau du-	11	Kf	48.45N	5.00 E
Barros, Lagoa dos-	55	Gi	29.56S	50.23W
Barros, Tierra de-	13	Ff	38.40N	6.25W
Barroso	55	Ke	21.11S	43.58W
Barrouallie	51n	Ba	13.14N	61.17W
Barrow [Ak.-U.S.]	39	Db	71.17N	156.47W
Barrow [Arg.]	55	Bn	38.18S	60.14W
Barrow/An Bhearú	9	Gi	52.10N	7.00W
Barrow, Point-	38	Db	71.23N	156.30W
Barrow Creek	58	Eg	21.33S	133.53 E
Barrow-in-Furness	9	Jg	54.07N	3.14W
Barrow Island	57	Cg	20.50S	115.25 E
Barrow Range	59	Fe	26.05S	127.30 E
Barrow Strait	38	Jb	74.21N	94.10W
Barru	26	Gg	4.25S	119.37 E
Barry	9	Jj	51.24N	3.18W
Barrytown	62	De	42.14S	171.20 E
Barsakelmes, Ostrov-	18	Bb	45.40N	59.55 E
Barsalogo	34	Ec	13.25N	1.03W
Barsatas	19	Hf	48.13N	78.33 E
Baršć/Forst	10	Ke	51.44N	14.38 E
Bārsi	25	Fe	18.14N	75.42 E
Barsinghausen	10	Fd	52.18N	9.27 E
Barstow	43	De	34.54N	117.01W
Bar-sur-Aube	11	Kf	48.14N	4.43 E
Bar-sur-Seine	11	Kf	48.07N	4.22 E
Baršyn	19	Gf	49.45N	69.36 E
Bārta/Barta	8	Ih	56.57N	20.57 E
Barta/Bārta	8	Ih	56.57N	20.57 E
Barṭallah	24	Jd	36.23N	43.25 E
Bartang	18	Hf	37.55N	71.33 E
Barth	10	Ib	54.22N	12.44 E
Bartholomew, Bayou-	45	Jj	32.43N	92.04W
Bartica	54	Gb	6.24N	58.37W
Bartın	24	Eb	41.38N	32.21 E
Bartle Frere, Mount-	57	Ff	17.23S	145.49 E
Bartlesville	43	Hd	36.45N	95.59W
Bartlett	45	Gf	41.53N	98.33W
Bartoszyce	10	Qb	54.16N	20.49 E
Bartow	44	Gl	27.54N	81.50W
Barú, Isla-	49	Jh	10.26N	75.35W
Barú, Volcán	47	Hg	8.48N	82.33W
Bārūd, Ra's-	24	Ei	26.47N	33.39 E
Barumini	14	Dk	39.42N	9.01 E
Barun-Bogdo-Ula	27	Hb	45.00N	100.20 E
Bāruni	25	Hc	25.29N	85.59 E
Barun-Šabartuj, Gora-	20	Fg	49.43N	109.58 E
Barun-Urt	27	Jb	46.40N	113.12 E
Barwice	10	Mc	53.45N	16.22 E
Barwon River	57	Fg	30.00S	148.05 E
Barycz	10	Me	51.42N	16.15 E
Baryš	7	Lj	53.40N	47.08 E
Baryš	7	Li	54.35N	46.47 E
Bāsa'īdū	24	Pi	26.39N	55.17 E
Basail	55	Ch	27.52S	59.18W
Basankusu	36	Cb	1.14N	19.48 E
Basaral, Ostrov-	18	Ib	45.25N	73.45 E
Basauri	13	Ja	43.13N	2.53W
Basavilbaso	55	Ck	32.22S	58.53W
Bas Champs	12	Dd	50.20N	1.41 E
Basco	26	Hb	20.27N	121.58 E
Bascuñán, Cabo-	56	Fc	28.51S	71.30W
Base	11	Gj	44.17N	0.18 E
Basel [2]	14	Bc	47.35N	7.40 E
Basel/Bâle	6	Gf	47.30N	7.30 E
Baselland [2]	14	Bc	47.30N	7.45 E
Basentello	14	Kj	40.40N	16.23 E
Basento	14	Kj	40.20N	16.49 E
Başeu	15	Kb	47.44N	27.15 E
Basey	26	Id	11.17N	125.04 E
Bashi Channel (EN)=Bashi Haixia	27	Lg	22.00N	121.00 E
Bashi Haixia=Bashi Channel (EN)	27	Lg	22.00N	121.00 E
Bāsht	24	Ng	30.21N	51.09 E
Ba Shui	28	Ci	30.25N	115.02 E
Basilan	21	Oi	6.34N	122.03 E
Basilan City (Isabela)	22	Oi	6.42N	121.58 E
Basilan Strait	26	He	6.49N	122.05 E
Basildon	9	Nj	51.34N	0.25 E
Basilicata [2]	14	Kj	40.30N	16.30 E
Basingstoke	9	Lj	51.16N	1.05W
Basjanovski	17	Jg	58.19N	60.44 E
Başkale	24	Jc	38.02N	44.00 E
Baskatong, Réservoir-	42	Jg	46.47N	75.50W
Baškaus	20	Df	51.09N	87.43 E
Baskil	24	Hc	38.35N	38.40 E
Baškortostan respublika	19	Fe	55.00N	56.00 E
Baskunčak, ozero	16	Oe	48.10N	46.55 E
Bašmakovo	16	Mc	53.12N	43.03 E
Bāsmenj	24	Ld	37.59N	46.29 E
Basoko	36	Db	1.14N	23.36 E
Basongo	36	Dc	4.20S	20.24 E
Basque Provinces (EN)= Euzkadi/Vascongadas	13	Ja	43.00N	2.30W
Basque Provinces (EN)= Vascongadas/Euzkadi	13	Ja	43.00N	2.30W
Basra (EN)=Al Başrah	22	Gf	30.30N	47.47 E
Bas Rhin [3]	11	Nf	48.35N	7.40 E
Bass, Ilots de-	57	Mg	27.55S	143.26W
Bassano	46	Ia	50.47N	112.28W
Bassano del Grappa	14	Fe	45.46N	11.44 E
Bassar	34	Fd	9.15N	0.47 E
Bassas da India	30	Lk	21.25S	39.42 E
Bassein → Pathein	22	Lh	16.47N	94.44 E
Bassein → Vasai	25	Ee	19.21N	72.48 E
Basse-Kotto [3]	35	Ce	5.00N	21.30 E
Basse-Pointe	51h	Ab	14.52N	61.07W
Basses, Pointe des-	51e	Bc	15.52N	61.17W
Basse-Sambre	12	Gd	50.27N	4.37 E
Basse Santa Su	34	Cc	13.19N	14.13W
Basse-Terre	50	Fd	16.10N	61.40W
Basse-Terre	47	Le	16.00N	61.44W
Basseterre	47	Le	17.18N	62.43W
Bassett	45	Ge	42.35N	99.32W
Bassigny	11	Lf	48.00N	5.30 E
Bassikounou	32	Ff	15.52N	5.58W
Bassila	34	Fd	9.01N	1.40 E
Bass Islands	63c	Ba	9.58S	167.17 E
Basso, Plateau de-	30	Jg	17.20N	22.40 E
Bass Strait	57	Fh	39.20S	145.30 E
Bassum	12	Kb	52.51N	8.44 E
Basswood Lake	45	Kb	48.05N	91.35W
Båstad	7	Ch	56.26N	12.51 E
Bastak	24	Pi	27.14N	54.22 E
Bastām	24	Pd	36.29N	55.04 E
Bastenaken/Bastogne	11	Le	50.00N	5.43 E
Bastia [Fr.]	6	Gg	42.42N	9.27 E
Bastia [It.]	14	Gg	43.04N	12.33 E
Bastogne/Bastenaken	11	Le	50.00N	5.43 E
Bastrop	45	Kj	32.47N	91.55W
Basudan Ula	27	Fe	33.05N	91.00 E
Basuo → Dongfang	27	Ih	19.14N	108.39 E
Basuto	37	Dc	19.52S	26.32 E
Bas-Zaïre [2]	36	Bd	5.30S	14.30 E
Bata	31	Hh	1.51N	9.45 E
Batabanó, Golfo de-	47	Hd	22.15N	82.30W
Batagaj	20	Ic	67.38N	134.38 E
Batagaj-Alyta	20	Ic	67.53N	130.31 E
Bataguaçu	54	Hh	21.42S	52.22W
Bataiporã	55	Ff	22.20S	53.17W
Batajnica	15	De	44.54N	20.17 E
Batajsk	19	Df	47.05N	39.46 E
Batak	15	Hh	41.57N	24.13 E
Bataklık Gölü	24	Ed	37.42N	33.07 E
Batala	25	Fb	31.48N	75.12 E
Batalha	13	De	39.39N	8.50W
Batama	36	Eb	0.56N	26.39 E
Batamaj	20	Hd	63.30N	129.25 E
Batamšinski	19	Fe	50.36N	58.17 E
Batan	26	Hb	20.30N	121.50 E
Batang	27	Ge	30.02N	99.10 E
Batanga	36	Ac	0.21S	9.18 E
Batangafo	35	Bd	7.18N	18.18 E
Batangas	22	Oh	13.45N	121.03 E
Batanghari	26	Mj	1.00S	104.00 E
Batan Islands	21	Og	20.30N	121.50 E
Batanta, Pulau-	26	Jg	0.50S	130.40 E
Bátaszék	10	Oj	46.11N	18.44 E
Batatais	55	Ie	20.53S	47.37W
Batavia	44	Hd	43.00N	78.11W
Bat-Cengel	27	Hb	47.47N	101.58 E
Batchawana	44	Eb	46.58N	84.34W
Batchelor	59	Gb	13.04S	131.01 E
Bătdâmbâng	22	Mh	13.06N	103.12 E
Batéké, Plateaux-	36	Cc	3.30S	15.45 E
Batel, Esteros del-	55	Ci	28.30S	58.20W
Batemans Bay	59	Kg	35.43S	150.11 E
Batesburg	44	Gi	33.56N	81.33W
Batesville [Ar.-U.S.]	45	Ki	35.46N	91.39W
Batesville [Ms.-U.S.]	45	Li	34.18N	90.00W
Bath [Eng.-U.K.]	9	Kj	51.23N	2.22W
Bath [Me.-U.S.]	44	Md	43.55N	69.49W
Bath [N.B.-Can.]	44	Nb	46.32N	67.33W
Bath [St.C.N.]	51c	Ab	17.08N	62.37W
Batha	35	Bc	14.00N	19.00 E
Bathinda	25	Fb	30.12N	74.57 E
Bá Thrá Li/Tralee Bay	9	Di	52.15N	9.59W
Bathsheba	50	Gf	13.13N	59.31W
Bá Thuath Reanna/ Liscannor Bay	9	Di	52.55N	9.25W
Bathurst	38	Ib	76.00N	100.30W
Bathurst [Austl.]	59	Jf	33.25S	149.35 E
Bathurst [N.B.-Can.]	39	Me	47.36N	65.39W
Bathurst, Cape-	38	Gb	70.35N	128.00W
Bathurst Inlet	38	Ic	68.10N	108.50W
Bathurst Inlet	39	Ic	66.50N	108.01W
Bathurst Island	57	Ef	11.35S	130.25 E
Bati	35	Gc	11.13N	40.01 E
Batié	34	Ed	9.53N	2.55W
Bāṭin, Wādī al-	23	Gc	30.25N	47.35 E
Batman	23	Fb	37.52N	41.07 E
Batman	24	Id	37.45N	41.00 E
Batna [3]	32	Ib	35.10N	6.00 E
Batna	31	He	35.34N	6.11 E
Ba To	25	Lf	14.46N	108.44 E
Bato Bato	26	Ge	5.06N	119.50 E
Batoka	36	Ef	16.47S	27.15 E
Baton Rouge	39	Jf	30.23N	91.11W
Batopilas	48	Fd	27.01N	107.44W
Batouri	34	He	4.26N	14.22 E
Batovi	55	Fb	15.53S	53.24W
Batovi, Coxilha de-	55	Ej	30.33S	54.27W
Båtsfjord	7	Ga	70.38N	29.44 E
Bat-Sumber	27	Ib	48.25N	106.42 E
Batticaloa	25	Gg	7.43N	81.42 E
Batti Maly	25	Ig	8.50N	92.51 E
Battipaglia	14	Ij	40.37N	14.58 E
Battle	12	Cd	50.55N	0.30 E
Battle	42	Gf	52.42N	108.15W
Battle Creek	46	Kb	48.36N	109.11W
Battle Creek	43	Jc	42.19N	85.11W
Battle Harbour	39	Nd	52.17N	55.35W
Battle Mountain	43	Dc	40.38N	116.56W
Battonya	10	Rj	46.17N	21.01 E
Battowia Island	51n	Bb	12.58N	61.09W
Batu	35	Fd	6.59N	39.37 E
Batu, Kepulauan-=Batu Islands (EN)	21	Lj	0.18S	98.28 E
Batuasa	26	Jg	3.32S	130.08 E
Batuata, Pulau-	26	Hh	6.12S	122.42 E
Batudaka, Pulau-	26	Hg	0.28S	121.48 E
Batui	26	Hg	1.17S	122.33 E
Batu Islands (EN)=Batu, Kepulauan-	21	Lj	0.18S	98.28 E
Batumi	6	Kg	41.38N	41.38 E
Batu Pahat	26	Df	1.51N	102.56 E
Baturaja	26	Dg	4.08S	104.10 E
Baturino	20	De	57.45N	85.12 E
Baturité	54	Kd	4.20S	38.53W
Batz, Ile de-	11	Bf	48.45N	4.01W
Bau	26	Ff	1.25N	110.09 E
Baubau	22	Oj	5.28S	122.38 E
Baucau	26	Ih	8.27S	126.27 E
Bauchi	31	Hg	10.19N	9.50 E
Bauchi [2]	34	Hc	10.40N	10.00 E
Bauchi Plateau	34	Gc	10.00N	9.30 E
Baud	11	Cg	47.52N	3.01W
Baudette	45	Ib	48.43N	94.36W
Baudo, Serrania de-	54	Cb	6.00N	77.05W
Baudour, Saint-Ghislain-	12	Fd	50.29N	3.49 E
Baugé	11	Fg	47.33N	0.06W
Bauges	11	Mi	45.38N	6.10 E
Baúl, Cerro-	48	Ii	17.38N	100.19W
Baula	26	Hg	4.09S	121.41 E
Bauld, Cape-	38	Nd	51.38N	55.25W
Bauman Fiord	42	Ia	77.45N	86.00W
Baume-les-Dames	11	Mg	47.21N	6.22 E
Baunach	10	Gg	49.59N	10.51 E
Baunani	63a	Ec	9.08S	160.51 E
Baunei	14	Dj	40.02N	9.40 E
Baures	54	Ff	13.35S	63.35W
Bauru	53	Lh	22.19S	49.04W
Baús	55	Fd	18.19S	53.10W
Baús, Serra dos-	55	Fd	18.20S	53.25W
Bauska	7	Fh	56.24N	24.13 E
Bautzen/Budyšin	10	Ke	51.11N	14.26 E
Bavaria (EN)=Bayern [2]	10	Hg	49.00N	11.30 E
Bavaria (EN)=Bayern	5	Hf	49.00N	11.30 E
Bavarian Forest (EN)= Bayerischer Wald	10	Ig	49.00N	12.55 E
Bavay	12	Fd	50.18N	3.47 E
Båven	8	Ge	59.00N	16.55 E
Bavispe	48	Eb	30.24N	108.50W
Bavispe, Rio de-	48	Ec	29.15N	109.11W
Bavly	7	Mi	54.26N	53.18 E
Bawah, Pulau-	26	Ef	2.31N	106.03 E
Bawal, Pulau-	26	Fg	2.44S	110.06 E
Bawe	58	Ee	2.59S	134.43 E
Bawean, Pulau-	26	Fh	5.46S	112.40 E
Bawku	34	Ec	11.03N	0.15W
Baxian	27	Kd	39.03N	116.24 E
Baxol	27	Ge	30.07N	96.56 E
Bay [3]	35	Ge	2.50N	43.30 E
Bay/Baicheng	27	Dc	41.46N	81.52 E
Bayamo	47	Id	20.23N	76.39W
Bayamón	49	Nd	18.24N	66.09W
Bayan	28	Ia	46.05N	127.24 E
Bayanbulak	27	Dc	43.05N	84.05 E
Bayanga	35	Be	2.53N	16.19 E
Bayan Gol	27	Gd	37.18N	96.50 E
Bayan Gol → Dengkou	22	Me	40.25N	106.59 E
Bayan Har Shan	21	Lf	34.20N	97.00 E
Bayan Har Shankou	27	Ge	34.06N	97.38 E
Bayan Hot → Alxa Zuoqi	27	Id	38.50N	105.32 E
Bayan Hure → Chen Barag Qi	27	Kb	49.21N	119.25 E
Bayan Huxu → Horqin Youyi Zhongqi	27	Lb	45.04N	121.27 E
Bayano, Lago de-	49	Hi	9.00N	78.30W
Bayan Obo	27	Ic	41.50N	109.58 E
Bayan Qagan	28	Ga	46.11N	123.59 E
Bayan Qagan → Qahar Youyi Houqi	28	Bd	41.28N	113.10 E
Bayan Ul Hot → Xi Ujimqin Qi	27	Kc	44.31N	117.33 E
Bayas	48	Gf	23.32N	104.50W
Bayat	24	Fb	40.39N	34.15 E
Bayauca	55	Bl	34.51S	61.18W
Bayawan	26	He	9.20N	123.00 E
Bayāẕ	24	Pg	30.42N	55.28 E
Bayāzeh	24	Pf	30.42N	55.28 E
Baybay	26	Hd	10.41N	124.48 E
Bayburt	23	Fa	40.16N	40.15 E
Bay City [Mi.-U.S.]	43	Kc	43.36N	83.53W
Bay City [Tx.-U.S.]	43	Hf	29.09N	95.39W
Bayerische Alpen	10	Hi	47.30N	11.30 E
Bayerischer Wald=Bavarian Forest (EN)	10	Ig	49.00N	12.55 E
Bayern=Bavaria (EN)	5	Hf	49.00N	11.30 E
Bayern=Bavaria (EN) [2]	10	Hg	49.00N	11.30 E
Bayes, Cap-	63b	Be	20.57S	165.25 E
Bayeux	11	Fe	49.16N	0.42W
Bayfield	45	Kc	46.49N	90.49W
Bay Fiord	42	Ja	79.00N	84.00W
Baygorria	55	Dk	32.52S	56.44W
Baygorria, Lago Artificial de-	55	Dk	33.05S	57.00W
Bayḩān al Qişāb	33	Ig	14.48N	45.44 E
Bayındır	24	Bc	38.13N	27.40 E
Bayjī	24	Je	34.56N	43.29 E
Bay Minette	44	Dj	30.53N	87.47W
Baynūnah	24	Ok	23.50N	52.50 E
Bayombong	26	Hc	16.29N	121.09 E
Bayona	13	Db	42.07N	8.51W
Bayonnaise Seamount (EN)	57	Jf	12.00S	179.30W
Bayonne	6	Fg	43.29N	1.29W
Bayou Bodcau Lake	45	Jj	32.58N	93.30W
Bayou D'Arbonne Lake	45	Jj	32.45N	92.27W
Bayramiç	15	Jj	39.48N	26.37 E
Bayreuth	10	Hg	49.57N	11.35 E
Bayrūt=Beirut (EN)	22	Ff	33.53N	35.30 E
Bay Saint Louis	45	Lk	30.19N	89.20W
Bay Springs	45	Lk	31.59N	89.17W
Bayt al Faqīh	23	Fg	14.31N	43.17 E
Baytik Shan	27	Fb	45.15N	90.50 E
Bayt Laḩm=Bethlehem (EN)	24	Fg	31.43N	35.12 E
Baytown	43	If	29.44N	94.58W
Bayuda Desert (EN)= Bayyūḑah, Şaḩrā'-	30	Kg	18.00N	33.00 E
Bayunglencir	26	Dg	2.03S	103.41 E
Bayview	46	Gc	48.00N	116.30W
Bay View	62	Gc	39.26S	176.52 E
Bayy al Kabīr	33	Cc	31.11N	15.53 E
Bayyūḑah, Şaḩrā'-=Bayuda Desert (EN)	30	Kg	18.00N	33.00 E
Baza	13	Jg	37.29N	2.46W
Baza, Sierra de-	13	Jg	37.15N	2.45W
Bazardjuzju, Gora-	5	Kg	41.13N	47.51 E
Bazaruto, Ilha do-	37	Fd	21.40S	35.25 E
Bazas	11	Fj	44.26N	0.13W
Bazhong	27	Ie	31.54N	106.42 E
Bazoches-sur-Vesle	12	Fe	49.19N	3.37 E
Baztán	13	Ka	43.09N	1.31W
Beach	43	Gb	46.55N	103.52W
Beachy Head	9	Nk	50.44N	0.16 E
Beacon	44	Ke	41.31N	73.59W
Beaconsfield [Austl.]	59	Jh	41.12S	146.48 E
Beaconsfield [Eng.-U.K.]	12	Bc	51.36N	0.38W
Beagle, Canal-	56	Gh	54.53S	68.10W
Beagle Gulf	59	Gb	12.00S	130.20 E
Bealach an Doirín/ Ballaghaderreen	9	Eh	53.55N	8.35W
Béalanana	37	Hb	14.33S	48.44 E
Béal an Átha/Ballina	9	Dg	54.07N	9.09W
Béal an Bheara/Gweebarra Bay	9	Eg	54.52N	8.20W
Béal Átha Fhirdhia/Ardee	9	Gh	53.52N	6.33W
Béal Átha hAmhnais/ Ballyhaunis	9	Eh	53.46N	8.46W

Index Symbols

[1] Independent Nation
[2] State, Region
[3] District, County
[4] Municipality
[5] Colony, Dependency
Continent
Physical Region
Historical or Cultural Region
Mount, Mountain
Volcano
Hill
Mountains, Mountain Range
Hills, Escarpment
Plateau, Upland
Pass, Gap
Plain, Lowland
Delta
Salt Flat
Valley, Canyon
Crater, Cave
Karst Features
Depression
Polder
Desert, Dunes
Forest, Woods
Heath, Steppe
Oasis
Cape, Point
Coast, Beach
Cliff
Peninsula
Isthmus
Sandbank
Island
Atoll
Rock, Reef
Islands, Archipelago
Rocks, Reefs
Coral Reef
Well, Spring
Geyser
River, Stream
Waterfall Rapids
River Mouth, Estuary
Lake
Salt Lake
Intermittent Lake
Reservoir
Swamp, Pond
Canal
Glacier
Ice Shelf, Pack Ice
Ocean
Sea
Gulf, Bay
Strait, Fjord
Lagoon
Bank
Seamount
Tablemount
Ridge
Shelf
Basin
Escarpment, Sea Scarp
Fracture
Trench, Abyss
National Park, Reserve
Point of Interest
Recreation Site
Cave, Cavern
Historic Site
Ruins
Wall, Walls
Church, Abbey
Temple
Scientific Station
Airport
Port
Lighthouse
Mine
Tunnel
Dam, Bridge

Index Symbols

① Independent Nation	▣ Historical or Cultural Region	◲ Pass, Gap	◰ Depression
② State, Region	▲ Mount, Mountain	◳ Plain, Lowland	◱ Polder
③ District, County	◭ Volcano	◬ Delta	◨ Cliff
⑤ Municipality	◔ Hill	◫ Salt Flat	◩ Desert, Dunes
◪ Colony, Dependency	◮ Mountains, Mountain Range	◧ Valley, Canyon	◦ Forest, Woods
■ Continent	◍ Hills, Escarpment	◌ Crater, Cave	◊ Heath, Steppe
◪ Physical Region	◐ Plateau, Upland	◒ Karst Features	◑ Oasis
			◉ Cape, Point

Index Symbols

[1] Independent Nation
[2] State, Region
[3] District, County
[4] Municipality
[5] Colony, Dependency
■ Continent
◨ Physical Region

Historical or Cultural Region
Mount, Mountain
Volcano
Hill
Mountains, Mountain Range
Hills, Escarpment
Plateau, Upland

Pass, Gap
Plain, Lowland
Delta
Salt Flat
Valley, Canyon
Crater, Cave
Karst Features

Depression
Polder
Desert, Dunes
Forest, Woods
Heath, Steppe
Oasis
Cape, Point

Coast, Beach
Cliff
Peninsula
Isthmus
Sandbank
Island
River, Stream

Rock, Reef
Islands, Archipelago
Rocks, Reefs
Coral Reef
Well, Spring
Geyser
Atoll

Waterfall Rapids
River Mouth, Estuary
Lake
Salt Lake
Intermittent Lake
Reservoir
Swamp, Pond

Canal
Glacier
Ice Shelf, Pack Ice
Ocean
Sea
Gulf, Bay
Strait, Fjord

Lagoon
Bank
Seamount
Tablemount
Ridge
Shelf
Basin

Escarpment, Sea Scarp
Fracture
Trench, Abyss
National Park, Reserve
Point of Interest
Recreation Site
Cave, Cavern

Historic Site
Ruins
Wall, Walls
Church, Abbey
Temple
Scientific Station
Airport

Port
Lighthouse
Mine
Tunnel
Dam, Bridge

Bingen 10 Dg 49.58N 7.54 E
Bingham [Me.-U.S.] 44 Mc 45.03N 69.53W
Bingham [N.M.-U.S.] 45 Cj 33.56N 106.17W
Binghamton 43 Lc 42.06N 75.55W
Bin Ghunaymah, Jabal- 30 If 25.00N 15.30 E
Bing Inlet 44 Gc 45.13N 80.30W
Bingöl 23 Fb 38.53N 40.29 E
Bingöl Dağlari 24 Ic 39.20N 41.20 E
Binhai (Dongkan) 27 Ke 34.00N 119.52 E
Binjai 26 Cf 3.36N 98.30 E
Binkiliç 15 Lh 41.25N 28.11 E
Binongko, Pulau- 26 Hh 5.57S 124.02 E
Bin Qirdān 32 Jc 33.08N 11.13 E
Bintan, Pulau- 26 Df 1.05N 104.30 E
Bintuhan 26 Dg 4.48S 103.22 E
Bintulu 26 Ff 3.10N 113.02 E
Bin Walīd, Jabal- 14 En 36.52N 10.47 E
Binxian 28 Df 37.22N 117.57 E
Binxian (Binzhou) [China] 27 Mb 45.45N 127.27 E
Binxian (Binzhou) [China] 27 Id 35.02N 108.06 E
Binzhou → Binxian [China] 27 Id 35.02N 108.06 E
Binzhou → Binxian [China] 27 Mb 45.45N 127.27 E
Bioara 25 Fd 23.58N 76.55 E
Biobío 56 Fe 36.49S 73.10W
Bio Bío [2] 56 Fe 37.45S 72.00W
Biograd na Moru 14 Jg 43.57N 15.27 E
Bioko [3] 34 Ge 3.00N 8.40 E
Bioko 30 Hh 4.30N 9.30 E
Biokovo 14 Lg 43.18N 17.02 E
Biorra/Birr 9 Fh 53.05N 7.54W
Bippen 12 Jb 52.35N 7.44 E
Bīr 25 Fe 18.59N 75.46 E
Bira 20 Ig 49.03N 132.27 E
Bi'r Abraq 33 Fe 23.35N 34.48 E
Bi'r Abū al Ḩuşayn 33 Ee 22.53N 29.55 E
Bi'r Abū Gharādiq 24 Cg 30.06N 28.06 E
Bi'r Abū Hashim 33 Fe 23.42N 34.08 E
Bi'r Abū Minqat 33 Ed 26.30N 27.35 E
Bīrah Kaprah 24 Kd 36.52N 44.01 E
Birāk 33 Bd 27.39N 14.17 E
Birakan 20 Ig 49.02N 131.40 E
Bi'r al 'Abd 24 Eg 31.22N 32.58 E
Bi'r al Ghuzaylah 33 Bd 28.50N 10.45 E
Bi'r al Ḩakīm 33 Dc 31.36N 23.29 E
Bi'r al Hasa 35 Fa 22.58N 35.40 E
Bi'r al Khamsah 33 Ec 30.57N 25.46 E
Bi'r 'Allāq 33 Bc 31.10N 11.55 E
Bi'r al Mushayqīq 32 Jc 30.53N 10.18 E
Bi'r al Qurayyah 24 Ei 26.22N 33.01 E
Bi'r al Uzam 33 Dc 31.46N 23.59 E
Bi'r al Wa'r 31 Be 22.39N 14.10 E
Bi'r al Washkah 33 Cd 28.52N 15.35 E
Birao 31 Jg 10.17N 22.47 E
Bi'r 'Arjā' 24 Ij 25.17N 40.58 E
Bi'r ar Rāh 24 If 33.27N 40.25 E
Bi'r ar Rūmān 32 Ic 32.31N 8.21 E
Birātnagar 25 Hc 26.29N 87.17 E
Biratori 28 Qc 42.35N 142.12 E
Bi'r Baylī 33 Ec 30.32N 25.08 E
Bi'r Bayzaḩ 24 Fj 25.10N 34.05 E
Bi'r Bū Ḩawsh 33 Dd 24.34N 22.07 E
Bi'r Bū Zurayyq 33 Dd 24.32N 22.38 E
Birca 15 Gf 43.58N 23.37 E
Birch 42 Ge 58.28N 112.17W
Birch Mountains 42 Ge 57.20N 112.55W
Bird 42 Ie 56.30N 94.14W
Bi'r Dibs 33 Ee 22.12N 29.32 E
Bird Island [Gren.] 51p Bb 12.12N 61.33W
Bird Island [Sey.] 37b Ca 3.43S 55.12 E
Birdsville 59 He 25.54S 139.22 E
Birdum 59 Gc 15.39S 133.13 E
Birecik 24 Gd 37.02N 37.58 E
Bir El Ater 32 Ic 34.44N 8.03 E
Bir el Mrabba'ab 24 He 34.30N 39.07 E
Bir Enzarān 32 Ee 23.53N 14.32W
Bireuen 26 Ce 5.12N 96.41 E
Bi'r Fajr 24 Gh 28.54N 37.54 E
Bi'r Fu'ād 33 Ec 30.27N 26.27 E
Bir Gandūs 32 De 21.38N 16.30W
Birganj 25 Gc 27.00N 84.52 E
Bir Gara 35 Bc 13.11N 15.58 E
Bir-Ghbalou 13 Ph 36.16N 3.35 E
Birgi 15 Lk 38.15N 28.05 E
Bi'r Ḩasanah 24 Eg 30.28N 33.47 E
Bi'r Ḩaymir 24 Hj 24.41N 38.04 E
Bi'r Ḩulayyī 24 Fj 24.06N 34.32 E
Birigui 55 Ge 21.18S 50.19W
Biriliussy 20 Ee 57.07N 90.42 E
Birīn 24 Ge 35.01N 36.40 E
Birine 13 Pi 35.37N 3.13 E
Birjand 22 Hf 32.53N 59.13 E
Birjusa 21 Ld 57.43N 95.24 E
Birjusinsk 20 Ee 55.55N 97.55 E
Bi'r Karawayn 24 Ci 27.06N 28.32 E
Birkeland 7 Bg 58.20N 8.14 E
Birkenfeld 10 Dg 49.39N 7.11 E
Birkenhead 9 Jh 53.24N 3.02W
Birkerød 8 Ei 55.50N 12.26 E
Bi'r Khālidah 24 Bg 30.50N 27.15 E
Birksgate Range 59 Fe 27.10S 129.45 E
Birlad 15 Kc 46.14N 27.40 E
Birlad 15 Kc 45.36N 27.31 E
Bir Lehlū 32 Fd 26.21N 9.34W
Bi'r Ma'sūr 24 Fj 24.31N 34.12 E
Birmingham [Al.-U.S.] 39 Kf 33.31N 86.49W
Birmingham [Eng.-U.K.] 6 Fe 52.30N 1.50W
Bi'r Misāḩah 33 Ee 22.12N 27.57 E
Bi'r Murr 33 Fe 23.21N 30.05 E
Bi'r Murrah 33 Fe 22.32N 33.54 E
Bi'r Nāhid 33 Ec 30.13N 28.52 E
Bi'r Naşīf 24 Ee 24.51N 39.11 E
Birnie Atoll [5] 57 Je 3.35S 171.31W
Birnin Gaouré 34 Fc 13.05N 2.54 E
Birnin Gwari 34 Gc 11.02N 6.47 E
Birnin Kebbi 34 Fc 12.28N 4.12 E
Birnin Nkonni 31 Hg 13.48N 5.15 E
Birnin Kudu 34 Gc 11.27N 9.30 E
Birni Yauri 34 Fc 10.47N 4.49 E
Bi'r Nukhaylah 24 Dj 24.01N 30.52 E
Birobidžan 22 Pe 48.48N 132.57 E
Birr/Biorra 9 Fh 53.05N 7.54W
Birs 14 Bc 47.26N 7.33 E
Bi'r Safājah 33 Fd 26.50N 34.54 E
Bi'r Sayyālah 24 Ei 26.07N 33.56 E
Bi'r Shalatayn 33 Ge 23.08N 35.36 E
Birsk 19 Fd 55.25N 55.32 E
Birštonas 8 Kj 54.33N 24.07 E
Bi'r Ţarfāwī 33 Ee 22.55N 28.53 E
Biru 27 Fe 31.30N 93.50 E
Bi'r Umm al 'Abbās 24 Ei 26.57N 32.34 E
Bi'r Umm Fawākhīr 24 Ei 26.01N 33.38 E
Bi'r Umm Sa'īd 24 Eh 29.40N 33.34 E
Bi'r Umm Ţunayḑibah 24 Ej 25.16N 33.06 E
Biruni 19 Gg 41.42N 60.45 E
Biržai/Biržaj 19 Cd 56.12N 24.48 E
Biržaj/Biržai 19 Cd 56.12N 24.48 E
Bîrzava 15 Ec 46.07N 21.59 E
Bîrzava 15 Dd 45.16N 20.49 E
Birzebbuga 14 Io 35.49N 14.32 E
Bisa, Pulau- 26 Ig 1.15S 127.28 E
Bisaccia 14 Ji 41.01N 15.22 E
Bisacquino 14 Hm 37.42N 13.15 E
Bisbee 43 Fe 31.27N 109.55W
Biscarrosse, Étang de- 11 Ej 44.21N 1.10W
Biscay, Bay of- (EN) =
Gascogne, Golfe de- 5 Fg 44.00N 4.00W
Bisceglie 14 Ki 41.14N 16.30 E
Bischofshofen 14 Hc 47.25N 13.13 E
Bischofswerda/Biskopicy 10 Ke 51.07N 14.11 E
Biscoe Islands 66 Qe 66.00S 66.30W
Biscotasi Lake 44 Fb 47.20N 82.05W
Biscucuy 50 Bh 9.22N 69.59W
Bisert 17 Hh 56.39N 57.59 E
Bisert 19 Fd 56.52N 59.03 E
Biševski Kanal 14 Kg 43.00N 16.03 E
Biševo 14 Kh 42.59N 16.01 E
Bisha 35 Fb 15.28N 37.33 E
Bishārah 33 De 22.58N 22.39 E
Bishārīyīn, Barq al- 35 Eb 19.26N 32.22 E
Bishnupur 25 Hd 23.05N 87.19 E
Bishop 43 Dd 37.22N 118.24W
Bishop Auckland 9 Lg 54.40N 1.40W
Bishop Rock 9 Gl 49.53N 6.25W
Bishop's Falls 42 Lg 49.01N 55.30W
Bishop's Stortford 9 Nj 51.53N 0.09 E
Bishop's Waltham 12 Ad 50.57N 1.13W
Bishrī, Jabal- 24 He 35.20N 39.20 E
Bishui 27 La 52.07N 123.43 E
Biškek (Frunze) 22 Je 42.54N 74.36 E
Biskra 31 He 34.51N 5.44 E
Biskra [3] 32 Ic 34.40N 6.00 E
Biskupiec 10 Qc 53.52N 20.27 E
Bislig 26 Ie 8.13N 126.19 E
Bismarck 39 Ie 46.48N 100.47W
Bismarck, Kap- 41 Kc 76.40N 18.40W
Bismarck Archipelago 57 Fe 5.00S 150.00 E
Bismarck Sea 60 Dh 4.00S 147.30 E
Bismark Range 60 Ci 5.30S 144.45 E
Bismil 24 Id 37.51N 40.40 E
Bison 45 Ed 45.31N 102.28W
Bīsotūn 24 Le 34.23N 47.26 E
Bispfors 8 Ga 63.02N 16.37 E
Bissau 31 Fg 11.51N 15.35W
Bissaula 34 Hd 7.01N 10.27 E
Bissett 44 Hb 46.13N 78.02W
Bisson, Banc du- 37 Hb 12.00S 46.25 E
Bistcho Lake 42 Fe 59.45N 118.50W
Bistineau, Lake- 45 Jj 32.25N 93.22W
Bistra 15 Fd 45.29N 22.11 E
Bistra 15 Dh 41.37N 20.44 E
Bistreţ 15 Gf 43.54N 23.30 E
Bistrica 15 Dg 42.09N 20.59 E
Bistrica 15 Cf 43.28N 19.42 E
Bistriţa 15 Hb 47.08N 24.29 E
Bistriţa [Rom.] 15 Jc 46.30N 26.57 E
Bistriţa [Rom.] 15 Hb 47.04N 24.25 E
Bistriţa-Năsăud [2] 15 Hb 47.05N 24.35 E
Bitam 36 Bb 2.05N 11.29 E
Bitam 13 Ri 35.15N 5.11 E
Bitburg 10 Cg 49.58N 6.32 E
Bitche 11 Ne 49.03N 7.26 E
Bitéa 35 Cc 13.11N 20.10 E
Bithia 14 Cl 38.55N 8.52 E
Bithynia 15 Mi 40.20N 29.30 E
Bitjug 16 Kd 50.37N 39.55 E
Bitkine 35 Bc 11.59N 18.13 E
Bitlis 23 Fb 38.22N 42.06 E
Bitola 6 Ig 41.02N 21.20 E
Bitonto 14 Ki 41.06N 16.41 E
Bitterfeld 10 Ie 51.37N 12.19 E
Bitterfontein 31 Il 31.00S 18.32 E
Bitterroot Range 38 He 47.06N 115.10W
Bitterroot River 46 Hc 46.52N 114.06W
Bitti 14 Dj 40.29N 9.23 E
Bitung 26 If 1.27N 125.11 E
Biu 31 Ig 10.37N 12.12 E
Bivolari 15 Kb 47.32N 27.26 E
Bivolu, Vîrful- 15 Ib 47.15N 25.56 E
Bivona 14 Hm 37.37N 13.26 E
Biwa-ko 28 Ng 35.13N 136.05 E
Bixad [Rom.] 15 Ic 46.06N 25.52 E
Bixad [Rom.] 15 Gb 47.56N 23.24 E
Bixby 45 Ii 35.57N 95.53W
Biyalā 24 Dg 31.10N 31.13 E
Biyang 27 Je 32.40N 113.21 E
Biyārjomand 24 Pd 36.06N 55.53 E
Biźbuljak 17 Gj 53.43N 54.16 E
Biže 18 Kb 45.10N 77.58 E
Bizen 28 Mg 34.44N 134.09 E
Bizerte (EN) = Banzart 31 He 37.17N 9.52 E
Bjala 15 If 43.27N 25.44 E
Bjala Slatina 15 Gf 43.28N 23.56 E
Bjargtangar 5 Db 65.30N 24.32W
Bjärna/Perniö 7 Ff 60.12N 23.08 E
Bjärnum 8 Eh 56.17N 13.42 E
Bjästa 8 Ha 63.12N 18.30 E
Bjelašnica 14 Mg 43.43N 18.09 E
Bjelašnica 14 Mh 42.51N 18.09 E
Bjelašnica 14 Mg 43.09N 18.23 E
Bjelolasica 14 Ie 45.16N 14.58 E
Bjelovar 14 Ke 45.54N 16.51 E
Bjerkvik 7 Db 68.33N 17.34 E
Bjerringbro 8 Ch 56.23N 9.40 E
Bjervamoen 8 Ce 59.25N 9.04 E
Bjeshkët e Nemuna 15 Cg 42.30N 19.50 E
Björdo 8 Fd 60.28N 14.42 E
Bjørkelangen 8 De 59.53N 11.34 E
Björkfors 8 Ff 58.01N 15.54 E
Björklinge 8 Gd 60.02N 17.33 E
Björkö 7 Eg 59.55N 19.00 E
Björna 7 Ee 63.34N 18.33 E
Bjørnafjorden 8 Ad 60.05N 5.20 E
Björneborg 8 Fe 59.15N 14.15 E
Björneborg/Pori 6 Ic 61.29N 21.47 E
Bjorne Peninsula 42 Ia 77.30N 87.00W
Bjornesfjorden 8 Bd 60.10N 7.40 E
Bjørnevatn 7 Gb 69.40N 30.00 E
Bjørnøya 67 Kd 74.30N 19.00 E
Bjørnöya = Bear Island (EN)
5 Ha 74.30N 19.00 E
Bjurholm 7 Ee 63.56N 19.13 E
Bjuröklubb 7 Ed 64.28N 21.35 E
Bjuv 8 Eh 56.05N 12.54 E
Bla 34 Dc 12.56N 5.45W
Blace 15 Ef 43.18N 21.18 E
Blackall 58 Gf 24.25S 145.28 E
Black Bank (EN) = Zwarte
Bank 12 Fa 53.15N 3.55 E
Black Bay 45 Lb 48.40N 88.30W
Blackburn 9 Kh 53.45N 2.29W
Blackburn, Mount- 38 Ec 61.44N 143.26W
Black Butte Lake 46 Dg 39.45N 122.20W
Black Coast 66 Qf 71.45S 62.00W
Blackdown Hills 9 Jk 50.57N 3.09W
Blackduck 45 Ic 47.44N 94.33W
Blackfoot 43 Ec 43.11N 112.20W
Blackfoot Reservoir 46 Je 42.55N 111.35W
Black Forest (EN) =
Schwarzwald 5 Gf 48.00N 8.15 E
Black Head 9 Hk 50.01N 5.03W
Black Hills 38 Ie 44.00N 104.00W
Black Isle 9 Id 57.35N 4.20W
Black Lake 42 Ge 59.11N 105.20W
Blackman's 51q Ab 13.11N 59.32W
Black Mesa 46 Jh 36.35N 110.20W
Blackmoor 9 Ik 50.23N 4.50W
Black Mountain 43 Kd 36.54N 82.54W
Black Mountain [U.S.] 46 Hi 35.30N 114.30W
Black Mountains
[Wales-U.K.] 9 Jj 51.57N 3.08W
Blackpool 9 Jh 53.50N 3.03W
Black Range 43 Fe 33.20N 107.50W
Black River 49 Id 18.01N 77.51W
Black River [Az.-U.S.] 46 Jj 33.44N 110.13W
Black River [Mi.-U.S.] 44 Fd 43.00N 82.25W
Black River [N.Y.-U.S.] 44 Id 43.59N 76.04W
Black River [U.S.] 45 Ki 35.38N 91.19W
Black River [Wi.-U.S.] 45 Ke 43.57N 91.22W
Black River (EN) = Babian
Jiang 21 Mg 20.17N 106.34 E
Black River (EN) = Da, Sông-
21 Mg 20.17N 106.34 E
Black River Falls 45 Kd 44.16N 90.52W
Black Rock 56 Lh 53.39S 41.48W
Black Rock [Ire.] 9 Cg 54.05N 10.20W
Black Rock [Phil.] 26 Ge 8.48N 119.50 E
Black Rock Desert 43 Dc 41.10N 119.00W
Blacksburg 44 Gg 37.15N 80.25W
Black Sea (EN) = Černoje
More 5 Jg 43.00N 35.00 E
Black Sea (EN) = Černo
More 5 Jg 43.00N 35.00 E
Black Sea (EN) =
Karadeniz 5 Jg 43.00N 35.00 E
Black Sea (EN) = Neagră,
Marea- 5 Jg 43.00N 35.00 E
Blacksod Bay/Cuan an
Fhóid Duibh 9 Dg 54.08N 10.00W
Blackstairs Mountains/Na
Staighri Dubha 9 Gi 52.33N 6.49W
Blackstone 44 Hg 37.04N 78.01W
Blackville 44 Ob 46.47N 65.54W
Black Volta 30 Gh 8.38N 1.30W
Black Volta (EN) = Volta
Noire 30 Gh 8.38N 1.30W
Black Volta (EN) = Volta
Noire [3] 34 Ec 12.30N 4.00W
Blackwater 12 Cc 51.43N 0.28 E
Blackwater/An Abhainn
Dubh 9 Gh 53.39N 6.43W
Blackwater/An Abhainn
Mhór [Ire.] 9 Fj 51.51N 7.50W
Blackwater/An Abhainn
Mhór [N.Ire.-U.K.] 9 Gg 54.30N 6.35W
Blackwell 45 Hh 36.48N 97.17W
Blackwood River 59 Df 34.35S 115.02 E
Blagnac 11 Hk 43.38N 1.24 E
Blagodarny 16 Mg 45.04N 43.24 E
Blagoevgrad 15 Gg 42.01N 23.06 E
Blagoevgrad [2] 15 Gh 41.45N 23.25 E
Blagoveščenka 20 Cf 52.50N 79.55 E
Blagoveščensk 17 Fd 55.01N 55.59 E
Blagoveščensk 22 Od 50.17N 127.32 E
Blåhø 8 Cb 62.45N 9.19 E
Blain 11 Eg 47.29N 1.45W
Blaine [Mn.-U.S.] 45 Jd 45.11N 93.14W
Blaine [Wa.-U.S.] 46 Db 48.59N 122.44W
Blair 45 Hf 41.33N 96.08W
Blair Athol 59 Jd 22.42S 147.33 E
Blairgowrie 9 Je 56.36N 3.21W
Blairmore 46 Hb 49.36N 114.26W
Blaise 11 Kf 48.38N 4.43 E
Blaj 15 Gc 46.11N 23.55 E
Blake Basin (EN) 43 Mf 29.00N 76.00W
Blakely 44 Ej 31.23N 84.56W
Blakeney Point 9 Ni 52.59N 1.00 E
Blake Plateau (EN) 38 Lf 31.00N 79.00W
Blake Ridge (EN) 38 Lg 29.00N 73.30W
Blakstad 7 Bg 58.30N 8.39 E
Blanc, Cape- (EN) = Abyaḑ,
Ra's al- 30 He 37.20N 9.50 E
Blanc, Cape- (EN) =
Nouâdhibou, Râs- 30 Ff 20.46N 17.03W
Blanc, Lac- 44 Kb 47.45N 73.12W
Blanc, Mont- 5 Gf 45.50N 6.52 E
Blanca, Bahía- 52 Ji 38.55S 62.10W
Blanca, Cerro- 49 Gi 8.40N 80.35W
Blanca, Cordillera- 54 Ce 9.10S 77.35W
Blanca, Costa- 13 Lg 37.38N 0.40W
Blanca, Isla- 48 Pg 21.24N 86.50W
Blanca, Punta- 48 Bc 29.05N 114.45W
Blancagrande 55 Bm 36.32S 60.53W
Blanca Peak [Co.-U.S.] 43 Fd 37.34N 105.29W
Blanca Peak [U.S.] 38 If 37.35N 105.29W
Blanche, Lake- [Austl.] 59 Ed 22.25S 123.15 E
Blanche, Lake- [Austl.] 59 He 29.15S 139.40 E
Blanche, Point- 51b Ac 18.00N 63.00W
Blanche Channel 63a Cc 8.30S 157.30 E
Blanc-Nez, Cap- 12 Dd 50.56N 1.42 E
Blanco, Cabo- [C.R.] 47 Gg 9.33N 85.06W
Blanco, Cabo- [Sp.] 13 Oe 39.22N 2.46 E
Blanco, Cape- 43 Cc 42.50N 124.34W
Blanco, Cerro- 48 Fe 25.43N 107.39W
Blanco, Río- 54 Ff 12.30S 64.18W
Blanco del Sur, Cayo- 49 Gb 22.02N 81.24W
Blanda 7a Bb 65.39N 20.18W
Blanding 46 Kh 37.37N 109.29W
Blanes 13 Oc 41.41N 2.48 E
Blangy-le-Château 12 Ce 49.14N 0.17 E
Blangy-sur-Bresle 11 He 49.56N 1.38 E
Blanice [Czech.] 10 Kg 49.48N 14.58 E
Blanice [Czech.] 10 Kg 49.17N 14.09 E
Blankaholm 8 Gg 57.35N 16.31 E
Blankenberge 11 Jc 51.19N 3.08 E
Blankenheim 12 Id 50.26N 6.39 E
Blanquilla, Isla- 54 Fa 11.51N 64.37W
Blanquillo 55 Ek 32.55S 55.40W
Blansko 10 Mg 49.22N 16.39 E
Blantyre 31 Ki 15.47S 35.00 E
Blantyre-Limbe 36 Gf 15.49S 35.03 E
Blåskavlen 8 Bd 60.58N 7.18 E
Błaszki 10 Oe 51.39N 18.27 E
Blatná 10 Jg 49.26N 13.53 E
Blato 14 Kh 42.56N 16.48 E
Blåvands Huk 5 Gd 55.33N 8.05 E
Blavet [Fr.] 11 Cf 48.13N 3.10W
Blavet [Fr.] 11 Cg 47.46N 3.18W
Blaye 11 Fi 45.08N 0.40W
Blaye-les-Mines 11 Ij 44.01N 2.08 E
Bled 14 Id 46.22N 14.08 E
Blefjell 8 Ce 59.48N 9.10 E
Bleialf 12 Id 50.14N 6.17 E
Blekinge [2] 7 Dh 56.20N 15.20 E
Blenheim 58 Ii 41.31S 173.57 E
Bletchley 9 Mj 52.00N 0.46W
Bleus, Monts- 36 Fb 1.30N 30.30 E
Blhārshāh 25 Fe 19.50N 79.22 E
Blida [3] 32 Hb 36.35N 2.30 E
Blida 31 He 36.34N 2.55 E
Blidö 8 He 59.35N 18.55 E
Blidsberg 8 Eg 57.56N 13.29 E
Blies 12 Je 49.07N 7.04 E
Blieskastel 12 Je 49.14N 7.15 E
Bligh Water 63d Ab 17.00S 178.00 E
Blind River 42 Jg 46.10N 82.58W
Blitar 26 Fh 8.06S 112.09 E
Blitta 34 Fd 8.19N 0.59 E
Block Island 44 Le 41.11N 71.35W
Bloemfontein 31 Jk 29.12S 26.07 E
Bloemhof 37 De 27.38S 25.32 E
Blois 11 Hg 47.35N 1.20 E
Blokhus 8 Cg 57.15N 9.35 E
Blomberg 12 Lc 51.56N 9.05 E
Blönduós 7a Bb 65.40N 20.18W
Bloody Foreland/Cnoc
Fola 9 Ef 55.09N 8.17W
Bloomfield [Ia.-U.S.] 45 Jf 40.45N 92.25W
Bloomfield [In.-U.S.] 44 Df 39.01N 86.56W
Bloomington [Il.-U.S.] 43 Jc 40.29N 88.59W
Bloomington [In.-U.S.] 43 Jd 39.10N 86.32W
Bloomington [Mn.-U.S.] 45 Jd 44.50N 93.17W
Bloomsburg 44 Ie 41.01N 76.27W
Blosseville Kyst 41 Je 68.45N 27.25W
Blötberget 8 Fd 60.07N 15.04 E
Blountstown 44 Ej 30.29N 85.03W
Bludenz 14 Dc 47.09N 9.49 E
Blue Earth 45 Ie 43.38N 94.06W
Bluefield 43 Kd 37.14N 81.17W
Bluefields 47 Hf 12.00N 83.45W
Bluefields, Bahía de- 49 Fg 12.02N 83.44W
Blue Mesa Reservoir 45 Cg 38.28N 107.15W
Blue Mountain 44 Ie 40.15N 77.30W
Blue Mountain [Or.-U.S.] 46 Ge 42.25N 117.50W
Blue Mountain [U.S.] 45 Ii 34.41N 94.03W
Blue Mountain Lake 44 Jd 43.53N 74.26W
Blue Mountain Pass 46 Ge 42.18N 117.45W
Blue Mountain Peak 47 Ie 18.03N 76.35W
Blue Mountains [Austl.] 57 Kf 33.35S 150.15 E
Blue Mountains [U.S.] 43 Ec 44.35N 118.25W
Blue Mud Bay 59 Hb 13.25S 135.55 E
Blue Nile (EN) = Abay 30 Kg 15.38N 32.31 E
Blue Nile (EN) = Azraq, Al
Baḩr al- 30 Kg 15.38N 32.31 E
Bluenose Lake 42 Fc 68.00N 121.00W
Blue Ridge 44 Eh 34.52N 84.20W
Blue Ridge 38 Kf 37.00N 82.00W
Blue Stack/Na Cruacha 9 Eg 54.45N 8.06W
Bluestone Lake 44 Gg 37.30N 80.50W
Bluff [N.Z.] 61 Ci 46.36S 168.21 E
Bluff [Ut.-U.S.] 46 Kh 37.17N 109.33W
Bluff Point 59 Ce 27.50S 114.05 E
Bluffton 44 Ee 40.44N 85.11W
Blumberg 10 Ei 47.50N 8.32 E
Blumenau 56 Kc 26.56S 49.03W
Blyth 12 Db 52.19N 1.41 E
Blyth 9 Lf 55.07N 1.30W
Blythe 43 Ee 33.37N 114.36W
Blytheville 43 Jd 35.56N 89.55W
Bø 7 Bg 59.25N 9.04 E
Bo 31 Fh 7.58N 11.45W
Boa 34 Dd 8.26N 7.10W
Boac 26 Hd 12.28N 122.28 E
Boaco [3] 49 Eg 12.35N 85.25W
Boaco 49 Eg 12.28N 85.40W
Boa Esperança 55 Je 21.05S 45.34W
Boa Esperança, Represa- 54 Je 6.50S 44.00W
Boa Esperançao, Serra da-
55 Je 20.57S 45.40W
Bo'ai 28 Bg 35.10N 113.03 E
Boal 13 Fa 43.26N 6.49W
Boali 35 Be 4.48N 18.07 E
Boano, Pulau- 26 Ig 2.56S 127.56 E
Boardman 46 Fd 45.51N 119.43W
Boa Sentença, Serra da- 55 Ed 19.13S 57.33W
Boa Vista 30 Eg 16.05N 22.50W
Boa Vista [Braz.] 55 Ec 17.51S 54.13W
Boa Vista [Braz.] 55 Ia 12.40S 46.51W
Boa Vista [Braz.] 53 Je 2.49N 60.40W
Bobai 27 Ig 22.15N 109.58 E
Bobali, Cerros de- 49 Ki 8.53N 73.28W
Bobali, Cerros de- 49 Ki 8.53N 73.28W
Bobbio 14 Df 44.46N 9.23 E
Bobigny 11 If 48.54N 2.27 E
Bobo Dioulasso 31 Gg 11.12N 4.18W
Bobojod, Gora- 18 Hd 40.50N 70.20 E
Bobolice 10 Mc 53.57N 16.36 E
Bobonong 37 Dd 21.58S 28.25 E
Bobovdol 15 Fg 42.22N 23.00 E
Bóbr 10 Ld 52.04N 15.04 E
Bobrik 16 Ec 52.08N 26.48 E
Bobrinec 16 He 48.04N 32.09 E
Bobrka 10 Ug 49.34N 24.20 E
Bobrov 19 Ee 51.06N 40.01 E
Bobrovica 16 Gd 50.43N 31.28 E
Bobrowniki 10 Tc 53.08N 23.50 E
Bobrujsk 6 Ie 53.09N 29.15 E
Bobures 54 Db 9.15N 71.11W
Boby, Pic- 37 Hd 22.12S 46.55 E
Boca del Rio 48 Ee 25.20N 108.25W
Boca de Pozo 50 Dg 11.00N 64.23W
Boca do Acre 53 Jf 8.45S 67.23W
Bocage, Cap- 63b Be 21.12S 165.37 E
Bocaina 55 Db 15.16S 56.45W
Bocaiúva 55 Kc 17.07S 43.49W
Bocajá 55 Ef 22.45S 55.13W
Bocaranga 35 Bd 6.59N 15.39 E
Boca Raton 43 Kf 26.21N 80.05W
Bocas del Toro 47 Hg 9.20N 82.15W
Bocas del Toro [3] 49 Fi 8.50N 82.10W
Bocas del Toro, Archipiélago
de- 49 Fi 9.20N 82.10W
Bocay 49 Ef 14.19N 85.10W
Bochaine 11 Lj 44.20N 5.50 E
Bochnia 10 Qg 49.58N 20.26 E
Bocholt [Bel.] 12 Hc 51.10N 5.35 E
Bocholt [Ger.] 10 Ce 51.50N 6.36 E
Bochum 10 De 51.29N 7.13 E
Bocognano 11a Ba 42.05N 9.04 E
Bocoio 36 Be 12.28S 14.08 E
Boconó 49 Li 9.15N 70.16W
Bocşa 15 Ed 45.23N 21.47 E
Boda 35 Be 4.19N 17.28 E
Boda 8 Fc 61.01N 15.13 E
Böda 8 Gg 57.15N 17.03 E
Bodafors 8 Fg 57.30N 14.42 E
Bodajbo 22 Nd 57.51N 114.10 E
Bodalangi 36 Db 3.14N 22.14 E
Bode 10 Hd 52.01N 11.12 E
Bödefeld-Freiheit,
Schmallenberg- 12 Kc 51.15N 8.24 E
Bodegraven 12 Gb 52.06N 4.44 E
Bodélé 30 Ig 16.30N 17.30 E
Boden 6 Ib 65.50N 21.42 E
Bodenheim 12 Ke 49.56N 8.18 E
Bodensee = Constance,
Lake- (EN) 5 Gf 47.35N 9.25 E
Boderg, Lough- 9 Fh 53.52N 8.00W
Bodmin 9 Ik 50.29N 4.43W
Bodmin Moor 9 Ik 50.35N 4.40W
Bodø 6 Hb 67.17N 14.23 E
Bodoquena 55 De 20.12S 56.48W
Bodoquena, Serra da- 54 Gh 21.00S 56.50W
Bodrog 10 Rh 48.07N 21.25 E
Bodrogköz 10 Rh 48.15N 21.45 E
Bodrum 23 Cb 37.02N 27.06 E
Bodrum Yarimadasi 15 Kl 37.05N 27.30 E
Bodva 10 Qh 48.12N 20.47 E
Boën 11 Ji 45.44N 4.00 E
Boende 31 Ji 0.13S 20.52 E
Boeo, Capo- (Lilibeo, Capo-)
14 Gm 37.34N 12.41 E
Boerne 45 Gl 29.47N 98.44W
Boesmanland = Bushman-
land (EN) 37 Be 29.30S 19.00 E
Boffa 34 Cc 10.10N 14.02W
Boga 15 Cg 42.24N 19.38 E
Bogale 25 Je 16.17N 95.24 E
Bogalusa 45 Lk 30.47N 89.52W
Bogandé 34 Ec 12.59N 0.08W
Bogangolo 35 Bd 5.34N 18.15 E
Bogatić 15 Ce 44.51N 19.29 E
Bogatynia 10 Kf 50.55N 14.59 E
Boğazkale 24 Fb 40.01N 34.35 E
Boğazlıyan 24 Fc 39.12N 35.15 E
Bogbonga 36 Cb 1.35N 19.25 E

Index Symbols

[1] Independent Nation
[2] State, Region
[3] District, County
[4] Municipality
[5] Colony, Dependency
Continent
Physical Region
Historical or Cultural Region
Mount, Mountain
Volcano
Hill
Mountains, Mountain Range
Hills, Escarpment
Plateau, Upland
Pass, Gap
Plain, Lowland
Delta
Salt Flat
Valley, Canyon
Crater, Cave
Karst Features
Depression
Polder
Desert, Dunes
Forest, Woods
Heath, Steppe
Oasis
Cape, Point
Coast, Beach
Cliff
Peninsula
Isthmus
Sandbank
Island
Atoll
Rock, Reef
Islands, Archipelago
Rocks, Reefs
Coral Reef
Well, Spring
Geyser
River, Stream
Waterfall Rapids
River Mouth, Estuary
Lake
Salt Lake
Intermittent Lake
Reservoir
Swamp, Pond
Canal
Glacier
Ice Shelf, Pack Ice
Ocean
Sea
Gulf, Bay
Strait, Fjord
Lagoon
Bank
Seamount
Tablemount
Ridge
Shelf
Basin
Escarpment, Sea Scarp
Fracture
Trench, Abyss
National Park, Reserve
Point of Interest
Recreation Site
Cave, Cavern
Historic Site
Ruins
Wall, Walls
Church, Abbey
Temple
Scientific Station
Airport
Port
Lighthouse
Mine
Tunnel
Dam, Bridge

Bogda Feng 27 Ec 43.45N 88.32 E
Bogdan 15 Hg 42.37N 24.28 E
Bogdanovka → Ninocminda 16 Mi 41.15N 43.36 E
Bogda Shan 21 Ke 43.35N 90.00 E
Bogen 7 Db 68.32N 17.00 E
Bogenfels 37 Be 27.23S 15.22 E
Bogense 8 Di 55.34N 10.06 E
Boggeragh Mountains/An Bhograch 9 Ei 52.05N 9.00W
Boggy Peak 51d Bb 17.03N 61.51W
Boghar 13 Oi 35.55N 2.43 E
Boghni 13 Ph 36.32N 3.57 E
Bogia 60 Ch 4.16S 144.58 E
Bognor Regis 12 Bd 50.47N 0.39W
Bogny-sur-Meuse 12 Ge 49.54N 4.43 E
Bogoduhov 16 Id 50.12N 35.31 E
Bogomila 15 Eh 41.36N 21.28 E
Bogor 22 Mj 6.35S 106.47 E
Bogoridick 19 De 53.50N 38.08 E
Bogorodčany 10 Uh 48.45N 24.40 E
Bogorodsk 7 Kh 56.09N 43.32 E
Bogorodskoje 7 Mh 57.51N 50.48 E
Bogorodskoje 20 Jf 52.22N 140.30 E
Bogotá → Santa Fe de Bogotá 53 Ie 4.36N 74.05W
Bogotol 20 De 56.17N 89.43 E
Bogøy 7 Dc 67.54N 15.11 E
Bogra 25 Hd 24.51N 89.22 E
Bogučany 20 Ee 58.23N 97.39 E
Bogučar 16 Le 49.57N 40.33 E
Bogué 32 Ef 16.36N 14.15W
Boguševsk 7 Hi 54.50N 30.13 E
Boguslav 19 Df 49.33N 30.54 E
Bo Hai=Chihli, Gulf of- (EN) 21 Nf 38.30N 120.00 E
Bohai Haixia 27 Ld 38.00N 121.30 E
Bohain-en-Vermandois 12 Fe 49.59N 3.27 E
Bohemia (EN)=Čechy 5 Hf 50.00N 14.30 E
Bohemia (EN)=Čechy 10 Kf 50.00N 14.30 E
Bohemian Forest (EN)= Böhmerwald 5 Hf 49.00N 13.30 E
Bohemian Forest (EN)= Český Les 10 Ig 49.50N 12.30 E
Bohemian Forest (EN)= Oberpfälzer Wald 10 Ig 49.50N 12.30 E
Bohemian Forest (EN)= Šumava 5 Hf 49.00N 13.30 E
Bohicon 34 Fd 7.12N 2.04 E
Bohmte 12 Kb 52.22N 8.19 E
Bohodoyou 34 Dd 9.46N 9.04W
Bohol 21 Oi 9.50N 124.10 E
Böhönye 10 Nj 46.24N 17.24 E
Bohor 14 Jd 46.04N 15.26 E
Bohu/Bagrax 27 Ec 41.58N 86.29 E
Bohus 8 Eg 57.51N 12.01 E
Bohuslän 8 Df 58.15N 11.50 E
Boiaçu 54 Fd 0.27S 61.46W
Boiano 14 Ii 41.29N 14.29 E
Boina 30 Lj 16.00S 46.30 E
Bois, Lac des - 42 Ec 66.50N 125.15W
Bois, Rio dos- [Braz.] 55 Gd 18.35S 50.02W
Bois, Rio dos- [Braz.] 55 Ha 13.55S 49.51W
Bois Blanc Island 44 Ec 45.45N 84.28W
Boischaut 11 Hb 46.40N 1.45 E
Boise 39 He 43.37N 116.13W
Boise City 45 Eh 36.44N 102.31W
Boise River 46 Ge 43.49N 117.01W
Boissay 12 De 49.31N 1.21 E
Boissevain 42 Hg 49.14N 100.03W
Boizenburg 10 Gc 53.23N 10.43 E
Bojador, Cabo- 30 Ff 26.08N 14.30W
Bojana 15 Ch 41.52N 19.22 E
Bojanowo 10 Me 51.42N 16.44 E
Bojarka 19 De 50.19N 30.20 E
Bojčinovci 15 Gf 43.28N 23.20 E
Bojnūrd 23 Ib 37.28N 57.19 E
Bojonegoro 26 Fh 7.09S 111.52 E
Bojuru 55 Gj 31.38S 51.26W
Bokatola 36 Cc 0.38S 18.46 E
Boké 34 Cc 10.56N 14.13W
Bokhara River 59 Je 29.55S 146.42 E
Bokn 8 Ae 59.15N 5.25 E
Boknafjorden 5 Gd 59.10N 5.35 E
Boko 36 Bc 4.47S 14.38 E
Bokol Mayo 35 Ge 4.31N 41.32 E
Bokoro 35 Bc 12.23N 17.03 E
Bokote 36 Dc 0.05S 20.08 E
Bokpyin 25 Jf 11.16N 98.46 E
Boksitogorsk 19 Dd 59.29N 33.52 E
Bokungu 36 Dc 0.41S 22.19 E
Bol [Chad] 35 Ac 13.30N 14.41 E
Bol 14 Kg 43.16N 16.40 E
Bola, Bahr- 35 Bd 9.50N 18.59 E
Bolama 34 Bc 11.35N 15.28W
Bolands 51d Bb 17.02N 61.53W
Bolaños, Rio- 48 Gg 21.14N 104.08W
Bolattau, Gora- 18 Ha 46.44N 71.54 E
Bolayir 15 Ji 40.31N 26.45 E
Bolbec 11 Ge 49.34N 0.29 E
Bolda 16 Pg 45.58N 48.35 E
Bole [Eth.] 35 Fd 6.37N 37.22 E
Bole [Ghana] 34 Ed 9.02N 2.29W
Bole/Bortala 27 Dc 44.59N 81.57 E
Bolehov 16 Ce 49.03N 23.50 E
Bolesławiec 10 Le 51.16N 15.34 E
Bolgatanga 31 Gg 10.47N 0.51W
Bolgrad 16 Fg 45.40N 28.38 E
Bolhov 19 De 53.30N 36.01 E
Boli 27 Nb 45.46N 130.31 E
Bolia 36 Cc 1.36S 18.23 E
Boliden 7 Ed 64.52N 20.23 E
Bolinao, Cape- 26 Gc 16.22N 119.50 E
Bolintin Vale 15 Ie 44.27N 25.46 E
Bolívar [Col.] [2] 54 Db 9.00N 74.40W
Bolivar [Mo.-U.S.] 45 Jh 37.37N 93.25W
Bolivar [Tn.-U.S.] 44 Ch 35.15N 88.59W
Bolívar [Ven.] [2] 54 Fb 6.20N 63.30W
Bolívar, Cerro- 54 Fb 7.28N 63.25W
Bolívar, Pico- 52 Ie 8.30N 71.02W
Bolivia [1] 53 Jg 17.00S 65.00W
Bolivia, Altiplano de- 52 Jg 18.00S 68.00W
Boljevac 15 Ef 43.50N 21.58 E
Bollendorf 12 Ie 49.51N 6.22 E
Bollène 11 Kj 44.17N 4.45 E
Bollnäs 7 Df 61.21N 16.25 E
Bollon 59 Je 28.02S 147.28 E
Bollstabruk 8 Ga 63.00N 17.41 E
Bollullos par del Condado 13 Fg 37.20N 6.32W
Bolmen 7 Ch 56.55N 13.40 E
Bolnisi 16 Ni 41.28N 44.31 E
Bolobo 36 Cc 2.10S 16.14 E
Bolodek 20 If 53.43N 133.09 E
Bologna 6 Hg 44.29N 11.20 E
Bolognesi 54 Df 10.01S 74.05W
Bologoje 6 Jd 57.54N 34.02 E
Bolohovo 16 Jb 54.05N 37.52 E
Bolomba 36 Cb 0.29N 19.12 E
Bolombo 36 Dc 3.59S 21.22 E
Bolon 20 Ig 49.58N 136.04 E
Bolotnoje 20 De 55.41N 84.33 E
Bolovens, Plateau des- 25 Le 15.20N 106.20 E
Bolšaja Balahnja 20 Fb 73.37N 107.05 E
Bolšaja Berestovica 10 Uc 53.09N 24.02 E
Bolšaja Černigovka 7 Mj 52.08N 50.48 E
Bolšaja Glušica 7 Mj 52.24N 50.29 E
Bolšaja Ižora 8 Me 59.55N 29.40 E
Bolšaja Kinel 7 Mj 53.14N 50.32 E
Bolšaja Koksaga 7 Lh 56.07N 47.48 E
Bolšaja Kuonamka 20 Gc 70.50N 113.20 E
Bolšaja Oju 17 Jb 69.42N 60.42 E
Bolšaja Rogovaja 17 Jc 66.30N 60.40 E
Bolšaja Synja 17 Id 65.58N 58.01 E
Bolšaja Tap 17 Lg 59.55N 65.42 E
Bolšaja Ussurka 20 Ig 46.00N 133.30 E
Bolšaja Vladimirovka 19 He 50.53N 79.30 E
Bolšakovo 8 Ij 54.50N 21.36 E
Bolsena 14 Fh 42.39N 11.59 E
Bolsena, Lago di- 14 Fh 42.35N 11.55 E
Bolšerečje 19 Hd 56.06N 74.38 E
Bolšereck 20 Kf 52.22N 156.24 E
Bolšeustikinskoje 17 Ii 55.57N 58.20 E
Bolševik 20 Jd 62.40N 147.30 E
Bolševik, Ostrov-=Bolshevik Island (EN) 21 Mb 78.40N 102.30 E
Bolšezemelskaja Tundra 19 Fb 67.30N 58.30 E
Bolshevik Island (EN)= Bolševik, Ostrov- 21 Mb 78.40N 102.30 E
Bolšije Uki 19 Hd 56.57N 72.37 E
Bolšoj Anjuj 20 Lc 68.30N 160.50 E
Bolšoj Begičev, Ostrov- 20 Gb 74.20N 112.30 E
Bolšoj Berezovy, Ostrov- 8 Md 60.15N 28.35 E
Bolšoj Boktybaj, Gora- [Kaz.-U.S.S.R.] 19 Ff 48.30N 58.20 E
Bolšoj Boktybaj, Gora- [U.S.S.R.] 16 Ue 48.30N 58.25 E
Bolšoj Bolvanski Nos, Mys- 17 Ia 70.27N 59.05 E
Bolšoj Čeremšan 7 Li 54.12N 49.40 E
Bolšoje Muraškino 7 Ki 55.47N 44.46 E
Bolšoje Vlasjevo 20 Jf 53.25N 140.55 E
Bolšoje Zagorje 8 Mg 57.47N 28.58 E
Bolšoj Gašun 16 Mf 47.22N 42.42 E
Bolšoj Ik 17 Hj 51.47N 56.20 E
Bolšoj Irgiz 19 Ee 52.01N 47.24 E
Bolšoj Jenisej 20 Ef 51.40N 94.26 E
Bolšoj Jugan 19 Hc 60.55N 73.40 E
Bolšoj Kamen 20 Ih 43.08N 132.28 E
Bolšoj Klimecki, Ostrov- 7 Ie 62.00N 35.15 E
Bolšoj Kujalnik 16 Gf 46.46N 30.38 E
Bolšoj Kumak 16 Ud 51.22N 58.55 E
Bolšoj Ljahovski, Ostrov- 20 Jb 73.35N 142.00 E
Bolšoj Murta 20 Ee 56.55N 93.10 E
Bolšoj Nimnyr 20 He 58.08N 125.45 E
Bolšoj Pit 20 Ee 59.02N 91.40 E
Bolšoj Tjuters, Ostrov- 8 Le 59.50N 27.10 E
Bolšoj Uluj 20 Ee 56.45N 90.46 E
Bolšoj Uvat, Ozero- 17 Oh 57.35N 70.30 E
Bolšoj Uzen 5 Kf 48.50N 49.40 E
Bolsón, Cerro del- 52 Jh 27.13S 66.06W
Bolšovcy 10 Ug 49.08N 24.47 E
Bolsward 12 Ha 53.04N 5.30 E
Boltaña 13 Mb 42.27N 0.04 E
Bolton 9 Kh 53.35N 2.26W
Bolu 23 Da 40.44N 31.37 E
Bolu Dağları 24 Eb 41.05N 32.05 E
Bolungarvik 7a Aa 66.09N 23.15W
Boluntay 27 Fd 36.29N 92.18 E
Bolva 16 Ic 53.17N 34.20 E
Bolvadin 24 Dc 38.42N 31.04 E
Bolzano/Bozen 6 Hf 46.31N 11.22 E
Bom, Rio- 55 Gf 23.56S 51.44W
Boma 31 Ii 5.51S 13.03 E
Bomassa 36 Cb 2.12N 16.12 E
Bombala 59 Jg 36.54S 149.14 E
Bombarral 13 Ce 39.16N 9.09W
Bombay 22 Jh 18.58N 72.50 E
Bomberai, Jazirah- 26 Jg 3.00S 133.00 E
Bombo 36 Fb 0.35N 32.32 E
Bomboma 36 Cb 2.26N 18.57 E
Bom Comércio 54 Ee 9.45S 65.54W
Bom Conselho 54 Ke 9.10S 36.41W
Bom Despacho 54 Ig 19.43S 45.15W
Bomdila 25 Ic 27.16N 92.23 E
Bomi/Bowo 27 Ge 30.02N 95.39 E
Bomi Hills 34 Cd 6.52N 10.45W
Bomili 36 Eb 1.40N 27.01 E
Bom Jardim de Goiás 55 Fc 16.17S 52.07W
Bom Jardim de Minas 55 Je 21.57S 44.11W
Bom Jesus 55 Gi 28.42S 50.24W
Bom Jesus da Lapa 53 Lg 13.15S 43.25W
Bom Jesus de Goiás 55 Hd 18.12S 49.37W
Bømlafjorden 8 Ae 59.40N 5.20 E
Bømlo 7 Ag 59.45N 5.10 E
Bomokandi 36 Eb 3.30N 26.08 E
Bomongo 36 Cb 1.22N 18.21 E
Bom Retiro 55 Hh 27.48S 49.31W
Bom Sucesso 55 Je 21.02S 44.46W
Bomu 30 Jh 4.08N 22.26 E
Bomu (EN)=Mbomou 30 Jh 4.08N 22.26 E
Bomu (EN)=Mbomou [3] 35 Cd 5.30N 23.30 E
Bon, Cape- (EN)=Ţib, Ra's At- 30 Ie 37.05N 11.03 E
Bona, Mount- 40 Kd 61.20N 141.50W
Bonaire 54 Ea 12.10N 68.15W
Bonaire Basin (EN) 50 Cg 11.25N 67.30W
Bonampak 48 Ni 16.43N 91.05W
Bonanza 49 Ef 14.01N 84.35W
Bonanza Peak 46 Eb 48.14N 120.52W
Bonao 49 Ld 18.56N 70.25W
Bonaparte, Mount- 46 Fb 48.45N 119.08W
Bonaparte Archipelago 57 Df 14.20S 125.20 E
Bonaparte Lake 46 Ea 51.16N 120.35W
Bonaparte Rocks 51p Cb 12.24N 61.30W
Bonasse 50 Fg 10.05N 61.52W
Bonavista 42 Mg 48.39N 53.07W
Bonavista Bay 42 Mg 49.00N 53.20W
Bon-Cagan-Nur 27 Gb 45.35N 99.15 E
Bondeno 14 Ff 44.53N 11.25 E
Bondo 31 Jh 3.49N 23.40 E
Bondoukou 34 Ed 8.02N 2.48W
Bondoukou [3] 34 Ed 8.20N 2.55W
Bondowoso 26 Fh 7.55S 113.49 E
Bone, Gulf of- (EN)=Bone, Teluk- 21 Oj 4.00S 120.40 E
Bone, Teluk-=Bone, Gulf of- (EN) 21 Oj 4.00S 120.40 E
Bone Bay 51a Db 18.45N 64.22W
Bonelohe 26 Hh 5.48S 120.27 E
Bönen 12 Jc 51.36N 7.46 E
Bone Rate, Kepulauan- 26 Hh 7.00S 121.00 E
Bone Rate, Pulau- 26 Hh 7.22S 121.08 E
Bonete, Cerro- 56 Gc 27.51S 68.47W
Bong 34 Cd 6.49N 10.19W
Bong [3] 34 Dd 7.00N 9.40W
Bonga 35 Fd 7.16N 36.14 E
Bongabong 26 Hd 12.45N 121.29 E
Bongandanga 36 Db 1.30N 21.03 E
Bongo, Massif des- 35 Cd 8.40N 22.25 E
Bongolava 37 Hc 18.35S 45.20 E
Bongor 31 Ig 10.17N 15.22 E
Bongouanou [3] 34 Ed 6.43N 4.12W
Bongouanou 34 Ed 6.39N 4.12W
Bonham 45 Hj 33.35N 96.11W
Bonheiden 12 Gc 51.02N 4.32 E
Bonhomme, Col du- 11 Nf 48.10N 7.06 E
Bonhomme, Pic- 49 Kd 19.05N 72.15W
Bonifacio 11a Bb 41.23N 9.09 E
Bonifacio, Bocche di-= Bonifacio, Strait of- (EN) 5 Gg 41.18N 9.15 E
Bonifacio, Strait of- (EN)= Bonifacio, Bocche di- 5 Gg 41.18N 9.15 E
Bonifati, Capo- 14 Jk 39.33N 15.52 E
Bonin Basin (EN) 60 Bb 29.00N 137.00 E
Bonin Islands (EN)= Ogasawara-Shotō 21 Qg 27.00N 142.10 E
Bonin Trench (EN) 3 If 30.00N 145.00 E
Bonita Springs 44 Gl 26.21N 81.47W
Bonito [Braz.] 55 Jb 15.20S 44.46W
Bonito [Braz.] 55 De 21.08S 56.28W
Bonito, Pico- 47 Ge 15.38N 86.55W
Bonito, Rio- [Braz.] 55 Hb 15.18S 49.36W
Bonito, Rio- [Braz.] 55 Gc 16.31S 51.23W
Bonn 6 Ge 50.44N 7.06 E
Bonn-Bad Godesberg 10 Df 50.41N 7.09 E
Bonnebosq 12 Ce 49.12N 0.05 E
Bonnechère River 44 Ic 45.31N 76.33W
Bonners Ferry 46 Gb 48.41N 116.18W
Bonnet, Lac du- 45 Ia 50.22N 95.55W
Bonnétable 11 Gf 48.11N 0.26 E
Bonnet Plume 42 Ec 65.33N 134.58W
Bonneval 11 Hf 48.11N 1.24 E
Bonneville 11 Mh 46.05N 6.25 E
Bonneville Salt Flats 46 If 40.45N 113.50W
Bonnières-sur-Seine 12 De 49.02N 1.35 E
Bonningues-lès-Ardres 12 Ed 50.47N 2.01 E
Bonny 34 Ge 4.25N 7.10 E
Bono 14 Dj 40.25N 9.02 E
Bō-no-Misaki 29 Bf 31.15N 130.13 E
Bonorva 14 Cj 40.25N 8.46 E
Bontang 26 Gf 0.08N 117.30 E
Bonthain 26 Gh 5.32S 119.56 E
Bonthe 34 Cd 7.32N 12.30W
Bontoc 26 Hc 17.05N 120.58 E
Bonyhád 10 Oj 46.18N 18.32 E
Boo, Kepulauan- 26 Ig 1.12S 129.24 E
Boola 34 Dd 8.22N 8.43W
Booligal 59 If 33.52S 144.53 E
Boone [Ia.-U.S.] 45 Je 42.04N 93.53W
Boone [N.C.-U.S.] 44 Gg 36.13N 81.41W
Booneville [Ar.-U.S.] 45 Ji 35.08N 93.55W
Booneville [Ms.-U.S.] 45 Li 34.39N 88.34W
Boon Point 51d Bb 17.10N 61.50W
Boonville [In.-U.S.] 44 Df 38.03N 87.16W
Boonville [Mo.-U.S.] 45 Jg 38.58N 92.44W
Boos 12 De 49.23N 1.12 E
Boothia, Gulf of- 38 Jb 71.00N 91.00W
Boothia Peninsula 38 Jb 70.30N 95.00W
Boot Reefs 60 Cj 10.00S 144.35 E
Booué 36 Bc 0.06S 11.56 E
Bophuthatswana 37 De 26.00S 25.30 E
Bopolu 34 Cd 7.04N 10.29W
Boppard 12 Jd 50.14N 7.36 E
Boquerón [3] 55 Bf 23.00S 61.00W
Boquerón 51a Ab 18.03N 67.09W
Boquilla, Presa de la- 48 Gd 27.30N 105.30W
Boquillas del Carmen 48 Hc 29.17N 102.53W
Bor [Czech.] 10 Ig 49.43N 12.47 E
Bor 7 Kh 56.23N 44.07 E
Bor [Sud.] 31 Kh 6.12N 31.33 E
Bor [Swe.] 8 Fg 57.07N 14.10 E
Bor [Tur.] 24 Fd 37.54N 34.34 E
Bor 15 Fe 44.06N 22.06 E
Bora-Bora, Ile- 57 Lf 16.30S 151.45W
Borah Peak 38 He 44.08N 113.14W
Boraldaj 18 Gc 42.30N 69.05 E
Bora Marina 14 Jm 37.56N 15.55 E
Bōramo 35 Gd 9.58N 43.07 E
Borås 7 Ch 57.43N 12.55 E
Borāzjān 24 Nh 29.16N 51.12 E
Borba [Braz.] 54 Gd 4.24S 59.35W
Borba [Port.] 13 Ef 38.48N 7.27W
Borborema, Planalto da- 52 Mf 7.00S 37.00W
Borca 15 Ib 47.11N 25.46 E
Borcea 15 Ke 44.20N 27.45 E
Borcea, Braţul- 15 Ke 44.40N 27.53 E
Borchgrevink Coast 66 Kf 73.00S 171.00 E
Borçka 24 Ib 41.22N 41.40 E
Borculo 12 Ib 52.07N 6.31 E
Borda da Mata, Serra- 55 Ie 21.18S 47.06W
Bordeaux 6 Fg 44.50N 0.34W
Borden 42 Ga 78.30N 110.30W
Borden Peninsula 38 Kb 73.00N 83.00W
Borders [3] 9 Kf 55.35N 3.00W
Bordertown 58 Fh 36.19S 140.47 E
Bordighera 14 Bg 43.46N 7.39 E
Bordj Bou Arreridj 32 Hb 36.04N 4.46 E
Bordj el Emir Abdelkader 13 Oi 35.52N 2.16 E
Bordj Fly Sainte Marie 32 Gd 27.18N 2.59W
Bordj-Menaiel 13 Ph 36.44N 3.43 E
Bordj Messouda 32 Ic 30.12N 9.25 E
Bordj Moktar 31 Hf 21.20N 0.56 E
Bordj Omar Driss 31 Hf 28.09N 6.49 E
Bord Khūn-e Now 24 Nh 28.03N 51.28 E
Bordon Camp 12 Bc 51.07N 0.51W
Boreal, Chaco- 52 Kh 23.00S 60.00W
Boren 8 Ff 58.35N 15.10 E
Borensberg 8 Ff 58.34N 15.17 E
Borgå/Porvoo 7 Ff 60.24N 25.40 E
Borgarnes 7a Bb 64.32N 21.55W
Børgefjell 7 Cd 65.23N 13.50 E
Borgentreich 12 Lc 51.34N 9.15 E
Borger [Neth.] 12 Ib 52.55N 6.48 E
Borger [Tx.-U.S.] 43 Gd 35.39N 101.24W
Borgholm 7 Dh 56.53N 16.39 E
Borghorst, Steinfurt- 12 Jb 52.08N 7.25 E
Borgia 14 Kl 38.49N 16.30 E
Borgloon 12 Hd 50.48N 5.20 E
Borgomanero 14 Ce 45.42N 8.28 E
Borgorose 14 Hh 42.11N 13.15 E
Borgo San Dalmazzo 14 Bf 44.20N 7.30 E
Borgo San Lorenzo 14 Fg 43.57N 11.23 E
Borgosesia 14 Ce 45.43N 8.16 E
Borgou [3] 34 Fc 10.30N 2.50 E
Borgo Val di Taro 14 Df 44.29N 9.46 E
Borgo Valsugana 14 Fd 46.03N 11.27 E
Borgu 30 Hg 10.35N 3.40 E
Borgworm/Waremme 11 Ld 50.42N 5.15 E
Bori 34 Ge 4.42N 7.21 E
Borinquen, Punta- 51a Ab 18.30N 67.10W
Borislav 19 Cf 49.18N 23.27 E
Borisoglebsk 6 Ke 51.23N 42.06 E
Borisov 19 Ce 54.15N 28.30 E
Borisovka 16 Jd 50.36N 36.06 E
Borispol 16 De 50.23N 30.59 E
Bo River 35 Dd 6.48N 27.55 E
Borja 14 Lf 44.31N 17.44 E
Borja [Peru] 54 Cd 4.26S 77.33W
Borja [Sp.] 13 Kc 41.50N 1.32W
Borjas Blancas/Les Borges Blanques 13 Mc 41.31N 0.52 E
Borken 12 Ce 51.51N 6.52 E
Borkou 30 Ig 18.15N 18.50 E
Borkou-Ennedi-Tibesti [3] 35 Bb 18.00N 19.00 E
Borkoviči 8 Mi 55.38N 28.23 E
Borkum 10 Cc 53.35N 6.41 E
Borlänge 7 Df 60.29N 15.25 E
Borlu 24 Cc 38.44N 28.27 E
Bormida 14 Cf 44.56N 8.40 E
Bormio 14 Ed 46.28N 10.22 E
Born 11 Fj 44.30N 1.00W
Borna 10 Ie 51.07N 12.30 E
Borndiep 12 Ha 53.25N 5.35 E
Borne 12 Ib 52.18N 6.45 E
Borneo/Kalimantan 21 Ni 1.00N 114.00 E
Bornheim 12 Id 50.46N 7.00 E
Bornholm 5 Hd 55.10N 15.00 E
Bornholm [2] 8 Fi 55.10N 15.00 E
Bornos 13 Gh 36.48N 5.44W
Bornova, İzmir- 24 Bc 38.27N 27.14 E
Bornu [2] 34 Hc 12.00N 12.40 E
Bornu 30 Ig 12.30N 13.00 E
Boro 30 Jh 8.52N 26.11 E
Borodino 7 Ii 55.32N 35.50 E
Borodino 20 Ee 55.57N 95.03 E
Borodinskoje 8 Md 61.00N 29.29 E
Borogoncy 20 Id 62.39N 131.08 E
Borohoro Shan 21 Ke 42.00N 85.00 E
Boromo 34 Ec 11.45N 2.56W
Borongan 26 Id 11.37N 125.26 E
Borotou 34 Dd 8.44N 7.30W
Borovan 15 Gf 43.26N 23.45 E
Borovec 15 Gg 42.16N 23.35 E
Boroviči 19 Dd 58.24N 33.56 E
Borovici 8 Mg 57.58N 29.47 E
Borovljanka 20 Df 52.38N 84.35 E
Borovo 14 Me 45.24N 18.59 E
Borovsk 19 Gd 57.03N 65.04 E
Borovskoj 19 Ge 53.48N 64.17 E
Borrachas, Islas- 50 Dg 10.18N 64.44W
Borrān 35 Hc 10.11N 48.53 E
Borrby 8 Fi 55.27N 14.10 E
Borroloola 58 Ef 16.04S 136.17 E
Borş 15 Eb 47.07N 21.49 E
Borşa 15 Hb 47.39N 24.40 E
Borščovočny Hrebet= Borshchovochny Range (EN) 20 Gf 52.00N 118.30 E
Borsec 15 Ic 46.57N 25.34 E
Borshchovochny Range (EN) =Borščovočny Hrebet 20 Gf 52.00N 118.30 E
Borsod-Abaúj-Zemplén [2] 10 Qh 48.15N 21.00 E
Bortala/Bole 27 Dc 44.59N 81.57 E
Bortala He 27 Dc 44.53N 82.45 E
Bort-les-Orgues 11 Ii 45.24N 2.30 E
Borūjen 24 Ng 31.59N 51.18 E
Borūjerd 23 Gc 33.54N 48.46 E
Borzja 22 Nd 50.24N 116.31 E
Borzna 16 Hd 51.15N 32.29 E
Boržomi 16 Mi 41.50N 43.25 E
Borzsöny 10 Oi 47.55N 19.00 E
Borzyszkowy 10 Nb 54.03N 17.22 E
Bosa 14 Cj 40.18N 8.30 E
Bosanska Dubica 14 Ke 45.11N 16.48 E
Bosanska Gradiška 14 Le 45.09N 17.15 E
Bosanska Krupa 14 Kf 44.53N 16.10 E
Bosanski Brod 14 Me 45.08N 18.01 E
Bosanski Novi 14 Ke 45.03N 16.22 E
Bosanski Petrovac 14 Kf 44.34N 16.21 E
Bosanski Šamac 14 Me 45.04N 18.28 E
Bosansko Grahovo 23 Ff 44.11N 16.22 E
Bōsāso 31 Lg 11.13N 49.08 E
Bosavi, Mount- 59 Ia 6.35S 142.50 E
Bosbeek 12 Hc 51.06N 5.48 E
Bose 22 Mg 24.01N 106.32 E
Boshan 27 Kd 36.30N 117.50 E
Boshrūyeh 24 Qf 33.53N 57.26 E
Bosilegrad 15 Fg 42.30N 22.28 E
Bosingfeld, Extertal- 12 Lb 52.04N 9.07 E
Bosna 14 Me 45.04N 18.28 E
Bosna 15 Kg 42.11N 27.27 E
Bosna=Bosnia (EN) 5 Hg 44.00N 18.00 E
Bosna = Bosnia (EN) 14 Lf 44.00N 18.00 E
Bosna i Hercegovina = Bosnia and Herzegovina (EN) 14 Lf 44.15N 17.50 E
Bosnia (EN) = Bosna 14 Lf 44.00N 18.00 E
Bosnia (EN) = Bosna 5 Hg 44.00N 18.00 E
Bosnia and Herzegovina (EN) = Bosna i Hercegovina 14 Lf 44.15N 17.50 E
Bosnik 26 Kg 1.10S 136.14 E
Bošnjakovo 20 Jg 49.41N 142.10 E
Bosobolo 36 Cb 4.11N 19.54 E
Bōsō-Hantō 28 Pg 35.20N 140.10 E
Bosporus (EN)=İstanbul Boğazi 5 Ig 41.00N 29.00 E
Bosque Bonito 48 Gb 30.42N 105.06W
Bossangoa 31 Ih 6.29N 17.27 E
Bossé Bangou 34 Fc 13.21N 1.18 E
Bossembélé 35 Bd 5.16N 17.39 E
Bossemtélé II 35 Bd 5.41N 16.38 E
Bossier City 43 Ie 32.31N 93.43W
Bosso 34 Hc 13.42N 13.19 E
Bosso, Dallol- 30 Hg 12.25N 2.50 E
Bossut, Cape- 59 Ec 18.43S 121.38 E
Bostān 25 Db 30.26N 67.02 E
Bostānābād 24 Ld 37.50N 46.50 E
Bosten/Bagrax Hu 21 Ke 42.00N 87.00 E
Boston [Eng.-U.K.] 9 Mi 52.59N 0.01W
Boston [Ma.-U.S.] 39 Le 42.21N 71.04W
Boston Bar 46 Eb 49.52N 121.26W
Boston Deeps 12 Ca 53.00N 0.15 E
Boston Mountains 43 Id 35.50N 93.20W
Botan 24 Id 37.44N 41.48 E
Botas, Ribeirão das- 55 Fe 20.26S 53.43W
Botesdale 12 Db 52.20N 1.01 E
Botev 5 Ig 42.43N 24.55 E
Botevgrad 15 Gg 42.54N 23.47 E
Bothnia, Gulf of- (EN)= Bottniska viken 5 Hc 63.00N 20.00 E
Bothnia, Gulf of- (EN)= Pohjanlahti 5 Hc 63.00N 20.00 E
Boticas 13 Ec 41.41N 7.40W
Botletle 37 Cd 21.07S 24.42 E
Botlih 16 Oh 42.41N 46.13 E
Botna 15 Mc 46.48N 29.30 E
Botoşani [2] 15 Jb 47.40N 26.43 E
Botoşani 15 Jb 47.45N 26.40 E
Botrange 11 Md 50.30N 6.08 E
Botswana [1] 31 Jk 22.00S 24.00 E
Botte Donato 14 Kk 39.17N 16.27 E
Bottineau 43 Gb 48.50N 100.27W
Bottniska viken=Bothnia, Gulf of- (EN) 5 Hc 63.00N 20.00 E
Bottrop 10 Ce 51.31N 6.55 E
Botucatu 56 Kb 22.52S 48.26W
Botucatu, Serra de- 55 Hf 23.00S 48.20W
Botwood 42 Lg 49.08N 55.21W
Bouaflé 34 Dd 6.59N 5.45W
Bouaflé [3] 34 Dd 7.03N 5.48W
Bouaké 31 Gh 7.41N 5.02W
Bouaké [3] 34 Dd 7.45N 5.02W
Bou Anane 32 Gc 32.02N 3.03W
Bouar 31 Ih 5.57N 15.36 E
Bou Arfa 32 Gc 32.32N 1.57W
Boubin 10 Jh 48.58N 13.50 E
Bouca 31 Ih 6.30N 18.17 E
Bouchain 12 Fd 50.17N 3.19 E
Bouchegouf 14 Bn 36.28N 7.44 E
Bouche Island 51k Bb 13.57N 60.53W
Bouches-du-Rhône [3] 11 Kk 43.30N 5.00 E
Boudenib 32 Gc 31.57N 3.36W
Boudeuse Cay 37b Bb 6.05S 52.51 E
Boû Djébéha 34 Eb 18.33N 2.45W
Bouenza [3] 36 Bc 3.00S 13.00 E
Boufarik 13 Oh 36.34N 2.55 E
Bougaa 13 Rh 36.20N 5.05 E
Bougainville Island 57 Ge 6.00S 155.00 E
Bougainville Reef 59 Jc 15.30S 147.05 E
Bougainville Strait [Ocn.] 63a Cb 6.40S 156.10 E
Bougainville Strait [Van.] 63b Cb 15.50S 167.10 E
Bougouni 31 Gg 11.25N 7.28W

Index Symbols

[1] Independent Nation
[2] State, Region
[3] District, County
[4] Municipality
[5] Colony, Dependency
Continent
Physical Region
Historical or Cultural Region
Mount, Mountain
Volcano
Hill
Mountains, Mountain Range
Hills, Escarpment
Plateau, Upland
Pass, Gap
Plain, Lowland
Delta
Salt Flat
Valley, Canyon
Crater, Cave
Karst Features
Depression
Polder
Desert, Dunes
Forest, Woods
Heath, Steppe
Oasis
Cape, Point
Coast, Beach
Cliff
Peninsula
Isthmus
Sandbank
Island
Atoll
Rock, Reef
Islands, Archipelago
Rocks, Reefs
Coral Reef
Well, Spring
Geyser
River, Stream
Waterfall Rapids
River Mouth, Estuary
Lake
Salt Lake
Intermittent Lake
Reservoir
Swamp, Pond
Canal
Glacier
Ice Shelf, Pack Ice
Ocean
Sea
Gulf, Bay
Strait, Fjord
Lagoon
Bank
Seamount
Tablemount
Ridge
Shelf
Basin
Escarpment, Sea Scarp
Fracture
Trench, Abyss
National Park, Reserve
Point of Interest
Recreation Site
Cave, Cavern
Historic Site
Ruins
Wall, Walls
Church, Abbey
Temple
Scientific Station
Airport
Port
Lighthouse
Mine
Tunnel
Dam, Bridge

Bougtob 32 Hc 34.02N 0.05 E
Bouguenais 11 Eg 47.11N 1.37W
Bougzoul 13 Oi 35.42N 2.51 E
Bou Hadjar 14 Cn 36.30N 8.06 E
Bouhalla, Jbel- 13 Gi 35.06N 5.07W
Bou Hamed 13 Hi 35.19N 4.58W
Bouillante 51e Ab 16.08N 61.46W
Bouillon 11 Le 49.48N 5.04 E
Bouira 32 Hb 36.23N 3.54 E
Bouira [3] 32 Hb 36.15N 4.10 E
Bou Ismaïl 13 Oh 36.38N 2.41 E
Bou Izakarn 32 Fd 29.10N 9.44W
Bou Kadir 13 Nh 36.04N 1.07 E
Boukombé 34 Fc 10.11N 1.06 E
Boû Lanouâr 32 De 21.16N 16.30W
Boulay-Moselle 12 Ie 49.11N 6.30 E
Boulder [Co.-U.S.] 39 Ie 40.01N 105.17W
Boulder [Mt.-U.S.] 46 Ic 46.14N 112.07W
Boulder City 46 Hi 35.59N 114.50W
Boulemane 32 Gc 33.22N 4.45W
Boulemane [3] 32 Gc 33.02N 4.04W
Boulevard Atlántico 55 Dn 38.19S 57.59W
Boulia 59 Hd 22.54S 139.54 E
Bouligny 11 Le 49.17N 5.45 E
Boulogne 11 Eg 47.05N 1.40W
Boulogne-Billancourt 11 If 48.50N 2.15 E
Boulogne-sur-Mer 11 Hd 50.43N 1.37 E
Boulonnais 11 Hd 50.42N 1.40 E
Bouloupari 63b Ce 21.52S 166.03 E
Boulsa 34 Ec 12.39N 0.34W
Boultoum 34 Hc 14.40N 10.18 E
Bou Maad, Djebel- 13 Oh 36.26N 2.08 E
Boumba 34 Ie 2.02N 15.12 E
Boumdeid 32 Ef 17.26N 11.21W
Boum Kabir 35 Bc 10.11N 19.24 E
Boumort 13 Nb 42.14N 1.08 E
Bouna 31 Gh 9.16N 3.00W
Bouna [3] 34 Ed 9.15N 3.20W
Boû Nâga 32 Ef 19.00N 13.13W
Bou Nasser, Adrar- 32 Gc 33.35N 3.53W
Boundary Peak 46 Fh 37.51N 118.21W
Boundiali [3] 34 Dd 9.23N 6.32W
Boundiali 34 Dd 9.31N 6.29W
Boundji 36 Cc 1.03S 15.22 E
Boungou 35 Cd 6.45N 22.06 E
Bountiful 43 Ec 40.53N 111.53W
Bounty Bay 64q Ab 25.03S 130.05W
Bounty Islands 57 Ii 47.45S 179.05 E
Bounty Trough (EN) 3 Jn 46.00S 178.00 E
Bourail 61 Cd 21.34S 165.30 E
Bourbon-Lancy 11 Jh 46.37N 3.47 E
Bourbonnais 11 Ih 46.30N 3.00 E
Bourbonne-les-Bains 11 Lg 47.57N 5.45 E
Bourbourg 12 Ed 50.57N 2.12 E
Bourbre 11 Li 45.47N 5.11 E
Bourem 34 Eb 16.58N 0.21W
Bouressa 34 Fa 20.01N 2.18 E
Bourg-Achard 12 Ce 49.21N 0.49 E
Bourganeuf 11 Hi 45.57N 1.45 E
Bourgar'oûn, Cap- 32 Ib 37.06N 6.28 E
Bourg-de-Péage 11 Li 45.02N 5.03 E
Bourg-en-Bresse 11 Lh 46.12N 5.13 E
Bourges 6 Gf 47.05N 2.24 E
Bourget, Lac du- 11 Li 45.44N 5.52 E
Bourgneuf, Baie de- 11 Dg 47.05N 2.13W
Bourgogne 12 Ge 49.21N 4.04 E
Bourgogne = Burgundy (EN) 5 Gf 47.00N 4.30 E
Bourgogne = Burgundy (EN) 11 Kg 47.00N 4.30 E
Bourgogne, Canal de- 11 Jg 47.58N 3.30 E
Bourgogne, Porte de- 11 Mg 47.38N 6.52 E
Bourgoin-Jallieu 11 Li 45.35N 5.17 E
Bourgtheroulde-Infreville 12 Ce 49.18N 0.53 E
Bourguébus 12 Be 49.07N 0.18W
Boû Rjeïmat 32 Df 19.04N 15.08W
Bourke 58 Fh 30.05S 145.56 E
Bourne 12 Bb 52.46N 0.23W
Bournemouth 9 Lk 50.43N 1.54W
Bourtanger Moor 12 Jb 52.50N 7.06 E
Bourth 12 Cf 48.46N 0.49 E
Bou Saâda 32 Hb 35.12N 4.11 E
Bou Salem 13 Qh 36.36N 4.34 E
Boussac 11 Ih 46.21N 2.13 E
Boussé 34 Ec 12.39N 1.53W
Boussens 11 Gk 43.11N 0.58 E
Bousso 35 Bc 10.29N 16.43 E
Bouthaleb, Djebel- 13 Ri 35.48N 5.12 E
Boutilimit 32 Ef 17.33N 14.42W
Bou-Tlélis 13 Li 35.34N 0.54W
Boutonne 11 Fi 45.55N 0.49W
Bouvet 66 Cd 54.26S 3.24 E
Bouxwiller 12 Jf 48.49N 7.29 E
Bouza 34 Gc 14.25N 6.02 E
Bouzanne 11 Hh 46.38N 1.28 E
Bouzghaïa 13 Nh 36.20N 1.15 E
Bouzonville 12 Ie 49.18N 6.32 E
Bovalino 14 Kl 38.09N 16.11 E
Bovec 14 Hd 46.20N 13.33 E
Bovenkarspel 12 Hb 52.42N 5.17 E
Boves 12 Ee 49.51N 2.23 E
Bovino 14 Ji 41.15N 15.20 E
Bovril 55 Cj 31.21S 59.26W
Bowa → Muli 27 Hf 27.55N 101.13 E
Bowen [Arg.] 56 Ge 35.02S 67.31W
Bowen [Austl.] 58 Fg 20.01S 148.15 E
Bowers Bank (EN) 40a Bb 54.00N 180.00
Bowers Ridge (EN) 40a Bb 54.30N 180.00
Bowie 45 Hj 33.34N 97.51W
Bowkān 24 Ld 36.31N 46.12 E
Bowland, Forest of- 9 Kh 54.00N 2.35W
Bowling Green [Ky.-U.S.] 43 Jd 37.00N 86.27W
Bowling Green [Oh.-U.S.] 44 Fe 41.22N 83.40W
Bowman 43 Gb 46.11N 103.24W
Bowman Bay 42 Kc 65.33N 73.40W
Bowman Island 66 He 65.17S 103.08 E
Bowman, Mount- 46 Ea 51.10N 121.55W
Bowo/Bomi 27 Ge 30.02N 95.39 E
Bowokan, Kepulauan- 26 Hg 2.05S 123.35 E
Bowral 59 Kf 34.28S 150.25 E
Bow River 42 Gg 49.56N 111.42W
Box Elder Creek 46 Kc 46.57N 108.04W
Boxelder Creek 46 Nd 45.59N 103.57W
Boxholm 7 Dg 58.12N 15.03 E
Boxian 27 Ke 33.46N 115.44 E
Boxing 27 Kd 37.07N 118.04 E
Boxmeer 12 Hc 51.39N 5.57 E
Boxtel 11 Lc 51.35N 5.20 E
Boyabat 24 Fb 41.28N 34.47 E
Boyabo 36 Cb 3.43N 18.46 E
Boyacá [2] 54 Db 5.30N 72.50W
Boyang 27 Kf 29.00N 116.41 E
Boyer, Cap- 63b De 21.37S 168.07 E
Boyer Ahmadī-e Kohkīlūyeh [3] 23 Hc 31.00N 50.30 E
Boyle/Mainistir na Búille 9 Eh 53.58N 8.18W
Boyne/An Bhóinn 9 Gh 53.43N 6.15W
Boyne City 44 Ec 45.13N 85.01W
Boynes, Iles de- 30 Nm 49.58S 69.59 E
Boynton Beach 44 Gl 26.32N 80.03W
Boysen Reservoir 46 Ke 43.19N 108.11W
Boz, Kūh-e- 24 Pi 27.46N 55.54 E
Bozburun 15 Li 40.32N 28.46 E
Bozburun 15 Lm 36.41N 28.04 E
Bozburun Dağı 24 Dd 37.18N 31.03 E
Bozcaada 24 Bc 39.50N 26.04 E
Bozcaada 24 Bc 39.49N 26.03 E
Bozdağ 15 Lk 38.20N 28.06 E
Boz Dağı [Tur.] 24 Cd 37.18N 29.12 E
Boz Dağı [Tur.] 24 Cc 38.19N 28.08 E
Boz Dağları 15 Kj 38.20N 27.45 E
Bozdoğan 15 Ll 37.40N 28.19 E
Bozeman 39 He 45.41N 111.02W
Bozen / Bolzano 6 Hf 46.31N 11.22 E
Bozene 36 Cb 2.56N 19.12 E
Bozhen 28 De 38.04N 116.34 E
Bozkol, Zaliv- 18 Cb 45.20N 61.45 E
Bozkurt 24 Fb 41.57N 34.01 E
Bozok Platosu 24 Fc 39.05N 35.05 E
Bozouls 11 Ij 44.28N 2.43 E
Bozoum 31 Ih 6.19N 16.23 E
Bozova 24 Hd 37.22N 38.31 E
Bozovici 15 Ee 44.56N 22.00 E
Bozqūsh, Kūh-e- 24 Ld 37.45N 47.40 E
Bra 14 Bf 44.42N 7.51 E
Braås 8 Fg 57.04N 15.03 E
Braathen, Cape- 66 Pf 71.48S 96.05W
Brabant 11 Lc 51.10N 5.05 E
Brabant [3] 12 Gd 50.45N 4.30 E
Brabant-les-Villers 12 Gf 48.51N 4.59 E
Brâbîch 34 Eb 17.30N 3.00W
Brač 14 Kg 43.19N 16.40 E
Bracadale, Loch- 9 Gd 57.20N 6.35W
Bracciano 14 Gh 42.06N 12.40 E
Bracciano, Lago di- 14 Gh 42.05N 12.15 E
Bräcke 7 De 62.43N 15.27 E
Brackettville 45 Fl 29.19N 100.24W
Bracki Kanal 14 Kg 43.24N 16.40 E
Brackley 12 Ab 52.02N 1.09W
Bracknell 9 Mj 51.26N 0.46W
Brackwede, Bielefeld- 12 Kc 51.59N 8.31 E
Brad 15 Fc 46.08N 22.47 E
Bradano 14 Kj 40.23N 16.51 E
Bradenton 43 Kf 27.29N 82.34W
Bradford [Eng.-U.K.] 9 Lh 53.48N 1.45W
Bradford [Pa.-U.S.] 44 He 41.57N 78.39W
Bradley Reef 60 Gi 6.52S 160.48 E
Brady 43 He 31.08N 99.20W
Brady Mountains 45 Gk 31.20N 99.40W
Brædstrup 8 Ci 55.58N 9.37 E
Braemar 9 Jd 57.01N 3.24W
Braga [2] 13 Dc 41.35N 8.25W
Braga 6 Fg 41.33N 8.26W
Bragadiru 15 If 43.46N 25.31 E
Bragado 56 He 35.08S 60.30W
Braganca [2] 13 Fc 41.30N 6.45W
Bragança [Braz.] 53 Lf 1.03S 46.46W
Bragança [Port.] 13 Fc 41.49N 6.45W
Bragança Paulista 55 If 22.57S 46.34W
Brahestad/Raahe 7 Fd 64.41N 24.29 E
Brāhmanbāria 25 Id 23.59N 91.07 E
Brahmapur 22 Kh 19.19N 84.47 E
Brahmaputra 21 Lg 24.02N 90.59 E
Brăila [2] 15 Kd 45.13N 27.48 E
Brăila 6 If 45.16N 27.59 E
Brăilei, Balta- 15 Ke 45.00N 28.00 E
Braine 12 Fe 49.20N 3.32 E
Braine-l'Alleud/Eigenbrakel 12 Gd 50.41N 4.22 E
Brainerd 43 Ib 46.21N 94.12W
Braintree 12 Cc 51.53N 0.34 E
Braithwaite Point 59 Gb 11.58S 134.00 E
Brake (Unterweser) 10 Ec 53.20N 8.29 E
Brakel [Bel.] 12 Fd 50.47N 3.45 E
Brakel [Ger.] 12 Lc 51.43N 9.11 E
Brakna [3] 32 Ef 17.30N 13.30W
Brålanda 8 Ef 58.34N 12.22 E
Bralorne 46 Da 50.47N 122.49W
Bramming 8 Ci 55.28N 8.42 E
Brämön 8 Gb 62.10N 17.40 E
Brampton 44 Hd 43.41N 79.46W
Bramsche 12 Jb 52.24N 7.59 E
Bran, Pasul- 15 Id 45.26N 25.17 E
Branco 32 Cf 16.39N 24.41W
Branco, Cabo- 52 Mf 7.09S 34.47W
Branco, Rio- [Braz.] 52 Jf 1.24S 61.51W
Branco, Rio- [Braz.] 55 De 21.00S 57.48W
Branco ou Cabixi, Rio- 55 Ba 13.55S 60.10W
Brandberg 30 Ik 21.08S 14.35 E
Brandbu 7 Cf 60.26N 10.28 E
Brande 7 Bi 55.57N 9.07 E
Brandenburg 10 Id 52.25N 12.33 E
Brandenburg 10 Jd 52.10N 13.30 E
Brändö 8 Id 60.25N 21.05 E
Brandon [Eng.-U.K.] 12 Cb 52.27N 0.37 E
Brandon [Fl.-U.S.] 44 Fl 27.56N 82.17W
Brandon [Man.-Can.] 39 Je 49.50N 99.57W
Brandon [Vt.-U.S.] 44 Kd 43.47N 73.05W
Brandon Head/Na Machairí 9 Ci 52.16N 10.15W
Brandon Mount/Cnoc Bréanainn 9 Ci 52.14N 10.15W
Brandval 8 Ed 60.19N 12.02 E
Brandvlei 37 Cf 30.25S 20.30 E
Brandýs nad Labem-Stará Boleslav 10 Kf 50.11N 14.40 E
Brăneşti 15 Je 44.27N 26.20 E
Braniewo 10 Pb 54.24N 19.50 E
Bransby Point 51c Bc 16.43N 62.14W
Bransfield Strait 66 Re 63.00S 59.00W
Brańsk 10 Sd 52.45N 22.51 E
Branson 45 Jh 36.39N 93.13W
Brantevik 8 Fi 55.31N 14.21 E
Brantford 42 Jh 43.08N 80.16W
Brantôme 11 Gi 45.22N 0.39 E
Bras d'Or Lake 42 Lg 45.50N 60.50W
Brasil = Brazil (EN) [1] 53 Kf 9.00S 53.00W
Brasil, Planalto do- = Brazilian Highlands (EN) 52 Lg 17.00S 45.00W
Brasiléia 54 Ef 11.00S 68.44W
Brasilia 53 Lg 15.47S 47.55W
Brasilia de Minas 55 Jc 16.12S 44.26W
Brasla 8 Kg 57.08N 24.50 E
Braslav 7 Gi 55.37N 27.05 E
Braşov [2] 15 Id 45.40N 25.10 E
Braşov 6 If 45.38N 25.35 E
Brass 34 Ge 4.19N 6.14 E
Brassac 11 Ik 43.38N 2.30 E
Brasschaat 12 Gc 51.17N 4.27 E
Brasstown Bald 44 Fh 34.52N 83.48W
Brastavăţu 15 Hf 43.55N 24.24 E
Brataj 15 Ci 40.16N 19.40 E
Bråte 8 De 59.43N 11.27 E
Bratea 15 Fc 46.56N 22.37 E
Bratislava 6 Hf 48.09N 17.07 E
Bratsk 22 Md 56.05N 101.48 E
Bratskoje Vodohranilišče = Bratsk Reservoir (EN) 20 Fe 56.30N 102.00 E
Bratsk Reservoir (EN) = Bratskoje Vodohranilišče 20 Fe 56.30N 102.00 E
Brattleboro 43 Mc 42.51N 72.36W
Brattvåg 8 Bb 62.36N 6.27 E
Braubach 12 Jd 50.17N 7.40 E
Braunau am Inn 14 Hb 48.16N 13.02 E
Braunschweig 10 Gd 52.16N 10.32 E
Brava 30 Eg 14.52N 24.43W
Brava, Costa- 13 Pc 41.45N 3.04 E
Bråviken 8 Gf 58.40N 16.30 E
Bravo del Norte, Rio- = Grande, Rio- (EN) 38 Jg 25.57N 97.09W
Brawley 43 De 32.59N 115.34W
Bray 42 Jc 69.20N 77.00W
Bray 37 Ce 25.26S 23.38 E
Bray/Brē 9 Gh 53.12N 6.06W
Bray, Pays de- 11 He 49.46N 1.26 E
Bray-Dunes 12 Ec 51.05N 2.31 E
Braye 11 Gg 47.45N 0.42 E
Bray Head 9 Cj 51.53N 10.25W
Bray-sur-Somme 12 Ee 49.56N 2.43 E
Brazi 15 Je 44.52N 26.01 E
Brazil 44 Df 39.32N 87.08W
Brazil (EN) = Brasil [1] 53 Kf 9.00S 53.00W
Brazil Basin (EN) 3 Dk 15.00S 25.00W
Brazilian Highlands (EN) = Brasil, Planalto do- 52 Lg 17.00S 45.00W
Brazos 38 Jg 28.53N 95.23W
Brazos Santiago Pass 45 Hm 26.05N 97.16W
Brazzaville 31 Ii 4.16S 15.17 E
Brčko 14 Mf 44.52N 18.49 E
Brda 10 Oc 53.07N 18.08 E
Brdy 10 Jg 49.35N 13.50 E
Bré/Bray 9 Gh 53.12N 6.06W
Brea, Punta- 51a Bc 17.54N 66.55W
Breaden, Lake- 59 Fe 25.45S 125.40 E
Breaksea Sound 62 Bf 45.35S 166.40 E
Breaza [Rom.] 15 Id 45.11N 25.40 E
Breaza [Rom.] 15 Ib 47.37N 25.20 E
Breaza, Vîrful- 15 Hb 47.22N 24.02 E
Brebes 26 Eh 6.53S 109.03 E
Brêche 12 Ee 49.16N 2.30 E
Brechin 9 Ke 56.44N 2.40W
Brecht 12 Gc 51.21N 4.38 E
Brechte 12 Jb 52.15N 7.10 E
Breckenridge [Mn.-U.S.] 45 Hc 46.16N 96.35W
Breckenridge [Tx.-U.S.] 45 Gj 32.45N 98.54W
Breckland 9 Ni 52.30N 0.35 E
Břeclav 10 Mh 48.46N 16.54 E
Brecon 9 Jj 51.57N 3.24W
Brecon Beacons 9 Jj 51.53N 3.31W
Breda 11 Kc 51.35N 4.46 E
Bredaryd 8 Eg 57.10N 13.44 E
Bredasdorp 31 Jl 34.32S 20.02 E
Brede 12 Cd 50.55N 0.43 E
Bredene 12 Ec 51.14N 2.58 E
Bredstedt 10 Eb 54.37N 8.59 E
Bredy 19 Ge 52.26N 60.21 E
Bree 12 Hc 51.08N 5.36 E
Breg 10 Ei 47.57N 8.31 E
Bregalnica 15 Eh 41.36N 21.56 E
Bregenz 14 Dc 47.30N 9.46 E
Bréhat, Ile de- 11 Df 48.51N 3.00W
Breiðafjörður 5 Db 65.15N 23.15W
Breimsvatnet 8 Bc 61.40N 6.25 E
Breisach am Rhein 10 Dh 48.02N 7.35 E
Breisund 8 Ab 62.30N 6.00 E
Breit Bridge 37 Dd 22.12S 29.59 E
Breivikbotn 7 Fa 70.37N 22.29 E
Brejão 55 Ia 12.59S 46.28W
Brekken 7 Ce 62.39N 11.53 E
Brekstad 7 Be 63.41N 9.41 E
Bremangerlandet 7 Af 61.50N 5.00 E
Brembana, Val- 14 De 45.55N 9.40 E
Brembo 14 De 45.35N 9.32 E
Bremen [2] 10 Ec 53.05N 8.50 E
Bremen [Ger.] 6 Ge 53.05N 8.48 E
Bremen [In.-U.S.] 44 De 41.27N 86.09W
Bremerhaven 6 Ge 53.33N 8.35 E
Bremerton 43 Cb 47.34N 122.38W
Bremervörde 10 Fc 53.29N 9.08 E
Brendel 46 Kg 38.57N 109.50W
Brenham 45 Hk 30.10N 96.24W
Brenne 11 Hh 46.44N 1.14 E
Brennero, Passo del- = Brenner Pass (EN) 5 Hf 47.00N 11.30 E
Brennerpaß = Brenner Pass (EN) 5 Hf 47.00N 11.30 E
Brenner Pass (EN) = Brennero, Passo del- 5 Hf 47.00N 11.30 E
Brenner Pass (EN) = Brennerpaß 5 Hf 47.00N 11.30 E
Brenta 14 Ge 45.11N 12.18 E
Brentwood 9 Nj 51.38N 0.18 E
Brescia 6 Hf 45.33N 10.15 E
Breskens 12 Fc 51.24N 3.33 E
Breslau (EN) = Wrocław 6 He 51.06N 17.00 E
Bresle 12 Hd 50.04N 1.22 E
Bressanone / Brixen 14 Fd 46.43N 11.39 E
Bressay 9 La 60.08N 1.05W
Bresse 11 Lh 46.30N 5.15 E
Bressuire 11 Fh 46.51N 0.29W
Brest 6 Ie 52.06N 23.42 E
Brest [Fr.] 6 Ff 48.24N 4.29W
Brestova 14 Ie 45.08N 14.14 E
Brestskaja Oblast [3] 19 Ce 52.20N 25.30 E
Bretagne = Brittany (EN) 11 Df 48.00N 3.00W
Bretagne = Brittany (EN) 5 Ff 48.00N 3.00W
Breţcu 15 Jc 46.03N 26.18 E
Breteuil [Fr.] 12 Cf 48.50N 0.55 E
Breteuil [Fr.] 11 Ie 49.38N 2.18 E
Breton, Marais- 11 Eh 46.56N 2.00W
Breton, Pertuis- 11 Eh 46.16N 1.22W
Breton Sound 45 Ll 29.30N 89.30W
Brett 12 Cc 51.58N 0.57 E
Brett, Cape- 62 Fa 35.10S 174.20 E
Bretten 12 Ke 49.03N 8.42 E
Bretteville-sur-Laize 12 Be 49.03N 0.20W
Breueh, Pulau- 26 Be 5.41N 95.05 E
Breuil Cervinia 14 Be 45.56N 7.38 E
Breukelen 12 Db 52.10N 5.01 E
Breuna 12 Lc 51.25N 9.11 E
Breves 54 Hd 1.40S 50.29W
Brevik 7 Bg 59.04N 9.42 E
Brevoort 42 Ld 63.30N 64.20W
Brewarrina 59 Je 29.57S 146.52 E
Brewerville 34 Cd 6.25N 10.47W
Brewster 46 Fb 48.06N 119.47W
Brewster, Kap- 67 Md 70.10N 21.30W
Brewton 43 Je 31.07N 87.04W
Brežice 14 Je 45.54N 15.35 E
Brézina 32 Hc 33.05N 1.16 E
Březnice 10 Jg 49.33N 13.57 E
Breznik 15 Fg 42.44N 22.54 E
Brezno 10 Ph 48.49N 19.39 E
Brezoi 15 Hd 45.21N 24.15 E
Brezolles 12 Df 48.41N 1.04 E
Brezovo 15 Ig 42.21N 25.05 E
Bria 31 Jh 6.32N 21.59 E
Briance 11 Hi 45.47N 1.12 E
Briançon 11 Mj 44.54N 6.39 E
Brianza 14 De 45.45N 9.15 E
Briare, Canal de- 11 If 48.02N 2.43 E
Bribie Island 59 Ke 27.00S 153.05 E
Bričany 15 Ka 48.18N 27.04 E
Bride 9 Fi 52.05N 7.50W
Bridgend 9 Jj 51.31N 3.35W
Bridgeport [Ca.-U.S.] 46 Fg 38.10N 119.13W
Bridgeport [Ct.-U.S.] 43 Mc 41.11N 73.11W
Bridgeport [Nb.-U.S.] 45 Ef 41.40N 103.06W
Bridge River 46 Ea 50.45N 121.55W
Bridger Peak 46 Lf 41.12N 107.02W
Bridges Point 64g Bb 1.58N 157.28W
Bridgeton 44 Jf 39.26N 75.14W
Bridgetown [Austl.] 59 Df 33.57S 116.08 E
Bridgetown [Bar.] 39 Nh 13.06N 59.37W
Bridgewater 42 Lh 44.23N 64.31W
Bridgwater 9 Kj 51.08N 3.00W
Bridgwater Bay 9 Jj 51.16N 3.12W
Bridlington 9 Mg 54.05N 0.12W
Bridlington Bay 9 Mg 54.04N 0.08W
Bridport 9 Kk 50.44N 2.46W
Brie 11 Jf 48.40N 3.30 E
Brielle 12 Gc 51.54N 4.10 E
Brienzer-See 14 Bd 46.45N 7.55 E
Briey 11 Le 49.15N 5.56 E
Brig 14 Bd 46.20N 8.00 E
Brigach 10 Ei 47.58N 8.30 E
Brigham City 43 Ec 41.31N 112.01W
Brighstone 12 Ad 50.38N 1.23W
Bright 59 Jg 36.44S 146.58 E
Brightlingsea 12 Dc 51.48N 1.02 E
Brighton [Co.-U.S.] 45 Dg 39.59N 104.49W
Brighton [Eng.-U.K.] 6 Fe 50.50N 0.10W
Brignoles 11 Mk 43.24N 6.04 E
Brihuega 13 Jd 40.45N 2.52W
Brijuni 14 Hf 44.55N 13.46 E
Brikama 34 Bc 13.16N 16.39W
Brilhante, Rio- 54 Hh 21.58S 54.18W
Brilon 12 Kc 51.24N 8.35 E
Brilon-Alme 12 Kc 51.27N 8.37 E
Brimstone Hill 51c Ab 17.21N 62.49W
Brindisi 6 Hg 40.38N 17.56 E
Brinkley 45 Ki 34.53N 91.12W
Brinkmann 55 Aj 30.52S 62.02W
Brionne 12 Ce 49.12N 0.43 E
Brioude 11 Ji 45.18N 3.24 E
Brisbane 58 Gg 27.28S 153.02 E
Brisighella 14 Ff 44.13N 11.46 E
Bristol 66 Ad 59.02S 26.31W
Bristol [Eng.-U.K.] 6 Fe 51.27N 2.35W
Bristol [Tn.-U.S.] 44 Fg 36.36N 82.11W
Bristol Bay 38 Dd 58.00N 159.00W
Bristol Channel 5 Fe 51.20N 4.00W
Bristol Lake 46 Hi 34.28N 115.41W
Bristow 45 Hi 35.50N 96.23W
Britannia Range 66 Jf 80.00S 158.00 E
British Columbia [3] 42 Fe 55.00N 125.00W
British Honduras → Belize 49 Ce 17.35N 88.35W
British Indian Ocean Territory [5] 22 Jj 7.00S 72.00 E
British Isles 5 Fd 54.00N 4.00W
British Mountains 40 Kc 69.20N 140.20W
British Solomon Islands → Solomon Islands [1] 58 Ge 8.00S 159.00 E
British Virgin Islands [5] 39 Mh 18.20N 64.50W
Brits 37 De 25.40S 27.46 E
Britstown 37 Cf 30.37S 23.30 E
Britt 45 Je 43.06N 93.48W
Brittany (EN) = Bretagne 5 Ff 48.00N 3.00W
Brittany (EN) = Bretagne 11 Df 48.00N 3.00W
Britton 45 Hd 45.48N 97.45W
Brive-la-Gaillarde 11 Hi 45.09N 1.32 E
Briviesca 13 Ib 42.33N 3.19W
Brixen / Bressanone 14 Fd 46.43N 11.39 E
Brixham 9 Jk 50.24N 3.30W
Brjansk 6 Je 53.15N 34.22 E
Brjanskaja Oblast [3] 19 De 52.50N 33.20 E
Brjuhoveckaja 16 Kg 45.46N 39.01 E
Brjukoviči 10 Jg 49.52N 24.00 E
Brno 6 Hf 49.12N 16.37 E
Broa, Ensenada de la- 49 Fb 22.35N 82.00W
Broad Bay 9 Gc 58.15N 6.15W
Broadford 9 Hd 57.14N 5.54W
Broad Sound 59 Jd 22.10S 149.45 E
Broadstairs 12 Dc 51.22N 1.27 E
Broadus 43 Fb 45.27N 105.25W
Brocēni/Broceny 8 Jh 56.41N 22.30 E
Broceny/Brocēni 8 Jh 56.41N 22.30 E
Brochet 42 He 57.53N 101.40W
Brochu, Lac- 44 Ja 48.26N 74.15W
Brock 42 Ga 77.55N 114.30W
Brocken 10 Ge 51.48N 10.36 E
Brockman, Mount- 59 Dd 22.28S 117.18 E
Brockton 44 Ld 42.05N 71.01W
Brockville 42 Jh 44.35N 75.41W
Brod 15 Eh 41.31N 21.14 E
Brodarevo 15 Cf 43.14N 19.43 E
Broderick Falls 36 Fb 0.37N 34.46 E
Brodeur Peninsula 38 Kb 73.00N 88.00W
Brodick 9 Hf 55.35N 5.09W
Brodnica 10 Pc 53.16N 19.23 E
Brody 16 Dd 50.04N 25.12 E
Broglie 12 Ce 49.01N 0.32 E
Brok 10 Rd 52.43N 21.52 E
Brok 10 Rd 52.38N 21.55 E
Broken Arrow 45 Ih 36.03N 95.48W
Broken Bow 45 Gf 41.24N 99.38W
Broken Bow Lake 45 Ii 34.10N 94.40W
Broken Hill 58 Fh 31.57S 141.27 E
Broken Ridge (EN) 3 Hm 31.30S 95.00 E
Brokind 8 Ff 58.13N 15.40 E
Brokopondo 54 Hb 5.04N 55.00W
Bromarv 8 Je 59.55N 23.00 E
Bromley, London- 12 Cc 51.25N 0.01 E
Bromölla 7 Dh 56.04N 14.28 E
Brønderslev 8 Cg 57.16N 9.58 E
Brong-Ahafo [3] 34 Ed 7.45N 1.30W
Bronnikovo 17 Ng 58.29N 68.27 E
Brønnøysund 7 Cd 65.28N 12.13 E
Bronte 14 Im 37.47N 14.50 E
Brooke's Point 26 Ge 8.47N 117.50 E
Brookfield 45 Jg 39.47N 93.04W
Brookhaven 45 Kk 31.35N 90.26W
Brookings [Or.-U.S.] 43 Cc 42.03N 124.17W
Brookings [S.D.-U.S.] 43 Hc 44.19N 96.48W
Brooks 42 Gf 50.35N 111.53W
Brooks Banks (EN) 60 Mc 24.05N 166.50W
Brooks Range 38 Dc 68.00N 154.00W
Brookston 45 Jc 46.50N 92.32W
Brooksville 44 Fk 28.33N 82.23W
Brookton 59 Df 32.22S 117.01 E
Brookville [In.-U.S.] 44 Ef 39.25N 85.01W
Brookville [Pa.-U.S.] 44 He 41.10N 79.06W
Broom 9 Hd 57.45N 5.05W
Broom, Loch- 9 Hd 57.55N 5.15W
Broome 58 Df 17.58S 122.14 E
Brora 9 Jc 58.00N 3.50W
Brora 9 Jc 58.01N 3.51W
Brosna/An Bhrosnach 9 Fh 53.13N 7.58W
Broşteni 15 Ib 47.14N 25.42 E
Brou 11 Hf 48.13N 1.11 E
Brough 9 Kg 54.32N 2.19W
Broughton Island 39 Mc 67.35N 63.50W
Broussard 45 Kk 30.09N 91.58W
Brovary 16 Gd 50.32N 30.48 E
Brovst 8 Cg 57.06N 9.32 E
Brown Bank (EN) = Bruine Bank 12 Fb 52.35N 3.20 E
Brownfield 43 Ge 33.11N 102.16W
Browning 46 Ib 48.34N 113.01W
Browns Bank (EN) 42 Kh 42.40N 66.05W
Brownsville [Tn.-U.S.] 44 Ch 35.36N 89.15W
Brownsville [Tx.-U.S.] 39 Jg 25.54N 97.30W
Brownwood 43 He 31.43N 98.59W
Browse Island 59 Eb 14.05S 123.35 E
Broye 14 Bd 46.55N 7.02 E
Bruay-en-Artois 11 Id 50.29N 2.33 E
Bruay-sur-l'Escaut 12 Fd 50.23N 3.32 E
Bruce 45 Lj 33.59N 89.21W
Bruce, Mount- 57 Cg 22.36S 118.08 E
Bruce Crossing 44 Cb 46.32N 89.10W
Bruce Peninsula 42 Jh 44.59N 81.20W
Bruce Rock 59 Df 31.53S 118.09 E
Bruche 11 Nf 48.34N 7.43 E

Index Symbols

[1] Independent Nation
[2] State, Region
[3] District, County
[4] Municipality
[5] Colony, Dependency
Continent
Physical Region
Historical or Cultural Region
Mount, Mountain
Volcano
Hill
Mountains, Mountain Range
Hills, Escarpment
Plateau, Upland
Pass, Gap
Plain, Lowland
Delta
Salt Flat
Valley, Canyon
Crater, Cave
Karst Features
Depression
Polder
Desert, Dunes
Forest, Woods
Heath, Steppe
Oasis
Cape, Point
Coast, Beach
Cliff
Peninsula
Isthmus
Sandbank
Island
Atoll
Rock, Reef
Islands, Archipelago
Rocks, Reefs
Coral Reef
Well, Spring
Geyser
River, Stream
Waterfall Rapids
River Mouth, Estuary
Lake
Salt Lake
Intermittent Lake
Reservoir
Swamp, Pond
Canal
Glacier
Ice Shelf, Pack Ice
Ocean
Sea
Gulf, Bay
Strait, Fjord
Lagoon
Bank
Seamount
Tablemount
Ridge
Shelf
Basin
Escarpment, Sea Scarp
Fracture
Trench, Abyss
National Park, Reserve
Point of Interest
Recreation Site
Cave, Cavern
Historic Site
Ruins
Wall, Walls
Church, Abbey
Temple
Scientific Station
Airport
Port
Lighthouse
Mine
Tunnel
Dam, Bridge

Bruchhausen Vilsen	12	Lb	52.50N	9.01 E
Bruchmühlbach Miesau	12	Je	49.23N	7.28 E
Bruchsal	10	Eg	49.08N	8.36 E
Bruck an der Leitha	14	Kb	48.01N	16.46 E
Bruck an der Mur	14	Jc	47.25N	15.17 E
Brue	9	Kj	51.13N	3.00W
Bruges/Brugge	11	Jc	51.13N	3.14 E
Brugg	14	Cc	47.29N	8.12 E
Brugge/Bruges	11	Jc	51.13N	3.14 E
Brugge-Assebroek	12	Fc	51.12N	3.16 E
Brüggen	12	Ic	51.15N	6.11 E
Brugge-Sint-Andries	12	Fc	51.12N	3.10 E
Brühl [Ger.]	12	Ke	49.24N	8.32 E
Brühl [Ger.]	12	Id	50.50N	6.54 E
Bruine Bank = Brown Bank (EN)	12	Fb	52.35N	3.20 E
Bruin Point	43	Ed	39.39N	110.22W
Brule River	44	Cc	45.57N	88.12W
Brumado	54	Jf	14.13S	41.40W
Brummen	12	Ib	52.06N	6.10 E
Brummo	8	Ef	58.50N	13.40 E
Brumunddal	7	Cf	60.53N	10.56 E
Bruna	14	Eh	42.45N	10.53 E
Brune	12	Fe	49.45N	3.47 E
Bruneau	46	He	42.53N	115.48W
Bruneau River	46	He	42.57N	115.58W
Bruneck / Brunico	14	Fd	46.48N	11.56 E
Brunehamel	12	Ge	49.46N	4.11 E
Brunei [5]	22	Ni	4.30N	114.40 E
Brunei, Teluk-	21	Ni	5.05N	115.18 E
Brunette Downs	59	Hc	18.38S	135.57 E
Brunflo	8	Fa	63.05N	14.49 E
Brunico / Bruneck	14	Fd	46.48N	11.56 E
Brunna	8	Ge	59.52N	17.25 E
Brunner	62	De	42.26S	171.19 E
Brunner, Lake-	62	De	42.35S	171.25 E
Brunnsberg	8	Ec	61.17N	13.55 E
Brunsbüttel	10	Fc	53.54N	9.07 E
Brunssum	12	Hd	50.57N	5.57 E
Brunswick [Ga.-U.S.]	43	Ke	31.10N	81.29W
Brunswick [Me.-U.S.]	43	Nc	43.55N	69.58W
Brunswick, Peninsula de-	52	Ik	53.30S	71.25W
Brunswick Lake	44	Fa	49.00N	83.23W
Bruntál	10	Ng	49.59N	17.28 E
Bruny Island	59	Jh	43.30S	147.05 E
Brus	15	Ef	43.23N	21.02 E
Brus, Laguna de-	49	Ef	15.50N	84.35W
Brush	43	Gc	40.15N	103.37W
Brus Laguna	49	Ef	15.47N	84.35W
Brusque	56	Kc	27.06S	48.56W
Brussel/Bruxelles = Brussels (EN)	6	Ge	50.50N	4.20 E
Brussels (EN) = Brussel/Bruxelles	6	Ge	50.50N	4.20 E
Brussels (EN) = Bruxelles/Brussel	6	Ge	50.50N	4.20 E
Brusset, 'Erg-	34	Hb	18.55N	10.30 E
Brusturi	15	Fb	47.09N	22.15 E
Brusy	10	Nc	53.53N	17.45 E
Bruxelles/Brussel = Brussels (EN)	6	Ge	50.50N	4.20 E
Bruzual	50	Bh	8.03N	69.19W
Bryan [Oh.-U.S.]	44	Ee	41.30N	84.34W
Bryan [Tx.-U.S.]	43	He	30.40N	96.22W
Bryan Coast	66	Pf	73.35S	84.00W
Bryne	7	Ag	58.44N	5.39 E
Brza Palanka	15	Fe	44.28N	22.27 E
Brzava kanal	15	Dd	45.16N	20.49 E
Brzeg	10	Nf	50.52N	17.27 E
Brzeg Dolny	10	Me	51.15N	16.40 E
Brzeziny	10	Pe	51.48N	19.46 E
Brzozów	10	Sg	49.42N	22.02 E
Bsharrī	24	Ge	34.15N	36.01 E
Bû	12	Df	48.48N	1.30 E
Bua	8	Eg	57.14N	12.07 E
Buada Lagoon	64e	Ab	0.32S	166.54 E
Buala	58	Ge	8.10S	159.35 E
Bū al Ḩīdān, Wādī-	33	Cd	27.25N	19.22 E
Buapinang	26	Hg	4.46S	121.34 E
Buatan	26	Df	0.44N	101.51 E
Bū aţ Tifl	33	Dd	28.54N	22.30 E
Bua Yai	25	Ke	15.34N	102.24 E
Bu'ayrāt al Ḩasūn	33	Cc	31.24N	15.44 E
Bubanza	36	Ec	3.06S	29.23 E
Bubaque	34	Bc	11.17N	15.50W
Būbīyan	24	Mh	29.45N	48.15 E
Bubu	36	Gd	6.03S	35.19 E
Bubye	37	Ed	22.20S	31.07 E
Buca	15	Kk	38.22N	27.11 E
Bučač	16	De	49.04N	25.23 E
Bucačača	20	Gf	52.59N	116.55 E
Bucak	24	Dd	37.28N	30.36 E
Bucaramanga	53	Ie	7.08N	73.09W
Bucas Grande	26	Ie	9.40N	125.58 E
Buccament Bay	51n	Ba	13.12N	61:17W
Buccaneer Archipelago	59	Ec	16.17S	123.20 E
Bucecea	15	Jb	47.46N	26.26 E
Buchanan	31	Fh	5.53N	10.03W
Buchanan, Lake- [Austl.]	59	Jd	21.30S	145.50 E
Buchanan, Lake- [Tx.-U.S.]	45	Gk	30.48N	98.25W
Buchanan Bay	42	Ka	78.55N	75.00W
Buchan Gulf	42	Kb	71.48N	74.06W
Buchardo	56	Hd	34.43S	63.31W
Bucharest (EN) = Bucureşti	6	Ig	44.26N	26.06 E
Buchen	10	Fg	49.31N	9.20 E
Buchholz in der Nordheide	10	Fc	53.20N	9.52 E
Buchon, Point-	46	Ei	35.15N	120.54W
Buchs	14	Dc	47.10N	9.30 E
Buchy	12	De	49.35N	1.22 E
Bückeburg	12	Lb	52.16N	9.03 E
Buckeye	46	Ij	33.22N	112.35W
Buckhaven	9	Je	56.11N	3.03W
Buckie	9	Kd	57.40N	2.58W
Buckingham [Eng.-U.K.]	12	Bb	52.00N	0.59W
Buckingham [Que.-Can.]	44	Jc	45.35N	75.25W
Buckingham Bay	59	Hb	12.10S	135.46 E
Buckinghamshire [3]	9	Mj	51.50N	0.55W
Buckland	40	Gc	66.16N	161.20W
Buckle Island	66	Ke	66.47S	163.14 E
Buckley Bay	66	Je	68.16S	148.12 E
Bucks	9	Mj	51.50N	0.55W
Bucksport	44	Mc	44.34N	68.48W
Buco Zau	36	Bc	4.50S	12.33 E
Bu Craa	32	Ed	26.17N	12.46W
Bucureşti [2]	15	Je	44.30N	26.05 E
Bucureşti = Bucharest (EN)	6	Ig	44.26N	26.06 E
Bucy-lès-Pierrepont	12	Fe	49.39N	3.54 E
Bucyrus	44	Fe	40.47N	82.57W
Bud	7	Be	62.55N	6.55 E
Budacu, Vîrful-	15	Ib	47.07N	25.41 E
Buda-Koševelo	16	Gc	52.43N	30.39 E
Budapest [2]	10	Pi	47.30N	19.05 E
Budapest	6	Hf	47.30N	19.05 E
Búdardalur	7a	Bb	65.07N	21.46W
Budaun	25	Fc	28.03N	79.07 E
Budbud	35	He	4.13N	46.31 E
Budd Coast	66	He	66.30S	113.00 E
Buddusò	14	Di	40.35N	9.15 E
Bude [Eng.-U.K.]	9	Ik	50.50N	4.33W
Bude [Ms.-U.S.]	45	Kk	31.28N	90.51W
Bude Bay	9	Ik	50.50N	4.37W
Budel	12	Hc	51.16N	5.30 E
Budennovsk	19	Eg	44.45N	44.08 E
Budeşti	15	Je	44.14N	26.27 E
Budia	13	Jd	40.38N	2.45W
Büdingen	10	Ff	50.18N	9.07 E
Búdir	7a	Cb	64.56N	14.01W
Budjala	36	Cb	2.39N	19.42 E
Budkowiczanka	10	Nf	50.52N	17.33 E
Budogošč	7	Hg	59.19N	32.29 E
Budrio	14	Ff	44.32N	11.32 E
Budslav	8	Lj	54.49N	27.32 E
Budva	15	Bg	42.17N	18.51 E
Budyšin/Bautzen	10	Ke	51.11N	14.26 E
Budžjak	15	Lc	46.15N	28.45 E
Buea	34	Ge	4.09N	9.14 E
Buech	11	Lj	44.12N	5.57 E
Buenaventura [Col.]	53	Ie	3.53N	77.04W
Buenaventura [Mex.]	47	Cc	29.51N	107.29W
Buenaventura, Bahia de-	54	Cc	3.45N	77.15W
Buenavista	48	Ef	23.39N	109.42W
Buena Vista [Co.-U.S.]	45	Cg	38.50N	106.08W
Buena Vista [Mex.]	48	Mi	16.05N	93.00W
Buena Vista [Mex.]	48	Bb	31.10N	115.40W
Buena Vista [Ven.]	50	Eh	9.02N	63.49W
Buenavista, Bahia de-	49	Hb	22.30N	79.08W
Buendia, Embalse de-	13	Jd	40.25N	2.43W
Buenópolis	55	Jc	17.54S	44.11W
Buenos Aires [2]	56	Ie	36.00S	60.00W
Buenos Aires [Arg.]	53	Ki	34.36S	58.27W
Buenos Aires [C.R.]	49	Fi	10.04N	84.26W
Buenos Aires, Lago-	52	Ij	46.30S	72.00W
Buffalo	42	Fe	60.52N	115.03W
Buffalo [N.Y.-U.S.]	39	Le	42.54N	78.53W
Buffalo [Ok.-U.S.]	45	Gh	36.50N	99.38W
Buffalo [S.D.-U.S.]	43	Gb	45.35N	103.33W
Buffalo [Tx.-U.S.]	45	Hk	31.28N	96.04W
Buffalo [Wy.-U.S.]	43	Fc	44.21N	106.42W
Buffalo Bill Reservoir	46	Kd	44.29N	109.13W
Buffalo Lake	42	Fd	60.12N	115.25W
Buffalo Narrows	42	Ge	55.51N	108.30W
Buffalo Pound Lake	46	Ma	50.38N	105.20W
Buffels	37	Be	29.41S	17.04 E
Bū Fīshah	14	En	36.18N	10.28 E
Buford	44	Fh	34.07N	84.00W
Buftea	15	Ie	44.34N	25.57 E
Bug	5	Ie	52.31N	21.05 E
Buga	54	Cc	3.55N	76.18W
Bugarach, Pech de-	11	Il	42.52N	2.23 E
Bugeat	11	Hi	45.36N	1.56 E
Bugene	36	Fc	1.35S	31.08 E
Bugey	11	Li	45.48N	5.30 E
Bugojno	23	Ff	44.03N	17.27 E
Bugøynes	7	Gb	69.58N	29.39 E
Bugrino	17	Db	68.48N	49.09 E
Bugsuk	26	Ge	8.15N	117.18 E
Bugt	27	Lb	48.47N	121.55 E
Bugulma	19	Fe	54.33N	52.48 E
Bugun	18	Hc	43.22N	70.10 E
Bugun	18	Gc	42.56N	68.36 E
Bügür/Luntai	27	Dc	41.46N	84.10 E
Buguruslan	19	Fe	53.39N	52.30 E
Buhara	22	If	39.49N	64.25 E
Buharskaja Oblast [3]	19	Gg	41.20N	64.20 E
Bū Ḩaşā'	24	Ok	23.20N	53.20 E
Buhera	37	Ec	19.18S	31.29 E
Buh He	27	Gd	36.58N	99.48 E
Buhl	46	He	42.36N	114.46W
Bühl	10	Eh	48.42N	8.09 E
Būhōdle	35	Hd	8.15N	46.20 E
Buhtarminskoje Vodohranilišče	19	If	49.10N	84.00 E
Bui Dam	34	Ed	8.22N	2.10W
Builth Wells	9	Ji	52.09N	3.24W
Buin [Chile]	56	Fd	33.44S	70.44W
Buin [Pap.N.Gui.]	60	Fi	6.50S	155.44 E
Buinsk	19	Ee	54.59N	48.17 E
Buir Nur	27	Kb	47.48N	117.42 E
Buitrago del Lozoya	13	Id	41.00N	3.38W
Buj	17	Gh	56.15N	54.12 E
Buj	19	Ed	58.29N	41.31 E
Bujalance	13	Hg	37.54N	4.22W
Bujanovac	15	Eg	42.28N	21.47 E
Bujaraloz	13	Lc	41.30N	0.09W
Buje	14	He	45.24N	13.40 E
Bujnaksk	19	Eg	42.49N	47.07 E
Bujukly	20	Jg	49.33N	142.55 E
Bujumbura	31	Ji	3.23S	29.22 E
Bujunda	20	Kd	62.00N	153.30 E
Buk	10	Md	52.22N	16.31 E
Bük	10	Mi	47.23N	16.45 E
Buk	10	Hb	54.10N	11.42 E
Buka Island	57	Ge	5.15S	154.35 E
Bukakata	36	Fc	0.18S	32.02 E
Bukama	31	Ji	9.12S	25.51 E
Buka Passage	63a	Ba	5.25S	154.41 E
Bukavu	31	Ji	2.30S	28.52 E
Bukene	36	Fc	4.14S	32.53 E
Bukhā	24	Qi	26.10N	56.09 E
Bukit Besi	26	Df	4.46N	103.12 E
Bukit Mertajam	26	De	5.22N	100.28 E
Bukittinggi	22	Mj	0.19S	100.22 E
Bükk	10	Qh	48.05N	20.30 E
Bukoba	31	Ki	1.20S	31.49 E
Bukovina	15	Ia	48.00N	25.30 E
Bukowiec	10	Ld	52.23N	15.20 E
Bukuru	34	Gd	9.48N	8.52 E
Būl, Kūh-e-	23	Hc	30.48N	52.45 E
Bulajevo	19	He	54.53N	70.26 E
Bulan	26	Hd	12.40N	123.52 E
Bulanaš	17	Kh	57.16N	62.02 E
Bulancak	24	Hb	40.57N	38.14 E
Bulanık	24	Jc	39.05N	42.15 E
Būlāq	33	Fd	25.12N	30.32 E
Bulawayo	31	Jk	20.09S	28.34 E
Buldan	24	Cc	38.03N	28.51 E
Bulgan [Mong.]	27	Hc	44.05N	103.32 E
Bulgan [Mong.]	27	Hb	48.45N	103.34 E
Bulgan [Mong.]	27	Fb	46.05N	91.34 E
Bulgar (Kujbyšev)	7	Li	55.01N	49.06 E
Bulgaria (EN) = Bălgarija [1]	6	Ig	43.00N	25.00 E
Buli	26	If	0.53N	128.18 E
Buli, Teluk-	26	If	0.45N	128.30 E
Buliluyan, Cape-	26	Ge	8.20N	117.11 E
Bulki	35	Fd	6.01N	36.36 E
Bullahār	35	Gc	10.23N	44.27 E
Bullange/Büllingen	12	Id	50.25N	6.16 E
Bullaque	13	Hf	38.59N	4.17W
Bulla Regia	14	Cn	36.33N	8.45 E
Bullas	13	Kf	38.03N	1.40W
Bulle	14	Bd	46.37N	7.04 E
Buller	62	Dd	41.44S	171.35 E
Bullfinch	59	Df	30.59S	119.06 E
Büllingen/Bullange	12	Id	50.25N	6.16 E
Bullion Mountains	46	Hi	34.25N	116.00W
Bulloo River	57	Fg	28.43S	142.30 E
Bull Point [Eng.-U.K.]	9	Ij	51.12N	4.10W
Bull Point [Falk.Is.]	56	Ih	52.19S	59.18W
Bulls	62	Fd	40.10S	175.23 E
Bulls Bay	44	Hi	32.59N	79.33W
Bull Shoals Lake	45	Jh	36.30N	92.50W
Bully Choop Mountain	46	Df	40.35N	122.45W
Bully-les-Mines	12	Ed	50.26N	2.43 E
Bulo Berde	35	He	3.52N	45.40 E
Bulolo	60	Di	7.12S	146.39 E
Bulqiza	15	Dh	41.30N	20.21 E
Bulter	45	Ig	38.16N	94.20W
Bultfontein	37	De	28.20S	26.05 E
Bulukumba	26	Hh	5.33S	120.11 E
Bulungu [Zaire]	36	Cc	4.33S	18.36 E
Bulungu [Zaire]	36	Dd	6.04S	21.54 E
Bumba	31	Jh	2.11N	22.28 E
Bumbah, Khalīj al-	33	Dc	32.25N	23.06 E
Buna	15	Ch	41.52N	19.22 E
Buna	36	Gb	2.47N	39.31 E
Bunbury	58	Ch	33.19S	115.38 E
Buncrana/Bun Cranncha	9	Ff	55.08N	7.27W
Bun Cranncha/Buncrana	9	Ff	55.08N	7.27W
Bunda	36	Fc	2.03S	33.52 E
Bundaberg	58	Gg	24.52S	152.21 E
Bünde	10	Ed	52.12N	8.35 E
Bundesrepublik Deutschland = Germany	6	Ge	51.00N	10.00 E
Bun Dobhráin/Bundoran	9	Eg	54.28N	8.17W
Bundoran/Bun Dobhráin	9	Eg	54.28N	8.17W
Bungay	12	Db	52.27N	1.27 E
Bungku	26	Hg	2.33S	121.58 E
Bungo	36	Cd	7.26S	15.24 E
Bungo Strait (EN) = Bungo-Suidō	28	Lh	32.40N	132.18 E
Bungo-Suidō = Bungo Strait (EN)	28	Lh	32.40N	132.18 E
Bungotakada	29	Be	33.33N	131.27 E
Bungsberg	10	Gb	54.12N	10.43 E
Buni	34	Hc	11.12N	12.02 E
Bunja	31	Kh	1.34N	30.15 E
Bunji	25	Ea	35.40N	74.36 E
Bunker	45	Kh	37.27N	91.13W
Bunker Group	59	Kd	23.50S	152.20 E
Bunkeya	36	Ee	10.24S	26.58 E
Bunkie	45	Jk	30.57N	92.11W
Bunnerfjällen	8	Ea	63.10N	12.34 E
Buñol	13	Le	39.25N	0.47W
Bunschoten	12	Hb	52.14N	5.24 E
Buntingford	12	Bc	51.57N	0.01W
Buntok	26	Fg	1.42S	114.48 E
Bünyan	24	Fc	38.51N	35.52 E
Bunyu, Pulau-	26	Gf	3.30N	117.50 E
Buon Me Thuot	25	Lf	12.40N	108.03 E
Buor-Haja, Guba-	20	Ib	71.00N	131.00 E
Buotama	20	Hd	61.17N	128.55 E
Buqayaq	23	Gd	25.56N	49.40 E
Buqda Kōsār	35	Ge	4.31N	44.49 E
Bur	20	Hb	71.40N	123.40 E
Bura	36	Gc	1.06S	39.57 E
Buram	31	Jg	10.49N	25.10 E
Buran	19	If	48.04N	85.15 E
Burang	27	De	30.18N	81.08 E
Burāq	24	Gf	33.10N	36.29 E
Buras	45	Ll	29.21N	89.32W
Buraydah	22	Gg	26.20N	43.59 E
Burbach	12	Kd	50.43N	8.03 E
Būrdab	35	Hd	9.05N	46.30 E
Burdekin River	59	Jc	19.39S	147.30 E
Burdēre	35	He	3.30N	45.37 E
Burdur	23	Db	37.43N	30.17 E
Burdur Gölü	24	Dd	37.44N	30.12 E
Burdwood Bank (EN)	56	Ih	54.15S	59.00W
Bure	12	Db	52.38N	1.45 E
Bure [Eth.]	35	Fd	8.20N	35.08 E
Bure [Eth.]	35	Fc	10.43N	37.03 E
Bureå	7	Ed	64.37N	21.12 E
Bureinski Hrebet = Bureya Range (EN)	21	Pd	50.40N	134.00 E
Bureja	20	Hg	49.43N	129.51 E
Bureja	21	Oe	49.25N	129.35 E
Büren	10	Ee	51.33N	8.34 E
Buren-Cogt	27	Jb	46.45N	111.30 E
Bureya Range (EN) = Bureinski Hrebet	21	Pd	50.40N	134.00 E
Burfjord	7	Fb	69.56N	22.03 E
Būr Gābo	35	Gf	1.10S	41.50 E
Burgas	6	Ig	42.30N	27.28 E
Burgas [2]	15	Kg	42.30N	27.20 E
Burgas, Gulf of- (EN) = Burgaski Zaliv	15	Kg	42.30N	27.33 E
Burgaski Zaliv = Burgas, Gulf of- (EN)	15	Kg	42.30N	27.33 E
Burg auf Fehmarn	10	Hb	54.26N	11.12 E
Burg auf Fehmarn-Puttgarden	10	Hb	54.30N	11.13 E
Burgaw	44	Ih	34.33N	77.56W
Burgaz Daği	15	Mk	38.25N	29.46 E
Burg bei Magdeburg	10	Hd	52.16N	11.51 E
Burgdorf [Ger.]	10	Gd	52.27N	10.01 E
Burgdorf [Switz.]	14	Bc	47.04N	7.37 E
Burgenland [2]	14	Kc	47.30N	16.25 E
Burgersdorp	37	Df	31.00S	26.20 E
Burgess Hill	12	Bd	50.58N	0.08W
Burgfjället	7	Dd	64.56N	15.03 E
Burghausen	10	Ih	48.10N	12.50 E
Burghūth, Sabkhat al-	24	Ie	34.58N	41.06 E
Burglengenfeld	10	Ig	49.12N	12.02 E
Burgos [3]	13	Ib	42.20N	3.40W
Burgos [Mex.]	48	Je	24.57N	98.57W
Burgos [Sp.]	6	Fg	42.21N	3.42W
Burg-Reuland	12	Id	50.12N	6.09 E
Burgsvik	7	Eh	57.03N	18.16 E
Burgundy (EN) = Bourgogne	5	Gf	47.00N	4.30 E
Burgundy (EN) = Bourgogne	11	Kg	47.00N	4.30 E
Burgwald	12	Kd	50.57N	8.48 E
Būr Hakkaba	35	Ge	2.43N	44.10 E
Burhaniye	24	Bc	39.30N	26.58 E
Burhānpur	22	Jg	21.18N	76.14 E
Burias	26	Hd	12.57N	123.08 E
Buribaj	17	Ij	51.57N	58.11 E
Burica, Punta-	47	Hg	8.03N	82.53W
Burien	46	Dc	47.27N	122.21W
Burin Peninsula	42	Lg	47.00N	55.40W
Buriram	25	Kf	14.59N	103.08 E
Buriti, Rio-	55	Ca	12.50S	58.28W
Buriti Alegre	55	Hd	18.09S	49.03W
Buriti Bravo	54	Je	5.50S	43.50W
Buriti dos Lopes	54	Jd	3.10S	41.52W
Buritis	55	Ib	15.37S	46.26W
Burj al Ḩaţţābah	32	Ic	30.20N	9.30 E
Burjasot	13	Le	39.31N	0.25W
Burjatija, respublika	20	Ff	53.00N	110.00 E
Burj Şāfītā	24	Ge	34.49N	36.07 E
Burkandja	20	Jd	63.27N	147.27 E
Burkburnett	45	Gi	34.06N	98.34W
Burke	45	Ge	43.11N	99.18W
Burke, Mount-	46	Ha	50.18N	114.30W
Burke Island	66	Of	73.08S	105.06W
Burke River	59	Hd	23.12S	139.33 E
Burketown	58	Ef	17.44S	139.22 E
Burkina Faso [1]	31	Gg	13.00N	2.00W
Burley	43	Ec	42.32N	113.48W
Burli	16	Rd	51.28N	52.44 E
Burlingame	45	Ig	38.45N	95.50W
Burlington [Co.-U.S.]	43	Gd	39.18N	102.16W
Burlington [Ia.-U.S.]	43	Ic	40.49N	91.07W
Burlington [Ks.-U.S.]	45	Ig	38.12N	95.45W
Burlington [N.C.-U.S.]	44	Hg	36.06N	79.26W
Burlington [Ont.-Can.]	44	Hd	43.19N	79.43W
Burlington [Vt.-U.S.]	43	Mc	44.28N	73.14W
Burlington [Wi.-U.S.]	45	Le	42.41N	88.17W
Burma [1]	22	Lg	22.00N	98.00 E
Burma [1] (Myanmar-Nainggan-Daw)	22	Lg	22.00N	98.00 E
Burnazului, Cîmpia-	15	Ie	44.10N	25.50 E
Burnett River	59	Kd	24.46S	152.25 E
Burney	46	Ef	40.53N	121.40W
Burnham Market	12	Cb	52.57N	0.44 E
Burnham-on-Crouch	12	Cc	51.37N	0.50 E
Burnie	59	Jh	41.04S	145.54 E
Burnley	9	Kh	53.48N	2.14W
Burns	43	Dc	43.35N	119.03W
Burnside	42	Gc	66.51N	108.04W
Burnside, Lake-	59	Ee	25.20S	123.10 E
Burns Lake	42	Ef	54.14N	125.46W
Burnsville	44	Fh	35.55N	82.18W
Burnt Lava Flow	46	Ef	41.35N	121.35W
Burnt River	44	Hc	44.35N	78.46W
Burntwood	42	He	56.08N	96.33W
Bur'o	31	Lh	9.30N	45.34 E
Burqin	27	Eb	47.43N	86.53 E
Burqin He	27	Eb	47.42N	86.50 E
Burqūm, Ḩarrat al-	33	He	20.54N	42.00 E
Burra	59	Hf	33.40S	138.56 E
Burragorang Lake	59	Kf	34.00S	150.25 E
Burreli	15	Ch	41.37N	20.00 E
Burrendong Reservoir	59	Jf	32.40S	149.10 E
Burriana	13	Le	39.53N	0.05W
Burro, Serranias del	48	Ic	28.50N	101.35W
Burrow Head	9	Ig	54.41N	4.24W
Bursa	22	Ee	40.11N	29.04 E
Būr Sa'īd = Port Said (EN)	31	Ke	31.16N	32.18 E
Burscheid	12	Jc	51.06N	7.07 E
Bürstadt	12	Ke	49.38N	8.27 E
Burštyn	16	De	49.16N	24.37 E
Būr Sūdān = Port Sudan (EN)	31	Kg	19.37N	37.14 E
Burt Lake	44	Ec	45.27N	84.40W
Burtnieku, Ozero-	8	Kg	57.35N	25.10 E
Burtnieku, Ozero-/Burtnieku Ezers	8	Kg	57.35N	25.10 E
Burtnieku Ezers	8	Kg	57.35N	25.10 E
Burtnieku Ezers/Burtnieku, Ozero-	8	Kg	57.35N	25.10 E
Burton	44	Fd	43.02N	83.36W
Burton Latimer	12	Bb	52.21N	0.40W
Burton-upon-Trent	9	Li	52.49N	1.36W
Burträsk	7	Ed	64.31N	20.39 E
Buru, Pulau-	57	De	3.24S	126.40 E
Burullus, Buḩayrat al-	24	Dg	31.30N	30.50 E
Burultokay/Fuhai	27	Eb	47.06N	87.23 E
Burum Gana	34	Hc	13.00N	11.57 E
Burūn, Ra's-	24	Eg	31.14N	33.04 E
Burundaj	19	Hg	43.20N	76.49 E
Burundi [1]	31	Ki	3.15S	30.00 E
Bururi	36	Ec	3.57S	29.37 E
Burutu	34	Gd	5.21N	5.31 E
Bury	9	Kh	53.36N	2.17W
Burylbajtal	18	Ib	44.56N	73.59 E
Buryn	16	Hd	51.13N	33.48 E
Bury Saint Edmunds	9	Ni	52.15N	0.43 E
Burzil Pass	25	Ff	34.54N	75.06 E
Busalla	14	Cf	44.34N	8.57 E
Busanga [Zaire]	36	Ee	10.12S	25.23 E
Busanga [Zaire]	36	Dc	0.51S	22.04 E
Busanga Swamp	36	Ee	14.10S	25.50 E
Buşayrah	24	Ie	35.09N	40.26 E
Būsh	24	Dh	29.09N	31.08 E
Būshehr [3]	23	Hd	28.00N	52.00 E
Būshgān	24	Nh	28.48N	51.42 E
Bushimaie	29	Ji	6.02S	23.45 E
Bushmanland (EN) = Boesmanland	37	Be	29.30S	19.00 E
Busia	36	Fb	0.28N	34.06 E
Busigny	12	Fd	50.02N	3.28 E
Businga	36	Db	3.20N	20.53 E
Busira	30	Ii	0.15S	18.59 E
Busk	16	Dd	50.01N	24.37 E
Buskerud [2]	7	Bf	60.30N	9.10 E
Busko-Zdrój	10	Qf	50.28N	20.44 E
Busoga [3]	36	Fb	0.45N	33.30 E
Buşrá ash Shām	24	Gf	32.31N	36.29 E
Busselton	59	Df	33.39S	115.20 E
Bussum	11	Lb	52.16N	5.10 E
Bustamante, Bahía-	56	Gg	45.07S	66.27W
Buşteni	15	Id	45.24N	25.32 E
Busto Arsizio	14	Ce	45.37N	8.51 E
Buštyna	10	Th	48.03N	23.28 E
Busuanga	26	Hd	12.05N	120.05 E
Busu-Djanoa	36	Db	1.43N	21.23 E
Büsum	10	Eb	54.08N	8.51 E
Buta	31	Jh	2.48N	24.44 E
Butajira	35	Fd	8.08N	38.27 E
Buta Ranquil	56	Ge	37.03S	69.50W
Butare	36	Ec	2.36S	29.44 E
Butaritari Atoll	57	Id	3.03N	172.49 E
Bute, Island of-	9	Hf	55.50N	5.05W
Bute Inlet	46	Ca	50.37N	124.53W
Butembo	31	Jh	0.09N	29.17 E
Butera	14	Im	37.11N	14.11 E
Butere	36	Fb	0.13N	34.30 E
Butha Qi (Zalantum)	27	Lb	48.02N	122.42 E
Buthidaung	25	Id	20.52N	92.32 E
Butiá	56	Jd	30.07S	51.58W
Butiaba	36	Fb	1.49N	31.19 E
Butler	44	He	40.51N	79.55W
Butser Hill	12	Bd	50.57N	0.59W
Butte	39	He	46.00N	112.32W
Butterworth [Mala.]	26	Df	5.25N	100.24 E
Butterworth [S.Afr.]	37	Df	32.23S	28.04 E
Button Bay	42	Ie	58.45N	94.25W
Butuan	22	Oi	8.57N	125.33 E
Butung, Palau-	21	Oj	5.00S	122.55 E
Buturlinovka	16	Ld	50.48N	40.45 E
Butzbach	12	Kd	50.26N	8.41 E
Bützow	10	Hc	53.50N	11.59 E
Buxtehude	10	Fc	53.27N	9.42 E
Buxton [Eng.-U.K.]	9	Lh	53.15N	1.55W
Buxton [N.C.-U.S.]	44	Jh	35.16N	75.32W
Buyo	34	Dd	6.16N	7.03W
Büyük Ağri Daği = Ararat, Mount- (EN)	21	Gf	39.40N	44.24 E
Büyükanafarta	15	Ji	40.17N	26.22 E
Büyükçekmece	15	Lh	41.01N	28.34 E
Büyükkarıştiran	15	Kh	41.18N	27.32 E
Büyük Kemikli Burun	15	Ji	40.18N	26.14 E
Büyük Mahya	15	Kh	41.47N	27.36 E
Büyük Menderes	23	Cb	37.57N	28.58 E
Büyükorhan	15	Lj	39.45N	28.55 E
Buyun Shan	27	Lc	40.06N	122.42 E
Buzači, Poluostrov-	19	Ff	45.00N	52.00 E
Buzan	16	Pf	46.18N	49.06 E
Buzançais	11	Hh	46.53N	1.25 E
Buzancy	12	Ge	49.25N	4.57 E
Buzău [2]	15	Jd	45.09N	26.50 E
Buzău	15	Jd	45.09N	26.50 E
Buzău	15	Kd	45.26N	27.44 E
Buzaymah	33	De	24.55N	22.02 E
Buzen	29	Be	33.37N	131.08 E
Buzet	14	He	45.24N	13.59 E
Būzhān	24	Le	34.09N	47.05 E
Búzi	37	Ec	19.51S	34.30 E
Búzi	37	Ec	19.52S	34.46 E
Buziaş	15	Ed	45.39N	21.36 E
Búzios, Ilha dos-	55	Jf	23.48S	45.08W
Bužora, Gora-	10	Th	48.24N	23.15 E
Buzuluk	19	Fe	52.46N	52.17 E
Buzuluk	16	Md	50.13N	42.12 E
Buzuluk	16	Rc	52.47N	52.16 E
Buzzards Bay	44	Le	41.33N	70.47W

Index Symbols

- [1] Independent Nation
- [2] State, Region
- [3] District, County
- [4] Municipality
- [5] Colony, Dependency
- Continent
- Physical Region
- Historical or Cultural Region
- Mount, Mountain
- Volcano
- Hill
- Mountains, Mountain Range
- Hills, Escarpment
- Plateau, Upland
- Pass, Gap
- Plain, Lowland
- Delta
- Salt Flat
- Valley, Canyon
- Crater, Cave
- Karst Features
- Depression
- Polder
- Desert, Dunes
- Forest, Woods
- Heath, Steppe
- Oasis
- Cape, Point
- Coast, Beach
- Cliff
- Peninsula
- Isthmus
- Sandbank
- Island
- Atoll
- Rock, Reef
- Islands, Archipelago
- Rocks, Reefs
- Coral Reef
- Well, Spring
- Geyser
- River, Stream
- Waterfall Rapids
- River Mouth, Estuary
- Lake
- Salt Lake
- Intermittent Lake
- Reservoir
- Swamp, Pond
- Canal
- Glacier
- Ice Shelf, Pack Ice
- Ocean
- Sea
- Gulf, Bay
- Strait, Fjord
- Lagoon
- Bank
- Seamount
- Tablemount
- Ridge
- Shelf
- Basin
- Escarpment, Sea Scarp
- Fracture
- Trench, Abyss
- National Park, Reserve
- Point of Interest
- Recreation Site
- Cave, Cavern
- Historic Site
- Ruins
- Wall, Walls
- Church, Abbey
- Temple
- Scientific Station
- Airport
- Port
- Lighthouse
- Mine
- Tunnel
- Dam, Bridge

Canakkale Boğazi= Dardanelles (EN) 5 Ig 40.15N 26.25 E
Canala 63b Be 21.32S 165.57 E
Canandaigua 44 Id 42.53N 77.19W
Cananea 47 Bb 30.57N 110.18W
Cananéia 55 Ig 25.01S 47.57W
Canapolis 55 Hd 18.44S 49.13W
Canarias, Islas-=Canary Islands (EN) [5] 31 Ff 28.00N 15.30W
Canarias, Islas-=Canary Islands (EN) 30 Ff 28.00N 15.30W
Canaries 51k Ab 13.55N 61.04W
Canaronero, Laguna- 48 Ff 21.00N 106.15W
Canarreos, Archipiélago de los- 47 Hd 21.50N 82.30W
Canary Basin (EN) 3 Dg 30.00N 25.00W
Canary Islands (EN)= Canarias, Islas- 30 Ff 28.00N 15.30W
Canary Islands (EN)= Canarias, Islas- [5] 31 Ff 28.00N 15.30W
Cañas [C.R.] 49 Eh 10.25N 85.07W
Cañas [Pan.] 49 Gj 7.27N 80.16W
Canastra, Serra da- 55 Ie 20.00S 46.20W
Canatlán 48 Ge 24.31N 104.47W
Cañaveral 13 Fe 39.47N 6.23W
Canaveral, Cape- 38 Kg 28.30N 80.35W
Canavese 14 Be 45.20N 7.40 E
Canavieiras 54 Kg 15.39S 38.57W
Canazei 14 Fd 46.28N 11.46 E
Canberra 58 Fh 35.17S 149.08 E
Canby [Mn.-U.S.] 45 Hd 44.43N 96.16W
Canby [Or.-U.S.] 46 Dd 45.16N 122.42W
Cance 11 Ki 45.12N 4.48 E
Canche 11 Hd 50.31N 1.39 E
Cancon 11 Gj 44.32N 0.37 E
Cancún 47 Gd 21.05N 86.46W
Cancún, Isla- 48 Pg 21.05N 86.46W
Çandarli 15 Jk 38.56N 26.56 E
Çandarli Körfezi 15 Jk 38.52N 26.55 E
Candé 11 Eg 47.34N 1.02W
Candela 48 Id 26.50N 100.40W
Candelaria 48 Nh 18.18N 91.21W
Candelaria, Cerro- 48 Hf 23.25N 103.43W
Candelaria, Río- [Bol.] 55 Cc 17.17S 58.39W
Candelaria, Río- [Mex.] 48 Nh 18.38N 91.15W
Candelaro 14 Ji 41.34N 15.53 E
Cândido de Abreu 55 Gg 24.35S 51.20W
Cândido Mendes 54 Id 1.27S 45.43W
Candlemas Islands 66 Ad 57.03S 26.40W
Candói 55 Fg 25.43S 52.11W
Çandyr 16 Jj 38.13N 55.44 E
Canela 56 Jc 29.22S 50.50W
Canelli 14 Cf 44.43N 8.17 E
Canelones [2] 55 El 34.35S 56.00W
Canelones 55 Dl 34.32S 56.17W
Canendiyu [3] 55 Eg 24.20S 55.00W
Cañete [Chile] 56 Fe 37.48S 73.24W
Cañete [Sp.] 13 Kd 40.03N 1.39W
Cangallo 55 Cm 37.13S 58.42W
Cangamba 36 Ce 13.44S 19.53 E
Cangas 13 Db 42.16N 8.47W
Cangas de Narcea 13 Fa 43.11N 6.33W
Cangas de Onis 13 Ga 43.21N 5.07W
Cangola 36 Cd 7.58S 15.53 E
Cangombe 36 Ce 14.24S 19.59 E
Cangshan (Bianzhuang) 28 Eg 34.51N 118.03 E
Canguçu 56 Fj 31.24S 52.41W
Canguçu, Serra do- 55 Fj 31.20S 52.40W
Canguinha 55 Eb 14.42S 55.40W
Cangumbe 36 Ce 12.00S 19.09 E
Cangyuan 27 Gg 23.10N 99.15 E
Cangzhou 27 Kd 38.14N 116.58 E
Cani, Iles- 14 Em 37.21N 10.07 E
Caniapiscau [5] 38 Md 57.40N 69.30W
Caniapiscau, Lac- 42 Kf 54.00N 70.10W
Canicatti 14 Hm 37.21N 13.51 E
Canigou, Pic du- 11 Il 42.31N 2.27 E
Canik Dağlari 24 Gb 40.50N 37.10 E
Canim Lake 46 Ea 51.52N 120.45W
Canindé 54 Kd 4.22S 39.19W
Canindé, Rio- 54 Je 6.15S 42.52W
Cañitas de Felipe Pescador 48 Hf 23.36N 102.43W
Çankaya 24 Ec 39.56N 32.52 E
Çankırı 23 Da 40.36N 33.37 E
Canna 9 Gd 57.03N 6.33W
Cannac 63a Ac 9.15S 153.29 E
Çannakale 23 Ca 40.09N 26.24 E
Cannanore 25 Ff 11.51N 75.22 E
Cannanore Islands 25 Ef 10.05N 72.10 E
Cannes 11 Nk 43.33N 7.01 E
Cannich 9 Id 57.20N 4.45W
Canning Basin 59 Ed 20.10S 123.00 E
Cannobio 14 Cd 46.04N 8.42 E
Cannock 9 Ki 52.42N 2.01W
Cannonball River 45 Fc 46.26N 100.38W
Cann River 59 Jg 37.34S 149.10 E
Caño, Isla del- 49 Fi 8.44N 83.53W
Canoas 56 Jc 29.56S 51.11W
Canoas, Punta- 48 Bc 29.25N 115.10W
Canoas, Rio- 56 Jc 27.36S 51.25W
Canoeiros 54 Ig 18.02S 45.31W
Canoinhas 55 Gh 26.10S 50.24W
Canoinhas, Rio- 55 Gh 26.07S 50.22W
Cañoles 13 Le 39.02N 0.29W
Canon City 43 Fd 38.27N 105.14W
Canon Fiord 42 Ja 80.15N 83.00W
Canonnier, Pointe du- 51b Ab 18.04N 63.10W
Canora 42 Hf 51.37N 102.26W
Canosa di Puglia 14 Ki 41.13N 16.04 E
Canouan Island 50 Ff 12.43N 61.20W
Canourgue 11 Jj 44.25N 3.13 E
Canso, Strait of - 42 Lg 45.35N 61.23W
Canta 54 Cf 11.25S 76.38W
Cantabrian Mountains (EN) =Cantábrica, Cordillera- 5 Fg 43.00N 5.00W
Cantábrica, Cordillera-= Cantabrian Mountains (EN) 5 Fg 43.00N 5.00W
Cantal 5 Gf 45.10N 2.50 E
Cantal [3] 11 Ii 45.05N 2.40 E
Cantalejo 13 Ic 41.15N 3.55W
Cantanhede 13 Dd 40.21N 8.36W
Cantaura 54 Fb 9.19N 64.21W
Cantavieja 13 Ld 40.32N 0.24W
Cantavir 15 Cd 45.55N 19.46 E
Canterbury [2] 62 De 43.30S 171.50 E
Canterbury 9 Oj 51.17N 1.05 E
Canterbury Bight 57 Ii 44.10S 172.00 E
Can Tho 22 Mi 10.02N 105.47 E
Cantiles, Cayo- 49 Fc 21.36N 82.02W
Canto do Buriti 54 Je 8.07S 42.58W
Canton [Il.-U.S.] 45 Kf 40.33N 90.02W
Canton [Mo.-U.S.] 45 Kf 40.08N 91.32W
Canton [Ms.-U.S.] 45 Kj 32.37N 90.02W
Canton [N.Y.-U.S.] 44 Jc 44.37N 75.11W
Canton [Oh.-U.S.] 43 Kc 40.48N 81.23W
Canton [S.D.-U.S.] 45 He 43.18N 96.35W
Canton (EN)=Guangzhou 22 Ng 23.07N 113.18 E
Cantù 14 De 45.44N 9.08 E
Cantwell 40 Jd 63.23N 148.57W
Cañuelas 55 Cl 35.03S 58.44W
Canumã, Rio- 52 Kf 3.55S 59.10W
Canutama 54 Fe 6.32S 64.20W
Canvey 12 Cc 51.31N 0.36 E
Čany 20 Ce 55.19N 76.56 E
Čany, Ozero- 21 Jd 54.50N 77.30 E
Cany-Barville 12 Ce 49.47N 0.38 E
Canyon [Mn.-U.S.] 45 Jc 47.02N 92.29W
Canyon [Tx.-U.S.] 43 Ge 34.59N 101.55W
Canyon [Wy.-U.S.] 46 Jd 44.44N 110.30W
Canyon Lake 45 Gl 29.52N 98.16W
Canzar 36 Dd 7.36S 21.33 E
Cao Bang 25 Ld 22.40N 106.15 E
Caojiahe → Qichun 28 Ci 30.15N 115.26 E
Caojian 27 Gf 25.38N 99.07 E
Caombo 36 Cd 8.42S 16.33 E
Caorle 14 Ge 45.36N 12.53 E
Caoxian 28 Cg 34.49N 115.33 E
Caozhou → Heze 27 Kd 35.14N 115.28 E
Capaccio 14 Jj 40.25N 15.05 E
Čapajev 19 Fe 50.14N 51.08 E
Čapajevsk 19 Ee 53.01N 49.36 E
Capanaparo, Río- 54 Eb 7.01N 67.07W
Capanema [Braz.] 54 Id 1.12S 47.11W
Capanema [Braz.] 55 Fg 25.40S 53.48W
Capanema, Serra do- 55 Fh 26.05S 53.16W
Capão Alto 55 Gh 27.56S 50.30W
Capão Bonito 55 Hf 24.01S 48.20W
Capão Doce, Morro do- 55 Gh 26.43S 51.25W
Caparo, Río- 49 Lj 7.46N 70.23W
Capatárida 49 Lh 11.11N 70.37W
Capbreton 11 Ek 43.38N 1.26W
Cap Breton Canyon (EN) 11 Ek 43.40N 1.50W
Čapčama, Pereval- 18 Hd 41.34N 70.50 E
Cap-Chat 44 Na 49.06N 66.42W
Capcir 11 Il 42.45N 2.10 E
Cap-de-la-Madeleine 42 Kg 46.22N 72.32W
Capdenac-Gare 11 Ij 44.34N 2.05 E
Cape Barren Island 59 Jh 40.25S 148.10 E
Cape Basin (EN) 3 Em 37.00S 7.00 E
Cape Breton Island 38 Me 46.00N 60.30W
Cape Charles 44 Jg 37.17N 76.00W
Cape Coast 31 Gh 5.06N 1.15W
Cape Cod Bay 44 Le 41.52N 70.22W
Cape Coral 44 Gl 26.33N 81.58W
Cape Dorset 39 Lc 64.14N 76.32W
Cape Dyer 39 Mc 66.30N 61.18W
Cape Fear River 44 Ii 33.53N 78.00W
Cape Girardeau 43 Jd 37.19N 89.32W
Cape Johnson Tablemount (EN) 57 Jc 17.08N 177.15W
Capel 12 Bc 51.08N 0.19W
Cape Lisburne 40 Fc 68.52N 166.05W
Capelka 8 Mf 58.02N 29.07 E
Capelongo 36 Ce 14.54S 15.05 E
Capem 55 Ea 13.15S 55.14W
Cape May 44 Jf 38.56N 74.54W
Cape Mount [3] 34 Cd 7.05N 10.50W
Cape Rise (EN) 3 En 42.00S 15.00 E
Cape Smith 42 Jd 60.44N 78.29W
Capesterre 51e Bc 15.54N 61.13W
Capesterre-Belle-Eau 50 Fd 16.03N 61.34W
Cape Town / Kaapstad 31 Il 33.55S 18.22 E
Cape Verde (EN)=Cabo Verde [1] 31 Eg 16.00N 24.00W
Cape Verde (EN)=Cap Vert [3] 34 Bc 14.45N 17.20W
Cape Verde Basin (EN) 3 Ch 15.00N 30.00W
Cape Verde Islands (EN)= Cabo Verde, Ilhas do- 30 Eg 16.00N 24.10W
Cape Yakataga 40 Kd 60.04N 142.26W
Cape York Peninsula 57 Ff 14.00S 142.30 E
Cap-Haïtien 39 Lh 19.45N 72.15W
Capiibary, Arroyo- 55 Dg 24.06S 56.26W
Capiibary, Río- 55 Eg 25.30S 55.33W
Capim, Rio- 52 Lf 1.40S 47.47W
Capinópolis 55 Hd 18.41S 49.35W
Capira 49 Hi 8.45N 79.53W
Capital Federal [2] 56 Id 34.36S 58.27W
Capitán Arturo Prat 66 Re 62.29S 59.39W
Capitán Bado 56 Ib 23.16S 55.32W
Capitán Bermúdez 55 Bk 32.49S 60.43W
Capitán Sarmiento 55 Cl 34.10S 59.48W
Capitão Noronha, Rio- 55 Ea 13.19S 54.36W
Capivara, Represa da- 55 Gf 22.40S 50.57W
Capivari, Rio- 55 Dd 19.16S 57.10W
Capivarita 55 Fj 30.18S 52.19W
Cap Lopez, Baie du- 36 Ac 0.40S 9.00 E
Čaplygin 16 Kc 53.17N 39.59 E
Cappeln (Oldenburg) 12 Kb 52.49N 8.07 E
Cap Point 50 Fe 14.07N 60.57W
Capraia 14 Dg 43.05N 9.50 E
Caprara, Punta- 14 Ci 41.07N 8.19 E
Capreol 44 Gb 46.43N 80.56W
Caprera 14 Di 41.10N 9.30 E
Capri 14 Ij 40.35N 14.15 E
Capri 14 Ij 40.33N 14.14 E
Capricorn, Cape- 59 Kd 23.30S 151.15 E
Capricorn Channel 59 Kd 22.15S 151.30 E
Capricorn Group 57 Gg 23.30S 152.00 E
Caprivi Strip (EN)=Caprivi Zipfel 30 Jj 18.00S 23.00 E
Caprivi Zipfel=Caprivi Strip (EN) 30 Jj 18.00S 23.00 E
Captain Cook 65a Fd 19.30N 155.55W
Captains Flat 59 Jg 35.35S 149.27 E
Captieux 11 Fj 44.17N 0.15W
Capua 14 Ii 41.06N 14.12 E
Capuchin, Cape- 51g Ba 15.38N 61.28W
Capunda 36 Ce 10.41S 17.23 E
Cap Vert=Cape Verde (EN) [3] 34 Bc 14.45N 17.20W
Caquetá [2] 54 Dc 1.00N 74.00W
Čara 21 Oc 60.17N 120.40 E
Čara 20 Ge 56.58N 118.17 E
Čara 20 Ge 58.54N 118.12 E
Carabobo [2] 54 Ea 10.10N 68.05W
Caracal 15 He 44.07N 24.21 E
Caracaraí 54 Fc 1.50N 61.08W
Caracas 53 Jd 10.30N 66.56W
Carache 49 Li 9.38N 70.14W
Caracol 55 De 21.59S 57.02W
Caracol, Rio- 55 Df 22.13S 57.03W
Caracollo 54 Eg 17.39S 67.10W
Cara Droma Rúisc/Carrick-on-Shannon 9 Eh 53.57N 8.05W
Caraguatá, Cuchilla- 55 Ek 32.05S 54.54W
Caraguatatuba 55 Jf 23.37S 45.25W
Caraïbe, Mer-/Antilles, Mer des-=Caribbean Sea (EN) 38 Lh 15.00N 73.00W
Carajas, Serra dos- 54 He 6.00S 51.20W
Caramoan Peninsula 26 Hd 13.48N 123.40 E
Caramulo, Serra do- 13 Dd 40.34N 8.11W
Caraná, Rio- 55 Ca 13.20S 59.17W
Carandai 55 Ke 20.57S 43.48W
Carandazal 55 Dd 19.50S 57.09W
Caransebeş 15 Fd 45.25N 22.13 E
Carapá, Río- 55 Eg 24.30S 54.20W
Carapelle 14 Ji 41.30N 15.55 E
Caraş 15 Ee 44.49N 21.20 E
Caraş Severin [2] 15 Ed 45.20N 22.00 E
Caratasca, Cayo- 49 Fe 16.02N 83.20W
Caratasca, Laguna de- 47 He 15.20N 83.50W
Caratinga 54 Jg 19.47S 42.08W
Carauari 54 Ed 4.52S 66.54W
Caraúbas 54 Ke 5.47S 37.34W
Caravaca 13 Kf 38.06N 1.51W
Caravelas 53 Mg 17.45S 39.15W
Caraveli 54 Dg 15.46S 73.22W
Caravelle, Presqu'île de la- 51h Bb 14.45N 60.55W
Caravelle, Rocher de la- 51h Bb 14.48N 60.53W
Caràzinho 56 Jc 28.18S 52.48W
Carazo [3] 49 Dh 11.45N 86.15W
Carballino 13 Db 42.26N 8.04W
Carballo 13 Da 43.13N 8.41W
Carberry 45 Gb 49.52N 99.20W
Carbet, Pitons du- 51h Ab 14.42N 61.07W
Carbon, Cap- [Alg.] 13 Rh 36.47N 5.06 E
Carbon, Cap- [Alg.] 13 Li 35.54N 0.20W
Carbonara, Capo- 14 Dk 39.06N 9.31 E
Carbondale [Il.-U.S.] 43 Jd 37.44N 89.13W
Carbondale [Pa.-U.S.] 44 Je 41.35N 75.31W
Carbonera, Cuchilla de la- 55 El 34.30S 54.00W
Carboneras 13 Kh 36.59N 1.54W
Carboneras, Cerro- 48 Ih 18.10N 101.10W
Carbones 13 Gg 37.36N 5.39W
Carbonia 14 Ck 39.10N 8.31 E
Carcans, Étang de- 11 Ei 45.06N 1.07W
Carcar 26 Hd 10.06N 123.38 E
Carcaraña, Río- 55 Bk 32.27S 60.48W
Carcassonne 11 Ik 43.13N 2.21 E
Carcross 42 Ed 60.10N 134.42W
Çardak [Tur.] 15 Ji 40.22N 26.43 E
Çardak [Tur.] 24 Cd 37.48N 29.40 E
Čardara 19 Gg 41.15N 68.01 E
Čardarinskoje Vodohranilišče 18 Gd 41.05N 68.15 E
Cárdenas [Cuba] 47 Hd 23.02N 81.12W
Cárdenas [Mex.] 47 Ed 22.00N 99.40W
Cárdenas [Mex.] 48 Mi 17.59N 93.22W
Cárdenas, Bahia de- 49 Gb 23.05N 81.10W
Cardener/Cardoner 13 Nc 41.41N 1.51 E
Cardiel, Lago- 56 Fg 48.55S 71.15W
Cardiff 6 Fe 51.30N 3.13W
Cardigan 9 Ii 52.06N 4.40W
Cardigan Bay 5 Fe 52.30N 4.20W
Cardona [Sp.] 13 Nc 41.55N 1.41 E
Cardona [Ur.] 55 Dk 33.54S 57.22W
Cardoner/Cardener 13 Nc 41.41N 1.51 E
Cardozo 55 Dk 32.38S 56.21W
Cardston 42 Gg 49.12N 113.18W
Čardžou 22 If 39.06N 63.34 E
Čardžouskaja Oblast [3] 19 Gh 39.00N 63.00 E
Carei 15 Fb 47.41N 22.28 E
Careiro 54 Gd 3.12S 59.45W
Carentan 11 Ee 49.18N 1.14W
Carey 46 Ie 43.20N 113.58W
Carey, Lake- 57 Dg 29.05S 122.15 E
Cargados Carajos Islands 30 Mj 16.35S 59.40 E
Cargese 11a Aa 42.08N 8.35 E
Carhaix-Plouguer 11 Cf 48.17N 3.35W
Cari 14 Hi 41.23N 13.50 E
Caria 15 Ll 37.30N 29.00 E
Cariacica 54 Jh 20.16S 40.25W
Cariaco 50 Eg 10.29N 63.33W
Cariaco, Golfo de- 50 Eg 10.30N 64.00W
Cariaco Basin (EN) 50 Dg 10.37N 65.10W
Cariati 14 Kk 39.30N 16.57 E
Caribana, Punta- 49 Ii 8.37N 76.52W
Caribbean Sea 38 Lh 15.00N 73.00W
Caribbean Sea (EN)= Antillas, Mar de las-/ Caribe, Mar- 38 Lh 15.00N 73.00W
Caribbean Sea (EN)= Antilles, Mer des-/Caraïbe, Mer- 38 Lh 15.00N 73.00W
Caribbean Sea (EN)= Caribe, Mar-/Antillas, Mar de las- 38 Lh 15.00N 73.00W
Caribe, Mar-/Antillas, Mar de las-=Caribbean Sea (EN) 38 Lh 15.00N 73.00W
Cariboo Mountains 42 Ff 53.00N 121.00W
Caribou 42 Ie 59.20N 94.45W
Caribou 44 Mb 46.52N 68.01W
Caribou Island 44 Eb 47.27N 85.52W
Caribou Lake 45 La 50.25N 89.00W
Caribou Mountains 38 Hd 59.12N 115.40W
Caribou Range 46 Je 43.05N 111.15W
Caričin Grad 15 Eg 42.57N 21.45 E
Carignan 11 Le 49.38N 5.10 E
Carignano 14 Bf 44.55N 7.40 E
Cariñena 13 Kc 41.20N 1.13W
Carinhanha 54 Jf 14.08S 43.47W
Carinhanha, Rio- 55 Kb 14.20S 43.47W
Carini 14 Hl 38.08N 13.11 E
Carinola 14 Hi 41.11N 13.58 E
Carinthia (EN) = Kärnten [2] 14 Hd 46.45N 14.00 E
Carinthia (EN) = Kärnten 14 Hd 46.45N 14.00 E
Caripe 50 Eg 10.21N 63.29W
Caripito 54 Fa 10.08N 63.06W
Caris, Rio- 50 Eh 8.09N 63.46W
Carlet 13 Le 39.14N 0.31W
Carleton Place 44 Ic 45.07N 76.08W
Carletonville 37 De 26.23S 27.22 E
Carlin 46 Gf 40.43N 116.07W
Carling 12 Ie 49.10N 6.43 E
Carlingford Lough/Loch Cairlinn 9 Gg 54.05N 6.14W
Carlinville 45 Lg 39.17N 89.53W
Carlisle [Eng.-U.K.] 6 Fe 54.54N 2.55W
Carlisle [Pa.-U.S.] 44 Ie 40.12N 77.12W
Carlisle Bay 51q Ab 13.05N 59.37W
Carloforte 14 Ck 39.08N 8.18 E
Carlos Beguerie 55 Cl 35.29S 59.06W
Carlos Casares 56 He 35.38S 61.21W
Carlos Chagas 54 Jg 17.43S 40.45W
Carlos Reyles 55 Dk 33.03S 56.29W
Carlos Tejedor 55 Al 35.23S 62.25W
Carlow/Ceatharlach 9 Gi 52.50N 6.55W
Carlow/Ceatharlach [2] 9 Gi 52.50N 7.00W
Carloway 9 Gc 58.17N 6.47W
Carlsbad [Ca.-U.S.] 46 Gj 33.10N 117.21W
Carlsbad [N.M.-U.S.] 39 If 32.25N 104.14W
Carlyle 42 Hg 49.38N 102.16W
Carlyle Lake 45 Lg 38.40N 89.18W
Carmacks 42 Dd 62.05N 136.18W
Carmagnola 14 Bf 44.51N 7.43 E
Carmarthen 9 Ij 51.52N 4.19W
Carmarthen Bay 9 Ij 51.40N 4.30W
Carmaux 11 Ij 44.03N 2.09 E
Carmel Head 9 Ih 53.24N 4.34W
Carmelita 49 Be 17.21N 90.10W
Carmelo 56 Id 34.00S 58.17W
Carmen 55 Dk 33.15S 56.01W
Carmen, Isla- 47 Bc 25.57N 111.12W
Carmen, Isla del- 48 Nh 18.42N 91.40W
Carmen, Laguna del- 48 Mh 18.15N 93.50W
Carmen, Río del- 48 Fb 30.42N 106.29W
Carmen, Sierra del- 48 Hc 29.00N 102.30W
Carmen de Patagones 56 Hf 40.48S 62.59W
Carmensa 56 Ge 35.08S 67.38W
Carmi 45 Lg 38.07N 88.10W
Carmichael 46 Eg 38.38N 121.19W
Carmo de Minas 55 Jf 22.07S 45.08W
Carmo do Paranaiba 55 Id 18.59S 46.21W
Carmona 13 Gg 37.28N 5.38W
Carnac 11 Cg 47.35N 3.05W
Carnamah 59 De 29.42S 115.53 E
Carnarvon [Austl.] 58 Cg 24.53S 113.40 E
Carnarvon [S.Afr.] 31 Jl 30.56S 22.08 E
Carnarvon Range 59 Ee 25.10S 121.00 E
Carnatic (EN) 21 Jh 10.30N 79.00 E
Carnegie, Lake- 57 Dg 26.10S 122.30 E
Carnegie Ridge (EN) 3 Nj 1.00S 85.00W
Carn Eige 9 Hd 57.30N 5.05W
Carney Island 66 Nf 73.57S 121.00W
Carnia 14 Gd 46.25N 13.00 E
Car Nicobar 25 Ig 9.10N 92.47 E
Carnot 35 Be 4.48N 16.03 E
Carnoustie 9 Ke 56.30N 2.44W
Carnsore Point/Ceann an Chairn 9 Gi 52.10N 6.22W
Carn Ui Néid/Mizen Head 5 Fe 51.27N 9.49W
Caro 44 Fd 43.29N 83.24W
Carol City 44 Gm 25.56N 80.16W
Carolina [Braz.] 53 Lf 7.20S 47.28W
Carolina [P.R.] 51a Cb 18.24N 65.57W
Carolina [S.Afr.] 37 Ee 26.05S 30.06 E
Carolina Beach 44 Ih 34.02N 77.54W
Carolinas, Puntan- 64b Bb 14.54N 145.38 E
Caroline Atoll 57 Le 9.58S 150.13W
Caroline Islands 57 Fd 8.00N 147.00 E
Carondelet Reef 57 Je 5.34S 173.51W
Caroni, Rio- 52 Je 8.21N 62.43W
Caronie→Nebrodi 14 Im 37.55N 14.35 E
Carora 54 Da 10.11N 70.05W
Carpathian Mountains (EN) 5 If 48.00N 24.00 E
Carpathian Mountains (EN) =Carpații Occidentali 15 Fc 46.30N 22.10 E
Carpathian Mountains (EN) =Carpații Orientali 15 Ib 47.30N 25.30 E
Carpații Meridionali= Transylvanian Alps (EN) 5 If 45.30N 22.10 E
Carpații Occidentali = Carpathian Mountains (EN) 15 Fc 46.30N 22.10 E
Carpații Orientali= Carpathian Mountains (EN) 15 Ib 47.30N 25.30 E
Carpen 15 Ge 44.20N 23.15 E
Carpentaria, Gulf of- 57 Ef 14.00S 139.00 E
Carpentras 11 Lj 44.03N 5.03 E
Carpi 14 Ef 44.47N 10.53 E
Carpina 54 Ke 7.51S 35.15W
Carr, Cape- 66 Ie 66.07S 130.51 E
Carraig Fhearghais/ Carrickfergus 9 Hg 54.43N 5.44W
Carraig na Siúire/Carrick-on-Suir
Carrara 14 Ef 44.05N 10.06 E
Carrauntoohil 5 Fe 52.00N 9.45W
Carreiro, Rio- 55 Gi 29.07S 51.43W
Carreño 13 Ga 43.35N 5.46W
Carreta, Punta- 54 Cf 14.13S 76.18W
Carretero, Puerto- 13 Ig 37.28N 3.40W
Carriacou 50 Ff 12.30N 61.27W
Carrick 9 If 55.15N 4.40W
Carrickfergus/Carraig Fhearghais 9 Hg 54.43N 5.44W
Carrick-on-Shannon/cara Droma Rúisc 9 Eh 53.57N 8.05W
Carrick-on-Suir/Carraig na Siúire 9 Fi 52.21N 7.25W
Carrington 43 Hb 47.27N 99.08W
Carrión 13 Hc 41.53N 4.32W
Carrión de los Condes 13 Hb 42.20N 4.36W
Carrizal 49 Kh 11.58N 72.12W
Carrizo Peak 45 Dj 33.20N 105.38W
Carrizos 48 Gc 29.58N 105.16W
Carrizo Springs 45 Gl 28.31N 99.52W
Carrizo Wash 46 Ki 34.36N 109.26W
Carrizozo 45 Dj 33.38N 105.53W
Carroll 45 Ie 42.04N 94.52W
Carroll Inlet 66 Qf 73.18S 78.30W
Carrollton [Ga.-U.S.] 44 Ei 33.35N 85.05W
Carrollton [Il.-U.S.] 45 Kg 39.18N 90.24W
Carrollton [Ky.-U.S.] 44 Ef 38.41N 85.11W
Carrollton [Mo.-U.S.] 45 Jg 39.22N 93.30W
Carron, Loch- 9 Hd 57.30N 5.40W
Carrot 42 Hf 53.50N 101.18W
Carrowmore Lough 9 Dg 54.12N 9.47W
Çarşamba 24 Gb 41.12N 36.44 E
Çarşamba 24 Ed 37.53N 32.37 E
Čaršanga 19 Gh 37.31N 66.03 E
Čarsk 19 If 49.35N 81.05 E
Carson 46 Ed 45.44N 121.49W
Carson City 39 Hf 39.10N 119.46W
Carson Lake 46 Fg 39.19N 118.43W
Carson Sink 46 Fg 39.45N 118.30W
Cartagena [Col.] 53 Id 10.25N 75.32W
Cartagena [Sp.] 6 Fh 37.36N 0.59W
Cartago [3] 49 Fi 9.50N 83.45W
Cartago [Col.] 54 Cc 4.46N 75.56W
Cartago [C.R.] 47 Hg 9.52N 83.55W
Cartaxo 13 De 39.09N 8.47W
Carter, Mount- 59 Ib 13.05S 143.15 E
Carteret 11 Ee 49.23N 1.47W
Cartersville 44 Eh 34.10N 85.05W
Carterton 62 Fd 41.01S 175.31 E
Carthage [Mo.-U.S.] 45 Ih 37.11N 94.19W
Carthage [Tx.-U.S.] 45 Ij 32.09N 94.20W
Cartier 44 Gb 46.42N 81.32W
Cartier Island 57 Df 12.30S 123.30 E
Caruaru 53 Mf 8.17S 35.58W
Carúpano 54 Fa 10.40N 63.14W
Carutapera 54 Id 1.13S 46.01W
Čarvak 18 Gd 41.38N 69.56 E
Carvin 12 Ed 50.29N 2.58 E
Carvoeiro, Cabo- 13 Ce 39.21N 9.24W
Čaryn 18 Lc 43.50N 79.12 E
Čaryš 20 Df 52.22N 83.45 E
Casablanca [2] 32 Fc 33.37N 7.35W
Casablanca 31 Ge 33.36N 7.37W
Casa Branca 55 Ie 21.46S 47.05W
Casa Grande 43 Ee 32.53N 111.45W
Casalbordino 14 Ih 42.09N 14.35 E
Casale Monferrato 14 Ce 45.08N 8.27 E
Casalmaggiore 14 Ef 44.59N 10.26 E
Casalvasco 55 Cb 15.19S 59.59W
Casal Velino 14 Jj 40.11N 15.06 E
Casamance 34 Bc 12.33N 16.46W
Casamance [3] 34 Bc 12.50N 15.00W
Casanare [2] 54 Db 5.20N 72.00W
Casanare, Rio- 54 Eb 6.02N 69.51W
Casanay 50 Eg 10.30N 63.25W
Casa Nova 54 Je 9.25S 41.08W
Casarano 14 Mj 40.00N 18.10 E
Casas Grandes, Rio- 48 Eb 30.22N 107.31W
Casas-Ibáñez 13 Ke 39.17N 1.28W
Casca, Rio da- 55 Eb 14.52S 55.52W
Cascade 46 Hd 44.31N 115.59W
Cascade Point 62 Cf 44.01S 168.22 E
Cascade Range 38 Ge 45.00N 121.30W
Cascais 13 Cf 38.42N 9.25W
Cascavel 56 Jb 24.57S 53.28W
Cascia 14 Hh 42.43N 13.01 E
Casciana Terme 14 Eg 43.32N 10.38 E
Cascina 14 Eg 43.41N 10.33 E
Casentino 14 Fg 43.40N 11.50 E

Index Symbols

[1] Independent Nation
[2] State, Region
[3] District, County
[4] Municipality
[5] Colony, Dependency
Continent
Physical Region
Historical or Cultural Region
Mount, Mountain
Volcano
Hill
Mountains, Mountain Range
Hills, Escarpment
Plateau, Upland
Pass, Gap
Plain, Lowland
Delta
Salt Flat
Valley, Canyon
Crater, Cave
Karst Features
Depression
Polder
Desert, Dunes
Forest, Woods
Heath, Steppe
Oasis
Cape, Point
Coast, Beach
Cliff
Peninsula
Isthmus
Sandbank
Island
Atoll
Rock, Reef
Islands, Archipelago
Rocks, Reefs
Coral Reef
Well, Spring
Geyser
River, Stream
Waterfall Rapids
River Mouth, Estuary
Lake
Salt Lake
Intermittent Lake
Reservoir
Swamp, Pond
Canal
Glacier
Ice Shelf, Pack Ice
Ocean
Sea
Gulf, Bay
Strait, Fjord
Lagoon
Bank
Seamount
Tablemount
Ridge
Shelf
Basin
Escarpment, Sea Scarp
Fracture
Trench, Abyss
National Park, Reserve
Point of Interest
Recreation Site
Cave, Cavern
Historic Site
Ruins
Wall, Walls
Church, Abbey
Temple
Scientific Station
Airport
Port
Lighthouse
Mine
Tunnel
Dam, Bridge

International Map Index

Case-Pilote 51h Ab 14.38N 61.08W
Caserta 14 Ii 41.04N 14.20 E
Casey 66 He 66.17S 110.32 E
Casey Bay 66 Ee 67.00S 48.00 E
Cashel/Caiseal 9 Fi 52.31N 7.53W
Casigua 49 Ki 8.46N 72.30W
Casilda 56 Hd 33.03S 61.10W
Casimcea 15 Le 44.24N 28.33 E
Casino 59 Ke 28.52S 153.03 E
Casiquiare, Brazo- 54 Ec 2.01N 67.07W
Čáslav 10 Lg 49.55N 15.25 E
Casma 54 Ce 9.28S 78.19W
Časnačorr, Gora- 7 Hc 67.45N 33.29 E
Čašniki 7 Gi 54.52N 29.08 E
Casoli 14 Ih 42.07N 14.18 E
Casoria 14 Ij 40.54N 14.17 E
Caspe 13 Lc 41.14N 0.02W
Casper 39 Ie 42.51N 106.19W
Caspian Depression (EN)=Prikaspijskaja Nizmennost 5 Lf 48.00N 52.00 E
Caspian Sea (EN)=Kaspijskoje More 5 Lg 42.00N 50.30 E
Caspian Sea (EN)=Māzandarān, Daryā-ye- 5 Lg 42.00N 50.30 E
Cassai 30 Ii 3.02S 16.57 E
Cassamba 36 De 13.04S 20.25 E
Cassange, Rio- 55 Dc 17.06S 57.23W
Cassano allo Ionio 14 Kk 39.47N 16.19 E
Cass City 44 Fd 43.36N 83.10W
Cassel 12 Ed 50.47N 2.29 E
Casselton 45 Hc 46.54N 97.13W
Cássia 55 Ie 20.36S 46.56W
Cassiar 42 Ee 59.16N 129.40W
Cassiar Mountains 38 Gd 59.00N 129.00W
Cassilândia 54 Hg 19.09S 51.45W
Cassino [Braz.] 55 Fk 32.11S 52.10W
Cassino [It.] 14 Hi 41.30N 13.49 E
Cassis 11 Lk 43.13N 5.32 E
Cass Lake 45 Ic 47.23N 94.36W
Cass River 44 Fd 43.23N 83.59W
Cassununga 55 Fc 16.03S 53.38W
Castagneto Carducci 14 Eg 43.10N 10.36 E
Castagniccia 11a Ba 42.25N 9.30 E
Castañar, Sierra del- 13 He 39.35N 4.10W
Castanhal 54 Id 1.18S 47.55W
Castaños 48 Id 26.47N 101.25W
Castelbuono 14 Im 37.56N 14.05 E
Castel di Sangro 14 Ii 41.47N 14.06 E
Castelfidardo 14 Hg 43.28N 13.33 E
Castelfranco Veneto 14 Fe 45.40N 11.55 E
Casteljaloux 11 Gj 44.19N 0.06 E
Castellabate 14 Ij 40.17N 14.57 E
Castellammare, Golfo di- 14 Gl 38.10N 12.55 E
Castellammare del Golfo 14 Gl 38.01N 12.53 E
Castellammare di Stabia 14 Ij 40.42N 14.29 E
Castellana Grotte 14 Lj 40.53N 17.10 E
Castellane 11 Mk 43.51N 6.31 E
Castellaneta 14 Kj 40.38N 16.56 E
Castelldefels 13 Nc 41.17N 1.58 E
Castelli [Arg.] 56 Hc 25.57S 60.37W
Castelli [Arg.] 55 Dm 36.06S 57.47W
Castelló de la Plana/Castellón de la Plana 6 Fh 39.59N 0.02W
Castellón [3] 13 Ld 40.10N 0.10W
Castellón de la Plana/Castelló de la Plana 6 Fh 39.59N 0.02W
Castellón de la Plana-El Grao 13 Me 39.58N 0.01 E
Castellote 13 Ld 40.48N 0.19W
Castelnaudary 11 Hk 43.19N 1.57 E
Castelnau-de-Médoc 11 Fi 45.02N 0.48W
Castelnovo ne' Monti 14 Ef 44.26N 10.24 E
Castelo Branco [2] 13 Ee 40.00N 7.30W
Castelo Branco 13 Ee 39.49N 7.30W
Castelo de Vide 13 Ee 39.25N 7.27W
Castelo do Piaui 54 Je 5.20S 41.33W
Castel San Giovanni 14 De 45.04N 9.26 E
Castelsardo 14 Cj 40.55N 8.43 E
Castelsarrasin 11 Hj 44.02N 1.06 E
Casteltermini 14 Hm 37.32N 13.39 E
Castelvetrano 14 Gm 37.41N 12.47 E
Castets 11 Ek 43.53N 1.09W
Castiglione del Lago 14 Gg 43.07N 12.03 E
Castiglione della Pescaia 14 Eh 42.46N 10.53 E
Castiglion Fiorentino 14 Fg 43.20N 11.55 E
Castilla la Nueva=New Castile (EN) 13 Id 40.00N 3.45W
Castilla la Vieja=Old Castile (EN) 13 Ic 41.30N 4.00W
Castillejo 13 Gc 41.14N 5.30W
Castillon-la-Bataille 11 Fj 44.51N 0.02W
Castillonnès 11 Gj 44.39N 0.36 E
Castillos 56 Jd 34.12S 53.50W
Castillos, Laguna de- 55 Fl 34.20S 53.54W
Castlebar/Caisleán an Bharraigh 9 Dh 53.52N 9.17W
Castle Bruce 51g Bb 15.26N 61.16W
Castle Dome Peak 46 Hj 33.05N 114.08W
Castle Douglas 9 Jg 54.57N 3.56W
Castlegar 42 Fg 49.19N 117.40W
Castleisland/Oiléan Ciarraí 9 Di 52.14N 9.27W
Castlemaine 59 Ig 37.04S 144.13 E
Castle Peak 46 Hd 44.03N 114.32W
Castlepoint 62 Gd 40.55S 176.13 E
Castlepollard 9 Fh 53.41N 7.17W
Castlerea/An Caisleán Riabhach 9 Eh 53.46N 8.29W
Castlereagh Bay 59 Hb 12.10S 135.10 E
Castle Rock Butte 45 Ed 45.00N 103.27W
Castle Rock Lake 45 Le 43.56N 89.58W
Častoozerje 17 Mi 55.34N 67.53 E
Castor 46 Ja 52.13N 111.53W
Castres 11 Ik 43.36N 2.15 E
Castricum 12 Gb 52.33N 4.42 E
Castries 39 Mh 14.01N 61.00W
Castrignano del Capo 14 Mk 39.50N 18.20 E
Castro [Braz.] 56 Jb 24.47S 50.03W
Castro [Chile] 56 Ff 42.29S 73.46W
Castro Alves 54 Kf 12.45S 39.26W
Castrocaro Terme e Terra del Sole 14 Ff 44.10N 11.57 E
Castro Daire 13 Ed 40.54N 7.56W
Castro del Río 13 Hg 37.41N 4.28W
Castrojeriz 13 Hb 42.17N 4.08W
Castropol 13 Ea 43.32N 7.02W
Castrop-Rauxel 12 Jc 51.33N 7.19 E
Castro Urdiales 13 Ia 43.23N 3.13W
Castro Verde 13 Dg 37.42N 8.05W
Castrovillari 14 Kk 39.49N 16.12 E
Castrovirreyna 54 Cf 13.16S 75.19W
Castuera 13 Gf 38.43N 5.33W
Častyje 17 Gh 57.19N 54.59 E
Casupá 55 El 34.09S 55.38W
Caswell Sound 62 Bf 45.00S 167.10 E
Çat 24 Ic 39.40N 41.02 E
Čata 10 Oi 47.58N 18.40 E
Catacamas 49 Ef 14.54N 85.56W
Catahoula Lake 45 Jk 31.30N 92.06W
Çatak 24 Jc 38.01N 43.07 E
Çatak 24 Jd 37.53N 42.39 E
Catalan Coastal Range (EN)=Cadena Costero Catalana/Serralada Litoral Catalana 5 Gg 41.35N 1.40 E
Catalan Coastal Range (EN)=Serralada Litoral Catalana/Cadena Costero Catalana 5 Gg 41.35N 1.40 E
Catalão 54 Ig 18.10S 47.57W
Čatal Balkan 15 Jg 42.46N 27.00 E
Çatalca 15 Lh 41.09N 28.27 E
Çatal Dağ 15 Lj 39.51N 28.20 E
Catalina 56 Gc 25.13S 69.43W
Catalina, Isla- 49 Md 18.21N 69.00W
Catalina, Punta- 56 Gh 52.32S 68.47W
Catalonia (EN)=Cataluña/Catalunya 5 Gg 42.00N 2.00 E
Catalonia (EN)=Cataluña/Catalunya 13 Nc 42.00N 2.00 E
Catalonia (EN)=Catalunya/Cataluña 5 Gg 42.00N 2.00 E
Catalonia (EN)=Catalunya/Cataluña 13 Nc 42.00N 2.00 E
Cataluña/Catalunya=Catalonia (EN) 5 Gg 42.00N 2.00 E
Cataluña/Catalunya=Catalonia (EN) 13 Nc 42.00N 2.00 E
Catalunya/Cataluña=Catalonia (EN) 13 Nc 42.00N 2.00 E
Catalunya/Cataluña=Catalonia (EN) 5 Gg 42.00N 2.00 E
Çatalzeytin 24 Fb 41.57N 34.13 E
Catamarca 53 Jh 28.30S 65.45W
Catamarca [2] 56 Gc 27.00S 67.00W
Catanduanes 21 Oh 13.45N 124.15 E
Catanduva 56 Kb 21.08S 48.58W
Catanduvas 55 Fg 25.12S 53.08W
Catania 6 Hh 37.30N 15.06 E
Catania, Golfo di- 14 Jm 37.25N 15.10 E
Catania, Piana di- 14 Im 37.25N 14.50 E
Catanzaro 6 Hh 38.54N 16.35 E
Catarman 26 Hd 12.30N 124.38 E
Catastrophe, Cape- 57 Eh 35.00S 136.00 E
Catatumbo, Río- 49 Li 9.21N 71.45W
Catbalogan 26 Hd 11.46N 124.53 E
Catemaco, Lago- 48 Lh 18.25N 95.05W
Catete 36 Bd 9.07S 13.41 E
Cathair na Mart/Westport 9 Dh 53.48N 9.32W
Cathair Saidhbhín/Cahersiveen 9 Cj 51.57N 10.13W
Cathcart 37 Df 32.18S 27.09 E
Catherine, Mount- 46 Ig 39.05N 112.04W
Catholic Island 51n Bb 12.40N 61.24W
Catio 34 Bc 11.17N 15.15W
Cat Island 38 Lg 24.30N 75.30W
Čatkal 18 Hd 41.36N 70.05 E
Čatkalski Hrebet 19 Hg 41.30N 70.50 E
Cat Lake 42 If 51.40N 91.52W
Catoche, Cabo- 38 Kg 21.36N 87.07W
Cato Island 57 Gg 23.15S 155.35 E
Catolé do Rocha 54 Ke 6.21S 37.45W
Catoute 13 Fb 42.45N 6.20W
Catria 14 Gg 43.28N 12.42 E
Catriló 56 He 36.26S 63.24W
Catrimani, Rio- 54 Fc 0.28N 61.44W
Catskill Mountains 44 Jd 42.10N 74.30W
Cattenom 12 Ie 49.25N 6.15 E
Cattolica 14 Gg 43.58N 12.44 E
Catu 54 Kf 12.21S 38.23W
Catuane 37 Ee 26.48S 32.14 E
Catumbela 36 Be 12.27S 13.29 E
Catur 37 Fb 13.45S 35.37 E
Catwick, Iles- 25 Lg 10.00N 109.00 E
Catwright 39 Nd 53.50N 56.45W
Catyrkël, Ozero- 18 Jd 40.35N 75.20 E
Catyrtaš 18 Kd 40.52N 76.23 E
Cauca [2] 54 Cc 2.30N 77.00W
Cauca, Río- 52 Ie 8.54N 74.28W
Caucasia 54 Cb 7.59N 75.13W
Caucasus (EN)=Kavkaz, Bolšoj- 5 Kg 42.30N 45.00 E
Caucete 56 Gd 31.38S 68.16W
Caudebec-en-Caux 12 Ce 49.32N 0.44 E
Caudete 13 Lf 38.42N 0.59W
Caudry 11 Jd 50.08N 3.25 E
Caulonia 14 Kl 38.23N 16.24 E
Caumont-l'Eventé 12 Be 49.05N 0.48W
Caungula 31 Ii 8.26S 18.37 E
Čaunskaja Guba 20 Lc 69.30N 170.00 E
Caupolican 54 Ef 13.30S 68.30W
Cauquenes 56 Fe 35.58S 72.21W
Caura, Río- 52 Je 7.38N 64.53W
Causapscal 44 Na 48.22N 67.14W
Caussade 11 Hj 44.10N 1.32 E
Čausy 16 Gc 53.50N 30.59 E
Cauterets 11 Fl 42.53N 0.07W
Cauto, Río- 49 Ic 20.33N 77.15W
Cauvery 21 Jh 11.09N 78.52 E
Caux, Pays de- 11 Ge 49.40N 0.40 E
Cávado 13 Dc 41.32N 8.48W
Cavaillon 11 Lk 43.50N 5.02 E
Cavalcante 55 Ia 13.48S 47.30W
Cavalese 14 Fd 46.17N 11.27 E
Cavalli Islands 62 Ea 35.00S 173.55 E
Cavallo, Isola- 11a Bb 41.22N 9.16 E
Cavallo Pass 45 Hl 28.25N 96.26W
Cavally 30 Gh 4.22N 7.32W
Cavan/An Cabhán 9 Fg 54.00N 7.21W
Cavan/An Cabhán [2] 9 Fh 53.55N 7.30W
Cavarzere 14 Ge 45.08N 12.05 E
Çavdarhisar 15 Mj 39.12N 29.37 E
Çavdir 15 Ml 37.09N 29.42 E
Caviana, Ilha- 54 Hc 0.10N 50.05W
Cavili 26 He 9.17N 120.50 E
Cavour, Canale- 14 Be 45.11N 7.54 E
Cavtat 14 Mh 42.35N 18.13 E
Caxambu 55 Je 21.59S 44.56W
Caxias 53 Lf 4.50S 43.21W
Caxias do Sul 53 Kh 29.10S 51.11W
Caxito 36 Bd 8.34S 13.40 E
Çay 24 Dc 38.35N 31.02 E
Cayambe 54 Cc 0.05N 78.08W
Cayambe, Volcán- 52 Ie 0.02N 77.59W
Cayastá 55 Bj 31.12S 60.10W
Cayce 44 Gi 33.59N 81.04W
Çaycuma 24 Eb 41.25N 32.05 E
Çayeli 24 Ib 41.05N 40.44 E
Cayenne 53 Ke 4.56N 52.20W
Cayeux-Sur-Mer 12 Dd 50.11N 1.29 E
Cayey 49 Nd 18.07N 66.10W
Çayırlı 24 Ic 39.48N 40.01 E
Çaykara 24 Ib 40.45N 40.19 E
Caylus 11 Hj 44.14N 1.47 E
Cayman Brac 47 Ie 19.43N 79.49W
Cayman Islands [5] 39 Kh 19.30N 80.30W
Cayman Islands 38 Kh 19.30N 80.30W
Cayman Ridge (EN) 47 He 19.30N 80.30W
Cayman Trench (EN) 3 Bh 19.00N 80.00W
Cayo 49 Ce 17.10N 88.50W
Cayon 51c Ab 17.21N 62.43W
Cayones, Cayos- 49 Fe 16.05N 83.12W
Cay Sal Bank 47 Hd 23.45N 80.00W
Cayuga Lake 44 Id 42.45N 76.45W
Cazalla de la Sierra 13 Gg 37.56N 5.45W
Caza Pava 55 Di 28.17S 56.07W
Cazaux, Étang de- 11 Ej 44.29N 1.10W
Cazombo 31 Jj 11.54S 22.53 E
Cazorla 13 Jg 37.55N 3.00W
Cazorla, Sierra de- 13 Jf 37.55N 2.55W
Cea 13 Gb 42.00N 5.36W
Ceahlău 15 Ib 47.03N 25.58 E
Ceanannas Mór/Kells 9 Gh 53.44N 6.53W
Ceanna Caillighe/Hags Head 9 Di 52.57N 9.28W
Ceann Acla/Achill Head 9 Ch 53.59N 10.13W
Ceann an Chairn/Carnsore Point 9 Gi 52.10N 6.22W
Ceann Chill Mhantáin/Wicklow Head 9 Hi 52.58N 6.00W
Ceann Gólaim/Slyne Head 9 Ch 53.24N 10.13W
Ceann Iorrais/Erris Head 5 Fe 54.19N 10.00W
Ceann Léime/Loop Head 9 Di 52.34N 9.56W
Ceann Ros Eoghain/Rossan Point 9 Eg 54.42N 8.48W
Ceann Sléibhe/Slea Head 9 Ci 52.06N 10.27W
Ceann Toirc/Kanturk 9 Ei 52.10N 8.55W
Ceará [2] 54 Kd 5.00S 39.30W
Ceará-Mirim 54 Ke 5.38S 35.26W
Ceatharlach/Carlow [2] 9 Gi 52.50N 7.00W
Ceatharlach/Carlow 9 Gi 52.50N 6.55W
Cébaco, Isla- 49 Gj 7.32N 81.09W
Ceballos 48 Gd 26.32N 104.09W
Čebarkul 17 Ji 54.58N 60.25 E
Čeboksary 6 Kd 56.09N 47.15 E
Cebollati 55 Fk 33.16S 53.47W
Cebollati, Río- 55 Fk 33.09S 53.38W
Cebollera, Sierra- 13 Jc 42.00N 2.40W
Ceboruco, Volcán- 48 Gg 21.09N 104.30W
Cebreros 13 Hd 40.27N 4.28W
Cebrikovo 15 Nb 47.09N 30.02 E
Cebu 21 Oh 10.20N 123.45 E
Cebu 22 Oh 10.18N 123.54 E
Cece 10 Oj 46.46N 18.39 E
Čečen, Ostrov- 16 Og 44.00N 47.45 E
Čečeno respublika 19 Eg 43.15N 45.30 E
Cecen-Ula 27 Gb 48.45N 95.55 E
Cecerleg 22 Me 47.30N 101.27 E
Čečersk 16 Gc 52.56N 30.58 E
Čechy=Bohemia (EN) 5 Hf 50.00N 14.30 E
Čechy=Bohemia (EN) 10 Kf 50.00N 14.30 E
Cecina 14 Eg 43.18N 10.29 E
Cecina 14 Eg 43.10N 10.31 E
Čečuisk 20 Fe 58.07N 108.32 E
Cedar City 39 Hf 37.41N 113.04W
Cedar Creek 45 Fc 46.07N 101.18W
Cedar Creek Reservoir 45 Hj 32.20N 96.10W
Cedar Falls 43 Ic 42.32N 92.27W
Cedar Grove 51d Bb 17.10N 61.49W
Cedar Lake 42 Hf 53.25N 100.00W
Cedar Rapids 39 Je 41.59N 91.40W
Cedar River [Nb.-U.S.] 45 Hf 41.22N 97.57W
Cedar River [U.S.] 43 Ic 41.17N 91.20W
Cedartown 44 Eh 34.01N 85.15W
Cedar-Tree Point 51d Ba 17.42N 61.53W
Cedeira 13 Da 43.39N 8.03W
Cedral 48 If 23.48N 100.44W
Cedrino 14 Dj 40.23N 9.44 E
Cedro 54 Ke 6.36S 39.03W
Cedrón 13 Ie 39.48N 3.33W
Cedros, Isla- [Mex.] 47 Ac 28.12N 115.15W
Cedros, Isla [Mex.]=Cedros Island (EN) 38 Hg 28.10N 115.15W
Cedros Island (EN)=Cedros, Isla [Mex.] 38 Hg 28.10N 115.15W
Cedros Trench (EN) 47 Ac 27.45N 115.45W
Ceduna 59 Gf 32.07S 133.40 E
Cedynia 10 Kd 52.50N 14.14 E
Cefalù 14 Il 38.02N 14.01 E
Cega 13 Hc 41.33N 4.46W
Čegdomyn 22 Pd 51.07N 133.05 E
Čegem 16 Mh 43.36N 43.48 E
Cegléd 10 Pi 47.10N 19.48 E
Ceglie Messapico 14 Lj 40.39N 17.31 E
Cehegin 13 Kf 38.06N 1.48W
Cehotina 15 Bf 43.31N 18.45 E
Čehov 7 Ii 55.11N 37.29 E
Čehov 20 Jg 47.24N 142.05 E
Ceica 15 Fc 46.51N 22.11 E
Çekerek 24 Fb 40.34N 35.46 E
Çekerek 24 Fb 40.04N 35.31 E
Čekmaguš 17 Gi 55.10N 54.40 E
Celano 14 Hh 42.05N 13.33 E
Celaya 47 Dd 20.31N 100.37W
Čelbas 16 Kf 46.06N 38.59 E
Célé 11 Hj 44.28N 1.38 E
Celebes/Sulawesi 21 Oj 2.00S 121.10 E
Celebes Basin (EN) 26 Hf 4.00N 122.00 E
Celebes Sea (EN)=Sulawesi, Laut- 21 Oj 3.00N 122.00 E
Čeleken 19 Fh 39.27N 53.10 E
Čeleken, Poluostrov- 16 Rj 39.25N 53.35 E
Celendín 54 Ce 6.52S 78.09W
Celerain, Punta- 48 Pg 20.16N 86.59W
Celeste 55 Dj 31.18S 57.04W
Celestún 48 Ng 20.52N 90.24W
Celinograd 22 Jd 51.10N 71.30 E
Celinogradskaja Oblast [3] 19 Gh 51.00N 70.00 E
Čeljabinsk 22 Id 55.10N 61.24 E
Čeljabinskaja Oblast [3] 19 Ge 54.00N 61.00 E
Celje 14 Jd 46.14N 15.16 E
Celjuskin, Mys- 21 Mb 77.45N 104.20 E
Čelkar 19 Ff 47.50N 59.29 E
Celldömölk 10 Ni 47.15N 17.09 E
Celle 10 Gd 52.37N 10.05 E
Celles 12 Fd 50.43N 3.27 E
Celles, Houyet- 12 Hd 50.19N 5.01 E
Cellina 14 Ge 46.02N 12.47 E
Celone 14 Ji 41.36N 15.41 E
Celorico da Beira 13 Ed 40.38N 7.23W
Celtic Sea 5 Fe 51.00N 7.00W
Celtic Sea (EN)=An Mhuir Cheilteach 5 Fe 51.00N 7.00W
Cemaes Head 9 Ii 52.07N 4.44W
Čemal 20 Df 51.25N 86.05 E
Čemdalsk 20 Fe 59.45N 103.18 E
Cemernica 14 Lf 44.30N 17.15 E
Cemerno 15 Df 43.36N 20.26 E
Çemişkezek 24 Hc 39.04N 38.55 E
Cenajo, Embalse de- 13 Kf 38.20N 1.55W
Cenderawasih, Teluk- 26 Kg 2.25S 135.10 E
Cengel 27 Eb 48.56N 89.10 E
Çengel Geçidi 24 Kc 39.45N 44.02 E
Ceno 14 Ef 44.41N 10.05 E
Centenary 37 Ec 16.44S 31.07 E
Centennial 46 Lf 41.51N 106.07W
Centennial Lake 44 Ic 45.15N 77.00W
Centennial Mountains 46 Jd 44.35N 111.55W
Center 45 Ik 31.48N 94.11W
Center Hill Lake 44 Eg 36.00N 85.45W
Centerville 45 Jf 40.43N 92.52W
Centinela, Farallón- 50 Cg 10.49N 66.05W
Centinela, Picacho del- 47 Dc 29.07N 102.27W
Cento 14 Ff 44.43N 11.17 E
Centrafrique=Central African Republic (EN) [1] 31 Jh 7.00N 21.00 E
Central [Bots.] [3] 37 Dd 21.30S 26.00 E
Central [Ghana] [3] 34 Ed 5.30N 1.00W
Central [Kenya] [3] 36 Gc 0.45S 37.00 E
Central [Mwi.] [3] 36 Fe 13.30S 34.00 E
Central [Par.] [3] 55 Dg 25.30S 57.30W
Central [Scot.-U.K.] [3] 9 Ie 56.15N 4.10W
Central [Ug.] [3] 36 Fb 0.10N 32.05 E
Central [Zam.] [3] 36 Ee 15.00S 29.00 E
Central, Chaco- 52 Kh 25.00S 59.45W
Central, Cordillera- [Dom.Rep.] 47 Je 18.45N 70.30W
Central, Cordillera- [P.R.] 49 Nd 18.10N 66.35W
Central, Massif- 5 Gf 45.00N 3.10 E
Central, Meseta- 38 Ig 23.00N 103.00W
Central African Republic (EN)=Centrafrique [1] 31 Jh 7.00N 21.00 E
Central Auckland [2] 62 Fb 36.45S 174.40 E
Central Brāhui Range 25 Dc 29.20N 66.55 E
Central City 45 Hf 41.07N 98.00W
Centralia [Il.-U.S.] 45 Lg 38.31N 89.08W
Centralia [Wa.-U.S.] 43 Cb 46.43N 122.58W
Central Lowland 38 Ke 40.20N 90.00W
Central Makrān Range 21 Ig 26.40N 64.30 E
Centralno Tungusskoje Plato 20 Fd 61.15N 102.00 E
Centralny-Kospašski 17 Hg 59.03N 57.50 E
Central Pacific Basin (EN) 3 Ki 5.00N 175.00W
Central Plateau 64e Bb 0.32S 166.56 E
Central Point 46 De 42.23N 122.57W
Central Range 57 Fe 5.00S 142.30 E
Central Russian Uplands (EN)=Srednerusskaja Vozvyšennost 5 Je 52.00N 38.00 E
Central Siberian Uplands (EN)=Srednesibirskoje Ploskogorje 21 Mc 65.00N 105.00 E
Central Urals (EN)=Sredni Ural 5 Ld 58.00N 59.00 E
Centre [Togo] [3] 34 Fd 9.15N 1.00 E
Centre [U.V.] [3] 34 Ec 12.00N 1.00W
Centre, Canal du- 11 Jh 46.28N 3.59 E
Centre-Est [3] 34 Ec 11.30N 0.20W
Centre-Nord [3] 34 Ec 13.20N 0.55W
Centre-Ouest [3] 34 Ec 12.00N 2.20W
Centre-Sud [3] 34 He 3.30N 11.50 E
Centro, Cayo- 48 Ph 18.35N 87.20W
Centuripe 14 Im 37.37N 14.44 E
Čepca 19 Fd 58.35N 50.05 E
Čepelare 15 Hh 41.44N 24.41 E
Cephalonia (EN)=Kefallinia 5 Ih 38.15N 20.35 E
Čepin 14 Me 45.32N 18.34 E
Ceplenița 15 Jb 47.23N 26.58 E
Cepu 26 Fh 7.09S 111.35 E
Cer 15 Ce 44.37N 19.28 E
Ceram Sea (EN)=Seram, Laut- 57 De 2.30S 128.00 E
Cerbatana, Serranía de la- 54 Eb 6.50N 66.15W
Cerbicales, Iles- 11a Bb 41.33N 9.22 E
Cercal 13 Dg 37.47N 8.42W
Čerchov 10 Rg 49.10N 21.05 E
Čerdakly 7 Li 54.23N 48.51 E
Čerdyn 17 Hf 60.25N 56.29 E
Cère 11 Hj 44.55N 1.49 E
Čereha 7 Gh 57.47N 28.22 E
Čeremhovo 22 Md 53.09N 103.05 E
Čerepanovo 20 Df 54.13N 83.32 E
Čerepovec 6 Jd 59.08N 37.54 E
Ceres [Arg.] 56 Hc 29.53S 61.57W
Ceres [Braz.] 54 Ig 15.17S 49.35W
Ceres [S.Afr.] 37 Bf 33.21S 19.18 E
Céret 11 Il 42.29N 2.45 E
Cereté 54 Cb 8.53N 75.47W
Cerf Island 30 Mi 9.31S 51.01 E
Cerfontaine 12 Gd 50.10N 4.25 E
Cergy 12 Ee 49.02N 2.04 E
Cerignola 14 Ji 41.16N 15.54 E
Čerikov 16 Gc 53.35N 31.25 E
Cérilly 11 Ih 46.37N 2.50 E
Čerkasskaja Oblast [3] 19 Df 49.15N 31.15 E
Čerkassy 19 Df 49.26N 32.04 E
Çerkeş 24 Eb 40.50N 32.54 E
Čerkessk 19 Eg 44.14N 42.04 E
Čerkesskaja respublika 19 Eg 43.45N 41.45 E
Çerkezköy 15 Kh 41.17N 28.00 E
Čerlak 19 He 54.09N 74.58 E
Čerlakski 19 He 53.47N 74.31 E
Čermasàn 17 Gi 55.10N 55.20 E
Cermei 15 Ec 46.33N 21.51 E
Çermenika 15 Dh 41.03N 20.20 E
Čermoz 17 Hg 58.47N 56.10 E
Cerna [Rom.] 15 Ge 44.37N 23.57 E
Cerna [Rom.] 15 Fd 44.42N 22.25 E
Cerna [Rom.] 15 Fe 45.53N 22.58 E
Černaja 17 Hb 68.35N 56.31 E
Černaja 17 Hb 68.35N 56.30 E
Černaja 15 Mb 47.39N 29.11 E
Černa Skala, Prohod- 15 Fg 42.02N 22.47 E
Černatica 15 Hh 41.53N 24.33 E
Černavčicy 10 Td 52.11N 23.47 E
Cernavoda 15 Le 44.22N 28.01 E
Cernay 11 Ng 47.49N 7.10 E
Cernay-en-Dormois 12 Ge 49.13N 4.46 E
Černevo 8 Mf 58.35N 28.23 E
Černigov 6 Je 51.30N 31.18 E
Černigovskaja Oblast [3] 19 De 51.20N 32.00 E
Černi Lom 15 If 43.33N 25.57 E
Černi vrăh 15 Gg 42.35N 23.15 E
Černjahovsk 19 Ce 54.38N 21.48 E
Černjanka 16 Jd 50.55N 37.49 E
Černobyl 19 De 51.17N 30.13 E
Černogorsk 20 Ef 53.45N 91.18 E
Černoje More=Black Sea (EN) 5 Jg 43.00N 35.00 E
Černo More=Black Sea (EN) 5 Jg 43.00N 35.00 E
Černomorskoje 16 Hg 45.31N 32.42 E
Černovcy 6 If 48.18N 25.56 E
Černovickaja Oblast [3] 19 Cf 48.20N 26.10 E
Černuška 19 Fd 56.31N 56.03 E
Černy Jar 16 Oe 48.03N 46.05 E
Černyje Zemli 16 Nf 45.55N 46.00 E
Černyšëva, Grjada- 17 Ic 66.20N 59.45 E
Černyševa, Zaliv- 18 Bb 45.50N 59.10 E
Černyševsk 20 Gf 52.35N 117.02 E
Černyševski 20 Gd 62.58N 112.15 E
Černyškovski 16 Me 48.27N 42.14 E
Cérou 11 Hj 44.08N 1.52 E
Cerralvo 48 Jd 26.06N 99.37W
Cerralvo, Isla- 47 Cd 24.15N 109.55W
Cerredo, Torre de- 13 Ha 43.13N 4.50W
Cerriku 15 Ch 41.02N 19.57 E
Cerrito [Col.] 54 Db 6.51N 72.42W
Cerrito [Par.] 55 Dh 27.19S 57.40W
Cerritos 47 Dd 22.26N 100.17W
Cerro Azul 48 Kg 21.12N 97.44W
Cêrro Azul 56 Kb 24.50S 49.15W
Cerro Chato 55 Ek 33.06S 55.08W
Cerro Colorado 55 Ek 33.52S 55.33W
Cerro de las Mesas 48 Kh 18.47N 96.05W
Cerro de Pasco 53 Ig 10.41S 76.16W
Cêrro Grande 55 Gj 30.36S 51.45W
Cerro Largo 56 Jc 28.09S 54.45W
Cerro Largo [2] 55 Ek 32.20S 54.20W
Cerron, Cerro- 49 Lh 10.19N 70.39W
Cerro San Valentín 52 Ij 46.36S 73.20W
Cerros Colorados, Embalse- 56 Ge 38.35S 68.40W
Cerro Vera 55 Dk 33.11S 57.28W
Cerrudo Cué 55 Dh 27.34S 57.57W
Čerski 22 Sc 68.45N 161.45 E
Čerskogo, hrebet- 20 Gf 52.00N 114.00 E
Čerskogo, hrebet-=Cherski Mountains 21 Qc 65.00N 145.00 E

Index Symbols

1 Independent Nation
2 State, Region
3 District, County
4 Municipality
5 Colony, Dependency
Continent
Physical Region
Historical or Cultural Region
Mount, Mountain
Volcano
Hill
Mountains, Mountain Range
Hills, Escarpment
Plateau, Upland
Pass, Gap
Plain, Lowland
Delta
Salt Flat
Valley, Canyon
Crater, Cave
Karst Features
Depression
Polder
Desert, Dunes
Forest, Woods
Heath, Steppe
Oasis
Cape, Point
Coast, Beach
Cliff
Peninsula
Isthmus
Sandbank
Island
Atoll
Rock, Reef
Islands, Archipelago
Rocks, Reefs
Coral Reef
Well, Spring
Geyser
River, Stream
Waterfall Rapids
River Mouth, Estuary
Lake
Salt Lake
Intermittent Lake
Reservoir
Swamp, Pond
Canal
Glacier
Ice Shelf, Pack Ice
Ocean
Sea
Gulf, Bay
Strait, Fjord
Lagoon
Bank
Seamount
Tablemount
Ridge
Shelf
Basin
Escarpment, Sea Scarp
Fracture
Trench, Abyss
National Park, Reserve
Point of Interest
Recreation Site
Cave, Cavern
Historic Site
Ruins
Wall, Walls
Church, Abbey
Temple
Scientific Station
Airport
Port
Lighthouse
Mine
Tunnel
Dam, Bridge

Certaldo 14 Fg 43.33N 11.02 E
Čertkovo 16 Le 49.20N 40.12 E
Cervaro 14 Ji 41.30N 15.52 E
Cervati 14 Jj 40.17N 15.29 E
Červeh 15 Jf 43.37N 26.02 E
Červen 16 Fc 53.43N 28.29 E
Červen brjag 15 Hf 43.16N 24.06 E
Cervera 13 Nc 41.40N 1.17 E
Cervera del Río Alhama 13 Kb 42.01N 1.57W
Cervera de Pisuerga 13 Hb 42.52N 4.30W
Cerveteri 14 Gh 42.00N 12.06 E
Cervia 14 Gf 44.15N 12.22 E
Cervin/Cervino 14 Be 45.58N 7.39 E
Cervino/Cervin 14 Be 45.58N 7.39 E
Cervione 11a Ba 42.20N 9.29 E
Červonoarmejsk 10 Vf 50.03N 25.18 E
Červonoarmejskoje 15 Ld 45.50N 28.38 E
Červonograd 19 Ce 50.24N 24.12 E
Cesano 14 Hg 43.45N 13.10 E
Cesar [2] 54 Db 9.50N 73.30W
César, Río- 49 Ki 9.00N 73.58W
Cesena 14 Gf 44.08N 12.15 E
Cesenatico 14 Gf 44.12N 12.24 E
Cēsis/Cesis 19 Cd 57.18N 25.18 E
Cesis/Cēsis 19 Cd 57.18N 25.18 E
Česká Lípa 10 Kf 50.42N 14.32 E
Česká Republika = Czech Republic (EN) 6 Hf 50.00N 13.00 E
Česká Třebová 10 Mg 49.54N 16.27 E
České Budějovice 10 Kh 48.58N 14.29 E
České středohoří 10 Jf 50.35N 14.00 E
České země [2] 10 Kg 49.45N 15.00 E
Českomoravská Vrchovina = Moravian Upland (EN) 5 Hf 49.20N 15.30 E
Český Krumlov 10 Kh 48.49N 14.19 E
Český Les = Bohemian Forest (EN) 10 Ig 49.50N 12.30 E
Cesma 14 Kf 45.35N 16.29 E
Česma 17 Jj 53.50N 60.40 E
Çeşme 24 Bc 38.18N 26.19 E
Çeşme Yarimadasi 15 Jk 38.30N 26.30 E
Češskaja Guba = Chesha Bay (EN) 5 Kb 67.20N 46.30 E
Cessnock 59 Kf 32.50S 151.21 E
Cestos 30 Gh 5.27N 9.35W
Cesvaine/Cesvajne 8 Lh 56.55N 26.20 E
Cesvajne/Cesvaine 8 Lh 56.55N 26.20 E
Cetate 15 Ge 44.06N 23.03 E
Cetina 14 Kg 43.27N 16.42 E
Cetinje 15 Bg 42.24N 18.55 E
Çetinkaya 24 Gc 39.15N 37.38 E
Cetraro 14 Jk 39.31N 15.56 E
Cetynia 10 Sd 52.33N 22.26 E
Ceuta [5] 31 Ge 35.53N 5.19W
Ceva-i-Ra (Conway Reef) 57 Ig 21.45S 174.35 E
Cevedale/Zufallspitze 14 Ed 46.27N 10.37 E
Cévennes 5 Gg 44.40N 4.00 E
Ceyhan 23 Eb 36.45N 35.42 E
Ceyhan 23 Eb 37.04N 35.47 E
Ceylanpinar 24 Id 36.51N 40.02 E
Ceylon → Srī Lanka [1] 22 Ki 7.40N 80.50 E
Cézallier 11 Ii 45.20N 3.00 E
Cèze 11 Kj 44.06N 4.42 E
Chaalis, Abbaye de- 12 Ee 49.10N 2.40 E
Cha-am 25 Jf 12.48N 99.58 E
Chabanais 11 Gi 45.52N 0.43 E
Chabjuwardoo Bay 59 Cd 22.55S 113.50 E
Chablais 11 Mh 46.20N 6.30 E
Chăboksar 24 Nd 36.58N 50.34 E
Chabówka 10 Pg 49.34N 19.58 E
Chacabuco 56 Hd 34.38S 60.29W
Chachan, Nevado- 54 Dg 16.12S 71.33W
Chachapoyas 54 Ce 6.13S 77.51W
Chachoengsao 25 Kf 13.41N 101.03 E
Chaco [2] 56 Hc 26.00S 60.30W
Chaco [3] 55 Bd 20.00S 60.30W
Chaco, Gran- 52 Jh 23.00S 60.00W
Chaco Mesa 45 Ci 35.50N 107.35W
Chaco River 45 Bh 36.46N 108.69W
Chad (EN) = Tchad [1] 31 Ig 15.00N 19.00 E
Chad, Lake- (EN) = Tchad, Lac- 30 Ig 13.20N 14.00 E
Chādegān 24 Nf 32.46N 50.38 E
Chadileuvú, Río- 56 Ee 38.49S 64.57W
Chadiza 36 Fe 14.04S 32.26 E
Chadron 43 Gc 42.50N 103.02W
Chaeryŏng 28 He 38.24N 125.37 E
Chafarinas, Islas- 13 Ji 35.11N 2.26W
Chāgai Hills 21 Ig 29.30N 64.15 E
Chagang-Do [2] 28 Ie 40.50N 126.30 E
Chaghcharān 22 If 34.31N 65.15 E
Chagny 11 Kh 46.55N 4.45 E
Chagos Archipelago 21 Jj 6.00S 72.00 E
Chagos-Laccadive Plateau (EN) 3 Gi 3.00N 73.00 E
Chagu, Serra do- 55 Fg 25.10S 52.40W
Chaguaramas 50 Ch 9.20N 66.16W
Chahār Borjak 23 Jc 30.17N 62.03 E
Chahār Maḥāl-e Bakhtīārī [3] 23 Hc 32.00N 50.00 E
Chahbounia 13 Oi 35.33N 2.36 E
Ch'aho 28 Jd 40.12N 128.38 E
Chai Badan 25 Ke 15.05N 101.04 E
Chaibāsa 25 Hd 22.34N 85.49 E
Chaigoubu → Huai'an 28 Cd 40.40N 114.25 E
Chai He 28 Gc 42.20N 123.51 E
Chaillu, Massif du- 30 Ii 2.32S 11.10 E
Chainat 25 Ke 15.10N 100.10 E
Chaitén 56 Ff 42.55S 72.43W
Chaiyaphum 25 Ke 16.09N 102.02 E
Chajul 49 Bf 15.30N 91.02W
Chakari 37 Dc 18.09S 29.52 E
Chak Chak 35 Dd 8.40N 26.54 E
Chake Chake 31 Ki 5.15S 39.46 E
Chakhānsūr 23 Jc 31.10N 62.04 E
Chala 54 Dg 15.52S 74.16W
Chalais 11 Gi 45.17N 0.02 E
Chalaltenango 49 Cf 14.03N 88.56W
Chalan Kanoa 64b Ba 15.08N 145.43 E
Chālūs 22 Gf 37.16N 49.36 E
Chalbi Desert 30 Kh 3.00N 37.20 E
Chalchuapa 49 Cg 13.59N 89.41W
Chalcidice (EN) = Khalkidhiki 5 Ig 40.25N 23.25 E
Chālesbān 24 Ne 35.18N 50.03 E
Chaleur Bay 42 Kg 47.50N 65.30W
Chalhuanca 54 Df 14.17S 73.15W
Chaling 27 Jf 26.47N 113.32 E
Chalky Inlet 62 Bg 46.05S 166.30 E
Challans 11 Eh 46.51N 1.53W
Challapata 54 Eg 18.54S 66.47W
Challis 46 Hd 44.30N 114.14W
Chalmette 45 Ll 29.56N 89.58W
Châlons-sur-Marne 11 Kf 48.57N 4.22 E
Chalon-sur-Saône 11 Kh 46.47N 4.51 E
Chaltubo 16 Mh 42.19N 42.34 E
Chālūs 23 Hb 36.38N 51.26 E
Châlus 11 Gi 45.39N 0.59 E
Cham 10 Ig 49.13N 12.40 E
Chama 36 Fe 11.12S 33.10 E
Chama, Rio- 45 Ch 36.03N 106.05W
Chama, Río- 49 Li 9.03N 71.37W
Chaman 25 Db 30.55N 66.27 E
Chaman Bīd 24 Qd 37.25N 56.38 E
Chamba [India] 25 Fb 32.34N 76.08 E
Chamba [Tan.] 36 Ge 11.35S 36.58 E
Chambal 21 Jg 26.29N 79.15 E
Chambaran, Plateau de- 11 Li 45.10N 5.20 E
Chambas 49 Hb 22.12N 78.55W
Chamberlain 45 Ge 43.49N 99.20W
Chamberlain Lake 44 Mb 46.17N 69.20W
Chamberlain River 59 Fc 15.35S 127.51 E
Chambersburg 44 If 39.57N 77.40W
Chambéry 11 Li 45.34N 5.56 E
Chambeshi 30 Jj 11.53S 29.48 E
Chambley-Bussières 12 He 49.03N 5.54 E
Chambly 12 Ee 49.10N 2.15 E
Chambois 12 Cf 48.48N 0.07 E
Chambon, Lac de- 11 Ih 45.35N 2.55 E
Chambord 11 Hg 47.37N 1.31 E
Chamchamal 24 Ke 35.32N 44.50 E
Chame, Punta- 49 Hi 8.39N 79.42W
Chamela 48 Gh 19.32N 105.05W
Chamela, Bahía- 48 Gh 19.30N 105.10W
Chamelecón, Río- 49 Df 15.51N 87.49W
Chamical 56 Gd 30.21S 66.19W
Chamiss Bay 46 Ba 50.07N 127.22W
Chamoli 25 Fb 30.24N 79.21 E
Chamonix-Mont-Blanc 11 Mi 45.55N 6.52 E
Chamouchouane, Rivière- 44 Ka 48.40N 72.20W
Champagne 5 Gf 49.00N 4.30 E
Champagne 11 Kf 49.00N 4.30 E
Champagne Berrichonne 11 Hh 47.00N 2.00 E
Champagne Humide 11 Kf 48.20N 4.30 E
Champagne Pouilleuse 11 Kf 48.40N 4.20 E
Champagnole 11 Lh 46.45N 5.55 E
Champaign 43 Jc 40.07N 88.14W
Champaquí, Cerro- 52 Ji 31.59S 64.56W
Champasak 25 Lf 14.53N 105.52 E
Champaubert 12 Ff 48.53N 3.47 E
Champdoré, Lac- 42 Ke 55.55N 65.45W
Champeigne 12 Gg 47.15N 0.50 E
Champerico 49 Bf 14.18N 91.55W
Champlain, Lake- 43 Mc 44.45N 73.15W
Champlitte-et-le-Prélot 11 Lg 47.37N 5.31 E
Champotón 47 Fe 19.21N 90.43W
Champsaur 11 Mj 44.45N 6.10 E
Chāmrājnagar 25 Ff 11.55N 76.57 E
Chañaral 56 Fc 26.21S 70.37W
Chança 13 Eg 37.33N 7.31W
Chan Chan 54 Ce 8.07S 79.02W
Chanco 56 Fe 35.44S 72.32W
Chandalar 40 Jc 66.36N 145.48W
Chandalar 40 Jc 67.30N 148.30W
Chandausi 25 Fc 28.27N 78.46 E
Chandeleur Islands 43 Jf 29.48N 88.51W
Chandeleur Sound 45 Ll 29.55N 89.10W
Chandīgarh 22 Jf 30.44N 76.55 E
Chandler 42 Lg 48.21N 64.41W
Chandless, Rio 54 Ee 9.08S 69.51W
Chāndpur 25 Id 23.13N 90.39 E
Chandragupta 25 Fe 16.11N 78.52 E
Chandrapur 22 Jh 19.57N 79.18 E
Chang, Ko- 25 Kf 12.00N 102.23 E
Changajn Nuruu → Hangaj, Hrebet- = Khangai Mountains (EN) 21 Le 47.30N 100.00 E
Chang'an → Rong'an 27 If 25.16N 109.23 E
Changane 30 Kk 24.43S 33.32 E
Changbai 28 Jd 41.25N 128.11 E
Changbai Shan 21 Oe 42.00N 128.00 E
Changchun 22 Oe 43.51N 125.20 E
Changdao (Sihou) 28 Ff 37.56N 120.42 E
Changde 22 Ng 29.04N 111.42 E
Ch'angdo 28 Ie 38.30N 127.45 E
Changfeng (Shuijiahu) 28 Dh 32.29N 117.10 E
Changge 28 Bg 34.12N 113.45 E
Changhang 28 If 36.01N 126.42 E
Chang He 28 Ei 31.21N 118.21 E
Changhowŏn 28 If 37.07N 127.38 E
Changhua 27 Lg 24.05N 120.32 E
Changhŭng 28 Ig 34.40N 126.54 E
Changji 27 Ec 44.01N 87.16 E
Chang Jiang 28 Dj 28.59N 116.42 E
Changjiang (Shiliu) 27 Ih 19.20N 109.03 E
Chang Jiang (Yangtze Kiang) 21 Of 31.48N 121.10 E
Changjiang Kou 27 Le 31.24N 121.59 E
Changjin-gang 28 Id 40.30N 127.12 E
Changjin-ho 28 Id 40.30N 127.12 E
Changjin-ŭp 27 Mc 40.23N 127.15 E
Changli 28 Ee 39.43N 119.10 E
Changling 27 Lc 44.15N 123.58 E
Changlung 25 Fb 34.56N 77.29 E
Changping 28 Dd 40.14N 116.13 E
Changsha 22 Ng 28.12N 113.02 E
Changshan 28 Ej 28.55N 118.31 E
Changshan Qundao 28 Ge 39.10N 122.34 E
Changshu 28 Fi 31.38N 120.44 E
Changsŏng 28 Ig 35.19N 126.48 E
Changting 28 Jb 44.27N 128.50 E
Changtu 28 Hc 42.47N 124.08 E
Changuillo 54 Cf 14.40S 75.12W
Changuinola 49 Fi 9.26N 82.31W
Changwu 27 Id 35.17N 107.52 E
Changxing 28 Ei 31.01N 119.55 E
Changxing Dao 28 Fe 39.35N 121.42 E
Changyi 28 Ef 36.52N 119.25 E
Changyŏn 27 Md 38.15N 125.05 E
Changyuan 28 Cg 35.12N 114.40 E
Changzhi 27 Jd 36.07N 113.10 E
Changzhou 28 Ei 31.46N 119.56 E
Channel Islands [5] 9 Kl 49.20N 2.20W
Channel Islands [Chan.Is.] 5 Ff 49.20N 2.20W
Channel Islands [U.S.] 38 Hf 34.00N 120.00W
Channel Port-aux-Basques 39 Ne 47.35N 59.11W
Channel Rock 49 Ib 23.00N 77.55W
Channing 45 Ei 35.41N 102.20W
Chantada 13 Eb 42.37N 7.46W
Chantengo, Laguna- 48 Ji 16.35N 99.10W
Chanthaburi 25 Kf 12.35N 102.06 E
Chantilly 11 Ie 49.12N 2.28 E
Chantonnay 11 Eh 46.41N 1.03W
Chantrey Inlet 38 Jc 67.48N 96.20W
Chanute 45 Ih 37.41N 95.27W
Chanza 13 Eg 37.33N 7.31W
Chao'an (Chaozhou) 27 Kg 23.41N 116.37 E
Chaobai Xinhe 28 De 39.07N 117.41 E
Chao He 28 Dd 40.36N 117.08 E
Chao Hu 28 Di 31.31N 117.33 E
Chao Phraya 21 Mh 13.32N 100.36 E
Chaor He 27 Lb 46.49N 123.45 E
Chaoxian 27 Ke 31.37N 117.49 E
Chaoyang [China] 22 Oe 41.35N 120.26 E
Chaoyang [China] 27 Kg 23.17N 116.37 E
Chaoyang → Huinan 28 Ic 42.41N 126.03 E
Chaoyang → Jiayin 27 Nb 48.52N 130.21 E
Chaoyangchuan 28 Jc 42.53N 129.23 E
Chaoyangcun 27 La 50.01N 124.22 E
Chaozhong 27 La 50.53N 121.23 E
Chaozhou → Chao'an 27 Kg 23.41N 116.37 E
Chapada dos Guimarães 54 Gg 15.26S 55.45W
Chapadinha 54 Jd 3.44S 43.21W
Chapais 44 Ja 49.47N 74.56W
Chapala 48 Hg 20.18N 103.12W
Chapala, Lago de- 38 Ig 20.15N 103.00W
Chaparral 54 Cc 3.43N 75.28W
Chapecó 56 Jc 27.06S 52.36W
Chapecó, Rio- 55 Fh 27.06S 53.01W
Chapecó, Serra do- 55 Gh 26.44S 51.54W
Chapel Hill 44 Hh 35.55N 79.04W
Chapicuy 55 Dj 31.40S 57.55W
Chapleau 42 Jg 47.50N 83.24W
Chaplin 46 La 50.28N 106.40W
Chaplin Lake 46 La 50.18N 106.35W
Chapman, Cape - 42 Ic 69.15N 89.27W
Chappell 45 Ef 41.06N 102.28W
Chāpra 25 Gc 25.46N 84.45 E
Chapultepec 48 Hf 23.27N 103.04W
Chaqui 54 Eg 19.36S 65.32W
Char 32 Ee 21.31N 12.51W
Charadai 55 Ch 27.38S 59.54W
Charagua 54 Fg 19.48S 63.13W
Charām 24 Ng 30.45N 50.44 E
Charaña 54 Eg 17.36S 69.28W
Charcas 48 If 23.08N 101.07W
Charco de la Aguja 48 Gc 28.25N 104.01W
Charcot Island 66 Qe 69.45S 75.15W
Chard [Alta.-Can.] 42 Ge 55.48N 111.10W
Chard [Eng.-U.K.] 9 Kk 50.53N 2.58W
Chardāvol 24 Lf 33.45N 46.38 E
Chardonnières 49 Jd 18.16N 74.10W
Charente [3] 11 Gi 45.40N 0.05 E
Charente 11 Ei 45.57N 1.05W
Charente-Maritime [3] 11 Fi 45.30N 0.45W
Charentonne 12 Ce 49.07N 0.44 E
Chari 30 Ig 12.58N 14.31 E
Chari-Baguirmi [3] 35 Bc 12.00N 17.00 E
Chārīkār 23 Kb 35.01N 69.11 E
Charing 12 Cc 51.12N 0.48 E
Chariton 45 Jf 41.00N 93.19W
Chariton River 45 Jg 39.19N 92.57W
Charity 54 Gb 7.24N 58.36W
Charleroi 11 Kd 50.25N 4.26 E
Charleroi-Jumet 11 Kd 50.27N 4.26 E
Charleroi-Marcinelle 12 Gd 50.25N 4.28 E
Charles 42 Kd 62.38N 74.15W
Charles, Cape- [Can.] 38 Nd 52.13N 55.40W
Charles, Cape- [Va.-U.S.] 43 Ld 37.08N 75.58W
Charles, Peak- 59 Ef 32.52S 121.11 E
Charlesbourg 44 Lb 46.52N 71.16W
Charles City 43 Ic 43.04N 92.40W
Charles de Gaulle, Aéroport- = Charles de Gaulle Airport (EN) 12 Ee 49.02N 2.35 E
Charles de Gaulle Airport (EN) = Charles de Gaulle, Aéroport- 12 Ee 49.02N 2.35 E
Charleston [Il.-U.S.] 45 Lg 39.30N 88.10W
Charleston [Mo.-U.S.] 45 Lh 36.55N 89.21W
Charleston [Ms.-U.S.] 45 Ki 34.01N 90.04W
Charleston [N.Z.] 62 Dd 41.54S 171.27 E
Charleston [S.C.-U.S.] 39 Lf 32.48N 79.57W
Charleston [W.V.-U.S.] 39 Kf 38.21N 81.38W
Charleston Peak 43 Dd 36.16N 115.42W
Charles Town 44 If 39.18N 77.52W
Charlestown 50 Ed 17.12N 62.35W
Charleval 12 De 49.22N 1.23 E
Charleville 58 Fg 26.24S 146.15 E
Charleville-Mézières 11 Ke 49.46N 4.43 E
Charleville Mézières-Mohon 12 Ge 49.46N 4.43 E
Charlevoix 44 Ec 45.19N 85.16W
Charlieu 11 Kh 46.09N 4.11 E
Charlotte [Mi.-U.S.] 44 Ed 42.34N 84.50W
Charlotte [N.C.-U.S.] 39 Kf 35.14N 80.50W
Charlotte Amalie 47 Le 18.21N 64.56W
Charlotte Bank (EN) 57 If 11.47S 173.13 E
Charlotte Harbor 44 Fl 26.45N 82.12W
Charlottenberg 8 Ee 59.53N 12.17 E
Charlottesville 43 Ld 38.02N 78.29W
Charlottetown 39 Me 46.14N 63.08W
Charlton 59 Ig 36.16S 143.21 E
Charlton 42 Jf 52.00N 79.26W
Charly 12 Ff 48.58N 3.17 E
Charmes 11 Mf 48.22N 6.17 E
Charnley River 59 Ec 16.20S 124.53 E
Charny-sur-Meuse 12 He 49.12N 5.22 E
Charollais 11 Kh 46.26N 4.16 E
Charouine 32 Gd 29.01N 0.16W
Charroux 11 Gh 46.09N 0.24 E
Chārsadda 25 Eb 34.09N 71.44 E
Charters Towers 58 Fg 20.05S 146.16 E
Chartres 11 Hf 48.27N 1.30 E
Charzykowskie, Jezioro- 10 Nc 53.47N 17.30 E
Chascomus 56 Ie 35.34S 58.01W
Chase 46 Fa 50.49N 119.41W
Chasŏng 28 Id 41.25N 126.35 E
Chassengue 36 Ce 10.26S 18.32 E
Chassezac 11 Kj 44.26N 4.19 E
Chassiron, Pointe de- 11 Eh 46.03N 1.24W
Chat 24 Pd 37.59N 55.16 E
Châtaigneraie 11 Ij 44.45N 2.20 E
Chātāl 24 Pd 37.40N 55.45 E
Château-Arnoux 11 Lj 44.06N 6.00 E
Châteaubelair 51n Ba 13.17N 61.15W
Châteaubriant 11 Eg 47.43N 1.23W
Château-Chinon 11 Jg 47.04N 3.56 E
Château-du-Loir 11 Gg 47.42N 0.25 E
Châteaudun 11 Hf 48.05N 1.20 E
Château-Gontier 11 Fg 47.50N 0.42W
Châteaulin 11 Bf 48.12N 4.05W
Châteaulin, Bassin de- 11 Cf 48.18N 3.50W
Châteaumeillant 11 Ih 46.34N 2.12 E
Châteauneuf-de-Randon 11 Jj 44.39N 3.04 E
Châteauneuf-sur-Cher 11 Ih 46.51N 2.19 E
Châteauneuf-sur-Loire 11 Ig 47.52N 2.14 E
Château-Porcien 12 Ge 49.32N 4.15 E
Châteaurenard 11 Kk 43.53N 4.51 E
Château-Renault 11 Gg 47.35N 0.54 E
Châteauroux 11 Hh 46.49N 1.42 E
Château-Salins 11 Mf 48.49N 6.30 E
Château-Thierry 11 Je 49.03N 3.24 E
Châteaux, Pointe des- 51e Bb 16.15N 61.11W
Châtelaillon-Plage 11 Eh 46.04N 1.05W
Châtelet 12 Gd 50.24N 4.31 E
Châtelguyon 11 Ji 45.55N 3.04 E
Châtellerault 11 Gh 46.48N 0.32 E
Chatelodo 55 De 21.19S 57.28W
Chatham [Eng.-U.K.] 9 Nj 51.23N 0.32 E
Chatham [N.B.-Can.] 42 Kg 47.02N 65.26W
Chatham [Ont.-Can.] 42 Jh 42.24N 82.11W
Chatham [Va.-U.S.] 44 Hg 36.49N 79.26W
Chatham Island 57 Ji 44.00S 176.30W
Chatham Islands 57 Ji 44.00S 176.30W
Chatham Rise (EN) 57 Ii 43.30S 180.00
Chatham Strait 40 Me 57.30N 134.45W
Châtillon-en-Bazois 11 Jg 47.03N 3.40 E
Châtillon-sur-Indre 11 Hh 46.59N 1.10 E
Châtillon-sur-Marne 12 Fe 49.06N 3.45 E
Châtillon-sur-Seine 11 Kg 47.51N 4.33 E
Chatom 44 Cj 31.28N 88.16W
Chatsworth 37 Ec 19.38S 30.50 E
Chattahoochee 44 Ej 30.42N 84.51W
Chattahoochee 38 Kf 30.52N 84.57W
Chattanooga 39 Kf 35.03N 85.19W
Chatteris 12 Cb 52.27N 0.03 E
Chaucas 55 Cc 16.46S 58.44W
Chaudfontaine 12 Hd 50.35N 5.38 E
Chaudière, Rivière- 44 Lb 46.43N 71.17W
Chauk 25 Id 20.53N 94.49 E
Chaulnes 12 Ee 49.49N 2.48 E
Chaumont 11 Lf 48.07N 5.08 E
Chaumont-en-Vexin 12 De 49.16N 1.53 E
Chaumont-Gistoux 12 Gd 50.41N 4.44 E
Chaumont-Porcien 12 Ge 49.39N 4.15 E
Chaumont-sur-Aire 12 Hf 48.56N 5.15 E
Chaumont-sur-Loire 12 Hg 47.29N 1.11 E
Chauny 11 Je 49.37N 3.13 E
Chau Phu 25 Lf 10.42N 105.07 E
Chausey, Iles- 11 Ef 48.53N 1.50W
Chauvigny 11 Gh 46.34N 0.39 E
Chavantina 54 Hf 14.40S 52.21W
Chavarria 55 Ci 28.57S 58.35W
Chaves [Braz.] 54 Id 0.10S 49.55W
Chaves [Port.] 13 Ec 41.44N 7.28W
Chavigny, Lac - 42 Je 58.00N 75.05W
Chavuma 36 De 13.05S 22.42 E
Chazelles-sur-Lyon 11 Ki 45.38N 4.23 E
Chbar 25 Lf 12.46N 107.10 E
Cheaha Mountain 44 Ei 33.30N 85.47W
Cheat River 44 Hf 39.45N 79.55W
Cheb 10 If 50.04N 12.23 E
Cheboygan 43 Kb 45.39N 84.29W
Chech, 'Erg- 30 Gf 25.00N 3.00W
Chechaouene [3] 32 Fb 35.00N 5.00W
Chechaouene 32 Fb 35.10N 5.16W
Checheng 27 Lg 22.05N 120.42 E
Che-Chiang Sheng → Zhejiang Sheng [2] 27 Kf 29.00N 120.00 E
Chech'ŏn 28 Jf 37.08N 128.12 E
Chęciny 10 Qf 50.48N 20.28 E
Cheddar Gorge 9 Kj 51.13N 2.47W
Cheduba 25 Ie 18.48N 93.38 E
Chée 12 Gf 48.45N 4.39 E
Cheektowaga 44 Hd 42.57N 78.38W
Chefu 37 Ed 22.27S 32.45 E
Chegga 31 Gf 25.22N 5.49W
Cheghelvandī 24 Mf 33.42N 48.25 E
Chehel Pāyeh 24 Qg 31.54N 57.14 E
Cheju 27 Me 33.31N 126.32 E
Cheju-Do 21 Of 33.25N 126.30 E
Cheju-Do [2] 28 Ih 33.25N 126.30 E
Cheju-Haehyŏp 28 Ih 33.40N 126.28 E
Chela, Serra da- 30 Ij 16.00S 13.10 E
Chelan 46 Ec 47.51N 120.01W
Chelan, Lake- 46 Eb 48.05N 120.30W
Chelforó, Arroyo- 55 Cm 36.55S 58.12W
Cheliff [3] 32 Hb 36.10N 1.45 E
Cheliff 30 He 36.02N 0.08 E
Cheliff 32 Hb 36.10N 1.20 E
Cheliff, Plaine du- 13 Mi 35.57N 0.45 E
Chellalat el Adhaouara 13 Pi 35.56N 3.25 E
Chelleh Khāneh, Kūh-e- 24 Md 36.52N 48.36 E
Chełm [2] 10 Te 51.10N 23.30 E
Chełm 10 Te 51.10N 23.28 E
Chelmer 12 Cc 51.44N 0.42 E
Chełmińskie, Pojezierze- 10 Oc 53.20N 19.00 E
Chełmno 10 Oc 53.22N 18.26 E
Chelmsford 9 Nj 51.44N 0.28 E
Chełmża 10 Oc 53.12N 18.37 E
Cheltenham 9 Kj 51.54N 2.04W
Chelva 13 Le 39.45N 0.59W
Chemainus 46 Db 48.55N 123.43W
Chemâma 32 Ef 16.50N 14.00 E
Chemba 37 Ec 17.09S 34.53 E
Chembe 36 Ee 11.58S 28.45 E
Chemillé 11 Fg 47.13N 0.43W
Chemnitz = Karl-Marx-Stadt 6 He 50.50N 12.55 E
Chemult 46 Ee 43.13N 121.47W
Chenachane 32 Gd 26.00N 4.15W
Chenārbāshi 24 Lf 33.20N 46.20 E
Chen Barag Qi (Bayan Hure) 27 Kb 49.21N 119.25 E
Chencha 35 Fd 6.17N 37.40 E
Chencoyi 48 Nh 19.48N 90.14W
Cheney 46 Gc 47.29N 117.34W
Cheney Reservoir 45 Hh 37.45N 97.50W
Cheng'an 28 Cf 36.27N 114.41 E
Chengde 27 Kc 41.00N 117.57 E
Chengdu 22 Mf 30.45N 104.04 E
Chengkou 27 Ie 31.54N 108.37 E
Chengmai 27 Ih 19.50N 109.59 E
Chengshan Jiao 27 Ld 37.24N 122.42 E
Chengxi Hu 28 Dh 32.22N 116.12 E
Chengzitan 27 Ld 39.31N 122.28 E
Chenhsiekali 16 Mh 42.06N 42.16 E
Chenjiagang 28 Eg 34.22N 119.48 E
Chenonceaux 11 Hg 47.20N 1.04 E
Chenxi 27 Jf 28.02N 110.15 E
Chenxian 27 Jf 25.49N 113.05 E
Chenying → Wannian 28 Dj 28.42N 117.04 E
Chépénéhé 63b Ce 20.47S 167.09 E
Chepes 56 Gd 31.21S 66.36W
Chepo 49 Hi 9.10N 79.06W
Cher [3] 11 Ig 47.00N 2.30 E
Cher 5 Gf 47.21N 0.29 E
Cheradi, Isole- 14 Lj 40.25N 17.10 E
Cherangany Hills 36 Gb 1.15N 35.27 E
Cheraw 44 Hh 34.42N 79.53W
Cherbaniani Reef 25 Ef 12.18N 71.53 E
Cherbourg 6 Ff 49.39N 1.39W
Cherchell 32 Hb 36.36N 2.12 E
Chère 11 Eg 47.42N 1.50W
Chergui, Chott Ech- 30 He 34.21N 0.30 E
Chéri 34 Hc 13.26N 11.21 E
Cherlen → Kerulen 21 Ne 48.48N 117.00 E
Cherokee 45 Ie 42.45N 95.33W
Cherokees, Lake O' the- 45 Ih 36.39N 94.49W
Cherksi Mountains (EN) = Čerskogo, hrebet- 21 Qc 65.00N 145.00 E
Chesterfield Inlet 39 Jc 63.21N 90.42W
Chertsey 12 Bc 51.23N 0.30W
Cherwell 9 Lj 51.44N 1.15W
Chesapeake 44 Ig 36.45N 76.15W
Chesapeake Bay 38 Lf 38.40N 76.25W
Chesapeake Bay Bridge-Tunnel 44 Ig 37.00N 76.02W
Chesha Bay (EN) = Češskaja Guba 5 Kb 67.20N 46.30 E
Chesham 12 Bc 51.42N 0.36W
Cheshire [3] 9 Kh 53.15N 2.30W
Cheshire Plain 9 Kh 53.20N 2.40W
Cheshunt 12 Bc 51.42N 0.02W
Chester 9 Kh 53.10N 2.55W
Chester [Eng.-U.K.] 9 Kh 53.12N 2.54W
Chester [Il.-U.S.] 45 Lh 37.55N 89.49W
Chester [Mt.-U.S.] 46 Jb 48.31N 110.58W
Chester [Pa.-U.S.] 44 Jf 39.50N 75.23W
Chester [S.C.-U.S.] 44 Gh 34.40N 81.12W
Chesterfield 9 Lh 53.15N 1.25W
Chesterfield, Ile- 37 Gc 16.20S 43.58 E
Chesterfield, Récifs et Iles- = Chesterfield Reefs and Islands (EN) 57 Gf 20.00S 159.00 E
Chesterfield Inlet 38 Jc 63.25N 90.45W
Chesterfield Reefs and Islands (EN) = Chesterfield, Récifs et Iles- 57 Gf 20.00S 159.00 E
Chesterton Range 59 Je 25.30S 147.30 E
Chestnut Ridge 44 He 40.10N 79.25W
Chesuncook Lake 44 Mb 46.00N 69.20W
Chetaibi 32 Ib 37.04N 7.23 E
Chetumal 39 Kh 18.35N 88.07W
Chetumal, Bahía de 47 Ge 18.20N 88.05W
Cheviot 62 Ee 42.49S 173.16 E
Chew Bahir = Stefanie, Lake- (EN) 30 Kh 4.38N 36.50 E
Chewelah 46 Gb 48.17N 117.43W
Cheyenne [Ok.-U.S.] 45 Gi 35.37N 99.40W

Index Symbols

[1] Independent Nation
[2] State, Region
[3] District, County
[4] Municipality
[5] Colony, Dependency
Continent
Physical Region
Historical or Cultural Region
Mount, Mountain
Volcano
Hill
Mountains, Mountain Range
Hills, Escarpment
Plateau, Upland
Pass, Gap
Plain, Lowland
Delta
Salt Flat
Valley, Canyon
Crater, Cave
Karst Features
Depression
Polder
Desert, Dunes
Forest, Woods
Heath, Steppe
Oasis
Cape, Point
Coast, Beach
Cliff
Peninsula
Isthmus
Sandbank
Island
Atoll
Rock, Reef
Islands, Archipelago
Rocks, Reefs
Coral Reef
Well, Spring
Geyser
River, Stream
Waterfall Rapids
River Mouth, Estuary
Lake
Salt Lake
Intermittent Lake
Reservoir
Swamp, Pond
Canal
Glacier
Ice Shelf, Pack Ice
Ocean
Sea
Gulf, Bay
Strait, Fjord
Lagoon
Bank
Seamount
Tablemount
Ridge
Shelf
Basin
Escarpment, Sea Scarp
Fracture
Trench, Abyss
National Park, Reserve
Point of Interest
Recreation Site
Cave, Cavern
Historic Site
Ruins
Wall, Walls
Church, Abbey
Temple
Scientific Station
Airport
Port
Lighthouse
Mine
Tunnel
Dam, Bridge

Cheyenne [Wy.-U.S.] 39 Ie 41.08N 104.49W
Cheyenne River 43 Gc 44.40N 101.15W
Cheyenne Wells 45 Eg 38.51N 102.11W
Cheyne Bay 59 Df 34.35S 118.50 E
Chhatarpur 25 Fd 24.54N 79.36 E
Chhindwāra 25 Fd 22.04N 78.56 E
Chi 25 Ke 15.11N 104.43 E
Chiamboni, Rās- 35 Gf 1.38S 41.36 E
Chiana, Val di- 14 Fg 43.15N 11.50 E
Chianciano Terme 14 Fg 43.02N 11.49 E
Chiang-hsi Sheng → Jangxi Sheng=Kiangsi (EN) [2] 27 Kf 28.00N 116.00 E
Chiang Mai 22 Lh 18.46N 98.58 E
Chiang Rai 22 Lh 19.54N 99.50 E
Chiang-su Sheng → Jiangsu Sheng=Kiangsu (EN) [2] 27 Ke 33.00N 120.00 E
Chiani 14 Gh 42.44N 12.07 E
Chianje 31 Ij 15.45S 13.54 E
Chianti 14 Fg 43.30N 11.25 E
Chiapa, Río- 48 Mj 16.30N 93.10W
Chiapas [2] 47 Fe 16.30N 92.30W
Chiapas, Meseta de- 47 Fe 16.30N 92.00W
Chiaramonte Gulfi 14 Im 37.02N 14.42 E
Chiaravalle 14 Hg 43.36N 13.19 E
Chiaromònte 14 Kj 40.07N 16.13 E
Chiautla de Tapia 48 Jh 18.17N 98.36W
Chiavari 14 Df 44.19N 9.19 E
Chiavenna 14 Dd 46.19N 9.24 E
Chiayi 27 Lg 23.29N 120.27 E
Chiba 27 Pd 35.36N 140.07 E
Chiba Ken [2] 28 Pg 35.40N 140.20 E
Chibemba 36 Bf 15.45S 14.06 E
Chibia 36 Bf 15.11S 13.41 E
Chibougamau 39 Le 49.53N 74.21W
Chibougamau, Lac- 44 Ja 49.50N 74.15W
Chibougamau, Rivière- 44 Ja 49.50N 74.25W
Chiburi-Jima 28 Lf 36.00N 133.02 E
Chibuto 37 Ed 24.42S 33.33 E
Chicago 39 Ke 41.53N 87.38W
Chicago Heights 45 Mf 41.30N 87.38W
Chicala 36 Ce 11.59S 19.30 E
Chicapa 30 Ji 6.25S 20.48 E
Chic-Chocs, Monts- 44 Na 48.55N 66.45W
Chicha 35 Bb 16.52N 18.33 E
Chichagof 40 Le 57.30N 135.30W
Chichancanab, Laguna de- 48 Oh 19.54N 88.46W
Chichaoua 32 Fc 31.32N 8.46W
Chichas, Cordillera de- 54 Eh 20.30S 66.30W
Chicheng 27 Kc 40.55N 115.47 E
Chichén Itzá 39 Kg 20.40N 88.35W
Chichester 9 Mk 50.50N 0.48W
Chichester Range 59 Dd 22.20S 119.20 E
Chichibu 28 Og 35.59N 139.05 E
Chichigalpa 49 Dg 12.34N 87.02W
Chichijma-Rettō 60 Cb 27.06N 142.12 E
Chichilla de Monte-Aragón 13 Kf 38.55N 1.43W
Chichiriviche 49 Mh 10.56N 68.16W
Chickasawhay River 45 Lk 31.00N 88.45W
Chickasha 43 Hd 35.02N 97.58W
Chicken 40 Kd 64.04N 141.56W
Chiclana de la Frontera 13 Fh 36.25N 6.08W
Chiclayo 53 If 6.46S 79.50W
Chico 43 Cd 39.44N 121.50W
Chico, Río- [Arg.] 52 Jj 43.48S 66.25W
Chico, Río- [Arg.] 52 Jj 49.56S 68.32W
Chicoana 56 Gc 25.06S 65.33W
Chicomo 37 Ed 24.31S 34.17 E
Chicoñono 37 Fb 12.57S 35.45 E
Chicopee 44 Kd 42.10N 72.36W
Chicote 36 Df 16.01S 21.48 E
Chicoutimi 39 Le 48.26N 71.04W
Chicoutimi Nord 44 La 48.29N 71.02W
Chicualacuala 37 Ed 22.05S 31.42 E
Chidenguele 37 Ed 24.55S 34.10 E
Chidley, Cape- 38 Mc 60.25N 64.30W
Chiemsee 10 Ii 47.54N 12.29 E
Chiengi 36 Ed 8.39S 29.10 E
Chienti 14 Hg 43.18N 13.45 E
Chieri 14 Be 45.01N 7.49 E
Chiers 12 He 49.39N 5.00 E
Chiese 14 Ee 45.08N 10.25 E
Chieti 14 Ih 42.21N 14.10 E
Chièvres 12 Fd 50.35N 3.48 E
Chifeng/Ulanhad 27 Kc 42.16N 118.57 E
Chifumage 36 De 12.10S 22.30 E
Chifwefwe 36 Fe 13.35S 29.35 E
Chigasaki 29 Fd 35.19N 139.24 E
Chignik 40 He 56.18N 158.23W
Chigombe 37 Ed 23.26S 33.19 E
Chigorodó 49 Ij 7.41N 76.41W
Chigubo 37 Ed 22.50S 33.31 E
Chigu Co 27 Ff 28.40N 91.50 E
Chi He 28 Dh 32.51N 117.59 E
Chihli, Gulf of- (EN)=Bo Hai 21 Nf 38.30N 120.00 E
Chihuahua [2] 47 Cc 28.30N 106.00W
Chihuahua 39 Ig 28.38N 106.05W
Chii-san 28 Ig 35.20N 127.44 E
Chikaskia River 45 Hh 36.37N 97.15W
Chikugo 29 Be 33.13N 130.30 E
Chikugo-Gawa 29 Be 33.10N 130.21 E
Chikuma-Gawa 29 Fc 37.00N 138.35 E
Chikwana 36 Ff 16.03S 34.48 E
Chilapa de Alvarez 48 Ji 17.36N 99.10W
Chilās 25 Ea 35.26N 74.05 E
Chilaw 25 Fg 7.34N 79.47 E
Chilcotin 42 Ff 51.46N 122.22W
Childers 59 Ke 25.14S 152.17 E
Childress 43 Ge 34.25N 100.13W
Chile [1] 53 Ii 30.00S 71.00W
Chile Basin (EN) 3 Mm 33.00S 90.00W
Chile Chico 56 Fg 46.33S 71.44W
Chilecito [Arg.] 56 Gd 33.53S 69.03W
Chilecito [Arg.] 56 Gc 29.10S 67.30W
Chile Rise (EN) 3 Mm 40.00S 90.00W
Chili 35 Cb 16.44N 20.53 E
Chilia, Bratul- 15 Md 45.13N 29.43 E
Chililabombwe 36 Ee 12.22S 27.50 E
Chi-lin Sheng → Jilin Sheng =Kirin (EN) [2] 27 Mc 43.00N 126.00 E
Chilko Lake 46 Ca 51.20N 124.05W
Chilko River 46 Da 52.00N 123.40W
Chillán 53 Ii 36.36S 72.07W
Chillar 56 Ie 37.18S 59.59W
Chillicothe [Il.-U.S.] 45 Lf 40.55N 89.29W
Chillicothe [Mo.-U.S.] 45 Jg 39.48N 93.33W
Chillicothe [Oh.-U.S.] 43 Kd 38.20N 82.59W
Chilliwack 46 Eb 49.10N 121.57W
Chiloé, Isla de- 52 Ij 42.30S 73.55W
Chilón 48 Mi 17.14N 92.25W
Chiloquin 46 Ee 42.35N 121.52W
Chilpancingo de los Bravos 47 Ee 17.33N 99.30W
Chiltern Hills 9 Mj 51.42N 0.48W
Chilton 45 Ld 44.02N 88.10W
Chiluage 36 Dd 9.31S 21.46 E
Chilumba 36 Fe 10.27S 34.16 E
Chilwa, Lake- 36 Fc 15.12S 35.50 E
Chimala 36 Fd 8.51S 34.01 E
Chimaltenango 49 Bf 14.39N 90.49W
Chimaltenango [3] 49 Bf 14.40N 90.55W
Chimán 49 Hi 8.42N 78.37W
Chimanas, Islas- 50 Dg 10.17N 64.38W
Chimay 12 Gd 50.03N 4.19 E
Chimborazo, Volcán- 52 If 1.28S 78.48W
Chimbote 53 If 9.05S 78.36W
Chimichagua 49 Ki 9.16N 73.49W
Chimoio 37 Ec 19.00S 33.23 E
Chimorra 13 Hf 38.18N 4.53W
Chin [2] 25 Id 22.00N 93.30 E
China [Jap.] 29b Bb 27.20N 128.36 E
China [Mex.] 48 Je 25.42N 99.14W
China (EN)=Zhonghua Renmin Gongheguo [1] 22 Mf 35.00N 105.00 E
Chinacates 48 Ge 25.00N 105.13W
China Lake 46 Gi 35.46N 117.39W
Chinandega 47 Gf 12.37N 87.09W
Chinandega [3] 49 Dg 12.45N 87.05W
Chinati Peak 45 Dl 29.57N 104.29W
Chincha Alta 54 Cf 13.27S 76.08W
Chinchaga 42 Fe 58.52N 118.19W
Chinchilla 59 Ke 26.45S 150.38 E
Chinchón 13 Id 40.08N 3.25W
Chinchorro, Banco- 47 Ge 18.35N 87.20W
Chincoteague 44 Jg 37.55N 75.23W
Chinde 31 Kj 18.34S 36.27 E
Chin-Do 28 Ig 34.25N 126.15 E
Chindu 27 Ge 33.30N 96.31 E
Chindwinn 21 Lg 21.26N 95.15 E
Ch'ing-hai Sheng → Qinghai Sheng=Tsinghai (EN) [2] 27 Gd 36.00N 96.00 E
Chingil 35 Bc 10.33N 18.57 E
Chingola 31 Jj 12.32S 27.52 E
Chinguar 36 Ce 12.33S 16.22 E
Chinguetti 32 Ee 20.27N 12.21W
Chinguetti, Dahr de- 32 Ee 20.43N 12.20W
Chinhae 28 Jg 35.08N 128.40 E
Chiniot 25 Eb 31.43N 72.59 E
Chínipas 48 Ed 27.23N 108.32W
Chinju 27 Md 35.11N 128.05 E
Chinko 30 Jh 4.50N 23.53 E
Chinle 46 Kh 36.09N 109.33W
Chinle Creek 46 Kh 37.12N 109.43W
Chinmen 27 Kg 24.25N 118.25 E
Chino 29 Fd 36.00N 138.09 E
Chinon 11 Gg 47.10N 0.15 E
Chinook 46 Kb 48.35N 109.14W
Chinquila 48 Pg 21.30N 87.25W
Chinsali 36 Fe 10.33S 32.04 E
Chinteche 36 Fe 11.50S 34.10 E
Chinú 54 Cb 9.06N 75.24W
Chinvali 19 Eg 42.13N 43.57 E
Chiny 12 He 49.44N 5.20 E
Chinyŏng 28 Jg 35.18N 128.44 E
Chioco 37 Ec 16.25S 32.50 E
Chioggia 14 Ge 45.13N 12.17 E
Chios (EN)=Khíos 5 Ih 38.22N 26.00 E
Chipata 31 Kj 13.39S 32.40 E
Chipepo 36 Ef 16.49S 27.50 E
Chipindo 36 Ce 13.48S 15.48 E
Chiping 28 Df 36.35N 116.16 E
Chipinge 37 Ed 20.12S 32.38 E
Chipman 44 Ob 46.11N 65.53W
Chippenham 9 Kj 51.28N 2.07W
Chippewa, Lake- 45 Kd 45.56N 91.13W
Chippewa Falls 43 Ic 44.56N 91.24W
Chippewa River [Wi.-U.S.] 45 Id 44.56N 95.44W
Chippewa River [U.S.] 45 Jd 44.25N 92.10W
Chipping Ongar 12 Cc 51.42N 0.15 E
Chiputneticook Lakes 44 Mc 45.45N 68.45W
Chiquián 54 Cf 10.09S 77.11W
Chiquimula [3] 49 Cf 14.40N 89.25W
Chiquimula 49 Cf 14.48N 89.33W
Chiquimulilla 49 Bf 14.05N 90.23W
Chiquinquirá 54 Db 5.37N 73.50W
Chiquitos, Llanos de- 54 Fg 18.00S 61.30W
Chīrāla 25 Ge 15.49N 80.21 E
Chiran 29 Bf 31.22N 130.27 E
Chiredzi 31 Kk 21.03S 31.45 E
Chirfa 34 Ha 20.57N 12.21 E
Chirgua, Río- 50 Bh 8.30N 68.01W
Chiricahua Peak 43 Fe 31.52N 109.20W
Chiriguaná 49 Ki 9.22N 73.37W
Chirikof 40 He 55.50N 155.35W
Chiriquí [3] 49 Fi 8.30N 82.00W
Chiriquí, Golfo de- 38 Ki 8.00N 82.20W
Chiriquí, Laguna de- 47 Hg 9.03N 82.00W
Chiriquí Grande 49 Fi 8.57N 82.07W
Chirnogi 15 Je 44.07N 26.84 E
Chiromo 36 Gf 16.33S 35.08 E
Chirripó, Cerro- 38 Ki 9.29N 83.29W
Chirripó, Río- [C.R.] 49 Fh 10.03N 83.16W
Chirripó, Río- [C.R.] 49 Fh 10.41N 83.41W
Chirundu 37 Dc 15.59S 28.54 E
Chisamba 36 Ee 14.59S 28.23 E
Chisāpāni Garhi 25 Hc 27.34N 85.08 E
Chisenga 36 Fd 9.56S 33.26 E
Chisasibi 39 Ld 53.50N 79.00W
Chishui 27 If 28.30N 105.44 E
Chişineu Criş 15 Ec 46.32N 21.31 E
Chisone 14 Bf 44.49N 7.25 E
Chitado 36 Bf 17.18S 13.54 E
Chita-Hantō 29 Ed 34.50N 136.50 E
Chitati 35 Ac 14.40N 14.30 E
Chitato 31 Jl 7.22S 20.49 E
Chita-Wan 29 Ed 34.50N 136.55 E
Chitembo 36 Ce 13.31S 16.45 E
Chitina 40 Kd 61.31N 144.27W
Chitipa 36 Fd 9.43S 33.16 E
Chitorgarh 25 Ed 24.53N 74.38 E
Chitose 28 Pc 42.49N 141.39 E
Chitradurga 25 Ff 14.14N 76.24 E
Chitrāl 25 Ea 35.51N 71.47 E
Chitré 47 Hg 7.58N 80.26W
Chittagong 22 Lg 22.20N 91.50 E
Chittoor 25 Ff 13.12N 79.07 E
Chiumbe 30 Ji 6.59S 21.12 E
Chiume 36 Df 15.08S 21.12 E
Chiusi 14 Fg 43.01N 11.57 E
Chiusi, Lago di- 14 Fg 43.05N 12.00 E
Chiva 13 Le 39.28N 0.43W
Chivacoa 50 Bg 10.10N 68.54W
Chivapuri, Río- 50 Ci 6.25N 66.23W
Chivasso 14 Be 45.11N 7.53 E
Chivay 54 Dg 15.38S 71.36W
Chivilcoy 56 Hd 34.53S 60.01W
Chixoy o Negro, Río- 49 Be 16.28N 90.33W
Chizou → Guichi 27 Ke 30.38N 117.30 E
Chizu 29 Dd 35.15N 134.14 E
Chŏâm Khsant 25 Kf 14.13N 104.56 E
Choapa, Río- 56 Fd 31.38S 71.34W
Chobe 30 Jj 17.47S 25.10 E
Choc Bay 51k Ba 14.03N 60.59W
Choch'iwŏn 28 If 36.36N 127.18 E
Chocó [2] 54 Cb 6.00N 77.00W
Chocolate Mountains 46 Hj 33.25N 114.10W
Chodecz 10 Pd 52.24N 19.01 E
Chodov 10 If 50.15N 12.45 E
Chodzież 10 Md 52.59N 16.56 E
Choele-Choel 56 Ge 39.16S 65.41W
Choique 56 He 38.28S 62.43W
Choiseul 51k Ab 13.47N 61.03W
Choiseul Island 57 Ge 7.00S 157.00 E
Choix 48 Ed 26.43N 108.17W
Chojna 10 Kd 52.58N 14.28 E
Chojnice 10 Nc 53.42N 17.34 E
Chojnów 10 Le 51.17N 15.56 E
Chōkai-San 21 Qf 39.10N 140.02 E
Choke 30 Kg 10.45N 37.35 E
Chókué 37 Ed 24.27S 32.55 E
Cho La 27 Ge 31.52N 98.51 E
Cholet 11 Fg 47.04N 0.53W
Chŏlla-Namdo [2] 28 Ig 34.45N 127.00 E
Chŏlla-Pukto [2] 28 Ig 35.45N 127.15 E
Cholo 36 Gf 16.04S 35.08 E
Cholula 48 Jh 19.04N 98.18W
Choluteca 47 Gf 13.18N 87.12W
Choluteca [3] 49 Dg 13.20N 87.10W
Choluteca, Río- 49 Dg 13.07N 87.19W
Choma 31 Jj 16.49S 26.59 E
Chomo/Yadong 27 Ef 27.38N 89.03 E
Chomo Lhari 27 Ef 27.50N 89.16 E
Chomutov 10 Jf 50.28N 13.25 E
Ch'ŏnan 27 Md 36.48N 127.09 E
Chon Buri 25 Kf 13.22N 100.59 E
Chone 54 Bd 0.42S 80.07W
Ch'ŏngch'ŏn-gang 28 He 39.35N 125.28 E
Ch'ŏngjin 22 Oe 41.46N 129.49 E
Ch'ŏngjin Si [2] 28 Jd 41.45N 129.45 E
Chŏngju 27 Md 39.51N 125.15 E
Ch'ŏngju 27 Md 36.38N 127.30 E
Chongli (Xiwanzi) 28 Cd 40.57N 115.12 E
Chongming 28 Fi 31.38N 121.24 E
Chongming Dao 28 Fi 31.36N 121.33 E
Chongoroi 36 Be 13.34S 13.55 E
Chongqing (Yuzhou)= Chungking (EN) 22 Mg 29.34N 106.27 E
Chongqing → Yuzhou= Chungking (EN) 22 Mg 29.34N 106.27 E
Ch'ŏngsan-Do 28 Ig 34.11N 126.54 E
Chŏngŭp 28 Ig 35.34N 126.51 E
Chongyang 28 Cj 29.32N 114.02 E
Chongzuo 27 Ig 12.29N 107.22 E
Chŏnju 27 Md 35.49N 127.09 E
Choni (Culukidze) 16 Mh 42.18N 42.25 E
Chonos, Archipiélago de los- 52 Ij 45.00S 74.00W
Chontaleña, Cordillera- 49 Eh 11.50N 85.00W
Chontales [3] 49 Eg 12.05N 85.10W
Chopim, Rio- 55 Fg 25.35S 53.05W
Chopinzinho 55 Fg 25.51S 52.30W
Chorito, Sierra del- 13 He 39.25N 4.25W
Choroszcz 10 Sc 53.09N 22.59 E
Chorreras, Cerro- 48 Fd 26.02N 106.21W
Ch'ŏrwŏn 27 Md 38.15N 127.13 E
Chorzele 10 Qc 53.16N 20.55 E
Chorzów 10 Of 50.19N 18.57 E
Ch'osan 28 Hd 40.45N 125.50 E
Chośebuz/Cottbus 10 Ke 51.46N 14.20 E
Chōshi 28 Pg 35.44N 140.50 E
Chos Malal 56 Fe 37.23S 70.16W
Chosŏn M.I.K.=North Korea (EN) [1] 22 Oe 40.00N 127.30 E
Chosŏn Minjuju-Inmin-Konghwaguk=Chosŏn M.I.K. [1] 22 Oe 40.00N 127.30 E
Choszczno 10 Lc 53.10N 15.26 E
Chota 54 Ce 6.33S 78.39W
Chotanagpur Plateau 21 Kg 22.00N 86.00 E
Choteau 46 Ic 47.49N 112.11W
Chotla, Cerro de- 48 Ii 17.55N 101.31W
Choukchot, Djebel- 13 Qh 36.01N 4.11 E
Choum 32 Ee 21.18N 12.59W
Chovd → Kobdo 27 Fb 48.06N 92.11 E
Chövsgöl nuur → Hubsugul Nur 21 Md 51.00N 100.30 E
Chowchilla 46 Eh 37.07N 120.16W
Chowra 25 Ig 8.27N 93.02 E
Chréa 13 Oh 36.25N 2.53 E
Chřiby 10 Ng 49.10N 17.20 E
Christchurch 58 Ii 43.32S 172.37 E
Christian, Cape - 42 Kb 70.32N 68.18W
Christian, Point- 64q Ab 25.04S 130.07W
Christiana 37 De 27.52S 25.08 E
Christian IV Gletscher 41 Ie 68.40N 30.20W
Christiansburg 44 Gg 37.07N 80.26W
Christiansfeld 8 Ci 55.21N 9.29 E
Christianshåb/Qasigiánguit 41 Ge 68.45N 51.30W
Christiansø 8 Fi 55.20N 15.10 E
Christian Sound 40 Me 55.56N 134.40W
Christiansted 50 Dd 17.45N 64.40W
Christiansted Harbor 51a Dc 17.46N 64.42W
Christie Bay 42 Gd 62.45N 110.15W
Christmas → Kiritimati Atoll 57 Ld 1.52N 157.20W
Christmas Creek 59 Fc 18.29S 125.23 E
Christmas Creek 59 Fc 18.53S 125.55 E
Christmas Island [5] 22 Mk 10.30S 105.40 E
Christmas Ridge (EN) 3 Ki 10.00N 165.00W
Chrudim 10 Lg 49.57N 15.47 E
Chrzanów 10 Pf 50.09N 19.24 E
Chrząstowa 10 Mc 53.35N 16.58 E
Chuansha 28 Fi 31.11N 121.42 E
Chūbar 24 Mc 38.11N 48.51 E
Chubut [2] 56 Gf 44.00S 69.00W
Chubut, Río- 52 Jj 43.20S 65.03W
Chugach Mountains 40 Jd 61.00N 145.00W
Chudžand (Leninabad) 22 Ie 40.17N 69.37 E
Chudžandskaja oblast 19 Gh 40.00N 69.10 E
Chu He 28 Eh 32.15N 119.03 E
Chuhuichupa 48 Ec 29.38N 108.22W
Chuí 55 Fk 33.41S 53.27W
Chuka 36 Gc 0.20S 37.39 E
Chukai 26 Df 4.15N 103.25 E
Chukchi Peninsula (EN)= Čukotski Poluostrov 21 Uc 66.00N 175.00W
Chukchi Plateau (EN) 67 Bd 78.00N 165.00W
Chukchi Sea 67 Bd 69.00N 171.00W
Chukchi Sea (EN)= Čukotskoje More 67 Bd 69.00N 171.00W
Chula Vista 46 Gj 32.39N 117.05W
Chulitna 40 Jd 62.55N 149.39W
Chullo 13 Jg 37.10N 2.57W
Chulucanas 54 Be 5.06S 80.10W
Chumbicha 56 Gc 28.52S 66.14W
Chumphon 25 Jf 10.32N 99.13 E
Chumunjin 28 Jf 37.53N 128.49 E
Ch'unch'ŏn 27 Md 37.52N 127.44 E
Chunga 36 Ef 15.03S 26.00 E
Ch'ungch'ŏng-Namdo [2] 28 If 36.30N 127.00 E
Ch'ungch'ŏng-Pukto [2] 28 Jf 36.45N 128.00 E
Ch'ungju 27 Md 36.58N 127.56 E
Chungking (EN)= Chongqing (Yuzhou) 22 Mg 29.34N 106.27 E
Chungking (EN)= Yuzhou → Chongqing 22 Mg 29.34N 106.27 E
Ch'ungmu 28 Jg 34.51N 128.26 E
Chunya 36 Fd 8.32S 33.25 E
Chuquibamba 54 Dg 15.50S 72.39W
Chuquibambilla 54 Df 14.07S 72.43W
Chuquicamata 56 Gb 22.19S 68.56W
Chuquisaca [2] 54 Fg 20.00S 64.20W
Chur/Cuera 14 Dd 46.50N 9.35 E
Churchill 39 Jd 58.46N 94.10W
Churchill [Can.] 38 Md 53.30N 60.10W
Churchill [Can.] 38 Jd 58.47N 94.12W
Churchill, Cape - 42 Ie 58.46N 93.12W
Churchill Falls 42 Lf 53.30N 64.10W
Churchill Lake 42 Ge 56.05N 108.15W
Churchill Peak 42 Ee 58.20N 125.02W
Churchill Range 66 Jg 81.30S 158.30 E
Chūru 25 Ec 28.18N 74.57 E
Churuguara 54 Ea 10.49N 69.32W
Churún Merú=Angel Falls (EN) 52 Je 5.57N 62.30W
Chuska Mountains 46 Kh 36.15N 108.50W
Chute-des Passes 42 Kg 49.50N 71.00W
Chuxian 27 Ke 32.16N 118.15 E
Chuxiong 27 Hf 25.02N 101.32 E
Chuy 55 Fk 33.41S 53.27W
Chyncĕšt'(Kotovsk) 16 Ff 46.49N 28.33 E
Ciamis 26 Eh 7.20S 108.21 E
Cianjur 26 Eh 6.49S 107.08 E
Ciarrai/Kerry [2] 9 Di 52.10N 9.30W
Čiatura 16 Mh 42.17N 43.15 E
Cibuta, Cerro- 48 Db 31.02N 110.58W
Ćićarija 14 He 45.28N 13.54 E
Ćićevac 15 Ef 43.43N 21.27 E
Cicicleja 15 Nb 47.23N 30.50 E
Cicolano 14 Hh 42.15N 13.10 E
Cidacos 13 Kb 42.19N 1.55W
Cide 24 Eb 41.54N 33.00 E
Cidlina 10 Lf 50.09N 15.12 E
Ciechanów 10 Qd 52.53N 20.38 E
Ciechanów [2] 10 Qd 52.55N 20.40 E
Ciechanowiec 10 Sd 52.42N 22.31 E
Ciechanowska, Wysoczyzna- 10 Qc 53.10N 20.30 E
Ciego de Ávila 47 Id 21.51N 78.46W
Ciego de Ávila [3] 49 Hb 22.00N 78.40W
Ciénaga 54 Da 11.00N 74.14W
Ciénaga de Flores 48 Ie 25.57N 100.11W
Ciénaga de Oro 49 Ji 8.53N 75.38W
Cieneguita 48 Fd 27.57N 106.59W
Cienfuegos [3] 49 Gb 22.15N 80.30W
Cienfuegos 39 Kg 22.09N 80.27W
Cíes, Islas de- 13 Db 42.13N 8.54W
Cieszanów 10 Tf 50.16N 23.08 E
Cieza 13 Kf 38.14N 1.25W
Çifteler 24 Dc 39.22N 31.03 E
Cifuentes 13 Jd 40.47N 2.37W
Čiganak 19 Hf 45.05N 73.58 E
Čigirin 16 He 49.03N 32.42 E
Cigüela 13 Ie 39.08N 3.44W
Cihanbeyli 24 Ec 38.40N 32.56 E
Cihanbeyli Platosu 24 Ec 38.40N 32.45 E
Čihareši 16 Mh 42.47N 43.02 E
Cihuatlán 48 Gh 19.14N 104.35W
Čiily 19 Gg 44.13N 66.46 E
Cijara, Embalse de- 13 He 39.18N 4.52W
Cijulang 26 Eh 7.44S 108.27 E
Čik 15 Dd 45.42N 20.04 E
Čikoj 20 Ff 51.02N 106.39 E
Cikurački, Vulkan- 20 Kf 50.15N 155.29 E
Cilacap 26 Eh 7.44S 109.00 E
Çıldır 24 Jb 41.08N 43.07 E
Çıldır Gölü 24 Jb 41.04N 43.15 E
Cilento 14 Jj 40.20N 15.20 E
Čilik 18 Lc 43.42N 78.14 E
Čilik 19 Hg 43.35N 78.12 E
Cill Airne/Killarney 9 Di 52.03N 9.30W
Cill Chainnigh/Kilkenny 9 Fi 52.39N 7.15W
Cill Chainnigh/Kilkenny [2] 9 Fi 52.40N 7.20W
Cill Chaoi/Kilkee 9 Di 52.41N 9.38W
Cill Dara/Kildare [2] 9 Gh 53.15N 6.45W
Cill Dara/Kildare 9 Gh 53.10N 6.55W
Cill Mhantáin/Wicklow 9 Gi 52.59N 6.03W
Cill Mhantain/Wicklow [2] 9 Gi 53.00N 6.30W
Cill Mocheallóg/Kilmallock 9 Ei 52.25N 8.35W
Cill Rois/Kilrush 9 Di 52.39N 9.29W
Cilma 17 Fd 65.25N 52.05 E
Cilo Dağı 24 Kd 37.30N 44.00 E
Cimaltepec, Sierra- 47 Ee 16.00N 96.40W
Cimarron 38 Jf 36.10N 96.17W
Cimarron 45 Dh 36.31N 104.55W
Čimbaj 19 Fg 42.59N 59.47 E
Cimini, Monti- 14 Gh 42.24N 12.12 E
Čimišlija 16 Ff 46.32N 28.46 E
Čimkent 22 Ie 42.18N 69.36 E
Čimkentskaja Oblast [3] 19 Gg 43.00N 68.40 E
Cimljansk 19 Ef 47.37N 42.04 E
Cimljanskoje Vodohranilišče =Tsimlyansk Reservoir (EN) 5 Kf 48.00N 43.00 E
Cimone 5 Hg 44.12N 10.40 E
Cîmpeni 15 Gc 46.22N 23.03 E
Cîmpia Turzii 15 Gc 46.33N 23.53 E
Cîmpina 15 Id 45.08N 25.44 E
Cîmpulung 15 Id 45.16N 25.03 E
Cîmpulung Moldovenesc 15 Ib 47.32N 25.34 E
Čimtarga, Gora- 18 Ge 39.14N 68.12 E
Cina, Tanjung- 26 Dh 5.55S 104.35 E
Çinar 24 Id 37.39N 40.06 E
Cinarcik 15 Mi 40.39N 29.06 E
Cinaruco, Río- 50 Ci 6.41N 67.07W
Cina Selatan, Laut-=South China Sea (EN) 21 Ni 10.00N 113.00 E
Cinaz 18 Gd 40.56N 68.45 E
Cinca 13 Mc 41.26N 0.21 E
Cincar 14 Lg 43.54N 17.04 E
Cincinnati 39 Kf 39.06N 84.31W
Cinco Irmãos, Serra dos- 55 Ff 22.55S 52.50W
Cinco Saltos 56 Ge 38.49S 68.04W
Cindrelu, Vîrful- 15 Gd 45.35N 23.48 E
Çine 24 Cd 37.36N 28.04 E
Çine 15 Kl 37.46N 27.49 E
Ciney 11 Ld 50.18N 5.06 E
Čingirlau 19 Fe 51.07N 54.05 E
Cingoli 14 Hg 43.22N 13.13 E
Cintalapa de Figueroa 48 Mi 16.44N 93.43W
Cinto, Monte- 5 Gg 42.23N 8.56 E
Cintra, Golfo de- 32 De 23.00N 16.15W
Cinzas, Rio das- 55 Gf 22.56S 50.32W
Ciociaria 14 Hi 41.45N 13.15 E
Cionn Mhálanna/Malin Head 5 Fd 55.23N 7.24W
Cionn tSáile/Kinsale 9 Ej 51.42N 8.32W
Ciorani 15 Je 44.49N 26.25 E
Čiovo 14 Kg 43.30N 16.18 E
Cipa 20 Ge 55.20N 115.55 E
Cipikan 20 Gf 54.58N 113.21 E
Cipó 54 Kf 11.06S 38.31W
Cipolletti 56 Ge 38.56S 67.59W
Čiprovci 15 Ff 43.23N 22.53 E
Čir 16 Me 48.35N 42.55 E
Circeo, Capo- 14 Hi 41.14N 13.03 E
Čirčik 19 Gg 41.28N 69.35 E
Circle [Ak.-U.S.] 40 Kc 65.50N 144.04W
Circle [Mt.-U.S.] 46 Mc 47.25N 105.35W
Circleville 44 Ff 39.36N 82.57W
Cirebon 22 Mj 6.44S 108.34 E
Cirencester 9 Lj 51.44N 1.59W
Ciriè 14 Be 45.14N 7.36 E
Čirinda 20 Fc 67.30N 100.35 E
Čirip, Vulkan- 20 Jg 45.20N 147.58 E
Čirka-Kem 7 Hd 64.45N 32.10 E
Cirò 14 Lk 39.23N 17.04 E
Cirò Marina 14 Lk 39.22N 17.08 E
Ciron 11 Fj 44.36N 0.18W
Čirpan 15 Ig 42.12N 25.20 E
Cirque Mountain 42 Le 58.55N 63.33W
Cisa, Passo della- 14 Df 44.28N 9.55 E
Ciscaucasia (EN) 5 Kf 45.00N 43.00 E
Cisco 45 Gj 32.23N 98.59W
Ciskei 37 Df 31.30S 26.40 E
Čišmy 19 Fe 54.35N 55.25 E
Cisnădie 15 Hd 45.43N 24.09 E
Cisne, Islas del- 47 He 17.22N 83.51W
Cistern Point 49 Ib 24.40N 77.45W
Cistierna 13 Gb 42.48N 5.07W
Čistoozernoje 20 Cf 54.43N 76.43 E
Čistopol 19 Fd 55.23N 50.39 E
Čita 22 Nd 52.03N 113.30 E
Çitak 15 Mk 38.08N 29.39 E

Index Symbols

[1] Independent Nation
[2] State, Region
[3] District, County
[4] Municipality
[5] Colony, Dependency
Continent
Physical Region
Historical or Cultural Region
Mount, Mountain
Volcano
Hill
Mountains, Mountain Range
Hills, Escarpment
Plateau, Upland
Pass, Gap
Plain, Lowland
Delta
Salt Flat
Valley, Canyon
Crater, Cave
Karst Features
Depression
Polder
Desert, Dunes
Forest, Woods
Heath, Steppe
Oasis
Cape, Point
Coast, Beach
Cliff
Peninsula
Isthmus
Sandbank
Island
Atoll
Rock, Reef
Islands, Archipelago
Rocks, Reefs
Coral Reef
Well, Spring
Geyser
River, Stream
Waterfall Rapids
River Mouth, Estuary
Lake
Salt Lake
Intermittent Lake
Reservoir
Swamp, Pond
Canal
Glacier
Ice Shelf, Pack Ice
Ocean
Sea
Gulf, Bay
Strait, Fjord
Lagoon
Bank
Seamount
Tablemount
Ridge
Shelf
Basin
Escarpment, Sea Scarp
Fracture
Trench, Abyss
National Park, Reserve
Point of Interest
Recreation Site
Cave, Cavern
Historic Site
Ruins
Wall, Walls
Church, Abbey
Temple
Scientific Station
Airport
Port
Lighthouse
Mine
Tunnel
Dam, Bridge

Index Symbols

Symbol	Meaning		Symbol	Meaning
[1]	Independent Nation		Historical or Cultural Region	
[2]	State, Region		Mount, Mountain	
[3]	District, County		Volcano	
[4]	Municipality		Hill	
[5]	Colony, Dependency		Mountains, Mountain Range	
■	Continent		Hills, Escarpment	
⬚	Physical Region		Plateau, Upland	

Pass, Gap	Depression	Coast, Beach	Rock, Reef	Waterfall, Rapids	Canal	Lagoon	Escarpment, Sea Scarp	Historic Site	Port
Plain, Lowland	Polder	Cliff	Islands, Archipelago	River Mouth, Estuary	Bank	Glacier	Fracture	Ruins	Lighthouse
Delta	Desert, Dunes	Peninsula	Rocks, Reefs	Lake	Ice Shelf, Pack Ice	Seamount	Trench, Abyss	Wall, Walls	Mine
Salt Flat	Forest, Woods	Isthmus	Coral Reef	Salt Lake	Tablemount	National Park, Reserve	Church, Abbey	Tunnel
Valley, Canyon	Heath, Steppe	Sandbank	Well, Spring	Ocean	Ridge	Point of Interest	Temple
Crater, Cave	Oasis	Island	Intermittent Lake	Sea	Shelf	Recreation Site	Dam, Bridge
Karst Features	Cape, Point	Atoll	Geyser	Reservoir	Gulf, Bay	Basin	Scientific Station
			River, Stream	Swamp, Pond	Strait, Fjord	Cave, Cavern	Airport

Index Symbols

Crest 11 Lj 44.44N 5.02 E
Crested Butte 45 Cg 38.52N 106.59W
Creston [B.C.-Can.] 46 Gb 49.06N 116.31W
Creston [Ia.-U.S.] 43 Ic 41.04N 94.22W
Crestone Peak 45 Dh 37.58N 105.36W
Crestview 43 Je 30.46N 86.34W
Creswell 44 Ih 35.52N 76.23W
Creswell Bay 42 Ib 72.40N 93.30W
Creswell Creek 59 Hc 18.10S 135.11 E
Crete 45 Hf 40.38N 96.58W
Crete (EN) = Kriti 5 Ih 35.15N 24.45 E
Crete (EN) = Kriti [2] 15 Hn 35.35N 25.00 E
Crete, Sea of- (EN) = Kritikón Pélagos 15 Hn 36.00N 25.00 E
Créteil 11 If 48.47N 2.28 E
Cretin, Cape- 60 Di 6.40S 147.52 E
Creus, Cabo de-/Creus, Cap de- 5 Gg 42.19N 3.19 E
Creus, Cap de-/Creus, Cabo de- 5 Gg 42.19N 3.19 E
Creuse [3] 11 Hh 46.05N 2.00 E
Creuse 11 Gg 47.00N 0.34 E
Creutzwald 11 Me 49.12N 6.41 E
Crevecoeur-en-Auge 12 Ce 49.07N 0.01 E
Crèvecoeur-le-Grand 12 Ee 49.36N 2.05 E
Crevillente 13 Lf 38.15N 0.48W
Crewe 9 Kh 53.05N 2.27W
Crézancy 12 Fe 49.03N 3.30 E
Criciúma 53 Lh 28.40S 49.23W
Cricket Mountains 46 Ig 38.50N 113.00W
Crieff 9 Je 56.23N 3.52W
Criel-sur-Mer 12 Dd 50.01N 1.19 E
Criel sur Mer-Mesnil Val 12 Dd 50.03N 1.20 E
Crikvenica 14 Ie 45.11N 14.42 E
Crillon 12 De 49.31N 1.56 E
Crimea (EN) = Krymski Poluostrov 5 Jf 45.00N 34.00 E
Crimean Mountains (EN) = Krymskije Gory 5 Jg 44.45N 34.30 E
Crimmitschau 10 If 50.49N 12.23 E
Criquetot-l'Esneval 12 Ce 49.39N 0.16 E
Crissolo 14 Bf 44.42N 7.09 E
Cristal, Monts de- 36 Bb 0.30N 10.30 E
Cristal, Sierra del- 49 Jc 20.33N 75.31W
Cristalândia 54 If 10.36S 49.11W
Cristalina 54 Ig 16.45S 47.36W
Cristalino, Rio- 54 Hf 12.40S 50.40W
Cristallo 14 Gd 46.34N 12.12 E
Cristóbal Colón, Pico 52 Id 10.50N 73.45W
Cristuru Secuiesc 15 Ic 46.35N 25.47 E
Crişu Alb 15 Ec 46.42N 21.16 E
Crişu Negru 15 Ec 46.42N 21.16 E
Crişu Repede 15 Dc 46.55N 20.59 E
Crixás 55 Hb 14.27S 49.58W
Crixás-Açu, Rio- 54 Hf 13.19S 50.36W
Crixás Mirim, Rio- 55 Ga 13.28S 50.36W
Crkvena Planina 15 Fg 42.48N 22.22 E
Crna Gora 15 Eg 42.16N 21.35 E
Crna Gora 15 Ce 44.05N 19.50 E
Crna Gora = Montenegro (EN) [2] 15 Cg 42.30N 19.18 E
Crna Gora = Montenegro (EN) 15 Cg 42.30N 19.18 E
Crna Reka 15 Ef 43.50N 21.55 E
Crna reka 15 Eh 41.33N 21.59 E
Crni Drim 15 Dg 42.05N 20.23 E
Crni Timok 15 Ff 43.55N 22.18 E
Črni Vrh 14 Jd 46.29N 15.14 E
Crni vrh 14 Kf 44.36N 16.30 E
Črnomelj 14 Je 45.34N 15.12 E
Croatia (EN) = Hrvatska 14 Jf 45.00N 15.30 E
Croatia (EN) = Hrvatska 5 Hf 45.00N 15.30 E
Croatia (EN) = Hrvatska 14 Je 45.00N 15.30 E
Crocker, Banjaran- 26 Ge 5.40N 116.20 E
Crockett 45 Ik 31.19N 95.28W
Crocq 11 Ii 45.52N 2.22 E
Crocus Bay 51b Ab 18.13N 63.05W
Croisette, Cap- 11 Lk 43.13N 5.20 E
Croisic, Pointe du- 11 Dg 47.17N 2.33W
Croisilles 12 Ed 50.12N 2.53 E
Croissy-sur-Celle 12 Ee 49.42N 2.11 E
Croix, Lac la- 45 Jb 48.21N 92.05W
Croix-Haute, Col de la- 11 Lj 44.43N 5.40 E
Croker, Cape- 59 Gb 10.58S 132.35 E
Croker Bay 42 Jb 74.38N 83.15W
Croker Island 59 Gb 11.10S 132.30 E
Cromarty 9 Id 57.40N 4.02W
Cromer 9 Oi 52.56N 1.18 E
Cromwell 62 Cf 45.03S 169.14 E
Crooked Island 47 Jd 22.45N 74.13W
Crooked Island Passage 47 Jd 22.55N 74.35W
Crooked River 46 Ed 44.34N 121.16W
Crookston 43 Hb 47.47N 96.37W
Crosby [Mn.-U.S.] 45 Jc 46.28N 93.57W
Crosby [N.D.-U.S.] 45 Eb 48.55N 103.18W
Cross 34 Ge 4.55N 8.15 E
Cross City 44 Fk 29.32N 83.07W
Crossett 45 Kj 33.08N 91.58W
Cross Fell 9 Kg 54.42N 2.29W
Cross Lake 42 Hf 54.47N 97.22W
Crossman Peak 46 Hi 34.32N 114.07W
Cross River [2] 34 Gd 5.40N 8.10 E
Cross Sound 40 Le 58.10N 136.30W
Crotone 14 Lk 39.05N 17.08 E
Crotto 55 Bm 36.35S 60.10W
Crouch 12 Cc 51.37N 0.53 E
Crow Agency 46 Ld 45.36N 107.27W
Crowborough 12 Cc 51.03N 0.09 E
Crow Creek 45 Df 40.23N 104.29W
Crowell 45 Gj 33.59N 99.43W
Crow Lake 45 Jb 49.12N 93.57W
Crowley 45 Jk 30.13N 92.22W
Crowley, Lake- 46 Fh 37.37N 118.44W
Crowley Ridge 45 Ki 35.45N 90.45W
Crownpoint 45 Bi 35.42N 108.07W
Crown Prince Frederik 42 Ic 70.05N 86.40W
Crowsnest Pass 42 Gg 49.00N 114.30W
Crows Nest Peak 45 Ed 44.03N 103.58W
Croydon 59 Ic 18.12S 142.14 E
Croydon, London- 9 Mj 51.23N 0.07W
Crozet, Iles- 30 Mm 46.30S 51.00 E
Crozet Basin (EN) 3 Gm 39.00S 60.00 E
Crozet Ridge (EN) 3 Fn 45.00S 45.00 E
Crozon 11 Bf 48.15N 4.29W
Crozon, Presqu'île de- 11 Bf 48.15N 4.25W
Crucero, Cerro- 48 Gg 21.41N 104.25W
Cruces 49 Gb 22.21N 80.16W
Crump Lake 46 Fe 42.17N 119.50W
Crumpton Point 51g Ba 15.35N 61.19W
Cruz, Cabo- 47 Ie 19.51N 77.44W
Cruz Alta [Arg.] 55 Bk 33.01S 61.49W
Cruz Alta [Braz.] 53 Kh 28.39S 53.36W
Cruz del Eje 56 Hd 30.44S 64.48W
Cruzeiro do Oeste 56 Jb 23.46S 53.04W
Cruzeiro do Sul 53 If 7.38S 72.36W
Cruzen Island 66 Mf 74.47S 140.42W
Cruz Grande 48 Ji 16.44N 99.08W
Crvanj 14 Mg 43.25N 18.11 E
Crvenka 15 Cd 45.39N 19.28 E
Crystal Brook 59 Hf 33.21S 138.13 E
Crystal City [Man.-Can.] 45 Gb 49.08N 98.57W
Crystal City [Tx.-U.S.] 45 Gl 28.41N 99.50W
Crystal Falls 44 Cb 46.06N 88.20W
Crystal Springs 45 Kk 31.59N 90.21W
Csákvár 10 Oi 47.24N 18.27 E
Cserhat 10 Pi 47.55N 19.30 E
Csongrád [2] 10 Qj 46.25N 20.15 E
Csongrad 10 Qj 46.42N 20.09 E
Csorna 10 Ni 47.37N 17.15 E
Csurgó 10 Nj 46.16N 17.06 E
Ctesiphon 24 Kf 33.05N 44.35 E
Ču 21 Ie 45.00N 67.44 E
Ču 22 Je 43.33N 73.45 E
Cuajinicuilapa 48 Ji 16.28N 98.25W
Cuale 36 Cd 7.40S 17.01 E
Cuamba 31 Kj 14.49S 36.33 E
Cuan an Fhóid Duibh/Blacksod Bay 9 Dg 54.08N 10.00W
Cuanavale 36 Cf 15.07S 19.14 E
Cuan Bhaile Átha Cliath/Dublin Bay 9 Gh 53.20N 6.06W
Cuan Chill Ala/Killala Bay 9 Dg 54.15N 9.10W
Cuan Dhun Dealgan/Dundalk Bay 9 Gh 53.57N 6.17W
Cuan Dhùn Droma/Dundrum Bay 9 Hg 54.13N 5.45W
Cuando 30 Jj 18.27S 23.32 E
Cuando-Cubango [3] 36 Df 16.00S 20.30 E
Cuan Eochaille/Youghal Harbour 9 Fj 51.52N 7.50W
Cuangar 36 Cf 17.36S 18.37 E
Cuango 30 Ii 3.14S 17.22 E
Cuango [Ang.] 36 Cd 9.07S 18.05 E
Cuango [Ang.] 36 Cd 6.17S 16.41 E
Cuan Loch Garman/Wexford Harbour 9 Gi 52.20N 6.25W
Cuan Mó/Clew Bay 9 Dh 53.50N 9.50W
Cuan na Gaillimhe/Galway Bay 5 Fe 53.10N 9.15W
Cuan na gCaorach/Sheep Haven 9 Ff 55.10N 7.52W
Cuan Phort Láirge/Waterford Harbour 9 Gi 52.10N 6.57W
Cuan Shligigh/Sligo Bay 9 Eg 54.20N 8.40W
Cuanza 30 Ii 9.19S 13.08 E
Cuanza Norte [3] 36 Bd 8.50S 14.30 E
Cuanza Sul [3] 36 Be 10.50S 14.50 E
Cuareim, Arroyo- 55 Dj 30.12S 57.36W
Cuaró 55 Dj 30.37S 56.54W
Cuaró Grande, Arroyo- 55 Dj 30.18S 57.12W
Cuarto, Rio- 56 Hd 33.25S 63.02W
Cuatir 36 Cf 17.01S 18.09 E
Cuatro Ciénegas de Carranza 48 Hd 26.59N 102.05W
Cuauhtémoc 47 Cc 28.25N 106.52W
Cuautitlán 48 Jh 19.40N 99.11W
Cuay Grande 55 Di 28.40S 56.17W
Cuba 38 Lg 21.30N 80.00W
Cuba [1] 39 Lg 21.30N 80.00W
Cuba [Mo.-U.S.] 45 Kg 38.04N 91.24W
Cuba [N.M.-U.S.] 45 Ch 36.01N 107.04W
Cuba [Port.] 13 Ef 38.10N 7.53W
Cubabi, Cerro- 48 Cb 31.42N 112.46W
Cubagua, Isla- 50 Dg 10.49N 64.11W
Cubal 36 Be 13.03S 14.15 E
Cubal [Ang.] 36 Be 11.29S 13.48 E
Cubal [Ang.] 36 Bf 15.22S 12.39 E
Cubango 30 Jj 18.53N 22.24 E
Çubuk 24 Eb 40.14N 32.05 E
Čubukulah, Gora- 20 Kc 66.23N 153.59 E
Cucalón, Sierra de- 13 Kd 40.59N 1.10W
Cuchi 36 Ce 14.40S 16.52 E
Cuchi 30 Ij 15.28S 17.21 E
Cuchibi 36 De 15.00S 20.45 E
Cuchilla Águila, Cerro- 49 Ig 21.27N 101.03W
Cuchivero, Rio- 50 Di 7.40N 65.57W
Cuchumatanes, Sierra de los- 49 Bf 15.35N 91.25W
Cuckfield 12 Bc 51.01N 0.08W
Cuckmere 12 Cd 50.45N 0.09 E
Cucui 54 Ec 1.12N 66.50W
Cucumbi 36 Ce 10.17S 19.03 E
Cucurpe 48 Db 30.20N 110.43W
Cúcuta 53 Ie 7.54N 72.31W
Cudahy 45 Me 42.57N 87.52W
Cudalbi 15 Kd 45.47N 27.42 E
Cuddalore 22 Jh 11.45N 79.45 E
Cuddapah 25 Ff 14.28N 78.49 E
Čudovo 19 Dd 59.08N 31.41 E
Čudskoje Ozero = Peipus, Lake- (EN) 5 Id 58.45N 27.30 E
Cue 59 De 27.25S 117.54 E
Cuebe 36 Cf 15.48S 17.30 E
Cuelei 36 Cf 15.33S 17.21 E
Cuéllar 13 Hc 41.29N 4.19W
Cuemba 36 Ce 12.09S 18.07 E
Cuenca [3] 13 Ke 40.00N 2.00W
Cuenca [Ec.] 53 If 2.53S 78.59W
Cuenca [Sp.] 13 Jd 40.04N 2.08W
Cuenca, Serrania de- 5 Fg 40.10N 1.55W
Cuencamé de Ceniceros 48 He 24.53N 103.42W
Cuera/Chur 14 Dd 46.50N 9.35 E
Cuerda del Pozo, Embalse de la- 13 Jc 41.51N 2.44W
Cuernavaca 39 Jh 18.55N 99.15W
Cuero 45 Hl 29.06N 97.18W
Cuevas del Almanzora 13 Kg 37.18N 1.53W
Cugir 15 Gd 45.50N 23.22 E
Cugo 36 Cd 7.22S 17.06 E
Čugujev 16 Je 49.50N 36.41 E
Čugujevka 28 Mb 44.08N 133.53 E
Čuhloma 19 Ed 58.47N 42.41 E
Cuiabá 53 Kg 15.35S 56.05W
Cuiabá, Rio- 52 Kg 17.05S 56.36W
Cuiabá Mirim, Rio- 55 Ec 16.20S 55.55W
Cuidado, Punta- 65d Bb 27.08S 109.19W
Cuijk, Cuijk en Sint Agatha- 12 Hc 51.44N 5.52 E
Cuijk en Sint Agatha-Cuijk 12 Hc 51.44N 5.52 E
Cuilapa 49 Bf 14.17N 90.18W
Cuillin Hills 9 Gd 57.14N 6.15W
Cuilo 30 Ii 3.22S 17.22 E
Cúil Raithin/Coleraine 9 Gf 55.08N 6.40W
Cuiluan 27 Mb 47.39N 128.34 E
Cuima 36 Ce 13.14S 15.38 E
Cuito 30 Jj 18.01S 20.48 E
Cuito Cuanavale 31 Ij 15.13S 19.08 E
Cuitzeo, Lago de- 48 Ih 19.55N 101.05W
Cuiuni, Rio- 54 Fd 0.45S 63.07W
Cujmir 15 Fe 44.13N 22.56 E
Čujskaja oblast 19 Hg 42.30N 73.50 E
Čukotski avtonomnyj okrug [3] 20 Mc 66.00N 172.30 E
Čukotski Poluostrov = Chukchi Peninsula (EN) 21 Uc 66.00N 175.00W
Čukotskoje More = Chukchi Sea (EN) 67 Bd 69.00N 171.00W
Çukurca 24 Jd 37.15N 43.37 E
Çukurdaği 15 Ll 37.58N 28.44 E
Čulakkurgan 19 Gg 43.48N 69.12 E
Culan 11 Ih 46.33N 2.21 E
Cu Lao, Hon- 25 Lf 10.30N 109.13 E
Culasi 26 Hd 11.26N 122.03 E
Culbertson 46 Mb 48.09N 104.31W
Culebra, Isla de- 49 Od 18.19N 65.17W
Culebra, Sierra de la- 13 Fc 41.55N 6.20W
Culebra Peak 45 Dh 37.06N 105.10W
Culemborg 12 Hc 51.57N 5.14 E
Culiacán, Rio de- 48 Fe 24.31N 107.41W
Culiacán Rosales 39 Ig 24.48N 107.24W
Culion 26 Gd 11.50N 119.55 E
Culion 26 Hd 11.53N 120.01 E
Culiseu, Rio- 54 Hf 12.14S 53.17W
Cullera 13 Le 39.10N 0.15W
Cullman 43 Je 34.11N 86.51W
Čulman 22 Od 56.52N 124.52 E
Culpeper 44 Hf 38.28N 78.01W
Culuene, Rio- 52 Kg 12.56S 52.51W
Culver, Point- 59 Ef 32.54S 124.43 E
Culverden 62 Ee 42.46S 172.51 E
Čulym 20 De 55.06N 80.58 E
Čulym 21 Kd 57.40N 83.50 E
Čulyšman 20 Df 51.20N 87.45 E
Cuma 36 Ce 12.52S 15.04 E
Cumaná 53 Jd 10.28N 64.10W
Cumanacoa 50 Eg 10.15N 63.55W
Cumaovası 15 Kk 38.15N 27.09 E
Cumbal, Volcán- 54 Cc 0.57N 77.52W
Cumberland 9 Kg 54.40N 2.50W
Cumberland 38 Kf 37.09N 88.25W
Cumberland [B.C.-Can.] 46 Cb 49.37N 125.01W
Cumberland [Md.-U.S.] 43 Ld 39.39N 78.46W
Cumberland [Va.-U.S.] 44 Hg 37.31N 78.16W
Cumberland, Cap- 63b Cb 14.39S 166.37 E
Cumberland, Lake- 44 Eg 36.57N 84.55W
Cumberland Bay 51n Ba 13.16N 61.17W
Cumberland Island 44 Gj 30.51N 81.27W
Cumberland Islands 59 Jd 20.40S 149.10 E
Cumberland Lake 42 Hf 54.00N 102.20W
Cumberland Peninsula 38 Mc 66.50N 64.00W
Cumberland Plateau 38 Kf 36.00N 85.00W
Cumberland Sound 38 Mc 65.10N 65.30W
Cumbernauld 9 Jf 55.58N 3.59W
Cumbre, Paso de la-/Bermejo, Paso- 52 Ii 32.50S 70.05W
Cumbria [3] 9 Kg 54.35N 2.45W
Cumbrian Mountains 9 Jg 54.30N 3.05W
Çumerna 15 Ig 42.47N 25.58 E
Čumikan 20 If 54.42N 135.19 E
Cummins 59 Hf 34.16S 135.44 E
Cumnock 9 If 55.27N 4.16W
Cumpas 48 Eb 30.02N 109.48W
Çumra 24 Ed 37.34N 32.48 E
Čumyš 20 Df 53.30N 83.10 E
Čuna 21 Ld 57.42N 95.35 E
Cunagua 49 Hb 22.05N 78.20W
Cuñapirú 55 Ej 31.32S 55.35W
Cuñapirú, Arroyo- 55 Ej 31.12S 55.31W
Cuñapirú, Cuchilla de- 55 Ej 31.12S 55.36W
Cunaviche, Rio- 50 Ci 7.19N 67.11W
Cunderdin 59 Df 31.39S 117.15 E
Cundinamarca [2] 54 Db 5.00N 74.00W
Čundža 19 Hg 43.32N 79.28 E
Cunene [3] 36 Cf 16.30S 15.00 E
Cunene = Kunene (EN) 30 Ij 17.20S 11.50 E
Cuneo 14 Bf 44.23N 7.32 E
Čunja 21 Lc 61.30N 96.20 E
Cunnamulla 58 Fg 28.04S 145.41 E
Čunski 20 Ee 56.03N 99.48 E
Čunski 20 Ee 57.23N 97.40 E
Cuorgné 14 Be 45.23N 7.39 E
Čupa 19 Db 66.17N 33.01 E
Cupar 9 Je 56.19N 3.01W
Cupica, Golfo de- 54 Cb 6.35N 77.30W
Cuprija 15 Ef 43.56N 21.22 E
Cupula, Pico- 48 De 24.47N 110.50W
Čur 7 Mh 57.11N 53.01 E
Curaçá 54 Ke 8.59S 39.54W
Curacao 52 Jd 12.11N 69.00W
Curacautin 56 Fe 38.26S 71.53W
Curá Malal, Sierra de- 55 Am 37.44S 62.16W
Curanilahue 56 Fe 37.28S 73.21W
Čurapča 20 Id 61.56N 132.18 E
Curaray, Rio- 54 Dd 2.20S 74.05W
Curcúbata, Vîrful- 15 Fc 46.25N 22.35 E
Curdimurka 58 Eg 29.30S 137.10 E
Curé 55 De 21.25S 56.25W
Cure 11 Jg 47.40N 3.41 E
Curepipe 37a Bb 20.19S 57.31 E
Curepto 56 Fe 35.05S 72.01W
Curiapo 54 Fb 8.33N 61.00W
Curicó 53 Ii 34.59S 71.14W
Curicuriari, Rio- 54 Ed 0.14S 66.48W
Curitabanos 56 Jc 27.18S 50.36W
Curitiba 53 Lh 25.25S 49.15W
Curoca 36 Bf 15.43S 11.55 E
Currais Novos 54 Ke 6.15S 36.31W
Curralinho 54 Id 1.48S 49.47W
Curral-Velho 32 Cf 15.59N 22.48W
Current River 45 Kh 36.15N 90.57W
Currie 59 Ig 39.56S 143.52 E
Curtea de Argeş 15 Hd 45.08N 24.41 E
Curtici 15 Ec 46.21N 21.18 E
Curtis 45 Ff 40.38N 100.31W
Curtis Channel 59 Kd 23.55S 152.05 E
Curtis Island [N.Z.] 57 Jh 30.35S 178.36W
Curtis Island [Austl.] 59 Kd 23.40S 151.10 E
Curuá, Rio- [Braz.] 55 Ga 13.26S 51.24W
Curuá, Rio- [Braz.] 54 Gd 1.55S 55.07W
Curuá, Rio- [Braz.] 52 Kf 5.23S 54.22W
Curuçá 54 Id 0.43S 47.50W
Curuçá, Rio- 54 Dd 4.27S 71.23W
Curuguaty 56 Ib 24.31S 55.42W
Curuguaty, Arroyo- 55 Dg 24.06S 56.02W
Curup 26 Dg 3.28S 102.32 E
Curupira, Sierra de- 54 Fc 1.25N 64.30W
Cururupu 54 Jd 1.50S 44.52W
Curuzú Cuatiá 56 Ic 29.47S 58.03W
Curvelo 54 Jg 18.45S 44.25W
Cusco → Cuzco 53 Ig 13.31S 71.59W
Cushing 45 Hi 35.59N 96.46W
Cushing, Mount- 42 Ee 57.36N 126.51W
Čusovaja 5 Ld 58.13N 56.30 E
Čusovoj 19 Fd 58.17N 57.50 E
Cusset 11 Jh 46.08N 3.28 E
Cusseta 44 Ei 32.18N 84.47W
Čust 18 Hd 41.00N 71.15 E
Custer 45 Ee 43.46N 103.36W
Cutato 36 Ce 10.33S 16.48 E
Cut Bank 43 Eb 48.38N 112.20W
Cutervo 54 Ce 6.22S 78.51W
Cuthbert 44 Ej 31.46N 84.48W
Cutral Có 56 Ge 38.56S 69.14W
Cutro 14 Kk 39.02N 16.59 E
Cuttack 22 Kg 20.30N 85.50 E
Čuvašskaja respublika 19 Ed 55.30N 47.10 E
Cuvelai 36 Cf 15.40S 15.47 E
Cuvette [3] 36 Cc 0.10S 15.30 E
Cuvier Basin (EN) 59 Cd 22.00S 111.00 E
Cuvier Island 62 Fb 36.25S 175.45 E
Cuvo ou Queve 30 Ij 10.50S 13.47 E
Cuxhaven 10 Ec 53.53N 8.42 E
Cuya 56 Fa 19.07S 70.08W
Cuyahoga Falls 44 Ge 41.08N 81.55W
Cuyo Islands 26 Hd 11.04N 120.57 E
Cuyubini, Rio- 50 Fh 8.20N 60.20W
Cuyuni, Rio 52 Ke 6.23N 58.41W
Cuyutlán, Laguna 48 Gh 19.00N 104.10W
Cuzco (Cusco) 53 Ig 13.31S 71.59W
Cuzco [2] 54 Df 12.30S 72.30W
Cuzna 13 Hf 38.04N 4.41W
Cvikov 10 Kf 50.48N 14.40 E
Čvrsnica 14 Lg 43.35N 17.35 E
Cyangugu 36 Ec 2.29S 28.54 E
Cybinka 10 Kd 52.12N 14.48 E
Cyclades (EN) = Kikládhes 5 Ih 37.00N 25.10 E
Čyjyrčyk, Pereval- 18 Id 40.15N 73.20 E
Cypress Hills 38 Ie 49.40N 109.30W
Cypress Lake 46 Kb 49.28N 109.29W
Cyprus (EN) = Kıbrıs/Kypros [1] 22 Ff 35.00N 33.00 E
Cyprus (EN) = Kıbrıs/Kypros 21 Ff 35.00N 33.00 E
Cyprus (EN) = Kypros/Kıbrıs [1] 22 Ff 35.00N 33.00 E
Cyprus (EN) = Kypros/Kıbrıs 21 Ff 35.00N 33.00 E
Cyrenaica (EN) = Barqah 33 Dc 31.00N 22.30 E
Cyrenaica (EN) = Barqah 30 Je 31.00N 23.00 E
Cyrene 33 Dc 32.48N 21.59 E
Cyrus Field Bay 42 Ld 62.50N 65.00W
Cysoing 12 Fd 50.34N 3.13 E
Cythera (EN) = Kíthira 15 Fm 36.09N 23.00 E
Czaplinek 10 Mc 53.34N 16.14 E
Czarna [Pol.] 10 Pe 51.12N 19.53 E
Czarna [Pol.] 10 Rf 50.30N 21.15 E
Czarna Białostocka 10 Tc 53.18N 23.19 E
Czarna Dąbrówka 10 Nb 54.20N 17.32 E
Czarna Hańcza 10 Tc 53.50N 23.47 E
Czarnków 10 Md 52.55N 16.34 E
Czchów 10 Qg 49.50N 20.39 E
Czechowice-Dziedzice 10 Og 49.54N 19.00 E
Czech Republic (EN) = Česká Republika 6 Hf 50.00N 13.00 E
Czeremcha 10 Td 52.32N 23.15 E
Czersk 10 Nc 53.48N 18.00 E
Częstochowa 6 He 50.49N 19.06 E
Częstochowa [2] 10 Pf 50.50N 19.05 E
Człopa 10 Mc 53.06N 16.08 E
Człuchów 10 Nc 53.41N 17.21 E

D

Da, Sông- = Black River (EN) 21 Mg 20.17N 106.34 E
Da'an (Dalai) 27 Lb 45.35N 124.16 E
Dabaga 36 Gd 8.07S 35.55 E
Dabakala 34 Ed 8.22N 4.26W
Dabakala [3] 34 Ed 8.27N 4.28W
Daban → Bairin Youqi 27 Kc 43.30N 118.37 E
Dabas 10 Pi 47.11N 19.19 E
Daba Shan 21 Mf 32.15N 109.00 E
Dabat 35 Fc 12.58N 37.45 E
Dabay Sima 35 Gc 12.43N 42.17 E
Dabba/Daocheng 27 Hf 29.01N 100.26 E
Dabbāgh, Jabal- 23 Ed 27.52N 35.45 E
Dabeiba 54 Cb 7.02N 76.16W
Dębie 10 Od 52.06N 18.49 E
Dąbie, Jezioro- 10 Kc 53.29N 14.40 E
Dabie Shan 21 Nf 31.15N 115.00 E
Dabl, Wādī- [Sau.Ar.] 24 Gh 28.35N 39.04 E
Dabl, Wādī- [Sau.Ar.] 24 Gh 29.05N 36.14 E
Dabnou 34 Gc 14.09N 5.22 E
Dabola 34 Cc 10.45N 11.07W
Daborow 35 Hd 6.11N 48.22 E
Dabou 34 Ed 5.19N 4.23W
Dabqig → Uxin Qi 27 Id 38.27N 109.08 E
Dabraš 15 Gh 41.40N 23.50 E
Dabrowa Białostocka 10 Tc 53.40N 23.20 E
Dąbrowa Górnicza 10 Pf 50.20N 19.11 E
Dąbrowa Tarnowska 10 Qf 50.11N 21.00 E
Dabsan Hu 27 Fd 36.58N 95.00 E
Dăbuleni 15 Hf 43.48N 24.05 E
Dabus 35 Fc 10.38N 35.10 E
Dacata 35 Gd 7.16N 42.15 E
Dacca → Dhaka 22 Lg 23.43N 90.25 E
Dachangzhen 28 Eh 32.13N 118.44 E
Dachau 10 Hh 48.16N 11.26 E
Dachen Dao 28 Fj 28.29N 121.53 E
Dachstein 14 Hc 47.30N 13.36 E
Dacia Seamount (EN) 5 Ei 31.10N 13.42W
Dačice 10 Lg 49.05N 15.26 E
Dac Lac, Caonguyen- 25 Lf 12.50N 108.05 E
Đacovica 15 Dg 42.23N 20.26 E
Dadali 63a Dc 8.07S 159.06 E
Dadanawa 54 Gc 2.50N 59.30W
Daday 24 Eb 41.28N 33.28 E
Dade City 44 Fk 28.22N 82.12W
Dadou 11 Hk 43.44N 1.49 E
Dādra and Nagar Haveli [3] 25 Ed 20.20N 72.50 E
Dadu 25 Dc 26.44N 67.47 E
Dadu He 21 Mg 29.32N 103.44 E
Dadukou 28 Di 30.30N 117.03 E
Dăeni 15 Le 44.50N 28.07 E
Daet 26 Hd 14.05N 122.55 E
Dafang 27 If 27.06N 105.32 E
Dafeng (Dazhongji) 28 Fh 33.11N 120.27 E
Dagana 34 Bb 16.31N 15.30W
Dagana 35 Bc 13.05N 16.00 E
Daga Post 35 Ed 9.13N 33.58 E
Dağardi 15 Lj 39.26N 29.00 E
Dagash 35 Eb 19.22N 33.24 E
Dagda 8 Lh 56.04N 27.36 E
Dagéla 35 Bc 10.40N 18.26 E
Dagestanskaja respublika 19 Eg 43.00N 47.00 E
Dagestanskije Ogni 19 Eg 42.06N 48.12 E
Dagu 28 De 38.58N 117.40 E
Daguan 27 Hf 27.48N 103.54 E
Dagu He 28 Ff 37.34N 121.17 E
Daguokui Shan 28 Jb 45.19N 129.50 E
Dagupan 26 Hc 16.03N 120.20 E
Dagxoi → Yidun 27 Ge 30.25N 99.28 E
Dagzê 27 Ff 29.41N 91.24 E
Dagzê Co 27 Ee 31.54N 87.29 E
Daheiding Shan 27 Mb 47.58N 129.10 E
Dahei He 28 Ad 40.34N 111.05 E
Da Hinggan Ling = Greater Khingan Range (EN) 21 Oe 49.00N 122.00 E
Dahlak Archipelago 30 Lg 15.40N 40.30 E
Dahlak Kebir 35 Gb 15.38N 40.11 E
Daḥl al Furayy 24 Li 26.45N 47.03 E
Dahlem 12 Id 50.23N 6.33 E
Dahlonega Plateau 44 Fh 34.30N 83.45W
Dahm, Ramlat- 33 If 16.25N 45.45 E
Dahme 10 Je 51.52N 13.26 E
Dahmouni 13 Ni 35.25N 1.29 E
Dahn 12 Je 49.09N 7.47 E
Dahomey → Bénin [1] 31 Hh 9.30N 2.15 E
Dahongliutan 27 Cd 36.00N 79.12 E
Dahra 13 Mh 36.18N 0.55 E
Dahra [Lib.] 33 Cd 29.40N 17.40 E
Dahra [Sen.] 34 Bb 15.21N 15.29W
Dahra, Massif de- 13 Oh 36.30N 2.05 E
Dahūk [3] 24 Jd 36.57N 43.00 E
Dahūk 24 Jd 36.52N 43.00 E
Dahushan 28 Gd 41.37N 122.09 E
Dahy, Nafūd ad- 33 Ie 22.00N 45.25 E
Dai 63a Eb 7.53S 160.37 E
Daia 15 If 44.00N 25.59 E
Daïa, Région des- 32 Hc 33.30N 3.25 E
Daicheng 28 De 38.42N 116.37 E
Daigo 28 Pf 36.46N 140.21 E
Dai Hai 28 Bd 40.31N 112.43 E
Dailekh 25 Gc 28.50N 81.44 E
Daimanji-San 29 Cc 36.15N 133.19 E
Daimiel 13 Ie 39.04N 3.37W

Index Symbols

[1] Independent Nation
[2] State, Region
[3] District, County
[4] Municipality
[5] Colony, Dependency
Continent
Physical Region
Historical or Cultural Region
Mount, Mountain
Volcano
Hill
Mountains, Mountain Range
Hills, Escarpment
Plateau, Upland
Pass, Gap
Plain, Lowland
Delta
Salt Flat
Valley, Canyon
Crater, Cave
Karst Features
Depression
Polder
Desert, Dunes
Forest, Woods
Heath, Steppe
Oasis
Cape, Point
Coast, Beach
Cliff
Peninsula
Isthmus
Sandbank
Island
Atoll
Rock, Reef
Islands, Archipelago
Rocks, Reefs
Coral Reef
Well, Spring
Geyser
River, Stream
Waterfall Rapids
River Mouth, Estuary
Lake
Salt Lake
Intermittent Lake
Reservoir
Swamp, Pond
Canal
Glacier
Ice Shelf, Pack Ice
Ocean
Sea
Gulf, Bay
Strait, Fjord
Lagoon
Bank
Seamount
Tablemount
Ridge
Shelf
Basin
Escarpment, Sea Scarp
Fracture
Trench, Abyss
National Park, Reserve
Point of Interest
Recreation Site
Cave, Cavern
Historic Site
Ruins
Wall, Walls
Church, Abbey
Temple
Scientific Station
Airport
Port
Lighthouse
Mine
Tunnel
Dam, Bridge

Index Symbols

- [1] Independent Nation
- [2] State, Region
- [3] District, County
- [4] Municipality
- [5] Colony, Dependency
- ■ Continent
- Physical Region
- Historical or Cultural Region
- Mount, Mountain
- Volcano
- Hill
- Mountains, Mountain Range
- Hills, Escarpment
- Plateau, Upland
- Pass, Gap
- Plain, Lowland
- Delta
- Salt Flat
- Valley, Canyon
- Crater, Cave
- Karst Features
- Depression
- Polder
- Desert, Dunes
- Forest, Woods
- Heath, Steppe
- Oasis
- Cape, Point
- Coast, Beach
- Cliff
- Peninsula
- Isthmus
- Sandbank
- Island
- Atoll
- Rock, Reef
- Islands, Archipelago
- Rocks, Reefs
- Coral Reef
- Well, Spring
- Geyser
- River, Stream
- Waterfall Rapids
- River Mouth, Estuary
- Lake
- Salt Lake
- Ocean
- Sea
- Gulf, Bay
- Strait, Fjord
- Canal
- Glacier
- Ice Shelf, Pack Ice
- Seamount
- Tablemount
- Ridge
- Shelf
- Basin
- Lagoon
- Escarpment, Sea Scarp
- Fracture
- Trench, Abyss
- National Park, Reserve
- Point of Interest
- Recreation Site
- Cave, Cavern
- Historic Site
- Ruins
- Wall, Walls
- Church, Abbey
- Temple
- Scientific Station
- Airport
- Port
- Lighthouse
- Mine
- Tunnel
- Dam, Bridge

Değirmendere 15 Kk 38.06N 27.09 E
De Gray Lake 45 Ji 34.15N 93.15W
De Grey River 59 Dd 20.12S 119.11 E
Degtarsk 17 Jh 56.42N 60.06 E
De Haan 12 Fc 51.16N 3.02 E
Dehaj 24 Pg 30.42N 54.53 E
Dehaq 24 Nf 32.55N 50.57 E
Deh Bārez 24 Qi 27.26N 57.12 E
Deh Bīd 24 Og 30.38N 53.13 E
Deh Dasht 24 Ng 30.47N 50.34 E
Dehdez 24 Ng 31.43N 50.17 E
Deh-e Namak 24 Oe 35.25N 52.50 E
Deh-e Shīr 24 Og 31.29N 53.45 E
Deh-e Ziyār 24 Qg 30.40N 57.00 E
Dehgolān 24 Le 35.17N 47.25 E
Dehiwala-Mount Lavinia 25 Fg 6.50N 79.52 E
Dehlorān 24 Lf 32.41N 47.16 E
Deh Now 24 Qf 33.01N 57.41 E
Dehra Dūn 25 Fb 30.19N 78.02 E
Dehui 27 Mc 44.33N 125.38 E
Deinze 11 Jd 50.59N 3.32 E
Dej 15 Gb 47.09N 23.52 E
Deje 8 Ee 59.36N 13.28 E
Dejen 35 Fc 10.05N 38.11 E
Dejés, Mali i- 15 Dh 41.42N 20.10 E
Dejnau 19 Gh 39.18N 63.11 E
De Jongs, Tanjung- 26 Kh 6.56S 138.32 E
De Kalb 45 Lf 41.56N 88.45W
Dekar 37 Cd 21.30S 21.58 E
Dekese 31 Ji 3.27S 21.24 E
Dekina 34 Gd 7.42N 7.01 E
Dékoa 35 Bd 6.19N 19.04 E
De Koog, Texel- 12 Ga 53.07N 4.46 E
De La Garma 55 Bm 37.58S 60.25W
De Land 44 Gk 29.02N 81.18W
Delano 43 Dd 35.41N 119.15W
Delano Peak 43 Ed 38.22N 112.23W
Delārām 23 Jc 32.11N 63.25 E
Delarof Islands 40a Cb 51.30N 178.45W
Delaware 44 Fe 40.18N 83.06W
Delaware 45 Ek 32.00N 104.00W
Delaware [2] 43 Ld 39.10N 75.30W
Delaware Bay 38 Lc 39.05N 75.15W
Delaware River 43 Ld 39.20N 75.25W
Delbrück 12 Kc 51.46N 8.34 E
Del Carril 55 Cl 35.31S 59.30W
Delčevo 15 Fh 41.58N 22.47 E
Del City 45 Hi 35.27N 97.27W
Delegate 59 Jg 37.03S 148.58 E
Delémont/Delsberg 14 Bc 47.22N 7.21 E
Delet/Teili 8 Id 60.15N 20.35 E
Delfinópolis 55 Ie 20.20S 46.51W
Delft 11 Kb 52.00N 4.21 E
Delfzijl 11 Ma 53.19N 6.56 E
Delgada, Punta- 52 Jj 42.46S 63.38W
Delgado, Cabo-=Delgado, Cape-(EN) 30 Lj 10.40S 40.38 E
Delgado, Cabo-=Delgado, Cape-(EN) [3] 37 Fb 12.30S 39.00 E
Delgado, Cape-(EN)= Delgado, Cabo- 30 Lj 10.40S 40.38 E
Delgado, Cape-(EN)= Delgado, Cabo- [3] 37 Fb 12.30S 39.00 E
Delger Muren 27 Hb 49.17N 100.40 E
Delhi [Co.-U.S.] 45 Eh 37.42N 103.58W
Delhi [India] 25 Jg 28.40N 77.13 E
Delhi [N.Y.-U.S.] 44 Jd 42.17N 74.57W
Deliblatska Peščara 15 Dd 45.00N 21.00 E
Delice 24 Fc 39.58N 34.02 E
Delicermak 24 Fb 40.28N 34.10 E
Delicias [Cuba] 49 Ic 21.11N 76.34W
Delicias [Mex.] 47 Cc 28.13N 105.28W
Delījān 24 Nf 33.59N 50.40 E
Delingha 27 Gd 37.26N 97.25 E
Dēliņkalns/Delinkalns, Gora- 8 Lg 57.30N 27.02 E
Delinkalns, Gora-/Dēliņkalns 8 Lg 57.30N 27.02 E
Delitzsch 10 Ie 51.32N 12.21 E
Deljatin 15 Ha 48.29N 24.45 E
Delle 11 Mg 47.30N 7.00 E
Dell Rapids 45 He 43.50N 96.43W
Dellys 32 Hb 36.55N 3.55 E
Delmarva Peninsula 38 Lf 38.50N 75.30W
Delme 12 Ka 53.05N 8.40 E
Delme 12 If 48.53N 6.24 E
Delmenhorst 10 Ec 53.03N 8.37 E
Delnice 14 Ie 45.24N 14.48 E
Delo 35 Fd 5.49N 37.57 E
De Long Strait (EN)= Longa, Proliv- 21 Tb 70.20N 178.00 E
De-Longa, Ostrova-=De Long Islands (EN) 21 Rb 76.30N 153.00 E
De Long Islands (EN)=De-Longa, Ostrova- 21 Rb 76.30N 153.00 E
De Long Mountains 40 Gc 68.20N 162.00W
Deloraine 59 Jh 41.31S 146.39 E
Delorme, Lac- 42 Kf 54.35N 69.55W
Delphi (EN) = Dhelfoi 15 Fk 38.29N 22.30 E
Del Rio 43 Gf 29.22N 100.54W
Delsberg/Delémont 14 Bc 47.22N 7.21 E
Delsbo 7 Dc 61.48N 16.35 E
Delta [Co.-U.S.] 43 Fd 38.44N 108.04W
Delta [Ut.-U.S.] 43 Ed 39.21N 112.35W
Delta Amacuro [2] 54 Fb 8.30N 61.30W
Delta Junction 40 Jd 64.02N 145.41W
Delvāda 25 Ed 20.46N 71.02 E
Del Valle 55 Bl 35.54S 60.43W
Delvina 15 Dj 39.57N 20.06 E
Dëma 17 Gi 54.42N 55.58 E
Demanda, Sierra de la- 13 Ib 42.15N 3.05W
Demba 36 Dd 5.30S 22.16 E
Dembi 35 Fd 8.05N 36.28 E
Dembia 35 Cd 5.07N 24.25 E
Dembi Dolo 35 Ed 8.32N 34.49 E
De Medinilla, Farallon- 57 Fc 16.01N 146.04 E
Demer 11 Kd 50.58N 4.45 E
Demerara Plateau (EN) 52 Le 4.30N 44.00W
Demerara River 50 Gi 6.48N 58.10W
Demidov 16 Gb 55.15N 31.29 E
Demidovka 10 Vf 50.20N 25.27 E
Deming 43 Fe 32.16N 107.45W
Demini, Rio- 54 Fd 0.46S 62.56W
Demirci 24 Cc 39.03N 28.40 E
Demir Kapija 15 Fh 41.25N 22.15 E
Demirköy 15 Kh 41.49N 27.15 E
Demirtaş 15 Mi 40.16N 29.06 E
Demjanka 19 Gd 59.34N 69.20 E
Demjansk 7 Hh 57.38N 32.29 E
Demjanskoje 19 Gd 59.36N 69.18 E
Demmin 10 Jc 53.54N 13.02 E
Demopolis 44 Di 32.31N 87.50W
Dempo, Gunung- 21 Mj 4.02S 103.09 E
Demta 26 Lg 2.20S 140.08 E
Denain 11 Jd 50.20N 3.23 E
Denan 35 Gd 6.30N 43.30 E
Denau 19 Gh 38.18N 67.55 E
Den Bosch/'s-Hertogenbosch 11 Lc 51.41N 5.19 E
Den Burg, Texel- 12 Ga 53.03N 4.47 E
Den Chai 25 Ke 17.59N 100.04 E
Dendang 26 Eg 3.05S 107.54 E
Dender/Dendre 11 Kc 51.02N 4.06 E
Dendermonde/Termonde 12 Gc 51.02N 4.07 E
Dendre/Dender 11 Kc 51.02N 4.06 E
Dendtler Island 66 Pf 72.58S 89.57W
Denekamp 12 Jb 52.23N 7.00 E
Deneżkin Kamen, Gora- 6 Fc 60.25N 59.31 E
Dengarh 25 Hd 23.50N 81.42 E
Dêngkagoin→Têwo 27 He 34.03N 103.21 E
Dengkou (Bayan Gol) 22 Me 40.25N 106.59 E
Dêngqên 27 Ge 31.29N 95.32 E
Dengzhou→Penglai 27 Ld 37.44N 120.45 E
Den Haag/'s-Gravenhage= The Hague (EN) 6 Ge 52.06N 4.18 E
Den Ham 12 Ib 52.28N 6.32 E
Denham→Shak Bay 59 Ce 25.55S 113.32 E
Denham, Mount- 49 Id 18.13N 77.32W
Denham Range 59 Jd 21.55S 147.45 E
Denham Sound 59 Ce 25.40S 113.15 E
Den Helder 11 Kb 52.54N 4.45 E
Denia 13 Mf 38.51N 0.07 E
Deniliquin 59 Ig 35.32S 144.58 E
Denio 46 Ff 41.59N 118.39W
Denis Island 37b Ca 3.48S 55.40 E
Denison [Ia.-U.S.] 43 Hc 42.01N 95.20W
Denison [Tx.-U.S.] 43 He 33.45N 96.33W
Denison, Mount- 40 Ie 58.25N 154.27W
Denizli 23 Cb 37.46N 29.06 E
Denklingen, Reichshof- 12 Jd 50.55N 7.39 E
Denman Glacier 66 Ge 66.45S 99.25 E
Denmark [Austl.] 59 Df 34.57S 117.21 E
Denmark [S.C.-U.S.] 44 Gi 33.19N 81.09W
Denmark (EN)=Danmark [1] 6 Gd 56.00N 10.00 E
Denmark Strait (EN)= Danmarksstraedet 38 Qc 67.00N 25.00W
Dennery 51k Bb 13.55N 60.54W
Den Oever, Wieringen- 12 Hb 52.56N 5.02 E
Denpasar 22 Nj 8.39S 115.13 E
Denton 43 He 33.13N 97.08W
D'Entrecasteaux, Point- 59 Df 34.50S 116.00 E
D'Entrecasteaux Islands 57 Ge 9.35S 150.40 E
Denver 39 If 39.43N 105.01W
Deoghar 25 Hd 24.29N 86.42 E
Deolāli 25 Ee 19.54N 73.50 E
De Pajaros, Farallon- 57 Fb 20.32N 144.54 E
De Panne/La Panne 12 Ec 51.06N 2.35 E
De Pere 45 Ld 44.27N 88.04W
Deputatski 20 Ic 69.13N 139.55 E
Dêqên 27 Gf 28.32N 98.50 E
Deqing 27 Jg 23.14N 111.42 E
De Queen 45 Ii 34.02N 94.21W
De Quincy 45 Jk 30.27N 93.26W
Dequing 28 Fi 30.34N 120.05 E
Dera, Lach- 35 Ge 0.15N 42.17 E
Dera, Lagh- 30 Lh 0.15N 42.17 E
Dera Bugti 25 Dc 29.02N 69.09 E
Dera Ghāzi Khan 22 Jf 30.03N 70.38 E
Dera Ismāil Khan 25 Eb 31.50N 70.54 E
Derbent 6 Kg 42.00N 48.18 E
Derbent [Tur.] 15 Lk 38.11N 28.33 E
Derby 9 Lh 53.05N 1.40W
Derby [Austl.] 58 Df 17.18S 123.38 E
Derby [Eng.-U.K.] 9 Li 52.55N 1.30W
Derby [Ks.-U.S.] 45 Hh 37.33N 97.16W
Derbyshire [3] 9 Lh 53.10N 1.35W
Đerdap 15 Fe 44.41N 22.10 E
Derecske 10 Ri 47.21N 21.34 E
Dereköy 15 Kh 41.56N 27.21 E
Dereli 24 Hb 40.45N 38.27 E
Derg/Abhainn na Deirge 9 Fg 54.40N 7.25W
Đerg, Lough-/Loch Deirgeirt 9 Ei 53.00N 8.20W
Dergači 16 Pd 51.13N 48.46 E
Dergači 16 Jd 50.09N 36.09 E
Der Grabow 10 Ib 54.23N 12.50 E
De Ridder 45 Jk 30.51N 93.17W
Derik 24 Id 37.22N 40.17 E
Derkul 16 Qd 51.17N 51.15 E
Dermott 45 Kj 33.32N 91.26W
Dernieres, Isles- 45 Kl 29.02N 90.47W
Derong 27 Gf 28.44N 99.18 E
De Rose Hill 59 Ge 26.25S 133.15 E
Déroute, Passage de la- 11 Ee 49.12N 1.51W
Dersa, Eglab- 32 Gd 26.45N 4.26W
Dersca 15 Jb 47.59N 26.12 E
Dersingham 12 Cb 52.51N 0.30 E
Derudeb 35 Fb 17.32N 36.06 E
Derventa 14 Lf 44.59N 17.55 E
Derwent [Eng.-U.K.] 9 Mg 54.10N 0.40W
Derwent [Eng.-U.K.] 12 Ab 52.53N 1.17W
Derwent River 59 Jh 43.03S 147.22 E
Deržavinsk 19 Ge 51.03N 66.19 E
Desaguadero, Rio- 52 Ji 34.13S 66.47W
Désappointement, Iles du- 57 Mf 14.10S 141.20W
Des Arc 45 Ki 34.58N 91.30W
Desborough 12 Bb 52.26N 0.49W
Descalvado 55 Ie 21.54S 47.37W
Descartes 11 Gh 46.58N 0.45 E
Deschambault Lake 42 Hf 54.50N 103.30W
Deschutes River 43 Cb 45.38N 120.54W
Descoberto, Rio- 55 Hc 16.20S 48.19W
Dese 31 Kg 11.07N 39.38 E
Deseado, Rio- 52 Jj 47.45S 65.54W
Desecheo, Isla- 51a Ab 18.25N 67.28W
Desengaño, Punta- 56 Gg 49.15S 67.37W
Desenzano del Garda 14 Ee 45.28N 10.32 E
Desert Center 46 Hj 33.42N 115.26W
Desert Peak 46 If 40.28N 112.38W
Deshaies [Guad.] 51e Ab 16.18N 61.48W
Deshaies [Guad.] 51e Ab 16.18N 61.47W
Desiderio, Rio- 55 Ja 12.20S 44.50W
Desmaraisville 44 Ia 49.31N 76.10W
De Smet 45 Hd 44.23N 97.33W
Desmochado 55 Ch 27.07S 58.06W
Des Moines 38 Je 40.22N 91.26W
Des Moines [Ia.-U.S.] 39 Je 41.35N 93.37W
Des Moines [N.M.-U.S.] 45 Eh 36.46N 103.50W
Desmoronado, Cerro- 47 Dd 20.21N 105.01W
Desna 5 Je 50.33N 30.32 E
Desnățui 15 Ge 43.53N 23.35 E
Desolación, Isla- 52 Ik 53.00S 74.10W
De Soto 45 Kg 38.08N 90.33W
Despeñaperros, Desfiladero de- 13 If 38.24N 3.30W
Des Roches, Ile- 37b Bb 5.41S 53.41 E
Dessau 10 Ie 51.50N 12.15 E
Destruction Bay 42 Dd 61.20N 139.00W
Desvres 11 Hd 50.40N 1.50 E
Deta 15 Ed 45.24N 21.14 E
Dete 37 Dc 18.37S 26.51 E
Detmold 10 Ee 51.56N 8.53 E
Detour, Point- 44 Dc 45.36N 86.37W
Detroit [Mi.-U.S.] 39 Ke 42.20N 83.03W
Detroit [Or.-U.S.] 46 Dd 44.42N 122.10W
Detroit Lakes 45 Ic 46.49N 95.51W
Dettifoss 7a Cb 65.49N 16.24W
Detva 10 Ph 48.34N 19.25 E
Deûle 12 Fd 50.44N 2.56 E
Deurdeur 13 Oh 36.14N 2.16 E
Deurne 12 Hc 51.28N 5.48 E
Deutsche Bucht 10 Db 54.30N 7.30 E
Deutsche Demokratische Republik = Germany 6 Ge 51.00N 10.00 E
Deutschlandsberg 14 Jd 46.49N 15.13 E
Deux-Bassins, Col des- 13 Ph 36.27N 3.18 E
Deux Sèvres [3] 11 Fh 46.30N 0.15W
Deva 15 Fd 45.53N 22.54 E
Dévaványa 10 Qi 47.02N 20.58 E
Deveci Dağları 24 Gb 40.05N 36.00 E
Devecser 10 Ni 47.06N 17.26 E
Develi 24 Fc 38.22N 35.06 E
Deventer 11 Mb 52.15N 6.10 E
Deverd, Cap- 63b Be 20.46S 164.22 E
Deveron 9 Kd 57.40N 2.30W
Devès, Monts du- 11 Jj 44.57N 3.46 E
Devetak 14 Mg 43.58N 19.00 E
Devil River Peak 62 Ed 40.58S 172.39 E
Devil's Hole 9 Ne 56.38N 0.40 E
Devil's Island (EN)=Diable, Ile du- 54 Hb 5.17N 52.35W
Devils Lake 43 Hb 48.07N 98.59W
Devils Lake 45 Gb 48.01N 98.52W
Devils Paw 40 Me 58.44N 133.50W
Devils River 45 Fl 29.39N 100.58W
Devils Tower 46 Md 44.31N 104.57W
Devin 15 Hh 41.45N 24.24 E
Devizes 9 Lj 51.22N 1.59W
Devnja 15 Kf 43.13N 27.33 E
Devodi Munda 25 Ge 17.37N 82.57 E
De Volet Point 51n Ba 13.22N 61.13W
Devolli 15 Ci 40.49N 19.51 E
Devolli 15 Di 40.30N 20.50 E
Dévoluy 11 Lj 44.39N 5.53 E
Devon [3] 9 Jk 50.50N 3.50W
Devon 9 Jk 50.50N 4.00W
Devon 38 Kb 75.00N 87.00W
Devon 12 Ba 53.04N 0.49W
Devonport 57 Fi 41.11S 146.21 E
Devoto 55 Aj 31.24S 62.19W
Devrek 24 Db 41.13N 31.57 E
Devrez 24 Fb 41.06N 34.25 E
Dewa 30 Lh 4.11N 42.06 E
Dewar Lakes 42 Kc 68.00N 73.00W
Dewās 25 Fd 22.58N 76.04 E
Dewa-Sanchi 29 Gb 39.30N 140.15 E
Dewey 45 Ih 36.48N 95.56W
De Witt 45 Ki 34.18N 91.20W
Dexemhare 35 Fb 15.04N 39.03 E
Dexing 28 Dj 28.55N 117.33 E
Dexter 45 Lh 36.48N 89.57W
Deyang 27 He 31.07N 104.25 E
Dey-Dey, Lake- 59 Ge 29.15S 131.05 E
Deyhūk 24 Qf 33.17N 57.30 E
Deyyer 23 Hd 27.50N 51.55 E
Dez 24 Mg 31.39N 48.52 E
Dezfūl 22 Gf 32.23N 48.24 E
Dez Gerd 24 Ng 30.45N 51.57 E
Dezhou 27 Kd 37.28N 116.18 E
Dháfni 15 Fl 37.46N 22.02 E
Dhahab 33 Fd 28.29N 34.32 E
Dhaka 22 Lg 23.43N 90.25 E
Dhamār 23 Fg 14.37N 44.23 E
Dhamtari 25 Gd 20.41N 81.34 E
Dhānbād 25 Hd 23.48N 86.27 E
Dhanushkodi 25 Fg 9.11N 79.24 E
Dhaulagiri 21 Kg 28.44N 83.25 E
Dhekeleia 24 Ee 35.03N 33.40 E
Dhelfoi = Delphi (EN) 15 Fk 38.29N 22.30 E
Dhelvinákion 15 Dj 39.56N 20.28 E
Dhenkanal 25 Hd 20.40N 85.36 E
Dheskáti 15 Ej 39.55N 21.49 E
Dhespotikó 15 Hm 36.58N 25.00 E
Dhiapóndioi Nisoi 15 Cj 39.50N 19.25 E
Dhībān 24 Fg 31.30N 35.47 E
Dhidhimótikhon 15 Jh 41.21N 26.30 E
Dhikti Óros 15 In 35.15N 25.30 E
Dhilos 15 Il 37.24N 25.16 E
Dhilos 15 Il 37.24N 25.16 E
Dhimitsána 15 Fl 37.36N 22.03 E
Dhionisiádhes, Nísoi- 15 Jn 35.21N 26.10 E
Dhiórix Potidhaia 15 Gi 40.10N 23.20 E
Dhī-Qar [3] 24 Lg 31.10N 46.10 E
Dhī-Qar 24 Kf 32.14N 44.22 E
Dhírfis Óros 15 Gk 38.38N 23.50 E
Dhísoron Óros 15 Fh 41.11N 22.57 E
Dhivounia 15 Jn 35.50N 26.28 E
Dhodhekánisos = Dodecanese (EN) 15 Jm 36.20N 27.00 E
Dhodhóni = Dodona (EN) 15 Dj 39.33N 20.46 E
Dholpur 25 Fc 26.42N 77.54 E
Dhomokós 15 Fj 39.08N 22.18 E
Dhone 25 Fe 15.25N 77.53 E
Dhonoúsa 15 Il 37.10N 25.50 E
Dhoráji 25 Ed 21.44N 70.27 E
Dhoxáton 15 Hh 41.06N 24.14 E
Dhragónisos 15 Il 37.27N 25.29 E
Dhuburi 25 Hc 26.02N 89.58 E
Dhule 22 Jg 20.54N 74.47 E
Dhuliān 25 Hd 24.41N 87.58 E
Dia 15 In 35.27N 25.13 E
Diable, Ile du-=Devil's Island (EN) 54 Hb 5.17N 52.35W
Diable, Morne au- 51g Ba 15.37N 61.27W
Diable, Pointe du- [Mart.] 51h Bb 14.47N 60.54W
Diable, Pointe du- [Van.] 63b Dc 16.01S 168.12 E
Diablo, Punta del- 55 Fl 34.22S 53.46W
Diablo, Puntan- 64b Ba 15.00N 145.34 E
Diablo Range 46 Eh 36.45N 121.20W
Diafarabé 34 Ec 14.10N 5.00W
Dialafara 34 Cc 13.27N 11.23W
Diamant, Pointe du- 51h Ac 14.27N 61.04W
Diamant, Rocher du- 51h Ac 14.27N 61.03W
Diamante [Arg.] 56 Hd 32.04S 60.39W
Diamante [It.] 14 Jk 39.41N 15.49 E
Diamante, Punta del- 48 Ji 16.47N 99.52W
Diamantina 54 Jg 18.15S 43.36W
Diamantina, Chapada- 52 Lg 11.30S 41.10W
Diamantina, Rio- 55 Fc 16.42S 52.45W
Diamantina Depth (EN) 3 Hm 33.30S 102.00 E
Diamantina Lakes 59 Id 23.46S 141.09 E
Diamantina River 57 Eg 26.45S 139.10 E
Diamantina Trench (EN) 3 Hm 36.00S 104.00 E
Diamantino 53 Kg 14.25S 56.27W
Diamantino, Rio- 55 Fc 16.08S 52.28W
Diamond Harbour 25 Hd 22.12N 88.12 E
Diamond Island 51p Bb 12.20N 61.35W
Diamond Jenness Peninsula 42 Fb 71.00N 117.00W
Diamond Peak [Nv.-U.S.] 46 Hg 39.40N 115.48W
Diamond Peak [Or.-U.S.] 46 De 43.33N 122.09W
Diamond Peak [U.S.] 46 Id 44.09N 113.05W
Diamond Peak [U.S.] 46 Gc 46.07N 117.32W
Diamou 34 Cc 14.05N 11.16W
Diana, Baie- 42 Kd 61.00N 70.00W
Dianbai 27 Jg 21.33N 110.58 E
Dianbu → Feidong 28 Di 31.53N 117.29 E
Diancang Shan 27 Hf 25.42N 100.02 E
Dian Chi 27 Hg 24.50N 102.45 E
Diane, Étang de- 11a Ba 42.07N 9.32 E
Dianjiang 27 Ie 30.19N 107.25 E
Diano Marina 14 Cg 43.54N 8.05 E
Dianópolis 54 If 11.38S 46.50W
Dianra 34 Dd 8.45N 6.18W
Diapaga 34 Fc 12.04N 1.47 E
Diaz 55 Bk 32.22S 61.05W
Dibā, Dawḥat- 24 Qk 25.38N 56.18 E
Dībagah 24 Je 35.52N 43.49 E
Dibang 25 Jc 27.50N 95.32 E
Dibaya 36 Dd 6.30S 22.57 E
Dibaya-Lubue 36 Cc 4.09S 19.52 E
Dibella 34 Hb 17.31N 12.59 E
Dibrugarh 22 Lg 27.29N 94.54 E
Dibs 24 Ke 35.40N 44.04 E
Dibsī Afnān 24 Ee 35.55N 38.16 E
Dickens 45 Fj 33.37N 100.50W
Dickinson 43 Gb 46.53N 102.47W
Dickins Seamount (EN) 40 Lf 54.30N 137.00W
Dickson 44 Dg 36.05N 87.23W
Dicle 24 Ic 38.22N 40.04 E
Dicle=Tigris (EN) 21 Gf 31.00N 47.25 E
Didam 12 Ic 51.56N 6.09 E
Didao 28 Kb 45.22N 130.48 E
Didcot 12 Ac 51.36N 1.15W
Didesa 35 Fd 9.30N 35.32 E
Didiéni 34 Dc 13.23N 8.05W
Didyma 15 Kl 37.21N 27.13 E
Die 11 Lj 44.45N 5.22 E
Dieburg 10 Eg 49.54N 8.51 E
Diecinueve de Abril 55 El 34.22S 54.04W
Dieciocho de Julio 55 Fk 33.41S 53.33W
Diefenbaker Lake 42 Gf 51.00N 107.00W
Diège 11 Ii 45.36N 2.16 E
Diego Garcia 21 Jj 6.20S 72.20 E
Diego Ramirez, Islas 56 Gi 56.30S 68.44W
Diekirch 11 Me 49.53N 6.10 E
Die Lewitz 10 Hc 53.30N 11.30 E
Diéma 34 Dc 14.33N 9.11W
Diemel 10 Fe 51.39N 9.27 E
Diemelsee 12 Kc 51.19N 8.43 E
Diemelstadt 12 Lc 51.27N 9.01 E
Dien Bien Phu 25 Kd 21.23N 103.01 E
Diepenbeek 12 Hd 50.54N 5.24 E
Diepholz 10 Ed 52.36N 8.22 E
Dieppe 11 He 49.56N 1.05 E
Dieppe Bay Town 51c Ab 17.25N 62.48W
Dierdorf 12 Jd 50.33N 7.40 E
Dieren, Rheden- 12 Ib 52.03N 6.08 E
Di'er Songhua Jiang 27 Lc 45.26N 124.39 E
Diest 12 Hd 50.59N 5.03 E
Dieulefit 11 Lj 44.31N 5.04 E
Dieulouard 12 If 48.51N 6.04 E
Dieuze 11 Mf 48.49N 6.43 E
Dieveniškes 8 Kj 54.10N 25.44 E
Die Ville 12 Id 50.40N 6.55 E
Diez 12 Kd 50.22N 8.01 E
Dif 36 Hb 0.59N 40.57 E
Diffa [2] 34 Hb 16.00N 13.30 E
Diffa 34 Hc 13.19N 12.37 E
Differdange/Differdingen 11 Le 49.32N 5.52 E
Differdingen/Differdange 11 Le 49.32N 5.52 E
Digby 42 Kh 44.40N 65.50W
Dighton 45 Fg 38.29N 100.28W
Digne 11 Mj 44.06N 6.14 E
Digoin 11 Jh 46.29N 3.59 E
Digora 16 Nh 43.07N 44.06 E
Digos 26 Ie 6.45N 125.20 E
Digranes 7a Ca 66.02N 14.45W
Digul 26 Kh 7.07S 138.42 E
Dihang 25 Jc 27.48N 95.30 E
Dijar 16 Tf 46.33N 56.05 E
Dijlah=Tigris (EN) 21 Gf 31.00N 47.25 E
Dijle 11 Kd 50.53N 4.42 E
Dijon 6 Gf 47.19N 5.01 E
Dik 35 Bd 9.58N 17.31 E
Dikanäs 7 Dd 65.14N 16.00 E
Dikhil 35 Gc 11.06N 42.22 E
Dikili 24 Bc 39.04N 26.53 E
Dikli 8 Kg 57.30N 25.00 E
Diksmuide/Dixmude 11 Ic 51.02N 2.52 E
Dikson 22 Kb 73.30N 80.35 E
Dikwa 34 Hc 12.02N 13.55 E
Dila 35 Fd 6.23N 38.19 E
Dilbeek 12 Gd 50.51N 4.16 E
Dili 22 Oj 8.33S 125.34 E
Di Linh 25 Lf 11.35N 108.04 E
Diližan 16 Ni 40.46N 44.55 E
Dilj 14 Me 45.16N 18.01 E
Dill 12 Kd 50.33N 8.29 E
Dillenburg 10 Ef 50.44N 8.17 E
Dillia 30 Ig 14.09N 12.50 E
Dilling 31 Jg 12.03N 29.39 E
Dillingen (Saar) 12 Ie 49.21N 6.44 E
Dillingham 39 Dd 59.02N 158.29W
Dillon [Mt.-U.S.] 43 Eb 45.13N 112.38W
Dillon [S.C.-U.S.] 44 Hh 34.25N 79.22W
Dilly 34 Dc 14.57N 7.43W
Dilolo 31 Jj 10.42S 22.20 E
Dilsen 12 Hc 51.02N 5.44 E
Dimashq=Damascus (EN) 22 Ff 33.30N 36.15 E
Dimbelenge 36 Dd 5.30S 23.53 E
Dimbokro [3] 34 Ed 6.50N 4.45W
Dimbokro 34 Ed 6.39N 4.42W
Dimboola 59 Ig 36.27S 142.02 E
Dîmbovița 15 Je 44.14N 26.27 E
Dîmbovița [2] 15 Ie 44.55N 25.30 E
Dîmbovnic 15 Ie 44.20N 25.40 E
Dimitrovgrad [Bul.] 15 Ig 42.03N 25.36 E
Dimitrovgrad 19 Ee 54.14N 49.42 E
Dimitrovgrad [Yugo.] 15 Fg 43.01N 22.47 E
Dimmitt 45 Ei 34.33N 102.19W
Dimona 24 Fg 31.04N 35.02 E
Dimovo 15 Ff 43.44N 22.44 E
Dinagat 26 Id 10.12N 125.35 E
Dinājpur 25 Hc 25.38N 88.38 E
Dinan 11 Df 48.27N 2.02W
Dinangourou 34 Ec 14.27N 2.14W
Dinant 11 Kd 50.16N 4.55 E
Dinar 24 Dc 38.04N 30.10 E
Dinar, Kūh-e- 24 Ng 30.50N 51.35 E
Dinara 14 Kf 44.04N 16.23 E
Dinara=Dinaric Alps (EN) 5 Hg 43.50N 16.35 E
Dinard 11 Df 48.38N 2.04W
Dinaric Alps (EN)= Dinara 5 Hg 43.50N 16.35 E
Dindar, Nahr ad- 35 Ec 14.06N 33.40 E
Dinder 35 Ec 14.06N 33.40 E
Dindigul 25 Ff 10.21N 77.57 E
Dindima 34 Hc 10.14N 10.09 E
Dinga 36 Cd 5.19S 16.34 E
Dingbian 27 Id 37.35N 107.37 E
Dingden, Hamminkeln- 12 Ic 51.46N 6.37 E
Dinggyê 27 Ef 28.25N 87.45 E
Dinghai 27 Le 30.05N 122.07 E
Dingle 8 Df 58.32N 11.34 E
Dingle/An Daingean 9 Ci 52.08N 10.15W
Dingle Bay/Bá an Daingin 9 Ci 52.05N 10.15W
Dingolfing 10 Ih 48.38N 12.30 E
Dingshuzhen 28 Ei 31.16N 119.50 E
Dingtao 28 Cg 35.04N 115.35 E
Dinguiraye 34 Cc 11.18N 10.43W
Dingwall 9 Id 57.35N 4.26W
Dingxi 27 Hd 35.33N 104.32 E
Dingxian 27 Jd 39.29N 115.00 E
Dingxiang 28 Be 38.32N 112.59 E
Dingxing 27 Kd 39.11N 115.48 E
Dingyuan 28 Dh 32.32N 117.41 E
Dingzi Gang 28 Ff 36.33N 120.59 E
Dinh, Mui- 21 Mh 11.22N 109.01 E
Dinkel 12 Ib 52.30N 6.58 E
Dinosaur 45 Bf 40.15N 109.01W
Dinskaja 16 Kg 45.09N 39.12 E
Dinslaken 12 Ic 51.34N 6.44 E
Dinsör 35 Ge 2.23N 42.58 E
Dintel 12 Gc 51.39N 4.24 E
Dinuba 46 Fh 36.36N 119.27W

Index Symbols

[1] Independent Nation
[2] State, Region
[3] District, County
[4] Municipality
[5] Colony, Dependency
Continent
Physical Region
Historical or Cultural Region
Mount, Mountain
Volcano
Hill
Mountains, Mountain Range
Hills, Escarpment
Plateau, Upland
Pass, Gap
Plain, Lowland
Delta
Salt Flat
Valley, Canyon
Crater, Cave
Karst Features
Depression
Polder
Desert, Dunes
Forest, Woods
Heath, Steppe
Oasis
Cape, Point
Coast, Beach
Cliff
Peninsula
Isthmus
Sandbank
Island
Atoll
Rock, Reef
Islands, Archipelago
Rocks, Reefs
Coral Reef
Well, Spring
Geyser
River, Stream
Waterfall Rapids
River Mouth, Estuary
Lake
Salt Lake
Intermittent Lake
Reservoir
Swamp, Pond
Canal
Glacier
Ice Shelf, Pack Ice
Ocean
Sea
Gulf, Bay
Strait, Fjord
Lagoon
Bank
Seamount
Tablemount
Ridge
Shelf
Basin
Escarpment, Sea Scarp
Fracture
Trench, Abyss
National Park, Reserve
Point of Interest
Recreation Site
Cave, Cavern
Historic Site
Ruins
Wall, Walls
Church, Abbey
Temple
Scientific Station
Airport
Port
Lighthouse
Mine
Tunnel
Dam, Bridge

Dinwiddie 44 Ig 37.05N 77.35W
Dioïla 34 Dc 12.28N 6.47W
Diois, Massif du- 11 Lj 44.35N 5.20 E
Dion 34 Dc 10.12N 8.39W
Diorama 55 Gc 16.21 S 51.14W
Dios 63a Ba 5.33 S 154.58 E
Diosig 15 Eb 47.18N 22.00 E
Dioura 34 Dc 14.51N 5.15W
Diourbel [3] 34 Bc 14.45N 16.10W
Diourbel 34 Bc 14.40N 16.15W
Dipkarpas 24 Fe 35.36N 34.23 E
Dipolog 22 Oi 8.35N 123.20 E
Dīr 25 Ea 35.12N 71.53 E
Dira, Djebel- 13 Ph 36.05N 3.38 E
Diré 34 Eb 16.15N 3.24W
Dire Dawa 31 Lh 9.35N 41.53 E
Diriamba 49 Dh 11.51N 86.14W
Dirico 36 Df 17.58 S 20.45 E
Dirj 33 Bc 30.09N 10.26 E
Dirk Hartog Island 59 Ce 25.45 S 113.00 E
Dirkou 34 Hb 19.01N 12.53 E
Dirranbandi 58 Fg 28.35 S 148.14 E
Dirty Devil River 46 Jh 37.53N 110.24W
Disappointment, Cape- [B.A.T.] 56 Mh 54.53 S 36.07W
Disappointment, Cape- [U.S.] 46 Cc 46.18N 124.03W
Disappointment, Lake- 57 Dg 23.30 S 122.50 E
Discovery Tablemount (EN) 30 Hm 42.00 S 0.10 E
Dishna 33 Fd 26.07N 32.28 E
Disko 67 Nc 69.50N 53.30W
Disko Bay (EN)=Disko Bugt 67 Nc 69.15N 52.30W
Disko Bugt=Disko Bay (EN) 67 Nc 69.15N 52.30W
Diskofjord 41 Ge 69.39N 53.45W
Disna 7 Gi 55.33N 28.12 E
Disna 7 Gi 55.34N 28.12 E
Disnaj, Ozero-/Dysnų Ežeras 7 Gi 55.35N 26.32 E
Dispur 25 Ic 26.07N 91.48 E
Diss 12 Db 52.23N 1.07 E
District of Columbia [2] 43 Ld 38.54N 77.01W
Distrito Federal [Braz.] [2] 54 Ig 15.45 S 47.45W
Distrito Federal [Mex.] [2] 47 Ee 19.15N 99.10W
Disūq 24 Dg 31.08N 30.39 E
Dithmarschen 10 Fb 54.10N 9.15 E
Ditrău 15 Ic 46.49N 25.31 E
Dittaino 14 Im 37.25N 15.00 E
Diu [3] 25 Ed 20.42N 70.59 E
Dīvāndarreh 24 Le 35.55N 47.02 E
Divénié 36 Bc 2.41 S 12.05 E
Divenskaja 8 Ne 59.09N 30.09 E
Dives 11 Fe 49.19N 0.05W
Dives-sur-Mer 12 Be 49.17N 0.06W
Diviaka 15 Ci 41.00N 19.32 E
Diviči 16 Pi 42.10N 49.01 E
Divin 10 Ue 51.57N 24.09 E
Divinópolis 53 Lh 20.09 S 44.54W
Divion 12 Ed 50.28N 2.30 E
Divisões, Serra das- 54 Hg 16.40 S 50.50W
Divisor, Serra de 54 De 8.00 S 73.50W
Divnogorsk 20 Ee 55.58N 92.32 E
Divnoje 19 Ef 45.53N 43.22 E
Divo [3] 34 Dd 5.57N 5.15W
Divo 34 Dd 5.50N 5.22W
Divoká Orlice 10 Mf 50.09N 16.06 E
Divor 13 Df 38.59N 8.29W
Divriği 24 Hc 39.23N 38.07 E
Dīvrūd 24 Nd 36.52N 49.34 E
Dixmude/Diksmuide 11 Ic 51.02N 2.52 E
Dixon [Il.-U.S.] 45 Lf 41.50N 89.29W
Dixon [N.M.-U.S.] 45 Dh 36.11N 105.53W
Dixon Entrance 38 Fd 54.25N 132.30W
Diyālā 21 Gf 33.14N 44.31 E
Diyālá [3] 24 Kf 34.00N 45.00 E
Diyarbakir 23 Fb 37.55N 40.14 E
Dizy 12 Fe 49.04N 3.58 E
Dizy-le-Gros 12 Ge 49.38N 4.01 E
Dja 30 Ih 2.02N 15.12 E
Djado 31 If 21.01N 12.18 E
Djado, Plateau du- 30 If 21.45N 12.50 E
Djakovo 10 Th 48.03N 23.01 E
Djamaa 32 Ic 33.32N 6.00 E
Djambala 31 Ii 2.33 S 14.45 E
Djanet 31 Hf 24.34N 9.29 E
Djaret 32 Hd 26.35N 1.38 E
Djatkovo 19 De 53.36N 34.20 E
Djatlovo 16 Dc 53.31N 25.24 E
Djaul Island 60 Eh 2.56 S 150.55 E
Djebel Ṭāriq, El Bōghāz-= Gibraltar, Strait of- (EN) 5 Fh 35.57N 5.36W
Djédaa 35 Bc 13.31N 18.34 E
Djedi 30 He 34.39N 5.55 E
Djedoug, Djebel- 13 Qi 35.53N 4.20 E
Djelfa 31 He 34.40N 3.15 E
Djelfa [3] 32 Hc 34.15N 3.30 E
Djéma 31 Jh 6.03N 25.19 E
Djember 35 Bc 10.25N 17.50 E
Djemila 32 Ib 36.19N 5.44 E
Djenane 13 Pi 35.43N 3.59 E
Djenné 34 Ec 13.55N 4.33W
Djerem 34 Hd 5.20N 13.24 E
Dji 35 Cd 6.47N 22.14 E
Djibo 34 Ec 14.06N 1.38W
Djibouti 31 Lg 11.35N 43.08 E
Djibouti (Afars and Issas) [1] 31 Lg 11.30N 43.00 E
Djokupunda 36 Dd 5.27 S 20.58 E
Djolu 31 Jh 0.37N 22.21 E
Djoua 36 Bb 1.13N 13.12 E
Djougou 34 Fd 9.42N 1.40 E
Djoum 34 He 2.40N 12.40 E
Djourab, Erg du- [Chad] 35 Bb 17.00N 19.30 E
Djourab, Erg du- [Chad] 35 Bb 16.40N 18.50 E
Djugu 36 Fb 1.55N 30.30 E
Djultydag, Gora- 16 Oi 41.58N 46.56 E
Djup 8 Bd 60.50N 8.00 E
Djúpi vogur 7a Cb 64.39N 14.17W
Djurbeldžin 18 Jd 41.10N 74.59 E
Djurdjura, Djebel- 13 Qh 36.27N 4.15 E
Djurmo 8 Fd 60.33N 15.10 E
Djurö 8 Ef 58.50N 13.30 E
Djursholm 8 He 59.24N 18.05 E
Djursland 8 Dh 56.20N 10.45 E
Djurtjuli 19 Fd 55.29N 54.55 E
Dmitrija Lapteva, Proliv-= Dmitri Laptev Strait (EN) 21 Qb 73.00N 142.00 E
Dmitrijev-Lgovski 16 Ic 52.08N 35.05 E
Dmitri Laptev Strait (EN)= Dmitrija Lapteva, Proliv- 21 Qb 73.00N 142.00 E
Dmitrov 7 Ih 56.26N 37.31 E
Dmitrovsk-Orlovski 16 Ic 52.31N 35.09 E
Dnepr 5 Jf 46.30N 32.18 E
Dneprodzeržinsk 19 Df 48.30N 34.37 E
Dneprodzeržinskoje Vodohranilišče 16 Ie 48.45N 34.10 E
Dnepropetrovsk 6 Jf 48.27N 34.59 E
Dnepropetrovskaja Oblast [3] 19 Df 48.15N 35.00 E
Dneprorudnoje 16 If 47.23N 35.01 E
Dneprovski Liman 16 Gf 46.35N 31.55 E
Dneprovsko-Bugski Kanal 16 Dc 52.03N 25.10 E
Dnepr Upland (EN)= Pridneprovskaja Vozvyšennost 5 Jf 49.00N 32.00 E
Dnestr 5 Jf 46.18N 30.17 E
Dnestrovsk 15 Mc 46.39N 29.48 E
Dnestrovski Liman 16 Gf 46.15N 30.15 E
Dno 19 Cd 57.49N 29.59 E
Doany 37 Hb 14.22 S 49.30 E
Doba 35 Bd 8.39N 16.51 E
Dobbiaco / Toblach 14 Gd 46.44N 12.14 E
Dobele 7 Fh 56.39N 23.16 E
Döbeln 10 Je 51.07N 13.07 E
Doberah, Jazirah- 26 Jg 1.30 S 132.30 E
Dobo 26 Jh 5.46 S 134.13 E
Doboj 14 Mf 44.44N 18.05 E
Dobra 10 Oe 51.54N 18.37 E
Dobre Miasto 10 Qc 53.59N 20.25 E
Dobreta Turnu Severin 6 Ig 44.38N 22.40 E
Dobrič (Tolbuhin) 15 Kf 43.34N 27.50 E
Dobrinka 16 Lc 52.08N 40.29 E
Dobříš 10 Kg 49.47N 14.10 E
Dobrjanka 19 Fd 58.29N 56.29 E
Dobrodzień 10 Of 50.44N 18.27 E
Dobrogea=Dobruja (EN) 15 Ke 44.00N 28.00 E
Dobrogea = Dobruja (EN) 5 Ig 44.00N 28.00 E
Dobrogean, Masivul- 15 Le 44.50N 28.30 E
Dobromil 10 Sg 49.34N 22.49 E
Dobropolje 16 Je 48.28N 37.02 E
Dobroteşti 15 He 44.17N 24.53 E
Dobrotvor 10 Uf 50.10N 24.27 E
Dobrudžansko Plato 15 Kf 43.32N 27.50 E
Dobruja (EN) = Dobrogea 5 Ig 44.00N 28.00 E
Dobruš 16 Gc 52.26N 31.19 E
Dobruška 10 Mf 50.18N 16.10 E
Dobrzyń nad Wisłą 10 Pd 52.38N 19.20 E
Dobrzyńskie, Pojezierze- 10 Pc 53.00N 19.20 E
Dobšiná 10 Qh 48.49N 20.22 E
Doce, Rio- [Braz.] 52 Mg 19.37 S 39.49W
Doce, Rio- [Braz.] 55 Gd 18.28 S 51.05W
Doce Leguas, Cayos de las- 49 Hc 20.55N 79.05W
Doce Leguas, Laberinto de las- 49 Hc 20.39N 78.35W
Docker River 59 Fd 24.58 S 129.03 E
Docksta 8 Ha 63.03N 18.20 E
Doctor Arroyo 48 If 23.40N 100.11W
Doctor Cecilio Baez 55 Dg 25.03 S 56.19W
Doctor Pedro P. Peña 56 Hb 22.26 S 62.22W
Doctor Petru Groza 15 Fc 46.37N 22.25 E
Doda 25 Fb 33.08N 75.34 E
Doda Betta 25 Ff 11.24N 76.44 E
Dodecanese (EN) = Dhodhekánisos 15 Jm 36.20N 27.00 E
Dodecanese (EN)= Nótioi Sporádhes 5 Ih 36.00N 27.00 E
Dodge City 43 Gd 37.45N 100.00W
Dodgeville 45 Ke 42.58N 90.08W
Dodman Point 9 Ik 50.13N 4.48W
Dodoma [3] 36 Gd 6.00 S 36.00 E
Dodoma 31 Ki 6.11 S 35.45 E
Dodona (EN) = Dhodhóni 15 Dj 39.33N 20.46 E
Dodurga 15 Mj 39.48N 29.55 E
Doesburg 12 Ib 52.01N 6.08 E
Doetinchem 11 Mc 51.58N 6.17 E
Dofa 26 Ig 1.47 S 125.22 E
Dogai Coring 27 Ee 34.30N 89.10 E
Doğanbey 15 Jk 38.04N 26.53 E
Doğanşehir 24 Gc 38.06N 37.53 E
Dog Creek 46 Da 51.35N 122.15W
Dogger Bank 5 Ge 55.00N 3.00 E
Dog Island 50 Ec 18.15N 63.13W
Dog Lake [Man.-Can.] 45 Ga 51.02N 98.30W
Dog Lake [Ont.-Can.] 44 Ea 48.18N 84.10W
Dog Lake [Ont.-Can.] 45 Lb 48.46N 89.32W
Dogliani 14 Bf 44.32N 7.56 E
Dōgo 28 Lf 36.15N 133.17 E
Dogonbadān 23 Hc 30.21N 50.48 E
Dogondoutchi 34 Fc 13.38N 4.02 E
Dōgo-San 29 Cd 35.04N 133.14 E
Dog Rocks 49 Ha 24.05N 79.51W
Doğubayazıt 24 Kc 39.32N 44.08 E
Dogwood Point 51c Ab 17.06N 62.38W
Doha (EN)=Ad Dawḩah 22 Hg 25.17N 51.32 E
Dohad 25 Ed 22.50N 74.16 E
Dohāzāri 25 Id 22.10N 92.04 E
Doi Luang Chinag Dao 25 Je 19.23N 98.54 E
Doilungdêqên 27 Ff 29.47N 90.49 E
Doire/Londonderry 6 Fd 55.00N 7.19W
Doire Baltée/Dora Baltea 14 Ce 45.11N 8.03 E
Doische 12 Gd 50.08N 4.45 E
Dojransko jezero 15 Fh 41.13N 22.44 E
Doka 35 Fc 13.31N 35.46 E
Dokhara, Dunes de- 32 Ic 32.50N 6.00 E
Dokka 8 Dd 60.49N 10.05 E
Dokka 7 Cf 60.50N 10.05 E
Dokkum 11 La 53.19N 6.00 E
Dokšicy 7 Gi 54.56N 27.46 E
Doksy 10 Kf 50.34N 14.40 E
Dokučajevsk 16 Jf 47.43N 37.47 E
Dolak, Pulau- 57 Ee 7.50 S 138.30 E
Dolbeau 42 Kg 48.52N 72.14W
Dol-de-Bretagne 11 Ef 48.33N 1.45W
Dôle 11 Lg 47.06N 5.30 E
Doleib Hill 35 Ed 9.22N 31.36 E
Dolenjsko 14 Je 45.50N 15.10 E
Dolgaja, Kosa- 16 Jf 46.40N 37.45 E
Dolgellau 9 Ji 52.44N 3.53W
Dolgi, Ostrov- 17 Ib 69.15N 59.05 E
Dolgi Most 20 Ee 56.45N 96.58 E
Dolianova 14 Dk 39.22N 9.10 E
Dolina 16 De 48.58N 24.01 E
Dolinsk 20 Jg 47.20N 142.50 E
Dolinskaja 19 Df 48.07N 32.44 E
Dolinskoje 15 Mb 47.33N 29.50 E
Dolj [2] 15 Ge 44.10N 23.40 E
Dollart 11 Na 53.17N 7.10 E
Dolly Cays 49 Ib 23.39N 77.22W
Dolni Dăbnik 15 Hf 43.24N 24.26 E
Dolní Dvořiště 10 Kh 48.39N 14.27 E
Dolnomoravský úval 10 Nh 49.00N 17.15 E
Dolnośląskie, Bory- 10 Le 51.25N 15.20 E
Dolný Kubín 10 Pg 49.12N 19.17 E
Dolo 31 Lh 4.11N 42.05 E
Dolomites (EN) = Dolomiti 5 Hf 46.23N 11.51 E
Dolomiti = Dolomites (EN) 5 Hf 46.23N 11.51 E
Dolon, Pereval- 18 Jd 41.48N 75.45 E
Dolonnur/Duolun 27 Kc 42.10N 116.30 E
Dolores [Arg.] 56 Ie 36.20 S 57.40W
Dolores [Guat.] 49 Ce 16.31N 89.25W
Dolores [Ur.] 56 Id 33.33 S 58.13W
Dolores River 46 Kg 38.49N 109.17W
Dolphin, Cape- 56 Ih 51.15 S 58.58W
Dolphin and Union Strait 42 Gc 69.00N 115.00W
Dom, Kūh-e- 24 Of 33.52N 53.00 E
Domačevo 10 Te 51.46N 23.37 E
Domaniç 24 Cc 39.48N 29.37 E
Domantai/Domantaj 8 Ji 55.57N 23.19 E
Domantaj/Domantai 8 Ji 55.57N 23.19 E
Domart-en-Ponthieu 12 Ed 50.04N 2.07 E
Domasa, údolná nádrž- 10 Rg 49.05N 21.47 E
Domažlice 10 Ig 49.27N 12.56 E
Dombaj-Ulgen, Gora- 16 Lh 43.14N 41.46 E
Dombarovski 19 Fe 50.47N 59.34 E
Dombås 6 Gc 62.05N 9.08 E
Dombe Grande 36 Be 12.56 S 13.07 E
Dombes 11 Lh 46.00N 5.03 E
Dombóvár 10 Oj 46.23N 18.07 E
Dombrád 10 Rh 48.14N 21.56 E
Domburg 12 Fc 51.34N 3.30 E
Dôme, Monts- 11 Ii 45.45N 2.55 E
Dôme, Puy de- 11 Ii 45.47N 2.58 E
Domérat 11 Ih 46.21N 2.32 E
Domeyko, Cordillera- 52 Jh 24.30 S 69.00W
Domfront 11 Ff 48.36N 0.39W
Domingo M. Irala 55 Eg 25.54 S 54.43W
Domingos Martins 54 Jh 20.22 S 40.40W
Dominica [1] 39 Mh 15.30N 61.20W
Dominica 38 Mh 15.30N 61.20W
Dominical 49 Fi 9.13N 83.51W
Dominicana, República-= Dominican Republic (EN) [1] 39 Lh 19.00N 70.40W
Dominican Republic (EN)= Dominicana, República- [1] 39 Lh 19.00N 70.40W
Dominica Passage 50 Fe 15.10N 61.15W
Dominica Passage (EN)= Dominique, Canal de la- 50 Fe 15.10N 61.15W
Dominion, Cape - 42 Kc 66.10N 74.30W
Dominique, Canal de la-= Dominica Passage (EN) 50 Fe 15.10N 61.15W
Domino 42 Lf 53.28N 55.46W
Domiongo 36 Dc 4.37 S 21.15 E
Dommartin-Varimont 12 Gf 48.59N 4.46 E
Domme 11 Hj 44.48N 1.13 E
Dommel 11 Lc 51.40N 5.20 E
Domneşti 15 Hd 45.12N 24.50 E
Domo 35 Hd 7.57N 46.51 E
Domodedovo 7 Ii 55.27N 37.47 E
Domodossola 14 Cd 46.07N 8.17 E
Domont 12 Ee 49.02N 2.20 E
Dom Pedrito 56 Jd 30.59 S 54.40W
Dom Pedro 54 Jd 5.00 S 44.27W
Dompierre-sur-Besbre 11 Jh 46.31N 3.41 E
Dompu 26 Gh 8.32 S 118.28 E
Domusnovas 14 Ck 39.19N 8.39 E
Domuyo, Volcán- 52 Ii 36.38 S 70.26W
Don 48 Ed 26.26N 109.02W
Don [Eng.-U.K.] 9 Mh 53.39N 0.59W
Don [Fr.] 11 Eg 47.40N 1.56W
Don 5 Jf 47.04N 39.18 E
Don [Scot.-U.K.] 9 Kd 57.10N 2.04W
Donaldsonville 45 Kk 30.06N 90.59W
Donau=Danube (EN) 5 If 45.20N 29.40 E
Donaueschingen 10 Ei 47.57N 8.30 E
Donaumoos 10 Hh 48.40N 11.15 E
Donauried 10 Gh 48.35N 10.40 E
Donauwörth 10 Gh 48.42N 10.48 E
Don Benito 13 Gf 38.57N 5.52W
Doncaster 9 Lh 53.32N 1.07W
Dondjušany 15 Ka 48.11N 27.31 E
Dondo [Ang.] 31 Ii 9.40 S 14.26 E
Dondo [Moz.] 37 Ec 19.36 S 34.44 E
Dondra Head 21 Ki 5.55N 80.35 E
Donec 5 Kf 47.40N 40.50 E
Doneck 16 Ke 48.21N 39.59 E
Doneck 6 Jf 48.00N 37.48 E
Doneckaja Oblast [3] 19 Df 48.00N 37.45 E
Donecki Krjaž=Donec Ridge (EN) 5 Kh 48.15N 38.45 E
Donec Ridge (EN)=Donecki Krjaž 5 Kh 48.15N 38.45 E
Donegal/Dún na nGall 9 Eg 54.39N 8.06W
Donegal/Dún na nGall [2] 9 Fg 54.50N 8.00W
Donegal Bay/Bá Dhún na nGall 5 Fe 54.30N 8.30W
Donegal Mountains 9 Eg 54.50N 8.10W
Donga 34 Hd 8.19N 10.01 E
Dongara 59 Ce 29.15 S 114.56 E
Dongbei Pingyuan 28 Gc 44.00N 124.00 E
Dongchuan (Tangdan) 27 Hf 26.07N 103.05 E
Dongcun → Lanxian 28 Ae 38.17N 111.38 E
Dong Dao 27 Jc 16.45N 113.00 E
Donge 12 Gc 51.41N 4.49 E
Dong'e (Tongcheng) 28 Df 36.19N 116.14 E
Dongen 12 Gc 51.37N 4.57 E
Donges 11 Dg 47.18N 2.04W
Dongfang (Basuo) 27 Ih 19.14N 108.39 E
Dongfanghong 28 La 46.15N 133.07 E
Dongfeng 28 Hc 42.41N 125.33 E
Donggala 26 Gg 0.40 S 119.44 E
Donggou 27 Ld 39.55N 124.08 E
Dongguang 28 Df 37.54N 116.32 E
Dong Hai=East China Sea (EN) 21 Og 29.00N 125.00 E
Donghai Dao 27 Jg 21.00N 110.25 E
Dong He 27 Hc 42.12N 101.10 E
Dong Hoi 25 Le 17.29N 106.36 E
Dong Jang 21 Ng 23.02N 113.31 E
Dongkala 26 Hh 5.18 S 122.03 E
Dongkan → Binhai 27 Ke 34.00N 119.52 E
Donglan 27 Ig 24.35N 107.22 E
Dongliao He 28 Gc 43.24N 123.42 E
Dongming 28 Cg 35.17N 115.04 E
Dongnan Qiuling 27 Jg 24.00N 113.00 E
Dongo 36 Ce 14.36 S 15.43 E
Dongola (EN)=Dunqulah 31 Kg 19.10N 30.29 E
Dongou 36 Cb 2.02N 18.04 E
Dongoun → Haiyang 28 Ff 36.46N 121.09 E
Dongping 27 Kd 35.51N 116.15 E
Dongping → Anhua 27 Jf 28.27N 111.15 E
Dong Rak, Phanom-= Dangrek Range (EN) 21 Mh 14.25N 104.30 E
Dongsha Dao 27 Kg 20.45N 116.45 E
Dongsha Qundao 21 Ng 20.42N 116.43 E
Dongsheng 27 Id 39.48N 110.00 E
Dongtai 27 Le 32.47N 120.18 E
Dong Taijnar Hu 27 Fd 37.25N 94.00 E
Dongtin Hu 21 Ng 29.18N 112.45 E
Dong Ujimqin Qi (Uliastai) 27 Kc 45.31N 116.58 E
Dongwe 36 De 13.56 S 23.53 E
Dongxiang 27 Kf 28.15N 116.38 E
Dongyang 28 Fj 29.16N 120.14 E
Dongying 27 Kd 37.30N 118.30 E
Dongzhi (Yaodu) 28 Di 30.06N 117.01 E
Donington 12 Bb 52.54N .0.12W
Doniphan 45 Kh 36.37N 90.50W
Donja Brela 14 Kg 43.23N 16.55 E
Donji Miholjac 14 Me 45.45N 18.10 E
Donji Vakuf 14 Lf 44.08N 17.24 E
Dønna 7 Cc 66.06N 12.35 E
Donnacona 44 Lb 46.40N 71.47W
Donner Pass 43 Cd 39.19N 120.20W
Donnersberg 12 Je 49.38N 7.55 E
Donner und Blitzen River 46 Fe 43.17N 118.49W
Donnybrook 59 Df 33.35 S 115.49 E
Donskaja Grjada=Don Upland (EN) 5 Kf 49.10N 42.00 E
Donskoj 16 Kb 54.01N 38.20 E
Don Upland (EN)=Donskaja Grjada 5 Kf 49.10N 42.00 E
Donuzlav, Ozero- 16 Hg 45.25N 33.10 E
Doolette Bay 66 Je 67.55 S 147.00 E
Doon 9 If 55.26N 4.38W
Doonerak, Mount- 40 Ic 67.56N 150.37W
Doorn 12 Hb 52.02N 5.19 E
Doornik/Tournai 11 Jd 50.36N 3.23 E
Door Peninsula 45 Md 44.55N 87.20W
Do Qu 27 He 31.48N 102.09 E
Dora, Lake- 59 Ed 22.05 S 122.56 E
Dora Baltea/Doire Baltée 14 Ce 45.11N 8.03 E
Dorada, Costa- 13 Nc 41.08N 1.10 E
Dora Riparia 14 Be 45.05N 7.44 E
Dorbiljin/Emin 27 Db 46.32N 83.39 E
Dorchester 9 Kk 50.43N 2.26W
Dorchester, Cape - 42 Jc 65.28N 77.30W
Dordabis 37 Bd 22.52 S 17.38 E
Dordogne 5 Ff 45.02N 0.35W
Dordogne [3] 11 Gi 45.10N 0.50 E
Dordrecht [Neth.] 12 Gc 51.48N 4.40 E
Dordrecht [Neth.] 11 Kc 51.49N 4.40 E
Dordrecht [S.Afr.] 37 Df 31.20 S 27.03 E
Dore 11 Ji 46.00N 3.28 E
Dore, Monts- 5 Gf 45.30N 2.45 E
Doré Lake 42 Gf 54.45N 107.20W
Dores do Indaia 54 Ig 19.27 S 45.36W
Dorgali 14 Dj 40.17N 9.35 E
Dori 31 Gg 14.02N 0.02W
Doring 30 Il 31.52 S 18.39 E
Dorking 12 Bc 51.13N 0.20W
Dormagen 12 Ic 51.06N 6.50 E
Dormans 11 Je 49.04N 3.38 E
Dormidontovka 20 Ig 47.45N 134.58 E
Dornbirn 14 Dc 47.25N 9.44 E
Dornoch 9 Id 57.52N 4.02W
Dornoch Firth 9 Id 57.52N 4.02W
Doro 34 Eb 16.09N 0.51W
Dorog 10 Oi 47.43N 18.44 E
Dorogobuž 16 Hb 54.56N 33.15 E
Dorohoi 15 Jb 47.57N 26.24 E
Dorotea 7 Dd 64.16N 16.24 E
Dorre Island 59 Ce 25.10 S 113.05 E
Dorrigo 59 Kf 30.20 S 152.45 E
Dorset [3] 9 Kk 50.50N 2.10W
Dorset 9 Kk 50.55N 2.15W
Dorsten 10 Ce 51.40N 6.58 E
Dortmund 6 Ge 51.31N 7.27 E
Dortmund-Ems-Kanal 10 De 51.32N 7.27 E
Do Rūd 23 Gc 33.28N 49.04 E
Doruma 36 Eb 4.44N 27.42 E
Dörverden 12 Lb 52.51N 9.14 E
Doseo, Bar- 35 Bd 9.01N 19.38 E
Dos Hermanas 13 Gg 37.17N 5.55W
Dos Lagunas 49 Ce 17.42N 89.36W
Dospat 15 Hh 41.39N 24.10 E
Dospat 15 Hh 41.23N 24.05 E
Dosse 10 Ic 53.13N 12.20 E
Dosso 31 Hg 13.03N 3.12 E
Dosso [2] 34 Fc 13.30N 3.30 E
Dossor 19 Ff 47.32N 53.01 E
Dostluk 18 Ef 37.45N 65.22 E
Dothan 43 Je 31.13N 85.24W
Dotnuva 8 Ji 55.18N 23.55 E
Dötyol 24 Gd 36.52N 36.12 E
Douai 11 Jd 50.22N 3.04 E
Douala 31 Hh 4.03N 9.42 E
Douaouir 34 Ea 20.45N 2.30W
Douarnenez 11 Bf 48.06N 4.20W
Douarnenez, Baie de- 11 Bf 48.10N 4.25W
Double Mountain Fork Brazos 45 Gj 33.15N 100.00W
Doubrava 10 Lf 50.03N 15.20 E
Doubs 11 Lh 46.54N 5.02 E
Doubs [3] 11 Mg 47.10N 6.25 E
Doubtful Sound 62 Bf 45.15 S 166.50 E
Doubtless Bay 62 Ea 34.55 S 173.25 E
Douchy-les-Mines 12 Fd 50.18N 3.23 E
Doudeville 12 Ce 49.43N 0.48 E
Doué-la-Fontaine 11 Fg 47.12N 0.17W
Douentza 34 Eb 15.03N 2.57W
Douera 13 Oh 36.40N 2.57 E
Dougga 32 Ib 36.24N 9.13 E
Douglas [Ak.-U.S.] 40 Me 58.16N 134.26W
Douglas [Az.-U.S.] 43 Fe 31.21N 109.33W
Douglas [Ga.-U.S.] 44 Fj 31.31N 82.51W
Douglas [S.Afr.] 37 Ce 29.04 S 23.46 E
Douglas [U.K.] 9 Ig 54.09N 4.28W
Douglas [Wy.-U.S.] 43 Fc 42.45N 105.24W
Douglas Lake 44 Fh 36.00N 83.22W
Douglas Range 66 Qf 70.00 S 69.35W
Doullens 11 Id 50.09N 2.21 E
Doumé 34 He 4.14N 13.27 E
Douna 34 Ec 14.39N 1.43W
Doupovské hory 10 Jf 50.13N 13.08 E
Dour 12 Fd 50.24N 3.47 E
Dourada, Serra- [Braz.] 55 Gb 16.00 S 50.05W
Dourada, Serra- [Braz.] 55 Ha 13.10 S 48.45W
Dourados 53 Kh 22.13 S 54.48W
Dourados, Rio- [Braz.] 55 Ee 21.58 S 54.18W
Dourados, Rio- [Braz.] 55 Id 18.17 S 47.36W
Dourbali 35 Bc 11.49N 15.52 E
Dourdan 11 If 48.32N 2.01 E
Douro 5 Fg 41.08N 8.40W
Douro Litoral 13 Dc 41.05N 8.20W
Doushi → Gong'an 27 Je 30.05N 112.12 E
Douve 11 Ee 49.19N 1.44W
Douvres-la-Delivrande 12 Be 49.17N 0.23W
Douze 11 Fk 43.54N 0.30W
Douzy 12 He 49.40N 5.03 E
Dove 9 Li 52.50N 1.35W
Dove Bugt 41 Jd 76.25N 21.00W
Dove Creek 45 Bh 37.46N 108.54W
Dover [De.-U.S.] 39 Lf 39.10N 75.32W
Dover [Eng.-U.K.] 6 Ge 51.08N 1.19 E
Dover [N.H.-U.S.] 44 Ld 43.12N 70.55W
Dover [Oh.-U.S.] 44 Ge 40.32N 81.30W
Dover, Strait of- 5 Ge 51.00N 1.30 E
Dover, Strait of- (EN)= Calais, Pas de- 5 Ge 51.00N 1.30 E
Dover Foxcroft 44 Mc 45.11N 69.13W
Dovey 9 Ji 52.34N 3.59W
Dovre 8 Cc 61.59N 9.15 E
Dovrefjell 5 Gc 62.10N 9.25 E
Dowa 36 Fe 13.39 S 33.56 E
Dowagiac 44 De 41.59N 86.06W
Dowlatābād 24 Qh 28.20N 57.13 E
Downey 46 Ie 42.26N 112.07W
Downhan Market 12 Cb 52.36N 0.22 E
Downieville 46 Eg 39.34N 120.50W
Downpatrick / Dún Pádraig 9 Hg 54.20N 5.43W
Dow Sar 24 Me 35.06N 48.02 E
Dōzen 29 Cc 36.05N 132.59 E
Dozois, Reservoir- 44 Ib 47.30N 77.00W
Dozulé 12 Be 49.14N 0.03W
Drâa 30 Ff 28.40N 11.07W
Drâa, Cap- 32 Ed 28.44N 11.05W
Drâa, Hamada du- 30 Gf 28.30N 7.30W
Draa el Baguel 32 Ic 30.17N 6.25 E
Draa el Mizan 13 Ph 36.32N 3.50 E
Drac 11 Li 45.13N 5.41 E
Dracena 55 Ge 21.32 S 51.29W
Drach, Cuevas del- 13 Pe 39.32N 3.15 E
Dragalina 15 Kc 44.26N 27.19 E
Dragan 7 Dd 64.00N 15.21 E
Drăgăneşti-Olt 15 He 44.09N 24.42 E
Drăgăneşti-Vlaşca 15 Ie 44.06N 25.36 E
Drăgăşani 15 He 44.39N 24.16 E
Dragobia 15 Cg 42.26N 19.59 E
Dragón, Bocas del-/ Dragon's Mouths 54 Fa 10.45N 61.46W
Dragonera, Isla-/Dragonera, Sa- 13 Oe 39.35N 2.19 E
Dragonera, Sa-/Dragonera, Isla- 13 Oe 39.35N 2.19 E

Index Symbols

[1] Independent Nation
[2] State, Region
[3] District, County
[4] Municipality
[5] Colony, Dependency
Continent
Physical Region
Historical or Cultural Region
Mount, Mountain
Volcano
Hill
Mountains, Mountain Range
Hills, Escarpment
Plateau, Upland
Pass, Gap
Plain, Lowland
Delta
Salt Flat
Valley, Canyon
Crater, Cave
Karst Features
Depression
Polder
Desert, Dunes
Forest, Woods
Heath, Steppe
Oasis
Cape, Point
Coast, Beach
Cliff
Peninsula
Isthmus
Sandbank
Island
Atoll
Rock, Reef
Islands, Archipelago
Rocks, Reefs
Coral Reef
Well, Spring
Geyser
River, Stream
Waterfall Rapids
River Mouth, Estuary
Lake
Salt Lake
Intermittent Lake
Reservoir
Swamp, Pond
Canal
Glacier
Ice Shelf, Pack Ice
Ocean
Sea
Gulf, Bay
Strait, Fjord
Lagoon
Bank
Seamount
Tablemount
Ridge
Shelf
Basin
Escarpment, Sea Scarp
Fracture
Trench, Abyss
National Park, Reserve
Point of Interest
Recreation Site
Cave, Cavern
Historic Site
Ruins
Wall, Walls
Church, Abbey
Temple
Scientific Station
Airport
Port
Lighthouse
Mine
Tunnel
Dam, Bridge

Dragon's Mouths/Dragón, Bocas del- 54 Fa 10.45N 61.46W
Dragør 8 Ei 55.36N 12.41 E
Draguignan 11 Mk 43.32N 6.28 E
Drahanska vrchovina 10 Mg 49.30N 16.45 E
Drain 46 De 43.40N 123.19W
Drake 45 Fc 47.55N 100.23W
Drake, Estrecho de-=Drake Passage (EN) 52 Jk 58.00S 70.00W
Drakensberg 30 Jk 29.00S 29.00 E
Drake Passage (EN)=Drake, Estrecho de- 52 Jk 58.00S 70.00W
Dráma 15 Hh 41.09N 24.09 E
Drammen 6 Hd 59.44N 10.15 E
Dramselva 8 De 59.44N 10.14 E
Drangajokull 7a Aa 66.09N 22.15W
Dranse 11 Mh 46.24N 6.30 E
Drau=Drava (EN) 5 Hf 45.33N 18.55 E
Dráva=Drava (EN) 5 Hf 45.33N 18.55 E
Drava (EN)=Drau 5 Hf 45.33N 18.55 E
Drava (EN)=Dráva 5 Hf 45.33N 18.55 E
Dravograd 14 Jd 46.35N 15.01 E
Drawa 10 Ld 52.52N 15.59 E
Drawno 10 Lc 53.13N 15.45 E
Drawsko, Jezioro- 10 Mc 53.33N 16.10 E
Drawsko Pomorskie 10 Lc 53.32N 15.48 E
Drayton Valley 42 Gf 53.13N 115.00W
Drean 14 Bn 36.41N 7.45 E
Dreieich 12 Ke 50.01N 8.43 E
Drenovci 14 Mf 44.55N 18.55 E
Drenthe [3] 12 Ib 52.45N 6.30 E
Dresden 6 He 51.03N 13.45 E
Dreux 11 Hf 48.44N 1.22 E
Drevsjø 7 Cf 61.54N 12.02 E
Drezdenko 10 Ld 52.51N 15.50 E
Dricēni/Driceni 8 Lh 56.39N 27.11 E
Driceni/Dricēni 8 Lh 56.39N 27.11 E
Driffield 9 Mg 54.01N 0.26W
Driggs 46 Je 43.44N 111.14W
Drina 5 Hg 44.53N 19.21 E
Drincea 15 Fe 44.07N 22.59 E
Drin Gulf (EN)=Drinit, Gjiri i- 15 Ch 41.45N 19.28 E
Drini 5 Hg 41.45N 19.34 E
Drini i Zi 15 Dg 42.05N 20.23 E
Drinit, Gjiri i-=Drin Gulf (EN) 15 Ch 41.45N 19.28 E
Drinjača 14 Nf 44.17N 19.10 E
Drinosi 15 Di 40.17N 20.02 E
Drissa 7 Gi 55.47N 27.57 E
Drisvjaty, Ozero-/Drūkšiu Ežeras 8 Lj 55.37N 26.45 E
Driva 8 Cb 62.40N 8.34 E
Drjanovo 15 Ig 42.58N 25.28 E
Drniš 14 Kg 43.52N 16.09 E
Drøbak 7 Cg 59.39N 10.39 E
Drocea, Vîrful- 15 Fc 46.12N 22.14 E
Drogheda/Droichead Átha 9 Gh 53.43N 6.21W
Drogičin 16 Dc 52.13N 25.10 E
Drogobyč 16 Ce 49.22N 23.33 E
Drohiczyn 10 Sd 52.24N 22.41 E
Droichead Átha/Drogheda 9 Gh 53.43N 6.21W
Droichead na Bandan/Bandon 9 Ej 51.45N 8.45W
Droichead na Banna/Banbridge 9 Gg 54.21N 6.16W
Drokija 16 Ee 48.01N 27.53 E
Drôme 12 Be 49.19N 0.45W
Drôme [3] 11 Lj 44.35N 5.10 E
Drömling 10 Hd 52.29N 11.04 E
Dronero 14 Bf 44.28N 7.22 E
Dronne 11 Fi 45.02N 0.09W
Dronning Fabiola-Fjella 66 Df 71.30S 35.40 E
Dronning Louise Land 41 Jc 76.45N 24.00W
Dronten 11 Lb 52.31N 5.42 E
Dropt 11 Fj 44.35N 0.06W
Drovjanoj 20 Cb 72.25N 72.45 E
Drowning River 45 Na 50.55N 84.35W
Druja 7 Gi 55.47N 27.29 E
Drūkšiu Ežeras/Drisvjaty, Ozero- 8 Lj 55.37N 26.45 E
Druk-Yul→Bhutan [1] 22 Lg 27.30N 90.30 E
Drulingen 12 Jf 48.52N 7.11 E
Drumheller 42 Gf 51.28N 112.42W
Drummond [Mt.-U.S.] 46 Ic 46.40N 113.09W
Drummond [Wi.-U.S.] 45 Kc 46.20N 91.15W
Drummond Island 44 Fb 46.00N 83.40W
Drummond Range 59 Jd 23.30S 147.15 E
Drummondville 42 Kg 45.50N 72.20W
Drummore 9 Ig 54.42N 4.54W
Drumochter, Pass of- 9 Ie 56.50N 4.12W
Drunen 12 Hc 51.41N 5.10 E
Druskininkai/Druskininkaj 7 Fi 54.04N 24.06 E
Druskininkaj/Druskininkai 7 Fi 54.04N 24.06 E
Drut 16 Gc 53.04N 30.35 E
Druten 12 Hc 51.54N 5.38 E
Družba 16 Hc 52.02N 33.59 E
Družba 19 If 45.18N 82.29 E
Družkovka 16 Je 48.36N 37.33 E
Družnaja Gorka 8 Ne 59.11N 30.10 E
Družnino 17 Ih 56.48N 59.29 E
Družno, Jezioro- 10 Pb 54.08N 19.30 E
Drvar 14 Kf 44.22N 16.23 E
Drvenik 14 Lg 43.09N 17.15 E
Drwęca 10 Oc 53.00N 18.42 E
Dryden 42 Ig 49.47N 92.50W
Dry Fork 46 Me 43.30N 105.24W
Drygalski Ice Tongue 66 Kf 75.24S 163.30 E
Drygalski Island 66 Ge 65.45S 92.30 E
Drysdale River 59 Fb 13.59S 126.51 E
Dry Tortugas 43 Kg 24.38N 82.55W
Drzewica 10 Qe 51.27N 20.28 E
Drzewiczka 10 Qe 51.33N 20.35 E
Dschang 34 Hd 5.27N 10.04 E
Dua 36 Db 3.20N 20.53 E
Duaca 54 Ea 10.18N 69.10W
Duancun→Wuxiang 28 Bf 36.50N 112.51 E
Duarte, Pico- 38 Lh 19.00N 71.00W
Duartina 55 Hf 22.24S 49.25W
Dubawnt 42 Hd 64.30N 100.06W
Dubawnt Lake 38 Ic 63.08N 101.30W
Ḍubay'ah, Ra's- 24 Pj 24.20N 54.09 E
Dubayy 22 Hg 25.18N 55.18 E
Dubbo 58 Fh 32.15S 148.36 E
Dübener Heide 10 Ie 51.40N 12.40 E
Dubenski 16 Td 51.29N 56.38 E
Dubesar' 16 Ff 47.17N 29.10 E
Dubh Artach 9 Ge 56.08N 6.39W
Dubica 14 Ke 45.13N 16.48 E
Dublin 43 Ke 32.32N 82.54W
Dublin/Baile Átha Cliath [2] 9 Gh 53.20N 6.15W
Dublin/Baile Átha Cliath 6 Fe 53.20N 6.15W
Dublin Bay/Cuan Bhaile Átha Cliath 9 Gh 53.20N 6.06W
Dubljany 10 Tg 49.26N 23.16 E
Dublon 64d Bb 7.23N 151.53 E
Dubna 8 Lh 56.20N 26.31 E
Dubna 19 Dd 56.47N 37.10 E
Dubnica nad Váhom 10 Oh 48.58N 18.10 E
Dubno 19 Ce 50.29N 25.46 E
Du Bois 44 He 41.06N 78.46W
Dubois [Id.-U.S.] 46 Id 44.10N 112.14W
Dubois [Wy.-U.S.] 46 Ke 43.33N 109.38W
Dubovka 19 Ef 49.03N 44.50 E
Dubovoje 10 Ih 48.08N 23.59 E
Dubreka 34 Cd 9.48N 13.31W
Dubrovica 16 Ed 51.34N 26.34 E
Dubrovnik 6 Hg 42.39N 18.07 E
Dubrovno 7 Hi 54.33N 30.41 E
Dubrovnoje 19 Gd 57.58N 69.25 E
Dubuque 43 Ic 42.30N 90.41W
Dubysa 8 Ji 55.02N 23.27 E
Duc de Gloucester, Iles du-=Duke of Gloucester, Islands (En) 57 Mg 20.38S 143.20W
Duchang 28 Dj 29.16N 116.11 E
Duchesne 46 Jf 40.10N 110.24W
Duchess 59 Hd 21.22S 139.52 E
Ducie Atoll 57 Og 24.40S 124.47W
Duck River 44 Dg 36.02N 87.52W
Duckwater Peak 46 Hg 38.58N 115.26W
Duclair 12 Ce 49.29N 0.53 E
Duc Lap 25 Lf 12.27N 107.38 E
Ducos 51h Bb 14.34N 60.58W
Dudelange/Düdelingen 12 Ie 49.28N 6.06 E
Duderstadt 10 Ge 51.31N 10.16 E
Dudinka 22 Kc 69.25N 86.15 E
Dudley 9 Ki 52.30N 2.05W
Ḍūḍo 35 Id 9.20N 50.14 E
Dudub 35 Hd 6.55N 46.42 E
Dudune 63b Ce 21.21S 167.44 E
Dudváh 10 Ni 47.58N 17.50 E
Dudweiler, Saarbrücken- 12 Je 49.17N 7.02 E
Düdwēyn 35 Gd 9.19N 44.53 E
Dudypta 20 Db 70.55N 89.50 E
Duékoué 34 Dd 6.45N 7.21W
Dueodde 8 Fj 54.59N 15.05 E
Duerna 13 Gb 42.19N 5.54W
Duero 5 Fg 41.08N 8.40W
Dufek Coast 66 Lg 84.30S 179.00W
Duffer Peak 46 Ff 41.40N 118.44W
Duff Islands 57 He 9.50S 167.10 E
Dugi Otok 14 Ii 44.00N 15.00 E
Dugo Selo 14 Ke 45.48N 16.15 E
Du Gué, Rivière- 42 Ke 57.20N 70.46W
Duhovnickoje 16 Pc 52.29N 48.15 E
Duijan Yan 27 He 31.01N 103.28 E
Duiru→Wuchuan 27 If 28.28N 107.57 E
Duisburg 10 Ce 51.26N 6.45 E
Duitama 54 Db 5.50N 73.02W
Dujūma 35 Ge 1.14N 42.34 E
Dukagjini 15 Cg 42.18N 19.45 E
Dūkān 24 Ke 35.56N 44.58 E
Dukan, Sad ad- 24 Kd 36.10N 44.56 E
Dukat 15 Fg 42.26N 22.21 E
Duke of Gloucester Islands (EN)=Duc de Gloucester, Iles du- 57 Mg 20.38S 143.20W
Duke of York 63a Aa 4.10S 152.28 E
Duke of York Bay 42 Jc 65.25N 84.50W
Duk Fadiat 35 Ed 7.45N 31.25 E
Duk Faiwil 35 Ed 7.30N 31.29 E
Dukhān 23 Hd 25.25N 50.48 E
Dukielska, Przełecz- 10 Rg 49.25N 21.42 E
Dukku 34 Hc 10.49N 10.46 E
Dukla 10 Rg 49.34N 21.41 E
Dukou 22 Mg 26.31N 101.44 E
Dūkštas/Dukštas 8 Li 55.32N 26.28 E
Dukštas/Dūkštas 8 Li 55.32N 26.28 E
Dulan (Qagan Us) 22 Lf 36.29N 98.29 E
Dulce, Bahía- 48 Ji 16.30N 98.50W
Dulce, Golfo- 47 Hg 8.36N 83.15W
Dulce, Río- 52 Ji 30.31S 62.32W
Dulce Nombre de Culmi 49 Ef 15.09N 85.37W
Duldurga 20 Gf 50.38N 113.35 E
Dulgalah 20 Ic 67.30N 133.20 E
Dulia 36 Db 2.57N 24.08 E
Dülmen 10 De 51.50N 7.18 E
Dulovka 8 Mg 57.27N 28.29 E
Dulovo 15 Kf 43.49N 27.09 E
Duluth 39 Je 46.47N 92.06W
Dūmā 24 Gf 33.35N 36.24 E
Dumaguete 26 He 9.18N 123.18 E
Dumai 26 Df 1.41N 101.27 E
Dumaran 26 Gd 10.33N 119.51 E
Dumaresq River 59 Ke 28.40S 150.28 E
Dumas [Ar.-U.S.] 45 Kj 33.53N 91.29W
Dumas [Tx.-U.S.] 45 Fi 35.52N 101.58W
Dumayr 24 Gf 33.38N 36.40 E
Dumbarton 9 If 55.57N 4.35W
Dumbéa 63b Cf 22.09S 166.27 E
Dumbrăveni [Rom.] 15 Jb 47.39N 26.25 E
Dumbrăveni [Rom.] 15 Hc 46.14N 24.34 E
Dumfries 9 Jf 55.04N 3.37W
Dumfries and Galloway [3] 9 Jf 55.10N 3.35W
Dumka 25 Hd 24.16N 87.15 E
Dumlupınar 15 Mk 38.52N 30.00 E
Dümmer 10 Ed 52.31N 8.19 E
Dumoine, Lac- 44 Ib 46.52N 77.52W
Dumoine, Rivière- 44 Ib 46.13N 77.50W
Dumont d'Urville 66 Je 66.40S 140.01 E
Dumont D'Urville Sea (EN) 66 Je 63.00S 140.00 E
Dumpu 58 Fe 5.52S 145.46 E
Dümrek 15 Lk 38.40N 28.24 E
Dumuhe 28 La 46.21N 133.33 E
Dumyāṭ=Damietta (EN) 31 Ke 31.25N 31.48 E
Dumyāṭ, Maṣabb- 24 Dg 31.27N 31.51 E
Duna=Danube (EN) 5 If 45.20N 29.40 E
Dunaföldvár 10 Oi 46.48N 18.56 E
Dunaharaszti 10 Pi 47.21N 19.05 E
Dunaj 20 Ih 42.57N 132.20 E
Dunaj=Danube (EN) 5 If 45.20N 29.40 E
Dunajec 10 Qf 50.15N 20.44 E
Dunajevcy 16 Ee 48.51N 26.44 E
Dunajská Streda 10 Ni 47.01N 17.38 E
Dunakeszi 10 Pi 47.38N 19.08 E
Dunántúl 10 Nj 47.00N 18.00 E
Dunărea=Danube (EN) 5 If 45.20N 29.40 E
Dunărea Veche 15 Ld 45.17N 28.02 E
Dunării, Delta-=Danube, Mouths of the- (EN) 5 If 45.30N 29.45 E
Duna-Tisza Köze 10 Pj 46.45N 19.30 E
Dunaújváros 10 Oj 46.58N 18.56 E
Dunav=Danube (EN) 5 If 45.20N 29.40 E
Dunavățu de Jos 15 Me 44.59N 29.13 E
Dunav-Tisa-Dunav kanal 15 Dd 45.10N 20.50 E
Dunback 62 Df 45.23S 170.38 E
Dunbar 9 Kf 56.00N 2.31W
Duncan [Az.-U.S.] 46 Kj 32.43N 109.06W
Duncan [B.C.-Can.] 46 Db 48.47N 123.42W
Duncan [Ok.-U.S.] 43 He 34.30N 97.57W
Duncan Passage 25 If 11.00N 92.00 E
Duncansby Head 5 Fd 58.39N 3.01W
Dundaga 8 Jg 57.31N 22.14 E
Dundalk 44 If 39.15N 76.31W
Dundalk/Dún Dealgan 9 Gg 54.01N 6.25W
Dundalk Bay/Cuan Dhun Dealgan 9 Gh 53.57N 6.17W
Dundas [Grld.] 41 Fc 76.30N 69.00W
Dundas [Ont.-Can.] 44 Hd 43.16N 79.58W
Dundas, Lake- 59 Ef 32.35S 121.50 E
Dundas Peninsula 42 Gb 74.40N 113.00W
Dundas Strait 59 Gb 11.20S 131.35 E
Dún Dealgan/Dundalk 9 Gg 54.01N 6.25W
Dundee [S.Afr.] 37 Ee 28.12S 30.16 E
Dundee [Scot.-U.K.] 6 Fd 56.28N 3.00W
Dund Hot→Zhenglan Qi 28 Cc 42.14N 115.59 E
Dundrum Bay/Cuan Dhún Droma 9 Hg 54.13N 5.45W
Dunedin [Fl.-U.S.] 44 Fk 28.02N 82.47W
Dunedin [N.Z.] 58 Ii 45.53S 170.31 E
Dunfanaghy 9 Ff 55.11N 7.59W
Dunfermline 9 Je 56.04N 3.29W
Dungannon/Dún Geanainn 9 Gg 54.31N 6.46W
Dún Garbhán/Dungarvan 9 Fi 52.05N 7.37W
Dūngarpur 25 Ed 23.50N 73.43 E
Dungarvan/Dún Garbhán 9 Fi 52.05N 7.37W
Dungas 34 Gc 13.04N 9.20 E
Dungau 10 Ih 48.45N 12.30 E
Dún Geanainn/Dungannon 9 Gg 54.31N 6.46W
Dungeness 9 Nk 50.55N 0.58 E
Dungu 36 Eb 3.42N 28.40 E
Dungu 36 Eb 3.37N 28.34 E
Dunhua 27 Mc 43.22N 128.12 E
Dunhuang 27 Fc 40.10N 94.50 E
Dunkerque 11 Ic 51.03N 2.22 E
Dunkery Beacon 9 Jj 51.11N 3.35W
Dunkirk 43 Lc 42.29N 79.21W
Dunkwa 34 Ed 5.58N 1.47W
Dún Laoghaire 9 Gh 53.17N 6.08W
Dún Mánmhai/Dunmanway 9 Dj 51.43N 9.07W
Dunmanway/Dún Mánmhai 9 Dj 51.43N 9.07W
Dunn 44 Hh 35.19N 78.37W
Dún na nGall/Donegal [2] 9 Fg 54.50N 8.00W
Dún na nGall/Donegal 9 Eg 54.39N 8.06W
Dunnellon 44 Fk 29.03N 82.28W
Dunnet Head 9 Jc 58.39N 3.23W
Dunning 45 Ff 41.50N 100.06W
Dún Pádraig/Downpatrick 9 Hg 54.20N 5.43W
Dunqulah=Dongola (EN) 31 Kg 19.10N 30.29 E
Dunqulah al Qadīmah 35 Eb 18.13N 30.45 E
Dunqunāb 35 Fa 21.06N 37.05 E
Dunqunāb, Khalīj- 35 Fa 21.05N 37.08 E
Dunrankin 44 Fa 48.39N 83.04W
Duns 9 Kf 55.47N 2.20W
Dünsberg 12 Kd 50.39N 8.35 E
Dunsmuir 46 Df 41.13N 122.16W
Dunstable 12 Bc 51.53N 0.31W
Dunstan Mountains 62 Cf 44.55S 169.30 E
Dun-sur-Auron 11 Ih 46.53N 2.34 E
Dun-sur-Meuse 12 He 49.23N 5.11 E
Duntroon 62 Df 44.51S 170.41 E
Dunvegan 9 Gd 57.26N 6.35W
Duobukur 27 La 50.19N 124.57 E
Duolun/Dolonnur 27 Kc 42.10N 116.30 E
Duong Dong 25 Kf 10.13N 103.58 E
Dupree 45 Fd 45.03N 101.36W
Duqm 22 Hf 19.41N 57.32 E
Duque de Bragança, Quedas- 30 Ii 9.05S 16.10 E
Duque de Caxias 54 Jh 22.47S 43.18W
Duque de York, Isla- 56 Eh 50.40S 75.20W
Du Quoin 45 Lg 38.01N 89.14W
Durack Range 59 Fc 17.00S 128.00 E
Durack River 59 Fc 15.33S 127.52 E
Durağan 24 Fb 41.25N 35.04 E
Durance 5 Gg 43.55N 4.44 E
Durand 45 Kd 44.38N 91.58W
Durand, Récif- 63b Df 22.02S 168.39 E
Durango [2] 47 Dd 24.50N 104.50W
Durango [Co.-U.S.] 39 If 37.16N 107.53W
Durango [Sp.] 13 Ja 43.10N 2.37W
Durañona 55 Bm 37.15S 60.31W
Durant 43 He 33.59N 96.23W
Duras 11 Gj 44.40N 0.11 E
Duratón 13 Hc 41.37N 4.07W
Durazno 56 Id 33.22S 56.31W
Durazno [2] 55 Dk 33.05S 56.05W
Durazno, Cuchilla Grande del- 55 Dk 33.15S 56.15W
Durazzo (EN)=Durresi 15 Ch 41.19N 19.26 E
Durban 31 Kk 29.55S 30.56 E
Durbe 8 Ih 56.39N 21.14 E
Durbet-Daba, Pereval- 27 Eb 49.37N 89.25 E
Ḍurbo 35 Ic 11.30N 50.18 E
Durbuy 12 Hd 50.21N 5.28 E
Đurđevac 14 Ld 46.02N 17.04 E
Düren 10 Cf 50.48N 6.29 E
Durg 25 Gd 21.11N 81.17 E
Durgapūr 25 Hd 23.30N 87.15 E
Durgen-Nur 27 Fb 47.40N 93.30 E
Durham 9 Lg 54.45N 1.45W
Durham [3] 9 Lg 54.45N 1.40W
Durham [Eng.-U.K.] 9 Lg 54.47N 1.34W
Durham [N.C.-U.S.] 43 Ld 35.59N 78.54W
Durkee 46 Gd 44.36N 117.28W
Durlas/Thurles 9 Fi 52.41N 7.49W
Ḍurmā 23 Ge 24.37N 46.08 E
Durmersheim 12 Kf 48.56N 8.16 E
Durmitor 5 Hg 43.09N 19.02 E
Durnford, Punta- 32 De 23.37N 16.00W
Durresi=Durazzo (EN) 15 Ch 41.19N 19.26 E
Durrësit, Gjiri- 15 Ch 41.16N 19.28 E
Dursey/Oiléan Baoi 9 Cj 51.36N 10.12W
Dursunbey 24 Cc 39.35N 28.38 E
Durtal 11 Fg 47.40N 0.15W
Duru→Wuchuan 27 If 28.28N 107.57 E
Duruksi 35 Hd 8.29N 45.38 E
Durusu Gölü 15 Lh 41.20N 28.38 E
Durūz, Jabal ad- 24 Gf 32.40N 36.44 E
D'Urville Island 61 Dh 40.50S 173.50 E
Dušak 18 Cf 37.15N 60.01 E
Dusa Mareb 35 Hd 5.31N 46.24 E
Dušanbe 22 If 38.35N 68.48 E
Dušeti 16 Nh 42.05N 44.42 E
Dusetos 8 Li 55.42N 26.02 E
Dushan 22 Mg 25.55N 107.36 E
Dushan Hu 28 Dg 35.06N 116.48 E
Dusios Ežeras/Dusja, Ozero- 8 Jj 54.15N 23.45 E
Dusja, Ozero-/Dusios Ežeras 8 Jj 54.15N 23.45 E
Dusky Sound 62 Bf 45.45S 166.30 E
Düsseldorf 6 Ge 51.13N 6.46 E
Dusti 18 Gf 37.22N 68.43 E
Dutch Harbor 40a Eb 53.53N 166.32W
Dutlwe 37 Cd 23.58S 23.54 E
Dutton, Mount- 46 Ig 38.01N 112.13W
Duved 8 Ea 63.24N 12.52 E
Duvergé 49 Ld 18.22N 71.31W
Düvertepe 15 Lj 39.14N 28.27 E
Duvno 14 Lg 43.43N 17.14 E
Duwayhin 23 He 24.16N 51.20 E
Duwayhin, Khawr- 24 Nj 24.20N 51.25 E
Duyfken Point 59 Ib 12.35S 141.40 E
Duyun 27 If 26.20N 107.28 E
Dūz 32 Ic 33.28N 9.01 E
Düzce 23 Da 40.50N 31.10 E
Dve Mogili 15 If 43.36N 25.52 E
Dvina (EN)=Daugava 19 Cd 57.04N 24.03 E
Dvina Gulf (EN)=Dvinskaja Guba 5 Jb 65.00N 39.45 E
Dvinskaja Guba=Dvina Gulf (EN) 5 Jb 65.00N 39.45 E
Dvor 14 Ke 45.04N 16.23 E
Dvuh Cirkov, Gora- 20 Lc 67.30N 168.20 E
Dvůr Králové nad Labem 10 Lf 50.26N 15.48 E
Dwārka 25 Dd 22.14N 68.58 E
Dworshak Reservoir 46 Hc 46.45N 116.00W
Dyer, Cape- 38 Mc 66.37N 61.18W
Dyero 34 Dc 12.50N 6.30W
Dyer Plateau 66 Qf 70.45S 65.30W
Dyersburg 43 Jd 36.03N 89.23W
Dyfed [3] 9 Ji 52.05N 4.00W
Dyhtau, Gora- 16 Mh 43.05N 43.12 E
Dyje 10 Mh 48.37N 16.56 E
Dyjsko-Svratecký úval 10 Mh 48.56N 16.25 E
Dyle 12 Gd 50.57N 4.40 E
Dylewska Góra 10 Pc 53.34N 19.57 E
Dynów 10 Sg 49.49N 22.14 E
Dyr, Djebel- 14 Cn 36.13N 8.46 E
Dyrhólaey 5 Ec 63.24N 19.08W
Dysnų Ežeras/Disnaj, Ozero- 7 Gi 55.35N 26.32 E
Dytike Rodhópi 15 Hh 41.45N 24.05 E
Dzabhan 21 Le 48.54N 93.23 E
Džalagaš 19 Gf 45.05N 64.40 E
Džalal-Abad 18 Id 40.56N 73.05 E
Džalal-Abadskaja oblast 18 Hd 41.40N 71.50 E
Džalilabad 19 Eh 39.12N 48.31 E
Džalinda 20 Hf 53.31N 123.59 E
Džambejty 16 Rd 50.14N 52.38 E
Džambul 22 Je 42.54N 71.22 E
Džambul 19 Hf 47.17N 71.42 E
Džambulskaja Oblast [3] 19 Hg 44.30N 72.30 E
Dzamyn-Ud 27 Jc 43.50N 111.45 E
Džanak 16 Si 40.30N 55.35 E
Džanga 19 Fg 40.01N 53.10 E
Džankoj 19 Df 45.42N 34.22 E
Džansugurov 19 Hf 45.23N 79.29 E
Džanybek 19 Ef 49.24N 46.50 E
Dzaoudzi 31 Lj 12.47S 45.17 E
Džardžan 20 Hc 68.55N 124.05 E
Džargalant 27 Gb 47.20N 99.35 E
Džargalant 27 Ib 48.35N 105.50 E
Džarkurgan 19 Gh 37.29N 67.25 E
Džava 16 Mh 42.24N 43.53 E
Džebariki-Haja 20 Id 62.23N 135.50 E
Džebel [Bul.] 15 Ih 41.30N 25.18 E
Džebel 16 Sj 39.37N 54.18 E
Džebrail 16 Oj 39.23N 47.01 E
Dzereg 27 Fb 47.08N 92.50 E
Džergalan 18 Lc 42.33N 79.02 E
Dzermuk 16 Nj 39.48N 45.39 E
Dzeržinsk 16 Ec 53.44N 27.08 E
Dzeržinsk 19 Ed 56.16N 43.32 E
Dzeržinsk 16 Je 48.22N 37.50 E
Dzeržinskaja, Gora- 8 Lk 53.53N 27.10 E
Dzeržinskoje 20 Ee 56.49N 95.18 E
Džetygara 22 Id 52.11N 61.12 E
Džetysaj 18 Gd 40.49N 68.20 E
Džezkazgan 19 Gf 47.53N 67.27 E
Džezkazgan 22 Ie 47.47N 67.46 E
Džezkazganskaja Oblast [3] 19 Gf 47.30N 70.00 E
Dzhugdzhur Range (EN)=Džugdžur, Hrebet- 21 Pd 58.00N 136.00 E
Działdówka 10 Qd 52.58N 20.05 E
Działdowo 10 Qc 53.15N 20.10 E
Działoszyce 10 Qf 50.22N 20.21 E
Dzibalchén 48 Oh 19.31N 89.45W
Dzibilchaltún 48 Og 21.05N 89.36W
Dzierzgoń 10 Pc 53.56N 19.21 E
Dzierżoniów 10 Mf 50.44N 16.39 E
Džirgatal 18 He 39.13N 71.12 E
Džizak 19 Gg 40.07N 67.52 E
Džizakskaja Oblast [3] 19 Gg 40.20N 67.40 E
Džugdžur, Hrebet-=Dzhugdzhur Range (EN) 21 Pd 58.00N 136.00 E
Džūkste/Džukste 8 Jh 56.45N 23.10 E
Džukste/Džūkste 8 Jh 56.45N 23.10 E
Džulfa 16 Nj 38.59N 45.35 E
Džuma 18 Fe 39.44N 66.39 E
Dzun-Bajan 27 Jc 44.26N 110.03 E
Dzungarian Basin (EN)=Junggar Pendi 21 Ke 45.00N 88.00 E
Dzungarian Gate (EN)=Alataw Shankou 21 Ke 45.25N 82.25 E
Dzungarian Gate (EN)=Džungarskije Vorota 21 Ke 45.25N 82.25 E
Džungarski Alatau, Hrebet- 21 Ke 45.00N 81.00 E
Džungarskije Vorota=Dzungarian Gate (EN) 21 Ke 45.25N 82.25 E
Dzun-Hara 27 Ib 48.40N 106.40 E
Dzun-Mod 27 Ib 47.50N 106.57 E
Džurak-Sal 16 Mf 47.18N 43.36 E
Džusaly 19 Gf 45.29N 64.05 E
Džvari 16 Mh 42.42N 42.02 E

E

Éadan Doire/Edenderry 9 Fh 53.21N 7.03W
Eads 45 Eg 38.29N 102.47W
Eagle 40 Kd 64.46N 141.16W
Eagle 42 Lf 53.35N 57.25W
Eagle Creek 46 La 52.22N 107.24W
Eagle Lake 44 Mb 47.02N 68.36W
Eagle Lake [Ca.-U.S.] 46 Ef 40.39N 120.44W
Eagle Lake [Me.-U.S.] 44 Mb 46.20N 69.20W
Eagle Lake [Ont.-Can.] 45 Jb 49.42N 93.13W
Eagle Mountain 45 Kc 47.54N 90.33W
Eagle Nest 45 Dh 36.35N 105.14W
Eagle Pass 43 Gf 28.43N 100.30W
Eagle Peak [Ca.-U.S.] 43 Cc 41.17N 120.12W
Eagle Peak [Tx.-U.S.] 45 Dk 30.56N 105.01W
Eagle River [Ak.-U.S.] 40 Jd 61.19N 149.34W
Eagle River [Wi.-U.S.] 45 Ld 45.55N 89.15W
Eagle Summit 40 Jc 65.30N 145.38W
Ealing, London- 12 Bc 51.30N 0.19W
Ear Falls 45 Ja 50.38N 93.13W
Earn 9 Je 56.25N 3.30W
Earn, Loch- 9 Ie 56.28N 4.10W
Earnslaw, Mount- 62 Cf 44.37S 168.25 E
Easley 44 Fh 34.50N 82.36W
East Alligator River 59 Gb 12.08S 132.42 E
East Anglia 9 Ni 52.25N 1.00 E
East Angus 44 Lc 45.29N 71.40W
East Bay [Can.] 42 Jd 64.05N 81.30W
East Bay [U.S.] 45 Ll 29.05N 89.15W
East Berlin = Berlin 6 He 52.31N 13.24 E
Eastbourne [Eng.-U.K.] 9 Nk 50.46N 0.17 E
Eastbourne [N.Z.] 62 Fd 41.17S 174.54 E
East Caicos 49 Lc 21.41N 71.30W
East Cape [Fl.-U.S.] 44 Gm 25.07N 81.05W
East Cape [N.Z.] 57 Ih 37.41S 178.33 E
East Caroline Basin (EN) 3 Ii 4.00N 146.45 E
East Chicago 44 De 41.38N 87.27W
East China Sea (EN)=Dong Hai 21 Og 29.00N 125.00 E
East China Sea (EN)=Higashi-Shina-Kai 21 Og 29.00N 125.00 E
East Coast [2] 62 Gc 38.20S 177.50 E
East Dereham 9 Ni 52.41N 0.56 E
Eastend 46 Kb 49.31N 108.48W
East Entrance 64a Bb 7.50N 134.40 E
Easter Island (EN)=Pascua, Isla de-/Rapa Nui 57 Qg 27.07S 109.22W
Easter Island (EN)=Rapa Nui/Pascua, Isla de- 57 Qg 27.07S 109.22W
Eastern [Ghana] [3] 34 Ed 6.30N 0.30W
Eastern [Kenya] [3] 36 Gb 0.05N 38.00 E
Eastern [S.L.] [3] 34 Cd 8.15N 11.00W
Eastern [Ug.] [3] 36 Fb 1.30N 33.50 E
Eastern [Zam.] [3] 36 Fe 13.00S 32.15 E
Eastern Fields 60 Dj 10.03S 145.22 E

Index Symbols

[1] Independent Nation
[2] State, Region
[3] District, County
[4] Municipality
[5] Colony, Dependency
Continent
Physical Region
Historical or Cultural Region
Mount, Mountain
Volcano
Hill
Mountains, Mountain Range
Hills, Escarpment
Plateau, Upland
Pass, Gap
Plain, Lowland
Delta
Salt Flat
Valley, Canyon
Crater, Cave
Karst Features
Depression
Polder
Desert, Dunes
Forest, Woods
Heath, Steppe
Oasis
Cape, Point
Coast, Beach
Cliff
Peninsula
Isthmus
Sandbank
Island
Atoll
Rock, Reef
Islands, Archipelago
Rocks, Reefs
Coral Reef
Well, Spring
Geyser
River, Stream
Waterfall Rapids
River Mouth, Estuary
Lake
Salt Lake
Intermittent Lake
Reservoir
Swamp, Pond
Canal
Glacier
Ice Shelf, Pack Ice
Ocean
Sea
Gulf, Bay
Strait, Fjord
Lagoon
Bank
Seamount
Tablemount
Ridge
Shelf
Basin
Escarpment, Sea Scarp
Fracture
Trench, Abyss
National Park, Reserve
Point of Interest
Recreation Site
Cave, Cavern
Historic Site
Ruins
Wall, Walls
Church, Abbey
Temple
Scientific Station
Airport
Port
Lighthouse
Mine
Tunnel
Dam, Bridge

Eastern Ghats 21 Jh 14.00N 78.50 E
Eastern Point 51b Ab 18.07N 63.01W
Eastern Sayans (EN) = Vostočny Sajan 21 Ld 53.00N 97.00 E
Eastern Siberia (EN) 21 Rc 65.00N 155.00 E
Eastern Sierra Madre (EN) = Madre Oriental, Sierra- 38 Jg 22.00N 99.30W
Eastern Turkistan (EN) 21 Jf 40.00N 80.00 E
East Falkland/Soledad, Isla- 52 Kk 51.45 S 58.50W
East Fork 45 Ie 42.41N 94.12W
East Friesland (EN) = Ostfriesland 10 Dc 53.20N 7.40 E
East Frisian Islands (EN) = Ostfriesische Inseln 10 Dc 53.45N 7.25 E
East Grand Forks 45 Hc 47.56N 97.01W
East Grand Rapids 44 Ed 42.56N 85.35W
East Greenland (EN) = Østgrønland [2] 41 Id 72.00N 35.00W
East Grinstead 9 Mj 51.08N 0.01W
East Ilsley 12 Ac 51.32N 1.17W
East Kilbride 9 If 55.46N 4.10W
East Lansing 44 Ed 42.44N 84.29W
East Las Vegas 46 Hh 36.07N 115.01W
Eastleigh 9 Lk 50.58N 1.22W
East London 31 Jl 33.00 S 27.55 E
East Lynn Lake 44 Ff 38.05N 82.20W
Eastmain 42 Jf 52.15N 78.34W
Eastmain 42 Jf 52.14N 78.31W
Eastman 44 Fi 32.12N 83.11W
East Mariana Basin (EN) 3 Jh 12.00N 153.00 E
East Midlands Airport 12 Ab 52.50N 1.20W
East Novaya Zemlya Trough (EN) 67 Hd 73.30N 61.00 E
Easton 44 Je 40.41N 75.13W
East Pacific Rise (EN) 3 Ml 20.00 S 110.00W
East Point 44 Ei 33.40N 84.27W
East Point [B.V.I.] 51a Db 18.43N 64.16W
East Point [V.I.U.S.] 51a Dc 17.46N 64.33W
Eastport 44 Nc 44.54N 67.00W
East Pryor Mountain 46 Kd 45.14N 108.30W
East Retford 9 Mh 53.19N 0.56W
East Road 12 Cd 51.00N 1.02 E
East Schelde (EN) = Oosterschelde 11 Jc 51.30N 4.00 E
East Scotia Basin (EN) 52 Mk 57.00 S 35.00W
East Siberian Sea (EN) = Vostočno Sibirskoje More 67 Cd 74.00N 166.00 E
East St. Louis 43 Id 38.38N 90.05W
East Sussex [3] 9 Nk 50.55N 0.15 E
East Tavaputs Plateau 46 Kg 39.45N 109.30W
East Wear Bay 12 Dc 51.08N 1.18 E
Eaton 44 Ef 39.44N 84.37W
Eatonia 46 Ka 51.13N 109.23W
Eatonton 44 Fi 33.20N 83.23W
Eatonville 46 Dc 46.51N 122.17W
Eau Claire 43 Ic 44.49N 91.31W
Eau-Claire, Lac à l' - 42 Ke 56.20N 74.00W
Eauripik Atoll 57 Fd 6.42N 143.03 E
Eauripik Ridge (EN) 60 Cg 3.00N 142.00 E
Eauze 11 Gk 43.52N 0.06 E
Ebano 48 Jf 22.13N 98.24W
Ebbegebirge 10 De 51.10N 7.45 E
Ebbw Vale 9 Jj 51.47N 3.12W
Ebebiyin 34 He 2.09N 11.20 E
Ebeltoft 8 Dh 56.12N 10.41 E
Ebensburg 44 He 40.28N 78.44W
Ebensee 14 Hc 47.48N 13.46 E
Eberbach 10 Eg 49.28N 8.59 E
Eber Gölü 24 Dc 38.38N 31.12 E
Ebersbach 10 Ke 51.01N 14.35 E
Eberswalde 10 Jd 52.50N 13.50 E
Ebetsu 28 Pc 43.07N 141.34 E
Ebino 28 Kh 32.02N 130.47 E
Ebinur Hu 21 Ke 44.55N 82.55 E
Ebla 23 Eb 35.42N 36.50 E
Ebo 36 Ce 11.02 S 14.40 E
Ebola 36 Db 3.20N 20.57 E
Eboli 14 Jj 40.36N 15.04 E
Ebolowa 31 Ih 2.54N 11.09 E
Ebombo 36 Ed 5.42 S 26.07 E
Ebon Atoll 57 Hd 4.38N 168.43 E
Ebre/Ebro 5 Gg 40.43N 0.54 E
Ebre, Delta de l'-/Ebro, Delta del- 13 Md 40.43N 0.54 E
Ebril, Récif- 61 Od 22.40 S 133.30W
Ebro/Ebre 5 Gg 40.43N 0.54 E
Ebro, Delta del-/Ebre, Delta de l'- 13 Md 40.43N 0.54 E
Ebro, Embalse del- 13 Ia 43.00N 3.58W
Ebschloh 10 Ef 50.58N 8.15 E
Ecaussines 12 Gd 50.34N 4.10 E
Ecbatana 24 Me 34.48N 48.30 E
Eceabat 15 Ji 40.11N 26.21 E
Echdeiria 32 Ed 27.14N 10.27W
Echegarate, Puerto de- 13 Jb 42.57N 2.14W
Echeng [China] 28 Ci 30.24N 114.52 E
Echeng [China] 27 Kd 36.10N 116.03 E
Echez 11 Gk 43.28N 0.02 E
Echigo-Sanmyaku 29 Fc 37.30N 139.15 E
Echizen-Misaki 29 Dd 35.59N 135.57 E
Echo Bay 39 Hc 66.04N 118.00W
Echo Seamount (EN) 32 Dd 25.23N 19.25W
Echt 12 Hc 51.06N 5.52 E
Echternach 12 Ie 49.49N 6.25 E
Echuca 59 Ig 36.10 S 144.45 E
Echzell 12 Kd 50.23N 8.52 E
Ecija 13 Gg 37.32N 5.05W
Eckernförde 10 Fb 54.28N 9.50 E
Eckerö 7 Ef 60.15N 19.35 E
Eclipse Sound 42 Jb 72.40N 79.30W
Ečmiadzin 19 Eg 40.09N 44.18 E
Ecommoy 11 Gg 47.50N 0.16 E
Ecos 12 De 49.10N 1.39 E
Ecouis 12 De 49.19N 1.26 E
Écouves, Forêt d'- 11 Gf 48.32N 0.04 E
Écrin, Barre des- 11 Mj 44.55N 6.22 E
Ecuador [2] 53 If 2.00 S 77.30W
Ecury-sur-Coole 12 Gf 48.54N 4.20 E
Ed 7 Cf 58.54N 11.56 E
Edam-Volendam 12 Hb 52.30N 5.03 E
Edane 8 Ee 59.38N 12.49 E
Eday 9 Kb 59.11N 2.47W
Edchera 32 Ed 27.02N 13.04W
Eddrachillis Bay 9 Hc 58.19N 5.15W
Eddystone Point 59 Jh 41.00 S 148.20 E
Eddystone Rocks 9 Ik 50.15N 4.10W
Eddyville 44 Cg 37.03N 88.04W
Ede [Neth.] 11 Lb 52.03N 5.40 E
Ede [Nig.] 34 Fd 7.44N 4.26 E
Edéa 31 Ih 3.48N 10.08 E
Ed Edd 35 Gc 13.56N 41.40 E
Edefors 7 Ec 66.13N 20.54 E
Edéia 55 Hc 17.18 S 49.55W
Edelény 10 Qh 48.18N 20.44 E
Eden 9 Jg 54.57N 3.01W
Eden [Austl.] 59 Jg 37.04 S 149.54 E
Eden [Tx.-U.S.] 45 Gk 31.13N 99.51W
Edenburg 37 De 29.45 S 25.56 E
Edenderry/Éadan Doire 9 Fh 53.21N 7.03W
Edenkoben 12 Ke 49.17N 8.09 E
Edenton 44 Ig 36.04N 76.39W
Eder 10 Fe 51.13N 9.27 E
Edersee 12 Lc 51.11N 9.03 E
Edertal 12 Lc 51.09N 9.09 E
Edewecht 12 Ja 53.08N 7.59 E
Edgar Ranges 59 Ec 18.43 S 123.25 E
Edgartown 44 Le 41.23N 70.31W
Edgecumbe 62 Gb 37.58 S 176.50 E
Edgeley 45 Gc 46.22N 98.43W
Edgell 42 Ld 61.50N 65.00W
Edgemont 45 Ee 43.18N 103.50W
Edgeøya 67 Jd 77.45N 22.30 E
Édhessa 15 Fi 40.48N 22.03 E
Edina 45 Jd 44.55N 93.20W
Edinburg 43 Hf 26.18N 98.10W
Edinburgh 6 Fd 55.57N 3.13W
Edinburgh, Arrecife- 49 Ff 14.50N 82.39W
Edincik 24 Bb 40.20N 27.51 E
Edingen/Enghien 12 Gd 50.42N 4.02 E
Edirne 24 Bb 41.40N 26.34 E
Edisto Island 44 Gi 32.35N 80.10W
Edisto River 44 Gi 32.39N 80.24W
Edith, Mount- 46 Jc 46.26N 111.11W
Edith Ronne Land (EN) 66 Qf 78.30 S 61.00W
Edjeleh 32 Id 27.42N 9.53 E
Edjereh 32 He 24.35N 4.30 E
Édjérir 34 Fb 18.06N 0.50 E
Edmond 45 Hi 35.39N 97.29W
Edmonds 46 Dc 47.48N 122.22W
Edmonton 39 Hd 53.33N 113.28W
Edmundston 42 Kg 47.22N 68.20W
Edna 45 Hl 28.42N 96.39W
Edremit 23 Cb 39.35N 27.01 E
Edremit, Gulf of- (EN) = Edremit Körfezi 24 Bc 39.30N 26.45 E
Edremit Körfezi = Edremit, Gulf of- (EN) 24 Bc 39.30N 26.45 E
Edsbro 7 Eg 59.54N 18.29 E
Edsbruk 8 Gf 58.02N 16.28 E
Edsbyn 8 Fc 61.23N 15.49 E
Edson 42 Ff 53.35N 116.26W
Edsvalla 8 Ee 59.26N 13.13 E
Eduardo Castex 56 He 35.54 S 64.18W
Eduni, Mount- 42 Ed 64.08N 128.10W
Edward, Lake- 30 Ji 0.25 S 29.30 E
Edward, Lake- (EN) = Rutanzige, Lac- 30 Ji 0.25 S 29.30 E
Edwards Creek 59 He 28.21 S 135.51 E
Edwards Plateau 38 If 31.20N 101.00W
Edward VIII Bay 66 Ee 66.50 S 57.00 E
Edward VII Peninsula 66 Mf 77.40 S 155.00W
Edzo 42 Fd 62.47N 116.08W
Eeklo 11 Jc 51.11N 3.34 E
Eelde 12 Ia 53.08N 6.33 E
Eel River 43 Cc 40.40N 124.20W
Eem 12 Hb 52.16N 5.20 E
Eems 11 Na 53.19N 7.03 E
Eemskanaal 12 Ia 53.19N 6.57 E
Eenrum 12 Ia 53.23N 6.25 E
Eersel 12 Hc 51.22N 5.19 E
Eesti = Estonskaja SSR 19 Cd 59.00N 26.00 E
Eesti Nõukogude Socialistlik Vabarijk/Estonskaja SSR → Eesti 19 Cd 59.00N 26.00 E
Eesti NSV → Eesti 19 Cd 59.00N 26.00 E
Efaté, Ile- 57 Hf 17.40 S 168.25 E
Eferding 14 Ib 48.19N 14.01 E
Efes = Ephesus (EN) 15 Kl 37.55N 27.20 E
Effingham 45 Lg 39.07N 88.33W
Eflâni 24 Eb 41.26N 32.57 E
Eforie 15 Le 44.01N 28.38 E
Ega 13 Kb 42.19N 1.55W
Egadi, Isole- = Egadi Islands (EN) 5 Hh 38.00N 12.15 E
Egadi Islands (EN) = Egadi, Isole- 5 Hh 38.00N 12.15 E
Egan Range 46 Hg 39.00N 115.00W
Eganville 44 Ic 47.33N 77.06W
Egbe 34 Gd 8.13N 5.31 E
Ege Denizi = Aegean Sea (EN) 5 Ih 39.00N 25.00 E
Egedesminde/Ausiait 67 Nc 68.50N 52.45W
Egegik 40 He 58.13N 157.22W
Egentliga Finland/Varsinais-Suomi 8 Jd 60.40N 22.30 E
Eger 10 Kf 50.32N 14.08 E
Eger 10 Qi 47.54N 20.23 E
Egersund 7 Ag 58.27N 6.00 E
Egerton, Mount- 59 Dd 24.45 S 117.45 E
Egeskov 8 Di 55.10N 10.30 E
Eggegebirge 10 Ee 51.40N 8.55 E
Eggenfelden 10 Ih 48.24N 12.46 E
Eggenstein Leopoldshafen 12 Ke 49.05N 8.23 E
Eggum 7 Cb 68.19N 13.42 E
Eghezée 12 Gd 50.36N 4.56 E
Egijn-Gol 27 Ha 49.24N 103.36 E
Egletons 11 Ii 45.24N 2.03 E
Eglinton 42 Fa 75.45N 118.50W
Egmont, Cape- 61 Dg 39.17 S 173.45 E
Egmont, Mount- 62 Fc 39.18 S 174.04 E
Egnazia 14 Lj 40.50N 17.25 E
Eğridir 24 Dd 37.52N 30.51 E
Eğridir Gölü 23 Db 38.02N 30.53 E
Eğrigöz Dağ 15 Mj 39.21N 29.07 E
Egtved 8 Ci 55.37N 9.18 E
Éguas ou Correntina, Rio das- 55 Ja 13.26 S 44.14W
Eguey 30 Ig 16.10N 16.10 E
Egvekinot 22 Tc 66.19N 179.10 E
Egypt (EN) = Mişr [1] 31 Jf 27.00N 30.00 E
Eha Amufu 34 Gd 6.40N 7.46 E
Ehen Hudag → Alxa Youqi 27 Hd 39.12N 101.40 E
Ehime Ken [2] 28 Lh 33.35N 132.40 E
Ehingen 10 Fh 48.17N 9.44 E
Ehrang, Trier- 12 Ie 49.49N 6.41 E
Ehrwald 14 Ec 47.24N 10.55 E
Ei 29 Bf 31.13N 130.30 E
Eiao, Ile- 57 Me 8.00 S 140.40W
Eibar 13 Ja 43.11N 2.28W
Eibergen 12 Ib 52.07N 6.40 E
Eichsfeld 10 Ge 51.25N 10.20 E
Eichstätt 10 Hh 48.53N 11.11 E
Eickelborn, Lippetal- 12 Kc 51.39N 8.13 E
Eide 8 Bb 62.55N 7.26 E
Eider 10 Eb 54.19N 8.58 E
Eiderstedt 10 Eb 54.22N 8.50 E
Eidet 7 Cd 64.27N 13.37 E
Eidfjord 7 Bf 60.28N 7.05 E
Eidfjorden 8 Bd 60.25N 6.45 E
Eidslandet 8 Ad 60.44N 5.45 E
Eidsvåg 7 Be 62.47N 8.03 E
Eidsvoll 7 Cf 60.19N 11.14 E
Eidsvollfiellet 41 Nc 79.00N 13.00 E
Eierlandse Gat 12 Ga 53.12N 4.52 E
Eifel 10 Cf 50.15N 6.45 E
Eiffel Flats 37 Dc 18.15 S 29.59 E
Eigenbrakel/Braine-l'Alleud 12 Gd 50.41N 4.22 E
Eigerøya 8 Af 58.25N 5.55 E
Eigg 9 Ge 56.54N 6.10W
Eight Degree Channel 21 Ji 8.00N 73.00 E
Eights Coast 66 Pf 73.30 S 96.00W
Eighty Mile Beach 59 Ec 19.45 S 121.00 E
Eigrim, Jabal- 35 Fb 19.22N 35.18 E
Eijsden 12 Hd 50.46N 5.42 E
Eikeren 8 Ce 59.40N 10.00 E
Eikesdalsvatnet 8 Cb 62.35N 8.10 E
'Eilai 35 Eb 16.33N 30.54 E
Eildon, Lake- 59 Jg 37.10 S 145.50 E
Eilenburg 10 Ie 51.28N 12.37 E
Eiler Rasmussen, Kap- 41 Kb 82.40N 20.00W
Eil Malk 64a Ac 7.09N 134.22 E
Eina 8 Dd 60.38N 10.36 E
Einasleigh 59 Ic 18.31 S 144.05 E
Einasleigh River 59 Ic 17.30 S 142.17 E
Einbeck 10 Fe 51.49N 9.52 E
Eindhoven 11 Lc 51.26N 5.28 E
Einsiedeln 14 Cc 47.08N 8.45 E
Éire/Ireland [1] 6 Fe 53.00N 8.00W
Eiriksjökull 7a Bb 64.46N 20.24W
Eirunepé 53 Jf 6.40 S 69.52W
Eisack/Isarco 14 Fd 46.27N 11.18 E
Eisacktal/Isarco, Valle- 14 Fd 46.45N 11.35 E
Eisacktal/Valle Isarco 14 Fd 46.45N 11.35 E
Eisenach 10 Gf 50.59N 10.19 E
Eisenberg 10 Hf 50.58N 11.54 E
Eisenberg 12 Kc 51.15N 8.50 E
Eisenberg (Pfalz) 12 Ke 49.33N 8.06 E
Eisenerz 14 Ic 47.32N 14.53 E
Eisenerzer Alpen 14 Ic 47.30N 14.40 E
Eisenhüttenstadt 10 Kd 52.10N 14.42 E
Eisenstadt 14 Kc 47.51N 16.31 E
Eisenwurzen 14 Jc 47.56N 15.02 E
Eišiškės/Ejšiškes 7 Fi 54.14N 25.02 E
Eisleben 10 He 51.32N 11.33 E
Eitorf 12 Jd 50.46N 7.27 E
Eivissa/Ibiza = Iviza (EN) 5 Gh 39.00N 1.25 E
Eje, Sierra del- 13 Fb 42.20N 6.55W
Ejea de los Caballeros 13 Kb 42.08N 1.08W
Ejeda 37 Gd 24.19 S 44.21 E
Ejido 54 Db 8.33N 71.14W
Ejido Insurgentes 48 De 25.12N 111.45W
Ejin Horo Qi (Altan Xiret) 27 Id 39.31N 109.45 E
Ejin Qi 22 Me 41.50N 100.50 E
Ejšiškes/Eišiškės 7 Fi 54.14N 25.02 E
Ejura 34 Ed 7.23N 1.22W
Ejutla de Crespo 47 Ee 16.34N 96.44W
Ekalaka 46 Md 45.53N 104.33W
Ekecek Dağı 24 Fc 38.39N 34.03 E
Ekenäs/Tammisaari 7 Fg 59.58N 23.26 E
Ekeren, Antwerpen- 11 Kc 51.17N 4.25 E
Eket 34 Ge 4.39N 7.56 E
Eketahuna 62 Fd 40.39 S 175.44 E
Ekhinádhes Nísoi 15 Ek 38.25N 21.02 E
Ekiatapski Hrebet 20 Mc 68.40N 177.50 E
Ekibastuz 19 He 51.42N 75.22 E
Ekimčan 20 If 53.07N 133.02 E
Ekoli 36 Dc 0.23 S 24.16 E
Ekoln 8 Ge 59.45N 17.35 E
Ekombe 36 Db 1.16N 21.36 E
Ekonda 20 Fc 65.47N 105.17 E
Eksjö 7 Dh 57.40N 14.57 E
Ekuma 37 Bc 18.10 S 15.47 E
Ekwan 42 Jf 53.12N 82.15W
El Aaiún 31 Ff 27.10N 13.12W
El Aargub 32 De 23.37N 15.52W
El Aatf 32 De 23.30N 15.30W
El Abadia 13 Nh 36.13N 1.40 E
El-Abd 13 Mi 35.29N 0.42 E
El Abiodh Sidi Cheikh 32 Hc 32.53N 0.34 E
El 'Açâba [3] 32 Ef 16.30N 12.00W
El 'Açâba 30 Fg 16.49N 12.05W
El Adeb Larache 32 Id 27.22N 8.52 E
El Affroun 13 Oh 36.28N 2.37 E
Elafónisi Channel (EN) = Elafonísou, Stenón- 15 Fm 36.25N 23.00 E
Elafónisos 15 Fm 36.29N 22.58 E
Elafonísou Stenón- = Elafónisi Channel (EN) 15 Fm 36.25N 23.00 E
El Agreb 32 Ic 30.48N 5.30 E
El Aguilar 56 Gb 32.12 S 65.42W
El Álamo 48 Ab 31.34N 116.02W
El Alia 32 Ic 32.42N 5.26 E
El-Amria 13 Ki 35.32N 1.01W
Elan 15 Lc 46.06N 28.04 E
El Andévalo 13 Fg 37.40N 7.00W
El Aouinet 14 Bo 35.52N 7.54 E
El Arahal 13 Gg 37.16N 5.33W
El Aricha 32 Gc 34.13N 1.16W
Elása 15 Jn 35.17N 26.20 E
Elassón 15 Fj 39.54N 22.11 E
Elat 22 Fg 29.33N 34.57 E
Eláti 15 Dk 38.43N 20.39 E
Elato Atoll 57 Fd 7.28N 146.10 E
El Attaf 13 Nh 36.13N 1.40 E
Elâziğ 23 Eb 38.41N 39.14 E
El Azúcar, Presa de- 48 Jd 26.15N 99.00W
Elba 44 Dj 31.25N 86.04W
Elba 5 Hg 42.45N 10.15 E
Elban 20 If 50.05N 136.30 E
El Banco 54 Db 9.01N 73.58W
El Barco de Ávila 13 Gd 40.21N 5.31W
El Barco de Valdeorras 13 Fb 42.25N 6.59W
Elbasani 15 Dh 41.06N 20.05 E
El Baúl 54 Eb 8.57N 68.17W
El Bayadh 32 Hc 33.41N 1.01 E
Elbe 5 Ge 53.50N 9.00 E
Elbe (EN) = Labe 5 Ge 53.50N 9.00 E
Elbe-Lübeck-Kanal 10 Gc 53.50N 10.36 E
Elbert, Mount- 38 If 39.07N 106.27W
Elberton 44 Fh 34.07N 82.52W
Elbe-Seitenkanal 10 Gd 52.22N 10.34 E
Elbeuf 11 Ge 49.17N 1.00 E
Elbeyl 23 Eb 36.41N 37.26 E
El Bierzo 13 Fb 42.40N 6.50W
Elbıstan 24 Gc 38.13N 37.12 E
Elbląg [2] 10 Pb 54.10N 19.25 E
Elbląg 6 He 54.10N 19.25 E
Elbląski, Kanał- 10 Pc 53.43N 19.53 E
El Bolsón 56 Ff 41.58 S 71.31W
El Bonillo 13 Jf 38.57N 2.32W
Elbow 46 La 51.07N 106.35W
Elbow Cays 49 Gb 23.57N 80.29W
Elbow Lake 45 Id 46.00N 95.58W
Elbrus 5 Kg 43.21N 42.26 E
Elbsandsteingebirge 10 Kf 50.50N 14.12 E
'Ēlbūr 35 He 4.40N 46.40 E
Elburg 11 Lb 52.26N 5.50 E
El Burgo de Osma 13 Ic 41.35N 3.04W
Elburgon 36 Gc .0.18 S 35.49 E
El Burro 48 Ic 29.16N 101.55W
Elburz Mountains (EN) = Alborz, Reshteh-ye Kūhhā-ye- 21 Hf 36.00N 53.00 E
El Cajon 43 De 32.48N 116.58W
El Callao 54 Fb 7.21N 61.49W
El Calvario 50 Ch 8.59N 67.00W
El Campo 45 Hl 29.12N 96.16W
El Canelo 48 Ie 24.19N 100.23W
El Cármen 55 Cd 18.49 S 58.33W
El Carmen de Bolívar 54 Cb 9.43N 75.07W
El Casco 48 Ge 25.34N 104.35W
El Castillo 49 Eh 11.01N 84.24W
El Centro 43 De 32.48N 115.34W
El Cerro 54 Fg 17.31 S 61.34W
El Chaparro 50 Dh 9.10N 65.01W
Elche 13 Lf 38.15N 0.42W
Elcho Island 59 Hb 11.55 S 135.45 E
El Cury 56 Ge 39.56 S 68.20W
Elda 13 Lf 38.29N 0.47W
Ēldab 35 Hd 8.58N 46.38 E
Elde 10 Ic 53.17N 12.40 E
'Ēl Ḍēre 31 Lh 3.55N 47.10 E
El Dere 35 Gd 5.07N 43.12 E
El Descanso 48 Aa 32.12N 116.55W
El Desemboque 47 Bb 30.30N 112.59W
El Dificil 49 Ji 9.51N 74.14W
Eldikan 20 Id 60.38N 135.07 E
El Djouf 30 Gf 21.25N 6.40W
El Doncello 54 Cc 1.43N 75.17W
Eldorado 45 Fk 30.52N 100.36W
Eldorado 56 Jc 26.24 S 54.38W
El Dorado [Ar.-U.S.] 43 Ie 33.13N 92.40W
El Dorado [Ks.-U.S.] 43 Hd 37.49N 96.52W
El Dorado [Mex.] 47 Cd 24.17N 107.31W
El Dorado [Ven.] 53 Je 6.44N 61.38W
Eldorado Paulista 55 Hg 24.32 S 48.06W
El Dorado Springs 45 Ih 37.52N 94.01W
Eldoret 36 Gb 0.31N 35.17 E
Eldsberga 8 Eh 56.36N 12.59 E
'Ēl Ḍubbo 35 Ge 3.52N 44.45 E
Eldžik 18 De 39.25N 63.01 E
Elefantes, Rio dos- 37 Ed 24.03 S 32.40 E
El Eglab 30 Gf 26.30N 5.00W
Elēja/Eleja 7 Fh 56.28N 23.41 E
Eleja/Elēja 7 Fh 56.28N 23.41 E
Elektrėnai/Elektrenaj 8 Kj 54.46N 24.47 E
Elektrenaj/Elektrėnai 8 Kj 54.46N 24.47 E
Elektrostal 19 Dd 55.48N 38.29 E
Elele 34 Gd 5.06N 6.49 E
Elena 15 Ig 42.56N 25.53 E
El Encanto [Bol.] 55 Cc 16.57 S 59.24W
El Encanto [Col.] 54 Dd 1.37 S 73.13W
Elephant Butte Reservoir 45 Cj 33.19N 107.10W
Elephant Island 66 Re 61.10 S 55.14W
Elephant Mountain 45 Ek 30.02N 103.30W
Elesbão Veloso 54 Je 6.13 S 42.08W
El Escorial 13 Hd 40.35N 4.10W
Eleşkirt 24 Jc 39.49N 42.40 E
El Estor 49 Cf 15.32N 89.21W
Eleuthera 38 Lg 25.15N 76.20W
Elevsís 15 Gk 38.02N 23.32 E
Elevtheroúpolis 15 Hi 40.55N 24.15 E
El Fendek 13 Gi 35.34N 5.35W
El Ferrol del Caudillo 13 Da 43.29N 8.14W
El Fud 35 Gd 7.15N 42.51 E
El Fuerte [Mex.] 48 Hf 23.50N 103.06W
El Fuerte [Mex.] 47 Cc 26.25N 108.39W
Elgåhogna 8 Eb 62.09N 12.04 E
'Ēl Gāl 35 Ic 11.23N 50.23 E
El Galhak 35 Ec 11.03N 32.42 E
El Gassi 32 Ic 30.55N 5.50 E
Elgen 20 Kd 62.45N 150.40 E
Elgepiggen 7 Ce 62.10N 11.22 E
El Ghomri 13 Mi 35.41N 0.12 E
Elgi 20 Jd 64.20N 142.05 E
Elgin [Il.-U.S.] 43 Jc 42.02N 88.17W
Elgin [N.D.-U.S.] 45 Fc 46.24N 101.51W
Elgin [Or.-U.S.] 46 Gd 45.34N 117.55W
Elgin [Scot.-U.K.] 9 Jd 57.39N 3.20W
Elginski 20 Jd 64.48N 141.50 E
Elgjaij 20 Gd 62.28N 117.37 E
El Goléa 31 He 30.34N 2.53 E
Elgon, Mont- 30 Kh 1.08N 34.33 E
Elgoran 35 Gd 5.04N 44.22 E
El Grao, Castellón de la Plana- 13 Me 39.58N 0.01 E
El Grao, Valencia- 13 Le 39.27N 0.20W
El Guapo 50 Dg 10.09N 65.58W
El Guayabo 49 Ki 8.37N 72.20W
El Hadjar 14 Bn 36.48N 7.45 E
El Hajeb 32 Fc 33.42N 5.22W
El-Ham 13 Qi 35.42N 4.52 E
El Hammam 13 Li 35.50N 0.15W
'Ēl Ḥamurre 35 Hd 7.11N 48.55 E
El Hank 30 Gf 24.00N 6.30W
El Harrach, Al Jazā'ir- 13 Ph 36.43N 3.08 E
Elhotovo 16 Nh 43.20N 44.13 E
Elhovo 15 Jg 42.10N 26.34 E
El Huecú 56 Fe 37.37 S 70.36W
Elida 45 Ej 33.57N 103.39W
Èliki, Vallée d'- 34 Gc 14.45N 7.15 E
Elila 36 Ec 2.43 S 25.53 E
Elila 30 Ji 2.45 S 25.53 E
Elimäki 8 Ld 60.43N 26.28 E
Elin Pelin 15 Gg 42.40N 23.36 E
Elisejna 15 Gf 43.05N 23.29 E
Elisenvaara 8 Mc 61.19N 29.47 E
Elista 6 Kf 46.16N 44.14 E
Elizabeth [Austl.] 58 Eh 34.45 S 138.39 E
Elizabeth [N.J.-U.S.] 44 Je 40.40N 74.13W
Elizabeth, Cape- 46 Cc 47.22N 124.22W
Elizabeth City 43 Ld 36.18N 76.14W
Elizabeth Reef 57 Gg 29.55 S 159.05 E
Elizabethton 44 Fg 36.21N 82.13W
Elizabethtown [Ky.-U.S.] 44 Eg 37.42N 85.52W
Elizabethtown [N.C.-U.S.] 44 Hh 34.38N 78.37W
El Jadida [3] 32 Fc 32.54N 8.30W
El Jadida 31 Ge 33.15N 8.30W
El Jícaro 49 Dg 13.43N 86.08W
'Ēl Jilib 35 He 3.48N 47.07 E
Ełk 10 Sc 53.50N 22.22 E
Ełk 10 Sc 53.32N 22.47 E
El Kala 32 Ib 36.54N 8.27 E
El Kantara 32 Ib 35.13N 5.43 E
El-Karimia 13 Nh 36.07N 1.33 E
Elk City [Id.-U.S.] 46 Hd 45.51N 115.29W
Elk City [Ok.-U.S.] 45 Gi 35.25N 99.25W
El Kelaa des Srarhna [3] 32 Fc 32.03N 7.30W
El Kelaa des Srarhna 32 Fc 32.03N 7.24W
El Kere 35 Gd 5.51N 42.06 E
Elkhart [In.-U.S.] 43 Jc 41.41N 85.58W
Elkhart [Ks.-U.S.] 45 Fh 37.00N 101.54W
El Khatt 32 Ef 19.00N 12.25W
Elkhead Mountains 45 Cf 40.50N 107.05W
El Khnâchîch 34 Ea 21.20N 3.45W
Elkhorn River 45 Hf 41.07N 96.19W
Elkins 44 Hf 38.56N 79.53W
Elk Lake 44 Gb 47.42N 80.11W
Elk Mountain 46 Lf 41.38N 106.32W
Elk Mountains 45 Cg 38.55N 106.50W
Elko 39 He 40.50N 115.46W
Elk Peak 46 Jc 46.27N 110.46W
Elk River 44 Gf 38.21N 81.38W
Elk River 45 Jd 45.18N 93.35W
Elku Kalns 8 Kg 57.04N 25.23 E
Ell, Lake- 59 Fe 29.15 S 127.45 E
Ellás = Greece (EN) [1] 6 Ih 39.00N 22.00 E
Ellé 11 Cg 47.52N 3.32W
Ellef Ringnes 38 Ib 78.30N 104.00W
Ellen, Mount- 43 Ed 38.07N 110.49W
Ellendale 43 Hb 46.06N 98.32W
Ellensburg 43 Cb 46.40N 120.32W
Ellenville 44 Je 41.43N 74.23W
Ellesmere 38 Kb 79.00N 82.00W
Ellesmere, Lake- 62 Ee 43.45 S 172.30 E
Ellice 42 Hc 68.02N 103.25W
Ellice Islands → Tuvalu [1] 58 Ie 8.00 S 178.00 E
Elliot [Austl.] 59 Gc 17.35 S 133.35 E
Elliot [S.Afr.] 37 Df 31.18 S 27.50 E
Elliot, Mount- 59 Jc 19.29 S 146.58 E
Elliot Lake 42 Jg 46.23N 82.39W
Ellisras 37 Dd 23.40 S 27.46 E
Elliston 59 Gf 33.39 S 134.55 E
Ellisville 45 Lk 31.36N 89.12W
Ellmau 14 Gc 47.31N 12.18 E
Ellös 7 Cg 58.11N 11.27 E
Ellsworth [Ks.-U.S.] 45 Gg 38.44N 98.14W
Ellsworth [Me.-U.S.] 44 Mc 44.33N 68.26W
Ellsworth [Nb.-U.S.] 45 Ee 42.04N 102.15W
Ellsworth, Lake- 45 Gi 34.48N 98.20W
Ellsworth Land (EN) 66 Pf 75.30 S 80.00W
Ellsworth Mountains 66 Pf 78.30 S 85.00W
Ellwangen 10 Gh 48.57N 10.08 E

Index Symbols

- [1] Independent Nation
- [2] State, Region
- [3] District, County
- Municipality
- Colony, Dependency
- Continent
- Physical Region
- Historical or Cultural Region
- Mount, Mountain
- Volcano
- Hill
- Mountains, Mountain Range
- Hills, Escarpment
- Plateau, Upland
- Pass, Gap
- Plain, Lowland
- Delta
- Salt Flat
- Valley, Canyon
- Crater, Cave
- Karst Features
- Depression
- Polder
- Desert, Dunes
- Forest, Woods
- Heath, Steppe
- Oasis
- Cape, Point
- Coast, Beach
- Cliff
- Peninsula
- Isthmus
- Sandbank
- Island
- Atoll
- Rock, Reef
- Islands, Archipelago
- Rocks, Reefs
- Coral Reef
- Well, Spring
- Geyser
- River, Stream
- Waterfall Rapids
- River Mouth, Estuary
- Lake
- Salt Lake
- Intermittent Lake
- Reservoir
- Swamp, Pond
- Canal
- Glacier
- Ice Shelf, Pack Ice
- Ocean
- Sea
- Gulf, Bay
- Strait, Fjord
- Lagoon
- Bank
- Seamount
- Tablemount
- Ridge
- Shelf
- Basin
- Escarpment, Sea Scarp
- Fracture
- Trench, Abyss
- National Park, Reserve
- Point of Interest
- Recreation Site
- Cave, Cavern
- Historic Site
- Ruins
- Wall, Walls
- Church, Abbey
- Temple
- Scientific Station
- Airport
- Port
- Lighthouse
- Mine
- Tunnel
- Dam, Bridge

Index Symbols

◩ Independent Nation	◨ Historical or Cultural Region	◻ Pass, Gap
② State, Region	▲ Mount, Mountain	▨ Plain, Lowland
③ District, County	▲ Volcano	▽ Delta
④ Municipality	△ Hill	▭ Salt Flat
⑤ Colony, Dependency	▨ Mountains, Mountain Range	▨ Valley, Canyon
■ Continent	▨ Hills, Escarpment	▨ Crater, Cave
◨ Physical Region	◿ Plateau, Upland	▨ Karst Features

▨ Depression	▨ Coast, Beach	▨ Rock, Reef
▨ Polder	▨ Cliff	▨ Islands, Archipelago
▨ Desert, Dunes	▨ Peninsula	▨ Rocks, Reefs
▨ Forest, Woods	▨ Isthmus	▨ Coral Reef
▨ Heath, Steppe	▨ Sandbank	▨ Well, Spring
▨ Oasis	▨ Island	▨ Geyser
▨ Cape, Point	▨ Atoll	▨ River, Stream

▨ Waterfall Rapids	▨ Canal	▨ Lagoon
▨ River Mouth, Estuary	▨ Glacier	▨ Bank
▨ Lake	▨ Ice Shelf, Pack Ice	▨ Seamount
▨ Salt Lake	▨ Ocean	▨ Tablemount
▨ Intermittent Lake	▨ Sea	▨ Ridge
▨ Reservoir	▨ Gulf, Bay	▨ Shelf
▨ Swamp, Pond	▨ Strait, Fjord	▨ Basin

▨ Escarpment, Sea Scarp	▨ Historic Site	▨ Port
▨ Fracture	▨ Ruins	▨ Lighthouse
▨ Trench, Abyss	▨ Wall, Walls	▨ Mine
▨ National Park, Reserve	▨ Church, Abbey	▨ Tunnel
▨ Point of Interest	▨ Temple	▨ Dam, Bridge
▨ Recreation Site	▨ Scientific Station	
▨ Cave, Cavern	▨ Airport	

Farīd, Qarāt al- 24 Ch 28.43N 28.21 E
Faridpur 25 Hd 23.36N 89.50 E
Fārila 7 Df 61.48N 15.51 E
Farilhões, Ilhas- 13 Ce 39.28N 9.34W
Farim 34 Bc 12.29N 15.13W
Farini d'Olmo 14 Df 44.43N 9.34 E
Fāris 24 Ej 24.37N 32.54 E
Fariš 18 Fd 40.33N 66.52 E
Fāris 35 Ia 20.11N 50.56 E
Faris Seamount (EN) 40 Jf 54.30N 147.15W
Färjestaden 7 Dh 56.39N 16.27 E
Farkadhón 15 Fj 39.36N 22.04 E
Farmahīn 24 Me 34.30N 49.41 E
Farmakonisi 15 Kl 37.18N 27.08 E
Farmerville 45 Jj 32.47N 92.24W
Farmington [Me.-U.S.] 44 Lc 44.40N 70.09W
Farmington [Mo.-U.S.] 45 Kh 37.47N 90.25W
Farmington [N.M.-U.S.] 43 Fd 36.44N 108.12W
Farmville 44 Hg 37.17N 78.25W
Färnäs 8 Fc 61.00N 14.38 E
Farnborough 12 Bc 51.16N 0.44W
Farne Deep 9 Mf 55.30N 0.50W
Farne Islands 9 Lf 55.38N 1.38W
Farnham [Eng.-U.K.] 12 Bc 51.12N 0.48W
Farnham [Que.-Can.] 44 Kc 45.17N 72.59W
Farnham, Mount- 46 Ga 50.29N 116.30W
Fårö 7 Eh 57.55N 19.10 E
Faro 34 Hd 9.21N 12.55 E
Faro [2] 13 Dg 37.12N 8.10W
Faro 6 Fh 37.01N 7.56W
Faro, Punta- 49 Jh 11.07N 74.51W
Faro, Sierra del- 13 Eb 42.37N 7.55W
Faro de Avión 13 Db 42.18N 8.16W
Faro de Chantada 13 Eb 42.37N 7.55W
Farofa, Serra da- 55 Gh 28.00S 50.10W
Farosund 8 Hg 57.55N 19.05 E
Fårösund 7 Eh 57.52N 19.03 E
Farquhar, Cape- 59 Cd 23.35S 113.35 E
Farquhar Group 30 Mj 10.10S 51.10 E
Farrar 9 Id 57.27N 4.35W
Farrāshband 24 Oh 28.53N 52.06 E
Farris 8 Ce 59.05N 10.00 E
Farruch, Cabo- 13 Pe 39.47N 3.21 E
Farrukhābād 25 Fc 27.24N 79.34 E
Fārs 21 Hg 29.00N 53.00 E
Fārs [3] 23 Hd 29.00N 53.00 E
Fārsābād 24 Mc 39.30N 48.05 E
Fársala 15 Fj 39.18N 22.23 E
Farshūţ 24 Ei 26.03N 32.09 E
Farsø 8 Ch 56.47N 9.21 E
Farsund 7 Bg 58.05N 6.48 E
Fartak, Ra's- 23 Hf 15.38N 52.15 E
Fartura, Rio- 56 Gc 16.29S 50.33W
Fartura, Serra da- [Braz.] 55 Hf 23.20S 49.25W
Fartura, Serra da- [Braz.] 55 Fh 26.21S 52.52W
Fārūj 24 Rd 37.14N 58.14 E
Farvel, Kap-/ Ūmánarssuaq 67 Nb 59.50N 43.50W
Farwell Island 66 Pf 72.49S 91.10W
Fāryāb [3] 23 Jb 36.00N 65.00 E
Fasā 24 Oh 28.56N 53.42 E
Fasano 14 Lj 40.50N 17.22 E
Fastnet Rock 9 Dj 51.24N 9.35W
Fastov 19 De 50.06N 30.01 E
Fataka Island 57 If 11.55S 170.12 E
Fatala 34 Cc 10.13N 14.00W
Fatehpur 25 Ec 28.01N 74.58 E
Fatež 16 Ic 52.06N 35.52 E
Father Lake 44 Ja 49.24N 75.18W
Fatick 34 Bc 14.20N 16.25W
Fátima 13 De 39.37N 8.39W
Faţīrah, Wādī- 24 Ei 26.39N 32.58 E
Fatsa 24 Gb 40.59N 37.24 E
Fatu Hiva, Ile- 57 Nf 10.28S 138.38W
Fatu Hutu, Ile- 57 Ne 9.00S 138.50W
Fatumanini, Passe- 64h Ab 13.14S 176.13W
Fatunda 36 Cc 4.08S 17.13 E
Fauabu 63a Ec 8.34S 160.43 E
Faucigny 11 Mh 46.05N 6.35 E
Faucille, Col de la- 11 Mh 46.22N 6.02 E
Faulkton 45 Gd 45.02N 99.08W
Faulquemont 12 Ie 49.03N 6.36 E
Fauquembergues 12 Ed 50.36N 2.05 E
Făurei 15 Kd 45.04N 27.14 E
Fauro 63a Cb 6.55S 156.07 E
Fauske 7 Dc 67.15N 15.24 E
Fauville-en-Caux 12 Ce 49.39N 0.35 E
Faux-Lap 37 He 25.32S 45.30 E
Fåvang 8 Dc 61.26N 10.13 E
Favara 14 Hm 37.19N 13.39 E
Faversham 12 Cc 51.19N 0.54 E
Favignana 14 Gm 37.55N 12.19 E
Favignana 14 Gm 37.56N 12.20 E
Favorite 12 Kf 48.49N 8.16 E
Fawley 12 Ad 50.49N 1.21W
Fawn 42 Ie 55.22N 88.20W
Fa'w Qiblī 24 Ei 26.07N 32.24 E
Faxaflói 5 Dc 64.24N 23.00W
Faxinal 55 Gf 23.59S 51.22W
Faya-Largeau 31 Ig 17.55N 19.07 E
Fayaoué 63b Ce 20.39S 166.32 E
Fayd 24 Ji 27.07N 42.31 E
Fayette [Al.-U.S.] 44 Di 33.42N 87.50W
Fayette [Oh.-U.S.] 44 Ee 41.41N 84.20W
Fayetteville [Ar.-U.S.] 43 Id 36.04N 94.10W
Fayetteville [N.C.-U.S.] 39 Lf 35.03N 78.54W
Fayetteville [Tn.-U.S.] 44 Dh 35.09N 86.35W
Faylakah, Jazīrat- 24 Mh 29.27N 48.20 E
Faysh Khābūr 24 Jd 37.04N 42.23 E
Fayu Island 57 Gd 8.35N 151.22 E
Fazenda de Cima 55 Db 15.56S 56.37W
Fazenda Nova 55 Gc 16.11S 50.48W
Fāzilka 25 Eb 30.24N 74.02 E
Fazrān 24 Mi 26.13N 49.12 E
Fazzān=Fezzan (EN) 33 Bd 25.30N 14.00 E
Fazzān=Fezzan (EN) 30 If 26.00N 14.00 E
Fdérick 31 Ff 22.39N 12.43W
Feale/An Fhéil 9 Di 52.28N 9.40W
Fear, Cape- 43 Le 33.50N 77.58W
Featherston 62 Fd 41.07S 175.19 E
Feathertop, Mount- 59 Jg 36.54S 147.08 E
Fécamp 11 Ge 49.45N 0.22 E
Fecht 11 Nf 48.11N 7.26 E
Federacion 56 Id 31.00S 57.54W
Federal 56 Id 30.55S 58.45W
Federated States of Micronesia [5] 58 Gd 6.30N 152.00 E
Federovka 19 Ge 53.38N 62.42 E
Federovka 17 Gj 53.10N 55.10 E
Federsee 10 Fh 48.05N 9.38 E
Fedje 7 Af 60.47N 4.42 E
Fedorovka 16 Qd 51.16N 52.00 E
Fefan 64d Bb 7.21N 151.51 E
Fegen 8 Eg 57.11N 13.09 E
Fegen 8 Eg 57.06N 13.02 E
Fehérgyarmat 10 Si 47.59N 22.31 E
Fehmarn 10 Hb 54.30N 11.10 E
Fehmarnbelt 8 Dj 54.35N 11.15 E
Fehrbellin 10 Id 52.48N 12.46 E
Feicheng 28 Df 36.15N 116.46 E
Feidong (Dianbu) 28 Di 31.53N 117.29 E
Fei Huang He 28 Fg 34.15N 120.17 E
Feijó 54 De 8.09S 70.21W
Feilding 61 Eh 40.12S 175.35 E
Feira 36 Ff 15.37S 30.25 E
Feira de Santana 53 Mg 12.15S 38.57W
Feiran Oasis 24 Eh 28.42N 33.38 E
Feistritz 14 Kc 47.01N 16.08 E
Feixi (Shangpaihe) 28 Di 31.42N 117.09 E
Feixian 28 Dg 35.16N 117.59 E
Feixiang 28 Cf 36.32N 114.47 E
Fejão Prêto ou Furtado, Rio- 55 Dc 17.33S 57.23W
Fejér [2] 10 Oi 47.10N 18.35 E
Fejø 8 Dj 54.55N 11.25 E
Feke 24 Fd 37.53N 35.58 E
Fekete-viz 10 Ok 45.47N 18.13 E
Felanitx 13 Pe 39.28N 3.08 E
Feldbach 14 Jd 46.57N 15.53 E
Feldioara 15 Id 45.49N 25.36 E
Feldkirch 14 Dc 47.14N 9.36 E
Feldkirchen 14 Id 46.43N 14.06 E
Feliciano, Arroyo- 55 Cj 31.06S 59.54W
Felidu Atoll [atoll] 25a Bb 3.30N 73.30 E
Felipe Carrillo Puerto 47 Ge 19.35N 88.03W
Felix, Cape - 42 Hc 69.55N 97.47W
Felixlândia 55 Jd 18.47S 44.55W
Felixstowe 9 Oj 51.58N 1.20 E
Felletin 11 Ii 45.53N 2.11 E
Feltre 14 Fd 46.01N 11.54 E
Femer Bælt 8 Dj 54.35N 11.15 E
Femø 8 Dj 54.55N 11.35 E
Femund 7 Ce 62.15N 11.50 E
Fena Valley Reservoir 64c Bb 13.20N 144.45 E
Fener Burnu 24 Hb 41.07N 39.25 E
Fénérive 37 Hc 17.22S 49.25 E
Fenerwa 35 Fc 13.05N 39.01 E
Fénétrange 12 Jf 48.51N 7.01 E
Fengcheng [China] 27 Lc 40.28N 124.01 E
Fengcheng [China] 27 Cj 28.11N 115.47 E
Fengdu 27 If 29.58N 107.39 E
Fenghua 28 Fj 29.40N 121.24 E
Fengjie 27 He 31.06N 104.30 E
Fenglingdu 27 Je 34.40N 110.19 E
Fengnan (Xugezhuang) 28 Ee 39.34N 118.05 E
Fengning (Dagezhen) 28 Dd 41.12N 116.39 E
Fengqing 27 Gg 24.41N 99.53 E
Fengqiu 28 Cg 35.02N 114.24 E
Fengrun 28 Ee 39.50N 118.09 E
Fengshui Shan 27 La 52.15N 123.30 E
Fengtai [China] 28 Dh 32.43N 116.43 E
Fengtai [China] 28 De 39.51N 116.17 E
Fengweiba→Zhenkang 27 Gg 23.54N 99.00 E
Fengxian 28 Dg 34.42N 116.35 E
Fengxian (Nanqiao) 28 Fi 30.55N 121.27 E
Fengxiang 27 Ie 34.32N 107.34 E
Fengxiang→Luobei 27 Nb 47.36N 130.58 E
Fengxin 28 Cj 28.42N 115.23 E
Fengyang 28 Dh 32.53N 117.33 E
Fengzhen 27 Jc 40.28N 113.09 E
Fen He [China] 27 Jd 35.36N 110.42 E
Fen He [China] 28 Ae 38.06N 111.52 E
Feni Islands 57 Ge 4.05S 153.42 E
Fennimore 45 Ke 42.59N 90.39W
Fensfjorden 8 Ad 60.50N 4.50 E
Fenshui Guan 27 Kf 27.56N 117.50 E
Fenton 44 Fd 42.48N 83.42W
Fenua Fu 64h Ac 13.23S 176.11W
Fenualoa 63c Bb 10.16S 166.15 E
Fenyang 27 Jd 37.17N 111.45 E
Feodosija 19 Df 45.02N 35.23 E
Fer, Cap de- 32 Ib 37.05N 7.10 E
Fer, Point au- 45 Kl 29.20N 91.21W
Feragen 8 Db 62.30N 11.55 E
Férai 15 Ji 40.54N 26.10 E
Ferdows 23 Ic 34.00N 58.09 E
Fère-Champenoise 11 Jf 48.45N 3.59 E
Fère-en-Tardenois 12 Fe 49.12N 3.31 E
Feren 8 Da 63.34N 11.50 E
Ferentino 14 Hi 41.42N 13.15 E
Ferfer [Eth.] 35 Hd 5.06N 45.09 E
Ferfer [Som.] 35 Hd 5.07N 45.07 E
Fergana 22 Je 40.23N 71.46 E
Fergana 21 Je 40.30N 71.00 E
Ferganskaja Oblast [3] 19 Hg 40.30N 71.20 E
Ferganski Hrebet 19 Hg 41.00N 74.00 E
Fergus Falls 43 Hb 46.17N 96.04W
Ferguson Lake 42 Hc 69.00N 105.00W
Fergusson Island 60 Ei 9.30S 150.40 E
Ferkéssédougou [3] 34 Ed 9.20N 4.55W
Ferkéssédougou 34 Dd 9.36N 5.12W
Ferlo 30 Fg 15.00N 14.00W
Ferlo 30 Fg 15.42N 15.30W
Fermo 14 Hg 43.09N 13.43 E
Fermoselle 13 Fc 41.19N 6.23W
Fermoy/Mainistir Fhear Mai 9 Ei 52.08N 8.16W
Fernandina, Isla- 52 Gf 0.25S 91.30W
Fernandina Beach 44 Gj 30.40N 81.27W
Fernando de Noronha, Ilha- 52 Mf 3.51S 32.25W
Fernando de Noronha, Território de- [2] 54 Ld 3.50S 33.00W
Fernandópolis 56 Kb 20.16S 50.00W
Fernán-Núñez 13 Hg 37.40N 4.43W
Fernelmont 12 Hd 50.35N 5.02 E
Fernie 46 Hb 49.30N 115.03W
Ferrandina 14 Kj 40.29N 16.27 E
Ferrara 14 Ff 44.50N 11.35 E
Ferrat, Cap- 13 Li 35.54N 0.23W
Ferrato, Capo- 14 Dk 39.18N 9.38 E
Ferré 55 Bl 34.08S 61.08W
Ferré, Cap- 51h Bc 14.28N 60.49W
Ferreira do Alentejo 13 Df 38.03N 8.07W
Ferreñafe 54 Ce 6.38S 79.48W
Ferret, Cap- 11 Ej 44.37N 1.15W
Ferriday 45 Kk 31.38N 91.33W
Ferrières 12 Hd 50.24N 5.36 E
Ferro, Capo- 14 Di 41.09N 9.31 E
Ferro, Rio- 55 Ea 12.27S 54.31W
Ferru, Monte- 14 Cj 40.08N 8.36 E
Ferry, Pointe- 51e Ab 16.17N 61.49W
Fertilia 14 Cj 40.36N 8.17 E
Fertő→Neusiedler See 10 Mi 47.50N 16.45 E
Fès 31 Ge 34.02N 4.59W
Fès [3] 32 Gc 34.00N 5.00W
Feshi 36 Cd 6.07S 18.10 E
Fessenden 45 Gc 47.39N 99.38W
Festieux 12 Fe 49.31N 3.45 E
Festus 45 Kg 38.13N 90.24W
Feteşti 15 Ke 44.23N 27.50 E
Fethiye 23 Cb 36.37N 29.07 E
Fethiye Körfezi 24 Cd 36.40N 29.00 E
Fetlar 9 Ma 60.37N 0.52W
Fetsund 7 Cg 59.56N 11.10 E
Feuchtwangen 10 Gg 49.10N 10.20 E
Feuilles, Baie aux - 42 Ke 58.55N 69.15W
Feuilles, Rivière aux- 42 Ke 58.46N 70.05W
Feurs 11 Ki 45.45N 4.14 E
Fevik 8 Cf 58.23N 8.42 E
Feyzābād 23 Jf 37.06N 70.34 E
Fezzan (EN)=Fazzān 33 Bd 25.30N 14.00 E
Fezzan (EN)=Fazzān 30 If 26.00N 14.00 E
Fezzane, Emi- 34 Ha 21.42N 14.15 E
Ffestiniog 9 Ji 52.58N 3.55W
Fiambalá 56 Gc 27.41S 67.38W
Fianarantsoa 31 Lk 21.28S 47.05 E
Fianarantsoa [3] 37 Hd 21.30S 47.05 E
Fianga 35 Bd 9.55N 15.09 E
Fiche 35 Fd 9.48N 38.44 E
Fichtelgebirge 5 He 50.00N 12.00 E
Ficksburg 37 De 28.57S 27.50 E
Fidenza 14 Ef 44.52N 10.03 E
Fieni 15 Id 45.08N 25.25 E
Fier 15 Ci 40.43N 19.34 E
Fife [3] 9 Je 56.05N 3.15W
Fife Ness 9 Ke 56.17N 2.36W
Fiffa 34 Dc 11.27N 9.52W
Fifth Cataract (EN)= Khāmis, Ash Shallāl al- 30 Kg 18.23N 33.47 E
Figalo, Cap- 13 Ki 35.35N 1.12W
Figeac 11 Ij 44.36N 2.02 E
Figeholm 8 Gg 57.22N 16.33 E
Figtree 37 Dd 20.22S 28.20 E
Figueira, Baia da- 55 Dc 16.33S 57.25W
Figueira da Foz 13 Dd 40.09N 8.52W
Figueira de Castelo Rodrigo 13 Fd 40.54N 6.58W
Figueras 13 Ob 42.16N 2.58 E
Figueras/Figueres 13 Ob 42.16N 2.58 E
Figueres 13 Ob 42.16N 2.58 E
Figueres/Figueras 13 Ob 42.16N 2.58 E
Figuig [3] 32 Gc 33.00N 2.01W
Figuig 31 Ge 32.06N 1.14W
Fiherenana 37 Gd 23.19S 43.37 E
Fijāj, Shaţţ al- 32 Ic 33.55N 9.10 E
Fiji [1] 58 If 18.00S 178.00 E
Fiji Islands 57 If 18.00S 178.00 E
Fik 35 Gd 8.08N 42.18 E
Filabres, Sierra de los- 13 Jg 37.15N 2.20W
Filabusi 37 Dd 20.32S 29.16 E
Filadelfia 54 Ie 7.21S 47.30W
Filadelfia [C.R.] 49 Eh 10.26N 85.34W
Filadelfia [It.] 14 Kl 38.47N 16.17 E
Filakara 63b Dc 16.49S 168.24 E
Filákovo 10 Ph 48.16N 19.50 E
Filamana 34 Dc 10.30N 7.57W
Filatova Gora 8 Mg 57.39N 28.21 E
Filchner Ice Shelf 66 Af 79.00S 40.00W
Filey 9 Mg 54.12N 0.17W
Filiaşi 15 Ge 44.33N 23.31 E
Filiátai 15 Dj 39.36N 20.49 E
Filiatrá 15 El 37.09N 21.35 E
Filicudi 14 Il 38.35N 14.35 E
Filingué 34 Fc 14.21N 3.19 E
Filiouri 15 Ih 40.57N 25.20 E
Filippiás 15 Dj 39.12N 20.53 E
Filippoi 15 Hh 41.02N 24.20 E
Filippoi = Philippi (EN) 15 Hh 41.02N 24.18 E
Filipstad 7 Dg 59.43N 14.10 E
Fillefjell 8 Cc 61.09N 8.15 E
Filliévres 12 Ed 50.19N 2.10 E
Fillmore 46 Ig 38.58N 112.20W
Fils 10 Fh 48.35N 9.29 E
Filtu 35 Gd 5.06N 40.40 E
Fimaina 15 Jl 37.35N 26.26 E
Fimi 30 Ii 3.01S 16.58 E
Fin [Iran] 24 Pi 27.38N 55.55 E
Fin [Iran] 24 Nf 33.57N 51.24 E
Finale Emilia 14 Ff 44.50N 11.17 E
Finale Ligure 14 Cf 44.10N 8.20 E
Findhorn 9 Jd 57.41N 3.32W
Fındıklı 24 Ib 41.17N 41.09 E
Findlay 43 Kc 41.02N 83.40W
Findlay, Mount- 46 Ga 50.04N 116.28W
Findlay Group 42 Ha 77.15N 104.00W
Fineveke 64h Ab 13.19S 176.12W
Fingoé 37 Ec 15.10S 31.53 E
Finike 24 Dd 36.18N 30.09 E
Finistère [3] 11 Cf 48.20N 4.00W
Finisterre, Cabo de- 5 Fg 42.53N 9.16W
Finisterre Range 59 Ja 5.50S 146.05 E
Finke 58 Eg 25.34S 134.35 E
Finke, Mount- 59 Gf 30.55S 134.02 E
Finke River 57 Eg 27.00S 136.10 E
Finland/Suomi [1] 6 Ic 64.00N 26.00 E
Finland, Gulf of- (EN)= Finski Zaliv 5 Ic 60.00N 27.00 E
Finland, Gulf of- (EN)= Soomenlaht 5 Ic 60.00N 27.00 E
Finland, Gulf of- (EN)= Suomenlahti 5 Ic 60.00N 27.00 E
Finlay 42 Fe 55.59N 123.50W
Finlay Mountains 45 Dk 31.30N 105.35W
Finne 10 He 51.13N 11.19 E
Finngrunden 8 Hc 61.00N 18.19 E
Finnigan, Mount- 59 Jc 15.50S 145.20 E
Finniss, Cape- 59 Gf 33.38S 134.51 E
Finnmark 7 Fa 70.00N 25.00 E
Finnmark [3] 7 Fb 69.50N 24.10 E
Finnmarksvidda 5 Ib 69.30N 24.20 E
Finnøy 8 Ae 59.10N 5.50 E
Finnskogen 8 Ed 60.40N 12.40 E
Finnsnes 7 Eb 69.14N 18.02 E
Finnveden 8 Eh 56.50N 13.40 E
Finote Selam 35 Fc 10.42N 37.12 E
Finschhafen 59 Ja 6.35S 147.50 E
Finse 8 Bd 60.36N 7.30 E
Finski Zaliv=Finland, Gulf of- (EN) 5 Ic 60.00N 27.00 E
Finspång 7 Dg 58.43N 15.47 E
Finstadåa 8 Dc 61.47N 11.10 E
Finsteraarhorn 14 Cd 46.32N 8.08 E
Finsterwalde 10 Je 51.38N 13.43 E
Finström 8 Hd 60.16N 19.50 E
Fiora 14 Fh 42.20N 11.34 E
Fiorenzuola d'Arda 14 Df 44.56N 9.55 E
Firat=Euphrates (EN) 21 Gf 31.00N 47.25 E
Firenze = Florence (EN) 6 Hg 43.46N 11.15 E
Firenzuola 14 Ff 44.07N 11.23 E
Firmat 55 Bk 33.27S 61.29W
Firminópolis 55 Gc 16.40S 50.19W
Firminy 11 Ki 45.23N 4.18 E
Firozābād 25 Fc 27.09N 78.25 E
Firozpur 25 Eb 30.55N 74.36 E
First Cataract (EN)=Aswān, Sadd al- 30 Kf 24.01N 32.52 E
Firūzābād 24 Oh 28.50N 52.36 E
Firūzābād 24 Pg 31.59N 54.20 E
Firūzābād 24 Le 34.09N 46.25 E
Firūz Kūk 24 Oe 35.45N 52.47 E
Fischbach 12 Je 49.44N 7.24 E
Fischbacher Alpen 14 Jc 47.25N 15.30 E
Fischland 10 Ib 54.22N 12.25 E
Fish [Nam.] 30 Ik 17.11S 28.08 E
Fish [S.Afr.] 37 Cf 31.14S 20.15 E
Fisher Glacier 66 Ef 73.15S 66.00 E
Fisher Peak 44 Gg 36.33N 80.50W
Fisher Strait 42 Jd 63.00N 84.00W
Fishguard 6 Fe 51.59N 4.59W
Fish River' Canyon 37 Be 27.35S 17.35 E
Fiskárdhon 15 Dk 38.28N 20.35 E
Fiskenaes Bank (EN) 41 Gf 63.18N 52.10W
Fiskenæsset 41 Gf 63.10N 50.45W
Fismes 11 Je 49.18N 3.41 E
Fišt, Gora- 19 Dg 43.57N 39.55 E
Fitchburg 44 Ld 42.35N 71.48W
Fitjar 7 Ag 59.55N 5.20 E
Fito, Mount- 65c Ba 13.55S 171.44W
Fitri, Lac- 35 Bc 12.50N 17.28 E
Fitzcarrald 54 Df 11.49S 71.48W
Fitzgerald [Alta.-Can.] 42 Ge 59.52N 111.40W
Fitzgerald [Ga.-U.S.] 44 Fj 31.43N 83.15W
Fitzroy Crossing 59 Fc 18.11S 125.35 E
Fitzroy River [Austl.] 59 Kc 23.32S 150.52 E
Fitzroy River [Austl.] 57 Df 17.31S 123.35 E
Fitzwilliam Island 44 Gc 45.30N 81.45W
Fiuggi 14 Hi 41.48N 13.13 E
Fiumicino 14 Gi 41.46N 12.14 E
Five Island Harbour 51d Bb 17.06N 61.54W
Fivizzano 14 Ef 44.14N 10.08 E
Fizi 31 Ji 4.18S 28.57 E
Fizuli 19 Eh 39.35N 47.11 E
Fjærlandsfjorden 8 Bc 61.15N 6.40 E
Fjällbacka 8 Df 58.36N 11.17 E
Fjärås 7 Ch 57.26N 12.09 E
Fjerritslev 8 Cg 57.05N 9.16 E
Fjöllum, Jökulsá á- 7a Ca 66.02N 16.27W
Fjugesta 8 Fe 59.10N 14.52 E
Flacq 37a Bb 20.12S 57.43 E
Flade Isblink 41 Kb 81.25N 16.00W
Fladen 8 Dg 57.07N 11.35 E
Fladen 8 Dg 57.10N 11.45 E
Flagler 45 Eg 39.18N 103.04W
Flagstaff 39 Hf 35.12N 111.39W
Flåm 7 Bf 60.50N 7.07 E
Flamborough Head 9 Mg 54.07N 0.04W
Fläming 10 Ie 52.00N 13.00 E
Flaming Gorge Reservoir 46 Kf 41.15N 109.30W
Flamingo 44 Gm 25.09N 80.56W
Flamingo, Teluk- 26 Kh 5.33S 138.00 E
Flanders (EN)=Flandres/ Vlaanderen 5 Ge 51.00N 3.20 E
Flanders (EN)=Flandres/ Vlaanderen 11 Jc 51.00N 3.20 E
Flanders (EN)=Vlaanderen/ Flandres 5 Ge 51.00N 3.20 E
Flanders (EN)=Vlaanderen/ Flandres 11 Jc 51.00N 3.20 E
Flanders Plain (EN)= Flandres, Plaine des- 11 Id 50.40N 2.50 E
Flanders Plain (EN)= Vlamse Vlakte 11 Id 50.40N 2.50 E
Flandreau 45 Hd 44.03N 96.36W
Flandres/Vlaanderen= Flanders (EN) 11 Jc 51.00N 3.20 E
Flandres/Vlaanderen= Flanders (EN) 5 Ge 51.00N 3.20 E
Flandres, Plaine des-= Flanders Plain (EN) 11 Id 50.40N 2.50 E
Flannan Isles 9 Fc 58.20N 7.35W
Flåren 8 Fh 57.00N 14.05 E
Flasher 45 Fc 46.27N 101.14W
Fläsjön 7 Dd 64.06N 15.51 E
Flat 40 Hd 62.27N 158.01W
Flatey 7a Ab 65.22N 22.56W
Flateyri 7a Aa 66.03N 23.31W
Flathead Lake 43 Eb 47.52N 114.08W
Flathead Range 46 Ib 48.05N 113.28W
Flathead River 46 Hc 47.22N 114.47W
Flat Point 51b Ab 18.15N 63.05W
Flat River 45 Kh 37.51N 90.31W
Flattery, Cape- 38 Ge 48.23N 124.43W
Flåvatnet 8 Ce 59.20N 8.50 E
Flaxton 45 Eb 48.54N 102.24W
Flaygreen Lake 42 Hf 53.50N 97.20W
Fleckenstein, Château de- 12 Je 49.05N 7.48 E
Fleet 12 Bc 51.17N 0.50W
Fleetwood 9 Jh 53.56N 3.01W
Flekkefjord 7 Bg 58.17N 6.41 E
Flémalle 12 Hd 50.36N 5.29 E
Flemish Bight [Eur.] 11 Dc 51.44N 2.30W
Flemish Bight [U.K.] 9 Pi 52.10N 2.50 E
Flemish Cap (EN) 38 Oe 47.00N 45.00W
Flemsøya 8 Bb 62.40N 6.20 E
Flen 7 Dg 59.04N 16.35 E
Flensborg Fjord 8 Cj 54.50N 9.45 E
Flensburg 6 Ge 54.47N 9.26 E
Flensburger Förde 8 Cj 54.50N 9.45 E
Flers 11 Ff 48.45N 0.34W
Flesberg 8 Ce 59.51N 9.27 E
Fleurance 11 Gk 43.50N 0.40 E
Fleury-sur-Andelle 12 De 49.22N 1.21 E
Fleuve [3] 34 Cb 16.00N 13.50W
Flevoland 11 Lb 52.25N 5.30 E
Flian 8 Ef 58.27N 13.05 E
Flims 14 Dd 46.50N 9.16 E
Flinders Bay 59 Df 34.25S 115.19 E
Flinders Island 57 Fi 40.00S 148.00 E
Flinders Passage 59 Jc 18.50S 149.00 E
Flinders Ranges 57 Eh 31.25S 138.45 E
Flinders Reefs 57 Ff 17.40S 148.30 E
Flinders River 57 Ff 17.36S 140.36 E
Flin Flon 39 Id 54.56N 101.53W
Flint [Mi.-U.S.] 39 Ke 43.01N 83.41W
Flint [Wales-U.K.] 9 Jh 53.15N 3.07W
Flint Hills 45 Hh 37.20N 96.35W
Flint Island 57 Lf 11.26S 151.48W
Flint River 43 Ke 30.52N 84.38W
Flisa 7 Cf 60.37N 12.04 E
Flisa 8 Ed 60.36N 12.01 E
Flisegga 8 Be 59.50N 7.50 E
Flitwick 12 Bb 52.00N 0.29W
Flix 13 Mc 41.14N 0.33 E
Flixecourt 12 Ed 50.01N 2.05 E
Flize 12 Ge 49.42N 4.46 E
Flobecq/Vloesberg 12 Fd 50.44N 3.44 E
Floby 8 Ef 58.08N 13.20 E
Floda [Swe.] 8 Fd 60.26N 14.49 E
Floda [Swe.] 8 Eg 57.48N 12.22 E
Flood Range 66 Nf 76.03S 134.00W
Flora [Il.-U.S.] 45 Lg 38.40N 88.29W
Flora [Nor.] 7 Af 61.36N 5.00 E
Florac 11 Jj 44.19N 3.36 E
Florala 44 Dj 31.00N 86.20W
Florange 12 Ie 49.20N 6.07 E
Florence [Al.-U.S.] 43 Je 34.49N 87.40W
Florence [Ks.-U.S.] 45 Hg 38.15N 96.56W
Florence [Or.-U.S.] 46 Cd 44.01N 124.07W
Florence [S.C.-U.S.] 43 Le 34.12N 79.44W
Florence (EN) = Firenze 6 Hg 43.46N 11.15 E
Florencia [Arg.] 55 Ci 28.02S 59.15W
Florencia [Col.] 53 Ie 1.36N 75.36W
Florencio Sánchez 55 Dk 33.53S 57.24W
Florennes 12 Gd 50.15N 4.37 E
Florentino Ameghino, Embalse- 56 Gf 43.48S 66.25W
Florenville 11 Le 49.42N 5.18 E
Flores [2] 55 Dk 33.35S 56.50W
Flores 30 De 39.26N 31.13W
Flores [Guat.] 49 Ce 16.56N 89.53W
Flores [Guat.] 47 Ge 16.58N 89.50W
Flores, Arroyo de las- 55 Cl 35.36S 59.01W
Flores, Laut-=Flores Sea (EN) 21 Oj 8.00S 121.00 E
Flores, Pulau- 21 Oj 8.30S 121.00 E
Flores Island 46 Bb 49.20N 126.10W
Flores Sea (EN)=Flores, Laut- 21 Oj 8.00S 121.00 E
Floreşty 16 Ff 47.55N 28.18 E
Floriano 53 Lf 6.47S 43.01W
Florianópolis 53 Lh 27.35S 48.34W
Florida [Braz.] 55 Ei 29.15S 54.36W
Florida [Cuba] 47 Id 21.32N 78.14W
Florida [U.S.] [2] 43 Kf 28.00N 82.00W
Florida [Ur.] [2] 55 Ek 33.50S 55.55W
Florida [Ur.] 56 Id 34.06S 56.13W
Florida, Estrecho de-= Florida, Straits of- (EN) 38 Kg 24.00N 81.00W
Florida, Straits of- 38 Kg 24.00N 81.00W
Florida, Straits of- (EN)= Florida, Estrecho de- 38 Kg 24.00N 81.00W
Florida Bay 44 Gm 25.00N 80.45W
Floridablanca 54 Db 7.04N 73.06W

Index Symbols

[1] Independent Nation
[2] State, Region
[3] District, County
[4] Municipality
[5] Colony, Dependency
Continent
Physical Region
Historical or Cultural Region
Mount, Mountain
Volcano
Hill
Mountains, Mountain Range
Hills, Escarpment
Plateau, Upland
Pass, Gap
Plain, Lowland
Delta
Salt Flat
Valley, Canyon
Crater, Cave
Karst Features
Depression
Polder
Desert, Dunes
Forest, Woods
Heath, Steppe
Oasis
Cape, Point
Coast, Beach
Cliff
Peninsula
Isthmus
Sandbank
Island
Atoll
Rock, Reef
Islands, Archipelago
Rocks, Reefs
Coral Reef
Well, Spring
Geyser
River, Stream
Waterfall Rapids
River Mouth, Estuary
Lake
Salt Lake
Intermittent Lake
Reservoir
Swamp, Pond
Canal
Glacier
Ice Shelf, Pack Ice
Ocean
Sea
Gulf, Bay
Strait, Fjord
Lagoon
Bank
Seamount
Tablemount
Ridge
Shelf
Basin
Escarpment, Sea Scarp
Fracture
Trench, Abyss
National Park, Reserve
Point of Interest
Recreation Site
Cave, Cavern
Historic Site
Ruins
Wall, Walls
Church, Abbey
Temple
Scientific Station
Airport
Port
Lighthouse
Mine
Tunnel
Dam, Bridge

Florida City 44 Gm 25.27N 80.29W
Florida Islands 60 Gi 9.00S 160.10E
Florida Keys 43 Kg 24.45N 81.00W
Floridia 14 Jm 37.05N 15.09E
Florido, Río- 48 Gd 27.43N 105.10W
Flórina 15 Ei 40.47N 21.24E
Flörsheim 12 Kd 50.01N 8.26E
Flotte, Cap de- 63b Ce 21.11S 167.24E
Floydada 45 Fj 33.59N 101.20W
Fluessen 11 Lb 52.57N 5.30E
Flumen 13 Lc 41.43N 0.09W
Flumendosa 14 Dk 39.26N 9.37E
Fluminimaggiore 14 Ck 39.26N 8.30E
Flumini Mannu 14 Ck 39.16N 9.00E
Flums 14 Dc 47.05N 9.20E
Fluvià 13 Pb 42.12N 3.07E
Flying Fish, Cape- 66 Of 72.06S 102.29W
Fly River 57 Fe 8.00S 142.21E
Fnideq 13 Gi 35.50N 5.22W
Fnjóská 7a Bb 65.54N 18.07W
Foa 65b Ba 19.45S 174.18W
Foam Lake 46 Na 51.39N 103.33W
Foça 15 Jk 38.39N 26.46E
Foča 14 Mg 43.31N 18.47E
Fochi 15 Bb 18.25N 15.40E
Fochi 35 Bb 18.56N 15.57E
Focşani 15 Kd 45.42N 27.11E
Fodda 13 Nh 36.14N 1.33E
Fodé 35 Cd 5.29N 23.18E
Føringehavn 41 Gf 63.45N 51.28W
Foga, Dallol- 34 Fc 12.05N 3.32E
Foggaret ez Zoua 32 Hd 27.22N 2.50E
Foggia 6 Hg 41.27N 15.34E
Foggo 34 Gc 11.23N 9.57E
Foglia 14 Gg 43.55N 12.54E
Föglö 8 Ie 60.00N 20.25E
Fogo [Can.] 42 Mg 49.40N 54.10W
Fogo [C.V.] 30 Eg 14.55N 24.25W
Fohnsdorf 14 Ic 47.12N 14.41E
Föhr 10 Eb 54.45N 8.30E
Föhren 12 Ie 49.51N 6.46E
Foix 11 Hl 42.58N 1.36E
Fojnica 23 Fg 43.58N 17.54E
Fokino 16 Ic 53.27N 34.26E
Folda 7 Dc 67.36N 14.50E
Folégandros 15 Hm 36.38N 24.54E
Foley 42 Kc 68.30N 75.00W
Foleyet 42 Jg 48.16N 82.30W
Folgefonni 7 Bf 60.00N 6.20E
Foligno 14 Gh 42.57N 12.42E
Folkestone 9 Oj 51.05N 1.11E
Folkingham 12 Bb 52.52N 0.24W
Folkston 44 Fj 30.50N 82.01W
Folldals verk 7 Bb 62.08N 10.00E
Follebu 7 Cf 61.14N 10.17E
Föllinge 7 De 63.40N 14.37E
Follo 8 De 59.55N 10.55E
Follonica 14 Eh 42.55N 10.45E
Follonica, Golfo di- 14 Eh 42.55N 10.40E
Folschviller 12 Ie 49.04N 6.41E
Fomboni 37 Gb 12.16S 43.45E
Fomento 49 Hb 22.06N 79.43W
Fond d'Or Bay 51k Bb 13.56N 60.54W
Fond-du-Lac 42 Ge 59.19N 107.10W
Fond-du-Lac 42 Ge 59.17N 106.00W
Fond du Lac 43 Jc 43.47N 88.27W
Fondi 14 Hi 41.21N 13.25E
Fongen 8 Da 63.11N 11.38E
Fongoro 35 Cc 11.30N 22.25E
Fonni 14 Dj 40.07N 9.15E
Fonoifua 65b Bb 20.17S 174.38W
Fonsagrada 13 Ea 43.08N 7.04W
Fonseca 54 Da 10.53N 72.50W
Fonseca, Golfo de- 38 Kh 13.08N 87.40W
Fonsecas, Serra dos- 55 Jc 17.02S 44.13W
Fontaine-Bellenger 12 De 49.11N 1.16E
Fontainebleau 11 If 48.24N 2.42E
Fontaine-Henry, Château de- 12 Be 49.17N 0.27W
Fontaine-le-Dun 12 Ce 49.49N 0.51E
Fontaine-l'Evêque 12 Gd 50.25N 4.19E
Fontas 42 Fe 58.17N 121.46W
Fonte Boa 54 Ed 2.32S 66.01W
Fontenay-le-Comte 11 Fh 46.28N 0.49W
Fontenay Trésigny 12 Ef 48.42N 2.52E
Fontenelle Reservoir 46 Je 42.05N 110.06W
Fontevraud-l'Abbaye 11 Gg 47.11N 0.03E
Fontur 5 Eb 66.23N 14.32W
Fonuafo'ou Falcon 61 Fd 20.19S 175.25W
Fonualei Island 57 Jf 18.01S 174.19W
Fonyód 10 Nj 46.44N 17.33E
Foraker, Mount- 40 Id 62.56N 151.26W
Forbach 11 Me 49.11N 6.54E
Forbes 59 Jf 33.23S 148.01E
Forbes, Mount- 46 Ga 51.52N 116.56W
Forcados 34 Gd 5.23N 5.19E
Forcados 34 Gd 5.21N 5.25E
Forcalquier 11 Lk 43.58N 5.47E
Forchheim 10 Hg 49.43N 11.04E
Ford City 46 Fi 35.09N 119.27W
Førde 7 Af 61.27N 5.52E
Førdefjorden 8 Ac 61.30N 5.40E
Ford Ranges 66 Mf 77.00S 145.00W
Fordyce 45 Jj 33.49N 92.25W
Forécariah 34 Cd 9.26N 13.06W
Forel, Mont- 67 Mc 67.05N 36.55W
Forelshogna 8 Db 62.41N 10.47E
Forest 45 Lj 32.22N 89.28W
Forest Park 44 Ei 33.37N 84.22W
Forestville 44 Ma 48.45N 69.06W
Forez, Monts du- 11 Ji 45.35N 3.48E
Forez, Plaine du- 11 Ki 45.50N 4.10E
Forfar 9 Ke 56.38N 2.54W
Forges-les-Eaux 11 He 49.37N 1.33E
Forggensee 10 Gi 47.36N 10.44E
Forks 46 Cc 47.57N 124.23W
Forlì 14 Gf 44.13N 12.03E
Forlì, Bocca di- 14 Ii 41.45N 14.10E
Formby Point 9 Jh 53.33N 3.06W
Formentera 5 Gh 38.42N 1.28E
Formentor, Cabo de-/ Formentor, Cap de- 13 Pe 39.58N 3.12E
Formentor, Cap de-/ Formentor, Cabo de- 13 Pe 39.58N 3.12E
Formerie 12 De 49.39N 1.44E
Formia 14 Hi 41.15N 13.37E
Formiga 54 Ih 20.27S 45.25W
Formigas 32 Cb 37.16N 24.47W
Formosa [2] 56 Ib 25.00S 60.00W
Formosa [Arg.] 53 Kh 26.10S 58.11W
Formosa [Braz.] 54 Ig 15.32S 47.20W
Formosa [Gui. Bis.] 34 Bc 11.45N 16.05W
Formosa [Tai.]→ Taiwan 21 Og 23.30N 121.00E
Formosa, Serra- 52 Kg 12.00S 55.00W
Formosa Bay 36 Hc 2.45S 40.20E
Formosa Strait (EN) = Taiwan Haixia 21 Ng 24.00N 119.00E
Formoso [Braz.] 55 Ib 14.57S 46.14W
Formoso [Braz.] 55 Ha 13.37S 48.54W
Formoso, Rio- [Braz.] 55 Ja 13.26S 44.14W
Formoso, Rio- [Braz.] 54 If 10.34S 49.59W
Formoso, Rio- [Braz.] 55 Fd 18.25S 52.28W
Fornæs 7 Ch 56.27N 10.58E
Fornosovo 8 Ne 59.31N 30.45E
Fornovo di Taro 14 Ef 44.42N 10.06E
Föroyar/Færøerne = Færoe Islands (EN) [5] 6 Fc 62.00N 7.00W
Föroyar/Færøerne = Færoe Islands (EN) 5 Fc 62.00N 7.00W
Forres 9 Jd 57.37N 3.38W
Forrest 59 Ff 30.51S 128.06E
Forrest City 45 Ki 35.01N 90.47W
Forrester Island 66 Nf 74.06S 132.00W
Forsayth 59 Ic 18.35S 143.36E
Forsbacka 8 Gd 60.37N 16.53E
Forserum 8 Fg 57.42N 14.28E
Forshaga 7 Cg 59.32N 13.28E
Forsnäs 7 Ec 66.14N 18.39E
Forssa 7 Ff 60.49N 23.38E
Forst/Baršć 10 Ke 51.44N 14.38E
Forsyth 46 Lc 46.16N 106.41W
Fort Albany 39 Kd 52.15N 81.37W
Fortaleza 53 Mf 3.43S 38.30W
Fortaleza, Ribeirão- 55 Fd 19.50S 53.25W
Fort Augustus 9 Id 57.09N 4.41W
Fort Beaufort 37 Df 32.46S 26.40E
Fort Benton 43 Eb 47.49N 110.40W
Fort Bragg 43 Cd 39.26N 123.48W
Fort Bridger 46 Jf 41.19N 110.23W
Fort-Carnot 37 Hd 21.53S 48.26E
Fort Chipewyan 42 Ge 58.42N 111.08W
Fort Cobb Reservoir 45 Gi 35.12N 98.29W
Fort Collins 43 Fc 40.35N 105.05W
Fort Collinson 42 Fb 71.37N 117.57W
Fort Coulogne 44 Ic 45.51N 76.44W
Fort Davis 45 Ek 30.35N 103.54W
Fort-de-France 39 Mh 14.36N 61.05W
Fort-de-France, Baie de- 51h Ab 14.34N 61.04W
Fort Dodge 43 Ic 42.30N 94.10W
Forte 55 Ib 14.16S 47.17W
Forte dei Marmi 14 Eg 43.57N 10.10E
Fortescue River 57 Cg 21.00S 116.06E
Fort Frances 39 Je 48.36N 93.24W
Fort Franklin 42 Fc 65.12N 123.26W
Fort Garland 45 Dh 37.26N 105.26W
Fort Gibson Lake 45 Ih 36.00N 95.18W
Fort Good-Hope 39 Gc 66.15N 128.38W
Forth 9 Je 56.04N 3.42W
Forth, Firth of- 5 Fd 56.05N 2.55W
Fort Hall 36 Gc 0.43S 37.09E
Fort Hope 42 If 51.32N 88.00W
Fortin Avalos Sanchez 55 Bf 23.28S 60.07W
Fortín Boquerón 55 Cf 22.47S 59.57W
Fortín Buenos Aires 55 Bf 22.57S 61.51W
Fortín Cadete Pastor Pando 55 Cg 24.20S 58.54W
Fortín Capitán Figari 55 Cf 23.12S 59.32W
Fortín Carlos A. Lopez 55 Ce 21.19S 59.44W
Fortín Comandante Nowak 55 Cg 24.51S 58.15W
Fortín Coronel Bogado 55 Ce 20.46S 59.09W
Fortín Coronel Eugenio Garay 56 Hb 20.31S 62.08W
Fortín Coronel Hermosa 55 Bf 22.33S 60.01W
Fortín Coronel Martinez 55 Cf 22.15S 59.09W
Fortín Florida 55 Ce 20.45S 59.17W
Fortín Galpón 55 Cd 19.51S 58.16W
Fortín Gaspar Rodriguez de Francia 55 Cf 23.01S 59.57W
Fortín General Caballero 55 Cg 24.08S 59.30W
Fortín General Delgado 55 Cg 24.28S 59.15W
Fortín General Diaz 56 Hb 23.31S 60.34W
Fortín Guarani 55 Cf 22.44S 59.30W
Fortín Hernandarias 55 Be 21.58S 61.30W
Fortín José M. López 55 Be 20.07S 60.15W
Fortín Lagerenza 55 Be 20.06S 61.03W
Fortín Madrejón 55 Ce 20.38S 59.52W
Fortín Mariscal López 55 Cf 23.39S 59.44W
Fortín Max Paredes 55 Cd 19.16S 59.58W
Fortín May Alberto Gardel 55 Af 22.46S 62.12W
Fortín Mayor Long 55 Ae 20.33S 62.01W
Fortín Mayor R. Santacruz 55 Be 20.15S 60.37W
Fortín Nueva Asunción 55 Be 20.42S 61.55W
Fortín Pikyrenda 55 Be 20.05S 61.48W
Fortín Pilcomayo [Par.] 55 Bf 23.44S 60.51W
Fortín Pilcomayo [Arg.] 55 Bf 23.52S 60.53W
Fortín Pratts Gill 55 Bf 22.41S 61.33W
Fortín Presidente Ayala 55 Cf 23.30S 59.46W
Fortín Ravelo 55 Bd 19.18S 60.35W
Fortín Suarez Arana 55 Bd 18.40S 60.09W
Fortín Teniente 1º Alfredo Stroessner 55 Bf 22.45S 61.32W
Fortín Teniente 1º H. Mendoza 55 Cd 19.54S 59.47W
Fortín Teniente 1º M. Cabello 55 Bf 23.28S 61.19W
Fortín Teniente 1º Ramiro Espinola 55 Be 21.28S 61.18W
Fortín Teniente Acosta 55 Bf 22.41S 60.32W
Fortín Teniente Agripino Enciso 55 Be 21.12S 61.34W
Fortín Teniente Américo Picco 55 Cd 19.35S 59.43W
Fortín Teniente Aristigueta 55 Bf 22.21S 60.38W
Fortín Teniente E. Ochoa 55 Be 21.42S 61.02W
Fortín Teniente Esteban Martinez 55 Cg 24.02S 59.51W
Fortín Teniente Juan E. López 55 Be 21.05S 61.48W
Fortín Teniente Montania 55 Cf 22.04S 59.57W
Fortín Teniente R. Rueda 55 Be 21.49S 60.49W
Fortín Toledo 55 Bf 22.20S 60.21W
Fortín Torres 55 Ce 21.01S 59.30W
Fortín Vanguardia 55 Cd 19.39S 58.10W
Fortín Vitiones 55 Cd 19.30S 58.06W
Fortín Zenteno 55 Cf 23.10S 59.59W
Fort Jeuedy, Point of- 51p Bb 12.00N 61.42W
Fort Kent 44 Mb 47.15N 68.36W
Fort Knox 44 Eg 37.53N 85.55W
Fort Lamy → N'djamena 31 Ig 12.07N 15.03E
Fort Lauderdale 43 Kf 26.07N 80.08W
Fort Liard 39 Gc 60.15N 123.28W
Fort-Liberté 49 Ld 19.38N 71.57W
Fort MacKay 42 Ge 57.08N 111.42W
Fort Macleod 42 Gg 49.43N 113.25W
Fort Mac Mahon 32 Hd 29.46N 1.37E
Fort Madison 45 Kf 40.38N 91.21W
Fort-Mahon-Plage 12 Dd 50.21N 1.34E
Fort McMurray 39 Hd 56.44N 111.23W
Fort McPherson 39 Fc 67.27N 134.53W
Fort Miribel 32 Hd 29.26N 3.00E
Fort Morgan 45 Ef 40.15N 103.48W
Fort Myers 39 Kg 26.37N 81.54W
Fort Myers Beach 44 Gl 26.27N 81.57W
Fort Nelson 39 Gd 58.49N 122.39W
Fort Nelson 42 Fe 59.33N 124.01W
Fort Norman 42 Ed 64.56N 125.22W
Fortore 14 Ji 41.55N 15.17E
Fort Payne 44 Eh 34.27N 85.43W
Fort Peck 46 Lb 48.01N 106.27W
Fort Peck Lake 43 Fb 47.45N 106.50W
Fort Pierce 43 Kf 27.27N 80.20W
Fort Pierre 43 Gc 44.21N 100.22W
Fort Portal 36 Fb 0.39N 30.17E
Fort Providence 39 Hc 61.21N 117.39W
Fort Qu'Appelle 46 Na 50.56N 103.09W
Fort Resolution 42 Gd 61.10N 113.40W
Fortrose 62 Cg 46.34S 168.48E
Fort Saint James 42 Ff 54.26N 124.15W
Fort Saint John 39 Gd 56.15N 120.51W
Fort Sandenam 25 Db 31.20N 69.27E
Fort Saskatchewan 42 Gf 53.43N 113.13W
Fort Scott 45 Ih 37.50N 94.42W
Fort-Ševčenko 19 Fg 44.30N 50.14E
Fort Severn 39 Kd 56.00N 87.38W
Fort Simpson 39 Gc 61.52N 121.23W
Fort Smith [Ar.-U.S.] 39 Jf 35.23N 94.25W
Fort Smith [N.W.T.-Can.] 39 Hd 60.00N 111.53W
Fort Stockton 43 Ge 30.53N 102.53W
Fort Sumner 45 Di 34.28N 104.15W
Fortuna 46 Cf 40.36N 124.09W
Fortuna, Rio de la- 55 Cc 16.36S 58.46W
Fortune Bay 42 Lg 47.15N 55.40W
Fort Vermilion 42 Fe 58.24N 116.00W
Fort Walton Beach 43 Je 30.25N 86.36W
Fort Washakie 46 Ke 43.00N 108.53W
Fort Wayne 39 Ke 41.04N 85.09W
Fort William 9 He 56.49N 5.07W
Fort Worth 39 Jf 32.45N 97.20W
Fort Yates 45 Fc 46.05N 100.38W
Fort Yukon 39 Ec 66.34N 145.17W
Forūr, Jazīreh-ye- 24 Pi 26.17N 54.32E
Foshan 22 Ng 22.59N 113.05E
Fosheim Peninsula 42 Ja 80.00N 84.30W
Fosnavåg 8 Ab 62.21N 5.39E
Fosnøy 8 Ad 60.45N 4.55E
Fossacesia 14 Ih 42.15N 14.29E
Fossano 14 Bf 44.33N 7.43E
Fossato, Colle di- 14 Gg 43.20N 12.49E
Fossberg 8 Cc 61.50N 8.34E
Fossil 46 Ed 44.59N 120.13W
Fossil Bluff 66 Qf 71.20S 68.17W
Fossombrone 14 Gg 43.41N 12.48E
Fosston 45 Ic 47.35N 95.45W
Fos-sur-Mer 11 Kk 43.26N 4.57E
Foster 59 Jg 38.39S 146.12E
Foster, Mount- 40 Le 59.48N 135.29W
Foster Bugt 41 Jd 73.40N 21.40W
Fostoria 44 Fe 41.10N 83.25W
Fotuha'a 65b Ba 19.49S 174.44W
Foucarmont 12 De 49.51N 1.34E
Fougamou 36 Bc 1.13S 10.36E
Fougères 11 Ef 48.21N 1.12W
Foul, Khalīj- 33 Ge 23.30N 35.40E
Foula 9 Ka 60.10N 2.05W
Foul Bay 51q Bb 13.06N 59.27W
Fouligny 12 Ie 49.06N 6.30E
Foulness 9 Nj 51.36N 0.55E
Foulness Point 12 Cc 51.37N 0.57E
Foulwind, Cape- 62 Dd 41.45S 171.28E
Foumban 34 Hd 5.43N 10.55E
Foumbouni 37 Gb 11.50S 43.30E
Foum Zguid 32 Fc 30.05N 6.52W
Foundation Ice Stream 66 Qg 83.15S 60.00W
Fountains Abbey 9 Lg 54.07N 1.34W
Fouquet Island 37b Bb 5.25S 53.20E
Fourchambault 11 Jg 47.01N 3.05E
Fourchue, Ile- 51b Bc 17.57N 62.55W
Fourmiers 11 Kd 50.00N 4.03E
Four Mountains, Islands of the- 40a Db 52.50N 170.00W
Foúrnoi 15 Jl 37.34N 26.30E
Fouron/Voeren 12 Hd 50.45N 5.48E
Fours 11 Jh 46.49N 3.43E
Fourth Cataract (EN) = Rabi', Ash Shallāl ar- 30 Kg 18.47N 32.03E
Fous, Pointe des- 51g Bb 15.12N 61.20W
Fouta 34 Cb 16.18N 14.48W
Fouta Djalon 30 Fg 11.30N 12.30W
Foutouna, Ile- 57 If 19.32S 170.13E
Foux, Cap-à- 49 Kd 19.45N 73.27W
Fouzon 11 Hg 47.16N 1.27E
Foveaux Strait 57 Hi 46.40S 168.10E
Fowler [Co.-U.S.] 45 Eg 38.08N 104.00W
Fowler [In.-U.S.] 44 De 40.37N 87.19W
Fowlers Bay 59 Gf 32.00S 132.25E
Fowman 24 Md 37.13N 49.19E
Foxe Basin 38 Lc 68.25N 77.00W
Foxe Channel 38 Lc 64.30N 80.00W
Foxen 8 De 59.25N 11.55E
Foxe Peninsula 38 Lc 65.00N 76.00W
Foxford/Béal Easa 9 Dh 53.59N 9.07W
Fox Glacier 61 Ch 43.28S 170.00E
Fox Islands 38 Cd 54.00N 168.00W
Fox Peak 62 De 43.50S 170.47E
Fox River 45 Lf 41.21N 88.50W
Foxton 62 Fd 40.28S 175.17E
Fox Valley 46 Ka 50.29N 109.28W
Foyle 9 Ff 55.04N 7.15W
Foyle, Lough-/Loch Feabhail 9 Ff 55.05N 7.10W
Foz do Cunene 36 Bf 17.15S 11.48E
Foz do Iguaçu 53 Kh 25.33S 54.35W
Fraga 13 Mc 41.31N 0.21E
Fragoso, Cayo 49 Hb 22.44N 79.30W
Fraire, Walcourt- 12 Gd 50.16N 4.30E
Fram 55 Eh 27.06S 55.58W
Fram Basin (EN) 67 He 88.00N 80.00E
Framlingham 12 Db 52.13N 1.20E
Franca 56 Kb 20.32S 47.24W
Franca-Josifa, Zemlja- = Franz Joseph Land (EN) 21 Ha 81.00N 55.00E
Francavilla al Mare 14 Ih 42.25N 14.17E
Francavilla Fontana 14 Lj 40.32N 17.35E
France [1] 6 Gf 46.00N 2.00E
Frances 42 Ed 60.16N 129.11W
Francés, Punta- 49 Fc 21.38N 83.12W
Francesi, Punta di li- 14 Di 41.08N 9.02E
Francés Viejo, Cabo- 49 Md 19.39N 69.55W
Franceville 31 Ii 1.38S 13.35E
Franche-Comté 11 Lh 47.00N 6.00E
Franches Montagnes/ Freiberge 14 Ac 47.15N 7.00E
Francia 55 Dk 32.34S 56.38W
Francia, Sierra de- 13 Fd 40.35N 6.05W
Francis Case, Lake- 38 Je 43.15N 99.00W
Francisco Beltrão 56 Jc 26.05S 53.04W
Francisco Escárcega 48 Nh 18.37N 90.43W
Francisco I. Madero 48 Ge 24.32N 104.22W
Francisco Madero 55 Al 35.52S 62.03W
Francisco Morazán [3] 49 Df 14.15N 87.15W
Francisco Sá 54 Jg 16.28S 43.30W
Franciscus Bay 37 Ae 25.00S 14.50E
Francistown 31 Jk 21.09S 27.31E
Francofonte 14 Im 37.14N 14.53E
Franconian Jura (EN) = Fränkische Alb 5 Hf 49.00N 11.30E
Francs Peak 43 Fc 43.58N 109.20W
Franeker 11 La 53.11N 5.32E
Frankenau 12 Kc 51.06N 8.56E
Frankenberg (Eder) 10 Ee 51.04N 8.40E
Frankenhöhe 10 Gg 49.15N 10.15E
Frankenthal (Pfalz) 12 Ke 49.32N 8.21E
Frankenwald 10 Hf 50.18N 11.36E
Frankfort [In.-U.S.] 44 De 40.17N 86.31W
Frankfort [Ky.-U.S.] 39 Kf 38.12N 84.52W
Frankfort [Mi.-U.S.] 44 Dc 44.38N 86.14W
Frankfort on the Main (EN) = Frankfurt am Main 6 Ge 50.07N 8.41E
Frankfurt 10 Kd 52.21N 14.33E
Frankfurt am Main = Frankfort on the Main (EN) 6 Ge 50.07N 8.41E
Fränkische Alb = Franconian Jura(EN) 5 Hf 49.00N 11.30E
Fränkische Saale 10 Ff 50.03N 9.42E
Fränkische Schweiz 10 Hg 49.45N 11.20E
Franklin [In.-U.S.] 44 Df 39.29N 86.03W
Franklin [Ky.-U.S.] 44 Dg 36.43N 86.35W
Franklin [La.-U.S.] 45 Kl 29.48N 91.30W
Franklin [N.C.-U.S.] 44 Fh 35.11N 83.23W
Franklin [N.H.-U.S.] 44 Ld 43.27N 71.39W
Franklin [Pa.-U.S.] 44 He 41.24N 79.49W
Franklin [Tn.-U.S.] 44 Dh 35.55N 86.52W
Franklin, District of- [3] 42 Hb 72.00N 96.00W
Franklin Bay 38 Gc 68.45N 125.35W
Franklin Delano Roosevelt Lake 43 Db 48.20N 118.10W
Franklin Island 66 Kf 76.05S 168.11E
Franklin Lake [Nv.-U.S.] 46 Hf 40.24N 115.12W
Franklin Lake [N.W.T.-Can.] 42 Hc 66.55N 96.05W
Franklin Mountains 38 Gc 63.15N 123.30W
Franklin Strait 42 Hb 71.30N 96.30W
Fransfontein 37 Bd 20.12S 15.01E
Frånsta 8 Gb 62.30N 16.09E
Franz Josef Glacier 62 De 43.23S 170.11E
Franz Joseph Land (EN) = Franca-Josifa, Zemlja- 21 Ha 81.00N 55.00E
Frascati 14 Gi 41.48N 12.41E
Fraser [Can.] 38 Ge 49.09N 123.12W
Fraser [Newf.-Can.] 42 Le 56.39N 63.08W
Fraserburg 37 Cf 31.55S 21.30E
Fraserburgh 9 Ld 57.42N 2.00W
Fraserdale 42 Jg 49.51N 81.38W
Fraser Island 57 Gg 25.15S 153.10E
Fraser Plateau 38 Gd 51.30N 122.00W
Fraser Range 59 Ef 32.03S 122.48E
Frasertown 62 Gc 38.58S 177.24E
Frasnes-les-Anvaing 12 Fd 50.40N 3.36E
Frauenfeld 14 Cc 47.35N 8.54E
Fray Bentos 56 Id 33.08S 58.18W
Frechen 12 Id 50.55N 6.49E
Frechilla 13 Hb 42.08N 4.50W
Fredericia 7 Bi 55.35N 9.46E
Frederick [Md.-U.S.] 44 If 39.25N 77.25W
Frederick [Ok.-U.S.] 45 Gi 34.23N 99.01W
Frederick E. Hyde Fjord 41 Jb 82.40N 25.45W
Frederick Reef 57 Gg 21.00S 154.25E
Fredericksburg [Tx.-U.S.] 45 Gk 30.17N 98.52W
Fredericksburg [Va.-U.S.] 44 If 38.18N 77.30W
Fredericktown 45 Kh 37.33N 90.18W
Frederico Westphalen 55 Fh 27.22S 53.24W
Fredericton 39 Me 45.58N 66.39W
Frederiksborg [2] 8 Ei 55.55N 12.15E
Frederiksdal 41 Hf 60.15N 45.30W
Frederikshåb/Pâmiut 41 Hf 62.00N 49.45W
Frederikshåbs Bank (EN) 41 Hf 62.16N 49.45W
Frederikshavn 6 Hd 57.26N 10.32E
Frederikssund 8 Ei 55.50N 12.04E
Fréderiksted 50 Dd 17.42N 64.48W
Frederiksværk 8 Ei 55.58N 12.02E
Fredonia 46 Ih 36.57N 112.32W
Fredrika 7 Ed 64.05N 18.24E
Fredriksberg 7 Df 60.08N 14.23E
Fredrikshamn/Hamina 7 Gf 60.34N 27.12E
Fredrikstad 7 Cg 59.13N 10.57E
Fredvang 7 Cb 68.05N 13.10E
Freeling Heights 59 Hf 30.10S 139.25E
Freels, Cape- 42 Mg 49.13N 53.29W
Freeport [Bah.] 47 Ic 26.30N 78.45W
Freeport [Il.-U.S.] 43 Jc 42.17N 89.36W
Freeport [N.Y.-U.S.] 44 Ke 40.40N 73.35W
Freeport [Tx.-U.S.] 43 Hf 28.55N 95.22W
Freer 45 Gm 27.53N 98.37W
Freetown [Atg.] 51d Bb 17.03N 61.42W
Freetown [S.L.] 31 Fh 8.30N 13.15W
Fregenal de la Sierra 13 Ff 38.10N 6.39W
Fregene 14 Gi 41.51N 12.12E
Frei 8 Ba 63.01N 7.48E
Freiberg 10 Jf 50.55N 13.22E
Freiberge/Franches Montagnes 14 Ac 47.15N 7.00E
Freiberger Mulde 10 Ie 51.10N 12.48E
Freiburg/Fribourg 14 Bd 46.50N 7.10E
Freiburg im Breisgau 6 Gf 48.00N 7.51E
Freilassing 10 Ii 47.51N 12.59E
Freirina 56 Fc 28.30S 71.06W
Freisen 12 Je 49.33N 7.15E
Freising 10 Hh 48.24N 11.44E
Freistadt 14 Ib 48.30N 14.30E
Freital 10 Je 51.01N 13.39E
Fréjus 11 Mk 43.26N 6.44E
Fréjus, Col du- 11 Mi 45.07N 6.40E
Fremantle, Perth- 59 Df 32.03S 115.45E
Fremont [Ca.-U.S.] 43 Cd 37.34N 122.01W
Fremont [Nb.-U.S.] 43 Hc 41.26N 96.30W
Fremont [Oh.-U.S.] 44 Fe 41.21N 83.08W
Fremont River 46 Jg 38.24N 110.42W
French Frigate Shoals 57 Kb 23.45N 166.10W
French Guiana (EN) = Guyane Française [5] 53 Ke 4.00N 53.00W
French Lick 44 Df 38.33N 86.37W
Frenchman Creek 45 Ff 40.13N 100.50W
Frenchman River 43 Fb 48.24N 107.05W
French Pass 62 Ed 40.55S 173.50E
French Plain (EN) 5 Gf 47.00N 1.00E
French Polynesia (EN) = Polynésie Française [5] 58 Mf 16.00S 145.00W
French River 44 Gc 45.56N 80.54W
Frenda 32 Hb 35.04N 1.02E
Frénel, Cap- 11 Df 48.42N 2.19W
Frentani, Monti dei- 14 Ii 41.55N 14.30E
Freren 12 Jb 52.29N 7.33E
Fresco 34 Dd 5.05N 5.34W
Fresco, Rio- 54 He 6.39S 52.00W
Freshfield, Cape- 66 Je 68.22S 151.05E
Fresnes-en-Woëvre 12 He 49.06N 5.37E
Fresnillo de Gonzales Echeverría 47 Dd 23.10N 102.53W
Fresno 39 Hf 36.45N 119.45W
Fresno, Portillo del- 13 Ib 42.35N 3.40W
Fresno River 46 Eh 37.05N 120.33W
Fresquel 11 Ik 43.14N 2.24E
Fresvikbreen 8 Bc 61.02N 6.45E
Freu, Cabo- 13 Pe 39.45N 3.27E
Freudenberg 12 Jd 50.54N 7.52E
Freudenstadt 10 Eh 48.26N 8.25E
Frévent 11 Id 50.16N 2.17E
Freycinet Estuary 59 Ce 26.25S 113.45E
Freycinet Peninsula 59 Jh 42.15S 148.20E
Freyming-Merlebach 12 Ie 49.09N 6.47E
Freyre 55 Aj 31.10S 62.02W
Freyung 10 Jh 48.48N 13.33E
Fri 15 Jn 35.25N 26.56E
Fria 34 Cc 10.27N 13.32W
Fria, Cape- 30 Ij 18.27S 12.01E
Frias 56 Gc 28.39S 65.09W
Fribourg [2] 14 Bd 46.40N 7.10E
Fribourg/Freiburg 14 Bd 46.50N 7.10E
Fridtjof Nansen, Mount- 66 Lg 85.21S 167.33W
Friedberg [Aus.] 14 Kc 47.26N 16.03E
Friedberg 10 Ef 50.21N 8.46E
Friedrichshafen 10 Fi 47.39N 9.29E
Friedrichsthal 12 Je 49.19N 7.06E
Friesach 14 Id 46.57N 14.24E
Friese Gat 12 Ia 53.30N 6.05E
Friese Wad 12 Ha 53.25N 5.50E
Friese Wad 12 Ha 53.24N 5.45E
Friesland [3] 12 Ha 53.03N 5.45E
Friesland 11 La 53.05N 6.00E
Friesland 5 Ge 53.05N 6.00E

Index Symbols

[1] Independent Nation
[2] State, Region
[3] District, County
[4] Municipality
[5] Colony, Dependency
Continent
Physical Region
Historical or Cultural Region
Mount, Mountain
Volcano
Hill
Mountains, Mountain Range
Hills, Escarpment
Plateau, Upland
Pass, Gap
Plain, Lowland
Delta
Salt Flat
Valley, Canyon
Crater, Cave
Karst Features
Depression
Polder
Desert, Dunes
Forest, Woods
Heath, Steppe
Oasis
Cape, Point
Coast, Beach
Cliff
Peninsula
Isthmus
Sandbank
Island
Atoll
Rock, Reef
Islands, Archipelago
Rocks, Reefs
Coral Reef
Well, Spring
Geyser
River, Stream
Waterfall Rapids
River Mouth, Estuary
Lake
Salt Lake
Intermittent Lake
Reservoir
Swamp, Pond
Canal
Glacier
Ice Shelf, Pack Ice
Ocean
Sea
Gulf, Bay
Strait, Fjord
Lagoon
Bank
Seamount
Tablemount
Ridge
Shelf
Basin
Escarpment, Sea Scarp
Fracture
Trench, Abyss
National Park, Reserve
Point of Interest
Recreation Site
Cave, Cavern
Historic Site
Ruins
Wall, Walls
Church, Abbey
Temple
Scientific Station
Airport
Port
Lighthouse
Mine
Tunnel
Dam, Bridge

Friesoythe 10 Dc 53.01N 7.51 E
Frigate Island 51p Cb 12.25N 61.29W
Friggesund 8 Gc 61.54N 16.32 E
Frignano 14 Ef 44.20N 10.50 E
Frindsbury Reef 63a Da 5.00S 159.07 E
Frinnaryd 8 Fg 57.55N 14.49 E
Frinton-on-Sea 12 Dc 51.50N 1.15 E
Frio, Cabo- 52 Lh 22.53S 42.00W
Frio, Rio- 49 Eh 11.08N 84.46W
Frio Draw 45 Ei 34.50N 102.08W
Friona 45 Ei 34.38N 102.43W
Frio River 45 Gl 28.30N 98.10W
Frisco Peak 46 Ig 38.31N 113.14W
Frisian Islands (EN) 5 Ge 54.00N 7.00 E
Fristad 8 Eg 57.50N 13.01 E
Fritsla 8 Eg 57.33N 12.47 E
Fritzlar 10 Fe 51.08N 9.17 E
Friuli 14 Ge 46.00N 13.00 E
Friuli-Venezia Giulia [2] 14 Gd 46.00N 13.00 E
Frobisher Bay 38 Mc 62.30N 66.00W
Frobisher Lake 42 Ge 56.20N 108.20W
Froidchapelle 12 Gd 50.09N 4.20 E
Froissy 12 Ee 49.34N 2.13 E
Frolovo 19 Ef 49.45N 43.39 E
Fromberg 46 Kd 45.23N 108.54W
Frombork 10 Pb 54.22N 19.41 E
Frome 9 Kj 51.14N 2.20W
Frome, Lake- 57 Eh 30.50S 139.50 E
Frondenberg 12 Jc 51.28N 7.46 E
Fronteira 13 Ee 39.03N 7.39W
Fronteiras 54 Je 7.05S 40.37W
Frontera 48 Mh 18.32N 92.38W
Frontera, Punta- 48 Mh 19.36N 92.42W
Fronteras 48 Eb 30.56N 109.31W
Frontignan 11 Jk 43.27N 3.45 E
Frontino, Paramo- 54 Cb 6.28N 76.04W
Front Range 38 If 39.45N 105.45W
Front Royal 44 Hf 38.56N 78.13W
Frosinone 14 Hi 41.38N 13.19 E
Frösö 8 Fa 63.11N 14.32 E
Frostburg 44 Hf 39.39N 78.56W
Frost Glacier 66 Ie 67.05S 129.00 E
Frövi 8 Fe 59.28N 15.22 E
Frøya 7 Be 63.43N 8.42 E
Frøysjøen 8 Ac 61.50N 5.05 E
Frozen Strait 42 Jc 65.50N 84.30W
Fruges 11 Id 50.31N 2.08 E
Frunze → Biškek 22 Je 42.54N 74.36 E
Frunze 18 Hd 40.06N 71.45 E
Frunzovka 15 Mb 47.20N 29.37 E
Fruška Gora 15 Cd 45.10N 19.35 E
Frutal 54 Ih 20.02S 48.55W
Frutigen 14 Bd 46.35N 7.40 E
Fry Canyon 46 Jh 37.38N 110.08W
Frýdek Mistek 10 Og 49.41N 18.22 E
Frylinckspan 37 Ce 26.46S 22.28 E
Ftéri 15 Ej 39.09N 21.33 E
Fua'amotu 65b Ac 21.15S 175.08W
Fua Mulaku Island 25a Bc 0.15S 73.30 E
Fu'an 27 Kf 27.10N 119.44 E
Fu-chien Sheng → Fujian Sheng = Fukien (EN) [2] 27 Kf 26.00N 118.00 E
Fuchskauten 10 Ef 50.40N 8.05 E
Fuchū [Jap.] 29 Cd 34.34N 133.14 E
Fuchū [Jap.] 29 Fd 35.41N 139.28 E
Fuchun-Jiang 28 Fi 30.15N 120.15 E
Fuchunjiang-Shuiku 28 Ej 29.29N 119.31 E
Fucino, Conca del- 14 Hj 42.01N 13.31 E
Fudai 29 Ga 40.01N 141.52 E
Fuding 27 Lf 27.19N 120.08 E
Fuengirola 13 Hh 36.32N 4.37W
Fuente Alto 56 Fd 33.37S 70.35W
Fuente del Maestre 13 Ff 38.32N 6.27W
Fuente-Obejuna 13 Gf 38.16N 5.25W
Fuentesaúco 13 Gc 41.14N 5.30W
Fuentes de Andalucía 13 Gg 37.28N 5.21W
Fuentes de Cantos 13 Ff 38.15N 6.18W
Fuerte 47 Cc 25.54N 109.22W
Fuerte, Isla- 49 Ii 9.23N 76.11W
Fuerte, Sierra del- 48 Hd 27.30N 102.45W
Fuerte Olimpo 56 Ib 21.02S 57.54W
Fuerteventura 30 Ff 28.20N 14.00W
Fuga 26 Hc 18.52N 121.22 E
Fugong 27 Gf 27.03N 98.57 E
Fugou 28 Cg 34.04N 114.23 E
Fugu 27 Jd 39.02N 111.03 E
Fuguo → Zhanhua 28 Ef 37.42N 118.08 E
Fuhai/Burultokay 27 Eb 47.06N 87.23 E
Fuhayrī, Wādī- 23 Hf 16.04N 52.11 E
Fu He 28 Dj 28.36N 116.04 E
Fuji 28 Og 35.09N 138.38 E
Fujian Sheng (Fu-chien Sheng) = Fukien (EN) [2] 27 Kf 26.00N 118.00 E
Fujieda 29 Fd 34.51N 138.15 E
Fuji-Gawa 29 Fd 35.07N 138.38 E
Fujin 27 Nb 47.15N 132.01 E
Fujinomiya 29 Fd 35.12N 138.38 E
Fujioka 29 Fc 36.15N 139.03 E
Fuji-San 21 Pf 35.26N 138.43 E
Fujisawa 29 Fd 35.21N 139.27 E
Fuji-yoshida 29 Fd 35.29N 138.47 E
Fukagawa 27 Pc 43.43N 142.03 E
Fūkah 24 Bg 31.04N 27.55 E
Fukang 27 Ec 44.10N 87.59 E
Fuka-Shima 29 Be 32.43N 131.56 E
Fukiage 29 Bf 31.30N 130.20 E
Fukien (EN) = Fu-chien Sheng → Fujian Sheng [2] 27 Kf 26.00N 118.00 E
Fukien (EN) = Fujian Sheng (Fu-chien Sheng) [2] 27 Kf 26.00N 118.00 E
Fukuchiyama 28 Mg 35.18N 135.07 E
Fukue 28 Jh 32.41N 128.50 E
Fukueichiao 27 Lf 25.19N 121.34 E
Fukue-Jima 28 Jh 32.41N 128.48 E
Fukui 27 Od 36.04N 136.13 E
Fukui Ken [2] 28 Ng 36.00N 136.20 E
Fukuma 29 Be 33.47N 130.28 E
Fukuoka 22 Pf 33.35N 130.24 E
Fukuoka Ken [2] 28 Kh 33.28N 130.45 E
Fukuroi 29 Ed 34.45N 137.54 E
Fukushima [Jap.] 27 Pd 37.45N 140.28 E
Fukushima [Jap.] 27 Pc 41.29N 140.15 E
Fukushima Ken [2] 28 Pf 37.25N 140.10 E
Fukuyama 27 Ne 34.29N 133.22 E
Fūlādī, Kūh-e- 23 Kc 34.38N 67.32 E
Fūlād Mahalleh 24 Od 36.02N 53.44 E
Fulanga 63d Cc 19.08S 178.34W
Fulda 5 Ge 51.25N 9.39 E
Fulda 10 Ff 50.33N 9.40 E
Fuliji 28 Dh 33.47N 116.59 E
Fulin → Hanyuan 27 Hf 29.25N 102.12 E
Fuling 27 If 29.40N 107.21 E
Fullerton 45 Hf 41.22N 97.58W
Fulton [Arg.] 55 Cm 37.25S 58.48W
Fulton [Il.-U.S.] 45 Kf 41.52N 90.11W
Fulton [Ky.-U.S.] 44 Cg 36.30N 88.53W
Fulton [Mo.-U.S.] 45 Kg 38.52N 91.57W
Fulton [N.Y.-U.S.] 44 Id 43.20N 76.26W
Fulufjället 8 Ec 61.33N 12.43 E
Fumaiolo 14 Gg 43.47N 12.04 E
Fumay 11 Kd 50.00N 4.42 E
Fumel 11 Gj 44.30N 0.58 E
Funabasi 28 Og 35.42N 139.59 E
Funabiki 29 Gc 37.26N 140.35 E
Funafuti 58 Ie 8.01S 178.00 E
Funafuti Atoll 57 Ie 8.31S 179.08 E
Funagata 29 Gb 38.42N 140.18 E
Funagata-Yama 29 Gb 38.27N 140.37 E
Funakoshi-Wan 29 Hb 39.25N 142.00 E
Funan 28 Ch 32.38N 115.35 E
Funäsdalen 7 Ce 62.32N 12.33 E
Funchal 31 Fe 32.38N 16.54W
Fundación 54 Da 10.29N 74.12W
Fundão 13 Ed 40.08N 7.30W
Fundy, Bay of- 38 Me 45.00N 66.00W
Funeral Peak 46 Gh 36.08N 116.37W
Fungalei 64h Bb 13.17S 176.07W
Funhalouro 37 Ed 23.05S 34.24 E
Funing [China] 27 Ig 23.39N 105.33 E
Funing [China] 28 Eh 33.48N 119.47 E
Funing [China] 28 Ee 39.56N 119.15 E
Funiu Shan 27 Je 33.40N 112.10 E
Funtua 34 Gc 11.32N 7.19 E
Fuping 28 Ce 38.49N 114.15 E
Fuqing 27 Kf 25.47N 119.24 E
Furancungo 37 Eb 14.54S 33.37 E
Furano 28 Qc 43.21N 142.23 E
Füren 29a Ca 44.17N 142.25 E
Furenai 29a Cb 42.43N 142.15 E
Füren-Ko 29a Db 43.20N 145.20 E
Fürg 24 Ph 28.18N 55.13 E
Fur Jiang 28 Hc 42.37N 125.33 E
Furmanov 7 Jh 57.16N 41.07 E
Furnas, Represa de- 54 Ih 21.20S 45.50W
Furnas, Serra das- 55 Fb 15.45S 53.20W
Furneaux Group 57 Fi 40.10S 148.05 E
Furnes/Veurne 11 Ic 51.04N 2.40 E
Furqlus 24 Ge 34.36N 37.05 E
Furrīyānah 32 Ic 34.57N 8.34 E
Fürstenau 12 Jb 52.31N 7.43 E
Fürstenauer Berge 12 Jb 52.35N 7.45 E
Fürstenfeld 14 Kc 47.03N 16.05 E
Fürstenfeldbruck 10 Hh 48.11N 11.15 E
Furstenlager 12 Ke 49.42N 8.38 E
Fürstenwalde 10 Kd 52.22N 14.04 E
Fürth [Ger.] 10 Gg 49.28N 11.00 E
Fürth [Ger.] 12 Ke 49.39N 8.47 E
Furth im Wald 10 Ig 49.18N 12.51 E
Furubira 29a Bb 43.16N 140.39 E
Furudal 7 Df 61.10N 15.08 E
Furukawa 27 Pd 38.34N 140.58 E
Furusund 8 He 59.40N 18.55 E
Fury and Hecla Strait 42 Jc 69.55N 84.00W
Fushan [China] 28 Ff 37.30N 121.15 E
Fushan [China] 28 Ag 35.58N 111.51 E
Fushë-Arëzi 15 Dg 42.04N 20.02 E
Fushë-Lura 15 Dh 41.48N 20.13 E
Fu Shui 28 Cj 29.52N 115.26 E
Fushun 22 Oe 41.46N 123.56 E
Fusong 27 Mc 42.20N 127.17 E
Füsselberg 12 Je 49.32N 7.14 E
Füssen 10 Gi 47.34N 10.42 E
Futa, Passo della- 14 Ff 44.05N 11.17 E
Futago-Yama 29 Be 33.35N 131.38 E
Futaoi-Jima 29 Bd 34.06N 130.47 E
Futog 15 Cd 45.15N 19.42 E
Futuna, Ile- 57 Jf 14.17S 178.09W
Fuwah 24 Dg 31.12N 30.33 E
Fuxian (Wafangdian) 27 Ld 39.38N 121.59 E
Fuxian Hu 27 Hg 24.30N 102.55 E
Fuxin 22 Oe 41.59N 121.38 E
Fuxin Monggolzu Zizhixian 28 Fc 42.06N 121.46 E
Fuyang 27 Ke 32.47N 115.46 E
Fuyang He 28 Dg 38.14N 116.05 E
Fuyang Zhang 28 Ch 32.56N 115.53 E
Fuyu [China] 27 Lb 45.10N 124.52 E
Fuyu [China] 27 Lb 47.48N 124.26 E
Fuyuan [China] 27 Lc 42.44N 124.57 E
Fuyuan [China] 27 Nb 48.21N 134.18 E
Fuyuan [China] 27 Hf 25.43N 104.20 E
Fuyun/Koktokay 22 Ke 47.13N 89.39 E
Füzesabony 10 Qi 47.45N 20.25 E
Fuzhou [China] 22 Ng 26.10N 119.20 E
Fuzhou [China] 27 Kf 27.58N 116.20 E
Fuzhou He 28 Fe 39.36N 121.35 E
Fyllas Bank (EN) 41 Gf 64.00N 53.00W
Fyn 5 Hd 55.20N 10.30 E
Fyn [2] 8 Di 55.20N 10.30 E
Fyne, Loch- 9 He 56.10N 5.20W
Fyresdal 7 Bg 59.11N 8.06 E
Fyresvatn 8 Ce 59.05N 8.10 E
Fzâra, Garaʻet- 14 Bn 36.47N 7.30 E

G

Gaasbeek 12 Gd 50.48N 4.10 E
Gaasterland 12 Hb 52.54N 5.36 E
Gaasterland 12 Hb 52.53N 5.35 E
Gaasterland-Balk 12 Hb 52.54N 5.36 E
Gabaru Reef 64a Bb 7.53N 134.31 E
Gabas 11 Fk 43.46N 0.42W
Gabba' 35 Id 8.02N 50.08 E
Gabbs 46 Gg 38.52N 117.55W
Gabela 31 Ij 10.52S 14.23 E
Gabel'a (Kutkašen) 16 Oi 40.58N 47.52 E
Gabès, Gulf of-(EN) = Qābis, Khalīj- 30 Ie 34.00N 10.25 E
Gabon 36 Ab 0.25N 9.20 E
Gabon [1] 31 Ii 1.00S 11.45 E
Gaborone 31 Jk 24.40S 25.55 E
Gabras 35 Dc 10.16N 26.14 E
Gabriel Strait 42 Kd 61.50N 65.40W
Gabriel y Galán, Embalse de- 13 Fd 40.15N 6.15W
Gabrovo 15 Ig 42.52N 25.19 E
Gabrovo [2] 15 Ig 42.52N 25.19 E
Gacé 11 Gf 48.48N 0.18 E
Gachsārān 24 Ng 30.12N 50.47 E
Gackle 45 Gc 46.38N 99.09W
Gacko 14 Mg 43.10N 18.32 E
Gadag 25 Fe 15.25N 75.37 E
Gäddede 7 Dd 64.30N 14.09 E
Gadê 27 Ge 34.13N 99.29 E
Gadjač 16 Id 50.22N 34.01 E
Gádor, Sierra de- 13 Jh 36.55N 2.45W
Gadsden 43 Je 34.02N 86.02W
Gadūk, Gardaneh-ye- 24 Oe 35.55N 52.55 E
Gadzi 35 Be 4.47N 16.42 E
Gael Hamkes Bugt 41 Jd 74.00N 22.00W
Găeşti 15 Ie 44.43N 25.19 E
Gaeta 14 Hi 41.12N 13.35 E
Gaeta, Golfo di- 14 Hi 41.05N 13.30 E
Gaferut Island 57 Fd 9.14N 145.23 E
Gaffney 44 Gh 35.05N 81.39W
Gagan 63a Ba 5.14S 154.37 E
Gagarin 19 Dd 55.35N 35.01 E
Gagarin 18 Gd 40.40N 68.05 E
Gagévésouva, Pointe- 63b Ca 13.04S 166.32 E
Gaggenau 12 Kf 48.48N 8.20 E
Gagnef 7 Df 60.35N 15.04 E
Gagnoa 31 Gh 6.08N 5.56W
Gagnoa [3] 34 Dd 6.03N 6.00W
Gagnon 42 Kf 51.55N 68.10W
Gagra 19 Eg 43.17N 40.15 E
Gahkom 24 Ph 28.12N 55.50 E
Gahkom, Kūh-e- 24 Ph 28.10N 55.57 E
Gaiba, Laguna- 55 Dc 17.45S 57.43W
Gail 14 Hd 46.36N 13.53 E
Gaillac 11 Hk 43.54N 1.55 E
Gaillefontaine 12 De 49.39N 1.37 E
Gaillimh/Galway 6 Fe 53.16N 9.03W
Gaillimh/Galway [2] 9 Eh 53.20N 9.00W
Gaillon 12 De 49.10N 1.20 E
Gailtaler Alpen 14 Gd 46.40N 13.00 E
Gaiman 56 Gf 43.17S 65.29W
Găineşti 15 Ib 47.25N 25.55 E
Gainesville [Fl.-U.S.] 39 Kg 29.40N 82.20W
Gainesville [Ga.-U.S.] 44 Fh 34.18N 83.50W
Gainesville [Mo.-U.S.] 45 Jh 36.36N 92.26W
Gainesville [Tx.-U.S.] 43 He 33.37N 97.08W
Gainsborough 9 Mh 53.24N 0.46W
Gairdner, Lake- 57 Eh 31.35S 136.00 E
Gairloch 9 Hd 57.43N 5.40W
Gaizina Kalns/Gajzinkalns 8 Kh 56.50N 25.59 E
Gaj 19 Fe 51.31N 58.30 E
Gajny 19 Fc 60.20N 54.15 E
Gajsin 19 Cf 48.50N 29.27 E
Gajvoron 16 Fe 48.22N 29.52 E
Galaasija 18 Ee 39.52N 64.27 E
Galâbovo 15 Ig 42.08N 25.51 E
Gala Gölü 15 Ji 40.45N 26.12 E
Galaico, Macizo- 13 Eb 42.30N 7.20W
Galán, Cerro- 56 Gc 25.55S 66.52W
Galana 30 Li 3.09S 40.08 E
Galanta 10 Nh 48.12N 17.44 E
Galap 64a Bb 7.38N 134.39 E
Galápagos, Islas-/Colón, Archipiélago de- = Galapagos Islands (EN) 52 Gf 0.30S 90.30W
Galapagos Fracture Zone (EN) 3 Mi 0.00 100.00W
Galapagos Islands (EN) = Colón, Archipiélago de-/Galápagos, Islas- 52 Gf 0.30S 90.30W
Galapagos Islands (EN) = Galápagos, Islas-/Colón, Archipiélago de- 52 Gf 0.30S 90.30W
Galarza 55 Di 28.06S 56.41W
Galashiels 9 Kf 55.37N 2.49W
Galați [2] 15 Kd 45.33N 27.56 E
Galați 6 If 45.27N 28.03 E
Galatina 14 Mj 40.10N 18.10 E
Galatone 14 Mj 40.09N 18.04 E
Galatzó 13 Oe 39.38N 2.29 E
Galdar 32 Dd 28.09N 15.39W
Galdhøpiggen 7 Bf 61.37N 8.17 E
Galeana [Mex.] 48 Fb 30.07N 107.38W
Galeana [Mex.] 48 Ie 24.50N 100.04W
Galeh Dār 24 Oi 27.38N 52.42 E
Galela 58 Dd 1.50N 127.50 E
Galena [Ak.-U.S.] 40 Hd 64.44N 156.57W
Galena [Il.-U.S.] 45 Ke 42.25N 90.26W
Galeota Point 50 Fg 10.08N 60.59W
Galera, Punta- 56 Fe 39.59S 73.43W
Galera, Rio- 55 Bb 14.25S 60.07W
Galera Point 50 Fg 10.49N 60.55W
Galesburg 43 Ic 40.57N 90.22W
Galga 10 Pi 47.33N 19.43 E
Gal Gaduud [3] 35 Hd 5.00N 47.00 E
Galheirão, Rio- 55 Ja 12.23S 45.05W
Galheiros 55 Ia 13.18S 46.25W
Gali 16 Lh 42.36N 41.42 E
Galič 19 Ed 58.23N 42.21 E
Galič 16 De 49.06N 24.43 E
Galicea Mare 15 Ge 44.06N 23.18 E
Galicia 5 Fg 43.00N 8.00W
Galicia 13 Eb 43.00N 8.00W
Galicia (EN) = Galicija 5 If 49.50N 21.00 E
Galicia (EN) = Galicija [Eur.] 10 Qg 49.50N 21.00 E
Galicia (EN) = Galicja 10 Qg 49.50N 21.00 E
Galicia (EN) = Galicja 5 If 49.50N 21.00 E
Galicija [Eur.] = Galicia (EN) 10 Qg 49.50N 21.00 E
Galicija 10 Jg 49.00N 24.00 E
Galicija = Galicia (EN) 5 If 49.50N 21.00 E
Galicja = Galicia (EN) 5 If 49.50N 21.00 E
Galicja = Galicia (EN) 10 Qg 49.50N 21.00 E
Galilee, Lake- 59 Jd 22.20S 145.55 E
Galimy 20 Kd 62.19N 156.00 E
Galina Point 49 Id 18.24N 76.53W
Galion 44 Fe 40.44N 82.46W
Galion, Baie du- 51h Bb 14.44N 60.57W
Galiton 14 Cm 37.30N 8.52 E
Galiuro Mountains 46 Jj 32.40N 110.20W
Gälka'yo 31 Lh 6.49N 47.23 E
Galkino 17 Ki 55.40N 62.55 E
Gallarate 14 Ce 45.40N 8.47 E
Gallatin 44 Dg 36.24N 86.27W
Gallatin Range 46 Jd 45.15N 111.05W
Gallatin River 46 Jd 45.56N 111.29W
Galle 22 Ki 6.02N 80.13 E
Gállego 13 Lc 41.39N 0.51W
Gallegos, Rio- 52 Jk 51.36S 68.59W
Gallinas, Punta- 52 Id 12.25N 71.40W
Gallinas Peak 45 Di 34.15N 105.45W
Gallipoli 14 Lj 40.03N 17.58 E
Gallipoli Peninsula (EN) = Gelibolu Yarimadasi 15 Ji 40.20N 26.30 E
Gallipolis 44 Ff 38.49N 82.14W
Gällivare 6 Ib 67.08N 20.42 E
Galljaaral 18 Fd 40.02N 67.35 E
Gallo 13 Jd 40.48N 2.09W
Gällö 7 De 62.55N 15.14 E
Gallo, Capo- 14 Hl 38.15N 13.19 E
Gallo Mountains 45 Bi 34.00N 108.15W
Galloway 9 If 55.00N 4.25W
Galloway, Mull of- 9 Ig 54.38N 4.50W
Gallup 39 If 35.32N 108.44W
Gallur 13 Kc 41.52N 1.19W
Gallura 14 Dj 41.00N 9.15 E
Galmaarden/Gammerages 12 Fd 50.45N 3.58 E
Galole 36 Hc 1.30S 40.02 E
Galt 44 Gd 43.22N 80.19W
Gal Tardo 35 He 3.37N 45.58 E
Galtasen 8 Eg 57.48N 13.30 E
Galty Mountains/Na Gaibhlte 9 Ei 52.23N 8.11W
Galut 27 Hb 46.43N 100.08 E
Galveston 39 Jg 29.18N 94.48W
Galveston Bay 38 Jg 29.36N 94.57W
Galveston Island 45 Il 29.13N 94.55W
Gálvez 56 Hd 32.02S 61.13W
Galway/Gaillimh [2] 9 Eh 53.20N 9.00W
Galway/Gaillimh 6 Fe 53.16N 9.03W
Galway Bay/Cuan na Gaillimhe 5 Fe 53.10N 9.15W
Gamaches 12 De 49.59N 1.33 E
Gamagōri 29 Ed 34.49N 137.13 E
Gamarra 54 Db 8.19N 73.44W
Gamba [China] 27 Ef 28.17N 88.31 E
Gamba [Gabon] 36 Ac 2.37S 10.00 E
Gambaga 34 Ec 10.32N 0.26W
Gambela 31 Kh 8.15N 34.36 E
Gambell 40 Ed 63.46N 171.46W
Gambia 30 Fg 13.28N 16.34W
Gambia [1] 31 Fg 13.25N 16.00W
Gambie 34 Bc 13.28N 16.34W
Gambier, Iles- = Gambier Islands (EN) 57 Ng 23.09S 134.58W
Gambier Islands (EN) = Gambier, Iles- 57 Ng 23.09S 134.58W
Gambo 35 Ce 4.39N 22.16 E
Gamboma 36 Cc 1.53S 15.51 E
Gamboula 35 Be 4.08N 15.09 E
Gamda → Zamtang 27 He 32.23N 101.05 E
Gamelão 55 Db 15.29S 57.50W
Gamkonora, Gunung- 26 If 1.21N 127.31 E
Gamlakarleby/Kokkola 6 Ic 63.50N 23.07 E
Gamla Uppsala 8 Ge 59.54N 17.38 E
Gamleby 7 Dh 57.54N 16.24 E
Gamo Gofa [3] 35 Fd 5.45N 37.20 E
Gamua 64h Bb 13.15S 176.08W
Gamud 35 Fe 4.05N 38.06 E
Gamvik 7 Ga 71.03N 28.14 E
Ganāne, Webi- = Juba (EN) 30 Lh 0.15S 42.38 E
Gananoque 44 Ic 44.20N 76.10W
Ganāveh 24 Nh 29.32N 50.31 E
Gancedo 55 Bh 27.30S 61.42W
Gancevići 16 Ec 52.45N 26.29 E
Gand/Gent = Ghent (EN) 11 Jc 51.03N 3.43 E
Ganda 36 Be 12.59S 14.40 E
Gandadiwata, Bulu- 26 Gg 2.42S 119.27 E
Gandajika 36 Dd 6.45S 23.57 E
Gandak 25 Hc 25.39N 85.13 E
Gander 39 Ne 48.57N 54.34W
Ganderkesee 12 Ka 53.04N 8.33 E
Gandesa 13 Mc 41.03N 0.26 E
Gandhinagar 22 Jg 23.21N 72.40 E
Gāndhi Sāgar 25 Fd 24.30N 75.30 E
Gandia 13 Lf 38.58N 0.11W
Gandia-Grao de Gandia 13 Lf 38.59N 0.09W
Gandisê Shan 21 Kf 31.00N 83.00 E
Gandu 54 Kf 13.45S 39.30W
Ganetti 35 Eb 17.58N 31.13 E
Ganga = Ganges (EN) 21 Lg 23.20N 90.30 E
Gangaw 25 Id 22.10N 94.08 E
Gangca (Shaliuhe) 27 Hd 37.30N 100.14 E
Ganges 11 Jk 43.56N 3.42 E
Ganges (EN) = Ganga 21 Lg 23.20N 90.30 E
Ganges, Mouths of the- (EN) 21 Lg 23.20N 90.30 E
Gangi 14 Im 37.48N 14.12 E
Gango 36 Cd 9.48S 15.40 E
Gangtok 22 Kg 27.20N 88.37 E
Gangu 27 Ie 34.45N 105.12 E
Gangziyao 28 Cf 36.17N 114.06 E
Gan He 27 Mb 49.12N 125.14 E
Ganhe 27 La 50.43N 123.00 E
Gani 26 Ig 0.47S 128.13 E
Ganjgah 24 Md 37.42N 48.16 E
Gan Jiang 21 Ng 29.12N 116.00 E
Ganjig → Horqin Zuoyi Houqi 27 Lc 42.57N 122.14 E
Gannan 27 Lb 47.53N 123.26 E
Gannat 11 Jh 46.06N 3.12 E
Gannett Peak 38 Ie 43.10N 109.40W
Gansbaai 37 Bf 34.35S 19.22 E
Gansu Sheng (Kan-su Sheng) = Kansu (EN) [2] 27 Hd 38.00N 102.00 E
Ganta 34 Dd 7.14N 8.59W
Gantang → Taiping 28 Ei 30.18N 118.07 E
Ganyu (Qingkou) 28 Eg 34.50N 119.07 E
Ganzhou 22 Ng 25.49N 114.56 E
Gao [3] 34 Eb 18.15N 1.00W
Gao [Mali] 31 Hg 16.15N 0.01 E
Gao [Niger] 34 Gb 15.25N 5.45 E
Gao'an 27 Kf 28.27N 115.24 E
Gaobeidian → Xincheng 28 Ce 39.20N 115.50 E
Gaocheng 28 Ce 38.02N 114.50 E
Gaolan (Shidongsi) 27 Hd 36.23N 103.55 E
Gaoliangjian → Hongze 27 Ke 33.10N 119.58 E
Gaoligong Shan 27 Gf 25.45N 98.45 E
Gaolou Ling 27 Ig 24.47N 106.48 E
Gaomi 28 Ef 36.23N 119.45 E
Gaoping 27 Jd 35.46N 112.55 E
Gaoqing (Tianzhen) 28 Df 37.10N 117.50 E
Gaotai 27 Gd 39.20N 99.58 E
Gaotingzhen → Daishan 28 Gi 30.15N 122.13 E
Gaoua 34 Ec 10.20N 3.11W
Gaoual 34 Cc 11.45N 13.12W
Gaoyang 28 Ce 38.42N 115.47 E
Gaoyi 28 Cf 37.37N 114.37 E
Gaoyou 28 Eh 32.46N 119.27 E
Gaoyou Hu 27 Ke 32.50N 119.15 E
Gaozhou 27 Jg 21.56N 110.47 E
Gap 11 Mj 44.34N 6.05 E
Gar 27 Ce 32.12N 79.57 E
Gara, Lough-/Loch Ui Ghadra 9 Eh 53.55N 8.30W
Gara'ad 35 Hd 6.54N 49.20 E
Garabato 55 Bi 28.56S 60.09W
Garachiné 49 Hi 8.04N 78.22W
Garachiné, Punta- 49 Hi 8.06N 78.25W
Gara Dragoman 15 Fg 42.55N 22.56 E
Ga'raet el Oubeira 14 Cn 36.50N 8.23 E
Gara Kostenec 15 Gg 42.18N 23.52 E
Garalo 34 Dc 11.00N 7.26W
Gara Muleta 35 Gd 9.05N 41.43 E
Garanhuns 53 Mf 8.54S 36.29W
Garapan 64b Ba 15.12N 145.43 E
Garapuava 55 Ic 16.06S 46.33W
Garavuti 18 Gf 37.36N 68.29 E
Garba 35 Cd 9.12N 20.30 E
Garbahārrey 35 Ge 3.20N 42.17 E
Garberville 46 Df 40.06N 123.48W
Gārbosh, Kūh-e- 24 Nf 32.36N 50.04 E
Garça 55 Hf 22.14S 49.37W
Garças, Rio das- 55 Fb 15.54S 52.16W
Garcias 55 Fe 20.34S 52.13W
Gard [3] 11 Jj 44.00N 4.00 E
Gard 11 Kk 43.51N 4.37 E
Garda 14 Ee 45.34N 10.42 E
Garda, Lago di- = Garda, Lake- (EN) 5 Hf 45.35N 10.35 E
Garda, Lake- (EN) = Garda, Lago di- 5 Hf 45.35N 10.35 E
Gardabani 16 Ni 41.29N 45.05 E
Garde, Cap de- 14 Bn 36.58N 7.47 E
Gardelegen 10 Hd 52.32N 11.22 E
Garden City [Ga.-U.S.] 44 Gi 32.06N 81.09W
Garden City [Ks.-U.S.] 43 Gd 37.58N 100.53W
Garden Grove 46 Gj 33.46N 117.57W
Garden Peninsula 44 Dc 45.40N 86.35W
Gardermoen 8 Dd 60.13N 11.06 E
Gardey 55 Cm 37.17S 59.21W
Gardēz 23 Kc 33.37N 69.07 E
Gardiner 46 Jd 45.02N 110.42W
Gardiner Range 59 Fc 19.15S 128.50 E
Gardner → Nikumaroro Atoll 57 Je 4.40S 174.32W
Gardner Pinnacles 57 Kb 25.00N 167.55W
Gardno, Jezioro- 10 Nb 54.43N 17.05 E
Gardone Riviera 14 Ee 45.37N 10.34 E
Gargždai/Gargždaj 7 Ei 55.43N 21.24 E
Gareloi 40a Cb 51.47N 178.48W
Garessio 14 Cf 44.12N 8.02 E
Garfagnana 14 Ef 44.05N 10.30 E
Gargaliánoi 15 El 37.04N 21.38 E
Gargano 5 Hg 41.50N 16.00 E
Gargano, Testa del- 14 Ki 41.35N 16.12 E
Gargantua, Cape- 44 Eb 47.36N 85.02W
Gargždaj/Gargždai 7 Ei 55.43N 21.24 E
Gari 19 Gd 59.28N 62.25 E
Garibaldi 55 Gi 29.15S 51.32W
Garibaldi, Mount- 46 Db 49.51N 123.01W
Garies 37 Bf 30.30S 18.00 E
Garigliano 14 Hi 41.13N 13.45 E
Garimpo 55 Ed 18.41S 54.50W
Garissa 31 Ki 0.28S 39.38 E

Index Symbols

[1] Independent Nation
[2] State, Region
[3] District, County
[4] Municipality
[5] Colony, Dependency
Continent
Physical Region
Historical or Cultural Region
Mount, Mountain
Volcano
Hill
Mountains, Mountain Range
Hills, Escarpment
Plateau, Upland
Pass, Gap
Plain, Lowland
Delta
Salt Flat
Valley, Canyon
Crater, Cave
Karst Features
Depression
Polder
Desert, Dunes
Forest, Woods
Heath, Steppe
Oasis
Cape, Point
Coast, Beach
Cliff
Peninsula
Isthmus
Sandbank
Island
Atoll
Rock, Reef
Islands, Archipelago
Rocks, Reefs
Coral Reef
Well, Spring
Geyser
River, Stream
Waterfall Rapids
River Mouth, Estuary
Lake
Salt Lake
Intermittent Lake
Reservoir
Swamp, Pond
Canal
Glacier
Ice Shelf, Pack Ice
Ocean
Sea
Gulf, Bay
Strait, Fjord
Lagoon
Bank
Seamount
Tablemount
Ridge
Shelf
Basin
Escarpment, Sea Scarp
Fracture
Trench, Abyss
National Park, Reserve
Point of Interest
Recreation Site
Cave, Cavern
Historic Site
Ruins
Wall, Walls
Church, Abbey
Temple
Scientific Station
Airport
Port
Lighthouse
Mine
Tunnel
Dam, Bridge

Garkida 34 Hc 10.25N 12.34 E
Garland 45 Hj 32.54N 96.39W
Garlasco 14 Ce 45.12N 8.55 E
Garliava/Garljava 8 Jj 54.46N 23.55 E
Garljava/Garliava 8 Jj 54.46N 23.55 E
Garm 18 He 39.02N 70.18 E
Garmisch-Partenkirchen 10 Hi 47.30N 11.06 E
Garmsar 24 Oe 35.20N 52.13 E
Garnet Bank (EN) 55 Hk 33.05S 49.25W
Garnet Range 46 Ic 46.45N 113.15W
Garnett 45 Ig 38.17N 95.14W
Garonne 5 Ff 45.02N 0.36W
Garonne, Canal latéral à la- 11 Fj 44.34N 0.09W
Garopába 55 Hi 28.04S 48.40W
Garoua 31 Ih 9.18N 13.24 E
Garoua Boulaï 35 Ad 5.53N 14.33 E
Garoubi 34 Fc 13.07N 2.18 E
Garöwe 31 Lh 8.25N 48.33 E
Garpenberg 8 Gd 60.19N 16.12 E
Garphyttan 8 Fe 59.19N 14.56 E
Garrel 12 Kb 52.57N 8.01 E
Garreru 64a Bc 7.20N 134.33 E
Garri, Kūh-e- 24 Mf 33.59N 48.25 E
Garrigues 11 Kj 44.10N 4.30 E
Garrison 45 Fc 47.40N 101.25W
Garron Point/An Gearran 9 Hf 55.05N 5.58W
Garrovillas 13 Fe 39.43N 6.33W
Garruchos 55 Ei 28.11S 55.39W
Garry 9 Je 56.45N 3.45W
Garry Bay 42 Ic 69.00N 85.10W
Garry Lake 38 Jc 66.00N 100.00W
Garsen 36 Hc 2.16S 40.07 E
Gartar/Qianning 27 He 30.27N 101.29 E
Gartempe 11 Gh 46.47N 0.50 E
Gartog → Markam 27 Gf 29.32N 98.33 E
Garut 26 Eh 7.13S 107.54 E
Garuva 55 Hh 26.01S 48.51W
Garvie Mountains 62 Cf 45.30S 168.50 E
Garwa 25 Gd 24.11N 83.49 E
Garwolin 10 Re 51.54N 21.37 E
Gary 43 Jc 41.36N 87.20W
Garyarsa 27 De 31.40N 80.26 E
Garzê 27 Ge 31.42N 99.58 E
Garzón [Col.] 54 Cc 2.13N 75.38W
Garzón [Ur.] 56 Jd 34.36S 54.33W
Gasan-Kuli 19 Fh 37.29N 53.59 E
Gascogne = Gascony (EN) 11 Gk 43.30N 0.10 E
Gasconade River 45 Kg 38.40N 91.33W
Gascony (EN) = Gascogne 11 Gk 43.30N 0.10 E
Gascoyne Junction 59 De 25.03S 115.12 E
Gascoyne River 57 Cg 24.52S 113.37 E
Gasefjord 41 Je 70.00N 27.30W
Gaseland 41 Jd 70.20N 29.00W
Gash 30 Kg 16.48N 35.51 E
Gas Hu 27 Fd 38.08N 90.45 E
Gashua 31 Ig 12.52N 11.03 E
Gaspar Strait (EN)=Kelasa, Selat- 26 Eg 2.40S 107.15 E
Gaspé 39 Me 48.50N 64.29W
Gaspé, Cap de - 42 Lg 48.45N 64.10W
Gaspé, Péninsule de-= Gaspe Peninsula (EN) 38 Me 48.30N 65.00W
Gaspe Peninsula (EN)= Gaspé, Péninsule de- 38 Me 48.30N 65.00W
Gassan 29 Gb 38.34N 140.01 E
Gassol 34 Hd 8.32N 10.28 E
Gaston, Lake- 44 Ig 36.35N 78.00W
Gastonia 43 Kd 35.16N 81.11W
Gastoúni 15 El 37.51N 21.15 E
Gastre 56 Gf 42.17S 69.14W
Gästrikland 8 Gd 60.30N 16.30 E
Gata, Akrōtērion- 24 Ee 34.34N 33.02 E
Gata, Cabo de- 5 Fh 36.43N 2.12W
Gata, Sierra de- 13 Fd 40.15N 6.45W
Gătaia 15 Ed 45.26N 21.26 E
Gatčina 19 Dd 59.34N 30.09 E
Gate 45 Fh 36.51N 100.01W
Gate City 44 Fg 36.38N 82.37W
Gateshead 9 Lg 54.58N 1.37W
Gateshead 42 Hb 70.35N 100.15W
Gathemo 12 Bf 48.46N 0.58W
Gâtinais 11 If 48.00N 2.20 E
Gâtine, Hauteurs de- 11 Fh 46.38N 0.38W
Gatineau, Rivière- 42 Jg 45.27N 75.42W
Gatlinburg 44 Fh 35.43N 83.31W
Gato, Cumbres del- 48 Fd 27.00N 106.35W
Gattinara 14 Ce 45.37N 8.22 E
Gatún 49 Hi 9.16N 79.55W
Gatún, Lago-=Gatun Lake (EN) 47 Ig 9.12N 79.55W
Gatun Lake (EN)=Gatún, Lago- 47 Ig 9.12N 79.55W
Gatvand 24 Mf 32.15N 48.50 E
Gatwick Airport 12 Bc 51.08N 0.12W
Gaucín 13 Gh 36.31N 5.19W
Gauhati → Guwāhāti 22 Lg 26.11N 91.44 E
Gauiena/Gaujiena 8 Lg 57.25N 26.28 E
Gauja 7 Fh 57.10N 24.16 E
Gaujiena/Gauiena 8 Lg 57.25N 26.28 E
Gaula [Nor.] 8 Da 63.21N 10.14 E
Gaula [Nor.] 8 Ac 61.22N 5.41 E
Gauldalen 8 Db 63.00N 11.00 E
Gauley River 44 Gf 38.10N 81.12W
Gau-Odernheim 12 Ke 49.46N 8.12 E
Gaurdak 19 Gh 37.49N 66.01 E
Gausdal 8 Cc 61.20N 9.55 E
Gausta 7 Bg 59.50N 8.39 E
Gāvbandī 24 Oi 27.12N 53.04 E
Gāvbūs, Kūh-e- 24 Oi 27.10N 54.00 E
Gavdhopoúla 15 Go 34.56N 24.00 E
Gávdhos 5 Ii 34.50N 24.05 E
Gāveh 24 Le 35.00N 46.58 E
Gavere 12 Fd 50.56N 3.40 E
Gavkhūnī, Bātlāq-e- 24 Of 32.06N 52.52 E
Gāv Kosh 24 Le 34.00N 48.00 E
Gävle 6 Hc 60.40N 17.10 E
Gävleborg [2] 7 Df 61.30N 16.15 E
Gävlebukten 8 Gd 60.40N 17.20 E
Gavorrano 14 Eh 42.55N 10.54 E
Gavri 8 Lh 56.49N 27.58 E
Gavrilov-Jam 7 Jh 57.19N 39.51 E
Gāw Koshi 23 Id 28.38N 57.12 E
Gawler 59 Hf 34.37S 138.44 E
Gawler Ranges 57 Eh 32.30S 136.00 E
Gaxun Nur 21 Me 42.25N 101.00 E
Gaya [India] 22 Kg 24.47N 85.00 E
Gaya [Niger] 34 Fc 11.53N 3.27 E
Gaya He 28 Jc 42.58N 129.52 E
Gaylord 44 Ec 45.02N 84.40W
Gayndah 59 Ke 25.37S 151.36 E
Gaz 24 Nf 32.48N 51.37 E
Gaza [3] 37 Ed 23.30S 33.00 E
Gaz-Ačak 19 Gg 41.11N 61.27 E
Gazalkent 18 Gd 41.33N 69.46 E
Gazaoua 34 Gc 13.32N 7.55 E
Gazelle, Récif de la- 63b Be 20.11S 165.27 E
Gaziantep 22 Ff 37.05N 37.22 E
Gaziemir 15 Kk 38.19N 27.10 E
Gazimağusa = Famagusta (EN) 23 Dc 35.07N 33.57 E
Gazipaşa 24 Ed 36.17N 32.20 E
Gazli 19 Gg 40.09N 63.23 E
Gbarnga 31 Gh 7.00N 9.29W
Gboko 34 Gd 7.21N 8.58 E
Gbon 34 Dd 9.50N 6.27W
Gdańsk [2] 10 Ob 54.25N 18.40 E
Gdańsk=Danzig (EN) 6 He 54.23N 18.40 E
Gdansk, Gulf of- (EN)= Gdanska, Zatoka- 5 He 54.40N 19.15 E
Gdov 7 Gg 58.47N 27.54 E
Gdynia 6 He 54.32N 18.33 E
Gearhart Mountain 46 Ee 42.30N 120.53W
Gêba 34 Bc 11.58N 15.00W
Gebe, Pulau- 26 Ig 0.05S 129.20 E
Gebze 24 Cb 40.48N 29.25 E
Gecha 35 Fd 7.29N 35.25 E
Geçitkale 25 Ee 35.15N 33.45 E
Gedi 36 Hc 3.18S 40.01 E
Gedinne 12 Ge 49.59N 4.56 E
Gediz 24 Cc 39.02N 29.25 E
Gedo 35 Ge 2.20N 41.20 E
Gedo [3] 35 Ge 3.00N 42.00 E
Gedo 35 Fd 9.00N 37.29 E
Gedser, Sydfalster- 7 Ci 54.35N 11.57 E
Gedser Odde 8 Dj 54.34N 11.59 E
Geel 11 Kc 51.10N 5.00 E
Geelong 58 Fh 38.08S 144.21 E
Geelvink Channel 59 Ce 28.30S 114.10 E
Geer 12 Hd 50.51N 5.42 E
Geeste 12 Jb 52.36N 7.16 E
Geesthacht 10 Gc 53.26N 10.22 E
Gê'gyai 27 De 32.29N 80.52 E
Ge Hu 28 Ei 31.36N 119.51 E
Geidam 34 Hc 12.53N 11.56 E
Geigar 35 Ec 11.59N 32.46 E
Geihoku 29 Cd 34.44N 132.17 E
Geikie 42 He 57.48N 103.46W
Geilo 7 Bf 60.31N 8.12 E
Geiranger 8 Bb 62.06N 7.12 E
Geisenheim 12 Je 49.59N 7.58 E
Geislingen an der Steige 10 Fh 48.37N 9.51 E
Geita 36 Fc 2.52S 32.10 E
Geithus 7 Bg 59.57N 9.59 E
Geiyo-Shotō 29 Cd 34.15N 132.45 E
Gejiu 22 Mg 23.22N 103.14 E
Gel [Sud.] 30 Jh 7.46N 29.36 E
Gel [Sud.] 35 Ed 6.08N 31.17 E
Gela 14 Im 37.04N 14.15 E
Gela, Golfo di- 14 Im 37.05N 14.10 E
Geladi 35 Hd 6.57N 46.25 E
Geldenaken/Jodoigne 12 Gd 50.43N 4.52 E
Gelderland [3] 12 Hb 52.10N 5.50 E
Geldermalsen 12 Hc 51.53N 5.19 E
Geldern 10 Ce 51.31N 6.20 E
Geldrop 12 Hc 51.25N 5.33 E
Geleen 11 Ld 50.58N 5.52 E
Gelembé 15 Kj 39.10N 27.50 E
Gelemso 35 Gd 8.48N 40.32 E
Gelendžik 19 Dg 44.33N 38.06 E
Gelengdeng 35 Bc 10.56N 15.32 E
Gelgaudiškis 8 Ji 55.02N 22.58 E
Gelibolu 24 Bb 40.24N 26.40 E
Gelibolu Yarimadası = Gallipoli Peninsula (EN) 15 Ji 40.20N 26.30 E
Gélise 11 Gj 44.11N 0.17 E
Gellinsör 35 Hd 6.24N 46.46 E
Gelnhausen 10 Ff 50.12N 9.11 E
Gelsenkirchen 10 De 51.31N 7.06 E
Gemena 31 Ih 3.15N 19.46 E
Gemerek 24 Gc 39.11N 36.05 E
Gemert 12 Hc 51.33N 5.41 E
Gemi, Jabal- 35 Ed 9.01N 34.09 E
Gemlik 24 Cb 40.26N 29.09 E
Gemlik Körfezi 24 Cb 40.25N 28.55 E
Gemona del Friuli 14 Hd 46.16N 13.09 E
Gemünden (Felda) 12 Ld 50.42N 9.03 E
Gemünden (Wohra) 12 Kd 50.58N 8.58 E
Gemünden am Main 10 Ff 50.03N 9.42 E
Genale 30 Lh 0.15S 42.38 E
Genç 24 Ic 38.46N 40.35 E
Gendringen 12 Ic 51.52N 6.23 E
Gendringen-Ulft 12 Ic 51.54N 6.24 E
Genemuiden 12 Ib 52.37N 6.02 E
General Acha 56 He 37.23S 64.36W
General Alvear [Arg.] 56 Gd 34.58S 67.42W
General Alvear [Arg.] 56 He 36.03S 60.01W
General Arenales 55 Bl 34.18S 61.18W
General Artigas 55 Dh 26.53S 56.17W
General Belgrano 56 Ie 35.46S 58.30W
General Belgrano Station 66 Af 77.50S 38.00W
General Bernardo O'Higgins 66 Re 63.19S 57.54W
General Bravo 48 Je 25.48N 99.10W
General Cabrera 56 Hd 32.48S 63.52W
General Capdevila 55 Bh 27.26S 61.28W
General Carneiro 55 Gh 26.28S 51.25W
General Carrera, Lago- 52 Ij 46.30S 72.00W
General Cepeda 48 Ie 25.23N 101.27W
General Conesa [Arg.] 55 Dm 36.30S 57.20W
General Conesa [Arg.] 56 Hf 40.06S 64.26W
General Enrique Martínez 55 Fk 33.12S 53.50W
General Galarza 55 Ck 32.43S 59.24W
General Güemes 56 Hb 24.40S 65.00W
General Guide 56 Ie 36.40S 57.46W
General José de San Martin 55 Ch 26.33S 59.21W
General Juan Madariaga 56 Ie 37.00S 57.09W
General La Madrid 56 He 37.16S 61.17W
General Lavalle 56 Ie 36.24S 56.58W
General Manuel Belgrano, Cerro- 52 Jh 29.01S 67.49W
General O'Brien 55 Bl 34.54S 60.45W
General Pico 56 He 35.40S 63.44W
General Pinedo 56 Hc 27.19S 61.17W
General Pinto 55 Bl 34.46S 61.53W
General Pirán 55 Dm 37.16S 57.45W
General Roca 56 Ge 39.02S 67.35W
General Salgado 55 Ge 20.39S 50.22W
General Santos 22 Oi 6.05N 125.10 E
General Sarmiento 55 Cl 34.33S 58.43W
General Terán 48 Je 25.16N 99.41W
General-Toševo 15 Lf 43.42N 28.02 E
General Treviño 48 Jd 26.14N 99.29W
General Trías 48 Fc 28.21N 106.22W
General Vargas 55 Ei 29.42S 54.40W
General Viamonte 55 Bl 35.01S 61.01W
General Villegas 56 He 35.02S 63.01W
Genesee River 44 Id 43.16N 77.36W
Geneseo 44 Id 42.46N 77.49W
Geneva [Al.-U.S.] 44 Ej 31.02N 85.52W
Geneva [Nb.-U.S.] 45 Hf 40.32N 97.36W
Geneva [N.Y.-U.S.] 44 Id 42.53N 76.59W
Geneva (EN) = Genève 6 Gf 46.10N 6.10 E
Geneva, Lake- (EN) = Léman, Lac- 5 Gf 46.25N 6.30 E
Genève [2] 14 Ad 46.10N 6.15 E
Genève = Geneva (EN) 6 Gf 46.10N 6.10 E
Genevois 11 Mh 46.00N 6.10 E
Genhe → Ergun Zuoqi 22 Od 50.47N 121.32 E
Geni 35 Ed 8.31N 33.10 E
Geničesk 19 Df 46.12N 34.48 E
Genil 13 Gg 37.42N 5.19W
Genk 11 Ld 50.58N 5.30 E
Genkai-Nada 29 Ae 33.45N 130.00 E
Gennargentu 5 Gg 40.00N 9.20 E
Gennep 12 Hc 51.42N 5.59 E
Genoa (EN) = Genova 6 Gg 44.25N 8.57 E
Genoa, Gulf of- (EN) = Genova, Golfo di- 5 Gg 44.10N 8.55 E
Genova = Genoa (EN) 6 Gg 44.25N 8.57 E
Genova, Golfo di- = Genoa, Gulf of- (EN) 5 Gg 44.10N 8.55 E
Genova-Nervi 14 Df 44.23N 9.02 E
Genova-Voltri 14 Cf 44.26N 8.45 E
Genovesa, Isla- 54a Ba 0.20N 89.58W
Gent/Gand=Ghent (EN) 11 Jc 51.03N 3.43 E
Gentbrugge, Gent- 12 Fc 51.03N 3.45 E
Gent-Gentbrugge 12 Fc 51.03N 3.45 E
Genthin 10 Id 52.24N 12.10 E
Gent-Sint-Amandsberg 12 Fc 51.04N 3.45 E
Genū, Kūhhā-ye- 23 Id 27.25N 56.09 E
Genyem 26 Lg 2.46S 140.12 E
Genzano di Lucania 14 Kj 40.51N 16.02 E
Genzano di Roma 14 Fi 41.42N 12.41 E
Geographe Bay 57 Ch 33.35S 115.15 E
Geographe Channel 59 Cd 24.40S 113.20 E
Geographical Society Øer 41 Jd 72.40N 22.20W
Geokčaj 16 Oi 40.40N 47.42 E
Geok-Tepe 19 Fh 38.10N 57.58 E
Geomagnetic Pole (1975) (EN) 66 Hf 78.40S 109.33 E
Georga, Zemlja- 21 Ga 80.30N 49.00 E
George 38 Md 58.30N 66.00W
George 37 Cf 33.58S 22.24 E
George, Lake- [Austl.] 59 Jg 35.05S 149.25 E
George, Lake- [Fl.-U.S.] 44 Gk 29.17N 81.36W
George, Lake- [Ug.] 36 Fc 0.00 30.12 E
George, Lake- [U.S.] 44 Kd 43.35N 73.35W
George Gill Range 59 Gd 24.15S 131.35 E
Georges Bank (EN) 43 Nc 41.15N 67.30W
George Sound 62 Bf 44.50S 167.20 E
George Town [Austl.] 58 Fi 41.06S 146.50 E
George Town [Cay.Is.] 47 He 19.18N 81.23W
George Town [Indon.] 22 Mi 5.25N 100.20 E
George Town [Tx.-U.S.] 45 Hk 30.38N 97.41W
Georgetown [Austl.] 58 Ff 18.18S 143.33 E
Georgetown [Bah.] 49 Jb 23.30N 75.46W
Georgetown [De.-U.S.] 44 Jf 38.42N 75.23W
Georgetown [Gam.] 31 Fg 13.32N 14.46W
Georgetown [Guy.] 53 Ke 6.48N 58.10W
Georgetown [Ky.-U.S.] 44 Ef 38.13N 84.33W
Georgetown [Oh.-U.S.] 44 Ff 38.52N 83.54W
Georgetown [S.C.-U.S.] 43 Le 33.23N 79.18W
Georgetown [St.Hel.] 31 Fi 7.56S 14.25W
Georgetown [St.Vin.] 50 Ff 13.16N 61.08W
George V Coast 66 Je 68.30S 147.30 E
George VI Sound 66 Qf 71.00S 68.00W
George West 45 Gl 28.20N 98.07W
Georgia [2] 43 Ke 32.50N 83.15W
Georgia (EN) [3] 5 Kg 42.00N 44.00 E
Georgia (EN) = Sakartvelo 19 Eg 42.00N 44.00 E
Georgia, Strait of 42 Fg 49.00N 123.20W
Georgia del Sur/South Georgia 66 Ad 54.15S 36.45W
Georgian Bay 38 Ke 45.15N 80.50W
Georgijevka 19 Hg 43.02N 74.43 E
Georgijevka 19 If 49.19N 81.35 E
Georgijevsk 16 Mg 44.09N 43.28 E
Georgina River 57 Eg 23.30S 139.47 E
Georgsmarienhütte 10 Ed 52.16N 8.02 E
Gera 10 Ge 51.08N 10.56 E
Gera 10 If 50.52N 12.05 E
Geraardsbergen/Grammont 12 Fd 50.46N 3.52 E
Gerais, Chapadão dos- 55 Jc 17.40S 45.35W
Geral, Serra- [Braz.] 55 Gi 29.10S 50.15W
Geral, Serra- [Braz.] 52 Kh 26.30S 50.30W
Geral, Serra- [Braz.] 55 Gf 23.54S 50.46W
Geral da Serra, Coxilha- 55 Ej 30.20S 55.15W
Geral de Goiás, Serra- 52 Lg 13.00S 46.15W
Geraldine 62 Df 44.05S 171.15 E
Geral do Paraná, Serra- 55 Ib 14.45S 47.30W
Geraldton [Austl.] 58 Cg 28.46S 114.36 E
Geraldton [Ont.-Can.] 42 Ig 49.44N 86.57W
Gérardmer 11 Mf 48.04N 6.53 E
Gerāsh 24 Pi 27.40N 54.06 E
Gerbiči, Gora- 20 Fe 66.39N 105.02 E
Gerca 15 Ja 48.10N 26.17 E
Gercüş 24 Id 37.34N 41.23 E
Gerecse 10 Oi 47.41N 18.29 E
Gerede 24 Eb 40.52N 32.39 E
Gerede 24 Eb 40.48N 32.12 E
Gerês, Serra do- 13 Ec 41.48N 8.00W
Gereshk 23 Jc 31.48N 64.34 E
Gérgal 13 Jg 37.07N 2.33W
Gering 45 Ef 41.50N 103.40W
Gerlachovský štít 10 Qg 49.12N 20.09 E
Gerlogubi 35 Hd 6.56N 45.03 E
Gerlos 14 Gc 47.14N 12.02 E
Gerlovo 15 Kf 43.03N 27.35 E
German Democratic Republic = Germany 6 Ge 51.00N 10.00 E
Germania 55 Al 34.34S 62.03W
Germania Land 41 Kc 76.50N 20.00W
Germany, Federal Republic of = Germany 6 Ge 51.00N 10.00 E
Germencik 15 Kl 37.51N 27.37 E
Germersheim 12 Ke 49.13N 8.22 E
Germī 23 Hc 33.32N 54.58 E
Germi 24 Mc 39.01N 48.03 E
Germiston 37 De 26.15S 28.05 E
Gernsbach 12 Kf 48.46N 8.19 E
Gernsheim 12 Ke 49.45N 8.29 E
Gero 28 Ng 35.48N 137.14 E
Gerolstein 12 Id 50.13N 6.40 E
Gerona [3] 13 Ob 42.10N 2.40 E
Gerona/Girona 13 Oc 41.59N 2.49 E
Gerpinnes 12 Gd 50.20N 4.31 E
Gers 11 Gj 44.09N 0.39 E
Gers [3] 11 Gk 43.40N 0.30 E
Gersprenz 12 Le 49.59N 9.04 E
Gêrzê 27 De 32.20N 84.04 E
Gerze 24 Fb 41.48N 35.12 E
Gescher 12 Jc 51.57N 7.00 E
Geseke 12 Kc 51.39N 8.31 E
Geser 26 Jg 3.53S 130.54 E
Gesunda 8 Fd 60.54N 14.32 E
Gesunden 8 Fa 63.10N 15.55 E
Geta 7 Ef 60.23N 19.50 E
Getafe 13 Id 40.18N 3.43W
Gete 11 Ld 50.55N 5.08 E
Getinge 7 Ch 56.49N 12.44 E
Gettysburg 45 Gd 45.01N 99.57W
Gettysburg Seamount (EN) 32 Eb 36.32N 11.37W
Getúlio Vargas 55 Fh 27.50S 52.16W
Getz Ice Shelf 66 Nf 74.15S 125.00W
Geul 12 Hd 50.40N 5.43 E
Gévaudan 11 Jj 44.27N 3.30 E
Gevelsberg 12 Jc 51.19N 7.20 E
Gevgelija 15 Fh 41.08N 22.31 E
Gévora 13 Ff 38.53N 6.57W
Gevsjön 8 Ea 63.25N 12.40 E
Gewane 35 Gc 10.10N 40.39 E
Gex 11 Mh 46.20N 6.04 E
Gexianzhuang → Qinghe 28 Cf 37.03N 115.39 E
Geyersberg 12 Fg 49.50N 9.30 E
Geyik Dağı 24 Ed 36.54N 32.10 E
Geyikli 15 Jj 39.48N 26.12 E
Geyser, Banc du- 37 Hb 12.25S 46.25 E
Geysir 5 Dc 64.19N 20.18W
Geyve 24 Db 40.30N 30.18 E
Ghabāri, Darb al- 24 Cj 25.10N 29.50 E
Ghadāmis 31 He 30.08N 9.30 E
Ghadduwah 33 Bd 26.26N 14.18 E
Ghaghara 21 Kg 24.52N 84.55 E
Ghaghe 63a Db 7.23S 158.12 E
Ghallah, Wādī al- 30 Jg 10.25N 27.32 E
Ghamrah, Wādī al- 24 Hj 25.47N 38.45 E
Ghana [1] 31 Gh 8.00N 2.00W
Ghanzi 31 Jk 21.42S 21.38 E
Ghanzi [3] 37 Cd 22.00S 23.00 E
Ghār ad Dimā' 14 Cn 36.27N 8.26 E
Gharaqābād 24 Me 35.06N 49.50 E
Gharbī, Al Hajar al- 24 Qj 24.10N 56.15 E
Gharbīyah, Aş Şaḩrā' al-= Western Desert (EN) 30 Jf 27.30N 28.00 E
Ghardaïa 31 He 32.29N 3.40 E
Ghārib, Jabal- 33 Fd 28.07N 32.54 E
Gharrāf, Shaţţ al- 24 Kf 32.30N 45.48 E
Gharsah, Shaţţ al- 32 Ic 34.06N 7.50 E
Gharyān 33 Bc 32.10N 13.01 E
Gharyān [3] 33 Bc 30.35N 12.00 E
Ghāt 31 If 24.58N 10.11 E
Ghatere 63a Db 7.58S 159.01 E
Ghattī 24 Gg 31.16N 37.31 E
Ghazāl, Baḩr al- 35 Ed 9.31N 30.25 E
Ghazal, Bahr el- 30 Ig 13.01N 15.28 E
Ghazal, Bahr el- 35 Bc 14.00N 16.30 E
Ghazaouet 32 Gb 35.06N 1.51W
Ghazipur 25 Gc 25.35N 83.34 E
Ghaznī 22 If 33.33N 68.26 E
Ghaznī [3] 23 Kc 33.00N 68.00 E
Ghent (EN) = Gand/Gent 11 Jc 51.03N 3.43 E
Gheorghe Gheorghiu-Dej → Onești 15 Jc 46.12N 26.46 E
Gheorghieni 15 Ic 46.43N 25.37 E
Gheorghiu-Dej → Liski 19 De 51.00N 39.31 E
Gherla 15 Gb 47.02N 23.55 E
Ghidigeni 15 Kc 46.03N 27.30 E
Ghidole (EN)=Gidole 35 Fd 5.37N 37.29 E
Ghilarza 14 Cj 40.07N 8.50 E
Ghimeş, Pasul- 15 Jc 46.33N 26.07 E
Ghisonaccia 11a Ba 42.00N 9.24 E
Ghizunabeana Islands 63a Db 7.33S 158.45 E
Ghowr [3] 23 Jc 34.00N 65.00 E
Ghriss 13 Mi 35.15N 0.10 E
Ghubbat al Qamar 21 Hh 16.00N 52.30 E
Ghudāf, Wādī al- 24 Jf 32.56N 43.30 E
Ghurāb, Jabal al- 24 Hf 34.00N 38.42 E
Ghurayrah 33 Hf 18.37N 42.41 E
Ghūriān 23 Jc 34.21N 61.30 E
Ghurrab, Jabal al- 14 Cn 36.36N 8.23 E
Ghuzayyil, Sabkhat- 33 Dd 29.50N 19.45 E
Giaginskaja 16 Lg 44.47N 40.05 E
Giala, Jabal- 24 Ei 27.20N 32.57 E
Gialo Oasis (EN)=Jālū, Wāḩāt- 30 Jf 29.00N 21.20 E
Gialoúsa 24 Fe 35.35N 34.15 E
Gia Nghia 25 Lf 11.59N 107.42 E
Giannutri 14 Fh 42.15N 11.05 E
Giant's Causeway/Clochán an Aifir 9 Gf 55.15N 6.35W
Giarre 14 Jm 37.43N 15.11 E
Gibara 49 Ic 21.07N 76.08W
Gibbon Point 51b Bb 18.14N 63.00W
Gibb River 59 Fc 16.25S 126.25 E
Gibbs Islands 66 Re 61.30S 55.31W
Gibellina 14 Gm 37.47N 12.58 E
Gibeon [3] 37 Bd 25.00S 18.30 E
Gibeon 37 Be 25.09S 17.43 E
Gibostad 7 Db 69.21N 18.00 E
Gibraleón 13 Fg 37.23N 6.58W
Gibraltar 6 Fh 36.11N 5.22W
Gibraltar [5] 6 Fh 36.11N 5.22W
Gibraltar, Estrecho de-= Gibraltar, Strait of- (EN) 5 Fh 35.57N 5.36W
Gibraltar, Strait of- (EN)= Djebel Ţāriq, El Bōghāz- 5 Fh 35.57N 5.36W
Gibraltar, Strait of- (EN)= Gibraltar, Estrecho de- 5 Fh 35.57N 5.36W
Gibson Desert 57 Dg 24.30S 126.00 E
Gidami 35 Ed 8.58N 34.40 E
Giddings 45 Hk 30.11N 96.56W
Gidigič 15 Jb 47.04N 28.38 E
Gidole=Ghidole (EN) 35 Fd 5.37N 37.29 E
Gien 11 Ig 47.42N 2.38 E
Giens, Presqu'île de- 11 Mk 43.02N 6.08 E
Gier 11 Ki 45.35N 4.46 E
Gießen 10 Ef 50.35N 8.39 E
Gieten 12 Ia 53.01N 6.48 E
Giethoorn 12 Ib 52.43N 6.07 E
Gifford 42 Jb 70.21N 83.05W
Gifford Seamount (EN) 52 Hi 39.00S 82.00W
Gifhorn 10 Gd 52.29N 10.33 E
Gift Lake 42 Fe 55.49N 115.57W
Gifu 22 Pf 35.25N 136.45 E
Gifu Ken [2] 28 Ng 35.50N 137.00 E
Gigant 16 Lf 46.29N 41.20 E
Giganta, Cerro- 47 Bc 26.07N 111.36W
Giganta, Sierra de la- 47 Bc 26.18N 111.39W
Gigante 54 Cc 2.24N 75.34W
Gigen 15 Hf 43.42N 24.29 E
Gigha 9 Hf 55.41N 5.44W
Giglio 14 Eh 42.20N 10.55 E
Gijón 6 Fg 43.32N 5.40W
Gikongoro 36 Ec 2.30S 29.35 E
Gila Bend 46 Ij 32.57N 112.43W
Gila Bend Mountains 46 Ij 33.10N 113.10W
Gīlān [3] 23 Gb 37.00N 49.50 E
Gīlān-e-Gharb 24 Ke 34.08N 45.55 E
Gila River 43 Ee 32.43N 114.33W
Gilbert, Mount- 46 Ca 50.51N 124.20W
Gilbert River 59 Ic 16.35S 141.15 E
Gilbert Seamount (EN) 40 If 52.50N 150.10W
Gilbués 54 Ie 9.50S 45.21W
Gile 37 Fc 16.09S 38.19 E
Giles Meteorological Station 59 Fe 25.02S 128.18 E
Gilford Island 46 Ba 50.45N 126.25W
Gilgandra 59 Jf 31.42S 148.39 E
Gilğau 15 Gb 47.17N 23.43 E
Gilgil 36 Gc 0.30S 36.19 E
Gilgit 25 Ea 35.44N 74.38 E
Gilgit 22 Jf 35.55N 74.18 E
Giljuj 20 Hf 54.17N 127.05 E
Gillam 42 Ie 56.21N 94.43W
Gilleleje 8 Eh 56.07N 12.19 E
Gillen, Lake- 59 Ee 26.10S 124.40 E
Gillenfeld 12 Id 50.07N 6.54 E
Gillette 43 Fc 44.18N 105.30W
Gillian, Lake - 42 Jc 69.30N 75.30W
Gillingham 9 Nj 51.24N 0.33 E
Gilo 35 Ed 8.10N 33.15 E
Gilort 15 Ge 44.36N 23.27 E
Gilroy 46 Eh 37.00N 121.34W
Giluwe, Mount- 60 Ci 6.04S 143.53 E
Gilvān 24 Md 36.47N 49.08 E
Gimån 8 Gb 62.28N 16.20 E
Gimbi 35 Fd 9.10N 35.51 E
Gimie, Mount- 50 Ff 13.52N 61.01W
Gimli 42 Hf 50.39N 97.00W
Gimo 8 Hd 60.11N 18.11 E
Gimolskoje, Ozero- 7 He 63.00N 32.15 E
Gimone 11 Hk 44.00N 1.06 E
Ginda 35 Fb 15.27N 39.06 E
Ginetu 63a Ac 9.30S 152.43 E

Index Symbols

[1] Independent Nation
[2] State, Region
[3] District, County
[4] Municipality
[5] Colony, Dependency
Continent
Physical Region
Historical or Cultural Region
Mount, Mountain
Volcano
Hill
Mountains, Mountain Range
Hills, Escarpment
Plateau, Upland
Pass, Gap
Plain, Lowland
Delta
Salt Flat
Valley, Canyon
Crater, Cave
Karst Features
Depression
Polder
Desert, Dunes
Forest, Woods
Heath, Steppe
Oasis
Cape, Point
Coast, Beach
Cliff
Peninsula
Isthmus
Sandbank
Island
Atoll
Rock, Reef
Islands, Archipelago
Rocks, Reefs
Coral Reef
Well, Spring
Geyser
River, Stream
Waterfall Rapids
River Mouth, Estuary
Lake
Salt Lake
Intermittent Lake
Reservoir
Swamp, Pond
Canal
Glacier
Ice Shelf, Pack Ice
Ocean
Sea
Gulf, Bay
Strait, Fjord
Lagoon
Bank
Seamount
Tablemount
Ridge
Shelf
Basin
Escarpment, Sea Scarp
Fracture
Trench, Abyss
National Park, Reserve
Point of Interest
Recreation Site
Cave, Cavern
Historic Site
Ruins
Wall, Walls
Church, Abbey
Temple
Scientific Station
Airport
Port
Lighthouse
Mine
Tunnel
Dam, Bridge

Gin Gin	59	Kd	25.00S	151.58 E
Gingin	59	Df	31.21S	115.42 E
Gingoog	26	Ie	8.50N	125.07 E
Ginir	35	Gd	7.08N	40.43 E
Ginosa	14	Kj	40.35N	16.45 E
Ginowan	29b	Ab	26.17N	127.45 E
Ginzo de Limia	13	Eb	42.03N	7.43W
Giofra Oasis (EN)=Jufrah, Wāḩāt al-	30	If	29.10N	16.00 E
Gioia, Golfo di-	14	Jl	38.30N	15.45 E
Gioia del Colle	14	Kj	40.48N	16.55 E
Gioia Tauro	14	Jl	38.25N	15.54 E
Gion	35	Fd	8.24N	37.55 E
Gióna Óros	15	Fk	38.35N	22.15 E
Giovi, Passo dei-	14	Cf	44.33N	8.57 E
Giraltovce	10	Rg	49.07N	21.31 E
Girardot	54	Dc	4.18N	74.49W
Girdle Ness	9	Kd	57.08N	2.02W
Giresun	23	Ea	40.55N	38.24 E
Giresun Dağları	24	Hb	40.40N	38.10 E
Giri	36	Cb	0.28N	17.59 E
Giridih	25	Hd	24.11N	86.18 E
Giriftu	36	Gb	2.00N	39.45 E
Girne	24	Ee	35.20N	33.19 E
Girón	54	Cd	3.10S	79.09W
Girona/Gerona	13	Oc	41.59N	2.49 E
Gironde	11	Fj	44.55N	0.30W
Gironde	5	Ff	45.35N	1.03W
Gironella	13	Nb	42.02N	1.53 E
Girou	11	Hk	43.46N	1.23 E
Girvan	9	If	55.15N	4.51W
Girvas	7	He	62.31N	33.44 E
Gisborne	58	Ih	38.39S	178.01 E
Gisenyi	36	Ec	1.42S	29.15 E
Gislaved	8	Eg	57.18N	13.32 E
Gisors	11	He	49.17N	1.47 E
Gissar	18	Ge	38.31N	68.36 E
Gissarski Hrebet	18	Ge	39.00N	68.40 E
Gistad	8	Ff	58.27N	15.55 E
Gistel	12	Ec	51.10N	2.57 E
Gistral	13	Ea	43.28N	7.35W
Gitarama	36	Ec	2.05S	29.16 E
Gitega	36	Ec	3.26S	29.56 E
Gitu	24	Me	35.20N	48.05 E
Giudicarie, Valli-	14	Ed	46.00N	10.40 E
Giulianova	14	Hh	42.45N	13.57 E
Giumalău, Vîrful-	15	Ib	47.26N	25.29 E
Giurgeni	15	Ke	44.35N	27.48 E
Giurgiu	15	If	43.53N	25.58 E
Give	8	Ci	55.51N	9.15 E
Givors	11	Ki	45.35N	4.46 E
Givry-en-Argonne	12	Gf	48.57N	4.53 E
Givry Island	64d	Bb	7.07N	151.53 E
Giwa	34	Gc	11.18N	7.27 E
Giza (EN)=Al Jīzah	31	Ke	30.01N	31.13 E
Gižduvan	19	Gg	40.06N	64.40 E
Gižiga	20	Ld	62.03N	160.30 E
Gižiginskaja Guba	20	Kd	61.10N	158.30 E
Gizo	63a	Cc	8.07S	156.50 E
Gizo	60	Fi	8.06S	156.51 E
Giżycko	10	Rb	54.03N	21.47 E
Gjalicës, Mali i-	15	Dg	42.01N	20.28 E
Gjamyš, Gora-	16	Oi	40.20N	46.25 E
Gjandža	6	Kg	40.40N	46.22 E
Gjerstad	8	Cf	58.52N	9.00 E
Gjevilvatn	8	Cb	62.40N	9.25 E
Gjirokastra	15	Di	40.05N	20.10 E
Gjoa Haven	39	Jc	68.38N	95.57W
Gjøvik	6	Hc	60.48N	10.42 E
Gjuhës, Kep i-	15	Ci	40.25N	19.18 E
Glace Bay	42	Lg	46.12N	59.57W
Glacier Bay	40	Le	58.40N	136.00W
Glacier Peak	43	Cb	48.07N	121.07W
Glacier Strait	42	Ja	76.15N	79.00W
Gladbeck	12	Ic	51.34N	6.59 E
Gladenbach	12	Kd	50.46N	8.34 E
Gladewater	45	Ij	32.33N	94.56W
Gladstone [Austl.]	58	Gg	23.51S	151.16 E
Gladstone [Man.-Can.]	45	Ga	50.15N	98.50W
Gladstone [Mi.-U.S.]	44	Dc	45.51N	87.03W
Gladstone [Mo.-U.S.]	45	Ig	39.13N	94.34W
Glafsfjorden	8	Ee	59.35N	12.35 E
Glåma	5	Hd	59.12N	10.57 E
Gláma	7a	Ab	65.48N	23.00W
Glamis Castle	9	Ke	56.37N	3.00W
Glamoč	23	Ff	44.03N	16.51 E
Glan	7	Dg	58.35N	15.55 E
Glan [Aus.]	14	Id	46.36N	14.25 E
Glan [Ger.]	10	Dg	49.47N	7.43 E
Glan-Münchweiler	12	Je	49.28N	7.26 E
Glarner Alpen	14	Cd	46.55N	9.00 E
Glärnisch	14	Cd	47.00N	9.00 E
Glarus	14	Dd	46.55N	9.05 E
Glarus	14	Dc	47.03N	9.04 E
Glasgow [Ky.-U.S.]	44	Eg	37.00N	85.55W
Glasgow [Mt.-U.S.]	43	Fb	48.12N	106.38W
Glasgow [Scot.-U.K.]	6	Fd	55.53N	4.15W
Glashütte	10	Jf	50.51N	13.47 E
Glass	9	Id	57.25N	4.30W
Glassboro	44	Jf	39.42N	75.07W
Glass Mountains	45	Ek	30.25N	103.15W
Glastonbury	9	Kj	51.09N	2.43W
Glauchau	10	If	50.49N	12.32 E
Glava	8	Ee	59.33N	12.34 E
Glazov	6	Ld	58.09N	52.40 E
Gleann Dá Loch/Glendalough	9	Gh	53.00N	6.20W
Gledićske Planine	15	Df	43.49N	20.55 E
Gleinalpe	14	Jc	47.10N	15.05 E
Gleisdorf	14	Jc	47.06N	15.43 E
Glen	12	Bb	52.50N	0.07W
Glénan, Iles de-	11	Cg	47.43N	4.00W
Glen Arbor	44	Ec	44.53N	85.58W
Glenavy	62	Df	44.55S	171.06 E
Glen Canyon	46	Jh	37.05N	111.41W
Glencoe [Mn.-U.S.]	45	Id	44.46N	94.09W
Glencoe [S.Afr.]	37	Ee	28.12S	30.07 E
Glendale [Az.-U.S.]	43	Ee	33.32N	112.11W
Glendale [Ca.-U.S.]	43	De	34.10N	118.17W
Glendalough/Gleann Dá Loch	9	Gh	53.00N	6.20W
Glendive	43	Gb	47.06N	104.43W
Glendo Reservoir	46	Me	42.31N	104.58W
Glenhope	61	Dh	41.39S	172.39 E
Glen Innes	58	Gg	29.44S	151.44 E
Glennallen	40	Jd	62.07N	145.33W
Glenner	14	Dd	46.46N	9.12 E
Glenns Ferry	46	He	42.57N	115.18W
Glenorchy	62	Cf	44.52S	168.24 E
Glenrock	46	Me	42.52N	105.52W
Glen Rose	45	Hj	32.14N	97.45W
Glenrothes	9	Je	56.12N	3.05W
Glens Falls	44	Kd	43.17N	73.41W
Glenville	44	Gf	38.57N	80.51W
Glenwood [Ia.-U.S.]	45	If	41.03N	95.45W
Glenwood [Mn.-U.S.]	45	Id	45.39N	95.23W
Glenwood Springs	43	Fd	39.32N	107.19W
Glibokaja	15	Ja	48.05N	26.00 E
Glina	14	Ke	45.20N	16.06 E
Glinjany	10	Ug	49.46N	24.33 E
Glittertinden	5	Gc	61.39N	8.33 E
Gliwice	10	Of	50.17N	18.40 E
Globe	43	Ee	33.24N	110.47W
Globino	16	He	49.24N	33.18 E
Głogów	10	Me	51.40N	16.05 E
Glomfjord	7	Cc	66.49N	13.58 E
Glommersträsk	7	Ed	65.16N	19.38 E
Glonn	10	Hh	48.11N	11.45 E
Glorieuses, Iles-	30	Lj	11.30S	47.20 E
Glottof, Mount-	40	Ie	57.30N	153.30W
Gloucester	9	Kj	51.55N	2.15W
Gloucester [Eng.-U.K.]	9	Kj	51.53N	2.14W
Gloucester [Ma.-U.S.]	44	Ld	42.41N	70.39W
Gloucester, Cape-	60	Di	5.27S	148.25 E
Gloucestershire	9	Lj	51.50N	1.55W
Glover Island	51p	Bb	11.59N	61.47W
Glover's Reef	49	De	16.49N	87.48W
Gloversville	44	Jd	43.03N	74.21W
Głowno	10	Pe	51.58N	19.44 E
Głubczyce	10	Nf	50.13N	17.49 E
Glubokoje	19	Cd	55.08N	27.41 E
Glubokoje	19	Ie	50.06N	82.19 E
Glubokoje, Ozero-	8	Md	60.30N	29.25 E
Głuchołazy	10	Nf	50.20N	17.22 E
Glücksburg	10	Fb	54.50N	9.33 E
Glückstadt	10	Fc	53.47N	9.25 E
Gluhov	19	De	51.43N	33.57 E
Gluša	16	Fc	53.06N	28.52 E
Glyngøre	8	Ch	56.46N	8.52 E
Gmünd [Aus.]	14	Hd	46.54N	13.32 E
Gmünd [Aus.]	14	Ib	48.46N	14.59 E
Gmunden	14	Hc	47.55N	13.48 E
Gnarp	7	De	62.03N	17.16 E
Gnesta	7	Dg	59.03N	17.18 E
Gniben	8	Dh	56.01N	11.18 E
Gniew	10	Oc	53.51N	18.49 E
Gniewkowo	10	Od	52.54N	18.25 E
Gniezno	10	Nd	52.31N	17.37 E
Gnjilane	15	Eg	42.28N	21.29 E
Gnosjö	7	Ch	57.22N	13.44 E
Gnowangerup	59	Df	33.56S	117.50 E
Goa, Damān and Diu	25	Ee	15.35N	74.00 E
Goageb	37	Be	26.44S	17.15 E
Goālpāra	25	Ic	26.10N	90.37 E
Goat	63b	Dd	18.42S	169.17 E
Goat Island	51d	Ba	17.44N	61.51W
Goat Point	51d	Ba	17.44N	61.51W
Goba	31	Kh	7.01N	39.59 E
Gobabis	31	Ik	22.30S	18.58 E
Gobabis	37	Bd	22.00S	19.00 E
Göbel	15	Lj	40.00N	28.09 E
Gober	34	Gc	13.48N	6.51 E
Gobernador Gregores	56	Fg	48.46S	70.15W
Gobernador Ingeniero Valentín Virasoro	56	Ic	28.03S	56.02W
Gobernador Mansilla	55	Ck	32.33S	59.22W
Gobi, Pustynja-=Gobi Desert (EN)	21	Me	43.00N	106.00 E
Gobi Altai (EN)=Gobijski Altaj	21	Me	44.00N	102.00 E
Gobi Desert (EN)=Gobi, Pustynja-	21	Me	43.00N	106.00 E
Gobijski Altaj=Gobi Altai (EN)	21	Me	44.00N	102.00 E
Gobō	28	Mh	33.53N	135.10 E
Göçbeyli	15	Kj	39.13N	27.25 E
Goceano	14	Dj	40.30N	9.15 E
Goceano, Catena del-	14	Cj	40.30N	9.00 E
Goce Delčev	15	Gh	41.33N	23.42 E
Goch	10	Ce	51.40N	6.10 E
Gochas	37	Bd	24.55S	18.55 E
Goczałkowickie, Jezioro-	10	Og	49.53N	18.50 E
Göd	10	Pi	47.42N	19.08 E
Godafoss	7a	Cb	65.41N	17.33W
Godalming	12	Bc	51.11N	0.36W
Godār	24	Qh	29.45N	57.30 E
Godār-e Shah	24	Me	34.45N	48.10 E
Godāvari	21	Kh	17.00N	81.45 E
Godbout, Rivière-	44	Na	49.21N	67.42W
Gode	35	Gd	5.55N	43.40 E
Godeč	15	Gf	43.01N	23.03 E
Godelbukta Breidvika	66	Df	70.15S	24.15 E
Goderich	44	Gd	43.45N	81.43W
Goderville	12	Ce	49.39N	0.22 E
Godhavn/Qeqertarssuaq	67	Nc	69.20N	53.35W
Godhra	25	Ed	22.45N	73.38 E
Godinlabe	35	Hd	5.54N	46.40 E
Gödöllő	10	Pi	47.36N	19.22 E
Godoy Cruz	56	Gd	32.55S	68.50W
Gods Lake	42	If	54.40N	94.09W
Gods Lake	42	If	54.40N	94.20W
Gods Mercy, Bay of -	42	Id	63.30N	86.10W
Gods River	42	Ie	56.22N	92.52W
Godthåb/Nûk	67	Nc	64.15N	51.40W
Godthåbfjord	41	Gf	64.20N	51.30W
Godwin Austen (EN)=K2	21	Jf	35.53N	76.30 E
Godwin Austen (EN)=Qogir Feng	21	Jf	35.53N	76.30 E
Goedereede	12	Fc	51.49N	3.58 E
Goéland, Lac au-	42	Jg	49.45N	76.50W
Goélands, Lac aux-	42	Le	55.30N	64.30W
Goële	12	Ee	49.10N	2.40 E
Goelette Island	37b	Bc	10.13S	51.08 E
Goeree	11	Jc	51.50N	3.55 E
Goes	11	Jc	51.30N	3.54 E
Gogama	42	Jg	47.40N	81.43W
Gō-Gawa	29	Cd	35.01N	132.13 E
Gogebic Range	44	Cb	46.45N	89.25W
Gogland, Ostrov-	7	Gf	60.05N	27.00 E
Gog Magog Hills	12	Cb	52.09N	0.11 E
Gogounou	34	Fc	10.50N	2.50 E
Gogrial	35	Dd	8.32N	28.07 E
Gogu, Vîrful-	15	Fd	45.12N	22.30 E
Gogui	34	Db	15.39N	9.21W
Goğu Karadeniz Dağları	24	Ib	40.40N	40.00 E
Gohelle	12	Ed	50.28N	2.45 E
Goiandira	54	Ig	18.08S	48.06W
Goianésia	54	Ig	15.19S	49.04W
Goiânia	53	Lg	16.40S	49.16W
Goianinha	54	Ke	6.16S	35.12W
Goiás	54	If	12.00S	48.00W
Goiás	54	Hg	15.56S	50.08W
Goiatuba	54	Ig	18.01S	49.22W
Goikul	64a	Bc	7.22N	134.36 E
Göinge	8	Eh	56.20N	13.50 E
Goio-Erê	56	Jb	24.12S	53.01W
Goioxim	55	Gg	25.14S	52.01W
Goirle	12	Hc	51.34N	5.05 E
Góis	13	Dd	40.09N	8.07W
Goito	14	Ee	45.15N	10.40 E
Gojam	35	Fc	10.33N	37.35 E
Gojō	29	Dd	34.21N	135.42 E
Gojōme	29	Gb	39.56N	140.07 E
Gojra	25	Eb	31.09N	72.41 E
Gojthski, Pereval-	16	Kg	44.15N	39.18 E
Gokase-Gawa	29	Be	32.35N	131.42 E
Gokasho-Wan	29	Ed	34.20N	136.40 E
Gökbel Dağı	15	Kl	37.28N	28.00 E
Gökçay	24	Ed	36.36N	33.23 E
Gökçeada	24	Ac	40.10N	25.50 E
Gökçeören	15	Lk	38.35N	28.32 E
Gökçeyazi	15	Kj	39.38N	27.39 E
Gökdere	24	Ed	36.39N	33.35 E
Gökırmak	24	Fb	41.24N	35.08 E
Göksu [Tur.]	24	Fd	36.20N	34.05 E
Göksu [Tur.]	24	Fd	37.37N	35.35 E
Göksu [Tur.]	15	Mi	40.23N	29.58 E
Göksun	24	Gc	38.03N	36.30 E
Gök Tepe	15	Mm	36.53N	29.17 E
Göktepe	15	Ll	37.16N	28.36 E
Gokwe	37	Dc	18.13S	28.55 E
Gol	7	Bf	60.42N	8.57 E
Golāghāt	25	Ic	26.31N	93.58 E
Golaja Pristan	16	Hf	46.29N	32.31 E
Gołańcz	10	Nd	52.57N	17.18 E
Golconda [Il.-U.S.]	45	Lh	37.22N	88.29W
Golconda [Nv.-U.S.]	46	Gf	40.57N	117.30W
Gölcük	24	Cb	40.44N	29.44 E
Golčův Jeníkov	10	Lg	49.49N	15.30 E
Gołdap	10	Sb	54.19N	22.19 E
Gold Beach	46	Ce	42.25N	124.25W
Gold Coast	58	Gg	27.58S	153.25 E
Gold Coast	30	Gh	5.20N	0.45W
Golden [B.C.-Can.]	42	Ff	51.18N	116.58W
Golden [Co.-U.S.]	45	Dg	39.46N	105.13W
Golden Bay	62	Ed	40.50S	172.50 E
Goldendale	4C	Ed	45.49N	120.50W
Goldene Aue	10	Ge	51.25N	11.00 E
Golden Gate	46	Dh	37.49N	122.29W
Golden Hinde	42	Eg	49.39N	125.45W
Golden Meadow	45	Kl	29.23N	90.16W
Golden Vale/Machaire na Mumhan	9	Fi	52.30N	8.00W
Goldfield	46	Gh	37.42N	117.14W
Gold River	46	Bb	49.41N	126.08W
Goldsboro	43	Ld	35.23N	77.59W
Goldsworthy	59	Dd	20.20S	119.30 E
Göle	24	Jb	40.48N	42.36 E
Golegã	13	De	39.24N	8.29W
Goleniów	10	Kc	53.36N	14.50 E
Golešnica	15	Eh	41.42N	21.33 E
Goleta, Cerro-	48	Ih	18.38N	100.04W
Golfito	47	Hg	8.38N	83.11W
Golfo Aranci	14	Dj	41.00N	9.37 E
Gölgeli Dağları	15	Ml	37.15N	29.06 E
Gölhisar	15	Ml	37.08N	29.30 E
Goliad	45	Hl	28.40N	97.23W
Golija [Yugo.]	15	Df	43.19N	20.18 E
Golija [Yugo.]	15	Bf	43.02N	18.47 E
Goljak	15	Eg	42.44N	21.31 E
Goljama Kamčija	15	Kf	43.03N	27.29 E
Goljama Sjutkja	15	Hh	41.54N	24.01 E
Goljamo Konare	15	Hg	42.16N	24.33 E
Goljam Perelik	15	Hh	41.36N	24.34 E
Goljam Persenk	15	Hh	41.49N	24.33 E
Gölköy	24	Gb	40.15N	37.26 E
Gölkük	15	Kj	39.19N	27.59 E
Göllheim	12	Ke	49.35N	8.03 E
Gölmarmara	15	Kk	38.42N	27.56 E
Golmud He	27	Gd	36.54N	95.11 E
Golo	11a	Ba	42.31N	9.32 E
Goloby	10	Ve	51.06N	25.06 E
Gologory	10	Ug	49.35N	24.30 E
Gololcha	35	Gd	8.12N	40.05 E
Golovin	40	Gd	64.33N	163.02W
Golovnin Seamount (EN)	20	Kg	46.50N	157.00 E
Golpāyegān	23	Hc	33.27N	50.18 E
Gölpazarı	24	Db	40.17N	30.19 E
Golšanka	10	Kb	54.00N	26.16 E
Golspie	9	Jd	57.58N	3.58W
Gol Tappeh	24	Kd	36.35N	45.45 E
Golubac	15	Ee	44.39N	21.38 E
Golub-Dobrzyń	10	Pc	53.08N	19.02 E
Golungo Alto	36	Bd	9.08S	14.47 E
Golyšmanovo	19	Gd	56.23N	68.23 E
Goma	31	Ji	1.37S	29.12 E
Gómara	13	Jc	41.37N	2.13W
Gombe	31	Ig	10.17N	11.10 E
Gombi	34	Hc	10.10N	12.44 E
Gomel	6	Je	52.25N	31.00 E
Gomelskaja Oblast	19	Ce	52.20N	29.40 E
Gomera	30	Ff	28.06N	17.08W
Gómez Farias	48	Ie	24.57N	101.02W
Gómez Palacio	47	Dc	25.34N	103.30W
Gomo Co	27	Ee	33.45N	85.35 E
Goms	14	Cd	46.25N	8.10 E
Gonābād	23	Ic	34.20N	58.42 E
Gonaïves	47	Je	19.27N	72.43W
Gonam	20	Ie	57.18N	131.20 E
Gonâve, Golfe de la-	47	Je	19.00N	73.30W
Gonâve, Ile de la-	47	Je	18.51N	73.03W
Gonbad-e Qābūs	23	Ib	37.15N	55.09 E
Gonda	25	Gc	27.08N	81.56 E
Gonder	35	Fc	12.00N	38.00 E
Gonder	31	Kg	12.38N	37.27 E
Gondia	25	Gd	21.27N	80.12 E
Gondo	30	Gg	14.20N	3.10W
Gondomar	13	Dc	41.09N	8.32W
Gondwana	21	Kg	23.00N	81.00 E
Gönen	24	Bb	40.06N	27.39 E
Gönen	24	Bb	40.06N	27.36 E
Gonfreville-l'Orcher	12	Ce	49.30N	0.14 E
Gong'an (Doushi)	27	Je	30.05N	112.12 E
Gongbo'gyamda	27	Ff	29.59N	93.25 E
Gonggar	27	Ff	29.17N	90.50 E
Gongga Shan	21	Mg	29.34N	101.53 E
Gonghe	27	Hd	36.21N	100.47 E
Gongliu/Tokkuztara	27	Dc	43.30N	82.15 E
Gongola	30	Ih	9.30N	12.04 E
Gongola	34	Hd	8.40N	11.20 E
Gongpoquan	27	Gc	41.50N	97.00 E
Gongshan	27	Gf	27.39N	98.35 E
Gongxian	27	Kf	26.05N	119.32 E
Gongzian (Xiaoyi)	28	Bg	34.46N	112.57 E
Gongzhuling → Huaide	27	Lc	43.30N	124.52 E
Goñi	55	Dk	33.31S	56.24W
Goniądz	10	Sc	53.30N	22.45 E
Gonīshān	24	Pd	37.04N	54.06 E
Gonjo	27	Ge	30.52N	98.20 E
Gonohe	29	Ga	40.31N	141.19 E
Go-no-ura	29	Ae	33.45N	129.41 E
Gönuk	24	Ic	39.00N	40.41 E
Gonzales	45	Hl	29.30N	97.27W
Gonzáles, Riacho-	55	Df	22.48S	57.54W
González	48	Jf	22.50N	98.27W
Goodenough, Cape-	66	Ie	66.16S	126.10 E
Goodenough Bay	59	Ja	9.55S	150.00 E
Goodenough Island	60	Ei	9.22S	150.16 E
Good Hope, Cape of-/Groeie Hoop, Kaap die-	30	Il	34.21S	18.28 E
Goodhouse	37	Be	28.57S	18.13 E
Gooding	46	He	42.56N	114.43W
Goodland	43	Gd	39.21N	101.43W
Goodnews Bay	40	Ge	59.07N	161.35W
Goodsir, Mount-	46	Ga	51.12N	116.20W
Good Spirit Lake	46	Na	51.34N	102.40W
Goodwin Sands	12	Dc	51.15N	1.35 E
Goodyear	46	Ij	33.26N	112.21W
Goole	9	Mh	53.42N	0.52W
Goomalling	59	Df	31.19S	116.49 E
Goondiwindi	58	Gg	28.32S	150.19 E
Goonyella	59	Jd	21.43S	147.58 E
Goor	12	Ib	52.14N	6.37 E
Goose Lake	43	Cc	41.57N	120.25W
Goose River	45	Hc	47.28N	96.52W
Gopło, Jezioro-	10	Od	52.35N	18.20 E
Göppingen	10	Fh	48.42N	9.40 E
Góra	10	Me	51.40N	16.33 E
Gora	15	Di	40.40N	20.30 E
Góra Kalwaria	10	Re	51.59N	21.12 E
Gorakhpur	22	Kg	26.45N	83.22 E
Goransko	15	Bf	43.07N	18.50 E
Gorata	15	Ih	41.45N	25.55 E
Goražde	14	Mg	43.40N	18.59 E
Gorda	46	Ei	35.55N	121.27W
Gorda, Cayo	49	Ff	15.55N	82.15W
Gorda, Punta- [Ca.-U.S.]	46	Cf	40.16N	124.20W
Gorda, Punta- [Cuba]	49	Fb	22.24N	82.10W
Gorda, Punta- [Nic.]	49	Ff	14.21N	83.12W
Gördes	15	Lk	38.54N	28.18 E
Gördes	15	Kj	38.46N	27.58 E
Gordil	35	Cd	9.44N	21.35 E
Gordior	24	Ec	39.37N	32.00 E
Gordon [Nb.-U.S.]	45	Ee	42.48N	102.12W
Gordon [Wi.-U.S.]	45	Kc	46.15N	91.47W
Gordon, Lake-	59	Jh	43.05S	146.05 E
Gordon Horne Peak	46	Fa	51.46N	118.50W
Gordonvale	59	Jc	17.05S	145.47 E
Goré	35	Bd	7.55N	16.38 E
Gore [Eth.]	35	Fd	8.09N	35.34 E
Gore [N.Z.]	62	Cg	46.06S	168.56 E
Görele	24	Hb	41.02N	39.00 E
Görenez Dağı	15	Lk	39.00N	28.01 E
Gorenjsko	14	Id	46.20N	14.10 E
Gorey/Guaire	9	Gi	52.40N	6.18W
Gorgān	24	Pd	36.59N	54.05 E
Gorgān	24	Jf	33.21N	43.40 E
Gorgān, Khalīj-e-	24	Od	36.40N	53.50 E
Gorgany	10	Jh	48.30N	24.15 E
Gorgin	24	Ld	36.15N	47.55 E
Gorgol	32	Ef	15.45N	13.00W
Gorgol el Abiod	32	Ef	16.14N	12.58W
Gorgona	14	Dg	43.25N	9.55 E
Gorgona, Isla-	54	Cc	2.59N	78.12W
Gorgora	35	Fc	12.14N	37.17 E
Gorham	44	Lc	44.23N	71.11W
Gori	19	Eg	42.00N	44.02 E
Gorinchem	11	Kc	51.50N	5.00 E
Goring	12	Ac	51.31N	1.08W
Goris	16	Oj	39.31N	46.22 E
Gorizia	14	He	45.57N	13.38 E
Gorj	15	Gd	45.00N	23.20 E
Gorjačegorsk	20	De	55.24N	88.55 E
Gorjači Kljuc	16	Kg	44.36N	39.07 E
Gorjanci	14	Je	45.45N	15.20 E
Gorki	16	Gb	54.17N	31.00 E
Gorki → Nižnij Novgorod	6	Kd	57.38N	45.05 E
Gorki	20	Bc	65.05N	65.15 E
Gorkovskoje Vodohranilišče =Gorky Reservoir (EN)	5	Kd	57.00N	43.10 E
Gorkum	10	Hf	50.10N	11.08 E
Gorky Reservoir (EN)= Gorkovskoje Vodohr.	5	Kd	57.00N	43.10 E
Gørlev	8	Di	55.32N	11.14 E
Gorlice	10	Rg	49.40N	21.10 E
Görlitz	10	Ke	51.10N	15.00 E
Gorlovka	6	Jf	48.18N	38.03 E
Gornalunga	14	Jm	37.24N	15.03 E
Gorna Orjahovica	15	If	43.07N	25.41 E
Gornjak	20	Df	51.00N	81.29 E
Gornjak	10	Uf	50.16N	24.13 E
Gornji Milanovac	15	De	44.02N	20.27 E
Gornji Vakuf	23	Fg	43.56N	17.36 E
Gorno-Altajsk	22	Kd	51.58N	85.58 E
Gorno-Badahšanskaja avtonomnaja respublika	19	Hh	38.15N	73.00 E
Gorno-Čujski	20	Ge	57.40N	111.40 E
Gornozavodsk	20	Jg	46.30N	141.55 E
Gornozavodsk	17	Ig	58.25N	58.20 E
Gorny	20	Ih	44.50N	133.56 E
Gorny	16	Pd	51.45N	48.34 E
Gorny	20	If	50.48N	136.26 E
Gornyj Altaj respublika	20	Df	51.00N	87.00 E
Gornyje Ključi	28	Lb	45.15N	133.30 E
Gorochan	35	Fd	9.26N	37.05 E
Gorodec	7	Kh	56.40N	43.30 E
Gorodec	8	Mf	58.30N	29.55 E
Gorodenka	16	De	48.42N	25.32 E
Gorodišče	10	Vc	53.16N	26.03 E
Gorodišče	16	Nc	53.16N	45.42 E
Gorodišče	16	Ge	49.17N	31.27 E
Gorodnica	16	Ed	50.49N	27.22 E
Gorodnja	16	Gd	51.55N	31.31 E
Gorodok	19	Cd	55.26N	29.59 E
Gorodok	16	Ee	49.10N	26.31 E
Gorodok	16	Ce	49.47N	23.39 E
Gorodovikovsk	19	Ef	46.05N	41.59 E
Gorohov	10	Uf	50.28N	24.47 E
Gorohovec	7	Kh	56.12N	42.42 E
Goroka	58	Fe	6.02S	145.22 E
Gorom-Gorom	34	Ec	14.26N	0.14W
Gorong, Kepulauan-	26	Jg	4.05S	131.20 E
Gorongosa, Serra da-	37	Ec	18.24S	34.06 E
Gorontalo	22	Oi	0.33N	123.03 E
Goroual	34	Fc	14.42N	0.53 E
Górowo Iławeckie	10	Qb	54.17N	20.30 E
Gorron	11	Ff	48.25N	0.49W
Goršečnoje	16	Kd	51.33N	38.09 E
Gorski Kotar	14	Ie	45.26N	14.40 E
Gorssel	12	Ib	52.12N	6.13 E
Gort	9	Eh	53.04N	8.50W
Goru, Vîrful-	15	Jd	45.48N	26.25 E
Görükle	15	Li	40.14N	28.50 E
Goryn	19	Ce	52.09N	27.17 E
Gorzów	10	Ld	54.25N	15.15 E
Gorzów Wielkopolski	10	Ld	52.44N	15.15 E
Goschen Strait	59	Kb	10.09S	150.56 E
Gosen	28	Of	37.44N	139.11 E
Gosford	59	Kf	33.26S	151.21 E
Goshen	44	Ee	41.35N	85.50W
Goshogawara	28	Pd	40.48N	140.27 E
Gosier	51e	Bb	16.12N	61.30W
Goslar	10	Ge	51.54N	10.26 E
Gospić	14	Jf	44.33N	15.23 E
Gosport	9	Lk	50.48N	1.08W
Gossen	8	Bb	62.50N	6.55 E
Gossi	34	Eb	15.47N	1.15W
Gossinga	35	Dd	8.39N	25.59 E
Gostivar	15	Dh	41.48N	20.54 E
Gostyń	10	Me	51.53N	17.00 E
Gostynin	10	Pd	52.26N	19.29 E
Gota älv	5	Hd	57.42N	11.52 E
Göta Kanal	5	Hd	58.50N	13.58 E
Götaland	5	Hd	57.30N	14.30 E
Götaland	7	Dg	57.30N	14.30 E
Göteborg	6	Hd	57.43N	11.58 E
Göteborg och Bohus	7	Cg	58.30N	11.30 E
Gotel Mountains	30	Ih	7.00N	11.40 E
Gotemba	29	Fd	35.18N	138.56 E
Götene	7	Cg	58.32N	13.29 E
Gotha	10	Gf	50.57N	10.43 E
Gothenburg	45	Ff	40.56N	100.09W
Gothèye	34	Fc	13.52N	1.34 E
Gotland	7	Eh	57.30N	18.30 E
Gotland	5	Hd	57.30N	18.30 E
Gotō-Nada	29	Ae	32.45N	129.30 E
Gotō-Rettō	27	Me	32.50N	129.00 E
Gotowasi	26	If	0.38N	128.26 E
Gotska Sandön	7	Eg	58.25N	19.15 E
Gōtsu	28	Lg	35.00N	132.14 E
Gttingen	10	Fe	51.32N	9.56 E
Gottwaldov → Zlín	10	Ng	49.13N	17.39 E
Goubangzi	28	Fd	41.23N	121.48 E
Gouda	11	Kc	52.01N	4.43 E
Goudiri	34	Cc	14.11N	12.43W
Gouet	11	Df	48.32N	2.45W
Gough Island	30	Gm	40.20S	10.00W
Gough Lake	46	Ia	52.02N	112.28W
Gouin, Réservoir-	42	Kg	48.35N	74.50W
Goulbin Kaba	34	Gc	13.42N	6.19 E
Goulburn	58	Fh	34.45S	149.43 E

Index Symbols

1 Independent Nation
2 State, Region
3 District, County
4 Municipality
5 Colony, Dependency
Continent
Physical Region
Historical or Cultural Region
Mount, Mountain
Volcano
Hill
Mountains, Mountain Range
Hills, Escarpment
Plateau, Upland
Pass, Gap
Plain, Lowland
Delta
Salt Flat
Valley, Canyon
Crater, Cave
Karst Features
Depression
Polder
Desert, Dunes
Forest, Woods
Heath, Steppe
Oasis
Cape, Point
Coast, Beach
Cliff
Peninsula
Isthmus
Sandbank
Island
Atoll
Rock, Reef
Islands, Archipelago
Rocks, Reefs
Coral Reef
Well, Spring
Geyser
River, Stream
Waterfall Rapids
River Mouth, Estuary
Lake
Salt Lake
Intermittent Lake
Reservoir
Swamp, Pond
Canal
Glacier
Ice Shelf, Pack Ice
Ocean
Sea
Gulf, Bay
Strait, Fjord
Lagoon
Bank
Seamount
Tablemount
Ridge
Shelf
Basin
Escarpment, Sea Scarp
Fracture
Trench, Abyss
National Park, Reserve
Point of Interest
Recreation Site
Cave, Cavern
Historic Site
Ruins
Wall, Walls
Church, Abbey
Temple
Scientific Station
Airport
Port
Lighthouse
Mine
Tunnel
Dam, Bridge

Goulburn Islands 59 Gb 11.50S 133.30 E
Gould Bay 66 Rf 78.10S 44.00W
Gould Coast 66 Mg 84.30S 150.00W
Goulia 34 Dc 10.01N 7.11W
Goulimine 32 Ed 28.59N 10.04W
Gouménissa 15 Fi 40.57N 22.27 E
Gouna 34 Hd 8.32N 13.34 E
Gounda 35 Cd 9.09N 21.15 E
Goundam 34 Eb 16.24N 3.38W
Goundi 35 Bd 9.22N 17.22 E
Goundoumaria 34 Hc 13.42N 11.10 E
Gounou Gaya 35 Bd 9.38N 15.31 E
Gourara 32 Hd 29.30N 0.40 E
Gouraya 13 Nh 36.34N 1.55 E
Gourcy 34 Ec 13.13N 2.21W
Gourdon 11 Hj 44.44N 1.23 E
Gouré 31 Ig 13.58N 10.18 E
Gourin 11 Cf 48.08N 3.36W
Gourma [Mali] 30 Gg 15.45N 2.00W
Gourma 30 Hg 12.20N 1.30 E
Gourma-Rharous 34 Eb 16.52N 1.55W
Gournay-en-Bray 11 He 49.29N 1.44 E
Gourniá 15 In 35.06N 25.48 E
Gouro 35 Bb 19.40N 19.28 E
Gourrama 32 Gc 32.20N 4.05W
Goussainville 12 Ee 49.01N 2.28 E
Gouyave 51p Bb 12.10N 61.44W
Gouzeaucourt 12 Fd 50.03N 3.07 E
Gouzon 11 Ih 46.11N 2.14 E
Govena, Mys- 20 Le 59.47N 166.02 E
Gove Peninsula 59 Hb 13.02S 136.50 E
Goverla, Gora- 19 Cf 48.10N 24.32 E
Governador Valadares 53 Lg 18.51S 41.56W
Governor's Harbour 47 Ic 25.10N 76.14W
Gowanda 44 Hd 42.28N 78.57W
Gower 9 Ij 51.36N 4.10W
Gowganda 44 Gb 47.38N 80.46W
Goya 53 Kh 29.10S 59.20W
Goyave 51e Ab 16.08N 61.34W
Goyaves, Ilets 'a- 51e Ab 16.10N 61.48W
Goyder River 59 Hb 12.38S 135.05 E
Göynücek 24 Fb 40.24N 35.32 E
Göynük 15 Ni 40.20N 30.05 E
Göynük 24 Db 40.24N 30.47 E
Gozaisho-Yama 29 Ed 35.01N 136.24 E
Goz Arian 35 Bc 14.35N 20.00 E
Goz Beïda 35 Cc 12.13N 21.25 E
Gozha Co 27 De 34.59N 81.06 E
Goz Kerki 35 Bb 15.30N 18.50 E
Gözlü Baba Dağı 15 Lk 38.15N 28.28 E
Gozo 5 Hh 36.05N 14.15 E
Graaff-Reinet 37 Cf 32.14S 24.32 E
Graafschap 11 Mb 52.05N 6.30 E
Graben Neudorf 12 Ke 49.10N 8.28 E
Grabia 10 Oe 51.26N 18.56 E
Grabière Point 51g Bb 15.30N 61.29W
Grabowa 10 Mb 54.26N 16.20 E
Gračac 14 Jf 44.18N 15.51 E
Gračanica 14 Mf 44.42N 18.18 E
Gračanica, Manastir- 15 Eg 42.36N 21.12 E
Gracias 49 Cf 14.35N 88.35W
Gracias a Dios 49 Ef 15.20N 84.20W
Gracias a Dios, Cabo 38 Kh 15.00N 83.08W
Graciosa [Azr.] 30 Ee 39.04N 28.00W
Graciosa [Can.Is.] 32 Ed 29.15N 13.30W
Gradačac 14 Mf 44.53N 18.26 E
Gradaús, Serra dos- 52 Kf 8.00S 50.45W
Grado [It.] 14 He 45.40N 13.23 E
Grado [Sp.] 13 Fa 43.23N 6.04W
Grænalon 7a Cb 64.10N 17.24W
Grænlandshaf = Greenland Sea (EN) 67 Ld 77.00N 1.00W
Grafenau 10 Jh 48.51N 13.24 E
Grafham Water 12 Bb 52.19N 0.10W
Grafing bei München 10 Hh 48.03N 11.58 E
Grafschaft Bentheim 12 Jb 52.30N 7.05 E
Grafton [Austl.] 59 Ke 29.41S 152.56 E
Grafton [N.D.-U.S.] 43 Hb 48.25N 97.25W
Grafton [W.V.-U.S.] 44 Hf 39.21N 80.00W
Grafton, Mount- 46 Hg 38.40N 114.45W
Graham 42 Ef 53.40N 132.30W
Graham [N.C.-U.S.] 44 Hg 36.05N 79.25W
Graham [Tx.-U.S.] 45 Gj 33.06N 98.35W
Graham, Mount- 43 Fe 32.42N 109.52W
Graham Land (EN) 66 Qe 66.00S 63.30W
Graham Moore, Cape - 42 Jb 72.51N 76.05W
Grahamstown 31 Jl 33.19S 26.31 E
Grain Coast 30 Gh 5.00N 9.00W
Graisivaudan 11 Li 45.15N 5.50 E
Grajaú 54 Ie 5.49S 46.08W
Grajaú, Rio- 54 Jd 3.41S 44.48W
Grajewo 10 Sc 53.39N 22.27 E
Gram 8 Ci 55.17N 9.04 E
Gramalote 49 Kj 7.54N 72.48W
Gramat 11 Hj 44.47N 1.43 E
Gramat, Causse de- 11 Hj 44.40N 1.50 E
Graminha, Represa da- 55 Ie 21.33S 46.38W
Grammerages/Galmaarden 12 Fd 50.45N 3.58 E
Grammichele 14 Im 37.13N 14.38 E
Grammont/Geraardsbergen 12 Fd 50.46N 3.52 E
Grámmos Óros 15 Di 40.20N 20.45 E
Grampian 9 Kd 57.25N 2.35W
Grampian Mountains 5 Fd 56.45N 4.00W
Gramshi 15 Di 40.52N 20.11 E
Gram 8 Dd 60.22N 10.34 E
Granada [Col.] 54 Dc 3.33N 73.44W
Granada [Nic.] 49 Eh 11.50N 86.00W
Granada [Nic.] 47 Gf 11.56N 85.57W
Granada [Sp.] 13 Ig 37.15N 3.15W
Granada [Sp.] 6 Fh 37.13N 3.41W
Granada, Vega de- 13 Ig 37.15N 4.00W
Grånard/Granard 9 Fh 53.47N 7.30W
Granard/Grånard 9 Fh 53.47N 7.30W
Granby 42 Kg 45.24N 72.43W
Gran Canaria 30 Ff 28.00N 15.36W
Gran Chaco 52 Jh 23.00S 60.00W
Grand Anse Bay 51p Bb 12.02N 61.45W
Grand Bahama 38 Lg 26.40N 78.20W
Grand Ballon 11 Ng 47.55N 7.08 E
Grand Bank 42 Lg 47.06N 55.47W
Grand Banks (EN) 38 Oe 45.00N 50.00W
Grand Bassa 34 Dd 6.10N 9.40W
Grand-Bassam 31 Gh 5.12N 3.44W
Grand Bay 51g Bb 15.14N 61.19W
Grand Bay 51p Cb 12.29N 61.23W
Grand-Bérêby 34 De 4.38N 6.55W
Grand-Bourg 50 Fe 15.53N 61.19W
Grand Cache 42 Ff 53.14N 119.00W
Grand Caille Point 51k Ab 13.52N 61.05W
Grandcamp-Maisy 12 Ae 49.23N 1.02W
Grand Canal 9 Gh 53.21N 6.14W
Grand Canal (EN) = Da Yunhe 21 Nf 39.54N 116.44 E
Grand Canyon 43 Ed 36.03N 112.09W
Grand Canyon 38 Hc 36.10N 112.45W
Grand' Case 51b Ab 18.06N 63.03W
Grand Cayman 47 He 19.20N 81.15W
Grand Cess 34 De 4.24N 8.13W
Grand Chartreuse 11 Li 45.22N 5.50 E
Grand Colombier 11 Li 45.54N 5.46 E
Grand Coulee 46 Fc 47.56N 119.00W
Grand-Couronne 12 De 49.21N 1.01 E
Grandcourt 12 De 49.55N 1.30 E
Grand Cul de Sac Bay 51k Ab 13.59N 61.02W
Grand Cul-de-Sac Marin 51e Ab 16.20N 61.35W
Grande, Arroyo- 55 Dm 37.32S 57.34W
Grande, Bahía- 52 Jk 50.45S 68.45W
Grande, Boca- 54 Fb 8.45N 60.35W
Grande, Cachoeira- 55 Gb 15.37S 51.48W
Grande, Cerro- 48 If 23.40N 100.40W
Grande, Ciénaga- 49 Ji 9.13N 75.46W
Grande, Corixa- 55 Cc 17.10S 58.20W
Grande, Cuchilla- [Arg.] 55 Cj 31.45S 58.35W
Grande, Cuchilla- [Ur.] 55 Ki 33.15S 55.07W
Grande, Ile- 11 Cf 48.48N 3.35W
Grande, Ilha 54 Jh 23.10S 44.10W
Grande, Rio- [Ven.] 54 Fb 8.39N 60.59W
Grande, Rio- [Braz.] 52 Lg 11.05S 43.09W
Grande, Rio- [N.Amer.] 38 Jg 25.57N 97.09W
Grande, Rio- (EN) = Bravo del Norte, Río- 38 Jg 25.57N 97.09W
Grande, Rio- o Guapay, Rio- 52 Jg 15.51S 64.39W
Grande, Serra- 52 Lf 6.00S 40.52W
Grande, Sierra- 48 Gc 29.40N 104.55W
Grande-Anse 51e Bb 16.18N 61.04W
Grande Anse 51k Ba 14.01N 60.54W
Grande Briere 11 Dg 47.22N 2.15W
Grande Casse 11 Mi 45.24N 6.50 E
Grande Cayemite 49 Kd 18.37N 73.45W
Grande Comore → Njazidja 30 Lj 11.35S 43.20 E
Grande de Santa Marta, Ciénaga- 49 Jh 10.50N 74.25W
Grande de Santiago, Rio- 38 Ig 21.36N 105.26W
Grande do Gurupa, Ilha- 54 Hd 1.00S 51.30W
Grande Inferior, Cuchilla- 55 Dk 33.50S 56.10W
Grande Kabylie 13 Ph 36.45N 4.00 E
Grande ou Sete Quedas, Ilha- 55 Ef 23.45S 54.03W
Grande Pointe [Guad.] 51b Bc 17.50N 62.50W
Grande Pointe [Guad.] 51e Ac 15.59N 61.38W
Grande Prairie 39 Hd 55.10N 118.48W
Grand Erg de Bilma 30 Ig 18.30N 13.50 E
Grand Erg Occidental 30 He 30.20N 0.01 E
Grand Erg Oriental 30 He 30.00N 7.00 E
Grande Rio- 52 Kh 20.06S 51.04W
Grande Rivière à Goyaves 51e Ab 16.18N 61.37W
Grande Rivière de la Baleine 38 Ld 55.15N 77.45W
Grande Rivière du Nord 49 Kd 19.35N 72.11W
Grande Ronde River 46 Gc 46.05N 116.59W
Grandes, Salinas- 52 Ji 30.05S 65.05W
Grande Sebkha d'Oran 13 Li 35.32N 0.48W
Grandes Rousse 11 Mi 45.06N 6.07 E
Grande-Synthe 12 Ec 51.01N 2.17 E
Grand Etang 51p Bb 12.06N 61.42W
Grande-Terre 50 Fd 16.20N 61.25W
Grande Vigie, Pointe de la- 51e Ba 16.31N 61.28W
Grand Falls [N.B.-Can.] 42 Kg 47.03N 67.44W
Grand Falls [Newf.-Can.] 39 Ne 48.56N 55.40W
Grand Forks [B.C.-Can.] 46 Fb 49.02N 118.27W
Grand Forks [N.D.-U.S.] 39 Je 47.55N 97.03W
Grand Found, Anse du- 51b Bc 17.53N 62.49W
Grand Gedeh 34 Dd 5.45N 8.05W
Grand Haven 44 Dd 43.04N 86.10W
Grand Ilet 51e Ac 15.50N 61.36W
Grand Island 39 Je 40.55N 98.21W
Grand Junction 39 If 39.05N 108.33W
Grand-Lahou 34 Dd 5.08N 5.01W
Grand Lake [La.-U.S.] 45 Kl 29.55N 91.35W
Grand Lake [La.-U.S.] 45 Jl 29.55N 92.47W
Grand Lake [N.B.-Can.] 44 Nc 45.42N 66.05W
Grand Lake [Newf.-Can.] 42 Lg 49.00N 57.20W
Grand Lake [Oh.-U.S.] 44 Ee 40.30N 84.32W
Grand Lake Victoria 44 Ib 47.35N 77.33W
Grand Lieu, Lac de- 11 Eg 47.05N 1.40W
Grand Manan Channel 44 Nc 44.45N 66.52W
Grand Manan Island 42 Kh 44.40N 66.50W
Grand Marais [Mi.-U.S.] 44 Eb 46.40N 85.59W
Grand Marais [Mn.-U.S.] 45 Kc 47.45N 90.20W
Grand-Mère 44 Kb 46.37N 72.41W
Grand Morin 11 If 48.54N 2.50 E
Grândola 13 Df 38.10N 8.34W
Grândola, Serra de- 13 Df 38.06N 8.38W
Grand Passage 63b Ad 18.45S 163.10 E
Grand-Popo 34 Fd 6.17N 1.50 E
Grand Portage 45 Lc 47.58N 89.41W
Grand Prairie 45 Hj 32.45N 96.59W
Grandpré 12 Ge 49.20N 4.52 E
Grand Rapids [Man.-Can.] 42 Hf 53.10N 99.17W
Grand Rapids [Mi.-U.S.] 39 Ke 42.58N 85.40W
Grand Rapids [Mn.-U.S.] 43 Ib 47.14N 93.31W
Grand Récif Sud 61 Cd 22.38S 167.00 E
Grand River [Mi.-U.S.] 44 Dd 43.04N 86.15W
Grand River [Mo.-U.S.] 45 Jg 39.23N 93.06W
Grand River [Ont.-Can.] 44 Hd 42.51N 79.34W
Grand River [S.D.-U.S.] 45 Fd 45.40N 100.32W
Grand'Rivière 51h Ab 14.52N 61.11W
Grand Roy 51p Bb 12.08N 61.45W
Grand-Sans-Toucher 51e Ab 16.06N 61.41W
Grand Teton 43 Ec 43.44N 110.48W
Grand Traverse Bay 43 Jb 45.02N 85.30W
Grand Turk 49 Lc 21.30N 71.10W
Grand Turk 47 Jd 21.28N 71.09W
Grand Union Canal 12 Bc 51.30N 0.02W
Grand Valley 45 Bg 39.27N 108.03W
Grandview [Man.-Can.] 45 Fa 51.10N 100.45W
Grandview [Mo.-U.S.] 45 Ig 38.53N 94.32W
Grandvilliers 12 De 49.40N 1.56 E
Grand Wash Cliffs 46 Ii 35.45N 113.45W
Grand Wintersberg 11 Ne 48.59N 7.37 E
Granger 46 Ke 41.35N 109.58W
Grängesberg 8 Fd 60.05N 14.59 E
Grangeville 46 Gd 45.56N 116.07W
Gran Guardia 56 Ic 25.52S 58.53W
Granite City 45 Kg 38.42N 90.09W
Granite Falls 45 Id 44.49N 95.33W
Granite Pass 46 Ld 44.38N 107.30W
Granite Peak [Nv.-U.S.] 43 Dc 41.40N 117.35W
Granite Peak [U.S.] 43 Fb 45.10N 109.48W
Granite Range 46 Ff 41.00N 119.35W
Granitola, Punta- 14 Gm 37.34N 12.41 E
Grankulla/Kauniainen 8 Kd 60.13N 24.45 E
Granma 49 Ic 20.30N 77.00W
Gran Malvina, Isla-/West Falkland 52 Kk 51.40S 60.00W
Gran Morelos [Mex.] 48 Eb 30.40N 108.35W
Gran Morelos [Mex.] 48 Fc 28.15N 106.30W
Gränna 8 Ff 58.01N 14.28 E
Granollers/Granollérs 13 Oc 41.37N 2.18 E
Granollérs/Granollers 13 Oc 41.37N 2.18 E
Gran Paradis/Gran Paradiso 14 Be 45.32N 7.16 E
Gran Paradiso/Gran Paradis 14 Be 45.32N 7.16 E
Gran Pilastro/Hochfeiler 14 Fd 46.58N 11.44 E
Gran San Bernardo 14 Be 45.50N 7.10 E
Gran Sasso d'Italia 5 Hg 42.25N 13.40 E
Grant 45 Ff 40.50N 101.56W
Grant, Mount- 46 Fg 38.34N 118.48W
Gran Tarajal 32 Ed 28.12N 14.01W
Grantham 9 Mi 52.54N 0.38W
Grant Island 66 Nf 74.24S 131.20W
Grantown-on-Spey 9 Jd 57.20N 3.38W
Grant Range 46 Hg 38.25N 115.30W
Grants 43 Fd 35.09N 107.52W
Grantsburg 45 Jd 45.47N 92.41W
Grants Pass 43 Cc 42.26N 123.19W
Granville 11 Ef 48.50N 1.36W
Granville Lake 42 He 56.00N 100.20W
Granvin 8 Bd 60.33N 6.43 E
Grao de Gandia, Gandia-Grao de Sagunto, Sagunto- 13 Lf 38.59N 0.09W
13 Le 39.40N 0.16W
Grappa, Monte- 14 Fe 45.52N 11.48 E
Grappler Bank (EN) 51a Cc 17.48N 65.55W
Graskop 37 Ed 24.58S 30.49 E
Gräsmark 8 Ee 59.57N 12.55 E
Gräsö 7 Ef 60.25N 18.25 E
Grasse 11 Mk 43.40N 6.55 E
Grasset,Lac- 44 Ha 49.58N 78.10W
Grassrange 46 Kc 47.01N 108.48W
Gråsten 7 Bi 54.55N 9.36 E
Grästorp 8 Ef 58.20N 12.40 E
Graubünden 14 Dd 46.35N 9.35 E
Graulhet 11 Hk 43.46N 2.00 E
Graus 13 Mb 42.11N 0.20 E
Grave 12 Hc 51.45N 5.45 E
Grave, Pointe de- 11 Ei 45.34N 1.04W
Gravedona 14 Dd 46.09N 9.18 E
Gravelbourg 46 Lb 49.53N 106.34W
Gravelines 11 Id 50.59N 2.07 E
Gravenhurst 44 Hc 44.55N 79.22W
Gravenor Bay 51d Ba 17.33N 61.45W
Graves 11 Fj 44.35N 0.30W
Gravesend 9 Nj 51.27N 0.24 E
Gravesend-Tilbury 9 Nj 51.28N 0.23 E
Gravina in Puglia 14 Kj 40.49N 16.25 E
Gravone 11a Ab 41.55N 8.47 E
Gray 11 Lg 47.27N 5.35 E
Gray Feather Bank (EN) 60 Df 8.00N 148.40 E
Grayling 44 Ec 44.40N 84.43W
Grays Harbor 46 Cc 46.56N 124.05W
Grayson 44 Ff 38.20N 82.57W
Grays Peak 43 Fd 39.37N 105.45W
Graz 6 Hf 47.04N 15.27 E
Grazalema 13 Gh 36.46N 5.22W
Grdelica 15 Fg 42.54N 22.04 E
Greåker 8 Df 59.16N 11.02 E
Great 51p Bb 12.10N 61.38W
Great Artesian Basin 57 Fg 25.00S 143.00 E
Great Astrolabe Reef 63d Bc 18.52S 178.31 E
Great Australian Bight 57 Eh 35.00S 130.00 E
Great Bacolet Point 51p Bb 12.05N 61.37W
Great Bahama Bank (EN) 38 Lg 23.15N 78.00W
Great Bardfield 12 Cc 51.56N 0.29 E
Great Barrier Island 57 Ih 36.10S 175.25 E
Great Barrier Reef 57 Ff 19.10S 149.00 E
Great Basin 38 Hf 40.00N 117.00W
Great Bay 44 Jf 39.30N 74.23W
Great Bear 42 Ed 64.54N 125.35W
Great Bear Lake 38 Hc 66.00N 120.00W
Great Belt (EN) = Store Bælt 5 Hd 55.30N 11.00 E
Great Bend 43 Hd 38.22N 98.46W
Great Blasket/An Blascaod Mór 9 Ci 52.05N 10.32W
Great Britain 5 Fd 54.00N 3.00W
Great Central Lake 46 Cb 49.27N 125.12W
Great Channel 21 Li 6.00N 94.00 E
Great Chesterford 12 Cb 52.04N 0.12 E
Great Dismal Swamp 44 Ig 36.30N 76.30W
Great Dividing Range 57 Fg 25.00S 147.00 E
Great Dunmow 12 Cc 51.53N 0.22 E
Greater Accra 34 Fd 5.45N 0.10 E
Greater Antilles (EN) = Antillas Mayores 38 Lh 20.00N 74.00W
Greater Khingan Range (EN) = Da Hinggan Ling 21 Oe 49.00N 122.00 E
Greater London 9 Mj 51.35N 0.05W
Greater Manchester 9 Kh 53.35N 2.10W
Greater Sunda Islands (EN) 21 Nj 3.52S 111.20 E
Great Exhibition Bay 61 Df 34.40S 173.00 E
Great Exuma Island 47 Id 23.32N 75.50W
Great Falls 39 He 47.30N 111.17W
Great Harbour Cay 44 Im 25.45N 77.52W
Great Inagua 38 Lg 21.02N 73.20W
Great Indian Desert/Thar 21 Ig 27.00N 70.00 E
Great Karasberge (EN) = Groot-Karasberge 30 Ik 27.20S 18.45 E
Great Karroo (EN) = Groot Karoo 30 Jl 33.00S 22.00 E
Great Lake 59 Jh 41.52S 146.45 E
Great Namaland/Groot Namaland 37 Be 26.00S 17.00 E
Great Nicobar 21 Li 7.00N 93.50 E
Great North East Channel 59 Ia 9.30S 143.25 E
Great Ormes Head 9 Jh 53.21N 3.52W
Great Ouse 9 Ni 52.44N 0.23 E
Great Plain of the Koukdjuak 42 Kc 66.25N 72.50W
Great Plains 38 Je 42.00N 100.00W
Great Reef 63c Bb 10.14S 166.02 E
Great Ruaha 30 Ki 7.56S 37.52 E
Great Sacandaga Lake 44 Jd 43.08N 74.10W
Great Sale Cay 44 Hl 27.00N 78.12W
Great Salt Lake 38 He 41.10N 112.30W
Great Salt Lake Desert 43 Ec 40.40N 113.30W
Great Salt Plains Lake 45 Gh 36.44N 98.12W
Great Salt Pond 51c Ab 17.15N 62.38W
Great Sandy Desert [Austl.] 57 Dg 21.30S 125.00 E
Great Sandy Desert [U.S.] 43 Cc 43.35N 120.15W
Great Sea Reef 63d Bb 16.15S 178.33 E
Great Shelford 12 Cb 52.07N 0.08 E
Great Sitkin 40a Cb 52.03N 176.07W
Great Slave Lake 38 Hd 61.30N 114.00W
Great Smoky Mountains 44 Fh 35.35N 83.30W
Great Stour 9 Oj 51.19N 1.15 E
Great Valley [U.S.] 44 Ie 40.15N 76.50W
Great Valley [U.S.] 43 Kd 36.30N 82.00W
Great Victoria Desert 57 Dg 28.30S 127.45 E
Great Yarmouth 9 Oi 52.37N 1.44 E
Grebbestad 7 Cg 58.42N 11.15 E
Grebenka 16 Hd 50.07N 32.25 E
Gréboun, Mont- 34 Gb 20.00N 8.35 E
Greci 15 Ld 45.11N 28.14 E
Gredos, Sierra de- 13 Gd 40.20N 5.05W
Greece (EN) = Elláς 6 Ih 39.00N 22.00 E
Greeley [Co.-U.S.] 43 Gc 40.25N 104.42W
Greeley [Nb.-U.S.] 45 Gf 41.33N 98.32W
Greely Fiord 42 Ja 80.40N 85.00W
Greem-Bell 21 Ia 81.10N 64.00 E
Green 46 De 43.07N 123.28W
Green Bay 43 Jb 45.00N 87.30W
Green Bay 39 Ke 44.30N 88.01W
Greencastle 44 Df 39.38N 86.52W
Green Cay 49 Ia 24.02N 77.11W
Greeneville 44 Fg 36.10N 82.50W
Greenfield [In.-U.S.] 44 Ef 39.47N 85.46W
Greenfield [Ma.-U.S.] 44 Kd 42.36N 72.36W
Greenhorn Mountain 45 Dh 37.57N 105.00W
Green Island 62 Df 45.54S 170.26 E
Green Island [Atg.] 51d Bb 17.03N 61.40W
Green Island [Gren.] 51p Bb 12.14N 61.35W
Green Islands 63a Bb 4.30S 154.10 E
Greenland 51q Ab 13.15N 59.34W
Greenland (EN) = Grønland/Kalaallit Nunaat 38 Pb 70.00N 40.00W
Greenland (EN) = Grønland/Kalaallit Nunaat 39 Pb 70.00N 40.00W
Greenland (EN) = Kalaallit Nunaat/Grønland 38 Pb 70.00N 40.00W
Greenland (EN) = Kalaallit Nunaat/Grønland 39 Pb 70.00N 40.00W
Greenland Basin (EN) 3 Gb 77.00N 0.00
Greenland Sea (EN) = Grænlandshaf 67 Ld 77.00N 1.00W
Greenland Sea (EN) = Grønlandshavet 67 Ld 77.00N 1.00W
Green Lookout Mountain 46 Dd 45.52N 122.08W
Green Mountains 38 Le 43.45N 72.45W
Greenock 9 If 55.57N 4.45W
Greenough River 59 Ce 28.51S 114.38 E
Green Peter Lake 46 Dd 44.28N 122.30W
Green River [U.S.] 44 Dg 37.55N 87.30W
Green River [U.S.] 38 If 38.11N 109.53W
Green River [Ut.-U.S.] 43 Ed 38.59N 110.10W
Green River [Wy.-U.S.] 43 Fc 41.32N 109.28W
Green River Lake 44 Eg 37.15N 85.15W
Greensboro 39 Lf 36.04N 79.47W
Greensburg [In.-U.S.] 44 Ef 39.20N 85.29W
Greensburg [Ks.-U.S.] 45 Gh 37.36N 99.18W
Greensburg [La.-U.S.] 45 Kk 30.51N 90.42W
Greenstone Point 9 Hd 57.55N 5.40W
Greenvale 59 Jc 18.55S 145.05 E
Greenville [Al.-U.S.] 44 Dj 31.50N 86.38W
Greenville [Il.-U.S.] 45 Lg 38.53N 89.25W
Greenville [Lbr.] 31 Gh 4.59N 9.02W
Greenville [Me.-U.S.] 44 Mc 45.28N 69.35W
Greenville [Ms.-U.S.] 43 Ie 33.25N 91.05W
Greenville [N.C.-U.S.] 43 Ld 35.37N 77.23W
Greenville [Oh.-U.S.] 44 Ee 40.06N 84.37W
Greenville [Pa.-U.S.] 44 Ge 41.24N 80.24W
Greenville [S.C.-U.S.] 39 Kf 34.51N 82.23W
Greenville [Tx.-U.S.] 43 He 33.08N 96.07W
Greenwich 44 Fe 41.02N 82.32W
Greenwich, London- 9 Mj 51.28N 0.00
Greenwood [Ms.-U.S.] 43 Ie 33.31N 90.11W
Greenwood [S.C.-U.S.] 44 Fh 34.12N 82.10W
Greenwood, Lake- 44 Gh 34.15N 82.00W
Greer 44 Fh 34.55N 82.14W
Greers Ferry Lake 45 Ji 35.30N 92.10W
Greeson, Lake- 45 Ji 34.10N 93.45W
Grefrath 12 Ic 51.18N 6.19 E
Gregoria Pérez de Denis 55 Bi 28.14S 61.32W
Gregório, Rio- 54 De 6.50S 70.46W
Gregório, Rio- 55 Ha 13.42S 49.58W
Gregory, Lake- 59 He 28.55S 139.00 E
Gregory Lake 59 Fd 20.10S 127.20 E
Gregory Range 57 Ff 19.00S 143.00 E
Gregory River 59 Hc 17.53S 139.17 E
Greifenburg 14 Hd 46.45N 13.11 E
Greifswald 10 Jb 54.06N 13.23 E
Greifswalder Bodden 10 Jb 54.15N 13.35 E
Greifswalder Oie 10 Jb 54.14N 13.55 E
Grein 14 Ib 48.13N 14.51 E
Greiz 10 If 50.39N 12.12 E
Grēko, Akrōtērion- 24 Fe 34.56N 34.05 E
Gremiha 6 Jb 68.03N 39.29 E
Gremjačinsk 17 Hg 58.34N 57.51 E
Grenå 7 Ch 56.25N 10.53 E
Grenada 39 Mh 12.07N 61.40W
Grenada 38 Mh 12.07N 61.40W
Grenada 45 Lj 33.47N 89.55W
Grenada Basin (EN) 47 Lf 13.30N 62.00W
Grenada Lake 45 Lj 33.50N 89.40W
Grenadines 47 Lf 12.40N 61.15W
Grenchen 14 Bc 47.11N 7.25 E
Grenen 5 Hd 57.44N 10.40 E
Grenfell 45 Ea 50.25N 102.56W
Grenoble 6 Gf 45.10N 5.43 E
Grenora 45 Eb 48.37N 103.56W
Grense-Jakobselv 7 Hb 69.47N 30.50 E
Grenville 50 Ff 12.07N 61.37W
Grenville, Cape- 59 Ib 12.00S 143.15 E
Gréoux-les-Bains 11 Lk 43.45N 5.53 E
Gresham 46 Dd 45.30N 122.26W
Gresik 26 Fh 7.09S 112.38 E
Gressoney-la-Trinité 14 Be 45.50N 7.49 E
Gretas Klackar 8 Gc 61.34N 17.50 E
Gretna 45 Kl 29.55N 90.03W
Grevelingen 12 Fc 51.45N 4.00 E
Greven 10 Dd 52.06N 7.37 E
Grevená 15 Ei 40.05N 21.25 E
Grevenbroich 10 Ce 51.05N 6.35 E
Grevenbrück, Lennestadt- 12 Kc 51.08N 8.01 E
Grevenmacher 12 Ie 49.41N 6.27 E
Grevesmühlen 10 Hc 53.52N 11.11 E
Grey 62 De 42.26S 171.11 E
Greybull 46 Kd 44.30N 108.03W
Greybull River 46 Kd 44.28N 108.03W
Grey Islands 42 Lf 50.50N 55.35W
Greymouth 61 Dh 42.27S 171.12 E
Grey Range 57 Fg 27.00S 143.35 E
Greystones/Ná Clocha Liatha 9 Gh 53.09N 6.04W
Greytow 37 Ee 29.07S 30.30 E
Greytown 62 Fd 41.05S 175.28 E
Gribanovski 16 Ld 51.29N 41.58 E
Gribb Bank (EN) 66 Ge 63.00S 90.30 E
Gribës, Mali i- 15 Ci 40.34N 19.34 E
Gribingui 35 Bd 7.00N 19.30 E
Gribingui 35 Bd 8.33N 19.05 E
Griend 12 Ha 53.15N 5.20 E
Griesheim 12 Ke 49.52N 8.33 E
Grieskirchen 14 Hb 48.14N 13.50 E
Griffin 43 Ke 33.15N 84.16W
Griffith 59 Jf 34.17S 146.03 E
Grigoriopol 15 Mb 47.09N 29.13 E
Grijalva 38 Jh 18.36N 92.39W
Grim, Cape- 59 Ih 40.41S 144.41 E
Grimari 35 Cd 5.44N 20.03 E
Grimbergen 12 Gd 50.56N 4.23 E
Grimma 10 Ie 51.14N 12.43 E
Grimmen 10 Jb 54.06N 13.03 E
Grimsby 9 Mh 53.35N 0.05W
Grimsey 7a Ca 66.33N 18.00W
Grimsstadir 7a Cb 65.39N 16.07W
Grimstad 7 Bg 58.20N 8.36 E
Grimsvotn 7a Cb 64.24N 17.22W
Grindavik 7a Ac 63.50N 22.30W
Grindelwald 14 Cd 46.38N 8.03 E
Grindsted 7 Bi 55.45N 8.56 E
Grinnell 45 Jf 41.45N 92.43W
Grinnel Peninsula 42 Ia 76.40N 95.00W
Grintavec 14 Id 46.22N 14.32 E
Griquatown 37 Ce 28.49S 23.15 E
Grise Fiord 39 Kb 76.10N 83.15W
Gris-Nez, Cap- 11 Hd 50.52N 1.35 E
Grisslehamn 8 Hd 60.06N 18.50 E
Grjazi 19 De 52.29N 39.57 E
Grjazovec 19 Ed 58.53N 40.15 E
Grmeč 14 Kf 44.43N 16.15 E
Grobiņa/Grobinja 7 Eh 56.33N 21.11 E
Grobinja/Grobiņa 7 Eh 56.33N 21.11 E
Groblersdal 37 De 25.15S 29.25 E
Grocka 15 De 44.41N 20.43 E
Grodk/Spremberg 10 Ke 51.33N 14.22 E
Grodków 10 Nf 50.43N 17.22 E
Grodnenskaja Oblast 19 Ce 53.45N 25.10 E
Grodno 6 Ie 53.42N 23.50 E
Grodzisk Mazowiecki 10 Qd 52.07N 20.37 E
Grodzjanka 16 Fc 53.34N 28.48 E
Groeie Hoop, Kaap die-/Good Hope, Cape of- 30 Il 34.21S 18.28 E

Index Symbols

- Independent Nation
- State, Region
- District, County
- Municipality
- Colony, Dependency
- Continent
- Physical Region
- Historical or Cultural Region
- Mount, Mountain
- Volcano
- Hill
- Mountains, Mountain Range
- Hills, Escarpment
- Plateau, Upland
- Pass, Gap
- Plain, Lowland
- Delta
- Salt Flat
- Valley, Canyon
- Crater, Cave
- Karst Features
- Depression
- Polder
- Desert, Dunes
- Forest, Woods
- Heath, Steppe
- Oasis
- Cape, Point
- Coast, Beach
- Cliff
- Peninsula
- Isthmus
- Sandbank
- Island
- Atoll
- Rock, Reef
- Islands, Archipelago
- Rocks, Reefs
- Coral Reef
- Well, Spring
- Geyser
- River, Stream
- Waterfall Rapids
- River Mouth, Estuary
- Lake
- Salt Lake
- Intermittent Lake
- Reservoir
- Swamp, Pond
- Canal
- Glacier
- Ice Shelf, Pack Ice
- Ocean
- Sea
- Gulf, Bay
- Strait, Fjord
- Lagoon
- Bank
- Seamount
- Tablemount
- Ridge
- Shelf
- Basin
- Escarpment, Sea Scarp
- Fracture
- Trench, Abyss
- National Park, Reserve
- Point of Interest
- Recreation Site
- Cave, Cavern
- Historic Site
- Ruins
- Wall, Walls
- Church, Abbey
- Temple
- Scientific Station
- Airport
- Port
- Lighthouse
- Mine
- Tunnel
- Dam, Bridge

Index Symbols

[1] Independent Nation
[2] State, Region
[3] District, County
[4] Municipality
[5] Colony, Dependency
■ Continent
[6] Physical Region

Historical or Cultural Region
Mount, Mountain
Volcano
Hill
Mountains, Mountain Range
Hills, Escarpment
Plateau, Upland

Pass, Gap
Plain, Lowland
Delta
Salt Flat
Valley, Canyon
Crater, Cave
Karst Features

Depression
Polder
Desert, Dunes
Forest, Woods
Heath, Steppe
Oasis
Cape, Point

Coast, Beach
Cliff
Peninsula
Isthmus
Sandbank
Island
Atoll

Rock, Reef
Islands, Archipelago
Rocks, Reefs
Coral Reef
Well, Spring
Geyser
River, Stream

Waterfall Rapids
River Mouth, Estuary
Lake
Salt Lake
Intermittent Lake
Reservoir
Swamp, Pond

Canal
Bank
Seamount
Tablemount
Ocean
Sea
Ridge
Shelf
Gulf, Bay
Strait, Fjord
Basin

Lagoon
Glacier
Ice Shelf, Pack Ice

Escarpment, Sea Scarp
Fracture
Trench, Abyss
National Park, Reserve
Point of Interest
Recreation Site
Cave, Cavern

Historic Site
Ruins
Church, Abbey
Temple
Scientific Station
Airport

Port
Lighthouse
Mine
Wall, Walls
Tunnel
Dam, Bridge

Index Symbols

Symbol group					
[1] Independent Nation	Historical or Cultural Region	Pass, Gap	Depression	Coast, Beach	Rock, Reef
[2] State, Region	Mount, Mountain	Plain, Lowland	Polder	Cliff	Islands, Archipelago
[3] District, County	Volcano	Delta	Desert, Dunes	Peninsula	Rocks, Reefs
[4] Municipality	Hill	Salt Flat	Forest, Woods	Isthmus	Coral Reef
[5] Colony, Dependency	Mountains, Mountain Range	Valley, Canyon	Heath, Steppe	Sandbank	Well, Spring
Continent	Hills, Escarpment	Crater, Cave	Oasis	Island	
Physical Region	Plateau, Upland	Karst Features	Cape, Point	Atoll	

Waterfall Rapids	Canal	Lagoon	Escarpment, Sea Scarp	Historic Site
River Mouth, Estuary	Glacier	Bank	Fracture	Ruins
Lake	Ice Shelf, Pack Ice	Seamount	Trench, Abyss	Wall, Walls
Salt Lake	Ocean	Tablemount	National Park, Reserve	Church, Abbey
Intermittent Lake	Sea	Ridge	Point of Interest	Temple
Reservoir	Gulf, Bay	Shelf	Recreation Site	Scientific Station
River, Stream	Strait, Fjord	Basin	Cave, Cavern	Airport
Swamp, Pond				

Port	
Lighthouse	
Mine	
Tunnel	
Dam, Bridge	

Hansen Mountains	66	Ee	68.16 S	58.47 E
Hanshan	28	Ei	31.43N	118.07 E
Hanshou	28	Aj	28.55N	111.58 E
Han Shui	21	Nf	30.34N	114.17 E
Hanstholm	8	Cg	57.07N	8.38 E
Han Sum	28	Eb	44.33N	119.58 E
Han-sur-Lesse, Rochefort-	12	Hd	50.08N	5.11 E
Han-sur-Nied	12	If	48.59N	6.26 E
Hantajskoje, Ozero-	20	Ec	68.25N	91.00 E
Hantau	19	Hg	44.13N	73.48 E
Hantengri Feng	27	Dc	42.03N	80.11 E
Hants	9	Lj	51.10N	1.10W
Hanty-Mansijsk	22	Ic	61.00N	69.06 E
Hanty-Mansijski avtonomnyj okrug	19	Hc	62.00N	72.30 E
Hantzsch	42	Kc	67.32N	72.26W
Hanušovice	10	Mf	50.05N	16.55 E
Hanwang	27	He	31.25N	104.13 E
Hanyang	28	Ci	30.34N	114.01 E
Hanyang, Wuhan-	28	Ci	30.33N	114.16 E
Hanyū	29	Fc	36.11N	139.32 E
Hanyuan (Fulin)	27	Hf	29.25N	102.12 E
Hanzhong [China]	22	Mf	32.59N	107.11 E
Hanzhong [China]	27	Ie	33.07N	107.00 E
Hanzhuang	28	Dg	34.38N	117.23 E
Hao Atoll	57	Mf	18.15 S	140.54W
Hāora	22	Kg	22.35N	88.20 E
Haoud el Hamra	32	Ic	31.58N	5.59 E
Haoxue	28	Bi	30.02N	112.25 E
Haparanda	7	Fd	65.50N	24.10 E
Hapčeranga	20	Gg	49.42N	112.20 E
Happy Valley-Goose Bay	39	Md	53.19N	60.24W
Hapsu	28	Jd	41.13N	128.51 E
Ḩaql	24	Fh	29.18N	34.57 E
Ḩaql al Barqan	24	Lh	28.55N	47.57 E
Ḩaql al Manāqīsh	24	Lh	29.02N	47.32 E
Ḩaql as Şābirīyah	24	Lh	29.48N	47.50 E
Hara, Zaliv-/Hara Laht	8	Ke	59.35N	25.30 E
Hara-Ajrag	27	Ib	45.50N	109.20 E
Harabali	19	Ef	47.25N	47.16 E
Ḩaraḑ	23	Ge	24.14N	49.11 E
Haraiki Atoll	57	Mf	17.28 S	143.27W
Hara Laht/Hara, Zaliv-	8	Ke	59.35N	25.30 E
Haramachi	28	Pf	37.38N	140.58 E
Haram Dāgh	23	Gb	37.35N	46.43 E
Harami, Pereval-	16	Oh	42.48N	46.12 E
Harand	24	Of	32.34N	52.26 E
Harani'ia Point	63a	Ed	10.21 S	161.16 E
Hara Nur	27	Fb	48.05N	93.12 E
Ḩarardēre	35	He	4.32N	47.53 E
Harare	31	Kj	17.50 S	31.10 E
Harat	35	Fb	16.05N	39.28 E
Hara-Tas, Krjaž-	20	Fb	72.00N	107.00 E
Haratini	64n	Bc	10.28 S	160.58W
Ḩarat Zuwayyah	31	Jf	24.14N	21.59 E
Hara-Us-Nur	27	Fb	48.00N	92.10 E
Haraz	35	Bc	13.57N	19.26 E
Harāz	24	Od	36.40N	52.43 E
Harāzah, Jabal-	35	Eb	15.03N	30.27 E
Haraze	35	Cd	9.55N	20.48 E
Harbel	34	Cd	6.16N	10.21W
Harbin	22	Oe	45.45N	126.37 E
Harbor Beach	44	Fd	43.51N	82.39W
Harbour Breton	42	Lg	47.29N	55.50W
Harbour Grace	42	Mg	47.41N	53.15W
Harburg, Hamburg-	10	Fc	53.28N	10.00 E
Harcourt	44	Ob	46.30N	65.15W
Harcuvar Mountains	46	Ii	34.00N	113.30W
Harcyzsk	16	Kf	47.59N	38.11 E
Hardanger	8	Bd	60.20N	6.30 E
Hardangerfjorden	5	Gc	60.10N	6.00 E
Hardangerjøkulen	8	Bd	60.35N	7.25 E
Hardangervidda	7	Bf	60.20N	7.30 E
Hardelot Plage, Neufchâtel Hardelot-	12	Dd	50.38N	1.35 E
Hardenberg	12	Ib	52.34N	6.37 E
Harderwijk	11	Lb	52.21N	5.36 E
Hardin	43	Fb	45.44N	107.37W
Harding	37	Df	30.34 S	29.58 E
Hardinsburg	44	Dg	37.47N	86.28W
Härdler	12	Kc	51.06N	8.14 E
Hardoi	25	Gc	27.25N	80.07 E
Hardy, Peninsula-	56	Gi	55.25 S	68.30W
Hareid	8	Bb	62.22N	6.02 E
Hareidlandet	7	Ae	62.20N	5.55 E
Hare Indian	42	Ec	66.18N	128.38W
Harelbeke	12	Fd	50.51N	3.18 E
Haren	12	Ia	53.11N	6.38 E
Haren (Ems)	12	Jb	52.47N	7.14 E
Harer	31	Lh	9.18N	42.08 E
Harerge [3]	35	Gd	9.00N	41.30 E
Harēri Mālinwarfā	35	He	4.34N	47.21 E
Harewa	35	Gd	9.54N	41.58 E
Harfleur	12	Ce	49.30N	0.12 E
Harg	8	Hd	60.11N	18.24 E
Hargeysa	31	Lh	9.30N	44.03 E
Harghiţa [2]	15	Ic	46.25N	25.45 E
Harghita, Munţii-	15	Ic	46.31N	25.33 E
Harghita, Vîrful-	15	Ic	46.27N	25.35 E
Hargla	8	Lg	57.31N	26.25 E
Harhorin	27	Hb	47.13N	102.50 E
Har Hu			38.15N	97.40 E
Ḩarīb	23	Gg	14.56N	45.30 E
Haridwār	25	Fc	29.58N	78.10 E
Harihari	62	De	43.09S	170.34 E
Hari Kurk	8	Je	59.00N	22.50 E
Harim	24	Gd	36.12N	36.31 E
Harīm, Jabal al-	24	Qj	25.58N	56.14 E
Harima-Nada	29	Dd	34.30N	134.35 E
Haringey, London-	12	Bc	51.36N	0.06W
Harīrūd	21	If	37.24N	60.38 E
Härjångsfjallet	8	Ea	63.01N	12.35 E
Harjavalta	7	Ff	61.19N	22.08 E
Härjedalen	8	Eb	62.20N	13.05 E
Härjehågna	8	Ec	61.44N	12.08 E
Hårkan	8	Fa	63.20N	14.55 E
Harkov	6	Je	50.00N	36.15 E
Harkovskaja Oblast [3]	19	Df	49.40N	36.30 E
Harlan [Ia.-U.S.]	45	If	41.39N	95.19W
Harlan [Ky.-U.S.]	44	Fg	36.51N	83.19W
Harlan County Lake	45	Gf	40.04N	99.16W
Harlech Castle	9	Ii	52.52N	4.07W
Harlem	46	Kb	48.32N	108.47W
Harleston	12	Db	52.24N	1.18 E
Harlingen [Neth.]	11	La	53.10N	5.24 E
Harlingen [Tx.-U.S.]	43	Hf	26.11N	97.42W
Harlovka	7	Ib	68.47N	37.20 E
Harlovka	7	Ib	68.47N	37.15 E
Harlow	9	Nj	51.47N	0.08 E
Harlowton	46	Kc	46.26N	109.50W
Harlu	7	Hf	61.51N	30.54 E
Hărman	15	Id	45.43N	25.41 E
Harmancık	24	Cc	39.41N	29.10 E
Harmånger	7	Df	61.56N	17.13 E
Harmanli	15	Ih	41.56N	25.54 E
Harmil	35	Gb	16.30N	40.12 E
Harmony	45	Ke	43.33N	91.59W
Harnai	25	Ee	17.48N	73.06 E
Harney Basin	38	Ge	43.15N	120.40W
Harney Lake	43	Dc	43.14N	119.07W
Harney Peak	43	Gc	44.00N	103.30W
Härnön	8	Gb	62.35N	18.00 E
Härnösand	6	Hc	62.38N	17.56 E
Haro	13	Jb	42.35N	2.51W
Harovsk	19	Ed	59.59N	40.11 E
Harøya	8	Bb	62.45N	6.25 E
Harøyfjorden	8	Bb	62.45N	6.35 E
Harpenden	12	Bc	51.48N	0.21W
Harper [Ks.-U.S.]	45	Gh	37.17N	98.01W
Harper [Lbr.]	31	Gh	4.22N	7.43W
Harper, Mount-	40	Kd	64.14N	143.50W
Harper Pass	62	De	42.44 S	171.53 E
Harplinge	8	Eh	56.45N	12.43 E
Harqin Qi (Jinshan)	28	Ed	41.57N	118.40 E
Harqin Zuoyi Monggolzu Zizhixian	28	Ed	41.05N	119.40 E
Ḩarrah	23	Hg	14.57N	50.19 E
Ḩarrat al 'Uwayrid	23	Ed	27.00N	37.30 E
Harricana	42	Jf	51.10N	79.47W
Harricana, Rivière-	44	Ha	51.10N	79.45W
Harrington-Harbour	42	Lf	50.26N	59.30W
Harris	9	Gd	57.53N	6.55W
Harris	51c	Bc	16.28N	62.10W
Harris, Lake-	44	Gk	28.46N	81.49W
Harris, Sound of-	9	Fd	57.45N	7.08W
Harrisburg	39	Le	40.16N	76.52W
Harrismith	37	De	28.18 S	29.03 E
Harrison [Ar.-U.S.]	45	Jh	36.14N	93.07W
Harrison [Mi.-U.S.]	44	Ec	44.01N	84.48W
Harrison [Nb.-U.S.]	45	Ee	42.41N	103.53W
Harrison, Cape -	42	Lf	54.56N	57.55W
Harrison Bay	40	Ib	70.30N	151.30W
Harrisonburg	44	Hf	38.27N	78.54W
Harrison Lake	46	Eb	49.31N	121.59W
Harrison Point	51q	Ab	13.18N	59.38W
Harrisonville	45	Ig	38.39N	94.21W
Harrisville [Mi.-U.S.]	44	Fc	44.39N	83.17W
Harrisville [W.V.-U.S.]	44	Gf	39.13N	81.04W
Harrodsburg	44	Eg	37.46N	84.51W
Harrogate	9	Lh	54.00N	1.33W
Harrow, London-	12	Bc	51.36N	0.20W
Harry S. Truman Reservoir	45	Jg	38.00N	93.45W
Har Sai Shan	27	Gd	35.26N	97.41 E
Harsewinkel	12	Kc	51.58N	8.14 E
Harshō	35	Hc	11.17N	47.30 E
Harsim	24	Lf	33.48N	46.50 E
Harsīn	24	Le	34.16N	47.35 E
Harstad	7	Db	68.47N	16.30 E
Harsvik	7	Cd	64.03N	10.02 E
Hart	44	Dd	43.42N	86.22W
Hart	42	Dc	65.51N	136.22W
Hartao	28	Gc	42.30N	122.08 E
Hartbees	30	Jk	28.45 S	20.33 E
Hartberg	14	Jc	47.17N	15.58 E
Hårteigen	8	Bd	60.12N	7.04 E
Hartford [Ct.-U.S.]	39	Le	41.46N	72.41W
Hartford [Ky.-U.S.]	44	Dg	37.27N	86.55W
Hartford City	44	Ee	40.29N	85.23W
Hartington	45	He	42.37N	97.16W
Hartland	44	Nb	46.18N	67.32W
Hartland Point	9	Ij	51.02N	4.31W
Hartlepool	9	Lg	54.42N	1.11W
Hartmannberge	37	Ac	17.30 S	12.23 E
Hartola	7	Gf	61.35N	26.01 E
Harts			28.24 S	24.18 E
Hartselle	44	Dh	34.27N	86.56W
Harts Range	59	Gd	23.05 S	134.55 E
Hartsville	44	Gh	34.23N	80.04W
Hartwell	44	Fh	34.21N	82.56W
Hartwell Lake	44	Fh	34.30N	82.55W
Harun, Bukit-	26	Gf	4.06N	115.46 E
Haruno	29	Ce	33.30N	133.30 E
Harves Bank (EN)	51c	Ac	16.52N	62.35W
Harvey [Austl.]	59	Df	33.05 S	115.54 E
Harvey [N.D.-U.S.]	43	Hb	47.47N	99.56W
Harvey Bay	59	Kd	25.00 S	153.00 E
Harwich	9	Oj	51.57N	1.17 E
Haryana [3]	25	Fc	29.30N	76.30 E
Harz	5	He	51.45N	10.30 E
Hasaki	29	Gd	35.44N	140.48 E
Hasama	29	Gb	38.42N	141.13 E
Hasan	20	Ih	42.26N	130.39 E
Ḩasanābād [Iran]	24	Ph	28.47N	54.19 E
Ḩasanābād [Iran]	24	Nd	36.28N	50.17 E
Hasan Dağı	23	Db	38.08N	34.12 E
Ḩasan Langī	24	Qi	27.22N	56.52 E
Hasavjurt	16	Oh	43.16N	46.35 E
Hāsbayyā	24	Ff	33.43N	33.52 E
Hasdo	25	Hd	21.44N	82.44 E
Hase	10	Dd	52.41N	7.18 E
Hasekijata	15	Kg	42.08N	27.30 E
Hasenkamp	55	Cj	31.31 S	59.51W
Hashimoto	29	Dd	34.19N	135.37 E
Hashtpar	24	Md	37.48N	48.55 E
Hasi Hausert	32	Ee	22.35N	14.18W
Haskell	43	He	33.10N	99.44W
Haskerland	12	Hb	52.58N	5.47 E
Haskerland-Joure	12	Hb	52.58N	5.47 E
Haskovo	15	Ih	41.56N	25.33 E
Haskovo [2]	15	Ih	41.50N	25.55 E
Hasle	8	Fi	55.11N	14.43 E
Haslemere	9	Mj	51.06N	0.43W
Haslev	8	Di	55.20N	11.58 E
Hăşmaşu Mare, Vîrful-	15	Ic	46.30N	25.50 E
Haspengouws Plateau/Hesbaye	11	Ld	50.35N	5.10 E
Haspres	12	Fd	50.15N	3.25 E
Hassa	24	Gd	36.50N	36.29 E
Hassan	25	Ff	13.00N	76.05 E
Hassberge	10	Gf	50.12N	10.29 E
Hassela	7	De	62.07N	16.42 E
Hassel Sound	42	Ha	78.30N	99.00W
Hasselt	11	Ld	50.56N	5.20 E
Hassi Bel Guebbour	32	Id	28.30N	6.41 E
Hassi el Ghella	13	Ki	35.27N	1.03W
Hassi-Mamèche	13	Mi	35.51N	0.04 E
Hassi Messaoud	31	He	31.43N	6.03 E
Hassi R'mel	32	Hc	32.55N	3.16 E
Hassi Serouenout	32	Ie	24.00N	7.50 E
Hässleholm	7	Ch	56.09N	13.46 E
Hasslö	8	Fh	56.05N	15.25 E
Haßloch	12	Ke	49.23N	8.16 E
Hastière	12	Gd	50.13N	4.50 E
Hastière-Hastière par-delà	12	Gd	50.13N	4.50 E
Hastière-par-delà, Hastière-	12	Gd	50.13N	4.50 E
Hastings [Bar.]	51q	Ab	13.04N	59.35W
Hastings [Eng.-U.K.]	9	Nk	50.51N	0.36 E
Hastings [Mi.-U.S.]	44	Ed	42.39N	85.17W
Hastings [Mn.-U.S.]	45	Jd	44.44N	92.51W
Hastings [Nb.-U.S.]	43	Hc	40.35N	98.23W
Hastings [N.Z.]	61	Eg	39.38 S	176.50 E
Hästveda	8	Eh	56.16N	13.56 E
Hašuri	16	Mi	41.59N	43.33 E
Hasvik	7	Fa	70.29N	22.09 E
Ḩasy al Qaţţār	33	Ec	30.14N	27.11 E
Ḩasy Hague	33	Bd	26.17N	10.31 E
Hat'ae-Do	28	Hg	34.23N	125.17 E
Hatanga	22	Mb	71.58N	102.30 E
Hatanga	21	Mb	72.55N	106.00 E
Hatch	45	Cj	32.40N	107.09W
Haţches Creek	59	Hd	20.56 S	135.12 E
Haţeg	15	Fd	45.37N	22.57 E
Hatgal	27	Ha	50.26N	100.09 E
Ḩaţībah, Ra's-	23	Ee	21.59N	38.55 E
Ha Tien	25	Kf	10.23N	104.29 E
Ha Tinh	25	Le	18.20N	105.54 E
Hato Mayor	49	Md	18.46N	69.15W
Ḩattá, Jabal-	24	Qj	24.45N	56.04 E
Hattem	12	Ib	52.28N	6.06 E
Hatten	12	Ka	53.03N	8.23 E
Hatteras, Cape-	38	Lf	35.13N	75.32W
Hatteras Inlet	44	Jh	35.00N	75.40W
Hatteras Island	43	Ld	35.25N	75.30W
Hattfjelldal	7	Cd	65.36N	14.00 E
Hattiesburg	43	Je	31.19N	89.16W
Hattingen	12	Jc	51.24N	7.10 E
Hatu Iti, Ile-	61	Ma	8.42 S	140.43W
Hatutaa, Ile-	57	Me	7.30 S	140.38W
Hatvan	10	Pi	47.40N	19.41 E
Hat Yai	25	Kg	7.01N	100.27 E
Hatyrka	20	Md	62.03N	175.05 E
Hau Bon	25	Lf	13.24N	108.27 E
Haubourdin	12	Ed	50.36N	2.59 E
Hauge	7	Bg	58.21N	6.17 E
Haugesund	6	Gd	59.25N	5.18 E
Hauho	8	Kc	61.10N	24.33 E
Hauhungaroa Range	62	Fc	38.40 S	175.35 E
Haukeligrend	7	Bg	59.51N	7.11 E
Haukipudas	7	Fd	65.15N	25.28 E
Haukivesi	5	Ic	62.05N	28.30 E
Haukivuori	8	Lb	62.01N	27.13 E
Hauraha	63a	Ed	10.49 S	161.57 E
Hauraki Gulf	61	Eg	36.35 S	175.00 E
Hauroko, Lake-	62	Bf	45.55 S	167.20 E
Hausa	32	Ed	27.06N	11.01W
Hausruck	14	Hb	48.07N	13.35 E
Haut, Isle au-	44	Mc	44.03N	68.38W
Haut Atlas=High Atlas (EN)	30	Ge	32.00N	6.00W
Haute-Champagne	12	Ge	49.18N	4.15 E
Haute-Corse [3]	11a	Aa	42.30N	9.00 E
Haute-Garonne [3]	11	Hk	43.25N	1.30 E
Haute-Guinée [3]	34	Dc	11.30N	10.00W
Haute-Kotto [3]	35	Cd	7.00N	23.00 E
Haute-Loire [3]	11	Ji	45.05N	4.00 E
Haute-Marne [3]	11	Lf	48.05N	5.10 E
Hauterive	44	Ma	49.11N	68.16W
Hautes-Alpes [3]	11	Mj	44.40N	6.30 E
Haute-Sangha [3]	35	Be	4.30N	16.00 E
Haute-Saône [3]	11	Mg	47.40N	6.10 E
Haute-Saône, Plateau de-	11	Lg	47.50N	6.00 E
Haute-Savoie [3]	11	Mi	46.00N	6.20 E
Hautes Fagnes/Hoge Venen	10	Bf	50.30N	6.00 E
Hautes-Pyrénées [3]	11	Gk	43.00N	0.10 E
Haute Vienne [3]	11	Hi	45.50N	1.10 E
Haute Volta→Burkina Faso	31	Gg	13.00N	2.00W
Haut-Mbomou [3]	35	Dd	6.00N	26.00 E
Hautmont	11	Jd	50.15N	3.56 E
Haut-Ogooué [3]	36	Bc	2.00 S	14.00 E
Haut Rhin [3]	11	Ng	48.00N	7.20 E
Hauts-Bassins [3]	34	Ec	12.30N	4.30W
Hauts-de-Seine [3]	11	If	48.50N	2.11 E
Hauts-Plateaux	30	He	34.00N	0.01 E
Haut-Zaïre [2]	36	Eb	2.30N	25.30 E
Hauula	65a		21.36N	157.54W
Hauz-Han	18	Cf	37.16N	61.15 E
Hauz-Hanskoje Vodohr.	18	Cf	37.10N	61.20 E
Havana	45	Kf	40.18N	90.04W
Havana (EN)=La Habana	39	Kg	23.08N	82.22W
Havant	9	Mk	50.51N	0.59W
Havast	18	Gd	40.16N	68.51 E
Havasu, Lake-	46	Hi	34.30N	114.20W
Havel	10	Hd	52.53N	11.58 E
Havelange	12	Hd	50.23N	5.14 E
Havelange-Méan	12	Hd	50.22N	5.20 E
Havelberg	10	Id	52.49N	12.05 E
Havelland	10	Id	52.25N	12.45 E
Havelländisches Luch	10	Id	52.40N	12.40 E
Havelock [N.C.-U.S.]	44	Ih	34.53N	76.54W
Havelock [N.Z.]	62	Ed	41.17 S	173.46 E
Havelock North	62	Gc	39.40 S	176.53 E
Havelte	12	Ib	52.46N	6.16 E
Haverfordwest	9	Ij	51.49N	4.58W
Haverhill [Eng.-U.K.]	9	Ni	52.05N	0.26 E
Haverhill [Ma.-U.S.]	44	Ld	42.47N	71.05W
Havering,-London-	12	Cc	51.36N	0.11 E
Havířov	10	Og	49.48N	18.27 E
Havlíčkův Brod	10	Lg	49.36N	15.34 E
Havøysund	7	Fa	71.03N	24.40 E
Havran	24	Bc	39.33N	27.06 E
Havre	39	Ie	48.33N	109.41W
Havre-Saint-Pierre	39	Md	50.15N	63.36W
Havsa	15	Jh	41.33N	26.49 E
Havza	24	Fb	41.05N	35.45 E
Hawaii [2]	58	Kb	24.00N	167.00W
Hawaiian Islands	57	Kb	24.00N	167.00W
Hawaiian Ridge (EN)	3	Kg	24.00N	165.00W
Hawaii Island	57	Lc	19.30N	155.30W
Ḩawallī	23	Gd	29.19N	48.02 E
Ḩawār	24	Nj	25.40N	50.45 E
Hawarden	62	Ee	42.56 S	172.39 E
Ḩawashīyah, Wādī-	24	Eh	28.31N	32.58 E
Hawaymī, Sha'īb al-	24	Kg	30.58N	44.15 E
Hawd	30	Lh	7.40N	47.43 E
Ḩawḑ Al Waqf	24	Ei	26.03N	32.22 E
Hawea, Lake-	62	Cf	44.30 S	169.20 E
Hawera	61	Dg	39.35 S	174.17 E
Hawi	58	Lb	20.14N	155.50W
Hawick	9	Kf	55.25N	2.47W
Ḩawīzah, Hawr al-	24	Lg	31.35N	47.38 E
Hawkdun Range	62	Cf	44.50 S	170.00 E
Hawke Bay	61	Eg	39.25 S	177.20 E
Hawke Harbour	42	Lf	53.01N	55.50W
Hawker	59	Hf	31.53 S	138.25 E
Hawkes, Mount-	66	Rg	83.55 S	56.05W
Hawke's Bay [2]	62	Gc	39.30 S	176.40 E
Hawkesbury	44	Jc	45.36N	74.37W
Hawkhurst	12	Cc	51.02N	0.30 E
Hawkinsville	44	Fi	32.17N	83.28W
Hawksbill	44	Hf	38.33N	78.23W
Hawk Springs	46	Mf	41.48N	104.09W
Ḩawmat as Sūq	32	Jc	33.53N	10.51 E
Hawng Tuk	25	Jd	20.28N	99.56 E
Ḩawrā'	35	Hb	15.43N	48.18 E
Hawrān, Wādī al-	23	Fc	33.58N	42.34 E
Ḩawsh 'Isá	24	Dg	30.55N	30.17 E
Hawthorne	43	Dd	38.32N	118.38W
Hawthorne, Mount-	66	Pf	72.10 S	98.39W
Haxtun	45	Ef	40.39N	102.38W
Hay	58	Fh	34.30 S	144.51 E
Hay	38	Hc	60.51N	115.44W
Hayachine-San	29	Gb	39.34N	141.29 E
Hayakita	29a	Bb	42.45N	141.48 E
Hayange	11	Me	49.20N	6.03 E
Hayastan = Armenia (EN)	19	Eg	40.00N	45.00 E
Hayato	29	Bf	31.45N	130.43 E
Haybān	35	Ec	11.13N	30.31 E
Haybān, Jabal-	35	Ec	11.15N	30.31 E
Hayden	46	Jj	33.00N	110.47W
Hayes [Man.-Can.]	42	Ie	57.00N	92.15W
Hayes [N.W.T.-Can.]	42	Hc	67.20N	95.02W
Hayes, Mount-	40	Jd	63.37N	146.43W
Hayes Halvø=Hayes Peninsula (EN)	67	Od	77.40N	64.30W
Hayes Peninsula (EN)=Hayes Halvø	67	Od	77.40N	64.30W
Ḩayl	24	Qj	24.33N	56.06 E
Hayl, Wādī al-	24	He	34.47N	39.18 E
Hayling Island	12	Bd	50.48N	0.58W
Haymana	24	Ec	39.27N	32.30 E
Haymana Platosu	24	Ec	39.25N	32.45 E
Haynin	23	Gf	15.50N	48.18 E
Hayrabolu	24	Bb	41.12N	27.06 E
Ḩayrān	33	Hf	16.02N	42.49 E
Hay River	59	Hd	25.00 S	138.00 E
Hay River	39	Hc	60.51N	115.40W
Hayrūt	35	Ib	15.59N	52.09 E
Hays	43	Hd	38.53N	99.20W
Hay Springs	45	Ee	42.41N	102.41W
Haystack Peak	46	Ig	39.50N	113.55W
Hayward [Ca.-U.S.]	46	Dh	37.40N	122.05W
Hayward [Wi.-U.S.]	45	Kc	46.01N	91.29W
Haywards Heath	12	Bc	51.00N	0.06W
Hazar, Wādī-	35	Hb	17.50N	49.07 E
Hazarasp	18	Cd	41.19N	61.08 E
Hazard	44	Fg	37.15N	83.12W
Hazar Gölü	24	Hc	38.30N	39.25 E
Hazāribāgh	25	Hd	23.59N	85.21 E
Hazebrouck	11	Id	50.43N	2.32 E
Hazelton	42	Ee	55.15N	127.40W
Hazen	45	Fc	47.18N	101.38W
Hazen Strait	42	Ga	77.15N	110.00W
Ḩaẕeva	24	Fg	30.48N	35.15 E
Hazlehurst [Ga.-U.S.]	44	Fj	31.52N	82.36W
Hazlehurst [Ms.-U.S.]	45	Kk	31.52N	90.24W
Hazleton	44	Je	40.58N	76.00W
Hazlett, Lake-	59	Fd	21.30 S	128.50 E
Hazrah, Ra's al-	24	Nj	24.22N	51.36 E
Hazro	24	Ic	38.15N	40.47 E
Heacham	12	Cb	52.55N	0.29 E
Headley	12	Bc	51.07N	0.49W
Healdsburg	46	Dg	38.37N	122.52W
Heanor	12	Aa	53.00N	1.18W
Heard Island	30	On	53.00 S	73.35 E
Hearne	45	Hk	30.53N	96.36W
Hearst	42	Jg	49.41N	83.40W
Heart River	45	Fc	46.47N	100.51W
Heathrow Airport London	12	Bc	51.28N	0.30W
Hebbronville	45	Gm	27.18N	98.41W
Hebei Sheng (Ho-pei Sheng) =Hopeh (EN) [2]	27	Kd	39.00N	116.00 E
Heber City	46	Jf	40.30N	111.25W
Hebi	27	Jd	35.53N	114.09 E
Hebian	27	Jd	38.35N	113.06 E
Hebiji	28	Cf	36.00N	114.08 E
Hebrides	5	Fd	57.00N	6.30W
Hebrides, Sea of the-	9	Ge	57.00N	7.00W
Hebron [N.D.-U.S.]	45	Ec	46.54N	102.03W
Hebron [Newf.-Can.]	42	Le	58.15N	62.35W
Heby	8	Ge	59.56N	16.53 E
Hecate Strait	42	Ef	53.20N	131.00W
Hecelchakán	48	Ng	20.10N	90.08W
Hechi (Jnchengjiang)	27	Ig	24.44N	108.02 E
Hechingen	10	Eh	48.21N	8.59 E
Hechuan	27	Ie	30.07N	106.15 E
Hecla	45	Gd	45.43N	98.09W
Hecla and Griper Bay	42	Ga	76.00N	111.30W
Hecla Island	45	Ha	51.08N	96.45W
Heddalsvatnet	8	Ce	59.30N	9.15 E
Hede	7	Ce	62.25N	13.30 E
Hede → Sheyang	28	Fh	33.47N	120.15 E
Hedemarken	8	Dd	60.50N	11.20 E
Hedemora	7	Df	60.17N	15.59 E
Hedensted	8	Ci	55.46N	9.42 E
Hedesunda	7	Df	60.25N	17.00 E
Hedesunda fjärdarna	8	Gd	60.20N	17.00 E
Hedmark [2]	7	Cf	61.30N	11.45 E
Hedo-Misaki	29b	Bb	26.52N	128.16 E
Heemskerk	12	Gb	52.30N	4.42 E
Heemstede	12	Gb	52.21N	4.37 E
Heerenveen	11	Lb	52.57N	5.55 E
Heerhugowaard	12	Gb	52.40N	4.50 E
Heerlen	11	Ld	50.54N	5.59 E
Hefa=Haifa (EN)	22	Ff	32.50N	35.00 E
Hefei	22	Nf	31.47N	117.15 E
Hefeng	27	Jf	29.49N	110.01 E
Hegang	22	Pe	47.20N	130.12 E
Hegau	10	Ei	47.50N	8.45 E
Hegura Jima	27	Od	37.50N	136.55 E
Heide	10	Fb	54.12N	9.06 E
Heidelberg	10	Eg	49.25N	8.42 E
Heidenheim an der Brenz	10	Gh	48.41N	10.09 E
Heidenreichstein	14	Jb	48.52N	15.07 E
Hei-Gawa	29	Gb	39.38N	141.58 E
Heigun-Tō	29	Ce	33.47N	132.15 E
Hei He	27	Hd	38.15N	100.15 E
Heihe→Aihui	22	Od	50.13N	127.26 E
Heilbron	37	De	27.21 S	27.58 E
Heilbronn	10	Fg	49.08N	9.13 E
Heiligenblut	14	Gd	47.02N	12.50 E
Heiligenhafen	10	Gb	54.22N	10.59 E
Heiligenhaus	12	Ic	51.19N	6.58 E
Heiligenstadt	10	Ge	51.23N	10.08 E
Heilinzi	28	Ib	44.33N	126.41 E
Heilong Jiang	21	Qd	52.56N	141.10 E
Heilongjiang Sheng (Hei-lung-chiang Sheng)= Heilungkiang (EN) [2]	27	Mb	48.00N	128.00 E
Heiloo	12	Gb	52.36N	4.43 E
Hei-lung-chiang Sheng→Heilongjiang Sheng=Heilungkiang (EN) [2]	27	Mb	48.00N	128.00 E
Heilungkiang (EN)= Heilongjiang Sheng (Hei-lung-chiang Sheng) [2]	27	Mb	48.00N	128.00 E
Heilungkiang (EN)=Hei-lung-chiang Sheng→Heilongjiang Sheng [2]	27	Mb	48.00N	128.00 E
Heimæy	7a	c	63.26N	20.17W
Heimbach	12	Id	50.38N	6.29 E
Heimdal	7	Ce	63.21N	10.22 E
Heimsheim	12	Kf	48.48N	8.51 E
Heinävesi	7	Ge	62.26N	28.36 E
Heinola	7	Gf	61.13N	26.02 E
Heinsberg	12	Ic	51.04N	6.05 E
Heishan	28	Gd	41.42N	122.07 E
Heishan Xia	27	Hd	37.18N	104.39 E
Heishui [China]	28	Ec	42.06N	119.22 E
Heishui [China]	27	He	32.03N	103.05 E
Heist, Knokke-	12	Fc	51.21N	3.15 E
Heist-op-den-Berg	12	Gc	51.05N	4.43 E
Hei-Zaki	29	Hb	39.39N	142.00 E
Hejgijaha	17	Pd	65.27N	72.50 E
Hejian	28	De	38.27N	116.05 E
Hejing	27	Ec	42.18N	86.18 E
Hejjaha	17	Kb	68.18N	62.32 E
Hekimhan	24	Gc	38.49N	37.56 E
Hekinan	29	Ed	34.52N	136.58 E
Hekla	5	Ec	64.00N	19.40W
Hekou	28	Ci	31.20N	114.25 E
Hekou → Yanshan	28	Dj	28.18N	117.41 E
Hel	10	Ob	54.37N	18.48 E
Helagsfjället	7	Ce	62.55N	12.27 E
Helan	27	Id	38.35N	106.16 E
Helan Shan	27	Id	39.00N	106.00 E
Helden's Point	51c	Ab	17.24N	62.50W
Helena [Ar.-U.S.]	43	Ie	34.32N	90.35W
Helena [Guy.]	54	Gb	6.41N	57.55W
Helena [Mt.-U.S.]	39	He	46.36N	112.01W
Helen Glacier	66	Ge	66.40 S	93.55 E
Helen Reef	57	Ed	2.53N	131.47 E
Helensburgh	9	Ie	56.01N	4.44W
Helensville	62	Fb	36.40 S	174.27 E
Helgaå	8	Fi	55.53N	14.08 E
Helgasjön	8	Fh	56.55N	14.45 E
Helgeland	7	Cd	66.15N	13.05 E
Helgoland	10	Db	54.12N	7.53 E

Index Symbols

[1] Independent Nation
[2] State, Region
[3] District, County
[4] Municipality
[5] Colony, Dependency
Continent
Physical Region
Historical or Cultural Region
Mount, Mountain
Volcano
Hill
Mountains, Mountain Range
Hills, Escarpment
Plateau, Upland
Pass, Gap
Plain, Lowland
Delta
Salt Flat
Valley, Canyon
Crater, Cave
Karst Features
Depression
Polder
Desert, Dunes
Forest, Woods
Heath, Steppe
Oasis
Cape, Point
Coast, Beach
Cliff
Peninsula
Isthmus
Sandbank
Island
Atoll
Rock, Reef
Islands, Archipelago
Rocks, Reefs
Coral Reef
Well, Spring
Geyser
River, Stream
Waterfall Rapids
River Mouth, Estuary
Lake
Salt Lake
Intermittent Lake
Reservoir
Swamp, Pond
Canal
Glacier
Ice Shelf, Pack Ice
Ocean
Sea
Gulf, Bay
Strait, Fjord
Lagoon
Bank
Seamount
Tablemount
Ridge
Shelf
Basin
Escarpment, Sea Scarp
Fracture
Trench, Abyss
National Park, Reserve
Point of Interest
Recreation Site
Cave, Cavern
Historic Site
Ruins
Wall, Walls
Church, Abbey
Temple
Scientific Station
Airport
Port
Lighthouse
Mine
Tunnel
Dam, Bridge

Helgoländer Bucht	10	Eb	54.10N	8.04 E
Helikón Óros	15	Fk	38.20N	22.50 E
Helixi	28	Ei	30.39N	119.01 E
Heljulja	8	Nc	61.37N	30.38 E
Hella	7a	Bc	63.50N	20.24W
Hellberge	10	Hd	52.34N	11.17 E
Hëlleh	24	Nh	29.10N	50.40 E
Hellendoorn	11	Mb	52.24N	6.26 E
Hellendoorn-Nijverdal	12	Ib	52.22N	6.27 E
Hellenic Trough (EN)	5	Ii	35.00N	24.00 E
Hellental	12	Id	50.29N	6.26 E
Hellesylt	7	Be	62.05N	6.54 E
Hellín	13	Kf	38.31N	1.41W
Hells Canyon	43	Db	45.20N	116.45W
Hellweg	12	Kc	51.40N	8.00 E
Helmand	21	If	31.12N	61.34 E
Helmand	23	Jc	31.00N	64.00 E
Helme	10	He	51.20N	11.20 E
Helmeringhausen	37	Be	25.54S	16.57 E
Helmond	11	Lc	51.29N	5.40 E
Helmsdale	9	Jc	58.10N	3.40W
Helmsdale	9	Jc	58.07N	3.40W
Helmstedt	10	Gd	52.14N	11.00 E
Helong	27	Mc	42.32N	129.00 E
Helpe Majeure	12	Fd	50.11N	3.47 E
Helpringham	12	Bb	52.56N	0.18W
Helpter Berge	10	Jc	53.30N	13.36 E
Helsingborg	6	Hd	56.03N	12.42 E
Helsinge	8	Eh	56.01N	12.12 E
Helsingfors/Helsinki	6	Ic	60.10N	24.58 E
Helsingør	7	Ch	56.02N	12.37 E
Helsinki/Helsingfors	6	Ic	60.10N	24.58 E
Helska, Mierzeja-	10	Ob	54.45N	18.39 E
Helston	9	Hk	50.05N	5.16W
Helvecia	55	Bj	31.06S	60.05W
Helwān (EN)=Ḩulwān	33	Fd	29.51N	31.20 E
Ḩemār	24	Qg	31.42N	57.31 E
Hemčik	20	Ef	51.40N	92.10 E
Hemel Hempstead	9	Mj	51.46N	0.28W
Hemer	12	Jc	51.23N	7.46 E
Hemnesberget	7	Cc	66.14N	13.38 E
Hemsby	12	Db	52.41N	1.42 E
Hemse	8	Hg	57.14N	18.22 E
Hemsedal	8	Cd	60.50N	8.40 E
Hemsö	7	Ee	62.45N	18.05 E
Hen	8	Dd	60.13N	10.14 E
Henan	27	He	34.33N	101.55 E
Hen and Chickens Islands	62	Fa	35.55S	174.45 E
Henan Sheng (Ho-nan Sheng)=Honan (EN)	27	Je	34.00N	114.00 E
Henares	13	Id	40.24N	3.30W
Henashi-Zaki	29	Fa	40.37N	139.51 E
Henbury	59	Gd	24.35S	133.15 E
Hendaye	11	Ek	43.22N	1.47W
Hendek	24	Db	40.48N	30.45 E
Henderson [Arg.]	55	Bm	36.18S	61.43W
Henderson [Ky.-U.S.]	44	Dg	37.50N	87.35W
Henderson [N.C.-U.S.]	44	Hg	36.20N	78.25W
Henderson [Nv.-U.S.]	43	Dd	36.02N	115.01W
Henderson [Tx.-U.S.]	45	Ij	32.09N	94.48W
Henderson Island	57	Og	24.22S	128.19W
Henderson Seamount (EN)	43	Df	25.34N	119.33W
Hendersonville [N.C.-U.S.]	44	Fh	35.19N	82.28W
Hendersonville [Tn.-U.S.]	44	Dg	36.18N	86.37W
Hendījān	24	Mg	30.14N	49.43 E
Hendorābī, Jazīreh-ye-	24	Oi	26.40N	53.37 E
Hendrik Verwderddam	30	Km	46.36S	37.55 E
Hengām, Jazīreh-ye-	24	Pi	26.39N	55.53 E
Hengduan Shan	21	Lg	27.30N	99.00 E
Hengelo [Neth.]	11	Mb	52.15N	6.45 E
Hengelo [Neth.]	12	Ib	52.03N	6.20 E
Heng Shan [China]	27	Jd	39.42N	113.45 E
Hengshan [China]	27	Jf	27.16N	112.51 E
Heng Shan [China]	27	Jf	27.18N	112.41 E
Hengshan [China]	27	Id	37.51N	109.20 E
Hengshan [China]	28	Kb	45.24N	131.01 E
Hengshui	27	Kd	37.39N	115.46 E
Hengxian	27	Ig	22.46N	109.15 E
Hengyang	22	Ng	26.56N	112.35 E
Henik Lakes	42	Hd	61.05N	97.20W
Hénin-Liétard	11	Id	50.25N	2.56 E
Henley-on-Thames	12	Bc	51.32N	0.54W
Hennan	8	Fb	62.05N	15.45 E
Hennan	7	De	62.02N	15.54 E
Hennebont	11	Cg	47.48N	3.17W
Hennef (Sieg)	12	Jd	50.47N	7.17 E
Hennigsdorf bei Berlin	10	Jd	52.38N	13.12 E
Henrietta Maria, Cape -	42	Je	55.09N	82.19W
Henrietty, Ostrov-	20	Ka	77.00N	157.00 E
Henry, Mount-	46	Hb	48.53N	115.31W
Henry Bay	66	Ie	66.40S	120.40 E
Henryetta	45	Ii	35.27N	95.59W
Henry Kater Peninsula	42	Kk	69.15N	67.30W
Henry Mountains	46	Jh	37.55N	110.50W
Henrys Fork River	46	Je	43.45N	111.56W
Henslow, Cape-	63a	Ec	9.56S	160.38 E
Hentej	21	Me	48.50N	109.00 E
Hentiesbaai	37	Ad	22.08S	14.18 E
Henzada	22	Lh	17.38N	95.28 E
Heping → Yanhe	27	If	28.31N	108.28 E
Heppenheim (Bergstraße)	12	Ke	49.38N	8.39 E
Heppner	46	Fd	45.21N	119.33W
Hepu (Lianzhou)	27	Ig	21.40N	109.12 E
Hequ	27	Jd	39.22N	111.15 E
Herakol Dağı	24	Id	37.45N	42.35 E
Heralds Cays	59	Jc	16.55S	149.10 E
Herāt	23	Jc	34.30N	62.00 E
Herāt	22	If	34.20N	62.12 E
Hérault	11	Jk	43.40N	3.30 E
Hérault	11	Jk	43.17N	3.26 E
Herbert [N.Z.]	62	Df	45.13S	170.46 E
Herbert [Sask.-Can.]	46	La	50.26N	107.12W
Herberton	59	Jc	17.23S	145.23 E
Herbert River	59	Jc	18.32S	146.17 E
Herborn	10	Ef	50.41N	8.19 E
Herby	10	Of	50.45N	18.40 E
Hercegnovi	15	Bg	42.27N	18.32 E
Hercegovina	14	Lg	43.00N	17.50 E
Herdubreid	7a	Cb	65.11N	16.21W
Heredia	49	Fh	10.30N	84.00W
Heredia	47	Hf	10.00N	84.07W
Hereford	9	Ki	52.15N	2.50W
Hereford [Eng.-U.K.]	9	Ki	52.04N	2.43W
Hereford [Tx.-U.S.]	43	Ge	34.49N	102.24W
Hereford and Worcester	9	Ki	52.10N	2.35W
Hereheretue Atoll	57	Mf	19.54S	144.58W
Hereke	15	Mi	40.48N	29.39 E
Herekino	62	Ea	35.16S	173.13 E
Herent	12	Gd	50.54N	4.40 E
Herentals	12	Gc	51.11N	4.50 E
Herfølge	8	Ei	55.25N	12.10 E
Herford	10	Ed	52.08N	8.41 E
Héricourt	11	Mg	47.35N	6.45 E
Herington	45	Hg	38.40N	96.57W
Heriot	61	Ci	45.51S	169.16 E
Herīs	24	Lc	38.14N	47.07 E
Herisau	14	Dc	47.24N	9.16 E
Herk	12	Hd	50.58N	5.07 E
Herk-de-Stad	12	Hd	50.56N	5.10 E
Herkimer	44	Jd	43.02N	74.59W
Herlen He	27	Kb	48.48N	117.00 E
Hermagor	14	Hd	46.37N	13.22 E
Hermanas	48	Id	27.14N	101.14W
Herma Ness	9	Ma	60.50N	0.54W
Hermano Peak	45	Bh	37.17N	108.48W
Hermansverk	8	Bc	61.11N	6.51 E
Hermanus	37	Bf	34.25S	19.16 E
Hermeskeil	12	Ie	49.39N	6.57 E
Hermiston	46	Fd	45.51N	119.17W
Hermitage	62	De	43.44S	170.05 E
Hermit Islands	57	Fe	1.32S	145.05 E
Hermosa de Santa Rosa, Sierra-	48	Id	28.00N	101.45W
Hermosillo	39	Hg	29.04N	110.58W
Hermoso Campo	55	Bh	27.36S	61.21W
Hérnad	10	Qh	48.00N	20.58 E
Hernandarias	56	Jc	25.22S	54.45W
Hernández [Arg.]	55	Bk	32.21S	60.02W
Hernández [Mex.]	48	Hf	23.02N	102.02W
Hernani	13	Ka	43.16N	1.58W
Herne	10	De	51.33N	7.13 E
Herne Bay	9	Oj	51.23N	1.08 E
Herning	6	Gd	56.08N	8.59 E
Heroica Alvarado	48	Lh	18.46N	95.46W
Heroica Tlapacoyan	48	Kh	19.58N	97.13W
Heroica Zitácuaro	48	Ih	19.24N	100.22W
Herouville-Saint-Clair	12	Be	49.12N	0.19W
Herowābād	24	Md	37.37N	48.32 E
Herradura	55	Ch	26.29S	58.18W
Herre	8	Ce	59.06N	9.34 E
Herrera	55	Ck	32.26S	58.38W
Herrera	49	Gj	7.54N	80.38W
Herrera del Duque	13	Ge	39.10N	5.03W
Herrera de Pisuerga	13	Hb	42.36N	4.20W
Herrero, Punta-	48	Ph	19.10N	87.30W
Herrljunga	8	Ef	58.05N	13.02 E
Hers	11	Hk	43.47N	1.20 E
Herschel	42	Dc	69.35N	139.05W
Herselt	12	Gc	51.03N	4.53 E
Herserange	12	He	49.31N	5.47 E
Hershey	44	Ie	40.17N	76.39W
Hersilia	55	Bj	30.00S	61.51W
Herson	6	Jf	46.38N	32.35 E
Hersonesski, Mys-	16	Hg	44.33N	33.25 E
Hersonskaja Oblast	19	Df	46.40N	33.30 E
Herstal	11	Ld	50.40N	5.38 E
Herten	12	Jc	51.36N	7.08 E
Hertford	9	Mj	51.50N	0.05W
Hertford	9	Mj	51.48N	0.05W
Hertfordshire	9	Mj	51.45N	0.20W
Hertugen Af Orleans Land	41	Jc	78.15N	21.12W
Hervás	13	Gd	40.16N	5.51W
Herve	12	Hd	50.38N	5.48 E
Herve, Plateau van-/Herveland	12	Hd	50.40N	5.50 E
Herveland/Herve, Plateau van-	12	Hd	50.40N	5.50 E
Hervey Bay	59	Ke	25.15S	152.50 E
Herzberg	10	Je	51.41N	13.14 E
Herzberg am Harz	10	Ge	51.39N	10.20 E
Herzebrock	12	Kc	51.53N	8.15 E
Herzegovina (EN)	5	Hg	43.00N	17.50 E
Herzele	12	Fd	50.53N	3.53 E
Herzliyya	24	Ff	32.10N	34.51 E
Herzogenrath	12	Id	50.52N	6.06 E
Herzog-Ernst-Bucht (Vahsel Bay)	66	Af	77.48S	34.39W
Hesāmābād	24	Me	35.52N	48.25 E
Hesbaye/Haspengouws Plateau	11	Ld	50.35N	5.10 E
Hesdin	11	Id	50.22N	2.02 E
Hesel	12	Ja	53.18N	7.36 E
Heshī	24	Md	37.30N	48.15 E
Heshun	27	Jd	37.18N	113.32 E
Hesse (EN)=Hessen	10	Ff	50.30N	9.15 E
Hesselberg	10	Gg	49.05N	10.35 E
Hesselø	8	Dh	56.10N	11.45 E
Hessen	12	Ke	49.47N	8.08 E
Hessen=Hesse (EN)	10	Ff	50.30N	9.15 E
Hess Tablemount (EN)	57	Jc	17.50N	174.15W
Heta	21	Mb	71.54N	102.00 E
Heta	20	Eb	71.35N	99.45 E
Hettange-Grande	12	Ie	49.24N	6.09 E
Hettinger	45	Ec	46.00N	102.39W
Heuberg	10	Eh	48.06N	8.55 E
Heuchin	12	Ed	50.28N	2.16 E
Heuru	63a	Ed	10.12S	161.25 E
Hève, Cap de la-	11	Fe	49.31N	0.04W
Heves	10	Qi	47.36N	20.17 E
Heves	10	Qi	47.50N	20.15 E
Hexham	9	Kg	54.58N	2.06W
Hexi	27	Hf	27.44N	102.09 E
Hexian	28	Ei	31.43N	118.22 E
Hexian (Babu)	27	Jg	24.28N	111.34 E
Hexigten Qi (Jingfeng)	27	Kc	43.15N	117.31 E
Heydarābād	24	Kd	37.06N	45.27 E
Heysham	9	Kg	54.02N	2.54W
Heyuan	27	Jg	23.41N	114.43 E
Heywood	59	Ig	38.08S	141.38 E
Heze (Caozhou)	27	Kd	35.14N	115.28 E
Hezuo	27	Hd	35.02N	102.57 E
Hialeah	44	Gm	25.49N	80.17W
Hiawatha	45	Ig	39.51N	95.32W
Hibara-Ko	29	Gc	37.42N	140.03 E
Hibbing	43	Ib	47.25N	92.56W
Hibernia Reef	59	Eb	12.00S	123.25 E
Hibiki-Nada	29	Bd	34.15N	130.40 E
Hibiny	7	Hc	67.40N	33.35 E
Hiburi-Jima	29	Ce	33.10N	132.18 E
Hickman	44	Cg	36.34N	89.11W
Hickory	44	Gh	35.44N	81.21W
Hick's Cay	49	Ce	17.39N	88.08W
Hida-Gawa	29	Ed	35.25N	137.03 E
Hidaka [Jap.]	28	Qc	42.53N	142.28 E
Hidaka [Jap.]	29	Dd	35.28N	134.47 E
Hidaka-Gawa	29	De	33.53N	135.08 E
Hidaka Sanmyaku	28	Qc	42.25N	142.50 E
Hidalgo	47	Ed	20.30N	99.00W
Hidalgo [Mex.]	47	Ed	24.15N	99.26W
Hidalgo [Mex.]	48	Jd	27.47N	99.52W
Hidalgo del Parral	39	Ig	26.56N	105.40W
Hida-Sanchi	29	Ec	36.20N	137.00 E
Hida-Sanmyaku	28	Nf	36.10N	137.30 E
Hiddensee	10	Jb	54.33N	13.07 E
Hidra	8	Bf	58.15N	6.35 E
Hidrolândia	55	Hc	16.58S	49.16W
Hidrolina	55	Hb	14.37S	49.25W
Hieflau	14	Ic	47.36N	14.44 E
Hiei-Zan	29	Dd	35.05N	135.50 E
Hienghène	61	Cd	20.35S	164.56 E
Hierro	30	Ff	27.45N	18.00W
Higashi	29b	b	26.38N	128.08 E
Higashihiroshima	29	Cd	34.25N	132.43 E
Higashi-izu	29	Fd	34.48N	139.02 E
Higashi-matsuyama	29	Fc	36.02N	139.22 E
Higashimuroran	29a	Bb	42.21N	141.02 E
Higashine	28	Pe	38.26N	140.24 E
Higashiōsaka	29	Dd	34.40N	135.37 E
Higashi Rishiri	29a	Ba	45.16N	141.15 E
Higashi-Shina-Kai=East China Sea (EN)	21	Og	29.00N	125.00 E
Higgins	45	Fh	36.07N	100.02W
Higham Ferrers	12	Bb	52.18N	0.35W
High Atlas (EN)=Haut Atlas	30	Ge	32.00N	6.00W
Highland	9	Id	57.30N	5.00W
Highland Park	45	Me	42.11N	87.48W
High Level	42	Fe	58.30N	117.05W
Highmore	45	Gd	44.31N	99.27W
High Plains	38	If	38.30N	103.00W
High Point	43	Ld	35.58N	79.59W
High Prairie	42	Fe	55.27N	116.30W
High River	42	Gf	50.35N	113.52W
Highrock Lake	42	He	55.49N	100.23W
High Springs	44	Fk	29.50N	82.36W
High Tatra (EN)=Vysoké Tatry	10	Pg	49.10N	20.00 E
High Willhays	9	Jk	50.41N	3.59W
Highwood Mountains	46	Jc	47.25N	110.30W
High Wycombe	9	Mj	51.38N	0.46W
Higuera de Zaragoza	48	Ee	25.59N	109.16W
Higüero, Punta-	49	Nd	18.22N	67.16W
Higuerote	50	Cg	10.29N	66.06W
Higüey	49	Md	18.37N	68.43W
Hiidenvesi	8	Kd	60.20N	24.10 E
Hii-Gawa	29	Cd	35.26N	132.52 E
Hiiraan	35	He	4.00N	45.30 E
Hiitola	7	Gf	61.16N	29.42 E
Hiiumaa/Hiuma	5	Id	58.50N	22.40 E
Hijar	13	Lc	41.10N	0.27W
Ḩijāz	23	Ee	24.30N	38.30 E
Hijāz, Jabal al-	33	Hf	19.45N	41.55 E
Hiji	29	Be	33.22N	131.32 E
Hiji-Gawa	29	Ce	33.36N	132.29 E
Hikami	29	Dd	35.11N	135.02 E
Hikari	28	Kh	33.58N	131.56 E
Hiketa	29	Dd	34.13N	134.24 E
Hikiä	8	Kd	60.45N	24.55 E
Hiki-Gawa	29	De	33.35N	135.26 E
Ḩikmah, Ra's al-	24	Bg	31.17N	27.44 E
Hikone	28	Ng	35.15N	136.15 E
Hiko-San	29	Be	33.29N	130.56 E
Hikueru Atoll	61	Mc	17.36S	142.37W
Hikurangi	62	Hb	37.55S	178.04 E
Hikurangi	62	Fa	35.36S	174.17 E
Hila	26	Ih	7.35S	127.24 E
Hilāl, Ra's al-	33	Dc	32.55N	22.11 E
Hiland	46	Le	43.08N	107.18W
Hilchenbach	12	Kc	51.00N	8.06 E
Hildburghausen	10	Gf	50.25N	10.45 E
Hilden	12	Ic	51.10N	6.56 E
Hildesheim	10	Fd	52.09N	9.58 E
Hillaby, Mount-	50	Gf	13.12N	59.35W
Hillared	8	Eg	57.38N	13.09 E
Hillary Coast	6	Kf	79.00S	161.00 E
Hill Bank	49	Ce	17.35N	88.42W
Hill City	45	Gg	39.22N	99.51W
Hillcrest Center	46	Fi	35.23N	118.57W
Hille	12	Kb	52.20N	8.45 E
Hillegom	12	Gb	52.18N	4.35 E
Hillekrog	8	Dj	54.36N	11.30 E
Hillerød	8	Ei	55.56N	12.19 E
Hillerstorp	8	Eg	57.19N	13.52 E
Hillesheim	12	Id	50.19N	6.41 E
Hillingdon, London-	12	Bc	51.31N	0.27W
Hillsboro [Il.-U.S.]	45	Lg	39.09N	89.29W
Hillsboro [N.D.-U.S.]	45	Hc	47.26N	97.03W
Hillsboro [Oh.-U.S.]	44	Ff	39.12N	83.37W
Hillsboro [Or.-U.S.]	46	Dd	45.31N	122.59W
Hillsboro [Tx.-U.S.]	45	Hj	32.01N	97.08W
Hillsborough	51p	Cb	12.29N	61.26W
Hillsdale	44	Ee	41.55N	84.38W
Hillsville	44	Gg	36.46N	80.44W
Hillswich	9	La	60.28N	1.30W
Hilo	58	Lc	19.44N	155.05W
Hilo Bay	65a	Fd	19.44N	155.05W
Hilok	21	Md	51.19N	106.59 E
Hilok	20	Gf	51.22N	110.30 E
Hilton Head Island	44	Gi	32.12N	80.45W
Hiltrup, Münster-	12	Jc	51.54N	7.38 E
Hilvan	24	Hd	37.30N	38.58 E
Hilvarenbeek	12	Hc	51.29N	5.08 E
Hilversum	11	Lb	52.14N	5.10 E
Himāchal Prādesh	25	Fb	31.00N	78.00 E
Himalaya=Himalayas (EN)	21	Kg	29.00N	83.00 E
Himalayas (EN)=Himalaya	21	Kg	29.00N	83.00 E
Himara	15	Ci	40.07N	19.44 E
Himeji	27	Ne	34.49N	134.42 E
Hime-Jima	29	Be	33.43N	131.40 E
Hime-Kawa	29	Ec	37.02N	137.50 E
Hime-Shima	29	Ae	32.49N	128.41 E
Hime-Zaki	29	Fb	38.05N	138.34 E
Himi	28	Nf	36.51N	136.59 E
Himki	7	Ii	55.56N	37.28 E
Himmelbjerget	8	Ch	56.06N	9.42 E
Himmerfjärden	8	Ge	59.00N	17.43 E
Himmerland	8	Ch	56.50N	9.45 E
Himo	36	Gc	3.23S	37.33 E
Ḩimş=Homs (E)	22	Ff	34.44N	36.43 E
Hims, Bahrat-	24	Ge	34.39N	36.34 E
Hinai	29	Ga	40.13N	140.35 E
Hinca Renancó	56	Hd	34.50S	64.23W
Hinche	49	Kd	19.09N	72.01W
Hinchinbrook	40	Jd	60.22N	146.30W
Hinchinbrook Island	59	Jc	18.25S	146.15 E
Hinckley	12	Ab	52.32N	1.22W
Hindås	8	Eg	57.42N	12.27 E
Hindhead	12	Bc	51.06N	0.44W
Hindi, Badwēynta-=Indian Ocean (EN)	3	Gl	21.00S	82.00 E
Hindmarsh, Lake-	59	Ig	36.05S	141.55 E
Hinds	62	Df	44.00S	171.34 E
Hindsholm	8	Di	55.33N	10.40 E
Hindukush	21	Jf	35.00N	71.00 E
Hindustan	21	Jg	25.00N	79.00 E
Hinesville	44	Gj	31.51N	81.36W
Hinganghāt	25	Fd	20.34N	78.50 E
Hınıs	24	Ic	39.22N	41.44 E
Hınıs	24	Jc	39.18N	42.12 E
Hinlopenstretet	41	Oc	79.15N	21.00 E
Hinnøya	5	Hb	68.30N	16.00 E
Hino-Gawa	29	Cd	35.27N	133.22 E
Hinojosa del Duque	13	Gf	38.30N	5.09W
Hinokage	29	Be	32.39N	131.24 E
Hi-no-Misaki	29	Cd	35.26N	132.38 E
Hino-Misaki	29	De	33.53N	135.04 E
Hinterrhein	14	Dd	46.49N	9.25 E
Hinton	42	Ff	53.25N	117.34W
Hi-Numa	29	Gc	36.16N	140.30 E
Hınzır Burun	24	Fb	36.22N	35.45 E
Hiou	63b	Ca	13.08S	166.33 E
Hipólito	48	Ie	25.41N	101.26W
Hippolytushoef, Wieringen-	12	Gb	52.54N	4.59 E
Hippone	14	Bn	36.52N	7.44 E
Hirado	28	Jh	33.22N	129.33 E
Hirado-Shima	28	Jh	33.19N	129.32 E
Hiraka	29	Gb	39.16N	140.29 E
Hirakata	29	Dd	34.48N	135.38 E
Hīrākud	25	Gd	21.15N	84.15 E
Hiraman	36	Gc	1.07S	39.55 E
Hiranai	29a	Bc	40.54N	140.57 E
Hirara	27	Mg	24.48N	125.17 E
Hira-Shima	29	Ae	33.01N	129.15 E
Hirata	29	Cd	35.26N	132.49 E
Hiratsuka	29	Fd	35.19N	139.19 E
Hirfanlı barajı Gölü	24	Ec	39.10N	33.32 E
Hirgis	27	Fb	49.32N	93.48 E
Hirgis-Nur	21	Le	49.12N	93.24 E
Hirhafok	32	Ie	23.29N	5.45 E
Hîrlău	15	Jb	47.26N	26.54 E
Hiromi	29	Ce	33.15N	132.38 E
Hiroo	27	Pc	42.17N	143.19 E
Hirosaki	27	Pc	40.35N	140.28 E
Hiroshima	22	Pf	34.24N	132.27 E
Hiroshima Ken	28	Lg	34.35N	132.50 E
Hiroshima-Wan	29	Cd	34.10N	132.20 E
Hirschhorn (Neckar)	12	Ke	49.27N	8.54 E
Hirson	11	Ke	49.55N	4.05 E
Hîrşova	15	Ke	44.41N	27.56 E
Hîrtibaciu	15	Hd	45.44N	24.14 E
Hirtshals	7	Bh	57.35N	9.58 E
Hirvensalmi	8	Lc	61.38N	26.48 E
Ḩīs	35	Hc	10.50N	46.54 E
Hisai	29	Ed	34.40N	136.28 E
Hisaka-Shima	29	Ae	32.48N	128.52 E
Hisar	15	Jg	42.35N	27.00 E
Hisar	25	Fc	29.10N	75.43 E
Hisarcik	15	Mj	39.15N	29.15 E
Hisarja	15	Hg	42.30N	24.42 E
Ḩismā	24	Fh	28.30N	35.50 E
Ḩişn al 'Abr	33	If	16.08N	47.14 E
Ḩişn aş Şaḩābī	33	Dc	30.01N	20.48 E
Hispaniola (EN)=La Española	38	Lh	19.00N	71.00W
Histon	12	Cb	52.15N	0.06 E
Histria	15	Le	44.30N	28.45 E
Hīt	24	Jf	33.38N	42.49 E
Hita	28	Kh	33.19N	130.56 E
Hitachi	28	Pf	36.36N	140.39 E
Hitachi-ōta	29	Gc	36.32N	140.31 E
Hitchin	12	Bc	51.57N	0.16W
Hitiaa	65e	Fc	17.36S	149.18W
Hitotsuse-Gawa	29	Be	32.03N	131.31 E
Hitoyoshi	28	Kh	32.15N	130.45 E
Hitra	5	Gc	63.30N	8.45 E
Hiuchi-ga-Take	29	Fc	36.57N	139.17 E
Hiuchi-Nada	29	Cd	34.05N	133.15 E
Hiuma/Hiiumaa	5	Id	58.50N	22.40 E
Hiv	16	Oi	41.46N	47.57 E
Hiva	19	Gg	41.25N	60.23 E
Hiva Oa, Ile-	57	Ne	9.45S	139.00W
Hiw	24	Ei	26.01N	32.16 E
Hjademeste/Häädemeeste	8	Uf	58.00N	24.28 E
Hjallerup	8	Dg	57.10N	10.09 E
Hjälmare kanal	8	Fe	59.25N	15.55 E
Hjälmaren	5	Hd	59.15N	15.45 E
Hjelm	8	Dh	56.10N	10.50 E
Hjelmelandsvågen	7	Bg	59.15N	6.10 E
Hjelmsøya	7	Fa	71.05N	24.43 E
Hjerkinn	8	Cb	62.13N	9.32 E
Hjo	7	Dg	58.18N	14.17 E
Hjørring	7	Bh	57.28N	9.59 E
Hlatikulu	37	Ee	26.58S	31.19 E
Hlavní město Praha	10	Kf	50.05N	14.25 E
Hlavní město SSR Bratislava	10	Nh	48.10N	17.10 E
Hlinsko	10	Lg	49.46N	15.54 E
Hlohovec	10	Nh	48.25N	17.48 E
Hluhluwe	37	Ee	28.02S	32.17 E
Hmelnickaja Oblast	19	Cf	49.30N	27.00 E
Hmelnicki	19	Cf	49.24N	26.57 E
Hmelnik	16	Ee	49.33N	27.59 E
Hnilec	10	Rh	48.53N	21.01 E
Ho	34	Fd	6.36N	0.28 E
Hoa Binh	25	Ld	20.50N	105.20 E
Hoai Nhon	25	Lf	14.26N	109.01 E
Hoanib	37	Ac	19.23S	13.06 E
Hoare Bay	42	Lc	65.30N	63.10W
Hoback Peak	46	Je	43.10N	110.33W
Hobart [Austl.]	58	Fi	42.53S	147.19 E
Hobart [Ok.-U.S.]	45	Gi	35.01N	99.06W
Hobbs	43	Ge	32.42N	103.08W
Hobbs Coast	66	Nf	74.50S	131.00W
Hobda	16	Sd	50.55N	54.38 E
Hoboken, Antwerpen-	12	Gc	51.10N	4.21 E
Hoboksar	27	Eb	46.47N	85.43 E
Hobq Shamo	27	Ic	40.30N	108.00 E
Hobro	7	Bh	56.38N	9.48 E
Hoburgen	7	Eh	56.55N	18.07 E
Hobyā	31	Lh	5.20N	48.38 E
Hocalar	15	Mk	38.37N	29.57 E
Hochalmspitze	14	Hc	47.01N	13.19 E
Hochfeiler/Gran Pilastro	14	Fd	46.58N	11.44 E
Hochgolling	14	Hc	47.16N	13.45 E
Hochschwab	14	Jc	47.36N	15.05 E
Höchstadt an der Aisch	10	Gg	49.42N	10.44 E
Hochstetters Forland	41	Kc	75.45N	20.00W
Höchst im Odenwald	12	Ke	49.48N	9.00 E
Hochtor	14	Gc	47.05N	12.48 E
Hockenheim	12	Ke	49.19N	8.33 E
Hodaka-Dake	29	Ec	36.17N	137.39 E
Hodda	35	Ic	11.30N	50.45 E
Hoddesdon	12	Cc	51.45N	0.00
Hodgenville	44	Eg	37.34N	85.44W
Hodh	30	Gg	16.10N	8.40W
Hodh ech Chargui	32	Ff	17.00N	7.15W
Hodh el Gharbi	32	Ff	16.30N	10.00W
Hódmezővásárhely	10	Qj	46.25N	20.20 E
Hodna, Chott el-	32	Hb	35.25N	4.45 E
Hodna, Monts du-	32	Hb	35.50N	4.50 E
Hodna, Plaine du-	13	Qi	35.35N	4.35 E
Hodonín	10	Nh	48.52N	17.08 E
Hodorov	16	De	49.25N	24.18 E
Hodžambas	18	Ee	38.06N	65.01 E
Hodža-Pirjah, Gora-	18	Fe	38.47N	67.35 E
Hodžejli	19	Fg	42.23N	59.20 E
Hœdic, Ile de-	11	Dg	47.20N	2.52W
Hoegaarden	12	Gd	50.47N	4.53 E
Hoei/Huy	11	Ld	50.31N	5.14 E
Hoë Karoo	30	Jl	30.00S	21.30 E
Hoek van Holland	11	Kc	51.59N	4.09 E
Hoeselt	12	Hd	50.51N	5.29 E
Hof	10	Hf	50.19N	11.55 E
Höfdakaupstadur	7a	Bb	65.50N	20.19W
Hofgeismar	10	Fe	51.29N	9.24 E
Hofheim	12	Kd	50.05N	8.27 E
Hofmeyr	37	Df	31.39S	25.50 E
Höfn	7a	Cb	64.15N	15.13W
Hofsjökull	5	Ec	64.49N	18.48W
Hōfu	28	Kg	34.03N	131.34 E
Höganäs	8	Eh	56.12N	12.33 E
Hogarth, Mount-	59	Hd	21.48S	136.58 E
Hogback Mountain	46	Id	44.54N	112.07W
Hog Cliffs	51d	Ba	17.38N	61.44W
Hoge Venen/Hautes Fagnes	10	Bf	50.30N	6.00 E
Högfors/Karkkila	7	Ff	60.32N	24.11 E
Hog Island	51p	Bb	12.00N	61.44W
Hogne, Somme-Leuze-	12	Hd	50.15N	5.17 E
Hog Point	51d	Ba	17.43N	61.48W
Högsby	7	Dh	57.10N	16.02 E
Høgste Breakulen	8	Bc	61.41N	7.02 E
Høgstegia	8	Db	62.23N	10.08 E
Hogsty Reef	49	Kc	21.41N	73.49W
Hŏhang-nyŏng	28	Jd	41.48N	128.20 E
Hohe Acht	10	Cf	50.23N	7.00 E
Hohe Eifel	12	Id	50.16N	6.50 E
Hohenau	55	Eh	27.05S	55.45W
Hohenems	14	Dc	47.22N	9.41 E
Hohenloher Ebene	10	Fg	49.20N	9.40 E
Hohes Venn	10	Bf	50.30N	6.00 E
Hohe Tauern	14	Gc	47.10N	12.30 E
Hohhot	22	Ne	40.51N	111.38 E
Hōhoku	29	Bd	34.17N	130.57 E
Höhr-Grenzhausen	12	Jd	50.26N	7.40 E
Höhtiäinen	8	Mb	62.50N	29.40 E
Hoh Xil Hu	27	Fd	35.35N	91.06 E
Hoh Xil Shan	21	Lf	35.20N	91.00 E
Hoi An	25	Le	15.52N	108.19 E

Index Symbols

1 Independent Nation	Historical or Cultural Region	Pass, Gap	Depression	Coast, Beach	Rock, Reef	Waterfall Rapids	Canal	Lagoon	Escarpment, Sea Scarp
2 State, Region	Mount, Mountain	Plain, Lowland	Polder	Cliff	Islands, Archipelago	River Mouth, Estuary	Glacier	Bank	Fracture
3 District, County	Volcano	Delta	Desert, Dunes	Peninsula	Rocks, Reefs	Lake	Ice Shelf, Pack Ice	Seamount	Trench, Abyss
4 Municipality	Hill	Salt Flat	Forest, Woods	Isthmus	Coral Reef	Salt Lake	Ocean	Tablemount	National Park, Reserve
5 Colony, Dependency	Mountains, Mountain Range	Valley, Canyon	Heath, Steppe	Sandbank	Well, Spring	Intermittent Lake	Sea	Ridge	Point of Interest
Continent	Hills, Escarpment	Crater, Cave	Oasis	Island	Geyser	Reservoir	Gulf, Bay	Shelf	Recreation Site
Physical Region	Plateau, Upland	Karst Features	Cape, Point	Atoll	River, Stream	Swamp, Pond	Strait, Fjord	Basin	Cave, Cavern

Historic Site, Ruins, Wall, Walls, Church, Abbey, Temple, Scientific Station, Airport, Port, Lighthouse, Mine, Tunnel, Dam, Bridge

Hoima 36 Fb 1.26N 31.21 E
Hoisington 45 Gg 38.31N 98.47W
Hoj, Vozvyšennost- 17 Ob 68.50N 71.30 E
Højer 8 Cj 54.58N 8.43 E
Hojniki 19 Ce 51.54N 29.56 E
Hōjō 28 Lh 33.58N 132.46 E
Hökensås 8 Ff 58.11N 14.08 E
Hokianga Harbour 62 Ea 35.30S 173.20 E
Hokitika 58 Ii 42.43S 170.58 E
Hok-Kai = Okhotsk, Sea of- (EN) 21 Qd 53.00N 150.00 E
Hokkaidō 21 Qe 43.00N 143.00 E
Hokkaidō Ken [2] 28 Qc 43.00N 143.00 E
Hokksund 7 Bg 59.47N 9.59 E
Hokmābād 24 Qd 36.37N 57.36 E
Hokota 29 Gc 36.10N 140.30 E
Hol 8 Cd 60.36N 8.22 E
Holap 64d Ba 7.39N 151.54 E
Holbæk 8 Di 55.43N 11.43 E
Holbeach 12 Cb 52.48N 0.01 E
Holbeach Marsh 12 Cb 52.52N 0.02 E
Holbox, Isla- 48 Pg 21.33N 87.15W
Holbrook 43 Ee 34.54N 110.10W
Holdenville 45 Hi 35.05N 96.24W
Holderness 9 Mh 53.47N 0.10W
Holdrege 45 Gf 40.26N 99.22W
Hold With Hope 41 Jd 73.40N 21.45W
Hole in the Wall 44 Im 25.51N 77.12W
Hølen 8 De 59.32N 10.45 E
Holešov 10 Ng 49.20N 17.33 E
Holetown 51q Ab 13.11N 59.39W
Holguin 39 Lg 20.53N 76.15W
Holguín [3] 49 Jc 20.40N 75.50W
Hol Hol 35 Gc 11.20N 42.50 E
Holitna 40 Hd 61.40N 157.12W
Höljes 7 Cf 60.54N 12.36 E
Hollabrunn 14 Kb 48.33N 16.05 E
Holland 44 Dd 42.47N 86.07W
Holland [Eng.-U.K.] 12 Bb 52.52N 0.10W
Holland [Neth.] 5 Ge 52.20N 4.45 E
Hollandale 45 Kj 33.10N 90.58W
Hollandsbird Island 37 Ad 24.45S 14.34 E
Hollands Diep 12 Gc 51.40N 4.30 E
Hollesley Bay 12 Db 52.04N 1.33 E
Hollick-Kenyon Plateau 66 Pf 79.00S 97.00W
Hollis 45 Gi 34.41N 99.55W
Hollister [Ca.-U.S.] 46 Eh 36.51N 121.24W
Hollister [Id.-U.S.] 46 He 42.23N 114.35W
Hollola 8 Kc 61.03N 25.26 E
Höllviksnäs 8 Ei 55.25N 12.57 E
Holly Springs 45 Li 34.41N 89.26W
Hollywood 43 Kf 26.00N 80.09W
Holm 7 Hh 57.09N 31.12 E
Holma 34 Hd 9.54N 13.03 E
Holman Island 42 Fb 70.40N 117.35W
Hólmavík 7a Bb 65.43N 21.41W
Holmes Reefs 57 Ff 16.30S 148.00 E
Holmestrand 8 De 59.29N 10.18 E
Holm Land 41 Kb 80.16N 18.20W
Holms 41 Gd 74.30N 57.00W
Holmsjö 8 Fh 56.25N 15.32 E
Holmsjön [Swe.] 7 De 62.25N 15.20 E
Holmsjön [Swe.] 8 Gb 62.40N 16.35 E
Holmsk 20 Jg 47.00N 142.03 E
Holmski 16 Kg 44.50N 38.24 E
Holmsland Klit 8 Ch 56.00N 8.10 E
Holmsund 7 Ee 63.42N 20.21 E
Holmsveden 8 Gc 61.07N 16.43 E
Holmudden 8 Hg 57.57N 19.21 E
Holod 15 Fc 46.47N 22.08 E
Holohit, Punta- 48 Og 21.37N 88.08W
Holothuria Banks (EN) 59 Fb 13.25S 126.00 E
Holsnøy 8 Ad 60.35N 5.05 E
Holstebro 7 Bh 56.21N 8.38 E
Holsted 8 Ci 55.30N 8.55 E
Holstein 45 Ie 42.29N 95.33W
Holsteinsborg/ Sisimiut 67 Nc 67.05N 53.45W
Holt 12 Db 52.54N 1.05 E
Holten 12 Ib 52.17N 6.27 E
Holton 45 Ig 39.28N 95.44W
Holtoson 20 Ff 50.18N 103.20 E
Holtyn-Daba 27 Ib 47.40N 107.20 E
Holwerd, Westdongeradeel- 12 Ha 53.22N 5.54 E
Holy Cross 40 Hd 62.12N 159.47W
Holyhead 9 Ih 53.20N 4.38W
Holy Island [Eng.-U.K.] 9 Lf 55.41N 1.48W
Holy Island [Wales-U.K.] 9 Ih 53.18N 4.37W
Holyoke [Co.-U.S.] 45 Ef 40.35N 102.18W
Holyoke [Ma.-U.S.] 44 Kd 42.12N 72.37W
Holýšov 10 Jg 49.36N 13.07 E
Homa Bay 36 Fc 0.31S 34.27 E
Homalin 25 Id 24.52N 94.55 E
Homathko River 46 Ca 50.55N 124.50W
Homberg (Ohm) 12 Kd 50.44N 8.59 E
Hombori 34 Eb 15.17N 1.42W
Hombre Muerto, Salar del- 56 Gc 25.23S 67.06W
Homburg 10 Dg 49.19N 7.20 E
Home Bay 38 Mc 68.45N 67.10W
Homecourt 12 He 49.14N 5.59 E
Home Hill 59 Jc 19.40S 147.25 E
Homer [Ak.-U.S.] 39 Dd 59.39N 151.33W
Homer [La.-U.S.] 45 Jj 32.48N 93.04W
Homert 12 Kc 51.16N 8.06 E
Homerville 44 Fj 31.02N 82.45W
Homestead 44 Gm 25.29N 80.29W
Homewood 44 Di 33.29N 86.48W
Hommelstø 7 Cd 65.25N 12.30 E
Hommersåk 8 Af 58.55N 5.50 E
Homoine 37 Fd 23.52S 35.08 E
Homoljske Planina 15 Ee 44.20N 21.45 E
Homonhon 26 Id 10.44N 125.43 E
Homosassa 44 Fk 28.47N 82.37W
Homs (EN) = Ḥimṣ 22 Ff 34.44N 36.43 E
Honan (EN) = Henan Sheng (Ho-nan Sheng) [2] 27 Je 34.00N 114.00 E
Honan (EN) = Ho-nan Sheng → Henan Sheng [2] 27 Je 34.00N 114.00 E
Ho-nan Sheng → Henan Sheng = Honan (EN) [2] 27 Je 34.00N 114.00 E
Honaz 15 Ml 37.45N 29.17 E
Honaz Daği 15 Ml 37.41N 29.18 E
Honbetsu 28 Qc 43.18N 143.33 E
Honda 54 Db 5.13N 74.45W
Honda, Bahía- 49 Lg 12.21N 71.47W
Hondeklipbaai 37 Bf 30.20S 17.18 E
Hòn Diên, Núi- 25 Lf 11.33N 108.38 E
Hondo 47 Ge 18.29N 88.19W
Hondo [Jap.] 28 Kh 32.27N 130.12 E
Hondo [N.M.-U.S.] 45 Dj 33.23N 105.16W
Hondo [Tx.-U.S.] 45 Gl 29.21N 99.09W
Hondo, Rio- 45 Dj 33.22N 104.24W
Hondschoote 12 Ed 50.59N 2.35 E
Hondsrug 11 Mb 52.50N 6.50 E
Honduras [1] 39 Kh 15.00N 86.30W
Honduras, Cabo de- 49 De 16.01N 86.01W
Honduras, Golfo de- = Honduras, Gulf of- (EN) 38 Kh 16.10N 87.50W
Honduras, Gulf of- 38 Kh 16.10N 87.50W
Honduras, Gulf of- (EN) = Honduras, Golfo de- 38 Kh 16.10N 87.50W
Hønefoss 7 Cf 60.10N 10.18 E
Honey Lake 46 Ef 40.16N 120.19W
Honfleur 11 Ge 49.25N 0.14 E
Hồng, Sông- = Red River (EN) 21 Mg 20.17N 106.34 E
Hong'an (Huang'an) 28 Ci 31.17N 114.37 E
Hongch'ŏn 28 If 37.41N 127.52 E
Hong-Do 28 Hg 34.41N 125.13 E
Hong He 28 Ch 32.24N 115.32 E
Honghton Lake 44 Ec 44.22N 84.43W
Hong Hu 27 Je 30.00N 113.25 E
Honghu (Xindi) 28 Bj 29.50N 113.28 E
Honghui 27 Id 36.46N 105.05 E
Hong Kong/Xianggang [5] 22 Ng 22.15N 114.10 E
Hongliuyuan 27 Gc 41.02N 95.24 E
Hongluoxian 28 Fd 41.01N 120.52 E
Hongning → Wulian 28 Eg 35.45N 119.13 E
Hongor 28 Bb 45.48N 112.45 E
Hongqizhen 27 Ih 18.48N 109.30 E
Hongshui He 21 Mg 23.47N 109.33 E
Hongsŏng 28 If 36.36N 126.40 E
Hongtong 28 Af 36.15N 111.41 E
Hongū 29 De 33.50N 135.46 E
Honguedo, Détroit d'- 42 Lg 49.30N 65.00W
Hongwansi → Sunan 27 Gd 38.59N 99.25 E
Hongwŏn 28 Id 40.02N 127.58 E
Hongyuan (Hurama) 27 He 32.45N 102.38 E
Hongze (Gaoliangjian) 27 Ke 33.10N 119.58 E
Hongze Hu 27 Ke 33.20N 118.40 E
Honiara 58 Ge 9.27S 159.57 E
Honikulu, Passe- 64h Ac 13.23S 176.11W
Honiton 9 Jk 50.48N 3.13W
Honjō 28 Pe 39.23N 140.03 E
Honkajoki 8 Jb 61.59N 22.16 E
Hon-kawane 29 Fd 35.07N 138.06 E
Honningsvåg 7 Ga 70.59N 26.01 E
Hönö 8 Dg 57.42N 11.39 E
Honokaa 65a Fc 20.05N 155.28W
Honokohau 65a Eb 21.01N 156.37W
Honolulu 58 Lb 21.19N 157.52W
Honomu 65a Fd 19.52N 155.07W
Honrubia 13 Je 39.37N 2.16W
Honshū 21 Pf 36.00N 136.00 E
Hontenisse 12 Gc 51.23N 4.00 E
Hontenisse-Kloosterzande 12 Gc 51.23N 4.00 E
Honuapo Bay 65a Fd 19.05N 155.33W
Honuu 20 Jc 66.27N 143.06 E
Honyō 29 Fc 36.14N 139.10 E
Hood 42 Gc 67.25N 108.53W
Hood, Mount- 38 Ge 45.23N 121.41W
Hood Point 59 Df 34.23S 119.34 E
Hood River 46 Ed 45.43N 121.31W
Hoogeveen 11 Mb 52.43N 6.29 E
Hoogezand-Sappemeer 12 Ia 53.09N 6.48 E
Hooglede 12 Fd 50.59N 3.05 E
Hoogstraten 12 Gc 51.24N 4.46 E
Hooker 45 Fh 36.52N 101.13W
Hooker, Cape- 66 Kf 70.38S 166.45 E
Hook Head/Rinn Dúain 9 Gi 52.07N 6.55W
Hook Island 59 Jc 20.10S 148.55 E
Hoolehua 65a Db 21.10N 157.05W
Hoonah 40 Le 58.07N 135.26W
Hooper, Cape- 42 Kc 68.24N 66.43W
Hooper Bay 40 Fd 61.31N 166.06W
Hoopeston 45 Mf 40.28N 87.40W
Höör 8 Ei 55.56N 13.32 E
Hoorn 11 Lb 52.38N 5.04 E
Hoornaar 12 Gc 51.53N 4.57 E
Hoover Dam 46 Hi 36.00N 114.27W
Hopa 24 Ib 41.25N 41.24 E
Hope [Ar.-U.S.] 45 Jj 33.40N 93.36W
Hope [Az.-U.S.] 46 Ij 33.44N 113.42W
Hope [B.C.-Can.] 46 Eb 49.23N 121.26W
Hope, Ben- 9 Ic 58.24N 4.36W
Hope, Lake- 59 Ef 32.50S 121.40 E
Hope, Point- 38 Cc 68.21N 166.50W
Hopedale 42 Le 55.50N 60.10W
Hopefield 37 Bf 33.04S 18.21 E
Hopeh (EN) = Hebei Sheng (Ho-pei Sheng) [2] 27 Kd 39.00N 116.00 E
Hopeh (EN) = Ho-pei Sheng → Hebei Sheng [2] 27 Kd 39.00N 116.00 E
Hopeh (EN) = Hu-pei Sheng → Hubei Sheng [2] 27 Je 31.00N 112.00 E
Ho-pei Sheng → Hebei Sheng = Hopeh (EN) [2] 27 Kd 39.00N 116.00 E
Hopelchén 48 Oh 19.46N 89.51W
Hopen 41 Oc 76.35N 25.10 E
Hopër 5 Kf 49.36N 42.19 E
Hopes Advance, Cap- 42 Kd 61.05N 69.33W
Hopetoun [Austl.] 59 Ig 35.44S 142.22 E
Hopetoun [Austl.] 58 Dh 33.57S 120.07 E
Hopetown 37 Ce 29.34S 24.03 E
Hopewell 44 Ig 37.17N 77.19W
Hopewell Islands 42 Je 58.20N 78.10W
Hopin 25 Jd 24.59N 96.31 E
Hopkins, Lake- 59 Fd 24.15S 128.50 E
Hopkinsville 43 Jd 36.52N 87.29W
Hopsten 12 Jb 52.23N 7.37 E
Hoptrup 8 Ci 55.11N 9.28 E
Hoquiam 43 Cb 46.59N 123.53W
Hor 20 Ig 47.48N 134.43 E
Hor 20 Ig 47.55N 135.01 E
Hōrai 29 Ed 34.55N 137.34 E
Hōrai-San 29 Dd 35.13N 135.53 E
Horasan 24 Jb 40.03N 42.11 E
Horaždovice 10 Jg 49.20N 13.42 E
Horb am Neckar 10 Eh 48.26N 8.41 E
Horconcitos 49 Fi 8.19N 82.10W
Hordaland [2] 7 Bf 60.15N 6.30 E
Hordogoj 20 Gd 62.32N 115.38 E
Horezmskaja Oblast [3] 19 Gg 41.30N 60.40 E
Horfors 7 Df 60.33N 16.17 E
Horgen 14 Cc 47.15N 8.36 E
Horgoš 15 Cc 46.09N 19.58 E
Horgos 19 Ig 44.10N 80.20 E
Hořice 10 Lf 50.22N 15.38 E
Horinger 28 Ad 40.24N 111.46 E
Horizon Tablemount (EN) 57 Kc 19.40N 168.30W
Horizontina 55 Eh 27.37S 54.19W
Horley 12 Bc 51.10N 0.10W
Horlick Mountains 66 Og 85.23S 121.00W
Hormigas 48 Gc 29.12N 105.45W
Hormoz [Iran] 24 Pi 27.32N 54.57 E
Hormoz [Iran] 23 Id 27.06N 56.28 E
Hormoz, Kūh-e- 23 Id 27.27N 55.10 E
Hormoz, Tangeh-ye- = Hormuz, Strait of- (EN) 21 Hg 26.34N 56.15 E
Hormozgān [3] 23 Id 27.30N 56.00 E
Hormūd-e Bāgh 24 Pi 27.30N 54.18 E
Hormuz, Strait of- (EN) = Hormoz, Tangeh-ye- 21 Hg 26.34N 56.15 E
Horn 42 Fd 61.30N 118.00W
Horn 5 Db 66.28N 22.30W
Horn [Aus.] 14 Jb 48.39N 15.39 E
Horn [Swe.] 8 Fg 57.54N 15.50 E
Horn, Cape- (EN) = Hornos, Cabo de- 52 Jk 55.59S 67.16W
Hornád 10 Qh 48.00N 20.58 E
Hornaday 42 Fc 69.22N 123.56W
Hornavan 7 Dc 66.14N 17.30 E
Hornbach 12 Je 49.12N 7.22 E
Horn-Bad Meinberg 12 Kc 51.54N 8.57 E
Hornby Bay 42 Fc 66.35N 117.50W
Horncastle 9 Mh 53.13N 0.07W
Horndal 8 Gd 60.18N 16.25 E
Horndean 12 Bd 50.55N 0.59W
Hörnefors 7 Ee 63.38N 19.54 E
Hornell 44 Id 42.19N 77.39W
Hornepayne 42 Jg 49.13N 84.47W
Hornindalsvatn 8 Bc 61.55N 6.25 E
Hornisgrinde 10 Eh 48.36N 8.12 E
Horn Islands (EN) = Horne, Iles de- 57 Jf 14.19S 178.05W
Hörnli 14 Cc 47.23N 8.56 E
Hornomoravský úval 10 Ng 49.25N 17.20 E
Hornos, Cabo de- = Horn, Cape- (EN) 52 Jk 55.59S 67.16W
Hornoy-le-Bourg 12 De 49.51N 1.54 E
Horn Plateau 42 Fd 62.10N 119.30W
Hornsea 9 Mh 53.55N 0.10W
Hornslandet 8 Gc 61.40N 17.30 E
Horns Rev 8 Bi 55.30N 8.00 E
Horns Rev 8 Bi 55.30N 7.45 E
Hornsund 41 Nc 76.58N 15.28 E
Hornsundtind 41 Nc 76.55N 16.10 E
Horog 22 Jf 37.31N 71.33 E
Horokanai 29a Ca 44.02N 142.09 E
Horol 16 He 49.29N 33.49 E
Horol 28 Lb 44.30N 132.03 E
Horol 16 He 49.47N 33.16 E
Horonobe 28 Pb 45.00N 141.51 E
Hořovice 10 Jg 49.50N 13.54 E
Horqin Youyi Qianqi (Ulan Hot) 22 Oe 46.04N 122.00 E
Horqin Youyi Zhongqi (Bayan Huxu) 27 Lb 45.04N 121.27 E
Horqin Zuoyi Houqi (Ganjig) 27 Lc 42.57N 122.14 E
Horqin Zuoyi Zhongqi (Baokang) 27 Lc 44.06N 123.19 E
Horqueta 56 Ib 23.24S 56.53W
Horred 8 Eg 57.21N 12.28 E
Horse Creek [Co.-U.S.] 45 Eg 38.05N 103.19W
Horse Creek [U.S.] 46 Nf 41.57N 103.58W
Horsehead Lake 45 Gc 47.02N 99.47W
Horsens 7 Bi 55.52N 9.52 E
Horsham [Austl.] 58 Fh 36.43S 142.13 E
Horsham [Eng.-U.K.] 9 Mj 51.04N 0.21W
Hørsholm 8 Ei 55.53N 12.30 E
Horšovský Týn 10 Ig 49.32N 12.57 E
Horst 12 Gd 50.56N 4.47 E
Horst 12 Ic 51.28N 6.03 E
Hörstel 12 Jb 52.19N 7.35 E
Horstmar 12 Jb 52.05N 7.19 E
Horsunlu 15 Ll 37.55N 28.36 E
Horta 32 Bb 38.32N 28.28W
Horta [3] 32 Bb 38.35N 28.40W
Horten 8 De 59.25N 10.30 E
Horton 42 Ec 70.01N 126.42W
Hörvik 8 Fh 56.03N 14.46 E
Ḥorvot 'Avedat 24 Fg 30.48N 34.46 E
Ḥorvot Meẕada 24 Fg 31.19N 35.21 E
Horwood Lake 44 Fa 48.03N 82.20W
Hosaina 35 Fd 7.33N 37.52 E
Hose Mountains 26 Ff 2.00N 114.10 E
Hosenofu 33 De 23.34N 21.15 E
Hoseynābād [Iran] 24 Ne 34.30N 50.59 E
Hoseynābād [Iran] 24 Le 35.33N 47.08 E
Hoseynīyeh 24 Mg 32.42N 48.14 E
Hoshāb 25 Cc 26.01N 63.56 E
Hosingen 12 Id 50.01N 6.05 E
Hoskins 60 Ei 5.30S 150.32 E
Hospet 25 Fe 15.16N 76.24 E
Hospital, Cuchilla del- 55 Ej 31.40S 54.53W
Hospitalet 13 Oc 41.22N 2.08 E
Hospitalet del Infante/ L'Hospitalet de l'Infant 13 Md 40.59N 0.56 E
Hoste, Isla- 52 Jk 55.15S 69.00W
Hot 25 Je 18.06N 98.35 E
Hotagen 7 De 63.53N 14.29 E
Hotaka 29 Ec 36.20N 137.53 E
Hotan 22 Jf 37.07N 79.55 E
Hotan He 21 Ke 40.30N 80.48 E
Hotazel 37 Ce 27.15S 23.00 E
Hotin 16 Ee 48.29N 26.29 E
Hoting 7 Dd 64.07N 16.10 E
Hotont 27 Hb 47.23N 102.30 E
Hot Springs 43 Gc 43.26N 103.29W
Hot Springs → Truth or Consequences 43 Fe 33.08N 107.15W
Hot Springs National Park 39 Jf 34.30N 93.03W
Hot Springs Peak 46 Gf 41.22N 117.26W
Hotspur Seamount (EN) 54 Kg 18.00S 36.00W
Hottah Lake 42 Fc 65.05N 118.36W
Hottentot Bay 37 Ae 26.07S 14.57 E
Hotton 12 Hd 50.16N 5.27 E
Hottstedt 10 He 51.39N 11.30 E
Houaïlou 61 Cd 21.17S 165.38 E
Houat, Ile de- 11 Dg 47.24N 2.58W
Houdan 11 Hf 48.47N 1.36 E
Houeillès 11 Gj 44.12N 0.02 E
Houffalize 12 Hd 50.08N 5.47 E
Houghton 43 Jb 47.06N 88.34W
Houillères, Canal des- 12 If 48.42N 6.55 E
Houji → Liangshan 28 Dg 35.48N 116.07 E
Houlgate 12 Be 49.18N 0.04W
Houlton 43 Nb 46.08N 67.51W
Houma [China] 27 Jd 35.36N 111.23 E
Houma [La.-U.S.] 43 If 29.36N 90.43W
Houndé 34 Ec 11.30N 3.31W
Hourtin, Étang d'- 11 Ei 45.10N 1.06W
House Range 46 Ig 39.30N 113.15W
Houston [Mo.-U.S.] 45 Kh 37.22N 91.58W
Houston [Tx.-U.S.] 39 Jg 29.46N 95.22W
Houthalen-Helchteren 12 Hc 51.02N 5.22 E
Houthulst 12 Ed 50.59N 2.57 E
Houthulst-Merkem 12 Ed 50.57N 2.51 E
Houtman Abrolhos 59 Ce 28.40S 113.50 E
Houtskär/Houtskari 8 Id 60.15N 21.20 E
Houtskari/Houtskär 8 Id 60.15N 21.20 E
Houyet 12 Hd 50.11N 5.01 E
Houyet-Celles 12 Hd 50.19N 5.01 E
Hov 8 Di 55.55N 10.16 E
Hova 8 Ff 58.52N 14.13 E
Hovden 8 Ac 61.40N 4.50 E
Hovden 8 Be 59.32N 7.21 E
Hove 9 Mk 50.49N 0.10W
Hovgaard 41 Kc 80.00N 18.45W
Hovmantorp 8 Fh 56.47N 15.08 E
Hovu-Aksy 20 Ef 51.01N 93.43 E
Howa 35 Db 17.30N 27.08 E
Howar 30 Jg 17.30N 27.08 E
Howard 45 Hd 44.01N 97.32W
Howe, Cape- 57 Fh 37.31S 149.59 E
Howell 44 Fd 42.36N 83.55W
Howick [N.Z.] 62 Fb 36.54S 174.56 E
Howick [S.Afr.] 37 Ee 29.28S 30.14 E
Howland 44 Mc 45.14N 68.40W
Howland Island 57 Jd 0.48N 176.38W
Howrah → Hāora 22 Kg 22.35N 88.20 E
Howth 9 Gh 53.23N 6.04W
Ḥowẓ Solṭān 24 Ne 35.06N 51.06 E
Hoxie 45 Fg 39.21N 100.26W
Höxter 10 Fe 51.46N 9.23 E
Hoxud 27 Ec 42.16N 86.51 E
Hoy 9 Jc 58.52N 3.18W
Hoya 12 Lb 52.48N 9.09 E
Høyanger 7 Bf 61.13N 6.05 E
Hoyerswerda/Wojerecy 10 Ke 51.26N 14.15 E
Hoyos 13 Fd 40.10N 6.43W
Hōyo-Shotō 29 Ce 33.50N 132.30 E
Hoytiäinen 7 Ge 62.48N 29.39 E
Hozat 24 Hc 39.07N 39.14 E
Hpunhpu 25 Jc 26.42N 97.17 E
Hradec Králové 10 Lf 50.13N 15.50 E
Hradiště 10 Jf 50.13N 13.08 E
Hrami 16 Ni 41.20N 45.07 E
Hrastnik 14 Jd 46.09N 15.06 E
Hřebeny 10 Kg 49.50N 14.10 E
Hristinovka 16 Fe 48.53N 29.56 E
Hroma 20 Jb 71.30N 144.49 E
Hromtau 19 Fe 50.18N 58.35 E
Hron 10 Oi 47.49N 18.45 E
Hrubieszów 10 Tf 50.49N 23.55 E
Hrubý Jeseník 10 Nf 50.05N 17.10 E
Hrustalny 20 Ih 44.24N 135.06 E
Hrvatska = Croatia (EN) 14 Jf 45.00N 15.30 E
Hrvatska = Croatia (EN) 14 Je 45.00N 15.30 E
Hrvatska = Croatia (EN) 5 Hf 45.00N 15.30 E
Hrvot Shivta 24 Fg 30.53N 34.38 E
Hsin-chiang-wei-wu-erh Tzu-chih-ch'ü → Xinjiang Uygur Zizhiqu = Sinkiang (EN) [2] 27 Ec 42.00N 86.00 E
Hsinchu 27 Lg 24.48N 120.58 E
Hsinying 27 Lg 23.25N 120.20 E
Hsipaw 25 Jd 22.37N 97.18 E
Hsi-tsang Tzu-chih-ch'ü → Xizang Zizhiqu [2] 27 Ee 32.00N 90.00 E
Hsuphāng 25 Jd 20.18N 98.42 E
Huab 37 Ad 20.49S 13.24 E
Huabei Pingyuan 21 Nf 37.00N 117.00 E
Huachacalla 54 Eg 18.45S 68.17W
Huachinera 48 Eb 30.15N 108.50W
Huacho 54 Cf 11.07S 77.37W
Huaco 56 Gd 30.09S 68.31W
Huacrachuco 54 Ce 8.39S 77.05W
Huade 27 Jc 41.50N 114.00 E
Huadian 27 Mc 42.59N 126.38 E
Hua Hin 25 Jf 12.34N 99.58 E
Huahine, Iles- 57 Lf 16.45S 151.00W
Huahine Iti 65e Eb 16.45S 151.00W
Huahine Nui 65e Eb 16.43S 151.00W
Huahuapán 48 Ge 24.31N 105.57W
Huai'an 28 Eh 33.30N 119.08 E
Huai'an (Chaigoubu) 28 Cd 40.40N 114.25 E
Huaibei 27 Ke 33.56N 116.48 E
Huaibin (Wulongji) 28 Ci 32.27N 115.23 E
Huaide (Gongzhuling) 27 Lc 43.30N 124.52 E
Huaidian → Shenqiu 27 Ke 33.27N 115.05 E
Huai He 21 Nf 33.12N 118.33 E
Huaiji 27 Jg 23.57N 112.12 E
Huailai (Shacheng) 27 Kc 40.29N 115.30 E
Huainan 22 Nf 32.32N 116.59 E
Huaining (Shipai) 28 Di 30.25N 116.39 E
Huairen 27 Jd 39.50N 113.07 E
Huairou 28 Dd 40.20N 116.37 E
Huaiyang 28 Ch 33.44N 114.52 E
Huaiyin (Wangying) 28 Eh 33.35N 119.02 E
Huaiyuan 28 Dh 32.58N 117.10 E
Huajuapan de León 47 Ee 17.48N 97.46W
Hualalai 65a Fd 19.41N 155.52W
Hualapai Mountains 46 Ii 34.40N 113.45W
Hualien 27 Lg 23.58N 121.36 E
Huallaga, Rio- 52 If 5.07S 75.30W
Huallanca 54 Ce 8.49S 77.52W
Huamachuco 54 Ce 7.48S 78.04W
Humahuaca 56 Gb 23.13S 65.23W
Huambo [3] 36 Ce 12.30S 15.40 E
Huambo 31 Ij 12.47S 15.43 E
Huanan 27 Nb 46.14N 130.33 E
Huancabamba [Peru] 54 Cf 10.21S 75.32W
Huancabamba [Peru] 54 Ce 5.14S 79.28W
Huancané 54 Eg 15.12S 69.46W
Huancapi 54 Df 13.41S 74.04W
Huancavelica [2] 54 Df 13.00S 75.00W
Huancavelica 53 Ig 12.46S 75.02W
Huancayo 53 Ig 12.04S 75.14W
Huanchaca, Serranía- 55 Bb 14.30S 60.39W
Huang'an → Hong'an 28 Ci 31.17N 114.37 E
Huangcaoba → Xingyi 27 Hf 25.03N 104.55 E
Huangchuan 27 Ke 32.00N 115.02 E
Huanggang 28 Ci 30.27N 114.53 E
Huanggangliang 27 Kc 43.33N 117.32 E
Huanggang Shan 27 Kf 27.50N 117.47 E
Huanggi Hai 28 Bd 40.51N 113.17 E
Huang Hai = Yellow Sea (EN) 21 Of 36.00N 124.00 E
Huang He = Yellow River (EN) 21 Nf 37.32N 118.19 E
Huanghe Kou 28 Ef 37.54N 118.48 E
Huangheyan → Madoi 22 Ll 35.00N 98.56 E
Huanghua 28 De 38.23N 117.21 E
Huanghuashi 28 Bj 28.14N 113.11 E
Huangliu 27 Ih 18.41N 108.46 E
Huangmao Jian 27 Kf 27.55N 119.11 E
Huangmei 28 Ci 30.05N 115.56 E
Huangnihe 28 Ic 43.33N 127.28 E
Huangpi 28 Ci 30.53N 114.22 E
Huangpu 27 Jg 23.05N 113.25 E
Huang Shan 27 Ke 30.10N 118.10 E
Huangshi 22 Nf 30.12N 115.00 E
Huang Shui 27 Hd 36.05N 103.20 E
Huangtu Gaoyuan 21 Mf 37.00N 108.00 E
Huanguelén 55 Bm 37.02S 61.57W
Huangxian 27 Ld 37.32N 120.30 E
Huangyan 27 Lf 28.39N 121.17 E
Huangyuan 27 Hd 36.40N 101.12 E
Huangzhai → Yangqu 28 Be 38.05N 112.37 E
Huangzhong 27 Hd 36.30N 101.30 E
Huanren 27 Mc 41.16N 125.22 E
Huan Shui 28 Ci 30.40N 114.21 E
Huanta 54 Df 12.56S 74.15W
Huantai (Suozhen) 28 Ef 36.57N 118.05 E
Huánuco [2] 54 Ce 9.30S 75.50W
Huánuco 53 If 9.55S 76.14W
Huanxian 27 Id 36.36N 107.06 E
Huaráz 53 If 9.32S 77.32W
Huarmey 54 Cf 10.04S 78.10W
Huarong 28 Bj 29.31N 112.33 E
Huascarán, Nevado- 52 If 9.07S 77.37W
Hua Shan 27 Je 34.27N 110.05 E
Huatabampo 47 Cc 26.50N 109.38W
Huatong 28 Fd 40.03N 121.56 E
Huatusco de Chiquellar 48 Kh 19.09N 96.57W
Huauchinango 48 Jg 20.11N 98.03W
Huautla de Jiménez 48 Kh 18.08N 96.51W
Huaxian (Daokou) 28 Cg 35.33N 114.30 E
Huayllay 54 Cf 11.01S 76.21W
Huaynamota, Rio- 48 Gg 21.51N 104.42W
Huaytara 54 Cf 13.36S 75.22W
Hubbard Creek Lake 45 Gj 32.45N 99.00W
Hubbard Lake 44 Fc 44.49N 83.34W
Hubei Sheng (Hu-pei Sheng) = Hupeh (EN) 27 Je 31.00N 112.00 E
Hubli-Dhārwār 22 Jh 15.21N 75.10 E
Hubsugul Nur (Chövsgöl nuur) 21 Md 51.00N 100.30 E
Hückelhoven 12 Ic 51.03N 6.13 E
Hückeswagen 12 Jc 51.09N 7.21 E
Hucknall 9 Lh 53.02N 1.11W
Hucqueliers 12 Dd 55.03N 1.54 E
Huczwa 10 Tf 50.49N 23.59 E
Hudat 16 Pi 41.34N 48.43 E
Hudat [Eth.] 35 Fe 4.45N 39.27 E
Huddersfield 9 Lh 53.39N 1.47W
Huddinge 8 Ge 59.14N 17.59 E
Huddun 35 Hd 9.08N 47.32 E
Huddur Hadama 35 Ge 4.07N 43.55 E

Index Symbols

[1] Independent Nation
[2] State, Region
[3] District, County
[4] Municipality
[5] Colony, Dependency
Continent
Physical Region
Historical or Cultural Region
Mount, Mountain
Volcano
Hill
Mountains, Mountain Range
Hills, Escarpment
Plateau, Upland
Pass, Gap
Plain, Lowland
Delta
Salt Flat
Valley, Canyon
Crater, Cave
Karst Features
Depression
Polder
Desert, Dunes
Forest, Woods
Heath, Steppe
Oasis
Cape, Point
Coast, Beach
Cliff
Peninsula
Isthmus
Sandbank
Island
Atoll
Rock, Reef
Islands, Archipelago
Rocks, Reefs
Coral Reef
Well, Spring
Geyser
River, Stream
Waterfall Rapids
River Mouth, Estuary
Lake
Salt Lake
Intermittent Lake
Reservoir
Swamp, Pond
Canal
Glacier
Ice Shelf, Pack Ice
Ocean
Sea
Gulf, Bay
Strait, Fjord
Lagoon
Bank
Seamount
Tablemount
Ridge
Shelf
Basin
Escarpment, Sea Scarp
Fracture
Trench, Abyss
National Park, Reserve
Point of Interest
Recreation Site
Cave, Cavern
Historic Site
Ruins
Wall, Walls
Church, Abbey
Temple
Scientific Station
Airport
Port
Lighthouse
Mine
Tunnel
Dam, Bridge

Name	Page	Grid	Lat.	Long.
Hude (Oldenburg)	12	Ka	53.07N	8.28 E
Huder	27	Lb	49.59N	121.30 E
Hudiksvall	6	Hc	61.44N	17.07 E
Hudson	38	Le	40.42N	74.02W
Hudson [Fl.-U.S.]	44	Fk	28.22N	82.42W
Hudson [N.Y.-U.S.]	44	Kd	42.15N	73.47W
Hudson, Lake-	45	Ih	36.20N	95.05W
Hudson Bay	42	Hf	52.52N	102.23W
Hudson Bay	38	Kd	60.00N	86.00W
Hudson Canyon (EN)	44	Kf	39.27N	72.12W
Hudson Hope	42	Fe	56.02N	121.55W
Hudson Land	41	Jd	73.45N	22.30W
Hudson Mountains	66	Pf	74.32S	99.20W
Hudson Strait	38	Lc	62.30N	72.00W
Hudžirt	27	Hb	47.05N	102.45 E
Hue	22	Mh	16.28N	107.36 E
Huebra	13	Fc	41.02N	6.48W
Huechucuicui, Punta-	56	Ff	41.47S	74.02W
Hueco Mountains	45	Dj	32.05N	105.55W
Huedin	15	Gc	46.52N	23.03 E
Huehuetenango [3]	49	Bf	15.40N	91.35W
Huehuetenango	47	Fe	15.20N	91.28W
Huejutla de Reyes	48	Jg	21.08N	98.25W
Huelgoat	11	Cf	48.22N	3.45W
Huelma	13	Ig	37.39N	3.27W
Huelva [3]	13	Fg	37.40N	7.00W
Huelva	6	Fh	37.16N	6.57W
Huelva, Ribera de-	13	Gg	37.27N	6.00W
Huércal Overa	13	Kg	37.23N	1.57W
Huerfano Mountain	45	Bh	36.30N	108.10W
Huertas, Cabo de-	13	Lf	38.21N	0.24W
Huerva	13	Lc	41.39N	0.52W
Huesca	13	Lb	42.08N	0.25W
Huesca [3]	13	Lb	42.10N	0.10W
Huéscar	13	Jg	37.49N	2.32W
Hueso, Sierra del-	48	Gb	30.15N	105.20W
Huesos, Arroyo de los-	55	Cm	36.30S	59.09W
Huetamo de Núñez	48	Ih	18.35N	100.53W
Huete	13	Jd	40.08N	2.41W
Ḫufrat an Naḥās	35	Cd	9.45N	24.19 E
Huftarøy	8	Ad	60.05N	5.15 E
Hugh Butler Lake	45	Ff	40.22N	100.42W
Hughenden	58	Fg	20.51S	144.12 E
Hughes	40	Ic	66.03N	154.16W
Hughes Range	46	Hb	49.55N	115.28W
Hugo	45	Ii	34.01N	95.31W
Huguan	28	Bf	36.05N	113.12 E
Huhur He	28	Fc	43.55N	120.47 E
Hui'an	27	Kf	25.07N	118.47 E
Huiarau Range	62	Gc	38.35S	177.10 E
Huib-Hochpiato	37	Be	27.10S	16.50 E
Huichang	27	Kf	25.33N	115.45 E
Huicheng → Shexian	28	Ej	29.53N	118.27 E
Huicholes, Sierra de los-	48	Gf	22.00N	104.00W
Huich'ŏn	27	Mc	40.10N	126.17 E
Huifa He	28	Ic	43.06N	126.53 E
Hui He [China]	27	Kb	48.51N	119.12 E
Hui He [China]	28	Be	39.21N	112.37 E
Huiji He	28	Ch	33.53N	115.37 E
Huila [2]	54	Cc	2.30N	75.45W
Huila [3]	36	Ce	15.00S	15.00 E
Huila, Nevado del-	52	Ie	3.00N	76.00W
Huilai	27	Kg	23.05N	116.18 E
Huili	27	Hf	26.37N	102.19 E
Huimanguillo	48	Mi	17.51N	93.23W
Huimin	27	Kd	37.29N	117.30 E
Huinan (Chaoyang)	28	Ic	42.41N	126.03 E
Huisne	11	Gg	47.59N	0.11 E
Huissen	12	Hc	51.56N	5.55 E
Huiten Nur	27	Fd	35.30N	91.55 E
Huittinen	8	Jc	61.11N	22.42 E
Huivuilay, Isla de-	48	Dd	27.03N	110.01W
Huixian [China]	28	Bg	35.27N	113.47 E
Huixian [China]	27	Ie	33.46N	106.06 E
Huixtla	47	Fe	15.09N	92.28W
Huize	27	Hf	26.28N	103.18 E
Huizen	12	Hb	52.18N	5.16 E
Huizhou	27	Jg	23.02N	114.28 E
Hukou	28	Dj	29.44N	116.14 E
Hu Kou	27	Jd	36.09N	110.20 E
Hŭksan-Chedo	27	Me	34.30N	125.20 E
Hukuntsi	37	Cd	23.59S	21.44 E
Hulan	27	Mb	46.03N	126.36 E
Hulan He	27	Mb	45.54N	126.42 E
Ḥulayfā'	23	Fd	26.00N	40.47 E
Hulett	46	Md	44.41N	104.36W
Hulga	17	Jd	64.15N	60.58 E
Hulin	27	Nb	45.52N	132.58 E
Hulin He	28	Hb	45.19N	124.06 E
Hull	42	Jg	45.26N	75.43W
Hull → Kingston-upon-Hull	6	Fe	53.45N	0.20W
Hull → Orona Atoll	57	Je	4.29S	172.10W
Hull Bay	66	Nf	74.55S	137.40W
Hull Glacier	66	Nf	75.05S	137.15W
Hull Mountain	46	Dg	39.31N	122.59W
Hüls, Krefeld-	12	Ic	51.22N	6.31 E
Hultsfred	7	Dh	57.29N	15.50 E
Huludao	27	Lc	40.44N	120.59 E
Hulun Nur	21	Ne	49.00N	117.30 E
Ḥulwān = Helwân (EN)	33	Fd	29.51N	31.20 E
Hulwät, Qūr al-	24	Hh	28.49N	38.50 E
Huma [China]	27	Ma	51.44N	126.36 E
Huma [Ton.]	65b	Bc	21.19S	174.56W
Humacao	49	Od	18.09N	65.50W
Huma He	27	Ma	51.42N	126.42 E
Humaitá [Braz.]	53	Jf	7.31S	63.02W
Humaitá [Par.]	56	Ic	27.03S	58.33W
Humansdorp	37	Cf	34.02S	24.46 E
Humbe	36	Bf	16.42S	14.54 E
Humber	5	Fe	53.40N	0.10W
Humberside [3]	9	Mh	53.55N	0.30W
Humboldt River	38	He	40.02N	118.31W
Humboldt	61	Cd	21.53S	166.25 E
Humboldt [Ia.-U.S.]	45	Ie	42.43N	94.13W
Humboldt [Nb.-U.S.]	45	If	40.10N	95.57W
Humboldt [Sask.-Can.]	42	Gf	52.12N	105.07W
Humboldt [Tn.-U.S.]	44	Ch	35.49N	88.55W
Humboldt Gletscher	41	Fc	79.40N	63.45W
Humboldt Range	46	Ff	40.15N	118.10W
Hume, Lake-	59	Jg	36.05S	147.05 E
Humenné	10	Rh	48.56N	21.55 E
Hummelfjell	8	Db	62.27N	11.17 E
Hümmling, Der-	10	Dd	52.52N	7.31 E
Humphreys Peak	38	Hf	35.20N	111.40W
Humppila	7	Ff	60.56N	23.22 E
Humuya, Río-	49	Df	15.13N	87.57W
Hūn	31	If	29.07N	15.56 E
Húnaflói	5	Db	65.50N	20.50W
Hunan Sheng (Hu-nan Sheng) [3]	27	Jf	28.00N	112.00 E
Hu-nan Sheng → Hunan Sheng [3]	27	Jf	28.00N	112.00 E
Hunchun	28	Kc	42.52N	130.21 E
Hundested	8	Di	55.58N	11.52 E
Hunedoara [2]	15	Fd	45.45N	22.52 E
Hünfeld	10	Ff	50.40N	9.46 E
Hünfelden	12	Kd	50.19N	8.11 E
Hunga Ha'apai	65b	Ab	20.33S	175.24W
Hungary (EN) = Magyarország [1]	6	Hf	47.00N	20.00 E
Hunga Tonga	65b	Ab	20.32S	175.23W
Hungen	12	Kd	50.28N	8.54 E
Hŭngnam	27	Md	39.50N	127.38 E
Hungry Horse Reservoir	46	Ib	48.15N	113.50W
Hun He [China]	28	Be	39.47N	113.15 E
Hun He [China]	28	Gd	40.41N	122.12 E
Hunhedoara	15	Fd	45.45N	22.54 E
Hunish, Rubha-	9	Gd	57.43N	6.20W
Hun Jiang	28	Hd	40.52N	125.42 E
Hunjiang	27	Mc	41.55N	126.27 E
Hunneberg	8	Ef	58.20N	12.27 E
Hunnebostrand	8	Df	58.27N	11.18 E
Hunsrück	10	Cg	49.50N	6.40 E
Hunstanton	9	Ni	52.57N	0.30 E
Hunte	10	Ed	52.30N	8.19 E
Hunter, Ile-	57	Ig	22.24S	172.03 E
Hunter Island	59	Ih	40.30S	144.45 E
Hunter Ridge (EN)	57	Ig	21.30S	174.30 E
Hunter River	59	Kf	32.30S	151.42 E
Hunterville	62	Fc	39.56S	175.34 E
Huntingdon	9	Mi	52.30N	0.10W
Huntingdon [Eng.-U.K.]	9	Mi	52.20N	0.12W
Huntingdon [Pa.-U.S.]	44	He	40.31N	78.02W
Huntingdon [Que.-Can.]	44	Jc	45.05N	74.08W
Huntington [In.-U.S.]	44	Ee	40.53N	85.30W
Huntington [W.V.-U.S.]	43	Kd	38.24N	82.26W
Huntly [N.Z.]	62	Fb	37.33S	175.10 E
Huntly [Scot.-U.K.]	9	Kd	57.27N	2.47W
Huntsville [Al.-U.S.]	39	Kf	34.44N	86.35W
Huntsville [Ont.-Can.]	42	Jg	45.20N	79.13W
Huntsville [Tx.-U.S.]	43	He	30.43N	95.33W
Hunucmá	48	Og	21.01N	89.52W
Hünxe	12	Ic	51.39N	6.47 E
Hunyani	37	Ec	15.37S	30.39 E
Hunyuan	27	Jd	39.38N	113.44 E
Hunza → Baltit	25	Ea	36.20N	74.40 E
Hunze	11	Ma	53.13N	6.40 E
Huocheng (Shuiding)	27	Dc	44.03N	80.49 E
Huojia	28	Bg	35.16N	113.39 E
Huolongmen	27	Mb	49.49N	125.49 E
Huolu	28	Ce	38.05N	114.18 E
Huon, Ile-	57	Hf	18.01S	162.57 E
Huon Gulf	59	Ja	7.10S	147.25 E
Huon Peninsula	60	Di	6.25S	147.30 E
Huonville	59	Jh	43.01S	147.02 E
Huoqin	28	Dh	32.21N	116.17 E
Huoshan	27	Ke	31.19N	116.20 E
Huo Shan [China]	27	Jd	37.00N	111.52 E
Huo Shan [China]	27	Ke	31.06N	116.12 E
Huoxian	27	Jd	36.39N	111.47 E
Hupeh (EN) = Hubei Sheng (Hu-pei Sheng) [2]	27	Je	31.00N	112.00 E
Hu-pei Sheng → Hubei Sheng → Hopeh (EN) [2]	27	Je	31.00N	112.00 E
Hūr	24	Qg	30.50N	57.07 E
Hurama → Hongyuan	27	He	32.45N	102.38 E
Hurānd	24	Lc	38.40N	47.20 E
Hurd, Cape-	44	Gc	45.13N	81.44W
Hurdalssjøen	8	Dd	60.20N	11.05 E
Hurd Deep = La Grande Trench (EN)	9	Kl	49.40N	3.00W
Hurdiyo	35	Ic	10.32N	51.08 E
Hurepoix	11	If	48.30N	2.10 E
Hure Qi	28	Fc	42.44N	121.44 E
Hurkett	45	Lb	48.50N	88.29W
Hurmuli	20	If	51.01N	136.56 E
Huroizumi	29a	Cb	42.01N	143.07 E
Huron	43	Hc	44.22N	98.13W
Huron, Lake-	38	Ke	44.30N	82.15W
Huron Mountains	44	Db	46.45N	87.45W
Hurricane	46	Ih	37.11N	113.17W
Hurricane Cliffs	46	Ih	37.00N	113.05W
Hurrungane	8	Bc	61.27N	7.51 E
Hursley	12	Ac	51.01N	1.24W
Hurst	45	Hj	32.49N	97.09W
Hurstpierpoint	12	Bd	50.55N	0.10W
Hürth	10	Cf	50.52N	6.52 E
Hurum	8	De	59.35N	10.35 E
Hurunui	62	Ee	42.54S	173.18 E
Hurup	8	Ch	56.45N	8.25 E
Huş	15	Lc	46.41N	28.04 E
Húsavik	7a	Ca	66.03N	17.21W
Hushan → Cixi	28	Fi	30.10N	121.14 E
Huskvarna	8	Fg	57.48N	14.16 E
Huslia	40	Hc	65.42N	156.25W
Husnes	8	Ae	59.52N	5.46 E
Husnesfjorden	8	Ae	59.50N	5.35 E
Hussigny-Godbrange	12	He	49.29N	5.52 E
Hust	16	Ce	48.10N	23.27 E
Hustadvika	8	Ba	63.00N	7.05 E
Husum [Ger.]	10	Fb	54.28N	9.03 E
Husum [Swe.]	7	Ee	63.20N	19.10 E
Hutag	27	Hb	49.23N	102.43 E
Hutchinson [Ks.-U.S.]	43	Hd	38.05N	97.56W
Hutchinson [Mn.-U.S.]	45	Id	44.54N	94.22W
Hutch Mountain	46	Ji	34.47N	111.22W
Hūth	33	Hf	16.14N	43.58 E
Hutou	27	Nb	46.00N	133.36 E
Hutte Sauvage, Lac de la-	42	Ke	55.57N	65.45W
Hutton, Mount-	59	Je	25.51S	148.20 E
Hutubi	27	Ec	44.07N	86.57 E
Hutuiti, Caleta-	65d	Bb	27.07S	109.17W
Hutuo He	28	De	38.14N	116.05 E
Huvhojtun, Gora-	20	Le	57.44N	160.45 E
Huxley, Mount-	62	Cf	44.04S	169.41 E
Huy	10	Ge	51.55N	10.55 E
Huy/Hoei	11	Ld	50.31N	5.14 E
Huzhou → Wuxing	27	Le	30.47N	120.07 E
Hvaler	8	De	59.05N	11.00 E
Hvalynsk	19	Ee	52.30N	48.07 E
Hvammstangi	7a	Bb	65.24N	20.57W
Hvannadalshnúkur	5	Ec	64.01N	16.41W
Hvar	14	Kg	43.07N	16.45 E
Hvar	14	Kg	43.11N	16.27 E
Hvarski kanal	14	Kg	43.15N	16.37 E
Hvatovka	16	Oc	52.21N	46.36 E
Hveragerdi	7a	Bb	64.00N	21.12W
Hveravellir	7a	Bb	64.54N	19.35W
Hvide Sande	8	Ci	55.59N	8.08 E
Hvitá [Ice.]	7a	Bb	64.35N	21.46W
Hvitá [Ice.]	7a	Bb	64.00N	20.58W
Hvittingfoss	8	De	59.29N	10.01 E
Hvojnaja	7	Ig	58.56N	34.31 E
Hwach'on-ni	28	Ie	38.58N	126.02 E
Hwang-Hae = Yellow Sea (EN)	21	Of	36.00N	124.00 E
Hwanghae-Namdo [2]	28	He	38.15N	125.30 E
Hwanghae-Pukto [2]	28	Ie	38.30N	126.25 E
Hwangju	28	He	38.40N	125.45 E
Hyannis [Ma.-U.S.]	44	Le	41.39N	70.17W
Hyannis [Nb.-U.S.]	45	Ff	42.00N	101.44W
Hybo	8	Gc	61.48N	16.12 E
Hyde Park	50	Gi	6.30N	58.16W
Hyderābād [India]	22	Jh	17.23N	78.28 E
Hyderābād [Pak.]	22	Ig	25.22N	68.22 E
Hyères	11	Mk	43.07N	6.07 E
Hyères, Iles d'-	11	Ml	43.00N	6.20 E
Hyesan	27	Mc	41.24N	128.10 E
Hyltebruk	7	Ch	57.00N	13.14 E
Hyndman Peak	46	He	43.50N	114.10W
Hyōgo Ken [2]	28	Mg	34.50N	134.48 E
Hyrov	10	Sg	49.32N	22.48 E
Hyrulä	8	Kd	60.24N	25.02 E
Hyrum	46	Jf	41.38N	111.51W
Hyrynsalmi	7	Gd	64.40N	28.32 E
Hysham	46	Lc	46.18N	107.14W
Hythe [Eng.-U.K.]	12	Ad	50.52N	1.24W
Hythe [Eng.-U.K.]	9	Oj	51.05N	1.05 E
Hyūga	28	Kh	32.25N	131.38 E
Hyūga-Nada	29	Be	32.25N	131.45 E
Hyvinge/Hyvinkää	7	Ff	60.38N	24.52 E
Hyvinkää/Hyvinge	7	Ff	60.38N	24.52 E
I				
Iaco, Rio-	54	Ee	9.03S	68.35W
Iacobeni	15	Ib	47.26N	25.19 E
Iakora	37	Hd	23.08S	46.38 E
Ialomiţa [2]	15	Ke	44.30N	27.30 E
Ialomiţa	15	Kd	44.42N	27.51 E
Ialomiţei, Balta-	15	Ke	44.30N	28.00 E
Iapó, Rio-	55	Gg	24.30S	50.24W
Iaşi	6	If	47.10N	27.36 E
Iaşi [2]	15	Kb	47.07N	27.39 E
Iba	26	Gc	15.20N	119.58 E
Ibadan	31	Hh	7.23N	3.54 E
Ibagué	53	Ie	4.27N	75.14W
Ibaiti	56	Jb	23.50S	50.10W
Iballja	15	Cg	42.11N	20.00 E
Ibans, Laguna de-	49	Ef	15.53N	84.52W
Ibar	15	Df	43.44N	20.45 E
Ibara	29	Cd	34.36N	133.28 E
Ibaraki	29	Dd	34.49N	135.34 E
Ibaraki Ken [2]	28	Pf	36.25N	140.30 E
Ibaré	55	Ej	30.49S	54.16W
Ibarra	53	Ie	0.21N	78.07W
Ibarreta	56	Ic	25.13S	59.51W
Ibb	22	Gh	13.58N	44.12 E
Ibba	35	De	4.48N	29.06 E
Ibba	35	Dd	7.09N	28.41 E
Ibbenbüren	10	Dd	52.16N	7.44 E
Ibdekkene	34	Fb	18.28N	0.38 E
Ibembo	36	Db	2.38N	23.37 E
Ibenga	36	Cb	2.20N	18.08 E
Iberá, Esteros del-	55	Di	28.05S	57.05W
Iberá, Laguna-	55	Di	28.30S	57.09W
Iberian Basin (EN)	3	De	40.00N	16.00W
Iberian Mountains (EN) = Sistema Ibérico	5	Fg	41.30N	2.30W
Iberian Peninsula (EN) = Peninsula Ibérica	5	Fg	40.00N	4.00W
Iberville, Lac d'-	42	Ke	56.00N	73.10W
Ibestad	7	Db	68.48N	17.08 E
Ibi [Nig.]	34	Gd	8.11N	9.45 E
Ibi [Sp.]	13	Lf	38.38N	0.34W
Ibiá	54	Ig	19.29S	46.32W
Ibiagui	55	Ja	13.03S	44.12W
Ibiai	55	Jc	16.51S	44.55W
Ibibobo	54	Fh	21.35S	62.58W
Ibicaraí	54	Kf	14.51S	39.36W
Ibicuí, Rio-	52	Kh	29.25S	56.47W
Ibicuí da Armada, Rio-	55	Ej	30.16S	54.54W
Ibicuy	55	Ck	33.44S	59.10W
Ibicuy, Rio-	55	Ck	33.48S	59.10W
Ibigawa	29	Ed	35.29N	136.34 E
Ibipetuba	54	Jf	11.00S	44.32W
Ibiraiaras	55	Gi	28.22S	51.39W
Ibirama	55	Hh	27.04S	49.31W
Ibirapuitã, Rio-	55	Ei	29.22S	55.57W
Ibirocai, Arroio-	55	Di	29.26S	56.43W
Ibiruba	55	Fi	28.38S	53.06W
Ibitinga	55	He	21.45S	48.49W
Ibitinga, Represa-	55	He	21.41S	49.05W
Ibity	37	Hd	20.10S	46.58 E
Ibiza	13	Nf	38.54N	1.26 E
Ibiza/Eivissa = Iviza (EN)	5	Gh	39.00N	1.25 E
Iblei, Monti-	14	Im	37.10N	14.55 E
Ibn Hāni', Ra's-	24	Fe	35.35N	35.43 E
Ibn Qawrah	35	Ib	15.43N	50.32 E
Ibo	37	Gb	12.22S	40.36 E
Ibo-Gawa	29	Dd	34.46N	134.35 E
Iboundji, Mont-	36	Bc	1.08S	11.48 E
Ibrā'	23	Ie	22.38N	58.40 E
Ibrah	35	Dc	10.36N	25.20 E
Ibrāhīm, Jabal-	21	Gg	20.27N	41.09 E
Ibresi	7	Li	55.18N	47.05 E
'Ibrī	23	Ie	23.16N	56.32 E
Ibrīm	33	Fe	22.39N	32.05 E
Ibshawāy	24	Dh	29.22N	30.41 E
Ibuki-Sanchi	29	Ed	35.35N	136.25 E
Ibuki-Yama	29	Ed	35.25N	136.24 E
Ibusuki	28	Ki	31.16N	130.39 E
Iča	20	Ke	55.28N	155.58 E
Ica [2]	54	Cf	14.20S	75.30W
Ica	53	Ig	14.04S	75.42W
Iça, Rio-	52	Jf	3.07S	67.58W
Icaiché	48	Oh	18.05N	89.10W
Icamaquã, Rio-	55	Ei	28.34S	56.00W
Icana, Rio-	54	Ec	0.26N	67.19W
Icara	55	Hi	28.42S	49.18W
Icaraima	55	Ff	23.23S	53.41W
İçel	23	Db	36.48N	34.38 E
Iceland (EN) = Island	5	Eb	65.00N	18.00W
Iceland Basin (EN)	3	Dc	60.00N	20.00W
Ichalkaranji	25	Ee	16.42N	74.28 E
Ichibusa-Yama	29	Be	32.19N	131.06 E
Ichihara	28	Pg	35.31N	140.05 E
Ichi-Kawa	29	Dd	34.46N	134.43 E
Ichikawa	29	Fd	35.44N	139.55 E
Ichinohe	28	Pd	40.13N	141.17 E
Ichinomiya	28	Ng	35.18N	136.48 E
Ichinoseki	28	Pe	38.55N	141.08 E
Ich'ŏn [N. Kor.]	28	Ie	38.29N	126.53 E
Ich'ŏn [S. Kor.]	28	If	37.17N	127.27 E
Ichtegem	12	Fc	51.06N	3.00 E
Ičigemski Hrebet	20	Ld	63.30N	164.00 E
Ičinskaja Sopka, Vulkan-	21	Rd	55.39N	157.40 E
Ičnja	19	De	50.52N	32.25 E
Icó	54	Ke	6.24S	38.51W
Icy Cape	40	Gb	70.20N	161.52W
Idaarderadeel	12	Ha	53.06N	5.50 E
Idaarderadeel-Grow	12	Ha	53.06N	5.50 E
Idabel	45	Ij	33.54N	94.50W
Idah	34	Gd	7.06N	6.44 E
Idaho [2]	43	Ec	45.00N	115.00W
Idaho Falls	39	He	43.30N	112.02W
Idalia	45	Eg	39.43N	102.14W
Idān	35	Hd	6.03N	49.01 E
Idanha-a-Nova	13	Ee	39.55N	7.14W
Idar-Oberstein	10	Dg	49.42N	7.18 E
Idarwald	12	Je	49.50N	7.13 E
Idel	7	Id	64.08N	34.12 E
Ideles	32	Ie	23.49N	5.55 E
Ider	27	Hb	49.16N	100.41 E
Idfū	33	Fe	24.58N	32.52 E
Idhi Óros	5	Ih	35.15N	24.45 E
Idhra	15	Gl	37.20N	23.30 E
Idhra	15	Gl	37.21N	23.28 E
Idhras, Kólpos-	15	Gl	37.22N	23.22 E
Idice	14	Ff	44.35N	11.49 E
İdil	24	Id	37.21N	41.54 E
Idíni	32	Df	17.58N	15.40W
Idiofa	36	Cc	4.59S	19.36 E
Idjil, Kédia d'-	32	Ee	22.38N	12.33W
Idkerberget	8	Fd	60.23N	15.14 E
Idle	9	Mh	53.27N	0.48W
Idlib	23	Eb	35.55N	36.38 E
Idokogo	36	Ab	0.35N	9.19 E
Idolo, Isla del-	48	Kg	21.25N	97.27W
Idre	8	Ec	61.52N	12.43 E
Idrica	8	Mh	56.18N	28.55 E
Idrija	14	Id	46.00N	14.02 E
Idro, Lago d'-	14	Ee	45.47N	10.30 E
Idstein	10	Ef	50.14N	8.16 E
Idževan	16	Ni	40.52N	45.04 E
Iecava	8	Jh	56.40N	23.40 E
Iecava	8	Kh	56.33N	24.11 E
Iepê	55	Gf	22.40S	51.05W
Ieper/Ypres	11	Id	50.51N	2.53 E
Ierápetra	15	In	35.01N	25.45 E
Ierisós	15	Gi	40.24N	23.53 E
Ierisoú, Kólpos-	15	Gi	40.26N	23.55 E
Iernut	15	Hc	46.27N	24.15 E
Ie-Shima	29b	Ab	26.43N	127.47 E
Ieshima-Shotō	29	Dd	34.40N	134.30 E
Iesolo	14	Ge	45.32N	12.38 E
Iezerul, Vîrful-	15	Hd	45.28N	24.57 E
Ifakara	36	Gd	8.08S	36.41 E
Ifaki	34	Gd	7.48N	5.14 E
'Ifāl, Wādī al-	24	Fh	28.07N	35.02 E
Ifalik Atoll	57	Fd	7.15N	144.27 E
Ifanadiana	37	Hd	21.17S	47.35 E
Ife	34	Fd	7.28N	4.34 E
Iferouâne	31	Hg	19.04N	8.24 E
Ifetesene	32	Hd	25.30N	4.33 E
Ifni	32	Ed	29.15N	10.08W
Ifon	34	Gd	6.58N	5.55 E
Iforas, Adrar des-	30	Hg	19.00N	2.00 E
Iga	29	Ed	34.49N	136.12 E
Igal	10	Nj	46.32N	17.57 E
Iganga	36	Fb	0.37N	33.29 E
Igara Paraná, Rio-	54	Dd	2.09N	71.47W
Igarapava	55	Ie	20.03S	47.47W
Igarapé-Açu	54	Id	1.07S	47.37W
Igarapé-Miri	54	Id	1.59S	48.58W
Igarka	22	Kc	67.28N	86.35 E
Igatimí	56	Ib	24.05S	55.30W
Igawa	36	Fd	8.46S	34.23 E
Igbetti	34	Fd	8.45N	4.08 E
Iğdır	24	Kc	39.56N	44.02 E
Iggesund	7	Df	61.38N	17.04 E
Iglesias	14	Ck	39.19N	8.32 E
Iglesiente	14	Ck	39.20N	8.40 E
Igli	32	Gc	30.27N	2.18W
Iglim al Janūbīyah = Southern Region (EN) [2]	35	Dd	6.00N	30.00 E
Iglino	17	Hi	54.50N	56.28 E
Igloolik	39	Kc	69.24N	81.49W
Ignace	42	Ig	49.26N	91.41W
Ignalina	7	Gi	55.22N	26.13 E
Ignatovo	7	If	60.49N	37.48 E
İğneada	24	Bb	41.50N	27.58 E
İğneada Burun	15	Lh	41.54N	28.03 E
Igombe	36	Fc	4.25S	31.58 E
Igoumenitsa	15	Dj	39.30N	20.16 E
Igra	19	Fd	57.33N	53.10 E
Igreja, Morro de-	55	Hi	28.08S	49.30W
Igren	16	Ie	48.29N	35.13 E
Igrim	19	Gc	63.12N	64.29 E
Iguaçu, Rio-	52	Kh	25.36S	54.36W
Igualada	13	Nc	41.35N	1.38 E
Iguala de la Independencia	47	Ee	18.21N	99.32W
Iguana, Sierra de la-	48	Id	26.30N	100.15W
Iguape	55	Ig	24.43S	47.33W
Iguariaça, Serra do-	55	Ei	29.03S	55.15W
Iguassu Falls (EN) = Iguazú, Cataratas del-	52	Kh	25.41S	54.26W
Iguatemi	54	If	14.35S	49.02W
Iguatemi, Rio-	55	Ef	23.55S	54.10W
Iguatu	53	Mf	6.22S	39.18W
Iguazú, Cataratas del- = Iguassu Falls (EN)	52	Kh	25.41S	54.26W
Iguéla	36	Ac	1.55S	9.19 E
Iguidi, 'Erg-	30	Gf	27.00N	6.00W
Ihavandiffulu Atoll	25a	Ba	7.00N	72.55 E
Iheya-Jima	29b	Ab	27.03N	127.57 E
Ih-Hajrhan	27	Ib	46.56N	105.56 E
Ihiala	34	Gd	5.51N	6.51 E
Ihirene	32	He	20.28N	4.37 E
Ihnāsiyat al Madīnah	24	Dh	29.05N	30.56 E
Ih-Obo-Ula	27	Gc	44.55N	95.20 E
Ihosy	31	Lk	22.25S	46.07 E
Ihotry, Lac-	37	Gd	21.56S	43.41 E
Ihrhove, Westoverledingen-	12	Ja	53.10N	7.27 E
Ihsaniye	24	Dc	36.55N	34.46 E
Ihtiman	15	Gg	42.26N	23.49 E
Ih-Ula	27	Hb	49.27N	101.27 E
Ii	7	Fd	65.19N	25.27 E
Iida	28	Ng	35.31N	137.50 E
Iide-San	29	Fc	37.52N	139.41 E
Iijoki	7	Fd	65.20N	25.17 E
Iisaku/Isaku	8	Le	59.14N	27.41 E
Iisalmi	7	Ge	63.34N	27.11 E
Iisvesi	8	Lb	62.45N	26.50 E
Iittala	8	Kc	61.04N	24.10 E
Iivaara	7	Gd	65.47N	29.40 E
Iiyama	29	Fc	36.52N	138.20 E
Iizuka	29	Be	33.38N	130.41 E
Ija	20	Fe	55.02N	101.00 E
Ijebu Ode	34	Fd	6.49N	3.56 E
IJmuiden, Velsen-	12	Gb	52.28N	4.35 E
Ijoubbâne, 'Erg-	34	Da	22.30N	6.00W
IJssel	11	Lb	52.30N	6.00 E
IJsselmeer	11	Lb	52.45N	5.25 E
IJsselmuiden	12	Hb	52.34N	5.56 E
IJsselstein	12	Hb	52.01N	5.02 E
Ijuí	56	Jc	28.23S	53.55W
Ijuí, Rio-	55	Eh	27.58S	55.20W
Ijūin	29	Bf	31.37N	130.24 E
Ijuizinho, Rio-	55	Ei	28.20S	54.28W
Ijuw	64e	Bb	0.31S	166.57 E
IJzendijke	12	Fc	51.20N	3.37 E
IJzer	11	Ic	51.09N	2.43 E
Ik	5	Ld	55.55N	52.36 E
Ikaalinen	7	Ff	61.46N	23.03 E
Ikalamavony	37	Hd	21.10S	46.32 E
Ikamatua	62	De	42.17S	171.42 E
Ikaria	15	Jl	37.35N	26.10 E
Ikarion Pélagos	15	Jl	37.30N	26.35 E
Ikast	8	Ch	56.08N	9.10 E
Ikatski Hrebet	20	Gf	54.00N	111.15 E
Ikawa	29	Fd	35.13N	138.14 E
Ikeda [Jap.]	29	Cd	34.01N	133.48 E
Ikeda [Jap.]	27	Pc	42.55N	143.27 E
Ikeda-Ko	29	Bf	31.14N	130.34 E
Ikej	20	Ff	54.12N	100.04 E
Ikeja	34	Fd	6.36N	3.21 E
Ikela	31	Ji	1.11S	23.16 E
Ikelemba	36	Cb	0.07N	18.17 E
Ikerre	34	Gd	7.30N	5.14 E
Ikerssuaq	41	Ie	65.10N	39.45W
Iki	29	Ae	33.45N	129.45 E
Iki-Kàikyō	28	Jh	33.45N	129.50 E
Ikitsuki-Shima	29	Ae	33.25N	129.25 E
İkizdere	24	Ib	40.47N	40.33 E
Ikom	34	Gd	5.58N	8.42 E
Ikongo	36	Gd	9.04S	36.51 E
Ikopa	37	Hc	16.50S	46.50 E
Ikot Ekpene	34	Gd	5.10N	7.43 E
Ikuno	29	Dd	35.10N	134.48 E
Ikurangi, Mount-	64p	Bb	21.12S	159.45W
Ila	34	Fd	7.40N	4.40 E
Ilaferh	32	He	21.50N	1.20 E
Ilagan	22	Oh	17.10N	121.54 E
Ilām	25	Hc	26.54N	87.56 E
Ilam	23	Gc	33.38N	46.26 E
Ilām	23	Gc	33.00N	47.00 E
Ilan	27	Lg	24.45N	121.44 E
Ilanski	20	Ee	56.10N	96.03 E
Ilaro	34	Fd	6.53N	3.01 E
Iława	10	Pc	53.37N	19.33 E

Index Symbols

[1] Independent Nation
[2] State, Region
[3] District, County
[4] Municipality
[5] Colony, Dependency
Continent
Physical Region
Historical or Cultural Region
Mount, Mountain
Volcano
Hill
Mountains, Mountain Range
Hills, Escarpment
Plateau, Upland
Pass, Gap
Plain, Lowland
Delta
Salt Flat
Valley, Canyon
Crater, Cave
Karst Features
Depression
Polder
Desert, Dunes
Forest, Woods
Heath, Steppe
Oasis
Cape, Point
Coast, Beach
Cliff
Peninsula
Isthmus
Sandbank
Island
Atoll
Rock, Reef
Islands, Archipelago
Rocks, Reefs
Coral Reef
Well, Spring
Geyser
River, Stream
Waterfall Rapids
River Mouth, Estuary
Lake
Salt Lake
Intermittent Lake
Reservoir
Swamp, Pond
Canal
Glacier
Ice Shelf, Pack Ice
Ocean
Sea
Gulf, Bay
Strait, Fjord
Lagoon
Bank
Seamount
Tablemount
Ridge
Shelf
Basin
Escarpment, Sea Scarp
Fracture
Trench, Abyss
National Park, Reserve
Point of Interest
Recreation Site
Cave, Cavern
Historic Site
Ruins
Wall, Walls
Church, Abbey
Temple
Scientific Station
Airport
Port
Lighthouse
Mine
Tunnel
Dam, Bridge

Ilbengja 20 Hd 62.55N 124.10 E
Ile-à-la-Crosse 42 Ge 55.27N 107.53W
Ilebo 31 Ji 4.44S 20.33 E
Ile de France 11 Ie 49.00N 2.20 E
Ile de France 41 Kc 77.45N 27.45W
Ile de France, Côte de l'- 11 Jf 48.55N 3.50 E
Ilek 19 Fe 51.32N 53.27 E
Ilek 5 Le 51.30N 53.20 E
Ileksa 7 Ie 62.30N 36.57 E
Ilerh 32 He 21.40N 2.22 E
Ileša 7 Le 62.37N 46.35 E
Ilesha [Nig.] 34 Fd 8.55N 3.25 E
Ilesha [Nig.] 34 Fd 7.37N 4.44 E
Ilet 7 Li 55.57N 48.14 E
Ilfov [2] 15 Je 44.30N 26.20 E
Ilfracombe 9 Ij 51.13N 4.08W
Ilgaz 24 Eb 40.56N 33.38 E
Ilgaz Dağlari 24 Eb 41.00N 33.35 E
Ilgın 24 Dc 38.17N 31.55 E
Ilha Grande 54 Ed 0.27S 65.02W
Ilha Grande, Baía da- 55 Jf 23.09S 44.30W
Ilhas Desertas 32 Dc 32.30N 16.30W
Ilhavo 13 Dd 40.36N 8.40W
Ilhéus 53 Mg 14.49S 39.02W
Ili 21 Je 45.24N 74.08 E
Ilia 15 Fd 45.56N 22.39 E
Iliamna 40 Ie 59.45N 154.54W
Iliamna Lake 40 He 59.30N 155.00W
Iliç 24 Hc 39.28N 38.34 E
Ilič 18 Gd 40.55N 68.29 E
Ilica 15 Kj 39.52N 27.46 E
Iličevsk 16 Nj 39.33N 44.59 E
Iličevsk 19 Df 46.18N 30.37 E
Ilidža 14 Mg 43.50N 18.19 E
Iligan 22 Oi 8.14N 124.14 E
Iligan Bay 26 He 8.25N 124.05 E
Ilim 20 Fe 56.50N 103.25 E
Ilimskoje Vodohranilišče 20 Fe 57.20N 102.30 E
Ilinski 7 Hf 61.02N 32.42 E
Ilinski 20 Jg 47.59N 142.21 E
Ilinski 17 Gg 58.35N 55.41 E
Ilion 44 Jd 43.01N 75.04W
Ilio Point 65a Db 21.13N 157.16W
Ilir 20 Fe 55.13N 100.45 E
Ilirska Bistrica 14 Ie 45.34N 14.16 E
Iljaly 18 Bd 41.53N 59.40 E
Ilkal 25 Fe 15.58N 76.08 E
Ilkeston 12 Ab 52.58N 1.18W
Ill 11 Nf 48.40N 7.53 E
Illampu, Nevado del- 54 Eg 15.50S 68.34W
Illana Bay 26 He 7.25N 123.45 E
Illapel 56 Fd 31.38S 71.10W
Illbillee, Mount- 59 Ge 27.02S 132.30 E
Ille 11 Ef 48.08N 1.40W
Ille-et-Vilaine [3] 11 Ef 48.10N 1.30W
Illéla 34 Gc 14.28N 5.15 E
Iller 10 Fh 48.23N 9.58 E
Illescas 13 Id 40.07N 3.50W
Ille-sur-Têt 11 Il 42.40N 2.37 E
Illi, Ba- 35 Bc 10.44N 16.21 E
Illimani, Nevado del- 52 Jg 16.39S 67.48W
Illingen 12 Je 49.22N 7.03 E
Illinois 38 Jf 38.58N 90.27W
Illinois [2] 43 Jd 40.00N 89.00W
Illinois Peak 46 Hc 47.02N 115.04W
Illizi 31 Hf 26.29N 8.28 E
Ilm 10 He 51.07N 11.40 E
Ilmajoki 8 Jb 62.44N 22.34 E
Ilmen, Ozero- 5 Jd 58.20N 31.20 E
Ilmenau 10 Gf 50.41N 10.54 E
Ilmenau 10 Gc 53.23N 10.10 E
Il Montello 14 Ge 45.49N 12.07 E
Ilo 54 Dg 17.38S 71.20W
Iloilo 22 Oh 10.42N 122.34 E
Ilok 14 Ne 45.13N 19.23 E
Ilomantsi 7 He 62.40N 30.55 E
Ilorin 31 Hh 8.30N 4.33 E
Iloron, Cerro- 48 Gg 20.57N 104.22W
Ilova 14 Ke 45.25N 16.45 E
Ilovik 14 If 44.27N 14.33 E
Ilovlja 16 Ne 49.18N 44.01 E
Ilovlja 16 Me 49.14N 43.54 E
Ilpyrski 20 Le 59.52N 164.12 E
Ilski 16 Kg 44.51N 38.32 E
Iltin 20 Nc 67.52N 178.48W
Ilubabor [3] 35 Ed 7.50N 35.00 E
Ilūkste/Ilukste 8 Li 55.58N 26.26 E
Ilukste/Ilūkste 8 Li 55.58N 26.26 E
Ilulissat/Jakobshavn 67 Nc 69.20N 50.50W
Ilwaki 26 Ih 7.56S 126.26 E
Ilyč 17 He 62.32N 56.40 E
Ilz 10 Jh 48.35N 13.30 E
Iłżanka 10 Re 51.14N 21.47 E
Imabari 28 Lg 34.03N 133.00 E
Imagane 28 Pc 42.26N 140.01 E
Imaichi 28 Of 36.43N 139.41 E
Imán, Sierra del- 55 Eh 27.42S 55.28W
Imanburluk 17 Mj 53.40N 67.15 E
Imandra, Ozero- 5 Jb 67.30N 33.00 E
Imano-Yama 29 Ce 32.51N 132.49 E
Imari 28 Jh 33.16N 129.53 E
Imarui 55 Hi 28.21S 48.49W
Imataca, Serranía de- 50 Fi 7.45N 61.00W
Imatra 7 Gf 61.10N 28.46 E
Imazu 29 Ed 35.24N 136.01 E
Imbabah, Al Qāhirah- 33 Fc 30.05N 31.13 E
Imba-Numa 29 Gd 35.45N 140.14 E
Imbert 49 Ld 19.45N 70.50W
Imbituba 56 Kc 28.14S 48.40W
Imeni 26 Bakinskih Komissarov 19 Eh 39.19N 49.12 E
Imeni 26 Bakinskih Komissarov 19 Fh 39.21N 54.12 E
Imeni Gastello 20 Jd 61.35N 147.59 E
Imeni Karla Liebknechta 16 Id 51.38N 35.29 E
Imeni Mariny Raskovoj 20 Jd 62.05N 146.30 E
Imeni Poliny Osipenko 20 If 52.23N 136.25 E
Imi 31 Lh 6.28N 42.11 E
Imilili 32 De 22.50N 15.54W
Imi n'Tanout 32 Fc 31.03N 8.08W
Imišli 19 Eh 39.53N 48.03 E
Imjin-gang 28 If 37.47N 126.40 E
Imlay 46 Ff 40.42N 118.07W
Immenstadt im Allgäu 10 Gi 47.34N 10.13 E
Imo [2] 34 Gd 5.30N 7.20 E
Imola 14 Ff 44.21N 11.42 E
Imotski 14 Lg 43.27N 17.13 E
Imperatriz 53 Lf 5.32S 47.29W
Imperia 14 Cg 43.53N 8.03 E
Imperial 45 Ff 40.31N 101.39W
Imperial de Aragón, Canal- 13 Kb 42.02N 1.33W
Imperial Valley 46 Hj 32.50N 115.30W
Impfondo 31 Ih 1.37N 18.04 E
Imphāl 22 Lg 24.49N 93.57 E
Imphy 11 Jh 46.56N 3.15 E
Impilanti 7 Hf 61.41N 31.12 E
Imrali Adasi 15 Li 40.32N 28.32 E
Imst 14 Ec 47.14N 10.44 E
Imtan 24 Gf 32.24N 36.49 E
Imuris 48 Db 30.47N 110.52W
Im-Zouren 13 Ii 35.04N 3.50W
Ina 28 Ng 35.50N 137.57 E
Ina 10 Kc 53.32N 14.38 E
I-n-Abanrherit 34 Gb 17.58N 6.05 E
Inabu 29 Ed 35.13N 137.30 E
Inaccessible Islands 66 Re 60.34S 46.44W
Inaccessible Island 30 Fi 37.17S 12.45W
I-n-Afaleleh 32 Ie 23.34N 9.12 E
I Naftan, Puntan- 64b Ba 15.05N 145.45 E
Ina-Gawa 29 Fc 37.23N 139.18 E
I-n-Amenas 31 Hf 28.03N 9.33 E
Inami 29 De 33.48N 135.12 E
Inanba-Jima 29 Fe 33.39N 139.18 E
Inangahua Junction 62 Dd 41.52S 171.56 E
Inanwatan 26 Jg 2.08S 132.10 E
Iñapari 54 Ef 10.57S 69.35W
Inarajan 64c Bb 13.16N 144.45 E
I-n-Arhâta 34 Ea 21.09N 0.18W
Inari 6 Ib 68.54N 27.01 E
Inari, Lake- (EN)= Inarijärvi 5 Ib 69.00N 28.00 E
Inarijärvi=Inari, Lake- (EN) 5 Ib 69.00N 28.00 E
Inawashiro 29 Gc 37.34N 140.05 E
Inawashiro-Ko 28 Pf 37.30N 140.03 E
I-n-Azaoua 34 Ga 20.47N 7.31 E
I-n-Azaoua 34 Ga 20.54N 7.28 E
Inazawa 29 Ed 35.15N 136.47 E
Inca 13 Oe 39.43N 2.54 E
Inca de Oro 56 Gc 26.45S 69.54W
Incaguasi 56 Fc 29.13S 71.03W
Ince Burun 15 Ki 40.28N 27.16 E
İnce Burun 23 Da 42.07N 34.56 E
İncekum Burun 24 Ed 36.13N 33.58 E
Inceler 15 Ml 37.42N 29.35 E
I-n-Chaouâg 34 Fb 16.23N 0.10 E
Inchcape (Bell Rock) 9 Ke 56.26N 2.24W
Inchiri [3] 32 Df 20.00N 15.00W
Inch'ŏn 22 Of 37.28N 126.38 E
Incirliova 15 Kl 37.50N 27.43 E
Incudine 11a Bb 41.51N 9.12 E
Indaiá, Rio- 55 Jd 18.27S 45.22W
Indaia Grande, Ribeirão- 55 Fd 19.31S 52.29W
Indaiatuba 55 If 23.05S 47.14W
Indal 8 Gb 62.34N 17.06 E
Indalsälven 7 De 62.31N 17.27 E
Inda Selase 35 Fc 14.06N 38.17 E
Indawgyi 25 Jc 25.08N 96.20 E
Indefatigable Banks 9 Ph 53.35N 2.20 E
Independence [Ca.-U.S.] 46 Fh 36.48N 118.12W
Independence [Ia.-U.S.] 45 Ke 42.28N 91.54W
Independence [Ks.-U.S.] 43 Hd 37.13N 95.42W
Independence [Mo.-U.S.] 45 Ig 39.05N 94.04W
Independence [Va.-U.S.] 44 Gg 36.38N 81.11W
Independence Fjord 67 Me 82.00N 30.25W
Independence Mountains 46 Gf 41.15N 116.05W
Independência [Braz.] 54 Je 5.23S 40.19W
Independência [Braz.] 55 Fa 13.34S 53.57W
Independenta 15 Kd 45.29N 27.45 E
Inder → Jalaid Qi 27 Lb 46.41N 122.52 E
Inder, Ozero- 16 Qe 48.25N 51.55 E
Inderborski 6 Lf 48.32N 51.47 E
India (EN) 21 Jh 20.00N 77.00 E
India (EN)=Bhārat Juktarashtra [1] 22 Jh 20.00N 77.00 E
India Muerta, Arroyo de la- 55 Fk 33.40S 54.04W
Indiana [2] 43 Jc 40.00N 86.15W
Indiana 44 He 40.39N 79.11W
Indianapolis 39 Kf 39.46N 86.09W
Indian Church 49 Ce 17.45N 88.40W
Indian Creek Point 51d Bb 17.00N 61.43W
Indian Harbour 42 Lf 54.27N 57.13W
Indian Head 42 Hf 50.32N 103.40W
Indian Ocean 3 Gl 21.00S 82.00 E
Indian Ocean (EN)=Hindi, Badwēynta- 3 Gl 21.00S 82.00 E
Indian Ocean (EN)=Indico, Oceano- 3 Gl 21.00S 82.00 E
Indian Ocean (EN)=Indien, Océan- 3 Gl 21.00S 82.00 E
Indian Ocean (EN)=Indiese Oseaan- 3 Gl 21.00S 82.00 E
Indian Ocean (EN)= Indonesia, Samudera- 3 Gl 21.00S 82.00 E
Indianola 45 Kj 33.27N 90.39W
Indianópolis 55 Id 19.02S 47.55W
Indian Peak 46 Ig 38.16N 113.53W
Indian Rock 46 Ec 46.01N 120.49W
Indian Springs 43 Dd 36.34N 115.40W
Indiantown 44 Gl 27.01N 80.28W
Indian Town Point 51d Bb 17.06N 61.40W
Indiapora 55 Gd 19.57S 50.17W
Indias Occidentales=West Indies (EN) 47 Je 19.00N 70.00W
Indico, Oceano-=Indian Ocean (EN) 3 Gl 21.00S 82.00 E
Indiese, Oseaan-=Indian Ocean (EN) 3 Gl 21.00S 82.00 E
Indiga 19 Eb 67.41N 49.00 E
Indigirka 21 Qb 70.48N 148.54 E
Indigskaja Guba 17 Dc 67.45N 48.20 E
Inđija 15 Dd 45.03N 20.05 E
Indio 43 De 33.43N 116.13W
Indio, Rio- 49 Fh 10.57N 83.44W
Indio Rico 55 Bn 38.19S 60.53W
Indispensable Reefs 57 Hf 12.40S 160.25 E
Indispensable Strait 63a Ec 9.00S 160.30 E
Indochina (EN) 21 Mh 16.00N 107.00 E
Indonesia [1] 22 Nj 5.00S 120.00 E
Indonesia, Samudera-=Indian Ocean (EN) 3 Gl 21.00S 82.00 E
Indore 22 Jg 22.43N 75.50 E
Indra 8 Li 55.53N 27.40 E
Indragiri 26 Dg 0.22S 103.26 E
Indramayu 26 Eh 6.20S 108.19 E
Indrāvati 25 Ge 18.44N 80.16 E
Indre 11 Gg 47.14N 0.11 E
Indre [3] 11 Hh 46.50N 1.40 E
Indre Arna 8 Ad 60.26N 5.30 E
Indre-et-Loire [3] 11 Gg 47.15N 0.45 E
Indus 21 Ig 24.20N 67.47 E
İnebolu 23 Da 41.58N 33.46 E
Inece 15 Kh 41.41N 27.04 E
Inecik 15 Ki 40.56N 27.16 E
İnegöl 23 Ca 40.05N 29.31 E
Inés Indart 55 Bl 34.24S 60.33W
Ineu 15 Ec 46.26N 21.51 E
Ineu, Vîrful- 15 Hb 47.32N 24.53 E
Inezgane 32 Fc 30.21N 9.32W
I-n-Ezzane 32 Je 23.29N 11.15 E
Inferior, Laguna- 48 Li 16.15N 94.45W
Infiernillo, Presa del- 47 De 18.35N 101.45W
Infiesto 13 Ga 43.21N 5.22W
Infreschi, Punta degli- 14 Jk 39.59N 15.25 E
Ingá 54 Ke 7.17S 35.36W
Inga 36 Bd 5.39S 13.39 E
Ingå/Inkoo 7 Ff 60.03N 24.01 E
Ingabu 25 Je 17.49N 95.16 E
Ingai, Rio- 55 Je 21.10S 44.52W
I-n-Gall 34 Gb 16.47N 6.56 E
Ingarö 8 He 59.15N 18.30 E
Ingavi 55 Bb 15.02S 60.29W
Ingelheim am Rhein 12 Ke 49.59N 8.02 E
Ingelmunster 12 Fd 50.55N 3.15 E
Ingelstad 8 Fh 56.45N 14.55 E
Ingende 36 Cc 0.15S 18.57 E
Ingeniero Guillermo N. Juarez 56 Hb 23.54S 61.51W
Ingeniero Jacobacci 56 Gf 41.18S 69.35W
Ingeniero Luiggi 56 He 35.25S 64.29W
Ingenio Santa Ana 56 Gc 27.28S 65.41W
Ingermanland (EN) 5 Id 59.00N 30.00 E
Ingham 58 Ff 18.39S 146.10 E
Ingička 18 Ee 39.47N 65.58 E
Inglefield Bredning 41 Fc 77.40N 65.00W
Inglefield Land 41 Fc 78.44N 68.20W
Inglewood [Austl.] 59 Ke 28.25S 151.05 E
Inglewood [Ca.-U.S.] 46 Fj 33.58N 118.21W
Inglewood [N.Z.] 62 Fc 39.09S 174.12 E
Ingolf Fjord 41 Kb 80.35N 17.35W
Ingólfshöfdi 7a Cc 63.48N 16.39W
Ingolstadt 10 Hh 48.46N 11.26 E
Ingrāj Bāzār 25 Hc 25.00N 88.09 E
I-n-Guezzâm 31 Hg 19.32N 5.42 E
Ingul 16 Gf 47.02N 31.59 E
Ingulec 16 Hf 46.41N 32.48 E
Ingulec 16 Df 47.43N 33.10 E
Inguri 16 Lh 42.24N 41.32 E
Ingušskaja respublika 19 Eg 43.15N 45.30 E
Inhaca, Ilha da- 30 Kk 26.02S 32.58 E
Inhambane 31 Kk 23.52S 35.23 E
Inhambane [3] 37 Ed 23.00S 34.30 E
Inhambane, Baía de- 37 Fd 23.50S 35.20 E
Inhaminga 37 Fc 18.25S 35.01 E
Inhanduí-Guaçu, Rio- 55 Fe 21.37S 52.59W
Inhanduizinho, Rio- 55 Fe 21.34S 53.36W
Inharrime 37 Fd 24.28S 35.01 E
Inhassoro 37 Fd 21.32S 35.12 E
Inhaúma 55 Ja 13.01S 44.39W
I-n-Hihaou 32 He 23.00N 2.00 E
Inhobi, Rio- 55 Ef 23.45S 54.40W
Inhumas 54 Ig 16.22S 49.30W
Iniö 8 Id 60.25N 21.25 E
Inírida, Rio- 52 Je 3.55N 67.52W
Inis/Ennis 9 Ei 52.50N 8.59W
Inis Airc/Inishark 9 Ch 53.37N 10.16W
Inis Bó Finne/Inishbofin 9 Ch 53.38N 10.12W
Inis Ceithleann/Enniskillen 9 Fg 54.21N 7.38W
Inis Córthaidh/Enniscorthy 9 Gi 52.30N 6.34W
Inis Díomáin/Ennistymon 9 Di 52.57N 9.13W
Inis Eoghain/Inishowen Peninsula 9 Ff 55.15N 7.20W
Inishark/Inis Airc 9 Ch 53.37N 10.16W
Inishbofin/Inis Bó Finne 9 Ch 53.38N 10.12W
Inisheer/Inis Oírr 9 Dh 53.03N 9.31W
Inishkea 9 Cg 54.08N 10.11W
Inishmaan/Inis Meáin 9 Dh 53.05N 9.35W
Inishmore/Árainn 9 Dh 53.07N 9.45W
Inishmurray/Inis Muirigh 9 Eg 54.26N 8.40W
Inishowen Peninsula/Inis Eoghain 9 Ff 55.15N 7.20W
Inishtranull 9 Ff 55.27N 7.14W
Inishturk/Inis Toirc 9 Ch 53.43N 10.05W
Inis Meáin/Inishmaan 9 Dh 53.05N 9.35W
Inis Muirigh/Inishmurray 9 Eg 54.26N 8.40W
Inis Oírr/Inisheer 9 Dh 53.03N 9.31W
Inis Toirc/Inishturk 9 Ch 53.43N 10.05W
Inja 20 Je 59.22N 144.50 E
Inja 20 Je 59.30N 144.48 E
Inja 20 Df 50.27N 86.42 E
Injeŭp 28 Je 38.04N 128.10 E
Injibara 35 Fc 10.55N 36.58 E
Injune 59 Je 25.51S 148.34 E
I-n-Kâk 34 Fb 16.20N 0.17 E
Inkisi 36 Bc 4.46S 14.52 E
Inkoo/Ingå 7 Ff 60.03N 24.01 E
Inland Kaikoura Range 62 Ee 42.00S 173.35 E
Inland Sea (EN)= Setonaikai 21 Pf 34.10N 133.00 E
Inn 5 Hf 48.35N 13.28 E
Innamincka 59 Ie 27.45S 140.44 E
Inner Hebrides 9 Ge 57.00N 6.45W
Inner Mongolia (EN)=Nei Monggol Zizhiqu (Nei-meng-ku Tzu-chih-ch'ü) [2] 27 Jc 44.00N 112.00 E
Inner Silver Pit 9 Nh 53.30N 0.40 E
Inner Sound 9 Hd 57.30N 5.55W
Innerste 10 Fd 52.15N 9.50 E
Innisfail [Alta.-Can.] 46 Ia 52.02N 113.57W
Innisfail [Austl.] 59 Jc 17.32S 146.02 E
Innokentjevka 20 Ig 49.42N 136.55 E
Innokentjevski 20 Jg 48.38N 140.12 E
Innoko 40 Hd 62.14N 159.45W
Innsbruck 6 Hf 47.16N 11.24 E
Innuksuac 42 Je 58.27N 78.08W
Innviertel 14 Hb 48.15N 13.15 E
Innvikfjorden 8 Bc 61.50N 6.35 E
Inny/An Eithne 9 Fh 53.35N 7.50W
Ino 29 Ce 33.33N 133.26 E
Inobonto 26 Hf 0.52N 123.57 E
Inongo 31 Ii 1.57S 18.16 E
Inoni 36 Cc 3.04S 15.39 E
Inönü 15 Nj 39.48N 30.09 E
I-n-Ouagar 34 Gb 16.12N 6.54 E
I-n-Ouzzal 32 He 21.34N 1.59 E
Inowrocław 10 Od 52.48N 18.15 E
I-n-Salah 31 Hf 27.13N 2.28 E
Insar 7 Ki 54.42N 45.18 E
Insar 7 Kj 53.52N 44.23 E
Inscription, Cape- 57 Cg 25.30S 112.59 E
Insjön 8 Fd 60.41N 15.05 E
Ińsko 10 Lc 53.27N 15.33 E
Instruč 8 Ij 54.39N 21.48 E
Insurăţei 15 Ke 44.55N 27.36 E
Inta 6 Mb 66.05N 60.08 E
I-n-Tabezas 34 Fb 17.54N 1.50 E
I-n-Tallak 34 Fb 16.19N 3.15 E
Intepe 15 Ji 40.00N 26.20 E
Interlaken 14 Bd 46.41N 7.52 E
International Falls 43 Ib 48.36N 93.25W
Interview 25 If 12.55N 92.43 E
Inthanon, Doi- 25 Je 18.35N 98.29 E
Intibucá [3] 49 Cf 14.20N 88.15W
Intiyaco 56 Hc 28.39S 60.05W
Intorsura Buzaului 15 Jd 45.41N 26.02 E
Intracoastal Waterway 45 Im 28.45N 95.40W
Inubō-Zaki 29 Gd 35.42N 140.52 E
Inukjuak 39 Ld 58.30N 78.15W
Inutil, Bahía- 56 Fh 52.45S 71.24W
Inuvik 39 Fc 68.25N 133.30W
Inuyama 29 Ed 35.23N 136.56 E
Inva 17 Gg 58.59N 55.40 E
Inveraray 9 He 56.13N 5.05W
Invercargill 58 Hi 46.25S 168.21 E
Inverell 59 Ke 29.47S 151.07 E
Inverness 6 Fd 57.27N 4.15W
Inverurie 9 Kd 57.17N 2.23W
Investigator Group 57 Eh 33.45S 134.30 E
Investigator Strait 59 Hg 35.25S 137.10 E
Inyangani 30 Kj 18.18S 32.51 E
Inyangani 37 Ec 18.13S 32.46 E
Inyati 37 Dc 19.40S 28.51 E
Inyazura 37 Ec 18.43S 32.10 E
Inyo Mountains 46 Gh 36.50N 117.45W
Inza 19 Ee 53.53N 46.28 E
Inzá 54 Cc 2.33N 76.04W
Inžavino 16 Mc 52.19N 42.31 E
Inzer 17 Hi 54.30N 56.28 E
Inzer 17 Hi 54.14N 57.34 E
Inzia 36 Cc 3.45S 17.57 E
Iō/Kazan-Rettō=Volcano Islands (EN) 21 Qg 25.00N 141.00 E
Ioánnina 6 Ih 39.40N 20.50 E
Ioanninon, Límni- 15 Dj 39.40N 20.53 E
Iokanga 7 Jb 68.03N 39.40 E
Iola 45 Ih 37.55N 95.24W
Iolotan 19 Gh 37.18N 62.21 E
Iona 9 Ge 56.19N 6.25W
Iona 36 Bf 16.52S 12.34 E
Ionava/Jonava 7 Fi 55.05N 24.17 E
Ion Corvin 15 Ke 44.07N 27.48 E
Ione 46 Eg 38.21N 120.56W
Ionia 44 Ed 42.59N 85.04W
Ionian Basin (EN) 5 Hh 36.00N 20.00 E
Ionian Islands (EN)=Iónioi Nísoi 5 Ih 38.30N 20.30 E
Ionian Sea (EN)=Ionio, Mar- 5 Hh 39.00N 19.00 E
Ionian Sea (EN)=Iónion Pélagos 5 Hh 39.00N 19.00 E
Ionio, Mar-=Ionian Sea (EN) 5 Hh 39.00N 19.00 E
Iónioi Nísoi [2] 15 Dk 38.40N 20.10 E
Iónioi Nísoi=Ionian Islands (EN) 5 Ih 38.30N 20.30 E
Iónion Pélagos=Ionian Sea (EN) 5 Hh 39.00N 19.00 E
Ioniškelis/Joniškėlis 8 Ki 56.00N 24.14 E
Ioniškis/Joniškis 7 Fh 56.16N 23.37 E
Iony, Ostrov- 20 Je 56.15N 143.20 E
Iori 16 Oi 41.03N 46.27 E
Ios 15 Im 36.44N 25.18 E
Ios 15 Im 36.42N 25.20 E
Iō-Shima 28 Ki 31.51N 130.13 E
Iowa [2] 43 Ic 42.15N 93.15W
Iowa City 43 Ic 41.40N 91.32W
Iowa Falls 45 Je 42.31N 93.16W
Iowa Park 45 Gj 33.57N 98.40W
Iowa River 45 Kf 41.10N 91.02W
Iō-Yama 29a Da 44.10N 145.10 E
Ipa 16 Fc 52.07N 29.12 E
Ipameri 54 Ig 17.43S 48.09W
Ipatovo 19 Ef 45.43N 42.53 E
Ipaumirim 54 Ke 6.47S 38.43W
Ipel' 10 Oi 47.49N 18.52 E
Ipiales 54 Cc 0.50N 77.37W
Ipiaú 54 Kf 14.08S 39.44W
Ipiranga 55 Gg 25.01S 50.35W
Ipiros [2] 15 Dj 39.30N 20.40 E
Ipiros=Epirus (EN) 15 Dj 39.30N 20.40 E
Ipiros=Epirus (EN) 5 Ih 39.30N 20.40 E
Ipixuma, Rio- 54 Fe 5.50S 63.00W
Ipixuna 54 De 7.34S 72.36W
Ipoh 22 Mi 4.35N 101.05 E
Ipoly 10 Oi 47.49N 18.52 E
Iporã 55 Ff 23.59S 53.37W
Iporá 54 Hg 16.28S 51.07W
Ippy 35 Cd 6.15N 21.12 E
Ipsala 24 Bb 40.55N 26.23 E
Ipsizonos Óros 15 Gi 40.28N 23.34 E
Ipswich [Austl.] 58 Gg 27.36S 152.46 E
Ipswich [Eng.-U.K.] 6 Ge 52.04N 1.10 E
Ipswich [S.D.-U.S.] 45 Gd 45.27N 99.02W
Ipu 54 Jd 4.20S 40.42W
Iqaluit 39 Mc 63.44N 68.28W
Iquique 53 Ih 20.13S 70.10W
Iquitos 53 If 3.50S 73.15W
Iraan 45 Fk 30.54N 101.54W
Ira Banda 35 Cd 5.57N 22.06 E
Irabu-Jima 27 Mg 24.50N 125.10 E
Iracoubo 54 Hb 5.29N 53.13W
Iraël 17 Gd 64.27N 55.08 E
Irago-Suidō 29 Ed 34.35N 136.55 E
Irago-Zaki 29 Ed 34.35N 137.01 E
Iráklia 15 Gh 41.10N 23.16 E
Iráklia 15 Im 36.50N 25.26 E
Iráklion 6 Ih 35.20N 25.08 E
Īrān=Iran (EN) [1] 22 Hf 32.00N 53.00 E
Iran (EN)=Īrān [1] 22 Hf 32.00N 53.00 E
Iran, Pegunungan-=Iran Mountains (EN) 21 Ni 2.05N 114.55 E
Iran, Plateau of- (EN) 21 Hf 32.00N 56.00 E
Irani, Serra do- 55 Fh 27.05S 52.12W
Iran Mountains (EN)=Iran, Pegunungan- 21 Ni 2.05N 114.55 E
Irānshahr 22 Ig 27.13N 60.41 E
Irapa 50 Eg 10.34N 62.35W
Irapuá, Arroio- 55 Fj 30.15S 53.10W
Irapuato 39 Ig 20.41N 101.28W
Iraq (EN)=Al 'Irāq [1] 22 Gf 33.00N 44.00 E
'Irāq al 'Arabi 24 Kg 31.50N 45.50 E
Irati 13 Kb 42.35N 1.16W
Irati 56 Jc 25.27S 50.39W
Irazú, Volcán- 38 Ki 9.59N 83.51W
Irbeni Väin 8 Ig 57.48N 22.05 E
Irbid 23 Ec 32.33N 35.51 E
Irbiktepe 15 Jh 41.00N 26.30 E
Irbit 17 Kh 57.42N 63.07 E
Irbit 19 Gd 57.41N 63.03 E
Irebu 36 Cc 0.37S 17.45 E
Irecê 54 Jf 11.18S 41.52W
Iregua 13 Jb 42.27N 2.24W
Ireland 5 Fe 53.00N 8.00W
Ireland/Éire [1] 6 Fe 53.00N 8.00W
Ireland Trough (EN) 5 Ed 55.00N 12.40W
Iren 17 Hh 57.25N 56.59 E
Ireng River 54 Gc 3.33N 59.51W
Irês Corações 54 Ih 21.42S 45.16W
Iretama 55 Fg 24.27S 52.02W
Irgiz 19 Gf 48.13N 62.08 E
Irgiz 19 Gf 48.36N 61.16 E
Irharhar [Alg.] 30 Hf 28.00N 6.15 E
Irharhar [Alg.] 32 Ie 21.01N 6.01 E
Irherm 32 Fc 30.04N 8.26W
Iri 28 Ig 35.56N 126.57 E
Iriba 31 Jg 15.07N 22.15 E
Irîgui 30 Gg 16.43N 5.30W
Iriklinski 16 Ud 51.39N 58.38 E
Iriklinskoje Vodohranilišče 16 Ud 51.45N 58.45 E
Iringa [3] 36 Gd 8.00S 35.30 E
Iringa 31 Ki 7.46S 35.42 E
Irinja, Gora- 20 Fe 58.20N 104.30 E
Iriomote Jima 27 Lg 24.20N 123.50 E
Iriona 49 Ef 15.57N 85.11W
Iriri, Rio- 52 Kf 3.52S 52.37W
Irish Sea 5 Fe 53.30N 5.20W
Irish Sea (EN)=Muir Eireann 5 Fe 53.30N 5.20W
Irituia 54 Id 1.46S 47.26W
Irkeštam 18 Ie 39.38N 73.55 E
Irkutsk 22 Md 52.16N 104.20 E
Irkutskaja Oblast [3] 20 Fe 56.00N 104.00 E
Irlir, Gora- 18 Dc 42.40N 63.30 E
Irminio 14 In 36.46N 14.36 E
Irnijärvi 7 Gd 65.36N 29.05 E
Iro, Lac- 35 Bc 10.06N 19.25 E
Iroise 11 Bf 48.15N 4.55W
Iron Gate (EN) = Portile de Fier 5 Ig 44.41N 22.31 E
Iron Knob 59 Hf 32.44S 137.08 E
Iron Mountain 43 Jb 45.49N 88.04W
Iron Mountains 9 Fg 54.15N 7.50W
Iron River [Mi.-U.S.] 43 Jb 46.05N 88.39W
Iron River [Wi.-U.S.] 45 Kc 46.34N 91.24W
Ironside Mountain 46 Fd 44.15N 118.08W
Ironton [Mo.-U.S.] 45 Kh 37.36N 90.38W
Ironton [Oh.-U.S.] 44 Ff 38.32N 82.40W
Ironwood 43 Ib 46.27N 90.10W
Iroquois Falls 42 Jg 48.46N 80.41W
Irō-Zaki 28 Og 34.35N 138.55 E

Index Symbols

[1] Independent Nation
[2] State, Region
[3] District, County
[4] Municipality
[5] Colony, Dependency
Continent
Physical Region
Historical or Cultural Region
Mount, Mountain
Volcano
Hill
Mountains, Mountain Range
Hills, Escarpment
Plateau, Upland
Pass, Gap
Plain, Lowland
Delta
Salt Flat
Valley, Canyon
Crater, Cave
Karst Features
Depression
Polder
Desert, Dunes
Forest, Woods
Heath, Steppe
Oasis
Cape, Point
Coast, Beach
Cliff
Peninsula
Isthmus
Sandbank
Island
Atoll
Rock, Reef
Islands, Archipelago
Rocks, Reefs
Coral Reef
Well, Spring
Geyser
River, Stream
Waterfall Rapids
River Mouth, Estuary
Lake
Salt Lake
Intermittent Lake
Reservoir
Swamp, Pond
Canal
Glacier
Ice Shelf, Pack Ice
Ocean
Sea
Gulf, Bay
Strait, Fjord
Lagoon
Bank
Seamount
Tablemount
Ridge
Shelf
Basin
Escarpment, Sea Scarp
Fracture
Trench, Abyss
National Park, Reserve
Point of Interest
Recreation Site
Cave, Cavern
Historic Site
Ruins
Wall, Walls
Church, Abbey
Temple
Scientific Station
Airport
Port
Lighthouse
Mine
Tunnel
Dam, Bridge

Irpen 19 De 50.31N 30.16 E
Irpinia 14 Ij 40.55N 15.00 E
Irrawaddy → Ayeyarwady 25 Ie 17.00N 95.00 E
Irrawaddy (EN) = Ayeyarwady 21 Lg 15.50N 95.06 E
Irrel 12 Ie 49.51N 6.28 E
Irsâva 10 Th 48.15N 23.05 E
Irsina 14 Kj 40.45N 16.14 E
Irtek 16 Rd 51.29N 52.42 E
Irthlingborough 12 Bb 52.19N 0.36W
Irtyš 21 Ic 61.04N 68.52 E
Irtyšsk 19 He 53.21N 75.27 E
Irumu 36 Eb 1.27N 29.52 E
Irún 13 Ka 43.21N 1.47W
Irurzun 13 Kb 42.55N 1.50W
Irves Šaurums 8 Ig 57.48N 22.05 E
Irvine 9 If 55.37N 4.40W
Irving 45 Hj 32.49N 96.56W
Is, Jabal- 35 Fa 21.49N 35.39 E
Isa, Ra's- 33 Hf 15.11N 42.39 E
Isabel 45 Fd 45.24N 101.26W
Isabel, Bahia- 54a Ab 0.38 S 91.25W
Isabela 51a Ab 18.31N 67.07W
Isabela → Basilan City 26 He 6.42N 121.58 E
Isabela, Cabo- 49 Ld 19.56N 71.01W
Isabela, Isla- [Ec.] 52 Gf 0.30 S 91.06W
Isabela, Isla- [Mex.] 48 Gg 21.51N 105.55W
Isabella, Cordillera- 47 Gf 13.30N 85.30W
Isabel Segunda 49 Od 18.09N 65.27W
Isabey 15 Ml 38.00N 29.24 E
Isaccea 15 Ld 45.16N 28.28 E
Isachsen 39 Ib 78.50N 103.30W
Ísafjörður 6 Db 66.03N 23.09W
Isahaya 28 Jh 32.50N 130.03 E
Isakov, Seamount (EN) 57 Ga 31.35N 151.07 E
Isana, Rio- 54 Ec 0.26N 67.19W
Isandja 36 Dc 2.59 S 22.00 E
Isanga 36 Dc 1.26 S 22.18 E
Isangi 36 Db 0.46N 24.15 E
Isanlu Makutu 34 Gd 8.16N 5.48 E
Isaouane-n-Irarraren 32 Id 27.15N 8.00 E
Isaouane-n-Tifernine 32 Id 27.00N 7.30 E
Isar 10 Ih 48.49N 12.58 E
Isarco/Eisack 14 Fd 46.27N 11.18 E
Isarco, Valle-/Eisacktal 14 Fd 46.45N 11.35 E
Isbergues 12 Ed 50.37N 2.27 E
Iscayachi 54 Eh 21.31 S 65.03W
Ischgl 14 Ec 47.01N 10.17 E
Ischia 14 Hj 40.45N 13.55 E
Ischia 14 Hj 40.44N 13.57 E
Ise 27 Oe 34.29N 136.42 E
Isefjord 8 Di 55.50N 11.50 E
Išejevka 7 Li 54.28N 48.17 E
Isen 10 Ih 48.20N 12.45 E
Isenach 12 Ke 49.38N 8.28 E
Isen-Zaki 29b Bb 27.39N 128.55 E
Iseo, Lago d'- 14 Ee 45.45N 10.05 E
Iseran, Col de l'- 11 Ni 45.25N 7.02 E
Isère 11 Kj 44.59N 4.51 E
Isère [3] 11 Li 45.10N 5.50 E
Išerit, Gora- 17 If 61.08N 59.10 E
Iserlohn 10 De 51.22N 7.42 E
Isernia 14 Ii 41.36N 14.14 E
Isesaki 29 Fc 36.19N 139.12 E
Iset 21 Id 56.36N 66.24 E
Isetskoje 17 Lh 56.29N 65.21 E
Ise-Wan 28 Ng 34.40N 136.42 E
Iseyin 34 Fd 7.58N 3.36 E
Isfahan (EN) = Eşfahān 22 Hf 32.40N 51.38 E
Isfana 18 Ge 39.51N 69.32 E
Isfara 18 Hd 40.07N 70.38 E
Isfendiyar Dağları 23 Da 41.45N 34.10 E
Isfjorden 41 Nc 78.15N 15.00 E
Isha Baydabo = Baidoa (EN) 31 Lh 3.04N 43.48 E
Ishasha River 36 Ec 0.50S 29.40 E
Ishavet = Arctic Ocean (EN) 67 Be 85.00N 170.00 E
Isherton 54 Gc 2.19N 59.22W
Ishigaki 27 Lg 24.20N 124.09 E
Ishikari 29a Bb 43.13N 141.18 E
Ishikari-Dake 29a Cb 43.33N 143.00 E
Ishikari-Gawa 29a Bb 43.15N 141.20 E
Ishikari-Heiya 29a Bb 43.00N 141.40 E
Ishikari-Wan 27 Pc 43.25N 141.00 E
Ishikawa [Jap.] 27 Mf 26.27N 127.50 E
Ishikawa [Jap.] 29 Gc 37.09N 140.27 E
Ishikawa Ken [2] 28 Nf 36.35N 136.40 E
Ishim Steppe (EN) = Išimskaja Step 21 Id 55.00N 67.30 E
Ishinomaki 27 Pd 38.25N 141.18 E
Ishinomaki-Wan 29 Gb 38.20N 141.15 E
Ishioka 28 Pf 36.11N 140.16 E
Ishitate-San 29 De 33.44N 134.03 E
Ishizuchi-Yama 29 Ce 33.45N 133.05 E
Ishodnaja, Gora- 20 Nd 64.50N 173.26W
Ishpeming 44 Db 46.30N 87.40W
Isidro Alves 55 Ee 20.09 S 55.12W
Isigny-sur-Mer 11 Ee 49.19N 1.06W
Isii 29 Dd 34.04N 134.26 E
Işıklar Dağı 24 Bb 40.50N 27.05 E
Işıkli 15 Mk 38.19N 29.51 E
Isikli Göl 15 Mk 38.14N 29.55 E
Isili 14 Dk 39.44N 9.06 E
Isilkul 19 He 54.55N 71.16 E
Išim 22 Id 56.09N 69.27 E
Išim 21 Jd 57.45N 71.12 E
Išimbaj 19 Fe 53.28N 56.02 E
Išimskaja Step = Ishim Steppe (EN) 21 Id 55.00N 67.30 E
Isinga 20 Gf 52.55N 112.00 E
Isiolo 36 Gb 0.21N 37.35 E
Isiro 31 Jh 2.48N 27.41 E
Isisford 59 Id 24.16 S 144.26 E
Isjangulovo 17 Hj 52.12N 56.36 E
Iskandar 18 Gd 41.35N 69.43 E
Iskăr, Jazovir- 15 Gg 42.25N 23.35 E
Iškašim 19 Hh 36.44N 71.39 E
İskenderun = Alexandretta (EN) 22 Ff 36.37N 36.07 E
İskenderun Körfezi = Alexandretta, Gulf of- (EN) 23 Eb 36.30N 35.40 E
İskilip 24 Fb 40.45N 34.29 E
Iski-Naukat 18 Id 40.14N 72.41 E
Iskininski 16 Rf 47.13N 52.36 E
Iskitim 20 Df 54.38N 83.18 E
Iskushuban 35 Ic 10.13N 50.14 E
Iskut 42 Ee 56.45N 131.48W
Isla-Cristina 13 Eg 37.12N 7.19W
Islâhiye 24 Gd 37.26N 36.41 E
Islāmābād 22 Jf 33.42N 73.10 E
Islāmābād → Anantnāg 25 Fb 33.44N 75.09 E
Isla Mujeres 48 Pg 21.12N 86.43W
Island = Iceland (EN) [1] 6 Eb 65.00N 18.00W
Island = Iceland (EN) 5 Eb 65.00N 18.00W
Island Harbour 51b Ab 18.16N 63.02W
Island Lagoon 59 Hf 31.30 S 136.40 E
Island Lake 42 If 53.45N 94.30W
Island Lake 42 If 53.58N 94.46W
Island Pond 44 Lc 44.50N 71.53W
Islands, Bay of - [Can.] 42 Lg 49.10N 58.15W
Islands, Bay of- [N.Z.] 62 Fa 35.10 S 174.10 E
Islao, Massif de l'- 30 Lk 22.30 S 45.20 E
Islas de la Bahia [3] 49 De 16.20N 86.30W
Islay 5 Fd 55.46N 6.10W
Islaz 15 Hf 43.44N 24.45 E
Isle 11 Fj 44.55N 0.15W
Isle of Man [5] 9 Ig 54.15N 4.30W
Isle of Wight [3] 9 Lk 50.40N 1.15W
Isleta 45 Ci 34.55N 106.42W
'Isle-Verte 44 Ma 48.01N 69.22W
Ismael Cortinas 55 Dk 33.56 S 57.08W
Ismailia (EN) = Al Ismā'īlīyah 33 Fc 30.35N 32.16 E
Ismailly 16 Pi 40.47N 48.13 E
Ismantorps Borg 8 Gh 56.45N 16.40 E
Isnā 31 Kf 25.18N 32.33 E
Isny im Allgäu 10 Gi 47.42N 10.02 E
Isojärvi 8 Ic 61.45N 21.45 E
Isojoki 7 Ee 62.07N 21.58 E
Isojoki/Storå 7 Ee 62.07N 21.58 E
Isoka 36 Fe 10.08 S 32.38 E
Isola del Liri 14 Hi 41.41N 13.34 E
Isola di Capo Rizzuto 14 Ll 38.58N 17.05 E
Isonzo 14 He 45.43N 13.33 E
Isonzo (EN) = Soča 14 He 45.43N 13.33 E
Isosyöte 7 Gd 65.37N 27.35 E
Isparta 23 Db 37.46N 30.33 E
Isperih 15 Jf 43.43N 26.50 E
Ispica 14 In 36.47N 14.55 E
İspir 24 Ib 40.29N 41.00 E
Ispiriz Dağı 24 Jc 38.03N 43.55 E
Israel (EN) = Yisra'el [1] 22 Ff 31.30N 35.00 E
Isratu 35 Fb 16.20N 39.55 E
Issa 8 Mh 56.55N 28.50 E
Issano 54 Gb 5.49N 59.25W
Issaran, Ra's- 24 Eh 28.50N 32.56 E
Issel 10 Cd 52.00N 6.10 E
Isser 13 Ph 36.51N 3.40 E
Issia [3] 34 Dd 6.30N 6.35W
Issia 34 Dd 6.29N 6.35W
Issoire 11 Ji 45.33N 3.15 E
Issoudun 11 Hh 46.57N 2.00 E
Issyk 18 Kc 43.20N 77.28 E
Issyk-Kul' (Rybačje) 19 Hg 42.28N 76.11 E
Issyk-Kul, Ozero- 21 Je 42.25N 77.15 E
Issyk-Kulskaja Oblast [3] 19 Hg 42.10N 78.00 E
Ist 14 If 44.17N 14.47 E
İstanbul 22 Ee 41.01N 28.58 E
İstanbul-Bakırköy 15 Li 40.59N 28.52 E
İstanbul-Beyoğlu 15 Lh 41.02N 28.59 E
İstanbul Boğazi = Bosporus (EN) 5 Ig 41.00N 29.00 E
İstanbul-Kadıköy 15 Mi 40.59N 29.01 E
Isteren 8 Db 62.00N 11.50 E
Istgâh-e Eqbāliyeh 24 Ne 35.50N 50.45 E
Isthilart 55 Dj 31.11 S 57.58W
Istiaia 15 Gk 38.57N 23.09 E
Istisu 16 Nj 39.57N 46.00 E
Istmina 54 Cb 5.09N 76.42W
Isto, Mount- 38 Ec 69.12N 143.48W
Istok 15 Dg 42.47N 20.29 E
Istokpoga, Lake- 44 Gl 27.22N 81.17W
Istra = Istria (EN) 14 Ge 45.00N 14.00 E
Istres 11 Kk 43.31N 4.59 E
Istria 15 Le 44.34N 28.43 E
Istria (EN) = Istra 5 Hf 45.00N 14.00 E
Isulan 26 He 7.02N 124.29 E
Itabaiana 54 Kf 10.41 S 37.26W
Itabaianinha 54 Kf 11.16 S 37.47W
Itaberá 55 Hf 23.51 S 49.09W
Itaberaba 54 Jf 12.32 S 40.18W
Itaberai 54 Ig 16.02 S 49.48W
Itabira 54 Jg 19.37 S 43.13W
Itabirito 55 Ke 20.15 S 43.48W
Itabuna 53 Mg 14.48 S 39.16W
Itacaiúna, Rio- 54 Ie 5.21 S 49.08W
Itacarambi 55 Jb 15.01 S 44.03W
Itacoatiara 53 Kf 3.08 S 58.25W
Itacolomi, Pico do- 55 Ke 20.26 S 43.29W
Itacuai, Rio- 54 Dd 4.20 S 70.12W
Itacumbi 55 Ei 28.44 S 55.08W
Itacurubi del Rosario 55 Dg 24.29 S 56.41W
Itaguari, Rio- 55 Jb 14.11 S 44.40W
Itaguaru 55 Hb 15.44 S 49.37W
Itagüi 54 Cb 6.12N 75.40W
Itaimbézinho 55 Gi 28.38 S 50.34W
Itaituba 53 Kf 4.17 S 55.59W
Itajai 53 Lh 26.53 S 48.39W
Itajai Açu, Rio- 55 Hh 26.54 S 48.33W
Itajubá 54 Ih 22.26 S 45.27W
Itajuípe 54 Kf 14.41 S 39.22W
Itaka 20 Gf 53.54N 118.42 E
Italia = Italy (EN) [1] 6 Hg 42.50N 12.50 E
Itálica 13 Fg 37.25N 6.05W
Italy (EN) = Italia [1] 6 Hg 42.50N 12.50 E
Itambacuri 54 Jg 18.01 S 41.42W
Itambé, Pico de- 52 Lg 18.23 S 43.21W
Itämeri = Baltic, Sea (EN) 5 Hd 57.00N 19.00 E
Itampolo 37 Gd 24.41 S 43.57 E
Itanagar 25 Ic 26.57N 93.15 E
Itanará, Rio- 55 Eg 24.00 S 55.53W
Itanhaém 56 Kb 24.11 S 46.47W
Itano 29 Dd 34.09N 134.28 E
Itapaci 55 Hb 14.57 S 49.34W
Itapagé 54 Kd 3.41 S 39.34W
Itapajipe 55 Hd 19.54 S 49.22W
Itaparaná, Rio- 54 Fe 5.47 S 63.03W
Itapebi 54 Kg 15.56 S 39.32W
Itapecerica 55 Je 20.28 S 45.07W
Itapecuru-Mirim 54 Jd 3.24 S 44.20W
Itapemirim 54 Jh 21.01 S 40.50W
Itaperina, Pointe- 30 Lk 24.59 S 47.06 E
Itaperuna 54 Jh 21.12 S 41.54W
Itapetinga 54 Jg 15.15 S 40.15W
Itapetininga 56 Kb 23.36 S 48.03W
Itapetininga, Rio- 55 Hf 23.35 S 48.27W
Itapeva 55 Hf 23.58 S 48.52W
Itapeva, Lagoa- 55 Hi 29.30 S 49.55W
Itapicuru, Rio- [Braz.] 54 Kf 11.47 S 37.32W
Itapicurú, Rio- [Braz.] 52 Lf 2.52 S 44.12W
Itapipoca 54 Kd 3.31 S 39.33W
Itapiranga [Braz.] 54 Gd 2.45 S 58.01W
Itapiranga [Braz.] 55 Fh 27.08 S 53.43W
Itapirapuã, Pico- 55 Hg 24.17 S 49.12W
Itápolis 55 He 21.35 S 48.46W
Itaporã 55 Ef 22.01 S 54.54W
Itaporanga [Braz.] 55 Hf 23.42 S 49.29W
Itaporanga [Braz.] 54 Ke 7.18 S 38.10W
Itapúa [3] 55 Eh 26.50 S 55.50W
Itapuã 55 Gj 30.16 S 51.01W
Itapuranga 54 Ig 15.35 S 49.59W
Itaqui 56 Ic 29.08 S 56.33W
Itaquyry 55 Eg 24.56 S 55.13W
Itararé 55 Hg 24.07 S 49.20W
Itararé, Rio- 55 Hf 23.10 S 49.42W
Itārsi 25 Fd 22.37N 77.45 E
Itarumã 55 Gd 18.42 S 51.25W
Itati 55 Ch 27.16 S 58.15W
Itatinga 55 Hf 23.07 S 48.36W
Itatski 20 De 56.07N 89.20 E
Itaum 55 Ef 22.00 S 55.20W
Itaúna 54 Jh 20.04 S 44.34W
Itaya-Tōge 29 Gc 37.50N 140.13 E
Itbāy 30 Kf 22.00N 35.30 E
Itbayat 26 Hb 20.46N 121.50 E
Itchen 12 Ad 50.57N 1.22W
Ite 54 Dg 17.50 S 70.58W
Itéa 15 Fk 38.26N 22.25 E
Ithaca 43 Lc 42.26N 76.30W
Ithaca (EN) = Itháki 15 Dk 38.24N 20.40 E
Itháki 15 Dk 38.22N 20.43 E
Itháki = Ithaca (EN) 15 Dk 38.24N 20.40 E
Ith Hils 10 Fd 52.05N 9.35 E
Ithnayn, Harrat- 24 Ii 26.40N 40.10 E
Itigi 36 Fd 5.42 S 34.29 E
Itimbiri 30 Jh 2.02N 22.44 E
Itiopya = Ethiopia (EN) [1] 31 Kh 9.00N 39.00 E
Itiquira 54 Hg 17.05 S 54.56W
Itiquira, Rio- 52 Kg 17.18 S 56.44W
Itirapina 55 If 22.15 S 47.49W
Itiúba 54 Kf 10.43 S 39.51W
Itivdleq 41 Ge 66.38N 53.51W
Itō 28 Og 34.58N 139.05 E
Itoigawa 28 Nf 37.02N 137.51 E
Itoko 36 Dc 1.00 S 21.45 E
Itoman 29b Ab 26.07N 127.40 E
Iton 11 Hf 49.09N 1.12 E
Itremo, Massif de l'- 37 Hd 20.45 S 46.30 E
Itsā 24 Dh 29.15N 30.48 E
Itsukaichi 29 Cd 34.22N 132.22 E
Itsuki 29 Be 32.24N 130.50 E
Ittiri 14 Cj 40.36N 8.34 E
Itu [Braz.] 55 If 23.16 S 47.19W
Itu [Nig.] 34 Gd 5.12N 7.59 E
Itu, Rio- 55 Ei 29.25 S 55.51W
Itui, Rio- 54 Dd 4.38 S 70.19W
Ituiutaba 54 Ig 18.58 S 49.28W
Itula 36 Ec 3.29 S 27.52 E
Itumbiara 54 Ig 18.25 S 49.13W
Itumkale 16 Nh 42.43N 45.35 E
Ituna 46 Na 51.10N 103.30W
Itungi Port 36 Fd 9.35 S 33.56 E
Itupiranga 54 Ie 5.09 S 49.20W
Iturama 55 Gd 19.44 S 50.11W
Iturbide 48 Oh 19.40N 89.37W
Ituri 30 Jh 1.40N 27.01 E
Iturregui 55 Bm 36.50 S 61.08W
Iturup, Ostrov- 21 Qe 44.54N 147.30 E
Iturup, Ostrov-/Etorofu Tō 21 Qe 44.54N 147.30 E
Itutinga 55 Je 21.18 S 44.40W
Ituverava 56 Kb 20.20 S 47.47W
Ituxi, Rio- 52 Jf 7.18 S 64.51W
Ituzaingó 55 Dh 27.36 S 56.41W
Itz 10 Gg 49.58N 10.52 E
Itzehoe 10 Fc 53.55N 9.31 E
Ivacevići 16 Dc 52.43N 25.21 E
Ivaí 55 Gg 25.01 S 50.52W
Ivai, Rio- [Braz.] 55 Fi 29.08 S 53.16W
Ivai, Rio- [Braz.] 52 Kh 23.18 S 53.42W
Ivaiporã 55 Gg 24.15 S 51.45W
Ivajlovgrad 15 Jh 41.32N 26.08 E
Ivakoany, Massif de l'- 37 Hd 23.50 S 46.25 E
Ivalojoki 7 Gc 68.43N 27.36 E
Ivančice 10 Mg 49.06N 16.22 E
Ivangorod 7 Gg 59.23N 28.20 E
Ivangrad 15 Cg 42.51N 19.52 E
Ivanhoe 58 Fh 32.54 S 144.18 E
Ivanić-Grad 14 Ke 45.42N 16.24 E
Ivaniči 10 Uf 50.38N 24.24 E
Ivanjica 15 Df 43.35N 20.14 E
Ivanjska 14 Lf 44.55N 17.04 E
Ivankov 16 Fd 50.57N 29.58 E
Ivano-Frankovo 10 Tg 49.52N 23.46 E
Ivano-Frankovsk 6 If 48.55N 24.43 E
Ivano-Frankovskaja Oblast [3] 19 Cf 48.40N 24.40 E
Ivanovka 20 Hf 50.18N 127.59 E
Ivanovka 16 Gf 46.57N 30.28 E
Ivanovo 16 Dc 52.10N 25.32 E
Ivanovo 6 Kd 57.00N 40.59 E
Ivanovskaja Oblast [3] 19 Ed 57.00N 41.50 E
Ivanovskoje 8 Me 59.12N 28.59 E
Ivanščica 14 Kd 46.11N 16.10 E
Ivdel 19 Gc 60.42N 60.28 E
Ivenec 8 Lk 53.55N 26.49 E
Ivigtut 41 Hf 61.15N 48.00W
Ivindo 30 Ii 0.09 S 12.09 E
Ivinheima 55 Ff 22.10 S 53.37W
Ivinheima, Rio- 54 Hh 23.14 S 53.42W
Ivinski razliv 7 If 61.10N 35.00 E
Iviza (EN) = Eivissa/Ibiza 5 Gh 39.00N 1.25 E
Iviza (EN) = Ibiza/Eivissa 5 Gh 39.00N 1.25 E
Ivje 10 Vc 53.55N 25.51 E
Ivohibe 37 Hd 22.29 S 46.52 E
Ivoire, Côte d'- = Ivory Coast (EN) [1] 30 Gh 5.00N 5.00W
Ivolândia 55 Gc 16.34 S 50.51W
Ivory Coast (EN) = Côte d'Ivoire [1] 31 Gh 8.00N 5.00W
Ivory Coast (EN) = Ivoire, Côte d'- 30 Gh 5.00N 5.00W
Ivösjön 8 Fh 56.05N 14.25 E
Ivrea 14 Be 45.28N 7.52 E
Ivrindi 15 Kj 39.34N 27.29 E
Ivry-la-Bataille 12 Df 48.53N 1.28 E
Ivry-sur-Seine 12 Ef 48.49N 2.23 E
Ivujivik 39 Lc 62.25N 77.54W
Iwai-Shima 29 Be 33.47N 131.58 E
Iwaizumi 28 Pe 39.50N 141.48 E
Iwaki 22 Qf 36.55N 140.48 E
Iwaki-Gawa 29 Ga 41.01N 140.22 E
Iwaki-Hisanohama 29 Gc 37.09N 140.59 E
Iwaki-Jōban 29 Gc 37.02N 140.50 E
Iwaki-Kawamae 29 Gc 37.12N 140.45 E
Iwaki-Miwa 29 Gc 37.09N 140.42 E
Iwaki-Nakoso 29 Gc 36.56N 140.48 E
Iwaki-Onahama 29 Gc 36.57N 140.53 E
Iwaki-San 29 Ga 40.40N 140.20 E
Iwaki-Taira 29 Gc 37.05N 140.55 E
Iwaki-Uchigō 29 Gc 37.04N 140.50 E
Iwaki-Yoshima 29 Gc 37.05N 140.50 E
Iwaki-Yotsukura 29 Gc 37.07N 140.58 E
Iwakuni 27 Ne 34.09N 132.11 E
Iwami 29 Dd 35.35N 134.20 E
Iwami-Kōgen 29 Cd 35.00N 132.30 E
Iwamizawa 27 Pc 43.12N 141.46 E
Iwanai 28 Pc 42.58N 140.30 E
Iwanuma 29 Gb 38.07N 140.52 E
Iwase 29 Gc 36.21N 140.06 E
Iwasuge-Yama 29 Fc 36.44N 138.32 E
Iwata 29 Ed 34.42N 137.48 E
Iwate 29 Gb 39.30N 141.30 E
Iwate Ken [2] 28 Pe 39.30N 141.15 E
Iwate San 28 Pe 39.49N 141.26 E
Iwo 34 Fd 7.38N 4.11 E
Iwŏn 27 Mc 40.19N 128.37 E
Iwuy 12 Fd 50.14N 3.19 E
Ixiamas 54 Ef 13.45 S 68.09W
Ixmiquilpan 48 Jg 20.29N 99.14W
Ixopo 37 Ef 30.08 S 30.00 E
Ixtapa, Punta- 48 Ii 17.39N 101.40W
Ixtepec 47 Ee 16.34N 95.06W
Ixtlahuacán del Río 48 Hg 20.52N 103.15W
Ixtlán del Río 47 Dd 21.02N 104.22W
Iyah 35 Hd 9.00N 49.38 E
Iyo 28 Lh 33.46N 132.42 E
Iyo-mishima 29 Ce 33.58N 133.33 E
Iyo-Nada 29 Ce 33.40N 132.15 E
Iž 7 Mh 56.00N 52.41 E
Iž 14 Jf 44.03N 15.06 E
Izabal [3] 49 Cf 15.30N 89.00W
Izabal, Lago de- 47 Ge 15.30N 89.10W
Izad Khvāst 24 Og 31.31N 52.07 E
Izamal 47 Gd 20.56N 89.01W
Izamal 48 Og 20.56N 89.01W
Izapa 47 Ff 14.55N 92.10W
'Izbat al Jājah 24 Dj 24.48N 30.35 E
'Izbat Dush 24 Dj 24.34N 30.42 E
Izberbaš 19 Eg 42.33N 47.52 E
Izbiceni 15 Hf 43.50N 24.39 E
Izborsk 8 Mg 57.39N 28.01 E
Izegem 12 Fd 50.55N 3.12 E
Izeh 24 Mg 31.50N 49.50 E
Izena-Shima 29b Ab 26.56N 127.56 E
Iževsk 6 Ld 56.51N 53.14 E
Izjaslav 16 Ed 50.09N 26.51 E
Izjum 19 Df 49.12N 37.17 E
Izki 23 Ie 22.57N 57.49 E
Izma 19 Fc 65.19N 52.54 E
Ižma 17 Fd 65.02N 53.55 E
Izmail 6 If 45.21N 28.50 E
İzmir = Smyrna (EN) 22 Ef 38.25N 27.09 E
İzmir, Gulf of- (EN) = İzmir Körfezi 24 Bc 38.30N 26.50 E
İzmir-Bornova 24 Bc 38.27N 27.14 E
İzmir Körfezi = Izmir, Gulf of- (EN) 24 Bc 38.30N 26.50 E
İzmit 22 Ee 40.46N 29.55 E
İzmit Körfezi 24 Cb 40.45N 29.35 E
İzmor 24 Ab 40.11N 25.55 E
Iznajar, Embalse de- 13 Hg 37.15N 4.30W
İznalloz 13 Ig 37.23N 3.31W
İznik 24 Cb 40.26N 29.43 E
İznik Gölü 23 Ca 40.26N 29.30 E
Izobilny 16 Lg 45.19N 41.42 E
Izola 14 He 45.32N 13.40 E
Izōrskaja Vozvyšennost 8 Me 59.35N 29.30 E
Izozog, Bañados del- 54 Fg 18.50 S 62.10W
Izra' 24 Gf 32.51N 36.15 E
Izsák 10 Pj 46.48N 19.22 E
Iztočni Rodopi 15 Ih 41.44N 25.31 E
Izúcar de Matamoros 48 Jh 18.36N 98.28W
Izu-Hantō 28 Og 34.55N 138.55 E
Izuhara 28 Jg 34.12N 129.17 E
Izu Islands (EN) = Izu-shotō 21 Pf 32.00N 140.00 E
Izumi [Jap.] 28 Kh 32.05N 130.22 E
Izumi [Jap.] 29 Dd 34.29N 135.26 E
Izumi [Jap.] 29 Gb 38.19N 140.51 E
Izumi-sano 29 Dd 34.24N 135.18 E
Izumo 28 Lg 35.22N 132.46 E
Izu-Shotō = Izu Islands (EN) 21 Pf 32.00N 140.00 E
Izvesti CIK, Ostrova- = Izvestiya Tsik Islands (EN) 20 Da 75.55N 82.30 E
Izvestiya Tsik Islands (EN) = Izvesti CIK, Ostrova- 20 Da 75.55N 82.30 E

J

Jaala 8 Lc 61.03N 26.29 E
Jaama/Jama 8 Lf 58.59N 27.45 E
Jääsjärvi 8 Lc 61.35N 26.05 E
Jaba 24 Qe 35.55N 56.35 E
Jabal, Baḩr al- = Mountain Nile (EN) 30 Kh 9.30N 30.30 E
Jabal Abū Rujmayn 24 Ge 34.50N 37.56 E
Jabal al Awliyā' 35 Eb 15.14N 32.30 E
Jabal aẓ Ẓannah 24 Oj 24.11N 52.38 E
Jabalón 13 Hf 38.53N 4.05W
Jabalpur 22 Jg 23.10N 79.57 E
Jabal Şabāyā 33 Hf 18.35N 41.03 E
Jabālyah 24 Fg 31.32N 34.29 E
Jabal Zuqar, Jazīrat- 33 Hg 14.00N 42.45 E
Jabbārah 33 Hf 19.27N 40.03 E
Jabbeke 12 Fc 51.11N 3.05 E
Jabjabah, Wādī- 35 Ea 22.37N 33.17 E
Jablah 24 Fe 35.21N 35.55 E
Jablanac 14 If 44.43N 14.53 E
Jablanica 15 Dh 41.15N 20.30 E
Jablanica [Bul.] 15 Hf 43.01N 24.06 E
Jablanica 14 Lg 43.39N 17.45 E
Jabločny 20 Jg 47.09N 142.03 E
Jablonec nad Nisou 10 Lf 50.44N 15.10 E
Jablonicki, Pereval- 5 If 48.18N 24.28 E
Jablonovo 20 Gf 51.51N 112.50 E
Jablonovy Hrebet = Yablonovy Range (EN) 21 Nd 53.30N 115.00 E
Jablunkovský průsmyk 10 Og 49.30N 18.45 E
Jaboatão 54 Ke 8.07 S 35.01W
Jaboti 55 De 20.48 S 56.23W
Jabrīn 24 Ni 27.51N 51.26 E
Jabuka 14 Jg 43.05N 15.28 E
Jabung, Tanjung- 26 Dg 1.01 S 104.22 E
Jabuticabal 56 Kb 21.16 S 48.19W
Jabuticatubas 55 Kd 19.30 S 43.45W
Jaca 13 Lb 42.34N 0.33W
Jacaltenango 49 Bf 15.40N 91.44W
Jacaré, Rio- 55 Je 21.03 S 45.16W
Jacarei 55 Jf 23.19 S 45.58W
Jacarezinho 56 Kb 23.09 S 49.59W
Jáchal, Rio- 52 Ji 30.44 S 68.08W
Jaciara [Braz.] 55 Ib 14.12 S 46.41W
Jaciara [Braz.] 55 Eb 15.59 S 54.57W
Jackman 44 Lc 45.38N 70.16W
Jack Mountain 46 Eb 48.47N 120.57W
Jackpot 46 Hf 41.59N 114.09W
Jacksboro 45 Gj 33.13N 98.10W
Jacks Mountain 44 Ie 40.45N 77.30W
Jackson [Al.-U.S.] 44 Dj 31.31N 87.53W
Jackson [Bar.] 51q Ab 13.10N 59.43W
Jackson [Ky.-U.S.] 44 Fg 37.33N 83.23W
Jackson [Mi.-U.S.] 43 Kc 42.15N 84.24W
Jackson [Mn.-U.S.] 45 Ie 43.37N 94.59W
Jackson [Mo.-U.S.] 45 Lh 37.23N 89.40W
Jackson [Ms.-U.S.] 39 Jf 32.18N 90.12W
Jackson [Oh.-U.S.] 44 Ff 39.03N 82.40W
Jackson [Tn.-U.S.] 43 Jd 35.37N 88.49W
Jackson [Wy.-U.S.] 46 Je 43.29N 110.38W
Jackson, Cape- 62 Fd 40.59 S 174.19 E
Jackson, Mount- [Ant.] 66 Qf 71.23 S 63.22W
Jackson, Mount- [Austl.] 59 Df 30.15 S 119.16 E
Jackson Bay 62 Ce 43.55 S 168.40 E
Jackson Head 62 Ce 43.58 S 168.37 E
Jackson Lake 46 Je 43.55N 110.40W
Jacksonville [Ar.-U.S.] 45 Ji 34.52N 92.07W
Jacksonville [Fl.-U.S.] 39 Kf 30.20N 81.40W
Jacksonville [Il.-U.S.] 45 Kg 39.44N 90.14W
Jacksonville [N.C.-U.S.] 45 Le 34.45N 77.26W
Jacksonville [Tx.-U.S.] 43 He 31.58N 95.17W
Jacksonville Beach 43 Ke 30.18N 81.24W
Jacmel 47 Je 18.14N 72.32W
Jacobābād 25 Dc 28.17N 68.26 E
Jacobina 54 Jf 11.11 S 40.31W
Jacob Lake 46 Ih 36.45N 112.13W
Jacobs 45 La 50.15N 89.46W
Jacona de Plancarte 48 Hh 19.57N 102.16W
Jacques-Cartier, Détroit de - 42 Lg 50.00N 63.30W
Jacques Cartier, Mont - 42 Kg 48.58N 65.57W
Jacuba, Rio- 55 Fd 18.25 S 52.28W
Jacuí, Rio- 52 Ki 30.02 S 51.15W
Jacuí-Mirim, Rio- 55 Fi 28.51 S 53.07W
Jacundá 54 Id 4.33 S 49.28W
Jacundá, Rio- 54 Hd 1.57 S 50.26W
Jacupiranga 56 Kb 24.42 S 48.00W
Jada 34 Hd 8.46N 12.09 E
Jadal 34 Fb 18.37N 5.00 E

Index Symbols

[1] Independent Nation
[2] State, Region
[3] District, County
[4] Municipality
[5] Colony, Dependency
Continent
Physical Region
Historical or Cultural Region
Mount, Mountain
Volcano
Hill
Mountains, Mountain Range
Hills, Escarpment
Plateau, Upland
Pass, Gap
Plain, Lowland
Delta
Salt Flat
Valley, Canyon
Crater, Cave
Karst Features
Depression
Polder
Desert, Dunes
Forest, Woods
Heath, Steppe
Oasis
Cape, Point
Coast, Beach
Cliff
Peninsula
Isthmus
Sandbank
Island
Atoll
Rock, Reef
Islands, Archipelago
Rocks, Reefs
Coral Reef
Well, Spring
Geyser
River, Stream
Waterfall Rapids
River Mouth, Estuary
Lake
Salt Lake
Intermittent Lake
Reservoir
Swamp, Pond
Canal
Glacier
Ice Shelf, Pack Ice
Ocean
Sea
Gulf, Bay
Strait, Fjord
Lagoon
Bank
Seamount
Tablemount
Ridge
Shelf
Basin
Escarpment, Sea Scarp
Fracture
Trench, Abyss
National Park, Reserve
Point of Interest
Recreation Site
Cave, Cavern
Historic Site
Ruins
Wall, Walls
Church, Abbey
Temple
Scientific Station
Airport
Port
Lighthouse
Mine
Tunnel
Dam, Bridge

Name	Page	Grid	Lat.	Long.
Jadar [Yugo.]	15	Ce	44.38N	19.16 E
Jaddi, Rās-	25	Cc	25.14N	63.31 E
Jade	10	Ec	53.25N	8.05 E
Jadebusen	10	Ec	53.30N	8.10 E
Jadīd Ra's al Fīl	35	Dc	12.40N	25.43 E
Jadito Wash	46	Ji	35.22N	110.50W
J.A.D. Jensens Nunatakker	41	Hf	62.45N	48.20W
Jädraås	8	Gd	60.51N	16.28 E
Jadransko More=Adriatic Sea (EN)	5	Hg	43.00N	16.00 E
Jadrin	7	Li	55.57N	46.11 E
Jādū	33	Bc	31.57N	12.01 E
Ja'ēl	35	Ic	10.56N	51.09 E
Jaén [3]	13	If	38.00N	3.30W
Jaén	13	Ig	37.46N	3.47W
Jæren	8	Af	58.45N	5.45 E
Jærens rev	8	Af	58.45N	5.29 E
Jaffa, Cape-	59	Hg	36.58S	139.40 E
Jaffna	22	Ji	9.40N	80.00 E
Jafr, Qā' al-	24	Gg	30.17N	36.20 E
Jägala Jõgi	8	Ke	59.28N	25.04 E
Jagdalpur	22	Kh	19.04N	82.02 E
Jagdaqi	27	La	50.26N	124.02 E
Jaghbūb, Wāḥāt al-=Jarabub Oasis (EN)	30	Jf	29.41N	24.43 E
Jagotin	16	Gd	50.17N	31.47 E
Jagst	10	Fg	49.14N	9.11 E
Jaguapitā	55	Gf	23.07S	51.33W
Jaguaquara	54	Kf	13.32S	39.58W
Jaguarão	56	Jd	32.34S	53.23W
Jaguarão, Rio-	55	Fk	32.39S	53.12W
Jaguarari	54	Jf	10.16S	40.12W
Jaguari	55	Ei	29.30S	54.41W
Jaguari, Rio- [Braz.]	55	Ei	29.42S	55.07W
Jaguari, Rio- [Braz.]	55	If	22.41S	47.17W
Jaguariaíva	56	Kb	24.15S	49.42W
Jaguaribe	54	Ke	5.53S	38.37W
Jaguaribe, Rio	52	Mf	4.25S	37.45W
Jaguaruana	54	Kd	4.50S	37.47W
Jagüey Grande	49	Gb	22.32N	81.08W
Jahadyjaha	17	Pc	67.03N	72.01 E
Jahām, 'Irq-	24	Li	26.12N	47.00 E
Jahorina	14	Mg	43.42N	18.35 E
Jahrom	23	Hd	28.31N	53.33 E
Jaice	23	Ff	44.21N	17.17 E
Jaicoa, Cordillera-	51a	Ab	18.25N	67.05W
Jaicós	54	Je	7.21S	41.08W
Jailolo	26	If	1.05N	127.30 E
Jailolo, Selat-	26	If	0.05N	129.05 E
Jaina, Isla de-	48	Ng	20.14N	90.40W
Jainca	27	Hd	35.57N	102.00 E
Jaipur	22	Jg	26.55N	75.49 E
Jaisalmer	25	Ec	26.55N	70.54 E
Jaja	20	De	56.12N	86.26 E
Jājarm	24	Qd	36.58N	56.27 E
Jajdúdorog	10	Ri	47.49N	21.30 E
Jajere	34	Hc	11.59N	11.26 E
Jajpan	18	Hd	40.23N	70.50 E
Jajsan	16	Td	50.51N	56.14 E
Jajva	19	Fd	59.20N	57.16 E
Jajva	17	Hg	59.16N	56.42 E
Jakarta	22	Mj	6.10S	106.46 E
Jakobshavn/Ilulissat	67	Nc	69.20N	50.50W
Jakobstad/Pietarsaari	7	Fe	63.40N	22.42 E
Jakoruda	15	Gg	42.02N	23.40 E
Jakupica	15	Eh	41.43N	21.26 E
Jakutsk	22	Oc	62.13N	129.49 E
Jakutskaja ASSR → Saha (Jakutija), respublika	20	Hc	67.00N	130.00 E
Jal	45	Ej	32.07N	103.12W
Jalaid Qi (Inder)	27	Lb	46.41N	122.52 E
Jalājil	24	Kj	25.41N	45.28 E
Jalālābād	23	Lc	34.26N	70.28 E
Jalālah al Baḥrīyah, Jabal al-	24	Eh	29.20N	32.20 E
Jalālah al Qiblīyah, Jabal al-	24	Eh	28.42N	32.22 E
Jalán, Rio-	49	Df	15.43N	87.34W
Jalandhar	22	Jf	31.19N	75.34 E
Jalapa [3]	49	Cf	14.35N	89.55W
Jalapa [Guat.]	47	Gf	14.38N	89.59W
Jalapa [Mex.]	48	Mi	17.43N	92.49W
Jalapa [Nic.]	47	Gf	13.55N	86.08W
Jalapa Enriquez	39	Jh	19.32N	96.55W
Jalasjarvi	7	Fe	62.30N	22.45 E
Jales	55	Ge	20.16S	50.33W
Jālgaon	25	Fd	21.01N	75.34 E
Jalhay	12	Hd	50.34N	5.58 E
Jalībah	24	Lg	30.35N	46.32 E
Jalib Shahab	24	Lg	30.23N	46.09 E
Jalingo	34	Hd	8.53N	11.22 E
Jalisco [2]	47	Dd	20.20N	103.40W
Jāliṭah=La Galite (EN)	30	He	37.32N	8.56 E
Jāliṭah, Canal de-	14	Cm	37.20N	9.00 E
Jallas	13	Cb	42.54N	9.08W
Jälna	25	Fe	19.50N	75.53 E
Jalón	13	Kc	41.47N	1.04W
Jalostotitlán	48	Hg	21.12N	102.28W
Jalpa	48	Hg	21.38N	102.58W
Jalpaiguri	25	Hc	26.31N	88.44 E
Jalpan	48	Jg	21.14N	99.29W
Jalpug, Ozero-	16	Fg	45.25N	28.40 E
Jalta	19	Dg	44.30N	34.10 E
Jaltepec, Rio-	48	Li	17.26N	94.59W
Jālū	33	Dd	28.30N	21.05 E
Jālū, Wāḥāt-=Gialo Oasis (EN)	30	Jf	29.00N	21.20 E
Jaluit Atoll	57	Hd	6.00N	169.35 E
Jalūlā'	24	Ke	34.16N	45.10 E
Jalutorovsk	19	Gd	56.40N	66.18 E
Jam [Iran]	24	Pe	35.45N	55.02 E
Jam [Iran]	24	Oi	27.50N	52.22 E
Jama/Jaama	8	Lf	58.59N	27.45 E
Jamaari	30	Ig	12.06N	10.14 E
Jamaica	49	Jc	20.12N	75.09W
Jamaica	38	Lh	18.15N	77.30W
Jamaica [1]	39	Lh	18.15N	77.30W
Jamaica Channel	47	Ie	18.00N	75.30W
Jamaica Channel (EN)=Jamaïque, Canal de-	49	Jd	18.00N	75.30W
Jamaïque, Canal de-=Jamaica Channel (EN)	49	Jd	18.00N	75.30W
Jamal, Poluostrov-=Yamal Peninsula (EN)	21	Ib	70.00N	70.00 E
Jamalo-Neneckij respublika	20	Cc	67.00N	75.00 E
Jamālpur	25	Hd	24.55N	89.56 E
Jamāme	31	Lh	0.04N	42.46 E
Jamantau, Gora-	5	Le	54.15N	58.06 E
Jamanxim, Rio-	52	Kf	4.43S	56.18W
Jamari, Rio-	54	Fe	8.27S	63.30W
Jamarovka	20	Gf	50.38N	110.16 E
Jambi	22	Oj	1.38S	123.42 E
Jambi [3]	26	Dg	1.36S	103.37 E
Jambol [2]	15	Jg	42.15N	26.35 E
Jambol	15	Jg	42.29N	26.30 E
Jambongan, Pulau-	26	Ge	6.41N	117.25 E
Jambuair, Tanjung-	26	Ce	5.16N	97.30 E
Jambusar	25	Ed	22.03N	72.48 E
James Bay	38	Kd	51.00N	80.30W
Jameson Land	41	Jd	70.45N	23.45W
James River [U.S.]	38	Je	42.52N	97.18W
James River [U.S.]	44	Ig	36.56N	76.27W
James Ross	66	Re	64.15S	57.45W
James Ross Strait	42	Hc	69.50N	96.30W
Jamestown [Austl.]	59	Hf	33.12S	138.36 E
Jamestown [N.D.-U.S.]	43	Hb	46.54N	98.42W
Jamestown [N.Y.-U.S.]	43	Lc	42.05N	79.15W
Jamestown [St.Hel.]	31	Gj	15.56S	5.43W
Jamestown Reservoir	45	Gc	47.15N	98.40W
Jamm	8	Mf	58.24N	28.15 E
Jammer Bugt	7	Bh	57.20N	9.30 E
Jammu	22	Jf	32.44N	74.52 E
Jammu and Kashmir [3]	25	Fb	34.00N	76.00 E
Jāmnagar	22	Jg	22.28N	70.04 E
Jamno, Jezioro-	10	Mb	54.15N	16.10 E
Jampol	16	Fe	48.15N	28.17 E
Jämsä	7	Ff	61.52N	25.12 E
Jamsah	24	Ei	27.38N	33.35 E
Jämsänkoski	8	Kc	61.55N	25.11 E
Jamshedpur	22	Kg	22.48N	86.11 E
Jamsk	20	Ke	59.37N	154.10 E
Jämtland [2]	7	De	63.00N	14.40 E
Jämtland	8	Fa	63.25N	14.05 E
Janā	24	Mi	27.22N	49.54 E
Jana	21	Pb	71.31N	136.32 E
Janakpur	25	Hc	26.42N	85.55 E
Janaucu, Ilha-	54	Hc	0.30N	50.10W
Janaul	17	Gh	56.16N	54.59 E
Janda, Laguna de la-	13	Gh	36.15N	5.51W
Jandaia	55	Gc	17.06S	50.07W
Jandaq	24	Pe	34.02N	54.26 E
Jandiatuba, Rio-	54	Ed	3.28S	68.42W
Jandowae	59	Ke	26.47S	151.06 E
Jandula	13	Hf	38.03N	4.06W
Jane Peak	62	Cf	45.20S	168.19 E
Janesville	43	Jc	42.41N	89.01W
Jangada	55	Db	15.14S	56.29W
Jangada, Rio-	55	Db	15.12S	56.24W
Jangao Shan	27	Gf	25.31N	98.08 E
Jange	27	Ie	31.59N	105.28 E
Jangijer	18	Gd	40.18N	68.50 E
Jangijul	19	Gg	41.07N	69.03 E
Jangirabad	18	Ed	40.03N	65.59 E
Jango	55	Ee	20.27S	55.29W
Jangxi Sheng (Chiang-hsi Sheng)=Kiangsi (EN) [2]	27	Kf	28.00N	116.00 E
Jangy-Bazar	18	Hd	41.40N	70.52 E
Janikowo	10	Od	52.45N	18.07 E
Janīn	24	Ff	32.28N	35.18 E
Janisjarvi, Ozero-	7	He	62.00N	31.00 E
Janja	14	Nf	44.40N	19.19 E
Jan Mayen	5	Fa	71.00N	8.30W
Jan Mayen Ridge (EN)	5	Fb	69.00N	8.00W
Jano-Indigirskaja Nizmennost	20	Ib	71.00N	139.30 E
Janos	47	Cb	30.56N	108.08W
Jánoshalma	10	Pj	46.18N	19.20 E
Jánosháza	10	Ni	47.07N	17.10 E
Janów Lubelski	10	Sf	50.43N	22.24 E
Janów Podlaski	10	Td	52.11N	23.11 E
Jansenville	37	Cf	32.56S	24.40 E
Jansha Jang	21	Mg	28.46N	104.38 E
Janski Zaliv	21	Pb	72.00N	136.00 E
Jantarny	8	Hj	54.53N	19.55 E
Jantra	15	If	43.38N	25.34 E
Januária	54	Jg	15.29S	44.22W
Janūbīyah, Aṣ Ṣaḥrā' al-=Southern Desert (EN)	30	Jf	24.00N	30.00 E
Janykurgan	19	Gg	43.55N	67.14 E
Janzhang Ansha	27	Ke	9.30N	116.59 E
Japan (EN)	21	Pf	35.00N	135.00 E
Japan (EN)=Nippon [1]	22	Pf	38.00N	137.00 E
Japan, Sea of- (EN)=Japonskoje More	21	Pf	40.00N	134.00 E
Japan, Sea of- (EN)=Nippon Kai	21	Pf	40.00N	134.00 E
Japan, Sea of- (EN)=Tong-Hae	21	Pf	40.00N	134.00 E
Japan Basin (EN)	27	Nc	40.00N	135.00 E
Japan Trench (EN)	3	If	37.00N	143.00 E
Japiim	54	De	7.37S	72.54W
Japonskoje More=Japan, Sea of- (EN)	21	Pf	40.00N	134.00 E
Jäppilä	8	Lb	62.23N	27.26 E
Japtiksale	17	Pb	69.25N	72.29 E
Japurá	54	Ed	1.24S	69.25W
Japurá, Rio-	52	Jf	3.08S	64.46W
Jaqué	49	Hj	7.31N	78.10W
Jaquet, Point-	51g	Ba	15.38N	61.26W
Jaquirana	55	Gi	28.54S	50.23W
Jar	7	Mg	58.17N	52.06 E
Jarabub Oasis (EN)=Jaghbūb, Wāḥāt al-	30	Jf	29.41N	24.43 E
Jarābulus	24	Hd	36.49N	38.01 E
Jaraguá [Braz.]	55	Hb	15.45S	49.20W
Jaraguá [Braz.]	55	Hh	26.29S	49.04W
Jaraguá, Serra do-	55	Hh	26.40S	49.15W
Jaraguari	55	Ee	20.09S	54.25W
Jaraiz de la Vera	13	Gd	40.04N	5.45W
Jarama	13	Id	40.02N	3.39W
Jaramillo	56	Gg	47.11S	67.09W
Jarandilla	13	Gd	40.08N	5.39W
Jaransk	19	Ed	57.18N	47.55 E
Jarānwāla	25	Eb	31.20N	73.26 E
Jarash	24	Ff	32.17N	35.54 E
Jarau, Cêrro do-	55	Dj	30.18S	56.32W
Jarbah	30	Ie	33.48N	10.54 E
Järbo	7	Df	60.43N	16.36 E
Jarcevo	16	Hb	55.05N	32.45 E
Jarcevo	20	Ed	60.15N	90.10 E
Jardāwīyah	24	Jj	25.24N	42.42 E
Jardim	54	Gh	21.28S	56.09W
Jardine River	59	Ib	11.10S	142.30 E
Jardines de la Reina, Archipiélago de los-	47	Id	20.50N	78.55W
Jardinópolis	55	Ie	21.02S	47.46W
Jarega	17	Fe	63.27N	53.31 E
Jaremča	16	De	48.31N	24.33 E
Jarenga	7	Le	62.08N	49.03 E
Jarez de Garcias Salinas	47	Dd	22.39N	103.00W
Järfälla	8	Ge	59.24N	17.50 E
Jargava	15	Lc	46.27N	28.27 E
Jari, Rio-	52	Kf	1.09S	51.54W
Jarīd, Shaṭṭ al-	30	He	33.42N	8.26 E
Jarīr, Wādī-	24	Jj	25.38N	42.30 E
Jarjīs	32	Jc	33.30N	11.07 E
Jarkovo	17	Mh	57.26N	67.05 E
Jarmah	33	Bd	26.32N	13.04 E
Järna	8	Ge	59.06N	17.34 E
Jarnac	11	Fi	45.41N	0.10W
Järnlunden	8	Ff	58.10N	15.40 E
Jarny	11	Le	49.09N	5.53 E
Jarocin	10	Ne	51.59N	17.31 E
Jaroměř	10	Lf	50.21N	15.55 E
Jaroměřice nad Rokytnou	10	Lg	49.06N	15.54 E
Jaroslavl	6	Jd	57.37N	39.52 E
Jaroslavskaja Oblast [3]	19	Dd	57.45N	39.15 E
Jaroslavski	28	Lb	44.10N	132.13 E
Jarosław	10	Sf	50.02N	22.42 E
Järpen	8	Ea	63.21N	13.29 E
Jarrāḥī	24	Mg	30.44N	48.46 E
Jarroto, Ozero-	17	Oc	67.55N	71.40 E
Jar-Sale	20	Cc	66.50N	70.50 E
Jartai	27	Id	39.45N	105.46 E
Jartai Yanchi	27	Id	39.45N	105.40 E
Jarudej	17	Od	65.50N	71.50 E
Jarud Qi (Lubei)	27	Lc	44.30N	120.55 E
Järva-Jaani/Jarva-Jani	8	Ke	59.00N	25.49 E
Jarva-Jani/Järva-Jaani	8	Ke	59.00N	25.49 E
Jarvakandi/Järvakandi	8	Kf	58.45N	24.44 E
Järvakandi/Jarvakandi	8	Kf	58.45N	24.44 E
Järvenpää	7	Ff	60.28N	25.06 E
Jarvis Island	57	Ke	0.23S	160.01W
Järvsö	7	Df	61.43N	16.10 E
Jaščera	8	Ne	59.05N	30.00 E
Jaselda	16	Ec	52.07N	26.29 E
Jasień	10	Le	51.46N	15.01 E
Jasikan	34	Fd	7.24N	0.28 E
Jasinja	10	Uh	48.14N	24.31 E
Jasinovataja	16	Je	48.05N	37.57 E
Jasiołka	10	Rg	49.47N	21.30 E
Jasīra	35	He	1.57N	45.16 E
Jasīred Mayd	35	Hc	11.12N	47.13 E
Jäsk	23	Id	25.38N	57.46 E
Jaškul	16	Nf	46.17N	45.10 E
Jaškul	16	Nf	46.11N	45.17 E
Jasło	10	Rg	49.45N	21.29 E
Jasmund	10	Jb	54.32N	13.35 E
Jasnogorsk	16	Jb	54.29N	37.42 E
Jasny	19	Fe	51.01N	59.59 E
Jasny	20	Hf	53.18N	128.03 E
Jason Islands	56	Hh	51.00S	61.00W
Jasper [Alta.-Can.]	39	Hd	52.53N	118.05W
Jasper [Al.-U.S.]	43	Je	33.50N	87.17W
Jasper [Fl.-U.S.]	44	Fj	30.31N	82.57W
Jasper [In.-U.S.]	44	Df	38.24N	86.56W
Jasper [Tn.-U.S.]	44	Eh	35.04N	85.38W
Jasper [Tx.-U.S.]	45	Jk	30.55N	93.59W
Jasper Seamount (EN)	38	Gf	30.32N	122.42W
Jaşşān	24	Kf	32.58N	45.53 E
Jastrebarsko	14	Je	45.40N	15.39 E
Jastrowie	10	Mc	53.26N	16.49 E
Jastrzebie Zdrój	10	Og	49.58N	18.34 E
Jászapáti	10	Qi	47.31N	20.09 E
Jászárokszállás	10	Pi	47.38N	19.59 E
Jászberény	10	Pi	47.30N	19.55 E
Jász-Nagykun-Szolnok	10	Qi	47.15N	20.30 E
Jászság	10	Pi	47.25N	20.00 E
Jatai	53	Kg	17.53S	51.43W
Jatapu, Rio-	54	Gd	2.30S	58.17W
Játiva/Xàtiva	13	Lf	38.59N	0.31W
Jatobá, Rio-	55	Ea	12.23S	54.07W
Jaú	56	Kb	22.18S	48.33W
Jaú, Rio-	54	Fd	1.55S	61.25W
Jaua, Cerro-	54	Fc	4.48N	64.26W
Jauaperi, Rio-	54	Fc	1.26S	61.35W
Jauja	54	Cf	11.48S	75.30W
Jaumave	48	Jf	23.25N	99.23W
Jaunanna	8	Lg	57.13N	27.10 E
Jaunelgava/Jaunjelgava	7	Fh	56.37N	25.06 E
Jaunfeld	14	Id	46.35N	14.45 E
Jaungulbene	8	Lh	57.00N	26.42 E
Jaunjelgava/Jaunelgava	7	Fh	56.37N	25.06 E
Jaunpiebalga	8	Lg	57.05N	26.03 E
Jaunpur	25	Gc	25.44N	82.41 E
Jauru	55	Ed	18.35S	54.17W
Jauru, Rio- [Braz.]	54	Hg	18.40S	54.36W
Jauru, Rio- [Braz.]	55	Dc	16.22S	57.46W
Java (EN)=Jawa	21	Mj	7.20S	110.00 E
Javalambre	13	Ld	40.06N	1.00W
Javalambre, Sierra de-	13	Ld	40.05N	1.00W
Javan	18	Ge	38.19N	69.01 E
Javānrūd	24	Le	34.48N	46.30 E
Javari, Rio-	52	If	4.21S	70.02W
Java Sea (EN)=Jawa, Laut-	21	Mj	5.00S	110.00 E
Java Trench (EN)	3	Hk	10.30S	110.00 E
Jávea	13	Mf	38.47N	0.10 E
Javier	13	Kb	42.36N	1.13W
Javor	14	Mf	44.07N	18.59 E
Javorie	10	Ph	48.27N	19.18 E
Javornik	10	Jh	48.10N	13.35 E
Javorníky	10	Og	49.20N	18.20 E
Javorov	16	Cd	50.00N	23.27 E
Javorová skála	10	Kg	49.31N	14.30 E
Jävre	7	Ed	65.09N	21.29 E
Jawa=Java (EN)	21	Mj	7.20S	110.00 E
Jawa, Laut-=Java Sea (EN)	21	Mj	5.00S	110.00 E
Jawa Barat [3]	26	Eh	7.00S	107.00 E
Jawa Tengah [3]	26	Eh	7.30S	110.00 E
Jawa Timur [3]	26	Fh	8.00S	113.00 E
Jawf, Wādī-	33	If	15.50N	45.30 E
Jawor	10	Me	51.03N	16.11 E
Jaworzno	10	Pf	50.13N	19.15 E
Jaya, Puncak-	57	Ee	4.10S	137.00 E
Jayapura	58	Fe	2.32S	140.42 E
Jayawijaya, Pegunungan-	26	Kg	4.30S	139.30 E
Jāyezān	24	Mg	30.50N	49.52 E
Jaypur	25	He	18.51N	82.35 E
Jazāyer va Banāder-e Khalīj-e Fārs va Daryā-ye Omān→Hormozgān	23	Id	27.30N	56.00 E
Jaz Mūriān, Hāmūn-e-	23	Id	27.20N	58.55 E
Jazva	17	Hf	60.23N	56.50 E
Jazvān	24	Md	36.58N	48.40 E
Jazykovo	7	Li	54.20N	47.22 E
Jazzīn	24	Ff	33.32N	35.34 E
Jdiouia	13	Mi	35.56N	0.50 E
Jeannetty, Ostrov-	20	Ka	76.45N	158.25 E
Jean-Rabel	49	Kd	19.52N	73.11W
Jebala	13	Gi	35.25N	5.30W
Jebal Bārez, Kūh-e-	23	Id	28.30N	58.20 E
Jebba	34	Fd	9.08N	4.50 E
Jebel	15	Ed	45.33N	21.14 E
Jebha	13	Hi	35.13N	4.40W
Jedincy	16	Ee	48.06N	27.19 E
Jedisa	16	Nh	42.32N	44.14 E
Jędrzejów	10	Qf	50.39N	20.18 E
Jeetze	10	Hc	53.09N	11.04 E
Jefferson	45	Ie	42.01N	94.23W
Jefferson, Mount- [Nv.-U.S.]	43	Dd	38.46N	116.55W
Jefferson, Mount- [Or.-U.S.]	46	Ed	44.40N	121.47W
Jefferson City	39	Jf	38.34N	92.10W
Jefferson River	46	Jd	45.56N	111.30W
Jeffersonville	44	Ef	38.17N	85.44W
Jef-Jef el Kebir	35	Ca	20.30N	21.25 E
Jefremov	19	De	53.11N	38.07 E
Jega	34	Fc	12.13N	4.23 E
Jegersfontein	37	De	29.44S	25.29 E
Jegorjevsk	7	Ji	55.25N	39.07 E
Jegorlyk	16	Lf	46.32N	41.52 E
Jegorlykskaja	16	Lf	46.34N	40.44 E
Jehegnadzor	16	Nj	39.47N	45.18 E
Jeja	16	Kf	46.39N	38.36 E
Jejsk	19	Df	46.40N	38.15 E
Jēkabpils	19	Cd	56.30N	25.59 E
Jekaterinburg (Sverdlovsk)	22	Id	56.51N	60.36 E
Jekaterinburgskaja oblast	19	Gd	59.00N	62.00 E
Jekaterinovka	16	Nc	52.04N	44.30 E
Jelabuga	19	Fd	55.48N	52.05 E
Jelai	26	Fg	2.59S	110.45 E
Jelan	16	Md	50.57N	43.43 E
Jelancy	20	Ff	52.44N	106.27 E
Jelanec	16	Gf	47.42N	31.50 E
Jelcz	10	Ne	51.01N	17.18 E
Jelec	6	Je	52.37N	38.30 E
Jeleckj	17	Lc	67.03N	64.15 E
Jelenia Góra	10	Lf	50.55N	15.46 E
Jelenia Góra [2]	10	Lf	50.55N	15.45 E
Jelgava	19	Cd	56.39N	23.41 E
Jelica	15	Df	43.47N	20.20 E
Jelin vrh	14	Lg	43.02N	19.27 E
Jelizavety, Mys-	5	Qd	54.30N	142.40 E
Jelizovo	16	Fc	53.24N	29.00 E
Jelizovo	20	Kf	53.06N	158.20 E
Jelling	8	Ci	55.45N	9.26 E
Jelnja	16	Hb	54.35N	33.12 E
Jeloguj	20	Dd	63.10N	87.45 E
Jelow Gīr	24	Lf	32.58N	47.48 E
Jeløy	8	De	58.30N	10.40 E
Jelsk	16	Fd	51.49N	29.13 E
Jelva	17	Ee	63.05N	50.50 E
Jemaja, Pulau-	26	Ef	2.55N	105.45 E
Jemanželinsk	19	Ge	54.45N	61.20 E
Jember	26	Fh	8.10S	113.42 E
Jemca	7	Je	63.32N	41.56 E
Jemca	7	Je	63.04N	40.18 E
Jemeppe-sur-Sambre	12	Gd	50.28N	4.40 E
Jeminay	27	Eb	47.28N	85.48 E
Jemnice	10	Lg	49.01N	15.35 E
Jena	10	Hf	50.56N	11.35 E
Jenakijevo	16	Ke	48.12N	38.18 E
Jenašimski Polkan, Gora-	20	Ee	59.50N	92.45 E
Jendyr	17	Mf	61.38N	67.20 E
Jeneponto	26	Gh	5.41S	119.42 E
Jenisej=Yenisey (EN)	21	Kb	71.50N	82.40 E
Jenisejsk	20	Ee	58.27N	92.10 E
Jenisejski Krjaž=Yenisey Ridge (EN)	21	Ld	59.00N	92.30 E
Jenisejski Zaliv=Yenisey Bay (EN)	20	Db	72.00N	81.00 E
Jennersdorf	14	Kd	46.56N	16.08 E
Jennings	45	Jk	30.13N	92.39W
Jenny Lind	42	Hc	68.50N	101.30W
Jenny Point	51g	Bb	15.28N	61.15W
Jensen	46	Kf	40.22N	109.17W
Jens Munk	42	Jc	69.40N	79.40W
Jequié	53	Lg	13.51S	40.05W
Jequitai	55	Jc	17.15S	44.28W
Jequitai, Rio	55	Jc	17.04S	44.50W
Jequitinhonha, Rio-	52	Mg	15.51S	38.53W
Jerada	32	Gc	34.19N	2.09W
Jeralijev	19	Fg	43.12N	51.43 E
Jerbogačën	20	Fd	61.15N	107.57 E
Jérémie	47	Je	18.39N	74.08W
Jeremoabo	54	Kf	10.04S	38.21W
Jerer	35	Gd	7.40N	43.48 E
Jerevan	6	Kg	40.11N	44.30 E
Jerez, Punta-	48	Kf	22.54N	97.46W
Jerez de la Frontera	13	Fh	36.41N	6.08W
Jerez de los Caballeros	13	Ff	38.19N	6.46W
Jergeni	5	Kf	47.00N	44.00 E
Jericho	59	Jd	23.36S	146.08 E
Jermak	19	He	52.02N	76.55 E
Jermakovskoje	20	Ef	53.16N	92.24 E
Jermentau	19	He	51.38N	73.10 E
Jermolajevo (Kumertau)	19	Fe	52.46N	55.47 E
Jeroaquara	55	Gb	15.23S	50.25W
Jerofej Pavlovič	20	Hf	53.58N	121.57 E
Jerome	46	He	42.43N	114.31W
Jersa	17	Fc	66.19N	52.32 E
Jersey	9	Kl	49.15N	2.10W
Jersey City	43	Mc	40.44N	74.04W
Jerseyville	45	Kg	39.07N	90.20W
Jeršov	19	Ee	51.20N	48.17 E
Jertarski	17	Lh	56.47N	64.25 E
Jerte	13	Fe	39.58N	6.17W
Jerusalem (EN)=Yerushalayim	22	Ff	31.46N	35.14 E
Jeruslan	16	Od	50.20N	46.25 E
Jervis Bay	59	Kg	35.05S	150.44 E
Jerzu	14	Dk	39.47N	9.31 E
Jesberg	12	Lc	51.00N	9.09 E
Jesenice	14	Jf	44.14N	15.34 E
Jesenice	14	Id	46.27N	14.04 E
Jesenik	10	Nf	50.14N	17.12 E
Jesi	14	Hg	43.31N	13.14 E
Jesil	19	Ge	51.58N	66.24 E
Jeskianhor, Kanal-	18	Fe	39.15N	66.00 E
Jessej	20	Fc	68.29N	102.10 E
Jessentuki	16	Mg	44.03N	42.51 E
Jessheim	7	Cf	60.09N	11.11 E
Jessore	25	Hd	23.10N	89.13 E
Ještěd	10	Kf	50.42N	14.59 E
Jestro, Wabe-	30	Lh	4.11N	42.09 E
Jesup	43	Ke	31.36N	81.53W
Jesús Carranza	48	Li	17.26N	95.02W
Jesús Maria	56	Hd	30.59S	64.06W
Jesús Maria, Boca de-	48	Ke	24.29N	97.40W
Jesús Maria, Rio-	48	Gg	21.55N	104.30W
Jetmore	45	Gg	38.03N	99.54W
Jever	10	Dc	53.35N	7.54 E
Jevgenjevka	18	Kc	43.27N	77.40 E
Jevišovka	10	Mh	48.52N	16.36 E
Jevlah	19	Eg	40.35N	47.10 E
Jevnaker	7	Cf	60.15N	10.28 E
Jevpatorija	19	Df	45.12N	33.18 E
Jeyḥūn	24	Pi	27.16N	55.12 E
Jeypore → Jaypur	25	He	18.51N	82.35 E
Jezercës	15	Cg	42.26N	19.49 E
Jezero	14	Lf	44.21N	17.10 E
Jeziorak, Jezioro-	10	Pc	53.50N	19.35 E
Jeziorany	10	Qc	53.58N	20.46 E
Jeziorka	10	Rd	52.10N	21.06 E
Jhang Sadar	25	Eb	31.16N	72.19 E
Jhānsi	22	Jg	25.26N	78.35 E
Jhelum	25	Eb	32.56N	73.44 E
Jhelum	21	Jf	31.12N	72.08 E
Jiaji → Qionghai	27	Jh	19.25N	110.28 E
Jialing Jiang	21	Mg	29.34N	106.35 E
Jiamusi	22	Pe	46.49N	130.21 E
Ji'an [China]	27	Mc	41.08N	126.10 E
Ji'an [China]	22	Ng	27.12N	114.59 E
Jianchang	28	Ed	40.49N	119.46 E
Jianchuan	27	Gf	26.32N	99.53 E
Jiande (Baisha)	27	Kf	29.31N	119.17 E
Jiang'an	27	If	28.40N	105.07 E
Jiangao Shan	27	Gf	25.31N	98.08 E
Jiangbiancun	27	Kf	27.13N	115.57 E
Jiangcheng	27	Hg	22.37N	101.48 E
Jiangdu (Xiannümiao)	28	Eh	32.30N	119.33 E
Jianghua (Shuikou)	27	Jg	24.58N	111.56 E
Jiangjin	27	If	29.15N	106.18 E
Jiangle	27	Kf	26.48N	117.29 E
Jiangling (Jingzhou)	27	Je	30.21N	112.10 E
Jiangmen	27	Jg	22.35N	113.02 E
Jiangpu	28	Eh	32.03N	118.37 E
Jiangshan	28	Ej	28.45N	118.37 E
Jiangsu Sheng (Chiang-su Sheng)=Kiangsu (EN) [2]	27	Ke	33.00N	120.00 E
Jiangyou (Zhongba)	27	He	31.48N	104.39 E
Jianhu	28	Eh	33.28N	119.47 E
Jianli	27	Jf	29.50N	112.55 E
Jian'ou	27	Kf	27.08N	118.20 E
Jianping (Yebaishou)	27	Kc	41.55N	119.37 E
Jianshi	27	Ie	30.32N	109.43 E
Jianshui	27	Hg	23.39N	102.46 E
Jianyang	27	Kf	27.23N	118.03 E
Jiaocheng	27	Jd	37.32N	112.09 E
Jiaoding Shan	27	Lc	41.11N	120.01 E
Jiaohe [China]	27	Mc	43.43N	127.20 E
Jiaohe [China]	28	De	38.01N	116.17 E
Jiaolai He [China]	28	Ef	37.07N	119.35 E
Jiaolai He [China]	27	Fc	43.02N	120.48 E
Jiaoliu He	28	Gb	45.21N	122.48 E
Jiaonan (Wanggezhuang)	28	Eg	35.53N	119.58 E

Index Symbols

- [1] Independent Nation
- [2] State, Region
- [3] District, County
- [4] Municipality
- [5] Colony, Dependency
- Continent
- Physical Region
- Historical or Cultural Region
- Mount, Mountain
- Volcano
- Hill
- Mountains, Mountain Range
- Hills, Escarpment
- Plateau, Upland
- Pass, Gap
- Plain, Lowland
- Delta
- Salt Flat
- Valley, Canyon
- Crater, Cave
- Karst Features
- Depression
- Polder
- Desert, Dunes
- Forest, Woods
- Heath, Steppe
- Oasis
- Cape, Point
- Coast, Beach
- Cliff
- Peninsula
- Isthmus
- Sandbank
- Island
- Atoll
- Rock, Reef
- Islands, Archipelago
- Rocks, Reefs
- Coral Reef
- Well, Spring
- Geyser
- River, Stream
- Waterfall Rapids
- River Mouth, Estuary
- Lake
- Salt Lake
- Intermittent Lake
- Reservoir
- Swamp, Pond
- Canal
- Glacier
- Ice Shelf, Pack Ice
- Ocean
- Sea
- Gulf, Bay
- Strait, Fjord
- Lagoon
- Bank
- Seamount
- Tablemount
- Ridge
- Shelf
- Basin
- Escarpment, Sea Scarp
- Fracture
- Trench, Abyss
- National Park, Reserve
- Point of Interest
- Recreation Site
- Cave, Cavern
- Historic Site
- Ruins
- Wall, Walls
- Temple
- Scientific Station
- Airport
- Port
- Lighthouse
- Mine
- Tunnel
- Dam, Bridge

Name	Pg	Grid	Lat	Long
Jiaoxian	27	Kd	36.20N	120.00 E
Jiaozhou-Wan [C]	28	Ff	36.10N	120.15 E
Jiaozuo	22	Nf	35.15N	113.18 E
Jiashan	28	Fi	30.51N	120.54 E
Jiashan (Mingguang)	28	Dh	32.47N	118.00 E
Jiashi/Payzawat	27	Cd	39.29N	76.39 E
Jiawang	28	Dg	34.27N	117.26 E
Jiaxian	28	Bh	33.58N	113.13 E
Jiaxing	27	Le	30.44N	120.46 E
Jiayin (Chaoyang)	27	Nb	48.52N	130.21 E
Jiayu	27	Jf	30.00N	113.57 E
Jiayuguan	27	Gd	39.49N	98.18 E
Jibalei	35	Ic	10.07N	50.47 E
Jibão, Serra do- [M]	55	Jb	14.48 S	45.15W
Jibiya	34	Gc	13.06N	7.14 E
Jibou	15	Gb	47.16N	23.15 E
Jicarón, Isla- [I]	49	Gj	7.16N	81.47W
Jičín	10	Lf	50.26N	15.22 E
Jiddah	22	Fg	21.29N	39.12 E
Jiddat al Ḥarāsīs [X]	23	Ie	20.05N	56.00 E
Jiehu → Yinan	28	Eg	35.33N	118.27 E
Jieshou	28	Ch	33.17N	115.22 E
Jiesjjavrre [L]	7	Fb	69.40N	24.12 E
Jiexiu	27	Jd	37.00N	112.00 E
Jieyang	27	Kg	23.32N	116.25 E
Jieznas/Eznas	8	Kj	54.34N	24.17 E
Jifn, Wādī al- [S]	24	Jj	25.48N	42.15 E
Jiftūn, Jazā'ir- [I]	24	Ei	27.13N	33.56 E
Jigley	35	He	4.25N	45.22 E
Jiguani	49	Ic	20.22N	76.26W
Jigüey, Bahía de- [C]	49	Hb	22.08N	78.05W
Jihlava [S]	10	Mh	48.55N	16.37 E
Jihlava	10	Lg	49.24N	15.34 E
Jihlavské vrchy [M]	10	Lg	49.15N	15.20 E
Jihočeský kraj [3]	10	Kg	49.05N	14.30 E
Jihomoravský kraj [3]	10	Mg	49.10N	16.40 E
Jijel	32	Ib	36.48N	5.46 E
Jijel [3]	32	Ib	36.45N	5.45 E
Jijia [S]	15	Lc	46.54N	28.05 E
Jijiga	35	Gd	9.21N	42.48 E
Jijona	13	Lf	38.32N	0.30W
Jikharrah	33	Dd	29.17N	21.38 E
Jilava	15	Je	44.20N	26.05 E
Jilf al Kabīr, Haḍabat al- [M]	33	Ee	23.30N	26.00 E
Jilib	31	Lh	0.29N	42.47 E
Jilin	27	Mc	43.51N	126.33 E
Jilin Sheng (Chi-lin Sheng) = Kirin (EN) [2]	27	Mc	43.00N	126.00 E
Jiliu He [S]	27	La	52.02N	120.41 E
Jiloca [S]	13	Kc	41.21N	1.39W
Jima = Jimma (EN)	31	Kh	7.39N	36.49 E
Jimāl, Wādī- [S]	24	Fj	24.40N	35.06 E
Jimani	49	Ld	18.28N	71.51W
Jimbe	36	Dh	11.05 S	24.00 E
Jimbolia	15	Dd	45.48N	20.43 E
Jimena	13	Ig	37.50N	3.28W
Jimena de la Frontera	13	Gh	36.26N	5.27W
Jiménez	47	Dc	27.08N	104.55W
Jiménez del Teul	48	Gf	23.10N	104.05W
Jimma (EN) = Jima	31	Kh	7.39N	36.49 E
Jimo	28	Ff	36.24N	120.27 E
Jimsar	27	Ec	43.59N	89.04 E
Jimulco [M]	48	He	25.20N	103.10W
Jinān	24	Dj	25.20N	30.31 E
Jinan = Tsinan (EN)	22	Nf	36.35N	117.00 E
Jincheng [China]	27	Jd	35.32N	112.53 E
Jincheng [China]	28	Fd	41.12N	121.25 E
Jinchuan /Quqên	27	He	31.02N	102.02 E
Jind	25	Fc	29.19N	76.19 E
Jindřichův Hradec	10	Kg	49.09N	15.00 E
Jinfo Shan [M]	27	If	29.01N	107.14 E
Jing'an	27	Dc	44.39N	82.50 E
Jingbian (Zhangjiapan)	27	Id	37.32N	108.45 E
Jingde	28	Ei	30.18N	118.30 E
Jingdezhen	22	Ng	29.18N	117.18 E
Jingfeng → Hexigten Qi	27	Kc	43.15N	117.31 E
Jinggang Shan [M]	27	Jf	26.42N	114.07 E
Jinggu	27	Hg	23.28N	100.39 E
Jinghai	28	De	38.57N	116.56 E
Jinghe/Jing	27	Dc	44.39N	82.50 E
Jinghong (Yunjinghong)	27	Hg	21.59N	100.48 E
Jinghong Dao [I]	27	Je	9.45N	114.28 E
Jingjiang	28	Fh	32.01N	120.15 E
Jingle	28	Ae	38.22N	111.56 E
Jingmen	27	Je	31.00N	112.11 E
Jingning	27	Id	35.30N	105.45 E
Jingpo Hu [C]	28	Be	39.32N	112.14 E
Jingpo Hu [S]	27	Mc	43.50N	128.53 E
Jingshan	28	Bi	31.04N	113.08 E
Jingtai	27	Hd	37.10N	104.08 E
Jingxian [China]	27	If	26.40N	109.37 E
Jingxian [China]	27	Ke	30.41N	118.29 E
Jingxing (Weishui)	28	Ce	38.03N	114.09 E
Jingyu	28	Ic	42.25N	126.48 E
Jingyuan	28	Jc	36.35N	104.40 E
Jingzhi	28	Ef	36.18N	119.22 E
Jingzhou → Jiangling	28	Bh	33.01N	119.01 E
Jinhua	28	Ei	29.07N	119.38 E
Jining [China]	22	Nf	37.26N	116.36 E
Jining [China]	22	Ne	41.02N	113.07 E
Jinja	31	Kh	0.26N	33.13 E
Jin Jiang [S]	28	Cj	28.23N	115.48 E
Jinkou	28	Ci	30.20N	114.07 E
Jinotega [3]	49	Eg	14.00N	85.25W
Jinotega	49	Eg	13.06N	86.00W
Jinotepe	47	Gf	11.51N	86.12W
Jinping	27	Hg	22.45N	103.15 E
Jinsha	27	If	27.18N	106.16 E
Jinsha → Nantong	28	Fh	32.06N	120.52 E
Jinshan	28	Fi	30.54N	121.09 E
Jinshan = Harqin Qi	28	Ed	41.57N	118.40 E
Jinshi	28	Aj	29.03N	111.53 E
Jinta	27	Gc	40.00N	99.00 E
Jintan	28	Ei	31.45N	119.34 E
Jinxi	27	Lc	40.46N	120.50 E
Jinxian [China]	27	Ld	39.06N	121.44 E
Jinxian [China]	28	Dj	28.21N	116.16 E
Jinxiang	28	Dg	35.04N	116.19 E
Jinyang	27	Hf	27.39N	103.12 E
Jinyun	28	Fj	28.39N	120.05 E
Jinzhai (Meishan)	28	Ci	31.40N	115.52 E
Jinzhou	22	Oe	41.09N	121.08 E
Jinzū-Gawa [S]	29	Ec	36.45N	137.13 E
Jiparaná, Rio- [S]	52	Jf	8.03 S	62.52W
Jipijapa	54	Bd	1.22 S	80.34W
Jiquilisco	49	Cg	13.19N	88.35W
Jiquilisco, Bahía de- [C]	49	Cg	13.10N	88.28W
Jirjā	33	Fd	26.20N	31.53 E
Jishou	27	If	28.18N	109.43 E
Jishu	28	Ib	44.16N	126.50 E
Jisr ash Shughur	24	Gc	35.48N	36.19 E
Jiu [S]	15	Gd	43.47N	23.48 E
Jiucai Ling [M]	27	Jf	25.33N	111.18 E
Jiucheng → Wucheng	28	Df	37.12N	116.04 E
Jiujiang	22	Ng	29.39N	116.00 E
Jiuling Shan [M]	27	Jf	28.55N	114.50 E
Jiulong/Gyaisi	28	Hf	28.58N	101.33 E
Jiuquan (Suzhou)	22	Lf	39.46N	98.34 E
Jiurongcheng	28	Gf	37.22N	122.33 E
Jiutai	27	Mc	44.10N	125.50 E
Jiwani, Rās- [P]	25	Cc	25.01N	61.44 E
Jixi [China]	28	Ei	30.04N	118.35 E
Jixi [China]	22	Pe	45.15N	130.55 E
Jixian [China]	28	Cg	35.23N	114.04 E
Jixian [China]	28	Df	37.34N	115.34 E
Jiyang	28	Dd	40.03N	117.24 E
Jiyuan	28	Df	36.59N	117.11 E
Jiyun He [S]	28	Dg	35.06N	112.35 E
Jiz, Wādī al- [S]	28	De	39.05N	117.45 E
Jīzān	35	Ib	16.12N	52.14 E
Jize	22	Gb	16.54N	42.32 E
Jizerá [S]	28	Cf	36.54N	114.52 E
Jizl, Wādī al- [S]	10	Kf	50.10N	14.43 E
Jizō-Zaki [P]	24	Hj	25.39N	38.25 E
Jmbe	28	Lg	35.33N	133.18 E
Jnchengjiang → Hechi	36	De	10.20 S	16.40 E
Joaçaba	27	Ig	24.44N	108.02 E
Joal-Fadiout	55	Gb	27.10 S	51.30W
João Câmara	34	Ke	5.32 S	35.48W
João Monlevade	55	Kd	19.50 S	43.08W
João Pessoa	53	Mf	7.07 S	34.52W
João Pinheiro	54	Ig	17.45 S	46.10W
Joaquín V. González	56	Hb	25.05 S	64.11W
Jobado	49	Ic	20.54N	77.17W
Jódar	13	Ig	37.50N	3.21W
Jodhpur	22	Jg	26.17N	73.02 E
Jodoigne/Geldenaken	12	Gd	50.43N	4.52 E
Joensuu	6	Ic	62.36N	29.46 E
Joerg Plateau [M]	66	Qf	75.00 S	69.30W
Joes Hill [M]	64g	Bb	1.48N	157.19W
Jõetsu	27	Od	37.06N	138.15 E
Joeuf	12	Ie	49.14N	6.01 E
Joffre, Mount- [M]	14	Hd	46.26N	13.26 E
Jogbani	46	Ha	50.32N	115.13W
Jogeva/Jyvega	25	Hc	26.25N	87.15 E
Joghatay	7	Gg	58.46N	26.26 E
Joghatāy, Kūh-e- [M]	24	Qd	36.36N	57.01 E
Jõhana	24	Qd	36.30N	57.00 E
Johannesburg	29	Ec	36.31N	136.54 E
Jõhen	31	Jk	26.15 S	28.00 E
John Day	29	Cc	32.57N	132.35 E
John Day River [S]	46	Fd	44.25N	118.57W
John H. Kerr Reservoir [S]	43	Cb	45.44N	120.39W
John Martin Reservoir [S]	44	Hg	36.31N	78.18W
John o' Groat's	45	Gg	38.05N	103.02W
Johnson	9	Jc	58.38N	3.05W
Johnson, Pico de- [M]	45	Fh	37.34N	101.45W
Johnson City [Tn.-U.S.]	48	Cc	29.13N	112.07W
Johnson City [Tx.-U.S.]	43	Kd	36.19N	82.21W
Johnsons Crossing	45	Gk	30.17N	98.25W
Johnstone, Lake- [S]	42	Ed	60.29N	133.17W
Johnstone Strait [S]	59	Ef	32.20 S	120.40 E
Johnston Island	46	Ca	50.25N	126.00W
Johnston Island [5]	57	Kc	17.00N	168.30W
Johnstown [N.Y.-U.S.]	58	Kc	17.00N	168.30W
Johnstown [Pa.-U.S.]	42	Jd	43.01N	74.22W
Johor Baharu	43	Lc	40.20N	78.56W
Joia	22	Mi	1.28N	103.45 E
Joigny	55	Ei	28.39 S	54.08W
Joinville	11	Jg	47.59N	3.24 E
Joinville Island [5]	53	Jh	26.18 S	48.50W
Jokau	11	Lf	48.27N	5.08 E
Jokela	66	Ra	63.15 S	55.45W
Jokelbugten [C]	35	Ed	8.24N	33.49 E
Jokioinen	8	Kd	60.33N	24.59 E
Jokkmokk	41	Kc	78.25N	19.00W
Jøkulegi [M]	8	Hd	60.49N	23.28 E
Jolfā	7	Ec	66.36N	19.51 E
Joliet	8	Cc	61.03N	8.12 E
Joliette	13	Jc	41.32N	88.05W
Jolo	42	Kg	46.01N	73.26W
Jolo Group [C]	26	He	6.00N	121.00 E
Jølstravatnet [S]	21	Oi	6.00N	121.09 E
Jomala	8	Hd	60.09N	6.15 E
Jombang	8	Ie	60.09N	19.58 E
Jomda	27	Ge	31.37N	98.20 E
Jönåker	58	Gf	58.44N	16.40 E
Jonava/Ionava	7	Fi	55.05N	24.17 E
Jonê	34	Hd	34.35N	103.32 E
Jones Bank [M]	12	Bg	48.58N	7.11W
Jonesboro [Ar.-U.S.]	43	Id	35.50N	90.42W
Jonesboro [La.-U.S.]	45	Ik	32.15N	92.43W
Jones Mountains [M]	66	Pf	73.32 S	94.00W
Jones Sound [S]	41	Kb	76.00N	85.00W
Jonesville	44	Fg	36.41N	83.06W
Jonglei [S]	35	Ed	7.20N	32.00 E
Jonglei	35	Ed	6.50N	31.18 E
Jonglei, Tur'ah-=Jonglei Canal (EN) [S]	35	Ed	9.22N	31.30 E
Jonglei Canal (EN)=Jonglei, Tur'ah-	35	Ed	9.22N	31.30 E
Joniškelis/Ioniškelis	8	Ki	56.00N	24.14 E
Joniškis/Ioniškis	7	Fh	56.16N	23.37 E
Jönköping	6	Hd	57.47N	14.11 E
Jönköping [2]	7	Dh	57.30N	14.30 E
Jonquière	42	Kg	48.25N	71.15W
Jonuta	48	Mh	18.05N	92.08W
Jonzac	11	Fi	45.27N	0.26W
Joplin	39	Jf	37.06N	94.31W
Jordan	43	Fb	47.19N	106.55W
Jordan [S]	23	Ec	31.46N	35.33 E
Jordan (EN)=Al Urdun [1]	22	Ff	31.00N	36.00 E
Jordan Valley	46	Ge	42.58N	117.03W
Jordão, Rio- [S]	55	Fg	25.46 S	52.07W
Jorhāt	22	Lg	26.45N	94.13 E
Jörn	7	Ed	65.04N	20.02 E
Joroinen	7	Ge	62.11N	27.50 E
Jørpeland	7	Bg	59.01N	6.03 E
Jos	31	Hh	9.55N	8.54 E
José A. Guisasola	55	Bn	38.40 S	61.05W
José Battle y Ordóñez	55	Ek	33.28 S	55.07W
José Bonifácio	55	He	21.03 S	49.41W
José de San Martín	56	Ff	44.02 S	70.29W
Joselandia	55	Dc	16.32 S	56.12W
José Otávio	55	Ej	31.17 S	54.07W
José Pedro Varela	55	Ek	33.27 S	54.32W
Joseph, Lake- [S]	44	Hc	45.14N	79.45W
Joseph Bonaparte Gulf [C]	57	Df	14.55 S	128.15 E
Josephine Seamount (EN) [S]	5	Eh	36.52N	14.20W
Joseph Lake	25	Kf	52.48N	65.17W
Joshimath	25	Fb	30.34N	79.34 E
Joškar-Ola	6	Kd	56.40N	47.55 E
Jos Plateau [M]	30	Hh	10.00N	9.30 E
Josselin	11	Dg	47.57N	2.33W
Jostedalen [M]	8	Bc	61.35N	7.20 E
Jostedalsbreen [M]	7	Bf	61.40N	7.00 E
Jostefonn [M]	8	Bc	61.26N	6.33 E
Jost Van Dyke [I]	51a	Db	18.28N	64.45W
Jotunheimen [M]	5	Gc	61.40N	8.20 E
Joubertberge [M]	37	Ac	18.45 S	13.55 E
Joué-lès-Tours	11	Gg	47.21N	0.40 E
Jouquara, Rio- [S]	55	Db	15.06 S	57.06W
Joure, Haskerland-	12	Hb	52.58N	5.47 E
Joutsa	7	Gf	61.44N	26.07 E
Joutseno	7	Gf	61.06N	28.30 E
Jovan, Deli- [M]	15	Fe	44.15N	22.13 E
Jovellanos	49	Gb	22.48N	81.12W
Joviânia	55	He	17.49 S	49.30W
Jowhar	31	Lh	2.46N	45.32 E
Jow Kär	24	Me	34.26N	48.42 E
Jowzjān [3]	23	Kb	36.30N	66.00 E
Joya, Laguna de la- [C]	48	Mj	15.55N	93.40W
Jreida	32	Ef	18.59N	16.03W
Jrian Jaya [3]	26	Kg	3.55 S	138.00 E
Juan Aldama	47	Dd	24.19N	103.21W
Juana Ramírez, Isla- [I]	48	Kj	21.50N	97.40W
Juan Blanquier	55	Cl	35.54 S	59.18W
Juancheng	28	Cg	35.33N	115.30 E
Juan de Fuca, Strait of- [S]	38	Ge	48.20N	124.00W
Juan de Nova, Ile- [I]	30	Lj	17.03 S	42.45 E
Juan E. Barra	55	Bm	37.48 S	60.29W
Juan Fernández, Archipiélago-=Juan Fernández, Islands (EN) [C]	52	Ii	33.00 S	80.00W
Juan Fernandez Islands (EN)=Juan Fernández, Archipiélago-	52	Ii	33.00 S	80.00W
Juan G. Bazán	55	Bg	24.33 S	60.50W
Juangriego	50	Fg	11.05N	63.57W
Juanjuy	54	Cf	7.11 S	76.45W
Juan L. Lacaze	55	Dl	34.26 S	57.27W
Juárez [Arg.]	56	Ie	37.40 S	59.48W
Juárez [Mex.]	48	Ld	27.37N	100.44W
Juárez, Sierra de- [M]	48	Bb	32.00N	115.50W
Juazeirinho	54	Dd	7.04 S	36.35W
Juázeiro	53	Lf	9.25 S	40.30W
Juázeiro do Norte	53	Mf	7.12 S	39.20W
Jūbā (EN)=Ganāne, Webi- [S]	31	Lh	0.15 S	42.38 E
Juba, Rio- [S]	55	Dl	14.59 S	57.44W
Jūbāl, Maḍīq- [S]	24	Ei	27.40N	33.55 E
Jubaland (EN) [X]	30	Lh	1.00N	42.00 E
Jubayl [Eg.]	24	Ei	28.12N	33.38 E
Jubayl [Leb.]	24	Fd	34.07N	35.39 E
Jubayt [Sud.]	35	Fb	18.57N	36.50 E
Jubayt [Sud.]	24	Fn	20.59N	36.18 E
Jubbada Dhexe [3]	35	Gf	0.30 S	42.40 E
Jubbada Hoose [3]	35	Gf	0.30 S	42.10 E
Jubbah	24	Hg	28.02N	40.56 E
Jubilee Lake [S]	59	Fe	29.10 S	126.40 E
Juby, Cap- [P]	37	Tf	27.57N	12.55W
Júcar/Xúquer [S]	5	Hg	39.09N	0.14W
Juçara	55	Cn	38.35 S	60.06W
Jucaro	49	Hc	21.37N	78.51W
Jüchen	12	Ic	51.06N	6.30 E
Juchipila	48	Hg	21.25N	103.07W
Juchipila, Rio- [S]	48	Hg	21.03N	103.25W
Juchitán de Zaragoza	48	Li	16.26N	95.01W
Jučugej	20	Jd	63.20N	142.15 E
Judas, Punta- [P]	49	Fi	9.31N	84.32W
Judayyidat 'Ar'ar	24	Hf	31.20N	41.12 E
Judenburg	14	Jc	47.10N	14.40 E
Juding Shan [M]	28	Dk	27.07N	117.00 E
Judith Mountains [M]	46	Kc	47.12N	109.15W
Judith River [S]	46	Kc	47.44N	109.40W
Judoma [S]	20	Ie	59.08N	135.03 E
Judomski Hrebet [M]	20	Ie	59.05N	141.30 E
Juegang → Rudong	28	Fh	32.19N	121.11 E
Juelsminde	8	Di	55.43N	10.01 E
Jufrah, Wāḥāt al-=Giofra Oasis (EN) [M]	30	If	29.10N	16.00 E
Jug [S]	5	Kc	60.45N	46.20 E
Jug	17	Hh	57.43N	56.12 E
Jugorski poluostrov	19	Kb	69.30N	62.30 E
Jugorski Šar, Proliv- [S]	19	Gb	69.45N	60.35 E
Jugoslavija = Yugoslavia (EN) [1]	6	Hg	44.00N	19.00 E
Jugo-Tala	20	Kc	66.03N	151.05 E
Jugydjan	17	Gf	61.42N	54.58 E
Juhaym	24	Kh	29.36N	45.24 E
Juhnov	16	Ib	54.43N	35.12 E
Juhor [S]	15	Ef	43.50N	21.15 E
Juhoslovenská nížina [M]	10	Ph	48.10N	19.40 E
Juhua Dao [I]	28	Fd	40.32N	120.48 E
Juigalpa	49	Eg	12.05N	85.24W
Juina, Rio- [S]	55	Ca	12.36 S	58.57W
Juine [S]	11	If	48.32N	2.23 E
Juininha, Rio- [S]	55	Ca	12.55 S	59.13W
Juist [I]	10	Cc	53.40N	7.00 E
Juiz de Fora	53	Lh	21.45 S	43.20W
Jujuy	56	Gb	23.00 S	66.00W
Jujuy [3]	56	Gb	23.00 S	66.00W
Jukagirskoje Ploskogorje [M]	20	Kc	66.00N	155.30 E
Jukonda [S]	17	Mg	59.38N	67.20 E
Juksejevo	17	Gg	59.52N	54.16 E
Jula [S]	7	Ke	63.48N	44.44 E
Juldybajevo	17	Hj	52.20N	57.52 E
Julesburg	45	Ef	40.59N	102.16W
Juli	54	Ig	16.13 S	69.27W
Juliaca	54	Dg	15.30 S	70.08W
Julia Creek	59	Id	20.39 S	141.45 E
Julian Alps (EN)=Julijske Alpe [M]	14	Hd	46.20N	13.45 E
Juliana Top [M]	54	Gc	3.41N	56.32W
Julianehāb/Qaqortoq	67	Nc	60.50N	46.10W
Jülich	10	Cf	50.56N	6.22 E
Jülicher Borde [M]	12	Id	50.50N	6.30 E
Julijske Alpe = Julian Alps (EN) [M]	14	Hd	46.20N	13.45 E
Julimes	48	Gc	28.25N	105.27W
Júlio de Castilhos	55	Fi	29.14 S	53.41W
Jullundur → Jalandhar	22	Jf	31.19N	75.34 E
Julong/New Kowloon	22	Ng	22.20N	114.09 E
Julu	28	Cf	37.13N	115.02 E
Juma [S]	7	Hd	65.05N	33.13 E
Juma He [S]	28	De	39.31N	116.08 E
Jumet, Charleroi-	11	Kd	50.27N	4.26 E
Jumièges	12	Gc	49.26N	0.49 E
Jumilla	13	Kf	38.29N	1.17W
Jümme [S]	12	Ja	53.13N	7.31 E
Junāgadh	25	Ed	21.31N	70.28 E
Junan (Shizilu)	28	Eg	35.10N	118.50 E
Junaynah, Ra's al-	24	Eh	29.01N	33.58 E
Juncal	48	De	24.50N	111.47W
Juncos	51a	Cb	18.13N	65.55W
Junction [Tx.-U.S.]	45	Gk	30.29N	99.46W
Junction [Ut.-U.S.]	46	Ih	38.14N	112.13W
Junction City	43	Hd	39.02N	96.50W
Jundiaí	56	Kb	23.11 S	46.52W
Jundiaí do Sul	55	Gf	23.27 S	50.17W
Jundūbah	32	Ib	36.30N	8.45 E
Jundūbah [3]	32	Ib	36.28N	8.41 E
Juneau	39	Fd	57.20N	134.27W
Junee	59	Jf	34.52 S	147.35 E
Jungar Qi (Shagedu)	27	Jd	39.37N	110.58 E
Jungfrau [M]	14	Bd	46.32N	7.58 E
Junggar Pendi = Dzungarian Basin [X]	21	Ke	45.00N	88.00 E
Junín [2]	54	Df	11.30 S	75.00W
Junín [Arg.]	53	Ji	34.35 S	60.57W
Junín [Peru]	54	Cf	11.10 S	76.00W
Junín, Lago de- [S]	54	Cf	11.02 S	76.05W
Junin de los Andes	56	Fe	39.56 S	71.05W
Juniville	12	He	49.24N	4.23 E
Jūniyah	24	Ff	33.59N	35.38 E
Junjaha	16	Kc	66.25N	62.00 E
Junlian	27	Hf	28.12N	104.34 E
Junsele	7	Dd	63.41N	16.54 E
Juntura	46	Fe	43.45N	118.05W
Junxian (Danjiang)	27	Je	32.31N	111.32 E
Juodupė	8	Kh	56.03N	25.44 E
Juojärvi [S]	7	Ge	62.45N	28.35 E
Juoksengi	7	Fc	66.34N	23.51 E
Jupiá, Reprêsa de- [S]	56	Jb	20.47 S	51.39W
Juquiá	55	Hg	24.19 S	47.38W
Juquiá, Rio- [S]	55	Hg	24.18 S	47.49W
Juquiá, Serra do- [M]	55	Gg	25.15 S	48.00W
Jur [S]	30	Jh	8.40N	29.18 E
Jura [3]	14	Ac	47.35N	6.15 E
Jura [M]	5	Gf	46.45N	6.30 E
Jura [I]	9	Ef	56.00N	5.50W
Jura [M]	11	Lh	46.50N	5.50 E
Jūra [S]	8	Hh	55.03N	22.10 E
Jūra/Jūra [S]	7	Fi	55.03N	22.10 E
Jura, Sound of- [S]	9	Ef	55.55N	5.45W
Juradó	54	Bb	7.07N	77.46W
Juratiški	8	Kj	54.02N	26.06 E
Juraybī'āt	24	Kh	29.08N	45.30 E
Juraybī'āt	24	Kh	29.08N	45.03 E
Jurbarkas	7	Fi	55.05N	22.47 E
Jurdī, Wādī- [S]	24	Ei	28.12N	32.44 E
Jurga	19	Li	55.25N	84.28 E
Jurgamyš	17	Lh	55.25N	64.28 E
Juribej [S]	19	Kb	68.55N	69.05 E
Jurien Bay [C]	59	Ee	30.15 S	115.00 E
Jurigue, Rio- [S]	55	Ec	16.29 S	54.37W
Jurilovca	15	Le	44.46N	28.52 E
Jurja	17	Li	54.52N	58.28 E
Jurjan	17	Li	59.20N	54.16 E
Jurmala/Jūrmala	19	Cd	56.59N	23.38 E
Jūrmala/Jurmala	19	Cd	56.59N	23.38 E
Jurmo	8	Ie	59.50N	21.35 E
Jurong	28	Ei	31.56N	119.10 E
Juruá	54	Ed	3.27 S	66.03W
Juruá, Rio- [S]	52	Jf	2.37 S	65.44W
Juruena, Rio- [S]	52	Kf	7.20 S	58.03W
Jurumirim, Reprêsa de- [S]	56	Kb	23.20 S	49.00W
Juruti	54	Gd	2.09 S	56.04W
Jurva	9	Ib	62.41N	21.59 E
Jusan-Kö [S]	29a	Bc	41.00N	140.20 E
Jusayrah	24	Nj	25.53N	50.36 E
Jusheng	27	Mb	48.44N	126.37 E
Ju Shui [S]	28	Ci	31.09N	114.52 E
Juškozero	19	Dc	64.45N	32.08 E
Jussarö	8	Ji	59.50N	23.35 E
Justo Daract	5c	Gd	33.52 S	65.11W
Jusva	17	Gg	58.59N	54.57 E
Jutaí	54	Ee	5.11 S	68.54W
Jutaí, Rio- [S]	52	Jf	2.43 S	66.57W
Jüterbog	10	Je	51.59N	13.05 E
Juti	55	Ef	22.52 S	54.37W
Jutiapa [3]	49	Bf	14.10N	89.50W
Jutiapa [Guat.]	47	Gf	14.17N	89.54W
Jutiapa [Hond.]	49	Df	15.46N	86.34W
Juticalpa	47	Gf	14.42N	86.15W
Jutland (EN)=Jylland [X]	5	Gd	56.00N	9.15 E
Juuka	7	Ge	63.14N	29.15 E
Juva	7	Gf	61.54N	27.51 E
Juventud, Isla de la- = Pines, Isle of- (EN) [I]	38	Kg	21.40N	82.50W
Juxian	27	Kd	35.33N	118.45 E
Jūybār	24	Od	36.38N	52.53 E
Juye	28	Dg	35.23N	116.05 E
Jüyom	24	Oh	28.10N	54.02 E
Juža	7	Kh	56.36N	42.01 E
Južnaja Keltma [S]	17	Gf	60.30N	55.40 E
Južna Morava [S]	15	Ef	43.41N	21.24 E
Južni Rodopi [M]	15	Jh	41.15N	25.30 E
Južnoje	20	Jg	46.13N	143.27 E
Južno-Jenisejski	20	Ee	58.48N	94.45 E
Južno-Kurilsk	20	Ah	44.05N	145.52 E
Južno-Sahalinsk	22	Qe	46.58N	142.42 E
Južno-Uralsk	19	Ge	54.26N	61.15 E
Južnyj, Mys- [P]	20	Ke	57.42N	156.55 E
Južnyj Bug [S]	5	Jf	46.59N	31.58 E
Južnyj Ural=Southern Urals (EN) [M]	5	Le	54.00N	58.30 E
Jygeva/Jõgeva	7	Gg	58.46N	26.26 E
Jylland=Jutland (EN) [X]	5	Gd	56.00N	9.15 E
Jylland Bank [S]	8	Bh	56.55N	7.20 E
Jyske [S]	8	Dg	57.15N	10.14 E
Jyväskylä	6	Ic	62.14N	25.44 E

K

Name	Pg	Grid	Lat	Long
K2=Godwin Austen (EN) [M]	21	Jf	35.53N	76.30 E
Ka [S]	34	Fc	11.39N	4.11 E
Kaabong	36	Fb	3.31N	34.09 E
Kaahka	19	Fh	37.21N	59.38 E
Kaala	65a	Cb	21.31N	158.09W
Kaala-Gomén	63b	Be	20.40 S	164.24 E
Kaalualu Bay [C]	65a	Fe	18.58N	155.37W
Kaamanen	7	Gb	69.06N	27.12 E
Kaap Kruis	37	Ad	21.46 S	13.58 E
Kaap Plateau (EN)= Kaapplato	30	Jk	27.30 S	23.45 E
Kaapplato=Kaap Plateau (EN) [M]	30	Jk	27.30 S	23.45 E
Kaapprovinsie/Cape Province [2]	37	Cf	32.00 S	22.00 E
Kaapstad/Cape Town	31	Il	33.55 S	18.22 E
Kaarst	12	Ic	51.15N	6.37 E
Kaarta [X]	34	Cc	14.35N	10.00W
Kaba/Habahe	8	Fe	47.53N	86.12 E
Kabaena, Pulau- [I]	26	Hh	5.15 S	121.55 E
Kabah [S]	48	Og	20.07N	89.29W
Kabala	34	Cd	9.35N	11.33W
Kabale	36	Ec	1.15 S	29.59 E
Kabalega Falls [S]	36	Fb	2.17N	31.41 E
Kabalo	31	Ji	6.08 S	24.29 E
Kabamba [S]	36	Gb	0.30N	35.45 E
Kabambare	36	Cf	3.06N	98.30 E
Kabardino-Balkarskaja respublika	19	Ej	43.30N	43.30 E
Kabare	36	Ec	2.29 S	28.48 E
Kabasalan	26	He	7.48N	122.45 E
Kaba-Shima [Jap.]	29	Af	32.45N	129.00 E
Kaba-Shima [Jap.]	29	Ae	32.34N	129.47 E
Kabba	34	Gd	7.50N	6.04 E
Kåbdalis	7	Ec	66.09N	20.00 E
Kaberamaido	36	Fb	1.45N	33.10 E
Kabetogama Lake [S]	45	Jb	48.28N	92.59W
Kabhegy [M]	10	Nf	47.03N	17.39 E
Kabinakagami Lake [S]	44	Ea	48.58N	84.25W
Kabinda	31	Ji	6.08 S	24.29 E
Kabīr, Wādī al- [S]	14	Dn	36.23N	9.52 E
Kabir Küh [M]	24	Lf	33.25N	46.45 E
Kableškovo	15	Kg	42.39N	27.34 E
Kabna	35	Eb	19.10N	32.41 E
Kabo	35	Bd	7.39N	18.38 E
Kabol	23	If	34.31N	69.12 E
Kābol [2]	24	Sf	34.30N	69.00 E
Kabompo [S]	36	Dg	13.36 S	24.12 E
Kabompo	36	Dg	13.36 S	24.12 E
Kabondo Dianda	36	Dg	8.53 S	25.60 E
Kabongo	36	Df	7.19 S	25.35 E
Kabūdīyah, Ra's- [P]	32	Jb	35.14N	11.10 E
Kabūd Rāhang	24	Me	35.12N	48.44 E
Kabunda	36	Eg	12.25 S	29.23 E
Kābul	21	Jf	33.55N	72.14 E

Index Symbols

- [1] Independent Nation
- [2] State, Region
- [3] District, County
- [4] Municipality
- [5] Colony, Dependency
- Continent
- [X] Physical Region
- Historical or Cultural Region
- Mount, Mountain
- Volcano
- Hill
- Mountains, Mountain Range
- Hills, Escarpment
- Plateau, Upland
- Pass, Gap
- Plain, Lowland
- Delta
- Desert, Dunes
- Forest, Woods
- Heath, Steppe
- Crater, Cave
- Karst Features
- Depression
- Polder
- Cliff
- Peninsula
- Isthmus
- Sandbank
- Oasis
- Cape, Point
- Coast, Beach
- Islands, Archipelago
- Rocks, Reefs
- Coral Reef
- Well, Spring
- Island
- Atoll
- Rock, Reef
- Waterfall Rapids
- River Mouth, Estuary
- Lake
- Salt Lake
- Intermittent Lake
- Reservoir
- Swamp, Pond
- Canal
- Glacier
- Ice Shelf, Pack Ice
- Ocean
- Sea
- Gulf, Bay
- Strait, Fjord
- River, Stream
- Lagoon
- Bank
- Seamount
- Tablemount
- Ridge
- Shelf
- Basin
- Escarpment, Sea Scarp
- Fracture
- Trench, Abyss
- National Park, Reserve
- Point of Interest
- Recreation Site
- Cave, Cavern
- Historic Site
- Ruins
- Wall, Walls
- Church, Abbey
- Temple
- Scientific Station
- Airport
- Port
- Lighthouse
- Mine
- Tunnel
- Dam, Bridge

Name	Page	Grid	Lat.	Long.
Kabunga	36	Ec	1.42 S	28.08 E
Kaburuang, Pulau-	26	If	3.48N	126.48 E
Kabwe	31	Jj	14.27 S	28.27 E
Kača	16	Hg	44.44N	33.32 E
Kačanik	15	Eg	42.14N	21.15 E
Kačanovo	8	Lg	57.24N	27.53 E
Kačergine	8	Jj	54.53N	23.49 E
Kachchh, Gulf of	21	Ig	22.36N	69.30 E
Kachchh, Rann of	25	Dd	23.51N	70.30 E
Kachia	34	Gd	9.52N	7.57 E
Kachikau	37	Cc	18.09 S	24.29 E
Kachin	25	Jc	26.00N	97.30 E
Kachul (Kagul)	19	Cf	45.53N	28.14 E
Kačiry	19	He	53.04N	76.07 E
Kačkanar	19	Fd	58.42N	59.35 E
Kačug	20	Ff	54.00N	105.52 E
Kaczawa	10	Me	51.18N	16.27 E
Kadada	16	Oc	53.09N	46.01 E
Kadaň	10	Jf	50.23N	13.16 E
Kadan Kyun	25	Jf	12.30N	98.22 E
Kadei	30	Ih	3.31N	16.03 E
Kadijevka	19	Df	48.32N	38.40 E
Kadiköy	24	Bb	40.51N	26.50 E
Kadıköy, İstanbul	15	Mi	40.59N	29.01 E
Kadina	59	Hf	33.58 S	137.43 E
Kadınhanı	24	Ec	38.15N	32.14 E
Kadiolo	34	Dc	10.34N	5.45W
Kadiri	25	Ff	14.07N	78.10 E
Kadirli	23	Eb	37.23N	36.05 E
Kadja	35	Cc	12.02N	22.28 E
Kadmat Island	25	Ef	11.14N	72.47 E
Kadnikov	7	Jg	59.30N	40.24 E
Kadoka	45	Fe	43.50N	101.31W
Kaduj	7	Ig	59.14N	37.09 E
Kaduna	34	Gc	11.00N	7.30 E
Kaduna	30	Hh	8.45N	5.48 E
Kaduna	34	Hg	10.31N	7.26 E
Kāduqlī	31	Jg	11.01N	29.43 E
Kadykčan	20	Jd	63.05N	146.58 E
Kadžaran	16	Oj	39.11N	46.10 E
Kadžerom	17	Gd	64.41N	55.54 E
Kadži-Saj	18	Kc	42.08N	77.10 E
Kaech'ŏn	28	He	39.42N	125.53 E
Kaédi	31	Fg	16.08N	13.31W
Kaélé	34	Hc	10.07N	14.27 E
Kaena Point	65a	Cb	21.35N	158.17W
Kaeo	62	Ea	35.06 S	173.47 E
Kaesŏng	22	Of	37.58N	126.33 E
Kaesŏng Si	28	Ie	38.05N	126.30 E
Kāf	24	Gg	31.24N	37.29 E
Kafakumba	36	Dd	9.41 S	23.44 E
Kafan	19	Eh	39.12N	46.28 E
Kafanchan	34	Gd	9.35N	8.18 E
Kaffrine	34	Bc	14.06N	15.33W
Kafia Kingi	35	Cd	9.16N	24.25 E
Kafiréos, Dhiékplous-	15	Hl	38.00N	24.40 E
Kafirévs, Ákra-	15	Hk	38.10N	24.35 E
Kafr ad Dawwār	24	Dg	31.08N	30.07 E
Kafr ash Shaykh	33	Fc	31.07N	30.56 E
Kafta	35	Fc	13.54N	37.11 E
Kafu	36	Fb	1.39N	32.05 E
Kafue	30	Ef	15.56 S	28.55 E
Kafue	31	Jj	15.47 S	28.11 E
Kafue Dam	36	Ef	15.45 S	28.28 E
Kafue Flats	36	Ef	15.40 S	26.25 E
Kafufu	36	Fd	7.12 S	31.31 E
Kaga	28	Nf	36.18N	136.18 E
Kaga Bandoro	35	Bd	7.02N	19.13 E
Kagalaska	40a	Cb	51.47N	176.23W
Kagalnik	16	Kf	47.04N	39.18 E
Kagami	29	Be	32.34N	130.40 E
Kagan	19	Gh	39.43N	64.32 E
Kagarlyk	16	Ge	49.53N	30.56 E
Kagawa Ken	28	Mg	34.15N	134.15 E
Kagera	30	Ki	0.57 S	31.47 E
Kağızman	24	Jb	40.09N	43.07 E
Kagoshima	22	Pf	31.36N	130.33 E
Kagoshima Bay (EN) = Kagoshima-Wan	28	Ki	31.27N	130.40 E
Kagoshima Ken	28	Ki	31.45N	130.40 E
Kagoshima-Taniyama	29	Bf	31.31N	130.31 E
Kagoshima-Wan = Kagoshima Bay (EN)	28	Ki	31.27N	130.40 E
Kagul → Kachul	19	Cf	45.53N	28.14 E
Kahal Tabelbala	32	Gd	28.45N	2.15W
Kahama	36	Fc	3.50S	32.36 E
Kahemba	31	Ii	7.17 S	19.00 E
Kahi	16	Oi	41.23N	46.59 E
Kahiu Point	65a	Eb	21.13N	156.58W
Kahler Asten	10	Ee	51.11N	8.29 E
Kahnūj	24	Qi	27.58N	57.47 E
Kahoku	29	Gb	38.30N	141.20 E
Kahoku-Gata	29	Ec	36.40N	136.40 E
Kahoolawe Island	57	Lb	20.33N	156.35W
Kahouanne, Ilet à-	51e	Ab	16.22N	61.47W
Kahovka	19	Df	46.47N	33.32 E
Kahovskoje Vodohranilišče = Kakhovka Reservoir (EN)	5	Jf	47.25N	34.10 E
Kahramanmaraş	23	Eb	37.36N	36.55 E
Kahrūyeh	24	Ng	31.43N	51.48 E
Kâhta	24	Hd	37.46N	38.36 E
Kahuku	65a	Db	21.41N	157.57W
Kahuku Point	65a	Db	21.43N	157.59W
Kahului	65a	Ec	20.53N	156.27W
Kahului Bay	65a	Ec	20.55N	156.30W
Kahurangi Point	62	Ed	40.46 S	172.13 E
Kai, Kepulauan-	57	Ee	5.35 S	132.45 E
Kaiama	34	Fd	9.36N	3.57 E
Kaiapoi	62	Ee	43.23 S	172.39 E
Kaibab Plateau	46	Ih	36.30N	112.15W
Kai Besar	26	Jh	5.35 S	133.00 E
Kaidu He/Karaxabar He	27	Ec	41.55N	86.38 E
Kaieteur Falls	54	Gc	5.10N	59.28W
Kaifeng	22	Nf	34.45N	114.25 E
Kaihua	28	Ej	29.10N	118.24 E
Kai Kecil	26	Jh	5.45 S	132.40 E
Kaikohe	62	Ea	35.24 S	173.48 E
Kaikoura	61	Dh	42.25 S	173.41 E
Kaili	27	If	26.35N	107.59 E
Kailu	27	Lc	43.37N	121.19 E
Kailua [Hi.-U.S.]	65a	Fd	19.39N	155.59W
Kailua [Hi.-U.S.]	65a	Db	21.23N	157.44W
Kaimana	26	Jg	3.39 S	133.45 E
Kaimanawa Mountains	62	Fc	39.15 S	176.00 E
Kaimon-Dake	29	Bf	31.10N	130.32 E
Kain, Tournai-	12	Fd	50.38N	3.22 E
Kainach	14	Jd	46.54N	15.31 E
Kainan [Jap.]	29	Dd	34.09N	135.12 E
Kainan [Jap.]	29	De	33.36N	134.22 E
Kainantu	60	Di	6.15 S	145.53 E
Kainji Dam	34	Fd	9.55N	4.40 E
Kainji Reservoir	34	Fc	10.30N	4.35 E
Kaipara Harbour	62	Fb	36.25 S	174.15 E
Kaiparowits Plateau	46	Jh	37.20N	111.15W
Kaiser Franz Josephs Fjord	41	Jd	73.30N	24.00W
Kaisersesch	12	Jd	50.14N	7.09 E
Kaiserslautern	10	Dg	49.27N	7.45 E
Kaiserstuhl	10	Dh	48.06N	7.40 E
Kaishantun	27	Mc	42.43N	129.37 E
Kaišiadorys/Kajšjadoris	7	Fi	54.53N	24.31 E
Kaita	29	Cd	34.20N	132.32 E
Kaitaia	62	Ea	35.07 S	173.14 E
Kaitangata	62	Cg	46.17 S	169.51 E
Kaithal	25	Fc	29.48N	76.23 E
Kaitong → Tongyu	27	Lc	44.47N	123.05 E
Kaituma River	50	Gh	8.11N	59.41W
Kaiwaka	61	Dg	36.10 S	174.26 E
Kaiwi Channel	60	Oc	21.13N	157.30W
Kaixian	27	Ie	31.10N	108.25 E
Kaiyuan [China]	27	Lc	42.33N	124.04 E
Kaiyuan [China]	27	Hg	23.47N	103.15 E
Kaiyuh Mountains	40	Hd	64.00N	158.00W
Kaja	30	Jg	12.02N	22.28 E
Kajaani	6	Ic	64.14N	27.41 E
Kajaapu	26	Dh	5.26 S	102.24 E
Kajabbi	58	Fg	20.02 S	140.02 E
Kajak	20	Fb	71.30N	103.15 E
Kajang	26	Df	2.59N	101.47 E
Kajdak, Sor-	16	Rg	44.40N	53.30 E
Kajerkan	20	Dc	69.25N	87.30 E
Kajiado	36	Gc	1.51 S	36.47 E
Kajiki	29	Bf	31.44N	130.40 E
Kajmakčalan	15	Ei	40.58N	21.48 E
Kajnar	15	Lb	47.50N	28.06 E
Kajo Kaji	35	Ee	3.53N	31.40 E
Kajrakkumskoje Vodohranilišče	18	Hd	40.20N	70.05 E
Kajrakty	19	Hf	48.31N	73.14 E
Kajšjadoris/Kaišiadorys	7	Fi	54.53N	24.31 E
Kajuru	34	Gc	10.19N	7.41 E
Kaka	35	Fd	7.28N	39.06 E
Käkä	35	Ec	10.36N	32.11 E
Kakagi Lake	45	Jb	49.13N	93.52W
Kakamas	37	Ce	28.45 S	20.33 E
Kakamega	36	Fb	0.17N	34.45 E
Kakamigahara	29	Ed	35.25N	136.50 E
Kakanj	14	Mf	44.08N	18.05 E
Kaka Point	65a	Ec	20.32N	156.33W
Kakata	34	Cd	6.32N	10.21W
Kake	29	Cd	34.36N	132.19 E
Kakegawa	29	Ed	34.46N	138.00 E
Kakenge	36	Dc	4.51 S	21.55 E
Kakeroma-Jima	29b	Ba	28.08N	129.15 E
Kakhovka Reservoir (EN) = Kahovskoje Vodohranilišče	5	Jf	47.25N	34.10 E
Kākī	24	Nh	28.19N	51.34 E
Kakināda	22	Kh	16.56N	82.13 E
Kakisa Lake	42	Fd	60.55N	117.40W
Kakizaki	29	Fc	37.16N	138.22 E
Kaklkan	24	Cd	36.15N	29.24 E
Kakogawa	29	Dd	34.46N	134.51 E
Kakpin	34	Ed	8.39N	3.48W
Kaktovik	40	Kb	70.08N	143.37W
Kakuda	29	Gc	37.58N	140.47 E
Kakuma	36	Fb	3.43N	34.52 E
Kakunodate	28	Pe	39.40N	140.32 E
Kakva	17	Jg	59.37N	60.50 E
Kakya	36	Gc	1.36 S	39.02 E
Kalaa	13	Mi	35.35N	0.20 E
Kalaa Khasba	14	Co	35.38N	8.36 E
Kalaallit Nunaat/Grønland = Greenland (EN)	39	Pb	70.00N	40.00W
Kalaallit Nunaat/Grønland = Greenland (EN)	38	Pb	70.00N	40.00W
Kalabahi	26	Hh	8.13 S	124.31 E
Kalabáka	15	Ej	39.42N	21.38 E
Kalabera	64b	Ba	15.14N	145.48 E
Kalabo	36	De	14.58 S	22.41 E
Kalābsha	33	Fe	23.33N	32.50 E
Kalač	19	Ee	50.23N	41.01 E
Kalačinsk	19	Hd	55.03N	74.34 E
Kalač-na-Donu	19	Ef	48.43N	43.32 E
Kaladan	12	Ed	20.09N	92.57 E
Ka Lae	60	Od	18.55N	155.41W
Kalahari Desert	30	Jk	23.00 S	22.00 E
Kalaheo	65a	Bb	21.56N	159.32W
Kalai-Mor	19	Gh	35.37N	62.31 E
Kalaj Humo	18	He	38.25N	70.47 E
Kalajoki	7	Fd	64.15N	23.57 E
Kalakan	20	Ge	55.10N	116.45 E
Kalaldi	34	Hd	6.30N	14.04 E
Kalaleh	24	Pd	37.25N	55.40 E
Kalāmai	6	Ih	37.02N	22.07 E
Kalamákion	15	Gl	37.55N	23.43 E
Kalamazoo	43	Jc	42.17N	85.32W
Kalambo Falls	36	Fd	8.36 S	31.14 E
Kalamitski Zaliv	16	Hg	45.00N	33.25 E
Kálamos	15	Dk	38.37N	20.55 E
Kalamunda, Perth-	59	Df	31.57 S	116.03 E
Kalan	23	Eb	39.07N	39.32 E
Kalanshiyū, Sarīr-	30	Jf	27.00N	21.30 E
Kalao, Pulau-	26	Hh	7.18 S	120.58 E
Kalaotoa, Pulau-	26	Hh	7.22 S	121.47 E
Kalapana	65a	Gd	19.21N	154.59W
Kalaraš	16	Ff	47.16N	28.16 E
Kalarne	8	Gb	62.59N	16.05 E
Kalarski Hrebet	20	Ge	56.30N	118.50 E
Kalasin [Indon.]	26	Ff	0.12N	114.16 E
Kalasin [Thai.]	25	Ke	16.29N	103.31 E
Kalāt	25	Dc	29.02N	66.35 E
Kalāteh	24	Pd	36.29N	54.10 E
Kalau	65b	Bc	21.28 S	174.57W
Kalaupapa	65a	Eb	21.12N	156.59W
Kalaus	16	Ng	45.43N	44.07 E
Kalavárdha	15	Km	36.20N	27.57 E
Kálavrita	15	Fk	38.02N	22.07 E
Kalbā'	24	Qj	25.03N	56.21 E
Kalbīyah, Sabkhat al-	14	Eo	35.51N	10.17 E
Kaldbakur	7a	Ab	65.49N	23.39W
Kaldygajty	16	Re	49.20N	52.38 E
Kale [Tur.]	24	Cd	37.26N	28.51 E
Kale [Tur.]	24	Cd	36.14N	29.59 E
Kalecik	24	Eb	40.06N	33.25 E
Kalehe	36	Ec	2.06 S	28.55 E
Kalemie	31	Ji	5.56 S	29.12 E
Kāl-e Shur	23	Jb	35.05N	60.59 E
Kalevala	19	Db	65.12N	31.10 E
Kalewa	25	Id	23.12N	94.18 E
Kaleybar	24	Lc	38.47N	47.02 E
Kalgoorlie	58	Dh	30.45 S	121.28 E
Kaliakoúdha	15	Ek	38.48N	21.46 E
Kaliakra, Nos-	15	Lf	43.18N	28.30 E
Kalibo	26	Hd	11.43N	122.22 E
Kali Limni	15	Kn	35.35N	27.08 E
Kalima	31	Ji	2.34 S	26.37 E
Kalimantan/Borneo	21	Ni	1.00N	114.00 E
Kalimantan Barat	26	Ff	0.01N	110.30 E
Kalimantan Selatan	26	Gg	2.30 S	115.30 E
Kalimantan Tengah	26	Fg	2.00 S	113.30 E
Kalimantan Timur	26	Gf	1.30N	116.30 E
Kálimnos	15	Jm	36.57N	26.59 E
Kalinin → Tver'	6	Jd	56.52N	35.55 E
Kalinin	19	Fg	42.07N	59.40 E
Kalininabad-	18	Gf	37.53N	68.57 E
Kaliningrad	6	Ie	54.43N	20.30 E
Kaliningrad	7	Ii	55.55N	37.57 E
Kaliningradskaja oblast	19	Ce	54.45N	21.20 E
Kalinino → Tašir	16	Ni	41.08N	44.14 E
Kalinino	16	Kg	45.05N	38.59 E
Kalininsk	15	Ka	48.07N	27.16 E
Kalininsk	16	Nd	51.30N	44.30 E
Kalinkoviči	19	Ce	52.07N	29.23 E
Kalino	17	Hg	58.15N	57.35 E
Kalinovik	14	Mg	43.31N	18.26 E
Kalinovka	16	Fe	49.29N	28.32 E
Kaliro	36	Fb	0.54N	33.30 E
Kalispell	39	He	48.12N	114.19W
Kalisz	10	Of	51.45N	18.05 E
Kalisz	10	Oe	51.46N	18.06 E
Kalisz Pomorski	10	Lc	53.19N	15.54 E
Kalitva	16	Le	48.10N	40.46 E
Kaliua	36	Fd	5.04 S	31.48 E
Kalix	7	Fd	65.51N	23.08 E
Kalixälven	7	Fd	65.47N	23.13 E
Kalja	17	Jf	60.20N	60.01 E
Kaljazin	19	Dd	57.15N	37.55 E
Kalkandere	24	Ib	40.55N	40.28 E
Kalkar	12	Ic	51.44N	6.18 E
Kalkaska	44	Ec	44.44N	85.11W
Kalkfeld	37	Bd	20.53 S	16.11 E
Kalkfontein	37	Cd	22.07 S	20.54 E
Kalkim	15	Kj	39.48N	27.13 E
Kalkrand	37	Bd	24.03 S	17.33 E
Kall	7	Ce	63.28N	13.15 E
Källands Halvö	8	Ef	58.35N	13.05 E
Källandsö	8	Ef	58.40N	13.10 E
Kallaste	7	Gg	58.41N	27.08 E
Kallavesi	5	Ic	62.50N	27.45 E
Kalletal	12	Kb	52.08N	8.57 E
Kallhäll	8	Ge	59.27N	17.48 E
Kallidhromon Óros	15	Fk	38.44N	22.34 E
Kallinge	7	Dh	56.14N	15.17 E
Kallonis, Kolpos-	15	Jj	39.07N	26.08 E
Kallsjön	7	Ce	63.35N	13.00 E
Kalmar	6	Hd	56.40N	16.22 E
Kalmar	7	Dh	57.20N	16.00 E
Kalmarsund	7	Dh	56.40N	16.25 E
Kalmit	12	Ke	49.19N	8.05 E
Kalmius	16	Jf	47.03N	37.34 E
Kalmthout	12	Gc	51.23N	4.28 E
Kalmykija, respublika	19	Ef	46.30N	45.30 E
Kalmykovo	16	Qe	49.05N	51.47 E
Kalnciems	8	Jh	56.48N	23.34 E
Kalnik	14	Kd	46.10N	16.30 E
Kalocsa	10	Oj	46.32N	19.00 E
Kalofer	15	Hg	42.37N	24.59 E
Kalohi Channel	65a	Ec	21.00N	156.56W
Kalole	36	Ec	3.42 S	27.22 E
Kaloli Point	65a	Gd	19.37N	154.57W
Kalomo	36	Ef	17.02 S	26.30 E
Kalpa	25	Fb	31.37N	78.10 E
Kalpákion	15	Dj	39.53N	20.35 E
Kalpeni Island	25	Ef	10.05N	73.38 E
Kalpin	27	Cc	40.31N	79.03 E
Kalsūbai	25	Jh	19.36N	73.43 E
Kaltern/Caldaro	14	Fd	46.25N	11.14 E
Kaltungo	34	Hd	9.49N	11.19 E
Kaluga	6	Je	54.31N	36.16 E
Kalulushi	36	Ee	12.50 S	28.05 E
Kalumburu Mission	59	Fb	14.18 S	126.39 E
Kalundborg	7	Ci	55.41N	11.06 E
Kaluš	19	Cf	49.03N	24.23 E
Kałuszyn	10	Rd	52.13N	21.49 E
Kalužskaja Oblast	19	De	54.20N	35.30 E
Kalvåg	8	Ac	61.46N	4.53 E
Kalvarija	7	Fi	54.27N	23.14 E
Kalya	36	Fd	6.28 S	30.03 E
Kalyān	25	Ee	19.15N	73.09 E
Kám	10	Mi	47.06N	16.53 E
Kama	36	Ec	3.32 S	27.07 E
Kama	17	Nf	60.27N	69.00 E
Kama	5	Ld	55.45N	52.00 E
Kamae	29	Be	32.48N	131.56 E
Kamaï	35	Ba	21.12N	17.30 E
Kamaing	25	Jc	25.31N	96.44 E
Kamaishi	28	Pe	39.16N	141.53 E
Kamakou	65a	Eb	21.07N	156.52W
Kamakura	29	Fd	35.19N	139.32 E
Kamālia	25	Eb	30.44N	72.39 E
Kamalo	65a	Eb	21.03N	156.53W
Kaman	24	Ec	39.25N	33.45 E
Kamand, Āb-e-	24	Mf	33.28N	49.04 E
Kamanjab	37	Ac	19.35 S	14.51 E
Kamanyola	36	Ec	2.46 S	29.00 E
Kamaran	23	Ff	15.12N	42.35 E
Kamarang	54	Fb	5.53N	60.35W
Kama Reservoir (EN) = Kamskoje Vodohranilišče	5	Ld	58.50N	56.15 E
Kamaši	19	Gh	38.48N	66.29 E
Kamativi	37	Dc	18.19 S	27.03 E
Kambalda	59	Ef	31.10 S	121.37 E
Kambalnaja Sopka, Vulkan-	20	Kf	51.17N	156.57 E
Kambara	29	Fd	35.07N	138.36 E
Kambara	63d	Cc	18.57 S	178.57W
Kambarka	7	Nh	56.18N	54.14 E
Kambia	34	Cd	9.07N	12.55W
Kambja	8	Lf	58.11N	26.43 E
Kambove	36	Ee	10.52 S	26.35 E
Kamčatka	20	Le	56.10N	162.30 E
Kamčatka, Poluostrov- = Kamchatka Peninsula (EN)	21	Rd	56.00N	160.00 E
Kamčatskaja Oblast	20	Kf	54.50N	159.00 E
Kamčatski Zaliv	20	Le	55.30N	163.00 E
Kamchatka Peninsula (EN) = Kamčatka, Poluostrov-	21	Rd	56.00N	160.00 E
Kamčija	15	Kf	43.02N	27.53 E
Kamčijska Plato	15	Kg	42.56N	27.32 E
Kameda [Jap.]	29	Fc	37.52N	139.06 E
Kameda [Jap.]	29a	Bc	41.49N	140.46 E
Kameda-Hantō	29a	Bc	41.45N	141.00 E
Káměiros	15	Km	36.18N	27.56 E
Kamelik	16	Pc	52.06N	49.30 E
Kamen	12	Jc	51.36N	7.40 E
Kaménai	15	Im	36.25N	25.25 E
Kamende	36	Dd	6.28 S	24.33 E
Kamenec	10	Td	52.23N	23.49 E
Kamenec-Podolski	19	Cf	48.39N	26.33 E
Kamenijak, Rt-	14	Hf	44.46N	13.56 E
Kamenka	16	Qd	51.07N	50.20 E
Kamenka	16	Fe	48.03N	28.45 E
Kamenka	16	Kd	50.43N	39.25 E
Kamenka	19	Ee	53.13N	44.03 E
Kamenka	7	Kd	65.54N	44.04 E
Kamenka	20	Nb	44.28N	136.01 E
Kamenka	16	Df	49.03N	32.06 E
Kamenka-Bugskaja	10	Uf	50.01N	24.25 E
Kamenka-Dneprovskaja	16	If	47.29N	34.29 E
Kamen-Kaširski	16	Dd	51.36N	24.59 E
Kamen-na-Obi	20	Df	53.47N	81.20 E
Kamennogorsk	7	Gf	60.59N	29.12 E
Kamennoje, Ozero-	7	Hd	64.30N	30.15 E
Kamennomostski	16	Lg	44.17N	40.12 E
Kamen-Rybolov	28	Kb	44.45N	132.04 E
Kamenskoje	20	Ld	62.30N	166.12 E
Kamensk-Šahtinski	16	Le	48.18N	40.16 E
Kamensk-Uralski	22	Id	56.28N	61.54 E
Kamenz/Kamjenc	10	Ke	51.16N	14.06 E
Kameoka	29	Dd	35.00N	135.35 E
Kameškovo	7	Jh	56.22N	41.01 E
Kamet	25	Fd	30.55N	79.35 E
Kameyama	29	Ed	34.51N	136.27 E
Kami-Agata	29	Ad	34.38N	129.25 E
Kamiah	46	Gc	46.14N	116.02W
Kamicharo	29a	Cb	43.11N	143.52 E
Kamienna	10	Re	51.06N	21.47 E
Kamienna Góra	10	Mf	50.47N	16.01 E
Kamień Pomorski	10	Kc	53.58N	14.46 E
Kamieńsk	10	Pe	51.12N	19.30 E
Kamieskroon	37	Bf	30.09 S	17.56 E
Kami-furano	29a	Cb	43.29N	142.27 E
Kamiiso	28	Pd	41.49N	140.39 E
Kamiita	29	Dd	34.08N	134.24 E
Kamiji	36	Dd	6.39 S	23.17 E
Kamikawa	29a	Cb	43.50N	142.47 E
Kami-Koshiki-Jima	29	Af	31.50N	129.55 E
Kamina	31	Ji	8.44 S	24.59 E
Kaminak Lake	42	Id	62.13N	95.00W
Kaminokuni	29a	Bc	41.48N	140.05 E
Kamino-Shima	29	Ad	34.30N	129.25 E
Kaminoyama	28	Pe	38.09N	140.17 E
Kaminuriak Lake	42	Hd	63.00N	95.45W
Kamioka	28	Nf	36.16N	137.18 E
Kami-shihoro	29a	Cb	43.13N	143.16 E
Kamisunagawa	29a	Bb	43.28N	141.58 E
Kamitsushima	29	Ad	34.39N	129.28 E
Kamituga	36	Ec	3.04 S	28.11 E
Kamiyama	29	De	33.58N	134.21 E
Kami-yūbetsu	29a	Ca	44.11N	143.34 E
Kamjenc/Kamenz	10	Ke	51.16N	14.06 E
Kamloops	39	Gd	50.40N	120.20W
Kamloops Plateau	46	Ea	50.10N	120.35W
Kamnik	14	Id	46.14N	14.37 E
Kamo	16	Ni	40.22N	45.05 E
Kamo [Jap.]	29	Fc	37.39N	139.03 E
Kamo [N.Z.]	62	Fa	35.41 S	174.17 E
Kamōda-Misaki	29	De	33.50N	134.45 E
Kamogawa	29	Gd	35.06N	140.05 E
Kamp	14	Jb	48.23N	15.48 E
Kampala	31	Kh	0.19N	32.35 E
Kampar	26	Df	4.18N	101.09 E
Kampar	26	Mi	0.32N	103.08 E
Kampen	11	Lb	52.33N	5.54 E
Kampene	36	Ec	3.36 S	26.40 E
Kamphaeng Phet	25	Je	16.26N	99.33 E
Kamp-Lintfort	12	Ic	51.30N	6.32 E
Kamp'o	28	Jg	35.48N	129.30 E
Kâmpóng Cham	22	Mh	12.00N	105.27 E
Kâmpóng Chhnăng	25	Kf	12.15N	104.40 E
Kâmpóng Saôm	22	Mh	10.38N	103.30 E
Kâmpóng Saôm, Chhâk-	25	Kf	10.50N	103.32 E
Kâmpóng Thum	25	Kf	12.42N	104.54 E
Kâmpôt	25	Kf	10.37N	104.11 E
Kampti	34	Ec	10.08N	3.27W
Kampuchea → Cambodia	22	Mh	13.00N	105.00 E
Kamrau, Teluk-	26	Jg	3.32 S	133.37 E
Kamsack	42	Hf	51.34N	101.54W
Kamsar	34	Cc	10.40N	14.36W
Kamskoje Ustje	7	Li	55.14N	49.16 E
Kamskoje Vodohranilišče = Kama Reservoir (EN)	5	Ld	58.50N	56.15 E
Kam Summa	35	Ge	0.21N	42.44 E
Kamuenai	29a	Bb	43.08N	140.26 E
Kamui-Dake	29a	Cb	42.25N	142.52 E
Kamui-Misaki	27	Pc	43.20N	140.20 E
Kámuk, Cerro-	49	Fi	9.17N	83.04W
Kamvoúnia Óri	15	Ei	40.00N	21.52 E
Kāmyārān	24	Le	34.47N	46.56 E
Kamyšin	6	Ke	50.06N	45.24 E
Kamyšlov	19	Gd	56.52N	62.43 E
Kamyšovaja Buhta	16	Hg	44.31N	33.33 E
Kamysty-Ajat	17	Jj	53.01N	61.35 E
Kamyzjak	19	Ef	46.06N	48.05 E
Kan	24	Ne	35.45N	51.16 E
Kan	20	Ee	56.31N	93.47 E
Kana	37	Dc	18.32 S	27.24 E
Kanaaupscow	42	Jf	54.01N	76.32W
Kanaaupscow	42	Jf	53.40N	77.08W
Kanab	43	Ed	37.03N	112.32W
Kanab Creek	46	Ih	36.24N	112.38W
Kanaga	40a	Cb	51.45N	177.10W
Kanagawa Ken	28	Og	35.30N	139.10 E
Kanaliasem	26	Dg	1.44S	103.35 E
Kanami-Zaki	29b	Bb	27.53N	128.58 E
Kananga	31	Ji	5.54 S	22.25 E
Kanariktok	42	Le	55.03N	60.10W
Kanaš	7	Li	55.31N	47.31 E
Kanathea	63d	Cb	17.16 S	179.09W
Kanaya	29	Fd	34.48N	138.07 E
Kanayama	29	Ed	35.39N	137.09 E
Kanazawa	22	Pf	36.34N	136.39 E
Kanbalu	25	Jd	23.12N	95.31 E
Kanbe	25	Je	16.42N	96.01 E
Kanchanaburi	25	Jf	14.02N	99.33 E
Kānchenjunga	21	Kg	27.42N	88.08 E
Kānchipuram	25	Ff	12.50N	79.43 E
Kandalakša	6	Jb	67.09N	32.21 E
Kandalaksha, Gulf of- (EN) = Kandalakšski Zaliv	5	Jb	66.35N	32.45 E
Kandalakšski Zaliv = Kandalaksha, Gulf of- (EN)	5	Jb	66.35N	32.45 E
Kandangan	26	Gg	2.47 S	115.16 E
Kándanos	15	Gn	35.20N	23.44 E
Kandava	7	Fh	57.03N	22.46 E
Kandavu Island	57	If	19.00 S	178.13 E
Kandavu Passage	63d	Ac	18.45 S	178.00 E
Kandel	12	Ke	49.05N	8.12 E
Kandel	10	Eh	48.04N	8.01 E
Kandheliousa	15	Jm	36.30N	26.58 E
Kandi	31	Hg	11.08N	2.56 E
Kandıra	24	Db	41.04N	30.09 E
Kandla	25	Ed	23.02N	70.14 E
Kando-Gawa	29	Cd	35.22N	132.40 E
Kandovān, Gardaneh-ye-	24	Nd	36.09N	51.18 E
Kandrian	60	Di	6.13 S	149.33 E
Kandry	17	Gi	54.34N	54.10 E
Kandy	22	Ki	7.18N	80.38 E
Kane	44	He	41.40N	78.48W
Kane Bassin	67	Od	79.35N	67.00W
Kaneh	24	Pi	27.04N	54.18 E
Kanem	35	Bc	15.00N	16.00 E
Kanem	10	Ig	14.45N	15.30 E
Kaneohe	60	Oc	21.25N	157.48W
Kaneohe Bay	65a	Db	21.28N	157.48W
Kánestron, Ákra-	15	Gj	39.56N	23.45 E
Kanev	16	Ge	49.42N	31.29 E
Kanevskaja	19	Df	46.06N	38.58 E
Kaneyama	29	Fc	37.27N	139.30 E
Kang	37	Cd	23.44 S	22.50 E
Kangaba	34	Dc	11.56N	8.25W
Kangal	24	Gc	39.15N	37.24 E
Kangalassy	20	Hd	62.17N	129.58 E
Kangâmiut	41	Ge	65.39N	53.55W
Kangān [Iran]	24	Oi	27.50N	52.03 E
Kangān [Iran]	24	Qj	25.48N	57.28 E
Kangar	26	De	6.26N	100.12 E
Kangaré	34	Dc	11.37N	8.08W
Kangaroo Island	57	Eh	35.50 S	137.05 E
Kangasala	8	Kc	61.28N	24.05 E
Kangasniemi	7	Gf	61.59N	26.38 E
Kangâtsiaq	41	Ge	68.20N	53.18W
Kangāvar	24	Le	34.30N	47.58 E
Kangbao	28	Cd	41.51N	114.37 E
Kangding/Dardo	27	He	30.01N	101.58 E
Kangean, Kepulauan- = Kangean Islands (EN)	26	Gh	6.55 S	115.30 E
Kangean, Pulau-	26	Gh	6.54 S	115.20 E
Kangean Islands (EN) = Kangean, Kepulauan-	26	Gh	6.55 S	115.30 E
Kangeeak Point	42	Lc	68.01N	64.45W
Kangen	30	Kh	6.47N	33.09 E
Kangerdlugssuaq	41	Ie	68.20N	31.40W
Kangetet	36	Gb	1.58N	36.06 E

Index Symbols

Independent Nation · State, Region · District, County · Municipality · Colony, Dependency · Continent · Physical Region · Historical or Cultural Region · Mount, Mountain · Volcano · Hill · Mountains, Mountain Range · Hills, Escarpment · Plateau, Upland · Pass, Gap · Plain, Lowland · Delta · Salt Flat · Valley, Canyon · Crater, Cave · Karst Features · Depression · Polder · Desert, Dunes · Forest, Woods · Heath, Steppe · Oasis · Cape, Point · Coast, Beach · Cliff · Peninsula · Isthmus · Sandbank · Island · Atoll · Rock, Reef · Islands, Archipelago · Rocks, Reefs · Coral Reef · Well, Spring · Geyser · River, Stream · Waterfall Rapids · River Mouth, Estuary · Lake · Salt Lake · Intermittent Lake · Reservoir · Swamp, Pond · Canal · Glacier · Ice Shelf, Pack Ice · Ocean · Sea · Gulf, Bay · Strait, Fjord · Lagoon · Bank · Seamount · Tablemount · Ridge · Shelf · Basin · Escarpment, Sea Scarp · Fracture · Trench, Abyss · National Park, Reserve · Point of Interest · Recreation Site · Cave, Cavern · Historic Site · Ruins · Wall, Walls · Church, Abbey · Temple · Scientific Station · Airport · Port · Lighthouse · Mine · Tunnel · Dam, Bridge

Kanggup'o 28 Id 41.07N 127.31 E
Kanggye 27 Mc 40.58N 126.36 E
Kangi 35 Dd 8.10N 27.39 E
Kangjin 28 Ig 34.38N 126.46 E
Kangiqsualujjuaq 39 Md 58.35N 65.59W
Kangiqsujuaq 42 Kd 61.36N 71.57W
Kangirsuk 39 Lc 60.00N 70.01W
Kangmar 27 Ef 28.32N 89.43 E
Kangnŭng 27 Md 37.44N 128.54 E
Kango 36 Bb 0.09N 10.08 E
Kangondu 36 Gc 1.06S 37.42 E
Kangping 28 Gc 42.45N 123.20 E
Kangrinboqê Feng 27 De 31.04N 81.30 E
Kangto 25 Ic 27.52N 92.30 E
Kangwŏn-Do [N.Kor.] [2] 28 Ie 38.45N 127.35 E
Kangwŏn-Do [S.Kor.] [2] 28 Jf 37.45N 128.15 E
Kani 34 Dd 8.29N 6.36W
Kaniama 36 Dd 7.31S 24.11 E
Kanibadam 18 Hd 40.17N 70.25 E
Kaniet Islands 57 Fe 0.53S 145.30 E
Kanija 15 Lc 46.16N 28.13 E
Kanimeh 18 Ed 40.18N 65.09 E
Kanina 15 Ci 40.26N 19.31 E
Kanin Kamen 17 Bb 68.15N 45.15 E
Kanin Nos 19 Eb 68.39N 43.14 E
Kanin Nos, Mys- 5 Kb 68.39N 43.16 E
Kanin Peninsula (EN)=
Kanin Poluostrov 5 Kb 68.00N 45.00 E
Kanin Poluostrov=Kanin
Peninsula (EN) 5 Kb 68.00N 45.00 E
Kanioumé 34 Eb 15.46N 3.09W
Kanita 29a Bc 41.02N 140.38 E
Kanjiža 15 Dc 46.04N 20.03 E
Kankaanpää 7 Ff 61.48N 22.25 E
Kankakee 43 Jc 41.07N 87.52W
Kankakee River 45 Lf 41.23N 88.16W
Kankalabé 34 Cc 11.00N 12.00W
Kankan 31 Gg 10.23N 9.18W
Kanker 25 Gd 20.17N 81.29 E
Kankesanturai 25 Gg 9.49N 80.02 E
Kankossa 32 Ef 15.55N 11.31W
Kankunski 20 He 57.39N 126.25 E
Kanla 10 Hf 50.48N 11.35 E
Kanmav Kyun 25 Jf 11.40N 98.28 E
Kanmon-Kaikyō 29 Bd 33.56N 130.57 E
Kanmuri-Yama 29 Cd 34.28N 132.05 E
Kannapolis 43 Kd 35.30N 80.37W
Kannone-Jima 28 Jj 28.51N 128.58 E
Kannonkoski 8 Kb 62.58N 25.15 E
Kannus 7 Fe 63.54N 23.54 E
Kano [2] 34 Gc 12.00N 9.00 E
Kano 31 Hg 12.00N 8.31 E
Kanona 36 Fe 13.04S 30.38 E
Kan'onji 28 Lg 34.07N 133.39 E
Kanoya 28 Ki 31.23N 130.51 E
Kanozero, Ozero- 7 Ic 67.00N 34.05 E
Kānpur 22 Kg 26.28N 80.21 E
Kansas 38 Jf 39.07N 94.36W
Kansas [2] 43 Hd 38.45N 98.15W
Kansas City [Ks.-U.S.] 39 Jf 39.07N 94.39W
Kansas City [Mo.-U.S.] 39 Jf 39.05N 94.35W
Kanshi 27 Kg 24.57N 116.52 E
Kansk 22 Ld 56.13N 95.41 E
Kansōng 28 Je 38.22N 128.28 E
Kansu (EN)=Gansu Sheng
(Kan-su Sheng) [2] 27 Hd 38.00N 102.00 E
Kansu (EN)=Kan-su
Sheng→Gansu Sheng [2] 27 Hd 38.00N 102.00 E
Kan-su Sheng→Gansu
Sheng=Kansu (EN) [2] 27 Hd 38.00N 102.00 E
Kansyat 26 Kg 2.15S 138.51 E
Kant 18 Jc 42.52N 74.50 E
Kantang 25 Jg 7.23N 99.32 E
Kantchari 34 Fc 12.29N 1.31 E
Kanté 34 Fd 9.57N 1.03 E
Kantemirovka 19 Df 49.45N 39.53 E
Kantō-Heiya 29 Fc 36.00N 139.30 E
Kanton Atoll 57 Je 2.50S 171.41W
Kantō-Sanchi 29 Fc 36.00N 138.45 E
Kantubek 18 Bb 45.06N 59.16 E
Kanturk/Ceann Toirc 9 Ei 52.10N 8.55W
Kanuma 29 Fc 36.34N 139.45 E
Kanye 31 Jk 24.58S 25.21 E
Kanyu 37 Cd 20.04S 24.36 E
Kanzenze 36 Ee 10.31S 25.12 E
Kao 65b Aa 19.40S 175.01W
Kaohsiung 22 Og 22.38N 120.17 E
Kaôk Nhêk 25 Lf 13.05N 107.04 E
Kaoko Otavi 37 Ac 18.15S 13.37 E
Kaokoveld [3] 37 Ac 18.00S 13.00 E
Kaokoveld 30 Ij 19.30S 13.30 E
Kaolack 31 Fg 14.09N 16.04W
Kao Neua, Col de- 25 Le 18.23N 105.10 E
Kaouadja 35 Cd 8.00N 23.14 E
Kaouar 34 Hb 19.05N 12.52 E
Kapaa 65a Ba 22.05N 159.19W
Kapanga 31 Ji 8.21S 22.35 E
Kapar 24 Ld 36.32N 47.30 E
Kapčagaj 19 Hg 43.52N 77.03 E
Kapčagajskoje
Vodohranilišče 18 Hg 43.45N 78.00 E
Kapchorwa 36 Fb 1.24N 34.27 E
Kap Dan 41 Ie 65.32N 37.30W
Kapelle 12 Fc 51.39N 3.57 E
Kapellskär 8 He 59.43N 19.04 E
Kapena 36 Ee 10.47S 28.20 E
Kapenguria 36 Gb 1.14N 35.07 E
Kapfenberg 14 Jc 47.26N 15.18 E
Kapidaği Yarimadası 15 Ki 40.28N 27.50 E
Kapiri Mposhi 36 Ee 13.58S 28.41 E
Kāpīsā [3] 23 Kc 34.45N 69.30 E
Kapit 26 Ff 2.01N 112.56 E
Kapiti Island 62 Fd 40.50S 174.55 E
Kapka, Massif du- 35 Cb 15.07N 21.45 E
Kapoeta 31 Kh 4.47N 33.35 E
Kapona 36 Ed 7.11S 29.09 E
Kapos 10 Oj 46.44N 18.29 E
Kaposvár 10 Nj 46.22N 17.48 E
Kapp 8 Dd 60.42N 10.52 E
Kappeln 10 Fb 54.40N 9.56 E
Kapša 7 Hg 59.52N 33.45 E
Kapsan 28 Jd 41.05N 128.18 E
Kapuas [Indon.] 26 Mj 0.25S 109.40 E
Kapuas [Indon.] 26 Fg 3.01S 114.20 E
Kapuas Hulu, Pegunungan-
=Kapuas Mountains (EN)
26 Ff 1.25N 113.15 E
Kapuas Mountains (EN)=
Kapuas Hulu,
Pegunungan 26 Ff 1.25N 113.15 E
Kapugargin 15 Lm 36.40N 28.50 E
Kapušany 10 Rg 49.03N 21.21 E
Kapuskasing 39 Ke 49.25N 82.26W
Kapustin Jar 16 Ne 48.35N 45.45 E
Kapustoje 7 Ic 67.17N 34.12 E
Kaputdžuh, Gora- 16 Oj 39.12N 46.01 E
Kapuvár 10 Ni 47.36N 17.02 E
Kara 17 Lb 69.10N 64.45 E
Kara 34 Fd 9.33N 1.12 E
Kara [3] 34 Fd 9.35N 1.05 E
Kara Ada [Tur.] 15 Km 36.58N 27.28 E
Kara Ada [Tur.] 15 Jk 38.25N 26.20 E
Kara-Balta 19 Hg 42.49N 73.57 E
Karabas 19 Hf 49.30N 73.00 E
Karabaš 17 Ji 55.29N 60.13 E
Karabekaul 19 Gh 38.28N 64.10 E
Karabiga 15 Ki 40.24N 27.18 E
Karabil, Vozvyšennost- 18 Df 36.20N 63.30 E
Kara-Bogaz-Gol 19 Fg 41.01N 52.59 E
Kara-Bogaz-Gol, proliv-
16 Ri 41.04N 52.59 E
Kara-Bogaz-Gol, Zaliv- 5 Lg 41.00N 53.15 E
Karabuk 23 Da 41.12N 32.37 E
Karabulak 18 Lb 44.54N 78.29 E
Karabulak 19 Gg 42.31N 69.47 E
Kara Burun 15 Km 36.32N 27.58 E
Karaburun [Tur.] 24 Cb 41.21N 28.40 E
Karaburun [Tur.] 24 Bc 38.37N 26.31 E
Karabutak 19 Gf 49.57N 60.08 E
Karacabey 24 Cb 40.13N 28.21 E
Karaca Dağ 24 Hd 37.40N 39.50 E
Karačajevo-Čerkesskaja
respublika 19 Eg 43.45N 41.45 E
Karačajevsk 16 Lh 43.44N 41.58 E
Karacaköy 24 Cb 41.22N 28.30 E
Karacaoğlan 15 Kh 41.32N 27.04 E
Karacasu 24 Cd 37.43N 28.37 E
Karačev 19 De 53.04N 34.59 E
Karāchi 22 Ig 24.52N 67.03 E
Kara Dağ [Tur.] 24 Jd 37.40N 43.42 E
Kara Dağ [Tur.] 24 Ed 37.23N 33.10 E
Karadah 16 Oh 42.29N 46.54 E
Karadeniz=Black Sea (EN)
5 Jg 43.00N 35.00 E
Kara Dong 27 Dd 38.26N 81.50 E
Karagajly 19 Hf 49.20N 75.48 E
Karaganda 22 Je 49.50N 73.10 E
Karagandinskaja Oblast [3] 19 Hf 50.00N 74.00 E
Karaginski, Ostrov- 21 Sd 58.48N 164.05 E
Karaginski Zaliv 21 Sd 58.50N 164.00 E
Kara Gölü 15 Mm 36.42N 29.50 E
Karagoš, Gora- 20 Df 51.44N 89.24 E
Karahalli 15 Mk 38.20N 29.32 E
Karaidelski 17 Hi 55.49N 57.05 E
Kara-Irtyš 21 Ke 47.52N 84.16 E
Karaisali 24 Fd 37.16N 35.03 E
Karaj 24 Ne 35.48N 50.59 E
Karaj 24 Ne 35.07N 51.35 E
Karak, Gora- 19 Gg 44.59N 63.05 E
Kara-Kala 19 Fh 38.28N 56.18 E
Karakalpakstan
respublika 19 Fg 43.30N 59.00 E
Karakax/Moyu 27 Cd 37.17N 79.42 E
Karakax He 27 Dd 38.06N 80.24 E
Karakaya Baraji 24 Hc 38.25N 38.45 E
Karakeçi 24 Hd 37.26N 39.26 E
Karakelong, Pulau- 26 If 4.15N 126.48 E
Karakoçan 24 Ic 38.02N 40.07 E
Karakoin, Ozero- 18 Ga 46.10N 68.40 E
Karakojsu 16 Oh 42.30N 47.05 E
Karakolka 18 Kd 41.29N 77.24 E
Karakoram 18 Je 34.00N 78.00 E
Karakoram Pass 21 Jf 35.30N 77.50 E
Karakore 35 Gc 10.25N 40.01 E
Karakoro 34 Cc 14.43N 12.03 E
Karakorum Shan 27 Cd 36.00N 76.00 E
Karakorum Shankou 27 Cd 35.30N 77.50 E
Karaköy 24 Ic 39.04N 41.42 E
Kara-Kul 18 Id 41.34N 72.47 E
Karakul, Ozero- 19 Hh 39.05N 73.25 E
Karakumski kanal imeni V.I.
Lenina 19 Gh 37.42N 64.20 E
Karakumy 21 Hf 39.00N 60.00 E
Karakuwisa 37 Bc 18.56S 19.40 E
Karam 20 Fe 55.09N 107.37 E
Karama 26 Gg 2.18S 119.06 E
Karaman 23 Db 37.11N 33.14 E
Karamanli 15 Ml 37.22N 29.49 E
Karamay 22 Ke 45.30N 84.55 E
Karamea 61 Dh 41.15S 172.06 E
Karamea Bight 62 Dd 41.25S 171.50 E
Karamet-Nijaz 19 Gh 37.43N 64.31 E
Karamiran He 27 Dd 37.50N 84.35 E
Karamiran Shankou 27 Ed 36.15N 87.05 E
Karamiševo 8 Mg 57.44N 28.50 E
Karamoja [3] 36 Fb 2.45N 34.15 E
Karamürsel 15 Mi 40.42N 29.36 E
Kara-myk 19 Hh 39.30N 71.51 E
Karamyš 16 Nd 51.18N 45.00 E
Karān 24 Mi 27.43N 49.49 E
Karaova 15 Kl 37.05N 27.40 E
Karapınar 24 Ed 37.43N 33.33 E
Kara-Saki 29 Ad 34.40N 129.29 E
Kara-Sal 16 Mf 47.18N 43.36 E
Karasay 27 Dd 36.48N 83.48 E
Karasburg 31 Ik 28.00S 18.43 E
Kara Sea (EN)=Karskoje
More 67 Hd 76.00N 80.00 E
Karašica 14 Me 45.36N 18.36 E
Karasjok 7 Fb 69.27N 25.30 E
Kara Strait (EN)=Karskije
Vorota, Proliv- 21 Hb 70.30N 58.00 E
Karasu 24 Db 41.04N 30.47 E
Karasu [Tur.] 21 Ff 38.52N 38.48 E
Karasu [Tur.] 24 Ic 38.49N 41.28 E
Karasu [Tur.] 24 Jc 38.32N 43.10 E
Karasu Dağları 24 Ic 39.30N 40.45 E
Karasuk 20 Cf 53.44N 78.08 E
Karasuk 20 Cf 53.35N 77.30 E
Karasuyama 29 Gc 36.39N 140.08 E
Karatá, Laguna- 49 Fg 13.56N 83.30W
Karatal 19 Hf 46.26N 77.10 E
Karataş [Tur.] 24 Fd 36.36N 35.21 E
Karataş [Tur.] 15 Lk 38.34N 28.17 E
Karataş Burun 24 Fb 36.35N 35.22 E
Karatau 19 Hg 43.10N 70.29 E
Karatau, Hrebet- 21 Ie 43.40N 69.00 E
Karatj 7 Ec 66.43N 18.33 E
Karatobe 16 Re 49.42N 53.33 E
Karaton 19 Ff 46.25N 53.34 E
Karatsu 28 Jh 33.26N 130.00 E
Karatsu-Wan 29 Be 33.30N 130.00 E
Kara-Turgaj 21 Ie 48.01N 62.45 E
Karaul 19 Hf 49.00N 79.20 E
Karaul 20 Db 70.10N 83.08 E
Karaulbazar 18 Ee 39.29N 64.47 E
Karaulkala 18 Bc 42.18N 58.41 E
Karāva 15 Ej 39.19N 21.36 E
Karavanke 14 Id 46.25N 14.25 E
Karavastase, Gjiri i- 15 Ci 40.55N 19.30 E
Karavastase, Laguna e- 15 Ci 40.55N 19.30 E
Karávi 15 Gm 36.45N 23.35 E
Karavonísia 15 Jn 35.59N 26.26 E
Karawa 36 Db 3.20N 20.18 E
Karaxabar He/Kaidu He 27 Ec 41.55N 86.38 E
Karažal 19 Hf 47.59N 70.53 E
Karbalā' 22 Gf 32.36N 44.02 E
Karbalā [3] 24 Jf 32.30N 43.45 E
Kårbole 7 Df 61.59N 15.19 E
Karcag 10 Qi 47.19N 20.56 E
Kardeljevo (Ploče) 14 Lg 43.04N 17.26 E
Kardhámaina 15 Km 36.47N 27.09 E
Kardhámila 15 Jk 38.31N 26.06 E
Kardhiotissa 15 Im 36.38N 25.01 E
Kardhítsa 15 Ej 39.22N 21.55 E
Kärdla/Kjardla 7 Fg 59.01N 22.42 E
Kărdžali 15 Ih 41.39N 25.22 E
Kărdžali [2] 15 Ih 41.30N 25.30 E
Kareha, Jbel- 13 Gi 35.15N 5.30W
Karelia (EN) 8 Jc 64.00N 32.00 E
Karelija, respublika 19 Dc 63.30N 33.30 E
Karema 36 Fd 6.49S 30.26 E
Karen → Kayin 25 Je 17.30N 97.45 E
Karen 25 If 12.51N 92.53 E
Karesuando 7 Fb 68.27N 22.29 E
Karêt 30 Gf 24.00N 7.30W
Kärevere/Kjarevere 8 Lf 58.23N 26.30 E
Kargala 16 Sd 51.59N 55.10 E
Kargapazari Daği 24 Ib 40.07N 41.35 E
Kargapolje 17 Li 55.57N 64.27 E
Kargasok 20 De 59.07N 81.01 E
Kargat 20 De 55.10N 80.17 E
Kargı 24 Fb 41.08N 34.30 E
Kargil 25 Fb 34.34N 76.06 E
Kargilik/Yecheng 22 Jf 37.54N 77.26 E
Kargopol 19 Dc 61.32N 38.58 E
Karhula 7 Gf 60.31N 26.57 E
Kari 34 Hc 11.14N 10.34 E
Kariai 6 Ig 40.15N 24.15 E
Kariba 31 Jj 16.30S 28.45 E
Kariba, Lake- 30 Jj 17.00S 28.00 E
Kariba-Dake 29a Ab 42.37N 139.56 E
Kariba Dam 37 Dc 16.30S 28.50 E
Karibib 31 Ik 21.58S 15.51 E
Karibib [3] 37 Bd 22.00S 16.00 E
Kariet-Arkmane 13 Ji 35.06N 2.45W
Karigasniemi 7 Fb 69.24N 25.50 E
Karijärvi 8 Jc 61.35N 22.30 E
Karikachi Tōge 29a Cb 43.10N 142.40 E
Kārikāl 25 Ff 10.55N 79.50 E
Karikari, Cape- 62 Ea 34.47S 173.24 E
Karima (EN)=Kuraymah 31 Kg 18.33N 31.51 E
Karimama 34 Fc 12.04N 3.11 E
Karimata, Kepulauan-=
Karimata Islands (EN) 26 Eg 1.25S 109.05 E
Karimata, Pulau- 26 Eg 1.36S 108.55 E
Karimata, Selat-=Karimata
Strait (EN) 21 Mj 2.05S 108.40 E
Karimata Islands (EN)=
Karimata, Kepulauan- 26 Eg 1.25S 109.05 E
Karimata Strait (EN)=
Karimata, Selat- 21 Mj 2.05S 108.40 E
Karīmganj 25 Id 24.42N 92.33 E
Karīmnagar 25 Fe 18.26N 79.09 E
Karimunjawa, Kepulauan-=
Karimunjawa Islands (EN) 26 Fh 5.50S 110.25 E
Karimunjawa Islands (EN)=
Karimunjawa, Kepulauan- 26 Fh 5.50S 110.25 E
Karin [Som.] 35 Hc 10.59N 49.13 E
Karin [Som.] 35 Hc 10.51N 45.45 E
Karis/Karjaa 7 Ff 60.05N 23.40 E
Karisimbi 30 Ji 1.30S 29.27 E
Káristos 15 Hk 38.01N 24.25 E
Karkār 35 Hd 9.57N 49.20 E
Karkaralinsk 19 Hf 49.23N 75.31 E
Karkar Island 57 Fe 4.40S 146.00 E
Karkas, Kūh-e 24 Nf 33.27N 51.48 E
Karkheh 23 Gc 31.31N 47.55 E
Karkinitski zaliv 5 Jf 45.55N 33.00 E
Karkkila/Högfors 7 Ff 60.32N 24.11 E
Karkku 8 Jc 61.25N 23.01 E
Kärkölä 8 Kd 60.55N 25.15 E
Kärla/Kjarla 8 Jf 58.16N 22.05 E
Karlholm 8 Gd 60.31N 17.37 E
Karlik Shan 21 Le 43.00N 94.30 E
Karlino 10 Lb 54.03N 15.51 E
Karliova 24 Ic 39.18N 41.01 E
Karl Marx, Pik- 19 Hh 37.08N 72.29 E
Karl-Marx-Stadt →
Chemnitz 6 He 50.50N 12.55 E
Karlö/Hailuoto 5 Ib 65.02N 24.42 E
Karlobag 14 Jf 44.32N 15.05 E
Karlovac 14 Je 45.29N 15.33 E
Karlovka 16 Ie 49.28N 35.08 E
Karlovo 15 Hg 42.38N 24.48 E
Karlovy Vary 10 If 50.14N 12.52 E
Karlsbad 12 Kf 48.55N 8.35 E
Karlsborg 7 Df 58.32N 14.31 E
Karlshamn 7 Dh 56.10N 14.51 E
Karlskoga 7 Dg 59.20N 14.31 E
Karlskrona 6 Hd 56.10N 15.35 E
Karlsöarna 8 Gg 57.15N 18.00 E
Karlsruhe 10 Eg 49.01N 8.24 E
Karlstad [Mn.-U.S.] 45 Hb 48.35N 96.31W
Karlstad [Swe.] 6 Hd 59.22N 13.30 E
Karluk 40 Ie 57.34N 154.28W
Karmah=Kerma (EN) 35 Eb 19.38N 30.25 E
Karmana 18 Ed 40.09N 65.15 E
Karmøy 7 Ag 59.15N 5.15 E
Karnāli 25 Gc 28.45N 81.16 E
Karnataka (Mysore) [3] 25 Ff 13.30N 76.00 E
Karnobat 15 Jg 42.39N 26.59 E
Kärnten = Carinthia (EN)
[2] 14 Hd 46.45N 14.00 E
Kärnten = Carinthia (EN)
14 Hd 46.45N 14.00 E
Karoi 37 Dc 16.50S 29.40 E
Karonga 31 Ki 9.56S 33.56 E
Karora 35 Fb 17.39N 38.22 E
Káros 15 Im 36.53N 25.39 E
Kárpathos 15 Kn 35.30N 27.14 E
Kárpathos=Karpathos (EN)
5 Ih 35.40N 27.10 E
Karpathos (EN)=
Kárpathos 5 Ih 35.40N 27.10 E
Karpáthou, Stenón- 15 Kn 35.50N 27.30 E
Karpenísion 15 Ek 38.55N 21.47 E
Karpinsk 17 Jg 59.45N 60.01 E
Karpuzlu 15 Kl 37.33N 27.50 E
Kars 23 Fa 40.37N 43.05 E
Karsakpaj 19 Gf 47.48N 66.45 E
Kärsämäki 7 Fe 64.00N 25.46 E
Kärsava/Kārsava 7 Gh 56.47N 27.42 E
Kārsava/Karsava 7 Gh 56.47N 27.42 E
Karši 22 If 38.53N 65.48 E
Karşiyaka 15 Ki 40.26N 28.00 E
Karşiyaka 15 Kk 38.27N 27.07 E
Karskije Vorota, Proliv-=
Kara Strait (EN) 21 Hb 70.30N 58.00 E
Karskoje More=Kara Sea
(EN) 67 Hd 76.00N 80.00 E
Kars Platosu 24 Jb 40.40N 43.07 E
Karst (EN)=Kras 5 Hf 45.48N 14.00 E
Kårsta 8 He 59.39N 18.14 E
Karstula 7 Fe 62.52N 24.47 E
Kartal 24 Cb 40.53N 29.10 E
Kartaly 19 Ge 53.03N 60.40 E
Kartaly-Ajat 17 Jj 53.01N 61.50 E
Karttula 8 Lb 62.53N 26.58 E
Kartuzy 10 Ob 54.20N 18.12 E
Karumai 29 Ga 40.20N 141.28 E
Karumba 59 Ic 17.29S 140.50 E
Karūn 21 Gf 30.25N 48.12 E
Karungi 7 Fc 66.03N 23.57 E
Karungu 36 Fc 0.51S 34.09 E
Karunki 7 Fc 66.02N 24.01 E
Karūr 25 Ff 10.57N 78.05 E
Karvia 7 Fe 62.08N 22.34 E
Karviná 10 Og 49.51N 18.32 E
Kārwār 25 Ef 14.48N 74.08 E
Karwendel Gebirge 14 Fc 47.28N 11.20 E
Karymskoje 20 Gf 51.37N 114.21 E
Kas 35 Cc 12.34N 24.14 E
Kaş 24 Cd 36.12N 29.38 E
Kasaba [Tur.] 15 Mm 36.18N 29.44 E
Kasaba [Zam.] 36 Ee 10.44S 29.43 E
Kasado-Shima 29 Be 33.57N 131.50 E
Kasah 16 Mi 40.03N 43.52 E
Kasai 29 Dd 34.56N 134.49 E
Kasai 30 Ii 3.02S 16.57 E
Kasai Occidental [2] 36 Dc 5.00S 21.30 E
Kasai Oriental [2] 36 Dc 3.00S 23.00 E
Kasaji 36 De 10.22S 23.27 E
Kasaku 36 Ec 1.55S 25.50 E
Kasama [Jap.] 29 Gc 36.22N 140.16 E
Kasama [Zam.] 31 Kj 10.13S 31.12 E
Kasan 18 Ee 39.01N 65.35 E
Kasane 31 Jj 17.48S 25.09 E
Kasanga 36 Fd 8.28S 31.09 E
Kasangulu 36 Bc 4.36S 15.10 E
Kasansaj 18 Hd 41.10N 71.32 E
Kasaoka 29 Cd 34.30N 133.29 E
Kāsaragod 25 Ef 12.30N 75.00 E
Kasari 29b Ba 28.27N 129.41 E
Kašary 16 Le 49.02N 41.03 E
Kasatori-Yama 29 Ce 33.33N 132.55 E
Kasba Lake 42 Hd 60.20N 102.10W
Kasba Tatla 32 Fc 32.36N 6.16W
Kaseda 28 Ki 31.25N 130.19 E
Kasempa 36 Ee 13.27S 25.50 E
Kasenga 31 Jj 10.22S 28.37 E
Kasenye 36 Fb 1.24N 30.26 E
Kasese [Ug.] 36 Fb 0.10N 30.05 E
Kasese [Zaire] 36 Ec 1.38S 27.07 E
Kashaf 23 Jb 35.58N 61.07 E
Kāshān 22 Hf 33.59N 51.29 E
Kashi 22 Jf 39.29N 75.58 E
Kashihara 29 Dd 34.31N 135.47 E
Kashima [Jap.] 29 Cd 35.31N 132.59 E
Kashima [Jap.] 29 Gd 35.58N 140.38 E
Kashima [Jap.] 29 Be 33.07N 130.07 E
Kashima-Nada 29 Gc 36.30N 140.45 E
Kashiobwe 36 Ed 9.39S 28.37 E
Kashiwazaki 28 Of 37.25N 138.30 E
Kashkū'īyeh 24 Qh 28.58N 56.37 E
Kāshmar 23 Ib 35.12N 58.27 E
Kashmir 21 Jf 34.00N 76.00 E
Kashmor 25 Dc 28.26N 69.35 E
Kasimov 19 Ee 54.59N 41.28 E
Kašin 19 Dd 57.23N 37.37 E
Kasindi 36 Eb 0.02N 29.43 E
Kašira 7 Ji 54.52N 38.11 E
Kasiruta, Pulau- 26 Ig 0.25S 127.12 E
Kasisty 20 Fb 73.40N 109.45 E
Kaškadarinskaja Oblast [3] 19 Gh 38.50N 66.10 E
Kaškadarja 18 Ee 39.35N 64.38 E
Kaskaskia River 45 Lh 37.59N 89.56W
Kaskelen 19 Hg 43.09N 76.37 E
Kaskö/Kaskinen 7 Ee 62.23N 21.13 E
Kasli 17 Ji 55.53N 60.48 E
Kaslo 46 Gb 49.55N 116.55W
Kasongo 31 Ji 4.27S 26.40 E
Kasongo-Lunda 36 Cd 6.28S 16.49 E
Kásos 15 Jn 35.25N 26.55 E
Kásou, Stenon- 15 Jn 35.25N 26.35 E
Kaspi 16 Ni 41.58N 44.25 E
Kaspičan 15 Kf 43.18N 27.11 E
Kaspijsk 19 Eg 42.57N 47.35 E
Kaspijski 19 Ef 45.25N 47.22 E
Kaspijskoje More=Caspian
Sea (EN) 5 Lg 42.00N 50.30 E
Kasplja 16 Gb 55.24N 30.43 E
Kasr, Ra's- 35 Fb 18.04N 38.33 E
Kassaar/Kassar 8 Jf 58.47N 22.40 E
Kassalā 31 Kg 15.28N 36.24 E
Kassalā [3] 35 Fc 14.40N 35.30 E
Kassándra 15 Gi 40.00N 23.30 E
Kassandra, Gulf of- (EN) =
Kassándras, Kólpos- 15 Gi 40.05N 23.30 E
Kassándras, Ákra- 15 Gj 39.57N 23.21 E
Kassándras, Kólpos- =
Kassandra, Gulf of- (EN)
15 Gi 40.05N 23.30 E
Kassel 10 Fe 51.19N 9.30 E
Kassiópi 15 Cj 39.47N 19.55 E
Kastamonu 23 Da 41.22N 33.47 E
Kastanéai 15 Jh 41.39N 26.28 E
Kastellaun 12 Jd 50.04N 7.27 E
Kastéllion [Grc.] 15 In 35.12N 25.20 E
Kastéllion [Grc.] 15 Gn 35.30N 23.39 E
Kastéllos, Ákra- 15 Kn 35.23N 27.09 E
Kasterlee 12 Gc 51.15N 4.57 E
Kastlösa 8 Gh 56.28N 16.25 E
Kastoria 15 Ei 40.31N 21.16 E
Kastorias, Límni- 15 Ei 40.31N 21.18 E
Kastornoje 16 Kd 51.51N 38.07 E
Kastós 15 Dk 38.35N 20.55 E
Kasuga 29 Be 33.32N 130.27 E
Kasugai 29 Ed 35.14N 136.58 E
Kasulu 36 Fc 4.34S 30.06 E
Kasumbalesa 36 Ee 12.13S 27.48 E
Kasumi 29 Dd 35.38N 134.38 E
Kasumi-ga-Ura 28 Pf 36.00N 140.25 E
Kasumkent 16 Pi 41.42N 48.10 E
Kasungan 26 Fg 1.58S 113.24 E
Kasungu 36 Fe 13.02S 33.29 E
Kasupe 36 Gf 15.10S 35.18 E
Kasūr 25 Eb 31.07N 74.27 E
Kaszuby 10 Ob 54.10N 18.15 E
Kataba 31 Jj 16.05S 25.10 E
Katahdin, Mount- 43 Nb 45.55N 68.55W
Katajsk 17 Kh 56.18N 62.35 E
Katako-Kombe 36 Dc 3.24S 24.25 E
Katanga 36 Ed 10.00S 25.30 E
Katanga 20 Fd 60.10N 102.10 E
Katangli 20 Jf 51.43N 143.16 E
Katanning 59 Df 33.42S 117.33 E
Katav-Ivanovsk 17 Ii 54.47N 58.15 E
Katchall 25 Ig 7.57N 93.22 E
Katchi 32 Ef 17.00N 13.55W
Katende, Chutes de- 36 Dd 6.30S 22.10 E
Katerini 15 Fi 40.16N 22.30 E
Katesh 36 Gc 4.31S 35.23 E
Katete 36 Fe 14.06S 32.05 E
Katha 25 Jd 24.11N 96.21 E
Katherine 58 Ef 14.28S 132.16 E
Katherine River 59 Gb 14.39S 131.42 E
Kāthiāwār 21 Jg 21.58N 70.30 E
Kāthmāndāū =
Kathmandu (EN) 22 Kg 27.43N 85.19 E
Kathmandu →
Kāthmāndāū 22 Kg 27.43N 85.19 E
Kathua 36 Gc 1.17S 39.03 E
Kati 34 Dc 12.43N 8.05W
Katihār 25 Hc 25.32N 87.35 E
Katiki, Volcán- 65d Bb 27.06S 109.16W
Katima Mulilo 36 Df 17.28S 24.14 E
Katiola 34 Dd 8.08N 5.06W
Katiola [3] 34 Dd 8.13N 5.02W
Katiu Atoll 61 Mc 16.26S 144.22W
Katla 7a Bc 63.38N 18.58W
Katlabuh, Ozero- 15 Ld 45.25N 29.00 E
Katlanovo 15 Eh 41.54N 21.41 E
Katmai, Mount- 40 Ie 58.17N 154.56W
Káto Akhaia 15 Ek 38.09N 21.33 E
Katofio 36 Ee 11.02S 28.01 E
Katompi 36 Ed 6.11S 26.20 E
Katonga 36 Fb 0.10N 30.40 E
Katon-Karagaj 19 If 49.11N 85.37 E
Káto Ólimbos 15 Fj 39.55N 22.28 E
Katoomba 59 Kf 33.42S 150.18 E
Katopasa, Gunung- 26 Hg 1.14S 121.25 E

Index Symbols

[1] Independent Nation
[2] State, Region
[3] District, County
[4] Municipality
[5] Colony, Dependency
Continent
Physical Region
Historical or Cultural Region
Mount, Mountain
Volcano
Hill
Mountains, Mountain Range
Hills, Escarpment
Plateau, Upland
Pass, Gap
Plain, Lowland
Delta
Salt Flat
Valley, Canyon
Crater, Cave
Karst Features
Depression
Polder
Desert, Dunes
Forest, Woods
Heath, Steppe
Oasis
Cape, Point
Coast, Beach
Cliff
Peninsula
Isthmus
Sandbank
Island
Atoll
Rock, Reef
Islands, Archipelago
Rocks, Reefs
Coral Reef
Well, Spring
Geyser
River, Stream
Waterfall Rapids
River Mouth, Estuary
Lake
Salt Lake
Intermittent Lake
Reservoir
Swamp, Pond
Canal
Glacier
Ice Shelf, Pack Ice
Ocean
Sea
Gulf, Bay
Strait, Fjord
Lagoon
Bank
Seamount
Tablemount
Ridge
Shelf
Basin
Escarpment, Sea Scarp
Fracture
Trench, Abyss
National Park, Reserve
Point of Interest
Recreation Site
Cave, Cavern
Historic Site
Ruins
Wall, Walls
Church, Abbey
Temple
Scientific Station
Airport
Port
Lighthouse
Mine
Tunnel
Dam, Bridge

Katowice [2] 10 Of 50.15N 19.00 E
Katowice 6 He 50.16N 19.00 E
Katrancık Dağı 24 Dd 37.27N 30.25 E
Kātrīnā, Jabal- 30 Kf 28.31N 33.57 E
Katrineholm 7 Dg 59.00N 16.12 E
Katsina 31 Hg 13.00N 7.36 E
Katsina Ala 34 Gd 7.48N 8.52 E
Katsumoto 28 Jh 33.51N 129.42 E
Katsuta 28 Pf 36.24N 140.32 E
Katsuura 28 Pg 35.08N 140.18 E
Katsuyama [Jap.] 28 Nf 36.03N 136.30 E
Katsuyama [Jap.] 29 Cd 35.06N 133.41 E
Kattakurgan 19 Gh 39.55N 66.15 E
Kattavia 15 Kn 35.57N 27.46 E
Kattegat 5 Hd 57.00N 11.00 E
Katthammarsvik 8 Hg 57.26N 18.50 E
Katulo, Lagh- 36 Hb 2.08N 40.56 E
Katumbi 36 Fe 10.49S 33.32 E
Katun 21 Kd 52.25N 85.05 E
Katwijk aan Zee 11 Kb 52.13N 4.24 E
Katwijk aan Zee, Katwijk- 12 Gb 52.12N 4.25 E
Katwijk-Katwijk aan Zee 12 Gb 52.12N 4.25 E
Katzenelnbogen 12 Jd 50.17N 7.57 E
Kau 26 If 1.11N 127.54 E
Kauai Channel 60 Oc 21.45N 158.50W
Kauai Island 57 Lb 22.03N 159.30W
Kaub 12 Jd 50.05N 7.46 E
Kauehi Atoll 61 Lc 15.51S 145.09W
Kaufbeuren 10 Gi 47.53N 10.37 E
Kauhajoki 7 Fe 62.26N 22.11 E
Kauhava 7 Fe 63.06N 23.05 E
Kauiki Head 60 Oc 20.46N 155.59W
Kaukauna 45 Ld 44.17N 88.17W
Kaukauveld 30 Jk 20.00S 21.50 E
Kaukonen 7 Fc 67.29N 24.54 E
Kaukura Atoll 57 Mf 15.45S 146.42W
Kaula Island 57 Kb 21.40N 160.32W
Kaulakahi Channel 65a Ba 22.02N 159.53W
Kaumalapau 65a Ec 20.47N 156.59W
Kaunakakai 60 Oc 21.05N 157.02W
Kaunas 6 Ie 54.54N 23.54 E
Kaunasskoje Vodohranilišče /Kauno Marios 8 Kj 54.50N 24.15 E
Kauniainen/Grankulla 8 Kd 60.13N 24.45 E
Kauno Marios/Kaunasskoje Vodohranilišče 8 Kj 54.50N 24.15 E
Kaunos 15 Lm 36.50N 28.35 E
Kaupanger 7 Bf 61.11N 7.14 E
Kau Paulatmada, Gunung- 26 Ig 3.15S 126.09 E
Kaura Namoda 34 Gc 12.36N 6.35 E
Kauriāla Ghāt 25 Gc 28.27N 80.59 E
Kaušany 16 Ff 46.39N 29.25 E
Kaustinen 7 Fe 63.32N 23.42 E
Kautokeino 7 Fb 68.59N 23.08 E
Kavacik 15 Lj 39.40N 28.30 E
Kavadarci 15 Fh 41.26N 22.01 E
Kavaja 15 Ch 41.11N 19.33 E
Kavak [Tur.] 15 Ji 40.36N 26.54 E
Kavak [Tur.] 24 Gb 41.05N 36.03 E
Kavaklidere 15 Ll 37.26N 28.22 E
Kavála 6 Ig 40.56N 24.25 E
Kavála, Kólpos- 15 Hi 40.52N 24.25 E
Kavalerovo 20 Ih 44.19N 135.05 E
Kavali 25 Ff 14.55N 79.59 E
Kavār 24 Oh 29.11N 52.44 E
Kavaratti 25 Jh 10.33N 72.38 E
Kavaratti Island 25 Ef 10.33N 72.38 E
Kavarna 15 Lf 43.25N 28.20 E
Kavarskas/Kovarskas 8 Ki 55.24N 25.03 E
Kavendou, Mont- 30 Fg 10.41N 12.12W
Kavieng 60 Eh 2.34S 150.48 E
Kavīr, Dasht-e- 21 Hf 34.40N 54.30 E
Kavkaz 16 Jg 45.21N 36.12 E
Kavkaz, Bolšoj-=Caucasus (EN) 5 Kg 42.30N 45.00 E
Kävlinge 8 Ei 55.48N 13.06 E
Kävlingeån 8 Ei 55.47N 13.06 E
Kawa 35 Eb 19.10N 30.39 E
Kawabe 29 Gb 39.39N 140.15 E
Kawachi-nagano 29 Dd 34.27N 135.34 E
Kawagoe 29 Fd 35.55N 139.28 E
Kawaguchi 29 Fd 35.48N 139.42 E
Kawaihae Bay 65a Fc 20.02N 155.51W
Kawaihoa Point 65a Ab 21.47N 160.12W
Kawakawa 62 Fa 35.23S 174.04 E
Kawalusu, Pulau- 26 If 4.15N 125.19 E
Kawamata 29 Gc 37.40N 140.36 E
Kawambwa 36 Ed 9.47S 29.05 E
Kawaminami 29 Be 32.12N 131.32 E
Kawamoto 29 Cd 34.59N 132.29 E
Kawanishi 29 Gc 37.59N 140.03 E
Kawanoe 29 Cd 34.01N 133.34 E
Kawartha Lakes 44 Hc 44.32N 78.30W
Kawasaki [Jap.] 29 Gb 38.10N 140.38 E
Kawasaki [Jap.] 28 Og 35.32N 139.43 E
Kawashiri-Misaki 29 Bd 34.26N 130.58 E
Kawauchi 29a Bc 41.12N 141.00 E
Kawau Island 62 Fb 36.25S 174.50 E
Kawaura 29 Be 32.21N 130.05 E
Kawerau 62 Gc 38.05S 176.42 E
Kawhia 62 Fc 38.04S 174.49 E
Kawich Range 46 Gh 37.40N 116.30W
Kawio, Kepulauan- 26 If 4.30N 125.30 E
Kawkareik 25 Je 16.33N 98.14 E
Kawm Umbū 35 Fe 24.28N 32.57 E
Kawthaung 25 Jg 9.59N 98.33 E
Kaxgar He 21 Jf 39.46N 78.15 E
Kax He 27 Dc 43.37N 81.48 E
Kaya 34 Ec 13.05N 1.05W
Kayah [2] 25 Je 19.15N 97.30 E
Kayak 40 Ke 59.52N 144.30W
Kayali Dağı 15 Jj 39.58N 26.38 E
Kayan 21 Ni 2.55N 117.35 E
Kayanga 34 Bc 11.58N 15.00W
Kayangel Islands 57 Ed 8.04N 134.43 E
Kayangel Passage 64a Ba 8.01N 134.42 E
Kaycee 46 Le 43.43N 106.38W
Kayenta 46 Jh 36.44N 110.17W
Kayes [3] 34 Cc 14.00N 11.00W
Kayes 31 Fg 14.26N 11.27W
Kayin 25 Je 17.30N 97.45 E
Kayoa, Pulau- 26 Ig 0.05S 127.25 E
Kayseri 22 Ff 38.43N 35.30 E
Kayuagung 26 Dg 3.24S 104.50 E
Kayu Ara, Pulau- 26 Ef 1.31N 106.26 E
Kazačje 20 Ib 70.40N 136.13 E
Kazah 16 Ni 41.05N 45.22 E
Kazahskaja Sovetskaja Socialističeskaja Respublika → Kazakhstan 19 Gf 48.00N 68.00 E
Kazahskaja SSR/Kazak Sovettik Socialistik Respublikasy → Kazakhstan 19 Gf 48.00N 68.00 E
Kazahskaja SSR → Kazakhstan 19 Gf 48.00N 68.00 E
Kazahski Melkosopočnik = Kazakh Hills (EN) 21 Je 49.00N 73.00 E
Kazahski Zaliv 16 Rh 42.40N 52.25 E
Kazakh Hills (EN) = Kazahski Melkosopočnik 21 Je 49.00N 73.00 E
Kazakhstan (EN) = Qazaqstan 19 Gf 48.00N 68.00 E
Kazakhstan (EN) 21 Ie 47.00N 65.00 E
Kazaklija 15 Lc 46.05N 28.38 E
Kazak SSR → Qazaqstan 19 Gf 48.00N 68.00 E
Kazalinsk 19 Gf 45.46N 62.07 E
Kazan 6 Kd 55.45N 49.08 E
Kazan 38 Jc 64.02N 95.30W
Kazandžik 19 Fh 39.17N 55.34 E
Kazanka 7 Li 55.48N 49.05 E
Kazanka 16 Hf 47.50N 32.49 E
Kazanlăk 15 Ig 42.37N 25.24 E
Kazan-Rettō/Iō=Volcano Islands (EN) 21 Qg 25.00N 141.00 E
Kazanskoje 19 Gd 55.38N 69.14 E
Kazarman 19 Hg 41.20N 74.02 E
Kazatin 19 Cf 49.43N 28.50 E
Kazbek, Gora- 5 Kg 42.42N 44.31 E
Kaz Dağı 23 Cb 39.42N 26.50 E
Kaz Dağı 15 Mk 38.35N 29.15 E
Kāzerūn 22 Hg 29.37N 51.38 E
Kažim 17 Ef 60.20N 51.32 E
Kazi-Magomed 16 Pi 40.02N 48.56 E
Kazimierza Wielka 10 Qf 50.16N 20.30 E
Kâzımkarabekir 24 Ed 37.14N 32.59 E
Kazincbarcika 10 Qh 48.15N 20.38 E
Kazinga Channel 36 Ec 0.13S 29.53 E
Kazlų-Rūda/Kazlu-Ruda 8 Jj 54.42N 23.32 E
Kazo 29 Fc 36.08N 139.36 E
Kaztalovka 16 Pe 49.46N 48.44 E
Kazumba 36 Dd 6.25S 22.02 E
Kazuno 28 Pd 40.14N 140.48 E
Kazym 19 Gc 63.54N 65.50 E
Kazyr 20 Ef 53.50N 92.53 E
Kcynia 10 Nd 53.00N 17.30 E
Kdyně 10 Jg 49.24N 13.02 E
Ké 35 Bb 18.32N 17.55 E
Kéa 15 Hl 37.37N 24.20 E
Kéa 15 Hl 37.39N 24.20 E
Keaau 65a Fd 19.37N 155.03W
Keahole Point 65a Ed 19.44N 156.04W
Kealaikahiki Channel 65a Ec 20.37N 156.50W
Kealaikahiki Point 65a Ec 20.32N 156.42W
Kealakekua Bay 65a Fd 19.28N 155.56W
Keams Canyon 46 Ji 35.49N 110.12W
Keanae 65a Ec 20.52N 156.09W
Keanapapa Point 65a Dc 20.54N 157.04W
Kearney 43 Hc 40.42N 99.05W
Kearns 46 Jf 40.39N 111.59W
Kéas, Stenón- 15 Hl 37.40N 24.12 E
Keats Bank (EN) 57 Id 5.23N 173.28 E
Keb 8 Mg 57.44N 28.38 E
Keban Barajı 24 Hc 38.53N 39.00 E
Kébémer 34 Bb 15.22N 16.27W
Kebir, Oued el- 14 Bn 36.51N 7.57 E
Kebnekaise 5 Hb 67.53N 18.33 E
Kebri Dehar 31 Lh 6.45N 44.17 E
Kebumen 26 Eh 7.40S 109.39 E
Kecel 10 Pj 46.32N 19.16 E
Kechika 42 Ee 59.38N 127.09W
Kecskemét 10 Pj 46.54N 19.42 E
Kėdainiai/Kedajnjaj 7 Fi 55.18N 23.59 E
Kedajnjaj/Kėdainiai 7 Fi 55.18N 23.59 E
Kedgwick 44 Nb 47.39N 67.21W
Kediri 22 Nj 7.49S 112.01 E
Kédougou 34 Cc 12.33N 12.11W
Kedva 17 Fd 64.14N 53.30 E
Kędzierzyn-Koźle 10 Of 50.20N 18.10 E
Keele 42 Fd 64.24N 124.47W
Keele Peak 38 Fc 63.26N 130.19W
Keeling Islands → Cocos Islands 21 Lk 12.10S 96.55 E
Keeling Islands → Cocos Islands [5] 22 Lk 12.10S 96.55 E
Keelung 22 Og 25.08N 121.44 E
Keene 44 Kd 42.55N 72.17W
Keer-Weer, Cape- 59 Ib 13.58S 141.30 E
Keetmanshoop 31 Ik 26.36S 18.08 E
Keetmanshoop [3] 37 Be 26.30S 18.30 E
Keewatin 42 Ig 49.46N 94.34W
Keewatin, District of- [3] 42 Hd 64.00N 96.00W
Kefa [3] 35 Fd 7.00N 36.00 E
Kefallinía=Cephalonia (EN) 5 Ih 38.15N 20.35 E
Kefamenanu 26 Hh 9.27S 124.29 E
Kefar Sava 24 Ff 32.10N 34.54 E
Keffi 34 Gd 8.51N 7.52 E
Keflavík 7a Ab 64.01N 22.34W
Kegen 19 Hg 42.58N 79.12 E
Kegums 8 Kh 56.41N 24.44 E
Kehdingen 10 Fc 53.45N 9.20 E
Kehl 10 Dh 48.35N 7.49 E
Kehra 7 Fg 59.19N 25.18 E
Keighley 9 Lh 53.52N 1.54W
Keila/Kejla 7 Fg 59.19N 24.27 E
Keila Jõgi/Kejla 8 Ke 59.25N 24.15 E
Keimoes 37 Ce 28.41S 21.00 E
Keipel Bank (EN) 59 Le 25.15S 159.30 E
Keita 34 Gc 14.46N 5.46 E
Kéita, Bahr- 35 Bd 9.14N 18.21 E
Keitele 5 Ic 62.55N 26.00 E
Keith [Austl.] 59 Ig 36.06S 140.21 E
Keith [Scot.-U.K.] 9 Kd 57.32N 2.57W
Keith Arm 42 Fc 65.20N 122.00W
Keiyasi 63d Ab 17.53S 177.45 E
Kejla/Keila 7 Fg 59.19N 24.27 E
Kejla/Keila Jõgi 8 Ke 59.25N 24.15 E
Kejvy 7 Ic 67.30N 37.45 E
Kekaha 65a Bb 21.58N 159.43W
Kekerengu 62 Ee 42.00S 174.00 E
Kékes 10 Qi 47.52N 20.01 E
Keklau 64a Bb 7.35N 134.39 E
Kelafo 35 Gd 5.37N 44.13 E
Kelakam 34 Hc 13.35N 11.44 E
Kela Met 35 Fb 15.50N 38.23 E
Kelan 27 Jd 38.44N 111.34 E
Kelang 22 Mi 3.02N 101.27 E
Kelasa, Selat-=Gaspar Strait (EN) 26 Eg 2.40S 107.15 E
Kelberg 12 Id 50.18N 6.55 E
Kélcyra 15 Di 40.19N 20.11 E
Kelefesia 65b Bb 20.30S 174.44W
Kelekçi 15 Ml 37.14N 29.28 E
Kelem 35 Fe 4.49N 35.59 E
Keles 15 Mj 39.55N 29.14 E
Keles 18 Gd 41.02N 68.37 E
Kelheim 10 Hh 48.55N 11.52 E
Kelifely, Causse du- 37 Hc 17.15S 45.30 E
Kelifski Uzboj 18 Ef 37.45N 64.40 E
Keli Hāji Ibrāhīm 24 Kd 36.42N 45.00 E
Kelkheim 12 Kd 50.08N 8.27 E
Kelkit 23 Ea 36.32N 40.46 E
Kelkit 24 Hb 40.08N 39.27 E
Kellé 36 Bc 0.06S 14.33 E
Kellerberrin 59 Df 31.38S 117.43 E
Kellerwald 10 Fe 51.03N 9.10 E
Kellett, Cape- 42 Eb 72.57N 125.27W
Kellett Strait 42 Fa 75.50N 117.40W
Kellog 20 Dd 62.27N 86.35 E
Kellogg 43 Db 47.32N 116.07W
Kelloselkä 7 Gc 66.56N 29.00 E
Kells/Ceanannas Mór 9 Gh 53.44N 6.53W
Kelmé/Kelme 7 Fi 55.39N 22.58 E
Kelme/Kelmé 7 Fi 55.39N 22.58 E
Kelmency 15 Ja 48.27N 26.47 E
Kelmis/La Calamine 12 Hd 50.43N 6.00 E
Kélo 35 Bd 9.15N 15.48 E
Kelowna 39 He 49.53N 119.29W
Kelsey 42 He 56.00N 97.00W
Kelsey Bay 42 Ef 50.24N 125.57W
Kelso 46 Dc 46.09N 122.54W
Kelso Bank 59 Ld 24.10S 159.10 E
Kelso Bank (EN) 59 Ld 24.10S 159.30 E
Kel Tepe [Tur.] 24 Eb 41.05N 32.27 E
Kel Tepe [Tur.] 15 Ni 40.39N 30.06 E
Keltie, Mount- 66 Jf 79.15S 159.00 E
Keluang 26 Df 2.02N 103.19 E
Kelvin Seamount (EN) 43 Od 38.50N 64.00W
Kelyehēd 35 Hd 8.44N 49.10 E
Kem 19 Dc 64.57N 34.31 E
Kema 7 If 60.19N 37.15 E
Ké Macina 34 Dc 13.57N 5.23W
Kemah 24 Hc 39.36N 39.02 E
Kemaliye 24 Hc 39.16N 38.29 E
Kemalpaşa 24 Cc 40.00N 28.20 E
Kemalpaşa 15 Kk 38.25N 27.26 E
Kembé 35 Ce 4.36N 21.54 E
Kemer [Tur.] 15 Mm 36.28N 29.21 E
Kemer [Tur.] 24 Dd 36.36N 30.34 E
Kemer Baraji 15 Ll 37.30N 28.35 E
Kemeri/Ķemeri 8 Jh 56.56N 23.25 E
Ķemeri/Kemeri 8 Jh 56.56N 23.25 E
Kemerovo 22 Kd 55.20N 86.05 E
Kemerovskaja Oblast [3] 20 De 55.00N 87.00 E
Kemi 6 Ib 65.44N 24.34 E
Kemijärvi 7 Gc 66.40N 27.25 E
Kemijärvi=Kenni, Lake- (EN) 7 Gc 66.36N 27.24 E
Kemijoki 5 Ib 65.47N 24.30 E
Kemiö 8 Jd 60.10N 22.40 E
Kemiö/Kimito 8 Jd 60.10N 22.40 E
Kemlja 7 Ki 54.43N 45.15 E
Kemmerer 46 Jf 41.48N 110.32W
Kémo-Gribingui [3] 35 Bd 6.00N 19.00 E
Kemp, Lake- 45 Gj 33.45N 99.13W
Kempaž 17 Jd 64.03N 61.02 E
Kempele 7 Fd 64.55N 25.30 E
Kempen 12 Ic 51.22N 6.25 E
Kempen/Campine 11 Lc 51.10N 5.20 E
Kempendjaj 20 Gd 62.02N 118.42 E
Kempenich 12 Jd 50.25N 7.08 E
Kemp Land 66 Ee 67.10S 58.00 E
Kemps Bay 49 Ia 24.02N 77.33W
Kempsey 59 Kf 31.05S 152.50 E
Kempston 12 Bb 52.06N 0.29W
Kempt, Lac- 42 Kg 47.25N 74.15W
Kempten 10 Gi 47.43N 10.19 E
Ken 25 Hc 25.46N 80.31 E
Ken, Loch- 9 If 55.02N 4.02W
Kena 7 Je 62.06N 39.05 E
Kenadsa 32 Gc 31.34N 2.26W
Kenai 39 Dc 60.33N 151.15W
Kenai Mountains 40 Ie 60.00N 150.00W
Kenai Peninsula 38 Ed 60.10N 150.00W
Kendal 9 Kg 54.20N 2.45W
Kendall 44 Gm 25.41N 80.19W
Kendall, Cape- 42 Id 63.36N 87.13W
Kendallville 44 Ee 41.27N 85.16W
Kendari 22 Oj 3.57S 122.35 E
Kendawangan 26 Fg 2.32S 110.12 E
Kenema 31 Fh 7.52N 11.12W
Kenge 31 Ii 4.52S 16.59 E
Kengere 36 Ee 11.10S 25.28 E
Keng Tung 25 Jd 21.17N 99.36 E
Kenhardt 37 Ce 29.19S 21.12 E
Kéniéba 34 Cc 12.50N 11.14W
Keningau 26 Ge 5.20N 116.10 E
Kenitra 31 Ge 34.16N 6.36W
Kenitra [3] 32 Fc 34.00N 6.00W
Kenli (Xishuanghe) 28 Ef 37.35N 118.30 E
Kenmare 43 Gb 48.40N 102.05W
Kenmare/Neidín 9 Dj 51.53N 9.35W
Kenmare River/An Ribhéar 9 Dj 51.50N 9.50W
Kennebunk 44 Ld 43.23N 70.33W
Kennedy Peak 25 Id 23.19N 93.46 E
Kennedy Range 59 Cd 24.30S 115.00 E
Kenner 45 Ki 29.59N 90.15W
Kennet 9 Mj 51.28N 0.57W
Kennett 45 Kh 36.14N 90.03W
Kennewick 46 Fc 46.12N 119.07W
Kenni, Lake- (EN)= Kemijärvi 7 Gc 66.36N 27.24 E
Kennington 12 Cc 51.09N 0.53 E
Kenn Reef 57 Gg 21.10S 155.50 E
Kénogami 44 La 48.26N 71.14W
Kénogami, Lac- 44 La 48.21N 71.28W
Kenogami River 42 Jf 51.06N 84.29W
Keno Hill 42 Dd 63.54N 135.18W
Kenora 39 Je 49.47N 94.29W
Kenosha 43 Jc 42.35N 87.49W
Kent 9 Nj 51.10N 0.55 E
Kent [3] 9 Nj 51.20N 0.55 E
Kent [S.L.] 34 Cd 8.10N 13.10W
Kent [Wa.-U.S.] 46 Dc 47.23N 122.14W
Kent, Vale of- 9 Nj 51.10N 0.30 E
Kentau 19 Gg 43.32N 68.33 E
Kent Group 59 Jg 39.30S 147.20 E
Kenton 44 Fe 40.38N 83.38W
Kent Peninsula 42 Gc 68.30N 107.00W
Kentucky [2] 43 Jd 37.30N 85.15W
Kentucky Lake 43 Jd 36.25N 88.05W
Kentucky River 44 Ef 38.41N 85.11W
Kenya [1] 31 Kh 1.00N 38.00 E
Kenya, Mount-/Kirinyaga 30 Ki 0.10S 37.20 E
Keokea 65a Ec 20.42N 156.21W
Keokuk 43 Ic 40.24N 91.24W
Keonjhargarh 25 Hd 21.38N 85.35 E
Keowee, Lake- 44 Fh 34.55N 82.50W
Kepe 7 Hd 65.09N 32.08 E
Kepi 26 Kh 6.32S 139.19 E
Kępno 10 Ne 51.17N 17.59 E
Kepsut 24 Cc 39.41N 28.09 E
Kerala [3] 25 Ff 11.00N 76.30 E
Kerama-Rettō 29b Ab 26.10N 127.15 E
Kerang 59 Ig 35.44S 143.55 E
Keratéa 15 Gl 37.48N 23.59 E
Kerava/Kervo 8 Kd 60.24N 25.07 E
Kerč 6 Jf 45.22N 36.27 E
Kerčenski Poluostrov 16 Ig 45.15N 36.00 E
Kerčenski Proliv 5 Jf 45.22N 36.38 E
Kerdhilion Óros 15 Gi 40.47N 23.39 E
Kerema 60 Di 7.58S 145.46 E
Keren 35 Fb 15.47N 38.27 E
Keret, Ozero- 7 Hd 65.50N 32.50 E
Kerewan 34 Bc 13.29N 16.06W
Kerguélen 30 Nm 49.20S 69.30 E
Kerguélen, Iles- 30 Nm 49.15S 69.10 E
Kerguelen Plateau (EN) 3 Go 55.00S 75.00 E
Kericho 36 Gc 0.22S 35.17 E
Keri Kera 35 Ec 12.21N 32.46 E
Kerimäki 8 Mc 61.55N 29.17 E
Kerinci, Gunung- 21 Mj 1.42S 101.16 E
Kerio 30 Kh 2.59N 36.07 E
Kerion 15 Dl 37.40N 20.49 E
Keriya/Yutian 22 Kf 36.52N 81.42 E
Keriya He 27 Dd 38.30N 82.10 E
Keriya Shankou 27 Dd 35.12N 81.44 E
Kerka 10 Mj 46.28N 16.36 E
Kerken 12 Ic 51.27N 6.26 E
Kerkennah Islands (EN)= Qarqannah, Juzur- 30 Ie 34.44N 11.12 E
Kerketevs Óros 15 Jl 37.44N 26.38 E
Kerki 19 Gh 37.50N 65.13 E
Kerkini Óros 15 Fh 41.21N 22.50 E
Kérkira 15 Cj 39.36N 19.55 E
Kérkira=Corfu (EN) 5 Hh 39.40N 19.45 E
Kerkiras, Stenón- = Corfu, Strait of- (EN) 15 Dj 39.35N 20.05 E
Kerkrade 12 Id 50.52N 6.04 E
Kerma (EN)=Karmah 35 Eb 19.38N 30.25 E
Kermadec Islands 57 Jh 30.00S 178.30W
Kermadec Ridge (EN) 57 Jh 30.30S 178.30W
Kermadec Trench (EN) 3 Km 30.00S 177.00W
Kermajarvi 8 Mb 62.30N 28.40 E
Kermān [3] 23 Ic 30.50N 57.50 E
Kermān 22 Hf 30.17N 57.05 E
Kermānshāh→ Bakhtarān 22 Gf 34.19N 47.04 E
Kermānshāhān 24 Pg 31.17N 54.55 E
Kerme 15 Kl 37.02N 28.00 E
Kerme Körfezi 24 Bd 36.50N 28.00 E
Kermit 45 Ek 31.51N 103.06W
Kern River 46 Fi 35.13N 119.17W
Kérouané 34 Dd 9.16N 9.01W
Kerpen 12 Id 50.52N 6.41 E
Kerrobert 42 Gf 51.55N 109.08W
Kerrville 43 He 30.03N 99.08W
Kerry/Ciarraí [2] 9 Di 52.10N 9.30W
Kerry, Mountains of- 9 Dj 51.55N 9.50W
Kertamulya 26 Eg 0.23N 109.09 E
Kerteh 26 Df 4.31N 103.27 E
Kerteminde 8 Di 55.27N 10.40 E
Kerulen (Cherlen) 21 Ne 48.48N 117.00 E
Kervo/Kerava 8 Kd 60.24N 25.07 E
Kerzaz 32 Gd 29.27N 1.25W
Keržеnec 7 Kh 56.04N 45.01 E
Kesagami Lake 42 Jf 50.23N 80.10W
Kesälahti 8 Mc 61.54N 29.50 E
Keşan 23 Ca 40.51N 26.37 E
Keşap 24 Hb 40.55N 38.31 E
Kesen'numa 28 Pe 38.54N 141.35 E
Kesen'numa-Wan 29 Gb 38.50N 141.35 E
Keshan 27 Mb 48.04N 125.51 E
Keskastel 12 Jf 48.58N 7.02 E
Keskin 24 Ec 39.41N 33.37 E
Keski-Suomi [2] 7 Fe 62.30N 25.30 E
Kestenga 7 Hd 65.53N 31.45 E
Keswick 9 Jg 54.37N 3.08W
Keszthely 10 Nj 46.46N 17.15 E
Ket 21 Kd 58.55N 81.32 E
Kéta 34 Fd 5.55N 0.59 E
Ketanda 20 Jd 60.38N 141.30 E
Ketapang 22 Mj 1.52S 109.59 E
Ketčenery (Sovetskoje) 19 Ef 47.17N 44.30 E
Ketchikan 39 Fd 55.21N 131.35W
Ketchum 43 Ec 43.41N 114.22W
Ketchum Mountain 45 Fk 31.15N 101.00W
Kete Krachi 34 Ed 7.46N 0.03W
Ketelmeer 12 Hb 52.35N 5.45 E
Ketlí, Jbel- 13 Gi 35.22N 5.17W
Ketmen, Hrebet- 18 Lc 43.20N 80.00 E
Kétou 34 Fd 7.22N 2.36 E
Kętrzyn 10 Rb 54.06N 21.23 E
Kettering [Eng.-U.K.] 9 Mi 52.24N 0.44W
Kettering [Oh.-U.S.] 44 Ef 39.41N 84.10W
Kettle River 46 Fb 48.42N 118.07W
Kettle River Range 46 Fb 48.30N 118.40W
Keuka Lake 44 Id 42.27N 77.10W
Keur Massène 32 Df 16.33N 16.14W
Keuruu 7 Fe 62.16N 24.42 E
Keuruunselkä 8 Kb 62.10N 24.40 E
Kevelaer 12 Ic 51.35N 6.15 E
Kew 49 Kc 21.54N 72.02W
Kewanee 43 Jc 41.14N 89.56W
Keweenaw Bay 44 Cb 46.56N 88.23W
Keweenaw Peninsula 43 Jb 47.12N 88.25W
Key, Lough-/Loch Cé 9 Eg 54.00N 8.15W
Keya Paha River 45 Ge 42.54N 99.00W
Keyhole Reservoir 46 Md 44.21N 104.51W
Key Largo 44 Gm 25.04N 80.28W
Keypel Bank (EN) 59 Le 25.15S 159.30 E
Keystone Lake 45 Hh 36.15N 96.25W
Key West 39 Kg 24.33N 81.48W
Kez 7 Mh 57.56N 53.43 E
Kezi 37 Dd 20.55S 28.29 E
Kežma 20 Fe 59.02N 101.09 E
Kežmarok 10 Qg 49.08N 20.25 E
Kgalagadi [3] 37 Ce 25.00S 22.00 E
Kgatleng [3] 37 Dd 24.28S 26.05 E
Kghoti 37 Cd 24.55S 21.59 E
Khabr, Kūh-e- 23 Id 28.50N 56.26 E
Khābūr, Nahr al- 24 Ie 35.08N 40.26 E
Khadari, Wādī al- 35 Dc 10.29N 27.00 E
Khādim, Shūshat al- 24 Bh 28.35N 27.43 E
Khadki (Kirkee) 25 Ee 18.34N 73.52 E
Khadra 13 Mh 36.15N 0.35 E
Khafs Banbān 24 Lj 25.31N 46.27 E
Khairónia 15 Fk 38.30N 22.51 E
Khairpur 25 Dc 27.32N 68.46 E
Khāīz, Kūh-e- 24 Nq 30.27N 50.55 E
Khakhea 37 Cd 24.42S 23.30 E
Khalatse 25 Fb 34.20N 76.49 E
Khalīj-e Fārs=Persian Gulf (EN) 21 Hg 27.00N 51.00 E
Khálki 15 Km 36.13N 27.37 E
Khálki 15 Km 36.14N 27.36 E
Khalkidhikí=Chalcidice (EN) 5 Ig 40.25N 23.25 E
Khalkís 15 Gk 38.28N 23.36 E
Khaluf 23 Ie 20.29N 57.59 E
Khambhāt 25 Ed 22.18N 72.37 E
Khambhāt, Gulf of- 21 Jg 21.00N 72.30 E
Khāmgaon 25 Fd 20.41N 76.34 E
Khamili 15 Jn 35.52N 26.14 E
Khamir 23 Ff 15.59N 43.57 E
Khāmis, Ash Shallāl al-= Fifth Cataract (EN) 30 Kg 18.23N 33.47 E
Khamīs Mushayţ 23 Ff 18.18N 42.44 E
Khammam 25 Ge 17.15N 80.09 E
Khamseh 24 Md 36.40N 48.50 E
Khan 37 Ad 22.42S 14.54 E
Khān 24 Qj 24.13N 56.20 E
Khānābād 23 Kb 36.41N 69.07 E
Khān al Baghdādī 24 Jf 33.51N 42.33 E
Khān al Hammād 24 Kf 32.19N 44.17 E
Khānaqīn 23 Gc 34.21N 45.22 E
Khān az Zabīb 24 Gg 31.28N 36.06 E
Khandwa 25 Fd 21.50N 76.20 E
Khāneh Sorkh, Gardaneh-ye- 24 Qh 29.49N 56.06 E
Khānewāl 25 Eb 30.18N 71.56 E
Khangai Mountains (EN)= Changajn Nuruu → Hangaj, Hrebet- 21 Le 47.30N 100.00 E
Khangai Mountains (EN)= Hangaj, Hrebet- (Changai Nuruu) 21 Le 47.30N 100.00 E
Khánia 6 Ih 35.31N 24.02 E
Khanion, Kólpos- 15 Gn 35.35N 23.50 E
Khanka, Lake- (EN)=Hanka, Ozero- 21 Pe 45.00N 132.24 E
Khanka Lake (EN)=Xingkai Hu 21 Pe 45.00N 132.24 E
Khānpur 25 Ec 28.39N 70.39 E
Khān Shaykhūn 24 Ge 35.26N 36.38 E
Khan Takhti 24 Kc 38.09N 44.55 E
Khān Yūnus 24 Fg 31.21N 34.19 E
Khānzīr, Rās- 35 Hc 10.50N 45.50 E

Index Symbols

[1] Independent Nation
[2] State, Region
[3] District, County
[4] Municipality
[5] Colony, Dependency
Continent
Physical Region
Historical or Cultural Region
Mount, Mountain
Volcano
Hill
Mountains, Mountain Range
Hills, Escarpment
Plateau, Upland
Pass, Gap
Plain, Lowland
Delta
Salt Flat
Valley, Canyon
Crater, Cave
Karst Features
Depression
Polder
Desert, Dunes
Forest, Woods
Heath, Steppe
Oasis
Cape, Point
Coast, Beach
Cliff
Peninsula
Isthmus
Sandbank
Island
Atoll
Rock, Reef
Islands, Archipelago
Rocks, Reefs
Coral Reef
Well, Spring
Geyser
River, Stream
Waterfall Rapids
River Mouth, Estuary
Lake
Salt Lake
Intermittent Lake
Reservoir
Swamp, Pond
Canal
Glacier
Ice Shelf, Pack Ice
Ocean
Sea
Gulf, Bay
Strait, Fjord
Lagoon
Bank
Seamount
Tablemount
Ridge
Shelf
Basin
Escarpment, Sea Scarp
Fracture
Trench, Abyss
National Park, Reserve
Point of Interest
Recreation Site
Cave, Cavern
Historic Site
Ruins
Wall, Walls
Church, Abbey
Temple
Scientific Station
Airport
Port
Lighthouse
Mine
Tunnel
Dam, Bridge

Name	Map	Grid	Lat.	Long.
Khao Laem	25	Kf	14.19N	101.11 E
Khao Miang	25	Ke	17.42N	101.01 E
Khao Mokochu	25	Je	15.56N	99.06 E
Khao Saming	25	Kf	12.16N	102.26 E
Khar	24	Me	35.53N	48.55 E
Kharagpur	22	Kg	22.20N	87.20 E
Khárakas	15	In	35.01N	25.07 E
Khārān	24	Qh	28.55N	57.09 E
Kharānaq	24	Pf	32.20N	54.39 E
Kharānaq, Kūh-e-	24	Pf	32.10N	54.39 E
Kharga Oasis (EN) = Khārijah, Waḩāt al-	30	Kf	25.20N	30.35 E
Khārijah, Wāḩāt al- = Kharga Oasis (EN)	30	Kf	25.20N	30.35 E
Kharīţ, Wādī al-	24	Ej	24.26N	33.03 E
Kharīţah, Shiqqat al-	33	If	17.10N	47.50 E
Khārk	24	Nh	29.15N	50.20 E
Khārk, Jazīreh-ye-	23	Hd	29.15N	50.20 E
Khār Khū	24	Og	31.39N	53.46 E
Kharmān, Kūh-e-	23	Hd	29.13N	53.35 E
Kharshah, Qārat al-	24	Bg	30.35N	27.25 E
Khartoum (EN) = Al Kharţūm	35	Eb	15.50N	33.00 E
Khartoum (EN) = Al Kharţūm	31	Kg	15.36N	32.32 E
Khartoum North (EN) = Al Kharţūm Baḩrī	31	Kg	15.38N	32.33 E
Khāsh	23	Jc	31.31N	62.52 E
Khāsh	23	Jc	31.11N	62.05 E
Khashm al Qirbah	35	Fc	14.58N	35.55 E
Khāsi Jaintia	21	Lg	25.35N	91.38 E
Khatikhon, Yam- = Mediterranean Sea (EN)	5	Hh	35.00N	20.00 E
Khaţţ	33	Dd	28.40N	22.40 E
Khātūn, Kūh-e-	24	Og	30.25N	53.38 E
Khawr al Fakkān	24	Qk	25.21N	56.22 E
Khawr āl Juḩaysh	35	Ia	20.36N	50.59 E
Khawr al Mufattaḩ	24	Mh	28.40N	48.25 E
Khawr Umm Qasr	24	Lg	30.02N	47.56 E
Khay'	23	Ff	18.45N	.41.24 E
Khaybar	23	Ed	25.42N	39.31 E
Khaybar, Ḩarrat-	24	Hj	25.30N	39.45 E
Khazzī, Qārat-	30	Jf	21.26N	24.30 E
Khemis	13	Qh	36.10N	4.04 E
Khemis Anjra	13	Gi	35.41N	5.32W
Khémis Beni Arouss	13	Gi	35.19N	5.38W
Khemis Miliana	32	Hb	36.16N	2.13 E
Khemissat	32	Fc	33.49N	6.04W
Khemisset	32	Fc	33.49N	6.00W
Khemmarat	25	Ke	16.03N	105.11 E
Khenchela	32	Ib	35.26N	7.08 E
Khenifra	32	Fc	32.56N	5.40W
Khenifra	32	Fc	33.00N	5.08W
Kherāmeh	24	Oh	29.32N	53.21 E
Khersan	24	Ng	31.33N	50.22 E
Khersónisos Akrotiri	15	Hn	35.35N	24.10 E
Kheyrābād [Iran]	24	Mg	31.49N	48.23 E
Kheyrābād [Iran]	24	Ph	29.26N	55.19 E
Khionótripa	15	Hh	41.18N	24.05 E
Khios	15	Jk	38.22N	26.08 E
Khios = Chios (EN)	5	Ih	38.22N	26.00 E
Khirbat Isrīyah	24	Ge	35.21N	37.46 E
Khirr, Nahr al-	24	Kf	33.17N	44.21 E
Khlomón Óros	15	Fk	38.36N	23.00 E
Khlong Yai	25	Kf	11.46N	102.53 E
Khokhropār	25	Ec	25.42N	70.12 E
Khok Kloi	25	Jg	8.17N	98.19 E
Khok Samrong	25	Ke	15.03N	100.44 E
Kholm	23	Kb	36.42N	67.41 E
Khomām	24	Md	37.22N	49.40 E
Khomas Highland (EN) = Khomas Hochland	30	Ik	22.40S	16.20 E
Khomas Hochland = Khomas Highland (EN)	30	Ik	22.40S	16.20 E
Khomeyn	24	Nf	33.38N	50.04 E
Khomeynīshahr	23	Hc	32.42N	51.27 E
Khon Kaen	25	Ke	16.26N	102.50 E
Khonsār	24	Nf	33.21N	50.19 E
Khóra	15	El	37.03N	21.43 E
Khor Anghar	35	Gc	12.27N	43.18 E
Khorāsān	21	Hf	34.00N	56.00 E
Khorāsān	23	Ic	35.00N	58.00 E
Khorāsānī, Godār-e	24	Qg	30.44N	57.03 E
Khóra Sfakion	15	Hn	35.12N	24.09 E
Khormūj, Kūh-e-	23	Hd	28.43N	51.22 E
Khorof Harar	36	Hb	2.14N	40.44 E
Khorramābād	23	Gc	33.30N	48.20 E
Khorramshahr	23	Gc	30.25N	48.11 E
Khorsābād	24	Jd	36.38N	43.17 E
Khoshyeylāq	24	Pd	36.53N	55.15 E
Khosrowābād	24	Mg	30.00N	48.25 E
Khosrowshah	24	Ld	37.57N	46.03 E
Khouribga	32	Fc	32.56N	6.36W
Khouribga	32	Fc	32.53N	6.54W
Khowst	23	Kc	33.22N	69.57 E
Khrisí	15	Io	34.52N	25.42 E
Khrisoúpolis	15	Hi	40.59N	24.42 E
Khristianá	15	Im	36.14N	25.13 E
Khu Dağı	24	Jc	38.35N	43.40 E
Khuff [Lib.]	33	Cd	28.17N	18.20 E
Khuff [Sau.Ar.]	23	Ed	25.20N	37.20 E
Khulna	22	Kg	22.48N	89.33 E
Khūrān	24	Pi	26.50N	55.40 E
Khurayş	23	Gd	25.05N	48.02 E
Khurayt	35	Dc	13.57N	26.02 E
Khurīyā Murīyā, Jazā'ir- = Kuria Muria Islands (EN)	21	Hh	17.30N	56.00 E
Khurr, Wādī al-	24	Jg	30.52N	42.10 E
Khursanīyah	24	Mi	27.18N	49.16 E
Khūshābar	24	Md	37.59N	48.54 E
Khutse	37	Cd	23.20S	24.34 E
Khuwayy	35	Dc	13.05N	29.14 E
Khuzdār	25	Dc	27.48N	66.37 E
Khūzestān	23	Gc	32.00N	48.30 E
Khūzestan	21	Gf	30.33N	50.00 E
Khvojeh Lāk, Kūh-e-	24	Le	35.43N	46.29 E
Khvor	24	Pf	33.47N	55.03 E
Khvorāsgān	24	Nf	32.39N	51.45 E
Khvormūj	24	Nh	28.39N	51.23 E
Khvoshkūh	24	Qi	27.37N	56.41 E
Khvoy	24	Kc	38.33N	44.58 E
Khyber Pass	25	Eb	34.05N	71.10 E
Kia	63a	Db	7.32S	158.26 E
Kia	63d	Bb	16.14S	179.05 E
Kiamba	26	He	5.59N	124.37 E
Kiambi	36	Ed	7.20S	28.01 E
Kiamichi River	45	Ij	33.57N	95.14W
Kiangarow, Mount-	59	Ke	26.49S	151.33 E
Kiangsi (EN) = Chiang-hsi Sheng → Jangxi Sheng	27	Kf	28.00N	116.00 E
Kiangsi (EN) = Jangxi Sheng (Chiang-hsi Sheng)	27	Kf	28.00N	116.00 E
Kiangsu (EN) = Chiang-su Sheng → Jiangsu Sheng	27	Ke	33.00N	120.00 E
Kiangsu (EN) = Jiangsu Sheng (Chiang-su Sheng)	27	Ke	33.00N	120.00 E
Kiantajärvi	7	Gd	65.03N	29.07 E
Kiáton	15	Fk	38.01N	22.45 E
Kibali	36	Eb	3.37N	28.34 E
Kibangou	36	Bc	3.27S	12.21 E
Kibartaj/Kybartai	8	Jj	54.38N	22.44 E
Kibasira Swamp	36	Gd	8.20S	36.18 E
Kibau	36	Gd	8.35S	35.17 E
Kibaya	36	Gd	5.18S	36.34 E
Kibbish	35	Fe	4.40N	35.53 E
Kiberg	7	Ha	70.17N	31.00 E
Kibikogen	29	Cd	34.45N	133.15 E
Kiboko	36	Gc	2.15S	37.42 E
Kibombo	36	Ec	3.54S	25.55 E
Kibondo	36	Fc	3.35S	30.42 E
Kibre Mengist	35	Fd	5.58N	39.00 E
Kıbrıs/Kypros = Cyprus (EN)	22	Ff	35.00N	33.00 E
Kıbrıs/Kypros = Cyprus (EN)	21	Ff	35.00N	33.00 E
Kibungo	36	Fc	2.10S	30.32 E
Kibuye	36	Ec	2.03S	29.21 E
Kibwezi	36	Gc	2.25S	37.58 E
Kičevo	15	Dh	41.31N	20.58 E
Kichi Kichi	35	Bb	17.36N	17.19 E
Kicking Horse Pass	42	Ff	51.50N	116.30W
Kidal	31	Hg	18.26N	1.24 E
Kidapawan	26	Ie	7.01N	125.03 E
Kidatu	36	Gd	7.42S	36.57 E
Kidira	34	Cc	14.28N	12.13W
Kidnappers, Cape-	62	Gc	39.38S	177.06 E
Kiekie	65a	Ab	21.53N	160.13W
Kiel	6	He	54.20N	10.08 E
Kiel Canal (EN) = Nord-Ostsee Kanal	5	Ge	53.53N	9.08 E
Kielce	6	Ie	50.52N	20.37 E
Kielce	10	Qf	50.50N	20.35 E
Kieler Bucht	10	Gb	54.35N	10.35 E
Kienge	36	Ee	10.33S	27.33 E
Kierspe	12	Jc	51.08N	7.35 E
Kieta	58	Ge	6.15S	155.37 E
Kietrz	10	Of	50.05N	18.01 E
Kiev (EN) = Kijev	6	Je	50.26N	30.31 E
Kiev Reservoir (EN) = Kijevskoje Vodohranilišče	5	Je	51.00N	30.25 E
Kiffa	31	Fg	16.36N	11.23W
Kifisiá	15	Gk	38.04N	23.49 E
Kifisós	15	Gk	38.26N	23.15 E
Kifrī	24	Ke	34.42N	44.58 E
Kigač	16	Pf	46.28N	49.08 E
Kigali	31	Ki	1.57S	30.04 E
Kiğı	24	Ic	39.19N	40.21 E
Kigille	35	Ed	8.40N	34.02 E
Kigoma	31	Ji	4.52S	29.38 E
Kigoma	36	Fc	4.50S	30.05 E
Kigosi	36	Fc	4.40S	31.27 E
Kihelkonna	8	If	58.20N	21.54 E
Kihniö	8	Jb	62.12N	23.11 E
Kihnu	7	Fg	58.10N	24.00 E
Kiholo	65a	Fd	19.51N	155.55W
Kiholo Bay	65a	Fd	19.52N	155.56W
Kihti/Skiftet	8	Id	60.15N	21.05 E
Kii-Hantō	27	Oe	34.00N	135.45 E
Kiikka	8	Jc	61.20N	22.46 E
Kiil	16	Se	49.27N	54.50 E
Kiiminki	7	Fd	65.08N	25.44 E
Kii-Sanchi	29	Dd	34.15N	135.50 E
Kii-Suido	28	Mh	34.00N	134.55 E
Kija	20	De	56.52N	86.40 E
Kijev = Kiev (EN)	6	Je	50.26N	30.31 E
Kijevka	19	He	50.16N	71.34 E
Kijevskaja Oblast	19	De	50.20N	30.45 E
Kijevskoje Vodohranilišče = Kiev Reservoir (EN)	5	Je	51.00N	30.25 E
Kijma	19	Ge	51.35N	67.34 E
Kikai-Jima	27	Mf	28.15N	130.00 E
Kikerino	8	Me	59.23N	29.38 E
Kikinda	15	Dd	45.50N	20.29 E
Kikládhes = Cyclades (EN)	5	Ih	37.00N	25.10 E
Kikonai	28	Pd	41.40N	140.26 E
Kikori	58	Fe	7.25S	144.13 E
Kikori River	57	Fe	7.23S	144.16 E
Kikuchi	29	Be	32.59N	130.49 E
Kikuma	29	Cd	34.03N	132.51 E
Kikvidze	16	Md	50.44N	43.03 E
Kikwit	31	Ii	5.02S	18.49 E
Kil [Nor.]	8	Cf	58.52N	9.19 E
Kil [Swe.]	7	Cg	59.30N	13.19 E
Kilafors	7	Df	61.15N	16.33 E
Kilambé, Cerro-	49	Eg	13.34N	85.42W
Kilauea	65a	Ba	22.13N	159.25W
Kilauea Crater	65a	Fd	19.24N	155.17W
Kilauea Point	65a	Ba	22.14N	159.24W
Kilbrannan Sound	9	Hf	55.40N	5.25W
Kilbuck Mountains	40	Hd	60.30N	159.45W
Kilchu	27	Mc	40.58N	129.20 E
Kilcoy	59	Ke	26.57S	152.33 E
Kildare/Cill Dara	9	Gh	53.15N	6.45W
Kildare/Cill Dara	9	Gh	53.10N	6.55W
Kildin, Ostrov-	7	Ib	69.20N	34.10 E
Kilembe	36	Cd	5.42S	19.55 E
Kilgore	45	Ij	32.23N	94.53W
Kilgoris	36	Fc	1.00S	34.53 E
Kiliao He	21	Oe	43.24N	123.42 E
Kiliç	15	Mi	40.40N	29.23 E
Kilifi	36	Gc	3.38S	39.51 E
Kili Island	57	Hd	5.39N	169.04 E
Kilija	19	Cf	45.27N	29.14 E
Kilijskoje girlo	15	Md	45.13N	29.43 E
Kilimanjaro	36	Gc	4.00S	37.40 E
Kilimanjaro, Mount-	30	Ki	3.04S	37.22 E
Kilimli	24	Db	41.29N	31.50 E
Kilinailau Islands	60	Fh	4.45S	155.20 E
Kilindoni	31	Ki	7.55S	39.39 E
Kilingi-Nõmme/Kilingi-Nymme	7	Fg	58.08N	24.59 E
Kilingi-Nymme/Kilingi-Nõmme	7	Fg	58.08N	24.59 E
Kilis	23	Eb	36.44N	37.05 E
Kilitbahir	24	Bb	40.12N	26.20 E
Kilkee/Cill Chaoi	9	Di	52.41N	9.38W
Kilkenny/Cill Chainnigh	9	Fi	52.39N	7.15W
Kilkenny/Cill Chainnigh	9	Fi	52.40N	7.20W
Kilkieran Bay	9	Dh	53.15N	9.45W
Kilkis	15	Fi	41.00N	22.52 E
Killala Bay/Cuan Chill Ala	9	Dg	54.15N	9.10W
Killarney/Cill Airne	9	Di	52.03N	9.30W
Killary Harbour/An Caoláire Rua	9	Dh	53.38N	9.55W
Killdeer	45	Ec	47.22N	102.45W
Killeen	43	He	31.08N	97.44W
Killinck	42	Ld	60.25N	64.40W
Killini	15	El	37.56N	21.09 E
Killini Óros	15	Fl	37.55N	22.26 E
Kilmallock/Cill Mocheallóg	9	Ei	52.25N	8.35W
Kilmarnock	9	If	55.37N	4.30W
Kilmez	7	Mh	56.58N	50.29 E
Kilmez	7	Mh	57.03N	51.24 E
Kilmore	59	Ig	37.18S	144.57 E
Kilombero	36	Gd	8.31S	37.22 E
Kilosa	31	Ki	6.50S	36.59 E
Kilpisjärvi	7	Eb	69.03N	20.48 E
Kilp-Javr	7	Hb	69.07N	32.28 E
Kilrush/Cill Rois	9	Di	52.39N	9.29W
Kilsbergen	8	Fe	59.20N	14.45 E
Kiltān Island	25	Ef	11.29N	73.00 E
Kilwa	36	Ed	9.17S	28.20 E
Kilwa Kisiwani	31	Ki	8.58S	39.30 E
Kilwa Kivinje	36	Gd	8.45S	39.24 E
Kilwa Masoko	36	Gd	8.56S	39.31 E
Kilyos → Kumköy	15	Mh	41.15N	29.02 E
Kim	45	Eh	37.15N	103.21W
Kimamba	36	Gd	6.47S	37.08 E
Kimba	59	Hf	33.09S	136.25 E
Kimball [Nb.-U.S.]	45	Ef	41.14N	103.40W
Kimball [S.D.-U.S.]	45	Ge	43.45N	98.57W
Kimball, Mount-	40	Kd	63.14N	144.39W
Kimbe	59	Ka	5.31S	150.12 E
Kimbe Bay	60	Ei	5.30S	150.30 E
Kimberley	57	Df	16.00S	126.00 E
Kimberley [B.C.-Can.]	42	Fg	49.41N	115.59W
Kimberley [S.Afr.]	31	Jk	28.43S	24.46 E
Kimberley Plateau	59	Fc	17.00S	127.00 E
Kimch'aek (Sŏngjin)	27	Mc	40.41N	129.12 E
Kimch'ŏn	27	Md	36.07N	128.07 E
Kimhandu	30	Ki	7.05S	37.35 E
Kími	15	Hk	38.38N	24.06 E
Kimito	8	Jd	60.10N	22.40 E
Kimito/Kemiö	8	Jd	60.10N	22.40 E
Kimje	28	Ig	35.48N	126.53 E
Kimobetsu	29a	Bb	42.47N	140.56 E
Kímolos	15	Hm	36.48N	24.34 E
Kimongo	36	Bc	4.29S	12.58 E
Kimovsk	19	De	54.01N	38.36 E
Kimpu-San	29	Fd	35.52N	138.37 E
Kimry	19	Dd	56.52N	37.24 E
Kimvula	36	Cd	5.44S	15.58 E
Kinabalu, Gunong-	21	Ni	6.05N	116.33 E
Kinabatangan	26	Ge	5.42N	118.23 E
Kinango	36	Gc	4.08S	39.19 E
Kinaros	15	Jm	36.59N	26.17 E
Kincardine	42	Jh	44.11N	81.38W
Kind	8	Eg	57.35N	13.25 E
Kinda	36	Ed	9.18S	25.04 E
Kinda	8	Ff	58.05N	15.40 E
Kindamba	36	Bc	3.44S	14.31 E
Kinder	45	Jk	30.29N	92.51W
Kinder Scout	9	Lh	53.23N	1.52W
Kindersley	42	Gf	51.27N	109.10W
Kindi	34	Ec	12.26N	2.01W
Kindia	31	Fg	10.04N	12.51W
Kindu	31	Ji	2.57S	25.56 E
Kinel	7	Mj	53.14N	50.40 E
Kinesi	36	Fc	1.28S	33.52 E
Kinešma	19	Ed	57.28N	42.16 E
King	63a	Aa	4.24S	152.43 E
King, Cayos-	49	Fg	12.45N	83.20W
Kingaroy	59	Ke	26.33S	151.50 E
King Christian	42	Ha	77.45N	102.00W
King Christian IX Land (EN) = Kong Christian IX Land	67	Mc	68.00N	36.30W
King Christian X Land (EN) = Kong Christian X Land	67	Md	72.20N	32.30W
King City	43	Cd	36.13N	121.08W
King Edward River	59	Fb	14.14S	126.35 E
Kingfisher	45	Hi	35.52N	97.56W
King Frederik VI Coast (EN) = Kong Frederik VI Kyst	67	Nc	63.00N	43.30W
King Frederik VIII Land (EN) = Kong Frederik VIII Land	67	Md	78.30N	28.00W
King George Island	66	Re	62.00S	58.15W
King George Islands	42	Je	57.15N	78.30W
King George Sound	59	Dg	35.10S	118.10 E
Kingisepp	7	Gg	59.23N	28.37 E
Kingissepp → Kuresaare	19	Cd	58.17N	22.29 E
King Island	57	Fh	39.50S	144.00 E
King Lear Peak	46	Ff	41.12N	118.34W
King Leopold Ranges	59	Fc	17.30S	125.45 E
Kingman [Az.-U.S.]	43	Ed	35.12N	114.04W
Kingman [Ks.-U.S.]	45	Gh	37.39N	98.07W
Kingman Reef	57	Kd	6.19N	162.28W
Kingombe [Zaire]	36	Ec	2.35S	26.37 E
Kingombe [Zaire]	36	Ec	3.52S	26.35 E
Kingoome Inlet	46	Ba	50.49N	126.13W
Kingoonya	58	Eh	30.54S	135.18 E
King Peninsula	66	Of	73.12S	101.00W
Kingsclere	12	Ac	51.19N	1.15W
Kingscote	59	Hg	35.40S	137.38 E
King's Lynn	9	Ni	52.45N	0.24 E
King Sound	57	Df	17.00S	123.30 E
Kings Peak [Ca.-U.S.]	46	Cf	40.10N	124.08W
Kings Peak [U.S.]	38	He	40.46N	110.22W
Kingsport	43	Kd	36.32N	82.33W
Kings River	46	Fh	36.03N	119.49W
Kingston [Jam.]	39	Lh	18.00N	76.50W
Kingston [Nor.I.]	58	Hg	29.04S	167.58 E
Kingston [N.Y.-U.S.]	43	Mc	41.55N	74.00W
Kingston [N.Z.]	61	Ci	45.20S	168.43 E
Kingston [Ont.-Can.]	39	Le	44.14N	76.30W
Kingston Peak	46	Hi	35.42N	115.52W
Kingston South East	58	Eh	36.50S	139.51 E
Kingston-upon-Hull (Hull)	6	Fe	53.45N	0.20W
Kingston-upon-Thames, London-	9	Mj	51.28N	0.19W
Kingstown	39	Mh	13.09N	61.14W
Kingsville	43	Hf	27.31N	97.52W
Kings Worthy	12	Ac	51.05N	1.18W
Kingussie	9	Id	57.05N	4.04W
King William	38	Jc	69.00N	97.30W
King William's Town	31	Jl	32.51S	27.22 E
Kiniama	36	Ee	11.26S	28.19 E
Kınık	24	Bc	39.05N	27.23 E
Kinkala	36	Bc	4.22S	14.46 E
Kinlochleven	9	Ie	56.43N	4.58W
Kinna	8	Eg	57.30N	12.41 E
Kinnairds Head	9	Ld	57.42N	2.00W
Kinnared	8	Eg	57.02N	13.06 E
Kinnekulle	8	Ef	58.35N	13.23 E
Kinneret, Yam-	24	Ff	32.48N	35.35 E
Kino-Kawa	29	Dd	34.13N	135.08 E
Kinomoto	29	Ed	35.31N	136.13 E
Kinoosao	42	He	57.06N	102.01W
Kinós Kefalaí	15	Fj	39.25N	22.34 E
Kinross	9	Je	56.13N	3.27W
Kinsale/cionn tSáile	9	Ej	51.42N	8.32W
Kinsale, Old Head of-/An Seancheann	9	Ej	51.36N	8.32W
Kinsangire	36	Gd	7.26S	38.35 E
Kinsarvik	7	Bf	60.23N	6.43 E
Kinshasa	36	Cc	4.00S	16.00 E
Kinshasa (Leopoldville)	31	Ii	4.18S	15.18 E
Kinsley	45	Gh	37.55N	99.25W
Kinston	43	Ld	35.16N	77.35W
Kintampo	34	Ed	8.03N	1.43W
Kintap	26	Gg	3.51S	115.13 E
Kintyre	9	Hf	55.32N	5.35W
Kin-Wan	29b	Ab	26.25N	127.54 E
Kinyan	34	Dc	11.51N	6.01W
Kinyeti	30	Kh	3.57N	32.54 E
Kinzig [Eur.]	10	Dh	48.37N	7.49 E
Kinzig [Ger.]	10	Ef	50.08N	8.54 E
Kioa	63d	Bb	16.39S	179.55 E
Kipaka	36	Ec	4.09S	26.30 E
Kiparissia	15	El	37.15N	21.40 E
Kiparissia, Gulf of- (EN) = Kiparissiakós Kólpos	15	El	37.30N	21.25 E
Kiparissiakós Kólpos = Kiparissia, Gulf of- (EN)	15	El	37.30N	21.25 E
Kipawa, Lac-	42	Jg	46.55N	79.00W
Kipembawe	36	Fd	7.39S	33.24 E
Kipengere Range	30	Ki	9.10S	34.15 E
Kiperčeny	15	Lb	47.32N	28.40 E
Kipili	36	Fd	7.26S	30.36 E
Kipini	36	Hc	2.32S	40.31 E
Kipling	45	Ea	50.10N	102.38W
Kippure	9	Gh	53.11N	6.20W
Kiprarenukk, Mys-/Undva Neem	8	If	58.25N	21.45 E
Kípros = Cyprus (EN)	23	Db	35.01N	33.00 E
Kipushi	36	Ee	11.46S	27.14 E
Kirakira	58	Hf	10.27S	161.56 E
Kiraz	24	Cc	39.21N	27.25 E
Kirazlı	24	Bb	40.01N	26.40 E
Kirbla	8	Jf	58.42N	23.49 E
Kircasalih	15	Jh	41.23N	26.48 E
Kirchberg (Hunsrüch)	12	Je	49.57N	7.24 E
Kirchhain	12	Kd	50.49N	8.58 E
Kirchheimbolanden	12	Ke	49.40N	8.01 E
Kirchheim unter Teck	10	Fh	48.39N	9.27 E
Kirchhundem	12	Kc	51.06N	8.06 E
Kirchhundem-Rahrbach	12	Jc	51.02N	7.59 E
Kirchlengern	12	Kb	52.12N	8.38 E
Kirdimi	35	Bb	18.11N	18.38 E
Kireç	15	Lj	39.33N	28.22 E
Kirenga	21	Md	57.47N	107.59 E
Kirensk	22	Md	57.46N	108.08 E
Kirghiz SSR (EN) → Kyrgyzstan	19	Hg	41.30N	75.00 E
Kirghiz Steppe (EN)	5	Lf	49.30N	50.30 E
Kirgizskaja Sovetskaja Socialističeskaja Respublika → Kyrgyzstan	19	Hg	41.30N	75.00 E
Kirgizskaja SSR/Kyrgyz Sovetik Socialistik Respublikasy → Kyrgyzstan	19	Hg	41.30N	75.00 E
Kirgizskaja SSR → Kyrgyzstan	19	Hg	41.30N	75.00 E
Kiri	36	Cc	1.27S	19.00 E
Kiribati	58	Je	0.01S	174.00 E
Kirikhan	24	Gd	36.32N	36.19 E
Kırıkkale	23	Db	39.50N	33.31 E
Kirillov	7	Jg	59.54N	38.27 E
Kirillovskoje	8	Md	60.28N	29.28 E
Kirin (EN) = Chi-lin Sheng → Jilin Sheng	27	Mc	43.00N	126.00 E
Kirin (EN) = Jilin Sheng (Chi-lin Sheng)	27	Mc	43.00N	126.00 E
Kirinyaga/Kenya, Mount-	30	Ki	0.10S	37.20 E
Kirishima-Yama	29	Bf	31.56N	130.52 E
Kiriši	19	Dd	59.27N	32.02 E
Kiritimati Atoll (Christmas)	57	Ld	1.52N	157.20W
Kirja	7	Li	55.05N	46.52 E
Kirkağaç	24	Bc	39.06N	27.40 E
Kirkby Lonsdale	9	Kg	54.13N	2.36W
Kirkcaldy	9	Je	56.07N	3.10W
Kirkcudbright	9	Ig	54.50N	4.03W
Kirkee → Khadki	25	Ee	18.34N	73.52 E
Kirkenær	7	Cf	60.28N	12.03 E
Kirkenes	6	Jb	69.43N	30.03 E
Kirkjubæjarklaustur	7a	Bc	63.47N	18.04W
Kirkkonummi/Kyrkslätt	8	Kd	60.07N	24.26 E
Kirkland	46	Dc	47.41N	122.12W
Kirkland Lake	39	Ke	48.09N	80.02W
Kırklareli	23	Ca	41.44N	27.12 E
Kirkpatrick, Mont-	66	Kg	84.20S	166.19 E
Kırkpınar Dağı	24	Fd	37.14N	34.15 E
Kirksville	43	Ic	40.12N	92.35W
Kirkūk	22	Gf	35.28N	44.23 E
Kirkwall	9	Kc	58.59N	2.58W
Kirkwood [Mo.-U.S.]	45	Kg	38.35N	90.24W
Kirkwood [S.Afr.]	37	Df	33.22S	25.15 E
Kırlangıç Burun	24	Dd	36.13N	30.25 E
Kirn	10	Dg	49.47N	7.27 E
Kirobasi	24	Ed	36.43N	33.52 E
Kirov	19	De	54.03N	34.21 E
Kirov	6	Kd	58.33N	49.42 E
Kirova, Zaliv-	16	Pj	39.05N	49.05 E
Kirovabad → Gjandža	6	Kg	40.40N	46.22 E
Kirovaken	19	Eg	40.48N	44.28 E
Kirovgrad	17	Jh	57.26N	60.04 E
Kirovo	18	Hd	40.28N	70.34 E
Kirovo-Čepeck	19	Fd	58.35N	50.03 E
Kirovograd	6	Jf	48.30N	32.18 E
Kirovogradskaja Oblast	19	Df	48.20N	31.50 E
Kirovsk	19	Db	67.37N	33.37 E
Kirovsk	7	Hg	59.53N	31.01 E
Kirovsk	18	Cf	37.43N	60.24 E
Kirovskaja Oblast	19	Ed	58.30N	50.00 E
Kirovski	19	Hg	44.53N	78.12 E
Kirovski	20	Ig	45.05N	133.27 E
Kirovski	16	Pg	45.48N	48.08 E
Kirovski	20	Kf	54.25N	155.37 E
Kirovski	20	Hf	54.26N	127.00 E
Kirovskoje	18	Hc	42.39N	71.35 E
Kirpilski Liman	16	Kg	45.50N	38.05 E
Kirriemuir	9	Je	56.41N	3.01W
Kirs	19	Fd	59.21N	52.18 E
Kirsanov	16	Mc	52.41N	42.45 E
Kırşşehir	23	Db	39.09N	34.10 E
Kīrthar Range	21	Ig	27.00N	67.20 E
Kirton	12	Bb	52.55N	0.03W
Kiruna	6	Ib	67.51N	20.13 E
Kirundu	36	Ec	0.44S	25.32 E
Kiryū	29	Fc	36.25N	139.20 E
Kiržač	7	Jh	56.11N	38.53 E
Kisa	7	Dh	57.59N	15.37 E
Kisabi	36	Ed	8.03S	29.11 E
Kisač	15	Cd	45.21N	19.44 E
Kisakata	29	Fb	39.14N	139.54 E
Kisaki	36	Gd	7.28S	37.36 E
Kisalföld	10	Mi	47.30N	17.00 E
Kisangani	31	Jh	0.25N	25.12 E
Kisarazu	29	Fd	35.23N	139.55 E
Kisbér	10	Oi	47.30N	18.02 E
Kiselevsk	20	Df	54.03N	86.49 E
Kiserawe	36	Gd	6.54S	39.05 E
Kishangarh	25	Ec	26.34N	74.52 E
Kishb, Harraţ al-	33	He	22.47N	41.30 E
Kishi	34	Fd	9.05N	3.51 E
Kishiwada	28	Mg	34.28N	135.22 E
Kisii	36	Fc	0.41S	34.46 E
Kisiju	36	Gd	7.24S	39.20 E
Kišinev	6	If	46.59N	28.52 E
Kısır Dağı	24	Jb	40.58N	43.04 E
Kiska	40a	Bb	52.00N	177.30 E
Kiska Volcano	40a	Bb	52.07N	177.36 E
Kisko	8	Jd	60.14N	23.29 E
Kiskörei Víztároló	10	Qi	47.44N	20.40 E
Kiskórös	10	Pj	46.37N	19.18 E
Kiskunfélegyháza	10	Pj	46.33N	19.51 E
Kiskunhalas	10	Pj	46.26N	19.30 E
Kiskunmajsa	10	Pj	46.29N	19.45 E
Kiskunság	10	Pj	46.35N	19.15 E
Kislovodsk	19	Eg	43.54N	42.42 E
Kismanyo	31	Li	0.22S	42.32 E
Kisofukushima	29	Ed	35.51N	137.41 E
Kiso-Gawa	28	Ng	35.05N	136.45 E
Kisoro	36	Ec	1.17S	29.41 E
Kiso-Sanmyaku	29	Ed	35.45N	137.45 E
Kisria, Daiet el-	13	Oi	35.44N	2.47 E
Kissámou, Kólpos-	15	Gn	35.35N	23.40 E
Kissidougou	34	Cd	9.11N	10.06W
Kissimmee	44	Gk	28.18N	81.24W
Kissimmee, Lake-	44	Gl	27.55N	81.16W
Kissū, Jabal-	35	Da	21.35N	25.09 E
Kistelek	10	Pj	46.28N	19.59 E
Kisterenye	10	Ph	48.01N	19.50 E

Index Symbols

Independent Nation · State, Region · District, County · Municipality · Colony, Dependency · Continent · Physical Region · Historical or Cultural Region · Mount, Mountain · Volcano · Hill · Mountains, Mountain Range · Hills, Escarpment · Plateau, Upland · Pass, Gap · Plain, Lowland · Delta · Salt Flat · Valley, Canyon · Crater, Cave · Karst Features · Depression · Polder · Desert, Dunes · Forest, Woods · Heath, Steppe · Oasis · Cape, Point · Coast, Beach · Cliff · Peninsula · Isthmus · Sandbank · Island · Atoll · Rock, Reef · Islands, Archipelago · Rocks, Reefs · Coral Reef · Well, Spring · Geyser · River, Stream · Waterfall Rapids · River Mouth, Estuary · Lake · Salt Lake · Intermittent Lake · Reservoir · Swamp, Pond · Canal · Glacier · Ice Shelf, Pack Ice · Ocean · Sea · Gulf, Bay · Strait, Fjord · Lagoon · Bank · Seamount · Tablemount · Ridge · Shelf · Basin · Escarpment, Sea Scarp · Fracture · Trench, Abyss · National Park, Reserve · Point of Interest · Recreation Site · Cave, Cavern · Historic Site · Ruins · Wall, Walls · Church, Abbey · Temple · Scientific Station · Airport · Port · Lighthouse · Mine · Tunnel · Dam, Bridge

Kisújszállás 10 Qi 47.13N 20.46 E
Kisuki 29 Cd 35.17N 132.54 E
Kisumu 31 Ki 0.06S 34.45 E
Kisvárda 10 Sh 48.13N 22.05 E
Kita 31 Gg 13.03N 9.30W
Kitab 19 Gh 39.08N 66.54 E
Kita-Daitō-Jima 27 Nf 25.55N 131.20 E
Kitaibaraki 28 Pf 36.48N 140.45 E
Kita-Iō-Jima 60 Cb 25.26N 141.17 E
Kitaj, Ozero- 15 Md 45.35N 29.15 E
Kitakami 27 Pd 39.30N 141.10 E
Kitakami-Gawa 29 Gb 38.25N 141.19 E
Kitakami-Sanchi 29 Gb 39.30N 141.30 E
Kitakata 28 Of 37.39N 139.52 E
Kitakyūshū 22 Pf 33.53N 130.50 E
Kitale 31 Kh 1.01N 35.00 E
Kitamaiaioi 29a Cb 43.33N 143.57 E
Kitami 27 Pc 43.48N 143.54 E
Kitami-Fuji 29a Cb 43.42N 143.14 E
Kitami-Sanchi 28 Qb 44.30N 142.30 E
Kitami Tōge 29a Cb 43.55N 142.55 E
Kitan-Kaikyō 29 Dd 34.15N 135.00 E
Kita-Taiheyō=Pacific Ocean (EN) 60 Ch 22.00N 167.00 E
Kita-Ura 29 Gc 36.00N 140.34 E
Kit Carson 45 Eg 38.46N 102.48W
Kitchener 42 Jh 43.27N 80.29W
Kitee 7 He 62.06N 30.09 E
Kitessa 35 Dd 5.22N 25.22 E
Kitgum 36 Fb 3.19N 32.53 E
Kithira=Cythera (EN) 15 Fm 36.09N 23.00 E
Kithira=Kythera (EN) 5 Ih 36.15N 23.00 E
Kithira Channel (EN)= Kithíron Dhiékplous 15 Fm 36.00N 23.00 E
Kithíron, Dhiékplous-= Kithira Channel (EN) 15 Fm 36.00N 23.00 E
Kíthnos 15 Hl 37.25N 24.26 E
Kíthnos 15 Hl 37.23N 24.25 E
Kíthnou, Stenón- 15 Hl 37.25N 24.30 E
Kitimat 39 Gd 54.05N 128.38W
Kitimat Ranges 42 Ef 53.58N 128.39W
Kitoushi-Yama 29a Cb 43.27N 143.25 E
Kitrianí 15 Hm 36.54N 24.44 E
Kitridge Point 51q Bb 13.09N 59.25W
Kitros 15 Fi 40.22N 22.35 E
Kitsuki 29 Be 33.25N 131.37 E
Kittanning 44 He 40.49N 79.31W
Kittery 44 Ld 43.05N 70.45W
Kittilä 7 Fc 67.40N 24.54 E
Kitui 31 Ki 1.22S 38.01 E
Kitunda 36 Fd 6.48S 33.13 E
Kitutu 36 Ec 3.17S 28.05 E
Kitwe-Nkana 31 Jj 12.49S 28.13 E
Kitzbühel 14 Gc 47.27N 12.23 E
Kitzbüheler Alpen 14 Gc 47.20N 12.20 E
Kitzingen 10 Gg 49.44N 10.10 E
Kiunga [Kenya] 36 Hc 1.45S 41.29 E
Kiunga [Pap.N.Gui.] 60 Ci 6.07S 141.18 E
Kiuruvesi 7 Ge 63.39N 26.37 E
Kivalina 40 Gc 67.59N 164.33W
Kivercy 16 Dd 50.50N 25.31 E
Kivijärvi [Fin.] 8 Ld 60.55N 27.40 E
Kivijärvi [Fin.] 7 Fe 63.10N 25.09 E
Kivik 7 Di 55.41N 14.15 E
Kiviõli/Kiviyli 7 Gg 59.23N 26.59 E
Kiviyli/Kiviõli 7 Gg 59.23N 26.59 E
Kivu [2] 36 Ec 2.30S 27.30 E
Kivu, Lac-=Kivu, Lake- (EN) 30 Ii 2.00S 29.10 E
Kivu, Lake- (EN)=Kivu, Lac- 30 Ii 2.00S 29.10 E
Kiwai Island 60 Ci 8.30S 143.25 E
Kiyāmakī Dāgh 24 Kc 38.47N 45.51 E
Kiyiköy 24 Cb 41.25N 28.01 E
Kiyosato 29a Db 43.51N 144.35 E
Kizel 19 Fd 59.03N 57.40 E
Kizema 7 Kf 61.09N 44.46 E
Kızılcabölük 15 Ml 37.37N 29.01 E
Kızılca Dağı 24 Cd 36.55N 29.52 E
Kızılcahaman 24 Eb 40.28N 32.39 E
Kızıl Dağ 24 Ed 36.25N 32.42 E
Kizilhisar 15 Ml 37.33N 29.18 E
Kızılırmak 21 Fe 41.45N 35.59 E
Kızılırmak 24 Eb 40.22N 33.59 E
Kiziljurt 16 Oh 43.13N 46.55 E
Kizilskoje 17 Ij 52.44N 58.54 E
Kızıltepe 24 Id 37.12N 40.36 E
Kizimen, Vulkan- 20 Le 55.03N 160.27 E
Kižinga 20 Ff 51.51N 109.55 E
Kizir 20 Ef 54.10N 93.30 E
Kizljar 19 Eg 43.50N 46.42 E
Kizljarski Zaliv 16 Og 44.35N 46.55 E
Kizukuri 29a Bc 40.48N 140.22 E
Kizyl-Arvat 19 Fh 39.01N 56.20 E
Kizyl-Atrek 19 Fh 37.38N 54.47 E
Kizyl-Su 19 Fh 39.46N 53.01 E
Kjahta 20 Ff 50.26N 106.25 E
Kjalvaz 16 Pj 38.38N 48.20 E
Kjardla/Kärdla 7 Fg 59.01N 22.42 E
Kjarevere/Kärevere 8 Lf 58.23N 26.30 E
Kjarla/Kärla 8 Jf 58.16N 22.05 E
Kjellerup 8 Ch 56.17N 9.26 E
Kjøllefjord 7 Ga 70.56N 27.27 E
Kjölur 7a Bb 64.50N 19.25W
Kjøpsvik 7 Db 68.06N 16.21 E
Kjubjume 20 Jd 63.28N 140.30 E
Kjurdamir 19 Eg 40.20N 48.07 E
Kjusjur 20 Hb 70.35N 127.45 E
Kjustendil 15 Fg 42.17N 22.41 E
Kjustendil [2] 15 Fg 42.17N 22.41 E
Kjyosumi-Yama 29 Gd 35.10N 140.09 E
Klabat, Gunung- 26 If 1.28N 125.02 E
Kladanj 23 Gf 44.14N 18.42 E
Kladno 10 Kf 50.09N 14.07 E
Kladovo 15 Fe 44.37N 22.37 E
Klagenfurt 6 Hf 46.38N 14.18 E
Klaipėda/Klajpeda 6 Id 55.43N 21.07 E
Klajpeda/Klaipėda 6 Id 55.43N 21.07 E
Klamath 46 Cf 41.32N 124.02W
Klamath Falls 39 Ge 42.13N 121.46W
Klamath Mountains 43 Cc 41.40N 123.20W
Klamath River 46 Cf 41.33N 124.04W
Klamono 26 Jg 1.08S 131.30 E
Klarälven 5 Hd 59.23N 13.32 E
Klaten 26 Fh 7.42S 110.35 E
Klatovy 10 Jg 49.24N 13.19 E
Klavreström 8 Fg 57.08N 15.08 E
Klawer 37 Bf 31.44S 18.36 E
Klazienaveen, Emmen- 12 Jb 52.44N 7.01 E
Kleck 16 Ec 53.03N 26.40 E
Klecko 10 Nd 52.38N 17.26 E
Kleinblittersdorf 12 Je 49.09N 7.02 E
Kleine Nete 12 Gc 51.08N 4.34 E
Kleine Sluis, Anna Paulowna- 12 Gb 52.52N 4.52 E
Klein-Karoo=Little Karroo (EN) 37 Cf 33.42S 21.20 E
Kleinsee 37 Be 29.40S 17.05 E
Klekovača 14 Kf 44.26N 16.31 E
Kléla 34 Dc 11.40N 5.40W
Kleppe 8 Af 58.46N 5.40 E
Klerksdorp 37 De 26.58S 26.39 E
Kletnja 19 De 53.27N 33.17 E
Kletski 16 Me 49.19N 43.04 E
Kleve 10 Ce 51.47N 6.09 E
Klibreck, Ben- 9 Ic 58.19N 4.30W
Klička 20 Gf 50.24N 118.01 E
Klimoviči 19 De 53.37N 32.01 E
Klimovo 16 Hc 52.23N 32.16 E
Klin 19 Dd 56.20N 36.42 E
Klina 15 Dg 42.37N 20.35 E
Klincy 19 De 52.46N 32.17 E
Klingbach 12 Ke 49.11N 8.24 E
Klingenthal 10 If 50.22N 12.28 E
Klinovec 10 If 50.24N 12.58 E
Klintehamn 7 Eh 57.24N 18.12 E
Klippan 8 Eh 56.08N 13.06 E
Klipplaat 37 Cf 33.02S 24.21 E
Kliškovcy 15 Ja 48.23N 26.13 E
Klisura 15 Hg 42.42N 24.27 E
Klitmøller 8 Cg 57.02N 8.31 E
Kljazma 5 Kd 56.10N 42.58 E
Ključevskaja Sopka, Vulkan- 21 Sd 56.04N 160.38 E
Kljuci 20 Le 56.14N 160.58 E
Kłobuck 10 Of 50.55N 18.57 E
Kłodawa 10 Od 52.16N 18.55 E
Kłodzka, Kotlina- 10 Mf 50.30N 16.35 E
Kłodzko 10 Mf 50.28N 16.40 E
Kløfta 8 Dd 60.04N 11.09 E
Kloga/Klooga 8 Ke 59.24N 24.10 E
Kłomnice 10 Pf 50.56N 19.21 E
Klondike Plateau 42 Dd 63.10N 139.55W
Klondike River 42 Dd 64.03N 139.26W
Klooga/Kloga 8 Ke 59.24N 24.10 E
Kloosteezande, Hontenisse- 12 Gc 51.23N 4.00 E
Klosi 15 Dh 41.29N 20.06 E
Klosterneuburg 14 Kb 48.18N 16.19 E
Klosters/Claustra 14 Dd 46.52N 9.52 E
Kloten 14 Cc 47.27N 8.35 E
Klotz, Lac - 42 Kd 60.40N 73.00W
Kluane Lake 42 Dd 61.15N 138.40W
Kluczbork 10 Of 50.59N 18.13 E
Knaben 8 Bf 58.39N 7.04 E
Knäred 8 Eh 56.32N 13.19 E
Kneža 15 Hf 43.30N 24.05 E
Knife River 45 Fc 47.20N 101.23W
Knin 14 Kf 44.02N 16.12 E
Knislinge 8 Fh 56.11N 14.05 E
Knittelfeld 14 Ic 47.13N 14.49 E
Knivsta 8 Ge 59.43N 17.48 E
Knjaževac 15 Ff 43.34N 22.15 E
Knobly Mountain 44 Hf 39.15N 79.05W
Knockmealdown Mountains/ Cnoc Mhaoldonn 9 Fi 52.15N 8.00W
Knokke-Heist [Bel.] 12 Fc 51.21N 3.15 E
Knokke-Heist [Bel.] 11 Jc 51.21N 3.17 E
Knokke-Westkapelle 12 Fc 51.19N 3.18 E
Knolls grund 8 Gg 57.30N 17.30 E
Knøsen 8 Dg 57.12N 10.18 E
Knosós = Cnossus (EN) 15 In 35.18N 25.10 E
Knox, Cape - 42 Ef 54.11N 133.05W
Knox Coast 66 He 66.30S 105.00 E
Knoxville [Ia.-U.S.] 45 Jf 41.19N 93.06W
Knoxville [Tn.-U.S.] 39 Kf 35.58N 83.56W
Knud Rasmussen Land 67 Nd 80.00N 55.00W
Knüllgebirge 10 Ff 50.50N 9.30 E
Knutsholstind 8 Cc 61.26N 8.34 E
Knysna 31 Jl 34.02S 23.02 E
Ko, Kut 25 Kf 11.40N 102.35 E
Koartac 42 Kd 60.50N 69.30W
Koba 26 Eg 2.29S 106.24 E
Koba, Pulau- 26 Jh 6.25S 134.28 E
Kobar Sink 35 Gc 14.00N 40.30 E
Kobayashi 28 Ki 31.59N 130.59 E
Kobdo 22 Le 48.01N 91.38 E
Kobdo (Chovd) 27 Fb 48.06N 92.11 E
Köbe 22 Pf 34.41N 135.10 E
Kobeljaki 16 Ie 49.08N 34.12 E
København [2] 8 Ei 55.40N 12.10 E
København=Copenhagen (EN) 6 Hi 55.40N 12.35 E
Kobenni 32 Ff 15.55N 9.25W
Kobern-Gondorf 12 Jd 50.19N 7.28 E
Kobjaj 20 Hd 63.30N 126.26 E
Koblenz 10 Df 50.21N 7.36 E
Kobo 35 Fc 12.09N 39.39 E
Koboldo 20 If 52.58N 132.42 E
Kobra 7 Mg 59.19N 50.54 E
Kobrin 19 Ce 52.13N 24.23 E
Kobrinskoje 8 Ne 59.22N 30.14 E
Kobroor, Pulau- 26 Jh 6.12S 134.32 E
Kobuk 38 Cc 66.45N 161.00W
Kobuleti 16 Li 41.47N 41.45 E
Koca 24 Eb 41.41N 32.15 E
Kocabaş 24 Bb 40.22N 27.19 E
Koca Çay 15 Lj 38.43N 28.30 E
Koca Çay [Tur.] 24 Bb 40.08N 27.57 E
Koca Çay [Tur.] 24 Cd 36.17N 29.16 E
Koca Çay/Orhaneli 15 Lj 39.56N 28.32 E
Kočani 15 Fh 41.55N 22.25 E
Kocasu 15 Mj 39.42N 29.31 E
Kočečum 20 Fd 64.17N 100.10 E
Kočetovka 16 Lc 53.01N 40.31 E
Kočevje 14 Ie 45.39N 14.51 E
Kočevski rog 14 Ie 45.41N 15.00 E
Koch 42 Jc 69.35N 78.20W
Kŏch'ang 28 Ig 35.41N 127.55 E
Ko Chang 25 Kf 12.00N 102.23 E
Koch Bihār 25 Hc 26.19N 89.26 E
Kochi 27 Ne 33.33N 133.33 E
Kōchi Ken [2] 28 Lh 33.20N 133.30 E
Kochisar Ovası 24 Ec 38.50N 33.30 E
Kock 10 Se 51.39N 22.27 E
Kočkorka 18 Jc 42.11N 75.45 E
Kočmar 15 Kf 43.41N 27.28 E
Kočubej 19 Eg 44.23N 46.31 E
Kočubejevskoje 16 Lg 44.41N 41.50 E
Kodiak 39 Dd 57.48N 152.23W
Kodiak 38 Dd 57.30N 153.30W
Kodino 7 Je 63.44N 39.40 E
Kodok 35 Ed 9.53N 32.07 E
Kodomari 29a Bc 41.08N 140.18 E
Kodori 16 Lh 42.49N 41.10 E
Kodry 15 Lb 47.15N 28.15 E
Kodyma 16 Ge 48.01N 30.48 E
Kodža Balkan 15 Jg 42.50N 27.00 E
Koekenaap 37 Bf 31.29S 18.19 E
Koes 37 Be 25.59S 19.08 E
Kofa Mountains 46 Ij 33.20N 114.00W
Koṭarli 15 Kl 37.45N 27.42 E
Kofaz 24 Bb 41.58N 27.12 E
Koffiefontein 37 Ce 29.30S 25.00 E
Kofiau, Pulau- 26 Ig 1.11S 129.50 E
Köflach 14 Jc 47.04N 15.05 E
Koforidua 31 Gh 6.05N 0.15W
Kōfu [Jap.] 29 Cd 35.18N 133.29 E
Kōfu [Jap.] 27 Od 35.39N 138.35 E
Koga 29 Fc 36.12N 139.42 E
Kogaluc 42 Je 59.38N 77.30W
Köge 29 Dd 35.24N 134.15 E
Køge 7 Ci 55.27N 12.11 E
Køge Bugt 8 Ei 55.30N 12.20 E
Kogel 17 He 62.38N 57.07 E
Kogilnik 15 Md 45.51N 29.38 E
Kogilnik (Kunduk) 15 Md 45.51N 29.38 E
Kogon 34 Cc 11.09N 14.42W
Kogota 29 Gb 38.32N 141.01 E
Kohala Mountains 65a Fc 20.05N 155.43W
Kohāt 25 Eb 33.35N 71.26 E
Kohila 8 Ke 59.11N 24.40 E
Kohima 25 Ic 25.40N 94.07 E
Koh-i Mārān 25 Dc 29.05N 66.50 E
Kohinggo 63a Cc 8.13S 157.10 E
Kohma 7 Jh 56.57N 41.07 E
Kohtla-Järve/Kohtla-Jarve 19 Cd 59.25N 27.14 E
Kohu Daği 15 Mm 36.30N 29.50 E
Kohunlich 48 Oh 18.30N 88.55W
Koide 29 Fc 37.14N 138.57 E
Koigi/Kojgi 8 Kf 58.49N 25.40 E
Koin 17 Ee 61.23N 51.15 E
Koindu 34 Cd 8.28N 10.20W
Koitere 7 He 62.58N 30.45 E
Kojā 23 Jd 25.34N 61.13 E
Kojandytau 18 Lb 44.20N 78.45 E
Kojda 7 Kc 66.23N 42.31 E
Koje-Do 28 Jg 34.52N 128.37 E
Kojetín 10 Ng 49.21N 17.20 E
Kojgi/Koigi 8 Kf 58.49N 25.40 E
Ko-Jima [Jap.] 29 Fe 33.07N 139.40 E
Ko-Jima [Jap.] 28 Od 41.22N 139.47 E
Kojō 27 Md 38.57N 127.52 E
Kojonup 59 Df 33.50S 117.09 E
Kojtaš 18 Fd 40.14N 67.22 E
Kojtezek, Pereval- 18 If 37.29N 72.45 E
Kojur 24 Nd 36.23N 51.43 E
Kojva 17 Ig 58.15N 58.14 E
Kokab 35 Cc 10.03N 22.04 E
Kokai-Gawa 29 Gd 35.52N 140.08 E
Kokand 22 Je 40.33N 70.57 E
Kökar 7 Eg 59.55N 20.55 E
Kokarsfjärden 8 Ie 59.55N 20.45 E
Kokas 26 Jg 2.42S 132.26 E
Kokava nad Rimavicou 10 Ph 48.34N 19.50 E
Kokawa 29 Dd 34.17N 135.26 E
Kokčetav 22 Id 53.17N 69.25 E
Kokčetavskaja Oblast [3] 19 Ge 53.30N 70.00 E
Kokemäenjoki 8 Ic 61.33N 21.42 E
Kokemäki/Kumo 7 Ff 61.15N 22.21 E
Kok-Jangak 18 Hd 40.59N 73.15 E
Kokkina 24 Ee 35.10N 32.36 E
Kokkola/Gamlakarleby 6 Ic 63.50N 23.07 E
Koko [Eth.] 35 Fc 10.20N 36.04 E
Koko [Nig.] 34 Fc 11.26N 4.30 E
Kokomo 43 Jc 40.29N 86.08W
Kokonau 26 Kg 4.43S 136.26 E
Kokong 37 Cd 24.27S 23.03 E
Koko Nor (EN)=Qinghai Hu 21 Mf 37.00N 100.20 E
Kokpekty 19 If 48.45N 82.24 E
Kokšaal-Tau, Hrebet- 19 Hg 41.00N 78.00 E
Kokšenga 7 Kf 61.27N 42.38 E
Koksijde 12 Ec 51.06N 2.39 E
Koksoak 42 Ke 58.31N 68.11W
Kokstad 31 Jl 30.32S 29.29 E
Koktal 18 Lb 44.05N 79.44 E
Koktokay/Fuyun 22 Ke 47.13N 89.39 E
Kokubu 28 Ki 31.44N 130.46 E
Kola 19 Db 68.53N 33.01 E
Kola, Pulau- 26 Jh 5.30S 134.35 E
Kolahun 34 Cd 8.17N 10.05W
Kolaka 26 Hg 4.03S 121.36 E
Kolamadulu Atoll 25a Bb 2.25N 73.10 E
Kola Peninsula (EN)=Kolski Poluostrov 5 Jb 67.30N 37.00 E
Kolār Gold Fields 25 Ff 12.55N 78.17 E
Kolari 7 Fc 67.20N 23.48 E
Kolarovo 10 Ni 47.55N 18.00 E
Kolašin 15 Cg 42.49N 19.32 E
Kolbäck 8 Ge 59.34N 16.15 E
Kolbäcksån 8 Ge 59.32N 16.16 E
Kolbio 36 Hc 1.09S 41.12 E
Kolbuszowa 10 Rf 50.15N 21.47 E
Kolby 8 Di 55.48N 10.33 E
Kolčugino 7 Jh 56.16N 39.23 E
Kolda 34 Cc 12.53N 14.57W
Kolding 6 Gd 55.31N 9.29 E
Kole [Zaire] 36 Dc 3.31S 22.27 E
Kole [Zaire] 36 Eb 2.07N 25.26 E
Koléa 13 Oh 36.38N 2.46 E
Kolendo 20 Jf 53.43N 142.57 E
Kolente 34 Cd 8.55N 13.08W
Kolesnoje 15 Mc 46.04N 29.45 E
Kolga 8 Ke 59.28N 25.29 E
Kolga, Zaliv-/Kolga Laht 8 Ke 59.30N 25.15 E
Kolga Laht/Kolga, Zaliv- 8 Ke 59.30N 25.15 E
Kolgompja, Mys- 8 Me 59.44N 28.35 E
Kolgujev, Ostrov- 5 Kb 69.05N 49.15 E
Kolhāpur 22 Jh 16.42N 74.13 E
Kolhozabad 18 Gf 37.35N 68.39 E
Kolhozbentskoje, Vodohranilišče- 18 Df 37.10N 62.30 E
Koli 7 Ge 63.06N 29.53 E
Kolimbiné 34 Cc 14.45N 11.00 E
Kolín 10 Lf 50.02N 15.13 E
Kolito 35 Fd 7.25N 38.07 E
Koljučinskaja Guba 20 Nc 66.50N 174.30W
Kolka 8 Jg 57.44N 22.27 E
Kolkasrags 7 Fh 57.46N 22.37 E
Kolki 16 Dd 51.07N 25.42 E
Kollinai 15 Fl 37.17N 22.22 E
Kollumúli 7a Cb 65.47N 14.21W
Kolmården 8 Gf 58.41N 16.35 E
Köln=Cologne (EN) 6 Ge 50.56N 6.57 E
Köln-Lövenich 12 Id 50.57N 6.50 E
Kolno 10 Rc 53.25N 21.56 E
Köln-Porz 10 Df 50.53N 7.03 E
Koło 10 Od 52.12N 18.38 E
Koloa 65a Bb 21.54N 159.28W
Kołobrzeg 10 Lb 54.12N 15.33 E
Kolodnja 16 Hb 54.49N 32.11 E
Kologriv 7 Kg 58.51N 44.17 E
Kolokani 34 Dc 13.34N 8.03W
Koloko 34 Dc 11.05N 5.19W
Kolokolkova Guba 17 Fb 68.30N 52.30 E
Kololo 35 Gd 7.27N 41.59 E
Kolombangara Island 60 Fi 8.00S 157.05 E
Kolomna 6 Jd 55.05N 38.49 E
Kolomyja 19 Cf 48.32N 25.01 E
Kolondiéba 34 Dc 11.06N 6.53W
Kolonga 65b Ac 21.08S 175.04W
Kolonodale 26 Hg 2.00S 121.19 E
Kolosovka 19 Hd 56.28N 73.36 E
Kolossa 34 Dc 13.52N 7.35W
Kolovai 65b Ac 21.06S 175.20W
Kolozero, Ozero- 7 Hb 68.15N 33.15 E
Kolp 7 Ig 59.20N 36.50 E
Kolpaševo 22 Kd 58.20N 82.50 E
Kolpino 7 Hg 59.45N 30.33 E
Kolpny 16 Jc 52.16N 37.00 E
Kolski Poluostrov=Kola Peninsula (EN) 5 Jb 67.30N 37.00 E
Koltubanovski 16 Rc 52.57N 52.02 E
Kolubara 15 De 44.40N 20.15 E
Koluszki 10 Pe 51.44N 19.49 E
Koluton 19 Ge 51.42N 69.25 E
Kolva 19 Fb 65.55N 57.20 E
Kolva 17 Hf 60.22N 56.33 E
Kolvickoje, Ozero- 7 Hc 67.05N 33.30 E
Kolvrå 8 Ch 56.18N 9.08 E
Kolwezi 31 Jj 10.43S 25.28 E
Kolyma 21 Sc 69.30N 161.00 E
Kolyma Plain (EN) = Kolymskaja Nizmennost 21 Rc 68.30N 154.00 E
Kolyma Range (EN) = Kolymskoje Nagorje 21 Rc 62.30N 155.00 E
Kolymskaja Nizmennost= Kolyma Plain (EN) 21 Rc 68.30N 154.00 E
Kolymskoje Nagorje= Kolyma Range (EN) 21 Rc 62.30N 155.00 E
Kolyšlej 16 Nc 52.40N 44.31 E
Kolžat 19 Ig 43.29N 80.37 E
Kom 15 Gf 43.10N 23.03 E
Kom 36 Gb 1.05N 38.02 E
Komádi 10 Rj 47.00N 21.30 E
Komadugu Gana 34 Hc 13.05N 12.24 E
Komadugu Yobe 30 Ig 13.42N 13.24 E
Komagane 29 Ed 35.43N 137.54 E
Koma-ga-Take [Jap.] 29 Fd 35.45N 138.13 E
Koma-ga-Take [Jap.] 29 Gb 39.47N 140.50 E
Koma-ga-Take [Jap.] 29a Bb 42.04N 140.40 E
Komandorski Islands (EN) =Komandorskije Ostrova 21 Sd 55.00N 167.00 E
Komandorskije Ostrova= Komandorski Islands (EN) 21 Sd 55.00N 167.00 E
Komandorskiye Basin (EN) 20 Le 57.00N 168.00 E
Komarin 16 Gd 51.27N 30.32 E
Komarno 10 Tg 49.34N 23.43 E
Komárno 10 Oi 47.46N 18.09 E
Komárom 10 Oi 47.44N 18.07 E
Komárom-Esztegom 10 Oi 47.40N 18.15 E
Komatipoort 37 Ee 25.25S 31.55 E
Komatsu 27 Od 36.24N 136.27 E
Komatsujima 29 Dd 34.01N 134.35 E
Komba, Pulau- 26 Hh 7.47S 123.35 E
Kombissiri 34 Ec 12.04N 1.20W
Kombolcha 35 Fc 11.05N 39.45 E
Komebail Lagoon 64a Ac 7.24N 134.27 E
Komen/Comines 12 Ed 50.46N 2.59 E
Komi respublika 19 Fc 64.00N 55.00 E
Komi-Permjackij avtonomnyj okrug 19 Fd 60.00N 54.30 E
Komló 10 Oj 46.12N 18.16 E
Kommunarsk (Alčevsk) 16 Ke 48.27N 38.52 E
Kommunary 8 Nd 60.55N 30.10 E
Kommunizma, Pik-= Communism Peak (EN) 21 Jf 38.57N 72.08 E
Komodo, Pulau- 26 Gh 8.36S 119.30 E
Komoé 30 Gh 5.12N 3.44W
Komoé [3] 34 Ec 10.25N 4.20W
Komono 36 Bc 3.15S 13.14 E
Komoran, Pulau- 26 Kh 8.18S 138.45 E
Komoro 29 Fc 36.19N 138.24 E
Komotini 15 Ih 41.07N 25.24 E
Komovi 15 Cg 42.41N 19.39 E
Kompasberg 30 Jl 31.46S 24.32 E
Komrat 16 Ff 46.17N 28.38 E
Komsa 20 Dd 61.40N 89.25 E
Komsomolec 17 Kj 53.45N 62.02 E
Komsomolec, Ostrov- 21 La 80.30N 95.00 E
Komsomolec, Zaliv- 16 Rg 45.30N 52.45 E
Komsomolsk 7 Jh 57.02N 40.22 E
Komsomolsk 20 De 57.25N 86.02 E
Komsomolski 19 Gh 39.02N 63.36 E
Komsomolski 19 Ff 47.20N 53.44 E
Komsomolski 16 Og 45.22N 46.01 E
Komsomolski 7 Ki 54.27N 45.45 E
Komsomolski 19 Gb 67.35N 63.47 E
Komsomolski 17 Kf 61.20N 63.15 E
Komsomolski 20 Mc 69.12N 172.55 E
Komsomolsk-na-Amure 22 Pd 50.36N 137.02 E
Komsomolsk-na-Ustjurte 19 Fg 44.07N 58.17 E
Komsomolskoje [Ukraine] 16 Je 49.36N 36.33 E
Komsomolskoje [Ukraine] 16 Kf 47.37N 38.05 E
Komsomolskoj Pravdy, Ostrova- 20 Fa 77.15N 107.30 E
Kōmun-Do 28 Ig 34.02N 127.19 E
Kömür Burun 15 Jk 38.39N 26.25 E
Komusan 27 Mc 42.07N 129.42 E
Kona 34 Ec 14.57N 3.53W
Kona Coast 65a Fd 19.35N 155.56W
Konakovo 19 Dd 56.42N 36.46 E
Konar 23 Lc 34.25N 70.32 E
Konārak 25 Hh 19.54N 86.07 E
Konarha [3] 23 Lb 35.15N 71.00 E
Konda 19 Gc 60.40N 69.46 E
Kondagaon 25 Ge 19.36N 81.40 E
Kondinin 59 Df 32.30S 118.16 E
Kondinskoje 17 Mg 59.40N 67.25 E
Kondoa 31 Ki 4.54S 35.47 E
Kondopoga 6 Jc 62.13N 34.17 E
Kondratjevo 8 Md 60.36N 28.02 E
Kondrovo 19 De 54.49N 35.55 E
Kondurča 7 Mj 53.31N 50.24 E
Koné 61 Bd 21.04S 164.52 E
Konečnaja 19 He 50.45N 78.27 E
Konevic, Ostrov- 8 Nd 60.50N 30.45 E
Kong 34 Ed 9.09N 4.37W
Kong 25 Lf 13.32N 105.58 E
Kŏng, Kaôh- 25 Kf 11.20N 103.00 E
Konga/Koonga 8 Jf 58.34N 24.00 E
Kongauru 64a Ac 7.04N 134.17 E
Kong Christian IX Land = King Christian IX Land (EN) 67 Mc 68.00N 36.30W
Kong Christian X Land = King Christian X Land (EN) 67 Md 72.20N 32.30W
Kongeå 8 Ci 55.23N 8.39 E
Kong Frederik VIII Land = King Frederik VIII Land (EN) 67 Md 78.30N 28.00W
Kong Frederik VI Kyst = King Frederik VI Coast (EN) 67 Nc 63.00N 43.30W
Konginkangas 8 Kb 62.46N 25.48 E
Kongju 28 If 36.27N 127.08 E
Kong Karls Land 41 Oc 78.50N 28.00 E
Kong Kong 35 Ed 7.26N 33.14 E
Kongolo 31 Ji 5.23S 27.00 E
Kongor 35 Ed 7.10N 31.21 E
Kong Oscars Fjord 67 Md 72.20N 23.00W
Kongoussi 34 Ec 13.19N 1.32W
Kongsberg 7 Bg 59.39N 9.39 E
Kongsøya 41 Oc 78.55N 28.40 E
Kongsvinger 7 Cf 60.12N 12.00 E
Kongur Shan 21 Jf 38.40N 75.21 E
Kongwa 36 Gd 6.12S 36.25 E
Kong Wilhelms Land 41 Jc 75.48N 23.15W
Koniecpol 10 Pf 50.48N 19.41 E
Königslutter am Elm 10 Gd 52.15N 10.49 E
Konigswinter 12 Jd 50.41N 7.11 E
Königs Wusterhausen 10 Jd 52.17N 13.37 E
Konin 10 Od 52.13N 18.16 E
Konin [2] 10 Od 52.15N 18.15 E
Konispoli 15 Dj 39.39N 20.10 E
Konitsa 15 Di 40.03N 20.45 E
Konj 14 Kg 43.43N 16.55 E
Konjed Jān 24 Nf 33.30N 50.27 E
Konjic 14 Lg 43.39N 17.58 E
Konjuh 14 Mf 44.18N 18.33 E
Konkan 25 Ee 18.05N 73.25 E
Konkiep 37 Be 28.00S 17.23 E
Konko 36 Ed 10.12S 27.27 E
Konkouré 34 Cd 9.58N 13.42W
Konnevesi 8 Lb 62.40N 26.35 E
Konnevesi 8 Lb 62.37N 26.19 E
Konnivesi 8 Lc 61.10N 26.10 E
Konoša 6 Kc 60.58N 40.15 E

Index Symbols

(1) Independent Nation
(2) State, Region
(3) District, County
(4) Municipality
(5) Colony, Dependency
Continent
Physical Region
Historical or Cultural Region
Mount, Mountain
Volcano
Hill
Mountains, Mountain Range
Hills, Escarpment
Plateau, Upland
Pass, Gap
Plain, Lowland
Delta
Salt Flat
Valley, Canyon
Crater, Cave
Karst Features
Depression
Polder
Desert, Dunes
Forest, Woods
Heath, Steppe
Oasis
Cape, Point
Coast, Beach
Cliff
Peninsula
Isthmus
Sandbank
Island
Atoll
Rock, Reef
Islands, Archipelago
Rocks, Reefs
Coral Reef
Well, Spring
Geyser
River, Stream
Waterfall Rapids
River Mouth, Estuary
Lake
Salt Lake
Intermittent Lake
Reservoir
Swamp, Pond
Canal
Glacier
Ice Shelf, Pack Ice
Ocean
Sea
Gulf, Bay
Strait, Fjord
Lagoon
Bank
Seamount
Tablemount
Ridge
Shelf
Basin
Escarpment, Sea Scarp
Fracture
Trench, Abyss
National Park, Reserve
Point of Interest
Recreation Site
Cave, Cavern
Historic Site
Ruins
Wall, Walls
Church, Abbey
Temple
Scientific Station
Airport
Port
Lighthouse
Mine
Tunnel
Dam, Bridge

Name	Page	Grid	Lat	Long
Kōnosu	29	Fc	36.04N	139.30 E
Konotop	6	Je	51.14N	33.12 E
Konqi He	21	Ke	41.48N	86.47 E
Konrei	64a	Bb	7.43N	134.37 E
Konsei-Tōge	29	Fc	36.52N	139.22 E
Konsen-Daichi	29a	Db	43.20N	144.50 E
Końskie	10	Qe	51.12N	20.26 E
Konstantinovka	16	Je	48.29N	37.43 E
Konstantinovsk	16	Lf	47.35N	41.05 E
Konstanz	10	Fi	47.40N	9.11 E
Kontagora	31	Hg	10.24N	5.29 E
Kontcha	34	Hd	7.58N	12.14 E
Kontich	12	Gc	51.08N	4.27 E
Kontiolahti	7	Ge	62.46N	29.51 E
Kontiomäki	7	Gd	64.21N	28.09 E
Kontum	25	Lf	14.21N	108.00 E
Kontum, Plateau de-	25	Lf	13.55N	108.05 E
Konusin, Mys-	7	Kc	67.10N	43.50 E
Konya	22	Ff	37.52N	32.31 E
Konya Ovası	24	Ed	37.30N	33.20 E
Konz	12	Ie	49.42N	6.35 E
Konza	36	Gc	1.45 S	37.07 E
Konžakovski Kamen, Gora-	5	Ld	59.38N	59.08 E
Koocanusa, Lake-	46	Hb	48.45N	115.15W
Kook, Punta-	65d	Ab	27.08 S	109.26W
Koolau Range	65a	Db	21.21N	157.47W
Koonga/Konga	8	Jf	58.34N	24.00 E
Koorda	59	Df	30.50 S	117.29 E
Koosa	8	Lf	58.33N	27.07 E
Kootenay Lake	46	Gb	49.35N	116.50W
Kootenay River	38	He	49.15N	117.39W
Kopa	18	Jc	43.31N	75.48 E
Kopaonik	15	Df	43.15N	20.50 E
Kópasker	7a	Ca	66.18N	16.27W
Kópavogur	7a	Bb	64.06N	21.55W
Kopejsk	19	Gd	55.08N	61.39 E
Koper	14	He	45.33N	13.44 E
Kopervik	7	Ag	59.17N	5.18 E
Kopetdag, Hrebet-	21	Hf	37.45N	58.15 E
Kop Geçidi	24	Ib	40.01N	40.28 E
Ko Phangan	25	Jg	9.45N	100.00 E
Köping	7	Dg	59.31N	16.00 E
Köpingsvik	8	Gh	56.53N	16.43 E
Kopjevo	20	Df	54.59N	89.55 E
Kopliku	15	Cg	42.13N	19.26 E
Köpmanholmen	7	Ee	63.10N	18.34 E
Koporje	8	Me	59.40N	29.08 E
Koporski Zaliv	8	Me	59.45N	28.45 E
Koppal	25	Fe	15.21N	76.09 E
Koppang	7	Cf	61.34N	11.04 E
Koppány	10	Oj	46.35N	18.26 E
Kopparberg	8	Fe	59.52N	14.59 E
Kopparberg [2]	7	Df	61.00N	14.30 E
Kopparstenarna	8	Hf	58.32N	19.20 E
Koppom	8	Ee	59.43N	12.09 E
Koprivnica	14	Kd	46.10N	16.50 E
Kopru	24	Dd	36.49N	31.10 E
Köprüören	15	Mj	39.30N	29.47 E
Korab	5	Ig	41.44N	20.32 E
Korablino	7	Jj	53.57N	40.00 E
Korahe	35	Gd	6.36N	44.16 E
Korak	64a	Bc	7.21N	134.34 E
Koralpe	14	Id	46.45N	15.00 E
Koramlik	27	Ed	37.32N	85.42 E
Korana	14	Je	45.30N	15.35 E
Korangi	25	Dd	24.47N	67.08 E
Koraput	25	Ge	18.49N	82.43 E
Korba	25	Gd	22.21N	82.41 E
Korbach	10	Ee	51.17N	8.52 E
Körby	8	Ei	55.51N	13.39 E
Korça	15	Di	40.37N	20.46 E
Korčula	14	Kh	42.57N	16.55 E
Korčula	14	Lh	42.58N	17.08 E
Korčulanski Kanal	14	Kg	43.03N	16.40 E
Kordān	24	Ne	35.56N	50.50 E
Kordel	12	Ie	49.50N	6.38 E
Kordestān [3]	23	Gb	35.30N	47.00 E
Kord Kūy	23	Hb	36.48N	54.07 E
Kordun	14	Je	45.10N	15.35 E
Korea Bay (EN)=Sŏjosŏn-man	21	Of	39.15N	125.00 E
Korean Peninsula (EN)	21	Of	35.30N	125.30 E
Korea Strait (EN)=Taehan-Haehyŏp	21	Of	34.40N	129.00 E
Korea Strait (EN)= Tsushima-Kaikyō	21	Of	34.40N	129.00 E
Korec	16	Ed	50.37N	27.10 E
Korem	35	Fc	12.30N	39.32 E
Korenovsk	19	Df	45.28N	39.28 E
Korf	20	Ld	60.18N	166.01 E
Korfovski	20	Ig	48.11N	135.04 E
Korgen	7	Cc	66.05N	13.50 E
Kõrgesaare/Kyrgesare	8	Je	59.00N	22.25 E
Korhogo	31	Gh	9.27N	5.38W
Korhogo [3]	34	Dd	9.35N	5.55W
Koribundu	34	Cd	7.43N	11.42W
Korienzé	34	Eb	15.24N	3.47W
Korinthiakós Kólpos= Corinth, Gulf of- (EN)	5	Ih	38.12N	22.30 E
Kórinthos	15	Fl	37.55N	22.53 E
Kórinthos = Corinth (EN)	15	Fl	37.55N	22.53 E
Korínthou, Dhiórix- = Corinth Canal (EN)	15	Fl	37.57N	22.58 E
Koriolei	31	Lh	1.48N	44.30 E
Kőrishegy	10	Ni	47.12N	17.49 E
Koritnik	15	Dg	42.05N	20.34 E
Kōriyama	27	Pd	37.24N	140.23 E
Korjakskaja Sopka, Vulkan-	21	Rd	53.20N	158.47 E
Korjakski avtonomnyj okrug	20	Le	60.00N	163.00 E
Korjakskoje Nagorje = Koryak Range (EN)	21	Tc	62.30N	172.00 E
Korjažma	19	Ec	61.18N	47.07 E
Korjukovka	16	Hd	51.47N	32.17 E
Korkino	17	Ji	54.54N	61.25 E
Korkodon	20	Kd	64.43N	154.05 E
Korkuteli	24	Dd	37.04N	30.13 E
Korla	22	Ke	41.44N	86.09 E
Körmend	10	Mi	47.01N	16.36 E
Kormy, Gora-	20	Fd	62.15N	106.08 E
Kornati	14	Jg	43.49N	15.20 E
Kornejevka	17	Ni	54.01N	68.27 E
Kornešty	15	Kb	47.23N	28.00 E
Korneuburg	14	Kb	48.21N	16.20 E
Kórnik	10	Nd	52.17N	17.04 E
Kornsjø	7	Cg	58.57N	11.39 E
Koro	34	Ec	14.05N	3.04W
Koroba	59	Ia	5.40 S	142.45 E
Koroča	16	Jd	50.50N	37.13 E
Köroğlu Dağları	23	Da	40.40N	32.35 E
Köroğlu Tepe	24	Db	40.31N	31.53 E
Korogwe	36	Gd	5.09 S	38.29 E
Koro Island	57	If	17.32 S	179.42 E
Koroit	59	Ig	38.17 S	142.22 E
Korolevo	10	Th	48.08N	23.07 E
Korolevu	63d	Ac	18.12 S	177.53 E
Korom, Bahr	35	Bc	10.35N	19.45 E
Koromiri	64p	Cc	21.15 S	159.43W
Koronadal	26	He	6.12N	125.01 E
Korónia, Límni-	15	Gi	40.40N	23.10 E
Koronowo	10	Nc	53.19N	17.57 E
Koronowski e, Jezioro-	10	Nc	53.22N	17.55 E
Koror	57	Ed	7.20N	134.30 E
Koror	58	Ed	7.20N	134.29 E
Körös	10	Qj	46.43N	20.12 E
Koro Sea	61	Ec	18.00 S	180.00
Korosten	6	Ie	50.57N	28.39 E
Korostyšev	16	Fd	50.18N	29.05 E
Korotaiha	17	Jb	68.55N	60.55 E
Koro Toro	31	Ig	16.05N	18.30 E
Korovin Volcano	40a	Db	52.22N	174.10W
Korpijärvi	8	Lc	61.15N	27.10 E
Korpilahti	7	Fe	62.01N	25.33 E
Korpo/Korppoo	8	Id	60.10N	21.35 E
Korppoo/Korpo	8	Id	60.10N	21.35 E
Korsakov	20	Jg	46.37N	142.51 E
Korshäs	7	Ee	62.47N	21.12 E
Korsholm/Mustasaari	8	Ia	63.05N	21.43 E
Korso	8	Kd	60.21N	25.06 E
Korsør	7	Ci	55.20N	11.09 E
Korsun-Ševčenkovski	16	Ge	49.26N	31.18 E
Korsze	10	Rb	54.10N	21.09 E
Kortemark	12	Fc	51.02N	3.02 E
Kortrijk/Courtrai	11	Jd	50.50N	3.16 E
Koruçam Burnu	24	Ee	35.24N	32.56 E
Korucu	15	Kj	39.28N	27.22 E
Koru Dağ	15	Ji	40.42N	26.45 E
Koryak Range (EN)= Korjakskoje Nagorje	21	Tc	62.30N	172.00 E
Korzybie	10	Mb	54.18N	16.50 E
Kos	15	Km	36.53N	27.18 E
Kos	15	Km	36.50N	27.10 E
Kosa	17	Gg	59.56N	55.01 E
Kosa	17	Gf	60.11N	55.10 E
Kosai	29	Ed	34.43N	137.30 E
Kosaja Gora	16	Jb	54.09N	37.31 E
Kosaka	29	Ga	40.20N	140.44 E
Kō-Saki	29	Ad	34.05N	129.13 E
Ko Samui	25	Jg	9.30N	99.58 E
Kosan-ŭp	27	Md	38.51N	127.25 E
Koščagyl	16	Rf	46.52N	53.47 E
Kościan	10	Md	52.06N	16.38 E
Kościerzyna	10	Nb	54.08N	18.00 E
Kosciusko	45	Lj	32.58N	89.35W
Kosciusko, Mount-	57	Fg	36.27 S	148.16 E
Kose/Koze	8	Ke	59.11N	25.05 E
Köse Dağ	24	Gb	40.06N	37.58 E
Kosha	35	Ea	20.49N	30.32 E
Koshigaya	29	Fd	35.55N	139.45 E
Koshiji	29	Fc	37.24N	138.45 E
Koshiki-Kaikyō	29	Bf	31.45N	130.05 E
Koshiki Rettō	27	Me	31.45N	129.45 E
Koshimizu	29a	Db	43.51N	144.25 E
Kōshoku	28	Of	36.38N	138.06 E
Kōshyū Seamount (EN)	29	Df	31.35N	135.50 E
Košice	6	If	48.43N	21.15 E
Kosjerić	15	Cf	44.00N	19.55 E
Kosju	17	Ic	66.18N	59.53 E
Kosju	17	Id	65.38N	58.59 E
Köşk	15	Ll	37.51N	28.03 E
Koski	8	Jd	60.39N	23.09 E
Koskolovo	8	Me	59.34N	28.30 E
Koslan	19	Ec	63.29N	48.52 E
Kosma	17	Dd	65.43N	49.50 E
Kosmaj	15	De	44.28N	20.33 E
Kosŏng	27	Md	38.40N	128.19 E
Kosov	15	Ia	48.15N	25.08 E
Kosovo	15	Eg	42.40N	21.05 E
Kosovo [3]	15	Dg	42.35N	21.00 E
Kosovska Mitrovica	15	Dg	42.53N	20.52 E
Kosrae (Kusaie)	57	Hd	5.19N	162.59 E
Kossol Passage	64a	Bb	7.52N	134.36 E
Kossol Reef	64a	Bb	7.57N	134.41 E
Kossou, Barrage de-	34	Dd	7.01N	5.29W
Kossovo	16	Dc	52.47N	25.10 E
Kostajnica	14	Ke	45.13N	16.33 E
Kostenec	15	Gg	42.16N	23.49 E
Koster	37	De	25.57 S	26.42 E
Kosteröarna	8	Df	58.55N	11.05 E
Kostjukoviči	16	Hc	53.23N	32.06 E
Kostjukovka	16	Gc	52.32N	30.58 E
Kostolac	15	Ee	44.44N	21.12 E
Kostopol	16	Ed	50.53N	26.29 E
Kostriževka	15	Ia	48.31N	25.45 E
Kostroma	6	Kd	57.47N	40.59 E
Kostromskaja Oblast [3]	19	Ed	58.30N	44.00 E
Kostrzyń	10	Nd	52.25N	17.14 E
Kostrzyn	10	Kd	52.37N	14.39 E
Kosva	17	Hg	58.50N	56.45 E
Koszalin	10	Mb	54.12N	16.09 E
Koszalin [2]	10	Mb	54.10N	16.10 E
Kőszeg	10	Mi	47.23N	16.33 E
Kota	22	Jg	25.16N	75.55 E
Kotaagung	26	Dh	5.30 S	104.38 E
Kota Baharu	22	Mi	6.08N	102.15 E
Kotabaru	26	Gg	3.14 S	116.13 E
Kotabumi	22	Mj	4.50 S	104.54 E
Kotadabok	26	Dg	0.30 S	104.33 E
Kota Kinabalu	22	Ni	5.59N	116.04 E
Kotamobagu	26	Hf	0.46N	124.19 E
Ko Tao	25	Jf	10.05N	99.52 E
Kotari	14	Jf	44.05N	15.30 E
Ko Tarutau	25	Jg	6.35N	99.40 E
Kota Tinggi	26	Df	1.44N	103.54 E
Kotel	15	Jg	42.53N	26.27 E
Kotelnič	19	Ed	58.20N	48.20 E
Kotelnikovo	16	Mf	47.38N	43.09 E
Kotelny, Ostrov-	21	Pb	75.45N	138.44 E
Kotelva	16	Id	50.03N	34.45 E
Köthen	10	He	51.45N	11.58 E
Kotido	36	Fb	3.00N	34.09 E
Kotjužany	29	Gb	47.50N	28.27 E
Kotka	7	Gf	60.28N	26.55 E
Kot Kapūra	25	Eb	30.35N	74.54 E
Kotlas	6	Kc	61.16N	46.35 E
Kotlenik	15	Df	43.51N	20.42 E
Kotlenski prohod	15	Jg	42.53N	26.27 E
Kotlik	40	Gd	63.02N	163.33W
Kotlin, Ostrov-	8	Md	60.00N	29.45 E
Kotly	8	Me	59.30N	28.48 E
Kotobi	34	Ed	6.42N	4.08W
Kotohira	29	Cd	34.11N	133.48 E
Koton Karifi	34	Gd	8.06N	6.48 E
Kotor	15	Bg	42.25N	18.46 E
Kotorosl	7	Jh	57.38N	39.57 E
Kotorska, Boka-	15	Bg	42.25N	18.40 E
Kotor Varoš	14	Lf	44.37N	17.22 E
Kotouba	34	Ed	8.41N	3.12W
Kotovo	19	Ee	50.18N	44.48 E
Kotovsk → Chynčešt'	16	Ff	46.49N	28.33 E
Kotovsk	19	Ee	52.35N	41.32 E
Kotovsk	19	Cf	47.43N	29.33 E
Kotra	10	Uc	53.32N	24.17 E
Kotri	25	Dc	25.22N	68.18 E
Kötschach	14	Gd	46.40N	13.00 E
Kottayam	25	Fg	9.35N	76.31 E
Kotto	30	Jh	4.14N	22.02 E
Kotton	35	Id	9.37N	50.32 E
Kotu	65b	Ba	19.57 S	174.48W
Kotu Group	57	Jg	20.00 S	174.45W
Kotuj	21	Mb	71.55N	102.05 E
Kotujkan	20	Fb	70.40N	103.25 E
Koturdepe	16	Rj	39.26N	53.40 E
Kotzebue	39	Cc	66.53N	162.39W
Kotzebue Sound	38	Cc	66.20N	163.00W
Kouandé	34	Fc	10.20N	1.42 E
Kouango	35	Be	4.58N	19.59 E
Kouba Modounga	35	Bb	15.40N	18.15 E
Koudougou	31	Gg	11.44N	4.31W
Kouéré	34	Ec	10.27N	3.59W
Koufália	15	Fi	40.47N	22.35 E
Koufonísion [Grc.]	15	Jo	34.56N	26.10 E
Koufonísion [Grc.]	15	Im	36.55N	25.35 E
Koufonísiou, Stenón-	15	Jo	35.00N	26.10 E
Kouilou [3]	36	Bc	4.00 S	12.00 E
Kouilou	30	Ii	4.28 S	11.41 E
Koukdjuak	42	Kc	66.47N	73.10W
Kouki	35	Bd	7.10N	17.18 E
Koukourou	35	Cd	7.12N	20.02 E
Koulamoutou	36	Bc	1.08 S	12.29 E
Koulikoro	34	Dc	12.51N	7.34W
Koulountou	34	Cc	13.15N	13.37W
Koumac	58	Hg	20.30 S	164.12 E
Koumac, Grand Récif de-	63b	Be	20.32 S	164.04 E
Koumbi-Saleh	32	Ff	15.47N	7.58W
Koumi	29	Fc	36.05N	138.28 E
Koumpentoum	34	Cc	13.59N	14.34W
Koumra	35	Bd	8.55N	17.33 E
Koundara	31	Fg	12.29N	13.18W
Koundian	34	Cc	13.08N	10.42W
Kounoúpoi	15	Jm	36.32N	26.27 E
Kounradski	19	Hf	46.57N	75.01 E
Kounta	34	Eb	17.30N	0.40W
Koupéla	34	Ec	12.11N	0.21W
Kouqian → Yongji	28	Ic	43.40N	126.30 E
Kourou	54	Hb	5.09N	52.39W
Kouroussa	34	Dc	10.39N	9.53W
Koury	34	Ec	12.10N	4.48W
Koussané	34	Cc	14.52N	11.15W
Kousséri	34	Ic	12.05N	15.02 E
Koussi, Emi-	30	Ig	19.55N	18.30 E
Koutiala	31	Gg	12.23N	5.27W
Koutoumo	63b	Cf	22.40 S	167.32 E
Koutous	34	Hc	14.30N	10.00 E
Kouvola	7	Gf	60.52N	26.42 E
Kouyou	36	Cc	0.45 S	16.38 E
Kova	20	Fe	58.20N	100.20 E
Kovač	15	Cf	43.31N	19.07 E
Kovačica	15	Dd	45.06N	20.38 E
Koval	10	Pd	52.31N	19.10 E
Kovalevka	15	Nc	46.42N	30.31 E
Kovarskas/ Kavarskas	8	Ki	55.24N	25.03 E
Kovdor	19	Db	67.33N	30.25 E
Kovdozero, Ozero-	7	Hc	66.47N	32.00 E
Kovel	19	Ce	51.13N	24.43 E
Kovenskaja	17	Mf	61.24N	67.39 E
Kovin	15	De	44.45N	20.59 E
Kovinskaja Grjada	20	Fe	57.15N	101.00 E
Kovrov	19	Ed	56.24N	41.20 E
Kovylkino	7	Ki	54.02N	43.58 E
Kowŏn	27	Md	39.26N	127.15 E
Kowtal-e Do Rāh	23	Lb	36.07N	71.15 E
Kowt-e 'Ashrow	23	Kc	34.27N	68.48 E
Kōyama	29	Bf	31.19N	130.57 E
Köyceğiz	24	Cd	36.55N	28.43 E
Köycegiz Gölü	15	Lm	36.55N	28.40 E
Koyoshi-Gawa	29	Gb	39.24N	140.01 E
Koyuk	40	Gd	64.56N	161.08W
Koyukuk	38	Dc	64.56N	157.30W
Kozaklı	24	Fc	39.13N	34.49 E
Kozan	24	Fd	37.27N	35.49 E
Kozáni	15	Ei	40.18N	21.47 E
Kozara	14	Ke	45.00N	16.55 E
Kozawa	29a	Bb	42.58N	140.40 E
Koze/Kose	8	Ke	59.11N	25.05 E
Kozelsk	19	De	54.01N	35.46 E
Koževnikovo	20	De	56.18N	84.00 E
Kozhikode → Calicut	22	Jh	11.19N	75.46 E
Kozienice	10	Re	51.35N	21.33 E
Kožim	17	Id	65.43N	59.31 E
Kožim	17	Id	65.45N	59.15 E
Kozima	14	He	45.37N	13.56 E
Kozjak	15	Eh	41.06N	21.54 E
Kozloduj	15	Gf	43.47N	23.44 E
Kozlovka	7	Li	55.52N	48.13 E
Kozlovščina	10	Vc	53.14N	25.20 E
Kozlu	24	Db	41.25N	31.46 E
Kozluk	24	Ic	38.11N	41.29 E
Koźmin	10	Ne	51.50N	17.28 E
Kozmodemjansk	7	Lh	56.20N	46.36 E
Kožozero, Ozero-	7	Je	63.05N	38.05 E
Kożuchów	10	Le	51.45N	15.35 E
Kožuf	15	Fh	41.09N	22.10 E
Kōzu-Shima	27	Oe	34.15N	139.10 E
Kožva	17	Hd	65.07N	56.57 E
Kožva	17	Hd	65.10N	57.00 E
Kozyrevsk	20	Ke	55.59N	159.59 E
Kpalimé	34	Fd	6.54N	0.38 E
Kpandu	34	Fd	7.00N	0.18 E
Kpessi	34	Fd	8.04N	1.16 E
Kra, Isthmus of- (EN)=Kra, Khokhok-	21	Lh	10.20N	99.00 E
Kra, Khokhok-=Kra, Isthmus of- (EN)	21	Lh	10.20N	99.00 E
Kraba	15	Ch	41.12N	19.59 E
Krabbfjärden	8	Gf	58.45N	17.40 E
Krabi	25	Jg	8.05N	98.53 E
Krabit, Mali i-	15	Cg	42.07N	19.59 E
Kra Buri	25	Jf	10.24N	98.47 E
Krâchéh	22	Mh	12.29N	106.01 E
Kragerø	7	Bg	58.52N	9.25 E
Kragujevac	15	De	44.01N	20.55 E
Kraichbach	12	Ke	49.22N	8.31 E
Kraichgau	10	Eg	49.10N	8.50 E
Kraichtal	12	Ke	49.07N	8.46 E
Krajina	14	Kf	44.45N	16.35 E
Krajina	15	Fe	44.10N	22.30 E
Krajište	15	Fg	42.35N	22.25 E
Krajnovka	16	Oh	43.57N	47.24 E
Kråka	8	Ca	63.28N	9.00 E
Krakatau, Gunung-	21	Mj	6.07 S	105.24 E
Krak des Chevaliers	24	Ge	34.46N	36.19 E
Krakovec	10	Tg	49.56N	23.13 E
Kraków [2]	10	Pf	50.05N	20.00 E
Kraków	6	He	50.03N	19.58 E
Kraków-Nowa Huta	10	Qf	50.04N	20.05 E
Krakowsko-Częstochowska, Wyżyna-	10	Pf	50.50N	19.15 E
Kralendijk	50	Bf	12.10N	68.16W
Kraljevica	14	Ie	45.16N	14.34 E
Kraljevo	15	Df	43.44N	20.43 E
Kralupy nad Vltavou	10	Kf	50.14N	14.19 E
Kramatorsk	16	Je	48.43N	37.32 E
Kramfors	7	De	62.56N	17.47 E
Krammer	12	Gc	51.38N	4.15 E
Kranenburg	12	Ic	51.47N	6.01 E
Kranídhion	15	Gl	37.23N	23.09 E
Kranj	14	Id	46.14N	14.22 E
Krapina	14	Jd	46.10N	15.53 E
Krapkowice	10	Nf	50.29N	17.56 E
Kras=Karst (EN)	5	Hf	45.48N	14.00 E
Krasavino	19	Ec	60.59N	46.28 E
Krasiczyn	10	Sg	49.48N	22.39 E
Krasilov	16	Ee	49.37N	26.59 E
Kraskino	28	Kc	42.44N	130.48 E
Kraslava/Krāslava	7	Gi	55.54N	27.10 E
Krāslava/Kraslava	7	Gi	55.54N	27.10 E
Krasnaja Poljana	16	Lh	43.40N	40.12 E
Kraśnik	10	Sf	50.56N	22.13 E
Kraśnik Fabryczny, Kraśnik-	10	Sf	50.58N	22.12 E
Kraśnik-Kraśnik Fabryczny	10	Sf	50.58N	22.12 E
Krasnoarmejsk	19	Ge	53.57N	69.43 E
Krasnoarmejsk	19	Ee	51.02N	45.42 E
Krasnoarmejsk	16	Je	48.11N	37.12 E
Krasnoarmejski	20	Mc	69.37N	172.02 E
Krasnodar	6	Jf	45.02N	39.00 E
Krasnodarski Kraj [3]	19	Df	45.20N	39.30 E
Krasnodon	16	Ke	48.17N	39.44 E
Krasnogorodskoje	8	Mh	56.47N	28.18 E
Krasnogorsk	20	Jg	48.26N	142.10 E
Krasnogorsk	7	Ii	55.51N	37.20 E
Krasnogorski	17	Ji	54.36N	61.15 E
Krasnograd	19	Df	49.22N	35.27 E
Krasnogvardejsk	18	Fe	39.45N	67.16 E
Krasnogvardejskoje	16	Lg	45.49N	41.31 E
Krasnoholmski	17	Gh	56.02N	55.05 E
Krasnoilsk	15	Ia	48.02N	25.48 E
Krasnojarsk	22	Ld	56.01N	92.50 E
Krasnojarski	17	Ij	51.58N	59.57 E
Krasnojarski Kraj [3]	20	Ee	57.30N	95.00 E
Krasnojarskoje Vodohranilišče	20	Ee	55.05N	91.30 E
Krasnoje	10	Ug	49.49N	24.39 E
Krasnoje Selo	7	Hg	59.43N	30.03 E
Krasnoje Znamja	18	Df	36.50N	62.29 E
Krasnokamensk	20	Gf	50.00N	118.05 E
Krasnokamsk	19	Fd	58.04N	55.45 E
Krasnokutsk	19	He	52.59N	75.59 E
Krasnolesje	8	Jj	54.23N	22.25 E
Krasnolesny	16	Kd	51.52N	39.35 E
Krasnooktjabrski	18	Jc	42.45N	74.20 E
Krasnooktjabrski	7	Lh	56.43N	47.37 E
Krasnooskolskoje Vodohranilišče	16	Je	49.25N	37.35 E
Krasnoostrovski	8	Md	60.12N	28.39 E
Krasnoperekopsk	19	Df	45.57N	33.47 E
Krasnorečenski	28	Mb	44.38N	135.15 E
Krasnoščelje	7	Ic	67.23N	37.02 E
Krasnoselki	10	Uc	53.14N	24.30 E
Krasnoselkup	20	Dc	65.41N	82.28 E
Krasnoslobodsk	16	Ne	48.40N	44.31 E
Krasnoslobodsk	7	Ki	54.27N	43.47 E
Krasnoturinsk	19	Gd	59.46N	60.18 E
Krasnoufimsk	19	Fd	56.37N	57.46 E
Krasnouralsk	19	Gd	58.24N	60.03 E
Krasnousolski	19	Fe	53.54N	56.29 E
Krasnovišersk	19	Fc	60.23N	57.03 E
Krasnovodsk	22	He	40.00N	53.00 E
Krasnovodski poluostrov	16	Rc	40.30N	53.15 E
Krasnovodski Zaliv	16	Rj	39.50N	53.15 E
Krasnozatonski	19	Fc	61.41N	51.01 E
Krasnozavodsk	7	Jh	56.29N	38.13 E
Krasnoznamensk	19	Ge	51.03N	69.30 E
Krasnoznamensk	8	Jj	54.52N	22.27 E
Krasny Čikoj	20	Ff	50.25N	108.45 E
Krasny Holm	7	Ig	58.04N	37.09 E
Krasny Jar	20	De	57.07N	84.40 E
Krasny Jar	19	Hd	55.14N	72.56 E
Krasnyje Barrikady	16	Of	46.13N	47.50 E
Krasnyje Okny	15	Mb	47.34N	29.23 E
Krasny Kut	19	Ee	50.58N	46.58 E
Krasny Liman	16	Je	48.59N	37.47 E
Krasny Luč	16	Ke	48.09N	38.57 E
Krasny Oktjabr	19	Gd	55.37N	64.48 E
Krasny Profintern	7	Jh	57.47N	40.29 E
Krasnystaw	10	Tf	50.59N	23.10 E
Krasny Sulin	16	Lf	47.53N	40.09 E
Kratovo	15	Fg	42.05N	22.12 E
Kraulshavn	41	Gd	74.10N	57.00W
Krâvanh, Chuŏr Phnum-	21	Mh	12.00N	103.15 E
Krawang	26	Eh	6.19 S	107.17 E
Krefeld	10	Ce	51.20N	6.34 E
Krefeld-Hüls	12	Ic	51.22N	6.31 E
Kremastá, Límni-	15	Ek	38.50N	21.30 E
Kremenchug Reservoir (EN) =Kremenčugskoje Vodohranilišče	5	Jf	49.20N	32.30 E
Kremenčug	6	Jf	49.04N	33.25 E
Kremenčugskoje Vodohranilišče= Kremenchug Reservoir (EN)	5	Jf	49.20N	32.30 E
Kremenec	16	Dd	50.06N	25.43 E
Kremennaja	16	Ke	49.03N	38.14 E
Kremmling	45	Cf	40.03N	106.24W
Krems	14	Jb	48.25N	15.36 E
Krems an der Donau	14	Jb	48.25N	15.36 E
Kremsmünster	14	Ib	48.03N	14.08 E
Krenitzin Islands	40a	Eb	54.08N	166.00W
Kresta, Zaliv-	20	Nc	65.30N	179.00W
Krestcy	7	Hg	58.15N	32.31 E
Krestovy, Pereval-	16	Nh	42.32N	44.30 E
Kretek	26	Fh	7.59 S	110.19 E
Kretinga	7	Ei	55.55N	21.17 E
Kreuzau	12	Id	50.45N	6.29 E
Kreuzberg	10	Ff	50.22N	9.58 E
Kreuzlingen	14	Dc	47.39N	9.10 E
Kreuztal	10	Df	50.58N	7.59 E
Kría Vrísi	15	Fi	40.41N	22.18 E
Kribi	31	Hh	2.57N	9.55 E
Kričev	19	De	53.43N	31.43 E
Kričim	15	Hg	42.08N	24.31 E
Krim	14	Ie	45.56N	14.28 E
Krimml	14	Gc	47.13N	12.11 E
Krimpen aan den IJssel	12	Gc	51.55N	4.35 E
Kriós, Ákra-	5	Ih	35.14N	23.35 E
Krishna	21	Kh	15.57N	80.59 E
Krishnanagar	25	Hd	23.24N	88.30 E
Kristdala	8	Gg	57.24N	16.11 E
Kristiansand	6	Gd	58.10N	8.00 E
Kristianstad	7	Dh	56.02N	14.08 E
Kristianstad [2]	7	Ch	56.15N	14.00 E
Kristiansund	6	Gc	63.07N	7.45 E
Kristiinankaupunki/ Kristinestad	7	Ee	62.17N	21.23 E
Kristineberg	7	Ed	65.04N	18.35 E
Kristinehamn	7	Dg	59.20N	14.07 E
Kristinestad/ Kristiinankaupunki	7	Ee	62.17N	21.23 E
Kríti = Crete (EN)	5	Ih	35.15N	24.45 E
Kríti = Crete (EN) [2]	15	Hn	35.35N	25.00 E
Kritikón Pélagos = Crete, Sea of- (EN)	15	Hn	36.00N	25.00 E
Krivaja	14	Mf	44.27N	18.10 E
Kriva Palanka	15	Fg	42.12N	22.21 E
Kriviči	8	Lj	54.44N	27.20 E
Krivodol	15	Gf	43.23N	23.29 E
Krivoje Ozero	16	Gf	47.57N	30.21 E
Krivoj Rog	6	Jf	47.54N	33.21 E
Križevci	14	Kd	46.02N	16.32 E
Krk	14	Ie	45.05N	14.35 E
Krk	14	Ie	45.02N	14.35 E
Krka	14	Jg	43.43N	15.51 E
Krka	14	Je	45.53N	15.36 E
Krkonoše	10	Lf	50.46N	15.35 E
Krn	14	Hd	46.16N	13.40 E
Krndija	14	Le	45.27N	17.55 E
Krnjača, Beograd-	15	De	44.52N	20.28 E
Krnov	10	Nf	50.05N	17.41 E
Krobia	10	Me	51.47N	16.58 E
Krøderen	8	Cd	60.15N	9.40 E
Krokeaí	15	Fm	36.53N	22.33 E
Krokek	8	Gf	58.40N	16.24 E
Kroken	7	Dd	65.22N	14.16 E

Index Symbols

[1] Independent Nation
[2] State, Region
[3] District, County
[4] Municipality
[5] Colony, Dependency
Continent
Physical Region
Historical or Cultural Region
Mount, Mountain
Volcano
Hill
Mountains, Mountain Range
Hills, Escarpment
Plateau, Upland
Pass, Gap
Plain, Lowland
Delta
Salt Flat
Valley, Canyon
Crater, Cave
Karst Features
Depression
Polder
Desert, Dunes
Forest, Woods
Heath, Steppe
Oasis
Cape, Point
Coast, Beach
Cliff
Peninsula
Isthmus
Sandbank
Island
Atoll
Rock, Reef
Islands, Archipelago
Rocks, Reefs
Coral Reef
Well, Spring
Geyser
River, Stream
Waterfall Rapids
River Mouth, Estuary
Lake
Salt Lake
Intermittent Lake
Reservoir
Swamp, Pond
Canal
Glacier
Ice Shelf, Pack Ice
Ocean
Sea
Gulf, Bay
Strait, Fjord
Lagoon
Bank
Seamount
Tablemount
Ridge
Shelf
Basin
Escarpment, Sea Scarp
Fracture
Trench, Abyss
National Park, Reserve
Point of Interest
Recreation Site
Cave, Cavern
Historic Site
Ruins
Wall, Walls
Church, Abbey
Temple
Scientific Station
Airport
Port
Lighthouse
Mine
Tunnel
Dam, Bridge

Krokom 7 De 63.20N 14.28 E
Krolevec 16 Hd 51.32N 33.30 E
Kroměříž 10 Ng 49.18N 17.22 E
Krompachy 10 Qh 48.56N 20.52 E
Kronach 10 Hf 50.14N 11.19 E
Krŏng Kaôh Kŏng 25 Kf 11.37N 102.59 E
Kronoberg [2] 7 Dh 56.40N 14.40 E
Kronockaja Sopka, Vulkan- 20 Lf 54.47N 160.35 E
Kronocki, Mys- 20 Lf 54.43N 162.07 E
Kronocki Zaliv 20 Lf 54.00N 161.00 E
Kronoki 20 Lf 54.33N 161.14 E
Kronprins Christian Land 41 Jb 80.45N 22.00W
Kronprinsesse Mærtha Kyst 66 Bf 72.00S 7.30W
Kronprins Frederiks Bjerge 41 Ie 67.20N 34.00W
Kronprins Olav Kyst 66 Ee 68.30S 42.30 E
Kronštadt 19 Cc 60.01N 29.44 E
Kroonstad 31 Jk 27.46S 27.12 E
Kropotkin 19 Ef 45.26N 40.34 E
Kropotkin 20 Ge 58.36N 115.27 E
Kroppefjäll 8 Ef 58.40N 12.13 E
Krośniewice 10 Pd 52.16N 19.10 E
Krosno 10 Rg 49.42N 21.46 E
Krosno [2] 10 Rg 49.40N 21.45 E
Krosno Odrzańskie 10 Ld 52.04N 15.05 E
Krossfjorden 8 Ad 60.10N 5.05 E
Krotoszyn 10 Ne 51.42N 17.26 E
Kroviga, Gora- 20 Ed 60.40N 91.30 E
Krško 14 Je 45.58N 15.28 E
Krstača 15 Dg 42.58N 20.08 E
Krugersdorp 31 Jk 26.05S 27.35 E
Krui 26 Dh 5.11S 103.56 E
Kruibeke 12 Gc 51.10N 4.19 E
Kruiningen 12 Gc 51.27N 4.02 E
Kruja 15 Ch 41.30N 19.48 E
Krulevščina 8 Li 55.03N 27.52 E
Krumbach 10 Gh 48.15N 10.22 E
Krumovgrad 15 Ih 41.28N 25.39 E
Krung Thep=Bangkok (EN) 22 Mh 13.45N 100.31 E
Krupanj 15 Ce 44.22N 19.22 E
Krupinica 10 Oh 48.05N 18.54 E
Krupinská vrchovina 10 Ph 48.20N 19.15 E
Kruså 8 Cj 54.50N 9.25 E
Krušedol 15 Cd 45.07N 19.57 E
Kruševac 15 Ef 43.35N 21.20 E
Kruševo 15 Eh 41.22N 21.15 E
Krušné Hory=Ore Mountains (EN) 5 He 50.30N 13.15 E
Krustpils 8 Lh 56.29N 26.00 E
Kruzof 40 Le 57.10N 135.40W
Krym 16 Jg 45.23N 36.36 E
Krym, respublika 19 Dg 45.15N 34.20 E
Krymsk 19 Dg 44.54N 37.57 E
Krymskije Gory=Crimean Mountains (EN) 5 Jg 44.45N 34.30 E
Krymski Poluostrov=Crimea (EN) 5 Jf 45.00N 34.00 E
Krynica 10 Qg 49.25N 20.56 E
Krzemieniucha 10 Sb 54.12N 22.54 E
Krzepice 10 Of 50.58N 18.44 E
Krzna 10 Td 52.08N 23.31 E
Krzywiń 10 Me 51.58N 16.49 E
Krzyż 10 Md 52.53N 16.01 E
Ksar el Boukhari 32 Hb 35.53N 2.45 E
Ksar el Kebir 32 Fc 35.00N 5.59W
Ksar es Srhir 13 Gi 35.51N 5.34W
Ksenjevka 20 Gf 53.34N 118.44 E
Kšenski 16 Jd 51.52N 37.44 E
Ksour, Monts des- 32 Gc 32.45N 0.10W
Kū', Wādī al- 35 Dc 12.12N 25.43 E
Kuai He 28 Dh 33.09N 117.32 E
Kuala Belait 26 Ff 4.35N 114.11 E
Kuala Dungun 26 Df 4.47N 103.26 E
Kuala Kangsar 26 Df 4.46N 100.56 E
Kualakapuas 26 Fg 3.01S 114.21 E
Kuala Kerai 26 De 5.32N 102.12 E
Kualakurun 26 Fg 1.07S 113.53 E
Kualalangsa 26 Cf 4.32N 98.01 E
Kuala Lipis 26 Df 4.11N 102.03 E
Kuala Lumpur 22 Mi 3.10N 101.42 E
Kuala Pilah 26 Df 2.44N 102.15 E
Kuala Rompin 26 Df 2.49N 103.29 E
Kuala Terengganu 22 Mi 5.20N 103.08 E
Kuancheng 28 Ed 40.37N 118.31 E
Kuandang 26 Hf 0.52N 122.55 E
Kuandian 27 Lc 40.45N 124.48 E
Kuang-hsi-chuang-tsu Tzu-chih-ch'ü→Guangxi Zhuangzu Zizhiqu=Kwangsi Chuang (EN) [2] 27 Ig 24.00N 109.00 E
Kuang-tun Sheng→Guangdong Sheng=Kwangtung (EN) [2] 27 Jg 23.00N 113.00 E
Kuantan 26 Df 3.48N 103.20 E
Kuba 19 Eg 41.20N 48.35 E
Kuban 5 Jf 45.20N 37.30 E
Kuba-Shima 29b b 26.10N 127.15 E
Kubaysah 24 Jf 33.35N 42.37 E
Kubbum 35 Cc 11.47N 23.47 E
Kubena 7 Jg 59.37N 39.48 E
Kubenskoje, Ozero- 7 Jg 59.40N 39.30 E
Kubnja 7 Li 55.32N 48.28 E
Kubokawa 28 Lh 33.12N 133.08 E
Kubolta 15 Lb 47.48N 28.03 E
Kubrat 15 Jf 43.48N 26.30 E
Kubumesaai 26 Gf 1.31N 115.06 E
Kučaj 15 Ef 43.53N 21.44 E
Kučevo 15 Ee 44.29N 21.41 E
Kutching 22 Ni 1.33N 110.20 E
Kuchinotsu 29 Be 32.36N 130.12 E
Kuçova (Qyteti Stalin) 15 Ci 40.48N 19.54 E
Küçükçekmece 15 Lh 40.59N 28.46 E
Küçükkerenköy 24 Ee 35.22N 33.45 E
Küçükkuyu 15 Jj 39.32N 26.36 E
Küçuk Menderes 15 Kl 37.57N 27.16 E
Kučurgan 15 Mc 46.35N 29.55 E
Kudaka-Jima 29b Ab 26.10N 127.54 E
Kudamatsu 29 Bd 34.01N 131.53 E
Kudat 26 Ge 6.53N 116.50 E
Kudeb 8 Mg 57.30N 28.16 E
Kudirkos-Naumiestis 8 Jj 54.43N 22.49 E
Kudowa-Zdrój 10 Mf 50.27N 16.20 E
Kudremukh 25 Ff 13.08N 75.16 E
Kudus 26 Fh 6.48S 110.50 E
Kudymkar 19 Fd 59.01N 54.37 E
Kuee Ruins 65a Fd 19.12N 155.23W
Kuei-chou Sheng→Guizhou Sheng=Kweichow (EN) [2] 27 If 27.00N 107.00 E
Kufi 24 Cc 38.10N 29.43 E
Kufrah, Wāḥāt al-=Kufra Oasis (EN) 30 Jf 24.10N 23.15 E
Kufra Oasis (EN)=Kufrah, Wāḥāt al- 30 Jf 24.10N 23.15 E
Kufstein 14 Gc 47.35N 12.10 E
Kuganavolok 7 Ie 62.16N 36.55 E
Kugmallit Bay 42 Ek 69.30N 133.20W
Kugojeja 16 Kf 46.33N 39.38 E
Kūh, Ra's al- 23 Id 25.48N 57.19 E
Kuḥaylī 35 Eb 19.29N 32.49 E
Kūhbonān 24 Qg 31.23N 56.19 E
Kūhdasht 24 Lf 33.32N 47.36 E
Kūh-e Būrh 24 Pi 27.22N 54.40 E
Kūh-e Gāvbūs 24 Oi 27.10N 54.00 E
Kūh-e Karkas 24 Nf 33.27N 51.48 E
Kūh-e Kārūn 24 Ng 31.27N 50.18 E
Kūhestak 24 Qi 26.47N 57.02 E
Kūhīn, Gardaneh-ye- 24 Md 36.23N 49.37 E
Kühlungsborn 10 Hb 54.09N 11.43 E
Kuhmo 7 Gd 64.08N 29.31 E
Kuhmoinen 8 Kc 61.34N 25.11 E
Kuhn 41 Kd 74.45N 19.45W
Kūhpāyeh 23 Ic 30.35N 57.15 E
Kūhpāyeh [Iran] 24 Of 32.43N 52.26 E
Kūhpāyeh [Iran] 24 Qg 30.43N 57.30 E
Kūhrān, Kūh-e- 23 Id 26.46N 58.12 E
Kuhtuj 20 Je 59.23N 143.10 E
Kuhva 8 Mg 57.17N 28.17 E
Kuiseb 37 Ad 23.00S 14.33 E
Kuishan Ding 27 Ig 22.32N 109.52 E
Kuito 31 Ij 12.23S 16.56 E
Kuiu 40 Me 57.45N 134.10W
Kuivaniemi 7 Fd 65.35N 25.11 E
Kujang 27 Md 39.52N 126.01 E
Kujawy 10 Od 52.45N 18.30 E
Kujawy 10 Od 52.45N 18.35 E
Kujbyšev → Samara 6 Le 53.12N 50.09 E
Kujbyšev → Bulgar 7 Li 55.01N 49.06 E
Kujbyšev 20 Ce 55.27N 78.29 E
Kujbyševskaja Oblast [3] 19 Fe 53.20N 50.30 E
Kujbyševski 19 Ge 53.15N 66.51 E
Kujbyševski 18 Gf 37.53N 68.44 E
Kujbyševskoje Vodohranilišče=Kuybyshev Reservoir (EN) 5 Ke 53.50N 49.00 E
Kujeda 17 Gh 56.26N 55.35 E
Kujgan 19 Hf 45.22N 74.10 E
Kuji 28 Pd 40.11N 141.46 E
Kuji-Gawa 29 Gc 36.30N 140.37 E
Kujtun 20 Ff 54.21N 101.35 E
Kujūkuri-Hama 29 Gd 35.40N 140.30 E
Kujū-San 28 Kh 33.09N 131.15 E
Kūkalār, Kūh-e- 24 Ng 31.50N 50.53 E
Kukalaya, Rio- 49 Fg 13.39N 83.37W
Kukësi 15 Dg 42.05N 20.24 E
Kukkia 8 Kc 61.20N 24.40 E
Kukmor 7 Mh 56.13N 50.52 E
Kükürt Dağı 24 Ib 41.07N 41.27 E
Kula [Bul.] 15 Ff 43.53N 22.31 E
Kula [Tur.] 24 Cc 38.30N 28.40 E
Kula [Yugo.] 15 Cd 45.37N 19.32 E
Kulai 26 Df 1.40N 103.36 E
Kulanak 18 Jd 41.18N 75.34 E
Kulandy 19 Ff 46.08N 59.31 E
Kular 20 Ib 70.32N 134.26 E
Kular, Hrebet- 20 Ic 69.00N 133.30 E
Kulata 15 Gh 41.23N 23.22 E
Kulautuva 8 Jj 54.55N 23.43 E
Kulbus 35 Cc 14.24N 22.31 E
Kuldīga/Kuldiga 19 Cd 56.59N 21.59 E
Kuldīga/Kuldiga 19 Cd 56.59N 21.59 E
Kuldur 20 Ig 49.10N 131.40 E
Kulebaki 7 Ki 55.26N 42.32 E
Kulenjin 24 Me 35.40N 49.30 E
Kulen Vakuf 14 Kf 44.33N 16.06 E
Kulgera 58 Eg 25.50S 133.18 E
Kulikov 10 Ug 49.55N 24.06 E
Kulim 26 De 5.22N 100.34 E
Kuljab 19 Gh 37.55N 69.47 E
Kuljabskaja Oblast [3] 19 Gh 38.00N 69.40 E
Kullaa 8 Jc 61.28N 22.10 E
Kullen 7 Ch 56.18N 12.26 E
Kulmasa 34 Ed 9.35N 2.27W
Kulmbach 10 Hf 50.06N 11.27 E
Kuloj 7 Kf 61.03N 42.30 E
Kuloj 19 Eb 66.00N 43.30 E
Kuloj 7 Kf 61.01N 42.12 E
Kulp 24 Ic 38.30N 41.02 E
Kulsary 19 Ff 46.57N 54.02 E
Kultuk 20 Ff 51.44N 103.42 E
Kulu 20 Jd 62.15N 147.45 E
Kulu [India] 25 Fb 31.58N 77.06 E
Kulu [Tur.] 24 Ec 39.06N 33.05 E
Kulumadau 63a Ac 9.03S 152.43 E
Kulunda 20 Cf 52.35N 78.57 E
Kulundinskaja Step 20 Cf 52.45N 79.00 E
Kulundinskoje, Ozero- 20 Cf 53.00N 79.30 E
Kum 24 Bc 38.38N 27.32 E
Kum, Kūh-e- 24 Oh 29.55N 53.45 E
Kuma 29 Ce 33.39N 132.54 E
Kuma 17 Mg 59.33N 66.40 E
Kuma 7 Hc 66.15N 31.02 E
Kuma 5 Kg 44.56N 47.00 E
Kumagaya 28 Of 36.08N 139.23 E
Kumai [Indon.] 26 Fg 2.44S 111.43 E
Kumai [Indon.] 26 Fg 3.23S 112.33 E
Kumaishi 29a Ab 42.08N 139.59 E
Kumajri (Leninakan) 6 Kg 40.47N 43.50 E
Kumak 16 Vd 51.13N 60.08 E
Kumamoto 22 Pf 32.48N 130.43 E
Kumamoto Ken [2] 28 Kh 32.30N 130.50 E
Kumano 28 Nh 33.54N 136.05 E
Kumano-Gawa 29 De 33.45N 135.59 E
Kumano-Nada 29 Ee 34.00N 136.30 E
Kumanovo 15 Eg 42.08N 21.43 E
Kumara [N.Z.] 62 De 42.38S 171.11 E
Kumara 20 Hf 51.35N 126.45 E
Kumasi 31 Gh 6.41N 1.37W
Kumba 34 Ge 4.38N 9.25 E
Kumbakonam 25 Ff 10.58N 79.23 E
Kumbe 26 Lh 8.21S 140.13 E
Kumbo 34 Hd 6.12N 10.40 E
Kumboro Cape 63a Cb 7.18S 157.32 E
Kŭmch'ŏn 28 Ie 38.10N 126.30 E
Kum-Dag 19 Fh 39.13N 54.40 E
Kumdah 33 Ie 20.23N 45.05 E
Kumertau → Jermolajevo 19 Fe 52.46N 55.47 E
Kumhwa 28 Ie 38.17N 127.28 E
Kumihama 29 Dd 35.36N 134.54 E
Kuminski 19 Gd 58.40N 65.55 E
Kumköy (Kilyos) 15 Mh 41.15N 29.02 E
Kumkuduk 27 Fc 40.15N 91.55 E
Kumkurgan 18 Ff 37.50N 67.35 E
Kumla 7 Dg 59.08N 15.08 E
Kumlinge 8 Id 60.15N 20.45 E
Kumluca 24 Dd 36.22N 30.18 E
Kummerower See 10 Ic 53.49N 12.52 E
Kumo/Kokemäki 7 Ff 61.15N 22.21 E
Kumo-Manyčski Kanal 16 Ng 45.27N 44.38 E
Kumon Taung 21 Lg 26.30N 96.50 E
Kumora 20 Ge 55.56N 111.13 E
Kumru 24 Gb 40.53N 37.17 E
Kumu 36 Eb 3.04N 25.09 E
Kumuh 16 Oh 42.11N 47.07 E
Kumukahi, Cape- 60 Od 19.31N 154.49W
Kumul/Hami 12 Le 42.48N 93.27 E
Kümüx 27 Ec 42.15N 88.10 E
Kumzār 24 Qj 26.20N 56.25 E
Kunashiri-Tō/Kunašir, Ostrov- 21 Qe 44.05N 145.51 E
Kunašir, Ostrov-/Kunashiri-Tō 21 Qe 44.05N 145.51 E
Kunaširski Proliv=Nemuro Strait (EN) 20 Jh 43.50N 145.30 E
Kunchaung 25 Jd 23.50N 96.35 E
Kunda 7 Gg 59.30N 26.30 E
Kunda Jõgi 8 Le 59.25N 26.27 E
Kundelungu, Monts- 36 Ed 9.30S 28.00 E
Kundiawa 59 Ia 6.00S 145.00 E
Kunduchi 36 Gd 6.40S 39.13 E
Kunduk 15 Md 45.51N 29.38 E
Kunduk → Kogilnik 15 Md 45.51N 29.38 E
Kunduk → Sasyk, Ozero- 16 Fg 45.45N 29.40 E
Kunene 30 Ij 17.20S 11.50 E
Kunene (EN)=Cunene 30 Ij 17.20S 11.50 E
Künes/Xinyuan 27 Dc 43.24N 83.18 E
Künes He 27 Dc 43.32N 82.29 E
Kungälv 7 Ch 57.52N 11.58 E
Kungej-Alatau, Hrebet- 19 Hg 42.50N 77.15 E
Küngmiut 41 Ie 65.50N 36.45W
Kungrad 19 Fg 43.06N 58.54 E
Kungsbacka 7 Ch 57.29N 12.04 E
Kungsbackafjorden 8 Eg 57.25N 12.04 E
Kungshamn 8 Df 58.21N 11.15 E
Kungsör 8 Ge 59.25N 16.05 E
Kungu 36 Cb 2.47N 19.12 E
Kungur 19 Fd 57.25N 56.57 E
Kunhegyes 10 Qi 47.22N 20.38 E
Kunhing 25 Jd 21.18N 98.26 E
Kunigami 29b Bb 26.45N 128.11 E
Kunigami-Misaki 29b Bb 27.26N 128.43 E
Kunimi-Dake 29 Be 32.33N 131.01 E
Kunisaki 29 Be 33.34N 131.45 E
Kunisaki-Hantō 29 Be 33.30N 131.40 E
Kunja 7 Hh 57.09N 31.10 E
Kunja-Urgenč 19 Fg 42.20N 59.12 E
Kunlong 25 Jd 23.25N 98.39 E
Kunlun Guan 27 Ig 23.06N 108.40 E
Kunlun Shan 21 Kf 36.00N 84.00 E
Kunlun Shankou 27 Fd 35.40N 94.03 E
Kunming 22 Mg 25.08N 102.43 E
Kunnui 29a Bb 42.26N 140.19 E
Kunovat 17 Ld 64.59N 65.35 E
Kunsan 27 Md 35.59N 126.43 E
Kunshan 28 Fi 31.22N 120.57 E
Kuntaur 34 Cc 13.40N 14.53W
Kununurra 59 Fc 15.47S 128.44 E
Kunyao 36 Gb 1.47N 35.03 E
Kunyu Shan 28 Ff 37.15N 121.46 E
Künzelsau 10 Fg 49.17N 9.41 E
Kuohijärvi 8 Kc 61.15N 24.55 E
Kuolimo 8 Lc 61.15N 27.35 E
Kuop Atoll 64d Bb 7.03N 151.56 E
Kuopio [2] 7 Ge 63.20N 27.35 E
Kuopio 6 Ic 62.54N 27.41 E
Kuorboaivi 7 Gb 69.41N 27.45 E
Kuortane 8 Jb 62.48N 23.30 E
Kupa 14 Ke 45.28N 16.24 E
Kupang 22 Ok 10.10S 123.35 E
Kupiano 60 Dj 10.10S 148.02 E
Kupičev 10 Uf 50.58N 24.52 E
Kupino 20 Cf 54.22N 77.18 E
Kupiškis 7 Fi 55.49N 25.01 E
Kupjansk 19 Df 49.42N 37.37 E
Kupjansk-Uzlovoj 16 Je 49.39N 37.45 E
Küplü [Tur.] 15 Jh 41.07N 26.21 E
Küplü [Tur.] 15 Mi 40.06N 30.00 E
Kuppenheim 12 Kf 48.50N 8.15 E
Kupreanof 40 Me 56.50N 133.30W
Kuqa 22 Ke 41.43N 82.57 E
Kura 16 Mh 44.05N 44.45 E
Kura 5 Kh 39.20N 49.25 E
Kuragaty 18 Ic 43.55N 73.34 E
Kuragino 20 Ef 53.53N 92.40 E
Kurahashi-Jima 29 Cd 34.08N 132.31 E
Kuraminski Hrebet 18 Hd 40.50N 70.30 E
Kurashiki 28 Lg 34.35N 133.46 E
Kurashiki-Kojima 29 Cd 34.28N 133.48 E
Kurashiki-Tamashima 29 Cd 34.33N 133.40 E
Kura-Take 29 Be 32.27N 130.20 E
Kuraymah=Karima (EN) 31 Kg 18.33N 31.51 E
Kurayoshi 28 Lg 35.28N 133.49 E
Kurbneshi 15 Dh 41.47N 20.05 E
Kurčatov 16 Id 51.41N 35.42 E
Kurdaj 18 Jc 43.18N 74.59 E
Kurdistan 21 Gf 37.00N 44.00 E
Kurdistan 23 Fb 37.00N 44.00 E
Kurdufān 30 Jg 13.00N 30.00 E
Kurdufān al Janūbīyah [3] 35 Dc 11.00N 29.30 E
Kurdufān ash Shamālīyah [3] 35 Dc 14.50N 29.40 E
Kure 28 Lg 34.14N 132.34 E
Küre 24 Eb 41.48N 33.43 E
Kure Island 57 Jb 28.25N 178.25W
Kurejka 21 Kc 66.25N 87.12 E
Kuresaare (Kingissepp) 19 Cd 58.17N 22.29 E
Kurgaldžinski 19 He 50.30N 70.03 E
Kurgan 22 Id 55.26N 65.18 E
Kurganinsk 16 Lg 44.57N 40.35 E
Kurganskaja Oblast [3] 19 Gd 55.00N 65.00 E
Kurgan-Tjube 19 Gh 37.51N 68.46 E
Kurgan-Tjubinskaja Oblast [3] 19 Gh 37.30N 68.30 E
Kuria Island 57 Id 0.14N 173.25 E
Kuria Muria Islands (EN)=Khurīyā Murīyā, Jazā'ir 21 Hh 17.30N 56.00 E
Kuri Bay 59 Ec 15.35S 124.50 E
Kurikka 7 Fe 62.37N 22.25 E
Kurikoma 29 Gb 38.50N 140.59 E
Kurikoma-Yama 29 Gb 38.57N 140.47 E
Kuril Basin (EN) 20 Jg 47.00N 150.00 E
Kuril Islands (EN)=Kurilskije Ostrova 21 Re 46.10N 152.00 E
Kurilo 15 Gg 42.49N 23.21 E
Kurilsk 20 Jg 45.16N 147.58 E
Kurilskije Ostrova=Kuril Islands (EN) 21 Re 46.10N 152.00 E
Kuril Trench (EN) 3 Je 47.00N 155.00 E
Kuring Kuru 37 Bc 17.38S 18.33 E
Kurino 29 Bf 31.57N 130.43 E
Kurinskaja Kosa 16 Pj 39.05N 49.10 E
Kurinwās, Rio- 49 Fg 12.49N 83.41W
Kuriyama 29a Bb 43.03N 141.45 E
Kürkhūd, Kūh-e- 24 Qd 37.15N 56.30 E
Kurkosa 16 Pj 38.59N 49.08 E
Kurkūmā, Ra's- 24 Gj 25.51N 36.39 E
Kurkur 24 Ek 23.54N 32.19 E
Kurlovski 7 Ji 55.29N 40.39 E
Kurmuk 35 Ec 10.33N 34.17 E
Kurnool 22 Jh 15.50N 78.03 E
Kurobe 28 Nf 36.51N 137.26 E
Kurobe-Gawa 29 Ec 36.55N 137.26 E
Kurogi 29 Be 33.14N 130.40 E
Kuroishi 28 Pd 40.38N 140.36 E
Kuroiso 28 Pf 36.58N 140.03 E
Kuromatsunai 28 Pc 42.43N 140.20 E
Kurono-Seto 29 Be 32.05N 130.10 E
Kurort Družba 15 Kf 43.12N 28.00 E
Kurort Slănčev brjag 15 Kg 42.40N 27.42 E
Kurort Zlatni pjasăci 15 Lf 43.16N 28.02 E
Kuro-Shima 28 Ji 31.52N 129.58 E
Kurovskoje 7 Ji 55.35N 38.59 E
Kurow 61 Dh 44.44S 170.28 E
Kurów 10 Se 51.25N 22.10 E
Kurpiowska, Puszcza- 10 Rc 53.20N 21.30 E
Kuršėnai/Kuršenaj 19 Cd 56.03N 22.58 E
Kuršenaj/Kuršėnai 19 Cd 56.03N 22.58 E
Kuršiu užurėkis 8 Ii 55.05N 21.00 E
Kursk 6 Je 51.42N 36.12 E
Kurskaja Kosa 7 Ei 55.18N 21.00 E
Kurskaja Oblast [3] 19 De 51.45N 36.15 E
Kurski zaliv 7 Ei 55.05N 21.00 E
Kuršumlija 15 Ef 43.09N 21.16 E
Kurtalan 24 Id 37.57N 41.42 E
Kurtamyš 19 Ge 54.55N 64.27 E
Kürtī 31 Kg 18.07N 31.33 E
Kurtistown 65 Fd 19.36N 155.04W
Kurty 18 Kb 44.19N 76.42 E
Kuru 8 Jc 61.52N 23.44 E
Kuru 35 Dd 9.08N 26.57 E
Kuruçaşile 24 Eb 41.51N 32.43 E
Kuruktag 27 Ec 41.30N 89.00 E
Kuruman 30 Jk 26.56S 20.39 E
Kuruman 31 Jk 27.28S 23.28 E
Kurume 28 Kh 33.19N 130.31 E
Kurunegala 25 Gg 7.29N 80.22 E
Kurur, Jabal- 35 Ea 20.31N 31.32 E
Kurzeme=Courland (EN) 8 Ih 56.50N 22.00 E
Kurzemes Augstiene/Kurzemskaja Vozvyšennost 8 Jh 56.45N 22.15 E
Kurzemskaja Vozvyšennost/Kurzemes Augstiene 8 Jh 56.45N 22.15 E
Kusa 17 Ii 55.20N 59.29 E
Kuşada Körfezi 15 Kl 37.50N 27.08 E
Kuşadasi 24 Bd 37.51N 27.15 E
Kusagaki-Guntō 27 Me 31.00N 129.00 E
Kusaie → Kosrae 57 Hd 5.19N 162.59 E
Kusalu/Kuusalu 8 Ke 59.23N 25.25 E
Kusary 16 Pi 41.24N 48.29 E
Kusatsu [Jap.] 29 Fc 36.37N 138.35 E
Kusatsu [Jap.] 29 Dd 35.03N 135.59 E
Kuščevskaja 16 Kf 46.33N 39.37 E
Kuščinski 16 Oi 40.33N 46.06 E
Kusel 12 Je 49.33N 7.24 E
Kuş Gölü 24 Bb 40.10N 27.59 E
Kushida-Gawa 29 Ed 34.36N 136.34 E
Kushikino 28 Ki 31.44N 130.16 E
Kushima 28 Ki 31.29N 131.14 E
Kushimoto 28 Mh 33.28N 135.47 E
Kushiro 22 Qe 42.58N 144.23 E
Kushiro-Gawa 29a Db 42.59N 144.23 E
Kushtia 25 Hd 23.55N 89.07 E
Kuška 18 Dg 35.16N 62.18 E
Kuskokwim 38 Cc 60.17N 162.27W
Kuskokwim Bay 38 Cd 59.45N 162.25W
Kuskokwim Mountains 38 Dc 62.30N 156.00W
Kušmurun 19 Ge 52.27N 64.40 E
Kušmurun, Ozero- 19 Ge 52.40N 64.45 E
Kušnarenkovo 17 Gi 55.06N 55.22 E
Kušnica 16 Ce 48.29N 23.20 E
Kusŏng 27 Md 39.59N 125.16 E
Kussharo Ko 28 Rc 43.35N 144.15 E
Kustanaj 22 Id 53.10N 63.35 E
Kustanajskaja Oblast [3] 19 Ge 53.00N 64.00 E
Kustavi 8 Id 60.30N 21.25 E
Kustavi/Gustavs 8 Id 60.30N 21.25 E
Küstenkanal 10 Dd 52.57N 7.18 E
Kūstī 31 Kg 13.10N 32.40 E
Kustvlakte=Coast Plain (EN) 11 Ic 51.00N 2.30 E
Kusu 29 Be 33.16N 131.09 E
Kušva 19 Fd 58.18N 59.45 E
Kut, Ko- 25 Kf 11.40N 102.35 E
Kūt 'Abdollāh 24 Mg 31.13N 48.39 E
Kutacane 26 Cf 3.30N 97.48 E
Kutahya 23 Cb 39.25N 29.59 E
Kutaisi 6 Kg 42.15N 42.40 E
Kutch, Gulf of- → Kachchh, Gulf of 21 Ig 22.36N 60.30 E
Kutch, Rann of- 25 Ed 24.05N 70.10 E
Kutchan 28 Pc 42.54N 140.45 E
Kutcharo-Ko 29a Ca 45.10N 142.20 E
Kutina 14 Ke 45.29N 16.47 E
Kutkai 25 Jd 23.27N 97.56 E
Kutkašen → Gabel'a 16 Oi 40.58N 47.52 E
Kutná Hora 10 Lg 49.57N 15.16 E
Kutno 10 Pd 52.15N 19.23 E
Kutse, Gora-/Kuutse Mägi 8 Lg 57.58N 26.24 E
Kuttara-Ko 29a Bb 42.30N 141.10 E
Kutu 31 Ii 2.44S 18.09 E
Kutum 35 Cc 14.12N 24.40 E
Küty 10 Nh 48.40N 17.01 E
Kuty 15 Ia 48.13N 25.15 E
Kuujjuaq 39 Md 58.10N 68.30W
Kuujjuarapik 42 Je 55.20N 76.50W
Kuuli-Majak 19 Fg 40.16N 52.45 E
Kuurne 12 Fd 50.51N 3.17 E
Kuusalu/Kusalu 8 Ke 59.23N 25.25 E
Kuusamo 6 Ib 66.00N 29.11 E
Kuusankoski 8 Ld 60.54N 26.38 E
Kuutse Mägi/Kutse, Gora- 8 Lg 57.58N 26.24 E
Kuvandyk 16 Td 51.29N 57.28 E
Kuvdlorssuaq 41 Gd 74.38N 56.40W
Kuvšinovo 7 Ih 57.03N 34.13 E
Kuwait (EN)=Al Kuwayt [1] 22 Gg 29.30N 47.45 E
Kuwait (EN)=Al Kuwayt 22 Gg 29.20N 47.59 E
Kuwana 29 Ed 35.04N 136.39 E
Kuybyshev Reservoir (EN)=Kujbyševskoje Vodohranilišče 5 Ke 53.50N 49.00 E
Küysanjaq 24 Kd 36.05N 44.38 E
Kuytun 27 Dc 44.25N 84.58 E
Kuyucak 15 Ll 37.55N 28.28 E
Kuzey Kibris = North Cyprus 23 Db 35.15N 33.40 E
Kuzneck 19 Ee 53.07N 46.36 E
Kuznecki Alatau 21 Kd 54.45N 88.00 E
Kuznečnoje 8 Mc 61.04N 29.58 E
Kuźnia Raciborska 10 Of 50.11N 18.15 E
Kuzomen 19 Db 66.18N 36.49 E
Kuzovatovo 7 Lj 53.33N 47.41 E
Kuzumaki 29 Ga 40.02N 141.26 E
Kuzuryū-Gawa 29 Ec 36.13N 136.08 E
Kvænangen 7 Ea 70.05N 21.13 E
Kvaløy 7 Eb 69.40N 18.30 E
Kvaløya 7 Fa 70.37N 23.52 E
Kvalsund 7 Fa 70.30N 24.00 E
Kvam 8 Cc 61.40N 9.42 E
Kvareli 16 Ni 41.57N 45.47 E
Kvarkeno 17 Ij 52.05N 59.40 E
Kvarnbergsvattnet 7 Dd 64.36N 14.03 E
Kvarner 14 If 44.45N 14.15 E
Kvarnerić 14 If 44.45N 14.35 E
Kvichak Bay 40 He 58.48N 157.30W
Kvemo-Kedi 16 Oi 41.22N 46.31 E
Kvenna 8 Bd 60.01N 7.56 E
Kvichak 40 He 59.10N 156.40W
Kvikkjokk 7 Dc 66.57N 17.47 E
Kvina 8 Bf 58.17N 6.56 E
Kvinesdal 8 Bg 58.19N 6.57 E
Kvissleby 8 Gb 62.17N 17.21 E
Kviteggja 8 Bb 62.05N 6.40 E
Kviteseid 8 Ce 59.24N 8.30 E
Kvitøya 67 Je 80.08N 32.35 E
Kwa 30 Ii 3.10S 16.11 E
Kwahu Plateau 34 Ed 6.30N 0.30W
Kwailibesi 63a Ec 8.20S 160.40 E
Kwajalein Atoll 57 Hd 9.05N 167.20 E
Kwakoegron 54 Gb 5.15N 55.20W
Kwale [Kenya] 36 Gc 4.11S 39.27 E
Kwale [Nig.] 34 Gd 5.45N 6.25 E
Kwamouth 36 Cc 3.10S 16.12 E
Kwa Mtoro 36 Gd 5.14S 35.26 E
Kwando 36 Df 18.27S 23.32 E
Kwangdae-ri 27 Mc 40.34N 127.33 E
Kwangju 22 Of 35.09N 126.55 E
Kwango 30 Ii 3.14S 17.22 E

Index Symbols

[1] Independent Nation
[2] State, Region
[3] District, County
[4] Municipality
[5] Colony, Dependency
Continent
Physical Region
Historical or Cultural Region
Mount, Mountain
Volcano
Hill
Mountains, Mountain Range
Hills, Escarpment
Plateau, Upland
Pass, Gap
Plain, Lowland
Delta
Salt Flat
Valley, Canyon
Crater, Cave
Karst Features
Depression
Polder
Desert, Dunes
Forest, Woods
Heath, Steppe
Oasis
Cape, Point
Coast, Beach
Cliff
Peninsula
Isthmus
Sandbank
Island
Atoll
Rock, Reef
Islands, Archipelago
Rocks, Reefs
Coral Reef
Well, Spring
Geyser
River, Stream
Waterfall Rapids
River Mouth, Estuary
Lake
Salt Lake
Intermittent Lake
Reservoir
Swamp, Pond
Canal
Glacier
Ice Shelf, Pack Ice
Ocean
Sea
Gulf, Bay
Strait, Fjord
Lagoon
Bank
Seamount
Tablemount
Ridge
Shelf
Basin
Escarpment, Sea Scarp
Fracture
Trench, Abyss
National Park, Reserve
Point of Interest
Recreation Site
Cave, Cavern
Historic Site
Ruins
Wall, Walls
Church, Abbey
Temple
Scientific Station
Airport
Port
Lighthouse
Mine
Tunnel
Dam, Bridge

Index Symbols

[1] Independent Nation	Historical or Cultural Region	Pass, Gap	Depression	Coast, Beach
[2] State, Region	Mount, Mountain	Plain, Lowland	Polder	Cliff
[3] District, County	Volcano	Delta	Desert, Dunes	Peninsula
[4] Municipality	Hill	Salt Flat	Forest, Woods	Isthmus
[5] Colony, Dependency	Mountains, Mountain Range	Valley, Canyon	Heath, Steppe	Sandbank
[6] Continent	Hills, Escarpment	Crater, Cave	Oasis	Island
[7] Physical Region	Plateau, Upland	Karst Features	Cape, Point	Atoll

Rock, Reef	Waterfall Rapids	Canal	Lagoon
Islands, Archipelago	River Mouth, Estuary	Glacier	Bank
Rocks, Reefs	Lake	Ice Shelf, Pack Ice	Seamount
Coral Reef	Salt Lake	Ocean	Tablemount
Well, Spring	Intermittent Lake	Sea	Ridge
Geyser	Reservoir	Gulf, Bay	Shelf
River, Stream	Swamp, Pond	Strait, Fjord	Basin

Escarpment, Sea Scarp	Historic Site
Fracture	Ruins
Trench, Abyss	Wall, Walls
National Park, Reserve	Church, Abbey
Point of Interest	Temple
Recreation Site	Scientific Station
Cave, Cavern	Airport

Port
Lighthouse
Mine
Tunnel
Dam, Bridge

Lamotte-Beuvron 11 Ig 47.36N 2.01 E
La Moure 45 Gc 46.21N 98.18W
Lampang 25 Je 18.16N 99.34 E
Lampasas 45 Gk 31.03N 98.12W
Lampazos de Naranjo 48 Id 27.01N 100.31W
Lampedusa 14 Go 35.30N 12.35 E
Lampertheim 10 Eg 49.36N 8.28 E
Lampeter 9 Ii 52.07N 4.05W
Lamphun 25 Je 18.35N 99.00 E
Lampione 14 Go 35.35N 12.20 E
Lampung [3] 26 Dg 5.00S 105.00 E
Lamu 31 Li 2.16S 40.54 E
Lamud 54 Ce 6.09S 77.55W
La Mure 11 Lj 44.54N 5.47 E
Lan 16 Ec 52.09N 27.18 E
Lana 14 Fd 46.37N 11.09 E
Lana, Rio de la- 48 Li 17.49N 95.09W
Lanai City 65a Ec 20.50N 156.55W
Lanaihale 65a Ec 20.49N 156.52W
Lanai Island 57 Lb 20.50N 156.55W
Lanaken 12 Hd 50.53N 5.39 E
Lanark 9 Jf 55.41N 3.48W
Lanbi Kyun 25 Jf 10.50N 98.15 E
Lancang (Menglangba) 27 Gg 22.37N 99.57 E
Lancang Jiang=Mekong (EN) 21 Mh 10.15N 105.55 E
Lancashire [3] 9 Kh 53.55N 2.40W
Lancashire Plain 9 Kh 53.40N 2.45W
Lancaster 9 Kh 53.45N 2.50W
Lancaster [Ca.-U.S.] 43 De 34.42N 118.08W
Lancaster [Eng.-U.K.] 9 Kg 54.03N 2.48W
Lancaster [Mo.-U.S.] 45 Jf 40.31N 92.32W
Lancaster [N.H.-U.S.] 44 Lc 44.29N 71.34W
Lancaster [Oh.-U.S.] 44 Ff 39.43N 82.37W
Lancaster [Ont.-Can.] 44 Jc 45.12N 74.30W
Lancaster [Pa.-U.S.] 43 Lc 40.01N 76.19W
Lancaster [S.C.-U.S.] 44 Gh 34.43N 80.47W
Lancaster Sound 38 Kb 74.13N 84.00W
Lançeiro 55 Fe 20.59S 53.43W
Lancelin 59 Df 31.01S 115.19 E
Lanciano 14 Ih 42.14N 14.23 E
Lančin 15 Ha 48.31N 24.49 E
Lancun 28 Ff 36.25N 120.11 E
Łańcut 10 Sf 50.05N 22.13 E
Land 8 Cd 60.45N 10.00 E
Lândana 36 Bd 5.15S 12.10 E
Landau an der Isar 10 Ih 48.41N 12.41 E
Landau in der Pfalz 10 Eg 49.12N 8.07 E
Land Bay 66 Mf 75.25S 141.45W
Landeck 14 Ec 47.08N 10.34 E
Landen 12 Hd 50.45N 5.05 E
Lander 43 Fc 42.50N 108.44W
Landerneau 11 Bf 48.27N 4.15W
Lander River 59 Gd 20.25S 132.00 E
Landeryd 8 Eg 57.05N 13.16 E
Landes 11 Fj 44.15N 1.00W
Landes [3] 11 Fj 44.00N 0.50W
Landesbergen 12 Lb 52.34N 9.08 E
Landeta 55 Ak 32.01S 62.04W
Landete 13 Ke 39.54N 1.22W
Landfallis 25 If 13.40N 93.02 E
Land Glacier 66 Mf 75.40S 141.45W
Landi Kotal 25 Eb 34.06N 71.09 E
Landless Corner 36 Ee 14.53S 28.04 E
Landrecies 12 Fd 50.08N 3.42 E
Landsberg am Lech 10 Gh 48.03N 10.52 E
Landsbro 8 Fg 57.22N 14.54 E
Land's End 5 Fe 50.03N 5.44W
Lands End 42 Fa 76.25N 122.45W
Landshut 10 Ih 48.32N 12.09 E
Landskrona 8 Ei 55.52N 12.50 E
Landsort 8 Gf 58.45N 17.50 E
Landsortsdjupet 8 Hf 58.40N 18.30 E
Landstuhl 12 Je 49.25N 7.34 E
Landusky 46 Kc 47.54N 108.37W
La Neuve-Lyre 12 Cf 48.54N 0.45 E
Lanfeng → Lankao 28 Cg 34.49N 114.48 E
Lang 46 Mb 49.56N 104.23W
La'nga Co 27 De 30.41N 81.17 E
Langadhás 15 Gi 40.45N 23.04 E
Langádhia 15 Fl 37.39N 22.03 E
Lången 7 De 63.19N 14.44 E
Langano, Lake- 35 Fd 7.36N 38.43 E
Langao 27 Ie 32.20N 108.53 E
Langara 26 Hg 4.02S 123.00 E
Langarfoss 7a Cb 65.35N 14.15W
Langasian 26 Ie 8.16N 125.39 E
Langdon 45 Gb 48.46N 98.22W
Langeac 11 Ji 45.06N 3.29 E
Langeais 11 Gg 47.20N 0.24 E
Langeb 35 Fb 17.46N 36.41 E
Langebaan 37 Bf 33.06S 18.02 E
Langeberg 37 Cf 33.56S 20.45 E
Langedijk 12 Gb 52.42N 4.48 E
Langeland 7 Ci 55.00N 10.50 E
Langelands Bælt 8 Dj 54.50N 10.55 E
Längelmävesi 8 Kc 61.30N 24.20 E
Langen 12 Ke 49.59N 8.40 E
Langenberg 12 Kc 51.17N 8.34 E
Langenburg 45 Fa 50.50N 101.43W
Langenfeld (Rheinland) 12 Ic 51.06N 6.57 E
Langenhagen 10 Fd 52.27N 9.45 E
Langenselbold 12 Ld 50.11N 9.02 E
Langenthal 14 Bc 47.13N 7.49 E
Langeoog 10 Dc 53.46N 7.32 E
Langeri 20 Jf 50.08N 143.20 E
Langesund 8 Ce 59.00N 9.45 E
Langesundsfjorden 8 Cf 59.00N 9.48 E
Langevåg 8 Bb 62.27N 6.12 E
Langfang → Anci 27 Kd 39.29N 116.40 E
Långfjället 8 Eb 62.10N 12.20 E
Langfjorden 8 Bb 62.45N 7.30 E
Langhe 14 Bf 44.30N 8.00 E
Langholm 9 Kf 55.09N 3.00W
Langjökull 5 Ec 64.39N 20.00W
Langkawi, Pulau- 26 Ce 6.22N 99.48 E
Langkon 26 Ge 6.32N 116.42 E
Langlade 44 Ja 48.12N 75.57W
Langnau im Emmental 14 Bd 46.56N 7.46 E
Langogne 11 Jj 44.43N 3.51 E
Langon 11 Fj 44.33N 0.15W
Langorūd 24 Md 37.11N 50.10 E
Langøya 7 Db 68.44N 14.50 E
Langreo 13 Ga 43.18N 5.41W
Langres 11 Lg 47.52N 5.20 E
Langres, Plateau de- 5 Gf 47.41N 5.03 E
Langrune-sur-Mer 12 Be 49.19N 0.22W
Langsa 22 Li 4.28N 97.58 E
Långsele 8 Ga 63.11N 17.04 E
Långshyttan 8 Gd 60.27N 16.01 E
Lang Son 25 Ld 21.50N 106.44 E
Lang Suan 25 Jg 9.55N 99.07 E
Languedoc 5 Gg 44.00N 4.00 E
Languedoc 11 Jj 44.00N 4.00 E
Langueyú, Arroyo- 55 Cm 36.39S 58.27W
Langwedel 12 Lb 52.58N 9.13 E
Langxi 28 Ei 31.08N 119.11 E
Langzhong 27 Ie 31.40N 106.04 E
Lan Hsu 27 Lg 22.00N 121.30 E
Laniel 44 Hb 47.06N 79.15W
Lanin, Volcán- 52 Ii 39.38S 71.30W
Lankao 27 Cd 35.12N 79.50 E
Lankao (Lanfeng) 27 Kg 21.00N 116.00 E
Lankao (Lanfeng) 28 Cg 34.49N 114.48 E
Länkipohja 8 Kc 61.44N 24.48 E
Lannemezan 11 Gk 43.08N 0.23 E
Lannemezan, Plateau de- 11 Gk 43.09N 0.27 E
Lannion 11 Cf 48.44N 3.28W
Lannion, Baie de- 11 Cf 48.43N 3.34W
La Noria 56 Gb 20.23S 69.53W
Lansdowne House 42 If 52.13N 87.53W
L'Anse 44 Cb 46.45N 88.27W
Lansing [Ia.-U.S.] 45 Ke 43.22N 91.13W
Lansing [Mi.-U.S.] 39 Ke 42.43N 84.34W
Lansjärv 7 Fc 66.39N 22.12 E
Łańskie, Jezioro- 10 Qc 53.33N 20.30 E
Lantar 20 Ie 56.05N 137.35 E
Lanta Yai, Ko- 25 Jg 7.35N 99.03 E
Lanteri 55 Ci 28.50S 59.39W
Lanterne 11 Mg 47.44N 6.03 E
Lanús 55 Cl 34.43S 58.24W
Lanusei 14 Dk 39.53N 9.32 E
Lanvaux, Landes de- 11 Dg 47.47N 2.36W
Lanxi [China] 28 Ej 29.13N 119.28 E
Lanxi [China] 28 Ha 46.15N 126.16 E
Lanxian (Dongcun) 28 Ae 38.17N 111.38 E
Lanyi He 28 Ae 38.40N 110.53 E
Lanzarote 30 Ff 29.00N 13.40W
Lanzhou 22 Mf 36.03N 103.41 E
Lanzo Torinese 14 Be 45.16N 7.28 E
Lao 14 Jk 39.47N 15.48 E
Laoag 22 Oh 18.12N 120.36 E
Laoang 26 Id 12.34N 125.00 E
Lao Cai 22 Mg 22.30N 103.57 E
Laocheng 28 Hc 42.37N 124.04 E
Laoha He 27 Lc 43.24N 120.39 E
Lao He 28 Cj 29.02N 115.47 E
Laohuanghe Kou 28 Ef 37.39N 119.02 E
Laois [2] 9 Fi 53.00N 7.30W
Laojunmiao → Yumen 22 Lf 39.50N 97.44 E
Laojun Shan 27 Je 33.45N 111.38 E
Lao Ling 28 Id 41.24N 126.10 E
Laon 11 Je 49.34N 3.37 E
Laona 45 Ld 45.34N 88.40W
Laonnois 12 Fe 49.35N 3.40 E
La Orchila, Isla- 54 Ea 11.48N 66.10W
La Oroya 53 Ig 11.32S 75.57W
Laos [1] 22 Mh 18.00N 105.00 E
Laoshan (Licun) 28 Ff 36.10N 120.25 E
Laotougou 28 Jc 42.54N 129.09 E
Laou 13 Gi 35.26N 5.05W
Laoye Ling 28 Kb 44.50N 130.10 E
Lapa 56 Kc 25.45S 49.42W
Lapai 34 Gd 9.03N 6.43 E
Lapalisse 11 Jh 46.15N 3.38 E
La Palma 30 Ff 28.40N 17.52W
La Palma [ElSal.] 49 Cf 14.19N 89.11W
La Palma [Pan.] 47 Ig 8.25N 78.09W
La Palma del Condado 13 Fg 37.23N 6.33W
La Paloma 55 El 34.40S 54.10W
La Pampa [2] 56 Ge 37.00S 66.00W
La Panne/De Panne 12 Ec 51.06N 2.35 E
La Paragua 54 Fb 6.50N 63.20W
La Partida, Isla- 48 De 24.30N 110.25W
La Paz [3] 49 Df 14.15N 87.50W
La Paz [2] 54 Eg 15.00S 68.00W
La Paz [Arg.] 56 Id 30.45S 59.39W
La Paz [Arg.] 56 Gd 33.28S 67.33W
La Paz [Bol.] 53 Jg 16.30S 68.09W
La Paz [Col.] 49 Kh 10.23N 73.10W
La Paz [Hond.] 47 Gf 14.16N 87.40W
La Paz [Mex.] 39 Hg 24.10N 110.18W
La Paz [Ur.] 55 Dl 34.46S 56.13W
La Paz [Ven.] 49 Lh 10.41N 72.00W
La Paz, Bahía de- 47 Bd 24.09N 110.25W
La Paz, Llano de- 48 De 24.00N 110.30W
La Paz Centro 49 Dg 12.20N 86.41W
La Pedrera 54 Ed 1.18S 69.40W
Lapeer 44 Fd 43.03N 83.19W
La Pelada 55 Bj 30.52S 60.59W
La Pérouse, Bahía- 65d Bb 27.04S 109.18W
La Perouse Strait (EN)=Laperuza, Proliv- 21 Qe 45.30N 142.00 E
La Perouse Strait (EN)=Sōya-Kaikyō 21 Qe 45.30N 142.00 E
Laperuza, Proliv-=La Perouse Strait (EN) 21 Qe 45.30N 142.00 E
La Pesca 47 Ed 23.47N 97.47W
La Petite Pierre 12 Jf 48.52N 7.19 E
La Picasa, Laguna- 55 Al 34.20S 62.14W
La Piedad Cavadas 48 Hg 20.21N 102.00W
La Pine 46 Ee 43.40N 121.30W
Lapinjärvi/Lappträsk 8 Ld 60.36N 26.09 E
Lapinlahti 7 Ge 63.22N 27.30 E
La Plaine 51g Bb 15.20N 61.15W
La Plana 13 Ld 40.00N 0.05W
Lapland (EN)=Lappi 5 Ib 66.50N 22.00 E
Lapland (EN)=Lappland 5 Ib 66.50N 22.00 E
La Plant 45 Fd 45.10N 100.38W
La Plata 53 Ki 34.55S 57.57W
La Pobla de Lillet 13 Nb 42.15N 1.59 E
La Pobla de Segur/Pobla de Segur 13 Mb 42.15N 0.58 E
La Pocatière 44 Lb 47.21N 70.02W
La Porte 44 De 41.36N 86.43W
Lapovo 15 Ee 44.11N 21.06 E
Lappajärvi 7 Fe 63.08N 23.40 E
Lappeenranta/Villmanstrand 6 Ic 61.04N 28.11 E
Lappfjärd/Lapväärtti 8 Ib 62.15N 21.32 E
Lappi [2] 7 Gc 67.40N 26.30 E
Lappi 8 Ic 61.06N 21.50 E
Lappi=Lapland (EN) 5 Ib 66.50N 22.00 E
Lappo/Lapua 7 Fe 62.57N 23.00 E
Lappträsk/Lapinjärvi 8 Ld 60.36N 26.09 E
Lapri 20 He 55.45N 124.59 E
Laprida 56 He 37.33S 60.49W
Lâpseki 24 Bb 40.20N 26.31 E
Lapta 24 Ee 35.20N 33.10 E
Laptev Sea (EN)=Laptevyh, More- 67 Fd 76.00N 126.00 E
Laptevyh, More-=Laptev Sea (EN) 67 Fd 76.00N 126.00 E
Lapua/Lappo 7 Fe 62.57N 23.00 E
La Puebla 13 Pe 39.46N 3.01 E
La Puebla de Cazalla 13 Gg 37.14N 5.19W
Lapuna 55 Ba 13.19S 60.28W
La Puntilla 52 Hf 2.11S 81.01W
La Purísima 48 Cd 26.10N 112.04W
Lăpuş 15 Hb 47.30N 24.01 E
Lăpuş 15 Gb 47.39N 23.24 E
La Push 46 Cc 47.55N 124.38W
Lapväärtti/Lappfjärd 8 Ib 62.15N 21.32 E
Łapy 10 Sd 53.00N 22.53 E
Laqīyat al Arba'in 35 Da 20.03N 28.02 E
La Quemada 48 Hf 22.27N 102.45W
La Quiaca 56 Gb 22.06S 65.37W
L'Aquila 6 Hg 42.22N 13.22 E
Lar 23 Hd 27.41N 54.17 E
Lara [2] 54 Ea 10.10N 69.50W
Larache 32 Fb 35.12N 6.09W
Laragne-Montéglin 11 Lj 44.19N 5.49 E
Lārak 23 Id 26.52N 56.22 E
La Rambla 13 Hg 37.36N 4.44W
Laramie 39 Ie 41.19N 105.35W
Laramie Mountains 43 Fc 42.00N 105.40W
Laramie Peak 46 Me 42.17N 105.27W
Laramie River 46 Me 42.12N 104.32W
Laranjal, Rio- 55 Ff 23.12S 53.45W
Laranjeiras do Sul 56 Jc 25.25S 52.25W
Larantuka 26 Hh 8.21S 122.59 E
Larat 26 Jh 7.09S 131.45 E
Larat, Pulau- 26 Jh 7.10S 131.50 E
La Raya 49 Ji 8.20N 74.34W
L'Arba 13 Ph 36.34N 3.09 E
L'Arbaa-Naït-Irathen 13 Qh 36.38N 4.12 E
L'Arbresle 11 Ki 45.50N 4.37 E
Lärbro 7 Eh 57.47N 18.47 E
Larche, Col de- 11 Mj 44.25N 6.53 E
Larde 37 Fc 16.28S 39.43 E
Larderello 14 Eg 43.14N 10.53 E
La Réale 11 Fj 44.35N 0.02W
Laredo [Sp.] 13 Ia 43.24N 3.25W
Laredo [Tx.-U.S.] 39 Jg 27.31N 99.30W
Laren 12 Hb 52.16N 5.16 E
Lārestān 21 Hg 27.00N 55.30 E
Larestan 24 Pi 27.00N 55.30 E
Large Island 51p Cb 12.24N 61.30W
Largentière 11 Kj 44.32N 4.18 E
L'Argentière-la-Bessée 11 Mj 44.47N 6.33 E
Largo, Cayo- 49 Gc 21.38N 81.28W
Largs 9 If 55.48N 4.52W
La Ribagorça/Ribagorza 13 Mb 42.15N 0.30 E
La Ribera 13 Kb 42.30N 2.00W
Larimore 45 Hc 47.54N 97.38W
Larino 14 Ii 41.48N 14.54 E
La Rioja [2] 56 Gc 30.00S 67.30W
La Rioja 13 Jb 42.20N 2.20W
La Rioja 53 Jh 29.25S 66.50W
Lárisa 6 Ih 39.38N 22.25 E
La Rivière-Thibouville, Nassandres- 12 Ce 49.07N 0.44 E
Lārkāna 25 Dc 27.33N 68.13 E
Larmor-Plage 11 Cg 47.42N 3.23W
Larnaka/Lárnax 23 Dc 34.55N 33.38 E
Lárnax/Larnaka 23 Dc 34.55N 33.38 E
Larne/Latharna 9 Hg 54.51N 5.49W
Larned 45 Gg 38.11N 99.06W
La Robla 13 Gb 42.48N 5.37W
La Roche 63b De 21.28S 168.02 E
La Roche-en-Ardenne 11 Ld 50.11N 5.35 E
La Rochefoucauld 11 Gi 45.44N 0.23 E
La Roche-Guyon 12 De 49.05N 1.38 E
La Rochelle 6 Ff 46.10N 1.09W
La Roche-sur-Yon 11 Eh 46.40N 1.26W
La Roda 13 Je 39.13N 2.09W
La Romana 47 Ke 18.25N 68.58W
La Ronge 42 Ge 55.06N 105.17W
La Ronge, Lac- 38 Id 55.05N 104.59W
Larose 45 Kl 29.35N 90.23W
La Rosita 48 Ic 28.24N 101.43W
Larouco 13 Ec 41.56N 7.40W
Larreynaga 49 Dg 12.40N 86.34W
Larrey Point 59 Dc 20.00S 119.10 E
Larrimah 58 Ef 15.35S 133.12 E
Larsa 24 Kg 31.16N 45.49 E
Lars Christensen Kyst 66 Fe 69.30S 68.00 E
Larsen, Mount- 66 Kf 74.51S 162.12 E
Larsen Ice Shelf 66 Qe 68.30S 62.30W
Lartijas Padomju Socialistiska Respublika → Latvija 19 Cd 57.00N 25.00 E
La Rumorosa 48 Aa 32.34N 116.06W
Laruns 11 Fk 43.00N 0.25W
Larvik 7 Bg 59.04N 10.00 E
La Sabana [Arg.] 55 Ch 27.52S 59.57W
La Sabana [Col.] 54 Ec 2.20N 68.32W
Las Adjuntas, Presa de- 48 Jf 23.55N 98.45W
La Sagra 13 Id 40.05N 4.00W
La Sagra 13 Jg 37.57N 2.34W
La Salle 45 Lf 41.20N 89.06W
La Salle, Pic- 47 Je 18.22N 71.59W
La Sal Mountains 46 Kg 38.30N 109.10W
Las Alpujarras 13 Ih 36.50N 3.25W
La Sanabria 13 Fb 42.08N 6.30W
Las Animas 45 Eg 38.04N 103.13W
Lās 'ānōd 35 Hd 8.26N 47.24 E
La Sarre 42 Jg 48.48N 79.12W
Las Aves, Islas- 54 Ea 11.58N 67.33W
Las Avispas 55 Bi 29.53S 61.18W
Las Bardenas 13 Kb 42.10N 1.25W
Las Bonitas 50 Di 7.52N 65.40W
Las Breñas 56 Hc 27.05S 61.05W
Las Cabezas de San Juan 13 Gh 36.59N 5.56W
Lascahobas 49 Ld 18.50N 71.56W
Lascano 55 Ek 33.40S 54.12W
Las Casitas, Cerro- 47 Cd 23.31N 109.53W
Lascaux, Grotte de- 11 Hi 45.03N 1.11 E
Las Cejas 56 Hc 26.53S 64.44W
Las Chilcas, Arroyo- 55 Cm 37.16S 58.26W
Las Choapas 47 Fe 17.55N 94.05W
Las Cinco Villas 13 Kb 42.05N 1.07W
Las Cruces 43 Fe 32.23N 106.29W
Läsdäred 35 Hc 10.10N 46.01 E
Lās Dawa'o 35 Hc 10.22N 49.03 E
La Segarra 13 Nc 41.30N 1.10 E
La Selva 13 Oc 41.40N 2.50 E
La Serena 13 Gf 38.45N 5.30W
La Serena 53 Ih 29.54S 71.16W
La Seu d'Urgell/Seo de Urgel 13 Nb 42.21N 1.28 E
La-Seyne-sur-Mer 11 Lk 43.06N 5.53 E
Las Flores 56 Ie 36.03S 59.07W
Lāsh-e Joveyn 23 Jc 31.43N 61.37 E
Las Heras 56 Gd 32.51S 68.49W
Lashkar Gāh 22 If 31.35N 64.21 E
Las Hurdes 13 Fd 40.20N 6.20W
La Sila 5 Hh 39.15N 16.30 E
Łasin 10 Pc 53.32N 19.05 E
Łask 10 Pe 51.36N 19.07 E
Las Lajas 56 Fe 38.31S 70.22W
Las Lomitas 56 Hb 24.42S 60.36W
Las Margaritas 48 Ni 16.19N 91.59W
Las Mariñas 13 Da 43.20N 8.15W
Las Marismas 13 Fg 37.00N 6.15W
Las Mercedes 54 Eb 9.07N 66.24W
Las Mestenas 48 Gc 28.13N 104.35W
Las Minas, Cerro- 47 Gf 14.33N 88.39W
Las Minas, Sierra de- 47 Ge 15.05N 90.00W
Las Mixtecas, Sierra del- 48 Ki 17.45N 97.15W
La Sola, Isla- 54 Fa 11.20N 63.34W
La Solana 13 If 38.56N 3.14W
Lasolo 26 Hg 3.29S 122.04 E
La Sorcière 51k Bb 13.59N 60.56W
La Souterraine 11 Hh 46.14N 1.29 E
Las Palmas [3] 32 Ed 28.20N 14.20W
Las Palmas de Gran Canaria 31 Ff 28.06N 15.24W
Las Petas 55 Cc 16.23S 59.11W
La Spezia 6 Gg 44.07N 9.50 E
Las Piedras 56 Id 34.45S 56.13W
Las Plumas 53 Jj 43.40S 67.15W
Lās Qoray 35 Hc 11.15N 48.22 E
Las Rosas 55 Bk 32.28S 61.34W
Lassen Peak 43 Cc 40.29N 121.31W
Lassigny 12 Ee 49.35N 2.51 E
Laßnitz 14 Jd 46.46N 15.32 E
Lasso 64b Ba 15.02N 145.38 E
Las Tablas 49 Gj 7.46N 80.17W
Last Mountain Lake 42 Gf 51.10N 105.15W
Las Toscas 55 Ci 28.21S 59.17W
Lastoursville 36 Bc 0.49S 12.42 E
Lastovo 14 Kh 42.46N 16.55 E
Lastovo 14 Kh 42.45N 16.50 E
Lastovski kanal 14 Kh 42.50N 16.59 E
Las Tres Virgenes, Volcán- 47 Bc 27.27N 112.34W
Las Tunas [3] 49 Ic 21.00N 77.00W
Las Tunas, Punta- 51a Bb 18.30N 66.37W
Las Varillas 56 Hd 31.52S 62.43W
Las Vegas [N.M.-U.S.] 43 Fd 35.36N 105.13W
Las Vegas [Nv.-U.S.] 39 Hf 36.11N 115.08W
Las Villuercas 13 Ge 39.33N 5.27W
Łaszczów 10 Tf 50.32N 23.40 E
Lata 65c Db 14.14S 169.29W
Latacunga 54 Cd 0.55S 78.37W
La Tagua 54 Dd 0.03S 74.40W
Latakia (EN)=Al Lādhiqīyah 22 Ff 35.31N 35.07 E
Latarc, Causse du- 11 Jk 43.57N 3.11 E
Late Island 61 Gc 18.48S 174.39W
Laterza 14 Kj 40.37N 16.48 E
La Teste 11 Ej 44.38N 1.09W
Latgale 8 Lh 56.45N 27.30 E
Latgales Augstiene/Latgalskaja Vozvyšennost 8 Lh 56.10N 27.30 E
Latgalskaja Vozvyšennost/Latgales Augstiene 8 Lh 56.10N 27.30 E
Latharna/Larne 9 Hg 54.51N 5.49W
Lathen 12 Jb 52.52N 7.19 E
La Tigra 55 Bh 27.06S 60.34W
Latina 14 Gi 41.28N 12.52 E
Latisana 14 Ge 45.47N 13.00 E
Latium (EN) = Lazio [2] 14 Gh 42.02N 12.23 E
La Toja 13 Db 42.27N 8.50W
La Toma 56 Gd 33.03S 65.37W
La Tontouta 63b Ce 22.00S 166.15 E
Latorica 10 Rh 48.28N 21.50 E
La Tortuga, Isla- 54 Ea 10.56N 65.20W
La-Tour-du-Pin 11 Li 45.34N 5.27 E
La Trimouille 11 Hh 46.28N 1.03 E
La Trinidad 49 Dg 12.58N 86.14W
La Trinidad de Orichuna 50 Bi 7.07N 69.45W
La Trinité 50 Fe 14.44N 60.58W
Latronico 14 Kj 40.05N 16.01 E
Lattari, Monti- 14 Ij 40.40N 14.30 E
La Tuque 42 Kg 47.27N 72.47W
Lātūr 25 Fe 18.24N 76.35 E
Latvia (EN) = Latvija 19 Cd 57.00N 25.00 E
Latvija = Latvia (EN) 19 Cd 57.00N 25.00 E
Latvijas PSR → Latvija 19 Cd 57.00N 25.00 E
Latvijskaja Sovetskaja Socialističeskaja Respublika → Latvija 19 Cd 57.00N 25.00 E
Latvijskaja SSR/Latvijas Padomju Socialistika Respublika → Latvija 19 Cd 57.00N 25.00 E
Lau 30 Kh 6.56N 30.16 E
Laubach 12 Kd 50.33N 8.59 E
Lauchert 10 Fh 48.05N 9.15 E
Lauchhammer 10 Je 51.30N 13.48 E
Lauenburg 10 Gc 53.22N 10.34 E
Lauf an der Pegnitz 10 Hg 49.31N 11.17 E
Laughlan Islands 63a Ac 9.15S 153.40 E
Laughlin Peak 45 Dh 36.38N 104.12W
Lau Group 57 Jf 18.20S 178.30W
Lauhanvuori 8 Jb 62.10N 22.10 E
Laujar de Andarax 13 Jh 36.59N 2.51W
Laukaa 7 Fe 62.25N 25.57 E
Laukuva 8 Ji 55.35N 22.08 E
Laulau, Bahia- 64b Ba 15.08N 145.46 E
Launceston [Austl.] 58 Fi 41.26S 147.08 E
Launceston [Eng.-U.K.] 9 Ik 50.38N 4.21W
La Unión [Bol.] 55 Bb 15.18S 61.05W
La Unión [Chile] 56 Ff 40.17S 73.05W
La Unión [Col.] 54 Cc 1.37N 77.08W
La Unión [ElSal.] 47 Gf 13.20N 87.51W
La Unión [Mex.] 48 Ii 17.58N 101.49W
La Unión [Peru] 54 Ce 9.46S 76.48W
La Unión [Sp.] 13 Lg 37.37N 0.52W
La Unión [Ven.] 49 Ni 8.13N 67.46W
Laura 59 Ic 15.34S 144.28 E
La Urbana 50 Ci 7.08N 66.56W
Laurel [Ms.-U.S.] 43 Je 31.42N 89.08W
Laurel [Mt.-U.S.] 43 Fb 45.40N 108.46W
Laureles 55 Ej 31.23S 55.52W
Laurel Hill 44 He 40.02N 79.17W
Laurel Mountain 44 Hf 39.20N 79.50W
Laurens 44 Fh 34.30N 82.01W
Laurentian Plateau (EN)=Laurentien, Plateau- 38 Md 50.00N 70.00W
Laurentian Scarp 44 Ic 45.50N 76.15W
Laurentide Scarp 44 Kb 46.38N 73.00W
Laurentien, Plateau-=Laurentian Plateau (EN) 38 Md 50.00N 70.00W
Lauria 14 Jj 40.02N 15.50 E
Lau Ridge (EN) 3 Kl 25.00S 179.00 E
Laurie River 42 He 56.00N 100.58W
Laurinburg 44 Hh 34.47N 79.27W
Laurium 44 Cb 47.14N 88.26W
Lauro Muller 55 Hi 28.24S 49.23W
Lausanne 6 Gf 46.30N 6.40 E
Lausitzer Gebirge 10 Kf 50.48N 14.40 E
Lausitzer Neiße 10 Kd 52.04N 14.46 E
Laut, Pulau- 26 Ef 4.43N 107.59 E
Laut, Pulau- 21 Nj 3.40S 116.10 E
Lautaret, Col du- 11 Mi 45.02N 6.24 E
Lautaro 56 Fe 38.31S 72.27W
Lautém 26 Ih 8.22S 126.54 E
Lauter 10 Eg 48.58N 8.11 E
Lauterbach 10 Ff 50.38N 9.24 E
Lauterbourg 12 Kf 48.59N 8.11 E
Lauterecken 12 Je 49.39N 7.36 E
Lauthala 63d Cb 16.45S 179.41W
Laut Kecil, Kepulauan- 26 Gg 4.50S 115.45 E
Lautoka 61 Ec 17.37S 177.27 E
Lauvergne Island 64d Cb 7.00N 152.00 E
Lauwersmeer 12 Ia 53.25N 6.15 E
Lauzerte 11 Hj 44.15N 1.08 E
Lauzon 44 Lb 46.50N 71.10W
Lauzoue 11 Gj 44.03N 0.15 E
Lava 10 Rb 54.37N 21.14 E
Lava, Nosy- [Mad.] 37 Hb 12.49S 48.41 E
Lava, Nosy- [Mad.] 37 Hb 14.33S 47.36 E
Lavaca River 45 Hl 28.50N 96.36W
Lava Flow 45 Bi 34.45N 108.20W
Laval 11 Ff 48.01N 0.46W
Lavalle 55 Ci 29.01S 59.11W
Lavalleja [2] 55 El 34.00S 55.00W
Lāvān, Jazīreh-ye- 23 Hd 26.48N 53.00 E
Lavanggu 63a Ed 11.37S 160.15 E
Lavant 14 Id 46.38N 14.56 E
Lavapié, Punta- 52 Ii 37.09S 73.35W
Lāvar Meydān 24 Pg 30.20N 54.30 E
Lavassaare 8 Kf 58.29N 24.16 E
Lavaur 11 Hk 43.42N 1.49 E
La Vecilla 13 Gb 42.51N 5.24W
La Vega 47 Je 19.13N 70.31W
La Vela de Coro 49 Mh 11.27N 69.34W
Lavelanet 11 Hl 42.56N 1.51 E
Lavello 14 Ji 41.03N 15.48 E
La Venta 47 Fe 18.08N 94.03W
Laventie 12 Ed 50.38N 2.46 E
La Ventura 48 Ie 24.37N 100.54W
La Vera 13 Gd 40.05N 5.30W
L'Averdy, Cape- 63a Ba 5.33S 155.04 E
Laverton 59 Ee 28.38S 122.25 E
Lavia 7 Ff 61.36N 22.36 E
La Victoria 54 Ea 10.14N 67.20W
La Vila Jojosa/Villajoyosa 13 Lf 38.30N 0.14W
La Villita, Presa- 48 Hh 18.05N 102.05W
La Viña 54 Ce 6.54S 79.28W

Index Symbols

[1] Independent Nation
[2] State, Region
[3] District, County
[4] Municipality
[5] Colony, Dependency
Continent
Physical Region
Historical or Cultural Region
Mount, Mountain
Volcano
Hill
Mountains, Mountain Range
Hills, Escarpment
Plateau, Upland
Pass, Gap
Plain, Lowland
Delta
Salt Flat
Valley, Canyon
Crater, Cave
Karst Features
Depression
Polder
Desert, Dunes
Forest, Woods
Heath, Steppe
Oasis
Cape, Point
Coast, Beach
Cliff
Peninsula
Isthmus
Sandbank
Island
Atoll
Rock, Reef
Islands, Archipelago
Rocks, Reefs
Coral Reef
Well, Spring
Geyser
River, Stream
Waterfall Rapids
River Mouth, Estuary
Lake
Salt Lake
Intermittent Lake
Reservoir
Swamp, Pond
Canal
Glacier
Ice Shelf, Pack Ice
Ocean
Sea
Gulf, Bay
Strait, Fjord
Lagoon
Bank
Seamount
Tablemount
Ridge
Shelf
Basin
Escarpment, Sea Scarp
Fracture
Trench, Abyss
National Park, Reserve
Point of Interest
Recreation Site
Cave, Cavern
Historic Site
Ruins
Wall, Walls
Church, Abbey
Temple
Scientific Station
Airport
Port
Lighthouse
Mine
Tunnel
Dam, Bridge

Index Symbols

- [1] Independent Nation
- [2] State, Region
- [3] District, County
- [4] Municipality
- [5] Colony, Dependency
- ■ Continent
- ⊡ Physical Region
- Historical or Cultural Region
- ▲ Mount, Mountain
- Volcano
- Hill
- Mountains, Mountain Range
- Hills, Escarpment
- Plateau, Upland
- Pass, Gap
- Plain, Lowland
- Delta
- Salt Flat
- Valley, Canyon
- Crater, Cave
- Karst Features
- Depression
- Polder
- Desert, Dunes
- Forest, Woods
- Heath, Steppe
- Oasis
- Cape, Point
- Coast, Beach
- Cliff
- Peninsula
- Isthmus
- Sandbank
- Island
- Atoll
- Rock, Reef
- Islands, Archipelago
- Rocks, Reefs
- Coral Reef
- Well, Spring
- Geyser
- Reservoir
- River, Stream
- Waterfall Rapids
- River Mouth, Estuary
- Lake
- Salt Lake
- Intermittent Lake
- Swamp, Pond
- Canal
- Glacier
- Ice Shelf, Pack Ice
- Ocean
- Sea
- Gulf, Bay
- Strait, Fjord
- Lagoon
- Bank
- Seamount
- Tablemount
- Ridge
- Shelf
- Basin
- Escarpment, Sea Scarp
- Fracture
- Trench, Abyss
- National Park, Reserve
- Point of Interest
- Recreation Site
- Cave, Cavern
- Historic Site
- Ruins
- Wall, Walls
- Church, Abbey
- Temple
- Scientific Station
- Airport
- Port
- Lighthouse
- Mine
- Tunnel
- Dam, Bridge

Name	Page	Grid	Lat.	Long.
Los Alamos	39	If	35.53N	106.19W
Los Amates	49	Cf	15.16N	89.06W
Los Amores	55	Ci	28.06S	59.59W
Los Angeles	39	Hf	34.03N	118.15W
Los Ángeles	53	Ii	37.28S	72.21W
Los Angeles Aqueduct	46	Fi	35.22N	118.05W
Losap Atoll	57	Gd	6.54N	152.44 E
Los Banos	46	Eh	37.04N	120.51W
Los Blancos	56	Hb	23.36S	62.36W
Los Charrúas	55	Cj	31.10S	58.11W
Los Chiles	49	Eh	11.02N	84.43W
Los Conquistadores	55	Cj	30.36S	58.28W
Los Frailes, Islas-	50	Eg	11.12N	63.45W
Los Frentones	55	Bh	26.25S	61.25W
Los Gatos	46	Eh	37.14N	121.59W
Losheim	12	Ie	49.31N	6.45 E
Los Hermanos, Islas-	54	Fa	11.45N	64.25W
Łosice	10	Sd	52.14N	22.43 E
Lošinj	14	If	44.35N	14.28 E
Los Islands (EN)=Los, Iles de-	34	Cd	9.30N	13.48W
Los Juries	55	Ai	28.28S	62.06W
Los Lagos	56	Fe	39.51S	72.50W
Los Lagos [2]	56	Ff	41.20S	73.00W
Los Llanos de Aridane	32	Dd	28.39N	17.54W
Los Médanos, Istmo de-	49	Mh	11.35N	69.45W
Los Mochis	39	Ig	25.45N	108.53W
Los Monegros	13	Lc	41.29N	0.03W
Los Monjes, Islas-	54	Da	12.25N	70.55W
Los Navalmorales	13	He	39.43N	4.38W
Loso	36	Ec	1.10S	27.10 E
Los Palacios	49	Fb	22.35N	83.12W
Los Palacios y Villafranca	13	Gg	37.10N	5.56W
Los Pedroches	13	Hf	38.27N	4.45W
Los Pirpintos	55	Ah	26.08S	62.05W
Los Remedios, Río de-	48	Fe	24.41N	106.28W
Los Reyes de Salgado	48	Hh	19.35N	102.29W
Los Roques, Islas-	54	Ea	11.50N	66.45W
Los Roques Basin (EN)	50	Cf	12.20N	67.40W
Los Santos [3]	49	Gj	7.45N	80.30W
Los Santos	49	Gj	7.56N	80.25W
Losser	12	Jb	52.16N	7.01 E
Lossiemouth	9	Jd	57.43N	3.18W
Lossnen	8	Eb	62.30N	12.50 E
Los Taques	49	Lh	11.50N	70.16W
Los Telares	56	Hc	28.59S	63.26W
Los Teques	54	Ea	10.21N	67.02W
Los Testigos, Islas-	54	Fa	11.23N	63.06W
Lost River	46	Ef	41.56N	121.30W
Lost River Range	46	Id	44.10N	113.35W
Lost Trail Pass	43	Eb	45.41N	113.57W
Los Vilos	56	Fd	31.55S	71.31W
Lot	5	Gg	44.18N	0.20 E
Lot [3]	11	Hj	44.30N	1.30 E
Lota	56	Fe	37.05S	73.10W
Lotagipi Swamp	35	Ee	4.36N	34.55 E
Løten	8	Dd	60.49N	11.19 E
Lot-et-Garonne [3]	11	Gj	44.20N	0.30 E
Lothair	37	Ee	26.23S	30.27 E
Lothian [3]	9	Jf	55.55N	3.30W
Lothian	9	Jf	55.55N	3.05W
Loto	36	Dc	2.47S	22.30 E
Lotofaga	65c	Ba	13.59S	171.50W
Lotoi	36	Cc	1.35S	18.30 E
Lotru	15	Hd	45.20N	24.16 E
Lotrului, Munţii-	15	Gd	45.30N	23.52 E
Lotta	7	Hb	68.39N	30.20 E
Lottefors	8	Gc	61.25N	16.24 E
Löttorp	8	Gg	57.10N	16.59 E
Lotuke, Jabal-	35	Ee	4.07N	33.48 E
Louang Namtha	25	Kd	20.57N	101.25 E
Louangphrabang	22	Mh	19.52N	102.08 E
Loubomo	31	Ii	4.12S	12.41 E
Loučná	10	Lf	50.06N	15.48 E
Loudéac	11	Df	48.10N	2.45W
Loudima	36	Bc	4.07S	13.04 E
Loudon	44	Eh	35.44N	84.20W
Loudun	11	Gh	47.00N	0.04 E
Loué	11	Fg	48.00N	0.09W
Loue	11	Lg	47.01N	5.27 E
Loufan	28	Ae	38.04N	111.47 E
Louga	34	Bb	15.37N	16.13W
Louga [3]	34	Bb	15.00N	15.30W
Louge	11	Hk	43.27N	1.20 E
Loughborough	9	Li	52.47N	1.11W
Lougheed	42	Ha	77.30N	105.00W
Loughrea/Baile Locha Riach	9	Eh	53.12N	8.34W
Louhans	11	Lh	46.38N	5.13 E
Louhi	19	Db	66.04N	33.01 E
Louisa	44	Ff	38.07N	82.36W
Louiseville	44	Kb	46.16N	72.57W
Louisiade Archipelago	57	Gf	11.00S	153.00 E
Louisiana	45	Kg	39.27N	91.03W
Louisiana [2]	43	Ie	31.15N	92.15W
Louis Trichardt	37	Dd	23.01S	29.43 E
Louisville [Ky.-U.S.]	39	Kf	38.16N	85.45W
Louisville [Ms.-U.S.]	45	Lj	33.07N	89.03W
Louis-XIV, Pointe-	42	Jf	54.50N	79.30W
Loukoléla	36	Cc	1.02S	17.07 E
Loulan Yiji	27	Ec	40.32N	89.50 E
Loulé	13	Dg	37.08N	8.02W
Loum	34	Ge	4.43N	9.44 E
Lount Lake	45	Ia	50.10N	94.20W
Louny	10	Jf	50.22N	13.49 E
Loup City	45	Gf	41.17N	98.58W
Loup River	45	Hf	41.24N	97.19W
Loups Marins, Lacs des-	42	Ke	56.40N	74.00W
Lourdes	11	Fk	43.06N	0.03W
Lourenço Marques→Maputo	31	Kk	25.58S	32.34 E
Lousa, Serra da-	13	Dd	40.04N	8.13W
Loushan Guan	27	If	28.02N	106.51 E
Louštín	10	Jf	50.12N	13.48 E
Louth [Austl.]	59	Jf	30.32S	145.07 E
Louth [Eng.-U.K.]	9	Mh	53.22N	0.01W
Louth/Lú [2]	9	Gh	53.55N	6.30W
Loutrá Aidhipsoú	15	Gk	38.51N	23.03 E
Loutrá Killínis	15	El	37.52N	21.07 E
Loutrákion	15	Fl	37.59N	23.00 E
Louvain/Leuven	11	Kd	50.53N	4.42 E
Louvet Point	51k	Bb	13.58N	60.53W
Louviers	11	He	49.13N	1.10 E
Lövånger	7	Ed	64.22N	21.18 E
Lovászi	10	Mj	46.33N	16.34 E
Lovat	5	Jd	58.14N	31.28 E
Lovćen	15	Bg	42.24N	18.49 E
Loveč [2]	15	Hf	43.08N	24.43 E
Loveč	15	Hf	43.08N	24.43 E
Loveland	45	Df	40.24N	105.05W
Lovell	43	Fc	44.50N	108.24W
Lovelock	43	Dc	40.11N	118.28W
Lövenich, Köln-	12	Id	50.57N	6.50 E
Lovenske Gorice	14	Jd	46.40N	16.00 E
Lovere	14	Ee	45.49N	10.04 E
Loviisa	7	Gf	60.27N	26.14 E
Loviisa/Lovisa	7	Gf	60.27N	26.14 E
Loving	45	Dj	32.17N	104.06W
Lovington	43	Ge	33.27N	103.21W
Lovisa	7	Gf	60.27N	26.14 E
Lovisa/Loviisa	7	Gf	60.27N	26.14 E
Lovoi	36	Ed	8.05S	26.40 E
Lovosice	10	Kf	50.31N	14.03 E
Lovozero	7	Ib	68.01N	35.01 E
Lovozero, Ozero-	7	Ic	67.50N	35.10 E
Lövstabruk	8	Gd	60.24N	17.53 E
Lövstabukten	8	Gd	60.35N	17.45 E
Lovua	36	Dd	6.07S	20.35 E
Lovua	36	De	11.31S	23.35 E
Low, Cape-	42	Id	63.06N	85.18W
Lowa	30	Ji	1.24S	25.52 E
Lowell	43	Mc	42.39N	71.18W
Löwenberg in der Mark	10	Jd	52.53N	13.09 E
Lower Arrow Lake	46	Fb	49.40N	118.08W
Lower Austria (EN) = Niederösterreich [2]	14	Jb	48.30N	15.45 E
Lower California (EN) — Baja California	38	Hg	28.00N	112.00W
Lower Hutt	62	Fd	41.13S	174.55 E
Lower Lake	46	Ef	41.15N	120.02W
Lower Lake	46	Dg	38.55N	122.36W
Lower Lough Erne/Loch Éirne Iochtair	9	Fg	54.30N	7.50W
Lower Post	42	Ee	59.55N	128.30W
Lower Red Lake	45	Ic	48.00N	94.50W
Lower Rhine (EN) = Neder-Rijn	11	Mc	51.59N	6.20 E
Lower Saxony (EN)= Niedersachsen [2]	10	Fd	52.00N	10.00 E
Lower Trajan's Wall (EN)= Nižni Trajanov Val	15	Ld	45.45N	28.30 E
Lower Tunguska (EN)= Nižnjaja Tunguska	21	Kc	65.48N	88.04 E
Lowestoft	9	Oi	52.29N	1.45 E
Lowestoft Ness	9	Oi	52.28N	1.44 E
Lowgar [3]	23	Kc	33.50N	69.00 E
Łowicz	10	Pd	52.07N	19.56 E
Lowlands	9	Jf	56.00N	4.00W
Lowrah	21	If	31.33N	66.33 E
Lowshān	24	Md	36.39N	49.32 E
Low Tatra (EN) = Nízke Tatry	10	Ph	48.54N	19.40 E
Lowther	42	Hb	74.35N	97.40W
Lowville	44	Jd	43.47N	75.30W
Loxton [Austl.]	59	If	34.27S	140.35 E
Loxton [S.Afr.]	37	Cf	31.30S	22.22 E
Loyalty Islands (EN)= Loyauté, Iles-	57	Hg	21.00S	167.00 E
Loyauté, Iles-=Loyalty Islands (EN)	57	Hg	21.00S	167.00 E
Loyoro	36	Fb	3.21N	34.17 E
Lozère [3]	11	Jj	44.30N	3.30 E
Lozère, Mont-	11	Jj	44.25N	3.46 E
Loznica	15	Ce	44.32N	19.13 E
Lozovaja	19	Df	48.53N	36.15 E
Lozva	19	Gd	59.36N	62.20 E
Lú/Louth [2]	9	Gh	53.55N	6.30W
Lua	36	Cb	2.46N	18.26 E
Luacano	36	De	11.16S	21.38 E
Luachimo	36	Dd	6.33S	20.59 E
Luaha-Sibuha	26	Cg	0.31S	98.28 E
Luahoko	65b	Ba	19.40S	174.24W
Luala	37	Fc	17.57S	36.30 E
Lualaba	29	Jh	0.26N	25.20 E
Luama	36	Ec	4.46S	26.53 E
Lua Makika	65a	Ec	20.35N	156.34W
Luampa	36	De	14.32S	24.10 E
Lu'an	27	Ke	31.44N	116.30 E
Luanda	31	Ii	8.50S	13.15 E
Luanda [3]	36	Bd	8.30S	13.20 E
Luando	30	Ij	10.19S	16.40 E
Luang, Khao-	25	Jg	8.31N	99.47 E
Luang, Thale-	25	Kg	7.30N	100.15 E
Luang Chiang Dao, Doi-	25	Je	19.23N	98.54 E
Luanginga	35	Cj	15.11S	22.55 E
Luang Prabang Range	25	Ke	18.30N	101.15 E
Luangue	36	Dc	4.17S	20.01 E
Luangwa	30	Kj	15.36S	30.25 E
Luan He	21	Nf	39.20N	119.10 E
Luaniva	64h	Bb	13.16S	176.07W
Luannan (Bencheng)	28	Ee	39.30N	118.42 E
Luanping (Anjiangying)	28	Dd	40.55N	117.19 E
Luanshya	31	Jj	13.08S	28.25 E
Luanxian	27	Kd	39.45N	118.44 E
Luanza	36	Ed	8.40S	28.40 E
Luapula	30	Ji	9.26S	28.33 E
Luapula [3]	36	Ee	10.40S	29.15 E
Luarca	13	Fa	43.32N	6.32W
Luashi	36	De	10.56S	23.37 E
Luba	34	Ge	3.28N	8.40 E
Lubaantum	49	Ce	16.17N	88.58W
Lubaczów	10	Tf	50.10N	23.07 E
Lubaczówka	10	Sf	50.08N	22.35 E
Lubalo	36	Cd	7.22S	19.20 E
Lubalo	36	Cd	9.07S	19.15 E
Lubamba	36	Ed	5.14S	26.02 E
Lubań	10	Le	51.08N	15.18 E
Lubāna/Lubana	8	Lh	56.49N	26.49 E
Lubana/Lubāna	8	Lh	56.49N	26.49 E
Lubanas, Ozero-/Lubānas Ezers	8	Lh	56.40N	27.00 E
Lubānas Ezers/Lubanas, Ozero-	8	Lh	56.40N	27.00 E
Lubang Islands	26	Hd	13.45N	120.15 E
Lubango	31	Ij	14.55S	13.28 E
Lubao	31	Ji	5.22S	25.45 E
Lubartów	10	Se	51.28N	22.46 E
Lubawa	10	Pc	53.30N	19.45 E
Lübbecke	10	Ed	52.18N	8.37 E
Lubbeek	12	Gd	50.53N	4.50 E
Lübben/Lubin	10	Je	51.57N	13.54 E
Lübbenau/Lubnjow	10	Je	51.52N	13.58 E
Lubbock	39	If	33.35N	101.51W
Lübeck	6	He	53.52N	10.42 E
Lübecker Bucht	10	Gb	54.00N	10.55 E
Lübeck-Travemünde	10	Gc	53.57N	10.52 E
Lubefu	36	Dc	4.10S	23.00 E
Lubefu	36	Dc	4.43S	24.25 E
Lubei→Jarud Qi	27	Lc	44.30N	120.55 E
Lubelska, Wyżyna-	10	Sf	51.00N	23.00 E
Lubenec	10	Jf	50.08N	13.20 E
Lubenka	16	Sd	50.28N	54.06 E
Lubero	36	Ec	0.06S	29.06 E
Lubéron, Montagne du-	11	Lk	43.48N	5.22 E
Lubi	36	Dc	4.59S	23.26 E
Lubie, Jezioro-	10	Lc	53.30N	15.50 E
Lubień Kujawski	10	Pd	52.25N	19.10 E
Lubij/Löbau	10	Ke	51.06N	14.40 E
Lubilash	29	Ji	6.02S	23.45 E
Lubin	10	Me	51.24N	16.13 E
Lubin/Lübben	10	Je	51.57N	13.54 E
Lublin	6	Ie	51.15N	22.35 E
Lublin [2]	10	Se	51.15N	22.35 E
Lubliniec	10	Of	50.40N	18.41 E
Lubnān=Lebanon (EN) [1]	22	Ff	33.50N	35.50 E
Lubnān, Jabal-=Lebanon Mountains (EN)	23	Ec	34.00N	36.30 E
Lubnjow/Lübbenau	10	Je	51.52N	13.58 E
Lubny	19	De	50.01N	33.00 E
Luboń	10	Md	52.23N	16.54 E
Lubraniec	10	Od	52.33N	18.50 E
Lubsko	10	Ke	51.46N	14.59 E
Lubsza	10	Ke	51.55N	14.45 E
Lubudi	29	Ji	9.13S	25.38 E
Lubudi	36	Ed	9.57S	25.58 E
Lubue	36	Dc	4.10S	19.53 E
Lubukklinggau	26	Dg	3.10S	102.52 E
Lubuksikaping	26	Df	0.08N	100.10 E
Lubumba	36	Ec	3.58S	29.06 E
Lubumbashi	31	Jj	11.40S	27.30 E
Lubuskie, Pojezierze-	10	Ld	52.18N	15.20 E
Lubutu	31	Ji	0.44S	26.35 E
Lucala	36	Bd	6.38S	12.34 E
Lucala	36	Cd	9.16S	15.16 E
Lucania, Mount-	42	Dd	61.01N	140.29W
Lucas	55	Ea	13.05S	55.56W
Lucca	14	Eg	43.50N	10.29 E
Lucea	49	Hd	18.27N	78.10W
Luce Bay	9	Ig	54.47N	4.50W
Lucedale	45	Lk	30.55N	88.35W
Lučegorsk	20	Ig	46.25N	134.20 E
Lucélia	55	Ge	21.44S	51.01W
Lucena [Phil.]	26	Hd	13.56N	121.37 E
Lucena [Sp.]	13	Hg	37.24N	4.29W
Lucena del Cid	13	Ld	40.08N	0.17W
Luc-en-Diois	11	Lj	44.37N	5.27 E
Lučenec	10	Ph	48.20N	19.41 E
Lucera	14	Ji	41.30N	15.20 E
Lucerne (EN) = Luzern	14	Cc	47.05N	8.20 E
Lucerne, Lake- (EN) = Vierwaldstätter-See	14	Cc	47.00N	8.30 E
Lucero	48	Fb	30.49N	106.30W
Lucheng	28	Bf	36.18N	113.15 E
Lucheringo	37	Fb	11.43S	36.15 E
Lucheux	12	Ed	50.12N	2.25 E
Luchico	30	Lj	12.15S	44.25 E
Luchico	36	Cd	6.12S	19.42 E
Lüchow	10	Hd	52.58N	11.09 E
Lüchun	27	Hg	23.02N	102.19 E
Lucipara, Kepulauan-	26	Ih	5.30S	127.33 E
Lucira	36	Be	13.52S	12.32 E
Luck	19	Ce	50.47N	25.20 E
Luckau	10	Je	51.51N	13.43 E
Luckenwalde	10	Jd	52.05N	13.10 E
Lucknow	22	Kg	26.51N	80.55 E
Luçon	11	Eh	46.27N	1.10W
Lucrecia, Cabo-	49	Jc	21.04N	75.37W
Luc-sur-Mer	12	Be	49.18N	0.21W
Lucunga	36	Bd	6.49S	14.35 E
Lucusse	36	De	12.33S	20.51 E
Lüda→Dalian=Dairan (EN)	22	Of	38.55N	121.39 E
Luda Kamčija	15	Kg	43.03N	27.29 E
Ludbreg	14	Kd	46.15N	16.37 E
Lüdenscheid	10	De	51.13N	7.37 E
Lüderitz	31	Ik	26.38S	15.10 E
Lüderitz [3]	37	Be	26.00S	15.00 E
Lüderitz Bay	37	Be	26.35S	15.10 E
Ludhiāna	22	Jf	30.54N	75.51 E
Ludinghausen	10	De	51.46N	7.28 E
Ludington	43	Jc	43.57N	86.27W
Ludlow	9	Ki	52.22N	2.43W
Ludogorije	15	Jf	43.46N	26.56 E
Ludogorsko Plato	15	Kf	43.36N	27.03 E
Luduş	15	Hc	46.29N	24.06 E
Ludvika	7	Df	60.09N	15.11 E
Ludwigsburg	10	Fh	48.54N	9.11 E
Ludwigshafen am Rhein	10	Eg	49.29N	8.27 E
Ludwigslust	10	Hc	53.19N	11.30 E
Ludza	7	Gh	56.32N	27.45 E
Luebo	31	Ji	5.21S	21.25 E
Lueki	36	Ec	3.24S	25.57 E
Lueki	36	Ec	3.22S	25.51 E
Luele	36	Dd	7.55S	20.00 E
Luembe	36	Dd	6.43S	24.11 E
Luembe	36	Dd	6.37S	21.06 E
Luena [Ang.]	36	De	12.31S	22.34 E
Luena [Ang.]	31	Ij	11.48S	19.55 E
Luena [Zaire]	36	Ed	9.27S	25.47 E
Luena [Zam.]	36	Df	15.20S	23.30 E
Luenguė	36	Df	16.54S	21.52 E
Luenha	37	Ec	16.24S	33.48 E
Luera Peak	45	Cj	33.47N	107.49W
Lueta	36	Dd	7.04S	21.40 E
Lueyang	27	Ie	33.25N	106.14 E
Lufeng	27	Kg	22.57N	115.41 E
Lufico	36	Bd	6.22S	13.30 E
Lufira	29	Ji	8.16S	26.27 E
Lufira, Chutes de la-	36	Ed	9.50S	27.30 E
Lufkin	43	Ie	31.20N	94.44W
Lug	15	De	44.23N	20.45 E
Luga	19	Cd	59.43N	28.18 E
Luga	19	Cd	58.44N	29.50 E
Lugano	14	Cd	46.00N	8.57 E
Lugano, Lago di-	14	Cd	46.00N	9.00 E
Lugansk = Vorošilovgrad	6	Jf	48.34N	39.20 E
Luganville	58	Hf	15.32S	167.10 E
Lügde	12	Lc	51.57N	9.15 E
Lugela	37	Fc	16.26S	36.39 E
Lugenda	30	Kj	11.26S	38.33 E
Lugnaquillia	9	Gi	52.58N	6.27W
Lugo [3]	13	Eb	43.00N	7.30W
Lugo [It.]	14	Ff	44.25N	11.54 E
Lugo [Sp.]	13	Ea	43.00N	7.34W
Lugoj	15	Ed	45.41N	21.55 E
Lugovoj	19	Hg	42.55N	72.47 E
Lugovoj	19	Gd	59.44N	65.55 E
Lugovski	20	Ge	58.05N	112.55 E
Lugulu	36	Ec	2.17S	26.32 E
Luh	7	Kh	56.14N	42.28 E
Luhe	10	Gc	53.18N	10.11 E
Luhe	28	Eh	32.21N	118.50 E
Luhin Sum	27	Kb	46.41N	118.38 E
Luhit	25	Jc	27.48N	95.28 E
Luhovicy	7	Ji	54.59N	39.02 E
Luhuo	27	He	31.21N	100.40 E
Lui	36	Cd	8.41S	17.56 E
Luia	36	Dd	8.26S	21.45 E
Luiana	36	Df	17.22S	22.59 E
Luiana	30	Jj	17.27S	23.14 E
Luie	36	Cc	4.33S	17.41 E
Luik/Liège	6	Ge	50.38N	5.34 E
Luilaka	30	Ji	0.52S	20.12 E
Luilu	36	Dd	6.22S	23.50 E
Luimneach/Limerick	6	Fe	52.40N	8.38W
Luimneach/Limerick [2]	9	Ei	52.30N	9.00W
Luing	9	He	56.13N	5.39W
Luino	14	Cd	46.00N	8.44 E
Luio	36	De	13.15S	21.39 E
Lui Pătru, Vîrful-	15	Gd	45.30N	23.30 E
Luis Correia	54	Jd	2.53S	41.40W
Luishia	36	Ee	11.13S	27.07 E
Luitpold Coast	66	Af	78.30S	32.00W
Luiza	36	Dd	7.12S	22.25 E
Luján [Arg.]	56	Gd	32.22S	65.57W
Luján [Arg.]	56	Id	34.34S	59.07W
Lujiang	28	Di	31.15N	117.17 E
Lukafu	36	Ee	10.30S	27.33 E
Lukanga Swamp	36	Ee	14.25S	27.45 E
Lukavac	14	Mf	44.33N	18.32 E
Lukengo	36	Ed	5.46S	29.06 E
Lukenie	30	Ii	2.44S	18.09 E
Lukeville	46	Ik	31.57N	112.50W
Lukojanov	19	Ed	55.02N	44.30 E
Lukolela	36	Cc	1.03S	17.12 E
Lukonzolwa	36	Ed	8.47S	28.39 E
Lukov	10	Ue	51.14N	24.25 E
Lukovit	15	Hf	43.12N	24.10 E
Łuków	10	Se	51.56N	22.23 E
Lukuga	30	Ji	5.40S	26.55 E
Lukula	36	Bd	5.23S	12.57 E
Lukulu	36	De	14.23S	23.15 E
Lukusashi	36	Fe	14.38S	30.00 E
Luleå	6	Ib	65.34N	22.10 E
Luleälven	5	Ib	65.35N	22.03 E
Lüleburgaz	23	Ca	41.24N	27.21 E
Lüliang Shan	21	Nf	37.45N	111.25 E
Lulimba	36	Ec	4.42S	28.38 E
Luling	45	Hl	29.41N	97.39W
Lulong	28	Ee	39.53N	118.52 E
Lulonga	36	Cb	0.37N	18.23 E
Lulonga	30	Ih	0.43N	18.23 E
Lulua	30	Ji	5.02S	21.07 E
Lulu Fakahega, Mount-	64h	Bb	13.16S	176.10W
Luma	65c	Db	14.14S	169.32W
Lumajang	26	Fh	8.08S	113.13 E
Lumajangdong Co	27	De	34.00N	81.37 E
Lumbala Kaquengue	31	Jj	14.06S	21.25 E
Lumbala N'guimbo	36	De	12.39S	22.32 E
Lumberton	43	Le	34.37N	79.00W
Lumbo	37	Gc	15.00S	40.44 E
Lumbrales	13	Fd	40.56N	6.43W
Lumbres	12	Ed	50.42N	2.08 E
Lumby	46	Fa	50.15N	118.58W
Lumding	25	Ic	25.45N	93.10 E
Lumege	36	De	11.34S	20.48 E
Lumesule	36	Ge	11.14S	38.06 E
Lumi	60	Ch	3.29S	142.03 E
Lummen	12	Hd	50.59N	5.15 E
Lumparland	8	Id	60.10N	20.15 E
Lumphăt	25	Lf	13.30N	106.59 E
Lumsden [N.Z.]	62	Cf	45.44S	168.26 E
Lumsden [Sask.-Can.]	46	Ma	50.34N	104.53W
Lumuna	36	Ec	3.46S	26.24 E
Lumut	26	Df	4.14N	100.38 E
Luna	13	Gb	42.40N	5.49W
Luna, Laguna de-	55	Di	28.06S	56.46W
Lunan Shan	27	Hf	27.00N	102.30 E
Lunayyr, Harrat-	24	Gj	25.10N	37.50 E
Lunca Ilvei	15	Hb	47.22N	24.59 E
Lund	7	Ci	55.42N	13.11 E
Lunda [3]	36	Cd	9.30S	20.00 E
Lundazi	31	Kj	12.19S	33.13 E
Lunde	8	Gb	62.53N	17.51 E
Lundevatn	8	Bf	58.20N	6.35 E
Lundi	30	Kk	21.19S	32.24 E
Lundu	26	Ef	1.40N	109.51 E
Lundy Island	9	Ij	51.10N	4.40W
Lüneburg	10	Gc	53.15N	10.24 E
Lüneburger Heide	10	Gc	53.10N	10.20 E
Lunel	11	Kk	43.41N	4.08 E
Lünen	10	De	51.37N	7.31 E
Lunéville	11	Mf	48.36N	6.30 E
Lunga	30	Jj	14.34S	26.26 E
Lungué-Bungo	37	Jj	28.38S	16.27 E
Lungwebungu	36	De	14.19S	23.14 E
Lūni	25	Ed	24.41N	71.14 E
Lūni	25	Ec	26.00N	73.00 E
Lunigiana	14	Df	44.20N	9.55 E
Luninec	19	Ce	52.16N	26.50 E
Lunino	16	Nc	53.35N	45.14 E
Lunsemfwa	36	Fe	14.54S	30.12 E
Luntai/Bügür	27	Dc	41.46N	84.10 E
Luobei (Fengxiang)	27	Nb	47.36N	130.58 E
Luobuzhuang	27	Ed	39.30N	88.15 E
Luocheng	27	Ig	24.51N	108.53 E
Luodian (Longping)	27	If	25.26N	106.47 E
Luoding	27	Jg	22.43N	111.33 E
Luohe	27	Je	33.30N	114.08 E
Luo He	27	Id	32.18N	109.12 E
Luoma Hu	28	Eg	34.10N	118.12 E
Luonteri	8	Lc	61.35N	27.45 E
Luoping	27	Hg	24.58N	104.19 E
Luopioinen	8	Kc	61.22N	24.40 E
Luoshan	28	Ch	32.13N	114.32 E
Luotian	28	Ci	30.48N	115.23 E
Luoxiao Shan	27	Jf	26.35N	114.00 E
Luoyang	22	Nf	34.41N	112.25 E
Luoyuan	27	Kf	26.31N	119.32 E
Luozi	36	Bc	4.57S	14.08 E
Lupa	36	Fd	8.39S	33.12 E
Lupane	37	Dc	18.56S	27.48 E
Łupawa	10	Nb	54.42N	17.07 E
Lupeni	15	Gd	45.21N	23.14 E
Luperón	49	Ld	19.54N	70.57W
Łupków	10	Sg	49.12N	22.06 E
Luputa	36	Dd	7.10S	23.42 E
Lūq	31	Lh	3.56N	42.32 E
Luqiao	28	Fj	28.39N	120.05 E
Luqu	27	He	34.36N	102.30 E
Luque	56	Ic	25.16S	57.34W
Luquillo	51a	Cb	18.22N	65.43W
Luray	44	Hf	38.40N	78.28W
Lure	11	Mg	47.41N	6.30 E
Lure, Montagne de-	11	Lj	44.07N	5.47 E
Luremo	36	Cd	8.30S	17.51 E
Lurgan/An Lorgain	9	Gg	54.28N	6.20W
Lurín	54	Cf	12.17S	76.52W
Lúrio	37	Gb	13.32S	40.30 E
Lúrio	30	Lj	13.31S	40.42 E
Lusaka	31	Jj	15.25S	28.17 E
Lusambo	31	Ji	4.58S	23.27 E
Lusanga	36	Cc	4.44S	18.58 E
Lusangi	36	Ec	4.37S	27.08 E
Lu Shan	27	Kf	29.30N	115.55 E
Lushan [China]	28	Cj	29.33N	115.58 E
Lushan [China]	28	Bh	33.44N	112.54 E
Lushi	27	Je	34.04N	111.02 E
Lushiko	36	Cd	6.12S	19.42 E
Lushnja	15	Ci	40.56N	19.42 E
Lushoto	36	Gc	4.47S	38.17 E
Lu Shui	28	Bj	29.54N	113.39 E
Lushui (Luzhangjie)	27	Gf	26.00N	98.50 E
Lüshun=Port Arthur (EN)	27	Ld	38.50N	121.13 E
Lusignan	11	Gh	46.26N	0.07 E
Lusk	43	Gc	42.46N	104.27W
Lussac-les-Châteaux	11	Gh	46.24N	0.43 E
Lustrafjorden	8	Bc	61.20N	7.20 E
Lūt, Dasht-e-=Lut, Dasht-i- (EN)	21	Hf	33.00N	57.00 E
Lut, Dasht-i- (EN)=Lūt, Dasht-e-	21	Hf	33.00N	57.00 E
Lu Tao	27	Lg	22.35N	121.30 E
Lutembo	36	De	13.28S	21.22 E
Luti	63a	Cb	7.14S	157.00 E
Lütjenburg	10	Gb	54.17N	10.35 E
Luton	9	Mj	51.53N	0.25W
Luton Airport	12	Bc	51.50N	0.22W
Lutong	26	Ff	4.28N	114.00 E
Lutshima	36	Cd	5.22S	18.59 E
Lutshima	36	Cd	5.22S	18.59 E
Lutterworth	12	Ab	52.27N	1.12W
Lutuai	36	De	12.40S	20.12 E
Lutugino	16	Ke	48.33N	39.13 E
Lützow-Holmbukta	66	De	69.10S	37.30 E
Lutzputs	37	Ce	28.22S	20.37 E
Luuk	26	He	5.58N	121.18 E
Luverne	45	He	43.39N	96.13W
Luvidjo	36	Ed	6.26S	26.59 E
Luvua	30	Ji	6.46S	26.58 E
Luvuei	36	De	13.06S	21.12 E
Luwegu	30	Ki	8.31S	37.23 E
Luwingu	36	Ee	10.15S	29.54 E
Luwuk	26	Hg	0.56S	122.47 E
Luxembourg [3]	12	He	50.00N	5.30 E
Luxembourg/Luxemburg [1]	6	Gf	49.45N	6.05 E
Luxembourg/Luxemburg	6	Gf	49.45N	6.05 E
Luxemburg/Luxembourg	6	Gf	49.45N	6.05 E
Luxemburg/Luxembourg [1]	6	Gf	49.45N	6.05 E
Luxeuil-les-Bains	11	Mg	47.49N	6.23 E
Luxi	22	Mg	24.34N	103.44 E
Luxi (Mangshi)	27	Gg	24.29N	98.40 E
Luxor (EN)=Al Uqşur	33	Fd	25.41N	32.39 E
Luy	11	Ek	43.39N	1.08W
Luy de Béarn	11	Fk	43.38N	0.47W

Index Symbols

- [1] Independent Nation
- [2] State, Region
- [3] District, County
- [4] Municipality
- [5] Colony, Dependency
- Continent
- Physical Region
- Historical or Cultural Region
- Mount, Mountain
- Volcano
- Hill
- Mountains, Mountain Range
- Hills, Escarpment
- Plateau, Upland
- Pass, Gap
- Plain, Lowland
- Delta
- Salt Flat
- Valley, Canyon
- Crater, Cave
- Karst Features
- Depression
- Polder
- Desert, Dunes
- Forest, Woods
- Heath, Steppe
- Oasis
- Cape, Point
- Coast, Beach
- Cliff
- Peninsula
- Isthmus
- Sandbank
- Island
- Atoll
- Rock, Reef
- Islands, Archipelago
- Rocks, Reefs
- Coral Reef
- Well, Spring
- Geyser
- River, Stream
- Waterfall Rapids
- River Mouth, Estuary
- Lake
- Salt Lake
- Intermittent Lake
- Reservoir
- Swamp, Pond
- Canal
- Glacier
- Ice Shelf, Pack Ice
- Ocean
- Sea
- Gulf, Bay
- Strait, Fjord
- Lagoon
- Bank
- Seamount
- Tablemount
- Ridge
- Shelf
- Basin
- Escarpment, Sea Scarp
- Fracture
- Trench, Abyss
- National Park, Reserve
- Point of Interest
- Recreation Site
- Cave, Cavern
- Historic Site
- Ruins
- Wall, Walls
- Church, Abbey
- Temple
- Scientific Station
- Airport
- Port
- Lighthouse
- Mine
- Tunnel
- Dam, Bridge

Index Symbols

- ① Independent Nation
- ② State, Region
- ③ District, County
- ④ Municipality
- ⑤ Colony, Dependency
- Continent
- Physical Region

- Historical or Cultural Region
- Mount, Mountain
- Volcano
- Hill
- Mountains, Mountain Range
- Hills, Escarpment
- Plateau, Upland

- Pass, Gap
- Plain, Lowland
- Delta
- Salt Flat
- Valley, Canyon
- Crater, Cave
- Karst Features

- Depression
- Polder
- Desert, Dunes
- Forest, Woods
- Heath, Steppe
- Oasis
- Cape, Point

- Coast, Beach
- Cliff
- Peninsula
- Isthmus
- Sandbank
- Island
- Atoll

- Rock, Reef
- Islands, Archipelago
- Rocks, Reefs
- Coral Reef
- Well, Spring
- Geyser
- River, Stream

- Waterfall Rapids
- River Mouth, Estuary
- Lake
- Salt Lake
- Intermittent Lake
- Reservoir
- Swamp, Pond

- Canal
- Glacier
- Ice Shelf, Pack Ice
- Ocean
- Sea
- Gulf, Bay
- River, Stream

- Lagoon
- Bank
- Seamount
- Tablemount
- Ridge
- Shelf
- Basin

- Escarpment, Sea Scarp
- Fracture
- Trench, Abyss
- National Park, Reserve
- Point of Interest
- Recreation Site
- Cave, Cavern

- Historic Site
- Ruins
- Wall, Walls
- Church, Abbey
- Temple
- Scientific Station
- Airport

- Port
- Lighthouse
- Mine
- Tunnel
- Dam, Bridge

Index Symbols

[1] Independent Nation
[2] State, Region
[3] District, County
[4] Municipality
[5] Colony, Dependency
■ Continent
▦ Physical Region

Historical or Cultural Region
Mount, Mountain
Volcano
Hill
Mountains, Mountain Range
Hills, Escarpment
Plateau, Upland

Pass, Gap
Plain, Lowland
Delta
Salt Flat
Valley, Canyon
Crater, Cave
Karst Features

Depression
Polder
Desert, Dunes
Forest, Woods
Heath, Steppe
Oasis
Cape, Point

Coast, Beach
Cliff
Peninsula
Isthmus
Sandbank
Island
Atoll

Rock, Reef
Islands, Archipelago
Rocks, Reefs
Coral Reef
Well, Spring
Geyser
River, Stream

Waterfall Rapids
River Mouth, Estuary
Lake
Salt Lake
Intermittent Lake
Reservoir
Swamp, Pond

Canal
Glacier
Ice Shelf, Pack Ice
Ocean
Sea
Gulf, Bay
Strait, Fjord

Lagoon
Bank
Seamount
Tablemount
Ridge
Shelf
Basin

Escarpment, Sea Scarp
Fracture
Trench, Abyss
National Park, Reserve
Point of Interest
Recreation Site
Cave, Cavern

Historic Site
Ruins
Wall, Walls
Church, Abbey
Temple
Scientific Station
Airport

Port
Lighthouse
Mine
Tunnel
Dam, Bridge

Manicoré, Rio- 54 Fe 5.51 S 61.19W
Manicouagan 42 Kg 49.10N 68.15W
Manicouagan 42 Kf 51.00N 68.20W
Manicouagan, Réservoir- 38 Md 51.30N 68.19W
Manigotagan 45 Ha 51.06N 96.18W
Manihi Atoll 57 Mf 14.24 S 145.56W
Manihiki Anchorage 64n Ab 10.23 S 161.03W
Manihiki Atoll 57 Kf 10.24 S 161.01W
Manika, Plateau de la- 36 Ed 10.00 S 26.00 E
Manila [Phil.] 22 Oh 14.35N 121.00 E
Manila [Ut.-U.S.] 46 Kf 40.59N 109.43W
Manila Bay 21 Oh 14.30N 120.45 E
Manilaid/Manilajd 8 Kf 58.08N 24.03 E
Manilajd/Manilaid 8 Kf 58.08N 24.03 E
Manily 20 Ld 62.30N 165.20 E
Maningrida Settlement 59 Gb 12.05 S 134.10 E
Maniouro, Pointe- 63b Dc 17.41 S 168.35 E
Manipa, Selat- 26 Ig 3.20 S 127.23 E
Manipur [3] 25 Id 25.00N 94.00 E
Manipur 25 Id 22.52N 94.05 E
Manisa 23 Cb 38.36N 27.26 E
Manisa Dağı 15 Kk 38.33N 27.28 E
Manises 13 Le 39.29N 0.27W
Manissau a-Missu, Rio- 54 Hf 10.58 S 53.20W
Manistee 44 Dc 44.15N 86.18W
Manistee River 44 Dc 44.15N 86.21W
Manistique 43 Jb 45.57N 86.15W
Manitique Lake 44 Eb 46.15N 85.45W
Manitoba [3] 42 Hf 55.00N 97.00W
Manitoba, Lake- 38 Jd 51.00N 98.45W
Manitou Islands 44 Ec 45.10N 86.00W
Manitou Lake 44 Gc 45.48N 82.00W
Manitoulin Island 42 Jg 45.45N 82.30W
Manitou Springs 45 Dg 38.52N 104.55W
Manitouwadge 45 Nb 49.08N 85.47W
Manitowoc 43 Jc 44.06N 87.40W
Manitsoq/Sukkertoppen 41 Ge 65.25N 53.00W
Maniwaki 42 Jg 46.23N 75.58W
Manizales 53 Ie 5.05N 75.32W
Manja 17 Jd 64.23N 60.50 E
Manja 37 Gd 21.23 S 44.20 E
Manjača 14 Lf 44.35N 17.05 E
Manjacaze 37 Ed 24.42 S 33.33 E
Manjakandriana 37 Hc 18.55 S 47.47 E
Manji 29a Bb 43.09N 141.59 E
Manjimup 59 Df 34.14 S 116.09 E
Mānjra 25 Fe 18.49N 77.52 E
Mān Kāt 25 Jd 22.05N 98.01 E
Mankato [Ks.-U.S.] 45 Gg 39.47N 98.12W
Mankato [Mn.-U.S.] 43 Ic 44.10N 94.01W
Mankono 34 Dd 8.04N 6.12W
Mankono [3] 34 Dd 7.58N 6.02W
Mankoya 31 Jj 14.50 S 25.00 E
Manley Hot Springs 40 Ic 65.00N 150.37W
Manlleu 13 Ob 42.00N 2.17 E
Manmād 25 Ed 20.15N 74.27 E
Manmanoc, Mount- 26 Hc 17.40N 121.06 E
Manna 26 Dh 4.27 S 102.55 E
Mannahill 59 Hf 32.26 S 139.59 E
Mannar 25 Fg 8.59N 79.54 E
Mannar, Gulf of- 21 Ji 8.30N 79.00 E
Mannheim 6 Gf 49.29N 8.28 E
Manning [Alta.-Can.] 42 Fe 56.55N 117.33W
Manning [S.C.-U.S.] 44 Gi 33.42N 80.12W
Manning, Cape- 64g Ba 2.02N 157.26W
Manning Strait 63a Db 7.24 S 158.04 E
Manningtree 12 Dc 51.57N 1.04 E
Mann Ranges 59 Fe 26.00 S 129.30 E
Mann River 59 Gb 12.20 S 134.07 E
Mannu, Capo- 14 Cj 40.02N 8.22 E
Mannu, Rio- [It.] 14 Cj 40.50N 8.23 E
Mannu, Rio- [It.] 14 Cj 40.41N 8.59 E
Mano 34 Cd 6.56N 11.31W
Mano [Jap.] 29 Fc 37.58N 138.20 E
Mano [S.L.] 34 Cd 7.55N 12.00W
Manoa 54 Ee 9.40 S 65.27W
Man of War, Cayos- 49 Fg 13.02N 83.22W
Manokwari 58 Ee 2.30 S 134.36 E
Manombo 37 Gd 22.55 S 43.28 E
Manompana 37 Hc 16.41 S 49.45 E
Manonga 36 Fc 4.08 S 34.12 E
Manono 31 Ji 7.18 S 27.25 E
Manono 65c Aa 13.50 S 172.05W
Manosque 11 Lk 43.50N 5.47 E
Manouane, Lac- 42 Kf 50.40N 70.45W
Manö-Wan 29 Fc 37.55N 138.15 E
Manp'ojin 28 Id 41.09N 126.17 E
Manra Atoll (Sydney) 57 Je 4.27 S 171.15W
Manresa 13 Nc 41.44N 1.50 E
Mansa 31 Jj 11.12 S 28.53 E
Mansa Konko 34 Bc 13.28N 15.33W
Mansel 38 Lc 62.00N 79.50W
Mansfield [Austl.] 59 Jg 37.03 S 146.05 E
Mansfield [Eng.-U.K.] 9 Lh 53.09N 1.11W
Mansfield [La.-U.S.] 45 Jj 32.02N 93.43W
Mansfield [Oh.-U.S.] 43 Kc 40.46N 82.31W
Mansfield [Pa.-U.S.] 44 Ie 41.47N 77.05W
Mansfield, Mount- 44 Kc 44.33N 72.49W
Mansle 11 Gi 45.52N 0.11 E
Manso, Rio- 55 Db 14.42 S 56.16W
Manso, Rio- ou Mortes, Rio das- 52 Kg 11.45 S 50.44W
Mansôa 34 Bc 12.04N 15.19W
Mansourah 13 Qh 36.04N 4.28 E
Mansourah, Djebel- 13 Qh 36.02N 4.28 E
Manta 54 Bd 0.57 S 80.42W
Manta, Bahía de- 54 Bd 0.50 S 80.40W
Mantalingajan, Mount- 26 Ge 8.48N 117.40 E
Manteca 46 Eh 37.48N 121.13W
Mantecal [Ven.] 50 Di 6.52N 65.38W
Mantecal [Ven.] 50 Bi 7.33N 69.09W
Manteigas 13 Ed 40.24N 7.32W
Manteo 44 Jh 35.55N 75.40W
Mantes-la-Jolie 11 Hf 48.59N 1.43 E
Manti 46 Jg 39.16N 111.38W
Mantiqueira, Serra da- 52 Lh 22.00 S 44.45W
Manto 49 Df 14.55N 86.23W
Manton 44 Ec 44.24N 85.24W
Mantova 14 Ee 45.09N 10.48 E
Mäntsälä 8 Kd 60.38N 25.20 E
Mänttä 7 Fe 62.02N 24.38 E
Mantua 49 Eb 22.17N 84.17W
Manturovo 19 Ed 58.22N 44.44 E
Mäntyharju 7 Gf 61.25N 26.53 E
Mäntyluoto 8 Ic 61.35N 21.29 E
Manu 54 Df 12.15 S 70.50W
Manuae Atoll 57 Lf 19.21 S 158.56W
Manua Islands 57 Kf 14.13 S 169.35W
Manuangi Atoll 57 Mf 19.12 S 141.16W
Manūbah 14 En 36.48N 10.06 E
Manuel 48 Jf 22.44N 98.19W
Manuel Alves, Rio- 54 If 11.19 S 48.28W
Manuel Bonavides 48 Hc 29.05N 103.55W
Manuel Derqui 55 Ch 27.50 S 58.48W
Manuel J. Cobo 55 Dl 35.49 S 57.54W
Manuel Ocampo 55 Bk 33.46 S 60.39W
Manuga Reefs 63a Ad 11.00 S 153.21 E
Manui, Pulau- 26 Hg 3.35 S 123.08 E
Manujān 24 Qi 27.24N 57.32 E
Manūk, Tell- 24 Hf 33.10N 38.50 E
Manukau 58 Ih 36.56 S 174.56 E
Manulu Lagoon 64g Bb 1.56N 157.20W
Manus Island 57 Fe 2.05 S 147.00 E
Many 45 Jk 31.34N 93.29W
Manyara, Lake- 36 Gc 3.35 S 35.50 E
Manyas 24 Bb 40.02N 27.58 E
Manyč 5 Kf 47.15N 40.00 E
Manyč-Gudilo, Ozero- 5 Kf 46.25N 42.35 E
Manyoni 36 Fd 5.45 S 34.50 E
Manzanal, Puerto del- 13 Fb 42.32N 6.10W
Manzanares 13 Ie 39.00N 3.22W
Manzaneda, Cabeza de- 13 Eb 42.20N 7.15W
Manzanilla 13 Fg 37.23N 6.25W
Manzanillo [Cuba] 39 Lg 20.21N 77.07W
Manzanillo [Mex.] 39 Ih 19.03N 104.20W
Manzanillo, Bahía de- [Dom.Rep.] 49 Ld 19.45N 71.46W
Manzanillo, Bahía de- [Mex.] 48 Gh 19.04N 104.25W
Manzanillo, Punta- 49 Hi 9.38N 79.32W
Manzano Mountains 45 Ci 34.45N 106.20W
Manzhouli 22 Ne 49.33N 117.28 E
Manzilah, Buḩayrat al- 24 Eg 31.15N 32.00 E
Manzil Bū Ruqaybah 32 Ib 37.10N 9.48 E
Manzil bū Zalafah 14 En 36.41N 10.35 E
Manzil Tamīn 14 En 36.47N 10.59 E
Manzini 37 Ee 26.29 S 31.22 E
Mao 63b Dc 17.29 S 168.29 E
Mao [Chad] 31 Ig 14.07N 15.19 E
Mao [Dom.Rep.] 47 Je 19.34N 71.05W
Mao/Mahón 13 Qe 39.53N 4.15 E
Maoke, Pegunungan- 57 Ee 4.00 S 138.00 E
Maomao Shan 27 Hd 37.12N 103.10 E
Maoming 22 Ng 21.41N 110.52 E
Maoniu Shan 27 He 32.50N 104.12 E
Maotou Shan 27 Hg 24.31N 100.38 E
Maouri, Dallol- 34 Fc 12.05N 3.32 E
Mapai 37 Ed 22.51 S 31.58 E
Mapanda 36 Dd 9.32 S 24.16 E
Mapati 36 Bc 3.38 S 13.21 E
Mapi 58 Ee 7.07 S 139.23 E
Mapi 26 Kh 7.00 S 139.16 E
Mapia, Kepulauan- 26 Jf 0.50N 134.20 E
Mapimí, Bolsón de- 38 Ig 27.30N 103.15W
Mapinhane 37 Fd 22.15 S 35.07 E
Mapire 50 Di 7.45N 64.42W
Mapiri 54 Eg 15.15 S 68.10W
Maple Creek 42 Gg 49.55N 109.27W
Maprik 60 Ch 3.38 S 143.03 E
Mapuera, Rio- 54 Gd 1.05 S 57.02W
Maputo [3] 37 Ee 26.00 S 32.30 E
Maputo (Lourenço Marques) 31 Kk 25.58 S 32.34 E
Maputo, Baía de- 30 Kk 26.05 S 33.00 E
Maqên (Dawu) 27 He 34.29N 100.01 E
Maqran, Wādī al- 33 Ie 20.55N 47.12 E
Maqu 27 He 34.05N 101.45 E
Maquan He/Damqog Kanbab 27 Df 29.36N 84.09 E
Maquela do Zombo 31 Ii 6.03 S 15.08 E
Maquinchao 56 Gf 41.15 S 68.44W
Maquoketa 45 Ke 42.04N 90.40W
Mar, Serra do- 52 Lh 25.00 S 48.00W
Mara 36 Fc 1.31 S 33.56 E
Mara [3] 36 Fc 2.30 S 34.00 E
Maraā 54 Ed 1.50 S 65.22W
Marab 35 Fc 14.54N 37.55 E
Marabá 54 Ie 5.21 S 49.07W
Marabahan 26 Fg 3.00 S 114.45 E
Marabá Paulista 55 Gf 22.06 S 51.56W
Maraca, Ilha de- 54 Hc 2.05N 50.25W
Maracaibo 53 Id 10.40N 71.37W
Maracaibo, Lago de- = Maracaibo, Lake- (EN) 52 Ie 9.50N 71.30W
Maracaibo, Lake- (EN) = Maracaibo, Lago de- 52 Ie 9.50N 71.30W
Maracaju 54 Gh 21.38 S 55.09W
Maracaju, Serra de- [Braz.] 52 Kh 21.00 S 55.00W
Maracaju, Serra de- [S.Amer.] 55 Ef 23.57 S 55.01W
Maracanã 54 Id 0.46 S 47.27W
Maracás 54 Jf 13.26 S 40.27W
Maracay 53 Jd 10.15N 67.36W
Marādah 33 Cd 29.14N 19.13 E
Maradi 31 Hg 13.29N 7.06 E
Maradi [3] 34 Gc 14.15N 7.15 E
Marāgheh 23 Gb 37.23N 46.40 E
Marāh 23 Gd 25.04N 45.28 E
Maraho 35 Bb 18.21N 17.28 E
Marahuaca, Cerro- 52 Je 3.34N 65.27W
Marajó, Baía de- 52 Lf 1.00 S 48.30W
Marajó, Ilha de- 52 Lf 1.00 S 49.30W
Marakei Atoll 57 Id 1.58N 173.25 E
Maralal 36 Gb 1.06N 36.42 E
Maralinga 59 Gf 30.13 S 131.35 E
Maralwexi/Bachu 27 Cd 39.46N 78.15 E
Maramag 26 He 7.46N 125.00 E
Maramasike Island 60 Gi 9.30 S 161.25 E
Maramba 31 Jj 17.51 S 25.52 E
Marampa 34 Cd 8.41N 12.28W
Maramureş [2] 15 Gb 47.40N 24.00 E
Maranchón 13 Jc 41.03N 2.12W
Marand 23 Gb 38.26N 45.46 E
Marang 26 De 5.12N 103.13 E
Maranhão [2] 54 Je 5.00 S 45.00W
Maranhão, Rio- 54 If 14.34 S 49.02W
Marano, Laguna di- 14 He 45.44N 13.10 E
Maranoa River 59 Je 27.50 S 148.37 E
Marañón, Rio- 52 If 4.30 S 73.35W
Marans 11 Fh 46.18N 1.00W
Marão 37 Ed 24.18 S 34.07 E
Marão, Serra do- 13 Ec 41.15N 7.55W
Maraoué 34 Dd 6.54N 5.31W
Marapanim 54 Id 0.42 S 47.42W
Marapi, Gunung- 26 Dg 0.23 S 100.28 E
Marargiu, Capo- 14 Cj 40.20N 8.23 E
Marari, Serra do- 55 Gh 27.30 S 51.00W
Mara Rosa 55 Ha 13.58 S 49.09W
Mărăşeşti 15 Kd 45.53N 27.14 E
Maratea 14 Jk 39.59N 15.43 E
Marathón 15 Gk 38.09N 23.58 E
Marathon 45 Ek 30.12N 103.15W
Marathon 42 Ig 48.46N 86.26W
Maratua, Pulau- 26 Gf 2.15N 118.36 E
Marau 55 Fi 28.27 S 52.12W
Maravari 63a Cb 7.54 S 156.44 E
Marāveh Tappeh 24 Pd 37.55N 55.57 E
Maravilha 55 Fh 26.47 S 53.09W
Maravillas Creek 45 El 29.34N 102.47W
Maravovo 63a Dc 9.17 S 159.38 E
Marāwah 33 Dc 32.29N 21.25 E
Marawi 26 He 8.13N 124.15 E
Marawī 35 Eb 18.29N 31.49 E
Marāwiḩ 24 Oj 24.18N 53.18 E
Marayes 56 Gd 31.29 S 67.20W
Marbella 13 Hh 36.31N 4.53W
Marble Bar 59 Dd 21.11 S 119.44 E
Marble Canyon 46 Jh 36.30N 111.50W
Marble Falls 45 Gk 30.34N 98.17W
Marble Hall 37 Dd 24.57 S 29.13 E
Marburg an der Lahn 10 Ef 50.49N 8.46 E
Marca, Ponta da- 30 Ij 16.31 S 11.42 E
Marcal 10 Ni 47.38N 17.32 E
Marcala 49 Df 14.07N 88.00W
Marçal Dağları 15 Kl 37.09N 28.00 E
Marcali 10 Nj 46.35N 17.25 E
March 10 Mh 48.10N 16.59 E
March 9 Ni 52.33N 0.06 E
Marche 11 Hh 46.10N 1.30 E
Marche = Marches (EN) [2] 14 Hh 43.30N 13.15 E
Marche, Plateau de la- 11 Hh 46.16N 1.30 E
Marche-en-Famenne 11 Ld 50.14N 5.20 E
Marchena 13 Gg 37.20N 5.24W
Marchena, Isla- 54a Aa 0.20N 90.30W
Marches (EN) = Marche [2] 14 Hh 43.30N 13.15 E
Marchesato 14 Kk 39.05N 17.00 E
Marchfeld 14 Kb 48.15N 16.40 E
Mar Chiquita, Laguna- 55 Dm 37.37 S 57.24W
Mar Chiquita, Laguna- 52 Ji 30.42 S 62.36W
Marciana Marina 14 Eh 42.48N 10.12 E
Marcigny 11 Kh 46.16N 4.02 E
Marcilly-sur-Eure 12 Df 48.49N 1.21 E
Marcinelle, Charleroi- 12 Gd 50.25N 4.28 E
Marck 12 Dd 50.57N 1.57 E
Marcoing 12 Fd 50.07N 3.11 E
Marcos Juaréz 56 Fd 32.42 S 62.06W
Marcus Baker, Mount- 40 Jd 61.26N 147.45W
Marcus Island (EN) = Minami-Tori-Shima 57 Gb 26.32N 142.09 E
Marcy, Mount- 43 Mc 44.07N 73.56W
Mardakert 16 Oi 40.12N 46.52 E
Mardakjan 16 Qi 40.29N 50.12 E
Mardān 25 Eb 34.09N 71.52 E
Mardarovka 15 Mb 47.30N 29.40 E
Mar del Plata 53 Ki 38.01 S 57.35W
Marden 12 Cc 51.10N 0.30 E
Mardin 23 Fb 37.18N 40.44 E
Mardin Dağları 24 Id 37.20N 41.00 E
Maré, Ile- 57 Hg 21.30 S 168.00 E
Mare, Muntele- 15 Gc 46.29N 23.14 E
Marechal Cândido Rondon 55 Eg 24.34 S 54.04W
Maree, Loch- 9 Hd 57.40N 5.30W
Mareeba 59 Jc 17.00 S 145.26 E
Marēg 35 He 3.47N 47.18 E
Maremma 14 Fh 42.30N 11.30 E
Marennes 11 Ei 45.49N 1.07W
Marettimo 14 Gm 37.56N 12.05 E
Mareuil-en-Brie 12 Ff 48.57N 3.45 E
Marfa 43 Ge 30.18N 104.01W
Marfil, Laguna- 55 Bb 15.30 S 60.20W
Margai Caka 27 Ed 35.10N 86.55 E
Marganec 19 Df 47.38N 34.40 E
Margaret River 59 Df 33.57 S 115.04 E
Margarida 55 De 21.41 S 56.44W
Margarita, Isla de- 54 Fa 11.00N 64.00W
Margarita Belén 55 Ch 27.16 S 58.58W
Margarition 15 Dj 39.21N 20.26 E
Margate [Eng.-U.K.] 9 Oj 51.24N 1.24 E
Margate [S.Afr.] 37 Ef 30.55 S 30.15 E
Marghera, Venezia- 14 Ge 45.28N 12.44 E
Margherita 30 Jh 0.23N 29.54 E
Margherita di Savoia 14 Ki 41.22N 16.09 E
Marghine, Catena del- 14 Cj 40.20N 8.50 E
Marghita 15 Fb 47.21N 22.20 E
Marghūb, Kūh-e- 24 Qf 33.06N 57.50 E
Margilan 19 Hg 40.28N 71.46 E
Margina 15 Fd 45.51N 22.16 E
Marguerite Bay 66 Qe 68.30 S 68.30W
Margut 12 He 49.35N 5.16 E
Marha 20 Hd 60.35N 123.10 E
Marha 21 Nc 63.20N 118.50 E
Mari 24 Ie 34.39N 40.53 E
Mari 24 Ee 34.44N 33.18 E
Maria Atoll [W.F.] 57 Ng 22.00 S 136.10W
Maria Atoll [W.F.] 57 Lg 21.48 S 154.41W
Maria Cleofas, Isla- 48 Fg 21.16N 106.14W
Maria Elena 56 Gb 22.21 S 69.40W
Mariager 8 Ch 56.39N 10.00 E
Mariager Fjord 8 Dh 56.40N 10.20 E
Maria Grande, Arroyo- 55 Ci 29.21 S 58.45W
Maria Ignacia 55 Cm 37.24 S 59.30W
Maria Island [Austl.] 59 Jh 42.40 S 148.05 E
Maria Island [Austl.] 59 Hb 14.55 S 135.40 E
Maria Island [St.Luc.] 51k Bb 13.44N 60.56W
Mariakani 36 Gc 3.52 S 39.28 E
Maria Laach 12 Jd 50.25N 7.15 E
Maria Madre, Isla- 48 Fg 21.35N 106.33W
Maria Magdalena, Isla- 48 Fg 21.25N 106.25W
Mariana Islands 57 Fc 16.00N 145.30 E
Marianao 47 Hd 23.05N 82.26W
Mariana Trench (EN) 3 Ih 14.00N 147.30 E
Marianna [Ar.-U.S.] 45 Ki 34.46N 90.46W
Marianna [Fl.-U.S.] 44 Ej 30.47N 85.14W
Mariannelund 8 Fg 57.37N 15.34 E
Mariano I. Loza 55 Ci 29.22 S 58.12W
Mariánské Lázně 10 Ig 49.58N 12.43 E
Marias, Islas- 38 Ig 21.25N 106.28W
Marias Pass 46 Ib 48.19N 113.21W
Marias River 43 Eb 47.56N 110.30W
Maria Theresa Reef 57 Lh 36.58 S 151.23W
Mariato, Punta- 47 Hg 7.13N 80.53W
Maria van Diemen, Cape- 62 Ea 34.29 S 172.39 E
Mariazell 14 Jc 47.46N 15.19 E
Ma'rib 23 Gf 15.30N 45.21 E
Maribo 8 Dj 54.46N 11.31 E
Maribor 14 Jd 46.33N 15.39 E
Marica 5 Ig 40.52N 26.12 E
Marica 15 Ig 42.02N 25.50 E
Maricao 51a Bb 18.10N 66.58W
Maricopa 46 Ij 33.04N 112.03W
Marīdī 35 Dd 6.05N 29.24 E
Marīdī 35 De 4.55N 29.28 E
Marié, Rio- 54 Ed 0.25 S 66.26W
Marie Byrd Land (EN) 66 Nf 80.00 S 120.00W
Mariec 7 Lh 56.31N 49.51 E
Marie Galante 47 Le 15.56N 61.16W
Marie-Galante, Canal de- 51e Bc 15.55N 61.25W
Mariehamn / Maarianhamina 7 Ef 60.06N 19.57 E
Marie Louise Island 37b Bb 6.11 S 53.09 E
Mariembourg, Couvin- 12 Gd 50.06N 4.31 E
Marienburg 12 Jd 50.04N 7.08 E
Marienmünster 12 Lc 51.50N 9.13 E
Marienstatt 12 Jd 50.40N 7.49 E
Mariental 31 Ik 24.36 S 17.59 E
Mariestad 7 Cg 58.43N 13.51 E
Marietta [Ga.-U.S.] 43 Ke 33.57N 84.33W
Marietta [Oh.-U.S.] 44 Gf 39.26N 81.27W
Mariga 34 Gd 9.36N 5.57 E
Marignac 11 Gl 42.55N 0.39 E
Marignane 11 Lk 43.25N 5.13 E
Marigot [Dom.] 50 Fe 15.32N 61.18W
Marigot [Guad.] 50 Ec 18.04N 63.06W
Marigot [Haiti] 49 Kd 18.14N 72.19W
Marigot [Mart.] 51h Ab 14.49N 61.02W
Marigot [St.Luc.] 51k Ab 13.58N 61.02W
Mariinsk 20 De 56.13N 87.45 E
Mariinski Posad 7 Lh 56.08N 47.48 E
Marinskoje 20 Jf 51.43N 140.19 E
Marijampole (Kapsukas) 7 Fi 54.33N 23.23 E
Marijskaja respublika 19 Ed 56.40N 48.00 E
Marilia 56 Jb 22.13 S 50.01W
Mariluz 55 Fg 24.02 S 53.13W
Marimba 36 Cd 8.22 S 17.02 E
Marimbondo, Cachoeira do- 55 He 20.18 S 49.10W
Marin 13 Db 42.23N 8.42W
Marin, Cul-de-Sac du- 51h Bc 14.27N 60.53W
Marina di Catanzaro 14 Kl 38.49N 16.36 E
Marina di Gioiosa Ionica 14 Kl 38.18N 16.20 E
Marina di Pisa 14 Eg 43.40N 10.16 E
Marina di Ravenna 14 Gf 44.29N 12.17 E
Marina Gorka 19 Ce 53.31N 28.12 E
Marinduque 26 Hd 13.24N 121.58 E
Marineland 44 Gk 29.43N 81.12W
Marines 12 De 49.09N 1.59 E
Marinette 43 Jb 45.06N 87.38W
Maringá 53 Kh 23.25 S 51.55W
Maringa 30 Ih 1.14N 19.48 E
Marinha Grande 13 De 39.45N 8.56W
Marino [It.] 14 Gi 41.46N 12.39 E
Marino [Van.] 63b Db 14.59 S 168.03 E
Marins, Pico dos- 55 Jf 22.27 S 45.10W
Marinsko 8 Mf 58.46N 28.39 E
Marion 30 Km 46.36 S 37.55 E
Marion [Al.-U.S.] 44 Di 32.32N 87.26W
Marion [Ia.-U.S.] 45 Ke 42.02N 91.36W
Marion [Il.-U.S.] 45 Lh 37.44N 88.56W
Marion [In.-U.S.] 44 Ee 40.33N 85.40W
Marion [Oh.-U.S.] 43 Kc 40.35N 83.08W
Marion [S.C.-U.S.] 44 Hh 34.11N 79.23W
Marion [Va.-U.S.] 44 Gg 36.51N 81.30W
Marion, Lake- 44 Gi 33.30N 80.25W
Marion Reefs 57 Gf 19.10 S 152.20 E
Maripa 54 Ea 7.26N 65.09W
Mariposa 46 Fh 37.29N 119.58W
Mariquita, Cerro- 48 Jf 23.13N 98.22W
Marisa 26 Hf 0.28N 121.56 E
Mariscala 55 El 34.03 S 54.47W
Mariscal Estigarribia 56 Hb 22.02 S 60.38W
Mariupol' 6 Jf 47.06N 37.33 E
Mariusa, Caño 50 Fh 9.43N 61.26W
Mariusa, Isla- 50 Fh 9.39N 61.19W
Marīvan 24 Le 35.31N 46.10 E
Märjamaa/Mar'jamaa 8 Kf 58.54N 24.21 E
Mar'jamaa/Märjamaa 8 Kf 58.54N 24.21 E
Marjanovka 19 He 54.58N 72.38 E
Marjanovka 10 Uf 50.23N 24.55 E
Mark 12 Gc 51.39N 4.39 E
Mark [Ger.] 12 Jc 51.13N 7.36 E
Mark [Swe.] 8 Eg 57.35N 12.35 E
Marka 31 Lh 1.43N 44.46 E
Markakol, Ozero- 19 If 48.45N 85.50 E
Markam (Gartog) 27 Gf 29.32N 98.33 E
Markaryd 7 Ch 56.26N 13.36 E
Markazi [3] 23 Hb 35.30N 51.30 E
Marken 12 Hb 52.27N 5.05 E
Markerwaard 12 Hb 52.31N 5.15 E
Market Deeping 12 Bb 52.40N 0.18W
Market Harborough 9 Mi 52.29N 0.55W
Markham, Mount- 66 Kg 82.51 S 161.21 E
Markham Bay 42 Kd 63.30N 71.40W
Markham River 59 Ja 6.35 S 146.25 E
Marki 10 Rd 52.20N 21.07 E
Märkische Schweiz 10 Jd 52.35N 14.00 E
Markit 27 Cd 38.53N 77.35 E
Markounda 35 Bd 7.37N 16.59 E
Markovac 15 Ee 44.14N 21.06 E
Markovka 16 Ke 49.31N 39.32 E
Markovo 22 Tc 64.40N 170.25 E
Markoye 34 Fc 14.39N 0.02 E
Marksburg 12 Jd 50.16N 7.40 E
Marksville 45 Jk 31.08N 92.04W
Marktoberdorf 10 Gi 47.47N 10.37 E
Marktredwitz 10 If 50.00N 12.05 E
Markulešty 15 Lb 47.51N 28.07 E
Marl 10 De 51.39N 7.05 E
Marlagne 12 Gd 50.25N 4.40 E
Marlborough [2] 62 Ed 41.50 S 173.40 E
Marlborough [Austl.] 59 Jd 22.49 S 149.53 E
Marlborough [Guy.] 50 Gi 7.29N 58.38W
Marle 11 Je 49.44N 3.46 E
Marlin 45 Hk 31.18N 96.53W
Marlinton 44 Gf 38.14N 80.06W
Marlow [Eng.-U.K.] 12 Bc 51.34N 0.46W
Marlow [Ok.-U.S.] 45 Hi 34.39N 97.57W
Marmande 11 Gj 44.30N 0.10 E
Marmara 24 Bb 40.35N 27.33 E
Marmara, Sea of- (EN) = Marmara Denizi 5 Ig 40.40N 28.15 E
Marmara Adasi 24 Bb 40.38N 27.37 E
Marmara Denizi = Marmara, Sea of- (EN) 5 Ig 40.40N 28.15 E
Marmara Ereğlisi 15 Ki 40.58N 27.57 E
Marmara Gölü 15 Lk 38.37N 28.02 E
Marmarica (EN) = Barqah al Bahrīyah 30 Je 31.40N 24.30 E
Marmaris 23 Cb 36.51N 28.16 E
Marmelos, Rio- 54 Fe 6.08 S 61.47W
Marmion Lake 45 Kb 48.54N 91.30W
Marmolada 14 Fd 46.26N 11.51 E
Marmora 44 Ic 44.29N 77.41W
Marmore, Cascata delle- 14 Gh 42.35N 12.45 E
Marne 10 Ec 53.57N 9.00 E
Marne 5 Gf 48.49N 2.24 E
Marne [3] 11 Kf 48.55N 4.10 E
Marne à la Saône, Canal de la- 11 Kf 48.44N 4.36 E
Marne au Rhin, Canal de la- 11 Nf 48.35N 7.47 E
Mårnes 7 Dc 67.09N 14.06 E
Marneuli 16 Ni 41.29N 44.45 E
Maro 35 Bd 8.25N 18.46 E
Maro 35 Bb 19.23N 16.38 E
Maroa 54 Ec 2.43N 67.33W
Maroantsetra 31 Lj 15.27 S 49.44 E
Marokau Atoll 61 Mc 18.02 S 142.17W
Marolambo 37 Hd 20.04 S 48.08 E
Maromandia 37 Hb 14.11 S 48.06 E
Maromme 11 He 49.28N 1.02 E
Maromokotro 37 Hb 14.01 S 48.58 E
Maroni, Fleuve- 52 Ke 5.45N 53.58W
Marōnia 15 Ii 40.55N 25.31 E
Maronne 11 Hi 45.04N 1.56 E
Maroochydore 59 Ke 26.39 S 153.06 E
Maro Reef 57 Jb 25.25N 170.35W
Maros 15 Dc 46.15N 20.12 E
Maros 26 Gg 5.00 S 119.34 E
Maroua 31 Ig 10.36N 14.20 E
Marovoay 37 Hc 16.06 S 46.37 E
Marowijne River 54 Hb 5.45N 53.58W
Marqādah 24 Ie 35.44N 40.46 E
Mar Qu 27 He 31.58N 101.54 E
Marquard 37 De 28.54 S 27.28 E
Marquenterre 12 Dd 50.20N 1.41 E
Marquesas Islands (EN) = Marquises, Iles- 57 Ne 9.00 S 139.30W
Marquette 43 Jb 46.33N 87.24W
Marquion 12 Fd 50.13N 3.05 E
Marquis [Gren.] 51p Bb 12.06N 61.37W
Marquis [St.Luc.] 51k Ba 14.02N 60.55W
Marquis, Cape- 51k Ba 14.03N 60.54W
Marquise 12 Dd 50.49N 1.42 E
Marquises, Iles- = Marquesas Islands (EN) 57 Ne 9.00 S 139.30W
Marracuene 37 Ee 25.44 S 32.41 E
Marradi 14 Ff 44.04N 11.37 E
Marrah, Jabal- 30 Jg 13.04N 24.21 E
Marrak 33 Hf 16.26N 41.54 E
Marrakech 31 Ge 31.38N 8.00W
Marrakech [3] 32 Fc 32.00N 8.00W
Marrawah 59 Ih 40.56 S 144.41 E
Marree 58 Eg 29.39 S 138.04 E
Marreh, Kūh-e- 24 Oh 29.15N 52.20 E
Marrero 45 Kl 29.54N 90.07W
Marresalja 17 Mb 69.44N 66.59 E
Marresalskije Koški, Ostrova- 17 Mb 69.30N 67.10 E
Marromeu 37 Fc 18.17 S 35.56 E
Marrti 7 Gc 67.28N 28.22 E
Marrupa 37 Fb 13.12 S 37.30 E
Marsá al 'Alam 33 Fd 25.05N 34.54 E
Marsá al Burayqah 33 Cc 30.25N 19.35 E

Index Symbols

[1] Independent Nation
[2] State, Region
[3] District, County
[4] Municipality
[5] Colony, Dependency
Continent
Physical Region
Historical or Cultural Region
Mount, Mountain
Volcano
Hill
Mountains, Mountain Range
Hills, Escarpment
Plateau, Upland
Pass, Gap
Plain, Lowland
Delta
Salt Flat
Valley, Canyon
Crater, Cave
Karst Features
Depression
Polder
Desert, Dunes
Forest, Woods
Heath, Steppe
Oasis
Cape, Point
Coast, Beach
Cliff
Peninsula
Isthmus
Sandbank
Island
Atoll
Rock, Reef
Islands, Archipelago
Rocks, Reefs
Coral Reef
Well, Spring
Geyser
River, Stream
Waterfall Rapids
River Mouth, Estuary
Lake
Salt Lake
Intermittent Lake
Reservoir
Swamp, Pond
Canal
Glacier
Ice Shelf, Pack Ice
Ocean
Sea
Gulf, Bay
Strait, Fjord
Lagoon
Bank
Seamount
Tablemount
Ridge
Shelf
Basin
Escarpment, Sea Scarp
Fracture
Trench, Abyss
National Park, Reserve
Point of Interest
Recreation Site
Cave, Cavern
Historic Site
Ruins
Wall, Walls
Church, Abbey
Temple
Scientific Station
Airport
Port
Lighthouse
Mine
Tunnel
Dam, Bridge

Marsá al Uwayjah 33 Cc 30.55N 17.52 E
Marsa Ben Mehidi 13 Ji 35.05N 2.11W
Marsabit 31 Kh 2.20N 37.59 E
Marsala 14 Gm 37.48N 12.26 E
Marsá Sha'b 35 Fa 22.52N 35.47 E
Marsá Umm Ghayj 24 Fj 25.38N 34.30 E
Marsberg 10 Ee 51.27N 8.51 E
Marsciano 14 Gh 42.54N 12.20 E
Marsdiep 12 Gb 52.58N 4.45 E
Marseille=Marseilles (EN) 6 Gg 43.18N 5.24 E
Marseille-en-Beauvaisis 11 He 49.35N 1.57 E
Marseilles (EN)=Marseille 6 Gg 43.18N 5.24 E
Marshall [Ak.-U.S.] 40 Gd 61.52N 162.04W
Marshall [Ar.-U.S.] 45 Ji 35.55N 92.38W
Marshall [Il.-U.S.] 45 Mg 39.23N 87.42W
Marshall [Lbr.] 34 Cd 6.09N 10.23W
Marshall [Mn.-U.S.] 45 Hc 44.27N 95.47W
Marshall [Mo.-U.S.] 45 Jg 39.07N 93.12W
Marshall [Tx.-U.S.] 43 Ie 32.33N 94.23W
Marshall Islands 58 Hd 9.00N 168.00 E
Marshall Islands 57 Hd 9.00N 168.00 E
Marshall River 59 Hd 22.59S 136.59 E
Marshalltown 43 Ic 42.03N 92.54W
Marshfield 45 Kd 44.40N 90.10W
Marsh Harbour 47 Ic 26.33N 77.03W
Mārshinān, Kūh-e- 24 Of 32.53N 52.24 E
Marsh Island 45 Kl 29.35N 91.53W
Marsica 14 Hi 41.55N 13.35 E
Marsico Nuovo 14 Jj 40.25N 15.44 E
Marsjaty 17 Jf 60.05N 60.29 E
Marsland 45 Ee 42.29N 103.16W
Mars-la-Tour 12 He 49.06N 5.54 E
Marson 12 Gf 48.55N 4.32 E
Märsta 8 Ge 59.37N 17.51 E
Marstal 8 Dj 54.51N 10.31 E
Marstrand 8 Dg 57.53N 11.35 E
Marta 14 Fh 42.14N 11.42 E
Martaban 25 Je 16.32N 97.37 E
Martaban, Gulf of- (EN) 21 Lh 16.30N 97.00 E
Martap 34 Hd 6.54N 13.03 E
Martapura [Indon.] 26 Dg 4.19S 104.22 E
Martapura [Indon.] 26 Fg 3.25S 114.51 E
Martelange/Martelingen 12 He 49.50N 5.44 E
Martelingen/Martelange 12 He 49.50N 5.44 E
Martés, Sierra de- 13 Le 39.20N 0.57W
Martha's Vineyard 43 Mc 41.25N 70.40W
Martigny 14 Bd 46.06N 7.05 E
Martigues 11 Lk 43.24N 5.03 E
Martil 13 Gi 35.37N 5.17W
Martim Vaz, Ilhas- 52 Nh 20.30S 28.51W
Martin 13 Lc 41.18N 0.19W
Martin [Czech.] 10 Og 49.04N 18.55 E
Martin [S.D.-U.S.] 43 Gc 43.10N 101.44W
Martin [Tn.-U.S.] 44 Cg 36.21N 88.51W
Martina Franca 14 Lj 40.42N 17.20 E
Martinez de Hoz 55 Bl 35.19S 61.37W
Martinez de la Torre 48 Kg 20.04N 97.03W
Martin Garcia, Isla- 55 Cl 34.11S 58.15W
Martin Hills 66 Pg 82.04S 88.01W
Martinho Campos 55 Jd 19.20S 45.13W
Martinique 38 Mh 14.40N 61.00W
Martinique 39 Mh 14.40N 61.00W
Martinique, Canal de la-= Martinique Passage (EN) 47 Le 15.10N 61.20W
Martinique Passage 50 Fe 15.10N 61.20W
Martinique Passage (EN)= Martinique, Canal de la- 47 Le 15.10N 61.20W
Martin Lake 44 Ei 32.50N 85.55W
Martin Peninsula 66 Of 74.25S 114.10W
Martinsburg 44 If 39.28N 77.59W
Martins Ferry 44 Ge 40.07N 80.45W
Martinsville [In.-U.S.] 44 Df 39.26N 86.25W
Martinsville [Va.-U.S.] 43 Ld 36.43N 79.53W
Marton 62 Fd 40.05S 175.23 E
Martos 13 Ig 37.43N 3.58W
Martre, Lac la- 42 Fd 63.20N 118.00W
Martuk 19 Fe 50.47N 56.31 E
Martuni 16 Ni 40.06N 45.18 E
Maru 34 Gc 12.21N 6.24 E
Marud 25 Ee 18.19N 72.58 E
Marudi 26 Ff 4.11N 114.19 E
Marudu, Teluk- 26 Ge 6.45N 116.55 E
Marugame 29 Cd 34.18N 133.47 E
Maruko 29 Fc 36.19N 138.15 E
Mārūn 24 Mg 31.02N 49.36 E
Marungu, Monts- 30 Ji 7.42S 30.00 E
Maruoka 29 Ec 36.09N 136.16 E
Maruseppu 29a Ca 44.01N 143.19 E
Marutea Atoll [W.F.] 57 Ng 21.30S 135.34W
Marutea Atoll [W.F.] 57 Mf 17.00S 143.10W
Maruyama-Gawa 29 Dd 35.40N 134.50 E
Marvão 13 Ee 39.24N 7.23W
Marvast 24 Pg 30.30N 54.15 E
Marvast, Kavīr-e- 24 Pg 30.20N 54.25 E
Mårvatn 8 Cd 60.10N 8.15 E
Marv-Dasht 23 Hd 29.50N 52.40 E
Marvejols 11 Jj 44.33N 3.17 E
Marvine, Mount- 46 Jg 38.40N 111.39W
Marx 16 Od 51.42N 46.46 E
Mary 22 If 37.36N 61.50 E
Maryborough [Austl.] 58 Gg 25.32S 152.42 E
Maryborough [Austl.] 59 Ig 37.03S 143.45 E
Marydale 37 Ce 29.23S 22.05 E
Maryjskaja Oblast 19 Gh 37.15N 62.30 E
Maryland 43 Ld 39.00N 76.45W
Maryland 34 De 4.45N 8.00W
Maryport 9 Jg 54.43N 3.30W
Mary River 59 Gb 12.53S 131.38 E
Marysville [Ca.-U.S.] 46 Eg 39.09N 121.35W
Marysville [Ks.-U.S.] 45 Hg 39.51N 96.39W
Marysville [N.B.-Can.] 44 Nc 45.59N 66.35W
Marysville [Oh.-U.S.] 44 Fe 40.13N 83.22W
Marysville [Wa.-U.S.] 46 Db 48.03N 122.11W
Maryville [Mo.-U.S.] 43 Ic 40.21N 94.52W
Maryville [Tn.-U.S.] 44 Fh 35.46N 83.58W
Marzūq 31 If 25.55N 13.55 E
Marzūq, Ḩamādat- 33 Bd 26.00N 12.30 E
Marzuq, Şaḩrā'- 30 If 24.30N 13.00 E
Masachapa 49 Dh 11.47N 86.31W
Masāhim, Kūh-e- 24 Pg 30.21N 55.20 E
Masai Steppe 30 Ki 4.45S 37.00 E
Masaka 36 Fc 0.20S 31.44 E
Masākin 32 Jb 35.44N 10.35 E
Masalembo, Kepulauan- 26 Fh 5.30S 114.26 E
Masally 19 Eh 39.01N 48.40 E
Masalog, Puntan- 64b Ba 15.01N 145.41 E
Masan 27 Md 35.11N 128.24 E
Masasi 31 Kj 10.43S 38.48 E
Masaya 49 Dh 12.00N 86.10W
Masaya 47 Gf 11.58N 86.06W
Masbate 21 Oh 12.15N 123.30 E
Masbate 26 Hd 12.10N 123.35 E
Mascara 32 Hb 35.24N 0.08 E
Mascara 32 Hb 35.30N 0.15 E
Mascareignes, Iles-/ Mascarene Islands 30 Mk 21.00S 57.00 E
Mascarene Basin (EN) 3 Fk 15.00S 56.00 E
Mascarene Islands/ Mascareignes, Iles- 30 Mk 21.00S 57.00 E
Mascarene Plateau (EN) 3 Gk 10.00S 60.00 E
Mascota 48 Gg 20.32N 104.49W
Masela, Pulau- 26 Ih 8.09S 129.50 E
Maseru 31 Jk 29.28S 27.29 E
Maşfūţ 24 Qk 24.48N 56.06 E
Mashābih 24 Gj 25.37N 36.32 E
Mashan 28 Kb 45.12N 130.32 E
Mashava 37 Ed 20.02S 30.29 E
Mashhad 22 Hf 36.18N 59.36 E
Mashike 28 Pc 43.51N 141.31 E
Mashiki 29 Be 32.47N 130.50 E
Mashīz 24 Qh 29.56N 56.37 E
Mashkel 21 Ig 28.02N 63.25 E
Mashonaland North 37 Ec 17.00S 31.00 E
Mashonaland South 37 Ec 18.00S 31.00 E
Mashra' ar Raqq 35 Dd 8.25N 29.16 E
Mashū-Ko 29a Db 43.35N 144.30 E
Masiaca 48 Ed 26.45N 109.18W
Masīlah, Wādī al- 21 Hh 15.10N 51.08 E
Masi-Manimba 36 Cc 4.46S 17.55 E
Masindi 36 Fb 1.42N 31.43 E
Maşīrah, Jazīrat- 21 Hg 20.29N 58.33 E
Maşīrah, Khalīj- 21 Hh 20.15N 57.40 E
Masisi 36 Ec 1.24S 28.49 E
Masjed-Soleymān 23 Gc 31.58N 49.18 E
Mask, Lough-/Loch Measca 9 Dh 53.35N 9.20W
Maskanah 24 Hd 36.01N 38.05 E
Maskelynes, Iles- 63b Cc 16.32S 167.49 E
Maslovare 14 Lf 44.34N 17.33 E
Masoala, Cap- 30 Mj 15.59S 50.13 E
Masoala, Presqu'île de- 37 Ic 15.40S 50.12 E
Mason 45 Gk 30.45N 99.14W
Mason Bay 62 Bg 46.55S 167.45 E
Mason City 39 Je 43.09N 93.12W
Masovia (EN)= Mazowsze 5 Ie 52.40N 20.20 E
Masparro, Rio- 49 Mi 8.04N 69.26W
Masqaţ=Muscat (EN) 22 Hg 23.29N 58.33 E
Massa 14 Ef 44.01N 10.09 E
Massachusetts 43 Mc 42.15N 71.50W
Massachusetts Bay 44 Ld 42.20N 70.50W
Massaciuccoli, Lago di- 14 Eg 43.50N 10.20 E
Massafra 14 Lj 40.35N 17.07 E
Massaguet 35 Bc 12.28N 15.26 E
Massakori 35 Bc 13.00N 15.44 E
Massa Marittima 14 Eg 43.03N 10.53 E
Massangano 36 Bd 9.37S 14.17 E
Massangena 37 Ed 21.32S 32.57 E
Massapê 54 Jd 3.31S 40.19W
Massawa (EN)=Mitsiwa 31 Kg 15.37N 39.39 E
Massena 43 Mc 44.56N 74.57W
Massénya 35 Bc 11.24N 16.10 E
Masset 42 Ef 54.02N 132.09W
Masseube 11 Gk 43.26N 0.35 E
Massey Sound 42 Ia 78.00N 94.00W
Massiac 11 Ji 45.15N 3.12 E
Massiaru 8 Kg 57.52N 24.27 E
Massillon 44 Ge 40.48N 81.32W
Massinga 37 Fd 23.20S 35.22 E
Masson Island 66 Ge 66.08S 96.34 E
Massuma 36 De 14.05S 22.00 E
Mastābah 33 Ge 20.49N 39.26 E
Maštaga 16 Pi 40.32N 49.59 E
Masterton 61 Eh 40.57S 175.39 E
Mastūrah 33 Ge 23.06N 38.50 E
Masuda 27 Ne 34.40N 131.51 E
Māsūleh 24 Md 37.10N 48.59 E
Masurai, Gunung- 26 Dg 2.30S 101.51 E
Masuria (EN) 5 Ie 53.50N 21.30 E
Masurian Lakes (EN) 5 Ie 53.45N 21.45 E
Maşyāf 24 Ge 35.03N 36.21 E
Maszewo 10 Lc 53.29N 15.02 E
Matabé, Cap- 63b Cb 15.38S 166.46 E
Matabeleland North 37 Dc 19.00S 27.30 E
Matabeleland South 37 Dd 21.00S 29.30 E
Matachel 13 Ff 38.50N 6.17W
Matachewan 42 Jg 47.56N 80.39W
Matacu 55 Bc 17.21S 61.28W
Matadi 31 Ii 5.49S 13.27 E
Matador 45 Fi 34.01N 100.49W
Matagalpa 49 Eg 13.00N 85.30W
Matagalpa 39 Kh 12.53N 85.57W
Matagami 42 Jg 49.45N 77.35W
Matagami, Lac- 44 Ia 49.54N 77.32W
Mata Gassile 35 Ge 2.30N 42.16 E
Matagorda Bay 45 Hl 28.35N 96.20W
Matagorda Island 43 Hf 28.15N 96.30W
Matagorda Peninsula 45 Hl 28.32N 96.07W
Mataiea 65e Fc 17.46S 149.25W
Mataiva Atoll 57 Mf 14.53S 148.40W
Mataj 19 Hf 45.51N 78.43 E
Matak, Pulau- 26 Ef 3.18N 106.16 E
Matakana Island 62 Gb 37.35S 176.05 E
Matala 36 Ce 14.43S 15.02 E
Matalaa, Pointe- 64h Bc 13.20S 176.08W
Matale 25 Gg 7.28N 80.37 E
Mataliele 37 Df 30.24S 28.43 E
Matam 34 Cb 15.40N 13.15W
Matamey 34 Gc 13.26N 8.28 E
Matamoros [Mex.] 47 Dc 25.32N 103.15W
Matamoros [Mex.] 39 Jg 25.53N 97.30W
Matana, Danau- 26 Hg 2.28S 121.20 E
Ma'ţan as Sarra 33 De 21.41N 21.52 E
Matancita 48 De 25.09N 111.59W
Matane 42 Kg 48.51N 67.32W
Matankari 34 Fc 13.46N 4.01 E
Matanza 55 Cl 34.33S 58.35W
Matanzas 39 Kg 23.03N 81.35W
Matanzas 49 Gb 22.40N 81.10W
Matão 55 He 21.35S 48.22W
Matapalo, Cabo- 49 Fi 8.23N 83.19W
Matapan, Cape- (EN)= Tainaron, Ákra- 5 Ih 36.23N 22.29 E
Matape, Rio- 48 Dc 28.17N 110.41W
Mata Point 64k Bb 19.07S 169.50W
Matara 35 Fc 14.35N 39.28 E
Matara 25 Gg 5.56N 80.33 E
Mataram 22 Nj 8.35S 116.07 E
Mataranka 59 Gb 14.56S 133.07 E
Mataró 13 Oc 41.32N 2.27 E
Matarraña/Matarranya 13 Mc 41.14N 0.22 E
Matarranya/Matarraña 13 Mc 41.14N 0.22 E
Matasso 63b Dc 17.15S 168.25 E
Matatula, Cape- 65c Cb 14.15S 170.34W
Mataura 62 Cg 46.34S 168.44 E
Mataura 62 Cg 46.12S 168.52 E
Mata-Utu 58 Jf 13.17S 176.08W
Mata-Utu, Baie de- 64h Bb 13.19S 176.07W
Matavai 61 Gb 13.28S 172.35W
Matavera 64p Cb 21.13S 159.44W
Mataverj 65d Ab 27.10S 109.27W
Matawai 62 Gc 38.21S 177.32 E
Matawin, Réservoir- 44 Kb 46.45N 73.50W
Matawin, Rivière- 44 Kb 46.55N 72.55W
Maţāy 24 Dh 28.25N 30.46 E
Maţbakhayn 33 Hf 17.29N 41.48 E
Matca 15 Kd 45.51N 27.32 E
Matemo, Ilha- 37 Gb 12.13S 40.36 E
Matera 14 Kj 40.40N 16.36 E
Matese 14 Ii 41.25N 14.20 E
Mátészalka 10 Si 47.57N 22.20 E
Matfors 7 De 62.21N 17.02 E
Matha 11 Fi 45.52N 0.19W
Mathematicians Seamounts (EN) 47 Be 15.30N 111.00W
Matheson 44 Ga 48.32N 80.28W
Mathis 45 Hl 28.06N 97.50W
Mathrákion 15 Cj 39.46N 19.31 E
Mathura 25 Fc 27.30N 77.41 E
Mati 15 Ch 41.39N 19.34 E
Mati 26 Ie 6.57N 126.13 E
Matias Cardoso 55 Kb 14.52S 43.56W
Matias Romero 47 Ee 16.53N 95.02W
Maticora, Rio- 49 Lh 11.01N 71.09W
Matina 49 Fh 10.05N 83.17W
Matinha 54 Id 3.06S 45.02W
Māţir 32 Ib 37.03N 9.40 E
Matiyure, Rio- 50 Ci 7.36N 67.39W
Matkaselkja 8 Nc 61.57N 30.33 E
Mātmāţah 32 Ic 33.33N 9.58 E
Matnog 26 Hd 12.35N 124.05 E
Mato, Cerro- 50 Di 7.15N 65.14W
Mato, Rio- 50 Di 7.09N 65.07W
Matočkin Šar, Proliv- 19 Fa 73.30N 54.55 E
Mato Grosso 54 Gf 14.00S 56.00W
Mato Grosso [Braz.] 55 Dd 18.18S 57.20W
Mato Grosso [Braz.] 53 Kg 15.00S 59.57W
Mato Grosso, Planalto do- = Mato Grosso, Plateau of- (EN) 52 Kg 15.30S 56.00W
Mato Grosso, Plateau of- (EN) = Mato Grosso, Planalto do- 52 Kg 15.30S 56.00W
Mato Grosso do Sul 54 Hg 20.00S 55.00W
Matos Costa 55 Gh 26.27S 51.09W
Matosinhos 13 Dc 41.11N 8.42W
Matou 28 Cj 29.50N 115.32 E
Matov→Qiuxian 28 Cf 36.47N 114.30 E
Mātra 5 Hf 47.53N 19.57 E
Maţraḩ 23 Ie 23.29N 58.31 E
Matrei in Osttirol 14 Gc 47.00N 12.32 E
Maţrūḩ 31 Je 31.21N 27.14 E
Matsiatra 37 Hd 21.25S 45.33 E
Matsudo 28 Og 35.48N 139.55 E
Matsue 27 Nd 35.28N 133.04 E
Matsukawa [Jap.] 29 Gc 37.40N 140.28 E
Matsukawa [Jap.] 29 Ed 35.36N 137.53 E
Matsu Liehtao 27 Kf 26.05N 119.56 E
Matsumae 29a Bc 41.26N 140.07 E
Matsumae-Hantō 29a Bc 41.40N 140.15 E
Matsumoto 27 Od 36.14N 137.58 E
Matsuo 29 Gb 39.58N 141.02 E
Matsu-Ōminato 29a Bc 41.16N 141.09 E
Matsusaka 28 Ng 34.34N 136.32 E
Matsushima 29 Gb 38.22N 141.04 E
Matsutō 29 Ec 36.31N 136.33 E
Matsuura 29 Ae 33.22N 129.42 E
Matsuyama 22 Pf 33.50N 132.45 E
Matsuzaki 29 Fd 34.44N 138.45 E
Mattagami Lake 44 Gb 47.57N 81.35W
Mattagami River 42 Jf 50.43N 81.30W
Mattawa 42 Jg 46.19N 78.42W
Matterhorn [Eur.] 14 Bd 45.58N 7.39 E
Matterhorn [Nv.-U.S.] 46 Hf 41.49N 115.23W
Matthew, Ile- 57 Ig 22.20S 171.20 E
Matthews Ridge 54 Fb 7.30N 60.10W
Matthew Town 47 Jd 20.57N 73.40W
Maţţī, Sabkhat- 35 Ia 23.30N 52.00 E
Mattighofen 14 Hb 48.06N 13.09 E
Mattoon 45 Lg 39.29N 88.22W
Matua, Ostrov- 20 Kg 48.00N 153.10 E
Matucana 54 Cf 11.51S 76.24W
Matuku Island 61 Ec 19.10S 179.46 E
Matundu 36 Db 4.21N 23.40 E
Matundu 36 Gd 8.50S 39.30 E
Maturin 53 Je 9.45N 63.11W
Matvejev Kurgan 16 Kf 47.34N 38.55 E
Maua 37 Fb 13.52S 37.09 E
Maubeuge 11 Jd 50.17N 3.58 E
Ma-ubin 25 Je 16.44N 95.39 E
Maudheimvidda 66 Bf 74.00S 8.00W
Maud Seamount (EN) 66 Ce 65.00S 2.35 E
Maués 54 Gd 3.24S 57.42W
Maués, Rio- 54 Gd 3.22S 57.44W
Mau Escarpment 36 Gc 0.40S 36.02 E
Maug Islands 57 Fb 20.01N 145.13 E
Maui Island 57 Lb 20.45N 156.20W
Mauke Island 57 Lg 20.09S 157.23W
Mau Kyun 25 Jf 12.45N 98.20 E
Mauldre 12 Df 48.59N 1.49 E
Maule 56 Fe 35.45S 72.15W
Mauléon 11 Fh 46.55N 0.45W
Mauléon-Licharre 11 Fk 43.14N 0.53W
Maullín 56 Ff 41.38S 73.37W
Maumee 44 Fe 41.34N 83.39W
Maumere 26 Hh 8.37S 122.14 E
Maun 31 Jj 19.58S 23.26 E
Maun 14 If 44.26N 14.55 E
Mauna Kea 57 Lc 19.50N 155.28W
Maunaloa 65a Db 21.08N 157.13W
Mauna Loa 65a Fd 19.28N 155.36W
Maunath 25 Gc 25.40N 82.38 E
Maunawili 65a Db 21.21N 157.47W
Maunga Roa 64p Bb 21.13S 159.48W
Maungdaw 25 Id 20.49N 92.22 E
Maunoir, Lac- 42 Fc 67.30N 125.00W
Maupihaa Atoll (Mopelia, Atoll-) 57 Lf 16.50S 153.55W
Maupin 46 Ed 45.11N 121.05W
Maupiti, Ile- 57 Lf 16.27S 152.15W
Maurepas, Lake- 45 Kk 30.15N 90.30W
Maures 11 Mk 43.16N 6.23 E
Mauriac 11 Ii 45.13N 2.20 E
Maurice, Lake- 59 Ge 29.30S 131.00 E
Maurienne 11 Mi 45.13N 6.30 E
Mauritania (EN)= Mūrītāniyā 31 Fg 20.00N 12.00W
Mauriti 54 Ke 7.23S 38.46W
Mauritius 30 Mk 20.17S 57.33 E
Mauritius 31 Mj 18.00S 57.40 E
Mauron 11 Df 48.05N 2.18W
Maurs 11 Ij 44.43N 2.12 E
Mauston 45 Ke 43.48N 90.05W
Mauthausen 14 Ib 48.14N 14.31 E
Mauzé-sur-le-Mignon 11 Fh 46.12N 0.40W
Mavinga 36 Df 15.47S 20.24 E
Mavita 37 Ec 19.32S 33.09 E
Mavrovoúni [Grc.] 15 Fj 39.37N 22.47 E
Mavrovoúni [Grc.] 15 Gh 41.07N 23.08 E
Mawchi 25 Je 18.49N 97.09 E
Mawei 27 Kf 26.02N 119.30 E
Mawlaik 25 Id 23.38N 94.25 E
Mawlamyine 22 Le 16.30N 97.38 E
Mawqaq 24 Ii 27.25N 41.08 E
Mawr, Wādī- 23 Ff 15.41N 42.42 E
Mawson 66 Fe 67.36S 62.53 E
Mawson Coast 66 Fe 67.40S 63.30 E
Mawson Escarpment 66 Ff 73.05S 68.10 E
Maxcanú 47 Fd 20.35N 90.01W
Maxixe 37 Fd 23.51S 35.21 E
Maxwell Bay 42 Ib 74.32N 89.00W
May, Isle of- 9 Ke 56.10N 2.30W
Maya, Pulau- 26 Eg 1.10S 109.35 E
Mayaguana Island 47 Jd 22.23N 72.57W
Mayaguana Passage 49 Kb 22.32N 73.15W
Mayagüez 47 Ke 18.12N 67.09W
Mayahi 34 Gc 13.58N 7.40 E
Mayama 36 Bc 3.51S 14.54 E
Mayāmey 24 Pd 36.24N 55.42 E
Maya Mountains 47 Ge 16.40N 88.50W
Mayapan 47 Gd 20.38N 89.27W
Mayari 49 Jc 20.40N 75.41W
Maybell 45 Bf 40.31N 108.05W
Maychew 35 Fc 12.46N 39.34 E
Mayd 35 Hc 10.57N 47.06 E
Maydān 24 Ke 34.55N 45.37 E
Maydena 59 Jh 42.55S 146.30 E
Maydī 23 Ff 16.18N 42.48 E
Mayen 10 Df 50.20N 7.13 E
Mayenne 11 Ff 48.18N 0.37W
Mayenne 11 Fg 47.30N 0.32W
Mayenne 11 Ff 48.05N 0.40W
Mayfa'ah 35 Hc 14.16N 47.35 E
Mayfield 44 Cg 36.44N 88.38W
May Glacier 66 Ie 67.00S 130.00 E
Mayi He 28 Jb 45.52N 128.46 E
Maymyo 25 Jd 22.02N 96.28 E
Maynas 54 Dd 3.00S 75.00W
Mayo 39 Fc 63.35N 135.54W
Mayo/Muigheo 9 Dh 53.50N 9.30W
Mayo, Mountains of- 9 Dg 54.05N 9.30W
Mayo, Rio- 48 Ed 26.45N 109.47W
Mayo Darlé 34 Hd 6.30N 11.55 E
Mayo-Kébbi 35 Ad 9.18N 13.33 E
Mayo-Kébbi 35 Bd 10.00N 15.30 E
Mayoko 36 Bc 2.18S 12.49 E
Mayon, Mount- 21 Oh 13.15N 123.41 E
Mayor, Puig-/Major, Puig- 13 Oe 39.48N 2.48 E
Mayor Island 62 Gb 37.15S 176.15 E
Mayor Pablo Lagerenza 56 Ha 19.58S 60.45W
Mayotte 31 Lj 12.50S 45.10 E
Mayotte/Mahoré 31 Lj 12.50S 45.10 E
May Pen 49 Id 17.58N 77.14W
Mayraira Point 26 Hc 18.39N 120.51 E
Mayran, Laguna de- 48 He 25.45N 102.45W
Mayreau Island 51n Bb 12.39N 61.23W
May-sur-Orne 12 Be 49.06N 0.22W
Maysville 44 Ff 38.39N 83.46W
Mayumba [Gabon] 31 Ii 3.25S 10.39 E
Mayumba [Zaire] 36 Ed 7.16S 27.03 E
Mayum La 27 De 30.35N 82.27 E
Mayville 44 Hd 42.15N 79.32W
Mayyit, Al Baḩr al-=Dead Sea (EN) 21 Ff 31.30N 35.30 E
Mazabuka 36 Ef 15.51S 27.46 E
Mazagão 54 Hd 0.07S 51.17W
Mazamet 11 Ik 43.30N 2.24 E
Māzandarān 23 Hb 36.00N 54.00 E
Māzandarān, Daryā-ye-= Caspian Sea (EN) 5 Lg 42.00N 50.30 E
Mazar 27 Cd 36.27N 77.03 E
Mazara del Vallo 14 Gm 37.39N 12.35 E
Mazār-e Sharīf 22 If 36.42N 67.06 E
Mazarrón, Golfo de- 13 Kg 37.30N 1.18W
Mazartag 27 Dd 38.29N 80.50 E
Mazaruni River 54 Gb 6.25N 58.38W
Mazatenango 47 Ff 14.32N 91.30W
Mazatlán 39 Ig 23.13N 106.25W
Mažeikiai/Mažejkjaj 7 Fh 56.20N 22.22 E
Mažejkjaj/Mažeikiai 7 Fh 56.20N 22.22 E
Mazhafah, Jabal- 24 Fh 28.48N 34.57 E
Mazhūr, 'Irq al- 24 Ji 27.25N 43.55 E
Mazinga 51c Ab 17.29N 62.58W
Mazirbe 8 Jg 57.40N 22.10 E
Mazoe 37 Ec 17.30S 30.58 E
Mazoe 30 Kj 16.32S 33.25 E
Mazomeno 36 Ec 4.55S 27.13 E
Mazong Shan 27 Gc 41.33N 97.10 E
Mazowsze 10 Qd 52.40N 20.20 E
Mazowsze=Masovia (EN) 5 Ie 52.40N 20.20 E
Mazsalaca 8 Kg 57.45N 24.59 E
Mazunga 37 Dd 21.44S 29.52 E
Mazurskie, Pojezierze- 10 Qc 53.40N 21.00 E
Mazzarino 14 Im 37.18N 14.13 E
Mba 63d Ab 17.32S 177.42 E
Mbabane 31 Kk 26.18S 31.07 E
Mbabo, Tchabal- 34 Hd 7.16N 12.09 E
Mbacké 34 Bc 14.48N 15.55W
Mbaéré 35 Be 3.47N 17.31 E
Mbaïki 31 Ih 3.53N 18.00 E
Mbakaou 34 Hd 6.19N 12.49 E
Mbakaou, Barrage de- 34 Hd 6.25N 13.00 E
Mbala 31 Ki 8.50S 31.22 E
Mbalam 34 He 2.13N 13.49 E
Mbale 31 Kh 1.05N 34.10 E
Mbali 35 Be 4.27N 18.20 E
Mbalmayo 34 He 3.31N 11.30 E
Mbam 30 Ih 4.24N 11.17 E
Mbamba Bay 36 Fe 11.17S 34.46 E
Mbandaka 31 Ih 0.04N 18.16 E
Mbanga 34 Ge 4.30N 9.34 E
Mbanika 63a Dc 9.05S 159.12 E
M'banza Congo 36 Bd 6.16S 14.15 E
Mbanza-Ngungu 31 Ii 5.35S 14.47 E
Mbarangandu 36 Gd 8.57S 37.24 E
Mbarara 36 Fc 0.36S 30.38 E
Mbari 35 Ce 4.34N 22.43 E
Mbatiki 63d Bb 17.46S 179.08 E
Mbava 63a Cb 7.49S 156.37 E
Mbé 34 Hd 7.51N 13.36 E
Mbengga 63d Bc 18.23S 178.08 E
Mbengwi 34 Hd 6.01N 10.00 E
Mbéré 35 Bd 9.07N 16.26 E
Mbeya 31 Ki 8.54S 33.27 E
Mbeya 36 Fd 8.00S 33.30 E
Mbi 35 Be 4.28N 18.07 E
Mbigou 36 Bc 1.53S 11.56 E
Mbinda 31 Ii 2.07S 12.52 E
Mbinga 36 Ge 10.56S 35.01 E
Mbingué 34 Dc 10.00N 5.54W
Mbini 34 Ge 1.34N 9.37 E
Mbini 34 He 1.30N 10.00 E
Mbini 30 Ih 1.30N 10.30 E
Mboki 35 Dd 5.19N 25.58 E
Mbokonimbeti 63a Ec 8.57S 160.05 E
Mbomo 36 Bb 0.24N 14.44 E
Mbomou=Bomu (EN) 35 Cd 5.30N 23.30 E
Mbomou=Bomu (EN) 30 Jh 4.08N 22.26 E
Mborokua 63a Dc 9.02S 158.44 E
Mbour 34 Bc 14.24N 16.58W
Mbout 32 Ef 16.01N 12.35W
Mbozi 36 Fd 9.02S 32.56 E
Mbrés 35 Bd 6.40N 19.48 E
M'Bridge 36 Bd 7.14S 12.52 E
Mbua 63d Bb 16.48S 178.37 E
Mbuji-Mayi 31 Ji 6.09S 23.33 E
Mbulo 63a Dc 8.46S 158.21 E
Mbulu 36 Gc 3.51S 35.32 E
Mburucuyá 55 Ci 28.03S 58.14W
Mbutha 63d Bb 16.39S 179.51 E
Mbuyuni 36 Gd 7.23S 36.32 E
Mbwemburu 36 Gd 9.29S 39.39 E
Mcalester 43 He 34.56N 95.46W
Mcensk 19 De 53.17N 36.32 E
M'Chedallah 13 Qh 36.22N 4.16 E
Mcherrah 32 Gd 27.00N 4.30W
Mchinga 36 Gd 9.44S 39.42 E
Mchinji 36 Fe 13.48S 32.54 E
Mdandu 36 Fd 9.09S 34.42 E
M'Daourouch 14 Bn 36.05N 7.49 E
Mdennah 32 Gd 25.00N 4.50W
Mdiq 13 Gi 35.41N 5.19W
Mead 44 Fa 49.29N 83.50W
Mead, Lake- 40 Ed 36.05N 114.25W
Meade 40 Hb 70.50N 156.25W
Meade 45 Fh 37.17N 100.20W
Meade Peak 46 Je 42.30N 111.15W
Meadow Lake 42 Gf 54.07N 108.20W
Meadville 44 Ge 41.38N 80.10W
Me-akan-Dake 29a Cb 43.23N 143.59 E
Mealhada 13 Dd 40.22N 8.27W

Index Symbols

1 Independent Nation
2 State, Region
3 District, County
4 Municipality
5 Colony, Dependency
Continent
Physical Region
Historical or Cultural Region
Mount, Mountain
Volcano
Hill
Mountains, Mountain Range
Hills, Escarpment
Plateau, Upland
Pass, Gap
Plain, Lowland
Delta
Salt Flat
Valley, Canyon
Crater, Cave
Karst Features
Depression
Polder
Desert, Dunes
Forest, Woods
Heath, Steppe
Oasis
Cape, Point
Coast, Beach
Cliff
Peninsula
Isthmus
Sandbank
Island
Atoll
Rock, Reef
Islands, Archipelago
Rocks, Reefs
Coral Reef
Well, Spring
Geyser
River, Stream
Waterfall Rapids
River Mouth, Estuary
Lake
Salt Lake
Intermittent Lake
Reservoir
Swamp, Pond
Canal
Glacier
Ice Shelf, Pack Ice
Ocean
Sea
Gulf, Bay
Strait, Fjord
Lagoon
Bank
Seamount
Tablemount
Ridge
Shelf
Basin
Escarpment, Sea Scarp
Fracture
Trench, Abyss
National Park, Reserve
Point of Interest
Recreation Site
Cave, Cavern
Historic Site
Ruins
Wall, Walls
Church, Abbey
Temple
Scientific Station
Airport
Port
Lighthouse
Mine
Tunnel
Dam, Bridge

Mealy Mountains	42	Lf	53.20N	59.30W
Meama	65b	Ba	19.45S	174.34W
Méan, Havelange-	12	Hd	50.22N	5.20 E
Meander Reef	26	Ge	8.09N	119.14 E
Meander River	42	Fe	59.02N	117.42W
Meanguera, Isla-	49	Dg	13.12N	87.43W
Mearim, Rio-	52	Lf	3.04S	44.35W
Meath/An Mhí	9	Gh	53.35N	6.40W
Meaux	11	If	48.57N	2.52 E
Mecca (EN)=Makkah	22	Fg	21.27N	39.49 E
Mechara	35	Gd	8.34N	40.28 E
Mechelen/Maasmechelen	12	Hd	50.57N	5.40 E
Mechelen/Malines	11	Kc	51.02N	4.29 E
Mecheraa-Asfa	13	Ni	35.24N	1.03 E
Mecheria	32	Gc	33.33N	0.17W
Mechernich	12	Id	50.36N	6.39 E
Mechongué	55	Cn	38.09S	58.13W
Mecidiye	15	Ji	40.38N	26.32 E
Mecitözü	24	Fb	40.31N	35.19 E
Mecklemburgischer Höhenrücken	10	Ic	53.40N	12.10 E
Mecklenburg	10	Hc	53.30N	12.00 E
Mecklenburger Bucht	10	Hb	54.20N	11.40 E
Mecklenburger Schweiz	10	Ic	53.45N	12.35 E
Mecoacán, Laguna-	48	Mh	18.20N	93.10W
Meconta	37	Fb	14.59S	39.50 E
Mecsek	10	Oj	46.10N	18.18 E
Mecubúri	37	Gb	14.10S	40.31 E
Mecúfi	37	Gb	13.17S	40.33 E
Mecula	37	Fb	12.05S	37.39 E
Médala	32	Ff	15.30N	5.37W
Medan	22	Li	3.35N	98.40 E
Médanos [Arg.]	56	He	38.50S	62.41W
Médanos [Arg.]	55	Ck	33.24S	59.05W
Medanosa, Punta-	56	Gg	48.06S	65.55W
Mede	14	Ce	45.06N	8.44 E
Médéa	32	Hb	36.16N	2.45 E
Médéa	32	Hb	36.20N	3.25 E
Medebach	12	Kc	51.12N	8.43 E
Medellin	26	Hd	11.08N	123.58 E
Medellín	53	Ie	6.15N	75.35W
Medelpad	8	Gb	62.35N	16.15 E
Medemblik	12	Hb	52.46N	5.06 E
Medenica	10	Tg	49.21N	23.45 E
Mederdra	32	Df	16.54N	15.40W
Medetzız	24	Fd	37.25N	34.40 E
Medford [Or.-U.S.]	39	Ge	42.19N	122.52W
Medford [Wi.-U.S.]	45	Kd	45.09N	90.20W
Medgidia	15	Le	44.15N	28.17 E
Medi	35	Ed	5.06N	30.44 E
Media Luna, Arrecife de la-	49	Ff	15.13N	82.36W
Medianeira	55	Eg	25.17S	54.05W
Mediaş	15	Hc	46.10N	24.21 E
Medical Lake	46	Gc	47.34N	117.41W
Medicine Bow	46	Lf	41.54N	106.12W
Medicine Bow Mountains	46	Lf	41.10N	106.25W
Medicine Butte	46	Jf	41.29N	110.48W
Medicine Hat	39	Hd	50.03N	110.40W
Medicine Lake	46	Mb	48.28N	104.24W
Medicine Lodge	45	Gh	37.17N	98.35W
Međimurje	14	Kd	46.25N	16.30 E
Medina (EN)=Al Madīnah [Sau.Ar.]	22	Fg	24.28N	39.36 E
Medina Az-Zahra	13	Hg	37.52N	4.50W
Medinaceli	13	Jc	41.10N	2.26W
Medina del Campo	13	Hc	41.18N	4.55W
Medina de Rioseco	13	Gc	41.53N	5.02W
Medina-Sidonia	13	Gh	36.27N	5.55W
Medininkai/Medininkaj	8	Kj	54.32N	25.46 E
Medinīpur	25	Hd	22.26N	87.20 E
Medio, Arroyo del-	55	Bk	33.16S	60.15W
Mediterranean Sea (EN)= Akdeniz	5	Hh	35.00N	20.00 E
Mediterranean Sea (EN)= Khatikhon, Yam-	5	Hh	35.00N	20.00 E
Mediterranean Sea (EN)= Méditerranée, Mer-	5	Hh	35.00N	20.00 E
Mediterranean Sea (EN)= Mediterraneo, Mar-	5	Hh	35.00N	20.00 E
Mediterranean Sea (EN)= Mediterráneo, Mar-	5	Hh	35.00N	20.00 E
Mediterranean Sea (EN)= Mesoyéios Thálassa	5	Hh	35.00N	20.00 E
Mediterranean Sea (EN)= Mutawassiţ, Al Baḩr al-	5	Hh	35.00N	20.00 E
Méditerranée, Mer-= Mediterranean Sea (EN)	5	Hh	35.00N	20.00 E
Mediterráneo, Mar-= Mediterranean Sea (EN)	5	Hh	35.00N	20.00 E
Mediterraneo, Mar-= Mediterranean Sea (EN)	5	Hh	35.00N	20.00 E
Medje	36	Eb	2.25N	27.18 E
Medjerda, Monts de la-	32	Ib	36.35N	8.15 E
Mednogorsk	19	Fe	51.26N	57.40 E
Medny, Ostrov-	20	Lf	54.40N	167.50 E
Médoc	11	Fi	45.00N	1.00W
Mêdog	27	Gf	29.18N	95.27 E
Médouneu	36	Bb	1.01N	10.48 E
Medveđa	15	Eg	42.51N	21.36 E
Medvedica	5	Kf	49.35N	42.41 E
Medvedica	7	Ih	57.05N	37.31 E
Medvednica	14	Je	45.55N	15.58 E
Medvedok	7	Mh	57.24N	50.06 E
Medvenka	16	Jd	51.27N	36.08 E
Medveži, Ostrova-=Bear Islands (EN)	21	Sb	70.52N	161.26 E
Medvežjegorsk	19	Dc	62.56N	34.29 E
Medway	12	Cc	51.23N	0.31 E
Medzilaborce	10	Rg	49.16N	21.55 E
Meekatharra	58	Cg	26.36S	118.29 E
Meeker	45	Cf	40.02N	107.55W
Meerane	10	If	50.51N	12.28 E
Meerbusch	12	Ic	51.16N	6.40 E
Meerut	25	Fc	28.59N	77.42 E
Meeteetse	46	Kd	44.09N	108.52W
Mefarlane, Lake-	59	Hf	32.00S	136.40 E
Mega [Eth.]	31	Kh	4.03N	38.20 E
Mega [Indon.]	26	Jg	0.41S	131.53 E
Mega, Pulau-	26	Dg	4.00S	101.02 E
Megalo	35	Gd	6.52N	40.47 E
Megálon Khorion	15	Km	36.27N	27.21 E
Megalópolis	15	Fl	37.24N	22.08 E
Megálo Sofráno	15	Jm	36.04N	26.25 E
Meganísion	15	Dk	38.38N	20.43 E
Meganom, Mys-	16	Ig	44.48N	35.05 E
Mégara	15	Gk	38.00N	23.21 E
Megève	11	Mi	45.52N	6.37 E
Meghalaya	25	Ic	26.00N	91.00 E
Megid	33	Dd	28.35N	22.10 E
Megion	19	Hc	61.00N	76.15 E
Megiscane, Lac-	44	Ia	48.30N	76.04W
Megri	16	Oj	38.55N	46.15 E
Mehadia	15	Fe	44.54N	22.22 E
Mehaigne	12	Hd	50.32N	5.13 E
Meharry, Mount-	59	Dd	23.00S	118.35 E
Mehdia	13	Ni	35.25N	1.45 E
Mehdīshahr	24	Oe	35.44N	53.22 E
Mehedinţi	15	Fe	44.30N	23.00 E
Mehetia, Ile-	61	Lc	17.52S	148.03W
Mehrabān	24	Lc	38.05N	47.08 E
Mehrān	24	Pi	26.52N	55.24 E
Mehrān	24	Lf	33.07N	46.10 E
Mehrenga	7	Je	63.17N	41.20 E
Mehrīz	24	Pg	31.35N	54.28 E
Mehtar Lām	23	Lc	34.39N	70.10 E
Mehun-sur-Yèvre	11	Ig	47.09N	2.13 E
Meia Meia	36	Gd	5.49S	35.48 E
Meia Ponte, Rio-	54	Ig	18.32S	49.36W
Meiganga	34	Hd	6.31N	14.18 E
Meighen	42	Ha	79.55N	99.00W
Meihekou → Hailong	27	Mc	42.32N	125.37 E
Meiktila	25	Jd	20.52N	95.52 E
Meilü → Wuchuan	27	Jg	21.28N	110.44 E
Meinerzhagen	12	Jc	51.07N	7.39 E
Meiningen	10	Gf	50.33N	10.25 E
Meio, Rio do-	55	Ja	13.20S	44.34W
Meisenheim	12	Je	49.43N	7.40 E
Meishan [China]	27	He	30.05N	103.48 E
Meishan [China]	28	Ei	31.06N	119.43 E
Meishan → Jinzhai	28	Ci	31.40N	115.52 E
Meißen	10	Je	51.09N	13.29 E
Meißner	10	Fe	51.12N	9.50 E
Meitan (Yiquan)	27	If	27.48N	107.32 E
Meixian	27	Kg	24.21N	116.07 E
Meiyukou	28	Bd	40.01N	113.08 E
Méjean, Causse-	11	Jj	44.16N	3.22 E
Mejillones	56	Fb	23.06S	70.27W
Mékambo	36	Bb	1.01N	13.56 E
Mekdela	35	Fc	11.28N	39.20 E
Mekele=Meqele (EN)	31	Kg	13.30N	39.28 E
Mékhé	34	Bb	15.07N	16.38W
Mekherrhane, Sebkha-	30	Hf	26.22N	1.20 E
Meknès	32	Fc	33.00N	5.30W
Meknès	31	Ge	33.54N	5.32W
Mekong (EN)=Lancang Jiang	21	Mh	10.15N	105.55 E
Mekong (EN)=Mae Nam Khong	21	Mh	10.15N	105.55 E
Mekong (EN)=Mékôngk	21	Mh	10.15N	105.55 E
Mekong (EN)=Mènam Khong	21	Mh	10.15N	105.55 E
Mekong Delta (EN)	21	Mi	10.20N	106.40 E
Mekongga, Gunung-	26	Hg	3.35S	121.15 E
Mékôngk=Mekong (EN)	21	Mh	10.15N	105.55 E
Mekoryuk	40	Fd	60.23N	166.12W
Mékrou	34	Fc	12.24N	2.49 E
Mel, Ilha do-	55	Hg	25.31S	48.20W
Melaab	13	Ni	35.43N	1.20 E
Mēladēn	35	Hc	10.25N	49.52 E
Melaka	22	Mi	2.12N	102.15 E
Melaka, Selat-=Malacca, Strait of- (EN)	21	Mi	2.30N	101.20 E
Melamo, Cabo-	30	Lj	14.24S	40.49 E
Melanesia	57	Hf	13.00S	164.00 E
Melanesian Basin (EN)	3	Jj	0.05S	160.35 E
Melawi	26	Ff	0.05N	111.29 E
Melbourne [Ar.-U.S.]	45	Kh	36.04N	91.54W
Melbourne [Austl.]	58	Fh	37.49S	144.58 E
Melbourne [Eng.-U.K.]	12	Ab	52.49N	1.26W
Melbourne [Fl.-U.S.]	43	Kf	28.05N	80.37W
Melbourne-Dandenong	59	Jg	37.59S	145.12 E
Melchor Múzquiz	47	Dc	27.53N	101.31W
Melchor Ocampo	48	Hi	17.59N	102.11W
Meldorf	10	Fb	54.05N	9.05 E
Mele, Capo-	14	Cg	43.57N	8.10 E
Melekeiok	64a	Bc	7.29N	134.38 E
Melela	37	Fc	17.04S	38.36 E
Melenci	15	Dd	45.31N	20.19 E
Melenki	19	Ed	55.23N	41.42 E
Meleto Dağı	24	Ic	38.35N	41.32 E
Meleuz	19	Fe	52.58N	55.59 E
Mélèzes, Rivière aux-	42	Ke	57.00N	69.00W
Melfa	14	Hi	41.30N	13.35 E
Melfi [Chad]	35	Bc	11.04N	17.56 E
Melfi [It.]	14	Jj	41.00N	15.39 E
Melfort	42	Hf	52.52N	104.36W
Melgaço	54	Hd	1.47S	50.44W
Melibocus	10	Eg	49.42N	8.40 E
Melilla	31	Ge	35.19N	2.58W
Melincué, Laguna-	55	Bk	33.42S	61.28W
Melipilla	56	Fd	33.42S	71.13W
Melita	45	Fb	49.16N	101.00W
Meliti	15	Ei	40.50N	21.35 E
Melito di Porto Salvo	14	Jm	37.55N	15.47 E
Melito di Porto Salvo, Punta di-	14	Jm	37.57N	15.45 E
Melitopol	6	Jf	46.50N	35.22 E
Melk	14	Jb	48.13N	15.19 E
Mella	14	Ee	45.13N	10.13 E
Mellakou	13	Ni	35.15N	1.14 E
Mellanfryken	8	Ee	59.40N	13.15 E
Melle [Fr.]	11	Fh	46.13N	0.08W
Melle [Ger.]	12	Kb	52.12N	8.21 E
Mellen	45	Kc	46.20N	90.40W
Mellerud	7	Cg	58.42N	12.28 E
Mellish Reef	59	Lc	17.25S	155.50 E
Mellish Seamount (EN)	57	Ia	34.00N	178.15 E
Mellit	35	Dc	14.08N	25.33 E
Mělník	10	Kf	50.21N	14.30 E
Melnik	15	Gh	41.31N	23.24 E
Melo	53	Ki	32.22S	54.11W
Melo, Río-	55	De	21.25S	57.55W
Melrhir, Chott-	30	He	34.20N	6.20 E
Melrose	46	Id	45.38N	112.40W
Melsungen	10	Fe	51.08N	9.33 E
Meltaus	7	Fc	66.54N	25.22 E
Melton Constable	12	Db	52.51N	1.02 E
Melton Mowbray	9	Mi	52.46N	0.53W
Meluco	37	Fb	12.33S	39.37 E
Meluli	37	Fc	16.28S	39.44 E
Melun	11	If	48.32N	2.40 E
Melville	38	Ib	75.15N	110.00W
Melville	46	Na	50.55N	102.48W
Melville, Cape-	59	Ib	14.10S	144.30 E
Melville, Lake-	42	Lf	53.42N	59.30W
Melville Bay	59	Hb	12.05S	136.45 E
Melville Bay (EN)=Melville Bugt	67	Od	75.35N	62.30W
Melville Bugt=Melville Bay (EN)	67	Od	75.35N	62.30W
Melville Hills	42	Fc	69.20N	123.00W
Melville Island	57	Ef	11.40S	131.00 E
Melville Peninsula	38	Kc	68.00N	84.00W
Melville Sound	42	Gc	68.05N	107.30W
Melvin, Lough-	9	Eg	54.25N	8.10W
Mélykút	10	Pj	46.13N	19.23 E
Memaliaj	15	Ci	40.20N	19.58 E
Memambetsu	29a	Db	43.55N	144.11 E
Memba, Baia de-	37	Gb	14.11S	40.35 E
Memberamo	26	Kg	1.28S	137.52 E
Memboro	26	Gh	9.22S	119.32 E
Mēmele	8	Kh	56.24N	24.10 E
Memmert	10	Cc	53.39N	6.53 E
Memmingen	10	Gi	47.59N	10.10 E
Mempawan	26	Ef	0.22N	108.58 E
Memphis	33	Fd	29.52N	31.15 E
Memphis [Mo.-U.S.]	45	Jf	40.28N	92.10W
Memphis [Tn.-U.S.]	39	Jf	35.08N	90.03W
Memphis [Tx.-U.S.]	45	Fi	34.44N	100.32W
Memrut Dağı	24	Jc	38.40N	42.12 E
Memuro	28	Qc	42.55N	143.03 E
Memuro-Dake	29a	Cb	42.52N	142.45 E
Mena	35	Gd	5.30N	41.06 E
Mena [Ar.-U.S.]	45	Ii	34.35N	94.15W
Mena	19	De	51.33N	32.14 E
Menabe	30	Lk	20.00S	44.40 E
Menai Strait	9	Ih	53.12N	4.12W
Ménaka	31	Hg	15.55N	2.26 E
Mènam Khong=Mekong (EN)	21	Mh	10.15N	105.55 E
Menangalaku	26	Gh	9.36S	119.01 E
Menard	45	Gk	30.55N	99.47W
Menawashei	35	Dc	12.40N	25.01 E
Menčul, Gora-	10	Th	48.16N	23.49 E
Mendala, Puncak-	26	Lg	4.44S	140.20 E
Mendanau, Pulau-	26	Eg	2.51S	107.26 E
Mendanha	55	Kd	18.06S	43.30W
Mende	11	Jj	44.31N	3.30 E
Mendebo	30	Kh	6.50N	39.40 E
Mendelejevsk	7	Mi	55.57N	52.22 E
Menden (Sauerland)	10	De	51.26N	7.48 E
Mendes	13	Mi	35.39N	0.52 E
Méndez	48	Je	25.07N	98.34W
Mendi [Eth.]	35	Fd	9.48N	35.05 E
Mendi [Pap.N.Gui.]	60	Ci	6.10S	143.40 E
Mendig	12	Jd	50.22N	7.16 E
Mendip Hills	9	Kj	51.15N	2.40W
Mendocino	46	Dg	39.19N	123.48W
Mendocino, Cape-	38	Ge	40.25N	124.25W
Mendocino Fracture Zone (EN)	3	Lf	40.00N	145.00W
Mendota [Ca.-U.S.]	46	Eh	36.45N	120.23W
Mendota [Il.-U.S.]	45	Lf	41.33N	89.07W
Mendoza	53	Ji	32.54S	68.50W
Mendoza	56	Gd	34.30S	68.30W
Mené, Landes du-	11	Df	48.15N	2.32W
Mene de Mauroa	49	Lh	10.43N	71.01W
Mene Grande	54	Db	9.49S	70.56W
Menemen	24	Bc	38.36N	27.04 E
Menen/Menin	11	Jd	50.48N	3.07 E
Meneng Point	64e	Bb	0.33S	166.57 E
Meneses	55	Dj	30.53S	56.30W
Ménez Hom	11	Bf	48.13N	4.16W
Menfi	14	Gm	37.36N	12.58 E
Mengcheng	27	Ke	33.11N	116.30 E
Mengdingjie	27	Gg	23.31N	99.07 E
Menggala	26	Eg	4.28S	105.17 E
Mengíbar	13	Ig	37.58N	3.48W
Mengjin	28	Bg	34.50N	112.26 E
Mengla	27	Hg	21.30N	101.35 E
Menglangba → Lancang	27	Gg	22.37N	99.57 E
Menglian	27	Gg	22.20N	99.27 E
Mengoun Huizu Zizhixian	28	De	38.04N	117.06 E
Mengyin	28	Dg	35.42N	117.56 E
Mengzi	22	Mg	23.23N	103.34 E
Menihek Lakes	42	Kf	54.00N	66.30W
Menin/Menen	11	Jd	50.48N	3.07 E
Menindee	59	If	32.24S	142.26 E
Menindee Lake	59	If	22.00S	142.23 E
Meningie	59	Hg	35.42S	139.20 E
Menjapa, Gunung-	26	Gf	1.05N	116.05 E
Menno	45	He	43.14N	97.34W
Menoíkion Óros	15	Gh	41.11N	23.48 E
Menominee	44	Dc	45.07N	87.39W
Menongue	31	Ij	14.40S	17.39 E
Menor, Mar-	13	Lg	37.43N	0.48W
Menorca=Minorca (EN)	5	Gg	40.00N	4.00 E
Menor do Araguaia, Braço-ou Javaes	54	He	9.50S	50.12W
Mentana	14	Gh	42.02N	12.38 E
Mentasta Lake	40	Kd	62.55N	143.45W
Mentawai, Kepulauan-= Mentawai Islands (EN)	21	Lj	2.00S	99.30 E
Mentawai, Selat-	21	Lj	2.00S	99.30 E
Mentawai Islands (EN)= Mentawai, Kepulauan-	21	Lj	2.00S	99.30 E
Menton	11	Nk	43.47N	7.30 E
Mentougou	28	De	39.56N	116.02 E
Menyuan	27	Hd	37.30N	101.35 E
Menzelinsk	7	Mi	55.45N	53.09 E
Menzies	59	Ee	29.41S	121.02 E
Menzies, Mount-	66	Ff	73.30S	61.50 E
Meon	12	Ad	50.49N	1.15W
Meoqui	47	Cc	28.17N	105.29W
Meponda	37	Eb	13.25S	34.52 E
Meppel	11	Mb	52.42N	6.11 E
Meppen	10	Dd	52.41N	7.19 E
Meqele(EN)=Mekele	31	Kg	13.30N	39.28 E
Mê Qu	27	He	33.58N	102.10 E
Mequinensa, Pantà de-/ Mequinenza, Embalse de-	13	Lc	41.15N	0.02W
Mequinenza, Embalse de-/ Mequinensa, Pantà de-	13	Lc	41.15N	0.02W
Mera	14	Dd	46.11N	9.25 E
Merabello, Gulf of- (EN) = Merabéllou, Kólpos-	15	In	35.14N	25.47 E
Merabéllou, Kólpos- = Merabello, Gulf of- (EN)	15	In	35.14N	25.47 E
Merak	26	Eh	5.56S	106.00 E
Meråker	7	Ce	63.26N	11.45 E
Méralab	63b	Db	14.27S	168.03 E
Meramangye, Lake-	59	Ge	28.25S	132.15 E
Meran / Merano	14	Fd	46.40N	11.09 E
Merano / Meran	14	Fd	46.40N	11.09 E
Meratus, Pegunungan-	26	Gg	2.45S	115.40 E
Merauke	58	Fe	8.28S	140.20 E
Mercadal	13	Qe	39.59N	4.05 E
Mercato Saraceno	14	Gg	43.57N	12.12 E
Merced	43	Cd	37.18N	120.29W
Mercedario, Cerro-	52	Ii	31.59S	70.14W
Mercedes [Arg.]	56	Id	34.39S	59.27W
Mercedes [Arg.]	56	Ic	29.12S	58.05W
Mercedes [Arg.]	53	Ji	33.40S	65.30W
Mercedes [Ur.]	53	Ki	33.16S	58.01W
Merchants Bay	42	Lc	67.10N	62.50W
Merchtem	12	Gd	50.58N	4.14 E
Mercury Islands	62	Fb	36.35S	175.50 E
Mercy, Cape -	42	Ld	64.56N	63.40W
Mercy Bay	42	Fb	74.15N	118.10W
Meredith, Cape-	56	Hh	52.12S	60.38W
Meredith, Lake-	45	Fi	35.36N	101.42W
Meredoua	32	Hd	25.20N	2.05 E
Merefa	19	Df	49.51N	36.00 E
Merelbeke	12	Fd	51.00N	3.45 E
Merenga	20	Kd	61.43N	156.05 E
Mergui	22	Lh	12.26N	98.36 E
Mergui Archipelago	21	Lh	12.00N	98.00 E
Méri	34	Hc	10.47N	14.06 E
Meriç	15	Jh	41.11N	26.25 E
Meriç	24	Bb	40.52N	26.12 E
Mérida	54	Db	8.30N	71.10W
Mérida [Mex.]	39	Kg	20.58N	89.37W
Mérida [Sp.]	13	Ff	38.55N	6.20W
Mérida [Ven.]	53	Ie	8.36N	71.08W
Merida, Cordillera de-	52	Ie	8.40N	71.00W
Meridian	39	Kf	32.22N	88.42W
Mérig	63b	Cb	14.19S	167.48 E
Mérignac	11	Fj	44.50N	0.38W
Merikarvia	7	Ef	61.51N	21.30 E
Merín, Laguna-	56	Jd	32.45S	52.50W
Meringur	59	If	34.24S	141.29 E
Merir Island	57	Ed	4.19N	132.19 E
Merizo	64c	Bb	13.16N	144.40 E
Merke	18	Ic	42.52N	73.12 E
Merkem, Houthulst-	12	Ed	50.57N	2.51 E
Merkine/Merkiné	8	Kj	54.07N	24.20 E
Merkiné/Merkine	8	Kj	54.07N	24.20 E
Merkis/Merkys	7	Fi	54.10N	24.11 E
Merksem, Antwerpen-	12	Gc	51.15N	4.27 E
Merksplas	12	Gc	51.22N	4.52 E
Merkys/Merkis	7	Fi	54.10N	24.11 E
Meroe	35	Eb	16.56N	33.59 E
Meroe	35	Eb	16.05N	33.55 E
Merouane, Chott-	32	Ic	34.00N	6.02 E
Merredin	59	Df	31.29S	118.16 E
Merrick	9	If	55.08N	4.29W
Merrill	43	Jb	45.11N	89.41W
Merriman	45	Fe	42.55N	101.42W
Merritt	42	Ff	50.07N	120.47W
Merritt Island	43	Kf	28.21N	80.42W
Merritt Reservoir	45	Fe	42.35N	100.55W
Mersa Fatma	35	Gc	14.53N	40.19 E
Mersa Teklay	35	Fb	17.25N	38.45 E
Mersea Island	12	Cc	51.47N	0.57 E
Merseburg	10	He	51.22N	12.00 E
Mers el Kebir	13	Li	35.44N	0.43W
Mersey	9	Kh	53.25N	3.00W
Merseyside	9	Kh	53.30N	3.00W
Mersin → Içel	23	Db	36.48N	34.38 E
Mersing	26	Df	2.26N	103.50 E
Mers-les-Bains	12	Dd	50.04N	1.23 E
Mērsrags/Mersrags	8	Jg	57.19N	23.01 E
Mersrags/Mērsrags	8	Jg	57.19N	23.01 E
Merta	25	Ec	26.39N	74.02 E
Merta Road	25	Ec	26.43N	73.55 E
Mertert	12	Ie	49.42N	6.29 E
Merthyr Tydfil	9	Jj	51.46N	3.23W
Merti	36	Gb	1.04N	38.40 E
Mértola	13	Eg	37.38N	7.40W
Mertule Maryam	35	Fc	10.50N	38.15 E
Mertvy Kultuk, Sor-	16	Rg	45.30N	53.40 E
Mertz Glacier	66	Je	67.40S	144.45 E
Meru	36	Gb	0.03N	37.39 E
Méru	11	Ie	49.14N	2.08 E
Meru, Mount-	36	Gc	3.14S	36.45 E
Merure	55	Fb	15.33S	53.05W
Merville	12	Ed	50.38N	2.38 E
Merzifon	23	Ea	40.53N	35.29 E
Merzig	10	Cg	49.27N	6.38 E
Meša	7	Li	55.34N	49.24 E
Mesa [Az.-U.S.]	39	Hf	33.25N	111.50W
Mesa [Co.-U.S.]	45	Bg	39.14N	108.08W
Mesabi Range	45	Jc	47.30N	92.50W
Mesagne	14	Lj	40.34N	17.48 E
Mescalero	45	Dj	33.09N	105.46W
Meščera=Moscow Basin	5	Kd	55.00N	40.30 E
Meschede	10	Ee	51.21N	8.17 E
Mescit Dağı	24	Ib	40.22N	41.11 E
Meščovsk	16	Ib	54.19N	35.18 E
Mesegon	64d	Bb	7.09N	151.55 E
Mesfinto	35	Fc	13.28N	37.23 E
Me-Shima	28	Jh	32.01N	128.25 E
Meshkīnshahr	24	Lc	38.24N	47.40 E
Mesima	14	Jl	38.30N	15.55 E
Mesjagutovo	17	Ii	55.35N	58.20 E
Meskiana	14	Bo	35.38N	7.40 E
Meskiana, Oued-	14	Bo	35.48N	7.53 E
Meslo	35	Fd	6.22N	39.50 E
Mesnil-Val, Criel-sur-Mer-	12	Dd	50.03N	1.20 E
Mesola	14	Gf	44.55N	12.14 E
Mesolóngion	15	Ek	38.22N	21.26 E
Mesopotamia	52	Kh	30.00S	58.00W
Mesopotamia (EN)	23	Fc	34.00N	44.00 E
Mesoyéios Thálassa= Mediterranean Sea (EN)	5	Hh	35.00N	20.00 E
Mesquite [Nv.-U.S.]	46	Hh	36.48N	114.04W
Mesquite [Tx.-U.S.]	45	Hj	32.46N	96.36W
Mesra	13	Mi	35.50N	0.10 E
Messaad	32	Hc	34.10N	3.30 E
Messalo	30	Lj	11.40S	40.46 E
Messará, Órmos-	15	Ho	35.00N	24.40 E
Messina [It.]	6	Hh	38.11N	15.34 E
Messina [S.Afr.]	31	Kk	22.23S	30.00 E
Messina, Strait of- (EN) = Messina, Stretto di-	5	Hh	38.15N	15.35 E
Messina, Stretto di- = Messina, Strait of- (EN)	5	Hh	38.15N	15.35 E
Messíni	15	El	37.15N	21.50 E
Messíni	15	Fl	37.03N	22.01 E
Messiniakós Kólpos	15	Fm	36.45N	22.10 E
Messojaha	20	Cc	67.52N	77.27 E
Mesta	15	Hi	40.51N	24.44 E
Mestecăniş, Pasul-	15	Ib	47.28N	25.20 E
Mesters Vig	41	Jd	72.15N	24.20W
Mestia	16	Mh	43.03N	42.43 E
Mestre, Espigão-	54	If	12.30S	46.00W
Mestre, Venezia-	14	Ge	45.29N	12.14 E
Mesuji	26	Eg	4.08S	105.52 E
Meta	54	Dc	3.30N	73.00W
Meta, Río-	52	Je	6.12N	67.28W
Meta Incognita Peninsula	38	Mc	62.40N	68.00W
Metairie	45	Kl	29.59N	90.09W
Metaliferi, Munţii-	15	Fc	46.10N	22.50 E
Metallifere, Colline-	14	Eg	43.10N	10.55 E
Metán	56	Hc	25.29S	64.57W
Metangula	37	Eb	12.43S	34.49 E
Metaponto	14	Kj	40.20N	16.50 E
Metauro	14	Hg	43.50N	13.03 E
Metautu	65c	Ba	13.57S	171.54W
Meteghan	44	Nc	44.11N	66.10W
Metelen	12	Jb	52.09N	7.12 E
Metéora	15	Ej	39.43N	21.40 E
Meteor Seamount (EN)	30	Hm	48.00S	8.30 E
Meteor Trench (EN)	3	Do	55.00S	27.00 E
Méthana	15	Gl	37.35N	23.23 E
Methánon, Khersónisos-	15	Gl	37.36N	23.22 E
Methven	62	De	43.38S	171.38 E
Methwold	12	Cb	52.31N	0.33 E
Metković	14	Lg	43.03N	17.39 E
Metlakatla	40	Me	55.08N	131.35W
Metlika	14	Je	45.39N	15.19 E
Metlili Chaamba	32	Hc	32.16N	3.38 E
Metmárfag	32	Ed	26.26N	13.26W
Metohija	15	Dg	42.40N	20.27 E
Metro	26	Eh	5.05S	105.20 E
Metropolis	45	Lh	37.09N	88.44W
Métsovon	15	Ej	39.46N	21.11 E
Métsovon, Zigós- = Métsovon Pass (EN)	15	Ej	39.47N	21.15 E
Métsovon Pass (EN) = Métsovon, Zigós-	15	Ej	39.47N	21.15 E
Mettet	12	Gd	50.19N	4.40 E
Mettingen	12	Jb	52.19N	7.47 E
Mettlach	12	Ie	49.30N	6.36 E
Mettmann	12	Ic	51.15N	6.58 E
Metu	31	Kh	8.20N	35.38 E
Metuje	10	Lf	50.20N	15.55 E
Metz	6	Gf	49.08N	6.10 E
Metzervisse	12	Ie	49.19N	6.17 E
Meu	11	Ef	48.02N	1.47W
Meulaboh	26	Cf	4.09N	96.08 E
Meulan	12	De	49.01N	1.54 E
Meulebeke	12	Fd	50.57N	3.17 E
Meureudu	26	Ce	5.16N	96.16 E
Meurthe	11	Mf	48.47N	6.09 E
Meurthe-et-Moselle	11	Mf	48.35N	6.10 E
Meuse	11	Lf	49.00N	5.30 E
Meuse	5	Ge	51.49N	5.01 E
Meuse (EN)=Maas	5	Ge	51.49N	5.01 E
Meuse, Côtes de-	11	Le	49.10N	5.30 E
Meuzenti	35	Bb	18.14N	17.06 E
Mexia	45	Hk	31.41N	96.29W
Mexiana, Ilha	54	Ic	0.00	49.35W
Mexicali	39	Hf	32.40N	115.29W
Mexicana, Altiplanicie-= Mexico, Plateau of- (EN)	38	Ig	25.30N	104.00W
Mexican Hat	46	Kh	37.09N	109.52W
Mexicanos, Laguna de los-	48	Fc	28.09N	106.57W
Mexico	45	Kg	39.10N	91.53W
México	39	Ig	23.00N	102.00W

Index Symbols

Independent Nation	Historical or Cultural Region	Pass, Gap	Depression	Coast, Beach	Rock, Reef	Waterfall Rapids	Canal	Lagoon	Escarpment, Sea Scarp	Historic Site	Port
State, Region	Mount, Mountain	Plain, Lowland	Polder	Cliff	Islands, Archipelago	River Mouth, Estuary	Glacier	Bank	Fracture	Ruins	Lighthouse
District, County	Volcano	Delta	Desert, Dunes	Peninsula	Rocks, Reefs	Lake	Ice Shelf, Pack Ice	Seamount	Trench, Abyss	Wall, Walls	Mine
Municipality	Hill	Salt Flat	Forest, Woods	Isthmus	Coral Reef	Salt Lake	Ocean	Tablemount	National Park, Reserve	Church, Abbey	Tunnel
Colony, Dependency	Mountains, Mountain Range	Valley, Canyon	Heath, Steppe	Sandbank	Well, Spring	Intermittent Lake	Sea	Ridge	Point of Interest	Temple	Dam, Bridge
Continent	Hills, Escarpment	Crater, Cave	Oasis	Island	Geyser	Reservoir	Gulf, Bay	Shelf	Recreation Site	Scientific Station	
Physical Region	Plateau, Upland	Karst Features	Cape, Point	Atoll	River, Stream	Swamp, Pond	Strait, Fjord	Basin	Cave, Cavern	Airport	

México [2] 47 Ee 19.20N 99.30W
México, Golfo de- = Mexico, Gulf of- (EN) 38 Kg 25.00N 90.00W
Mexico, Gulf of- (EN) = México, Golfo de- 38 Kg 25.00N 90.00W
Mexico, Plateau of- (EN) = Mexicana, Altiplanicie- 38 Ig 25.30N 104.00W
Mexico Basin (EN) 3 Bg 25.00N 92.00W
Mexico City (EN) = Ciudad de México 39 Jh 19.24N 99.09W
Meybod 24 Of 32.16N 53.59 E
Meydān-e Gel 24 Ph 29.04N 54.50 E
Meyïsti 15 Mm 36.08N 29.34 E
Meyisti 15 Mm 36.09N 29.40 E
Meymaneh 22 If 35.55N 64.47 E
Meymeh 24 Nf 33.27N 51.10 E
Meymeh 24 Lf 32.05N 47.16 E
Meža 7 Hi 55.43N 31.30 E
Mezcala 48 Ji 17.56N 99.37W
Mezcalapa, Rio- 48 Mh 18.36N 92.39W
Mezdra 15 Gf 43.09N 23.42 E
Meždurečenski 19 Gd 59.36N 65.53 E
Meždušarski, Ostrov- 19 Fa 71.20N 53.00 E
Mèze 11 Jk 43.25N 3.36 E
Mezen 5 Kb 66.00N 43.59 E
Mezen 6 Kb 65.50N 44.13 E
Mézenc, Mont- 11 Kj 44.55N 4.11 E
Meženin 10 Sc 53.07N 22.29 E
Mezenskaja Guba 5 Kb 66.40N 43.45 E
Mezenskaja Pižma 7 Ld 64.30N 48.32 E
Mežgorje 10 Th 48.30N 23.37 E
Mežica 14 Id 46.31N 14.52 E
Mézidon-Canon 12 Be 49.05N 0.04W
Mézin 11 Gj 44.03N 0.16 E
Mezőberény 10 Rj 46.49N 21.02 E
Mezőcsát 10 Qi 47.49N 20.55 E
Mezőföld 10 Oj 46.55N 18.35 E
Mezőkovácsháza 10 Qj 46.24N 20.55 E
Mezőkövesd 10 Qi 47.49N 20.35 E
Mezőtúr 10 Qi 47.00N 20.38 E
Mežozerny 17 Ii 54.10N 59.25 E
Mežpjanje 7 Ki 55.25N 45.00 E
Mezquital 48 Gf 23.29N 104.23W
Mezquital, Rio- 48 Gf 22.55N 104.54W
Mezquitic 48 Hf 22.23N 103.41W
Mgači 20 Jf 51.02N 142.18 E
Mglin 16 Hc 53.04N 32.53 E
Mhow 25 Fd 22.33N 75.46 E
Miahuatlán de Porfirio Díaz 48 Ki 16.20N 96.36W
Miajadas 13 Ge 39.09N 5.54W
Miaméré 35 Bd 9.02N 19.55 E
Miami [Az.-U.S.] 46 Jj 33.24N 110.52W
Miami [Fl.-U.S.] 39 Kg 25.46N 80.12W
Miami [Ok.-U.S.] 43 Id 36.53N 94.53W
Miami Beach 43 Kf 25.47N 80.08W
Miānābād 24 Qd 37.02N 57.27 E
Miāndowāb 23 Gb 36.58N 46.06 E
Miandrivazo 37 Hc 19.30S 45.28 E
Mianduhe 27 Lb 49.12N 121.09 E
Miāneh 23 Gb 37.26N 47.42 E
Miang, Khao- 25 Ke 17.42N 101.01 E
Miangas, Pulau- 26 Ie 5.35N 126.35 E
Mianning 27 Hf 28.31N 102.10 E
Miānwāli 25 Eb 32.35N 71.33 E
Mianyang 27 He 31.23N 104.49 E
Mianyang (Xiantaozhen) 28 Bi 30.22N 113.27 E
Miaodao Qundao 27 Ld 38.10N 120.45 E
Miao'er Shan 27 Jf 25.50N 110.22 E
Miao Ling 27 If 26.05N 108.00 E
Miarinarivo 37 Hc 18.56S 46.54 E
Miass 19 Gd 55.01N 60.06 E
Miass 19 Gd 56.06N 64.30 E
Miasskoje 17 Ji 55.15N 61.55 E
Miasteczko Krajeńskie 10 Nc 53.06N 17.01 E
Miastko 10 Mb 54.01N 17.00 E
Michael, Mount- 59 Ja 6.25S 145.20 E
Michajlova Island 66 Ge 66.30S 85.00 E
Michalovce 10 Rh 48.46N 21.55 E
Michelstadt 12 Le 49.41N 9.01 E
Miches 49 Md 18.59N 69.03W
Michigan [2] 43 Jc 44.00N 85.00W
Michigan, Lake- 38 Ke 44.00N 87.00W
Michigan City 43 Jc 41.43N 86.54W
Michipicoten Bay 44 Eb 47.55N 84.56W
Michipicoten Island 42 Ig 47.45N 85.45W
Michoacán [2] 47 De 19.10N 101.50W
Michów 10 Se 51.32N 22.19 E
Mico, Rio- 49 Eg 12.11N 84.16W
Micoud 51k Bb 13.50N 60.54W
Micronesia 57 Gc 11.00N 159.00 E
Micronesia, Federated States of- [5] 58 Gd 6.30N 152.00 E
Mičurin 15 Kg 42.10N 27.51 E
Mičurinsk 6 Ke 52.54N 40.31 E
Midai, Pulau- 26 Ef 3.00N 107.47 E
Midar 32 Gc 34.57N 3.32W
Mid-Atlantic Ridge (EN) 3 Di 0.00 20.00W
Middelburg [Neth.] 11 Jc 51.30N 3.37 E
Middelburg [S.Afr.] 37 Cf 31.30S 25.00 E
Middelburg [S.Afr.] 37 De 25.47S 29.28 E
Middelfart 7 Bi 55.30N 9.45 E
Middelharnis 12 Gc 51.45N 4.12 E
Middelkerke 12 Ec 51.11N 2.49 E
Middelkerke-Westende 12 Ec 51.10N 2.46 E
Middle Alkali Lake 46 Ef 41.28N 120.04W
Middle America Trench (EN) 3 Mh 15.00N 95.00W
Middle Andaman 25 If 12.30N 92.50 E
Middle Atlas (EN) = Moyen Atlas 30 Ge 33.30N 4.30W
Middlebury 44 Kc 44.01N 73.10W
Middle Caicos 49 Lc 21.47N 71.43W
Middle Fork Feather River 46 Eg 38.47N 121.36W
Middle Island 37b Ab 9.22S 46.21 E
Middle Loup River 45 Gf 41.17N 98.23W
Middlemarch 62 Df 45.30S 170.07 E
Middle Reef 63a Ee 12.35S 160.30 E
Middlesboro 43 Kd 36.36N 83.43W
Middlesbrough 9 Lg 54.35N 1.14W
Middlesex 49 Ce 17.02N 88.31W
Middlesex 12 Bc 51.35N 0.10W
Middlesex 9 Mj 51.30N 0.05W
Middleton 40 Je 59.25N 146.25W
Middleton Reef 57 Gg 29.30S 159.10 E
Middletown [Ct.-U.S.] 44 Ke 41.33N 72.39W
Middletown [N.Y.-U.S.] 44 Je 41.26N 74.26W
Middletown [Oh.-U.S.] 44 Ef 39.31N 84.25W
Midelt 32 Gc 32.41N 4.45W
Mid Glamorgan [3] 9 Jj 51.35N 3.35W
Midhordland 8 Ad 60.15N 5.55 E
Midhurst 12 Bd 50.59N 0.44W
Midi, Canal du- 5 Gg 43.36N 1.25 E
Midi de Bigorre, Pic du- 11 Gl 42.56N 0.08 E
Midi d'Ossau, Pic du- 11 Fl 42.51N 0.26W
Mid-Indian Basin (EN) 3 Gj 10.00S 80.00 E
Mid-Indian Ridge (EN) 3 Gj 3.00S 75.00 E
Midland [Mi.-U.S.] 43 Kc 43.37N 84.14W
Midland [Ont.-Can.] 42 Jh 44.45N 79.53W
Midland [S.D.-U.S.] 45 Fd 44.04N 101.10W
Midland [Tx.-U.S.] 43 Ge 32.00N 102.05W
Midlands [3] 37 Dc 19.00S 30.00 E
Midlands 9 Li 52.40N 1.50W
Midleton/Mainistir na Corann 9 Ej 51.55N 8.10W
Midnapore → Medinīpur 25 Hd 22.26N 87.20 E
Midongy du Sud 37 Hd 23.34N 47.01 E
Midou 11 Fk 43.54N 0.30W
Midouze 11 Fk 43.48N 0.51W
Mid-Pacific Mountains (EN) 3 Jg 20.00N 170.00 E
Midway Islands [5] 58 Jb 28.13N 177.22W
Midway Islands 57 Jb 28.13N 177.22W
Midwest 46 Le 43.25N 106.16W
Midwest City 45 Hi 35.27N 97.24W
Midyat 24 Id 37.25N 41.23 E
Midžor 5 Ig 43.24N 22.40 E
Miechów 10 Qf 50.23N 20.01 E
Miedwie, Jezioro- 10 Kc 53.15N 14.55 E
Międzychód 10 Ld 52.36N 15.53 E
Międzylesie 10 Mf 50.10N 16.40 E
Międzyrzec Podlaski 10 Se 52.00N 22.47 E
Międzyrzecz 10 Ld 52.27N 15.34 E
Międzyrzecze Łomżyńskie 10 Rd 52.45N 21.45 E
Miehikkälä 8 Ld 60.40N 27.42 E
Mie Ken [2] 28 Ng 34.35N 136.25 E
Miekojärvi 7 Fc 66.36N 24.23 E
Mielan 11 Gk 43.26N 0.19 E
Mielec 10 Rf 50.18N 21.25 E
Mielno 10 Mb 54.16N 16.01 E
Mien 8 Fh 56.25N 14.50 E
Mier 48 Jd 26.26N 99.09W
Miercurea Ciuc 15 Ic 46.21N 25.48 E
Mieres 13 Ga 43.15N 5.46W
Miersig 15 Ec 46.53N 21.51 E
Mier y Noriega 48 If 23.25N 100.07W
Miesbach 10 Hi 47.47N 11.50 E
Mieso 35 Gd 9.15N 40.45 E
Mifune 29 Be 32.43N 130.48 E
Migang Shan 27 Id 35.32N 106.13 E
Miguel Alamán, Presa- 48 Kh 18.13N 96.32W
Miguel Auza 48 He 24.18N 103.25W
Miguel Hidalgo, Presa- 48 Ed 26.40N 108.45W
Miha Chakaja → Senaki 19 Eg 42.17N 42.02 E
Mihăileşti 15 Ie 44.20N 25.54 E
Mihail Kogălniceanu 15 Le 44.22N 28.27 E
Mihajlov 19 De 54.16N 39.03 E
Mihajlovgrad 15 Gf 43.25N 23.13 E
Mihajlovgrad [2] 15 Gf 43.25N 23.13 E
Mihajlovka 18 Hc 43.01N 71.31 E
Mihajlovka 19 Ee 50.05N 43.15 E
Mihajlovsk 17 Ih 56.29N 59.07 E
Mihalıççık 24 Dc 39.52N 31.30 E
Mihara 29 Cd 34.24N 133.05 E
Mihara-Yama 29 Fd 34.43N 139.23 E
Mi He 28 Ef 37.12N 119.10 E
Mihonoseki 29 Cd 35.34N 133.18 E
Miho-Wan 29 Cd 35.30N 133.20 E
Miiraku 29 Ae 32.45N 128.40 E
Mijaly 16 Re 48.54N 53.50 E
Mijares/Millars 13 Le 39.55N 0.01W
Mijdaḥah 35 Hc 14.00N 48.26 E
Mijdrecht 12 Gb 52.12N 4.52 E
Mijirtein (EN) = Majërtën 30 Lh 9.00N 50.00 E
Mikasa 28 Pc 43.20N 141.40 E
Mikata 29 Dd 35.34N 135.54 E
Miki 29 Dd 34.17N 134.07 E
Mikínai = Mycenae (EN) 15 Fl 37.43N 22.45 E
Mikindani 36 Ge 10.17S 40.07 E
Mikkeli [2] 7 Ge 62.00N 27.30 E
Mikkeli/Sankt Michel 6 Ic 61.41N 27.15 E
Mikomoto-Jima 29 Fd 34.34N 138.56 E
Mikonoš 15 Il 37.27N 25.23 E
Mikonos 15 Il 37.27N 25.20 E
Mikonou, Stenón- 15 Il 37.30N 25.20 E
Mikrá Préspa, Límni- 15 Ei 40.45N 21.06 E
Mikre 15 Hf 43.02N 24.31 E
Mikró Sofráno 15 Jm 36.05N 26.24 E
Mikulov 10 Mh 48.49N 16.39 E
Mikumi 36 Gd 7.24S 36.59 E
Mikun 19 Fc 62.21N 50.05 E
Mikuni 29 Ec 36.13N 136.09 E
Mikuni-Sanmyaku 28 Of 36.55N 138.40 E
Mikuni-Tōge 29 Fc 36.46N 138.50 E
Mikuni-Yama 29 Dd 35.21N 134.01 E
Mikura-Jima 27 Oe 33.50N 139.35 E
Milaca 45 Jd 45.45N 93.39W
Miladummadulu Atoll 25a Ba 6.15N 73.15 E
Milagro 54 Cd 2.07S 79.36W
Milåjerd 24 Me 34.37N 49.12 E
Milan [Mo.-U.S.] 45 Jf 40.12N 93.07W
Milan [Tn.-U.S.] 44 Ch 35.55N 88.46W
Milan (EN) = Milano 6 Gf 45.28N 9.12 E
Milange 37 Fc 16.05S 35.47 E
Milano = Milan (EN) 6 Gf 45.28N 9.12 E
Milâs 24 Bd 37.19N 27.47 E
Milazzo 14 Jl 38.13N 15.14 E
Milazzo, Capo di- 14 Jl 38.16N 15.14 E
Milazzo, Golfo di- 14 Jl 38.15N 15.20 E
Milbank 43 Hb 45.13N 96.38W
Mildenhall 12 Cb 52.21N 0.31 E
Mildura 58 Fh 34.12S 142.09 E
Mile 27 Hg 24.28N 103.26 E
Mile 35 Gc 11.08N 40.55 E
Miléai 15 Gj 39.20N 23.09 E
Miles 58 Gg 26.40S 150.11 E
Miles City 43 Fb 46.25N 105.51W
Milet = Miletus (EN) 15 Kl 37.30N 27.16 E
Miletus (EN) = Milet 15 Kl 37.30N 27.16 E
Milevec 15 Fg 42.34N 22.27 E
Milevsko 10 Kg 49.27N 14.22 E
Milford 46 Ig 38.24N 113.01W
Milford Haven 9 Hj 51.44N 5.02W
Milford Lake 45 Hg 39.15N 97.00W
Milford Sound 61 Ch 44.40S 167.55 E
Milford Sound 62 Bf 44.35S 167.50 E
Milgis 36 Gb 1.48N 38.06 E
Milḥ, Baḥr al- 23 Fc 32.40N 43.35 E
Milḥ, Ra's al- 33 Ec 31.55N 25.02 E
Miliana 13 Oh 36.17N 2.14 E
Mili Atoll 57 Id 6.08N 171.55 E
Milicz 10 Ne 51.32N 17.17 E
Milkovo 20 Kf 54.43N 158.43 E
Milk River 43 Eb 49.09N 112.05W
Milk River 46 Ib 49.09N 112.05W
Milkūh 23 Jc 32.45N 61.55 E
Mill 42 Jd 63.57N 78.00W
Millars/Mijares 13 Le 39.55N 0.01W
Millau 11 Jj 44.06N 3.05 E
Milledgeville 44 Fi 33.04N 83.14W
Mille Lacs, Lac des - 42 Ig 48.50N 90.30W
Mille Lacs Lake 43 Ib 46.15N 93.40W
Millen 44 Gi 32.48N 81.57W
Miller [Nb.-U.S.] 45 Gf 40.57N 99.26W
Miller [S.D.-U.S.] 45 Gd 44.31N 98.59W
Millerovo 19 Ef 48.52N 40.25 E
Miller Seamount (EN) 40 Kf 53.30N 144.20W
Millerton 62 Dd 41.38S 171.52 E
Millevaches, Plateau de- 11 Ii 45.45N 2.11 E
Millicent 59 Ig 37.36S 140.22 E
Millington 44 Ch 35.20N 89.54W
Millinocket 44 Mc 45.39N 68.43W
Mill Island 66 He 65.30S 100.40 E
Millmerran 59 Ke 27.52S 151.16 E
Mills Lake 42 Fd 61.28N 118.15W
Millstatt 14 Hd 46.48N 13.35 E
Millville 44 Jf 39.24N 75.02W
Millwood Lake 45 Jj 33.45N 94.00W
Milne Land 41 Jd 71.20N 27.30W
Milo 30 Gg 11.04N 9.14W
Milolii 65a Fd 19.11N 155.55W
Milos 15 Hm 36.45N 24.26 E
Milos = Milos (EN) 15 Hm 36.41N 24.25 E
Milos (EN) = Milos 15 Hm 36.41N 24.25 E
Milparinka 59 Ie 29.44S 141.53 E
Miltenberg 10 Fg 49.42N 9.15 E
Milton [Fl.-U.S.] 44 Dj 30.38N 87.03W
Milton [N.Z.] 62 Cg 46.07S 169.58 E
Milton-Freewater 46 Fd 45.56N 118.23W
Milton Keynes 9 Mi 52.03N 0.42W
Miltou 35 Bc 10.14N 17.26 E
Milumbe, Monts- 36 Ed 8.00S 27.30 E
Miluo 28 Bj 28.51N 113.05 E
Miluo Jiang 27 Jf 28.51N 112.59 E
Milwaukee 39 Ke 43.02N 87.55W
Milwaukee Depth (EN) 3 Do 55.10S 26.00W
Milwaukee Seamounts (EN) 57 Ia 32.28N 171.55 E
Milwaukie 46 Dd 45.27N 122.38W
Mimi-Gawa 29 Be 32.20N 131.37 E
Mimizan 11 Ej 44.12N 1.14W
Mimoň 10 Kf 50.40N 14.44 E
Mimongo 36 Bc 1.38S 11.39 E
Mimoso 55 Hb 15.10S 48.05W
Mîna 13 Mi 35.58N 0.31 E
Mina [Mex.] 48 Id 26.01N 100.32W
Mina [Nv.-U.S.] 46 Fg 38.24N 118.07W
Mina, Cerro- 49 Ki 8.21N 73.10W
Mīnā' Abd Allāh 24 Mh 29.01N 48.10 E
Mīnā' al Aḥmadī 24 Mh 29.04N 48.09 E
Mīnāb 24 Qi 27.09N 57.05 E
Mīnāb 24 Qi 27.01N 56.53 E
Mīnā' Barānīs 33 Ge 23.55N 35.28 E
Minahassa = Minahassa Peninsula (EN) 21 Oi 1.00N 124.35 E
Minahassa Peninsula (EN) = Minahassa 21 Oi 1.00N 124.35 E
Minakuchi 29 Ed 34.59N 136.11 E
Minamata 28 Kh 32.13N 130.24 E
Minami-Daitō-Jima 27 Nf 25.50N 131.15 E
Minami-furano 29a Cb 43.10N 142.32 E
Minami-Iō-Jima 60 Cc 24.14N 141.28 E
Minami-kayabe 29a Bc 41.53N 141.01 E
Minami-Tori-Shima = Marcus Island (EN) 57 Gb 26.32N 142.09 E
Minas [Cuba] 49 Ic 21.29N 77.37W
Minas [Indon.] 26 Df 0.50N 101.29 E
Minas [Ur.] 53 Ki 34.23S 55.14W
Minas de Ríotinto 13 Fg 37.42N 6.35W
Minas Gerais [2] 54 Jg 18.00S 44.30W
Mīnā' Su'ūd 24 Mh 28.44N 48.24 E
Minatitlán [Mex.] 47 Fe 17.59N 94.31W
Minatitlán [Mex.] 48 Gh 19.22N 104.04W
Minaya 13 Je 39.17N 2.19W
Minbu 25 Id 20.09N 94.53 E
Minbya 25 Id 20.22N 93.16 E
Minchinmávida, Volcan- 56 Ff 42.49S 72.28W
Mincio 14 Ee 45.04N 10.59 E
Mindanao 21 Oi 8.00N 125.00 E
Mindanao Sea 21 Oi 9.15N 123.40 E
Mindel 10 Gh 48.31N 10.23 E
Mindelheim 10 Gh 48.03N 10.29 E
Mindelo 31 Eg 16.53N 25.00W
Minden [Ger.] 10 Ed 52.17N 8.55 E
Minden [La.-U.S.] 45 Jj 32.37N 93.17W
Minden [Nb.-U.S.] 45 Gf 40.30N 98.57W
Mindif 34 Hc 10.24N 14.26 E
Mindoro 21 Oh 12.50N 121.05 E
Mindoro Strait 26 Hd 12.20N 120.40 E
Mindouli 36 Bc 4.17S 14.21 E
Mindszent 10 Qj 46.32N 20.12 E
Mine 29 Bd 34.12N 131.11 E
Minehead 9 Jj 51.13N 3.29W
Mine Head 9 Fj 52.00N 7.35W
Mineiros 54 Hg 17.34S 52.34W
Mineral del Monte 48 Jg 20.08N 98.40W
Mineralnyje Vody 19 Eg 44.12N 43.08 E
Mineral Wells 43 He 32.48N 98.07W
Minerva Reefs 57 Jg 23.50S 179.00W
Minervino Murge 14 Ki 41.05N 16.05 E
Minervois 11 Ik 43.25N 2.45 E
Minfeng/Niya 27 Dd 37.04N 82.46 E
Minga 36 Ee 11.08S 27.56 E
Mingala 35 Cd 5.06N 21.49 E
Mingan 42 Lf 50.18N 64.01W
Mingečaur 16 Oi 40.46N 47.02 E
Mingečaurskoje Vodohranilišče 16 Oi 40.55N 46.45 E
Mingenew 59 De 29.11S 115.26 E
Minggang 28 Ci 32.27N 114.02 E
Mingguang → Jiashan 28 Dh 32.47N 118.00 E
Ming He 28 Cf 37.14N 114.47 E
Minglanilla 13 Ke 39.32N 1.36W
Mingoyo 36 Ge 10.06S 39.38 E
Mingshui 27 Mb 47.15N 125.53 E
Mingshui → Zhangqiu 28 Df 36.44N 117.33 E
Mingteke 27 Bd 37.09N 74.58 E
Mingteke Daban 27 Bd 37.00N 74.50 E
Minguez, Puerto- 13 Ld 40.50N 0.59W
Mingulay 9 Fe 56.50N 7.40W
Mingyuegou 28 Jc 43.08N 128.55 E
Minhe 27 Hd 36.20N 102.50 E
Minho 13 Dc 41.52N 8.51W
Minho 13 Dc 41.40N 8.30W
Minicoy Island 21 Ji 8.17N 73.02 E
Minigwal, Lake- 59 Ee 29.35S 123.10 E
Minija 8 Ii 55.20N 21.12 E
Minilya 59 Cd 23.51S 113.58 E
Minilya River 59 Cd 23.56S 113.51 E
Minipi Lake 42 Lf 52.28N 60.50W
Ministra, Sierra- 13 Jc 41.07N 2.30W
Minjar 17 Hi 55.04N 57.33 E
Min Jiang 21 Mg 28.46N 104.38 E
Minmaya 28 Pd 41.10N 140.28 E
Minna 31 Hh 9.37N 6.33 E
Minna Bluff 66 Kf 78.32S 166.30 E
Minneapolis [Ks.-U.S.] 45 Hg 39.08N 97.42W
Minneapolis [Mn.-U.S.] 39 Je 44.59N 93.13W
Minnedosa 42 Hf 50.14N 99.51W
Minnedosa River 45 Fb 49.53N 100.08W
Minnesota [2] 43 Ib 46.00N 94.15W
Minnesota River 43 Ic 44.54N 93.10W
Miño 5 Fg 41.52N 8.51W
Mino 29 Ed 35.32N 136.54 E
Minobu 29 Fd 35.22N 138.24 E
Minobu-Sanchi 29 Fd 35.15N 138.20 E
Minokamo 29 Ed 35.26N 137.00 E
Mino-Mikawa-Kōgen 29 Ed 35.10N 137.25 E
Minorca (EN) = Menorca 5 Gg 40.00N 4.00 E
Minot 39 Ie 48.14N 101.18W
Minqin 27 Hd 38.42N 103.11 E
Minqing 27 Kf 26.15N 118.52 E
Minquan 28 Cg 34.39N 115.08 E
Min Shan 27 He 33.35N 103.00 E
Minsk 6 Ie 53.54N 27.34 E
Minskaja Oblast [3] 19 Ce 53.50N 27.40 E
Minskaja Vozvyšennost 8 Lj 54.00N 27.10 E
Mińsk Mazowiecki 10 Rd 52.11N 21.34 E
Minta 34 He 4.35N 12.48 E
Minto, Lac - 42 Ke 57.15N 74.50W
Minto, Mount- 66 Kf 71.47S 168.45 E
Minto Inlet 42 Fb 71.19N 117.00W
Minto Reef 57 Gd 8.08N 154.17 E
Minturn 45 Cg 39.35N 106.26W
Minūdasht 24 Pd 37.10N 55.25 E
Minuf 24 Dg 30.28N 30.56 E
Minusinsk 20 Ef 53.43N 91.48 E
Minvoul 36 Bb 2.09N 12.08 E
Minwakh 35 Hb 16.48N 48.06 E
Minxian 27 He 34.26N 104.02 E
Miory 7 Gi 55.39N 27.41 E
Mios Num 26 Kg 1.30S 135.10 E
Miquan 27 Ec 44.05N 87.33 E
Miquelon 42 Jg 49.00N 76.00W
Mira 13 Dg 37.43N 8.47W
Mira [It.] 14 Ge 45.26N 12.08 E
Mira [Port.] 13 Dd 40.26N 8.44W
Mira, Peña- 13 Fc 41.55N 6.28W
Mīrābād 23 Jc 30.25N 61.50 E
Mirabela 55 Jc 16.15S 44.11W
Miracatu 55 Ig 24.17S 47.28W
Miracema 54 Jh 21.25S 42.11W
Miracema do Tocantins 54 Ie 9.33S 48.24W
Mirador, Serra do- 55 Hh 26.45S 49.50W
Miraflores [Col.] 54 Db 5.12N 73.12W
Miraflores [Col.] 54 Dc 1.30N 72.16W
Miraj 25 Ee 16.50N 74.38 E
Miramar 56 Ie 38.16S 57.51W
Miramar, Laguna- 48 Ni 16.20N 91.20W
Miramas 11 Kk 43.35N 5.00 E
Mirambeau 11 Fi 45.22N 0.34W
Miramichi Bay 42 Kg 47.07N 65.10W
Miramont-de-Guyenne 11 Gj 44.36N 0.22 E
Miran 27 Ed 39.15N 88.50 E
Miranda [2] 54 Ea 10.15N 66.25W
Miranda [Arg.] 55 Cm 36.32S 59.09W
Miranda [Braz.] 54 Gh 20.14S 56.22W
Miranda de Corvo 13 Dd 40.06N 8.20W
Miranda de Ebro 13 Jb 42.41N 2.57W
Miranda do Douro 13 Fc 41.30N 6.16W
Mirande 11 Gk 43.31N 0.25 E
Mirandela 13 Ec 41.29N 7.11W
Mirandola 14 Ff 44.53N 11.04 E
Mirandópolis 55 Ge 21.09S 51.06W
Mirante do Paranapanema 55 Gf 22.17S 51.54W
Mira Por Vos 49 Jb 22.04N 74.38W
Mirapuxi, Rio- 55 Ga 13.06S 51.10W
Mirassol 55 He 20.46S 49.28W
Miravalles 13 Fb 42.45N 6.53W
Miravalles, Volcán- 38 Kh 10.45N 85.10W
Miravete, Puerto de- 13 Ge 39.43N 5.43W
Mir-Bašir → Terter 16 Oi 40.19N 46.58 E
Mirbāṭ 23 Hf 16.58N 54.50 E
Mirdita 15 Ch 41.49N 19.56 E
Mirebalais 49 Kd 18.50N 72.06W
Mirebeau 11 Gh 46.47N 0.11 E
Mirecourt 11 Mf 48.18N 6.08 E
Mirepoix 11 Hk 43.05N 1.53 E
Mirgorod 19 Df 50.00N 33.40 E
Miri 22 Ni 4.23N 113.59 E
Miria 34 Gc 13.43N 9.07 E
Mirim, Lagoa- 52 Ki 32.45S 52.50W
Mirina 15 Ij 39.52N 25.04 E
Miriñay, Esteros del- 55 Di 28.50S 57.10W
Miriñay, Rio- 55 Dj 30.10S 57.39W
Mirny 66 Ge 66.33S 93.01 E
Mirny 22 Nc 62.33N 113.53 E
Mironovka 16 Ge 49.40N 31.01 E
Mirosławiec 10 Mc 53.21N 16.05 E
Mirpur 25 Eb 33.11N 73.46 E
Mirpur Khās 22 Ig 25.32N 69.00 E
Mirqah Sūr 24 Kd 36.50N 44.19 E
Mirsāle 35 Hd 5.58N 47.54 E
Mirşani 15 He 44.01N 24.01 E
Mirtóön Pélagos 15 Gm 37.00N 24.00 E
Miryang 28 Jg 35.29N 128.45 E
Mirzāpur 25 Gc 25.09N 82.35 E
Misaki 29 Ce 33.23N 132.07 E
Misawa 28 Pd 40.41N 141.24 E
Misery, Mount- 51c Ab 17.22N 62.48W
Mishan 27 Nb 45.34N 131.50 E
Mishawaka 44 De 41.40N 86.11W
Mi-Shima 28 Kg 34.47N 131.10 E
Mishima 29 Fd 35.07N 138.54 E
Mishraq, Khashm- 24 Lj 24.13N 46.18 E
Misilmeri 14 Hl 38.02N 13.27 E
Misima Island 60 Ej 10.40S 152.45 E
Misiones [3] 55 Dh 27.00S 57.00W
Misiones [2] 56 Jc 27.00S 55.00W
Misiones, Sierra de- 55 Eh 26.45S 54.20W
Miski, Enneri- 35 Bb 18.10N 17.45 E
Miškino 17 Ki 55.20N 63.55 E
Miskitos, Cayos- 47 Hf 14.23N 82.46W
Miskolc [2] 10 Qh 48.06N 20.43 E
Miskolc 6 If 48.06N 20.47 E
Mismār 35 Fb 18.13N 35.38 E
Misool, Pulau- 26 Jg 1.52S 130.10 E
Misquah Hills 43 Ib 47.50N 92.00W
Miṣr = Egypt (EN) [1] 31 Jf 27.00N 30.00 E
Miṣr al Jadīdah, Al Qāhirah- 33 Fc 30.06N 31.20 E
Miṣrātah 31 Ie 32.23N 15.06 E
Miṣrātah [3] 33 Cd 29.00N 16.00 E
Miṣrātah, Ra's- 30 Ie 32.25N 15.05 E
Misserghin 13 Li 35.37N 0.44W
Missinaibi 42 Jf 50.44N 81.30W
Missinaibi Lake 44 Fa 48.23N 83.40W
Missinipe 42 He 55.36N 104.45W
Mission [S.D.-U.S.] 45 Fe 43.18N 100.40W
Mission [Tx.-U.S.] 45 Gm 26.13N 98.20W
Mission City 46 Db 49.08N 122.18W
Mission Range 46 Ic 47.30N 113.55W
Mississippi 38 Kg 29.00N 89.15W
Mississippi [2] 43 Je 32.50N 89.30W
Mississippi Delta 38 Kg 29.10N 89.15W
Mississippi Fan (EN) 43 Jf 26.45N 88.30W
Mississippi River 44 Ic 45.26N 76.16W
Mississippi Sound 45 Lk 30.15N 89.00W
Misso 8 Lg 57.33N 27.23 E
Missoula 39 He 46.52N 114.01W
Missour 32 Gc 33.03N 3.59W
Missouri 38 Jf 38.50N 90.08W
Missouri [2] 43 Id 38.30N 93.30W
Missouri, Coteau du- 45 Gc 46.00N 99.30W
Missouri Valley 45 If 41.33N 95.53W
Mistassibi 42 Kg 48.53N 72.13W
Mistassini 44 Ka 48.58N 72.40 E
Mistassini 42 Kf 50.30N 74.00W
Mistassini, Rivière- 42 Kg 48.42N 72.20W
Mistelbach an der Zaya 14 Kb 48.34N 16.34 E
Misterhult 8 Gg 57.28N 16.33 E
Mistrás 15 Fl 37.04N 22.22 E
Mistretta 14 Im 37.56N 14.22 E
Misugi 29 Ed 34.33N 136.15 E
Misumi [Jap.] 29 Bd 34.46N 131.58 E
Misumi [Jap.] 29 Be 32.37N 130.29 E
Mita, Punta- 48 Gg 32.04N 105.33W
Mitare, Rio- 49 Mh 11.28N 69.56W
Mitchell [Austl.] 59 Je 26.29S 147.58 E
Mitchell [Or.-U.S.] 46 Ed 44.34N 120.09W
Mitchell [S.D.-U.S.] 43 Hc 43.40N 98.01W
Mitchell, Mount- 38 Kf 35.46N 82.16W
Mitchell Range 59 Hb 12.50S 135.35 E
Mitchell River 57 Ff 15.12S 141.35 E
Mitchell River Mission 59 Ic 15.28S 141.44 E
Mitchelstown/Baile Mhistéala 9 Ei 52.16N 8.16W
Mithimna 15 Jj 39.22N 26.10 E
Mitiaro Island 57 Lf 19.49S 157.43W
Mitidja, Plaine de la- 13 Oh 36.36N 3.00 E
Mitilini 15 Jj 39.06N 26.33 E
Mitilinis, Stenón- 15 Jj 39.10N 26.35 E
Mitla 47 Ee 16.55N 96.17W
Mitla, Laguna- 48 Ii 17.03N 100.25W
Mito 27 Pd 36.22N 140.28 E
Mitomoni 36 Ge 11.32S 35.19 E

Index Symbols

- [1] Independent Nation
- [2] State, Region
- [3] District, County
- [4] Municipality
- [5] Colony, Dependency
- Continent
- Physical Region
- Historical or Cultural Region
- Mount, Mountain
- Volcano
- Hill
- Mountains, Mountain Range
- Hills, Escarpment
- Plateau, Upland
- Pass, Gap
- Plain, Lowland
- Delta
- Salt Flat
- Valley, Canyon
- Crater, Cave
- Karst Features
- Depression
- Polder
- Desert, Dunes
- Forest, Woods
- Heath, Steppe
- Oasis
- Cape, Point
- Coast, Beach
- Cliff
- Peninsula
- Isthmus
- Sandbank
- Island
- Atoll
- Rock, Reef
- Islands, Archipelago
- Rocks, Reefs
- Coral Reef
- Well, Spring
- Geyser
- River, Stream
- Waterfall Rapids
- River Mouth, Estuary
- Lake
- Salt Lake
- Intermittent Lake
- Reservoir
- Swamp, Pond
- Canal
- Glacier
- Ice Shelf, Pack Ice
- Ocean
- Sea
- Gulf, Bay
- Strait, Fjord
- Lagoon
- Bank
- Seamount
- Tablemount
- Ridge
- Shelf
- Basin
- Escarpment, Sea Scarp
- Fracture
- Trench, Abyss
- National Park, Reserve
- Point of Interest
- Recreation Site
- Cave, Cavern
- Historic Site
- Ruins
- Wall, Walls
- Church, Abbey
- Temple
- Scientific Station
- Airport
- Port
- Lighthouse
- Mine
- Tunnel
- Dam, Bridge

Mitsamiouli 37 Gb 11.23S 43.18 E
Mitsinjo 37 Hc 16.00S 45.52 E
Mitsio, Nosy- 37 Hb 12.54S 48.36 E
Mitsiwa=Massawa (EN) 31 Kg 15.37N 39.39 E
Mitsiwa Channel 35 Fb 15.30N 40.00 E
Mitsuishi 29a Cb 42.15N 142.33 E
Mitsukaido 29 Fc 36.01N 139.59 E
Mitsuke 29 Fc 37.32N 138.56 E
Mitsushima 29 Ad 34.16N 129.20 E
Mittelfranken 10 Gg 49.20N 10.40 E
Mittelland 14 Bd 46.50N 7.05 E
Mittellandkanal 5 He 52.16N 11.41 E
Mittelmark 10 Jd 52.20N 13.20 E
Mittenwald 10 Hi 47.27N 11.15 E
Mittersheim 12 If 48.52N 6.56 E
Mittersill 14 Gc 47.16N 12.29 E
Mittweida 10 If 50.59N 12.59 E
Mitú 53 Ie 1.08N 70.03W
Mitumba, Monts-=Mitumba Range (EN) 30 Ji 6.00S 29.00 E
Mitumba Range (EN)= Mitumba, Monts- 30 Ji 6.00S 29.00 E
Mituva 8 Jj 55.00N 22.45 E
Mitwaba 36 Ed 8.38S 27.20 E
Mitzic 36 Bb 0.47N 11.34 E
Miura 29 Fd 35.08N 139.37 E
Miura-Hantō 29 Fd 35.15N 139.40 E
Mixco Viejo 49 Bf 14.52N 90.40W
Mixian 28 Bg 34.31N 113.22 E
Mixteco, Río- 48 Jh 18.11N 98.30W
Miya-Gawa 29 Ed 34.32N 136.42 E
Miyagi Ken [2] 28 Pe 38.30N 140.50 E
Miyagusuku-Jima 29b Ab 26.22N 127.59 E
Miyāh, Wādī al- [Eg.] 24 Ej 25.00N 33.23 E
Miyāh, Wādī al- [Sau. Ar.] 24 Gi 26.06N 36.31 E
Miyāh, Wādī al- [Syr.] 24 He 34.44N 39.57 E
Miyake-Jima 27 Oe 34.05N 139.30 E
Miyako 27 Pd 39.38N 141.57 E
Miyako-Jima 27 Mg 24.45N 125.20 E
Miyakonojō 28 Ki 31.44N 131.04 E
Miyako-Rettō 27 Lg 24.25N 125.00 E
Miyako-Wan 29 Hb 39.40N 142.00 E
Miyama 29 Dd 35.17N 135.34 E
Miyanojō 29 Bf 31.54N 130.27 E
Miyanoura-Dake 28 Ki 30.20N 130.29 E
Miyata 29 Be 33.45N 130.45 E
Miyazaki 27 Ne 31.54N 131.26 E
Miyazaki Ken [2] 28 Kh 32.05N 131.20 E
Miyazu 28 Mg 35.32N 135.11 E
Miyazuka-Yama 29 Fd 34.24N 139.16 E
Miyazu-Wan 29 Dd 35.35N 135.13 E
Miyoshi 28 Lg 34.48N 132.51 E
Miyun 27 Kc 40.22N 116.53 E
Miyun Shuiku 28 Dd 40.31N 116.58 E
Mizan Teferi 35 Fd 6.53N 35.28 E
Mizdah 33 Bc 31.26N 12.59 E
Mizen Head/Carn Ui Néid 5 Fe 51.27N 9.49W
Mizil 15 Je 45.01N 26.27 E
Mizorām [3] 25 Id 23.00N 93.00 E
Mizque 54 Eg 17.56S 65.19W
Mizuho 29 Cd 34.50N 132.29 E
Mizuho 66 Ef 70.43S 40.20 E
Mizunami 29 Ed 35.22N 137.15 E
Mizusawa 28 Pe 39.08N 141.08 E
Mjadel 8 Lj 54.54N 27.03 E
Mjakiševo 8 Mh 56.30N 28.54 E
Mjakit 20 Kd 61.23N 152.10 E
Mjällom 8 Ha 62.59N 18.26 E
Mjaundža 20 Jd 63.02N 147.13 E
Mjölby 7 Dg 58.19N 15.08 E
Mjøndalen 8 De 59.45N 10.01 E
Mjorn 8 Eg 57.54N 12.25 E
Mjøsa 5 Hc 60.40N 11.00 E
Mkoani 36 Gd 5.22S 39.39 E
Mkokotoni 36 Gd 5.52S 39.15 E
Mkushi Bona 36 Ee 13.37S 29.23 E
Mkushi River 36 Fe 13.33S 29.40 E
Mkuze 37 Ee 27.10S 32.00 E
Mladá Boleslav 10 Kf 50.21N 14.54 E
Mladenovac 15 De 44.26N 20.42 E
Mlava 15 Ee 44.45N 21.14 E
Mława 10 Qc 53.06N 20.23 E
Mljet 14 Lh 42.45N 17.30 E
Mljetski kanal 14 Lh 42.48N 17.35 E
Mmadinare 37 Dd 21.53S 27.45 E
Mnichovo Hradiště 10 Kf 50.32N 14.59 E
Mnogoveršinny 20 If 53.55N 139.50 E
Moa 49 Jc 20.40N 74.56W
Moa 34 Cd 6.59N 11.36W
Moa, Pulau- 26 Ih 8.10S 127.56 E
Moab 43 Fd 38.35N 109.33W
Moabi 36 Bc 2.24S 10.59 E
Moala 63d Bc 18.36S 179.53 E
Moamba 37 Ee 25.36S 32.15 E
Moanda [Gabon] 36 Bc 1.34S 13.11 E
Moanda [Zaire] 36 Bd 5.56S 12.21 E
Moatize 37 Ec 16.10S 33.46 E
Moba 31 Ji 7.03S 29.47 E
Mobara 29 Gd 35.25N 140.17 E
Mobārakeh 24 Nf 32.20N 51.30 E
Mobaye 31 Jh 4.19N 21.11 E
Mobayi-Mbongo 36 Db 4.18N 21.11 E
Mobeka 36 Cb 1.53N 19.46 E
Moberly 43 Id 39.25N 92.26W
Mobile 39 Kf 30.42N 88.05W
Mobile Bay 43 Je 30.25N 88.00W
Mobridge 43 Gb 45.32N 100.26W
Mobuto Sese Seko, Lac-= Albert, Lake- (EN) 30 Kh 1.40N 31.00 E
Moca 49 Ld 19.24N 70.31W
Moçambique= Mozambique (EN) [1] 31 Kj 18.15S 35.00 E
Moçambique= Mozambique (EN) 31 Lk 15.03S 40.45 E
Moçambique, Canal de-= Mozambique Channel (EN) 30 Lk 20.00S 43.00 E
Moçâmedes → Namibe 36 Bf 15.20S 12.30 E
Moçâmedes → Namibe 31 Ij 15.12S 12.10 E
Mocapra, Río- 50 Ci 7.56N 66.46W
Mocha, Isla- 56 Fe 38.22S 73.56W
Moc Hoa 25 Lf 10.46N 105.56 E
Mochudi 37 Dd 24.23S 26.08 E
Mocímboa da Praia 31 Lj 11.20S 40.21 E
Möckeln 8 Fh 56.40N 14.10 E
Mockfjärd 8 Fd 60.30N 14.58 E
Môco, Serra- 30 Ij 12.28S 15.10 E
Mocoa 54 Cc 1.09N 76.38W
Mococa 55 Ie 21.28S 47.01W
Mocoví 55 Ci 28.24S 59.42W
Moctezuma [Mex.] 47 Cc 29.48N 109.42W
Moctezuma [Mex.] 48 If 22.45N 101.05W
Moctezuma [Mex.] 48 Fb 30.12N 106.26W
Moctezuma, Río [Mex.] 48 Ec 29.09N 109.40W
Moctezuma, Río- [Mex.] 48 Jg 21.59N 98.34W
Mocuba 31 Kj 16.51S 36.56 E
Mocubúri 37 Fb 14.39S 38.54 E
Močurica 15 Jg 42.31N 26.32 E
Modane 11 Mi 45.12N 6.40 E
Modderrivier 37 Ce 29.02S 24.37 E
Modena [It.] 14 Ef 44.40N 10.55 E
Modena [Ut.-U.S.] 46 Ih 37.49N 113.55W
Moder 11 Of 48.49N 8.06 E
Modesto 43 Cd 37.39N 120.59W
Modica 14 In 36.52N 14.46 E
Modjamboli 36 Db 2.28N 22.06 E
Modjigo 34 Hb 17.09N 13.12 E
Mödling 14 Kb 48.05N 16.28 E
Modriča 14 Mf 44.58N 18.18 E
Modum 8 Ce 59.55N 10.00 E
Moe 59 Jg 38.10S 146.15 E
Moelv 7 Cf 60.56N 10.42 E
Moen 64d Bb 7.26N 151.52 E
Moengo 54 Hb 5.37N 54.24W
Moen-jo-Daro 25 Dc 27.19N 68.07 E
Moenkopi Wash 46 Ji 35.54N 111.26W
Moerbeke 12 Fc 51.10N 3.56 E
Moers 10 Ce 51.27N 6.39 E
Moeskroen/Mouscron 11 Jd 50.44N 3.13 E
Moffat 9 Jf 55.20N 3.27W
Moga 36 Ec 2.21S 26.49 E
Mogadishu (EN)= Muqdisho 31 Lh 2.03N 45.22 E
Mogadouro 13 Fc 41.20N 6.43W
Mogadouro, Serra do- 13 Fc 41.19N 6.40W
Mogāl 24 Nd 36.35N 50.35 E
Mogalakwena 37 Dd 22.27S 28.55 E
Mogami 29 Gb 38.45N 140.30 E
Mogami-Gawa 28 Oe 38.54N 139.50 E
Mogami Trench (EN) 29 Fb 39.00N 139.00 E
Mogaung 25 Jc 25.18N 96.56 E
Mogho 35 Ge 4.49N 40.19 E
Mogielnica 10 Qe 51.42N 20.43 E
Mogilev 6 Je 53.56N 30.18 E
Mogilev-Podolski 16 Ee 48.27N 27.48 E
Mogilevskaja Oblast [3] 19 De 53.45N 30.30 E
Mogilno 10 Nd 52.40N 17.58 E
Mogincual 37 Gc 15.34S 40.24 E
Mogoča 22 Nd 53.44N 119.44 E
Mogočin 20 De 57.43N 83.40 E
Mogogh 35 Ed 8.26N 31.19 E
Mogojto 20 Gf 54.25N 110.27 E
Mogojtuj 20 Gf 51.15N 114.58 E
Mogok 25 Jd 22.55N 96.30 E
Mogollon Rim 43 Ee 34.20N 111.00W
Mogotes, Punta- 55 Dn 38.06S 57.33W
Mogotón, Pico- 49 Dg 13.45N 86.23W
Mogreïn 31 Ff 25.13N 11.34W
Mogroum 35 Bc 11.06N 15.25 E
Moguer 13 Fg 37.16N 6.50W
Mogzon 20 Gf 51.42N 111.59 E
Mohács 10 Ok 45.59N 18.42 E
Mohaka 62 Gc 39.07S 177.12 E
Mohaka 62 Gc 39.07S 177.12 E
Mohales Hoek 37 Df 30.15S 27.25 E
Mohall 45 Fb 48.46N 101.31W
Moḩammadābād 24 Pg 31.47N 54.27 E
Mohammadia 13 Mi 35.35N 0.04 E
Mohammedia 32 Fc 33.42N 7.24W
Mohanganj 25 Id 24.54N 90.59 E
Mohang-ni 28 If 36.46N 126.08 E
Mohave, Lake- 43 Ed 35.25N 114.38W
Mohawk Mountains 46 Ij 32.25N 113.25W
Mohe 22 Od 53.27N 122.18 E
Moheda 8 Fh 57.00N 14.34 E
Mohéli → Mwali 30 Lj 12.15S 43.45 E
Moher, Cliffs of-/Aillte an Mhothair 9 Di 52.58N 9.27W
Mohican, Cape- 40 Fd 60.12N 167.28W
Mohinora 38 Ig 26.06N 107.04W
Möhnesee 12 Kc 51.29N 8.05 E
Mohns Ridge (EN) 5 Ga 73.00N 5.00 E
Moholm 8 Ff 58.37N 14.02 E
Mohon, Charleville-Mézierès- 12 Ge 49.46N 4.43 E
Mohon Peak 46 Ii 34.57N 113.15W
Mohoro 36 Gd 8.08S 39.10 E
Mohotani, Ile- 61 Na 9.59S 138.49W
Mohovaja 20 Kf 53.01N 158.38 E
Moi 8 Bf 58.28N 6.32 E
Moikovac 15 Cg 42.58N 19.35 E
Moimenta da Beira 13 Ed 40.59N 7.37W
Moindou 63b Be 21.42S 165.41 E
Moineşti 15 Jc 46.28N 26.29 E
Moírai 15 Hn 35.03N 24.52 E
Mo i Rana 6 Hb 66.18N 14.08 E
Mõisaküla/Myjzakjula 7 Fg 58.07N 25.10 E
Moisés Ville 55 Bj 30.43S 61.29W
Moisie 42 Kf 50.13N 66.06W
Moisie 42 Kf 50.11N 66.06W
Moissac 11 Hj 44.06N 1.05 E
Moïssala 35 Bd 8.21N 17.46 E
Moitaco 50 Dh 8.01N 61.21W
Mõja 8 He 59.25N 18.55 E
Mojácar 13 Kg 37.08N 1.51W
Mojada, Sierra- 48 Hd 27.15N 103.45W
Mojana, Caño- 49 Ji 9.02N 74.46W
Mojave 43 Dd 35.03N 118.10W
Mojave Desert 38 Hf 35.00N 117.00W
Mojiguaçu, Rio- 55 He 20.53S 48.10W
Moji Mirim 55 If 22.26S 46.57W
Mojjero 20 Fc 68.44N 103.30 E
Mojo 35 Fd 8.36N 39.09 E
Mojo 35 Gd 8.00N 41.50 E
Mojos, Llanos de- 52 Jg 15.00S 65.00W
Moju, Rio- 54 Id 1.40S 48.25W
Mojynty 19 Hf 47.10N 73.18 E
Mokambo 36 Ee 12.25S 28.21 E
Mokapu Peninsula 65a Db 21.26N 157.45W
Mokau 62 Fc 38.42S 174.35 E
Mokau 61 Dg 38.41S 174.37 E
Mokhotlong 37 De 29.17S 29.05 E
Mokil Atoll 57 Gd 6.40N 159.47 E
Moklakan 20 Gf 54.48N 118.56 E
Möklinta 8 Gd 60.05N 16.32 E
Mokochu, Khao- 25 Je 15.56N 99.06 E
Mokohinau Islands 62 Fa 35.55S 175.05 E
Mokolo 34 Hc 10.45N 13.48 E
Mokp'o 22 Of 34.47N 126.23 E
Mokra Gora 15 Dg 42.50N 20.25 E
Mokrany 10 Ue 51.48N 24.23 E
Mokrin 15 Dd 45.56N 20.25 E
Mokša 5 Ke 54.44N 41.53 E
Mokwa 34 Gd 9.17N 5.03 E
Mol 11 Lc 51.11N 5.07 E
Mola di Bari 14 Li 41.04N 17.05 E
Molango 48 Jg 20.47N 98.43W
Moláoi 15 Fm 36.48N 22.51 E
Molara 14 Dj 40.50N 9.45 E
Molas, Punta- 48 Pg 20.35N 86.44W
Molat 14 If 44.13N 14.50 E
Molatón 13 Kf 38.59N 1.24W
Moldau (EN)=Vltava 5 He 50.21N 14.30 E
Moldava nad Bodvou 10 Qh 48.37N 21.00 E
Moldavia (EN) = Moldova 15 Jc 46.30N 27.00 E
Moldavia (EN)=Moldova 5 If 46.30N 27.00 E
Moldavia (EN) = Moldova 19 Cf 47.00N 29.00 E
Moldavskaja Sovetskaja Socialističeskaja Respublika → Moldova 19 Cf 47.00N 29.00 E
Moldavskaja SSR/ Respublika Sovetike Sočialiste Moldovenjaske → Moldova 19 Cf 47.00N 29.00 E
Moldavskaja SSR → Moldova 19 Cf 47.00N 29.00 E
Molde 6 Gc 62.44N 7.11 E
Moldefjorden 8 Bb 62.45N 7.05 E
Moldova 19 Cf 47.00N 29.00 E
Moldova 15 Jc 46.54N 26.58 E
Moldova = Moldavia (EN) 15 Jc 46.30N 27.00 E
Moldova = Moldavia (EN) 5 If 46.30N 27.00 E
Moldova Nouă 15 Ee 44.44N 21.41 E
Moldoveanu, Vîrful- 5 If 45.36N 24.44 E
Moldoviţa 15 Ib 47.41N 25.32 E
Mole 12 Bc 51.24N 0.20W
Moléne, Ile de- 11 Bf 48.24N 4.58W
Molens van Kinderdijk 12 Gc 51.52N 4.40 E
Molepolole 31 Jk 24.25S 25.30 E
Môle Saint-Nicolas 49 Kd 19.47N 73.22W
Moletai/Moletaj 8 Ki 55.13N 25.36 E
Moletaj/Moletai 8 Ki 55.13N 25.36 E
Molfetta 14 Ki 41.12N 16.36 E
Molihong Shan 28 Hc 42.11N 124.43 E
Molina, Parameras de- 13 Jd 40.55N 2.01W
Molina de Aragón 13 Kd 40.51N 1.53W
Molina de Segura 13 Kf 38.03N 1.12W
Moline 45 Kf 41.30N 90.31W
Moliniere Point 51p Bb 12.05N 61.45W
Molise [2] 14 Ii 41.40N 14.30 E
Molkābād 24 Oe 34.32N 52.35 E
Molkom 8 Ee 59.36N 13.43 E
Möll 14 Hd 46.50N 13.26 E
Moll 55 Cl 35.04S 59.39W
Mollafeneri 15 Mi 40.54N 29.30 E
Mölle 8 Eh 56.17N 12.29 E
Mollendo 53 Ig 17.02S 72.01W
Molliens-Dreuil 12 Ee 49.52N 2.01 E
Mölln 10 Gc 53.38N 10.41 E
Mollösund 8 Df 58.04N 11.28 E
Mölndal 7 Ch 57.39N 12.01 E
Mölnlycke 8 Ef 57.39N 12.09 E
Moločansk 16 If 47.10N 35.36 E
Moločny, Liman- 16 If 46.30N 35.20 E
Molócuè 37 Fc 17.03S 38.52 E
Molodečno 19 Ce 54.19N 26.53 E
Molodežnaja 66 Ee 67.40S 45.51 E
Molodi 8 Mf 58.00N 28.52 E
Molodogvardejskoje 19 He 54.07N 70.50 E
Mologa 5 Jd 58.50N 37.11 E
Molokai Island 57 Lb 21.08N 157.00W
Moloma 7 Lg 58.20N 48.28 E
Molong 9 Jf 33.06S 148.52 E
Molopo 30 Jk 28.31S 20.13 E
Moloundou 34 Ie 2.02N 15.13 E
Molteno 37 Df 31.24S 26.22 E
Molu, Pulau- 26 Jh 6.45S 131.33 E
Moluccas (EN)=Maluku, Kepulauan- 57 De 2.00S 128.00 E
Molucca Sea (EN)=Maluku, Laut- 21 Oj 0.05S 125.00 E
Molygino 20 Ee 58.11N 94.45 E
Moma 20 Jc 66.20N 143.06 E
Moma 37 Fc 16.44S 39.14 E
Mombaça 54 Ke 5.45S 39.28W
Mombasa 31 Ki 4.03S 39.40 E
Mombo 36 Gc 4.53S 38.17 E
Momboyo 36 Cc 0.16S 19.00 E
Mombuca, Serra da- 55 Fd 18.15S 52.26W
Momčilgrad 15 Ih 41.32N 25.25 E
Mömling 12 Le 49.50N 9.09 E
Momotombo, Volcán- 49 Dg 12.26N 86.33W
Mompono 36 Db 0.04N 21.48 E
Mompós 54 Db 9.14N 74.27W
Momski Hrebet 20 Jc 66.00N 145.00 E
Mon [2] 25 Je 17.22N 97.20 E
Møn 7 Ci 55.00N 12.20 E
Mona, Canal de la-=Mona Passage (EN) 38 Mh 18.30N 67.45W
Mona, Isla- 47 Ke 18.05N 67.54W
Mona, Punta- 49 Fi 9.38N 82.37W
Monach Islands 9 Fd 57.32N 7.40W
Monaco [1] 6 Gg 43.42N 7.23 E
Monadhliath Mountains 9 Id 57.15N 4.10W
Monagas [2] 54 Fb 9.20N 63.00W
Monaghan/Muineachán [2] 9 Gg 54.10N 7.00W
Monaghan/Muineachán 9 Gg 54.15N 6.58W
Monahans 45 Ek 31.36N 102.54W
Mona Passage (EN)=Mona, Canal de la- 38 Mh 18.30N 67.45W
Monapo 37 Gb 14.55S 40.18 E
Monarch Mountain 42 Ef 51.54N 125.54W
Monashee Mountains 42 Ff 51.00N 118.43W
Monastyrščina 16 Gb 54.19N 31.48 E
Monatélé 34 He 4.16N 11.12 E
Monbetsu [Jap.] 28 Qc 42.28N 142.07 E
Monbetsu [Jap.] 27 Pc 44.21N 143.22 E
Monbetsu-Shokotsu 29a Ca 44.23N 143.16 E
Moncalieri 14 Be 45.00N 7.41 E
Moncalvo 14 Ce 45.03N 8.16 E
Monção [Braz.] 54 Id 3.30S 45.15W
Monção [Port.] 13 Db 42.05N 8.29W
Moncayo 13 Kc 41.46N 1.50W
Moncayo, Sierra del- 13 Kc 41.45N 1.50W
Mončegorsk 19 Db 67.56N 32.58 E
Mönchengladbach 10 Ce 51.12N 6.26 E
Mönchengladbach-Rheydt 12 Ic 51.10N 6.27 E
Mönchengladbach-Wickrath 12 Ic 51.08N 6.25 E
Mönchgut 10 Jb 54.20N 13.40 E
Monchique 13 Dg 37.19N 8.33W
Monchique, Serra de- 13 Dg 37.19N 8.36W
Monclova 39 Ig 26.54N 101.25W
Moncton 39 Me 46.06N 64.07W
Mondai 55 Fh 27.05S 53.25W
Mondego 13 Dd 40.09N 8.52W
Mondego, Cabo- 13 Dd 40.11N 8.55W
Mondeville 12 Be 49.10N 0.19W
Mondjoko 36 Dc 1.41S 21.12 E
Mondo 35 Bc 13.43N 15.32 E
Mondoñedo 13 Ea 43.26N 7.22W
Mondorf-les-Bains/Bad Mondorf 12 Ie 49.30N 6.17 E
Mondoubleau 11 Gg 47.59N 0.54 E
Mondoví 14 Bf 44.23N 7.49 E
Mondragone 14 Hi 41.07N 13.53 E
Mondy 20 Ff 51.40N 100.59 E
Monemvasía 15 Gm 36.41N 23.03 E
Monessen 44 He 40.09N 79.53W
Monett 45 Jh 36.55N 93.55W
Monfalcone 14 He 45.49N 13.32 E
Monferrato 14 Cf 44.55N 8.05 E
Monforte 13 Ee 39.03N 7.26W
Monforte de Lemos 13 Eb 42.31N 7.30W
Monga 36 Db 4.12N 22.49 E
Mongala 36 Cb 1.53N 19.46 E
Mongalla 35 Ed 5.12N 31.46 E
Mongbwalu 36 Fb 1.57N 30.02 E
Mong Cai 25 Ld 21.32N 107.58 E
Monger, Lake- 59 De 29.15S 117.05 E
Mongga 63a Cb 7.57S 156.59 E
Monggolküre/Zhaosu 27 Dc 43.10N 81.07 E
Monghyr → Munger 25 Hc 25.23N 86.28 E
Monginevro, Colle del- 11 Mj 44.56N 6.44 E
Mongo 31 Ig 12.11N 18.42 E
Mongo 34 Cd 9.34N 12.11W
Mongol Altajn Nuruu → Mongolski Altaj= Mongolian Altai (EN) 21 Le 46.30N 93.00 E
Mongol Ard-Uls=Mongolia (EN) [1] 22 Me 47.00N 104.00 E
Mongolia (EN)=Mongol Ard-Uls [1] 22 Me 47.00N 104.00 E
Mongolian Altai (EN)= Mongol Altajn Nuruu → Mongolski Altaj 21 Le 46.30N 93.00 E
Mongolian Altai (EN)= Mongolski Altaj (Mongol Altajn Nuruu) 21 Le 46.30N 93.00 E
Mongolski Altaj (Mongol Altajn Nuruu)=Mongolian Altai (EN) 21 Le 46.30N 93.00 E
Mongonu 34 Hc 12.41N 13.36 E
Mongororo 35 Cc 12.01N 22.28 E
Mongoumba 35 Be 3.38N 18.36 E
Möng Pan 25 Jd 20.19N 98.22 E
Mongrove, Punta- 48 Hi 17.56N 102.11W
Mongu 31 Jj 15.17S 23.08 E
Monguel 32 Ef 16.25N 13.08W
Möng Yai 25 Jd 22.25N 98.02 E
Monheim 12 Ic 51.05N 6.53 E
Mönichkirchen 14 Kc 47.30N 16.02 E
Mon Idée, Auvillers-lès-Forges- 12 Ge 49.52N 4.21 E
Monigotes 55 Bj 30.30S 61.39W
Moní Hosiou Louká 15 Fk 38.24N 22.49 E
Monistrol-sur-Loire 11 Ki 45.17N 4.10 E
Monito, Isla- 51a Ab 18.09N 67.56W
Monitor Peak 46 Gg 38.50N 116.32W
Monitor Range 46 Gg 38.45N 116.40W
Monjolos 55 Jd 18.18S 44.05W
Monkayo 26 Ie 7.50N 126.00 E
Monkey Bay 36 Fe 14.05S 34.55 E
Monkey Point 49 Fg 11.36N 83.39W
Monkey River 49 Ce 16.22N 88.29W
Mońki 10 Sc 53.24N 22.49 E
Monkoto 36 Dc 1.38S 20.39 E
Monmouth [Il.-U.S.] 45 Kf 40.55N 90.39W
Monmouth 9 Kj 51.45N 3.00W
Monmouth [Or.-U.S.] 46 Dd 44.51N 123.14W
Monmouth [Wales-U.K.] 9 Kj 51.50N 2.43W
Monmouth Mountain 46 Da 51.00N 123.47W
Mönne 10 De 51.28N 7.30 E
Monnikendam 12 Hb 52.27N 5.02 E
Monnow 9 Kj 51.48N 2.42W
Mono 63a Bb 7.20S 155.35 E
Mono [3] 34 Fd 6.45N 1.50 E
Monobe-Gawa 29 Ce 33.32N 133.42 E
Mono Lake 43 Dd 38.00N 119.00W
Monólithos 15 Km 36.07N 27.45 E
Monopoli 14 Lj 40.57N 17.18 E
Monor 10 Pi 47.21N 19.27 E
Monou 35 Cb 16.24N 22.11 E
Monóvar 13 Lf 38.26N 0.50W
Monowai, Lake- 62 Bf 45.55S 167.25 E
Monreal 12 Jd 50.18N 7.10 E
Monreal del Campo 13 Kd 40.47N 1.21W
Monreale 14 Hl 38.05N 13.17 E
Monroe [Ga.-U.S.] 44 Fi 33.47N 83.43W
Monroe [La.-U.S.] 39 Jf 32.33N 92.07W
Monroe [Mi.-U.S.] 44 Fe 41.55N 83.24W
Monroe [N.C.-U.S.] 44 Gh 34.59N 80.33W
Monroe [Or.-U.S.] 46 Dd 44.19N 123.18W
Monroe [Wi.-U.S.] 45 Le 42.36N 89.38W
Monroe, Lake- 44 Df 39.05N 86.25W
Monroe City 45 Kg 39.39N 91.44W
Monroeville 44 Dj 31.31N 87.20W
Monrovia 31 Fh 6.19N 10.48W
Mons/Bergen 11 Jd 50.27N 3.56 E
Monsanto 13 Ed 40.02N 7.07W
Monschau 10 Cf 50.33N 6.15 E
Monselice 14 Fe 45.14N 11.45 E
Monserrate, Isla- 48 De 25.41N 111.05W
Monsheim 12 Ke 49.38N 8.12 E
Møns Klint 8 Ej 54.58N 12.33 E
Mönsterås 7 Dh 57.02N 16.26 E
Montabaur 10 Df 50.26N 7.50 E
Montagna Grande 14 Gm 37.56N 12.44 E
Montagne 11 Jh 46.10N 3.40 E
Montagu 66 Ad 58.25S 26.20W
Montague 40 Je 60.00N 147.30W
Montague, Isla- 48 Bb 31.45N 114.48W
Montaigu 11 Eh 46.59N 1.19W
Montalbán 13 Ld 40.50N 0.48W
Montalbano Ionico 14 Kj 40.17N 16.34 E
Montalcino 14 Fg 43.03N 11.29 E
Montalegre 13 Ec 41.49N 7.48W
Montalto di Castro 14 Fh 42.21N 11.37 E
Montalto Uffugo 14 Kk 39.24N 16.09 E
Montalvânia 55 Jb 14.28S 44.32W
Montana [2] 43 Eb 47.00N 110.00W
Montana 14 Bd 46.18N 7.30 E
Montánchez 13 Fe 39.13N 6.09W
Montánchez, Sierra de- 13 Ge 39.15N 5.55W
Montargis 11 Ig 48.00N 2.45 E
Montataire 12 Ee 49.16N 2.26 E
Montauban [Fr.] 11 Hj 44.01N 1.21 E
Montauban [Fr.] 11 Df 48.12N 2.03W
Montauk Point 44 Le 41.04N 71.52W
Montbard 11 Kg 47.37N 4.20 E
Montbéliard 11 Mg 47.31N 6.48 E
Montblanc 13 Nc 41.22N 1.10 E
Mont Blanc 5 Gf 45.50N 6.52 E
Montbrison 11 Ki 45.36N 4.03 E
Montceau-les-Mines 11 Kh 46.40N 4.22 E
Mont Cenis, Col du- 5 Gf 45.15N 6.54 E
Montchanin 11 Kh 46.45N 4.27 E
Mont Darwin 37 Ec 16.46S 31.35 E
Mont-de-Marsan 11 Fk 43.53N 0.30W
Montdidier 11 Ie 49.39N 2.34 E
Mont Dore 11 Ii 45.34N 2.49 E
Mont-Dore 63b Cf 22.17S 166.35 E
Monte, Laguna del- 55 Am 37.00S 62.28W
Monteagudo 54 Fg 19.49S 63.59W
Monte Alban 39 Jh 17.02N 96.45W
Monte Alegre 54 Hd 2.01S 54.04W
Monte Alegre, Rio- 55 Gc 17.16S 50.41W
Monte Alegre de Goiás 55 Ia 13.14S 47.10W
Montealegre del Castillo 13 Kf 38.47N 1.19W
Monte Alegre de Minas 55 Hd 18.52S 48.52W
Monte Azul 54 Jg 15.09S 42.53W
Montebello 44 Jc 45.39N 74.56W
Monte Bello Islands 59 Dd 20.25S 115.30 E
Monte Carlo 11 Nk 43.44N 7.25 E
Montecarlo 55 Eh 26.34S 54.47W
Monte Carmelo 55 Id 18.43S 47.29W
Monte Caseros 56 Id 30.15S 57.39W
Montecatini Terme 14 Eg 43.23N 10.45 E
Montecchio Maggiore 14 Fe 45.30N 11.24 E
Monte Comán 56 Gd 34.36S 67.54W
Montecristi 49 Ld 19.52N 71.39W
Montecristo 14 Eh 42.20N 10.20 E
Monte Cristo 55 Bb 14.43S 61.14W
Monte Ermoso 55 Bn 38.55S 61.33W
Monte Escobedo 48 Hf 22.18N 103.35W
Montefalco 14 Gh 42.52N 12.39 E
Montefeltro 14 Gg 43.55N 12.15 E
Montefiascone 14 Gh 42.32N 12.02 E
Montefrío 13 Hg 37.19N 4.01W
Montego Bay 39 Lh 18.30N 77.55W
Monteiro 54 Ke 7.53S 37.07W
Montelíbano 49 Ji 8.02N 75.29W
Montélimar 11 Kj 44.34N 4.45 E
Monte Lindo, Arroyo- 55 Cg 25.28S 59.25W
Monte Lindo, Río- 56 Ib 23.56S 57.12W
Monte Lindo Chico, Riacho- 55 Dg 25.53S 57.53W

Index Symbols

[1] Independent Nation
[2] State, Region
[3] District, County
[4] Municipality
[5] Colony, Dependency
Continent
Physical Region
Historical or Cultural Region
Mount, Mountain
Volcano
Hill
Mountains, Mountain Range
Hills, Escarpment
Plateau, Upland
Pass, Gap
Plain, Lowland
Delta
Salt Flat
Valley, Canyon
Crater, Cave
Karst Features
Depression
Polder
Desert, Dunes
Forest, Woods
Heath, Steppe
Oasis
Cape, Point
Coast, Beach
Cliff
Peninsula
Isthmus
Sandbank
Island
Atoll
Rock, Reef
Islands, Archipelago
Rocks, Reefs
Coral Reef
Well, Spring
Geyser
River, Stream
Waterfall Rapids
River Mouth, Estuary
Lake
Salt Lake
Intermittent Lake
Reservoir
Swamp, Pond
Canal
Glacier
Ice Shelf, Pack Ice
Ocean
Sea
Gulf, Bay
Strait, Fjord
Lagoon
Bank
Seamount
Tablemount
Ridge
Shelf
Basin
Escarpment, Sea Scarp
Fracture
Trench, Abyss
National Park, Reserve
Point of Interest
Recreation Site
Cave, Cavern
Historic Site
Ruins
Wall, Walls
Church, Abbey
Temple
Scientific Station
Airport
Port
Lighthouse
Mine
Tunnel
Dam, Bridge

Monte Lindo Grande, Riacho-	55	Cg	25.45 S	58.06W
Montello [Nv.-U.S.]	46	Hf	41.16N	114.12W
Montello [Wi.-U.S.]	45	Le	43.48N	89.20W
Montemorelos	47	Ec	25.12N	99.49W
Montemor-o-Novo	13	Df	38.39N	8.13W
Montemor-o-Velho	13	Dd	40.10N	8.41W
Montemuro, Serra de-	13	Dc	40.58N	8.01W
Montenegro	56	Jc	29.42 S	51.28W
Montenegro (EN) = Crna Gora [2]	15	Cg	42.30N	19.18 E
Montenegro (EN)=Crna Gora	15	Cg	42.30N	19.18 E
Monte Plata	49	Md	18.48N	69.47W
Montepuez	37	Gb	12.32 S	40.27 E
Montepuez	37	Fb	13.07 S	39.00 E
Montepulciano	14	Fg	43.05N	11.47 E
Monte Quemado	56	Hc	25.48 S	62.52W
Monte Real	13	De	39.51N	8.52W
Montereale, Passo di-	14	Hh	42.31N	13.13 E
Montereau-Faut-Yonne	11	If	48.23N	2.57 E
Monterey	43	Cd	36.37N	121.55W
Monterey Bay	43	Cd	36.45N	121.55W
Montería	53	Ie	8.46N	75.53W
Montero	54	Fg	17.20S	63.15W
Monteros	56	Gc	27.10S	65.30W
Monterotondo	14	Gh	42.03N	12.37 E
Monterrey	39	Ig	25.40N	100.19W
Montesano	46	Dc	46.59N	123.36W
Monte San Savino	14	Fg	43.20N	11.43 E
Monte Sant'Angelo	14	Ji	41.42N	15.57 E
Monte Santu, Capo di-	14	Dj	45.05N	9.44 E
Montes Claros	53	Lg	16.43S	43.52W
Montes Claros de Goiás	55	Gb	15.54S	51.13W
Montesilvano	14	Ih	42.31N	14.09 E
Montevarchi	14	Fg	43.31N	11.34 E
Montevideo [2]	55	Dl	34.50S	56.10W
Montevideo [Mn.-U.S.]	45	Id	44.57N	95.43W
Montevideo [Ur.]	53	Ki	34.53S	56.11W
Monte Vista	45	Ch	37.35N	106.09W
Montfaucon	12	He	49.17N	5.08 E
Montfort-l'Amaury	12	Df	48.47N	1.49 E
Montfort-sur-Risle	12	Ce	49.18N	0.40 E
Montgenèvre, Col de-	11	Mj	44.56N	6.44 E
Montgomery	39	Kf	32.23N	86.18W
Montgomery Pass	46	Fh	38.00N	118.20W
Montguyon	11	Fi	45.13N	0.11W
Monthermé	12	Ge	49.53N	4.44 E
Monthey	14	Ad	46.15N	6.56 E
Monthois	12	Ge	49.19N	4.43 E
Monticello [Ar.-U.S.]	45	Kj	33.38N	91.47W
Monticello [Fl.-U.S.]	44	Fj	30.33N	83.52W
Monticello [Ia.-U.S.]	45	Ke	42.15N	91.12W
Monticello [In.-U.S.]	44	De	40.45N	86.46W
Monticello [Ky.-U.S.]	44	Eg	36.50N	84.51W
Monticello [N.Y.-U.S.]	44	Je	41.39N	74.41W
Monticello [Ut.-U.S.]	43	Fd	37.52N	109.21W
Montiel	13	Jf	38.42N	2.52W
Montiel, Campo de-	13	Jf	38.46N	2.44W
Montiel, Cuchilla de-	55	Cj	31.05S	59.10W
Montignac	11	Hi	45.04N	1.10 E
Montigny-le-Roi	11	Lf	48.00N	5.30 E
Montigny-les-Metz	11	Me	49.06N	6.09 E
Montigny-le-Tilleul	12	Gd	50.23N	4.22 E
Montijo [Pan.]	49	Gj	7.59N	81.03W
Montijo [Port.]	13	Df	38.42N	8.58W
Montijo [Sp.]	13	Ff	38.55N	6.37W
Montijo, Golfo de-	49	Gj	7.40N	81.07W
Montilla	13	Hg	37.35N	4.38W
Montividiu	55	Gc	17.24S	51.14W
Montivilliers	11	Ge	49.33N	0.12 E
Mont Joli	42	Kg	48.35N	68.11W
Mont-Laurier	42	Jg	46.33N	75.30W
Mont Louis	44	Oa	49.15N	65.43W
Mont-Louis	11	Il	42.31N	2.07 E
Montluçon	11	Ih	46.20N	2.36 E
Montmagny	42	Kg	46.59N	70.33W
Montmarault	11	Ih	46.19N	2.57 E
Montmédy	11	Le	49.31N	5.22 E
Montmirail	11	Jf	48.52N	3.32 E
Montmorency	12	Ef	49.00N	2.20 E
Montmorillon	11	Gh	46.26N	0.52 E
Montmort-Lucy	12	Ff	48.55N	3.49 E
Monto	59	Kd	24.52S	151.07 E
Montoire-sur-le-Loir	11	Gg	47.45N	0.52 E
Montone	14	Gf	44.24N	12.14 E
Montoro	13	Hf	38.01N	4.23W
Montpelier [Id.-U.S.]	43	Ec	42.19N	111.18W
Montpelier [Vt.-U.S.]	43	Le	44.16N	72.35W
Montpellier	6	Gg	43.36N	3.53 E
Montpon-Ménestérol	11	Gi	45.01N	0.10 E
Montréal	39	Le	45.31N	73.34W
Montréal Lake	42	Gf	54.20N	105.40W
Montreal River	44	Hb	47.08N	79.27W
Montréjeau	11	Gk	43.05N	0.35 E
Montreuil [Fr.]	11	Hd	50.28N	1.46 E
Montreuil [Fr.]	12	Ef	48.52N	2.26 E
Montreuil-l'Argillé	12	Cf	48.56N	0.29 E
Montreux	14	Ad	46.26N	6.55 E
Montrose [Co.-U.S.]	43	Fd	38.29N	107.53W
Montrose [Scot.-U.K.]	9	Ke	56.43N	2.29W
Monts, Pointe des-	44	Na	49.19N	67.23W
Mont-Saint-Aignan	12	De	49.28N	1.05 E
Mont-Saint-Michel, Baie du-	11	Ef	48.40N	1.40W
Montsalvy	11	Ij	44.42N	2.30 E
Montsant, Serra del-/ Montsant, Sierra de-	13	Mc	41.17N	0.50 E
Montsant, Sierra de-/ Montsant, Serra del-	13	Mc	41.17N	0.50 E
Montsec, Serra del-/ Montsech, Sierra del-	13	Mb	42.02N	0.50 E
Montsech, Sierra del-/ Montsec, Serra del-	13	Mb	42.02N	0.50 E
Montseny/Pallars, Montsent de-	13	Nb	42.29N	1.02 E
Montseny, Sierra de-	13	Oc	41.48N	2.24 E
Montserrado [3]	34	Cd	6.35N	10.35W
Montserrat [5]	39	Mh	16.45N	62.12W
Montserrat, Monasterio de-	13	Nc	41.35N	1.49 E
Montserrat, Monasterio de-/ Montserrat, Monèstir de-	13	Nc	41.35N	1.49 E
Montserrat, Monèstir de-	13	Nc	41.35N	1.49 E
Montserrat, Monèstir de-/ Montserrat, Monasterio de-	13	Nc	41.35N	1.49 E
Montuosa, Isla-	49	Fj	7.28N	82.14W
Montville	12	De	49.33N	1.07 E
Monument Peak	46	He	42.07N	114.14W
Monument Valley	46	Jh	36.50N	110.20W
Monveda	36	Db	2.57N	21.27 E
Monviso	5	Gg	44.40N	7.07 E
Monywa	25	Jd	22.07N	95.08 E
Monza	14	De	45.35N	9.16 E
Monze	36	Ef	16.16S	27.29 E
Monzen	29	Ec	37.17N	136.46 E
Monzón	13	Mc	41.55N	0.12 E
Mo'oka	29	Fc	36.27N	139.59 E
Moonbeam	44	Fa	49.25N	82.11W
Moonie	59	Ke	27.40S	150.19 E
Moonie River	59	Je	29.19S	148.43 E
Moonta	59	Hf	34.04S	137.35 E
Moora	58	Ch	30.39S	116.00 E
Moorcroft	46	Md	44.16N	104.57W
Moore	45	Hi	35.20N	97.29W
Moore, Lake-	57	Cg	29.50S	117.35 E
Moorea, Ile-	57	Mf	17.32S	149.50W
Moore's Island	44	Il	26.18N	77.33W
Moorhead	43	Hb	46.53N	96.45W
Moormerland	12	Ja	53.18N	7.26 E
Moormerland-Neermoor	12	Ja	53.18N	7.26 E
Moorreesburg	37	Bf	33.09S	18.40 E
Moosburg an der Isar	10	Hh	48.28N	11.56 E
Moose	38	Kd	50.48N	81.18W
Moosehead Lake	43	Nb	45.40N	69.40W
Moose Jaw	39	Id	50.23N	105.32W
Moose Jaw River	46	Ma	50.34N	105.17W
Moose Lake	45	Jc	46.25N	92.45W
Mooselookmeguntic Lake	44	Lc	44.53N	70.48W
Moose Mountain	45	Eb	49.45N	102.37W
Moose Mountain Creek	45	Eb	49.12N	102.10W
Moosomin	42	Hf	50.09N	101.40W
Moosonee	39	Kd	51.17N	80.39W
Mopeia	37	Fc	17.59S	35.43 E
Mopelia, Atoll-→ Maupihaa Atoll	57	Lf	16.50S	153.55W
Mopti	31	Gg	14.30N	4.12W
Mopti [3]	34	Ec	14.40N	4.15W
Moqokorei	35	He	4.04N	46.08 E
Moquegua [2]	54	Dg	16.50S	70.55W
Moquegua	53	Ig	17.12S	70.56W
Mór	10	Oi	47.23N	18.12 E
Mor, Glen-	9	Id	57.10N	4.40W
Mora [Cam.]	34	Hc	11.03N	14.09 E
Mora [Port.]	13	Df	38.56N	8.10W
Mora [Sp.]	13	Ie	39.41N	3.46W
Mora [Swe.]	7	Df	61.00N	14.33 E
Moraća	15	Cg	42.16N	19.09 E
Moraća, Manastir-	15	Cg	42.46N	19.24 E
Morādābād	22	Jg	28.50N	78.47 E
Morada Nova de Minas	55	Jd	18.25S	45.22W
Móra d'Ebre/Mora de Ebro	13	Mc	41.05N	0.38 E
Mora de Ebro/Móra d'Ebre	13	Mc	41.05N	0.38 E
Mora de Rubielos	13	Ld	40.15N	0.45W
Morafenobe	37	Gc	17.49S	44.55 E
Morąg	10	Pc	53.56N	19.56 E
Mórahalom	10	Pj	46.13N	19.53 E
Moraleda, Canal-	56	Ff	44.30S	73.30W
Moraleja	13	Fd	40.04N	6.39W
Morales [Col.]	49	Ki	8.17N	73.52W
Morales [Guat.]	49	Cf	15.29N	88.49W
Morales, Laguna-	48	Kf	23.35N	97.45W
Moramanga	37	Hc	18.57S	48.11 E
Moran	46	Je	43.50N	110.28W
Morane Atoll	57	Ng	23.10S	137.07W
Morangas, Ribeirão-	55	Fd	19.39S	52.19W
Morant Bay	49	Ie	17.53N	76.25W
Morant Cays	47	Ie	17.24N	75.59W
Morant Point	49	Ie	17.55N	76.10W
Morar, Loch-	9	He	56.58N	5.45W
Morarano	37	Hc	17.46S	48.10 E
Mora River	45	Di	35.44N	104.23W
Moraska, Góra-	10	Md	52.30N	16.52 E
Morat/Murten	14	Bd	46.56N	7.08 E
Morata, Puerto de-	13	Kc	41.29N	1.31W
Moratalla	13	Kf	38.12N	1.53W
Moratuwa	25	Fg	6.46N	79.53 E
Morava	5	Hf	48.10N	16.59 E
Morava=Moravia (EN)	5	Hf	49.30N	17.00 E
Morava=Moravia (EN)	10	Mg	49.30N	17.00 E
Moravia (EN)=Morava	5	Hf	49.30N	17.00 E
Moravia (EN)=Morava	10	Mg	49.30N	17.00 E
Moravian Gate (EN)= Moravská Brána	5	Hf	49.33N	17.42 E
Moravian Upland (EN)= Českomoravská Vrchovina	5	Hf	49.20N	15.30 E
Moravica	15	Df	43.51N	20.05 E
Moravská Brána=Moravian Gate(EN)	5	Hf	49.33N	17.42 E
Moravské Budějovice	10	Lg	49.03N	15.49 E
Morawa	59	De	29.13S	116.00 E
Morawhanna	54	Gb	8.16N	59.45W
Moray Firth	5	Fd	57.50N	3.30W
Morbach	12	Je	49.49N	7.07 E
Morbihan [3]	11	Dg	47.55N	2.50W
Morbihan	11	Dg	47.35N	2.48W
Morbylånga	7	Dh	56.31N	16.23 E
Morcenx	11	Fj	44.02N	0.55W
Mordāb	24	Md	37.26N	49.25 E
Mordaga	27	La	51.14N	120.43 E
Morden	42	Hg	49.11N	98.05W
Mordovo	16	Lc	52.05N	40.46 E
Mordovskaja respublika	19	Ee	54.20N	44.30 E
Möre	8	Fh	56.25N	15.55 E
More, Ben-	9	Ie	56.23N	4.31W
Morea	37	Bd	22.41S	15.54 E
More Assynt, Ben-	9	Ic	58.07N	4.51W
Moreau River	43	Gb	45.18N	100.43W
Morecambe	9	Kg	54.04N	2.53W
Morecambe Bay	9	Kg	54.07N	3.00W
Moree	58	Fg	29.28S	149.51 E
Morehead [Ky.-U.S.]	44	Ff	38.11N	83.25W
Morehead [Pap.N.Gui.]	60	Ci	8.50S	141.57 E
Morehead City	39	Lf	34.43N	76.43W
Moreiz, Gora-	19	Gb	69.30N	62.05 E
Moreju	17	Ib	68.20N	59.45 E
Morelia	39	Ih	19.42N	101.07W
Morella	13	Ld	40.37N	0.06W
Morelos	48	Ic	28.25N	100.53W
Morelos [2]	47	Ee	18.45N	99.00W
Morena, Sierra-	5	Fh	38.00N	5.00W
Moreni	15	Ie	44.59N	25.39 E
Møre og Romsdal [2]	7	Be	62.40N	7.50 E
Moresby	42	Ef	52.45N	131.50W
Moreton Bay	59	Ke	27.20S	153.15 E
Moreton Island	59	Ke	27.10S	153.25 E
Moret-sur-Loing	11	If	48.22N	2.49 E
Moreuil	11	Ie	49.46N	2.29 E
Morez	11	Mh	46.31N	6.02 E
Morezu	15	Hd	45.09N	24.01 E
Mörfelden	12	Ke	49.59N	8.34 E
Morgan City	45	Kl	29.42N	91.12W
Morganfield	44	Dg	37.41N	87.55W
Morganton	44	Gh	35.45N	81.41W
Morgantown [Ky.-U.S.]	44	Dg	37.14N	86.41W
Morgantown [W.V.-U.S.]	44	Hf	39.38N	79.57W
Morges	14	Ad	46.31N	6.30 E
Morghāb	23	Jb	38.18N	61.12 E
Morhange	11	Mf	48.55N	6.38 E
Mori [China]	27	Fc	43.49N	90.11 E
Mori [Jap.]	28	Pc	42.06N	140.35 E
Moriarty	45	Ci	34.59N	106.03W
Morichal Largo, Río-	50	Eh	9.27N	62.25W
Moriguchi	29	Dd	34.44N	135.34 E
Morin Dawa (Nirji)	27	Lb	48.30N	124.28 E
Morioka	22	Qf	39.42N	141.09 E
Moriyoshi	29	Ga	40.07N	140.22 E
Moriyoshi-Yama	29	Gb	39.59N	140.33 E
Morjärv	7	Fc	66.04N	22.43 E
Morki	7	Lh	56.28N	49.00 E
Morko	8	Gf	59.00N	17.40 E
Morkoka	20	Gc	65.03N	115.40 E
Morkøv	8	Di	55.40N	11.32 E
Morlaix	11	Cf	48.35N	3.50W
Morlanwelz	12	Gd	50.27N	4.14 E
Mörlunda	8	Fg	57.19N	15.51 E
Mormanno	14	Jk	39.53N	15.59 E
Morne-à-l'Eau	50	Fd	16.21N	61.31W
Morne Diablotin	47	Le	15.30N	61.24W
Mornington, Isla-	56	Eg	49.45S	75.23W
Mornington Island	59	Hc	16.35S	139.24 E
Moro	46	Ed	45.29N	120.44W
Morobe	58	Fe	7.45S	147.37 E
Morocco (EN)=Al Maghrib [1]	31	Ge	32.00N	5.50W
Morogoro	31	Ki	6.49S	37.40 E
Morogoro [3]	36	Gd	8.20S	37.00 E
Moro Gulf	26	He	6.51N	123.00 E
Moroleón	48	Ig	20.08N	101.12W
Morombe	31	Lk	21.44S	43.23 E
Morón [Arg.]	55	Cl	34.39S	58.37W
Morón [Cuba]	47	Id	22.06N	78.38W
Morón [Ven.]	54	Ea	10.29N	68.11W
Morona, Río-	54	Cd	4.45S	77.04W
Morondava	31	Lk	20.15S	44.17 E
Morón de la Frontera	13	Gg	37.08N	5.27W
Morones, Sierra-	48	Hg	21.55N	103.05W
Moroni	31	Lj	11.41S	43.16 E
Moron Us He	21	Lf	34.42N	94.50 E
Morotai, Pulau-	57	Dd	2.20N	128.25 E
Moroto	31	Kh	2.32N	34.39 E
Morovița	15	Ed	45.16N	21.16 E
Morozov	15	Ig	42.30N	25.10 E
Morozovsk	19	Ef	48.20N	41.50 E
Morpeth	9	Lf	55.10N	1.41W
Morphou → Güzelyurt	24	Ee	35.12N	32.59 E
Morrilton	45	Ji	35.09N	92.45W
Morrinhos	54	Ig	17.44S	49.07W
Morrinsville	62	Fb	37.39S	175.32 E
Morris [Il.-U.S.]	45	Lf	41.22N	88.26W
Morris [Man.-Can.]	42	Hg	49.21N	97.22W
Morris [Mn.-U.S.]	45	Id	45.35N	95.55W
Morris, Mount-	59	Ge	26.09S	131.04 E
Morrisburg	44	Jc	44.54N	75.11W
Morris Jesup, Kap-	67	Me	83.45N	35.50W
Morrison Dennis Cays	49	Ff	14.28N	82.53W
Morristown	44	Fg	36.13N	83.18W
Morrito	49	Eh	11.37N	85.05W
Morro, Punta del-	48	Kh	19.51N	96.27W
Morro Bay	43	Cd	35.22N	120.51W
Morro do Chapéu	54	Jf	11.33S	41.09W
Morrosquillo, Golfo de-	49	Ji	9.35N	75.40W
Morro Vermelho, Serra do-	55	Jc	17.45S	45.20W
Mörrum	8	Fh	56.11N	14.45 E
Morrumbala	37	Fc	17.20S	35.35 E
Morrumbene	37	Fd	23.39S	35.20 E
Mörrumsån	8	Fh	56.09N	14.44 E
Mors	8	Ch	56.50N	8.45 E
Moršansk	19	Ee	53.26N	41.49 E
Morsbach	12	Jd	50.52N	7.45 E
Morsberg	12	Ke	49.43N	8.54 E
Mörsil	7	Ce	63.19N	13.38 E
Mörskom/Myrskylä	8	Kd	60.40N	25.51 E
Morsott	14	Co	35.40N	8.01 E
Mortagne	11	Mf	48.33N	6.27 E
Mortagne-au-Perche	11	Gf	48.31N	0.33 E
Mortagne-sur-Sèvre	11	Fg	47.00N	0.57W
Mortain	11	Ff	48.39N	0.56W
Mortara	14	Ce	45.15N	8.44 E
Mortcha	30	Jg	16.00N	21.10 E
Morteau	11	Mg	47.04N	6.37 E
Morteaux-Couliboeuf	12	Bf	48.56N	0.04W
Morteros	56	Hd	30.42S	62.00W
Mortes, Rio das-	55	Je	21.09S	44.53W
Mortesoro	35	Ec	10.12N	34.09 E
Mortlock Islands	57	Gd	5.27N	153.40 E
Morton	46	Dc	46.33N	122.17W
Mortsel	12	Gc	51.10N	4.28 E
Morumbi	55	Ef	23.46S	54.06W
Morvan	11	Jg	47.05N	4.00 E
Morven	59	Je	26.25S	147.07 E
Morvern	9	He	56.35N	5.50W
Morvi	25	Ed	22.49N	70.50 E
Morwell	58	Fh	38.14S	146.24 E
Morzine	11	Mh	46.11N	6.43 E
Moržovec, Ostrov-	7	Kc	66.45N	42.35 E
Moša	7	Je	62.25N	39.48 E
Mosbach	10	Fg	49.21N	9.09 E
Mosby	8	Bf	58.14N	7.54 E
Mošćny, Ostrov-	7	Gg	60.00N	27.50 E
Mosconi	55	Bl	35.44S	60.34W
Moscos Islands	25	Jf	14.00N	97.45 E
Moscow [Id.-U.S.]	43	Db	46.44N	116.59W
Moscow (EN)=Moskva	5	Jd	55.08N	38.50 E
Moscow (EN) = Moskva	6	Jd	55.45N	37.35 E
Moscow Basin (EN) = Meščera	5	Kd	55.00N	40.30 E
Moscow Canal (EN)= Moskvy, kanal imeni-	5	Jd	56.43N	37.08 E
Moscow Upland (EN)= Moskovskaja Vozvyšennost	5	Jd	56.30N	37.30 E
Mosel=Moselle (EN)	5	Ge	50.22N	7.36 E
Moselberge	12	Ie	49.57N	6.56 E
Moselle [3]	11	Me	49.00N	6.30 E
Moselle	5	Ge	50.22N	7.36 E
Moselle (EN)=Mosel	5	Ge	50.22N	7.36 E
Moses Lake	43	Db	47.08N	119.17W
Mosgiel	61	Di	45.53S	170.22 E
Moshi	31	Ki	3.21S	37.20 E
Mosina	10	Md	52.16N	16.51 E
Mosjøen	7	Cd	65.50N	13.12 E
Moskalvo	20	Jf	53.39N	142.37 E
Moskenesøy	7	Cc	67.59N	13.00 E
Moskovskaja Oblast [3]	19	Dd	55.45N	37.45 E
Moskovskaja Vozvyšennost =Moscow Upland (EN)	5	Jd	56.30N	37.30 E
Moskovski	18	Gf	37.40N	69.39 E
Moskva Moscow (EN)	6	Jd	55.45N	37.35 E
Moskva	18	Ee	38.27N	64.24 E
Moskva=Moscow (EN)	5	Jd	55.08N	38.50 E
Moskva, Pik-	18	He	38.55N	71.52 E
Moskvy, kanal imeni-= Moscow Canal (EN)	5	Jd	56.43N	37.08 E
Moslavačka Gora	14	Ke	45.38N	16.42 E
Moso	63b	Dc	17.32S	168.15 E
Mosomane	37	Dd	24.01S	26.19 E
Mosoni-Duna	10	Ni	47.44N	17.47 E
Mosonmagyaróvár	10	Ni	47.52N	17.17 E
Mosor	14	Kg	43.30N	16.40 E
Mosquero	45	Ei	35.47N	103.58W
Mosquito, Baie -	42	Jd	60.40N	78.00W
Mosquito Coast (EN)= Mosquitos, Costa de-	38	Kh	13.00N	83.45W
Mosquito, Riacho-	55	Cf	22.12S	57.57W
Mosquitos, Costa de-= Mosquito Coast (EN)	38	Kh	13.00N	83.45W
Mosquitos, Golfo de los-	38	Ki	9.00N	81.20W
Moss	6	Hd	59.26N	10.42 E
Mossaka	36	Cc	1.13S	16.48 E
Mossâmedes	55	Gc	16.07S	50.11W
Mossbank	46	Mb	49.55N	105.59W
Mossburn	61	Ci	45.41S	168.15 E
Mosselbaai	31	Jl	34.11S	22.08 E
Mossendjo	36	Bc	2.57S	12.44 E
Mossman	58	Ff	16.28S	145.22 E
Mosso	8	Ch	56.05N	9.50 E
Mossoró	53	Mf	5.11S	37.20W
Moss Point	45	Lk	30.25N	88.29W
Mossuril	37	Gb	14.58S	40.40 E
Most	10	Jf	50.32N	13.39 E
Mostaganem [3]	32	Hb	35.40N	0.30 E
Mostaganem	31	He	35.56N	0.05 E
Mostar	14	Lg	43.21N	17.49 E
Mostardas	55	Gj	31.06S	50.57W
Møsting, Kap-	41	Hf	63.45N	41.00W
Mostiska	16	Ce	49.48N	23.09 E
Mostiștea	15	Je	44.15N	26.54 E
Most na Soci	14	Hd	46.09N	13.45 E
Mostovskoj	16	Lg	44.22N	40.48 E
Mosty	19	Ce	53.27N	24.33 E
Mosul (EN)=Al Mawșil	22	Gf	36.20N	43.08 E
Møsvatn	7	Bg	59.50N	8.05 E
Mota	63b	Ca	13.40S	167.42 E
Mota	35	Fc	11.05N	37.53 E
Motaba	36	Cb	2.03N	18.03 E
Motacusito	55	Bc	17.35S	61.31W
Mota del Marques	13	Gc	41.38N	5.10W
Motagua	38	Kh	15.44N	88.14W
Motajica	14	Le	45.04N	17.40 E
Motala	7	Dg	58.33N	15.03 E
Motala ström	8	Gf	58.38N	16.10 E
Motatán	49	Li	9.24N	70.36W
Motatán, Río-	49	Li	9.32N	71.02W
Motegi	29	Gc	36.32N	140.10 E
Motehuala	47	Dd	23.39N	100.39W
Mothe	63d	Cc	18.40S	178.30W
Motherwell	9	Jf	55.48N	4.00W
Motīhāri	25	Gc	26.39N	84.55 E
Motilla del Palancar	13	Ke	39.34N	1.53W
Motiti Island	62	Gb	37.40S	176.25 E
Motlav	63b	Ca	13.40S	167.40 E
Motobu	29b	Ab	26.40N	127.55 E
Motol	10	Vd	52.17N	25.40 E
Motovski Zaliv	7	Hb	69.30N	32.30 E
Motoyoshi	29	Gb	38.48N	141.31 E
Motozintla de Mendoza	48	Mj	15.22N	92.14W
Motril	13	Ih	36.45N	3.31W
Motru	15	Ge	44.33N	23.27 E
Motru	15	Fe	44.48N	23.00 E
Motsuta-Misaki	29a	Ab	42.36N	139.49 E
Mott	45	Ec	46.22N	102.20W
Motteville	12	Ce	49.38N	0.51 E
Motu	62	Gb	37.51S	177.35 E
Motueka	62	Ed	41.07S	173.01 E
Motuhora Island	62	Gb	37.50S	177.00 E
Motu-Iti	65d	Ac	27.11S	109.27W
Motu-Iti → Tupai Atoll	61	Kc	16.17S	151.50W
Motul	47	Gd	21.06N	89.17W
Motu-Nui	65d	Ac	27.12S	109.28W
Motu One Atoll	57	Lf	15.48S	154.33W
Motupae	64n	Ac	10.27S	161.02W
Motupena Point	63a	Bb	6.32S	155.09 E
Moturiki	63d	Bb	17.46S	178.45 E
Motutapu	64p	Cb	21.14S	159.43W
Motu Tautara	65d	Ab	27.05S	109.26W
Motutunga Atoll	57	Mf	17.06S	144.22W
Moubray Bay	66	Kf	72.11S	170.15 E
Mouchard	11	Lh	46.58N	5.48 E
Mouchoir Bank (EN)	47	Jd	20.57N	70.42W
Mouchoir Passage	49	Lc	21.10N	71.00W
Moudjéria	32	Ef	17.52N	12.20W
Mouila	31	Ii	1.52S	11.01 E
Mouka	35	Cd	7.16N	21.52 E
Moul	34	Hb	15.03N	13.18 E
Mould Bay	39	Hb	76.15N	119.30W
Moule	50	Fd	16.20N	61.21W
Moule à Chique, Cap-	51k	Bb	13.43N	60.57W
Moulins	11	Jh	46.34N	3.20 E
Moulmein → Mawlamyine	22	Le	16.30N	97.38 E
Moulouya	30	Ge	35.06N	2.20W
Moult	12	Be	49.07N	0.10W
Moultrie	44	Fj	31.11N	83.47W
Moultrie, Lake-	44	Gi	33.20N	80.05W
Mouly, Pointe de-	63b	Ce	20.43S	166.23 E
Moúnda, Ákra-	15	Dk	38.03N	20.47 E
Moundou	31	Ih	8.34N	16.05 E
Moundsville	44	Gf	39.54N	80.44W
Mo'unga'one	65b	Ba	19.38S	174.29W
Moungoudou	36	Bc	2.40S	12.41 E
Mountainair	45	Ci	34.31N	106.15W
Mountain Grove	45	Jh	37.08N	92.16W
Mountain Home [Ar.-U.S.]	45	Jh	36.21N	92.23W
Mountain Home [Id.-U.S.]	43	Dc	43.08N	115.41W
Mountain Nile (EN)=Jabal, Baḥr al-	30	Kh	9.30N	30.30 E
Mountain Village	40	Gd	62.05N	163.44W
Mount Airy	44	Gg	36.31N	80.37W
Mount Barker	59	Df	34.38S	117.40 E
Mount Carmel	45	Mf	38.25N	87.46W
Mount Desert Island	44	Mc	44.20N	68.20W
Mount Douglas	58	Fg	21.30S	146.50 E
Mount Eba	59	Hf	30.12S	135.40 E
Mount Forest	44	Gd	43.59N	80.44W
Mount Frere	37	Df	31.00S	28.58 E
Mount Gambier	58	Fh	37.50S	140.46 E
Mount Hagen	60	Ci	5.52S	144.13 E
Mount Hope	59	Hf	34.07S	135.23 E
Mount Isa	58	Eg	20.44S	139.30 E
Mountlake Terrace	46	Dc	47.47N	122.18W
Mount Lebanon	44	Ge	40.23N	80.03W
Mount Lofty Ranges	59	Hg	35.15S	138.50 E
Mount Magnet	58	Cg	28.04S	117.49 E
Mount Maunganui	61	Eg	37.38S	176.12 E
Mount Morgan	59	Kd	23.39S	150.23 E
Mountnorris Bay	59	Gb	11.20S	132.45 E
Mount Peck	46	Ha	50.10N	115.02W
Mount Pleasant [Ia.-U.S.]	45	Kf	40.58N	91.33W
Mount Pleasant [Mi.-U.S.]	44	Ed	43.35N	84.47W
Mount Pleasant [S.C.-U.S.]	44	Hi	32.47N	79.52W
Mount Pleasant [Tx.-U.S.]	45	Ij	33.09N	94.58W
Mount Pleasant [Ut.-U.S.]	46	Jg	39.33N	111.27W
Mount's Bay	9	Hk	50.03N	5.25W
Mount Somers	62	De	43.42S	171.25 E
Mount Sterling [Il.-U.S.]	45	Kg	39.59N	90.45W
Mount Sterling [Ky.-U.S.]	44	Ff	38.04N	83.56W
Mount Vancouver	42	Dd	60.20N	139.41W
Mount Vernon [Al.-U.S.]	44	Cj	31.05N	88.01W
Mount Vernon [Austl.]	59	Dd	24.13S	118.14 E
Mount Vernon [Il.-U.S.]	43	Jd	38.19N	88.55W
Mount Vernon [In.-U.S.]	44	Dg	37.56N	87.54W
Mount Vernon [Ky.-U.S.]	44	Eg	37.21N	84.20W
Mount Vernon [Oh.-U.S.]	44	Fe	40.23N	82.30W
Mount Vernon [Wa.-U.S.]	43	Cb	48.25N	122.20W
Moura [Austl.]	59	Jd	24.35S	150.00 E
Moura [Port.]	13	Ef	38.08N	7.27W
Mourão	13	Ef	38.23N	7.21W
Mourdi	35	Cb	17.50N	22.25 E
Mourdi, Dépression du-= Mourdi Depression (EN)	30	Jg	18.10N	23.00 E
Mourdiah	34	Dc	14.26N	7.31W
Mourdi Depression (EN)= Mourdi, Dépression du-	30	Jg	18.10N	23.00 E
Mourmelon-le-Grand	12	Ge	49.08N	4.22 E
Mourne Mountains/Beanna Boirche	9	Gg	54.10N	6.04W
Mouscron/Moeskroen	11	Jd	50.44N	3.13 E
Moussoro	31	Ig	13.39N	16.29 E
Moustiers-Sainte-Marie	11	Mk	43.51N	6.13 E
Moutier/Münster	14	Bc	47.16N	7.22 E
Moutiers	11	Mi	45.29N	6.32 E
Moutong	26	Hf	0.28N	121.13 E
Mouy	12	Ee	49.19N	2.19 E
Mouydir	30	Hf	25.00N	4.10 E
Mouyondzi	36	Bc	3.58S	13.57 E
Mouzaia	13	Oh	36.28N	2.41 E
Mouzon	12	He	49.36N	5.05 E
Movas	48	Ec	28.10N	109.25W

Index Symbols

[1] Independent Nation; [2] State, Region; [3] District, County; [4] Municipality; [5] Colony, Dependency; Continent; Physical Region; Historical or Cultural Region; Mount, Mountain; Volcano; Hill; Mountains, Mountain Range; Hills, Escarpment; Plateau, Upland; Pass, Gap; Plain, Lowland; Delta; Salt Flat; Valley, Canyon; Crater, Cave; Karst Features; Depression; Polder; Desert, Dunes; Forest, Woods; Heath, Steppe; Oasis; Cape, Point; Coast, Beach; Cliff; Peninsula; Isthmus; Sandbank; Island; Atoll; Rock, Reef; Islands, Archipelago; Rocks, Reefs; Coral Reef; Well, Spring; Geyser; River, Stream; Waterfall Rapids; River Mouth, Estuary; Lake; Salt Lake; Intermittent Lake; Reservoir; Swamp, Pond; Canal; Glacier; Ice Shelf, Pack Ice; Ocean; Sea; Gulf, Bay; Strait, Fjord; Lagoon; Bank; Seamount; Tablemount; Ridge; Shelf; Basin; Escarpment, Sea Scarp; Fracture; Trench, Abyss; National Park, Reserve; Point of Interest; Recreation Site; Cave, Cavern; Historic Site; Ruins; Wall, Walls; Church, Abbey; Temple; Scientific Station; Airport; Port; Lighthouse; Mine; Tunnel; Dam, Bridge

Moxico [3]	36	De	12.00S	20.00 E
Moxico	36	De	11.51S	20.01 E
Moy/An Mhuaidh	9	Dg	54.12N	9.08W
Moyahua	48	Hg	21.16N	103.10W
Moyale [Eth.]	31	Kh	3.32N	39.04 E
Moyale [Kenya]	36	Gb	3.32N	39.03 E
Moyamba	34	Cd	8.10N	12.26W
Moÿ-de-l'Aisne	12	Fe	49.45N	3.22 E
Moyen Atlas=Middle Atlas (EN)	30	Ge	33.30N	4.30W
Moyen-Chari [3]	35	Bd	9.00N	18.00 E
Moyenne Guinée [3]	34	Cc	11.15N	12.30W
Moyenneville	12	Dd	50.04N	1.45 E
Moyen-Ogooué [3]	36	Bc	0.30S	10.30 E
Moyeuvre-Grande	12	Ie	49.15N	6.02 E
Moyo	36	Fb	3.40N	31.43 E
Moyo, Pulau-	26	Gh	8.15S	117.34 E
Moyobamba	53	If	6.02S	76.58W
Moyowosi	36	Fc	4.50S	31.24 E
Moyto	35	Bc	12.35N	16.33 E
Moyu/Karakax	27	Cd	37.17N	79.42 E
Možajsk	7	Ii	55.32N	36.02 E
Mozambique (EN)=Moçambique [1]	31	Kj	18.15S	35.00 E
Mozambique (EN)=Moçambique	31	Lk	15.03S	40.45 E
Mozambique, Canal de-=Mozambique Channel (EN)	30	Lk	20.00S	43.00 E
Mozambique Channel (EN)=Moçambique, Canal de-	30	Lk	20.00S	43.00 E
Mozambique Channel (EN)=Mozambique, Canal de-	30	Lk	20.00S	43.00 E
Mozambique Plateau (EN)	30	Kl	32.00S	35.00 E
Mozdok	19	Eg	43.44N	44.38 E
Možga	19	Fd	56.28N	52.13 E
Mozuli	8	Mh	56.32N	28.14 E
Mozyr	19	Ce	52.02N	29.16 E
Mpala	36	Ed	6.45S	29.31 E
Mpanda	31	Ki	6.22S	31.02 E
Mpigi	36	Fb	0.15N	32.20 E
Mpika	31	Kj	11.50S	31.27 E
Mpoko	35	Be	4.19N	18.33 E
Mporokoso	36	Fd	9.23S	30.08 E
Mpouia	36	Cc	2.37S	16.13 E
Mpui	36	Fd	8.21S	31.50 E
Mpulungu	36	Fd	8.46S	31.07 E
Mpwapwa	36	Gd	6.21S	36.29 E
Mrągowo	10	Rc	53.52N	21.19 E
Mrakovo	17	Hj	52.43N	56.38 E
Mrkonjić Grad	14	Lf	44.25N	17.06 E
Mrocza	10	Nc	53.14N	17.36 E
Mroga	10	Pd	52.09N	19.42 E
Msangesi	36	Ge	11.40S	36.45 E
Msid, Djebel-	14	Cn	36.25N	8.04 E
Msif	13	Qi	35.23N	4.45 E
M'Sila	13	Qi	35.31N	4.30 E
M'Sila [3]	32	Hb	35.00N	4.30 E
M'Sila	32	Hb	35.42N	4.33 E
Mšinskaja	8	Nf	58.55N	30.03 E
Msta	5	Jd	58.25N	31.20 E
Mstislavl	16	Gc	53.59N	31.45 E
Mszana Dolna	10	Qg	49.42N	20.05 E
Mtakuja	36	Fd	7.22S	30.37 E
Mtama	36	Ge	10.18S	39.22 E
Mtelo	36	Gb	1.39N	35.23 E
Mtera Reservoir	36	Gd	7.01S	35.55 E
Mtito Andei	36	Gc	2.41S	38.10 E
Mtubatuba	37	Ee	28.30S	32.08 E
Mtwara [3]	36	Ge	10.40S	39.00 E
Mtwara	31	Lj	10.16S	40.11 E
Mu, Cerro-	49	Ki	9.29N	73.07W
Mua	64h	Ac	13.21S	176.10W
Mu'a	65b	Ac	21.11S	175.07W
Mua, Baie de-	64h	Bc	13.23S	176.09W
Muaná	54	Id	1.32S	49.13W
Muang Huon	25	Kd	20.09N	101.27 E
Muang Khammouan	25	Ke	17.24N	104.48 E
Muang Không	25	Lf	14.07N	105.51 E
Muang Khôngxédôn	25	Le	15.34N	105.49 E
Muang Khoua	25	Kd	21.05N	102.31 E
Muang Pak Lay	25	Ke	18.12N	101.25 E
Muang Pakxan	25	Ke	18.22N	103.39 E
Muang Pakxong	25	Le	15.11N	106.14 E
Muang Sing	25	Kd	21.11N	101.09 E
Muang Tahoi	25	Le	16.10N	106.38 E
Muang Thai=Thailand (EN) [1]	22	Lh	15.00N	100.00 E
Muang Vangviang	25	Ke	18.56N	102.27 E
Muang Xaignabouri	25	Ke	19.15N	101.45 E
Muang Xay	25	Kd	20.42N	101.59 E
Muang Xépôn	25	Le	16.41N	106.14 E
Muanzanza	36	Dd	6.32S	20.51 E
Muar	26	Df	2.02N	102.34 E
Muaraaman	26	Dg	3.07S	102.12 E
Muarabungo	26	Dg	1.28S	102.07 E
Muaraenim	26	Dg	3.39S	103.48 E
Muaralasan	26	Gf	1.48N	117.12 E
Muarapajang	26	Gg	1.32S	115.48 E
Muarasiberut	26	Cg	1.36S	99.11 E
Muarasiram	26	Gg	0.46S	116.11 E
Muaratebo	26	Dg	1.30S	102.26 E
Muaratewe	26	Fg	0.57S	114.53 E
Muarawahau	26	Gf	1.02N	116.52 E
Mubarek	18	Ee	39.16N	65.07 E
Mubende	36	Fb	0.35N	31.23 E
Mubi	31	Ig	10.16N	13.16 E
Much	12	Jd	50.55N	7.24 E
Muchinga Escarpment	36	Fe	13.40S	34.00 E
Muchinga Mountains	30	Kj	12.00S	31.45 E
Muck	9	Ge	56.50N	6.14W
Mücke	12	Ld	50.37N	9.02 E
Mucojo	37	Gb	12.04S	40.28 E
Muconda	36	De	10.34S	21.20 E
Mucua	37	Ec	18.09S	34.58 E
Mucubela	37	Fc	16.54S	37.49 E
Mucuchies	49	Li	8.45N	70.55W
Mucumbura	37	Ec	16.10S	31.42 E
Mucur	24	Fc	39.04N	34.23 E
Mucusso	36	Df	18.00S	21.25 E
Mudan Jang	21	Oe	46.18N	129.31 E
Mudanjiang	22	Oe	44.35N	129.34 E
Mudanya	24	Cb	40.22N	28.52 E
Muddy Gap	46	Le	42.22N	107.27W
Mudgee	59	Jf	32.36S	149.35 E
Mud Lake	46	Ie	43.53N	112.24W
Mud Lake	46	Gh	37.55N	117.05W
Mudon	25	Je	16.15N	97.44 E
Mudug [3]	35	Hd	6.30N	48.00 E
Mudug	35	Hd	6.20N	47.00 E
Mudurnu	24	Db	40.28N	31.13 E
Muecate	37	Fb	14.53S	39.38 E
Mueda	37	Fb	11.39S	39.33 E
Muerto, Cayo-	49	Ff	14.34N	82.44W
Muerto, Mar-	48	Li	16.10N	94.10W
Mufulira	31	Jj	12.33S	28.14 E
Mufu Shan	27	Jf	29.15N	114.20 E
Mufu Shan	27	Jf	29.00N	113.50 E
Mugello	14	Fg	43.55N	11.25 E
Múggia	14	He	45.36N	13.46 E
Mughshin, Wādī-	35	Ib	19.44N	55.00 E
Mugi	29	De	33.40N	134.25 E
Mu Gia, Deo-	25	Le	17.40N	105.47 E
Mugila, Monts-	36	Ed	6.49S	29.08 E
Muğla	23	Cb	37.12N	28.22 E
Mugodžary	21	He	49.00N	58.40 E
Mugur an Na'ām	24	Ig	31.56N	40.30 E
Muhaiwir	24	If	33.28N	40.59 E
Muḩammad, Ra's-	33	Fd	27.42N	34.13 E
Muḩammad Oawl	35	Fa	20.54N	37.05 E
Muhen	20	Ig	48.10N	136.08 E
Muheza	36	Gd	5.10S	38.47 E
Muhīt, Al Baḩr al-=Atlantic Ocean (EN)	3	Di	2.00N	25.00W
Mühlacker	10	Eh	48.57N	8.50 E
Mühldorf am Inn	10	Ih	48.15N	12.32 E
Mühlhausen in Thüringen	10	Ge	51.13N	10.27 E
Mühlig-Hofmann Gebirge	66	Cf	72.00S	5.20 E
Mühlviertel	14	Ib	48.30N	14.10 E
Muhoršibir → Taksimo	20	Ff	51.01N	107.50 E
Muhos	7	Gd	64.50N	26.01 E
Muhu	7	Fg	58.35N	23.15 E
Muhu	8	Jf	58.37N	23.05 E
Muhu, Proliv-/Muhu Väin	8	Jf	58.45N	23.15 E
Muhulu	36	Ec	1.03S	27.17 E
Muhu Väin/Muhu, Proliv-	8	Jf	58.45N	23.15 E
Muhuwesi	36	Ge	11.16S	37.58 E
Muiderslot	12	Hb	52.20N	5.06 E
Muigheo/Mayo [2]	9	Dh	53.50N	9.30W
Muikamachi	28	Of	37.04N	138.53 E
Muineachán/Monaghan [2]	9	Gg	54.10N	7.00W
Muineachán/Monaghan	9	Gg	54.15N	6.58W
Muine Bheag	9	Gi	52.42N	6.57W
Muir Bhreatan=Saint George's Channel (EN)	5	Fe	52.00N	6.00W
Muir Eireann=Irish Sea (EN)	5	Fe	53.30N	5.20W
Muiron Islands	59	Cd	21.35S	114.20 E
Muir Seamount (EN)	38	Mf	33.41N	63.32W
Muite	37	Fb	14.02S	39.02 E
Mujeres, Isla-	48	Pg	21.13N	86.43W
Mujezerski	7	He	63.57N	32.01 E
Muji	27	Cd	37.27N	78.33 E
Mujnak	19	Fg	43.44N	59.02 E
Mujnakski Zaliv	18	Bc	43.50N	58.40 E
Mujunkum, Peski-	21	Je	44.00N	70.30 E
Mukačevo	19	Cf	48.26N	22.45 E
Mukah	26	Ff	2.54N	112.06 E
Mukawa	29a	Bb	42.35N	141.55 E
Mu-Kawa	29a	Bb	42.33N	141.53 E
Mukawwar	35	Fa	20.48N	37.13 E
Mukdahan	25	Ke	16.31N	104.42 E
Mukden → Shenyang	22	Oe	41.48N	123.24 E
Mukeru	64a	Bc	7.25N	134.30 E
Mukho	28	Jf	37.33N	129.07 E
Mukinbudin	59	Df	30.54S	118.13 E
Mukojima-Rettō	60	Cb	27.37N	142.10 E
Mukomuko	26	Dg	2.35S	101.07 E
Muksu	18	He	39.17N	71.25 E
Mula	25	Dc	27.57N	67.36 E
Mula	13	Kf	38.03N	1.30W
Mulainagiri	25	Ff	13.24N	75.43 E
Mulaku Atoll	25a	Bb	2.57N	73.34 E
Mulaly	19	Hf	45.27N	78.20 E
Mulan	27	Mb	46.00N	128.02 E
Mulanje	30	Kj	16.03S	35.31 E
Mulanje	36	Gf	16.02S	35.30 E
Mulatre, Point-	51g	Bb	15.17N	61.15W
Mulatupo Sasardí	49	Ii	8.57N	77.45W
Mulchatna	40	Hd	59.39N	157.08W
Mulchén	56	Fe	37.34S	72.14W
Mulda	17	Kc	67.28N	63.34 E
Mulde	10	Ie	51.48N	12.10 E
Mulebreen	66	Ee	67.28S	59.21 E
Mulegé	47	Bc	26.53N	112.01W
Mulegé, Sierra de-	47	Bc	37.30N	112.40W
Mulenda	36	Dc	4.18S	24.58 E
Muleshoe	45	Ei	34.13N	102.43W
Mulgrave Island	59	Ib	10.05S	142.10 E
Mulhacén	5	Fh	37.03N	3.19W
Mülheim an der Ruhr	12	Ic	51.26N	6.53 E
Mülheim-Kärlich	12	Jd	50.23N	7.30 E
Mulhouse	6	Gf	47.45N	7.20 E
Muli (Bowa)	27	Hf	27.55N	101.13 E
Mulifanua	65c	Aa	13.50S	172.02W
Muling	28	Kb	44.34N	130.12 E
Muling (Bamiantong)	28	Kb	44.55N	130.32 E
Muling Guan	28	Ef	36.10N	118.46 E
Muling He	28	Lb	45.53N	133.30 E
Mull, Island of-	5	Fd	56.27N	6.00W
Mull, Sound of-	9	He	56.35N	5.50W
Mullen	45	Fe	42.03N	101.01W
Mullens	44	Gg	37.35N	81.25W
Muller, Pegunungan-	26	Ff	0.40N	113.50 E
Mullet Peninsula/An Muirthead	9	Cg	54.15N	10.04W
Mullett Lake	44	Ec	45.30N	84.30W
Mullewa	59	De	28.33S	115.31 E
Müllheim	10	Di	47.48N	7.38 E
Mullingar/An Muileann gCearr	9	Fh	53.32N	7.20W
Mullsjö	8	Eg	57.55N	13.53 E
Mulobezi	36	Ef	16.47S	25.10 E
Mulock Glacier	66	Jf	79.03S	159.10 E
Mulongo	36	Ed	7.50S	26.57 E
Multān	22	Jf	30.11N	71.29 E
Multé	48	Ni	17.41N	91.24W
Multia	8	Kb	62.25N	24.47 E
Multien	12	Ee	49.05N	2.55 E
Mulu, Gunong-	26	Ff	4.03N	114.56 E
Mulvane	45	Hh	37.29N	97.14W
Mulymja	17	Lf	60.12N	64.32 E
Mumbué	36	Ce	13.53S	17.19 E
Mumbwa	36	Ee	14.59S	27.04 E
Mumhan/Munster	9	Ei	52.30N	9.00W
Mumra	16	Og	45.43N	47.41 E
Mun	21	Mh	15.19N	105.30 E
Muna	48	Og	20.29N	89.43W
Muna	21	Oc	67.52N	123.10 E
Muna, Pulau-	26	Hg	5.00S	122.30 E
Munābāo	25	Ec	25.45N	70.17 E
Munamägi/Munamjagi	8	Lg	57.38N	27.10 E
Munaybarah, Sharm-	24	Gi	26.04N	36.38 E
Muncar	26	Fh	8.29S	114.21 E
Münchberg	10	Hf	50.12N	11.47 E
München=Munich (EN)	6	Hf	48.09N	11.35 E
Münchhausen	12	Kd	50.57N	8.43 E
Muncho Lake	42	Ee	58.56N	125.46W
Munch'ŏn	28	Ie	39.14N	127.22 E
Muncie	43	Jc	40.11N	85.23W
Munda	63a	Cc	8.19S	157.15 E
Mundaring, Perth-	59	Df	31.54S	116.10 E
Munday	45	Gj	33.27N	99.38W
Mundemba	34	Ge	4.59N	8.40 E
Münden	10	Fe	51.25N	9.41 E
Mundesley	12	Db	52.52N	1.25 E
Mundford	12	Cb	52.30N	0.39 E
Mundiwindi	58	Dg	23.52S	120.09 E
Mundo	13	Kf	38.19N	1.40W
Mundo Novo	54	Jf	11.52S	40.28W
Munellës, Mali i-	15	Dh	41.58N	20.06 E
Munera	13	Je	39.02N	2.28W
Mungana	59	Ic	17.07S	144.24 E
Mungbere	31	Jh	2.38N	28.30 E
Munger	25	Hc	25.23N	86.28 E
Mungindi	59	Je	28.58S	148.59 E
Munhango	36	Ce	12.10S	18.34 E
Munh-Hajrhan-Ula	21	Le	46.40N	91.30 E
Munich (EN)=München	6	Hf	48.09N	11.35 E
Muniesa	13	Lc	41.02N	0.48W
Munīfah	23	Gd	27.38N	49.00 E
Munising	44	Db	46.25N	86.40W
Munkedal	7	Cg	58.29N	11.41 E
Munkfors	7	Cg	59.50N	13.32 E
Munku Sardik, Gora-	21	Md	51.45N	100.20 E
Muñoz Gamero, Peninsula-	56	Fh	52.30S	73.10W
Munsan	28	If	37.55N	126.22 E
Münsingen	10	Fh	48.25N	9.30 E
Munster	11	Nf	48.03N	7.08 E
Münster [Ger.]	10	De	51.58N	7.38 E
Münster [Ger.]	12	Ke	49.55N	8.52 E
Münster/Moutier	14	Bc	47.16N	7.22 E
Munster/Mumhan	9	Ei	52.30N	9.00W
Münster-Hiltrup	12	Jc	51.54N	7.38 E
Münsterland [Ger.]	10	De	52.00N	7.30 E
Münsterland [Ger.]	12	Kb	52.45N	8.10 E
Münstermaifeld	12	Jd	50.15N	7.22 E
Muntenia	15	Ie	44.00N	26.00 E
Munteni Buzău	15	Je	44.38N	26.59 E
Muntok	26	Eg	2.04S	105.11 E
Munzur Dağları	24	Hc	39.30N	39.10 E
Muojärvi	7	Gd	65.56N	28.36 E
Muong Sen	25	Ke	19.24N	104.08 E
Muonio	6	Ib	67.57N	23.42 E
Muonioälven Muonionijoki	5	Ib	67.11N	23.34 E
Muping	28	Ff	37.23N	121.36 E
Muqaddam	35	Eb	18.04N	31.30 E
Muqayshiț	24	Oj	24.10N	53.45 E
Muqdisho=Mogadishu (EN)	31	Lh	2.03N	45.22 E
Mur	5	Hf	46.18N	16.55 E
Mura	5	Hf	46.18N	16.55 E
Muradiye [Tur.]	15	Kk	38.39N	27.24 E
Muradiye [Tur.]	24	Jc	39.00N	43.43 E
Murafa	16	Fe	48.13N	28.14 E
Murakami	28	Oe	38.14N	139.29 E
Murallón, Cerro-	52	Ij	49.48S	73.25W
Muráň	10	Qh	48.45N	20.02 E
Mur'aňyo	35	Ic	11.41N	50.27 E
Muraši	19	Ed	59.24N	48.59 E
Murat	21	Ff	38.52N	38.48 E
Murat	11	Ii	45.07N	2.52 E
Murat Dağı	23	Cb	38.55N	29.43 E
Muratlı [Tur.]	24	Ib	41.29N	41.41 E
Muratlı [Tur.]	15	Kh	41.10N	27.30 E
Murau	14	Ic	47.06N	14.10 E
Muravera	14	Dk	39.25N	9.34 E
Murayama	29	Gb	38.29N	140.23 E
Mūrchen Khvort	24	Nf	33.06N	51.30 E
Murchison	62	Ed	41.48S	172.20 E
Murchison, Mount- [Austl.]	59	De	26.46S	116.25 E
Murchison, Mount- [N.Z.]	62	De	43.01S	171.17 E
Murchison River	57	Cg	27.50S	114.00 E
Murcia	6	Fh	37.59N	1.07W
Murcia [3]	13	Kg	38.00N	1.30W
Murcia	13	Kf	38.30N	1.45W
Mur-de-Barrez	11	Ij	44.51N	2.39 E
Murdo	45	Fe	43.53N	100.43W
Mürefte	15	Ki	40.40N	27.14 E
Muren	22	Me	49.38N	100.10 E
Mureş	5	If	46.15N	20.12 E
Mureş [2]	15	Hc	46.30N	24.40 E
Muret	11	Hk	43.28N	1.21 E
Murfreesboro	43	Jd	35.51N	86.23W
Murg	10	Eh	48.55N	8.10 E
Murgab	21	If	38.18N	61.12 E
Murgab	19	Hh	38.10N	73.59 E
Murgab	18	Df	37.32N	62.01 E
Murgaš	15	Gg	42.50N	23.40 E
Murgeni	15	Lc	46.12N	28.01 E
Murgon	59	Ke	26.15S	151.57 E
Muri	64p	Cc	21.15S	159.43W
Muriaé	54	Jh	21.08S	42.22W
Murici	54	Ke	9.19S	35.56W
Muriege	36	Dd	9.53S	21.13 E
Murihiti	64n	Ab	10.23S	161.02W
Murilo Atoll	57	Gd	8.40N	152.11 E
Mūrītāniyā=Mauritania (EN) [1]	31	Fg	20.00N	12.00W
Müritz	10	Ic	53.25N	12.43 E
Murkong Selek	25	Jc	27.44N	95.18 E
Murmansk	6	Jb	68.58N	33.05 E
Murmanskaja Oblast [3]	19	Db	68.00N	35.30 E
Murmaši	19	Db	68.49N	32.49 E
Murnau	10	Hi	47.41N	11.12 E
Muro	13	Pe	39.44N	3.03 E
Muro, Capo di-	11a	Ab	41.44N	8.40 E
Muro Lucano	14	Jj	40.45N	15.29 E
Murom	6	Kd	55.34N	42.02 E
Muromcevo	19	Hd	56.23N	75.14 E
Muroran	22	Qe	42.18N	140.59 E
Muros	13	Cb	42.47N	9.02W
Muros y Noya, Ría de-	13	Db	42.45N	9.00W
Muroto	27	Ne	33.18N	134.09 E
Muroto Zaki	28	Mh	33.16N	134.10 E
Murowana Goślina	10	Nd	52.35N	17.01 E
Murphy [Id.-U.S.]	46	Ge	43.13N	116.33W
Murphy [N.C.-U.S.]	44	Eh	35.05N	84.01W
Murphysboro	45	Lh	37.46N	89.20W
Murrah al Kubrá, Al Buḩayrah al-	24	Eg	30.20N	32.23 E
Murray [Ky.-U.S.]	44	Cg	36.37N	88.19W
Murray [Ut.-U.S.]	46	Jf	40.40N	111.53W
Murray, Lake- [Pap.N.Gui.]	60	Ci	7.00S	141.30 E
Murray, Lake- [S.C.-U.S.]	44	Gh	34.04N	81.23W
Murray Bridge	59	Hg	35.07S	139.17 E
Murray Fracture zone (EN)	3	Lf	34.00N	135.00W
Murray Islands	59	Ia	9.55S	144.05 E
Murray Ridge (EN)	3	Gg	21.00N	61.50 E
Murray River	57	Eh	35.22S	139.22 E
Murraysburg	37	Cf	31.58S	23.47 E
Murro di Porco, Capo-	14	Jm	37.00N	15.20 E
Murrumbidgee River	57	Fh	34.43S	143.12 E
Murrupula	37	Fc	15.27S	38.47 E
Murska Sobota	14	Kd	46.40N	16.10 E
Murten/Morat	14	Bd	46.56N	7.08 E
Murter	14	Jg	43.47N	15.37 E
Murtle Lake	46	Fa	52.08N	119.38W
Murud, Gunong-	26	Gf	3.52N	115.30 E
Murupara	62	Gc	38.27S	176.42 E
Mururoa Atoll	57	Ng	21.52S	138.55W
Murwāra	25	Gd	23.51N	80.24 E
Murwillumbah	59	Ke	28.19S	153.24 E
Mürz	14	Jc	47.24N	15.17 E
Mürzzuschlag	14	Jc	47.36N	15.41 E
Muş	23	Fb	38.44N	41.30 E
Muša/Mūša	7	Fh	56.24N	24.12 E
Mūša/Muša	7	Fh	56.24N	24.12 E
Mūsa, Jabal-=Sinai, Mount- (EN)	24	Eh	28.32N	33.59 E
Musa Ali	35	Gc	12.30N	42.27 E
Musāfī	24	Qk	25.18N	56.10 E
Musā'id	33	Ed	31.36N	25.03 E
Musala	5	Ig	42.11N	23.34 E
Musallam	24	Lg	31.53N	46.56 E
Musan	27	Mc	42.14N	129.13 E
Musandam Peninsula	24	Qi	26.18N	56.24 E
Musay'īd	24	Nj	25.00N	51.33 E
Musaymir	33	Hg	13.27N	44.37 E
Muscat (EN)=Masqaț	22	Hg	23.29N	58.33 E
Muscat and Oman (EN) → Oman (EN) [1]	22	Hg	21.00N	57.00 E
Muscatine	45	Kf	41.25N	91.03W
Musgrave	58	Ff	14.47S	143.30 E
Musgrave Ranges	57	Eg	26.10S	131.50 E
Mūshā	24	Di	27.07N	31.14 E
Mus-Haja, Gora-	21	Qc	62.35N	140.50 E
Mushāsh al 'Ashawī	24	Mj	24.12N	48.50 E
Mushāsh Ramlān	24	Mj	24.25N	49.15 E
Mushayrib, Ra's-	24	Nj	24.18N	51.44 E
Mushie	36	Cc	3.01S	16.54 E
Mūsi	25	Ge	15.20N	80.06 E
Musi	21	Mj	2.20S	104.56 E
Mūsiān	24	Lf	32.28N	47.26 E
Musicians Seamounts (EN)	57	Kb	29.00N	162.00W
Muskegon	43	Jc	43.14N	86.16W
Muskegon Heights	44	Dd	43.12N	86.12W
Muskegon River	44	Dd	43.14N	86.20W
Muskö	8	He	59.00N	18.05 E
Muskogee	43	Hd	35.45N	95.22W
Muskoka, Lake-	44	Hc	45.00N	79.25W
Musoma	31	Ki	1.30S	33.48 E
Musone	14	Hg	43.28N	13.38 E
Mussaţţaḩah, Al Jazīrah al-	14	Em	37.11N	10.20 E
Mussau Island	60	Dh	1.25S	149.38 E
Musselkanaal, Stadskanaal-	12	Jb	52.56N	7.02 E
Musselshell River	43	Fb	47.21N	107.58W
Mussende	36	Ce	10.31S	16.02 E
Mussidan	11	Gi	45.02N	0.22 E
Mussòmeli	14	Hm	37.35N	13.45 E
Must	27	Fb	46.40N	92.40 E
Muşţafá, Ra's-	14	Fn	36.50N	11.07 E
Mustafakemalpaşa	24	Cb	40.02N	28.24 E
Mustahil	35	Gd	5.15N	44.44 E
Mustāng	25	Gc	29.11N	83.58 E
Mustang Draw	45	Fj	32.00N	101.40W
Mustang Island	45	Hm	28.00N	96.55W
Mustasaari/Korsholm	8	Ia	63.05N	21.43 E
Musters, Lago-	56	Gg	45.27S	69.13W
Mustique Island	50	Ff	12.39N	61.15W
Mustjala	8	Jf	58.25N	22.04 E
Mustla	7	Fg	58.14N	25.52 E
Mustvee	7	Gg	58.52N	26.59 E
Musu-dan	28	Jd	40.50N	129.43 E
Muswellbrook	59	Kf	32.16S	150.53 E
Muszyna	10	Qg	49.21N	20.54 E
Mut	24	Ed	36.39N	33.27 E
Mūţ	33	Ed	25.29N	28.59 E
Mūtaf, Ra's al-	23	Hd	27.41N	51.27 E
Mutalau	64k	Ba	18.56S	169.50W
Mutarara	31	Kj	17.27S	35.04 E
Mutatá	54	Cb	7.16N	76.32W
Mutawassiţ, Al Baḩr al-=Mediterranean Sea (EN)	5	Hh	35.00N	20.00 E
Mutha	36	Gc	1.48S	38.26 E
Muting	26	Lh	7.23S	140.20 E
Mutis, Gunung-	26	Hh	9.34S	124.14 E
Mutoraj	20	Fd	61.20N	100.20 E
Mutsamudu	31	Lj	12.09S	44.25 E
Mutshatsha	36	De	10.39S	24.27 E
Mutsu	27	Pc	41.05N	140.55 E
Mutsu-Wan	28	Pd	41.10N	140.55 E
Muttaburra	59	Id	22.36S	144.33 E
Mutterstadt	12	Ke	49.27N	8.21 E
Mutton/Oiléan Coarach	9	Di	52.49N	9.31W
Mutton Bird Islands	62	Bg	47.15S	167.25 E
Mutuali	37	Fb	14.53S	37.00 E
Mutún	55	Dd	19.10S	57.54W
Mutunópolis	55	Ha	13.40S	49.15W
Mutusjärvi	7	Gb	69.31N	26.57 E
Muurame	8	Kb	62.08N	25.40 E
Mu Us Shamo=Ordos Desert (EN)	21	Mf	[illegible]	109.10 E
Muxima	36	Bd	9.32S	13.57 E
Muyinga	36	Fc	2.51S	30.20 E
Muy Muy	49	Eg	12.46N	85.38W
Muzaffarābād	25	Eb	34.22N	73.28 E
Muzaffargarh	25	Eb	30.04N	71.12 E
Muzaffarnagar	25	Fc	29.28N	77.41 E
Muzaffarpur	25	Hc	26.07N	85.24 E
Muzambinho	55	Ie	21.22S	46.32W
Muzat He	27	Dc	41.15N	83.27 E
Muži	20	Bc	65.27N	64.40 E
Muzillac	11	Dg	47.33N	2.29W
Mužlja	15	Dd	45.21N	20.25 E
Muztag [China]	21	Kf	35.55N	80.20 E
Muztag [China]	21	Kf	36.25N	87.25 E
Muztagata	27	Cd	38.17N	75.07 E
Mvolo	35	Dd	6.03N	29.56 E
Mvomero	36	Gd	6.20S	37.25 E
Mvoung	36	Bb	0.04N	12.18 E
Mwadingusha	36	Ee	10.45S	27.15 E
Mwali	30	Lj	12.15S	43.45 E
Mwanza [3]	36	Fc	2.30S	32.30 E
Mwanza [Mwi.]	36	Ff	15.37S	34.31 E
Mwanza [Tan.]	31	Ki	2.31S	32.54 E
Mwanza [Zaire]	36	Ed	7.54S	26.45 E
Mwatate	36	Gc	3.30S	38.23 E
Mweelrea	9	Dh	53.38N	9.50W
Mweka	31	Ji	4.51S	21.34 E
Mwene Ditu	31	Ji	7.03S	23.27 E
Mwenga	36	Ec	3.02S	28.26 E
Mweru, Lake-	30	Ji	9.00S	28.45 E
Mweru Wantipa, Lake-	36	Ed	8.42S	29.46 E
Mwimbi	36	Fd	8.39S	31.40 E
Mwinilunga	36	De	11.44S	24.26 E
Mya	30	He	31.40N	5.15 E
Myaing	25	Id	21.37N	94.51 E
Myanaung	25	Je	18.17N	95.19 E
Myanmar-Nainggan-Daw → Burma [1]	22	Lg	22.00N	98.00 E
Myaungmya	25	Ie	16.36N	94.56 E
Mycenae (EN) = Mikínai	15	Fl	37.43N	22.45 E
Myebon	25	Id	20.03N	93.22 E
Myingyan	22	Lg	21.28N	95.23 E
Myinmoletkat Taung	25	Jf	13.28N	98.48 E
Myitta	25	Jf	14.10N	98.31 E
Myjava	10	Mh	48.33N	16.58 E
Myjzakjula/Mõisaküla	7	Fg	58.07N	25.10 E
Mykulkin, Mys-	17	Cc	67.48N	46.40 E
Mylius Erichsens Land	41	Jb	81.40N	24.00W
Myltkyinā	22	Lg	25.23N	97.24 E
Mymensingh	25	Id	24.45N	90.24 E
Mynämäki	7	Ef	60.40N	22.00 E
Mynaral	19	Hf	45.22N	73.39 E
Myōkō-Zan	29	Fc	36.52N	138.06 E
Mýrdalsjökull	7a	Bc	63.40N	19.06W
Myre	7	Db	68.51N	15.05 E
Myrskylä/Mörskom	8	Kd	60.40N	25.51 E
Myrtle Beach	43	Le	33.42N	78.54W
Myrtle Point	46	Ce	43.04N	124.08W
Mysen	7	Cg	59.33N	11.20 E
Mysia	15	Kj	39.30N	28.00 E
Myśla	10	Kd	52.40N	14.29 E
Myślenice	10	Pg	49.51N	19.56 E
Myślibórz	10	Kd	52.55N	14.52 E
Mysore	22	Jh	12.18N	76.39 E
Mysore → Karnataka [3]	25	Ff	13.30N	76.00 E
Mys Saryč	16	Hg	44.23N	33.45 E
Myszków	10	Pf	50.36N	19.20 E
Myszyniec	10	Rc	53.24N	21.21 E
My Tho	22	Mh	10.21N	106.21 E
Mytišči	7	Ii	55.56N	37.46 E
Mývatn	7a	Cb	65.36N	17.00W

Index Symbols

[1] Independent Nation
[2] State, Region
[3] District, County
[4] Municipality
[5] Colony, Dependency
Continent
Physical Region
Historical or Cultural Region
Mount, Mountain
Volcano
Hill
Mountains, Mountain Range
Hills, Escarpment
Plateau, Upland
Pass, Gap
Plain, Lowland
Delta
Salt Flat
Valley, Canyon
Crater, Cave
Karst Features
Depression
Polder
Desert, Dunes
Forest, Woods
Heath, Steppe
Oasis
Cape, Point
Coast, Beach
Cliff
Peninsula
Isthmus
Sandbank
Island
Atoll
Rock, Reef
Islands, Archipelago
Rocks, Reefs
Coral Reef
Well, Spring
Geyser
River, Stream
Waterfall Rapids
River Mouth, Estuary
Lake
Salt Lake
Intermittent Lake
Reservoir
Swamp, Pond
Canal
Glacier
Ice Shelf, Pack Ice
Ocean
Sea
Gulf, Bay
Strait, Fjord
Lagoon
Bank
Seamount
Tablemount
Ridge
Shelf
Basin
Escarpment, Sea Scarp
Fracture
Trench, Abyss
National Park, Reserve
Point of Interest
Recreation Site
Cave, Cavern
Historic Site
Ruins
Wall, Walls
Church, Abbey
Temple
Scientific Station
Airport
Port
Lighthouse
Mine
Tunnel
Dam, Bridge

Myzeqeja 15 Ci 41.01N 19.36 E
M'Zab 32 Hc 32.35N 3.20 E
Mže 10 Jg 49.46N 13.24 E
Mziha 36 Gd 5.54S 37.47 E
Mzimba 36 Fe 11.54S 33.36 E
Mzuzu 31 Kj 11.27S 33.55 E

N

Naab 10 Ig 49.01N 12.02 E
Naaldwijk 12 Gc 51.59N 4.12 E
Naalehu 65a Fd 19.04N 155.35W
Naantali/Nådendal 7 Ff 60.27N 22.02 E
Naarden 12 Hb 52.18N 5.10 E
Naas/An Nás 9 Gh 53.13N 6.39W
Nabadid 35 Gd 9.38N 43.29 E
Nabão 13 De 39.31N 8.21W
Nabari 29 Ed 34.37N 136.05 E
Naberera 36 Gc 4.12S 36.56 E
Naberežnyje Čelny 6 Ld 55.42N 52.19 E
Nabileque, Rio- 55 De 20.55S 57.49W
Nabire 58 Ee 3.22S 135.29 E
Nabī Shu'ayb, Jabal an- 21 Gh 15.17N 43.59 E
Nabq 24 Fh 28.04N 34.25 E
Nābul 31 Ie 36.27N 10.44 E
Nābul [3] 32 Jb 36.45N 10.45 E
Nābulus 24 Ff 32.13N 35.16 E
Nabusanke 36 Fb 0.01N 32.03 E
Nacala 37 Gb 14.33S 40.40 E
Nacala-a-Velha 31 Lj 14.33S 40.36 E
Nacaome 49 Dg 13.31N 87.30W
Nacaroa 37 Fb 14.23S 39.55 E
Nacereddine 13 Ph 36.08N 3.26 E
Nachikatsuura 29 De 33.39N 135.55 E
Nachingwea 36 Ge 10.23S 38.46 E
Nachi-San 29 De 33.42N 135.51 E
Náchod 10 Mf 50.26N 16.10 E
Nachuge 25 If 10.35N 92.28 E
Nachvak Fiord 42 Le 59.03N 63.45W
Nacka 7 Ee 59.18N 18.10 E
Ná Clocha Liatha/
Greystones 9 Gh 53.09N 6.04W
Nacogdoches 45 Ik 31.36N 94.39W
Na Comaraigh/Comeragh
Mountains 9 Fi 52.13N 7.35W
Nacori, Sierra- 48 Ec 29.50N 108.50W
Nacozari, Rio- 48 Ec 29.48N 109.42W
Nacozari de Garcia 47 Cb 30.24N 109.39W
Na Cruacha/Blue Stack 9 Eg 54.45N 8.06W
Na Cruacha Dubha/
Macgillycuddy's Reeks 9 Di 52.00N 9.50W
Nacunday, Rio- 55 Eh 26.03S 54.45W
Nada → Danxian 27 Ih 19.38N 109.32 E
Nådendal/Naantali 7 Ff 60.27N 22.02 E
Nadiād 25 Ed 22.42N 72.52 E
Nădlac 15 Dc 46.10N 20.45 E
Nador [3] 32 Gb 35.00N 3.00W
Nador 32 Gb 35.11N 2.56W
Nádusa 15 Fi 40.38N 22.04 E
Nadvoicy 19 Dc 63.52N 34.20 E
Nadvornaja 16 De 48.38N 24.34 E
Nadym 22 Jc 65.35N 72.42 E
Naeba-San 29 Fc 36.51N 138.41 E
Nærbø 8 Af 58.40N 5.39 E
Næstved 7 Ci 55.14N 11.46 E
Nafada 34 Hc 11.06N 11.20 E
Näfels 14 Dc 47.06N 9.04 E
Naftah 14 Dn 36.57N 9.04 E
Naftan Rock 64b Bb 14.50N 145.32 E
Naft-e-Safid 24 Mg 31.40N 49.17 E
Naft-e-Shāh 24 Kf 33.59N 45.30 E
Naft Khāneh 24 Ke 34.02N 45.28 E
Nafūsah, Jabal- 30 Ie 31.50N 12.00 E
Nāg 25 Dc 27.24N 65.08 E
Naga 22 Oh 13.28N 123.39 E
Nāga, Kreb en- 32 Fe 24.00N 6.00W
Nagagami Lake 44 Ea 49.28N 85.02W
Nagagami River 45 Na 50.25N 84.20W
Nagahama [Jap.] 29 Ed 35.23N 136.16 E
Nagahama [Jap.] 29 Ce 33.36N 132.29 E
Nagai 29 Gb 38.06N 140.02 E
Nagai 40 Ge 55.11N 159.55W
Na Gaibhlte/Galty
Mountains 9 Ei 52.23N 8.11W
Nāgāland [3] 25 Ic 26.30N 94.00 E
Nagano 22 Pf 36.39N 138.11 E
Nagano Ken [2] 28 Nf 36.10N 138.00 E
Nagano-Matsushiro 29 Fc 36.34N 138.10 E
Nagano-Shinonoi 29 Fc 36.35N 138.06 E
Nagaoka 27 Od 37.27N 138.51 E
Nāgappattinam 25 Ff 10.46N 79.50 E
Nagara-Gawa 29 Ed 35.02N 136.43 E
Nagarote 49 Dg 12.16N 86.34W
Nagarzê 27 Ff 28.59N 90.28 E
Nagasaki 22 Of 32.47N 129.56 E
Nagasaki-Hantō 29 Ae 32.40N 129.45 E
Nagasaki Ken [2] 28 Jh 33.00N 129.50 E
Naga-Shima 29 Ce 33.50N 132.05 E
Nagashima 29 Ed 34.12N 136.19 E
Nagashima 29 Be 32.10N 130.10 E
Naga-Shima-Kaikyō 29 Be 32.15N 130.10 E
Nagato 28 Kg 34.21N 131.10 E
Nagayo 29 Ae 32.50N 129.52 E
Nāgda 25 Fd 23.27N 75.25 E
Nāgercoil 25 Fg 8.10N 77.26 E
Naghora Point 60 Gj 10.50S 162.24 E
Nagichot 35 Ee 4.16N 33.34 E
Nagi-San 29 Dd 35.10N 134.10 E
Nagiso 29 Ed 35.36N 137.36 E
Nago 27 Mf 26.35N 128.01 E
Nagold 10 Eh 48.52N 8.42 E
Nagorno-Karabakh 19 Eh 39.55N 46.45 E
Nagorny 20 He 55.45N 124.58 E
Nagorny 20 Md 63.10N 179.05 E
Nagorsk 7 Mg 59.21N 50.48 E
Nago-Wan 29b Ab 26.35N 127.55 E
Nagoya 22 Pf 35.10N 136.55 E
Nāgpur 22 Jg 21.09N 79.06 E
Nagqu 22 Lf 31.30N 92.00 E
Nag's Head 51c Ab 17.13N 62.38W
Nagua 49 Md 19.23N 69.50W
Naguabo 51a Cb 18.13N 65.44W
Nagyatád 10 Nj 46.13N 17.22 E
Nagybajom 10 Mj 46.23N 16.31 E
Nagyecsed 10 Si 47.52N 22.24 E
Nagyhalász 10 Rh 48.08N 21.46 E
Nagykálló 10 Ri 47.53N 21.51 E
Nagykanizsa 10 Mj 46.27N 16.59 E
Nagykáta 10 Pi 47.25N 19.45 E
Nagykőrös 10 Pi 47.02N 19.47 E
Nagykunság 10 Qj 46.55N 20.15 E
Nagy-Milic 10 Rh 48.35N 21.28 E
Naha 22 Og 26.13N 127.40 E
Nahanni Butte 42 Fd 61.04N 123.24W
Nahari 29 De 33.25N 134.01 E
Naharyya 24 Ff 33.00N 35.05 E
Nahāvand 23 Gc 34.12N 48.22 E
Nahe 10 Dg 49.58N 7.57 E
Nahičevan 6 Kh 39.13N 45.27 E
Nahičevanskaja respublika 19 Eh 39.15N 45.35 E
Na'hīmābād 24 Qg 30.51N 56.31 E
Nahodka 22 Pe 42.48N 132.52 E
Nahr al 'Āṣī = Orontes (EN) 23 Eb 36.02N 35.58 E
Nahr Quassel 13 Oi 35.45N 2.46 E
Nahuala, Laguna- 48 Ji 16.50N 99.40W
Nahuel Huapi, Lago- 56 Ff 40.58S 71.30W
Nahunta 44 Gj 31.12N 81.59W
Naie 29a Bb 43.24N 141.52 E
Naiguatá, Pico- 54 Ea 10.33N 66.46W
Naila 10 Hf 50.19N 11.42 E
Naiman Qi (Daqin Tal) 27 Lc 42.49N 120.38 E
Nain 39 Md 57.00N 61.40W
Nā'īn 24 Of 32.52N 53.05 E
Na'īnābād 24 Pd 36.14N 54.39 E
Nairai 63d Bb 17.49S 179.24 E
Nairn 9 Jd 57.35N 3.53W
Nairobi 31 Kl 1.17S 36.49 E
Nairobi [3] 36 Gc 1.17S 36.50 E
Naissaar/Najssar 8 Ke 59.35N 24.25 E
Naitamba 63d Cb 17.01S 179.17W
Naizishan 28 Ic 43.41N 127.27 E
Najafābād 23 Hc 32.37N 51.21 E
Najd 23 Fe 25.00N 44.30 E
Najd 21 Gg 25.00N 44.30 E
Nájera 13 Jb 42.25N 2.44W
Najerilla 13 Jb 42.31N 2.42W
Naj' Ḩammādī 33 Fd 26.03N 32.15 E
Najibābād 25 Fc 29.58N 78.10 E
Najin 27 Nc 42.15N 130.18 E
Najō 29 Ec 35.47N 136.12 E
Najrān 33 Hf 17.30N 44.10 E
Najrān 33 Hf 17.30N 44.10 E
Najssar/Naissaar 8 Ke 59.35N 24.25 E
Najstenjarvi 7 He 62.18N 32.42 E
Naju 28 Ig 35.02N 126.43 E
Najzataš, Pereval- 18 If 37.52N 73.46 E
Nakadōri-Jima 28 Jh 32.58N 129.05 E
Nakagawa 29a Ca 44.47N 142.05 E
Naka-Gawa [Jap.] 29 Gc 36.20N 140.36 E
Naka-Gawa [Jap.] 29 De 33.56N 134.42 E
Nakagusuku-Wan 29b Ab 26.15N 127.50 E
Nakahechi 29 De 33.47N 135.29 E
Naka-lō-Jima 60 Cc 24.47N 141.20 E
Naka-Jima 29 Ce 33.58N 132.37 E
Nakajō 28 Oe 38.03N 139.24 E
Naka-Koshiki-Jima 29 Af 31.48N 129.50 E
Nakalele Point 65a Eb 21.02N 156.35W
Nakama 29 Be 33.50N 130.43 E
Nakaminato 29 Gc 36.22N 140.36 E
Nakamura 28 Lh 32.59N 132.56 E
Nakanai Mountains 59 Ka 5.35S 151.10 E
Nakano 29 Fc 36.45N 138.22 E
Naka-no-Dake 29 Fc 37.04N 139.06 E
Nakanojō 29 Fc 36.35N 138.51 E
Naka-no-Shima 28 Lf 36.05N 133.04 E
Naka-no-Shima 27 Mf 29.50N 129.50 E
Nakasato 29a Bc 40.58N 140.26 E
Naka-satsunai 29a Cb 42.42N 143.08 E
Nakashibetsu 28 Rc 43.36N 145.00 E
Nakasongola 36 Fb 1.19N 32.28 E
Nakatonbetsu 29a Ca 44.58N 142.17 E
Nakatsu 28 Kh 33.34N 131.13 E
Nakatsugawa 28 Ng 35.29N 137.30 E
Nakfa 35 Fb 16.40N 38.30 E
Nakhon Pathom 25 Kf 13.49N 100.06 E
Nakhon Phanom 25 Mh 17.22N 104.46 E
Nakhon Ratchasima 22 Mh 14.57N 102.09 E
Nakhon Sawan 22 Mh 15.42N 100.06 E
Nakhon Si Thammarat 22 Li 8.26N 99.58 E
Nakijin 29b Ab 26.42N 127.59 E
Nakina 43 Kd 50.10N 86.42W
Nakkila 8 Ic 61.22N 22.00 E
Nakło nad Notecia 10 Nc 53.08N 17.35 E
Naknek 40 He 58.44N 157.02W
Nakonde 36 Fd 9.19S 32.46 E
Nakskov 7 Ci 54.50N 11.09 E
Näkten 8 Fb 62.50N 14.40 E
Naktong-gang 28 Jg 35.07N 128.57 E
Nakuru 31 Ki 0.20S 35.56 E
Nakusp 46 Ga 50.15N 117.48W
Nāl 25 Dc 26.02N 65.29 E
Nalajch → Nalajha 27 Ib 47.45N 107.16 E
Nalajha (Nalajch) 27 Ib 47.45N 107.16 E
Nal'čik 6 Kg 43.29N 43.37 E
Nallıhan 24 Db 40.11N 31.21 E
Nalón 13 Fa 43.32N 6.04W
Nālūt 31 Ie 31.52N 10.59 E
Nalwasha 36 Gc 0.43S 36.26 E
Na Machairí/Brandon
Head 9 Ci 52.16N 10.15W
Namacurra 37 Fc 17.29S 37.01 E
Namai Bay 64a Bb 7.32N 134.39 E
Namak, Daryācheh-ye- =
Namak Lake (EN) 21 Hf 34.45N 51.36 E
Namak Lake (EN)=
Namak, Daryācheh-ye- 21 Hf 34.45N 51.36 E
Namakan Lake 45 Jb 48.27N 92.35W
Namak-e Mighān, Kavīr-e- 24 Me 34.13N 49.49 E
Namakia 37 Hc 15.56S 45.48 E
Namakwaland = Little
Namamland (EN) 37 Be 29.00S 17.00 E
Namanga 36 Gc 2.33S 36.47 E
Namangan 22 Je 41.00N 71.40 E
Namanganskaja Oblast [3] 19 Hg 41.00N 71.20 E
Namanyere 36 Fd 7.31S 31.03 E
Namapa 37 Fb 13.43S 39.50 E
Namaqua Seamount (EN) 37 Af 31.30S 11.20 E
Namarrói 37 Fc 15.57S 36.51 E
Namasagali 36 Fb 1.01N 32.57 E
Namasale 36 Fb 1.30N 32.37 E
Namatanai 60 Eh 3.40S 152.27 E
Namathu 63d Bb 17.21S 179.26 E
Nambavatu 63d Bb 16.36S 178.55 E
Namber 26 Jg 1.04S 134.49 E
Nambour 59 Ke 26.38S 152.58 E
Nambouwalu 61 Ec 16.59S 178.42 E
Nam Can 25 Kg 8.46N 104.59 E
Namche Bazar 25 Hc 27.49N 86.43 E
Nam Co 21 Lf 30.45N 90.35 E
Namčy 20 Hd 62.35N 129.40 E
Namdalen 7 Cd 64.38N 12.35 E
Nam Dinh 22 Mg 20.25N 106.10 E
Namdö 8 He 59.10N 18.40 E
Nam Du, Quan Dao- 25 Kg 9.42N 104.22 E
Naméche, Andenne- 12 Hd 50.28N 5.00 E
Namelakl Passage 64a Bc 7.24N 134.38 E
Namen/Namur 11 Kd 50.28N 4.52 E
Namerikawa 29 Ec 36.45N 137.20 E
Náměšt nad Oslavou 10 Mg 49.12N 16.09 E
Nametil 37 Fc 15.43S 39.21 E
Namib Desert/
Namibwoestyn 30 Ik 23.00S 15.00 E
Namibia (South West
Africa) 31 Ik 22.00S 17.00 E
Namibe 31 Ij 15.12S 12.10 E
Namibe 36 Bf 15.20S 12.30 E
Namie 28 Pf 37.29N 140.59 E
Namīn 24 Mc 38.25N 48.30 E
Namioka 29 Ga 40.42N 140.35 E
Namiquipa 48 Fc 29.15N 107.40W
Namiranga 37 Gb 10.33S 40.30 E
Namjagbarwa Feng 21 Lg 29.38N 95.04 E
Namja La 27 Df 29.58N 82.34 E
Namkham 25 Jd 23.50N 97.41 E
Namlea 26 Ig 3.18S 127.06 E
Namling 27 Ef 29.44N 89.05 E
Namnoi, Khao- 25 Jf 10.36N 98.38 E
Namoi River 59 Je 30.00S 148.07 E
Namoluk Island 57 Gd 5.55N 153.08 E
Namonuito Atoll 57 Gd 8.46N 150.02 E
Namorik Atoll 57 Hd 5.36N 168.07 E
Namous 32 Gc 30.28N 0.14W
Nampa 43 Dc 43.34N 116.34W
Nampala 34 Db 15.17N 5.33W
Nam Phan = Cochin China
(EN) 21 Mg 11.00N 107.00 E
Nam Phong 25 Ke 16.45N 102.52 E
Nampi 28 De 38.02N 116.42 E
Namp'o 27 Md 38.44N 125.25 E
Nampula [3] 37 Fb 15.00S 39.30 E
Nampula 31 Kj 15.07S 39.15 E
Namsê Shankou 27 Df 29.58N 82.34 E
Namsos 6 Hc 64.30N 11.30 E
Namtu 25 Jd 23.05N 97.24 E
Namu 46 Ba 51.49N 127.52W
Namu Atoll 57 Hd 8.00N 168.10 E
Namuka-I-Lau 63d Cc 18.51S 178.38W
Namùli, Serra- 30 Kj 15.21S 37.00 E
Namuno 37 Fb 13.37S 38.48 E
Namur [3] 12 Gd 50.20N 4.50 E
Namur/Namen 11 Kd 50.28N 4.52 E
Namur-Saint Servais 12 Gd 50.28N 4.50 E
Namuruputh 36 Gb 4.34N 35.57 E
Namur-Wépion 12 Gd 50.25N 4.52 E
Namutoni 37 Bc 18.30S 17.55 E
Namwala 36 Ef 15.45S 26.26 E
Namwŏn 28 Ig 35.24N 127.23 E
Namysłow 10 Ne 51.05N 17.42 E
Nan 21 Mh 15.42N 100.09 E
Nan 25 Ke 18.48N 100.46 E
Nana 35 Bd 5.00N 15.50 E
Nana Barya 35 Bd 7.59N 17.43 E
Nanae 29a Bc 41.53N 140.41 E
Nanaimo 42 Fg 49.10N 123.56W
Nanakuli 65a Cb 21.23N 158.08W
Nana-Mambéré [3] 35 Bd 6.00N 16.00 E
Nanango 59 Ke 26.40S 152.00 E
Nanao 27 Od 37.03N 136.58 E
Nanao-Wan 29 Ec 37.10N 137.00 E
Nanatsu-Shima 29 Ec 37.35N 136.50 E
Nancha 27 Mb 47.08N 129.09 E
Nanchang 22 Ng 28.40N 115.58 E
Nancheng 27 Kf 27.32N 116.36 E
Nanchong 22 Mf 30.47N 106.03 E
Nancowry 25 Ig 7.59N 93.32 E
Nancy 6 Gf 48.41N 6.12 E
Nanda Devi 21 Jf 30.23N 79.59 E
Nandaime 49 Dh 11.46N 86.03W
Nandan [China] 27 Ig 24.59N 107.31 E
Nandan [Jap.] 28 Mg 34.15N 134.43 E
Nandaran → Qingyuan 28 Ge 38.46N 115.29 E
Nanded 22 Jh 19.09N 77.20 E
Nandewar Range 59 Kf 30.40S 151.10 E
Nandi 61 Ec 17.48S 177.25 E
Nandu Jiang 27 Jg 20.04N 110.22 E
Nanduri 63d Bb 16.27S 179.09 E
Nandyāl 25 Fe 15.29N 78.29 E
Nanfen 28 Gd 41.06N 123.45 E
Nanfeng 27 Kf 27.15N 116.30 E
Nanga-Eboko 34 He 4.41N 12.22 E
Nanga Parbat 21 Jf 35.15N 74.36 E
Nangapinoh 26 Fg 0.20S 111.44 E
Nangarhār [3] 23 Lc 34.15N 70.30 E
Nangatayap 26 Fg 1.32S 110.34 E
Nangis 11 If 48.33N 3.00 E
Nangnim-san 28 Id 40.21N 126.55 E
Nangnim-Sanmaek 28 Id 40.30N 127.00 E
Nangong 27 Kd 37.22N 115.23 E
Nangqên 27 Ge 32.15N 96.13 E
Nanguan 28 Af 36.42N 111.41 E
Nanguantao → Guantao 28 Cf 36.33N 115.18 E
Nangweshi 36 Df 16.26S 23.20 E
Nan Hai = South China Sea
(EN) 21 Ni 10.00N 113.00 E
Nanhaoqian → Shangyi 28 Bd 41.06N 113.58 E
Nanhe 28 Cf 36.58N 114.41 E
Nanhua 27 Hf 25.16N 101.18 E
Nanhui 28 Fi 31.03N 121.46 E
Nan Hulsan Hu 27 Gd 36.45N 95.45 E
Nanjian 27 Hf 25.05N 100.32 E
Nanjiang 27 Ie 32.22N 106.45 E
Nanjing = Nanking (EN) 22 Nf 31.59N 118.51 E
Nankai Trough (EN) 27 Ne 32.00N 135.00 E
Nanking (EN) = Nanjing 22 Nf 31.59N 118.51 E
Nankoku 28 Lh 33.39N 133.44 E
Nanle 28 Cf 36.06N 115.12 E
Nanling 28 Ei 30.55N 118.19 E
Nan Ling 21 Ng 25.00N 112.00 E
Nanlou Shan 28 Ic 43.24N 126.40 E
Nanma → Yiyuan 28 Ef 36.11N 118.10 E
Nanning 22 Mg 22.50N 108.18 E
Nannup 59 Df 33.59S 115.45 E
Nanortalik 41 Hf 60.32N 45.45W
Nanpan Jiang 27 Ig 24.56N 106.12 E
Nānpāra 25 Gc 27.52N 81.30 E
Nanping [China] 22 Ng 26.42N 118.09 E
Nanping [China] 27 He 33.15N 104.13 E
Nanpu 28 Ee 39.16N 118.12 E
Nanqiao → Fengxian 28 Fi 30.55N 121.27 E
Nansei-Shotō = Ryukyu
Islands (EN) 21 Og 26.30N 128.00 E
Nansen Cordillera (EN) 67 Ge 87.00N 90.00 E
Nansen Land 41 Hb 83.20N 46.00W
Nanshan Islands (EN) =
Nansha Qundao 21 Ni 9.40N 113.30 E
Nansha Qundao =
Nanshan Islands (EN) 21 Ni 9.40N 113.30 E
Nansio 36 Fc 2.08S 33.03 E
Nant 11 Jj 44.01N 3.18 E
Nantais, Lac - 42 Kd 61.00N 73.50W
Nanterre 11 If 48.54N 2.12 E
Nantes 6 Ff 47.13N 1.33W
Nantes à Brest, Can. de- 11 Bf 48.12N 4.06W
Nanteuil-le-Haudouin 12 Ee 49.08N 2.48 E
Nanticoke 44 Je 41.13N 76.00W
Nantō 29 Ed 34.17N 136.29 E
Nantong 27 Le 32.00N 120.52 E
Nantong (Jinsha) 28 Fh 32.06N 120.52 E
Nantou 27 Lg 23.54N 120.51 E
Nantua 11 Lh 46.09N 5.37 E
Nantucket 44 Le 41.17N 70.06W
Nantucket Island 43 Mc 41.16N 70.03W
Nantucket Sound 44 Le 41.30N 70.15W
Nanuku Passage 63d Cb 16.45S 179.15W
Nanuku Reef 63d Cb 16.40S 179.26W
Nanumanga Island 57 Ie 6.18S 176.20 E
Nanumea Atoll 57 Ie 5.43S 176.00 E
Nanuque 54 Jg 17.50S 40.21W
Nanusa, Pulau-Pulau- 26 If 4.42N 127.06 E
Nanwan Shuiku 28 Bh 32.02N 113.57 E
Nanwei Dao =
Spratly Islands 26 Fe 8.42N 111.40 E
Nanxian 28 Bj 29.22N 112.25 E
Nanxiang 28 Fi 31.18N 121.17 E
Nanxiong 27 Jf 25.13N 114.18 E
Nanxun 28 Fi 30.53N 120.26 E
Nanyandang Shan 27 Lf 27.37N 120.06 E
Nanyang 22 Nf 32.56N 112.32 E
Nanyang Hu 28 Dg 35.15N 116.39 E
Nanyō 28 Pe 38.03N 140.10 E
Nanyuki 31 Kh 0.01N 37.04 E
Nanzhang 27 Je 31.45N 111.53 E
Nanzhao 27 Je 33.28N 112.29 E
Nao, Cabo de la- 5 Gh 38.44N 0.14 E
Naococane, Lac- 42 Kf 52.50N 70.40W
Naoero/Nauru [1] 58 He 0.31S 166.56 E
Naoetsu 29 Fc 37.11N 138.14 E
Não-me-Toque 55 Fi 28.28S 52.49W
Naours, Souterrains de- 12 Ed 50.05N 2.17 E
Napa 46 Dg 38.18N 122.17W
Napanee 44 Ic 44.15N 76.57W
Napassoq 41 Ge 65.45N 52.38W
Napata 35 Eb 18.29N 31.51 E
Na-Peng 25 Lg 23.10N 98.26 E
Napf 14 Bc 47.01N 7.57 E
Napier 58 Ih 39.30S 176.54 E
Napier, Mount- 59 Fc 17.32S 129.10 E
Napier Mountains 66 Ee 66.30S 53.40 E
Naples [Fl.-U.S.] 43 Kf 26.08N 81.48W
Naples [Id.-U.S.] 46 Gb 48.34N 116.24W
Naples (EN) = Napoli 6 Hg 40.50N 14.15 E
Naples, Gulf of- (EN) =
Napoli, Golfo di- 14 Ij 40.45N 14.10 E
Napo 27 Ig 23.25N 105.49 E
Napo, Rio- 52 If 3.20S 72.40W
Napoleon 45 Gc 46.30N 99.46W
Napoli = Naples (EN) 6 Hg 40.50N 14.15 E
Napoli, Golfo di- = Naples,
Gulf of- (EN) 14 Ij 40.45N 14.10 E
Napostá 55 An 38.26S 62.15W
Napuka, Ile- 57 Mf 14.12S 141.15W
Naqa 35 Eb 16.16N 33.17 E
Naqadeh 23 Gb 36.57N 45.23 E
Naqsh-e-Rostam 24 Og 30.01N 52.50 E
Nar 9 Ni 52.45N 0.24 E
Nāra 25 Dc 24.07N 69.07 E
Nara [Jap.] 27 Oe 34.41N 135.50 E
Nara [Mali] 34 Db 15.11N 7.15W
Naračenskibani 15 Hh 41.54N 24.45 E
Naracoorte 59 Ig 36.58S 140.44 E
Nara-Ken [2] 28 Mg 34.20N 135.55 E
Naranjo 48 Ee 25.48N 108.31W
Naranjos [Bol.] 55 Cd 18.38S 59.09W
Naranjos [Mex.] 48 Kg 21.21N 97.41W
Narao 29 Ae 32.52N 129.04 E
Narathiwat 25 Kg 6.25N 101.48 E
Nārāyanganj 25 Id 23.37N 90.30 E
Narbonne 11 Ik 43.11N 3.00 E
Narca, Ponta da- 36 Bd 6.07S 12.16 E
Narcea 13 Fa 43.28N 6.06W
Narcondam 25 If 13.15N 94.30 E
Nardò 14 Mj 40.11N 18.02 E
Naré 55 Bj 30.58S 60.28W
Nares Land 41 Hb 82.25N 47.30W
Nares Strait 38 Lb 78.50N 73.00W
Narew 10 Td 52.55N 23.29 E
Narew 10 Qd 52.26N 20.42 E
Narian, Pointe- 63b Be 20.05S 164.00 E
Narin Gol 27 Fd 36.54N 92.51 E
Nariño [2] 54 Cc 1.30N 78.00W
Narita 29 Gd 35.47N 140.18 E
Narjan-Mar 6 Lb 67.39N 53.00 E
Närke 8 Ff 59.05N 15.05 E
Narlı 24 Gd 37.27N 37.09 E
Narmada 21 Jg 21.38N 72.36 E
Narman 24 Ib 40.21N 41.52 E
Nārnaul 25 Fc 28.03N 76.06 E
Narni 14 Gh 42.31N 12.31 E
Naroč 8 Lj 54.27N 26.45 E
Naroč 8 Lj 54.57N 26.49 E
Naroč, Ozero- 16 Eb 54.50N 26.45 E
Naroda 17 Jd 64.15N 61.00 E
Narodnaja, Gora- 5 Mb 65.04N 60.09 E
Naro-Fominsk 19 Dd 55.24N 36.43 E
Narok 36 Gc 1.05S 35.52 E
Narovlja 16 Fd 51.48N 29.31 E
Närpes/Närpio 8 Ib 62.28N 21.20 E
Närpio/Närpes 8 Ib 62.28N 21.20 E
Narrabri 59 Jf 30.19S 149.47 E
Narrandera 59 Jf 34.45S 146.33 E
Narrogin 59 Df 32.56S 117.10 E
Narromine 59 Jf 32.14S 148.15 E
Narrows, The- 51c Ab 17.12N 62.38W
Narryer, Mount- 59 De 26.30S 116.25 E
Narsimhapur 25 Fd 22.57N 79.12 E
Narssalik 41 Hf 61.42N 49.11W
Narssaq [Grld.] 41 Hf 61.00N 46.00W
Narssaq [Grld.] 41 Gf 64.00N 51.33W
Narssarssuaq 41 Hf 61.10N 45.15W
Narthákion 15 Fj 39.14N 22.22 E
Nartkala 16 Mh 43.32N 43.47 E
Narubis 37 Be 26.55S 18.35 E
Narugo 29 Gb 38.44N 140.43 E
Năruja 15 Jd 45.50N 26.47 E
Naru-Shima 29 Ae 32.50N 128.56 E
Naruto 28 Mg 34.11N 134.37 E
Naruto-Kaikyō 29 Dd 34.15N 134.40 E
Narva 7 Gg 59.29N 28.02 E
Narva 6 Id 59.23N 28.11 E
Narva Jõesuu/Narva-Jyesuu 8 Me 59.21N 28.04 E
Narva-Jyesuu/Narva Jõesuu 8 Me 59.21N 28.04 E
Narva laht 7 Gg 59.30N 27.40 E
Narvik 6 Hb 68.26N 17.25 E
Narvski Zaliv 7 Gg 59.30N 27.40 E
Narvskoje Vodohranilišče 8 Me 59.10N 28.30 E
Narym 20 De 58.58N 81.40 E
Naryn 21 Je 40.54N 71.45 E
Naryn 22 Je 41.26N 75.59 E
Naryncol 19 Ig 42.43N 80.08 E
Narynskaja Oblast [3] 19 Hg 41.20N 75.40 E
Nås 7 Df 60.27N 14.29 E
Na Sailti/Saltee Islands 9 Gi 52.07N 6.36W
Näsåker 7 De 63.23N 16.54 E
Nasarawa 34 Gd 8.32N 7.43 E
Năsăud 15 Hb 47.17N 24.24 E
Nasawa 63b Db 15.12S 168.06 E
Na Sceirí/Skerries 9 Gh 53.35N 6.07W
Nāshik 22 Jg 20.05N 73.48 E
Nash Point 9 Jj 51.24N 3.27W
Nashtārud 24 Nd 36.45N 51.02 E
Nashua 44 Ld 42.44N 71.28W
Nashville [Ar.-U.S.] 45 Jj 33.57N 93.51W
Nashville [Ga.-U.S.] 44 Fj 31.12N 83.15W
Nashville [Il.-U.S.] 45 Lg 38.21N 89.23W
Nashville [In.-U.S.] 44 Df 39.12N 86.15W
Nashville [Tn.-U.S.] 39 Kf 36.09N 86.48W
Nashville Seamount (EN) 38 Nf 35.00N 57.20W
Našice 14 Me 45.30N 18.06 E
Nasielsk 10 Qd 52.36N 20.48 E
Näsijärvi 5 Ic 61.35N 23.40 E
Nāşir 35 Ed 8.36N 33.04 E
Naskaupi 42 Lf 53.47N 60.51W
Nasorolevu 63d Bb 16.38S 179.24 E
Naşr [Eg.] 24 Dg 30.36N 30.23 E
Naşr [Lib.] 33 Dd 28.59N 21.13 E
Naşrābād 24 Of 32.09N 52.08 E
Nass 42 Ee 55.00N 129.50W
Nassandres 12 Ce 49.07N 0.44 E
Nassandres-La Rivière
Thibouville 12 Ce 49.07N 0.44 E
Nassau [Bah.] 39 Lg 25.05N 77.21W
Nassau [Ger.] 12 Jd 50.19N 7.48 E
Nassau, Bahía- 56 Gi 55.25S 67.40W
Nassau Island 57 Kf 11.33S 165.25W
Nassau River 59 Ic 15.58S 141.30 E
Nasser, Birkat- = Nasser,
Lake-(EN) 30 Kf 22.40N 32.00 E

Index Symbols

[1] Independent Nation
[2] State, Region
[3] District, County
[4] Municipality
[5] Colony, Dependency
Continent
Physical Region
Historical or Cultural Region
Mount, Mountain
Volcano
Hill
Mountains, Mountain Range
Hills, Escarpment
Plateau, Upland
Pass, Gap
Plain, Lowland
Delta
Salt Flat
Valley, Canyon
Crater, Cave
Karst Features
Depression
Polder
Desert, Dunes
Forest, Woods
Heath, Steppe
Oasis
Cape, Point
Coast, Beach
Cliff
Peninsula
Isthmus
Sandbank
Island
Atoll
Rock, Reef
Islands, Archipelago
Rocks, Reefs
Coral Reef
Well, Spring
Geyser
River, Stream
Waterfall Rapids
River Mouth, Estuary
Lake
Salt Lake
Intermittent Lake
Reservoir
Swamp, Pond
Canal
Glacier
Ice Shelf, Pack Ice
Ocean
Sea
Gulf, Bay
Strait, Fjord
Lagoon
Bank
Seamount
Tablemount
Ridge
Shelf
Basin
Escarpment, Sea Scarp
Fracture
Trench, Abyss
National Park, Reserve
Point of Interest
Recreation Site
Cave, Cavern
Historic Site
Ruins
Wall, Walls
Church, Abbey
Temple
Scientific Station
Airport
Port
Lighthouse
Mine
Tunnel
Dam, Bridge

Nasser, Lake-(EN)=Nasser, Birkat- 30 Kf 22.40N 32.00 E
Nassian 34 Ed 9.24N 4.29W
Nässjö 7 Dh 57.39N 14.41 E
Nassogne 12 Hd 50.08N 5.21 E
Na Staighri Dubha/Blackstairs Mountains 9 Gi 52.33N 6.49W
Nastapoka Islands 42 Je 56.50N 76.50W
Nastätten 12 Jd 50.12N 7.52 E
Nastola 8 Kd 60.57N 25.56 E
Nasu 29 Gc 37.02N 140.06 E
Nasu-Dake 29 Fc 37.07N 139.58 E
Näsviken 8 Gc 61.45N 16.52 E
Natá 49 Gi 8.20N 80.31W
Nata 30 Jk 20.14S 26.10 E
Nata 37 Dd 20.13S 26.11 E
Natal [2] 37 Ee 29.00S 30.00 E
Natal [B.C.-Can.] 46 Hb 49.44N 114.50W
Natal [Braz.] 53 Mf 5.47S 35.13W
Natal [Indon.] 26 Cf 0.33N 99.07 E
Natal Basin (EN) 3 Fm 30.00S 40.00 E
Natanz 24 Nf 33.31N 51.54 E
Natashquan 42 Lf 50.09N 61.37W
Natashquan 42 Lf 50.11N 61.49W
Natchez 43 Ie 31.34N 91.23W
Natchitoches 43 Ie 31.46N 93.05W
Natewa Bay 63d Bb 16.35S 179.40 E
Nathorsts Land 41 Jd 72.20N 27.00W
Nathula 63d Ab 16.53S 177.25 E
Natitingou 31 Hg 10.19N 1.22 E
Natityāy, Jabal- 33 Fe 23.01N 34.22 E
Natividad, Isla- 48 Bd 27.55N 115.10W
Natividade 54 If 11.43S 47.47W
Natori 28 Pe 38.11N 140.58 E
Natron, Lake- 30 Ki 2.25S 36.00 E
Naṭrūn, Wādī an- 24 Dg 30.25N 30.13 E
Natsudomari-Zaki 29a Bc 41.00N 140.53 E
Nättarö 8 Hf 58.50N 18.10 E
Nättraby 8 Fh 56.12N 15.31 E
Natuna Besar, Pulau- 26 Ef 4.00N 108.15 E
Natuna Islands (EN)=Bunguran, Kepulauan- 21 Mi 2.45N 109.00 E
Naturaliste, Cape- 57 Ch 33.32S 115.01 E
Naturaliste Channel 57 Ce 25.25S 113.00 E
Naturita 45 Bg 38.14N 108.34W
Naturno / Naturns 14 Ed 46.39N 11.00 E
Naturns / Naturno 14 Ed 46.39N 11.00 E
Nau 18 Gd 40.09N 69.22 E
Nau, Cap de la-/Nao, Cabo de la- 5 Gh 38.44N 0.14 E
Naucelle 11 Ij 44.12N 2.21 E
Nauėji-Akmjane/Naujoji-Akmenė 7 Fh 56.21N 22.50 E
Naugo/Nauvo 8 Id 60.10N 21.50 E
Nauhcampatépetl→Cofre de Perote, Cerro- 48 Kh 19.29N 97.08W
Nauja Bay 42 Kc 68.58N 75.00W
Naujamiestis/Naujamiestis 8 Ki 55.41N 24.09 E
Naujamiestis/Naujamiestis 8 Ki 55.41N 24.09 E
Naujoji-Akmenė/Nauėji-Akmjane 7 Fh 56.21N 22.50 E
Naukluft 37 Bd 24.10S 16.10 E
Naumburg [Ger.] 12 Lc 51.15N 9.10 E
Naumburg [Ger.] 10 He 51.09N 11.49 E
Nā'ūr 24 Fg 31.53N 35.50 E
Nauru 57 He 0.31S 166.56 E
Nauru/Naoero [1] 58 He 0.31S 166.56 E
Nauški 20 Ff 50.28N 106.07 E
Nausori 61 Ec 18.02S 178.32 E
Nauta 54 Dd 4.32S 73.33W
Nautanwa 25 Gc 27.26N 83.25 E
Nautla 48 Kg 20.13N 96.47W
Nauvo/Naugo 8 Id 60.10N 21.50 E
Nava 48 Ic 28.25N 100.45W
Navacerrada, Puerto de- 13 Id 40.47N 4.00W
Nava del Rey 13 Gc 41.20N 5.05W
Navahermosa 13 He 39.38N 4.28W
Navajo Mountain 46 Jh 37.02N 110.52W
Navajo Reservoir 45 Ch 36.55N 107.30W
Navalmoral de la Mata 13 Ge 39.54N 5.32W
Navan/An Uaimh 9 Gh 53.39N 6.41W
Navarin, Mys- 21 Tc 62.16N 179.10 E
Navarino, Isla- 52 Jk 55.05S 67.40W
Navarra [3] 13 Kb 42.45N 1.40W
Navarra=Navarre (EN) 13 Kb 43.00N 1.30W
Navarre (EN)=Navarra 13 Kb 43.00N 1.30W
Navarro 55 Cl 35.01S 59.16W
Navarro Mills Lake 45 Hk 31.56N 96.45W
Navašino 7 Ki 55.33N 42.12 E
Navasota 45 Hk 30.23N 96.05W
Navasota River 45 Hk 30.20N 96.09W
Navassa 47 Ie 18.24N 75.01W
Navaste Jõgi/Navesti 8 Kf 58.56N 24.58 E
Nävekvarn 8 Gf 58.38N 16.49 E
Naver 9 Ic 58.30N 4.15W
Navesti/Navaste Jõgi 8 Kf 58.56N 24.58 E
Navia 13 Fa 43.32N 6.43W
Navia 13 Fa 43.33N 6.44W
Navidad, Bahía de- 48 Gh 19.10N 104.45W
Navidad Bank (EN) 49 Mc 20.00N 68.50W
Naviti 63d Ab 17.07S 177.15 E
Navlja 16 Ic 52.42N 34.03 E
Navlja 19 De 52.50N 34.31 E
Năvodari 15 Le 44.19N 28.36 E
Navoi 19 Gg 40.10N 65.15 E
Navoja 47 Cc 27.06N 109.26W
Navolato 48 Fe 24.47N 107.42W
Navoloki 7 Jh 57.28N 41.59 E
Návpaktos 15 Ek 38.24N 21.50 E
Návplion 15 Fl 37.34N 22.48 E
Navrongo 34 Ec 10.54N 1.06W
Navsāri 25 Ed 20.51N 72.55 E
Navtilos 15 Gn 35.57N 23.13 E
Navua 63d Bc 18.13S 178.10 E
Navy Board Inlet 42 Jb 73.30N 81.00W
Nawa 24 Gf 32.53N 36.03 E
Nawābshāh 25 Dc 26.15N 68.25 E
Nawāṣīf, Ḩarrat- 33 He 21.20N 42.10 E
Ṉaws, Ra's- 23 If 17.18N 55.16 E
Náxos 15 Il 37.06N 25.23 E
Naxos 14 Jm 37.49N 15.15 E
Náxos=Naxos (EN) 5 Ih 37.02N 25.35 E
Naxos (EN)=Náxos 5 Ih 37.02N 25.35 E
Nayarit [2] 47 Cd 22.00N 105.00W
Nayarit, Sierra- 47 Dd 22.00N 103.50W
Nayau 63d Cb 17.58S 179.03W
Nāy Band [Iran] 24 Oi 27.23N 52.38 E
Nāy Band [Iran] 24 Qf 32.20N 57.34 E
Nāy Band, Ra's-e- 24 Oi 27.23N 52.34 E
Nayoro 27 Pc 44.21N 142.28 E
Nazaré [Braz.] 54 Kf 13.02S 39.00W
Nazaré [Port.] 13 Ce 39.36N 9.04W
Nazareth (EN)=Naẓerat 24 Ff 32.42N 35.18 E
Nazarovo 20 Ee 56.01N 90.36 E
Nazas 48 Ge 25.14N 104.08W
Nazas, Rio- 38 Ig 25.35N 105.00W
Nazca 53 Ig 14.50S 74.55W
Nazca Ridge (EN) 3 Nl 22.00S 82.00W
Naze 27 Mf 28.23N 129.30 E
Naẓerat=Nazareth (EN) 24 Ff 32.42N 35.18 E
Nazilli 23 Cb 37.55N 28.21 E
Nazimiye 24 Hc 39.11N 39.50 E
Nazimovo 20 Ee 59.30N 90.58 E
Nazino 20 Cd 60.15N 78.58 E
Nazlū 24 Kd 37.42N 45.16 E
Nazran 16 Nh 43.15N 44.46 E
Nazret 35 Fd 8.34N 39.18 E
Nazw'a 23 Ie 22.54N 57.31 E
Nazym 17 Nf 61.12N 68.57 E
Nazyvajevsk 19 Hd 55.34N 71.21 E
Nbâk 32 Ef 17.15N 14.59W
Nchanga 36 Ee 12.31S 27.52 E
Ncheu 36 Fe 14.49S 34.38 E
Ndala 36 Fc 4.46S 33.16 E
N'dalatando 36 Bd 9.18S 14.54 E
Ndali 34 Fd 9.51N 2.43 E
Ndélé 31 Jh 8.24N 20.39 E
Ndélélé 34 He 4.02N 14.56 E
Ndendé 36 Bc 2.23S 11.23 E
Ndindi 36 Bc 3.46S 11.09 E
N'Djamena (Fort-Lamy) 31 Ig 12.07N 15.03 E
Ndola 31 Jj 12.58S 28.38 E
Ndouana, Pointe- 63b Dc 16.35S 168.09 E
Ndrhamcha, Sebkha de- 32 Df 18.45N 15.48W
Nduindui 60 Fi 9.48S 159.58 E
Ndui Ndui 63b Cb 15.24S 167.46 E
Né 11 Fi 45.40N 0.23W
Nea 63c Ab 10.51S 165.47 E
Nea 7 Ce 63.13N 11.02 E
Néa Alikarnassós 15 In 35.20N 25.09 E
Néa Artáki 15 Gk 38.31N 23.38 E
Neagari 29 Ec 36.26N 136.26 E
Neagh, Lough-/Loch nEathach 5 Fe 54.38N 6.24W
Neagră, Marea-=Black Sea (EN) 5 Jg 43.00N 35.00 E
Neah Bay 46 Cb 48.22N 124.37W
Néa Ionía 15 Fj 39.23N 22.56 E
Neajlov 15 Je 44.11N 26.12 E
Neale, Lake- 59 Fd 24.20S 130.00 E
Neamț [2] 15 Jb 47.00N 26.20 E
Neápolis [Grc.] 15 In 35.15N 25.37 E
Neápolis [Grc.] 15 Ei 40.19N 21.23 E
Neápolis [Grc.] 15 Gm 36.31N 23.04 E
Near Islands 38 Bd 52.40N 173.30W
Neath 9 Jj 51.37N 3.50W
Neath 9 Jj 51.40N 3.48W
Néa Zíkhni 15 Gh 41.02N 23.50 E
Nebaj 49 Bf 15.24N 91.08W
Nebbou 34 Ec 11.18N 1.53W
Nebit-Dag 22 Hf 39.30N 54.22 E
Neblina, Pico da- 52 Je 1.08N 66.10W
Nebo 59 Jd 21.40S 148.39 E
Nebo, Mount- 46 Jg 39.49N 111.46W
Neboľči 7 Hg 59.08N 33.21 E
Nebraska [2] 43 Gc 41.30N 100.00W
Nebraska City 43 Hc 40.41N 95.52W
Nebrodi (Caronie) 14 Im 37.55N 14.35 E
Necedah 45 Kd 44.02N 90.03W
Nechako 42 Ff 53.55N 122.44W
Nechako Reservoir 42 Ef 53.00N 126.10W
Nechar, Djebel- 13 Qi 35.52N 4.59 E
Neches River 45 Jl 29.55N 93.52W
Nechi 49 Ji 8.07N 74.46W
Nechi, Rio- 49 Ji 8.08N 74.46W
Neckako Plateau 42 Ff 53.25N 124.40W
Neckar 10 Eg 49.31N 8.26 E
Neckarsulm 10 Fg 49.11N 9.14 E
Necker Island 57 Kb 23.35N 164.42W
Necochea 53 Ki 38.34S 58.45W
Necy 12 Bf 48.50N 0.07W
Nedeley 35 Bb 15.34N 18.10 E
Nederland 45 Jl 29.58N 93.59W
Nederland=Netherlands (EN) [1] 6 Ge 52.15N 5.30 E
Nederlandse Antillen [5] 50 Ec 18.06N 63.10W
Nederlandse Antillen = Netherlands Antilles (EN) [5] 53 Jd 12.15N 69.00W
Neder-Rijn = Lower Rhine (EN) 11 Mc 51.59N 6.20 E
Nédong 22 Lg 29.14N 91.46 E
Nedstrand 8 Ae 59.21N 5.51 E
Nedstrandefjorden 8 Ae 59.20N 5.50 E
Neede 12 Ib 52.08N 6.37 E
Needham Market 12 Db 52.09N 1.02 E
Needham's Point 51q Ab 13.05N 59.36W
Needles 43 Ee 34.51N 114.37W
Neembucú [3] 55 Dh 27.00S 58.00W
Neenah 45 Ld 44.11N 88.28W
Neepawa 45 Ga 50.13N 99.29W
Neermoor, Moormerland- 12 Ja 53.18N 7.26 E
Neeroeteren, Maaseik- 12 Hc 51.05N 5.42 E
Neerpelt 12 Hc 51.13N 5.25 E
Nefasit 35 Fb 15.18N 39.04 E
Nefedova 19 Hd 58.48N 72.34 E
Né Finn/Nephin 9 Dg 54.01N 9.22W
Neftah 32 Ic 33.52N 7.53 E
Neftečala 16 Pj 39.19N 49.13 E
Neftegorsk 16 Kg 44.22N 39.42 E
Neftegorsk 20 Jf 53.00N 143.00 E
Neftegorsk 19 Fe 52.45N 51.13 E
Neftejugansk 19 Hc 61.05N 72.45 E
Neftekamsk→Nikolo-Berjozovka 19 Fd 56.06N 54.17 E
Neftekumsk 19 Eg 44.43N 44.59 E
Neftjanyje Kamin 16 Qi 40.15N 50.49 E
Negage 36 Cd 7.46S 15.18 E
Negara 26 Fh 8.22S 114.37 E
Negele=Neghelle (EN) 31 Kh 5.20N 39.37 E
Negev Desert (EN)=Hanegev 24 Fg 30.30N 34.55 E
Neghelle (EN)=Negele 31 Kh 5.20N 39.37 E
Negola 36 Be 14.10S 14.30 E
Negomano 37 Fb 11.26S 38.33 E
Negombo 25 Fg 7.13N 79.50 E
Negonego Atoll 57 Mf 18.47S 141.48W
Negotin 15 Fe 44.13N 22.32 E
Negotino 15 Fh 41.29N 22.06 E
Negra, Cordillera- 54 Ce 9.25S 77.40W
Negra, Coxilha- 55 Ej 31.02S 55.45W
Negra, Peña- 13 Fb 42.11N 6.30W
Negra, Ponta- 55 Jf 23.21S 44.36W
Negra, Punta- 52 Hf 6.06S 81.10W
Negra, Serra- 55 Fc 16.30S 52.10W
Negra o de los Difuntos, Laguna- 55 Fl 34.03S 53.40W
Negreira 13 Db 42.54N 8.44W
Negreni 15 He 44.34N 24.36 E
Negrești 15 Gb 47.52N 23.26 E
Negrine 32 Ic 34.29N 7.31 E
Negrinho, Rio- 55 Ed 19.20S 55.05W
Negro, Cabo- 13 Gi 35.41N 5.17W
Negro, Rio- [Arg.] 55 Ch 27.27S 58.54W
Negro, Rio- [Arg.] 52 Jj 41.02S 62.47W
Negro, Rio- [Bol.] 54 Ff 14.11S 63.07W
Negro, Rio- [Braz.] 54 Gg 19.13S 57.17W
Negro, Rio- [Braz.] 56 Jc 26.01S 50.30W
Negro, Rio- [Par.] 56 Ib 24.23S 57.11W
Negro, Rio- [S.Amer.] 52 Kf 3.08S 59.55W
Negro, Rio- [S.Amer.] 55 Ce 20.11S 58.10W
Negro, Rio- [Ur.] 52 Ki 33.24S 58.22W
Negros 21 Oi 10.00N 123.00 E
Negru, Rîu- 15 Id 45.45N 25.46 E
Negru Vodă 15 Lf 43.49N 28.12 E
Nehajevski 16 Ld 50.27N 41.46 E
Nehalem River 46 Dd 45.40N 123.56W
Nehāvand 24 Me 35.56N 49.31 E
Nehe 27 Lb 48.28N 124.53 E
Nehoiu 15 Jd 45.26N 26.17 E
Néhoué, Baie de- 63b Be 20.21S 164.09 E
Neiba 49 Ld 18.28N 71.25W
Neiba, Bahía de- 49 Ld 18.15N 71.02W
Neidín/Kenmare 9 Dj 51.53N 9.35W
Neige, Crêt de la- 11 Lh 46.16N 5.56 E
Neiges, Piton des- 30 Mk 21.05S 55.29 E
Neijiang 22 Mg 29.38N 104.58 E
Neilton 46 Dc 47.25N 123.52W
Nei-meng-ku Tzu-chih-ch'ü→Nei Monggol Zizhiqu 27 Jc 44.00N 112.00 E
Nei Monggol Gaoyuan 21 Ne 42.00N 111.00 E
Nei Monggol Zizhiqu (Nei-meng-ku Tzu-chih-ch'ü)=Inner Mongolia (EN) [2] 27 Jc 44.00N 112.00 E
Neiqiu 28 Cf 37.17N 114.30 E
Neiva 53 Ie 2.56N 75.18W
Neja 19 Ed 58.19N 43.52 E
Nejanilini Lake 42 He 59.30N 97.50W
Nejdek 10 If 50.19N 12.44 E
Nejo 35 Fd 9.30N 35.32 E
Nejva 17 Kh 57.54N 62.18 E
Nekemt=Leqemt (EN) 31 Kh 9.05N 36.33 E
Nekså 8 Fi 55.04N 15.09 E
Nelemnoje 20 Kc 65.23N 151.08 E
Nelgese 20 Ic 66.40N 136.30 E
Nelichu 35 Ed 6.08N 34.25 E
Nelidovo 19 Dd 56.13N 32.50 E
Neligh 45 Ge 42.08N 98.02W
Neljaty 20 Ge 56.29N 115.50 E
Nelkan 20 Jd 64.15N 143.03 E
Nellore 22 Jh 12.56N 79.08 E
Nelma 20 Ig 47.40N 139.08 E
Nelson [2] 62 Ed 41.45S 172.30 E
Nelson 38 Jd 57.04N 92.30W
Nelson [B.C.-Can.] 42 Fg 49.29N 117.17W
Nelson [N.Z.] 58 Ii 41.16S 173.15 E
Nelson, Cape- [Austl.] 57 Fh 38.26S 141.33 E
Nelson, Cape- [Pap.N.Gui.] 59 Ja 9.00S 149.15 E
Nelson Island 40 Gd 60.35N 164.45W
Nelson's Dockyard 51d Bb 17.00N 61.46W
Nelspruit 31 Kk 25.30S 30.58 E
Néma 31 Gg 16.36N 7.15W
Néma, Dahr- 32 Ff 16.14N 7.30W
Neman 5 Id 55.18N 21.23 E
Neman 7 Fi 55.03N 22.01 E
Nembrala 26 Hi 10.53S 122.50 E
Nemda 7 Kh 57.31N 43.15 E
Neméa 15 Fl 37.49N 22.39 E
Neméa 15 Fl 37.49N 22.40 E
Neměckes, Mali i- 15 Di 40.08N 20.24 E
Nemenčinė 8 Kj 54.50N 25.39 E
Neměrçkes, Mali i- 15 Di 40.08N 20.24 E
Nemira, Vîrful- 15 Jc 46.15N 26.19 E
Nemirov 10 Tf 50.08N 23.28 E
Nemirov 16 Fe 48.59N 28.50 E
Némiscau 42 Jf 51.30N 77.00W
Nemjuga 7 Kd 65.29N 43.40 E
Nemours 11 If 48.16N 2.42 E
Nemunas 5 Id 55.18N 21.23 E
Nemunėlis 8 Kh 56.24N 24.10 E
Nemuro 27 Qc 43.20N 145.35 E
Nemuro-Hantō 29a Db 43.20N 145.35 E
Nemuro-Kaikyō=Nemuro Strait (EN) 20 Jh 43.50N 145.30 E
Nemuro Strait (EN)=Kunaširskij Proliv 20 Jh 43.50N 145.30 E
Nemuro Strait (EN)=Nemuro-Kaikyō 20 Jh 43.50N 145.30 E
Nemuro-Wan 29a Db 43.25N 145.25 E
Nenagh/An tAonach 9 Ei 52.52N 8.12W
Nenana 40 Jd 64.30N 149.00W
Nenana 40 Jd 64.34N 149.07W
Nendo Island 57 Hf 10.40S 165.54 E
Nene 9 Ni 52.48N 0.13 E
Neneckij avtonomnaja respublika 19 Fb 67.30N 54.00 E
Nenjiang 22 Oe 49.10N 125.12 E
Nen Jiang 21 Oe 45.26N 124.39 E
Neo 29 Ed 35.38N 136.37 E
Neodesha 45 Ih 37.25N 95.41W
Néon Karlovásion 15 Jl 37.47N 26.42 E
Neosho 45 Ih 36.52N 94.22W
Neosho River 45 Ih 35.48N 95.18W
Néouvielle, Massif de- 11 Gl 42.51N 0.07 E
Nepal [1] 22 Kg 28.00N 84.00 E
Nepalganj 25 Gc 28.03N 81.37 E
Nephi 43 Ed 39.43N 111.50W
Nephin/Né Finn 9 Dg 54.01N 9.22W
Nepisiguit River 44 Ob 47.37N 65.38W
Nepoko 30 Jh 1.40N 27.01 E
Nepomuk 10 Jg 49.29N 13.34 E
Ner 10 Od 52.10N 18.40 E
Nera [It.] 14 Gh 42.26N 12.24 E
Nera [Rom.] 15 Ee 44.49N 21.22 E
Nérac 11 Gj 44.08N 0.21 E
Neratovice 10 Kf 50.16N 14.31 E
Nerău 15 Dd 45.58N 20.34 E
Nerča 20 Gf 51.54N 116.30 E
Nerčinsk 20 Gf 51.58N 116.35 E
Nerčinski Zavod 20 Gf 51.17N 119.30 E
Nerehta 19 Ed 57.28N 40.34 E
Nereju 15 Jd 45.42N 26.43 E
Nereta 8 Kh 56.12N 25.24 E
Neretva 14 Lg 43.02N 17.27 E
Neretvanski kanal 14 Lg 43.03N 17.11 E
Nerica 17 Fd 65.20N 52.45 E
Neringa 7 Ei 55.24N 21.05 E
Neringa 7 Ei 55.18N 21.00 E
Neringa-Juodkrante/Neringa-Juodkranté 8 Ii 55.35N 21.01 E
Neringa-Juodkranté/Neringa-Juodkrante 8 Ii 55.35N 21.01 E
Neringa-Nida 8 Ii 55.18N 20.53 E
Neringa-Preila/Neringa-Prejla 8 Ii 55.20N 20.59 E
Neringa-Prejla/Neringa-Preila 8 Ii 55.20N 20.59 E
Neriquinha 36 Df 15.45S 21.33 E
Neris/Njaris 8 Kj 54.55N 25.45 E
Nerja 13 Ih 36.44N 3.52W
Nerjungri 20 He 56.40N 124.47 E
Nerl 7 Jh 56.11N 40.34 E
Nerl 7 Ih 57.07N 37.39 E
Nerpio 13 Jf 38.09N 2.18W
Nerussa 16 Hc 52.33N 33.47 E
Nerva 13 Fg 37.42N 6.32W
Nervi, Genova- 14 Df 44.23N 9.02 E
Nervión 13 Ja 43.14N 2.53W
Nes 8 Cd 60.34N 9.59 E
Nes, Ameland- 12 Ha 53.26N 5.48 E
Nesbyen 7 Bf 60.34N 9.06 E
Nesebăr 15 Kg 42.39N 27.44 E
Nesjøen 8 Db 63.00N 12.00 E
Neskaupstaður 7a Db 65.09N 13.42W
Nesle 12 Ee 49.46N 2.45 E
Nesna 7 Cc 66.12N 13.02 E
Ness City 45 Gg 38.27N 99.54W
Nesterov 7 Fi 54.42N 22.34 E
Nesterov 16 Cd 50.03N 24.00 E
Néstos 15 Hi 40.51N 24.44 E
Nesttun 8 Ad 60.19N 5.20 E
Nesviž 16 Ec 53.13N 26.39 E
Netanya 24 Ff 32.20N 34.51 E
Netcong 44 Je 40.54N 74.43W
Nete 11 Kc 51.10N 4.15 E
Nethe 12 Lc 51.44N 9.23 E
Netherdale 59 Jd 21.08S 148.32 E
Netherlands (EN)=Nederland [1] 6 Ge 52.15N 5.30 E
Netherlands Antilles (EN) = Nederlandse Antillen [5] 53 Jd 12.15N 69.00W
Neto 14 Lk 39.12N 17.09 E
Netphen 12 Kd 50.55N 8.06 E
Nettebach 12 Jd 50.26N 7.28 E
Nettersheim 12 Id 50.30N 6.38 E
Nettetal 12 Ic 51.18N 6.12 E
Nettilling Lake 38 Lc 66.30N 70.40W
Nettuno 14 Gi 41.27N 12.39 E
Netzahualcóyotl, Presa- 48 Mi 17.00N 93.30W
Neubourg, Campagne du- 11 Ge 49.08N 1.00 E
Neubrandenburg 10 Jc 53.34N 13.16 E
Neuburg an der Donau 10 Hh 48.44N 11.11 E
Neuchâtel [2] 14 Ac 47.05N 6.50 E
Neuchâtel/Neuenburg 14 Ad 46.59N 6.56 E
Neuchâtel, Lac de-/Neuenburger See 14 Ad 46.55N 6.55 E
Neuenbürg 12 Kf 48.50N 8.35 E
Neuenburg/Neuchâtel 14 Ad 46.59N 6.56 E
Neuenburger See/Neuchâtel, Lac de- 14 Ad 46.55N 6.55 E
Neuenhaus 12 Ib 52.30N 6.58 E
Neuenkirchen 12 Jb 52.15N 7.22 E
Neuerburg 12 Id 50.01N 6.18 E
Neufchâteau [Bel.] 11 Le 49.51N 5.26 E
Neufchâteau [Fr.] 11 Lf 48.21N 5.42 E
Neufchâtel-en-Bray 11 He 49.44N 1.27 E
Neufchâtel-Hardelot 12 Dd 50.37N 1.38 E
Neufchâtel Hardelot-Hardelot Plage 12 Dd 50.38N 1.35 E
Neufchâtel-sur-Aisne 12 Ge 49.26N 4.02 E
Neuffossé, Canal de- 12 Ed 50.45N 2.15 E
Neuhaus am Rennweg 10 Hf 50.31N 11.09 E
Neuilly-en-Thelle 12 Ee 49.13N 2.17 E
Neuilly-Saint-Front 12 Fe 49.10N 3.16 E
Neu-Isenburg 12 Kd 50.03N 8.42 E
Neukirchen-Vluyn 12 Ic 51.27N 6.35 E
Neum 14 Lh 42.55N 17.38 E
Neumagen Dhron 12 Ie 49.51N 6.54 E
Neumarkter Sattel 14 Id 47.06N 14.22 E
Neumarkt in der Oberpfalz 10 Hg 49.17N 11.28 E
Neumünster 10 Fb 54.04N 9.59 E
Neunkirchen [Aus.] 14 Kc 47.43N 16.05 E
Neunkirchen [Ger.] 10 Dg 49.21N 7.11 E
Neunkirchen [Ger.] 12 Kd 50.48N 8.00 E
Neunkirchen [Ger.] 12 Jd 50.51N 7.20 E
Neuquén 53 Ji 39.00S 68.05W
Neuquén [2] 56 Ge 39.00S 70.00W
Neuquén, Río- 52 Ji 38.59S 68.00W
Neurupping 10 Id 52.56N 12.48 E
Neuse River 44 Ih 35.06N 76.30W
Neusiedl am See 14 Kc 47.56N 16.50 E
Neusiedler See (Fertö) 10 Mi 47.50N 16.45 E
Neuß 10 Ce 51.12N 6.42 E
Neustadt (Hessen) 12 Ld 50.51N 9.07 E
Neustadt am Rübenberge 10 Fd 52.30N 9.28 E
Neustadt an der Aisch 10 Gg 49.35N 10.36 E
Neustadt an der Orla 10 Hf 50.44N 11.45 E
Neustadt an der Weinstraße 10 Eg 49.21N 8.09 E
Neustadt bei Couburg 10 Hf 50.19N 11.07 E
Neustadt in Holstein 10 Gb 54.06N 10.49 E
Neustrelitz 10 Jc 53.22N 13.05 E
Neu-Ulm 10 Gh 48.24N 10.01 E
Neuville-les-Dieppe 12 De 49.55N 1.06 E
Neuville-sur-Saône 11 Ki 45.52N 4.51 E
Neuwerk 10 Ec 53.55N 8.30 E
Neuwied 10 Df 50.26N 7.28 E
Neva 5 Jd 59.55N 30.15 E
Nevada [2] 43 Dd 39.00N 117.00W
Nevada [Ia.-U.S.] 45 Je 42.01N 93.27W
Nevada [Mo.-U.S.] 43 Id 37.51N 94.22W
Nevada, Sierra- [Sp.] 5 Fh 37.05N 3.10W
Nevada, Sierra- [U.S.] 38 Hf 38.00N 119.15W
Nevada del Cocuy, Sierra- 52 Ie 6.10N 72.15W
Nevada de Santa Marta, Sierra- 52 Id 10.50N 73.40W
Nevado, Cerro- 52 Ie 3.59N 74.04W
Nevado de Ampato 52 Ig 15.50S 71.52W
Neve, Serra da- 30 Ij 13.52S 13.26 E
Nevel 19 Cd 56.02N 29.55 E
Nevele 12 Fc 51.02N 3.33 E
Nevelsk 20 Jg 46.37N 141.57 E
Neverkino 16 Oc 52.47N 46.48 E
Nevers 11 Jg 46.59N 3.10 E
Nevesinje 14 Mg 43.16N 18.07 E
Nevinnomyssk 19 Eg 44.38N 41.58 E
Nevis 47 Le 17.10N 62.34W
Nevis, Ben- 5 Fd 56.48N 5.01W
Nevis Peak 51c Ab 17.10N 62.34W
Nevjansk 19 Gd 57.32N 60.13 E
Nevşehir 23 Db 38.38N 34.43 E
Nevskoje 28 Lb 45.42N 133.40 E
Newala 36 Ge 10.56S 39.18 E
New Albany [In.-U.S.] 43 Jd 38.18N 85.49W
New Albany [Ms.-U.S.] 45 Li 34.29N 89.00W
New Alresford 12 Ac 51.05N 1.10W
New Amsterdam 53 Ke 6.17N 57.36W
Newark [De.-U.S.] 44 Jf 39.41N 75.45W
Newark [N.J.-U.S.] 43 Mc 40.44N 74.11W
Newark [N.Y.-U.S.] 44 Id 43.03N 77.06W
Newark [Oh.-U.S.] 43 Kc 40.03N 82.25W
Newark-on-Trent 9 Mh 53.05N 0.49W
New Bedford 43 Mc 41.38N 70.56W
New Bern 43 Ld 35.07N 77.03W
Newberry [Mi.-U.S.] 44 Eb 46.21N 85.30W
Newberry [S.C.-U.S.] 44 Gh 34.17N 81.37W
New Braunfels 43 Hf 29.42N 98.08W
New Britain 44 Ke 41.40N 72.47W
New Britain Island 57 Ge 5.40S 151.00 E
New Britain Trench (EN) 60 Ei 6.00S 153.00 E
New Brunswick 44 Je 40.29N 74.27W
New Brunswick [3] 42 Kg 46.30N 66.45W
New Buckenham 12 Db 52.28N 1.05 E
New Buffalo 44 De 41.47N 86.45W
Newburgh 43 Mc 41.30N 74.00W
Newbury 9 Lj 51.25N 1.20W
New Caledonia (EN) = Nouvelle-Calédonie [5] 58 Hg 21.30S 165.30 E
New Caledonia (EN)=Nouvelle-Calédonie 57 Hg 21.30S 165.30 E
New Caledonia Basin (EN) 3 Jm 30.00S 165.00 E
New Carlisle 44 Oa 48.01N 65.20W
New Castile (EN)=Castilla la Nueva 13 Id 40.00N 3.45W
New Castle [In.-U.S.] 44 Ef 39.55N 85.22W
New Castle [Pa.-U.S.] 43 Kc 41.00N 80.22W
Newcastle [Austl.] 58 Gh 32.56S 151.46 E
Newcastle [N.B.-Can.] 42 Kg 47.00N 65.34W
Newcastle [N.Ire.-U.K.] 9 Hg 54.12N 5.54W
Newcastle [S.Afr.] 37 De 27.49S 29.55 E
Newcastle [St.C.N.] 51c Ab 17.13N 62.34W
Newcastle/An Caisleán Nua 9 Hg 54.12N 5.54W
Newcastle Creek 59 Gc 17.20S 133.23 E
Newcastle-under-Lyme 9 Kh 53.00N 2.14W

Index Symbols

[1] Independent Nation
[2] State, Region
[3] District, County
[4] Municipality
[5] Colony, Dependency
Continent
Physical Region
Historical or Cultural Region
Mount, Mountain
Volcano
Hill
Mountains, Mountain Range
Hills, Escarpment
Plateau, Upland
Pass, Gap
Plain, Lowland
Delta
Salt Flat
Valley, Canyon
Crater, Cave
Karst Features
Depression
Polder
Desert, Dunes
Forest, Woods
Heath, Steppe
Oasis
Cape, Point
Coast, Beach
Cliff
Peninsula
Isthmus
Sandbank
Island
Atoll
Rock, Reef
Islands, Archipelago
Rocks, Reefs
Coral Reef
Well, Spring
Geyser
River, Stream
Waterfall Rapids
River Mouth, Estuary
Lake
Salt Lake
Intermittent Lake
Reservoir
Swamp, Pond
Canal
Glacier
Ice Shelf, Pack Ice
Ocean
Sea
Gulf, Bay
Strait, Fjord
Lagoon
Bank
Seamount
Tablemount
Ridge
Shelf
Basin
Escarpment, Sea Scarp
Fracture
Trench, Abyss
National Park, Reserve
Point of Interest
Recreation Site
Cave, Cavern
Historic Site
Ruins
Wall, Walls
Church, Abbey
Temple
Scientific Station
Airport
Port
Lighthouse
Mine
Tunnel
Dam, Bridge

Index Symbols

- [1] Independent Nation
- [2] State, Region
- [3] District, County
- [4] Municipality
- [5] Colony, Dependency
- ■ Continent
- Physical Region
- Historical or Cultural Region
- Mount, Mountain
- Volcano
- Hill
- Mountains, Mountain Range
- Hills, Escarpment
- Plateau, Upland
- Pass, Gap
- Plain, Lowland
- Delta
- Salt Flat
- Valley, Canyon
- Crater, Cave
- Karst Features
- Depression
- Polder
- Desert, Dunes
- Forest, Woods
- Heath, Steppe
- Oasis
- Cape, Point
- Coast, Beach
- Cliff
- Peninsula
- Isthmus
- Sandbank
- Island
- Islands, Archipelago
- Rock, Reef
- Rocks, Reefs
- Coral Reef
- Well, Spring
- Geyser
- Reservoir
- River, Stream
- Waterfall Rapids
- River Mouth, Estuary
- Lake
- Salt Lake
- Intermittent Lake
- Swamp, Pond
- Canal
- Bank
- Seamount
- Tableland
- Ridge
- Basin
- Lagoon
- Glacier
- Ice Shelf, Pack Ice
- Ocean
- Sea
- Shelf
- Gulf, Bay
- Strait, Fjord
- Escarpment, Sea Scarp
- Fracture
- Trench, Abyss
- National Park, Reserve
- Point of Interest
- Recreation Site
- Cave, Cavern
- Historic Site
- Ruins
- Wall, Walls
- Church, Abbey
- Temple
- Scientific Station
- Airport
- Port
- Lighthouse
- Mine
- Tunnel
- Dam, Bridge

International Map Index

Name	Map	Grid	Lat	Long
Nižni Oseredok, Ostrov- ▣	16	Pg	45.45N	48.35 E
Nižni Tagil	6	Ld	57.55N	59.57 E
Nižni Trajanov Val = Lower Trajan's Wall (EN) ▦	15	Ld	45.45N	28.30 E
Nižnjaja Omra	17	Ge	62.46N	55.46 E
Nižnjaja Pojma	19	Eb	66.43N	47.36 E
Nižnjaja Pojma	20	Ee	56.08N	97.18 E
Nižnjaja Salda	17	Jg	58.05N	60.48 E
Nižnjaja Tavda	19	Gd	57.40N	66.12 E
Nižnjaja Tojma ◨	7	Ke	62.22N	44.15 E
Nižnjaja Tunguska = Lower Tunguska (EN) ◨	21	Kc	65.48N	88.04 E
Nižnjaja Tura	17	Ig	58.37N	59.49 E
Nižnjaja Zolotica	7	Jd	65.41N	40.13 E
Nižny Pjandž	18	Gf	37.14N	68.35 E
Nizza Monferrato	14	Cf	44.46N	8.21 E
Njajs ◨	17	Je	62.25N	60.47 E
Njamunas ◨	5	Id	55.18N	21.23 E
Njandoma	19	Ec	61.43N	40.12 E
Njaris/Neris ◨	8	Kj	54.55N	25.45 E
Njazepetrovsk	17	Ih	56.03N	59.38 E
Njazidja ▨	30	Lj	11.35S	43.20 E
Njegoš ▨	15	Bg	42.53N	18.45 E
Njinjo	36	Gd	8.48S	38.54 E
Njombe ◨	30	Ki	6.56S	35.06 E
Njombe	31	Ki	9.20S	34.46 E
Njudung ▣	8	Fg	57.25N	14.50 E
Njuja	20	Gd	60.32N	116.25 E
Njuk, Ozero- ▱	7	Hd	64.25N	31.45 E
Njuksenica	7	Kf	60.28N	44.15 E
Njukža ◨	20	He	56.30N	121.40 E
Njunes ▨	7	Eb	68.45N	19.30 E
Njurba	22	Nc	63.17N	118.20 E
Njurundabommen	7	De	62.16N	17.22 E
Njutånger	8	Gc	61.37N	17.03 E
Njuvčim	17	Ef	61.22N	50.42 E
Nkambe	34	Hd	6.38N	10.40 E
Nkawkaw	34	Ed	6.33N	0.46W
Nkayi [Con.]	31	Ii	4.05S	13.18 E
Nkayi [Zimb.]	37	Dc	19.00S	28.54 E
Nkhata Bay	36	Fe	11.36S	34.18 E
Nkongsamba	31	Hh	4.57N	9.56 E
Nkota Kota	31	Kj	12.55S	34.18 E
Nkululu ◨	36	Fd	6.26S	32.49 E
Nkusi ◨	36	Fb	1.07N	30.40 E
Nkwalini	37	Ee	28.45S	31.30 E
'Nmai ◨	25	Jc	25.42N	97.30 E
Nmaki ◨	24	Pg	31.16N	55.29 E
Nnewi	34	Gd	6.01N	6.55 E
Nô	29	Ec	37.05N	137.59 E
Noailles	12	Ie	49.20N	2.12 E
Noākhāli ▣	25	Id	22.49N	91.06 E
Noatak	40	Gc	67.34N	162.59W
Nobel	44	Gc	45.25N	80.06W
Nobeoka	27	Ne	32.35N	131.40 E
Noblesville	44	Ee	40.03N	86.00W
Noboribetsu	28	Pc	42.25N	141.11 E
Noce ◨	14	Fd	46.09N	11.04 E
Nocra ◨	35	Fc	15.40N	39.55 E
Nodaway River ◨	45	Ig	39.54N	94.58W
Noën	27	Hc	43.15N	102.20 E
Noeuf, Île- ◨	37b	Bb	6.14S	53.03 E
Noeux-les-Mines	12	Ed	50.29N	2.40 E
Nogajskaja Step ◪	16	Ng	44.15N	46.00 E
Nogales [Az.-U.S.]	43	Ee	31.21N	110.56W
Nogales [Mex.]	39	Hf	31.20N	110.56W
Nogaro	11	Fk	43.46N	0.02W
Nogat ◨	10	Pb	54.11N	19.15 E
Nōgata	29	Be	33.44N	130.44 E
Nogent-le-Rotrou	11	Gf	48.19N	0.50 E
Nogent-sur-Marne	12	Ef	48.50N	2.29 E
Nogent-sur-Oise	12	Ee	49.16N	2.28 E
Nogent-sur-Seine	11	Jf	48.29N	3.30 E
Noginsk	20	Ed	64.25N	91.10 E
Noginsk	19	Dd	55.54N	38.28 E
Nogliki	20	Jf	51.45N	143.15 E
Nōgo-Hakusan ▲	29	Ed	35.46N	136.31 E
Nogoyá	56	Id	32.24S	59.48W
Nogoya, Arroyo- ◨	55	Ck	32.55S	59.59W
Nógrád ▣	10	Ph	48.00N	19.35 E
Nogueira, Serra da- ▨	13	Fc	41.42N	6.52W
Noguera Pallaresa ◨	13	Mb	42.15N	0.54 E
Noguera Ribagorçana/ Noguera Ribagorzana ◨	13	Mc	41.40N	0.43 E
Noguera Ribagorzana/ Noguera Ribagorçana ◨	13	Mc	41.40N	0.43 E
Noh, Laguna- ▱	48	Nh	18.40N	90.20W
Nohain ◨	11	Jf	47.24N	2.55 E
Noheji	28	Pd	40.52N	141.08 E
Nohfelden	12	Je	49.35N	7.09 E
Noidore, Rio- ◨	55	Fb	14.50S	52.34W
Noir, Causse- ▨	11	Jj	44.09N	3.15 E
Noire, Montagne- ▲	11	Ik	43.28N	2.18 E
Noires, Montagnes- ▲	11	Cf	48.09N	3.40W
Noirétable	11	Jj	45.49N	3.46 E
Noirmoutier, Île de- ◨	11	Dh	46.58N	2.12W
Noirmoutier-en-l'Île	11	Dg	47.00N	2.15W
Nojima-Zaki ▸	29	Fd	34.54N	139.50 E
Nojiri-Ko ▱	29	Ec	36.49N	138.13 E
Noka	63c	Bb	10.40S	166.03 E
Nokaneng	37	Cc	19.40S	22.12 E
Nokia	7	Ff	61.28N	23.30 E
Nok Kundi	25	Cc	28.48N	62.46 E
Nokomis	46	Ma	51.30N	105.00W
Nokou	35	Ac	14.35N	14.47 E
Nokra	35	Fb	15.42N	39.56 E
Nol	8	Eg	57.55N	12.03 E
Nola [C.A.R.]	35	Be	3.32N	16.04 E
Nola [It.]	14	Ij	40.55N	14.33 E
Nolin Lake ▱	44	Dg	37.20N	86.10W
Nolinsk	17	Fd	57.33N	50.02 E
Nomad	58	Fe	6.21S	142.12 E
Noma Omuramba ◨	37	Cc	19.10S	22.16 E
Noma-Zaki ▸	29	Bf	31.25N	130.06 E
Nombre de Dios	48	Gf	23.51N	104.14W
Nome	39	Cc	64.30N	165.24W
Nomeny	12	Jf	48.54N	6.14 E

Name	Map	Grid	Lat	Long
Nomo-Saki ▸	29	Ae	32.35N	129.45 E
Nomozaki	29	Ae	32.35N	129.45 E
Nomuka ◨	65b	Bb	20.15S	174.48W
Nomuka Group ◪	57	Jg	20.20S	174.45W
Nomuka Iki ◨	65b	Bb	20.17S	174.49W
Nomwin Atoll ◉	57	Gd	8.32N	151.47 E
Nonacho Lake ▱	42	Gd	62.40N	109.30W
Nonancourt	12	Df	48.46N	1.12 E
Nonette ◨	12	Ee	49.12N	2.24 E
Nong'an	27	Mc	44.24N	125.08 E
Nong Han ▱	25	Ke	17.21N	103.06 E
Nong Khai	22	Mh	17.52N	102.45 E
Nongoma	37	Ee	27.53S	31.38 E
Nonoava	48	Fd	27.28N	106.44W
Nonouti Atoll ◉	57	Ie	0.40S	174.21 E
Nonsan	28	If	36.12N	127.05 E
Nonsuch Bay ◨	51d	Bb	17.03N	61.42W
Nontron	11	Gi	45.32N	0.40 E
Noord-Beveland ◨	12	Fc	51.35N	3.45 E
Noord-Brabant ▣	12	Gc	51.30N	5.00 E
Noord-Holland ▣	12	Gb	52.40N	4.50 E
Noordoewer	37	Be	28.45S	17.37 E
Noordoostpolder ▣	11	Lb	52.40N	5.45 E
Noordoostpolder	12	Hb	52.42N	5.44 E
Noordoostpolder- Emmeloord	12	Hb	52.42N	5.44 E
Noordwijk aan Zee	11	Kb	52.14N	4.26 E
Noordwijk aan Zee, Noordwijk-Noordwijk aan Zee	12	Gb	52.14N	4.26 E
Noordwijk-Noordwijk aan Zee	12	Gb	52.14N	4.26 E
Noordzee = North Sea (EN) ▦	5	Gd	55.20N	3.00 E
Noordzeekanaal ◨	11	Kb	52.30N	4.52 E
Noormarkku/Norrmark	8	Ic	61.35N	21.52 E
Noorvik	40	Gc	66.50N	161.12W
Nootka Island ◨	46	Bb	49.32N	126.42W
Nootka Sound ◨	46	Bb	49.33N	126.38W
Nóqui	36	Bd	5.50S	13.27 E
Nora [It.]	14	Dk	39.00N	9.02 E
Nora [Swe.]	7	Dg	59.31N	15.02 E
Noraskog ▣	8	Fe	59.40N	14.50 E
Norberg	8	Fd	60.04N	15.56 E
Norcia	14	Hh	42.48N	13.05 E
Nord	41	Kb	81.45N	17.30W
Nord [Cam.] ▣	34	Hd	9.00N	13.50 E
Nord [Fr.] ▣	11	Jd	50.20N	3.40 E
Nord [Burkina]	34	Ec	13.40N	2.30W
Nord, Canal du- ◨	11	Id	49.57N	2.55 E
Nord, Mer du- = North Sea (EN) ▦	5	Gd	55.20N	3.00 E
Nordausques	12	Ed	50.49N	2.05 E
Nordaustlandet ◨	67	Jd	79.48N	22.24 E
Nordborg	8	Ci	55.03N	9.45 E
Nordby	8	Ci	55.27N	8.25 E
Norddeutsches Tiefland = North German Plain (EN)	5	He	53.00N	11.00 E
Norden	10	Dc	53.36N	7.12 E
Nordenham	10	Ec	53.29N	8.29 E
Nordenskjöld Archipelago (EN) = Nordenskjölda, Archipelago (EN) ◪	20	Ea	76.50N	96.00 E
Nordenskjöld Archipelago (EN) = Nordenskjölda, Ostrova- ◪	20	Ea	76.50N	96.00 E
Norderney ◨	10	Dc	53.42N	7.10 E
Norderstedt	10	Ec	53.41N	9.58 E
Nordfjord ◨	8	Bc	61.50N	6.15 E
Nordfjord ◨	7	Af	61.55N	5.10 E
Nordfjordeid	7	Af	61.54N	6.00 E
Nordfold	7	Dc	67.46N	15.12 E
Nordfriesische Inseln = North Frisian Islands (EN) ◪	10	Ea	54.50N	8.30 E
Nordfriesland ▣	10	Eb	54.40N	8.55 E
Nordgau ▣	10	Hg	49.15N	11.50 E
Nordgrønland = North Greenland (EN) ▣	41	Gc	79.30N	50.00W
Nordhausen	10	Ff	51.31N	10.48 E
Nordhordland ▣	8	Ad	60.50N	5.50 E
Nordhorn	10	Dd	52.26N	7.05 E
Nord-Jylland ▣	8	Cg	57.15N	10.00 E
Nordkapp [Nor.] = North Cape (EN) = North Cape (EN) ▸	5	Ia	71.11N	25.48 E
Nordkapp [Sval.] ▸	41	Nb	80.31N	20.00 E
Nordkinn	5	Ia	71.08N	27.39 E
Nordkinnhalvøya ◨	7	Ga	70.55N	27.45 E
Nord-Kvaløy ◨	7	Ea	70.10N	19.11 E
Nordland ▣	7	Cc	67.06N	13.20 E
Nördlingen	10	Gh	48.51N	10.30 E
Nordloher Tief ◨	12	Ja	53.10N	7.45 E
Nordmark	8	Fe	59.50N	14.06 E
Nordmøre ▣	8	Ca	63.00N	8.30 E
Nordostrundingen ▸	67	Le	81.30N	11.00W
Nord-Ostsee Kanal = Kiel Canal (EN) ◨	10	Eb	54.04N	9.23 E
Nord-Ouest ▣	34	Hd	6.30N	10.30 E
Nordoyane ◨	8	Bb	62.40N	6.15 E
Nordreisa	7	Fb	69.46N	21.03 E
Nordre Rønner ◨	8	Dg	57.22N	10.56 E
Nordrhein-Westfalen = North Rhine-Westphalia (EN) ▣	10	De	51.30N	7.30 E
Nordsee = North Sea (EN) ▦	5	Gd	55.20N	3.00 E
Nordsøen = North Sea (EN) ▦	5	Gd	55.20N	3.00 E
Nordsjøen = North Sea (EN) ▦	5	Gd	55.20N	3.00 E
Nordsjøbotn	7	Eb	69.13N	19.34 E
Nordstrand ◨	10	Eb	54.30N	8.55 E
Nordtiroler Kalkalpen ▲	10	Hi	47.30N	11.20 E
Nord-Trøndelag ▣	7	Cd	64.25N	12.00 E
Nordvestfjord ◨	41	Jd	71.30N	26.30W
Nore/An Fheoir ◨	9	Gi	52.26N	6.58W
Norefjell ▲	8	Cd	60.16N	9.29 E

Name	Map	Grid	Lat	Long
Norefjorden ▱	8	Cd	60.10N	9.00 E
Norfolk ▣	9	Oi	52.40N	1.05 E
Norfolk ▦	9	Mi	52.45N	0.40W
Norfolk [Nb.-U.S.]	43	Hc	42.02N	97.25W
Norfolk [Va.-U.S.]	39	Lf	38.40N	76.14W
Norfolk Island ▣	58	Hg	29.05S	167.59 E
Norfolk Island ▣	42	Gd	62.40N	109.30W
Norfolk Ridge (EN) ▦	57	Hg	29.00S	168.00 E
Norfolk Lake ▱	45	Je	36.25N	92.10W
Norg	12	Ia	53.04N	6.32 E
Norheimsund	7	Bf	60.22N	6.08 E
Norikura-Dake ▲	29	Ec	36.06N	137.33 E
Norilsk	22	Kc	69.20N	88.06 E
Normal	45	Lf	40.31N	88.59W
Norman	43	Hd	35.15N	97.26W
Norman, Lake- ▱	44	Gh	35.35N	81.00W
Normanby Island ◨	60	Ej	10.00S	151.00 E
Normanby River ◨	59	Ib	14.25S	144.08 E
Normand, Bocage- ▲	11	Ef	49.00N	1.10W
Normandie = Normandy (EN) ▨	11	Gf	49.00N	0.10 E
Normandie, Collines de- = Normandy Hills (EN) ▲	5	Gf	49.00N	0.10 E
Normandin	44	Ka	48.52N	72.30W
Normandy (EN) = Normandie ▨	11	Gf	49.00N	0.10 E
Normandy (EN) = Normandie ▣	5	Gf	49.00N	0.10 E
Normandy Hills (EN) = Normandie, Collines de- ▲	5	Ff	48.50N	0.40W
Norman Island ◨	51a	Db	18.20N	64.37W
Norman River ◨	59	Ic	17.28S	140.39 E
Normanton	58	Ff	17.40S	141.05 E
Norman Wells	39	Gc	65.17N	126.51W
Norquinco	56	Ff	41.51S	70.54W
Norra Dellen ▱	8	Gc	61.55N	16.40 E
Norrahammar	8	Fg	57.42N	14.06 E
Norrala	8	Gc	61.22N	16.59 E
Norra Midsjöbanken ▦	8	Gh	56.10N	17.30 E
Norra Ny	8	Fe	60.24N	13.15 E
Norra Storfjället ▲	7	Dd	65.53N	15.14 E
Norrbotten ▣	7	Ec	67.26N	19.35 E
Norre Åby	8	Ci	55.27N	9.54 E
Nørre Alslev	8	Dj	54.54N	11.54 E
Nørre-Nebel	8	Bi	55.47N	8.18 E
Norrent-Fontes	12	Ed	50.35N	2.24 E
Nørresundby	7	Bh	57.04N	9.55 E
Norrhult	7	Fh	57.08N	15.10 E
Norris Lake ▱	44	Fg	36.20N	83.55W
Norristown	44	Je	40.07N	75.20W
Norrköping	6	Hd	58.36N	16.11 E
Norrland ▣	5	Hc	64.27N	17.20 E
Norrland ▣	7	Dd	65.00N	18.00 E
Norrmark/Noormarkku	8	Ic	61.35N	21.52 E
Norrsundet	8	Gd	60.56N	17.08 E
Norrtälje	7	Eg	59.46N	18.42 E
Norseman	58	Dh	32.12S	121.46 E
Norsewood	62	Gd	40.04S	176.13 E
Norsjö	7	Ed	64.55N	19.29 E
Norsjø ▱	8	Ce	59.20N	9.20 E
Norsk	20	Hf	52.20N	129.59 E
Norske Havet = Norwegian Sea (EN) ▦	5	Gc	70.00N	2.00 E
Norske Øer ▣	41	Kc	79.00N	18.00W
Norsoup	63b	Cc	16.04S	167.23 E
Norte, Baía- ◨	55	Hh	27.30S	48.35W
Norte, Cabo- [Braz.] ▸	54	Ic	1.40N	50.00W
Norte, Cabo- [Pas.] ▸	65d	Ab	27.03S	109.24W
Norte, Canal do- ◨	54	Hc	0.30N	50.50W
Norte, Punta- ▸	56	Hf	42.04S	63.45W
Norte, Serra do- ▲	54	Gf	11.00S	59.00W
Norte del Cabo San Antonio, Punta- ▸	56	Ie	36.17S	56.47W
Norte de Santander ▣	54	Db	8.00N	73.00W
Nortelândia	54	Gf	14.25S	56.48W
Norte, Cape- ▸	42	Lg	47.02N	60.25W
North Adams	44	Kd	42.42N	73.02W
Northallerton	9	Lf	54.20N	1.26W
Northam [Austl.]	58	Ch	31.39S	116.40 E
Northam [S.Afr.]	37	Dd	24.58S	27.11 E
North America (EN) ▲	38	Jf	40.00N	95.00W
North American Basin (EN) ▦	3	Cf	30.00N	60.00W
Northampton [Austl.]	58	Bg	28.21S	114.37 E
Northampton [Eng.-U.K.]	9	Mi	52.14N	0.54W
Northampton [Ma.-U.S.]	44	Kd	42.19N	72.38W
Northampton Seamounts (EN) ▦	57	Jb	25.20N	172.04W
Northamptonshire ▣	9	Mi	52.25N	0.55W
North Andaman ◨	25	If	13.15N	92.55 E
North Arm ◨	42	Gd	62.10N	114.30W
North Astrolabe Reef ▨	63d	Bc	18.39S	178.32 E
North Augusta	43	Kd	33.30N	81.58W
North Aulatsivik ◨	42	Le	59.45N	64.04W
North Australian Basin (EN) ▦	3	Hk	14.30S	116.00 E
North Battleford	39	Hc	52.47N	108.17W
North Bay	39	Le	46.19N	79.28W
North Belcher Islands ◪	42	Je	56.45N	79.45W
North Berwick	9	Ke	56.04N	2.44W
North Buganda ▣	36	Fb	0.50N	32.10 E
North Caicos ◨	49	Lc	21.56N	71.59W
North Canadian River ◨	43	Gd	35.30N	95.31W
North Cape ▸	57	Ih	34.25S	173.03 E
North Cape (EN) = Nordkapp [Nor.] ▸	5	Ia	71.11N	25.48 E
North Caribou Lake ▱	42	If	52.48N	90.45W
North Carolina ▣	43	Kd	35.30N	80.00W
North Channel ▦	42	Jg	46.02N	82.50W
North Channel/Sruth na Maoile ▦	5	Fd	55.00N	5.40W
North Charleston	43	Kd	32.53N	80.00W
North Chicago	45	Me	42.20N	87.51W

Name	Map	Grid	Lat	Long
North Cove	46	Cc	46.47N	124.06W
North Cyprus	22	Ff	35.15N	33.40 E
North Dakota	43	Gb	47.30N	100.15W
North Downs ▲	9	Nj	51.20N	0.10 E
North East	44	Hd	42.13N	79.51W
North-East ▣	37	Dd	21.00S	27.30 E
Northeast Cape	40	Fd	63.18N	168.42W
North-Eastern ▣	36	Hb	1.00N	40.15 E
Northeast Islands ▣	64d	Ba	7.36N	151.57 E
▣	3	Lg	20.00N	140.00W
Northeast Pass ▦	64d	Ba	7.30N	151.59 E
North East Point [Bah.] ▸	64g	Bb	1.57N	157.16W
Northeast Point [Bah.] ▸	49	Kb	21.18N	72.54W
Northeast Point [Bah.] ▸	49	Kb	22.43N	73.50W
Northeast Providence Channel ▦	47	Ic	25.40N	77.09W
Northeim	10	Fe	51.42N	10.00 E
North Entrance ▦	64a	Bb	7.59N	134.37 E
North Esk ◨	9	Ke	56.45N	2.25W
Northern [Ghana] ▣	34	Ed	9.30N	1.00W
Northern [Mwi.] ▣	36	Fe	11.00S	34.00 E
Northern [S.L.] ▣	34	Cd	9.15N	11.45W
Northern [Ug.] ▣	36	Fb	2.45N	32.45 E
Northern [Zam.] ▣	36	Fe	11.00S	31.00 E
Northern Cay ▨	49	De	17.27N	87.28W
Northern Cook Islands ◪	57	Kf	10.00S	161.00W
Northern Dvina (EN) = Severnaja Dvina ◨	5	Kc	64.32N	40.30 E
Northern Guinea ◨	30	Gh	8.30N	1.00W
Northern Indian Lake ▱	42	He	57.20N	97.17W
Northern Ireland ▣	9	Gg	54.40N	6.45W
Northern Mariana Islands ▣	58	Fc	16.00N	145.30 E
Northern Sporades (EN) = Vórioi Sporádhes, Nisoi- ◪	5	Ih	39.15N	23.55 E
Northern Territory	59	Gc	20.00S	134.00 E
Northern Urals (EN) = Severny Ural ▲	5	Lc	62.00N	59.00 E
Northern Uvals (EN) = Severnyje Uvaly ▲	5	Kd	59.30N	49.00 E
Northfield	45	Kd	44.27N	93.09W
North Fiji Basin (EN) ▦	3	Jk	16.00S	174.00 E
North Foreland ▸	9	Oj	51.23N	1.27 E
North Fork Grand River ◨	45	Gd	45.47N	102.16W
North Fork John Day River ◨	46	Fd	44.45N	119.38W
North Fork Moreau River ◨	45	Gd	45.09N	102.50W
North Fork Pass ▦	42	Dd	64.00N	138.00W
North Fork Powder River ◨	46	Le	43.40N	106.30W
North Fork Red ◨	43	Gd	35.24N	99.14W
North Fort Myers	44	Gl	26.40N	81.54W
North Frisian Islands (EN) = Nordfriesische Inseln ◪	10	Ea	54.50N	8.30 E
North German Plain (EN) = Norddeutsches Tiefland	5	He	53.00N	11.00 E
North Greenland (EN) = Nordgrønland ▣	41	Gc	79.30N	50.00W
North Highlands	46	Eg	38.40N	121.23W
North Horr	36	Gb	3.19N	37.04 E
North Island [N.Z.]	57	Ih	39.00S	176.00 E
North Island [Sey.]	37b	Bc	10.07S	51.11 E
North Kent ▣	42	Ia	76.40N	90.15W
North Korea (EN) = Chosŏn ▣	22	Oe	40.00N	127.30 E
North Lakhimpur	25	Ic	27.14N	94.07 E
North Las Vegas	46	Hh	36.12N	115.07W
North Lincoln Land ▣	42	Ja	76.15N	80.00W
North Little Rock	43	Ie	34.46N	92.14W
North Loup River ◨	45	Gf	41.17N	98.23W
North Magnetic Pole (1980)	67	Qd	77.03N	101.08W
North Malosmadulu Atoll ▨	25a	Ba	5.35N	72.55 E
North Mayreau Channel ▦	51b	Bb	12.41N	61.20W
North Miami	44	Gl	25.56N	80.09W
North Minch ▦	5	Fd	58.05N	5.55W
North Palisade ▲	46	Gg	37.06N	118.31W
North Pass [F.S.M.] ▦	64d	Ba	7.41N	151.48 E
North Pass [U.S.] ▦	45	Ll	29.10N	89.15W
North Platte	43	Gc	41.08N	100.46W
North Platte ◨	38	Le	41.15N	100.45W
North Point ▸	29	Bf	22.18N	114.12 E
North Point [Bar.] ▸	64n	Ab	10.22S	161.02W
North Point [Bar.] ▸	51a	Ab	13.20N	59.36W
North Pole	67	Ge	90.00	0.00
North Powder	46	Gd	45.03N	117.55W
North Raccoon River ◨	45	Jf	41.39N	93.31W
North Reef ▨	63a	Ee	12.13S	160.04 E
North Rhine-Westphalia (EN) = Nordrhein-Westfalen ▣	5	Ge	51.30N	7.30 E
North Rim	46	Ih	36.12N	112.03W
North River	42	Ie	58.53N	94.42W
North Rona ◨	9	Hb	59.10N	5.40W
North Ronaldsay ◨	9	Kb	59.25N	2.30W
North Saskatchewan ◨	38	Id	53.15N	105.06W
North Sea ▦	5	Gd	55.20N	3.00 E
North Sea (EN) = ▦	5	Gd	55.20N	3.00 E
North Sea (EN) = Nord, Mer du- ▦	5	Gd	55.20N	3.00 E
North Sea (EN) = ▦	5	Gd	55.20N	3.00 E
Nordsee ▦	5	Gd	55.20N	3.00 E
Nordsøen ▦	5	Gd	55.20N	3.00 E
Nordsjøen ▦	5	Gd	55.20N	3.00 E
North Sentinel ◨	25	If	11.33N	92.15 E
North Shoshone Peak ▲	46	Gg	39.10N	117.29W
North Siberian Plain (EN) = Severo-Sibirskaja Niz. ▲	21	Mb	72.00N	104.00 E
North Sound ▦	51	Bc	17.07N	61.45W
North Sound ▦	49	Gd	19.25N	81.26W
North Stradbroke Island ◨	62	Fc	38.50S	174.25 E
North Taranaki Bight ◨	62	Fc	38.50S	174.25 E
North Thompson ◨	42	Ff	50.41N	120.11W

Name	Map	Grid	Lat	Long
North Tokelau Trough (EN) ▦	3	Kj	3.00S	165.00W
North Tonawanda	44	Hd	43.02N	78.54W
North Trap ▸	62	Bg	47.20S	167.55 E
North Tyne ◨	9	Kg	54.59N	2.08W
North Uist ◨	9	Fd	57.37N	7.22W
Northumberland ▣	9	Kf	55.15N	2.10W
Northumberland ▣	9	Kf	55.15N	2.05W
Northumberland Islands ◪	57	Gg	21.40S	150.00 E
Northumberland Strait ▦	42	Lg	46.00N	63.30W
North Umpqua River ◨	46	De	43.18S	123.24W
North Vancouver	46	Bb	49.19N	123.04W
North Walsham	12	Db	52.49N	1.23 E
Northway	40	Kd	62.59N	141.43W
North West Bluff ▨	51c	Bc	16.49N	62.12W
North West Cape	57	Cf	21.45S	114.10 E
North-Western ▣	36	Ee	13.00S	25.00 E
Northwest Frontier ▣	25	Eb	33.00N	70.30 E
North West Highlands ▲	5	Fd	57.30N	5.00W
Northwest Pacific Basin (EN) ▦	3	Je	40.00N	155.00 E
North West Point ▸	64g	Ab	2.02N	157.30W
Northwest Providence Channel ▦	44	Hl	26.10N	78.20W
Northwest Reef ▨	64a	Bb	7.59N	134.33 E
North West River	42	Lf	53.32N	60.09W
Northwest Territories ▣	42	Hc	66.00N	102.00W
Northwich	9	Kh	53.16N	2.32W
North York Moors ▲	9	Mg	54.25N	0.50W
North Yorkshire ▣	9	Lg	54.15N	1.40W
Norton [Ks.-U.S.]	43	Gd	39.50N	100.01W
Norton [Va.-U.S.]	44	Fg	36.56N	82.37W
Norton [Zimb.]	37	Ec	17.53S	30.41 E
Norton Bay ◨	40	Gd	64.45N	161.15W
Norton Sound ▦	38	Gc	64.45N	161.15W
Norvegia, Kapp- ▸	66	Bf	71.25S	12.18W
Norwalk [Ct.-U.S.]	44	Ke	41.07N	73.27W
Norwalk [Oh.-U.S.]	44	Fe	41.14N	82.37W
Norway	44	Dc	45.47N	87.55W
Norway (EN) = Norge ▣	6	Gc	62.00N	10.00 E
Norway Bay ◨	42	Hb	71.00N	104.35W
Norway House	42	Hf	53.58N	97.50W
Norwegian Basin (EN) ▦	3	Dc	68.00N	2.00W
Norwegian Bay ▦	42	Ij	77.45N	90.30W
Norwegian Sea (EN) = Norske Havet ▦	5	Gc	70.00N	2.00 E
Norwegian Trench (EN) ▦	5	Gd	59.00N	4.30 E
Norwich [Eng.-U.K.]	6	Ge	52.38N	1.18 E
Norwich [N.Y.-U.S.]	44	Jd	42.33N	75.33W
Norwich Airport ▸	12	Db	50.40N	1.18 E
Norwood	44	Ef	39.10N	84.28W
Nosappu-Misaki ▸	29a	Db	43.23N	145.47 E
Noshappu-Misaki ▸	29a	Ba	45.27N	141.39 E
Noshiro	27	Pc	40.12N	140.02 E
Nosovaja	19	Fb	68.15N	54.31 E
Nosovka	19	De	50.54N	31.37 E
Nosratābād	23	Id	29.54N	59.59 E
Nossa Senhora das Candeias	54	Kf	12.40S	38.33W
Nossa Senhora do Livramento	55	Db	15.48S	56.22W
Noss Head ▸	9	Jc	58.30N	3.05W
Nossob ▨	30	Jk	26.55S	20.40 E
Nossop ◨	37	Cc	26.55S	20.40 E
Nosy-Be ◨	30	Lj	13.20S	48.15 E
Nosy-Be	31	Lj	13.23S	48.16 E
Nosy-Varika	37	Hd	20.35S	48.30 E
Nota ◨	7	Hb	68.00N	30.10 E
Notch Peak ▲	46	Ig	39.08N	113.24W
Noteć ◨	10	Mc	52.44N	15.26 E
Notecka, Puszcza- ▨	10	Lc	52.45N	16.00 E
Notengo, Laguna de- ▱	48	Ji	16.15N	98.10W
Notia Pindhos ▲	15	Ej	39.30N	21.20 E
Nótioi Sporádhes = Dodecanese (EN) ◪	5	Ih	36.00N	27.00 E
Nótios Evvoïkós Kólpos ▦	15	Gk	38.20N	23.50 E
Nōtō ◨	8	Ie	60.00N	21.45 E
Noto [It.]	14	Ja	36.53N	15.04 E
Noto [Jap.]	28	Nf	37.18N	137.09 E
Noto, City do- ◨	14	Ja	36.50N	15.10 E
Notodden	7	Bg	59.34N	9.17 E
Noto-Hantō ◨	27	Od	37.20N	137.00 E
Noto-Jima ◨	29	Ec	37.07N	137.00 E
Notoro-Ko ▱	29a	Da	44.05N	144.10 E
Notoro-Misaki ▸	29a	Da	44.07N	144.15 E
Notranjsko ▨	14	Je	45.46N	14.26 E
Notre-Dame, Monts- ▲	38	Me	48.00N	69.00W
Notre Dame Bay ◨	42	Mg	49.50N	55.00W
Notre-Dame-de-Courson	12	Cf	49.59N	0.16 E
Notre-Dame-de-Gravenchon	12	Ce	49.29N	0.35 E
Notre-Dame-du-Lac	44	Ma	47.38N	68.49W
Notre-Dame-du-Nord	44	Hb	47.36N	79.29W
Notsé	34	Fd	6.59N	1.12 E
Nottawasaga Bay ◨	44	Gc	44.40N	80.30W
Nottaway ◨	38	Ld	51.25N	79.50W
Nottawasaga ◨	44	Gc	44.24N	79.53W
Nottaway ◨	42	Je	51.25N	79.50W
Notterøy ◨	8	De	59.15N	10.25 E
Nottingham ▣	9	Li	52.58N	1.10W
Nottingham	42	Jd	63.00N	78.00W
Nottinghamshire ▣	9	Mh	53.05N	1.00W
Nottoway River ◨	44	Ig	36.33N	76.55W
Nottuln	12	Lc	51.56N	7.21 E
Notukeu Creek ◨	46	Lb	49.55N	106.30W
Nouâdhibou	31	Ff	20.54N	17.01W
Nouâdhibou, Dakhlet- ◨	32	Dc	20.46N	16.50W
Nouâdhibou, Râs- = Blanc, Cape- (EN) ▸	30	Ff	20.46N	17.03W
Nouakchott	31	Fg	18.07N	15.59W
Nouakchott, District de- ▣	32	Df	18.07N	15.57W
Nouamrhar	32	Df	19.22N	16.31W
Nouméa	58	Hg	22.16S	166.26 E
Nouna	34	Ec	12.44N	3.52W
Noupoort	37	Cf	31.10S	24.57 E

Index Symbols

① Independent Nation	◨ Historical or Cultural Region	◗ Pass, Gap	▱ Depression	◣ Coast, Beach	▨ Rock, Reef
② State, Region	▲ Mount, Mountain	◗ Plain, Lowland	◗ Polder	◢ Cliff	▨ Islands, Archipelago
③ District, County	▲ Volcano	◗ Delta	◗ Desert, Dunes	◗ Peninsula	▨ Rocks, Reefs
④ Municipality	▲ Hill	◗ Salt Flat	◗ Forest, Woods	◗ Isthmus	◗ Coral Reef
⑤ Colony, Dependency	▲ Mountains, Mountain Range	◗ Valley, Canyon	◗ Heath, Steppe	◗ Sandbank	◗ Well, Spring
◗ Continent	▲ Hills, Escarpment	◗ Crater, Cave	◗ Oasis	◗ Island	◗ Geyser
◗ Physical Region	◗ Plateau, Upland	◗ Karst Features	◗ Cape, Point	◗ Atoll	◗ River, Stream
◗ Waterfall Rapids	◗ Canal	◗ Lagoon	◗ Escarpment, Sea Scarp	◗ Historic Site	◗ Port
◗ River Mouth, Estuary	◗ Glacier	◗ Bank	◗ Fracture	◗ Ruins	◗ Lighthouse
◗ Lake	◗ Ice Shelf, Pack Ice	◗ Seamount	◗ Trench, Abyss	◗ Wall, Walls	◗ Mine
◗ Salt Lake	◗ Ocean	◗ Tablemount	◗ National Park, Reserve	◗ Church, Abbey	◗ Tunnel
◗ Intermittent Lake	◗ Sea	◗ Ridge	◗ Point of Interest	◗ Temple	◗ Dam, Bridge
◗ Reservoir	◗ Shelf	◗ Recreation Site	◗ Scientific Station		
◗ Swamp, Pond	◗ Gulf, Bay	◗ Basin	◗ Cave, Cavern	◗ Airport	

Nouveau-Comptoir 42 Jf 52.35N 78.40W
Nouveau-Québec, Cratère du- = New Quebec Crater (EN) 42 Kd 61.30N 73.55W
Nouvelle-Calédonie = New Caledonia (EN) [5] 58 Hg 21.30S 165.30 E
Nouvelle-Calédonie = New Caledonia (EN) 57 Hg 21.30S 165.30 E
Nouvelle-France, Cap de- 42 Kd 62.33N 73.35W
Nouvelles Hébrides/New Hebrides 57 Hf 16.01S 167.01 E
Nouvion 12 Dd 50.12N 1.47 E
Nouzonville 11 Ke 49.49N 4.45 E
Novabad 18 He 39.01N 70.09 E
Nová Baňa 10 Oh 48.26N 18.39 E
Nová Bystřice 10 Lg 49.02N 15.06 E
Nova Cruz 54 Ke 6.28S 35.26W
Nova Esperança 55 Ff 23.08S 52.13W
Nova Friburgo 54 Jh 22.16S 42.32W
Nova Gaia 36 Ce 10.05S 17.32 E
Nova Gorica 14 He 45.57N 13.39 E
Nova Gradiška 14 Le 45.16N 17.23 E
Nova Granada 55 He 20.29S 49.19W
Nova Iguaçu 53 Lh 22.45S 43.27W
Novaja Igirma 20 Fe 57.10N 103.55 E
Novaja-Ivanovka 15 Md 45.59N 29.04 E
Novaja Kahovka 16 Hf 46.43N 33.23 E
Novaja Kazanka 16 Pe 48.58N 49.37 E
Novaja Ladoga 7 Hf 60.05N 32.16 E
Novaja Ljalja 19 Gd 59.03N 60.36 E
Novaja Odessa 16 Gf 47.18N 31.47 E
Novaja Sibir, Ostrov- = New Siberia (EN) 21 Qb 75.00N 149.00 E
Novaja Vodolaga 16 Ie 49.45N 35.52 E
Novaja Zemlja = Novaya Zemlya (EN) 21 Hb 74.00N 57.00 E
Nova Lamego 34 Cc 12.17N 14.13W
Nova Lima 54 Jh 19.59S 43.51W
Nova Londrina 55 Ff 22.45S 53.00W
Nova Mambone 37 Fd 20.58S 35.00 E
Nova Olinda do Norte 54 Gd 3.45S 59.03W
Nová Paka 10 Lf 50.29N 15.31 E
Nova Prata 55 Gi 28.47S 51.36W
Novara 14 Ce 45.28N 8.38 E
Nova Roma 55 Ia 13.51S 46.57W
Nova Russas 54 Jd 4.42S 40.34W
Nova Scotia [3] 42 Lh 45.00N 63.00W
Nova Scotia 38 Me 45.00N 63.00W
Nova Sintra 32 Cf 14.54N 24.40W
Nova Sofala 37 Ed 20.10S 34.44 E
Novato 46 Dg 38.06N 122.34W
Nova Varoš 15 Cf 43.28N 19.49 E
Nova Venécia 54 Jg 18.43S 40.24W
Novaya Zemlya (EN) = Novaja Zemlja 21 Hb 74.00N 57.00 E
Nova Zagora 15 Jg 42.29N 26.01 E
Novelda 13 Lf 38.23N 0.46W
Novellara 14 Ef 44.51N 10.44 E
Nové Mesto nad Váhom 10 Nh 48.46N 17.50 E
Nové Zámky 10 Oi 47.59N 18.11 E
Novgorod 6 Jd 58.31N 31.17 E
Novgorodka 8 Mg 57.00N 28.37 E
Novgorod-Severski 19 De 52.01N 33.16 E
Novgorodskaja Oblast [3] 19 Dd 58.20N 32.40 E
Novi Bečej 15 Dd 45.36N 20.08 E
Novigrad 14 He 45.19N 13.34 E
Novigrad 14 Jf 44.11N 15.33 E
Novi Kričim 15 Hg 42.03N 24.28 E
Novi Ligure 14 Cf 44.46N 8.47 E
Novillero 48 Gf 22.21N 105.39W
Novion-Porcien 12 Ge 49.36N 4.25 E
Novi Pazar [Bul.] 15 Kf 43.21N 27.12 E
Novi Pazar [Yugo.] 15 Df 43.08N 20.31 E
Novi Sad 6 Hf 45.15N 19.50 E
Novi Travnik 14 Lf 44.10N 17.39 E
Novi Vinodolski 14 Ie 45.08N 14.47 E
Novoaleksandrovsk 16 Lg 45.24N 41.14 E
Novoalekseevka 16 Sd 50.08N 55.42 E
Novoalekseevka 16 If 46.16N 34.39 E
Novoaltajsk 20 Df 53.24N 83.58 E
Novoanninski 19 Ee 50.31N 42.45 E
Novoarhangelsk 16 Ge 48.39N 30.50 E
Novo Aripuanã 54 Fe 5.08S 60.22W
Novoazovsk 16 Kf 47.05N 38.05 E
Novobirjusinski 20 Ee 56.58N 97.55 E
Novobogdanovka 16 If 47.05N 35.18 E
Novočeboksarsk 7 Lh 56.08N 47.29 E
Novočeremšansk 7 Mi 54.23N 50.10 E
Novočerkassk 19 Ef 47.25N 40.03 E
Novodevičje 7 Lj 53.35N 48.51 E
Novograd-Volynski 19 Ce 50.36N 27.36 E
Novogrudok 16 Dc 53.37N 25.50 E
Nôvo Hamburgo 56 Jc 29.41S 51.08W
Novohopërsk 16 Ld 51.06N 41.37 E
Novo Horizonte 55 He 21.28S 49.13W
Novoizborsk 8 Mg 57.43N 28.05 E
Novojenisejsk 20 Ee 58.19N 92.27 E
Novojerudinski 20 Ee 59.47N 93.30 E
Novokačalinsk 20 Ig 45.05N 131.59 E
Novokazalinsk 22 Ie 45.50N 62.10 E
Novokubansk 16 Lg 45.06N 41.01 E
Novokujbyševsk 19 Ee 53.08N 49.58 E
Novokuzneck 22 Kd 53.45N 87.06 E
Novolazarevskaja 66 Cf 70.46S 11.50 E
Novolukoml 7 Gi 54.38N 29.07 E
Novo Mesto 14 Je 45.48N 15.10 E
Novomičurinsk 7 Ji 54.02N 39.48 E
Novomihajlovka 20 Ih 44.17N 133.50 E
Novo Miloševo 15 Dd 45.43N 20.18 E
Novomirgorod 16 Ge 48.45N 31.39 E
Novomoskovsk 16 Je 54.05N 38.13 E
Novomoskovsk 19 Df 48.37N 35.16 E
Novonikolajevski 16 Md 50.55N 42.24 E
Novoorsk 19 Fe 51.24N 58.59 E
Novopokrovskaja 16 Lg 45.56N 40.42 E
Novopolock 19 Cd 55.31N 28.40 E
Novorossijsk 6 Jg 44.45N 37.45 E
Novorybnaja 20 Fb 72.50N 105.45 E
Novoržev 19 Cd 57.02N 29.20 E
Novo-Šahtinsk 19 Df 47.47N 39.54 E
Novoselica 15 Ja 48.13N 26.17 E
Novoselje 8 Mf 58.05N 29.00 E
Novoselki 10 Ud 52.04N 24.25 E
Novoselovo 20 Ef 54.55N 91.00 E
Novosergijevka 19 Fe 52.03N 53.39 E
Novosibirsk 22 Kd 55.02N 82.55 E
Novosibirskaja Oblast [3] 20 Ce 55.30N 80.00 E
Novosibirskije Ostrova = New Siberian Islands (EN) 21 Qb 75.00N 142.00 E
Novosibirskoje Vodohranilišče 20 Df 54.40N 82.35 E
Novosil 16 Jc 52.59N 37.01 E
Novosineglazovski 17 Ji 55.05N 61.25 E
Novosokolniki 19 Dd 56.19N 30.12 E
Novospasskoje 7 Lj 53.09N 47.44 E
Novotroick 19 Fe 51.12N 58.35 E
Novotroickoje 19 Hg 43.39N 73.45 E
Novoukrainka 16 Ge 48.19N 31.32 E
Novouljanovsk 7 Li 54.10N 48.23 E
Novouzensk 19 Ee 50.29N 48.08 E
Novovjatsk 7 Lg 58.31N 49.43 E
Novovolynsk 19 Ce 50.46N 24.09 E
Novovoronežski 16 Kd 51.17N 39.16 E
Novozybkov 19 De 52.32N 32.00 E
Novska 14 Ke 45.20N 16.59 E
Novy Bug 16 Hf 47.43N 32.29 E
Nový Bydžov 10 Lf 50.15N 15.29 E
Novy Jaričev 10 Ug 49.50N 24.21 E
Novyje Aneny 15 Mc 46.53N 29.13 E
Novyje Burasy 16 Oc 52.06N 46.06 E
Nový Jičín 10 Og 49.36N 18.01 E
Novy Oskol 19 De 50.43N 37.54 E
Novy Pogost 8 Li 55.30N 27.32 E
Novy Port 22 Jc 67.40N 72.52 E
Novy Tap 17 Mh 56.55N 67.15 E
Novy Terek 16 Oh 43.37N 47.25 E
Novy Uzen 19 Fg 43.19N 52.55 E
Novy Vasjugan 20 Ce 58.34N 76.29 E
Novy Zaj 7 Mi 55.17N 52.02 E
Nowa Dęba 10 Rf 50.26N 21.46 E
Nowa Huta, Kraków- 10 Qf 50.04N 20.05 E
Nowa Ruda 10 Mf 50.35N 16.31 E
Nowa Sarzyna 10 Sf 50.23N 22.22 E
Nowa Sól 10 Le 51.48N 15.44 E
Now Bandegān 24 Oh 28.52N 53.53 E
Nowbarān 24 Me 35.08N 49.42 E
Nowdesheh 24 Le 35.11N 46.15 E
Nowe 10 Oc 53.40N 18.43 E
Nowe Miasto Lubawskie 10 Pc 53.27N 19.35 E
Nowe Miasto-nad-Pilicą 10 Qe 51.38N 20.35 E
Nowe Warpno 10 Kc 53.44N 14.20 E
Nowfel low Shātow 24 Ne 34.27N 50.55 E
Nowgong 25 Ic 26.21N 92.40 E
Nowogard 10 Lc 53.40N 15.08 E
Nowogród 10 Rc 53.15N 21.53 E
Nowood River 46 Ld 44.17N 107.58W
Nowra 59 Kf 34.53S 150.36 E
Nowshahr 24 Nd 36.39N 51.31 E
Nowy Dwór Gdański 10 Pb 54.13N 19.06 E
Nowy Dwór Mazowiecki 10 Qd 52.26N 20.43 E
Nowy Korczyn 10 Qf 50.20N 20.50 E
Nowy Sącz [2] 10 Qg 49.40N 20.40 E
Nowy Sącz 10 Qg 49.38N 20.42 E
Nowy Targ 10 Qg 49.29N 20.02 E
Nowy Tomyśl 10 Md 52.20N 16.07 E
Noya 13 Db 42.47N 8.53W
Noya/Anoia 13 Nc 41.28N 1.56 E
Noyant 11 Gg 47.31N 0.08 E
Noyon 11 Ie 49.35N 3.00 E
Nozaki-Jima 29 Ae 33.11N 129.08 E
Nozay 11 Eg 47.34N 1.38W
Nsanje 36 Gf 16.55S 35.16 E
Nsawan 34 Ed 5.48N 0.21W
Nschodnia 10 Rf 50.30N 21.18 E
Nsefu 36 Fe 13.03S 32.07 E
Nsukka 34 Gd 6.52N 7.23 E
Ntadembele 36 Cc 2.11S 17.08 E
Ntchisi 36 Fe 13.22S 34.00 E
Ntem 30 Hh 2.10N 9.57 E
Ntoum 36 Ab 0.22N 9.47 E
Ntui 34 He 4.27N 11.38 E
Ntusi 36 Fb 0.03N 31.13 E
Nuageuses, Iles- 30 Nm 48.40S 68.58 E
Nuanetsi 30 Kk 22.40S 31.49 E
Nūbah, Jibāl an- 30 Kg 12.00N 30.45 E
Nubian Desert (EN) = Nūbiyah, Aş Şaḩrā' an- 30 Kf 20.30N 33.00 E
Nūbiyah, Aş Şaḩrā' an- = Nubian Desert (EN) 30 Kf 20.30N 33.00 E
Nudha 63a Ec 9.32S 160.48 E
Nueces Plain 43 Hf 28.30N 99.15W
Nueces River 43 Hf 27.50N 97.30W
Nueltin Lake 38 Jc 60.50N 99.30W
Nü'er He 28 Fd 41.06N 121.09 E
Nueva Asunción [3] 55 Be 21.00S 60.20W
Nueva Ciudad Guerrero 48 Jd 26.35N 99.15W
Nueva Esparta [2] 54 Fa 11.00N 64.00W
Nueva Germania 55 Df 23.54S 56.34W
Nueva Gerona 47 Hd 21.53N 82.48W
Nueva Imperial 56 Fe 38.44S 72.57W
Nueva Italia de Ruiz 48 Hh 19.01N 102.06W
Nueva Ocotepeque 49 Cf 14.24N 89.13W
Nueva Palmira 55 Ck 33.53S 58.25W
Nueva Rosita 39 Ig 27.57N 101.13W
Nueva San Salvador 47 Gf 13.41N 89.17W
Nueva Segovia [3] 49 Dg 13.40N 86.10W
Nueve de Julio 56 He 35.27S 60.52W
Nuevitas 47 Id 21.33N 77.16W
Nuevitas, Bahía de- 49 Ic 21.30N 77.12W
Nuevo, Cayo- 48 Mg 21.51N 92.05W
Nuevo, Golfo- 52 Jj 42.42S 64.36W
Nuevo Berlín 55 Ck 32.59S 58.03W
Nuevo Casas Grandes 39 If 30.25N 107.55W
Nuevo Laredo 39 Jg 27.30N 99.31W
Nuevo León [2] 47 Ec 25.40N 100.00W
Nuevo Mundo, Cerro- 54 Eh 21.55S 66.53W
Nuevo Rocafuerte 54 Cd 0.56S 75.25W
Nugaal [3] 35 Hd 8.30N 48.00 E
Nugālēd, Dēh- 30 Lh 7.58N 49.51 E
Nugālēd, Dōho- 35 Hd 8.35N 48.35 E
Nûgâtsiaq 41 Gd 71.39N 53.45W
Nugget Point 62 Cg 46.27S 169.49 E
Nûgssuaq 41 Gd 70.30N 51.30W
Nuguria Islands 57 Ge 3.20S 154.45 E
Nuguš 17 Gj 53.05N 56.00 E
Nuhaka 62 Gc 39.02S 177.45 E
Nui Atoll 57 Ie 7.15S 177.10 E
Nuijama 8 Md 60.58N 28.32 E
Nuiqsut 40 Ib 70.20N 151.00W
Nu Jiang 21 Lh 16.31N 97.37 E
Nûk/Godthåb 67 Nc 64.15N 51.40W
Nukapu 63c Ab 10.07S 165.59 E
Nukey Bluff 59 Hf 32.35S 135.40 E
Nukhayb 23 Fc 32.02N 42.15 E
Nukhaylak 31 Jg 19.08N 26.20 E
Nukiki 63a Cb 6.45S 156.29 E
Nukuaéta 64h Ac 13.22S 176.11W
Nuku'alofa 58 Jg 21.08S 175.12W
Nukufetau Atoll 57 Ie 8.00S 178.22 E
Nukufotu 64h Bb 13.11S 176.10W
Nukuhifala 64h Bb 13.17S 176.05W
Nukuhione 64h Bb 13.16S 176.06W
Nuku Hiva, Ile- 57 Me 8.54S 140.06W
Nukulaelae Atoll 57 Ie 9.23S 179.52 E
Nukuloa 64h Bb 13.11S 176.09W
Nukumanu Islands 57 Ge 4.30S 159.30 E
Nukumbasanga 63d Cb 16.18S 179.15W
Nukunonu Atoll 57 Je 9.10S 171.53W
Nukuoro Atoll 57 Gd 3.51N 154.58 E
Nukus 22 He 42.50N 59.29 E
Nukutapu 64h Bb 13.13S 176.08W
Nukuteatea 64h Bb 13.12S 176.08W
Nulato 40 Hd 64.43N 158.06W
Nules 13 Le 39.51N 0.09W
Nullagine 58 Dg 21.53S 120.06 E
Nullagine River 59 Ed 20.43S 120.33 E
Nullarbor 59 Gf 31.26S 130.55 E
Nullarbor Plain 57 Dh 31.00S 129.00 E
Nulu'erhu Shan 27 Kc 41.40N 119.50 E
Numakawa 29a Ba 45.15N 141.51 E
Numan 34 Hd 9.28N 12.02 E
Numancia [Phil.] 26 Ie 9.52N 125.58 E
Numancia [Sp.] 13 Jc 41.47N 2.30W
Numanohata 29a Bb 42.40N 141.41 E
Numata [Jap.] 29a Bb 43.49N 141.55 E
Numata [Jap.] 28 Of 36.38N 139.03 E
Numatinna 35 Dd 7.14N 27.37 E
Numazu 28 Og 35.06N 138.52 E
Nümbrecht 12 Jd 50.54N 7.33 E
Numedal 7 Bf 60.05N 9.05 E
Numena 36 Ee 11.46S 26.31 E
Número Cinco, Canal- 55 Cm 37.14S 58.06W
Número Doce, Canal- 55 Cm 36.30S 59.08W
Número Dos, Canal- 55 Cm 36.51S 58.03W
Número Nueve, Canal- 55 Cm 37.00S 58.36W
Número Once, Canal- 55 Bm 36.28S 60.01W
Número Quince, Canal- 55 Dl 35.55S 57.45W
Número Uno, Canal- 55 Cm 36.40S 58.35W
Numfoor, Pulau- 26 Jg 1.03S 134.54 E
Nuneaton 9 Li 52.32N 1.28W
Nungarin 59 Df 31.11S 118.06 E
Nungnain Sum 27 Kb 45.45N 118.56 E
Nungo 37 Fb 13.25S 37.46 E
Nunivak 38 Cd 60.00N 166.30W
Nunkirchen, Wadern- 12 Ie 49.32N 6.53 E
Nunn 45 Df 40.45N 104.46W
Nunspeet 12 Hb 52.22N 5.46 E
Nunukan Timur, Pulau- 26 Gf 4.05N 117.40 E
Nuomin He 27 Lb 48.21N 124.32 E
Nuorgam 7 Ga 70.05N 27.51 E
Nuoro 6 Gg 40.19N 9.20 E
Nupani 63c Ab 10.04S 165.40 E
Nūq 24 Pg 30.55N 55.35 E
Nuqayr 24 Mi 27.48N 48.21 E
Nuqrah 24 Ij 25.34N 41.24 E
Nuqruş, Jabal- 33 Fe 24.49N 34.36 E
Nuqui 54 Cb 5.43N 77.16W
Nür 24 Od 36.15N 52.20 E
Nür 24 Pg 31.25N 54.20 E
Nura 19 Gf 48.57N 62.20 E
Nura 21 Id 50.30N 69.59 E
Nūrābād 24 Ng 30.48N 51.27 E
Nuraghe Santu Antine 14 Cj 40.29N 8.45 E
Nurata 19 Gg 40.34N 65.35 E
Nur Dağları 24 Gd 36.45N 36.20 E
Nure 14 De 45.03N 9.49 E
Nurek 19 Gh 38.25N 69.20 E
Nurhak Dağı 23 Eb 38.04N 37.29 E
Nūrī 35 Eb 18.30N 32.02 E
Nurki 20 Ie 56.42N 138.28 E
Nurlat 19 Fe 54.28N 50.48 E
Nurlati 7 Li 55.38N 48.17 E
Nurmes 7 Ge 63.33N 29.07 E
Nurmijärvi 8 Kd 60.28N 24.48 E
Nurmo 8 Jb 62.50N 22.54 E
Nürnberg 6 Hf 49.27N 11.05 E
Nurra 14 Cj 40.45N 8.15 E
Nurri, Mount- 59 Jf 31.42S 146.02 E
Nurugas 37 Bc 19.11S 18.54 E
Nurzec 10 Sd 52.33N 22.28 E
Nusa Tenggara Barat [3] 26 Gh 8.50S 117.30 E
Nusa Tenggara Timur [3] 26 Hh 9.30S 122.00 E
Nusaybin 24 Id 37.03N 41.13 E
Nushagak 40 He 58.57N 158.29W
Nushan 27 Gf 25.00N 99.00 E
Nu-Shima 29 Dd 34.10N 134.50 E
Nutak 42 Le 57.31N 62.00W
Nuttal 25 Dc 28.45N 68.08 E
Nuutele 65c Bb 14.02S 171.22W
Nuwākot 25 Gc 28.08N 83.53 E
Nuwara 25 Gg 6.58N 80.46 E
Nuwaybi 'al Muzayyinah 33 Fd 28.58N 34.39 E
Nyabing 59 Df 33.32S 118.09 E
Nyagquka/Yajiang 27 He 30.07N 100.58 E
Nyagrong/Xinlong 27 He 30.57N 100.12 E
Nyahanga 36 Fc 2.23S 33.33 E
Nyahua 36 Fd 4.58S 33.34 E
Nyainqêntanglha Feng 27 Fe 30.12N 90.33 E
Nyainqêntanglha Shan 21 Kf 30.10N 90.00 E
Nyakanazi 36 Fc 3.00S 31.15 E
Nyala 31 Jg 12.03N 24.53 E
Nyalam 27 Ef 28.15N 85.55 E
Ny-Ålesund 41 Nc 78.56N 11.57 E
Nyalikungu 36 Fc 3.11S 33.47 E
Nyamandhlovu 37 Dc 19.51S 28.16 E
Nyamapanda 37 Ec 16.55S 32.52 E
Nyamlell 35 Dd 9.07N 26.58 E
Nyamtumbo 36 Ge 10.30S 36.06 E
Nyanding 35 Ed 8.40N 32.41 E
Nyanga 30 Ii 2.58S 10.15 E
Nyanga [3] 36 Bc 3.00S 11.00 E
Nyanza [3] 36 Fc 0.30S 34.30 E
Nyanza-Lac 36 Ec 4.21S 29.36 E
Nyasa, Lake- (EN) = Niassa, Lago- 30 Kj 12.00S 34.30 E
Nyaunglebin 25 Je 17.57N 96.44 E
Nyborg 7 Ci 55.19N 10.48 E
Nybro 7 Dh 56.45N 15.54 E
Nyda 17 Pc 66.40N 72.50 E
Nyda 20 Cc 66.36N 72.54 E
Nyeboe Land 41 Gb 81.45N 56.40W
Nyêmo 27 Ff 29.30N 90.07 E
Nyeri 36 Gc 0.25S 36.57 E
Nyerol 35 Ed 8.41N 32.02 E
Ny Friesland 41 Nc 79.30N 17.00 E
Nyhammar 8 Fd 60.17N 14.58 E
Nyhem 8 Fb 62.54N 15.40 E
Nyika 30 Ki 2.37S 38.44 E
Nyika Plateau 30 Kj 10.40S 33.50 E
Nyikog Qu 27 He 30.24N 100.40 E
Nyimba 36 Fe 14.33S 30.48 E
Nyingchi 27 Ff 29.38N 94.23 E
Nyírbátor 10 Si 47.50N 22.08 E
Nyíregyháza 10 Ri 47.57N 21.43 E
Nyiri Desert 36 Gc 2.20S 37.20 E
Nyiro, Mount- 36 Gb 2.08N 36.51 E
Nyírség 10 Ri 47.50N 21.55 E
Nykøbing [Den.] 7 Ci 54.46N 11.53 E
Nykøbing [Den.] 7 Ci 55.55N 11.41 E
Nykøbing [Den.] 8 Ch 56.48N 8.52 E
Nyköping 7 Dg 58.45N 17.00 E
Nyköpingsån 8 Gf 58.45N 17.01 E
Nykroppa 8 Fe 59.38N 14.18 E
Nyland 8 Ga 63.00N 17.46 E
Nylstroom 37 Dd 24.42S 28.20 E
Nymburk 10 Lf 50.11N 15.03 E
Nymphe Bank (EN) 9 Fj 51.30N 7.05W
Nynäshamn 7 Dg 58.54N 17.57 E
Nyngan 58 Fh 31.34S 147.11 E
Nyon 14 Ad 46.23N 6.15 E
Nyong 30 Hh 3.17N 9.54 E
Nyonga 36 Fd 6.43S 32.04 E
Nyons 11 Lj 44.22N 5.08 E
Nyřany 10 Jg 49.43N 13.13 E
Nyrob 17 Hf 60.42N 56.45 E
Nyš 20 Jf 51.30N 142.49 E
Nysa 10 Nf 50.29N 17.20 E
Nysa Kłodzka 10 Nf 50.49N 17.50 E
Nysa Łużycka 10 Kd 52.04N 14.46 E
Nyslott/Savonlinna 7 Gf 61.52N 28.53 E
Nyssa 46 Ge 43.53N 117.00W
Nystad/Uusikaupunki 7 Ef 60.48N 21.25 E
Nysted 8 Dj 54.40N 11.45 E
Nytva 19 Fd 57.56N 55.20 E
Nyūdō-Zaki 28 Od 40.00N 139.35 E
Nyunzu 36 Ed 5.57S 28.01 E
Nyūzen 29 Ec 36.56N 137.30 E
Nzambi 36 Bc 3.58S 11.16 E
Nzara 35 De 4.40N 28.14 E
Nzega 36 Fc 4.13S 33.11 E
Nzérékoré 31 Gh 7.45N 8.49W
N'zeto 36 Bd 7.05S 12.50 E
Nzi 30 Gh 5.57N 4.50W
Nzilo, Barrage de- 36 Ee 10.35S 25.30 E
Nzo 34 Dd 6.16N 7.03W
Nzoro 36 Eb 3.18N 29.26 E
Nzwani 30 Lj 12.15S 44.25 E

O

Oa, Mull of- 9 Gf 55.35N 6.20W
Oahe, Lake- 38 Ie 45.30N 100.25W
Oahu Island 57 Lb 21.30N 158.00W
O-akan-Dake 29a Db 43.27N 144.10 E
Oakdale [Ca.-U.S.] 46 Eh 37.46N 120.51W
Oakdale [La.-U.S.] 45 Jk 30.49N 92.40W
Oakham 9 Mi 52.40N 0.44W
Oak Harbor 46 Db 48.18N 122.39W
Oak Lake 45 Fb 49.40N 100.45W
Oakland [Ca.-U.S.] 39 Gf 37.47N 122.13W
Oakland [Md.-U.S.] 44 Hf 39.25N 79.24W
Oakley [Id.-U.S.] 46 Ie 42.15N 113.53W
Oakley [Ks.-U.S.] 43 Gd 39.08N 100.51W
Oak Park 45 Mf 41.53N 87.48W
Oak Ridge 43 Kd 36.01N 84.16W
Oakridge 46 De 43.45N 122.28W
Oakville 44 Hd 43.27N 79.41W
Oamaru 61 Di 45.05S 170.59 E
Oancea 15 Ld 45.55N 28.06 E
Oani-Gawa 29 Ga 40.12N 140.16 E
Ōarai 29 Gc 36.18N 140.33 E
Oaro 62 Ee 42.31S 173.30 E
Oasis 46 Hf 41.01N 114.37W
Oasis 32 Hd 26.00N 5.00 E
Oates Coast 66 Jf 70.00S 160.00 E
Oaxaca [2] 47 Ee 17.00N 96.30W
Oaxaca, Sierra Madre de- 48 Ki 17.30N 96.30W
Oaxaca de Juárez 39 Jh 17.03N 96.43W
Ob 21 Ic 66.45N 69.30 E
Oba 42 Jg 48.55N 84.17W
Obala 34 He 4.10N 11.32 E
Obama [Jap.] 28 Mg 35.30N 135.45 E
Obama [Jap.] 29 Be 32.43N 130.13 E
Obama-Wan 29 Dd 35.30N 135.40 E
Oban [N.Z.] 61 Ci 46.52S 168.10 E
Oban [Scot.-U.K.] 9 He 56.25N 5.29W
Obanazawa 28 Pe 38.36N 140.24 E
Obando 53 Je 4.07N 67.45W
Oban Hills 34 Gd 5.30N 8.35 E
Obeliai/Obeljaj 8 Ki 55.58N 25.59 E
Obeljaj/Obeliai 8 Ki 55.58N 25.59 E
Oberá 56 Ic 27.29S 55.08W
Oberbayern 10 Hi 47.50N 11.50 E
Oberderdingen 12 Ke 49.04N 8.48 E
Oberfranken 10 Hf 50.10N 11.30 E
Oberhausen 10 Ce 51.28N 6.51 E
Oberkirchen, Schmallenberg- 12 Kc 51.09N 8.18 E
Oberland [Switz.] 14 Bd 46.35N 7.30 E
Oberland [Switz.] 14 Dd 46.45N 9.05 E
Oberlausitz 10 Ke 51.15N 14.30 E
Oberlin 45 Fg 39.49N 100.32W
Obermoschel 12 Je 49.44N 7.46 E
Obernkirchen 12 Lb 52.16N 9.08 E
Oberösterreich = Upper Austria (EN) [2] 14 Hb 48.15N 14.00 E
Oberpfalz 10 Ig 49.30N 12.10 E
Oberpfälzer Wald = Bohemian Forest (EN) 10 Ig 49.50N 12.30 E
Oberpullendorf 14 Kc 47.30N 16.31 E
Ober-Ramstadt 12 Ke 49.50N 8.45 E
Oberstdorf 10 Gi 47.24N 10.16 E
Oberursel (Taunus) 12 Kd 50.12N 8.35 E
Obervellach 14 Hd 46.56N 13.12 E
Oberwesel 12 Jd 50.06N 7.44 E
Ob Gulf (EN) = Obskaja Guba 21 Jc 69.00N 73.00 E
Obi, Kepulauan- 26 Ig 1.30S 127.45 E
Obi, Pulau- 57 De 1.30S 127.45 E
Obi, Selat- 26 Ig 0.52S 127.33 E
Óbidos [Braz.] 53 Kf 1.55S 55.31W
Óbidos [Port.] 13 Ce 39.22N 9.09W
Obihiro 27 Pc 42.55N 143.12 E
Obilić 15 Eg 42.41N 21.05 E
Obira 29a Ba 44.01N 141.38 E
Obispos 49 Li 8.36N 70.05W
Obispo Trejo 56 Hd 30.46S 63.25W
Obitočnaja Kosa 16 Jf 46.35N 36.15 E
Obluče 20 Ig 48.59N 131.05 E
Obninsk 19 Dd 55.05N 36.37 E
Obo 31 Jh 5.24N 26.30 E
Obock 35 Gc 11.57N 43.17 E
Obojan 19 De 51.13N 36.16 E
Obokote 36 Ec 0.52S 26.19 E
Obol 7 Gi 55.24N 29.01 E
Oborniki 10 Md 52.39N 16.51 E
Obouya 36 Cc 0.56S 15.43 E
Obozerski 19 Ec 63.28N 40.20 E
Obra 10 Ld 52.36N 15.28 E
Obrenovac 15 De 44.39N 20.12 E
Obrovac 14 Jf 44.12N 15.41 E
Obrovo 10 Vd 52.27N 25.43 E
Obruchev Rise (EN) 20 Lf 52.30N 166.00 E
Obruk Platosu 24 Ec 38.02N 33.30 E
Obšči Syrt 5 Le 51.50N 51.00 E
Obskaja Guba = Ob Gulf (EN) 21 Jc 69.00N 73.00 E
Ob' Tablemount (EN) 30 Ln 52.30S 42.00 E
Ōbu 29 Ed 35.01N 136.58 E
Obuasi 34 Ed 6.12N 1.40W
Obudu 34 Gd 6.40N 9.10 E
Obuhov 16 Gd 50.07N 30.37 E
Obva 16 Gg 58.35N 55.25 E
Obzor 15 Kg 42.49N 27.53 E
Oca 13 Ib 42.46N 3.26W
Oca, Montes de- 13 Ib 42.20N 3.15W
Očakov 19 Df 46.38N 31.33 E
Ocala 43 Kf 29.11N 82.07W
Očamčira 16 Lh 42.46N 41.27 E
Ocampo [Mex.] 48 Hd 27.20N 102.21W
Ocampo [Mex.] 48 Ee 28.11N 108.23W
Ocaña [Col.] 54 Db 8.15N 73.20W
Ocaña [Sp.] 13 Ie 39.56N 3.31W
Occhito, Lago di- 14 Ii 41.35N 14.55 E
Ocean Bight 49 Kc 21.15N 73.15W
Ocean City [Md.-U.S.] 43 Ld 38.20N 75.05W
Ocean City [N.J.-U.S.] 44 Jf 39.16N 74.35W
Ocean Falls 42 Ef 52.21N 127.40W
Oceania 57 Ie 5.00S 175.00E
Ocean Point 44 Il 26.16N 77.03W
Oceanside 43 Dd 33.12N 117.23W
Ocean Springs 45 Lk 30.25N 88.50W
Ocejón, Pico- 13 Ic 41.07N 3.15W
Očenyrd, Gora- 17 Mb 68.05N 66.20 E
Očer 19 Fd 57.53N 54.45 E
Ochagavia 13 Kb 42.55N 1.05W
Ochiai 29 Cd 35.02N 133.45 E
Ochi-Gata 29 Ec 36.55N 136.48 E
Ochiishi-Misaki 29a Db 43.10N 145.28 E
Ochil Hills 9 Je 56.23N 3.35W
Och'ŏnjang 28 Jd 40.55N 128.50 E
Ocho Rios 49 Id 18.25N 77.07W
Ochsenfurt 10 Gg 49.39N 10.05 E
Ochtrup 12 Jb 52.13N 7.11 E
Ockelbo 7 Dd 60.53N 16.43 E
Öckerö 8 Dg 57.43N 11.39 E
Ocmulgee River 44 Fj 31.58N 82.32W
Ocna Mureş 15 Gc 46.23N 23.51 E

Index Symbols

[1] Independent Nation
[2] State, Region
[3] District, County
[4] Municipality
[5] Colony, Dependency
Continent
Physical Region
Historical or Cultural Region
Mount, Mountain
Volcano
Hill
Mountains, Mountain Range
Hills, Escarpment
Plateau, Upland
Pass, Gap
Plain, Lowland
Delta
Salt Flat
Valley, Canyon
Crater, Cave
Karst Features
Depression
Polder
Desert, Dunes
Forest, Woods
Heath, Steppe
Oasis
Cape, Point
Coast, Beach
Cliff
Peninsula
Isthmus
Sandbank
Island
Atoll
Rock, Reef
Islands, Archipelago
Rocks, Reefs
Coral Reef
Well, Spring
Geyser
River, Stream
Waterfall Rapids
River Mouth, Estuary
Lake
Salt Lake
Intermittent Lake
Reservoir
Swamp, Pond
Canal
Glacier
Ice Shelf, Pack Ice
Ocean
Sea
Gulf, Bay
Strait, Fjord
Lagoon
Bank
Seamount
Tablemount
Ridge
Shelf
Basin
Escarpment, Sea Scarp
Fracture
Trench, Abyss
National Park, Reserve
Point of Interest
Recreation Site
Cave, Cavern
Historic Site
Ruins
Wall, Walls
Church, Abbey
Temple
Scientific Station
Airport
Port
Lighthouse
Mine
Tunnel
Dam, Bridge

Ocna Sibiului 15 Hc 45.53N 24.03 E
Ocoa, Bahia de- ◄◘ 49 Ld 18.22N 70.39W
Oconee River ◥ 44 Fj 31.58N 82.32W
Oconto 45 Md 44.55N 87.52W
Ocosingo 48 Mi 17.04N 92.15W
Ocotal 49 Dg 13.38N 86.29W
Ocotepeque [3] 49 Cf 14.30N 89.00W
Ocotlán 47 Dd 20.21N 102.46W
Ocotlán de Morelos 48 Ki 16.48N 96.43W
Ocracoke Inlet ◄ 44 Jh 35.10N 76.05W
Ocracoke Island ◘ 44 Jh 35.09N 75.53W
Ocreza ◥ 13 Ee 39.32N 7.50W
Octeville-sur-Mer 12 Ce 49.33N 0.07 E
October Revolution Island
   (EN) = Oktjabrskoj
   Revoljuci, Ostrov- ◘ 21 Lb 79.30N 97.00 E
Ocú 49 Gj 7.57N 80.47W
Ocumare del Tuy 50 Cg 10.07N 66.46W
Oda [Ghana] 34 Ed 5.55N 0.59W
Oda [Jap.] 29 Ce 33.34N 132.48 E
Ōda 28 Lg 35.11N 132.30 E
Oda, Jabal- ▲ 35 Fa 20.21N 36.39 E
Odádahraun ◄◘ 7a Cb 65.09N 17.00W
Ōdai 29 Ed 34.24N 136.24 E
Odaigahara-San ▲ 29 Ed 34.11N 136.06 E
Odalen [Ⅹ] ◘ 8 Dd 60.15N 11.40 E
Ōdate 28 Pd 40.16N 140.34 E
Odawara 28 Og 35.15N 139.10 E
Odda 7 Bf 60.04N 6.33 E
Odder 8 Di 55.58N 10.10 E
Odeleite ◥ 13 Eg 37.21N 7.27W
Odemira 13 Dg 37.36N 8.38W
Ödemiş 24 Bc 38.13N 27.59 E
Odendaalsrus 37 De 27.48S 26.45 E
Odense 6 Hd 55.24N 10.23 E
Odenthal 12 Jc 51.02N 7.07 E
Odenwald ▲ 10 Eg 49.40N 9.00 E
Oder [Eur.] ◥ 5 He 53.40N 14.33 E
Oder [Ger.] ◥ 10 Ge 51.40N 10.02 E
Oderbruch 10 Kd 52.40N 14.15 E
Oderské vrchy ▲ 10 Ng 49.40N 17.45 E
Oderzo 14 Ge 45.47N 12.29 E
Ödeshög 7 Dg 58.14N 14.39 E
Odessa [Tx.-U.S.] 39 If 31.51N 102.22W
Odessa 6 Jf 46.28N 30.44 E
Odessa [Wa.-U.S.] 46 Fc 47.20N 118.41W
Odesskaja Oblast [3] 19 Df 46.45N 30.30 E
Odet ◥ 11 Bg 47.52N 4.06W
Odiel ◥ 13 Fg 37.10N 6.54W
Odienné 31 Gh 9.30N 7.34W
Odienné [3] 34 Dd 9.45N 7.45W
Odivelas ◥ 13 Df 38.12N 8.18W
Ödmården ◄◘ 8 Gc 61.05N 16.40 E
Odobeşti 15 Kd 45.46N 27.03 E
Ödöngk 25 Kf 11.48N 104.45 E
Odoorn 12 Ib 52.51N 6.50 E
Odorheiu Secuiesc 15 Ic 46.18N 25.18 E
Ōdose-Zaki ◄ 29a Bc 40.46N 140.03 E
Odra ◥ 5 He 53.40N 14.33 E
Ödwéyne 35 Hd 9.23N 45.04 E
Odžaci 15 Cd 45.31N 19.16 E
Odžak 14 Me 45.01N 18.18 E
Odzi ◥ 37 Ec 19.47S 32.24 E
Oeiras ◥ 13 Eg 37.38N 7.40W
Oeiras [Braz.] 54 Je 7.01S 42.08W
Oeiras [Port.] 13 Cf 38.41N 9.19W
Oelde 12 Kc 51.49N 8.09 E
Oelerbeek ◥ 12 Ib 52.21N 6.38 E
Oelrichs 45 Ee 43.15N 103.10W
Oelsnitz 10 If 50.25N 12.10 E
Oelwein 45 Ke 42.41N 91.55W
Oeno Island ◘ 57 Ng 23.56S 130.44W
Oer-Erkenschwick 12 Jc 51.38N 7.15 E
Oeste, Punta- ◄ 51a Ab 18.05N 67.57W
Oeventrop, Arnsberg- ◥ 12 Kc 51.24N 8.08 E
Ōe-Yama ▲ 29 Dd 35.27N 135.06 E
Of 24 Ib 40.57N 40.16 E
O'Fallon Creek ◥ 46 Mc 46.50N 105.09W
Ofanto ◥ 14 Ki 41.21N 16.13 E
Ofaqim 24 Fg 31.17N 34.37 E
Offa 34 Fd 8.09N 4.43 E
Offaly/Uibh Fhaili [2] 9 Fh 53.20N 7.30W
Offenbach am Main 10 Ef 50.06N 8.46 E
Offenbach-Hundheim 12 Je 49.37N 7.33 E
Offenburg 10 Dh 48.29N 7.56 E
Offida 14 Hh 42.56N 13.41 E
Offoué ◥ 36 Cc 0.04S 11.44 E
Offranville 12 De 49.52N 1.03 E
Ofidhoúsa ◘ 15 Jm 36.33N 26.09 E
Ofólanga ◘ 65b Ba 19.36S 174.27W
Ofu ◘ 65c Db 14.11S 169.42W
Ōfunato 28 Pe 39.04N 141.43 E
Oga 28 Oe 40.43N 141.18 E
Ogachi 29 Gb 39.05N 140.28 E
Ogaden ◄◘ 30 Lh 7.30N 45.00 E
Oga-Hantō ◄ 28 Oe 39.55N 139.56 E
Ōgaki 28 Ng 35.21N 136.37 E
Ogallala 43 Gc 41.08N 101.43W
Ogasawara-Shotō = Bonin
   Islands (EN) ◘ 21 Og 27.00N 142.10 E
Ogawara-Ko ◄ 29a Bc 40.45N 141.20 E
Ogden 39 Hc 41.14N 111.58W
Ogdensburg 44 Jc 44.42N 75.31W
Ogeechee River ◥ 44 Gj 31.51N 81.06W
Oghāsh 34 Fc 39.10N 46.55 E
Ogi 29 Fc 37.50N 138.16 E
Ogilvie Mountains ▲ 42 Dc 65.00N 140.00W
Ogi-no-Sen ▲ 29 Dd 35.26N 134.26 E
Oginski Kanal ◥ 16 Dc 52.20N 25.55 E
Oglanly 16 Sj 39.50N 54.33 E
Oglethorpe 44 Ei 31.28N 84.04W
Ogliastra [3] 14 Ee 40.00N 9.35 E
Oglio ◥ 14 Ee 45.02N 10.39 E
Ognon ◥ 11 Lg 42.00 5.26 E
Ogo ◘ 35 Hd 9.48N 45.35 E
Ogoamas, Bulu- ▲ 26 Hf 0.40N 120.12 E

Ogodźa 20 If 52.48N 132.40 E
Ogoja 34 Gd 6.40N 8.48 E
Ogoki 42 If 51.38N 85.56W
Ogoki ◥ 42 If 51.38N 85.55W
Ogoki Reservoir ◘ 42 If 51.35N 86.00W
Ogonëk 20 Ie 59.40N 138.01 E
Ogooué ◥ 30 Hi 0.49S 9.00 E
Ogooué-Ivindo [3] 36 Bb 0.30N 13.00 E
Ogooué-Lolo [3] 36 Bc 1.00S 13.00 E
Ogooué-Maritime [3] 36 Ac 2.00S 9.30 E
Ogôri [Jap.] 29 Bd 34.06N 131.25 E
Ogôri [Jap.] 29 Be 33.24N 130.34 E
Ogosta ◥ 15 Gf 43.45N 23.51 E
Ograżden ▲ 15 Fh 41.50N 24.39 E
Ogre 8 Kh 56.42N 24.33 E
Ogre ◥ 7 Hh 56.50N 24.39 E
Ogulin 14 Je 45.16N 15.14 E
Ogun [2] 34 Fd 7.00N 3.40 E
Oguni [Jap.] 29 Be 33.04N 139.45 E
Oguni [Jap.] 29 Gb 33.07N 131.04 E
Ogurčinski, Ostrov- ◘ 16 Rj 38.55N 53.05 E
Oguzeli 24 Gd 37.00N 37.30 E
Oha 22 Qd 53.34N 142.56 E
Ohai 62 Bf 45.56S 167.57 E
Ohakune 62 Fc 39.25S 175.25 E
Ōhama 32 Id 28.40N 8.50 E
Ohansk 17 Gh 57.42N 55.25 E
Ohanet 29 Gd 35.15N 140.23 E
Ōhasama 29 Gb 39.28N 141.17 E
Ōhata 20 Ie 59.20N 143.05 E
Ōhata 28 Pd 41.24N 141.10 E
Ohau, Lake- ◄ 62 Cf 44.15S 169.50 E
Ohey 12 Hd 50.26N 5.08 E
Ohio [2] 43 Kc 40.15N 82.45W
Ohm ◥ 10 Ef 50.51N 8.48 E
Ohmberge ▲ 10 Ge 51.30N 10.28 E
'Ohonua 65b Bc 21.20S 174.57W
Ohopoho 31 Ij 18.03S 13.45 E
Ohotsk 22 Qd 59.23N 143.18 E
Ohotskoje More = Okhotsk,
   Sea of- (EN) ◘ 21 Qd 53.00N 150.00 E
Ohre ◥ 10 Hd 52.18N 11.47 E
Ohře ◥ 10 Kf 50.32N 14.08 E
Ohrid 15 Dh 41.07N 20.48 E
Ohrid, Lake- (EN) =
   Ohridsko Jezero ◘ 5 Ig 41.00N 20.45 E
Ohrid, Lake- (EN) = Ohrit,
   Liqen i- ◘ 5 Ig 41.00N 20.45 E
Ohridsko Jezero = Ohrid,
   Lake- (EN) ◘ 5 Ig 41.00N 20.45 E
Öhringen 10 Fg 49.12N 9.30 E
Ohrit, Liqen i- = Ohrid,
   Lake- (EN) ◘ 5 Ig 41.00N 20.45 E
Ohura 62 Fc 38.51S 174.59 E
Oiapoque 54 Hc 3.50N 51.50W
Oich ◥ 9 Id 57.10N 4.45W
Oi-Gawa ◥ 29 Fd 34.46N 138.17 E
Oil City 44 Hd 41.26N 79.44W
Oildale 46 Fi 35.25N 119.01W
Oiléan Baoi/Dursey ◘ 9 Cj 51.36N 10.12W
Oiléan Ciarrai/Castleisland 9 Di 52.14N 9.27W
Oiléan Coarach/Mutton ◘ 9 Di 52.49N 9.31W
Oiléan Mhic Aodha/Magee,
   Island- ◘ 9 Hg 54.50N 5.50W
Oinoúsai ◘ 15 Jk 38.32N 26.13 E
Oinoúsai, Nisoi- ◘ 15 Jk 38.31N 26.14 E
Oirschot 11 Mi 45.02N 6.02 E
Oisans [3] 11 Mi 45.02N 6.02 E
Oise [3] 11 Ie 49.30N 2.30 E
Oise ◥ 11 Ie 49.00N 2.04 E
Oise à l'Aisne, Canal de l'-
   11 Je 49.36N 3.11 E
Oisemont 12 De 49.57N 1.46 E
Oissel 12 De 49.20N 1.06 E
Oisterwijk 12 Hc 51.35N 5.11 E
Oistins 51q Ab 13.04N 59.32W
Oistins Bay ◄ 51q Ab 13.03N 59.33W
Ōita 27 Ne 33.14N 131.36 E
Ōita Ken [2] 29 Bd 33.15N 131.20 E
Ōiti Óros ▲ 15 Fk 38.49N 22.17 E
Oituz, Pasul- ◄ 15 Jc 46.03N 26.23 E
Oiwake 29a Bb 42.52N 141.48 E
Ojat ◥ 7 Hf 60.31N 33.05 E
Öje 8 Ed 60.49N 13.51 E
Ojestos de Jalisco 48 Jg 21.50N 101.35W
Ōjika-Jima ◘ 29 Ae 33.13N 129.03 E
O-Jima ◘ 29 Be 34.00N 130.45 E
Ojinaga 47 Dc 29.34N 104.25W
Ojiya 29 Of 37.18N 138.48 E
Ojmjakon 22 Jd 63.28N 142.49 E
Ojocaliente 48 Hf 22.34N 102.15W
Ojo Caliente 48 Fb 30.25N 106.33W
Ojos del Salado, Nevado- ▲ 52 Jh 27.06S 68.32W
Ojos Negros 13 Kd 40.44N 1.30W
Oka ◥ 19 Hg 42.54N 73.21 E
Oka ◥ 21 Md 55.00N 102.3 E
Oka ◥ 5 Kc 56.20N 43.59 E
Okaba 26 Kh 8.06S 139.42 E
Okahandja [3] 37 Bd 21.30S 17.30 E
Okahandja 31 Ik 21.59S 16.58 E
Okahukura 62 Fc 38.47S 175.14 E
Okak Islands ◘ 42 Le 57.28N 61.48W
Okanagan Lake ◘ 42 Ff 49.55N 119.30W
Okano ◥ 36 Bc 0.05S 10.57 E
Okanogan River ◥ 46 Fb 48.06N 119.43W
Okapa 59 Ja 6.31S 145.32 E
Okarem 25 Be 30.49N 73.27 E
Okato 62 Ec 39.12S 173.53 E
Okaukuejo 31 Jj 18.53N 22.24 E
Okavango ◥ 30 Jj 18.53N 22.24 E
Okavango ◥ 31 Jj 19.30S 23.00 E
Okavango Swamp ◘ 30 Jj 19.30S 23.00 E
Ōkawa 29 Be 33.12N 130.23 E

Okaya 28 Of 36.03N 138.03 E
Okayama 22 Pf 34.39N 133.55 E
Okayama Ken [2] 28 Lg 34.50N 133.45 E
Okazaki 28 Ng 34.57N 137.10 E
Okeechobee 44 Gl 27.15N 80.50W
Okeechobee, Lake- ◘ 38 Kg 26.55N 80.45W
Okefenokee Swamp ◘ 44 Fj 30.42N 82.20W
Okehampton 9 Jk 50.44N 4.00W
Okene 34 Gd 7.33N 6.14 E
Oketo 10 Gd 52.30N 10.22 E
Okha 29a Cb 43.41N 143.32 E
Okha 25 Dd 22.27N 69.04 E
Ókhi Óros ▲ 15 Hk 38.04N 24.28 E
Okhotsk, Sea of- (EN) =
   Hok-Kai ◘ 21 Qd 53.00N 150.00 E
Okhotsk, Sea of- (EN) =
   Ohotskoje More ◘ 21 Qd 53.00N 150.00 E
Okhthonia, Ákra- ◄ 15 Hk 38.32N 24.14 E
Oki-Daitō-Jima ◘ 27 Ng 24.30N 131.00 E
Okiep 37 Be 29.39S 17.53 E
Okinawa 29b Ab 26.20N 127.47 E
Okinawa Islands (EN) =
   Okinawa-Shotō ◘ 27 Mf 26.40N 128.00 E
Okinawa-Jima ◘ 27 Mf 26.40N 128.20 E
Okinawa Ken [2] 29b Ab 26.31N 127.59 E
Okinawa-Shotō = Okinawa
   Islands (EN) ◘ 21 Og 26.40N 128.00 E
Okinoerabu-Jima ◘ 27 Mf 27.20N 128.35 E
Okino-Shima [Jap.] ◘ 29 Ce 32.44N 132.33 E
Okino-Shima [Jap.] ◘ 29 Bd 34.15N 130.08 E
Okino-Tori-Shima ◘ 21 Pg 20.25N 136.00 E
Oki-Shotō ◘ 27 Mf 37.00N 135.00 E
Okitipupa 34 Fd 6.30N 4.48 E
Oki Trench (EN) ◘ 29 Dc 37.00N 135.30 E
Oklahoma [2] 43 Hd 35.30N 98.00W
Oklahoma City 39 Jf 35.28N 97.32W
Okmulgee 45 Ii 35.37N 95.58W
Oknica 15 Ka 48.22N 27.24 E
Okoko 35 Fa 22.20N 35.56 E
Okolo 36 Fb 2.06N 33.53 E
Okolona 44 Ef 38.08N 85.41W
Okondja 36 Bc 0.41S 13.47 E
Okonek 10 Mc 53.35N 16.50 E
Okoppe 28 Qb 44.28N 143.08 E
Okotoks 46 Ia 50.44N 113.59W
Okoyo 36 Cc 1.28S 15.04 E
Okrzeika ◥ 10 Re 51.40N 21.30 E
Øksfjord 7 Fa 70.14N 22.22 E
Oksino 17 Fc 67.33N 52.10 E
Øxstindane ▲ 5 Hb 66.02N 14.10 E
Oktemberjan 16 Ni 40.09N 44.03 E
Oktjabrsk 6 Lf 48.40N 57.11 E
Oktjabrsk 7 Lj 53.13N 48.40 E
Oktjabrsk 16 Fc 52.38N 28.54 E
Oktjabrski 17 Kj 52.37N 62.43 E
Oktjabrski 22 Ee 56.05N 99.25 E
Oktjabrski 19 Fe 54.31N 53.28 E
Oktjabrski 17 Hh 54.31N 57.12 E
Oktjabrski 17 Kf 61.05N 43.08 E
Oktjabrski 20 Hf 53.00N 128.42 E
Oktjabrski 20 Kd 52.38N 156.15 E
Oktjabrski 16 Mf 47.56N 43.38 E
Oktjabrskoje 19 Gc 62.28N 66.01 E
Oktjabrskoj Revoljuci,
   Ostrov- = October
   Revolution Island (EN) ◘ 21 Lb 79.30N 97.00 E
Oku 29b Bb 26.50N 128.17 E
Ōkuchi 28 Kh 32.04N 130.37 E
Okulovka 7 Hg 58.24N 33.18 E
Okushiri 28 Oc 42.09N 139.29 E
Okushiri-Kaikyō ◘ 29a Ab 42.15N 139.40 E
Okushiri-Tō ◘ 27 Od 42.10N 139.25 E
Okuta 34 Fd 9.13N 3.11 E
Oku Tango-Hantō ◄ 29 Dd 35.40N 135.10 E
Okwa ◥ 30 Jk 22.26S 22.58 E
Ola 20 Ke 59.37N 151.20 E
Ólafsfjördur 7a Ba 66.04N 18.39W
Ólafsvik 7a Ab 64.53N 23.43W
Ola Grande, Punta- ◄ 51a Bc 17.55N 66.08W
Olaine/Olajne 7 Fh 56.49N 23.59 E
Olajne/Olaine 7 Fh 56.49N 23.59 E
Olanchito 46 Jh 36.17N 117.59W
Olancho [3] 49 Df 15.30N 86.35W
Olancho [3] 49 Ef 14.45N 86.00W
Öland ◘ 6 Hd 56.45N 16.40 E
Ölands norra udde ◄ 8 Gg 57.22N 17.05 E
Ölands södra grund ◘ 8 Gh 55.40N 16.53 E
Ölands södra udde ◄ 8 Gh 56.11N 16.24 E
Olanga ◥ 7 Hc 66.08N 30.38 E
Olathe 45 Jg 38.53N 94.49W
Olavarria 53 Ji 36.53S 60.20W
Oława 10 Nf 50.57N 17.17 E
Oława ◥ 10 Nf 50.57N 17.17 E
Olbernhau 10 Jf 50.40N 13.21 E
Olbia 5 Gg 40.55N 9.31 E
Olbia, Golfo di- ◘ 14 Dj 40.55N 9.35 E
Old Bahama Channel ◘ 49 Ib 22.30N 78.05W
Old Bahama Channel (EN) =
   Bahamas, Canal Viejo de-
   ◘ 49 Ib 22.30N 78.05W
Old Castile (EN) = Castilla la
   Vieja ◄◘ 13 Ic 41.30N 4.00W
Old Crow 39 Fc 67.35N 139.50W
Oldeani 36 Fc 3.21S 35.33 E
Oldebroek 12 Hb 52.26N 5.53 E
Oldenburg 10 Ec 53.10N 8.12 E
Oldenburg in Holstein 10 Gb 54.18N 10.53 E
Oldenzaal 11 Mc 52.19N 6.55 E
Old Faithful Geyser ◘ 46 Jd 44.30N 110.45W
Old Fletton 12 Kh 52.33N 2.07W
Old Hickory Lake ◘ 44 Df 36.18N 86.35W
Oldman River ◥ 46 Jb 49.56N 111.42W
Old Marsh Bed ◘ 59 Gd 20.55S 130.30 E

Ōmachi 28 Nf 36.30N 137.52 E
Old Mkuski 36 Ee 14.22S 29.22 E
Old Road 51d Bb 17.01N 61.50W
Old Road Town 51c Ab 17.19N 62.48W
Olds 42 Gf 51.47N 114.06W
Old Town 44 Mc 44.56N 68.39W
Old Wives Lake ◘ 46 Ma 50.06N 106.00W
Olean 44 Hd 42.05N 78.26W
Olecko 10 Sb 54.03N 22.30 E
Olekma ◥ 13 Ee 39.55N 7.55W
Olëkma ◥ 22 Oc 60.22N 120.42 E
Olëkminsk 22 Oc 60.30N 120.15 E
Olëkminski Stanovik ◄◘ 20 Gf 54.00N 119.00 E
Ølen 7 Ag 59.36N 5.48 E
Olenegorsk 19 Db 68.10N 33.13 E
Olenëk ◥ 20 Hb 73.10N 121.00 E
Olenëkski Zaliv ◘ 21 Nb 73.00N 119.55 E
Olenj, Ostrov- ◘ 20 Cb 72.25N 77.45 E
Olenty ◥ 16 Re 49.45N 52.10 E
Oléron, Ile d'- ◘ 5 Ff 45.56N 1.18W
Olesko 10 Ug 49.53N 24.58 E
Oleśnica 10 Ne 51.13N 17.23 E
Olesno 10 Of 50.53N 18.25 E
Olevsk 16 Ed 51.13N 27.41 E
Olga 20 Ih 43.46N 135.21 E
Olga, Mount- ▲ 59 Ge 25.19S 130.46 E
Olgastretet ◘ 41 Oc 78.30N 24.00 E
Ølgod 8 Ci 55.49N 8.37 E
Olhão 13 Eg 37.02N 7.50W
Olhovatka 16 Kd 50.17N 39.17 E
Oli ◥ 34 Fd 9.40N 4.29 E
Oliana 13 Kb 42.04N 1.19 E
Olib ◘ 14 If 44.23N 14.47 E
Oliena 14 Dj 40.16N 9.24 E
Olifants (Afr.) ◥ 30 Kk 24.03S 32.40 E
Olifants (Nam.) ◥ 37 Be 25.30S 19.30 E
Olifantshoek 37 Ce 27.57S 22.42 E
Olimarao Atoll ◘ 57 Fd 7.42N 145.53 E
Olímbia ◘ 15 Fl 39.39N 21.38 E
Ólimbos ▲ 15 Kn 35.44N 27.13 E
Ólimbos, Óros-=Olympus,
   Mount- (EN) ▲ 5 Ig 40.05N 22.21 E
Ólimbos Óros ▲ 15 Jj 39.05N 26.20 E
Olinda 55 He 24.55 48.54W
Olinda 54 Le 8.01S 34.51W
Oliva [Arg.] 56 Md 32.03S 63.34W
Oliva [Sp.] 13 Lf 38.55N 0.07W
Oliva, Monasterio de la- ◄ 13 Ff 38.16N 6.55W
Oliva de la Frontera 13 Ff 38.16N 6.55W
Oliveira dos Brejinhos 54 Jf 12.19S 42.54W
Olivença 37 Fb 11.46S 40.43 E
Olivenza 13 Ef 38.41N 7.06W
Olivet 11 Ie 47.52N 1.54 E
Olivia 45 Id 44.46N 94.59W
Olja ◥ 16 Og 45.47N 47.35 E
Olji Moron He ◥ 28 Fb 44.16N 121.42 E
Ojutorski, Mys- ◄ 21 Sd 59.55N 170.25 E
Oljutorski Zaliv ◘ 20 Ld 60.00N 168.00 E
Olkusz 10 Pf 50.17N 19.35 E
Ollan ◘ 64d Bb 7.14N 151.38 E
Ollerton 12 Aa 53.13N 1.01W
Olmedo 13 Hc 41.17N 4.41W
Olmos 54 Ce 5.59S 79.46W
Olney [Eng.-U.K.] 12 Bb 52.09N 0.42W
Olney [Il.-U.S.] 45 Lg 38.44N 88.05W
Olney [Tx.-U.S.] 45 Hj 33.22N 98.45W
Oločí 20 Gf 51.20N 119.53 E
Olofström 7 Dh 56.16N 14.30 E
Oloitokitok 36 Gc 2.56S 37.30 E
Oloj ◥ 20 Kc 66.20N 159.29 E
Olojskoj Hrebet ▲ 20 Lc 65.50N 162.30 E
Olombo 36 Cc 1.18S 15.53 E
Olomburi 63a Ec 8.59S 161.09 E
Olomouc 6 Hf 49.36N 17.16 E
Olona ◥ 14 Dc 45.26N 9.21 E
Olonec 7 Hf 60.59N 32.58 E
Olonešty 15 Mc 46.29N 29.52 E
Olongapo 26 Gb 14.50N 120.16 E
Oloron, Gave d'- ◥ 11 Ek 43.33N 1.05W
Oloron-Sainte-Marie 11 Fk 43.12N 0.36W
Olosega ◘ 65c Db 14.11S 169.39W
Olot 13 Nb 42.11N 2.29 E
Olovjannaja 20 Gf 50.56N 115.35 E
Olovo 14 Mf 44.07N 18.35 E
Olpe 12 Jc 51.02N 7.51 E
Oloyd River ◥ 59 Ia 14.10S 141.50 E
Olsberg 12 Kc 51.21N 8.30 E
Olshammar 8 Ff 58.45N 14.48 E
Olst 12 Hb 52.20N 6.08 E
Olsztyn 6 Ie 53.48N 20.29 E
Olsztynek 10 Qc 53.36N 20.17 E
Olt [2] 15 Ih 44.25N 24.30 E
Olt ◥ 6 If 43.43N 24.51 E
Oltedal 8 Bf 58.50N 6.02 E
Olten 14 Bc 47.21N 7.55 E
Olteni 15 Ih 44.11N 25.17 E
Oltenia ◄◘ 15 Ge 44.30N 23.30 E
Olteniţa 15 Je 44.05N 26.38 E
Oltet ◥ 15 He 44.14N 24.27 E
Oltu 24 Ib 40.33N 41.59 E
Oluanpi 28 Fg 21.54N 120.51 E
Olutanga ◘ 26 Hf 7.22N 122.52 E
Olvera 13 Gg 36.56N 5.16W
Olympia 39 Hb 47.03N 122.53W
Olympic Mountains ▲ 38 Gc 47.48N 123.43W
Olympus, Mount- (EN) =
   Ólimbos, Óros- ▲ 5 Ig 40.05N 22.21 E
Oma 29a Bc 41.30N 140.55 E
Ōma ◥ 17 Cc 66.45N 46.20 E
Oma ◥ 29a Bc 41.30N 140.55 E
Ōma-Zaki ◄ 29a Bc 41.32N 140.55 E
Ōma-Zaki ◄ 29 Bd 41.32N 140.55 E
Ōma-Zaki ◄ 28 Od 41.32N 140.55 E

Ōmachi 28 Nf 36.30N 137.52 E
Omae-Zaki ◄ 29 Fd 34.36N 138.14 E
Ōmagari 28 Pe 39.27N 140.29 E
Omagh/An Ōmaigh 9 Fg 54.36N 7.18W
Omaha 39 Je 41.16N 95.57W
Omak 46 Fb 48.24N 119.31W
Omakau 62 Cf 45.06S 169.36 E
Omak Lake ◘ 46 Fb 48.16N 119.23W
Oman (EN) = 'Umān [1] 22 Hg 21.00N 57.00 E
Oman, Gulf of- (EN) =
   'Umān, Khalīj- ◄◘ 21 Hg 25.00N 58.00 E
Omarama 61 Ch 44.29S 169.58 E
Omar Gambon 35 He 3.10N 45.47 E
Omaru-Gawa ◥ 29 Be 32.07N 131.34 E
Omaruru 37 Bd 21.28S 15.56 E
Omaruru ◥ 37 Bd 21.33S 15.00 E
Omatako ◥ 37 Bd 21.28S 16.43 E
Omatako, Omuramba- ◥ 30 Jj 17.57S 20.25 E
Omate 54 Dg 16.41S 70.59W
Ōma-Zaki ◄ 29a Bc 41.32N 140.55 E
Ombai, Selat- ◘ 26 Hh 8.30S 125.00 E
Ombella-Mpoko [3] 35 Bd 5.00N 18.00 E
Omberg ▲ 8 Ff 58.20N 14.39 E
Ombo ◘ 8 Ae 59.15N 6.00 E
Omboué 36 Ac 1.34S 9.15 E
Ombrone ◥ 14 Fh 42.39N 11.01 E
Ombu 27 Je 31.18N 86.33 E
Omčak 20 Jd 61.38N 147.55 E
Omdurman (EN) = Umm
   Durmān 31 Kg 15.38N 32.30 E
Ōme 29 Fd 35.47N 139.15 E
Omegna 14 Ce 45.53N 8.24 E
Omeo 59 Jg 37.06S 147.38 E
Ōmerköy 15 Ij 39.50N 28.04 E
Ometepe, Isla de- ◘ 47 Gf 11.30N 85.35W
Ometepec 47 Ee 16.41N 98.25W
Omhajer 35 Fc 14.19N 36.40 E
Ōmihachiman 29 Ed 35.08N 136.05 E
Omihi 62 Ed 43.01S 172.51 E
Omineca ◥ 42 Fe 56.05N 124.05W
Omineca Mountains ▲ 42 Ec 56.35N 125.55W
Omiš 14 Kg 43.27N 16.42 E
Ōmi-Shima [Jap.] ◘ 29 Bd 34.25N 131.15 E
Ōmi-Shima [Jap.] ◘ 29 Cd 34.15N 133.00 E
Omitara 37 Bd 22.18S 18.01 E
Ōmiya 27 Of 35.54N 139.38 E
Ommanney Bay ◘ 42 Hb 73.00N 101.00W
Omme Å ◥ 8 Ci 55.55N 8.25 E
Ommen 12 Ib 52.31N 6.25 E
Omo ◥ 30 Kh 4.32N 36.04 E
Ōmoa ◘ 8 Di 55.01N 11.10 E
Omoa, Bahía de- ◘ 49 Cf 15.50N 88.10W
Omodeo, Lago- ◘ 14 Cj 40.10N 8.51 E
Omoloj ◥ 20 Ib 71.08N 132.01 E
Omolon 21 Rc 68.42N 158.36 E
Omolon ◥ 20 Lc 65.12N 160.27 E
Omono-Gawa ◥ 29 Gb 39.44N 140.04 E
Omont 12 Ge 49.36N 4.44 E
Omoto-Gawa ◥ 29 Gb 39.51N 141.58 E
Omsk 22 Bd 55.00N 73.24 E
Omskaja Oblast [3] 19 Hd 56.00N 72.30 E
Omsukčan 20 Kd 63.00N 155.10 E
Omsukčanski Hrebet ▲ 20 Kd 63.00N 155.10 E
Ōmu 29 Qb 44.34N 142.58 E
Omu, Virful- ▲ 15 Id 45.26N 25.25 E
Omulew ◥ 10 Rc 53.05N 21.32 E
Omuo 34 Gd 7.51S 5.32W
Ōmura 29 Ae 33.00N 129.57 E
Ōmura-Wan ◘ 29 Ae 33.00N 129.50 E
Omurtag 15 Jf 43.06N 26.25 E
Ōmuta 28 Kh 33.02N 130.27 E
Omutinski 19 Hd 56.31N 67.45 E
Omutninsk 19 Fd 58.43N 52.12 E
Oña 13 Ib 42.44N 3.24W
Onagawa 29 Gb 38.26N 141.27 E
Onakayale 37 Bc 17.30S 15.01 E
Onaman Lake ◘ 45 Ma 50.00N 87.29W
Onamia 45 Jc 46.04N 93.40W
Onamue ◘ 64d Bb 7.21N 151.31 E
Onaping Lake ◘ 44 Bb 46.57N 81.30W
Onatchiway, Lac- ◘ 44 La 49.03N 71.03W
Onawa 45 Id 42.02N 96.06W
Onch'ŏn 28 He 38.49N 125.13 E
Oncócua 36 Bf 16.40S 13.24 E
Onda 13 Le 39.58N 0.15W
Ondangua 31 Ij 17.55S 16.00 E
Ondarroa 13 Ja 43.19N 2.25W
Ondo 34 Fd 7.06N 4.50 E
Ondo [Jap.] 29 Cd 34.12N 132.32 E
Ondo [Nig.] 34 Fd 7.06N 4.50 E
Ondor Sum 28 Bc 42.30N 113.00 E
Ondozero, Ozero- ◘ 7 Hd 63.40N 33.15 E
One and Half Degree
   Channel ◘ 21 Ji 1.30N 73.10 E
Oneata ◘ 63d Cc 18.27S 178.29W
Oneata Passage ◘ 63d Cc 18.32S 178.28W
Onega 6 Jc 63.55N 38.05 E
Onega ◥ 5 Jc 63.58N 37.55 E
Onega, Lake- (EN) =
   Onežskoje Ozero- ◘ 5 Jc 61.30N 35.45 E
Onežskoje Ozero ◘ 5 Jc 61.30N 35.45 E
Onehunga 62 Fb 36.56S 174.48 E
One Hundred Mile House 42 Ff 51.38N 121.16W
Oneida 44 Jd 43.05N 75.40W
Oneida Lake ◘ 44 Jd 43.13N 76.00W
O'Neil 43 Hc 42.27N 98.39W
Onekotan, Ostrov- ◘ 21 Rd 49.25N 154.45 E
Oneonta [Al.-U.S.] 44 Di 33.57N 86.28W
Oneonta [N.Y.-U.S.] 44 Jd 42.28N 75.04W
Oneroa ◘ 64p Cb 21.15S 159.43W
Oneşti (Gheorghe
   Gheorghiu-Dej) 15 Jc 46.12N 26.46 E
Onežskaja guba ◘ 5 Jc 64.20N 36.30 E
Onežskoje Ozero=Onega,
   Lake- (EN) ◘ 5 Jc 61.30N 35.45 E
Ongea Levu ◘ 63d Cc 19.08S 178.24W

Ongijn-Gol 27 Hc 44.30N 103.40 E
Ongjin 27 Md 37.56N 125.22 E
Ongniud Qi (Wudan) 27 Kc 42.58N 119.01 E
Ongole 25 Ge 15.30N 80.03 E
Ongon 27 Jb 45.49N 113.08 E
Onhaye 12 Gd 50.15N 4.50 E
Oni 16 Mh 42.35N 43.27 E
Onigajō-Yama 29 Ce 33.07N 132.41 E
Onilany 30 Lk 23.34S 43.45 E
Onishibetsu 29a Ca 45.21N 142.06 E
Onitsha 31 Hh 6.10N 6.47 E
Ono 29 Dd 34.51N 134.57 E
Ono 63d Bc 18.54S 178.29 E
Ōno [Jap.] 28 Ng 35.59N 136.29 E
Ōno [Jap.] 29 Cd 34.18N 132.17 E
Onoda 29 Be 33.59N 131.11 E
Ōno-Gawa 29 Be 33.15N 131.43 E
Ōnohara-Jima 29 Fd 34.02N 139.23 E
Onohoj 20 Ff 51.55N 108.01 E
Ono-i-Lau Islands 57 Jg 20.39S 178.42W
Onojō 29 Be 33.34N 130.29 E
Onomichi 28 Lg 34.25N 133.12 E
Onon 21 Nd 51.42N 115.50 E
Onoto 50 Dh 9.36N 65.12W
Onotoa Atoll 57 Ie 1.52S 175.34 E
Ons, Isla de- 13 Db 42.23N 8.56W
Onsala 7 Ch 57.25N 12.01 E
Onseepkans 37 Be 28.45S 19.17 E
Onslow 58 Cg 21.39S 115.06 E
Onslow Bay 43 Le 34.20N 77.20W
On-Take 29 Bf 31.35N 130.39 E
Ontake-San 29 Ed 35.53N 137.29 E
Ontario [3] 42 If 50.00N 86.00W
Ontario [Ca.-U.S.] 46 Gi 34.04N 117.39W
Ontario [Or.-U.S.] 43 Dc 44.02N 116.58W
Ontario, Lake- 38 Le 43.40N 78.00W
Ontario Peninsula 38 Ke 43.50N 81.00W
Onteniente/Ontinyent 13 Lf 38.49N 0.37W
Ontinyent/Onteniente 13 Lf 38.49N 0.37W
Ontojärvi 7 Gd 64.08N 29.09 E
Ontonagon 44 Cb 46.52N 89.19W
Ontong Java Atoll 57 Ge 5.20S 159.30 E
Ō-Numa 29a Bc 41.59N 140.41 E
Oodnadatta 58 Eg 27.33S 135.28 E
Ooidonk 12 Fc 51.01N 3.35 E
Ookala 65a Fc 20.01N 155.17W
Ooldea 58 Eh 30.27S 131.50 E
Oologah Lake 45 Ih 36.39N 95.36W
Ooltgensplaat, Oostflakkee- 12 Gc 51.41N 4.21 E
Oostburg 12 Fc 51.20N 3.30 E
Oostelijk Flevoland 12 Hb 52.30N 5.40 E
Oostende/Ostende 11 Ic 51.14N 2.55 E
Oosterhout 11 Kc 51.38N 4.51 E
Oosterschelde=East Schelde (EN) 11 Jc 51.30N 4.00 E
Oosterwolde, Ooststellingwerf- 12 Ha 53.00N 6.18 E
Oosterzele 12 Fd 50.57N 3.48 E
Oostflakkee 12 Gc 51.41N 4.21 E
Oostflakkee-Ooltgensplaat 12 Gc 51.41N 4.21 E
Oostkamp 12 Fc 51.09N 3.14 E
Oost-Souburg, Vlissingen- 12 Fc 51.28N 3.36 E
Ooststellingwerf 12 Ib 53.00N 6.18 E
Ooststellingwerf-Oosterwolde 12 Ha 53.00N 6.18 E
Oost Vieland, Vieland- 12 Ha 53.17N 5.06 E
Oost-Vlaanderen [3] 12 Fc 51.00N 3.40 E
Ootmarsum 12 Ib 52.25N 6.54 E
Opala 36 Dc 0.37S 24.21 E
Opalenica 10 Md 52.19N 16.23 E
Opanake 25 Gg 6.36N 80.37 E
Opari 35 Ee 3.56N 32.03 E
Oparino 7 Lg 59.53N 48.25 E
Opasatika 44 Fa 49.31N 82.58W
Opasatika Lake 44 Fa 49.06N 83.08W
Opasatika River 44 Fa 50.15N 82.25W
Opatija 14 Ie 45.20N 14.19 E
Opatów 10 Rf 50.49N 21.26 E
Opatówka 10 Rf 50.42N 21.50 E
Opava 10 Ng 49.57N 17.54 E
Opava 10 Og 49.51N 18.17 E
Opelika 43 Je 32.39N 85.23W
Opelousas 45 Jk 30.32N 92.05W
Opémisca, Lac- 44 Ja 49.58N 74.57W
Opheim 46 Lb 48.51N 106.24W
Ophir 40 Hd 63.10N 156.31W
Ophthalmia Range 59 Dd 23.15S 119.30 E
Opienge 36 Eb 0.12N 27.30 E
Opihikao 65a Gd 19.26N 154.53W
Opinaca 42 Jf 52.14N 78.02W
Opiscotéo, Lac- 42 Kf 53.09N 68.10W
Opladen, Leverkusen- 10 De 51.04N 7.01 E
Opobo 34 Ge 4.34N 7.27 E
Opočka 19 Cd 56.42N 28.41 E
Opoczno 10 Qe 51.23N 20.17 E
Opole [2] 10 Nf 50.40N 17.55 E
Opole 10 Nf 50.41N 17.55 E
Opole Lubelskie 10 Re 51.09N 21.58 E
Oporny 19 Ff 46.13N 54.29 E
Opotiki 62 Gc 38.01S 177.17 E
Opp 44 Dj 31.17N 86.22W
Oppa-Wan 29 Gb 38.35N 141.30 E
Oppdal 7 Be 62.36N 9.40 E
Oppenheim 10 Eg 49.51N 8.21 E
Oppland [2] 7 Bf 61.10N 9.40 E
Opportunity 46 Gc 47.39N 117.15W
Opsa 8 Li 55.31N 26.54 E
Opsterland 12 Ia 53.03N 6.04 E
Opsterland-Beetsterzwaag 12 Ia 53.03N 6.04 E
Opua 61 Dg 35.18S 174.07 E
Opunake 62 Ec 39.27S 173.51 E
Oputo 48 Eb 30.03N 109.20W
Oquossoc 44 Lc 45.04N 70.44W
Or 16 Ud 51.12N 58.33 E
Ōra 33 Cd 28.20N 19.35 E
Oradea 6 If 47.04N 21.56 E
Orahovac 15 Dg 42.24N 20.40 E
Orahovica 14 Le 45.32N 17.53 E
Orai 25 Fc 25.59N 79.28 E
Oraibi Wash 46 Ji 35.26N 110.49W
Oran 31 Ge 35.42N 0.38W
Oran [3] 32 Gb 36.00N 0.35W
Orange [Austl.] 58 Fh 33.17S 149.06 E
Orange [Fr.] 11 Kj 44.08N 4.48 E
Orange [Tx.-U.S.] 43 Ie 30.01N 93.44W
Orange [Va.-U.S.] 44 Hf 38.14N 78.07W
Orange/Oranje 30 Ik 28.38S 16.27 E
Orange, Cabo- 52 Ke 4.24N 51.33W
Orangeburg 43 Ke 33.30N 80.52W
Orange Free State/Oranje Vrystaat [2] 37 De 29.00S 26.00 E
Orange Lake 44 Fk 29.25N 82.13W
Orange Park 44 Gj 30.10N 81.42W
Orangeville 44 Gd 43.55N 80.06W
Orange Walk 47 Ge 18.06N 88.33W
Orango 30 Fg 11.05N 16.08W
Oranienburg 10 Jd 52.45N 13.14 E
Oranje/Orange 30 Ik 28.38N 16.27 E
Oranje Gebergte 54 Hc 3.00N 55.00W
Oranjemund 37 Be 28.38S 16.24 E
Oranjestad 54 Da 12.33N 70.06W
Oranje Vrystaat/Orange Free State [2] 37 De 29.00S 26.00 E
Oranžerei 16 Og 45.50N 47.36 E
Orapa 37 Dd 21.16S 25.22 E
Orăştie 15 Gd 45.50N 23.12 E
Orava 10 Pg 49.08N 19.10 E
Oravita 15 Ed 45.02N 21.42 E
Orayská Priehradni Nádrž 10 Pg 49.20N 19.35 E
Orb 11 Jk 43.15N 3.18 E
Orba 14 Cf 44.53N 8.37 E
Orba Co 27 De 34.33N 81.06 E
Ørbæk 8 Di 55.16N 10.41 E
Orbec 12 Ce 49.01N 0.25 E
Orbetello 14 Fh 42.27N 11.13 E
Orbetello, Laguna di- 14 Fh 42.25N 11.15 E
Orbigo 13 Gc 41.58N 5.40W
Orbiquet 12 Ce 49.09N 0.14 E
Orbost 59 Jg 37.42S 148.27 E
Örbyhus 8 Gd 60.14N 17.42 E
Orcas Island 46 Db 48.39N 122.55W
Orchej (Orgejev) 19 Cf 47.23N 28.50 E
Orchies 12 Fd 50.28N 3.14 E
Orcia 14 Fh 42.58N 11.21 E
Orco 14 Be 45.10N 7.52 E
Ord, Mount- 59 Fc 17.20S 125.35 E
Ordenes 13 Da 43.04N 8.24W
Ordos Desert (EN)=Mu Us Shamo 21 Mf 38.45N 109.10 E
Ord River 57 Df 15.30S 128.21 E
Ordu 23 Ea 41.00N 37.53 E
Ordubad 16 Oj 38.55N 46.01 E
Ordynskoje 20 Df 54.22N 81.58 E
Ordžonikidze 16 If 47.40N 34.04 E
Ordžonikidze 17 Jj 52.25N 61.45 E
Ordžonikidze Vladikavkaz 6 Kg 43.03N 44.40 E
Ordžonikidzeabad 19 Gh 38.34N 69.02 E
Ore älv 8 Fc 61.08N 14.35 E
Orebić 14 Lh 42.58N 17.11 E
Örebro 6 Hd 59.17N 15.13 E
Örebro [2] 7 Dg 59.30N 15.00 E
Oredež 8 Nf 58.50N 30.13 E
Oregon 44 Fe 41.38N 83.28W
Oregon [2] 43 Cc 44.00N 121.00W
Oregon City 43 Cb 45.21N 122.36W
Oregon Inlet 44 Jh 35.50N 75.35W
Öregrund 8 Hd 60.20N 18.26 E
Orehov 16 If 47.34N 35.47 E
Orehovo-Zujevo 6 Jd 55.49N 38.59 E
Orel 6 Je 52.59N 36.05 E
Orel 16 Ie 48.31N 34.55 E
Orel, Gora- 20 Jf 53.55N 140.01 E
Orellana [Peru] 54 Ce 6.54S 75.04W
Orellana [Peru] 54 Cd 4.40S 78.10W
Orem 43 Ec 40.19N 111.42W
Ore Mountains (EN)=Erzgebirge 5 He 50.30N 13.15 E
Ore Mountains (EN)=Krušné Hory 5 He 50.30N 13.15 E
Ören 24 Bd 37.18N 29.17 E
Orenbel 24 Hb 40.00N 39.10 E
Orenburg 6 Le 51.54N 55.06 E
Orenburgskaja Oblast [3] 19 Fe 52.00N 55.00 E
Orencik 24 Cc 39.16N 29.34 E
Orense [3] 13 Eb 42.10N 7.30W
Orense [Arg.] 56 Ie 38.40S 59.47W
Orense [Sp.] 13 Eb 42.20N 7.51W
Oreón, Dhíavlos- 15 Fk 38.54N 22.55 E
Orepuki 62 Bg 46.17S 167.44 E
Orestiás 15 Jh 41.30N 26.31 E
Øresund 5 Hd 55.50N 12.40 E
Oreti 62 Cg 46.28S 168.17 E
Orewa 62 Fb 36.35S 174.42 E
Orford 12 Db 52.05N 1.32 E
Orford Ness 9 Oi 52.05N 1.34 E
Organá/Organyà 13 Nb 42.13N 1.20 E
Organ Needle 45 Cj 32.21N 106.33W
Organyà/Organá 13 Nb 42.13N 1.20 E
Orgaz 13 Ie 39.39N 3.54W
Orgejev → Orchej 19 Cf 47.23N 28.50 E
Orgelet 11 Lh 46.31N 5.37 E
Orgon Tal 28 Bc 43.20N 112.40 E
Orgosolo 14 Dj 40.12N 9.21 E
Orgūn 23 Kc 32.57N 69.11 E
Orhaneli 15 Lj 39.54N 29.00 E
Orhaneli/Koca Çay 15 Lj 39.56N 28.32 E
Orhangazi 15 Mi 40.30N 29.18 E
Orhomenós 15 Fk 38.35N 22.54 E
Orhon (Orchon) 21 Md 50.21N 106.05 E
Orhy, Pico de- 13 La 42.59N 1.00W
Oria 13 Ja 43.17N 2.08W
Orichuna, Rio- 50 Bi 7.30N 68.13W
Orick 46 Cf 41.17N 124.04W
Oriental 48 Kh 19.22N 97.37W
Oriéntal, Cordillera- 49 Md 18.55N 69.15W
Oriente 56 He 38.44S 60.37W
Orihuela 13 Lf 38.05N 0.57W
Oriku 15 Ci 40.17N 19.25 E
Óri Lekánis 15 Hh 41.08N 24.33 E
Orillia 42 Jh 44.37N 79.25W
Orimattila 7 Ff 60.48N 25.45 E
Orinoco, Rio- 52 Je 8.37N 62.15W
Oripää 8 Jd 60.51N 22.41 E
Orissa [3] 25 Gd 21.00N 84.00 E
Orissaare/Orissare 7 Fg 58.34N 23.05 E
Oristano 14 Ck 39.54N 8.36 E
Oristano, Golfo di- 14 Ck 39.50N 8.30 E
Orituco, Rio- 50 Ch 8.45N 67.27W
Orivesi 5 Ic 62.15N 29.25 E
Orivesi 7 Ff 61.41N 24.21 E
Oriximiná 54 Gd 1.45S 55.52W
Orizaba 39 Jh 18.51N 97.06W
Orizaba, Pico de- (Citlaltépetl, Volcán-) 38 Jh 19.01N 97.16W
Orizona 55 Hc 17.03S 48.18W
Orjahovo 15 Gf 43.44N 23.58 E
Ørje 8 De 59.29N 11.39 E
Orjen 15 Bg 42.34N 18.33 E
Orjiva 13 Ih 36.54N 3.25W
Orkanger 7 Be 63.19N 9.52 E
Orkdalen 8 Ca 63.15N 9.50 E
Örkelljunga 8 Eh 56.17N 13.17 E
Orkla 8 Ca 63.18N 9.50 E
Orkney 37 De 27.00S 26.39 E
Orkney [3] 9 Kb 59.00N 3.00W
Orkney Islands 5 Fd 59.00N 3.00W
Orlândia 55 Ie 20.43S 47.53W
Orlando 39 Kg 28.32N 81.23W
Orlando, Capo d'- 14 Il 38.10N 14.45 E
Orlanka 10 Td 52.52N 23.12 E
Orléanais 11 Hf 48.40N 1.20 E
Orléans 6 Gf 47.55N 1.54 E
Orlice 10 Lf 50.12N 15.49 E
Orlické Hory 10 Mf 50.10N 16.30 E
Orlik 20 Ef 52.30N 99.55 E
Orlov (Halturin) 19 Ed 58.35N 48.55 E
Orlovskaja oblast 19 De 52.45N 36.30 E
Orlovski 16 Mf 46.52N 42.06 E
Orlovski, mys- 7 Jc 67.16N 41.18 E
Orly 11 If 48.45N 2.24 E
Ormāra 25 Cc 25.12N 64.38 E
Ormes 12 Ce 49.03N 0.59 E
Ormoc 26 Hd 11.00N 124.37 E
Ormond 62 Gc 38.33S 177.55 E
Ormond Beach 44 Gk 29.17N 81.02W
Ornain 11 Kf 48.46N 4.47 E
Ornans 11 Mg 47.06N 6.09 E
Ornäs 8 Fd 60.31N 15.32 E
Orne 11 Gf 48.40N 0.05 E
Orne [Fr.] 11 Ie 49.17N 6.11 E
Orne [Fr.] 11 Be 49.19N 0.14W
Orne Seamount (EN) 61 Je 27.30S 157.30W
Orneta 10 Qb 54.08N 20.08 E
Ornö 7 Eg 59.05N 18.25 E
Örnsköldsvik 7 Ee 63.18N 18.43 E
Oro 28 Id 40.01N 127.27 E
Oro, Rio de- 55 Ch 27.04S 58.34W
Oro, Rio del- 48 Ge 25.35N 105.03W
Orocué 54 Dc 4.48N 71.20W
Orodara 34 Ec 10.59N 4.55W
Orofino 46 Gc 46.29N 116.15W
Orogrande 45 Cj 32.23N 106.08W
Orohena, Mont- 65e Fc 17.31S 149.28W
Oroluk Atoll 57 Gd 7.32N 155.18 E
Orom 36 Fb 3.20N 33.40 E
Oromocto 44 Ng 45.51N 66.29W
Oron 34 Ge 4.50N 8.14 E
Orona Atoll (Hull) 57 Je 4.29S 172.10W
Orongo 65d Ac 27.10S 109.26W
Oronsay 9 Ge 56.01N 6.14W
Orontes (EN)=Nahr al 'Āṣī 23 Eb 36.02N 35.58 E
Oropesa [Sp.] 13 Ge 39.55N 5.10W
Oropesa [Sp.] 13 Ld 40.06N 0.09W
Oroqen Zizhiqi (Alihe) 27 La 50.35N 123.42 E
Oroquieta 26 He 8.29N 123.48 E
Orós 54 Ke 6.15S 38.55W
Orós, Açude- 54 Ke 6.15S 39.05W
Orosei 14 Dj 40.23N 9.42 E
Orosei, Golfo di- 14 Dj 40.15N 9.45 E
Orosháza 10 Qj 46.34N 20.40 E
Oro-Shima 29 Be 33.52N 130.02 E
Oroszlány 10 Oi 47.29N 18.19 E
Orote Peninsula 64c Bb 13.26N 144.38 E
Orote Point 64c Bb 13.27N 144.37 E
Orotukan 20 Kd 62.17N 151.50 E
Oroville [Ca.-U.S.] 46 Eg 39.31N 121.33W
Oroville [Wa.-U.S.] 46 Fb 48.56N 119.26W
Orp-Jauche 12 Gd 50.40N 4.57 E
Orqohan 27 Lb 49.36N 121.23 E
Orr 45 Jb 48.03N 92.50W
Orrefors 8 Fh 56.50N 15.45 E
Orri, Pic d'-/Llorri 13 Nb 42.23N 1.12 E
Orša 6 Je 54.30N 30.24 E
Orsa 7 Df 61.07N 14.37 E
Orsasjön 8 Fc 61.05N 14.35 E
Orsay 12 Ef 48.42N 2.11 E
Orsjön 8 Gc 61.35N 16.20 E
Orsk 6 Le 51.12N 58.34 E
Orsova 15 Fe 44.42N 22.25 E
Ørsta 7 Be 62.12N 6.09 E
Örsundsbro 8 Ge 59.44N 17.18 E
Orta, Lago d'- 14 Ce 45.50N 8.25 E
Ortaca 24 Cd 36.49N 28.47 E
Ortakent 15 Kl 37.02N 27.21 E
Ortaklar 15 Kl 37.53N 27.30 E
Orta Nova 14 Ji 41.19N 15.42 E
Orte 14 Gh 42.27N 12.23 E
Ortegal, Cabo- 13 Ea 43.45N 7.53W
Ortenberg 12 Ld 50.21N 9.03 E
Orthez 11 Fk 43.29N 0.46W
Orthon, Rio- 54 Ef 10.50S 66.04W
Ortigueira [Braz.] 56 Jb 24.12S 50.55W
Ortigueira [Sp.] 13 Fa 43.34N 6.44W
Ortisei / Sankt Ulrich 14 Fd 46.34N 11.40 E
Ortiz [Mex.] 48 Dc 28.15N 110.43W
Ortiz [Ven.] 50 Ch 9.37N 67.17W
Ortlergruppe/Ortles 14 Ed 46.30N 10.40 E
Ortles/Ortlergruppe 14 Ed 46.30N 10.40 E
Ortolo 11a Ab 41.30N 8.55 E
Ortona 14 Ih 42.21N 14.24 E
Ortonville 45 Hd 45.19N 96.27W
Orto-Tokoj 18 Kc 42.20N 76.02 E
Örtze 10 Fd 52.40N 9.57 E
Orukuizu 64a Ac 7.10N 134.17 E
Orūmīyeh 22 Gf 37.33N 45.04 E
Orūmīyeh, Daryācheh-ye-= Urmia, Lake- (EN) 21 Gf 37.40N 45.30 E
Oruro [2] 54 Eg 18.40S 67.30W
Oruro 53 Jg 17.59S 67.09W
Orust 8 Df 58.10N 11.38 E
Orūzgān [3] 23 Kc 33.15N 66.00 E
Orūzgān 23 Kc 32.56N 66.38 E
Orval, Abbaye d'- 12 He 49.38N 5.22 E
Orvault 11 Eg 47.16N 1.37W
Orvieto 14 Gh 42.43N 12.07 E
Orville Escarpment 66 Qf 75.45S 65.30W
Orvilos, Óros- 15 Gh 41.23N 23.36 E
Orwell 12 Dc 51.58N 1.18 E
Orxois 12 Fe 49.08N 3.12 E
Orz 10 Rd 52.50N 21.30 E
Orzinuovi 14 De 45.24N 9.55 E
Orzyc 10 Rd 52.47N 21.13 E
Orzysz 10 Rc 53.49N 21.56 E
Oš 19 Hg 40.32N 72.50 E
Os 7 Ce 62.30N 11.12 E
Osa 19 Fd 57.17N 55.26 E
Oša 8 Lh 56.21N 26.29 E
Osa 10 Oc 53.33N 18.45 E
Osa, Peninsula de- 47 Hg 8.35N 83.33W
Osage 45 Je 43.17N 92.49W
Osage River 43 Id 38.35N 91.57W
Osaka 29 Ed 35.57N 137.14 E
Ōsaka 22 Pf 34.40N 135.30 E
Osaka Bay (EN)=Ōsaka-Wan 28 Mg 34.36N 135.27 E
Ōsaka-Fu [2] 28 Mg 34.45N 135.35 E
Osakarovka 19 He 50.32N 72.39 E
Ōsaka-Wan=Osaka Bay (EN) 28 Mg 34.36N 135.27 E
Osām 15 Hf 43.42N 24.51 E
Osan 28 If 37.09N 127.04 E
Osasco 55 If 23.32S 46.46W
Osat 14 Nf 44.02N 19.20 E
Osawatomie 45 Ig 38.31N 94.57W
Osborne 45 Gg 39.26N 98.42W
Osburger Hochwald 12 Ie 49.40N 6.50 E
Osby 7 Ch 56.22N 13.59 E
Osceola [Ar.-U.S.] 45 Li 35.42N 89.58W
Osceola [Ia.-U.S.] 43 Ic 41.02N 93.46W
Osceola [Mo.-U.S.] 45 Jh 38.03N 93.42W
Oschatz 10 Je 51.18N 13.07 E
Oschersleben 10 Hd 52.02N 11.15 E
Oschiri 14 Dj 40.43N 9.06 E
Osen 7 Cd 64.18N 10.31 E
Osered 16 Ld 50.01N 40.48 E
Osetr 16 Kb 55.00N 38.45 E
Ōse-Zaki 28 Jh 32.38N 128.42 E
Oshamanbe 28 Pc 42.30N 140.22 E
Oshawa 42 Jh 43.54N 78.51W
Oshekehia Lake 37 Bc 18.08S 15.45 E
Oshika 29 Gb 38.17N 141.31 E
Oshika-Hantō 28 Pe 38.22N 141.27 E
Oshikango 37 Bc 17.22S 15.55 E
Oshima 29 Ce 33.55N 132.11 E
Ō-Shima [Jap.] 29 De 33.28N 135.50 E
Ō-Shima [Jap.] 29 Ae 33.30N 129.33 E
Ō-Shima [Jap.] 29 Ae 32.34N 128.54 E
Ō-Shima [Jap.] 29 Be 33.54N 130.27 E
Ō-Shima [Jap.] 27 Oe 34.45N 139.30 E
Ōshima [Jap.] 29 Fd 34.44N 139.20 E
Ō-Shima [Jap.] 29 Bf 31.32N 131.25 E
Ō-Shima [Jap.] 29 De 33.38N 134.30 E
Ō-Shima [Jap.] 29 Cd 34.10N 133.05 E
Ōshima [Jap.] 29 Ae 33.04N 129.36 E
Ō-Shima [Jap.] 28 Od 41.30N 139.15 E
Ō-Shima [Jap.] 28 Jh 32.04N 128.26 E
Oshima-Hantō 28 Pd 41.40N 140.30 E
Ōshima-Kaikyō 29b Ba 28.10N 129.15 E
Oshkosh [Nb.-U.S.] 45 Ef 41.24N 102.21W
Oshkosh [Wi.-U.S.] 43 Jc 44.01N 88.33W
Oshnaviyeh 24 Kd 37.02N 45.06 E
Oshogbo 31 Hh 7.46N 4.34 E
Oshtorān Kūh 23 Gc 33.20N 49.16 E
Oshtorīnān 24 Me 34.01N 48.38 E
Oshwe 36 Cc 3.24S 19.30 E
Osich'ŏn-ni 28 Jd 41.25N 128.16 E
Osijek 6 Hf 45.33N 18.42 E
Osilo 14 Cj 40.45N 8.40 E
Osimo 14 Hg 43.28N 13.29 E
Osinki 7 Lj 52.52N 49.31 E
Osinniki 20 Df 53.37N 87.31 E
Osipaonica 15 Ee 44.33N 21.04 E
Osipoviči 16 Fc 53.19N 28.40 E
Osječenica 14 Kf 44.29N 16.17 E
Oskaloosa 45 Jf 41.18N 92.39W
Oskarshamn 7 Dh 57.16N 16.26 E
Oskarström 8 Eh 56.48N 12.58 E
Oskélanéo 44 Ja 48.08N 75.05W
Oskino 20 Fd 60.48N 107.58 E
Öskjuvatn 7a Cb 65.02N 16.45W
Oskol 16 Je 49.06N 37.25 E
Oskū 24 Ld 37.55N 46.06 E
Oslava 10 Mg 49.05N 16.22 E
Ösling 11 Le 49.55N 6.00 E
Osljanka, Gora- 17 Ig 59.10N 58.33 E
Oslo [2] 7 Cg 59.55N 10.45 E
Oslo 6 Hd 59.55N 10.45 E
Oslofjorden 5 Hd 59.20N 10.35 E
Osmānābād 25 Fe 18.10N 76.03 E
Osmancık 24 Fb 40.59N 34.49 E
Osmaneli 15 Ni 40.22N 30.01 E
Osmaniye 23 Eb 37.05N 36.14 E
Osmino 8 Mf 58.54N 29.15 E
Ošmjanskaja Vozvyšennost 8 Kj 54.30N 26.00 E
Ošmjany 16 Db 54.27N 25.57 E
Ösmo 8 Gf 58.59N 17.54 E
Osmussaar/Osmussar 8 Je 59.20N 23.15 E
Osmussar/Osmussaar 8 Je 59.20N 23.15 E
Osnabrück 6 Ge 52.16N 8.03 E
Osning 12 Kb 52.10N 8.05 E
Oso, Sierra del- 48 Gd 26.00N 105.25W
Osobłoga 10 Nf 50.27N 17.58 E
Osogovske Planine 15 Fg 42.10N 22.30 E
Osor 14 If 44.42N 14.24 E
Osório 56 Jc 29.54S 50.16W
Osorno 53 Ij 40.34S 73.09W
Osoyoos 42 Fg 49.02N 119.28W
Osøyra 7 Af 60.11N 5.28 E
Ospino 50 Bh 9.18N 69.27W
Osprey Reef 57 Ff 13.55S 146.40 E
Oss 11 Lc 51.46N 5.31 E
Ossa, Mount- 57 Fi 41.54S 146.01 E
Óssa, Óros- 15 Fj 39.49N 22.40 E
Ossabaw Island 44 Gj 31.47N 81.06W
Ossa de Montiel 13 Jf 38.58N 2.45W
Osse 11 Gj 44.07N 0.17 E
Ossining 44 Ke 41.10N 73.52W
Ossjøen 8 Dc 61.15N 11.55 E
Ošskaja Oblast [3] 19 Hg 40.45N 73.20 E
Ossora 20 Le 59.15N 163.02 E
Östanvik 8 Fc 61.10N 15.13 E
Ostaškov 19 Dd 57.09N 33.07 E
Ostbevern 12 Jb 52.03N 7.51 E
Oste 10 Fc 53.33N 9.10 E
Ostende/Oostende 11 Ic 51.14N 2.55 E
Oster 16 Gd 50.55N 30.57 E
Oster 16 Gd 50.53N 30.55 E
Oster 16 Gc 53.47N 31.45 E
Osterburg in der Altmark 10 Hd 52.47N 11.44 E
Österbybruk 8 Gd 60.12N 17.54 E
Österdalälven 7 Df 60.33N 15.08 E
Østerdalen 7 Cf 62.00N 10.40 E
Osterfjorden 8 Ad 60.30N 5.20 E
Österforse 8 Ga 63.09N 17.01 E
Östergarnsholm 8 Hg 57.25N 19.00 E
Östergötland 8 Ff 58.25N 15.35 E
Östergötland [2] 7 Dg 58.25N 15.45 E
Osterholz Scharmbeck 10 Ec 53.14N 8.48 E
Österlen 8 Fi 55.30N 14.10 E
Ostermark/Teuva 7 Ee 62.29N 21.44 E
Osterode am Harz 10 Ge 51.44N 10.11 E
Osterøya 7 Af 60.35N 5.35 E
Österreich = Austria (EN) [1] 6 Hf 47.30N 14.00 E
Östersjön=Baltic Sea (EN) 5 Hd 57.00N 19.00 E
Østersøen=Baltic Sea (EN) 5 Hd 57.00N 19.00 E
Östersund 6 Hc 63.11N 14.39 E
Osterwick, Rosendahl- 12 Jb 52.01N 7.12 E
Østfold [2] 7 Cg 59.20N 11.30 E
Ostfriesische Inseln=East Frisian Islands (EN) 10 Dc 53.45N 7.25 E
Ostfriesland=East Friesland (EN) 10 Dc 53.20N 7.40 E
Østgrønland=East Greenland (EN) [2] 41 Id 72.00N 35.00W
Östhammar 7 Ed 60.16N 18.22 E
Osthofen 12 Ke 49.42N 8.20 E
Östmark 8 Ed 60.17N 12.45 E
Ostrach 10 Fh 48.05N 9.25 E
Östra Silen 8 Ee 59.15N 12.20 E
Ostrava 6 Hf 49.50N 18.17 E
Ostrhauderfehn 12 Ja 53.08N 7.37 E
Oströda 10 Pc 53.43N 19.59 E
Ostrog 16 Ed 50.19N 26.32 E
Ostrogožsk 19 De 50.52N 39.05 E
Ostrołęka [2] 10 Rc 53.05N 21.35 E
Ostrołęka 10 Rc 53.06N 21.34 E
Ostrošicki Gorodok 8 Lj 54.03N 27.46 E
Ostrov 10 Vd 52.48N 26.01 E
Ostrov [Czech.] 10 If 50.18N 12.57 E
Ostrov [Rom.] 15 Ke 44.07N 27.22 E
Ostrov 19 Cd 57.23N 28.22 E
Ostrov 8 Mf 58.28N 28.44 E
Ostrovec 8 Lj 54.38N 26.06 E
Ostrovicës, Mali i- 15 Di 40.34N 20.27 E
Ostrovskoje 7 Kh 57.50N 42.13 E
Ostrov Zmeiny 16 Gg 45.15N 30.12 E
Ostrowiec Świętokrzyski 10 Rf 50.57N 21.23 E
Ostrów Lubelski 10 Se 51.30N 22.52 E
Ostrów Mazowiecka 10 Rd 52.49N 21.54 E
Ostrów Wielkopolski 10 Ne 51.39N 17.49 E
Ostryna 10 Uc 53.41N 24.37 E
Ostrzeszów 10 Ne 51.25N 17.57 E
Ostsee=Baltic Sea (EN) 5 Hd 57.00N 19.00 E
Oststeirisches Hügelland 14 Jd 47.00N 15.45 E
Osttirol [2] 14 Gd 46.55N 12.30 E
Ostuni 14 Lj 40.44N 17.35 E
Osumi 15 Ci 40.48N 19.52 E
Ōsumi 29 Bf 31.36N 130.59 E
Ōsumi-Hantō 29 Bf 31.15N 130.50 E
Osumi Islands (EN)=Ōsumi-Shotō 21 Pf 30.35N 130.59 E
Ōsumi-Shotō=Osumi Islands (EN) 21 Pf 30.35N 130.59 E
Osuna 13 Gg 37.14N 5.07W
Osveja 8 Mi 55.59N 28.10 E
Osvejskoje, Ozero- 8 Mh 56.00N 28.15 E
Oswego 43 Lc 43.27N 76.31W
Oswestry 9 Ji 52.52N 3.04W

Index Symbols

[1] Independent Nation
[2] State, Region
[3] District, County
[4] Municipality
[5] Colony, Dependency
Continent
Physical Region
Historical or Cultural Region
Mount, Mountain
Volcano
Hill
Mountains, Mountain Range
Hills, Escarpment
Plateau, Upland
Pass, Gap
Plain, Lowland
Delta
Salt Flat
Valley, Canyon
Crater, Cave
Karst Features
Depression
Polder
Desert, Dunes
Forest, Woods
Heath, Steppe
Oasis
Cape, Point
Coast, Beach
Cliff
Peninsula
Isthmus
Sandbank
Island
Atoll
Rock, Reef
Islands, Archipelago
Rocks, Reefs
Coral Reef
Well, Spring
Geyser
River, Stream
Waterfall Rapids
River Mouth, Estuary
Lake
Salt Lake
Intermittent Lake
Reservoir
Swamp, Pond
Canal
Glacier
Ice Shelf, Pack Ice
Ocean
Sea
Gulf, Bay
Strait, Fjord
Lagoon
Bank
Seamount
Tablemount
Ridge
Shelf
Basin
Escarpment, Sea Scarp
Fracture
Trench, Abyss
National Park, Reserve
Point of Interest
Recreation Site
Cave, Cavern
Historic Site
Ruins
Wall, Walls
Church, Abbey
Temple
Scientific Station
Airport
Port
Lighthouse
Mine
Tunnel
Dam, Bridge

Oświęcim 10 Pf 50.03N 19.12 E
Osyka 45 Kk 31.00N 90.28W
Ōta 29 Fc 36.18N 139.22 E
Ota 29 Ec 35.56N 136.03 E
Otago [2] 62 Cf 45.00 S 169.10 E
Otago Peninsula 62 Df 45.50 S 170.45 E
Ōtake 28 Lg 34.12N 132.13 E
Otakeho 62 Fc 39.33 S 174.03 E
Otaki 62 Fd 40.45 S 175.08 E
Ōtakime-Yama 29 Gc 37.22N 140.42 E
Otanoshike 29a Db 43.01N 144.16 E
Otar 19 Hg 43.31N 75.12 E
Otaru 27 Pc 43.13N 141.00 E
Otautau 62 Bg 46.09 S 168.00 E
Otava 10 Kg 49.26N 14.12 E
Otava 8 Lc 61.39N 27.04 E
Otavi 37 Bc 19.39 S 17.20 E
Ōtawara 28 Pf 36.52N 140.02 E
Otelu Roşu 15 Fd 45.32N 22.22 E
Otematata 62 Df 44.37 S 170.11 E
Otepää/Otepja 7 Gg 58.03N 26.30 E
Otepää, Vozvyšennost-/
Otepää Kõrgustik 8 Lf 58.00N 26.40 E
Otepää Kõrgustik/Otepää,
Vozvyšennost- 8 Lf 58.00N 26.40 E
Otepja/Otepää 7 Gg 58.03N 26.30 E
Oteros 47 Cc 26.55N 108.30W
Othain 12 He 49.31N 5.23 E
Othello 46 Fc 46.50N 119.10W
Othonoí 15 Cj 39.50N 19.25 E
Óthris Óros 15 Fj 39.02N 22.37 E
Oti 30 Hh 7.48N 0.08 E
Otira 62 De 42.51 S 171.33 E
Otish, Monts- 38 Md 52.45N 69.15W
Otjikondo 37 Bc 19.50 S 15.23 E
Otjimbingwe 37 Bd 22.21 S 16.08 E
Otjiwarongo 31 Ik 20.29 S 16.36 E
Otjiwarongo [3] 37 Bd 20.30 S 17.30 E
Otjosondjou, Omuramba- 30 Ij 19.55 S 20.00 E
Otjosondu 37 Bd 21.12 S 17.58 E
Otmuchowskie, Jezioro- 10 Nf 50.27N 17.15 E
Otnes 7 Cf 61.46N 11.12 E
Otobe 29a Bc 41.57N 140.08 E
Otočac 14 Jf 44.52N 15.14 E
Otofuke 29a Cb 42.59N 143.10 E
Otofuke-Gawa 29a Cb 42.56N 143.12 E
Otog Qi (Ulan) 27 Id 39.07N 108.00 E
Otoineppu 29a Ca 44.43N 142.16 E
Otok 14 Me 45.09N 18.53 E
Otopeni 15 Je 44.33N 26.04 E
Otorohanga 62 Fc 38.11 S 175.12 E
Otorten, Gora- 17 If 61.50N 59.13 E
Ōtoyo 29 Ce 33.46N 133.40 E
Otra 5 Gd 58.09N 8.00 E
Otradnaja 16 Lg 44.23N 41.31 E
Otradnoje, Ozero- 8 Nd 60.50N 30.25 E
Otradny 7 Mj 53.23N 51.24 E
Otranto 14 Mj 40.09N 18.30 E
Otranto, Canale d'-=
Otranto, Strait of- (EN) 5 Hg 40.00N 19.00 E
Otranto, Capo d'- 14 Mj 40.06N 18.31 E
Otranto, Strait of- (EN)=
Otranto, Canale d'- 5 Hg 40.00N 19.00 E
Otranto, Strait of- (EN)=
Otrantos, Kanali i- 15 Bi 40.00N 19.00 E
Otranto, Terra d'- 14 Mj 40.20N 18.15 E
Otrantos, Kanali i-=Otranto,
Strait of- (EN) 15 Bi 40.00N 19.00 E
Ötscher 14 Jc 47.51N 15.12 E
Ōtsu 28 Mg 35.00N 135.52 E
Ōtsuchi 28 Pe 39.21N 141.54 E
Ōtsuki [Jap.] 29 Fd 35.36N 138.54 E
Ōtsuki [Jap.] 29 Ce 32.50N 132.41 E
Otta 8 Cc 61.46N 9.31 E
Otta 7 Bf 61.46N 9.32 E
Otta 64d Bb 7.09N 151.54 E
Ottadalen 8 Bc 61.55N 8.00 E
Ottana 14 Dj 40.15N 9.05 E
Otta Pass 64d Bb 7.09N 151.53 E
Ottawa [Il.-U.S.] 45 Lf 41.21N 88.51W
Ottawa [Ks.-U.S.] 43 Hd 38.37N 95.16W
Ottawa [Oh.-U.S.] 44 Ee 41.02N 84.03W
Ottawa [Ont.-Can.] 39 Le 45.25N 75.42W
Ottawa Islands 38 Kd 59.30N 80.10W
Ottawa River 38 Le 45.20N 73.58W
Ottemby 7 Dh 56.16N 16.24 E
Otterberg 12 Je 49.30N 7.46 E
Otter Creek 44 Fk 29.19N 82.48W
Otterndorf 10 Ec 53.48N 8.54 E
Otteroy 8 Bb 62.40N 6.50 E
Otter Rapids 44 Ga 50.15N 81.45W
Otterup 8 Di 55.31N 10.24 E
Ottumwa 43 Ic 41.01N 92.25W
Ottweiler 12 Je 49.23N 7.10 E
Otukpa 34 Gd 7.05N 7.40 E
Otumpa 55 Ah 27.19 S 62.13W
Otuquis, Bañados de- 54 Gg 19.20 S 58.30W
Otuquis, Río- 55 Cd 19.41 S 58.20W
Oturkpo 34 Gd 7.13N 8.09 E
Otu Tolu Group 65b Bb 20.21 S 174.32W
Otuzco 54 Ce 7.54 S 78.35W
Otway, Cape- 59 Ig 38.52 S 143.31 E
Otwock 10 Rd 52.07N 21.16 E
Otynja 10 Uh 48.40N 24.57 E
Ötz 14 Ec 47.12N 10.54 E
Ötztaler Ache 14 Ec 47.14N 10.50 E
Ötztaler Alpen 10 Gi 46.45N 10.55 E
Ou 25 Kd 20.04N 102.13 E
'O'ua 65b Bb 20.02 S 174.41W
Oua 63b Ce 21.14 S 167.05 E
Ouachita, Lake- 45 Ji 34.40N 93.25W
Ouachita Mountains 38 Jf 34.40N 94.25W
Ouachita River 43 Ie 31.38N 91.49W
Ouadane 31 Ff 20.57N 11.35W
Ouaddaï [3] 35 Cc 13.00N 21.00 E
Ouaddaï 30 Jg 13.00N 21.00 E
Ouagadougou 31 Gg 12.22N 1.31W
Ouahigouya 31 Gg 13.35N 2.25W
Ouaka [3] 35 Cd 6.00N 21.00 E
Ouaka 30 Ih 4.59N 19.56 E
Oualata 32 Ff 17.18N 7.00W
Oualata, Dahr- 32 Ff 17.48N 7.24W
Oualidia 32 Fc 32.44N 9.02W
Ouallam 34 Fc 14.19N 2.05 E
Ouallene 32 He 24.35N 1.17 E
Ouanda-Djallé 35 Cd 8.54N 22.48 E
Ouandjia 35 Cd 8.35N 23.12 E
Ouandjia 35 Cd 9.35N 21.43 E
Ouango 35 Ce 4.19N 22.33 E
Ouangolodougou 34 Dd 9.58N 5.09W
Ouanne 11 Ig 47.57N 2.47 E
Ouarane 30 Ff 21.00N 10.00W
Ouargaye 34 Fc 11.32N 0.01 E
Ouargla 31 He 31.57N 5.20 E
Ouargla [3] 32 Id 30.00N 6.30 E
Ouarkziz, Jbel- 30 Gf 28.00N 8.20W
Ouarra 30 Jh 5.05N 24.26 E
Ouarsenis, Djebel- 13 Ni 35.53N 1.38 E
Ouarsenis, Massif de l'- 32 Hb 35.50N 2.05 E
Ouarzazate [3] 32 Fc 31.00N 6.30W
Ouarzazate 32 Fc 30.55N 6.55W
Oubangui 30 Ii 0.30 S 17.42 E
Ouborré, Pointe- 63b Dd 18.47 S 169.16 E
Ouche, Pays d'- 11 Gf 48.55N 0.45 E
Ōuchi 29 Gb 39.27N 140.06 E
Oud Beijerland 12 Gc 51.50N 4.26 E
Oude IJssel 12 Ic 52.00N 6.10 E
Oudenaarde/Audenarde 11 Jd 50.51N 3.36 E
Oudenbosch 12 Gc 51.35N 4.34 E
Oude Rijn 11 Kb 52.05N 4.20 E
Oudon 11 Fg 47.37N 0.42W
Oudtshoorn 31 Jl 33.35 S 22.14 E
Oued Ben Tili 32 Fd 25.48N 9.32W
Oued el Abtal 13 Mi 35.27N 0.41 E
Oued Fodda 13 Nh 36.11N 1.32 E
Oued Lili 13 Ni 35.31N 1.16 E
Oued Rhiou 32 Hb 35.58N 0.55 E
Oued-Taria 13 Mi 35.07N 0.05 E
Oued Tlelat 13 Li 35.33N 0.27W
Oued Zem 31 Ge 32.52N 6.34W
Ouégoa 63b Be 20.21 S 164.26 E
Ouéllé 34 Ed 7.18N 4.01W
Ouémé 30 Hh 6.29N 2.32 E
Ouémé [3] 34 Fd 7.00N 2.35 E
Ouen 63b Cf 22.26 S 166.48 E
Ouenza 32 Ib 35.57N 8.07 E
Ouenza, Djebel- 14 Co 35.57N 8.05 E
Ouessa 34 Ec 11.03N 2.47W
Ouessant, Ile d'- 11 Af 48.28N 5.05W
Ouesso 31 Ih 1.37N 16.04 E
Ouest [3] 34 Hd 5.20N 10.30 E
Ouest, Baie de l'- 64h Ab 13.15 S 176.13W
Ouezzane 32 Fc 34.48N 5.36W
Oughter, Lough- 9 Fg 54.00N 7.29W
Ouham [3] 35 Bd 7.00N 18.00 E
Ouham 30 Ih 9.18N 18.14 E
Ouham-Pendé [3] 35 Bd 7.00N 16.00 E
Ouidah 34 Fd 6.22N 2.05 E
Ouistreham 11 Fe 49.17N 0.15W
Ouistreham-Riva Bella 12 Be 49.17N 0.16W
Oujda [3] 32 Gc 33.00N 2.00W
Oujda 31 Ge 34.40N 1.54W
Oujeft 32 Ee 20.02N 13.03W
Oulainen 7 Fd 64.16N 24.57 E
Oulchy-le-Château 12 Fe 49.12N 3.21 E
Ouled Djellal 32 Ic 34.25N 5.04 E
Ouled Naïl, Monts des- 32 Hc 34.40N 3.25 E
Oulou, Bahr- 35 Cd 9.48N 21.32 E
Oulu [2] 7 Gd 65.00N 27.00 E
Oulu/Uleåborg 6 Ib 65.01N 25.30 E
Oulu, Lake- (EN)=
Oulujärvi 5 Ic 64.20N 27.15 E
Oulujärvi=Oulu, Lake- (EN) 5 Ic 64.20N 27.15 E
Oulujoki 5 Ib 65.01N 25.25 E
Oum Chalouba 31 Jg 15.48N 20.46 E
Oumé [3] 34 Dd 6.25N 5.30W
Oumé 34 Dd 6.23N 5.25W
Oum el Bouaghi [3] 32 Ib 35.30N 7.10 E
Oum el Bouaghi 32 Ib 35.53N 7.07 E
Oum er Rbia 30 Ge 33.19N 8.20W
Oum Hadjer 35 Bc 13.18N 19.41 E
Oumm ed Droûs Guebli,
Sebkhet- 32 Ee 24.03N 11.45W
Oumm ed Droûs Telli,
Sebkhet- 32 Ee 24.20N 11.30W
Ounasjoki 5 Ib 66.30N 25.45 E
Oundle 12 Bb 52.29N 0.28W
Ounianga 35 Cb 19.10N 20.30 E
Ounianga Kébir 31 Jg 19.04N 20.29 E
Ountivou 34 Fd 7.21N 1.34 E
Ouolossébougou 34 Dc 12.00N 7.55W
Oupeye 12 Hd 50.42N 5.39 E
Oupu 27 Ma 52.45N 126.00 E
Our 12 Ie 49.53N 6.18 E
Ouray 45 Cg 38.01N 107.40W
Ouray, Mount- 45 Cg 38.25N 106.14W
Ource 11 Kf 48.06N 4.23 E
Ourcq 11 Je 49.01N 3.01 E
Ourcq, Canal de l'- 11 If 48.51N 2.22 E
Ourém 54 Id 1.33 S 47.06W
Ouricuri 54 Je 7.35 S 40.05W
Ourinhos 53 Lh 22.59 S 49.52W
Ouro, Rio do- 55 Ha 13.20 S 48.59W
Ouro Fino 55 If 22.17 S 46.22W
Ouro Prêto 54 Jh 20.23 S 43.30W
Ourthe [Bel.] 11 Ld 50.38N 5.35 E
Ourville-en-Caux 12 Ce 49.44N 0.36 E
Ous 19 Gc 60.55N 61.31 E
Ōu-Sanmyaku 28 Pe 39.00N 141.00 E
Ouse [Eng.-U.K.] 9 Nk 50.47N 0.03 E
Ouse [Eng.-U.K.] 9 Mh 53.42N 0.41W
Oust 11 Dg 47.35N 2.06W
Outagouna 34 Fb 15.11N 0.43 E
Outaouais, Rivière- 38 Le 45.20N 73.58W
Outardes, Rivière aux- 42 Kg 49.05N 68.23W
Outat Oulad El Hajj 32 Gc 33.21N 3.42W
Outer Dowsing 9 Oh 53.25N 1.05 E
Outer Hebrides 9 Fd 57.50N 7.32W
Outer Santa Barbara
Passage 46 Fj 33.10N 118.30W
Outer Silver Pit 9 Og 54.05N 2.00 E
Outjo 31 Ik 20.08 S 16.08 E
Outjo [3] 37 Ac 19.30 S 14.30 E
Outlook 46 La 51.30N 107.03W
Outokumpu 7 Ge 62.44N 29.01 E
Outram Mountain 46 Eb 49.19N 121.05W
Outreau 12 Dd 50.42N 1.35 E
Out Skerries 9 Ma 60.30N 0.50W
Outwell 12 Cb 52.37N 0.14 E
Ouvéa, Ile- 57 Hg 20.35 S 166.35 E
Ouvèze 11 Kk 43.59N 4.51 E
Ouxian 28 Ej 28.58N 118.53 E
Ouyen 59 Ig 35.04 S 142.20 E
Ouyou Bézédinga 34 Hb 16.32N 13.15 E
Ouzera 13 Oh 36.15N 2.51 E
Ovacık [Tur.] 24 Ed 36.11N 33.40 E
Ovacık [Tur.] 24 Hc 39.22N 39.13 E
Ovada 14 Cf 44.38N 8.38 E
Ova Gölü 15 Mm 36.16N 29.22 E
Ovakent 15 Lk 38.06N 28.02 E
Ovalau Island 63d Bb 17.40 S 178.48 E
Ovalle 53 Ii 30.36 S 71.12W
Oval Peak 46 Eb 48.15N 120.25W
Ovamboland 37 Bc 18.30 S 16.00 E
Ovamboland [3] 37 Bc 18.00 S 16.00 E
Ovan 36 Bb 0.30N 12.10 E
Ovanåker 7 Df 61.21N 15.54 E
Ovar 13 Dd 40.52N 8.38W
Ovau 63a Cb 6.48 S 156.02 E
Ovejas 49 Ji 9.32N 75.14W
Overath 12 Jd 50.57N 7.18 E
Øverbygd 7 Eb 69.01N 19.18 E
Overflakke 11 Kc 51.45N 4.10 E
Overhalla 7 Cd 64.30N 12.00 E
Overije 12 Gd 50.46N 4.32 E
Overijssel [3] 12 Ib 52.25N 6.30 E
Överkalix 7 Fc 66.19N 22.50 E
Overland Park 45 Ig 38.59N 94.40W
Övermark/Ylimarkku 8 Ib 62.37N 21.28 E
Overpelt 12 Hc 51.12N 5.25 E
Overri 34 Gd 5.29N 7.02 E
Overton 46 Hh 36.33N 114.27W
Övertorneå 7 Fc 66.23N 23.40 E
Överum 8 Gg 57.59N 16.19 E
Ovidiu 15 Le 44.16N 28.34 E
Oviedo [3] 13 Ga 43.20N 6.00W
Oviedo [Dom.Rep.] 49 Le 17.47N 71.22W
Oviedo [Sp.] 6 Fg 43.22N 5.50W
Oviši 8 Ig 57.34N 21.35 E
Ovo, Capo dell'- 14 Lj 40.18N 17.30 E
Øvre Årdal 7 Bf 61.19N 7.48 E
Övre Fryken 8 Ed 60.00N 13.05 E
Övre Soppero 7 Eb 68.05N 21.41 E
Ovruč 19 Ce 51.19N 28.50 E
Ovsjanka 20 Hf 53.32N 126.58 E
Owaka 62 Cg 46.27 S 169.40 E
Owando 31 Ii 0.29 S 15.55 E
Ōwani 28 Pd 40.31N 140.35 E
Owase 28 Ng 34.04N 136.12 E
Owatonna 43 Ic 44.05N 93.14W
Owego 44 Id 42.06N 76.16W
Owen, Mount- 62 Ed 41.33 S 172.32 E
Owendo 36 Ab 0.17N 9.30 E
Owen Falls Dam 36 Fb 0.24N 33.11 E
Owensboro 43 Jd 37.46N 87.07W
Owens Lake 46 Gh 36.25N 117.56W
Owen Sound 42 Jh 44.34N 80.56W
Owens River 46 Gh 36.31N 117.57W
Owen Stanley Range 57 Fe 9.20 S 148.00 E
Owl Creek Mountains 46 Ke 43.30N 108.35W
Ownay, Kowlal-e- 23 Kc 34.27N 68.22 E
Owo 34 Gd 7.11N 5.35 E
Owosso 44 Ed 43.00N 84.10W
Owyhee 46 Gf 41.57N 116.06W
Owyhee, Lake- 46 Ge 43.28N 117.20W
Owyhee Mountains 46 Ge 43.00N 116.45W
Owyhee River [U.S.] 46 Ge 43.40N 117.16W
Owyhee River [U.S.] 43 Dc 43.46N 117.02W
Oxberg 8 Fc 61.07N 14.10 E
Oxbow 45 Eb 49.14N 102.11W
Oxelösund 7 Dg 58.40N 17.06 E
Oxford 9 Lj 51.50N 1.30W
Oxford [Eng.-U.K.] 6 Fe 51.46N 1.15W
Oxford [Ms.-U.S.] 45 Li 34.22N 89.32W
Oxford [N.C.-U.S.] 44 Hg 36.19N 78.35W
Oxford [N.Z.] 62 Ee 43.17 S 172.11 E
Oxford Lake 42 Hf 54.50N 95.35W
Oxfordshire [3] 9 Lj 51.50N 1.20W
Oxia 15 Ek 38.18N 21.06 E
Oxkutzcab 48 Og 20.18N 89.25W
Oxnard 43 De 34.12N 119.11W
Ox or Slieve Gamph
Mountains/Sliabh
Gamh 9 Eg 54.10N 8.50W
Oxted 12 Bc 51.14N 0.01W
Oyabe 29 Ec 36.40N 136.52 E
Oyahue 53 Jh 21.08 S 68.45W
O-Yama 29 Fd 34.04N 139.31 E
Oyama 28 Of 36.21N 139.50 E
Ōyama 29 Ec 36.35N 137.18 E
Ōyano 29 Be 32.35N 130.27 E
Oyapock, Fleuve- 52 Ke 4.08N 51.40W
Oyem 31 Ih 1.37N 11.35 E
Oyen 46 Ja 51.22N 110.28W
Øyeren 8 De 59.50N 11.14 E
Oykel 9 Id 57.50N 4.25W
Oyo [2] 34 Fd 8.00N 3.50 E
Oyo [Nig.] 34 Fd 7.51N 3.56 E
Oyo [Sud.] 35 Fa 21.55N 36.06 E
Oyodo-Gawa 29 Bf 31.55N 131.28 E
Oyonnax 11 Lh 46.15N 5.40 E
Oyster Bay 59 Jh 42.10 S 148.10 E
Øystese 8 Bd 60.23N 6.13 E
Özalp 24 Jc 38.39N 43.59 E
Ozamiz 26 He 8.08N 123.50 E
Ozark 44 Ej 31.28N 85.38W
Ozark Plateau 38 Jf 37.00N 93.00W
Ozark Reservoir 45 Ii 35.25N 94.05W
Ozarks, Lake of the- 43 Id 37.39N 92.50W
Ózd 10 Qh 48.13N 20.18 E
Ozeblin 14 Jf 44.35N 15.53 E
Ozernoj, Zaliv- 20 Le 57.00N 163.20 E
Ozernovski 20 Kf 51.21N 156.32 E
Ozerny 16 Vd 51.08N 60.55 E
Ozersk 8 Ij 54.24N 21.59 E
Ozery 10 Uc 53.38N 24.18 E
Ozery 7 Ji 54.54N 38.32 E
Ožezdy 19 Gf 48.03N 67.09 E
Ozieri 14 Cj 40.35N 9.00 E
Ozinki 19 Ee 51.12N 49.47 E
Ožogina 20 Kc 66.12N 151.05 E
Ozona 43 Ge 30.43N 101.12W
Ozorków 10 Pe 51.58N 19.19 E
Ozouri 36 Ac 0.55 S 8.55 E
Ozren 14 Mf 44.37N 18.15 E
Ozren 14 Mg 43.59N 18.30 E
Ozren [Yugo.] 15 Ef 43.36N 21.54 E
Ōzu [Jap.] 29 Be 32.52N 130.52 E
Ōzu [Jap.] 28 Lh 33.30N 132.23 E
Ozurgeti (Maharadze) 19 Eg 41.53N 42.01 E

P

Pääjärvi 8 Kb 62.50N 24.45 E
Paama 63b Dc 16.28 S 168.13 E
Pa-an → Pha-an 25 Je 16.53N 97.38 E
Paar 10 Hh 48.45N 11.35 E
Paarl 31 Il 33.45S 18.56 E
Paauilo 65a Fc 20.03N 155.22W
Paavola 7 Fd 64.36N 25.12 E
Pabbay 9 Fd 57.47N 7.20W
Pabellón, Ensenada del- 48 Fe 24.27N 107.36W
Pabianice 10 Pe 51.40N 19.22 E
Pābna 25 Hd 24.00N 89.15 E
Pabradé/Pabrade 7 Fi 54.59N 25.50 E
Pabrade/Pabradé 7 Fi 54.59N 25.50 E
Pacaás Novos, Serra dos- 54 Ff 10.50 S 64.00W
Pacajá, Rio- 54 Hd 1.56 S 50.55W
Pacajus 54 Kd 4.10 S 38.28W
Pacaraima, Serra- 52 Je 4.30N 60.40W
Pacasmayo 54 Ce 7.24 S 79.34W
Paceco 14 Gm 37.59N 12.33 E
Pachala 35 Ed 7.10N 34.06 E
Pacheco 48 Eb 30.06N 108.21W
Pachino 14 Jn 36.43N 15.05 E
Pachitea, Río- 54 De 8.46 S 74.32W
Pachuca de Soto 47 Ed 20.07N 98.44W
Pacific-Antarctic Ridge (EN) 3 Kp 62.00 S 157.00W
Pacific City 46 Dd 45.12N 123.57W
Pacific Grove 46 Eh 36.38N 121.56W
Pacific Islands, Trust
Territory of the- 58 Ed 7.30N 134.30 E
Pacifico, Océano- = Pacific
Ocean (EN) 3 Ki 5.00N 155.00W
Pacific Ocean 3 Ki 5.00N 155.00W
Pacific Ocean (EN)=Kita-
Taiheiyō 60 Ch 22.00N 167.00 E
Pacific Ocean (EN)=
Pacífico, Océano- 3 Ki 5.00N 155.00W
Pacific Ocean (EN)=
Pacifique, Océan- 3 Ki 5.00N 155.00W
Pacific Ocean (EN)=
Taiheiyō 3 Ki 5.00N 155.00W
Pacific Ocean (EN)=Tihi
Okean 3 Ki 5.00N 155.00W
Pacific Ranges 42 Ef 50.55N 125.10W
Pacifique, Océan-=Pacific
Ocean (EN) 3 Ki 5.00N 155.00W
Packsattel 14 Id 46.58N 14.58 E
Pacuí, Rio- 55 Jc 16.46 S 45.01W
Pacuneiro, Rio- 55 Fa 13.02 S 53.25W
Pacy-sur-Eure 12 De 49.01N 1.23 E
Paczków 10 Mf 50.27N 17.00 E
Padana, Pianura-=Po
Valley (EN) 5 Gf 45.20N 10.00 E
Padang 22 Mj 0.57 S 100.21 E
Padangsidempuan 26 Cf 1.22N 99.16 E
Padangtikar, Pulau- 26 Eg 0.50 S 109.30 E
Padany 7 He 63.19N 33.25 E
Padasjoki 8 Kc 61.21N 25.17 E
Padauiri, Rio- 54 Fd 0.15 S 64.05W
Paddle Prairie 42 Fe 58.02N 117.50W
Paderborn 10 Ee 51.43N 8.46 E
Paderborn-Elsen 12 Kc 51.44N 8.41 E
Paderborn-Schloß Neuhaus 12 Kc 51.44N 8.42 E
Padeş, Vîrful- 15 Fd 45.40N 22.20 E
Padilla 54 Fg 19.19 S 64.20W
Padina 15 Ke 44.50N 27.07 E
Padornelo, Portillo del- 13 Fb 42.03N 6.50W
Padova = Padua (EN) 14 Fe 45.25N 11.53 E
Padre, Morro do- 55 Ic 16.48 S 47.35W
Padre Bernardo 55 Hb 15.21 S 48.30W
Padre Island 43 Hf 27.00N 97.15W
Padrón 13 Db 42.44N 8.40W
Padua (EN) = Padova 14 Fe 45.25N 11.53 E
Paducah [Ky.-U.S.] 39 Kf 37.05N 88.36W
Paducah [Tx.-U.S.] 45 Fi 34.01N 100.18W
Padula 14 Jj 40.20N 15.39 E
Paea 65e Fc 17.41 S 149.35W
Paegam-san 28 Id 40.35N 126.15 E
Paengnyong-Do 27 Ld 38.00N 124.40 E
Paeroa 61 Eg 37.23 S 175.41 E
Paestum 14 Jj 40.25N 15.01 E
Paeu 63c Bb 11.22 S 166.50 E
Pafuri 37 Ed 22.26 S 31.20 E
Pag 14 Jf 44.27N 15.03 E
Pag 14 If 44.30N 15.00 E
Pagadian 26 He 7.49N 123.25 E
Pagai, Kepulauan-=Pagi
Islands (EN) 21 Lj 2.45 S 100.00 E
Pagai Selatan 26 Dg 3.00 S 100.20 E
Pagai Utara 26 Cg 2.42 S 100.07 E
Pagan Island 57 Fc 18.07N 145.46 E
Pagasitikós Kólpos 15 Fj 39.15N 23.00 E
Pagatan 26 Gg 3.36 S 115.56 E
Pagat Point 64c Bb 13.30N 144.53 E
Page 46 Jh 36.57N 111.27W
Pagégiai 8 Ii 55.09N 21.54 E
Paget, Mount- 66 Ad 54.26 S 36.33W
Pagi Islands (EN)=Pagai,
Kepulauan- 21 Lj 2.45 S 100.00 E
Paglia 14 Gh 42.42N 12.11 E
Pago Bay 64c Bb 13.25N 144.48 E
Pagoda Point 21 Lh 15.57N 94.15 E
Pāgodār 24 Qh 28.10N 57.22 E
Pago Pago 58 Jf 14.16 S 170.42W
Pago Pago Harbor 65c Cb 14.17 S 170.40W
Pago Redondo 55 Ci 29.35 S 59.13W
Pagosa Springs 45 Ch 37.16N 107.01W
Pagoua Bay 51g Ba 15.32N 61.17W
Pagwa River 45 Na 50.01N 85.10W
Pahači 20 Ld 60.30N 169.00 E
Pahala 65a Fd 19.12N 155.29W
Pàhara, Laguna- 49 Ff 14.18N 83.15W
Pahiatua 62 Fd 40.27 S 175.50 E
Pahkāing Bum 21 Lg 26.00N 95.30 E
Pahoa 65a Gd 19.30N 154.57W
Pahokee 44 Gl 26.49N 80.40W
Pahtakor 18 Fd 40.16N 67.55 E
Pahute Mesa 46 Gh 37.20N 116.40W
Païa 63b Dc 16.35 S 168.12 E
Paide/Pajde 7 Fg 58.57N 25.35 E
Paignton 9 Jk 50.28N 3.30W
Päijänne 5 Ic 61.35N 23.30 E
Päïkon Óros 15 Fi 40.56N 22.21 E
Paila 48 He 25.39N 102.07W
Pailîn 25 Kf 12.51N 102.36 E
Pailitas 49 Ki 8.58N 73.38W
Pailolo Channel 65a Eb 21.05N 156.42W
Paimio/Pemar 8 Jd 60.27N 22.42 E
Paimionjoki 8 Jd 60.25N 22.40 E
Paimpol 11 Cf 48.46N 3.03W
Painan 26 Dg 1.21 S 100.34 E
Paine, Mount- 66 Mg 86.46 S 147.32W
Painel 55 Gh 27.55 S 50.06W
Painesville 44 Ge 41.43N 81.15W
Painted Desert 43 Ed 36.00N 111.20W
Paintsville 44 Fg 37.49N 82.48W
Pais do Vinho 13 Ec 41.15N 7.55W
Paisley 9 If 55.50N 4.26W
Paita 54 Be 5.06 S 81.07W
Païta 63b Cf 22.08 S 166.22 E
Paiva 13 Dc 41.04N 8.16W
Paj 7 If 61.43N 34.28 E
Pajala 7 Fc 67.12N 23.22 E
Pajares, Puerto de- 13 Ga 43.00N 5.46W
Pajaros, Punta- 48 Ph 19.36N 87.25W
Pajaros Point 51a Db 18.31N 64.18W
Pajatén 54 Ce 7.29 S 77.22W
Pajde/Paide 7 Fg 58.57N 25.35 E
Pajęczno 10 Oe 51.09N 19.00 E
Pajer, Gora- 19 Gb 66.40N 64.20 E
Paj-Hoj 5 Mb 69.00N 62.30 E
Pajule 36 Fb 2.58N 32.56 E
Pakanbaru 22 Mi 0.32N 101.27 E
Pakaraima Mountains 54 Fb 4.05N 61.30W
Pakch'on 28 He 39.44N 125.35 E
Pakhiá 15 Im 36.16N 25.50 E
Pakhna 24 Ee 34.46N 32.48 E
Pákhnes 15 Gn 35.18N 23.58 E
Paki 34 Gc 11.30N 8.09 E
Pakima 36 Dc 3.21 S 24.06 E
Pakin Atoll 57 Gd 7.04N 157.48 E
Pakistan [1] 22 Ig 30.00N 70.00 E
Pakleni Otoci 14 Kg 43.10N 16.23 E
Pakokku 25 Jd 21.17N 95.06 E
Pakowki Lake 46 Jb 49.22N 110.57W
Pak Phanang 25 Kg 8.21N 100.12 E
Pakrac 14 Le 45.26N 17.12 E
Pakruois/Pakruojis 7 Fi 55.57N 23.50 E
Pakruojis/Pakruois 7 Fi 55.57N 23.50 E
Paks 10 Oj 46.38N 18.52 E
Paktīā [3] 23 Kc 33.30N 69.30 E
Pakwach 36 Fb 2.28N 31.30 E
Pakxé 22 Mh 15.07N 105.47 E
Pakxèng 25 Kd 20.10N 102.40 E
Pala 35 Ad 9.22N 14.54 E
Palacca Point 49 Kc 21.15N 73.26W
Palacios [Arg.] 55 Bj 30.43 S 61.37W
Palacios [Tx.-U.S.] 45 Hl 28.42N 96.13W
Palafrugell 13 Pc 41.55N 3.10 E
Palagruža 14 Kh 42.24N 16.15 E
Palaiokastrítsa 15 Cj 39.40N 19.41 E
Palaiokhóra 15 Gn 35.14N 23.41 E
Palaiseau 12 Ef 48.43N 2.15 E
Palamás 15 Fj 39.28N 22.05 E
Palamós 13 Pc 41.51N 3.08 E
Palamuse/Palamuze 8 Lf 58.39N 26.35 E
Palamut 15 Kk 38.59N 27.41 E
Palamuze/Palamuse 8 Lf 58.39N 26.35 E
Palana 22 Rd 59.07N 159.58 E
Palancia 13 Le 39.40N 0.12W
Palanga 19 Cd 55.57N 21.05 E
Palangkaraya 26 Fg 2.16 S 113.56 E
Pālanpur 25 Ed 24.10N 72.26 E

Index Symbols

[1] Independent Nation
[2] State, Region
[3] District, County
[4] Municipality
[5] Colony, Dependency
Continent
Physical Region
Historical or Cultural Region
Mount, Mountain
Volcano
Hill
Mountains, Mountain Range
Hills, Escarpment
Plateau, Upland
Pass, Gap
Plain, Lowland
Delta
Salt Flat
Valley, Canyon
Crater, Cave
Karst Features
Depression
Polder
Desert, Dunes
Forest, Woods
Heath, Steppe
Oasis
Cape, Point
Coast, Beach
Cliff
Peninsula
Isthmus
Sandbank
Island
Atoll
Rock, Reef
Islands, Archipelago
Rocks, Reefs
Coral Reef
Well, Spring
Geyser
River, Stream
Waterfall Rapids
River Mouth, Estuary
Lake
Salt Lake
Intermittent Lake
Reservoir
Swamp, Pond
Canal
Glacier
Ice Shelf, Pack Ice
Ocean
Sea
Gulf, Bay
Strait, Fjord
Lagoon
Bank
Seamount
Tablemount
Ridge
Shelf
Basin
Escarpment, Sea Scarp
Fracture
Trench, Abyss
National Park, Reserve
Point of Interest
Recreation Site
Cave, Cavern
Historic Site
Ruins
Wall, Walls
Church, Abbey
Temple
Scientific Station
Airport
Port
Lighthouse
Mine
Tunnel
Dam, Bridge

Palaoa Point	65a Ec	20.44N	156.58W	
Palapye	31 Jk	22.33S	27.08 E	
Palasa	26 Hf	0.29N	120.24 E	
Palatka [Fl.-U.S.]	43 Kf	29.39N	81.38W	
Palatka	20 Kd	60.05N	151.00 E	
Palau (EN) = Belau	58 Ed	7.30N	134.30 E	
Palau [5]	58 Ed	7.30N	134.30 E	
Palau Islands	57 Ed	7.30N	134.30 E	
Palauli	65c Aa	13.44S	172.16W	
Palauli Bay	65c Aa	13.47S	172.14W	
Palau Trench (EN)	60 Af	6.30N	134.30 E	
Palavas-les-Flots	11 Jk	43.32N	3.56 E	
Palaw	25 Jf	12.58N	98.39 E	
Palawan	21 Ni	9.30N	118.30 E	
Palawan Passage	26 Gd	10.00N	118.00 E	
Palayan	26 Hc	15.33N	121.06 E	
Pālayankottai	25 Fg	8.43N	77.44 E	
Palazzo, Punta-	11a Aa	42.22N	8.33 E	
Palazzolo Acreide	14 Im	37.04N	14.54 E	
Palazzolo sull'Oglio	14 De	45.36N	9.53 E	
Paldiski	19 Cd	59.20N	24.06 E	
Pale di San Martino	14 Fd	46.14N	11.53 E	
Paleleh	26 Hf	1.04N	121.57 E	
Palembang	22 Mj	2.55S	104.45 E	
Palena	14 Ii	41.59N	14.08 E	
Palencia [3]	13 Hb	42.25N	4.30W	
Palencia	13 Hb	42.01N	4.32W	
Palen Lake	46 Hj	33.46N	115.12W	
Palenque	39 Jh	17.30N	92.00W	
Palenque [Mex.]	48 Ni	17.31N	91.58W	
Palenque [Pan.]	49 Hi	9.13N	79.41W	
Palenque, Punta-	49 Ld	18.14N	70.09W	
Palermo	6 Hh	38.07N	13.22 E	
Palermo, Golfo di-	14 Hl	38.10N	13.25 E	
Palestine	43 He	31.46N	95.38W	
Palestine (EN)	23 Dc	32.15N	34.47 E	
Palestrina	14 Gi	41.50N	12.53 E	
Pālghāt	25 Ff	10.47N	76.39 E	
Palgrave Point	37 Ad	20.28S	13.16 E	
Palhoça	55 Hh	27.38S	48.40W	
Pāli	25 Ec	25.46N	73.20 E	
Palinuro	14 Jj	40.02N	15.17 E	
Palinuro, Capo-	14 Jj	40.02N	15.16 E	
Palisades Reservoir	46 Je	43.04N	111.26W	
Paliseul	12 He	49.54N	5.08 E	
Palivere	8 Jf	59.00N	23.45 E	
Palizada	48 Mh	18.15N	92.05W	
Paljakka	7 Gd	64.45N	28.07 E	
Paljavaam	20 Mc	68.50N	170.50 E	
Paljenik	5 Hg	44.15N	17.36 E	
Pälkäne	8 Kc	61.20N	24.16 E	
Palkino	8 Mg	57.29N	28.10 E	
Palk Strait	21 Ji	10.00N	79.45 E	
Palla Bianca/Weißkugel	14 Ed	46.48N	10.44 E	
Pallars	13 Mb	42.25N	0.55 E	
Pallars, Montsent de-/Montseny	13 Nb	42.29N	1.02 E	
Pallasovka	19 Ee	50.03N	46.55 E	
Pallastunturi	7 Fb	68.06N	24.02 E	
Palliser, Cape-	61 Eh	41.37S	175.16 E	
Palliser, Iles-	57 Mf	15.30S	146.30W	
Palma [Moz.]	37 Gb	10.46S	40.28 E	
Palma [Sp.]	6 Gh	39.34N	2.39 E	
Palma, Badia de-/Palma, Bahia de-	13 Oe	39.27N	2.35 E	
Palma, Bahía de-/Palma, Badia de-	13 Oe	39.27N	2.35 E	
Palma, Rio-	54 If	12.33S	47.52W	
Palma, Sierra de la-	48 Id	26.00N	101.35W	
Palma del Rio	13 Gg	37.42N	5.17W	
Palma di Montechiaro	14 Hm	37.11N	13.46 E	
Palmar, Laguna del-	55 Bi	29.35S	60.42W	
Palmar, Rio-	49 Lh	10.11N	71.52W	
Palmar, Salto-	55 Cg	24.18S	59.18W	
Palmares	54 Ke	8.41S	35.36W	
Palmares do Sul	55 Gj	30.16S	50.31W	
Palmarito	54 Db	7.37N	70.10W	
Palmarola	14 Gj	40.55N	12.50 E	
Palmar Sur	47 Hg	8.58N	83.29W	
Palmas	56 Jc	26.30S	52.00W	
Palmas, Cape-	30 Gh	4.22N	7.44W	
Palmas, Golfo di-	14 Cl	39.00N	8.30 E	
Palmas Bellas	49 Gi	9.14N	80.05W	
Palma Soriano	47 Id	20.13N	76.00W	
Palm Bay	44 Gk	28.01N	80.35W	
Palm Beach	43 Kf	26.42N	80.02W	
Palmdale	46 Fi	34.35N	118.07W	
Palmeira	55 Gg	25.25S	50.00W	
Palmeira das Missões	56 Jc	27.55S	53.17W	
Palmeira dos Indios	54 Ke	9.25S	36.37W	
Palmeirais	54 Je	5.58S	43.04W	
Palmeiras, Rio-	55 Gb	15.25S	51.10W	
Palmeiras de Goiás	55 Hc	16.47S	49.53W	
Palmeirinhas, Ponta das-	30 Ii	9.05S	13.00 E	
Palmela	13 Df	38.34N	8.54W	
Palmer	40 Jd	61.36N	149.07W	
Palmer Archipelago	66 Qe	64.10S	62.00W	
Palmer Land (EN)	66 Qf	71.30S	65.00W	
Palmer Station	66 Qe	64.46S	64.05W	
Palmerston	57 Df	45.29S	170.43 E	
Palmerston Atoll	57 Kf	18.04S	163.10W	
Palmerston North	62 Ii	40.28S	175.17 E	
Palmetto Point	51d Ba	17.35N	61.52W	
Palmi	14 Jl	38.21N	15.51 E	
Palmira [Col.]	53 Ie	3.32N	76.16W	
Palmira [Cuba]	49 Gb	22.14N	80.23W	
Palm Islands	59 Jc	18.40S	146.30 E	
Palmital	55 Fg	24.39S	52.16W	
Palmitas	55 Dk	33.27S	57.48W	
Palmito	55 Cd	18.53S	58.22W	
Palmitos	55 Fh	27.05S	53.08W	
Palm Springs	43 De	33.50N	116.33W	
Palmyra	23 Ec	34.33N	38.17 E	
Palmyra Atoll	57 Kd	5.52N	162.06W	
Palo Alto	43 Cd	37.27N	122.09W	
Paloh	26 Ef	1.43N	109.18 E	
Paloich	35 Ec	10.28N	32.32 E	
Palomani, Nevado-	52 Jg	14.38S	69.14W	
Palomar Mountain	43 De	33.22N	116.50W	
Palomera, Sierra-	13 Kd	40.40N	1.12W	
Palopo	22 Oj	3.00S	120.12 E	
Palos, Cabo de-	5 Fh	37.38N	0.41W	
Palo Santo	55 Cg	25.34S	59.21W	
Palotina	55 Fg	24.17S	53.50W	
Palouse River	46 Fc	46.35N	118.13W	
Palpa	54 Cf	14.32S	75.11W	
Palsa	8 Lg	57.23N	26.24 E	
Pålsboda	8 Fe	59.04N	15.20 E	
Paltamo	7 Gd	64.25N	27.50 E	
Palu [Indon.]	22 Nj	0.53S	119.53 E	
Palu [Tur.]	24 Hc	38.42N	39.57 E	
Palu, Pulau-	26 Hh	8.20S	121.43 E	
Pam	63b Be	20.15S	164.17 E	
Pama	34 Fc	11.15N	0.42 E	
Pâmark/Pomarkku	8 Ic	61.42N	22.00 E	
Pambarra	37 Fd	21.56S	35.06 E	
Pambeguwa	34 Gc	10.40N	8.17 E	
Pamekasan	26 Fh	7.10S	113.28 E	
Pamiers	11 Hk	43.07N	1.36 E	
Pamir	21 Jf	38.00N	73.00 E	
Pamir	19 Hh	37.01N	72.41 E	
Pâmiut/Frederikshåb	41 Hf	62.00N	49.45W	
Pamlico Sound	43 Ld	35.20N	75.55W	
Pampa	43 Gd	35.32N	100.58W	
Pampa del Indio	55 Ch	26.02S	59.55W	
Pampa del Infierno	55 Bh	26.31S	61.10W	
Pampa de los Guanacos	56 Hc	26.14S	61.51W	
Pampas	54 Df	12.24S	74.54W	
Pampas	52 Ji	35.00S	63.00W	
Pampeiro	55 Ej	30.38S	55.16W	
Pamplona [Col.]	54 Db	7.23N	72.38W	
Pamplona [Sp.]	6 Fg	42.49N	1.38W	
Pamukkale	15 Ml	37.47N	29.04 E	
Pamukova	15 Ni	40.31N	30.09 E	
Pamunkey River	44 Ig	37.32N	76.48W	
Pan, Tierra del-	13 Gc	41.50N	6.00W	
Pana	36 Bc	1.41S	12.39 E	
Panagjurište	15 Hg	42.30N	24.11 E	
Panaitan, Pulau-	26 Eh	6.36S	105.12 E	
Panaitolikón Óros	15 Ek	38.43N	21.39 E	
Panaji (Panjim)	22 Jh	15.29N	73.50 E	
Panakhaïkón Óros	15 Ek	38.12N	21.54 E	
Panamá [1]	39 Li	9.00N	80.00W	
Panamá = Panama (EN) [3]	49 Hi	9.00N	79.00W	
Panamá = Panama City (EN)	39 Li	8.58N	79.31W	
Panama (EN) = Panamá [3]	49 Hi	9.00N	79.00W	
Panamá, Bahia de-	49 Hi	8.50N	79.15W	
Panamá, Canal de- = Panama Canal (EN)	47 Ig	9.20N	79.55W	
Panamá, Golfo de- = Panama, Gulf of- (EN)	38 Li	8.00N	79.10W	
Panama, Gulf of- (EN) = Panamá, Golfo de-	38 Li	8.00N	79.10W	
Panama, Isthmus of- (EN) = Panamá, Istmo de-	38 Li	9.20N	79.30W	
Panamá, Istmo de- = Panama, Isthmus of- (EN)	38 Li	9.20N	79.30W	
Panama Canal (EN) = Panamá, Canal de-	47 Ig	9.20N	79.55W	
Panama City [La.-U.S.]	39 Kf	30.10N	85.41W	
Panama City (EN) = Panamá	39 Li	8.58N	79.31W	
Panamá La Vieja	49 Hi	9.00N	79.29W	
Panambi	55 Fi	28.18S	53.30W	
Panamint Range	46 Gh	36.30N	117.20W	
Panao	54 Ce	9.49S	76.00W	
Panarea	14 Jl	38.40N	15.05 E	
Panaro	14 Ff	44.55N	11.25 E	
Pana Tinai	63a Ad	11.14S	153.10 E	
Pana-Wina	63a Ad	11.11S	153.01 E	
Panay	21 Oh	11.15N	122.30 E	
Pancake Range	46 Hg	39.00N	115.45W	
Pančevo	15 De	44.52N	20.39 E	
Pančičev vrh	15 Df	43.15N	20.45 E	
Panciu	15 Kd	45.54N	27.05 E	
Pancros	63b Db	15.58S	168.12 E	
Panda	37 Ed	24.03S	34.43 E	
Panda ma Tenga	37 Dc	18.32S	25.38 E	
Pandan	26 Hd	11.43N	122.06 E	
Pan de Azúcar	55 El	34.48S	55.14W	
Pandeiros, Ribeirão-	55 Jb	15.42S	44.36W	
Pandelis/Pandėlys	8 Kh	56.01N	25.21 E	
Pandėlys/Pandelis	8 Kh	56.01N	25.21 E	
Pandharpur	25 Fe	17.40N	75.20 E	
Pándheon	15 Fi	40.05N	22.20 E	
Pāndhurna	25 Fd	21.36N	78.31 E	
Pandivere Kõrgustik/Pandivere Vozvyšennost	8 Le	59.00N	26.15 E	
Pandivere Vozvyšennost/Pandivere Kõrgustik	8 Le	59.00N	26.15 E	
Pando	56 Id	34.43S	55.57W	
Pando [2]	54 Ef	11.20S	67.40W	
Pandokrátor	15 Cj	39.45N	19.52 E	
Pandora	49 Fi	9.45N	82.57W	
Pandrup	8 Cg	57.14N	9.41 E	
Pandu	36 Cb	4.59N	19.16 E	
Panevežis/Panevėžys	19 Cd	55.44N	24.22 E	
Panevėžys/Panevežis	19 Cd	55.44N	24.22 E	
Panfilov	19 Ig	44.08N	80.01 E	
Panga	36 Eb	1.51N	26.25 E	
Pangai	65b Ba	19.48S	174.21W	
Pangaion Óros	15 Hi	40.50N	24.05 E	
Pangalanes, Canal de-	30 Lk	22.48S	47.50 E	
Pangani	36 Gd	5.26S	38.58 E	
Pangani or Ruvu	36 Gc	5.26S	38.58 E	
Pange	12 Ie	49.05N	6.22 E	
Panggoe	58 Ge	7.01S	157.05 E	
Pangi	36 Ec	3.11S	26.38 E	
Pangkajene	26 Gg	4.50S	119.32 E	
Pangkalanberandan	26 Cf	4.01N	98.17 E	
Pangkalanbuun	26 Fg	2.41S	111.37 E	
Pangkalaseang, Tanjung-	26 Hg	0.42S	123.26 E	
Pangkalpinang	26 Eg	2.08S	106.08 E	
Pangnirtung	39 Mc	66.08N	65.44W	
Pang-Pang	63b Dc	17.41S	168.32 E	
Panguitch	43 Ed	37.49N	112.26W	
Panguma	34 Cd	8.24N	11.13W	
Pangutaran Group	26 He	6.15N	120.30 E	
Panhandle	45 Fi	35.21N	101.23W	
Pania Mutombo	36 Dd	5.11S	23.51 E	
Paniau	65a Ab	21.57N	160.05W	
Panié, Mont-	61 Bd	20.36S	164.46 E	
Pānīpat	25 Fc	29.23N	76.58 E	
Paniza, Puerto de-	13 Kc	41.15N	1.20W	
Panjang	26 Eh	5.29S	105.18 E	
Panjang, Pulau-	26 Ef	2.44N	108.55 E	
Panjgūr	25 Cc	26.58N	64.06 E	
Panjim → Panaji	22 Jh	15.29N	73.50 E	
Panjwin	24 Ke	35.36N	45.58 E	
Pankow, Berlin-	10 Jd	52.34N	13.24 E	
Pankshin	34 Gd	9.20N	9.27 E	
P'anmunjŏm	28 If	37.57N	126.40 E	
Panopah	26 Fg	1.56S	111.11 E	
Panorama	56 Jb	21.21S	51.51W	
Panshan	28 Gd	41.12N	122.03 E	
Panshi	27 Mc	42.56N	126.02 E	
Pant	12 Cc	51.53N	0.39 E	
Pantanal	52 Kg	18.00S	56.00W	
Pantar, Pulau-	26 Hh	8.25S	124.07 E	
Pantego	44 Ih	35.34N	76.36W	
Pantelleria	14 Fn	36.50N	11.57 E	
Pantelleria	5 Hh	36.45N	12.00 E	
Pantelleria, Canale di-	14 Fn	36.40N	11.45 E	
Pante Makassar	26 Hh	9.12S	124.23 E	
Pantoja	54 Cd	0.58S	75.10W	
Pánuco	48 Jf	22.03N	98.10W	
Pánuco	38 Jg	22.16N	97.47W	
Panxian	27 Hf	25.45N	104.39 E	
Panyam	34 Gd	9.25N	9.13 E	
Panzi	36 Cd	7.13S	17.58 E	
Panzós	49 Cf	15.24N	89.40W	
Pao, Rio- [Ven.]	50 Bh	8.33N	68.01W	
Pao, Rio- [Ven.]	50 Dh	8.06N	64.17W	
Paola [It.]	14 Kk	39.21N	16.03 E	
Paola [Ks.-U.S.]	45 Ig	38.35N	94.53W	
Paoli	44 Df	38.33N	86.28W	
Paopao	65e Fc	17.30S	149.49W	
Paoua	35 Bd	7.15N	16.26 E	
Pápa	10 Ni	47.20N	17.28 E	
Papa	65a Fd	19.13N	155.52W	
Papaaloa	65a Fd	19.59N	155.13W	
Papagaios	55 Jd	19.32S	44.45W	
Papagayo, Golfo del-	47 Gf	10.45N	85.45W	
Papaikou	65a Fd	19.47N	155.06W	
Papakura	62 Fb	37.03S	174.57 E	
Papaloapan, Rio-	48 Lh	18.42N	95.38W	
Papanduva	55 Gh	26.25S	50.09W	
Papangpanjang	26 Dg	0.27S	100.25 E	
Papantla de Olarte	47 Ed	20.27N	97.19W	
Papar	26 Ge	5.44N	115.56 E	
Paparoa Range	62 De	42.05S	171.35 E	
Papa Stour	9 La	60.30N	1.40W	
Papa Westray	9 Kb	59.22N	2.54W	
Papeete	58 Mf	17.32S	149.34W	
Papenburg	10 Dc	53.04N	7.24 E	
Papenburg-Aschendorf (Ems)	12 Ja	53.04N	7.22 E	
Papenoo	65e Fc	17.30S	149.25W	
Papes Ezers/Papes Ozero	8 Ih	56.15N	20.55 E	
Papes Ozero/Papes Ezers	8 Ih	56.15N	20.55 E	
Papetoai	65e Fc	17.30S	149.52W	
Papey	7a Cb	64.36N	14.11W	
Paphos/Baf	24 Ee	34.50N	32.35 E	
Papija	15 Kg	42.07N	27.51 E	
Papikion Óros	15 Ih	41.15N	25.18 E	
Papilé/Papilė	8 Jh	56.09N	22.45 E	
Papilė/Papilé	8 Jh	56.09N	22.45 E	
Papillion	45 Hf	41.09N	96.03W	
Papua, Gulf of-	57 Fe	8.32S	145.00 E	
Papua New Guinea [1]	58 Fe	6.00S	150.00 E	
Papua Passage	64p Bc	21.15S	159.47W	
Papuk	14 Le	45.31N	17.39 E	
Papun	25 Je	18.04N	97.27 E	
Para	7 Ji	54.23N	40.53 E	
Pará [2]	54 Hd	4.00S	53.00W	
Pará, Rio-	55 Jd	19.13S	45.07W	
Para, Rio-	52 Lf	1.30S	48.55W	
Parabel	20 De	58.40N	81.30 E	
Parabel	20 De	58.43N	81.31 E	
Paraburdoo	59 Dd	23.15S	117.45 E	
Paracas	54 Cf	13.49S	76.16W	
Paracatu	54 Ig	17.13S	46.52W	
Paracatu, Rio- [Braz.]	55 Ic	17.30S	46.32W	
Paracatu, Rio- [Braz.]	55 Jc	16.30S	45.04W	
Paracel Islands (EN) = Xisha Qundao	21 Nh	16.30N	112.15 E	
Pārachinār	25 Eb	33.54N	70.06 E	
Paraćin	15 Ef	43.52N	21.25 E	
Paracuru	54 Kd	3.24S	39.04W	
Parada Km 329	55 Ek	32.30S	55.25W	
Paradip	25 Hd	20.19N	86.42 E	
Paradise [Ca.-U.S.]	46 Eg	39.46N	121.37W	
Paradise [Mi.-U.S.]	44 Eb	46.38N	85.03W	
Paragould	45 Kh	36.03N	90.29W	
Paragua, Rio-	54 Fb	6.55N	62.55W	
Paraguá, Rio-	54 Ff	13.34S	61.53W	
Paraguaçu, Rio-	52 Mg	12.45S	38.54W	
Paraguaçu Paulista	55 Gf	22.25S	50.34W	
Paraguai, Rio	52 Kh	27.18S	58.38W	
Paraguaipoa	49 Lh	11.21N	71.57W	
Paraguaná, Peninsula de	54 Da	11.55N	70.00W	
Paraguari [3]	55 Dg	26.00S	57.10W	
Paraguari	56 Ic	25.38S	57.09W	
Paraguay [1]	53 Kh	23.00S	58.00W	
Paraguay, Rio-	52 Kh	27.18S	58.38W	
Paraiba [2]	54 Ke	7.10S	36.30W	
Paraíba do Sul, Rio-	52 Lh	21.37S	41.03W	
Paraibuna, Represa do-	55 Jf	23.25S	45.35W	
Paraibuna, Rio-	55 Jf	23.22S	45.40W	
Parainen/Pargas	7 Ff	60.18N	22.18 E	
Paraíso [Braz.]	55 Fd	19.03S	52.59W	
Paraíso [Mex.]	48 Mh	18.24N	93.14W	
Paraíso, Rio-	55 Bb	15.08S	61.52W	
Parakou	31 Hh	9.21N	2.37 E	
Param	64d Bb	7.22N	151.48 E	
Paramaribo	53 Ke	5.50N	55.10W	
Paramera, Sierra de la-	13 Hd	40.30N	4.46W	
Paramithiá	15 Dj	39.28N	20.31 E	
Paramušir, Ostrov-	21 Rd	50.25N	155.50 E	
Paraná	53 Ji	31.45S	60.30W	
Paraná [2]	56 Jb	24.00S	51.00W	
Paraná, Pico-	55 Hg	25.14S	48.48W	
Paraná, Rio-	52 Ki	33.43S	59.15W	
Paranã, Rio-	52 Lg	12.30S	48.14W	
Paraná de las Palmas, Rio-	55 Cl	34.18S	58.33W	
Paranaguá	53 Lh	25.31S	48.30W	
Paraná-Guazú, Rio-	55 Ck	34.00S	58.25W	
Paranaíba	54 Hg	19.40S	51.11W	
Paranaíba, Rio-	52 Kh	20.07S	51.05W	
Paranaiguara	55 Gd	18.53S	50.28W	
Paranapanema, Rio-	52 Kh	22.40S	53.09W	
Paranapiacaba, Serra do-	52 Lh	24.20S	49.00W	
Paranapuã-Guaçu, Ponta do-	55 Ig	24.24S	47.00W	
Paranavai	56 Jb	23.04S	52.28W	
Parandak	24 Ne	35.21N	50.42 E	
Paranéstion	15 Hh	41.16N	24.30 E	
Paranhos	55 Ef	23.55S	55.25W	
Paraoa Atoll	57 Mf	19.09S	140.43W	
Paraopeba	55 Jd	19.18S	44.25W	
Paraopeba, Rio-	55 Jd	18.50S	45.11W	
Parapara	63b Ca	13.32S	167.20 E	
Paraparaumu	62 Fd	40.55S	175.00 E	
Paraspóri	15 Kn	35.54N	27.14 E	
Parati	55 Jf	23.13S	44.43W	
Paratodos, Serra-	55 Jb	14.40S	44.50W	
Paratunka	20 Kf	52.52N	158.12 E	
Pārāu, Kūh-e-	24 Le	34.37N	47.05 E	
Paraúna	55 Gc	17.02S	50.26W	
Paravae	64n Bc	10.27S	160.58W	
Paray-le-Monial	11 Kh	46.27N	4.07 E	
Parbati	25 Fc	25.51N	76.36 E	
Parbhani	25 Fe	19.16N	76.47 E	
Parchim	10 Hc	53.26N	11.51 E	
Parczew	10 Se	51.39N	22.54 E	
Pardo	55 Cm	36.15S	59.22W	
Pardo, Rio- [Braz.]	55 Fi	29.59S	52.23W	
Pardo, Rio- [Braz.]	54 Hh	21.46S	52.09W	
Pardo, Rio- [Braz.]	55 He	20.10S	48.38W	
Pardo, Rio- [Braz.]	55 Hf	22.55S	49.58W	
Pardo, Rio- [Braz.]	55 Jb	15.48S	44.48W	
Pardo, Rio- [Braz.]	54 Kg	15.39S	38.57W	
Pardubice	10 Lf	50.02N	15.45 E	
Parea	65e Eb	16.49S	150.58W	
Parecis, Chapada dos-	52 Kg	13.00S	60.00W	
Parecis, Rio-	55 Da	12.56S	56.43W	
Paredes de Nava	13 Hb	42.09N	4.41W	
Parelhas	54 Ke	6.41S	36.39W	
Paren	20 Ld	62.28N	163.05 E	
Parent	42 Kg	47.55N	74.37W	
Parentis-en-Born	11 Ej	44.21N	1.04W	
Pareora	62 Df	44.29S	171.13 E	
Parepare	22 Nj	4.01S	119.38 E	
Párga	15 Dj	39.17N	20.24 E	
Pargas/Parainen	7 Ff	60.18N	22.18 E	
Pargolovo	8 Nd	60.03N	30.30 E	
Parham	51d Bb	17.05N	61.46W	
Parhar	19 Gh	37.31N	69.23 E	
Pari, Rio-	55 Db	15.36S	56.08W	
Paria, Golfo de-/Paria, Gulf of-	54 Fa	10.20N	62.00W	
Paria, Gulf of-/Paria, Golfo de-	54 Fa	10.20N	62.00W	
Paria, Peninsula de-	50 Eg	10.40N	62.30W	
Pariaguán	54 Fb	8.51N	64.43W	
Pariaman	26 Dg	0.38S	100.08 E	
Paria River	46 Jh	36.52N	111.36W	
Paricutin, Volcán-	48 Hh	19.28N	102.15W	
Parida, Isla-	49 Fi	8.07N	82.20W	
Pari das Pedras	55 Ja	12.45S	44.47W	
Parigi	26 Hg	0.48S	120.10 E	
Parika	54 Gb	6.52N	58.25W	
Parikkala	7 Gf	61.33N	29.30 E	
Parima, Serra-	52 Je	3.00N	64.20W	
Parinacota	56 Ga	18.12S	69.16W	
Pariñas, Punta-	52 Hf	4.40S	81.20W	
Paringul Mare, Vîrful-	15 Gd	45.20N	23.30 E	
Parintins	53 Kf	2.36S	56.44W	
Paris [Fr.]	6 Gf	48.52N	2.20 E	
Paris [Il.-U.S.]	45 Mg	39.36N	87.42W	
Paris [Kir.]	64g Ab	1.56N	157.31W	
Paris [Ky.-U.S.]	44 Ef	38.13N	84.14W	
Paris [Tn.-U.S.]	44 Cg	36.19N	88.20W	
Paris [Tx.-U.S.]	43 He	33.40N	95.33W	
Paris Basin (EN) = Parisien, Bassin-	5 Gf	49.00N	2.00 E	
Parisien, Bassin- = Paris Basin (EN)	5 Gf	49.00N	2.00 E	
Parita	49 Gi	8.00N	80.31W	
Parita, Bahia de-	49 Gi	8.08N	80.24W	
Parit Buntar	26 De	5.07N	100.30 E	
Parkano	7 Fe	62.01N	23.01 E	
Parkent	18 Gd	41.18N	69.40 E	
Parker	46 Hi	34.09N	114.17W	
Parker, Mount-	59 Fc	17.10S	128.20 E	
Parkersburg	43 Kd	39.17N	81.33W	
Parker Seamount (EN)	40 If	52.35N	151.15W	
Parkes	58 Fh	33.08S	148.11 E	
Park Falls	45 Kd	45.56N	90.32W	
Parkland	46 Dc	47.09N	122.26W	
Park Range	43 Fc	40.00N	106.30W	
Park Rapids	45 Ic	46.55N	95.04W	
Park River	45 Hb	48.24N	97.45W	
Park Valley	46 If	41.50N	113.21W	
Parma	14 Ef	44.56N	10.26 E	
Parma [It.]	6 Hg	44.48N	10.20 E	
Parma [Oh.-U.S.]	44 Ge	41.24N	81.44W	
Parnaguá	54 Jf	10.13S	44.38W	
Parnaíba	53 Lf	2.54S	41.47W	
Parnaíba, Rio-	52 Lf	3.00S	41.50W	
Parnamirim [Braz.]	54 Ke	8.05S	39.34W	
Parnamirim [Braz.]	54 Ke	5.55S	35.15W	
Parnarama	54 Je	5.41S	43.06W	
Parnassós Óros = Parnassus (EN)	5 Ih	38.30N	22.37 E	
Parnassus	62 Ee	42.43S	173.17 E	
Parnassus (EN) = Parnassós Óros	5 Ih	38.30N	22.37 E	
Párnis Óros	15 Gk	38.10N	23.40 E	
Párnon Óros	15 Fl	37.12N	22.38 E	
Pärnu/Pjarnu	6 Id	58.24N	24.32 E	
Pärnu-Jaagupi/Pjarnu-Jagupi	8 Kf	58.36N	24.25 E	
Pärnu Jõgi/Pjarnu	7 Fg	58.23N	24.34 E	
Pärnu Laht/Pjarnu, Zaliv-	7 Fg	58.15N	24.25 E	
Parola	8 Kc	61.03N	24.22 E	
Paroo River	57 Fh	31.28S	143.32 E	
Paropamisus/Salseleh-ye Safid Kūh	21 If	34.30N	63.30 E	
Páros	15 Il	37.05N	25.09 E	
Páros	15 Il	37.06N	25.12 E	
Parowan	46 Ih	37.51N	112.57W	
Parpaillon	11 Mj	44.35N	6.40 E	
Parque Industrial	55 Jd	19.57S	44.01W	
Parral	56 Fe	36.09S	71.50W	
Parral, Rio-	48 Gd	27.35N	105.25W	
Parras, Sierra de-	48 He	25.25N	102.00W	
Parras de la Fuente	47 Dc	25.25N	102.11W	
Parravicini	55 Dm	36.27S	57.46W	
Parrett	9 Jj	51.13N	3.01W	
Parrita	49 Ei	9.30N	84.19W	
Parry, Cape-	42 Fb	70.12N	124.35W	
Parry, Kap- [Grld.]	41 Jd	72.28N	22.00W	
Parry, Kap- [Grld.]	41 Ec	77.00N	71.00W	
Parry Bay	42 Jc	68.00N	82.00W	
Parry Islands	38 Ib	76.00N	110.00W	
Parry Peninsula	42 Fc	69.45N	124.35W	
Parry Sound	42 Jg	45.21N	80.02W	
Parsęta	10 Lb	54.12N	15.33 E	
Parsons [Ks.-U.S.]	43 Hd	37.20N	95.16W	
Parsons [W.V.-U.S.]	44 Hf	39.06N	79.43W	
Parsons Range	59 Hb	13.30S	135.15 E	
Partanna	14 Gm	37.43N	12.53 E	
Parthenay	11 Fh	46.39N	0.15W	
Partille	8 Eg	57.44N	12.07 E	
Partinico	14 Hl	38.03N	13.07 E	
Partizansk	20 Ih	43.13N	133.05 E	
Partizánske	10 Oh	48.38N	18.23 E	
Partizanskoje	20 Ee	55.30N	94.30 E	
Paru, Rio-	52 Kf	1.33S	52.38W	
Paru de Este, Rio-	54 Hc	1.10N	54.40W	
Paru de Oeste, Rio-	52 Kf	1.30S	56.00W	
Paruru	63a Ec	9.51S	160.49 E	
Parvān [3]	23 Kb	35.15N	69.30 E	
Pārvomaj	15 Ig	42.06N	25.13 E	
Parys	37 De	27.04S	27.16 E	
Paša	7 Hf	60.28N	32.55 E	
Pasadena [Ca.-U.S.]	39 Hf	34.09N	118.09W	
Pasadena [Tx.-U.S.]	45 Il	29.42N	95.13W	
Paşaeli Yarimadası	15 Lh	41.20N	28.25 E	
Paşalimani Adası	15 Ki	40.28N	27.37 E	
Pasangkaju	26 Gg	1.10S	119.20 E	
Pāsārgād	24 Og	30.17N	52.55 E	
Pasarwajo	26 Hh	5.29S	122.50 E	
Pascagoula	43 Je	30.23N	88.31W	
Paşcani	15 Jb	47.15N	26.44 E	
Pasco	43 Db	46.14N	119.06W	
Pasco [2]	54 Cf	10.30S	75.15W	
Pascoal	55 Ba	13.38S	61.06W	
Pascoal, Monte-	54 Kg	16.54S	39.24W	
Pascua, Isla de-/Rapa Nui = Easter Island (EN)	57 Qg	27.07S	109.22W	
Pas-de-Calais [3]	11 Id	50.30N	2.20 E	
Pas-en-Artois	12 Ed	50.09N	2.30 E	
Pasewalk	10 Jc	53.31N	13.59 E	
Pasinler	24 Ib	40.00N	41.41 E	
Pašino	20 De	55.11N	83.02 E	
Pasión, Rio de la-	49 Be	16.28N	90.33W	
Pasir Mas	26 De	6.02N	102.08 E	
Pasirpengarayan	26 Df	0.51N	100.16 E	
Pasir Puteh	26 De	5.50N	102.24 E	
Påskallavik	8 Gg	57.10N	16.27 E	
Paškovski	16 Kg	45.01N	39.05 E	
Pasłęk	10 Pb	54.05N	19.39 E	
Pasłęka	10 Pb	54.25N	19.50 E	
Pašman	14 Jg	43.57N	15.21 E	
Pasni	22 Ig	25.16N	63.28 E	
Paso de Indios	56 Gf	43.52S	69.06W	
Paso del Cerro	55 Ej	31.31S	55.46W	
Paso de los Libres	56 Ic	29.43S	57.05W	
Paso de los Toros	56 Id	32.49S	56.31W	
Paso Tranqueras	55 Ej	31.12S	55.45W	
Passamaquoddy Bay	44 Nc	45.06N	66.59W	
Passa Três, Serra-	55 Hb	14.40S	49.30W	
Passau	10 Jh	48.35N	13.29 E	
Passero, Capo-	14 Jn	36.40N	15.10 E	
Passo Fundo	53 Kh	28.15S	52.24W	
Passo Fundo, Rio-	55 Fh	27.16S	52.42W	
Passos	54 Ig	20.43S	46.37W	
Pastaza, Rio-	52 If	4.50S	76.25W	
Pasteur	56 He	35.08S	62.14W	
Pasto	53 Ie	1.13N	77.17W	
Pastora Peak	46 Kh	36.47N	109.10W	
Pastoria, Laguna de-	48 Ki	16.00N	97.40W	
Pastos Bons	54 Je	6.36S	44.05W	
Pastrana	13 Jd	40.25N	2.55W	
Paštrik	15 Dg	42.14N	20.32 E	
Pasubio	14 Fe	45.47N	11.10 E	
Pasvalis/Pasvalys	7 Fh	56.02N	24.28 E	
Pasvalys/Pasvalis	7 Fh	56.02N	24.28 E	
Pásztó	10 Pi	47.55N	19.42 E	

Index Symbols

[1] Independent Nation; [2] State, Region; [3] District, County; [4] Municipality; [5] Colony, Dependency; Continent; Physical Region; Historical or Cultural Region; Mount, Mountain; Volcano; Hill; Mountains, Mountain Range; Hills, Escarpment; Plateau, Upland; Pass, Gap; Plain, Lowland; Delta; Salt Flat; Valley, Canyon; Crater, Cave; Karst Features; Depression; Polder; Desert, Dunes; Forest, Woods; Heath, Steppe; Oasis; Cape, Point; Coast, Beach; Cliff; Peninsula; Isthmus; Sandbank; Island; Atoll; Rock, Reef; Islands, Archipelago; Rocks, Reefs; Coral Reef; Well, Spring; Geyser; River, Stream; Waterfall Rapids; River Mouth, Estuary; Lake; Salt Lake; Intermittent Lake; Reservoir; Swamp, Pond; Canal; Glacier; Ice Shelf, Pack Ice; Ocean; Sea; Gulf, Bay; Strait, Fjord; Lagoon; Bank; Seamount; Tablemount; Ridge; Shelf; Basin; Escarpment, Sea Scarp; Fracture; Trench, Abyss; National Park, Reserve; Point of Interest; Recreation Site; Cave, Cavern; Historic Site; Ruins; Wall, Walls; Church, Abbey; Temple; Scientific Station; Airport; Port; Lighthouse; Mine; Tunnel; Dam, Bridge

Pervari 24 Jd 37.54N 42.36 E
Pervomajsk 19 Ee 54.52N 43.48 E
Pervomajsk 16 Ke 48.36N 38.32 E
Pervomajsk 19 Df 48.03N 30.52 E
Pervomajski 10 Vc 53.52N 25.33 E
Pervomajskij 19 Ie 50.15N 81.59 E
Pervomajskij 16 Lc 53.18N 40.15 E
Pervomajskij 19 Ec 64.26N 40.48 E
Pervomajskij 17 Ji 54.52N 61.08 E
Pervomajskij 16 Sd 51.34N 54.59 E
Pervomajskij 16 Je 49.24N 36.15 E
Pervouralsk 19 Fd 57.00N 60.00 E
Pervy Kurilski Proliv 20 Kf 50.50N 156.50 E
Perwez/Perwijs 12 Gd 50.37N 4.49 E
Perwijs/Perwez 12 Gd 50.37N 4.49 E
Pes 7 Ig 59.10N 35.18 E
Peša 17 Cc 66.50N 47.32 E
Pesaro 14 Gg 43.54N 12.55 E
Pescadores (EN)=Penghu Liehtao 27 Kg 23.30N 119.30 E
Pescadores, Punta- 48 Ef 23.45N 109.45W
Pesčany, Mys- 16 Qh 43.10N 51.18 E
Pesčany, Ostrov 20 Gb 74.20N 115.55 E
Pescara 14 Ih 42.28N 14.13 E
Pescara 6 Hg 42.28N 14.13 E
Pescasseroli 14 Hi 41.48N 13.47 E
Peschici 14 Ki 41.57N 16.01 E
Pescia 14 Eg 43.54N 10.41 E
Pescocostanzo 14 Ii 41.53N 14.04 E
Peshāwar 22 Jf 34.01N 71.33 E
Peshkopia 15 Dh 41.41N 20.26 E
Pesio 14 Bf 44.28N 7.53 E
Peskovka 7 Mg 59.03N 52.22 E
Pesmes 11 Lg 47.17N 5.34 E
Pesočny 8 Nd 60.05N 30.20 E
Peso da Régua 13 Ec 41.10N 7.47W
Pesqueira 54 Ke 8.22S 36.42W
Pesquería, Río- 48 Je 25.54N 99.11W
Pessac 11 Fj 44.48N 0.37W
Pest [2] 10 Pi 47.25N 19.20 E
Pešter 15 Df 43.05N 20.02 E
Peštera 15 Hg 42.02N 24.18 E
Pestovo 19 Dd 58.36N 35.47 E
Petacalco, Bahía de- 47 De 17.57N 102.05W
Petah Tiqwa 24 Ff 32.05N 34.53 E
Petäjävesi 8 Kb 62.15N 25.12 E
Petal 45 Lk 31.21N 89.17W
Petalioi 15 Hl 38.01N 24.17 E
Petalioi, Gulf of- (EN) = Petalión, Kólpos- 15 Hk 38.00N 24.05 E
Petalión, Kólpos- = Petalioi, Gulf of- (EN) 15 Hk 38.00N 24.05 E
Petaluma 46 Dg 38.14N 122.39W
Pétange/Petingen 12 He 49.33N 5.53 E
Petare 54 Ea 10.29N 66.49W
Petatlán 48 Ii 17.31N 101.16W
Petatlán, Río- 48 Fd 26.09N 107.45W
Petauke 36 Fe 14.15S 31.20 E
Petén 47 Fe 16.15N 89.50W
Petén [3] 49 Be 16.50N 90.00W
Petén Itzá, Lago- 49 Ce 16.59N 89.50W
Petenwell Lake 45 Ld 44.05N 89.45W
Peterborough [Austl.] 59 Hf 32.58S 138.50 E
Peterborough [Eng.-U.K.] 9 Mi 52.35N 0.15W
Peterborough [Ont.-Can.] 42 Jh 44.18N 78.19W
Peterhead 9 Ld 57.30N 1.46W
Peter I, Oy- 66 Pe 68.47S 90.35W
Peter Island 51a Db 18.22N 64.35W
Peterlee 9 Lg 54.46N 1.19W
Petermann Gletscher 41 Fb 80.45N 61.00W
Petermann Ranges 59 Fd 25.00S 129.45 E
Petermanns Bjerg 67 Md 73.10N 28.00W
Peter Pond Lake 42 Ge 55.55N 108.40W
Petersberg 10 He 51.35N 11.57 E
Petersburg [Ak.-U.S.] 40 Me 56.49N 132.57W
Petersburg [In.-U.S.] 44 Df 38.30N 87.16W
Petersburg [Va.-U.S.] 43 Ld 37.14N 77.24W
Petersburg [W.V.-U.S.] 44 Hf 39.01N 79.09W
Petersfield 9 Mk 51.00N 0.56W
Petershagen 12 Kb 52.23N 8.58 E
Peter the Great Bay (EN)= Petra Velikogo, Zaliv- 21 Pe 42.40N 132.00 E
Petilia Policastro 14 Kk 39.07N 16.47 E
Petingen/Pétange 12 He 49.33N 5.53 E
Petit-Bourg 51e Ab 16.12N 61.36W
Petit-Canal 51e Bb 16.23N 61.29W
Petit Canouan 51n Bb 12.47N 61.17W
Petit Cul-de-Sac Marin 51e Ab 16.12N 61.33W
Petite Kabylie 13 Rh 36.35N 5.25 E
Petite Rivière de l'Artibonite 49 Kd 19.08N 72.29W
Petites Pyrénées 11 Hk 43.05N 1.10 E
Petite-Terre, Iles de la- 51e Bb 16.10N 61.07W
Petit-Goâve 49 Kd 18.26N 72.52W
Petit Martinique Island 51p Ca 12.32N 61.22W
Petit-Mécatina, Rivière du- 42 Lf 50.39N 59.25W
Petit Morin 11 Jf 48.56N 3.07 E
Petit Mustique Island 51n Bb 12.51N 61.13W
Petit Nevis Island 51n Bb 12.58N 61.15W
Petitot 42 Fd 60.14N 123.29W
Petit Saint-Bernard, Col du- 14 Ae 45.40N 6.55 E
Petit Saint Vincent Island 51n Bb 12.33N 61.23W
Petit Savanne 51g Bb 15.15N 61.17W
Petitsikapau Lake 42 Kf 54.40N 66.25W
Petkula 7 Gc 67.40N 26.41 E
Petlalcingo 48 Kh 18.05N 97.54W
Peto 47 Gd 20.08N 88.55W
Petorca 56 Fd 32.15S 71.00W
Petoskey 44 Ec 45.22N 84.57W
Petra 24 Fg 30.19N 35.29 E
Petralia Soprana 14 Im 37.47N 14.06 E
Petra Pervogo, Hrebet- 18 He 39.00N 71.10 E
Petra Velikogo, Zaliv-= Peter the Great Bay (EN) 21 Pe 42.40N 132.00 E
Petre, Point- 44 Id 43.50N 77.09W
Petre Bay 62 Je 43.55S 176.40W
Petrel 66 Re 63.28S 56.17W
Petrela 15 Ch 41.15N 19.51 E
Petrella Tifernina 14 Ii 41.41N 14.42 E
Petrič 15 Gh 41.24N 23.13 E
Pétrie, Récif- 61 Bc 18.30S 164.20 E
Petrikov 16 Fc 52.08N 28.31 E
Petrila 15 Gd 45.27N 23.25 E
Petrinja 14 Ke 45.27N 16.17 E
Petrodvorec 7 Gg 59.53N 29.50 E
Petrólea 54 Db 8.30N 72.35W
Petrolia 44 Fd 42.52N 82.09W
Petrolina 54 Je 9.24S 40.30W
Petrolina de Goiás 55 Hc 16.06S 49.20W
Petronanski prohod 15 Gf 43.08N 23.08 E
Petronell 14 Kb 48.07N 16.51 E
Petropavlovka 20 Ff 50.38N 105.19 E
Petropavlovsk 22 Id 54.54N 69.06 E
Petropavlovsk-Kamčatski 22 Rd 53.01N 158.39 E
Petrópolis 53 Lh 22.31S 43.10W
Petroşani 15 Gd 45.25N 23.22 E
Petrovac [Yugo.] 15 Bg 42.12N 18.57 E
Petrovac [Yugo.] 15 Ee 44.22N 21.25 E
Petrova Gora 14 Je 45.17N 15.47 E
Petrovaradin 15 Cd 45.15N 19.53 E
Petrovka 15 Nc 46.55N 30.40 E
Petrovsk 19 Ee 52.18N 45.23 E
Petrovski Jam 7 Ie 63.18N 35.15 E
Petrovsk-Zabajkalski 22 Md 51.17N 108.50 E
Petrov Val 16 Nd 50.10N 45.12 E
Petrozavodsk 6 Jc 61.47N 34.20 E
Petuhovo 19 Gd 55.06N 67.58 E
Petuški 7 Ji 55.59N 39.28 E
Petworth 12 Bd 50.59N 0.36W
Peuetsagoe, Gunung- 26 Cf 4.55N 96.20 E
Peumo 56 Fd 34.24S 71.10W
Peureulak 26 Cf 4.48N 97.53 E
Pevek 22 Tc 69.42N 170.17 E
Pevensey 12 Cd 50.48N 0.21 E
Pevensey Bay 12 Cd 50.48N 0.22 E
Peza 7 Kd 65.34N 44.33 E
Pézenas 11 Jk 43.27N 3.25 E
Pezinok 10 Nh 48.18N 17.16 E
Pfaffenhofen an der Ilm 10 Hh 48.32N 11.31 E
Pfaffenhoffen 12 Jf 48.51N 7.37 E
Pfalz 12 Je 49.20N 7.57 E
Pfalzel, Trier- 12 Ie 49.46N 6.41 E
Pfälzer Bergland 10 Dg 49.35N 7.30 E
Pfälzer Wald 10 Dg 49.15N 7.50 E
Pfarrkirchen 10 Ih 48.26N 12.52 E
Pfinz 12 Ke 49.11N 8.25 E
Pfinztal 12 Ke 49.02N 8.30 E
Pforzheim an der Enz 10 Eh 48.53N 8.42 E
Pfrimm 12 Ke 49.39N 8.22 E
Pfullendorf 10 Fi 47.55N 9.15 E
Pfunds 14 Ed 46.58N 10.33 E
Pfungstadt 12 Ke 49.48N 8.36 E
Phalaborwa 37 Ed 23.55S 31.13 E
Phalodi 25 Ec 27.08N 72.22 E
Pha-an 25 Je 16.53N 97.38 E
Phangnga 25 Jg 8.28N 98.32 E
Phan Ly Cham 25 Lf 11.13N 108.31 E
Phanom 25 Jg 8.49N 98.50 E
Phan Rang 25 Lf 11.34N 108.59 E
Phan Thiet 25 Lf 10.56N 108.06 E
Pharr 45 Gm 26.12N 98.11W
Phatthalung 25 Kg 7.38N 100.04 E
Phayao 25 Ke 18.07N 100.11 E
Phenix City 43 Je 32.29N 85.01W
Phet Buri 25 Jf 13.06N 99.56 E
Phetchabun, Thiu Khao- 25 Ke 16.20N 100.55 E
Phichit 25 Ke 16.24N 100.21 E
Philadelphia [Ms.-U.S.] 45 Lj 32.46N 89.07W
Philadelphia [Pa.-U.S.] 39 Lf 39.57N 75.07W
Philae 33 Fe 23.35N 32.52 E
Philip 45 Fd 44.02N 101.40W
Philippeville 11 Kd 50.12N 4.33 E
Philippi 44 Gf 39.08N 80.03W
Philippi (EN) = Filippoi 15 Hh 41.02N 24.18 E
Philippi, Lake- 59 Hd 24.20S 139.00 E
Philippi Glacier 66 Ge 66.45S 88.20 E
Philippine Basin (EN) 3 Ih 17.00N 132.00 E
Philippine Islands (EN) = Pilipinas 21 Oh 13.00N 122.00 E
Philippines (EN)=Pilipinas [1] 22 Oh 13.00N 122.00 E
Philippine Sea (EN) 21 Oh 20.00N 130.00 E
Philippine Trench (EN) 3 Ii 9.00N 127.00 E
Philippsburg 12 Ke 49.14N 8.27 E
Philipsburg [Mt.-U.S.] 46 Ic 46.20N 113.08W
Philipsburg [Neth.Ant.] 50 Ec 18.01N 63.04W
Philip Smith Mountains 40 Jc 68.30N 148.00W
Philipstown 37 Cf 30.26S 24.29 E
Phillipsburg 45 Gg 39.45N 99.19W
Philpots 42 Jb 74.55N 80.00W
Phitsanulok 22 Mh 16.49N 100.15 E
Phnom Penh (EN)=Phnum Pénh 22 Mh 11.33N 104.55 E
Phnum Penh=Phnom Penh (EN) 22 Mh 11.33N 104.55 E
Phoenix 39 Hf 33.27N 112.05W
Phoenix→Rawaki Atoll 57 Je 3.43S 170.43W
Phoenix Islands 57 Je 4.00S 172.00W
Phôngsali 25 Kd 21.41N 102.06 E
Phrae 25 Ke 18.07N 100.11 E
Phra Nakhom Si Ayutthaya 22 Mh 14.21N 100.33 E
Phrygia 15 Mk 38.30N 29.50 E
Phu Cuong 25 Lf 10.58N 106.39 E
Phuket 22 Li 7.54N 98.24 E
Phuket, Ko- 21 Li 8.00N 98.20 E
Phulbani 25 Gd 20.28N 84.14 E
Phumĭ Mlu Prey 25 Lf 13.48N 105.16 E
Phumĭ Sâmraông 25 Kf 14.11N 103.31 E
Phu My 25 Lf 14.10N 109.03 E
Phuoc Binh 25 Lf 11.50N 106.58 E
Phu Quoc, Dao- 25 Kf 10.12N 104.00 E
Phu Tho 25 Ld 21.24N 105.13 E
Phu Vinh → Tra Vinh 25 Lg 9.56N 106.20 E
Piaanu Pass 64d Ab 7.20N 151.26 E
Piacenza 14 De 45.01N 9.40 E
Piana degli Albanesi 14 Hm 37.59N 13.17 E
Piana Mwanga 36 Ed 7.40S 28.10 E
Piancó 54 Ke 7.12S 37.57W
Pianguan 27 Jd 39.28N 111.32 E
Pianosa [It.] 14 Jh 42.15N 15.45 E
Pianosa [It.] 14 Eh 42.35N 10.05 E
Piaseczno 10 Rd 52.05N 21.01 E
Piaski 10 Se 51.08N 22.51 E
Piątek 10 Pd 52.05N 19.28 E
Piatra 15 If 43.49N 25.10 E
Piatra Neamţ 15 Jc 46.55N 26.20 E
Piatra Olt 15 He 44.22N 24.16 E
Piauí [2] 54 Je 7.00S 43.00W
Piauí, Rio- 52 Lf 6.38S 42.42W
Piave 5 Hf 45.32N 12.44 E
Piaxtla, Punta- 48 Ff 23.38N 106.50W
Piaxtla, Río- 48 Ff 23.42N 106.49W
Piazza Armerina 14 Im 37.23N 14.22 E
Pibor 35 Ed 8.26N 33.13 E
Pibor Post 35 Ed 6.48N 33.08 E
Pica 56 Gb 20.30S 69.21W
Picachos, Cerro dos- 48 Bc 29.25N 114.10W
Picardie = Picardy (EN) 11 Je 50.00N 3.30 E
Picardy (EN) = Picardie 11 Je 50.00N 3.30 E
Picayune 45 Lk 30.26N 89.41W
Picentini, Monti- 14 Jj 40.45N 15.10 E
Pichanal 53 Jh 23.20S 64.15W
Pichilemu 56 Fd 34.23S 72.00W
Pichilingue 48 De 24.20N 110.20W
Pichna 10 Oe 51.50N 18.40 E
Pichones, Cayos- 49 Ff 15.45N 82.55W
Pichucalco 48 Mi 17.31N 93.04W
Pickering 9 Mg 54.14N 0.46W
Pickering, Vale of- 9 Mg 54.10N 0.45W
Pickle Lake 42 If 51.29N 90.10W
Pickwick Lake 44 Ch 34.55N 88.10W
Pico 30 Ee 38.28N 28.20W
Picos 53 Lf 7.05S 41.28W
Pico Truncado 56 Gg 46.48S 67.58W
Picquigny 11 Ie 49.57N 2.09 E
Picton 61 Dh 41.18S 174.00 E
Pictou 42 Lg 45.41N 62.43W
Picunda 16 Lh 43.12N 40.21 E
Pidurutalagala 21 Ki 7.00N 80.46 E
Piedecuesta 54 Db 6.59N 73.03W
Piedimonte Matese 14 Ii 41.20N 14.22 E
Piedmont [Al.-U.S.] 44 Ei 33.55N 85.37W
Piedmont [Mo.-U.S.] 45 Kh 37.09N 90.42W
Piedmont (EN) = Piemonte [2] 14 Be 45.00N 8.00 E
Piedmont Plateau 43 Kf 35.00N 81.00W
Piedra 13 Kc 41.19N 1.48W
Piedra, Monasterio de- 13 Kc 41.10N 1.50W
Piedrabuena 13 He 39.02N 4.10W
Piedrafita, Puerto de- 13 Fb 42.36N 6.57W
Piedrahita 13 Gd 40.28N 5.19W
Piedras 54 Cd 3.38S 79.54W
Piedras, Punta- 55 Ie 35.25S 57.08W
Piedras, Rio de las- 54 Ef 12.30S 69.14W
Piedras Negras 39 Ig 28.42N 100.31W
Piedras Negras 49 Be 17.12N 91.15W
Piedra Sola 56 Id 32.04S 56.21W
Piekary Śląskie 10 Of 50.24N 18.58 E
Pieksämäki 7 Ge 62.18N 27.08 E
Pielach 14 Jb 48.15N 15.22 E
Pielavesi 7 Ge 63.14N 26.45 E
Pielinen 5 Ic 63.15N 29.40 E
Piemonte = Piedmont (EN) [2] 14 Be 45.00N 8.00 E
Pieniężno 10 Qb 54.15N 20.08 E
Pieni Salpausselkä 8 Lc 61.10N 27.20 E
Piennes 12 He 49.19N 5.47 E
Pienza 14 Fg 43.04N 11.41 E
Pierce 46 Hc 46.29N 115.48W
Pieria Óri 15 Fi 40.12N 22.07 E
Pierre 39 Ie 44.22N 100.21W
Pierrefitte-sur-Aire 12 Hf 48.54N 5.20 E
Pierrefonds 12 Ee 49.21N 2.59 E
Pierrelatte 11 Kj 44.23N 4.42 E
Pieskehaure 7 Dc 66.57N 16.30 E
Piešt'any 10 Nh 48.36N 17.50 E
Pietarsaari/Jakobstad 7 Fe 63.40N 22.42 E
Pietermaritzburg 31 Kk 29.37S 30.16 E
Pietersburg 31 Jk 23.54S 29.25 E
Pietraperzia 14 Im 37.25N 14.08 E
Pietrasanta 14 Eg 43.57N 10.14 E
Piet Retief 37 Ee 27.01S 30.50 E
Pietrii, Vîrful- 15 Fd 45.23N 22.40 E
Pietroşani 15 If 43.43N 25.38 E
Pietrosu, Vîrful- [Rom.] 15 Ib 47.08N 25.11 E
Pietrosu, Vîrful- [Rom.] 5 If 47.23N 25.33 E
Pieve di Cadore 14 Gd 46.26N 12.22 E
Pigeon Island 51k Ba 14.06N 60.58W
Pigeon River 45 Lb 48.02N 89.41W
Piggott 45 Kh 36.23N 90.11W
Pigg's Peak 37 Ee 25.58S 31.15 E
Pigs, Bay of- (EN)= Cochinos, Bahía de- 49 Gb 22.07N 81.10W
Pigüé 55 Am 37.37S 62.25W
Pi He 28 Dh 32.26N 116.34 E
Pihkva järv=Pskov, Lake- (EN) 7 Gg 58.00N 28.00 E
Pihlajavesi 7 Gf 61.45N 28.45 E
Pihlava 8 Ic 61.33N 21.36 E
Pihtipudas 7 Fe 63.23N 25.34 E
Piikkiö 8 Jd 60.26N 22.31 E
Piirisaar/Pirissar 8 Lf 58.23N 27.40 E
Pijijiapan 48 Mj 15.42N 93.14W
Pijol, Pico- 49 Df 15.06N 87.35W
Pikalevo 7 Ig 59.32N 34.03 E
Pikangikum 42 If 51.49N 94.00W
Pikelot Island 57 Fd 8.05N 147.38 E
Pikes Peak 43 Fd 38.51N 105.03W
Piketberg 37 Bf 32.54S 18.46 E
Pikiutdleq 41 Hf 64.45N 40.10W
Pikou 28 Ge 39.24N 122.21 E
Pikounda 36 Cb 0.33N 16.42 E
Piła 10 Mc 53.10N 16.44 E
Piła [2] 10 Mc 53.10N 16.45 E
Pila 55 Cm 36.01S 58.08W
Pila, Sierra de la- 13 Kf 38.16N 1.11W
Pilar [Arg.] 55 Bj 31.27S 61.15W
Pilar [Braz.] 54 Ke 9.36S 35.56W
Pilar [Par.] 56 Ic 26.52S 58.23W
Pilas Group 26 He 6.45N 121.35 E
Pilat, Mont- 11 Ki 45.23N 4.35 E
Pilatus 14 Cd 46.59N 8.20 E
Pilaya, Río- 54 Fh 20.55S 64.04W
Pilcaniyeu 56 Ff 41.08S 70.40W
Pilcomayo, Río- 52 Kh 25.21S 57.42W
Pile, Jezioro- 10 Mc 53.35N 16.30 E
Pili 15 Ej 39.28N 21.37 E
Pilibhit 25 Fc 28.38N 79.48 E
Pilica 10 Re 51.52N 21.17 E
Pilion Óros 15 Gj 39.24N 23.05 E
Pilipinas=Philippine Islands (EN) 21 Oh 13.00N 122.00 E
Pilipinas=Philippines (EN) [1] 22 Oh 13.00N 122.00 E
Pilis 10 Oi 47.41N 18.53 E
Pillahuincó, Sierra de- 55 Bn 38.18S 60.45W
Pillar, Cape- 59 Jh 43.15S 148.00 E
Pilna 7 Ki 55.33N 45.55 E
Pilões, Rio- 55 Gc 16.14S 50.54W
Pilões, Serra dos- 55 Ic 17.50S 47.13W
Pilón, Río- 48 Je 25.32N 99.32W
Pilos 15 Em 36.55N 21.42 E
Pilos = Pylos (EN) 15 Em 36.56N 21.40 E
Pilot Peak 46 Hf 41.02N 114.06W
Pilot Rock 46 Fd 45.29N 118.50W
Pilsen (EN)=Plzeň 6 Hf 49.45N 13.24 E
Piltene 7 Eh 57.15N 21.42 E
Pilzno 10 Rg 49.59N 21.17 E
Pim 19 Hc 61.18N 71.57 E
Pimba 59 Hf 31.15S 136.47 E
Pimenteiras 54 Je 6.14S 41.25W
Pimža Jõgi 8 Lg 57.57N 27.59 E
Pina 13 Lc 41.29N 0.32W
Pinacate, Cerro- 48 Cb 31.45N 113.31W
Pinaki Atoll 57 Nf 19.22S 138.44W
Pinamar 55 Dm 37.07S 56.50W
Piñami, Arroyo- 48 Cd 27.44N 113.47W
Pinar 13 Gh 36.46N 5.26W
Pinarbaşi 24 Gc 38.50N 36.30 E
Pinar del Rio 39 Kg 22.25N 83.42W
Pinar del Rio [3] 49 Eb 22.35N 83.40W
Pinarello 11a Bb 41.41N 9.22 E
Pinarhisar 15 Kh 41.37N 27.30 E
Pinchbeck 12 Bb 52.48N 0.09W
Pincher Creek 42 Gg 49.30N 113.48W
Pinçon, Mont- 11 Ff 48.58N 0.37W
Pîncota 15 Ec 46.20N 21.42 E
Pindaíba, Ribeirão 55 Gb 14.48S 52.00W
Pindaré, Rio- 54 Jd 3.17S 44.47W
Pindaré-Mirim 54 Id 3.37S 45.21W
Pindaval 55 Dc 17.08S 56.09W
Pindhos Óros=Pindus Mountains (EN) 5 Ih 39.45N 21.30 E
Pindus Mountains (EN)= Pindhos Óros 5 Ih 39.45N 21.30 E
Pine Bluff 43 Ie 34.13N 92.01W
Pine Bluffs 46 Mf 41.11N 104.04W
Pine Creek 59 Gb 13.49S 131.49 E
Pine Falls 42 Hf 50.35N 96.15W
Pinega 19 Ec 64.42N 43.22 E
Pinega 5 Kc 64.08N 41.54 E
Pine Island Glacier 66 Of 75.00S 101.00W
Pineland 45 Jk 31.15N 93.58W
Pine Mountain [Ga.-U.S.] 44 Ei 32.51N 84.47W
Pine Mountain [U.S.] 44 Fg 36.55N 83.20W
Pine Pass 42 Fe 55.50N 122.30W
Pine Point 39 Hc 61.01N 114.15W
Pine Ridge 45 Ee 43.02N 102.33W
Pinerolo 14 Bf 44.53N 7.21 E
Pines, Isle of- (EN)= Juventud, Isla de la- 38 Kg 21.40N 82.50W
Pines, Isle of- (EN)=Pins, Ile des- 57 Hg 22.37S 167.30 E
Pines, Lake O' The 45 Ij 32.46N 94.35W
Pinetown 37 Ee 29.52S 30.46 E
Ping 21 Mh 15.42N 100.09 E
Pingbian 27 Hg 22.56N 103.46 E
Pingchang 27 Ie 31.38N 107.06 E
Pingding 28 Bf 37.48N 113.37 E
Pingdingbu → Guyuan 28 Cd 41.40N 115.41 E
Pingding Shan 27 Mb 46.39N 128.30 E
Pingdingshan 27 Je 33.41N 113.27 E
Pingdu 28 Ef 36.47N 119.57 E
Pingelap Atoll 57 Hd 6.13N 160.42 E
Pingelly 59 Df 32.32S 117.05 E
Pinggu 28 Dd 40.08N 117.07 E
Pingguo 27 Ig 23.21N 107.34 E
Pinghu 28 Fi 30.42N 121.02 E
Pingjiang 28 Bj 28.45N 113.37 E
Pingle 27 Jg 24.43N 110.42 E
Pingli 27 Ie 32.27N 109.21 E
Pingliang 22 Mf 35.32N 106.41 E
Pinglu (Jingping) 28 Be 39.32N 112.14 E
Pingluo 22 Mf 38.56N 106.34 E
Pingma → Tiandong 27 Ig 23.40N 107.09 E
Pingnan 27 Jg 23.38N 110.23 E
Pingouins, Ile des- 30 Mm 46.25S 50.19 E
Pingquan 27 Kc 41.00N 118.36 E
Pingshan 28 Ce 38.21N 114.01 E
Pingshun 28 Bf 36.12N 113.26 E
Pingtan 27 Kf 25.31N 119.48 E
Pingtung 27 Lg 22.40N 120.29 E
Pingüicas, Cerro- 48 Jg 21.10N 99.42W
Pingvallavatn 7a Bb 64.15N 21.09W
Pingvellir 7a Bb 64.17N 21.06W
Pingwu 27 He 32.27N 104.35 E
Pingxiang [China] 27 Ig 22.11N 106.46 E
Pingxiang [China] 27 Jf 27.43N 113.48 E
Pingyang 27 Lf 27.40N 120.30 E
Pingyao 27 Jd 37.12N 112.13 E
Pingyi 28 Dg 35.30N 117.38 E
Pingyin 28 Df 36.17N 116.26 E
Pingyu 28 Ci 32.58N 114.36 E
Pingyuan 28 Df 37.10N 116.25 E
Pinhal 55 If 22.12S 46.45W
Pinhão 55 Gg 25.43S 51.38W
Pinheir Machado 55 Fj 31.34S 53.23W
Pinhel 13 Ed 40.46N 7.04W
Pini, Pulau- 26 Cf 0.08N 98.40 E
Piniós [Grc.] 15 Fj 39.53N 22.44 E
Piniós [Grc.] 15 El 37.48N 21.14 E
Pinipel 63a Ba 4.24S 154.08 E
Pinjug 7 Lf 60.16N 47.54 E
Pinka 10 Mi 47.00N 16.35 E
Pink Mountain 42 Fe 56.06N 122.35W
Pinnaroo 59 Ig 35.16S 140.55 E
Pinneberg 10 Fc 53.39N 9.48 E
Pínnes, Ákra- 15 Hi 40.07N 24.18 E
Pinolosean 26 Hf 0.23N 124.07 E
Pinos 48 If 22.18N 101.34W
Pinos, Mount- 38 Hf 34.50N 119.09W
Pinos-Puente 13 Ig 37.15N 3.45W
Pinrang 26 Gg 3.48S 119.38 E
Pins, Cap des- 63b Ce 21.04S 167.28 E
Pins, Ile des-=Pines, Isle of- (EN) 57 Hg 22.37S 167.30 E
Pins, Pointe aux- 44 Gd 42.15N 81.51W
Pinsk 19 Ce 52.08N 26.06 E
Pinta, Isla- 54a Aa 0.35N 90.44W
Pintas, Sierra de las- 48 Bb 31.40N 115.10W
Pinto [Arg.] 56 Hc 29.09S 62.39W
Pinto [Sp.] 13 Id 40.14N 3.41W
Pintwater Range 46 Hh 36.55N 115.30W
Pio 63a Ed 10.12S 161.42 E
Pioche 46 Hh 37.56N 114.27W
Piombino 14 Eh 42.55N 10.32 E
Piombino, Canale di- 14 Eh 42.55N 10.30 E
Pioneer Mountains 46 Id 45.40N 113.00W
Pioner, Ostrov- 21 Lb 79.50N 92.30 E
Pionerski 19 Gc 61.12N 62.57 E
Pionerski 7 Ei 54.57N 20.13 E
Pionki 10 Re 51.30N 21.27 E
Piorini, Lago- 54 Fd 3.35S 63.15W
Piorini, Rio- 54 Fd 3.23S 63.30W
Piotrków [2] 10 Pe 51.25N 19.40 E
Piotrków Trybunalski 10 Pe 51.25N 19.42 E
Piove di Sacco 14 Ge 45.18N 12.02 E
Pipa Dingzi 27 Mc 43.57N 128.14 E
Pipéri 15 Hj 39.19N 24.21 E
Pipestone 45 Hd 44.01N 96.19W
Pipestone Creek 45 Fb 49.42N 100.45W
Pipi 35 Cd 7.27N 22.48 E
Pipinas 55 Dl 35.32S 57.20W
Pipmouacan, Réservoir - 42 Kg 49.40N 70.20W
Piqan→Shanshan 27 Fc 42.52N 90.10 E
Piqua 44 Ee 40.08N 84.14W
Piqueras, Puerto de- 13 Jb 42.03N 2.32W
Piquiri, Rio- 56 Jb 24.03S 54.14W
Piquiri, Serra do- 55 Fg 24.53S 52.25W
Piracanjuba 55 Hc 17.18S 49.01W
Piracanjuba, Rio- [Braz.] 55 Hd 18.14S 48.48W
Piracanjuba, Rio- [Braz.] 55 Hc 17.18S 48.13W
Piracema 55 Je 20.31S 44.29W
Piracicaba 56 Kb 22.43S 47.38W
Piracicaba, Rio- 55 Hf 22.36S 48.19W
Piraçununga 55 Ie 21.59S 47.25W
Piracuruca 54 Jd 3.56S 41.42W
Piraeus (EN) = Piraiévs 6 Ih 37.57N 23.38 E
Pirai do Sul 55 Hg 24.31S 49.56W
Piraiévs = Piraeus (EN) 6 Ih 37.57N 23.38 E
Piraju 55 Hf 23.12S 49.23W
Pirajuí 55 He 21.59S 49.29W
Piramide, Cerro- 52 Ij 49.01S 73.32W
Piran 14 He 45.32N 13.34 E
Piranè 56 Ic 25.43S 59.06W
Piranhas 55 Gc 16.31S 51.51W
Piranhas, Rio- 55 Gc 16.01S 54.52W
Pirān Shahr 24 Kd 36.40N 45.05 E
Pirapora 53 Lg 17.21S 44.56W
Piraraja 55 Ek 33.44S 54.45W
Pirate Well 49 Kb 22.26N 73.04W
Piratini 55 Fj 31.27S 53.06W
Piratini, Rio- 55 Fk 32.01S 52.25W
Piratinim, Rio- 55 Ei 28.06S 55.27W
Pirdop 15 Hg 42.42N 24.11 E
Pirenópolis 55 Hb 15.51S 48.57W
Pires do Rio 54 Ig 17.18S 48.17W
Pirgos 15 El 37.41N 21.27 E
Pirgós 15 Fi 40.38N 22.44 E
Piriápolis 55 El 34.54S 55.17W
Pirin 15 Gh 41.40N 23.30 E
Pirineos=Pyrenees (EN) 5 Gg 42.40N 1.00 E
Pirineus, Serra dos- 55 Hc 16.15S 49.10W
Piripiri 54 Jd 4.16S 41.47W
Pirissar/Piirisaar 8 Lf 58.23N 27.40 E
Piritu 50 Bh 9.23N 69.12W
Piritu, Islas- 50 Dg 10.10N 64.56W
Pirizal 55 Dc 16.16S 56.23W
Pirjatin 16 Hd 50.14N 32.30 E
Pirmasens 10 Dg 49.12N 7.36 E
Pirna 10 Jf 50.58N 13.56 E
Piron 63a Ad 11.20S 153.27 E
Pirón 13 Hc 41.23N 4.31W
Pirot 15 Ff 43.09N 22.36 E
Pirre, Cerro- 49 Ij 7.49N 77.43W
Pirrit Hills 66 Pg 81.17S 85.21W
Pirsagat 16 Pj 39.53N 49.19 E
Pīr Tāj 24 Me 35.45N 48.07 E
Pirttikyla/Pörtom 8 Ib 62.42N 21.37 E
Piru 26 Ig 3.04S 128.12 E
Pis 64d Ba 7.41N 151.46 E
Pisa 14 Eg 43.43N 10.23 E
Pisa 10 Rc 53.15N 21.52 E
Pisagua 56 Fa 19.36S 70.13W

Index Symbols

[1] Independent Nation
[2] State, Region
[3] District, County
[4] Municipality
[5] Colony, Dependency
Continent
Physical Region
Historical or Cultural Region
Mount, Mountain
Volcano
Hill
Mountains, Mountain Range
Hills, Escarpment
Plateau, Upland
Pass, Gap
Plain, Lowland
Delta
Salt Flat
Valley, Canyon
Crater, Cave
Karst Features
Depression
Polder
Desert, Dunes
Forest, Woods
Heath, Steppe
Oasis
Cape, Point
Coast, Beach
Cliff
Peninsula
Isthmus
Sandbank
Island
Atoll
Rock, Reef
Islands, Archipelago
Rocks, Reefs
Coral Reef
Well, Spring
Geyser
River, Stream
Waterfall Rapids
River Mouth, Estuary
Lake
Salt Lake
Intermittent Lake
Reservoir
Swamp, Pond
Canal
Glacier
Ice Shelf, Pack Ice
Ocean
Sea
Gulf, Bay
Strait, Fjord
Lagoon
Bank
Seamount
Tablemount
Ridge
Shelf
Basin
Escarpment, Sea Scarp
Fracture
Trench, Abyss
National Park, Reserve
Point of Interest
Recreation Site
Cave, Cavern
Historic Site
Ruins
Wall, Walls
Church, Abbey
Temple
Scientific Station
Airport
Port
Lighthouse
Mine
Tunnel
Dam, Bridge

Pisano	14	Eg	43.46N	10.33 E
Pisar	64d	Cb	7.19N	152.01 E
Pisciotta	14	Jj	40.06N	15.14 E
Pisco	53	Ig	13.42S	76.13W
Pişcolt	15	Fb	47.35N	22.18 E
Písek	10	Kg	49.19N	14.10 E
Pishan/Guma	27	Cd	37.38N	78.19 E
Pīsh Qal'eh	24	Qd	37.35N	57.05 E
Pīshvā	24	Ne	35.18N	51.44 E
Piso Firme	55	Ba	13.41S	61.52W
Pissa	7	Ei	54.39N	21.50 E
Pisshiri-Dake	29a	Ba	44.20N	141.55 E
Pista	7	Hd	65.28N	30.45 E
Pisticci	14	Kj	40.23N	16.33 E
Pistoia	14	Eg	43.55N	10.54 E
Pisuerga	13	Hc	41.33N	4.52W
Pisz	10	Rc	53.38N	21.49 E
Pita	34	Cc	11.05N	12.24W
Pitalito	54	Cc	1.53N	76.02W
Pitanga	56	Jb	24.46S	51.44W
Pitanga, Serra da-	55	Gg	24.52S	51.48W
Pitangui	55	Jd	19.40S	44.54W
Pitcairn [5]	58	Og	24.00S	129.00W
Pitcairn Island	57	Ng	25.04S	130.05W
Piteå	7	Ed	65.20N	21.30 E
Piteälven	5	Ib	65.14N	21.32 E
Piteşti	6	Ig	44.51N	24.52 E
Pithiviers	11	If	48.10N	2.15 E
Pithorāgarh	25	Gc	29.35N	80.13 E
Piti	36	Fd	7.00S	32.44 E
Piti	64c	Bb	13.28N	144.41 E
Pitiquito	48	Cb	30.42N	112.02W
Pitkjaranta	19	Dc	61.35N	31.31 E
Pitkkala	8	Jc	61.28N	23.34 E
Pitljar	20	Bc	65.52N	65.55 E
Pitlochry	9	Je	56.43N	3.45W
Pitomača	14	Le	45.57N	17.14 E
Piton, Pointe du-	51e	Ba	16.30N	61.27W
Pit River	43	Cc	40.45N	122.22W
Pitrufquén	56	Fe	38.59S	72.39W
Pitt	42	Ef	53.40N	129.50W
Pitt Island	57	Ji	44.20S	176.10W
Pittsburg	43	Id	37.25N	94.42W
Pittsburgh	39	Le	40.26N	80.00W
Pittsfield [Il.-U.S.]	45	Kg	39.36N	90.48W
Pittsfield [Ma.-U.S.]	44	Kd	42.27N	73.15W
Pittsfield [Me.-U.S.]	44	Mc	44.47N	69.23W
Pitt Strait	62	Jf	44.10S	176.20W
Pitu	26	If	1.41N	128.01 E
Piũi	55	Je	20.28S	45.58W
Piura	53	Hf	5.12S	80.38W
Piura [2]	54	Be	5.00S	80.20W
Piuthán	25	Gc	28.06N	82.52 E
Piva	15	Bf	43.21N	18.51 E
Pivan	20	If	50.27N	137.05 E
Pivijay	49	Jh	10.28N	74.38W
Pižma	7	Lh	57.36N	48.58 E
Pižma	17	Fd	65.24N	52.05 E
Pizzo	14	Kl	38.44N	16.40 E
Pjakupur	20	Cd	65.00N	77.48 E
Pjalica	7	Jc	66.12N	39.32 E
Pjalma	19	Dc	62.27N	35.53 E
Pjana	7	Ki	55.37N	45.58 E
Pjandž	19	Gh	37.15N	69.07 E
Pjandž	21	If	37.06N	68.20 E
Pjaozero, Ozero-	5	Jb	66.05N	30.55 E
Pjarnu/Pärnu	6	Id	58.24N	24.32 E
Pjarnu/Pärnu Jõgi	7	Fg	58.23N	24.34 E
Pjarnu, Zaliv-/Pärnu Laht	7	Fg	58.15N	24.25 E
Pjarnu-Jagupi/Pärnu-Jaagupi	8	Kf	58.36N	24.25 E
Pjasina	21	Kb	73.47N	87.01 E
Pjasino, Ozero-	20	Dc	69.45N	87.30 E
Pjasinski Zaliv	20	Db	74.00N	85.00 E
Pjatigorsk	6	Kg	44.03N	43.04 E
Pjatihatki	16	He	48.27N	33.40 E
Pjórsá	5	Dc	63.45N	20.50W
Pjussi/Püssi	8	Le	59.17N	26.57 E
Pkulagalid	64a	Bb	7.36N	134.33 E
Pkulagasemieg	64a	Ac	7.08N	134.23 E
Pkurengel	64a	Ac	7.27N	134.28 E
Plá	55	Bl	35.07S	60.13W
Placentia	42	Mg	47.14N	53.58W
Placentia Bay	38	Ne	47.15N	54.30W
Placer	26	Hd	11.52N	123.55 E
Placerville	46	Eg	38.43N	120.48W
Placetas	47	Id	22.19N	79.40W
Plácido Rosas	55	Fk	32.45S	53.44W
Plačkovci	15	Ig	42.49N	25.28 E
Plačkovica	15	Fh	41.46N	22.32 E
Plainfield	44	Je	40.37N	74.25W
Plains [Mt.-U.S.]	46	Hc	47.27N	114.53W
Plains [Tx.-U.S.]	45	Ej	33.11N	102.50W
Plainview [Nb.-U.S.]	45	He	42.21N	97.47W
Plainview [Tx.-U.S.]	43	Ge	34.11N	101.43W
Plainville	45	Gg	39.14N	99.18W
Pláka, Ákra-	15	Ii	40.02N	25.25 E
Plake	15	Eh	41.14N	21.02 E
Plampang	26	Gh	8.48S	117.48 E
Planá	10	Ig	49.52N	12.44 E
Plana Cays	49	Kb	22.37N	73.33W
Plana o Nueva Tabarca, Isla-	13	Lf	38.10N	0.28W
Planco, Peñón-	48	Ge	24.35N	104.15W
Plane, Ile-	13	Li	35.46N	0.54W
Planeta Rica	54	Cb	8.25N	75.35W
Planet Depth (EN)	3	Hi	10.20S	110.30 E
Planézes	11	Ij	45.00N	2.50 E
Plankinton	45	Ge	43.43N	98.29W
Plantation	44	Gl	26.05N	80.14W
Plantaurel	11	Hk	43.04N	1.30 E
Plant City	44	Fk	28.01N	82.08W
Plasencia	13	Fd	40.02N	6.05W
Plast	19	Ge	54.22N	60.55 E
Plaster Rock	44	Nb	46.54N	67.24W
Plastun	20	Ih	44.48N	136.17 E
Plasy	10	Jg	49.56N	13.24 E
Plata, Río de la- [P.R.]	51a	Bb	18.30N	66.14W
Plata, Río de la- [S.Amer.]	52	Ki	35.00S	57.00W
Plataiaí	15	Gk	38.13N	23.16 E
Platani	14	Hm	37.24N	13.16 E
Plateau [2]	34	Gd	8.50N	9.00 E
Plateau [3]	36	Cc	2.10S	15.00 E
Plateau, Khorat-	21	Mh	15.30N	102.50 E
Plateaux [3]	34	Fd	7.30N	1.10 E
Platen, Kapp-	41	Ob	80.31N	22.48 E
Platí	15	Fi	40.39N	22.32 E
Plato	54	Db	9.47N	74.47W
Platte	45	Ge	43.23N	98.51W
Platte	38	Je	43.23N	98.51W
Platte Island	30	Mi	5.52S	55.23 E
Platte River	45	Ig	39.16N	94.50W
Platteville	45	Ke	42.44N	90.29W
Plattsburgh	43	Mc	44.42N	73.29W
Plattsmouth	45	If	41.01N	95.53W
Plau	10	Ic	53.27N	12.16 E
Plauen	10	If	50.30N	12.08 E
Plauer See	10	Ic	53.30N	12.20 E
Plav	15	Cg	42.36N	19.57 E
Plavecký Mikuláš	10	Nh	48.30N	17.18 E
Pļaviņas/Pljavinjas	7	Fh	56.38N	25.46 E
Plavsk	16	Jc	53.43N	37.18 E
Playa Azul	47	De	17.59N	102.24W
Playa Noriega, Laguna-	48	Dc	29.10N	111.50W
Playa Vicente	48	Li	17.50N	95.49W
Playón Chico	49	Hi	9.18N	78.14W
Pleasanton [Ks.-U.S.]	45	Ig	38.11N	94.43W
Pleasanton [Tx.-U.S.]	45	Gl	28.58N	98.29W
Pleasant Point	62	Df	44.16S	171.08 E
Pleasant Valley	45	Fi	35.15N	101.48W
Plechý	10	Jh	48.49N	13.53 E
Pleiku	25	Lf	13.59N	108.00 E
Pleiße	10	Ie	51.20N	12.22 E
Plekinge	8	Fh	56.20N	15.05 E
Pleniţa	15	Ge	44.13N	23.11 E
Plenty, Bay of-	57	Ih	37.45S	177.10 E
Plentywood	43	Gb	48.47N	104.34W
Plešcenicy	16	Eb	54.29N	27.55 E
Pleseck	19	Ec	62.44N	40.18 E
Plešivec	10	Qh	48.33N	20.25 E
Pleşu, Vîrful-	15	Fc	46.32N	22.11 E
Pleszew	10	Ne	51.54N	17.48 E
Plétipi, Lac -	42	Kf	51.42N	70.08W
Plettenberg	12	Jc	51.13N	7.53 E
Plettenbergbaai	37	Cf	34.03S	23.22 E
Pleven [2]	15	Hf	43.25N	24.37 E
Pleven	6	Ig	43.25N	24.37 E
Plibo	34	De	4.35N	7.40W
Pliska	15	Kf	43.22N	27.07 E
Pliszka	10	Kd	52.15N	14.40 E
Plitvice	14	Jf	44.54N	15.36 E
Pljavinjas/Pļaviņas	7	Fh	56.38N	25.46 E
Plješevica	14	Jf	44.45N	15.45 E
Pljevlja	15	Cf	43.21N	19.21 E
Pljusa	7	Gg	58.25N	29.20 E
Pljusa	7	Gg	59.13N	28.11 E
Ploča, Rt-	14	Jg	43.30N	15.58 E
Ploče → Kardeljevo	14	Lg	43.04N	17.26 E
Płock	10	Pd	52.35N	19.45 E
Płock	10	Pd	52.33N	19.43 E
Ploërmel	11	Dg	47.56N	2.24W
Ploieşti	6	Ig	44.57N	26.01 E
Plomárion	15	Jk	38.59N	26.22 E
Plomb du Cantal	11	Ii	45.03N	2.46 E
Plön	10	Gb	54.10N	10.26 E
Płonia	10	Kc	53.25N	14.36 E
Płonka	10	Qd	52.37N	20.30 E
Płońsk	10	Qd	52.38N	20.23 E
Plopana	15	Kc	46.41N	27.13 E
Płoty	10	Lc	53.50N	15.16 E
Plouguerneau	11	Bf	48.36N	4.30W
Plovdiv [2]	15	Hg	42.09N	24.45 E
Plovdiv	6	Ig	42.09N	24.45 E
Plummer	46	Gc	47.20N	116.53W
Plumridge Lakes	59	Fe	29.30S	125.25 E
Plumtree	37	Dd	20.31S	27.48 E
Plungé/Plunge	7	Ei	55.56N	21.48 E
Plunge/Plungé	7	Ei	55.56N	21.48 E
Plymouth [Eng.-U.K.]	6	Fe	50.23N	4.10W
Plymouth [In.-U.S.]	44	De	41.21N	86.19W
Plymouth [Ma.-U.S.]	44	Le	41.58N	70.41W
Plymouth [Mont.]	47	Le	16.42N	62.13W
Plymouth Sound	9	Ik	50.25N	4.05W
Plzeň=Pilsen (EN)	6	Hf	49.45N	13.24 E
Plzeňská pahorkatina	10	Jg	49.50N	13.15 E
Pniewy	10	Md	52.31N	16.15 E
Pô	34	Ec	11.10N	1.09W
Po	5	Hg	44.57N	12.05 E
Po, Colline del-	14	Be	45.05N	7.50 E
Po, Foci del-=Po, Mouths of the- (EN)	14	Gf	44.52N	12.30 E
Po, Mouths of the- (EN)=Po, Foci del-	14	Gf	44.52N	12.30 E
Poarta de Fier a Transilvaniei, Pasul-	15	Fd	45.25N	22.40 E
Poarta Orientală, Pasul-	15	Fd	45.08N	22.20 E
Poás, Volcán-	49	Eh	10.11N	84.13W
Pobé	34	Fd	6.58N	2.41 E
Pobeda, Gora-	21	Qc	65.12N	146.12 E
Pobeda Ice Island	66	Ge	64.30S	97.00 E
Pobedy, Pik-	21	Ke	42.02N	80.05 E
Pobla de Segur/La Pobla de Segur	13	Mb	42.15N	0.58 E
Poblet, Monasterio de-/Poblet, Monèstir de-	13	Nc	41.20N	1.05 E
Poblet, Monèstir de-/Poblet, Monasterio de-	13	Nc	41.20N	1.05 E
Pobrežije	15	Jf	43.56N	26.21 E
Pocahontas	45	Kh	36.16N	90.58W
Pocatello	39	He	42.52N	112.27W
Počep	16	Hc	52.57N	33.28 E
Pocerina	15	Ce	44.38N	19.35 E
Počinok	19	De	54.23N	32.29 E
Počitelj	14	Lg	43.08N	17.44 E
Pocito, Sierra del-	13	He	39.20N	4.05W
Pocito Casas	48	Dc	28.32N	111.06W
Pocklington Reef	60	Fj	11.00S	155.00 E
Poções	54	Jf	14.31S	40.21W
Poço Fundo, Cachoeira-	55	Jc	16.10S	45.51W
Poconé	54	Gg	16.15S	56.37W
Pocono Mountains	44	Je	41.10N	75.20W
Poços de Caldas	54	Ih	21.48S	46.34W
Pocri	49	Gj	7.40N	80.07W
Podborovje	8	Mg	57.51N	28.46 E
Podborovje	7	Ig	59.32N	35.01 E
Podbrezová	10	Ph	48.49N	19.31 E
Podčerje	17	He	63.55N	57.30 E
Poděbrady	10	Lf	50.09N	15.07 E
Podgajcy	10	Vg	49.12N	25.12 E
Podgorica (Titograd)	6	Hg	42.26N	19.16 E
Po di Volano	14	Gf	44.49N	12.15 E
Podjuga	7	Jf	61.07N	40.54 E
Podkamennaja Tunguska=Stony Tunguska (EN)	21	Lc	61.36N	90.18 E
Podlasie	10	Sd	52.30N	23.00 E
Podlaska, Nizina-	10	Sc	53.00N	22.45 E
Podlužje	15	Ce	44.45N	19.55 E
Podolia (EN)=Podolskaja Vozvyšennost	5	If	49.00N	28.00 E
Podolsk	19	Dd	55.27N	37.33 E
Podolskaja Vozvyšennost=Podolia (EN)	5	If	49.00N	28.00 E
Podor	34	Cb	16.40N	14.57W
Podporožje	19	Dc	60.54N	34.09 E
Podravina	14	Le	45.40N	17.40 E
Podravska Slatina	14	Le	45.42N	17.42 E
Podrima	15	Dg	42.24N	20.33 E
Podromanija	14	Mg	43.54N	18.46 E
Podsvilje	8	Mi	55.09N	28.01 E
Podujevo	15	Eg	42.55N	21.12 E
Podunajská nížina	10	Nh	48.00N	17.40 E
Podvološino	20	Fe	58.15N	108.25 E
Poel	10	Hb	54.00N	11.26 E
Poeniţa, Vîrful-	15	Gc	46.15N	23.20 E
Pofadder	37	Be	29.10S	19.22 E
Pogăniş	15	Ed	45.41N	21.21 E
Pogar	16	Hc	52.33N	33.16 E
Poggibonsi	14	Fg	43.28N	11.09 E
Pöggstall	14	Jb	48.19N	15.11 E
Pogibi	20	Jf	52.15N	141.45 E
Pogny	12	Gf	48.52N	4.29 E
Pogoanele	15	Je	44.55N	27.00 E
Pogórze Karpackie	10	Qg	49.52N	21.00 E
Pogradeci	15	Di	40.54N	20.39 E
Pograničny	20	Ih	44.26N	131.20 E
Pogrebišče	16	Fe	49.29N	29.14 E
Poguba Xoréu, Rio-	55	Ec	16.29S	54.58W
P'ohang	27	Md	36.02N	129.22 E
Pohja/Pojo	8	Jd	60.06N	23.31 E
Pohjankangas	8	Jc	62.00N	22.30 E
Pohjanlahti=Bothnia, Gulf of- (EN)	5	Hc	63.00N	20.00 E
Pohjanmaa	8	Jb	63.00N	22.30 E
Pohjois-Karjala [2]	7	Ge	63.00N	30.00 E
Pohlheim	12	Kd	50.32N	8.42 E
Pohorje	14	Jd	46.32N	15.28 E
Po Hu	28	Di	30.15N	116.32 E
Pohue Bay	65a	Fd	19.01N	155.48W
Pohvistnevo	19	Fe	53.40N	52.08 E
Poiana Mare	15	Gf	43.55N	23.04 E
Poiana Ruscă, Munţii	15	Fd	45.41N	22.30 E
Pöide/Pëjde	8	Jf	58.30N	22.50 E
Poie	36	Dc	2.55S	23.10 E
Poindimié	61	Cd	20.56S	165.20 E
Poindo → Lhünzhub	27	Fe	30.17N	91.20 E
Poinsett, Cape-	66	He	65.42S	113.18 E
Poinsett, Lake-	45	Hd	44.34N	97.05W
Point Arena	46	Dg	38.55N	123.41W
Point au Fer Island	45	Kl	29.15N	91.15W
Pointe-à-Pitre	47	Le	16.14N	61.32W
Pointe Duble	51e	Bb	16.20N	61.00W
Pointe-Noire	51e	Ab	16.14N	61.47W
Pointe Noire	31	Ii	4.48S	11.51 E
Point Hope	40	Fc	68.21N	166.41W
Point Lake	42	Gc	65.15N	113.00W
Point Lay	40	Gc	69.45N	163.03W
Point Pleasant [N.J.-U.S.]	44	Je	40.06N	74.02W
Point Pleasant [W.V.-U.S.]	44	Ff	38.53N	82.07W
Poisson-Blanc, Lac-	44	Jc	46.00N	75.44W
Poissonnier Point	59	Dc	20.00S	119.10 E
Poissy	11	If	48.56N	2.03 E
Poitevin, Marais-	11	Eh	46.22N	1.06W
Poitiers	6	Gf	46.35N	0.20 E
Poitou	11	Fh	46.40N	0.30W
Poitou, Plaines et Seuil du-	11	Gh	46.26N	0.17 E
Poivre Islands	37b	Bb	5.46S	53.19 E
Poix-de-Picardie	11	He	49.47N	1.59 E
Poix-Terron	12	Ge	49.39N	4.39 E
Pojarkovo	20	Hg	49.42N	128.50 E
Pojkovski	19	Hc	60.59N	72.00 E
Pojo/Pohja	8	Jd	60.06N	23.31 E
Pojuba, Rio-	55	Ec	16.30S	54.59W
Pokaran	25	Ec	26.55N	71.55 E
Pokhara	25	Gc	28.14N	83.59 E
Poko	36	Eb	3.09N	26.53 E
Pokoinu	64p	Bb	21.12S	159.49W
Pokój	10	Nf	50.56N	17.50 E
Pokrovka	18	Lc	42.19N	78.01 E
Pokrovsk	20	Hd	61.29N	129.10 E
Pokrovskoje	16	Jc	52.38N	36.51 E
Pokrovskoje	16	Jf	47.59N	36.13 E
Pokšenga	7	Kd	64.01N	44.15 E
Pokutje	15	Ia	48.20N	25.05 E
Pola	7	Hg	58.05N	31.40 E
Polabí	10	Lf	50.10N	15.10 E
Polacca	46	Ji	35.50N	110.23W
Pola de Laviana	13	Ga	43.15N	5.34W
Pola de Lena	13	Ga	43.10N	5.49W
Pola de Siero	13	Ga	43.23N	5.40W
Polanco	55	Ek	33.54S	55.09W
Poland	64g	Ab	1.52N	157.33W
Poland (EN)=Polska [1]	6	He	52.00N	19.00 E
Polanów	10	Mb	54.08N	16.39 E
Polar Plateau	66	Cg	90.00S	0.00
Polar Urals (EN)=Poljarny Ural	5	Mb	66.55N	64.30 E
Polatlı	23	Db	39.36N	32.09 E
Polch	12	Jd	50.18N	7.19 E
Połczyn Zdrój	10	Mc	53.46N	16.06 E
Pol-e Khomrī	23	Kb	35.56N	68.43 E
Pole of Inaccessibility (EN)	66	Eg	82.06S	54.58 E
Pol-e-Safīd	24	Od	36.06N	53.01 E
Polesella	14	Ff	44.58N	11.45 E
Polesie Lubelskie	10	Te	51.30N	23.20 E
Polesine	14	Fe	45.00N	11.45 E
Polesje=Polesye (EN)	5	Ie	52.00N	27.00 E
Polessk	8	Ij	54.51N	21.02 E
Polesskoje	16	Fd	51.16N	29.27 E
Polesye (EN)=Polesje	5	Ie	52.00N	27.00 E
Polevskoj	19	Gd	56.28N	60.11 E
Polewali	26	Gg	3.25S	119.20 E
Poležan	15	Gh	41.43N	23.30 E
Polgár	10	Ri	47.52N	21.07 E
Pŏlgyo	28	Ig	34.51N	127.21 E
Poli	34	Hd	8.29N	13.15 E
Políaigos	15	Hm	36.46N	24.38 E
Poliçani	15	Di	40.08N	20.21 E
Policastro, Golfo di-	14	Jk	40.00N	15.35 E
Police	10	Kc	53.33N	14.35 E
Policoro	14	Kj	40.13N	16.41 E
Poligny	11	Lh	46.50N	5.43 E
Poligus	20	Ed	61.58N	94.40 E
Polikastron	15	Fh	41.00N	22.34 E
Polikhnitos	15	Jj	39.05N	26.11 E
Polillo Islands	21	Oh	14.50N	122.05 E
Pólis	24	Ee	35.02N	32.25 E
Polist	7	Hg	58.07N	31.32 E
Polistena	14	Kl	38.24N	16.04 E
Polýiros	15	Gi	40.23N	23.27 E
Poljarny	19	Db	69.13N	33.28 E
Poljarny	20	Mc	69.01N	178.45 E
Poljarny Ural=Polar Urals (EN)	5	Mb	66.55N	64.30 E
Polkowice	10	Me	51.32N	16.06 E
Pöllau	14	Jc	47.18N	15.50 E
Polle	64d	Bb	7.20N	151.15 E
Pollença/Pollensa	13	Pe	39.53N	3.01 E
Pollensa/Pollença	13	Pe	39.53N	3.01 E
Pollino	5	Hh	39.55N	16.10 E
Polochic, Río-	49	Cf	15.28N	89.22W
Polock	19	Cd	55.29N	28.52 E
Polog	15	Dh	42.00N	21.00 E
Pologi	19	Df	47.28N	36.15 E
Polonina	10	Jh	48.30N	23.30 E
Polonnaruwa	25	Gg	7.56N	81.00 E
Polonnoje	16	Ed	50.06N	27.29 E
Polousny Krjaž	20	Jc	69.30N	144.00 E
Polska=Poland (EN) [1]	6	He	52.00N	19.00 E
Polski Gradec	15	Jg	42.11N	26.06 E
Polski Trămbeš	15	If	43.22N	25.38 E
Polson	46	Hc	47.41N	114.09W
Poltár	10	Ph	48.27N	19.48 E
Poltava	6	Jf	49.35N	34.34 E
Poltavka	19	He	54.22N	71.45 E
Poltavskaja Oblast [3]	19	Df	49.45N	33.50 E
Põltsamaa/Pyltsamaa	8	Lf	58.23N	26.08 E
Põltsamaa/Pyltsamaa	7	Fg	58.39N	25.59 E
Poluj	20	Bc	66.30N	66.31 E
Polunočnoje	19	Gc	60.52N	60.25 E
Polūr	24	Oe	32.52N	52.03 E
Põlva/Pylva	7	Gg	58.04N	27.06 E
Polvijärvi	7	Ge	62.51N	29.22 E
Polynesia	57	Le	4.00S	156.00W
Polynésie Française=French Polynesia (EN) [5]	58	Mf	16.00S	145.00W
Pom, Laguna de-	48	Mh	18.35N	92.15W
Pomarance	14	Eg	43.18N	10.52 E
Pomarkku/Påmark	8	Ic	61.42N	22.00 E
Pombal [Braz.]	54	Ke	6.46S	37.47W
Pombal [Port.]	13	De	39.55N	8.38W
Pombo, Rio-	55	Fe	20.53S	52.23W
Pomerania (EN)=Pommern	5	He	54.00N	16.00 E
Pomerania (EN)=Pommern	10	Lc	54.00N	16.00 E
Pomeranian Bay (EN)=Pommersche Bucht	10	Kb	54.20N	14.20 E
Pomeranian Bay (EN)=Pomorska, Zatoka-	10	Kb	54.20N	14.20 E
Pomeroy	44	Ff	39.03N	82.03W
Pomio	58	Ge	5.32S	151.30 E
Pomme de Terre Reservoir	45	Jh	37.51N	93.19W
Pommern=Pomerania (EN)	10	Lc	54.00N	16.00 E
Pommern=Pomerania (EN)	5	He	54.00N	16.00 E
Pommersche Bucht=Pomeranian Bay (EN)	10	Kb	54.20N	14.20 E
Pommersfelden	10	Gg	49.46N	10.49 E
Pomona	46	Gi	34.04N	117.45W
Pomona Lake	45	Ig	38.40N	95.35W
Pomorije	15	Kg	42.33N	27.39 E
Pomorska, Zatoka-=Pomeranian Bay (EN)	10	Kb	54.20N	14.20 E
Pomorski Bereg	7	Id	64.00N	36.15 E
Pomorskie, Pojezierze-	10	Mc	53.30N	16.30 E
Pomorski Proliv	19	Eb	68.40N	50.00 E
Pomošnaja	16	Ge	48.14N	31.29 E
Pompano Beach	44	Gl	26.15N	80.07W
Pompei	14	Ij	40.45N	14.30 E
Pompeu	55	Jd	19.12S	44.59W
Ponape	58	Gd	6.52N	158.15 E
Ponape Island	57	Gd	6.55N	158.15 E
Ponca City	43	Hd	36.42N	97.05W
Ponce	39	Mh	18.01N	66.37W
Poncheville, Lac-	44	Ia	50.12N	76.55W
Pondcreek	45	Hh	36.40N	97.48W
Pondicherry	25	Ff	11.56N	79.53 E
Pondicherry [3]	25	Ff	11.55N	79.45 E
Pond Inlet	39	Lb	72.41N	78.00W
Pond Inlet	42	Jb	72.48N	77.00W
Ponea	64n	Ac	10.28S	161.01W
Ponente, Riviera di-	14	Cf	44.10N	8.20 E
Ponérihouen	63b	Be	21.05S	165.24 E
Pones	64d	Bb	7.12N	151.59 E
Ponferrada	13	Fb	42.33N	6.35W
Pongaroa	62	Gd	40.33S	176.11 E
Pongo	30	Jh	8.42N	27.40 E
Pongola	37	Ee	26.52S	32.20 E
Pong Qu	27	Ef	26.49N	87.09 E
Poniatowa	10	Se	51.11N	22.05 E
Ponoj	6	Kb	67.05N	41.07 E
Ponoj	5	Kb	66.59N	41.10 E
Ponomarevka	16	Sc	53.09N	54.12 E
Ponorogo	26	Fh	7.52S	111.27 E
Pons	11	Fi	45.35N	0.33W
Pons/Ponts	13	Nc	41.55N	1.12 E
Ponsul	13	Ee	39.40N	7.31W
Pont-à-Celles	12	Gd	50.30N	4.21 E
Ponta Delgada	31	Ee	37.44N	25.40W
Ponta Delgada [3]	32	Bb	37.48N	25.30W
Ponta Grossa	53	Kh	25.05S	50.09W
Pont-à-Mousson	11	Mf	48.54N	6.04 E
Ponta Porá	53	Kh	22.32S	55.43W
Pontarlier	11	Mh	46.54N	6.22 E
Pontassieve	14	Fg	43.46N	11.26 E
Pont-Audemer	11	Ge	49.21N	0.31 E
Pontaut	55	Bm	37.44S	61.20W
Pontávert	12	Fe	49.25N	3.49 E
Pontchartrain, Lake-	43	Ie	30.10N	90.10W
Pontchâteau	11	Dg	47.26N	2.05W
Pont-de-l'Arche	12	De	49.18N	1.10 E
Pont de Suert	13	Mb	42.24N	0.45 E
Pont-de-Vaux	11	Kh	46.26N	4.56 E
Ponte Alta	55	Gh	27.29S	50.23W
Ponte Alta, Serra da-	55	Id	19.42S	47.40W
Ponte Branca	55	Fc	16.27S	52.40W
Pontecorvo	14	Hi	42.27N	13.40 E
Ponte de Lima	13	Dc	41.46N	8.35W
Ponte de Pedra	55	Ec	17.06S	54.23W
Ponte de Pedrã	55	Da	13.35S	57.21W
Pontedera	14	Eg	43.40N	10.38 E
Ponte de Sor	13	De	39.15N	8.01W
Ponte Firme, Chapada da-	55	Id	18.05S	46.25W
Ponteix	46	Lb	49.49N	107.30W
Ponte Nova	54	Jh	20.24S	42.54W
Pontés e Lacerda	55	Cb	15.11S	59.21W
Pontevedra [3]	13	Db	42.30N	8.30W
Pontevedra	13	Db	42.26N	8.38W
Pontevedra, Ría de-	13	Db	42.22N	8.45W
Ponte Vermelha	55	Ed	19.29S	54.25W
Pont-Farcy	12	Af	48.56N	1.02W
Pontfaverger-Moronvilliers	12	Ge	49.18N	4.19 E
Ponthieu	11	Hd	50.10N	1.55 E
Pontiac [Il.-U.S.]	45	Lf	40.53N	88.38W
Pontiac [Mi.-U.S.]	44	Fd	42.37N	83.18W
Pontianak	22	Mj	0.02S	109.20 E
Pontian Kechil	26	Df	1.29N	103.23 E
Pontine Islands (EN) = Ponziane, Isole-	14	Gj	40.55N	13.00 E
Pontivy	11	Df	48.04N	2.59W
Pontivy, Pays de-	11	Dg	48.00N	3.00W
Pont-l'Abbé	11	Bg	47.52N	4.13W
Pont-l'Evêque	12	Ce	49.18N	0.11 E
Pontoise	11	Ie	49.03N	2.06 E
Pontorson	11	Ef	48.33N	1.31W
Pontremoli	14	Df	44.22N	9.53 E
Pontresina	14	Dd	46.28N	9.53 E
Ponts/Pons	13	Nc	41.55N	1.12 E
Pont-Sainte-Maxence	12	Ee	49.18N	2.36 E
Pont-Saint-Esprit	11	Kj	44.15N	4.39 E
Pontypool	9	Jj	51.43N	3.02W
Ponza	14	Gj	40.54N	12.58 E
Ponza	14	Gj	40.55N	12.55 E
Ponziane, Isole- = Pontine Islands (EN)	14	Gj	40.55N	13.00 E
Pool [3]	36	Bc	3.30S	15.00 E
Poole	9	Lk	50.43N	1.59W
Poona → Pune	22	Jh	18.32N	73.52 E
Poopó	54	Eg	18.23S	66.59W
Poopó, Lago de- = Poopó, Lake- (EN)	52	Jg	18.45S	67.07W
Poopó, Lake- (EN) = Poopó, Lago de-	52	Jg	18.45S	67.07W
Poor Knights Islands	62	Fa	35.30S	174.45 E
Põõsaspea Neem/Pyzaspea	8	Je	59.15N	23.25 E
Popakai	54	Gc	3.22N	55.25W
Popayán	53	Ie	2.27N	76.36W
Poperinge	11	Id	50.51N	2.43 E
Poperinge-Watou	12	Ed	50.51N	2.37 E
Popigaj	20	Gb	71.55N	110.47 E
Popigaj	20	Fb	72.55N	106.00 E
Poplar	46	Mb	48.07N	105.12W
Poplar	42	Hf	53.00N	97.18W
Poplar Bluff	43	Id	36.45N	90.24W
Poplar River	46	Mb	48.05N	105.11W
Popocatépetl, Volcán-	38	Jh	19.02N	98.38W
Popokabaka	36	Cd	5.42S	16.35 E
Popoli	14	Hh	42.10N	13.50 E
Popomanaseu, Mount-	63a	Ec	9.42S	160.03 E
Popondetta	60	Di	8.46S	148.14 E
Popovo	15	Jf	43.21N	26.14 E
Poppberg	10	Hg	49.20N	11.45 E
Poppel, Ravels-	12	Hc	51.27N	5.02 E
Poprad	10	Qg	49.38N	20.42 E
Poprad	6	If	49.03N	20.19 E
Poptún	49	Ce	16.21N	89.26W
Por	10	Tf	50.48N	23.01 E
Porangahau	62	Gd	40.18S	176.38 E

Index Symbols

[1] Independent Nation
[2] State, Region
[3] District, County
[4] Municipality
[5] Colony, Dependency
Continent
Physical Region
Historical or Cultural Region
Mount, Mountain
Volcano
Hill
Mountains, Mountain Range
Hills, Escarpment
Plateau, Upland
Pass, Gap
Plain, Lowland
Delta
Salt Flat
Valley, Canyon
Crater, Cave
Karst Features
Depression
Polder
Desert, Dunes
Forest, Woods
Heath, Steppe
Oasis
Cape, Point
Coast, Beach
Cliff
Peninsula
Isthmus
Sandbank
Island
Atoll
Rock, Reef
Islands, Archipelago
Rocks, Reefs
Coral Reef
Well, Spring
Geyser
River, Stream
Waterfall Rapids
River Mouth, Estuary
Lake
Salt Lake
Intermittent Lake
Reservoir
Swamp, Pond
Canal
Glacier
Ice Shelf, Pack Ice
Ocean
Sea
Gulf, Bay
Strait, Fjord
Lagoon
Bank
Seamount
Tablemount
Ridge
Shelf
Basin
Escarpment, Sea Scarp
Fracture
Trench, Abyss
National Park, Reserve
Point of Interest
Recreation Site
Cave, Cavern
Historic Site
Ruins
Wall, Walls
Church, Abbey
Temple
Scientific Station
Airport
Port
Lighthouse
Mine
Tunnel
Dam, Bridge

Porangatu	55	Ha	13.26S	49.10W
Porbandar	25	Dd	21.38N	69.36 E
Porcien	12	Ge	49.40N	4.20 E
Porcos, Rio dos-	55	Ja	12.42S	45.07W
Porcuna	13	Hg	37.52N	4.11W
Porcupine	38	Ec	66.35N	145.15W
Porcupine	44	Ga	48.32N	81.10W
Porcupine Bank (EN)	5	Ee	53.20N	13.30W
Porcupine Hills	46	Ha	50.05N	114.10W
Porcupine Plain	42	Dc	67.30N	137.30W
Pordenone	14	Ge	45.57N	12.39 E
Poreč	14	He	45.13N	13.37 E
Poreč	15	Fe	44.20N	22.05 E
Porecatu	55	Gf	22.43S	51.24W
Porečje	8	Kk	53.53N	24.08 E
Poreckoje	7	Li	55.13N	46.19 E
Porhov	19	Cd	57.45N	29.32 E
Pori/Björneborg	6	Ic	61.29N	21.47 E
Porion	15	Gn	35.58N	23.16 E
Porirua	61	Dh	41.08S	174.50 E
Pörisvatn	7a	Bb	64.20N	18.55W
Porjus	7	Ec	66.57N	19.49 E
Porkkala	8	Ke	59.55N	24.25 E
Porlamar	54	Fa	10.57N	63.51W
Porma	13	Gb	42.29N	5.28W
Pornic	11	Dg	47.07N	2.06W
Poronajsk	22	Qe	49.14N	143.04 E
Poronin	10	Qg	49.20N	20.04 E
Póros	15	Gl	37.30N	23.31 E
Póros	15	Gl	37.30N	23.27 E
Poroshiri-Dake	28	Qc	42.42N	142.35 E
Porosozero	7	He	62.44N	32.42 E
Porozovo	10	Ud	52.54N	24.27 E
Porpoise Bay	66	Ie	66.30S	128.30 E
Porquis Junction	44	Ga	48.43N	80.52W
Porrentruy	14	Bc	47.25N	7.10 E
Porreras	13	Oe	39.31N	3.00 E
Porretta, Passo della-	14	Ef	44.02N	10.56 E
Porretta Terme	14	Ef	44.09N	10.59 E
Porsangen	5	Ia	70.50N	26.00 E
Porsangerhalvøya	7	Fa	70.50N	25.00 E
Porsgrunn	7	Bg	59.09N	9.40 E
Pórshöfn	7a	Ca	66.10N	15.20W
Porsuk	24	Dc	39.42N	31.59 E
Portachuelo	54	Fg	17.21S	63.24W
Portadown/Port an Dúnáin	9	Gg	54.26N	6.27W
Portage	45	Le	43.33N	89.28W
Portage la Prairie	42	Hg	49.57N	98.18W
Port Alberni	42	Fg	49.14N	124.48W
Portalegre	13	Ee	39.17N	7.26W
Portalegre [2]	13	Ee	39.15N	7.35W
Portales	43	Ge	34.11N	103.20W
Port-Alfred	42	Kg	48.20N	70.53W
Port Alfred	37	Df	33.36S	26.55 E
Port Alice	42	Ef	50.23N	127.27W
Port Allegany	44	He	41.48N	78.18W
Port an Dúnáin/Portadown	9	Gg	54.26N	6.27W
Port Angeles	43	Cb	48.07N	123.27W
Port Antonio	47	Ie	18.11N	76.28W
Port Arthur [Austl.]	59	Jh	43.09S	147.51 E
Port Arthur [Tx.-U.S.]	39	Jg	29.55N	93.55W
Port Arthur (EN)=Lüshun	27	Ld	38.50N	121.13 E
Port Augusta	58	Eh	32.30S	137.46 E
Port-Au-Prince	39	Lh	18.32N	72.20W
Port-au-Prince, Baie de-	49	Kd	18.40N	72.30W
Port Austin	44	Fc	44.03N	83.01W
Port aux Français	31	Om	49.25S	70.10 E
Porta Westfalica	12	Kb	52.15N	8.56 E
Port-Bergé-Vao Vao	37	Hc	15.33S	47.38 E
Port Blair	22	Lh	11.36N	92.45 E
Port-Bou/Portbou	13	Pb	42.25N	3.10 E
Portbou/Port-Bou	13	Pb	42.25N	3.10 E
Port Burwell [Newf.-Can.]	39	Mc	60.25N	64.49W
Port Burwell [Ont.-Can.]	44	Gd	42.39N	80.49W
Port-Cartier	42	Kf	50.01N	66.53W
Port Chalmers	62	Df	45.49S	170.37 E
Port Charlotte	43	Kf	26.59N	82.06W
Port Clinton	44	Fe	41.30N	82.58W
Port Coquitlam	46	Db	49.16N	122.46W
Port-de-Bouc	11	Kk	43.24N	4.59 E
Port-de-Paix	49	Kd	19.57N	72.50W
Port Dickson	26	Df	2.31N	101.48 E
Port Edward	37	Ef	31.03S	30.13 E
Portel [Braz.]	54	Hd	1.57S	50.49W
Portel [Port.]	13	Ef	38.18N	7.42W
Port Elgin	44	Gc	44.26N	81.24W
Port Elizabeth [S.Afr.]	31	Jl	33.58S	25.40 E
Port Elizabeth [St.Vin.]	51n	Ba	13.00N	61.16W
Port Ellen	9	Gf	55.39N	6.12W
Port-en-Bessin-Huppain	11	Fe	49.21N	0.45W
Port Erin	9	Ig	54.05N	4.43W
Porter Point	51n	Ba	13.23N	61.11W
Porterville [Ca.-U.S.]	43	Dd	36.04N	119.01W
Porterville [S.Afr.]	37	Bf	33.00S	19.00 E
Portete, Bahía de-	49	Lg	12.13N	71.55W
Port Fairy	59	Ig	38.23S	142.14 E
Port Fitzroy	62	Fb	36.10S	175.21 E
Port-Gentil	31	Hi	0.43S	8.47 E
Port Gibson	45	Kk	31.58N	90.58W
Port Harcourt	31	Hh	4.46N	7.01 E
Port Hardy	42	Ef	50.43N	127.29W
Port Hawkesbury	42	Lg	45.37N	61.21W
Porthcawl	9	Jj	51.29N	3.43W
Port Hedland	58	Cg	20.19S	118.34 E
Port Heiden	40	He	56.55N	158.41W
Port Hope Simpson	42	Lf	52.30N	56.17W
Port Huron	43	Kc	42.58N	82.27W
Portile de Fier = Iron Gate (EN)	5	Ig	44.41N	22.31 E
Port-Ilič	16	Pj	38.53N	48.51 E
Portimão	13	Dg	37.08N	8.32W
Port Isabel	45	Hm	26.04N	97.13W
Portiţa	15	Le	44.41N	29.00 E
Port Láirge/Waterford [2]	9	Fi	52.10N	7.40W
Port Láirge/Waterford	6	Fe	52.15N	7.06W
Portland [Austl.]	59	Ig	38.21S	141.36 E
Portland [Eng.-U.K.]	9	Kk	50.33N	2.27W
Portland [In.-U.S.]	44	Ee	40.26N	84.59W
Portland [Me.-U.S.]	39	Le	43.39N	70.17W
Portland [N.D.-U.S.]	45	Hc	47.30N	97.22W
Portland [N.Z.]	62	Fa	35.48S	174.20 E
Portland [Or.-U.S.]	39	Ge	45.33N	122.36W
Portland [Tx.-U.S.]	45	Hm	27.53N	97.20W
Portland, Bill of-	9	Kk	50.31N	2.28W
Portland, Promontoire -	42	Je	58.41N	78.33W
Portland Bight	49	Ie	17.57N	77.08W
Portland Island	62	Gc	39.20S	177.50 E
Portland Point	49	Ie	17.42N	77.11W
Port-la-Nouvelle	11	Jk	43.01N	3.03 E
Portlaoise/Port Laoise	9	Fh	53.02N	7.17W
Port Laoise/Portlaoise	9	Fh	53.02N	7.17W
Port Lavaca	43	Hf	28.37N	96.38W
Port Lincoln	58	Eh	34.44S	135.52 E
Port Loko	34	Cd	8.46N	12.47W
Port Louis	50	Fd	16.25N	61.32W
Port-Louis	31	Mk	20.10S	57.30 E
Port Macquarie	59	Kf	31.26S	152.44 E
Portmadoc	9	Ii	52.55N	4.08W
Port Maria	49	Id	18.22N	76.54W
Port-Menier	42	Lg	49.49N	64.20W
Port Moller	40	Ge	55.59N	160.34W
Port Moody	46	Db	49.17N	122.51W
Port Moresby	58	Fe	9.30S	147.07 E
Port Nelson	42	Ie	57.04N	92.30W
Portneuf, Rivière-	44	Ma	48.37N	69.05W
Port Nolloth	31	Ik	29.17S	16.51 E
Porto	13	Dc	41.15N	8.20W
Porto [Fr.]	11a	Aa	42.16N	8.42 E
Porto [Port.]	6	Fg	41.09N	8.37W
Porto, Golfe de-	11a	Aa	42.16N	8.37 E
Pôrto Acre	54	Ee	9.34S	67.31W
Porto Alegre [Braz.]	53	Ki	30.04S	51.11W
Porto Alegre [SaoT.P.]	34	Ge	0.02N	6.32 E
Porto Amboim	31	Ij	10.44S	13.45 E
Porto Azzurro	14	Eh	42.46N	10.24 E
Portobelo	49	Hi	9.33N	79.39W
Porto Cedro	55	Ed	18.17S	55.02W
Porto Cervo	14	Di	41.08N	9.35 E
Porto Curupai	55	Ff	22.50S	53.53W
Porto de Moz	53	Kf	1.45S	52.14W
Porto Empedocle	14	Hm	37.17N	13.32 E
Porto Esperança [Braz.]	55	Dd	19.37S	57.27W
Porto Esperança [Braz.]	55	Db	14.02S	56.06W
Porto Esperança [Braz.]	55	Dc	17.47S	57.07W
Porto Esperidião	55	Cb	15.51S	58.28W
Porto Estrêla	55	Db	15.20S	57.14W
Portoferraio	14	Eh	42.49N	10.19 E
Port of Ness	9	Gc	58.30N	6.15W
Porto Franco	54	Ie	6.20S	47.24W
Port of Spain	53	Jd	10.39N	61.31W
Porto Fundação	55	Ea	13.39S	55.18W
Portogruaro	14	Ge	45.47N	12.50 E
Porto Lucena	55	Eh	27.51S	55.01W
Portöm/Pirttikyla	8	Ib	62.42N	21.37 E
Portomaggiore	14	Ff	44.42N	11.48 E
Porto Mendes	55	Eg	24.30S	54.20W
Porto Moniz	32	Dc	32.51N	17.10W
Porto Moroco	55	Ea	13.24S	55.35W
Porto Morrinho	55	Dc	16.38S	57.49W
Porto Murtinho	53	Kh	21.42S	57.52W
Porto Novo [Ben.]	31	Hh	6.29N	2.37 E
Porto Novo [C.V.]	32	Bf	17.07N	25.04W
Port Orford	46	Ce	42.45N	124.30W
Porto San Giorgio	14	Hg	43.11N	13.48 E
Porto Santana	54	Hd	0.03S	51.11W
Porto Sant'Elpidio	14	Hg	43.15N	13.45 E
Porto Santo	30	Fe	33.04N	16.20W
Porto Santo Stefano	14	Fh	42.26N	11.07 E
Portoscuso	14	Ck	39.12N	8.23 E
Pôrto Seguro	54	Kg	16.26S	39.05W
Porto Tolle	14	Gf	44.56N	12.22 E
Porto Torres	14	Cj	40.50N	8.24 E
Porto União	55	Gh	26.15S	51.05W
Pôrto Válter	54	De	8.15S	72.45W
Porto Vecchio	11a	Bb	41.35N	9.17 E
Porto Velho	53	Jf	8.46S	63.54W
Portoviejo	53	Hf	1.03S	80.27W
Porto Xavier	55	Eh	27.54S	55.08W
Port Phillip Bay	59	Ig	38.05S	144.50 E
Port Pirie	58	Eh	33.11S	138.01 E
Portree	9	Gd	57.24N	6.12W
Port Renfrew	46	Cb	48.33N	124.25W
Port Rois/Portrush	9	Gf	55.12N	6.40W
Port Royal	44	If	38.10N	77.12W
Portrush/Port Rois	9	Gf	55.12N	6.40W
Port Said (EN)=Būr Sa'īd	31	Ke	31.16N	32.18 E
Port Saint Joe	43	Jf	29.49N	85.18W
Port Saint Johns	37	Df	31.38S	29.33 E
Port-Saint-Louis-du-Rhône	11	Kk	43.23N	4.48 E
Port-Salut	49	Kd	18.05N	73.55W
Port Saunders	42	Lf	50.39N	57.18W
Port Shepstone	31	Kl	30.46S	30.22 E
Portsmouth [Dom.]	50	Fe	15.35N	61.28W
Portsmouth [Eng.-U.K.]	9	Lk	50.48N	1.05W
Portsmouth [N.H.-U.S.]	43	Mc	43.03N	70.47W
Portsmouth [Oh.-U.S.]	43	Kd	38.45N	82.59W
Portsmouth [Va.-U.S.]	43	Ld	36.50N	76.26W
Portsmouth City Airport	12	Ad	50.46N	1.04W
Port Sudan (EN)=Būr Sūdān	31	Kg	19.37N	37.14 E
Port Sulphur	45	Ll	29.29N	89.42W
Port Talbot	9	Jj	51.36N	3.47W
Porttipahdantekojärvi	7	Gb	68.06N	26.33 E
Port Townsend	46	Db	48.07N	122.46W
Portugal [1]	6	Fh	39.30N	8.00W
Portugalete	13	Ia	43.19N	3.01W
Portuguesa [2]	54	Eb	9.10N	69.15W
Portuguesa, Rio-	54	Eb	7.57N	67.32W
Portuguesa, Sierra de-	50	Bh	9.35N	69.45W
Portuguese Guinea (EN) → Guinea Bissau (EN) [1]	31	Fg	12.00N	15.00W
Portús, Coll del-/Perthus, Col de-	13	Ob	42.28N	2.51 E
Port-Vendres	11	Jl	42.31N	3.07 E
Port-Vila	58	Hf	17.44S	168.19 E
Port Wakefield	59	Hf	34.11S	138.09 E
Port Washington	45	Me	43.23N	87.53W
Porvenir [Bol.]	54	Ef	11.15S	68.41W
Porvenir [Bol.]	55	Ba	13.59S	61.39W
Porvenir [Chile]	56	Fh	53.18S	70.22W
Porvenir [Ur.]	55	Dk	32.23S	57.59W
Porvoo/Borgå	7	Ff	60.24N	25.40 E
Porvoonjoki	8	Kd	60.23N	25.40 E
Porz, Köln-	10	Df	50.53N	7.03 E
Posada, Fiume di-	14	Dj	40.39N	9.45 E
Posadas [Arg.]	53	Kh	27.25S	55.50W
Posadas [Sp.]	13	Gg	37.48N	5.06W
Posavina	15	De	44.33N	20.04 E
Poschiavo	14	Ed	46.20N	10.04 E
Pošehonje	7	Jg	58.30N	39.08 E
Posht-e Bādām	24	Pf	33.02N	55.23 E
Posio	7	Gc	66.06N	28.09 E
Posjet	28	Kc	42.39N	130.48 E
Poskam/Zepu	27	Cd	38.12N	77.18 E
Poso	22	Oj	1.23S	120.44 E
Poso, Danau-	26	Hg	1.52S	120.35 E
Posof	24	Jb	41.31N	42.42 E
Posŏng	28	Ig	34.46N	127.05 E
Pospeliha	20	Df	52.02N	81.56 E
Posse	54	If	14.05S	46.22W
Possession, Ile de la-	30	Mm	46.14S	49.55 E
Possession Island	37	Be	27.01S	15.30 E
Pössneck	10	Hf	50.42N	11.36 E
Post	45	Fj	33.12N	101.23W
Posta de San Martín	55	Bk	33.09S	60.31W
Postavy	19	Cd	55.07N	26.50 E
Poste Maurice Cortier/Bidon V	32	He	22.18N	1.05 E
Poste Weygand	32	He	24.29N	0.40 E
Postmasburg	37	Ce	28.18S	23.05 E
Postojna	14	Ie	45.47N	14.14 E
Posto Simões Lopes	55	Eb	14.14S	54.41W
Postville [Ia.-U.S.]	45	Ke	43.05N	91.34W
Postville [Newf.-Can.]	42	Lf	54.55N	59.58W
Potchefstroom	37	De	26.46S	27.01 E
Poteau	45	Ii	35.03N	94.37W
Potenza	14	Hg	43.25N	13.40 E
Potenza	14	Jj	40.38N	15.48 E
Poteriteri, Lake-	62	Bg	46.05S	167.05 E
Potes	13	Ha	43.09N	4.37W
Potgietersrus	37	Dd	24.15S	28.55 E
Potholes Reservoir	46	Fc	47.01N	119.19W
Poti	6	Kg	42.08N	41.39 E
Poti, Rio-	54	Je	5.02S	42.50W
Potigny	12	Bf	48.58N	0.14W
Potiskum	31	Ig	11.43N	11.04 E
Potnarhvin	63b	Dd	18.45S	169.12 E
Potomac	38	Lf	38.00N	76.18W
Potosí [2]	54	Eh	20.40S	67.00W
Potosi [Bol.]	53	Jg	19.35S	65.45W
Potosi [Mex.]	47	Dd	24.51N	100.19W
Potosi, Bahía-	48	Ii	17.35N	101.30W
Potosi, Cerro-	48	Ie	24.52N	100.13W
Pototan	26	Hd	10.55N	122.40 E
Potrerillos	56	Gc	26.26S	69.29W
Potrero, Río-	55	Bc	17.32S	61.35W
Potsdam [Ger.]	10	Jd	52.24N	13.04 E
Potsdam [N.Y.-U.S.]	44	Jc	44.40N	75.01W
Pott	63b	Ad	19.35S	163.36 E
Potters Bar	12	Bc	51.41N	0.10W
Pottstown	44	Je	40.15N	75.38W
Pottsville	44	Ie	40.42N	76.13W
Pouancé	11	Eg	47.45N	1.10W
Pouébo	63b	Be	20.24S	164.34 E
Pouembout	63b	Be	21.08S	164.54 E
Poughkeepsie	44	Ke	41.43N	73.56W
Poulaphuca Reservoir/Loch Pholl an Phúca	9	Gh	53.10N	6.30W
Poum	63b	Be	20.14S	164.01 E
Pourtalé	55	Bm	37.02S	60.36W
Pouso Alegre	55	Ih	22.13S	45.56W
Pouss	34	Ic	10.51N	15.03 E
Poutasi	65c	Bb	14.01S	171.41W
Poŭthĭsăt	25	Kf	12.32N	103.55 E
Poutrincourt, Lac-	44	Ja	49.13N	74.04W
Po Valley (EN)=Padana, Pianura-	5	Gf	45.20N	10.00 E
Považská Bystrica	10	Og	49.07N	18.28 E
Považský Inovec	10	Nh	48.35N	18.00 E
Povenec	7	Ie	62.51N	34.45 E
Poverty Bay	62	Gc	38.45S	178.00 E
Povlen	15	Ce	44.09N	19.44 E
Póvoa de Varzim	13	Dc	41.23N	8.46W
Povorino	16	Md	51.12N	42.17 E
Povungnituk	42	Jd	60.03N	77.16W
Povungnituk	39	Lc	60.02N	77.10W
Powassan	44	Hb	46.05N	79.22W
Powder River [U.S.]	43	Fb	46.44N	105.26W
Powder River [Or.-U.S.]	46	Gd	44.45N	117.03W
Powell	46	Kd	44.45N	108.46W
Powell, Lake- [U.S.]	43	Ed	37.25N	110.45W
Powell Lake [Can.]	46	Ca	50.11N	124.24W
Powell River	42	Fg	49.52N	124.33W
Powers	44	Dc	45.39N	87.32W
Powers Lake	45	Eb	48.34N	102.39W
Powidzkie, Jezioro-	10	Nc	52.24N	17.57 E
Powys [3]	9	Ji	52.25N	3.20W
Poxoréu	54	Hg	15.50S	54.23W
Poxoréu, Rio- [Braz.]	55	Ec	16.32S	54.46W
Poxoréu, Rio- [Braz.]	55	Ec	16.08S	54.14W
Poya	63b	Be	21.21S	165.09 E
Poyang Hu	21	Ng	29.00N	116.25 E
Poza de la Sal	13	Ib	42.40N	3.30W
Pozanti	24	Fd	37.25N	34.52 E
Požarevac	15	Ee	44.37N	21.12 E
Poza Rica de Hidalgo	39	Jg	20.33N	97.27W
Požarskoje	28	Ma	46.16N	134.04 E
Požega	15	Df	43.51N	20.02 E
Poznań [2]	10	Pd	52.25N	19.55 E
Poznań	6	He	52.25N	16.55 E
Pozoblanco	13	Hf	38.22N	4.51W
Pozo Borrado	55	Bi	28.56S	61.41W
Pozo Colorado	55	Cf	23.22S	58.55W
Pozo del Mortero	55	Bg	24.24S	61.02W
Pozo del Tigre	55	Bc	17.34S	61.59W
Pozo Dulce	55	Ai	29.04S	62.02W
Pozos, Punta-	56	Gg	47.57S	65.47W
Pozuelos	54	Fa	10.11N	64.39W
Pozzallo	14	In	36.43N	14.51 E
Pozzuoli	14	Ij	40.49N	14.07 E
Pra [Ghana]	34	Ed	6.27N	1.47W
Pra	7	Ji	54.45N	41.01 E
Prabuty	10	Pc	53.46N	19.10 E
Prachatice	10	Jg	49.01N	14.00 E
Prachin Buri	25	Kf	14.02N	101.22 E
Prachuap Khiri Khan	25	Jf	11.48N	99.47 E
Praděd	10	Nf	50.06N	17.14 E
Prades	11	Il	42.37N	2.26 E
Prado	54	Kg	17.21S	39.13W
Præstø	8	Ei	55.07N	12.03 E
Prague (EN)=Praha	6	He	50.05N	14.26 E
Praha=Prague (EN)	6	He	50.05N	14.26 E
Prahova [2]	15	Id	45.10N	26.00 E
Praia	31	Eg	14.55N	23.31W
Praia a Mare	14	Jk	39.54N	15.47 E
Praia da Rocha	13	Dg	37.07N	8.32W
Praia Rica	55	Eb	14.51S	55.33W
Praid	15	Ic	46.33N	25.08 E
Prainha	54	Hd	1.48S	53.29W
Prairie Dog Town Fork	45	Gi	34.26N	99.21W
Prairie du Chien	45	Ke	43.03N	91.09W
Prangli	8	Ke	59.38N	24.50 E
Pránhita	25	Fe	18.49N	79.55 E
Prapat	26	Cf	2.40N	98.56 E
Prasat	25	Kf	14.38N	103.24 E
Praslin	51k	Bb	13.53N	60.54W
Praslin, Port-	51k	Bb	13.53N	60.54W
Praslin Island	37b	Ca	4.19S	55.44 E
Prasonisíon	15	Kn	35.52N	27.46 E
Prat, Isla-	56	Fg	48.15S	75.00W
Prata	55	Ig	19.18S	48.55W
Prata, Rio da-	55	Hd	18.49S	49.54W
Pratapgarh	25	Ed	24.02N	74.47 E
Prat de Llobregat/El Prat de Llobregat	13	Oc	41.20N	2.06 E
Prato	14	Fg	43.53N	11.06 E
Pratomagno	14	Fg	43.40N	11.40 E
Pratt	43	Hd	37.39N	98.44W
Prättigau	14	Dd	46.55N	9.40 E
Pratt Seamount (EN)	40	Ke	56.10N	142.30W
Prattville	44	Di	32.28N	86.29W
Pratudinho, Rio-	55	Ja	13.58S	45.10W
Pravda	18	Cf	36.50N	60.33 E
Pravda Coast	66	Ge	67.00S	94.00 E
Pravdinsk	8	Ij	54.28N	21.00 E
Pravdinsk	7	Kh	56.33N	43.33 E
Pravia	13	Fa	43.29N	6.07W
Praxedis G. Guerrero	48	Gb	31.22N	106.00W
Praya	26	Gh	8.42S	116.17 E
Prealpi Venete	14	Fd	46.25N	11.50 E
Predazzo	14	Fd	46.19N	11.36 E
Predeal	15	Id	45.30N	25.34 E
Predeal, Pasul-	15	Id	45.28N	25.36 E
Predel	14	Hd	46.25N	13.35 E
Predivinsk	20	Ee	57.04N	93.37 E
Predporožny	20	Jd	65.00N	143.20 E
Pré-en-Pail	11	Ff	48.27N	0.12W
Preetz	10	Gb	54.14N	10.17 E
Pregolia	7	Ei	54.42N	20.24 E
Pregradnaja	16	Lh	43.58N	41.12 E
Preilj/Prejli	7	Gh	56.19N	26.48 E
Preissac, Lac-	44	Ha	48.25N	78.28W
Prejli/Preilj	7	Gh	56.19N	26.48 E
Prekmurje	14	Kd	46.45N	16.15 E
Prekornica	15	Cg	42.40N	19.12 E
Prekule/Priekulė	8	Ii	55.36N	21.12 E
Přelouč	10	Lf	50.02N	15.33 E
Premià de Mar/Premiá de Mar	13	Oc	41.29N	2.22 E
Premiá de Mar/Premià de Mar	13	Oc	41.29N	2.22 E
Premnitz	10	Id	52.32N	12.20 E
Premuda	14	If	44.21N	14.37 E
Prenaj/Prienai	7	Fi	54.39N	23.59 E
Prenj	14	Lg	43.32N	17.52 E
Prenjasi	15	Dh	41.04N	20.32 E
Prentice	45	Kd	45.33N	90.17W
Prentiss	45	Lk	31.36N	89.52W
Prenzlau	10	Jc	53.19N	13.52 E
Preobraženije	20	Ih	42.58N	133.55 E
Preobraženka	20	Fd	60.04N	107.58 E
Preparis Island	25	If	14.52N	93.41 E
Preparis North Channel	25	Ie	15.27N	94.05 E
Preparis South Channel	25	If	14.45N	94.05 E
Přerov	10	Ng	49.27N	17.27 E
Prescelly, Mynydd-	9	Ij	51.58N	4.42W
Prescott [Ar.-U.S.]	45	Jj	33.48N	93.23W
Prescott [Az.-U.S.]	43	Ee	34.33N	112.28W
Preševo	15	Eg	42.19N	21.39 E
Presho	45	Fe	43.53N	100.04W
Presicce	14	Mk	39.54N	18.16 E
Presidencia Roque Sáenz Peña	53	Jh	26.50S	60.30W
Presidente Epitácio	56	Jb	21.46S	52.06W
Presidente Frei	66	Re	62.12S	58.55W
Presidente Hayes [3]	55	Cf	24.00S	59.00W
Presidente Juscelino	55	Jd	18.39S	44.05W
Presidente Murtinho	55	Fb	15.39S	53.54W
Presidente Olegário	55	Id	18.25S	46.25W
Presidente Prudente	56	Jb	22.07S	51.22W
Presidente Venceslau	55	Ge	21.52S	51.50W
President Thiers Seamount (EN)	57	Lg	24.39S	145.51W
Presidio	43	Gf	29.33N	104.23W
Presidio, Rio del-	48	Ff	23.06N	106.17W
Preslav	15	Jf	43.10N	26.49 E
Presnovka	17	Mi	54.40N	67.09 E
Prešov	10	Rh	49.00N	21.14 E
Prespa	15	Hh	41.43N	24.53 E
Prespa, Lake- (EN)=Prespansko jezero	5	Ig	40.55N	21.00 E
Prespansko jezero=Prespa, Lake- (EN)	5	Ig	40.55N	21.00 E
Presque Isle	43	Nb	46.41N	68.01W
Prestea	34	Ed	5.26N	2.09W
Přeštice	10	Jg	49.35N	13.21 E
Preston [Eng.-U.K.]	9	Kh	53.46N	2.42W
Preston [Id.-U.S.]	43	Ec	42.06N	111.53W
Preston [Ont.-Can.]	44	Gd	43.23N	80.21W
Prestonsburg	44	Fg	37.40N	82.46W
Preststranda	8	Ce	59.06N	9.04 E
Prestwick	9	If	55.30N	4.37W
Prêto, Rio- [Braz.]	54	Jf	11.21S	43.52W
Prêto, Rio- [Braz.]	55	Gd	18.44S	50.23W
Prêto, Rio- [Braz.]	55	Ic	17.00S	46.12W
Prêto, Rio- [Braz.]	55	Ha	13.37S	48.06W
Preto do Igapó Açu, Rio-	54	Gd	4.26S	59.48W
Pretoria	31	Jk	25.45S	28.10 E
Pretty Rock Butte	45	Fc	46.10N	101.42W
Preußisch-Oldendorf	12	Kb	52.18N	8.30 E
Préveza	15	Dk	38.57N	20.45 E
Prey	12	Df	48.58N	1.13 E
Prey Vêng	25	Lf	11.29N	105.19 E
Priangarskoje Plato	20	Ee	57.30N	97.00 E
Priargunsk	20	Gf	50.27N	119.00 E
Pribelski	17	Hi	54.24N	56.29 E
Pribilof Islands	38	Cd	57.00N	170.00W
Priboj	15	Cf	43.35N	19.32 E
Příbram	10	Kg	49.42N	14.01 E
Price [Que.-Can.]	44	Ma	48.39N	68.12W
Price [Ut.-U.S.]	46	Jg	39.36N	110.48W
Price River	46	Jg	39.10N	110.06W
Prichard	44	Cj	30.44N	88.05W
Prickly Pear Cays	51b	Ab	18.16N	63.11W
Prickly Point	51p	Bc	11.59N	61.45W
Pridneprovskaja Vozvyšennost=Dnepr Upland (EN)	5	Jf	49.00N	32.00 E
Priego	13	Jd	40.27N	2.18W
Priego de Córdoba	13	Hg	37.26N	4.11W
Priei, Măgura-	15	Fc	46.58N	22.50 E
Priekule	7	Eh	56.29N	21.37 E
Priekulė/Prekule	8	Ii	55.36N	21.12 E
Prienai/Prenaj	7	Fi	54.39N	23.59 E
Priene	24	Bd	37.40N	27.13 E
Prieska	31	Jk	29.40S	22.42 E
Priest Lake	46	Gb	48.34N	116.52W
Prieta, Peña-	13	Ha	43.01N	4.44W
Prieta, Sierra-	48	Cb	31.15N	112.55W
Prievidza	10	Oh	48.46N	18.39 E
Prignitz	10	Hc	53.00N	12.00 E
Prijedor	14	Kf	44.59N	16.42 E
Prijepolje	15	Cf	43.24N	19.39 E
Prijutovo	19	Fe	53.58N	53.58 E
Prikaspijskaja Nizmennost=Caspian Depression (EN)	5	Lf	48.00N	52.00 E
Prilenskoje Plato = Lena Mountains (EN)	21	Oc	60.45N	125.00 E
Prilep	15	Eh	41.21N	21.34 E
Priluki	19	De	50.36N	32.24 E
Primavera	66	Qe	64.09S	60.57W
Primeira Cruz	54	Jd	2.30S	43.26W
Primorje	8	Hj	54.56N	20.00 E
Primorsk	7	Gf	60.22N	28.36 E
Primorsk	16	Jf	46.43N	36.22 E
Primorski Hrebet	20	Ff	52.30N	106.00 E
Primorski Kraj [3]	20	Ig	45.30N	135.30 E
Primorsko	15	Kg	42.16N	27.46 E
Primorsko-Ahtarsk	19	Df	46.03N	38.11 E
Primorskoje	8	Ld	60.32N	27.56 E
Primorskoje	15	Nd	45.59N	30.15 E
Primošten	14	Jg	43.36N	15.55 E
Primrose Lake	42	Gf	54.55N	109.45W
Prims	10	Cg	49.20N	6.44 E
Prince Albert	39	Id	53.12N	104.46W
Prince Albert Mountains	66	Jf	76.00S	161.30 E
Prince Albert Peninsula	42	Fb	72.30N	116.00W
Prince Albert Road	37	Cf	33.13S	22.02 E
Prince Albert Sound	42	Gb	70.25N	115.00W
Prince Alfred, Cape -	42	Fb	74.05N	124.29W
Prince Charles	38	Lc	67.50N	76.00W
Prince Charles Mountains	66	Ff	72.00S	67.00 E
Prince-de-Galles, Cap -	42	Kd	61.36N	71.30W
Prince Edward	30	Km	46.33S	37.57 E
Prince Edward Island [3]	42	Lg	46.30N	63.00W
Prince Edward Island	38	Me	46.30N	63.00W
Prince Edward Islands	30	Km	46.35S	37.56 E
Prince George	39	Gd	53.55N	122.49W
Prince Gustaf Adolf Sea	38	Ib	78.30N	107.00W
Prince of Wales [Ak.-U.S.]	40	Me	55.47N	132.50W
Prince of Wales [Can.]	38	Jb	72.40N	99.00W
Prince of Wales, Cape-	38	Cc	65.40N	168.05W
Prince of Wales Island	59	Ib	10.40S	142.10 E
Prince of Wales Mountains	42	Ja	77.45N	78.00W
Prince of Wales Strait	42	Fb	72.45N	118.00W
Prince Patrick	38	Hb	76.45N	119.30W
Prince Regent Inlet	42	Ib	72.45N	90.30W
Prince Rupert	39	Fd	54.19N	130.19W
Prince Rupert Bay	51g	Ba	15.34N	61.29W
Prince Rupert Bluff	51g	Ba	15.35N	61.29W
Princes Risborough	12	Bc	51.43N	0.49W
Princess Anne	44	Jf	38.12N	75.41W
Princess Charlotte Bay	59	Ib	14.25S	144.00 E
Princess Elizabeth Land	66	Ff	70.00S	80.00 E

Index Symbols

[1] Independent Nation
[2] State, Region
[3] District, County
[4] Municipality
[5] Colony, Dependency
Continent
Physical Region
Historical or Cultural Region
Mount, Mountain
Volcano
Hill
Mountains, Mountain Range
Hills, Escarpment
Plateau, Upland
Pass, Gap
Plain, Lowland
Delta
Salt Flat
Valley, Canyon
Crater, Cave
Karst Features
Depression
Polder
Desert, Dunes
Forest, Woods
Heath, Steppe
Oasis
Cape, Point
Coast, Beach
Cliff
Peninsula
Isthmus
Sandbank
Island
Atoll
Rock, Reef
Islands, Archipelago
Rocks, Reefs
Coral Reef
Well, Spring
Geyser
River, Stream
Waterfall Rapids
River Mouth, Estuary
Lake
Salt Lake
Intermittent Lake
Reservoir
Swamp, Pond
Canal
Glacier
Ice Shelf, Pack Ice
Ocean
Sea
Gulf, Bay
Strait, Fjord
Lagoon
Bank
Seamount
Tablemount
Ridge
Shelf
Basin
Escarpment, Sea Scarp
Fracture
Trench, Abyss
National Park, Reserve
Point of Interest
Recreation Site
Cave, Cavern
Historic Site
Ruins
Wall, Walls
Church, Abbey
Temple
Scientific Station
Airport
Port
Lighthouse
Mine
Tunnel
Dam, Bridge

Princess Margaret Range 42 Ia 79.00N 88.30W
Princess Royal 42 Ef 52.55N 128.50W
Princeton [B.C.-Can.] 42 Fg 49.27N 120.31W
Princeton [Il.-U.S.] 45 Lf 41.23N 89.28W
Princeton [In.-U.S.] 44 Df 38.21N 87.34W
Princeton [Ky.-U.S.] 44 Dg 37.07N 87.53W
Princeton [Mo.-U.S.] 45 Jf 40.24N 93.35W
Prince William Sound 38 Ec 60.40N 147.00W
Principe 30 Hh 1.37N 7.25 E
Prineville 46 Ed 44.18N 120.51W
Prineville Reservoir 46 Ed 44.08N 120.42W
Prins Christians Sund 41 Hf 60.00N 43.10W
Prinsesse Astrid Kyst 66 Cf 70.45S 12.30 E
Prinsesse Ragnhild Kyst 66 Df 70.15S 27.30 E
Prins Harald Kyst 66 De 69.30S 36.00 E
Prins Karls Forland 41 Nc 78.32N 11.10 E
Prinzapolka 47 Hf 13.24N 83.34W
Prinzapolka, Río- 49 Fg 13.24N 83.34W
Priora, Mount- 59 Ja 6.51S 145.58 E
Priozersk 19 Dc 61.04N 30.07 E
Pripet Marshes (EN) 5 Ie 52.00N 27.00 E
Pripjat 5 Je 51.21N 30.09 E
Pripoljarny Ural=Subpolar Urals (EN) 5 Lb 65.00N 60.00 E
Prírečny 19 Db 69.02N 30.15 E
Prišib 16 Pj 39.06N 48.38 E
Prislop, Pasul- 15 Hb 47.37N 24.55 E
Pristan-Prževalsk 16 Lc 42.33N 78.18 E
Pristen 16 Jd 51.15N 36.42 E
Priština 15 Eg 42.40N 21.10 E
Pritzwalk 10 Ic 53.09N 12.11 E
Privas 11 Kj 44.44N 4.36 E
Priverno 14 Hi 41.28N 13.11 E
Privolžkaja Vozvyšennost=Volga Hills (EN) 5 Ke 52.00N 46.00 E
Privolžsk 7 Jh 57.27N 41.16 E
Privolžski 16 Od 51.23N 46.02 E
Prizren 15 Dg 42.13N 20.45 E
Prizzi 14 Hm 37.43N 13.26 E
Prjaža 7 Hf 61.43N 33.37 E
Prnjavor 14 Lf 44.52N 17.40 E
Probolinggo 26 Fh 7.45S 113.13 E
Prochowice 10 Me 51.17N 16.22 E
Procida 14 Hj 40.45N 14.00 E
Proctor Reservoir 45 Gj 32.02N 98.32W
Proddatur 25 Ff 14.44N 78.33 E
Profitis Ilias [Grc.] 15 Fm 36.53N 22.22 E
Profitis Ilias [Grc.] 15 Fj 39.50N 22.38 E
Profondeville 12 Gd 50.23N 4.52 E
Progonati 15 Ci 40.13N 19.56 E
Prograničnik 18 Dg 35.43N 63.12 E
Progreso [Mex.] 39 Kg 21.17N 89.40W
Progreso [Mex.] 48 Id 27.28N 101.04W
Progress 20 Hg 49.41N 129.40 E
Prohladny 16 Nh 43.45N 44.01 E
Prohorovka 16 Jd 51.02N 36.42 E
Prokopjevsk 22 Kd 53.53N 86.45 E
Prokuplje 15 Ef 43.15N 21.36 E
Proletari 7 Hg 58.26N 31.43 E
Proletarsk 19 Ef 46.41N 41.44 E
Proletarsk 18 Gd 40.10N 69.31 E
Proletarski 16 Id 50.51N 35.46 E
Proletarskoje Vodohranilišče 16 Mf 46.30N 42.10 E
Proliv Soela/Soela Väin 8 Jf 58.40N 22.30 E
Prome 22 Lh 18.49N 95.13 E
Promissão, Represa- 56 Kb 21.32S 49.52W
Promissão 55 He 21.32S 49.52W
Promyšlenny 17 Kc 67.35N 63.55 E
Pronja 16 Gc 53.27N 31.03 E
Pronja 16 Lb 54.21N 40.24 E
Pronsfeld 12 Id 50.10N 6.20 E
Prophet 42 Fe 58.46N 122.45W
Propriá 54 Kf 10.13S 36.51W
Propriano 11a Ab 41.40N 8.54 E
Prorva 16 Rg 45.57N 53.13 E
Proserpine 59 Jd 20.24S 148.34 E
Prosna 10 Nd 52.10N 17.39 E
Prosotsáni 15 Gh 41.11N 23.59 E
Prosperidad 26 Ie 8.34N 125.52 E
Prospihino 20 Ee 58.37N 99.20 E
Prosser 46 Fc 46.12N 119.46W
Prostějov 10 Ng 49.29N 17.07 E
Proszowice 10 Qf 50.12N 20.18 E
Próti 15 El 37.03N 21.33 E
Protoka 16 Jg 45.43N 37.46 E
Protva 7 Ii 54.51N 37.16 E
Provadija 15 Kf 43.11N 27.26 E
Prøven 41 Gd 72.15N 55.40W
Provence 11 Lk 44.00N 6.00 E
Provence 5 Gg 44.00N 6.00 E
Providence [Ky.-U.S.] 44 Dg 37.24N 87.39W
Providence [R.I.-U.S.] 39 Le 41.50N 71.25W
Providence, Cape- 62 Bg 46.01S 166.28 E
Providence Bay 44 Fc 45.44N 82.18W
Providence Island 30 Mi 9.14S 51.02 E
Providencia, Isla de- 47 Hf 13.21N 81.22W
Providenciales 49 Kc 21.49N 72.15W
Providenija 22 Uc 64.23N 173.18W
Provincetown 44 Ld 42.03N 70.11W
Provins 11 Jf 48.33N 3.18 E
Provo 39 He 40.14N 111.39W
Prozor 14 Lg 43.49N 17.37 E
Prudentópolis 55 Gg 25.12S 50.57W
Prudhoe Bay 39 Eb 70.20N 148.25W
Prudnik 10 Nf 50.19N 17.34 E
Prüm 12 Ie 49.49N 6.28 E
Prüm 10 Cf 50.13N 6.25 E
Prune Island 51n Bb 12.35N 61.24W
Prussia (EN) 10 Pc 53.45N 20.00 E
Pruszcz Gdański 10 Ob 54.16N 18.36 E
Pruszków 10 Qd 52.11N 20.48 E
Prut 5 If 45.28N 28.14 E
Pružany 19 Ce 52.36N 24.28 E
Prvić 14 If 44.54N 14.48 E
Prydz Bay 66 Fe 69.00S 76.00 E
Pryor 45 Ih 36.19N 95.19W
Przasnysz 10 Qc 53.01N 20.55 E
Przedbórz 10 Pe 51.06N 19.53 E
Przemyśl [2] 10 Sg 49.45N 22.45 E
Przemyśl 10 Sg 49.47N 22.47 E
Prževalsk 22 Je 42.29N 78.24 E
Przeworsk 10 Sf 50.05N 22.29 E
Przysucha 10 Qe 51.22N 20.38 E
Psakhná 15 Gk 38.35N 23.38 E
Psará 15 Ik 38.35N 25.37 E
Psathoúra 15 Hj 39.30N 24.11 E
Pščiš 16 Kg 45.03N 39.25 E
Psebaj 16 Lg 44.07N 40.47 E
Psël 5 Jf 49.05N 33.30 E
Psérimos 15 Km 36.56N 27.09 E
Psina 10 Of 50.02N 18.16 E
Pšiš, Gora- 16 Lh 43.24N 41.14 E
Pskem 18 Hd 41.38N 70.01 E
Pskent 18 Gd 40.54N 69.23 E
Pskov 6 Id 57.50N 28.20 E
Pskov, Lake- (EN)=Pihkva järv 7 Gg 58.00N 28.00 E
Pskov, Lake- (EN)=Pskovskoje Ozero 5 Id 58.00N 28.00 E
Pskova 8 Mg 57.47N 28.30 E
Pskovskaja Oblast [3] 19 Cd 57.20N 29.20 E
Pskovskoje Ozero=Pskov, Lake- (EN) 5 Id 58.00N 28.00 E
Psunj 14 Le 45.24N 17.20 E
Ptič 16 Fc 52.09N 28.52 E
Ptolemaïs 15 Ei 40.31N 21.41 E
Ptuj 14 Jd 46.25N 15.52 E
Pua-a, Cape- 65c Aa 13.26S 172.43W
Puah, Pulau- 26 Hg 0.30S 122.34 E
Puapua 65c Aa 13.34S 172.09W
Pucallpa 53 If 8.20S 74.30W
Pučež 7 Kh 56.59N 43.11 E
Pucheng [China] 27 Kf 27.55N 118.30 E
Pucheng [China] 27 Id 35.00N 109.38 E
Pucho 36 Cf 17.35S 16.30 E
Pucioasa 15 Id 45.05N 25.25 E
Pučišća 14 Kg 43.21N 16.44 E
Puck 10 Ob 54.44N 18.27 E
Pucka, Zatoka- 10 Ob 54.40N 18.35 E
Pudasjärvi 7 Gd 65.23N 27.00 E
Pudož 19 Dc 61.50N 36.32 E
Pudukkottai 25 Ff 10.23N 78.49 E
Puebla [2] 47 Ee 18.50N 98.00W
Puebla, Sierra de- 48 Kh 19.50N 97.00W
Puebla de Alcocer 13 Gf 38.59N 5.15W
Puebla de Don Fabrique 13 Jg 37.58N 2.26W
Puebla de Guzmán 13 Eg 37.37N 7.15W
Puebla de Sanabria 13 Fb 42.03N 6.38W
Puebla de Trives 13 Eb 42.20N 7.15W
Puebla de Zaragoza 39 Jh 19.03N 98.12W
Pueblo 39 If 38.16N 104.37W
Pueblo Libertador 55 Cj 30.13S 59.23W
Pueblo Nuevo [Mex.] 48 Gf 23.23N 105.23W
Pueblo Nuevo [Ven.] 49 Mh 11.58N 69.55W
Pueblo Nuevo Tiquisate 49 Bf 14.17N 91.22W
Pueblo Viejo, Laguna de- 48 Kf 22.10N 97.55W
Puelches 56 Ge 38.09S 65.55W
Puenteáreas 13 Db 42.11N 8.30W
Puente de la Reina 13 Kb 42.40N 1.49W
Puentedeume 13 Da 43.24N 8.10W
Puente-Genil 13 Hg 37.23N 4.47W
Puentelarrá 13 Ib 42.45N 3.03W
Pueo Point 65a Ab 21.54N 160.04W
Pu'er 27 Hg 23.00N 101.00 E
Puerca, Punta- 51a Cb 18.15N 65.35W
Puerco, Río- 45 Ci 34.22N 107.50W
Puerco River 46 Ji 34.52N 110.05W
Puerto Abente 55 Df 22.55S 57.43W
Puerto Acosta 54 Eg 15.32S 69.15W
Puerto Adela 55 Eg 24.33S 54.22W
Puerto Aisén 53 Ij 45.24S 72.42W
Puerto Alegre 54 Ff 13.53S 61.36W
Puerto Ángel 47 Ee 15.40N 96.29W
Puerto Arista 48 Mj 15.56N 93.48W
Puerto Armuelles 47 Hg 8.17N 82.52W
Puerto Asís 54 Cc 0.29N 76.32W
Puerto Ayacucho 53 Je 5.40N 67.35W
Puerto Ayora 54a Ab 0.45S 90.23W
Puerto Barrios 39 Kh 15.43N 88.36W
Puerto Bermejo 55 Ch 26.56S 58.30W
Puerto Berrío 54 Db 6.30N 74.25W
Puerto Boyacá 54 Db 5.45N 74.29W
Puerto Caballo 55 Ce 20.12S 58.12W
Puerto Cabello 53 Jd 10.28N 68.01W
Puerto Cabezas 47 Hf 14.02N 83.23W
Puerto Carreño 54 Eb 6.12N 67.22W
Puerto Casado 56 Ib 20.20S 57.55W
Puerto Colombia 49 Jh 10.59N 74.57W
Puerto Colón 55 Df 23.11S 57.33W
Puerto Constanza 55 Ck 33.50S 59.03W
Puerto Cooper 56 Ib 23.03S 57.43W
Puerto Cortés [C.R.] 49 Fi 8.58N 83.32W
Puerto Cortés [Hond.] 39 Kh 15.48N 87.56W
Puerto Cumarebo 54 Ea 11.29N 69.21W
Puerto de Eten 54 Ce 6.56S 79.52W
Puerto de la Cruz 32 Dd 28.23N 16.33W
Puerto de Lajas, Cerro- 47 Cc 28.59N 107.02W
Puerto del Rosario 32 Ed 28.30N 13.52W
Puerto de Mazarrón 13 Kg 37.34N 1.15W
Puerto de San José 47 Ff 13.55N 90.49W
Puerto Deseado 53 Jj 47.45S 65.55W
Puerto de Sóller 13 Oe 39.48N 2.41 E
Puerto Escondido [Mex.] 47 Ee 15.48N 96.57W
Puerto Escondido [Mex.] 48 De 25.48N 111.20W
Puerto Esperanza [Arg.] 55 Eh 26.01S 54.39W
Puerto Esperanza [Par.] 55 Ce 20.26S 58.06W
Puerto Estrella 49 Lg 12.14N 71.13W
Puerto Fonciere 55 Df 22.29S 57.48W
Puerto Francisco de Orellana 54 Cd 0.27S 76.57W
Puerto Frey 55 Bb 14.42S 61.10W
Puerto Gaitán 54 Dc 4.20N 72.10W
Puerto General Díaz 55 Eg 25.12S 54.32W
Puerto Goya 55 Ci 29.09S 59.20W
Puerto Grether 54 Fg 17.12S 64.21W
Puerto Guarani 55 De 21.18S 57.55W
Puerto Heath 54 Ef 12.30S 68.40W
Puerto Huasco 56 Fc 28.28S 71.14W
Puerto Huitoto 54 Dc 0.18N 74.03W
Puerto Iguazú 56 Jc 25.34S 54.34W
Puerto Indio 55 Eg 24.52S 54.29W
Puerto Ingeniero Ibañez 56 Fg 46.18S 71.56W
Puerto Isabel 55 Dd 18.11S 57.37W
Puerto Jesús 49 Eh 10.07N 85.16W
Puerto Juárez 39 Kg 21.11N 86.49W
Puerto la Concordia 54 Dc 2.38N 72.47W
Puerto la Cruz 53 Jd 10.13N 64.38W
Puerto Leguízamo 53 If 0.12S 74.46W
Puerto Lempira 49 Ff 15.15N 83.46W
Puerto Libertad 47 Bc 29.55N 112.43W
Puerto Limón [Col.] 54 Cc 1.02N 76.32W
Puerto Limón [Col.] 54 Dc 3.23N 73.30W
Puertollano 13 Hf 38.41N 4.07W
Puerto López 47 Jh 4.06N 72.58W
Puerto López 49 Lh 11.56N 71.17W
Puerto Lumbreras 13 Kg 37.34N 1.49W
Puerto Madero 48 Mj 14.44N 92.25W
Puerto Madryn 56 Gf 42.46S 65.03W
Puerto Magdalena 48 Ce 24.35N 112.05W
Puerto Maldonado 53 Jg 12.36S 69.11W
Puerto Marangatú 55 Eg 24.39S 54.21W
Puerto Mayor Otaño 55 Eh 26.19S 54.44W
Puerto Mihanovich 55 De 20.52S 57.59W
Puerto Monte Lindo 55 Df 23.57S 57.12W
Puerto Montt 53 Ij 41.28S 72.57W
Puerto Morelos 48 Pg 20.50N 86.52W
Puerto Mutis 54 Cb 6.14N 77.25W
Puerto Naranjito 55 Eh 26.57S 55.18W
Puerto Nariño 54 Ec 4.56N 67.48W
Puerto Natales 53 Ik 51.44S 72.31W
Puerto Nuevo 55 Ce 20.33S 58.03W
Puerto Nuevo, Punta- 51a Bb 18.30N 66.21W
Puerto Ordaz 54 Fb 8.22N 62.41W
Puerto Padre 49 Ic 21.12N 76.36W
Puerto Páez 54 Eb 6.13N 67.28W
Puerto Peñasco 47 Bb 31.20N 113.33W
Puerto Piña 49 Hj 7.35N 78.10W
Puerto Pinasco 56 Ib 22.43S 57.50W
Puerto Píritu 50 Dg 10.04N 65.03W
Puerto Plata 47 Je 19.48N 70.41W
Puerto Presidente Stroessner 55 Eg 25.33S 54.39W
Puerto Princesa 22 Ni 9.44N 118.44 E
Puerto Quijarro 55 Dc 17.47S 57.46W
Puerto Real 13 Fh 36.32N 6.11W
Puerto Rico [5] 39 Mh 18.15N 66.30W
Puerto Rico 38 Mh 18.15N 66.30W
Puerto Rico [Arg.] 56 Jc 26.48S 54.59W
Puerto Rico [Bol.] 54 Ef 11.05S 67.38W
Puerto Rico [Col.] 54 Cc 1.54N 75.10W
Puerto Rico Trench (EN) 3 Bg 20.00N 66.00W
Puerto Rondón 54 Db 6.18N 71.06W
Puerto San José 55 Eg 26.32S 54.50W
Puerto Santa Cruz 53 Jk 50.09S 68.30W
Puerto Sastre 56 Ib 22.06S 57.59W
Puerto Siles 54 Ef 12.48S 65.05W
Puerto Suárez 53 Kg 18.57S 57.51W
Puerto Tacurú Pytá 55 Df 23.49S 57.09W
Puerto Tirol 55 Ch 27.23S 59.05W
Puerto Tres Palmas 55 De 21.43S 57.58W
Puerto Triunfo 55 Eg 26.45S 55.06W
Puerto Vallarta 47 Cd 20.37N 105.15W
Puerto Varas 56 Ff 41.19S 72.59W
Puerto Victoria 55 Eh 26.20S 54.39W
Puerto Viejo 49 Eh 10.26N 83.59W
Puerto Villamizar 49 Ki 8.19N 72.26W
Puerto Villazón 55 Ba 13.32S 61.57W
Puerto Wilches 54 Db 7.20N 73.54W
Puerto Ybapobó 55 Df 23.42S 57.12W
Pueu 65e Fc 17.44S 149.13W
Pugačev 19 Ee 52.03N 48.48 E
Puget Sound 46 Dc 48.00N 122.30W
Puglia=Apulia (EN) [2] 14 Ki 41.15N 16.15 E
Pu He 28 Gd 41.21N 122.47 E
Puhja 8 Lf 58.13N 26.17 E
Puigcerdá 13 Nb 42.26N 1.56 E
Puigmal 13 Ob 42.23N 2.07 E
Puir 20 Jf 53.10N 141.25 E
Puisaye, Collines de la- 11 Jg 47.35N 3.18 E
Puisieux 12 Ed 50.07N 2.42 E
Pujehun 34 Cd 7.21N 11.42W
Pujeşti 15 Kc 46.25N 27.29 E
Puji → Wugong 27 Ie 34.15N 108.14 E
Pujiang 28 Ei 29.28N 119.53 E
Pujili 54 Cd 0.57S 78.42W
Puka 15 Cg 42.03N 19.54 E
Pukaki, Lake- 62 Df 44.05S 170.10 E
Pukalani 65a Ec 20.50N 156.21W
Pukapuka Atoll 57 Kf 10.53S 165.49W
Pukapuka Atoll [W.F.] 57 Nf 14.49S 138.48W
Pukaruha Atoll 57 Nf 18.20S 137.02W
Pukatawagan 42 He 55.44N 101.19W
Pukchin 28 Hd 40.12N 125.45 E
Pukch'ŏng 27 Mc 40.14N 128.19 E
Pukega, Pointe- 64h Ab 13.17S 176.13W
Pukekohe 62 Fb 37.12S 174.54 E
Pukemiro 62 Fb 37.37S 175.01 E
Pukeuri Junction 62 Df 45.02S 171.02 E
Pukšenga 7 Je 63.36N 41.55 E
Puksoozero 19 Ec 62.38N 40.32 E
Puksubaek-san 28 Id 40.42N 127.15 E
Pula [It.] 14 Ck 39.01N 9.00 E
Pula 14 Hf 44.52N 13.50 E
Pula, Capo di- 14 Dl 38.59N 9.01 E
Pulandian → Xinjin 27 Ld 39.24N 121.59 E
Pulap Atoll 57 Fd 7.39N 149.25 E
Pulaski [Tn.-U.S.] 44 Dh 35.12N 87.02W
Pulaski [Va.-U.S.] 44 Gg 37.03N 80.47W
Pulau 26 Kh 5.50S 138.15 E
Pulau Halura 26 Hi 10.19S 120.11 E
Pulau Irian/New Guinea 57 Fe 5.00S 140.00 E
Pulau Sapudi 26 Fh 7.06S 114.20 E
Puławy 10 Re 51.25N 21.57 E
Pulborough 12 Bd 50.57N 0.31W
Pulheim 12 Ic 51.00N 6.48 E
Pulkau 14 Kb 48.43N 16.21 E
Pulkkila 7 Fd 64.16N 25.52 E
Pullman 43 Db 46.44N 117.10W
Pulo Anna Island 57 Ed 4.40N 131.58 E
Pulog, Mount- 21 Oh 16.36N 120.54 E
Pulpito, Punta- 48 Dd 26.30N 111.30W
Pulsano 14 Lj 40.23N 17.21 E
Pułtusk 10 Rd 52.43N 21.05 E
Pülümür 24 Hc 39.30N 39.54 E
Pulusuk Island 57 Fd 6.42N 149.19 E
Puluwat Atoll 57 Fd 7.22N 149.11 E
Puma Yumco 27 Ff 28.35N 90.20 E
Pumpénai/Pumpenaj 8 Ki 55.53N 24.25 E
Pumpenaj/Pumpénai 8 Ki 55.53N 24.25 E
Pumpkin Creek 46 Mc 46.15N 105.45W
Puná, Isla- 54 Bd 2.50S 80.10W
Punākha 25 Hc 27.37N 89.52 E
Punaluu 65a Fd 19.08N 155.30W
Pūnch 25 Eb 33.46N 74.06 E
Punda Milia 37 Ed 22.40S 31.05 E
Pune (Poona) 22 Jh 18.32N 73.52 E
Punel 24 Md 37.33N 49.07 E
Pungan 18 Hd 40.45N 70.50 E
P'unggi 28 Jf 36.52N 128.32 E
Pungoè 37 Ec 19.50S 34.48 E
P'ungsan 28 Jd 40.40N 128.05 E
Punia 36 Ec 1.28S 26.27 E
Punitaqui 56 Fd 30.50S 71.16W
Punjab [3] 25 Fb 31.00N 76.00 E
Punjab 21 Jf 30.00N 74.00 E
Punjab [3] 25 Eb 30.00N 74.00 E
Punkaharju 8 Mc 61.48N 29.24 E
Punkalaidun 8 Jc 61.07N 23.06 E
Puno 53 Ig 15.50S 70.02W
Puno [2] 54 Ef 15.00S 70.00W
Punta, Cerro de- 47 Ke 18.10N 66.36W
Punta Alta 53 Ji 38.53S 62.04W
Punta Arenas 53 Ik 53.09S 70.55W
Punta Cardón 54 Da 11.38N 70.14W
Punta de Mata 50 Eh 9.43N 63.38W
Punta Gorda [Blz.] 47 Ge 16.07N 88.48W
Punta Gorda [Fl.-U.S.] 44 Fl 26.56N 82.03W
Punta Gorda [Nic.] 49 Fh 11.31N 83.47W
Punta Gorda, Bahía de- 49 Fh 11.15N 83.45W
Punta Gorda, Río- 49 Fh 11.30N 83.47W
Punta Indio 55 Dl 35.16S 57.14W
Punta Prieta 47 Bc 28.58N 114.17W
Puntarenas [3] 49 Ei 9.00N 83.15W
Puntarenas 39 Ki 9.58N 84.50W
Punta Róbalo 49 Fi 9.02N 82.15W
Punto Fijo 54 Da 11.42N 70.13W
Puolanka 7 Gd 64.52N 27.40 E
Puolo Point 65a Bb 21.54N 159.36W
Puqi 27 Jf 29.43N 113.52 E
Puquio 54 Df 14.42S 74.08W
Purace, Volcán- 54 Cc 2.21N 76.23W
Purari 60 Ci 7.52S 145.10 E
Purcell Mountains 42 Fg 49.55N 116.15W
Purdy Islands 57 Fe 2.53S 146.20 E
Purgatoire River 45 Eg 38.04N 103.10W
Puri 25 He 19.48N 85.51 E
Purificación 47 Ed 23.58N 98.42W
Purikari Neem/Purikarinem 8 Ke 59.36N 25.35 E
Purikarinem/Purikari Neem 8 Ke 59.36N 25.35 E
Purmani/Puurmani 8 Lf 58.30N 26.14 E
Purmerend 11 Kb 52.31N 4.57 E
Purna [India] 25 Fe 19.07N 77.02 E
Purna [India] 25 Fd 21.05N 76.00 E
Purnač 7 Jc 67.00N 40.15 E
Pūrnia 25 Hc 25.47N 87.28 E
Purukcahu 26 Fg 0.35S 114.35 E
Puruliya 25 Hd 23.20N 86.22 E
Puruni River 50 Gi 6.00N 59.12W
Purus, Rio- 52 Jf 3.42S 61.28W
Puruvesi 7 Gf 61.50N 29.25 E
Purwakarta 26 Eh 6.34S 107.26 E
Purwokerto 26 Eh 7.25S 109.14 E
Pusala Daği 24 Ed 37.12N 32.54 E
Pusan 22 Of 35.06N 129.03 E
Pusan Si [2] 28 Jg 35.10N 129.05 E
Pushi He 28 Hd 40.17N 124.43 E
Puškin 19 Dd 59.43N 30.24 E
Puškino 16 Od 51.14N 46.59 E
Puškino 7 Ih 56.02N 37.53 E
Puškinskije Gory 8 Mh 56.59N 28.59 E
Pušlahta 7 Id 64.48N 36.33 E
Püspökladány 10 Ri 47.19N 21.07 E
Püssi/Pjussi 8 Le 59.17N 26.57 E
Pusteci 15 Di 40.47N 20.54 E
Pusteria, Val-/Pustertal 14 Gd 46.45N 12.20 E
Pustertal/Pusteria, Val- 14 Gd 46.45N 12.20 E
Pustomyty 10 Tg 49.37N 23.59 E
Pustoška 7 Gh 56.20N 29.22 E
Putao 25 Jc 27.21N 97.24 E
Putaruru 62 Fc 38.03S 175.47 E
Putian 27 Kf 25.32N 119.01 E
Putignano 14 Lj 40.51N 17.07 E
Putila 15 Ip 48.00N 25.07 E
Putivl 16 Hd 51.22N 33.55 E
Putjatin 28 Lc 42.52N 132.25 E
Putla de Guerrero 48 Ki 17.02N 97.56W
Putna 15 Kd 45.34N 27.30 E
Putna 15 Ib 47.52N 25.37 E
Putnok 10 Qh 48.18N 20.26 E
Puto 63a Ba 5.41S 154.43 E
Putorana, Plato-=Putoran Mountains (EN) 21 Lc 69.00N 95.00 E
Putoran Mountains (EN)=Putorana, Plato- 21 Lc 69.00N 95.00 E
Puttalam 25 Fg 8.02N 79.49 E
Putte 12 Gc 51.04N 4.38 E
Puttelange-aux-Lacs 12 Ie 49.03N 6.56 E
Putten 12 Hb 52.16N 5.35 E
Putten 12 Gc 51.50N 4.15 E
Puttgarden, Burg auf Fehmarn- 10 Hb 54.30N 11.13 E
Püttlingen 12 Ie 49.17N 6.53 E
Putumayo [2] 54 Cc 0.30N 76.00W
Putumayo, Río- 52 Jf 3.07S 67.58W
Putuo (Shenjiamen) 28 Gj 29.57N 122.18 E
Putussibau 26 Ff 0.50N 112.56 E
Puu Kukui 65a Ec 20.54N 156.35W
Puulavesi 5 Ic 61.50N 26.40 E
Puumala 7 Gf 61.32N 28.11 E
Puu o Umi 65a Fc 20.05N 155.42W
Puurmani/Purmani 8 Lf 58.30N 26.14 E
Puurs 12 Gc 51.05N 4.17 E
Puuwai 65a Ab 21.54N 160.12W
Puyallup 46 Dc 47.11N 122.18W
Puyang 27 Jd 35.41N 115.00 E
Puy-de-Dôme [3] 11 Ii 45.40N 3.00 E
Puy-l'Evêque 11 Hj 44.30N 1.08 E
Puymorens, Col de- 11 Hl 42.34N 1.49 E
Puyo 54 Cd 1.29S 77.58W
Puysegur Point 62 Bg 46.10S 166.37 E
Pwani [3] 36 Gd 7.30S 39.00 E
Pweto 31 Ji 8.28S 28.54 E
Pwllheli 9 Ii 52.53N 4.25W
Pyapon 25 Je 16.17N 95.41 E
Pyhäjärvi 7 Fe 63.40N 25.59 E
Pyhäjärvi [Fin.] 7 Ff 61.00N 22.20 E
Pyhäjärvi [Fin.] 7 Fe 63.35N 25.57 E
Pyhäjärvi [Fin.] 8 Kc 62.45N 25.25 E
Pyhäjärvi [Fin.] 8 Jc 61.30N 23.35 E
Pyhäjoki 7 Fd 64.28N 24.13 E
Pyhäjoki 7 Fd 64.28N 24.14 E
Pyhäntä 7 Gd 64.06N 26.19 E
Pyhäranta 8 Id 60.57N 21.27 E
Pyhäselkä 7 Ge 62.30N 29.40 E
Pyhäselkä 8 Mb 62.26N 29.58 E
Pyhätunturi 7 Gc 67.01N 27.09 E
Pyhävesi 8 Lc 61.25N 26.35 E
Pyhävuori 8 Ib 62.17N 21.38 E
Pyhrnpaß 14 Ic 47.38N 14.18 E
Pyhtää/Pyttis 7 Gf 60.29N 26.32 E
Pyinmana 22 Lh 19.44N 96.13 E
Pylos (EN)=Pilos 15 Em 36.56N 21.40 E
Pyltsamaa/Põltsamaa 8 Lf 58.23N 26.08 E
Pyltsamaa/Põltsamaa 7 Fg 58.39N 25.59 E
Pylva/Põlva 7 Gg 58.04N 27.06 E
Pymatuning Reservoir 44 Ge 41.37N 80.30W
P'yŏngan-Namdo [2] 28 Ie 39.20N 126.00 E
P'yŏngan-Pukto [2] 28 Hd 40.00N 125.15 E
P'yŏnggang 27 Md 38.25N 127.17 E
P'yŏngsan 28 Md 38.20N 126.24 E
P'yongt'aek 28 If 36.59N 127.05 E
P'yŏngyang 22 Of 39.01N 125.45 E
P'yŏngyang Si [2] 28 He 39.04N 125.50 E
Pyramiden 41 Nc 77.54N 16.41 E
Pyramid Lake 43 Dc 40.00N 119.35W
Pyramid Mountains 45 Bj 32.00N 108.30W
Pyrénées=Pyrenees (EN) 5 Gg 42.40N 1.00 E
Pyrenees (EN)=Pirineos 5 Gg 42.40N 1.00 E
Pyrenees (EN)=Pyrénées 5 Gg 42.40N 1.00 E
Pyrenees (EN)=Serralada Pirinenca 5 Gg 42.40N 1.00 E
Pyrénées-Atlantiques [3] 11 Fk 43.15N 0.50W
Pyrénées-Orientales [3] 11 Il 42.30N 2.20 E
Pyrzyce 10 Kc 53.10N 14.55 E
Pyšma 19 Gd 57.08N 66.18 E
Pytalovo 7 Gh 57.06N 27.59 E
Pyttegga 8 Bd 62.13N 7.42 E
Pyttis/Pyhtää 7 Gf 60.29N 26.32 E
Pyu 25 Je 18.29N 96.26 E
Pyzaspea/Pöösaspea Neem 8 Je 59.15N 23.25 E
Pyzdry 10 Nd 52.11N 17.41 E

Q

Qā', Wādī al- 24 Hi 27.04N 38.34 E
Qābis [3] 32 Ic 33.00N 9.30 E
Qābis 31 Ie 33.53N 10.07 E
Qābis, Khalīj-=Gabès, Gulf of-(EN) 30 Ie 34.00N 10.25 E
Qabr Hūd 35 Hb 16.09N 49.34 E
Qāderābād 24 Og 30.17N 53.16 E
Qādir Karam 24 Ke 35.12N 44.53 E
Qāḑub 23 Hg 12.38N 53.57 E
Qā'emshahr 24 Od 36.30N 52.55 E
Qafşah 31 He 34.25N 8.48 E
Qafşah [3] 32 Ic 34.30N 9.00 E
Qa'fūr 14 Dn 36.20N 9.19 E
Qagan 27 Kb 49.16N 118.04 E
Qagan Moron He 28 Ec 43.13N 119.02 E
Qagan Nur 27 Jc 43.20N 112.58 E
Qagan Nur [China] 28 Bd 41.33N 113.48 E
Qagan Nur [China] 27 Jc 43.25N 114.50 E
Qagan Nur [China] 28 Hb 45.14N 124.17 E
Qagan Nur→Zhengxiangbai Qi 27 Jc 42.16N 114.59 E
Qagan Us→Dulan 22 Lf 36.29N 98.29 E
Qagchêng/Xiangcheng 27 Gf 28.56N 99.46 E
Qahar Youyi Houqi (Bayan Qagan) 28 Bd 41.28N 113.10 E
Qahar Youyi Qianqi (Togrog Ul) 28 Bd 40.46N 113.13 E
Qahar Youyi Zhongqi 28 Bd 41.15N 112.36 E
Qahd, Wādī- 24 Ii 26.13N 40.49 E
Qaidam He 27 Gd 36.48N 95.50 E
Qaidam Pendi=Tsaidam Basin (EN) 27 Fd 37.00N 95.00 E

Index Symbols

[1] Independent Nation
[2] State, Region
[3] District, County
[4] Municipality
[5] Colony, Dependency
Continent
Physical Region
Historical or Cultural Region
Mount, Mountain
Volcano
Hill
Mountains, Mountain Range
Hills, Escarpment
Plateau, Upland
Pass, Gap
Plain, Lowland
Delta
Salt Flat
Valley, Canyon
Crater, Cave
Karst Features
Depression
Polder
Desert, Dunes
Forest, Woods
Heath, Steppe
Oasis
Cape, Point
Coast, Beach
Cliff
Peninsula
Isthmus
Sandbank
Island
Atoll
Rock, Reef
Islands, Archipelago
Rocks, Reefs
Coral Reef
Well, Spring
Geyser
River, Stream
Waterfall Rapids
River Mouth, Estuary
Lake
Salt Lake
Intermittent Lake
Reservoir
Swamp, Pond
Canal
Glacier
Ice Shelf, Pack Ice
Ocean
Sea
Gulf, Bay
Strait, Fjord
Lagoon
Bank
Seamount
Tablemount
Ridge
Shelf
Basin
Escarpment, Sea Scarp
Fracture
Trench, Abyss
National Park, Reserve
Point of Interest
Recreation Site
Cave, Cavern
Historic Site
Ruins
Wall, Walls
Church, Abbey
Temple
Scientific Station
Airport
Port
Lighthouse
Mine
Tunnel
Dam, Bridge

Name	Sheet	Grid	Lat	Long
Qala'an Naḥl	35	Ec	13.38N	34.57 E
Qalāt	23	Kc	32.07N	66.54 E
Qal'at Abū Ghār	24	Lg	30.25N	46.09 E
Qal'at al Akhḍar	23	Ed	28.06N	37.05 E
Qal'at al Marqab	24	Fe	35.09N	35.57 E
Qal'at al Mu'azzam	24	Gi	27.45N	37.31 E
Qal'at Bīshah	22	Gh	20.00N	42.36 E
Qal'at Dīzah	24	Kd	36.11N	45.07 E
Qal'at Ṣāliḥ	24	Lg	31.31N	47.16 E
Qal'at Sukkar	24	Lg	31.53N	46.56 E
Qal'eh Asgar	24	Qh	29.30N	56.35 E
Qal'eh Kūh	24	Mf	33.00N	49.10 E
Qal'eh Mūreh	24	Pe	35.35N	55.58 E
Qal'eh-ye Now	23	Jc	34.59N	63.08 E
Qal'eh-ye Sahar	24	Mg	31.40N	48.33 E
Qalīb ash Shuyūkh	23	Gd	29.12N	47.55 E
Qallābāt	35	Fc	12.58N	36.09 E
Qalmarz, Godār-e-	24	Qf	33.26N	56.14 E
Qalyūb	24	Dg	30.11N	31.13 E
Qamata	37	Df	31.58S	27.24 E
Qamdo	22	Lf	31.15N	97.12 E
Qaminis	33	Dc	31.40N	20.01 E
Qamsar	24	Nf	33.45N	51.26 E
Qamūdah	32	Ic	35.00N	9.21 E
Qamūdah [3]	32	Ic	34.50N	9.20 E
Qânâq/Thule	67	Od	77.35N	69.40W
Qandahār	23	Kc	31.00N	65.45 E
Qandahār	22	If	31.35N	65.45 E
Qandala	35	Hc	11.23N	49.53 E
Qangdin Gol	28	Cc	43.27N	115.03 E
Qanțarat al Faḥs	14	Dn	36.23N	9.54 E
Qapqal	27	Dc	43.48N	80.47 E
Qaqortoq/Julianehåb	67	Nc	60.50N	46.10W
Qarā Dâgh	24	Lc	38.48N	47.13 E
Qārah	33	Ed	29.37N	26.30 E
Qarah Būlāq	24	Ke	34.32N	45.12 E
Qarah Dagh	24	Jd	37.00N	43.30 E
Qarah Tappah	24	Ke	34.25N	44.56 E
Qaranqū	24	Ld	37.23N	47.43 E
Qardo	31	Lh	9.30N	49.03 E
Qareh Āghāj	24	Ld	36.46N	48.46 E
Qareh Sū [Iran]	23	Ib	37.00N	56.50 E
Qareh Sū [Iran]	23	Hc	34.52N	51.25 E
Qareh Ziā'Od Dîn	24	Kc	38.53N	45.02 E
Qarkilik/Ruoqiang	22	Kf	39.02N	88.00 E
Qarnayn, Jazirat al-	24	Oj	24.56N	52.52 E
Qarnayt, Jabal-	23	Fc	21.02N	40.22 E
Qarqan/Qiemo	22	Kf	38.08N	85.32 E
Qarqan He	21	Kf	39.30N	88.15 E
Qarqannah, Juzur-=				
Kerkennah Islands (EN)	30	Ie	34.44N	11.12 E
Qartãjannah	14	En	36.51N	10.20 E
Qaryat Abū Nujaym	33	Fd	29.28N	30.40 E
Qaryat al Gharab	33	Cc	30.35N	15.24 E
Qaryat al Gharab	24	Kg	31.27N	44.48 E
Qaryat al Qaddāḥīyah	33	Cc	31.22N	15.14 E
Qaryat al 'Ulyā	23	Gd	27.33N	47.42 E
Qaryat az Zarrūq	33	Cc	32.22N	15.09 E
Qaryat az Zuwaytīnah	33	Dc	30.58N	20.07 E
Qaṣabah, Ra's al-	24	Fh	28.02N	34.38 E
Qaṣabât, Hanshir al-	14	Dn	36.24N	9.54 E
Qasigiánguit/Christianshåb	41	Ge	68.45N	51.30W
Qaṣr al Azraq	24	Gg	31.53N	36.49 E
Qaṣr Al Hayr	24	Ge	34.23N	37.36 E
Qaṣr al Qarahbullī	33	Bc	32.45N	13.43 E
Qaṣr 'Amij	24	If	33.30N	41.45 E
Qaṣr Bū Hādī	33	Cc	31.03N	16.40 E
Qaṣr Burqu'	24	Gf	32.37N	37.58 E
Qaṣr-e Shīrīn	23	Gc	34.31N	45.35 E
Qaṣr Farāfirah	31	Jf	27.15N	28.10 E
Qaṣr Ḥamān	23	Ge	20.50N	45.50 E
Qaṣr Qārūn	24	Dh	29.25N	30.25 E
Qaṣṣ Abū Sa'īd	24	Bi	27.00N	27.35 E
Qatana	24	Gf	33.26N	36.05 E
Qaṭar	21	Hg	25.30N	51.15 E
Qaṭar [1]	22	Hg	25.30N	51.15 E
Qatlīsh	24	Qd	37.50N	57.19 E
Qaṭrāni, Jabal-	24	Dh	29.41N	30.35 E
Qaṭrūyeh	24	Ph	29.09N	54.43 E
Qattara Depression (EN) =				
Qaṭṭârah, Munkhafaḍ al-				
	30	Je	30.00N	27.30 E
Qawām al Hamzah	24	Kg	31.43N	44.58 E
Qaw Abu Qulū'	35	Eb	16.55N	32.30 E
Qawz Rajab	35	Fb	16.04N	35.34 E
Qaysān	35	Fc	10.45N	34.48 E
Qayyārah	24	Je	35.48N	43.17 E
Qazaqstan =				
Kazakhstan (EN)	19	Gf	48.00N	68.00 E
Qazvīn [Iran]	22	Gf	36.16N	50.00 E
Qazvīn [Iraq]	24	Ja	34.21N	42.05 E
Qeqertarssuaq/Godhavn	67	Nc	69.20N	53.35W
Qeshm	24	Qi	26.58N	56.16 E
Qeshm	23	Id	26.45N	55.45 E
Qeydār	24	Md	36.07N	48.35 E
Qeys, Jazīreh-ye-	23	Hd	26.32N	53.58 E
Qezel Owzan	23	Gb	36.45N	49.22 E
Qian'an [China]	28	Ed	40.01N	118.42 E
Qian'an [China]	28	Hb	44.58N	124.01 E
Qianfangzi	28	Af	40.01N	111.23 E
Qian Gorlos (Qianguozhen)	27	Lb	45.05N	124.52 E
Qian He	28	Dh	32.55N	117.10 E
Qianjiang [China]	27	Jd	32.13N	108.58 E
Qianjiang [China]	28	Bi	30.25N	112.54 E
Qianjiang [China]	27	Hd	29.31N	108.46 E
Qianning/Gartar	27	He	30.27N	101.29 E
Qian Shan	28	Ff	36.55N	123.00 E
Qianwei	27	Hf	25.27N	100.41 E
Qianxi [China]	28	Hf	29.08N	103.56 E
Qianxi [China]	28	Ed	40.08N	118.19 E
Qianyang (Anjiang)	27	Jf	27.19N	110.13 E
Qiaojia	27	Hf	27.00N	103.00 E
Qiaowan	27	Gc	40.36N	96.42 E
Qibili	32	Ic	33.42N	8.58 E
Qichun (Caojiahe)	28	Ci	30.15N	115.26 E
Qidaogou	28	Id	41.31N	126.18 E
Qidong	28	Fi	31.48N	121.39 E
Qiemo/Qarqan	22	Kf	38.08N	85.32 E
Qift	24	Ei	26.00N	32.49 E
Qijiang	27	If	29.00N	106.39 E
Qijiaojing	27	Fc	43.28N	91.36 E
Qike → Xunke	27	Mb	49.34N	128.28 E
Qili → Shitai	28	Di	30.12N	117.28 E
Qilian (Babao)	27	Hd	38.14N	100.15 E
Qilian Shan	27	Gd	39.12N	98.35 E
Qilian Shan	21	Lf	38.30N	100.00 E
Qimantag	27	Fd	37.00N	91.00 E
Qimen	27	Kf	29.57N	117.39 E
Qinā	31	Kf	26.10N	32.43 E
Qinā, Wādī-	24	Ei	26.12N	32.44 E
Qin'an	27	Ie	34.50N	105.35 E
Qingchengzi	28	Gd	40.44N	123.36 E
Qingchuan	27	Ie	32.32N	105.11 E
Qingduizi	28	Of	36.05N	120.21 E
Qingfeng	28	Fd	41.27N	121.52 E
Qinggang	27	Mb	46.41N	126.03 E
Qinggil/Qinghe	27	Fb	46.43N	90.24 E
Qinghai Hu = Koko Nor (EN)				
	21	Mf	37.00N	100.20 E
Qinghai Sheng (Ch'ing-hai				
Sheng) = Tsinghai (EN) [2]	27	Gd	36.00N	96.00 E
Qinghe/Qinggil	27	Fb	46.43N	90.24 E
Qinghe (Gexianzhuang)	28	Cf	37.03N	115.39 E
Qinghemen	28	Ed	41.45N	121.25 E
Qingjian	27	Jd	37.10N	110.09 E
Qingjiang	22	Nf	33.31N	119.03 E
Qingjiang	27	Je	30.24N	111.30 E
Qingjiang				
(Zhangshuzhen)	27	Kf	28.02N	115.31 E
Qingkou → Ganyu	28	Eg	34.50N	119.07 E
Qinglong	28	Ed	40.26N	118.58 E
Qinglong He	28	Ee	39.51N	118.51 E
Qingshan	28	Ci	30.39N	114.27 E
Qingshuihe	27	Jd	39.56N	111.41 E
Qingshui Jiang	27	If	27.11N	109.48 E
Qingtian	27	Lf	28.12N	120.17 E
Qingxian	28	De	38.35N	116.48 E
Qingxu	28	Bf	37.36N	112.21 E
Qingyang [China]	27	Id	36.01N	107.48 E
Qingyang [China]	28	Di	30.38N	117.50 E
Qingyuan (Nandaran)	27	Lc	42.06N	124.56 E
Qingyuan (Xiejiaji)	28	Ce	38.46N	115.29 E
Qing Zang Gaoyuan = Tibet,				
Plateau of- (EN)	21	Kf	32.30N	87.00 E
Qin He	28	Bg	35.01N	113.25 E
Qinhuangdao	28	Kg	40.00N	119.32 E
Qin Ling	21	Mf	34.00N	108.00 E
Qinshui	28	Bg	35.41N	112.10 E
Qintong	28	Fh	32.39N	120.06 E
Qinxian	28	Bf	36.46N	112.42 E
Qinyang	28	Bg	35.05N	112.58 E
Qinyuan	28	Bf	36.29N	112.20 E
Qinzhou	27	Ig	22.02N	108.30 E
Qionghai (Jiaji)	27	Jh	19.25N	110.28 E
Qionglai	27	He	30.24N	103.28 E
Qiongzhou Haixia	21	Ng	20.10N	110.15 E
Qipan Guan	27	Ie	32.45N	106.11 E
Qiqihar	22	Oe	47.21N	123.58 E
Qīr	24	Oh	28.29N	53.04 E
Qira	27	Dd	37.00N	80.53 E
Qiryat Gat	24	Fg	31.36N	34.46 E
Qiryat Shemona	24	Ff	33.13N	35.34 E
Qiryat Yam	24	Ff	32.51N	35.04 E
Qishn	23	Hf	15.26N	51.40 E
Qi Shui	28	Ci	30.09N	115.22 E
Qishuyan	28	Fi	31.41N	120.04 E
Qitai	22	Ke	44.01N	89.28 E
Qitaihe	27	Nb	45.49N	130.51 E
Qiuxian (Matou)	28	Cf	36.50N	115.10 E
Qixia	28	Fe	37.18N	120.50 E
Qixian [China]	28	Bf	37.23N	112.21 E
Qixian [China]	28	Cg	34.33N	114.46 E
Qixian (Zhaoge)	28	Cg	35.35N	114.12 E
Qiyang	27	Jf	26.44N	111.50 E
Qizhou	28	Ci	30.04N	115.20 E
Qogir Feng = Godwin Austen				
(EN)	21	Jf	35.53N	76.30 E
Qog Qi	27	Ic	41.31N	107.00 E
Qog Ui	27	Kc	40.50N	116.19 E
Qohrūd, Kūhhā-ye-	21	Hf	32.40N	53.00 E
Qoltag	27	Ec	42.20N	88.45 E
Qom	22	Gf	34.39N	50.54 E
Qomolangma Feng = Everest,				
Mount- (EN)	21	Kg	27.59N	86.56 E
Qomrud	24	Ne	34.43N	51.04 E
Qomsheh	23	Hc	32.00N	51.50 E
Qondūz [3]	23	Kb	36.45N	68.30 E
Qondūz	22	If	36.45N	68.51 E
Qoqek/Tacheng	22	Ke	46.45N	82.57 E
Qôrnoq	41	Gd	64.30N	51.19W
Qorveh	24	Le	35.10N	47.48 E
Qoşbeh-ye Naşşâr	24	So	30.02N	48.27 E
Qoţbābād [Iran]	24	Oh	28.39N	53.37 E
Qoţbābād [Iran]	24	Qi	27.46N	56.06 E
Qoţūr	24	Kc	38.28N	44.25 E
Qoţūr	24	Kc	38.46N	45.16 E
Quadda	24	Kh	22.24 E	
Quadros, Lagoa dos-	55	Gi	29.42S	50.05W
Quairading	59	Df	32.01S	117.25 E
Quakenbrück	11	Fi	52.41N	7.57 E
Quanah	45	Gi	34.18N	99.44W
Quanbao Shan	28	Bh	33.50N	111.24 E
Quang Ngai	25	Le	15.07N	108.48 E
Quang Tri	25	Ld	16.45N	107.11 E
Quan He	28	Eh	33.52N	117.26 E
Quanjiao	28	Eh	32.09N	118.16 E
Quan Long	25	Lg	9.11N	105.08 E
Quanzhou [China]	22	Ng	24.57N	118.35 E
Quanzhou [China]	27	Jf	26.01N	111.04 E
Qu'Appelle River	42	Hf	50.27N	101.19W
Quarai	56	Id	30.23S	56.27W
Quaraí, Rio-	55	Dj	30.12S	57.36W
Quaregnon	12	Fd	50.26N	3.51 E
Quartu Sant'Elena	14	Dk	39.14N	9.11 E
Quartz Lake	42	Jb	70.57N	80.40W
Quartz Mountain	46	De	43.10N	122.40W
Quartzsite	46	Hj	33.40N	114.13W
Quatre, Isle-	51n Bb		12.57N	61.15W
Quatsino Sound	46	Aa	50.25N	128.10W
Qüchān	22	Hf	37.06N	58.30 E
Qué	36	Ce	14.43S	15.06 E
Queanbeyan	59	Jg	35.21S	149.14 E
Québec	39	Le	46.49N	71.13W
Québec [3]	42	Kf	54.00N	72.00W
Quebó	30	Db	11.46N	14.56W
Quebra Anzol, Rio-	55	Id	19.09S	47.38W
Quebracho	55	Dj	31.57S	57.57W
Quebradillas	51a	Bb	18.28N	66.56W
Quedas do Iguaçu	55	Fg	25.31S	52.54W
Quedlinburg	10	He	51.47N	11.09 E
Queen, Cape-	42	Jd	64.43N	78.18W
Queen Alexandra Range	66	Jg	84.00S	168.00 E
Queen Bess, Mount -	42	Ff	51.18N	124.33W
Queenborough	12	Cc	51.25N	0.46 E
Queen Charlotte Islands	38	Gf	51.30N	129.00W
Queen Charlotte Sound	42	Ef	51.30N	129.30W
Queen Charlotte Strait	38	Gf	50.40N	127.25W
Queen Elizabeth Islands	38	Ib	79.00N	105.00W
Queen Elizabeth Range	66	Kg	83.20S	162.00 E
Queen Mary Land	66	Ge	69.00S	96.00 E
Queen Maud Gulf	42	Id	68.25N	102.30W
Queen Maud Land	66	Cf	72.30S	12.00 E
Queen Maud Range	66	Jg	86.00S	160.00W
Queens Channel [Austl.]	59	Fb	14.45S	129.25 E
Queens Channel				
[N.W.T.-Can.]	42	Ha	76.11N	96.00W
Queensland	58	Id	22.00S	145.00 E
Queenstown [Austl.]	59	Jh	42.05S	145.33 E
Queenstown [Guy.]	50	Gi	7.12N	58.29W
Queenstown [N.Z.]	62	Cf	45.02S	168.40 E
Queenstown [S.Afr.]	31	Jl	31.52S	26.52 E
Queguay, Cuchilla del-	55	Dj	31.50S	57.30W
Queguay Grande, Rio-	55	Ck	32.09S	58.09W
Queich	12	Ke	49.14N	8.21 E
Queimadas	54	Kf	10.58S	39.38W
Queiros	55	Ge	21.49S	50.13W
Quela	36	Cd	9.15S	17.05 E
Quelimane	31	Kj	17.51S	36.52 E
Quemado	45	Bi	34.20N	108.30W
Quemado de Güines	49	Gb	22.48N	80.15W
Quembo	36	Ce	14.57S	20.22 E
Quemú-Quemú	56	He	36.03S	63.33W
Quequén	56	Ie	38.32S	58.42W
Quequén Grande, Rio-	55	Cn	38.34S	58.43W
Quequén Salado, Rio-	55	Ck	32.09S	60.31W
Quercy	11	Hj	44.15N	1.15 E
Querétaro	47	Ed	21.00N	99.55W
Querétaro [3]	39	Ig	20.36N	100.23W
Querobabi	48	Db	30.03N	111.01W
Quesada [C.R.]	49	Eh	10.19N	84.26W
Quesada [Sp.]	13	Ig	37.51N	3.04W
Queshan	28	Ch	32.42N	114.04 E
Quesnel	42	Ff	52.59N	122.30W
Quesnel Lake	42	Ff	52.32N	121.05W
Questa	45	Dh	36.42N	105.36W
Quetena	54	Eh	22.10S	67.25W
Quetico Lake	45	Kb	48.37N	91.52W
Quetta	22	If	30.12N	67.00 E
Quevas, Cerro-	48	Dc	29.15N	111.20W
Quevedo	54	Cd	1.02S	79.27W
Queyras	11	Mj	44.44N	6.49 E
Quezaltenango	39	Jh	14.50N	91.31W
Quezaltenango [3]	49	Bf	14.45N	91.40W
Quezon	26	Ge	9.14N	117.56 E
Quezon City	22	Oh	14.38N	121.00 E
Qufu	28	Dg	35.35N	116.59 E
Quiangguoshen →				
Qian Gorlos	27	Lb	45.05N	124.52 E
Quianshan	28	Di	30.38N	116.35 E
Quibala	36	Cd	10.44S	14.59 E
Quibaxe	36	Bd	8.30S	14.36 E
Quibdó	54	Cb	5.42N	76.39W
Quiberon, Baie de-	11	Dg	47.30N	3.00W
Quiberon, Presqu'île de-	11	Cg	47.30N	3.08W
Quibor	51	Mh	9.56N	69.37W
Quiché [3]	49	Bf	15.30N	90.55W
Quierschied	12	Je	49.19N	7.03 E
Quiha	35	Fc	13.28N	39.33 E
Quiindy	55	Dh	25.58S	57.16W
Quijarro	54	Cd	19.26S	58.08W
Quilá	48	Ee	24.23N	107.13W
Quilán, Cabo-	56	Cf	43.16S	74.23W
Quillabamba	54	Df	12.49S	72.43W
Quillacollo	54	Eg	17.26S	66.17W
Quillagua	56	Eb	21.39S	69.33W
Quillan	11	Il	42.52N	2.11 E
Quilleco	56	Ce	37.26S	71.56W
Quillebeuf-sur-Seine	12	Be	49.28N	0.31 E
Quillota	56	Td	32.53S	71.16W
Quilon	25	Ig	8.53N	76.36 E
Quilpie	59	Ie	26.37S	144.15 E
Quilpué	56	Td	33.03S	71.27W
Quimari, Alto de-	49	Ii	8.07N	76.23W
Quimili	56	Hc	27.36S	62.25W
Quimome	54	Fg	17.48S	61.14W
Quimome, Rio-	55	Bc	17.36S	61.09W
Quimper	11	Bf	48.00N	4.06W
Quimperlé	11	Cg	47.52N	3.33W
Quinault River	46	Cc	47.23N	124.18W
Quincy [Ca.-U.S.]	46	Eg	39.56N	120.57W
Quincy [Fl.-U.S.]	44	Ej	30.37N	84.32W
Quincy [Il.-U.S.]	43	Id	39.56N	91.23W
Quincy [Ma.-U.S.]	44	Ld	42.15N	71.01W
Quincy [Wa.-U.S.]	46	Fc	47.14N	119.51W
Quindío [2]	54	Cc	4.30N	75.40W
Quingey	11	Lg	47.06N	5.53 E
Quinhagak	40	Ge	59.45N	161.43W
Qui Nhon	22	Mh	13.46N	109.14 E
Quiñihual	55	Bm	37.47S	61.36W
Quinilubán Group	26	Hd	11.27N	120.48 E
Quinn River	46	Ff	40.25N	119.00W
Quiñones	48	De	24.22N	111.25W
Quintanar de la Orden	13	Ie	39.34N	3.03W
Quintana Roo [2]	47	Ge	19.40N	88.30W
Quinze, Lac des-	44	Hb	47.30N	79.00W
Quionga	37	Gb	10.35S	40.33 E
Quipongo	36	Be	14.45S	14.05 E
Quirigua	49	Cf	15.18N	89.07W
Quirihue	56	Fe	36.17S	72.32W
Quirima	36	Ce	10.48S	18.09 E
Quirinópolis	54	Hg	18.32S	50.30W
Quiroga	13	Eb	42.29N	7.16W
Quiros, Cap-	63b Cb		14.56S	167.01 E
Quisiro	49	Lh	10.53N	71.17W
Quissanga	37	Gb	12.25S	40.29 E
Quissico	37	Ed	24.43S	34.45 E
Quita Sueno Bank	47	Ih	14.20N	81.15W
Quitengues	36	Be	14.06S	14.05 E
Quiteria, Rio-	55	Ge	20.16S	51.08W
Quitilipi	55	Bh	26.52S	60.13W
Quitman [Ga.-U.S.]	44	Fj	30.47N	83.33W
Quitman [Ms.-U.S.]	45	Lj	32.03N	88.43W
Quito	53	Ff	0.13S	78.30W
Quitovac	48	Cb	31.32N	112.42W
Quixadá	54	Kd	4.58S	39.01W
Quixeramobim	54	Ke	5.12S	39.17W
Qujiang	28	Cj	28.14N	115.46 E
Qu Jiang [China]	27	Kf	29.32N	119.31 E
Qu Jiang [China]	27	Ie	30.01N	106.24 E
Qujing	27	Hf	25.31N	103.45 E
Qul'ân, Jazâ'ir-	24	Fj	24.22N	35.23 E
Qulansiyah	23	Hg	12.41N	53.29 E
Qulaybīah	32	Jb	36.51N	11.06 E
Qulbān al 'Isāwīyah	24	Qg	30.38N	37.53 E
Qulbān an Nabk al Gharbī	24	Qg	31.15N	37.26 E
Qumar He	21	Lf	34.44N	94.50 E
Qumarlêb	27	Ge	34.35N	95.18 E
Qunayfidhah, Nafūd-	24	Kj	24.45N	45.30 E
Quoi	64d Ba		7.32N	151.59 E
Quoich	42	Id	63.56N	93.25W
Quorn	59	Hf	32.21S	138.03 E
Quṣen/Jinchuan	27	He	31.02N	102.02 E
Quraitu	24	Ke	34.36N	45.30 E
Qurayyât, Juzur-	32	Jb	35.48N	11.02 E
Qurbah	14	En	36.35N	10.52 E
Qurdūd	35	Dc	10.17N	29.56 E
Qūr Laban	24	Cg	30.23N	28.59 E
Qurunbūliyah	14	En	36.36N	10.30 E
Qūş	33	Fd	25.55N	32.45 E
Qusay'ir	35	Ic	14.55N	50.20 E
Qutdligssat	41	Gd	70.12N	53.00W
Quthing	37	Df	30.24S	27.42 E
Qutū	33	Hf	18.30N	41.04 E
Quwaiz	33	He	20.27N	44.53 E
Quxian	27	Kf	28.54N	118.53 E
Qüxü	27	Ff	29.23N	90.45 E
Quyang	28	Ce	38.37N	114.41 E
Quy Chau	25	Le	19.33N	105.06 E
Quzhou	27	Lf	36.47N	114.56 E
Qyteti Stalin → Kuçova	15	Ci	40.48N	19.54 E

R

Name	Sheet	Grid	Lat	Long
Raab	10	Ni	47.41N	17.38 E
Raahe/Brahestad	7	Fd	64.41N	24.29 E
Rääkkylä	8	Mb	62.19N	29.37 E
Raalte	12	Gb	52.23N	6.17 E
Raamsdonk	12	Gc	51.41N	4.54 E
Raanes Peninsula	42	Ia	78.20N	86.20W
Raasay, Island of-	9	Gd	57.25N	6.04W
Raasay, Sound of-	9	Gd	57.25N	6.05W
Raasiku/Raziku	8	Kc	59.22N	25.11 E
Rab	14	If	44.46N	14.46 E
Rab	14	If	44.45N	14.46 E
Rāba	10	Ni	47.41N	17.38 E
Rabā	10	Of	50.40N	8.52 E
Rabaçal, Rio-	13	Ec	41.30N	7.12W
Rabah	30	Kg	18.47N	32.03 E
Rabak	35	Ec	13.11N	32.44 E
Rabaraba	60	Og	10.02S	149.50 E
Rabat [Malta]	14	Im	35.50N	14.29 E
Rabat [Mor.]	31	Ge	34.02N	6.50W
Rabat-Salé [2]	32	Fc	34.02N	6.50W
Rabaul	58	Ga	4.12S	152.12 E
Rabca	10	Ni	47.41N	17.37 E
Rabi, Ash Shallâl ar-=				
Fourth Cataract (EN)	35	Eb	18.47N	32.03 E
Rabiah	13	Fg	37.12N	6.55W
Rábida, Monasterio de-	13	Dg	37.12N	6.55W
Rābigh	22	Fg	22.48N	39.02 E
Rabinal	49	Bf	15.06N	90.27W
Rabka	10	Pg	49.36N	19.56 E
Rabočeostrovsk	7	Gd	64.59N	34.44 E
Rabyânah, Şaḥrā'-	31	If	24.30N	21.00 E
Rabyânah, Wâḩat al-=				
Rebiana Oasis (EN)	31	If	24.14N	21.59 E
Răcăciuni	15	Ic	46.20N	26.50 E
Racalmuto	14	Hm	37.24N	13.44 E
Răcășdia	15	Cd	45.00N	21.36 E
Racconigi	14	Bf	44.46N	7.46 E
Race, Cape-	42	Mg	46.40N	53.10W
Race Point	44	Ld	42.04N	70.14W
Rach Gia	22	Lh	10.01N	105.05 E
Rachid	32	Ef	18.48N	11.41W
Raciąż	10	Qd	52.47N	20.06 E
Racibórz	10	Of	50.06N	18.13 E
Racine	43	Jc	42.43N	87.48W
Räckeve	10	Oi	47.10N	18.57 E
Racos	15	Ic	46.03N	25.30 E
Râda	8	Ed	60.00N	13.36 E
Radama, Iles-	37	Hb	14.00S	47.47 E
Radan	15	Ef	43.02N	21.30 E
Rădăuți	15	Ib	47.51N	25.55 E
Radbuza	10	Jg	49.46N	13.24 E
Radeberg	10	Ie	51.07N	13.55 E
Radebeul	10	Ie	51.06N	13.39 E
Radeče	14	Jd	46.04N	15.11 E
Radehov	10	Uf	50.13N	24.43 E
Radenthein	14	Hd	46.48N	13.43 E
Radevormwald	12	Jc	51.12N	7.22 E
Radew	10	Lb	54.07N	15.50 E
Radford	44	Gg	37.07N	80.34W
Radnevo	15	Ig	42.18N	25.56 E
Radolfzell	10	Ei	47.44N	8.58 E
Radom [2]	10	Re	51.25N	21.10 E
Radom	6	Ie	51.25N	21.10 E
Radomir	15	Fg	42.33N	22.58 E
Radomka	10	Re	51.43N	21.26 E
Radomsko	10	Pe	51.05N	19.25 E
Radomyšl	16	Fd	50.29N	29.14 E
Radomyśl Wielki	10	Rf	50.12N	21.16 E
Radošković	8	Lj	54.12N	27.17 E
Radotin	10	Kg	49.59N	14.22 E
Radovanu	15	Je	44.12N	26.31 E
Radoviš	15	Fh	41.38N	22.28 E
Radøy	8	Ad	60.40N	5.00 E
Radstadt	14	Hc	47.23N	13.27 E
Radun	10	Vb	54.02N	25.07 E
Radunia	10	Ob	54.25N	18.45 E
Raduša	14	Lg	43.52S	17.29 E
Radvaniči	10	Ue	51.59N	24.09 E
Radviliškis	7	Fi	55.50N	23.33 E
Radymno	10	Sg	49.57N	22.48 E
Radziejów	10	Od	52.38N	18.32 E
Radzyń Podlaski	10	Se	51.48N	22.38 E
Rae	42	Fd	62.50N	116.00W
Räe Bareli	25	Gc	26.13N	81.14 E
Rae Isthmus	42	Ic	66.55N	86.10W
Raesfeld	12	Ic	51.46N	6.51 E
Raeside, Lake-	59	Ee	29.30S	121.50 E
Raetihi	62	Fc	39.26S	175.17 E
Raevavae, Ile-	57	Mg	23.52S	147.40W
Raevski, Groupe-	61	Mc	16.45S	144.14W
Râf, Jabal-	24	Hh	29.12N	39.48 E
Rafaela	53	Ji	31.17S	61.30W
Rafaï	35	Ce	4.58N	23.56 E
Rafḥā'	23	Gd	29.42N	43.30 E
Rafi	34	Fc	13.28N	4.10 E
Râfkâ	24	Ge	35.55N	37.36 E
Rafsanjän	23	Ic	30.24N	56.01 E
Rafsö/Reposaari	8	Ic	61.37N	21.27 E
Raga	31	Jh	8.28N	25.41 E
Ragay Gulf	26	Hd	13.30N	122.65 E
Ragged Island	49	Jb	22.12N	75.44W
Ragged Island Range	47	Id	22.42S	75.45W
Ragged Point	51q Bb		13.10N	59.25W
Raglan	62	Fb	37.48S	174.52 E
Raguencau	44	Ma	49.04N	68.32W
Ragusa	14	In	36.55N	14.44 E
Raguva	6	Ki	55.30N	24.45 E
Raha	26	Hg	4.51S	122.43 E
Raḥa, Ḥarrat ar-	24	Gi	27.40N	36.40 E
Rahad al Bardî	35	Cc	11.18N	23.53 E
Rahama	34	Gc	10.25N	8.41 E
Rahaṭ, Ḥarrat-	36	Be	23.00N	40.05 E
Rahat Daği	15	Ml	37.08N	29.49 E
Rahden	12	Kb	52.26N	8.37 E
Râhgâmâti	25	Ie	22.38N	92.12 E
Rahimyar Khan	25	Eb	28.25N	70.18 E
Rahmanovskije Ključi	19	Jf	49.35N	86.35 E
Rahmet	19	Gf	49.19N	65.10 E
Råholt	8	Dd	60.16N	11.11 E
Rahouia	14	Jn	35.32N	1.01 E
Rahov	16	De	48.02N	24.18 E
Rahrbach,				
Kirchhundem	12	Kc	51.02N	7.59 E
Raia	13	Df	39.00N	8.17W
Raiatea, Ile-	57	Lf	16.50S	151.25W
Raices	55	Cj	31.54S	59.16W
Räichür	22	Jh	16.12N	77.22 E
Raiganj	25	Hc	25.37N	88.07 E
Raigarh	22	Kg	21.54N	83.24 E
Raijua, Pulau-	26	Hi	10.37S	121.36 E
Rainbow Peak	46	Ha	44.55N	115.17W
Rainier, Mount-	38	Ge	46.52N	121.46W
Rainy Lake	43	Ib	48.42N	93.10W
Rainy River	45	Ja	48.43N	94.29W
Raipur	22	Kg	21.14N	81.38 E
Raisi, Punta-	14	Hl	38.11N	13.06 E
Raisio/Reso	7	Ff	60.29N	22.11 E
Raja Ampat, Kepulauan-	26	Jg	0.50S	130.25 E
Rajahmundry	22	Kh	16.59N	81.47 E
Rajakoski	8	Mb	68.59N	29.07 E
Rajang	21	Ni	2.07N	111.12 E
Rájasthân [3]	22	Jg	27.00N	74.00 E
Rájasthân Canal	25	Eb	31.10N	75.00 E
Rajbiraj	25	Hc	26.36N	86.50 E
Rajčihinsk	20	Hg	49.43N	129.27 E
Rajevski	17	Gi	54.04N	54.56 E
Rajgarh	25	Fc	28.38N	75.23 E
Rajka	10	Ni	48.00N	17.12 E
Rájgródzkie, Jezioro-	10	Sc	53.45N	22.38 E
Raj Nandgaon	25	Gd	21.06N	81.02 E
Rajonny respublikanskogo				
podčinenija =				
Čujskaja oblast	19	Hg	42.30N	73.50 E

Index Symbols

- [1] Independent Nation
- [2] State, Region
- [3] District, County
- [4] Municipality
- [5] Colony, Dependency
- Continent
- Physical Region
- Historical or Cultural Region
- Mount, Mountain
- Volcano
- Hill
- Mountains, Mountain Range
- Hills, Escarpment
- Plateau, Upland
- Pass, Gap
- Plain, Lowland
- Delta
- Salt Flat
- Valley, Canyon
- Crater, Cave
- Karst Features
- Depression
- Polder
- Desert, Dunes
- Forest, Woods
- Heath, Steppe
- Oasis
- Cape, Point
- Coast, Beach
- Cliff
- Peninsula
- Isthmus
- Sandbank
- Island
- Atoll
- Rock, Reef
- Islands, Archipelago
- Rocks, Reefs
- Coral Reef
- Well, Spring
- Geyser
- River, Stream
- Waterfall Rapids
- River Mouth, Estuary
- Lake
- Salt Lake
- Intermittent Lake
- Reservoir
- Swamp, Pond
- Canal
- Glacier
- Ice Shelf, Pack Ice
- Ocean
- Sea
- Gulf, Bay
- Strait, Fjord
- Lagoon
- Bank
- Seamount
- Tablemount
- Ridge
- Shelf
- Basin
- Escarpment, Sea Scarp
- Fracture
- Trench, Abyss
- National Park, Reserve
- Point of Interest
- Recreation Site
- Cave, Cavern
- Historic Site
- Ruins
- Wall, Walls
- Church, Abbey
- Temple
- Scientific Station
- Airport
- Port
- Lighthouse
- Mine
- Tunnel
- Dam, Bridge

Rājshāhi	25	Hd	24.22N	88.36 E
Rakahanga Atoll	57	Kl	10.02S	161.05W
Rakaia	62	Ee	43.54S	172.13 E
Rakaia	62	Ee	43.45S	172.01 E
Rakan, Ra's-	24	Ni	26.10N	51.13 E
Rakata, Pulau-	26	Eh	6.10S	105.26 E
Raka Zangbo	27	Ef	29.24N	87.58 E
Rakhawt, Wādī-	35	Ib	18.16N	51.50 E
Rakht-e Shāh	24	Mf	33.17N	49.23 E
Rakitnoje	28	Mb	45.36N	134.17 E
Rakitovo	15	Hh	41.59N	24.05 E
Rakkestad	8	De	59.26N	11.21 E
Rakoniewice	10	Md	52.10N	16.16 E
Rakops	37	Cd	21.01S	24.20 E
Rakovnicka panev	10	Jf	50.10N	13.30 E
Rakovník	10	Jf	50.06N	13.43 E
Rakovski	15	Hg	42.18N	24.58 E
Raków	10	Rf	50.42N	21.03 E
Rakušečny, Mys-	16	Qh	42.52N	51.55 E
Råkvåg	7	Ce	63.46N	10.05 E
Rakvere	7	Gg	59.22N	26.22 E
Raleigh [N.C.-U.S.]	39	Lf	35.47N	78.39W
Raleigh [Ont.-Can.]	45	Kb	49.31N	91.56W
Raleigh Bay	44	Ih	35.00N	76.20W
Ralik Chain	57	Hd	8.00N	167.00 E
Rama	47	Hf	12.09N	84.15W
Rama, Rio-	49	Eg	12.08N	84.13W
Ramādah	32	Jc	32.19N	10.24 E
Ramağin, Wādī-	24	Ej	24.57N	32.34 E
Ramales de la Victoria	13	Ia	43.15N	3.27W
Ramalho, Serra do-	55	Ja	13.45S	44.00W
Ramapo Bank (EN)	57	Fb	27.15N	145.10 E
Ramatlabama	37	De	25.37S	25.30 E
Ramberg	10	He	51.45N	11.05 E
Rambervillers	11	Mf	48.21N	6.38 E
Rambi	63d	Cb	16.30S	179.59W
Rambouillet	11	Hf	48.39N	1.50 E
Rambutyo Island	57	Fe	2.18S	147.48 E
Rāmhormoz	24	Mg	31.16N	49.36 E
Ramigala/Ramygala	8	Ki	55.28N	24.23 E
Ramis	35	Gd	8.02N	41.36 E
Ramla	24	Fg	31.55N	34.52 E
Ramlīyah, 'Aqabat ar-	24	Di	26.01N	30.42 E
Ramlu	35	Gc	13.20N	41.45 E
Ramm, Jabal-	24	Fh	29.35N	35.24 E
Rammāk, Ghurd ar-	24	Ch	29.40N	29.20 E
Rāmnagar	25	Fc	29.24N	79.07 E
Ramnäs	8	Ge	59.46N	16.12 E
Ramón				
Santamarina	55	Cn	38.26S	59.20W
Ramos	63a	Ec	8.16S	160.11 E
Ramos, Rio-	48	Ge	25.35N	105.03W
Ramotswa	37	Dd	24.52S	25.50 E
Rāmpur	25	Fc	28.49N	79.02 E
Ramree	25	Ie	19.06N	93.48 E
Rams	24	Oj	25.53N	56.02 E
Ramsele	7	De	63.33N	16.29 E
Ramsey [Eng.-U.K.]	12	Bb	52.27N	0.07W
Ramsey [Ont.-Can.]	44	Fb	47.29N	82.24W
Ramsey [U.K.]	9	Ig	54.20N	4.21W
Ramsey Lake	42	Jg	47.20N	83.00W
Ramsgate	9	Oj	51.20N	1.25 E
Rāmshīr	24	Mg	30.50N	49.30 E
Ramsjö	7	De	62.11N	15.39 E
Ramstein-Miesenbach	12	Je	49.27N	7.32 E
Ramsund	7	Db	68.29N	16.32 E
Ramu	60	Di	4.02S	144.41 E
Ramu	36	Hb	3.56N	41.13 E
Ramvik	7	De	62.49N	17.51 E
Ramville, Ilet-	51h	Bb	14.42N	60.53W
Ramygala/Ramigala	8	Ki	55.28N	24.23 E
Rana	7	Dc	66.20N	14.08 E
Rañadoiro, Sierra del-	13	Fa	43.20N	6.45W
Ranai	26	Ef	3.55N	108.23 E
Ranakah, Potjo-	26	Hh	8.38S	120.31 E
Rana Kao, Volcán-	65d	Ac	27.11S	109.27W
Rana Roi, Volcán-	65d	Ab	27.05S	109.23W
Rana Roraka, Volcán-	65d	Bb	27.07S	109.18W
Ranau	26	Ge	5.58N	116.41 E
Ranča	14	Lf	44.24N	17.22 E
Rancagua	53	Ii	34.10S	70.45W
Rance	11	Ef	48.31N	1.59W
Rance, Sivry-Rance-	12	Gd	50.09N	4.16 E
Rancharia	55	Gf	22.15S	50.55W
Rancheria, Rio-	49	Kh	11.34N	72.54W
Rānchī	22	Kg	23.21N	85.20 E
Ranchos	55	Cl	35.32S	58.22W
Ranco, Lago-	56	Ff	40.14S	72.24W
Randa	35	Gc	11.51N	42.40 E
Randaberg	8	Ae	59.00N	5.36 E
Randazzo	14	Im	37.53N	14.57 E
Randers	7	Ch	56.28N	10.03 E
Randers Fjord	8	Dh	56.35N	10.20 E
Randijaure	7	Ec	66.42N	19.18 E
Randow	10	Kc	53.41N	14.04 E
Randsfjorden	7	Cf	60.25N	10.25 E
Ranérou	34	Cb	15.18N	13.58W
Ranfurly	62	Df	45.08S	170.06 E
Rangasa, Tanjung-	26	Gg	3.33S	118.56 E
Ranger	45	Gj	32.28N	98.41W
Rangiora	62	Ee	43.18S	172.36 E
Rangiroa Atoll	57	Mf	15.10S	147.35W
Rangitaiki	62	Gb	37.55S	176.53 E
Rangitata	62	Df	44.10S	171.30 E
Rangitikei	62	Fd	40.17S	175.13 E
Rangkasbitung	26	Eh	6.21S	106.15 E
Rangoon (EN) =				
Yangon	22	Lh	16.47N	96.10 E
Rangpur	25	Hc	25.44N	89.16 E
Rāniyah	24	Kd	36.15N	44.53 E
Rankin Inlet	39	Jc	62.45N	92.10W
Rankoshi	29a	Bb	42.47N	140.31 E
Rannoch, Loch-	9	Ie	56.41N	4.20W
Ranobe	37	Gc	17.10S	44.08 E
Ranon	63b	Dc	16.09S	168.07 E
Ranong	25	Jg	9.59N	98.40 E
Ranongga Island	60	Fi	8.05S	156.34 E
Ranova	16	Lb	54.07N	40.14 E
Ransaren	7	Dd	65.14N	14.59 E
Rantabe	37	Hc	15.42S	49.39 E
Rantasalmi	8	Mb	62.04N	28.18 E
Rantaupanjang	26	Fg	1.23S	112.04 E
Rantauprapat	26	Cf	2.06N	99.50 E
Rantekombola, Bulu-	21	Oj	3.21S	120.01 E
Rantoul	45	Lf	40.19N	88.09W
Ranua	7	Gd	65.55N	26.32 E
Ranyah, Wādī-	33	He	21.18N	43.20 E
Raohe	27	Nb	46.48N	133.58 E
Raon-l'Étape	11	Mf	48.24N	6.51 E
Raoui, Erg er-	32	Gd	29.15N	2.45W
Raoul Island	57	Jg	29.15S	177.52W
Raoyang	28	Ce	38.14N	115.44 E
Raoyang He	28	Gd	41.13N	122.12 E
Rapa, Ile-	57	Mg	27.36S	144.20W
Rapallo	14	Df	44.21N	9.14 E
Rapang	26	Gg	3.50S	119.48 E
Rapa Nui/Pascua, Isla de- =				
Easter Island (EN)	57	Qg	27.07S	109.22W
Raper, Cape-	42	Kc	69.41N	67.24W
Rapid City	39	Ie	44.05N	103.14W
Rapid Creek	45	Ee	43.54N	102.37W
Rapid River	44	Dc	45.58N	86.59W
Räpina/Rjapina	8	Lf	58.03N	27.35 E
Rapla	7	Fg	59.02N	24.47 E
Rappahannock River	44	Ig	37.34N	76.18W
Rápulo, Rio-	52	Jg	13.43S	65.32W
Rāqūbah	31	If	28.58N	19.02 E
Raraka Atoll	57	Mf	16.10S	144.54W
Raroia Atoll	57	Mf	16.05S	142.26W
Rarotonga Island	57	Lg	21.14S	159.46W
Rasa, Punta-	52	Jj	40.51S	62.19W
Ra's Abū Daraj	24	Eh	29.23N	32.33 E
Ra's Abū Rudays	24	Eh	28.53N	33.11 E
Ra's Abū Shajarah	35	Fa	21.04N	37.14 E
Ra's Ajdīr	33	Bc	33.09N	11.34 E
Ra's al 'Ayn	24	Id	36.51N	40.04 E
Ra's al-Barr	24	Dg	31.31N	31.50 E
Ra's al Ḩikmah	24	Bg	31.08N	27.50 E
Ra's al Jabal	14	Em	37.13N	10.08 E
Ra's al Khafjī	24	Mh	28.25N	48.30 E
Ra's al Khaymah	23	Id	25.47N	55.57 E
Ra's al Mish'āb	24	Mh	28.12N	48.37 E
Ra's al Unūf	33	Cc	30.31N	18.34 E
Ra's an Naqb	24	Fh	30.00N	35.29 E
Ra's as Sidr	24	Eh	29.36N	32.40 E
Ra's at Tannūrah	24	Ni	26.42N	50.10 E
Ras Beddouza	30	Ge	32.22N	9.18W
Ras Dashen	30	Kg	13.19N	38.20 E
Raseiniai/Rasejnjaj	7	Fi	55.23N	23.07 E
Rasejnjaj/Raseiniai	7	Fi	55.23N	23.07 E
Râs el Mâ	34	Eb	16.37N	4.27W
Ras-el-Ma	13	Ji	35.08N	2.29W
Ras el Oued	13	Ri	35.57N	5.02 E
Ra's Ghārib	33	Fd	28.21N	33.06 E
Rashād	35	Ec	11.51N	31.04 E
Rāshayyā	24	Ff	33.30N	35.51 E
Rashīd=Rosetta (EN)	33	Fc	31.24N	30.25 E
Rashīd, Maşabb-	24	Dg	31.30N	30.20 E
Rasht	22	Gf	37.16N	49.36 E
Rāsiga 'Alūla	35	Ic	11.59N	50.50 E
Rās Jumbo	35	Gf	1.37S	41.31 E
Raška	15	Df	43.18N	20.38 E
Ra's Madhar, Jabal-	24	Gj	25.46N	37.32 E
Ra's Matārimah	24	Eh	29.27N	32.43 E
Rasmussen Basin	42	Hc	67.56N	95.15W
Rason Lake	59	Ee	28.45S	124.20 E
Rasskazovo	19	Ee	52.39N	41.57 E
Rassua, Ostrov-	20	Kg	47.40N	153.00 E
Rassvet	20	Ee	57.00N	91.32 E
Ras-Tarf, Cap-	13	Ii	35.17N	3.41W
Rastatt	10	Eh	48.51N	8.12 E
Rastede	12	Ka	53.15N	8.12 E
Rastigaissa	7	Ga	70.03N	26.18 E
Råstojaure	7	Eb	68.45N	20.30 E
Ra's Ţurunbī	24	Fj	25.40N	34.35 E
Rasūl	24	Pi	27.10N	55.30 E
Ra's Zayt	33	Fd	27.56N	33.31 E
Rat	40a	Bb	51.55N	178.20 E
Ratak Chain	57	Id	9.00N	171.00 E
Ratangarh	25	Ec	28.05N	74.36 E
Rätansbyn	7	De	62.29N	14.32 E
Rat Buri	25	Jf	13.32N	99.49 E
Rathbun Lake	45	Jf	40.54N	93.05W
Ráth Droma/Rathdrum	9	Gi	52.56N	6.13W
Rathdrum/				
Ráth Droma	9	Gi	52.56N	6.13W
Rathenow	10	Id	52.36N	12.20 E
Rathlin Island/				
Reachlainn	9	Gf	55.18N	6.13W
Ráth Luirc/An Ráth	9	Ei	52.21N	8.41W
Rathor, Pik-	18	If	37.55N	72.14 E
Rätikon	14	Dc	47.03N	9.40 E
Ratingen	12	Ic	51.18N	6.51 E
Rätische Alpen=Rhaetian				
Alps (EN)	14	Dd	46.30N	10.00 E
Rat Islands	38	Ad	52.00N	178.00 E
Ratlām	25	Fd	23.19N	75.04 E
Ratmanova, Ostrov-	20	Lc	65.45N	169.00W
Ratnāgiri	25	Ee	16.59N	73.18 E
Ratnapura	25	Gg	6.41N	80.24 E
Ratno	16	Dd	51.42N	24.31 E
Raton	43	Gd	36.54N	104.24W
Ratqh, Wādī ar-	24	Ie	34.25N	40.55 E
Ratta	20	Dd	63.35N	84.05 E
Rattlesnake Hills	46	Le	42.45N	107.10W
Rattray Head	9	Ld	57.38N	1.46W
Rättvik	7	Df	60.53N	15.06 E
Ratz, Mount-	38	Fd	57.23N	132.19W
Ratzeburg	10	Gc	53.42N	10.46 E
Raub	26	Df	3.48N	101.52 E
Rauch	56	Ie	36.46S	59.06W
Raucourt-et-Flaba	12	Ge	49.36N	4.57 E
Raudeberg	8	Ab	61.59N	5.09 E
Rauer Islands	66	Fe	68.51S	77.50 E
Raufarhöfn	7a	Ca	66.27N	15.57W
Raufjellet	8	Dc	61.15N	11.00 E
Raufoss	7	Cf	60.43N	10.37 E
Raukotaha	64n	Ac	10.28S	161.01W
Raukumara Range	62	Gc	38.00S	178.00 E
Rauland	8	Be	59.44N	8.00 E
Raúl Leoni, Represa- (Guri)				
	54	Fb	7.30N	63.00W
Rauma	7	Be	62.33N	7.43 E
Rauma/Raumo	7	Ef	61.08N	21.30 E
Raumo/Rauma	7	Ef	61.08N	21.30 E
Rauna	8	Kg	57.14N	25.39 E
Raunds	12	Bb	52.20N	0.32W
Raurimu	62	Fc	39.07S	175.24 E
Raurkela	22	Kg	22.13N	84.53 E
Rausu	28	Rb	44.01N	145.12 E
Rausu-Dake	29a	Da	44.06N	145.07 E
Rautalampi	8	Lb	62.38N	26.50 E
Ravahere Atoll	57	Mf	18.14S	142.09W
Ravan	14	Mf	44.15N	18.16 E
Ravanica, Manastir-	15	Ef	43.58N	21.30 E
Ravānsar	24	Le	34.43N	46.40 E
Ravanusa	14	Hm	37.16N	13.58 E
Rāvar	24	Qg	31.12N	56.53 E
Rava-Russkaja	16	Cd	50.13N	23.37 E
Ravels	12	Gc	51.22N	4.59 E
Ravelsbach	14	Jb	48.30N	15.50 E
Ravels-Poppel	12	Hc	51.27N	5.02 E
Ravenna [It.]	14	Gf	44.25N	12.12 E
Ravenna [Nb.-U.S.]	45	Gf	41.02N	98.55W
Ravensburg	10	Fi	47.47N	9.37 E
Ravenshoe	58	Ff	17.37S	145.29 E
Ravensthorpe	59	Ef	33.35S	120.02 E
Ravi	21	Jf	30.35N	71.49 E
Ravnina	19	Gh	37.57N	62.42 E
Rawaki Atoll (Phoenix)	57	Je	3.43S	170.43W
Rāwalpindi	22	Jf	33.35N	73.03 E
Rawa Mazowiecka	10	Qe	51.46N	20.16 E
Rawāndūz	24	Kd	36.37N	44.31 E
Rawdah	24	Ie	35.15N	41.05 E
Rawene	62	Ea	35.24S	173.30 E
Rawicz	10	Me	51.37N	16.52 E
Rawka	10	Qd	52.07N	20.08 E
Rawlinna	58	Dh	31.01S	125.20 E
Rawlins	43	Fc	41.47N	107.14W
Rawlinson Range	59	Fd	24.50S	128.00 E
Rawson [Arg.]	55	Bl	34.36S	60.04W
Rawson [Arg.]	53	Jj	43.18S	65.06W
Rawura, Ras-	36	He	10.20S	40.30 E
Raxaul	25	Gc	26.59N	84.51 E
Ray, Cape-	42	Lg	47.37N	59.19W
Raya, Bukit-	21	Nj	1.32S	111.05 E
Rayadrug	25	Ff	14.42N	76.52 E
Rayāt	24	Kd	36.40N	44.58 E
Rayleigh	12	Cc	51.35N	0.37 E
Raymond [Alta.-Can.]	46	Ib	49.27N	112.39W
Raymond [Wa.-U.S.]	46	Dc	46.41N	123.44W
Raymondville	43	Hf	26.29N	97.47W
Rayne	45	Jk	30.14N	92.16W
Rayón [Mex.]	48	Jg	21.51N	99.40W
Rayón [Mex.]	48	Dc	29.43N	110.35W
Rayones	48	Ie	25.01N	100.05W
Rayong	25	Kf	12.40N	101.17 E
Raysūt	23	Hf	16.54N	54.02 E
Raytown	45	Ig	39.00N	94.28W
Raz, Pointe du-	11	Bf	48.02N	4.44W
Razan	24	Me	35.23N	49.02 E
Razdan	16	Ni	40.28N	44.43 E
Razdelnaja	16	Gf	46.50N	30.05 E
Razdolinsk	20	Ee	58.25N	94.44 E
Razdolnaja	28	Kc	43.20N	131.49 E
Razdolnoje	28	Kc	43.33N	131.55 E
Razdolnoje	16	Hg	45.47N	33.30 E
Razgrad	15	Jf	43.32N	26.31 E
Razgrad [2]	15	Jf	43.32N	26.31 E
Razī	24	Mc	38.32N	48.08 E
Raziku/Raasiku	8	Ke	59.22N	25.11 E
Razlog	15	Gh	41.53N	23.28 E
Razo	32	Cf	16.37N	24.36W
Ré, Ile de-	5	Ff	46.12N	1.25W
Reachlainn	9	Gf	55.18N	6.13W
Reachlainn/Rathlin				
Island	9	Gf	55.18N	6.13W
Reachrainn/Lambay	9	Gh	53.29N	6.01W
Read	42	Gc	69.12N	114.30W
Reading [Eng.-U.K.]	9	Mj	51.28N	0.59W
Reading [Pa.-U.S.]	43	Lc	40.20N	75.55W
Real, Cordillera- [Bol.]	54	Eg	16.30S	68.30W
Real, Cordillera- [Ec.]	52	If	3.00S	78.00W
Real Audiencia	55	Cm	36.11S	58.35W
Real del Castillo	48	Aa	31.58N	116.19W
Realicó	56	He	35.02S	64.15W
Réalmont	11	Ik	43.47N	2.12 E
Reao Atoll	57	Nf	18.31S	136.23W
Reatini, Monti-	14	Gh	42.35N	12.50 E
Rebais	12	Ff	48.51N	3.14 E
Rebecca, Lake-	59	Ee	29.55S	122.10 E
Rebiana Oasis (EN) =				
Rabyānah, Wāḩāt al-	33	De	24.14N	21.59 E
Rebollera	13	Hf	38.25N	4.02W
Reboly	7	He	63.52N	30.47 E
Rebord Manamblen	37	Hd	24.05S	46.30 E
Rebun	28	Pb	45.23N	141.02 E
Rebun-Dake	29a	Ba	45.22N	141.01 E
Rebun-Suidō	29a	Ba	45.15N	141.05 E
Rebun-Tō	27	Pb	45.23N	141.10 E
Recalde	55	Bm	36.39S	61.05W
Recanati	14	Hg	43.24N	13.32 E
Recaş	15	Ed	45.48N	21.30 E
Recherche, Archipelago of				
the-	57	Dh	34.06S	122.45 E
Rečica	19	De	52.22N	30.25 E
Recife	53	Mf	8.03S	34.54W
Recife, Cape-	30	Jl	34.02S	25.45 E
Recke	12	Jb	52.23N	7.43 E
Recklinghausen	10	De	51.37N	7.12 E
Recknitz	10	Ib	54.14N	12.28 E
Recoaro Terme	14	Fe	45.42N	11.13 E
Reconquista	56	Ic	29.09S	59.39W
Recovery Glacier	66	Ag	81.10S	28.00W
Recreo	56	Gc	29.16S	65.04W
Recz	10	Lc	53.16N	15.33 E
Reda	10	Ob	54.38N	18.30 E
Redange	12	He	49.46N	5.54 E
Red Bank	44	Eh	35.07N	85.17W
Red Bay	42	Lf	51.44N	56.25W
Red Bluff	43	Cc	40.11N	122.15W
Red Bluff Reservoir	45	Ek	31.57N	103.56W
Redbridge, London-	12	Cc	51.35N	0.08 E
Red Butte	46	Ii	35.55N	112.03W
Redcar	9	Lg	54.37N	1.04W
Red Cliff	51c	Ab	17.05N	62.32W
Redcliff	37	Dc	19.02S	29.50 E
Redcliffe, Mount-	59	Ee	28.25S	121.32 E
Red Cloud	45	Gf	40.05N	98.32W
Red Deer	39	Hd	52.16N	113.48W
Red Deer [Can.]	42	Hf	52.55N	101.27W
Red Deer [Can.]	38	Id	50.56N	109.54W
Redding	39	Ge	40.35N	122.24W
Redditch	9	Li	52.19N	1.56W
Rede	9	Kf	55.08N	2.13W
Redenção	54	Kd	4.13S	38.43W
Redfield	43	Hc	44.53N	98.31W
Red Hill	65a	Ec	20.43N	156.15W
Red Hills	45	Gh	37.25N	99.25W
Redkino	7	Ih	56.40N	36.19 E
Red Lake	42	If	51.05N	93.55W
Red Lake	42	If	51.03N	93.49W
Red Lake River	45	Hc	47.55N	97.01W
Red Lakes	43	Ib	48.05N	94.45W
Redlands	46	Gi	34.03N	117.11W
Red Lodge	46	Kd	45.11N	109.15W
Redmond	43	Cc	44.17N	121.11W
Red Mountain [Ca.-U.S.]	46	Df	41.35N	123.06W
Red Mountain [Mt.-U.S.]	46	Ic	47.07N	112.44W
Red Oak	45	If	41.01N	95.14W
Redon	11	Dg	47.39N	2.05W
Redonda	50	Ed	16.55N	62.19W
Redondela	13	Db	42.17N	8.36W
Redondo	13	Ef	38.39N	7.33W
Redondo Beach	46	Fj	33.51N	118.23W
Redoubt Volcano	38	Dc	60.29N	152.45W
Red River [N.Amer.]	38	Jd	50.24N	96.48W
Red River [U.S.]	38	Jf	31.00N	91.40W
Red River (EN)=Hông,				
Sông-	21	Mg	20.17N	106.34 E
Red River (EN)=Yuan Jiang				
[Asia]	21	Mg	20.17N	106.34 E
Red Rock, Lake-	45	Jf	41.30N	93.20W
Red Rock River	46	Id	44.59N	112.52W
Redruth	9	Hk	50.13N	5.14W
Red Sea (EN)=Aḩmar, Al				
Baḩr al-	30	Kf	25.00N	38.00 E
Redstone	42	Fd	64.17N	124.33W
Redstone	46	Da	52.08N	123.42W
Red Volta (EN)=Volta				
Rouge	30	Gh	10.34N	0.30W
Redwater Creek	46	Mb	48.03N	105.13W
Red Wing	43	Ic	44.34N	92.31W
Redwood City	46	Dh	37.29N	122.13W
Redwood Falls	45	Id	44.32N	95.07W
Ree, Lough-/Loch Rí	9	Fh	53.35N	8.00W
Reed City	44	Ed	43.53N	85.31W
Reedley	46	Fh	36.24N	119.37W
Reeds Peak	45	Cj	33.09N	107.51W
Reedsport	43	Cc	43.42N	124.06W
Reedy Glacier	66	Ng	85.30S	134.00W
Reef Islands	57	Hf	10.15S	166.10 E
Reefton	62	De	42.07S	171.52 E
Reepham	12	Db	52.45N	1.07 E
Rees	12	Ic	51.46N	6.24 E
Reese River	46	Gf	40.39N	116.54W
Refahiye	24	Hc	39.54N	38.46 E
Reforma, Rio-	48	Ed	26.56N	108.12W
Reftele	8	Eg	57.11N	13.35 E
Reftinski	17	Jh	57.10N	61.43 E
Refugio	45	Hl	28.18N	97.17W
Refugio, Punta-	48	Cc	29.30N	113.30W
Rega	10	Lb	54.10N	15.18 E
Regar	19	Gh	38.34N	68.13 E
Regen	10	Jh	48.58N	13.08 E
Regen	10	Ig	49.01N	12.06 E
Regensburg	6	Hf	49.01N	12.06 E
Reggane	31	Hf	26.42N	0.10 E
Regge	12	Ib	52.26N	6.29 E
Reggio di Calabria	6	Hh	38.06N	15.39 E
Reggio nell'Emilia	14	Ef	44.43N	10.36 E
Reghin	15	Hc	46.46N	24.42 E
Regina [Fr.Gui.]	54	Hc	4.19N	52.08W
Regina [Sask.-Can.]	39	Id	50.25N	104.39W
Registan (EN)=Rīgestān	21	If	31.00N	65.00 E
Registro	55	Ig	24.30S	47.50W
Registro do Araguaia	55	Gb	15.44S	51.50W
Regnitz	10	Gg	49.54N	10.49 E
Regocijo	48	Gf	23.35N	105.11W
Reguengos de Monsaraz	13	Ef	38.25N	7.32W
Rehburg-Loccum	12	Lb	52.28N	9.14 E
Rehoboth [3]	37	Bd	23.50S	17.00 E
Rehoboth	37	Bd	23.18S	17.03 E
Reḩovot	24	Fg	31.54N	34.49 E
Reichelsheim (Odenwald)	12	Ke	49.43N	8.51 E
Reichenbach	10	If	50.37N	12.18 E
Reichshoffen	12	Jf	48.56N	7.40 E
Reichshof	12	Jd	50.55N	7.39 E
Reichshof-Denklingen	12	Jd	50.55N	7.39 E
Reidsville	44	Hg	36.21N	79.40W
Reigate	9	Mj	51.14N	0.13W
Reims	6	Gf	49.15N	4.02 E
Rein=Rhine (EN)	5	Ge	51.52N	6.02 E
Reina Adelaida,				
Archipiélago-	52	Ik	52.10S	74.25W
Reindeer	42	He	55.34N	103.10W
Reindeer Bank (EN)	51p	Ac	11.50N	62.05W
Reindeer Lake	38	Id	57.15N	102.40W
Reineskarvet	8	Cd	60.47N	8.13 E
Reinga, Cape-	62	Ea	34.25S	172.41 E
Reinhardswald	10	Fe	51.30N	9.30 E
Reinheim	12	Je	49.08N	7.11 E
Reinosa	13	Ha	43.00N	4.08W
Reisa	7	Eb	69.48N	21.00 E
Reitoru Atoll	57	Mf	17.52S	143.05W
Reitz	37	De	27.53S	28.31 E
Rejmyra	8	Ff	58.50N	15.55 E
Rejowiec Fabryczny	10	Te	51.08N	23.13 E
Reka Devnja	15	Kf	43.13N	27.36 E
Rekarne	8	Ge	59.20N	16.25 E
Reken	12	Jc	51.48N	7.03 E
Reliance	39	Ic	62.42N	109.08W
Relizane	32	Hb	35.45N	0.33 E
Remagen	12	Jd	50.34N	7.14 E
Remarkable, Mount-	59	Hf	32.48S	138.10 E
Rembang	26	Fh	6.42S	111.20 E
Remedios	49	Gi	8.14N	81.51W
Remedios, Punta-	49	Cg	13.31N	89.49W
Remedios, Rio-	49	Mh	11.01N	69.15W
Remich	12	Ie	49.32N	6.22 E
Rémire	54	Hc	4.53N	52.17W
Remiremont	11	Mf	48.01N	6.35 E
Remire Reef	37b	Bb	5.05S	53.22 E
Remontnoje	16	Mf	46.33N	43.40 E
Remoulins	11	Kk	43.56N	4.34 E
Remscheid	10	De	51.11N	7.12 E
Rena	7	Cf	61.08N	11.22 E
Rena	8	Dc	61.08N	11.23 E
Renaix/Ronse	11	Jd	50.45N	3.36 E
Renana, Fossa-	5	Gf	48.40N	7.50 E
Renard Islands	63a	Ad	10.50S	153.00 E
Renaud Island	66	Qe	65.40S	66.00W
Rende	14	Kk	39.20N	16.11 E
Rendezvous Bay	51b	Ab	18.10N	63.07W
Rend Lake	45	Lg	38.05N	88.58W
Rendova Island	60	Fi	8.32S	157.20 E
Rendsburg	10	Fb	54.18N	9.40 E
Renfrew	42	Jg	45.28N	76.41W
Rengat	26	Dg	0.24S	102.33 E
Rengo	56	Fd	34.25S	70.52W
Reni	16	Fg	45.29N	28.18 E
Renko	8	Kd	60.54N	24.17 E
Renkum	12	Hc	51.58N	5.45 E
Renland	41	Jd	71.15N	27.20W
Renmark	58	Fh	34.11S	140.45 E
Rennell, Islas-	56	Fh	52.00S	74.00W
Rennell Island	57	Hf	11.40S	160.10 E
Rennes	6	Ff	48.05N	1.41W
Rennes, Bassin de-	11	Ef	48.05N	1.40W
Rennesøy	8	Ae	59.05N	5.40 E
Rennick Glacier	66	Kf	70.30S	161.45 E
Rennie Lake	42	Gd	61.10N	105.30W
Reno	39	Hf	39.31N	119.48W
Reno	14	Gf	44.38N	12.16 E
Renqiu	28	De	38.42N	116.06 E
Rensselaer [In.-U.S.]	44	De	40.57N	87.09W
Rensselaer [N.Y.-U.S.]	44	Kd	42.37N	73.44W
Renteria	13	Ka	43.19N	1.54W
Renton	46	Dc	47.30N	122.11W
Renwez	12	Ge	49.50N	4.36 E
Renxian	28	Cf	37.07N	114.41 E
Reo	26	Hh	8.19S	120.30 E
Repartimento, Serra do-	55	Jc	17.40S	44.50W
Repino	8	Md	60.10N	29.58 E
Repong, Pulau-	26	Ef	2.22N	105.53 E
Reposaari/Räfsö	8	Ic	61.37N	21.27 E
Republic	46	Fb	48.39N	118.44W
Republican	38	Jf	39.03N	96.48W
Repulse Bay	42	Kc	66.32N	86.15W
Repulse Bay [Austl.]	59	Jd	20.35S	148.45 E
Repulse Bay [Can.]	42	Ic	66.20N	86.00W
Repvåg	7	Fa	70.45N	25.41 E
Requena [Peru]	54	Dd	5.00S	73.50W
Requena [Sp.]	13	Ke	39.29N	1.06W
Requin Bay	51p	Bb	12.02N	61.38W
Réquista	11	Ij	44.02N	2.32 E
Reşadiye Yarimadası	15	Km	36.40N	27.45 E
Reschenpass/Resia, Passo				
di-	14	Ed	46.50N	10.30 E
Resen	15	Eh	41.05N	21.01 E
Reserva	55	Gg	24.38S	50.52W
Reserve	45	Bj	33.43N	108.45W
Rešetilovka	16	Ie	49.33N	34.05 E
Reshui	27	Hd	37.38N	100.30 E
Resia, Passo di-/				
Reschenpass	14	Ed	46.50N	10.30 E
Resistencia	53	Kh	27.30S	58.59W
Reşiţa	15	Ed	45.18N	21.55 E
Resko	10	Lc	53.47N	15.25 E
Reso/Raisio	7	Ff	60.29N	22.11 E
Resolute	39	Jb	74.41N	94.54W
Resolution	38	Mc	61.30N	65.00W
Resolution Island	42	Ld	61.35N	64.39W
Resolution Island	62	Bf	45.40S	166.35 E
Respublikai Soveth				
Socialisti Todžikiston/				
Tadžikskaja SSR →				
Tajikistan	19	Hh	39.00N	71.00 E
Respublika Sovetike				
Socialiste Moldovenjaske/				
Moldavskaja SSR →				
Moldova	19	Cf	47.00N	29.00 E
Ressons-sur-Matz	12	Ee	49.33N	2.45 E
Restigouche River	44	Na	48.04N	66.20W
Restinga de Sefton, Isla-	52	Hi	37.00S	83.50W
Restinga Sêca	55	Fi	29.49S	53.23W
Reszel	10	Rb	54.04N	21.09 E
Retalhuleu [3]	49	Bf	14.20N	91.50W
Retalhuleu	47	Ff	14.32N	91.41W
Retavas/Rietavas	8	Ii	55.43N	21.49 E
Retezatului, Munţii-	15	Fd	45.25N	23.00 E
Rethel	11	Ke	49.31N	4.22 E
Rethem (Aller)	12	Lb	52.47N	9.23 E
Réthimnon	15	Hn	35.22N	24.28 E
Retie	12	Hc	51.17N	5.05 E

Index Symbols

[1] Independent Nation
[2] State, Region
[3] District, County
[4] Municipality
[5] Colony, Dependency
Continent
Physical Region
Historical or Cultural Region
Mount, Mountain
Volcano
Hill
Mountains, Mountain Range
Hills, Escarpment
Plateau, Upland
Pass, Gap
Plain, Lowland
Delta
Salt Flat
Valley, Canyon
Crater, Cave
Karst Features
Depression
Polder
Desert, Dunes
Forest, Woods
Heath, Steppe
Oasis
Cape, Point
Coast, Beach
Cliff
Peninsula
Isthmus
Sandbank
Island
Atoll
Rock, Reef
Islands, Archipelago
Rocks, Reefs
Coral Reef
Well, Spring
Geyser
River, Stream
Waterfall Rapids
River Mouth, Estuary
Lake
Salt Lake
Intermittent Lake
Reservoir
Swamp, Pond
Canal
Glacier
Ice Shelf, Pack Ice
Ocean
Sea
Gulf, Bay
Strait, Fjord
Lagoon
Bank
Seamount
Tablemount
Ridge
Shelf
Basin
Escarpment, Sea Scarp
Fracture
Trench, Abyss
National Park, Reserve
Point of Interest
Recreation Site
Cave, Cavern
Historic Site
Ruins
Wall, Walls
Church, Abbey
Temple
Scientific Station
Airport
Port
Lighthouse
Mine
Tunnel
Dam, Bridge

Index Symbols

Symbol	Meaning	Symbol	Meaning	Symbol	Meaning	Symbol	Meaning	Symbol	Meaning	Symbol	Meaning
①	Independent Nation	▭	Historical or Cultural Region	▭	Pass, Gap	▭	Depression	▨	Coast, Beach	▨	Rock, Reef	⌐	Waterfall Rapids	▭	Canal	▭	Lagoon	▭	Escarpment, Sea Scarp	▲	Historic Site	▨	Port
②	State, Region	▲	Mount, Mountain	▲	Plain, Lowland	▭	Polder	▭	Cliff	▨	Islands, Archipelago	⌐	River Mouth, Estuary	▭	Bank	▭	Glacier	▨	Fracture	▨	Ruins	▨	Lighthouse
③	District, County	▲	Volcano	▭	Delta	▭	Desert, Dunes	▶	Peninsula	▨	Rocks, Reefs	⌐	Lake	▭	Seamount	▭	Ice Shelf, Pack Ice	▭	Trench, Abyss	▨	Wall, Walls	▨	Mine
④	Municipality	▲	Hill	▭	Salt Flat	▭	Forest, Woods	⌐	Isthmus	▨	Coral Reef	⌐	Salt Lake	▭	Ocean	▭	National Park, Reserve	▨	Church, Abbey	▨	Tunnel
⑤	Colony, Dependency	▲	Mountains, Mountain Range	⌐	Valley, Canyon	▭	Heath, Steppe	▭	Sandbank	⌐	Well, Spring	⌐	Intermittent Lake	▭	Sea	▲	Point of Interest	▨	Temple	▭	Dam, Bridge
▬	Continent	▭	Hills, Escarpment	⌐	Crater, Cave	▭	Oasis	⌐	Island	⌐	Geyser	▭	Reservoir	▭	Ridge	▲	Recreation Site	▨	Scientific Station	
▭	Physical Region	▭	Plateau, Upland	⌐	Karst Features	▶	Cape, Point	⊙	Atoll	⌐	River, Stream	⌐	Swamp, Pond	▭	Basin	▭	Cave, Cavern	▨	Airport	

Rödeby	8	Fh	56.15N	15.36 E
Rodeio Bonito	55	Fh	27.28S	53.10W
Roden	12	Ia	53.09N	6.26 E
Rodeo [Arg.]	56	Gd	30.12S	69.06W
Rodeo [Mex.]	48	Ge	25.11N	104.34W
Rodeo [N.M.-U.S.]	45	Bk	31.50N	109.02W
Röder	10	Je	51.30N	13.25 E
Rodez	11	Ij	44.20N	2.34 E
Rodgau	12	Kd	50.01N	8.53 E
Rodholivos	15	Gi	40.56N	23.59 E
Ródhos = Rhodes (EN)	6	Ih	36.26N	28.13 E
Ródhos = Rhodes (EN)	5	Ih	36.10N	28.00 E
Rodi Garganico	14	Ji	41.55N	15.53 E
Roding	9	Nj	51.31N	0.06 E
Rodna	15	Hb	47.25N	24.49 E
Rodnei, Munţii-	15	Hb	47.35N	24.40 E
Rodney, Cape-	40	Fd	64.39N	166.24W
Rodniki	7	Jh	57.07N	41.48 E
Rodonit, Gjiri i-	15	Ch	41.35N	19.30 E
Rodonit, Kep i-	15	Ch	41.35N	19.27 E
Rodopi = Rhodope Mountains (EN)	5	Ig	41.30N	24.30 E
Rodrigues Island	30	Nj	19.42S	63.25 E
Roebourne	59	Dd	20.47S	117.09 E
Roebuck Bay	59	Ec	18.05S	122.15 E
Roer	10	Be	51.12N	5.59 E
Roermond	11	Lc	51.12N	6.00 E
Roeselare/Roulers	11	Jd	50.57N	3.08 E
Roes Welcome Sound	42	Id	64.30N	86.45W
Roetgen	12	Id	50.39N	6.12 E
Rogačev	16	Gc	53.09N	30.06 E
Rogačevka	16	Kd	51.31N	39.34 E
Rogagua, Laguna-	54	Ef	13.45S	66.55W
Rogaguado, Laguna-	54	Ef	12.55S	65.45W
Rogaland [2]	7	Bg	59.00N	6.15 E
Rogaška Slatina	14	Jd	46.15N	15.38 E
Rogatica	14	Ng	43.48N	19.01 E
Rogatin	10	Ug	49.19N	24.40 E
Rogers	45	Ih	36.20N	94.07W
Rogers, Mount-	44	Gg	36.39N	81.33W
Rogers City	44	Fc	45.25N	83.49W
Rogers Lake	46	Gi	34.52N	117.51W
Rogers Peak	46	Jg	38.04N	111.32W
Rogersville	44	Fg	36.25N	82.59W
Roggan	42	Jf	54.24N	79.30W
Roggeveldberge	37	Bf	31.50S	19.50 E
Roggewein, Cabo-	65d	Bb	27.07S	109.15W
Rognan	7	Dc	67.06N	15.23 E
Rogozhina	15	Ch	41.05N	19.40 E
Rogozna	15	Df	43.04N	20.40 E
Rogoźno	10	Md	52.46N	17.00 E
Rogue River	46	Ce	42.26N	124.25W
Rohan, Plateau de-	11	Dd	48.10N	3.00W
Rohl	35	Dd	7.05N	29.46 E
Rohrbach in Oberösterreich	14	Hb	48.34N	13.59 E
Rohrbach-lès-Bitche	12	Je	49.03N	7.16 E
Rohri	25	Dc	27.41N	68.54 E
Rohtak	25	Fc	28.54N	76.34 E
Roi, Le Bois du-	11	Kh	46.59N	4.02 E
Roi Et	25	Ke	16.05N	103.42 E
Roi Georges, Iles du-	57	Mf	14.32S	145.08W
Roine	8	Kc	61.25N	24.05 E
Roisel	12	Fe	49.57N	3.06 E
Roja	7	Fh	57.30N	22.51 E
Rojas	56	Hd	34.12S	60.44W
Rojo, Cabo- [Mex.]	47	Ed	21.33N	97.20W
Rojo, Cabo- [P.R.]	49	Nd	18.01N	67.15W
Rokan	26	Df	2.00N	100.52 E
Rokiškis	7	Fi	55.59N	25.37 E
Rokitnoje	16	Ed	51.21N	27.14 E
Rokkasho	29a	Bc	40.58N	141.21 E
Rokycany	10	Jg	49.45N	13.36 E
Rokytná	10	Mg	49.05N	16.21 E
Rola Co	27	Ed	35.25N	88.25 E
Rolândia	55	Gf	23.18S	51.22W
Rolla [Mo.-U.S.]	43	Id	37.57N	91.46W
Rolla [N.D.-U.S.]	45	Gb	48.52N	99.37W
Rolleston	62	Ee	43.35S	172.23 E
Rolvsøya	7	Fa	71.00N	24.00 E
Roma [Austl.]	58	Fg	26.35S	148.47 E
Roma [It.] = Rome (EN)	6	Hg	41.54N	12.29 E
Roma [Swe.]	7	Eh	57.32N	18.26 E
Romagna	14	Gf	44.30N	12.15 E
Romaine	42	Lf	50.18N	63.48W
Roman	15	Jc	46.55N	26.55 E
Romanche	11	Li	45.05N	5.43 E
Romanche Gap (EN)	3	Dj	0.10S	18.15W
Romang	55	Ci	29.30S	59.46W
Romang, Pulau-	26	Ih	7.35S	127.26 E
România = Romania (EN) [1]	6	If	46.00N	25.30 E
Romania (EN) = România [1]	6	If	46.00N	25.30 E
Romanija	14	Mg	43.51N	18.43 E
Roman Koš, Gora-	19	Dg	44.36N	34.16 E
Romano, Cayo-	49	Ib	22.04N	77.50W
Romanovka	20	Gf	53.14N	112.46 E
Romans-sur-Isère	11	Li	45.03N	5.03 E
Romanzof, Cape-	38	Cc	61.49N	166.09W
Romanzof Mountains	40	Kc	69.00N	144.00W
Rombas	12	Ie	49.15N	6.05 E
Romblon	26	Hd	12.35N	122.15 E
Rome [Ga.-U.S.]	43	Je	34.16N	85.11W
Rome [N.Y.-U.S.]	44	Jd	43.13N	75.28W
Rome [Or.-U.S.]	46	Ge	42.50N	117.37W
Rome (EN) = Roma [It.]	6	Hg	41.54N	12.29 E
Romeleåsen	8	Ei	55.34N	13.33 E
Romerike	8	Dd	60.05N	11.10 E
Romilly-sur-Seine	11	Jf	48.31N	3.43 E
Rommani	32	Fc	33.32N	6.36W
Romme	8	Fd	60.26N	15.30 E
Rommerskirchen	12	Ic	51.02N	6.41 E
Romney Marsh	12	Cc	51.02N	0.55 E
Romny	19	De	50.45N	33.29 E
Rømø	7	Bi	55.10N	8.30 E
Romodanovo	7	Ki	54.28N	45.18 E
Romont	14	Ad	46.42N	6.55 E
Romorantin-Lanthenay	11	Hg	47.22N	1.45 E
Romsdal	8	Bb	62.35N	7.50 E
Romsdalen	8	Bb	62.30N	7.55 E
Romsdalsfjorden	8	Bb	62.40N	7.15 E
Romsdalshorn	8	Bd	62.29N	7.50 E
Romsey	9	Lk	50.59N	1.30W
Ronas Hill	9	La	60.38N	1.20W
Ronave	64e	Ba	0.29S	166.56 E
Roncador, Cayos de-	47	Hf	13.32N	80.03W
Roncador, Serra do-	52	Kg	13.00S	51.50W
Roncador Reef	57	Ge	6.13S	159.22 E
Roncesvalles	13	Ka	43.01N	1.19W
Roncesvalles o Ibañeta, Puerto de-	13	Ka	43.01N	1.19W
Ronciglione	14	Gh	42.17N	12.13 E
Ronco	14	Gf	44.24N	12.12 E
Ronda	13	Gh	36.44N	5.10W
Ronda, Serrania de-	13	Gh	36.44N	5.05W
Ronda do Sul	55	Cb	15.57S	59.42W
Rondane	7	Bf	61.55N	9.45 E
Rønde	7	Ch	56.18N	10.29 E
Ronde, Point-	51g	Ba	15.33N	61.29W
Ronde Island	50	Ff	12.18N	61.31W
Rondeslottet	8	Cc	61.55N	9.46 E
Rondon	55	Ff	23.23S	52.48W
Rondón, Pico-	54	Fc	1.36N	63.08W
Rondônia	53	Jg	10.52S	61.57W
Rondônia	54	Ff	11.00S	63.00W
Rondonópolis	53	Kg	16.28S	54.38W
Rong'an (Chang'an)	27	If	25.16N	109.23 E
Rongcheng	28	Ce	39.03N	115.52 E
Rongcheng (Yatou)	28	Gf	37.10N	122.25 E
Rongelap Atoll	57	Hc	11.09N	166.50 E
Rongerik Atoll	57	Hc	11.21N	167.26 E
Rongjiang (Guzhou)	27	If	25.58N	108.30 E
Rongxian	27	Jg	22.48N	110.30 E
Rongzhag/Danba	27	He	30.48N	101.54 E
Rønne	7	Di	55.06N	14.42 E
Ronne Bay	66	Qf	72.30S	74.00W
Ronneby	7	Dh	56.12N	15.18 E
Ronnebyån	8	Fh	56.10N	15.18 E
Ronne Ice Shelf	66	Qf	78.30S	61.00W
Ronse/Renaix	11	Jd	50.45N	3.36 E
Ronuro, Rio-	52	Kg	11.56S	53.33W
Roodepoort	37	De	26.11S	27.54 E
Roof Butte	43	Fd	36.28N	109.05W
Rooiboklaagte	37	Cd	20.20S	21.15 E
Roon, Pulau-	26	Jg	2.23S	134.33 E
Rooniu, Mont-	65e	c	17.49S	149.12W
Roorkee	25	Fc	29.52N	77.53 E
Roosendaal	11	Kc	51.32N	4.28 E
Roosevelt [Az.-U.S.]	46	Jj	33.40N	111.09W
Roosevelt [Ut.-U.S.]	46	Kf	40.18N	109.59W
Roosevelt, Mount-	42	Ee	58.23N	125.04W
Roosevelt, Rio-	52	Jf	7.35S	60.20W
Roosevelt Island	66	Lf	79.30S	162.00W
Root Portage	45	Ka	50.53N	91.18W
Ropa	10	Rg	49.46N	21.29 E
Ropar	25	Fb	30.58N	76.20 E
Ropaži	8	Kh	56.58N	24.26 E
Ropczyce	10	Rf	50.03N	21.37 E
Rope, The-	64q	Ab	25.04S	130.05W
Roper River	57	Ef	14.43S	135.27 E
Roquefort	11	Fj	44.02N	0.19W
Roque Pérez	55	Cl	35.25S	59.20W
Roquetas de Mar	13	Jh	36.46N	2.36W
Roraima, Monte-	52	Je	5.12N	60.44W
Roraima	54	Fc	1.30N	61.00W
Røros	7	Ce	62.35N	11.24 E
Rorschach	14	Dc	47.30N	9.30 E
Rørvik	7	Cd	64.51N	11.14 E
Ros	16	Ge	49.39N	31.35 E
Rosa, Cap-	14	Cn	36.57N	8.14 E
Rosa, Lake-	49	Kc	20.55N	73.20W
Rosa, Monte-	5	Gf	45.55N	7.53 E
Rošal	7	Ji	55.41N	39.55 E
Rosala	8	Je	59.50N	22.25 E
Rosalia	46	Gc	47.14N	117.22W
Rosalia, Punta-	65d	Bb	27.03S	109.19W
Rosalie	51g	Bb	15.22N	61.16W
Rosalind Bank (EN)	49	Ge	16.30N	80.30W
Rosamond Lake	46	Fi	34.50N	118.04W
Rosamorada	48	Gf	22.08N	105.12W
Rosana	55	Ff	22.36S	53.01W
Rosario [Arg.]	53	Ji	32.57S	60.40W
Rosario [Braz.]	54	Jd	2.57S	44.14W
Rosario [Mex.]	48	Dd	26.27N	111.38W
Rosario [Mex.]	47	Cd	23.00N	105.52W
Rosario [Par.]	56	Ib	24.27S	57.03W
Rosario [Ven.]	49	Kh	10.19N	72.19W
Rosario, Arroyo-	48	Bb	30.03N	115.45W
Rosario, Bahía-	48	Bc	29.50N	115.45W
Rosario, Cayo del-	49	Gc	21.38N	81.53W
Rosario, Islas de-	49	Jh	10.10N	75.46W
Rosario, Sierra del-	48	He	25.35N	103.50W
Rosario de Arriba	47	Ab	30.01N	115.40W
Rosario de la Frontera	56	Hc	25.48S	64.58W
Rosario de Lerma	56	Gb	24.59S	65.35W
Rosario del Tala	55	Ck	32.18S	59.09W
Rosário do Sul	56	Jd	30.15S	54.55W
Rosário Oeste	54	Gf	14.50S	56.25W
Rosarito	48	Bc	28.38N	114.04W
Rosarno	14	Jl	38.29N	15.58 E
Rosas/Roses	13	Pb	42.16N	3.11 E
Rosas, Golfo de-/Roses, Golf de-	13	Pb	42.10N	3.15 E
Rosa Seamount (EN)	47	Bc	26.12N	114.58W
Rosa Zarate	54	Cc	0.18N	79.27W
Roščino	8	Md	60.13N	29.43 E
Roscoe Glacier	66	Ge	66.30S	95.20 E
Ros Comáin/Roscommon [2]	9	Eh	53.40N	8.30W
Ros Comáin/Roscommon	9	Eh	53.38N	8.11W
Roscommon	44	Ec	44.30N	84.35W
Roscommon/Ros Comáin	9	Eh	53.38N	8.11W
Roscommon/Ros Comáin [2]	9	Eh	53.40N	8.30W
Ros Cré/Roscrea	9	Fi	52.57N	7.47W
Roscrea/Ros Cré	9	Fi	52.57N	7.47W
Rose, Pointe de la-	51h	Bb	14.33N	61.03W
Roseau [Dom.]	39	Mh	15.18N	61.24W
Roseau [Dom.]	51g	Bb	15.18N	61.24W
Roseau [Mn.-U.S.]	45	Ib	48.51N	95.46W
Roseau [St.Luc.]	51k	Ab	13.58N	61.02W
Roseau River	45	Hb	49.08N	97.14W
Rosebery	59	Jh	41.46S	145.32 E
Rosebud	46	Lc	46.16N	106.27W
Rosebud Creek	46	Lc	46.16N	106.28W
Rosebud River	46	Ia	51.25N	112.37W
Roseburg	43	Cc	43.13N	123.20W
Rosemary Bank (EN)	9	Cb	59.15N	10.10W
Rosenberg	43	Hf	29.33N	95.48W
Rosendahl	12	Jb	52.01N	7.12 E
Rosendahl-Osterwick	12	Jb	52.01N	7.12 E
Rosendal	7	Bf	59.59N	6.01 E
Rosenheim	10	Ii	47.51N	12.08 E
Rosental	14	Id	46.33N	14.15 E
Roses/Rosas	13	Pb	42.16N	3.11 E
Roses, Golf de-/Rosas, Golfo de-	13	Pb	42.10N	3.15 E
Roseţi	15	Ke	44.13N	27.26 E
Roseto degli Abruzzi	14	Ih	42.41N	14.01 E
Rosetown	42	Gf	51.33N	108.00W
Rosetta (EN) = Rashīd	33	Fc	31.24N	30.25 E
Roseville	46	Eg	38.45N	121.17W
Roshage	7	Bh	57.07N	8.38 E
Rosica	15	If	43.15N	25.42 E
Rosières-en-Santerre	12	Ee	49.49N	2.43 E
Rosignano Solvay	14	Eg	43.23N	10.26 E
Rosignol	54	Gb	6.17N	57.32W
Roşiori de Vede	15	He	44.07N	24.59 E
Roskilde [2]	8	Ei	55.35N	12.10 E
Roskilde	7	Ci	55.39N	12.05 E
Roslagen	8	He	59.30N	18.40 E
Ros Láir/Rosslare	9	Gi	52.17N	6.23W
Roslavl	19	De	53.58N	32.53 E
Roslyn	46	Ec	47.13N	120.59W
Ros Mhic Thriúin/New Ross	9	Gi	52.24N	6.56W
Rosnæs	8	Di	55.45N	10.55 E
Rosny-sur-Seine	12	Df	49.00N	1.38 E
Rösrath	12	Jd	50.54N	7.12 E
Ross	42	Ed	62.00N	132.25W
Ross [Austl.]	59	Jh	42.02S	147.29 E
Ross	10	Uc	53.16N	24.29 E
Ross [N.Z.]	62	De	42.54S	170.49 E
Ross, Cape-	26	Gd	10.56N	119.13 E
Ross, Mount-	30	Nm	49.25S	69.08 E
Rossano	14	Kk	39.34N	16.38 E
Rossan Point/Ceann Ros Eoghain	9	Eg	54.42N	8.48W
Ross Barnett Reservoir	45	Lj	32.30N	90.00W
Rosseau Lake	44	Hc	45.10N	79.35W
Rossel Island	57	Gf	11.26S	154.07 E
Rossell, Cap-	63b	Ce	20.23S	166.36 E
Ross Ice Shelf	66	Lg	81.30S	175.00W
Rossija = Russia (EN)	19	Jc	60.00N	100.00 E
Ross Island	66	Kf	77.30S	168.00 E
Ross Lake	46	Eb	48.53N	121.04W
Rossland	46	Gb	49.05N	117.48W
Rosslare/Ros Láir	9	Gi	52.17N	6.23W
Roßlau	10	Ie	51.53N	12.15 E
Rosso	31	Fg	16.31N	15.49W
Ross-on-Wye	9	Kj	51.55N	2.35W
Rossony	8	Mi	55.53N	28.49 E
Rossoš	19	De	50.11N	39.39 E
Ross River	42	Ed	61.59N	132.27W
Ross Sea (EN)	66	Lf	76.00S	175.00W
Røssvatn	7	Cd	65.45N	14.00 E
Røst	7	Cc	67.31N	12.07 E
Rosta	7	Eb	69.02N	18.40 E
Rostamī	24	Nh	28.52N	51.02 E
Rostan Kalā	24	Od	36.42N	53.27 E
Rösterkopf	12	Ie	49.40N	6.50 E
Rosthern	42	Gf	52.40N	106.20W
Rostock	6	He	54.05N	12.08 E
Rostock-Warnemünde	10	Ib	54.10N	12.05 E
Rostov	19	Dd	57.13N	39.25 E
Rostov-na-Donu	6	Jf	47.14N	39.42 E
Rostovskaja Oblast [3]	19	Ef	47.45N	41.15 E
Roswell [Ga.-U.S.]	44	Eh	34.03N	84.22W
Roswell [N.M.-U.S.]	39	If	33.24N	104.32W
Rot	8	Fc	61.15N	14.02 E
Rota	13	Fh	36.37N	6.21W
Rota Island	57	Fc	14.10N	145.12 E
Rotenburg (Wümme)	10	Fc	53.07N	9.24 E
Rotenburg an der Fulda	10	Ff	50.59N	9.43 E
Roter Main	10	Hf	50.03N	11.27 E
Roth	10	Hg	49.15N	11.06 E
Rothaargebirge	10	Ee	51.05N	8.15 E
Rothenburg ob der Tauber	10	Gg	49.23N	10.11 E
Rother [Eng.-U.K.]	9	Nk	50.57N	0.45 E
Rother [Eng.-U.K.]	12	Bd	50.57N	0.22W
Rothera	66	Qe	67.46S	68.54W
Rotherham	9	Lh	53.26N	1.20W
Rothesay	9	Hf	55.51N	5.03W
Rothorn	14	Cd	46.47N	8.03 E
Rothschild Island	66	Qe	69.25S	72.30W
Rothwell	12	Bb	52.25N	0.48W
Roti, Pulau-	21	Ok	10.45S	123.10 E
Roti, Selat-	26	Hi	10.25S	123.25 E
Rotja, Punta-	13	Nf	38.38N	1.34 E
Rotnes	8	Dd	60.04N	10.53 E
Roto	59	Jf	33.03S	145.29 E
Rotoiti, Lake-	62	Ed	41.50S	172.50 E
Rotondella	14	Kj	40.10N	16.31 E
Rotondo, Monte-	11a	Ba	42.13N	9.03 E
Rotoroa, Lake-	62	Ed	41.50S	172.40 E
Rotorua	61	Eg	38.09S	176.15 E
Rotorua, Lake-	62	Gc	38.05S	176.15 E
Rotselaar	12	Gd	50.57N	4.43 E
Rott	10	Jh	48.25N	13.20 E
Rottenburg am Neckar	10	Eh	48.28N	8.56 E
Rotterdam	6	Ge	51.55N	4.28 E
Rottnaälven	8	Ed	59.48N	13.07 E
Rottnen	8	Fh	56.45N	15.05 E
Rottneros	8	Ee	59.48N	13.07 E
Rottnest Island	59	Df	32.00S	115.30 E
Rottumerplaat	11	Ma	53.35N	6.30 E
Rottweil	10	Eh	48.10N	8.37 E
Rotuma Island	57	If	12.30S	177.05 E
Roubaix	11	Jd	50.42N	3.10 E
Roubion	11	Kj	44.31N	4.42 E
Roudnice nad Labem	10	Kf	50.26N	14.16 E
Rouen	6	Gf	49.26N	1.05 E
Rouergue	11	Ij	44.30N	2.56 E
Rouge, Rivière-	44	Jc	45.38N	74.42W
Rouillac	11	Fi	45.47N	0.04W
Roulers/Roeselare	11	Jd	50.57N	3.08 E
Roumois	11	Ge	49.30N	0.30 E
Roundup	43	Fb	46.27N	108.33W
Rousay	9	Jb	59.01N	3.02W
Roussillon	11	Ki	45.22N	4.49 E
Roussillon	11	Il	42.30N	2.30 E
Roussin, Cap-	63b	Ce	21.21S	167.59 E
Routot	12	Ce	49.23N	0.44 E
Rouyn-Noranda	39	Le	48.14N	79.01W
Rovaniemi	6	Ib	66.30N	25.43 E
Rovenskaja Oblast [3]	19	Ce	51.00N	26.30 E
Rovereto	14	Fe	45.53N	11.02 E
Rovigo	14	Fe	45.04N	11.47 E
Rovinari	15	Ge	44.55N	23.11 E
Rovinj	14	He	45.05N	13.38 E
Rovkulskoje, Ozero-	7	Hd	64.00N	31.00 E
Rovno	6	Ie	50.37N	26.15 E
Rovnoje	16	Od	50.47N	46.05 E
Rovuma = Ruvuma (EN)	30	Lj	10.29S	40.28 E
Rowa, Iles-	63b	Ca	13.37S	167.32 E
Rowley	42	Jc	69.05N	78.55W
Rowley Shoals	57	Cf	17.30S	119.00 E
Roxas [Phil.]	26	Gd	10.28N	119.30 E
Roxas [Phil.]	26	Hd	11.35N	122.45 E
Roxboro	44	Hg	36.24N	78.59W
Roxburgh	62	Cf	45.33S	169.19 E
Roxen	8	Ff	58.30N	15.40 E
Roxo, Cap-	30	Fg	12.20N	16.43W
Roy [N.M.-U.S.]	45	Di	35.57N	104.12W
Roy [Ut.-U.S.]	46	If	41.10N	112.02W
Roya	11	Nk	43.48N	7.35 E
Royal Canal	9	Gh	53.21N	6.15W
Royale, Isle-	43	Jb	48.00N	89.00W
Royal Leamington Spa	9	Li	52.18N	1.31W
Royal Society Range	66	Jf	78.10S	162.36 E
Royal Tunbridge Wells	9	Nj	51.08N	0.16 E
Royan	11	Ei	45.38N	1.02W
Royat	11	Ji	45.46N	3.03 E
Royaumont, Abbaye de-	12	Ee	49.17N	2.28 E
Roye	11	Ie	49.42N	2.48 E
Roy Hill	59	Dd	22.38S	119.57 E
Røyken	8	Je	59.45N	10.23 E
Royston	9	Mi	52.03N	0.01W
Rožaj	15	Dg	42.51N	20.10 E
Różan	10	Rd	52.53N	21.25 E
Rozdol	10	Ug	49.24N	24.08 E
Rozewie, Przylądek-	10	Ob	54.51N	18.21 E
Rožišče	16	Dd	50.54N	25.19 E
Rožňava	10	Qh	48.40N	20.32 E
Rožniatov	10	Uh	48.51N	24.14 E
Roznov	15	Jc	46.50N	26.31 E
Rožnov pod Radhoštěm	10	Og	49.28N	18.09 E
Rożnów	10	Qg	49.46N	20.42 E
Rożnowskie, Jezioro-	10	Qg	49.48N	20.45 E
Rozoy-sur-Serre	12	Ge	49.43N	4.08 E
Roztocze	5	Ie	50.30N	23.20 E
Rrësheni	15	Ch	41.47N	19.54 E
RSFSR — Russia (EN)	19	Jc	60.00N	100.00 E
RSFSR — Rossija	19	Jc	60.00N	100.00 E
Rtanj	15	Ef	43.47N	21.54 E
Rtiščevo	19	Ee	52.16N	43.52 E
Ruacana, Quedas-	30	Jj	17.23S	14.15 E
Ruahine Range	62	Gc	39.50S	176.05 E
Ruapehu	57	Ih	39.17S	175.34 E
Ruapuke Island	61	Ci	46.45S	168.30 E
Rua Sura	63a	Ec	9.30S	160.36 E
Ruatahuna	62	Gc	38.38S	176.58 E
Rubbestadneset	8	Ae	59.49N	5.17 E
Rubcovsk	22	Kd	51.33N	81.10 E
Rubeho Mountains	36	Gd	6.55S	36.30 E
Rubeshibe	28	Qc	43.47N	143.38 E
Rubežnoje	16	Ke	48.59N	38.26 E
Rubi	36	Db	2.48N	23.54 E
Rubiataba	55	Hb	15.08S	49.48W
Rubiku	15	Ch	41.46N	19.45 E
Rubio	54	Db	7.43N	72.22W
Rubio	13	Ic	41.26N	3.47W
Ruby	40	Hd	64.44N	155.30W
Ruby Lake	46	Hf	40.15N	115.30W
Ruby Mountains	46	Hf	40.25N	115.35W
Ruby Range	46	Id	45.15N	112.15W
Rucăr	15	Id	45.24N	25.10 E
Rucava	8	Ih	56.10N	21.00 E
Ruciane Nida	10	Rc	53.39N	21.35 E
Ruda	10	Of	50.10N	18.18 E
Rudabánya	10	Qh	48.23N	20.38 E
Rūdak	24	Nh	35.51N	51.33 E
Rūdān	24	Qi	27.17N	57.13 E
Ruda Śląska	10	Of	50.18N	18.51 E
Rūdbār [Afg.]	23	Jc	30.09N	62.36 E
Rūdbār [Iran]	24	Md	36.48N	49.24 E
Rüdersdorf bei Berlin	10	Jd	52.27N	13.47 E
Rüdesheim am Rhein	12	Je	49.59N	7.55 E
Rudiškes/Rūdiškės	8	Kj	54.30N	24.58 E
Rūdiškės/Rudiškes	8	Kj	54.30N	24.58 E
Rudki	10	Tg	49.34N	23.30 E
Rudkøbing	7	Ci	54.56N	10.43 E
Rudnaja-Pristan	20	Ih	44.25N	135.49 E
Rudničny	7	Mg	59.38N	52.29 E
Rudnik	15	De	44.08N	20.30 E
Rudnik [Bul.]	15	Kg	42.57N	27.46 E
Rudnik [Pol.]	10	Sf	50.28N	22.15 E
Rudnik [Yugo.]	15	De	44.08N	20.31 E
Rudnjå	16	Nd	50.49N	44.36 E
Rudnja	19	De	54.57N	31.07 E
Rudno	10	Tg	49.44N	23.57 E
Rudny	19	Ge	52.57N	63.07 E
Rudny	28	Mb	44.28N	135.00 E
Rudolf, Lake-/Turkana, Lake-	30	Kh	3.30N	36.00 E
Rudolstadt	10	Hf	50.43N	11.20 E
Rudong (Juegang)	28	Fh	32.19N	121.11 E
Rudozem	15	Hh	41.29N	24.51 E
Rūd Sar	23	Hb	37.08N	50.18 E
Rudyard	46	Jb	48.34N	110.33W
Rue	11	Hd	50.16N	1.40 E
Ruecas	13	Ge	39.00N	5.55W
Ruelle-sur-Touvre	11	Gi	45.41N	0.14 E
Rufā'ah	35	Ec	14.46N	33.22 E
Ruffec	11	Gh	46.01N	0.12 E
Ruffing Point	51a	Db	18.45N	64.25W
Rufiji	30	Ki	8.00S	39.20 E
Rufino	56	Hd	34.16S	62.42W
Rufisque	34	Bc	14.43N	17.17W
Rufunsa	36	Ef	15.05S	29.40 E
Rugao	28	Fh	32.24N	120.34 E
Rugby [Eng.-U.K.]	9	Li	52.23N	1.15W
Rugby [N.D.-U.S.]	43	Gb	48.22N	99.59W
Rügen	5	He	54.25N	13.24 E
Rugles	12	Cf	48.49N	0.42 E
Ru He	28	Ch	32.55N	114.24 E
Ruhea	25	Hc	26.10N	88.25 E
Ruhengeri	36	Ec	1.30S	29.38 E
Rühlertwist	12	Jb	52.39N	7.06 E
Ruhner Berge	10	Hc	53.17N	11.55 E
Ruhnu, Ostrov-/Ruhnu Saar	7	Fh	57.50N	23.15 E
Ruhnu Saar/Ruhnu, Ostrov-	7	Fh	57.50N	23.15 E
Ruhr	10	Ce	51.27N	6.44 E
Rui'an	27	Lf	27.48N	120.38 E
Ruichang	28	Cj	29.41N	115.38 E
Ruiena/Rūjiena	7	Fh	57.54N	25.17 E
Ruijin	27	Kf	25.59N	116.03 E
Ruili	27	Gg	24.03N	97.46 E
Ruiselede	12	Fc	51.03N	3.24 E
Ruiz	48	Gg	21.57N	105.09W
Ruiz, Nevado del-	54	Cc	4.54N	75.18W
Ruj	15	Fg	42.51N	22.35 E
Ruja/Rūja	8	Kg	57.38N	25.10 E
Rūja/Ruja	8	Kg	57.38N	25.10 E
Rujan	15	Eg	42.23N	21.49 E
Rujen	15	Fg	42.10N	22.31 E
Rūjiena/Ruiena	7	Fh	57.54N	25.17 E
Ruki	36	Cc	0.05N	18.17 E
Rukwa [3]	36	Fd	7.00S	31.20 E
Rukwa, Lake-	30	Ki	8.00S	32.15 E
Rūl Dadnah	24	Qk	25.33N	56.21 E
Rülzheim	12	Ke	49.10N	8.18 E
Ruma	15	Cd	45.01N	19.49 E
Rumaylah	35	Fc	12.57N	35.02 E
Rumbek	31	Jh	6.48N	29.41 E
Rumberpon, Pulau-	26	Jg	1.50S	134.15 E
Rum Cay	47	Jd	23.40N	74.53W
Rumes	12	Fd	50.33N	3.18 E
Rumford	44	Lc	44.33N	70.33W
Rumia	10	Ob	54.35N	18.25 E
Rumigny	12	Ge	49.48N	4.16 E
Rumija	15	Cg	42.06N	19.12 E
Rumilly	11	Li	45.52N	5.57 E
Rum Jungle	59	Gb	13.01S	131.00 E
Rummah, Wādī ar-	24	Ki	26.38N	44.18 E
Rumoi	27	Pc	43.56N	141.39 E
Rumphi	36	Fe	11.01S	33.52 E
Run	12	Hc	51.40N	5.20 E
Runan	28	Ci	33.00N	114.21 E
Runanga	62	De	42.24S	171.15 E
Runaway, Cape-	62	Gb	37.32S	177.59 E
Rundēni/Rundeni	8	Lh	56.14N	27.52 E
Rundeni/Rundēni	8	Lh	56.14N	27.52 E
Rundu	31	Ij	17.55S	19.45 E
Rungu	36	Eb	3.11N	27.52 E
Rungwa	31	Ki	6.57S	33.31 E
Rungwa	36	Fd	7.36S	31.50 E
Runmarö	8	He	59.15N	18.45 E
Runn	8	Fd	60.35N	15.40 E
Ruokolahti	7	Gf	61.17N	28.50 E
Ruoqiang/Qarkilik	22	Kf	39.02N	88.00 E
Ruo Shui	21	Le	40.20N	99.40 E
Ruotsalainen	8	Kc	61.15N	25.55 E
Ruotsinpyhtää/Strömfors	8	Ld	60.32N	26.27 E
Ruovesi	7	Ff	61.59N	24.05 E
Ruovesi	8	Kc	61.55N	24.10 E
Rupanco	56	Ff	40.46S	72.42W
Rupea	15	Ic	46.02N	25.13 E
Rupel	12	Gc	51.07N	4.19 E
Rupert	42	Jf	51.30N	78.48W
Rupert	46	Ie	42.37N	113.41W
Rupert, Baie de-	42	Jf	51.35N	79.00W
Ruppert Coast	66	Mf	75.45S	141.00W
Rur	10	Be	51.12N	5.59 E
Rurrenabaque	53	Jg	14.28S	67.34W
Rurstausee	12	Id	50.38N	6.24 E
Rurutu, Ile-	57	Lg	22.26S	151.20W
Rušan	19	Hh	37.57N	71.31 E
Rusape	37	Ec	18.32S	32.07 E
Ruşayriş, Khazzān ar- = Rusayris, Lake- (EN)	35	Ec	11.40N	34.20 E
Rusayris, Lake- (EN) = Ruşayriş, Khazzān ar-	35	Ec	11.40N	34.20 E
Ruse	6	Ig	43.50N	25.57 E
Ruse [2]	15	If	43.50N	25.57 E
Ruşeţu	15	Ke	44.57N	27.13 E
Rushan (Xiacun)	28	Ff	36.55N	121.30 E
Rushden	12	Bb	52.17N	0.35W
Rushville	45	Kf	40.07N	90.34W
Rusk	45	Ik	31.48N	95.09W

Index Symbols

- [1] Independent Nation
- [2] State, Region
- [3] District, County
- [4] Municipality
- [5] Colony, Dependency
- Continent
- Physical Region
- Historical or Cultural Region
- Mount, Mountain
- Volcano
- Hill
- Mountains, Mountain Range
- Hills, Escarpment
- Plateau, Upland
- Pass, Gap
- Plain, Lowland
- Delta
- Salt Flat
- Valley, Canyon
- Crater, Cave
- Karst Features
- Depression
- Polder
- Desert, Dunes
- Forest, Woods
- Heath, Steppe
- Oasis
- Cape, Point
- Coast, Beach
- Cliff
- Peninsula
- Isthmus
- Sandbank
- Island
- Atoll
- Rock, Reef
- Islands, Archipelago
- Rocks, Reefs
- Coral Reef
- Well, Spring
- Geyser
- River, Stream
- Waterfall Rapids
- River Mouth, Estuary
- Lake
- Salt Lake
- Intermittent Lake
- Reservoir
- Swamp, Pond
- Canal
- Glacier
- Ice Shelf, Pack Ice
- Ocean
- Sea
- Gulf, Bay
- Strait, Fjord
- Lagoon
- Bank
- Seamount
- Tablemount
- Ridge
- Shelf
- Basin
- Escarpment, Sea Scarp
- Fracture
- Trench, Abyss
- National Park, Reserve
- Point of Interest
- Recreation Site
- Cave, Cavern
- Historic Site
- Ruins
- Wall, Walls
- Church, Abbey
- Temple
- Scientific Station
- Airport
- Port
- Lighthouse
- Mine
- Tunnel
- Dam, Bridge

Index Symbols

[1] Independent Nation	Historical or Cultural Region	Pass, Gap
[2] State, Region	Mount, Mountain	Plain, Lowland
[3] District, County	Volcano	Delta
[4] Municipality	Hill	Salt Flat
[5] Colony, Dependency	Mountains, Mountain Range	Valley, Canyon
Continent	Hills, Escarpment	Crater, Cave
Physical Region	Plateau, Upland	Karst Features

Depression	Coast, Beach	Rock, Reef
Polder	Cliff	Islands, Archipelago
Desert, Dunes	Peninsula	Rocks, Reefs
Forest, Woods	Isthmus	Coral Reef
Heath, Steppe	Sandbank	Well, Spring
Oasis	Island	Geyser
Cape, Point	Atoll	River, Stream

Waterfall Rapids	Canal	Lagoon
River Mouth, Estuary	Glacier	Bank
Lake	Ice Shelf, Pack Ice	Seamount
Salt Lake	Ocean	Tablemount
Intermittent Lake	Sea	Ridge
Reservoir	Gulf, Bay	Shelf
Swamp, Pond	Strait, Fjord	Basin

Escarpment, Sea Scarp	Historic Site	Port
Fracture	Ruins	Lighthouse
Trench, Abyss	Wall, Walls	Mine
National Park, Reserve	Church, Abbey	Tunnel
Point of Interest	Temple	Dam, Bridge
Recreation Site	Scientific Station	
Cave, Cavern	Airport	

Saint Helena Sound ⋍	44	Gi	32.27N	80.25W
Saint Helens [Austl.]	59	Jh	41.20S	148.15 E
Saint Helens [Eng.-U.K.]	9	Kh	53.28N	2.44W
Saint Helens [Or.-U.S.]	46	Dd	45.52N	122.48W
Saint Helens, Mount- ▲	46	Dc	46.12N	122.11W
Saint Helier	9	Kl	49.12N	2.07W
Saint-Hubert	12	Hd	50.03N	5.23 E
Saint-Hyacinthe	44	Kc	45.38N	72.57W
Saint Ignace Island ◆	45	Mb	48.48N	87.55W
Saint Ignatius	46	Hc	47.19N	114.06W
Saint Ives [Eng.-U.K.]	9	Hk	50.12N	5.29W
Saint Ives [Eng.-U.K.]	12	Bb	52.18N	0.04W
Saint James	45	Ie	43.59N	94.38W
Saint James, Cape - ►	42	Ef	51.57N	131.01W
Saint-Jean	42	Kg	45.13N	73.15W
Saint-Jean, Baie de- ◧	51b	Bc	17.55N	62.51W
Saint-Jean, Lac- ◍	38	Le	48.35N	72.00W
Saint-Jean-d'Angély	11	Fi	45.57N	0.31W
Saint-Jean-de-Luz	11	Ek	43.23N	1.40W
Saint-Jean-de-Maurienne	11	Mi	45.17N	6.21 E
Saint-Jean-de-Monts	11	Dh	46.47N	2.04W
Saint-Jean-du-Gard	11	Jj	44.06N	3.53 E
Saint-Jean-Pied-de-Port	11	Ek	43.10N	1.14W
Saint-Jérôme [Que.-Can.]	42	Kg	45.46N	74.00W
Saint-Jérôme [Que.-Can.]	44	La	48.26N	71.52W
Saint Joe River ∿	46	Gc	47.21N	116.42W
Saint John ◆	50	Dc	18.20N	64.42W
Saint John [Can.] ∿	38	Me	45.15N	66.04W
Saint John [Ks.-U.S.]	45	Gh	38.00N	98.46W
Saint John [Lbr.] ∿	34	Cd	5.55N	10.05W
Saint John [N.B.-Can.]	39	Me	45.16N	66.03W
Saint John's [Atg.]	47	Le	17.06N	61.51W
Saint Johns [Az.-U.S.]	46	Ki	34.30N	109.22W
Saint Johns [Mi.-U.S.]	44	Ed	43.00N	84.33W
Saint John's [Mont.]	51c	Bc	16.48N	62.11W
Saint John's [Newf.-Can.]	39	Ne	47.34N	52.43W
Saint Johnsbury	44	Kc	44.25N	72.01W
Saint Johns River ∿	44	Gj	30.24N	81.24W
Saint Joseph [Dom.]	51g	Bb	15.24N	61.26W
Saint Joseph [La.-U.S.]	45	Kk	31.55N	91.14W
Saint-Joseph [Mart.]	51h	Ab	14.40N	61.03W
Saint Joseph [Mi.-U.S.]	44	Dd	42.06N	86.29W
Saint Joseph [Mo.-U.S.]	43	Id	39.46N	94.51W
Saint-Joseph [New Caledonia]	63b	Ce	20.27S	166.36 E
Saint-Joseph [Reu.]	37a	Bb	21.22S	55.37 E
Saint Joseph, Lake- ◍	42	If	51.06N	90.36W
Saint Joseph Island ◆	44	Fb	46.13N	83.57W
Saint Joseph River ∿	44	Dd	42.06N	86.29W
Saint-Junien	11	Gi	45.53N	0.54 E
Saint-Just-en-Chaussée	12	Ee	49.30N	2.26 E
Saint Kilda ◆	9	Ed	57.49N	8.36W
Saint Kitts/Saint Christopher ◆	38	Mh	17.21N	62.48W
Saint-Lary-Soulan	11	Gl	42.49N	0.19 E
Saint Laurent	53	Ke	5.30N	54.02W
Saint Laurent = Saint Lawrence (EN) ∿	38	Me	49.15N	67.00W
Saint Lawrence ◆	38	Bc	63.30N	170.30W
Saint Lawrence ∿	38	Me	49.15N	67.00W
Saint Lawrence (EN) = Saint Laurent ∿	38	Me	49.15N	67.00W
Saint Lawrence, Gulf of- ◧	38	Me	48.00N	62.00W
Saint-Léger-en-Yvelines	12	Df	48.43N	1.46 E
Saint-Léonard	44	Nb	47.10N	67.56W
Saint-Léonard-de-Noblat	11	Hi	45.50N	1.29 E
Saint-Lewis ∿	42	Lf	52.22N	55.58W
Saint-Lô	11	Ee	49.07N	1.05W
Saint Louis	39	Jf	38.38N	90.11W
Saint-Louis [Guad.]	51e	Bc	15.57N	61.20W
Saint-Louis [Sen.]	31	Fg	16.02N	16.30W
Saint-Loup-sur-Semouse	11	Mg	47.53N	6.16 E
Saint Lucia	37	Ee	28.23S	32.25 E
Saint Lucia ①	39	Mh	13.53N	60.58W
Saint Lucia ◆	38	Mh	13.53N	60.58W
Saint Lucia, Cape- ►	30	Kk	28.32S	32.24 E
Saint Lucia, Lake- ◍	37	Ee	28.00S	32.30 E
Saint Lucia Channel ⋍	50	Fe	14.09N	60.57W
Saint Lucia Channel (EN) = Sainte-Lucie, Canal de- ⋍	50	Fe	14.09N	60.57W
Saint Magnus Bay ◧	9	La	60.25N	1.35W
Saint-Maixent-l'Ecole	11	Fh	46.25N	0.12W
Saint-Malo	6	Ff	48.39N	2.01W
Saint-Malo, Golfe de- ◧	5	Ff	48.45N	2.00W
Saint-Marc	47	Je	19.06N	72.43W
Saint-Marc, Canal de- ⋍	49	Kd	18.50N	72.45W
Saint Margaret's at Cliffe	12	Dc	51.09N	1.19 E
Saint Margaret's Hope	9	Kc	58.49N	2.57W
Saint Maries	46	Gc	47.19N	116.35W
Saint Martin ◆	47	Le	18.04N	63.04W
Saint Martin, Cap- ►	51h	Ab	14.52N	61.13W
Saint-Martin-Boulogne	12	Dd	50.43N	1.40 E
Saint-Martin-de-Ré	11	Eh	46.12N	1.22W
Saint-Martin-des-Besaces	12	Be	49.01N	0.51W
Saint Martins	44	Oc	45.21N	65.32W
Saint-Martin-Vésubie	11	Nj	44.04N	7.15 E
Saint Mary, Cape- ►	44	Nc	44.05N	66.13W
Saint Mary Peak [Austl.] ▲	59	Hf	31.30S	138.35 E
Saint Mary Peak [U.S.] ▲	46	Hc	46.40N	114.20W
Saint Mary's ◆	9	Gl	49.55N	6.20W
Saint Marys [Austl.]	59	Jh	41.35S	148.10 E
Saint Marys [Oh.-U.S.]	44	Ee	40.32N	84.22W
Saint Marys [W.V.-U.S.]	44	Gf	39.24N	81.13W
Saint Mary's, Cape - ►	42	Mg	46.49N	54.12W
Saint Mary's Bay [N.S.-Can.] ◧	44	Nc	44.25N	66.10W
Saint Mary's Bay [N.W.T.-Can.] ◧	42	Mg	46.50N	53.47W
Saint Marys River ∿	44	Gj	30.45N	81.30W
Saint-Mathieu, Pointe de- ►	5	Ff	48.20N	4.46W
Saint Matthew ◆	38	Bb	60.30N	172.45W
Saint Matthias Group ◈	57	Fe	1.30S	149.48 E
Saint-Maur-des-Fossés	11	If	48.48N	2.30 E
Saint-Maurice, Rivière- ∿	42	Kg	46.21N	72.31W
Saint Michael	40	Gd	63.29N	162.02W
Saint Michaels	46	Ki	35.46N	109.04W
Saint-Michel	12	Ge	49.55N	4.08 E
Saint-Mihiel	11	Lf	48.54N	5.33 E
Saint-Nazaire	11	Dg	47.17N	2.12W
Saint Neots	12	Bb	52.13N	0.16W
Saint-Nicolas/Sint Niklaas	11	Kc	51.10N	4.08 E
Saint-Nicolas-d'Aliermont	12	De	49.53N	1.13 E
Saint-Nicolas-de-Port	11	Mf	48.38N	6.18 E
Saint-Omer	11	Id	50.45N	2.15 E
Saintonge ⊟	11	Fi	45.50N	0.30W
Saint Patrick's	51c	Bc	16.41N	62.12W
Saint Paul ∿	34	Cd	6.23N	10.48W
Saint-Paul	37a	Bb	21.00S	55.16 E
Saint Paul ◆	30	Ol	38.55S	77.41 E
Saint Paul [Ak.-U.S.] ◆	40	Ee	57.07N	170.17W
Saint Paul [Alta.-Can.]	42	Gf	53.59N	111.17W
Saint Paul [Mn.-U.S.]	39	Je	44.58N	93.07W
Saint Paul [Nb.-U.S.]	45	Gf	41.13N	98.27W
Saint Paul, Cape- ►	34	Fd	5.49N	0.57 E
Saint-Paul-lès-Dax	11	Ek	43.44N	1.03W
Saint Paul's	51c	Ab	17.24N	62.49W
Saint Paul's Point ►	64q	Ab	25.04S	130.05W
Saint-Péray	11	Kj	44.57N	4.50 E
Saint Peter	45	Jd	44.17N	93.57W
Saint Peter Port	9	Kl	49.27N	2.32W
Saint Peter's	51	Bc	16.46N	62.12W
Saint Petersburg (EN) → Sankt-Peterburg	6	Jc	59.55N	30.15 E
Saint Petersburg	39	Kg	27.46N	82.38W
Saint Petersburg Beach	44	Fl	27.45N	82.45W
Saint-Pierre [Mart.]	50	Fe	14.45N	61.11W
Saint-Pierre [May.]	31	Mk	21.19S	55.29 E
Saint-Pierre [St.P.M.]	42	Lg	46.46N	56.12W
Saint-Pierre, Lac- ◍	44	Kb	46.10N	72.50W
Saint Pierre and Miquelon (EN) = Saint-Pierre et Miquelon ⑤	39	Ne	46.55N	56.10W
Saint-Pierre-en-Port	12	Ce	49.48N	0.29 E
Saint-Pierre et Miquelon ◈	38	Ne	46.55N	56.10W
Saint-Pierre et Miquelon = Saint Pierre and Miquelon (EN) ⑤	39	Ne	46.55N	56.10W
Saint Pierre Island ◆	37b	Bb	9.19S	50.43 E
Saint-Pierre-sur-Dives	12	Be	49.01N	0.02W
Saint-Pol-de-Léon	11	Cf	48.41N	3.59W
Saint-Pol-sur-Mer	12	Ec	51.02N	2.21 E
Saint-Pol-sur-Ternoise	11	Id	50.23N	2.20 E
Saint-Pons	11	Ik	43.29N	2.46 E
Saint-Pourçain-sur-Sioule	11	Jh	46.18N	3.17 E
Saint-Quentin	11	Je	49.51N	3.17 E
Saint-Quentin, Canal de- ═	12	Fe	49.36N	3.11 E
Saint-Raphaël	11	Mk	43.25N	6.46 E
Saint-Rémy-de-Provence	11	Kk	43.47N	4.50 E
Saint-Rigaux, Mont- ▲	11	Kh	46.12N	4.29 E
Saint-Riquier	12	Dd	50.08N	1.57 E
Saint Roch Basin ⊔	42	Ic	68.50N	95.00W
Saint-Romain-de-Colbosc	12	Ce	49.32N	0.22 E
Saint-Saëns	12	De	49.40N	1.17 E
Saint Sauflieu	12	Ee	49.47N	2.15 E
Saint-Savin	11	Gh	46.34N	0.52 E
Saint-Sébastien, Cap- ►	37	Hb	12.26S	48.44 E
Saint-Seine-l'Abbaye	11	Kg	47.26N	4.47 E
Saint-Servais, Namur-	12	Gd	50.28N	4.50 E
Saint Simon	12	Fe	49.45N	3.10 E
Saint Simons Island ◆	44	Gj	31.14N	81.21W
Saint Stanislas Bay ◧	64g	Bb	1.53N	157.30W
Saint Stephen	42	Kg	45.12N	67.17W
Saint-Sylvain	12	Be	49.03N	0.13W
Saint Teresa Beach	44	Ek	29.58N	84.28W
Saint Thomas	44	Gd	42.47N	81.12W
Saint Thomas ◆	47	Le	18.21N	64.55W
Saint-Trond/Sint-Truiden	11	Ld	50.49N	5.12 E
Saint-Tropez	11	Mk	43.16N	6.38 E
Saint-Tropez, Golfe de- ◧	11	Mk	43.17N	6.38 E
Saint-Valéry-en-Caux	11	Ge	49.52N	0.44 E
Saint-Valery-sur-Somme	11	Hd	50.11N	1.38 E
Saint-Vallier	11	Ki	45.10N	4.49 E
Saint-Venant	12	Ed	50.37N	2.33 E
Saint Vincent	14	Be	45.45N	7.39 E
Saint Vincent ◆	38	Mh	13.15N	61.12W
Saint-Vincent, Baie de- ◧	63b	Cf	22.00S	166.05 E
Saint Vincent, Cap- ►	30	Lk	21.57S	43.16 E
Saint Vincent, Gulf- ◧	59	Hf	35.00S	138.05 E
Saint Vincent and the Grenadines ①	39	Mh	13.15N	61.12W
Saint-Vincent-de-Tyrosse	11	Ek	43.40N	1.18W
Saint Vincent Island ◆	44	Ek	29.40N	85.07W
Saint Vincent Passage ⋍	50	Ff	13.30N	61.00W
Saint-Wandrille-Rançon	12	Ce	49.32N	0.46 E
Saint-Yrieix-la-Perche	11	Hi	45.31N	1.12 E
Saipan	64a	Ad	6.54N	134.08 E
Saipan Channel ⋍	64b	Ba	15.05N	145.41 E
Saipan Island ◆	57	Fc	15.12N	145.45 E
Saira	55	Ak	32.24S	62.06W
Sairecabur, Cerro- ▲	54	Eh	22.43S	67.54W
Saitama Ken ②	28	Of	36.00N	139.50 E
Saito	28	Kh	32.06N	131.24 E
Sajak	19	Hf	46.55N	77.22 E
Sajama	54	Eg	18.07S	69.00W
Sajama, Nevado de- ▲	52	Jg	18.06S	68.54W
Sajānan	14	Dm	37.03N	9.14 E
Sajat	18	De	38.49N	63.51 E
Sajīd ◆	33	Hf	16.52N	41.55 E
Sajir, Ra's- ►	35	Ib	16.45N	53.35 E
Sajmenski Kanal = Saimaa Canal (EN) ═	8	Mc	61.05N	28.18 E
Sajn-Sand	22	Ne	44.55N	110.11 E
Sajó ∿	10	Ri	47.56N	21.08 E
Sajószentpéter	10	Qh	48.13N	20.43 E
Sajram	18	Gc	42.18N	69.45 E
Sajzī	24	Of	32.41N	52.07 E
Saka	36	Gc	0.09S	39.20 E
Sakai	28	Mg	34.35N	135.28 E
Sakaide	29	Cd	34.19N	133.51 E
Sakaiminato	29	Cd	35.33N	133.15 E
Sakākah	23	Fd	29.59N	40.06 E
Sakakawea, Lake- ◍	43	Gb	47.50N	102.20W
Sakala, Vozvyšennost-/Sakala Kõrgustik ⊤	8	Kf	58.00N	25.30 E
Sakala Kõrgustik/Sakala, Vozvyšennost- ⊤	8	Kf	58.00N	25.30 E
Sakami ∿	42	Jf	53.18N	76.45W
Sakami, lac- ◍	42	Jf	53.15N	76.45W
Sâkâne, 'Erg i-n- ∴	34	Ea	20.40N	0.51W
Sakania	36	Ee	12.43S	28.33 E
Sakao ◆	63b	Cb	14.58S	167.07 E
Sakar ⛰	15	Jh	41.59N	26.16 E
Sakar	18	De	38.59N	63.45 E
Sakaraha	37	Gd	22.54S	44.32 E
Sakar-Čaga	18	Cf	37.39N	61.40 E
Sakartvelo = Georgia (EN)	19	Eg	42.00N	44.00 E
Sakartvelos Sabčata Socialisturi Respublica/Gruzinskaja SSR → Sakartvelo	19	Eg	42.00N	44.00 E
Sakata	27	Od	38.55N	139.50 E
Sakchu	28	Hd	40.23N	125.02 E
Sakhalin (EN) = Sahalin, Ostrov- ◆	21	Qd	51.00N	143.00 E
Saki	16	Hg	45.07N	33.37 E
Šakiai/Šakjaj	7	Fi	54.57N	23.01 E
Sakishima Islands (EN) = Sakishima-Shotō ◈	21	Og	24.30N	125.00 E
Sakishima-Shotō = Sakishima Islands (EN) ◈	21	Og	24.30N	125.00 E
Sakito	29	Ae	33.02N	129.34 E
Sakiz Boğazı ⋍	15	Jk	38.20N	26.12 E
Šakjaj/Šakiai	7	Fi	54.57N	23.01 E
Sakmara ∿	5	Le	51.46N	55.01 E
Sakon Nakhon	25	Ke	17.10N	104.01 E
Sakrivier	37	Cf	30.54S	20.28 E
Šakša	17	Hi	54.47N	56.15 E
Saksaulski	19	Gf	47.05N	61.13 E
Sakskøbing	8	Dj	54.48N	11.39 E
Saku	28	Of	36.09N	138.26 E
Sakuma	29	Ed	35.05N	137.47 E
Sakura	29	Gd	35.43N	140.13 E
Sakurai	29	Dd	34.31N	135.50 E
Sakura-Jima ◆	29	Bf	31.35N	130.40 E
Säkylä	8	Jc	61.02N	22.20 E
Sal ◆	30	Eg	16.45N	22.55W
Sal ∿	19	Ef	47.31N	40.45 E
Sal, Cay- ◆	49	Gb	23.42N	80.24W
Sal, Punta- ►	49	Df	15.53N	87.37W
Sala ∿	35	Cb	17.00N	20.53 E
Šalá	10	Nh	48.09N	17.53 E
Sala	7	Dg	59.55N	16.36 E
Salabangka, Kepulauan- ◈	26	Hg	3.02S	122.25 E
Salaca ∿	8	Kg	57.39N	24.15 E
Salacgriva/Salacgrīva	7	Fh	57.46N	24.27 E
Salacgrīva/Salacgriva	7	Fh	57.46N	24.27 E
Sala Consilina	14	Jj	40.23N	15.36 E
Salada	48	Hc	28.36N	103.28W
Salada, Laguna- ◍	48	Ba	32.20N	115.40W
Saladas	56	Ic	28.15S	58.38W
Saladillo	56	Ie	35.38S	59.46W
Saladillo, Arroyo- ∿	55	Bj	31.22S	60.30W
Saladillo Amargo, Arroyo- ∿	55	Ci	31.01S	60.19W
Saladillo Dulce, Arroyo- ∿	55	Bj	31.01S	60.19W
Salado, Arroyo- [Arg.] ∿	55	Bm	36.27S	61.06W
Salado, Arroyo- [Mex.] ∿	48	De	24.25N	111.30W
Salado, Riacho- ∿	55	Ch	26.30S	58.18W
Salado, Rio- ∿	45	Ci	34.16N	106.52W
Salado, Rio- ∿	47	Ec	26.52N	99.19W
Salado, Rio- [Arg.] ∿	52	Ji	31.42S	60.44W
Salado, Rio- [Arg.] ∿	56	Ee	38.49S	64.57W
Salado, Rio- [Arg.] ∿	52	Ki	35.44S	57.21W
Salado, Valle- ∨	48	He	24.47N	102.50W
Salaga	34	Ed	8.33N	0.31W
Salagle	35	Ge	1.50N	42.18 E
Salāhuddīn ③	24	Je	34.40N	44.00 E
Salailua	65c	Aa	13.41S	172.34W
Salairski Krjaž ⛰	20	Df	54.00N	85.00 E
Sălaj ②	15	Fb	47.10N	23.00 E
Šalakuša	7	Je	62.15N	40.18 E
Salal	35	Bc	14.51N	17.13 E
Salālah [Oman]	22	Hh	17.05N	54.10 E
Salālah [Sud.]	35	Fa	21.19N	36.13 E
Salamá	49	Bf	15.06N	90.16W
Salamanca ③	13	Gd	40.50N	6.00W
Salamanca [Chile]	56	Fd	31.47S	70.58W
Salamanca [Mex.]	47	Dd	20.34N	101.12W
Salamanca [N.Y.-U.S.]	44	Hd	42.11N	78.43W
Salamanca [Sp.]	6	Fg	40.58N	5.39W
Salamat ③	35	Cc	11.00N	20.30 E
Salamat, Bahr- ∿	35	Bd	9.27N	18.06 E
Salamina	49	Jh	10.30N	74.48W
Salamís	15	Gl	37.58N	23.29 E
Salamis ⍝	24	Ee	35.10N	33.54 E
Salamís ◆	15	Gl	37.55N	23.30 E
Sālang, Tūnel-e- ⋂	23	Kb	35.19N	69.02 E
Salani	65c	Bb	14.00S	171.34W
Salantai/Salantaj	8	Ih	56.05N	21.30 E
Salantaj/Salantai	8	Ih	56.05N	21.30 E
Salas	13	Fa	43.24N	6.16W
Salas de los Infant	13	Ib	42.01N	3.17W
Salat ◆	64d	Cb	7.14N	152.01 E
Salat ∿	11	Gk	43.10N	0.58 E
Salatiga	26	Fh	7.19S	110.30 E
Salavat	6	Le	53.25N	55.58 E
Salawati, Pulau- ◆	26	Jg	1.07S	130.52 E
Saia y Gómez ◆	57	Qg	26.28S	105.28W
Sala y Gómez Ridge (EN) ⋀	3	Ml	25.00S	98.00W
Salazar	55	Am	36.18S	62.12W
Salbris	11	Ig	47.26N	2.03 E
Salcantay, Nevado de- ▲	52	Ig	13.22S	72.34W
Šalčininkai/Salčininkaj	8	Kj	54.18N	25.30 E
Salčininkaj/Šalčininkai	8	Kj	54.18N	25.30 E
Salda Gölü ◍	15	Ml	37.33N	29.42 E
Saldaña	13	Hb	42.31N	4.44W
Saldanha	31	Il	33.00S	17.56 E
Saldungaray	55	Bn	38.12S	61.47W
Saldus	19	Cd	56.40N	22.31 E
Sale	59	Jg	38.06S	147.04 E
Salé	32	Fc	34.04N	6.48W
Salebabu, Pulau- ◆	26	If	3.55N	126.40 E
Şāleḩābād	24	Me	34.56N	48.20 E
Salehard	22	Ic	66.33N	66.40 E
Saleimoa	65c	Ba	13.48S	171.52W
Salelologa	65c	Aa	13.44S	172.10W
Salem [Fl.-U.S.]	44	Fk	29.58N	83.28W
Salem [Il.-U.S.]	45	Lg	38.38N	88.57W
Salem [India]	22	Jh	11.39N	78.10 E
Salem [In.-U.S.]	44	Df	38.36N	86.06W
Salem [Ma.-U.S.]	44	Ld	42.31N	70.55W
Salem [Mont.]	51c	Bc	16.45N	62.13W
Salem [Mo.-U.S.]	45	Kh	37.39N	91.32W
Salem [N.J.-U.S.]	44	Jf	39.35N	75.28W
Salem [Oh.-U.S.]	44	Ge	40.54N	80.52W
Salem [Or.-U.S.]	39	Ge	44.57N	123.01W
Salem [S.D.-U.S.]	45	He	43.44N	97.23W
Salem [Va.-U.S.]	44	Gg	37.17N	80.03W
Salemi	14	Gm	37.49N	12.48 E
Sälen	8	Ec	61.10N	13.16 E
Salentine Peninsula (EN) = Penisola Salentina ⊂	5	Hg	40.30N	18.00 E
Sale Pit ◍	9	Oh	53.40N	1.30 E
Salerno	6	Hg	40.41N	14.47 E
Salerno, Golfo di- ◧	14	Ij	40.30N	14.40 E
Salers	11	Ii	45.08N	2.30 E
Salève, Mont- ▲	11	Mh	46.07N	6.10 E
Salgir ∿	16	Ig	45.38N	35.01 E
Salgótarján	10	Ph	48.07N	19.49 E
Salgueiro	54	Ke	8.04S	39.06W
Salher ▲	25	Ed	20.41N	73.52 E
Salhus	7	Af	60.30N	5.16 E
Sali	14	Jg	43.56N	15.10 E
Šali	16	Nh	43.06N	45.56 E
Salice Terme	14	Df	44.55N	9.01 E
Salida	43	Fd	38.32N	106.00W
Salies-de-Béarn	11	Fk	43.29N	0.55W
Salihli	23	Cb	38.29N	28.09 E
Salima	36	Fe	13.47S	34.26 E
Salīma, Wāḩāt- = Salimah Oasis (EN)	31	Jf	21.22N	29.19 E
Salimah Oasis (EN) = Salīma, Wāḩāt-	31	Jf	21.22N	29.19 E
Salina ◆	14	Il	38.35N	14.50 E
Salina [Ks.-U.S.]	39	Jf	38.50N	97.37W
Salina [Ut.-U.S.]	46	Jg	38.58N	111.51W
Salina Cruz	47	Ee	16.10N	95.12W
Salinas [Ca.-U.S.]	39	Gf	36.40N	121.38W
Salinas [Ec.]	54	Bd	2.13S	80.58W
Salinas [P.R.]	51a	Bc	17.59N	66.17W
Salinas, Bahía de- ◧	49	Eh	11.03N	85.43W
Salinas, Cabo de-/Ses Salines, Cap de- ►	13	Pe	39.16N	3.03 E
Salinas, Punta- [Dom.Rep.] ►	49	Ld	18.12N	70.34W
Salinas, Punta- [P.R.] ►	51a	Bb	18.29N	66.10W
Salinas, Río- ∿	49	Be	16.28N	90.33W
Salinas de Hidalgo	48	If	22.38N	101.43W
Salinas Peak ▲	45	Cj	33.18N	106.31W
Saline, Point- ►	50	Fg	12.00N	61.48W
Saline Island ◆	51p	Cb	12.26N	61.29W
Saline River [Ks.-U.S.] ∿	45	Hg	38.51N	97.30W
Saline River [U.S.] ∿	45	Jj	33.10N	92.08W
Salines, Pointe des- ►	51h	Bc	14.24N	60.53W
Salinópolis	54	Id	0.37S	47.20W
Salins-les-Bains	11	Lh	46.57N	5.53 E
Salisbury ◆	42	Jd	63.35N	77.00W
Salisbury [Dom.]	51g	Bb	15.26N	61.27W
Salisbury [Eng.-U.K.]	9	Lj	51.05N	1.48W
Salisbury [Md.-U.S.]	43	Ld	38.22N	75.36W
Salisbury [N.C.-U.S.]	44	Gh	35.40N	80.29W
Salisbury Plain ▭	9	Lj	51.15N	1.55W
Săliște	15	Gd	45.47N	23.53 E
Šalja	19	Fd	57.15N	58.43 E
Saljany	19	Eh	39.35N	48.59 E
Šalkar, Ozero- ◍	16	Qd	50.35N	51.40 E
Šalkar-Jega-Kara, Ozero- ◍	16	Vd	50.45N	60.55 E
Salkhad	24	Gf	32.29N	36.43 E
Salla	7	Gc	66.50N	28.40 E
Sallent de Gállego	13	Lb	42.46N	0.20W
Salling ⊂	8	Ch	56.40N	9.00 E
Salliqueló	56	He	36.45S	62.56W
Sallisaw	45	Ii	35.28N	94.47W
Salluit	39	Lc	62.12N	75.38W
Sallūm, Khalīj as- = Salum, Gulf of- (EN) ◧	33	Ec	31.40N	25.20 E
Sallyana	25	Gc	28.22N	82.10 E
Salm ∿	12	Ie	49.51N	6.51 E
Salmās	23	Fb	38.11N	44.47 E
Salmi	7	Hf	61.24N	31.54 E
Salmo	46	Gb	49.12N	117.17W
Salmon	43	Eb	45.11N	113.54W
Salmon Arm	42	Ff	50.42N	119.16W
Salmon Bank (EN) ⊓	60	Kb	26.56N	176.28W
Salmon Falls Creek Reservoir ⊏	46	He	42.05N	114.45W
Salmon Mountain ▲	46	Hd	45.38N	114.50W
Salmon Mountains ⛰	46	Df	41.00N	123.00W
Salmon River ∿	38	He	45.51N	116.46W
Salmon River Mountains ⛰	43	Dc	44.45N	115.30W
Salmtal	12	Ie	49.56N	6.48 E
Salmyš ∿	16	Sc	52.01N	55.21 E
Salò	14	Ee	45.36N	10.31 E
Salo [C.A.R.]	35	Be	3.12N	16.07 E
Salo [Fin.]	7	Ff	60.23N	23.08 E
Salobra, Rio- ∿	55	De	20.12S	56.29W
Salobreña	13	Ih	36.44N	3.35W
Salomon, Cap- ►	51h	Ab	14.30N	61.06W
Salon-de-Provence	11	Lk	43.38N	5.06 E
Salonga ∿	30	Ii	0.10S	19.50 E
Salonika (EN) = Thessaloníki	6	Ig	40.38N	22.56 E
Salonika, Gulf of- (EN) = Thermaïkós Kólpos ◧	5	Ig	40.20N	22.45 E
Salonta	15	Ec	46.48N	21.39 E
Salop ③	9	Ki	52.40N	2.50W
Salop ⊟	9	Ki	52.40N	2.50W
Salor ∿	13	Ee	39.39N	7.03W
Salou	13	Nc	41.04N	1.08 E
Salouël	12	Ee	49.52N	2.15 E
Saloum ═	34	Bc	13.50N	16.45W
Salpausselkä ⛰	5	Ic	61.00N	26.30 E
Sal-Rei	32	Cf	16.11N	22.55W
Salsbruket	7	Cd	64.48N	11.52 E
Salseleh-ye Safīd Kūh/Paropamisus ⛰	21	If	34.30N	63.30 E
Salsipuedes, Canal de- ⋍	48	Cc	28.40N	113.00W
Salsipuedes, Punta- ►	49	Fi	8.28N	83.37W
Salsk	19	Ef	46.28N	41.29 E
Šalski	7	If	61.48N	36.03 E
Salso [It.] ∿	14	Hm	37.06N	13.57 E
Salso [It.] ∿	14	Im	37.39N	14.49 E
Salsola ∿	14	Ji	41.37N	15.40 E
Salsomaggiore Terme	14	Df	44.49N	9.59 E
Salt	13	Oc	41.59N	2.47 E
Salta ②	56	Hb	25.00S	64.30W
Salta	53	Jh	24.47S	65.24W
Saltash	9	Ik	50.24N	4.12W
Salt Basin ≋	45	Dk	31.50N	105.00W
Saltburn by the Sea	9	Mg	54.35N	0.58W
Salt Cay ◆	49	Lc	21.20N	71.11W
Salt Creek ∿	46	Gh	36.15N	116.49W
Salt Draw ∿	45	Ek	31.19N	103.28W
Saltee Islands/Na Sailtí ◈	9	Gi	52.07N	6.36W
Salten ⊠	7	Dc	67.45N	15.31 E
Salt Fork Arkansas River ∿	45	Hh	36.36N	97.03W
Salt Fork Brazos ∿	45	Gj	33.15N	100.00W
Salt Fork Red ∿	45	Gi	34.30N	99.22W
Saltholm ◆	8	Ei	55.40N	12.45 E
Saltillo	39	Ig	25.25N	101.01W
Salt Lake City	39	He	40.46N	111.53W
Salto ②	55	Dj	31.25S	57.00W
Salto ∿	14	Gh	42.23N	12.54 E
Salto [Arg.]	56	Hd	34.17S	60.15W
Salto [Ur.]	53	Ki	31.23S	57.58W
Salto da Divisa	54	Kg	16.00S	39.57W
Salto Grande	55	Hf	22.54S	49.59W
Salton Sea ◍	38	Hf	33.20N	115.50W
Salt River ∿	43	Ee	33.23N	112.18W
Saltsjöbaden	8	He	59.17N	18.18 E
Saltvik	7	Ef	60.17N	20.03 E
Saluafata Harbour	65c	Ba	13.55S	171.38W
Saluda	44	Ig	37.36N	76.36W
Salum, Gulf of- (EN) = Sallūm, Khalīj as- ◧	33	Ec	31.40N	25.20 E
Saluzzo	14	Bf	44.39N	7.29 E
Salvación, Bahía- ◧	56	Eh	50.55S	75.05W
Salvador [Braz.]	53	Mg	12.59S	38.31W
Salvador [Niger]	34	Ha	23.14N	12.05 E
Salvador, Lake- ◍	45	Kl	29.45N	90.15W
Salvador Maza	56	Hb	22.10S	63.43W
Salvaterra de Magos	13	De	39.01N	8.48W
Salvatierra [Mex.]	48	Ig	20.13N	100.53W
Salvatierra [Sp.]	13	Jb	42.51N	2.23W
Salwa, Dawḩat as- ◧	24	Nj	25.30N	50.40 E
Salwá Baḩrī	33	Fe	24.44N	32.56 E
Salween (EN) = Thanlwin	21	Lg	16.31N	97.37 E
Salyersville	44	Fg	37.45N	83.04W
Salza ∿	14	Ic	47.40N	14.43 E
Salzach ∿	10	Ih	48.12N	12.56 E
Salzburg	6	Hf	47.48N	13.02 E
Salzburg ②	14	Gc	47.20N	13.00 E
Salzburger Kalkalpen ⛰	14	Gc	47.35N	12.55 E
Salzgitter	10	Gd	52.05N	10.20 E
Salzkammergut ⊠	14	Hc	47.45N	13.30 E
Salzkotten	12	Kc	51.40N	8.36 E
Salzwedel	10	Hd	52.51N	11.09 E
Samadāy, Ra's- ►	24	Fj	25.00N	34.56 E
Samagaltaj	20	Ef	50.36N	95.03 E
Samaḩ [Lib.]	33	Cd	28.10N	19.10 E
Samaḩ [Sau.Ar.]	24	Kh	28.52N	45.30 E
Samaipata	54	Fg	18.09S	63.52W
Samalayuca	48	Fb	31.21N	106.28W
Samales Group ◈	26	He	6.00N	121.45 E
Samalga Pass ⋍	40a	Eb	52.48N	169.25W
Samālūt	33	Fd	28.18N	30.42 E
Samambaia, Rio- ∿	55	Ff	22.45S	53.21W
Samaná	49	Md	19.13N	69.19W
Samaná, Bahía de- ◧	47	Ke	19.10N	69.25W
Samaná, Cabo- ►	49	Md	19.18N	69.09W
Samana Cay ◆	49	Kb	23.06N	73.42W
Samandağı	24	Fd	36.07N	35.56 E
Samangān ③	23	Kb	36.15N	67.40 E
Samani	27	Pc	42.07N	142.56 E
Samanli Dağlari ⛰	15	Mi	40.32N	29.10 E
Samar ◆	21	Oh	12.00N	125.00 E
Samara (Kujbyšev)	6	Le	53.12N	50.09 E
Samara	5	Le	53.10N	50.04 E
Samarai	58	Gf	10.36S	150.39 E
Samarinda	22	Nj	0.30S	117.09 E
Samarkand	22	If	39.40N	66.58 E
Samarkandskaja Oblast ③	19	Gg	40.10N	66.20 E
Sāmarrā'	23	Fc	34.12N	43.52 E
Samar Sea ▦	26	Hd	11.50N	124.32 E
Samaru	34	Gc	11.10N	7.38 E
Samatan	11	Gk	43.30N	0.56 E
Samate	26	Jg	0.58S	131.04 E
Samba [Zaire]	36	Ec	4.38S	26.22 E
Samba [Zaire]	36	Db	0.14N	21.19 E
Samba Caju	36	Cd	8.45S	15.25 E
Sambalpur	25	Gd	21.27N	83.58 E
Sambar, Tanjung- ►	26	Fg	2.59S	110.19 E
Sambas	26	Ef	1.20N	109.15 E
Sambava	37	Ib	14.15S	50.10 E
Samber ∿	11	Kd	50.28N	4.52 E
Sāmbhar	25	Fc	26.55N	75.12 E
Sambiase	14	Kl	38.58N	16.17 E
Samboja	26	Gg	1.02S	117.02 E
Sambor	19	Cf	49.32N	23.11 E
Samborombón, Bahía- ◧	56	Ie	36.00S	57.12W
Samborombón, Río- ∿	55	Dl	35.43S	57.20W
Sambre ∿	11	Kd	50.28N	4.52 E
Sambre à l'Oise, Canal de la- ═	11	Je	49.39N	3.20 E
Samburg	20	Cc	67.00N	78.25 E

Index Symbols

① Independent Nation
② State, Region
③ District, County
④ Municipality
⑤ Colony, Dependency
■ Continent
⊠ Physical Region
⊟ Historical or Cultural Region
▲ Mount, Mountain
△ Volcano
∩ Hill
⛰ Mountains, Mountain Range
◠ Hills, Escarpment
⊤ Plateau, Upland
⌣ Pass, Gap
▭ Plain, Lowland
◣ Delta
≡ Salt Flat
∨ Valley, Canyon
◡ Crater, Cave
⌘ Karst Features
⌄ Depression
⊞ Polder
∴ Desert, Dunes
♣ Forest, Woods
⁂ Heath, Steppe
⊕ Oasis
► Cape, Point
⌇ Coast, Beach
◨ Cliff
⊂ Peninsula
⋈ Isthmus
∷ Sandbank
◆ Island
○ Atoll
✲ Rock, Reef
◈ Islands, Archipelago
❊ Rocks, Reefs
❋ Coral Reef
◉ Well, Spring
⇡ Geyser
∿ River, Stream
⤓ Waterfall Rapids
⊳ River Mouth, Estuary
◍ Lake
◌ Salt Lake
◔ Intermittent Lake
⊏ Reservoir
≋ Swamp, Pond
═ Canal
❄ Glacier
❅ Ice Shelf, Pack Ice
◼ Ocean
▦ Sea
◧ Gulf, Bay
⋍ Strait, Fjord
◒ Lagoon
⊓ Bank
⊼ Seamount
⏏ Tablemount
⋀ Ridge
⊥ Shelf
⊔ Basin
⌒ Escarpment, Sea Scarp
ϟ Fracture
∇ Trench, Abyss
♠ National Park, Reserve
✪ Point of Interest
☼ Recreation Site
◓ Cave, Cavern
⌂ Historic Site
⍝ Ruins
▥ Wall, Walls
✝ Church, Abbey
⛩ Temple
⚗ Scientific Station
✈ Airport
⚓ Port
☨ Lighthouse
⚒ Mine
⋂ Tunnel
⫽ Dam, Bridge

Index Symbols

[1] Independent Nation	⊟ Historical or Cultural Region	⟋ Pass, Gap	⊟ Depression	⊟ Coast, Beach	⊟ Rock, Reef
[2] State, Region	▲ Mount, Mountain	▲ Plain, Lowland	⊟ Polder	▲ Cliff	⊟ Rocks, Reefs
[3] District, County	▲ Volcano	▲ Delta	▲ Desert, Dunes	▲ Peninsula	⊟ Coral Reef
[4] Municipality	▲ Hill	▲ Salt Flat	▲ Forest, Woods	▲ Isthmus	⊟ Well, Spring
[5] Colony, Dependency	▲ Mountains, Mountain Range	▲ Valley, Canyon	▲ Heath, Steppe	⊟ Sandbank	⊟ Geyser
● Continent	▲ Hills, Escarpment	▲ Crater, Cave	⊟ Oasis	⊟ Island	⊟ River, Stream
⊟ Physical Region	▲ Plateau, Upland	▲ Karst Features	⊟ Cape, Point	⊟ Atoll	

⊟ Waterfall Rapids	⊟ Canal	⊟ Lagoon	⊟ Escarpment, Sea Scarp	⊟ Historic Site	⊟ Port
⊟ River Mouth, Estuary	⊟ Glacier	⊟ Bank, Shoal	⊟ Fracture	⊟ Ruins	⊟ Lighthouse
⊟ Lake	⊟ Ice Shelf, Pack Ice	⊟ Seamount	⊟ Trench, Abyss	⊟ Wall, Walls	⊟ Mine
⊟ Salt Lake	⊟ Ocean	⊟ Tablemount	⊟ National Park, Reserve	⊟ Church, Abbey	⊟ Tunnel
⊟ Intermittent Lake	⊟ Sea	⊟ Ridge	⊟ Point of Interest	⊟ Temple	⊟ Dam, Bridge
⊟ Reservoir	⊟ Gulf, Bay	⊟ Shelf	⊟ Recreation Site	⊟ Scientific Station	
⊟ Swamp, Pond	⊟ Strait, Fjord	⊟ Basin	⊟ Cave, Cavern	⊟ Airport	

San Marcial, Punta- ►	48	De	25.30N	111.00W
San Marco, Capo- ►	14	Hm	37.30N	13.01 E
San Marcos [3]	49	Bf	15.00N	91.55W
San Marcos [Col.]	54	Cb	8.39N	75.08W
San Marcos [Guat.]	49	Bf	14.58N	91.48W
San Marcos [Hond.]	49	Cf	14.24N	88.56W
San Marcos [Mex.]	48	Gg	20.47N	104.11W
San Marcos [Mex.]	48	Ji	16.48N	99.21W
San Marcos [Nic.]	49	Dh	11.55N	86.12W
San Marcos [Tx.-U.S.]	43	Hf	29.53N	97.57W
San Marcos, Isla- ◆	48	Cd	27.13N	112.06W
San Marcos, Sierra de- ⛰	48	Hd	26.30N	101.55W
San Marino	14	Gg	43.55N	12.28 E
San Marino [1]	6	Hg	43.55N	12.28 E
San Martín	56	Gd	33.04S	68.28W
San Martín ⊠	66	Qe	68.11S	67.00W
San Martín ◆	48	Ab	30.30N	116.05W
San Martín [2]	54	Ce	7.00S	76.50W
San Martín, Cerro- ▲	48	Lh	18.19N	94.48W
San Martín, Lago- ◍	56	Fg	48.52S	72.40W
San Martín, Río- ≈	54	Ff	13.08S	63.43W
San Martín de los Andes	56	Ff	40.10S	71.21W
San Martín de Valdeiglesias	13	Hd	40.21N	4.24W
San Martino di Castrozza	14	Fd	46.16N	11.48 E
San Mateo [Ca.-U.S.]	46	Dh	37.35N	122.19W
San Mateo [Ven.]	50	Dh	9.45N	64.33W
San Mateo/Sant Mateu del Maestrat	13	Md	40.28N	0.11 E
San Mateo Ixtatán	49	Bf	15.50N	91.29W
San Mateo Mountains ⛰	45	Cj	33.10N	107.20W
San Matias	55	Cc	16.22S	58.24W
San Matías, Golfo- ◧	52	Jj	41.30S	64.15W
Sanmen (Haiyou)	27	Lf	29.08N	121.22 E
Sanmen Wan ◧	28	Fj	29.00N	121.45 E
Sanmenxia	27	Je	34.44N	111.19 E
San Miguel [Arg.]	55	Dh	27.59S	57.36W
San Miguel [Bol.]	55	Bc	16.42S	61.01W
San Miguel [Ca.-U.S.]	46	Ei	35.45N	120.42W
San Miguel [ElSal.]	39	Kh	13.29N	88.11W
San Miguel [Pan.]	49	Hi	8.27N	78.56W
San Miguel, Golfo de- ◧	49	Hi	8.22N	78.17W
San Miguel, Río- [Bol.] ≈	52	Jg	13.52S	63.56W
San Miguel, Río- [Mex.] ≈	48	Dc	29.16N	110.53W
San Miguel, Río- [Mex.] ≈	48	Fd	26.59N	107.58W
San Miguel, Río- [S.Amer.] ≈	55	Cd	19.25S	58.20W
San Miguel, Salinas de- ◍	55	Bd	19.12S	60.45W
San Miguel, Volcán de- 🌋	47	Gf	13.26N	88.16W
San Miguel Bay ◧	26	Hd	13.50N	123.10 E
San Miguel de Allende	48	Ig	20.55N	100.45W
San Miguel de Horcasitas	48	Dc	29.29N	110.45W
San Miguel del Monte	55	Cl	35.27S	58.48W
San Miguel del Padrón	49	Fb	23.05N	82.19W
San Miguel de Tucumán	53	Jh	26.49S	65.13W
San Miguel Island ◆	46	Ei	34.02N	120.22W
San Miguel Islands ⁂	26	Ge	7.45N	118.28 E
San Miguelito	55	Bc	17.20S	60.59W
San Miguel River ≈	45	Bg	38.23N	108.48W
San Miguel Sola de Vega	48	Ki	16.31N	96.59W
San Millán ▲	13	Ib	42.18N	3.12W
Sanming	27	Kf	26.11N	117.37 E
San Miniato	14	Eg	43.41N	10.51 E
Sannan	29	Dd	35.04N	135.03 E
Sannār	31	Kg	13.33N	33.38 E
Sannicandro Garganico	14	Ji	41.50N	15.34 E
San Nicolás, Río- [Bol.] ≈	55	Bc	17.08S	61.17W
San Nicolás, Río- [Mex.] ≈	48	Gh	19.40N	105.14W
San Nicolas de los Arroyos	56	Hd	33.20S	60.13W
San Nicolás de los Garzas	48	Ie	25.45N	100.18W
San Nicolas Island ◆	46	Fj	33.15N	119.31W
Sannikova, Proliv- ⇌	20	Ib	74.30N	140.00 E
Sannio ⧗	14	Ii	41.20N	14.30 E
San'nohe	29	Ga	40.22N	141.15 E
San'nō-Tōge ⌣	29	Fc	37.06N	139.44 E
Sannūr, Wādī- ≈	24	Dh	28.59N	31.03 E
Sanok	10	Sg	49.34N	22.13 E
Sanok-Zagórz	10	Sg	49.31N	22.17 E
San Onofre	54	Cb	9.45N	75.32W
San Pablo	22	Oh	14.04N	121.19 E
San Pablo, Punta- ►	48	Bd	27.15N	114.30W
San Pedro	56	Ib	24.07S	56.59W
San-Pédro	34	De	4.44N	6.37W
San Pedro [3]	55	Dg	24.15S	56.30W
San Pedro [Arg.]	56	Hb	24.14S	64.52W
San Pedro [Arg.]	55	Ck	33.40S	59.40W
San Pedro [Arg.]	56	Jc	26.38S	54.08W
San Pedro, Río- [Guat.] ≈	49	Be	17.46N	91.26W
San Pedro, Río- [Mex.] ≈	48	Gg	21.45N	105.30W
San Pedro, Sierra de- ⛰	13	Fe	39.20N	6.35W
San Pedro Carchá	49	Bf	15.29N	90.16W
San Pedro Channel ⇌	46	Fj	33.43N	118.23W
San Pedro de Alcántara	13	Hh	36.29N	5.00W
San Pedro de Atacama	56	Gb	22.55S	68.13W
San Pedro de Lloc	54	Ce	7.26S	79.31W
San Pedro de Macorís	49	Md	18.27N	69.18W
San Pedro Martir, Sierra de- ⛰	47	Ab	30.45N	115.13W
San Pedro Nolasco, Isla- ◆	48	Dd	27.58N	111.25W
San Pedro Pochutla	48	Kj	15.44N	96.28W
San Pedros de las Colonias	47	Dc	25.45N	102.59W
San Pedro Sula	39	Kh	15.27N	88.02W
San Pedro Tapanatepec	48	Li	16.21N	94.12W
San Pedro Tututepec	48	Ki	16.09N	97.38W
San Pellegrino Terme	14	De	45.50N	9.40 E
San Pietro ◆	14	Ck	39.10N	8.15 E
San Quentin, Bahía de- ◧	48	Ab	30.20N	116.00W
San Quintín	47	Ab	30.29N	115.57W
San Rafael [Arg.]	53	Ji	34.40S	68.21W
San Rafael [Bol.]	55	Bc	16.45S	60.34W
San Rafael [Ca.-U.S.]	46	Dg	38.00N	122.31W
San Rafael [Mex.]	48	He	24.40N	102.01W
San Rafael [Mex.]	48	Ie	25.01N	100.33W
San Rafael [Ven.]	49	Lh	10.58N	71.44W
San Rafael, Cabo- ►	49	Md	19.01N	68.57W
San Rafael, Río- ≈	55	Cd	18.26S	59.37W
San Rafael de Atamaica	50	Ci	7.32N	67.24W
San Rafael del Norte	49	Dg	13.12N	86.06W
San Rafael Knob ▲	46	Jg	38.50N	110.48W
San Rafael Mountains ⛰	46	Fi	34.45N	119.50W
San Rafael River ≈	46	Jg	38.47N	110.07W
San Ramón [Peru]	54	Cf	11.08S	75.20W
San Ramón [Ur.]	55	El	34.18S	55.58W
San Ramón, Río- ≈	55	Bb	14.03S	61.35W
San Ramón de la Nueva Oran	56	Hb	23.08S	64.20W
San Raymundo, Arroyo- ≈	48	Cd	26.21N	112.37W
San Remo	14	Bg	43.49N	7.46 E
Sanriku	29	Gb	39.08N	141.48 E
San Román, Cabo- ►	54	Ea	12.12N	70.00W
San Roque [Arg.]	55	Ci	28.34S	58.43W
San Roque [Sp.]	13	Gh	36.13N	5.24W
San Saba	45	Gk	31.12N	98.43W
Sansalé	34	Cc	11.07N	14.51W
San Salvador ▲	13	Pe	39.27N	3.11 E
San Salvador [Arg.]	55	Di	29.16S	57.31W
San Salvador [Arg.]	56	Id	31.37S	58.30W
San Salvador [ElSal.]	39	Kh	13.42N	89.12W
San Salvador [Par.]	55	Dg	25.51S	56.28W
San Salvador (Watling) ◆	47	Jd	24.02N	74.28W
San Salvador, Cuchilla- ⛰	55	Dk	33.56S	57.45W
San Salvador, Isla- ◆	52	Gf	0.14S	90.45W
San Salvador, Río- ≈	55	Ck	33.29S	58.23W
San Salvador de Jujuy	53	Jh	24.10S	65.20W
Sansanné-Mango	34	Fc	10.21N	0.28 E
San Sebastián [Col.]	49	Ji	9.13N	74.18W
San Sebastián [P.R.]	51a	Bb	18.21N	67.00W
San Sebastián [Sp.]	6	Fg	43.19N	1.59W
San Sebastián, Bahía- ◧	56	Gh	53.15S	68.23W
San Sebastián, Isla- ◆	49	Cg	13.11N	88.26W
San Sebastián de la Gomera	32	Dd	28.06N	17.06W
Sansepolcro	14	Gg	43.34N	12.08 E
San Severo	14	Ji	41.41N	15.23 E
San Silvestre	49	Li	8.15N	70.02W
San Simeon	46	Ei	35.39N	121.11W
Sanski Most	14	Kf	44.46N	16.40 E
Santa Agueda	48	Cd	27.13N	112.20W
Santa Ana ◆	63a	Fd	10.50S	162.28 E
Santa Ana [Arg.]	55	Eh	27.22S	55.34W
Santa Ana [Bol.]	55	Bc	16.37S	60.43W
Santa Ana [Bol.]	54	Eg	15.31S	67.30W
Santa Ana [Bol.]	55	Cd	18.43S	58.44W
Santa Ana [Ca.-U.S.]	43	De	33.43N	117.54W
Santa Ana [ElSal.]	39	Kh	13.59N	89.34W
Santa Ana [Mex.]	47	Bb	30.33N	111.07W
Santa Ana [Ven.]	50	Dh	9.19N	64.39W
Santa Ana, Río- ≈	49	Li	9.30N	71.57W
Santa Ana, Volcán de- 🌋	38	Kh	13.50N	89.39W
Santa Bárbara [3]	49	Cf	15.10N	88.20W
Santa Barbara	39	Hf	34.03N	118.15W
Santa Bárbara [Hond.]	49	Cf	14.53N	88.14W
Santa Bárbara [Mex.]	47	Cc	26.48N	105.49W
Santa Bárbara [Ven.]	49	Lj	7.47N	71.10W
Santa Bárbara, Puerto de- ⌣	13	Lb	42.30N	0.50W
Santa Bárbara, Serra de- ⛰	55	Fe	21.45S	53.23W
Santa Barbara Channel ⇌	46	Fi	34.15N	119.55W
Santa Catalina ◆	63a	Fd	10.54S	162.27 E
Santa Catalina [Col.]	49	Jh	10.37N	75.33W
Santa Catalina [Ven.]	50	Fh	8.33N	61.51W
Santa Catalina, Gulf of- ◧	46	Gj	33.20N	117.45W
Santa Catalina, Isla- ◆	48	De	25.40N	110.45W
Santa Catalina Island ◆	46	Fj	33.23N	118.24W
Santa Catarina	48	Ie	25.41N	100.28W
Santa Catarina [2]	56	Kc	27.00S	50.00W
Santa Catarina, Ilha de- ◆	52	Lh	27.36S	48.30W
Santa Catarina, Sierra- ⛰	48	Fc	29.40N	107.30W
Santa Cecília	55	Gh	26.56S	50.27W
Santa Cesarea Terme	14	Mj	40.02N	18.28 E
Santa Clara [Ca.-U.S.]	46	Eh	37.21N	121.59W
Santa Clara [Cuba]	39	Lg	22.24N	79.58W
Santa Clara [Gabon]	36	Ab	0.34N	9.17 E
Santa Clara [Mex.]	48	Fc	29.17N	107.01W
Santa Clara [Ur.]	55	Ek	32.55S	54.58W
Santa Clara, Barragem do- ⊜	13	Dg	37.30N	8.20W
Santa Clara, Isla- ◆	56	Ed	33.42S	79.00W
Santa Clara de Saguier	55	Bj	31.21S	61.50W
Santa Coloma de Farners/Santa Coloma de Farnés	13	Oc	41.52N	2.40 E
Santa Coloma de Farnés/Santa Coloma de Farners	13	Oc	41.52N	2.40 E
Santa Coloma de Gramanet	13	Oc	41.27N	2.13 E
Santa Coloma de Queralt	13	Nc	41.32N	1.23 E
Santa Comba	13	Da	43.02N	8.49W
Santa Croce Camerina	14	In	36.50N	14.31 E
Santa Cruz [Arg.] [2]	56	Gg	49.00S	70.00W
Santa Cruz [Azr.]	32	Bb	39.05N	28.01W
Santa Cruz [Azr.]	32	Ab	39.27N	31.07W
Santa Cruz [Bol.]	53	Jg	17.48S	63.10W
Santa Cruz [Bol.] [2]	54	Fg	17.30S	61.30W
Santa Cruz [Braz.]	54	Id	0.36S	49.11W
Santa Cruz [Braz.]	55	Dd	18.32S	57.12W
Santa Cruz [Ca.-U.S.]	43	Cd	36.58N	122.01W
Santa Cruz [Chile]	56	Fd	34.38S	71.22W
Santa Cruz [C.R.]	49	Eh	10.01N	84.02W
Santa Cruz [Phil.]	26	Hd	14.01N	121.21 E
Santa Cruz, Isla- ◆	52	Gf	0.38S	90.23W
Santa Cruz, Isla de- ◆	48	De	25.17N	110.43W
Santa Cruz, Río- ≈	56	Gh	50.08S	68.20W
Santa Cruz, Serra da- ⛰	55	Jc	17.05S	45.17W
Santa Cruz Cabrália	54	Kg	16.17S	39.02W
Santa Cruz de la Palma	32	Dd	28.41N	17.45W
Santa Cruz de la Zarza	13	Ie	39.58N	3.10W
Santa Cruz del Quiché	49	Bf	15.02N	91.08W
Santa Cruz del Sur	47	Id	20.43N	78.00W
Santa Cruz de Mudela	13	If	38.38N	3.28W
Santa Cruz de Tenerife [3]	32	Dd	28.10N	17.20W
Santa Cruz de Tenerife	31	Ff	28.27N	16.14W
Santa Cruz do Rio Pardo	55	Hf	22.55S	49.37W
Santa Cruz do Sul	56	Jc	29.43S	52.26W
Santa Cruz Island ◆	46	Fi	34.01N	119.45W
Santa Cruz Islands ⁂	57	Hf	10.45S	165.55 E
Santadi	14	Ck	39.05N	8.43 E
Santa Elena [Arg.]	55	Bm	37.21S	60.37W
Santa Elena [Arg.]	56	Id	30.57S	59.48W
Santa Elena [Ec.]	54	Bd	2.14S	80.52W
Santa Elena, Bahía de- [C.R.] ◧	49	Eh	10.59N	85.50W
Santa Elena, Bahía de- [Ec.] ◧	54	Bd	2.05S	80.55W
Santa Elena, Cabo- ►	47	Gf	10.55N	85.57W
Santa Elena de Uairén	54	Fc	4.37N	61.08W
Santa Eulalia	13	Kd	40.34N	1.19W
Santa Eulalia del Río	13	Nf	38.59N	1.31 E
Santa Fé	49	Fc	21.45N	82.45W
Santa Fe [2]	56	Hd	31.00S	61.00W
Santafé	13	Ig	37.11N	3.43W
Santa Fe [Arg.]	53	Ji	31.40S	60.40W
Santa Fe [N.M.-U.S.]	39	If	35.42N	106.57W
Santa Fe de Bogotá (Bogotá)	53	Ie	4.36N	74.05W
Santa Fé de Minas	55	Jc	16.41S	45.28W
Santa Fé do Sul	55	Ge	20.13S	50.56 N
Sant'Agata di Militello	14	Il	38.04N	14.38 E
Santa Helena [Braz.]	55	Eg	24.56S	54.23W
Santa Helena [Braz.]	54	Id	2.14S	45.18W
Santa Helena de Goiás	54	Hg	17.43S	50.35W
Santa Inês	54	Id	3.39S	45.22W
Santa Inés	49	Mh	10.37N	69.18W
Santa Ines, Bahía- ◧	48	Dd	27.00N	111.55W
Santa Inés, Isla- ◆	52	Ik	53.45S	72.45W
Santa Isabel [Arg.]	55	Bk	33.54S	61.42W
Santa Isabel [Arg.]	56	Ge	36.15S	66.56W
Santa Isabel [Braz.]	55	Ba	13.40S	60.44W
Santa Isabel [P.R.]	51a	Bc	17.58N	66.25W
Santa Isabel, Pico de- ▲	34	Ge	3.35N	8.46 E
Santa Isabel Island ◆	57	Ge	8.00S	159.00 E
Santa Izabel do Ivaí	55	Ff	22.58S	53.14W
Santa Juliana	55	Id	19.19S	47.32W
Santa Lucía [Arg.]	56	Gd	31.32S	68.29W
Santa Lucía [Ur.]	55	Dl	34.27S	56.24W
Santa Lucía, Esteros del- ⩩	55	Ci	28.15S	58.20W
Santa Lucía, Río- [Arg.] ≈	55	Ci	29.05S	59.13W
Santa Lucía, Río- [Ur.] ≈	55	Dl	34.48S	56.22W
Santa Lucía Cotzumalguapa	49	Bf	14.20N	91.01W
Santa Lucia Range ⛰	43	Cd	36.00N	121.20W
Santa Luzia ◆	32	Cf	16.46N	24.45W
Santa Luzia, Ribeirão- ≈	55	Fe	21.31S	53.53W
Santa Margarita	55	Bi	28.18S	61.33W
Santa Margarita, Isla de- ◆	47	Bd	24.27N	111.50W
Santa Margherita Ligure	14	Df	44.20N	9.12 E
Santa Maria [Braz.]	53	Kh	29.41S	53.48W
Santa Maria ◆	30	Ee	36.58N	25.06W
Santa Maria [Ca.-U.S.]	43	Ce	34.57N	120.26W
Santa María	56	Gc	26.41S	66.02W
Santa Maria ≈	47	Cb	31.00N	107.14W
Santa María	55	Bc	17.08S	61.01W
Santa Maria, Bahía de- ◧	48	Ee	25.05N	108.10W
Santa Maria, Cabo de- [Ang.] ►	30	Ij	13.25S	12.32 E
Santa Maria, Cabo de- [Port.] ►	13	Eh	36.58N	7.54W
Santa Maria, Cape- ►	49	Jb	23.41N	75.19W
Santa María, Cayo- ◆	49	Hb	22.40N	79.00W
Santa María, Isla- [Chile] ◆	56	Fe	37.02S	73.33W
Santa María, Isla- [Ec.] ◆	54a	Ab	1.15S	90.25W
Santa María, Laguna de- ◍	48	Fb	31.10N	107.15W
Santa María, Río- [Mex.] ≈	48	Jg	21.37N	99.15W
Santa María, Río- [Pan.] ≈	49	Gi	8.06N	80.29W
Santa Maria, Rio- [Braz.] ≈	55	Ee	21.50S	54.53W
Santa Maria, Rio- [Braz.] ≈	55	Ib	14.19S	46.49W
Santa María Asunción Tlaxiaco	48	Ki	17.16N	97.41W
Santa Maria Capua Vetere	14	Ii	41.05N	14.15 E
Santa Maria da Vitória	55	Ja	13.24S	44.12W
Santa María de Cuevas	48	Fd	27.55N	106.23W
Santa María de Ipire	50	Dh	8.49N	65.19W
Santa María del Oro	48	Ge	25.56N	105.22W
Santa María del Río	48	Ig	21.48N	100.45W
Santa María la Real de Nieva	13	Hc	41.04N	4.24W
Santa María Zacatepec	48	Ki	16.46N	98.00W
Santa Marinella	14	Fh	42.02N	11.51 E
Santa Marta	53	Id	11.15N	74.13W
Santa Marta, Cabo de- ►	36	Be	13.52S	12.25 E
Santa Marta, Ría de- ⩤	13	Ea	43.42N	7.51W
Santa Marta Grande, Cabo de- ►	55	Hi	28.38S	48.45W
Santa Monica	43	De	34.01N	118.30W
Santan	26	Gg	0.03S	117.28 E
Santana	55	Ja	12.59S	44.03W
Santana, Coxilha de- ⛰	55	Ej	31.15S	55.15W
Santana, Rio- ≈	55	Gd	19.43S	51.02W
Santana da Boa Vista	55	Fj	30.52S	53.07W
Santana do Livramento	56	Id	30.53S	55.31W
Santander [3]	13	Ia	43.10N	4.00W
Santander [2]	54	Db	6.35N	73.20W
Santander [Col.]	54	Cc	3.01N	76.29W
Santander [Phil.]	26	He	9.25N	123.20 E
Santander [Sp.]	6	Fg	43.28N	3.48W
Santander, Bahía de- ◧	13	Ia	43.27N	3.48W
Santander Jiménez	47	Ed	24.13N	98.28W
Sant'Andrea ◆	14	Lj	40.05N	17.55 E
Sant'Antioco	14	Ck	39.04N	8.27 E
Sant'Antioco ◆	5	Gh	39.05N	8.25 E
Sant Antoni, Cap-/San Antonio, Cabo de- ►	13	Mf	38.48N	0.12 E
Santañy	13	Pe	39.22N	3.07 E
Santa Olalla	13	Hd	40.01N	4.26W
Santa Olalla del Cala	13	Fg	37.54N	6.13W
Santa Paula	46	Fi	34.21N	119.04W
Santa Pola	13	Lf	38.11N	0.33W
Sant'Arcangelo	14	Kj	40.15N	16.16 E
Santarcangelo di Romagna	14	Gf	44.04N	12.27 E
Santarém [2]	13	De	39.15N	8.35W
Santarém [Braz.]	53	Kf	2.26S	54.42W
Santarém [Port.]	13	De	39.14N	8.41W
Santaren Channel ⇌	47	Id	24.00N	79.30W
Santa Rita [Braz.]	55	Cc	16.15S	59.00W
Santa Rita [Col.]	54	Ec	4.55N	68.20W
Santa Rita [Guam]	64c	Bb	13.23N	144.40 E
Santa Rita [Hond.]	49	Df	15.09N	87.53W
Santa Rita [Ven.]	50	Ch	8.08N	66.16W
Santa Rita [Ven.]	49	Lh	10.32N	71.32W
Santa Rita do Araguaia	55	Fc	17.20S	53.12W
Santa Rosa [3]	49	Bf	14.10N	90.18W
Santa Rosa [Arg.]	56	Gd	31.31S	65.04W
Santa Rosa [Arg.]	53	Ji	36.40S	64.15W
Santa Rosa [Braz.]	56	Jc	27.52S	54.29W
Santa Rosa [Ca.-U.S.]	43	Cd	38.26N	122.43W
Santa Rosa [Ec.]	54	Cd	3.27S	79.58W
Santa Rosa [N.M.-U.S.]	43	Ge	34.57N	104.41W
Santa Rosa [Par.]	55	Dh	26.52S	56.49W
Santa Rosa [Ven.]	49	Mi	8.26N	69.42W
Santa Rosa [Ven.]	50	Dh	9.38N	64.18W
Santa Rosa, Mount- △	64c	Ba	13.32N	144.55 E
Santa Rosa de Copán	49	Cf	14.47N	88.46W
Santa Rosa de la Roca	55	Bc	16.04S	61.32W
Santa Rosa Island ◆	46	Ej	33.58N	120.06W
Santa Rosalia	39	Hg	27.19N	112.17W
Santa Rosalía	50	Bh	9.02N	69.01W
Santa Rosalia, Punta- ►	48	Bc	28.40N	114.20W
Santa Rosa Range ⛰	46	Gf	41.00N	117.40W
Santa Rosa Wash ≈	46	Ij	33.10N	112.05W
Šantarskije Ostrova = Shantar Islands (EN) ⁂	21	Pd	55.00N	137.36 E
Santas Creus/Santes Creus ∴	13	Nc	41.19N	1.18 E
Santa Sylvina	56	Hc	27.49S	61.09W
Santa Teresa [Arg.]	55	Bk	33.26S	60.47W
Santa Teresa [Mex.]	48	Ke	25.17N	97.51W
Santa Teresa [Peru]	54	Df	13.01S	72.39W
Santa Teresa, Rio- ≈	55	Ha	12.40S	48.47W
Santa Teresa di Riva	14	Jm	37.57N	15.22 E
Santa Teresa Gallura	14	Di	41.14N	9.11 E
Santa Teresita	55	Dm	36.32S	56.41W
Santa Vitória do Palmar	56	Jd	33.31S	53.21W
Santa Vitória	55	Gd	18.50S	50.08W
Sant Barbara Island ◆	46	Fj	33.23N	119.01W
Sant Boi de Llobregat/San Baudilio de Llobregat	13	Oc	41.21N	2.03 E
Sant Carles de la Ràpita/San Carlos de la Rápita	13	Md	40.37N	0.36 E
Santee River ≈	43	Le	33.14N	79.28W
Santeh	24	Ld	36.10N	46.32 E
San Telmo	48	Ab	30.58N	116.06W
San Telmo, Bahía de- ◧	48	Hh	18.45N	103.40W
San Telmo, Punta- ►	47	De	18.19N	103.30W
Santerno ≈	14	Ff	44.34N	11.58 E
Santerre ⧗	11	Ie	49.55N	2.30 E
Santes Creus/Santas Creus ⫽	13	Nc	41.19N	1.18 E
Sant'Eufemia, Golfo di- ◧	14	Kl	38.50N	16.05 E
Sant'Eufemia Lamezia	14	Kl	38.55N	16.15 E
Sant Feliu de Llobregat/San Feliú de Llobregat	13	Oc	41.23N	2.03 E
Santhià	14	Ce	45.22N	8.10 E
Santiago [2]	56	Fd	33.30S	70.50W
Santiago [Bol.]	54	Gg	18.19S	59.34W
Santiago [Bol.]	55	Bd	19.22S	60.51W
Santiago [Braz.]	56	Jc	29.11S	54.53W
Santiago [Chile]	53	Ii	33.27S	70.40W
Santiago [Dom.Rep.]	39	Lh	19.27N	70.42W
Santiago [Mex.]	48	Ie	25.25N	100.09W
Santiago [Mex.]	48	Cd	27.32N	112.49W
Santiago [Pan.]	39	Ki	8.05N	80.59W
Santiago [Par.]	55	Dh	27.09S	56.47W
Santiago, Cerro- ▲	49	Gi	8.33N	81.44W
Santiago, Río- ≈	54	Cd	4.27S	77.36W
Santiago, Río de- ≈	48	Ge	25.11N	105.26W
Santiago, Serranía- ⛰	55	Cd	18.25S	59.25W
Santiago de Chuco	54	Ce	8.09S	78.11W
Santiago de Compostela	13	Db	42.53N	8.33W
Santiago de Cuba	39	Lg	20.01N	75.49W
Santiago de Cuba [3]	49	Ic	20.10N	76.10W
Santiago de la Ribera	13	Lg	37.48N	0.48W
Santiago del Estero	53	Jh	27.50S	64.15W
Santiago del Estero [2]	56	Hc	28.00S	63.30W
Santiago de Papasquiaro	48	Ge	25.03N	105.25W
Santiago do Cacém	13	Df	38.01N	8.42W
Santiago Ixcuintla	47	Cd	21.49N	105.13W
Santiago Mountains ⛰	45	El	29.40N	103.15W
Santiago Pinotepa Nacional	47	Ee	16.19N	98.01W
Santiaguillo, Isla- ◆	48	Lh	19.05N	95.50W
Santiaguillo, Laguna de- ◍	48	Ge	24.50N	104.50W
Santiam River ≈	46	Dd	44.42N	123.55W
Santillana	13	Ha	43.23N	4.06W
San Timoteo	49	Li	9.48N	71.04W
Säntis ▲	14	Dc	47.15N	9.20 E
Santisteban del Puerto	13	If	38.15N	3.12W
Sant Jordi, Golf de-/San Jorge, Golfe de- ◧	13	Md	40.53N	1.00 E
Sant Mateu del Maestrat/San Mateo	13	Md	40.28N	0.11 E
Santo, Ile- ◆	57	Hf	15.15S	166.50 E
Santo Anastácio	55	Ge	21.58S	51.39W
Santo André	55	If	23.40S	46.31W
Santo Ângelo	56	Jc	28.18S	54.16W
Santo Antão ◆	30	Eg	17.05N	25.10W
Santo Antônio	56	Jc	26.03S	53.12W
Santo Antonio	34	Ge	1.39N	7.25 E
Santo Antônio de Jesus	54	Kf	12.58S	39.16W
Santo Antônio do Içá	54	Ed	3.05S	67.57W
Santo Antônio do Leverger	54	Gg	15.52S	56.05W
Santo Corazón	54	Gg	17.59S	58.51W
Santo Corazón, Río- ≈	55	Cc	17.23S	58.23W
Santo Domingo [Cuba]	49	Gb	22.35N	80.15W
Santo Domingo [Dom.Rep.]	39	Mh	18.28N	69.54W
Santo Domingo [Mex.]	48	Bb	30.43N	115.56W
Santo Domingo [Mex.]	48	Bc	28.12N	114.02W
Santo Domingo [Mex.]	48	If	23.20N	101.44W
Santo Domingo [Nic.]	49	Eg	12.16N	85.05W
Santo Domingo, Cay- ◆	49	Jc	21.42N	75.46W
Santo Domingo, Punta- ►	48	Cd	26.20N	112.40W
Santo Domingo, Río- [Mex.] ≈	48	Kh	18.10N	96.08W
Santo Domingo, Río- [Ven.] ≈	49	Mi	8.01N	69.33W
Santo Domingo de la Calzada	13	Jb	42.26N	2.57W
Santo Domingo de los Colorados	54	Cd	0.15S	79.10W
Santo Domingo de Silos	13	Ic	41.58N	3.25W
Santo Domingo Pueblo	45	Ci	35.31N	106.22W
San Tomé	50	Dh	8.58N	64.08W
Santoña	13	Ia	43.27N	3.27W
Santos	53	Lh	23.57S	46.20W
Santos, Sierra de los- ⛰	13	Gf	38.15N	5.20W
Santos Dumont	55	Ke	21.28S	43.34W
Santos Unzué	55	Bl	35.45S	60.51W
Santo Tirso	13	Dc	41.21N	8.28W
Santo Tomás [Bol.]	55	Cc	17.46S	58.55W
Santo Tomás [Mex.]	48	Ab	31.33N	116.24W
Santo Tomás [Nic.]	49	Eg	12.04N	85.05W
Santo Tomás, Punta- ►	48	Ab	31.34N	116.42W
Santo Tomé	56	Ic	28.33S	56.03W
Santu Lussurgiu	14	Cj	40.08N	8.39 E
Santurce-Antiguo	13	Ia	43.20N	3.02W
Sanuki-Sanmyaku ⛰	29	Cd	34.05N	134.00 E
San Valentín, Cerro- ▲	52	Ij	46.36S	73.20W
San Vicente [Arg.]	55	Cl	35.01S	58.25W
San Vicente [Mex.]	48	Ab	31.20N	116.15W
San Vicente [Phil.]	26	Hc	18.30N	122.09 E
San Vicente, Sierra de- ⛰	13	Hd	40.10N	4.45W
San Vicente de Cañete	54	Cf	13.05S	79.24W
San Vicente de la Barquera	13	Ha	43.26N	4.24W
San Vicente del Caguán	54	Dc	2.07N	74.46W
San Vicente de Raspeig	13	Lf	38.24N	0.31W
San Vincente	47	Gf	13.38N	88.48W
San Vincenzo	14	Eg	43.06N	10.32 E
San Vito [C.R.]	49	Fi	8.50N	82.58W
San Vito [It.]	14	Dk	39.26N	9.32 E
San Vito, Capo- ►	14	Gl	38.11N	12.44 E
Sanya → Yaxian	22	Mh	18.27N	109.28 E
Sanyati ≈	37	Dc	16.49S	28.45 E
San'yō	29	Bd	34.03N	131.10 E
Sanza	14	Jj	40.15N	15.33 E
Sanza Pombo	36	Cd	7.20S	16.00 E
São Bartoloméu, Rio- ≈	55	Ic	16.48S	47.55W
São Benedito	54	Jd	4.03S	40.53W
São Bento	54	Jd	2.42S	44.50W
São Bento do Sul	55	Hh	26.15S	49.23W
São Borja	56	Ic	28.39S	56.00W
São Brás de Alportel	13	Eg	37.09N	7.53W
São Caetano do Sul	56	Kb	23.36S	46.34W
São Carlos [Braz.]	56	Kb	22.01S	47.54W
São Carlos [Braz.]	55	Ej	33.47N	55.30W
São Domingos [Braz.]	55	Ia	13.24S	46.19W
São Domingos [Gui.Bis.]	34	Bc	12.24N	16.12W
São Domingos, Rio- [Braz.] ≈	55	Fe	20.03S	53.13W
São Domingos, Rio- [Braz.] ≈	55	Ia	13.24S	47.12W
São Domingos, Rio- [Braz.] ≈	55	Gd	19.13S	50.44W
São Domingos, Rio- [Braz.] ≈	55	Ib	15.37S	46.14W
São Felix	54	Hf	11.36S	50.39W
São Félix do Xingu	54	He	6.38S	51.59W
São Filipe	32	Cf	14.54N	24.31W
São Francisco [Braz.]	54	Jg	15.57S	44.52W
São Francisco [Braz.]	55	Dd	18.45S	56.55W
São Francisco, Ilha de- ◆	52	Lh	26.18S	48.37W
São Francisco, Rio- ≈	52	Mg	10.30S	36.24W
São Francisco de Assis	55	Ei	29.33S	55.08W
São Francisco de Paula	55	Gi	29.27S	50.35W
São Francisco de Sales	55	Hd	19.52S	49.46W
São Francisco do Sul	56	Kc	26.14S	48.39W
São Gabriel	56	Jd	30.20S	54.19W
São Gonçalo	54	Jh	22.51S	43.04W
São Gonçalo, Canal de- ═	55	Fk	32.10S	52.38W
São Gonçalo do Abaete	55	Jd	18.20S	45.49W
São Gonçalo do Sapucaí	55	Je	21.54S	45.36W
São Gotardo	55	Id	19.19S	46.03W
Sao Hill	36	Gd	8.20S	35.12 E
São Jerônimo, Serra de- ⛰	55	Ec	16.20S	54.55W
São João da Barra	54	Jh	21.38S	41.03W
São João da Boa Vista	55	Ie	21.58S	46.47W
São João d'Aliança	55	Ib	14.42S	47.31W
São João da Madeira	13	Dd	40.54N	8.30W
São João da Ponte	55	Kb	15.56S	44.01W
São João del Rei	54	Jh	21.09S	44.16W
São João de Meriti	55	Kf	22.48S	43.22W
São João do Araguaia	54	Ie	5.23S	48.46W
São João do Piauí	54	Je	8.21S	42.15W
São João dos Patos	54	Je	6.30S	43.42W
São João do Triunfo	55	Gg	25.41S	50.18W
São Joaquim	56	Kc	28.18S	49.56W
São Joaquim da Barra	55	Ie	20.35S	47.53W
São Jorge ◆	30	Ee	38.38N	28.03W
São José da Serra	55	Eb	15.40S	55.18W
São José do Cerrito	55	Gh	27.40S	50.35W
São José do Norte	55	Fk	32.01S	52.03W
São José do Rio Pardo	56	Kb	21.36S	46.54W
São José do Rio Prêto	53	Lh	20.48S	49.23W
São José dos Campos	56	Kb	23.11S	45.53W
São José dos Dourados, Rio- ≈	55	Ge	20.22S	51.21W
Saolat, Buku- ▲	26	If	0.45N	127.59 E
São Leopoldo	56	Jc	29.46S	51.09W
São Lourenço	55	Ec	16.32S	55.02W
São Lourenço, Pantanal de- ⩩	54	Gg	17.45S	56.15W
São Lourenço, Rio- ≈	54	Gg	17.53S	57.27W
São Lourenço, Serra de- ⛰	55	Ec	17.30S	54.50W
São Lourenço do Sul	56	Jd	31.22S	51.58W
São Luís	53	Lf	2.31S	44.16W
São Luís Gonzaga	56	Jc	28.24S	54.58W
São Mamede, Serra de- ⛰	13	Ee	39.19N	7.19W
São Manuel	55	Hf	22.44S	48.34W
São Marcos	55	Gi	28.58S	51.04W
São Marcos, Baía de- ◧	52	Lf	2.30S	44.30W
São Marcos, Rio- ≈	55	Id	18.15S	47.37W
São Mateus [Braz.]	54	Kg	18.44S	39.51W
São Mateus [Braz.]	55	Gg	25.52S	50.23W

Index Symbols

- [1] Independent Nation
- [2] State, Region
- [3] District, County
- [4] Municipality
- [5] Colony, Dependency
- ■ Continent
- ⧗ Physical Region
- ▣ Historical or Cultural Region
- ▲ Mount, Mountain
- 🌋 Volcano
- △ Hill
- ⛰ Mountains, Mountain Range
- ⌒ Hills, Escarpment
- ▬ Plateau, Upland
- ⌣ Pass, Gap
- ▭ Plain, Lowland
- ◣ Delta
- ▤ Salt Flat
- ∨ Valley, Canyon
- ◠ Crater, Cave
- ⊛ Karst Features
- ⊔ Depression
- ⊓ Polder
- ◢ Desert, Dunes
- ♣ Forest, Woods
- ⋙ Heath, Steppe
- 🌴 Oasis
- ► Cape, Point
- ⌇ Coast, Beach
- ▐ Cliff
- ⊏ Peninsula
- ⋈ Isthmus
- ⋯ Sandbank
- ◆ Island
- ◎ Atoll
- ✱ Rock, Reef
- ⁂ Islands, Archipelago
- ⁑ Rocks, Reefs
- ✾ Coral Reef
- ⊙ Well, Spring
- ⛲ Geyser
- ≈ River, Stream
- ⋎ Waterfall Rapids
- ⩤ River Mouth, Estuary
- ◍ Lake
- ◌ Salt Lake
- ◔ Intermittent Lake
- ⊜ Reservoir
- ⩩ Swamp, Pond
- ═ Canal
- ❄ Glacier
- ⛆ Ice Shelf, Pack Ice
- 🌊 Ocean
- ≋ Sea
- ◧ Gulf, Bay
- ⇌ Strait, Fjord
- ◯ Lagoon
- ⌗ Bank
- ⩓ Seamount
- ⏏ Tablemount
- ⋀ Ridge
- ⌂ Shelf
- ◡ Basin
- ⊿ Escarpment, Sea Scarp
- ⚡ Fracture
- ∪ Trench, Abyss
- ♠ National Park, Reserve
- ★ Point of Interest
- ⚑ Recreation Site
- ◓ Cave, Cavern
- ⌘ Historic Site
- ∴ Ruins
- ⊞ Wall, Walls
- ✝ Church, Abbey
- ⛩ Temple
- ⊠ Scientific Station
- ✈ Airport
- ⚓ Port
- ⛯ Lighthouse
- ⚒ Mine
- ∩ Tunnel
- ⫽ Dam, Bridge

Index Symbols

- Independent Nation
- State, Region
- District, County
- Municipality
- Colony, Dependency
- Continent
- Physical Region
- Historical or Cultural Region
- Mount, Mountain
- Volcano
- Hill
- Mountains, Mountain Range
- Hills, Escarpment
- Plateau, Upland
- Pass, Gap
- Plain, Lowland
- Delta
- Salt Flat
- Valley, Canyon
- Crater, Cave
- Karst Features
- Depression
- Polder
- Desert, Dunes
- Forest, Woods
- Heath, Steppe
- Oasis
- Cape, Point
- Coast, Beach
- Cliff
- Peninsula
- Isthmus
- Sandbank
- Island
- Atoll
- Rock, Reef
- Islands, Archipelago
- Rocks, Reefs
- Coral Reef
- Well, Spring
- Intermittent Lake
- Reservoir
- Swamp, Pond
- Waterfall Rapids
- River Mouth, Estuary
- Lake
- Salt Lake
- Ocean
- Sea
- Gulf, Bay
- Strait, Fjord
- Canal
- Glacier
- Ice Shelf, Pack Ice
- Seamount
- Tablemount
- Ridge
- Shelf
- Basin
- Lagoon
- Escarpment, Sea Scarp
- Fracture
- Trench, Abyss
- National Park, Reserve
- Point of Interest
- Recreation Site
- Scientific Station
- Historic Site
- Ruins
- Wall, Walls
- Church, Abbey
- Temple
- Cave, Cavern
- Airport
- Port
- Lighthouse
- Mine
- Tunnel
- Dam, Bridge

Schwäbisch Gmünd 10 Fh 48.48N 9.47 E
Schwäbisch Hall 10 Fg 49.06N 9.44 E
Schwalbach (Saar) 12 Ie 49.18N 6.49 E
Schwalm 12 Lc 51.07N 9.24 E
Schwalm 10 Ff 50.45N 9.25 E
Schwalmstadt 10 Ff 50.55N 9.12 E
Schwalmtal 12 Ic 51.15N 6.15 E
Schwandorf 10 Ig 49.20N 12.07 E
Schwaner, Pegunungan- 26 Fg 0.40S 112.40 E
Schwanewede 12 Ka 53.14N 8.36 E
Schwarzach 10 Ig 49.30N 12.10 E
Schwarzbach 12 Je 49.17N 7.40 E
Schwarze Elster 10 Ie 51.49N 12.51 E
Schwarzer Mann 12 Id 50.15N 6.22 E
Schwarzrand 37 Be 26.00S 17.10 E
Schwarzwald=Black Forest (EN) 5 Gf 48.00N 8.15 E
Schwarzwalder Hochwald 12 Ie 49.39N 6.55 E
Schwatka Mountains 40 Hc 67.25N 157.00W
Schwaz 14 Fc 47.20N 11.42 E
Schwechat 14 Kb 48.08N 16.28 E
Schwechat 14 Kb 48.08N 16.28 E
Schwedt 10 Kc 53.04N 14.18 E
Schweich 12 Ie 49.49N 6.45 E
Schweinfurt 10 Gf 50.03N 10.14 E
Schweiz / Suisse / Svizra / Svizzera = Switzerland (EN) 6 Gf 46.00N 8.30 E
Schweizer-Reneke 37 De 27.11S 25.18 E
Schwelm 12 Jc 51.17N 7.17 E
Schwerin 10 Hc 53.38N 11.23 E
Schweriner See 10 Hc 53.45N 11.28 E
Schwerte 12 Jc 51.27N 7.34 E
Schwetzingen 12 Ke 49.23N 8.34 E
Schwielochsee 10 Kd 52.03N 14.12 E
Schwyz [2] 14 Cc 47.10N 8.50 E
Schwyz 14 Cc 47.03N 8.40 E
Sciacca 14 Hm 37.31N 13.03 E
Scicli 14 In 36.47N 14.42 E
Ščigry 19 De 51.53N 36.55 E
Scilly, Isles of- 5 Ff 49.57N 6.15W
Scioto River 44 Ff 38.44N 83.01W
Ščirec 10 Tg 49.34N 23.54 E
Scobey 46 Mb 48.47N 105.25W
Scordia 14 Im 37.18N 14.51 E
Scoresby Land 41 Jd 71.45N 26.30W
Scoresbysund 67 Md 70.35N 21.40W
Scoresby Sund 67 Md 70.20N 23.30W
Scorff 11 Cg 47.46N 3.21W
Ščors 19 De 51.48N 31.59 E
Scotia Ridge (EN) 3 Co 57.00S 45.00W
Scotia Sea (EN) 52 Mk 57.00S 40.00W
Scotland [2] 9 Ie 56.30N 4.30W
Scotland 5 Fd 56.30N 4.30W
Scotlandville 45 Kk 30.31N 91.11W
Scotstown 44 Lc 45.31N 71.17W
Scott 42 Gf 52.27N 108.23W
Scott, Cape- [Austl.] 59 Fb 13.30S 129.50 E
Scott, Cape - [B.C.-Can.] 42 Ef 50.47N 128.25W
Scott, Mount- 46 De 42.56N 122.01W
Scott Base 66 Kf 77.51S 166.46 E
Scottburgh 37 Ef 30.19S 30.40 E
Scott Channel 46 Aa 50.45N 128.30W
Scott City 45 Fg 38.29N 100.54W
Scott Coast 66 Kf 76.30S 162.30 E
Scott Glacier [Ant.] 66 He 66.15S 100.05 E
Scott Glacier [Ant.] 66 Mg 85.45S 153.00W
Scott Inlet 42 Kb 71.05N 71.05W
Scott Island 66 Le 67.24S 179.55W
Scott Islands 46 Aa 50.48N 128.40W
Scott Peak 46 Id 44.21N 112.50W
Scott Reef 59 Eb 14.00S 121.50 E
Scottsbluff 39 Ie 41.52N 103.40W
Scottsboro 44 Dh 34.40N 86.01W
Scottsburg 44 Ef 38.41N 85.46W
Scottsdale [Austl.] 59 Jh 41.10S 147.31 E
Scottsdale [Az.-U.S.] 43 Ee 33.30N 111.56W
Scotts Head 51g Bb 15.13N 61.23W
Scottsville 44 Dg 36.45N 86.11W
Scottville 44 Dd 43.59N 86.17W
Scranton 39 Le 41.24N 75.40W
Scrivia 14 Ce 45.03N 8.54 E
Scrub Cays 49 Ia 24.07N 76.55W
Scrub Island 51b Bb 18.17N 62.57W
Ščučin 16 Dc 53.39N 24.48 E
Ščučinsk 19 He 53.00N 70.11 E
Ščučja 17 Nc 66.45N 68.20 E
Ščučje 19 Gd 55.15N 62.43 E
Scugog, Lake- 44 Hc 44.10N 78.51W
Ščugor 17 Hd 64.12N 57.32 E
Scunthorpe 9 Mh 53.36N 0.38W
Scuol / Schuls 14 Ed 46.48N 10.17 E
Scutari, Lake- (EN)= Shkodrës, Liqen i- 5 Hg 42.10N 19.20 E
Scutari, Lake- (EN)= Skadarsko Jezero 5 Hg 42.10N 19.20 E
Seaford 9 Nk 50.46N 0.06 E
Seahorse Point 42 Jd 63.47N 80.10W
Sea Islands 43 Ke 31.20N 81.20W
Seal 42 Ie 59.04N 94.47W
Seal Island 44 Nd 43.30N 66.01W
Sealpunt 30 Jl 34.06S 23.24 E
Searcy 45 Ki 35.15N 91.44W
Searles Lake 46 Gi 35.43N 117.20W
Seaside [Ca.-U.S.] 46 Eh 36.37N 121.50W
Seaside [Or.-U.S.] 46 Dc 46.01N 123.55W
Seattle 39 Ge 47.36N 122.20W
Seaward Kaikoura Range 62 Ee 42.15S 173.35 E
Seba 26 Hi 10.29S 121.50 E
Sébaco 49 Dg 12.51N 86.06W
Sebago Lake 44 Ld 43.50N 70.35W
Sebaiera 32 Ee 24.51N 13.02W
Sebaou 13 Ph 36.55N 3.51 E
Sebastian, Cape- 46 Ce 42.19N 124.26W
Sebastián Vizcaíno, Bahía- 38 Hg 28.00N 114.30W
Sebastopol 46 Dg 38.24N 122.49W
Sebatik, Pulau- 26 Gf 4.10N 117.45 E
Sebba 34 Fc 13.26N 0.32 E
Sebderat 35 Fb 15.27N 36.39 E
Sébé 36 Bc 1.02S 13.06 E
Šebekino 19 De 50.27N 37.00 E
Sébékoro 34 Dc 12.49N 8.50W
Seberi 55 Fh 27.29S 53.24W
Sebeş 15 Gd 45.58N 23.34 E
Sebeş 15 Gd 46.00N 23.34 E
Sebes-Körös 15 Dc 46.55N 20.59 E
Sebeşului, Munţii- 15 Gd 45.38N 23.27 E
Sebewaing 44 Fd 43.44N 83.27W
Sebež 19 Cd 56.19N 28.31 E
Sebha Oasis (EN)=Sabhā, Wāḥāt 30 If 27.00N 14.25 E
Şebinkarahisar 24 Hb 40.18N 38.26 E
Sebiş 15 Fc 46.22N 22.07 E
Sebou 30 Ge 34.16N 6.41W
Sebring 44 Gl 27.30N 81.26W
Sebugal 13 Ed 40.21N 7.05W
Sebuku, Pulau- 26 Gg 3.30S 116.22 E
Šebunino 20 Jg 46.24N 141.56 E
Secas, Islas- 49 Gi 7.58N 82.02W
Secchia 14 Ee 45.04N 11.00 E
Sechura 54 Be 5.33S 80.51W
Sechura, Bahía de- 54 Be 5.40S 81.00W
Sechura, Desierto de- 54 Be 6.00S 80.30W
Seckau 14 Ic 47.16N 14.47 E
Seclin 12 Fd 50.33N 3.02 E
Secondigny 11 Fh 46.37N 0.25W
Secos, Ilhéus- 32 Cf 14.58N 24.40W
Secretary Island 62 Bf 45.15S 166.55 E
Sécure, Río- 54 Fg 15.10S 64.52W
Seda 8 Kg 57.38N 25.12 E
Sêda 13 Df 38.56N 8.03W
Seda [Lat.] 8 Kg 57.32N 25.43 E
Seda [Lith.] 8 Jh 56.10N 22.00 E
Sedalia 43 Id 38.42N 93.14W
Sedan 11 Ke 49.42N 4.57 E
Sedanka 40a Eb 53.50N 166.10W
Sedano 13 Ib 42.43N 3.45W
Sedbergh 9 Kg 54.20N 2.31W
Seddenga 35 Ea 20.33N 30.18 E
Seddon 62 Fd 41.40S 174.04 E
Seddon, Kap- 41 Gc 75.20N 58.45W
Seddonville 62 Dd 41.33S 171.59 E
Seddülbahir 15 Ji 40.03N 26.10 E
Sedelnikovo 19 Hd 56.57N 75.18 E
Séderon 11 Lj 44.12N 5.32 E
Sédhiou 34 Bc 12.44N 15.33W
Sedini 14 Ci 40.51N 8.49 E
Šedok 16 Lg 44.13N 40.52 E
Sedom 24 Fg 31.04N 35.24 E
Sedona 46 Ji 34.52N 111.46W
Sedrada 14 Bn 36.08N 7.32 E
Šédro 14 Kg 43.05N 16.42 E
Sedro Woolley 46 Db 48.30N 122.14W
Šeduva 7 Fi 55.48N 23.45 E
Sée 11 Ef 48.39N 1.26W
Seeheim [Ger.] 12 Ke 49.46N 8.40 E
Seeheim [Nam.] 37 Be 26.50S 17.45 E
Seeis 37 Bd 22.29S 17.39 E
Seeland 14 Bc 47.05N 7.05 E
Seeling, Mount- 66 Og 82.28S 103.00W
Seelow 10 Kd 52.31N 14.23 E
Sées 11 Gf 48.36N 0.10 E
Seesen 10 Ge 51.54N 10.11 E
Seewarte Seamounts (EN) 30 Ee 33.00N 28.30W
Şefaatli 24 Fc 39.31N 34.46 E
Sefadu 34 Cd 8.39N 10.59W
Seferihisar 24 Bc 38.11N 26.51 E
Séféto 34 Dc 14.08N 9.51W
Sefid Dasht 24 Nf 32.09N 51.10 E
Sefrou 32 Gc 33.50N 4.50W
Sefuri-San 29 Be 33.26N 130.22 E
Segaf, Kepulauan- 26 Jg 2.10S 130.28 E
Ségalas 11 Hj 44.09N 2.30 E
Segamat 26 Df 2.30N 102.49 E
Segangane 13 Ii 35.10N 3.01W
Şegarcea 15 Ge 44.06N 23.45 E
Şegarka 20 De 57.16N 84.02 E
Segbana 34 Fc 10.56N 3.42 E
Segeg 35 Gd 7.40N 42.50 E
Segesta 14 Gm 37.55N 12.50 E
Segeža 6 Jc 63.44N 34.19 E
Seghe 63a Cc 8.25S 157.51 E
Seglinge 8 Id 60.15N 20.40 E
Segmon 8 Ee 59.17N 13.01 E
Segorbe 13 Le 39.51N 0.29W
Ségou [3] 34 Dc 14.00N 6.20W
Ségou 31 Gg 13.27N 6.15W
Segovia 13 Hd 40.57N 4.07W
Segovia [3] 13 Ic 41.10N 4.00W
Segozero, Ozero- 5 Jc 63.18N 33.45 E
Segré 11 Fg 47.41N 0.52W
Segre 13 Mc 41.40N 0.43 E
Seguam 40a Db 52.17N 172.30W
Séguédine 34 Ha 20.12N 12.59 E
Séguéla 34 Dd 7.57N 6.40W
Séguéla [3] 34 Dd 8.05N 6.32W
Seguin 43 Hf 29.34N 97.58W
Segula 40a Bb 52.01N 178.07 E
Segura 13 Lf 38.06N 0.38W
Segura, Sierra de- 13 Jf 38.00N 2.45W
Segura de la Sierra 13 Jf 38.18N 2.39W
Sehithwa 37 Cd 20.27S 22.42 E
Seia 13 Ed 40.25N 7.42W
Seibal 49 Be 16.27N 90.05W
Seiche 11 Eg 48.00N 1.46W
Seiland 7 Fa 70.25N 23.15 E
Seiling 45 Gh 36.09N 98.56W
Seille [Fr.] 11 Me 49.07N 6.11 E
Seille [Fr.] 11 Kh 46.31N 4.56 E
Sein, Ile de- 11 Bf 48.02N 4.51W
Seinäjoki 7 Fe 62.47N 22.50 E
Seine 5 Gf 49.26N 0.26 E
Seine, Baie de la-=Seine, Bay of the- (EN) 5 Ff 49.30N 0.30W
Seine, Bay of the- (EN)= Seine, Baie de la- 5 Ff 49.30N 0.30W
Seine, Val de- 11 Jf 48.30N 3.20 E
Seine-et-Marne [3] 11 If 48.30N 3.00 E
Seine-Maritime [3] 11 Ge 49.45N 1.00 E
Seine-Saint-Denis [3] 11 If 48.55N 2.30 E
Seine Seamount (EN) 5 Ei 33.45N 14.25W
Seini 15 Gb 47.45N 23.17 E
Seistan (EN)=Sīstān 21 If 30.30N 62.00 E
Seixal 13 Cf 38.38N 9.06W
Sējaha 20 Cb 70.10N 72.30 E
Sejerø 8 Di 55.55N 11.10 E
Sejerø Bugt 8 Di 55.50N 11.15 E
Sejm 5 Je 51.27N 32.34 E
Sejmčan 20 Kd 62.52N 152.27 E
Sejny 10 Tb 54.07N 23.20 E
Sekakes 37 Df 30.04S 28.21 E
Sekenke 36 Fc 4.16S 34.10 E
Šeki 19 Eg 41.10N 47.11 E
Seki [Jap.] 29 Ed 35.28N 136.54 E
Seki [Tur.] 24 Cd 36.44N 29.33 E
Sekincau, Gunung- 26 Dh 5.05S 104.18 E
Seki-Zaki 29b Be 33.16N 131.54 E
Sekoma 37 Cd 24.36S 23.58 E
Sekondi-Takoradi 31 Gh 4.53N 1.45W
Sekota 35 Fc 12.37N 39.03 E
Šeksna 19 Dd 59.13N 38.32 E
Šelagski, Mys- 20 Mb 70.10N 170.45 E
Selah 46 Ec 46.39N 120.32W
Selajar, Pulau- 26 Hh 6.05S 120.30 E
Selajar, Selat- 26 Hh 5.42S 120.28 E
Selaön 8 Ge 59.25N 17.10 E
Selaru, Pulau- 26 Jh 8.09S 131.00 E
Selatan, Cape- (EN)= Selatan, Tanjung- 21 Nj 4.10S 113.48 E
Selatan, Tanjung-=Selatan, Cape- (EN) 21 Nj 4.10S 113.48 E
Selawik 40 Gc 66.37N 160.03W
Selawik Lake 40 Hc 66.30N 160.40W
Selb 10 If 50.10N 12.08 E
Selbjørn 8 Ae 60.00N 5.10 E
Selbjørnsfjorden 8 Ae 59.55N 5.10 E
Selbu 8 Da 63.13N 11.02 E
Selbukta 66 Bf 71.40S 12.25W
Selbusjøen 8 Da 63.15N 10.55 E
Selby [Eng.-U.K.] 9 Lh 53.48N 1.04W
Selby [S.D.-U.S.] 45 Fd 45.31N 100.02W
Selco 16 Ic 53.23N 34.05 E
Selçuk 24 Bd 37.56N 27.22 E
Seldovia 40 Ie 59.27N 151.43W
Sele 14 Ij 40.29N 14.56 E
Sele, Piana del- 14 Ij 40.30N 14.55 E
Selebi-Pikwe 31 Jk 22.13S 27.58 E
Selečka Planina 15 Eh 41.05N 21.35 E
Šelehov 20 Ff 52.10N 104.01 E
Selemdža 21 Od 51.49N 128.53 E
Selencia 24 Kf 33.04N 44.33 E
Selendi 15 Lk 38.40N 28.41 E
Selendi 15 Lk 38.45N 28.53 E
Selenduma 20 Ff 50.55N 106.10 E
Selenga (Selenge) 21 Md 52.16N 106.16 E
Selenge [Mong.] 27 Hb 49.25N 103.59 E
Selenge [Zaire] 36 Cc 1.58S 18.11 E
Selenge → Selenga 21 Md 52.16N 106.16 E
Selenginsk 20 Ff 51.59N 106.57 E
Selenica 15 Ci 40.32N 19.38 E
Selennjah 20 Jc 67.55N 145.00 E
Sélestat 11 Nf 48.16N 7.27 E
Selety 19 He 53.06N 73.00 E
Seletyteniz, Ozero- 19 He 53.15N 73.15 E
Selevac 15 De 44.30N 20.53 E
Seleznevo 8 Md 60.44N 28.37 E
Selfoss 7a Bc 63.56N 21.00W
Seli 34 Cd 8.33N 12.48W
Sélibabi 32 Ef 15.10N 12.11W
Seliger, Ozero- 19 Dd 57.20N 33.05 E
Seligman 46 Ii 35.20N 112.53W
Šelihova, Zaliv-=Shelikhov Gulf (EN) 21 Rc 60.00N 158.00 E
Selimağa 15 Lj 39.35N 28.33 E
Selimiye 24 Bd 37.24N 27.40 E
Selingenstadt 12 Kd 50.03N 8.59 E
Selinunte 14 Gm 37.35N 12.48 E
Seližarovo 7 Hh 56.51N 33.29 E
Seljatin 15 Ib 47.52N 25.14 E
Selje 8 Ab 62.03N 5.22 E
Seljord 7 Bg 59.29N 8.37 E
Selkirk [Man.-Can.] 45 Ha 50.09N 96.52W
Selkirk [Scot.-U.K.] 9 Kf 55.33N 2.50W
Selkirk Mountains 42 Ff 50.00N 117.00W
Sella 13 Ga 43.28N 5.04W
Sellasia 15 Fl 37.10N 22.25 E
Selle 12 Fd 50.19N 3.23 E
Selles-sur-Cher 11 Hg 47.16N 1.33 E
Sells 46 Jk 31.55N 111.53W
Selm 12 Jc 51.42N 7.28 E
Selma [Al.-U.S.] 43 Je 32.25N 87.01W
Selma [Ca.-U.S.] 46 Fh 36.34N 119.37W
Selmer 44 Ch 35.11N 88.36W
Selmeţ Wielki, Jezioro- 10 Sc 53.50N 22.30 E
Šelon 7 Hg 58.14N 30.50 E
Selong 26 Gh 8.39S 116.32 E
Selsey 12 Bd 50.44N 0.47W
Selsey Bill 9 Mk 50.43N 0.48W
Seltz 12 Kf 48.53N 8.06 E
Selu, Pulau- 26 Jh 7.32S 130.54 E
Sélune 11 Ef 48.39N 1.26W
Selva 55 Ai 29.46S 62.03W
Selvagens, Ilhas- 30 Fe 30.05N 15.55W
Selvānā 24 Kd 37.25N 44.51 E
Selvas 52 Jf 5.00S 68.00W
Selway River 46 Hc 46.08N 115.36W
Selwyn, Détroit de- 63b Dc 16.04S 168.11 E
Selwyn Lake 42 He 60.00N 104.30W
Selwyn Mountains 38 Fc 63.10N 130.20W
Selwyn Range 57 Fg 21.35S 140.35 E
Selz 12 Ke 49.59N 8.02 E
Šemaha 16 Pi 40.39N 48.38 E
Semani 15 Ci 40.54N 19.26 E
Semara 31 Ff 26.44N 11.41W
Semarang 22 Nj 6.58S 110.25 E
Sematan 26 Ef 1.48N 109.46 E
Semau, Pulau- 26 Hi 10.13S 123.22 E
Sembakung 26 Gf 3.47N 117.30 E
Sembé 36 Bb 1.39N 14.36 E
Semberija 14 Nf 44.45N 19.10 E
Sembuan 26 Gg 0.19S 115.30 E
Semenicului, Munţii- 15 Fd 45.05N 22.05 E
Semenov 7 Kh 56.49N 44.29 E
Semenovka 16 Hc 52.11N 32.40 E
Semeru, Gunung- 21 Nj 7.58S 113.35 E
Semichi Islands 40a Db 52.42N 174.00 E
Semidi Islands 40 He 56.07N 156.44W
Semiluki 19 De 51.43N 39.02 E
Semily 10 Lf 50.36N 15.20 E
Seminoe Reservoir 46 Le 42.00N 106.50W
Seminole [Ok.-U.S.] 45 Hi 35.14N 96.14W
Seminole [Tx.-U.S.] 45 Ej 32.43N 102.39W
Seminole, Lake- 43 Ke 30.46N 84.50W
Semipalatinsk 22 Kd 50.28N 80.13 E
Semipalatinskaja Oblast [3] 19 If 48.30N 80.10 E
Semirara Islands 26 Hd 11.57N 121.27 E
Semirom 24 Ng 31.22N 51.47 E
Semisopochnoi 40a Cb 52.00N 179.35 E
Semitau 26 Ff 0.33N 111.58 E
Semiun, Pulau- 26 Ef 4.31N 107.44 E
Semizbugy 19 He 50.12N 74.48 E
Semliki 30 Kh 1.14N 30.28 E
Semmering 14 Jc 47.38N 15.49 E
Semnām [3] 23 Hb 35.00N 53.30 E
Semnān 22 Hf 35.33N 53.24 E
Semnon 11 Eg 47.54N 1.45W
Semois 11 Ke 49.53N 4.45 E
Šemonaiha 19 Ie 50.39N 81.54 E
Semporna 26 Gf 4.28N 118.36 E
Semuda 26 Fg 2.51S 112.58 E
Semur-en-Auxois 11 Kg 47.29N 4.20 E
Senador Mourão 55 Kc 17.51S 43.22W
Senador Pompeu 54 Ke 5.35S 39.22W
Senaja 26 Ge 6.45N 117.03 E
Senaki (Miha Chakaja) 19 Eg 42.17N 42.02 E
Sena Madureira 54 Ee 9.04S 68.40W
Senanga 36 Df 16.07S 23.16 E
Senarpont 12 De 49.53N 1.43 E
Senatobia 45 Li 34.39N 89.58W
Sendai [Jap.] 28 Ki 31.49N 130.18 E
Sendai [Jap.] 22 Qf 38.15N 140.53 E
Sendai-Gawa [Jap.] 29 Bf 31.51N 130.12 E
Sendai-Gawa [Jap.] 29 Dd 35.34N 134.11 E
Sendai-Wan 28 Pe 38.10N 141.15 E
Senden 12 Jc 51.51N 7.30 E
Sendenhorst 12 Jc 51.50N 7.50 E
Senderg 24 Qi 26.52N 57.37 E
Seneca 45 Hg 39.50N 96.04W
Seneca Lake 44 Id 42.40N 76.57W
Sénégal=Senegal (EN) 30 Fg 15.48N 16.32W
Sénégal=Senegal (EN) [1] 31 Fg 14.00N 14.00W
Senegal (EN)=Sénégal [1] 31 Fg 14.00N 14.00W
Senegal (EN)=Sénégal 30 Fg 15.48N 16.32W
Sénégal Oriental [3] 34 Cc 13.30N 13.00W
Senekal 37 De 28.30S 27.32 E
Senetosa, Punta di- 11a Ab 41.33N 8.47 E
Seney 44 Eb 46.21N 85.56W
Senftenberg/Zły Komorow 10 Ke 51.31N 14.01 E
Sengata 22 Ni 0.28N 117.33 E
Sengilej 7 Lj 53.58N 48.46 E
Senguerr, Río- 56 Gg 45.32S 68.54W
Sengwa 37 Dc 17.05S 28.03 E
Senhor do Bonfim 53 Lg 10.27S 40.11W
Senica 10 Nh 48.41N 17.23 E
Senigallia 14 Hg 43.43N 13.13 E
Senirkent 24 Dc 38.07N 30.33 E
Senj 14 If 45.00N 14.54 E
Senja 5 Hb 69.20N 17.30 E
Senjsko Bilo 14 Jf 44.55N 15.03 E
Senkaku-Shotō 27 Lf 25.45N 124.00 E
Şenkaya 24 Jb 40.35N 42.21 E
Senkevičevka 10 Vf 50.29N 25.05 E
Šenkursk 19 Ec 62.08N 42.53 E
Senlin Shan 28 Kc 43.12N 130.38 E
Senlis 11 Ie 49.12N 2.35 E
Senmonorom 25 Lf 12.27N 107.12 E
Senn, Dahr Ou- 32 Ef 17.55N 11.00W
Sennestadt, Bielefeld- 12 Kc 51.57N 8.35 E
Senneterre 42 Jg 48.24N 77.14W
Senno 7 Gi 54.47N 29.41 E
Sennoj 16 Oc 52.07N 46.59 E
Senorbì 14 Dk 39.32N 9.08 E
Senqu 37 Be 28.38S 16.27 E
Sens 11 Jf 48.12N 3.17 E
Sensée 12 Fd 50.16N 3.06 E
Sensuntepeque 49 Cg 13.52N 88.38W
Senta 15 Dd 45.56N 20.05 E
Sentinel Peak 42 Ff 54.58N 122.00W
Sentinel Range 66 Pf 78.10S 85.30W
Senyavin Islands 57 Gd 6.55N 158.00 E
Şenyurt 24 Id 37.06N 40.40 E
Senzaki-Wan 29 Bd 34.25N 131.20 E
Senžarka 17 Mi 54.45N 67.50 E
Seo de Urgel/La Seu d'Urgell 13 Nb 42.21N 1.28 E
Seoni 25 Fd 22.05N 79.32 E
Seoul (EN)=Sŏul 22 Of 37.34N 127.00 E
Séoune 11 Gj 44.10N 0.41 E
Sepanjang, Pulau- 26 Gh 7.10S 115.50 E
Separation Point 62 Ed 40.47S 173.00 E
Sepetovka 19 Ce 50.12N 27.04 E
Sepik River 57 Fe 3.51S 144.34 E
Sępólno Krajeńskie 10 Nc 53.28N 17.32 E
Sępopol 10 Qb 54.15N 21.00 E
Sępopolska, Nizina- 10 Rb 54.15N 21.10 E
Septemvri 15 Hg 42.13N 24.06 E
Septentrional, Cordillera- 49 Ld 19.35N 70.45W
Septeuil 12 Df 48.54N 1.41 E
Sept-Iles 39 Md 50.12N 66.23W
Sepúlveda 13 Ic 41.18N 3.45W
Sequeros 13 Fd 40.31N 6.01W
Sequillo 13 Gc 41.45N 5.30W
Sera 29 Cd 34.36N 133.01 E
Sera, Pulau- 26 Jh 7.40S 131.05 E
Šerabad 19 Gh 37.43N 66.59 E
Šerabad 18 Ff 37.22N 67.03 E
Serafettin Dağları 24 Ic 39.05N 41.10 E
Serafimović 16 Me 49.36N 42.47 E
Serahs 19 Gh 36.30N 61.13 E
Seraidi 14 Bn 36.55N 7.40 E
Seraing 11 Ld 50.36N 5.31 E
Seram 57 De 3.00S 129.00 E
Seram, Laut-=Ceram Sea (EN) 57 De 2.30S 128.00 E
Serang 26 Eh 6.07S 106.09 E
Serasan, Pulau- 26 Ef 2.30N 109.03 E
Serasan, Selat- 26 Ef 2.20S 109.00 E
Serbia (EN) = Srbija [2] 15 Df 44.00N 21.00 E
Serbia (EN) = Srbija 5 Ig 43.00N 21.00 E
Serbia (EN)=Srbija 15 Df 44.00N 21.00 E
Şercaia 15 Id 45.50N 25.08 E
Serchio 14 Eg 43.47N 10.16 E
Serdo 35 Gc 11.58N 41.18 E
Serdoba 16 Nc 52.34N 44.01 E
Serdobsk 19 Ee 52.29N 44.16 E
Sereba 35 Gc 13.12N 40.32 E
Serebrjansk 19 If 49.43N 83.20 E
Serebrjanski 7 Ib 68.52N 35.32 E
Sered' 10 Nh 48.17N 17.45 E
Seredka 8 Mf 58.10N 28.25 E
Şereflikoçhisar 24 Ec 38.56N 33.33 E
Serein 11 Jg 47.55N 3.31 E
Seremban 26 Df 2.43N 101.56 E
Serengeti Plain 36 Fc 2.50S 35.00 E
Serenje 36 Fe 13.14S 30.14 E
Šereševo 10 Ud 52.31N 24.19 E
Seret 16 De 48.38N 25.52 E
Serfopoúla 15 Hl 37.15N 24.36 E
Sergač 19 Ed 55.33N 45.28 E
Sergeievka 28 Lc 43.23N 133.22 E
Sergeja Kirova, Ostrova- 20 Da 77.10N 90.00 E
Sergejevka 19 Ge 53.51N 67.28 E
Sergejevka 28 Kb 44.20N 131.40 E
Sergijev Posad (Zagorsk) 6 Jd 56.18N 38.08 E
Sergino 22 Ic 62.30N 65.40 E
Sergipe [2] 54 Kf 10.30S 37.10W
Sergokala 16 Oh 42.30N 47.40 E
Sergozero, Ozero- 7 Ic 66.45N 36.50 E
Seria 26 Ff 4.37N 114.19 E
Serian 26 Ff 1.10N 110.34 E
Seriana, Val- 14 De 45.50N 9.50 E
Seribu, Kepulauan- 26 Eh 5.36S 106.33 E
Sérifontaine 12 De 49.21N 1.46 E
Sérifos 15 Hl 37.09N 24.30 E
Sérifos 15 Hl 37.10N 24.30 E
Serifou, Stenón- 15 Hl 37.15N 24.30 E
Serik 24 Dd 36.55N 31.06 E
Seringapatam Reef 59 Eb 13.40S 122.05 E
Serio 14 De 45.16N 9.45 E
Šerlovaja Gora 20 Gf 50.34N 116.18 E
Sermata, Kepulauan- 26 Ih 8.10S 128.40 E
Sermilik 41 Ie 66.00N 38.45W
Sernovodsk 7 Mj 53.54N 51.09 E
Sernur 7 Lh 56.57N 49.11 E
Sernyje Vody 7 Mj 53.53N 50.59 E
Sero 24 Kd 37.33N 44.40 E
Serock 10 Rd 52.31N 21.03 E
Serodino 55 Bk 32.37S 60.57W
Serov 22 Id 59.29N 60.31 E
Serowe 31 Jk 22.23S 26.43 E
Serpa 13 Eg 37.56N 7.36W
Serpent, Vallée du- 34 Dc 14.50N 8.00W
Serpentine Lakes 59 Fe 28.30S 129.10 E
Serpent's Mouth/Serpiente, Boca de la- 54 Fa 10.10N 61.58W
Serpiente, Boca de la-/ Serpent's Mouth 54 Fa 10.10N 61.58W
Serpnevoje 15 Lc 46.23N 28.59 E
Serpuhov 6 Je 54.55N 37.25 E
Serra, Aparados da- 55 Hi 28.45S 49.45W
Serra Bonita 55 Ib 15.13S 46.49W
Serra das Araras 55 Jb 15.30S 45.21W
Serra do Navio 53 Ke 0.59N 52.03W
Serra do Salitre 55 Id 19.06S 46.41W
Serra Dourada 55 Ka 12.50S 43.56W
Sérrai 15 Gh 41.05N 23.33 E
Serralada Litoral Catalana/ Cadena Costero Catalana= Catalan Coastal Range (EN) 5 Gg 41.35N 1.40 E
Serralada Pirinenca= Pyrenees (EN) 5 Gg 42.40N 1.00 E
Serrana Bank 47 Hf 14.23N 80.12W
Serranilla Bank 47 Ie 15.50N 79.50W
Serranópolis 55 Fd 18.16S 52.00W
Serra San Bruno 14 Kl 38.35N 16.20 E
Serrat, Cap- 32 Ib 37.14N 9.13 E
Serra Talhada 54 Ke 7.59S 38.18W
Serre 11 Je 49.41N 3.23 E
Serre, Massif de la- 11 Lg 47.10N 5.35 E
Serre-Ponçon, Réservoir de- 11 Mj 44.27N 6.16 E
Serres 11 Lj 44.26N 5.43 E
Serrezuela 56 Gd 30.38S 65.23W
Serrinha 54 Kf 11.39S 39.00W
Serriola, Bocca- 14 Gg 43.31N 12.21 E
Serro 55 Kd 18.37S 43.23W
Serrota 13 Gd 40.30N 5.04W
Serrote, Rio- 55 Ee 21.27S 54.40W

Index Symbols

[1] Independent Nation
[2] State, Region
[3] District, County
[4] Municipality
[5] Colony, Dependency
Continent
Physical Region
Historical or Cultural Region
Mount, Mountain
Volcano
Hill
Mountains, Mountain Range
Hills, Escarpment
Plateau, Upland
Pass, Gap
Plain, Lowland
Delta
Salt Flat
Valley, Canyon
Crater, Cave
Karst Features
Depression
Polder
Desert, Dunes
Forest, Woods
Heath, Steppe
Oasis
Cape, Point
Coast, Beach
Cliff
Peninsula
Isthmus
Sandbank
Island
Atoll
Rock, Reef
Islands, Archipelago
Rocks, Reefs
Coral Reef
Well, Spring
Geyser
River, Stream
Waterfall Rapids
River Mouth, Estuary
Lake
Salt Lake
Intermittent Lake
Reservoir
Swamp, Pond
Canal
Glacier
Ice Shelf, Pack Ice
Ocean
Sea
Gulf, Bay
Strait, Fjord
Lagoon
Bank
Seamount
Tablemount
Ridge
Shelf
Basin
Escarpment, Sea Scarp
Fracture
Trench, Abyss
National Park, Reserve
Point of Interest
Recreation Site
Cave, Cavern
Historic Site
Ruins
Wall, Walls
Church, Abbey
Temple
Scientific Station
Airport
Port
Lighthouse
Mine
Tunnel
Dam, Bridge

Sersou, Plateau du- 13 Ni 35.30N 2.00 E
Sertã 13 De 39.48N 8.06W
Sertão 52 Lg 10.00S 41.00W
Sertãozinho 55 Ie 21.08S 47.59W
Sêrtar 27 He 32.20N 100.20 E
Serti 34 Hd 7.30N 11.22 E
Serua, Pulau- 26 Jh 6.18S 130.01 E
Serui 26 Kg 1.53S 136.14 E
Serule 37 Dd 21.55S 27.19 E
Sérvia 15 Ei 40.11N 22.00 E
Sêrxü 27 Ge 32.56N 98.02 E
Seryitsi 15 Ii 40.00N 25.10 E
Seryševo 20 Hf 51.02N 128.25 E
Sesayap 26 Gf 3.36N 117.15 E
Sese 36 Eb 2.11N 25.47 E
Seseganaga Lake 45 Ka 50.10N 90.15W
Sese Islands 36 Fc 0.20S 32.20 E
Sesfontein 37 Ac 19.07S 13.39 E
Sesheke 36 Df 17.29S 24.18 E
Sesia 14 Ce 45.05N 8.37 E
Sesibi 35 Ea 20.05N 30.31 E
Sesimbra 13 Cf 38.26N 9.06W
Šešma 7 Mi 55.20N 51.12 E
Sesnut 8 Be 59.42N 7.21 E
Sessa Aurunca 14 Hi 41.14N 13.56 E
Ses Salines, Cap de-/
Salinas, Cabo de- 13 Pe 39.16N 3.03 E
Sestao 13 Ja 43.18N 3.00W
Sesto Fiorentino 14 Fg 43.50N 11.12 E
Sesto San Giovanni 14 De 45.32N 9.14 E
Sestriere 14 Af 44.57N 6.53 E
Sestri Levante 14 Df 44.16N 9.24 E
Sestroreck 7 Gf 60.06N 29.59 E
Šešupė 7 Fi 55.00N 22.10 E
Šešuvis 8 Ji 55.12N 22.31 E
Sesvenna, Piz- 14 Ed 46.42N 10.25 E
Sesvete 14 Ke 45.50N 16.07 E
Šeta/Šėta 8 Ki 55.14N 24.18 E
Šėta/Šeta 8 Ki 55.14N 24.18 E
Setaka 29 Be 33.09N 130.28 E
Setana 28 Oc 42.26N 139.51 E
Sète 11 Jk 43.24N 3.41 E
Sete de Setembro,
Rio- 55 Fa 12.56S 52.51W
Sete Lagoas 54 Jg 19.27S 44.14W
Setenil 13 Gh 36.51N 5.11W
Sete Quedas, Saltos das- =
Guaira Falls (EN) 56 Jb 24.02S 54.16W
Setermoen 7 Eb 68.52N 18.28 E
Setesdal 7 Bg 59.05N 7.35 E
Setesdalsheiane 8 Be 59.30N 7.10 E
Seti 25 Gc 28.58N 81.06 E
Sétif [3] 32 Ib 36.05N 5.00 E
Sétif 31 He 36.12N 5.24 E
Seto 29 Ed 35.13N 137.05 E
Setonaikai=Inland
Sea (EN) 21 Pf 34.10N 133.00 E
Setouchi 29b Ba 28.08N 129.20 E
Šetpe 19 Fg 44.06N 52.02 E
Settat 32 Fc 33.00N 7.37W
Settat [3] 32 Fc 33.00N 7.30W
Setté Cama 36 Ac 2.32S 9.45 E
Sette-Daban, Hrebet- 20 Id 62.00N 138.00 E
Settle 9 Kg 54.04N 2.16W
Setúbal [2] 13 Df 38.20N 8.30W
Setúbal 6 Fh 38.32N 8.54W
Setúbal, Baia de- 13 Df 38.27N 8.53W
Setúbal o de Guadalupe,
Laguna- 55 Bj 31.33S 60.35W
Seudre 11 Ei 45.48N 1.09W
Seugne 11 Fi 45.42N 0.32W
Seui 14 Dk 39.50N 9.19 E
Seuil-d'Argonne 12 Hf 48.58N 5.03 E
Seul, Lac- 38 Jd 50.20N 92.30W
Seulles 12 Be 49.20N 0.27W
Seurre 11 Lg 47.00N 5.09 E
Sevan 19 Eg 40.32N 44.57 E
Sevan, Lake- (EN)=Sevan,
Ozero- 5 Kg 40.20N 45.20 E
Sevan, Ozero-=Sevan,
Lake- (EN) 5 Kg 40.20N 45.20 E
Sévaré 34 Ec 14.32N 4.06W
Sevastopol 6 Jg 44.36N 33.32 E
Ševčenko → Aktau 22 He 43.35N 51.05 E
Ševčenko, Zaliv- 18 Ca 46.30N 60.15 E
Sevenoaks 9 Nj 51.16N 0.12 E
Sever 13 Ee 39.40N 7.32W
Sévérac-le-Château 11 Jj 44.19N 3.04 E
Severn 9 Kj 51.20N 3.10W
Severn [Can.] 38 Kd 56.02N 87.36W
Severn [U.K.] 9 Kj 51.35N 2.40W
Severnaja Dvina=Northern
Dvina (EN) 5 Kc 64.32N 40.30 E
Severnaja Keltma 17 Ff 61.30N 54.00 E
Severnaja Pseašho,
Gora- 16 Lh 43.47N 40.30 E
Severnaja Sosva 19 Gc 64.10N 65.28 E
Severnaja Zemlja=
Severnaya Zemlya (EN) 21 Lb 79.30N 98.00 E
Severnaya Zemlya (EN)=
Severnaja Zemlja 21 Lb 79.30N 98.00 E
Severn Lake 42 If 53.52N 90.58W
Severnoje 16 Rb 54.05N 52.32 E
Severnoje 20 Ce 56.21N 78.23 E
Severny 19 Gb 67.38N 64.06 E
Severnyje Uvaly=Northern
Uvals (EN) 5 Kd 59.30N 49.00 E
Severny Kommunar 17 Gg 58.23N 54.02 E
Severny Ledovity Okean=
Arctic Ocean (EN) 67 Be 85.00N 170.00 E
Severny Ural=Northern
Urals (EN) 5 Lc 62.00N 59.00 E
Severobajkalsk 20 Fe 55.40N 109.25 E
Severočeský kraj [3] 10 Kf 50.35N 14.15 E
Severodoneck 16 Ke 48.57N 38.31 E
Severodvinsk 6 Jc 64.34N 39.50 E
Severo-Jenisejski 20 Ed 60.28N 93.01 E
Severo-Kazahstanskaja
Oblast [3] 19 Ge 54.30N 68.00 E
Severo-Krymski Kanal 16 Ig 45.30N 34.35 E
Severo-Kurilsk 22 Rd 50.40N 156.08 E
Severomoravský kraj [3] 10 Ng 49.45N 17.50 E
Severomorsk 19 Db 69.04N 33.24 E
Severo-Osetinskaja
respublika 19 Eg 43.00N 44.10 E
Severo-Sibirskaja
Nizmennost=North
Siberian Plain (EN) 21 Mb 72.00N 104.00 E
Severouralsk 19 Gc 60.09N 60.01 E
Sevier 46 Ig 38.35N 112.14W
Sevier Bridge Reservoir 46 Jg 39.21N 111.57W
Sevier Desert 46 Ig 39.25N 112.50W
Sevier Lake 43 Ed 38.55N 113.09W
Sevier River 43 Ed 39.04N 113.06W
Sevilla [3] 13 Gg 37.30N 5.30W
Sevilla [Col.] 54 Cc 4.16N 75.53W
Sevilla [Sp.] =
Seville (EN) 6 Fh 37.23N 5.59W
Sevilla, Isla- 49 Fi 8.14N 82.24W
Seville (EN)=Sevilla [Sp.] 6 Fh 37.23N 5.59W
Sevlijevo 15 If 43.01N 25.06 E
Sèvre Nantaise 11 Eg 47.12N 1.33W
Sèvre Niortaise 11 Eh 46.18N 1.08W
Sevron 11 Lh 46.32N 5.16 E
Sevsk 16 Ic 52.08N 34.30 E
Sewa 34 Cd 7.18N 12.08W
Seward [Ak.-U.S.] 39 Ec 60.06N 149.26W
Seward [Nb.-U.S.] 45 Hf 40.55N 97.06W
Seward Peninsula 38 Cc 65.00N 164.00W
Sewell 56 Fd 34.05S 70.21W
Seyāhkal 24 Md 37.09N 49.52 E
Seybaplaya 48 Nh 19.39N 90.40W
Seybaplaya, Punta- 48 Nh 19.45N 90.42W
Seybouse, Oued- 14 Bn 36.53N 7.46 E
Seychelles [1] 31 Mi 8.00S 55.00 E
Seychelles Islands 30 Mi 4.35S 55.40 E
Seydān 24 Og 30.01N 53.01 E
Seydişehir 24 Dd 37.25N 31.51 E
Seyðisfjörður 6 Eb 65.16N 14.00W
Seyfe Gölü 24 Fc 39.13N 34.23 E
Seyf Ţāleh 24 Le 35.57N 46.19 E
Seyhan 23 Db 36.43N 34.53 E
Seyitgazi 24 Dc 39.27N 30.43 E
Seyitömer 15 Mj 39.34N 29.52 E
Seyla' 35 Gc 11.21N 43.30 E
Seymour [Austl.] 59 Jg 37.02S 145.08 E
Seymour [In.-U.S.] 44 Ef 38.58N 85.53W
Seymour [Mo.-U.S.] 45 Jh 37.09N 92.46W
Seymour [S.Afr.] 37 Df 32.33S 26.46 E
Seymour [Tx.-U.S.] 43 He 33.35N 99.16W
Sezana 14 He 45.42N 13.52 E
Sézanne 11 Jf 48.43N 3.43 E
Sfaktiria 15 Em 36.56N 21.40 E
Sfax (EN)=Şafāqis [3] 32 Jc 34.30N 10.30 E
Sfax (EN)=Şafāqis 31 Ie 34.44N 10.46 E
Sferracavallo, Capo- 14 Dk 39.43N 9.40 E
Sfîntu Gheorghe [Rom.] 15 Me 44.53N 29.26 E
Sfîntu Gheorghe [Rom.] 15 Id 45.52N 25.47 E
Sfîntu Gheorghe, Braţul- 15 Me 44.53N 29.36 E
Sfîntu Gheorghe, Ostrovul-
15 Md 45.07N 29.22 E
Sfizef 13 Li 35.14N 0.15W
's-Gravenhage/Den Haag=
The Hague (EN) 6 Ge 52.06N 4.18 E
's-Gravenhage-
Scheveningen 11 Kb 52.06N 4.18 E
Shaanxi Sheng (Shaan-hsi
Sheng)=Shensi (EN) [2] 27 Id 36.00N 109.00 E
Shaba [2] 36 Ed 8.30S 25.00 E
Sha'bah, Wādī ash- 24 Ij 25.59N 41.55 E
Shabeellaha Dhexe [3] 35 He 3.00N 46.00 E
Shabellaha Hoose [3] 35 Ge 2.00N 44.40 E
Shabēlle, Webi-=Shebeli
Webi (EN) 30 Lh 0.12S 42.45 E
Shabestar 24 Kc 38.11N 45.42 E
Shabunda 36 Ec 2.42S 27.20 E
Shache/Yarkant 27 Cd 38.24N 77.15 E
Shacheng → Huailai 27 Kc 40.29N 115.30 E
Shackleton Coast 66 Kg 82.00S 162.00 E
Shackleton Glacier 66 Lg 84.35S 176.15W
Shackleton Ice Shelf 66 He 66.00S 101.00 E
Shackleton Range 66 Ag 80.40S 26.00W
Shaddādī 24 Id 36.02N 40.45 E
Shādegān 24 Mg 30.40N 48.38 E
Shadwān, Jazīrat- 33 Fd 27.30N 33.55 E
Shaftesbury 9 Kk 51.01N 2.12W
Shagedu → Jungar Qi 27 Jd 39.37N 110.58 E
Shāghir Bazar 24 Id 36.52N 40.53 E
Shag Rocks 66 Rd 54.26S 36.33W
Shāh'Abbās 24 Oe 34.44N 52.10 E
Shah Alam 26 Df 3.05N 101.29 E
Shahdol 25 Gd 23.13N 81.18 E
Sha He [China] 28 Ch 33.39N 114.38 E
Sha He [China] 28 Cf 37.09N 114.46 E
Shahezhen → Linze 27 Hd 39.10N 100.21 E
Shah Jahān, Kūh-e- 24 Qd 37.02N 57.54 E
Shahjahānpur 25 Fc 27.53N 79.55 E
Shah Kūh 23 Hb 36.35N 54.31 E
Shahmīrzād 24 Oe 35.47N 53.20 E
Shāhpūr 24 Nh 32.50N 51.45 E
Shāhpūr 24 Nh 29.39N 51.03 E
Shahrak 24 Nd 36.14N 50.40 E
Shahr-e-Bābak 24 Pg 30.10N 55.09 E
Shahr-e Khafr 24 Oh 28.56N 53.14 E
Shahr Kord 23 Hc 32.19N 50.50 E
Shāhrūd 24 Md 37.17N 48.43 E
Shahu, Kūh-e- 24 Le 34.45N 46.30 E
Shāh Zeyd 24 Od 36.13N 52.22 E
Shā'ib al Banāt, Jabal- 30 Kf 26.59N 33.29 E
Sha'īt, Wādī- 24 Ej 24.33N 33.01 E
Shakaga-Dake 29 Be 33.11N 130.53 E
Shakawe 31 Ji 18.23S 21.51 E
Shak Bay (Denham) 59 Ce 25.55S 113.32 E
Shaker Heights 44 Ge 41.29N 81.36W
Shaki 34 Fd 8.40N 3.23 E
Shakotan-Dake 29a Bb 43.16N 140.26 E
Shakotan-Hantō 29a Bb 43.15N 140.30 E
Shakotan-Misaki 29a Bb 43.23N 140.28 E
Shaktoolik 40 Gd 64.20N 161.09W
Shāl 24 Me 35.54N 49.46 E
Shala, Lake- 35 Fd 7.29N 38.32 E
Shalamzār 24 Nf 32.02N 50.49 E
Shalānbōd 35 Ge 1.40N 44.42 E
Shaler Mountains 42 Gb 71.45N 111.00W
Shaliuhe → Gangca 27 Hd 37.30N 100.14 E
Shaluli Shan 21 Lf 30.45N 99.45 E
Shām, Bādiyat ash-=Syrian
Desert (EN) 21 Ff 32.00N 40.00 E
Shām, Jabal ash- 21 Hg 23.10N 57.20 E
Shamattawa 42 Ie 55.52N 92.05W
Shambe 35 Ed 7.07N 30.46 E
Shambu 35 Fd 9.33N 37.07 E
Shamīl 24 Qi 27.30N 56.53 E
Shāmīyah 21 Ff 34.00N 39.59 E
Shammar, Jabal- 21 Gg 27.20N 41.45 E
Shamo, Lake- 35 Fd 5.50N 37.40 E
Shamokin 44 Ie 40.47N 76.34W
Shamrock 45 Fi 35.13N 100.15W
Shams 24 Pg 31.04N 55.02 E
Shamsī 35 Db 19.03N 29.54 E
Shamwa 37 Ec 17.18S 31.34 E
Shan [2] 25 Jd 22.00N 98.00 E
Shandī 31 Kg 16.42N 33.26 E
Shandian He 28 Dc 42.20N 116.20 E
Shandong Bandao=
Shantung Peninsula (EN)
21 Of 37.00N 121.00 E
Shandong Sheng
(Shan-tung Sheng)=
Shantung (EN) [2] 27 Kd 36.00N 119.00 E
Shandūr Pass 25 Ea 36.04N 72.31 E
Shangani 37 Dc 19.42S 29.22 E
Shangani 37 Dc 18.30S 27.11 E
Shangbahe 28 Ci 30.39N 115.06 E
Shangcai 28 Ch 33.16N 114.15 E
Shangcheng 28 Ci 31.49N 115.24 E
Shangdu 27 Jc 41.31N 113.32 E
Shanggao 28 Cj 28.15N 114.55 E
Shanghai 22 Of 31.14N 121.28 E
Shanghai Shi (Shang-hai
Shih) [4] 27 Le 31.14N 121.28 E
Shang-hai Shih → Shanghai
Shi [4] 27 Le 31.14N 121.28 E
Shanghang 27 Kf 25.04N 116.21 E
Shanghe 28 Df 37.19N 117.09 E
Shanghekou 27 Lc 40.26N 124.51 E
Shangpaihe → Feixi 28 Di 31.42N 117.09 E
Shangqiu (Zhuji) 27 Ke 34.24N 115.37 E
Shangrao 27 Kf 28.29N 117.59 E
Shan Guan 27 Kf 27.28N 117.05 E
Shangxian 27 Ie 33.55N 109.57 E
Shangyi (Nanhaoqian) 28 Bd 41.06N 113.58 E
Shangyu (Baiguan) 28 Fi 30.01N 120.53 E
Shangzhi 27 Mb 45.13N 127.55 E
Shanhaiguan 28 Ed 40.01N 119.45 E
Shanhetun 28 Ib 44.43N 127.14 E
Shan-hsi Sheng → Shanxi
Sheng=Shansi (EN) [2] 27 Jd 37.00N 112.00 E
Shanklin 12 Ad 50.37N 1.11W
Shanmatang Ding 27 Jg 24.45N 111.50 E
Shannon 41 Kc 75.20N 18.10W
Shannon 62 Fd 40.33S 175.25 E
Shannon/Aerfort na
Sionainne 9 Ei 52.42N 8.57W
Shannon/An tSionainn 5 Fe 52.36N 9.41W
Shannon, Mount- 59 Ie 29.58S 141.30 E
Shannon, Mouth of the- 9 Di 52.30N 9.53W
Shanshan (Piqan) 27 Fc 42.52N 90.10 E
Shansi (EN)=Shan-hsi
Sheng → Shanxi Sheng [2] 27 Jd 37.00N 112.00 E
Shansi (EN)=Shanxi Sheng
(Shan-hsi Sheng) [2] 27 Jd 37.00N 112.00 E
Shansonggang 28 Ic 42.30N 126.13 E
Shanţah, Ra's- 24 Qi 26.22N 56.26 E
Shantar Islands (EN)=
Šantarskije Ostrova 21 Pd 55.00N 137.36 E
Shantou 22 Ng 23.26N 116.42 E
Shantung (EN)=Shandong
Sheng (Shan-tung Sheng)
[2] 27 Kd 36.00N 119.00 E
Shantung (EN)=Shan-tung
Sheng → Shandong
Sheng [2] 27 Kd 36.00N 119.00 E
Shantung Peninsula (EN)=
Shandong Bandao 21 Of 37.00N 121.00 E
Shan-tung
Sheng → Shandong Sheng
=Shantung (EN) [2] 27 Kd 36.00N 119.00 E
Shanxian 28 Dg 34.47N 116.05 E
Shanxi Sheng (Shan-hsi
Sheng)=Shansi (EN) [2] 27 Jd 37.00N 112.00 E
Shanyin (Daiyue) 28 Be 39.30N 112.48 E
Shanyincheng 28 Be 39.27N 112.56 E
Shaoguan 22 Ng 24.57N 113.34 E
Shaoshan 27 Jf 27.55N 112.32 E
Shaowu 27 Kf 27.21N 117.29 E
Shaoxing 22 Og 30.00N 120.30 E
Shaoyang 22 Ng 27.13N 111.31 E
Shapinsay 9 Kb 59.03N 2.51W
Shaqlāwah 24 Kd 36.23N 44.18 E
Shaqq al Ju'ayfir 35 Db 15.16N 26.00 E
Shaqrā' 23 Gg 13.21N 45.42 E
Shaqū 24 Qi 27.14N 56.22 E
Sharāf 24 Jg 30.37N 43.45 E
Sharafah 35 Dc 12.04N 27.07 E
Sharafkhāneh 24 Kc 38.11N 45.29 E
Sharāh, Jibāl ash- 24 Fg 30.10N 35.30 E
Sharā 'Iwah 24 Oj 25.02N 52.14 E
Shareh 24 Kd 37.38N 44.50 E
Shari 27 Pc 43.55N 144.40 E
Shārī, Buḩayrat- 24 Ke 34.23N 44.07 E
Shari-Dake 29a Db 43.46N 144.43 E
Sharifābād [Iran] 24 Nd 36.12N 50.08 E
Sharifābād [Iran] 24 Ne 35.25N 51.47 E
Shark Bay 57 Cg 25.30S 113.30 E
Sharm ash Shaykh 33 Fd 27.50N 34.16 E
Sharon 44 Ge 41.16N 80.30W
Sharon Springs 45 Fg 38.54N 101.45W
Sharp 9 Fc 58.05N 7.05W
Sharqīyah, Aş Şaḩrā' ash-=
Arabian Desert (EN) 30 Kf 28.00N 32.00 E
Sharshar, Jabal- 24 Dk 23.52N 30.20 E
Shary 23 Fd 27.15N 43.27 E
Shashe 37 Dd 21.24S 27.27 E
Shashemene 35 Fd 7.13N 38.36 E
Shashi 22 Nf 30.22N 112.11 E
Shashi 30 Jk 22.12S 29.21 E
Shasta, Mount- 38 Ge 41.20N 122.20W
Shasta Lake 43 Cc 40.50N 122.25W
Shāţi', Wādī ash- 33 Bd 27.10N 13.25 E
Shattuck 45 Gh 36.16N 99.53W
Shaunavon 42 Gg 49.40N 108.25W
Shawan 27 Ec 44.21N 85.37 E
Shawano 45 Ld 44.47N 88.36W
Shawinigan 42 Kg 46.33N 72.45W
Shawnee 43 Hd 35.20N 96.55W
Shawneetown 45 Lh 37.42N 88.08W
Shaw River 59 Dd 20.20S 119.17 E
Shāwshāw, Jabal- 24 Ci 26.03N 28.56 E
Shayang 28 Bi 30.42N 112.34 E
Shaybārā 24 Gj 25.25N 36.51 E
Shaykh Aḩmad 24 Lf 32.53N 46.26 E
Shaykh Fāris 24 Lf 32.05N 47.36 E
Shaykh Sa'd 24 Lf 32.34N 46.17 E
Shaykh 'Uthmān 23 Fg 12.52N 44.59 E
Shebar, Kowtal-e- 23 Kc 34.54N 68.14 E
Shebele, Wabe-=Shebeli
Webi (EN) 30 Lh 0.12S 42.45 E
Shebeli Webi (EN)=
Shabēlle, Webi- 30 Lh 0.12S 42.45 E
Shebeli Webi (EN)=
Shebele, Wabe- 30 Lh 0.12S 42.45 E
Sheberghān 22 If 36.41N 65.45 E
Sheboygan 45 Me 43.46N 87.44W
Shebshi Mountains 30 Ih 8.30N 11.45 E
Shedin Peak 42 Ee 55.50N 127.00W
Sheelin, Lough-/Loch
Sileann 9 Fh 53.48N 7.20W
Sheenjek 40 Kc 66.45N 144.33W
Sheep Haven/Cuan na
gCaorach 9 Ff 55.10N 7.52W
Sheep Mountain 46 Hj 32.32N 114.14W
Sheep Range 46 Hh 36.45N 115.05W
s'Heerenberg, Bergh- 12 Ic 51.53N 6.16 E
Sheerness 9 Nj 51.27N 0.45 E
Sheffield [Al.-U.S.] 44 Dh 34.46N 87.40W
Sheffield [Eng.-U.K.] 6 Fe 53.23N 1.30W
Sheffield [Tx.-U.S.] 45 Fk 30.43N 101.50W
Shefford 12 Bb 52.02N 0.20W
Shek Hasan 35 Fc 12.04N 35.53 E
Shek Husen 35 Gd 7.45N 40.42 E
Shelburne [N.S.-Can.] 42 Kh 43.46N 65.19W
Shelburne [Ont.-Can.] 44 Gc 44.04N 80.12W
Shelby [Mt.-U.S.] 43 Eb 48.30N 111.51W
Shelby [N.C.-U.S.] 44 Gh 35.17N 81.32W
Shelbyville [Il.-U.S.] 45 Lg 39.24N 88.48W
Shelbyville [In.-U.S.] 44 Ef 39.31N 85.47W
Shelbyville [Tn.-U.S.] 44 Dh 35.29N 86.27W
Shelbyville, Lake- 45 Lg 39.30N 88.40W
Sheldon 45 Ie 43.11N 95.51W
Sheldon Point 40 Gd 63.32N 164.52W
Shelikhov Gulf (EN)=
Šelihova, Zaliv- 21 Rc 60.00N 158.00 E
Shelikof Strait 40 Ie 57.30N 155.00W
Shell 46 Ld 44.33N 107.44W
Shellbrook 42 Gf 53.13N 106.24W
Shellharbour 58 Gh 34.35S 150.52 E
Shelter Point 62 Cg 47.06S 168.13 E
Shelton 46 Dc 47.13N 123.06W
Shenandoah 45 If 40.46N 95.22W
Shenandoah Mountain 44 Hf 38.58N 79.00W
Shenandoah Valley 44 Hf 38.45N 78.45W
Shenchi 28 Be 39.05N 112.11 E
Shendam 34 Gd 8.53N 9.32 E
Shending Shan 27 Nb 46.34N 133.27 E
Shenge 34 Cd 7.55N 12.57W
Shëngjini 15 Ch 41.49N 19.35 E
Shengsi (Caiyuanzhen) 28 Gi 30.42N 122.29 E
Shengsi Liedao 27 Le 30.45N 122.40 E
Shengxian 27 Lf 29.35N 120.45 E
Shengze 28 Fi 30.55N 120.39 E
Shenjiamen → Putuo 28 Gj 29.57N 122.18 E
Shenmu 27 Jd 38.52N 110.35 E
Shenqiu (Huaidian) 27 Ke 33.27N 115.05 E
Shensi (EN)=Shaan-hsi
Sheng → Shaanxi Sheng [2] 27 Id 36.00N 109.00 E
Shensi (EN)=Shaanxi
Sheng (Shaan-hsi Sheng)
[2] 27 Id 36.00N 109.00 E
Shenton, Mount- 59 Ee 28.00S 123.22 E
Shenxian 28 Ce 38.01N 115.33 E
Shenyang (Mukden) 22 Oe 41.48N 123.24 E
Shenze 28 Ce 38.11N 115.11 E
Shepherd, Iles-=Shepherd
Islands (EN) 63b Dc 16.55S 168.35 E
Shepherd Islands (EN)=
Shepherd, Iles- 63b Dc 16.55S 168.35 E
Shepparton 58 Fh 36.23S 145.25 E
Sheppey 9 Nj 51.24N 0.50 E
Shepshed 12 Ab 52.45N 1.17W
Sheqi 28 Bh 33.04N 112.56 E
Sherard, Cape - 42 Jb 74.36N 80.10W
Sherard Osborn Fjord 41 Gb 82.10N 51.30W
Sherborne 9 Kk 50.57N 2.31W
Sherbro Island 30 Fh 7.33N 12.42W
Sherbrooke 39 Le 45.24N 71.54W
Sherda 35 Ba 20.08N 16.45 E
Shere Hill 34 Gd 9.57N 9.03 E
Sheridan [Mt.-U.S.] 46 Id 45.27N 112.12W
Sheridan [Wy.-U.S.] 39 Ie 44.48N 106.58W
Sheridan Lake 45 Eg 38.30N 102.15W
Sheringham 9 Oi 52.57N 1.12 E
Sherman 43 He 33.38N 96.36W
Sherman Station 44 Mc 45.54N 68.26W
Sherridon 42 He 55.07N 101.05W
's-Hertogenbosch/Den
Bosch 11 Lc 51.41N 5.19 E
Sherwood Forest 9 Lh 53.10N 1.10W
She Shui 28 Ci 30.52N 114.22 E
Shetland [3] 9 La 60.30N 1.30W
Shetland Islands (Zetland)
5 Fc 60.30N 1.30W
Shewa [3] 35 Fd 9.20N 38.55 E
Shewa Gimira 35 Fd 7.00N 35.50 E
Shexian 28 Bf 36.33N 113.40 E
Shexian (Huicheng) 28 Ej 29.53N 118.27 E
Sheyang (Hede) 28 Fh 33.47N 120.15 E
Sheyenne River 43 Hb 47.05N 96.50W
Shiant Islands 9 Gd 57.54N 6.30W
Shibām 35 Hb 15.56N 48.38 E
Shibamīnah, Wādī- 23 Ie 22.12N 55.30 E
Shibata [Jap.] 28 Of 37.57N 139.20 E
Shibata [Jap.] 29 Gb 38.05N 140.50 E
Shibayama-Gata 29 Ec 36.21N 136.23 E
Shibazhan 27 Ma 42.28N 125.20 E
Shibecha 28 Rc 43.17N 144.36 E
Shibetsu [Jap.] 28 Rc 43.40N 145.08 E
Shibetsu [Jap.] 27 Pc 44.10N 142.23 E
Shibetsu-Gawa 29a Db 43.40N 145.06 E
Shibīn al Kawm 33 Fc 30.33N 31.01 E
Shibiutan 29a Ca 44.47N 142.35 E
Shibi-Zan 29 Bf 31.59N 130.22 E
Shīb Kūh 23 Hd 27.20N 52.40 E
Shibukawa 28 Of 36.29N 139.00 E
Shibushi 29 Bf 31.28N 131.07 E
Shibushi-Wan 28 Ki 31.25N 131.12 E
Shichinohe 29 Ga 40.41N 141.10 E
Shichiyo Islands 64d Bb 7.23N 151.40 E
Shidao 27 Ld 36.51N 122.18 E
Shido 29 Dd 34.19N 134.10 E
Shidongsi → Gaolan 27 Hd 36.23N 103.55 E
Shiel, Loch- 9 He 56.50N 5.50W
Shiga Ken [2] 28 Ng 35.15N 136.10 E
Shigu 27 Gf 26.54N 99.44 E
Shi He 28 Ch 32.32N 115.52 E
Shihezi 27 Ec 44.18N 86.02 E
Shiiba 29 Be 32.28N 131.09 E
Shijaku 15 Ch 41.20N 19.34 E
Shijiazhuang 22 Nf 38.00N 114.30 E
Shijiusuo 28 Eg 35.24N 119.32 E
Shika 29 Ec 37.01N 136.46 E
Shikabe 29a Bb 42.02N 140.47 E
Shikārpur 25 Dc 27.57N 68.38 E
Shiki Islands 64d Bb 7.24N 151.53 E
Shikine-Jima 29 Fd 34.19N 139.13 E
Shikoku 21 Pf 33.30N 133.30 E
Shikoku Basin (EN) 27 Oe 30.00N 135.30 E
Shikoku-Sanchi 29 Ce 33.45N 133.35 E
Shilabo 35 Gd 6.05N 44.45 E
Shiliguri 22 Kg 26.42N 88.26 E
Shiliu → Changjiang 27 Ih 19.20N 109.03 E
Shilla 25 Fb 32.24N 78.12 E
Shillong 22 Lg 25.34N 91.53 E
Shimabara 28 Kh 32.47N 130.22 E
Shimabara-Hantō 29 Be 32.45N 130.15 E
Shimabara-Wan 29 Be 32.50N 130.30 E
Shimada 29 Fd 34.49N 138.09 E
Shima-Hantō 29 Ed 34.25N 136.45 E
Shimane-Hantō 29 Cd 35.30N 133.00 E
Shimane Ken [2] 28 Lg 35.00N 132.20 E
Shimanto-Gawa 29 Ce 32.56N 133.00 E
Shimaura-Tō 29 Bd 34.50N 131.50 E
Shimian 27 Hf 29.10N 102.26 E
Shimizu [Jap.] 29a Cb 43.01N 142.51 E
Shimizu [Jap.] 28 Og 35.01N 138.29 E
Shimla 22 Jf 31.06N 77.10 E
Shimoda 28 Og 34.40N 138.57 E
Shimodate 29 Fc 36.19N 139.58 E
Shimoga 22 Jh 13.55N 75.34 E
Shimo-Jima 29 Be 32.25N 130.05 E
Shimokawa 29a Ca 44.18N 142.38 E
Shimokita-Hantō 29a Bc 41.15N 141.05 E
Shimo-Koshiki-Jima 29 Af 31.40N 129.40 E
Shimo la Tewa 36 Gc 3.57S 39.44 E
Shimoni 36 Gc 4.39S 39.23 E
Shimonoseki 27 Ne 33.57N 130.57 E
Shimono-Shima 29 Ad 34.15N 129.15 E
Shimotsu 29 Dd 34.07N 135.08 E
Shimotsuma 29 Fc 36.11N 139.58 E
Shin, Loch- 9 Ic 58.07N 4.32W
Shinano 29 Fc 36.47N 138.10 E
Shinano-Gawa 29 Fc 37.57N 139.04 E
Shināş 24 Qj 24.43N 56.27 E
Shindand 23 Jc 33.18N 62.08 E
Shinga 36 Dc 3.16S 24.38 E
Shingbwiyang 25 Jc 26.41N 96.13 E
Shingū 27 Oe 33.44N 135.59 E
Shingwidzi 37 Ed 23.01S 30.43 E
Shinji 29 Cd 35.24N 132.54 E
Shinji-Ko 28 Lg 35.27N 133.02 E
Shinjō 27 Pd 38.46N 140.18 E
Shinkafe 34 Gc 13.05N 6.31 E
Shinminato 29 Ec 36.47N 137.04 E
Shinnanyō 29 Bd 34.05N 131.45 E
Shinshiro 29 Ed 34.53N 137.30 E
Shintoku 28 Qc 43.12N 142.55 E
Shintotsugawa 29a Bb 43.32N 141.40 E
Shinyanga 31 Ki 3.40S 33.26 E
Shinyanga [3] 36 Fc 3.30S 33.00 E
Shiogama 29 Gb 38.19N 141.01 E
Shiojiri 28 Nf 36.06N 137.58 E
Shiokubi-Misaki 29a Bc 41.43N 140.57 E
Shio-no-Misaki 27 Oe 33.25N 135.45 E
Shipai → Huaining 28 Di 30.25N 116.39 E

Index Symbols

[1] Independent Nation
[2] State, Region
[3] District, County
[4] Municipality
[5] Colony, Dependency
Continent
Physical Region
Historical or Cultural Region
Mount, Mountain
Volcano
Hill
Mountains, Mountain Range
Hills, Escarpment
Plateau, Upland
Pass, Gap
Plain, Lowland
Delta
Salt Flat
Valley, Canyon
Crater, Cave
Karst Features
Depression
Polder
Desert, Dunes
Forest, Woods
Heath, Steppe
Oasis
Cape, Point
Coast, Beach
Cliff
Peninsula
Isthmus
Sandbank
Island
Atoll
Rock, Reef
Islands, Archipelago
Rocks, Reefs
Coral Reef
Well, Spring
Geyser
River, Stream
Waterfall Rapids
River Mouth, Estuary
Lake
Salt Lake
Intermittent Lake
Reservoir
Swamp, Pond
Canal
Glacier
Ice Shelf, Pack Ice
Ocean
Sea
Gulf, Bay
Strait, Fjord
Lagoon
Bank
Seamount
Tablemount
Ridge
Shelf
Basin
Escarpment, Sea Scarp
Fracture
Trench, Abyss
National Park, Reserve
Point of Interest
Recreation Site
Cave, Cavern
Historic Site
Ruins
Wall, Walls
Church, Abbey
Temple
Scientific Station
Airport
Port
Lighthouse
Mine
Tunnel
Dam, Bridge

Shiping 27 Hg 23.44N 102.28 E
Shipki La 27 Ce 31.49N 78.45 E
Shippegan 42 Lg 47.45N 64.42W
Shiprock 45 Bh 36.47N 108.41W
Shipshaw, Rivière- 44 La 48.30N 71.15W
Shipu 28 Fj 29.17N 121.57 E
Shipugi Shankou 27 Ce 31.49N 78.45 E
Shiquan 27 Ie 33.05N 108.15 E
Shiquanhe 22 Jf 32.24N 79.52 E
Shiquan He 27 Ce 32.28N 79.44 E
Shiragami Dake 29 Ga 40.30N 140.01 E
Shiragami-Misaki 28 Pd 41.25N 140.12 E
Shirahama 29 De 33.40N 135.20 E
Shirakawa [Jap.] 29 Ed 35.36N 137.12 E
Shirakawa [Jap.] 29 Ec 36.17N 136.53 E
Shirakawa [Jap.] 28 Pf 37.07N 140.13 E
Shirane-San [Jap.] 27 Od 36.48N 139.22 E
Shirane-San [Jap.] 29 Fd 35.40N 138.13 E
Shirane-San [Jap.] 29 Fc 36.38N 138.32 E
Shiranuka 28 Rc 42.57N 144.05 E
Shiraoi 28 Pc 42.31N 141.16 E
Shirase Coast 66 Mf 78.30S 156.00W
Shirataka 29 Gb 38.11N 140.06 E
Shirataki 29a Cb 43.53N 143.09 E
Shīrāz 22 Hg 29.36N 52.32 E
Shirbīn 24 Dg 31.11N 31.32 E
Shire 30 Kj 17.42S 35.19 E
Shiren 28 Id 41.54N 126.34 E
Shiretoko-Dake 29a Da 44.15N 145.14 E
Shiretoko-Hantō 29a Da 44.00N 145.00 E
Shiretoko-Misaki 27 Qc 44.21N 145.20 E
Shīrgāh 24 Od 36.17N 52.54 E
Shiribetsu-Gawa 29a Bb 42.52N 140.21 E
Shiriha-Misaki 29a Db 42.56N 144.45 E
Shirikishinai 29a Bc 41.48N 141.05 E
Shīrīn 24 Qi 27.10N 56.41 E
Shīrīn sū 24 Me 35.29N 48.27 E
Shiriya-Zaki 27 Pc 41.26N 141.28 E
Shīr Kūh 21 Hf 31.37N 54.04 E
Shirley Mountains 46 Le 42.15N 106.30W
Shiroishi 28 Pe 38.00N 140.37 E
Shirone 29 Fc 37.46N 139.00 E
Shirotori 29 Ed 35.53N 136.52 E
Shirouma-Dake 29 Ec 36.45N 137.46 E
Shirshov Ridge (EN) 20 Me 57.30N 171.00 E
Shīrvān 24 Lf 33.33N 46.49 E
Shirwan Mazin 24 Kd 37.03N 44.10 E
Shishaldin Volcano 38 Cd 54.45N 163.57W
Shishi-Jima 28 Be 32.17N 130.15 E
Shishmaref 40 Fc 66.14N 166.09W
Shishou 27 Jf 29.42N 112.23 E
Shitai (Qili) 28 Di 30.12N 117.28 E
Shitara 29 Ed 35.05N 137.34 E
Shitou Shan 27 Ma 51.02N 125.12 E
Shivwits Plateau 46 Ih 36.10N 113.40W
Shiwa 28 Pe 39.33N 141.35 E
Shiwan Dashan 27 Ig 21.45N 107.35 E
Shiwa Ngandu 26 Ff 11.12S 31.43 E
Shiwpuri 25 Fc 25.26N 77.39 E
Shixian 28 Jc 43.05N 129.46 E
Shiyan 27 Je 32.34N 110.48 E
Shiyang He 27 Hd 39.00N 103.25 E
Shizilu → Junan 28 Eg 35.10N 118.50 E
Shizugawa 29 Gb 38.40N 141.28 E
Shizui 28 Ic 43.03N 126.09 E
Shizuishan (Dawukou) 27 Id 39.03N 106.24 E
Shizukuishi 29 Gb 39.42N 140.59 E
Shizunai 28 Qc 42.20N 142.22 E
Shizunai-Gawa 29a Cb 42.20N 142.22 E
Shizuoka 22 Pf 34.58N 138.23 E
Shizuoka Ken [2] 29 Gd 35.00N 138.25 E
Shkodra 6 Hg 42.05N 19.30 E
Shkodrës, Liqen i-=Scutari, Lake- (EN) 5 Hg 42.10N 19.20 E
Shkumbini 15 Ch 41.01N 19.26 E
Shoal Lake 45 Fa 50.26N 100.34W
Shoal Lake 45 Ib 49.32N 95.00W
Shoal Lakes 45 Ha 50.20N 97.40W
Shōbara 28 Lg 34.51N 133.01 E
Shodo-Shima 29 Dd 34.30N 134.15 E
Shō-Gawa 29 Ec 36.47N 137.04 E
Shokanbetsu-Dake 29a Bb 43.43N 141.31 E
Shokotsu-Gawa 29a Ca 44.23N 143.17 E
Sholāpur → Solāpur 22 Jh 17.41N 75.55 E
Shoqān 24 Qd 37.20N 56.58 E
Shorānūr 25 Ff 10.46N 76.17 E
Shoreham-by-Sea 9 Mk 50.49N 0.16W
Shortland Islands 60 Fi 6.55S 155.53 E
Shosambetsu 29a Ba 44.32N 141.46 E
Shoshone 46 He 42.56N 114.24W
Shoshone Mountains 43 Dd 39.15N 117.25W
Shoshone Peak 46 Gh 36.56N 116.16W
Shoshone River 46 Kd 44.52N 108.11W
Shoshong 37 Dd 23.02S 26.31 E
Shoshoni 46 Ke 43.14N 108.07W
Shotor Khūn 23 Jc 34.20N 64.55 E
Shouchang 28 Ej 29.23N 119.12 E
Shouguang 28 Ef 36.53N 118.44 E
Shouxian (Shouyang) 28 Dh 32.35N 116.47 E
Shouyang → Shouxian 28 Dh 32.35N 116.47 E
Shōwa 29 Gb 39.51N 140.03 E
Show Low 46 Ji 34.15N 110.02W
Shqiperia=Albania (EN) [1] 6 Hg 41.00N 20.00 E
Shreveport 39 Jf 32.30N 93.45W
Shrewsbury 9 Ki 52.43N 2.45W
Shuangcheng 27 Mb 45.21N 126.17 E
Shuangjiang 27 Gg 23.27N 99.50 E
Shuangjiang → Tongdao 27 If 26.14N 109.45 E
Shuangliao 27 Lc 43.30N 123.30 E
Shuangyang 27 Mc 43.31N 125.28 E
Shuangyashan 27 Pe 46.37N 131.10 E
Shucheng 28 Di 31.28N 116.57 E
Shufu 27 Cd 39.27N 75.52 E
Shuguri Falls 36 Gd 8.31S 37.23 E
Shu He 28 Eg 34.07N 118.30 E
Shuicheng 27 Hf 26.34N 104.52 E
Shuiding → Huocheng 27 Dc 44.03N 80.49 E
Shuiji → Laixi 28 Ff 36.52N 120.31 E
Shuijiahu → Changfeng 28 Dh 32.29N 117.10 E
Shuikou → Jianghua 27 Jg 24.58N 111.56 E
Shuiye 28 Cf 36.08N 114.06 E
Shuizhai → Xiangcheng 28 Ch 33.27N 114.53 E
Shūl 24 Ng 30.10N 51.38 E
Shulan 27 Mc 44.26N 126.55 E
Shule 27 Cd 39.25N 76.06 E
Shule He 21 Le 40.20N 92.50 E
Shulu (Xinji) 28 Cf 37.56N 115.14 E
Shumagin Islands 40 He 55.07N 159.45W
Shumarinai-Ko 29a Ca 44.20N 142.13 E
Shunayn, Sabkhat- 33 Dc 30.10N 21.00 E
Shungnak 40 Hc 66.53N 157.02W
Shunyi 28 Dd 40.09N 116.38 E
Shuolong 27 Ig 22.51N 106.55 E
Shuoxian 27 Jd 39.18N 112.25 E
Shūr [Iran] 24 Pi 26.59N 55.47 E
Shūr [Iran] 24 Oh 28.12N 52.09 E
Shūr [Iran] 24 Ne 35.09N 51.30 E
Shūr [Iran] 24 Oh 28.33N 53.12 E
Shūr Āb 24 Pg 31.45N 55.15 E
Shurāb 23 Ic 33.07N 55.18 E
Shūsf 23 Jc 31.48N 60.01 E
Shūsh 24 Mf 32.12N 48.17 E
Shushica 15 Ci 40.34N 19.34 E
Shūshtar 23 Gc 32.03N 48.51 E
Shuswap Lake 46 Fa 50.57N 119.15W
Shūt 24 Oe 34.44N 52.53 E
Shuwak 35 Fc 14.23N 35.52 E
Shuyang 27 Ke 34.01N 118.52 E
Shuzenji 29 Fd 34.58N 138.55 E
Shwebo 25 Jd 22.34N 95.42 E
Shwell 25 Jd 23.56N 96.17 E
Shyok 25 Fa 35.13N 75.53 E
Sia 26 Jh 6.49S 134.19 E
Siagne 11 Mk 43.32N 6.57 E
Siāh Band 23 Kc 33.25N 65.21 E
Sīāh-Chashmeh 24 Kc 39.04N 44.23 E
Sīāh-Kūh 24 Oe 34.38N 52.16 E
Siak 26 Df 1.13N 102.09 E
Sialkot [Pak.] 25 Ea 35.15N 73.17 E
Sialkot [Pak.] 22 Jf 32.30N 74.31 E
Sianów 10 Mb 54.15N 16.16 E
Siantan, Pulau- 26 Ef 3.10N 106.15 E
Siargao 26 Ie 9.53N 126.02 E
Šiaškotan, Ostrov- 21 Re 48.49N 154.06 E
Siátista 15 Ei 40.16N 21.33 E
Siau, Pulau- 26 If 2.42N 125.24 E
Šiauliai/Šjauljaj 6 Id 55.53N 23.19 E
Siavonga 37 Ef 16.32S 28.43 E
Siazan 19 Eg 41.04N 49.06 E
Sibā'i, Jabal as- 33 Fd 25.43N 34.09 E
Sibaj 19 Fe 52.42N 58.39 E
Sibari 14 Kk 39.45N 16.27 E
Sibasa 37 Ed 22.56S 30.29 E
Šibenik 14 Jg 43.44N 15.53 E
Siberimanua 26 Cg 2.09S 99.34 E
Siberut, Pulau- 21 Lj 1.20S 98.55 E
Siberut, Selat- 26 Cg 0.42S 98.35 E
Sibi 25 Dc 29.33N 67.53 E
Sibigo 26 Cf 2.51N 95.55 E
Sibillini, Monti- 14 Hh 42.55N 13.15 E
Sibircatajaha 17 Lb 69.05N 64.43 E
Sibircevo 28 Ih 44.16N 132.20 E
Sibirjakova, Ostrov- 20 Cb 72.50N 79.00 E
Sibiti 36 Bc 3.41S 13.21 E
Sibiu [2] 15 Hd 45.46N 24.12 E
Sibiu 6 If 45.48N 24.09 E
Sibolga 22 Li 1.45N 98.48 E
Sibsāgar 25 Ic 26.59N 94.38 E
Sibu 22 Ni 2.18N 111.49 E
Sibuguey Bay 26 He 7.30N 122.40 E
Sibut 31 Ih 5.44N 19.05 E
Sibutu Islands 26 Gf 4.45N 119.20 E
Sibutu Passage 26 Gf 4.56N 119.36 E
Sibuyan 26 Hd 12.25N 122.34 E
Sibuyan Sea 26 Hd 12.50N 122.40 E
Siby 34 Dc 12.22N 8.22W
Sibyllenstein 10 Ke 51.12N 14.05 E
Sicani, Monti- 14 Hm 37.40N 13.15 E
Sicasica 54 Eg 17.22S 67.45W
Si Chon 25 Jg 9.00N 99.56 E
Sichuan Pendi 21 Mf 30.01N 105.00 E
Sichuan Sheng (Ssu-ch'uan Sheng)=Szechwan (EN) [2] 27 He 30.00N 103.00 E
Sicilia [2] 14 Im 37.45N 14.15 E
Sicilia = Sicily (EN) 5 Hh 37.30N 14.00 E
Sicilia, Canale di-=Sicily, Strait of- (EN) 5 Hh 37.20N 11.20 E
Sicilia, Mar di- 14 Gn 36.30N 13.00 E
Sicily (EN) = Sicilia 5 Hh 37.30N 14.00 E
Sicily, Strait of- (EN)= Sicilia, Canale di- 5 Hh 37.20N 11.20 E
Sicily, Strait of- (EN)= Tūnis, Canal de- 5 Hh 37.20N 11.20 E
Sico Tinto, Río- 49 Ef 15.58N 84.58W
Sicuani 53 Ig 14.15S 71.15W
Šid 15 Cd 45.08N 19.14 E
Sidamo [3] 35 Fd 5.48N 38.50 E
Siddipet 25 Fe 18.06N 78.51 E
Side 24 Dd 36.46N 31.22 E
Sidéradougou 34 Ec 10.40N 4.15W
Siderno 14 Kl 38.16N 16.18 E
Siders/Sierre 14 Bd 46.17N 7.32 E
Siderty 19 He 52.32N 74.50 E
Siderty 19 He 51.40N 74.50 E
Sidheros, Ákra- 15 Jn 35.19N 26.19 E
Sidhirókastron 15 Gh 41.14N 23.23 E
Sīdī 'Abd ar Raḥmān 24 Cg 30.58N 28.44 E
Sidi Aich 13 Qh 36.37N 4.41 E
Sidi-Akacha 13 Nh 36.28N 1.18 E
Sidi Ali 13 Mh 36.06N 0.25 E
Sīdī'Alī al Makkī, Ra's- 14 Em 37.11N 10.17 E
Sīdī Barrānī 33 Ec 31.36N 25.55 E
Sidi Bel Abbes [3] 32 Gc 34.45N 0.35W
Sidi Bel Abbes 32 Gb 35.12N 0.38W
Sidi Bennour 32 Fc 32.39N 8.26W
Sidi di Daoud 13 Ph 36.51N 3.52 E
Sidi Ifni 31 Ff 29.33N 10.10W
Sidi Kacem 32 Fc 34.13N 5.42W
Sidikalang 26 Cf 2.45N 98.19 E
Sidi Lakhdar 13 Mh 36.10N 0.27 E
Sīdī Zayd, Jabal- 14 En 36.29N 10.20 E
Sidlaw Hills 9 Ke 56.30N 3.00W
Sidmouth 9 Jk 50.41N 3.15W
Sidney [B.C.-Can.] 42 Fg 48.39N 123.24W
Sidney [Mt.-U.S.] 43 Gb 47.43N 104.09W
Sidney [Nb.-U.S.] 43 Gc 41.09N 102.59W
Sidney [Oh.-U.S.] 44 Ee 40.16N 84.10W
Sidney Lanier, Lake- 44 Fh 34.15N 83.57W
Sidobre 11 Ik 43.40N 2.30 E
Sidorovsk 20 Dc 66.35N 82.30 E
Sidra 10 Tc 53.33N 23.30 E
Sidra, Gulf of-(EN)=Surt, Khalīj- 30 Ie 31.30N 18.00 E
Sidrolândia 55 Ee 20.55S 54.58W
Siedlce [2] 10 Sd 52.10N 22.15 E
Siedlce 10 Sd 52.11N 22.16 E
Siedlecka, Wysoczyzna- 10 Sd 52.10N 22.15 E
Sieg [Ger.] 10 Df 50.45N 7.05 E
Sieg [Ger.] 12 Kd 50.55N 8.01 E
Siegburg 10 Df 50.48N 7.12 E
Siegen 10 Ef 50.52N 8.02 E
Siemiatycze 10 Sd 52.26N 22.53 E
Siĕmréab 25 Kf 13.22N 103.51 E
Siena 14 Fg 43.19N 11.21 E
Sieniawa 10 Sf 50.11N 22.36 E
Sienne 11 Ee 49.00N 1.34W
Sieradz 10 Oe 51.36N 18.45 E
Sieradz [2] 10 Oe 51.35N 18.45 E
Sieradzka, Niecka- 10 Oe 51.35N 18.50 E
Sierck-les-Bains 12 Ie 49.26N 6.21 E
Sierpc 10 Pd 52.52N 19.41 E
Sierra Blanca 45 Dk 31.11N 105.21W
Sierra Blanca Peak 43 Fe 33.23N 105.48W
Sierra Colorada 56 Gf 40.35S 67.48W
Sierra Leone [1] 31 Fh 8.30N 11.30W
Sierra Leone Basin (EN) 3 Di 5.00N 17.00W
Sierra Leone Rise (EN) 3 Di 5.30N 21.00W
Sierra Madre 21 Oh 16.20N 122.00 E
Sierra Mojada 47 Dc 27.17N 103.42W
Sierre/Siders 14 Bd 46.17N 7.32 E
Siete Palmas 55 Cg 25.13S 58.20W
Siete Puntas, Río- 55 Df 23.34S 57.20W
Sieu 15 Hb 47.11N 24.13 E
Sifié 34 Dd 7.59N 6.55W
Sífnos 15 Hm 37.00N 24.40 E
Sig 32 Gb 35.32N 0.11W
Siğacik Körfezi 15 Jk 38.12N 26.45 E
Sigean 11 Ik 43.02N 2.59 E
Sighetu Marmaţiei 15 Gb 47.56N 23.53 E
Sighişoara 15 Hc 46.13N 24.48 E
Sigli 26 Ce 5.23N 95.57 E
Siglufjördur 7a Ba 66.09N 18.55W
Sigmaringen 10 Fh 48.05N 9.13 E
Signal Peak 46 Hj 33.22N 114.03W
Signy Island 66 Re 60.43S 45.38W
Signy-l'Abbaye 12 Ge 49.42N 4.25 E
Signy-le-Petit 12 Ge 49.54N 4.17 E
Sigtuna 7 Dg 59.37N 17.43 E
Siguanea, Ensenada de la- 49 Fc 21.38N 83.05W
Siguatepeque 49 Df 14.32N 87.49W
Sigüenza 13 Jc 41.04N 2.38W
Siguiri 31 Gg 11.25N 9.10W
Sigulda 7 Fh 57.09N 24.53 E
Si He 28 Dg 35.11N 116.42 E
Sihong 28 Eh 33.28N 118.13 E
Sihote-Alin 21 Pe 48.00N 138.00 E
Sihou → Changdao 28 Ff 37.56N 120.42 E
Sihuas 54 Ce 8.34S 77.37W
Siikainen 8 Ic 61.52N 21.50 E
Siilinjärvi 7 Ge 63.02N 27.40 E
Siirt 23 Fb 37.56N 41.57 E
Sijunjung 26 Dg 0.42S 100.58 E
Sikaiana 63a Fc 8.22S 162.45 E
Sikakap 26 Dg 2.46S 100.13 E
Sikanni Chief 42 Fe 58.17N 121.46W
Sīkar 25 Fc 27.37N 75.09 E
Sikasso 31 Gg 11.20N 5.40W
Sikasso [3] 34 Dc 10.55N 7.00W
Sikéa [Grc.] 15 Fm 36.46N 22.56 E
Sikéa [Grc.] 15 Gi 40.03N 23.58 E
Sikeston 43 Jd 36.53N 89.35W
Síkinos 15 Im 36.50N 25.05 E
Sikkim [3] 25 Hc 27.50N 88.30 E
Siklós 10 Ok 45.51N 18.18 E
Sikonge 36 Fd 5.38S 32.46 E
Šikotan, Ostrov/Tō, Shikotan- 20 Jh 43.47N 146.45 E
Siktjah 20 Hc 69.55N 125.10 E
Sil 13 Eb 42.27N 7.43W
Sila Grande 14 Kk 39.20N 16.30 E
Sila Greca 14 Kk 39.30N 16.30 E
Šilale/Šilalé 7 Fi 55.29N 22.12 E
Šilalé/Šilale 7 Fi 55.29N 22.12 E
Silao 48 Ig 20.56N 101.26W
Silaogou 28 Be 39.59N 113.03 E
Sila Piccola 14 Kk 39.05N 16.35 E
Silba 14 If 44.23N 14.42 E
Silchar 25 Id 24.49N 92.48 E
Silda 16 Ud 51.47N 59.50 E
Sildagapet 8 Ab 62.05N 5.10 E
Sile 14 Ge 45.28N 12.35 E
Şile 24 Cb 41.05N 29.35 E
Silega 19 Ec 64.03N 44.02 E
Silesia (EN)=Śląsk 10 Me 51.00N 16.45 E
Silesia (EN)=Śląsk 10 Me 51.00N 16.45 E
Silet 32 He 22.39N 4.35 E
Silhouette Island 37b Ca 4.29S 55.14 E
Silifke 23 Db 36.22N 33.56 E
Siligir 20 Gc 68.27N 114.50 E
Siling Co 21 Kf 31.50N 89.00 E
Siling Jiao 27 Ke 8.20N 115.27 E
Silisili, Mauga- 65c Aa 13.35S 172.27W
Silistra [2] 15 Kf 44.07N 27.16 E
Silistra 15 Ke 44.07N 27.16 E
Silivri 24 Cb 41.04N 28.15 E
Siljan 7 Df 60.50N 14.45 E
Šilka 20 Gf 51.51N 116.02 E
Šilka 21 Od 53.22N 121.32 E
Silkeborg 7 Bh 56.10N 9.34 E
Sillamäe/Sillamjae 7 Gg 59.24N 27.43 E
Sillamjae/Sillamäe 7 Gg 59.24N 27.43 E
Sillaro 14 Ff 44.34N 11.51 E
Silleiro, Cabo- 13 Db 42.07N 8.54W
Sillé-le-Guillaume 11 Ff 48.12N 0.08W
Sillian 14 Gd 46.45N 12.25 E
Silil 35 Gc 11.00N 43.26 E
Siloam Springs 45 Ih 36.11N 94.32W
Siloana Plains 36 Df 17.15S 23.10 E
Šilovo 19 Ee 54.24N 40.52 E
Silsbee 45 Ik 30.21N 94.11W
Siltou 35 Bb 16.52N 15.43 E
Šilutė/Šilute 19 Cd 55.21N 21.30 E
Šilute/Šilutė 19 Cd 55.21N 21.30 E
Silvan 24 Ic 38.08N 41.01 E
Silvassa 25 Ed 20.20N 73.05 E
Silver Bank (EN) 49 Mc 20.30N 69.45W
Silver Bay 43 Ib 47.17N 91.16W
Silver City 43 Fe 32.46N 108.17W
Silverdalen 8 Fg 57.32N 15.44 E
Silver Lake 46 Ee 43.06N 120.53W
Silver Spring 44 If 39.02N 77.03W
Silver Springs 46 Fg 39.25N 119.13W
Silverthrone Mountain 46 Ba 51.31N 126.06W
Silverton [Co.-U.S.] 45 Ch 37.49N 107.40W
Silverton [Tx.-U.S.] 45 Fi 34.28N 101.19W
Silves [Braz.] 54 Gd 2.54S 58.27W
Silves [Port.] 13 Dg 37.11N 8.26W
Silvi 14 Ih 42.34N 14.06 E
Silvia 54 Cc 2.37N 76.24W
Silviers River 46 Fe 43.22N 118.48W
Silvretta 14 Ed 46.50N 10.15 E
Silyānah [3] 32 Ib 36.00N 9.30 E
Silyānah 32 Ib 36.05N 9.22 E
Silyānah, Wādī- 14 Dn 36.33N 9.25 E
Sim 17 Hi 54.59N 57.40 E
Sim 17 Hi 54.32N 56.30 E
Sim, Cap- 32 Fc 31.23N 9.51W
Simanggang 26 Ff 1.15N 111.26 E
Šimanovsk 20 Hf 52.01N 127.36 E
Simao 27 Hg 22.40N 101.02 E
Simard, Lac- 44 Hb 47.38N 78.40W
Simareh 24 Mf 32.08N 48.03 E
Simav 23 Ca 40.23N 28.31 E
Simav 24 Cc 39.05N 28.59 E
Simav Dağ 15 Lj 39.04N 28.54 E
Simav Gölü 15 Lj 39.09N 28.55 E
Simayama-Jima 29 Ae 32.40N 128.38 E
Simba 36 Db 0.36N 22.55 E
Simbo 36 Fc 4.53S 29.44 E
Simbo 63a Cc 8.18S 156.34 E
Simbruini, Monti- 14 Hj 41.55N 13.15 E
Simcoe 44 Gd 42.50N 80.18W
Simcoe, Lake - 42 Jh 44.27N 79.20W
Simen 35 Fc 13.25N 38.00 E
Simenti 34 Cc 13.00N 13.25W
Simeria 15 Gd 45.51N 23.01 E
Simeto 14 Jm 37.24N 15.06 E
Simeulue, Pulau- 21 Li 2.35N 96.05 E
Simferopol 6 Jf 44.57N 34.06 E
Simhah, Jabal- 23 Hf 17.20N 54.50 E
Simi 15 Km 36.36N 27.50 E
Simi 15 Km 36.35N 27.50 E
Simiti 49 Kj 7.58N 73.58W
Simitli 15 Gh 41.53N 23.06 E
Šimleu Silvaniei 15 Fb 47.14N 22.48 E
Simmental 14 Bd 46.35N 7.25 E
Simmerath 12 Id 50.36N 6.18 E
Simmerbach 12 Je 49.48N 7.31 E
Simmern 10 Dg 49.59N 7.31 E
Simmertal 12 Je 49.48N 7.33 E
Simnas 8 Jj 54.20N 23.45 E
Simo 7 Fd 65.39N 24.55 E
Simojärvi 7 Gc 66.06N 27.03 E
Simojoki 7 Fd 65.37N 25.03 E
Simojovel de Allende 48 Mi 17.12N 92.38W
Simonstown 37 Bf 34.14S 18.26 E
Simpele 7 Gf 61.26N 29.22 E
Simpelejärvi 8 Mc 61.30N 29.25 E
Simplon 14 Bd 46.15N 8.00 E
Simpson Desert 57 Eg 25.00S 137.00 E
Simpson Hill 59 Fe 26.30S 126.30 E
Simpson Peninsula 42 Ic 68.45N 89.10W
Simrishamn 7 Di 55.33N 14.20 E
Simsonbaai 51b Ab 18.02N 63.08W
Simušir, Ostrov- 21 Re 46.58N 152.02 E
Sina 25 Fe 17.22N 75.54 E
Sīnā'=Sinai Peninsula (EN) 30 Kf 29.30N 34.00 E
Sinabang 26 Cf 2.29N 96.23 E
Sinadogo 35 Hd 5.22N 46.22 E
Sinai, Mount- (EN)=Mūsa, Jabal- 24 Eh 28.32N 33.59 E
Sinaia 15 Id 45.21N 25.33 E
Sinai Peninsula (EN)= Sīnā' 30 Kf 29.30N 34.00 E
Sinajana 64c Bb 13.28N 144.45W
Sinaloa [2] 47 Cc 25.00N 107.30W
Sinaloa, Llanos de- 47 Cc 25.00N 107.30W
Sinaloa, Río- 48 Ee 25.18N 108.30W
Sinaloa de Leyva 48 Ee 25.50N 108.14W
Sinalunga 14 Fg 43.12N 11.44 E
Sinamaica 54 Da 11.05N 71.51W
Sinan 27 If 27.56N 108.11 E
Sinara 17 Kh 56.17N 62.23 E
Sināwin 33 Bc 31.02N 10.36 E
Sinazongwe 36 Ef 17.15S 27.28 E
Şincai 15 Hc 46.39N 24.23 E
Sincanli 24 Dc 38.45N 30.15 E
Sincé 49 Ji 9.14N 75.06W
Sincelejo 53 Ie 9.18N 75.24W
Sinch'am 28 Jc 42.07N 129.25 E
Sinch'ang 28 Jd 40.07N 128.28 E
Sinch'on 28 He 38.28N 125.27 E
Sinclair, Lake- 44 Fi 33.11N 83.16W
Sind [3] 25 Cc 25.30N 69.00 E
Sind 21 Ig 25.30N 69.00 E
Sindal 8 Dg 57.28N 10.13 E
Sindangbarang 26 Eh 7.27S 107.08 E
Sindara 36 Bc 1.02S 10.40 E
Sindelfingen-Böblingen 10 Fh 48.41N 9.01 E
Sindfeld 12 Kc 51.32N 8.48 E
Sindi 7 Fg 58.24N 24.42 E
Sındırgı 24 Cc 39.14N 28.10 E
Sindirgi Geçidi 15 Lj 39.10N 28.04 E
Sindominic 15 Ic 46.35N 25.47 E
Sindri 25 Hd 23.42N 86.29 E
Sinegorje 20 Kd 62.03N 150.25 E
Sinegorski 16 Le 48.00N 40.53 E
Šine-Ider 27 Gb 48.56N 99.33 E
Sinekli 15 Lh 41.14N 28.12 E
Sinelnikovo 16 Ie 48.18N 35.31 E
Sines 13 Dg 37.57N 8.52W
Sines, Cabo de- 13 Dg 37.57N 8.53W
Sine-Saloum [3] 34 Bc 14.00N 15.50W
Singako 35 Bd 9.50N 19.29 E
Singapore / Singapura 22 Mi 1.17N 103.51 E
Singapore Strait (EN)= Singapura, Selat- 26 Df 1.15N 104.00 E
Singapura / Singapore 22 Mi 1.17N 103.51 E
Singapura, Selat-= Singapore Strait (EN) 26 Df 1.15N 104.00 E
Singaraja 26 Gh 8.07S 115.06 E
Singatoka 63d Ac 18.08S 177.30 E
Sing Buri 25 Kf 14.53N 100.25 E
Singen 10 Ei 47.46N 8.50 E
Sîngeroz Băi 15 Hb 47.22N 24.41 E
Singida [3] 36 Fd 5.30S 34.30 E
Singida 31 Ki 4.49S 34.45 E
Singitic Gulf (EN) = Singitikós Kólpos 15 Gi 40.10N 23.55 E
Singitikós Kólpos = Singitic Gulf (EN) 15 Gi 40.10N 23.55 E
Singkaling Hkamti 25 Jc 26.00N 95.42 E
Singkang 26 Hg 4.08S 120.01 E
Singkawang 26 Ef 0.54N 109.00 E
Singkep, Pulau- 26 Dg 0.30S 104.25 E
Singkil 26 Cf 2.17N 97.49 E
Singleton [Austl.] 59 Kf 32.34S 151.10 E
Singleton [Eng.-U.K.] 12 Bd 50.55N 0.44W
Singleton, Mount- 59 De 29.28S 117.18 E
Singö 8 Hd 60.10N 18.45 E
Siniscola 14 Dj 40.34N 9.41 E
Sini vrăh 15 Ih 41.51N 25.01 E
Sinj 14 Kg 43.42N 16.38 E
Sinjah 35 Ec 13.09N 33.56 E
Sinjai 26 Hh 5.07S 120.15 E
Sinjaja 8 Mg 57.05N 28.33 E
Sinjajevina 15 Cf 43.00N 19.18 E
Sinjār 24 Id 36.19N 41.52 E
Sinjār, Jabal- 24 Id 36.23N 41.52 E
Sinjuža 16 Ge 48.03N 30.50 E
Sinkiang (EN)= Hsin-chiang-wei-wu-erh Tzu-chih-ch'ü → Xinjiang Uygur Zizhiqu [2] 27 Ec 42.00N 86.00 E
Sinkiang (EN)= Xinjiang Uygur Zizhiqu (Hsin-chiang-wei-wu-erh Tzu-chih-ch'ü) [2] 27 Ec 42.00N 86.00 E
Sin-le-Noble 12 Fd 50.22N 3.07 E
Sinmi-Do 28 He 39.33N 124.53 E
Sinn 12 Kd 50.39N 8.20 E
Sinn al Kadhdhāb 33 Fe 23.30N 32.05 E
Sinnamary 54 Hb 5.23N 53.00W
Sinni 14 Kj 40.08N 16.41 E
Sinnicolau Mare 15 Dc 46.05N 20.38 E
Sinnūris 24 Dh 29.25N 30.52 E
Sinnyŏng 28 Jf 36.02N 128.47 E
Sinoe [3] 34 Dd 5.20N 8.40W
Sinoe, Lacul- 15 Le 44.38N 28.53 E
Sinop 23 Ea 41.59N 35.09 E
Sinop Burun 24 Fa 42.02N 35.12 E
Sinp'o 28 Jd 40.02N 128.12 E
Sinsang 28 Ie 39.39N 127.25 E
Sinsheim 10 Eg 49.15N 8.53 E
Sint-Amandsberg, Gent- 12 Fc 51.04N 3.45 E
Sîntana 15 Ec 46.21N 21.30 E
Sint-Andries, Brugge- 12 Fc 51.12N 3.10 E
Sîntang 26 Ff 0.04N 111.30 E
Sint Eustatius 47 Le 17.30N 62.59W
Sint-Gillis-Waas 12 Gc 51.13N 4.08 E
Sint Kruis 50 Bf 12.18N 69.08W
Sint Laureins 12 Fc 51.15N 3.31 E
Sint Maarten 50 Ec 18.04N 63.04W
Sint Nicolaas 50 Bf 12.26N 69.55W
Sint Niklaas/Saint-Nicolas 11 Kc 51.10N 4.08 E
Sint-Oedenrode 12 Hc 51.34N 5.28 E
Sinton 45 Hl 28.02N 97.33W
Sint-Pieters-Leeuw 12 Gd 50.47N 4.14 E
Sintra 13 Cf 38.48N 9.23W
Sint-Truiden/Saint-Trond 11 Ld 50.49N 5.12 E
Sintu 35 Fd 8.12N 36.56 E
Sinú, Río- 49 Ji 9.24N 75.49W
Sinŭiju 22 Oe 40.06N 124.24 E
Sinujīf 35 Hd 8.30N 48.59 E
Sinzig 12 Jd 50.33N 7.15 E
Sió 10 Oj 46.23N 18.40 E
Siocon 26 He 7.42N 122.08 E
Siófok 10 Oj 46.54N 18.03 E
Sioma 36 Df 16.40S 23.35 E

Index Symbols

[1] Independent Nation
[2] State, Region
[3] District, County
[4] Municipality
[5] Colony, Dependency
Continent
Physical Region
Historical or Cultural Region
Mount, Mountain
Volcano
Hill
Mountains, Mountain Range
Hills, Escarpment
Plateau, Upland
Pass, Gap
Plain, Lowland
Delta
Salt Flat
Valley, Canyon
Crater, Cave
Karst Features
Depression
Polder
Desert, Dunes
Forest, Woods
Heath, Steppe
Oasis
Cape, Point
Coast, Beach
Cliff
Peninsula
Isthmus
Sandbank
Island
Atoll
Rock, Reef
Islands, Archipelago
Rocks, Reefs
Coral Reef
Well, Spring
Geyser
River, Stream
Waterfall Rapids
River Mouth, Estuary
Lake
Salt Lake
Intermittent Lake
Reservoir
Swamp, Pond
Canal
Glacier
Ice Shelf, Pack Ice
Ocean
Sea
Gulf, Bay
Strait, Fjord
Lagoon
Bank
Seamount
Tablemount
Ridge
Shelf
Basin
Escarpment, Sea Scarp
Fracture
Trench, Abyss
National Park, Reserve
Point of Interest
Recreation Site
Cave, Cavern
Historic Site
Ruins
Wall, Walls
Church, Abbey
Temple
Scientific Station
Airport
Port
Lighthouse
Mine
Tunnel
Dam, Bridge

Index Symbols

- Independent Nation
- State, Region
- District, County
- Municipality
- Colony, Dependency
- Continent
- Physical Region

- Historical or Cultural Region
- Mount, Mountain
- Volcano
- Hill
- Mountains, Mountain Range
- Hills, Escarpment
- Plateau, Upland

- Pass, Gap
- Plain, Lowland
- Delta
- Salt Flat
- Valley, Canyon
- Crater, Cave
- Karst Features

- Depression
- Polder
- Desert, Dunes
- Forest, Woods
- Heath, Steppe
- Oasis
- Cape, Point

- Coast, Beach
- Cliff
- Peninsula
- Isthmus
- Sandbank
- Island
- Atoll

- Rock, Reef
- Islands, Archipelago
- Rocks, Reefs
- Coral Reef
- Well, Spring
- Geyser
- River, Stream

- Waterfall Rapids
- River Mouth, Estuary
- Lake
- Salt Lake
- Intermittent Lake
- Sea
- Swamp, Pond

- Canal
- Lagoon
- Bank
- Seamount
- Tablemount
- Ridge
- Shelf
- Strait, Fjord
- Gulf, Bay
- Basin

- Escarpment, Sea Scarp
- Glacier
- Ice Shelf, Pack Ice
- Ocean
- National Park, Reserve
- Point of Interest
- Recreation Site
- Cave, Cavern
- Fracture
- Trench, Abyss

- Historic Site
- Ruins
- Wall, Walls
- Church, Abbey
- Temple
- Scientific Station
- Airport
- Port
- Lighthouse
- Mine
- Tunnel
- Dam, Bridge

Sob 16 Fe 48.41N 29.17 E
Soba 34 Gc 10.59N 8.04 E
Sobaek-Sanmaek 28 Jf 36.00N 128.00 E
Sobat (EN)=Sawbā 30 Kh 9.45N 31.45 E
Sobernheim 12 Je 49.48N 7.39 E
Soběslav 10 Kg 49.16N 14.44 E
Sōbetsu 29a Bb 42.33N 140.51 E
Sobinka 7 Jh 56.01N 40.07 E
Sobolevo 16 Qd 51.59N 51.48 E
Sobolevo 20 Kf 54.17N 156.00 E
Sobolew 10 Re 51.41N 21.40 E
Sobo-San 29 Be 32.47N 131.21 E
Sobradinho 55 Fi 29.24S 53.03W
Sobral 53 Lf 3.42S 40.21W
Sobrarbe 13 Mb 42.20N 0.05 E
Soca 55 El 34.41S 55.41W
Soča=Isonzo (EN) 14 He 45.43N 13.33 E
Sochaczew 10 Qd 52.14N 20.14 E
Soči 6 Jg 43.35N 39.45 E
Société, Iles de la-=Society Islands (EN) 57 Lf 17.00S 150.00W
Society Islands (EN)=Société, Iles de la- 57 Lf 17.00S 150.00W
Socompa, Paso- 52 Jh 24.27S 68.18W
Socorro [Col.] 54 Db 6.27N 73.16W
Socorro [N.M.-U.S.] 43 Fe 34.04N 106.54W
Socotra (EN) = Suqutrá 21 Hh 12.30N 54.00 E
Soc Trang 25 Lg 9.36N 105.58 E
Socuéllamos 13 Je 39.17N 2.48W
Soda Lake 46 Gi 35.08N 116.04W
Sodankylä 7 Gc 67.25N 26.36 E
Soda Springs 46 Je 42.39N 111.36W
Söderåsen 8 Eh 56.04N 13.05 E
Söderfors 7 Df 60.23N 17.14 E
Söderhamn 7 Df 61.18N 17.03 E
Söderköping 8 Gf 58.29N 16.18 E
Södermanland 8 Ge 59.10N 16.50 E
Södermanland [2] 7 Dg 59.15N 16.40 E
Söderslätt 8 Ei 55.30N 13.15 E
Södertälje 7 Dg 59.12N 17.37 E
Södertörn 8 Ge 59.05N 18.00 E
Sodo 35 Fd 6.51N 37.45 E
Södra Dellen 8 Gc 61.50N 16.45 E
Södra Gloppet 8 Ia 63.05N 21.00 E
Södra Kvarken 8 Hd 60.20N 19.08 E
Södra-Midsjöbanken 8 Gi 55.40N 17.20 E
Södra Vi 8 Fg 57.45N 15.48 E
Soe 26 Hh 9.52S 124.17 E
Soekmekaar 37 Dd 23.28S 29.58 E
Soela, proliv-/Soela Väin 8 Jf 58.40N 22.30 E
Soela Väin/Soela, proliv- 8 Jf 58.40N 22.30 E
Soest [Ger.] 10 Ee 51.35N 8.07 E
Soest [Neth.] 12 Hb 52.10N 5.20 E
Soeste 12 Ja 53.10N 7.44 E
Soester Borde 12 Kc 51.38N 8.03 E
Soestwetering 12 Ib 51.30N 6.09 E
Sofádhes 15 Fj 39.20N 22.06 E
Sofala [3] 37 Ec 19.30S 34.40 E
Sofala, Baia de- 30 Kk 20.11S 34.45 E
Sofia 37 Hc 15.27S 47.23 E
Sofia [Bul.] [2] 15 Gg 42.43N 23.25 E
Sofia [Grc.] [2] 15 Gg 42.41N 23.19 E
Sofia (EN)=Sofija 6 Ig 42.41N 23.19 E
Sofija=Sofia (EN) 6 Ig 42.41N 23.19 E
Sofijsk 20 If 52.20N 134.01 E
Sofporog 19 Db 65.48N 31.28 E
Sofrána, Nisídhes- 15 Jm 36.04N 26.24 E
Sōfu-Gan 27 Pf 29.50N 140.20 E
Sogamoso 54 Db 5.43N 72.56W
Soganlı 24 Eb 41.11N 32.38 E
Sogara, Lake- 36 Fd 5.15S 31.00 E
Sogda 20 If 50.24N 132.18 E
Sögel 10 Dd 52.51N 7.31 E
Sogeri 60 Di 9.10S 147.32 E
Sogn 8 Ac 61.05N 5.55 E
Sogndalsfjøra 8 Bc 61.14N 7.06 E
Søgne 8 Bf 58.05N 7.49 E
Sognefjell 8 Bc 61.35N 7.55 E
Sognefjorden 5 Gc 61.05N 5.10 E
Sognesjøen 8 Ac 61.05N 5.00 E
Sogn og Fjordane [2] 7 Bf 61.30N 6.50 E
Sogod 26 Hd 10.23N 124.59 E
Sogo Nur 27 Hc 42.20N 101.20 E
Sogoža 7 Jg 58.30N 39.06 E
Söğüt 15 Nj 40.00N 30.11 E
Söğütalan 15 Li 40.03N 28.34 E
Söğüt Gölü 24 Cd 37.03N 29.53 E
Sog Xian 27 Fe 31.51N 93.42 E
Soh 18 He 39.57N 71.08 E
Sohag (EN)=Sawhāj 31 Kf 26.33N 31.42 E
Sohano 60 Ei 5.29S 154.41 E
Sohŭksan-Do 28 Hg 34.04N 125.07 E
Soignies/Zinnik 11 Kd 50.35N 4.04 E
Soini 8 Kb 62.52N 24.13 E
Soisalo 8 Mb 62.40N 28.10 E
Soissonnais, Plateau du- 11 Je 49.15N 3.10 E
Soissons 11 Je 49.22N 3.20 E
Sōja 29 Cd 34.40N 133.44 E
Sojana 7 Kd 65.53N 43.30 E
Sojma 17 Ec 67.00N 51.00 E
Šojna 17 Bc 67.52N 44.08 E
Sŏjosŏn-man=Korea Bay (EN) 21 Of 39.15N 125.00 E
Sojuznoje 16 Vd 50.50N 60.10 E
Sok 19 Fe 53.25N 50.10 E
Sokal 16 Dd 50.29N 24.17 E
Šokalskogo, Proliv- 20 Ea 79.00N 100.00 E
Sokch'o 27 Md 38.12N 128.36 E
Söke 23 Cb 37.45N 27.24 E
Sokele 36 Dd 9.55S 24.36 E
Sokirjany 16 Ee 48.28N 27.25 E
Sokna 7 Bf 60.14N 9.54 E
Soko Banja 15 Ef 43.39N 21.53 E
Sokodé 31 Hh 8.59N 1.08 E
Sokol 19 Ed 59.29N 40.13 E
Sokol 15 Ce 44.18N 19.25 E
Sokółka 10 Tc 53.25N 23.31 E
Sokolo 34 Dc 14.44N 6.07W
Sokolov 10 If 50.11N 12.38 E
Sokołów Podlaski 10 Sd 52.25N 22.15 E
Sokone 34 Bc 13.53N 16.22W
Sokosti 7 Gb 68.20N 28.01 E
Sokoto 30 Hg 11.24N 4.07 E
Sokoto [2] 34 Gc 12.20N 5.20 E
Sokoto 31 Hg 13.04N 5.15 E
Sokourala 34 Dd 9.13N 8.05W
Sōl 35 Hd 9.20N 49.25 E
Sōl 35 Hd 9.40N 48.30 E
Sol, Costa del- 13 Ih 36.46N 3.55W
Sol, Pico do- 55 Ke 20.07S 43.28W
Soła 10 Pf 50.04N 19.13 E
Sola 63b Ca 13.53S 167.33 E
Solai 36 Gb 0.02N 36.09 E
Solakrossen 8 Af 58.53N 5.36 E
Solander Island 61 Ci 46.35S 166.50 E
Solanet 55 Cm 36.51S 58.31W
Solāpur 22 Jh 17.41N 75.55 E
Solbad Hall in Tirol 14 Fc 47.17N 11.31 E
Solcy 19 Dd 58.09N 30.20 E
Sölden 14 Ed 46.58N 11.00 E
Soldier Point 51d Bb 17.02N 61.41W
Soldotna 40 Id 60.29N 151.04W
Solec Kujawski 10 Oc 53.06N 18.14 E
Soledad [Arg.] 55 Bj 30.37S 60.55W
Soledad [Ca.-U.S.] 46 Eh 36.26N 121.19W
Soledad [Col.] 54 Da 10.55N 74.46W
Soledad [Ven.] 54 Fb 8.10N 63.34W
Soledad, Boca de- 48 Ce 25.17N 112.09W
Soledad, Isla-/East Falkland 52 Kk 51.45S 58.50W
Soledade 56 Jc 28.50S 52.30W
Sølen 8 Dc 61.55N 11.30 E
Sølensjøen 8 Dc 61.55N 11.35 E
Solentiname, Archipiélago de- 49 Fh 11.10N 85.00W
Solenzara 11a Bb 41.51N 9.24 E
Solesmes 12 Fd 50.11N 3.30 E
Solferino 14 Ee 45.23N 10.34 E
Solgen 8 Fg 57.33N 15.07 E
Solgne 12 Ie 48.58N 6.18 E
Soligalič 7 Kg 59.07N 42.13 E
Soligorsk 19 Ce 52.49N 27.31 E
Solihull 9 Li 52.25N 1.45W
Solikamsk 19 Fd 59.39N 56.47 E
Sol-Ileck 6 Le 51.12N 55.03 E
Solimán, Punta- 48 Ph 19.50N 87.27W
Solimoes → Amazonas, Rio-=Amazon (EN) 52 Lf 0.10S 49.00W
Solingen 10 De 51.11N 7.05 E
Solińskie, Jezioro- 10 Sg 49.22N 22.30 E
Solis, Presa- 48 Ig 20.05N 100.36W
Sollebrunn 8 Ef 58.07N 12.32 E
Sollefteå 7 De 63.10N 17.16 E
Sollentuna 8 Ge 59.28N 17.54 E
Sóller 13 Oe 39.46N 2.42 E
Sollerön 8 Fd 60.55N 14.37 E
Solling 10 Fe 51.45N 9.35 E
Solms 12 Kd 50.46N 9.36 E
Solna 8 He 59.22N 18.01 E
Solnečnogorsk 7 Ih 56.10N 37.00 E
Solnečny 20 Id 60.10N 137.35 E
Sologne 11 Hg 47.50N 2.00 E
Sologne Bourbonnaise 11 Jh 46.40N 3.30 E
Solok 26 Dg 0.48S 100.39 E
Sololá [3] 49 Bf 14.40N 91.15W
Sololá 49 Bf 14.46N 91.11W
Solomon Islands [1] 58 Ge 8.00S 159.00 E
Solomon Islands 57 Ge 8.00S 159.00 E
Solomon Islands (British Solomon Islands) [1] 58 Ge 8.00S 159.00 E
Solomon River 43 Hd 38.54N 97.22W
Solomon Sea 57 Ge 8.00S 155.00 E
Solon Springs 45 Kc 46.22N 91.48W
Solør 8 Dd 60.30N 11.55 E
Solor, Kepulauan- 26 Hh 8.25S 123.30 E
Solothurn 14 Bc 47.15N 7.30 E
Solothurn [2] 14 Bc 47.20N 7.40 E
Solotvin 10 Uh 48.38N 24.31 E
Soloveckije Ostrova 7 Id 65.05N 35.45 E
Solovjevka 8 Nd 60.44N 30.20 E
Solovjevsk 20 Hf 54.15N 124.30 E
Solovjevsk 20 Gg 49.54N 115.43 E
Sölöz 15 Mi 40.23N 29.25 E
Solre-le-Château 12 Gd 50.10N 4.05 E
Solsona 13 Nc 41.59N 1.31 E
Solt 10 Oj 46.48N 19.00 E
Solta 14 Kg 43.23N 16.17 E
Soltānābād [Iran] 24 Mg 31.03N 49.42 E
Soltānābād [Iran] 24 Rd 36.23N 58.02 E
Solṭānī, Khowr-e- 24 Nh 29.00N 50.50 E
Soltāniyeh 24 Md 36.26N 48.48 E
Soltau 10 Fd 52.59N 9.50 E
Soltvadkert 10 Pj 46.35N 19.23 E
Solvang 46 Ei 34.36N 120.08W
Sölvesborg 7 Dh 56.03N 14.33 E
Solvyčegodsk 7 Lf 61.21N 46.52 E
Solway Firth 9 Jg 54.50N 3.35W
Solwezi 31 Jj 12.11S 26.24 E
Sōma 28 Pf 37.48N 140.57 E
Soma 24 Bc 39.10N 27.36 E
Somain 12 Fd 50.22N 3.17 E
Somalia (EN)=Soomaaliya [1] 31 Lh 10.00N 49.00 E
Somali Basin (EN) 3 Fi 0.00 52.00 E
Sombo 36 Dd 8.42S 20.57 E
Sombor 15 Cd 45.46N 19.07 E
Sombrereta 47 Dd 23.38N 103.39W
Sombrero 47 Le 18.36N 63.26W
Sombrero Channel 25 Ig 7.41N 93.35 E
Sombrio 55 Hi 29.07S 49.40W
Sombrio, Lagoa do- 55 Hi 29.12S 49.42W
Somcuṭa Mare 15 Gb 47.31N 23.28 E
Someren 12 Hc 51.23N 5.43 E
Somero 8 Jd 60.37N 23.32 E
Somerset 38 Jb 73.30N 93.30W
Somerset [3] 9 Jk 51.10N 3.10W
Somerset 9 Kj 51.00N 3.00W
Somerset [Austl.] 59 Ib 10.35S 142.15 E
Somerset [Ky.-U.S.] 43 Kd 37.05N 84.36W
Somerset [Pa.-U.S.] 44 He 40.02N 79.05W
Somerset East 37 Df 32.42S 25.35 E
Somerton 46 Hj 32.36N 114.43W
Somerville Lake 45 Hk 30.18N 96.40W
Someş 15 Fa 48.07N 22.20 E
Someşu Mare 15 Gb 47.09N 23.55 E
Someşu Mic 15 Gb 47.09N 23.55 E
Somme [3] 11 Id 49.55N 2.30 E
Somme 11 Hd 50.11N 1.39 E
Somme, Baie de- 12 Dd 50.14N 1.33 E
Somme, Bassurelle de la- 12 Dd 50.15N 1.10 E
Somme, Canal de la- 11 He 50.11N 1.39 E
Somme-Leuze 12 Hd 50.20N 5.22 E
Somme-Leuze-Hogne 12 Hd 50.15N 5.17 E
Sommen 7 Dh 58.00N 15.15 E
Sommen 8 Ff 58.08N 14.58 E
Sommepy-Tahure 12 Ge 49.15N 4.33 E
Sömmerda 10 He 51.09N 11.06 E
Somogy [2] 10 Nj 46.25N 17.35 E
Somontano 13 Lc 42.02N 0.20W
Somosierra, Puerto de- 13 Ic 41.09N 3.35W
Somosomo Strait 63d Bb 16.47S 179.58 E
Somotillo 49 Dg 13.02N 86.53W
Somoto 47 Gf 13.28N 86.35W
Somovo 16 Kd 51.45N 39.25 E
Sompolno 10 Od 52.24N 18.31 E
Somport, Puerto de- 13 Lb 42.48N 0.31W
Son 21 Kg 25.50N 84.55 E
Sona 10 Qd 52.33N 20.35 E
Soná 49 Gi 8.01N 81.19W
Sonaguera 49 Df 15.38N 86.20W
Sonári, Ákra 15 Lm 36.27N 28.13 E
Sönch'on 28 He 39.48N 124.55 E
Søndeled 7 Bg 58.46N 9.05 E
Sønderborg 7 Bi 54.55N 9.47 E
Sonder-Jylland [2] 8 Ci 55.00N 9.00 E
Sønder-Omme 8 Ci 55.50N 8.54 E
Sondershausen 10 Ge 51.22N 10.52 E
Søndre Strømfjord 67 Nc 66.59N 50.40W
Søndre Strømfjord 41 Ge 66.10N 53.10W
Søndre Upernavik 41 Gd 72.10N 55.38W
Sondrio 14 Dd 46.10N 9.52 E
Sonepat 25 Fc 28.59N 77.01 E
Song 34 Hd 9.50N 12.37 E
Songa 8 Be 59.47N 7.43 E
Songavatn 8 Be 59.50N 7.35 E
Song Cau 25 Lf 13.27N 109.13 E
Songe 8 Cf 58.41N 9.01 E
Songea 31 Kj 10.41S 35.39 E
Songeons 12 De 49.33N 1.52 E
Songhua Hu 28 Ic 43.30N 126.51 E
Songhua Jiang=Sungari (EN) 21 Pe 47.42N 132.30 E
Songjiang 27 Le 31.01N 121.14 E
Songjiang → Antu 28 Jc 42.33N 128.20 E
Songjianghe 28 Ic 42.10N 127.30 E
Sŏngjin → Kimch'aek 27 Mc 40.41N 129.12 E
Songjŏng 28 Ig 35.08N 126.48 E
Songkhla 22 Mi 7.13N 100.34 E
Songling 27 Lb 48.02N 121.08 E
Songnim 28 He 38.44N 125.38 E
Songo [Ang.] 36 Bd 7.21S 14.50 E
Songo [Moz.] 37 Ec 15.33S 32.48 E
Songololo 36 Bd 5.42S 14.02 E
Songpan (Sungqu) 27 He 32.37N 103.34 E
Songsa-dong 28 Hd 39.49N 124.49 E
Song Shan 27 Je 34.31N 113.00 E
Sungshuzhen 28 Ic 42.01N 127.09 E
Songueur 13 Ni 35.11N 1.30 E
Songxian 28 Bg 34.12N 112.09 E
Songzi (Xinjiangkou) 28 Ai 30.10N 116.46 E
Sonid Youqi (Saihan Tal) 27 Jc 42.45N 112.36 E
Sonid Zuoqi (Mandalt) 27 Kc 43.50N 116.45 E
Sonkari 8 Lb 62.50N 26.35 E
Sonkël, Ozero- 18 Jd 41.50N 75.10 E
Sonkovo 7 Ih 57.47N 37.09 E
Son La 22 Mg 21.19N 103.54 E
Sonmiāni Bay 25 Dc 25.15N 66.30 E
Sonneberg 10 Hf 50.21N 11.10 E
Sono, Rio do- [Braz.] 55 Jc 17.02S 45.32W
Sono, Rio do- [Braz.] 54 Ie 9.00S 48.11W
Sonobe 29 Dd 35.07N 135.28 E
Sonoita 47 Bb 31.51N 112.50W
Sonoma Peak 46 Gf 40.52N 117.36W
Sonora [2] 47 Bc 29.20N 110.40W
Sonora 47 Bc 28.48N 111.49W
Sonora [Ca.-U.S.] 46 Eh 37.59N 120.23W
Sonora [Tx.-U.S.] 45 Fk 30.34N 100.39W
Sonqor 24 Le 34.47N 47.36 E
Sonsbeck 12 Ic 51.37N 6.22 E
Sonsonate 47 Gf 13.43N 89.44W
Sonsorol Islands 57 Ed 5.20N 132.13 E
Sonthofen 10 Gi 47.31N 10.17 E
Sontra 10 Fe 51.04N 9.56 E
Soomaaliya=Somalia (EN) [1] 31 Lh 10.00N 49.00 E
Soomenlaht=Finland, Gulf of- (EN) 5 Ic 60.00N 27.00 E
Soonwald 12 Je 49.56N 7.35 E
Søorværøy 7 Cc 67.38N 12.40 E
Sopi, Tanjung- 26 If 2.39N 128.34 E
Sopo 35 Dd 8.51N 26.11 E
Sopockin 10 Tc 53.50N 23.42 E
Sopot [Bul.] 15 Hg 42.39N 24.45 E
Sopot [Pol.] 10 Ob 54.28N 18.34 E
Sopron 10 Mi 47.41N 16.36 E
Sopur 25 Eb 34.18N 74.28 E
Sor 13 De 39.00N 8.17W
Sora 14 Hi 41.43N 13.37 E
Sorachi-Gawa 29a Bb 43.32N 141.52 E
Söråker 8 Gb 62.31N 17.30 E
Sorak-san 27 Md 38.07N 128.28 E
Sorano 14 Fh 42.41N 11.43 E
Soratteld 12 Kc 51.40N 8.55 E
Sorbas 13 Jg 37.07N 2.07W
Sorbe 13 Id 40.51N 3.08W
Sörberget 8 Gb 62.31N 17.22 E
Sore 11 Fj 44.19N 0.35W
Sorel 42 Kg 46.03N 73.07W
Sorell, Cape- 59 Jh 42.10S 145.10 E
Soresina 14 De 45.17N 9.51 E
Sorezaru Point 63a Cb 7.37S 156.38 E
Sørfjorden 8 Bd 60.25N 6.40 E
Sørfold 7 Dc 67.28N 15.28 E
Sorgues 11 Kj 44.00N 4.52 E
Sorgun 24 Fc 39.50N 35.19 E
Soria [3] 13 Jc 41.40N 2.40W
Soria 13 Jc 41.46N 2.28W
Soriano [2] 55 Dk 33.30S 57.45W
Sørkapp 67 Kd 76.28N 16.36 E
Sorkh, Godār-e- 24 Pf 33.05N 55.05 E
Sorkh, Kūh-e- 24 Pf 33.05N 55.05 E
Sorkheh 24 Oe 35.28N 53.13 E
Sorø 8 Di 55.26N 11.34 E
Sorocaba 53 Lh 23.29S 47.27W
Soroči Gory 7 Li 55.24N 49.55 E
Soročinsk 19 Fe 52.26N 53.10 E
Soroka 16 Fe 48.07N 28.16 E
Sorol Atoll 57 Fd 8.08N 140.23 E
Sorong 58 Ee 0.53S 131.15 E
Soroti 31 Kh 1.43N 33.37 E
Sørøya 5 Ia 70.36N 22.46 E
Sørøyane 8 Ab 62.20N 5.45 E
Sorraia 13 Df 38.56N 8.53W
Sørreisa 7 Eb 69.09N 18.10 E
Sorrentina, Penisola- 14 Ij 40.35N 14.30 E
Sorrento 14 Ij 40.37N 14.22 E
Sør Rondane 66 Df 72.00S 25.00 E
Sorsatunturi 7 Gc 67.24N 29.38 E
Sorsavesi 8 Lb 62.30N 27.35 E
Sorsele 7 Dd 65.32N 17.30 E
Sorsk 20 Ef 54.00N 90.20 E
Sorso 14 Cj 40.48N 8.34 E
Sorsogon 26 Hd 12.58N 124.00 E
Sort 13 Nb 42.24N 1.08 E
Šortandi 19 He 51.42N 71.05 E
Sortavala 19 Dc 61.44N 30.41 E
Sortland 7 Db 68.42N 15.24 E
Sør-Trøndelag [2] 7 Ce 63.00N 10.40 E
Sorum 17 Ne 63.50N 68.05 E
Sørumsand 8 De 59.58N 11.15 E
Šoša 7 Ih 56.33N 36.09 E
Sōsan 28 If 36.47N 126.27 E
Sösdala 8 Eh 56.02N 13.40 E
Sos del Rey Católico 13 Kb 42.30N 1.13W
Sosna 16 Kc 52.42N 38.55 E
Sosnogorsk 6 Lc 63.37N 53.51 E
Sosnovka 16 Lc 53.14N 41.22 E
Sosnovka 7 Mh 56.18N 51.17 E
Sosnovka 7 Jc 66.31N 40.33 E
Sosnovka 16 Dd 50.15N 24.13 E
Sosnovo 8 Nd 60.31N 30.29 E
Sosnovo-Ozerskoje 20 Gf 52.31N 111.35 E
Sosnovy Bor 8 Me 59.48N 29.10 E
Sosnowiec 10 Pf 50.18N 19.08 E
Sospel 11 Nk 43.53N 7.27 E
Šostka 19 De 51.52N 33.31 E
Sosumav 37 Hb 13.03S 48.54 E
Sosva 19 Gd 59.32N 62.20 E
Sosva 19 Gc 63.40N 62.02 E
Sosva 19 Gd 59.10N 61.50 E
Sotavento [3] 32 Cf 14.40N 23.25W
Sotavento, Islas de- = Windward Islands (EN) 52 Jd 11.10N 67.00W
Sotik 36 Gc 0.41S 35.07 E
Sotkamo 7 Gd 64.08N 28.25 E
Soto la Marina 48 Jf 23.48N 98.13W
Soto la Marina, Río- 48 Kf 23.45N 97.45W
Sotonera, Embalse de la- 13 Lb 42.05N 0.48W
Sotouboua 34 Fd 8.34N 0.59 E
Sotra 8 Ad 60.20N 5.05 E
Sotsudaka-Zaki 29b Ba 28.15N 129.10 E
Sottern 8 Fe 59.05N 15.30 E
Sotteville-lès-Rouen 11 He 49.25N 1.06 E
Sottrum 12 La 53.07N 9.14 E
Sottunga 8 Id 60.10N 20.40 E
Sotuf, Adrar- 32 De 21.42N 15.36W
Sotuta 48 Og 20.36N 89.01W
Souanké 36 Bb 2.05N 14.03 E
Soubré 34 Dd 5.47N 6.36W
Soubré [3] 34 Dd 5.47N 6.38W
Soúdha 15 Hn 35.29N 24.04 E
Souf 30 He 33.25N 6.50 E
Soufflenheim 12 Jf 48.50N 7.58 E
Souflion 15 Jh 41.12N 26.18 E
Soufrière 50 Ff 13.52N 61.04W
Soufrière [Guad.] 47 Le 16.03N 61.40W
Soufrière [St.Vin.] 47 Lf 13.21N 61.11W
Soufrière Bay 51g Bb 15.13N 61.22W
Soufrière Hills 51c Bc 16.43N 62.10W
Souillac 11 Hj 44.54N 1.29 E
Souilly 11 Le 49.01N 5.17 E
Souk Ahras 32 Ib 36.17N 7.57 E
Souk el Arba du Rharb 32 Fc 34.41N 5.59W
Sŏul=Seoul (EN) 22 Of 37.34N 127.00 E
Soulac-sur-Mer 11 Ei 45.30N 1.06W
Sŏul Si [2] 28 If 37.35N 127.00 E
Soultz-sous-Forêts 12 Jf 48.56N 7.53 E
Soumagne 12 Hd 50.37N 5.45 E
Soummam 13 Rh 36.44N 5.04 E
Sounding Creek 46 Ja 52.06N 110.28W
Soúnion 15 Hl 37.39N 24.02 E
Soúnion, Ákra- 15 Hl 37.39N 24.01 E
Sources, Mont aux- 30 Jk 28.46S 28.52 E
Soure [Braz.] 54 Id 0.44S 48.31W
Soure [Port.] 13 Dd 40.03N 8.38W
Sour el Ghozlane 32 Hb 36.09N 3.41 E
Souris 42 Hg 49.38N 100.15W
Souris 38 Je 49.39N 99.34W
Sous 32 Fc 30.22N 9.37W
Sous 32 Fc 30.25N 9.30W
Sousa 53 Mf 6.45S 38.14W
Sousel 13 Ef 38.57N 7.40W
Sous le Vent, Iles-=Leeward Islands (EN) 57 Lf 16.38S 151.30W
Sousse (EN)=Sūsah [3] 32 Jb 35.45N 10.30 E
Sousse (EN)=Sūsah [Tun.] 31 Ie 35.49N 10.38 E
Sout 37 Cf 33.03S 23.29 E
South Africa / Suid Africa [1] 31 Jl 30.00S 26.00 E
South Alligator River 59 Gb 12.15S 132.24 E
Southam 12 Ab 52.15N 1.23W
South America (EN) 52 Jg 15.00S 60.00W
Southampton 38 Kc 64.20N 84.40W
Southampton [Eng.-U.K.] 6 Fe 50.55N 1.25W
Southampton [N.Y.-U.S.] 44 Ke 40.54N 72.23W
Southampton, Cape - 42 Jd 62.08N 83.44W
Southampton Airport 12 Ad 50.55N 1.23W
Southampton Water 12 Ad 50.52N 1.20W
South Andaman 25 If 11.45N 92.45 E
Southard, Cape- 66 Ie 66.33S 122.04 E
South Auckland-Bay of Plenty [2] 62 Fb 38.00S 176.00 E
South Aulatsivik 42 Le 56.47N 61.30W
South Australia [2] 59 Ge 30.00S 135.00 E
South Australian Basin (EN) 3 Im 40.00S 128.00 E
Southaven 45 Li 35.00N 90.00W
South Baldy 45 Cj 33.59N 107.11W
South Bay 42 Jd 64.00N 83.25W
South Bend 43 Jc 41.41N 86.15W
South Benfleet 12 Cc 51.32N 0.33 E
Southborough 12 Cc 51.09N 0.15 E
South Boston 44 Hg 36.42N 78.58W
Southbridge 62 Ee 43.48S 172.15 E
South Buganda [3] 36 Fc 0.30S 32.00 E
South Caicos 49 Lc 21.31N 71.30W
South Carolina [2] 43 Ke 34.00N 81.00W
South China Basin (EN) 3 Hh 15.00N 115.00 E
South China Sea (EN)=Bien Dong 21 Ni 10.00N 113.00 E
South China Sea (EN)=Cina Selatan, Laut- 21 Ni 10.00N 113.00 E
South China Sea (EN)=Nan Hai 21 Ni 10.00N 113.00 E
South Dakota [2] 43 Gc 44.15N 100.00W
South Downs 9 Mk 50.55N 0.25W
South-East [3] 37 De 25.00S 25.45 E
South East Cape 57 Fi 43.39S 146.50 E
Southeast Indian Ridge (EN) 3 Ho 50.00S 110.00 E
Southeast Pacific Basin (EN) 3 Mp 60.00S 115.00W
South East Point [Austl.] 57 Fh 39.00S 146.20 E
South East Point [Kir.] 64g Bb 1.40N 157.10W
Southend 42 He 56.20N 103.14W
Southend-on-Sea 9 Nj 51.33N 0.43 E
Southern [Mwi.] [3] 36 Gf 15.30S 35.00 E
Southern [S.L.] [3] 34 Cd 7.40N 12.15W
Southern [Ug.] [3] 36 Fc 0.30S 30.30 E
Southern [Zam.] [3] 36 Ef 16.00S 27.00 E
Southern Alps 57 Ii 43.30S 170.35 E
Southern Cook Island 57 Lg 20.00S 159.00W
Southern Cross 58 Ch 31.13S 119.19 E
Southern Desert (EN)=Janūbīyah, Aş Şaḩrā' al- 30 Jf 24.00N 30.00 E
Southern Ghats 25 Ff 10.00N 76.50 E
Southern Gilbert Islands 60 Jh 1.30S 175.30 E
Southern Indian Lake 38 Jd 57.10N 98.40W
Southern Pines 44 Hh 35.11N 79.24W
Southern Region (EN)=Iglim al Janūbīyah [2] 35 Dd 6.00N 30.00 E
Southern Sierra Madre (EN)=Madre del Sur, Sierra- 38 Jj 17.00N 100.00W
Southern Uplands 5 Fd 55.30N 3.30W
Southern Urals (EN)=Južny Ural 5 Le 54.00N 58.30 E
Southern Yemen (EN) → Yemen, People's Democratic Republic of- (EN) [1] 22 Gh 14.00N 46.00 E
South Esk 9 Ke 56.43N 2.28W
South Fiji Basin (EN) 3 Jl 26.00S 175.00 E
South Foreland 9 Oj 51.09N 1.23 E
South Fork 46 Ge 42.26N 116.53W
South Fork Flathead River 46 Ib 48.07N 113.45W
South Fork Grand River 45 Ed 45.43N 102.17W
South Fork Kern River 46 Fi 35.40N 118.27W
South Fork Moreau River 45 Ed 45.09N 102.50W
South Fork Powder River 46 Le 43.40N 106.30W
South Fork Republican River 45 Ff 40.03N 101.31W
South Georgia/Georgia del Sur, Islas- 66 Ad 54.15S 36.45W
South Glamorgan [3] 9 Jj 51.30N 3.15W
South Haven 44 Dd 42.24N 86.16W
South Honshu Ridge (EN) 3 Ig 24.00N 142.00 E
South Horr 36 Gb 2.06N 36.55 E
South Indian Basin (EN) 3 Ho 60.00S 120.00 E
South Island [F.S.M.] 64d Bc 6.59N 151.59 E
South Island [Kenya] 36 Gb 2.38N 36.36 E
South Island [N.Z.] 57 Ii 44.00S 171.00 E
South Island [Sey.] 37b Ab 9.26S 46.23 E
South Island [Sey.] 37b Bc 10.10S 51.10 E

Index Symbols

[1] Independent Nation
[2] State, Region
[3] District, County
[5] Municipality
[9] Colony, Dependency
Continent
Physical Region
Historical or Cultural Region
Mount, Mountain
Volcano
Hill
Mountains, Mountain Range
Hills, Escarpment
Plateau, Upland
Pass, Gap
Plain, Lowland
Delta
Salt Flat
Valley, Canyon
Crater, Cave
Karst Features
Depression
Polder
Desert, Dunes
Forest, Woods
Heath, Steppe
Oasis
Cape, Point
Coast, Beach
Cliff
Peninsula
Isthmus
Sandbank
Island
Atoll
Rock, Reef
Islands, Archipelago
Rocks, Reefs
Coral Reef
Well, Spring
Geyser
River, Stream
Waterfall Rapids
River Mouth, Estuary
Lake
Salt Lake
Intermittent Lake
Reservoir
Swamp, Pond
Canal
Glacier
Ice Shelf, Pack Ice
Ocean
Sea
Gulf, Bay
Strait, Fjord
Lagoon
Bank
Seamount
Tablemount
Ridge
Shelf
Basin
Escarpment, Sea Scarp
Fracture
Trench, Abyss
National Park, Reserve
Point of Interest
Recreation Site
Cave, Cavern
Historic Site
Ruins
Wall, Walls
Church, Abbey
Temple
Scientific Station
Airport
Port
Lighthouse
Mine
Tunnel
Dam, Bridge

South Korea (EN)=Taehan-Min'guk [1] 22 Of 38.00N 127.30 E
South Lake Tahoe 46 Eg 38.57N 120.01W
Southland [2] 62 Bf 45.45S 168.00 E
South Loup River 45 Gf 41.04N 98.40W
South Lueti 36 Df 16.14S 23.12 E
South Magnetic Pole (1980) 66 Ie 65.08S 139.03 E
South Malosmadulu Atoll 25a Ba 5.10N 72.58 E
South Mountain 46 Ge 42.44N 116.54W
South Nahanni 42 Fd 61.03N 123.22W
South Negril Point 47 Ie 18.16N 78.22W
South Orkney Islands 66 Re 60.35S 45.30W
South Pass 38 Ie 42.22N 108.55W
South Pass [F.S.M.] 64d Bb 7.14N 151.48 E
South Pass [U.S.] 45 Ll 28.55N 89.20W
South Platte 38 Ie 41.07N 100.42W
South Point 51q Ab 13.02N 59.31W
South Pole 66 Bg 90.00S 0.00
South Porcupine 44 Ga 48.28N 81.13W
Southport [Eng.-U.K.] 9 Jh 53.39N 3.01W
Southport [N.C.-U.S.] 44 Hi 33.55N 78.01W
South Reef 63a Ee 13.00S 160.32 E
South Ronaldsay 9 Kc 58.46N 2.50W
South Rukuru 36 Fe 10.44S 34.14 E
South Saint Paul 45 Jd 44.52N 93.02W
South Sandwich Islands 66 Ad 56.00S 26.30W
South Sandwich Trench (EN) 3 Do 56.30S 25.00W
South Saskatchewan River 38 Id 53.15N 105.05W
South Shetland Islands 66 Re 62.00S 58.00W
South Shields 9 Lg 55.00N 1.25W
South Sioux City 45 He 42.28N 96.24W
South Sister 46 Ed 44.12N 121.45W
South Taranaki Bight 62 Fc 39.40S 174.15 E
South Trap 62 Bg 47.30S 167.55 E
South Tyne 9 Kg 54.59N 2.08W
South Uist 9 Fd 57.15N 7.24W
South Umpqua River 46 De 43.20N 123.25W
Southwell 12 Ba 53.04N 0.57W
South Wellesley Islands 59 Hc 17.05S 139.25 E
South West Africa→Namibia [1] 31 Ik 22.00S 17.00 E
Southwest Cape 57 Hi 47.17S 167.27 E
South West Cape 59 Jh 43.34S 146.02 E
Southwest Cape 51a Dc 17.42N 64.53W
Southwest Indian Ridge (EN) 3 Fm 32.00S 55.00 E
Southwest Miramichi River 44 Ob 46.50N 65.45W
Southwest Pacific Basin (EN) 3 Km 40.00S 150.00W
Southwest Pass 45 Ll 29.00N 89.20W
Southwest Point 49 Jb 22.10N 74.10W
South West Point 69g Ab 1.52N 157.33W
South West Point 51p Cb 12.27N 61.30W
Southwold 9 Oi 52.20N 1.40 E
South Yorkshire [3] 9 Lh 53.30N 1.25W
Soutpansberg 37 Dd 22.58S 29.50 E
Soverato 14 Kl 38.41N 16.33 E
Sovetabad 18 Gd 40.14N 69.42 E
Sovetsk 19 Ed 57.36N 48.58 E
Sovetsk 19 Cd 55.05N 21.52 E
Sovetskaja Gavan 22 Qe 48.58N 140.18 E
Sovetski 7 Lh 56.47N 48.30 E
Sovetski 8 Md 60.29N 28.40 E
Sovetski 19 Gc 61.20N 63.29 E
Şowghān 24 Qh 28.20N 56.54 E
Sowie, Góry- 10 Mf 50.38N 16.30 E
Sōya 29a Ba 45.28N 141.53 E
Sōya-Kaikyō=La Perouse Strait (EN) 21 Qe 45.30N 142.00 E
Sōya-Misaki 27 Pb 45.31N 141.56 E
Soyatita 48 Fe 25.45N 107.22W
Soyo 36 Bd 6.05S 12.20 E
Sož 5 Je 51.57N 30.48 E
Sozopol 15 Kg 42.25N 27.42 E
Spa 11 Ld 50.29N 5.52 E
Spain (EN)=España [1] 6 Fg 40.00N 4.00W
Špakovskoje 16 Lg 45.06N 42.00 E
Spalding 9 Mi 52.47N 0.10W
Spanish Fork 46 Jf 40.07N 111.39W
Spanish Peak 46 Fd 44.24N 119.46W
Spanish Point 51d Ba 17.33N 61.44W
Spanish Sahara (EN) → Western Sahara (EN) [5] 31 Ff 24.30N 13.00W
Spanish Town [B.V.I.] 51a Db 18.27N 64.26W
Spanish Town [Jam.] 47 Ie 17.59N 76.57W
Sparbu 7 Ce 63.55N 11.28 E
Spargi, Isola- 14 Di 41.15N 9.20 E
Sparks 43 Dd 39.32N 119.45W
Sparreholm 8 Ge 59.04N 16.49 E
Sparta [Il.-U.S.] 45 Lg 38.07N 89.42W
Sparta [N.C.-U.S.] 44 Gg 36.30N 81.07W
Sparta [Tn.-U.S.] 44 Eh 35.56N 85.29W
Sparta [Wi.-U.S.] 45 Ke 43.57N 90.47W
Sparta (EN) = Spárti 15 Fl 37.05N 22.26 E
Spartanburg 43 Ke 34.57N 81.55W
Spartel, Cap- 32 Ge 35.48N 5.56W
Spárti = Sparta (EN) 15 Fl 37.05N 22.26 E
Spartivento, Capo- [It.] 14 Cl 38.53N 8.50 E
Spartivento, Capo- [It.] 5 Hh 37.55N 16.04 E
Spas-Demensk 16 Ib 54.24N 34.01 E
Spas-Klepiki 7 Ji 55.10N 40.13 E
Spassk-Rjazanski 7 Ji 54.27N 40.22 E
Spátha, Akra- = Spatha, Cape- (EN) 15 Gn 35.42N 23.44 E
Spatha, Cape- (EN) = Spátha, Ákra- 15 Gn 35.42N 23.44 E
Spearfish 43 Gc 44.30N 103.52W
Spearman 45 Fh 36.12N 101.12W
Speedway 44 Df 39.47N 86.15W
Speicher 12 Ie 49.56N 6.38 E
Speightstown 50 Gf 13.15N 59.39W
Speke Gulf 36 Fc 2.20S 33.15 E
Spello 14 Gh 42.59N 12.40 E
Spenard 40 Jd 61.11N 149.55W
Spence Bay 39 Jc 69.32N 93.31W
Spencer [Ia.-U.S.] 43 Hc 43.09N 95.09W
Spencer [In.-U.S.] 44 Df 39.17N 86.46W
Spencer [Nb.-U.S.] 45 Ge 42.53N 98.42W
Spencer [W.V.-U.S.] 44 Gf 38.48N 81.22W
Spencer, Cape- 59 Hg 35.18S 136.53 E
Spencer Gulf 57 Eh 34.00S 137.00 E
Spenge 12 Kb 52.08N 8.29 E
Spenser Mountains 62 Ee 42.10S 172.35 E
Sperillen 8 Dd 60.30N 10.05 E
Sperkhiós 15 Fk 38.52N 22.34 E
Sperlonga 14 Hi 41.15N 13.26 E
Sperone, Capo- 14 Cl 38.55N 8.25 E
Sperrin Mountains/Sliabh Speirin 9 Fg 54.50N 7.05W
Spessart 10 Fg 49.55N 9.30 E
Spétsai 15 Gl 37.16N 23.09 E
Spétsai 15 Gl 37.16N 23.08 E
Spey 9 Jd 57.40N 3.06W
Spey Bay 9 Jd 57.40N 3.05W
Speyer 10 Eg 49.19N 8.26 E
Speyer-bach 12 Ke 49.19N 8.27 E
Speyside 50 Fg 11.18N 60.32W
Spezzano Albanese 14 Kk 39.40N 16.19 E
Spicer Islands 42 Jc 68.10N 79.00W
Spiekeroog 10 Dc 53.46N 7.42 E
Spiez 14 Bd 46.41N 7.42 E
Spijkenisse 12 Gc 51.51N 4.21 E
Spilimbergo 14 Gd 46.07N 12.54 E
Spilion 15 Hn 35.13N 24.32 E
Spilsby 12 Ca 53.11N 0.06 E
Spina 14 Gf 44.42N 12.08 E
Spinazzola 14 Kj 40.58N 16.05 E
Spincourt 12 He 49.20N 5.40 E
Spirit River 42 Fe 55.47N 118.50W
Spirovo 7 Ih 57.27N 35.01 E
Spiš 10 Qg 49.05N 20.30 E
Spišská Nová Ves 10 Qh 48.57N 20.34 E
Spitak 16 Ni 40.49N 44.14 E
Spitsbergen 67 Kd 78.00N 19.00 E
Spitsbergen 67 Kd 78.45N 16.00 E
Spittal an der Drau 14 Hd 46.48N 13.30 E
Spitzbergen Bank (EN) 41 Oc 76.00N 23.00 E
Spjelkavik 7 Be 62.28N 6.23 E
Split 6 Hg 43.31N 16.26 E
Split Lake 42 He 56.10N 96.10W
Spluga, Passo dello- 14 Dd 46.29N 9.20 E
Splügenpaß 14 Dd 46.29N 9.20 E
Spógi/Špogi 8 Lh 56.02N 26.52 E
Špogi/Spógi 8 Lh 56.02N 26.52 E
Spokane 39 He 47.40N 117.23W
Spokane, Mount- 46 Gc 47.55N 117.07W
Spokane River 46 Fc 47.44N 118.20W
Špola 19 Df 49.01N 31.24 E
Spoleto 14 Gh 42.44N 12.44 E
Spooner 45 Kd 45.50N 91.53W
Spoon River 45 Kf 40.18N 90.04W
Sporovo 10 Vd 52.25N 25.27 E
Spotsylvania 44 If 38.12N 77.35W
Sprague 46 Gc 47.18N 117.59W
Sprague River 46 Ee 42.34N 121.51W
Spratly (EN) → Nanwei Dao 26 Fe 8.42N 111.40 E
Spray 46 Fd 44.50N 119.48W
Spreewald 10 Je 51.55N 14.00 E
Spremberg/Grodk 10 Ke 51.33N 14.22 E
Sprengisandur 7a Bb 64.40N 18.07W
Springbok 31 Ik 29.43S 17.15 E
Spring Creek 45 Fd 45.45N 100.18W
Springdale 45 Ih 36.11N 94.08W
Springe 10 Fd 52.13N 9.33 E
Springer 45 Dh 36.22N 104.36W
Springer, Mount- 44 Ja 49.48N 74.51W
Springerville 46 Ki 34.08N 109.17W
Springfield [Co.-U.S.] 45 Eh 37.24N 102.37W
Springfield [Il.-U.S.] 39 Kf 39.47N 89.40W
Springfield [Ma.-U.S.] 43 Mc 42.07N 72.36W
Springfield [Mn.-U.S.] 45 Id 44.14N 94.59W
Springfield [Mo.-U.S.] 39 Jf 37.14N 93.17W
Springfield [N.Z.] 62 De 43.20S 171.56 E
Springfield [Oh.-U.S.] 43 Kd 39.55N 83.48W
Springfield [Or.-U.S.] 43 Cc 44.03N 123.01W
Springfield [S.D.-U.S.] 45 He 42.49N 97.54W
Springfield [Tn.-U.S.] 44 Dg 36.31N 86.52W
Springfontein 37 Df 30.19S 25.36 E
Spring Garden 54 Gb 6.59N 58.31W
Spring Hall 51q Ab 13.19N 59.36W
Springhill [La.-U.S.] 45 Jj 33.00N 93.28W
Springhill [N.S.-Can.] 42 Lg 45.39N 64.03W
Spring Mountains 46 Hh 36.10N 115.40W
Springs 37 De 26.13S 28.25 E
Springsure 59 Jd 24.07S 148.05 E
Spring Valley 46 Hg 39.10N 114.30W
Spring Valley 45 Je 43.41N 92.23W
Springville 46 Jf 40.10N 111.37W
Spruce Knob 38 Lf 38.42N 79.32W
Spruce Mountain [Az.-U.S.] 46 Ii 34.28N 112.24W
Spruce Mountain [Nv.-U.S.] 46 Hf 40.33N 114.49W
Spulico, Capo- 14 Kk 39.58N 16.38 E
Spurn Head 9 Nh 53.34N 0.07 E
Squamish 42 Fg 49.42N 123.09W
Squillace 14 Kl 38.47N 16.31 E
Squillace, Golfo di- 14 Kl 38.45N 16.50 E
Squinzano 14 Mj 40.26N 18.02 E
Srbica 15 Dg 42.45N 20.47 E
Srbija=Serbia (EN) 15 Df 44.00N 21.00 E
Srbija = Serbia (EN) [2] 15 Df 44.00N 21.00 E
Srbija = Serbia (EN) 5 Ig 43.00N 21.00 E
Srbobran 15 Cd 45.33N 19.48 E
Srē Âmběl 25 Kf 11.07N 103.46 E
Sredinny Hrebet 21 Rd 56.00N 158.00 E
Sredna Gora 15 Hg 42.30N 25.00 E
Srednekolymsk 20 Kc 67.27N 153.41 E
Srednerusskaja Vozvyšennost=Central Russian Uplands (EN) 5 Je 52.00N 38.00 E
Srednesatyginski Tuman, Ozero- 17 Lg 59.45N 65.25 E
Srednesibirskoje Ploskogorje =Central Siberian Uplands (EN) 21 Mc 65.00N 105.00 E
Sredni Kujto, Ozero- 7 Hd 65.05N 31.30 E
Sredni Ural=Central Urals (EN) 5 Ld 58.00N 59.00 E
Sredni Urgal 20 If 51.13N 132.58 E
Sredni Verecki, Pereval- 16 Ce 48.49N 23.07 E
Srednjaja Ahtuba 16 Ne 48.43N 44.52 E
Srednjaja Olëkma 20 He 55.26N 120.40 E
Śrem 10 Nd 52.08N 17.01 E
Sremska Mitrovica 15 Ce 44.58N 19.37 E
Sremski Karlovci 15 Cd 45.12N 19.56 E
Sretensk 22 Nd 52.15N 117.43 E
Sri Gangānagar 25 Ec 29.55N 73.53 E
Sri Jayawardenepura 25 Gg 6.54N 80.02 E
Srijem 15 Cd 45.00N 19.40 E
Srīkākulam 25 Ge 18.18N 83.54 E
Sri Lanka (Ceylon) [1] 22 Ki 7.40N 80.50 E
Srinagar 22 Jf 34.05N 74.49 E
Srivardhan 25 Ee 18.02N 73.01 E
Środa Śląska 10 Me 51.10N 16.36 E
Środa Wielkopolska 10 Nd 52.14N 17.17 E
Srpska Crnja 15 Dd 45.43N 20.42 E
Sruth na Maoile/North Channel 5 Fd 55.10N 5.40W
Ssu-ch'uan Sheng → Sichuan Sheng = Szechwan (EN) [2] 27 He 30.00N 103.00 E
Staaten River 59 Ic 16.24S 141.17 E
Stabroek 12 Gc 51.20N 4.22 E
Stack Skerry 9 Ib 59.02N 4.30W
Stade 10 Fc 53.36N 9.29 E
Staden 12 Fd 50.59N 3.01 E
Stadhavet 8 Ab 62.15N 5.05 E
Städjan 8 Ec 61.58N 12.52 E
Stadlandet 8 Ab 62.05N 5.20 E
Stadskanaal 11 Ma 53.00N 6.55 E
Stadskanaal-Musselkanaal 12 Jb 52.56N 7.02 E
Stadthagen 12 Lb 52.19N 9.12 E
Stadtkyll 12 Id 50.21N 6.32 E
Stadtlohn 12 Ic 51.59N 6.56 E
Stadtoldendorf 10 Fe 51.54N 9.39 E
Staffa 9 Ge 56.25N 6.10W
Staffanstorp 8 Ei 55.38N 13.13 E
Staffelsee 10 Hi 47.42N 11.10 E
Staffora 14 De 45.00N 9.01 E
Stafford 9 Li 52.50N 2.00W
Stafford 9 Ki 52.48N 2.07W
Staffordshire [3] 9 Li 52.55N 2.00W
Staicele/Stajcele 8 Kg 57.44N 24.39 E
Stainach 14 Ic 47.32N 14.06 E
Staines 12 Bc 51.26N 0.31W
Stakčin 10 Sg 49.00N 22.13 E
Stalać 15 Ef 43.40N 21.25 E
Stalham 12 Db 52.46N 1.31 E
Stalingrad → Volgograd 6 Kf 48.44N 44.25 E
Ställdalen 8 Fe 59.56N 14.56 E
Stalowa Wola 10 Sf 50.35N 22.02 E
Stamberger See 10 Ii 47.55N 12.20 E
Stamford [Ct.-U.S.] 44 Ke 41.03N 73.32W
Stamford [Eng.-U.K.] 9 Mi 52.39N 0.29W
Stamford [Tx.-U.S.] 45 Gj 32.57N 99.48W
Stamford, Lake- 45 Gj 33.05N 99.35W
Stampriet 37 Bd 24.20S 18.28 E
Stamsund 7 Cb 68.08N 13.51 E
Stanberry 45 If 40.13N 94.35W
Stancija Jakkabag 18 Fe 38.59N 66.42 E
Stancija-Karakul 19 Gh 39.30N 63.50 E
Standerton 37 De 26.58S 29.07 E
Standish 44 Fd 44.00N 83.57W
Stanford 46 Jc 47.09N 110.13W
Stånga 8 Hg 57.17N 18.28 E
Stångån 8 Ff 58.27N 15.37 E
Stange 8 Dd 60.43N 11.11 E
Stanger 37 Ee 29.27S 31.14 E
Stanke Dimitrov 15 Gg 42.16N 23.07 E
Stanley [Austl.] 59 Jh 40.46S 145.18 E
Stanley [Falk. Is.] 53 Kk 51.42S 57.51W
Stanley [N.D.-U.S.] 45 Eb 48.19N 102.23W
Stanley Falls (EN)=Ngaliema, Chutes- 30 Jh 0.30N 25.30 E
Stann Creek 49 Ce 16.50N 88.30W
Stanovoje Nagorje=Stanovoy Upland (EN) 21 Nd 56.00N 114.00 E
Stanovoj Hrebet=Stanovoy Range (EN) 21 Od 56.20N 126.00 E
Stanovoy Upland (EN)=Stanovoje Nagorje 21 Nd 56.00N 114.00 E
Stans 14 Cd 46.58N 8.22 E
Stansted Airport 12 Cc 51.54N 0.13 E
Stansted Mountfitchet 12 Cc 51.54N 0.12 E
Stanthorpe 59 Ke 28.39S 151.57 E
Stanton Banks 9 Fe 56.15N 7.50W
Staphorst 12 Ib 52.38N 6.14 E
Staples 45 Ic 46.21N 94.48W
Stapleton 45 Ff 41.29N 100.31W
Stąporków 10 Qe 51.09N 20.34 E
Starachowice 10 Re 51.03N 21.04 E
Staraja Majna 7 Li 54.36N 48.59 E
Staraja Russa 19 Dd 57.59N 31.23 E
Staraja-Vyževka 10 Ue 51.27N 24.34 E
Stará L'ubovňa 10 Qg 49.18N 20.42 E
Stara Moravica 15 Cd 45.52N 19.28 E
Stara Pazova 15 De 44.59N 20.10 E
Stara Planina = Balkan Mountains (EN) 5 Ig 43.15N 25.00 E
Stara Zagora [2] 15 Ig 42.25N 25.38 E
Stara Zagora 6 Ig 42.25N 25.38 E
Starbuck Island 57 Le 5.37S 155.53W
Staretina 14 Kf 44.02N 16.43 E
Stargard Szczeciński 10 Lc 53.20N 15.02 E
Stari Begejski kanal 15 Dd 45.29N 20.25 E
Starica 7 Ih 56.30N 34.56 E
Starigrad 14 Kg 43.11N 16.36 E
Stari Vlah 15 Df 43.23N 20.10 E
Starke 44 Fk 29.57N 82.07W
Starkville 45 Lj 33.28N 88.48W
Starnberg 10 Hh 48.00N 11.21 E
Starobelsk 19 Df 49.15N 38.58 E
Starodub 19 De 52.35N 32.46 E
Starogard Gdański 10 Oc 53.59N 18.33 E
Starokonstantinov 16 Ee 49.43N 27.13 E
Starominskaja 19 Df 46.31N 39.06 E
Staroščerbinovskaja 16 Kf 46.37N 38.42 E
Starosubhangulovo 17 Hj 53.06N 57.20 E
Starotimoškino 7 Lj 53.43N 47.32 E
Start Point 9 Jk 50.13N 3.38W
Staryje Dorogi 16 Fc 53.02N 28.17 E
Stary Krym 16 Ig 45.02N 35.05 E
Stary Oskol 19 De 51.18N 37.51 E
Stary Sambor 16 Ce 49.29N 23.01 E
Stary Terek 16 Og 44.01N 47.24 E
Staßfurt 10 He 51.52N 11.35 E
Staszów 10 Rf 50.34N 21.10 E
State College 44 Ie 40.48N 77.52W
Staten Island (EN)=Estados, Isla de los- 52 Jk 54.47S 64.15W
Statesboro 44 Gi 32.27N 81.47W
Statesville 44 Gh 35.47N 80.53W
Stathelle 8 Ce 59.03N 9.41 E
Stathmós Krioneriou 15 Ek 38.20N 21.35 E
Statland 7 Cd 64.30N 11.08 E
Staunton 43 Ld 38.10N 79.05W
Stavanger 6 Gd 58.58N 5.45 E
Stavelot 12 Hd 50.23N 5.56 E
Staveren 11 Lb 52.53N 5.22 E
Stavern 8 Df 59.00N 10.02 E
Stavnoje 10 Sh 48.59N 22.45 E
Stavropol 6 Kf 45.02N 41.59 E
Stavropolskaja Vozvyšennost 16 Mg 45.10N 43.00 E
Stavropolski Kraj [3] 19 Eg 45.00N 43.15 E
Stavrós [Grc.] 15 Fj 39.19N 22.14 E
Stavrós [Grc.] 15 Gi 40.40N 23.42 E
Stavroúpolis 15 Hh 41.12N 24.42 E
Stawell 59 Ig 37.04S 142.46 E
Stawiski 10 Sc 53.23N 22.09 E
Stawiszyn 10 Oe 51.55N 18.07 E
Stayton 46 Dd 44.48N 122.48W
Steamboat Springs 43 Fc 40.29N 106.50W
Stebnik 10 Tg 49.14N 23.34 E
Stedingen 12 Ka 53.10N 8.30 E
Steele 45 Gc 46.51N 99.55W
Steelpoort 37 Ed 24.48S 30.12 E
Steenbergen 12 Gc 51.35N 4.19 E
Steen River 42 Fe 59.38N 117.06W
Steensby Inlet 42 Jb 70.10N 78.25W
Steenstrups Gletscher 41 Gc 75.15N 57.30W
Steenvoorde 12 Ed 50.48N 2.35 E
Steenwijk 11 Mb 52.47N 6.08 E
Ştefăneşti 15 Kb 47.48N 27.12 E
Stefanie, Lake- (EN)=Chew Bahir 30 Kh 4.38N 36.50 E
Stefansson 42 Gb 73.30N 105.30W
Ştefleşti, Vîrful- 15 Gd 45.32N 23.48 E
Stege 8 Ej 54.59N 12.18 E
Steiermark = Styria (EN) 14 Ic 47.15N 15.00 E
Steiermark = Styria (EN) [2] 14 Ic 47.15N 15.00 E
Steigerwald 10 Gg 49.40N 10.20 E
Steilrandberge 37 Ac 17.53S 13.20 E
Steinach 14 Fc 47.05N 11.28 E
Steinbach 42 Hg 49.32N 96.41W
Steinen, Rio- 54 Hf 12.05S 53.46W
Steinfeld (Oldenburg) 12 Kb 52.36N 8.13 E
Steinfort/Steinfurt 12 He 49.40N 5.55 E
Steinfurt 10 Dd 52.09N 7.20 E
Steinfurt/Steinfort 12 He 49.40N 5.55 E
Steinfurt-Borghorst 12 Jb 52.08N 7.25 E
Steinhagen 12 Kb 52.01N 8.24 E
Steinhausen 37 Bd 21.49S 18.20 E
Steinheim 12 Lc 51.51N 9.06 E
Steinhuder Meer 10 Fd 52.28N 9.19 E
Steinkjer 7 Cd 64.01N 11.30 E
Steinkopf 37 Be 29.18S 17.43 E
Steinshamn 8 Bb 62.47N 6.29 E
Steinsøy 7 Ac 61.00N 4.30 E
Steirisch-Niederösterreichische Kalkalpen 14 Jc 47.45N 15.30 E
Stekene 12 Gc 51.12N 4.02 E
Stekolny 20 Ke 60.00N 150.50 E
Stella 37 Ce 26.33S 24.53 E
Stellenbosch 37 Bf 33.58S 18.50 E
Stello 11a Ba 42.47N 9.25 E
Stelvio, Passo dello-/Stilfser Joch 14 Ed 46.32N 10.27 E
Stemwede 12 Kb 52.26N 8.26 E
Stenay 11 Le 49.29N 5.11 E
Stendal 10 Hd 52.36N 11.51 E
Stende 8 Jg 57.10N 22.28 E
Stende 10 Ig 57.40N 21.57 E
Stenhouse Bay 59 Hg 35.17S 136.56 E
Stenstorp 8 Ef 58.16N 13.43 E
Stenungsund 7 Cg 58.05N 11.49 E
Stepanakert 6 Kh 39.49N 46.44 E
Stepanavan 16 Ni 40.59N 44.20 E
Stephens, Cape- 62 Ed 40.42S 173.57 E
Stephens, Mount- 66 Rg 83.23S 51.27W
Stephens Passage 40 Me 57.50N 133.50W
Stephenville [Newf.-Can.] 42 Lg 48.33N 58.35W
Stephenville [Tx.-U.S.] 45 Gj 32.13N 98.12W
Steps Point 65c Cb 14.22S 170.45W
Sterea Ellás kai Évvoia [2] 15 Hk 38.20N 24.30 E
Sterkstroom 37 Df 31.32S 26.32 E
Sterlibaševo 17 Gj 53.28N 55.15 E
Sterling [Co.-U.S.] 43 Gc 40.37N 103.13W
Sterling [Il.-U.S.] 45 Lf 41.48N 89.42W
Sterling City 45 Fk 31.50N 100.59W
Sterlitamak 6 Le 53.37N 55.58 E
Šternberk 10 Ng 49.44N 17.19 E
Sterzing / Vipiteno 14 Fd 46.54N 11.26 E
Stettin (EN)=Szczecin 6 He 53.24N 14.32 E
Stettiner Haff 10 Kc 53.46N 14.14 E
Stettler 42 Gf 52.19N 112.43W
Steubenville 43 Kc 40.22N 80.39W
Stevenage 9 Mj 51.54N 0.11W
Stevenson Entrance 40 Ie 57.45N 152.20W
Stevens Point 43 Jc 44.31N 89.34W
Stewart 42 Dd 63.18N 139.24W
Stewart 42 Ee 55.56N 129.59W
Stewart Crossing 42 Dd 63.19N 136.33W
Stewart Island 57 Hi 47.00S 167.50 E
Stewart Islands 57 He 8.20S 162.40 E
Steyerberg 12 Lb 52.34N 9.02 E
Steyning 12 Bd 50.53N 0.20W
Steynsburg 37 Df 31.15S 25.49 E
Steyr 14 Ib 48.02N 14.25 E
Steyr 14 Ib 48.03N 14.25 E
Štiavnické vrchy 10 Oh 48.15N 18.50 E
Stidia 13 Li 35.50N 0.05W
Stiene 8 Kg 57.19N 24.28 E
Stiens, Leeuwarderadeel- 12 Ha 53.16N 5.46 E
Stigliano 14 Kj 40.24N 16.14 E
St. Ignace 43 Kb 45.52N 84.43W
Stigtomta 8 Gf 58.48N 16.47 E
Stikine 38 Fd 56.40N 132.30W
Stikine Ranges 42 Ee 57.35N 131.00W
Stilfer Joch/Stelvio, Passo dello- 14 Ed 46.32N 10.27 E
Stilfontein 37 De 26.50S 26.50 E
Stilis 15 Fk 38.55N 22.37 E
Stillwater [Mn.-U.S.] 45 Jd 45.04N 92.49W
Stillwater [Ok.-U.S.] 43 Hd 36.07N 97.04W
Stillwater Range 46 Fg 39.50N 118.15W
Stilo 14 Kl 38.29N 16.28 E
Stilo, Punta- 14 Kl 38.27N 16.35 E
Štimlje 15 Eg 42.26N 21.03 E
Stînişoarei, Munţii- 15 Ib 47.20N 26.00 E
Stinnett 45 Fi 35.50N 101.27W
Štip 15 Fh 41.44N 22.12 E
Stirling 9 Je 56.07N 3.57W
Stirling Range 59 Df 34.25S 117.50 E
Stjernøya 7 Fa 70.18N 22.45 E
Stjørdalshalsen 7 Ce 63.28N 10.44 E
Stobi 15 Eh 41.33N 21.59 E
Stobrawa 10 Nf 50.50N 17.32 E
Stocka 8 Gc 61.54N 17.20 E
Stockach 10 Fi 47.51N 9.01 E
Stockbridge 12 Ac 51.06N 1.29W
Stockerau 14 Kb 48.23N 16.13 E
Stockholm [2] 7 Dg 59.20N 18.00 E
Stockholm 6 Hd 59.20N 18.03 E
Stockport 9 Kh 53.25N 2.10W
Stocks Seamount (EN) 52 Mg 12.15S 32.00W
Stockton [Ca.-U.S.] 39 Gf 37.57N 121.17W
Stockton [Mo.-U.S.] 45 Jh 37.42N 93.48W
Stockton Lake 45 Jh 37.40N 93.45W
Stockton-on-Tees 9 Lg 54.34N 1.19W
Stockton Plateau 43 Ge 30.30N 102.30W
Stoczek Łukowski 10 Re 51.58N 21.58 E
Stöde 7 De 62.25N 16.35 E
Stoĕng Trĕng 25 Lf 13.31N 105.58 E
Stoer, Point of- 9 Hc 58.20N 5.25W
Stogovo 15 Dh 41.29N 20.39 E
Stohod 10 Ve 51.52N 25.44 E
Stoholm 8 Ch 56.29N 9.10 E
Stoj, Gora- 16 Ce 48.39N 23.15 E
Stojba 22 Pd 52.49N 131.43 E
Stoke-on-Trent 9 Kh 53.00N 2.10W
Stokksnes 7a Cb 64.14N 14.58W
Stokmarknes 7 Db 68.34N 14.55 E
Stol 15 Fe 44.11N 22.09 E
Stolac 14 Lg 43.05N 17.58 E
Stolbcy 16 Ec 53.31N 26.43 E
Stolberg 10 Cf 50.46N 6.14 E
Stolbovoj, Ostrov- 20 Ib 74.05N 136.00 E
Stolin 16 Ed 51.57N 26.52 E
Stolzenau 12 Lb 52.31N 9.04 E
Ston 14 Lh 42.50N 17.42 E
Stone 9 Ki 52.54N 2.10W
Stonehaven 9 Ke 56.58N 2.13W
Stonehenge 9 Lj 51.11N 1.49W
Stonehenge 59 Id 24.22S 143.17 E
Stoner 45 Bh 37.37N 108.19W
Stonewall 45 Ha 50.09N 97.21W
Stony 40 Hd 61.45N 156.35W
Stony Rapids 42 Ge 59.16N 105.50W
Stony River 40 Hd 61.47N 156.41W
Stony Stratford 12 Bb 52.03N 0.51W
Stony Tunguska (EN)=Podkamennaja Tunguska 21 Lc 61.36N 90.18 E
Stör 10 Fc 53.50N 9.25 E
Storå 8 Ch 56.19N 8.19 E
Storå 8 Fe 59.43N 15.08 E
Storå/Isojoki 7 Ee 62.07N 21.58 E
Stora Gla 8 Ee 59.30N 12.30 E
Stora Le 8 De 59.05N 11.55 E
Stora Lulevatten 7 Ec 67.08N 19.20 E
Storavan 7 Ed 65.42N 18.12 E
Storby 8 Hd 60.13N 19.34 E
Stord 7 Ag 59.55N 5.25 E
Storða 7 Ee 62.07N 21.58 E
Stordal 8 Bb 62.23N 7.01 E

Index Symbols

[1] Independent Nation
[2] State, Region
[3] District, County
[4] Municipality
[5] Colony, Dependency
Continent
Physical Region
Historical or Cultural Region
Mount, Mountain
Volcano
Hill
Mountains, Mountain Range
Hills, Escarpment
Plateau, Upland
Pass, Gap
Plain, Lowland
Delta
Salt Flat
Valley, Canyon
Crater, Cave
Karst Features
Depression
Polder
Desert, Dunes
Forest, Woods
Heath, Steppe
Oasis
Cape, Point
Coast, Beach
Cliff
Peninsula
Isthmus
Sandbank
Island
Atoll
Rock, Reef
Islands, Archipelago
Rocks, Reefs
Coral Reef
Well, Spring
Geyser
River, Stream
Waterfall Rapids
River Mouth, Estuary
Lake
Salt Lake
Intermittent Lake
Reservoir
Swamp, Pond
Canal
Glacier
Ice Shelf, Pack Ice
Ocean
Sea
Gulf, Bay
Strait, Fjord
Lagoon
Bank
Seamount
Tablemount
Ridge
Shelf
Basin
Escarpment, Sea Scarp
Fracture
Trench, Abyss
National Park, Reserve
Point of Interest
Recreation Site
Cave, Cavern
Historic Site
Ruins
Wall, Walls
Church, Abbey
Temple
Scientific Station
Airport
Port
Lighthouse
Mine
Tunnel
Dam, Bridge

Name	Page	Grid	Lat.	Long.
Store Bælt=Great Belt (EN)	5	Hd	55.30N	11.00 E
Storebro	8	Fg	57.35N	15.51 E
Storefiskbank	9	Qe	56.50N	4.00 E
Store Heddinge	8	Ei	55.19N	12.25 E
Store Hellefiske Bank (EN)	41	Ge	67.30N	55.00W
Store Koldewey	41	Kc	76.20N	18.30W
Store Kvien	8	Dc	61.34N	10.33 E
Støren	7	Ce	63.02N	10.18 E
Store Nupsfonn	8	Be	59.54N	7.08 E
Store Sølnkletten	8	Dc	61.59N	10.18 E
Storfjorden [Nor.]	8	Bb	62.25N	6.30 E
Storfjorden [Sval.]	41	Nc	77.30N	20.00 E
Storfors	8	Fe	59.32N	14.16 E
Storis Passage	42	Hc	67.40N	98.30W
Storkerson Bay	42	Fb	73.00N	124.00W
Storkerson Peninsula	42	Gb	73.00N	106.30W
Storlien	7	Ce	63.19N	12.06 E
Stormarn	10	Gc	53.45N	10.20 E
Storm Bay	59	Jh	43.10S	147.30 E
Storm Lake	43	Hc	42.39N	95.13W
Stornoway	9	Gc	58.12N	6.23W
Storøya	41	Ob	80.08N	27.50 E
Storožinec	16	De	48.10N	25.46 E
Storsjøen [Nor.]	8	Dd	60.25N	11.40 E
Storsjøen [Nor.]	8	Dd	61.35N	11.15 E
Storsjön [Swe.]	8	Gd	60.35N	16.45 E
Storsjön [Swe.]	5	Hc	63.15N	14.20 E
Storsteinfjellet	7	Db	68.14N	17.52 E
Storstrøm [2]	8	Dj	55.00N	11.50 E
Storstrømmen	41	Jc	77.20N	23.00W
Storsudret	8	Hh	57.00N	18.15 E
Storuman	7	Dd	65.14N	16.54 E
Storuman	6	Hb	65.06N	17.06 E
Storvätteshågna	8	Eb	62.07N	12.27 E
Storvigelen	8	Eb	62.32N	12.04 E
Storvik	8	Gd	60.35N	16.32 E
Storvreta	8	Ge	59.58N	17.42 E
Stöttingfjället	7	Dd	64.38N	17.44 E
Stoughton	46	Nb	49.41N	103.03W
Stour [Eng.-U.K.]	9	Lk	50.43N	1.46W
Stour [Eng.-U.K.]	9	Oj	51.52N	1.16 E
Stourbridge	9	Ki	52.27N	2.09W
Støvring	8	Ch	56.53N	9.51 E
Stowmarket	12	Cb	52.11N	0.59 E
Strabane/An Srath Bán	9	Fg	54.49N	7.27W
Stradella	14	De	45.05N	9.18 E
Straelen	12	Ic	51.27N	6.16 E
Strakonice	10	Jg	49.16N	13.55 E
Straldža	15	Jg	42.36N	26.41 E
Stralsund	6	He	54.18N	13.06 E
Strand	37	Bf	34.06S	18.50 E
Stranda	7	Be	62.19N	6.54 E
Strand Bay	42	Ia	79.00N	94.00W
Strangford Lough/Loch Cuan	9	Hg	54.26N	5.36W
Strängnäs	8	Ge	59.23N	17.02 E
Stranraer	9	Hg	54.54N	5.02W
Strasbourg [Fr.]	6	Gf	48.35N	7.45 E
Strasbourg [Sask.-Can.]	46	Ma	51.04N	104.57W
Strašeny	16	Ff	47.06N	28.34 E
Straßwalchen	14	Hc	47.59N	13.15 E
Stratford [N.Z.]	62	Fc	39.21S	174.17 E
Stratford [Ont.-Can.]	44	Gd	43.22N	80.57W
Stratford [Tx.-U.S.]	45	Eh	36.20N	102.04W
Stratford-upon-Avon	9	Li	52.12N	1.41W
Strathclyde [3]	9	If	55.50N	4.50W
Strathgordon	59	Jh	42.54S	146.10 E
Strathmore	9	Je	56.40N	3.05W
Strathmore	46	Ia	51.03N	113.23W
Strathroy	44	Gd	42.57N	81.38W
Strathy Point	9	Ic	58.35N	4.01W
Straubenhardt	12	Kf	48.50N	8.34 E
Straubing	10	Ih	48.53N	12.34 E
Straumnes	7a	Aa	66.26N	23.08W
Straumsjøen	7	Db	68.41N	14.30 E
Strausberg	10	Jd	52.35N	13.53 E
Strawberry Mountain	46	Fd	44.19N	118.43W
Strawberry River	46	Jf	40.10N	110.24W
Straža	15	Fg	42.15N	22.14 E
Stražica	15	If	43.14N	25.58 E
Strážiště	10	Kg	49.32N	14.58 E
Stražovské vrchy	10	Oh	48.55N	18.30 E
Streaky Bay	59	Gf	32.48S	134.13 E
Streaky Bay	59	Gf	32.35S	134.10 E
Streator	45	Lf	41.07N	88.50W
Středočeská pahorkatina	10	Kg	49.30N	14.15 E
Středočeský kraj [3]	10	Kg	49.55N	14.30 E
Středoslovenský kraj [3]	10	Ph	48.50N	19.10 E
Strehaia	15	Ge	44.37N	23.12 E
Strei	15	Gd	45.51N	23.03 E
Střela	10	Jg	49.54N	13.32 E
Strelasund	10	Jb	54.20N	13.05 E
Strelka	20	Ee	58.03N	93.05 E
Strelna	7	Jc	66.04N	38.39 E
Strenči	7	Fh	57.39N	25.38 E
Stresa	14	Ce	45.53N	8.32 E
Streževoj	20	Cd	60.42N	77.35 E
Stříbro	10	Ig	49.46N	13.00 E
Strickland River	59	Ia	6.00S	142.05 E
Strîmbeni	15	He	44.28N	24.58 E
Strimón	15	Gi	40.47N	23.51 E
Strimonikós Kólpos	15	Gi	40.40N	23.50 E
Strjama	15	Hg	42.10N	24.56 E
Strofádhes, Nísoi-	15	Dl	37.15N	21.00 E
Ströhen, Wagenfeld-	12	Kb	52.32N	8.39 E
Stromberg	12	Je	49.57N	7.46 E
Stromboli	14	Jl	38.45N	15.15 E
Strömfors/Ruotsinpyhtää	8	Ld	60.32N	26.27 E
Stromness	9	Jc	58.57N	3.18W
Strömsbro	8	Gd	60.42N	17.10 E
Strömsbruk	7	Dc	61.53N	17.19 E
Strömsnäsbruk	8	Eh	56.33N	13.43 E
Strömstad	7	Cf	58.56N	11.10 E
Strömsund	7	De	63.51N	15.35 E
Strongíli	15	Hm	36.58N	24.55 E
Stròngoli	14	Lk	39.16N	17.03 E
Stronsay	9	Kb	59.08N	2.38W
Stropkov	10	Rg	49.12N	21.40 E
Stroud	9	Kj	51.45N	2.12W
Struer	7	Bh	56.29N	8.37 E
Struga	15	Dh	41.11N	20.41 E
Strugi-Krasnyje	7	Gg	58.17N	29.08 E
Strule	9	Fg	54.40N	7.20W
Struma	5	Ig	40.47N	23.51 E
Strumble Head	9	Hi	52.02N	5.04W
Strumica	15	Fh	41.26N	22.39 E
Stry	16	De	49.24N	24.13 E
Stry	19	Cf	49.14N	23.49 E
Strydenburg	37	Ce	29.58S	23.40 E
Stryn	7	Bf	61.55N	6.47 E
Strynsvatn	8	Bc	61.55N	7.05 E
Strzegom	10	Mf	50.57N	16.21 E
Strzegomka	10	Me	51.08N	16.50 E
Strzelce Krajeńskie	10	Ld	52.53N	15.32 E
Strzelce Opolskie	10	Of	50.31N	18.19 E
Strzelin	10	Nf	50.47N	17.03 E
Strzelno	10	Od	52.38N	18.11 E
Strzyzów	10	Rg	49.52N	21.47 E
Stuart	40	Gd	63.35N	162.30W
Stuart, Mount-	46	Ec	47.29N	120.54W
Stuart Bluff Range	59	Gd	22.45S	132.15 E
Stuart Lake	42	Ff	54.33N	124.35W
Stuart Range	59	Ge	29.10S	134.55 E
Stubaier Alpen	14	Fc	47.10N	11.05 E
Stubbekøbing	8	Ej	54.43N	12.03 E
Stubbenkammer	10	Jb	54.35N	13.40 E
Stubbs Bay	51n	Ba	13.08N	61.10W
Štubik	15	Fe	44.18N	22.21 E
Studenica, Manastir-	15	Df	43.28N	20.37 E
Studholme Junction	62	Df	44.44S	171.08 E
Stugun	7	De	63.10N	15.36 E
Stuhr	12	Ka	53.02N	8.45 E
Stupino	7	Ji	54.57N	38.03 E
Stura di Demonte	14	Bf	44.40N	7.53 E
Stura di Lanzo	14	Be	45.06N	7.44 E
Sturge Island	66	Ke	67.27S	164.18 E
Sturgeon Bay	45	Md	44.50N	87.23W
Sturgeon Falls	42	Jg	46.22N	79.55W
Sturgeon Lake	45	Kb	50.00N	90.45W
Sturgis [Mi.-U.S.]	44	Ee	41.48N	85.25W
Sturgis [S.D.-U.S.]	45	Ed	44.25N	103.31W
Sturkö	8	Fh	56.05N	15.40 E
Sturt Creek	59	Fd	20.08S	127.24 E
Sturt Desert	59	Ie	28.30S	141.00 E
Stutterheim	37	Df	32.33S	27.28 E
Stuttgart [Ar.-U.S.]	45	Ki	34.30N	91.33W
Stuttgart [Ger.]	6	Gf	48.46N	9.11 E
Stviga	16	Ec	52.04N	27.55 E
Stykkishólmur	7a	Ab	65.04N	22.44W
Styr	19	Ce	52.07N	26.35 E
Styria (EN) = Steiermark	14	Ic	47.15N	15.00 E
Styria (EN) = Steiermark [2]	14	Ic	47.15N	15.00 E
Styrsö	8	Dg	57.37N	11.46 E
Suafa Point	63a	Ec	8.19S	160.41 E
Suai	26	Ih	9.21S	125.17 E
Suakin Archipelago (EN)= Sawākin, Jazā'ir-	30	Kg	19.07N	37.20 E
Suao	27	Lg	24.36N	121.51 E
Suardi	55	Bj	30.32S	61.58W
Suavanao	60	Fi	7.34S	158.44 E
Subačius/Subačjus	8	Ki	55.44N	24.53 E
Subačjus/Subačius	8	Ki	55.44N	24.53 E
Subang	26	Eh	6.34S	107.45 E
Subansiri	25	Jc	26.48N	93.49 E
Subao Ding	27	Jf	27.10N	110.18 E
Šubarkuduk	19	Ff	49.09N	56.31 E
Šubarši	16	Te	48.38N	57.12 E
Subate	8	Lh	56.01N	26.04 E
Subay', 'Urūq-	33	He	22.15N	43.05 E
Subaytilah	32	Ib	35.14N	9.08 E
Subbético, Sistema-	13	Jf	38.30N	2.30W
Subei (Dangchengwan)	27	Fd	39.36N	94.58 E
Subi, Pulau-	26	Ef	2.55N	108.50 E
Subiaco	14	Hi	41.55N	13.06 E
Sublette	45	Fh	37.29N	100.50W
Submeseta Norte	5	Fg	42.20N	4.50W
Submeseta Sur	5	Fh	39.30N	3.30W
Subotica	15	Cc	46.06N	19.40 E
Subpolar Urals (EN)= Pripoljarny Ural	5	Lb	65.00N	60.00 E
Subugo	36	Gc	1.40S	35.49 E
Suceava	15	Jb	47.32N	26.32 E
Suceava [2]	15	Ib	47.40N	25.45 E
Suceava	15	Jb	47.38N	26.15 E
Sucha Beskidzka	10	Pg	49.44N	19.36 E
Süchbaatar → Suhe-Bator	22	Md	50.15N	106.12 E
Suchedniów	10	Qe	51.03N	20.51 E
Suchiapa, Río-	48	Mi	16.36N	93.01W
Suchitepéquez [3]	49	Bf	14.25N	91.20W
Sucía, Bahía-	51a	Ac	17.57N	67.10W
Sucio, Río-	49	Ij	7.27N	77.07W
Suck/An tSuca	9	Eh	53.16N	8.03W
Suckling, Mount-	59	Ja	9.45S	148.55 E
Sucre [Bol.]	53	Jg	19.02S	65.17W
Sucre [Col.] [2]	54	Db	9.00N	75.00W
Sucre [Col.]	54	Db	8.50N	74.43W
Sucre [Ven.] [2]	54	Fa	10.25N	63.30W
Suçuarana, Serra da-	55	Jb	14.25S	45.00W
Sucunduri, Rio-	54	Ge	5.30S	59.40W
Sućuraj	14	Lg	43.08N	17.12 E
Sucuriú, Rio-	54	Hh	20.47S	51.38W
Sud, Canal du-	49	Kd	18.40N	73.05W
Sud, Massif du-	49	Kd	18.25N	73.55W
Suda	7	Ig	59.11N	37.33 E
Suda	7	Ig	59.12N	37.30 E
Sudak	19	Dg	44.50N	34.59 E
Sudan	30	Ig	11.30N	15.00 E
Sudan (EN)=As Sūdān [1]	31	Jg	15.00N	30.00 E
Sudbury [Eng.-U.K.]	9	Ni	52.02N	0.44 E
Sudbury [Ont.-Can.]	39	Ke	46.30N	81.00W
Suddie	50	Gi	7.07N	58.29W
Sude	10	Gc	53.22N	10.45 E
Sudeten (EN)	5	He	50.30N	16.00 E
Sudirman, Pegunungan-	26	Kg	4.12S	137.00 E
Sudočje, Ozero-	18	Bc	43.25N	58.30 E
Sudogda	7	Ji	55.59N	40.50 E
Sudost	16	Hc	52.19N	33.24 E
Sud-Ouest [Cam.] [3]	34	Gd	5.20N	9.20 E
Sud-Ouest [U.V.] [3]	34	Ec	10.30N	3.15W
Sudovaja Višnja	10	Tg	49.43N	23.26 E
Südradde	12	Jb	52.41N	7.34 E
Südtirol / Trentino-Alto Adige [2]	14	Fd	46.30N	11.20 E
Sudža	16	Id	51.13N	35.16 E
Sue	30	Jh	7.41N	28.03 E
Sueca	13	Le	39.12N	0.19W
Suess Land	41	Jd	72.45N	26.00W
Suez (EN)=As Suways	31	Kf	29.58N	32.33 E
Suez, Gulf of-(EN)= Suways, Khalīj as-	30	Kf	28.10N	33.27 E
Suez Canal (EN)=Suways, Qanāt as-	30	Ke	29.55N	32.33 E
Suffolk	9	Ni	52.25N	1.00 E
Suffolk	43	Ld	36.44N	76.37W
Suffolk [3]	9	Li	52.10N	1.05W
Sufiān	24	Kc	38.17N	45.59 E
Sugana, Val-	14	Fd	46.00N	11.40 E
Suga-no-Sen	29	Dd	35.22N	134.31 E
Sugar Island	44	Eb	46.25N	84.12W
Sugarloaf Mountain	44	Lc	45.01N	70.22W
Suğla Gölü	24	Ed	37.20N	32.02 E
Sugoj	20	Kd	64.15N	154.29 E
Suguta	36	Gb	2.03N	36.33 E
Suha	15	Ke	44.08N	27.36 E
Suhai Hu	27	Fd	38.55N	94.05 E
Şuḩār	23	Ie	24.22N	56.45 E
Suhe-Bator (Süchbaatar)	22	Md	50.15N	106.12 E
Suhiniči	16	Ib	54.06N	35.20 E
Suhl	10	Gf	50.36N	10.42 E
Suhodolskoje, Ozero-	8	Nd	60.35N	30.30 E
Suhoj Log	17	Kh	56.55N	62.01 E
Suhona	5	Kc	60.46N	46.24 E
Suhr	14	Cc	47.25N	8.04 E
Suhumi	6	Kg	43.01N	41.02 E
Suhurlui	15	Kd	45.25N	27.35 E
Suiá-Missu, Rio-	54	Hf	11.13S	53.15W
Suibara	29	Fc	37.50N	139.12 E
Suichang	27	Kf	28.34N	119.15 E
Suid Africa / South Africa [1]	31	Jl	30.00S	26.00 E
Suide	27	Jd	37.28N	110.15 E
Suifen He	28	Kc	43.20N	131.49 E
Suifenhe	27	Nc	44.25N	131.09 E
Sui He	28	Eh	33.29N	118.06 E
Suihua	27	Mb	46.38N	126.57 E
Suijiang	27	Hf	28.37N	104.00 E
Suileng	27	Mb	47.17N	127.08 E
Suining [China]	27	Ie	30.30N	105.34 E
Suining [China]	28	Dh	33.54N	117.56 E
Suipacha	55	Cl	34.45S	59.41W
Suiping	28	Bh	33.09N	113.59 E
Suippe	11	Je	49.25N	3.57 E
Suippes	11	Ke	49.08N	4.32 E
Suir/An tSiúir	9	Gi	52.15N	7.00W
Suisse / Svizra / Svizzera / Schweiz = Switzerland (EN) [1]	6	Gf	46.00N	8.30 E
Suisse Normande	12	Bf	48.53N	0.50W
Suita	29	Dd	34.45N	135.32 E
Suixi	28	Dh	33.55N	116.47 E
Suixian [China]	28	Cg	34.25N	115.04 E
Suixian [China]	27	Je	31.44N	113.25 E
Suiyang	28	Kb	44.26N	130.53 E
Suizhong	27	Lc	40.21N	120.20 E
Suj	27	Ic	42.12N	108.01 E
Šuja	7	If	61.54N	34.15 E
Šuja	7	If	61.59N	34.15 E
Šuja	19	Ed	56.52N	41.23 E
Sujer	17	Li	55.59N	65.47 E
Suji → Haixing	28	De	38.10N	117.29 E
Sujstamo	8	Nc	61.49N	31.05 E
Sukabumi	26	Eh	6.55S	106.56 E
Sukadana	26	Eg	1.15S	109.57 E
Sukagawa	28	Pf	37.17N	140.23 E
Sukaja	26	Fg	7.27S	108.12 E
Sukeva	7	Ge	63.54N	27.26 E
Sukhothai	25	Je	17.01N	99.49 E
Suki	35	Ec	13.23N	33.58 E
Sukkertoppen/Manitsoq	41	Ge	65.25N	53.00W
Sukkozero	19	Dc	63.09N	32.23 E
Sukkur	22	Ig	27.42N	68.52 E
Sukon	26	Hg	0.56S	123.10 E
Sukses	37	Bd	21.01S	16.52 E
Suksun	17	Hh	57.07N	57.24 E
Sukumo	27	Ne	32.56N	132.44 E
Sukumo-Wan	29	Ce	32.55N	132.40 E
Sul, Baía-	55	Hh	27.40S	48.35W
Sul, Canal do-	54	Id	0.10S	49.30W
Sula [Nor.]	7	Af	61.10N	4.55 E
Sula [Nor.]	8	Bb	62.25N	6.10 E
Sula	7	Ld	64.41N	47.46 E
Sula	17	Fc	67.16N	52.07 E
Sula	16	He	49.40N	32.43 E
Sula, Kepulauan-=Sulu Islands (EN)	57	De	1.52S	125.22 E
Sulaimāniya	23	Gb	35.33N	45.26 E
Sūlaimaniya [3]	24	Ke	35.40N	45.30 E
Sulaimān Range	21	Jf	30.30N	70.10 E
Sulak	16	Oh	43.17N	47.31 E
Sulak	19	Eg	43.17N	47.34 E
Sula Sgeir	9	Gb	59.05N	6.10W
Sulawesi/Celebes	21	Oj	2.00S	121.10 E
Sulawesi, Laut-=Celebes Sea (EN)	21	Oj	3.00N	122.00 E
Sulawesi Selatan [3]	26	Gg	4.00S	120.00 E
Sulawesi Tengah [3]	26	Hg	1.00S	121.00 E
Sulawesi Tenggara [3]	26	Hg	4.00S	122.30 E
Sulawesi Utara [3]	26	Hf	1.00N	123.00 E
Sulaymān	14	En	36.42N	10.30 E
Sulb	35	Ea	20.26N	30.20 E
Sulcis	14	Ck	39.05N	8.40 E
Suldalsvatn	8	Be	59.35N	6.45 E
Sūldeh	24	Od	36.34N	52.01 E
Sulechów	10	Ld	52.06N	15.37 E
Sulęcin	10	Ld	52.26N	15.08 E
Suleja	17	Ii	55.11N	58.50 E
Sulejów	10	Pe	51.22N	19.53 E
Süleoğlu	15	Jh	41.46N	26.55 E
Sule Skerry	9	Ib	59.10N	4.10W
Sulima	34	Cd	6.58N	11.35W
Sulina	15	Md	45.09N	29.40 E
Sulina, Braţul-	15	Md	45.09N	29.41 E
Sulingen	10	Ed	52.41N	8.48 E
Sulitjelma	7	Dc	67.09N	16.03 E
Sulitjelma	7	Dc	67.08N	16.24 E
Suljukta	19	Gh	39.56N	69.37 E
Sulkava	7	Gf	61.47N	28.23 E
Sullana	53	Hf	4.53S	80.42W
Süller	15	Mk	38.09N	29.29 E
Sullivan [In.-U.S.]	44	Df	39.06N	87.24W
Sullivan [Mo.-U.S.]	45	Kg	38.13N	91.10W
Sullivan Lake	46	Ja	52.00N	112.00W
Sully-sur-Loire	11	Ig	47.46N	2.22 E
Sulmona	14	Hh	42.03N	13.55 E
Sulphur [La.-U.S.]	45	Jk	30.14N	93.23W
Sulphur [Ok.-U.S.]	45	Hi	34.31N	96.58W
Sulphur Creek	45	Ed	44.46N	102.25W
Sulphur River	45	Jj	33.07N	93.52W
Sulphur Springs	45	Ij	33.08N	95.36W
Sulphur Springs Draw	45	Fj	32.12N	101.36W
Sultandağı	24	Dc	38.32N	31.14 E
Sultan Dağları	24	Dc	38.20N	31.20 E
Sultanhanı	24	Ec	38.15N	33.33 E
Sultanhisar	15	Ll	37.53N	28.10 E
Sultānpur	25	Gc	26.16N	82.04 E
Sulu Archipelago	21	Oi	6.00N	121.00 E
Sulu Basin (EN)	26	Ge	8.00N	121.30 E
Sulu Islands (EN)=Sula, Kepulauan-	57	De	1.52S	125.22 E
Suluova	24	Fb	40.47N	35.42 E
Sulūq	33	Dc	31.40N	20.15 E
Sulu Sea	21	Ni	9.00N	120.00 E
Sulz am Neckar	10	Eh	48.21N	8.37 E
Sulzbach (Saar)	12	Je	49.18N	7.04 E
Sulzbach-Rosenberg	10	Hg	49.30N	11.45 E
Sulzberger Bay	66	Mf	77.00S	152.00W
Šumadija	15	De	44.20N	20.40 E
Sumalata	26	Hf	0.59N	122.30 E
Sumāmus	24	Nd	36.50N	50.30 E
Šumanaj	18	Bc	42.37N	58.55 E
Sumatera=Sumatra (EN)	21	Mj	0.01N	102.00 E
Sumatera Barat [3]	26	Dg	1.00S	100.30 E
Sumatera Selatan [3]	26	Dg	3.30S	104.00 E
Sumatera Utara [3]	26	Cf	2.00N	99.00 E
Sumatra (EN)= Sumatera	21	Mj	0.01N	102.00 E
Šumava=Bohemian Forest (EN)	5	Hf	49.00N	13.30 E
Sumayr	33	Hf	17.47N	41.26 E
Sumba, Pulau-	21	Nj	10.00S	120.00 E
Sumba, Selat-=Sumba Strait (EN)	26	Hh	9.05S	120.00 E
Sumbar	16	Jj	38.00N	55.15 E
Sumba Strait (EN)=Sumba, Selat-	26	Hh	9.05S	120.00 E
Sumbawa, Pulau-	21	Nj	8.40S	118.00 E
Sumbawa Besar	26	Gh	8.30S	117.26 E
Sumbawanga	36	Fd	7.58S	31.37 E
Sumber	27	Ib	46.21N	108.20 E
Sumbi Point	63a	Cb	7.19S	157.04 E
Sumbu	36	Fd	8.31S	30.29 E
Sumburgh Head	9	Lb	59.51N	1.16W
Sumedang	26	Eh	6.52S	107.55 E
Şūme'eh Sarā	24	Md	37.18N	49.19 E
Sümeg	10	Nj	46.59N	17.17 E
Šumen	15	Jf	43.16N	26.55 E
Šumen [2]	15	Jf	43.20N	27.00 E
Sumenep	26	Fh	7.01S	113.52 E
Šumerlja	6	Kd	55.30N	46.26 E
Sumgait	16	Pi	40.37N	49.37 E
Sumgait	6	Kg	40.33N	49.40 E
Sumidouro, Rio-	55	Da	13.28S	56.39W
Šumiha	19	Gd	55.14N	63.19 E
Sumkino	19	Gd	58.09N	68.21 E
Summer, Lake- [N.M.-U.S.]	45	Di	34.38N	104.26W
Summer, Lake- [N.Z.]	62	Ee	42.40S	172.15 E
Summer Lake	46	Ee	42.50N	120.45W
Summerland	46	Fb	49.39N	119.33W
Summerside	42	Lg	46.24N	63.47W
Summersville	44	Gf	38.17N	80.52W
Summerville	44	Eh	34.29N	85.21W
Summit Lake	42	Fe	54.17N	122.38W
Summit Mountain	46	Gg	39.23N	116.28W
Summit Peak	45	Ch	37.21N	106.42W
Sumoto	29	Dd	34.20N	134.54 E
Šumperk	10	Mg	49.58N	16.59 E
Sumprabum	25	Jc	26.33N	97.34 E
Sumsar	18	Hd	41.13N	71.23 E
Sumskaja Oblast [3]	19	De	51.00N	34.15 E
Šumšu, Ostrov-	20	Kf	50.45N	156.20 E
Sumter	43	Ke	33.55N	80.20W
Sumusţā al Waqf	24	Dh	28.55N	30.51 E
Sumy	6	Je	50.54N	34.48 E
Suna	7	Mh	57.53N	50.07 E
Suna	7	Ie	62.08N	34.12 E
Sunagawa	28	Pc	43.29N	145.55 E
Šunak, Gora-	19	Hf	47.05N	72.35 E
Sunan	28	He	39.15N	125.40 E
Sunan (Hongwansi)	27	Gd	38.59N	99.25 E
Sunart, Loch-	9	He	56.45N	5.45W
Sunaysilah	24	Ie	35.35N	41.53 E
Sunburst	46	Jb	48.53N	111.55W
Sunbury	44	Ie	40.52N	76.47W
Sunchales	56	Hd	30.56S	61.34W
Suncho Corral	56	Hc	27.56S	63.27W
Sunch'ŏn [N. Kor.]	27	Me	34.57N	127.29 E
Sunch'ŏn [S. Kor.]	27	Md	39.25N	125.56 E
Sun City	46	Ij	33.36N	112.17W
Suncun → Xinwen	27	Kd	35.49N	117.38 E
Sunda, Selat-=Sunda Strait (EN)	21	Mj	6.00S	105.45 E
Sundance	46	Md	44.24N	104.23W
Sundarbans	25	Hd	22.00N	89.00 E
Sundargarh	25	Gd	22.07N	84.02 E
Sunda Strait (EN)=Sunda, Selat-	21	Mj	6.00S	105.45 E
Sunday Strait	59	Ec	16.20S	123.15 E
Sundborn	8	Fd	60.39N	15.46 E
Sundbron	8	Ha	63.01N	18.11 E
Sundbyberg	8	Ge	59.22N	17.58 E
Sunde	7	Ag	59.50N	5.43 E
Sunderland	9	Lg	54.55N	1.23W
Sundern (Sauerland)	12	Kc	51.20N	8.00 E
Sundgau	11	Ng	47.40N	7.15 E
Sündiken Dağları	24	Dc	39.55N	31.00 E
Sundridge	44	Hc	45.46N	79.24W
Sundsvall	6	Hc	62.23N	17.18 E
Sundsvallsbukten	8	Gb	62.20N	17.35 E
Sunflower, Mount-	45	Eg	39.04N	102.01W
Sungaidareh	26	Dg	0.58S	101.30 E
Sungaigerong	26	Dg	2.59S	104.52 E
Sungaiguntung	26	Df	0.18N	103.37 E
Sungai Kolok	25	Kg	6.02N	101.58 E
Sungai Lembing	26	Df	3.55N	103.02 E
Sungailiat	26	Eg	1.51S	106.08 E
Sungaipenuh	26	Dg	2.05S	101.23 E
Sungai Petani	26	De	5.39N	100.30 E
Sungai Siput	26	Df	4.49N	101.04 E
Sungari (EN)=Songhua Jiang	21	Pe	47.42N	132.30 E
Sungqu → Songpan	27	He	32.37N	103.34 E
Sungurlu	24	Fb	40.10N	34.23 E
Sunharon Roads	64b	Bb	14.57N	145.36 E
Suning	28	Ce	38.25N	115.50 E
Sunja	14	Ke	45.21N	16.33 E
Sunjiapuzi	28	Ic	42.02N	126.34 E
Sunkar, Gora-	18	Ib	44.12N	73.55 E
Sun Kosi	25	Hc	26.55N	87.09 E
Sunnadalsøra	7	Be	62.40N	8.33 E
Sunnan	7	Cd	64.04N	11.38 E
Sunndalen	8	Cb	62.40N	8.45 E
Sunndalsfjorden	8	Cb	62.45N	8.25 E
Sunne	7	Cg	59.50N	13.09 E
Sunnerbo	8	Eh	56.45N	13.50 E
Sunnersta	8	Ge	59.48N	17.39 E
Sunnfjord	8	Ac	61.25N	5.20 E
Sunnhordland	8	Ae	59.55N	6.00 E
Sunnmøre	8	Bb	62.20N	6.40 E
Sunnyside	46	Fc	46.20N	120.00W
Sunnyvale	46	Dh	37.23N	122.01W
Su-no-Zaki	29	Fd	34.58N	139.45 E
Sun River	46	Jc	47.30N	111.25W
Sunsas, Serranía de-	55	Cc	17.57S	59.35W
Suntar	20	Gd	62.04N	117.40 E
Suntar-Hajata, Hrebet-= Suntar-Khayata Range (EN)	21	Qc	62.00N	143.00 E
Suntar-Khayata Range (EN) =Suntar-Hajata, Hrebet-	21	Qc	62.00N	143.00 E
Suntaži	8	Kh	56.49N	24.57 E
Sun Valley	43	Ec	43.42N	114.21W
Sunwu	27	Mb	49.27N	127.19 E
Sunyani	31	Gh	7.20N	2.20W
Sunža	16	Oh	43.26N	46.08 E
Suojarvi	19	Dc	62.04N	32.21 E
Suokonmäki	8	Kb	62.47N	24.30 E
Suolahti	7	Fe	62.34N	25.52 E
Suomenlahti=Finland, Gulf of- (EN)	5	Ic	60.00N	27.00 E
Suomenniemi	8	Lc	61.19N	27.27 E
Suomenselkä	5	Ic	62.50N	25.00 E
Suomi/Finland [1]	6	Ic	64.00N	26.00 E
Suomussalmi	7	Gd	64.54N	29.00 E
Suō-Nada	29	Be	33.50N	131.30 E
Suonenjoki	7	Ge	62.37N	27.08 E
Suontee	8	Lc	61.40N	26.35 E
Suordah	20	Ic	66.43N	132.04 E
Suozhen → Huantai	28	Ef	36.57N	118.05 E
Supamo, Río-	50	Fi	6.48N	61.50W
Superior [Az.-U.S.]	46	Jj	33.18N	110.06W
Superior [Mt.-U.S.]	46	Hc	47.12N	114.53W
Superior [Nb.-U.S.]	45	Gf	40.01N	98.04W
Superior [Wi.-U.S.]	39	Je	46.44N	92.05W
Superior, Lake-	38	Ke	48.00N	88.00W
Suphan Buri	25	Kf	14.29N	100.10 E
Süphan Dağı	23	Fb	38.54N	42.48 E
Supiori, Pulau-	26	Kg	0.45S	135.30 E
Supoj	16	Ge	49.38N	31.50 E
Support Force Glacier	66	Rg	83.05S	47.30W
Supraśl	10	Tc	53.13N	23.20 E
Supraśl	10	Sc	53.12N	22.55 E
Sup'ung	27	Lc	40.27N	124.57 E
Sup'ung-chosuji	28	Hd	40.30N	125.05 E
Suq ash Shuyūkh	24	Lg	30.53N	46.28 E
Suqian	27	Ke	33.55N	118.13 E
Sūq Suwayq	24	Hj	24.23N	38.27 E
Suquṭrá=Socotra (EN)	21	Hh	12.30N	54.00 E
Sūr	22	Hg	22.31N	59.30 E
Şūr	23	Ec	33.16N	35.11 E
Sur, Cabo-	65d	Ac	27.12S	109.26W
Sur, Point-	46	Eh	36.18N	121.54W
Sura	16	Nc	53.53N	45.44 E
Sura	5	Kd	56.06N	46.00 E
Šurab	18	Hd	40.03N	70.33 E
Surabaya	22	Nj	7.15S	112.45 E

Index Symbols

[1] Independent Nation
[2] State, Region
[3] District, County
[4] Municipality
[5] Colony, Dependency
Continent
Physical Region
Historical or Cultural Region
Mount, Mountain
Volcano
Hill
Mountains, Mountain Range
Hills, Escarpment
Plateau, Upland
Pass, Gap
Plain, Lowland
Delta
Salt Flat
Valley, Canyon
Crater, Cave
Karst Features
Depression
Polder
Desert, Dunes
Forest, Woods
Heath, Steppe
Oasis
Cape, Point
Coast, Beach
Cliff
Peninsula
Isthmus
Sandbank
Island
Atoll
Rock, Reef
Islands, Archipelago
Rocks, Reefs
Coral Reef
Well, Spring
Geyser
River, Stream
Waterfall Rapids
River Mouth, Estuary
Lake
Salt Lake
Intermittent Lake
Reservoir
Swamp, Pond
Canal
Glacier
Ice Shelf, Pack Ice
Ocean
Sea
Gulf, Bay
Strait, Fjord
Lagoon
Bank
Seamount
Tablemount
Ridge
Shelf
Basin
Escarpment, Sea Scarp
Fracture
Trench, Abyss
National Park, Reserve
Point of Interest
Recreation Site
Cave, Cavern
Historic Site
Ruins
Wall, Walls
Church, Abbey
Temple
Scientific Station
Airport
Port
Lighthouse
Mine
Tunnel
Dam, Bridge

T

Index Symbols

International Map Index

Tahat ▲ 30 Hf 23.18N 5.32 E
Tahe 27 La 52.22N 124.48 E
Ţāherī 24 Oi 27.42N 52.21 E
Tahgong, Puntan- ► 64b Ba 15.06N 145.39 E
Tahiataš 18 Bc 42.20N 59.33 E
Tahifet 32 Ie 22.56N 5.59 E
Tahir Geçidi ⊔ 24 Jc 39.52N 42.20 E
Tahiti, Ile- �''' 57 Mf 17.37S 149.27W
Tahkuna Neem/Takuna, Mys- ► 8 Je 59.05N 22.30 E
Tahlequah 45 Ii 35.55N 94.58W
Tahoe, Lake- ▭ 46 Fg 38.54N 120.00W
Tahoua ② 34 Gb 16.00N 5.30 E
Tahoua 31 Hg 14.54N 5.16 E
Ţaḩţā 33 Fd 26.46N 31.28 E
Tahta-Bazar 18 Dg 35.55N 62.55 E
Tahtabrod 19 Ge 52.40N 67.35 E
Tahtakarača Pereval ⊔ 18 Fe 39.17N 66.55 E
Tahtaköprü 15 Mj 39.57N 29.39 E
Tahtakupyr 19 Gg 43.01N 60.22 E
Tahtali Dağları ▲ 24 Gc 38.46N 36.47 E
Tahtamygda 20 Hf 54.09N 123.38 E
Tahuata, Ile- ➐ 57 Ne 9.57S 139.05W
Tahulandang, Pulau- ➐ 26 If 2.20N 125.25 E
Tahuna 26 If 3.37N 125.29 E
Tai 34 Dd 5.52N 7.27W
Tai'an [China] 28 Gd 41.24N 122.27 E
Tai'an [China] 27 Kd 36.09N 117.05 E
Taiarapu, Presqu'île de- 65e Fc 17.47S 149.14W
Taibai Shan ▲ 27 Ie 33.57N 107.40 E
Taibilla, Canal del- ⊏ 13 Kg 37.43N 1.22W
Taibilla, Sierra de- ▲ 13 Jf 38.10N 2.10W
Taibus Qi (Baochang) 27 Kc 41.55N 115.22 E
Taicang 28 Fi 31.26N 121.06 E
Taichung 22 Og 24.09N 120.41 E
Taieri ◁ 62 Dg 46.03S 170.12 E
Taiga 20 De 56.04N 85.37 E
Taigonos Peninsula (EN) = Taigonos, Poluostrov- ► 20 Ld 61.35N 161.00 E
Taigu 28 Bf 37.26N 112.33 E
Taihang Shan ▲ 21 Nf 37.00N 114.00 E
Taihape 62 Fc 39.41S 175.48 E
Taihe [China] 28 Ch 33.11N 115.38 E
Taihe [China] 27 Jf 26.50N 114.52 E
Taiheiyō = Pacific Ocean (EN) ▭ 3 Ki 5.00N 155.00W
Tai Hu ▭ 21 Of 31.15N 120.10 E
Taihu 30 Ke 30.26N 116.10 E
Taikang 27 Je 34.00N 114.56 E
Taiki 29a Cb 42.30N 143.16 E
Tailai 27 Lb 46.24N 123.26 E
Tailles, Plateau des- ▭ 12 Hd 50.15N 5.45 E
Taim 55 Fk 32.30S 52.35W
Tain 9 Ld 57.48N 4.04W
Tainan 22 Og 23.00N 120.11 E
Tainaron, Ákra-=Matapan, Cape- (EN) ⊳ 25 Ih 36.23N 22.29 E
Taiof ⊟ 63a Ba 5.31S 154.39 E
Taipei 22 Og 25.03N 121.30 E
Taiping 26 Df 4.51N 100.44 E
Taipingchuan 28 Ei 30.18N 118.07 E
Taiping Dao ➐ 28 Gb 44.24N 123.11 E
Taiping Ling ▲ 27 Jd 10.15N 113.42 E
Tairadate 27 Lf 47.36N 120.12 E
Tairadate-Kaikyō ≋ 29a Bc 41.09N 140.38 E
Taisei 29a Bc 41.10N 140.40 E
Taisetsu-Zan ▲ 29a Ab 42.14N 139.49 E
Taisha 21 Qe 43.40N 142.48 E
Taishaku-San ▲ 29 Cd 35.24N 132.40 E
Tai Shan ▲ 29 Fc 36.58N 139.28 E
Taishō 21 Nf 36.30N 117.20 E
Taitao Peninsula (EN) = 29 Ce 33.12N 132.57 E
Taitao, Península de- ► 52 Ij 46.30S 74.25W
Taitung 27 Lg 22.45N 121.09 E
Taiwa 29 Gb 38.26N 140.52 E
Taiwan ① 22 Og 23.30N 121.00 E
Taiwan Haixia = Taiwan Strait (EN) 21 Ng 24.00N 119.00 E
Taixian 28 Fh 32.31N 120.08 E
Taixing 28 Fh 32.10N 120.00 E
Taiyang Shan ▲ 27 Ie 33.37N 106.26 E
Taiyetos Óros- ▲ 15 Fl 37.06N 22.18 E
Taiyuan 22 Nf 37.50N 112.37 E
Taiyue Shan ▲ 28 Bf 36.48N 112.00 E
Taizhou 28 Eh 32.29N 119.55 E
Taizhou → Linhai 27 Lf 28.52N 121.08 E
Taizhou Wan ◁ 28 Fj 28.40N 121.37 E
Taizi He ◁ 28 Gd 41.00N 122.23 E
Ta'izz 22 Gh 13.38N 44.02 E
Tājābād 24 Pg 30.02N 54.24 E
Tajarhī 33 Be 24.21N 14.28 E
Tajgonos, Mys- ► 20 Ld 60.35N 160.10 E
Tajgonos, Poluostrov-= Taigonos Peninsula (EN) ► 20 Ld 61.35N 161.00 E
Tajikistan (EN) = Tojikiston 19 Hh 39.00N 71.00 E
Tajima 28 Of 37.12N 139.46 E
Tajimi 29 Ed 35.19N 137.08 E
Tājirwīn 14 Co 35.54N 8.33 E
Tajito 48 Cb 30.58N 112.18W
Tajmba 28 Ed 60.22N 98.50 E
Tajmyr 20 Ea 76.05N 98.55 E
Tajmyr, Ozero- ▭ 21 Mb 74.30N 102.30 E
Tajmyr, Poluostrov-= Taymyr Peninsula (EN) ► 76.00N 104.00 E
Tajmyra 21 Lb 76.00N 99.40 E
Tajmylyr 20 Hb 72.30N 121.39 E
Tajo = Tagus (EN) ◁ 5 Fh 38.40N 9.24W
Tajo-Segura, Canal de Trasvase- ⊏ 13 Ja 39.30N 2.05W
Tajrish 23 Hb 38.48N 51.25 E
Tajšet 22 Ld 55.57N 98.00 E

Tajumulco, Volcán- ▲ 38 Jh 15.02N 91.54W
Tajuña ◁ 13 Id 40.07N 3.35W
Tak 25 Je 16.52N 99.08 E
Taka Atoll ⊙ 3 Ii 4.00N 146.45 E
Takāb 24 Ld 36.24N 47.07 E
Takaba 36 Hb 3.27N 40.14 E
Takahagi 28 Pf 36.42N 140.41 E
Takahama 29 Dd 35.29N 135.33 E
Takahara-Gawa ◁ 29 Ec 36.27N 137.15 E
Takaharu 28 Lg 31.55N 130.59 E
Takahashi 28 Lg 34.47N 133.37 E
Takahashi-Gawa ◁ 29 Cd 34.32N 133.42 E
Takahata 29 Gc 38.00N 140.12 E
Takahe, Mount- ▲ 66 Of 76.17S 112.05W
Takaka 62 Ed 40.51S 172.48 E
Takakuma-Yama ▲ 29 Bf 31.28N 130.49 E
Takalar 26 Lh 5.28S 119.24 E
Takalous ◁ 32 Ie 23.25N 7.02 E
Takamatsu 27 Ne 34.21N 134.03 E
Takamori 28 Be 32.48N 131.08 E
Takanabe 28 Be 32.08N 131.31 E
Takanawa-Hantō ► 29 Ce 34.00N 132.55 E
Takanawa-San ▲ 29 Ce 33.57N 132.50 E
Takanosu 29 Ga 40.14N 140.22 E
Takaoka [Jap.] 28 Nf 36.45N 137.01 E
Takaoka [Jap.] 29 Bf 31.57N 131.17 E
Takapoto Atoll ⊙ 61 Lb 15.00S 148.10W
Takapuna 62 Fb 36.48S 174.47 E
Takara-Jima ➐ 27 Mf 29.10N 129.05 E
Takarazuka 29 Dd 34.49N 135.21 E
Takaroa Atoll ⊙ 61 Mb 14.28S 144.58W
Takasaki 27 Of 36.20N 139.01 E
Taka-Shima [Jap.] ➐ 29 Be 32.40N 131.50 E
Taka-Shima [Jap.] ➐ 28 Af 31.26N 129.45 E
Takatshwane 37 Cd 22.36S 21.55 E
Takatsu-Gawa ◁ 29 Bd 34.42N 131.49 E
Takatsuki 29 Mg 34.51N 135.37 E
Takayama 28 Nf 36.08N 137.15 E
Takebe 29 Cd 34.53N 133.54 E
Takefu 28 Ng 35.54N 136.10 E
Takehara 28 Cd 34.21N 132.54 E
Takeo 29 Ae 33.12N 130.00 E
Täkern ▭ 8 Ff 58.20N 14.50 E
Take-Shima ➐ 28 Kf 37.22N 131.58 E
Täkestān 23 Gb 36.05N 49.14 E
Taketa 29 Be 32.58N 131.24 E
Takêv 25 Kf 10.59N 104.47 E
Takhādīd 24 Kh 29.59N 44.30 E
Takhār ③ 23 Kb 36.30N 69.30 E
Takhmaret 13 Mi 35.06N 0.41 E
Takht-e Soleimān ▲ 24 Nd 36.20N 51.00 E
Taki [Jap.] 29 Cd 35.16N 132.38 E
Taki [Pap.N.Gui.] 63a Bb 6.29S 155.50 E
Takijuq Lake ▭ 42 Gc 66.05N 113.00W
Takikawa 21 Pc 43.33N 141.54 E
Takingeun 26 Cf 4.38N 96.50 E
Takinoue 29a Ca 44.13N 143.03 E
Takko 29 Ga 40.20N 141.09 E
Takla Lake ▭ 42 Ee 55.30N 126.00W
Takla Landing 42 Ee 55.29N 125.58W
Takla Makan (EN) = Taklimakan Shamo ⊟ 21 Kf 39.00N 83.00 E
Takob 18 Ge 38.51N 69.00 E
Tako-Bana ► 29 Cd 35.35N 133.05 E
Takolokouzet, Massif de- ▲ 34 Gb 18.40N 9.30 E
Taksimo (Muhoršibir) 20 Ff 51.01N 107.50 E
Taku 29 Be 33.19N 130.06 E
Takua Pa 25 Jg 8.52N 98.21 E
Takum 34 Gd 7.16N 9.59 E
Takuma 29 Cd 34.14N 133.40 E
Takume Atoll ⊙ 57 Mf 15.49S 142.12W
Takuna, Mys-/Tahkuna Neem- ► 8 Je 59.05N 22.30 E
Takutea Island ⊟ 57 Lf 19.49S 158.18W
Tala 48 Hg 20.40N 103.42W
Tālah 32 Jb 35.35N 8.40 E
Talaimannar 25 Fg 9.05N 79.44 E
Talaīyeh 24 Kd 37.50N 45.00 E
Talaja 20 Kd 61.03N 152.30 E
Talak ③ 34 Fb 18.20N 6.00 E
Talamanca, Cordillera de- 49 Fi 9.30N 83.40W
Talara 53 Hf 4.35S 81.25W
Talas 19 Hg 42.29N 72.14 E
Talas ◁ 18 Ic 44.05N 70.20 E
Talasea 59 Aa 5.20S 150.05 E
Talasskaja oblast 19 Hg 42.25N 72.15 E
Talasski Alatau, hrebet- 18 Hc 42.10N 72.00 E
Talata Mafara 34 Gc 12.34N 6.04 E
Talaud, Kepulauan-=Talaud Islands (EN) ⊡ 21 Oi 4.20N 126.50 E
Talaud Islands (EN) = Talaud, Kepulauan- ⊡ 21 Oi 4.20N 126.50 E
Talavera, Isla- ⊟ 55 Dh 27.32S 56.26W
Talavera de la Reina 13 Hd 39.57N 4.50W
Talawdī 35 Ec 10.38N 30.23 E
Talbot Inlet ◁ 42 Jf 77.55N 77.35W
Talca 53 Ii 35.26S 71.40W
Talcahuano 53 Hi 36.43S 73.07W
Tālcher 25 Hd 20.57N 85.13 E
Taldom 7 Hh 56.45N 37.32 E
Taldy-Kurgan 22 Kd 44.59N 78.23 E
Taldy-Kurganskaja Oblast ③ 19 Hf 44.00N 78.00 E
Talēḩ 35 Hd 9.09N 48.26 E
Tal-e-Khosravī 24 Ng 30.47N 51.29 E
Talence 11 Hf 44.49N 0.36W
Ţalḩa, Kūhhā-Ye- ▲ 24 Md 37.35N 48.38 E
Talgar 19 Hg 43.18N 77.13 E
Taliabu, Pulau- ➐ 26 If 1.45S 124.48 E
Talica 19 Gf 57.01N 63.43 E
Talimardžan 18 Fe 38.38N 65.31 E
Tali Post 35 Ed 5.54N 30.47 E
Talisajan 22 Ni 1.37N 118.11 E
Taliwang 26 Lh 8.45S 116.52 E
Talkeetna 40 Id 62.20N 150.07W

Talkeetna Mountains ▲ 40 Jd 62.10N 148.15W
Talkheh ◁ 24 Kd 37.40N 45.46 E
Talladega 44 Di 33.26N 86.06W
Tall 'Afar 23 Fb 36.22N 42.27 E
Tallah 24 Dh 28.05N 30.44 E
Tallahassee 39 Kf 30.25N 84.16W
Tallahatchie River ◁ 45 Kj 33.33N 90.10W
Tall al Abyaḏ 24 Hd 36.41N 38.57 E
Tallapoosa River ◁ 44 Di 32.30N 86.16W
Tallard 11 Mj 44.28N 6.03 E
Tällberg 8 Fd 60.49N 15.00 E
Tall Birāk at Taḩtānī 24 Id 36.38N 41.05 E
Tallinn 6 Id 59.25N 24.45 E
Tall Kayf 24 Jd 36.48N 42.04 E
Tall Kūshik 45 Kj 32.25N 91.11W
Tall Lullah 15 Hd 45.39N 24.16 E
Tālmaciu 20 Df 53.51N 83.45 E
Talmest 32 Fc 31.09N 9.00W
Talnah 20 Dc 69.30N 88.15 E
Talnoje 16 Ge 48.53N 30.42 E
Talo 30 Kg 10.44N 37.55 E
Talofofo 64c Bb 13.20N 144.46 E
Talon 29 Ga 59.48N 148.50 E
Tālogān 23 Kb 36.44N 69.33 E
Talovaja 16 Ld 51.06N 40.48 E
Talpa de Allende 48 Gg 20.23N 104.51W
Talsi 7 Hh 57.17N 22.37 E
Taltal 53 Ih 25.24S 70.29W
Taltson ◁ 42 Gd 61.24N 112.45W
Taluk 26 Dg 0.32S 101.35 E
Talvik 7 Fa 70.03N 22.58 E
Talwār ◁ 24 Md 36.00N 48.00 E
Tama ⊡ 35 Ic 14.45N 22.25 E
Tama ③ 32 Ic 34.23N 7.57 E
Tamaghzah 16 Mc 52.33N 43.18 E
Tamala 49 Ki 8.52N 73.38W
Tamalameque 31 Gh 9.24N 0.50W
Tamale 13 Hd 40.39N 6.06W
Tamames 29 Be 32.55N 130.33 E
Tamana 50 Dh 9.25N 65.23W
Tamanaco, Río- 57 Ie 2.29S 175.59 E
Tamana Island ➐ 28 Lg 34.30N 133.56 E
Tamano 29 Ae 32.38N 128.37 E
Tamanoura 30 Hf 22.03N 0.10 E
Tamanrasset 31 Hf 22.47N 5.31 E
Tamanrasset 32 Ie 23.00N 5.30 E
Tamanrasset ③ 15 Ik 50.22N 4.10W
Tamar ◁ 9 Lk 50.22N 4.10W
Tamara 15 Cg 42.27N 19.33 E
Tamara 54 Db 5.50N 72.10W
Tamarite de Llitera/Tamarite de Litera 13 Mc 41.52N 0.26 E
Tamarite de Litera/Tamarit de Llitera 13 Mc 41.52N 0.26 E
Tamarro 14 Ii 41.59N 14.59 E
Tamarugal, Pampa del- 56 Gb 21.00S 69.25W
Tamási 10 Jj 46.38N 18.17 E
Tamassoumit 32 Ef 18.35N 12.39W
Tamaulipas ② 47 Ed 24.00N 98.45W
Tamaulipas, Llanos de- ▭ 47 Ed 25.00N 98.25W
Tamaulipas, Sierra de- 48 Jf 23.30N 98.30W
Tamayama 29 Gb 39.50N 141.11 E
Tamazula de Gordiano 48 Hh 19.38N 103.15W
Tamazunchale 47 Ed 21.16N 98.47W
Tambach 36 Db 0.36N 35.31 E
Tambacounda 31 Fg 13.12N 15.48W
Tambara 37 Ec 16.44S 34.15 E
Tambelan, Kepulauan-= Tambelan Islands (EN) ⊡ 26 Ef 1.00N 107.30 E
Tambelan, Pulau- ➐ 26 Ef 0.58N 107.34 E
Tambelan Islands (EN) = Tambelan, Kepulauan- ⊡ 26 Ef 1.00N 107.30 E
Tambo 59 Jd 24.53S 146.15 E
Tambohorano 37 Gc 17.29S 43.58 E
Tambora, Gunung- ▲ 23 Gh 8.14S 117.55 E
Tambores 55 Dj 31.55S 56.16W
Tambov 6 Ke 52.43N 41.27 E
Tambovskaja Oblast ③ 19 Ee 52.45N 41.40 E
Tambre ◁ 13 Db 42.49N 8.53W
Tambunan 26 Ge 5.40N 116.22 E
Tambura 31 Jh 5.36N 27.28 E
Tamchaket 32 Ef 17.20N 10.40W
Tame 54 Db 6.27N 71.45W
Tâmega ◁ 13 Dc 41.05S 8.21W
Tâmega ◁ 13 Dc 41.05S 8.21W
Tamel Aike 56 Fg 48.19S 70.58W
Tamesi ◁ 47 Ed 22.13N 97.52W
Tamesnar ⊡ 32 Hf 19.11N 8.42 E
Tamgak, Monts- 34 Gb 19.00N 8.35 E
Tamgue, Massif du- 34 Ec 12.00N 12.18W
Tamiahua 47 Ed 21.16N 97.27W
Tamiahua, Laguna de- ▭ 47 Ed 21.35N 97.35W
Tamianglajang 26 Gg 2.07S 115.10 E
Tamil Nādu ③ 25 Ff 11.00N 78.00 E
Tamiš ◁ 15 Dd 44.51N 20.39 E
Tamise/Temse 12 Gc 51.08N 4.13 E
Tamitatoala, Río- 54 Hf 11.56S 53.36W
Ţāmiyah 33 Fc 29.30N 30.58 E
Tam Ky 25 Le 15.34N 108.29 E
Tammela 8 Jd 60.48N 23.46 E
Tammerfors/Tampere 6 Ic 61.30N 23.45 E
Tammisaari/Ekenäs 7 Gc 59.58N 23.26 E
Tämnaren ▭ 8 Gd 60.10N 17.20 E
Tamou 34 Fc 12.45N 2.11 E
Tampa 39 Kg 27.57N 82.27W
Tampa Bay ◁ 43 Kf 27.45N 82.35W
Tampakan-Misaki ► 29a Ab 43.43N 141.20 E
Tampere/Tammerfors 6 Ic 61.30N 23.45 E
Tampico 39 Jg 22.13N 97.51W
Tampin 26 Df 2.28N 102.14 E
Tamri 32 Ic 30.43N 9.50 E
Tamsag-Bulak 27 Kb 47.14N 117.21 E
Tamsalu 7 Gg 59.10N 26.07 E
Tamsweg 14 Hc 47.08N 13.48 E
Tamu 25 Je 24.13N 94.18 E
Tamuin 48 Jg 21.59N 98.45W

Tamuin ⊡ 47 Ed 22.00N 98.44W
Tamuin, Rio- ◁ 24 Kd 37.40N 45.46 E
Tamworth [Austl.] 58 Gh 31.05S 150.55 E
Tamworth [Eng.-U.K.] 9 Li 52.39N 1.40W
Tamyang 31 Jg 35.19N 126.59 E
Tana [Eur.] ◁ 5 Ia 70.28N 28.18 E
Tana [Kenya] ◁ 30 Li 2.32S 40.31 E
Tana, Lake- ▭ 30 Kg 12.00N 37.20 E
Tanabe 28 Mh 33.42N 135.44 E
Tana bru 7 Ga 70.16N 28.10 E
Tanacross 40 Kd 63.23N 143.21W
Tanafjorden ◁ 7 Ga 70.54N 28.40 E
Tanaga ⊟ 40a Cb 51.50N 178.00W
Tanagro ◁ 14 Jj 40.38N 15.14 E
Tanagura 29 Gc 37.02N 140.23 E
Tanahbala, Pulau- ➐ 26 Cg 0.25S 98.25 E
Tanahgrogot 26 Gg 1.55S 116.12 E
Tanahjampea, Pulau- ➐ 26 Hh 7.05S 120.42 E
Tanahmasa, Pulau- ➐ 26 Cg 0.12S 98.27 E
Tanah Merah 26 De 5.48N 102.09 E
Tanahmerah 26 Lh 6.05S 140.17 E
Tanakpur 25 Gc 29.05N 80.07 E
Tanalyk ◁ 17 Ij 51.6N 58.45 E
Tanami 59 Fc 19.59S 129.43 E
Tanami Desert ⊟ 57 Gg 20.00S 132.00 E
Tan An 25 Lf 10.32N 106.25 E
Tanana 40 Ic 65.10N 152.05W
Tanana ◁ 38 Dc 65.09N 151.55W
Tanapag 64b Ba 15.14N 145.45 E
Tanaqib, Ra's at- ► 24 Mi 27.50N 48.53 E
Tanaro ◁ 14 Ce 45.01N 8.47 E
Tanba-Sanchi ▲ 29 Dd 35.15N 135.35 E
Tancheng 28 Eg 34.37N 118.20 E
Tanch'ŏn 27 Mc 40.25N 128.57 E
Tanda 47 De 19.26N 102.18W
Tanda, Lac- ▭ 34 Eb 15.45N 4.42W
Tandag 13 He 9.04N 126.12 E
Tandaltí 35 Ec 13.01N 31.52 E
Tāndārei 15 He 44.39N 27.40 E
Tandijungbalai 26 Cf 2.58N 99.48 E
Tandil 53 Ki 37.20S 59.09W
Tandil, Sierras del- ▲ 55 Cm 37.24S 59.06W
Tandjilé ③ 35 Bd 9.30N 16.30 E
Tando Ādam 25 Dc 25.46N 68.40 E
Tandsjöborg 7 Df 61.42N 14.43 E
Tanḏūbāyah 35 Db 18.40N 28.37 E
Taneatua 62 Gc 38.04S 177.00 E
Tane-Ga-Shima ➐ 27 Me 30.40N 131.00 E
Taneichi 29 Ga 40.24N 141.43 E
Tanew ◁ 10 Sf 50.27N 22.16 E
Tanezrouft ⊟ 33 Bd 25.51N 10.19 E
Tanezzuft ◁ 32 Gd 24.00N 0.45W
Tanf, Jabal at- ▲ 24 Hf 33.30N 38.42 E
Tanga ③ 36 Gd 5.30S 38.00 E
Tanga 33 Ki 5.04S 39.06 E
Tangail 25 Hd 24.15N 89.55 E
Tanga Islands ⊡ 57 Se 3.30S 153.15 E
Tangalla 25 Gg 6.01N 80.48 E
Tanganyika 36 Fd 6.00S 35.00 E
Tanganyika, Lac-= Tanganyika, Lake- (EN) ▭ 30 Ji 6.00S 29.30 E
Tanganyika, Lake- ▭ 30 Ji 6.00S 29.30 E
Tanganyika, Lake- (EN) = Tanganyika, Lac- ▭ 30 Ji 6.00S 29.30 E
Tangará 54 Ke 6.11S 35.49W
Tangarare 63a Dc 9.35S 159.39 E
Tangdan → Dongchuan 27 Hf 26.07N 103.05 E
Tângețbغul 27 Pd 37.25N 55.50 E
Tanger = Tangier (EN) ③ 32 Fb 35.45N 5.45W
Tanger = Tangier (EN) 31 Gc 35.48N 5.48W
Tangerang 26 Eh 6.11S 106.37 E
Tangermünde 10 Hd 52.33N 11.57 E
Tanggu 27 Kd 39.00N 117.36 E
Tanggula Shan (Dangla Shan) ▲ 19 Ee 33.00N 92.00 E
Tanggula Shankou ⊔ 27 Ff 32.42N 92.27 E
Tanggulashanqu/Tuotuohe 21 Lf 34.15N 92.29 E
Tang He ◁ 28 Bg 32.10N 112.20 E
Tanghe 27 Je 32.37N 112.57 E
Tangier (EN) = Tanger 31 Gc 35.48N 5.48W
Tang La ⊔ 21 Kg 28.00N 89.15 E
Tango 29 Dd 35.05N 135.05 E
Tangra Yumco ▭ 21 Kf 31.00N 86.25 E
Tangshan 27 Kd 39.38N 118.09 E
Tanguiéta 34 Fc 10.37N 1.16 E
Tanguro, Río- 55 Fa 12.36S 52.56W
Tangxian 27 Jd 38.46N 114.58 E
Tangyin 28 Cg 35.54N 114.21 E
Tangyuan 27 Mb 46.45N 129.53 E
Tanhoj 20 Ff 51.33N 105.07 E
Tanhuijo, Arrecife- ⊟ 48 Kg 21.07N 97.17W
Taniantaweng Shan ▲ 27 Ge 30.00N 98.00 E
Tanimbar Islands (EN) ⊡ 57 Ee 7.30S 131.30 E
Tanimbar Islands (EN) = Tanimbar, Kepulauan- ⊡ 57 Ee 7.30S 131.30 E
Taninthayri 25 Jf 13.00N 99.00 E
Tanjung [Indon.] 26 Gg 2.11S 115.23 E
Tanjung [Indon.] 26 Dg 1.23S 103.58 E
Tanjungpinang 26 Df 0.55N 104.27 E
Tanjungredep 26 Gf 2.09N 117.29 E
Tanjungselor 26 Gf 2.51N 117.22 E
Tankenberg 12 Ib 52.21N 6.58 E
Tanna, Ile- ➐ 57 He 19.30S 169.20 E
Tännäs 7 Ce 62.27N 12.40 E
Tanner, Mount- 46 Fb 49.40N 118.84 E
Tannis Bugt ◁ 8 Eg 57.40N 10.15 E
Tannu-Ola ▲ 20 Ef 51.00N 94.00 E
Tano ◁ 34 Ee 5.07N 2.56W
Tanout 31 Hg 14.58N 8.53 E
Ţanţā 33 Fb 30.47N 31.00 E
Tan Tan 32 Ec 28.30N 11.02W
Tan-Tan ③ 32 Ed 28.30N 11.00W

Tan Tan Plage 32 Ed 28.26N 11.15W
Tantoyuca 48 Jg 21.21N 98.14W
Tanum 7 Cg 58.43N 11.20 E
Tanzania ① 31 Ki 6.00S 35.00 E
Tao, Ko- ➐ 25 Jf 10.05N 99.52 E
Tao'an (Taonan) 27 Lb 45.20N 122.46 E
Tao'er He ◁ 21 Oe 45.42N 124.05 E
Taoghe ◁ 37 Cd 20.37S 22.35 E
Taohe ◁ 27 Hd 35.50N 103.20 E
Taojiang 28 Bj 28.33N 112.05 E
Taonan → Tao'an 27 Lb 45.20N 122.46 E
Taongi Atoll ⊙ 57 Hc 14.37N 168.58 E
Taormina 14 Jm 37.51N 15.17 E
Taos 43 Fd 36.24N 105.24W
Taoudenni 31 Gf 22.42N, 3.56W
Taougrite 13 Mh 36.15N 0.55 E
Taounate 32 Gc 34.33N 4.39W
Taourirt ③ 32 Gc 34.04N 4.06W
Taoura 14 Cn 36.10N 8.02 E
Taourirt 32 Gc 34.25N 2.54W
Taouz 32 Gc 31.00N 4.00W
Taoyuan 27 Lg 25.00N 121.18 E
Tapa 19 Dc 59.15N 25.59 E
Tapa 39 Jh 14.54N 92.17W
Tapachula 65c Bb 14.01S 171.23W
Tapaga, Cape- ► 65c Bb 14.01S 171.23W
Tapah 26 Df 4.11N 101.16 E
Tapajera 55 Fi 28.09S 52.01W
Tapajós, Río- ◁ 52 Kf 2.24S 54.41W
Tapaktuan 26 Cf 3.16N 97.11 E
Tapalqué 55 Bm 36.21S 60.01W
Tapan 26 Dg 2.10S 101.04 E
Tapanahoni Rivier ◁ 54 Hc 4.22N 54.27W
Tapanlieh 21 Ng 21.58N 120.47 E
Tapanui 62 Cf 45.57S 169.16 E
Tapauà 54 Fe 5.45S 64.23W
Tapauá, Río- ◁ 52 Jf 5.40S 64.21W
Tapa 28 Bc 28.04S 59.10W
Taperas 55 Bc 17.54S 60.23W
Tapes 56 Jd 30.40S 51.23W
Tapera, Serra do- 55 Fj 30.25S 51.55W
Taphan Hin 25 Ke 16.12N 100.26 E
Tapili 36 Eb 3.25N 27.40 E
Tapini 60 Di 8.19S 146.59 E
Tapiola, Espoo- 8 Kd 60.11N 24.49 E
Tapirai 19 Je 19.52S 46.01W
Tapirapuã 55 Db 14.51S 57.45W
Tapolca 10 Nj 46.53N 17.26 E
Tappahannock 44 Ig 37.55N 76.54W
Tappi-Zaki ► 28 Pd 41.18N 140.22 E
Tappu 29a Ba 44.04N 141.52 E
Tapsuj ◁ 17 Je 62.20N 61.30 E
Tápti ◁ 21 Jg 21.06N 72.41 E
Tapul Group ⊡ 26 He 5.30N 121.00 E
Tapurucuara 54 Ed 0.24S 65.02W
Taputapu, Cape- ► 65c Cb 14.19S 170.50W
Tâqbostãn 24 Le 34.30N 46.58 E
Taquara 56 Jc 29.39S 50.47W
Taquaral, Serra do- 55 Fb 15.42S 52.30W
Taquari ◁ 55 Fc 17.50S 53.17W
Taquari, Pantanal de- ▭ 54 Gg 18.10S 56.30W
Taquari, Rio- [Braz.] ◁ 55 Gi 29.56S 51.44W
Taquari, Rio- [Braz.] ◁ 55 Hf 23.16S 49.12W
Taquari, Rio- [Braz.] ◁ 52 Kg 19.15S 57.17W
Taquari, Serra do- ▲ 55 Fd 18.18S 53.49W
Taquaritinga 55 He 21.24S 48.30W
Taquaruçu, Río- 55 He 23.31S 49.15W
Tara ▲ 10 Sf 21.35S 52.08W
Tara ◁ 15 Cf 43.55N 19.25 E
Tara [Austl.] 59 Ke 27.17S 150.28 E
Tara [Jap.] 29 Be 33.02N 130.11 E
Tara 10 Hd 52.33N 11.57 E
Tara 19 Hd 56.40N 74.50 E
Tara [Yugo.] ◁ 15 Bf 43.21N 18.51 E
Taraba 58 Hd 8.34N 10.15 E
Ţarābulus (Leb.)=Tripoli (EN) ③ 33 Bc 32.40N 13.15 E
Ţarābulus (Leb.)=Tripoli (EN) 31 Ec 34.26N 35.51 E
Ţarābulus (Lib.)=Tripoli (EN) 31 Ie 32.54N 13.11 E
Ţarābulus=Tripolitania (EN) ③ 30 Ie 31.00N 14.00 E
Ţarābulus=Tripolitania (EN) ⊡ 30 Ie 31.00N 14.00 E
Taradale 62 Gc 39.32S 176.51 E
Tarāghin 33 Bd 25.59N 14.28 E
Tarahumara, Sierra- 47 Cc 28.26N 106.50W
Tarakan 22 Ni 3.18N 117.38 E
Tarakan, Pulau- ➐ 26 Gf 3.21N 117.36 E
Taraklija 16 Fg 45.57N 28.41 E
Taranga Jima ➐ 27 La 24.40N 124.40 E
Tarancón 13 Jd 40.01N 3.00W
Taranga Island ⊟ 62 Fb 36.00S 174.45 E
Taransay ⊟ 9 Fd 57.55N 7.10W
Taranto 6 Hg 40.28N 17.14 E
Taranto, Golfo di- (EN) ◁ 5 Hg 40.10N 17.20 E
Taranto, Gulf of- (EN) = Taranto, Golfo di- ◁ 5 Hg 40.10N 17.20 E
Tarapacá 56 Ga 20.00S 69.20W
Tarapainã 54 Ga 19.55S 69.31W
Tarapoto 54 Ec 6.30S 76.25W
Taraqua 54 Ec 0.06N 68.28W
Tarare 11 Ki 45.54N 4.26 E
Tararua Range ▲ 62 Fd 40.40S 175.25 E
Tarašča 16 Ge 49.34N 30.31 E
Tarascon 11 Kk 43.48N 4.40 E
Tarascon-sur-Ariège 11 Ig 42.51N 1.36 E
Tarat 32 Id 26.08N 9.21 E
Tarata 54 Dg 17.27S 70.02W

Index Symbols

① Independent Nation	Historical or Cultural Region	Pass, Gap
② State, Region	Mount, Mountain	Plain, Lowland
③ District, County	Volcano	Delta
④ Municipality	Hill	Salt Flat
⑤ Colony, Dependency	Mountains, Mountain Range	Valley, Canyon
■ Continent	Hills, Escarpment	Crater, Cave
⊡ Physical Region	Plateau, Upland	Karst Features

Depression	Coast, Beach	Rock, Reef
Polder	Cliff	Islands, Archipelago
Desert, Dunes	Peninsula	Rocks, Reefs
Forest, Woods	Isthmus	Coral Reef
Heath, Steppe	Sandbank	Well, Spring
Oasis	Island	Geyser
Cape, Point	Atoll	River, Stream

Waterfall Rapids	Canal	Lagoon
River Mouth, Estuary	Glacier	Ice Shelf, Pack Ice
Lake	Bank	Ocean
Salt Lake	Seamount	Sea
Intermittent Lake	Tablemount	Gulf, Bay
Sea	Ridge	Strait, Fjord
Swamp, Pond	Shelf	Basin

Escarpment, Sea Scarp	Historic Site	Port
Fracture	Ruins	Lighthouse
Trench, Abyss	Wall, Walls	Mine
National Park, Reserve	Church, Abbey	Tunnel
Point of Interest	Temple	Dam, Bridge
Recreation Site	Scientific Station	
Cave, Cavern	Airport	

Tarauacá 54 De 8.10S 70.46W
Tarauacá, Rio 52 Jf 6.42S 69.48W
Taravao 65eFc 17.44S 149.19W
Taravao, Baie de- 65eFc 17.43S 149.17W
Taravo 11a Ab 41.42N 8.48 E
Tarawa Atoll 57 Id 1.25N 173.00 E
Tarawera 62 Gc 39.02S 176.35 E
Tarazi 24 Mg 31.05N 48.18 E
Tarazona 13 Kc 41.54N 1.44W
Tarazona de la Mancha 13 Ke 39.15N 1.55W
Tarbagataj, Hrebet 21 Ke 47.10N 83.00 E
Tarbagatay Shan 27 Db 47.10N 83.00 E
Tarbat Ness 9 Jd 57.50N 3.40W
Tarbert [Scot.-U.K.] 9 Gd 57.54N 6.49W
Tarbert [Scot.-U.K.] 9 Hf 55.52N 5.26W
Tarbes 11 Gk 43.14N 0.05 E
Tarboro 44 Ih 35.54N 77.32W
Tarcăului, Munţii- 15 Jc 46.45N 26.20 E
Tarcoola 59 Gf 30.41S 134.33 E
Tardenois 12 Fe 49.12N 3.40 E
Tardienta 13 Lc 41.59N 0.32W
Tardoire 11 Gi 45.52N 0.14 E
Tardoki-Jani, Gora- 20 Ig 48.50N 137.55 E
Taree 58 Gh 31.54S 152.28 E
Taremert-n-Akli 32 Id 25.53N 5.18 E
Tarentaise 11 Mi 45.30N 6.30 E
Ţarfā', Ra's aţ- 33 Hf 17.02N 42.22 E
Ţarfā', Wādī aţ- 24 Dh 28.38N 30.43 E
Ţarfah, Jazīrat aţ- 33 Hg 14.37N 42.55 E
Tarfaya 31 Ff 27.57N 12.55W
Targa 13 Qi 35.41N 4.09 E
Târgovişki prohod 15 Jf 43.12N 26.30 E
Târgovište 15 Jf 43.15N 26.34 E
Târgovište [2] 15 Jf 43.15N 26.34 E
Tarhankut, Mys- 16 Hg 45.21N 32.30 E
Tarhăus, Vîrful- 15 Jc 46.38N 26.10 E
Tarhūnah 33 Bc 32.26N 13.38 E
Tarhūnī, Jabal at- 33 De 22.12N 22.25 E
Táriba 49 Kj 7.49N 72.13W
Tarīf 23 He 24.01N 53.45 E
Tarifa 13 Gh 36.01N 5.36W
Tarifa, Punta de- 13 Ih 36.00N 3.37W
Tarija 53 Jh 21.31S 64.45W
Tarija [2] 54 Fh 21.30S 64.00W
Tarik 64d Bb 7.21N 151.47 E
Tariku 26 Kg 2.55S 138.26 E
Tarīm [Yem.] 23 Gf 16.03N 49.00 E
Tarīm [Sau.Ar.] 24 Fi 27.54N 35.24 E
Tarim Basin (EN) = Tarim Pendi 21 Ke 41.00N 84.00 E
Tarime 36 Fc 1.21S 34.22 E
Tarim He 21 Ke 41.05N 86.40 E
Tarim Pendi = Tarim Basin (EN) 21 Ke 41.00N 84.00 E
Tarin Kowt 23 Kc 32.52N 65.38 E
Taritatu 26 Kg 2.54S 138.27 E
Tarjalan 27 Hb 49.38N 101.59 E
Tarjannevesi 8 Kb 62.10N 24.05 E
Tarjat 27 Gb 48.10N 99.40 E
Tarka, Vallée de- 34 Gc 14.30N 6.30 E
Tarkastad 37 Df 32.00S 26.16 E
Tarkio 45 If 40.27N 95.23W
Tarko-Sale 20 Cd 64.55N 78.05 E
Tarkwa 34 Ed 5.18N 1.59W
Tarlac 22 Oh 15.29N 120.35 E
Tarm 8 Ci 55.55N 8.32 E
Tarma 54 Cf 11.25S 75.42W
Tarn 11 Hj 44.06N 1.02 E
Tarn [3] 11 Hk 43.50N 2.00 E
Tarna 10 Pi 47.31N 19.59 E
Tärnaby 7 Dd 65.43N 15.16 E
Tarn-et-Garonne [3] 11 Hj 44.00N 1.10 E
Tarnica 10 Sg 49.06N 22.47 E
Tarnobrzeg 10 Rf 50.35N 21.41 E
Tarnobrzeg [2] 10 Rf 50.35N 21.40 E
Tarnogród 10 Sf 50.23N 22.45 E
Tarnos 11 Ek 43.32N 1.28W
Tarnów 6 Ie 50.01N 21.00 E
Tarnów [2] 10 Qf 50.00N 21.00 E
Tarnowskie Góry 10 Of 50.27N 18.52 E
Tärnsjö 8 Gd 60.09N 16.56 E
Taro 14 Ef 45.00N 10.15 E
Taron 63a Aa 4.28S 153.04 E
Taroom 58 Fg 25.39S 149.49 E
Taroudant 32 Fc 30.29N 8.52W
Tarpon Springs 44 Fk 28.09N 82.45W
Tarquinia 14 Fh 42.15N 11.45 E
Tarra, Rio- 49 Ki 9.04N 72.27W
Tarrafal 32 Cf 15.17N 23.46W
Tarragona 6 Gg 41.07N 1.15 E
Tarragona [3] 13 Mc 41.10N 1.00 E
Tarraleah 59 Jh 42.10S 146.30 E
Tarrant 44 Di 33.38N 86.46W
Tarrasa 13 Oc 41.34N 2.01 E
Tàrrega 13 Nc 41.39N 1.09 E
Tarsus 23 Db 36.55N 34.53 E
Tart 27 Fd 37.07N 92.57 E
Tartagal 56 Hb 22.32S 63.49W
Tartaro 14 Fe 45.02N 11.30 E
Tartas 11 Fk 43.50N 0.48W
Tartas 20 Ce 55.37N 76.44 E
Tartu 6 Id 58.23N 26.45 E
Tartūs 23 Ec 34.53N 35.53 E
Tarumae-Yama 29a Bb 42.41N 141.23 E
Tarumizu 28 Ki 31.29N 130.42 E
Tarusa 16 Jb 54.43N 37.11 E
Tārūt 24 Ni 26.34N 50.04 E
Tarutau, Ko- 25 Jg 6.35N 99.40 E
Tarutino 16 Ff 46.12N 29.09 E
Tarutung 26 Cf 2.01N 98.58 E
Tarvisio 14 Hd 46.30N 13.35 E
Tarvo 55 Bb 15.06S 60.34W
Tarvo, Rio- 55 Bb 14.57S 61.03W
Tasajera, Sierra- 48 Gc 29.35N 105.35W
Tašanta 20 Dg 49.43N 89.11 E
Tasaral, Ostrov- 18 Ja 46.15N 74.05 E
Tašauz 19 Fg 41.52N 59.59 E
Tašauzskaja Oblast [3] 19 Fg 41.00N 58.40 E
Tasāwah 33 Bd 25.59N 13.29 E
Tasbuget 19 Gg 44.48N 65.38 E
Tasejeva 20 Ee 58.06N 94.01 E
Taseko Lake 46 Da 51.15N 123.35W
Tasendjanet 32 Hd 25.40N 0.59 E
Tashk, Daryācheh-ye- 23 Hd 29.45N 53.35 E
Tasikmalaya 22 Mj 7.20S 108.12 E
Tåsinge 8 Di 55.00N 10.36 E
Tašir (Kalinino) 16 Ni 41.08N 44.14 E
Tasiussaq 41 Gd 73.18N 56.00W
Taskan 20 Kd 62.58N 150.20 E
Taškent 22 Ie 41.20N 69.18 E
Taškentskaja Oblast [3] 19 Gg 41.20N 69.40 E
Taškepri 19 Gh 36.17N 62.38 E
Taškeprinskoje, Vodohranilišče- 18 Df 36.15N 62.40 E
Tasker 34 Hb 15.04N 10.42 E
Taşköprü 24 Fb 41.30N 34.14 E
Taš-Kumyr 19 Hg 41.20N 72.14 E
Taşlıçay 24 Jc 39.38N 43.23 E
Tasman, Mount- 62 De 43.34S 170.09 E
Tasman Basin (EN) 3 Jn 43.00S 158.00 E
Tasman Bay 61 Dh 41.10S 173.15 E
Tasmania 59 Jh 43.00S 147.00 E
Tasmania 57 Fi 43.00S 147.00 E
Tasman Peninsula 59 Jh 43.05S 147.50 E
Tasman Plateau (EN) 3 In 48.00S 148.00 E
Tasman Sea 57 Hh 40.00S 163.00 E
Tăşnad 15 Fb 47.29N 22.35 E
Taşova 24 Gb 40.46N 36.20 E
Tassah, Wādī- 14 Cn 36.35N 8.54 E
Tassara 34 Gb 16.01N 5.39 E
Taštagol 20 Df 52.47N 88.00 E
Tåstrup 8 Ei 55.39N 12.19 E
Tastūr 14 Dn 36.33N 9.27 E
Tasty-Taldy 19 Ge 50.47N 66.31 E
Ţasūj 24 Kc 38.19N 45.21 E
Taşucu 24 Ed 36.19N 33.53 E
Tata [3] 32 Fd 29.40N 8.00W
Tata [Hun.] 10 Oi 47.39N 18.19 E
Tata [Mor.] 32 Fd 29.45N 7.59W
Tataba 26 Hg 1.18S 122.49 E
Tatabánya 10 Oi 47.34N 18.25 E
Tatakoto Atoll 57 Nf 17.20S 138.23W
Tata Mailau 26 Ih 8.55S 125.30 E
Tatarbunary 16 Fg 45.49N 29.35 E
Tatarsk 22 Jd 55.13N 75.58 E
Tatarstan, respublika 19 Fd 55.20N 50.50 E
Tatar Strait (EN) = Tatarskì Proliv 21 Qd 50.00N 141.15 E
Tatau 26 Ff 2.53N 112.51 E
Taţāwīn 32 Jc 32.56N 10.27 E
Tateyama 28 Og 34.59N 139.52 E
Tathlina Lake 42 Fd 60.30N 117.30W
Tathlīth 23 Ff 19.32N 43.30 E
Tatiščevo 16 Nd 51.40N 45.35 E
Tatla Lake 46 Ca 51.58N 124.25W
Tatla Lake 46 Ca 51.55N 124.36W
Tatlow, Mount- 46 Da 51.23N 123.52W
Tatnam, Cape - 42 Ie 57.16N 91.00W
Tatra Mountains (EN) 5 Hf 49.15N 20.00 E
Tatsuno [Jap.] 29 Dd 34.52N 134.33 E
Tatsuno [Jap.] 29 Ed 35.58N 137.58 E
Tatsuruhama 29 Ec 37.04N 136.53 E
Tatta 25 Dd 24.45N 67.55 E
Tatuí 55 If 23.21S 47.51W
Tatum 45 Ej 33.16N 103.19W
Tatvan 23 Fb 38.30N 42.16 E
Tau 8 Ae 59.04N 5.54 E
Tau [Am.Sam.] 65c Db 14.15S 169.30W
Tau [Ton.] 65b Bc 21.01S 175.00W
Tauá 54 Je 6.01S 40.26W
Taubaté 53 Lh 23.02S 45.33W
Tauberbischofsheim 10 Fg 49.37N 9.40 E
Taučik 19 Fg 44.15N 51.20 E
Tauere Atoll 57 Mf 17.22S 141.30W
Tauern 4 Ff 47.15N 13.15 E
Taufstein 10 Ff 50.31N 9.14 E
Tauhunu 64n Ac 10.25S 161.03W
Tauhunu 64n Ac 10.25S 161.03W
Taujsk 20 Je 59.46N 149.20 E
Taujskaja Guba 20 Je 59.15N 150.00 E
Taukum 18 Jb 44.50N 75.30 E
Taumako 63c Ba 9.57S 167.13 E
Taumarunui 62 Fc 38.52S 175.15 E
Taum Sauk Mountain 45 Kh 37.34N 90.44W
Taunay 55 De 20.18S 56.05W
Taung 37 Ce 27.33S 24.47 E
Taungdwingyi 25 Jd 20.01N 95.33 E
Taunggyi 25 Jd 20.47N 97.02 E
Taungthonlon 25 Jd 24.58N 95.48 E
Taungup 25 Ie 18.51N 94.14 E
Taunton [Eng.-U.K.] 9 Jj 51.01N 3.06W
Taunton [Ma.-U.S.] 44 Le 41.54N 71.06W
Taunus 10 Ef 50.10N 8.15 E
Taunusstein 12 Kd 50.08N 8.10 E
Taupo 61 Eg 38.41S 176.05 E
Taupo, Lake- 61 Eg 38.50S 175.55 E
Tauragé/Taurage 7 Fi 55.16N 22.19 E
Taurage/Tauragé 7 Fi 55.16N 22.19 E
Tauranga 58 Ih 37.42S 176.10 E
Taurianova 14 Kl 38.21N 16.01 E
Taurion 11 Hi 45.53N 1.24 E
Taurisano 14 Mk 39.57N 18.13 E
Tauroa Point 62 Ea 35.10S 173.04 E
Taurus Mountains (EN) = Toros Dağları 21 Ff 37.00N 33.00 E
Tauste 13 Kc 41.55N 1.15W
Tauu Islands 57 Ge 4.45S 157.00 E
Tauz 19 Eg 41.01N 45.35 E
Ţavālesh, Kūhhā-Ye- 24 Mc 38.42N 48.18 E
Tavas [Tur.] 24 Dc 39.54N 30.03 E
Tavas [Tur.] 24 Cd 37.34N 29.04 E
Tavas Ovasi 15 Ll 37.30N 28.55 E
Tavastehus/Hämeenlinna 7 Ff 61.00N 24.27 E
Tavau/Davos 14 Dd 46.47N 9.50 E
Tavda 19 Gd 58.03N 65.15 E
Tavda 21 Id 57.47N 67.16 E
Tavendroua 63b Cc 16.21S 167.22 E
Taveta 36 Gc 3.24S 37.41 E
Taveuni Island 61 Fc 16.51S 179.58W
Taviano 14 Mk 39.59N 18.05 E
Tavignano 11a Ba 42.06N 9.33 E
Tavira 13 Eg 37.07N 7.39W
Tavistock 9 Ik 50.33N 4.08W
Tavolara 14 Dj 40.55N 9.40 E
Tavoliere 14 Ji 41.35N 15.25 E
Tavolžan 19 He 52.44N 77.30 E
Tavoy → Dawei 22 Lh 14.05N 98.12 E
Tavričanka 28 Kc 43.20N 131.52 E
Tavropóu, Tekhnití Límni- 15 Ej 39.15N 21.40 E
Tavşan Adaları 15 Jj 39.55N 26.05 E
Tavşanlı 24 Cc 39.35N 29.30 E
Tavua 61 Ec 17.27S 177.51 E
Taw 9 Ij 51.04N 4.11W
Tawakoni, Lake- 45 Ij 32.55N 96.00W
Tawas City 43 Kc 44.16N 83.31W
Tawau 22 Ni 4.15N 117.54 E
Tawfiqīyah 35 Ed 9.26N 31.37 E
Ţawīlah, Juzur- 24 Ei 27.35N 33.46 E
Tawitawi Group 26 Ge 5.10N 120.15 E
Ţawkar 31 Kg 18.26N 37.44 E
Ţāwūq 24 Ke 35.08N 44.27 E
Tawūq Chāy 24 Ke 34.35N 44.31 E
Tāwurghā', Sabkhat- 33 Cc 31.10N 15.15 E
Tawzar 32 Ic 33.55N 8.08 E
Taxco de Alarcón 48 Jh 18.33N 99.36W
Taxkorgan 27 Cd 37.47N 75.14 E
Tay 9 Je 56.30N 3.30W
Tay, Firth of- 9 Ke 56.28N 3.00W
Tay, Loch- 9 Ie 56.30N 4.10W
Tayandu, Kepulauan- 26 Jh 5.30S 132.15 E
Tayëgle 35 Ge 4.02N 44.36 E
Taylor [Nb.-U.S.] 45 Gf 41.46N 99.23W
Taylor [Tx.-U.S.] 43 He 30.34N 97.25W
Taylor, Mount- 43 Fd 35.14N 107.37W
Taylorville 45 Lg 39.33N 89.18W
Taymā' 23 Ed 27.38N 38.29 E
Taymyr Peninsula (EN) = Tajmyr, Poluostrov- 21 Mb 76.00N 104.00 E
Tay Ninh 25 Lf 11.18N 106.06 E
Tayside [3] 9 Je 56.30N 3.40W
Taytay 26 Gd 10.49N 119.31 E
Taza [3] 32 Gc 34.00N 4.00W
Taza [Mor.] 31 Ge 34.13N 4.01W
Taza 20 Gf 54.55N 111.05 E
Tāzah Khurmātū 24 Ke 35.18N 44.20 E
Tazawa-Ko 29 Gb 39.43N 140.40 E
Tazawako 29 Gb 39.42N 140.44 E
Tazenakht 32 Fc 30.35N 7.12W
Tazerbo Oasis (EN) = Tāzirbū, Wāḩāt al- 30 Jf 25.45N 21.00 E
Tazewell [Tn.-U.S.] 44 Fg 36.27N 83.34W
Tazewell [Va.-U.S.] 44 Gg 37.07N 81.34W
Tāzīāzet 32 De 20.55N 15.40W
Tazin Lake 42 Ge 59.48N 109.05W
Tāzirbū, Wāḩāt al- = Tazerbo Oasis (EN) 30 Jf 25.45N 21.00 E
Tazlău 15 Jc 46.16N 26.47 E
Tazmalt 13 Qh 36.43N 4.08 E
Tazouikert 34 Ea 21.46N 1.13W
Tazovskaja Guba 17 Qb 69.05N 76.00 E
Tazovski 20 Cc 67.28N 78.42 E
Tazrouk 32 Ie 23.27N 6.14 E
Tazumal 49 Cg 14.00N 89.40W
Tbilisi 6 Kg 41.43N 44.49 E
Tchad = Chad (EN) [1] 31 Ig 15.00N 19.00 E
Tchad, Lac- = Chad, Lake- (EN) 30 Ig 13.20N 14.00 E
Tchamba [Cam.] 34 Hd 8.37N 12.48 E
Tchamba [Togo] 34 Fd 9.02N 1.25 E
Tchibanga 36 Bc 2.51S 11.02 E
Tchien 34 Dd 6.04N 8.08W
Tchigaï, Plateau du- 35 If 21.30N 14.50 E
Tchin Tabaraden 34 Gb 15.58N 5.50 E
Tcholliré 34 Hd 8.24N 14.10 E
Tczew 10 Ob 54.06N 18.47 E
Tea, Rio- 54 Ed 0.30S 65.09W
Teaca 15 Hc 46.55N 24.31 E
Teacapán 48 Gf 22.33N 105.45W
Teaiti Point 64p Bb 21.11S 159.47W
Te Anau 62 Bf 45.25S 167.43 E
Te Anau, Lake- 61 Ci 45.15S 167.45 E
Teano 14 Ii 41.15N 14.04 E
Teapa 48 Mi 17.33N 92.57W
Te Araroa 61 Eg 37.38S 178.22 E
Te Aroha 62 Fb 37.32S 175.42 E
Tea Tree 59 Gd 22.11S 133.17 E
Te Atu Kura 64p Bb 21.14S 159.45W
Te Awamutu 62 Fc 38.00S 175.19 E
Teberda 16 Lh 43.28N 41.43 E
Tébessa 31 He 35.24N 8.07 E
Tébessa [3] 32 Ic 35.00N 7.45 E
Tébessa, Oued- 14 Bo 35.48N 7.53 E
Tebicuary, Rio- [Par.] 55 Ch 26.36S 58.16W
Tebicuary, Rio- [Par.] 55 Dh 26.26S 56.51W
Tebingtinggi [Indon.] 26 Dg 3.36S 103.05 E
Tebingtinggi [Indon.] 26 Cf 3.20N 99.09 E
Tebulosmta, Gora- 16 Nh 42.33N 45.16 E
Teča 17 Kh 56.17N 62.59 E
Tecate 47 Ab 32.34N 116.38W
Tecer Dağları 24 Gc 39.27N 37.11 E
Techirghiol 15 Le 44.03N 28.36 E
Tecka 56 Ff 43.29S 70.48W
Tecklenburg 12 Jb 52.13N 7.50 E
Tecomán 47 De 18.55N 103.53W
Tecomate, Laguna- 48 Ji 16.45N 99.25W
Tecoripa 48 Ec 28.37N 109.57W
Tecpan de Galeana 47 De 17.15N 100.41W
Tecuala 47 Cd 22.23N 105.27W
Tecuci 15 Kd 45.52N 27.25 E
Tedegra 35 Ba 20.46N 19.34 E
Tedori-Gawa 29 Ec 36.29N 136.28 E
Tedžen 21 If 37.24N 60.38 E
Tedženstroj 19 Gh 36.54N 60.53 E
Teeli 20 Ef 50.57N 90.18 E
Teenuse Jõgi/Tenuze 7 Jf 58.44N 23.58 E
Tees 9 Lg 54.34N 1.16W
Tees Bay 9 Lg 54.35N 1.05W
Teesside → Middlesbrough 6 Fe 54.35N 1.14W
Tefé 53 Jf 3.22S 64.42W
Tefé, Rio- 54 Fd 3.35S 64.47W
Tefedest 32 Ie 24.40N 5.30 E
Tefenni 24 Cd 37.18N 29.47 E
Tegal 22 Mj 6.52S 109.08 E
Tegea (EN) = Teyéa 15 Fl 37.27N 22.25 E
Tegelen 12 Ic 51.20N 6.08 E
Tegernsee 10 Hi 47.43N 11.46 E
Tegina 34 Gc 10.04N 6.11 E
Tégoua 63b Ca 13.15S 166.37 E
Tegucigalpa 39 Kh 14.06N 87.13W
Teguidda I-n-Tessoum 34 Gb 17.26N 6.39 E
Teguldet 20 De 57.20N 88.20 E
Tehachapi 46 Fi 35.08N 118.27W
Tehachapi Mountains 46 Fi 34.56N 118.40W
Tehamiyam 35 Fb 18.20N 36.32 E
Te Hapua 61 Df 34.30S 172.55 E
Tehaupoo 65eFc 17.49S 149.18W
Tehek Lake 42 Hd 64.55N 95.30W
Téhini 34 Ed 9.36N 3.40W
Tehi-n-Isser 32 Ie 24.48N 8.08 E
Tehoru 26 Ig 3.23S 129.30 E
Tehrān 22 Hf 35.40N 51.26 E
Tehrān → Markazi [3] 23 Hb 35.30N 51.30 E
Tehuacán 47 Ee 18.27N 97.23W
Tehuantepec 47 Ee 16.20N 95.14W
Tehuantepec, Golfo de- = Tehuantepec, Gulf of- (EN) 38 Jh 16.00N 94.50W
Tehuantepec, Gulf of- (EN) = Tehuantepec, Golfo de- 38 Jh 16.00N 94.50W
Tehuantepec, Isthmus of- (EN) = Tehuantepec, Istmo de- 38 Jh 17.00N 94.30W
Tehuantepec, Istmo de- = Tehuantepec, Isthmus of- (EN) 38 Jh 17.00N 94.30W
Tehuantepec Ridge (EN) 47 Ef 13.30N 98.00W
Tehuata Atoll 57 Mf 16.50S 141.55W
Teiga Plateau 35 Db 15.38N 25.40 E
Teignmouth 9 Jk 50.33N 3.30W
Teili/Delet 8 Id 60.15N 20.35 E
Teith 9 Ie 56.14N 4.20W
Teiuş 15 Gc 46.12N 23.41 E
Teixeira Pinto 34 Bc 12.04N 16.02W
Teja 20 Ed 60.27N 92.38 E
Tejkovo 19 Ed 56.50N 40.34 E
Tejo = Tagus (EN) 5 Fh 38.40N 9.24W
Teju 25 Jc 27.55N 96.10 E
Te Kaha 62 Gb 37.44S 177.41 E
Te Kao 62 Ea 34.39S 172.58 E
Tekapo, Lake- 62 De 43.50S 170.30 E
Te Karaka 62 Gc 38.28S 177.52 E
Tekax 48 Og 20.12N 89.17W
Teke 15 Mh 41.04N 29.39 E
Teke 15 Jh 41.21N 26.57 E
Teke Burun [Tur.] 15 Ji 40.02N 26.10 E
Teke Burun [Tur.] 15 Jk 38.05N 26.36 E
Tekeli 19 Hg 44.48N 78.57 E
Tekes 27 Dc 43.10N 81.43 E
Tekes He 27 Dc 43.35N 82.30 E
Tekeze 35 Fc 14.20N 35.50 E
Tekija 15 Fe 44.41N 22.25 E
Tekiliktag 27 Dd 36.35N 80.20 E
Tekirdağ 23 Ca 40.59N 27.31 E
Tekman 24 Ic 39.38N 41.31 E
Te Kopuru 62 Eb 36.02S 173.55 E
Te Kou 64p Bb 21.14S 159.46W
Tekouiat 32 He 22.20N 2.30 E
Tekro 35 Cb 19.34N 20.57 E
Te Kuiti 62 Fc 38.20S 175.10 E
Tela 47 Ge 15.44N 87.27W
Telagh 32 Gc 34.47N 0.34W
Telataï 34 Fb 16.31N 1.30 E
Telavåg 7 Af 60.16N 4.49 E
Telavi 19 Eg 41.55N 45.29 E
Tel Aviv-Yafo 22 Ff 32.04N 34.46 E
Telč 10 Lg 49.11N 15.27 E
Telchac Puerto 48 Og 21.21N 89.16W
Telciu 15 Hb 47.26N 24.24 E
Tele 36 Db 2.48N 23.54 E
Teleac 15 Hc 46.41N 24.48 E
Telečkoje Ozero 20 Df 51.30N 87.45 E
Telefomin 60 Ci 5.08S 141.31 E
Telegraph Creek 42 Ee 57.54N 131.09W
Telekitonga 65b Bb 20.24S 174.32W
Telekivavu'u 65b Bb 20.19S 174.32W
Telêmaco Borba 55 Gg 24.23S 50.28W
Telemark [2] 7 Bg 59.30N 8.40 E
Telemark 8 Ce 59.30N 8.45 E
Telén 56 Ge 36.16S 65.30W
Telen 26 Gf 0.26N 116.42 E
Telenešty 15 Lb 47.30N 28.16 E
Teleno 13 Fb 42.21N 6.23W
Teleorman 15 If 43.52N 25.26 E
Teleorman [2] 15 If 44.10N 25.15 E
Telerhteba, Djebel- 32 Ie 24.10N 6.51 E
Telescope Peak 46 Gh 36.10N 117.05W
Telescope Point 51p Bb 12.08N 61.36W
Telese 14 Ii 41.13N 14.32 E
Teles Pires, Rio- o São Manuel, Rio- 52 Kf 7.21S 58.03W
Telfān, Hadjer- 35 Bc 12.05N 18.57 E
Telford 9 Ki 52.40N 2.30W
Telgte 12 Jc 51.59N 7.47 E
Télimélé 34 Cc 10.54N 13.02W
Teljo, Jabal- 35 Dc 14.42N 25.56 E
Tell al Ubaid 24 Lg 30.59N 46.01 E
Tellaro 14 Jn 36.50N 15.06 E
Tell Atlas (EN) = Atlas Tellien 30 He 36.00N 2.00 E
Tell City 44 Dg 37.57N 86.46W
Teller 40 Fc 65.16N 166.22W
Telok Anson 26 Df 4.02N 101.01 E
Teloloapan 48 Jh 18.21N 99.51W
Telposiz, Gora- 5 Lc 63.54N 59.10 E
Telsen 56 Gf 42.24S 66.57W
Telšiai/Telšjaj 19 Cd 55.59N 22.17 E
Telšjaj/Telšiai 19 Cd 55.59N 22.17 E
Teltow 10 Jd 52.24N 13.16 E
Telukbetung 22 Mj 5.27S 105.16 E
Telukbutun 26 Ef 4.13N 108.12 E
Telukdalem 26 Cf 0.34N 97.49 E
Têma 31 Gh 5.37N 0.01W
Temacine 32 Ic 33.01N 6.01 E
Te Manga 64p Bb 21.13S 159.45W
Tematangi Atoll 57 Mg 21.41S 140.40W
Tembenči 20 Ed 64.36N 99.58 E
Témbi 15 Fj 39.53N 22.35 E
Tembilahan 26 Dg 0.19S 103.09 E
Temblador 50 Eh 8.59N 62.44W
Tembleque 13 Ie 39.42N 3.30W
Temblor Range 46 Fi 35.30N 119.55W
Tembo 36 Cd 7.42S 17.17 E
Tembo, Chutes- 30 Ii 8.50S 15.20 E
Tembo, Mont- 36 Bb 1.50N 12.00 E
Tembué 37 Eb 14.51S 32.50 E
Teme 9 Ki 52.09N 2.18W
Temerin 15 Cd 45.25N 19.53 E
Temerloh 26 Df 3.27N 102.25 E
Teminabuan 26 Jg 1.26S 132.01 E
Temir 19 Ff 49.08N 57.09 E
Temir 16 Te 48.31N 57.29 E
Temirlanovka 18 Gc 42.36N 69.17 E
Temirtau 22 Jd 50.05N 72.56 E
Témiscaming 44 Hb 46.44N 79.06W
Témiscouata, Lac- 44 Mb 47.40N 68.50W
Temki 35 Bc 11.29N 18.13 E
Temnikov 7 Ki 54.40N 43.13 E
Temo 14 Cj 40.17N 8.28 E
Temoe, Ile- 57 Ng 23.20S 134.29W
Temores 48 Ed 27.16N 108.15W
Tempe 46 Jj 33.25N 111.56W
Tempio Pausania 14 Dj 40.54N 9.06 E
Temple 43 He 31.06N 97.21W
Templeman, Mount- 46 Ga 50.43N 117.14W
Templemore/An Teampall Mór 9 Fi 52.48N 7.50W
Templin 10 Jc 53.07N 13.30 E
Tempoal, Rio- 48 Jg 21.47N 98.27W
Tempué 36 Ce 13.27S 18.53 E
Temrjuk 16 Jg 45.15N 37.23 E
Temse/Tamise 12 Gc 51.08N 4.13 E
Temuco 53 Ii 38.44S 72.36W
Temuka 62 Df 44.15S 171.16 E
Tena 54 Cd 0.59S 77.48W
Tenacatita, Bahia de- 48 Gh 19.10N 104.50W
Tenala/Tenhola 8 Jd 60.04N 23.18 E
Tenāli 25 Ge 16.15N 80.35 E
Tenancingo de Degollado 48 Jh 18.58N 99.36W
Tenasserim 25 Jf 12.05N 99.01 E
Tenasserim 25 Jf 12.24N 98.37 E
Tenasserim 21 Lh 12.35N 97.52 E
Tenby 9 Ij 51.41N 4.43W
Tence 11 Ki 45.07N 4.17 E
Tench Island 60 Eh 1.38S 150.42 E
Tenda, Col di- 14 Bf 44.09N 7.34 E
Tendaho 35 Gc 11.38N 41.00 E
Tende 11 Nj 44.05N 7.36 E
Tende, Col de- 14 Bf 44.09N 7.34 E
Ten Degree Channel 21 Lh 10.00N 92.30 E
Tendō 29 Gb 38.22N 140.22 E
Tendrara 32 Gc 33.03N 2.00W
Tendre, Mont- 14 Ad 46.36N 6.19 E
Tendrovskaja Kosa 16 Gf 46.15N 31.45 E
Ténénkou 34 Ec 14.28N 4.55W
Tenente Lira, Rio- 55 Db 15.56S 57.39W
Ténéré 30 Ig 17.35N 10.55 E
Ténéré, 'Erg du- 34 Hb 17.35N 10.55 E
Tenerife 30 Ff 28.19N 16.34W
Ténès 32 Hb 36.31N 1.18 E
Ténès, Cap- 13 Nh 36.33N 1.21 E
Teng 25 Je 19.52N 97.45 E
Tengah, Kepulauan- 26 Gh 7.30S 117.30 E
Tengchong 27 Gg 24.59N 98.32 E
Te Nggano, Lake- 60 Gj 11.45S 160.25 E
Tenggarong 26 Gg 0.24S 116.58 E
Tengger Shamo 21 Mf 38.00N 104.10 E
Tengiz, Ozero- 21 Id 50.25N 69.00 E
Tengréla 34 Dc 10.29N 6.24W
Tengréla [3] 34 Dc 10.27N 6.25W
Tengxian [China] 27 Jg 23.18N 110.49 E
Tengxian [China] 28 Dg 35.07N 117.10 E
Tenhola/Tenala 8 Jd 60.04N 23.18 E
Teniente General Rosendo M. Fraga 55 Af 23.45S 62.09W
Tenkāsi 25 Fg 8.58N 77.18 E
Tenke 36 Ee 10.33S 26.08 E
Tenkeli 20 Jb 70.01N 140.55 E
Tenkodogo 34 Ec 11.47N 0.22W
Tenna 14 Hg 43.14N 13.47 E
Tennant Creek 58 Ef 19.40S 134.10 E
Tennessee 38 Kf 37.04N 88.33W
Tennessee [2] 43 Jd 35.50N 85.30W
Tenneville 12 Hd 50.06N 5.32 E
Tenoïoki 7 Gb 70.28N 28.18 E
Tenom 26 Ge 5.08N 115.57 E
Tenosique de Pino Suárez 47 Fe 17.29N 91.26W
Tenri 29 Dd 34.36N 135.49 E
Tenryū 29 Ed 34.52N 137.47 E
Tenryū-Gawa 28 Ng 34.35N 137.48 E
Tensift 32 Fc 32.02N 9.21W
Ten Sleep 46 Ld 44.02N 107.27W
Tenterden 12 Cc 51.03N 0.42 E

Index Symbols

- [1] Independent Nation
- [2] State, Region
- [3] District, County
- [4] Municipality
- [5] Colony, Dependency
- Continent
- Physical Region
- Historical or Cultural Region
- Mount, Mountain
- Volcano
- Hill
- Mountains, Mountain Range
- Hills, Escarpment
- Plateau, Upland
- Pass, Gap
- Plain, Lowland
- Delta
- Salt Flat
- Valley, Canyon
- Crater, Cave
- Karst Features
- Depression
- Polder
- Desert, Dunes
- Forest, Woods
- Heath, Steppe
- Oasis
- Cape, Point
- Coast, Beach
- Cliff
- Peninsula
- Isthmus
- Sandbank
- Island
- Atoll
- Rock, Reef
- Islands, Archipelago
- Rocks, Reefs
- Coral Reef
- Well, Spring
- Geyser
- River, Stream
- Waterfall Rapids
- River Mouth, Estuary
- Lake
- Salt Lake
- Intermittent Lake
- Reservoir
- Swamp, Pond
- Canal
- Glacier
- Ice Shelf, Pack Ice
- Ocean
- Sea
- Gulf, Bay
- Strait, Fjord
- Lagoon
- Bank
- Seamount
- Tablemount
- Ridge
- Shelf
- Basin
- Escarpment, Sea Scarp
- Fracture
- Trench, Abyss
- National Park, Reserve
- Point of Interest
- Recreation Site
- Cave, Cavern
- Historic Site
- Ruins
- Wall, Walls
- Church, Abbey
- Temple
- Scientific Station
- Airport
- Port
- Lighthouse
- Mine
- Tunnel
- Dam, Bridge

Tenterfield	59	Ke	29.03 S	152.01 E
Tenuku	25	Ge	81.40N	16.45 E
Tenuze/Teenuse Jõgi	7	Jf	58.44N	23.58 E
Ten-Zan	29	Be	33.20N	130.08 E
Teocaltiche	48	Hg	21.26N	102.35W
Teodelina	55	Bl	34.11 S	61.32W
Teodoro Sampaio	55	Ff	22.31 S	52.10W
Teófilo Otoni	53	Lg	17.51 S	41.30W
Teotepec, Cerro-	38	Ih	16.50N	100.50W
Teotihuacan	47	Ee	19.44N	98.50W
Teotilán del Camino	48	Kh	18.08N	97.05W
Tepa [Indon.]	26	Ih	7.52 S	129.31 E
Tepa [W.F.]	64h	Bb	13.19 S	176.09W
Te Pae Roa Ngake o Tuko	64n	Bb	10.23 S	161.00W
Tepako, Pointe-	64h	Bb	13.16 S	176.08W
Tepalcatepec, Río-	48	Ih	18.35N	101.59W
Tepa Point	64k	Bb	19.07 S	169.56W
Tepatitlán de Morelos	48	Hg	20.49N	102.44W
Tepehuanes	47	Cc	25.21N	105.44W
Tepehuanes, Río-	48	Ge	25.11N	105.26W
Tepehuanes, Sierra de-	47	Cc	25.00N	105.40W
Tepelena	15	Di	40.18N	20.01 E
Tepi	35	Fd	7.03N	35.30 E
Tepic	39	Ig	21.30N	104.54W
Teplá	10	Ig	49.59N	12.52 E
Teplá	10	If	50.14N	12.52 E
Teplice	10	Jf	50.39N	13.50 E
Tepoca, Bahía de-	48	Cb	30.15N	112.50W
Tepopa, Cabo-	48	Cc	29.20N	112.25W
Te Puka	64n	Ac	10.26 S	161.02W
Te Puke	62	Gb	37.47 S	176.20 E
Tequepa, Bahía de-	48	Ii	17.17N	101.05W
Tequila	48	Hg	20.54N	103.47W
Tequisquiapan	48	Jg	20.31N	99.52W
Ter	13	Pb	42.01N	3.12 E
Téra	34	Fc	14.01N	0.45 E
Tera [Port.]	13	Df	38.56N	8.03W
Tera [Sp.]	13	Gc	41.54N	5.44W
Teradomari	29	Fc	37.38N	138.45 E
Terai	21	Kg	26.30N	85.15 E
Teraina Island (Washington)	57	Kd	4.43N	160.24W
Terakeka	35	Ed	5.26N	31.45 E
Teramo	14	Hh	42.39N	13.42 E
Terampa	26	Ef	3.14N	106.14 E
Ter Apel, Vlagtwedde-	12	Jb	52.52N	7.06 E
Terborg, Wisch-	12	Ic	51.55N	6.22 E
Tercan	24	Ic	39.47N	40.24 E
Terceira	30	Ee	38.43N	27.13W
Tercero, Río-	56	Hd	32.55 S	62.19W
Terebovlja	16	De	49.18N	25.42 E
Terehovka	28	Kc	43.38N	131.55 E
Terek	16	Nh	43.29N	44.08 E
Terek	5	Kg	43.44N	47.30 E
Térékolé	34	Cb	15.07N	10.53W
Terek-Saj	18	Hd	41.29N	71.13 E
Terenos	55	Ee	20.26 S	54.50W
Teresa Cristina	55	Gg	24.48 S	51.07W
Teresina	53	Lf	5.05 S	42.49W
Teresinha	54	Hc	0.58N	52.02W
Tereška	16	Od	51.50N	46.45 E
Terespol	10	Td	52.05N	23.36 E
Teressa	25	Ig	8.15N	93.10 E
Teresva	16	Cf	47.59N	23.15 E
Terevaka, Cerro-	65d	Ab	27.05 S	109.23W
Tergnier	11	Je	49.39N	3.18 E
Terhazza	34	Ea	23.36N	4.56W
Teriberka	7	Ib	69.10N	35.10 E
Teriberka	7	Ib	69.09N	35.08 E
Terlingua Creek	45	El	29.10N	103.36W
Termas de Río Hondo	56	Hc	27.29 S	64.52W
Terme	24	Gb	41.12N	36.59 E
Termez	22	If	37.14N	67.16 E
Termini Imerese	14	Hm	37.59N	13.42 E
Termini Imerese, Golfo di-	14	Hl	38.00N	13.45 E
Terminillo	14	Hh	42.28N	13.01 E
Términos, Laguna de-	47	Fe	18.37N	91.33W
Termit, Massif de-	34	Hb	16.15N	11.17 E
Termit-Kaoboul	34	Hb	15.43N	11.37 E
Termoli	14	Ii	42.00N	15.00 E
Termonde/Dendermonde	12	Gc	51.02N	4.07 E
Ternaard, Westdongeradeel-	12	Ha	53.23N	5.58 E
Ternate	25	If	0.48N	127.24 E
Ternej	20	Ig	45.05N	136.35 E
Terneuzen	11	Jc	51.20N	3.50 E
Terni	14	Gh	42.34N	12.37 E
Ternitz	14	Kc	47.43N	16.02 E
Ternois	12	Ed	50.25N	2.19 E
Ternopol	6	If	49.34N	25.38 E
Ternopolskaja Oblast	19	Cf	49.20N	25.35 E
Terpenija, Mys-	20	Jg	48.38N	144.40 E
Terpenija, Zaliv-	21	Qe	49.00N	143.30 E
Terrace	42	Ef	54.31N	128.35W
Terrace Bay	45	Mb	48.47N	87.09W
Terracina	14	Hi	41.17N	13.15 E
Terra de Basto	13	Ec	41.25N	8.00W
Terra Firma	37	Ce	25.36 S	23.24 E
Terråk	7	Cd	65.05N	12.25 E
Terralba	14	Ck	39.43N	8.39 E
Terra Rica	55	Ff	22.43 S	52.38W
Terrebonne Bay	45	Kl	29.09N	90.35W
Terre-de-Bas	51e	Ac	15.51N	61.39W
Terre-de-Haut	51e	Ac	15.58N	61.35W
Terre Froides	11	Li	45.30N	5.30 E
Terre Haute	43	Jd	39.28N	87.24W
Terrell	45	Hj	32.44N	96.17W
Terre Plaine	11	Jg	47.25N	4.00 E
Terril	13	Gh	37.00N	5.11W
Territoire de Belfort	11	Mg	47.45N	7.00 E
Terruca	13	Fc	41.45N	6.25W
Terry	46	Mc	46.47N	105.19W
Tersa	16	Nd	50.46N	44.42 E
Terschelling	12	Ha	53.21N	5.13 E
Terschelling	11	La	53.24N	5.20 E
Terschelling-West-Terschelling	12	Ha	53.21N	5.13 E
Tersef	35	Bc	12.55N	16.49 E
Terskej-Alatau, Hrebet-	19	Hg	42.10N	78.45 E
Terski Bereg	7	Jc	66.10N	39.30 E
Tersko-Kumski Kanal	16	Ng	44.47N	44.37 E
Terter (Mir-Bašir)	16	Oi	40.19N	46.58 E
Teruel	13	Kd	40.21N	1.06W
Teruel	13	Ld	40.40N	0.40W
Tervakoski	8	Kd	60.48N	24.37 E
Tervel	15	Kf	43.45N	27.24 E
Tervo	8	Lb	62.57N	26.45 E
Tervola	7	Fc	66.05N	24.48 E
Tes	27	Fa	50.27N	93.30 E
Teša	7	Ki	55.38N	42.10 E
Tesalia	54	Cc	2.29N	75.44W
Tesaret	32	Hd	25.40N	2.43 E
Tesdrero, Cerro-	48	Hf	22.47N	103.04W
Teseney	35	Fb	15.07N	36.40 E
Teshekpuk Lake	40	Ib	70.35N	153.30W
Teshikaga	28	Rc	43.29N	144.28 E
Teshio	28	Pb	44.53N	141.44 E
Teshio-Dake	28	Qc	43.58N	142.50 E
Teshio-Gawa	28	Pb	44.53N	141.44 E
Teshio-Sanchi	29a	Ba	44.20N	142.00 E
Tesijn → Tesijn Gol	21	Ld	50.28N	93.04 E
Tesijn Gol (Tesijn)	21	Ld	50.28N	93.04 E
Teslić	14	Lf	44.37N	17.52 E
Teslin	42	Ed	61.34N	134.50W
Teslin	42	Ed	60.09N	132.45W
Teslin Lake	42	Ed	60.00N	132.30W
Tesluí	15	He	44.09N	24.29 E
Tesocoma	48	Ed	27.41N	109.16W
Tesouras, Rio-	55	Gb	14.36 S	50.51W
Tesouro	55	Fc	16.04 S	53.34W
Tessala, Monts du-	13	Li	35.15N	0.45W
Tessalit	31	Hf	20.14N	0.59 E
Tessaoua	34	Gc	13.45N	7.59 E
Tessenderlo	12	Hc	51.04N	5.05 E
Test	9	Lk	50.55N	1.29W
Test, Tizi n'-	32	Fc	30.50N	8.20W
Testa, Capo-	14	Di	41.14N	9.08 E
Têt	11	Jl	42.44N	3.02 E
Tetari, Cerro-	49	Ki	9.59N	72.55W
Tetas, Punta-	56	Fc	23.31 S	70.38W
Tete	31	Kj	16.10 S	33.36 E
Tete	37	Ec	15.30 S	33.00 E
Te Teko	62	Gc	38.02 S	176.48 E
Tetepare Island	63a	Cc	8.45 S	157.35 E
Téterchen	12	Ie	49.14N	6.34 E
Tetere	63a	Ec	9.25 S	160.15 E
Teterev	16	Gd	51.01N	30.08 E
Teterow	10	Ic	53.47N	12.34 E
Teteven	15	Hg	42.55N	24.16 E
Tetiaroa Atoll	57	Mf	17.05 S	149.32W
Tetijev	16	Fe	49.23N	29.41 E
Tetjuši	7	Li	54.57N	48.49 E
Teton Peak	46	Ic	47.55N	112.48W
Teton Range	46	Je	43.50N	110.55W
Teton River	46	Jc	47.56N	110.31W
Tétouan	31	Ge	35.34N	5.22W
Tétouan	32	Fb	35.35N	5.30W
Tetovo	15	Dg	42.01N	20.59 E
Tetri-Ckaro	16	Ni	41.33N	44.27 E
Teuco, Río-	55	Bg	25.38 S	60.12W
Teufelskopf	12	Ie	49.36N	6.49 E
Teulada	14	Cl	38.58N	8.46 E
Teulada, Capo-	5	Gh	38.52N	8.38 E
Téul de Gonzales Ortega	48	Hg	21.28N	103.29W
Teun, Pulau-	26	Ih	6.59 S	129.08 E
Teupasenti	49	Df	14.13N	86.42W
Teuquito, Río-	55	Bg	24.22 S	61.09W
Teuri-Tō	29a	Ba	44.25N	141.20 E
Teutoburger Wald	10	Ee	52.10N	8.15 E
Teuva/Östermark	7	Ee	62.29N	21.44 E
Teuz	15	Ec	46.39N	21.33 E
Tevai	63c	Bb	11.37 S	166.55 E
Tevaitoa	65e	Db	16.46 S	151.28W
Tevere = Tiber (EN)	5	Hg	41.44N	12.14 E
Teverya	24	Ff	32.47N	35.32 E
Teviot	9	Kf	55.36N	2.26W
Tevli	10	Ud	52.19N	24.23 E
Tevriz	19	Hd	57.34N	72.24 E
Tevšruleh	27	Hb	47.25N	101.55 E
Te Waewae Bay	62	Bg	46.15 S	167.30 E
Tewkesbury	9	Kj	51.59N	2.09W
Têwo (Dêngkagoin)	27	He	34.03N	103.21 E
Texada Island	46	Cb	49.40N	124.24W
Texarkana [Ar.-U.S.]	43	Ie	33.26N	94.02W
Texarkana [Tx.-U.S.]	39	Jf	33.26N	94.03W
Texas	59	Ke	28.51 S	151.11 E
Texas	43	He	31.30N	99.00W
Texas City	43	If	29.23N	94.54W
Texcoco	48	Jh	19.31N	98.53W
Texel	12	Ga	53.03N	4.47 E
Texel	11	Ka	53.05N	4.45 E
Texel-De Koog	12	Ga	53.07N	4.46 E
Texel-Den Burg	12	Ga	53.03N	4.47 E
Texoma, Lake-	43	He	33.55N	96.37W
Teyéa = Tegea (EN)	15	Fl	37.27N	22.25 E
Teza	7	Jh	56.32N	41.57 E
Teze-Jel	19	Gh	37.55N	60.22 E
Teziutlán	47	Ee	19.49N	97.21W
Tezpur	25	Ic	26.38N	92.48 E
Tha-anne	42	Id	60.31N	94.37W
Thabana Ntlenyana	30	Jk	29.30 S	29.15 E
Thabazimbi	37	Dd	24.41 S	27.21 E
Thai, Ao- = Thailand, Gulf of- (EN)	21	Mh	10.00N	102.00 E
Thai Binh	25	Ld	20.27N	106.20 E
Thailand (EN) = Muang Thai	22	Mh	15.00N	100.00 E
Thailand, Gulf of- (EN) = Thai, Ao-	21	Mh	10.00N	102.00 E
Thai Nguyen	25	Ld	21.36N	105.50 E
Thal	25	Eb	31.30N	71.40 E
Thālith, Ash Shallāl ath- = Third Cataract (EN)	30	Kg	19.49N	30.19 E
Thamad Bū Ḩashīshah	33	Cd	25.50N	18.05 E
Thamarīd	35	Ib	17.39N	54.02 E
Thame	12	Bc	51.45N	0.59W
Thames	61	Eg	37.08 S	175.33 E
Thames	5	Ge	51.28N	0.43 E
Thames River	44	Fd	42.19N	82.28W
Thamūd	23	Gf	17.15N	49.54 E
Thāna	22	Jh	19.12N	72.58 E
Thandaung	25	Je	19.04N	96.41 E
Thanh Hoa	22	Mh	19.48N	105.46 E
Thanh Pho Ho Chi Minh (Saigon)	22	Mh	10.45N	106.40 E
Thanjāvūr	25	Ff	10.48N	79.08 E
Thanlwin = Salween (EN)	21	Lg	16.31N	97.37 E
Thann	11	Ng	47.49N	7.05 E
Thaon-les-Vosges	11	Mf	48.15N	6.25 E
Thap Sakae	25	Jf	11.14N	99.31 E
Thar/Great Indian Desert	21	Ig	27.00N	70.00 E
Thargomindah	59	Ie	28.00 S	143.49 E
Tharrawaddy	25	Je	17.39N	95.48 E
Tharros	14	Ck	39.54N	8.28 E
Tharthār, Baḩr ath-	23	Fc	33.59N	43.12 E
Tharthār, Wādī ath-	23	Fc	33.59N	43.12 E
Thasi Gang Dzong	25	Ic	27.19N	91.34 E
Thásos	5	Ig	40.49N	24.42 E
Thásos	15	Hi	40.47N	24.43 E
Thásou, Dhiavlos-	15	Hi	40.49N	24.42 E
Thathlīth, Wādī-	33	He	20.25N	44.55 E
Thau, Bassin de-	11	Jk	43.23N	3.36 E
Thaxted	12	Cc	51.57N	0.22 E
Thaya	10	Mh	48.37N	16.56 E
Thayetchaung	25	Jf	13.52N	98.16 E
Thayetmyo	25	Je	19.19N	95.11 E
Thaywthadangyi Kyun	25	Jf	12.20N	98.00 E
The Alberga River	59	He	27.06 S	135.33 E
The Aldermen Islands	62	Gb	37.00 S	176.05 E
Thebai = Thebes (EN)	33	Fd	25.43N	32.35 E
Thebes (EN) = Thebai	33	Fd	25.43N	32.35 E
Thebes (EN) = Thívai	15	Gk	38.19N	23.19 E
The Black Sugarloaf	59	Kf	31.20 S	151.33 E
The Borders	9	Kf	55.35N	2.50W
The Bottom	50	Ed	17.38N	63.15W
The Broads	9	Oi	52.40N	1.30 E
The Cheviot	9	Kf	55.28N	2.09W
The Cheviot Hills	9	Kf	55.30N	2.10W
The Crane	51q	Bb	13.06N	59.26W
The Dalles	43	Cb	45.36N	121.10W
Thedford	43	Gc	41.59N	100.35W
The Entrance	59	Kf	33.21 S	151.30 E
The Everglades	43	Kf	26.00N	81.00W
The Fens	9	Mi	5.24N	0.02W
The Gap	46	Jh	36.25N	111.30W
The Granites	59	Gd	20.35 S	130.21 E
The Hague (EN) = Den Haag /'s-Gravenhage	6	Ge	52.06N	4.18 E
The Little Minch	9	Gd	57.35N	6.55W
Thelle	12	De	49.23N	1.51 E
Thelon	38	Jc	64.16N	96.05W
The Macumba River	57	Eg	27.45 S	136.50 E
The Merse	9	Kf	55.50N	2.10W
The Naze	12	Dc	51.42N	1.47 E
The Neales River	59	He	28.08 S	136.47 E
The Needles	9	Lk	50.39N	1.34W
Theniet el Had	13	Oi	35.32N	2.01 E
Theodore	59	Kd	24.57 S	150.05 E
Theológos	15	Hi	40.40N	24.42 E
The Pas	39	Id	53.50N	101.15W
The Pillories	51n	Bb	12.54N	61.12W
Thérain	11	Ie	49.15N	2.27 E
Thermaïkós Kólpos = Salonika, Gulf of- (EN)	5	Ig	40.20N	22.45 E
Thermopílai = Thermopylae (EN)	15	Fk	38.48N	22.32 E
Thermopolis	43	Fc	43.39N	108.13W
Thermopylae (EN) = Thermopílai	15	Fk	38.48N	22.32 E
Thérouanne	12	Ed	50.38N	2.15 E
The Round Mountain	59	Kf	30.27 S	152.16 E
The Sandlings	9	Oi	52.10N	1.30 E
Thesiger Bay	42	Fb	71.30N	124.00W
The Slot → New Georgia Sound	60	Fi	8.00 S	158.10 E
The Solent Spithead	9	Lk	50.46N	1.20W
Thessalia	15	Fj	39.30N	22.10 E
Thessalia = Thessaly (EN)	5	Ih	39.30N	22.10 E
Thessalia = Thessaly (EN)	15	Fj	39.30N	22.10 E
Thessalon	44	Fb	46.15N	83.34W
Thessaloniki = Salonika (EN)	6	Ig	40.38N	22.56 E
Thessaly (EN) = Thessalia	15	Fj	39.30N	22.10 E
Thessaly (EN) = Thessalia	5	Ih	39.30N	22.10 E
The Stevenson River	59	He	27.06 S	135.33 E
Thet	12	Cb	52.24N	0.45 E
Thetford	9	Ni	52.25N	0.45 E
Thetford Mines	44	Lb	46.05N	71.18W
The Twins	62	Ed	41.14 S	172.40 E
Theux	12	Hd	50.33N	5.49 E
The Valley	47	Le	18.03N	63.04W
The Warburton River	59	He	27.55 S	137.28 E
The Wash	9	Ni	52.55N	0.15 E
The Weald	9	Nj	51.05N	0.05 E
The Witties	49	Ff	14.10N	82.45W
The Wolds	9	Mh	53.20N	0.10W
Thiaucourt-Regniéville	12	Hf	48.57N	5.52 E
Thiberville	12	Ce	49.08N	0.27 E
Thibodaux	45	Kl	29.48N	90.49W
Thief River Falls	43	Hb	48.07N	96.10W
Thiel Mountains	66	Pg	85.15 S	91.00W
Thiene	14	Fe	45.42N	11.29 E
Thiérache, Collines de la-	11	Je	49.48N	3.55 E
Thiers	11	Ji	45.51N	3.34 E
Thiès	31	Fg	14.48N	16.56W
Thiès	34	Bc	14.45N	16.50W
Thiesi	14	Cj	40.31N	8.43 E
Thika	36	Gc	1.03 S	37.05 E
Thikombia	61	Fc	15.44 S	179.55W
Thimerais	11	Hf	48.40N	1.20 E
Thimphu	22	Kg	27.28N	89.39 E
Thio	61	Cd	21.37 S	166.14 E
Thionville	11	Me	49.22N	6.10 E
Thiou	34	Ec	13.48N	2.40W
Thira	15	Im	36.25N	25.26 E
Thira = Thira (EN)	15	Im	36.24N	25.26 E
Thira (EN) = Thira	15	Im	36.24N	25.26 E
Thirasia	15	Im	36.25N	25.20 E
Third Cataract (EN) = Thālith, Ash Shallāl ath-	30	Kg	19.49N	30.19 E
Thirsk	9	Lg	54.14N	1.20W
Thisted	7	Bh	56.57N	8.42 E
Thithia	63d	Cb	17.45 S	179.18W
Thiu Khao Phetchabun	25	Ke	16.20N	100.55 E
Thívai = Thebes (EN)	15	Gk	38.19N	23.19 E
Thiviers	11	Gi	45.25N	0.55 E
Thlewiaza	42	Id	60.28N	94.42W
Thoa	42	Gd	60.31N	109.45W
Tho.Chu, Dao-	25	Kg	9.00N	103.50 E
Thoen	25	Je	17.41N	99.14 E
Tholen	12	Gc	51.32N	4.13 E
Tholen	11	Kc	51.35N	4.05 E
Tholey	12	Je	49.29N	7.04 E
Thomasset, Rocher-	57	Nf	10.21 S	138.25W
Thomaston	44	Ei	32.54N	84.20W
Thomasville [Al.-U.S.]	44	Dj	32.18N	87.47W
Thomasville [Ga.-U.S.]	43	Ke	30.50N	83.59W
Thomasville [N.C.-U.S.]	44	Gh	35.53N	80.05W
Thompson	42	He	55.45N	97.45W
Thompson Falls	46	Hc	47.36N	115.21W
Thompson River	45	Jg	39.45N	93.36W
Thompson Sound	62	Bf	45.10 S	167.00 E
Thomsen	42	Fb	73.40N	119.30W
Thomson	44	Fi	33.28N	82.30W
Thomson River	59	Ie	25.11 S	142.53 E
Thomson's Falls	36	Gb	0.02N	36.22 E
Thon	12	Fe	49.53N	3.55 E
Thon Buri	22	Mh	13.43N	100.24 E
Thong Pha Phum	25	Jf	14.44N	98.38 E
Thongwa	25	Je	16.46N	96.32 E
Thonon-les-Bains	11	Mh	46.22N	6.29 E
Thoreau	45	Bi	35.24N	108.13W
Thornaby-on-Tees	9	Lg	54.34N	1.18W
Thornbury	61	Ci	46.17 S	168.06 E
Thorney	12	Bb	52.37N	0.06W
Thornhill	9	Jf	55.18N	3.40W
Thorshavn	6	Fc	62.01N	6.46W
Thouars	11	Fh	46.58N	0.13W
Thouet	11	Fg	47.17N	0.06W
Thrace (EN) = Thráki	15	Jh	41.20N	26.45 E
Thrace (EN) = Thráki	5	Ig	41.20N	26.45 E
Thrace (EN) = Trakya	15	Jh	41.20N	26.45 E
Thrace (EN) = Trakya	5	Ig	41.20N	26.45 E
Thráki	15	Ih	41.10N	25.30 E
Thráki = Thrace (EN)	5	Ig	41.20N	26.45 E
Thráki = Thrace (EN)	15	Jh	41.20N	26.45 E
Thrakikón Pélagos	15	Hi	40.30N	25.00 E
Thrapston	12	Bb	52.24N	0.32W
Three Forks	43	Eb	45.54N	111.33W
Three Kings Islands	57	Ih	34.10 S	172.10 E
Three Kings Trough (EN)	3	Jm	32.00 S	170.30 E
Three Points, Cape-	30	Gh	4.45N	2.06W
Three Rivers	44	Ee	41.57N	85.38W
Three Sisters Islands	63a	Ed	10.10 S	161.57 E
Throckmorton	45	Gj	33.11N	99.11W
Throssel, Lake-	59	Ee	27.25 S	124.15 E
Thua	36	Gc	1.17 S	40.00 E
Thuin	11	Kd	50.20N	4.17 E
Thule	66	Ad	59.27 S	27.19W
Thule/Qânâq	67	Od	77.35N	69.40W
Thule, Mount-	42	Jb	73.00N	78.27W
Thun	14	Bd	46.45N	7.40 E
Thunder Bay	39	Ke	48.23N	89.15W
Thunder Bay [Mi.-U.S.]	44	Fc	45.04N	83.25W
Thunder Bay [Ont.-Can.]	45	Lb	48.24N	89.00W
Thunder Butte	45	Fd	45.19N	101.53W
Thuner See	14	Bd	46.40N	7.45 E
Thung Song	25	Jg	8.11N	99.41 E
Thur	14	Cc	47.36N	8.35 E
Thurgau	14	Dc	47.40N	9.10 E
Thüringen	10	Gf	50.40N	11.00 E
Thüringer Wald = Thuringian Forest (EN)	5	He	50.30N	11.00 E
Thuringian Forest (EN) = Thüringer Wald	5	He	50.30N	11.00 E
Thurles/Durlas	9	Fi	52.41N	7.49W
Thurrock	9	Nj	51.28N	0.20 E
Thursday Island	59	Ib	10.35 S	142.13 E
Thurso	6	Fd	58.35N	3.32W
Thurso	9	Jc	58.35N	3.30W
Thurston Island	66	Pf	72.06 S	99.00W
Thury-Harcourt	12	Bf	48.59N	0.29W
Thusis/Tusaun	14	Dd	46.42N	9.26 E
Thuwayrāt, Nafūd ath-	24	Kj	26.00N	44.50 E
Thuy Phong	25	Lf	11.14N	108.43 E
Thwaites Iceberg Tongue	66	Of	74.00 S	108.30W
Thy	8	Ch	57.00N	8.30 E
Thyborøn	8	Ch	56.42N	8.13 E
Tianbaoshan	28	Jc	42.57N	128.57 E
Tianchang	27	Ke	32.37N	119.00 E
Tiandong (Pingma)	27	Ig	23.40N	107.09 E
Tian'e (Liupai)	27	If	25.05N	107.12 E
Tianguá	54	Jd	3.44 S	40.59W
Tianjin = Tientsin (EN)	22	Nf	39.08N	117.12 E
Tianjin Shi (T'ien-chin Shih)	27	Kd	39.08N	117.12 E
Tianjun (Xinyuan)	22	Lf	37.18N	99.15 E
Tianlin (Leli)	27	Ig	24.22N	106.11 E
Tian Ling	28	Kb	44.24N	130.10 E
Tianmen	27	Je	30.40N	113.10 E
Tianmu Shan	28	Ei	30.31N	119.36 E
Tianmu Xi	28	Ej	29.59N	119.24 E
Tianqiaoling	27	Mc	43.35N	129.35 E
Tian Shan	21	Ke	42.00N	80.01 E
Tianshan → Ar Horqin Qi	27	Lc	43.55N	120.05 E
Tianshifu	27	Lc	41.15N	124.20 E
Tianshui	22	Mf	34.35N	105.43 E
Tiantal	28	Fj	29.08N	121.00 E
Tianwangsi	28	Ei	31.45N	119.12 E
Tianyi → Ningcheng	27	Kc	41.34N	119.25 E
Tianzhen	28	Cd	40.24N	114.05 E
Tianzhen → Gaoqing	28	Df	37.10N	117.50 E
Tianzhuangtai	28	Gd	40.49N	122.06 E
Tiaraju	55	Ej	30.15 S	54.23W
Tiarei	65e	Fc	17.32 S	149.20W
Tiaret	32	Hc	34.50N	1.30 E
Tiaret	31	He	35.20N	1.14 E
Tiaret, Monts de-	13	Ni	35.26N	1.15 E
Tiassalé	34	Ed	5.54N	4.50W
Tiavea	65c	Ba	13.57 S	171.24W
Ţīb, Ra's Aţ- = Bon, Cape- (EN)	30	Ie	37.05N	11.03 E
Tibagi	55	Gg	24.30 S	50.24W
Tibaji, Rio-	55	Gf	22.47 S	51.01W
Tibasti, Sarīr-	30	If	24.00N	17.00 E
Tibati	31	Ih	6.28N	12.38 E
Tiber (EN) = Tevere	5	Hg	41.44N	12.14 E
Tiberina, Val-	14	Gg	43.30N	12.10 E
Tibesti	30	If	21.30N	17.30 E
Tibet (EN) = Xizang Zizhiqu (Hsi-tsang Tzu-chih-ch'ü)	27	Ee	32.00N	90.00 E
Tibet, Plateau of- (EN) = Qing Zang Gaoyuan	21	Kf	32.30N	87.00 E
Tibidabo	13	Oc	41.25N	2.07 E
Tibni	24	He	35.35N	30.49 E
Tibro	8	Ff	58.26N	14.10 E
Tibú	49	Ki	8.40N	72.42W
Tibugà, Golfo de-	54	Cb	5.45N	77.20W
Tiburón, Capo-	49	Ii	8.42N	77.21W
Tiburon, Isla-	47	Bc	29.00N	112.25W
Ticao	26	Hd	12.31N	123.42 E
Tice	44	Gl	26.41N	81.49W
Tichá Orlice	10	Mf	50.09N	16.05 E
Tichît	31	Gg	18.26N	9.31W
Tichît, Dahr-	32	Ff	18.30N	9.25W
Tichka, Tizi n'-	32	Fc	31.17N	7.21W
Tichla	32	Ee	21.36N	14.58W
Ticino	14	Cd	46.20N	9.00 E
Ticino	14	De	45.09N	9.14 E
Ticul	47	Gd	20.24N	89.32W
Tidaholm	7	Cg	58.11N	13.57 E
Tidan	8	Ef	58.42N	13.48 E
Tiddim	25	Id	23.22N	93.40 E
Tidikelt, Plaine du-	30	Hf	27.00N	1.30 E
Tidirhine	32	Gc	34.51N	4.31W
Tidjikja	31	Fg	18.32N	11.27W
Tidore	26	If	0.40N	127.26 E
Tidra, Ile-	30	Fg	19.44N	16.24W
Tiebissou	34	Dd	7.10N	5.13W
Tiechang	28	Id	41.40N	126.12 E
Tiel	11	Lc	51.54N	5.25 E
Tieli	27	Mb	47.04N	128.02 E
Tieling	28	Gc	42.18N	123.51 E
Tielt	11	Jc	51.00N	3.20 E
Tienba	34	Dd	8.30N	7.10W
T'ien-chin Shih → Tianjin Shi	27	Kd	39.08N	117.12 E
Tienen/Tirlemont	12	Gd	50.48N	4.57 E
Tiengemeten	12	Gc	51.45N	5.20 E
Tientsin (EN) = Tianjin	22	Nf	39.08N	117.12 E
Tieroko, Tarso-	35	Ba	20.45N	17.52 E
Tierp	7	Df	60.20N	17.30 E
Tierra Amarilla [Chile]	56	Fc	27.29 S	70.17W
Tierra Amarilla [N.M.-U.S.]	45	Ch	36.42N	106.33W
Tierra Blanca	47	Ee	18.27N	96.21W
Tierra Colorada	48	Ji	17.10N	99.35W
Tierra del Fuego	56	Gh	54.00 S	67.00W
Tierra del Fuego (EN) = Tierra del Fuego, Isla Grande de-	52	Jk	54.00 S	69.00W
Tierra del Fuego, Isla Grande de- = Tierra del Fuego (EN)	52	Jk	54.00 S	69.00W
Tierralta	54	Cb	8.10N	76.04W
Tiétar	13	Fe	39.50N	6.01W
Tietê, Rio-	52	Kh	20.40 S	51.35W
Tietjerksteradeel	12	Ia	53.12N	6.00 E
Tietjerksteradeel-Bergum	12	Hb	52.17N	5.58 E
Tifariti	32	Ed	26.09N	10.33W
Tiffany Mountain	46	Fb	48.40N	119.56W
Tiffin	44	Fe	41.07N	83.11W
Tifton	43	Ke	31.27N	83.31W
Tiga	63b	Ce	21.08 S	167.49 E
Tigalda	40a	Fb	54.05N	165.05W
Tigăneşti	15	If	43.54N	25.22 E
Tighennif	13	Mi	35.25N	0.15 E
Tigil	20	Ke	57.57N	158.20 E
Tigil	20	Ke	57.48N	158.40 E
Tignère	34	Hd	7.22N	12.39 E
Tigray	35	Fc	14.00N	39.00 E
Tigre	48	Hh	19.53N	102.59W
Tigre, Cerro del-	48	Jf	23.03N	99.16W
Tigre, Rio- [S.Amer.]	52	If	4.30 S	74.10W
Tigre, Rio- [Ven.]	50	Eh	9.20N	62.30W
Tigris (EN) = Dicle	21	Gf	31.00N	47.25 E
Tigris (EN) = Dijlah	21	Gf	31.00N	47.25 E
Tigrovy Hvost, Mys-	18	Bc	43.57N	58.45 E
Tiguent	32	Df	17.15N	16.00W
Tiguentourine	32	Id	27.43N	9.33 E
Tigui	35	Bb	18.38N	18.47 E
Tigzirt	13	Qh	36.54N	4.07 E
Tih, Jabal at-	33	Fd	29.35N	34.00 E
Tih, Şahrā' at- = At Tih Desert (EN)	33	Fc	30.05N	34.00 E
Tihāmat	23	Ff	18.30N	41.30 E
Tihāmat Ash Shām	33	Hf	19.15N	41.10 E

Index Symbols

1 Independent Nation
2 State, Region
3 District, County
4 Municipality
5 Colony, Dependency
Continent
Physical Region
Historical or Cultural Region
Mount, Mountain
Volcano
Hill
Mountains, Mountain Range
Hills, Escarpment
Plateau, Upland
Pass, Gap
Plain, Lowland
Delta
Salt Flat
Valley, Canyon
Crater, Cave
Karst Features
Depression
Polder
Desert, Dunes
Forest, Woods
Heath, Steppe
Oasis
Cape, Point
Coast, Beach
Cliff
Peninsula
Isthmus
Sandbank
Island
Atoll
Rock, Reef
Islands, Archipelago
Rocks, Reefs
Coral Reef
Well, Spring
Geyser
River, Stream
Waterfall Rapids
River Mouth, Estuary
Lake
Salt Lake
Intermittent Lake
Reservoir
Swamp, Pond
Canal
Glacier
Ice Shelf, Pack Ice
Ocean
Sea
Gulf, Bay
Strait, Fjord
Lagoon
Bank
Seamount
Tablemount
Ridge
Shelf
Basin
Escarpment, Sea Scarp
Fracture
Trench, Abyss
National Park, Reserve
Point of Interest
Recreation Site
Cave, Cavern
Historic Site
Ruins
Wall, Walls
Church, Abbey
Temple
Scientific Station
Airport
Port
Lighthouse
Mine
Tunnel
Dam, Bridge

Tihāmat 'Asīr ⬚	33 Hf	17.30N	42.20 E
Tihi Okean = Pacific Ocean			
(EN) ▦	3 Ki	5.00N	155.00W
Tihoreck	6 Kf	45.51N	40.09 E
Tihuṭa, Pasul- ⬚	15 Hb	47.15N	25.00 E
Tihvin	19 Dd	59.38N	33.31 E
Tiirismaa ▲	8 Kc	61.01N	25.31 E
Tiji	33 Bc	32.01N	11.22 E
Tijirīt ⬚	32 Ee	20.30N	15.00W
Tijuana	39 Hf	32.32N	117.01W
Tijucas	55 Hh	27.14S	48.38W
Tijucas, Baía do- ◧	55 Hh	27.15S	48.31W
Tijucas, Rio- ◺	55 Hh	27.15S	48.38W
Tijucas, Serra do- ▲	55 Hh	27.16S	49.10W
Tijucas do Sul	55 Hg	25.56S	49.10W
Tijuco, Rio- ◺	55 Gd	18.40S	50.05W
Tikal ⬚	39 Kh	17.20N	89.39W
Tikanlik	27 Ec	40.42N	87.38 E
Tikchik Lakes ▨	40 Hd	60.07N	158.35W
Tikehau Atoll [○]	61 Lb	15.00S	148.10W
Tikei, Île- ▣	61 Mb	14.58S	144.32W
Tikitiki	62 Hb	37.47S	178.25 E
Tikkakoski	8 Kb	62.24N	25.38 E
Tikkurila	8 Kd	60.18N	25.03 E
Tiko	34 Ge	4.05N	9.22 E
Tikopia Island ▣	57 Hf	12.19S	168.49 E
Tikrīt	23 Fc	34.36N	43.42 E
Tikšeozero, Ozero- ◺	7 Hc	66.15N	31.45 E
Tiksi	22 Ob	71.36N	128.48 E
Tiladummati Atoll [○]	25a Ba	6.50N	73.05 E
Tilamuta	26 Hf	0.30N	122.20 E
Tilburg	11 Lc	51.34N	5.05 E
Tilbury, Gravesend- ▣	9 Nj	51.28N	0.23 E
Tilcara	56 Gb	23.34S	65.22W
Til-Châtel	11 Lg	47.31N	5.10 E
Tileagd	15 Fh	47.04N	22.12 E
Tilemsès	34 Fb	15.37N	4.44 E
Tilemsi, Vallée du- ⬚	30 Hg	19.00N	0.02 E
Tilia ◺	32 Gd	27.22N	0.02W
Tiličiki	20 Ld	60.20N	166.03 E
Tiligul ◺	16 Gf	47.07N	30.57 E
Tiligulskij Liman ▨	16 Gf	46.50N	31.10 E
Till ◺	9 Kf	55.41N	2.12W
Tillabéry	34 Fc	14.13N	1.27 E
Tillamook	46 Dd	45.27N	123.51W
Tillamook Bay ◧	46 Dd	45.30N	123.53W
Tillanchong ▣	25 Ig	8.30N	93.37 E
Tillberga	8 Ge	59.41N	16.37 E
Tille ◺	11 Lg	47.07N	5.21 E
Tillia	34 Fb	16.08N	4.47 E
Tillières-sur-Avre	12 Df	48.46N	1.04 E
Tillingham ◺	12 Cd	50.58N	0.44 E
Tillsonburg	44 Gd	42.51N	80.44W
Tilly-sur-Seulles	12 Be	49.11N	0.37W
Tiloa	34 Fb	15.04N	2.03 E
Tilos ▣	15 Km	36.25N	27.25 E
Tilpa	59 If	30.57S	144.24 E
Tim	16 Jd	51.37N	37.11 E
Tim ◺	16 Jc	52.15N	37.22 E
Ṭimā	33 Fd	26.54N	31.26 E
Timagami	44 Gb	47.00N	80.05W
Timagami, Lake - ▨	42 Ja	46.57N	80.05W
Timane, Rio- ◺	55 Be	20.16S	60.08W
Timan Ridge (EN) =			
Timanskij Krjaž ▲	5 Lc	65.00N	51.00 E
Timanski Bereg ▨	17 Eb	68.20N	51.45 E
Timanski Krjaž = Timan			
Ridge (EN) ▲	5 Lc	65.00N	51.00 E
Timaru	58 Ii	44.24S	171.15 E
Timaševsk	19 Df	45.35N	38.58 E
Timbalier Bay ◧	45 Kl	29.10N	90.20W
Timbalier Island ▣	45 Kl	29.04N	90.28W
Timbaúba	54 Ke	7.31S	35.19W
Timbédra	32 Ff	16.14N	8.10W
Timbó	55 Hh	26.50S	49.18W
Timbuktu (EN) =			
Tombouctou	31 Gg	16.46N	2.59W
Timedouine, Ras- ▲	33 Qh	36.28N	4.09 E
Timétrine ⬚	34 Eb	19.20N	0.42W
Timétrine ⬚	34 Eb	19.27N	0.26W
Timfi Óros ▲	15 Dj	39.57N	20.50 E
Timfristós ▲	15 Ek	38.57N	21.49 E
Timia	34 Gb	18.04N	8.40 E
Timimoun	31 Hf	29.15N	0.15 E
Timimoun, Sebkha de- ▨	32 Hd	29.00N	0.05 E
Timiris, Cap- ▶	30 Fg	19.23N	16.32W
Timirjazevo	19 Sa	53.45N	66.33 E
Timiş ◺	15 De	44.51N	20.39 E
Timiş ⬚	15 Ed	45.38N	21.13 E
Timiskaming, Lake- ▨	44 Hb	47.35N	79.35W
Timişoara	6 If	45.45N	21.13 E
Ti-m-Merhsoi ◺	34 Gb	18.00N	5.40 E
Timmins	39 Ke	48.28N	81.20W
Timmoudi	32 Gd	29.19N	1.08W
Timms Hill ▲	45 Kd	45.27N	90.11W
Timok ◺	15 Fe	44.13N	22.40 E
Timon	54 Je	5.06S	42.49W
Timor, Laut- = Timor Sea			
(EN) ▬	57 Df	11.00S	128.00 E
Timor, Pulau- ▣	21 Oj	8.50S	126.00 E
Timor Sea (EN) = Timor,			
Laut- ▬	57 Df	11.00S	128.00 E
Timor Timur ⬚	21 Oj	8.35S	126.00 E
Timor Trough ◺	3 Ij	9.50S	126.00 E
Timote	56 He	35.21S	62.14W
Timotes	54 Db	8.59N	70.44W
Timpton ▶	20 He	58.43N	127.12 E
Timrå	7 De	62.29N	17.18 E
Tims Ford Lake ▨	44 Dh	35.15N	86.10W
Tin, Ra's at- ▶	33 Dc	32.37N	23.08 E
Tinaca Point ▶	21 Oi	5.33N	125.20 E
Tinaco	50 Bh	9.42N	68.26W
Tinakula ▣	63c Ab	10.24S	165.47 E
Ti-n-Alkoum	32 Je	24.34N	10.11 E
Ti-n-Amzi [Alg.] ◺	32 Je	24.34N	9.53 E
Ti-n-Amzi [Niger] ◺	34 Fb	17.54N	4.32 E
Tinaquillo	50 Bh	9.55N	68.18W

Tinchebray	12 Bf	48.46N	0.44W
Tindalo	35 Ed	5.39N	31.03 E
Tindari ⬚	14 Jl	38.10N	15.04 E
Tindila	34 Dc	10.16N	8.15W
Tindouf	31 Gf	27.42N	8.09W
Tindouf, Hamada de- ▨	32 Ff	27.45N	8.25W
Tindouf, Sebkha de- ▨	32 Fd	27.45N	7.35W
Tinée ◺	11 Nk	43.55N	7.11 E
Tineo	13 Fa	43.20N	6.25W
Ti-n-Essako	34 Fb	18.27N	2.29 E
Tin Fouye	32 Id	28.15N	7.45 E
Tinghert, Ḥamādat- ⬚	30 Hf	28.50N	10.00 E
Tinglev	8 Cj	54.56N	9.15 E
Tingmiarmiut	41 Hf	62.25N	42.15W
Tingo Maria	54 Ce	9.10S	76.00W
Tingri (Xêgar)	27 Ef	28.41N	87.00 E
Tingsryd	7 Dh	56.32N	14.59 E
Tingstäde	8 Hg	57.44N	18.36 E
Tingvoll	7 Be	62.54N	8.12 E
Tinharé, Ilha de- ▣	64b Bb	14.54N	145.37 E
Tinian Island ▣	57 Fc	15.00N	145.38 E
Tini Wells	35 Cb	15.02N	22.48 E
Tinkisso ◺	34 Dc	11.21N	9.10W
Tinniswood, Mount- ▲	46 Da	50.19N	123.50W
Tinnoset	8 Ce	59.43N	9.02 E
Tinnsjø ▨	8 Ce	59.54N	8.55 E
Tinogasta	56 Gc	28.04S	67.34W
Tinos ▣	15 Il	37.35S	25.10 E
Tinos	15 Il	37.32N	25.10 E
Tínou, Stenón- ▬	15 Il	37.38N	25.10 E
Tinrhert, Hamada de- ▨	30 Hf	28.50N	10.00 E
Tinrhir	32 Fc	31.31N	5.32W
Tinsukia	25 Jc	27.30N	95.22 E
Tintagel Head ▶	9 Ik	50.41N	4.46W
Tintamarre, Île- ▣	51b Bb	18.07N	63.00W
Ti-n-Tarabine ◺	32 Ie	21.16N	7.24 E
Tintáreni	15 Ge	44.36N	23.29 E
Tinto ◺	13 Fg	37.12N	6.55W
Ti-n-toumma ⬚	30 Ig	16.04N	12.00 E
Tinwald	62 De	43.55S	171.43 E
Ti-n-Zaouâtene	31 Hg	19.56N	2.55 E
Tiobraid Árann/Tipperary	9 Ei	52.29N	8.10W
Tiobraid Árann/Tipperary [2]	9 Ei	52.40N	8.20W
Tioga	45 Bb	48.24N	102.56W
Tioman, Pulau- ▣	26 Df	2.48N	104.11 E
Tione di Trento	14 Ed	46.02N	10.43 E
Tioro, Selat- = Tioro, Strait			
(EN) ▬	26 Hg	4.40S	122.20 E
Tioro Strait (EN) = Tioro,			
Selat- ▬	26 Hg	4.40S	122.20 E
Tiotta	7 Cd	65.50N	12.24 E
Tiouilit	32 Df	18.52N	16.10W
Tipasa	32 Hb	36.35N	2.27 E
Tipitapa	47 Gf	12.12N	86.06W
Tipperary/Tiobraid Árann	9 Ei	52.29N	8.10W
Tipperary/Tiobraid Árann [2]	9 Ei	52.40N	8.20W
Tipton, Mount- ▲	46 Hi	35.32N	114.12W
Tip Top Mountain ▲	45 Nb	48.16N	85.59W
Tiptree	12 Cc	51.49N	0.45 E
Tiracambu, Serra do- ▲	54 Id	3.15S	46.30W
Tirahart ◺	32 He	23.45N	2.30 E
Tirân	24 Nf	32.42N	51.09 E
Tīrān, Maḍīq- ▬	24 Fi	27.55N	34.28 E
Tirana	6 Hj	41.20N	19.50 E
Tiranía ▨	32 Ie	23.08N	9.01 E
Tirano	14 Ed	46.13N	10.10 E
Tiraspol	17 Cf	46.50N	29.37 E
Tirat Karmel	24 Fg	32.46N	34.58 E
Tire	23 Cb	38.04N	27.45 E
Tirebolu	24 Hh	41.00N	38.50 E
Tiree ▣	9 Ge	56.30N	6.49W
Tiree, Passage of- ▬	9 Ge	56.30N	6.30W
Tírgovişte	15 Ie	44.56N	25.27 E
Tîrgu Bujor	15 Kd	45.52N	27.54 E
Tîrgu Cărbuneşti	15 Ge	44.57N	23.31 E
Tîrgu Frumos	15 Jb	47.12N	27.00 E
Tîrgu Jiu	15 Gd	45.03N	23.17 E
Tîrgu Lăpuş	15 Gc	47.27N	23.52 E
Tîrgu Mureş	6 If	46.33N	24.34 E
Tîrgu Neamţ	15 Jc	47.12N	26.22 E
Tîrgu Ocna	15 Jc	46.17N	26.37 E
Tîrgu Secuiesc	15 Jd	46.00N	26.08 E
Tîrguşor	15 Le	44.27N	28.25 E
Tirich Mir ▲	21 Jf	36.15N	71.50 E
Tirins ⬚	15 Fl	37.36N	22.48 E
Tiririca, Serra da- ▲	55 Ic	17.06S	47.06W
Tiris ⬚	30 Ff	23.10N	13.30W
Tiris Zemmour [3]	32 Fe	24.00N	10.00W
Tirlemont/Tienen	12 Gd	50.48N	4.57 E
Tirljanski	17 Lh	54.12N	58.33 E
Tîrnava Mare ◺	15 Gc	46.09N	23.42 E
Tîrnava Mică ◺	15 Hc	46.11N	23.55 E
Tîrnăveni	15 Hc	46.20N	24.17 E
Tirnavos	15 Fj	39.45N	22.17 E
Tiro	34 Cd	9.45N	10.39W
Tirol/Tirolo = Tyrol (EN) ▣	14 Fc	47.00N	11.20 E
Tirol = Tyrol (EN) [2]	14 Fc	47.00N	11.25 E
Tirolo/Tirol = Tyrol (EN) ▣	14 Fc	47.00N	11.20 E
Tiros	55 Jd	19.00S	45.58W
Tirreno, Mar- = Tyrrhenian			
Sea (EN) ▬	5 Hh	40.00N	12.00 E
Tirschenreuth	10 Ig	49.53N	12.21 E
Tirso ◺	14 Ck	39.53N	8.32 E
Tirstrup	8 Dh	56.18N	10.42 E
Tirua Point ▶	62 Fc	38.23S	174.38 E
Tiruchchirappalli	21 Ji	10.49N	78.41 E
Tiruliai/Tiruliąǐ ▨	8 Ji	55.49N	23.18 E
Tiruliai/Tiruliąǐ ▨	8 Ji	55.44N	23.18 E
Tiruliąǐ/Tiruliai ▨	8 Ji	55.49N	23.18 E
Tirunelveli	21 Ji	8.44N	77.42 E
Tirupati	25 Ff	13.39N	79.25 E
Tirza ◺	8 Kh	57.09N	26.15 E
Tis Åbay ◺	5 If	45.15N	20.17 E
Tisdale	42 Hf	52.51N	104.04W
Tisnaren ▨	8 Ff	58.55N	15.55 E

Tisovec	10 Ph	48.42N	19.57 E
Tissemsilt	32 Hb	35.36N	1.49 E
Tisse ◺	8 Di	55.35N	11.20 E
Tisza ◺	5 If	45.15N	20.17 E
Tisza (EN) = Tisa ◺	5 If	45.15N	20.17 E
Tiszaföldvár	10 Oj	46.59N	20.15 E
Tiszafüred	10 Oi	47.37N	20.46 E
Tiszakécske	10 Oj	46.56N	20.06 E
Tiszántúl ⬚	10 Oj	47.00N	21.00 E
Tiszaújváros			
(Leninváros)	10 Ri	47.56N	21.05 E
Tiszavasvári	10 Ri	47.58N	21.21 E
Titao	34 Ec	13.46N	2.04W
Titarísios ◺	15 Fj	39.47N	22.23 E
Tit-Ary	20 Hb	71.55N	127.01 E
Titicaca, Lago- ▨	52 Jg	15.50S	69.20W
Titikaveka	64p Bc	21.15S	159.45W
Titlagarh	25 Gd	20.18N	83.09 E
Titlis ▲	14 Cd	46.47N	8.26 E
Titograd → Podgorica	6 Hg	42.26N	19.16 E
Titova Korenica	14 Jf	44.45N	15.42 E
Titovo Užice → Užice	15 Cf	43.52N	19.51 E
Titov Veles	15 Eh	41.42N	21.48 E
Titov vrh ▲	15 Dh	41.58N	20.50 E
Titran	7 Be	63.40N	8.18 E
Titteri ▲	13 Pi	35.59N	3.15 E
Titule	36 Eb	3.17N	25.32 E
Titusville [Fl.-U.S.]	43 Kf	28.37N	80.49W
Titusville [Pa.-U.S.]	44 He	41.37N	79.42W
Tituvenaj/Tytuvėnai	8 Ji	55.33N	23.09 E
Tiva ◺	36 Gc	2.20S	39.55 E
Tivaouane	34 Bc	14.57N	16.49W
Tiveden ⬚	8 Ff	58.45N	14.40 E
Tiverton	9 Jk	50.55N	3.29W
Tivoli [Gren.]	51p Bb	12.10N	61.37W
Tivoli [It.]	14 Gi	41.58N	12.48 E
Ṭīwāl ◺	35 Cc	10.22N	22.43 E
Tiwi	36 Gc	4.14S	39.35 E
Tiyo	35 Cc	14.41N	40.57 E
Tizatlán ⬚	48 Jh	19.21N	98.15W
Tizimín	47 Gd	21.09N	88.09W
Tizi Ouzou	32 Hb	36.35N	4.05 E
Tizi Ouzou [3]	32 Hb	36.42N	4.03 E
Tiznados, Rio- ◺	50 Ch	8.16N	67.47W
Tiznit	32 Fc	29.43N	9.43W
Tiznit [3]	32 Fd	29.07N	9.04W
Tjačev	10 Th	48.02N	23.36 E
Tjanšan ▲	27 Dc	42.00N	80.01 E
Tjasmin ◺	16 He	49.03N	32.50 E
Tjeggelvas ▨	7 Dc	66.35N	17.40 E
Tjeukemeer ▨	11 Lb	52.54N	5.50 E
Tjøme ▣	8 De	59.10N	10.25 E
Tjorn ▣	8 Df	58.00N	11.38 E
Tjub-Karagan, Mys- ▶	16 Qg	44.38N	50.20 E
Tjubuk	17 Jh	56.03N	60.58 E
Tjuhtet	20 De	56.32N	89.29 E
Tjukalinsk	19 Hd	55.52N	72.12 E
Tjuleni, Ostrov- ▣	16 Qg	44.30N	47.30 E
Tjuleni, Ostrova- ◧	16 Qg	44.55N	50.10 E
Tjulgan	19 Fe	52.22N	56.12 E
Tjumen	22 Id	57.09N	65.32 E
Tjumenskaja Oblast [3]	19 Gd	57.00N	69.00 E
Tjung ◺	20 Hd	63.42N	121.30 E
Tjup	18 Lc	42.44N	78.20 E
Tjuri/Türi	7 Fg	58.50N	25.27 E
Tjust ⬚	8 Gf	57.50N	16.15 E
Tjuters Maly, Ostrov- ▣	8 Le	59.45N	26.53 E
Tjuzaşu, Pereval- ▨	18 Ic	42.19N	73.50 E
Tkibuli	16 Mh	42.19N	42.59 E
Tkvarčeli	16 Mg	42.52N	41.40 E
Tlacolula	48 Ki	16.57N	96.29W
Tlacotalpan	48 Jh	18.37N	95.40W
Tlahualilo,			
Sierra del- ▲	48 Hd	26.30N	103.20W
Tlainepantla	48 Jh	19.33N	99.12W
Tlapa de Comonfort	48 Ji	17.33N	98.33W
Tlapaneco, Rio- ◺	48 Jh	18.00N	98.48W
Tlaquepaque	48 Hg	20.39N	103.19W
Tlaxcala	47 Ee	19.25N	98.10W
Tlaxcala	48 Jh	19.19N	98.14W
Tlemcen	32 Gc	34.52N	1.19W
Tlemcen [3]	32 Gc	34.45N	1.30W
Tleń	10 Oc	53.38N	18.20 E
Tleta Rissana	13 Ig	35.14N	5.59W
Tletat ed Douair	13 Oi	35.59N	2.55 E
Tljarata	16 Oh	42.06N	46.22 E
Tlumač	10 Vh	48.46N	25.06 E
Tłuszcz	10 Rd	52.26N	21.26 E
Tmassah	33 Cd	26.22N	15.48 E
Tō, Shikotan-/Šikotan,			
Ostrov- ▣	20 Jh	43.47N	146.45 E
Toaca, Vîrful- ▲	15 Ic	46.55N	25.59 E
Toagel Mlungui ▬	64a Ab	7.32N	134.28 E
Toamasina	31 Lj	18.10S	49.24 E
Toamasina [3]	37 Hc	18.00S	48.40 E
Toau Atoll [○]	61 Lc	15.55S	146.00W
Toay	56 He	36.40S	64.21W
Toba	28 Ng	34.29N	136.51 E
Toba, Danau- = Toba, Lake-			
(EN) ▨	26 Li	2.35N	98.50 E
Tobago ▣	52 Jd	11.15N	60.40W
Tobago Basin (EN) ◺	50 Ff	12.30N	60.30W
Tobago Cays ▨	51b Bb	12.39N	61.22W
Toba Kākar Range ▲	25 Db	31.15N	68.00 E
Tobarra	13 Kf	38.35N	1.41W
Tobe	28 Gc	33.44N	132.47 E
Tobejuba, Isla- ▣	50 Fh	9.20N	60.52W
Tobelo	21 Of	1.25N	127.31 E
Tobermory [Ont.-Can.]	44 Gc	45.15N	81.40W
Tobermory [Scot.-U.K.]	9 Ge	56.37N	6.05W
Tōbetsu	29a Bb	43.14N	141.29 E
Tobi Island ▣	57 Ec	3.00N	131.10 E
Tobin, Kap- ▶	41 Id	70.25N	21.58W
Tobin, Mount- ▲	46 Hf	40.22N	117.32W
Tobin Lake [Austl.] ▨	59 Gd	21.45S	125.50 E
Tobin Lake [Sask.-Can.] ▨	42 Hf	53.40N	103.20W
Tobi-Shima ▣	29 Fb	39.12N	139.32 E

Toblach / Dobbiaco	14 Gd	46.44N	12.14 E
Toboali	26 Eg	3.00S	106.30 E
Tobol	19 Ge	52.40N	62.39 E
Tobol ◺	21 Id	58.10N	68.12 E
Tobolsk	22 Id	58.12N	68.16 E
Tobruk (EN) = Ṭubruq	31 Je	32.05N	23.59 E
Tobseda	19 Fb	68.36N	52.20 E
Tocantinópolis	53 Lf	6.20S	47.25W
Tocantins	54 If	10.30S	48.00W
Tocantins, Rio- ◺	52 Lf	1.45S	49.10W
Tocantinzinho, Rio- ◺	55 Ha	13.57S	48.20W
Toccoa	44 Fh	34.35N	83.19W
Toce ◺	14 Ce	45.56N	8.29 E
Tochigi	29 Fc	36.23N	139.44 E
Tochigi Ken [2]	28 Of	36.50N	139.50 E
Tochio	29 Fc	37.29N	138.58 E
Toco	50 Fg	10.50N	60.57W
Tocoa	49 Df	15.41N	86.03W
Toconao	56 Gb	23.11S	68.01W
Tocopilla	53 Ih	22.05S	70.12W
Tocumen	49 Hi	9.05N	79.23W
Tocuyo, Rio- ◺	50 Mh	11.03N	68.20W
Todd Mountain ▲	44 Nb	46.32N	66.43W
Todi	14 Gh	42.47N	12.24 E
Tödi ▲	14 Cd	46.49N	8.55 E
Todo-ga-Saki ▶	27 Pd	39.33N	142.05 E
Todos os Santos, Baía de-			
◧	52 Mg	12.48S	38.38W
Todos Santos	47 Bd	23.27N	110.13W
Todos Santos, Bahía de-			
◧	48 Ab	31.48N	116.42W
Tofino	42 Mg	49.09N	125.54W
Tofte	8 Ce	59.33N	10.34 E
Toftlund	8 Ci	55.11N	9.04 E
Tofua Island ▣	61 Fc	19.45S	175.05W
Toga ▣	63b Ca	13.26S	166.41 E
Tōgane	29 Gc	35.33N	140.21 E
Tog Ḍarōr ⬚	35 Hc	10.25N	50.00 E
Togdere ◺	35 Hd	9.01N	47.07 E
Tog-Dheer [3]	35 Hd	9.50N	45.50 E
Togi	29 Ec	37.08N	136.43 E
Togiak	40 Se	59.04N	160.24W
Togian Islands (EN) =			
Togian, Kepulauan- ◧	26 Hg	0.20S	122.00 E
Togliatti	6 Ke	53.31N	49.26 E
Togni	35 Fb	18.05N	35.10 E
Togo Ul ▣	31 Hh	8.00N	1.10 E
Togrog Ul → Qahar Youyi			
Qianqi	28 Bd	40.46N	113.13 E
Togtoh	27 Jc	40.17N	111.15 E
Toguçin	20 De	55.16N	84.33 E
Toguzak ◺	17 Ki	54.05N	62.48 E
Tohamiyam	35 Fb	18.26N	36.48 E
Tohatchi	43 Ee	43.45N	110.04W
Tohen	35 Ic	11.44N	51.15 E
Tohma ◺	24 Hc	38.31N	38.25 E
Tohmajärvi	7 Fe	62.11N	30.23 E
Tohopekaliga, Lake- ▨	44 Gk	28.12N	81.23W
Toi	29 Fd	34.54N	138.47 E
Toijala	7 Ff	61.10N	23.52 E
Toi-Misaki ▶	28 Ki	31.26N	131.19 E
Toisvesi ▨	8 Jb	62.20N	23.45 E
Tojikiston =			
Tajikistan (EN)	19 Hh	39.00N	71.00 E
Tōjō	29 Cd	34.53N	133.16 E
Tojtepa	18 Gd	41.03N	69.22 E
Tok ▲	19 Jg	49.43N	13.50 E
Tok ◺	16 Rc	52.46N	52.22 E
Tok	40 Kd	63.20N	142.59W
Tokachi-Dake ▲	29a Cb	43.25N	142.41 E
Tokachi-Gawa ◺	29a Cb	42.41N	143.37 E
Tokachi-Heiya ⬚	29a Cb	43.00N	143.20 E
Tokachimitsumata	29a Cb	43.31N	143.07 E
Tōkai [Jap.]	29 Gc	36.27N	140.34 E
Tōkai [Jap.]	29 Ec	35.01N	136.51 E
Tokaj	10 Ri	48.08N	21.25 E
Tōkamachi	28 Of	37.08N	138.46 E
Tokanui	62 Gg	46.34S	168.57 E
Tokara Islands (EN) =			
Tokara-Rettō ◧	21 Qg	29.35N	129.45 E
Tokara-Kaikyō ▬	28 Ki	30.10N	130.15 E
Tokara-Rettō = Tokara			
Islands (EN) ◧	21 Qg	29.35N	129.45 E
Tokashiki-Jima ▣	29b Ab	26.13N	127.21 E
Tokat	23 Ea	40.19N	36.34 E
Tŏkch'ŏn	28 Ie	39.45N	126.15 E
Toku-Do ▣	28 Kf	37.22N	131.58 E
Tokelau [5]	58 Kd	9.00S	171.45W
Tokelau/Union Islands ◧	57 Id	9.00S	171.45W
Toki	29 Ec	35.22N	137.11 E
Tokke	8 Ce	59.00N	9.15 E
Tokke ◺	8 Be	59.27N	7.58 E
Tokkuztara/Gongliu	27 Dc	43.30N	82.15 E
Tokmak	19 Jg	42.49N	75.19 E
Tokmak	16 If	47.13N	35.43 E
Tokomaru Bay	62 Hb	38.08S	178.20 E
Tokoname	29 Ec	34.53N	136.49 E
Tokoro	29a Da	44.08N	144.03 E
Tokoro-Gawa ◺	29a Da	44.08N	144.04 E
Toksoko	8 Nd	60.10N	30.42 E
Toksu/Xinhe	27 Dc	41.34N	82.38 E
Toksun	27 Ec	42.47N	88.38 E
Toktogul	19 Hg	41.50N	73.01 E
Toktogulskoje			
Vodohranilišče ▨	18 Id	41.45N	73.00 E
Tokuji	28 Bd	34.11N	131.39 E
Tokulu ◺	65b Bb	20.05N	174.48W
Toku-no-Shima ▣	28 Jg	27.45N	129.00 E
Tokunoshima	29b Bb	27.45N	128.59 E
Tokur	20 If	53.09N	132.56 E
Tokushima	28 Mf	34.04N	134.34 E
Tokushima Ken [2]	28 Mf	33.53N	134.12 E
Tokuyama [Jap.]	28 Mf	35.43N	136.17 E
Tokuyama [Jap.]	28 Kg	34.03N	131.49 E
Tokwe ◺	37 Ec	20.09S	31.54 E
Tōkyō	21 Pf	35.40N	139.46 E

Tokyo Bay (EN) = Tōkyō-			
Wan ◧	28 Og	35.38N	139.57 E
Tōkyō To [2]	28 Og	35.40N	139.20 E
Tōkyō-Wan = Tokyo Bay			
(EN) ◧	28 Og	35.38N	139.57 E
Tola	21 Me	48.57N	104.48 E
Tolaga Bay	62 Hc	38.22S	178.18 E
Tolbazy	17 Gi	54.02N	55.59 E
Tolbuhin → Dobrič	15 Kf	43.34N	27.50 E
Tolbuhin = Dobrič	15 Kf	43.34N	27.50 E
Toledo	13 Ie	39.50N	4.00W
Toledo [Blz.]	49 Ce	16.25N	88.50W
Toledo [Braz.]	56 Jb	24.44S	53.45W
Toledo [Oh.-U.S.]	39 Ke	41.39N	83.32W
Toledo [Phil.]	26 Hd	10.23N	123.38 E
Toledo [Sp.]	6 Fh	39.52N	4.01W
Toledo, Montes de- ▲	13 He	39.35N	4.20W
Toledo Bend Reservoir			
▨	43 Ie	31.30N	93.45W
Tolentino ⬚	14 Hg	43.12N	13.17 E
Tolfa	14 Fh	42.09N	11.56 E
Tolfa, Monti della- ▲	14 Fh	42.10N	11.55 E
Tolga	7 Ce	62.25N	11.00 E
Toli	27 Db	45.57N	83.37 E
Toliara	37 Gd	22.00S	44.00 E
Toliara	31 Lk	23.21S	43.39 E
Tolima [2]	54 Cc	3.45N	75.15W
Tolima, Nevado del- ▲	52 Ie	4.40N	75.19W
Toling → Zanda	27 Ce	31.28N	79.50 E
Tolitoli	26 Hf	1.02N	120.49 E
Toll ▶	64d Bb	7.22N	151.37 E
Tollarp	8 Ei	55.56N	13.59 E
Tollja, Zaliv- ◧	20 Ea	76.40N	100.00 E
Tolmačevo	8 Nf	58.48N	30.01 E
Tolmezzo	14 Hd	46.24N	13.01 E
Tolmin	14 Hd	46.11N	13.44 E
Tolna	10 Oj	46.26N	18.47 E
Tolna [2]	10 Oj	46.30N	18.35 E
Tolo	36 Cc	2.56S	18.34 E
Tolo, Gulf of- (EN) = Tolo,			
Teluk- ◧	21 Oj	2.00S	122.30 E
Tolo, Teluk- = Tolo, Gulf of-			
(EN) ◧	21 Oj	2.00S	122.30 E
Toločin	7 Gi	54.25N	29.41 E
Tolosa	13 Ja	43.08N	2.04W
Tolstoj, Mys- ▶	5 Rd	59.10N	155.05 E
Toltén	56 Fe	39.13S	73.14W
Tolú	54 Cb	9.32N	75.34W
Toluca, Nevado de- ▲	38 Jh	19.09N	99.44W
Toluca de Lerdo	39 Jh	19.17N	99.40W
Tom ◺	21 Kd	56.50N	84.27 E
Toma	34 Ec	12.46N	2.53W
Tomah	45 Ke	43.59N	90.30W
Tomakomai	27 Pc	42.38N	141.36 E
Tomamae	29a Ba	44.18N	141.39 E
Tomanivi ▲	63d Bb	17.37S	178.01 E
Tomar	13 De	39.36N	8.25W
Tómaros ▲	15 Dj	39.32N	20.45 E
Tomaševka	16 Cd	51.33N	23.40 E
Tomás Young	55 Ai	28.36S	62.11W
Tomaszów Lubelski	10 Tf	50.28N	23.25 E
Tomaszów Mazowiecki	10 Qe	51.33N	20.01 E
Tomatlán	48 Gh	19.56N	105.15W
Tombador, Serra dos- ▲	54 Gf	12.00S	57.40W
Tombigbee River ◺	43 Je	31.04N	87.58W
Tomboco	36 Bd	6.45S	13.18 E
Tombouctou = Timbuktu			
(EN)	31 Gg	16.46N	2.59W
Tombstone	46 Jk	31.43N	110.04W
Tombua	31 Ij	15.48S	11.52 E
Tomé	56 Fe	36.37S	72.57W
Tomé-Açu	54 Id	2.25S	48.09W
Tomelilla	7 Ci	55.33N	13.57 E
Tomelloso	13 Je	39.10N	3.01W
Tomichi Creek ◺	45 Jg	38.31N	106.58W
Tomie	28 Ae	32.37N	128.46 E
Tomini, Gulf of- (EN) =			
Tomini, Teluk- ◧	21 Oj	0.20S	121.00 E
Tomini, Teluk- = Tomini, Gulf			
of- (EN) ◧	21 Oj	0.20S	121.00 E
Tominian	34 Ec	13.17N	4.35W
Tomioka [Jap.]	29 Gc	37.20N	140.59 E
Tomioka [Jap.]	29 Fc	36.15N	138.52 E
Tomkinson Ranges ▲	59 Fe	26.11S	129.05 E
Tomma ▣	7 Cc	66.15N	12.48 E
Tommo, Rio- ◺	54 Eb	5.20N	67.48W
Tomochic	48 Fc	28.20N	107.51W
Tomorit, Mali i- ▲	15 Di	40.40N	20.09 E
Tomotu Neo ▣	63c Ab	10.51S	165.47 E
Tomotu Noi ▣	63c Bb	10.45S	166.02 E
Tompa	10 Pj	46.12N	19.33 E
Tompe	8 Be	59.27N	7.58 E
Tompo	20 Id	64.00N	136.00 E
Tom Price	59 Dd	22.40S	117.55 E
Tomsk	22 Kd	56.30N	84.58 E
Tomskaja Oblast [3]	20 De	58.20N	81.30 E
Tomtabacken ▲	8 Fg	57.30N	14.28 E
Tomur Feng ▲	21 Ke	42.02N	80.05 E
Tom White, Mount- ▲	40 Kd	60.40N	143.40W
Tonaki-Shima ▣	29b Ab	26.21N	127.09 E
Tonalá	39 Ih	16.04N	93.45W
Tonale, Passo del- ▨	14 Ed	46.16N	10.35 E
Tonami	29 Dc	36.38N	136.57 E
Tonara	14 Dj	40.02N	9.10 E
Tonasket	46 Fb	48.42N	119.26W
Tonate	51 Pa	4.50N	52.30W
Tonawanda	44 He	43.01N	78.53W
Tonbe-Bozorg ▲	24 Og	26.15N	55.03 E
Tonbetsu-Gawa ◺	29a Ca	45.08N	142.23 E
Tonbridge	9 Nj	51.12N	0.16 E
Tondano	26 Hf	1.19N	124.54 E
Tondela	13 De	40.31N	8.05W
Tønder	7 Bi	54.56N	8.54 E
Tone-Gawa ◺	29 Gc	35.44N	140.51 E
Tonekābon	24 Mc	36.50N	50.56 E
Tonga	66 Df	75.48S	115.48W
Tonga [1]	58 Jf	20.00S	175.00W
Tonga	35 Ed	9.28N	31.03 E

Tongaat 37 Ee 29.37S 31.03 E
Tonga Islands 57 Jf 20.00S 175.00W
Tonga Ridge (EN) 57 Jg 21.00S 175.00W
Tongariki 63b Dc 17.01S 168.37 E
Tongatapu Group 57 Jg 21.10S 175.10W
Tongatapu Island 61 Fd 21.10S 175.10W
Tonga Trench (EN) 3 Kl 20.00S 173.00W
Tongbai 28 Bh 32.21N 113.24 E
Tongbai Shan 27 Je 32.20N 113.14 E
Tongcheng [China] 28 Bj 29.15N 113.49 E
Tongcheng [China] 28 Di 31.04N 116.56 E
Tongcheng → Dong'e 28 Df 36.19N 116.14 E
Tongchuan 27 Id 35.10N 109.03 E
Tongdao (Shuangjiang) 27 If 26.14N 109.45 E
Tongde 27 Hd 35.29N 100.32 E
Tongeren/Tongres 11 Ld 50.47N 5.28 E
Tonggu 28 Cj 28.33N 114.21 E
Tongguzbasti 27 Dd 38.23N 82.00 E
Tonggu Zhang 27 Kg 24.12N 116.22 E
Tong-Hae = Japan, Sea of- (EN) 21 Pf 40.00N 134.00 E
Tonghai 22 Mg 24.15N 102.45 E
Tonghe 27 Mb 46.01N 128.42 E
Tonghua 22 Oe 41.43N 125.55 E
Tongjiang 27 Nb 47.39N 132.30 E
Tongjosŏn-man 21 Of 39.30N 128.00 E
Tongliao 22 Oe 43.37N 122.15 E
Tongling 27 Ke 30.49N 117.47 E
Tonglu 28 Ej 29.48N 119.39 E
Tongmun'gŏ-ri 27 Mc 40.58N 127.08 E
Tongoa 63b Dc 16.54S 168.33 E
Tongoy 56 Fd 30.15S 71.30W
Tongren [China] 27 If 27.45N 109.09 E
Tongren [China] 27 Hd 35.40N 102.07 E
Tongres/Tongeren 11 Ld 50.47N 5.28 E
Tongsa Dzong 25 Ic 27.31N 90.30 E
Tongshan 28 Cj 29.36N 114.30 E
Tongta 25 Jd 21.20N 99.16 E
Tongtian He/Zhi Qu 21 Lf 33.26N 96.36 E
Tongue 9 Ic 58.28N 4.25W
Tongue of the Ocean 49 Ia 24.12N 77.10W
Tongue River 43 Fb 46.24N 105.52W
Tongxian 27 Kd 39.52N 116.38 E
Tongxin 27 Id 36.59N 105.50 E
Tongxu 28 Cg 34.29N 114.27 E
Tongyu (Kaitong) 27 Lc 44.47N 123.05 E
Tongyu Yunhe 28 Eg 34.46N 119.51 E
Tongzi 27 If 28.09N 106.50 E
Tonichi 48 Ec 28.35N 109.34W
Tõnisvorst 12 Ic 51.19N 6.28 E
Tonj 35 Dd 7.17N 28.45 E
Tonj 30 Jh 7.31N 29.25 E
Tonk 25 Fc 26.10N 75.47 E
Tonkin (EN) = Bac-Phan 21 Mg 22.00N 105.00 E
Tonkin, Gulf of- (EN) = Beibu Wan 21 Mh 20.00N 108.00 E
Tonkin, Gulf of- (EN) = Vinh Bac Phan 21 Mh 20.00N 108.00 E
Tônlé Sab, Bœng- = Tonle Sap (EN) 21 Mh 13.00N 104.00 E
Tonle Sap (EN) = Tônlé Sab, Bœng- 21 Mh 13.00N 104.00 E
Tonnay-Charente 11 Fi 45.57N 0.54W
Tonneins 11 Gj 44.23N 0.19 E
Tönning 10 Eb 54.19N 8.57 E
Tōno 28 Pe 39.19N 141.32 E
Tonopah 43 Dd 38.04N 117.14W
Tonoshō 29 Dd 34.29N 134.11 E
Tonosí 49 Gj 7.24N 80.27W
Tønsberg 7 Cg 59.17N 10.25 E
Tonstad 7 Bg 58.40N 6.43 E
Tonumeia 65b Bb 20.28S 174.46W
Tonya 24 Hb 40.53N 39.16 E
Tooele 43 Ec 40.32N 112.18W
Toora-Hem 20 Ef 52.28N 96.22 E
Tootsi 8 Kf 58.34N 24.43 E
Toowoomba 58 Gg 27.33S 151.57 E
Topalú 15 Le 44.33N 28.03 E
Topa Taung 25 Jd 21.08N 95.12 E
Topeka 39 Jf 39.03N 95.41W
Topki 20 De 55.18N 85.40 E
Topko, Gora- 20 Ie 57.00N 137.23 E
Topl'a 10 Rh 48.45N 21.45 E
Toplet 15 Fe 44.48N 22.24 E
Toplica 15 Ef 43.13N 21.51 E
Toplița 15 Ic 46.55N 25.20 E
Topola 15 De 44.16N 20.42 E
Topol'čany 10 Oh 48.34N 18.10 E
Topolnica 15 Hg 42.11N 24.18 E
Topolobampo 47 Cc 25.36N 109.03W
Topolobampo, Bahía de- 48 Ee 25.30N 109.05W
Topolog 15 Hd 44.56N 24.16 E
Topolovgrad 15 Jg 42.05N 26.20 E
Topozero, Ozero- 5 Jb 65.40N 32.00 E
Toppenish 46 Ec 46.23N 120.19W
Toprakkale 24 Gd 37.06N 36.07 E
Top Springs 59 Gc 16.38S 131.50 E
Toquepala 54 Eg 17.38S 69.56W
Tor 35 Ed 7.51N 33.36 E
Tora 64d Ba 7.39N 151.53 E
Toraigh/Tory Island 9 Ef 55.16N 8.13W
Tora Island Pass 64d Ba 7.39N 151.53 E
Toråker 8 Gd 60.31N 16.29 E
Torbalı 24 Bc 38.10N 27.21 E
Torbat-e Heydarīyeh 22 Hf 35.16N 59.13 E
Torbat-e Jam 23 Jb 35.14N 60.36 E
Torbay 9 Jk 50.28N 3.30W
Torbert, Mount- 40 Id 61.25N 152.24W
Torch Lake 44 Ec 45.00N 85.19W
Torčin 10 Vf 50.44N 25.05 E
Tordesillas 13 Hc 41.30N 5.00W
Tordino 14 Hh 42.44N 13.59 E
Töre 7 Fd 65.54N 22.39 E
Töreboda 7 Dg 58.43N 14.08 E
Torekov 8 Eh 56.26N 12.37 E
Torenberg 11 Lb 52.15N 5.55 E
Torez 16 Kf 47.59N 38.41 E
Torgau 10 Ie 51.34N 13.00 E
Torgelow 10 Kc 53.38N 14.01 E
Torgun 16 Od 50.10N 46.20 E
Torhamn 8 Fh 56.05N 15.50 E
Torhout 11 Jc 51.04N 3.06 E
Toribulu 26 Hg 0.19S 120.01 E
Torigni-sur-Vire 12 Be 49.05N 0.59W
Torii-Tōge 29 Ed 35.59N 137.49 E
Tori-Jima 29b Ab 26.35N 126.50 E
Torino = Turin (EN) 6 Gf 45.03N 7.40 E
Toriparu 55 Fc 16.20S 53.55W
Tori-Shima [Jap.] 27 Pe 30.25N 140.15 E
Tori-Shima [Jap.] 29b Bb 27.52N 128.14 E
Torit 35 Ee 4.24N 32.34 E
Torixoreu 54 Hg 16.15S 52.26W
Torkoviči 7 Hg 58.53N 30.20 E
Törmänen 7 Gb 68.36N 27.29 E
Tormes 13 Fc 41.18N 6.29W
Tornado Mountain 46 Hb 49.58N 114.39W
Tornavacas, Puerto de- 13 Gd 40.16N 5.37W
Torneå/Tornio 7 Fd 65.51N 24.08 E
Torneälven 5 Ib 65.48N 24.08 E
Torneträsk 7 Eb 68.22N 19.06 E
Torngat Mountains 38 Md 59.00N 64.00W
Tornio/Torneå 7 Fd 65.51N 24.08 E
Tornionjoki 5 Ib 65.48N 24.08 E
Tornquist 55 An 38.06S 62.14W
Toro 13 Gc 41.31N 5.24W
Toro 8 Gf 58.50N 17.50 E
Toro, Cerro del- 52 Jh 29.08S 69.48W
Toro, Isla del- 48 Kg 21.35N 97.32W
Toro, Monte- 13 Qe 39.59N 4.07 E
Toroiaga, Vîrful- 15 Hb 47.44N 24.43 E
Torokina 63a Bb 6.14S 155.03 E
Tōro-Ko 29a Db 43.08N 144.30 E
Törökszentmiklós 10 Qi 47.11N 20.25 E
Torola, Río- 49 Cg 13.52N 88.30W
Toronto 39 Le 43.39N 79.23W
Toropec 19 Dd 56.31N 31.39 E
Tororo 36 Fb 0.41N 34.11 E
Toros Dağları = Taurus Mountains (EN) 21 Ff 37.00N 33.00 E
Torquato Severo 55 Ej 31.02S 54.11W
Torquay 9 Jk 50.29N 3.29W
Torrá, Cerro- 52 Ie 4.38N 76.15W
Torrance 46 Fj 33.50N 118.19W
Torre Annunziata 14 Ij 40.45N 14.27 E
Torreblanca 13 Md 40.13N 0.12 E
Torrecilla 13 Hh 36.41N 5.00W
Torrecilla en Cameros 13 Jb 42.16N 2.37W
Torre del Greco 14 Ij 40.47N 14.22 E
Torre del Mar 13 Hh 36.44N 4.06W
Torredembarra 13 Nc 41.09N 1.24 E
Torre de Moncorvo 13 Ec 41.10N 7.03W
Torre de' Passeri 14 Hh 42.14N 13.56 E
Torredonjimeno 13 Ig 37.46N 3.57W
Torrejón de Ardoz 13 Id 40.27N 3.29W
Torrelaguna 13 Id 40.50N 3.32W
Torrelavega 13 Ha 43.21N 4.03W
Torre Miró, Puerto de- 13 Ld 40.42N 0.05W
Torremolinos 13 Hh 36.37N 4.30W
Torrens, Lake- 57 Eh 31.00S 137.50 E
Torrens Creek 59 Jd 20.46S 145.02 E
Torrent de l'Horta/Torrente 13 Le 39.26N 0.28W
Torrente/Torrent de l'Horta 13 Le 39.26N 0.28W
Torrenueva 13 If 38.38N 3.22W
Torreón 39 Ig 25.33N 103.26W
Torre-Pacheco 13 Lg 37.44N 0.57W
Torre Pellice 14 Bf 44.49N 7.13 E
Torres 64d Ab 7.19N 151.27 E
Tôrres 56 Kc 29.21S 49.44W
Torrès, Iles- = Torres Islands (EN) 57 Hf 13.15S 166.37 E
Torres Islands (EN) = Torrès, Iles- 57 Hf 13.15S 166.37 E
Torres Novas 13 De 39.29N 8.32W
Torres Strait 57 Ff 10.25S 142.10 E
Torres Vedras 13 Ce 39.06N 9.16W
Torrevieja 13 Lg 37.59N 0.41W
Torridon, Loch- 9 Hd 57.35N 5.50W
Torriglia 14 Df 44.31N 9.10 E
Torrijos 13 He 39.59N 4.17W
Torrington [Ct.-U.S.] 44 Ke 41.48N 73.08W
Torrington [Wy.-U.S.] 43 Gc 42.04N 104.11W
Torroella de Montgri 13 Pb 42.02N 3.08 E
Torröjen 7 Cf 63.55N 12.56 E
Torrox 13 Ih 36.46N 3.58W
Torsås 7 Dh 56.24N 16.00 E
Torsby 7 Cf 60.08N 13.00 E
Torshälla 8 Ge 59.25N 16.28 E
Torsken 7 Db 69.20N 17.06 E
Torsö 7 Cg 58.50N 13.50 E
Torto 14 Hm 37.58N 13.46 E
Tortola 47 Le 18.27N 64.36W
Tortoli 14 Dk 39.55N 9.39 E
Tortona 14 Cf 44.54N 8.52 E
Tortorici 14 Il 38.02N 14.49 E
Tortosa 13 Md 40.48N 0.31 E
Tortosa, Cabo de-/Tortosa, Cap de- 13 Md 40.43N 0.55 E
Tortosa, Cap de-/Tortosa, Cabo de- 13 Md 40.43N 0.55 E
Tortue, Ile de la- 47 Jd 20.04N 72.49W
Tortuga, Isla- 48 Dd 27.26N 111.55W
Tortum 24 Ib 40.19N 41.35 E
Torud 24 Pe 35.26N 55.07 E
Torugart, Pereval- 21 Je 40.32N 75.24 E
Torul 24 Hb 40.35N 39.18 E
Toruń [2] 10 Oc 53.00N 18.35 E
Toruń 10 Oc 53.02N 18.35 E
Torunos 49 Li 8.30N 70.04W
Toruńska, Kotlina- 10 Oc 53.00N 18.30 E
Torup 7 Ch 56.58N 13.05 E
Tõrva/Tyrva 7 Fg 58.01N 25.59 E
Tory Island/Toraigh 9 Ef 55.16N 8.13W
Torysa 10 Rh 48.39N 21.21 E
Toržok 19 Dd 57.03N 35.01 E
Tosa 28 Lh 33.29N 133.25 E
Tosas, Puerto de-/Toses, Port de- 13 Ob 42.20N 2.01 E
Tosashimizu 28 Lh 32.46N 132.57 E
Tosa-Wan 28 Lh 33.25N 133.35 E
Tosa-yamada 29 Ce 33.36N 133.40 E
Toscana = Tuscany (EN) [2] 14 Eg 43.25N 11.00 E
Toses, Port de-/Tosas, Puerto de- 13 Ob 42.20N 2.01 E
Toshibetsu-Gawa [Jap.] 29a Cb 42.54N 143.25 E
Toshibetsu-Gawa [Jap.] 29a Ab 42.25N 139.48 E
Tōshi-Jima 29 Ed 34.31N 136.52 E
To-Shima 29 Fd 34.31N 139.17 E
Tosno 7 Hg 59.34N 30.50 E
Toson-Cengel 27 Gb 48.47N 98.15 E
Toson Hu 27 Gd 37.08N 96.52 E
Töss 14 Cc 47.33N 8.33 E
Tossa de Mar 13 Oc 41.43N 2.56 E
Tostado 56 Hc 29.14S 61.46W
Tõstamaa/Tystama 8 Jf 58.17N 23.52 E
Tosu 29 Be 33.22N 130.30 E
Tosya 24 Fb 41.01N 34.02 E
Totak 8 Be 59.40N 7.55 E
Totana 13 Kg 37.46N 1.30W
Toten 8 Dd 60.40N 10.50 E
Toteng 37 Cd 20.23S 22.59 E
Tôtes 12 Ce 49.41N 1.03 E
Totes Gebirge 14 Hc 47.42N 13.55 E
Tōtias 35 Ge 3.57N 43.58 E
Totland 12 Ad 50.40N 1.32W
Totma 19 Ed 60.00N 42.45 E
Totness 54 Gb 5.53N 56.19W
Toto 36 Bd 7.10S 14.25 E
Totonicapán [3] 49 Bf 15.00N 91.20W
Totonicapán 47 Ff 14.55N 91.22W
Totora 54 Eg 17.42S 65.09W
Totoras 55 Bk 32.35S 61.11W
Totota 34 Dd 6.49N 9.56W
Totoya 63d Cc 18.57S 179.50W
Totten Glacier 66 He 66.45S 116.10 E
Totton 12 Ad 50.55N 1.29W
Tottori 27 Nd 35.30N 134.14 E
Tottori Ken [2] 28 Lg 35.25N 133.50 E
Tou, Motu- 64p Bb 21.11S 159.48W
Touâjil 32 Ee 21.45N 12.35W
Touat 30 Gf 27.40N 0.01W
Touba [3] 34 Dd 8.15N 7.45W
Touba 34 Dd 8.17N 7.41W
Toubkal, Jebel- 30 Ge 31.03N 7.55W
Touch 11 Hk 43.38N 1.24 E
Toucy 11 Jg 47.44N 3.18 E
Tougan 34 Ec 13.04N 3.04W
Touggourt 31 He 33.06N 6.04 E
Tougué 34 Cc 11.27N 11.41W
Touho 63b Be 20.47S 165.14 E
Touil 32 Hb 35.33N 2.36 E
Toûil 13 Oi 35.33N 2.36 E
Toukoto 34 Dc 13.28N 9.52W
Toul 11 Lf 48.41N 5.54 E
Toulépleu 34 Dd 6.35N 8.25W
Toulon 6 Gg 43.07N 5.56 E
Toulouse 6 Gg 43.36N 1.26 E
Toulumne River 46 Eh 37.36N 121.10W
Toumodi 34 Dd 6.33N 5.01W
Tounassine, Hamada- 32 Fd 28.36N 5.10W
Toungo 34 Hd 8.07N 12.03 E
Toungoo 22 Lh 18.56N 96.26 E
Touques 12 Ce 49.22N 0.06 E
Toura 35 Bc 10.30N 15.19 E
Touraine 11 Hg 47.12N 1.30 E
Touraine, Val de- 11 Hg 47.20N 1.30 E
Tourcoing 11 Jd 50.43N 3.09 E
Touriñan, Cabo de- 13 Ca 43.03N 9.18W
Tourine 32 Ee 22.00N 12.15W
Tournai/Doornik 11 Jd 50.38N 3.23 E
Tournai-Kain 12 Fd 50.38N 3.22 E
Tournon 11 Ki 45.04N 4.50 E
Tournus 11 Kh 46.34N 4.54 E
Touros 54 Ke 5.12S 35.28W
Tours 6 Gf 47.23N 0.41 E
Tourteron 12 Ge 49.32N 4.39 E
Toury 11 Hf 48.12N 1.56 E
Touside, Pic- 35 Ba 21.02N 16.25 E
Toussoro 35 Cd 9.02N 23.55 E
Toutouba 63b Cb 15.34S 167.16 E
Touwsrivier 37 Cf 33.20S 20.00 E
Toužim 10 If 50.04N 12.59 E
Tovar 49 Li 8.20N 71.46W
Tovarkovski 16 Kc 53.43N 38.13 E
Tovdalselva 8 Cf 58.12N 8.06 E
Tove 12 Bb 52.04N 0.50W
Tõwa 29 Gb 39.23N 141.15 E
Towada 28 Pd 40.35N 141.13 E
Towada-Kō 29 Ga 40.28N 140.55 E
Towanda 44 Ie 41.46N 76.27W
Tower 45 Jc 47.48N 92.17W
Towner 45 Fb 48.21N 100.25W
Townsend 46 Jc 46.19N 111.31W
Townshend, Cape- 59 Kd 22.15S 150.30 E
Townsville 58 Ff 19.16S 146.48 E
Towot 35 Ed 6.12N 34.25 E
Towson 44 If 39.24N 76.36W
Towuti, Danau- 26 Hg 2.45S 121.32 E
Toxkan He 27 Dc 41.08N 80.11 E
Tōya 29a Bb 42.39N 140.48 E
Toyah Creek 45 Ek 31.18N 103.27W
Tōya-Ko 28 Pc 42.33N 140.50 E
Toyama 22 Pf 36.41N 137.13 E
Toyama Ken [2] 28 Nf 36.35N 137.10 E
Toyama Trench (EN) 29 Ec 38.00N 138.00 E
Toyama-Wan 28 Nf 37.00N 137.15 E
Tōyō 28 Mh 33.22N 134.18 E
Toyohashi 27 Oe 34.46N 137.23 E
Toyokoro 29a Cb 42.48N 143.28 E
Toyonaka 29 Dd 34.47N 135.28 E
Toyo'oka 27 Od 35.33N 137.54 E
Toyosaka 29 Fc 37.55N 139.12 E
Toyota 28 Ng 35.05N 137.09 E
Toyotama 29 Ad 34.27N 129.19 E
Toyotomi 29a Ba 45.08N 141.47 E
Toyoura 29 Bd 34.10N 130.55 E
Trabancos 13 Gc 41.27N 5.11W
Traben Trabach 12 Je 49.57N 7.07 E
Trabzon 22 Fe 40.59N 39.43 E
Traer 45 Je 42.12N 92.28W
Trafalgar, Cabo- 13 Fh 36.11N 6.02W
Tragacete 13 Kd 40.21N 1.51W
Traiguén 56 Fe 38.15S 72.41W
Trail 39 He 49.06N 117.43W
Traill 41 Jd 72.45N 24.00W
Trairas, Rio- 55 Hb 14.07S 48.31W
Trairi 54 Kd 3.17S 39.15W
Traisen 14 Jb 48.22N 15.46 E
Trakai/Trakaj 7 Fi 54.38N 24.57 E
Trakaj/Trakai 7 Fi 54.38N 24.57 E
Trakt 17 Ee 62.44N 51.11 E
Trakya = Thrace (EN) 15 Jh 41.20N 26.45 E
Trakya = Thrace (EN) 5 Ig 41.20N 26.45 E
Tralee/Trá Lí 9 Di 52.16N 9.42W
Tralee Bay/Bá Thrá Lí 9 Di 52.15N 9.59W
Trá Lí/Tralee 9 Di 52.16N 9.42W
Trá Mhór/Tramore 9 Fi 52.10N 7.10W
Tramore/Trá Mhór 9 Fi 52.10N 7.10W
Tramping Lake 46 Ka 52.10N 108.48W
Trân 15 Fg 42.50N 22.39 E
Tranås 7 Dg 58.03N 14.59 E
Trancoso 13 Ed 40.47N 7.21W
Tranebjerg 8 Di 55.50N 10.36 E
Tranemo 8 Eg 57.29N 13.21 E
Trang 22 Li 7.33N 99.36 E
Trani 14 Ki 41.17N 16.25 E
Transantarctic Mountains (EN) 66 Lg 85.00S 175.00W
Transcaucasia (EN) 5 Kg 41.00N 45.00 E
Transilvania = Transylvania (EN) 15 Hc 46.30N 25.00 E
Transilvania = Transylvania (EN) 5 If 46.30N 25.00 E
Transkei [1] 30 Jl 31.30S 29.00 E
Transkei 37 Df 32.45S 28.30 E
Transtrand 8 Ec 61.05N 13.19 E
Transtrandsfjällen 8 Ec 61.15N 12.58 E
Transylvania (EN) = Transilvania 15 Hc 46.30N 25.00 E
Transylvania (EN) = Transilvania 5 If 46.30N 25.00 E
Transylvanian Alps (EN) = Carpații Meridionali 5 If 45.30N 24.15 E
Trants Bay 51c Bc 16.46N 62.09W
Trapani 6 Hh 38.01N 12.29 E
Trapper Peak 46 Hd 45.54N 114.18W
Trappes 12 Ef 48.47N 2.01 E
Traralgon 59 Jg 38.12S 146.32 E
Trarza [3] 32 Ef 18.00N 15.00W
Trarza 30 Fg 17.20N 14.40W
Trașcăului, Munții- 15 Gc 46.23N 23.33 E
Trasimeno, Lago- 14 Gg 43.10N 12.05 E
Trässlövsläge 8 Eg 57.04N 12.16 E
Trás os Montes e Alto Douro 13 Ec 41.30N 7.15W
Trat 25 Kf 12.13N 102.16 E
Traun 14 Ib 48.13N 14.14 E
Traun 14 Ib 48.16N 14.22 E
Traunsee 14 Hc 47.52N 13.48 E
Traunstein 10 Ii 47.53N 12.39 E
Trave 10 Gc 53.54N 10.50 E
Travemünde, Lübeck- 10 Gc 53.57N 10.52 E
Travers, Mount- 61 Dh 42.01S 172.44 E
Traverse, Lake- 45 Hd 45.43N 96.40W
Traverse City 43 Jc 44.46N 85.37W
Traverse Islands 66 Ad 56.36S 27.43W
Travers Reservoir 46 Ia 50.14N 112.51W
Tra Vinh 25 Lg 9.56N 106.20 E
Travis, Lake- 45 Hk 30.27N 98.00W
Travnik 23 Ff 44.14N 17.40 E
Travo 11a Bb 41.54N 9.24 E
Trbovlje 14 Jd 46.10N 15.03 E
Treasurers 63c Ba 9.53S 167.09 E
Treasury Islands 63a Bb 7.22S 155.37 E
Trebbia 14 De 45.04N 9.41 E
Třebíč 10 Lg 49.13N 15.53 E
Trebinje 14 Mh 42.43N 18.21 E
Trebisacce 14 Kk 39.52N 16.32 E
Trebišnjica 14 Lg 43.01N 17.47 E
Trebišov 10 Rh 48.40N 21.43 E
Treblinka 10 Sd 52.40N 22.03 E
Trebnje 14 Je 45.54N 15.01 E
Třeboň 10 Kg 49.01N 14.48 E
Třeboňska pánev 10 Kg 49.00N 14.50 E
Trégorrois 11 Cf 48.45N 3.15W
Tregrosse Islets 57 Gf 17.40S 150.45 E
Tréguier 11 Cf 48.47N 3.14W
Treherne 45 Gb 49.38N 98.41W
Treignac 11 Hi 45.32N 1.48 E
Treinta y Tres [2] 55 Ek 33.00S 54.15W
Treinta y Tres 56 Jd 33.14S 54.23W
Treis-Karden 12 Jd 50.11N 7.17 E
Trélazé 11 Fg 47.27N 0.28W
Trelew 56 Gf 43.15S 65.18W
Trelleborg 6 Hd 55.22N 13.10 E
Trélon 12 Gd 50.04N 4.06 E
Tremadoc Bay 9 Ii 52.40N 4.10W
Tremblant, Mount- 38 Le 46.15N 74.34W
Tremiti, Isole- = Tremiti Islands (EN) 5 Hg 42.10N 15.30 E
Tremiti Islands (EN) = Tremiti, Isole- 5 Hg 42.10N 15.30 E
Tremonton 46 If 41.43N 112.10W
Tremp 13 Mb 42.10N 0.54 E
Třemšín 10 Jg 49.33N 13.48 E
Trenche, Rivière- 44 Kb 47.35N 72.58W
Trenčín 10 Oh 48.54N 18.04 E
Trenque Lauquen 56 He 35.58S 62.42W
Trent 9 Mh 53.42N 0.41W
Trent, Vale of- 9 Li 52.45N 1.50W
Trentino-Alto Adige / Südtirol [2] 14 Fd 46.30N 11.20 E
Trento 14 Fd 46.04N 11.08 E
Trenton [Mo.-U.S.] 45 Jf 40.05N 93.37W
Trenton [N.J.-U.S.] 39 Le 40.13N 74.45W
Trenton [Ont.-Can.] 44 Ic 44.06N 77.35W
Tréon 12 Df 48.41N 1.20 E
Trepassey 42 Mg 46.44N 53.22W
Tres Arboles [Ur.] 56 Id 32.24S 56.43W
Tres Arroyos 53 Ji 38.22S 60.15W
Tres Bocas 55 Ck 32.44S 59.45W
Tres Caraçoes 54 Ih 21.42S 45.16W
Tres Cruces, Cerro- 48 Mj 15.28N 92.24W
Três de Maio 55 Eh 27.47S 54.14W
Tres Esquinas 54 Cc 0.43N 75.15W
Tres Isletas 55 Bh 26.21S 60.26W
Treska 15 Eh 41.59N 21.19 E
Treskavica 14 Mg 43.35N 18.24 E
Três Lagoas 53 Kh 20.48S 51.43W
Três Marias, Represa- 54 Ig 18.15S 45.15W
Tres Montes, Península- 56 Eg 46.50S 75.30W
Três Passos 56 Jc 27.27S 53.56W
Tres Picos, Cerro- [Arg.] 52 Ji 38.09S 61.57W
Tres Picos, Cerro- [Mex.] 48 Li 16.36N 94.13W
Três Pontas 55 Je 21.22S 45.31W
Tres Puntas, Cabo- [Arg.] 52 Jj 47.06S 65.53W
Tres Puntas, Cabo- [Guat.] 49 Cf 15.58N 88.37W
Três Ranchos 55 Id 18.22S 47.47W
Três Rios 55 Kf 22.07S 43.12W
Třešť 10 Lg 49.18N 15.28 E
Tres Valles 48 Kh 18.15N 96.08W
Tres Zapotes 47 Ee 18.28N 95.24W
Tretten 7 Cf 61.19N 10.19 E
Treuer Range 59 Gd 22.15S 130.50 E
Treungen 8 Ce 59.02N 8.33 E
Trêve, Lac la- 44 Ja 49.58N 75.31W
Trevi 14 Gh 42.52N 12.45 E
Trévières 12 Be 49.19N 0.54W
Treviglio 14 De 45.31N 9.35 E
Trevinca, Peña- 13 Fb 42.15N 6.46W
Treviño 13 Jb 42.44N 2.45W
Treviso 14 Ge 45.40N 12.15 E
Trevose Head 9 Hk 50.33N 5.01W
Trgovište 15 Fg 42.21N 22.06 E
Triánda 15 Lm 36.24N 28.10 E
Triangle 37 Ed 21.02S 31.28 E
Triángulos, Arrecifes- 48 Mg 20.57N 92.16W
Trianísia 15 Jm 36.18N 26.45 E
Tribeč 10 Oh 48.27N 18.15 E
Tribune 45 Fg 38.28N 101.45W
Tricarico 14 Kj 40.37N 16.09 E
Tricase 14 Mk 39.56N 18.22 E
Trichūr 25 Ff 10.31N 76.13 E
Tri City 46 De 43.02N 123.15W
Trie-Château 12 De 49.17N 1.50 E
Triel-sur-Seine 12 Ef 48.59N 2.01 E
Trier 10 Cg 49.45N 6.38 E
Trier-Ehrang 12 Ie 49.49N 6.41 E
Trier-Pfalzel 12 Ie 49.46N 6.41 E
Trieste 6 Hf 45.40N 13.46 E
Trieste, Golfo di- 14 He 45.40N 13.30 E
Trieux 11 Cf 48.50N 3.03W
Trifels 12 Je 49.11N 7.59 E
Triglav 5 Hf 46.23N 13.50 E
Trigno 14 Ih 42.04N 14.48 E
Trikala 15 Ej 39.33N 21.46 E
Trikhonis, Límni- 15 Ek 38.34N 21.30 E
Trikomo → Yeniboğaziçi 24 Ee 35.17N 33.52 E
Trikomon → Yeniboğaziçi 24 Ee 35.17N 33.52 E
Trikora, Puncak- 26 Kg 4.15S 138.45 E
Trilport 12 Ef 48.57N 2.57 E
Trim/Baile Átha Troim 9 Gh 53.34N 6.47W
Trincheras 48 Gc 28.55N 104.18W
Trincomalee 22 Ki 8.34N 81.14 E
Trindade 54 Ig 16.40S 49.30W
Trindade, Ilha da- 52 Nh 20.31S 29.19W
Třinec 10 Og 49.41N 18.42 E
Tring 12 Bc 51.47N 0.39W
Tringia 15 Ej 39.38N 21.25 E
Trinidad 52 Jd 10.30N 61.15W
Trinidad [Bol.] 53 Jg 14.47S 64.47W
Trinidad [Ca.-U.S.] 46 Cf 41.07N 124.07W
Trinidad [Co.-U.S.] 39 If 37.10N 104.31W
Trinidad [Cuba] 47 Id 21.48N 79.59W
Trinidad [Mex.] 48 Ec 28.25N 109.06W
Trinidad [Ur.] 56 Id 33.32S 56.54W
Trinidad, Golfo- 56 Eg 49.55S 75.25W
Trinidad, Isla- 55 Bn 39.08S 61.58W
Trinidad, Laguna- 55 Be 20.21S 61.35W
Trinidad and Tobago [1] 53 Jd 11.00N 61.00W
Trinidade Spur (EN) 3 Cl 21.00S 35.00W
Trinitapoli 14 Ki 41.21N 16.05 E
Trinity 45 Ik 30.57N 95.22W
Trinity 38 Jg 29.47N 94.42W
Trinity Bay [Austl.] 59 Jc 16.25S 145.35 E
Trinity Bay [Can.] 42 Mg 48.15N 53.10W
Trinity Islands 40 Ie 56.33N 154.25W
Trinity Range 46 Ff 40.20N 118.45W
Trinity River 46 Df 41.11N 123.42W
Trinkitat 35 Fb 18.41N 37.43 E
Trino 14 Ce 45.12N 8.18 E
Trionto 14 Kk 39.37N 16.45 E
Trionto, Capo- 14 Kk 39.37N 16.45 E
Triora 14 Bf 43.59N 7.46 E
Tripoli (EN) = Țarābulus [3] 33 Bc 32.40N 13.15 E
Tripoli (EN) = Țarābulus [Leb.] 23 Ec 34.26N 35.51 E
Tripoli (EN) = Țarābulus [Lib.] 31 Ie 32.54N 13.11 E
Tripolis 15 Fl 37.31N 22.22 E
Tripolitania (EN) = Tarābulus 30 Ie 31.00N 14.00 E
Tripolitania (EN) = Țarābulus 33 Bc 30.00N 15.00 E

Index Symbols

[1] Independent Nation
[2] State, Region
[3] District, County
[4] Municipality
[5] Colony, Dependency
Continent
Physical Region
Historical or Cultural Region
Mount, Mountain
Volcano
Hill
Mountains, Mountain Range
Hills, Escarpment
Plateau, Upland
Pass, Gap
Plain, Lowland
Delta
Salt Flat
Valley, Canyon
Crater, Cave
Karst Features
Depression
Polder
Desert, Dunes
Forest, Woods
Heath, Steppe
Oasis
Cape, Point
Coast, Beach
Cliff
Peninsula
Isthmus
Sandbank
Island
Atoll
Rock, Reef
Islands, Archipelago
Rocks, Reefs
Coral Reef
Well, Spring
Geyser
River, Stream
Waterfall Rapids
River Mouth, Estuary
Lake
Salt Lake
Intermittent Lake
Reservoir
Swamp, Pond
Canal
Glacier
Ice Shelf, Pack Ice
Ocean
Sea
Gulf, Bay
Strait, Fjord
Lagoon
Bank
Seamount
Tablemount
Ridge
Shelf
Basin
Escarpment, Sea Scarp
Fracture
Trench, Abyss
National Park, Reserve
Point of Interest
Recreation Site
Cave, Cavern
Historic Site
Ruins
Wall, Walls
Church, Abbey
Temple
Scientific Station
Airport
Port
Lighthouse
Mine
Tunnel
Dam, Bridge

Name	Page	Grid	Lat.	Long.
Tripura [3]	25	Id	24.00N	92.00 E
Trisanna	14	Ec	47.07N	10.30 E
Tristan da Cunha	30	Fi	37.05S	12.17W
Tristan da Cunha Group	30	Fi	37.15S	12.30W
Triste, Golfo-	50	Bg	10.40N	68.10W
Triunfo	55	Ee	20.46S	55.47W
Trivandrum	22	Ji	8.29N	76.55 E
Trivento	14	Ii	41.47N	14.33 E
Trjavna	15	Ig	42.52N	25.30 E
Trnava	10	Nh	48.22N	17.35 E
Troarn	12	Be	49.11N	0.11W
Trobriand Islands	57	Ge	8.30S	151.05 E
Trödje	8	Gd	60.49N	17.12 E
Trofors	7	Cd	65.34N	13.25 E
Trögd	8	Ge	59.30N	17.15 E
Trogir	14	Kg	43.32N	16.15 E
Troglav	14	Kg	43.58N	16.36 E
Troglav	14	Mg	43.02N	18.33 E
Trøgstad	8	De	59.38N	11.18 E
Troia	14	Ji	41.22N	15.18 E
Troick	22	Id	54.06N	61.35 E
Troick	20	Ee	57.23N	94.55 E
Troickoje	20	Df	52.58N	84.45 E
Troickoje	20	Ig	49.30N	136.32 E
Troickoje	15	Nb	47.38N	30.12 E
Troicko Pečorsk	19	Fc	62.44N	56.06 E
Troina	14	Im	37.47N	14.36 E
Troisdorf	12	Jd	50.49N	7.10 E
Trois Fourches, Cap des-	32	Gb	35.26N	2.58W
Trois-Pistoles	44	Ma	48.07N	69.10W
Trois Pitons, Morne-	51g	Bb	15.22N	61.20W
Trois-Ponts	12	Hd	50.22N	5.52 E
Trois-Rivières [Guad.]	51e	Ac	15.59N	61.39W
Trois-Rivières [Que.-Can.]	39	Le	46.21N	72.33W
Troissereux	12	Ee	49.29N	2.03 E
Troisvierges/Ulflingen	12	Hd	50.07N	6.00 E
Trojah	15	Hg	42.53N	24.43 E
Trojanovka	10	Ve	51.21N	25.25 E
Trojanski Manastir	15	Hg	42.53N	24.48 E
Trojanski prohod	15	Hg	42.48N	24.40 E
Trojebratski	19	Ge	54.25N	66.03 E
Trollhättan	7	Cg	58.16N	12.18 E
Trollheimen	7	Be	62.50N	9.05 E
Trollhetta	8	Cb	62.51N	9.19 E
Trolltindane	8	Bd	62.29N	7.43 E
Tromba	55	Ha	13.28S	48.45W
Trombetas, Rio-	52	Kf	1.55S	55.35W
Tromelin	30	Mj	15.52S	54.25 E
Tromøya	8	Cf	58.30N	8.50 E
Troms [3]	7	Eb	69.07N	19.15 E
Tromsø	6	Hb	69.40N	19.00 E
Tron	8	Db	62.10N	10.43 E
Tronador, Monte-	52	Ij	41.10S	71.54W
Trondheim	6	Hc	63.25N	10.25 E
Trondheimsfjorden	5	Hc	63.40N	10.50 E
Tronto	14	Hh	42.54N	13.55 E
Tropea	14	Jl	38.41N	15.54 E
Tropeiros, Serra dos-	55	Jb	14.43S	44.33W
Tropoja	15	Dg	42.24N	20.10 E
Trosa	7	Dg	58.54N	17.33 E
Troškūnai/Troškunaj	8	Ki	55.32N	24.59 E
Troškunaj/Troškūnai	8	Ki	55.32N	24.59 E
Trostberg	10	Ih	48.02N	12.33 E
Trostjanec	16	Id	50.29N	34.59 E
Trotuş	15	Kc	46.03N	27.14 E
Trou Gras Point	51k	Bb	13.52N	60.53W
Troumasse	51k	Bb	13.49N	60.54W
Trout Lake [Mi.-U.S.]	44	Eb	46.12N	85.01W
Trout Lake [N.W.T.-Can.]	42	Fd	60.35N	121.10W
Trout Lake [Ont.-Can.]	42	If	51.12N	93.19W
Trout Lake [Ont.-Can.]	42	If	53.54N	89.56W
Trout Peak	46	Kd	44.36N	109.32W
Trout River	42	Lg	49.29N	58.08W
Trouville-sur-Mer	11	Ge	49.22N	0.05 E
Trowbridge	9	Kj	51.20N	2.13W
Troy [Al.-U.S.]	43	Je	31.48N	85.58W
Troy [Mo.-U.S.]	45	Kg	38.59N	90.59W
Troy [Mt.-U.S.]	46	Hb	48.28N	115.53W
Troy [N.Y.-U.S.]	43	Mc	42.43N	73.40W
Troy [Oh.-U.S.]	44	Ee	40.02N	84.12W
Troy (EN)=Truva	24	Bc	39.57N	26.15 E
Troyes	6	Gf	48.18N	4.05 E
Troy Peak	43	Dd	38.19N	115.30W
Trstenik	15	Df	43.37N	21.00 E
Trubčevsk	19	De	52.36N	33.46 E
Truc Giang	25	Lf	10.14N	106.23 E
Truchas Peak	45	Di	35.58N	105.39W
Trucial Coast (EN)	21	Hg	24.00N	53.00 E
Trucial States (EN)→United Arab Emirates (EN)	22	Hg	24.00N	54.00 E
Truckee	46	Eg	39.20N	120.11W
Trudfront	16	Og	45.56N	47.41 E
Trudovoje	20	Ih	43.18N	132.05 E
Trufanova	7	Kd	64.29N	44.05 E
Trujillo [2]	54	Db	9.25N	70.30W
Trujillo [Hond.]	47	Ge	15.55N	86.00W
Trujillo [Peru]	53	If	8.10S	79.02W
Trujillo [Sp.]	13	Ge	39.28N	5.53W
Trujillo [Ven.]	54	Db	9.22N	70.26W
Trujillo, Rio-	48	Hf	23.39N	103.08W
Truk Islands	57	Gd	7.25N	151.47 E
Trumann	45	Ki	35.41N	90.31W
Trumbull, Mount-	43	Ed	36.25N	113.10W
Trun	12	Gf	48.51N	0.02 E
Trung Phan=Annam (EN)	21	Me	15.00N	108.00 E
Truro [Eng.-U.K.]	9	Hk	50.16N	5.03W
Truro [N.S.-Can.]	39	Me	45.22N	63.16W
Truskavec	16	Ce	49.17N	23.34 E
Truth or Consequences (Hot Springs)	43	Fe	33.08N	107.15W
Trutnov	10	Lf	50.34N	15.54 E
Truva=Troy (EN)	24	Bc	39.57N	26.15 E
Truyère	11	Ij	44.38N	2.34 E
Trysil	8	Ec	61.25N	12.25 E
Trysil	7	Cf	61.18N	12.16 E
Trysilelva	5	Hd	59.23N	13.32 E
Trysilfjellet	8	Ec	61.18N	12.11 E
Trzcianka	10	Mc	53.03N	16.28 E
Trzcińsko Zdrój	10	Kd	52.58N	14.35 E
Trzebiatów	10	Lb	54.04N	15.14 E
Trzebież	10	Kc	53.42N	14.31 E
Trzebinia-Siersza	10	Pf	50.11N	19.25 E
Trzebnica	10	Ne	51.19N	17.03 E
Trzebnicki, Wał-	10	Me	51.30N	16.20 E
Trzebnickie, Wzgórza-	10	Me	51.15N	17.00 E
Trzemeszno	10	Nd	52.35N	17.50 E
Tsaidam Basin (EN)=Qaidam Pendi	27	Fd	37.00N	95.00 E
Tsamandá, Óri-	15	Dj	39.48N	20.21 E
Tsarap	25	Fb	33.31N	76.56 E
Tsaratanana	37	Hc	16.46S	47.38 E
Tsaratanana (EN)=Tsaratanana, Massif du-	30	Lj	14.00S	49.00 E
Tsaratanana, Massif du-=Tsaratanana (EN)	30	Lj	14.00S	49.00 E
Tsau	37	Cd	20.10S	22.27 E
Tsavo	36	Gc	2.59S	38.28 E
Tses	37	Be	25.58S	18.08 E
Tsévié	34	Fd	6.25N	1.13 E
Tshabong	31	Jk	26.02S	22.06 E
Tshane	31	Jk	24.01S	21.43 E
Tshangalele, Lac-	36	Ee	10.55S	27.03 E
Tshela	31	Ii	4.59S	12.56 E
Tshesebe	37	Dd	20.43S	27.37 E
Tshibala	36	Dd	6.56S	21.28 E
Tshibamba	36	Dd	9.06S	22.34 E
Tshikapa	31	Ji	6.25S	20.48 E
Tshilenge	36	Dd	6.15S	23.46 E
Tshimbalanga	36	Dd	9.43S	23.06 E
Tshimbulu	36	Dd	6.29S	22.51 E
Tshinsenda	36	Ee	12.16S	27.55 E
Tshofa	36	Ed	5.14S	25.15 E
Tshopo	36	Eb	0.33N	25.07 E
Tshuapa	30	Ji	0.14S	20.42 E
Tshwaane	37	Cd	22.38S	22.05 E
Tsiafajavona	37	Hc	19.21S	47.15 E
Tsihombe	37	He	25.17S	45.30 E
Tsimlyansk Reservoir (EN)=Cimljanskoje Vodohranilišče	5	Kf	48.00N	43.00 E
Tsinan (EN)=Jinan	22	Nf	36.35N	117.00 E
Tsinghai (EN)=Ch'ing-hai Sheng→Qinghai Sheng [2]	27	Gd	36.00N	96.00 E
Tsinghai (EN)=Qinghai Sheng (Ch'ing-hai Sheng) [2]	27	Gd	36.00N	96.00 E
Tsingtao (EN)=Qingdao	22	Of	36.05N	120.21 E
Tsiribihina	37	Gc	19.42S	44.31 E
Tsiroanomandidy	37	Hc	18.50S	46.00 E
Tsis	64d	Bb	7.18N	151.50 E
Tsjokkarassa	7	Fb	69.59N	24.32 E
Tsodilo Hill	37	Cc	18.50S	21.45 E
Tsu	27	Oe	34.43N	136.31 E
Tsubame	29	Fc	37.39N	138.56 E
Tsubata	28	Nf	36.40N	136.44 E
Tsubetsu	29a	Db	43.43N	144.01 E
Tsuchiura	28	Pf	36.05N	140.12 E
Tsugaru-Hantō	29a	Bc	41.00N	140.30 E
Tsugaru-Kaikyō=Tsugaru Strait (EN)	21	Qe	41.40N	140.55 E
Tsugaru Strait (EN)=Tsugaru-Kaikyō	21	Qe	41.40N	140.55 E
Tsuken-Jima	29b	Ab	26.15N	127.57 E
Tsukidate	29	Gb	38.44N	141.01 E
Tsukigata	29a	Bb	43.20N	141.39 E
Tsukuba-San	29	Gc	36.13N	140.06 E
Tsukumi	29	Be	33.04N	131.52 E
Tsukura-Se	29	Af	31.18N	129.47 E
Tsukushi-Sanchi	29	Be	33.25N	130.30 E
Tsumeb	31	Ij	19.13S	17.42 E
Tsumeb [3]	37	Bc	19.00S	17.30 E
Tsumkwe	37	Cc	19.32S	20.30 E
Tsuna	29	Dd	34.26N	134.54 E
Tsuno-Shima	29	Bd	34.22N	130.52 E
Tsuru	29	Fd	35.35N	138.50 E
Tsuruga	27	Od	35.39N	136.04 E
Tsuruga-Wan	29	Ed	35.45N	136.05 E
Tsurugi	29	Ec	36.26N	136.37 E
Tsurugi-San	29	De	33.51N	134.03 E
Tsurui	29a	Db	43.14N	144.21 E
Tsurumi-Dake	29	Be	33.18N	131.27 E
Tsurumi-Saki	29	Ce	32.56N	132.05 E
Tsuruoka	28	Oe	38.44N	139.50 E
Tsuruta	29	Ga	40.44N	140.26 E
Tsushima	21	Of	34.30N	129.20 E
Tsushima [Jap.]	29	Ce	33.07N	132.30 E
Tsushima [Jap.]	29	Ed	35.10N	136.43 E
Tsushima-Kaikyō=Korea, Strait (EN)	21	Of	34.40N	129.00 E
Tsuwano	29	Bd	34.28N	131.46 E
Tsuyama	28	Lg	35.03N	134.00 E
Tua	13	Ec	41.13N	7.26W
Tuai	28	Gc	38.49S	177.08 E
Tuaim/Tuam	9	Eh	53.31N	8.50W
Tuakau	62	Fb	37.15S	174.57 E
Tual	26	Jh	5.40S	132.45 E
Tuam/Tuaim	9	Eh	53.31N	8.50W
Tuamotu, Iles-=Tuamotu Archipelago (EN)	57	Mf	19.00S	142.00W
Tuamotu Archipelago (EN)=Tuamotu, Iles-	57	Mf	19.00S	142.00W
Tuamotu Ridge (EN)	3	Ll	20.00S	145.00W
Tuapa	64k	Ba	18.57S	169.54W
Tuapse	6	Jg	44.07N	39.05 E
Tuaran	26	Ge	6.11N	116.14 E
Tuasivi	65c	Aa	13.40S	172.07W
Tuasivi, Cape-	65c	Aa	13.40S	172.07W
Tuatapere	61	Ci	46.08S	167.41 E
Tuba	62	Ef	54.00N	91.40 E
Tuba City	46	Jh	36.08N	111.14W
Tubai, Ile-	57	Mg	23.18S	149.30W
Tubai-Manu→Maiao, Ile-	57	Lf	17.34S	150.35W
Tubal, Wādī at-	24	Jf	32.19N	42.13 E
Tuban	26	Fh	6.54S	112.03 E
Tubarão	56	Kc	28.30S	49.01W
Ṭubayq, Jabal at-	24	Gh	29.32N	37.30 E
Tubbataha Reefs	26	Ge	8.51N	119.56 E
Tubeke/Tubize	12	Gd	50.41N	4.12 E
Tübingen	10	Fh	48.32N	9.03 E
Tubize/Tubeke	12	Gd	50.41N	4.12 E
Ṭubruq=Tobruk (EN)	31	Je	32.05N	23.59 E
Tubuai, Iles-/Australes, Iles-=Tubuai Islands (EN)	57	Lg	23.00S	150.00W
Tubuai Islands (EN)=Australes, Iles-/Tubuai, Iles-	57	Lg	23.00S	150.00W
Tubuai Islands (EN)=Tubuai, Iles-/Australes, Iles-	57	Lg	23.00S	150.00W
Tubutama	48	Db	30.53N	111.29W
Tucacas	54	Ea	10.48N	68.19W
Tucacas, Punta-	49	Mh	10.52N	68.13W
Tucavaca	55	Cd	18.36S	58.55W
Tucavaca, Rio-	55	Cd	18.37S	58.59W
Tuchola	10	Nc	53.35N	17.50 E
Tucholska, Równina-	10	Oc	53.40N	18.30 E
Tuchów	10	Rg	49.54N	21.03 E
Tucker Glacier	66	Kf	72.35S	169.20 E
Tucson	39	Hf	32.13N	110.58W
Tucuarembó	56	Id	31.44S	55.59W
Tucumán [2]	56	Gc	27.00S	65.30W
Tucumcari	43	Gd	35.10N	103.44W
Tucunuí	54	Id	3.42S	49.27W
Tucupido	54	Eb	9.17N	65.47W
Tucupita	54	Fb	9.04N	62.03W
Tudela	13	Kb	42.05N	1.36W
Tudia, Sierra de-	13	Ff	38.05N	6.20W
Tudmur	23	Ec	34.33N	38.17 E
Tudora	15	Jb	47.31N	26.38 E
Tuela	13	Ec	41.30N	7.12W
Tuensang	25	Ic	26.17N	94.40 E
Tuerto	13	Gb	42.18N	5.53W
Tufanbeyli	24	Gc	38.18N	36.11 E
Tufi	58	Fe	9.08S	149.20 E
Tugela	30	Kk	29.14S	31.30 E
Tug Fork	44	Ff	38.25N	82.35W
Tuguegarao	26	Hc	17.37N	121.44 E
Tugulym	17	Lh	57.04N	64.39 E
Tugur	20	If	53.51N	136.52 E
Tuhai He	28	Ee	38.05N	118.13 E
Tujiabu→Yongxiu	27	Kf	29.05N	115.49 E
Tujmazy	19	Fe	54.36N	53.42 E
Tukan	17	Hj	53.50N	57.31 E
Tukangbesi, Kepulauan-=Tukangbesi Islands (EN)	26	Hh	5.40S	123.50 E
Tukangbesi Islands (EN)=Tukangbesi, Kepulauan-	26	Hh	5.40S	123.50 E
Tukayel	35	Hd	8.05N	45.20 E
Tukayyid	24	Kh	29.47N	45.36 E
Tukituki	62	Gc	39.36S	176.56 E
Tuko Village	64n	Ab	10.22S	161.02W
Tūkrah	33	Dc	32.32N	20.34 E
Tuktoyaktuk	39	Fc	69.27N	133.02W
Tukums	7	Fh	56.59N	23.10 E
Tukuringra, Hrebet-	20	Hf	54.30N	126.00 E
Tukuyu	36	Fd	9.15S	33.39 E
Tula	47	Ed	20.06N	99.19W
Tula	36	Gc	0.50S	39.51 E
Tula [Mex.]	48	Jf	23.00N	99.43W
Tula	6	Je	54.12N	37.37 E
Tula de Allende	48	Jg	20.03N	99.21W
Tula Mountains	66	Ee	66.54S	51.06 E
Tulancingo	47	Ed	20.05N	98.22W
Tulare	46	Fh	36.13N	119.21W
Tulare Lake Bed	46	Fh	36.03N	119.49W
Tularosa	45	Cj	33.04N	106.01W
Tularosa Valley	45	Cj	32.45N	106.10W
Tulcán	54	Cc	0.48N	77.43W
Tulcea [2]	15	Md	45.12N	29.10 E
Tulcea	15	Ld	45.10N	28.48 E
Tulčin	16	Fe	48.39N	28.52 E
Tulelake	46	Ef	41.57N	121.29W
Tulemalu Lake	42	Hd	62.55N	99.25W
Tulgheş	15	Ic	46.57N	25.46 E
Tuli	37	Dd	21.55S	29.12 E
Tuli	37	Dd	21.48S	29.04 E
Tulia	45	Fi	34.32N	101.46W
Tulihe	27	La	50.30N	121.51 E
Tullahoma	44	Dh	35.22N	86.11W
Tullamore/An Tulach Mhór	9	Fh	53.16N	7.30W
Tulle	11	Hi	45.16N	1.46 E
Tulln	14	Kb	48.22N	16.03 E
Tulln	14	Kb	48.20N	16.03 E
Tullner Becken	14	Jb	48.25N	15.55 E
Tullow/An Tulach	9	Gi	52.48N	6.44W
Tullus	35	Cc	11.03N	24.33 E
Tully	59	Jc	17.56S	145.56 E
Ṭulmaythah	33	Dc	32.43N	20.57 E
Tuloma	5	Jb	68.52N	32.49 E
Tulos, Ozero-	7	He	63.35N	30.35 E
Tulsa	39	Jf	36.09N	95.58W
Tulskaja Oblast [3]	19	De	54.00N	37.30 E
Tuluá	54	Cc	4.05N	76.12W
Tuluksak	40	Gd	61.06N	160.58W
Tulum	47	Gd	20.15N	87.27W
Tulum	48	Pg	20.13N	87.28W
Tulun	22	Md	54.35N	100.33 E
Tulungagung	26	Fh	8.04S	111.54 E
Tuma	7	Jh	55.10N	40.36 E
Tuma, Rio-	49	Eg	13.03N	84.44W
Tumaco	53	Ie	1.49N	78.46W
Tumaco, Rada de-	54	Cc	1.50N	78.40W
Tumacuarí, Pico-	54	Fc	1.15N	64.40W
Tuman-gang	28	Kc	42.18N	130.41 E
Tumba	8	Ge	59.12N	17.49 E
Tumbarumba	59	Jg	35.47S	148.01 E
Tumbes [2]	54	Bd	3.50S	80.30W
Tumbes	53	Hf	4.05S	80.35W
Tumča	7	Hc	66.35N	31.45 E
Tumd Youqi	27	Jc	40.33N	110.32 E
Tumd Zuoqi	27	Jc	40.43N	111.06 E
Tumen	22	Oe	42.58N	129.49 E
Tumen Jiang	28	Kc	42.18N	130.41 E
Tumeremo	54	Fb	7.18N	61.30W
Tumkur	25	Ff	13.21N	77.05 E
Tummel	9	Je	56.43N	3.44W
Tummo	33	Be	23.00N	14.10 E
Tumon Bay	64c	Ba	13.31N	144.48 E
Tumpat	26	De	6.12N	102.10 E
Tumu	34	Ec	10.52N	1.59W
Tumucumaque, Serra-	52	Ke	2.20N	55.00W
Tumwater	46	Dc	47.01N	122.54W
Tuna, Punta-	51a	Cc	18.00N	65.52W
Tunapuna	50	Fg	10.38N	61.23W
Tunas	55	Hg	24.58S	49.06W
Tunas, Sierra de las-	48	Fc	29.40N	107.15W
Tunas Chicas, Laguna-	55	Am	36.01S	62.20W
Tunaydah	24	Cj	25.31N	29.21 E
Tunçbilek	15	Mj	39.37N	29.29 E
Tunduma	36	Fd	9.18S	32.46 E
Tunduru	36	Ge	11.07S	37.21 E
Tundža	15	Jh	41.40N	26.34 E
Tunga	34	Gd	8.07N	9.12 E
Tungabhadra	25	Fe	15.57N	78.15 E
Tungaru	35	Ec	10.14N	30.42 E
Tungnaá	7a	Bb	64.10N	19.34W
Tungokočen	20	Gf	53.33N	115.34 E
Tungsten	42	Ed	62.05N	127.42W
Tungua	65b	Bb	20.01S	174.46W
Tuni	25	Ge	17.21N	82.33 E
Tūnis=Tunis (EN) [3]	32	Jb	36.30N	10.00 E
Tūnis=Tunis (EN)	31	Ie	36.48N	10.11 E
Tūnis=Tunisia (EN)	31	He	34.00N	9.00 E
Tunis (EN)=Tūnis	31	Ie	36.48N	10.11 E
Tunis (EN)=Tūnis [3]	32	Jb	36.30N	10.00 E
Tūnis, Canal de-=Sicily, Strait of- (EN)	5	Hh	37.20N	11.20 E
Tūnis, Khalīj-	32	Jb	37.00N	10.30 E
Tunisia (EN)=Tūnis	31	He	34.00N	9.00 E
Tunja	53	Ie	5.31N	73.22W
Tunkhannock	44	Je	41.32N	75.57W
Tunliu	28	Bf	36.18N	112.53 E
Tunnhovdfjorden	8	Cd	60.25N	8.55 E
Tunø	8	Di	55.55N	10.25 E
Tunumuk	42	Ec	69.00N	134.57W
Tununak	40	Fd	60.35N	165.16W
Tunungayualok	42	Le	56.05N	61.05W
Tunxi	27	Kf	29.45N	118.15 E
Tuo He	28	Dh	33.16N	117.45 E
Tuo Jang	27	If	28.55N	105.26 E
Tuostah	20	Ic	67.50N	135.40 E
Tuotuo He	27	Fe	34.03N	92.46 E
Tuotuohe/Tanggulashanqu	22	Lf	34.15N	92.29 E
Tupā	56	Jb	21.56S	50.30W
Tupaciguara	55	Hd	18.35S	48.42W
Tupai Atoll (Motu-Iti)	61	Kc	16.17S	151.50W
Tupanciretã	56	Jc	29.05S	53.51W
Tupelo	43	Je	34.16N	88.43W
Tupik	20	Gf	54.28N	119.57 E
Tupinambarana, Ilha-	54	Gd	3.00S	58.00W
Tupiraçaba	55	Hb	14.29S	48.34W
Tupper Lake	44	Jc	44.13N	74.29W
Tupungato, Cerro-	56	Gd	33.22S	69.47W
Tuquan	27	Lb	45.22N	121.33 E
Túquerres	54	Cc	1.06N	77.37W
Tur	15	Fa	48.04N	22.33 E
Tura	19	Gd	57.12N	66.56 E
Tura [India]	25	Ic	25.31N	90.13 E
Tura	22	Mc	64.17N	100.15 E
Turabah [Sau.Ar.]	23	Fe	21.13N	41.39 E
Turabah [Sau.Ar.]	23	Fd	28.13N	42.59 E
Turagua, Serranías-	50	Di	7.20N	64.35W
Turakina	62	Fd	40.02S	175.13 E
Turān	24	Qe	35.40N	56.50 E
Turan	20	Ef	52.08N	93.55 E
Turana, Hrebet-	20	If	51.30N	132.00 E
Turangi	62	Fc	38.59S	175.48 E
Turano	14	Gh	42.26N	12.47 E
Turanskaja Nizmennost	21	Ie	44.30N	63.00 E
Turawa	10	Of	50.45N	18.05 E
Turawskie, Jezioro-	10	Of	50.43N	18.10 E
Turbaco	49	Jh	10.19N	75.25W
Turbat	25	Cc	25.59N	63.04 E
Turbo	53	Ie	8.06N	76.43W
Turcoaia	15	Ld	45.07N	28.11 E
Turda	15	Gc	46.34N	23.47 E
Tureh	24	Me	34.02N	49.17 E
Tureia Atoll	57	Ng	20.50S	138.32W
Turek	10	Od	52.02N	18.30 E
Turenki	8	Kd	60.55N	24.38 E
Turfan Depression (EN)=Turpan Pendi	21	Ke	42.30N	89.30 E
Turgai Gates (EN)=Turgajskaja Ložbina	21	Id	51.00N	64.30 E
Turgai Upland (EN)=Turgajskoje Plato	21	Id	51.00N	64.00 E
Turgaj	19	Gf	49.38N	63.28 E
Turgaj	21	Ie	48.01N	62.45 E
Turgajskaja Ložbina=Turgai Gates (EN)	21	Id	51.00N	64.30 E
Turgajskaja Oblast [3]	19	Ge	50.30N	66.00 E
Turgajskoje Plato=Turgai Upland (EN)	21	Id	51.00N	64.00 E
Turgeon, Rivière-	44	Ha	50.00N	78.55W
Turgutlu	24	Bc	38.30N	27.50 E
Turhal	24	Gb	40.24N	36.06 E
Türi/Tjuri	7	Fg	58.50N	25.27 E
Turia	13	Le	39.27N	0.19W
Turiaçu, Baia de-	54	Id	1.30S	45.15W
Turiec	10	Og	49.06N	18.52 E
Turijsk	10	Ue	51.10N	24.37 E
Turimiquire, Cerro-	54	Fa	10.03N	64.00W
Turin (EN) = Torino	6	Gf	45.03N	7.40 E
Turinsk	19	Gd	58.03N	63.42 E
Turja	16	Dd	51.48N	24.52 E
Turka	20	Ff	52.57N	108.13 E
Turka	10	Tg	49.07N	23.01 E
Turkana [3]	36	Gb	4.00N	35.30 E
Turkana, Lake-/Rudolf, Lake-	30	Kh	3.30N	36.00 E
Türkeli	24	Fb	41.57N	34.21 E
Turkenstanski Hrebet	19	Gh	39.35N	69.00 E
Turkestan	22	Ie	43.18N	68.15 E
Türkeve	10	Qi	47.06N	20.45 E
Turkey (EN)=Türkiye [1]	22	Fg	39.00N	35.00 E
Turkey Creek	59	Fc	17.02S	128.12 E
Turki	16	Mc	52.01N	43.16 E
Türkiye=Turkey (EN) [1]	22	Fg	39.00N	35.00 E
Türkmenistan	19	Fh	40.00N	60.00 E
Turkmenistan Sovet Socialistik Respublikasy/Turkmenskaja SSR → Türkmenistan	19	Fh	40.00N	60.00 E
Turkmen-Kala	18	Df	37.26N	62.19 E
Turkmenskaja Sovetskaja Socialističeskaja Respublika → Türkmenistan	19	Fh	40.00N	60.00 E
Turkmenskaja SSR/Türkmenistan Sovet Socialistik Respublikasy → Türkmenistan	19	Fh	40.00N	60.00 E
Turkmenski zaliv	16	Rj	39.00N	53.30 E
Türkoğlu	24	Gd	37.31N	36.49 E
Turks and Caicos Islands [5]	39	Lg	21.45N	71.35W
Turks Island Passage	49	Lc	21.25N	71.19W
Turks Islands	47	Jd	21.24N	71.07W
Turku/Åbo	6	Ic	60.27N	22.17 E
Turku-Pori [2]	7	Ff	61.00N	22.30 E
Turkwel	36	Gb	3.06N	36.06 E
Turlock	46	Eh	37.30N	120.51W
Turmantas	8	Li	55.42N	26.34 E
Turnagain, Cape-	62	Gd	40.30S	176.37 E
Turneffe Islands	47	Ge	17.22N	87.51W
Turnhout	11	Kc	51.19N	4.57 E
Turnov	10	Lf	50.35N	15.09 E
Turnu Roşu, Pasul-	15	Hd	45.33N	24.16 E
Turnu Măgurele	15	Hf	43.45N	24.52 E
Turočak	20	Df	52.16N	87.05 E
Turó de l'Home	13	Oc	41.45N	2.25 E
Turopolje	14	Ke	45.38N	16.07 E
Turpan	22	Ke	42.56N	89.10 E
Turpan Pendi=Turfan Depression (EN)	21	Ke	42.30N	89.30 E
Turquino, Pico-	47	Ie	19.59N	76.51W
Turrialba	49	Fi	9.54N	83.41W
Tursuntski Tuman, Ozero-	17	Kf	60.35N	63.55 E
Turtas	17	Ng	58.57N	69.10 E
Turtas	17	Ng	59.06N	68.50 E
Turtkul	19	Gg	41.35N	61.00 E
Turtle Mountain	45	Fb	49.05N	100.15W
Turugart Shankou	21	Je	40.32N	75.24 E
Turuhan	20	Dc	65.56N	87.42 E
Turuhansk	20	Dc	65.49N	87.59 E
Turvânia	55	Gc	16.39S	50.09W
Turvo	55	Hi	28.56S	49.41W
Turvo, Rio- [Braz.]	55	Hd	19.56S	49.55W
Turvo, Rio- [Braz.]	55	Gc	17.46S	50.12W
Tusaun/Thusis	14	Dd	46.42N	9.26 E
Tuscaloosa	43	Je	33.13N	87.33W
Tuscan Archipelago (EN)=Arcipelago Toscano	5	Hg	42.45N	10.20 E
Tuscania	14	Fh	42.25N	11.52 E
Tuscany (EN) = Toscana [2]	14	Eg	43.25N	11.00 E
Tuscarora Mountain	44	Ie	40.10N	77.45W
Tuscarora Mountains	46	Gf	41.00N	116.20W
Tuščibas, Zaliv-	18	Ba	46.10N	59.45 E
Tuscola	45	Lg	39.48N	88.17W
Tusenøyane	41	Oc	77.05N	22.00 E
Tuskar	16	Jd	51.40N	36.15 E
Tuskegee	44	Ei	32.26N	85.42W
Tuşnad Băi	15	Ic	46.09N	25.51 E
Tustna	8	Ca	63.10N	8.05 E
Tuszymka	10	Rf	50.09N	21.30 E
Tuszyn	10	Pe	51.37N	19.34 E
Tutajev	19	Dd	57.52N	39.32 E
Tutak	24	Jc	39.32N	42.46 E
Tuticorin	25	Fg	8.47N	78.08 E
Tutira	62	Gc	39.12S	176.53 E
Tutóia	54	Jd	2.45S	42.16W
Tutoko Peak	62	Bf	44.36S	167.58 E
Tutončana	20	Ed	64.05N	93.50 E
Tutova	15	Kc	46.06N	27.32 E
Tutrakan	15	Je	44.03N	26.37 E
Tuttle Creek Lake	45	Hg	39.22N	96.40W
Tuttlingen	10	Ei	47.59N	8.49 E
Tutuala	26	Ih	8.24S	127.15 E
Tutuila Island	57	Jf	14.18S	170.42W
Tutupaca, Volcán-	54	Dg	17.01S	70.22W
Tuupovaara	8	Nb	62.29N	30.36 E
Tuusniemi	7	Ge	62.49N	28.30 E
Tuva, respublika	20	Ef	51.30N	94.00 E
Tuvalu (Ellice Islands) [1]	58	Ie	8.00S	178.00 E
Tuvalu Islands	57	Ie	8.00S	178.00 E
Tuvana-i-Ra Island	61	Fd	21.00S	178.43W
Tuvana-i-Tholo Island	57	Ig	21.02S	178.49W
Tuvutha	63d	Cb	17.40S	178.48W
Tuwayq, Jabal-	21	Gg	25.30N	46.20 E
Tuxer Alpen	14	Fc	47.10N	11.45 E
Tuxford	12	Ba	53.13N	0.53W
Tuxpan	48	Hh	19.33N	103.24W
Tuxpán	47	Cd	21.57N	105.18W
Tuxpan, Arrecife-	48	Kg	21.02N	97.13W
Tuxpan, Rio-	48	Kg	20.53N	97.18W
Tuxpán de Rodriguez Cano	47	Ed	20.57N	97.24W
Tuxtla Gutiérrez	39	Jh	16.45N	93.07W
Túy	13	Db	42.03N	8.38W
Tuy, Rio-	50	Dg	10.24N	65.59W
Tuy An	25	Lf	13.17N	109.16 E

Index Symbols

- [1] Independent Nation
- [2] State, Region
- [3] District, County
- [4] Municipality
- [5] Colony, Dependency
- Continent
- Physical Region
- Historical or Cultural Region
- Mount, Mountain
- Volcano
- Hill
- Mountains, Mountain Range
- Hills, Escarpment
- Plateau, Upland
- Pass, Gap
- Plain, Lowland
- Delta
- Salt Flat
- Valley, Canyon
- Crater, Cave
- Karst Features
- Depression
- Polder
- Desert, Dunes
- Forest, Woods
- Heath, Steppe
- Oasis
- Cape, Point
- Coast, Beach
- Cliff
- Peninsula
- Isthmus
- Sandbank
- Island
- Atoll
- Rock, Reef
- Islands, Archipelago
- Rocks, Reefs
- Coral Reef
- Well, Spring
- Geyser
- River, Stream
- Waterfall Rapids
- River Mouth, Estuary
- Lake
- Salt Lake
- Intermittent Lake
- Reservoir
- Swamp, Pond
- Canal
- Glacier
- Ice Shelf, Pack Ice
- Ocean
- Sea
- Gulf, Bay
- Strait, Fjord
- Lagoon
- Bank
- Seamount
- Tablemount
- Ridge
- Shelf
- Basin
- Escarpment, Sea Scarp
- Fracture
- Trench, Abyss
- National Park, Reserve
- Point of Interest
- Recreation Site
- Cave, Cavern
- Historic Site
- Ruins
- Wall, Walls
- Church, Abbey
- Temple
- Scientific Station
- Airport
- Port
- Lighthouse
- Mine
- Tunnel
- Dam, Bridge

Tuy Hoa 25 Lf 13.05N 109.18 E
Tūyserkān 24 Me 34.33N 48.27 E
Tuz, Lake- (EN)=Tuz Gölü 21 Ff 38.45N 33.25 E
Tuzkan, Ozero- 18 Fd 40.35N 67.30 E
Tūz Khurmātū 23 Fc 34.53N 44.38 E
Tuzla 14 Mf 44.33N 18.41 E
Tuzlov 16 Lf 47.23N 40.08 E
Tuzluca 24 Jb 40.03N 43.39 E
Tuzly 15 Nd 45.56N 30.05 E
Tvååker 8 Eg 57.03N 12.24 E
Tvărdica 15 Ig 42.42N 25.54 E
Tvedestrand 7 Bg 58.37N 8.55 E
Tver' (Kalinin) 6 Jd 56.52N 35.55 E
Tver'skaja oblast 19 Dd 57.20N 34.40 E
Tweed 9 Lf 55.46N 2.00W
Tweedsmuir Hills 9 Jf 55.30N 3.22W
Tweerivier 37 Be 25.35S 19.37 E
Twello, Voorst- 12 Ib 52.14N 6.07 E
Twente 11 Mb 52.17N 6.40 E
Twentekanaal 12 Ib 52.13N 6.53 E
Twilight Cove 59 Ff 32.20S 126.00 E
Twin Buttes Reservoir 45 Fk 31.20N 100.35W
Twin Falls 39 He 42.34N 114.28W
Twin Islands 42 Jf 53.50N 80.00W
Twin Peaks 46 Hd 44.35N 114.29W
Twisp 46 Eb 48.22N 120.07W
Twiste 12 Lc 51.29N 9.09 E
Twistringen 10 Ed 52.48N 8.39 E
Two Butte Creek 45 Eg 38.02N 102.08W
Two Harbors 45 Kc 47.01N 91.40W
Two Rivers 45 Md 44.09N 87.34W
Two Thumb Range 62 De 43.45S 170.40 E
Tychy 10 Of 50.09N 18.59 E
Tyczyn 10 Sg 49.58N 22.02 E
Tydal 7 Ce 63.04N 11.34 E
Tygda 20 Hf 53.07N 126.20 E
Tyin 8 Cc 61.15N 8.15 E
Tyin 8 Cc 61.14N 8.14 E
Tyler 43 He 32.21N 95.18W
Tylertown 45 Kk 31.07N 90.09W
Tylösand 8 Eh 56.39N 12.44 E
Tylöskog 8 Ff 58.40N 15.10 E
Tym 20 De 59.30N 80.07 E
Tymovskoje 20 Jf 50.50N 142.41 E
Tympákion 15 Hn 35.06N 24.45 E
Tynda 22 Od 53.07N 126.20 E
Tyne 9 Lf 55.01N 1.26W
Tyne and Wear [3] 9 Lg 55.00N 1.35W
Tynemouth 9 Lf 55.01N 1.24W
Týn nad Vltavou 10 Kg 49.14N 14.26 E
Tynset 7 Ce 62.17N 10.47 E
Tyra, Cayos- 49 Fg 12.50N 83.20W
Tyrifjorden 8 De 60.05N 10.10 E
Tyringe 8 Eh 56.10N 13.35 E
Tyrma 20 If 50.01N 132.10 E
Tyrnyauz 16 Mh 43.23N 42.56 E
Tyrol (EN)=Tirol [2] 14 Fc 47.10N 11.25 E
Tyrol (EN)=Tirol/Tirolo 14 Fd 47.00N 11.20 E
Tyrol (EN)=Tirolo/Tirol 14 Fd 47.00N 11.20 E
Tyrone 44 He 40.41N 78.15W
Tyrrell, Lake- 59 Ig 35.20S 142.50 E
Tyrrel Lake 42 Gd 63.05N 105.30W
Tyrrhenian Basin (EN) 5 Hh 40.00N 13.00 E
Tyrrhenian Sea (EN)= Tirreno, Mar- 5 Hh 40.00N 12.00 E
Tyrva/Tõrva 7 Fg 58.01N 25.59 E
Tyrvää 8 Jc 61.21N 22.53 E
Tysmenica 10 Uh 48.49N 24.56 E
Tyśmienica 10 Se 51.33N 22.30 E
Tysnesøy 7 Af 60.00N 5.35 E
Tysse 8 Ad 60.22N 5.45 E
Tyssedal 8 Bd 60.07N 6.34 E
Tystama/Tõstamaa 8 Jf 58.17N 23.52 E
Tystberga 8 Gf 58.52N 17.15 E
Tyszowce 10 Tf 50.36N 23.41 E
Tytuvėnai/Tituvenaj 8 Ji 55.33N 23.09 E
Tywyn 9 Ii 52.35N 4.05W
Tzanconeja, Río- 48 Ni 16.51N 91.47W
Tzaneen 37 Ed 23.50S 30.09 E
Tzintzuntzan 48 Ih 19.38N 101.34W
Tzucacab 48 Og 20.04N 89.05W

U

Uaboe 64e Ab 0.31S 166.54 E
Uacurizal, Ilha do- 55 Dc 16.25S 56.05W
Ua Huka, Ile- 57 Ne 8.54S 139.33W
Uanukuhahaki 65b Ba 19.58S 174.29W
Ua Pou, Ile- 57 Me 9.23S 140.03W
Uaroo 59 Dd 23.00S 115.10 E
Uatumã, Rio- 52 Kf 2.26S 57.37W
Uaupés 53 Jf 0.08S 67.05W
Uaupés, Rio- 52 Je 0.02N 67.16W
Uaxactún 47 Ge 17.25N 89.29W
Ub 15 De 44.27N 20.05 E
Ubá 54 Jh 21.07S 42.56W
Übach-Palenberg [Ger.] 10 Cf 50.56N 6.05 E
Ubagan 19 Ge 54.23N 64.40 E
Ubaila 24 If 33.06N 40.15 E
Ubaitaba 54 Kf 14.18S 39.20W
Ubajay 55 Cj 31.47S 58.18W
Ubangi 30 Ii 0.30S 17.42 E
Ubatuba 55 Jf 23.26S 45.04W
Ubay 26 Hd 10.03N 124.28 E
Ubaye 11 Mj 44.28N 6.18 E
Ubayyiḑ, Wādī al- 23 Fc 32.34N 43.48 E
Ube 28 Kh 33.56N 131.15 E
Ubeda 13 If 38.01N 3.22W
Ubekendt Ejland 41 Gd 71.10N 53.45W
Uberaba 53 Lg 19.45S 47.55W
Uberaba, Lagoa- 55 Dc 17.30S 57.45W
Uberlândia 53 Lg 18.56S 48.18W
Überlingen 10 Fi 47.46N 9.10 E
Ubiaja 34 Gd 6.39N 6.23 E
Ubiña, Peña- 13 Ga 43.01N 5.57W
Ubiratã 55 Fg 24.32S 52.56W
Ubon Ratchathani 22 Mh 15.15N 104.54 E
Ubort 16 Fc 52.06N 28.30 E
Ubrique 13 Gh 36.41N 5.27W
Ubsu-Nur (Uvs nuur) 21 Ld 50.20N 92.45 E
Ubundu 31 Ji 0.21S 25.29 E
Učaly 19 Fe 54.20N 59.31 E
Učami 22 Dd 63.50N 96.39 E
Učaral 19 If 46.08N 80.52 E
Ucayali, Río- 52 If 4.30S 73.30W
Uccle/Ukkel 12 Gd 50.48N 4.19 E
Üçdoruk Tepe 24 Ib 40.45N 41.05 E
Ucero 13 Ic 41.31N 3.04W
Uchiko 29 Ce 33.34N 132.38 E
Uchi Lake 45 Ja 51.05N 92.35W
Uchinomi 29 Dd 34.30N 134.19 E
Uchinoura 29 Bf 31.16N 131.05 E
Uchiura-Wan 28 Pc 42.18N 140.35 E
Uchte 10 Ed 52.30N 8.55 E
Učka 14 Ie 45.17N 14.12 E
Uckange 12 Ie 49.18N 6.09 E
Uckermark 10 Jc 53.10N 13.35 E
Uckfield 12 Cd 50.58N 0.06 E
Učkuduk 19 Gg 42.10N 63.30 E
Učkurgan 18 Id 41.01N 72.04 E
Ucrainskaja Sovetskaja Socialističeskaja Respublika — Ukrayina 19 Df 49.00N 32.00 E
Ucross 46 Ld 44.33N 106.31W
Ucua 36 Bd 8.40S 14.12 E
Učur 21 Pd 58.48N 130.35 E
Uda 21 Pd 54.42N 135.14 E
Uda 20 Ff 51.45N 107.25 E
Uda 20 Ee 56.05N 99.34 E
Udačny 20 Gc 66.25N 112.20 E
Udaipur 22 Jg 24.35N 73.41 E
Udaj 16 Hd 50.05N 33.07 E
Udaquiola 55 Cm 36.34S 58.31W
Udbina 14 Jf 44.32N 15.46 E
Uddevalla 7 Cg 58.21N 11.55 E
Uddjaure 5 Hb 65.58N 17.50 E
Uden 12 Hc 51.40N 5.37 E
Udgīr 25 Fe 18.23N 77.07 E
Udhampur 25 Fb 32.56N 75.08 E
Udimski 7 Kf 61.09N 45.52 E
Udine 14 Hd 46.03N 13.14 E
Udipi 25 Ef 13.21N 74.45 E
Udmurtskaja respublika 19 Fd 57.20N 52.50 E
Udoha 8 Mg 57.58N 29.50 E
Udomlja 7 Ih 57.56N 35.02 E
Udone-Jima 29 Fd 34.28N 139.17 E
Udon Thani 25 Ke 17.25N 102.48 E
Udot 64d Bb 7.23N 151.43 E
Udskaja Guba 21 Pd 55.00N 136.00 E
Udskoje 20 If 54.36N 134.30 E
Udy 16 Je 49.47N 36.35 E
Udžary 16 Oi 40.31N 47.40 E
Udzungwa Range 36 Gd 8.05S 35.50 E
Uebonti 26 Hg 0.55S 121.38 E
Uecker 10 Kc 53.45N 14.04 E
Ueckermünde 10 Kc 53.44N 14.03 E
Ueda 27 Od 36.24N 138.16 E
Uele 30 Jh 4.09N 22.26 E
Uelen 20 Oc 66.13N 169.48W
Uelzen 10 Gd 52.58N 10.34 E
Ueno 29 Ed 34.46N 136.06 E
Uere 30 Jh 3.42N 25.24 E
Ufa 5 Le 54.50N 56.00 E
Ufa 6 Le 54.44N 55.56 E
Uftjuga 7 Lf 61.28N 46.12 E
Ugab 30 Ik 21.12S 13.38 E
Ugale/Ugāle 8 Ig 57.19N 21.52 E
Ugāle/Ugale 8 Ig 57.19N 21.52 E
Ugalla 36 Fd 5.08S 30.42 E
Uganda [1] 31 Kh 1.00N 32.00 E
Ugărčin 15 Hf 43.06N 24.25 E
Ugashik 40 He 57.32N 157.25W
Ughelli 34 Gd 5.30N 5.59 E
Ugijar 13 Ih 36.57N 3.03W
Uglegorsk 20 Jg 49.05N 142.06 E
Uglekamensk 20 Ih 43.18N 133.08 E
Ugleural'ski 17 Hg 58.59N 57.38 E
Uglič 19 Dd 57.33N 38.23 E
Ugljan 14 Jf 44.05N 15.10 E
Uglovoje 28 Lc 43.20N 132.06 E
Ugnev 10 Tf 50.20N 23.45 E
Ugo 29 Gb 39.13N 140.23 E
Ugol'nyje Kopi 20 Md 64.42N 177.50 E
Ugoma 36 Ec 4.55S 26.50 E
Ugra 19 De 54.30N 36.07 E
Ugtal-Cajdam 27 Ib 48.25N 105.30 E
Uh 10 Rh 48.33N 22.00 E
Uherské Hradiště 10 Ng 49.04N 17.27 E
Úhlava 10 Jg 49.45N 13.23 E
Uhlenhorst 37 Bd 23.45S 17.55 E
Uhta 6 Lc 63.33N 53.40 E
Uibh Fhaili/Offaly [2] 9 Fh 53.20N 7.30W
Uig 9 Gd 57.30N 6.20W
Uige 31 Ii 7.35S 15.04 E
Uige [3] 36 Cd 7.00S 15.30 E
'Uiha 65b Ba 19.54S 174.25W
Uijec 64d Bb 7.10N 151.57 E
Ŭijŏngbu 28 If 37.44N 127.02 E
Uiju 28 Hd 40.12N 124.32 E
Uil 19 Ff 48.36N 52.30 E
Uil 19 Ff 49.04N 54.42 E
Uilpata, Gora- 16 Mh 42.47N 43.44 E
Uinta Mountains 43 Ec 40.45N 110.05W
Uinta River 46 Kf 40.14N 109.51W
Uis 37 Ad 21.08S 14.49 E
Ŭisŏng 28 Jf 36.21N 128.42 E
Uitenhage 31 Jl 33.40S 25.28 E
Uithoorn 12 Gb 52.14N 4.52 E
Uithuizen 12 Ia 53.25N 6.42 E
Uithuizerwad 12 Ia 53.30N 6.40 E
Ujae Atoll 57 Hd 9.05N 165.40 E
Ūjān 24 Og 30.45N 52.05 E
Ujandina 20 Jc 68.23N 145.50 E
Ujar 20 Ee 55.48N 94.20 E
Ujarrás 49 Fi 9.50N 83.40W
Ujedinenija, Ostrov- 20 Da 77.30N 82.30 E
Ujelang Atoll 57 Hd 9.49N 160.55 E
Újfehértó 10 Ri 47.48N 21.41 E
Uji 29 Dd 34.53N 135.47 E
Uji 19 Ge 54.20N 63.58 E
Uji-Guntō 28 Ji 31.10N 129.28 E
Ujiie 29 Fc 36.41N 139.57 E
Ujiji 31 Ji 4.55S 29.41 E
Ujjain 22 Jg 23.11N 75.46 E
Ujunglamuru 26 Gg 4.40S 119.58 E
Ujung Pandang (Makasar) 22 Nj 5.07S 119.24 E
Uk 20 Ee 55.04N 98.52 E
Ukata 34 Gc 10.50N 5.50 E
Ukeng, Bukit- 26 Gf 1.45N 115.08 E
Ukerewe Island 36 Fc 2.03S 33.00 E
Uke-Shima 29b Ba 28.02N 129.15 E
Ukhaydir 24 Jf 32.26N 43.36 E
Ukiah [Ca.-U.S.] 43 Cd 39.09N 123.13W
Ukiah [Or.-U.S.] 46 Fd 45.08N 118.56W
Uki Ni Masi 63a Ed 10.15S 161.44 E
Ukkel/Uccle 12 Gd 50.48N 4.19 E
Ukmergė/Ukmerge 7 Fi 55.14N 24.47 E
Ukmerge/Ukmergė 7 Fi 55.14N 24.47 E
Ukraine (EN) [1] 5 Jf 49.00N 32.00 E
Ukraine (EN) = Ukrayina 19 Df 49.00N 32.00 E
Ukrainskaja SSR/Ukrainska Radyanska Socialistična Respublika — Ukrayina 19 Df 49.00N 32.00 E
Ukrainska Radyanska Socialistična Respublika/ Ukrainskaja SSR — Ukrayina 19 Df 49.00N 32.00 E
Ukrayina = Ukraine (EN) 19 Df 49.00N 32.00 E
Ukrina 14 Le 45.05N 17.56 E
Uku-Jima 29 Ae 33.16N 129.07 E
Ula 24 Cd 37.05N 28.26 E
Ulah Lake 45 Hh 36.58N 96.10W
Ulaidh/Ulster 9 Gg 54.30N 7.00W
Ulalu 64d Bb 7.25N 151.40 E
Ulan (Xiligou) 27 Gd 36.55N 98.16 E
Ulan → Otog Qi 27 Id 39.07N 108.00 E
Ulanbaatar → Ulan-Bator 22 Me 47.55N 106.53 E
Ulan-Badrah 28 Ac 43.58N 110.37 E
Ulan-Bator (Ulaanbaatar) 22 Me 47.55N 106.53 E
Ulanbel 19 Hg 44.49N 71.10 E
Ulan-Burgasy, Hrebet- 20 Ff 52.30N 108.30 E
Ulangom 22 Le 49.58N 92.02 E
Ulanhad/Chifeng 27 Kc 42.16N 118.57 E
Ulan Hol 19 Ef 45.27N 46.46 E
Ulan Hot/Horqin Youyi Qianqi 22 Oe 46.04N 122.00 E
Ulan Hua → Siziwang Qi 28 Ad 41.31N 111.41 E
Ulan-Hus 27 Eb 49.02N 89.23 E
Ulanów 10 Sf 50.30N 22.16 E
Ulansuhai Nur 27 Ic 40.56N 108.49 E
Ulan-Tajga 27 Ga 50.45N 98.30 E
Ulan-Ude 22 Md 51.50N 107.37 E
Ulan Ul Hu 27 Fe 34.45N 90.25 E
Ulas 24 Gc 39.27N 37.03 E
Ulawa Island 60 Gi 9.46S 161.57 E
Ulbeja 20 Je 59.20N 144.25 E
Ulchin 28 Jf 36.59N 129.24 E
Ulcinj 15 Ch 41.56N 19.13 E
Uleåborg/Oulu 6 Ib 65.01N 25.30 E
Ulefoss 7 Bg 59.17N 9.16 E
Ulegej 22 Ke 48.56N 89.57 E
Ulety 20 Gf 51.22N 112.30 E
Uleza 15 Ch 41.40N 19.53 E
Ulfborg 8 Ch 56.16N 8.20 E
Ulflingen/Troisvierges 12 Hd 50.07N 6.00 E
Ulft, Gendringen- 12 Ic 51.54N 6.24 E
Ulgain Gol 27 Kb 45.31N 117.50 E
Ulhāsnagar 25 Ee 19.10N 73.07 E
Uliastai → Dong Ujimqin Qi 27 Kc 45.31N 116.58 E
Uliga 58 Id 7.09N 171.13 E
Ulindi 30 Ji 1.40S 25.52 E
Ulithi Atoll 57 Ed 9.58N 139.40 E
Ulja 20 Je 58.48N 141.40 E
Uljanovka 8 Ne 59.37N 30.55 E
Uljanovka 16 Ge 48.20N 30.13 E
Uljanovsk 6 Ke 54.20N 48.24 E
Uljanovskaja Oblast [3] 19 Ee 54.00N 48.00 E
Uljanovski 19 He 50.05N 73.45 E
Uljasutaj 22 Le 47.45N 96.49 E
Ulkan 20 Fe 55.55N 107.55 E
Ulla 13 Db 42.39N 8.44W
Ullapool 9 Hd 57.54N 5.10W
Ullared 7 Ch 57.08N 12.43 E
Ulldecona 13 Md 40.36N 0.27 E
Ullsfjorden 7 Eb 69.58N 20.00 E
Ullswater 9 Kg 54.34N 2.54W
Ullŭng-Do 28 Kf 37.29N 130.52 E
Ullvettern 8 Fe 59.25N 14.15 E
Ulm 10 Fh 48.25N 10.00 E
Ulmen 12 Id 50.13N 6.59 E
Ulmeni 15 Jd 45.04N 26.39 E
Ulmu 15 Je 44.16N 26.55 E
Ulongwé 37 Eb 14.43S 34.21 E
Ulricehamn 7 Ch 57.47N 13.25 E
Ulrichstein 12 Ld 50.35N 9.12 E
Ulrum 12 Ia 53.22N 6.20 E
Ulrum-Zoutkamp 12 Ia 53.20N 6.18 E
Ulsan 27 Md 35.33N 129.19 E
Ulsteinvik 7 Ae 62.20N 5.53 E
Ulster 10 Ff 50.51N 9.59 E
Ulster/Ulaidh 9 Gg 54.30N 7.00W
Ulster Canal 9 Gg 54.27N 6.40W
Ulu 35 Ec 10.43N 33.29 E
Ulu/Uulu 8 Kf 58.13N 24.29 E
Ulüa, Río- 47 Ge 15.56N 87.43W
Ulubat Gölü 24 Cb 40.10N 28.35 E
Ulubey 24 Cc 38.09N 29.33 E
Uludağ 23 Ca 40.04N 29.13 E
Uludere 24 Jd 37.27N 42.51 E
Ulugqat/Wuqia 27 Cd 39.40N 75.07 E
Ulukışla 24 Fd 37.33N 34.30 E
Ulungur He 21 Ke 46.58N 87.28 E
Ulungur Hu 27 Eb 47.20N 87.10 E
Ulus 24 Eb 41.35N 32.39 E
Ulus Dağ 15 Lj 39.18N 28.24 E
Ulva 9 Ge 56.28N 6.12W
Ulverston 9 Jg 54.12N 3.06W
Ulverstone 59 Jh 41.09S 146.10 E
Ulvik 8 Bd 60.34N 6.54 E
Ulvön 8 Ha 63.05N 18.40 E
Ulysses 45 Fh 37.35N 101.22W
Ulytau 19 Gf 48.35N 67.05 E
Ulytau, Gora- 19 Gf 48.45N 67.00 E
Uly-Žilanšik 19 Gf 48.51N 63.47 E
Uma 27 La 52.36N 120.38 E
Umag 14 He 45.25N 13.32 E
Umala 54 Eg 17.24S 67.58W
Umán 48 Og 20.53N 89.45W
Uman 64d Bb 7.18N 151.53 E
Uman 19 Df 48.47N 30.09 E
'Umān 21 Hg 22.10N 58.00 E
'Umān=Oman (EN) [1] 22 Hg 21.00N 57.00 E
'Umān, Khalīj-=Oman, Gulf of- (EN) 21 Hg 25.00N 58.00 E
Umanak 41 Gd 70.36N 52.15W
Ūmánarssuaq/Farvel, Kap- 67 Nb 59.50N 43.50W
Umatac 64c Bb 13.18N 144.40 E
Umba 19 Db 66.41N 34.17 E
Umbelasha 35 Cd 9.51N 24.50 E
Umbertide 14 Gg 43.18N 12.20 E
Umberto de Campos 54 Jd 2.37S 43.27W
Umboi Island 57 Fe 5.36S 148.00 E
Umbozero, Ozero- 7 Ic 67.45N 34.20 E
Umbria [2] 14 Gh 43.00N 12.30 E
Ume 37 Dc 17.15S 28.20 E
Umeå 6 Ic 63.50N 20.15 E
Umeälven 5 Ic 63.47N 20.16 E
Umm al Arānib 33 Bd 26.08N 14.45 E
Umm al Hayf, Wādī- 23 Hf 18.37N 53.59 E
Umm al Jamaājim 24 Ki 26.59N 45.19 E
Umm al Qaywayn 23 Id 25.35N 55.34 E
Ummanz 10 Jb 54.30N 13.10 E
Umm ar Rizam 33 Dc 32.32N 23.00 E
Umm as Samīm 23 Ie 21.30N 56.45 E
Umm Bāb 24 Nj 25.12N 50.48 E
Umm Bel 35 Dc 13.32N 28.04 E
Umm Buru 35 Cb 15.01N 23.36 E
Umm Dhibbān 35 Dc 14.14N 29.37 E
Umm Durmān=Omdurman (EN) 31 Kg 15.38N 32.30 E
Umm Inderaba 35 Eb 15.12N 31.54 E
Umm Kaddādah 35 Dc 13.36N 26.42 E
Umm Lajj 23 Ed 25.04N 37.13 E
Umm Naqqāt, Jabal- 24 Fj 25.30N 34.14 E
Umm Qam'ul 24 Pj 24.47N 54.42 E
Umm Ruwābah 31 Kg 12.54N 31.13 E
Umm Sayyālah 35 Ec 14.25N 31.00 E
Umm Urūmah 24 Gj 25.46N 36.33 E
Umnak 38 Cd 53.25N 168.10W
Umne-Gobi 27 Fb 49.06N 91.43 E
Umpqua River 46 Ce 43.42N 124.03W
Umpulu 36 Ce 12.42S 17.40 E
Umsini, Gunung- 26 Jg 1.35S 133.30 E
Umtata 31 Jl 31.35S 28.47 E
Umuarama 56 Jb 23.45S 53.20W
Umurbey 15 Ji 40.14N 26.36 E
Umvukwes 37 Ec 17.01S 30.52 E
Umvuma 37 Ec 19.19S 30.35 E
Umzingwani 37 Dd 22.12S 29.56 E
Una 14 Ke 45.16N 16.55 E
Unabetsu-Dake 29a Db 43.52N 144.51 E
Unac 14 Kf 44.29N 16.08 E
Unai 54 Ig 16.23S 46.53W
Unalakleet 40 Gd 63.53N 160.47W
Unalaska 38 Cd 53.45N 166.45W
Unare, Río- 50 Dg 10.06N 65.12W
Unauna, Pulau- 26 Hg 0.10S 121.35 E
'Unayzah [Jor.] 24 Fg 30.29N 35.48 E
'Unayzah [Sau. Ar.] 22 Gg 26.06N 43.56 E
Uncia 54 Eg 18.27S 66.37W
Uncompahgre Peak 43 Fd 38.04N 107.28W
Uncompahgre Plateau 45 Bg 38.30N 108.25W
Unden 8 Ff 58.45N 14.25 E
Underberg 37 De 29.50S 29.22 E
Under-Han 22 Ne 47.19N 110.39 E
Undjuljung 20 Hc 66.20N 124.40 E
Undu Point 63d Cb 16.08S 179.57W
Undva Neem/Kiprarenukk, Mys- 8 If 58.25N 21.45 E
Uneča 16 Hc 52.50N 32.44 E
'Ung, Jabal al- 24 Dn 36.45N 9.35 E
Unga 40 Ge 55.15N 160.45W
Ungava, Péninsule d'-= Ungava Peninsula (EN) 38 Lc 60.00N 74.00W
Ungava Bay 38 Md 59.30N 67.30W
Ungava Peninsula (EN)= Ungava, Péninsule d'- 38 Lc 60.00N 74.00W
Ungen' 16 Ef 47.13N 27.50 E
Unggi 28 Kc 42.21N 130.23 E
Ungureni 15 Jb 47.53N 26.47 E
Ungwatiri 35 Fb 16.55N 36.05 E
União 54 Jd 4.35S 42.52W
União da Vitória 56 Jc 26.13S 51.05W
União dos Palmares 54 Ke 9.10S 36.02W
Uničov 10 Ng 49.49N 17.07 E
Uniejów 10 Oe 51.58N 18.49 E
Unije 14 If 44.38N 14.15 E
Unimak 38 Cd 54.50N 164.00W
Unimak Pass 40 Gf 54.35N 164.43W
Unini, Rio- 54 Fd 1.41S 61.30W
Union [Mo.-U.S.] 45 Kg 38.27N 91.00W
Union [S.C.-U.S.] 44 Gh 34.42N 81.37W
Union City 44 Cg 36.26N 89.03W
Uniondale 37 Cf 33.40S 23.08 E
Unión de Reyes 49 Gb 22.48N 81.32W
Unión de Tula 48 Gh 19.58N 104.16W
Union Island 50 Ff 12.36N 61.26W
Union Islands/Tokelau 57 Je 9.00S 171.45W
Union Seamount (EN) 42 Eg 49.35N 132.45W
Union Springs 44 Ei 32.09N 85.49W
Uniontown 44 Hf 39.54N 79.44W
Unionville 45 Jf 40.29N 93.01W
United Arab Emirates (EN) =Al Imārāt al 'Arabīyah al Muttaḥidah [1] 22 Hg 24.00N 54.00 E
United Arab Republic (EN) → Egypt (EN) [1] 31 Jf 27.00N 30.00 E
United Kingdom [1] 6 Fe 54.00N 2.00W
United Kingdom of Great Britain and Northern Ireland [1] 6 Fe 54.00N 2.00W
United States [1] 39 Jf 38.00N 97.00W
United States of America [1] 39 Jf 38.00N 97.00W
Unity [Or.-U.S.] 46 Fd 44.29N 118.13W
Unity [Sask.-Can.] 42 Gf 52.27N 109.10W
Universales, Montes- 13 Kd 40.18N 1.33W
University City 45 Kg 38.39N 90.19W
Unna 10 De 51.32N 7.41 E
Unnāb, Wādī al- 24 Gg 30.11N 36.39 E
Unnukka 8 Lb 62.25N 27.55 E
Unst 5 Fc 60.45N 0.55W
Unstrut 10 He 51.10N 11.48 E
Unterfranken 10 Fg 50.00N 10.00 E
Unterwalden-Nidwalden [2] 14 Cd 46.55N 8.30 E
Unterwalden-Obwalden [2] 14 Cd 46.50N 8.20 E
Unuli Horog 27 Fd 35.12N 91.58 E
Ünye 23 Ea 41.08N 37.17 E
Unža 5 Kd 57.20N 43.08 E
Unzen-Dake 29 Be 32.45N 130.17 E
Uoleva 65b Ba 19.51S 174.24W
Uozu 28 Nf 36.48N 137.24 E
Úpa 10 Lf 50.22N 15.54 E
Upata 54 Fb 8.01N 62.24W
Upemba, Lac- 36 Ed 8.36S 26.26 E
Upernavik 41 Gd 72.20N 56.00W
Upin 26 Ig 2.56S 129.11 E
Upington 31 Jk 28.25S 21.15 E
Upland 12 Kc 51.18N 8.42 E
Upolu Island 57 Jf 13.55S 171.45W
Upolu Point 60 Oc 20.16N 155.52W
Upper [3] 34 Ec 10.30N 1.30W
Upper Arlington 44 Fe 40.01N 83.03W
Upper Arrow Lake 46 Ga 50.30N 117.55W
Upper Austria (EN) = Oberösterreich [2] 14 Hb 48.15N 14.00 E
Upper Hutt 62 Fd 41.07S 175.04 E
Upper Klamath Lake 43 Cc 42.23N 122.00W
Upper Lake 46 Ef 41.44N 120.08W
Upper Lough Erne/Loch Éirne Uachtair 9 Fg 54.20N 7.30W
Upper Red Lake 45 Ib 48.10N 94.40W
Upper Sandusky 44 Fe 40.48N 83.17W
Upper Sheik 35 Hd 9.57N 45.09 E
Upper Thames Valley 9 Lj 51.40N 1.40W
Upper Trajan's Wall (EN)= Verhni Trajanov Val 15 Lc 46.40N 29.00 E
Upper Volta→ Burkina Faso [1] 31 Gg 13.00N 2.00W
Uppingham 12 Bb 52.35N 0.43W
Uppland 8 Gd 60.00N 17.50 E
Upplands Väsby 8 Ge 59.31N 17.54 E
Uppsala [2] 7 Df 60.00N 17.45 E
Uppsala 6 Hd 59.52N 17.38 E
Upsala 45 Kb 49.02N 90.29W
Upshi 25 Fb 33.50N 77.49 E
Upton 46 Md 44.06N 104.38W
Uqbān 33 Hf 15.30N 42.23 E
'Uqlat aş Şuqūr 24 Jj 25.53N 42.15 E
Uqturpan/Wushi 27 Cc 41.10N 79.16 E
Ur 23 Gc 30.58N 46.06 E
Urabá, Golfo de- 54 Cb 8.25N 77.00W
Uracoa 50 Eh 9.00N 62.21W
Uracoa, Río- 50 Eh 9.08N 62.20W
Uradarja 18 Fe 38.51N 66.02 E
Urad Qianqi 27 Ic 40.39N 108.37 E
Urad Zhonghou Lianheqi (Haliut) 27 Ic 41.34N 108.32 E
Uraga-Suido 29 Fd 35.15N 139.45 E
Ura-Guba 7 Hb 69.18N 32.48 E
Urahoro 29a Cb 42.48N 143.38 E
Urahoro-Gawa 29a Cb 42.44N 143.40 E
Uraj 19 Gc 60.08N 64.40 E
Urakawa 28 Qc 42.09N 142.47 E
Ural 5 Lf 47.00N 51.48 E
Ural Mountains (EN)= Uralskije Gory 5 Ld 57.00N 60.00 E
Uralsk 6 Le 51.14N 51.22 E
Uralskaja Oblast [3] 19 Ff 49.45N 51.00 E
Uralskije Gory=Ural Mountains (EN) 5 Ld 57.00N 60.00 E
Urambo 36 Fd 5.04S 32.03 E
Uranium City 39 Id 59.34N 108.36W
Uraricoera 54 Fc 3.26N 60.59W
Uraricoera, Rio- 52 Je 3.02N 60.30W
Ura-Tjube 19 Gh 39.53N 69.01 E
Urawa 28 Og 35.51N 139.39 E
'Uray'irah 24 Mj 25.57N 48.53 E
Urayq, Nafūd al- 24 Jj 25.17N 42.25 E
Urbana [Il.-U.S.] 45 Lf 40.07N 88.12W
Urbana [Oh.-U.S.] 44 Fe 40.06N 83.45W
Urbandale 45 Jf 41.38N 93.48W
Urbania 14 Gg 43.40N 12.31 E

Index Symbols

[1] Independent Nation
[2] State, Region
[3] District, County
Municipality
Colony, Dependency
Continent
Physical Region
Historical or Cultural Region
Mount, Mountain
Volcano
Hill
Mountains, Mountain Range
Hills, Escarpment
Plateau, Upland
Pass, Gap
Plain, Lowland
Delta
Salt Flat
Valley, Canyon
Crater, Cave
Karst Features
Depression
Polder
Desert, Dunes
Forest, Woods
Heath, Steppe
Oasis
Cape, Point
Coast, Beach
Cliff
Peninsula
Isthmus
Sandbank
Island
Atoll
Rock, Reef
Islands, Archipelago
Rocks, Reefs
Coral Reef
Well, Spring
Geyser
River, Stream
Waterfall Rapids
River Mouth, Estuary
Lake
Salt Lake
Intermittent Lake
Reservoir
Swamp, Pond
Canal
Glacier
Ice Shelf, Pack Ice
Ocean
Sea
Gulf, Bay
Strait, Fjord
Lagoon
Bank
Seamount
Tablemount
Ridge
Shelf
Basin
Escarpment, Sea Scarp
Fracture
Trench, Abyss
National Park, Reserve
Point of Interest
Recreation Site
Cave, Cavern
Historic Site
Ruins
Wall, Walls
Church, Abbey
Temple
Scientific Station
Airport
Port
Lighthouse
Mine
Tunnel
Dam, Bridge

Index Symbols

[1] Independent Nation	[◪] Historical or Cultural Region	[◳] Pass, Gap	[▱] Depression
[2] State, Region	[▲] Mount, Mountain	[◱] Plain, Lowland	[▱] Polder
[3] District, County	[▲] Volcano	[◲] Delta	[▭] Desert, Dunes
[4] Municipality	[◭] Hill	[▭] Salt Flat	[▭] Forest, Woods
[5] Colony, Dependency	[▲] Mountains, Mountain Range	[◻] Valley, Canyon	[▭] Heath, Steppe
[■] Continent	[◰] Hills, Escarpment	[◌] Crater, Cave	[▭] Oasis
[⊠] Physical Region	[▱] Plateau, Upland	[◊] Karst Features	[▭] Cape, Point

[▭] Coast, Beach	[▭] Rock, Reef	[▭] Waterfall Rapids	[▭] Canal
[▭] Cliff	[▭] Islands, Archipelago	[▭] River Mouth, Estuary	[▭] Glacier
[▭] Peninsula	[▭] Rocks, Reefs	[▭] Lake	[▭] Ice Shelf, Pack Ice
[▭] Isthmus	[▭] Coral Reef	[▭] Salt Lake	[▭] Ocean
[▭] Sandbank	[⊙] Well, Spring	[▭] Intermittent Lake	[▭] Sea
[▭] Island	[◉] Geyser	[▭] Reservoir	[C] Gulf, Bay
[◉] Atoll	[≋] River, Stream	[▭] Swamp, Pond	[▭] Shelf

[⊠] Lagoon	[⊠] Escarpment, Sea Scarp	[▲] Historic Site	[▭] Port
[⊠] Bank	[⊠] Fracture	[:] Ruins	[⊠] Lighthouse
[⊠] Seamount	[⊠] Trench, Abyss	[:] Wall, Walls	[⊠] Mine
[⊠] Tablemount	[▲] National Park, Reserve	[:] Church, Abbey	[⊠] Tunnel
[⊠] Ridge	[:] Point of Interest	[:] Temple	[⊠] Dam, Bridge
[⊠] Basin	[▲] Recreation Site	[⊠] Scientific Station	
	[◌] Cave, Cavern	[⊠] Airport	

Index Symbols

◻ Independent Nation	◫ Historical or Cultural Region
◫ State, Region	◫ Mount, Mountain
◳ District, County	◫ Volcano
◲ Municipality	◫ Hill
◲ Colony, Dependency	◫ Mountains, Mountain Range
◲ Continent	◫ Hills, Escarpment
◲ Physical Region	◫ Plateau, Upland

◲ Pass, Gap	◲ Depression
◲ Plain, Lowland	◲ Polder
◲ Delta	◲ Desert, Dunes
◲ Salt Flat	◲ Forest, Woods
◲ Valley, Canyon	◲ Heath, Steppe
◲ Crater, Cave	◲ Oasis
◲ Karst Features	◲ Cape, Point

◲ Coast, Beach	◲ Rock, Reef
◲ Cliff	◲ Islands, Archipelago
◲ Peninsula	◲ Rocks, Reefs
◲ Isthmus	◲ Coral Reef
◲ Sandbank	◲ Well, Spring
◲ Island	◲ Geyser
◲ Atoll	◲ River, Stream

◲ Waterfall Rapids	◲ Canal
◲ River Mouth, Estuary	◲ Glacier
◲ Lake	◲ Ice Shelf, Pack Ice
◲ Salt Lake	◲ Bank
◲ Ocean	◲ Ridge
◲ Intermittent Lake	◲ Shelf
◲ Sea	◲ Gulf, Bay
◲ Swamp, Pond	◲ Strait, Fjord
	◲ Basin

◲ Lagoon	◲ Escarpment, Sea Scarp	◲ Historic Site	◲ Port
◲ Bank	◲ Fracture	◲ Ruins	◲ Lighthouse
◲ Trench, Abyss	◲ Wall, Walls	◲ Mine
◲ Tablemount	◲ Church, Abbey	◲ Tunnel
◲ National Park, Reserve	◲ Temple	◲ Dam, Bridge
◲ Point of Interest	◲ Scientific Station
◲ Recreation Site	◲ Airport
◲ Scientific Station	
◲ Cave, Cavern	

Vetlužski	7	Kh	57.11N	45.07 E
Vetlužski	7	Kg	58.26N	45.28 E
Vetreny	20	Jd	61.43N	149.40 E
Vetreny Pojas, Krjaž-	7	Ie	63.20N	37.30 E
Vetrino	8	Mi	55.25N	28.31 E
Vetschau/Wětošow	10	Ke	51.47N	14.04 E
Vettore	14	Hh	42.49N	13.16 E
Vetzstein	10	Hf	50.25N	11.25 E
Veules-les-Roses	12	Ce	49.52N	0.48 E
Veulettes-sur-Mer	12	Ce	49.51N	0.36 E
Veurne/Furnes	11	Ic	51.04N	2.40 E
Vevey	14	Ad	46.28N	6.50 E
Vevis/Vievis	8	Kj	54.45N	24.58 E
Vexin	11	He	49.10N	1.40 E
Veynes	11	Lj	44.32N	5.49 E
Vézelay	11	Jg	47.28N	3.44 E
Vežen	15	Hg	42.45N	24.24 E
Vézère	11	Gj	44.53N	0.53 E
Vezirköprü	24	Fb	41.09N	35.28 E
Viadana	14	Ef	44.56N	10.31 E
Viale	55	Bj	31.53S	60.01W
Viana	54	Jd	3.13S	45.00W
Viana del Bollo	13	Eb	42.11N	7.06W
Viana do Alentejo	13	Ef	38.20N	8.00W
Viana do Castelo	13	Dc	41.42N	8.50W
Viana do Castelo [2]	13	Dc	41.55N	8.25W
Vianden	12	Ie	49.55N	6.16 E
Viangchan (Vientiane)	22	Mh	17.58N	102.36 E
Vianópolis	55	Hc	16.45S	48.32W
Viar	13	Gg	37.36N	5.50W
Viareggio	14	Eg	43.52N	10.14 E
Viarmes	12	Ee	49.08N	2.22 E
Viaur	11	Hj	44.08N	1.58 E
Viborg [2]	8	Ch	56.30N	9.30 E
Viborg	7	Bh	56.26N	9.24 E
Vibo Valentia	14	Kl	38.40N	16.06 E
Vic	13	Oc	41.56N	2.15 E
Vicari	14	Hm	37.49N	13.34 E
Vicecomodoro Marambio	66	Re	64.16S	56.44W
Vicente Guerrero	47	Dd	23.45N	103.59W
Vicenza	14	Fe	45.33N	11.33 E
Vichada [2]	54	Ec	5.00N	69.30W
Vichada, Río-	52	Je	4.55N	67.50W
Vichadero	55	Ej	31.48S	54.43W
Vichy	11	Jh	46.07N	3.25 E
Vicksburg	43	Ie	32.14N	90.56W
Vico, Lago di-	14	Gh	42.19N	12.10 E
Vic-sur-Aisne	12	Fe	49.24N	3.07 E
Vic-sur-Cère	11	Ij	44.59N	2.37 E
Victor Bay	66	Ie	66.20S	136.30 E
Victor Harbour	59	Hg	35.34S	138.37 E
Victoria	38	Hb	71.00N	114.00W
Victoria [Arg.]	56	Hd	32.37S	60.10W
Victoria [Austl.]	59	Ig	38.00S	145.00 E
Victoria [B.C.-Can.]	39	Ge	48.25N	123.22W
Victoria [Cam.]	34	Ge	4.01N	9.12 E
Victoria [Chile]	56	Fe	38.13S	72.20W
Victoria [Gren.]	50	Ff	12.12N	61.42W
Victoria [Mala.]	26	Ge	5.17N	115.15 E
Victoria [Malta]	14	In	36.02N	14.14 E
Victoria [Rom.]	15	Hd	45.44N	24.41 E
Victoria [Sey.]	31	Mi	4.38S	55.27 E
Victoria [Tx.-U.S.]	39	Jg	28.48N	97.00W
Victoria/Ying zhan	22	Ng	22.17N	114.09 E
Victoria, Lake- [Afr.]	30	Ki	1.00S	33.00 E
Victoria, Lake- [Austl.]	59	If	34.00S	141.15 E
Victoria, Mount- [Bur.]	21	Lg	21.14N	93.55 E
Victoria, Mount- [Pap.N.Gui.]	57	Fe	8.53S	147.33 E
Victoria, Sierra de la-	55	Fg	25.55S	54.00W
Victoria and Albert Mountains	42	Ka	79.00N	75.00W
Victoria de Durango	39	Ig	24.02N	104.40W
Victoria de las Tunas	47	Id	20.58N	76.57W
Victoria Falls	31	Jj	17.56S	25.50 E
Victoria Falls	30	Jj	17.55S	25.21 E
Victoria Fjord	41	Hb	82.20N	48.00W
Victoria Land (EN)	66	Jf	75.00S	159.00 E
Victoria Nile	36	Kh	2.14N	31.26 E
Victoria Peak [B.C.-Can.]	46	Ba	50.03N	126.06W
Victoria Peak [Blz.]	49	Ce	16.48N	88.37W
Victoria River	57	Df	15.12S	129.43 E
Victoria River Downs	59	Gc	16.24S	131.00 E
Victoria Strait	42	Hc	69.30N	100.00W
Victoriaville	42	Kg	46.03N	71.58W
Victoria West	37	Cf	31.25S	23.04 E
Victorija	41	Pb	80.10N	36.45 E
Victorville	46	Gi	34.32N	117.18W
Victory, Mount-	59	Ja	9.10S	149.05 E
Vičuga	19	Ed	57.15N	42.00 E
Vicuña	56	Fc	29.59S	70.44W
Vicuña Mackenna	56	Hd	33.54S	64.23W
Vidå	8	Cj	54.58N	8.41 E
Vidal	46	Hi	34.11N	114.34W
Vidalia	45	Kk	31.34N	91.26W
Videbæk	8	Ch	56.05N	8.38 E
Videira	56	Jc	27.00S	51.08W
Videla	55	Bj	30.56S	60.39W
Videle	15	Ie	44.17N	25.31 E
Vidigueira	13	Ef	38.13N	7.48W
Vidin [2]	15	Ff	43.59N	22.52 E
Vidin	15	Ff	43.59N	22.52 E
Vidisha	25	Fd	23.42N	77.47 E
Vidlič	15	Ff	43.08N	22.47 E
Vidojevica	15	Ef	43.10N	21.32 E
Vidöstern	8	Fg	57.04N	14.01 E
Vidourle	11	Kk	43.32N	4.08 E
Vidra [Rom.]	15	Jd	45.55N	26.54 E
Vidra [Rom.]	15	Je	44.16N	26.09 E
Vidsel	7	Ed	65.49N	20.31 E
Viduša	14	Mh	42.54N	18.18 E
Vidzeme	8	Kg	57.10N	26.00 E
Vidzemes Augstiene/Vidzemskaja Vozvyšennost	8	Kh	56.45N	26.00 E
Vidzemskaja Vozvyšennost/Vidzemes Augstiene	8	Kh	56.45N	26.00 E
Vidzy	8	Li	55.23N	26.47 E
Vie	12	Be	49.09N	0.04W
Viechtach	10	Ig	49.05N	12.53 E
Viedma	53	Jj	40.50S	63.00W
Viedma, Lago-	52	Ij	49.35S	72.35W
Vieille Case	51g	Ba	15.36N	61.24W
Vieja, Sierra-	45	Dk	30.30N	104.40W
Viejo, Cerro-	47	Bb	30.20N	112.15W
Viekšniai/Viekšnjai	8	Jh	56.14N	22.28 E
Viekšnjai/Viekšniai	8	Jh	56.14N	22.28 E
Viella	13	Mb	42.42N	0.48 E
Vielsalm	12	Hd	50.17N	5.55 E
Viels-Maisons	12	Ff	48.54N	3.24 E
Vienna [Mo.-U.S.]	45	Kg	38.11N	91.57W
Vienna [W.V.-U.S.]	44	Gf	39.20N	81.33W
Vienna (EN) = Wien	6	Hf	48.12N	16.22 E
Vienna Woods (EN) = Wienerwald	14	Jb	48.10N	16.00 E
Vienne	11	Ki	45.31N	4.52 E
Vienne [3]	11	Gh	46.30N	0.30 E
Vienne	5	Gf	47.13N	0.05 E
Vientiane → Viangchan	22	Mh	17.58N	102.36 E
Vientos, Paso de los- = Windward Passage (EN)	38	Lh	20.00N	73.50W
Vieques, Isla de-	47	Ke	18.08N	65.25W
Vieques, Pasaje de-	51a	Cb	18.08N	65.40W
Vieques, Sonda de-	51a	Cb	18.17N	65.25W
Vierge Point	51k	Bb	13.49N	60.53W
Viersen	10	Ce	51.15N	6.23 E
Vierville-sur-Mer	12	Be	49.22N	0.54W
Vierwaldstätter-See = Lucerne, Lake- (EN)	14	Cc	47.00N	8.30 E
Vierzon	11	Ig	47.13N	2.05 E
Viesca	48	He	25.21N	102.48W
Viesite/Viesīte	8	Kh	56.20N	25.38 E
Viesīte/Viesite	8	Kh	56.20N	25.38 E
Vieste	14	Ki	41.53N	16.10 E
Viet Nam [1]	22	Mh	13.00N	108.00 E
Viet Tri	25	Ld	21.18N	105.26 E
Vieux Fort	50	Ff	13.44N	60.57W
Vieux-Fort, Pointe du-	51e	Ac	15.57N	61.43W
Vieux Fort Bay	51k	Bb	13.44N	60.58W
Vieux-Habitants	51e	Ab	16.04N	61.46W
Vievis/Vevis	8	Kj	54.45N	24.58 E
Viga	7	Kg	59.15N	43.42 E
Vigala	8	Kf	58.43N	24.22 E
Vigan	26	Hc	17.34N	120.23 E
Vigeland	8	Bf	58.05N	7.18 E
Vigevano	14	Ce	45.19N	8.51 E
Vigia	54	Id	0.48S	48.08W
Vigia Chico	48	Ph	19.46N	87.35W
Vignacourt	12	Ed	50.01N	2.12 E
Vignemale	13	Lb	42.46N	0.08W
Vigneulles-lès-Hattonchâtel	12	Hf	48.59N	5.43 E
Vignoble	11	Lh	46.50N	5.30 E
Vignola	14	Ef	44.29N	11.00 E
Vigny	12	De	49.05N	1.56 E
Vigo	6	Fg	42.14N	8.43W
Vigo, Ria de-	13	Db	42.15N	8.45W
Vigra	8	Bb	62.30N	6.05 E
Vigrestad	8	Af	58.34N	5.42 E
Vihanti	7	Fd	64.30N	25.00 E
Vihiers	11	Fg	47.09N	0.32W
Vihorevka	20	Fe	56.12N	101.09 E
Vihorlat	10	Sh	48.55N	22.10 E
Vihren	15	Gh	41.46N	23.24 E
Vihti	7	Ff	60.25N	24.20 E
Viiala	8	Jc	61.13N	23.47 E
Viinijärvi	8	Mb	62.45N	29.15 E
Viinijärvi	8	Mb	62.39N	29.14 E
Viitasaari	7	Fe	63.04N	25.52 E
Viivikonna/Vijvikonna	8	Le	59.14N	27.41 E
Vijayawāda	22	Kh	16.31N	80.37 E
Vijvikonna/Viivikonna	8	Le	59.14N	27.41 E
Vik	7a	Bc	63.25N	19.01W
Vika	8	Fd	60.57N	14.27 E
Vikarbyn	8	Fd	60.55N	15.01 E
Vikbolandet	8	Gf	58.30N	16.40 E
Viken	8	Eh	56.09N	12.34 E
Viken	8	Ff	58.40N	14.20 E
Vikenara Point	63a	Dc	8.34S	159.53 E
Vikersund	8	De	59.59N	10.02 E
Vikingbanken	9	Pa	60.20N	2.30 E
Vikmanshyttan	8	Fd	60.17N	15.49 E
Vikna	7	Cd	64.53N	10.58 E
Vikna	7	Cd	64.54N	11.00 E
Viksøyri	7	Bf	61.05N	6.34 E
Vila da Bispo	13	Dg	37.05N	8.55W
Vila da Maganja	37	Fc	17.18S	37.31 E
Vila de Rei	13	De	39.40N	8.09W
Vila do Conde	13	Dc	41.21N	8.45W
Vila do Porto	32	Bb	36.56N	25.09W
Vila Flor	13	Ec	41.18N	7.09W
Vilafranca del Penedès/Villafranca del Panadés	13	Nc	41.21N	1.42 E
Vila Franca de Xira	13	Df	38.57N	8.59W
Vila Franca do Campo	32	Bb	37.43N	25.26W
Vila Franca do Save	37	Ed	21.09S	34.32 E
Vila Gamito	37	Eb	14.10S	32.59 E
Vila Gouveia	37	Ec	18.03S	33.11 E
Vilaine	11	Dg	49.23N	2.27W
Viļaka/Viljaka	7	Gh	57.14N	27.46 E
Vila Machado	37	Ec	19.17S	34.12 E
Vilanculos	31	Kk	22.00S	35.19 E
Viļani/Viljani	7	Gh	56.33N	26.59 E
Vila Nova da Cerveira	13	Dc	41.56N	8.45W
Vila Nova de Famalicao	13	Dc	41.25N	8.32W
Vila Nova de Foz Côa	13	Ec	41.05N	7.12W
Vila Nova de Gaia	13	Dc	41.08N	8.37W
Vilanova i la Geltrú/Villanueva y Geltrú	13	Nc	41.14N	1.44 E
Vila Paiva de Andrada	37	Ec	18.41S	34.04 E
Vila Pouca de Aguiar	13	Ec	41.30N	7.39W
Vila Real [2]	13	Ec	41.35N	7.35W
Vila Real	13	Ec	41.18N	7.45W
Vila-Real de los Infantes/Villarreal de los Infantes	13	Le	39.56N	0.06W
Vila Real de Santo António	13	Eg	37.12N	7.25W
Vilar Formoso	13	Fd	40.37N	6.50W
Vila Velha	54	Jh	20.20S	40.17W
Vila Velha de Ródão	13	Ee	39.40N	7.42W
Vila Viçosa	13	Ef	38.47N	7.25W
Vîlcea [2]	15	He	45.10N	24.10 E
Vilches	13	If	38.12N	3.30W
Vildbjerg	8	Ch	56.12N	8.46 E
Viled	7	Lf	61.22N	47.15 E
Vilejka	19	Ce	54.30N	26.53 E
Vilhelmina	7	Dd	64.37N	16.39 E
Vilhena	53	Jg	12.43S	60.07W
Vilija	16	Db	54.55N	25.40 E
Viljaka/Viļaka	7	Gh	57.14N	27.46 E
Viljandi	19	Cd	58.22N	25.35 E
Viljany/Viļani	7	Gh	56.33N	26.59 E
Viljuj	21	Oc	64.24N	126.26 E
Viljujsk	20	Hd	63.40N	121.33 E
Viljujskoje Plato = Vilyui Range (EN)	21	Mc	66.00N	108.00 E
Viljujskoje Vodohranilišče	20	Gd	62.30N	111.00 E
Vilkaviškis	7	Fi	54.43N	23.02 E
Vilkickogo, ostrov-	20	Cb	73.30N	76.00 E
Vilkickogo, ostrov-	20	Ka	75.40N	152.30 E
Vilkickogo, proliv- = Vilkitski Strait (EN)	21	Mb	77.55N	103.00 E
Vilkija	7	Fi	55.03N	23.35 E
Vilkitski Strait (EN) = Vilkickogo, Proliv-	21	Mb	77.55N	103.00 E
Vilkovo	16	Fg	45.23N	29.35 E
Villa Aberastain	56	Gd	31.39S	68.35W
Villa Ahumada	47	Cb	30.37N	106.31W
Villa Altagracia	49	Ld	18.40N	70.10W
Villa Ana	55	Ci	28.29S	59.37W
Villa Angela	56	Hc	27.35S	60.43W
Villa Atuel	56	Gd	34.50S	67.54W
Villa Berthet	55	Bh	27.17S	60.25W
Villablino	13	Fb	42.56N	6.19W
Villa Bruzual	54	Eb	9.20N	69.06W
Villa Cañás	55	Bk	34.00S	61.36W
Villacañas	13	Ie	39.38N	3.20W
Villacarrillo	13	If	38.07N	3.05W
Villacastín	13	Hd	40.47N	4.25W
Villach	14	Hd	46.36N	13.50 E
Villacidro	14	Ck	39.27N	8.44 E
Villa Clara	55	Cj	31.50S	58.49W
Villaclara [3]	49	Hb	22.30N	80.00W
Villa Constitución [Arg.]	56	Hd	33.14S	60.20W
Villa Constitución [Mex.]	47	Bc	25.09N	111.43W
Villa Coronado	48	Gd	26.45N	105.10W
Villada	13	Hb	42.15N	4.58W
Villa de Arriaga	48	Ig	21.54N	101.23W
Villa de Cos	48	Hf	23.17N	102.21W
Villa de Cura	50	Cg	10.02N	67.29W
Villa de Maria	56	Hc	29.54S	63.43W
Villa de Reyes	48	Ig	21.48N	100.56W
Villa de San Antonio	49	Df	14.16N	87.36W
Villadiego	13	Ib	42.31N	4.00W
Villa Dolores	56	Gd	31.56S	65.12W
Villa Elisa	55	Ck	32.10S	58.24W
Villa Flores	48	Mi	16.14N	93.14W
Villa Florida	55	Dh	26.23S	57.09W
Villafranca del Bierzo	13	Fb	42.36N	6.48W
Villafranca del Cid	13	Ld	40.25N	0.15W
Villafranca de los Barros	13	Ff	38.34N	6.20W
Villafranca del Panadés/Vilafranca del Penedès	13	Nc	41.21N	1.42 E
Villafranca di Verona	14	Ee	45.21N	10.50 E
Villa Frontera	47	Dc	26.56N	101.27W
Villagarcia de Arosa	13	Db	42.36N	8.45W
Villa General Roca	56	Gd	32.39S	66.28W
Villa Gesell	55	Dm	37.15S	56.55W
Villagrán	48	Je	24.29N	99.29W
Villaguay	56	Id	31.51S	59.01W
Villa Guillermina	55	Ci	28.14S	59.28W
Villa Hayes	56	Ic	25.06S	57.34W
Villa Hermandarias	55	Cj	31.13S	59.59W
Villahermosa	39	Jh	17.59N	92.55W
Villa Hidalgo	48	Gd	26.16N	104.54W
Villa Huidobro	56	Hd	34.50S	64.35W
Villajoyosa/La Vila Jojosa	13	Lf	38.30N	0.14W
Villalba	13	Ea	43.18N	7.41W
Villaldama	48	Id	26.30N	100.26W
Villalón de Campos	13	Gb	42.06N	5.02W
Villalpando	13	Gc	41.52N	5.24W
Villamalea	13	Ke	39.22N	1.35W
Villamanrique	13	Jf	38.33N	3.00W
Villa Maria	53	Ji	32.25S	63.15W
Villamartin	13	Gh	36.52N	5.38W
Villa Matamoros	48	Gd	26.50N	105.35W
Villa Media Agua	56	Gd	31.59S	68.25W
Villamil	54a	Ab	0.56S	91.01W
Villa Minetti	55	Bi	28.37S	61.39W
Villa Montes	53	Jh	21.15S	63.30W
Villandraut	11	Fj	44.28N	0.22W
Villa Nueva	56	Gd	32.54S	68.47W
Villanueva	49	Kh	10.37N	72.59W
Villanueva [Mex.]	48	Hf	22.21N	102.53W
Villanueva [N.M.-U.S.]	45	Di	35.17N	105.23W
Villanueva de Córdoba	13	Hf	38.20N	4.37W
Villanueva del Arzobispo	13	Jf	38.10N	3.00W
Villanueva de la Serena	13	Gf	38.58N	5.48W
Villanueva del Fresno	13	Ef	38.23N	7.10W
Villanueva de los Infantes	13	If	38.44N	3.01W
Villanueva del Rio y Minas	13	Gg	37.39N	5.42W
Villanueva y Geltrú/Vilanova i la Geltrú	13	Nc	41.14N	1.44 E
Villa Ocampo [Arg.]	56	Ic	28.28S	59.22W
Villa Ocampo [Mex.]	47	Cc	26.27N	105.31W
Villa Ojo de Agua	56	Hc	29.31S	63.42W
Villa Oliva	55	Dh	26.01S	57.53W
Villa Pesqueira	48	Ec	29.08N	109.58W
Villaputzu	14	Dk	39.26N	9.34 E
Villa Ramirez	55	Bk	32.11S	60.12W
Villarcayo	13	Ib	42.56N	3.34W
Villar del Arzobispo	13	Le	39.44N	0.49W
Villa Regina	56	Ge	39.06S	67.04W
Villarica [Chile]	56	Fe	39.16S	72.16W
Villarica [Par.]	53	Kh	25.45S	56.26W
Villa Rosario	54	Db	7.50N	72.29W
Villarreal de los Infantes/Vila-Real de los Infantes	13	Le	39.56N	0.06W
Villarrobledo	13	Je	39.16N	2.36W
Villasalto	14	Dk	39.29N	9.23 E
Villa San Giovanni	14	Jl	38.13N	15.38 E
Villa San Martin	56	Hc	28.18S	64.12W
Villasimius	14	Dk	39.08N	9.31 E
Villatoro, Puerto de-	13	Gd	40.33N	5.10W
Villa Unión [Mex.]	47	Cd	23.12N	106.16W
Villa Unión [Mex.]	48	Ic	28.15N	100.43W
Villaverde, Madrid-	13	Id	40.21N	3.42W
Villavicencio	53	Ie	4.09N	73.37W
Villaviciosa	13	Ga	43.29N	5.26W
Villazón	54	Eh	22.06S	65.36W
Ville-de-Laval	44	Kc	45.33N	73.44W
Ville de Paris [3]	11	If	48.52N	2.20 E
Ville de Toulouse Bank (EN)	38	Hh	11.30N	117.00W
Villedieu-les-Poêles	11	Ef	48.50N	1.13W
Ville-en-Tardenois	12	Fe	49.11N	3.48 E
Villefranche-de-Lauragais	11	Hk	43.24N	1.44 E
Villefranche-de-Rouergue	11	Ij	44.21N	2.03 E
Villefranche-sur-Saône	11	Ki	45.59N	4.43 E
Ville-Marie	44	Hb	47.20N	79.26W
Villemur-sur-Tarn	11	Hk	43.52N	1.31 E
Villena	13	Lf	38.38N	0.51W
Villeneuve d'Ascq	12	Fd	50.38N	3.09 E
Villeneuve-Saint-Georges	12	Ef	48.44N	2.27 E
Villeneuve-sur-Lot	11	Gj	44.24N	0.43 E
Villeneuve-sur-Yonne	11	Jf	48.05N	3.18 E
Ville Platte	45	Jk	30.42N	92.16W
Villers-Bocage [Fr.]	12	Be	49.05N	0.39W
Villers-Bocage [Fr.]	12	Ee	50.00N	2.20 E
Villers-Bretonneux	12	Ee	49.52N	2.31 E
Villers-Carbonnel	12	Ee	49.52N	2.54 E
Villers-Cotterêts	12	Fe	49.15N	3.05 E
Villers-la-Ville	12	Gd	50.35N	4.32 E
Villers-sur-Mer	12	Be	49.19N	0.01W
Villerupt	11	Le	49.28N	5.56 E
Villerville	12	Ce	49.24N	0.08 E
Ville-sur-Tourbe	12	Ge	49.11N	4.47 E
Villeurbanne	11	Ki	45.59N	4.43 E
Villiersdorp	37	Bf	33.59S	19.17 E
Villingen-Schwenningen	10	Eh	48.04N	8.28 E
Villmanstrand/Lappeenranta	6	Ic	61.04N	28.11 E
Villmar	12	Kd	50.23N	8.12 E
Vilnius/Vilnjus	6	Ie	54.41N	25.19 E
Vilnjus/Vilnius	6	Ie	54.41N	25.19 E
Vilok	10	Sh	48.08N	22.50 E
Vilppula	8	Kb	62.01N	24.31 E
Vils [Ger.]	10	Hg	49.10N	11.59 E
Vils [Ger.]	10	Jh	48.35N	13.10 E
Vilsandi	8	If	58.20N	21.45 E
Vilsbiburg	10	Ih	48.27N	12.21 E
Vilshofen	10	Jh	48.38N	13.11 E
Vilusi	15	Bg	42.44N	18.36 E
Vilvoorde/Vilvorde	11	Kd	50.56N	4.26 E
Vilvorde/Vilvoorde	11	Kd	50.56N	4.26 E
Vilyui Range (EN) = Viljujskoje Plato	21	Mc	66.00N	108.00 E
Vimeu	12	Dd	50.05N	1.35 E
Vimianzo	13	Ca	43.07N	9.02W
Vimmerby	7	Dh	57.40N	15.51 E
Vimoutiers	11	Gf	48.55N	0.12 E
Vimperk	10	Jg	49.03N	13.47 E
Vimy	12	Ed	50.22N	2.49 E
Vina	34	Id	7.45N	15.36 E
Viña del Mar	53	Ii	33.02S	71.34W
Vinalhaven Island	44	Mc	44.05N	68.52W
Vinalopo	13	Lf	38.11N	0.36W
Vinaros/Vinaroz	13	Md	40.28N	0.29 E
Vinaroz/Vinaros	13	Md	40.28N	0.29 E
Vînători	15	Hc	46.14N	24.56 E
Vincennes	43	Jd	38.41N	87.32W
Vincennes Bay	66	He	66.30S	109.30 E
Vincente, Puntan-	64b	Bb	14.56N	145.40 E
Vinci	14	Eg	43.47N	10.55 E
Vindafjorden	8	Ae	59.20N	5.55 E
Vindelälven	7	Ee	63.54N	19.52 E
Vindeln	7	Ed	64.12N	19.44 E
Vinderup	8	Ch	56.29N	8.47 E
Vindhya Range	21	Kg	24.37N	82.00 E
Vindö	8	He	59.20N	18.40 E
Vineland	44	Jf	39.29N	75.02W
Vingåker	7	Dg	59.02N	15.52 E
Vingeanne	11	Lg	47.45N	5.18 E
Vinh	22	Mh	18.40N	105.40 E
Vinhais	13	Fc	41.50N	7.00W
Vinh Bac Phan = Tonkin, Gulf of- (EN)	21	Mh	20.00N	108.00 E
Vinh Linh	25	Le	17.04N	107.02 E
Vinica [Yugo.]	14	Jg	45.28N	77.00 E
Vinica [Yugo.]	15	Fh	41.53N	22.30 E
Vinita	45	Ih	36.39N	95.09W
Vînju Mare	15	Fe	44.25N	22.52 E
Vinkovci	14	Me	45.17N	18.49 E
Vinnica	6	If	49.14N	28.29 E
Vinnickaja Oblast [3]	19	Cf	49.00N	28.50 E
Vinniki	16	De	49.48N	24.11 E
Vino, Tierra del-	13	Gc	41.30N	5.30W
Vinogradov	16	Ce	48.09N	23.02 E
Vinslöv	8	Eh	56.06N	13.55 E
Vinson Massif	66	Pf	78.35S	85.25W
Vinstervatn	8	Cc	61.20N	9.00 E
Vinstra	7	Bf	61.36N	9.45 E
Vinstra	8	Cc	61.36N	9.45 E
Vintilă Vodă	15	Jd	45.28N	26.43 E
Vintjärn	8	Gd	60.50N	16.03 E
Vinton	45	Ke	42.10N	92.00W
Vintschgau/Venosta, Val-	14	Ed	46.40N	10.35 E
Vipiteno / Sterzing	14	Fd	46.54N	11.26 E
Vipya Plateau	36	Fe	11.09S	34.00 E
Viqueque	26	Ih	8.52S	126.22 E
Vir	14	Jf	44.18N	15.03 E
Virac	26	Hd	13.35N	124.15 E
Viramgām	25	Ed	23.07N	72.02 E
Virandozero	7	Id	64.01N	36.03 E
Viranşehir	24	Hd	37.13N	39.45 E
Virbalis	8	Jj	54.37N	22.49 E
Vircava	8	Jh	56.35N	23.43 E
Virden	42	Hg	49.51N	100.55W
Virdois/Virrat	7	Fe	62.14N	23.47 E
Vire	11	Ff	48.50N	0.53W
Vire	11	Ee	49.20N	1.07W
Virei	36	Bf	15.43S	12.54 E
Vireux-Wallerand	12	Gd	50.05N	4.44 E
Virgenes, Cabo-	52	Jk	52.19S	68.21W
Virgin Gorda	50	Dc	18.30N	64.25W
Virginia [2]	43	Ld	37.30N	78.45W
Virginia [Mn.-U.S.]	43	Ib	47.31N	92.32W
Virginia [S.Afr.]	37	De	28.12S	26.49 E
Virginia Beach	43	Ld	36.51N	75.59W
Virginia City	46	Fg	39.19N	119.39W
Virgin Islands	38	Mg	18.20N	66.45W
Virgin Islands of the United States [5]	39	Mh	18.20N	64.52W
Virgin Mountains	46	Ih	36.40N	113.50W
Virgin Passage	51a	Cb	18.20N	65.10W
Virgin River	46	Hh	36.35N	114.18W
Virihaure	7	Dc	67.22N	16.33 E
Virkby/Virkkala	8	Kd	60.13N	24.01 E
Virkkala/Virkby	8	Kd	60.13N	24.01 E
Virmasvesi	8	Lb	62.50N	26.55 E
Virôchey	25	Lf	13.59N	106.49 E
Viroin	11	Kd	50.05N	4.43 E
Viroinval	12	Gd	50.05N	4.33 E
Viroinval-Nismes	12	Gd	50.05N	4.33 E
Virojoki	7	Gf	60.35N	27.42 E
Viroqua	45	Ke	43.34N	90.53W
Virovitica	14	Le	45.50N	17.23 E
Virpazar	15	Cg	42.15N	19.06 E
Virrat/Virdois	7	Fe	62.14N	23.47 E
Virserum	7	Dh	57.19N	15.35 E
Virsko More	14	If	44.20N	15.00 E
Virton	11	Le	49.34N	5.32 E
Virton-Ethe	12	He	49.35N	5.35 E
Virtsu	7	Fg	58.37N	23.31 E
Virudanagar	25	Fg	9.36N	77.58 E
Virvičja/Virvyčia	8	Jh	56.14N	22.30 E
Virvyčia/Virvičja	8	Jh	56.14N	22.30 E
Vis	14	Kg	43.02N	16.10 E
Vis	14	Kg	43.03N	16.12 E
Visalia	43	Dd	36.20N	119.18W
Visayan Sea	26	Hd	11.35N	123.51 E
Visby	7	Eh	57.38N	18.18 E
Viscount Melville Sound	38	Hb	74.10N	113.00W
Visé/Wezet	12	Hd	50.44N	5.42 E
Višegrad	15	Jh	41.59N	26.20 E
Višegrad	14	Ng	43.48N	19.17 E
Višera	19	Fc	61.57N	52.25 E
Višera	5	Ld	59.55N	56.50 E
Viseu [2]	13	Ed	40.45N	7.50W
Viseu [Braz.]	54	Id	1.12S	46.07W
Viseu [Port.]	13	Ed	40.39N	7.55W
Vişeu de Sus	15	Hb	47.43N	24.26 E
Vishākhapatnam	22	Kh	17.42N	83.18 E
Visingsö	8	Ff	58.03N	14.20 E
Viskafors	8	Eg	57.38N	12.50 E
Viskan	7	Cg	57.14N	12.12 E
Viški Kanal	14	Kg	43.07N	16.17 E
Vislanda	7	Dh	56.47N	14.27 E
Vislinski Zaliv	10	Pb	54.27N	19.40 E
Visnes	8	Ae	59.21N	5.14 E
Višnevka	15	Lc	46.22N	28.27 E
Visoki Dečani	15	Dg	42.33N	20.16 E
Visoko	14	Mg	43.59N	18.11 E
Visokoi	66	Ad	56.42S	27.12W
Visonggo	63d	Bb	16.13S	179.40 E
Visp	14	Bd	46.17N	7.53 E
Vissefjärda	8	Fh	56.32N	15.35 E
Vista	46	Gj	33.12N	117.15W
Visten	8	Ee	59.40N	13.20 E
Vistonias, Órmos-	15	Ii	40.58N	25.05 E
Vistonis, Limni-	15	Ih	41.03N	25.07 E
Vistula (EN) = Wisła	5	He	54.22N	18.55 E
Vištytis	8	Jj	54.27N	22.44 E
Visuvisu Point	63a	Cb	7.57S	157.31 E
Vit	15	Hf	43.41N	24.45 E
Vitebsk	6	Jd	55.12N	30.11 E
Vitebskaja Oblast [3]	19	Cd	55.20N	29.00 E
Viterbo	14	Gh	42.25N	12.06 E
Vithkuqi	15	Di	40.31N	20.35 E
Vitichi	54	Eh	20.13S	65.29W
Vitigudino	13	Fc	41.01N	6.26W
Viti Levu	57	If	18.00S	178.00 E
Vitim	20	Ge	59.33N	112.28 E
Vitim	21	Nd	59.26N	112.34 E
Vitimski	20	Ge	58.18N	113.18 E
Vitimskoje Ploskogorje	20	Gf	54.00N	114.00 E
Vitinja	15	Gg	42.47N	23.45 E
Vitjaz Strait	60	Di	5.35S	147.00 E
Vitolište	15	Eh	41.11N	21.50 E
Vitoria	13	Jb	42.51N	2.40W
Vitória	53	Lh	20.19S	40.21W
Vitória da Conquista	53	Lg	14.51S	40.51W
Vitória de Santo Antão	54	Ke	8.07S	35.18W
Vitorog	14	Lf	44.08N	17.03 E
Vitosa	15	Gg	42.33N	23.15 E
Vitré	11	Ef	48.08N	1.12W
Vitry-en-Artois	12	Ed	50.20N	2.59 E
Vitry-le-François	11	Kf	48.44N	4.35 E
Vitsi	15	Ei	40.39N	21.23 E

Index Symbols

- [1] Independent Nation
- [2] State, Region
- [3] District, County
- [4] Municipality
- [5] Colony, Dependency
- Continent
- Physical Region
- Historical or Cultural Region
- Mount, Mountain
- Volcano
- Hill
- Mountains, Mountain Range
- Hills, Escarpment
- Plateau, Upland
- Pass, Gap
- Plain, Lowland
- Delta
- Salt Flat
- Valley, Canyon
- Crater, Cave
- Karst Features
- Depression
- Polder
- Desert, Dunes
- Forest, Woods
- Heath, Steppe
- Oasis
- Cape, Point
- Coast, Beach
- Cliff
- Peninsula
- Isthmus
- Sandbank
- Island
- Atoll
- Rock, Reef
- Islands, Archipelago
- Rocks, Reefs
- Coral Reef
- Well, Spring
- Geyser
- River, Stream
- Waterfall Rapids
- River Mouth, Estuary
- Lake
- Salt Lake
- Intermittent Lake
- Reservoir
- Swamp, Pond
- Canal
- Glacier
- Ice Shelf, Pack Ice
- Ocean
- Sea
- Gulf, Bay
- Strait, Fjord
- Lagoon
- Bank
- Seamount
- Tablemount
- Ridge
- Shelf
- Basin
- Escarpment, Sea Scarp
- Fracture
- Trench, Abyss
- National Park, Reserve
- Point of Interest
- Recreation Site
- Cave, Cavern
- Historic Site
- Ruins
- Wall, Walls
- Church, Abbey
- Temple
- Scientific Station
- Airport
- Port
- Lighthouse
- Mine
- Tunnel
- Dam, Bridge

Vittangi 7 Ec 67.41N 21.39 E
Vitteaux 11 Kg 47.24N 4.32 E
Vittel 11 Lf 48.12N 5.57 E
Vittinge 8 Ge 59.54N 17.04 E
Vittoria 14 In 36.57N 14.32 E
Vittorio Veneto 14 Ge 45.59N 12.18 E
Vityaz Depth (EN) 3 Je 44.00N 151.00 E
Vityaz ı Depth (EN) 3 Ih 11.20N 141.30 E
Vityaz II Depth (EN) 3 Kl 23.27 S 175.00W
Vityaz III Depth (EN) 3 Km 32.00 S 178.00W
Vityaz Seamount (EN) 57 Jc 13.30N 173.15W
Vityaz Trench (EN) 3 Jj 10.00 S 170.00 E
Vivarais, Monts du- 11 Ki 44.55N 4.15 E
Vivarais, Plateaux du- 11 Kj 44.50N 4.45 E
Viver 13 Le 39.55N 0.36W
Vivero 13 Ea 43.40N 7.35W
Viverone, Lago di- 14 Ce 45.25N 8.05 E
Vivi 20 Ed 63.52N 97.50 E
Vivian 45 Jj 32.53N 93.59W
Viviers 11 Kj 44.29N 4.41 E
Vivo 37 Dd 23.03 S 29.17 E
Vivoratá 55 Dm 37.40 S 57.39W
Vivorillo, Cayos- 49 Ff 15.50N 83.18W
Viwa 63d Ab 17.08 S 176.56 E
Vizcaíno, Desierto de- 47 Bc 27.40N 114.40W
Vizcaíno, Sierra- 48 Bd 27.20N 114.00W
Vizcaya 13 Ja 43.15N 2.55W
Vizcaya, Golfo de- 5 Fg 44.00N 4.00W
Vize 15 Kh 41.34N 27.45 E
Vize, Ostrov 21 Jb 79.30N 77.00 E
Vizianagaram 25 Ge 18.07N 83.25 E
Vizille 11 Li 45.05N 5.46 E
Vizinga 19 Fc 61.05N 50.10 E
Viziru 15 Kd 45.00N 27.42 E
Vižnica 16 De 48.14N 25.12 E
Vizzini 14 Im 37.10N 14.45 E
Vjaike-Maarja/Väike-Maarja 8 Le 59.04N 26.12 E
Vjajke-Pakri/Väike-Pakri 8 Je 59.50N 23.50 E
Vjajke-Vjajn/Väik Vain 8 Jf 58.30N 23.10 E
Vjalje, Ozero- 8 Ne 59.00N 30.20 E
Vjalozero, Ozero- 7 Ic 66.50N 35.10 E
Vjandra/Vändra 7 Fg 58.40N 25.01 E
Vjartsilja 7 He 62.10N 30.48 E
Vjatka 5 Ld 55.36N 51.30 E
Vjatskije Poljany 19 Fd 56.14N 51.04 E
Vjatski Uval 7 Lg 58.00N 49.45 E
Vjazemski 20 Ig 47.31N 134.45 E
Vjazma 6 Jd 55.13N 34.18 E
Vjazniki 7 Kh 56.15N 42.12 E
Vjeio, Río- 49 Dg 12.17N 86.54W
Vjosa 15 Ci 40.37N 19.20 E
Vlaamse Banken 12 Ec 51.15N 2.30 E
Vlaanderen/Flandres=Flanders (EN) 11 Jc 51.00N 3.20 E
Vlaardingen 11 Kc 51.54N 4.21 E
Vlădeasa, Vîrful- 15 Fc 46.45N 22.48 E
Vlădeni 15 Kb 47.25N 27.20 E
Vladičin Han 15 Fg 42.43N 22.04 E
Vladikavkaz (Ordžonikidze) 6 Kg 43.03N 44.40 E
Vladimir 6 Kd 56.10N 40.25 E
Vladimirskaja Oblast 19 Ed 56.00N 40.40 E
Vladimirski Tupik 16 Hb 55.42N 33.18 E
Vladimir-Volynski 19 Ce 50.51N 24.22 E
Vladivostok 22 Pe 43.10N 131.56 E
Vlad Ţepeş 15 Ke 44.21N 27.05 E
Vlagtwedde 12 Ja 53.02N 7.08 E
Vlagtwedde-Ter Apel 12 Jb 52.52N 7.06 E
Vlahina 15 Fi 41.54N 22.52 E
Vlăhiţa 15 Ic 46.21N 25.31 E
Vlamse Vlakte=Flanders Plain (EN) 11 Id 50.40N 2.50 E
Vlasenica 14 Mf 44.11N 18.57 E
Vlašic [Yugo.] 14 Lf 44.19N 17.40 E
Vlašim 10 Kg 49.42N 14.54 E
Vlasotince 15 Fg 42.58N 22.08 E
Vlasovo 20 Ib 70.40N 134.35 E
Vlieland 11 Ka 53.15N 5.00 E
Vlieland 12 Ha 53.17N 5.06 E
Vlieland-Oost Vlieland 12 Ha 53.17N 5.06 E
Vliestroom 12 Ha 53.17N 5.10 E
Vlissingen 11 Jc 51.26N 3.35 E
Vlissingen-Oost-Souburg 12 Fc 51.28N 3.36 E
Vloesberg/Flobecq 12 Fd 50.44N 3.44 E
Vlora 6 Hg 40.27N 19.30 E
Vlorës, Gjiri i- 15 Ci 40.25N 19.25 E
Vlotho 12 Kb 52.10N 8.51 E
Vltava=Moldau (EN) 5 He 50.21N 14.30 E
Vöcklabruck 14 Hb 48.01N 13.39 E
Vodice 14 Jg 43.46N 15.47 E
Vodla 7 If 61.49N 36.00 E
Vodlozero, Ozero- 7 Ie 62.20N 37.00 E
Vodňany 10 Kg 49.09N 14.11 E
Vodnjan 14 Hf 44.57N 13.51 E
Vodny 17 Fe 63.32N 53.20 E
Voerde (Niederrhein) 10 Ce 51.35N 6.41 E
Voeren/Fouron 12 Hd 50.45N 5.48 E
Vogel Peak 34 Hd 8.24N 11.47 E
Vogelsberg 10 Ff 50.30N 9.15 E
Voghera 14 Df 44.59N 9.01 E
Vogtland 10 If 50.30N 12.05 E
Voh 63b Be 20.58 S 164.42 E
Võhandu Jõgi/Vyhandu 8 Lf 58.03N 27.40 E
Vohémar 37 Ib 13.22 S 50.00 E
Vohipeno 37 Hd 22.20 S 47.52 E
Vöhl 12 Kc 51.12N 8.56 E
Vohma 7 Lg 58.45N 46.36 E
Vohma 19 Ed 58.58N 46.45 E
Voi 31 Ki 3.23 S 38.34 E
Voikoski 8 Lc 61.16N 26.48 E
Voinjama 31 Gh 8.25N 9.45W
Vóïon Óros 15 Ei 40.15N 21.03 E
Voire 11 Kf 48.27N 4.25 E
Voiron 11 Li 45.22N 5.35 E
Voitsberg 14 Jc 47.02N 15.09 E
Voïviïs, Límni- 15 Fj 39.32N 22.45 E
Vojens 8 Ci 55.15N 9.19 E
Vojkar 17 Ld 65.38N 64.40 E
Vojmsjön 7 Dd 65.00N 16.24 E
Vojnić 14 Je 45.19N 15.42 E
Vojnilov 10 Ug 49.04N 24.33 E
Vojvodina 15 Cd 45.00N 20.00 E
Voj-Vož 19 Fc 62.56N 54.59 E
Voknavolok 7 Hd 64.57N 30.31 E
Vokré, Hoséré- 30 Ih 8.21N 13.15 E
Volary 10 Jh 48.55N 13.54 E
Volcán 49 Fi 8.46N 82.38W
Volcanica, Cordillera- 38 Ih 18.00N 101.00W
Volcano 65a Fd 19.26N 155.20W
Volcano Islands (EN)=Iō/Kazan-Rettō 21 Qg 25.00N 141.00 E
Volcano Islands (EN)=Kazan-Rettō/Iō 21 Qg 25.00N 141.00 E
Volcán Rana Roi 65d Ab 27.05 S 109.23W
Volčansk 17 Jg 59.59N 60.04 E
Volčansk 16 Jd 50.16N 37.01 E
Volčiha 20 Df 52.02N 80.23 E
Volda 7 Be 62.09N 6.06 E
Voldafjorden 8 Ab 62.10N 6.00 E
Volga 5 Kf 45.55N 47.52 E
Volga 7 Jh 57.57N 38.25 E
Volga-Baltic Canal (EN)=Volgo-Baltijski vodny put imeni V. I. Lenina 5 Jd 59.58N 37.10 E
Volga Delta (EN) 5 Kf 46.30N 47.00 E
Volga Hills (EN)=Privolžkaja Vozvyšennóst 5 Ke 52.00N 46.00 E
Volgo-Baltijski vodny put imeni V.I. Lenina=Volga-Baltic Canal (EN) 5 Jd 59.58N 37.10 E
Volgodonsk 19 Ef 47.33N 42.08 E
Volgo-Donskoj sudohodny kanal imeni V. I. Lenina=Lenin Canal (EN) 5 Kf 48.40N 43.37 E
Volgograd (Stalingrad) 6 Kf 48.44N 44.25 E
Volgograd Reservoir (EN)=Volgogradskoje Vodohranilišče 5 Kf 49.20N 45.00 E
Volgogradskaja Oblast 19 Ef 49.30N 44.30 E
Volgogradskoje Vodohranilišče=Volgograd Reservoir (EN) 5 Kf 49.20N 45.00 E
Volhov 5 Jc 60.08N 32.20 E
Volhov 6 Jd 59.55N 32.20 E
Volhynia 5 Ie 51.00N 25.00 E
Volissós 15 Ik 38.29N 25.55 E
Volja 17 Je 63.11N 61.16 E
Volka 10 Vd 52.43N 25.43 E
Völkermarkt 14 Id 46.39N 14.38 E
Völklingen 10 Cg 49.15N 6.51 E
Volkmarsen 12 Lc 51.24N 9.07 E
Volkovysk 16 Dc 53.10N 24.31 E
Volkovysskaja Vozvyšennost 10 Kc 53.10N 24.30 E
Volksrust 37 De 27.24 S 29.53 E
Vollenhove 12 Hb 52.40N 5.57 E
Vollsjö 8 Ei 55.42N 13.46 E
Volme 12 Jc 51.24N 7.27 E
Volmunster 12 Je 49.07N 7.21 E
Volna, Gora- 20 Kd 63.30N 154.57 E
Volnjansk 16 If 47.54N 35.29 E
Volnovaha 16 Jf 47.37N 37.36 E
Voločajevka 2-ja 20 Ig 48.36N 134.36 E
Voločisk 16 Ee 49.31N 26.13 E
Volodarsk 7 Kh 56.14N 43.13 E
Volodarski 16 Pf 46.26N 48.31 E
Volodarskoje 19 Ge 53.18N 68.08 E
Vologda 6 Jd 59.12N 39.55 E
Vologodskaja Oblast 19 Ed 60.00N 41.00 E
Volokolamsk 7 Ih 56.03N 35.58 E
Volokonovka 16 Jd 50.29N 37.52 E
Vólos 6 Ih 39.22N 22.57 E
Vološka 7 Jf 61.42N 39.15 E
Vološka 7 Jf 61.21N 40.03 E
Volosovo 7 Gg 59.28N 29.31 E
Volovec 10 Jh 48.42N 23.17 E
Volovo 16 Kc 53.35N 38.01 E
Voložin 16 Eb 54.06N 26.32 E
Volquart Boons Kyst 41 Jd 70.20N 24.20W
Volsini, Monti- 14 Fh 42.40N 11.55 E
Volsk 19 Ee 52.02N 47.23 E
Volta 30 Hh 5.46N 0.41 E
Volta 34 Fd 7.00N 0.30 E
Volta Blanche=White Volta (EN) 30 Gh 8.38N 0.59W
Volta Lake 30 Hh 7.30N 0.15 E
Volta Noire=Black Volta (EN) 30 Gh 8.38N 1.30W
Volta Noire=Black Volta (EN) 34 Ec 12.30N 4.00W
Volta Redonda 53 Lh 22.32 S 44.07W
Volta Rouge=Red Volta (EN) 30 Gh 10.34N 0.30W
Volterra 14 Eg 43.24N 10.51 E
Voltoya 13 Hc 41.13N 4.31W
Voltri, Genova- 14 Cf 44.26N 8.45 E
Volturino 14 Jj 40.25N 15.48 E
Volturno 14 Hi 41.01N 13.55 E
Volubilis 32 Fc 34.04N 5.33W
Vólvi, Límni- 15 Gi 40.41N 23.28 E
Volynskaja Grjada 10 Ue 51.05N 25.00 E
Volynskaja Oblast 19 Ce 51.10N 25.00 E
Volynskaja Vozvyšennost 16 Dd 50.30N 25.00 E
Volžsk 19 Ed 55.55N 48.19 E
Volžski 6 Kf 48.48N 44.44 E
Volžski 7 Mj 53.28N 50.08 E
Voma 63d Bc 18.00 S 178.08 E
Vomano 14 Ih 42.39N 14.02 E
Vonavona 63a Cc 8.12 S 157.05 E
Vondrozo 37 Hd 22.47 S 47.17 E
Von Frank Mountain 40 Id 63.33N 154.20W
Vónitsa 15 Dk 38.55N 20.53 E
Vonne 11 Gh 46.25N 0.15 E
Võnnu/Vynnu 8 Lf 58.15N 27.10 E
Voorne 12 Gc 51.52N 4.05 E
Voorschoten 12 Gb 52.08N 4.28 E
Voorst 12 Ib 52.10N 6.09 E
Voorst-Twello 12 Ib 52.14N 6.07 E
Vop 16 Hb 54.56N 32.44 E
Vopnafjördur 7a Cb 65.45N 14.50W
Vora 15 Ch 41.23N 19.40 E
Vörå/Vöyri 8 Ja 63.09N 22.15 E
Vorarlberg 14 Dc 47.15N 9.50 E
Vóras Óros 15 Ei 41.00N 21.50 E
Vorau 14 Jc 47.24N 15.53 E
Vorden 12 Ib 52.06N 6.20 E
Vorderrhein 14 Dd 46.49N 9.26 E
Vordingborg 7 Ci 55.01N 11.55 E
Voreifel 12 Jd 50.10N 7.00 E
Vorga Šor 17 Kc 67.35N 63.40 E
Voría Píndhos 15 Dj 40.20N 20.55 E
Vórioi Sporádhes, Nísoi-=Northern Sporades (EN) 5 Ih 39.15N 23.55 E
Vórios Evvoïkós Kólpos=Évvoia, Gulf of- (EN) 15 Gk 38.45N 23.10 E
Vorkuta 6 Mb 67.27N 63.58 E
Vorma 7 Cf 60.09N 11.27 E
Vormsi 8 Je 59.02N 23.05 E
Vormsi 7 Fg 59.00N 23.15 E
Vorniceni 15 Jb 47.59N 26.40 E
Vorogovo 20 Dd 60.58N 89.28 E
Vorona 16 Md 51.22N 42.03 E
Voroncovo 20 Db 71.40N 83.40 E
Voroncovo 8 Mg 57.15N 28.49 E
Voronež 6 Je 51.40N 39.10 E
Voronež 16 Kd 51.31N 39.05 E
Voronežskaja Oblast 19 Ee 51.00N 40.15 E
Voronin Trough (EN) 67 Ge 80.00N 85.00 E
Voronja 7 Ib 69.09N 35.47 E
Voronovo 8 Kj 54.09N 25.19 E
Voropajevo 8 Li 55.07N 27.19 E
Vorošilovgrad → Lugansk 6 Jf 48.34N 39.20 E
Vorošilovgradskaja Oblast 19 Df 49.00N 39.10 E
Vorotan 16 Oj 39.15N 46.43 E
Vorotynec 7 Kh 56.02N 45.52 E
Vorožba 16 Id 51.10N 34.11 E
Vorskla 16 Ie 48.52N 34.05 E
Vorsma 7 Ki 55.58N 43.17 E
Võrts Järv/Vyrtsjarv, Ozero- 7 Gg 58.15N 26.05 E
Võru/Vyru 19 Cd 57.52N 27.05 E
Voruh 18 He 39.52N 70.35 E
Vosges 5 Gf 48.30N 7.10 E
Vosges 11 Mf 48.10N 6.20 E
Voskresensk 7 Ji 55.22N 38.42 E
Voskresenskoje 7 Kh 56.51N 45.27 E
Voss 8 Bd 60.40N 6.30 E
Vossa 8 Ad 60.39N 5.42 E
Vossevangen 7 Bd 60.39N 6.26 E
Vostočno-Kazahstanskaja Oblast 19 If 49.00N 84.00 E
Vostočno-Kounradski 19 Hf 46.58N 75.07 E
Vostočno Sibirskoje More=East Siberian Sea (EN) 67 Cd 74.00N 166.00 E
Vostočny 20 Jg 48.19N 142.40 E
Vostočny 17 Jg 58.48N 61.52 E
Vostočny, Hrebet- 20 Lf 55.00N 160.30 E
Vostočny Sajan=Eastern Sayans (EN) 21 Ld 53.00N 97.00 E
Vostok 66 Hf 78.28 S 106.48 E
Vostok Island 57 Lf 10.06 S 152.23W
Vostrecovo 20 Ig 45.56N 134.59 E
Vošu/Vyzu 8 Ke 59.30N 25.50 E
Votkinsk 19 Fd 57.05N 53.59 E
Votkinskoje Vodohranilišče = Votkinsk Reservoir (EN) 5 Ld 57.30N 55.10 E
Votkinsk Reservoir (EN) = Votkinskoje Vodohranilišče 5 Ld 57.30N 55.10 E
Votuporanga 55 He 20.24 S 49.59W
Vouga 13 Dd 40.41N 8.40W
Vouillé 11 Gh 46.38N 0.10 E
Voulgára 15 Ej 39.06N 21.54 E
Vouliagméni 15 Gl 37.49N 23.47 E
Voúrinos Óros 15 Ei 40.11N 21.40 E
Voúxa, Ákra- 15 Gn 35.38N 23.36 E
Vouziers 11 Ke 49.24N 4.42 E
Voves 11 Hf 48.16N 1.38 E
Vovodo 35 Cd 5.40N 24.21 E
Voxna 8 Fc 61.21N 15.34 E
Voxnan 8 Gc 61.17N 16.26 E
Voyeykov Ice Shelf 66 Ie 66.20 S 124.38 E
Vöyri/Vörå 8 Ja 63.09N 22.15 E
Vože, Ozero- 7 Jf 60.35N 39.05 E
Vožega 7 Jf 60.33N 39.13 E
Vožega 7 Jf 60.30N 40.12 E
Voznesenje 7 If 61.01N 35.27 E
Voznesensk 19 Df 47.35N 31.20 E
Vozroždenija, Ostrov- 18 Bb 45.05N 59.15 E
Vraca 15 Gf 43.12N 23.33 E
Vraca 15 Dh 41.54N 20.45 E
Vraca 15 Gf 43.12N 23.33 E
Vradijevka 16 Gf 47.51N 30.34 E
Vrakhiónas 15 Dl 37.48N 20.45 E
Vran 14 Lg 43.39N 17.27 E
Vrancea 15 Jd 45.50N 26.42 E
Vranica 14 Lg 43.57N 17.44 E
Vranje 15 Eg 42.33N 21.54 E
Vranov nad Topl'ou 10 Rh 48.54N 21.41 E
Vrăška čuka, Prohod- 15 Ff 43.50N 22.23 E
Vratnica 15 Eg 42.08N 21.07 E
Vratnik, prohod- 15 Jg 42.49N 26.10 E
Vrbas 14 Le 45.07N 17.31 E
Vrbas 15 Cd 45.34N 19.39 E
Vrbno pod Pradědem 10 Nf 50.08N 17.23 E
Vrbovsko 14 Je 45.22N 15.05 E
Vrchlabí 10 Lf 50.38N 15.37 E
Vrede 37 De 27.30 S 29.06 E
Vreden 12 Ib 52.02N 6.50 E
Vredenburg 37 Bf 32.54 S 17.59 E
Vredendal 37 Bf 31.41 S 18.35 E
Vresse, Vresse-sur-Semois- 12 Ge 49.52N 4.56 E
Vresse-sur-Semois 12 Ge 49.52N 4.56 E
Vresse-sur-Semois-Vresse 12 Ge 49.52N 4.56 E
Vretstorp 8 Fe 59.02N 14.52 E
Vrhnika 14 Ie 45.58N 14.18 E
Vries 12 Ia 53.05N 6.36 E
Vriezenveen 12 Ib 52.26N 6.36 E
Vrigstad 8 Fg 57.21N 14.28 E
Vron 12 Dd 50.19N 1.45 E
Vršac 15 Ed 45.07N 21.18 E
Vryburg 31 Jk 26.55 S 24.45 E
Vryheid 37 Ee 27.52 S 30.38 E
Vsetín 10 Ng 49.21N 18.00 E
Vsevidof, Mount- 40a Eb 53.07N 168.43W
Vsevoložsk 7 Hf 60.04N 30.41 E
Vstrečny 20 Lc 68.00N 165.58 E
Vtačnik 10 Oh 48.42N 18.37 E
Vuanggava 63d Cc 18.52 S 178.54W
Vučitrn 15 Dg 42.49N 20.58 E
Vučjak 15 Fh 41.28N 22.20 E
Vuka 14 Me 45.21N 19.00 E
Vukovar 14 Me 45.21N 19.00 E
Vuktyl 19 Fc 63.50N 57.25 E
Vulavu 63a Dc 8.31 S 159.48 E
Vulcan 15 Gd 45.23N 23.16 E
Vulcan, Vîrful- 15 Fc 46.14N 22.58 E
Vulcano 14 Il 38.25N 15.00 E
Vulkanešty 16 Fg 45.38N 28.27 E
Vulture 14 Jj 40.57N 15.38 E
Vung Tau 25 Lf 10.21N 107.04 E
Vunindawa 63d Bb 17.49 S 178.19 E
Vunisea Station 61 Ec 19.03 S 178.09 E
Vuohijarvi 8 Lc 61.10N 26.40 E
Vuoksa 8 Nd 60.35N 30.42 E
Vuoksa, ozero- 8 Mc 61.00N 30.00 E
Vuoksa, ozero- 8 Md 60.38N 29.55 E
Vuollerim 7 Ec 66.25E 20.36 E
Vuosjärvi 8 Ka 63.00N 25.30 E
Vuotso 7 Gb 68.06N 27.08 E
Vuranimala 63a Ec 9.05 S 160.51 E
Vyborg 6 Ic 60.42N 28.45 E
Vyčegda 5 Kc 61.18N 46.36 E
Vyčegodski 7 Lf 61.17N 46.48 E
Vychodočeský kraj 10 Lf 50.10N 16.00 E
Východoslovenska nížina 10 Rh 48.35N 21.50 E
Východoslovenský kraj 10 Rg 49.00N 21.15 E
Vyg 7 Ie 63.17N 35.17 E
Vygoda 15 Nc 46.38N 30.24 E
Vygoda 10 Uh 48.52N 24.01 E
Vygozero, Ozero- 5 Jc 63.35N 34.45 E
Vyhandu/Võhandu Jõgi 8 Lf 58.03N 27.40 E
Vyja 7 Le 62.57N 46.42 E
Vyksa 19 Ed 55.20N 42.12 E
Vym 19 Fc 62.13N 50.25 E
Vynnu/Võnnu 8 Lf 58.15N 27.10 E
Vyrica 19 Dd 59.24N 30.19 E
Vyrnwy 9 Ki 52.45N 2.50W
Vyrtsjarv, Ozero-/Võrts Järv 7 Gg 58.15N 26.05 E
Vyru/Võru 19 Cd 57.52N 27.05 E
Vyša 16 Mb 54.03N 42.06 E
Vyšgorod 16 Gd 50.38N 30.29 E
Vyšgorodok 8 Mh 56.55N 28.05 E
Vyškov 10 Mg 49.17N 17.00 E
Vyškovsk, pereval 10 Th 48.38N 23.45 E
Vyšni Voloček 19 Dd 57.37N 34.32 E
Vysock 7 Gf 60.36N 28.36 E
Vysoké Tatry=High Tatra (EN) 10 Pg 49.10N 20.00 E
Vysokogorny 20 If 50.07N 139.10 E
Vysokogorsk 28 Mb 44.23N 135.23 E
Vysokoje 10 Td 52.22N 23.26 E
Vysokovsk 7 Ih 56.21N 36.29 E
Vyšši Brod 10 Kh 48.37N 14.18 E
Vytebet 16 Ic 53.53N 35.38 E
Vytegra 19 Dc 61.01N 36.28 E
Vyvenka 20 Ld 60.10N 165.20 E
Vyzu/Vošu 8 Ke 59.30N 25.50 E
Vzmorje 20 Jg 47.45N 142.30 E

W

Wa 34 Ec 10.03N 2.29W
Waal 11 Kc 51.55N 4.30 E
Waalre 12 Hc 51.23N 5.27 E
Waalwijk 12 Hc 51.41N 5.04 E
Waar, Meos- 26 Jg 2.05 S 134.23 E
Waardgronden 12 Ha 53.12N 5.05 E
Waarschoot 12 Fc 51.09N 3.36 E
Wabana 42 Mg 47.38N 52.57W
Wabao, Cap- 63b Ce 21.36 S 167.51 E
Wabasca 42 Ge 56.00N 113.53W
Wabasca 42 Fe 58.21N 115.20W
Wabash 38 Kf 37.46N 88.02W
Wabash 44 Ee 40.48N 85.49W
Wabasha 45 Jd 44.23N 92.02W
Wabash River 45 Lh 37.46N 88.02W
Wabowden 42 Hf 54.55N 98.38W
Wąbrzeźno 10 Oc 53.17N 18.57 E
Wabu Hu 27 Ke 32.20N 116.55 E
Wachau 14 Jb 48.20N 15.25 E
Wachile 35 Fe 4.33N 39.03 E
Wachusett Seamount (EN) 57 Lh 32.00 S 151.20W
Waco 39 Jf 31.55N 97.08W
Waconda Lake 45 Gg 39.30N 98.30W
Wadayama 29 Dd 35.20N 134.51 E
Wad Bandah 35 Dc 13.06N 27.57 E
Waddān 33 Cd 29.10N 16.08 E
Waddān, Jabal- 33 Cd 29.20N 16.20 E
Waddeneilanden=West Frisian Islands (EN) 11 Ka 53.30N 5.00 E
Waddenzee 12 Ha 53.20N 5.30 E
Waddington, Mount- 38 Gd 51.23N 125.15W
Wadena 45 Ic 46.26N 95.08W
Wadern 12 Ie 49.32N 6.53 E
Wadern-Nunkirchen 12 Ie 49.32N 6.53 E
Wadersloh 12 Kc 51.44N 8.15 E
Wadersloh-Liesborn 12 Kc 51.43N 8.16 E
Wadesboro 44 Gh 34.58N 80.04W
Wadhams 46 Ba 51.30N 127.31W
Wādī Bīshah 23 Fe 21.24N 43.26 E
Wādī Fajr 23 Ec 30.17N 38.18 E
Wādī Ḩalfā' 31 Kf 21.56N 31.20 E
Wādī Jimāl, Jazīrat- 24 Fj 24.40N 35.10 E
Wādī Mūsá 24 Fg 30.19N 35.29 E
Wādī Shiḩan 35 Ib 18.10N 52.57 E
Wad Madanī 31 Kg 14.24N 33.32 E
Wad Nimr 35 Ec 14.32N 32.08 E
Wadowice 10 Pg 49.53N 19.30 E
Wadsworth 46 Fg 39.38N 119.17W
Wafangdian → Fuxian 27 Ld 39.38N 121.59 E
Wafrah 23 Gd 28.25N 47.56 E
Waga-Gawa 29 Gb 39.18N 141.07 E
Wagenfeld 12 Kb 52.33N 8.35 E
Wagenfeld-Ströhen 12 Kb 52.32N 8.39 E
Wageningen 12 Hc 51.57N 5.41 E
Wagēr, Qar- 35 Hc 10.01N 45.30 E
Wager Bay 38 Kc 65.26N 88.40W
Wagga Wagga 58 Fh 35.07 S 147.22 E
Waghäusel 12 Ke 49.15N 8.30 E
Wagin 58 Ch 33.18 S 117.21 E
Waginger See 10 Ii 47.58N 12.50 E
Wagoner 45 Ii 35.58N 95.22W
Wagon Mound 45 Dh 36.01N 104.42W
Wagontire Mountain 46 Fe 43.21N 119.53W
Wagrien 10 Gb 54.15N 10.45 E
Wągrowiec 10 Nd 52.49N 17.11 E
Wah 25 Eb 33.48N 72.42 E
Waha 31 If 28.10N 19.57 E
Wahai 26 Ig 2.48 S 129.30 E
Wahiawa 60 Oc 21.30N 158.02W
Wahoo 45 Hf 41.13N 96.37W
Wahpeton 43 Hb 46.16N 96.36W
Waialeale, Mount- 65a Ba 22.04N 159.30W
Waialua 65a Cb 21.35N 158.08W
Waianae 65a Cb 21.27N 158.12W
Waiau 62 Ee 42.47 S 173.22 E
Waiau 61 Dh 42.39 S 173.03 E
Waiblingen 10 Fh 48.50N 9.18 E
Waibstadt 12 Ke 49.18N 8.56 E
Waidhofen an der Thaya 14 Jb 48.49N 15.17 E
Waidhofen an der Ybbs 14 Ic 47.58N 14.46 E
Waigame 26 Ig 1.50 S 129.49 E
Waigeo, Pulau- 57 Ee 0.14 S 130.45 E
Waihi 62 Fb 37.24 S 175.50 E
Waihou 62 Fb 37.10 S 175.33 E
Waikabubak 26 Gh 9.38 S 119.25 E
Waikare, Lake- 62 Fb 37.25 S 175.10 E
Waikaremoana, Lake- 61 Eg 38.45 S 177.05 E
Waikato 62 Fb 37.23 S 174.43 E
Waikawa 62 Cg 46.38 S 169.08 E
Waikouaiti 62 Df 45.36 S 170.41 E
Wailangilala 63d Cb 16.45 S 179.06W
Wailua 65a Ba 22.03N 159.20W
Wailuku 60 Oc 20.53N 156.30W
Waimamaku 62 Ea 35.34 S 173.29 E
Waimanalo Beach 65a Db 21.20N 157.42W
Waimangaroa 62 Dd 41.43 S 171.46 E
Waimate 62 Df 44.45 S 171.03 E
Waimea 65a Fc 20.02N 155.40W
Waimes 12 Id 50.25N 6.07 E
Wainfleet All Saints 12 Ca 53.06N 0.15 E
Wainganga 21 Jh 19.36N 79.48 E
Waingapu 26 Hh 9.39 S 120.16 E
Waini Point 50 Gh 8.24N 59.49W
Waini River 50 Gh 8.24N 59.51W
Wainwright [Ak.-U.S.] 40 Gb 70.38N 160.01W
Wainwright [Alta.-Can.] 42 Gf 52.49N 110.52W
Waiouru 61 Eg 39.29 S 175.40 E
Waipahu 65a Cb 21.23N 158.01W
Waipara 62 Ee 43.03 S 172.45 E
Waipawa 62 Gc 39.56 S 176.35 E
Waipiro 62 Hc 38.02 S 178.20 E
Waipu 62 Fa 35.59 S 174.26 E
Waipukurau 62 Gd 40.00 S 176.33 E
Wairakei 62 Gc 38.37 S 176.05 E
Wairarapa, Lake- 62 Fd 41.15 S 175.15 E
Wairau 62 Fd 41.31 S 174.03 E
Wairoa 61 Eg 39.03 S 177.26 E
Wairoa 62 Fb 36.11 S 174.02 E
Waitaki 62 Df 44.56 S 171.09 E
Waitangi 61 Fh 43.56 S 176.34W
Waitara 61 Dg 39.00 S 174.14 E
Waitati 62 Df 45.45 S 170.34 E
Waitemata 62 Fb 36.50 S 174.40 E
Waitotara 62 Fc 39.48 S 174.44 E
Waiuku 62 Fb 37.15 S 174.44 E
Waiwerang 26 Hh 8.23 S 123.09 E
Waiyevo 61 Fc 16.48 S 179.59W
Wājid 35 Ge 3.50N 43.14 E
Wajima 28 Nf 37.24N 136.54 E
Wajir 31 Ih 1.42N 40.04 E
Waka [Eth.] 35 Fd 7.09N 37.19 E
Waka [Zaire] 36 Db 1.01N 20.13 E
Wakamatsu-Shima 29 Ae 32.54N 129.00 E
Wakasa-Wan 27 Od 35.45N 135.40 E
Wakatipu, Lake- 61 Ci 45.05 S 168.35 E
Wakaya 63d Bb 17.37 S 179.00 E
Wakayama 22 Pf 34.13N 135.11 E
Wakayama Ken 28 Mh 33.55N 135.20 E
Wake 29 Dd 34.48N 134.08 E
Wa Keeney 45 Gg 39.01N 99.53W
Wakefield [Eng.-U.K.] 9 Lh 53.42N 1.29W
Wakefield [N.Z.] 62 Ed 41.24 S 173.03 E

Index Symbols

1 Independent Nation
2 State, Region
3 District, County
4 Municipality
5 Colony, Dependency
Continent
Physical Region
Historical or Cultural Region
Mount, Mountain
Volcano
Hill
Mountains, Mountain Range
Hills, Escarpment
Plateau, Upland
Pass, Gap
Plain, Lowland
Delta
Salt Flat
Valley, Canyon
Crater, Cave
Karst Features
Depression
Polder
Desert, Dunes
Forest, Woods
Heath, Steppe
Oasis
Cape, Point
Coast, Beach
Cliff
Peninsula
Isthmus
Sandbank
Island
Atoll
Rock, Reef
Islands, Archipelago
Rocks, Reefs
Coral Reef
Well, Spring
Geyser
River, Stream
Waterfall Rapids
River Mouth, Estuary
Lake
Salt Lake
Intermittent Lake
Reservoir
Swamp, Pond
Canal
Glacier
Ice Shelf, Pack Ice
Ocean
Sea
Gulf, Bay
Strait, Fjord
Lagoon
Bank
Seamount
Tablemount
Ridge
Shelf
Basin
Escarpment, Sea Scarp
Fracture
Trench, Abyss
National Park, Reserve
Point of Interest
Recreation Site
Cave, Cavern
Historic Site
Ruins
Wall, Walls
Church, Abbey
Temple
Scientific Station
Airport
Port
Lighthouse
Mine
Tunnel
Dam, Bridge

Wake Island [5] 58 Jd 19.18N 166.36W
Wake Island 57 Hc 19.18N 166.36 E
Wakkanai 22 Qe 45.25N 141.40 E
Wakunai 63a Ba 5.52S 155.13 E
Wakuya 29 Gb 38.33N 141.05 E
Wala 36 Fd 5.46S 32.04 E
Walachia (EN) = Valahia 5 Ig 44.00N 25.00 E
Walachia (EN) = Valahia 15 He 44.00N 25.00 E
Wałbrzych [2] 10 Mf 50.45N 16.15 E
Wałbrzych 6 He 50.46N 16.17 E
Walchensee 10 Hi 47.35N 11.20 E
Walcheren 11 Jc 51.33N 3.35 E
Walcott, Lake- 46 Ie 42.40N 113.23W
Walcourt 12 Gd 50.15N 4.25 E
Walcourt-Fraire 12 Gd 50.16N 4.30 E
Wałcz 10 Mc 53.17N 16.28 E
Waldböckelheim 12 Je 49.49N 7.43 E
Waldbröl 10 Df 50.53N 7.37 E
Waldeck 12 Kc 51.17N 8.50 E
Waldeck 12 Lc 51.12N 9.05 E
Waldems 12 Kd 50.15N 8.18 E
Walden 45 Cf 40.44N 106.17W
Waldfischbach-Burgalben 12 Je 49.17N 7.40 E
Waldkirchen 10 Jh 48.44N 13.36 E
Waldkraiburg 10 Ih 48.12N 12.25 E
Wald-Michelbach 12 Ke 49.34N 8.49 E
Waldnaab 10 Ig 49.35N 12.07 E
Waldorf 44 If 38.37N 76.54W
Waldrach 12 Ie 49.45N 6.45 E
Waldron 45 Ii 34.54N 94.05W
Waldshut 10 Ei 47.37N 8.13 E
Waldviertel 14 Jb 48.30N 15.30 E
Waleabahi, Pulau- 26 Hg 0.15S 122.20 E
Wales 40 Fc 65.36N 168.05W
Wales 42 Ic 67.50N 86.40W
Wales 5 Fe 52.30N 3.30W
Wales [2] 9 Ji 52.30N 3.30W
Walewale 34 Ec 10.21N 0.48W
Walferdange 12 Ie 49.39N 6.08 E
Walgett 58 Fh 30.01S 148.07 E
Walgreen Coast 66 Of 75.15S 105.00W
Walhalla 45 Hb 48.55N 97.55W
Walikale 36 Ec 1.25S 28.03 E
Walker 45 Ic 47.06N 94.35W
Walker Lake 43 Dd 38.40N 118.43W
Walkerston 59 Jd 21.10S 149.10 E
Wall 45 Ed 44.01N 102.14W
Wallace 46 Hc 47.28N 115.56W
Wallaceburg 44 Fd 42.36N 82.23W
Wallangarra 59 Ke 28.56S 151.56 E
Wallaroo 59 Hf 33.56S 137.38 E
Wallary Island 59 Ic 15.05S 141.50 E
Wallasey 9 Jh 53.26N 3.03W
Walla Walla 43 Db 46.08N 118.20W
Walldorf 12 Ke 49.20N 8.39 E
Wallenhorst 12 Kb 52.21N 8.01 E
Wallibu 51n Ba 13.19N 61.15W
Wallingford 12 Ac 51.36N 1.08W
Wallis, Iles- = Wallis Islands (EN) 57 Jf 13.18S 176.10W
Wallis and Futuna (EN) = Wallis-et-Futuna, Iles- [5] 58 Jf 14.00S 177.00W
Walliser Alpen/Alpes Valaisannes 14 Bd 46.10N 7.30 E
Wallis-et-Futuna, Iles- = Wallis and Futuna (EN) [5] 58 Jf 14.00S 177.00W
Wallis Islands (EN) = Wallis, Iles- 57 Jf 13.18S 176.10W
Wallowa 46 Gd 45.34N 117.32W
Wallowa Mountains 46 Gd 45.10N 117.30W
Walmer 12 Dc 51.12N 1.24 E
Walney, Isle of- 9 Jg 54.07N 3.15W
Walnut Ridge 43 Id 36.04N 90.57W
Walpole, Ile- 57 Hg 22.37S 168.57 E
Walrus Islands 40 Ge 58.45N 160.20W
Walsall 9 Li 52.35N 1.58W
Walsenburg 43 Gd 37.37N 104.47W
Walsrode 10 Fd 52.52N 9.35 E
Walterboro 44 Gi 32.54N 80.39W
Walter F. George Lake 44 Ej 31.49N 85.08W
Walter Lake 43 Dd 38.44N 118.43W
Walters 45 Gi 34.22N 98.19W
Waltershausen 10 Gf 50.54N 10.34 E
Waltham 44 Lc 45.58N 76.57W
Walton-on-the-Naze 12 Dc 51.51N 1.17 E
Waltrop 12 Jc 51.38N 7.24 E
Walvisbaai/Walvis Bay [3] 37 Ad 23.00S 14.30 E
Walvisbaai = Walvis Bay (EN) 31 Ik 22.59S 14.31 E
Walvisbaai = Walvis Bay (EN) [5] 31 Ik 22.59S 14.31 E
Walvisbaai = Walvis Bay (EN) 30 Ik 22.57S 14.30 E
Walvis Bay/Walvisbaai [3] 37 Ad 23.00S 14.30 E
Walvis Bay (EN) = Walvisbaai 30 Ik 22.57S 14.30 E
Walvis Bay (EN) = Walvisbaai 31 Ik 22.59S 14.31 E
Walvis Ridge (EN) 3 El 28.00S 3.00 E
Wamba 30 Ii 3.56S 17.12 E
Wamba [Kenya] 36 Gb 0.59N 37.19 E
Wamba [Nig.] 34 Gd 8.56N 8.36 E
Wamba [Zaire] 36 Eb 2.09N 28.00 E
Wamena 26 Kg 4.00S 138.57 E
Wami 30 Ki 6.08S 38.49 E
Wampusirpi 49 Ef 15.15N 84.37W
Wamsutter 46 Lf 41.40N 107.58W
Wan 26 Kh 8.23S 137.56 E
Wana 25 Db 32.17N 69.35 E
Wanaka 58 Hi 44.42S 169.08 E
Wanaka, Lake- 62 Cf 44.30S 169.10 E
Wan'an 27 Jf 26.32N 114.48 E
Wanapiri 26 Kg 4.33S 135.59 E
Wanapitei Lake 44 Gb 46.45N 80.45W
Wandel Hav = Wandel Sea (EN) 41 Gb 83.00N 15.00W
Wandel Sea (EN) = Wandel Hav 41 Gb 83.00N 15.00W
Wandsworth, London- 12 Bc 51.27N 0.12W
Wanganui 62 Fc 39.58S 175.00 E
Wanganui 61 Eg 39.56S 175.02 E
Wangaratta 59 Jg 36.22S 146.20 E
Wangcun [China] 28 Df 36.41N 117.42 E
Wangcun [China] 27 Jd 39.58N 112.53 E
Wangda/Zogang 27 Gf 29.37N 97.58 E
Wangdu 28 Ce 38.43N 115.09 E
Wangen in Allgäu 10 Fi 47.41N 9.50 E
Wangerooge 10 Dc 53.46N 7.55 E
Wanggameti, Gunung- 26 Hi 10.07S 120.14 E
Wanggezhuang → Jiaonan 28 Eg 35.53N 119.58 E
Wangiwangi, Pulau- 26 Hh 5.20S 123.35 E
Wangjiang 28 Di 30.08N 116.41 E
Wangkui 27 Mb 46.50N 126.29 E
Wangpan Yang 21 Of 30.33N 121.26 E
Wangping 27 Mc 43.18N 129.46 E
Wangying → Huaiyin 28 Eh 33.35N 119.02 E
Wani, Laguna- 49 Ff 14.50N 83.25W
Wanie-Rukula 36 Eb 0.14N 25.34 E
Wanitsuka-Yama 29 Bf 31.45N 131.17 E
Wanlewëyn 35 Ge 2.35N 44.55 E
Wan Namton 25 Jd 22.03N 99.33 E
Wannian (Chenying) 28 Dj 28.42N 117.04 E
Wanning 27 Jh 18.59N 110.24 E
Wanquan 28 Cd 40.52N 114.44 E
Wansbeck 9 Lf 55.10N 1.34W
Wan Shui 28 Di 30.30N 117.01 E
Wanxian 22 Mf 30.48N 108.21 E
Wanyuan 27 Ie 32.03N 108.04 E
Wanzai 28 Cj 28.06N 114.27 E
Wanzhi → Wuhu 28 Ei 31.21N 118.23 E
Wapato 46 Ec 46.27N 120.25W
Wapiti 46 Kd 44.28N 109.28W
Wapiti 42 Fe 55.08N 118.19W
Wapsipinicon River 45 Kf 41.44N 90.20W
Waqooyi Galbeed [3] 35 Gc 10.00N 44.00 E
Warangal 22 Jh 18.18N 79.35 E
Waratah Bay 59 Jg 38.50S 146.05 E
Warburg 10 Fe 51.30N 9.10 E
Warburger Borde 12 Lc 51.35N 9.12 E
Warburg-Scherfede 12 Lc 51.32N 9.02 E
Warburton Bay 42 Gd 63.50N 111.30W
Warburton Mission 59 Fe 26.10S 126.35 E
Warburton Range 59 Fe 26.10S 126.40 E
Ward 62 Fd 41.50S 174.08 E
Warden 37 De 27.56S 29.00 E
Wardenburg 12 Ka 53.04N 8.12 E
Wardha 25 Fd 20.45N 78.37 E
Ward Hunt Strait 59 Ja 9.25S 149.55 E
Ware [B.C.-Can.] 42 Ee 57.27N 125.38W
Ware [Eng.-U.K.] 12 Bc 51.49N 0.01W
Waregem 12 Fd 50.53N 3.25 E
Waremme/Borgworm 11 Ld 50.42N 5.15 E
Waren [Ger.] 10 Ic 53.31N 12.41 E
Waren [Indon.] 58 Ee 2.16S 136.20 E
Warendorf 10 De 51.57N 7.59 E
Warin Chamrap 25 Ke 15.14N 104.52 E
Warka 10 Re 51.47N 21.10 E
Warkworth 62 Fb 36.24S 174.40 E
Warmbad [3] 37 Be 28.00S 18.30 E
Warmbad [Nam.] 37 Be 28.29S 18.41 E
Warmbad [S.Afr.] 37 Dd 24.53S 28.17 E
Warming Land 41 Gb 81.50N 52.45W
Warmington 12 Ab 52.08N 1.24W
Warminster 9 Kj 51.13N 2.12W
Warm Springs [Nv.-U.S.] 46 Gg 38.13N 116.20W
Warm Springs [Or.-U.S.] 46 Ed 44.46N 121.16W
Warnemünde, Rostock- 10 Ib 54.10N 12.05 E
Warner, Mount- 46 Da 51.03N 123.12W
Warner Mountains 43 Cc 41.40N 120.20W
Warner Peak 46 Fe 42.27N 119.44W
Warner Robins 43 Ke 32.37N 83.36W
Warner Valley 46 Fe 42.30N 119.55W
Warnes 54 Fg 17.30S 63.10W
Warnow 10 Ib 54.06N 12.09 E
Waroona 59 Df 32.50S 115.55 E
Warragul 59 Jg 38.10S 145.56 E
Warrego Range 59 Je 25.00S 145.45 E
Warrego River 57 Fh 30.24S 145.21 E
Warren [Ar.-U.S.] 45 Jj 33.38N 92.05W
Warren [Mi.-U.S.] 44 Fd 42.28N 83.01W
Warren [Mn.-U.S.] 45 Hb 48.12N 96.46W
Warren [Oh.-U.S.] 44 Gd 41.15N 80.49W
Warren [Pa.-U.S.] 44 He 41.52N 79.09W
Warrenpoint/An Pointe 9 Gg 54.06N 6.15W
Warrensburg 45 Jg 38.46N 93.44W
Warrenton 37 Ce 28.09S 24.47 E
Warri 34 Gd 5.31N 5.45 E
Warrington [Eng.-U.K.] 9 Kh 53.24N 2.37W
Warrington [Fl.-U.S.] 44 Dj 30.23N 87.16W
Warrior Reefs 59 Ia 9.35S 143.10 E
Warrnambool 58 Fh 38.23S 142.29 E
Warroad 45 Hb 48.54N 95.19W
Warrumbungle Range 59 Jf 31.30S 149.40 E
Warsaw [In.-U.S.] 44 Ee 41.14N 85.51W
Warsaw [Mo.-U.S.] 45 Jg 38.15N 93.23W
Warsaw [N.Y.-U.S.] 44 Hd 42.45N 78.07W
Warsaw (EN) = Warszawa 6 Ie 52.15N 21.00 E
Warshikh 35 He 2.18N 45.48 E
Warstein 12 Kc 51.27N 8.22 E
Warstein-Belecke 12 Kc 51.29N 8.20 E
Warszawa [2] 10 Qd 52.15N 21.00 E
Warszawa = Warsaw (EN) 6 Ie 52.15N 21.00 E
Warta 5 He 52.35N 14.39 E
Waru 26 Jg 3.24S 130.40 E
Warwich 59 Ke 28.13S 152.02 E
Warwick 9 Li 52.25N 1.30W
Warwick [Eng.-U.K.] 9 Li 52.17N 1.34W
Warwick [R.I.-U.S.] 44 Le 41.42N 71.23W
Warwickshire [3] 9 Li 52.10N 1.35W
Wasagu 34 Gc 11.22N 5.48 E
Wasatch Range 38 He 41.15N 111.30W
Wascana Creek 46 Ma 50.40N 104.55W
Wasco 46 Fi 35.36N 119.20W
Waseca 45 Jd 44.05N 93.30W
Washburn 45 Fc 47.17N 101.02W
Washess Bay 64g Ab 1.49N 157.31W
Wāshim 25 Fd 20.10N 76.58 E
Washington [2] 43 Cb 47.30N 120.30W
Washington [D.C.-U.S.] 39 Lf 38.54N 77.01W
Washington [Eng.-U.K.] 9 Lg 54.54N 1.31W
Washington [Ga.-U.S.] 44 Fi 33.44N 82.44W
Washington [Ia.-U.S.] 45 Kf 41.18N 91.42W
Washington [In.-U.S.] 44 Df 38.40N 87.10W
Washington [N.C.-U.S.] 44 Ih 35.33N 77.03W
Washington [Pa.-U.S.] 44 Ge 40.11N 80.16W
Washington → Teraina Island 57 Kd 4.43N 160.24W
Washington, Mount- 38 Le 44.15N 71.15W
Washington Court House 44 Ff 39.32N 83.29W
Washington Island 45 Md 45.23N 86.55W
Washington Land 41 Fb 80.15N 65.00W
Washita River 45 Hi 34.12N 96.50W
Washtucna 46 Fc 46.45N 118.19W
Wasile 26 If 1.04N 127.59 E
Wasilków 10 Tc 53.12N 23.12 E
Wasior 26 Jg 2.43S 134.30 E
Wāsit [3] 24 Lf 32.35N 46.00 E
Waskaganish 39 Ld 51.25N 78.45W
Wąsosz 10 Me 51.34N 16.42 E
Waspán 47 Hf 14.44N 83.58W
Wassamu 29a Ca 44.02N 142.24 E
Wassenaar 12 Gb 52.09N 4.24 E
Wassenberg 12 Ic 51.06N 6.09 E
Wasserburg am Inn 10 Ih 48.04N 12.14 E
Wasserkuppe 10 Ff 50.30N 9.56 E
Wassigny 12 Fd 50.01N 3.36 E
Wassuk Range 46 Fg 38.40N 118.50W
Wassy 11 Kf 48.30N 4.57 E
Waswanipi, Lac- 44 Ia 49.32N 76.29W
Watampone 22 Oj 4.32S 120.20 E
Watansoppeng 26 Gg 4.21S 119.53 E
Watari 29 Gb 38.02N 140.51 E
Waterbeach 12 Cb 52.16N 0.12 E
Waterberg 37 Bd 20.25S 17.15 E
Waterbury 43 Mc 41.33N 73.02W
Water Cays 49 Ib 23.40N 77.45W
Wateree Pond 44 Gh 34.25N 80.50W
Waterford/Port Láirge 6 Fe 52.15N 7.06W
Waterford/Port Láirge [2] 9 Fi 52.10N 7.40W
Waterford Harbour/Cuan Phort Láirge 9 Gi 52.10N 6.57W
Wateringues 12 Ec 51.00N 2.30 E
Waterloo [Bel.] 11 Kd 50.43N 4.24 E
Waterloo [Ia.-U.S.] 43 Ic 42.30N 92.20W
Waterloo [Il.-U.S.] 45 Kg 38.20N 90.09W
Waterlooville 12 Ad 50.52N 1.01W
Watersmeet 44 Cb 46.18N 89.11W
Watertown [N.Y.-U.S.] 43 Lc 43.57N 75.56W
Watertown [S.D.-U.S.] 43 Hc 44.54N 97.07W
Watertown [Wi.-U.S.] 45 Le 43.12N 88.43W
Waterville 43 Nc 44.33N 69.38W
Watford 9 Mj 51.40N 0.25W
Watford City 45 Ec 47.48N 103.17W
Wa'th 35 Ed 8.10N 32.07 E
Watheroo 59 Df 30.17S 116.04 E
Watīr, Wādī- 24 Fh 29.01N 34.40 E
Watkins Glen 44 Id 42.23N 76.53W
Watling → San Salvador 47 Jd 24.02N 74.28W
Watlington 12 Ac 51.38N 1.00W
Watonga 45 Gi 35.51N 98.25W
Watou, Poperinge- 12 Ed 50.51N 2.37 E
Watrous 42 Gf 51.40N 105.28W
Watsa 31 Jh 3.03N 29.32 E
Watseka 45 Mf 40.47N 87.44W
Watsi [C.R.] 49 Fi 9.37N 82.52W
Watsi [Zaire] 36 Dc 0.19S 21.04 E
Watsi Kengo 36 Dc 0.48S 20.33 E
Watson Lake 39 Gc 60.07N 128.48W
Watsonville 46 Eh 36.55N 121.45W
Watt, Morne- 51g Bb 15.19N 61.19W
Watton 12 Cb 52.34N 0.50 E
Watts Bar Lake 44 Eh 35.48N 84.39W
Wattwil 14 Dc 47.18N 9.05 E
Watubela, Kepulauan- 26 Jg 4.35S 131.40 E
Wau 59 Ja 7.20S 146.45 E
Waubay Lake 45 Hd 45.25N 97.25W
Wauchope 59 Kf 31.27S 152.44 E
Wauchula 44 Gl 27.33N 81.49W
Waucoba Mountain 46 Fh 37.00N 118.01W
Waukara, Gunung- 26 Gg 1.15S 119.42 E
Waukarlycarly, Lake- 59 Ed 21.25S 121.50 E
Waukegan 43 Jc 42.22N 87.50W
Waukesha 45 Le 43.01N 88.14W
Waupaca 45 Ld 44.21N 89.05W
Wausau 43 Jc 44.59N 89.39W
Wauseon 44 Ee 41.33N 84.09W
Wauwatosa 45 Me 43.03N 88.00W
Wave Hill 59 Gc 17.29S 130.57 E
Waveney 9 Oi 52.28N 1.45 E
Waver/Wavre 11 Kd 50.43N 4.37 E
Waverly [Ia.-U.S.] 45 Je 42.44N 92.29W
Waverly [Oh.-U.S.] 44 Ff 39.07N 82.59W
Waverly [Tn.-U.S.] 44 Dg 36.05N 87.48W
Waves 44 Jh 35.37N 75.29W
Wavre/Waver 12 Kd 50.43N 4.37 E
Wāw 31 Jh 7.42N 28.00 E
Wawa [Nig.] 34 Fd 9.55N 4.27 E
Wawa [Ont.-Can.] 42 Jg 47.59N 84.47W
Wawa, Rio- 49 Fg 13.53N 83.28W
Wāw al Kabīr 31 If 25.20N 16.43 E
Wāw an Nāmūs 33 Ce 24.55N 19.45 E
Wāw Nahr 35 Dd 7.03N 27.13 E
Wawo 26 Hg 3.41S 121.02 E
Wawotobi 26 Hg 3.51S 122.06 E
Waxahachie 45 Hj 32.24N 96.51W
Waxweiler 12 Id 50.06N 6.22 E
Waxxari 27 Ed 38.37N 87.22 E
Way, Lake- 59 Ee 26.50S 120.20 E
Waya 63d Ab 17.18S 177.08 E
Wayabula 26 If 2.17N 128.12 E
Wayan 46 Je 43.00N 111.22W
Waycross 43 Ke 31.13N 82.21W
Wayne [Nb.-U.S.] 45 He 42.14N 97.01W
Wayne [W.V.-U.S.] 44 Ff 38.14N 82.27W
Waynesboro [Ga.-U.S.] 44 Fi 33.06N 82.01W
Waynesboro [Ms.-U.S.] 45 Lk 31.40N 88.39W
Waynesboro [Pa.-U.S.] 44 If 39.45N 77.36W
Waynesboro [Va.-U.S.] 44 Hf 38.04N 78.54W
Waynesville [Mo.-U.S.] 45 Jh 37.50N 92.12W
Waynesville [N.C.-U.S.] 44 Fh 35.29N 83.00W
Waynoka 45 Gh 36.35N 98.53W
Waziers 12 Fd 50.23N 3.07 E
Wda 10 Oc 53.25N 18.29 E
Wdzydze, Jezioro- 10 Nc 54.00N 17.50 E
Wé 61 Cd 20.55S 167.16 E
We, Pulau- 26 Ce 5.51N 95.18 E
Wear 9 Lg 54.55N 1.22W
Weatherford [Ok.-U.S.] 45 Gi 35.32N 98.42W
Weatherford [Tx.-U.S.] 43 He 32.46N 97.48W
Weaverville 46 Df 40.44N 122.56W
Weber 62 Gd 40.24S 176.20 E
Webster 45 Hd 45.20N 97.31W
Webster City 45 Je 42.28N 93.49W
Webster Springs 44 Gf 38.29N 80.25W
Weda 26 If 0.21N 127.52 E
Weda, Teluk- 26 If 0.20N 128.00 E
Weddell Island 56 Hh 51.50S 61.00W
Weddell Sea (EN) 66 Rf 72.00S 45.00W
Wedel 10 Fc 53.35N 9.41 E
Wedgeport 44 Od 43.44N 65.59W
Wedza 37 Ec 18.35S 31.35 E
Weed 46 Df 41.25N 122.27W
Weener 10 Dc 53.10N 7.21 E
Weerdinge, Emmen- 12 Ib 52.49N 6.57 E
Weert 11 Lc 51.15N 5.43 E
Weesp 12 Hb 52.18N 5.02 E
Wegberg 12 Ic 51.09N 6.16 E
Węgliniec 10 Le 51.17N 15.13 E
Węgorzewo 10 Rb 54.14N 21.44 E
Węgrów 10 Sd 52.25N 22.01 E
Wehni 35 Fc 12.40N 36.42 E
Weichang (Zhuizishan) 28 Kc 41.55N 117.45 E
Weida 10 If 50.46N 12.04 E
Weiden in der Oberpfalz 10 Ig 49.41N 12.10 E
Weifang 22 Nf 36.43N 119.06 E
Weihai 27 Ld 37.27N 122.02 E
Weihe 28 Jh 44.55N 128.23 E
Wei He 21 Nf 34.36N 110.10 E
Weilburg 10 Ef 50.29N 8.15 E
Weilerbach 12 Je 49.29N 7.38 E
Weilerswist 12 Id 50.46N 6.50 E
Weilheim in Oberbayern 10 Hi 47.50N 11.09 E
Weilmünster 12 Kd 50.26N 8.21 E
Weimar [Ger.] 12 Kd 50.46N 8.43 E
Weimar [Ger.] 10 Hf 50.59N 11.19 E
Weinan 27 Ie 34.30N 109.34 E
Weingarten 10 Fi 47.48N 9.38 E
Weinheim 10 Eg 49.33N 8.40 E
Weining 27 Hf 26.46N 104.18 E
Weinsberger Wald 14 Ib 48.25N 15.00 E
Weinstraße 12 Ke 49.20N 8.05 E
Weinviertel 14 Kb 48.35N 16.30 E
Weipa 58 Ff 12.41S 141.52 E
Weirton 44 Ge 40.24N 80.37W
Weiser 46 Gd 44.15N 116.58W
Weiser River 46 Gd 44.15N 116.59W
Weishan Hu 27 Ke 34.35N 117.15 E
Weishi 28 Cg 34.25N 114.10 E
Weishui → Jingxing 28 Ce 38.03N 114.09 E
Weiße Elster 10 He 51.26N 11.57 E
Weißenberg 12 Je 49.15N 7.49 E
Weißenburg in Bayern 10 Gg 49.02N 10.59 E
Weißenfels 10 He 51.12N 11.58 E
Weißer Main 10 Hf 50.05N 11.24 E
Weißerstein 12 Id 50.24N 6.22 E
Weißkugel/Palla Bianca 14 Ed 46.48N 10.44 E
Weiss Lake 44 Eh 34.15N 85.35W
Weißwasser/Běła Woda 10 Ke 51.31N 14.38 E
Weitra 14 Ib 48.42N 14.53 E
Weixi 27 Gf 27.13N 99.19 E
Weixian 28 Cf 36.59N 115.15 E
Weixin (Zhaxi) 27 If 27.46N 105.04 E
Weiz 14 Jc 47.13N 15.37 E
Wejherowo 10 Ob 54.37N 18.15 E
Welbourn Hill 58 Eg 27.21S 134.06 E
Welch 44 Gg 37.26N 81.36W
Weldiya 35 Fc 11.48N 39.35 E
Weld Range 59 De 26.55S 117.25 E
Welega [3] 35 Fd 8.38N 35.40 E
Welel 35 Ed 8.56N 34.52 E
Weligama 25 Gg 5.58N 80.25 E
Welkenraedt 12 Hd 50.39N 5.58 E
Welker Seamount (EN) 40 Ke 55.07N 140.20W
Welkite 35 Fd 8.17N 37.49 E
Welkom 31 Jk 27.59S 26.45 E
Welland 42 Jh 42.59N 79.15W
Welland 9 Ni 52.53N 0.02 E
Welland Canal 44 Hd 43.14N 79.13W
Wellesley Islands 57 Ef 16.45S 139.30 E
Wellin 12 Hd 50.05N 5.07 E
Wellingborough 9 Mi 52.19N 0.42W
Wellington [2] 62 Fd 40.10S 175.30 E
Wellington [Austl.] 59 Jf 32.33S 148.57 E
Wellington [Eng.-U.K.] 9 Jk 50.59N 3.14W
Wellington [Ks.-U.S.] 45 Hh 37.16N 97.24W
Wellington [Nv.-U.S.] 46 Fg 38.45N 119.22W
Wellington [N.Z.] 58 Ii 41.17S 174.46 E
Wellington, Isla- 52 Ij 49.20S 74.40W
Wellington, Lake- 59 Jg 38.10S 147.15 E
Wellington Channel 42 Ia 75.10N 93.00W
Wells [Eng.-U.K.] 9 Kj 51.13N 2.39W
Wells [Nv.-U.S.] 43 Dc 41.07N 115.01W
Wells, Lake- 59 Ee 26.45S 123.15 E
Wells, Mount- 59 Fc 17.26S 127.14 E
Wellsboro 44 Ie 41.45N 77.18W
Wellsford 62 Fb 36.18S 174.31 E
Wells-next-the-Sea 9 Ni 52.58N 0.51 E
Wellton 46 Hj 32.40N 114.08W
Welmel 35 Gd 5.35N 40.55 E
Welna 10 Md 52.36N 16.50 E
Welo [3] 35 Fc 12.00N 40.00 E
Wels 14 Ib 48.10N 14.02 E
Welshpool 9 Ji 52.40N 3.09W
Welver 12 Jc 51.37N 7.58 E
Welwitschia 37 Ad 20.21S 14.57 E
Welwyn Garden City 9 Mj 51.48N 0.13W
Wema 36 Dc 0.26S 21.38 E
Wemding 10 Gh 48.52N 10.43 E
Wen'an 28 De 38.52N 116.30 E
Wenatchee 43 Cb 47.25N 120.19W
Wenatchee Mountains 46 Ec 47.20N 120.45W
Wenchang 27 Jh 19.43N 110.44 E
Wenchi 34 Ed 7.44N 2.06W
Wenchit 35 Fc 10.03N 38.35 E
Wenden 12 Jd 50.58N 7.52 E
Wendeng 27 Ld 37.10N 122.01 E
Wendland 10 Gc 53.10N 11.00 E
Wendo 35 Fd 6.37N 38.25 E
Wengyuan (Longxian) 27 Jg 24.21N 114.13 E
Wen He 28 Ef 37.06N 119.29 E
Wenling 27 Lf 28.23N 121.22 E
Wenquan 27 Fe 33.15N 91.55 E
Wenquan/Arixang 27 Dc 44.59N 81.04 E
Wenshan 27 Hg 23.22N 104.23 E
Wenshui 28 Bf 37.26N 112.01 E
Wensu 27 Dc 41.15N 80.14 E
Wensum 12 Db 52.37N 1.22 E
Wentworth 59 If 34.07S 141.55 E
Wenxian 27 He 32.52N 104.40 E
Wenzhou 22 Og 27.57N 120.38 E
Wenzhu 27 Jf 27.00N 114.00 E
Wepener 37 De 29.46S 27.00 E
Wépion, Namur- 12 Gd 50.25N 4.52 E
Werda 37 Ce 25.16S 23.17 E
Werder 31 Lh 7.00N 45.21 E
Werder 10 Jc 53.40N 13.25 E
Werdohl 12 Jc 51.16N 7.46 E
Were Ilu 35 Fc 10.38N 39.23 E
Werkendam 12 Gc 51.49N 4.55 E
Werl 12 Jc 51.33N 7.55 E
Werlte 12 Jb 52.51N 7.41 E
Wermelskirchen 12 Jc 51.09N 7.13 E
Werne 12 Jc 51.40N 7.38 E
Wernigerode 10 Ge 51.50N 10.47 E
Werra 5 Ge 51.26N 9.39 E
Werribee 59 Ig 37.54S 144.40 E
Werris Creek 59 Kf 31.21S 150.39 E
Werse 12 Jb 52.02N 7.41 E
Wertach 10 Gh 48.24N 10.53 E
Wertheim 10 Fg 49.45N 9.31 E
Wesel 12 Ce 51.40N 6.37 E
Weser 5 Ge 53.32N 8.34 E
Weserbergland 10 Fe 51.55N 9.30 E
Wesergebirge 10 Fd 52.15N 9.10 E
Weslaco 45 Gm 26.09N 98.01W
Wesley 51g Ba 15.34N 61.19W
Wesleyville 42 Mg 49.09N 53.34W
Wessel, Cape- 59 Hb 11.00S 136.45 E
Wesseling 12 Id 50.50N 6.59 E
Wessel Islands 57 Ef 12.00S 136.45 E
Wessington Springs 45 Gd 44.05N 98.34W
West Allis 45 Me 43.01N 88.00W
West Baines River 59 Gc 15.26S 130.08 E
West Bay 45 Ll 29.00N 89.30W
West Bend 45 Le 43.25N 88.11W
West Bengal [3] 25 Hd 24.00N 88.00 E
West Berlin (EN) = Berlin 6 He 52.31N 13.24 E
West Branch 44 Ec 44.17N 84.14W
West Bridgford 12 Ab 52.55N 1.07W
West Bromwich 9 Li 52.31N 1.59W
Westbrook 44 Ld 43.41N 70.21W
West Burra 9 La 60.05N 1.10W
West Caicos 49 Kc 21.47N 72.17W
West Cape 57 Hi 45.55S 166.26 E
West Caroline Basin (EN) 3 Ii 4.00N 138.00 E
West Carpathians (EN) = Západné Karpaty 10 Og 49.30N 19.00 E
West Des Moines 45 Jf 41.35N 93.43W
Westdongeradeel 12 Ha 53.23N 5.58 E
Westdongeradeel-Holwerd 12 Ha 53.22N 5.54 E
Westdongeradeel-Ternaard 12 Ha 53.23N 5.58 E
Westeinderplassen 12 Gb 52.15N 4.30 E
West Elk Mountains 45 Cg 38.40N 107.15W
West End 44 Hl 26.41N 78.58W
Westende, Middelkerke- 12 Ec 51.10N 2.46 E
West End Village 51b Ab 18.11N 63.09W
West Entrance 64a Bb 7.57N 134.30 E
Westerbork 12 Ib 52.51N 6.36 E
Westerburg 12 Jd 50.34N 7.59 E
Westerland 10 Eb 54.54N 8.18 E
Westerlo 12 Gc 51.05N 4.55 E
Western [Ghana] [3] 34 Ed 5.30N 2.30W
Western [Kenya] [3] 36 Fb 0.30N 34.35 E
Western [S.L.] [3] 34 Cd 8.20N 13.00W
Western [Ug.] [3] 36 Fb 1.00N 31.00 E
Western [Zam.] [3] 36 Df 15.00S 24.00 E
Western Australia [2] 59 Ed 25.00S 122.00 E
Western Desert (EN) = Gharbīyah, Aş Şaḩrā' al- 30 Jf 27.30N 28.00 E
Western Dvina (EN) = Zapadnaja Dvina 5 Id 57.04N 24.03 E
Western Entrance 63a Bb 6.55S 155.40 E
Western Ghats/Sahyadri 21 Jh 14.00N 75.00 E
Western Isles [3] 9 Fd 57.40N 7.10W
Western Port 59 Jg 38.25S 145.10 E
Western River 42 Gc 66.22N 107.15W
Western Sahara (EN) [5] 31 Ff 24.30N 13.00W

Index Symbols

[1] Independent Nation
[2] State, Region
[3] District, County
[4] Municipality
[5] Colony, Dependency
Continent
Physical Region
Historical or Cultural Region
Mount, Mountain
Volcano
Hill
Mountains, Mountain Range
Hills, Escarpment
Plateau, Upland
Pass, Gap
Plain, Lowland
Delta
Salt Flat
Valley, Canyon
Crater, Cave
Karst Features
Depression
Polder
Desert, Dunes
Forest, Woods
Heath, Steppe
Oasis
Cape, Point
Coast, Beach
Cliff
Peninsula
Isthmus
Sandbank
Island
Atoll
Rock, Reef
Islands, Archipelago
Rocks, Reefs
Coral Reef
Well, Spring
Geyser
River, Stream
Waterfall Rapids
River Mouth, Estuary
Lake
Salt Lake
Intermittent Lake
Reservoir
Swamp, Pond
Canal
Glacier
Ice Shelf, Pack Ice
Ocean
Sea
Gulf, Bay
Strait, Fjord
Lagoon
Bank
Seamount
Tablemount
Ridge
Shelf
Basin
Escarpment, Sea Scarp
Fracture
Trench, Abyss
National Park, Reserve
Point of Interest
Recreation Site
Cave, Cavern
Historic Site
Ruins
Wall, Walls
Church, Abbey
Temple
Scientific Station
Airport
Port
Lighthouse
Mine
Tunnel
Dam, Bridge

Western Samoa (EN) = Samoa I Sisifo [1] 58 Jf 13.40S 172.30W
Western Sayans (EN) = Zapadny Sajan 21 Ld 53.00N 94.00E
Western Sierra Madre (EN) = Madre Occidental, Sierra- 38 Ig 25.00N 105.00W
Western Turkistan (EN) 21 He 41.00N 60.00E
Westerschelde = West Schelde (EN) 11 Jc 51.25N 3.45E
Westerschouwen 12 Fc 51.41N 3.43E
Westerschouwen-Haamstede 12 Fc 51.42N 3.45E
Westerstede 10 Dc 53.15N 7.56E
Westerwald 10 Df 50.40N 7.55E
Westerwoldse A 12 Ja 53.10N 7.10E
West European Basin (EN) 3 De 47.00N 15.00W
West Falkland 52 Kk 51.40S 60.00W
West Falkland/Gran Malvina, Isla- 52 Kk 51.40S 60.00W
West Fayu Island 57 Fd 8.05N 146.44E
West Fork Big Blue River 45 Hf 40.42N 96.59W
Westfriesland = West Friesland (EN) 11 Kb 52.45N 4.50E
West Friesland (EN) = Westfriesland 11 Kb 52.45N 4.50E
West Frisian Islands (EN) = Waddeneilanden 11 Ka 53.30N 5.00E
Westgate-on-Sea 12 Dc 51.22N 1.21E
West Glacier 46 Ib 48.30N 113.59W
West Glamorgan [3] 9 Jj 51.40N 3.55W
West Grand Lake 44 Nc 45.15N 67.52W
West Greenland (EN) = Vestgrønland [2] 41 He 69.00N 49.30W
West Helena 45 Ki 34.33N 90.39W
West Hollywood 44 Gm 25.59N 80.11W
Westhope 45 Fb 48.55N 101.01W
West Ice Shelf 66 Ge 67.00S 85.00E
West Indies 47 Je 19.00N 70.00W
West Indies (EN) = Indias Occidentales 47 Je 19.00N 70.00W
West Island 37b Ab 9.22S 46.13E
Westkapelle 12 Fc 51.31N 3.26E
Westkapelle, Knokke- 12 Fc 51.19N 3.18E
West Lafayette 44 De 40.27N 86.55W
Westland [2] 62 De 43.10S 170.30E
West Liberty 44 Fg 37.55N 83.16W
Westlock 42 Gf 54.09N 113.52W
West Lunga 36 De 13.06S 24.39E
Westmalle 12 Gc 51.18N 4.41E
West Mariana Basin (EN) 3 Ih 15.00N 137.00E
Westmeath/An Iarmhi [2] 9 Fh 53.30N 7.30W
West Melanesian Trench (EN) 60 Dh 1.00S 150.00E
West Memphis 43 Id 35.08N 90.11W
West Mersea 12 Cc 51.46N 0.54E
West Midlands [3] 9 Li 52.30N 2.00W
Westminster 44 If 39.35N 76.59W
Westminster, London- 12 Bc 51.30N 0.07W
West Monroe 45 Jj 32.31N 92.09W
Westmorland 9 Kg 54.30N 2.40W
West Nicholson 31 Jk 21.03S 29.22E
West Nueces River 45 Gl 29.16N 99.56W
Weston [Mala.] 26 Ge 5.13N 115.36E
Weston [W.V.-U.S.] 44 Gf 39.03N 80.28W
Weston [Wy.-U.S.] 46 Md 44.42N 105.18W
Weston-super-Mare 9 Kj 51.21N 2.59W
Westoverledingen 12 Ja 53.10N 7.27E
Westoverledingen - Ihrhove 12 Ja 53.10N 7.27E
West Palm Beach 39 Kg 26.43N 80.04W
West Pensacola 44 Dj 30.27N 87.15W
West Plains 43 Id 36.44N 91.51W
West Point [Ms.-U.S.] 45 Lj 33.36N 88.39W
West Point [Nb.-U.S.] 45 Hf 41.51N 96.43W
Westport 58 Ii 41.45S 171.36E
Westport/Cathair na Mart 9 Dh 53.48N 9.32W
Westray 9 Kb 59.20N 3.00W
Westree 44 Gb 47.27N 81.32W
Westrich 12 Je 49.20N 7.25E
West Road 12 Cd 50.52N 0.50E
West Schelde (EN) = Westerschelde 11 Jc 51.25N 3.45E
West Scotia Basin (EN) 52 Kk 57.00S 53.00W
West Siberian Plain (EN) = Zapadno Sibirskaja Ravnina 21 Jc 60.00N 75.00E
Weststellingwerf 12 Ib 52.53N 6.00E
Weststellingwerf-Wolvega 12 Ib 52.53N 6.00E
West Sussex [3] 9 Mk 51.00N 0.40W
West Tavaputs Plateau 46 Jf 40.00N 110.25W
West-Terschelling, Terschelling- 12 Ha 53.21N 5.13E
West Union [Ia.-U.S.] 45 Ke 42.57N 91.49W
West Union [Oh.-U.S.] 44 Ff 38.48N 83.33W
West Virginia [2] 43 Kd 38.45N 80.30W
West-Vlaanderen [3] 12 Ec 51.00N 3.00E
Westwood 46 Ef 40.18N 121.00W
West Wyalong 59 Jf 33.55S 147.13E
West Yellowstone 43 Eb 44.30N 111.05W
West Yorkshire [3] 9 Lh 53.40N 1.30W
Wetar, Pulau- 57 De 7.48S 126.18E
Wetaskiwin 42 Gf 52.58N 113.22W
Wete 36 Gd 5.04S 39.43E
Wětošow/Vetschau 10 Ke 51.47N 14.04E
Wetter 12 Kd 50.18N 8.49E
Wetter (Hessen) 12 Kd 50.54N 8.43E
Wetter (Ruhr) 12 Jc 51.23N 7.24E
Wetterau 10 Ef 50.15N 8.50E
Wetteren 11 Jc 51.00N 3.53E
Wetzlar 10 Ef 50.33N 8.30E
Wevelgem 12 Fd 50.48N 3.10E
Wewahitchka 44 Ej 30.07N 85.12W
Wewak 58 Fe 3.34S 143.38E
Wexford/Loch Garman [2] 9 Gi 52.20N 6.40W
Wexford/Loch Garman 6 Fe 52.20N 6.27W
Wexford Harbour/Cuan Loch Garman 9 Gi 52.20N 6.25W
Wey 9 Mj 51.23N 0.28W
Weyburn 42 Hg 49.41N 103.52W
Weyhe 12 Kb 52.59N 8.52E
Weyhe-Leeste 12 Kb 52.59N 8.50E
Weymouth 9 Kk 50.36N 2.28W
Wezet/Visé 12 Hd 50.44N 5.42E
Whakatane 61 Eg 37.58S 177.00E
Whale Cove 42 Id 62.14N 92.10W
Whalsay 9 Ma 60.22N 0.59W
Whangarei 58 Ih 35.43S 174.19E
Wharfe 9 Lh 53.51N 1.07W
Wharton 45 Hl 29.19N 96.06W
Wharton Basin (EN) 3 Hk 19.00S 100.00E
Wharton Lake 42 Hd 64.00N 99.55W
Whataroa 62 De 43.16S 170.22E
Wheatland 46 Me 42.03N 104.57W
Wheat Ridge 45 Dg 39.46N 105.07W
Wheeler 42 Ke 57.02N 67.14W
Wheeler 46 Dd 45.42N 123.52W
Wheeler Lake 44 Dh 34.40N 87.05W
Wheeler Peak [N.M.-U.S.] 43 Fd 36.34N 105.25W
Wheeler Peak [U.S.] 38 Hf 38.59N 114.19W
Wheeling 43 Kc 40.05N 80.43W
Whidbey Island 46 Db 48.15N 122.40W
Whitby 9 Mg 54.29N 0.37W
Whitchurch [Eng.-U.K.] 9 Ki 52.58N 2.41W
Whitchurch [Eng.-U.K.] 12 Bc 51.53N 0.50W
Whitchurch [Eng.-U.K.] 12 Ac 51.13N 1.20W
White 42 Jc 65.50N 85.00W
White, Lake- 59 Fd 21.05S 129.00E
White Bay 38 Nd 50.00N 56.30W
White Bear Lake 45 Jd 45.04N 93.01W
White Butte 45 Ec 46.23N 103.19W
White Carpathians (EN) = Bílé Karpaty 10 Nh 48.55N 17.50E
White Cliffs 59 If 30.51S 143.05E
White Cloud 44 Ed 43.33N 85.46W
Whitecourt 42 Ff 54.09N 115.41W
Whitefish 43 Eb 48.25N 114.20W
Whitefish Bay 43 Kb 46.40N 84.50W
Whitefish Point 43 Eb 46.45N 85.00W
Whitefish Range 46 Hb 48.40N 114.26W
Whitehall [Mi.-U.S.] 44 Dd 43.24N 86.21W
Whitehall [Mt.-U.S.] 46 Id 45.52N 112.06W
Whitehall [Oh.-U.S.] 44 Ff 39.58N 82.54W
Whitehall [Wi.-U.S.] 45 Kd 44.22N 91.19W
Whitehaven 9 Jg 54.33N 3.35W
Whitehorse 39 Fc 60.43N 135.03W
White Island [Ant.] 66 Ee 66.44S 48.35E
White Island [N.Z.] 62 Gb 37.30S 177.10E
White Lake 45 Jl 29.45N 92.30W
White Lake (EN) = Beloje Ozero 5 Jc 60.11N 37.35E
Whiteman Range 59 Ja 5.50S 149.55E
Whitemark 59 Jh 40.07S 148.01E
White Mountain 40 Db 64.35N 163.04W
White Mountain Peak 43 Dd 37.38N 118.15W
White Mountains [Ak.-U.S.] 40 Jc 65.30N 147.00W
White Mountains [U.S.] 46 Fh 37.30N 118.15W
White Mountains [U.S.] 43 Mc 44.10N 71.35W
Whitemouth Lake 45 Ib 49.14N 95.40W
Whitemouth River 45 Ha 50.07N 96.02W
White Nile (EN) = Abyaḍ, Al Baḥr al- 30 Kg 15.38N 32.31E
White Nile (EN) = Abyaḍ, Al Baḥr al- [3] 35 Ec 12.40N 32.30E
White Pass [N.Amer.] 40 Le 59.37N 135.08W
White Pass [Wa.-U.S.] 46 Ec 46.38N 121.24W
Whiteriver 46 Kj 33.50N 109.58W
White River [In.-U.S.] 44 Df 38.25N 87.44W
White River [Nv.-U.S.] 46 Hh 37.18N 115.08W
White River [Ont.-Can.] 42 Ig 48.35N 85.17W
White River [S.D.-U.S.] 45 Fe 43.34N 100.45W
White River [Tx.-U.S.] 45 Fj 33.14N 100.56W
White River [U.S.] 46 Kf 40.04N 109.41W
White River [U.S.] 45 Hc 43.45N 99.30W
White River [U.S.] 38 Jf 33.53N 91.03W
White River [Yuk.-Can.] 42 Dd 63.10N 139.32W
White Salmon 46 Ed 45.44N 121.29W
Whitesand Bay 9 Ik 50.20N 4.35W
White Sea (EN) = Beloje More 5 Kb 66.00N 44.00E
White sea-Baltic Canal (EN) = Belomorsko-Baltijski Kanal 5 Jc 63.30N 34.48E
White Settlement 45 Hj 32.45N 97.27W
White Sulphur Springs 46 Jc 46.33N 110.54W
Whiteville 44 Hh 34.20N 78.42W
White Volta 30 Gh 8.38N 0.59W
White Volta (EN) = Volta Blanche 30 Gh 8.38N 0.59W
Whitewater 45 Bg 38.59N 108.27W
Whitewater Baldy 45 Bj 33.20N 108.39W
Whitewater Bay 44 Gm 25.16N 81.00W
Whitewater Lake 45 La 50.50N 89.10W
Whitewood 45 Ea 50.20N 102.15W
Whitianga 62 Fb 36.50S 175.42E
Whitmore Mountains 66 Og 82.35S 104.30W
Whitney 44 Hc 45.30N 78.14W
Whitney, Lake- 45 Hk 31.55N 97.23W
Whitney, Mount- 38 Hf 36.35N 118.18W
Whitstable 12 Dc 51.21N 1.06E
Whitsunday Island 59 Jd 20.15S 149.00E
Whittier 40 Jd 60.46N 148.41W
Whittlesea 59 Jg 37.31S 145.07E
Whittlesey 12 Bb 52.33N 0.08W
Wholdaia Lake 42 Hd 60.45N 104.10W
Whyalla 59 Hf 33.02S 137.35E
Wiarton 44 Gc 44.45N 81.09W
Wiawso 34 Ed 6.12N 2.29W
Wibaux 46 Mc 46.59N 104.11W
Wichita 39 Jf 37.41N 97.20W
Wichita Falls 39 Jf 33.54N 98.30W
Wichita Mountains 45 Gi 34.45N 98.40W
Wichita River 45 Gi 34.07N 98.10W
Wick 9 Jc 58.26N 3.06W
Wick 9 Jc 58.25N 3.05W
Wickenburg 46 Ij 33.58N 112.44W
Wickepin 59 Df 32.46S 117.30E
Wickham 12 Ad 50.54N 1.10W
Wickham Market 12 Db 52.09N 1.22E
Wickiup Reservoir 46 Ee 43.40N 121.43W
Wickliffe 44 Cg 36.58N 89.05W
Wicklow/Cill Mhantáin [2] 9 Gi 53.00N 6.30W
Wicklow/Cill Mhantáin 9 Gi 52.59N 6.03W
Wicklow Head/Ceann Chill Mhantáin 9 Hi 52.58N 6.00W
Wicklow Mountains/Sléibhte Chill Mhantáin 9 Gh 53.02N 6.24W
Wicko, Jezioro- 10 Mb 54.33N 16.35E
Wickrath, Mönchengladbach- 12 Ic 51.08N 6.25E
Widawa 10 Me 51.13N 16.55E
Wide Bay 59 Ka 5.05S 152.05E
Widefield 45 Dg 38.42N 104.40W
Widgiemooltha 59 Ef 31.30S 121.34E
Wi-Do 28 Ig 35.38N 126.17E
Więcbork 10 Nc 53.22N 17.30E
Wied 12 Jd 50.27N 7.28E
Wiedenbrück 12 Kc 50.51N 8.19E
Wiehengebirge 12 Ed 52.20N 8.40E
Wiehl 12 Jd 50.57N 7.32E
Wieliczka 10 Qg 49.59N 20.04E
Wielimie, Jezioro- 10 Mc 53.47N 16.50E
Wielki Dział 10 Tf 50.18N 23.25E
Wielkopolska 10 Ne 51.50N 17.20E
Wielkopolskie-Kujawskie, Pojezierze- 10 Md 52.25N 16.30E
Wieluń 10 Oe 51.14N 18.34E
Wien [2] 14 Kb 48.15N 16.25E
Wien = Vienna (EN) 6 Hf 48.12N 16.22E
Wiener Becken 14 Kc 48.00N 16.28E
Wiener Neustadt 14 Kc 47.48N 16.15E
Wienerwald = Vienna Woods (EN) 14 Jb 48.10N 16.00E
Wieprz 10 Re 51.32N 21.49E
Wieprza 10 Mb 54.26N 16.22E
Wieprz-Krzna, Kanał- 10 Se 51.56N 22.56E
Wierden 12 Ib 52.22N 6.36E
Wieringen 12 Hb 52.56N 5.02E
Wieringen-Den Oever 12 Hb 52.56N 5.02E
Wieringen-Hippolytushoef 12 Gb 52.54N 4.59E
Wieringermeer 12 Hb 52.51N 5.01E
Wieringermeer Polder 12 Gb 52.50N 5.00E
Wieringermeer-Wieringerwerf 12 Hb 52.51N 5.01E
Wieringerwerf, Wieringermeer- 12 Hb 52.51N 5.01E
Wieruszów 10 Oe 51.18N 18.08E
Wierzchowo, Jezioro- 10 Mc 53.50N 16.45E
Wierzyca 10 Oc 53.51N 18.50E
Wiesbaden 6 Ge 50.05N 8.15E
Wiese 10 Di 47.35N 7.35E
Wieslautern 12 Je 49.05N 7.49E
Wiesloch 10 Eg 49.18N 8.42E
Wietingsmoor 12 Kb 52.39N 8.39E
Wietmarschen 12 Jb 52.32N 7.08E
Wieżyca 10 Ob 54.17N 18.10E
Wigan 9 Kh 53.32N 2.35W
Wigger 14 Bc 47.15N 7.55E
Wiggins 45 Lk 30.51N 89.08W
Wight, Isle of- 5 Fe 50.40N 1.20W
Wigry, Jezioro- 10 Tb 54.05N 23.07E
Wigston 12 Ab 52.35N 1.06W
Wigtown 9 Ig 54.52N 4.26W
Wigtown Bay 9 Ig 54.46N 4.15W
Wijchen 12 Hc 51.48N 5.44E
Wijdefjorden 41 Nc 79.50N 15.30E
Wijk bij Duurstede 12 Hc 51.59N 5.22E
Wil 14 Dc 47.27N 9.05E
Wilbur 46 Fc 47.46N 118.42W
Wilburton 45 Ii 34.55N 95.19W
Wilcannia 58 Fh 31.34S 143.23E
Wild Coast 30 Jl 32.00S 29.50E
Wilder Seamount (EN) 57 Jd 9.00N 173.00W
Wildeshausen 10 Ed 52.54N 8.26E
Wild Horse 46 Jb 49.01N 110.12W
Wildspitze 14 Ed 46.53N 10.52E
Wilga 10 Re 51.50N 21.20E
Wilhelm-II-Land 66 Ge 69.00S 90.00E
Wilhelminakanaal 12 Gc 51.43N 4.53E
Wilhelmshaven 10 Ec 53.31N 8.08E
Wilhelmstal 37 Bd 21.54S 16.20E
Wilkes-Barre 43 Lc 41.15N 75.50W
Wilkesboro 44 Gg 36.09N 81.09W
Wilkes Land (EN) 66 Hf 71.00S 120.00E
Wilkins Coast 66 Qe 69.40S 63.00W
Wilkins Sound 66 Qf 70.15S 73.00W
Willamette River 46 Dd 45.39N 122.46W
Willandra Billabong Creek 59 If 33.08S 144.06E
Willapa Bay 46 Cc 46.37N 124.00W
Willard 45 Ci 34.36N 106.02W
Willards, Punta- 48 Cc 28.50N 112.35W
Willcox 46 Kj 32.15N 109.50W
Willebadessen 12 Lc 51.38N 9.02E
Willebadessen-Peckelsheim 12 Lc 51.36N 9.08E
Willebroek 12 Gc 51.04N 4.22E
Willemstad [Neth.] 12 Gc 51.41N 4.26E
Willemstad [Neth.Ant.] 53 Jd 12.06N 68.56W
Willeroo 59 Gc 15.17S 131.35E
William Bill Dannelly Reservoir 44 Di 32.15N 86.45W
Williams 43 Ed 35.15N 112.11W
Williamsburg [Ky.-U.S.] 44 Eg 36.44N 84.10W
Williamsburg [Va.-U.S.] 44 Ig 37.17N 76.43W
Williams Lake 42 Ff 52.08N 122.09W
Williamson Glacier 66 He 66.30S 114.30E
Williamsport 43 Lc 41.16N 77.03W
Williamston 44 Ih 35.50N 77.06W
Williamstown 44 Ef 38.38N 84.34W
Willich 12 Ic 51.16N 6.33E
Willikie's 51d Bb 17.03N 61.42W
Willingdon, Mount- 46 Ga 51.48N 116.17W
Willis Group 57 Gf 16.20S 150.00E
Williston [N.D.-U.S.] 43 Gb 48.09N 103.37W
Williston [S.Afr.] 37 Cf 31.20S 20.53E
Williston Lake 38 Gd 50.57N 122.23W
Willits 46 Dg 39.25N 123.21W
Willmar 43 Hb 45.07N 95.03W
Willoughby Bay 51d Bb 17.02N 61.44W
Willow Bunch Lake 46 Mb 49.27N 105.28W
Willowlake 42 Fd 62.42N 123.08W
Willowmore 37 Cf 33.17S 23.29E
Willows 46 Dg 39.31N 122.12W
Willow Springs 45 Kh 36.59N 91.58W
Wills, Lake- 59 Fd 21.20S 128.40E
Wills Point 45 Ij 32.43N 95.57W
Wilma Glacier 66 Ee 67.12S 56.00E
Wilmington [De.-U.S.] 43 Ld 39.44N 75.33W
Wilmington [N.C.-U.S.] 39 Lf 34.13N 77.55W
Wilmington [Oh.-U.S.] 44 Ff 39.28N 83.50W
Wilnsdorf 12 Kd 50.49N 8.06E
Wilseder Berg 10 Fc 53.10N 9.56E
Wilson 43 Ld 35.44N 77.55W
Wilson, Cape- 42 Jc 66.59N 81.27W
Wilson, Mount- 45 Ch 37.51N 107.59W
Wilson Bluff 66 Ff 74.20S 66.47E
Wilson Lake [Al.-U.S.] 44 Dh 34.49N 87.30W
Wilson Lake [Ks.-U.S.] 45 Gg 38.57N 98.40W
Wilsons Promontory 59 Jg 38.55S 146.20E
Wilton River 59 Gb 14.45S 134.33E
Wilts 9 Lj 51.20N 2.00W
Wiltshire [3] 9 Lj 51.30N 2.00W
Wiltz 11 Le 49.58N 5.55E
Wiluna 58 Dg 26.36S 120.13E
Wimereux 12 Dd 50.46N 1.37E
Winamac 44 De 41.03N 86.36W
Winburg 37 De 28.37S 27.00E
Winchelsea 12 Cd 50.55N 0.43E
Winchester [Eng.-U.K.] 9 Lj 51.04N 1.19W
Winchester [In.-U.S.] 44 Ee 40.10N 84.59W
Winchester [Ky.-U.S.] 44 Ef 38.01N 84.11W
Winchester [Va.-U.S.] 43 Ld 39.11N 78.12W
Windeck 12 Jd 50.49N 7.34E
Windemin, Pointe- 63b Cc 16.34S 167.27E
Winder 44 Fi 34.00N 83.47W
Windermere 9 Kg 54.22N 2.56W
Windermere [B.C.-Can.] 46 Ha 50.30N 115.58W
Windermere [Eng.-U.K.] 9 Kg 54.23N 2.54W
Windhoek 31 Ik 22.34S 17.06E
Windhoek [3] 37 Bd 22.30S 17.00E
Windischgarsten 14 Ic 47.43N 14.20E
Wind Mountain 45 Dj 32.02N 105.34W
Windom 45 Ie 43.52N 95.07W
Windom Mountain 45 Ch 37.37N 107.35W
Windorah 59 Ie 25.26S 142.39E
Window Rock 46 Ki 35.41N 109.03W
Wind River 46 Ke 43.08N 108.12W
Wind River Peak 46 Ke 42.42N 109.07W
Wind River Range 43 Fc 43.05N 109.25W
Windrush 9 Lj 51.42N 1.25W
Windsor [Eng.-U.K.] 9 Mj 51.29N 0.38W
Windsor [N.S.-Can.] 42 Lh 44.59N 64.09W
Windsor [Ont.-Can.] 42 Jh 42.18N 83.01W
Windsor Forest 44 Gj 31.58N 81.10W
Windward Islands 47 Lf 13.00N 61.00W
Windward Islands (EN) = Barlovento, Islas de- 38 Mh 15.00N 61.00W
Windward Islands (EN) = Sotavento, Islas de- 52 Jd 11.10N 67.00W
Windward Islands (EN) = Vent, Iles du- 57 Mf 17.30S 149.30W
Windward Passage (EN) = Vent, Canal du- 49 Lh 20.00N 73.50W
Windward Passage (EN) = Vientos, Paso de los- 38 Lh 20.00N 73.50W
Winfield [Al.-U.S.] 44 Di 33.56N 87.49W
Winfield [Ks.-U.S.] 43 Hd 37.15N 96.59W
Wingene 12 Fc 51.04N 3.16E
Wingen-sur-Moder 12 Jf 48.55N 7.22E
Winisk 38 Kd 55.17N 85.05W
Winisk 39 Kd 55.15N 85.12W
Winisk Lake 42 If 52.55N 87.20W
Winkler 45 Hb 49.11N 97.56W
Winklern 14 Gd 46.52N 12.52E
Winneba 34 Ed 5.20N 0.37W
Winnebago, Lake- 43 Jc 44.00N 88.25W
Winnemucca 43 Dc 40.58N 117.44W
Winnemucca Lake 46 Ff 40.10N 119.20W
Winner 43 Hc 43.22N 99.51W
Winnett 46 Kc 47.00N 108.21W
Winnfield 45 Jk 31.55N 92.38W
Winnibigoshish, Lake- 45 Ic 47.27N 94.12W
Winnipeg 39 Je 49.53N 97.09W
Winnipeg 38 Jd 50.38N 96.19W
Winnipeg, Lake- 38 Jd 52.00N 97.00W
Winnipeg Beach 45 Ha 50.31N 96.58W
Winnipegosis 42 Hf 51.39N 99.56W
Winnipegosis, Lake- 38 Jd 52.30N 100.00W
Winnipesaukee, Lake- 44 Ld 43.35N 71.20W
Winnsboro 45 Kj 32.10N 91.43W
Winnweiler 12 Je 49.34N 7.51E
Winona [Mn.-U.S.] 43 Ic 44.03N 91.39W
Winona [Mo.-U.S.] 45 Kh 37.06N 91.19W
Winona [Ms.-U.S.] 45 Lj 33.29N 89.44W
Winschoten 11 Na 53.08N 7.02E
Winsen 10 Gc 53.22N 10.13E
Winslow [Az.-U.S.] 43 Ed 35.01N 110.42W
Winslow [Eng.-U.K.] 12 Bc 51.57N 0.52W
Winslow Reef 57 Je 1.36S 174.57W
Winston-Salem 43 Kd 36.06N 80.15W
Winterberg 10 Ee 51.12N 8.32E
Winter Harbour 42 Gb 74.46N 110.40W
Winter Haven 43 Kf 28.01N 81.44W
Winter Park [Co.-U.S.] 45 Dg 39.47N 105.45W
Winter Park [Fl.-U.S.] 44 Gk 28.36N 81.20W
Winters 45 Gk 31.57N 99.58W
Winterset 45 If 41.20N 94.01W
Winterswijk 11 Mc 51.58N 6.44E
Winterthur 14 Cc 47.30N 8.45E
Winton [Austl.] 58 Fg 22.23S 143.02E
Winton [N.C.-U.S.] 44 Ig 36.24N 76.56W
Winton [N.Z.] 62 Cg 46.09S 168.20E
Wipper [Ger.] 10 He 51.20N 11.10E
Wipper [Ger.] 10 He 51.47N 11.42E
Wisbech 9 Ni 52.40N 0.10E
Wiscasset 44 Mc 44.00N 69.40W
Wisch 12 Ic 51.55N 6.22E
Wisch-Terborg 12 Ic 51.55N 6.22E
Wisconsin [2] 43 Jc 44.45N 89.30W
Wisconsin 38 Je 43.00N 91.15W
Wisconsin Range 66 Ng 85.45S 125.00W
Wisconsin Rapids 43 Jc 44.23N 89.49W
Wiseman 40 Ic 67.25N 150.06W
Wisła 10 Og 49.39N 18.50E
Wisła = Vistula (EN) 5 He 54.22N 18.55E
Wiślana, Mierzeja- 10 Pb 54.25N 19.30E
Wiślane, Żuławy- 10 Ob 54.10N 19.00E
Wiślany, Zalew- 10 Pb 54.27N 19.40E
Wisłok 10 Sf 50.13N 22.32E
Wisłoka 10 Rf 50.27N 21.23E
Wismar 10 Hc 53.54N 11.28E
Wismarbucht 10 Hc 53.57N 11.25E
Wissant 12 Dd 50.53N 1.40E
Wissembourg 11 Ne 49.02N 7.57E
Wissen 10 Df 50.47N 7.45E
Wissenkerke 12 Fc 51.35N 3.45E
Wissey 12 Cb 52.34N 0.21E
Witbank 31 Jk 25.56S 29.07E
Witchekar Lake 45 Fb 49.15N 100.16W
Witdraai 37 Ce 26.58S 20.41E
Witham 12 Cc 51.47N 0.38E
Witham 9 Ni 52.56N 0.04E
Withernsea 9 Nh 53.44N 0.02E
Witkowo 10 Nd 52.27N 17.47E
Witmarsum, Wonseradeel- 12 Ha 53.06N 5.28E
Witney 9 Lj 51.48N 1.29W
Witnica 10 Kd 52.40N 14.55E
Witputz 37 Be 27.37S 16.42E
Witten 10 De 51.26N 7.20E
Wittenberg [Ger.] 10 Ie 51.52N 12.39E
Wittenberg [Wi.-U.S.] 45 Ld 44.49N 89.10W
Wittenberge 10 Hc 53.00N 11.45E
Wittenoom 59 Dd 22.17S 118.19E
Wittingen 10 Gd 52.44N 10.43E
Wittlich 10 Cg 49.59N 6.53E
Wittmund 10 Dc 53.34N 7.47E
Wittow 10 Jb 54.38N 13.19E
Wittstock 10 Ic 53.09N 12.30E
Witu 36 Hc 2.23S 40.26E
Witu Islands 60 Dh 4.40S 149.18E
Witvlei 37 Bd 22.23S 18.32E
Witzenhausen 10 Fe 51.20N 9.52E
Wivenhoe 12 Cc 51.51N 0.58E
Wizard Reef 30 Mi 8.57S 51.01E
Wizna 10 Sc 53.13N 22.26E
Widawka 10 Oe 51.32N 18.52E
W. J. Van Blommestein Meer 54 Hc 4.45N 55.00W
Wkra 10 Qd 52.27N 20.44E
Władysławowo 10 Ob 54.49N 18.25E
Włocławek 10 Pd 52.39N 19.02E
Włocławek [2] 10 Od 52.40N 19.00E
Włodawa 10 Te 51.34N 23.32E
Włoszczowa 10 Pf 50.25N 19.59E
Wodonga 59 Jg 36.17S 146.54E
Wodzisław Śląski 10 Of 50.00N 18.28E
Woensdrecht 12 Gc 51.25N 4.18E
Woerden 12 Gb 52.05N 4.52E
Woerth 12 Jf 48.56N 7.45E
Woëvre, Plaine de la- 11 Le 49.15N 5.50E
Wohlthat-Massif 66 Cf 71.35S 12.20E
Woippy 12 Ie 49.09N 6.09E
Wojerecy/Hoyerswerda 10 Ke 51.26N 14.15E
Wokam, Pulau- 26 Jh 5.37S 134.30E
Woken He 28 Ja 46.19N 129.34E
Woking 9 Mj 51.20N 0.34W
Wokingham 12 Bc 51.25N 0.50W
Wolbrom 10 Pf 50.24N 19.46E
Wolcott 44 Id 43.13N 76.42W
Wołczyn 10 Oe 51.01N 18.03E
Woldberg 12 Hb 52.25N 5.55E
Woleai Atoll 57 Fd 7.21N 143.52E
Woleu-Ntem [3] 36 Bb 2.00N 12.00E
Wolf, Isla- 54a Aa 1.23N 91.49W
Wolf, Volcán- 54a Ab 0.01S 91.20W
Wolfach 10 Eh 48.18N 8.13E
Wolf Creek 45 Gh 36.35N 99.30W
Wolf Creek 46 Ic 47.00N 112.04W
Wolfen 10 Ie 51.40N 12.17E
Wolfenbüttel 10 Gd 52.10N 10.33E
Wolfhagen 10 Fe 51.19N 9.10E
Wolf Point 43 Fb 48.05N 105.39W
Wolfratshausen 10 Hi 47.54N 11.25E
Wolf River 45 Ld 44.11N 88.44W
Wolfsberg 14 Id 46.50N 14.50E
Wolfsburg 10 Gd 52.26N 10.48E
Wolfstein 12 Je 49.35N 7.36E
Wolgast 10 Jb 54.03N 13.46E
Wolica 10 Tf 50.54N 23.12E
Wolin 10 Kc 53.51N 14.38E
Wolin 10 Kc 53.50N 14.35E
Wollaston 12 Bb 52.15N 0.40W
Wollaston, Islas- 56 Gi 55.40S 67.30W
Wollaston Forland 41 Jd 74.35N 20.15W
Wollaston Lake 38 Id 58.15N 103.20W
Wollaston Lake 42 He 58.05N 103.38W
Wollaston Peninsula 38 Hc 70.00N 115.00W
Wollongong 58 Gh 34.25S 150.54E
Wöllstein 12 Je 49.49N 7.58E
Wolmaransstad 37 De 27.12S 26.13E
Wołomin 10 Rd 52.21N 21.14E
Wołów 10 Me 51.29N 16.55E

Index Symbols

[1] Independent Nation
[2] State, Region
[3] District, County
[4] Municipality
[5] Colony, Dependency
Continent
Physical Region
Historical or Cultural Region
Mount, Mountain
Volcano
Hill
Mountains, Mountain Range
Hills, Escarpment
Plateau, Upland
Pass, Gap
Plain, Lowland
Delta
Salt Flat
Valley, Canyon
Crater, Cave
Karst Features
Depression
Polder
Desert, Dunes
Forest, Woods
Heath, Steppe
Oasis
Cape, Point
Coast, Beach
Cliff
Peninsula
Isthmus
Sandbank
Island
Atoll
Rock, Reef
Islands, Archipelago
Rocks, Reefs
Coral Reef
Well, Spring
Geyser
River, Stream
Waterfall Rapids
River Mouth, Estuary
Lake
Salt Lake
Intermittent Lake
Reservoir
Swamp, Pond
Canal
Glacier
Ice Shelf, Pack Ice
Ocean
Sea
Gulf, Bay
Strait, Fjord
Lagoon
Bank
Seamount
Tablemount
Ridge
Shelf
Basin
Escarpment, Sea Scarp
Fracture
Trench, Abyss
National Park, Reserve
Point of Interest
Recreation Site
Cave, Cavern
Historic Site
Ruins
Wall, Walls
Church, Abbey
Temple
Scientific Station
Airport
Port
Lighthouse
Mine
Tunnel
Dam, Bridge

Wolseley 42 Hf 50.25N 103.19W
Wolstenholme, Cap - 42 Jd 62.34N 77.30W
Wolstenholme Fjord 41 Ec 76.40N 69.45W
Wolsztyn 10 Md 52.08N 16.06 E
Wolvega, Weststellingwerf- 12 Ib 52.53N 6.00 E
Wolverhampton 9 Ki 52.36N 2.08W
Wolverton 9 Mi 52.04N 0.50W
Wŏnju 27 Md 37.21N 127.58 E
Wŏnsan 22 Of 39.10N 127.26 E
Wonseradeel 12 Ha 53.06N 5.28 E
Wonseradeel-Witmarsum 12 Ha 53.06N 5.28 E
Wonthaggi 59 Jg 38.36S 145.35 E
Woodall Mountain 45 Li 34.45N 88.11W
Woodbridge 9 Oi 52.06N 1.19 E
Woodbridge Bay 51g Bb 15.19N 61.25W
Woodhall Spa 12 Ba 53.09N 0.13W
Woodland [Ca.-U.S.] 46 Eg 38.41N 121.46W
Woodland [Wa.-U.S.] 46 Dd 45.54N 122.45W
Woodlark Island 57 Ge 9.05S 152.50 E
Wood Mountain 46 Lb 49.14N 106.20W
Woodridge 45 Hb 49.17N 96.09W
Wood River 46 Lb 50.08N 106.10W
Wood River Lakes 40 He 59.30N 158.45W
Woodroffe, Mount- 59 Ge 26.20S 131.45 E
Woods, Lake- 59 Gc 17.50S 133.30 E
Woods, Lake of the- 38 Je 49.15N 94.45W
Woods Hole 44 Le 41.31N 70.40W
Woodside 46 Jg 39.21N 110.18W
Woodstock [Eng.-U.K.] 9 Lj 51.52N 1.21W
Woodstock [N.B.-Can.] 42 Kg 46.09N 67.34W
Woodstock [Ont.-Can.] 44 Gd 43.08N 80.45W
Woodstock [Vt.-U.S.] 44 Kd 43.37N 72.31W
Woodville [Ms.-U.S.] 45 Kk 31.01N 91.18W
Woodville [N.Z.] 62 Fd 40.20S 175.52 E
Woodville [Tx.-U.S.] 45 Ik 30.46N 94.25W
Woodward 43 Hd 36.26N 99.24W
Wooler 9 Kf 55.33N 2.01W
Woomera 59 Hf 31.11S 137.10 E
Wooramel River 59 Ce 25.47S 114.10 E
Wooster 44 Ge 40.46N 81.57W
Worcester [■] 9 Ki 52.15N 2.10W
Worcester [Eng.-U.K.] 9 Ki 52.11N 2.13W
Worcester [Ma.-U.S.] 43 Mc 42.16N 71.48W
Worcester [S.Afr.] 31 Il 33.39S 19.27 E
Worcester Range 66 Jf 78.50S 161.00 E
Wörgl 14 Gc 47.29N 12.04 E
Workai, Pulau- 26 Jh 6.40S 134.40 E
Workington 9 Jg 54.39N 3.33W
Worksop 9 Lh 53.18N 1.07W
Workum 12 Hb 52.59N 5.27 E
Worland 43 Fc 44.01N 107.57W
Wormer 12 Gb 52.30N 4.52 E
Wormhout 12 Ed 50.53N 2.28 E
Worms 10 Eg 49.38N 8.21 E
Worms Head 9 Ij 51.34N 4.20W
Wörrstadt 12 Ke 49.50N 8.06 E
Wörth am Rhein 12 Ke 49.03N 8.16 E
Wörther-See 14 Id 46.37N 14.10 E
Worthing 9 Mk 50.48N 0.23W
Worthington 43 Hc 43.37N 95.36W
Wosi 26 Ig 0.11S 127.58 E
Wotho Atoll 57 Hc 10.06N 165.59 E
Wotje Atoll 57 Id 9.27N 170.02 E
Woudenberg 12 Hb 52.05N 5.25 E
Wounnioné, Pointe- 63b Db 14.54S 168.02 E
Wounta, Laguna de- 49 Fg 13.38N 83.34W
Wour 35 Ba 21.21N 15.57 E
Wousi 63b Cb 15.22S 166.39 E
Wowoni, Pulau- 26 Hg 4.08S 123.06 E
Woy Woy 59 Kf 33.30S 151.20 E
Wrangel, Ostrov-=Wrangel Island (EN) 21 Tb 71.00N 179.30 E
Wrangel Island (EN)= Wrangel, Ostrov- 21 Tb 71.00N 179.30 E
Wrangell 39 Fd 56.28N 132.23W
Wrangell, Cape- 40a Ab 52.50N 172.26 E
Wrangell Mountains 38 Ec 62.00N 143.00W
Wrath, Cape- 5 Fd 58.37N 5.01W
Wray 43 Gc 40.05N 102.13W
Wreake 12 Ab 52.41N 1.05W
Wreck Reef 57 Gg 22.15S 155.10 E
Wrecks, Bay of- 64g Bb 1.52N 157.17W
Wrexham 9 Kh 53.03N 3.00W
Wright Island 66 Of 74.03S 116.45W
Wright Patman Lake 45 Ij 33.16N 94.14W
Wrightson, Mount- 46 Jk 31.42N 110.50W
Wrigley 42 Fd 63.19N 123.38W
Wrigley Gulf 66 Nf 74.00S 129.00W
Wrocław [2] 10 Me 51.05N 17.00 E
Wrocław=Breslau (EN) 6 He 51.06N 17.00 E
Wronki 10 Md 52.43N 16.23 E
Wrotham 12 Cc 51.18N 0.19 E
Wroxham 12 Db 52.42N 1.24 E
Września 10 Nd 52.20N 17.34 E
Wschowa 10 Me 51.48N 16.19 E
Wu'an 28 Cf 36.42N 114.12 E
Wuchale 35 Fc 11.31N 39.37 E
Wuchang 28 Ib 44.55N 127.11 E
Wuchang, Wuhan- 28 Ci 30.32N 114.18 E
Wucheng (Jiucheng) 28 Df 37.12N 116.04 E
Wuchiu Hsu 27 Kg 25.00N 119.27 E
Wuchuan 28 Ad 41.08N 111.25 E
Wuchuan (Duru) 27 If 28.28N 107.57 E
Wuchuan (Meilü) 27 Jg 21.28N 110.44 E
Wuda 27 Id 39.30N 106.33 E
Wudan → Ongniud Qi 27 Kc 42.58N 119.01 E
Wudao 27 Ld 39.28N 121.30 E
Wudaoliang 27 Fd 35.15N 93.14 E
Wudi 28 Df 37.44N 117.36 E
Wudil 34 Gc 11.49N 8.51 E
Wuding 27 Hf 25.36N 102.27 E
Wudu 27 He 33.24N 105.00 E
Wugang 27 Jf 26.48N 110.32 E
Wugong (Puji) 27 Ie 34.15N 108.14 E
Wuhai 27 Id 39.32N 106.55 E
Wuhan 22 Nf 30.30N 114.20 E
Wuhan-Hankou 28 Ci 30.35N 114.16 E
Wuhan-Hanyang 28 Ci 30.33N 114.16 E
Wuhan- Wuchang 28 Ci 30.32N 114.18 E
Wuhe 27 Ke 33.08N 117.51 E
Wuhu 22 Nf 31.18N 118.27 E
Wuhu (Wanzhi) 28 Ei 31.21N 118.23 E
Wujia He 27 Ic 40.56N 108.52 E
Wu Jiang 21 Mg 29.43N 107.24 E
Wujiang 28 Fi 31.09N 120.38 E
Wukari 31 Hh 7.51N 9.47 E
Wukro 35 Fc 13.48N 39.37 E
Wular 25 Eb 34.30N 74.30 E
Wulff Land 41 Hb 82.19N 50.00W
Wulian (Hongning) 28 Eg 35.45N 119.13 E
Wuliang Shan 27 Hg 24.00N 101.00 E
Wuliaru, Pulau- 26 Jh 7.27S 131.04 E
Wuling Shan 21 Mg 28.20N 110.00 E
Wulongbei 28 Hd 40.15N 124.16 E
Wulongji → Huaibin 28 Ci 32.27N 115.23 E
Wulur 26 Ih 7.09S 128.39 E
Wum 34 Hd 6.23N 10.04 E
Wumei Shan 28 Cj 28.47N 114.50 E
Wümme 12 Ka 53.10N 8.40 E
Wuning 28 Cj 29.17N 115.05 E
Wünnenberg 12 Kc 51.31N 8.42 E
Wünnenberg-Haaren 12 Kc 51.34N 8.44 E
Wunnummin Lake 42 If 52.55N 89.10W
Wun Rog 35 Dd 9.00N 28.21 E
Wunstrof 10 Fd 52.26N 9.25 E
Wuntho 25 Jd 23.54N 95.41 E
Wupper 10 Ce 51.05N 7.00 E
Wuppertal 10 De 51.16N 7.11 E
Wuqi 27 Id 36.57N 108.15 E
Wuqia/Ulugqat 27 Cd 39.40N 75.07 E
Wuqiao (Sangyuan) 28 Df 37.38N 116.23 E
Wuqing (Yangcun) 28 De 39.23N 117.04 E
Würm 12 Kf 48.53N 8.42 E
Wurno 34 Gc 13.18N 5.26 E
Würselen 12 Id 50.49N 6.08 E
Würzburg 6 Gf 49.48N 9.56 E
Wurzen 10 Ie 51.22N 12.44 E
Wu Shan 27 Ie 31.00N 110.00 E
Wushaoling 27 Hd 37.15N 102.50 E
Wuski/Uqturpan 27 Cc 41.10N 79.16 E
Wusong 28 Fi 31.23N 121.29 E
Wüst Seamount (EN) 30 Gl 34.00S 3.40W
Wusuli Jiang 27 Ob 48.28N 135.02 E
Wutach 12 Ke 47.37N 8.15 E
Wutai [China] 28 Be 38.43N 113.14 E
Wutai [China] 27 Dc 44.38N 82.06 E
Wutai Shan 27 Jd 39.04N 113.28 E
Wuustwezel 12 Gc 51.23N 4.36 E
Wuvulu Island 57 Fe 1.43S 142.50 E
Wuwei 28 Di 31.17N 117.54 E
Wuwei (Liangzhou) 22 Mf 37.58N 102.48 E
Wuxi [China] 22 Of 31.32N 120.18 E
Wuxi [China] 27 Ie 31.27N 109.34 E
Wu Xia 27 Je 31.02N 110.10 E
Wuxiang (Duancun) 28 Bf 36.50N 112.51 E
Wuxing (Huzhou) 27 Le 30.47N 120.07 E
Wuxue → Guangji 27 Kf 29.58N 115.32 E
Wuyang [China] 28 Bh 33.26N 113.35 E
Wuyang [China] 28 Jd 36.29N 113.07 E
Wuyang → Zhenyuan 27 If 27.05N 108.26 E
Wuyi [China] 28 Cf 37.49N 115.54 E
Wuyi [China] 28 Ej 28.54N 119.50 E
Wuyiling 27 Mb 48.37N 129.20 E
Wuyi Shan 21 Ng 27.00N 117.00 E
Wuyuan [China] 22 Me 41.08N 108.17 E
Wuyuan [China] 28 Dj 29.15N 117.52 E
Wuyuanzhen → Haiyan 28 Fi 30.31N 120.56 E
Wuzhai 28 Ae 38.54N 111.49 E
Wuzhen 28 Ai 31.42N 112.00 E
Wuzhi Shan [China] 28 Ed 40.31N 118.02 E
Wuzhi Shan [China] 27 Ih 18.54N 109.40 E
Wuzhong 27 Id 38.00N 106.10 E
Wuzhou 22 Ng 23.32N 111.21 E
Wyalkatchem 59 Df 31.10S 117.22 E
Wyandotte 44 Fd 42.12N 83.10W
Wyandra 59 Je 27.15S 145.59 E
Wye 9 Kj 51.37N 2.39W
Wye 12 Cc 51.11N 0.56 E
Wyemandoo, Mount- 59 De 28.31S 118.32 E
Wyk auf Föhr 10 Eb 54.42N 8.34 E
Wylie, Lake- 44 Gh 35.07N 81.02W
Wymondham 9 Oi 52.34N 1.07 E
Wyndham [Austl.] 58 Df 15.28S 128.06 E
Wyndham [N.Z.] 62 Cg 46.20S 168.51 E
Wyndmere 45 Hc 46.16N 97.08W
Wynne 45 Ki 35.14N 90.47W
Wynniatt Bay 42 Gb 72.50N 111.00W
Wynyard [Austl.] 59 Jh 40.59S 145.41 E
Wynyard [Sask.-Can.] 42 Hf 51.47N 104.10W
Wyoming 44 Ed 42.54N 85.42W
Wyoming [2] 43 Fc 43.00N 107.30W
Wyoming Peak 43 Ec 42.36N 110.37W
Wyśmierzyce 10 Qe 51.38N 20.49 E
Wysoka 10 Nc 53.11N 17.05 E
Wysokie Mazowieckie 10 Sd 52.56N 22.32 E
Wyszków 10 Rd 52.36N 21.28 E
Wyszogród 10 Qd 52.23N 20.11 E
Wytheville 44 Gg 36.57N 81.07W
Wyville Thomson Ridge (EN) 9 Fa 60.10N 8.00W
Wyvis, Ben- 9 Id 57.42N 4.30W

X

Xaintrie 11 Ii 45.00N 2.10 E
Xainza 27 Ee 30.50N 88.37 E
Xaitongmoin 27 Ef 29.26N 88.08 E
Xai-Xai 31 Kk 25.04S 33.39 E
Xamba → Hanggin Houqi 27 Ic 40.59N 107.07 E
Xam Nua 25 Kd 20.25N 104.02 E
Xangongo 31 Ij 16.46S 14.59 E
Xang Qu 27 Ef 29.22N 89.09 E
Xanten 10 Ce 51.40N 6.27 E
Xánthi 15 Hh 41.08N 24.53 E
Xanthos 24 Cd 36.20N 29.20 E
Xanxerê 56 Jc 26.53S 52.23W
Xapuri 54 Ef 10.39S 68.31W
Xar Hudag 27 Jb 45.06N 114.30 E
Xar Moron 28 Ac 42.37N 111.02 E
Xar Moron He 27 Lc 43.24N 120.39 E
Xarrama 13 Df 38.14N 8.20W
Xàtiva/Játiva 13 Lf 38.59N 0.31W
Xau, Lake- 37 Cd 21.15S 24.44 E
Xavantes, Represa de- 55 Hf 23.20S 49.35W
Xavantina 55 Fe 21.15S 52.48W
Xayar 27 Dc 41.15N 82.50 E
Xebert 28 Fc 44.00N 122.00 E
Xêgar → Tingri 27 Ef 28.41N 87.00 E
Xenia 44 Ff 39.41N 83.56W
Xiabin Ansha 27 Ke 9.48N 116.38 E
Xiachengzi 28 Kb 44.41N 130.26 E
Xiacun → Rushan 28 Ff 36.55N 121.30 E
Xiaguan 27 Hf 25.32N 100.12 E
Xiahe (Labrang) 28 Hd 35.18N 102.30 E
Xiajin 28 Cf 36.57N 116.00 E
Xiamen 22 Ng 24.32N 118.06 E
Xi'an 22 Mf 34.15N 108.50 E
Xianfeng 27 If 29.41N 109.09 E
Xiangcheng 28 Bh 33.51N 113.29 E
Xiangcheng/Qagchêng 27 Gf 28.56N 99.46 E
Xiangcheng (Shuizhai) 28 Ch 33.27N 114.53 E
Xiangfan 22 Nf 32.03N 112.05 E
Xianggang/Hong Kong [5] 22 Ng 22.15N 114.10 E
Xianghua Ling 27 Jf 25.26N 112.32 E
Xianghuang Qi (Xin Bulag) 27 Jc 42.12N 113.59 E
Xiang Jang 21 Ng 29.26N 113.08 E
Xiangkhoang 25 Ke 19.20N 103.22 E
Xiangkhoang, Plateau de- 25 Ke 19.30N 103.10 E
Xiangquan He 27 Ce 32.05N 79.20 E
Xiangshan (Dancheng) 27 Lf 29.29N 121.52 E
Xiangshan Gang 28 Fj 29.35N 121.38 E
Xiangtan 22 Ng 27.54N 112.55 E
Xiangtang 28 Cj 28.26N 115.59 E
Xiangyin 28 Bj 28.41N 112.53 E
Xiangyuan 28 Bf 36.32N 113.02 E
Xianju 27 Lf 28.50N 120.42 E
Xianning 28 Cj 29.52N 114.17 E
Xiannümiao → Jiangdu 28 Eh 32.30N 119.33 E
Xiantaozhen → Mianyang 28 Bi 30.22N 113.27 E
Xianxia Ling 27 Kf 28.24N 118.40 E
Xianxian 28 De 38.12N 116.07 E
Xianyang 27 Ie 34.26N 108.40 E
Xiaobole Shan 27 La 51.46N 124.09 E
Xiao'ergou 27 Lb 49.10N 123.43 E
Xiaogan 28 Bi 30.52N 113.58 E
Xiao He 28 Bf 37.38N 112.24 E
Xiao Hinggan Ling=Lesser Khingan Range (EN) 21 Oe 48.45N 127.00 E
Xiaoling He 28 Fd 40.55N 121.12 E
Xiaoluan He 28 Dd 41.36N 117.05 E
Xiaoqing He 28 Ef 37.19N 118.59 E
Xiaowutai Shan 28 Ce 39.57N 114.59 E
Xiaoxian 28 Dg 34.11N 116.56 E
Xiaoyi 28 Af 37.07N 111.48 E
Xiaoyi → Gongxian 28 Bg 34.46N 112.57 E
Xiapu 27 Kf 26.57N 119.59 E
Xiawa 28 Fc 42.36N 120.33 E
Xiayi 28 Dg 34.14N 116.07 E
Xiazhuang → Linshu 28 Eg 34.56N 118.38 E
Xicalango, Punta- 48 Nh 19.41N 92.00W
Xichang 22 Mg 27.52N 102.15 E
Xicheng → Yangyuan 28 Cd 40.08N 114.10 E
Xicoténcatl 47 Ed 23.00N 98.56W
Xicotepec de Juárez 48 Kg 20.17N 97.57W
Xiejiaji → Qingyun 28 Df 37.46N 117.22 E
Xifei He 28 Dh 32.38N 116.39 E
Xifeng 28 Hc 42.45N 124.44 E
Xifengzhen 27 Id 35.40N 107.42 E
Xigazê 22 Kg 29.15N 88.52 E
Xi He [China] 27 Hc 42.23N 101.03 E
Xi He [China] 28 Dj 29.38N 116.53 E
Xiheying 28 Ce 39.53N 114.42 E
Xihua 28 Ch 33.48N 114.31 E
Xi Jiang 21 Ng 23.05N 114.23 E
Xiji [China] 27 Id 35.52N 105.35 E
Xiji [China] 28 Ia 46.09N 127.08 E
Xi Jiang 27 Jg 23.05N 114.23 E
Xijir,Ulan Hu 27 Fd 35.12N 90.18 E
Xikouzi 27 La 52.46N 120.29 E
Xiligou → Ulan 27 Gd 36.55N 98.16 E
Xilin 27 Ig 24.30N 105.05 E
Xilin Gol 28 Dc 43.55N 116.05 E
Xilin Hot → Abagnar Qi 22 Ne 43.58N 116.08 E
Xilitla 48 Jg 21.20N 98.58W
Xilókastron 15 Fk 38.05N 22.38 E
Ximiao 27 Hc 41.04N 100.14 E
Xin'an 28 Bg 34.43N 112.09 E
Xin'anjiang 28 Ei 29.27N 119.15 E
Xin'anjiang Shuiku 27 Kf 29.25N 119.05 E
Xin'anzhen → Guannan 28 Eg 34.04N 119.21 E
Xin'anzhen → Xinyi 27 Ke 34.17N 118.14 E
Xin Barag Youqi (Altan-Emel) 27 Kb 48.41N 116.47 E
Xin Barag Zuoqi (Amgalang) 27 Kb 48.13N 118.14 E
Xinbin 28 Hd 41.44N 125.02 E
Xin Bulag → Xianghuang Qi 27 Jc 42.12N 113.59 E
Xincai 27 Je 32.40N 114.57 E
Xinchang 28 Fj 29.30N 120.54 E
Xincheng [China] 28 Bf 37.57N 112.33 E
Xincheng [China] 27 Ig 24.04N 108.39 E
Xincheng [China] 27 Id 38.33N 106.10 E
Xincheng (Gaobeidian) 28 Ce 39.20N 115.50 E
Xindi → Honghu 28 Bj 29.50N 113.28 E
Xing'an → Ankang 22 Mf 32.37N 109.03 E
Xingcheng 28 Fd 40.38N 120.43 E
Xingguo 27 Kf 26.22N 115.21 E
Xinghai 27 Gd 35.45N 99.59 E
Xinghe 27 Jc 40.52N 113.56 E
Xinghua 28 Eh 32.56N 119.49 E
Xingkai Hu=Khanka Lake (EN) 21 Pe 45.00N 132.24 E
Xinglong 28 Dd 40.25N 117.31 E
Xinglongzhen 28 Ia 46.26N 127.03 E
Xingren 27 If 25.26N 105.08 E
Xingtai 22 Nf 37.00N 114.30 E
Xingtang 28 Ce 38.26N 114.33 E
Xingu, Rio- 52 Kf 1.30S 51.53W
Xingxingxia 27 Gc 41.47N 95.07 E
Xingyang 28 Bg 34.47N 113.21 E
Xinryi (Huangcaoba) 27 Hf 25.03N 104.55 E
Xingzi 28 Dj 29.28N 116.03 E
Xinhe 28 Cf 37.32N 115.14 E
Xinhe/Toksu 27 Dc 41.34N 82.38 E
Xin Hot → Abag Qi 27 Jc 44.01N 114.59 E
Xinhuai He 28 Fg 34.23N 120.05 E
Xinhui → Aohan Qi 28 Ec 42.18N 119.53 E
Xining 22 Mf 36.37N 101.46 E
Xinji → Shulu 28 Cf 37.56N 115.14 E
Xinjian 28 Cj 28.41N 115.50 E
Xin Jiang 28 Dj 28.37N 116.40 E
Xinjiangkou → Songzi 28 Ai 30.10N 116.46 E
Xinjiang Uygur Zizhiqu (Hsin-chiang-wei-wu-erh Tzu-chih-ch'ü)=Sinkiang (EN) [2] 27 Ec 42.00N 86.00 E
Xinjin 27 He 30.25N 103.46 E
Xinjin (Pulandian) 27 Ld 39.24N 121.59 E
Xinkai He 28 Gc 43.36N 122.31 E
Xinle 28 Ce 38.15N 114.40 E
Xinlin 28 Ec 43.58N 118.03 E
Xinlitun [China] 27 Ma 50.58N 126.39 E
Xinlitun [China] 28 Gc 42.01N 122.11 E
Xinlong/Nyagrong 27 He 30.57N 100.12 E
Xinmin 28 Gc 42.00N 122.50 E
Xinpu → Lianyungang 22 Nf 34.34N 119.15 E
Xinqing 27 Mb 48.15N 129.31 E
Xintai 28 Dg 35.54N 117.44 E
Xinwen (Suncun) 27 Kd 35.49N 117.38 E
Xinxian [China] 27 Jd 38.24N 112.43 E
Xinxian [China] 28 Ci 31.42N 114.50 E
Xinxiang 22 Nf 35.17N 113.50 E
Xinyang 27 Je 32.05N 114.07 E
Xinye 28 Bh 32.30N 112.22 E
Xinyi (Xin'anzhen) 27 Ke 34.17N 118.14 E
Xinyi He 28 Eg 34.29N 119.49 E
Xinyuan/Künes 27 Dc 43.24N 83.18 E
Xinyuan → Tianjun 22 Lf 37.18N 99.15 E
Xinzhan 28 Ic 43.52N 127.20 E
Xin Zhen → Hanggin Qi 27 Id 39.54N 108.55 E
Xinzheng 28 Bg 34.25N 113.46 E
Xinzhou 28 Ci 30.51N 114.49 E
Xioashan 28 Fi 30.10N 120.16 E
Xiong Xian 28 De 38.59N 116.06 E
Xionyuecheng 28 Gd 40.12N 122.08 E
Xiping [China] 28 Ej 28.27N 119.29 E
Xiping [China] 28 Bh 33.22N 114.00 E
Xisha Qundao=Paracel Islands (EN) 21 Nh 16.30N 112.15 E
Xishuangbanna 27 Gg 22.15N 100.00 E
Xishuanghe → Kenli 28 Ef 37.35N 118.30 E
Xishui 28 Ci 30.28N 115.15 E
Xitianmu Shan 27 Ke 30.21N 119.25 E
Xiuanzi → Chongli 28 Cd 40.57N 115.12 E
Xi Ujimqin Qi (Bayan Ul Hot) 27 Kc 44.31N 117.33 E
Xiuning 28 Ej 29.47N 118.11 E
Xiushan 27 If 28.29N 108.58 E
Xiu Shui 28 Cj 29.13N 116.00 E
Xiushui 27 Jf 29.02N 114.33 E
Xiuwu 28 Bg 35.13N 113.27 E
Xiuyan 27 Lc 40.18N 123.10 E
Xiwanzi → Chongli 28 Cf 36.50N 115.10 E
Xixabangma Feng 27 Ef 28.21N 85.47 E
Xixian 28 Ch 32.21N 114.43 E
Xixiang 27 Ie 32.58N 107.45 E
Xiyang 28 Bf 37.38N 113.41 E
Xizang Zizhiqu (Hsi-tsang Tzu-chih-ch'ü)=Tibet (EN) [2] 27 Ee 32.00N 90.00 E
Xizhong Dao 28 Fe 39.25N 121.18 E
Xi Taijnar Hu 27 Fd 37.15N 93.30 E
Xochicalco 48 Jh 18.45N 99.20W
Xochimilco 48 Jh 19.16N 99.06W
Xorkol 27 Fd 39.04N 91.05 E
Xpujil 48 Oh 18.35N 89.25W
Xuancheng 28 Ei 30.56N 118.44 E
Xuande Qundao 26 Fc 17.08N 111.30 E
Xuan'en 27 Ie 30.02N 109.30 E
Xuanhan 27 Ie 31.23N 107.39 E
Xuanhua 27 Kc 40.39N 115.05 E
Xuanwei 27 Hf 26.19N 104.05 E
Xuchang 22 Nf 34.00N 113.58 E
Xuecheng (Lincheng) 28 Dg 34.38N 117.14 E
Xuefeng Shan 27 Jf 27.35N 110.50 E
Xue Shan 27 Gf 27.30N 99.55 E
Xugezhuang → Fengnan 28 Ee 39.34N 118.05 E
Xugou 28 Eg 34.37N 119.08 E
Xugui 27 Gd 35.45N 96.08 E
Xuguit Qi (Yakeshi) 27 Lb 49.16N 120.41 E
Xümatang 27 Ge 33.57N 97.00 E
Xun Jiang 23 Hf 23.28N 111.18 E
Xunke (Qike) 27 Mb 49.34N 128.28 E
Xunwu 27 Kg 24.59N 115.33 E
Xunxian 28 Cg 35.40N 114.33 E
Xupu 27 Jf 27.54N 110.35 E
Xúquer/Júcar 5 Fh 39.09N 0.14W
Xushui 28 Ce 39.02N 115.40 E
Xuwen 27 Jg 20.22N 110.10 E
Xuyi 27 Ke 32.58N 118.33 E
Xuyong (Yongning) 27 If 28.13N 105.26 E
Xuzhou 22 Nf 34.12N 117.13 E

Y

Ya'an 22 Mg 30.00N 102.57 E
Yabassi 34 Ge 4.28N 9.58 E
Yabe 29 Be 32.42N 130.59 E
Yabebyry 55 Dh 27.24S 57.11W
Yabelo 35 Fe 4.53N 38.07 E
Yablonovy Range (EN)= Jablonovy Hrebet 21 Nd 53.30N 115.00 E
Yabrai Shan 27 Hc 40.00N 103.10 E
Yabrīn 35 Ha 23.15N 48.59 E
Yabrūd 24 Gf 33.58N 36.40 E
Yabucoa 51a Cb 18.03N 65.53W
Yabuli 27 Mc 44.56N 128.37 E
Yabulu 59 Jc 19.00S 146.40 E
Yacaré Cururú, Cuchilla- 55 Dj 30.30S 56.33W
Yacaré Norte, Riacho- 55 Cf 22.43S 58.14W
Yacaré Sur, Riacho- 55 Cf 22.43S 58.14W
Yachats 46 Cd 44.20N 124.03W
Yacuma, Rio- 54 Ef 13.38S 65.23W
Yacyretá, Isla- 55 Dh 27.25S 56.30W
Yadé, Massif du- 35 Bd 7.00N 15.30 E
Yādgīr 25 Fe 16.46N 77.08 E
Yadong/Chomo 27 Ef 27.38N 89.03 E
Yae-Dake 29b Ab 26.38N 127.56 E
Yaeyama-Rettō 27 Lg 24.20N 124.00 E
Yafran 33 Bc 32.04N 12.31 E
Yağcilar 15 Lj 39.25N 28.23 E
Yagishiri-Tō 29a Ba 44.26N 141.25 E
Yagoua 34 Ic 10.20N 15.14 E
Yagradagzê Shan 27 Gd 35.09N 95.39 E
Yaguajay 49 Hb 22.19N 79.14W
Yaguarí 55 Ej 31.31S 54.58W
Yaguari, Arroyo- 55 Di 29.44S 57.37W
Yahalica de Gonzáles Gallo 48 Hg 21.08N 102.51W
Yahuma 36 Db 1.06N 23.10 E
Yaita 29 Fc 36.50N 139.55 E
Yaizu 29 Fd 34.51N 138.19 E
Yajiang/Nyagquka 27 He 30.07N 100.58 E
Yakacik 24 Ed 36.05N 32.45 E
Yake-Dake 29 Ec 36.14N 137.35 E
Yakeishi-Dake 29 Gb 39.10N 140.50 E
Yakeshi → Xuguit Qi 27 Lb 49.16N 120.41 E
Yake-Yama 29 Gb 39.58N 140.48 E
Yakima 39 Ge 46.36N 120.31W
Yakima River 46 Fc 46.15N 119.02W
Yako 34 Ec 12.58N 2.16W
Yakumo 27 Pc 42.15N 140.16 E
Yaku-Shima 27 Ne 30.20N 130.30 E
Yakutat 40 Le 59.33N 139.44W
Yakutat Bay 40 Ke 59.45N 140.45W
Yala 25 Kg 6.32N 101.19 E
Yalahán, Laguna de- 48 Pg 21.30N 87.15W
Yalcubul, Punta- 48 Og 21.35N 88.35W
Yale Point 46 Kh 36.25N 109.48W
Yalewa Kalou 63d Ab 16.40S 177.46 E
Yalgoo 59 De 28.20S 116.41 E
Yalikavak 15 Kl 37.06N 27.18 E
Yaliköy 15 Lh 41.29N 28.17 E
Yalinga 35 Cd 6.31N 23.13 E
Yaloké 35 Bd 5.19N 17.05 E
Yalong Jiang 21 Mg 26.37N 101.48 E
Yalova 24 Cb 40.39N 29.15 E
Yalu Jiang 21 Of 39.55N 124.20 E
Yalvaç 24 Dc 38.17N 31.11 E
Yām, Ramlat- 33 If 17.42N 45.09 E
Yamada [Jap.] 28 Pe 39.28N 141.57 E
Yamada [Jap.] 29 Be 33.33N 130.45 E
Yamada-Wan 29 Hb 39.30N 142.00 E
Yamaga 29 Be 33.01N 130.41 E
Yamagata 27 Pd 38.15N 140.15 E
Yamagata Ken [2] 28 Pe 38.30N 140.00 E
Yamagawa 29 Bf 31.12N 130.39 E
Yamaguchi 27 Ne 34.10N 131.29 E
Yamaguchi Ken [2] 28 Kh 34.10N 131.30 E
Yamakuni 29 Be 33.24N 131.02 E
Yamal Peninsula (EN)= Jamal, Poluostrov- 21 Ib 70.00N 70.00 E
Yamamoto 29 Ga 40.06N 140.03 E
Yamanaka 29 Ec 36.15N 136.22 E
Yamanashi Ken [2] 28 Og 35.30N 138.45 E
Yamashiro 29 Ce 33.57N 133.43 E
Yamato Rise (EN) 28 Me 39.30N 134.30 E
Yamatsuri 29 Gc 36.53N 140.25 E
Yamazaki 29 Dd 35.00N 134.33 E
Yambi, Mesa de- 54 Dc 1.30N 71.20W
Yambio 31 Jh 4.34N 28.23 E
Yambo 35 Fd 8.25N 36.00 E
Yambu Head 51n Ba 13.09N 61.09W
Yambuya 36 Db 1.16N 24.33 E
Yame 29 Be 33.13N 130.34 E
Yamethin 25 Jd 20.26N 96.09 E
Yamma Yamma, Lake- 59 Ie 26.20S 141.25 E
Yamoto 29 Gb 38.25N 141.13 E
Yamoussoukro 34 Dd 6.49N 5.17W
Yampa River 43 Fc 40.32N 108.59W
Yampi Sound 59 Ec 16.11S 123.40 E
Yamuna 21 Kg 25.30N 81.53 E
Yamunanagar 25 Fb 30.08N 76.59 E
Yamzho Yumco 27 Ff 29.00N 90.40 E
Yanagawa 29 Be 33.10N 130.24 E
Yanahara 29 Dd 34.57N 134.05 E
Yanahuanca 54 Cf 10.30S 76.30W
Yanai 29 Ce 33.58N 132.07 E
Yanam 25 Ge 16.51N 82.15 E
Yan'an 22 Mf 36.36N 109.30 E
Yanaoca 54 Df 14.13S 71.26W
Yanbian 27 Hf 26.51N 101.32 E
Yanbu' 23 Ee 24.05N 38.03 E
Yanchang 27 Jd 36.39N 110.03 E
Yancheng [China] 28 Bh 33.35N 114.00 E
Yancheng [China] 27 Le 33.16N 120.10 E
Yanchi 27 Id 37.49N 107.24 E
Yandé 63b Ae 20.03S 163.48 E
Yandina 63a Dc 9.07S 159.13 E
Yandja 36 Cc 1.41S 17.43 E

Index Symbols

[1] Independent Nation; [2] State, Region; [3] District, County; [4] Municipality; [5] Colony, Dependency; Continent; Physical Region; Historical or Cultural Region; Mount, Mountain; Volcano; Hill; Mountains, Mountain Range; Hills, Escarpment; Plateau, Upland; Pass, Gap; Plain, Lowland; Delta; Salt Flat; Valley, Canyon; Crater, Cave; Karst Features; Depression; Polder; Desert, Dunes; Forest, Woods; Heath, Steppe; Oasis; Cape, Point; Coast, Beach; Cliff; Peninsula; Isthmus; Sandbank; Island; Atoll; Rock, Reef; Islands, Archipelago; Rocks, Reefs; Coral Reef; Well, Spring; Geyser; River, Stream; Waterfall Rapids; River Mouth, Estuary; Lake; Salt Lake; Intermittent Lake; Reservoir; Swamp, Pond; Canal; Glacier; Ice Shelf, Pack Ice; Ocean; Sea; Gulf, Bay; Strait, Fjord; Lagoon; Bank; Seamount; Tablemount; Ridge; Shelf; Basin; Escarpment, Sea Scarp; Fracture; Trench, Abyss; National Park, Reserve; Point of Interest; Recreation Site; Cave, Cavern; Historic Site; Ruins; Wall, Walls; Church, Abbey; Temple; Scientific Station; Airport; Port; Lighthouse; Mine; Tunnel; Dam, Bridge

Index Symbols

[1] Independent Nation
[2] State, Region
[3] District, County
[4] Municipality
[5] Colony, Dependency
■ Continent
▣ Physical Region

◨ Historical or Cultural Region
▲ Mount, Mountain
▲ Volcano
◭ Hill
▲ Mountains, Mountain Range
◣ Hills, Escarpment
▨ Plateau, Upland

▨ Pass, Gap
▨ Plain, Lowland
▨ Delta
▨ Salt Flat
▨ Valley, Canyon
▨ Crater, Cave
▨ Karst Features

▨ Depression
▨ Polder
▨ Desert, Dunes
▨ Forest, Woods
▨ Heath, Steppe
▨ Oasis
▨ Cape, Point

▨ Coast, Beach
▨ Cliff
▨ Peninsula
▨ Isthmus
▨ Sandbank
▨ Island
◉ Atoll

▨ Rock, Reef
▨ Islands, Archipelago
▨ Rocks, Reefs
▨ Coral Reef
▨ Well, Spring
▨ Geyser
▨ River, Stream

▨ Waterfall Rapids
▨ River Mouth, Estuary
▨ Lake
▨ Salt Lake
▨ Intermittent Lake
▨ Sea
▨ Swamp, Pond

▨ Canal
▨ Glacier
▨ Ice Shelf, Pack Ice
▨ Ocean
▨ Gulf, Bay
▨ Strait, Fjord

▨ Lagoon
▨ Bank
▨ Seamount
▨ Tablemount
▨ Ridge
▨ Shelf
▨ Basin

▨ Escarpment, Sea Scarp
▨ Fracture
▨ Trench, Abyss
▨ National Park, Reserve
▨ Point of Interest
▨ Recreation Site
▨ Cave, Cavern

▨ Historic Site
▨ Ruins
▨ Wall, Walls
▨ Church, Abbey
▨ Temple
▨ Scientific Station
▨ Airport

▨ Port
▨ Lighthouse
▨ Mine
▨ Tunnel
▨ Dam, Bridge

Index Symbols

[1] Independent Nation   Historical or Cultural Region   Pass, Gap   Depression   Coast, Beach   Rock, Reef   Waterfall Rapids   Canal   Lagoon   Escarpment, Sea Scarp   Historic Site   Port
[2] State, Region   Mount, Mountain   Plain, Lowland   Polder   Cliff   Islands, Archipelago   River Mouth, Estuary   Glacier   Bank   Fracture   Ruins   Lighthouse
[3] District, County   Volcano   Delta   Desert, Dunes   Peninsula   Rocks, Reefs   Lake   Ice Shelf, Pack Ice   Seamount   Trench, Abyss   Wall, Walls   Mine
[4] Municipality   Hill   Salt Flat   Forest, Woods   Isthmus   Coral Reef   Salt Lake   Ocean   Tablemount   National Park, Reserve   Church, Abbey   Tunnel
[5] Colony, Dependency   Mountains, Mountain Range   Valley, Canyon   Heath, Steppe   Sandbank   Well, Spring   Intermittent Lake   Sea   Ridge   Point of Interest   Temple   Dam, Bridge
■ Continent   Hills, Escarpment   Crater, Cave   Oasis   Island   Geyser   Reservoir   Gulf, Bay   Shelf   Recreation Site   Scientific Station
Physical Region   Plateau, Upland   Karst Features   Cape, Point   Atoll   River, Stream   Swamp, Pond   Strait, Fjord   Basin   Cave, Cavern   Airport

Index Symbols

[1] Independent Nation	Historical or Cultural Region	Pass, Gap	Depression
[2] State, Region	Mount, Mountain	Plain, Lowland	Polder
[3] District, County	Volcano	Delta	Salt Flat
[4] Municipality	Hill	Salt Flat	Forest, Woods
[5] Colony, Dependency	Mountains, Mountain Range	Valley, Canyon	Heath, Steppe
Continent	Hills, Escarpment	Crater, Cave	Oasis
Physical Region	Plateau, Upland	Karst Features	Cape, Point

Coast, Beach	Rock, Reef	Waterfall Rapids	Canal
Cliff	Islands, Archipelago	River Mouth, Estuary	Glacier
Desert, Dunes	Rocks, Reefs	Ice Shelf, Pack Ice	Lake
Forest, Woods	Coral Reef	Salt Lake	Ocean
Heath, Steppe	Well, Spring	Intermittent Lake	Sea
Sandbank	Geyser	Reservoir	Gulf, Bay
Island	River, Stream	Swamp, Pond	Strait, Fjord

Lagoon	Escarpment, Sea Scarp	Historic Site	Port
Bank	Fracture	Ruins	Lighthouse
Seamount	Trench, Abyss	Wall, Walls	Mine
Tablemount	National Park, Reserve	Church, Abbey	Tunnel
Ridge	Point of Interest	Temple	Dam, Bridge
Shelf	Recreation Site	Scientific Station	
Basin	Cave, Cavern	Airport	